AMERICAN
BOTTLES
&
FLASKS
and Their Ancestry

Also by Helen McKearin:
BOTTLES, FLASKS, AND DR. DYOTT

By George S. and Helen McKearin:
TWO HUNDRED YEARS OF AMERICAN BLOWN GLASS
AMERICAN GLASS

Also by Kenneth M. Wilson:
NEW ENGLAND GLASS AND GLASSMAKING

AMERICAN BOTTLES & FLASKS

FLASKS
and *Their Ancestry*

BY
HELEN McKEARIN
AND
KENNETH M. WILSON

CROWN PUBLISHERS, INC. NEW YORK

Library of Congress Cataloging in Publication Data

McKearin, Helen.
    American bottles & flasks and their ancestry.

    Bibliography: p.
    Includes index.
    1. Bottles—United States. I. Wilson, Kenneth M.,
joint author.   II.   Title.
NK5440.B6M29   666'.19   78-18520
ISBN 0-517-53147-X

CONTENTS

PART VIII

FIGURED FLASKS AND CALABASH BOTTLES: DECORATIVE, MASONIC, HISTORICAL, PICTORIAL, AND LETTERED

PART IX

20th-CENTURY FIGURED BOTTLES AND FLASKS
by Kenneth M. Wilson

GLASSHOUSE SKETCHES
Nos. 1 through 44 by Helen McKearin

ACKNOWLEDGMENTS

Tis there
The instinctive theorizing whence a fact
Looks to the eye as the eye likes the look.

It was nearly 60 years ago that I first read those cautionary lines by Robert Browning. Before long they began to have a particular significance for me in connection with American glass. My father's insurance business necessitated periodic trips to Boston. Once business calls were over, he would pursue one of his hobbies—American glass. When he stayed in the city overnight, I often joined in his round of visits to the Charles Street antique shops or with one or another of his collector-friends. Escape from the college campus to dinner at the Parker House or the Touraine followed by the theatre was more than compensation for a few afternoon hours of boring talk about pieces of old glass. Then forced feeding took effect: glass became interesting and glass talk fascinating. Gradually I too became a collector—not of glass but of information about it. (Perhaps compulsive possession of objects turned me to study of and research about them.) Along the way Browning's lines became a warning of pitfalls; for we collectors

tend to be subjective rather than objective about what we collect, be it data or objects. And those who collect and pass along data should have a special dedication to objectivity. ". . . As the eye likes the look" may cloud one's judgment or, in other words, the *wish* often fathers an opinion, conclusion, or, above all, an attribution.

Another warning, one that came to my mind as my father, George S. McKearin, Sr., and I were working on *American Glass*: "Today's fact may become tomorrow's fiction." In glass studies, as in nearly if not all fields, conclusions drawn from the data available may be logical, even inescapable, but as research continues to unearth further information, those conclusions may become invalid. And so it may be in the case of some of the opinions given and conclusions drawn in *American Bottles & Flasks and Their Ancestry*.

Hence this book, like its predecessors, is but a stepping-stone toward more complete knowledge about glass bottles. It gives, we hope, meaningful glimpses of the evolution of a tiny bottle into a large family of many species and specialized uses, in many social, economic, and historical contexts, and, too, the evolution of an ancient craft, or, if you will, art, into a widespread industry. It is an industry in which the art has survived in spite of, or perhaps in part because of, the economic benefits of automation in the production of glass to meet the present demands.

The authors' names on the book's title page are Helen McKearin and Kenneth M. Wilson. Certainly much of our own harvests of research are present, and we have sifted chaff from earlier reapings of the field as some future writer will from ours. Nevertheless, this book is in essence a synthesis, the work of many collectors, dealers, writers, and researchers down the years from 1900, when Edwin Atlee Barber's slim volume *American Glassware* first called attention (as far as I know) to "historical" flasks.

Many scholars have delved deeply into the nature and history of Ancient, Continental, and—of particular interest to most American collectors— English and Irish glass. Although few have confined their studies and research to the bottle family, all whose works I have read contributed in one way or another to our knowledge of the evolution and history of bottles. The names of those to whom I am gratefully indebted are in the bibliography of this book, in its footnotes and references, and often in the text.

The same is true of writers about American glass and glass imported into the colonies and the United States. Nevertheless, special mention must be made of four whose pioneer and scholarly works were a tremendous stimulus to the collecting of American glass, of bottles especially, and who also laid the foundations upon which my father, George S. McKearin, I, and other students who followed them have built. They were Frederick William Hunter, Stephen Van Rensselaer, Harry Hall White, and Rhea Mansfield Knittle.

In 1914 Frederick William Hunter's *Stiegel Glass*, in which John B. Kerfoot was a silent partner in the research and preparation, was published. Their spotlights of research had been turned not only on Stiegel and his wares but also on the Wistars and theirs. Of course bottles and flasks, free-blown and pattern-molded, were the only categories examined. These types had already caught the interest of a few collectors, as had Barber's "Historical flasks." Now they had a native context and a romantic one. Ipso facto, all bottles and flasks patterned in ribbed or reticulated designs became Stiegel. It would be nearly, if not, a decade before a few collectors and students questioned the blanket attribution, and many more

years were to pass before Stiegel-type was rooted in most informed collectors' vocabularies of glass terms. And it would be several years before a vista would be opened to midwestern glass pattern-molded in the "Stiegel tradition."

In 1921 Stephen Van Rensselaer published *Early American Bottles and Flasks*, a book that quickly accelerated bottle collecting and research into the past of our bottles and flasks and their makers. It was eclipsed by his 1926 revised edition in which the categories of bottles were expanded. Also, the number of American glassworks producing bottles and, in particular, the number of reported "Historical" flasks far exceeded any previous record. From that time to the present, Figured Flasks in the Masonic, Historical, Decorative, and Pictorial groups have been in the forefront of bottle collecting. For many years Van Rensselaer's book was the bible of bottle collectors, my father of course among them. It brought "law and order" into the collecting of American bottles and flasks. Before *American Glass* was published in 1941, making available my father's charts of flasks dating from about 1815 through the 1850s and including varieties and variants not known in 1926, "V.R." group numbers were indispensable in identifying and cataloguing those flasks. And "V.R." numbers have continued in use for the hitherto uncharted Pike's Peak, Shield and Clasped Hands, and many other pictorial flasks.

Even before the publication of Mr. Van Rensselaer's first edition, a few students of American glass—dealers and collectors—were gleaning information about midwestern bottles and flasks and their makers. Among them was Harry Hall White, whose articles on the Kentucky Glass Works and one on early Pittsburgh glasshouses were published in ANTIQUES in 1926. Ten more equally important articles appeared in ANTIQUES over the next 15 years; and in conversation and correspondence as well, Mr. White gave generously of his knowledge. His evidence derived not only from documents and various archives, from well-weighed family and local histories, but also from excavations on the sites of several glassworks—in Ohio, one at Mantua and one near Kent; in New York, on the site of the Mt. Vernon Glass Works at Vernon and of its successor on Mt. Pleasant, Saratoga; in Connecticut, that of the Coventry Glass Works; and in New Hampshire, of the Marlboro-Street works in Keene. Among the quantities of shards unearthed were not only those of various bottle-types but also of Figured Flasks in numbers adequate to justify attribution of the flasks to the glassworks. The shards were the first physical evidence tying a flask design in a particular mold to a specific glassworks.

Rhea Mansfield Knittle was another of the early investigators of midwestern glassmaking. Although her activities did not precede Mr. White's, her first article, "Muskingham County, Ohio, Glass" appeared in ANTIQUES in 1924, two years before his first article. It was followed by five others, the last in 1933. In the meantime the scope of her researches broadened, radiating from the local to the national scene. Her *Early American Glass,* published in 1927, was a comprehensive study of glass and glassmaking in the colonies and the United States east of the Mississippi. It too became a bible for collectors of American glass.

My indebtedness to many scholars is not just for their books and for articles but also for unpublished data so generously given to me. And it is equaled by my indebtedness to even more bottle enthusiasts who have never committed their studies to print but have unstintingly shared them through word-of-mouth and correspondence.

When I was assembling my data for Part II, Historical Background, and was confronted with a few contradictory opinions regarding ancient glass production, Dr. Sidney Goldstein, Associate Curator, Ancient Glass, at The Corning Museum of Glass, came to my aid, resolving the problems. Invaluable, too, were not only articles by Robert J. Charleston who, before his recent retirement, was Keeper of the Department of Ceramics, the Victoria and Albert Museum, London, but also his informative letters, especially concerning early English bottles.

Although, undoubtedly, there is much still to be discovered about our glassworks, glassmakers, and their products, their history has become more accurate over the past few decades. Some of the data has been published by its discoverers, much has not. One such instance is that of the various Baltimore glassworks. The greatly enlarged picture presented in this book is due to the generosity of Richard H. Wood and of Delverne D. Dressell, who surpassed previous students in his searching of documentary sources and archives. Both have given the results of their researches to me. Another who has not published his important findings through searches in documentary and other primary sources is J. E. Pfeiffer. To him, I am very grateful for facts hitherto unknown to me about several South Jersey glasshouses. Also, through his "digs" on the site of the Crowleytown glassworks, he determined many sorts

of bottles produced there, including a Dyottville-type Washington-Taylor Figured Flask. Still another to shed light on an early glassworks that has long been important to the collector of Figured Flasks is Carl Flowers, Jr., historian and collector. His scholarly and continuing researches have already changed into fiction or only probabilities some "facts" about the Keene-Marlboro-Street glassworks, its products, and the men who operated it. I am also indebted to him for a new historical perspective of the New England Washington-Jackson flasks. His conclusion, derived from the history of men and events, that these flasks were brought out in 1832 primarily in celebration of Washington's 100th birthday and secondarily to boost Andrew Jackson's presidential campaign seems too logical not to be accepted.

In the vast field of utilitarian bottles and jars I am grateful to Olive Talbot of London and Ed Fletcher of York, England, for their information about the origin and use of the soda water bottle called the "egg bottle" and "egg mineral." Vernon L. McCord and Preston Bassett gave me much appreciated material on soda bottles and Fenton Keyes on Saratoga Spring Water bottles. Mr. Bassett also sent data on the varieties of the long-lived bottle for Turlington's Balsam. Professor James Harvey Young's information about that famous patent medicine as well as sources of material on Dr. Dyott were invaluable.

The section on Figured Flasks presented several obstacles. Inasmuch as my main interest had been in historical, social, and economic contexts—the why, when, and where—I was woefully deficient in knowledge of degrees of commonness and rarity, of details such as the colors in which a flask occurred, of unrecorded flasks falling in the groups charted in *American Glass*, and of later flasks other than those in my father's private collection. Even with that collection and his material for expanding the charts, I could not have attempted to follow in his footsteps without the ungrudging, even enthusiastic cooperation given to me by many students and collectors. My good friends George Austin and the late Charles B. Gardner made their collections available for study, and—as did Sam Laidacker—gave me the benefit of their opinions and experience. They added flasks to groups XI, XII, XIII, XIV, and XV in the new charts. They answered the questions about rarity of both charted and previously unrecorded flasks. Many collectors and students reported unlisted colors of flasks falling in the original ten charted groups: George Austin, the late Earl Dambach, the late Charles B. Gardner, Matthew G. Knapp, Jr., Dr.

Michael B. Krassner, Helen C. Hickman, Sam Laidacker (who had kept a list of new colors since the 1941 publication of *American Glass*), Warren Lane, Kenneth R. Lewis, L. D. McCullough, Robert Rodgers, Neil N. Sayles, Orin Summerville, Charles Vuono, Sterling Watlington, the late Crawford Wettlaufer, Jack Whistance, Robert H. Wise, and Richard Wood. Moreover, unlimited thanks are due Fred R. Salisbury, whose scroll flasks collection is doubtless the largest ever assembled and whose knowledge about them is the most comprehensive, for indispensable assistance in revising Group IX scroll flasks in the original charts and integrating the scrolls recorded since 1941.

To read and to advise on pattern-molded bottles and flasks, I turned to the late James H. Rose, who knew so much and committed so little to print but was a willing mentor to so many of us, especially about midwestern glass. Lowell Innes, too, generously gave me the benefit of his knowledge of the glass produced in that area, particularly the glass from the Pittsburgh area and its environs.

Above all, I am forever and gratefully obligated to Kenneth M. Wilson of the Henry Ford Museum. When ill health and eye problems ended my researches and writing, Ken came to the rescue of this book. He not only gave generously of his time and expertise to read and evaluate the parts I had completed but also took on the task of finishing the book. In addition, he succeeded in adding color, which so enhances the value of the illustrations in a book on the arts and crafts.

It is said that a picture is worth a thousand words. Certainly words are merely words insofar as a material object is concerned—unless, of course, one sees or has seen the thing to which the words relate. Conversely, whether in color or black and white, an object is only an image unless one has the words to explain and identify it. As in the case of heredity vs. environment, can either be said to be the more important? Be that as it may, we have tried to include as much pictorial evidence and guidance as possible. Unless otherwise stated, the photographs for the book were taken by Taylor and Dull of New York City and the line drawings were made by the late James McCreery, who also drew those used in *American Glass*. All the pieces that were photographed by Taylor and Dull and that served as models for Mr. McCreery's line drawings were in the private collection of George S. McKearin.

Last but not least, to use an overworked but valid cliché, I am forever indebted and grateful to my friend and editor, Kathryn Pinney. Among her numerous problems, perhaps the greatest were the reorganization of the charts and the rearranging of photographs and photostats, which had been planned for one format and had to be adjusted to the needs of a quite different one. I am grateful too that in the accomplishment of her tasks she had two able assistants, Ellen Lerner, followed by Peter Burford.

HELEN McKEARIN
Nantucket, Massachusetts

As Helen McKearin has indicated above, through their contributions to the history of glass and glassmaking many scholars, historians, and collectors have provided the basis for this book. Though a number of them have been recognized in the bibliography and reference notes, I too would like to thank them here.

In addition, numerous other colleagues, collectors, and friends have unstintingly shared their knowledge, their research efforts, time, and special skills, all of which have contributed significantly to this work. I am grateful to all these generous people, but the following persons and institutions deserve special mention: The Corning Museum of Glass and some of my colleagues there—Raymond Errett for his excellent photography, especially those color plates that picture objects from the Corning collection; the librarians, Norma Jenkins and Virginia Wright, for their conscientious response to my inquiries; Adrian Baer and Clifford Olmsted, for their help in providing the objects I needed to examine and have photographed; Jane Shadel Spillman, for her responses to my requests; Jane Lanahan, and particularly Priscilla Price, registrar, for long and continued help in many respects.

I am also indebted to the Henry Ford Museum and its resources, as well as to some of its staff: Christina Nelson, curator of glass and ceramics; Robert G. Wheeler, vice-president, collections and presentation; Rudy Ruzicska and Carl Malotka, photographers. I am especially grateful for the patience, cooperation, and skill of Mr. Malotka in producing many of the black-and-white illustrations for this book, as well as the color plates of bottles and flasks from the collection of the Henry Ford Museum.

Librarians, historians, and other staff members and volunteers at numerous museums, libraries, historical societies, and other institutions are due my sincere thanks for the time and effort they expended on my behalf: Walter Dunn, director of the Buffalo and Erie County Historical Society, and his wife,

Jean N. Dunn, gave me much information relating to the Lancaster and Lockport glasshouses. James D. Billota permitted me to use material from his graduate-seminar paper on the Lockport Glasshouse Company. Kay Fox, historian and author of the *History of Stoddard, New Hampshire,* supplied data about the several Stoddard glasshouses. Roy C. Horner contributed details on the Fislerville Glass Works, and Harold M. Lyn gave me a copy of his unpublished paper on the glassworks in Ravenna, Ohio. Cy Plough, director of the Portage County Historical Society, also contributed knowledge about this factory. Roland Salada furnished unpublished information and photocopies of various documents about the New Hampshire glasshouses, and Kenneth Usher, who has researched the Newburgh Glass Company, provided much information about that factory, as did Helen Ver Nooy Gearn, city historian of Newburgh, New York. Mrs. Helen Wilson, assistant librarian of the Historical Society of Western Pennsylvania, made available detailed information about several glasshouses in Pittsburgh and the vicinity that was particularly useful. Elizabeth B. Knox, secretary and curator of the New London County Historical Society, deserves thanks for valuable data about the glasshouses of New London, Connecticut. Al G. Smith, retired director of corporate information and archivist and historian for Owens-Illinois; Karol Schmiegel, assistant registrar, and Arlene Palmer, curator of glass and ceramics, of the Henry Francis duPont Winterthur Museum—all these helpful people provided valuable data and numerous photographs. Barry Taylor, director of Wheaton Village, supplied many facts about and numerous photographs of the products of Wheaton Industries.

I want to give special thanks to John Morrill Foster, author of *Old Bottle Foster and His Glassmaking Descendants* and great-grandson of Joseph Foster, of Stoddard glasshouse fame, and to James Frank, descendant of William Frank of the Frankstown and Wormser glasshouses, for material from family diaries and memoirs, as well as photographs relating to these respective factories.

Among other colleagues who generously gave valued help are Lura Woodside Watkins, Malcolm Watkins, and James Gergat. I owe special thanks to Mr. Gergat, curator of the York County Historical Society and formerly curator of the Valentine Museum in Richmond, Virginia, for sharing with me the results of his documentary and archaeological research into the several glasshouses in Richmond, and for permitting me to publish the results of his work in the historical sketch about the Richmond glasshouses.

Numerous collectors opened their houses and collections to me, and shared their knowledge about the specimens in their collections. Included among these were George Austin, Edwin and Jane Blaske, the late Charles B. Gardner and his wife, Nina, Lowell Innes, Eddie J. Pfeiffer, Fred R. Salisbury, Duncan Wolcott, and Joseph W. Wood. Eddie Pfeiffer and Fred Salisbury gave me extended help on the subjects of the New Jersey glasshouses and scroll flasks respectively—and I cannot say enough about the generous help, hospitality, and friendship that has been extended to me over the years by Charlie and Nina Gardner. The late Dr. Julian H. Toulouse, glass technologist, collector, and friend, was also the source of a good deal of information.

I too am indebted to our editor, Kay Pinney, and her two assistants, Ellen Lerner and Peter Burford, not only for their excellent work but also for their understanding and patience.

I also wish to acknowledge the numerous contributions made to this book by Peggy Haar Wilson, who typed and proofread much of my manuscript and edited it to a degree. My sincere thanks are due—and gratefully given—her.

And, finally, I want to express my indebtedness and gratitude to Helen McKearin, my mentor and valued friend. Since our first meeting in the cold March of 1955 when she came to evaluate the glass collection at Old Sturbridge Village, where I was a young assistant curator who knew virtually nothing about glass, she has been my guide, source of inspiration, valued counsel, and critic. She has always shared her knowledge wholeheartedly and fully, as well as given me carefully considered opinions in response to many and varied queries, encouraged my study of glass, and promoted my development and recognition in this field. One is always pleased to have his efforts recognized and applauded by a respected teacher, and so I felt greatly honored when Micky (as her close friends know her) and Crown Publishers asked me to help in completing this book. After some unfortunate delays, I have finally done so, but not without her continuing aid and understanding. It would have been almost impossible to carry out the task without the lifelong accumulation of notes, photographs, and other related materials that she so generously gave me, and on which I have drawn heavily. I appreciate her acknowledgment of my interest and help; I am even more grateful to her for the opportunity to share in this work.

KENNETH M. WILSON
Dearborn, Michigan

Part I

NOTES FOR THE CURIOUS

1

BOTTLE COLLECTING

Collecting is as instinctive in man as in the magpie, and it can be a fruitfully absorbing hobby. Whether ridden at random or guided along a well-marked course to an ordered destination, it is good therapy for those of us who need escape from the strains of business life, who need change from demanding routines, who need an interest to fill leisure hours. Too hard riding of a hobby is to be avoided, however: it may lead to a complex, that psychological state in which the hobby rides the collector and cunningly, by tortuous paths, forces back to itself all thoughts and conversation no matter how far afield they may have strayed. Thus the collector runs the risk of becoming a bore—except perhaps to fellow collectors. And of course, exciting as the hunt may be, since few collectors are misers gloating over a secret hoard, the ecstatic heights of collecting can be reached only by sharing the fruits of pursuit with like-minded companions, not only through the collection itself but also through the spoken and printed word. Inevitably, the things man collects inspire their own literature, and old bottles have inspired this stepping-stone in the stream of writings about bottles collected by Americans yesterday and today.

Bottles, as congenial esthetic companions gravitate into fit arrangements upon close acquaintance, as easily and readily as familiar friends around a hearth in studio or library. . . . Considered singly or blended in a collection, the bottle, antique, beautiful or curious, proves itself to have great resources for entertainment and artistic gratification.

Thus did Emma Carleton write of glass bottles in 1902,[1] two years after the budding interest in bottles made in the United States found expression in a slim little book listing 86 "historical flasks."[2] Her appreciative tribute may seem extravagant to the uninitiated, but the numerous company of bottle collectors today can but agree. Although each member of that company cherishes his own individual conception of "fit arrangements," of "great resources for entertainment," and of "artistic gratification," he will not deny that the ancient family of glass bottles offers certain satisfaction and gratification to any collector who has been caught in the web of fascination woven by the marvelous man-made substance, glass.

Many approaches to the rich field of glass bottles are open to the collector—as in all fields of collecting. He may be lured quite accidentally, perhaps snared by the eye appeal of a bottle's shape or color glimpsed through a shop window, by the historical significance of a Figured Flask, by the quaintness of a molded inscription. Any number of features may arrest his attention or arouse his curiosity. He may enter the field deliberately, his interest quickened by bottles in a friend's collection of glass, a museum display, or those seen while browsing in an antique shop. Once in, he may wander leisurely, gathering specimens without a method to his madness, or he may ride straight to a goal of specialization in one or more of the many species. But, generalized or specialized, the collection that results from his pursuit will depend upon his philosophy of collecting, which, if he be not indoctrinated by a seasoned collector, will evolve as he collects. If he is that rarity among bottle collectors, one activated mainly by a compulsion to collect, wedded to the zest of competition with rival collectors, his collection can be but a sterile physical possession of which he can boast. To others it may afford many "resources of entertainment" and deeper significance.

As physical objects, bottles have many tentacles of attraction drawing collectors to them: their great variety of free-blown and blown-molded forms; of decoration by a multitude of molded designs, by glass applied to itself and tooled into simple devices, by engraving and cutting; and a Lucullan feast of colors. The colors seem limitless in their hues, shades, tints, and tones, whether they are natural to glass, arising from its basic ingredients, or produced artificially by the addition of coloring agents to the batch. And the colors defy absolute descriptive terms, for so chameleonlike is glass that its color changes with the natural lights of day and with man-made lights. A bottle's color is also subtly influenced by that of its companions on a window shelf or in a cabinet. In bottles with molded decoration, the pattern, even simple ribbing, so planes the surface of the glass that lights and shades are created, enhancing the color charm and the brilliance of the glass much as cutting facets brings forth the brilliance latent in the rough diamond.

Although for some collectors the physical charms inherent in glass bottles suffice as the objective in collecting bottles, for the majority these are but one aspect of interest and achievement. Quite apart from the possible aesthetic qualities, each species can,

and usually does, exert the lure of variety, spiced by the uncertainty of when the end may be reached. Consequently, the aim of nearly every collector, whether he chooses to concentrate on one or on more than one species, becomes assembling as complete a representation as possible. Naturally, he is ambitious to heighten the importance of his collection by the known rarities in color and design. He may wait patiently for years, for the time when a collection containing such desirables will be broken up and he may be able to add coveted specimens to his own. Too, he cherishes a hope, infrequently fulfilled in these days, of discovering a hitherto unknown variant or an entirely new variety or color.

Although the hunt, the physical appeals, and the corralling of a species may remain the motivating stimuli, or may dominate in the early days of pursuing the hobby, other aspects eventually command the attention of the serious collector and arouse intellectual curiosity, the satisfying of which is as exciting as forming the collection itself. "The eye is not satisfied with seeing," nor the mind with the material possession and catalog of specimens. Almost inevitably, the question of how, when, where, and by whom his bottles were produced leads him to the literature on glass. If, as often happens, the information he seeks cannot be found in the writings of his predecessors or contemporaries, he may turn to research himself. Aroused interest in the techniques of fabrication and decoration by which his bottles were made and ornamented leads him to a study of these phases, a familiarity with the art and nature of glass, and hence to a deeper appreciation of his bottles. His curiosity may lead him to determining how, for what, and by whom his bottles were used, and hence into bypaths such as the historical role of glass containers, bottling and preserving, medicine, cosmetics, even advertising. For him the bottle becomes far more than a hollow glass vessel with long or short neck, narrow or wide mouth, a thing of beauty, or one in a long series of specimens: it becomes a social document in three dimensions, a tangible bit of Western culture and of an industry's development, evidence of how and with what our people lived. And so large, so heterogeneous, so universal has the family of glass vessels we call bottles become, that the possibilities for studying its background, for diversification or specialization in collecting, stretch toward infinity.

2
BOTTLE FAMILY NAMES

Quite some time ago, I realized that not only were the names of glass compositions and other glassmakers' cant terms a source of confusion, but also many of the names of bottles. Not being able to answer questions put to me about some of them by beginners in the field, I grew curious myself about the derivation and use of familiar and taken-for-granted names. As other students must also have wondered about them, included here are the results of my investigation and conclusions up to the present, beginning of course with "bottle" itself.

Apparently, like so many words entering the English language during the Middle Ages, *bottle* derived from a French word—*bouteille*—not necessarily a 1066 Norman invader but certainly integrated by Chaucer's time. Its spelling, like that of many English words, was unsettled for centuries—*botel*, *bottel*, and *bottell* preceding *bottle*. At first the new word was applied to the leather "bottles" so long used in the East and from one end of the Western world to the other.[3] Perhaps not until the 1300s did it embrace any vessel of glass. Be that as it may, by the 1500s *bottle* was being used synonymously with *flagon*: two lexicons (1573, 1580) gave "flagon or bottle"; one (1617), "bottles or flaggons of glass, vitreae ampulla."[4] Though lexicographers, always conservative, were slow to admit new words and meanings to their lexicons, it is surprising that, whereas bottle appeared in definitions of flask and vial before 1724, apparently not until then was it dignified by inclusion in its own right, and then it was defined simply as "a vessel to contain liquids." Starting in the mid-1700s, other features were given, such as "a narrow mouth," "a small vessel," "generally made of glass," "when made of glass a glass bottle." By then, *bottle* also signified "the quantity of liquor usually put in a bottle: a quart."[5] Today, the definitions are broad and detailed. For meaning 1, *Oxford* gives "a vessel with a narrow neck for holding liquids"; meaning 1, *Webster's*, ends with the observation: "Bottle is so loosely used that its limit of application is not well defined." For those of us who collect glass bottles, a generic definition could be: a vessel whose neck and mouth are considerably narrower than its body, used for packaging and containing liquid and dry preparations.

However defined, in the glass collector's lexicon, *bottle* is the class name of an ancient and prolific glass family with many species and subspecies of which several are known by names other than bottle. Among the latter are *vial* and *phial*, which actually preceded *bottle* in application to glass vessels. These might be called surnames. Later, other surnames, such as *decanter*, *flask*, and *demijohn*, were engendered by particular forms, sizes, and uses. As packaging in glass bottles increased, the contents led to many particularizing names, "first" names, such as *wine*, *snuff*, and *mustard*.

Presumably the vial or phial was the first of the bottle family; it probably was blown in England in the Middle Ages before Chaucer's time.[6] The English words seemingly derived from the old French *phiole* and *fiole*.[7] *Phial* appears to have been consistent in spelling, but *vial* has had many variations—*viole*, *violi* (defined as "a little Bottell or flagon"), *voyall*, *violl*, *viol*, *fiol*, and *vial*. Ben Jonson's *Volpone*, disguised as a mountebank, offered his nostrum at six crowns an "ampulla or viol," so evidently in the 1600s the Latin name was still a familiar one for containers of medicines. Occasionally in the 1500s and 1600s, probably earlier, large bottles were called *violles*. And a cruet or cruce "viz . . . Glass bottle with a round foot, handle, couer . . . a crooked slender pipe on the side" was called *viall*. *Viall* and *viol* persisted into the 1700s. In 1744, for instance, Benjamin Wheat, a druggist in Norwich, Connecticut, used both *viol* and *phial*: "viol of drops at 8s" and "oyl of amber phial and cork at 2s."[8] *Phial* also was applied to large and small vessels used by alchemists and in chemical and scientific laboratories.[9]

Not until the 1700s was *vial* or *phial* reserved primarily for small bottles. By then most lexicographers, as did N. Bailey in 1724, stated each was "a small glass bottle." Early 19th-century definitions of *vial* include their particular use by apothecaries and druggists for liquid medicines and, for *phial*, "a small bottle of cylindrical form."[10] In newspaper advertisements—from the mid-1700s on—*vials* and *phials*, white and green, narrow and wide-mouth, empty or filled (usually with some medical preparation), were offered for sale to Americans. Apparently the two names were interchangeable, a matter of personal habit or speech or preference. Whatever called, excepting the occasional 16th- and 17th-century applications mentioned above and the infrequent 18th-century use of *vial* for bottles for condiments such as mustard flour,[11] the vessel was a small or moderate-sized plain container mainly for medicinal and toilet preparations.

Flasks are another large species of the bottle family. *Flask*, as a word, has been given diverse meanings; as a name, assigned to a wide variety of bottle forms. Two main derivations have been given for *flask*, spelled also *flasque* and *flaske* at times: (1) Old-English *flasce* or *flaxe*, for a vessel for carrying liquids; (2) French *flasque*, a powder flask.[12] Definitions have varied also. In the early 1600s *flaske* was defined as "a flaggon, a soldier's flaske"—a vessel for powder is still one of the meanings of flask. Apparently not until late in the century did a definition include a glass vessel, and then one of *flasque* ended with "Also a Bottle of Florence Wine, containing 2 Quarts our Measure." In many 18th-century lexicons the glass bottle took precedence over the soldier's powder flask, usually as "a sort of bottle wrought over with wicker."[13] Thus it would seem that, however it was spelled, its first application to glass bottles may have been in the 1600s—and to the wickered Italian bottles for wines of Florence. While Johnson, in 1755, limited his definition "1" to an incontrovertible "A Bottle, a vessel," for many of his successors a glass flask continued to be the covered wine bottle, "a thin bottle with a long narrow neck, generally covered with wicker or withes." Such bottles, especially when used for oils, were also called *bettées* or *betties*.[14] The association with bottles for Florence wines and also oils has not been found in present-day American dictionaries but has been in the *Oxford*. It may be that this was the type of "half gallon flasks" for which, about 1752, Matthew Earnest and his New York partners agreed to pay Johan Martin Greiner, a glassman from Saxe Weimar, "3 gilders Hollands mony" for every one hundred he produced.[15]

The bottle form for which the name *flask* is reserved here is one whose cross section is elliptical or ovate, whose convex or flat sides rise to a shoulder or taper directly into a narrow short neck, and whose capacity is rarely over a quart and usually not over a pint. This type may not have been introduced until the 1600s, and then presumably it was called a *pocket bottle*. W. A. Thorpe believes that the "fflint pocket bottle 0.1.0" for which the Earl of Bedford was billed April 26, 1690, "probably was similar to the flat pear-shaped pocket-bottles with diamond-nipped, trailed or other decoration" of which 1 and 3 in Ill. 121 are later types. Certainly, being flint glass, the Earl's bottle must have been a luxury item at that time. And it was the only pocket bottle Mr. Thorpe

found in thirty bills dating from March 1651/2 to March 16, 1691/2, which suggests that pocket bottles were not yet in common usage. In fact, having one's own pocket glass container for liquor, or a less ardent potable, seems not to have become a fashion until well into the 18th century. In 1751 Tobias Smollett wrote of "a sportsman" taking a small flask out of his pocket and applying "it to his mouth." At that time *flask* was not the usual name; into the early 1800s, *pocket bottle* continued to be the common term for flasks from a dram to a pint in capacity, though *dram bottle* ran a close second for a while. This latter term presumably arose from the fact that a dram meant both a unit of measure and a small drink. An occasional name was *hunting bottle*, obviously stemming from the sportsman's habit of carrying a flask when on foot or riding to the hounds. There was at least one whimsical name: on June 29, 1763, the Reverend James Woodforde paid one shilling for "a Pocket Pistol, alias a dram bottle, to carry in one's pocket, it being necessary on a Journey."[16]

In my researches, none of these names appeared in *American* sources before the mid-1700s, though it would not surprise me to find them earlier in a further search. In 1745, "Gentlemen's hunting bottles" were advertised in Boston, and hunting bottles appeared sporadically into the early 1800s; in 1750, "green and white pocket bottles." Thenceforth through 1825 *pocket bottle* occurred in advertisements and price lists of importers and American bottle manufacturers. *Dram-bottle* appeared from 1758 through 1805—"suitable to carry the comfort of life into the fields," in the opinion of a Hartford merchant in 1790. The first mention of *flask* was in 1775: "pint and half pint green glass flasks"; the second, in 1799, ". . . country made bottles and flasks."[17] Between 1800 and 1825, *pocket flask* occurred occasionally, *flask* nearly as often as *pocket bottle*. Thereafter *flask* was the common name. Of course, one must be mindful that future research may shift these names, any bottle names, backward and forward in time. In any event, the type of bottle called *flask* today was for *carrying* potables as well as *containing* them.

Besides *pocket bottle*, a few other new and differentiating names for bottles appeared in the 1600s: *wine-bottle*, *sucking-glass* or *-bottle*, *water-bottle*, and *decanter*. Perhaps *wine-bottle* initiated the practice of giving first names to bottles that custom or bottle producers intended primarily for special purposes or contents. The name was given to an entirely new type of bottle created in England—a free-blown thick-walled bottle competing in strength with the popular stoneware and stronger than the also popular delft bottles for serving wine in home and tavern. Mr. Thorpe says *wine-bottle* was the right name chosen about 1630 by two men in Mansell & Company, by whom the bottles were first made; Ivor Noel Hume places the date about 1650. *Water-bottles* were mentioned in 1686 in the Glass Seller's Bills at Woburn Abbey, and *sucking-glasses*, which Mr. Thorpe concluded from the price were green-glass sucking bottles, in 1672.[18] The latter name was familiar by 1684, if not before, for Dryden uses it in the Prologue to "The Disappointment of the Mother of Fashion":

Betwixt them both for milk and sugar candy,
Your sucking-bottles were well stor'd with brandy.

Seemingly *sucking-bottle* was not supplanted by *nursing-bottle* until sometime in the 19th century.[19]

Decanter was a new surname given to bottles for table service. After anglicizing the French verb *decanter* (to decant), the English quite logically restored the *er* to *decant* to name vessels from which the decanted wine, spirits, and other potables were served. The new word was defined in 1708 as "a bottle of clear flint glass for holding the wine etc. to be pour'd off into a Drinking Glass."[20] However, it would appear that decades passed before *decanter* was taken into the vernacular as a name for colorless flint-glass serving vessels, though it probably was first given to them shortly after the rise, about 1685, of the custom of serving wine from "lead crystal" bottles, rather than from the black glass wine bottles, at fashionable English tables. Though the name and the type of glass were 17th-century inventions, colorless or nearly colorless bottles for serving wine were not an innovation—as is evident from even a brief survey of banquets and simple meals depicted by painters and illuminators of manuscripts from the 13th century on. And, it is interesting to note, decanters as well as ordinary bottles were appurtenances of some American taverns and inns in the late 18th and early 19th centuries. Merchants advertised them for taverns and called attention of tavern keepers to new shipments of even cut-glass decanters.[21] John Lewis Krimmel's *Interior of an American Inn* (Toledo Museum of Art), painted in 1813, shows colorless taper-shaped decanters behind the bar and one on a table. However, though decanters—and water bottles (carafes) too—belong to the bottle family, they fall into the collector's category of table glass, and as such do not come within the purview of this book.

But to return to names of bottles that do: Some-

time about the middle of the 18th century, two new names entered the language to designate large glass bottles, usually wickered and used for transport of liquids. They were *demijohn* and *carboy*, which were used sporadically by merchants and bottle manufacturers before the 19th century. *Carboy* was used far less often than *demijohn*, at least in advertisements. Also, it would seem, neither was admitted to a dictionary until well into the 19th century. According to accepted derivation, *carboy* was a corruption of the Persian *garabah*; *demijohn*, of the old French *dame jeanne*, as large bottles were called.[22] Though the spelling of *carboy* apparently was consistent, that of *demijohn*, perhaps because it was spelled mainly from its sound when spoken, was most unsettled before 1815; *demi-john, demi jeanne, Dame John, dime-john, Demie-John, Demi John, Demy John, dimijohn,* and *demijohn*.[23] *Demijohn*, which became official, occurred most frequently. In the newspaper advertisements covered, the name was not found until 1762, but in 1753 "wickered bottles that will hold 5 gallon" were advertised—demijohns, of course—which suggests that *demijohn*, however spelled, was unfamiliar before the 1760s. In fact, *The Oxford English Dictionary* (1933) gives 1769 as the date of its first appearance in print, and for *carboy*, 1753, fourteen years before it was found in the advertisements. In 1767, carboys ranging from a quart to seven gallons in size were offered to the public, and in 1792 demijohns of eight and nine gallons containing spirits of turpentine.[24] The two names, it would seem, were used interchangeably in the 18th century, and for the same sizes of bottle. Afterward, the majority of demijohns were bottles from a quart to five gallons in capacity, a few up to ten gallons; carboys were principally a gallon to twenty gallons, with sizes from six gallons predominating. And demijohns, wickered, were destined to contain noncorrosive and bland liquids, whereas carboys, set in very heavy wicker "tubs," were for acids and chemicals. Although these were the only new surnames found in 18th-century sources, from the midcentury on many first names were given to bottles.

In the main, the first names bottle manufacturers and merchants gave to various types of bottles were indicative of the intended contents and uses. The practice stemmed naturally from the expanding use of glass bottles in packaging a great variety of liquids and dry preparations. Also, it reflects the developing commercial production of many commodities, merchandising, and, of course, growth in the bottle industry. The names of this sort occurred mainly in the newspaper advertisements covered, but some, if not all, had been coined before they appeared in this medium of print. For instance, *snuff bottle* was entered in a merchant's Day Book in 1752, eight years before the first advertisement I found of snuff bottles for sale, though snuff *in* bottles was advertised as early as 1731. The 18th-century names, listed in the order of their appearance between 1750 and 1800, were Hungary (water), snuff, smelling, case, essence, champagne, lavender, beer, spice, ink, claret, porter, olive, caper, and anchovies; the early 19th-century names, between 1800 and 1830, were seltzer, blacking, cayenne, oil, gin (a tapered square or case bottle), cologne, mineral water, varnish (japan blacking), castor oil, soda, and mead.[25] Most of these names continued in use, and new ones appeared later. In few instances were there clues to type or form of the bottles so named. Presumably prospective buyers were well acquainted with the bottle, and so there was no need for advertisers to be more specific. However, since there were more names than general forms, more than one name must have been given to a particular type of bottle, and in some cases differences in size and proportion of the basic types doubtless determined specific uses.

Perhaps *junk bottle*, an 18th-century name, has puzzled collectors and students more than any other and has caused the most conjecture. *Junk* in itself gives no hint as to the usual contents or function, and these cannot be interpreted from the dictionary definitions of the word. The earliest reference I have that, by any stretch of the imagination, possibly may be to a bottle called *junk* was in Madam Knight's journal of her journey from Boston to New York in 1704: ". . . John sat down in the corner, fumbled out his black Junk, and saluted that instead of Debb. . . ." The earliest known reference to *junk bottles* was in William Henry Stiegel's 1769/70 account book of his Manheim (Pennsylvania) glassworks. Though without clue to form or function, this entry led to the generally accepted opinion, still current, that *junk bottle* may have been the name of the 18th- and early 19th-century common free-blown globular and chestnut bottles, often carelessly fashioned and, in capacity, ungoverned by a strict standard of liquid measure. In the newspaper advertisements culled, *junk bottles* appeared first in 1786. The adjective *black* was added in 1817; "Patent Moulded Bristol . . . Stamped Bottoms," in 1823 (produced in the Phoenix Glass Works of H. Ricketts & Co., Bristol, England, under Henry Ricketts's 1821 patent); and quart and pint, first and second quality, from the New-England Glass-Bottle Company, in 1830.[26] Today *Webster's* states that a *junk bottle* is "a stout

bottle of thick dark glass." These references seem to dispel the chestnut-bottle theory, at least in regard to 19th-century junk bottles.

Also, I have been fortunate in finding evidence of their use. In his 1790 appeal to the Connecticut Assembly for aid in establishing his New Haven Glass Works, Mark Leavenworth said the works was planned "principally for making bottles, particularly the Junk Bottle for the purpose of shipping cyder to the West Indies and Southern States." In Hartford, Connecticut, in 1820, black junk bottles were advertised as "suitable for spring water and cider." In his 1848 *Dictionary of Americanisms* Bartlett included *junk-bottle*, defining it as "the ordinary black glass porter bottle." From all these, it seems logical to conclude that by the end of the 18th century *junk bottle* was a trade name for black- and green-glass bottles of quart and pint sizes, used primarily for beers, porter, cider, and spring water. They must have been used also for other popular potables such as mead and metheglin when these were bottled commercially. And, of course, that they were used, at least occasionally, for whatever contents they were judged suitable is evident from the advertisements found of cayenne, Anis cordials, rosewater, and macassar oil "in junk bottles."[27]

Jar and *jug* are included here also because some jars are, in fact, wide-mouth bottles, and jugs are essentially bottles and flasks with handles. It was probably about the beginning of the 19th century that these familiar names for certain pottery and stoneware vessels were extended to similar forms in glass containers. *Jug*, like *flask*, has had a varied career as a name for a vessel. "A great pot to drink in" was the earliest definition found—1573. And *jug* was identified as a drinking vessel, not as a container or serving vessel, in most lexicons before Noah Webster's of 1828. Webster gave Swift as authority for "a vessel usually earthen, with a swelling body and narrow mouth, used for holding and carrying liquor," a description which, with addition of "handled," fits the concept of a glass jug. However, two 18th-century lexicographers did define *jug* as "an earthen Pot or Pitcher to hold Drink." In England *jug* is still applied to pitchers, but its use in this sense seems to have been only occasional in America. Just when handled glass bottles were called jugs by American manufacturers and the public is uncertain. There was no mention of a glass jug in the hundreds of 18th- and early 19th-century advertisements read, nor in the few available price lists and catalogs of glass manufacturers before the 1860s. In 1862 the Whitney

Brothers of Glassboro, New Jersey, listed "jugs with handles."[28] Whatever called, they were made in American glasshouses long before 1862.

Jar is the familiar name for some of the wide-mouth bottles and vessels with very wide short neck, or nearly no neck at all, and very wide mouth—forms reaching back to Roman glassmaking after the advent of the blowpipe. They were not intended as containers of potables or other liquids, but for such things as preserves, pickles, honey, condiments, and powdered preparations. In the 17th century it would appear they were usually called simply *glasses*. For instance, W. A. Thorpe concluded that the "mar-melet glasses" purchased for Woburn Abbey in 1678 and 1691 probably were green-glass jam jars of cylindrical or square shape. It is uncertain when *jar* was first applied to glass containers as well as to pottery and stoneware. In the many sources consulted, references to jars that *possibly* were glass occurred infrequently before the 19th century. Hunter found "Blue Flower Jars" listed in Stiegel's 1769–April 1, 1770, account books for his second Manheim glasshouse, and his conclusion that these were vases—not a housewife's container for some sort of flour (often spelled *flower*)—is still generally accepted. In my records the next unmistakable use of *jar* for a glass vessel was in a May 20, 1777, announcement in the *Pennsylvania Evening Post* of the public sale of "all the Glass Ware belonging to the Philadelphia Glass Works." Inasmuch as green as

well as flint glass was made there, the jars probably were green-glass containers. Not again until 1800 did *jar*, undoubtedly of glass, occur in the records and advertisements. In that year the Pittsburgh Glass Works advertised its "pickling jars," certainly of green glass. But since their form was not mentioned, it is impossible to say whether they were wide-mouth bottles or jars having a very wide neck and very wide mouth. Into the mid-19th century at least, *bottle* and *jar* were often used interchangeably for some wide-mouth bottles—for example, those for snuff and pickles. Also, in the early 19th century, *jar* acquired first names of its own, such as *pickling, preserve, fruit*, and *jelly*.[29]

The reader will note that I have frequently used *container*, the term adopted by the Glass Container Manufacturers Institute, Inc., and its members, producers of commercial bottles and jars for packaging all sorts of products today. It is a convenient all-embracing term. But, of course, names in themselves—no matter how they came about—are merely conventions, significant for the collector only when identified with particular types and forms. However, before that problem and the various types of bottles are discussed, it seems fitting to turn our attention to the compositions of the glass commonly used for bottles, to how bottles were blown, and to the framework within which they evolved—the ancestry of bottles made and used in America and the development of our bottle industry.

3
COLORS AND COMPOSITIONS OF GLASS

Almost invariably, the first questions prompted by the curiosity of the serious collector of bottles or of any glass objects pertain to the nature of glass itself and its colors. These are usually followed by questions as to the kinds of glass from which the objects of his collecting were made. To many of us, glass itself seems almost an alchemist's magical transmutation of base materials, through subjection to fire's intense heat, into a precious one. The only absolutely essential ingredients for this wonderful man-made substance are silica and alkali. The silica usually is sand, but other forms can be and have been used, such as flint (impure quartz) and pebbles. The alkalis are such substances as soda, lime, and potash or pearl ash (refined potash). And, at one time or

another in many places, ashes of bracken (fern) and of many other vegetables were a commonly used alkali. One or more other ingredients, as will be seen, are usually called for in most recipes. The ingredients mixed together in the designated proportions are called the *batch*. This, when gradually melted at a very high temperature to a vitreous molten state, is called the *metal*, which in its plastic and ductile stage is fashioned into objects and, when cold, becomes solid. The term *metal* is also applied to glass in its final solid state, as when the glass is said to be of good or bad metal.

As the glassmakers' names for the basic kinds of glass or metal are often confusing, especially to the neophyte, it may be helpful to explain them briefly before considering the glasses used for bottles. The principal names or terms used throughout the discussion of bottles and their history are *green, white, flint, lead*, and *black*.

1. *Green glass* refers to a composition of glass, *not* a color. Although in glassmakers' parlance this term does not mean a color, its application to compositions and their recipes doubtless derived from the fact that so many greens and greenish colors resulted from the ingredients of early recipes, when the glassman took no hand in what came naturally.

2. *White glass* means a composition, not a "color," as one thinks of white, but rather a lack of color or colorlessness. It may also be a decolorized green glass.

3. *Flint glass* originally meant only that glass in which the silica was in the form of calcined flint. In the late 17th century the term was given to lead glass also, and later to other types of glass containing neither flint nor lead—for instance, the lime glass perfected in 1864 by William L. Leighton of Hobbs, Brockunier & Company, Wheeling, West Virginia. It always implies fine quality.

4. *Lead glass* or glass of lead means glass containing oxide of lead; it was usually called *flint glass*.

5. *Black glass* is a species of green glass so dense in natural color as to appear black, especially in reflected light.

This last brings us to the terms *natural* and *artificial* as applied to colors, which—although they would seem self-explanatory—are often perplexing to those unfamiliar with the cant of glassmaking and collecting. Natural colors are those that result naturally from the nature of the ingredients in the batch. Artificial colors are those intentionally produced by the addition of various substances, mainly metallic oxides, in metal purged of its natural colors.

Probably bottles of one sort or another have been fashioned from all the kinds of glass devised by glassmen; they display nearly every possible color, natural or man-made. Certainly the recipes for the glass used for bottles varied so much in the proportions of even the basic silica and alkali, as well as in special ingredients, that they would run into the hundreds and perhaps, if assembled between two covers, would form as thick a tome as Fanny Farmer's cookbook. Possibly chief among them would be those for *green glass* from which ordinary containers of all kinds were made. And among the green-glass recipes would be several producing that particular green glass called *black*, so desirable for wine and

beverage bottles—in fact, bottles for any liquid needing protection from light. There would also be recipes for white glass, which—in the bottle family until about 1870—was used mainly for apothecary vials, druggists' and chemists' bottles, often for smelling bottles, sometimes for pocket bottles. Lead glass, the aristocrat of glasses (usually called *flint*), would also be represented—not that it would be the metal of common bottles—but it was sometimes used for the best apothecary vials, smelling bottles, and the finest of the pocket bottles. Even some of the Figured Flasks in the Masonic and Sunburst Groups were blown from lead glass in the early 19th century.

There would be recipes for coloring glass with ingredients producing artificial colors and recipes with ingredients for decolorizing, producing a colorless metal, which also might be called artificial. In the 18th and early 19th centuries, the bottle family members fashioned from artificially colored metal, principally blues, amethysts, and rich greens, were mainly the so-called pocket bottles and smelling bottles—that is, the members to be discussed later. Prior to the 1840s, intentionally colored and colorless metals were used occasionally for some of the Figured Flasks, particularly in the Masonic and Historical Groups. However, it apparently was not until late in the decade that the use of artificially colored metal ceased to be *unusual*, though it never predominated. By the next decade a narrow range, mainly blues and greens, was popular for soda and mineral-water bottles and some other commercial containers. By the 1870s, it is said, colorless or near colorless containers were increasingly favored for packaging many products, both liquid and dry.

Green glass, probably the oldest term for ordinary glass used for bottles of all kinds, was often also called *bottle glass*, and recipes appear under each name in publications and manuscripts. Although some of our glassmakers doubtless owned books containing recipes, perhaps more had their own notebooks in which they recorded recipes from books along with those handed down from one glassman to another or used in the houses where they had worked. In some of our earliest houses, probably only sand and ashes—basic essentials—were the ingredients of the metal. Benjamin Franklin, replying in 1746/47 to questions of Thomas Darling of New Haven, Connecticut, about glassmaking and the glassworks in South Jersey (Wistarburgh), wrote: "The ingredients of common Window and Bottle Glass are only Sand and Ashes."[30] Robert Dossie wrote in the mid-18th century: "It [bottle glass] is formed of sand of any kind, fluxed by ashes of burnt wood or any part of vegetables."[31] The vegetables used included such plants as bracken and saltwort. However, other ingredients, called for in most recipes evolving over the years, were added for various purposes, such as strengthening the metal, speeding the melting, or enabling melting to occur at lower temperatures. Normally the green-glass ingredients themselves produced the colors natural to them—a variety of olive-greens, greens, olive-ambers, and ambers. The tone, shade, or tint of color was occasioned by the quantity of so-called impurities in the materials and the chemical nature of the materials. But since the use of green glass was not confined to ordinary bottles and containers, a decolorizing agent that weakened or eliminated the natural color was added to the batch when the metal was to be made into window glass, vials, and other vessels. Cullet (that is, broken glass) was not mentioned in all early recipes for green glass, though for any kind of glass it was a normal addition to the batch as a valuable aid to more perfect vitrification and to producing a quality metal. Of the bottles illustrated, most of those in the widely varied hues, tints, and shades of amber and of green from aquamarine to black would be classified as green glass. How many different compositions were used for their metals it is impossible to say; only by chemical analysis could that be determined.

Following here are a few of the many recipes for green glass:

Composition of green or bottle glass. Take of wood-ashes two hundred pounds, and of sand one hundred pounds. Mix them thoroughly well by grinding together.

This is of due proportion where the sand is good and the wood-ashes are used without other addition; but there are instances of sand of so kindly a nature for vitrification that a greater proportion of it may be added.

This recipe and the next two were given by Dossie, so presumably were favored in the mid-18th century, and probably earlier.

No. 1. Composition of green or bottle glass with the addition of scoria or clinkers. Take of wood-ashes one hundred and seventy pounds, of sand one hundred pounds, and of scoria or clinkers fifty pounds. Mix the whole well by grinding them together.

The clinkers should be well ground before they are used if they admit of it; but frequently they are too

hard and in that case they should be broken into small bits as can be done conveniently, and mixt with the other matter without grinding.

No. 2. Cheapest composition of the green or common phial glass. Take of the cheapest kind of white sand one hundred and twenty pounds, of pearl ashes twenty pounds, of common salt fifteen pounds, of arsenic [decolorizer] one pound.

This will be green but tolerably transparent, and will work with a moderate fire, and vitrify quickly with a strong one.

No. 3. Composition of Common Green or Window Glass. Sixty pounds of white Sand, unpurified Pearl Ashes thirty pounds, Common Salt ten pounds, Arsenic two pounds and Magnesia two ounces [the last two, decolorizers]. This is a cheap composition and will not appear much green or be very deficient in transparency.

The preceding recipe was recorded about 1815 in the notebook of an anonymous American glassman. The one following appeared in a midwestern book on art and sciences published in 1824:

No. 40. Green without Pot or Pearl Ashes. 15 bu. sand, 25 of wood ashes, 8 of salt, 12 of broken glass.

Morris Holmes, who started working as a carrying boy in the Saratoga Mountain glassworks in 1856 and became a full-fledged blower in 1867, gave me this recipe many years ago: "Light green [color] green glass—about 12 measures of sand, 5 of soda, 3 of lime and 10 of sandstone." According to Mr. Holmes, the sandstone, burned and powdered, was substituted for ashes containing some lime, which acts as a stabilizer, in a usual composition for aquamarine bottle glass made at the Saratoga works in his time. It was the ingredient determining that the color would be light green, or aquamarine, instead of dark green.[32]

Perhaps the most important of the green glasses was the black, which, as has been pointed out, was of so deep a color as to appear black in reflected light and even in direct light when the walls of bottles were very thick. The dense color was a protective one for contents such as wines and other potables affected by light. It would seem, too, that it was a metal tougher than most, a quality that, of course, meant effective resistance to the pressure of effervescing or fermenting contents and increased safety in shipping. Naturally such a metal was considered a vital contribution to the development of the bottle industry, and black-glass bottles were considered superior to others for wines, porter, ales, beers, and cider. It would appear that the first of the tough, deeply colored metals was that invented in England sometime between 1630 and 1650 and introduced for the new English wine bottles, such as 1, 2, and 3 in Ill. 44. Though it is doubtful that the new metal was dubbed *black glass*, it is so called today. In fact, it seems likely the term may have been adopted in the mid-1700s, and then as a status term for the bottles rather than the composition of their metal. At least I have not found it before the 1740s, when "black-glass bottles" were being advertised in American newspapers.[33]

Nevertheless, although no recipes in the various 17th- and 18th-century treatises and books I have read were designated for *black glass*, many of the green-glass recipes must have produced a black glass. The proportions of the ingredients in the first two of Dossie's green- or bottle-glass recipes given above would indicate they made a metal that would be dense in color. And the scoria or clinkers in the one presumably would contribute to toughness as well as density of color. According to Morris Holmes, the usual recipe for the Saratoga Mountain dark olive-green glass called for about 12 measures of sand, 5 of soda, 3 of lime, and 10 of ashes, and the ashes gave the color—"the more ashes the darker the color."[34] Thus it appears that the proportion of ashes to other ingredients could be a prime factor in causing the dark, dense olive-amber and olive-green called black. Many of the spring-water bottles and individual free-blown pieces from the Mountain works·testify to ashes often having been used in sufficient quantity to make a very black glass.

In two sources only have I found recipes specifically for black glass. One was for "Black Bottles at the Mount Vernon Glass Factory," which operated from 1810 to 1844 at Vernon, New York. This recipe, recorded about 1815 by the previously mentioned anonymous glassman, called for "six and one-half bushels of sand, nine bushels of ashes, three bushels of salt, and one-half bushel of Black Salts." The amount was for six small pots.[35] The other source was the patent for "Improvement in the Manufacture of Black Bottle-Glass" granted to John F. McCully, Gonzales County, Texas. Mr. McCully states:

The ordinary ingredients for the manufacture of black glass are sand, (for the silica,) common salt, and slaked lime. The quantity of each of the ingredients to be used varies with the quality of the articles themselves and the kind of furnace, and the exact proportion is regulated better by practice than by theory.

"Lime in excess" was "necessary in the ordinary .

mixes to produce the color." His mix consisted of "sand, one hundred parts; soda-ash, fourty-one and one-half to twenty-eight parts; common salt, seven and one-half to twelve parts, and clay-slate, thirty to thirty-eight parts." The first proportions he had found most useful for a large furnace; the second, better suited for a small furnace. It was the clay-slate, found in the neighborhood of Pittsburgh and various other places, that caused the black color and was most desirable because it both furnished "the coloring matter" and formed "one of the bases of the glass itself." It contained silicate, oxide of iron, alumina, carbonate of lime, phosphate of lime, peroxide manganese, and oxide of manganese.[36]

White glass, as I have mentioned already, means colorless or near colorless glass, which is often called *clear*. (Until around 1953 I always used clear in this sense. Then, realizing it was often as misleading as *white*, I adopted *colorless*.) When added in the proper proportions, arsenic and magnesia or manganese, singly or in combination, were the usual decolorizers. Oxide of manganese so used came to be called the glassmaker's soap, doubtless because, as Merret said in his 1662 translation of Neri's *The Art of Glass*, "Manganese consumes the natural greenness of glass."[37] Under white glass, Dossie, whose treatise came out in 1764, included flint glass (lead glass) and "German Chrystal" that were used mainly for fine table and ornamental wares. But generally, in England and America, the term meant colorless nonlead glass used for inexpensive common wares.

Probably most white glass could be described as "a kind betwixt the flint glass and the common bottle or green glass," as Dossie said of a white glass of which "phials for the use of apothecaries, ink-bottles and many other vessels are made." "For the best phial glass" his recipe was as follows: "No. 3 Composition of Common Green or Window Glass": "Take of white sand one hundred and twenty pounds, of unpurified pearl-ashes fifty pounds, of common salt ten pounds, of arsenic five pounds and of magnesia five ounces." This phial glass, for which a moderate heat could be used, took some time to clear but could be brought "very near to the crystal glass."[38] It will be noted that, though differing in quantities and comment, the ingredients and also the number of this recipe are the same as the No. 3 quoted earlier, indicating the unknown glassman's direct or indirect familiarity with Dossie. The colorless or nearly colorless medicine bottles shown in Ills. 77 and 78 doubtless would have been advertised as "white glass." The bottles in the medicine chest,

Ill. 79, may be either the best white glass or lead glass. They have not been tested for lead content. Nor have the other illustrated flasks, nor the smelling and cologne bottles blown from colorless or near colorless metal, with the exception of the "F. Stenger" flask, Ill. 51, and the three blown three-mold flasks, Ill. 121. The former is nonlead glass; the latter are lead glass. Probably the two English flasks 4 and 6 in Ill. 121, the cut-glass decanter-flask 16 in Ill. 121, and the cut-glass decanter-flask 6 in Ill. 100 are lead glass; possibly a few of the smelling bottles are also. All the other colorless bottles, it seems safe to say, are white glass.

In the last quarter of the 17th century, after the Englishman George Ravenscroft perfected the use of lead as a flux, the glass par excellence became glass of lead, which was tougher yet softer than other glasses, firmer and with higher refractive quality— and it has never lost its standing. Previously, true flint glass ranked highest in quality, and doubtless because of this quality status its name, *flint glass*, was given to lead glass by the glassmakers and dealers in fine glasswares, English and American. Again, there were a great many recipes. Dossie alone gives four apparently favored in the 18th century. One, the "Composition of the most perfect kind of flint glass," called for 120 pounds of white sand, 50 pounds of red lead, 40 pounds of the best pearl ashes, 20 pounds of nitre, and 5 ounces of magnesia. All four recipes required the same amount of white sand, but the second, a composition producing a glass harder in texture than No. 1 and "with less of the refractive play of light," called for 54 pounds of the best pearl ashes, 36 of red lead, 12 of nitre, and 6 ounces of magnesia. The third, a "cheaper composition of flint glass with arsenic," called for 35 pounds of the best pearl ashes, 40 of red lead, 13 of nitre, 6 of arsenic, and 4 ounces of magnesia. In the fourth, a still cheaper composition, 15 pounds of common salt were substituted for the arsenic in the third.[39] Though, of course, lead glass was not used to make *ordinary* bottles, in glassworks producing lead-glass tablewares it might be used for the best apothecary vials and for bottles to outfit fine medicine chests, as well as for the most elegant smelling bottles and pocket flasks. Of the American bottles in categories covered in this book, those blown from lead glass were products of works specializing in fine flint tablewares, or attempting to do so. As mentioned above, the blown-three-mold flasks in Ill. 121 are the only illustrated bottles that have been proven by spot test to be lead glass.

Last, it should be noted that the name *flint glass* has never ceased to be a status symbol for the makers and users of glass. After William Leighton of Hobbs, Brockunier & Company, Wheeling, West Virginia, perfected a new lime glass in 1864, it too was called flint glass.[40] Today, in the container industry, the manufacturers of bottles and other containers use the term *flint glass* for their colorless glass—as white glass was used in the 18th and 19th centuries. However, in the 1948 "Glass Glossary" of the American Ceramic Society, the first definition of flint glass is "a lead containing glass," and "a term used by container industry for colorless glass" comes second.

Although colorless glasses were, and are, the most functional in affording an immediate view of a vessel's contents and their level, the artificially colored glasses have always had an irresistible fascination for most collectors. And the means and process of coloring glass have an equal fascination for most students of glass. Of coloring glass, Dossie wrote, "The substances employed for tinging glass are for the most part metallic and other fossile bodies. . . ."[41] Incidentally, the principal reason I have chosen to quote Dossie so often rather than any earlier writers is because his treatise on glass in his *The Handmaid to the Arts*, 1764, probably was available in the colonies and young United States and copies may have accompanied British glassmen emigrating to this country. Many of Dossie's recipes seem to have been copied by later writers, and sometimes practical glassmen transcribed them into their notebooks. The following short list of colors and the substances producing them was taken from the previously quoted notebook of the anonymous glassman, who apparently either took his list of colors direct from Dossie's treatise or obtained them from someone who had used Dossie:

Opaque whiteness: calcined tin (commonly called putty), calcined antimony, arsenic, calcined horns or bones and sometimes common salt.

Red: Gold, iron, copper, magnesia or antimony.

Blue: Zaffer [impure oxide of cobalt] and copper.

Yellow: Silver, iron, antimony and magnesia with tartar.

Greens: Copper, Bohemian granite and those that will produce yellow and blue.

Purple: Such as will produce red and blue.

Orange: Antimony, and all those which will produce red and yellow.

Black: Zaffer, magnesia, copper and iron in various combinations.

The coloring agents were used in combinations as well as singly to produce innumerable colors, of which the hues, tints, and shades varied according to the amounts used in a batch and the composition of the metal. Among those given by the English glass manufacturer Apsley Pellatt were 2 pounds of oxide of cobalt for blue transparent glass, about 6 pounds of copper for azure blue, 12 pounds of copper scales or 12 pounds of iron ore for emerald green, 20 pounds of oxide of manganese for amethyst or purple.[42] The last, it will be recalled, when used in limited amounts, purged metal of its natural colors. Probably the much-sought-after amethystine Figured Flasks were blown from glass intended to be color-less but in which a bit too much manganese had been used. Stiegel-type artificially colored bottles of the 18th century are shown in Color Plate 2 and by 1, 2, and 3 in Ill. 90. Possibly the unique sapphire-blue diamond-daisy in the Color Plate was colored by cobalt from the deposit in Pennsylvania not far from Manheim, where Stiegel built two of his glasshouses. Many of the smelling bottles in Ills. 101 through 106 and the cologne bottles in Ills. 111, 113, and 114 were blown from artificially colored glass. They, however, fall in the fancy goods category; for the vast majority of common containers, naturally colored glass was good enough.

4

NOTES ON THE FABRICATION OF FREE-BLOWN AND BLOWN-MOLDED BOTTLES AND FLASKS.

After the batch (mixed ingredients called for in a glass formula) had vitrified, "melted," the stopped-up working space in the furnace wall before each pot was opened, to give access to the pot of molten glass (metal). Until the last quarter of the 17th century, all glass compositions were melted in open-top pots, usually of inverted-cone shape. After Ravenscroft's development of English lead glass, ca. 1675, and the discovery that smoke from burning coal had a deleterious effect upon lead metal, the hooded straight-sided pot with shielded opening at one side near the top was evolved to protect the melting batch and molten lead glass from the fumes.[43] Use of open-top pots continued for green-glass bottle production and, where wood was the fuel, possibly for lead glass also. Doubtless both hooded and open-top pots were used in those United States glassworks producing lead-glass and green-glass wares in coal-burning furnaces—for instance, the Pittsburgh Flint Glass Works of the Bakewells, Pittsburgh, and Dr. Dyott's vial and bottle factories, Dyottville, Kensington, and Philadelphia, Pennsylvania.

(1.) The first step in blowing a bottle, or any article, was gathering the requisite amount of metal on the blowpipe—an iron tube of small bore, wider and thicker at the gathering end than at the blowing end. The blowpipe, passed through the working arch and inserted into the pot of red-hot metal, was twisted to secure a gather on the end. As the Englishman Christopher Merret wrote in 1662, ". . . the metal sticks to the Iron like some glutinous or clammy juice, much like but more firmly than Turpentine or Treacle taken by Tradesmen out of their pots."[44]

(2.) Although, sometimes for very ordinary bottles, the blower might simply rotate the pipe slowly, allowing the red-hot gather to cool slightly on the outside and to sag, usually the gather was rolled on the marver (from the French *marbre*) to give a cylindrical or ovoid form as the outer surface cooled slightly. In 1662, Christopher Merret described the step ". . . whilst 'tis red hot [the gather] the servitor rouls it to and fro on a marble that the parts thereof may be more firmly united."[45] The earliest marvers apparently were flat stones or marble slabs placed on the ground or floor. By the 18th century, if not earlier, the marver, commonly a metal slab, was placed on a supporting pillar or on a frame.

(3.) The next step was the "puff." The gatherer blew into the pipe to form an internal central bubble.

(4.) Next the gather was further expanded, and (*a*) to ensure uniformity was sometimes turned in a

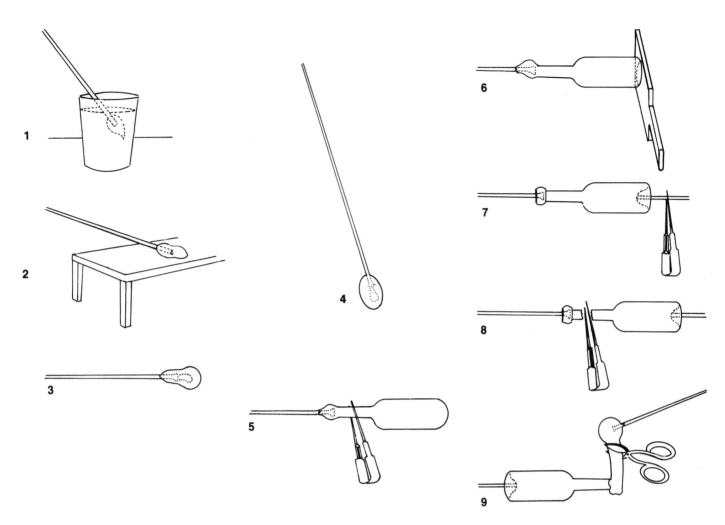

wooden block that had been dipped in cold water to retard charring by the hot metal, or again marvered. Or (b) if the bottle was to have a pattern-molded reticulated design, such as a diamond diaper, was placed in a small two-piece mold, and the leaves closed upon it, thus impressing the design in the soft metal; or, if a large piece mold was used, the gather was expanded against the patterned sides of the mold by blowing. Or (c) if a ribbed pattern was desired, the gather might be expanded in a fluted dip-mold or, more likely, the gather was forced into the mold before expansion. (See Ills. 92 and 93A & B.)

(5.) Then, by blowing and manipulation, the body form and neck were fashioned and the bottom of the bottle flattened, usually with a wooden paddle called a battledore.

(6.) Next, one of the irons was attached to the center bottom of the bottle and the bottle whetted, or cracked, off the blowpipe by touching the hot glass near the end of the pipe with a tool dipped in cold water. At this point, too, by pushing inward when attaching the iron, a kick-up could be formed in the bottom of the bottle. When the bare pontil was used, it might leave an oxide deposit on the bottom when

separated from the bottle; or before attaching the pontil, its end might be dipped in the pot to coat it with molten glass, in which case it would leave a rough mark or scar; or the glass-tipped end of the pontil might be lightly coated with sand, and so leave a slight grainy matte mark when it was cracked off.

When the blowpipe itself was used as a pontil, the bottle was first cracked off into a "cradle" or onto sand. The moile (glass left on the end of the pipe when the bottle was cracked off) served to make a bond with the bottom of the bottle; it left a rough ring of glass.

When a device was used to hold a molded bottle during the neck-finishing process, the bottom of the bottle was not marked in any way.

It is said that the earliest of the holding devices was used in France in the 1830s and shortly afterward in England. One, a sort of "spring cradle" at the end of an iron rod, was illustrated in 1849 by Apsley Pellatt in his *Curiosities of Glass Blowing.* [46] As described to me by Dr. Julian Toulouse, it was

a simple cage made of 2 pieces of strap iron crossing each other at right angles . . . with the four ends at a distance from their common center of half a bottle-diameter, turned upward at right angles for about 5 in. . . . This cage movable enough to clasp the bottle firmly was fastened into the end of an iron rod.[47]

Simple devices of this kind were followed about 1850[48] by the snap, which—to paraphrase Dr. Toulouse—had a short central post . . . ending in a heavy cup which encircles the bottom of the bottle . . . and two parallel matching side bars that extend beyond the cup several inches, ending in two right-angled wings, slightly curved. "They spring outwards, and are compressed together by a sliding sleeve which is pushed along the bar toward the cup, so as to squeeze the side bars together and toward the central part." Dr. Toulouse also informed me that, between August 11, 1857, and November 26, 1867, the United States Patent Office issued six patents for improvements on the snap or "snap dragon." Two of the improvements were movable and changeable parts so that the snap could be used for vessels of varying diameters and shapes.[49]

(7.) Next, with the bottle held on an iron (pontil or blowpipe) or in a holder, the blower reheated the neck to polish the lip (flashing or fire-polishing), and usually further smoothed it by tooling. If quite thick-walled, the lip was sheared before being tooled. The neck might be finished further by using the pucellas to evert the lip or to form a collar-like rib. Also, it might be finished with a variety of "applied and tooled" rings and collars. For these a "thread" of glass, gathered on a pontil or "ring iron," was laid on the neck. (*Ring iron* is an English term used in the 19th century, if not earlier. In France such a tool was described [1772] as *"une légère tringle de fer"* [light iron rod]. Merret [1662] called "those irons which make the Ring at the mouth of *Glass Bottles*" ferrets. They were used also to "try whether the Metall be fit to work.")[50] After attaching the end of the "thread" of glass to the neck of the bottle, the blower turned the iron or holder, thus revolving the bottle so that the "thread" encircled the neck. The amount of glass laid on depended upon the type of finish desired—a "string ring," a rounded or a flat ring, or a collar. Rings were usually about a quarter to a half inch below the mouth of the bottle; collars started at the mouth and their length down the neck varied. Typical neck finishes are seen in Ills. 52 and 135. See Ill. 53A & B for types of special tools used in the early 1840s (probably earlier) to late 19th century in fashioning collars.

(8.) Next, a stick or iron was inserted in the neck of the bottle, or the bottle was held by tongs, over a pan or tray, while the pontil was being struck from it. The bottle was then carried to the leer. Christopher Merret (1662) defined irons so used as "Fascets . . . *Irons thrust into the bottle to* carry them to anneal."[51]

(9.) If the bottle was to be *molded for body form*, after the marvering, puff, and a little expanding, the gather (now called the parison) was inserted in a mold and further expanded to take on the shape of the interior of the mold—mainly cylindrical, square, or polygonal. The molds were usually of clay or metal. Wood may have been used on occasion, but it was the least durable, so the more durable clay was used extensively. The most durable—and essential for lettered and figured bottles—were metal molds. Molds were either dip molds (a block having inner body-forming sides with a slight inward taper from top to bottom) or piece molds having two pieces or leaves hinged together, which left a basal bisecting mold seam. The shoulders, neck, and lip were fashioned by blowing and tooling, as in the case of free-blown bottles. On square bottles that I have seen, the shoulders rise from a plain spandrellike section at the corners. Copper, brass, iron, and wood were used, but predominantly iron in the 19th century. Dip molds might be sunk in the ground or let into or set on the floor. In some glasshouses molds were placed on the floor close to the platform on which the blower stood, which was on the level of the working furnace. Piece molds, too, could be let into the floor (see Ill. 54, Ricketts's apparatus), but usually they were either operated with a foot pedal by the blower or opened and shut by a boy or journeyman.

(10.) After the marvering, puff, and forming of the parison—if a bottle was to be molded for body, shoulder, and part of, or the entire, neck—the gather was further expanded in one of several types of piece molds. The earliest types, going back to the 1st century A.D. and probably to sometime in the 1st century B.C. after the invention of the blowpipe, were two-piece molds that left a bisecting mold seam and three-piece hinged molds having one leaf attached to the base, which left three vertical mold seams. A common type by the 1820s and possibly by the late 18th century had a one-piece (dip) body part and two-piece upper part forming the shoulder and lower neck, a type of which Ricketts's was an elaboration. The variety in mold construction, especially at the base, is evident from the base types shown in Ill. 136.

Part II

HISTORICAL BACKGROUND

1
ANCESTRY OF BOTTLES USED AND MADE IN AMERICA

By the middle of the 1st century B.C. some glassmakers in Mideastern glassworks along the Phoenecian coast had adopted a new tool and brought a new technique to glassmaking. The tool was the blowpipe—a hollow metal rod; the revolutionary technique was blowing glass. Over the years opinions and conclusions of scholars have varied as to when and where the blowpipe was introduced in the fabrication of glass objects. For many years following the 1798 excavations of XII Dynasty tombs at Beni Hasan, it was thought to have occurred in Egypt in the 1800s B.C. Wall paintings in Tomb No. 2 depicted scenes of crafts and occupations, and one was thought to represent glassblowing. In the scene, a craftsman, seated on a substantial block at the left, holds in his right hand a rod through which he appears to be blowing. At the end of the rod is an ovoid form licked by flames from a small "crucible." Another craftsman, seated on a very low block at the right, uses both hands to hold a similar rod, and the ovoid form at its end is near the outer edge of the "crucible." The ovoid forms were thought to be gathers of molten glass. By the 1890s, if not before, scholars had determined that the scene depicted

metalworkers, *not* glassblowers. For example, in 1893, as I learned from Dr. Sidney M. Goldstein, Associate Curator, Ancient Glass, at The Corning Museum of Glass, Percy E. Newberry noted in *Beni Hasan*, Part I, *Archeological Survey of Egypt*, that these men are involved in goldsmithing. Dr. Goldstein pointed out also Anton Kisas's statement in his "monumental" *Das Glas* (1908) that the scene must have been an illustration of metalworking, since glassblowing was not known at the time of the tomb paintings. Most familiar to students and collectors of American glass is the statement of Sir W. M. Flinders Petrie, the famous British Egyptologist, in his *Arts and Crafts of Ancient Egypt* (1909): ". . . the figures of smiths blowing in a fire with rods tipped with clay have been quoted as figures blowing glass, though no blown glass is known in Egypt before Roman times." These details have been resurrected here because the misinterpretation of the scene has been resurrected in the past few years. In a clipping from one of the current so-called tabloids for glass collectors (the title was not given) was the statement that "on the Wall of the Beni Hassan tomb" there were "figures of glassblowers with blowpipes, marvers, crucibles and furnace," and this information was said to be "From 1880 Egyptian Magazine." In 1940 when I was writing "A Note for the Curious" for *American Glass*, the scholars whose works I had read thought the blowpipe was introduced sometime before the 3rd century B.C., though apparently no firmly datable blown vessels were known. By 1948, the Roman Period or mid-1st century B.C. was being accepted. Since then, there has been growing evidence that glassblowing matured about 50 B.C. The famous Portland vase and other cameo vessels had to be blown in order to be cased, and they were produced toward the end of the Roman Republic or early in the Augustan period of the Roman Empire. During exploration of the Judean Desert in 1961, a small bottle blown in the years 40–37 B.C. was found. Later a deposit of blown material that could be no later than 50–40 B.C. was unearthed in the Jewish quarter of the Old City of Jerusalem![1]

Whenever or wherever the blowpipe became part of the glassmaker's equipment may always remain a tantalizing question, but the tool's importance lay in making possible "bubble blowing"—that is, "free-blowing" in the glassman's cant, and blowing molten glass into a mold for shape and sometimes decoration as well. Thereby it liberated certain properties of glass. Without it, the innumerable expansions of glass forms and uses that have been indispensable to the evolution of our Western civilization could not have been realized. Too, it liberated Mesopotamian and Egyptian glassmakers from tedious press-molding and sand-core processes of fabrication practiced for about 15 centuries. Hollow glass vessels had been formed by the sand-core process: a body shape, modeled around a metal rod, either was dipped and redipped in molten glass or softened canes or strips of glass were painstakingly wound around it, after which it was "marvered" for a smooth finish. And then the core had to be dug out. The vessels were time-absorbing in fabrication, and they were luxury items. Among them were small jars and bottles serving mainly as containers for oils and unguents, cosmetics and perfumes.[1a] Glassblowing meant quick and, comparatively speaking, cheap production. Equally, if not more important, it meant the possibility of making vessels and bottles of any desired size and capacity.

It may be that "free-blowing of glass developed from the discovery that the press-molding process could be facilitated by blowing the metal (molten glass) into the mold instead of manipulating it by hand."[2] Since shallow molds had long been used for

shaping and ornamentation, it would be surprising if the blowpipe had not soon been followed by deeper molds—today called dip molds—to impress ribs on unformed gathers of glass, molds of two pieces to give square or polygonal body form, and full-sized molds of two or more pieces for other shapes and for low-relief decoration. The winter of the press-molding process was followed by the spring of free-blowing. But blowing would not have been possible had there not been development in the size of furnaces and pots providing the means for melting larger batches of raw materials into metal than was possible in the small crucibles presumably used before the new era.[3] Then, as today in free-blowing, the blower dipped his pipe into a pot of molten viscous metal, turning it to gather a glob on the pipe's end. He could give symmetry to the gather by rolling it on a flat stone or other marver. Blowing gently into the pipe, he inflated the gather and expanded the resultant bubble to the size desired—or limited by the amount of metal in the gather. He could elongate it by swinging the pipe, and fashion it into its final shape with a tonglike spring tool. The new method led naturally to an expanded range of glass articles—luxury table glass and, above all, utilitarian wares, which may have been the backbone of the industry as they were to be in later times.

It was not long, perhaps less than a century, before the entire Roman world appreciated that glass could be impervious to most outside influences and, in turn, exercised no influences upon the flavor or nature of that which it contained. Sometime before A.D. 66, Gais Petronius testified through the lips of his Trimachio to the desirability of glass as a material, and also to the snobbish attitude of the wealthy Roman toward its presence on his table. Trimachio felt that the only thing really against glass was its cheapness. Nevertheless, had it not broken so easily, he would have preferred it to gold for "There's no tang to it."[4] The result of this property and of its low cost was that utilitarian vessels for everyday use became common even before the end of the first century.

That jars and bottles, especially bottles, of many sizes were foremost among the utilitarian wares seems evident from the numbers preserved under the volcanic ash that buried Pompeii during the catastrophic eruption of Vesuvius in A.D. 79. On exhibition in four cases of the Museo di Napoli alone are over 440 bottles (of which 165 have handles), 85 jars, and a few amphorae used by the doomed citizens of Pompeii. Jars: cylindrical and square, with short neck flaring to a plain lip, or with body constricted below a wide flanged mouth, or with short wide and collared neck. Small ampullae or phials: cylindrical and onion-shaped body and long neck. Bottles: piriform, conical, globular, and square; short and tall, slender and squat, with long or short, wide or narrow neck, with everted, flanged, or collared lips. Frequently conical, globular, and square bottles were given stiff angular ribbed handles. The square bodies apparently were shaped both by manipulation and, as they were in some of our own 18th- and early 19th-century glasshouses, by use of a two-piece clay mold.[5] Eventually these types, and others, were made in the glasshouses established in western parts of the Empire. Actually, in the heyday of the Roman Empire, bottles and jars were in more common usage than at any period before the 19th century. In fact, since about A.D. 1, no article of glass has served man more continuously through his life-span than the glass bottle, although before the blowpipe it was a luxury and doubtless, from the Dark through the Middle Ages, familiar only to privileged groups and unknown to the commonality of the Western world.

Toward the end of the 4th century the Roman Empire divided against itself, with the proverbial result. In the West, as it gradually fragmented under the impact of successive barbarian assaults, a slow attrition spread to the arts and crafts, and quickened when Islam took over the Mediterranean Sea. It has been believed that during the Merovingian period, from about the 5th to well into the 8th centuries, only a *germ* of glassmaking was kept alive in a *few* small and isolated forest furnaces where blowers evolved their own idiom from "Roman" practices; that gradually glass vessels became no longer the rule but the rare exception; that at the end of the Carolingian period, in the 10th century, glassmaking was practically an extinct art, which revived very slowly in the service of the medieval church. There is truth, but not the whole truth, in these beliefs.

As so often results when the spotlight of research is focused upon "established facts," the dim picture of Western glassmaking has been enlarged and brightened and details brought out in recent years. It now appears that the studies of scholars in the field are well on the research road to proof that glassmaking, though limited in quantity, may have been continuous in the Low Countries and France and, if not uninterrupted in Italy, begun at L'Altare in the 9th century and revived in Venice by the 10th at least. It is perhaps safe to conjecture that the same was true of the Germanic Rhineland. While glassmaking was still centuries from being a flourishing industry, the glass furnaces were more numerous than glass his-

tory has hitherto recorded.[6] After all, the production of glass demanded only a simple furnace and a few simple tools, and the raw materials and the wood to fire the furnaces were available in abundance. Above all, glass was so convenient a material it is difficult to believe it was not made wherever possible, or that so perfect a container as the glass bottle was entirely abandoned for those of leather, pottery, or metal. It is interesting to note that medieval Italian glassmen called themselves *philolarii* and bottles *phiella* and *fiole*.[7]

As has been believed, the role played by the Western church in glassmaking was indeed a vital one. It was the church, not the nobility of Europe, that preserved and nourished the seeds of science and literature, arts and crafts, in the abbeys and monasteries, particularly those of the Benedictines, eventually strewn throughout Europe from England to southern Italy, to the heart of Germany. Not surprisingly, glassmaking was one of the arts fostered, perhaps even more widely than has been determined as yet. Be that as it may, for some time, it would appear, early medieval glassmakers practiced their art almost—if not entirely—within the bounds of some of the monasteries. Window glass seems to have been the principal product; it was considered the most essential, and, as nearly everyone knows, much of it was for the marvelous stained-glass windows, which have never been surpassed. However, some glassware was blown also—simple drinking vessels and bottles, reliquaries and ecclesiastical vessels, including Eucharistic chalices. The last, though banned by Pope Leon IV in the mid-9th century, were still being used in the 11th, if not later. Besides meeting the needs of the church and clergy, glassworkers undoubtedly supplied some table glass and bottles to royalty and nobility, but presumably to serfdom the use of glass would have been unknown.[8]

However, the yeast of change was working slowly. By the 11th century, or during it, glassmakers were able to break monastic bonds and establish outside furnaces, many under the auspices of the nobility. Though glassmaking was still a parochial manufacture and window glass doubtless the principal product, there were more customers: a middle class had been developing as economic prosperity increased with the resurgence of commerce between the parts of Europe, the Mediterranean centers, and the Middle East. And naturally the multiplying merchant and middle class continued to broaden the base of demand for glassware. Though not keeping pace with the general economic development in the period from the 12th to the 15th centuries, glassmaking did take forward strides, so that not only quantity gradually increased but also variety and usages. In the case of Venice, at least, the geographical limits of her market were pushed outward by 1279, when her glass was "sufficiently well known to attract German pedlar-purchasers," who presumably peddled the Venetian wares in the states north of Italy. Though certainly no other Western wares traveled so far from home or so early as those of Venice, it does not seem improbable that, before the end of the 1400s, products of glass furnaces elsewhere in the West were sold to other than strictly local markets.[9]

Evidence of medieval glass is abundant in illuminated manuscripts from the 10th through the 14th centuries, and in frescoes from the 13th, especially a few types of bottles and drinking vessels. It is present also in some contemporary texts. Among the latter is a book written between the last half of the 10th and beginning of the 12th century by Theophilus, a monk in the monastery of Saint Pantaleon of Cologne. The chapters devoted to the fabrication of glass seem written from familiarity with the processes, not just theory. One, Chapter XI, gives instructions for blowing "FLASKS WITH A LONG NECK":

But if you wish to make flasks with a long neck act thus. When you have blown the hot glass in the form of a large bladder, close the opening of the tube with your thumb so that the air may not escape, swinging the tube, with the glass which hangs from it above your head, in such a manner as if you wish to throw it off, and presently its neck being extended in length, your hand being raised upright, allow the tube, with its vase below it to hang down, that the neck may not become curved; and thus separating it with a moist piece of wood, place it in the cooling oven.[10]

Though the only bottles for which Theophilus gave instructions were flasks with a long neck, phials and bottles with stable bases must also have been made in his period if not before. It seems inconceivable that they were not: a bottle that would stand by itself was so desirable and practical, so easily achieved by simply flattening the bottom of the "bladder" and perhaps pushing it into a kick-up. However, only the bladder, or balloon bottle, as it is also called, fitting Theophilus's description seems to have been depicted in the banqueting scenes in 10th and 11th century manuscripts (Ill. 1). In some, a diner is shown lifting the large bottle to his lips or actually drinking from it. And a servant is sometimes shown holding one in his hand, the base resting in his palm. The various depictions suggest three conclusions: (1)

the bottles were light in weight, since drinking from so large a bottle presented no difficulties; light in color and thin-walled, since their contents showed through their walls; (2) the bladder bottles functioned mainly as drinking and serving vessels; (3) bottles that were stable-based probably were purely utilitarian vessels having no place in the banqueting and religious scenes depicted by the illuminators.

Whenever it was first made, the bladder-type bottle with long neck and unstable base has had a long career. Down the centuries, ovoid, piriform, globular, and chestnut-shaped, these bottles served as containers of wines, waters, and oils. By the 17th century, possibly earlier, when set on the table they were held upright by twisted straw supports or bases of wood, stone, marble, or slate. However, long before—by the 15th century, at least—their thin walls were often protected by straw or osier coats, as Chianti bottles are today. Thus covered, they appear to have been used in the transport of liquids, oil in particular, from the 17th century. In the 18th and early 19th centuries, unstable bottles with straw covering were the common shipping containers for olive and sweet oils; they were called *betées* or *betties*. Belgian mineral-water bottles of the 18th century were also long necked, ovoid, and unstable bottles.[11]

By the last half of the 12th century, unstable bottles for serving beverages were joined by more elegant and practical types, blown from green (bottle) glass and the metal used for window glass. The form most often depicted had an ovoid or globular body on a pedestal foot, and usually a long neck and flanged mouth—a form today called decanter or carafe. In the art of the next two centuries, bottles of similar shape, with and without a flat circular foot, were shown on the tables. In the 14th century, bottles in the shape of a small cask appeared, and large bottles, such as those called demijohns, were sometimes used in the transport of wine.[12] And, of course, among the articles produced in larger quantities and forms would have been phials and bottles for apothecaries and alchemists, and for domestic use. But, as in previous centuries, there seems to have been no place for utilitarian bottles, with the exception of the urinal, in the pictorial art of the times, which remained religious in theme. The urinal, which had evolved by the second half of the 13th century at least, was a short-necked version of the Theophilus bottle. As depicted in manuscripts and paintings, it was a thin-walled bottle with either a more or less ovoid body or a spherical one, a com-

1. Bottles like those from which guests are drinking in this depiction of the feast of Balshazzar undoubtedly were the type Theophilus described as "flasks with a long neck." Similar bottles are depicted in several manuscripts of the 9th through 11th centuries, such as a commentary on the Apocalypse by the Monk Beatus dated A.D. 975, in which, in "the Feast of Balshazzar," a servant is shown with one of the long-necked unstable bottles in each hand. The scene illustrated here is from the 11th-century Catalonian Bible of San Pedro de Roda at the Bibliothèque Nationale, Paris (Latin 6 [11 D]). *Bibliothèque Nationale* and *The Corning Museum of Glass*

paratively short neck, and a wide-flanged mouth. It soon became the symbol of the doctor, and also a practically necessary article in the medical equipment of the apothecary, the doctor, and many households.[13]

Still, though the more plentiful and varied bottles were being used for beverages and, in the 14th century (if not sooner), for wine in some taverns and for oil in some shops, neither domestic nor commercial usage of *ordinary* glass bottles was as yet *ordinary*. Apparently, use of glass bottles for beverages did not approach being customary before the 15th century in some Continental areas, the 16th in others, and still later in England. Even then they were used mainly for serving beverages rather than for storing and shipping them.[14] Nevertheless, both production and usage were to be considerably accelerated during the Renaissance, that period of an almost phoenixlike reawakening in all fields of Western man's intellectual and artistic activities, when literature and science, arts and crafts, rediscovered by the laity, were stimulated to heights not achieved since the golden days of Greece and Rome. In the art of

glass, there were a revival of old forms and the creation of new ones, a rebirth of many decorative techniques and the birth of new ones. The attainment of superlative craftsmanship first reached its acme in Italy, particularly in Venice, whence it spread slowly to other regions.[15]

Although, to most of us, Renaissance glass means remarkable and beautiful table and ornamental objects, the resurgent glassmaking was not confined to the fashioning of such pieces for the princely of church and laity, the wealthy, and the well-to-do. Simple wares and the utilitarian were not neglected. In these categories, old forms were joined by new ones, some of which were created to meet new and also revived uses of glass vessels. In the 15th century, if not before, globular bottles were being decorated again with pattern-molded ribs, vertical and twisted, of which our midwestern bottles like those in Ill. 96 are reminiscent. The molds for impressing ribs on the unformed gathers of metal probably were similar to those shown on the floor of the 16th-century glasshouse in a woodcut in Agricola's *De Re Metallica*. (See Ill. 2.) The plain globular bottles shown and the quantity in the packing box suggest that they were staple products and in common usage. By the 15th century the previously mentioned variants of Theophilus's bladder bottle entered the stream of glass bottles. In stable-based bottles, the pear shape and double cone as well as globulars were being blown in Germany (that is, the area east of the Rhine) and in the Low Countries. Among their variants were sizes like those in the detail from a painting of the next century attributed to the Flemish painter Jan van Hemessen, detail 2, Ill. 3. Clearly, the covering, probably sized cloth, tied over the mouth shows that bottles were used in the home as containers of liquids as well as for serving vessels. Also in the 15th century, the annular flasks (canteens) made their debut, and they were still popular in France in the 18th century.[16]

Diversity and wider usage of glass bottles continued in the 16th century. As already mentioned, there were peddlers of Venetian glass by 1279. Robert Charleston has cited evidences of hawkers of glass in England in the late 15th century. If peddlers did not carry bottles then, they certainly did in France early in the next century. In his *La Verrerie en France*, James Barrelet shows an early 17th-century picture of a *crieur de verres* with two baskets of glasses, one of which includes small and large globular and ovoid bottles. For beverages, bottles were still used mainly for serving, and were often covered. In his *Cena in casa Levi*, Paolo Veronese (1528–88) depicted "colorless" decanterlike bottles and a large straw-covered wine bottle, the latter held by a serving man. In 1559 at a banquet given by Catherine de Medici in Paris, six and a half dozen glass bottles covered with osiers were used for the table wine. In England the use of glass bottles was likewise spreading, and not only among the upper classes, doctors, and apothecaries. One item in a 1588 inventory of a trader's widow at Salford was "Two glasse Bottles, at 1s. 4d." The use of glass bottles as containers of beverages (that is, "bottling") was advocated in *The Secretes of the Reverende Maister Alexis of Piermont*, which was translated into English in 1588. Among the glass vessels mentioned in connection with making a "precious liquor" was "a great and thick violle or glass, wel coured or bound in wicker or osiers." After being filled, it was to be stopped "Wel with waxe or bombase, and above that with a double parchment." Likewise, there was a revival—if they had ever gone out—of square bottles blown in a mold for body form, and also of rectangular and polygonal. On the Continent, at least in the Low Countries, slightly tapering, nearly cylindrical, tall wine bottles were introduced.[17]

2. Interior of a 16th-century German glasshouse. Typical beehive furnace. Five glassmen: at right, one taking a gather from the melting pot and, partially obscured by furnace, one blowing; at left, one raising a gather above his head; at right center, one marvering a gather, and at left center, one ready with another to serve as a pontil. Note the short blowpipes with long heavy wooden sheaths; in foreground the pattern-molds E and imperfect globular bottles, also bottles and laboratory vessels in bins at right, and the glass peddler outside the entrance with his box of wares on his back. (Agricola, *De Re Metallica.* Hoover translation of the 1556 edition, p. 476.) *New York Public Library*

Naturally the 17th century brought still more extensive use of ordinary glass bottles. Contemporary references to bottles were more frequent. Among them, one of particular interest is that of Merret, the Englishman who in 1662 published his translation from the Italian of Neri's treatise on glass and added pertinent observations of his own. In his section "On the Uses of Glass" he lists "Bottles and other vessels to keep Wine, Beer, Spirits, Oyls, Powders, wherein you may see their Fermentations, Separations and whatsoever other changes nature in time worketh in any liquors, the clearness and goodness of them."[18] More enlightening is the *variety* of forms and sizes recorded in the paintings of the period, particularly those of Dutch and Flemish artists, and the indication of common usage by their very presence in both religious and lay scenes and in still lifes. It is axiomatic that a glass bottle can be no younger than the time it served as an artist's model, but it can be much older, either in actual age or, as in the case of the pear-shape, double-cone, and globular bottles mentioned above, in type. Many of the bottles in 17th-century paintings were long-known types that had not been depicted in previous centuries when art was dominated by religious themes, scenes, and conventions. The details from the paintings in Ills. 3 and 4 show types frequently depicted, and—it will be noted—several are similar to bottles used and made in America in the 18th and early 19th centuries before the use of the full-size piece mold became the principal method of production. As a matter of fact, since with the 17th century our own historical period begins, such bottles must have found their way to the colonies, albeit in small numbers. And it is probable that some of them were blown in the short-lived mid-17th-century glasshouses at Salem, Massachusetts, and New Amsterdam, New York.

Although so many good functional types persisted from previous times, new types did emerge in the 17th century. Among them, as has already been mentioned in Bottle Names, was the thick-walled sturdy bottle for wine and other potables. It was invented in England by the midcentury, possibly not long after 1630, though archaeological evidence from those bearing seals with crests, initials, names, and dates places the date nearer 1650 (see Ills. 44 and 52). There can be no question that these wine bottles, as they were called, were used in America, for excavations in Virginia have yielded proof of their presence in Jamestown and later communities.[19] Bottles of Types 1 and 1a (Ill. 52) have been found in Indian graves in Rhode Island and Connecticut, and it may be that some of these were blown in the Salem glassworks. Another 17th-century innovation evidently was the pocket bottle, which seems to have appeared late in the century, at least in England.[20] However, in general, it can be said that whenever and wherever the various types of bottles originated, many became common to most European areas,

though some were more popular in one country or section than in another, and naturally minor variations evolved. This apparently maintained also in the 18th century.

By the early 1700s, to most people *bottle* had come to mean a glass bottle. The glass bottle had come into its own again as a perfect container. Its production had attained an important economic role in many areas as its use for storing and shipping beverages expanded, and also as its commercial use in packaging other products became customary. In America, the isolated attempts to root the industry did not result in a large output of bottles, and even imports failed to meet the eager demand. However, because of England's trade laws and the orientation of most colonists through commerce or heritage, or both, to England, nearly all *imported* bottles must have been of English manufacture. Nevertheless Continental bottles, especially those filled with such necessities as wines, spirits, and oils, reached American shores.

Inevitably, when the colonists ventured into glassmaking, they had both English and Continental bottles as models. Moreover, the majority of glassmen who were persuaded to come to America before the 19th century were Continentals, and of course saturated with the traditions and techniques followed in the glasshouses where they were trained and practiced their art. In the natural course of glass events, they would have had a practical influence upon the types of bottles produced in colonial and early 19th-century glasshouses. In the light of Ivor Noel Hume's statement that although "multi-sided moulds" were used in the late 16th century, "their use seemed to die out in the mid-17th century and never really became popular in England again,"[21] it seems likely that such bottles found here probably were of either Continental or American origin. Continental influence would be especially true in the case of many-sided bottles like 1 through 5, 7, and 8 in Ill. 73. Consequently our tendency to think of American-made bottles of the 18th and early 19th century as of purely English derivation—with two exceptions—has been too parochial. The exceptions are the "Pitkin" flasks, such as those shown in Ills. 87 through 89, which were blown by the so-called German half-post method, and the chunky bottles like those shown in Color Plate II that have long been accepted as 18th-century Continental types. Inevitably, the ancestry and inspiration of our early bottles were mixed. Although the family tree of American bottles put out many branches—some English, some Continental, and some hybrid—it was not until the 19th century that it developed national branches.

3. GLASS VESSELS IN DETAILS FROM 16th- AND 17th-CENTURY PAINTINGS

The ordinary green-glass bottles and jars depicted were typical Continental glass containers of the artists' periods. Excepting the Roman-type vials with small body and very long neck in Nos. 3 and 6, the 15th- to early-16th-century "double cone" in No. 2, the vaselike decanter-bottle in No. 3, and the decanter-bottle in No. 9, they will seem familiar to most collectors of glass containers made in America and imported, from colonial times into the 19th century. The "squares" and the rectangular bottles with chamfered corners were blown in molds for body form *only* and completed by the techniques of free-blowing. The others were free-blown.

Also illustrated are a few contemporary methods of closure. The reddish material over the mouth of the 15th- through 16th-century bottles in Nos. 1 and 2 probably was either sarsenet or sized cloth; on two bottles, it is tied down by packthread. Beneath the covering may have been a stopper of wax or bombase. A cork was used for the Spanish square bottle in No. 5 and probably in the flattened bottle in No. 9. The material depicted in the other paintings (I have seen only photographs of them) is a matter of conjecture. That tied over the wide mouth of the square bottle (or jar) on the table in No. 3 may have been sized cloth or parchment or leather. Also, parchment or paper doubtless was used to make the spills stopping some of the bottles in Nos. 3, 6, 7 and 9.

1. From *The Virgin and Child with St. Joseph* by Joos van Cleve (ca. 1490–1540), Flemish School. In form, Van Cleve's globular bottle, also Steen's in No. 8, reminds one of some early-19th-century midwestern bottles with nearly spherical bodies—for example, Nos. 2 and 3, Ill. 96. *Metropolitan Museum of Art, The Michael Friedsam Collection, 1931, New York City*

2. From *Woman at a Clavichord*, attributed to Jan van Hemessen, Flemish School, 16th century (about 1525, according to Chambon). The large pear-shaped bottle (*left*) is a "natural" form and one to which the presumably American 18th- to early-19th-century bottle, No. 5, Ill. 46, is similar. The "double cone" bottle, an early-15th-century innovation (*right*) apparently did not survive into the 17th century. *Worcester Art Museum, Worcester, Massachusetts*

3. From *The Village Doctor* by David Teniers, the younger (1610–90), Flemish School. Note the similarity between the mid-19th-century wide-mouth bottle, No. 9, Ill. 74, and the covered one depicted by Teniers on the table. The small square on the floor appears to be about the size of 19th-century blacking bottles Nos. 3 and 4, Ill. 75, but its light color suggests a medicine vial of white glass (green glass decolorized, usually with traces of color in thick parts of the article). *Staatliche Kunsthalle, Karlsruhe, Germany*

4. From *The Merry Fish Merchant* by Ary de Vois (1631–41—1680–95), Dutch School. The rectangular bottle appears to be about half-pint size and has counterparts in American bottles of a century and two later. *Rijksmuseum, Amsterdam, Netherlands.*

5. From *Winter* by Miguel March (1633–70), Spanish School. (Museo Provincial de Pinturas, Valencia, Spain.) *Frick Art Reference Library, New York City*

6. From *The Alchemist* by David Teniers, the younger (1610–90), Flemish School. Note the small globular bottles (depicted in this detail and in No. 9) which are distant relatives of the four small 18th- through early-19th-century globulars in Ill. 47. (State Picture Gallery, Dresden, Germany.) *Frick Art Reference Library, New York City*

7. From *The Apothecary Shop*, painted, probably about the end of the 17th century, by William van Mieris (1662–1747), Dutch School. The apothecary's bottles appear to be similar to the Belgian type evolving at the end of the 17th century (Chambon, No. 3, Planche T). Note the longer neck and more globular body than on the contemporary English wine bottle. Since wine was retailed by apothecaries, it seems likely that the bottles on the shelves and the one being sold to a customer held wine or perhaps a medicinal concoction in a wine vehicle. *Frick Art Reference Library, New York City*

8. From *The Quack* by Jan H. Steen (1626–79), Dutch School. Note the similarity of the rectangular bottle with chamfered corners to the 18th- and early-19th-century bottle No. 1, Ill. 72. *Rijksmuseum, Amsterdam, Netherlands*

9. From *An Alchemist* by David Teniers, the younger (1610–90), Flemish School. The tall long-necked square, a type apparently introduced in Flemish glassworks in the mid-16th century from Germany (Chambon, Planche R), appears to be blown from much darker metal than the one depicted in No. 6. Less frequently found in art is the long-necked flattened bottle or flask, possibly a forerunner of the large flat quart bottles advertised in the Boston *News Letter*, Feb. 1, 1728. *Frick Art Reference Library, New York City*

1

2

3

4

5

6

7

8

9

4. GLASS BOTTLES IN DETAILS FROM 17th- AND 18th-CENTURY PAINTINGS

1. From *A Woman Asleep and a Man Smoking* by Jan H. Steen (1626–79), Dutch School. The leather-covered large oval bottle doubtless held the wine or spirit that perhaps put the woman to sleep. The form became a common one for bottles, usually "wickered," used to transport liquids. By the mid-18th century such bottles ranged from 1 to 20 gallons in size and were being called *demijohns* and *carboys* in England and America. (The Hermitage, Leningrad, Russia.) *Frick Art Reference Library, New York City*

2. From *Peasant Interior* by David Teniers, the younger (1610–90), Flemish School. Teniers's interest in depicting glass is shown again here by the small globular bottle and the square, each apparently stopped with a paper or parchment spill. Their presence in the humble home suggests a widespread use of glass bottles in the 17th century on the Continent. *The Nelson Gallery—Atkins Museum (Nelson Fund), Kansas City, Missouri*

3. From *A Brandy Dealer and His Old Wife* by P. J. Quast (1605/6–47), Dutch School. Note that the square spirits bottles appear to have screw caps. (National Museum, Brunswick, Germany.) *Frick Art Reference Library, New York City*

4. From *The Sick Lady* by Jan H. Steen (1626–79), Dutch School. The covering of wine and of oil flasks with woven straw or osiers probably originated in Italy, possibly Florence, two centuries or so before Steen's lifetime. Such covered flasks were later called Florence bottles. Probably, without its covering, the bottle depicted by Steen was similar to that illustrated by No. 7 Ill. 50. (The Frans von Pannwitz Collection.) *Rijksmuseum, Amsterdam, Netherlands*

5. From *Luncheon in the Country* by Francesco Bayeu y Subias (1734–95), Spanish School. Probably the black-glass wine bottles represent Spanish types of the mid-to-late 18th century. They are unlike typical English wine bottles of that period. (The Prado, Madrid, Spain.) *Frick Art Reference Library, New York City*

6. From *Group of Men in a Tavern* by Léonard Defrance (1735–1805), Flemish School. The wine bottle depicted by Defrance is similar to the Belgian wine bottle of the mid-18th century as shown by Chambon's No. 6, Planche T. (Dr. A. Bredin's Collection, The Hague, Netherlands.) *Frick Art Reference Library, New York City*

7. From *Le Panier de Raisins* by J.B.S. Chardin (1699–1779), French School. The handsome black-glass bottle appears similar to the English wine bottle (Types 4a and 5, Ill. 52) of the period from about 1700 to 1740. (The Louvre, Paris, France.) *Frick Art Reference Library, New York City*

8. From *Beer Street*, 1751 engraving, by William Hogarth (1697–1764), English School. Hogarth gave his sign painter an English black-glass wine bottle (Type 6, Ill. 52) of the period from about 1730 to 1750. *The Brooklyn Museum, Brooklyn, New York*

9. From *Still Life with Cork Cask* by Luis Menendez (1716–80), Spanish School. The black-glass wine bottle, probably of Spanish origin, appears similar to the English wine bottle (Type 4, Ill. 52) of the period from about 1700 to 1740 but with a wide and rounded collar below the plain lip. (Collection of P. Smidt van Gelder.) *Frick Art Reference Library, New York City*

1

2

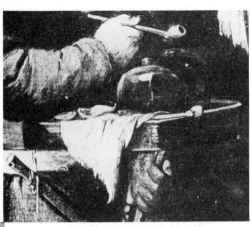

3

4

5

6

7

8

9

THE BOTTLE INDUSTRY IN AMERICA

Behind the billions of bottles produced in the United States today lies the colorful history of glassmaking in America,[1] interwoven with that of the country itself, of the artisans and men of business and trade who risked their capital to establish and nourish glasshouses, of the glassmen and mechanics who exercised their skills and ingenuity to extend the uses of glass and to perfect glassmaking, even evolving revolutionary methods and compositions. It is a history of struggle, failure, and success, but also of development from small primitive furnaces in shed-like glasshouses to huge perfected furnaces and tanks in giant factories, from handicraft to automation, from often painfully short-lived, small, and sporadic ventures to a successful industry of importance in the economy of the country. And if, as has been said, window glass has been the backbone of our glass industry, perhaps it may be said that bottles have been its spinal cord. Possibly it was a bottle that was blown at the dawn of our glassmaking history nearly 375 years ago in the infant Virginia colony of Jamestown when the first batch of metal was melted in a small primitive glass furnace. The date was 1608, only a little over a year after the first band of colonists had landed and begun their tragic struggle for existence.[2] From this abortive venture stems the claim of our glass manufacturers that theirs was the first industry in America.

The individual stories of the hundreds of proposed and actual glasshouses since 1608 are still unfolding as research progresses. Of some, little or nothing is known beyond the fact of intent or existence: they are merely statistics. Of others, a skeletal story can be told. And a few, very few, of the total number have been the object of intensive research and study. Even were all the facts known, it would not be possible in the space of this book to give a detailed history of each of the recorded glasshouses. I have tried to give a thumbnail sketch, where possible, of those in which bottles were, or probably were, blown in colonial days and in the critical years of the infant industry in the half-century after Independence, and of a few later works in which Figured Flasks were blown.[3]

A. 17th Century

That there were even six or seven adventures in glassmaking in the 17th century is surprising; that the first was at Jamestown in 1608 is astonishing. To us, with history's hindsight into New World conditions and the perils of transplantation from an Old World "modern society" to a virgin wilderness as yet unraped by civilization, an undertaking such as a glassworks seems utter foolhardiness. And so it proved to be. However, to the Virginia Company of London, reports of abundant raw materials for glassmaking near *unlimited* wood for the cutting, coupled with visions of profits from supplying the growing glass needs at home, must have seemed an invitation from Providence to establish glassworks. True, England did have glassworks, supplying mainly windowpanes and bottles, but expansion of the industry was handicapped by a paucity of skilled glassblowers. Moreover, the ravage of England's forests to satisfy the voracious appetite of glassmaking for firewood and potash was such that by 1617 the use of wood for fuel was prohibited by law—fortunately, the use of coal to fire the furnaces had already started in a few works. Not only would there be no fuel problem in Virginia, but money could be kept in English pockets instead of going into those of foreigners if glassware was made and sold by Englishmen. Hence, even though the glass would have to be transported across 3,000 or more miles of ocean, a flourishing glasshouse in Jamestown would benefit country and company alike.

The Jamestown ventures are unique in the annals of our glassmaking. Not only were they the first attempts in the colonies to manufacture this man-made material, but the products were to be for the benefit of England and, of course, the Virginia Company of London. Exported to England, the glassware would augment the profits anticipated from tapping the virginal raw materials of Virginia. In addition, the glasshouses were started in or near not a well-rooted settlement but one barely surviving under perilous conditions. The 1608 glasshouse, presumably an open-sided structure with shielding roof and small primitive furnaces, was manned by glassmen among the "eight Dutchmen and Poles" who were sent over that spring. Though glass was among the "tryals" of products taken back to London by Captain Newport late that year, it is probable all efforts to blow glass had ceased by the fall of 1609. According to the records of the Virginia Company, Captain William Norton persuaded it in June 1621 to join him in another attempt, and on a fifty-fifty profit basis.

However, shortage of funds led to taking private "Adventurers" into the project and the formation of a joint-stock company in July 1621. Their agreement specified that "round Glasse, Drincking Glasses and Beads" (the last to be currency of trade with the Indians) were to be made by the six Italian glassblowers who were to man the works, and also that Captain Norton was to have complete charge of the glassmen and of all operations. This glasshouse, probably on the site of the first one, was erected early in 1622. It was as ill-starred as its predecessor. Complete defeat of the project was accepted in the spring of 1624.

There has long been speculation about glass made in these two houses—that is, other than beads, which until a little over a decade ago were unquestioned as articles definitely made at Jamestown. Today even production of beads is rejected as improbable. In fact, so far as is known at present, not even samples were sent back to the proprietors from the 1622 house, and present evidence leads to the conclusion that probably no glass whatever was blown. As for the samples the London Company received from the 1608 furnace, we shall probably never know just what they were. The thorough archaeological investigations carried on by the National Park Service in 1948 and 1949 on the site of the first glasshouse established that glass had indeed been melted. However, the shards among the evidence uncovered were too small to reveal the form of the original objects. *Not a single bead or evidence of bead making was found.* Chemical analysis of the shards, drippings, and metal still adhering to parts of melting pots proved the metal was common green glass, though "one very small pot . . . showed evidence of having been used to melt blue glass."[3a] The objects blown between 1608 and the fall of 1609 remain in the realm of conjecture. If, as seems likely, bottles were among the glassware, it is a logical assumption they would have been small apothecary vials characteristic of the period and thin-walled globular bottles for wine and other liquids—for instance, like that in detail 1 of Ill. 3 from Joos Van Cleve's painting of the Holy Family.

Not for a decade and a half, so far as is known, was there another attempt to establish a glasshouse, although the new Americans needed window glass and bottles acutely. Imports did not meet the demand and were very dear, for the mercantile philosophy of England included the premise that English colonies existed for the sole benefit of England, and profits from highly priced manufactured products were the inalienable rights of English industries. (Seemingly the Dutch in New Amsterdam did not face the same problem.) As the colonies grew and prospered, the desirability of local glassworks must have occurred often to the builders of homes and public buildings, for which window glass was scarce; to brewers and cider makers, apothecaries and doctors, housewives, and many others who wanted bottles of glass.

But, quite apart from the colonists' grim problems of sustaining themselves, securing their settlements and means of livelihood, many other factors existed that were not conducive to such projects as glassmaking or to their success. The communities in which business and trade gradually flourished were few and, except for Boston and Salem in New England, far separated—in fact, more isolated than those of medieval Europe. They had little or no friendly contact with or interest in each other. Since, by land, only trails led from one to another, trade depended upon water carriage. And, by water, trade was mainly with England and the West Indies, except, of course, that of New Amsterdam, which was oriented to the Netherlands before the English took the colony in 1664. Thus it was only a restricted, almost local, market for which a glassmaker could reasonably hope. Furthermore, a glassworks demanded trained glassmen, skilled in more than blowing glass—men with practical knowledge of furnace building, pot making, mixing and cooking the batch, and of the proper materials for furnace, pots, and glass. Such men were jealously guarded craftsmen in Europe, where glass also was still in short supply in the 17th century. If not a sufficient deterrent in itself, this situation certainly must have contributed to the fact that, so far as is known at present, plans for glassworks were made in only three places between 1639 and 1732.

Significantly, the three towns were well-rooted centers of business activity—namely, Salem in the Province of Massachusetts Bay, New Amsterdam on Manhattan Island, and Philadelphia in the Province of Pennsylvania. Contemporary information about the glassworks, glassmen, and promoters in these communities is teasingly fragmentary. The Salem glassworks was erected on land granted by the town in 1639 to Obadiah Holmes, Lawrence Southwick, and a practical glassman, Ananias Concklin. The next year they were joined in the venture by John Concklin, also a glassman and the brother of Ananias, both of whom apparently were already citizens of the town and not "imports" for the purpose of producing glass. Whatever glass was produced, it did not bring in enough money to maintain the works, and as further capital was not forthcoming, the works was idle for three years. In 1645, the Concklins, having secured financial support, revived the works. The terminal date has been generally accepted as about 1661, but actually there is no proof as to how long operations continued.[4] In the meantime in New Amsterdam, where the Netherlanders were snugly settled on Manhattan living well-ordered lives, at least two glasshouses were established in the mid-1650s—one by Everett Duycking and one by Johannas Smedes, who presumably were Dutch, as doubtless were their glassblowers. Apparently they prospered. After Smedes sold his business in 1664 and Duycking retired in 1674, both houses were conducted by new proprietors, though for how long has not been determined.[5] Whereas the New Amsterdam and Salem glassworks were private colonial enterprises, the glasshouse erected by 1682 about a mile and a half from Philadelphia and "conveniently posted for water carriage" was a project of London's Free Society of Traders. The intent was to blow window glass and bottles under the direction of Joshua Tittery, a "broad glass maker" and "servant to Ye Society Board." Also, Francis Daniel Pastorious, agent of the Frankfort Land Company of England, reported a glassworks in 1684 at the company's new town of Frankfort about five miles above Philadelphia. Neither works was destined to prosper. A 1685 account of the city and its environs does not include a glassworks.[6]

What of the glass blown in these various glassworks? Little is known. Most historians have doubted any was blown in the works of the Free Society of Traders or at Frankfort. Still, it seems more likely to me that some batches were melted for trials, at least, of window glass and that some metal may have been fashioned into bottles of the period, possibly including the English wine bottles, such as 6 in Ill. 44. Also, perhaps thin-walled globular bottles and bottles like those shown in the details from 17th-century paintings, Ill. 3, were blown at Philadelphia and Salem, most certainly at New Amsterdam. It seems quite likely that Duycking, who specialized in window and stained glass, did not produce any bottles commercially, but his successors may have, and without doubt Smedes and his successors blew many bottles. After the English takeover in 1664, English-type wine bottles like 4 in Ill. 44 may have been ordered and, if glass production continued into the late century, like 6 in the same illustration. Possibly bottles like 1, 2, and 3 in Ill. 44 were blown at Salem (if, as I believe, the glasshouse survived from 1645 into the 1660s), for not only were the community, prospective customers, and the two

glassmen English, but also the new English heavy wine bottles, full and empty, were being imported into the colonies from about 1650. Some of these bottles that have been found in Indian graves in Rhode Island and Connecticut may be from the Salem glassworks.

B. 18th Century

During the 18th century the momentum of colonial development accelerated. The population of native-born citizens increased and was continually augmented by immigrants: freemen and indentured servants, who—whatever the motive sparking emigration from their homelands—anticipated security and profit in America from land, business, craft, or profession. Settlements spread along the Atlantic seaboard and inland—more land was cleared for new farms and plantations; new villages grew up and old centers crept outward to new boundaries. Though still Spartan for many, especially in the recent penetrations of virgin areas, life on most southern plantations and at northern country seats, in urban and semiurban communities, was increasingly easier, more gently and graciously lived by the people of substance among the "Better Sort" and the "Middling Classes."

And the more comfortable, sometimes luxurious, material life was possible because of the crescendo in business activities, reaching a high peak of prosperity during the French and Indian War. But, though there was commercial intercourse with a few European port cities—presumably in accordance with England's regulations of such affairs—in the main, trade continued to be with Britain and the West Indies. Intercolony trade developed too—principally a coastal trade, for transportation of goods and wares by land was still either almost impossible or very costly. Boston, Salem, New York, Philadelphia, and Charleston, already important and rival ports, thrived. So too, on a smaller scale, did Portsmouth, New London, New Haven, and Baltimore. From these active ports flowed American furs, tobacco, grains, raw materials vital to England's industries, rum, beer, and cider, and into them, via England and her other colonies, came many of the necessities of life and most of the luxuries.

However, the growth of the colonies and their enterprises was neither an unbroken stream nor uninhibited. Among many handicaps were lack of specie, indebtedness to English manufacturers and merchants, lack of free trade between the colonies,

English regulations of trade (when enforced), and a ban on colonial manufactures that might compete with England's. The prevailing English attitude, which had crystalized by the turn of the 17th century into the 18th, and was endorsed by most Englishmen of substance, was baldly expressed by Lord Cornbury in his 1705 report from New York to the Lords of Trade and Plantations in London:

. . . all these Colloneys which are but twigs belonging to the Main Tree [England] ought to be Kept entirely dependent upon and subservient to England and that can never be if they are suffered to goe on in the notion they have that as they are Englishmen, soe they may set up the same manufactures here as people do in England.[7]

The concept that the colonists were mere servants and the colonies a vast reservoir of raw materials to be siphoned off for the benefit of Englishmen in England, and refilled by English goods or supplied by England at exorbitant prices, was not shared by most Americans.

In New England and the Middle States, colonists did set up manufactures, among them glassworks. True, glass bottles of various kinds, window glass, and table glass were imported in continually greater quantities, but not sufficient to meet the growing demand. Housewives and tavern-keepers, grocers and confectioners, doctors and druggists, manufacturers of snuff and mustard, brewers and cider makers were among the principal users of bottles, and at times the last two needed them desperately for bottling their potables for export as well as for local consumption. Not unnaturally, many businessmen and wealthy men, even manufacturers of other commodities, and craftsmen with idle capital to invest, were seduced into glassmaking adventures by the obvious need for glass. Some of their projects never got beyond the stage of plans and patents granted by colonial assemblies; others materialized. Of at least 17 planned between 1732[8] and the eve of the Revolution, only 9 glasshouses, 3 of them Stiegel's, are more than statistics in our glass history; in all of them some bottles were blown.

The would-be glass manufacturers were not without support in their defiance of the manufacturing ban: several governors and assemblies recognized the desirability of some colonial manufacturing, including that of bottles and window glass, and condoned it. Connecticut, in 1747, and Rhode Island, in 1752, granted monopolies in glassmaking, but it would seem the petitioners never exercised their privilege. In 1752, Governor Belcher of the

Province of Jersey, replying to inquiries from a Boston friend, wrote a letter reflecting certain attitudes and conditions of the time and containing the following, the flavor of which is too piquant to be diluted by paraphrase:

I am fully in opinion with you and my other Friends in New England, that there is no Wiser or better Measure to go into for retrieving the Miserable Circumstances of your Province than to promote Manufactures among Your Selves and at the same time to be practicing Economy and all possible Frugality and I have often wondered that gentlemen of Substance have not long before set up a Glass House for which you are much better Accommodated than any one can be in this Province where such work [Wistarburgh] has already turn'd out to great Profit.
  But you put me upon a Hard Task to procure you and Tolerable Information as to Carrying on of these Works here in which the Managers are very close and secret however, I will take all the prudent Steps I can to make you an Answer in this matter and to get a Sample of the Clay you mention but as I am here a great distance from those works it will require time to Obtain what I desire for you . . .[9]

In Pennsylvania too there was sympathy with domestic production of glass. In 1771, but a year after he petitioned for financial aid for his Manheim glassworks about 80 miles from Philadelphia, the Provincial Council of Pennsylvania gave William Henry Stiegel a sop of £150 as a "Public Encouragement to his late Manufacture of White Flint Glass in this Province." Two years later, both Stiegel and the Philadelphia Glass Works were allowed to conduct lotteries in hopes of raising funds.[10]

Of course all the doings in and for glassmaking were not entirely unknown to Parliament, the Lords of Trade and Plantations, and the English glass manufacturers: reports on any colonial manufacture were required, and made—albeit sometimes reluctantly it would seem. Nevertheless, so far as is now known, though the official club always cast its shadow, it was not wielded to prevent the building and operation of colonial glasshouses. Probably this leniency stemmed in part from the tenor of the reports made to London and from the nature of the glass reported. Perhaps the controlling mercantile interests and the English government would have tolerated the scattered small works for ordinary window glass and bottles even if colonial reports on them had not lulled the English fears of a possible menace to imports from England. For instance, John Penn's report on manufactures in Pennsylvania,

January 1, 1767, contained the following, which must have referred to Stiegel's glassworks:

The other is a glass house which was erected about four years ago in Lancaster, seventy miles from this city [Philadelphia] by a private person. It is still carried on, tho' to a very inconsiderable extent, there being no other vent for their ware, which is very ordinary quality but to supply the small demands of the villages and farmers in the adjacent country.[11]

Penn might have added "successfully," though at the time Stiegel's glass *was* ordinary and not widely sold.

However, if discovered, any production of fine table glass that might affect the market for English and Anglo-Irish wares without doubt would have been ruthlessly quashed. But although there were several plans for flint-glass houses, there was nothing so alarming to report before Stiegel built his American Flint Glass Manufactory (second Manheim glasshouse) in 1769 and the Philadelphia Glass Works, built in 1771, was acquired by the Elliots and Gray in 1772.[12] By then English attempts to stop them probably would have been as futile as the proprietors' efforts to maintain them. Be that as it may, it appears that disturbing rumors reached England, and, in that period of strained relations, some governors were negligent in reporting on colonial manufactures. In 1768 three failed to send any report at all, and those of some others, stating that there was virtually no manufacturing in their provinces, were suspected of less than the truth by Prime Minister Grenville. Benjamin Franklin, writing to his son William, Governor of Jersey, about Grenville's complaints, suggested the tack to be taken to spill the disturbing winds of rumor: "You have only to report a Glass house, coarse window glass and bottles, all the finer goods coming from England and the like. I believe you will be puzzled to find any other, though I see great puffs in the papers." Governor Franklin took and elaborated on his father's hints. On glass in his province he reported:

A Glass House [Wistarburgh] was erected about twenty years ago in Salem County, which makes Bottles, and a very coarse Green Glass for windows used only in some of the houses of the poorer Sort of People. The Profits made by this Work have not hitherto been sufficient it seems to induce any Persons to set up more of the kind in this Colony: but since the late Act of Parliament laying a Duty on Glass exported to the Colonies, there had been a Talk of erecting others, but I cannot learn that any are yet begun. It seems probable that notwithstanding the

Duty, Fine Glass can still be imported into America cheaper than it can be made here.[13]

Governor Franklin might have added that the factory at Wistarburgh had been in successful operation for 29 years, supplying window glass and bottles to many citizens besides the "poorer Sort," and had contributed to the not inconsiderable fortune left by Caspar Wistar when he died in 1752. As Governor Belcher, who knew Caspar well, told his Boston friend, the works "turn'd out to great Profit. . . ." But perhaps the Franklins were unaware of such facts, or conveniently forgot them.

Governor Franklin was referring to the hateful Townshend Act of 1767, the third trespass upon colonial "rights" since the end of the French and Indian War in 1763, when England, depleted in purse and burdened with debts, decided her pampered wealthy colonies should contribute to parental support. And these restrictions came when colonial business was acutely depressed after nearly seven years of war-bred prosperity. First, the Sugar Act of 1764 had threatened, so those affected by it believed, to smother the vital West Indian trade. Then the Stamp Act of 1765 had so heightened growing resentment that violent opposition and a widespread boycott of English goods brought its repeal, and also further temptation to colonial manufacturing. *Now*, not only were existing trade regulations to be *strictly* enforced but TAXES were to be levied. Glass, an increasingly lucrative English export, was among the articles designated for "tax": on crown, flint, and white glass, a duty of 4s. 8d. per hundredweight, and on green glass 1/2d. Indignant citizens vowed to buy American goods or go without. And, of course, glass was among the specified articles in the Non-Importation Agreements signed by many citizens and most merchants—some reluctantly, carried along by the militant.

But nonimportation hurt: personal comfort and desires took precedence over adherence to cold principle, and by mid-1771, though some associations for nonimportation retained the ban on tea, paper, glass, and painters' colors,[14] the agreements were being buried quietly under wares imported by merchants in the port cities. As a result, at least in part, American glass manufacturers appealed in their advertisements to consumers' pocketbooks and in language calculated to deepen resentment against English policies and also perhaps to shame backsliders into buying home products. (An advertisement in a New York City or Philadelphia newspaper, or that of any port city, was read in many another and smaller community.) In 1769 Richard Wistar mildly pointed out that his glass was "clear of the Duties the Americans so justly complain of" and that it seemed "peculiarly the Interest of America to encourage her own manufactories, more especially those upon which duties have been imposed for the sole purpose of raising Revenue." The following summer, Stiegel, in emphatically worded advertisements, expressed both a conviction and a hope—a conviction that ". . . at this crisis it is the indispensable duty, as well as interest of every well wisher of America, to promote and encourage manufactures amongst ourselves"; a hope of approbation and encouragement "from the glorious spirit of patriotism at present voluntarily and virtuously existing here. . . ." In 1771, he told New Yorkers that he knew well "the patriotic spirit of Americans" and flattered himself that they would encourage their own country's manufactures. In 1773 the proprietors of the Philadelphia Glass Works were still hoping

the inhabitants of these provinces and of this city in particular, will in purchasing, give preference to Goods manufactured by their fellow citizens. Whereby they may be likely to receive again the money they expend, which it is in vain to expect when sent beyond the sea.[15]

Whatever the success of such appeals, it was not enough in itself to keep the glassworks in operation. By and large, it would be some decades before most Americans ceased to believe that glass, including wine and porter bottles, made abroad was not far superior, especially if English.

Even had political, commercial, and general economic conditions been favorable to colonial glasshouses, there were other obstacles to be hurdled before even a single glasshouse could be established, to say nothing of bringing up an infant industry. Financing and the continued paucity of expert glassmen were the most formidable, though materials and fuel, transportation, and marketing often were problems. Chronically the amount of capital needed was underestimated: the men who launched the enterprises had but limited conception of the expenses entailed. There had to be facilities for storing and preparing the ingredients; for melting, blowing, and annealing glass; for preparing the clay, making and storing melting pots; for cutting and curing the firewood; repairing the furnace, making and mending the irons and other tools; for housing workmen; for stabling oxen and horses; for boxes and hogsheads in which to pack the glass for shipment. Moreover, production was not year-round.

Usually it lasted from fall to spring, with the hot summer months between used for any necessary furnace repairs and pot making. If the glassmen did not participate in such activities, they had to be tided over the time the furnace was not in blast. All these things and others too *could* increase costs, and the farther a glasshouse was located from an established town, the more self-sufficient its community had to be; and, of course, the more diversified the skills of employees, besides the essential glassmen, had to be for all the ancillary activities. All wages were high, compared with those of Europe.

Equally vital to the success or failure of a glasshouse were expert glassmen with knowledge of furnace building and repair, glass composition and mixing a batch, glassblowing, pots, and pot making. And such glassmen were to be found only in Britain and on the Continent, where emigration of these craftsmen was forbidden or carefully discouraged. The majority who were persuaded to leave their homes and secure jobs came from Germany, most of them German Protestants lured by not only bright material prospects but more freedom and status than they enjoyed at home. Then, too, glassmen imported at great expense sometimes proved to have less practical and comprehensive knowledge than had been claimed. Some who may have been skilled blowers proved to know little more about pot making and furnace construction than a good cook would know about making her pots, pans, and stove. Apprentices were needed as well, but though some sons and nephews of glassmen tended to follow the family craft, native-born boys were not easily persuaded into so long and demanding an apprenticeship. Moreover, glassmen and apprentices sometimes absconded before, or defected when, their terms expired, drawn to less seasonal and exacting occupations or to the easily acquired land with its mantling of dignity and independence. The shortages of skilled glassmen, reluctance of boys to enter the craft, and tendency of both craftsmen and apprentices to abandon glassmaking were to bedevil glass manufacturers well into the 19th century.

The bottles blown in the colonial and also later 18th-century glasshouses would have been some or all of the kinds imported and typical of those made during the life-span of the glasshouse. However, in few instances can specimens be attributed to a specific glasshouse. Still, it is generally conceded that a large proportion, perhaps the vast majority, would have been free-blown, shaped by expansion and manipulation, with lips formed by "the tool," as glassblowers called their versatile pucellas. There probably was a large production of the so-called chestnut bottles and of globular bottles, even of demijohns, like and similar to the examples of Ills. 46 and 47. Also, I feel confident, some of the English wine bottles, sometimes sealed, were blown, following the forms (Ill. 52) prevailing during the years of a works' operation. Apothecary vials would have been similar to those in the doctor's saddlebag kit, Ill. 79, and when blown from white glass and lead glass, some doubtless were square and stoppered similar to those in the medicine chest in the same illustration. Some vials probably were similar, like 1 through 4, 14 through 17, and 19 in Ill. 77.

Still, molds must have been used in many of the glassworks. Probably they were used to some extent to give preliminary form to the parison destined to become a globular or cylindrical bottle. Certainly they were used for a straight-sided body. Definitely, they were used to impress a pattern on some gathers: for instance, one to be fashioned by free-blowing into a pocket bottle. Among the molds for a pattern might be a ribbed dip mold similar to Ill. 92 or to 2 in 93B, and ribbed two-piece molds similar to 3 in 93B. Others for reticulated designs might be small piece molds similar to Ill. 93A or two-piece molds similar to 93B. One or another of these types probably was used to pattern the gathers for the Pitkin-type flasks, Ill. 87, and 17 in Ill. 89, and the pocket bottles, 1 through 4 in Ill. 100. However, perhaps the type of mold most frequently used in the 18th-century glasshouses would have been the clay, or possibly wooden, mold to give body form, particularly to square, rectangular, and polygonal bottles like those in Ill. 72 and 1, 6 through 8, and 10 through 13 in Ill. 75. The square case bottles made in most of the houses would have been so shaped, and similar to 9, 10, or 13 in Ill. 47. Actually, any of the bottles in Ills. 46, 47, 51, 87, 88, 89, 90, and 100 attributed to the 18th and early 19th centuries could be types blown in more than one of the houses operating between 1739 and 1800. As we shall see, only a few of the 18th-century glasshouses survived into the 19th century, or were revived then, to produce bottles and containers of later fashions.

GLASSHOUSE SKETCHES

1. WISTARBURGH, *Salem County, New Jersey*

The glasshouse and community called Wistarburgh (sometimes spelled Wistarburg or Wistarberg) was founded by Caspar Wistar, a brass button manufacturer of Philadelphia. Though he was not a practical glassman, having found sand that seemed to him suitable for glassmaking in West (South) Jersey, Wistar decided to establish a glasshouse there. As his own capital was insufficient to finance the acquisition of the necessary land and to import glassmen, he supplemented it by money borrowed from wealthy acquaintances.[16] He then arranged with four expert glassmen to come to America from the Low Countries. According to the agreement, Wistar was to pay the glassmen's passage and advance the money for all expenses, including their support. It was stipulated that Wistar was to provide the necessary money for "land, fuel, servants, food and materials for a glassworks" and the glassmen, who were to teach the art only to Wistar and his young son Richard, to provide the know-how; Wistar was to receive two-thirds of any proceeds and the glassmen one-third. Apparently it was the first American cooperative venture of labor and capital in glassmaking. However, that there was a time limit to the copartnership and that it was to expire sometime after 1752 seem evident from Caspar Wistar's will, filed in March of that year.[17] The glassmen arrived in America in the spring of 1739.

In the meantime, Caspar Wistar had acquired some 2,000 acres of well-wooded land for his project. The glasshouse, completed by the fall of 1739, was so located that a small community, nearly sufficient unto itself, was necessary, but it was also strategically located for marketing the products as well as obtaining the essential sand, potash, firewood, and also a clay that would do for pots. It was about eight miles by good road from Salem and a mile and a half from two navigable creeks down which the glass could go by water on its way to Philadelphia or New York. The furnace, as Benjamin Franklin informed Thomas Darling of New Haven in 1747, was a small rectangular type about twelve feet long, eight wide, and six high, with three to four pots along the long side, and the fire was built on the floor. Some 2,400 cords of wood, cut in *three*-foot lengths, were consumed during the seven months the furnace was in blast during the year, a fact that points up the vital importance of wood holdings. However, the ashes provided the potash for the glass from which the window glass and bottles were blown. From one small furnace and only six glassmen at the time of Franklin's correspondence with Darling,[18] the works was expanded by the addition of a second furnace and the importation of more German glassmen.

When Caspar Wistar died in March 1752, he left his Jersey property, including the glassworks, tools, utensils, household goods, cattle, and so on, to Richard, who was to pay a third part of all proceeds to his mother. Also, each year he was to provide his brother Caspar with certain amounts of window glass and in addition ". . . Three Dozen of half Gallon Case Bottels and Six Dozen of Pocket Bottels one Groce of Quart Bottels half a Groce of half Gallon Bottels and three Dozen of Gallon Bottels." Richard continued the brass button business but maintained a shop for the sale of glass (some of which he apparently imported) in Philadelphia; he had experts to manage the glassworks at Wistarburgh. Also, like his father, he never overexpanded. Both trimmed their sails to the winds of their market, which was mainly the Philadelphia and Pennsylvania-German areas, nearby Jersey villages, and, in later years, New York City. And they prospered. Though in the troubled years between 1767 and 1775 a few "servants" deserted, it would seem there were no serious difficulties until the Revolution. War caused the fires to be drawn, but in what year has not been definitely determined. In October 1780 Richard offered for sale the glasshouse and all its property, which at that time included two furnaces, ovens for annealing glass and drying wood, two flattening ovens for window glass, a storehouse, pot house, house for cutting the window glass, stamping and rolling mills for preparing clay for pots, houses for workmen, a large mansion with bakehouse and "washhouse," and a storehouse with retail shop.[19] The following year Richard died, and so far as is known at present, glassmaking was never resumed at Wistarburgh.

Undoubtedly jars, pitchers, bowls, and other articles were blown from window-glass and bottle-glass metal for use of the glassmen's families and other Wistarburgh employees, and probably for sale in the "well assorted retail shop . . . kept above 30 years . . . as good a stand for the sale of goods as any in the county. . . .'" But the commercial products were window glass and bottles. That case bottles, pocket bottles, and bottles of quart, half-gallon, and gallon sizes were in the regular output seems indicated by Caspar's will, mentioned above, and also the fact that these were the sorts in demand. Quart bottles—as continued to be true—were in greater demand than the larger sizes. According to a 1765 advertisement, "Most sorts of bottles" were blown. However, no shapes were mentioned in the advertisements and no clues were given as to exactly what the sorts were, other than the following: pocket bottles, snuff and mustard bottles, bottles from a gallon to half-pint; full-measure half-gallon case bottles.[20] That the English-type wine bottles were among the sorts is indicated not only by high probability but also by fragments and bottoms of such bottles found on the Wistarburgh site by Frederick Hunter, John B. Kerfoot, and Harry Hall White. In the period of the works' production, possibly bottles of Types 4, 4a, and 5 were blown and almost certainly of Types 6, 7, and 8 (5 through 10 in Ill. 52). Also, at least one seal with initials has been unearthed, and a bottle with the seal of William Savery of Philadelphia has been tentatively attributed to Wistar. Personally, I believe it would be surprising if wine bottles were not sealed for some of Wistar's customers.

2. GERMANTOWN GLASSWORKS, *Braintree, Massachusetts*

The creation of a new manufacturing community to be manned by "imported" German Protestants was conceived by a visionary, optimistic German emigré, Joseph Crellius. Sometime in 1750 he found Bostonians with capi-

J OSEPH PALMER of *Ger-*
mantown in *Braintree*, makes (equal to any imported) Snuff Bottles, Pint, Quart, two Quart and Gallon Bottles, &c. Also Pots for Pickles, Conferves, &c. of all fizes : Likewife moft forts of Chymical Veffels, &c. And alfo the very beft Wool-Cards. Any Perfon wanting any large Quantity of any of thefe, may be fupply'd if they give feafonable Orders. The Cafh to be paid on Delivery of the Glafs, &c. ☞ N. B. He gives a Piftareen per Hundred Weight for broken green and black Glafs ; and two Coppers per Pound for white Glafs.
TO BE SOLD,
F IVE Lotts of choice Land, with three Dwelling Houfes thereon, fituar ..

5. Advertisement of wares made by Joseph Palmer in the Germantown glassworks, Braintree Township, Massachusetts. (*Boston News Letter,* Apr. 10, 1760.) *The New-York Historical Society, New York City*

tal to invest, and willing to risk it, in his project—John Franklin, brother of Benjamin and a tallow chandler; Peter Etter, a German stocking weaver; Norton Quincy, a prosperous merchant. The site selected in Braintree township was on the edge of Quincy at Shed's Neck, where they rented 100 acres of land from John Quincy. New capital was needed in 1752 when the village, appropriately called Germantown, was only partly completed. However, trees and shrubs had been planted! A pot house and furnace of a glasshouse had also been built.[21] In the meantime Crellius had gone to Germany in search of desirable settlers. His success and his return on September 19, 1752, occasioned the following news item: "Last Tuesday arrived here [Boston] a Ship from Holland, in which came Mr. Crellius with near 300 Germans, Men, Women and Children, some of whom are to settle at Germantown, and the others in the Eastern Parts of this Province. . . ." Among them were "artificers skilled in making glass of various sorts." Apparently they arrived none too soon, as about a month before that, Joseph Palmer, an Englishman of means and not a practical glassman, had leased the works, and his agreement with the proprietors stipulated an immediate start of production and expansion of the facilities.[22]

By November, when the president of Harvard, the Reverend Edward Holyoke, visited the glassworks (noted in his diary as established by a company of German Protestants), capital was again needed. At this point, Crellius and Etter seem to have dropped out of the venture, and so perhaps did Joseph Palmer—at least, in the scant documentary evidence known to me, he does not appear again until 1755. In any event, it was a new company (Franklin and Norton Quincy, joined by three merchants—Isaac Winslow, Thomas Flucker, and John Smith) that petitioned the assembly on November 27, 1752, to grant them a "Patent for making Glass for a Term of Years, and such further encouragement as shall be judged Reasonable for the Reasons mentioned." The reasons were the past expenditure of some hundreds of pounds Sterling and anticipated additional costs of £2,000 Sterling before they would be able "to reap any Advantage thereby." The bill for the sole privilege of making glass, which they were given permission to draft, was read by the assembly on December 1 and ordered "to lie on the Table." Monopoly or no monopoly, glassmaking progressed at Germantown, attracting curious visitors, even from miles away—so many, in fact, that the following notice appeared in two Boston newspapers:

Notice is hereby given, That for the future none will be admitted to see the new Manufactory at Germantown, unless they pay at least *One Shilling* lawful money and they are then desired not to ask above three or four Questions, and not to be offended if they have not a satisfactory Answer to all or any of them.
Note. The Manufactory has received considerable Damage and been very much retarded by the great number of People who constantly resort to the House.[23]

Far more hazardous to glasshouses than parties of visitors was fire, and fire destroyed the Germantown glasshouse, not from the frequent carelessness inside but from the elements outside. About 3 o'clock in the morning of May 29, 1755, the glasshouse was struck by lightning during a heavy thunderstorm and burned to the ground. Rebuilding must have started promptly, for by July 14 Jonathan Williams of Boston, who had "undertaken to carry on the Glass-Works . . . during one Fire [blast] at least," could advertise that glassblowing would start in a month or five weeks and orders could be sent to him or to Joseph Palmer.[24]

Just how long Palmer had been back in the picture, if he was ever entirely out of it, I have not ascertained. However, from sometime in 1755 until glassmaking ceased, Palmer seems to have had the management of the glassworks, possibly sole ownership toward the end. In fact, since he had a financial interest in other Germantown manufactories, he undoubtedly had in the glasshouse also, even before 1756. In April of that year he petitioned the assembly for assistance "by way of a Lottery or otherwise" because of the great expenditures in carrying on manufactures in Germantown, great losses by fire and otherwise suffered by himself and others "whereby they are wholly discouraged from proceeding any further in Company concerns." But it was February 11, 1757, before the Assembly considered a bill for "raising a Sum of Money by Lottery for the Encouragement of the Settlement called German-Town." On April 15 a bill was enacted allowing "John Quincy, Thomas Flucker and Isaac Winslow, Esqrs. [members of the company] with Mr. Edward Jackson, merchant. . . to set up a lottery or lotteries. . . ." Although the glass manufactory was specifically mentioned in the act as recorded in the *Acts and Resolves of the Province of Massachusetts Bay,* only the potash and cider manufactories were mentioned in the *Journals of the House of Representatives,* and only cider in the advertisements of the lottery. Whether or not the glasshouse profited by the lottery, it seems to have profited sufficiently from its output to have been kept in operation over a decade longer.[25] Another fire, late in 1768 or very early in 1769, coupled with lack of funds, apparently was the direct cause of the end of glassmaking in Germantown.

Until I found Joseph Palmer's notice published in the *Boston Gazette* of February 20, 1769, I had no definite evidence as to when the works closed. The notice seems to imply also that at some time after 1756 Palmer had acquired the sole or main interest in the works. So far as is known now, he found no one with enough "Public Vertue" and cash to lend, even at interest, so his notice becomes a curious epitaph for a brave venture:

To the PUBLIC

The Proprietor of the Glass Works at Germantown having met with great Losses by Fire, is himself unable to renew that Manufacture without Injury to another in which he is now engaged, or Assistance from some other Quarter; —He therefore invites such as are possess'd of Public Vertue and Ready Money, to assist him with Cash upon Interest, upon such Terms as may be more fully known by applying to *Charles Miller* on *Minot's* T.

As the Propriety of this Advertisement may be call'd in Question, considering the present distressing Situation of our public Affairs, which loudly call upon us to act with Vigor, instead of making Abundance of vain Pretences; an Excuse is made to the Public by assuring them that Application was made in a more private Way, to several Gentlemen of great Influence in the Town of *Boston*, who discouraged this Affair, under the mistaken narrow Notion that public Good here, meant only the Good of that particular Town, and expressly refused Encouragement, because the Manufactory was not to be carried on there.
Germantown, February 17, 1769.

Bottles of various kinds were the main product of Germantown, though some "Chymical" glass was made and, briefly, window glass. In their November 1752 memorial, Winslow and associates pointed out that the works would

be the means of supplying it [the Province] with Window Glass & Glass Bottles at a cheaper rate than they [could] be imported at, but also encourage . . . the manufacture of cyder which may be transported to the West Indies in great Quantities as Bottles may be so easily had and the Orchards of our Farmers thereby become as valuable as so many vineyards.

For a brief period, probably 1753/54, the company did make window glass, in part because it was then more profitable than their bottles. However, bottle production was not neglected: some days better than five gross were blown, commonly 80 or 90 from each of six or ten pots. Under Palmer, "Chymical" glass was made, as well as bottles for shipping cider to the West Indies in exchange for various commodities. Undoubtedly, as at Wistarburgh, the bottles were of most sorts. Specifically mentioned in 1755 were bottles and case bottles; in 1760, pint, quart, and gallon bottles, snuff bottles, pots for pickles, conserves, and the like (Ill. 5), round and square bottles from one to four quarts, cases of bottles (case bottles) of all sizes. It is probable that the bottles advertised by Jonathan Williams in 1756 were blown at Germantown. They were square case and round bottles from a pint to a gallon; pickle bottles, pint and quart black bottles.[26] These last may well have been heavy wine bottles, for it is likely that English wine bottles of Type 7 (9 in Ill. 52) were blown, possibly even Type 8 (10 in Ill. 52). In the form of glass drippings and small solid chunks, clear evidence of the production of light- and deep-green metal and light olive-amber was found by Richmond Morcom in his excavation on the glasshouse site. He found also part of an olive-green square or case bottle, six-sided bottles, cylindrical long-body vials, and also cylindrical, "rounds," wine bottles.

3. & 4. NEW WINDSOR, *Ulster County,* and NEWFOUNDLAND, *New York City*

The glasshouse at New Windsor in Ulster County, State of New York, and that at Newfoundland, on the outskirts of New York City, were treated by Hunter as distinctly separate ventures; by Knittle, as promoted by the same group of men, forming the Glass-House Company. In *American Glass* my father and I followed Knittle's interpretation of the meager evidence. Today, in the light of a few scraps of evidence unknown to me in 1941 and of reevaluation of the old, I incline to believe they probably were separate enterprises, although one or more of the same men were in each. I believe, too, that the New Windsor glassworks preceded the Newfoundland. Possibly sometime more data will be discovered that will either completely unravel the enmeshment—or tighten it. In any event the earliest known document in the case, a draft of an agreement between four New Yorkers and a German glassman, indicates that at the time of its drafting the site of the glassworks had not been determined. Also, the date of the agreement, February 1, 1752, and the fact that communication with Europe was a matter of months, not seconds, suggest that the plans for establishing a glassworks were well under way some time in 1751, and also the preliminary negotiations with the glassman.[27]

The men who formed the company were Matthew Earnest or Ernest, Samuel Bayard, Lodewyck Bamper or Bemper (merchants), and Christian Hertell (mariner); the glassman was Johan Martin Greiner of Saxe-Weimar. The draft stipulated that the company agree to provide the necessary monies for establishing the works and securing labor and glassmen, an expenditure anticipated to amount to £1,000 Sterling. A proper vessel was to be provided for the voyage to New York and money advanced for all expenses of the trip, but it was to be repaid by Greiner, without interest if paid within a year. Once he was in America, all his expenses of transport and for victuals and lodging—actually, a house was to be found for his

family—were to be paid by the company until a month after blowing began at the glasshouse. The company also was to grant him the privilege of using enough of the cleared land belonging to the glasshouse to raise garden stuff for his family and hay to feed a cow or two. After the glasshouse was completed and in production, the company was to pay him according to the glass delivered to it: "for every hundred Quart Bottles . . . twenty four styvers hollands money and for every hundred half gallon flasks 3 Gilders Hollands Mony & in proportion for all other Glass. . . ."

On Greiner's part, the agreement stipulated he should leave Rotterdam on February 1, 1752, or when any member of the Company thought proper. Greiner was to "assist from Sun Rise to Sun Set in helping erect a Glass Work and allso to make the Ovens, Potts & all other appurtenances there unto belonging, Nothing Excepted." (An accomplished glassman, indeed.) Also, he was to remain with the works at "City of N: York or at such place as the said Glass work shall be Erected" for 20 years from the day the glasswork began. During his term he was to instruct Earnest and his associates in the "whole Art and Mistery of Making a Glass house and Blowing Glass No Particular Excepted"; to assist in blowing glass, preparing and making all necessary tools; and in case of needed repairs to oven and pots, to "assist as much as in me lys." The absence of Greiner's name from any New York City records suggests that, if the agreement was implemented, he did not remain in New York but went to New Windsor.[28]

New Windsor, I now believe, was the site chosen for the glasshouse, which was built in 1752. On January 1, 1752, Samuel Bayard and Company (the same men who drew the agreement with Greiner) paid £360 for 10,360 acres of land in Orange and Ulster Counties for the purpose of establishing a glasshouse. Clearing the land and building the works probably began the following spring, or very early summer. In the meantime, arrangements to import glassmen besides Greiner apparently had been made, for a New York City news item dated the third of August, which appeared in the *Maryland Gazette* for August 20, 1752, mentioned the arrival of "a number of Glassmen, to work in a Glass Manufactory now erecting on the North River in the County of Orange." (Manhattan was never included in Orange County; even above Manhattan, the Hudson River was called North River by New Yorkers—as it is today in maritime insurance.)

Bamper was representing the company in New York in 1755. In July of that year, he advertised a £3 reward and all reasonable charges for apprehension of "a German Servant Man named Christian Medsher" who had run away from "the Glass-House at New-Windsor." In another advertisement he announced that "All Persons having demands on the Company of the Glass-House at New-Windsor" should bring their accounts to him as speedily as possible. As yet, the latest specific reference to the New Windsor works that I have seen was in a 1756 advertisement by the pewterer Johanes Will. Whether or not he ever had an interest in the works, at the time he sold "glassware made at New Windsor" and apparently bought "good Wood Ashes and broken Window and Bottle-glass" for use as cullet at the works.[29] Local history and tradition maintain that the glassworks operated until about 1785; if so, it fared better than the Newfoundland glasshouse.

If one accepts the assumption that the two glasshouses were entirely separate enterprises, then whether or not the Newfoundland glasshouse was built long before October 1754, or later, depends upon whether it was the one at New Windsor or the one at Newfoundland that was operated by the Glass House Company whose store on Sir Peter Warren's North River dock was kept by Thomas Lepper. Unfortunately, in his advertisement of October 14, 1754 (Ill. 6), Lepper did not mention the location of the *glasshouse*. However, in February 1757, Matthew Earnest (one of the New Windsor group also) was granted permission by the Common Council of the City of New York to build a dock "fronting his land . . . commonly called and known by the name New found Land," which was bounded on the south by the Warren land, and lay between the present 35th and 40th streets. In October 1758 Earnest advertised as follows:

This is to inform the Publick, That the new erected Glass-House, at Newfoundland, within four Miles of this City; is now at Work, and that any Gentleman may be suppl'd with Bottles, Flasks, or any sort of Glass agreeable to their Direction.

N.B. Any Persons that has Oak Wood to dispose of, by bringing it to the above-mentioned Place, will receive the New-York Price upon Delivery, by *Matthew Ernest.*

Of course, to its owners, a glasshouse only about three or four years old may have still seemed "new erected," though it seems unlikely to me, as does the necessity to advertise for oak wood if the company had an interest in New Windsor's many acres.

The next one hears of the Newfoundland glasshouse is of its being offered for sale, with the outhouses and all the implements, by Nicholas Bayard and Matthew Earnest in July 1762. By the spring of 1763 it had become a place of public entertainment, and off and on for five years or so was a popular tavern. The main cause of failure may have been loss of key glassmen, particularly to the land, if Governor Moore was referring to Newfoundland when he wrote in 1767:

The Master of a Glasshouse; which was set up here a few years ago now a Bankrupt, assured me that his ruin was owing to no other cause than being deserted in this manner [i.e., abandoning glassmaking for land] by the Servants which he Imported at great expense and that many others had suffered and been reduced as he was, by the same kind of misfortune.[30]

As for the products, it seems safe at present to assume that at both New Windsor and Newfoundland the main products were bottles, though Lepper's 1754 advertisement (Ill. 6) mentions a "variety of other glassware" and

6A. Advertisement of glassware made at New Windsor or Newfoundland works, for sale by Thomas Lepper, "Store-Keeper to the Glass House Company." Note that, on order, "Gentlemen" could have their names on their bottles. (*The New York Gazette or Weekly Post Boy,* Nov. 4, 1754.) *The New-York Historical Society, New York City*

6B. Advertisement of wares produced in 1798 by Christopher Trippel & Co., at the Old Glass Manufactory at Kensington, undoubtedly the old Philadelphia Glass Works rented from Thomas Leiper. (*Claypoole's American Advertiser* [formerly *Pennsylvania Packet*], Apr. 12, 1798.) *The New-York Historical Society, New York City*

Earnest's of 1758, "any sort of glass agreeable to their [Gentlemen's] Directions." Undoubtedly "all sorts of Bottles from 1 Quart to 3 Gallons and upward" and "flasks" of some sorts were blown at both. And whether Lepper served New Windsor or Newfoundland, the English wine bottles of the period (Types 7 and 9 in Ill. 52) doubtless could be had with or without a personalized seal bearing the name or initials of the owner. If New Windsor did indeed continue until or after the Revolution, then wine bottles of Type 8 (10 in Ill. 52) probably were blown there.

5. HILLTOWN TOWNSHIP, *Bucks County, Pennsylvania*

The existence of a glasshouse in Bucks County was unknown to students of glass until a few years ago. That from 1755 to about 1784 one was operated by glassmen in a section of Hilltown Township settled by Germans was discovered by Rudolf P. Hommel, who has searched various records for information and conducted excavations on the glassworks site. From at least 1776 to 1784, the works was run by a Peter Mason (Mr. Hommel suggests the name possibly was originally Maurer). Mason worked either for himself on rented land (which was not unusual in America and usual in Europe) or for the owner of the land on which the glasshouse stood. In 1772, that landowner was a Frederick Kern. From the fragments recovered, it was apparent that the metal was green glass and the main products were window glass and bottles, though there was evidence that household articles such as milk pans and some footed vessels were blown. The bottles apparently were case bottles with very short necks and globular bottles, which, like the square bottles, had no kick-up. The necks were finished with an everted lip. Probably all were the familiar Continental types. And, as no necks were found with an applied string-ring, it is probable no English or Continental type of heavy-walled wine bottles was blown.[31]

6. ELIZABETH FURNACE and MANHEIM,
Pennsylvania, glasshouses of Henry William Stiegel[32]

No name connected with American glass is more famous or better known than *Stiegel*, in no small degree because the man and his rise and fall as an entrepreneur are so fascinatingly portrayed in *Stiegel Glass*. However, insofar as glass is concerned, the association for most of us has not been with ordinary bottles and flasks but with flint and nonlead glass tableware of which, presumably, Stiegel was the first colonial manufacturer. Yet ordinary bottles and flasks and window glass were his principal products from the fall of 1763 to that of 1769. He was not a practical glassman: he was part owner of a successful iron furnace at Elizabeth Furnace and another at Charming Forge, not far from the busy market center of Lancaster; he also owned a local store and brewery. Capital for his new venture undoubtedly was to come from the profits of the old. In 1763 he built the Elizabeth Furnace glasshouse, which started production in September 1763 with just three glassmen blowing—Christian Nasel, Benjamin Misky, and Martin Grenier. As Martin's last name was spelled "Greiner" in later account books, one wonders whether, having dropped the Johan, he was the Greiner of Saxe-Weimar with whom Matthew Earnest and his copartners made the agreement about 1752 and if he had "deserted" to Stiegel.

By the following year, Stiegel and his staunch Tory partners in Philadelphia had planned and laid out the town of Manheim, also near Lancaster and about 80 miles from Philadelphia. There his first Manheim glasshouse was started in October 1764, and on February 7, 1765, Stiegel advertised in the *Pennsylvania Gazette* that "the Business of Glass-making in it is carried on."[33] In the fall, or possibly early the next year, the fires were drawn at the Elizabeth Furnace works. In the meantime, Stiegel had made a trip to England. Though the ostensible purpose may have been the orders he secured for the iron furnaces, his objectives must have included gathering information about the man-

ufacture of flint glass and making contacts through which he later succeeded in obtaining blowers—English, Irish, and Italian—for his second Manheim glasshouse, the American Flint Glass Manufactory. A consuming desire to be an entrepreneur worthy of his cherished soubriquet "Baron," a passion to make flint glassware equal to that imported from England, and an optimistic confidence (unwarranted) in the durability of nonimportation observances by American merchants and citizens doubtless were strong motivations in building this largest of his glasshouses. In April 1769 production ceased at the first house, as all hands were drafted to assist in finishing the second. This was said to have been "90 feet high, dome-like in shape and walls built of red brick imported from England and brought from Lancaster, Pa. to Manheim, Pa. on Connestoga wagons." Probably it was in production by late fall, and Hunter believes that blowing ceased then for all time at the first Manheim house, though for some reason a new roof was put on in 1773.

Although they made ordinary glass, as the previously quoted report to London stated, the Elizabeth Furnace and the first Manheim glasshouses were moderately successful, not making Stiegel a millionaire but perhaps yielding a modest profit, or at least breaking even. But he was not content with these two. He overexpanded at an economically impossible period of colonial upheaval. And he lived in a more and more princely, extravagant fashion, far beyond his means. The £150 granted by the Pennsylvania Council in 1771 was no more effective than a single log in a glasshouse furnace would have been. The lottery in 1773 was a disastrous failure. His American Flint Glass Manufactory proved to be a Moloch, consuming all his resources and those he could borrow. On May 7, 1774, Stiegel wrote in his account book: "Glass House shut down." In November, when all efforts to raise money for his creditors had failed, he was thrown into debtor's prison. Stiegel was released just before Christmas, only to slip back gradually into the obscurity from which he had erupted; there he remained for over a hundred years.

At least one attempt was made to revive the works as a green-glass house, but it seems not to have been successful. In February 1775, the glasshouse and all other Stiegel property in Manheim were bought at sheriff's sale by Michael Dieffenderfer, one of the Lancastrians who had handled Stiegel's output. Dieffenderfer, Paul Zantiziner (another Lancaster merchant who had sold Stiegel's glass), and three other partners undertook to carry on the "Glass Manufactory." On October 21, according to their advertisement in the *Pennsylvania Gazette*, they had "a large Quantity of green glass upon hand," and they flattered themselves that gentlemen, merchants, and shopkeepers would favor them with their custom. Though they offered 2d. a pound for broken flint glass and half-penny a pound for broken green glass, it would seem they made only green glass and probably their products were mainly bottles. It would seem also that too few patriotic gentlemen, merchants, and shopkeepers responded to their advertisement.

As I have said, until his American Flint Glass Manufactory was in operation, Stiegel's production consisted mainly of window glass and bottles. Like so many other manufacturers, he used the blanket phrase "All sorts of bottles" in his advertisements. Some of the "sorts" were specified in his ledger for the first Manheim works for October 1765 to April 1767—pocket bottles, pocket pints, case bottles, snuff bottles, bottles from half-pint to three gallons. It seems safe to assume that before 1765, and for as long as ordinary bottles were produced, the same sorts of bottles were blown. However, after the flint-glass house was in operation, the quantity of green-glass containers probably was reduced. Still, junk bottles and mustard bottles, presumably of green glass, appear in the 1769/70 list compiled by Hunter. Phials do too, and "all sorts of phials for druggists" were advertised in 1772, as were "enamelled smelling bottles, common and twisted ditto."[34] The twisted smelling bottles are believed to have been like those shown in Ill. 103, which led to attribution of *all* such pattern-molded ribbed smelling bottles to Stiegel until it was learned that they were made well into the 19th century, and also in Britain. Now they are usually called *Stiegel-type*. Also attributed to Stiegel are the choice pattern-molded bottles like 2 and 4 through 6 in Color Plate II, which have never yet been associated with any other glasshouse. It is believed at present that they were blown only in his last glasshouse. As for the English wine bottles, no one, so far as I know, has ever attributed any of them to Stiegel. If, by chance, some were blown in his glasshouse, they would have been Types 7 and 8 (9 and 10 in Ill. 52). For a further discussion, see Part VI: 1. Pattern Molds and Pattern Molding; 2. Pitkin-Type Bottles and Flasks; and 3. Stiegel-Type Bottles and Flasks.

7. PHILADELPHIA GLASS WORKS, *Kensington, Philadelphia, Pennsylvania*

In 1771, few if any American colonials anticipated that the current unpleasantness with the Mother Country would lead to a shooting war for independence. And Henry William Stiegel, proprietor of the Manheim glassworks, was not alone in believing competition possible in the glass market, and in placing too much faith in patriotic abstinence from English wares. Among the optimistic were a skinner and a watchmaker in Philadelphia—Robert Towars and Stephen Leacock—whose trades apparently had provided money to invest. On October 3, 1771, for a yearly rental of £15 "lawful money of Pennsylvania," they leased a plot of land in the township of Richmond near Philadelphia, a plot bounded on one side by the Delaware River, thus ensuring cheap and convenient water carriage for their glasswares. There they erected a "Glass house furnace and other improvements." That their intent was to make flint glassware is suggested by a January 23, 1772, advertisement: "the best Price is paid for broken Flint glass." This was repeated on January 30, with the addition of "good Alkaline Salts." It had also been announced on January 23 that "one or two workmen and Servitors will

meet with good Encouragement"; and on January 30 that "one workman and two Servitors [were] wanted at the Factory."[35] Where did they, and their successors, secure any glassmen? None were imported by them so far as is known at present; probably a few were lured from Stiegel and Wistar. Possibly some ex-glassmen returned to their art. However, doubtless there were too few glassmen and production was not extensive.

Anyway, whether from lack of funds or of workmen, or other causes, Towars and Leacock soon lost their eagerness to be glass manufacturers: on November 5, 1772, they sold the glasshouse with all its utensils and tools, including molds, and auxiliary buildings for £400, with the land still subject to the £15 ground rent, to Isaac Gray (merchant), John Elliott, Sr. (merchant), John Elliott, Jr. (brush-maker), and Samuel Elliott (tanner). John Elliott, Sr., had long maintained a looking-glass store, The Sign of the Bell and Looking Glass, where he sold all sorts of imported mirrors and other articles, supplied and silvered new glasses, replaced broken glass in bookcase doors, and the like. Isaac Gray dealt in wines and spirits, sugar and spices, tea and coffee, and featured "Choice Philadelphia Bottled Beer and Cyder" for foreign and domestic consumption. He also bought and sold beer bottles by the dozen or the gross. Thus glass produced in the Philadelphia Glass Works (also referred to as "made at Kensington") could be sold in his store and used by him. In fact, Gray's need for bottles for beer and cider may well have been a factor in his joining the company. And if sheet window-glass was made, Elliott too would have been a customer.[36]

In January 1773, the new proprietors advised the public that, "Having compleated" their works, they were ready to supply white and green glass of any kinds, including window glass, in any quantities, and as good as and as cheap as British imports. At the same time they found "it necessary to admit none but purchasers to the value of five shillings each," so inconvenienced had they been by the great resort of spectators to the glasshouse. Then, or soon afterward, the property was "inclosed on all sides with a good strong fence seven feet high, chiefly cedar." As described later, the buildings consisted of a brick (38′ by 42′) glasshouse with air furnace and annealing oven and, contiguous to it, a long narrow (24′ by 12′) brick "Shrow house" and mixing room; cedar-shingled (16′ by 24′) storehouse with one brick end; cedar-shingled two-story (26′ by 27′) dwelling; a grinding mill, and blacksmith shop; "several convenient shades, a well of water with a good pump, a baking oven &c." Upwards of £1,000 had been expended, but at a time when materials cost "less than one half the present [1777] prices."[37] Some, if not all, of these buildings and improvements contributed to the company's need for funds in the spring of 1773.

Funds were obtained, and John Elliott & Company operated the Philadelphia Glass Works for another three years or so. As has been previously mentioned, the proprietors resorted to that favorite means of raising money for all kinds of projects, a lottery. It was conducted from spring into the late fall of 1773, and at the same time as that for Stiegel's Manheim works. Moreover, each seems to have been called the American Flint Glass Manufactory Lottery. Whether or not the public paid attention to, or was influenced by, the dispute over which one rightfully claimed priority in flint-glass manufacture, the lottery for the Philadelphia Glass Works seemingly was at least fairly successful, whereas Stiegel's was not.[38] Though apparently the lottery's returns were a timely financial transfusion, sales must have improved also, especially after Stiegel's production ceased in April 1774. Possibly because a "sett of good workmen" (probably from Manheim) was obtained late in that year, the long roster of articles, cut and plain, on hand in February 1775 rivaled the earlier ones of Stiegel and exceeded those of importers. It is also interesting to note that those wishing to gratify their curiosity about the mysteries of glassmaking no longer had to buy 5s. worth of glass, though they did pay an admittance fee of 2s. at the gate, a sum at which the proprietors hoped no one would take umbrage and which was "very inadequate to the hindrance occasioned" by visitors' presence. War, with its shackles for trade and manufacturing, was but a few months away when, in the same February advertisement, the company offered to cheerfully and duly execute "Orders or patterns for any sorts of glasses for Apothecaries, Virtuosi, or others."[39]

For reasons not mentioned, but imaginable, all the property of the Philadelphia Glass Works was offered for sale at public vendue in April 1777, and in May, all glassware on hand when the works closed. There was no buyer, but possibly the works was rented by Felix Farrell and George Bakeoven. Perhaps both men, almost surely Farrell, had been employed at the glasshouse. It was the logical place for Farrell to have sought employment if he followed his craft after he went to Philadelphia from the Manheim glassworks. This he did in 1771 because, as he said, Stiegel failed to pay the wages required by their articles of agreement. That Farrell and Bakeoven erected a glasshouse in the Kensington area when a fully equipped one was available seems utterly unlikely. However, at present nothing definite is known of their career except that, in August 1777, they *were* blowing glass that was for sale at their Kensington warehouse or at Abraham Cloathing's in Philadelphia, and they were offering to buy broken flint and window glass. (Significantly, perhaps, green glass was not mentioned.) That the operation was on a small scale is suggested by the few items listed—decanters and tumblers of quart and pint sizes, wineglasses and phials—though other sorts of glass could be had on special order.[40] Possibly there were no orders, since by fall the British occupied Philadelphia and then English goods flowed in freely through 1778.

About a year and a half after Howe and his troops left Philadelphia, the Philadelphia Glass Works found a buyer. In the meantime, in October 1779, Samuel Elliott had transferred to Isaac Gray his quarter-share in the glassworks and property, along with his responsibility for a quarter of the ground rent. So it was Gray and the two John Elliotts who sold the property on May 5, 1780, to Thomas

Leiper, a Philadelphia tobacconist. The terms reflect the complicated money difficulties of the times: £425 lawful Pennsylvania money in gold or silver at the rate of 7s. 6d. for a hard dollar, and so in proportion for other specie in hand, and of course the perpetual £15 yearly ground rent. Doubtless Leiper was prompted as much by his own need for containers as by visions of a wide market. I have found no evidence to indicate he prospered greatly as a glass manufacturer. In fact, it seems probable no glass was made between 1783, when a Pennsylvania glasshouse was reported as operating, and 1789 or the 1790s. When Philadelphians celebrated their state's adoption of the Constitution in 1787, no glassmen were among the many craftsmen and tradesmen in the long triumphal "Constitution" parade; and none in the July 4, 1788, parade in which Leiper carried the tobacconists' standard. Moreover, in that year, he was buying bottles from the Dowesborough glassworks near Albany, New York.[41]

Presumably, in the light of present evidence, the glasshouse was idle until 1798, except for a rental in 1789 to one Philip Stimel, who "Wanted for Glass-Works, Two or Three Bottle-Blowers." Unfortunately, Stimel did not give the glassworks a name in his advertisement in the *Pennsylvania Packet* of September 10, 1789, but the Philadelphia Glass Works was the only one existing there at the time, so far as is now known. If Stimel did operate the works, it would seem to have been for a brief period. The works were then idle until 1798, when apparently Leiper rented them to a Christopher Trippel & Company, which announced in April that they now had "in blast and good order the OLD GLASS MANUFACTORY AT KENSINGTON, in Northern Liberties of Philadelphia" (Ill. 6A). A notice appearing in *Claypoole's American Daily Advertiser* on December 12, 1798, indicates that George, Basil, and Levi Fertner (glass manufacturers) had been members of the firm; an "N B" said: "The glass manufactory in all its branches is still carried on by Christopher Trippel and Co." The following January (1799) the firm opened a store in Philadelphia at the southwest corner of Vine and Third streets, which apparently was managed by Michael Fortune, who also took orders for Kensington wares and gave the "highest price" for old glass.[42] Probably the firm operated the works throughout the year, or until James Butland & Company took possession.

It has been thought that glass was made at this glasshouse site for over a century after Leiper sold the property in 1800, and also that the various proprietors and their dates were definitely established. However, if my interpretation is correct, data from recent research in newspapers and land records, though still incomplete, necessitates removing several of the old pieces of the jigsaw history and supplies some hitherto missing pieces. To begin with 1800, the property, still subject to the ground rent, and all the equipment were purchased on March 6 for $2,333 "lawful money of the United States" by Joseph Roberts, Jr., James Rowland, and James Butland, who formed a partnership to operate the glassworks under the firm name of James Butland & Company. In January 1802 the partnership was dissolved; Rowland and Butland purchased Roberts's entire interest for $2,548.70 to be paid, with lawful interest, in yearly installments through January 1, 1807. As Roberts "died intestate without making legal provision for the performance of the said contract," it was his administrators who instituted the necessary legal procedures, but not until February 29, 1804, was the indenture finally drawn and signed. On the sixteenth of the following March, Rowland and Butland gave "full satisfaction of & for the consideration monies . . ." and, for the consideration of $1.00, Roberts's widow signed a complete release on the same day.[43]

I have found no evidence that Butland sold out to Rowland in 1804, which suggests that possibly a misreading of the 1804 indenture led to Weeks's statement in 1880 (followed by later writers, including myself) that James Butland sold his interest to James Rowland for $2,548 in that year. Actually, it was on September 1, *1815*, that Rowland acquired Butland's interest, presumably for $3,500. This was the amount for which he mortgaged the property to one Anthony Williams when he bought out Butland. The next transfer occurred after James Rowland's death in 1832. On September 29, 1832, in a division of the estate, James Rowland, Jr., took the still mortgaged property, along with "three steel furnaces" on it, and bought his brother Joseph's share for $2,750. The following year, July 10, 1833, James, Jr., sold the property to Thomas W. Dyott, M.D. (glass manufacturer, already owner of abutting land and glassworks, which he called Dyottville), for $12,000.[44] No mean profit. Either the dollar had greatly depreciated or land values had soared.

Much more research is necessary if we are to learn exactly what happened on and to this 18th-century glasshouse site after 1800. As usual, there are a few facts and many conjectures. From 1800 through 1804, the shop of James Butland & Company was listed in the city directories at 80 North 4th Street in Philadelphia; in 1805 only James Butland was listed at that address, and as a glass manufacturer. Also in that year, Nicholas Swerer was manager of the Kensington Glass Works—at least he was referred to as such in a letter written April 19, 1805, by James O'Hara, proprietor of the Pittsburgh Glass Works. From 1806 through 1809 Butland was listed as a glassblower, surely an error as to occupation. James Rowland was listed as an iron merchant until his death in 1832, and without reference to any connection with a glassworks or glass. However, in August 1808, Rowland advertised that about the twentieth of the month the Kensington Glass Works would be in operation and orders for bottles would be "executed as usual, on application at the Glasshouse, or to the subscriber, No. 95 N Second-str." Since, in an 1810 letter, General O'Hara mentioned a blower whom he might obtain from Kensington, apparently the factory was operating that year. The last reference to ware of which I have record was in *Poulson's American Daily Advertiser* of February 7, 1812: John Dorsey's advertisement of coming auctions announced that on "the 11th inst. at 2 o'clock at Kensington Glass Works / 3000 Bushels of first quality Virginia Coals in lots to suit purchasers, / Seltzer Bottles do / Snuff bottles do . . ." would be sold. That does not sound as though the glassworks was in flourishing production—quite the contrary.[45]

Moreover, it seems significant that neither glasshouse nor glassmakers' equipment was mentioned among the buildings, appurtenances, et cetera, in 1832 and 1833 as in previous indentures, but steel furnaces were. Though it is unlikely that furnaces and ovens of the old 18th-century glasshouse had survived, Butland and Rowland may have repaired and restored them. In any event, it seems likely that (1) Rowland and Butland had ceased making glass between 1812 and 1815, when Rowland bought out Butland, and (2) Rowland's steel furnaces were those operated by Rowland, possibly including the works originally constructed for glassmaking. Certainly the works was *not* the Kensington Glass Works for which Dyott had been sole agent and which he acquired about 1821; that works was established in 1816 *on the lot next* to the "old Glass Works" by Hewson, Connell & Company, whose lot abutted the one on which the original Philadelphia Glass Works was built.[46] However, since an 1821 advertisement referred to "Kensington Glass Factories," possibly the old works had been rented from James Rowland, Jr., and reconverted to glass production.

Although, with one possible exception, I have found no direct reference to ordinary green-glass bottles before 1798, they must have been in the Philadelphia Glass Works' neat assortment of white and green glassware advertised in 1773. It would be extraordinary if no bottles were blown for the beer and cider sold by Isaac Gray or no snuff bottles were made for Thomas Leiper and other tobacconists. A few sorts of bottles were named specifically in 1773, 1775, and 1777. Case bottles were among the "home made White flint glass" offered by Isaac Gray in 1773 and bottles (flint or green or both) for cases by John Elliott & Company in 1775. Gray's advertisement ended with "Also a few groce of black Bottles," which possibly were of Type 8 (10 in Ill. 52). Since he had long dealt in bottles for potables, possibly the "home made" did not include the black bottles. Pocket bottles and smelling bottles were in the 1775 roster. "Phials of all sizes" appeared also, and again in the short list of Farrell and Bakeoven glassware. Some of these, almost certainly, were white glass, possibly flint glass, or both, and probably among them were stoppered square phials like those in the medicine chest in Ill. 79. As yet I have found no advertisement of bottles produced by Leiper, or by James Butland & Company; only the one by James Rowland referred to above. But among the wares specifically mentioned by Christopher Trippel & Company in their April 1798 advertisement were "green bottles of all sizes, claret bottles, olive bottles, caper bottles, anchovies bottles and snuff bottles *of all patterns*." (The italics are mine.) Incidentally, this is the earliest mention I have as yet of "olive," "caper," and "anchovies bottles." However, it is known that olives, capers, and anchovies were put up in bottles by 1771, and doubtless much earlier. The firm's next advertisement,

January 23, 1799, listed fewer bottles—only "snuff and mustard bottles of all sizes, half gallon, quart and pint bottles."[47]

During the Revolution there were a few attempts to establish new glasshouses, for—war or no war—bottles and window glass were essentials in far too limited supply to meet the continual and expanding demand. Among the factors contributing to the shortage were the disruption of business and blockage of the channels of commerce. Though American ports were open to any ship except a British one, England's blockade of the ports not in her hands was too effective. As the tide of foraging and fighting, which had engulfed so much business activity, receded from an area, however, local commerce, trade, and manufacturing started growing again. A few men looked to glassmaking. Besides Leiper's intent to revive the Philadelphia Glass Works, at least three other projects were planned before 1783 in war-free localities. In October 1779, a group of Connecticut Yankees obtained a 25-year monopoly from the state; they expended considerable sums, and asked for further aid in June 1780. This time the assembly granted a 15-year monopoly provided they started by November 1, 1781.[48] Nothing more is known of the venture at present. Two glasshouses were built: one at Temple, New Hampshire; the other in South Jersey. Both failed, but the Jersey house was rescued by new capital and administrative ability.

8. THE NEW ENGLAND GLASS WORKS *of Robert Hewes, New Hampshire*

In 1780, the year Leiper bought the Philadelphia Glass Works and Richard Wistar offered his for sale, Robert Hewes of Boston started glassmaking near Temple, not far from Boston as the crow flies. In his case, as in most others, glassmaking was a far cry from the source of his livelihood and capital—a prosperous shop near the Liberty Pump for the sale of crown glass, hard and soft soap, hair powder, Poland starch, glue, neat's-foot oil, candles, and so on, and in Pleasant Street, a glue manufactory and slaughterhouse.[49] Also, like his colonial predecessors who had launched glasshouses, he was not a practical glassman; but unlike them, he *was* a theoretical one, having read and studied available treatises on the subject. He was fascinated particularly by crown window glass, the best and the most expensive and difficult kind to make. It was that kind he hoped to produce at Temple, and at the time, as Deming Jarves commented later, window glass was "called for by the immediate wants of the people."

Choosing a site in the forest on a mountainside, he "carried his works to his fuel." As he told Jarves years later, the spot was so remote that during the building of the glasshouse the tracks of bears were frequently seen around it in the morning. Again a glasshouse was manned by Germans—not, as has been believed, by deserters from the British Army but, as Kenneth M. Wilson discovered, by glassmen who had been at Germantown until that works closed in 1769 and were glad to return to their craft. Shortly after the works, called the New England Glass Works, was finished, it was consumed by fire. Then, though rebuilt immediately, its furnace collapsed at the first melt, so we are told. Hewes appealed to town and state for aid. Although the town voted a loan in March 1781, the conditions were unacceptable to Hewes. Also in March, the state General Court authorized a "Glass-Works Lottery" in which the First Class consisted of "12,000 TICKETS at 2 dollars of the Emission cash of which 3500 [were] Prizes." Tickets were still available in Boston on May 31, 1781, but apparently neither the country's advantage in having a glassworks nor Temple's need of encouragement occasioned the anticipated rapid sale. The venture died of lack of money and a bad location.[50] But Hewes's enthusiasm was not killed. His vision was a factor in rooting Boston's glass industry and in his association with the Pitkins' East Hartford glassworks. However, his was not a Midas touch—neither project prospered during his association with it.

Hewes did realize his dream of making crown glass during the brief operation of the Temple works before the fire, but apparently only samples were made. Excavations on the site, though, have unearthed fragments of only ordinary window glass and bottle glass—colorless, light aquamarine to clear medium green, olive-amber, and olive-greens. Bottle necks and bases found two decades or so ago by John Gayton indicate that so-called chestnut bottles of various sizes were blown, thus supporting the local and family attributions of some of these bottles to Temple. Gayton found also part of a circular seal bearing the letters "PLE"—suggesting that seals with "TEMPLE" were affixed to the shoulder of chestnut bottles or English wine bottles of Type 8 (10 in Ill. 52), or both. Since Mr. Gayton's discoveries, further evidence of sealed bottles and also of the probable use of pattern molds for ribbing has been unearthed by Richmond Morcom. In the summer of 1963 Mr. Morcom (whose collecting has led him to delving on several New England glasshouse sites and that at Clementon, New Jersey) made a most exciting and fortuitous find. In a letter about his excavations he wrote: "When I stepped over the [glasshouse] wall at Temple I wasn't too optimistic and yet less than ten seconds after my arrival I was holding the Hewes seal. Somebody else had uncovered it and left it on the side of a small hole." The seal is much pitted as a result of being buried in the earth so long, but within a now-faint circle of fine beading are four lines of inscription. The first two are clearly discernible: "ROB.[T] / HEWES"; the next two, indistinct: "MANU[?]", possibly an abbreviation of "manufacturer," and below, presumably, "1781". All the letters are capitals with serifs. Among other shards recovered by Mr. Morcom were dark green thick-walled bottle fragments and one thick-walled corroded top of a bottle neck with everted lip and crude string-ring, which lend support to a supposition that some English wine bottles of the period were blown. Possibly square bottles of case and smaller sizes were made also. There is at least one slender dark bottle about 2⅛″ square and 9″ tall attributed to Temple by family history.[51]

9. THE NEW-JERSEY GLASS MANUFACTORY, *the first Stanger glasshouse, later called the Olive Glass Works, Glassboro, New Jersey*

The second glasshouse built during the Revolution was the second in New Jersey. Being the first built after the last of the 13 colonies signed the Articles of Confederation, it was the first *United States* glasshouse. It was also the first United States cooperative venture of practical glassmen combining ownership, management, and production—a proud estate from which financial difficulties soon returned them to their familiar roles as craftsmen. By May 1780, Solomon Stanger (also spelled Stinger and Stenger) had acquired a large tract of unimproved land in "a healthy part of Gloucester County and in a plentiful neighborhood for fuel . . . seven miles from the navigable waters of Mantua Creek and 20 miles from Philadelphia." There he, with Daniel, Francis, Peter, and Philip Stanger (said to be his brothers), started a little community of dwellings and a glasshouse with auxiliary buildings. Soon they were joined by Adam and Christian Stanger in the capacity of glassblowers. The community, first known simply as the Glass House, was called Glassborough by 1802 (later shortened to Glassboro), a name said to have been chosen by the Gloucester Fox Hunting Club in honor of the glassworks.[52]

By October 1784, about two years after the first blast, all the Stangers' interest had been acquired by men of means and business ability, under whom the glassworks prospered. In the next 30 years before ownership merged with that of the 19th-century Harmony Glass Works, several changes occurred in the operating firms, also changes in products, plant, and name. By 1786, if not when taken over by Colonel Thomas Heston and Thomas Carpenter, it was called the New-Jersey Glass Manufactory. In 1810, Edward Carpenter and Peter Wickoff changed the name to the Olive Glass Works, possibly because by then at least three other New Jersey glasshouses were operating. It is said that Edward Carpenter's death precipitated a crisis in 1813, and the works gradually fell into disuse until David Wolf acquired an interest about 1815. However, from December 1814 through February 1815, advertisements of Carpenter's half-interest, to be sold at auction by decree of the Orphans' Court of Gloucester County, speak of the works as "now in blast and in full operation." They mention also a partly completed second glasshouse that could "be finished at small expense." Doubtless it was in this period that Thomas W. Dyott, M.D., acquired an interest: he wrote that he became interested during the War (1812) and "so early as 1815" in a New Jersey glassworks, "the first that continued in operation for any number of years." It

7A. Advertisement of the products of the New-Jersey Glass Manufactory of Heston & Carpenter, proprietors of the glassworks started by the Stangers about 1781 in Gloucester County near Woodbury, New Jersey. Note that the advertisement is dated *(lower left corner)* "November 28 [1798]. (*New York Mercantile Advertiser,* Dec. 6, 1799.) *The New-York Historical Society, New York City*

7B. In 1808, under Carpenter & Wickoff, the name "New-Jersey Glass Manufactory" was changed to "Olive Glass Works." In 1816 Thomas W. Dyott became the sole agent in Philadelphia. This advertisement, the earliest we have found as yet of the Olive Glass Works, is dated September 26, so it must have first appeared in the newspaper by September 1816. (*True American and Commercial Advertiser,* Jan. 17–20, 1817.) *The New-York Historical Society, New York City*

would appear that the firm of David Wolf & Company was formed in 1816, and its agent was T. W. Dyott & Company in Philadelphia. From 1817, apparently into 1822, T. W. Dyott was the sole agent, at least according to advertisements. Seemingly he was retained in that capacity by Isaac Thorne, who acquired the Olive Glass Works in 1821. In

1824 Thorne sold the works to Jeremiah Foster, who merged them with the nearby Harmony Glass Works.[53]

Various sorts of bottles were the principal commercial output. However, the bad New Jersey window glass reported by Lord Sheffield in 1783 probably was blown at Glassboro. Also, tradition asserts that, in addition to their green glass, Heston and Carpenter made not only window glass but also flint glass. Although there are doubts still about flint glass, there are none about good white-glass production. In June 1788 it was widely reported that "A WHITE GLASS manufactory has lately been set on foot in New Jersey. . . ." (The only known glassworks operating there at that time was at Glassboro.) The glass was pronounced "equal to English white glass" and said to sell cheaper than imports. Possibly for a few months, or years, some tableware was blown: certainly white glass would have been used for the retorts, receivers, and tincture bottles advertised by Heston & Carpenter in 1799 (Ill. 7A). The assorted vials probably were of both white and green metal. It will be noted too that the bottles, undoubtedly of green glass, were snuff and mustard bottles, pocket bottles, quart and two-quart farmers' bottles (possibly chestnut bottles), and claret and lavender-water bottles. The advertisement in Ill. 7A, dated November 28 (1798), is the only one I have found as yet in which names and sizes of this glassworks' bottles were given, and I found few instances in which the products of the 19th-century Olive Glass Works were named specifically. In 1813, Wickoff & Carpenter sold Jeremiah Emlen, a Philadelphia druggist, phials, sweet oil bottles, and bottles of pint, quart, and half-gallon sizes. In 1816 (see Ill. 7B) the following bottles could be obtained at the store of T. W. Dyott & Co.: half- to eight-ounce vials, patent medicine vials of every description, mustards, Kians, capers, anchovies, Rupee and other snuff bottles, seltzers of half-pint, pint, and quart sizes, and the usual pint, quart, and half-gallon bottles.[54]

The end of the Revolution was not the end of an unfavorable manufacturing climate, nor the beginning of a new prosperity and national unity. Like an overblown bubble of glass, the United States flew into 13 "free republics,"[55] each jealous of its sovereign rights and commerce. Instead of fighting the Mother Country, the new family bickered. Instead of husbanding the scarce specie, they spent it abroad. The urge to "Buy American" lost its potency, though in some northern states societies were formed to encourage their own state's manufactures and the useful arts. Instead of ports blockaded by English ships, ports were open to all, and a vast influx of cash-draining goods, especially English, dwarfed exports.[56] Instead of England's home and colonial ports being as free to us as ours to her, our exports were prohibited or "loaded with most rigorous exactions"; and in port cities of the United States, factors of British manufacturers freely set up business in competition with unprotected Ameri-

cans.[57] These were among the just complaints in petitions asking Congress to regulate trade. But, though deluged with petitions from individuals and groups seeking federal remedies for the country's economic ills, Congress lacked the power and—worse—the cooperation of the states to legislate for the individual or common good. Not until the last of the states, except little Rhode Island, adopted the Constitution in 1789, not until the national government could regulate trade, levy taxes and duties, and assume proper financial responsibility, did the health of the economy begin to improve, and with it the climate for manufacturing.

Of course, glass manufacturers were among those who suffered before the Constitution was adopted, and were hopeful afterward. But not all the troubles in connection with the six or seven glasshouses planned or built during the transition period from 1783 to 1790, nor of the seven of the decade of the 1790s, stemmed from general economic conditions. Establishment of glasshouses presented the same endemic problems as before Independence—location so vital for easy access to materials, fuel, and markets; scarcity of expert glassmen and willing apprentices; overestimation of the demand for American-made glass and underestimation of the necessary capital. These hazards were topped by the tendency to build too large a works—a works, as a Hartford gentleman wrote in 1789, "calculated to cover all that part of the country with glass which was not covered by the house." Apparently he had observed that in large works an error that could be fatal to a moderate capital would scarcely be noticed in small ones and that "new works" (that is, manufactures new or unfamiliar to the proprietors) were prone to losses from inexperienced owners and workmen. One wonders whether he was associated with the Pitkins' East Hartford glassworks in Connecticut, which, first planned in 1783, was still not self-supporting in 1789. Whoever he was, he knew whereof he spoke, and his hints, available to the many readers of the *American Museum* as well as some newspapers, ended with sound advice to start with "a small works, and add what by experience is found necessary."[58]

Whether or not proprietors of works already started, or about to be, heeded his advice, most of them had to seek new funds and also turn to state and federal government for other types of assistance, particularly protection against foreign competition. Where, for lack of cash or from caution, private investors could not be found, permission to conduct lotteries or government loans were sought by some glass manufacturers, and with varied success. In the northern states, self-interest honed to a keen edge the awareness that manufactures would free the country from costly dependence upon foreign wares *and* keep money working at home. Legislatures in Massachusetts, Connecticut, New York, and Maryland, where glassworks existed or were planned, implemented their sympathy with the projects in various degrees and ways, including monopolies for a term of years if certain conditions were met, premiums on glass, secured loans of money, permission to conduct lotteries, exemption from taxation for a few years, and exemption of workmen from military or other duty so long as they were employed at the works.[59] However, at the federal level, congressmen's conflicting social and economic philosophies, sectional interests, and other factors militated against aid to individuals or particular manufactures. Although, when John Frederick Amelung petitioned for aid for the New Bremen Glassmanufactory in 1790, his cause was pleaded by eloquent friends in Congress and the committee recommended a secured loan of $8,000, the House did not concur, not only because of reluctance to single out for aid one of many languishing enterprises but because many representatives shared Thomas Johnson's aversion to a "partial encouragement, particularly of foreigners in preference to our own citizens." Amelung's 1791 petition, referred to committee, remained there.[60]

Mainly, manufacturers' petitions and memorials pleaded for trade regulations and protective tariffs. Still, without a compelling revenue need, tariff measures, like manufactures, would have languished: for decades, adherents of "Tariff for Revenue Only" outnumbered those for protection of infant industries, as did the proponents of agriculture instead of manufactures. Nevertheless, the Tariff Act of 1789 carried the germ of intent to foster embryonic industries. The duty on all glass, *except black quart bottles,* was 10 percent *ad valorem,* raised 2½ percent in 1790 and again in 1792 to a total of 15 percent, and more if imports arrived in foreign vessels. Until 1792, when increased 2½ percent, the 1789 duty of 5 percent levied on all goods "not otherwise provided for" applied to the black bottles. The 1794 petitions for higher duties or other encouragement sent to Congress by the proprietors of the Albany Glass House, the proprietors of the Boston Glass Manufactory, and John Frederick Amelung and James Labes, joined by Thomas Johnson, possibly influenced the June tariff act. Though window glass remained at 15 percent, black bottles were raised to 10 percent and all other glass (which, of course, included the general

run of bottles and vials) to 20 percent *ad valorem.* The following year, filled bottles paid the same duty as though empty. However, the infection of importation was not arrested, nor were the duties a panacea for all the glassworks' other complaints. And one, the high cost of labor, was considered more of an obstacle to glass manufactories than lack of government aid and protection—at least, Congress concurred in that majority opinion reported by the Committee on Commerce and Manufactures after considering the Boston group's 1797 petition.[61]

Whether or not duties were adequate, the debates on the subject of glass manufactories and the state actions in their behalf, along with reports on manufactures, pamphlets, and newspaper items reaching even into small villages and to farms, were arousing more general interest in glassworks. One aspect in particular was being drawn in sharper lines: namely, the potential economic importance of glassworks to the United States. As Alexander Hamilton, who had been well briefed, pointed out in his famous December 1790 "Report on Manufactures," the essential materials were to be found everywhere in the United States, and the country enjoyed the particular advantage of an extraordinary abundance of wood for fuel. Over two years before, an advocate of glassworks whose comments were reported in a March 31, 1789, Philadelphia news item stressed that one reason the United States should establish glasshouses was that wood was an encumbrance in many places. Doubtless it never occurred to anyone that—as in France, where in the 1780s want of wood was discouraging glassworks[62]—the day would come when eastern American glasshouses that did not, or could not, convert to coal would close because of the expense of wood and exhaustion of a works' woodlots.

Not unnaturally, when glassworks were advocated, the emphasis was on the two most essential products, window glass and bottles. Window glass was the more essential of the two, but on the chances for success and profit, some men considered bottles a better bet than window glass, which *could* be more costly to make than to import and at times *was* cheaper to import than were bottles. Mark Leavenworth of New Haven, Connecticut, pointed out in his 1787 "Hints to Manufacturers" that a box of window glass worth £3 or £4 cost only about 3s. or 3s. 3d. in freight charges to Connecticut, whereas bottles of the same worth cost £4 for freight. Also, and quite rightly, Leavenworth maintained that bottles were easier to blow than window glass, and bottle blowers were easier to obtain than were window-glass and flint-glass blowers. In another piece, "Upon the Manufacture of Glass," which also had wide circulation in the summer of 1789, the GLASSMAKER (as the writer signed it) had the following to say about bottles:

BOTTLES, black or green, are the most simple of all the glass manufactured—the profit in making which depends upon the greatest number of workmen being employed at the smallest expense of fuel. From eight to sixteen blowers can work all at once, at one melting furnace, six feet diameter, which will take six cords of wood every twenty-four hours. The best constructed green glass furnace in this country is in New-Jersey [New-Jersey Glass Manufactory] where the whole business of smelting, blowing and cooling is done with one fire, by the particular construction of the furnace.[63]

Of course, wherever ardent spirits, cider, beer, and ale were an important domestic and export commodity, or could be, there was concern about bottles. Though strong tough bottles were the most desirable for shipping any liquids, they were especially necessary for cider and other fermented potables. Consequently, their economic importance was stressed and, for the same reason, the tariff was lower on black quart bottles. It is interesting to note that in Hamilton's 1790 report, although he felt the tariff duty then in effect afforded considerable encouragement to glass manufacturers, he also felt that, if judged eligible, a direct bounty on window glass and black bottles would appear proper. "The first," he said, "recommends itself as an object of general convenience; the last adds to that character, the circumstance of being an important item in breweries." His last comment was that "Complaint is made of great deficiency in this respect." Three years earlier, in 1787, the new Pennsylvania Society for the Encouragement of Manufactures and the Useful Arts offered a plate of gold worth $20 "To the person who will manufacture in Pennsylvania the greatest quantity of glass bottles, strong and fit to contain fermentable liquors, or produce . . . the best specimen of sheet glass manufactured by him in this state," and exhibited on or before December 1, 1788. As yet I have no evidence of either being exhibited (one reason for believing Leiper's Philadelphia Glass Works was idle at the time). And, according to the correspondent quoted in the Philadelphia 1789 news item cited above:

No factory is more wanted . . . than a capital glass manufactory for bottles similar to those of Bristol in Great-Britain. Considerable orders for Philadelphia beer and porter are now in the city, some of which cannot be executed for want of proper bottles. . . .

In Massachusetts, it will be recalled, in their 1752 memorial to the assembly, the proprietors of the Germantown glassworks made a point of the advantage of home-made bottles to cider importation. In Connecticut, benefit to farmers and the probability of shipping cider to the West Indies and also to the southern states (where a pistareen a bottle was paid for the famous Bristol cider) were among the advantages foreseen in Leavenworth's "Hints." Moreover, "might not," he asked, "a plenty of bottles prevent the extravagance of drinking London bottled porter, and thereby make a demand for a greater number of bottles?"[64]

Still, important as were bottles, window glass certainly was even more essential to comfortable living and working conditions. Also, the demand was growing for table glass, which, whether blown from white or flint metal, was deemed the acme of commercial glass achievement. Perhaps, aside from practical reasons such as price, a few manufacturers were tempted to try making fine glassware because bottles and window glass were pedestrian compared to tableware—like the nicely browned loaf of bread, less exciting and praise-provoking than the handsomely iced cake. Nevertheless, bottles of one kind or another were produced commercially in all the known glasshouses of this period, with the possible exception of the Boston Glass Manufactory. Yet it will not be surprising to learn one day that apothecary vials and chemical and philosophical apparatus were blown at this Boston works before the 1800s. After all, there was a cavernous need to be filled, and also bottles *were* the simplest, quickest, and cheapest objects to fashion. So, too, was the metal for ordinary commercial bottles. Moreover, the materials not only were simple and easy to obtain, but also did not require the refining and decolorizing for ordinary containers that were essential for white glass and even good green glass for windowpanes. However, ordinary window (green) glass, white glass, and flint too were used for apothecary vials.

Between 1783 and 1800, either 13 or 14 glasshouses were projected; the New-Jersey Glass Manufactory was operating during the period and, part of that time, the Philadelphia Glass Works also. As would be expected, most of the new glasshouses were, or were planned to be, built near the seaboard in northern states. However, in the troubled and astringent economic waters in the wake of war, there had been a westward wave of population. Many of the adventurous, the economically distressed, and the discontented in the East were lured by the siren call to opportunity and a fresh start in life in the valley of New York's Mohawk River and in the western lands along the Allegheny, Monongahela, and Ohio rivers, of which Pittsburgh was the commercial heart. Spreading population and settlement meant spreading demands for glass. In New York, glassworks were built far inland from a port city for the first time: one, about eight miles from Albany, and the other, very short-lived, at Peterborough, Madison County, in the wilderness not far from the Mohawk River.[65] West of the Alleghenies, the cost and hazards of transporting merchandise over the mountains increased the prospects for profitable glassmaking. Just before the turn of the century two glasshouses were established: one at New Geneva and the other at Pittsburgh—born so close to 1800, they were to grow up in the 19th century. At Pittsburgh coal was used in a glass furnace for the first time in America. It did not seem a momentous event, but, as I have written before, "Right then the doom of many as yet unplanned eastern wood-burning glassworks was sealed and the future hub of the American glass industry was determined." Besides these two glassworks and the works at Kensington, four or five others of the 1789/99 decade survived into the next century, after the usual initial difficulties; one, the now famous New Bremen Glassmanufactory, lasted only ten years, until 1795. Little is known of the others.[66]

10. NEW BREMEN GLASSMANUFACTORY of John Frederick Amelung & Co.,[67] and other glassworks in Frederick County, Maryland

The glassworks and its community, about eight miles from Frederick-Town, were naturally christened New Bremen: the ambitious project was conceived in Bremen, Germany, and launched by John Frederick Amelung, a German glassmaker, and "some of the most capital houses" in that city. In the promotional pamphlet printed for Amelung in 1787, he recorded that the company was formed with a capital of £10,000 early in 1784, and was led by Benjamin Crockett, Baltimore merchant then in Bremen, to choose the state of Maryland for the venture. Probably it was Crockett who enabled Amelung to obtain from John Adams at The Hague, and Benjamin Franklin and Thomas Barclay (our consul general) in Paris, the letters of recommendation that Amelung claimed he brought with him to well-known mercantile houses and wealthy influential men—Thomas Mifflin, president of Congress; William Paca, governor of Maryland; Charles Carroll of Carrollton. Thus encouraged by his American contacts in Europe, and coming from Germany where—as

elsewhere in Europe—princes and governments wisely fostered manufactures, Amelung naturally expected similar attitudes, aid, and encouragement in America. There were no gloomy forebodings when, on August 31, 1784, he and his family landed at Baltimore with "68 hands" and "instruments for three different Glass Ovens."[68]

No time was lost in launching the enterprise. Aided by Abraham Faw of Frederick-Town and Messrs. Crockett and Harris of Baltimore, Amelung purchased 2,100 acres of land, through which Bennett's Creek ran to the nearby Monocacy River. From his published account, one concludes that he almost immediately started building the glassworks as well as accommodations for those who formed the nucleus of the new glasshouse community. However, as has been discovered by Dwight P. Lanmon of The Corning Museum of Glass and Arlene M. Palmer of the Henry Francis duPont Winterthur Museum, Amelung started with a glasshouse already in existence, and later built his own. It had been built by Baltaser (Baltazar) and Martin Kramer and Conrad Waltz (Foltz), former employees of Stiegel, and it was operating in 1774. In November Amelung's force was augmented by 14 more "hands" from Germany, whom his agent, not without difficulty, had brought to Amsterdam through Freisland to avoid detention. By February 1785 the glasshouse with "glass ovens for bottles, window and flint glass" was ready,[69] and orders could be sent to agents in New York, Philadelphia, Baltimore, or Frederick-Town or to John Frederick Amelung & Company at the glassworks. This was announced at the end of a long, sanguine, and enlightening advertisement appearing on February 11, 1785, and reading in part as follows:

A Company of German Manufacturers, being lately arrived in the State of Maryland, and having made a plan of establishing a compleat Glass Manufactory, in the United States of America, the present will inform the Public, that said Glass Manufactory, will consist in making all kinds of Glass-Wares. Viz. Window-Glass from the lowest to the finest sorts, *white and green Bottles*, Wine and other Drinking-Glasses, as also Optical Glasses, and Looking-Glasses finished compleat.

In the accomplishing of this plan, a beginning is already made, by having acquired a considerable tract of land, . . . where, at present, buildings fit for that purpose, are erected, and Window Glasses of two sorts, as also green and white hollow ware, are actually prepared. *As there is not the least doubt said plan will arrive in a short time to its full perfection, if assisted by the lawful power of the United States of America, and by means of the good advices of some gentlemen of this Country*, the Public may be assured that what kind of glass soever they may be in want of, their commissions given for them will be executed to their satisfaction, and afforded at the most reasonable prices. *In case any able Glass-Makers are willing to engage themselves at this new growing and truly large and extensive Fabrick, on reasonable conditions,* [they] *may find employment.* [The italics are mine.]

It may have been this advertisement that drew Baltaser

(Baltazar) Kramer to New Bremen, and perhaps other glassmen who had worked at Manheim and probably also at the Philadelphia Glass Works. In any event, Amelung did not have so large a staff as he thought necessary and, so he wrote, sent again to Germany for workmen in the fall of 1785. Wherever they came from, the number of blowers and other employees continued to increase. By 1788 Amelung claimed he employed 342 persons; in 1790, he stated more glassmakers were about to come from Germany and that between 400 and 500 persons were already working at the manufactory.[70] After the project failed, many of his glassmen were to play an important role in establishing glassworks in nearby Baltimore and far away west of the Alleghenies.

Possibly, had Amelung been content to start in a small instead of princely way, and to produce only window glass and bottles, until he was established, instead of seeking to capture the tableware market, New Bremen might have thrived and he could have enjoyed his handsome commodious mansion to the end of his days. He was not. By the time he wrote his pamphlet, he had sunk £5,000 in addition to the £10,000 subscribed in Germany. Since comparatively little could have come from sales of glass, most of the new money must have been obtained from American investors. Part of it went toward building a second glasshouse and acquiring more land, holdings of which totaled some 3,000 acres before 1790. By the spring of 1788, he turned to the Maryland Assembly for financial aid and was granted a £1,000 loan and five years' tax exemption. In the next two years he must have managed to raise another £5,000 and more, if, as he told Congress in his May 1790 petition, upward of £20,000 had been expended. His need for assistance, as set forth in the petition, arose from great losses by fire, "the unforseen high prices of Grain" (presumably for sustenance of the livestock and people at New Bremen), the small demand for glass, of which he had £4,000 worth on hand, the difficulty of collecting debts, of which he had nearly the same sum outstanding, the employment of between 400 and 500 people, *and* the erection of additional works to complete the original design for the enterprise. Just as it never occurred to Amelung to husband his resources, so refusal of his request failed to kill his optimistic belief that Congress would eventually see its duty to manufactures. In June he sent a second and futile petition presenting an ambitious scheme to establish glassworks in Virginia and the Carolinas as well as Maryland, and requesting higher tariffs on imports as well as a loan.[71]

The New Bremen Glassmanufactory and community was kept barely afloat for five more years, in part by mortgaging some of the land. About 1793 the firm became Amelung and Labes. (It will be recalled that James Labes [one holder of a mortgage], Amelung, and also Thomas Johnson of the Johnson and the Aetna Glass Works sought increased tariffs in 1794.) Like Stiegel's, Amelung's projects had continued to expand, whereas the demand for his wares had not. In March 1795, the works with "all the Buildings . . . wanted to carry on the manufactory of blow-ing Glass, on a large and extensive plan," and 2,000 acres of land were offered for sale. In September his unmortgaged interests were deeded to his son, John Frederick Magnus. On December 24, Amelung and Labes were among the insolvent debtors whose bankruptcy petitions were found reasonable by the Maryland legislature. Though it has been said that J.F.M. Amelung and James Labes attempted to keep the works in operation, as far as I know now, little if any glass was again blown in either of Amelung's glasshouses—unless the second one was taken over by Adam Kohlenberg and John Christian Gabler in 1799.[72]

However, there were three other glasshouses in Frederick County operating during part or all of the 1790s. Two of those are said to have been built by Thomas Johnson and his brothers—Baker, Roger, and James. But if the brothers were interested, apparently they were silent partners. As previously mentioned, Thomas, ex-governor of Maryland and member of Congress, to whom Amelung had had a letter of recommendation, joined with Amelung and Labes in the 1794 petition for higher tariffs on imported glass. Both glasshouses are said also to have been started for the production of window glass and bottles. One was called the Aetna Glass Works; the other, on Tuscarora Creek, simply Johnson's glassworks. The latter was on a thousand-acre tract of Johnson land that was offered for sale in October 1793. There was no buyer then, but in 1800 William Goldsborough purchased several acres, including the portion on which the glasshouse stood. Also unsold in 1793 was the Aetna Glass Works, advertised on November 15 as follows:

To be Sold, Etna Glass-House, with ten good dwelling-houses, brick or stone chimnies, two large flattening houses, and flattening ovens, stables, and other convenient houses all new, with about 1700 acres of land—They stand about two miles from Monacasy and one from the Baltimore road . . . —There are not more than 150 acres of land cut down, and it is chiefly wooded for Glass-Works—Any cords now remain from the finishing a blast, of nine months, the only one made at this work. A full set of good hands may be engaged who are very comfortably settled and like this place. A purchase may be indulged with time, if he desires it, on paying interest, and giving security. Thomas Johnson.

It seems unlikely that Johnson himself wrote that advertisement, at least as printed. A second advertisement on November 29 gave the location as "on Bush Creek, about five miles from Frederick-Town." At the time, apparently, the superintendent was the Johnsons' nephew Benjamin, but, before 1799, he was replaced by Lewis Repart (Reppert), one of the German family of glassblowers, several of whom were brought to Maryland by Amelung and who subsequently contributed so much to our glass industry. Whether the Aetna Glass Works was sold around 1800 or 1804, or continued to operate until about 1810, has not been definitely established. Each of these two Johnson glassworks is designated on Varle's 1808 map of Frederick County as "Old Glass Works," and the symbol for the

Aetna Glass Works appears to be a globular bottle instead of a building.[73]

The other glassworks are shown on the map. One, as "Old Glass Works," is the site of the first New Bremen glasshouse; the second, not far away but on the south side of Bennett's Creek, is designated "A. Kohlenberg / New Glass Works." This may be the site of Amelung's second glasshouse. According to Mrs. Quynn's findings, the Amelung land purchased in 1799 by Adam Kohlenberg and John Christian Gabler "lay along the stream, probably on the south bank where at least one of the Glass Ovens was located," and the oven site was that of the Kohlenberg works as indicated on the map. It is interesting to note that apparently no cash changed hands; the payment, Mrs. Quynn found, was to be in glass—"725 boxes of good merchantable eight-by-ten window glass." However, this apparently was not Kohlenberg's first venture. E. Ralston Goldsborough, whose interest in Frederick County glasshouses led him to studying land deeds, vital statistics, and other records, found that Adam Kohlenberg (Kohlenburgh), a skilled blower who came to Maryland with Amelung, purchased property on Bear Creek (a tributary of Bennett's Creek) about 1796, and built a glasshouse there, not far from Amelung's first. Perhaps this was the "New Glass House" that is indicated on Varle's map near a creek running into Bennett's Creek. Probably it was his works that was reported in the county in 1810 as having two furnaces producing 40,000 square feet of window glass and 4,000 bottles a year.[74] At present, I know of no specific evidence identifying the types of bottles produced in the Kohlenberg glassworks or in Johnson's. But it seems most likely that only ordinary utilitarian bottles typical of the time were blown and from ordinary "bottle" glass. Possibly some apothecary vials were blown from window-glass metal.

That ordinary bottles probably were important items of output, at least in the early years of the New Bremen Glassmanufactory, may surprise many collectors and students of American glass—to most of us, Amelung and his glass are synonymous with the finest and most elegant American-made 18th-century tableware. Although there is no rich lode of evidence as to the types and varieties of New Bremen bottles and flasks, two advertisements contain tantalizingly slight clues, and fragments excavated on the glassworks site offer some tangible evidence. The first known advertisement of John F. Amelung & Company, February 1785, listed white and green bottles. The white probably included case bottles such as those made for Baker Johnson, one of which, now owned by the Maryland Historical Society, is illustrated by 2 of Plate 40 in *American Glass*. "Phials assorted" were advertised in March 1788 for sale at the Baltimore shop of Andrew Keener, Amelung's son-in-law. These doubtless were blown from both green and white glass. It seems probable any white-glass phials were blown from the glass used for window glass, which apparently was produced throughout the lifetime of the glassworks. Green bottles from pints to gallons were also listed. No bottles were mentioned in the two known 1789 advertisements, which suggests that possibly their production was more limited than previously, that neither Amelung nor Labes considered bottles of great importance as compared with their tableware, and that sales of bottles may have been comparatively local. However, it should be noted that "Maryland Bottles" were advertised in the *Massachusetts Centinel*, July 22, 1789, by Abraham Hunt of Boston. Since Amelung's works was the only one operating in Maryland at that time, insofar as is known, it would appear Mr. Hunt's Maryland bottles must have been blown there. In the 1789 advertisements of John Frederick Amelung (no "& Co") and of James Labes, the ready-money scarcity of the time is interestingly reflected in the conditions of payment for orders— conditions that must have prevailed before and were not uncommon anywhere in the country. Labes, whose shop was one of New Bremen's Baltimore outlets, stated he would "sell low for Cash or Country Produce"; Amelung said Abraham Faw, agent at his Frederick-Town warehouse, would sell "as low as possibly . . . for Cash, good Bills on Philadelphia, or Baltimore, or would Barter for assorted Merchandise, either in Dry or Wet Goods Line, or any Kind of Country Produce. . . ."[75]

Although the scant newspaper evidence is barren of identifying details, pick-and-shovel excavations and bulldozing(!) prior to 1962 on the site of the first works unearthed some evidence as to types of metal and a few products. There were many fragments of bottle glass in its natural colors, colorless metal (both quite pure and of various tints), and a few of amethyst and of blue glass. Some shards were large enough to be identified as green-glass square bottles of sizes for medicine vials and snuff, and others as ordinary chestnut bottles. Some fragments showed that pattern molds were used for ribbing and diamond designs. One pattern-molded design, the so-called German checkered-diamond design, had been attributed previously to New Bremen by tradition bolstered by geographical distribution of many pieces so patterned. Martin and Elizabeth Stohlman unearthed a dark-tinted colorless fragment in this pattern that in color and design exactly matched those of a flask in their collection.[76] Other fragments of this particular design as well as ribbed and diamond patterns were among the great many fragments. Because of tradition, distribution, and the fragment of the Stohlmans, it is believed that pocket bottles like 1 and 3 in Color Plate II were blown at New Bremen.

Other fragments in the checkered-diamond pattern as well as rib and diamond patterns were among the great many fragments uncovered in the fall of both 1962 and 1963, in the first scientific archaeological examination of the site. It was a joint project of The Corning Museum of Glass and the Smithsonian Institution, under the direction of Ivor Noël Hume, archaeologist of Colonial Williamsburg. Mr. Hume reported the fragments included parts of bottles and flasks in greens, ambers, green to blue, amethyst, and colorless. Fragments of an amethyst bottle showed it had been patterned in ribs. There were also parts of green-glass square case bottles and smaller squares molded for body form and of phials blown from the window-glass metal. Of particular interest to collectors of wine bottles is the fact that, at the present stage of exploration, there is no evidence that any English-type wine bottles or common black-glass bottles were produced at the New Bremen Glassmanufactory.[77]

11. DOWESBOROUGH or DOWESBURGH
glassworks, later the Albany Glass House; then Hamilton Glass Factory, near Albany, New York

"The celebrated John De Neufville," Elkanah Watson recorded in his *Journal*,

negotiated a secret treaty with his country and was especially instrumental in producing war between England and France in 1781 and lived with the splendor of a Prince, as well in Amsterdam as at his County residence. He commenced his life with hereditary capital of a half million sterling. But alas his attachment to the American cause has ruined him and the wreck of his fortune has been committed to this hopeless enterprise [glassworks].

In hopes of salvaging some of the monies owed to them for supplies they had secured for the Americans, John De Neufville and his son Leonard had emigrated to the United States after our Revolutionary War. While waiting to collect from their impoverished—or forgetful—debtors, they decided the young country's obvious need for glass was favorable to the establishment of a glassworks. Consequently, on May 12, 1785, just a few months after Amelung started glassmaking at New Bremen, near Frederick, Maryland, Leonard, who then handled all the family affairs, signed an agreement with Ferdinand Walfahrt and Jan Heefke whereby Walfahrt would manage the works and Heefke would be business agent. With an advance of 1,400 Dutch guilders, Heefke was also to go to Germany to engage 24 or 25 workmen. The site selected for the glasshouse was on a tract of "barren sandy country" in Guilderland Township, eight miles from Albany and not far from the western turnpike to nearby Schenectady.[78] Though exactly when the glasshouse was completed and the necessary glassmen arrived has not been determined, present evidence indicates it was probably sometime before the end of 1786.

Dogged problems such as finances, materials, and marketing were present from the beginning, and some six years of effort to establish a profitable glassworks went unrewarded. In 1786 the state legislature refused a request for aid, and in December, while Leonard was in New York City, he received from John Van Schaick in Albany the distressing news that "The glass house is fallen down in a snow storm." Though it was rebuilt before May 1787, the poor clay on hand (presumably for pots) caused the workmen such uneasiness that, so Van Schaick reported, the green- and white-glass makers went to New York seeking "Verte Clay." By May 16 they had returned; satisfactory clay had come from Amboy (New Jersey); and Heefke

expected glass would be made in three or four weeks.[79] Though some window glass, as the reference to white-glass makers foreshadows, and hollow ware were produced in 1787, the earliest advertisement as yet found appeared in the *New York Packet* on May 27, 1788:

Dowesburgh, May 13, 1788.

Window & Green Hollow
G L A S S

Being the first that has been brought to that perfection within this State, and not without great expence. The Proprietors therefore, would solicit the public for a generous encouragement of their infant manufactory, wherein not so much themselves as the community is interested.

Leond. De Neufville,
Jan Heefke,
Ferdinand Walfahrt.

N.B. Said Glass is sold wholesale and retail, at the house of the said Heefke, in Cortlandt Street [New York City].

The same advertisement, but headed "Dowesborough, May 3, 1789" and without the *N.B.*, appeared in the *Albany Gazette* through August 24, 1789 at least. The advertisements and other sales efforts brought encouraging results during the year, probably not only locally but in New York City and Philadelphia, Pennsylvania. Not only a favorable New York market is evident from a December 1789 letter from Heefke to De Neufville, but also the handicap of marketing arising from lack of adequate roads and year-round water carriage: Heefke urged that glass be sent as soon as possible

as I believe the boats make but one trip more this season, it will be of great Damage to us if we do not get glass this winter for we may sell a great quantity if we have it as glass is high at present which makes people run to us for glass as our Comes somthing cheaper.[80]

Though engendering hope, sales were inadequate to the needs and funds were now scarce. De Neufville turned again to the state. In his petition of January 1, 1789 (his second), he expressed gratitude for "the early and unsollicited step taken last year by the Legislature in favor of this undertaking" that gave him "confidence to rely on further protection of the State to his infant establishment." (Though the state laws and records of the 1788 sessions have been searched, the nature of that aid is still to be learned.) Believing that, though a total loss to date, the works could become self-supporting, De Neufville now asked for a loan and for a grant of unlocated lands (doubtless for firewood and potash), and suggested that the fatherly protection of the state might extend to exemption from taxes and exemptions of the workmen from military duty entirely or at least when the furnace was in blast. By a tiny margin, on the last day of the session in March, the legislature passed a resolve authorizing the state treasurer, on such security as he thought proper, to advance £1,500 to De Neufville. No mention was made of the request for land or of the exemptions, which—incidentally—were soon to become common practice continuing into the early years of the next century. Since I have found no further record regarding the loan, it seems likely the treasurer did not take the chance of being indemnified at a future session, as the legislature's resolve provided. Be that as it may, in a little less than a year De Neufville again petitioned, praying for state aid in money. This petition of March 20, 1790, was referred to committee, where it went the way of so many good causes, perhaps because De Neufville was a foreigner—an accident of birth that, it will be recalled, aroused the opposition of several representatives when John Frederick Amelung petitioned the United States Congress for a loan. Nevertheless, somehow the proprietors managed to operate a while longer, and window glass, presumably from Dowesborough, was advertised by John (Jan) Heefke until the end of 1792 at least.[81]

Probably fairly early in 1792 the glassworks was taken over by three Albany merchants—James Caldwell, Robert McClellan, and Robert MacGregor—and Christopher Batterman, who, though he may also have been a businessman, had charge of the works, now called the Albany Glass-House or Albany Glass Factory. By September the new firm of McClellan, MacGregor & Co. had begun to advertise window glass and bottles, even in Vermont newspapers, and making the familiar appeal for "patriotic support of the public." The same advertisement reveals also that little time had been lost in soliciting state aid, which had not been granted as yet: "want of a legislative loan, which was fully expected by the public and the proprietors in particular, [prevented] their giving that credit to their friends they otherwise would wish and compelled them to sell for cash only. . . ." However, perhaps because they were local, not foreign, businessmen, they were to fare better with the legislature than did De Neufville: On March 9, 1793, the firm was granted a £3,000 loan without interest for three years and at 5 percent for five years, secured by a mortgage on unencumbered real estate.[82]

Probably it was the 27th of the previous month that two new partners, Elkanah Watson and Jeremiah Van Rensselaer of the great Van Rensselaer patroon family, had brought in new capital. Possibly then, certainly before mid-1795, Thomas and Samuel Mather and Frederick A. De Zeng became copartners. In any event, the firm of McClellan, MacGregor & Co., with an expanded "company" and a substantial loan in its coffers, promptly expanded the enterprise and with it their problems. By March 1793, if not before, a glass warehouse was established on Market Street in Albany, which by January 1, 1794, was moved to No. 4 North Side of Bloodgood's Slip, near the quay and on Dock Street. It was a much-needed adjunct, inasmuch as the glasshouse, though moderately convenient for the slowly growing market in the Mohawk Valley, was eight miles from a settled community and the Hudson River. The warehouse was not only convenient for local sales but, more important, for shipping to the wider market courted by the firm, as shown by advertisements in newspapers of Troy, New York City, Hartford, and Philadelphia.[83] The following enlightening advertisement appeared in the Philadelphia *American Daily Advertiser* of May 16, 1794 (similar ones probably appeared in newspapers of other cities where there were, or had been, glassworks):

> Albany Glass Factory
> In consequence of the liberal aid we have received from the Legislature of this State the public are notified that we have lately expanded the scale of our manufactory greatly, and shall continue to pursue the business with vigor and animation.
> *Wanted*, several window-glass and bottle makers, to whom great encouragement will be given, and their wages paid monthly in Cash.
>   M'Clellan, MacGregor & Co.
> Albany, 23 April, 1794.

Apparently they were undeterred in their expansion by such setbacks as the failure of Congress to increase the tariff on their principal product, window glass, in response to the aforementioned February 1794 petition, or by the breakdown "in the dead of winter" of two of the three furnaces in blast, which, so Watson recorded in his *Journal*, remained stopped until sandstone to repair them could be obtained after the ice left the river in March.

An idea of the three-year growth of the glassworks and its community is afforded by partial, and nearly identical, statements of the company's affairs as of July 12 and December 9, 1794. McClellan, MacGregor & Co. had acquired considerably more land: 4,000 acres in the Staatsburgh patent, a perpetual lease on two farms, and a 41-year lease on another 955 acres. In the glasshouse community, besides two glasshouses in which two of three furnaces had been in blast *11* months, there were a sawmill, stamping mill, and one called a "cross-cut," a store, and 24 houses, of which most were new and some double. (Unless some of the houses served as dormitories for unmarried workmen, it would seem that not all the nearly 200 employees reported by Watson in 1794 lived in company houses.) Also among the assets listed were six oxen, six horses, and three wagons.[84]

However, the profits from the sales of glass and the debts owed to the firm were less than half the sums loaned to it or invested by the copartners. Actually, so Watson wrote in February 1796 to Nathaniel Lawrence of the New York Assembly, nearly double the amount of the state's £3,000 loan had been spent in improvements, and part of the loan itself had been used to buy land. A financial statement and petition accompanied Watson's letter seeking Lawrence's "friendly Countenance and support in the object of our Petition vis—a premium on Glass to enable us to encounter present obstacles occasioned by the present high price of Labor and Provisions. . . ." "Without such aid," he wrote, "we are in danger of losing a Most Important Manufactory. . . ." If Watson was not permitting himself a bit of expedient exaggeration, the manufactory had indeed become an important source of glass for a large area; not, however, of income to its proprietors. Watson claimed that Albany glass, almost exclusively, supplied all the northern and western parts of the state (New York) and most of the western part of Vermont, and that, lately, considerable quantities had gone to upper Canada. Presumably he was referring to window glass, but equally presumably bottles had been widely sold also. The legislature did not concede a premium on glass, but did pass an act in April 1796 exempting "everything appertaining in and to carrying on the Albany Glass Factory from taxation for five years and all agents, superintendents, artificiers and workmen of every kind from working on highways, jury and military duty while employed at said factory." In March 1809 the number so exempted was limited to 20, but none from militia duty in case of insurrection or invasion.[85]

Also in the year 1796, the Hamilton Manufacturing Society replaced the old firm, the name of the works became the Hamilton Glass Factory, and expansion plans became more ambitious. The following year, on March 30, the society was incorporated for 14 years, a term extended to 1821 by legislative act in 1809. From a communication to the *Albany Register* in 1796, which the editor of the *Albany Chronical or Journal* considered so newsworthy he reprinted it on April tenth, it would appear that Republican objections to manufactures had been marshalled to defeat the act of incorporation: at least, the writer sarcastically observed, the act had been passed, "the busy opposition of some liberal minded patriotic gentleman to the contrary not withstanding." It seems probable, too, that there had been disagreements, possibly over plans for expansion, among the copartners in the months before the official dissolution of McClellan, MacGregor & Co. on June 6, 1796. None of the original partners was a member of the new society. However, one of the later partners, Frederick A. De Zeng, was agent at the glassworks. Another was factor in Albany—Abraham Ten Eyck, who had replaced Thomas Mather & Company in March.[86]

And, as early as April 22, 1796, a news item went out from Albany to various newspapers reporting that the proprietors had determined to found a permanent manufacturing town, "of late named HAMILTON, in honor of that celebrated Patron of American manufactories." Already surveyors were laying out streets and house lots; plans were made for an octagon church and a schoolhouse, and a nursery of fruit trees and shrubs had been started. If the tavern did not exist then, doubtless it too was started at this time. Hamilton village, which could boast of a third glasshouse and 32 more dwellings by 1813, also of stores and inns, not just *a* store and *a* tavern, was then at the peak of its growth. Within two years or a little longer, cessation of glassmaking brought on its decline, and by 1824 it could "hardly be called a Village."[87]

In the meantime, while glass was produced in large quantities, the Hamilton Manufacturing Society and Hamilton were far from realizing a "peaceable kingdom." Letters and other documents in the Van Rensselaer Papers at the New-York Historical Society reveal that, through 1805, finances were complicated and ramified; conduct of the glassworks and marketing of the glassware were unsatisfactory; and the society's changing membership was honeycombed by animosities. Present evidence indicates a continuance of disturbing situations. One of the disrupting rows, understandably, was over the establishment by some society members and ex-members of a rival window-glass house, the Rensselaer Glass Factory, which was located east of the Hudson River at Sand (Glass) Lake about ten miles from both Troy and Albany, and was in operation by the fall of 1805. Another involved James Kane, a stockholder and agent of the works, and Lawrence Schoolcraft, superintendent after the death in 1802 of John Van Rensselaer, lessor of the works. In April 1810, two years after going to the Oneida Glass Factory at Vernon, New York, Schoolcraft wrote to his son Henry Rowe, who had apprenticed at Hamilton under his father:

From the works at Hamilton, we have unfavorable accounts. Some of the workmen, late from that place give a sad account of things both there and at Rensselaer. They thought to injure me, but are now, by their heavy losses and bad luck, reaping the just reward of their iniquitous proceedings.[88]

Apparently Schoolcraft had left Hamilton to the relief, if not with the blessings, of the proprietors. Usually the glassmen who were willing to risk arrest for breaking their contracts and were lured away in hopes of more material gain brought down curses upon their heads.

According to local history, it was about five years later, sometime in 1815, that lack of wood for fuel forced the closing of the glasshouses. However, on May 8, 1815, members of the society recorded, at Albany, an indenture drawn *January 1811* granting the society for a "term of seven years [from January 1] full liberty and license to cut away and carry away such timber or wood . . . as shall be necessary for the use of the Glass Works...." The tract of land involved was on the west side of the Hudson in the Manor of Rensselaerwyck, as given in earlier indentures. Possibly that supply was near exhaustion in 1815, and evidently no effort was made to extend the privilege beyond the termination date (1818) or to secure another source of wood. Still, if glassmaking did cease in 1815, there could have been other factors of as much, or more, immediacy in the final equation of causes: internal strife, insufficient profits, competition from the Rensselaer glassworks across the river, possibly lack of new investors, and doubtless the defection of blowers and other essential workmen or their disinclination to renew contracts. Although a dividend, payable by the factor in Albany, was announced in December 1820 and the society's affairs were still unsettled in 1823, I have found no evidence as to the final dissolution or actual drawing of the furnace fires.[89] In any event, for about 30 years the glassworks was one of the most significant of its period in the struggle to root an American glass industry. Elkanah Watson recorded in his *Journal* in 1821 that the works had been "the nursery for workers in all our other glass works in the state." That influence spread into Vermont and New Hampshire as well.

The principal product of the glassworks under De Neufville, the copartnership of McClellan, MacGregor & Co., and the Hamilton Manufacturing Society was window glass. Nevertheless, in 1792 the copartners planned to produce flint glass, and in his 1808 account, Thomas Fessenden stated that it was made, as well as window glass and bottles. However, the fact that no flint glassware was mentioned in any of the records or advertisements known to me suggests that, if it was actually made, the quantity was very limited. On the other hand, there is little doubt that bottles of various sorts were an important line in the early years but, under the society, were too secondary to warrant mention in the many advertisements of "Albany" glass that I have read. In fact, the latest reference to bottles was in the previously cited one of September 1792, according to which orders for bottles from half-pint to five gallons would be thankfully received and punctually executed. Moreover, I found only one record of bottle production in the Van Rensselaer Papers. That was in 1797, when Christian Emison and son blew 3,426 *pocket bottles*, 180 pint bottles, and 1,182 half-pint *mustard bottles* in the months of September, October, and November. It is probable some of those pocket bottles were pattern-molded, single-gather or double-gather Pitkin-type similar to those in Ills. 87 and 88.[90] The mustard bottles doubtless were rectangular, with or without chamfered corners, or square, molded for body form—probably similar to the bottle in Ill. 69.

Snuff bottles, probably of the same shapes as the mustards, certainly were blown: Thomas Leiper of Philadelphia purchased snuff bottles from De Neufville in 1788. James Caldwell, one of the original partners in McClellan, MacGregor & Co., would surely have been a customer, since he was a tobacconist and also dealt in powdered substances other than snuff, usually packaged in glass bottles, as did other merchants interested in the copartnership and the society. It is not impossible that some wine bottles of Types 8 and 9 (10 and 11 in Ill. 52) were blown. Possibly it was for such bottles that 5s. per cwt. for broken black glass bottles were offered in 1792.[90a] Nearby production of black bottles for beer surely would have been welcomed by the local brewers. Also, demijohns with wicker coats (said by tradition to have been woven by Indians) were a good item for several years at least, and blown for a wider than local market, as shown by the following advertisement found in the *New York Packet* from June 9, 1789, through August 8, 1790:

FOR SALE,
A PARCEL of *Brown Wickered Demie John's* fit for shipping, made at Wicken, in Albany county, by
JOHN HEEFKE,
Cortlandt-Street
Five or six *SMART BOYS*, from 14 to 16 years old, wishing to engage apprentices in the Glass business, may apply to the same.

12. BOSTON GLASS MANUFACTORY, *Boston, Massachusetts*

The Boston Glass Manufactory was a vital step forward in establishing our glass industry, in particular crown window-glass production. There, after a few years of the inevitable trials, errors, and technical difficulties, crown glass was at last successfully produced in America. At least some of the credit must go to Robert Hewes of the abortive Temple venture—although, apparently having withdrawn from the company before marketable glass was made, he did not participate in the achievement. With his ambition undented by the Temple experience, he had been the instrument of persuasion in founding the Boston Glass Company or, as it was also called, the Boston Crown Glass Company. In 1787, four years after being granted a seven-year monopoly and permission for a lottery to raise £3,000 to start a glassworks, Hewes finally interested four merchants and six "Esquires" of Boston, in whom the speculative temperature of the times was raised by idle capital. On July 6, the General Court of Massachusetts, repealing the barren 1783 Act, gave the new copartnership a fine start with five years' tax exemption on capital stock; exemption of their artificers and workmen from military duty while employed; and a 15-year monopoly on glassmaking, upon which an unauthorized infringement carried a £500 penalty. The string binding the christening gifts was a proviso that the company carry through with its plans and manufacture at least 500 pounds of glass a year.[91]

Six eventful years were to pass before the conditions could be met. The erection of a pyramidal brick glasshouse was started at the foot of Essex Street sometime in 1788, and was reported in September as being prosecuted with the utmost vigor and the promise of soon being completed. Late in October construction had reached the point where the staging inside the building could be removed, and it was reported in the *Independent Chronicle* of October 23 that the previous day three of the carpenters engaged in the removal had fallen "30 feet from the stages." Fortunately one escaped any injury and the other two would recover from theirs. Although the interior and furnaces may have been completed before midsummer of 1789, apparently no glass was made until then. On August 10, a Boston news item informed the public that "The Workmen of the Glass Works in this town, began blowing a few days since—and, it is said, have produced as good ware &c as any ever made." The report was premature. Although Frederick E. A. Kupfer, a competent German glassman from Brunswick, was put in charge in 1790, he was handicapped by technical problems and, until the fall of 1792, by blowers unskilled in crown-glass blowing. In October it could be said that "The almost impracticability of procuring suitable workmen, which . . . hitherto impeded the design, is at last happily overcome, by the arrival of European workmen, well acquainted with the business. . . ." After a few attempts to make crown glass, the new German workmen declared the furnace unsuited to producing that kind of glass. As a result, all operation was "interrupted by the transformation of the building," thus solving a major technical problem.[92] Not surprisingly the company, which had lost some of the original members, including Robert Hewes, and gained others, appealed to the assembly for aid, which was given in June 1793.

During the next 34 years the fortunes of the Boston Glass Manufactory gradually climbed to a peak of satisfying prosperity, then descended rapidly into failure's pit. Calculated to ease the climb was the General Court's act of June 1793 (mentioned above) replacing that of 1787: five-year exemptions from all land and building taxes and of workmen from military duty while employed; ten-year monopoly on "window and plate glass" on which, for three years, the state treasury would pay sixpence for each merchantable sheet equal to British crown glass in quality, up to 10,000 sheets, provided 4,000 sheets 36 inches in diameter were made yearly, and a £500 penalty would be imposed on any infringer if the company "employed" not less than £2,000 a year; a ten-year monopoly on all sorts of hollow ware if within three years £1,000 worth of hollow ware, including bottles of all sorts, was made yearly. Though the petitions for higher tariffs that were submitted in 1794 and 1797 indicate the company felt a need for greater protection from foreign competition, the failure of Congress to heed its prayers did not result in fatal financial anemia. In 1802, two of the partners, Jonathan Hunnewell and Samuel Gore, established a cylinder-glass house in Middlesex Village—later Chelmsford, Massachusetts. In the improved manufacturing climate preceding and during the War of 1812 the Boston project was expanded: in 1811, a second crown-glass house was started, built in South Boston; and late in 1812 or very early in 1813, the latter became the birthplace of our eastern flint-glass industry. It was fathered by Thomas Cains, an exceptionally skilled glassman recruited from England in April 1812, who persuaded the company to erect a six-pot flint-glass furnace in the South Boston house.[93]

The descent from success started after the Treaty of Ghent officially ended the war. Probably it was the loss of three of their most able craftsmen in 1815 and a devastating accident in September that caused the first downward slip. In May 1816 Lawrason & Fowle, evidently the company's agents in Alexandria, Virginia, published an announcement reading in part as follows: "The proprietors of the Boston and Chelmsford Glass Manufactories inform the public that their Manufactory which was destroyed by the hurricane in September last is rebuilt with many improvements and in full operation. . . ." In their notice of September 27, the proprietors did not mention which of their Boston glasshouses was the victim, incapacitated for about seven months though the owners had expected repairs to be made "in a few weeks." In addition to loss of income, rebuilding any one of the houses entailed substantial expenditures just at a time when the country's fabric of commerce and business was beginning to shrink. Nor did the company escape the ensuing epidemic distress of the postwar depression; in 1819 production nearly ceased. The bad management that followed was the more virulent to an enterprise already weakened by lack of nourishing sales. Then internecine struggles within the firm ended with the departure of the invaluable Kupfer and Cains and the formation of a new firm, which soon failed. Operations ceased in June 1827. The South Boston house, known for over a decade as the South Boston Flint Glass Works, was operated about two years by lessees. At the Chelmsford works, another firm produced cylinder window glass for a dozen years before moving the plant to Suncook, New Hampshire, where it ran for another decade.[94]

I know of no evidence that the Boston Glass Company qualified for the 1793 hollow-ware monopoly by producing £1,000 worth within three years, or ever made any dark glass wine bottles, chestnut bottles, or other ordinary containers as a regular line of the Essex-Street, South Boston, or the Chelmsford works. However, doubtless chemical glass apothecaries' bottles and furniture (glass vessels) were blown from 1793 on, though probably such wares were unimportant as a commercial line before 1812, the first year of which I have found mention of any output other than window glass. And according to a February 6, 1813, advertisement, which ran well over a year, application could be made to "C. F. Kupfer, Superintendent at the Glass-House Essex-Street" for "Retorts for Chymists—Apothecaries Furniture and Bottles made to pattern or demensions at short notice." It may well be that, as in the case of flint-glass wares, this line was promoted by Thomas Cains. An advertisement in the *Columbian Centinel*, January 17, 1816, listed traveling bottles, nursing bottles, phials, and smelling and perfumery bottles. And it is evident from a study of four price lists—one undated (judged by the prices to be ca. 1813 to 16, with penciled reductions in 1817), one each in 1818, 1819, and 1822—that a wide range of bottles was produced in the company's South Boston or, as it was then called, South Boston Flint Glass House. Besides white (window glass) metal and flint (lead) metal, some green glass was produced, though whether it was left in its natural colors is uncertain since the term *green* could mean the type of metal, its color, or both. The roster of wares typifies the production of many houses of the period, including flint-glass houses. Under APOTHECARIES & CHEMICAL GLASS WARE, on one or more of the lists, are the following bottles of types with which we will be concerned:

Mustard, square
Essence of mustard
Essence, ½, 1, 2, 3, 6 oz.

Phials assorted, ½, 1, 2, 4, 6, 8 oz. [probably both green and white glass]
Square, stopper'd, ½, 1, 2, 4, 8, 12, 16, 24 oz. [probably similar to those in the medicine chest, Ill. 79]

Square, Liquors, same as stopper Rounds, ½ oz. to 2 gal.
Perfumery

Lavender or Honey Water, 1, 1½, 2, 3, 4, 6 oz.
Hungary or cologne

Durable inks
Macassar oils [hair oil]

Caper, green [probably color & metal]
PATENT MEDICINE BOTTLES [undoubtedly blown in full-size piece molds; for the first five below, molds probably lettered]:

British Oil
Turlington's [see Ill. 79 for type]

Opodeldocs, best and inferior
Bateman's Drops
Peppermint
Magnesias

Pungents, white

Pungents, fancy colored
best

Pungents, richly cut
[probably lead glass]

Smelling or Pungents
Fancy

Smelling molded and
twisted [probably Stiegel
type, see Ill. 103]

Pungents, enameled

Godfrey's Elixer

Cephalic snuffs [probably
similar to Ills. 67 & 68]

Whitwells Snuff [probably
similar to Ills. 67 & 68]

Jesuits Bark

Hills Balsam

Balsam of Honey

Squires Elixer

Nursing bottles

In an invoice book of Jeremiah Emlen, Philadelphia drug-gist, a June 1818 entry of pungents purchased from the Boston Glass Works suggests that "twisted," presumably the so-called Stiegel type, were among the "common" varieties: one gross of "Best pungents" was $15 and one of "Inferior twisted," $7.50.[95]

Under "CUT, PLAIN AND MOULDED FLINT GLASS WARE," various sorts of bottles for table use—decanters, cruets, and the like—are listed, and "Flasks, Pocket and Hunting," which, of course, are the ones of particular interest to bottle collectors. The wholesale prices, subject to an attractive discount on orders of suffi-cient size, were $2 a dozen for half-pints and $3 for pints in 1818; $1.33 a dozen for half-pints and $2 for pints and quarts in 1819; $.80 for half-pints, $1 for pints, and $1.67 for quarts in 1822. On the last two price lists, the flasks were designated as "green," referring, I believe, to the metal. Some of the flasks doubtless were aquamarine in color, possibly deeper natural colors also. The absence of "green" on the 1818 list suggests that, as was not unusual for the *best* pocket-flasks produced in flint-glass houses, those flasks were blown from flint glass. On the other hand, the prices were so little more than 1819, when the depression was still forcing reductions of prices in general, that to me they do not necessarily suggest a better quality of glass than that of the "green" flasks. Be that as it may, the data on the Boston flasks are too meager for more than speculation as to possibilities in the light of known current types, except that a diamond-diapered salt in the company of objects illustrating the company's billhead of the period testifies to pattern-molded wares.[96] Among the pocket flasks, there may have been some blown from flint metal and of the English type like 3 in Ill. 100, with which Thomas Cains and his English craftsmen must have been familiar, as would be the other flattened unstable pocket bottles in the same illustration. Also, whether of flint or green glass or both, chestnut flasks similar to 5 in Ill. 91 probably were blown, doubtless patterned in ribbed and diamond de-signs.

Further speculation has been stimulated by the fact that molded tableware and bottles for Turlington's Balsam were regular products. The Turlingtons (see Ill. 79) would have been blown in lettered full-size two-piece molds. Some, at least, of the molded glass probably fell in the category that today is called blown-three-mold glass, and was blown in full-size piece molds. In fact, it is possible Thomas Cains

may have introduced this type of molded ware; perhaps the "liquor bottles with stands" advertised in the *Columbian Centinel*, February 3, 1819, were blown-three-mold square decanter-bottles in the geometric pattern GII–28, having a wide band of vertical ribbing below one of diamond diaper-ing on the body and fan flutes on the shoulder. If so, then pocket-bottles similar to 1 and 2 in Ill. 97, and blown from flint glass, would be a possibility. There is also the strong likelihood some of the early Figured Flasks were pro-duced, though none has ever been attributed to the Boston Glass Manufactory's South Boston Flint Glass Works. In this connection (and with the New England Glass Com-pany also) present candidates for consideration are some—one or more—of the early and very heavy Masonic flasks among GIV–5 through GIV–14 and their variants, GIV–8a, GIV–10a and 10b, and GIV–13a, and Sunbursts, possibly GVIII–2 and GVIII–4 (see Charts).

Hitherto these particular Masonic flasks have been at-tributed to the Keene-Marlboro-Street glassworks, called the Flint Glass Works in its early years, and the Sunburst GVIII–2 to Keene and the Mt. Vernon. The basis for at-tributing the Masonic flasks was the extremely close simi-larity in design and physical characteristics to the "HS" Masonic GIV–2 and "IP" Masonic GIV–1, of which Harry Hall White excavated fragments in quantity at the Keene glasshouse site. And the attribution of the Sun-bursts was based on similar likeness to GVIII–1, of which he found fragments on both sites. In other words, the obvious kinship in all important features was taken as evidence of common origin, and the possibility of a com-mon source of molds was not considered. Perhaps one or two of the heavy Masonics without initials were Keene products, but it seems unreasonable and highly doubtful that so small a glassworks as the Keene-Marlboro-Street would have so large a market for Masonic flasks as to require 20 different molds, or that either Keene or the Mt. Vernon Glass Works would need several Sunburst molds. Quite apart from other possible reasons, I believe there were other sources of these flasks, the weight of which suited them for a decanter's function, but definitely not for a pocket container. I believe that among the strong prob-abilities is the South Boston Flint Glass Works.

13. THE PITKIN GLASSWORKS, *East Hartford, Connecticut*

Connecticut's first successful works has always been known locally and to collectors and students as the Pitkin Glassworks. Located not far from the navigable Connec-ticut River, in the township of East Hartford (formed Oc-tober 1783), parish of Orford, it became Manchester in May 1823. Like that of our other early glassworks, the history of the Pitkin works and its products still has many blank pages, and today changes have to be made in the compound of fact, tradition, and conjecture written on the old pages. The Pitkins' interest in a glassworks is scarcely surprising, as they were a large, old, influential, and landed family of which most members had fingers in lucrative pre-

GLASS MANUFACTORY.

AS Mr. HEWES has had the pleasure a fecond time to exhibit a fpecimen of his CROWN GLASS in this town, he takes this method to inform his friends and the publick, that they may be fupplied with whole fheets of CROWN GLASS, DIME-JOHNS, or any other large Bottles, by leaving their names, and the fize and form of faid Bottles, with Mr. WILLIAM CUNNINGHAM, near *Liberty Pole*, where a fample of his Sheets of Crown Glafs is to be feen. *Dec.* 17, 1788.

8A. Announcement of crown glass and bottle manufacture that appeared in the Boston *Massachusetts Centinel* December 17, and in the *Independent Chronicle* December 18, 1788, by Robert Hewes, Bostonian and superintendent of the "Pitkin" East Hartford glassworks. Two weeks earlier, December 4, a news item in the *Independent Chronicle* had announced the first exhibit of bottles and crown glass "manufactured at East Hartford," commenting, "This manufactory is conducted by Mr. Robert Hewes, late of this town." *The New-York Historical Society, New York City*

East-Hartford Glafs-Works LOTTERY,

For the purpofe of encouraging and carrying on the Glafs Manufactory in Eaft-Hartford, confifts of 5000 Tickets, at 1 Dollar each, is 5000 Dollars.

	Prize of		Dollars, is	
1	Prize of	300	Dollars, is	300
1		200		200
1		100		100
2		50		100
3		30		90
4		20		80
10		10		100
10		6		60
20		4		80
25		3		75
1241		2		2482

                            3667

For the benefit of the Factory   1333

                     —— 5000 Dol.

This Lottery was generoufly granted by the General Affembly, for the purpofe of encouraging and carrying on the Glafs manufactory in Eaft-Hartford, and have ordered the Lottery to be drawn within one year—The adventurers may rely upon the Managers purfuing their directions, and commence the drawing as fpeedily as poffible. The great defire people in general have manifefted to have the factory carried on, the price of the Tickets being low, and there being but about two blanks and half to a prize, and fubject to no deduction, induces the managers to hope the Tickets will meet with a quick fale. A Lift of the Prizes will be publifhed in the Connecticut Courant. Thofe Prizes not called for in fix months from the Drawing, will be deemed as generoufly given for the benefit of the Factory, and appropriated accordingly.

        ELISHA PITKIN,
        SHUBAEL GRISWOLD.
TICKETS may be had of the Managers.
Eaft-Hartford, Nov. 12, 1789.

8B. Advertisement in the *Connecticut Courant*, December 7, 1789, of the East-Hartford Glass-Works Lottery. The "Drawing" did not occur before June 1790. As the returns to the glassworks were below expectations, the General Assembly granted permission for another lottery, subject to 12½ percent deduction. It was launched in August 1791. Of 3,334 tickets at $2.00 each, 1,179 were "Prizes." (*Connecticut Courant*, Sept. 12, 1791.) *Connecticut State Library, Hartford, Connecticut*

and post-Revolutionary industrial pies, among them gunpowder, guns, tobacco, and snuff. The fact that the glass manufactory was planned by William Pitkin, his cousin Elisha Pitkin, and Samuel Bishop is established by their tactful memorial to the General Assembly on January 28, 1783: "Money out of the Public Treasury in this distressing day" they did not expect, but as the expense of erecting a glasshouse was great, they asked for an exclusive right to glassmaking for "such length of time as [might] be thought proper." Neither memorial, nor report of the committee appointed to consider the request, nor the final act of the assembly mentions the Pitkins' services to the patriots' cause, to which tradition has attributed the favorable response. In any event, in line with the committee's recommendations, the assembly granted "Liberty & Privelege" to erect works, a 25-year sole privilege (dating from the first blast) to make any kind of glass, and a 10-year exemption from assessments on any profits *provided* that manufacturing began within three years (that is, 1786) from the session's end. The partners never qualified for the sole privilege, as the condition was not met, though three years would seem to be ample time in which to build a glasshouse and to secure a staff of glassmen.[97]

However, the lack of a monopoly was not important, since during the struggle for survival from 1787 into the early 1790s, no successful competitor appeared in Connecticut—in fact, none did until John Mather built his glassworks in 1805. Presumably the glasshouse, built of native granite, "four stories high, and wide enough to admit of any length," and the necessary glassmen were ready to operate sometime in 1787. At least, there was no other known glass project in the state of which Mark Leavenworth could have written, as he did in August of that year: "the grantees have never made any glass because they did not understand their own business, not because they wanted workmen who understood theirs." And he predicted that the grant was or would be forfeited before any glass was made. But "trials" probably were made, and one wonders whether perhaps it was to supply the works with cullet that, also in August 1787, Thomas

Tinsdale, Hartford merchant and dealer in fine imported glassware, advertised he would allow the value on purchases or would pay for broken glass, if not in too small pieces, of the kinds (double flint and tale) he had for sale. Be that as it may, apparently hopes were not sanguine until the spring of 1788, by which time it was reported by an East Hartford gentleman to a friend in Boston that the proprietors planned to increase their £14,000 capital to £20,000 and that Robert Hughes (Hewes) of Boston was "chief artisan and superintendent."[98]

Just when or why Hewes left the Boston group (No. 12) less than a year after it had secured state encouragement is still one of the mysteries of our glass industry history; possibly he found the East Hartford adventurers more amenable to his grand plans. Although under his supervision some glass was blown before December, it was not until then that bottles and crown glass were exhibited in Boston. The news item of December 4, 1788, in the Boston

Independent Chronicle is quoted in full below, as it preceded the announcement in Ill. 8. Also, it was this news item which confirmed my belief that the "Robert Hughes" mentioned in connection with the Pitkin Glassworks was indeed Robert Hewes of Boston.

Several bottles and a piece of crown glass manufactured at East-Hartford, have been brought to this town.—Some of these a correspondent has seen, and for smoothness, elegance of form, and transparency, he is of opinion, are very little inferior to the best imported. This manufactory is conducted by Mr. ROBERT HEWES, late of this town.

Probably even before the gentleman in East Hartford wrote his widely published letter of May 1788, the proprietors of the Pitkin Glassworks had changed: Elisha Pitkin and Samuel Bishop seem to have dropped out, and the partnership had nine members before the advent of Robert Hewes—one from Glastonbury, three from East Windsor, and five Pitkins: namely, George, Sr. and Jr.; Richard, Sr. and Jr.; and William. During the ensuing months after Hewes was taken into partnership, they were to become quite disenchanted with him as a partner, as glassman, and as manager of the glassworks. The connection, one would expect, was severed sometime before October 1789, when they petitioned the General Assembly for permission to raise funds by a lottery. While admitting the usual "difficulties and unforeseen expenses" attendant upon starting a new manufactory, they claimed also to have been "subjected to great losses and disappointments by means of Mr. Hughes." He, they set forth, had engaged to procure a large proportion of the needed stock (apparently stock meant materials), and persuaded them he was well skilled in glassmaking, but he failed utterly in the matter of stock and "also proved by his subsequent conduct to be totally unskilled in the business of said Factory." One doubts that *all* the blame should have been piled on poor Hewes, who must have been striving to cope with the all-too-familiar problems of production and incompetent blowers. It seems likely, almost axiomatic, that two conditions emphasized in the 1791 petition—the imposition by "pretended workmen mere impostors," and the delay and postponement of glassmaking "at sundry times for want of able workmen"—prevailed before and during Hewes's regime and until early 1791, when presumably their "Excellent set of Workmen" was secured. Also, the proprietors seemed to resent Hewes because they had allowed themselves to be persuaded into an expenditure of $2,000 for improvements "to no good purpose and wholly lost" to them.[99]

In their petitions of October 5, 1789, and May 10, 1791, each asking permission to conduct a lottery, the proprietors stressed not only their misfortunes but their expenses in erecting the works, providing the materials, and securing workmen, their perseverance in spite of setbacks, and the importance of the glassworks to the public. The General Assembly responded quickly and favorably. The 1789 lottery for £400 was to be conducted at the petitioners' own risk and expense, and was to be completed within a year from the end of that session. This lottery "for the encouragement of the Glass Manufactory at East Hartford" was being advertised by November 12, 1789 (Ill. 9), and the 5,000 tickets at $1 each were for sale in many towns. The fact that the tickets were "being scattered to a great distance" was a reason for postponing the drawing until June 21, 1790. Also, in the June 1 notice of postponement, the managers requested that any tickets unsold by the day of drawing be sealed up and returned to them (Elisha Pitkin and Shubael Griswold) at East Hartford or to Mess'rs Hudson & Goodwin, Printers, in Hartford. That a disappointingly large number remained unsold is evidenced by a statement in the 1791 petition that, owing to the scarcity of money and dullness of business, the 1789 lottery "proved of very small consequence to us." Therefore, the proprietors prayed for the privilege of another lottery, one for £300. Permission was granted to raise £250 including expenses, provided the state treasurer was given a $1,000 bond within two months from the session's end. In this lottery the tickets, sold at $2 each, amounted to $6,668, subject to 12½ percent deduction. Called the "East-Hartford Glass-Works Lottery," it was advertised in August by the managers—Elisha Pitkin, Shubael Griswold, and George Pitkin, Jr.—who had met the bond requirements. The persuasive ending of the advertisement is reminiscent of the colonial period:

The favorable prospect which their Scheme presents to those who are willing to venture a small sum to gain a larger, will, we trust, be a sufficient inducement for them to become adventurers.—To those who act from patriotic principles the object in view will be sufficient motive for them to purchase a Ticket. The drawing will commence on or before the 20th of December next.

Prizes not called for in six months after drawing will be deemed as generously given for the use of the Factory, and appropriated Accordingly.[100]

Whether or not the 1791 lottery was lucrative, the glassworks is believed to have operated successfully for nearly another four decades. However, its life history is still a skeletal one of family and local traditional history and a very few documented facts. Strangely, neither the glassworks' formal title (if it had one) nor those of the operating firms have been discovered. So far "East Hartford Glass Works" has been found only in the 1791 lottery advertisements, which suggests the name was no more than a temporary convenience. Although *East Hartford "manufactured"* (or *"made"*), or *"glass bottles,"* or just *East Hartford bottles* were advertised by more than one Hartford merchant into 1821 (doubtless until the name Manchester was adopted in 1823), only those offered before 1805 necessarily were from the Pitkin Glassworks; those advertised afterward could have been either the Pitkins' or John Mather's bottles.[101]

It has been said that about 1810 a J. P. Foster, who had been superintendent, "took over" the works; another account has it that he became "active manager." The latter seems more probable since, as yet, no evidence is known pointing to the absence of one or more of the Pitkins from the operating firms. If, by any chance, Foster rented the works, it doubtless was for a brief period, since there is evidence suggesting that, from May 1815 into 1817 at least, the firm was Pitkin, Woodbridge & Company (Richard and Horace Pitkin and Dudley Woodbridge). Through records of a suit brought in 1817 against a customer, Kenneth M. Wilson has established that this firm ran a general store in East Hartford, and two credits ($.32 for cutting 1⅝ cords of chestnut wood, and $.58 for a day's work at the glassworks) against the debt seem to point to their ownership of the glassworks also, a quite common duality of businesses. At this writing I know of no later documented date of the works' operation than Mr. Wilson's 1817 reference. That year, it will be recalled, saw the beginning of a long deep depression out of which several glassworks were unable to climb. Still, insofar as I know now, there is no evidence refuting the family tradition that glassmaking continued until about 1830, or that lack or the cost of wood for fuel caused the permanent shutdown of the Pitkin Glassworks.[102]

The Pitkin Glassworks has always been considered a bottle glasshouse of which the commercial products consisted only of bottles, flasks, and other containers blown from green glass. But such is the tentativeness of knowledge that new "facts" necessitate expunging old ones and lead to new interpretations, especially in so partially explored a field as American glassworks. Today it is known that window glass of decolorized green glass and/or white glass was produced also in the early years. Under Hewes, as revealed by Ill. 8 and the earlier notice quoted above, some crown glass was made, and later that excellent set of workmen, so the 1791 petition states, had already blown a "Considerable Quantity of Window Glass of an excellent Quality." Also, though the bottles they had blown probably were mainly green glass, the clock glasses surely were blown from the window-glass metal, as undoubtedly were the cups and pitchers. However, as no window glass or hollow ware other than bottles was mentioned in any of the advertisements I have found, probably production of window glass was discontinued by 1795 and with it that of window-glass metal. Possibly the line had been unprofitable because of competition from the Boston Glass Manufactory. One would conjecture too that any cups, pitchers, bowls, and the like that might have been blown later were not a commercial line but were individual pieces for families of the workers and friends, and possibly for strictly local consumption.

On the other hand, bottles must have been blown in vast quantities throughout the active life of the works, which was of about the same span as Wistarburgh's, and they doubtless were of "all sorts" characteristic of the late 18th and early 19th centuries. In my research, none of the documents examined gave clues, and merchants advertising in the late 1790s were content with such phrases as "a good assortment of E. Hartford manufactured Glass Bottles," "East Hartford do [that is, clean junk bottles] different sizes, ½ pint drums do." "East Hartford manufac-

tured Bottles of all sizes," "East Hartford Glass Bottles," and later just "East Hartford bottles." Consequently, information about the output is still general and traditional rather than specific or proven. Judged by Hewes's mention of "Dimejohns" (Ill. 8), demijohns were blown from the beginning and, according to Mrs. Knittle, their wicker coats were woven by the wives and children of the workers.[103] Possibly the "½ pint drams" advertised were pattern-molded flasks blown by the German half-post method. Such pocket bottles and other containers, like 1 and 2 of Ill. 87 and 2, 3, 4, and 6 through 11 in Ill. 88, have long been attributed to the Pitkin Glassworks, and for many years were erroneously thought to be products of that glassworks only. Certainly the type was a natural one to have been blown there, and doubtless it was. A few excavated fragments indicate that these containers were blown at the Pitkin works as well as at Coventry and Glastenbury in Connecticut, at the Keene-Marlboro-Street works in New Hampshire, and at the Gloucester Glass Works at Clementon, New Jersey. (See Part VI: Pattern-molded Bottles, Flasks, and Jugs.) Hence *Pitkin-type* is used by most collectors, dealers, and writers when they do not succumb to an old habit. Still, the name *Pitkin* and the attribution persist: when tradition attributes a piece of glass or a type to a particular glassworks, it is an adhesive forming an almost indissoluble bond.

The Figured Flask is another type of molded flask probably produced at the Pitkin Glassworks, but until a few years ago there was no tangible evidence. Now, because of a *few* but significant fragments found close to the factory site, it seems probable that the Sunburst flasks, GVII–5, GVII–5A, GVII–7, and GVII–16, were Pitkin products. The last has long been attributed to Coventry. Previously only five flasks had been attributed, tentatively or confidently, to the works. These five (listed in the Charts of Figured Bottles and Flasks) are the pint Eagle-Cornucopia with initials "J.P.F." and "CONN." (GII–57), its twin in design except for absence of lettering (GII–58), the pint Decorative flask with "JARED SPENCER" and "MANCHESTER/CON." (GX–24), and two unlettered pints closely akin to GX–24 in design (GX–25 and 26). The early confident assumption by Stephen Van Rensselaer that "J.P.F." stood for J. P. Foster and that GII–57 was a Pitkin product arose quite naturally from the information about Foster's connection with the glassworks. The attribution of the half-pint GII–58 stemmed from the likeness in design to the "J.P.F." Though, by 1940, students were qualifying the attribution to "possibly," today I feel it must be more tentative, in part because Foster's role and the duration of his tenure are uncertain, as is the exact year of the first Figured Flask in the Historical category. Also, the mold for the "J.P.F." might well have been a private mold, not a glassworks mold with initials of a manager or lessee. And if it was a private mold used in a Connecticut glassworks, as geographical distribution of this extremely rare flask suggests, the flask might be Pitkin or Mather, possibly Coventry.

The same possibilities of origin apply also to the Jared

Spencer flasks, which definitely were blown in a private mold, and to their close kin. The "MANCHESTER/CON." places the earliest possible date as 1823, after the May incorporation of the village in that year. It also localizes the flask safely as to the owner's place of abode, and—in 1940—the Pitkin Glassworks seemed the probable source, particularly as John Mather's glassworks was unknown then. However, although land records show transactions between Jared Spencer of East Hartford (before 1823) and Richard and Horace Pitkin, and also Dudley Woodbridge, there is no *proof* as yet that he bought any flasks and bottles from the Pitkin Glassworks. On the other hand, Mr. Wilson found documentary evidence that Spencer had bought bottles from John Mather's glassworks in East Hartford, also from the Glastenbury, the Coventry, and the Willington Glass Works. Possibly, but perhaps improbably, since the flasks are so rare, Spencer sent his mold to more than one of the glassworks for orders to be filled. Though I lean toward the Pitkin or Mather attribution, I must admit it is an inclination without visible support. Anyway, whether made at the Pitkin Glassworks or not, the flasks are choice collector's items today and the Pitkin Glassworks is still as important in the history of our glass industry.[104]

14. NEW-HAVEN GLASS WORKS *of Mark Leavenworth, New Haven, Connecticut*

Although, so far as I know at present, the New-Haven Glass Works was so short-lived that probably no glass whatever was actually produced, its aura of mystery and the revealing information in the few known documents in the case are too intriguing to permit its omission from the thumbnail sketches of 18th-century glasshouses.

When in New Haven on Sunday, October 18, 1789, George Washington was informed "that a Glass Work [was] on foot here for the Manufacture of Bottles." This must have been the project of Mark Leavenworth, Esq., New Havenite, who evidently still felt about bottle production as he had in 1787 when he wrote his previously quoted "Hints to Manufacturers," and who seems to have been a theoretical rather than practical glassman. The "on foot" suggests that the glasshouse was in the process of building, or about to be so. According to Leavenworth's own statements in his "Memorial to the General Assembly," he had "erected a House built furnaces and prepared every Implement & Material necessary for making Glass" by March of 1790. The first blast, he said, was in that month, and was an utter failure "owing to one of those accidents which generally attend New Works." Whether or not that blast was also the last is one of the mysteries. Another is why, by May, Leavenworth planned to expand into the field of window glass and flint glass. It was on May 17, 1790, that he submitted his "Memorial," explaining his plans and problems and requesting "some proper aid either by Lottery or otherwise." Possibly because he was a man of some property and not without influence (he was elected to the

Common Council in June 1790 and was Clerk of the District Court of Connecticut in 1791), he seems to have anticipated a quick and favorable response. Possibly, too, members of the assembly were well primed with facts and arguments. Whatever the background circumstances, the affair moved swiftly to a conclusion satisfactory to Leavenworth. The day his "Memorial" was presented and read, a committee was appointed to consider and report on it. His own report, giving many details not in the "Memorial," may have been already prepared; it was in the committee's hands the next day, May 18.[105]

Leavenworth's exceedingly frank exposition of the situation and problems, including naïve admissions that make one wonder at the assembly's "encouragement," is, to me, one of the most interesting of all the documents I have read pertaining to our 18th-century glass industry. The report to the committee ran as follows:

The Glass House was originally designed principally for... making Bottles, particularly the Junk Bottles for the purpose of Shiping Cyder to the West Indies and Southern States. Bottles are still a principle [*sic*] object but the plan is enlarged. A Contract is made for building a furnace for ten Pots,—The proposal is to use two Pots for Window Glass One or two for Flint Glass and the remainder for Bottles. It is neither necessary nor practicable without the aid of accounts not here & never yet computed to estimate with any accuracy the expense which . . . has already arisen. It has been great from many causes among which the High Price of Wood is one, and the Expence has been increased at one time by the misfortune of an unusual Storm and Tide which damaged the Works and materials, and at an other time by an unfortunate attempt to make Glass in a furnace which was altogether improper for the business. Before it be put in blast there must be a farther sum advanced of probably six or seven Hundred Pounds, beside the Expence of procuring from Europe several Workmen—What the expence of obtaining those Men from Europe may be is altogether uncertain—With respect to the probability of success, I doubt not I shall succeed, but can not calculate that all my mistakes in the Business are at an End. I fully believe that I am enough acquainted with the business to direct every part of the Work untill the Glass is ready to be blown, but without the advice of workmen I might do the business to disadvantage.

The works will proceed if no Workmen are obtained from Europe, for in that case we must make use of such as we have and make such Glass as they understand.

It is for blowing the Glass that we want Workmen & in that business they are exceedingly wanted. The few workmen we have are in such demand that they obtain very high pay and there are few if any of them who are expert in the trade—There is not one in America who is in *any degree* a Workman at the Crown Window Glass. There are none except at the Works in Maryland [Amelung's New Bremen works] who well understand the flint Glass Works, and even at bottles they are so slow as to do little more than half what is usual in Europe—There are several who make what is called Dutch Window Glass in what perfection I can not judge.—

As to the sum I believe that four Hundred Pound would

enable me to go thro' the business free from great embarrasment.

M Leavenworth[106]

Because of Mr. Leavenworth's enterprising and industrious turn, the committee had little doubt of his success as a glass manufacturer, and almost immediately recommended he be allowed to raise the £400 "by lottery, or otherwise [to] grant him that sum out of the Publick Treasury." On May 19, 1790, the assembly chose to authorize a lottery consisting of two classes, provided certain conditions were met. As a safeguard, a £3,000 bond, with one or more securities approved by the state treasurer, was to be given as assurance the lottery would be properly managed and the prize money duly paid. The drawing of the "Class First" tickets for prizes was to start by June 1, 1790, and the £400, of course, was to be used for completing and operating the glassworks. Presumably the tickets for "Class First" of the lottery were printed and distributed for sale as soon as possible after the bond was posted. This class consisted of 2,500 tickets at 9s. each, and the first prize was $400 ($100 more than that of the Pitkin 1789 lottery but the same as their 1791). By December 15 few tickets remained unsold, and the managers, Jonas Prentice and Peter DeWitt, announcing that the drawing of these would commence on January 1, 1791, warned that "those persons who wish to become adventurers must strike while the 'Iron's hot!' " Before the end of January, "Class Second" was launched. As the managers told the public, "FORTUNE FAVORS THE BRAVE": *one* of the 3,600 tickets at 15s. ($2.50) each would pay $1,000. All the prizes, subject to 15 percent deduction, were higher than they had been in "Class First." The tickets were available in at least 20 towns besides New Haven, and from two post riders. And Timothy Phelps of New Haven would insure them. Though the drawing was set for May, the rapid sale of tickets so exceeded the managers' "most sanguine Calculations" that it was advanced a month, to Monday, April 4. On April 20 the list of fortunate numbers was published in New Haven's *Connecticut Journal*.[107]

Though I have found no statement to that effect, it would appear that the lottery was a financial success, which should have benefited the New-Haven Glass Works. However, the records so far discovered are silent as to what, if anything, occurred at the glassworks. Moreover, it seems the General Assembly was uninformed as to the disposition of the money realized after the payment of prizes. After about two years the assembly appointed one Moses Cleveland, Esq., to find out whether "the Money raised by Mark Leavenworth Esq. . . . by a Lottery granted him . . . to enable him to compleat and carry on the Glass Manufactory in New Haven [had] been applied according to the conditions of the Grant." Mr. Cleveland was to report to the assembly in May 1793.[108] And so the matter stands at present. What happened to the glassworks and to the lottery money and whether those so-necessary junk bottles or other kinds of glass were ever blown at New Haven remains a mystery. One guess would be that, in spite of the

funds, Mark Leavenworth had been unable to get competent glassmen from Europe or in America, where he would be competing for craftsmen with the Pitkin Glassworks in East Hartford, the Boston Glass Manufactory, the New-Jersey Glass Manufactory, and the Albany Glass Works.

15. NICHOLSON'S GLASS FACTORY, *at the Falls of the Schuylkill, Philadelphia, Pennsylvania*

The history of the first glasshouse to be built near the Schuylkill River is still fragmentary. Nevertheless, the known fragments of contemporary evidence, the traditions, and secondary reports about the works are tantalizingly suggestive. For more than 80 years it has been accepted as fact that the glassworks was established by Robert Morris, the wealthy Philadelphia merchant famed as financier of the Continental Congress, and John Nicholson, presumably a man with capital to invest and a belief in the future of American manufactures. In his history of the Falls published in 1869, Charles V. Hagner recorded that sometime between 1780 and 1786 John Nicholson and Robert Morris built a glasshouse near the Falls opposite Governor Mifflin's dwelling and, lower down the river, a row of stone houses for the workmen. In 1880, Weeks drew upon Hagner's brief account, and subsequent writers about our glass history drew upon Weeks. However, the few bits of contemporary evidence known to me at present contain only Nicholson's name. Still, absence of Morris's name does not preclude the possibility that he had a financial interest in the project. Nor is it impossible such an interest contributed to the financial difficulties of his later years. Whatever the extent of Nicholson's interest, whether he was sole or part owner, he was manager of the glassworks in 1796, according to a letter written in that year by the superintendent, William Peter (or Peter William) Eichbaum.[109]

It may be that although Morris and Nicholson planned the project in the first years of the 1780s, its execution was wisely postponed because of the unfavorable economic climate of that decade. Be that as it may, the scant primary evidence dated 1795 and 1796 seems to indicate that no part of the plan materialized until after 1790. Moreover, the plan was for an extensive enterprise, not limited to glassmaking, and, it would seem, far from fully realized in 1795. In April of that year, the Duc de la Rochefoucauld Liancourt visited the project and recorded the following observations:

Above the falls, a Mr. Nicholson possesses large iron-works, a button manufactory and a glass-house. But none of these works are yet completed. The buildings, however, which appear to be well constructed, are nearly all finished. A particular building is assigned to every different branch of labour; and the largest is designed for the habitation of the workmen, of whom Mr. Nicholson will be obliged to keep at least a hundred. These buildings are on the right bank, and the warehouse, which is to receive the manufactures is on the opposite side. The pieces of rock, which occasion the falls, form an easy communication across the river, and could greatly facilitate the construction of a bridge, were such a project to be carried into execution. . . .

There is in America a scarcity of persons capable of conducting a business of this kind. There is also but few good workmen, who are with difficulty obtained, and whose wages are exorbitant. The conductors of Mr. Nicholson's manufactories are said to be very able men. But then a whole year may elapse, before the workmen fall into a proper train of business, so that Mr. Nicholson's situation does not afford the most flattering prospects of success, if his returns be not rapid as well as large.[110]

Had Mr. Nicholson not been away the day of the visit, La Rochefoucauld Liancourt doubtless would have obtained more information to record in his *Travels*.

Although the above remarks seem to indicate that the glasshouse may not have been entirely finished, it was far enough along so that operation of the furnace was practical. Sand for the glasshouse, so La Rochefoucauld Liancourt said, was being brought from the Delaware banks, so it is evident that glass, even if limited in quantity, was being produced. In a February 10, 1795, advertisement, John Nicholson advised the public that glass of various kinds was for sale, wholesale and retail, at "the Store of American Manufactures at the Falls of the Schuylkill on the Wissahickon road." On April 25, 1790, he announced prices given for broken glass "for use of his Glass Manufactory . . . viz. For White Glass—1 dol. 10 cents per cwt. Window Glass ⌐dol. per do. Black Bottles 25 cents per do. . . .'' He ran the same advertisement again in December. It may be that glass was blown earlier if, as is said, William Peter Eichbaum (a cultured German, "Formerly glass cutter to Louis XVI, late King of France" and immediately an emigré from the French Revolution) was engaged in 1793 as superintendent. Presumably the glasshouse with its necessary furnaces could have been planned, built, and ready for operation in less than a year.[111]

How long, if at all, production continued after Eichbaum's departure in 1797 is not known as yet. The last bits of evidence of operation I have at this writing are two 1796 advertisements. One, which ran from January 25 through February 23, 1796, was almost the same in wording as that of February 1795. The other, running from April 25, 1796, through July 1 was for "Two boys to take glass from the manufacturers and blowers" (that is, carry the finished pieces to the leer). According to Weeks, about 1808 the works was converted for calico printing and was still standing in 1856. I have found no evidence of a reconversion for glassmaking, but have found that this 18th-century works seems to have been confused with the early 19th-century Schuylkill Glass Works—or Philadelphia Glass-House, as it was first called (No. 19)—established on South Street.[112]

Of course, there has been much speculation about the output of the glassworks at the Falls of the Schuylkill, the role of Eichbaum, and his influence upon the products. How much, if any, previous experience Eichbaum had had in construction of furnaces and in composition, mixing,

and melting batch is not known, but subsequent events in Pittsburgh would seem to indicate these facets of glassmaking were not his forte. On the other hand, it is well established that he was an accomplished glass cutter. Therefore students have conjectured that an objective of the proprietors of the works on the Schuylkill was fine glassware, and that some cut and engraved tableware may have been made, at least during Eichbaum's tenure. This is still a very "iffy" question. However, if any wares of this kind were made, it is most likely the metal was white glass, for which—as the advertisement quoted above shows—cullet was sought; not flint glass. Obviously, inasmuch as the same April 25, 1795, advertisement stated that "Orders will be executed . . . for glass of any size to 24 by 30 inches," window glass was an available product. Also obviously, and not surprisingly, bottles were an important product. The February 10, 1795, advertisement of glassware mentioned specifically "claret bottles, snuff bottles, square and round, pound and half pound mustard bottles, pint, quart, two quart bottles *black* and *white* [the italics are mine]." The January–February 1796 advertisement listed the same bottles from claret through mustard bottles, which were then followed by "pocket bottles, pint, quart, two quart and three quart bottles black and white."[113] The pocket bottles may have included patternmolded flasks blown from single and from Pitkin-type double gathers, and doubtless were of pint and half-pint sizes. Possibly, too, among the black bottles were English wine bottles of Type 9 (11 in Ill. 52). If and when a further search of Philadelphia newspapers of the 1790s can be made, it is possible further light will be thrown on the products of Nicholson's Glass Factory.

16. PITTSBURGH GLASS WORKS, *Pittsburgh, Pennsylvania*

The first of many Pittsburgh glassworks was the brainchild of James O'Hara, a gentleman of means and enterprise, keenly alive to the potentialities of the country west of the Allegheny Mountains. His acquaintance with the country started in 1773 at Fort Pitt, and after serving in the Revolutionary War, he returned to settle in Pittsburgh. In the decade that followed the war he acquired vast acreages of land, by purchase and government grant, and had a financial finger in more that one business pie. It is not surprising that the growing local and westward-creeping market for window glass and also bottles was an invitation to establish glassmaking. Doubtless a prime factor in his decision to do so was the fact that imports of these necessities from the East, mainly from Baltimore and Philadelphia, were inadequate and expensive, in part because of costly and hazardous transportation. Such fragile commodities usually came over the Allegheny Mountains during the summer months when the roads were at their poor best. But whatever the reason, the loaded wagons, dragged by five or six teams laboriously to the top of steep mountain ridges, had to be kept upright and braked on the perilously sharp descents by the combined strength of all available hands.[114] Thus, from the point of view of supply and demand, prospects of success were pleasing.

However, for O'Hara as for eastern manufacturers, there was the bedeviling problem of incompetent glassmen. Unversed in glassmaking himself, O'Hara had to obtain glassmen and depend on their advice in the construction of furnaces as well as for manning the works. Who his glassmen were, or whence they came, is not known at present, though it would seem they were not too expert. A frame glasshouse was built beyond the village of Allegheny on a tract along the Ohio River that O'Hara acquired in 1790. The first blast, so he wrote later, produced just one bottle, "a very ordinary one" that cost him $10,000. Inasmuch as the heat attainable in the woodburning furnace was deemed insufficient for bottle production; possibly the first one was the last bottle. However, cylinder window glass was blown for a few months before the glasshouse was pulled down. And in 1796, O'Hara, with Major Isaac Craig as partner, laid plans for a new venture at Coal Hill.[115] The new glassworks with its eight-pot coal-burning furnace, the first in the United States, was producing window glass and bottles in 1797, though how successfully is questioned by some students.

In taking a partner, O'Hara may have welcomed additional capital, but possibly more important to him at the time was having a financially interested man watch over the project during O'Hara's absences from Pittsburgh, occasioned by his duties as colonel (later general) in the Army Quartermaster Corps. His friend Isaac Craig was such a man—a landowner, owner of a successful distillery, and doubtless also a man convinced that a glassworks would be a profitable investment.

By 1804, not only had Craig's faith begun to waver, but he was pushed to doubt and withdrawal—mainly, it is said, by the alarms of his wife and brother-in-law. In September of that year, when the partnership was dissolved, Craig's interest was $13,034.80, representing three-eighths of the business and property. On the other hand, O'Hara—so he wrote in 1805—had sunk $32,000 (probably including the sum paid to Craig), of which only $2,000 had been paid back to him.[116]

What had happened was the usual result when men with capital but neither experience nor knowledge of the business attempted a "new manufactory," especially in a new or young community. The glassmen had to be lured to the West by tempting material prospects. Usually their traveling expenses were paid, as were those of their families, if they were married. And even in 1812, a glassblower might expect "a House rent free, plenty of fuel at his door and privilege of making a garden," in addition to substantial wages. Then too, as Craig told a correspondent in 1803, the expense of the extensive buildings necessarily erected to house the numerous employees and their families (O'Hara said they bred like mink) was greater than estimated. Further unexpected expense was occasioned by the "ignorance of some people in whose skill . . . we reposed too much confidence." Also, in the beginning, there was a considerable cost in getting those vital materials that were scarce in the vicinity of Pittsburgh. Surprisingly, in the light of his fears at the time of writing, a year later Craig said the manufacture had been brought to comparative perfection by perseverance and attention. Possibly one factor was the closing of the nearby infant Ohio Glass Works, probably in 1801, when the Pittsburgh Glass Works not only was relieved of local competition but was enabled to acquire the defunct works' best workmen and many of its tools.[117]

From the inception of the partnership almost to its end, it was Craig who conducted affairs in Pittsburgh while O'Hara was on military service elsewhere. As to the site and construction of the new glasshouse, Craig was advised by Peter William Eichbaum, who had been persuaded to leave Nicholson's Glass Factory (No. 15) in Philadelphia to supervise the building and operation of America's first glasshouse with a coal-burning furnace. From the standpoint of economy, the plan to use coal instead of wood as fuel called for a location convenient to a coal vein. One was soon found. On June 12, 1797, Craig reported to O'Hara (then in Detroit) that, as Eichbaum had approved a site on Coal Hill near Ward's pits, he had purchased one lot of the necessary land and was buying two more. Already lime and building stone were being quarried; a carpenter had been hired and scantling for the main buildings was being sawed; timber for the other buildings was being prepared by four log-house carpenters; and negotiations for the stonework were being conducted with a mason. Presumably the melting pots for the first blast, which may have been late in the year, were made during the summer, since "the clay [would] not bear handling in cold weather and no good workman [wished] to employ pots in less than six months after they were made."[118]

Pot clay undoubtedly was in Craig's mind when he mentioned the considerable expense caused by scarcity of some materials, and it was perhaps the most critical. The first pots were made from local clay, samples of which had been sent to Eichbaum while he was still in Philadelphia. Inasmuch as he had reported the clay did "not look amiss" except for "some roots," several tons had been dug and prepared according to instructions sent by him. Unfortunately the clay was quite unsuitable for the melting pots. Probably at the first blast it became evident that the pots could not withstand the intense heat. As soon as possible, arrangements were made to purchase proven eastern clay by the barrel and tierce, thus inflating overhead by the high cost of transportation over the mountains and the higher prices for eastern clay. Moreover, sometimes delays in shipments caused shortages of pots acute enough to halt melting, thereby contributing to loss of income—as in 1807, when production had to stop in May at an expense of "2 or 3000 dollars." Little wonder that in 1802, from May into December, the proprietors advertised a $100 reward to anyone finding a bed of suitable clay near Pittsburgh that appeared to contain 50 tons. Apparently no one earned that reward. However, good pot clay was obtained from New Jersey beds and shipped from Bordentown, and pots made from it "stood in the fire 3 to 13 weeks, when old and well managed." Even better clay, a fine white Delaware clay, was shipped from Newcastle, and the best, an imported German clay, was purchased in Baltimore from J. Labes (probably the James Labes who had been associated with Amelung). Later, the delays and cost of hauling barrel-loaded wagons over the mountains were cut by the discovery of excellent pot clay in Missouri.[119] Initially the other midwestern houses—in fact, almost if not all early glassworks—were afflicted by losses from poor clay and improperly made and aged melting pots, which cracked and broke under fire.

More difficult of solution were the problems of production and of the glassmen themselves. Of course a scarcity of glassmen was endemic to the industry at the time, but even more discouraging was the fact that some of the glassmen in key positions possessed less all-round knowledge and experience than glassmaking demanded. Also complicating the problem were personality conflicts and the intemperate and ornery behavior of some of the men. Trouble probably was brewing even before December 1798, when Eichbaum, Frederick Wendt, who had accompanied him to Pittsburgh, and at least two other glassmen formed Eichbaum, Wendt & Company, and leased the works on a percentage basis but guaranteeing the proprietors a minimum rental. By October 1799, Craig was "apprehensive of the glass manufactory [going] well the ensuing year under the direction of Eichbaum or any of the people now engaged as his partners," who were disinclined to renew the lease. Although both Eichbaum and Wendt were to play leading, but quite different, roles in the drama of Pittsburgh glass, they clashed in this appearance together. The gentle Eichbaum may have felt Wendt was upstaging him; the ambitious Wendt certainly felt Eichbaum was miscast. Not only did an "implacable enmity" develop between them; Wendt, supported by a chorus of other glassmen, maintained Eichbaum was not qualified to be superintendent. This would not be unlikely, since he was a glass cutter whose art and profession were the decoration of finished pieces, not their fabrication. Naturally it was in this field that he made his contribution to Pittsburgh glass, establishing the city's first glass-cutting shop, where presumably Bakewell's famous cut glassware was decorated before that firm added its own cutting and engraving department. But in 1800 Eichbaum started with only a small cutting shop, merely an adjunct to his noted tavern, The Sign of the Indian Queen, which he established in that year when he eased the situation at the Pittsburgh Glass Works by withdrawing.[120]

For nearly four years following Eichbaum's departure, the glassworks was the scene of much activity without measurable progress toward profits. Though O'Hara and Craig placed little trust in Wendt, apparently necessity dictated that they make him superintendent under Craig's management. In March 1800, the proprietors' rather glowing advertisement, more cheerfully worded than circumstances seem to have warranted, appeared in Pittsburgh and Philadelphia newspapers. It claimed their glass was made from the "best materials" by a "number of the most approved European glass manufacturers" and sold "at least 25 per cent lower than articles of the same quality brought from any of the sea ports in the United States." Orders could be sent to either O'Hara or Craig, or to Prather & Smilie, whose Market Street shop evidently was a Pittsburgh retail outlet at the time. The advertisement ran in the Philadelphia papers off and on for a year, perhaps because the contract covered that period. Nevertheless, by August, the works had been leased to F. Wendt & Company, formed by Wendt and his supporters among the glassmen. Probably the only reason the arrangement prevailed for about four years was that the proprietors found no competent superintendent to operate the works for them. They were not, however, absentee landlords; a close contact was kept.[121]

In August of 1800, a proposal to produce "white glass" was made to Craig by William Price, an English glassman "immediately from London." Price, who had left England's famous and nearly two-centuries-old Stourbridge glassmaking center, evidently hoped to better himself in one of America's new glassworks. He had been drawn to Pittsburgh by the above-mentioned advertisement, which he read in a Philadelphia newspaper after his arrival there. Presumably he was a competent glassman, familiar with the composition of most kinds of glass—in 1816 he obtained the first United States patent for a composition of glass. Craig and Mrs. O'Hara consulted with Wendt, who agreed to let Price have one pot in the furnace and assistance for the experiment. His first attempt failed because, he said, green and white glass could not be successfully made at the same time in the furnace. However, Price convinced the proprietors that he was as good a "white glass" maker as he professed to be, provided he had a proper furnace and equipment. After Craig learned that further experimentation involved extra expense estimated at $600, he lost most of his enthusiasm for expansion in that direction. Not so O'Hara. Experiments were resumed, and the necessary facilities are said to have been ready in 1802. If so, successful production was still a few years away. Possibly O'Hara's persistent pursuit of his ambition to produce white-glass wares contributed to the uneasiness leading to Craig's withdrawal in September 1804.[122]

With Craig's departure, O'Hara became the sole proprietor of the Pittsburgh Glass Works; as he emphasized in more than one letter, "no person [was] concerned with him in the works." As quickly as possible he gathered the reins of management into his own hands, installing Price as superintendent and Wendt as "foreman maker." Demoted to this status, several rungs below his desire for another rental of the glasshouse or a yearly salary, Wendt became a foreman mischief-maker. It probably was shortly before April 19, 1805, when, not bringing O'Hara to his way of thinking, Wendt deserted, taking Price and two others with him. On that date O'Hara wrote to a customer in Kentucky:

your suspicion respecting your glass was wrong, it was duly ordered and reported to be on hand, but find that owing to the perfidy of Price, my superintendent and Wendt the foreman maker in plotting to abandon the works, the large size of glass is not made, nor do I expect it can be made before September.

Price must have been involved, as adviser at least, in plans for the furnaces and ovens of a stone glasshouse and other improvements then under way. Also, though he had been struggling with the white-glass problem, no white-glass ware appeared in the roster of glass advertised in April 1804 and, even in 1806, white glass was not yet made in quantity.[123] Possibly Price's failure to meet O'Hara's expectations in this field influenced him to defect as much as did Wendt's persuasion. Perhaps, too, he had an inkling that O'Hara might be casting his eyes eastward for another superintendent, as he certainly did for skilled blowers.

In any event, it would appear that the chronic need for competent glassmen prompted O'Hara's April 19, 1805, letter to (John) Frederick M. Amelung, who apparently had been retained as superintendent of the Baltimore Glass Works (No. 18) when Philip R. J. Freize took over the works after Amelung and his partners failed in 1803. Doubtless O'Hara assumed Frederick M. Amelung was skilled in glassmaking, since he was the son of John Frederick Amelung of New Bremen (No. 10), and perhaps he believed that Amelung's failure in Baltimore was due more to misfortune than mismanagement. Amelung's willingness to go to the Pittsburgh Glass Works must have seemed to forecast certain solution of the production problems. However, he did not leap at the change. From O'Hara's letters, one gets the impression that, quite apart from matters of salary and position, Amelung asked probing questions to satisfy himself that the Pittsburgh works was well equipped and important enough to warrant his leaving Baltimore. Also, his opinions and desires counted so much with O'Hara that Wendt was rehired in spite of past behavior, and the arrangements completed with one Nicholas Swerer to leave the Kensington Glass Works (Philadelphia Glass Works [No. 7]) of Butland and Rowland. As O'Hara desired, Amelung must have arrived in Pittsburgh in plenty of time for the fall blast to start in September. His tenure was brief, ending possibly in October 1809 and certainly before April 1810—the whys and wherefores are conjectural. Anyway, on April 29, 1810, O'Hara wrote to Joseph Carson in Philadelphia saying that Amelung was managing "the glassworks down the Delaware" and was then "employed in endeavors to get my glassblowers to desert my works." O'Hara added, "I wish you could get me 2 or 3 of his best, mine receive commonly 100 dollars a month for their work."[124]

Perhaps, during most of the next eight or nine years, O'Hara derived nearly as much satisfaction as disappointment from his glassworks, though not substantial profits. Like other manufacturers he lost some of his glassmen to competitors, and a few left to start their own works. On the other hand, he continued to entice glassmen from other works. (Incidentally, the German background of so many of our blowers is highlighted by O'Hara's

request in 1810 that advertisements for blowers be placed in the "Dutch" as well as English language newspapers in Baltimore.) On the production side his output increased: in 1806 its value reached $18,000 a year, $5,500 more than in 1803. Probably it continued to rise until the depression after the War of 1812. Also, he achieved his ambition to make white glass and probably finished the erection of a large white-glass house in 1810. That, by October 1816, his white-glass production had become somewhat of an annoyance to Bakewell, Page & Bakewell is suggested by an agreement entered into by O'Hara and Benjamin Page whereby O'Hara's white-glass furnaces would be turned to green-glass production, he would withdraw entirely from the white-glass field, and Page would attend to sales of the Pittsburgh Glass Works' green-glass wares in the western market and collect the money for them. Two years later, O'Hara wrote a firm of commission merchants in New Orleans that his glassworks was in "flourishing order" and he had a quantity of glass on hand. The former condition seems remarkable in that time of depression; the latter, quite likely.[125]

In the meantime O'Hara's health, which had been failing since 1812, caused him to rely more and more on his practical glassmen, presumably chief among them Charles Impson (Ihmsen) and Frederick Rudolph Jaocim Lorenz, both of whom were to establish glassmaking dynasties in Pittsburgh. In fact, Lorenz started with the Pittsburgh Glass Works itself. However, if, as has been said, he took over soon after O'Hara's death in December 1819, it must have been on a lease for about one year, for "NO MONOPOLIST," whose letter appeared in the March 3, 1821, issue of *The Statesman*, refers to the revival, under the auspices of Messrs. Page and Gray, of the glassworks owned by the estate of the late Col. O'Hara. Probably it was not long afterward that Lorenz did buy the works, operating alone until 1841, when he joined with William McCully & Company, operators of three other glassworks. In 1851 Frederick Lorenz and Thomas Wightman, as Lorenz & Wightman, took over the works, and when Frederick died in 1854, his son Frederick R. Lorenz entered the firm. For a short time the glassworks was rented to Fahnstock, Albree & Company—the lease is said to have run from sometime in 1860—until a new firm of Lorenz & Wightman was formed in 1863 by Moses A. Lorenz, Thomas Wightman, and Alexander W. K. Nimick. The next change was in 1871, and the new firm was Thomas Wightman & Company, which was still manufacturing window glass in 1886, a decade short of 100 years after James O'Hara and Isaac Craig made plans for our first coal-burning glass furnace. And for most of those years, bottles and other containers had been products of the Pittsburgh Glass Works.[126]

As long as O'Hara held the reins, probably the green-glass hollow ware produced at the Pittsburgh Glass Works, though plentiful, ranked second to the window glass. Probably little of the white-glass metal was blown into bottles—or any at all if it was flint (lead) glass, except possibly for apothecaries' use. (Today I, personally, feel that the nature of O'Hara's white glass should be explored further before acceptance of the long-held conclusion that it was flint glass.) However, as at other glassworks, the bottles and other containers produced during the long lifetime of the works must have been typical of the various periods in which they were made. But, again, information is meager. At present I know of only two years in which O'Hara & Craig products were advertised. In 1800, in the previously referred to advertisement, "Bottles of all kinds, pocket flasks, pickling jars and apothecary shop furniture" represented the hollow ware. In April 1804, and for several months afterward, the following advertisement appeared in the *Pittsburgh Gazette*:

The Pittsburgh Glass Works, Having been in successful operation for some time past, the Proprietors are induced to inform their former customers and others, that they have now on hand a large assortment of WINDOW GLASS and HOLLOW WARE, of a superior quality to any hitherto manufactured in this country, and that they have determined to reduce the price this season as follows:

HOLLOW WARE

Gallon Bottles		400 cents a dozen
Half Gal.	do.	240 do.
Quart	do.	160 do.
Pint	do.	120 do.
Porter		
& Claret	do.	133 do.

From O'Hara's Letter Book, it seems evident that there had been no change in the price of pint flasks and quart bottles by 1809, but in that year quart jars were $2 a dozen; half gallon, $3; and gallon, $4.80. Gallon bottles had gone up $.80 a dozen.[127] It is my guess that at least some of the pocket bottles and pint flasks were pattern-molded in ribbing, possibly in reticulated designs also, and that among the ribbed were Pitkin-type flasks as well as chestnut flasks. Since Frederick M. Amelung was to take molds with him to Pittsburgh, it may be that checkered-diamond flasks, like 1 in Color Plate II but in light green glass, were blown in the Pittsburgh Glass Works. Doubtless quantities of chestnut bottles from small to gallon sizes were blown as well, and it would be very strange if molds for body form had not been used, especially for the important porter bottles, which O'Hara himself needed for his Pittsburgh Point Brewery in the early 1800s. Probably they were similar to 11 (Type 9) and 12 (Type 10) in Ill. 52.

Likewise, it would be strange if none of the 19th-century Figured Flasks, blown in full-size two-piece molds, was produced in the Pittsburgh Glass Works. In fact, a few have been attributed as possibilities on the basis of initials molded in the glass. It seems to me likely that, accepting the initials "F. L." as standing for Frederick Lorenz, three rare Figured Flasks in the Historical category may have been produced by Lorenz at the Pittsburgh Glass Works, as well as at his Sligo window-glass works. In the Charts these are (1) GI–7, "G.GEO.WASHINGTON"—Eagle, "F.L." in beaded oval frame, pint; (2) GI–8,

"G.G.WASHINGTON"—Eagle, "F.L." in beaded oval frame, pint; number 20 in Group A of the "Most Desirable Flasks"; and (3) GII–15, Eagle, "F.L." in beaded oval frame—Cornucopia, half pint; number 16 in Group B of the "Most Desirable Flasks." These flasks, of which none has been recorded in dark bottle-green colors, probably were first blown in the 1820s.[128]

Not until the Civil War period are more Figured Flasks found that, if the initials marking them have been correctly interpreted, may have been blown in the Pittsburgh Glass Works. There are five possibilities, all falling in the Historical category and in Group XII, which is called Shield and Clasped Hands after the design on the obverse. Two have a flying eagle on the reverse and "L & W" on the base. In the charts they are GXII–4 and GXII–18. Presumably "L & W" stands for Lorenz & Wightman, probably the second firm of that title to operate the Pittsburgh Glass Works. The other three flasks have "F A & Co." in the frame in the lower part of the shield and, on the reverse, a cannon design. In the Charts they are (1) GXII–40, pint; (2) GXII–42, half-pint; and (3) GXII–42a, half-pint. Since, as yet, the only recorded firm fitting "F A & Co." is Fahnstock, Albree & Company, Van Rensselaer's attribution of the three flasks to it is still accepted. As stated above, this firm is supposed to have rented the Pittsburgh Glass Works from sometime in 1860 into 1863. Therefore, as is likely, if the flasks were brought out in those years, they would have been produced in the Pittsburgh Glass Works, and of course the molds would doubtless have continued in use at Fahnstock, Albree & Company's Temperanceville factory. It is unlikely that no other flasks were blown at the works and perhaps in time some of the many other flasks attributed to the area or marked "PITTSBURGH" will be found to have emanated from this first of the successful glassworks in the Midwest.

17. NEW GENEVA GLASS WORKS, *"Gallatin Glass Works," New Geneva and Greensburgh (later Greensboro), Pennsylvania*

Until about 1950 the history of the New Geneva Glass Works remained sketchy and was based mainly on secondary sources of information. The new evidence, especially various documents including letters and account sheets, began enlarging and altering the traditional picture of the works and the people involved in them. Consequently, in *Two Hundred Years of American Blown Glass*[129] it was possible to both expand and, in some respects, correct the accepted history. Inasmuch as more information from documents and vital statistics has come my way since 1950, it seems safe to say that as research into primary sources progresses, further details will emerge, and perhaps even change some of the present conclusions. One feels almost as though a superimposed impressionistic sketch is being gradually scraped from the canvas to reveal a detailed original picture.

Among the details that I believe do not belong in the original picture is the tradition about the inception of the glassworks. The romance-flavored accounts, long accepted locally and transmitted from one generation to another in the family of more than one New Geneva glassblower, agree that the glassworks was conceived at a fortuitous meeting between Albert Gallatin and a group of former New Bremen glassmen in a tavern, where they were taking an overnight break in their respective journeys. The glassmen—headed for Kentucky in search of a suitable site for a glassworks, or returning from a fruitless search there—discussed their plans with Gallatin, who persuaded them to go to New Geneva. Besides differing as to whether the group was headed east or west, the accounts vary also as to date, tavern location, number of glassmen, and the names of those in the first glassworks company. However, all the versions I know of include John Gabler, presumed to be the John Christian Gabler associated at the time with Adam Kohlenberg in Frederick County, near New Bremen (No. 10), and Baltazar Kramer, who had blown glass for Stiegel, presumably for Amelung, and later for Kohlenberg. As yet, though, no Gabler has appeared in original documents before the summer of 1806, and then it was in connection with the new works at Greensburgh. Baltazar Kramer, after selling his Maryland property in June 1800, settled in New Geneva, where he bought land from George Kramer in November of that year. In the glassworks accounts I have seen, his name first appeared in 1801.[130]

These facts and other documentary evidence fed my doubts of a meeting at some indefinite time and in some tavern, doubts sparked by the postscript of a May 1797 letter to Gallatin. As a result, I branded the tradition as probably apocryphal, a judgment considered debatable by some collectors and some descendants of New Geneva glassblowers. The argument is advanced that Gallatin, en route to or from Congress, where he represented Washington County, was so busy a man, with his mind so full of congressional and personal business, that he could have forgotten the episode entirely or forgotten to notify his partners in Albert Gallatin & Company. To me this does not jibe with Gallatin's neat methods, keen business sense, and constant concern with developing New Geneva, as revealed by his steady correspondence with his partners at that time. Moreover, if *he* failed to inform his partners that a group of glassblowers would arrive to make or discuss plans for establishing a glasshouse, does it seem likely the *glassmen* would fail to mention the meeting? Gallatin's sending them would have been not only a mark of his approval, but a natural and important introduction to his partners; failure to mention it, peculiar and unnatural. Yet had the partners been informed, surely the announcement to Gallatin in the postscript quoted below would have been expressed in different words.

Be that as it may, the first documentary evidence of which I know now in connection with the New Geneva Glass Works is the *postscript* to a May 10, 1797, letter to Gallatin at Philadelphia, written by his close friend and business associate John Badollet about disturbing company affairs:

Since signing my letter we three [Badollet, Bourdillon, and Cazenova, all members of Albert Gallatin & Company] *unanimously* have begun an affair which can furnish the counterpart to the preceding reflexions and afford some comfort. It is no less than an undertaking of glassworks. Six Germans containing all the necessary workmen we are trying to deal with and have a well grounded hope of success. Such an undertaking considered either in a public or private point of view ought to supercede every other we will attend to it with the utmost of our abilities and by report inform you of the success.[131]

Five of the six blowers decided to stay for the project; the sixth departed, whether to return east or possibly go a little farther westward to Pittsburgh has not been learned. Nor has his name. Possibly it was Baltazar Kramer.

Presumably plans for the works were well developed by the time Gallatin returned to New Geneva. His biographer, Henry Adams, states that "glassmaking was begun during Mr. Gallatin's absence in the spring of 1797" and that Gallatin returned to New Geneva immediately after Congress adjourned on July 10. In records owned by Charles Lilley Horn there is a receipt signed on July 14 by George Kramer and Adolph Eberhart for $350 advanced by Gallatin for the use of the glassworks. However, not until September 20, 1797, were formal Articles of Agreement drawn and signed. The agreement to associate and to form a copartnership to erect a glasshouse and establish glass manufacturing was between Albert Gallatin & Company in the persons of Albert Gallatin, Louis Bourdillon, John Badollet, John W. Nicholson (Gallatin's brother-in-law), and Charles Casanova (Casenove) of the first part and, of the second part, the group of glassblowers—namely, George Kramer (seemingly the spokesman and leader), Adolphus Eberhart, Ludowitz Reitz, Christian Kramer, and George Reppert. In brief, the conditions of the agreement required the following:

(1) a copartnership for six years from the date of signing (that is, to September 20, 1803),
(2) Albert Gallatin & Company to advance the "monies necessary to erect the buildings" on the selected tract of the company's land on George Creek near town, and to carry on the glassworks,
(3) the glassmakers to "attend to & work at the said manufacture for six years" and to be paid the usual rate for "such labour and work,"
(4) the "neat profit," after deduction of expenses including the glassmen's pay, to be equally divided between Albert Gallatin & Company and "George Kramer and the other Workmen his associates." From the glassmen's half share of profits, Albert Gallatin & Company was to be reimbursed, without interest, for half of the capital invested by that company. In other words the glassmen would receive only their wages until their debt to the company was paid.[132]

About four months later, on January 17, 1798, Badollet wrote to Gallatin: "The first glass will appear Saturday. On a first appe[arance?] the expenses do not amount so high as we first calculated, please to G. it may hold true and that we may have been deceived." But they were deceived, and Gallatin was to be discouraged more than once to the point of contemplating abandonment of the infant industry. Probably difficulties with the melting pots and production arose at the first blast, as had happened to so many others; if not, they did soon afterward. A little less than three months after the furnace was fired, Gallatin, upset by Nicholson's reports, wrote his brother-in-law:

the result I form is that the works must be abandoned by us at all[?] events even in case of finding clay in the Country . . . if only 65 boxes window glass have been made in 5 weeks there must have been some strange deception by the Glass-Makers either upon themselves or upon us. For God's sake reject every plan that tends to involve us. Rent or sell or abandon the works but let us not melt away everything we have in the attempt.

However, nothing so drastic occurred then or later, though threatened. Yet if, as is presumable from 65 boxes, only 6,500 feet of window glass had been finished in five weeks, Gallatin had cause to wonder.[133]

The previous November, 1797, Gallatin had returned to Congress, of necessity leaving the affairs of Albert Gallatin & Company largely in the hands of his partners and, of course, the practical work of the glasshouse to the glassmen. Actually, personal participation in the conduct of the various New Geneva and Greensburgh projects was seldom possible for Gallatin because of his years of public service — in Congress, as Jefferson's Secretary of the Treasury, and as Madison's before becoming a member of the Peace Commission that finally signed the Treaty of Ghent, later as Minister to France, and still later as Envoy Extraordinary to Great Britain. Nevertheless it was Gallatin who retained an interest in the New Geneva Glass Works for 20 or more years after the last of the others in Albert Gallatin & Company had withdrawn. And apparently he came to think of the glassworks as primarily *his*: in 1816, replying to inquiries about starting glassworks, he wrote, "I commenced mine with about ten thousand dollars and made no profit during the first years, not until the capital amounted to near twenty thousand." Just when his financial interest ceased, I have not learned. S. Jones in his *Pittsburg in 1826* refers to Gallatin's New Geneva Glass Works. Possibly Gallatin or his son Albert R. was in B. F. Black & Company, the firm that took over in or about 1830. And letters written in February and May 1832 indicate Albert R. Gallatin was in some way connected with the glassworks.[134]

The *first* ownership change occurred sometime prior to February 1798, when financial disappointments and disagreements on business policies led to the premature dissolution of Albert Gallatin & Company. Gallatin was to become an Atlas bearing the load of the company's affairs and problems, settlement of which weighed upon him for years. Though Nicholson joined him in taking over the half-interest in the glassworks, Gallatin seems to have

been the partner making the vital decisions, albeit he usually had to do so at long distance. In 1799, he was no happier about the works and workmen than he had been in 1798. He felt that the glassmen's labor and board, also the wood cutting and hauling, were "extremely extravagant and pernicious." And, as cash was very scarce, he told Nicholson that wages — in fact, everything except clay and salt (presumably for the glass) — should be paid for in goods and provisions, which also would be acceptable in payment for glass, if necessary. In addition, he wrote that Nicholson "must try to get Agents to sell for us at Pittsburgh and all our other country towns." By the end of July, while he was again considering a rental or sale, he had "formed no fixed resolution . . . except that of taking Direction of the Business" into his own hands.[135]

This he did by putting the glassworks under "Ami Mussard," who firmly applied remedies to keep the infant alive, and to improve both the quality and quantity of window glass and hollow ware during the next two years. However, the change was not achieved without opposition: as Mussard wrote to Gallatin, he was too new in the business for his opinion to have much weight with people led by their prejudices and old customs. The glassmen had been accustomed to using coarse big pieces of potash that, Mussard found, neither mixed well nor melted properly but stuck to the pots, necessitating opening before the melt was done. Also, they had been using improperly cleaned sand (that is, not thoroughly washed) or too much sand because it made mixing easier, and both prolonged the melting time. Moreover, too much sand made the batch "too hard." Apparently Mussard succeeded in persuading the glassmen to use a finer potash and the proper amount of clean sand. He found, too, that the glassmen had been careless in curing the firewood sufficiently or had failed to have it cut long enough in advance of the need for it. As a result, sometimes green and wet wood expensively slowed melting or made it impossible. One such occasion was not a total loss, however, as the glassmen rebuilt the crown of the furnace while the fire was out.

Added to the production problems was the glassmen's dissatisfaction with sales. They felt that poor sales were due to ineffectual methods of selling. To meet this problem, Mussard allowed the glassmen to try selling the glass, but their three or four attempts were disappointing, resulting in dissatisfyingly irregular sales. Perhaps this conflict lay behind Gallatin's January 1800 intentions to first "settle all personal accounts with the glass blowers at the end of the [current] blast, paying full balance in glass," which they could sell as they pleased and, second, to rent the works to the blowers. It would seem the glassmen were not so minded, so one concludes differences were smoothed over.[136]

Possibly an uneasy truce on vital matters prevailed for the next three years. Whatever the atmosphere of the situation, in May 1803, four months before the Articles of Agreement were to expire, Gallatin and Nicholson advertised an auction sale of "One undivided half of the NEW-GENEVA GLASS WORKS," as well as the property of the defunct Albert Gallatin & Company. If ever held, the auction evidently was unsuccessful, for Gallatin bought Nicholson's interest in the glassworks and the old company in May. Perhaps some degree of rapport had been attained as sales increased and the glassmen became more proficient in aspects of glassmaking other than blowing. In any event, Gallatin made a new four-year agreement with the glassmen, presumably along the lines of the first, as he had suggested to Nicholson the previous January.[137]

Before this copartnership expired—in fact, by June 1806—the glassmen were hatching a plan for a glasshouse across the Monongehela at Greensburgh. Dubious about the plan at first, Gallatin would have attempted to continue operating the glasshouse on George Creek by himself had he been able to be in New Geneva. However, since absentee management of what he considered would be "tantamount to a new establishment" was impractical, he decided to join the glassblowers. His argument for "merely agreement to buy land and erect the works at joint expense" without an article of copartnership seems to have prevailed, at the time at least. Acting for the group, George Reppert purchased the necessary land in the fall of 1806. In February 1807 the agreement was signed by Gallatin, George Reppert (who seems to have replaced George Kramer as leader of the glassblowers), Lewis (Ludowitz) Reitz, Christian Kramer, and Adolph (Adolphus) Eberhart of the original copartnership, and two later arrivals at New Geneva, Baltazar Kramer, Sr., and Christian Gabler. (In the account sheets I have seen, *Christian* Gabler does not appear but *John* and *J. C.* do.)[138]

Exactly when the Greensburgh glasshouse, still called the New Geneva Glass Works, was finished, when blowing started there and ceased at the George Creek furnace, and how long the Greensburgh glasshouse operated are unanswerable questions at this time. However, account-book sheets seem to indicate blowing started late in 1807 or early in 1808. Gallatin had hoped to persuade the glassmen to continue production at George Creek for a year or more, but they probably stopped as soon as the new works was ready for operation. Though present documentary evidence indicates that Nicholson had no financial interest, as Gallatin's attorney he was to maintain contact with the glassmen and the works for years. Consequently, when *The Navigator* stated in 1810 that the glassworks, "now removed to the Greensburgh side," was "carried on by Messrs. N. Nicholson & Co.," it seems probable the glassworks was confused with Nicholson's store. Another "fact" seemingly in error is that coal was used as fuel from the start, and the choice of Greensburgh was determined by the discovery in 1804 of coal nearby. In the Gallatin records owned by Mr. Horn, an entry on January 24, 1816, states: "The experiment made with coal at the new glass works has exceeded our expectation. It makes glass of equal good quality as formerly and the saving of expense will be very very great." At the end of that year, it is interesting to note, a profit of $8,000 was netted on a capital investment that had reached $40,000. As previously noted, in or about 1830 the firm became B. F. Black & Company.

Later history is even more veiled than the early: it is said (1) the glasshouse was "rebuilt" in 1837 by Andrew and Theophilus Kramer, sons of one of the founders; (2) the two Kramer sons and Philip Reitz, also a founder's son, built a second works in 1837 and ran it to 1857; (3) the works burned down in 1847 and was never rebuilt.[139] Whatever the fact, for half at least—possibly most—of its lifetime, Albert Gallatin was financially interested in the New Geneva Glass Works.

The commercial products of the New Geneva Glass Works were window glass and hollow ware blown from a simple green-glass metal of which the ingredients apparently were only sand, potash or ashes, and salts. Of course, it was decolorized for the window glass. Presumably the colorless metal was used also for some of the hollow ware, *but* I have as yet found no documentary evidence to support the tradition and family history of either engraving or cutting at either house. The most important item of output was always the window glass, and since only data on window glass was given by B. F. Black & Company in its 1832 report to the federal government, it may have been the only commercial product after about 1830. Though bowls, pitchers, tumblers, and the like were blown, bottles were the important items of hollow ware. Mussard's reports give the principal sizes in 1799 and 1800 as pint, quart, and half-gallon. The same sizes were being sent to Wheeling in 1826. Gallon bottles and jars were also blown. Surprisingly, during Mussard's tenure at least, pints were "the most called for." Perhaps more surprising was the production of black bottles. In his February 28, 1800, letter to Gallatin, Mussard reported that two of the men, Graham and Reppert, had left with boxes of window glass and bottles to sell downriver, and among the bottles were "600 black and green for cider." On April 12, 1800, he reported that from a new blast he would have "some thousands of black bottles blown for the french market" ready by the end of the month, and that one Kendall had asked for a thousand. It seems probable these bottles were like or similar to Type 9 (11 in Ill. 52). At Greensburgh possibly Types 10 and 11 (12 and 14 in Ill. 52) were blown.[140]

That pattern-molded bottles, flasks, and other hollow ware were blown at both the George Creek and Greensburgh glasshouses is well established. Three of the molds, handed down in the family of the Christian Kramer who was a partner in the George Creek and also the Greensburgh works, were until recently owned by Logan Ross, one of his descendants. They are now in The Corning Museum of Glass. These are a small two-piece mold in diamond diaper above flutes, a small 16-rib dip mold, and a larger 20-rib dip mold. The first two are shown in Ills. 92 and 93A, drawn from photographs and descriptions supplied by Mr. Ross, and in the case of the piece mold, an impression as well. There is also sound reason to believe that a 24-rib dip mold was in the New Geneva equipment. A few bottles and other pieces of hollow ware, the gather for which was patterned in such a mold, have been attributed to the glassworks on the basis of geographical distribution and/or family history, supported by form and color. It is believed by many students that so-called grandfather flasks, like 10 in Ill. 98, were blown in the New Geneva Glass Works as well as elsewhere in the Midwest. Among the bottles were some closely similar in form, pattern, and lip finish to 1 and 9 in Ill. 46 and 6 in Ill. 95. The last is very like an aquamarine swirl bottle illustrated by C. Malcolm Watkins in an article in *Antiques*, February 1963. It was patterned in a 24-rib mold and said to have been blown between 1803 and 1806 by the Adolph Eberhart, Sr., who was interested in both houses. Ribbed small bottles, in shape like 1 in Ill. 91 and called cruets in the Midwest, are likewise attributed to New Geneva. To me it seems axiomatic that Pitkin-type flasks were blown at both houses, and I believe that 2 in Ill. 89 may have been blown at the George Creek glasshouse.

During the 1790s the climate of the American economy slowly improved. The turning point, as previously indicated, was the adoption of the Constitution, coupled with the federal government's immediate institution of stabilizing measures, including assumption of fiscal responsibility, and passage of a tariff measure for revenue but still the first faltering step toward a protective tariff. States too, it will be recalled, were extending a helping hand to industry. But there was more: trade, blown our way by Europe's ill winds of war—particularly in shipping and in agricultural products—was forming a healthy reservoir of capital, and "good business" was nourishing the whole economy. Fortunately, though far short of the need, some of the capital was wisely used for internal improvements—bridges and turnpikes so desperately needed to bind the parts of the country in trade and neighborliness. However, investments promising more immediate returns were more alluring, among them manufactories for various materials and commodities. As we have seen, the glasshouses at Boston, East Hartford, Albany, and Glassboro got their second financial wind to carry them along into the 19th century, and American glassmaking was putting down its midwestern roots at New Geneva and Pittsburgh as the new century started. The small Kohlenberg glassworks near New Bremen had survived and the old Philadelphia (Kensington) Glass Works was being revived. Although as an industry American glassmaking could not be called a husky infant in 1800, the signs did point to the survival of window-glass and bottle manufacture.

C. 19th Century

While compiling my present data on the United States bottle industry, I found it still true for me that the history of the growth of our glass industry should be punctuated mainly by chronological commas, not periods. To mark the end of a phase, there always seem to be sound reasons to select a date other than the one chosen. Then too, as shown by the thumbnail histories of 18th-century glassworks, the lifetime of an individual glassworks often overlaps chronological periods. Therefore, it is mainly for convenience that the 1800s are divided here into two general periods, and that the last is extended into 1903, when full automation of bottle production was made possible by Michael Owens's bottle machine: (1) 1800 through 1832, when the glass industry became firmly rooted, and (2) 1833 through 1903, by which time glass manufacture had become one of the country's largest and most important industries. Also, because the gargantuan proportions attained by the industry demand a canvas too unwieldy for a country-wide panorama, even if sketchily drawn, the country is divided into three main glassmaking regions: the Middle Atlantic States, New England, and the Midwest. As previously explained, in the glass collector's geography the Midwest embraces the so-called Pittsburgh–Monongehela area of western Pennsylvania, Ohio, the Wheeling–Wellsburg area of West Virginia, and parts of Kentucky. Concerning the more western states with glassworks producing green glass and lime glass (flint glass in the trade) containers in the last half of the 1800s—for instance, Missouri, California, Indiana, and Illinois—my present information is largely statistical. Few specific bottles and flasks made in any one of them are known to me at this time.

It will be recalled that when the new century began in 1800 only eight glassworks were operating, so far as is known at present. And not one was exactly robust. During the first 32 years of the new century, there were at least 102 schemes to establish new glassworks, more than half of them conceived between 1800 and 1815. Most of the others were planned or started in the 1820s, mainly rushing in the wake of the 1824 protective tariff. However, out of all the glassworks—over 100 including the 18th-century survivors—that operated for long or short periods, only 71 remained by 1832, and in at least 39 of these bottles were blown either as the main output or as a sideline. Many of the works had been rescued by new capital. Even higher were the financial fatalities among the many firms—more than double the number of glassworks—building and operating or taking over glassworks. And the firms were, of course, formed by a far greater number of glassmen, merchants, and other businessmen who, undisillusioned by their predecessors' losses, thought they saw in the stormy times a rainbow arcing from their invested capital into a pot of golden profits. Even such bare statistical data indicate a time of crisis. In fact, or so it seems to me, the events of the period make it the most critical in our glass industry's history, and as such it demands special attention.

In a large measure the trends favorable to manufacturing in the United States were due directly or indirectly to war. Certainly the fragile mushroom growth of glassworks during the first 16 years was germinated and nourished by political and economic events leading to war and by war-bred conditions—and its shrinkage was quickened by the aftermath of war. For about three years after England and France resumed their maritime conflict in 1803, handsome profits from shipping and commerce flowed our way, as they had in the 1790s. Then, as our "Mediterranean War" with the Barbary pirates was ending, both countries thrust spikes into our wheel of fortune: each decreed blockades to stop the commerce of the other; both took our ships as prizes. England stepped up impressment of seamen on American vessels (a right claimed since 1792, for many were indeed deserters from her fleet), giving rise to the succinct American rallying cry "Free Trade and Sailors' Rights," which in a later context appeared on one of Dr. Dyott's Kensington pocket bottles (GIV–34). Soon there was talk of war against England, for her acts seemed the more heinous to most Americans, including some politically powerful ones, a few of whom were beginning to ogle Canada with an imperialistic gleam in their eyes.[1]

But war was preceded by retaliatory acts against both England and France, acts harmful to our commerce and shipping but stimulating to our infant manufactories. Not surprisingly the United States hit back first at England and, being nearly her best customer, with a Non-Importation Act prohibiting import of enumerated articles—"window glass and other manufactures of glass," among them—from any port or place in Great Britain, Ireland, any of her colonies or dependencies, or via any foreign port. This act, signed on April 18, 1806, was followed on December 22, 1807, by an embargo laid on all ships and vessels in our ports and harbors and limiting our use of the seas to fishing and domestic coastwise trade, both under severe restrictions. The Long Embargo, as it was called, by which our ships were "Now doom'd to decay . . . fallen prey / To Jefferson, worms and Embargo" was lifted March 1, 1809, but replaced by Madison's Non-Intercourse Act prohibiting all commercial intercourse with not only

Great Britain and her dependencies but also France and hers. Neither Great Britain nor France was brought to heel. On June 12, 1812, Madison declared war against "the United Kingdom of Great Britain and Ireland and the dependencies thereof. . . ." Another embargo was laid in December 1813. In the meantime tariffs had been raised 100 percent, not as protection for any industries but to strengthen our financial sinews for war. Throughout the years from 1806 on, there flowed a stream of petitions, memorials, and debates for and against the various restrictive measures. So too, as the situation of the moment seemed to demand or warrant, did the pattern of easing and tightening the leash on trade and shipping. Whether in force or suspension, the laws restricting trade "hung up," as one congressman put it, "like a rod in terroem,"[2] whereas they were luring carrots dangling ahead of would-be manufacturers.

On the one hand, the various measures and war itself were injurious to all, fatal to many, of our merchants and importers as well as shippers. As the flow of commerce dwindled to a trickle, the demand for domestic manufactures ballooned. So, on the other hand, idle American funds were channeled into manufacturing and desperately needed internal improvements—toll bridges, turnpikes, and canals. Even the federal government started a national road, which was to extend from Washington through Cumberland to Wheeling, and eventually to St. Louis, *and* be toll free. Given a hungry market, promises of transporation facilities, and higher tariffs, it was inevitable that more capital would be attracted to glass manufacture, which was already tempting investors, among whom were merchants and druggists who needed glassware in their businesses. Though a few of the adventures were planned for flint-glass works, most of them were for window glass and bottles, or bottles were added to their output. The need for bottles, particularly vials and beverage bottles, was especially acute. For instance, imports of the nearly indispensable black glass bottle had dropped from *24,594 gross* in the year from October 1, 1806, to September 30, 1807, to *2,574 gross* in the same period of 1812/13.

But glass manufacturers had two, sometimes crippling, handicaps—lack of skilled glassmen and of apprentices and, especially when located outside urban areas and not on or close to navigable water trade-routes, lack of transportation. Idling capital was available and the demand urgent, and so there were raids or attempts to raid the staff of one glassworks to secure workmen for another. Some were in the form of frank advertisements in communities where, or near where, there was an established glassworks, as when Justus Perry of the Keene-Marlboro-Street glassworks, New Hampshire, advertised in the Hartford *Connecticut Courant* in 1817. More often personal persuasion was the means; for example, in 1810, Henry Rowe Schoolcraft as superintendent lured glassblowers into breaking their contracts to join the force of the Ontario Glass Manufacturing Company at Geneva, New York. Of course the main sources of mature trained glassmen were Great Britain, Ireland, and the Continent. However, obtaining them was not a simple matter of offering a job in America at enticing pay and conditions. In England and some other countries it was a crime to engage craftsmen to go to America, and recruitment was a hazardous venture, one undertaken in great secrecy. It was also expensive. Not until well after the Napoleonic Wars, of which our 1812 war was an offshoot, was there anything like free emigration of skilled glassmen from Europe. All countries were jealous of their glassmen, none more so than England.[3]

Still, even had there been a surplus rather than a shortage of glassmen and willing apprentices capable of producing all the glass the country required, there still had to be adequate transportation and distribution facilities. But fruition of the many plans for internal improvement was too slow. It took time to build bridges, canals, and roads. The national road did not reach Wheeling until 1818; the Erie Canal, plans for which undoubtedly influenced the choice of several glasshouse sites in 1809 and 1810, did not reach across New York from Lake Erie to the Hudson until 1825. In fact, though dozens of projects for new and better facilities linking communities and trade centers were stimuli to new manufactories, it was another generation that would reap the full benefits, not the 1800–1829 one. This was true also, of course, of the revolutionary steamboat, which had been proved practical when the *Clermont* steamed up the Hudson from New York City to Albany in 1807. Another mode of transportation that would speed up distribution of merchandise even more than the steamboat was the railroad, born near the end of our 33-year period.

Many of the transportation projects probably would have matured earlier had it not been for the postwar conditions of trade and economy. Even before Americans as a whole were aware that the war had ended officially on December 24, 1814, the first of the commercial armadas was on its way to the United States bearing merchandise, including glassware, that had been dammed up for so long.

Americans quickly forgave all the past in their eagerness to purchase once more their fill of foreign manufactures, especially those of England. This was one of the prime causes of the country's economic state, in 1816, of being in what today would be called a recession. The recession slipped into a depression in 1817, one that plumbed the depths in 1819, carrying many glasshouses with it. In 1820 the economy began its slow climb back to a prosperous level.

As usual when economic disaster fell upon them, the affected businessmen turned to Congress, demanding it *do* something to save the situation. The first line of defense for manufacturers was, of course, a higher tariff. Congress's response was the 1816 tariff under which the black-glass bottles so needed by brewers and bottlers paid a duty of $1.44 a gross, only $.24 more than under the war tariff but $.84 more than prior to 1812. All other glass paid 20 percent *ad valorem.* Congress apparently intended to give a measure of protection, but it proved ineffectual. Not until 1824 was there a really protective tariff for manufactures, among them glass. Then more categories of bottles were provided for specifically: apothecaries' vials of 4 ounces or less paid $1, and over 4 ounces but not over 8, $1.25 a gross; black-glass bottles not over a quart paid $2; over a quart but not over two quarts, $2.50, and over two quarts but not over a gallon, $3 a gross; demijohns (bottles over a gallon), $.25 each. All other glass paid $.02 a pound plus 20 percent *ad valorem.* In the opinion of bottle and vial manufacturers the duties were inadequate in the face of continued foreign imports and stronger domestic competition. Competition from both outside and inside the country forced prices down. Apothecary vials, for instance, were higher during the depression years than in 1828. Assorted vials had dropped from $3.50 a gross in 1815/18 to $3 in 1819/23, and further to $2.50 in 1824/27. Though prices fell another $.25 a gross in 1828, the rise in duty to $1.75 a gross on vials and bottles not over six ounces, $1.25 on all bottles over six ounces, and $1.25 on all bottles over six ounces but not over eight was deemed sufficient by some producers.[4] Competition was not quite so sharp and general economic conditions were favorable. Our glass industry was at last rooted. The added protection of the 1832 tariff was not a necessity to the industry but, nevertheless, fed the well-established roots.

As previously stated, around 71 glassworks were operating as the new decade came in. However, not all would survive and new ones would be established. Even had I the data for detailed historical sketches of each of the glassworks planned and operated successfully and unsuccessfully during the years from 1800 through 1832, or the rest of the century, their scope would be beyond the limitations of this book. Therefore, with few exceptions, I shall content myself with historical sketches mainly of those glassworks in which the most distinctive bottles of the 19th century were produced—namely, the Figured Flasks: Decorative, Masonic, Historical, and Pictorial.

18. BALTIMORE GLASS WORKS, *Baltimore, Maryland, 1800–1880s*

The truth as to when, where, and by whom Baltimore's first glassworks was started has long lain "somewhere behind the mists of tradition and contradictory information"—to quote myself. Today it can be reported that in recent years the mists have been blown away, mainly by the researches of Delverne A. Dressel and of Richard H. Wood, of Baltimore. Over all, their researches confirmed in some instances, and in many others disproved, hitherto accepted "facts." Through land records and other contemporary sources, Mr. Dressel has untangled most of the threads of chronology and ownership, including those of glassworks particularly interesting to bottle and flask collectors—namely, the Baltimore Glass Works, the Spring Garden Glass Works, and John Lee Chapman's Maryland Glass Works. Both Mr. Dressel and Mr. Wood have most generously shared their information with me. The first glasshouse *was* the Baltimore Glass Works of Frederick M. Amelung & Company, and it *was* built and operating in 1800: the company announced on June 27, 1800, that making "all kinds of glassware and bottles" would start on July 1.[5]

It will be remembered that, in September 1795, John Frederick Amelung deeded his unmortgaged property interests in and near New Bremen to his son, John Frederick Magnus, and that on December 24 of that year his petition of bankruptcy was granted by the Maryland legislature, after which probably little or no glass was produced at the New Bremen Glassmanufactory (see No. 10, New Bremen . . .). Frederick M. Amelung, as John Frederick Magnus styled himself, not only reaped no lasting profit from his father's deed, but his father's potage of debts and mortgages as well as his own was to ruin his hopes of becoming a successful glass manufacturer. Perhaps he turned to glassmaking either because it was the only branch of manufacture and business with which he had any familiarity or because he had acquired a liking for it during his experience at New Bremen—or both. Be that as it may, apparently he believed himself sufficiently well schooled to superintend the establishment and management of a profitable glassworks. At least three other men who had capital and/or glass experience to invest were convinced that his faith in his own ability was not mis-

placed. The first doubtless was Alexander Furnival, a prominent Baltimore merchant whose daughter Sophia married Frederick in May 1797. The other two were Lewis or Louis (Adolph) Reppert, a practical glassman, and Jacob Anhurtz, a Baltimore painter and glazier who, with Furnival, probably advanced most of the needed capital and who would have a practical objective in fostering window-glass production. Incidentally, I was informed by Cloyde A. Reppert, a descendant of George Reppert, that Lewis was the oldest of the Reppert brothers who were descendants of Adam Reppert, a glass manufacturer at Clarenthal on the river Saar in 1688. All were born in Germany and emigrated to Baltimore, presumably in the early 1790s, and worked first in the New Bremen Glassmanufactory and then at the Baltimore Glass Manufactory. Though Lewis's brothers George and Jacob may have acquired a direct financial interest in the Baltimore Glass Manufactory or just a brotherly partnership, only Lewis "acted as owner" (to quote Mr. Dressel), joining with Amelung, Furnival, and Anhurtz to form Frederick M. Amelung & Company.[6]

On November 16, 1799, a little over two years after he became Furnival's son-in-law, Frederick M. Amelung leased from a George Prestman of Baltimore about an acre of land on which to build the projected glassworks. The lease was in Amelung's name, not the company's, and was not to become effective until January 1, 1800. From that date it was to run for 99 years at $400 yearly rent, with an option to buy.[7] As Mr. Dressel and Mr. Wood both point out, the land was strategically located for a manufacturing enterprise: it was on the south shore of the northwest branch of the navigable Patapsco River and at the foot of Federal Hill (Hughes Street between Henry and Covington streets). At hand was suitable sand in quantity. And the riverfront ensured docking facilities and inexpensive water carriage of raw materials, fuel, and wood for potash and building to the glassworks, and for shipping glass away from it. The members of Frederick M. Amelung & Company had very sound reasons to anticipate financial rewards from their enterprise when their glassworks went into operation the following July.

Contrary to the bright expectations, Frederick M. Amelung & Company was ill-starred, destined to fold in fewer than three years. Evidently, by 1801, all rapport between Amelung and his father-in-law had turned to discord. Furnival had been sucked into the Amelung family financial quicksands; he resorted to the extreme measure of law, securing a judgment ordering Amelung to turn over properties due him. Not surprisingly, only about two years after the first blast at the young glassworks, Alexander Furnival desired to move to the country and dispose of his interest in the "Baltimore Glass Manufactory." Presumably no one responded to his advertisement of August 11, 1802, and being at the end of his resources by May 1803, he became a bankrupt. In less than a month the same business fate overtook Frederick M. Amelung, designated a "merchant." Perhaps not all blame should be laid on the New Bremen legacies of financial troubles and the investment in and needs of the new glassworks: Furnival and Amelung were but two of 61 merchants who failed between 1800 and 1805 during Baltimore's brief recession caused by the painful curtailment of trade with the old Hanseatic port cities and Holland, while England and France joined in a short uneasy peace and Napoleon set out on European conquests. No doubt contributing in no small measure to Frederick's financial difficulties was his style of more than comfortable living. Mr. Dressel found the following November 8, 1802, advertisement from which Amelung's "need for funds becomes readily apparent."

To Be Rented. That convenient & pleasant house & lot in Camden Street, next door to Mr. Mayer, within a hundred yards of Hanover market house. The house affords all desireable accommodations for a genteel family; in the yard are erected a milk house, smoak-house, stable & couch [coach] house, wood shed, etc. There is a pump of excellent water before the kitchen door; an extensive garden on the premises, planted with flowers, shrubs & vegetables of all sorts; upwards of a hundred of the best grafted fruit trees from Europe; two asparagus beds, with a roomy summer house enclosed by Venitian [sic] blinds. Unites with pleasures of a rural retreat to the convenience of town life. Enquire of Frederick M. Amelung, on the premises.[8]

In any event, the firm of Frederick M. Amelung & Company was unable to survive the Furnival-Amelung conflict and lack of funds. The firm dissolved by November 2, 1802, about six months before Furnival's and Amelung's bankruptcies. Three days later Amelung, again designated as merchant, assigned his lease on the Prestman land—"the glasshouse property"—to Philip R. J. Friese "for a recited payment of $2500.00." Mr. Dressel suggests that this sum probably was the actual price paid for Furnival's and Amelung's interests because of the conflict between these two members of the firm, and was also the cost of the improvements (glasshouse, et al.) on the rented lot.[9]

Thus the Friese majority interest, whether Philip's alone or in association with family members, in the Baltimore Glass Works was acquired. As for the members of the original firm, Lewis (Louis) Reppert retained his interest until his death in 1822. Jacob Anhurtz apparently did not retain his. It may have been acquired by Lewis or have been held in Lewis's name for himself and his brothers George and Jacob, also practical glassmen. Furnival left the scene permanently; Amelung remained, not as a partner but as superintendent, until 1805, when, it will be recalled, he accepted Colonel James O'Hara's invitation to the Pittsburgh Glass Works. Incidentally, in 1805 Philip Friese and O'Hara were corresponding. As a matter of fact, Amelung carried one of Friese's letters to O'Hara when he went to Pittsburgh sometime after June of that year. Therefore Friese doubtless knew all about the negotiations and plans. Perhaps he was not reluctant to see Amelung leave Baltimore, especially as Lewis Reppert was not only quite capable of taking Amelung's place as superintendent, but—if he had not already done so—did, in 1805. Actu-

ally, Reppert apparently was a more stable, practical glassman than Frederick Magnus Amelung ever was. It would appear that George Reppert also was advanced, becoming "vice master"—foreman.[10]

The Friese regime that began in November 1802 seems to have prospered during the years of the embargoes and the War of 1812, as did so many manufacturers. Philip R. J. Friese, who had followed his brother John H. to Baltimore from Germany and, like John, had become a successful merchant, must have believed in the future of glass manufacturing in the United States. After surveying the situation of the Baltimore Glass Works in particular, he decided to invest in the works. However, local history recorded that salvage of the works was suggested to him by members of Baltimore's German colony. "Their racial pride" wounded by the failure of two German glassmaking projects, they hoped Philip Friese would "redeem the credit of the German name." From Philip's "Journal Ledger Account Book," Mr. Dressel learned that others besides Philip were involved in the undertaking. He found financial transactions that suggested Philip was "handling matters for the 'old firm,' e.g., with his brother, John H. Friese, who returned to Europe, with a H. C. [Henry Christ] Friese." But the possibility remains that "he [Philip] purchased the business for his *own* account." In any event, according to local history, one of Philip's first acts was to secure skilled glassmen from Germany. A December 25, 1810, advertisement for apprentices testifies to the continued Germanness of the enterprise: "3 or 4 young men of 21 years or strong healthy boys of about 15 years" were wanted, and it was "required they should understand the German language." Philip also started improvements and additions, which were completed in 1897.[11]

In effect and action, he was the proprietor of the Baltimore Glass Works, but he was not so listed in the directories until 1810. In that year, also, he exercised the option in the 1799 lease, purchasing the land from Prestman for $5,800. And it is noteworthy that he needed no mortgage to finance the purchase: the "money apparently came from his account in Bremen," Germany. By then, 500,000 feet of window glass valued at $65,000 were being produced; at least, such was the information sent to the Treasury Department for Albert Gallatin's 1810 Census of Manufactures. Perhaps because of the two new glasshouses at nearby Vernon, the editor of the Utica (N.Y.) *Columbian Gazette* felt that the "Glass Works of Mr. Friese" would be of interest to his readers, and so he published a news item about it on May 10, 1810. The capital, it was said, was then [1810] $40,000. A decade later the invested capital had risen to "$70–80,000," but yearly production had dropped 160,000 feet, or from 5,000 boxes to 3,400. In 1811 a box of the 8 x 10 window glass commanded $14.50; in 1820, the price per box ranged from $8 to $10. "Sales dull, prices low" was the report.[12] In short, the Baltimore Glass Works and its owners had been floundering in the ruinous depression following the War of 1812.

From the midst of that depression through "Jackson's Panics" of the 1830s, stresses and strains from illnesses, deaths, and money problems afflicted the owners of the Baltimore Glass Works. The first firm change occurred between 1817 and 1819 with the entrance of Philip Friese's younger brother, John Frederick, who as early as November 1802 had been associated with him as merchant. Philip retired insofar as the glassworks was concerned, but only into the wings. When Lewis Reppert died on January 1, 1822, George and Jacob Reppert acquired a half-interest in the works. They and John F. Friese became sole proprietors. Philip kept the land, glasshouse, and its ancillary buildings, becoming the landlord. The Repperts seem to have been more canny and practical in money matters than John F. Friese, for he became deeply indebted to them—to the amount of $20,000 or more—which was to lead to complications and lawsuits a few years after his death. In, or during, 1829 it became evident that John F. Friese was an ill man. "He was afflicted in his intellect," was declared a lunatic July 1, 1830, and died the following December. To his nephew Frederick Schetter, "if inclined to carry on for himself the glassworks," John F. bequeathed his interest in the works "at a fair valuation, on credit of five years without interest," provided Schetter decided to carry on and made his decision within three months of John F.'s death. Schetter did not so choose.[13]

In the meantime, John's illness had drawn Philip Friese back into the glasshouse affairs. Philip and his nephew Frederick Schetter had been appointed John F.'s trustees in July, though it would appear that not until March 1831 were they required to give bond. At that time the partnership of John F. Friese and George and Jacob Reppert was dissolved, and—as the Repperts were made responsible for John F.'s half of the partnership—it would appear they had full management of the glassworks for a short time. The exact date of Philip's becoming proprietor again is uncertain, but there is no uncertainty about financial difficulties from at least 1833 throughout the depression. Mr. Dressel has concluded, from his present evidence, that around 1835 the Repperts forced Philip to buy their interest—George apparently wished to retire from glass manufacturing and Jacob, who died in 1837, was already failing in health. In any event, heavy indebtedness to his brother John H. in Germany and borrowing from the Repperts necessitated Philip's putting various mortgages on his properties. Failure to pay his debts in full led to foreclosures. In his need for financial backing, Philip turned to William Baker, a judge in the Orphans Court of the City of Baltimore and a son of the William Baker, who had founded William Baker & Sons, a dry goods house.[14] An interest in the Baltimore Glass Works was natural, for, according to an 1837 Baltimore directory, William Baker had a glass warehouse on Hanover Street.

So it was that the years 1837 to 1842 saw the ending of the Friese regime and the beginning of the Baker. William Baker made his entrance on the scene in March 1837. In September of the following year, when the second mortgage on the glasshouse and five dwellings owned by Philip Friese was foreclosed, he bought them for $5,650, subject to the first mortgage held by John H. Friese in Germany.

When John H. foreclosed about three months later, Baker acquired the entire property at public sales for $18,000, but he did not execute the bill of sale until January 1845. In the meantime, the Baltimore Glass Works had been incorporated by William Baker and five associates, none of whom had previously been connected with glass manufacture, and 50,000 shares of stock to the amount of $100,000 were authorized. By the mid-1840s Baker's two sons, Charles J. and Henry J., were established as dealers in paint, oil, and glass. They were agents not only for the Baltimore Glass Works but also for the "New Jersey Glass Works" (apparently the works of Coffin, Hay & Bowdle in Winslow, Camden County). Their firm was listed as C. J. and H. J. Baker in 1845; "Baker & Bro.," commission merchants and agents by 1850; and as "Baker Bros. & Co." from 1851 through July 1865, the period during which Joseph Rogers, Jr., was a member of the firm. The enterprise of the Baker brothers was further demonstrated in 1851 by the establishment of a New York City house, run by Henry J. Baker under the firm name "H. J. Baker & Bro."[15]

The years 1849 to 1865 were eventful ones in the history of the Baltimore Glass Works and those associated with it. About 1849 William Baker decided, as had Philip Friese before him, to retire from the scene as an active participant in the Baltimore Glass Works but to retain ownership of the physical property. There is still some confusion regarding "the exact relationship and persons [responsible] for operating the Company from 1837/38 through 1850." However, directory listings for 1849/50 indicate operation of the works was briefly in the hands of Schaum Reitz and Company, a firm presumably headed by Lewis (Louis) Schaum and Lewis Reitz, both of whom had been glassblowers at the works since around 1837. The 1851 listings indicate that F. & L. Schaum were the operators—Frederick and Lewis Schaum.[16]

Late in 1850—and apparently with the blessing of the Bakers—plans for a new cooperative bottle glassworks (See No. 43, Spring Garden . . .) were completed by a group of blowers in the bottle department of the Baltimore Glass Works. Among them were Lewis Schaum's sons, Frederick and Lewis; also William Swindell, who had arrived at Baltimore via the Excelsior Glass Works in Camden, New Jersey, and previous association with the Union Glass Works of Kensington, Philadelphia. According to the plan, window glass would be the Baltimore Glass Works' product, and the new Spring Garden Glass Works' bottles would be handled by Baker Brothers & Company. Nevertheless, in 1854 the Spring Garden group decided to market its own output. Tradition asserts that William Swindell, disagreeing with the new policy, withdrew from the group, immediately returned to the Baltimore Glass Works, and became superintendent there. Moreover, Baker Brothers & Company announced their intention to manufacture "druggists' ware, jars, bottles"—"all kinds of Glassware." As a result, within about two years, the cooperative glassworks failed; the blower-founders returned to the Federal Hill works, and the Spring Garden Glass Works and property were purchased by Baker

Brothers & Company. Sometime between the acquisition of the Spring Garden works and 1859, the Baltimore Glass Works' bottle department was moved permanently to the newer works, which by 1863 was no longer called the Spring Garden Glass Works but the Baltimore Glass Works, and the firm was Baker Brothers & Company. In 1865 the interests of Henry J. Baker and Joseph Rogers, Jr., were bought by Charles J. Baker, who took his sons William and Charles E. and his nephew George B. Baker into a firm called Baker Brothers Company. The following year the firm purchased the original Baltimore Glass Works at Federal Hill from Charles J.'s father, William, for $45,000.[17]

However, apparently some financial transfusion had been needed, or else Baker Brothers & Company had decided to concentrate upon their huge and widespread oil, paint, and glass business. In any event, from directory listings it appears that even before the purchase of the Federal Hill works, some interest in the Baltimore Glass Works was obtained by Philip Reitz and possibly by the other Reitz glassmen along with him. At least Philip Reitz was listed as a glass manufacturer in 1864, as were Baker Brothers and Company; in 1867 the listing was Philip Reitz and Company. About 1870, or shortly afterward, all production in the Federal Hill branch, the original works, ceased. Whether or not henceforth the manufacturing at the works on Eutaw Street (ex-Spring Garden) was under Philip Reitz & Company or Baker Brothers & Company has not been learned. But over the next decade or so, insofar as window-glass production was concerned, that glassworks was becoming obsolete because of changes in technique and equipment. About 1890, Baker Brothers & Company drew their fires in the Baltimore Glass Works and, as did so many glass manufacturers, went west. In Findlay, Ohio, they established a "modern" window-glass plant, one using natural gas as fuel.[18]

From the announcement by Frederick M. Amelung & Company on June 27, 1800, it would appear that initially the firm had planned to specialize in "all kinds of glassware and bottles"—certainly not in window glass. On June 1, 1802 (five months before the dissolution of the firm), friends and the public were informed that the Baltimore Glass Manufactory was now in blast and orders would be taken for "all kinds white hollow glass, black and green bottles [doubtless including the porter and wine bottles of the period] and window glass" that would be "cut to any size or shape." With the entrance of Philip R. J. Friese a few months later, apparently emphasis was to be on the production of window glass, and it was for its window glass the works became best known. Nevertheless, bottles continued to be an important sideline, except for the brief period during which Baker Brothers & Company were exclusive agents for the cooperative Spring Garden Works. After the bottle department was reconstituted at Federal Hill, the following announcement was made in 1854:

NOTICE. / The undersigned would respectfully inform their customers and the public generally that they intend manufacturing DRUGGIST' GLASSWARE: PICKLE JARS: MINERAL, PORTER AND WINE BOTTLES, &c at the BALTIMORE GLASS WORKS, Federal Hill and are now prepared to supply the trade with all kinds of Glassware from their present stock on the most favorable terms. Private Mould Ware made with particular care and attention. / BAKER & BRO., 32 and 34 S. Charles Street.[19]

Although as yet no newspaper advertisement or other contemporary source has been found in which flasks, with or without molded designs, were mentioned, inscribed Figured Flasks testify to their production by the Baltimore Glass Works at Federal Hill and, after 1856, at Eutaw Street. Of 24 flasks long associated with the Baltimore Glass Works in the period from the late 1820s to 1850, only four were inscribed with the name of the glassworks. Fourteen were attributed to the works on the basis of the designs and inscriptions, which were of more intense local than regional or national interest: Baltimore's two early monuments (see Ills. 128 and 129)—the Battle Monument "to those brave citizens who fell on the 12th and 13th Sept. 1814, at North Point and Fort M'Henry"[20] in battle with the British invaders, and the Washington Monument, which was the first to be raised to honor "The Father of His Country" (see Part VIII, 4B); Baltimore's chamber-of-commerce-like slogan "Corn for the World," along with an ear of corn and cornstalk symbolic of the port's role in grain exportation; "Fells Point," the name of the famed shipping area of the port; and Major Samuel Ringgold, Baltimore's special Mexican War hero.

The extremely rare Locomotive Railroad flask GV–12 was attributed to the Baltimore Glass Works by Van Rensselaer, though one wonders why he did not attribute it to a South Jersey glassworks, since he apparently believed it to have been inspired by the acquisition, and installation in November 1831, of an English steam engine by New Jersey's first railroad company, the Camden & Amboy. My own feeling is that if the Baltimore Glass Works produced this flask, it did so because of the keen interest not only of all Baltimoreans in their own railroad, but of the whole country in the Baltimore & Ohio. The B. & O., incorporated in 1827, was destined to run 121 miles from Baltimore to Pittsburgh—a matter of very practical concern to Baltimore merchants, grain dealers, and exporters, who were seeing too much western trade following the Erie Canal to New York City. Although, by 1831, the B. & O. had in use only the 13 miles of track between Baltimore and Endicott Mills, it carried some 5,931 tons of freight in the first six months of that year. Moreover, by July, it had in operation an *American*-built steam locomotive. Even the citizens of Cincinnati, Ohio, knew, if they read their local newspapers carefully, that the B. & O.'s locomotive was ". . . fully capable of transporting 20 tons (including the weight of the cars) or 150 passengers, at the requisite or desirable rate of velocity."[21] (See also Part VIII, 5, Railroads.)

On the other hand, though the B. & O. was of almost national interest and, not surprisingly, was newsworthy in the Midwest and New England as well as the Mid-Atlantic

States, another railroad, planned about the same time, may have had more immediate interest in the Baltimore-Philadelphia area—namely, the New Castle and Frenchtown Railroad. Mr. Dressel believes that if flask GV–12 was indeed made by the Baltimore Glass Works, it may well have been inspired by this railroad, which became a connecting link for trade between Baltimore and Philadelphia. According to his findings, the route had been an avenue of trade as early as 1799 on which ships, the "French-town packet," left Baltimore for Frenchtown, then a busy seaport on the Elk River. Thence an overland route of some 17 miles was followed to New Castle, where cargoes were reloaded and passengers boarded another packet for Philadelphia. The Frenchtown packet lines were merged into the "Union Line" sometime prior to 1827, when the decision to build a railroad between Frenchtown and New Castle was made and a charter was granted by the Maryland legislature in its 1827/28 session. In 1831 the railroad was completed, two years after the opening of the Delaware & Chesapeake Canal. Mr. Dressel learned also that

it was constructed with wooden rails 6 inches square and 12 inches long, placed on blocks of stone 10–12 inches square, with iron bars attached to the wooden rails. Horses pulled each car and they were changed at Glass Co[unty] and Baer. *In 1833 the first locomotive steam engine was acquired by the Railroad and it was made in England.*

It was first called The Delaware, but about a year later, after being rebuilt, it was renamed The Phoenix. In visits to the Railroad Museum of the Baltimore & Ohio Railroad Mr. Dressel has never seen an engine similar to that depicted on the flask. Therefore he believes that as the engine on the flask is undoubtedly of foreign make, it is more reasonable to attribute the depicted engine to the documented foreign engine purchased by the Union Line for the Frenchtown and New Castle Railroad—a well-taken point.

However, it is sensible to keep in mind Richard Wood's observation that the flask "could have been made anywhere where [figured] flasks were produced."

Restudy of the present data on glassworks in Baltimore and the flasks long attributed to the Baltimore Glass Works has led to the conclusion that the dating of four of the flasks and their definite factory attribution should be reexamined and perhaps reconsidered. The four flasks are the pint GI–20 with profile bust of Washington in uniform, quart GI–21 with classical bust of Washington, pint GI–73 with profile bust of an army officer and inscription "GEN^L TAYLOR," and half-pint with Chesapeake oysterman's and fisherman's sloop or shallop. (See Charts, Groups I and VI.) It is important to note—and keep in mind—that common to all four are inscriptions "FELLS POINT" and BALT^O" *and*, on one side, Baltimore's Washington Monument. The consensus is that these features are sufficient evidence for unqualified attribution to *a* Baltimore glass works. Moreover, the technique and treatment of

the designs leave little doubt that one and the same moldmaker created all four molds. Although there are variations in details in the monument, they are very slight, indeed unimportant. What may be of the utmost importance, raising the question of dating the four molds, is the *absence of the statue of Washington at the top.* That ultimate ornament was lifted into its present position, amid appropriate ceremonies, on November 19, 1829, 14 years after the cornerstone was laid, an event widely publicized through the country's newspapers.[22] Hence the absence of Washington from his pinnacle may indicate that the molds were made before November 1829, instead of in the late 1830s or the Mexican War period.

Moreover, it may be significant that the flasks themselves have a form, lines, and proportions typical of those designed in the late 1820s and early 1830s, not around 1840 and later. For instance, the curve of the end from base to neck of the pint and half-pint is similar to that of the New England Washington–Jacksons GI–31 through 34 of the early 1830s, ca. 1828–36, rather than to that of the Taylor–Ringgold GI–71 and 72, ca. 1846–47; the curve of the quart is more like the Dyott–Franklins GI–96 through 98, ca. 1825–36, than the Dyottville Washington–Taylors GI–37 and 38. Coupled with line, there is the depth from front to back, which varies from later designs. The planes of the sides from which the designs rise are a little less curved than on the Taylor–Ringgold and more curved than on the Taylor–Cornstalk GI–74 and 75, which have nearly flat planes. This is not to say that *no flasks* of the earlier period were produced after the 1830s; rather, that it seems unlikely *molds* for them were. It has been demonstrated that sometimes molds made in the late 1820s and 1830s bearing designs of proved popularity continued in use for many years. The mold for the Mount Vernon Glass Works' Railroad flask GV–5 is a case in point: Harry Hall White's excavations on the factory sites showed that when the Vernon glassworks was moved to Saratoga, New York, in 1844 or 1845, the mold for GV–5 was used at the Mountain glassworks to produce the Railroad flasks.[23]

Nevertheless, it was only a few years ago that serious consideration was given to the possibilities suggested by the statueless monument and the details of the flask type. In fact, it was not until the early 1950s that distinction was made even between the two obviously different monuments—the Battle and the Washington—on Baltimore flasks,[24] to say nothing of the Washington with and without statue. Collectors and students, including myself, blindly accepted Van Rensselaer's "Baltimore Monument" for each. If noticed at all, the differences were brushed aside as designers' or moldmakers' aberrations. However, since that pre-November 1829 monument, combined with other features of the flask, assumed probable significance, ca. 1829 dating has been batted back and forth in flask discussions, only to fall out of court because of the inscription "GEN^L TAYLOR" on GI–73. Though a consensus has arisen that, inasmuch as the officer appears to be a much younger man than Zachary Taylor was in the late 1840s, the flask probably was not brought out then, as were the Taylor–Ringgolds and Dyottville-type Washington–Taylors, but may have commemorated Taylor's being breveted Brigadier General early in 1838 in Florida. That event, however, was scarcely noticed outside military and government circles. (See Part VIII, 4C, Zachary Taylor.) Also, it was nearly a decade after the statue was placed. Hence, some argue, the model for the monument, chosen by or given to the moldmaker, was an old picture, one drawn or painted before the late fall of 1829. This explanation seems reasonable; that is, if no one—designer, moldmaker, or glass manufacturer—cared whether or not representation of the Washington Monument was out of date and if all were indifferent to and untouched by the ineradicable civic pride in that monument. Therefore, because of doubt that an old model would have been used, because of the flask form, because of the "younger Taylor" so utterly unlike any of the many portraits of Taylor examined, because of the uniform so like that of Washington on GI–20, I incline to dissent from not only the 1838 dating, but also identification, in spite of the present inability to give an identity to the officer. In other words, the present supposition is that the bust was *not* intended to represent Zachary Taylor; that the mold was made without any identifying inscription about 1829; that the mold may have been in use for many years, and was probably acquired by the Baltimore Glass Works; that the inscription "GEN^L TAYLOR" was cut in the mold during the Mexican War, probably soon after Taylor's forces went into action and made news. It would seem that, in general, Baltimoreans were for the annexation of Texas.

And so we come to the matter of factory attribution. These four flasks were attributed to the Baltimore Glass Works by Van Rensselaer in the 1920s and the consensus is that the attribution was, and is, well founded. I also believe that flasks probably were blown there in the molds for GI–20 and 21 and GVI–2, as well as GI–73. However, I now believe that it is possible, if only barely so, that the molds were made originally *not* for the Baltimore Glass Works but for the short-lived Baltimore Flint Glass Works. This glassworks, located at the west end of Lancaster Street, Fells Point, apparently was built in 1828 and was operating by the end of November. At least the company's first known advertisement was dated November 28 (1828). It stated that "able and experienced workmen . . . fully competent to manufacture all kinds of hollow DOUBLE FLINT GLASSWARE" were employed. Mr. Dressel found that several organizers and stockholders of the company were druggists or were closely connected with apothecary shops. Consequently one may feel confident that not only double or single flint (lead) glass was produced, but also good white glass for apothecaries' furniture and bottles. And it seems more than likely—especially because of the various druggists concerned—that, like many other flint-glass works of the period, they produced green-glass wares. After all, druggists' shops were normal sources of many liquid preparations *and* whiskey. Unless the Baltimore druggists were rare exceptions, they needed bottles for ink and blacking, for in-

stance, as demijohns and carboys, and certainly bottles for retail sales of spirits. Like most druggists, they probably supplied flasks and pocket bottles, full and empty. Of course they probably bought many from the Baltimore Glass Works, but those druggists with a financial interest in the Baltimore Flint Glass Works may have saved on the cost of their glassware by having it made in their own factory during the period of its operation, from 1828 to 1834.[25] If the four molds were made for the Baltimore Flint Glass Works, they could have been acquired by the Baltimore Glass Works when production ceased at the Fells Point glassworks. I believe that may have happened.

There remains another question of identity, that of the army officer on GI–17 who was identified as Zachary Taylor by Van Rensselaer. That the bust was supposed to be of Taylor has not been questioned, though, again because of the general appearance and uniform, it has been suggested it represented a "younger Taylor" and dated around 1838. Again I have come to dissent. I believe the flask was of the period ca. 1828–32, and that the military gentleman was supposed to be Andrew Jackson. (See Part VIII, 4C, Taylor.)

The Figured Flasks associated with the Baltimore Glass Works are listed below in two groups: those inscribed with the name of that glassworks, and those attributed to the Federal Hill glasshouse. The dates and periods given are those in which I believe the flasks were *first* produced. I say "first" because the mold for a popular flask might be used over a number of years.

I. INSCRIBED FLASKS:

GI–17. *Obverse:* "WASHINGTON" in arc above profile bust, in uniform. *Reverse:* "BALTIMORE GLAS^S WORK^S in arch above profile bust of an army officer in uniform. Pint. Bust on reverse was identified as Zachary Taylor by Van Rennselaer. I now believe it was intended to represent General Jackson. ca. 1828–32. See above. The cramping of *Glass* and *Works* suggests that the inscription may have been an afterthought.

GI–18. *Obverse*: "WASHINGTON" in arc above profile bust in uniform. *Reverse*: "BALTIMORE GLASS WORKS" in horseshoe arch above Battle Monument. Pint. Probably late 1820–1830s.

GI–19. Like GI–18 but with smooth edges.

GI–22. *Obverse*: "BALTIMORExGLASS.WORKS." in uneven arch above classical bust of Washington (the S's in GLASS are reversed). *Reverse*: Profile classical bust of Henry Clay (?). Quart. ca. 1832(?)–early 1840s(?). No. 36 of Most Desirable Flasks, Group B.

GI–23. *Obverse*: Washington, profile classical bust. *Reverse*: "BALTIMORExGLASS.WOKS." in arch above profile classical bust of Henry Clay (?). Quart. ca. 1832 (?)–early 1840s (?). No. 37 of Most Desirable Flasks, Group B.

GXIII–48. *Obverse*: Pennants inscribed "BALTIMORE GLASS WORKS" and an anchor. *Reverse*: Sheaf of grain, crossed rake and pitchfork. Quart. 1850s.

GXIII–48a. Like GXIII–48. Pint. I know of no one who has seen a specimen of this flask, listed by Van Rensselaer in 1926.

GXIII–49. *Obverse*: Pennants inscribed "BALTI-MORE/GLASS Works". *Reverse*: Sheaf of grain, crossed rake and pitchfork. Half-pint. 1850s.

GXIII–50. Similar to GXIII–49.

GXIII–51. Similar to GXIII–49.

GXIII–52. Calabash bottle. Same decorative designs and inscriptions as preceding. "Quart." ca. 1850.

GXIII–53. *Obverse*: Similar to preceding. *Reverse*: Phoenix above bar inscribed "RESURGAM". Pint. ca. 1850.

GXIII–54. Similar to GXIII–53, but phoenix has no crest and "flames" are of same length instead of graduated.

II. FLASKS ATTRIBUTED TO THE FEDERAL HILL GLASS-HOUSE:

GI–20. *Obverse*: "FELLS" above profile bust of Washington in uniform, "POINT" below. *Reverse*: "BALT^O" below Washington Monument *without statue*. Pint. Possibly brought out ca. 1829 by the Baltimore Flint Glass Works. See discussion above.

GI–21. *Obverse*: "FELLS" above profile classical bust of Washington, "POINT" below. *Reverse*: "BALT^O." below Washington monument *without statue*. Quart. Possibly brought out ca. 1829 by the Baltimore Flint Glass Works. See discussion above.

GI–71. *Obverse*: "ROUGH AND READY" in semi-oval below profile bust of Zachary Taylor in uniform. *Reverse*: "MAJOR" above profile bust of Samuel Ringgold in uniform, "RINGGOLD" below. Pint. 1846–1847.

GI–72. Like GI–71 but with smooth edge.

GI–73. *Obverse*: "GEN^L TAYLOR." in arc above profile bust of army officer in uniform. *Reverse*: "FELLS POINT" above Washington Monument *without statue*; "BALT^O" below. Pint. Possibly brought out ca. 1829 by the Baltimore Flint Glass Works; the mold acquired later by Baltimore Glass Manufactory or Works, and inscription added during Mexican War. See discussion above.

GI–74. *Obverse*: "ZACHARY TAYLOR" in semi-oval above profile bust of Taylor in uniform. "ROUGH & READY" in reverse semi-oval below. *Reverse*: "CORN FOR THE WORLD" and cornstalk. Pint. ca. 1850. No. 34 of Most Desirable Flasks, Group B.

GI–75. Like GI–74 but with smooth edges.

GV–12. *Obverse*: Steam locomotive and fuel car. *Reverse*: "Symbolical" figure. Pint. ca. 1831. See discussion above. No. 36 in Most Desirable Flasks, Group B.

GVI–1. *Obverse*: Battle Monument. *Reverse*: "A LITTLE MORE GRAPE CAP^T BRAG" in oval frame of grapes and vine. Half-pint. ca. 1847–48.

GVI–1a. Like GVI–1 except edges ribbed.

GVI–2. *Obverse*: "BALT^O" below Washington Monument *without statue*. *Reverse*: "FELLS" above shallop, "POINT" below. Half-pint. Possibly brought out ca. 1829 by the Baltimore Flint Glass Works. See discussion above.

GVI–3. *Obverse*: "BALTIMORE" in arc above the Battle Monument. *Reverse*: "LIBERTY & UNION". Pint. Probably 1840s. No. 38 of Most Desirable Flasks, Group B.

GVI–4. *Obverse*: "BALTIMORE" below Washington Monument with statue. *Reverse*: "CORN FOR THE WORLD" in arch above large ear of corn. Quart. 1840s.

GVI–4a. Similar to GVI–4; no inscription on monument side.

GVI–5. Similar to GVI–4. Quart. 1840s.

GVI–6. Similar to GVI–4. Pint. 1840s.

GVI–7. Similar to GVI–4. Half-pint.

GX–4. *Obverse*: "GENERAL TAYLOR NEVER SUR-RENDERS." arching over cannon (lengthwise). *Reverse*: "A LITTLE MORE GRAPE CAP^T BRAGG" in frame of grapes and vine. Pint. 1847–48. No. 35 of Most Desirable Flasks. Group B.

GX–5. Like GX–4 but with smooth edges.

GX–6. Similar to GX–4 but half-pint size.

19. PHILADELPHIA GLASS-HOUSE, *later the* SCHUYLKILL GLASS WORKS, *on the Schuylkill River, Philadelphia, Pennsylvania, 1807–ca. 1823*

There has long been considerable confusion about the glassworks on the Schuylkill River, Philadelphia, and about glassworks called Philadelphia and Schuylkill. Accepting the history as presented by Van Rensselaer in 1926 and Knittle in 1927, later writers believed the glassworks that operated there in the 19th century was the one supposedly established by Morris and Nicholson in the 18th. (See No. 15. Nicholson's Glass Factory.) Today, further research has established that they were entirely different glasshouses and enterprises. However, I still do not have a complete chronological history of this 19th-century works, in part because I was unable to complete my search of land records, a search I fervently hope another student will pursue. Still, land records and newspaper advertisements have yielded many facts as to its inception, events of the early years, and the nature of the glass produced during that time. The works was called at first the "Philadelphia Glass-House," and the intention of its proprietors was to manufacture both green- and flint-glass wares.[26]

It would appear that by 1806 two Philadelphia tailors, Thomas Harrison and William McIlhenney, and an umbrella maker, Philip Jones, had been sufficiently successful in their trades to have money to invest in another enterprise. Perhaps they decided upon glassmaking because they believed that the nonimportation plans afoot would increase the demand for domestic glass and, fortuitously, one or all knew John Encell, an unemployed glass manufacturer "late of the Kingdom of Great Britain now of Philadelphia." In any event, on December 3, 1806, the three Philadelphians, forming a copartnership styled Thomas Harrison & Company, and John Encell leased from James Pemberton and his wife land in Passyunk on which to build a glasshouse. The site was a good location—100 feet on Water Street along the Schuylkill River with 100 foot "depth into the river to low water mark" and 60 feet on "Cedar or South Street." The lease, to become effective January 1, 1807, called for a yearly rent of $100 in *current silver* to be paid in two $50 installments on January 1 and July 1, but at any time within ten years the full sum of $1,666.67 could be paid. Also, "Harrison et al" were to pay all taxes or charges assessed on the land and the buildings erected or to be erected. As usual in such arrangements, if the taxes were not paid, land and buildings would revert to the lessor. Probably the partners lost no time in starting construction of their glasshouse, which was followed by a warehouse, mill, small house, and stable. Bricks "of the most substantial kind" were used in the construction. The glasshouse was 43 feet square and equipped "with every convenience for carrying on the Glass-Blowing." The warehouse was about 50 feet by 43 feet.[27]

The years 1808 and 1809 apparently were ones in which the Philadelphia Glass-House suffered the usual new glasshouse growing pains, especially with skilled workmen hard to find and with changes in ownership. Late in June 1808 William McIlhenney sold his rights and interests in the copartnership of Thomas Harrison & Company for $3,921.03 to Robert C. Martin, a Philadelphia saddler. On the last day of December 1808, John Encell deeded all his "Estate Rights Title and Interest of and all and Singular the lot of ground and premises for a valuable consideration to [him] in hand paid." It is tantalizing not to know just how much that *valuable* consideration was, and—above all—*why* Encell, who must have been the superintendent of the works, left. Perhaps his associates were easing him out, for possibly his claim, like that of some other glassmen, to the all-embracing title of "glass manufacturer" was exaggerated, and his skill limited to blowing. More likely, perhaps, he preferred a paying job in hand rather than waiting for possible profits from a job and interest in a glassworks. If he was the John Encell—and he may be—who, with John B. Trevor in 1812, started a flint-glass works in Pittsburgh, Pennsylvania, then he doubtless left Philadelphia in 1809 for Pittsburgh, where he certainly would have been welcomed as a flint-glass blower.[28] In any event, a November 1808 advertisement suggests that Encell's associates, having had fair warning,

knew he was leaving and had arranged to purchase his interests before then. Inasmuch as the advertisement, occasioned by the lack of skilled craftsmen, was symptomatic of the period when glassworks proprietors attempted to raid each other's work forces by luring advertisements in newspapers publishing near successful glassworks, it is quoted below in its entirety. This particular advertisement was directed at the Hamilton Glass Factory near Albany, New York, primarily a window-glass factory. (See No. 11. Dowesborough . . .)

PHILADELPHIA
GLASS-HOUSE
Flint and Green Glass-Blowers
WANTED
The subscribers have erected a Glass-House on Schuylkill, South-Street in the City of Philadelphia, so calculated, that the workmen can be comfortably employed all the year—

Sober, steady, good workmen, in either of the above branches, will meet with good encouragement, constant work and good wages—Also a person well qualified to manage the Flint Glass Manufactory, will be treated with on liberal terms, by applying at the GLASS HOUSE or to either of the subscribers in Philadelphia.

Thomas Harrison
Philip Jones
Robert C. Martin

N.B. A good POT maker will meet with constant employ. Workmen wishing for further information or assistance may obtain it by applying to THOS. P. JONES, or leaving a line directed to him, at Macaulay and Campbell's, Jewelers, Court-Street Albany.
November 4, 1808[29]

It is probable that the response to the Albany advertisement was disappointing. (Incidentally, the same advertisement may have appeared in the newspapers in other areas where glassworks were established.) It is probable, too, that with Encell's departure all plans to produce flint-glass ware were abandoned. It is certain that on June 17, 1809, Thomas Passmore, auctioneer of T. B. Freeman Commission Merchant of Philadelphia, announced an auction June 20 "to close a concern" by selling "the glassware and mill houses," the land on which they stood, and "all the materials and utensils for carrying on the glass business." And the location described was that of the Philadelphia Glass-House. It would appear that there were no bidders or that the works had been withdrawn from auction, for on June 21 Thomas Harrison sold his one-third ground in Passyunk for $1,511.67 to Philip Jones and Robert C. Martin, who formed the firm of Philip Jones & Company and changed the name of the works to the Schuylkill Glass Works. Unless there was an error in recording the footage in the 1808 indenture, the new company acquired more land that extended their 60 feet to 600 "more or less" on the south side of South Street. At least that was the figure given in 1810, when the glassworks property was again advertised for sale at auction. Again there seem to have been no bidders. In the summer of 1813 Jones and Martin advertised that the works was for rent. Their announcement stated that the glasshouse had "every convenience for carrying on Glass Blowing [but] would answer as well for a Foundry, Distillery, Cotton Manufactory or any Manufacturing Business requiring extensive room."[30] Once more a gap yawns in my data; I do not know what happened, but I shall make a tentative guess.

According to Weeks, the Schuylkill Glass Works was in operation in 1819, in which year a drug and color merchant, Edward Lower, was selling window glass from the Schuylkill Glass Works. However, two bits of evidence suggest that although Philip Jones & Company may not have sold the glassworks, they may have rented it to Mark Richards, an iron merchant, or to associates of Richards, who changed the name to the Philadelphia Glass Works. On November 4, 1814, Mark Richards, as agent, advertised that the Philadelphia Glass Works was in complete operation; that he always had window glass on hand in the usual sizes, from 7 by 9 to 10 by 15, in whole and half boxes; that orders for extra sizes of superior-quality glass could be filled at very short notice, and as an "N.B.," that any kind of glass orders would be executed. The last suggests that although window glass was the regular product, the works still had the blowers and equipment for blowing bottles and other containers, and probably did. A strong reason for believing that this Philadelphia Glass Works was the works of Philip Jones & Company on Water and South streets is an 1823 notice that George and Jacob Peterman had the "agency of the Schuylkill Glass Works at South Street wharf, recently called the 'Philadelphia Glass Works.'"[31] It should be noted that "Philadelphia" appeared in a glassworks name three times—the first glassworks in the area, that built in 1771 and later called the Kensington Glass Works (see No. 7. Philadelphia Glass Works); the works at South and Water streets on the Schuylkill; and in No. 20 (following).

Exactly how long the Philadelphia Glass Works for which Richards was agent operated I have not learned. It is not unlikely that it failed to recover from the post-War of 1812 depression. In any event, in 1819 there must have been a new firm, and the name became the Schuylkill Glass Works again, or Schuylkill Window Glass Works. Possibly the new owners were H. & W. Lawrence, who advertised in 1822 that the glassworks were to let. Whoever the proprietors were in 1820 and 1821, George and Jacob Peterman were the sole agents, always having on hand various qualities and sizes (up to 22 inches by 28 inches) of window glass. No other kind of glass from the Schuylkill Glass Works was offered. Their 1823 notice, when the glassworks was owned by a Luther Frank, is the latest evidence I have found indicating the works was in operation.[32] It seems probable the works failed from inability to compete with the nearby Kensington Glass Works and the South Jersey window-glass works.

It would appear that the containers which are our primary concern were not produced, at least in noticeable quantity, after 1813. An advertisement in January of that year is my only definite information about the bottle output of the Schuylkill Glass Works and, presumably, of its predecessor, the Philadelphia Glass-House. One can assume only that the bottles offered the public were of the same types as those being made by competitors of the period. Two bottles listed below could be purchased *at* the glassworks from Captain Thomas Hewett, or from John Holmes at No. 6 South Wharves, who also had for sale Bristol (England) porter bottles and gallon demijohns. The Schuylkill's bottles itemized and followed by "etc etc" were

> Gallon and half-gallon case bottles
> Porter Bottles
> Quart and pint Flasks
> Half gallon, quart and pint Jars
> Snuff Bottles
> Blacking Bottles.[33]

20. KENSINGTON GLASS WORKS: PHILADELPHIA AND KENSINGTON GLASS FACTORIES OF THOMAS W. DYOTT, M.D.; DYOTTVILLE GLASS FACTORIES, *Kensington, Philadelphia, Pennsylvania*

In the chronology of Philadelphia glassworks, that on the Schuylkill (see No. 19. Philadelphia . . .) was followed by the Kensington Glass Works, the second to be established in the area called Kensington. It was, also, the second to have Kensington in its name, for, contrary to long-accepted glass history, it was not a continuation of the 18th-century glassworks built by Towars and Leacock late in 1771. (See No. 7. Philadelphia . . .) In August 1816, Hewson, Connell & Company announced that they had built a new glassworks "at considerable expense . . . on the lot adjoining the Old Glass Works in Kensington." The same announcement informed those in the iron business that there was also a furnace for converting iron into steel, and ended with an "N.B." that John Hewson had his calico printing business at the same place. From a second advertisement, one in October 1819, it is evident that the firm name had been changed to Hewson & Connell.[34] Apparently the "Company" had withdrawn; perhaps a reorganization resulted from the effects of the depression.

Strangely, or so it seems to me, the Philadelphia City Directories have no listing of the Kensington Glass Works—the very fact that the new glassworks was called the Kensington Glass Works seems sufficient evidence that the old one was not in operation—or of the two firms. However, John H. Connell (the Connell of John H. Connell & Co., iron manufacturers) was listed as a glass manufacturer at Kensington in all city directories from 1817 through 1822. John H. Hewson, Jr., was listed in 1816 as a calico printer in Kensington, as was a Robert Hewson, who perhaps was his brother and a member of the original company. There is little doubt that they were sons of the John Hewson who, in 1781, opened a "Linen Printing Manufactory" (cotton, calicoes, and silk too) "joining the Glass-House" in Kensington—that is, the 18th-century works built by Towars and Leacock. It doubtless was this calico printing establishment that John Hewson, Jr., was running at the time he joined with John H. Connell to start a glassworks. And it apparently was Hewson who was superintendent of the glassworks, at least through 1822.[35] Such is the meager data so far found pertaining to the founders of the 19th-century Kensington Glass Works and of the works before Dr. Dyott's association with it.

Thomas W. Dyott, M.D., was a prominent, prosperous druggist, patent medicine vendor, and physician, though in the last capacity some of the Philadelphia medical profession censured him for quackery. He came to Philadelphia from England, perhaps via the West Indies, and was practicing in 1805. Presumably starting from scratch as a physician and patent medicine vendor, he had a patent medicine warehouse in time to be listed in the 1807 city directory. In less than a decade he was occupying "No. 137, the northeast corner of Second and Race streets," the adjacent house on Second Street, and had built a large Drug Warehouse (Ill. 9A). He needed the space, for the sales of his medicines were galloping. He was advertising from Maine to Louisiana, from the Atlantic to the Mississippi, and had agents in almost innumerable towns and cities. His later claim to representation everywhere in the United States was not an idle one.[36]

By 1809, if not earlier, Dr. Dyott had his private mold for bottles for Dr. Robertson's medicine, and was perhaps the first American druggist to do so. They were, he said, "square flint glass bottles" inscribed "Dʳ ROBERTSON'S / FAMILY MEDICINES / PREPARED / ONLY BY T.W.DYOTT" and American-made. As the only known bottles—three—so inscribed are green glass of medium aquamarine color and rectangular in form, either he was using "flint glass" as a status term or had had to accept green-glass substitutes. It is frustrating that he left no record of who produced them for him. It was said by "an intimate" that he obtained his blacking bottles (like so many druggists, he made shoe blacking, at least in his early years in Philadelphia) at the *old* Kensington Glass Works. Possibly he bought all his bottles there as long as it was in operation. However, as present evidence indicates that this works ceased operating between 1812 and 1815, Dr. Dyott would have been forced to go elsewhere for bottles, especially as the war created a shortage of imports. Inasmuch as he required bottles of many sizes and vials literally by the thousands, he wisely acquired—as did many druggists and merchants—a financial interest in a glassworks, doubtless both as an investment and a source of indispensable bottles and vials at a saving. The glassworks must have been the Olive Glass Works, for according to his own account "so early as 1815" he became interested in "a factory in New Jersey . . . the first that continued in operation for any number of years," and that statement fits only the Olive Glass Works at Glassboro. Naturally he became the agent for the works, and apparently he continued in that capacity even after he had become interested in the new Kensington Glass Works.[37]

According to his own statements, Dr. Dyott became interested in the Kensington Glass Works in 1818 or 1819. At one time, around 1833, he stated that "since the year 1818" he had been "owner of a . . . Glass Factory in the district of Kensington." At another, in 1839, he said he had had the "glassworks twenty years." Definite proof of his connection is an October 1819 advertisement signed by "David Wolf & Co. / Olive Glass Works / Jona. Haines / Gloucester Glass Works [Clementon, New Jersey] / Hewson & Connell / Kensington Glass Works," naming "Dr. T. W. Dyott, Druggist," as their sole agent. All their glass, as it was produced, was to be deposited with the doctor for sale. Next, from a series of advertisements, it would certainly appear that Dr. Dyott had become the sole owner of, or had a controlling interest in, the Kensington Glass Works by 1821. For instance, besides being the only agent, Dr. Dyott was the one who advertised for broken bottles for cullet, for 4,000 to 5,000 bushels of stone lime to be delivered to the works as wanted, for seasoned pine for fuel and oak wood for boards for making boxes, to be delivered to the glassworks. Of especial importance is a July 24, 1821, advertisement in *The Union for the Country* referring to *factories* instead of *factory*. This is evidence of more than one glasshouse, and although possibly a second one had been built by Hewson & Connell, it seems to me most probable that they rented the old glassworks next door, reconverting it to glassmaking or restoring and repairing it. It seems probable, too, that this occurred after Dr. Dyott became interested, and that he was the force moving to expansion. I say "rented" because the property was still owned by James Rowland, Sr., and was not sold by James, Jr., until 1833, when Dyott acquired it.[38]

From March 5 through November 1, 1822, Dr. Dyott ran an advertisement that is particularly noteworthy for two quite disparate reasons. He listed products of *his* glass factories for sale at *his* "American Glass Ware House." Thus, his use of the possessive seems to establish definite ownership by 1822. The advertisement was illustrated in some newspapers by two boxes—and in others by one box—of window glass labeled "KENSINGTON GLASS." In two lines of the bottle products named below the boxes, this advertisement was made even more significant to bottle collectors than Thomas Mather's 1817 advertisement of "figured pocket bottles"—Dyott listed "American Eagle, ship Franklin, Agricultural and Masonic pocket bottles." (See GI–40, GII–42, and GIV–37 in the Charts.) This is the earliest known evidence of Historical Figured Flasks, and it appeared without emphasis or heralding as though they were nothing new in pocket bottles. Consequently one wonders if perhaps they had first appeared before March of 1822.[39]

The year 1822 was also that in which Dr. Dyott's extravagances in living and business expansions brought him to the edge of bankruptcy. Unable to collect monies owed to him and overwhelmingly in debt to many men, he had so stretched his credit and his creditors' patience that they snapped. His businesses, however, being basically sound,

North East Corner of Second & Race Streets, Philadelphia.

9A. Thomas W. Dyott's Drug Store and Warehouse, N.E. Corner of Second and Race streets, Philadelphia, engraved by R. Tiller from a watercolor or drawing by George Strickland, Philadelphia artist. The engraving is closely similar to the illustration heading Dyott's two-column advertisement dated November 24 (1819) and one of four columns dated March 22 (1820), both appearing in *The Union*. One interesting difference in detail is that, whereas no name appears on the covered wagon in the advertisement, Strickland inscribed the cover of his wagon "JACOB SLOUCH/PITTSBURGH". The engraving probably dates in the early 1820s. *Worcester Art Museum, Worcester, Massachusetts*

GLASS WARE.

Vials from 1 dram to 12 ounces	Specie Bottles with covers from 4 ounces to 4 gallons	Nipple shells	Pocket Bottles
Tincture Bottles from half pint to two gallons	Patent Medicine Vials of every description	Sucking Bottles	Mustard do.
		Urinals	Seltzer Water do.
		Graduated Measures	Snuff do.
Salt Mouths from 4 ounces to 2 gallons	Vials with ground stoppers	Funnels	Window Glass of all sizes
Breast Pipes		Mortars and Pestles	zes
		Smelling Bottles	Putty, &c. &c.

T. W DYOTT, *Druggist,*
Corner of Race and Second streets.

N. B.   An assortment of the above goods will be given in barter for any of the following articles, by applying as above, for which the highest market prices will always be given, viz: first quality bright Rosin, Turpentine, Lamp Black, Pink Root, Rice, Cotton, Tobacco, Sugar, Molasses, Coffee, Rum, Bees Wax, Castor Oil, Wheat Flower, Rye Meal, Buck Wheat Meal, Rye and Apple Whiskey, Peach Brandy, Hams, Pork, Butter, Lard, Beef, Mackarel, Shad, Pearl and Pot Ashes, Soap, Flaxseed, Flaxseed Oil, Paper, Lead, Nails, Glue, Furs, Domestic Goods generally, Logwood, Fire wood, &c. &c.

☞ Wanted two Apprentices to the Drug Business. Boys from the country will be preferred, they will require to be of good moral habits, of respectable connexions, have a good English education, and a knowledge of the German language.   Nov. 24—dtf

9B. The advertisement dated November 24 (1819) headed by an illustration similar to that in 9A. ended with a list of glassware and "NB". Its successor dated March 22 (also in *The Union*) gave a more detailed list of "FLINT AND OTHER GLASS WARE," naming 11 patent medicine bottles and "Pint Pocket" followed by "Half pint." In both advertisements the offer to barter reflected the lingering effects of the postwar (1812) depression and was, so Dyott stated in the March advertisement, "In consequence of the great depreciation of Country Bank Paper and the general scarcity of good money." (Philadelphia, *The Union*, Mar. 24, 1820.) *The New-York Historical Society, New York City*

PRICES CURRENT.

GLASS WARE OF THE

PHILADELPHIA AND KENSINGTON VIAL AND BOTTLE FACTORIES.

ARTICLES.	PRICES. Dol.	Cts.	Per
VIALS, assorted from ½ to 8 ounces in 5 and 10 Gross Packages	2	50	gro.
Do. ½ Drachm	3	00	"
Do. 1 Do.	3	00	"
Do. ½ oz.	2	00	"
Do. 1 "	2	00	"
Do. 1½ "	2	25	"
Do. 2 "	2	25	"
Do. 3 "	2	50	"
Do. 4 "	2	87½	"
Do. 6 "	3	25	"
Do. 8 "	3	50	"
Do. 1 " wide mouths	2	50	"
Do. 2 " Do.	3	00	
Do. 3 " Do.	3	25	
Do. 4 " Do.	3	50	"
Do. 6 " Do.	3	75	"
Do. 8 " Do.	4	00	"
Do. Bateman's	2	25	"
Do. British Oil	2	25	"
Do. Stoughton's	2	25	"
Do. Turlington's	2	25	"
Do. Peppermint	2	12½	"
Do. Godfrey's	2	62½	"
Do. Haarlem Oil	2	00	"
Do. Dalby's	2	50	"
Do. Opodeldoc	3	50	"
Do. Ditto (small size)	3	50	"
Do. Dafly's	5	00	"
Do. Cephalic Snuff	3	50	"
Do. Lemon Acid	3	00	"
Do. Balsam Honey	3	50	"
Do. Jesuits	3	00	"
Do. Ess. Mustard (Whitehead's)	5	00	"
Do. Clarke's Ink Mordant	3	50	"
Do. Clout's Do. Do.	3	00	"
Do. Durable Ink	3	00	"
Do. Liquid Opodeldoc	3	50	"
Do. Calcined Magnesia	3	50	"
Do. Cologne Water	3	50	"
Do. Ditto Do. (6 sided)	5	00	"
Do. Mustard (plain)	3	25	"
Do. Ditto (London)	3	50	"
Do. Cayenne	3	25	"
BOTTLES, Long Neck, White Rounds, Small Quarts	1	00	doz.
Do. Do. Do. Pint		75	"
Do. Do. Do. ½ Pint		62½	"
Do. CASTOR OIL (rounds)	1	00	"
Do. Ditto (octagon) Small Pint		75	"
Do. Ditto (ditto) ½ Pint		62½	"
Do. Ditto (ditto) ¼ Pint		50	"
Do. Seltzer Water		50	"
Do. Blacking ½ Pint		50	"
Do. Varnish ½ do.		50	"
Do. Sweet Oil 1 do.		75	"

ARTICLES.	PRICES. Dol.	Cts.	Per
TINCTURES, Gro. Stoppers, ½ Pint	1	50	doz.
Do. " 1 Pint	1	75	"
Do. " 1 Quart	2	00	"
Do. " 2 Quarts	3	00	"
Do. " 1 Gallon	5	00	"
Do. " 2 Gallons	12	00	"
SPECIES, with Lacquered Covers, ½ Pint	1	50	"
Do. " " " 1 Pint	1	75	"
Do. " " " 1 Quart	2	00	"
Do. " " " 2 Quarts	3	00	"
Do. " " " 1 Gallon	5	00	"
Do. " " " 6 Quarts	8	00	"
Do. " " " 2 Gallons	10	00	"
SALT MOUTHS, Gro. Stoppers, ½ Pint	2	00	"
Do. " " 1 Pint	2	50	"
Do. " " 1 Quart	3	00	"
Do. " " 2 Quarts	4	50	"
Do. " " 1 Gallon	7	50	"
Do. " " 6 Quarts	10	50	"
Do. " " 2 Gallons	15	00	"
DRUGGISTS Packing Bottles, white and black, wide and narrow Mouths ½ Pint		50	"
Do. " " 1 Pint		75	"
Do. " " 1 Quart	1	00	"
Do. " " 3 Pints	1	50	"
Do. " " 2 Quarts	2	00	"
Do. " " 3 Quarts	3	00	"
Do. " " 1 Gallon	4	00	"
Do. " " 2 Gallons	7	00	"
ACID BOTTLES, Gro. Stoppers	3	00	"
CARBOYS packed in Tubs	1	25	each
DEMIJOHNS, 2 Gallons	9	00	doz.
Do. 1 Gallon	6	00	"
Do. ½ Gallon	4	00	"
Do. 1 Quart	3	00	"
FLASKS, Fancy Quart		87½	"
Do. Assorted patterns, Pints		62½	"
Do. Eagle and Washington, do.		62½	"
Do. Eagle and Lafayette, do.		62½	"
Do. Lafayette and Washington, do.		62½	"
Do. Eagle and Ship Franklin, do.		62½	"
Do. Franklin and Dyott, do.		62½	"
Do. Ship Franklin & Agricultural, do.		62½	"
Do. Eagle and Cornucopiæ, ½ Pint		50	"
BOTTLES, Quarts		87½	"
Do. ½ Gallons	1	75	"
JARS, Straight or turned over Tops, ½ Pint		62½	"
Do. " " " Pint		75	"
Do. " " " Quart	1	00	"
Do. " " " 2 Quarts	2	00	"
Do. " " " 3 Quarts	3	00	"
Do. " " " 1 Gallon	4	00	"
SNUFFS, Scotch ½ pound		50	"
Do. Ditto pound		60	"
Do. Maccouba, ½ pound		50	"
Do. Ditto pound		60	"

***** The quality of the Glass made at the above Factories, is but little inferior to English Flint, and is warranted superior to any other Ware, of the same description, made in this country.**

☞ **Every description of Vials, Bottles, &c. made to order, on the most reasonable terms.**

"Address,"

T. W. DYOTT, *Proprietor,*

Corner of Second and Race streets, Philadelphia. or

Hickson W. Field agent

New York.

Terms.

For an amount above	$100
" " "	200
" " "	300
" " "	500

9C. Though undated, Dr. Dyott's "Prices Current" can be assigned by the vial prices and portrait flasks to the period from 1824 to the passage of the 1828 tariff act, after which vial prices dropped. Portrait flasks, first advertised in the fall of 1824, possibly were produced earlier in the year. Except for the flasks, the articles listed were nearly the same as those of other manufacturers of bottles and druggists' wares. No Lafayette–Washington flask, a natural combination of heroes, has ever been found. (From the Bella C. Landauer Collection [Vol. 8].) *The New-York Historical Society, New York City* were valuable assets which, if properly conducted, could pay off the doctor's obligations. Consequently, on October 19, 1822, an indenture was drawn placing Dyott's entire estate in trust for the benefit of his creditors, and transferring it to his three principal creditors, who were to act as trustees. On the same day, in the realization that all hope of payment lay in the profitable operation of the glass factories and the wholesale and retail businesses, a second indenture was drawn whereby Dr. Dyott, as representative of the trustees, was given the sole management of his businesses with the power to sell out the stock and work up the "raw materials" (presumably including the ingredients of the patent and other medicines) and to collect the debts. He was also to "carry on the Glass Works as heretofore to purchase all such materials and employ such hands as might be necessary." Of course, he was to turn over all monies to the trustees except that for his services, for which he was allowed "whatever commission for settling said estate . . . the assignees [trustees] would be entitled to."[40] Apparently the estate prospered under his management, and indications are that in 1823 or early in 1824 Dr. Dyott had been able to pay off not only the 17 creditors named in the indenture of trusteeship but also those who were unnamed.

In any event, his own man once more by the fall of 1824, Dr. Dyott began a decade of expansion. He was again advertising widely and lavishly, not only his drugs and medicines but also his glassware. One noteworthy article was advertised by itself. Like so many other forehanded manufacturers who created objects commemorating General Lafayette's visit to the United States, Dr. Dyott, too, produced one in glass, a Lafayette flask. (See GI–91 in the Charts.) Early in September 1824, a bit over a month after Lafayette's arrival at Castle Garden, New York City, Dr. Dyott was offering "pint LaFayette pocket bottles now blowing at the Kensington Glass Works." He even presented one of the flasks to Lafayette at a concert given for the general. In mid-October, editors throughout the United States with whom he had a long-term contract were asked to run "until forbid" his advertisement of vials and bottles of every description. No window glass was mentioned, which suggests that that line had been discontinued. In the same advertisement, he first used the title Philadelphia and Kensington Vial and Bottle Factories (Ill. 9C). The new name, so a contemporary local historian recorded, derived from the factories' location about a mile from Philadelphia and at the farther end of Kensington. Though he protested that his glass factories had "struggled hard for existence against foreign competition" until the 1828 tariff became effective in August, that struggle produced an extensive and comprehensive line of bottles and vials. It must also have produced them at an ample profit, for by June of 1828 he had added a third factory. By June 1829, there were four distinct factories, and a fifth and last one was built in the fall of 1833 after the founding of Dyottville. Also, Dr. Dyott acquired ownership of the land that all the previous years had been rented, and extended his waterfront.[41]

Even before Dyottville was formally proclaimed, the name Dyottville Factories or Dyottville Glass Factories instead of "Philadelphia and Kensington Glass Factories" had been chosen. Moreover, most of the "little village," as Dr. Dyott considered his creation, already existed, making the establishment "on a more extensive scale than any other of the kind in the United States." Just how complex it was even by 1831 is detailed in Thomas Porter's *Picture of Philadelphia* for that year. In addition to the four glass houses with furnaces, annealing ovens, and ovens for drying wood, there were the following:

2 mill houses for grinding clay and pot ashes	Superintendent's Dwelling
Clay house for burning clay	50 brick dwellings for workmen
Lime and sand houses	2 counting houses
Pounding house	Store
Batch house	Stablery and outhouses
Pot house	Wicker shop, for demijohn covering and basketry
2 smitherys in which tools and blowpipes were forged	
Carpenter's shop	Mill and work shop for glass paper
2 packing houses	
Fire-Engine house and apparatus.	

Porter mentioned also that a wharf of 100-foot front and extending 150 feet into the Delaware River was in the process of being built. Obviously a large staff was required by so large an establishment, and by the fall of 1831, according to Dr. Dyott, 250 to 300 men and boys were employed.[42]

In the 1828–31 period there were also important events immediately affecting production. The first was to reduce costs of production and contribute to improvement in the durable strength and quality of the wares. Since Dyott himself was not a practical glassman, probably one or more of his "first rate workmen" contributed to the experiments leading to Dyott's patent of October 10, 1828, for "an *improvement* in the Art of Melting and Fusing Glass and the materials for making and forming glass." The improvement in melting and fusing consisted "in using the resin of pine commonly called rosin as fuel either alone, or together with other fuel." Unfortunately the 1836 fire in the United States Patent Department consumed the original specifications, and the report of the patent in the *Journal of the Franklin Institute* does not tell what the improvement in materials was. However, the result doubtless was the "Patent Flint Glass" that Dr. Dyott was advertising by 1831. Although it has been assumed that this glass was a superior white glass given the status-quality name by Dyott, the tons of red lead among the materials he reported using leave no doubt that his white flint glass was indeed lead glass. And the Washington–Eagle flask GI–16a (see No. 1, Ill. 124) was blown from colorless lead glass. Next, perhaps late in 1830, certainly before March 1831, Dr. Dyott's brother Michael arrived from England—where, it was said, he had had considerable experience—and became superintendent of the glass factories.[43] Michael Dyott must have contributed also to the initial success of the doctor's Dyottville experiment in a glass-factory system based on "moral and mental" as well as physical labor within a self-contained glassworks community.

Of course, a glassworks community was nothing new or revolutionary, but Dr. Dyott's kind was. His years of experience with glassworkers and glass manufacturing made him acutely aware of factory-created social, economic, and business problems, and certainly more concerned about them than his peers. His humanism allied with self-interest prompted him to *do* something about conditions. In the case of "mechanics," he entertained no hope of reforming the Europeans "tainted by habits of a degenerate caste" or of reforming the Americans also habitually saturated with alcohol, but he could cull his staff, keeping only those willing to take the pledge. However, the real solution, he believed, lay in the establishment of a model community in which temperance and industry replaced intemperance and irresponsibility; education and piety replaced ignorance and profanity; thrifty use of time and money, spendthrift habits. Also, the system should improve his own profit. In an establishment such as he planned, he wrote, "Moral principles should operate with the force of Law, to elevate the character of the Mechanical classes, at the same time that they should produce the largest amount of comfort to the operative and profit to the proprietor."[44] In his day, Dr. Dyott was a very rare species of factory owner.

And so in 1833 Dr. Dyott formed Dyottville, which he did not succeed in incorporating as he wished to do, largely because of the bitter opposition of glass manufacturers and others in the business community and their influence on the state legislature. The rules and regulations governing Dyottville, in particular some 130 apprentices ranging from seven to their teens, were comparatively few but strict. There was to be no swearing or improper or abusive language. There was to be no gambling of any species. There was to be no liquor on the premises, and a $5 fine or—optional with the proprietor, Dr. Dyott—dismissal for breaking the rule. There was to be a $5 fine for striking or mistreating an apprentice—a far too common practice, prevention of which was another revolutionary step. On the other hand, there was a $5 fine for disobeying the orders of a superior. *All fines were to be used to buy books for the Dyottville Apprentices' Library.* Illnesses were to be reported immediately: apprentices were to report to the principal teacher and journeymen to the superintendent, so that another could take his station in the glassworks. Personal cleanliness was recommended, and "necessary ablution" was expected before meals, school, and church. Given a leave of absence, usually on a Sunday afternoon, apprentices were expected back before sundown unless the permission included an extension of time. Every apprentice was to abide by his articles of indenture, to attend school during the instruction hours and chapel on the Sabbath punctually. In general all employees were "solicited" to attend public worship on Sunday at the Dyottville church, where there were three services on Sunday and one on Wednesday evening, to which strangers were also admitted.[45]

The Dyottville daily and Sunday routines would not be tolerated today, but in 1833 they were an improvement. The weekday routine stretched from the first bell at daylight, when all rose, washed, and attended prayers before breakfast, to bedtime—8:30 P.M. for the younger boys, 9:00 P.M. for the older. A half hour later the gates were closed and the watchman went on duty. Working hours were from 7:00 A.M. to noon and 1:00 P.M. to 6:00 P.M., *but* there was an unprecedented break for a "cracker" and rest in the morning and a break for a "biscuit" and rest in the afternoon—10 hours' work instead of the usual 12, *and* year round. Though Dyott, so far as I have learned, was the only glass manufacturer to introduce the practice of rest and refreshment, he definitely was not alone in his belief that

It would be the utmost cruelty to endow an apprentice to a mechanical occupation, with the knowledge that begets exquisite sensibility, and creates appetites for distinctions and attainments, that under ordinary circumstances, never can be realized . . . as cruel to bestow an ill-proportioned education on the boys of a Factory as it would be to withhold it altogether.

Therefore, when a short after-supper playtime was followed by classes, the subjects were the three fundamentals—reading, writing, and arithmetic. The Sunday routine began at 8:00 A.M. with prayers. After breakfast and the arrival of Dr. Dyott, there was singing. School exercises replaced some of the weekly work. Incidentally, until they were vigorous and grown up enough, the youngest boys worked in the wicker shop, covering demijohns and making baskets. From Sunday noon until suppertime or, if given special permission, until sometime in the evening, boys (in rotation) could visit family or friends outside Dyottville.[46]

Dr. Dyott's apprentices apparently were extraordinarily well housed, clothed, fed, and paid compared with other apprentices and factory workers. The boys' dormitory over the chapel and schoolroom could accommodate 150 boys and their teachers—four beds to each room; two boys to each bed. Their washroom, heated by a large coal stove in winter, was on the ground floor of another large building. Each boy was provided with clothes, changes of which were kept in his "pigeonhole" in the wardrobe room. Through a window into the dressing room, the principal teacher received soiled garments and passed out clean ones. The diet, Dr. Dyott said, was balanced, but roast beef, being the favorite of most, was the meat served most often. Each one could eat his fill of abundant food, which included products of the 300-acre farm adjoining the glass factory and of its dairy of 40 cows. This apparently applied also to the single workers who boarded with Dr. Dyott. If a boy or other worker became ill, there was a medical department with an apothecary and surgical shop in the charge of a doctor and a "sickroom" in the charge of an elderly woman acting as nurse under the physician's directions. Any apprentice wishing to do more than the regulated amount of work received a journeyman's wages for the extra quantity. (Payment by the piece rather than by the hour was customary in glassworks.) Pocket money, out of which Sunday clothes and the like were bought, came from "overwork" pay, and if a boy wished, savings were credited to his account, to be paid him when he came of age.[47]

Inevitably, creation of this unorthodox community entailed more buildings, facilities, operations, and employees than were noted by Porter in 1831. Besides the brick dwellings rented to married employees, there was a building for the bachelors who boarded with the "proprietor." The women employees—15 or 20 engaged in cooking, laundering, tailoring, and working at the dairy—could have sleeping accommodations in the superintendent's dwelling. New were a bakery, a shoe shop where footgear was made and repaired, a tailor shop where the boys' clothes were made and mended. The chapel was also the meeting place for the boy choir of the Dyottville Temperance Society, founded by Dr. Dyott. Among the additions to the glass factories were a third forge in the blacksmith shop, a turner's shop, a wheelwright's shop, a cooper's shop, and a cutting and grinding shop where stoppers for druggists' bottles were "ground to an air-excluding firmness." There was a separate department for the manufacture of the clay "moulds for forming the various sizes of bottles, vials, jars," which probably was adjoining the pothouse. And there were also new docks and wharves. Probably new were the dairy and some of the farm buildings. Needless to say, the whole establishment required a small-town-size population—besides the glassblowers and apprentices there were nearly 200 other employees:

Wood	Packers
choppers	Carpenters
Rosin	Blacksmiths
pounders	Bricklayers
Fire tenders	Shoemakers
Sand washers	Tailors
Batch makers	Bakers
Moulders	Butchers
Clay pickers	Farmers
Pot and Mold	Boat and
makers	scowmen
Bottle grinders	&c.[48]
Basket makers	

For nearly five years the Dyottville community and factories appear to have been a success, at least from Dr. Dyott's viewpoint, and they might have survived the money panics and depressions of the late 1830s had not the doctor caught the epidemic banking fever. As local historians put it, "his ambition went far beyond his prudence." As indeed it did, for Dr. Dyott was totally ignorant about banking and he relied on his cashier, Stephen Simpson, who was said to have the entire management of the bank. It was said that his reason for opening a bank was his desire to encourage saving habits, and that, doubtless, was a primary factor. One reason he gave was the hope of escaping "shaving" by those who charged him usurious interest in

discounting his notes. The bank funds, he said, would be invested in American manufactures. In any event, on February 2, 1836, he opened the Manual Labor Bank, a purely private bank (he failed to secure a charter of incorporation), at the "N. E. Corner" of Second and Race streets, from which he moved his drugstore. According to the legend on his bank notes, his capitalization was $500,000 "Secured in trust on Real Estate and Publicly Recorded." Large deposits were lured into his bank by promises of attractive interest payments. Naturally, Manual Labor Bank notes were the medium of payment and exchange in Dyottville; they were also in general circulation.[49]

For a little over a year the bank apparently was as successful as his other enterprises. But a money panic lurked in the wings. There were weak runs on banks in the early spring; then, in May 1837, there was a strong run resulting in countrywide suspension of specie payments. In Philadelphia alone 11 banks suspended payments on the eleventh of May. Dyott managed to weather the crisis. In fact, the next few months were to be profitable and eventful ones. First, although it was illegal, in response to the demands for "promises to pay" of small denominations—and with the blessings of the "mechanics" and businessmen—Dyott issued desperately needed notes "in amounts of one, two and three dollars and also of the fractional parts (5, 6½, 10, 25, and 50 cents)." Also, in July, in order to devote more of his time to the bank, which had "increased in business and profit," he leased the Dyottville Glass Factories to his brother Michael at a yearly rental of $25,000. (He had been drawing $25,000 to $30,000 a year.) The glassware was to be disposed of through the new firm of C. W. and J. B. Dyott—Charles W., his nephew, and John B., his elder son. Shortly afterward, Thomas W. Dyott, Jr., and Company was formed, though Thomas, Jr., was only 16 at the time. Dr. Dyott himself maintained a countinghouse and retail dry goods and clothing store. In these three stores at 139, 141, and 143 Second Street, Manual Labor Bank notes were exchanged for drugs, medicines, glassware, groceries, and a wide variety of merchandise.[50]

There was fair business weather for Dr. Dyott until November 1837, when, following a rumor that the Manual Labor Bank was about to fail, an unexpected but determined run on the bank began. Dr. Dyott countered on November 4 with "a system of special deposits for redemption of his bank notes in the bank and by merchandise in the various stores," and on November 6 he offered a $500 reward for the detection of the one responsible for the false report. His confidence that, given enough time, he could work clear without loss to anyone, as he had in 1822/23, sustained him for several months as his affairs became more and more tangled and fragile, until finally in the fall of 1838 he pleaded bankruptcy. He had no incorporation behind which to take refuge; he was solely responsible for the bank's debts. Though money was realized through a sheriff's sale of some real estate and through sales and auctions of merchandise from the stores, which had closed also, it was insufficient to the need. Before long his creditors' angry charges of fraudulent insolvency brought him to court. On March 30, 1839, the grand jury returned a true bill against him.[51]

The trial in the criminal court lasted from April 30 through June 1, 1839. In summing up, the judge told the jury:

Nor should it be forgotten that there is a great difference between the moral culpability of the prosperous and deliberate actor of the various unfair acts of trade and the desperate insolvent reeling, confused, and terrified amid the wreck of a fallen fortune.

Nevertheless, "the Jury returned a verdict of 'guilty' on all counts" and recommended imprisonment at "hard labor, in solitary confinement, from one to seven years, at the discretion of the Court." Evidently the judge was not so convinced of Dr. Dyott's guilt as was the jury, for on August 31, 1839, he imposed a sentence of three years, but did not accede to the hard labor and solitary confinement. However, Dr. Dyott served only about a year and a half before receiving an absolute pardon from Governor Porter in May 1841. His freedom was almost momentary; he was arrested as a debtor and sent to Moyamensing prison, from which he was quickly rescued by one of his principal creditors, who assumed security on all the judgments against the doctor for his appearance before the insolvent court in June.[52] Another important event was the formation on May 11, 1841, of a trusteeship: Dr. Dyott assigned all his remaining estate, real and personal, to four trustees empowered to dispose of it for the benefit of his creditors. Having lost all his other business, he himself returned to the drug and medicine business, soon joining his sons John B. and Thomas W., Jr., at 143 Second Street and forming Thomas W. Dyott and Sons. By and large, he was received back into respectable society and served the community "faithfully and honorably" until he died in January 1861 in the eighty-fourth year of his life.[53]

During all this time the Dyottville Glass Factories had been idle. It seems probable that they were closed down about the same time as the Dyott stores in Philadelphia, September 1838. Michael B. Dyott—who, it will be recalled, had rented them in July 1837—was gravely ill. He died on December 31, 1838, so his listing as a glass manufacturer in the 1839 city directory must have been owing to the fact that data for that year had been compiled in 1838, before his death. At a sheriff's sale, the date of which I have not learned, Daniel Man bought 40 brick dwellings at Dyottville. And, perhaps at the same time, the Lehigh Coal and Navigation Company purchased a large portion of Dyottville, including the waterfront with its wharves, which the company had used as a coal depot.[54]

Before turning to the Dyottville Glass Factories after Dr. Dyott, I shall turn briefly to the glassware he produced. Excepting the Figured Flasks, the articles produced were those one would expect all manufacturers of glass containers and druggists' glassware to make. Dyott's "Prices Current," ca. 1824/25, Ill. 9C, shows the general regular output kept on hand, and says that any other "description" of vial or bottle would be "made to order, on the most reasonable terms." Of course it shows, too, the wholesale prices prevailing at the time, and comparing it with his "Prices Current" published in the *Democratic Herald* (his newspaper) of January 16, 1836, indicates that few changes had taken place in prices. The 1836 "Prices Current" listed the same articles as the earlier one and several additional items, among them a long roster of fancy colognes and pungents (see Part VII), and "Prescriptions" were listed separately. Figured Flasks were no longer named, but undoubtedly were the "FLASKS, Fancy" in quart sizes and "assorted patterns" in pint and half-pint sizes. The prices were the same as those for half-pint, pint, and quart flasks in 1824/25, as they were for most of the articles. The 1825 advertisement, Ill. 117, gives an excellent idea of the vast quantities of various kinds of bottles and flasks produced by Dyott.

Dr. Dyott left us no descriptions of the shapes of his various bottles and vials, but he did partially describe bottle blowing at Dyottville. In his *Exposition* . . . he stated that, after separation of the bottle from the blowpipe, "the pipe is now pressed against the bottom of the article." In other words, the usual method of empontilling at Dyottville was to use the blowpipe as a pontil to hold the vessel during the neck-finishing operation—a common practice in bottle manufacture. Consequently, the scar left on the bottom of the bottle was in the form of a rough ring of glass, or a portion of such a ring. Perhaps one reason for so using the blowpipe was that one less workman was needed. That the same method was used at the Philadelphia and Kensington factories is evident from the ring scar on many of Dr. Dyott's Figured Flasks, the only Dyott products that are identifiable as such today. However, as shown by the rough glass scar on some of these flasks, the pontil was used also, at least occasionally.

After the establishment of Dyottville, perhaps before, the molds for most of the output were made in Dr. Dyott's mold department and, he said, were clay,[55] quite probably the same high heat-resistant clay as the melting pots. I say "most" because it seems probable that the more durable metal molds were used for lettered vials and bottles—for example, Turlington vials and London mustard bottles, both of which were blown by the thousands. Still, the cost of frequently replacing simple lettered ceramic molds would not have been prohibitive in one's own mold department. However, in the case of the Figured Flasks with relief designs—for instance, the Washington–American Eagle GI–14—the consensus of knowledgeable students is that metal molds were used and were necessary to the well-defined designs on flasks produced by the thousands. It is believed that the molds were cast and refined by tooling, and that they probably were made for Dr. Dyott by a Philadelphia moldmaker.

Alteration of bottle and flask molds was a normal and common practice, arising in part perhaps from economy (metal full-size piece molds with intaglio designs, purchased from a moldmaker, were and still are expensive).

One alteration of a Dyott Kensington mold was recorded in *American Glass* in 1941; namely, that of the mold for the Washington–Eagle GI–16 by the addition of the edge inscriptions and "E PLURIBUS UNUM" above the eagle, thus making GI–14, occasioned by the deaths of Thomas Jefferson and John Adams on July 4, 1826. Study of my flask data and the line drawings of the remaining Dyott flasks led me to tentative conclusions that other molds were changed too. Since I was unable to make the comparative study of the actual flasks, Kenneth M. Wilson made it for me, giving unstintingly of his time and knowledge of molds and moldmaking. His studies confirmed not only the alterations postulated but also two unsuspected ones: (1) the same "Masonic and Agricultural" leaf was half of the mold for three flasks—GIV–34, 35, and 37 charted in the Masonic Group IV; and (2) the same Benjamin Franklin leaf was half of the mold for GI–97 and, with added inscription, for GI–96.

The various mold changes are given in the following list of flasks blown in Dr. Dyott's Kensington Glass Works or attributed to it. Also, the flasks are listed in the order in which they were charted by my father, George S. McKearin, in *American Glass* (1941). However, evidence points to their having been marketed in a quite different order. The dates given are those of the year or period in which I believe them to have been first produced.

GI–14. "GENERAL WASHINGTON" above bust of Washington; "ADAMS & JEFFERSON JULY 4. A.D. 1776" followed by 3 small stars on edge. *Reverse*: American Eagle with sun rays above head; "E PLURIBUS UNUM. T.W.D" in oval frame; "KENSINGTON GLASS WORKS PHILADELPHIA" on edge. Pint. Inscriptions on reverse and on edge of obverse cut in GI–16 mold in 1826.

GI–16. "GENERAL WASHINGTON" above bust of Washington. *Reverse*: American Eagle, "T.W.D" in oval frame. Pint. 1824. Mold changed after July 4, 1826, for GI–14.

GI–16a. "GENERAL WASHINGTON." above bust of Washington. *Reverse*: American Eagle, no sun rays as on preceding, 3 arrows instead of 5 in talon. Pint. Mold probably made between 1826 and 1828 or 1831. High lead content (20 to 30 percent) of the one known flask from this mold indicates it was blown in or soon after 1831, the year Dr. Dyott introduced his patent white flint glass.

GI–90. "GENERAL LA FAYETTE" above bust of Lafayette; "REPUBLICAN GRATITUDE" on edge. *Reverse*: American Eagle, "T.W.D" in oval frame; "KENSINGTON GLASS WORKS PHILADELPHIA" on edge. Pint. ca. 1826. Inscriptions on edges here were added to the mold of GI–91.

GI–91. "GENERAL LA FAYETTE" above bust of Lafayette. *Reverse*: American Eagle. Pint. 1824. Inscriptions added to edges to make GI–90.

GI–94. "BENJAMIN FRANKLIN" above bust of Franklin; "WHERE LIBERTY DWELLS THERE IS MY COUNTRY" on edge. *Reverse*: "T.W.DYOTT, M.D." above bust of Dyott; "KENSINGTON GLASS WORKS PHILADELPHIA" on edge. Pint. ca. 1826. Inscriptions on edges added to mold for GI–95.

GI–95. "BENJAMIN FRANKLIN" above bust of Franklin. *Reverse*: "T.W.DYOTT, M.D." above bust of Dyott. Pint. 1824.

GI–96. "BENJAMIN FRANKLIN" above bust of Franklin; "ERIPUIT COELO FULMEN SCEPTRUMQUE TYRANNIS" on edge. *Reverse*: "T.W.DYOTT, M.D." above bust of Dyott; "KENSINGTON GLASS WORKS PHILADELPHIA" on edge. Quart. ca. 1826–28. Inscriptions added to one leaf of mold for GI–97; other Franklin leaf of GI–97 replaced by Dyott leaf. ca. 1826–28.

GI–97. Bust of Franklin each side. Quart. Probably 1824.

GII–40. Eagle each side. Pint. 1822. Mr. Wilson found that originally the initials "T.W.D." had been in the oval frame on one side and had been filled in.

GII–41. Eagle—Tree. Pint. Attributed to Kensington. 1822–24.

GII–42. Eagle, "T.W.D" in oval frame. *Reverse*: "FRANKLIN" below ship *Franklin*. Pint. 1822.

GII–43. Eagle, "T.W.D" in oval frame, "E PLURIBUS UNUM ONE OF MANY" on edge. *Reverse*: Cornucopia. "KENSINGTON GLASS WORKS PHILADELPHIA" on edge. Half-pint. ca. 1826–28. Inscriptions on edges added to mold for GII–44.

GII–44. Eagle—Cornucopia. Half-pint. 1824.

GII–45. Eagle—Cornucopia. Half-pint. Attributed to Kensington. ca. 1824–25.

GIV–34. [Masonic and] Agriculture; "KENSINGTON GLASS WORKS" on edge. *Reverse*: "FRANKLIN" below ship *Franklin*; "FREE TRADE AND SAILORS RIGHTS" on edge. Pint, ca. 1826–28. Inscriptions on edges here were added to mold for GIV–35.

GIV–35. [Masonic and] Agriculture. *Reverse*: "FRANKLIN" below ship *Franklin*. Pint. 1825. Inscriptions added to edges to make GIV–34.

GIV–37. Masonic and Agricultural. *Reverse*: Eagle, "T.W.D." Pint. 1822. Masonic and Agricultural leaf combined with ship *Franklin* leaf to make GIV–35, and called "Agriculture"

The history of the Dyottville Glass Factories after the Dyott regime is skeletal, still derived mainly from the account in the *History of Philadelphia 1609–1884* by John T. Scharf and Thompson Westcott, and the city directory listings. In 1842 the Lehigh Coal and Navigation Company rented the factory (probably one, or possibly two, of the five individual units) to one Henry Seybert. Apparently Seybert was inspired on the one hand by the 1842 tariff act, passed August 30, restoring to bottles and vials, plain and fancy, and jars the protection that had seeped away by gradual reductions from 1833 to 1842, and on the other hand by the flourishing demand for mineral and soda water bottles, especially small ones like 1 through 4 of Ill. 49. Seybert repaired the furnaces and, except for one reserved for flint-glass production, "started them for the making of bottles, principally for the use of Eugene Roussel, mineral water manufacturer." In 1844 Henry Seybert sold out to H. B. Benners (who had worked under him), S. Decatur Smith, and Quinton Campbell, Jr., forming the firm of Benners, Smith and Campbell. This firm dissolved in 1852, when H. B. & J. M. Benners was formed by Henry Benners and his brother James. Four years later another brother, George, joined them, and the firm became H. B. & J. M. Benners & Company. James and George, being wine merchants, undoubtedly had been good customers for such wine and other bottles as they required. Four years later, 1860, James withdrew and Henry B. and George W. continued as H. B. & G. W. Benners. The next important event was the acquisition, in 1869, of that part of the Dyottville property not used by the Lehigh Coal and Navigation Company. In September of the following year George W. Benners died. From then until his own death about 1893, Henry B. Benners operated the glassworks; thereafter it belonged to his estate. It was last listed in the city directories in 1923.[56]

The glassware produced at Dyottville under Henry Seybert and then the various Benners firms and finally the estate of Henry B. Benners is not identifiable unless the factory name was molded into the glass. Hence, except for a tiny fraction, the output is anonymous. Though reports of the Franklin Institute Exhibitions and Premiums state that in 1845, 1846, and 1847 Dyottville flint and colored glassware was exhibited, and won an award and special mention in the first two years, they give no clue to the character of the ware. Moreover, as 1847 was the last year in which the glassware was exhibited, and no further mention of flint glass has been found as yet, it seems probable that line was discontinued by Benners, Smith and Campbell. Their 1848 advertisement, Ill. 64, states they were "Manufacturers of Carboys, Demijohns of all sizes, Wine, Porter, Soda and Mineral Water, Lemon Syrup and Ink Bottles, Jars and Druggists' Bottles and Vials of every description." Like other bottle manufactuers, they also made all kinds of bottles and vials to order in private molds. An 1860 advertisement in the city directory omitted lemon syrup and ink bottles and included pickle and preserve bottles. One can conclude only that all were of the currently popular forms.

The roster of bottles and flasks marked on the side or base with the name of the works, I am confident, is very incomplete. As yet, only marked Dyottville mineral water, porter, and wine bottles have been recorded; a few of these are listed in Part III. WINE, SPIRIT, AND BEVERAGE BOTTLES. Wine bottle 9 in Ill. 45 is one of the marked

wines of the period ca. 1850–60 or 1880. In the Figured Flask category three are inscribed "DYOTTVILLE GLASS WORKS PHILADA"—an eagle flask, GII–38, and two Washington–Taylors, GI–37 and 38. However, attributed to Dyottville in the past were all the flasks of form 20 (Ill. 133) having on each side an unframed panel —one side with profile classical bust of Washington and, on the reverse of 23 flasks, Zachary Taylor in uniform; of three, a sheaf of grain with crossed rake and pitchfork. Though it seems probable to me that Dyottville did produce the half-pint with the Taylorism "GEN. TAYLOR NEVER SURRENDERS"—as well as flasks with the Taylorisms "A LITTLE MORE GRAPE CAPT. BRAGG" and "I HAVE ENDEAVORED TO DO MY DUTY"—it seems highly improbable that Dyottville produced all 26 unmarked varieties: GI–39 through GI–59, GI–40a, b, and c, 55a, and 56a in the Charts. Actually, at this time, only of the three flasks listed below can it be said without qualification that they *are* Dyottville.

GII–38. American eagle with "E PLURIBUS UNUM" pennant and American shield. *Reverse*: "DYOTT-VILLE GLASS WORKS" on horseshoe arch and "PHILADA" below. "Pint." Probably second quarter of the 19th century.

GI–37. "THE FATHER OF HIS COUNTRY" arching over Washington. *Reverse*: "GEN. TAYLOR NEVER SURRENDERS" arching over Zachary Taylor; "DYOTTVILLE GLASS WORKS PHILAD.A" in arch following the line at top of panel. Quart. Probably first produced in 1847 by Benners, Smith & Campbell.

GI–38. Like GII–37, but pint size.

21. UNION GLASS WORKS, *Kensington, Philadelphia, Pennsylvania. 1826–ca. 1880*

For many years, 1820 was believed to be the year in which the Union Glass Works was established at Kensington, Philadelphia: Deming Jarves stated that it was founded in that year by workmen who had left the New England Glass Company. And the venture was thought to have been a short-lived failure, since Jarves disposed of it quite summarily as ill-starred, passing into other hands as the company's ranks were thinned by death and its funds depleted by mismanagement. Actually, the Union Glass Company, called also the Union Flint Glass Company, was not formed until late in 1825. The founders of the company were William Granville, William Swindell, William Bennett, Richard Synar, and William Emmett, all of Kensington, and Joseph Capewell of Cambridge and James Venables of Boston, Massachusetts. Venables and Granville apparently were businessmen, not glassmen like the others.

On November 1, 1825, it was Granville who, acting for the group, purchased for $3,600 a tract of land in Kensington for the glassworks site. This was well chosen, being bounded on one side by the Delaware River and on the opposite side by a main road into Philadelphia. In the same month, erection of the glassworks began. The year 1826 was an eventful one: early in the year the glassworks was completed and in blast; late in the year, Granville and Swindell withdrew from the firm and Charles Baldren Austin, an English glass cutter, who was to guide the works through 14 profitable years, joined the company. The new firm of Charles B. Austin & Company was formed, and so long as Austin was head of the firm and agent for the glassworks, it throve. But when Austin died in 1840, the management passed to William Bennett, who was handicapped by strife within the firm and litigation with Austin's widow. The firm was dissolved in 1844. The works was shut down.[57]

The Union Glass Works was one of the successful works producing flint (lead) glass and cut-glass wares that was established after the 1824 tariff proved to be protective. It is mentioned here because it may have been the source of the comparatively scarce Columbia flask GI–117 and the very rare GI–118, each having "UNION CO" on the eagle side and "KENSINGTON" on the side with a profile bust of Columbia. The flasks were charted in 1941 with the Columbia side as the obverse and the eagle side as the reverse, and since then they have been referred to as "Kensington Union Company." However, no factory of that name has ever been identified. To me, the logical explanation is that to the producer of the flasks the eagle side seemed the more significant—and was the obverse—and the Columbia the less important, the reverse. Regarded that way, the reading becomes Union Company Kensington. Having chosen the name "Union," the proprietors might well have decided to bring out flasks decorated with two symbols of the Union, the American eagle and Columbia. I have found no record of any other Union Glass Works Company located in Kensington. If this one did produce these two Columbia–Eagle flasks, it would not be the first works specializing in fine flint-glass tableware to produce Figured Flasks. The famous Bakewell's Pennsylvania Flint Glass Works in Pittsburgh did too—in fact, added green-glass to its output in 1811. And the Union Glass Works wares were advertised in Baltimore in 1828 as "all descriptions of Flint & Table Hollow glassware."[58]

In 1847, three years after the fires at the Union Glass Works had been drawn, the glassworks was reopened by the firm of Hartell & Lancaster, primarily for the production of bottles. Little is known about this firm, or its successor Hartell & Letchworth, aside from the listings in the Philadelphia city directories. And I found the listings a bit confusing. However, it appears that the first Hartell in the firm was William, and he was joined about 1850 by Thomas R. Hartell. The Lancaster appears to have been John or Joseph, who died in 1857. In 1858 the firm became Hartell & Letchworth—Thomas R. Hartell and John Letchworth. Thomas R. Hartell was listed as a glass manufacturer up through 1880; John Letchworth mainly as "Glassware" at the address of their warehouse, 1867–72. Apparently Hartell & Letchworth maintained an auction

house from 1878 through 1881. In October at least four years after the Union Glass Works was taken over by Hartell & Lancaster, its wares were shown at the exhibitions sponsored by the Franklin Institute of the State of Pennsylvania for the Promotion of the Mechanical Arts: Hartell & Lancaster exhibited in 1847 and 1848; Hartell & Letchworth in 1874. In 1858, the year the latter firm was formed, the Report of the Committee of Premiums and Exhibitions listed "T. R. Hartell. Philadelphia. Colored Glass." The only advertisement I have found is the following:

UNION GLASS WORKS,
Queen street, Kensington
Philadelphia
DRUGGIST' GLASS
of superior quality
Carboys, Wine, Porter and Mineral Water Bottles,
Also, Bohemia and Coloured Glass,

Ruby,	Emeralds,	Amethyst,
Canary,	Blues,	Amarite,
Turquoise,	Greens,	Black,
Opal,	Ambers,	White Agate,
Victoria Emerald,	Purples,	Chameleon,

ALSO, ENAMELS OF EVERY COLOUR,
PATENT MEDICINE BOTTLES,
And all other articles made in Private Moulds, will receive particular attention.

W. HARTELL
J. LANCASTER Proprietors.[59]

In the first 32 years of the 1800s, the southern area of New Jersey became a center of glass manufacture that endures to the present. One glassworks, the Olive Glass Works at Glassboro, survived from the 18th century and at least 13 others were started, seven of them before 1820. With the exception of the Jersey Glass Works, a flint-glass works established in 1824 in Jersey City, they were located in the flat, thickly wooded southern part of New Jersey, where suitable sand for glass and wood for potash and building were available in abundance. Another factor in determining their locations was that they could be built on or near waterways and turnpikes, not far from the important Philadelphia market, where most of the glass manufacturing firms were to have agents or their own outlets. In many instances, a community grew up around the glasshouse and its ancillary activities, as at Wistarburgh (Alloyways Town) and Glassboro.

The majority were window-glass houses, but in many, if not all, bottles and vials were a sideline at least part of the time. For the most part, the output of one was similar to that of another—unmarked, anonymous. One was the Eagle Glass Works at Port Elizabeth, established by a group of Philadelphians, including James Lee (manager through 1815) and probably James Josiah. The works suffered over the years from the common ills of depression, and there were many changes in ownership before it was abandoned in 1885.[60] That in its early years bottles were a sideline is evidenced by two advertisements in which window glass was headlined but bottles were mentioned specifically. In 1819, Josiah & Lee offered mustard, pocket, and claret bottles, half-gallon and gallon bottles, quart and half-gallon jars. It seems likely that the pocket bottles were Pitkin-type. In 1817, J. Josiah, Harrison & Lee offered a more extensive line: "vials assorted from 1 oz. to 8 oz. / Patent Vials [patent medicine bottles] of all kinds / Pint, Quart, half Gallon and Gallon Black Bottles / Olive Bottles and Sweet Oil Bottles; Mustard Bottles / Jars for Pickles &c &c."[61]

In another early house the blowing of window glass is said to have alternated with the blowing of bottles. This was the Gloucester Glass Works, which, according to local history, was built at Clementon around 1800 by Jonathan Haines. However, since Richmond Morcom learned Haines was only ten in 1800, either Haines established the works later or acquired them sometime prior to 1817. They were sold to Samuel Clement around 1820 and closed before 1825.[62] The works is noteworthy for bottle students and collectors on two counts. One is that Jonathan Haines appointed "T. W. Dyott, Druggist" as his sole agent by the fall of 1817. From advertising it would appear that Dr. Dyott served the glassworks in that capacity into 1822,[63] even though by then he was himself owner of a glassworks, the Kensington Glass Works, Philadelphia. The second count is that, in excavations on the site of the works, Richmond Morcom found ample evidence that the Gloucester Glass Works was another early 19th-century source of Pitkin-type pocket bottles. The many shards revealed that the flasks were blown from aquamarine, olive-amber, and olive-green colored glass. Some were decorated with vertical ribbing; some with the broken swirl. Though students have long believed that Pitkin-type flasks must have been blown in South Jersey glassworks, this is the first tangible evidence of the fact.

In 1806 a glassworks was started at Millville, a new village on the Maurice River, which emptied into Delaware Bay; the riverbanks were composed of so superior a sand that eventually it was "exported" to glassworks outside the state of New Jersey. In the next 20 years the works had three owners—the group of men, including James Lee of Port Elizabeth's Eagle Glass Works, who built it; a Gideon

Smith; and a group of glassblowers with Nathaniel Solomon as manager. In, or by, 1827, Burgin & Wood, Philadelphia druggists, acquired the works. Like many other glass manufacturers, they advertised "window, coach and picture glass, carboys, demijohns, bottles and vials of every description." In 1829 the Burgin member of the firm—Dr. George Burgin—received a patent for the "Use of Salts or Alkalies obtained from the spent ley of soap makers as a flux in the Manufacture of Glass." The same year the firm became Burgin, Wood & Pearsall, and two years later, Burgin & Pearsall. Sometime between 1833 and 1844 Burgin & Pearsall sold the New Jersey glassworks to Scattergood, Haverstock & Company, perhaps because they were planning to establish one in Kensington, Philadelphia, one that was to produce green-glass wares from around 1844 until 1910. In 1844 the Whitall regime began when Whitall Brothers acquired the Millville Glass Works. Five years later the firm became Whitall Brothers & Company, and in 1853 it increased its furnace and pot capacity by the South Millville glassworks established in 1832 by Frederick Schetter of Baltimore, nephew of Philip R. J. Friese and John F. Friese of the Baltimore Glass Works. In the panic year 1857, Whitall, Tatum & Company was formed, perhaps because, like many others, the firm was embarrassed for funds. For about 81 years Whitall, Tatum & Company were leading manufacturers of "Chemist, druggists and perfumers wares of lime [white] and green glass," for which an award was won at the Centennial Exposition of 1876. About 1938 the works became, and still is, a unit of the Armstrong Cork Company. The only marked articles of which I know are insulators; opaque white apothecary jars inscribed "WHITALL TATUM CO PHILA & N.Y." on the base; and, listed by Dr. Julian H. Toulouse, fruit jars marked "WHITALL-TATUM PAT'D JUNE 11, 1895" on the lid.[64] One category apparently was never produced—Figured Bottles and Flasks. As yet none have been identified, even tentatively, with the Millville Glass Works.

The following sketches are of New Jersey glassworks established between 1800 and 1832 in which Figured Bottles and/or Flasks were blown.

22. HARMONY GLASS WORKS, 1813, later
    WHITNEY GLASS WORKS, *Glassboro, N.J.; 1918,*
    acquired by the Owens Bottle Company

Glassboro's second glassworks was one of many started in the War of 1812 period. In 1813 a group of glassmen—among them Lewis Stanger of the large and now famous South Jersey family of glassmen—left the Olive Glass

Works and joined with John Rink of Philadelphia to form Rink, Stanger & Company to manufacture bottles and window glass. The glassmen tended to the "inside" work, as all the production functions were sometimes called, under the management of Daniel Focer (Pfotzer). Rink, as agent, took care of all "outside" business—finances, purchase of all supplies, and sale of the output. Their glassworks, located about 1,200 feet south of the Olive Glass Works, was called the Harmony Glass Works. Whether due to disharmony in the company or decline of business after the war, it would appear that Rink, Stanger & Company was not long-lived. John Rink's December 1818 advertisement (Ill. 10) in which he notified "his Customers and the public in general" that *he* had appointed new handlers—Thather & Tompson of Philadelphia—of the wares of the Harmony Glass Works suggests that the firm had been dissolved and Rink had either become owner of the glassworks or had a controlling interest. When he died late in 1822 or early in 1823, his seven-eighths part of the tract of land on which the Harmony Glass Works stood was put up to be sold at public vendue in September 1823. At the time the glassworks, so the advertisement stated, consisted of a "large Glass House, Pot House, Mill House, Packing House, Store House, several dwelling Houses, etc."[65] One assumes the dwellings were for the workers.

Perhaps it was at the auction in 1823 that Rink's interest in the Harmony Glass Works was bought by Daniel H. Miller, owner of the Franklin Glass Works, a Malaga, New Jersey, green-glass works purchased by Miller in 1820 from Christian Stanger and associates, who had founded it in 1814. The following year, 1824, Miller extended his ventures in glass manufacture: the Olive Glass Works then owned by Jeremiah Foster and the Harmony Glass Works were merged, and the name of Foster's works was dropped. Whether or not Foster retained an interest in the merged business is not clear. However, from an advertisement which ran for several years—1829 through 1835—it would appear that Daniel Miller was the proprietor. It ran as follows:

WINDOW GLASS/BOTTLES, VIALS &/THE SUBSCRIBER MANUFACTURES/AT THE/"FRANKLIN" AND "HARMONY"/GLASS MANUFACTORIES/IN NEW JERSEY/AND HAS CONSTANTLY FOR SALE/ *at No. 177 North Second Street near New Street/ Philadelphia*/Plain Window, Picture and Coach/GLASS/of various sizes/ALSO VIALS OF ALL DESCRIPTIONS/ PLAIN AND LETTERED/COMMON QUART, AND PACKING BOTTLES/CASTOR OIL BOTTLES, FLASKS, JARS & &c./Warrented [*sic*] to be as good Quality as any sold in the City/*and at the very lowest Prices./*Vials and Bottles made *to order* at the shortest notice. D. H. MILLER.[66]

One wonders whether any of the flasks was figured. None has ever been identified with the works before midcentury. The Whitney connection with the Glassboro glassworks, one lasting over 80 years, began in 1834 or 1835 (Pepper says 1834), when a one-third interest was acquired by

Thomas H. Whitney, grandson of Colonel Heston of Heston & Carpenter, one-time owners of the first Glassboro glassworks. (See No. 9. New-Jersey Glass Manufactory.) Two years later during the depression, having bought out his partners, Whitney took his sons Eben and Samuel into the business, forming the firm of Whitney and Brothers. In the 1860s Samuel was to obtain two patents: one in 1861 for a bottle and flask with screw-in stopper (see Ill. 55 and flask GXV–26 in the Flask Charts); one in 1867 for a pickle or preserve bottle design. In 1839 Whitney and Brothers expanded their interest in glass manufactories by joining John G. Rosenbaum in the operation of the Franklin Glass Works in Malaga, which Rosenbaum had purchased from Daniel H. Miller. The Malaga works, running into financial troubles in the depression of the late 1850s, was closed in 1858. (It was revived in 1861 by the heirs of John G. Rosenbaum, who had died in 1860, and operated for many years as a window-glass works.) It seems probable that the financial embarrassment at Malaga extended also to Glassboro, for at some time prior to 1857 Thomas E. and Samuel A. Whitney were joined by S. D. Smith, and the firm became Whitney, Smith & Company. A circular now in the archives of The Corning Museum of Glass announced the dissolution of that firm on September 1, 1857, and a new firm name of Whitney Brothers, Thomas H. and Samuel A. When the name Harmony Glass Works was dropped has not been determined, but the marked Wharton's Chestnut Grove handled whiskey flask, 6 in Ill. 48, suggests it also may have been in 1857. In 1882 the Whitney Brothers formed the Whitney Glass Works, which was incorporated in 1887.[67]

Not surprisingly, the Whitney Glass Works, was one of the first of the eastern factories to adopt modern mechani-

10. Advertisement of John Rink's Harmony Glass Works, Glassboro, N.J., dated December 31 (1818). (Philadelphia, *American Centinel and Mercantile Advertiser*, Jan. 14, 1819.) *Camden County Historical Society, Camden, New Jersey*

Harmony Glass Works.

The Subscriber respectfully informs his Customers and the public in general, that he has transferred the business of selling the Ware manufactured at the above Works, to Messrs. THATCHER & THOMPSON, North-West corner of Market and Second streets, by whom all orders will in future be received. The Subscriber acknowledges with gratitude the favors heretofore received, and pledges himself that every exertion shall be made at the Manufactory to have the quality of the Glass such as shall continue to give satisfaction.

John Rink.

WINDOW GLASS & VIALS.

VIALS, from ½ oz. to 8 oz. and for Patent Medicines of all kinds. Also, Snuff, Mustard and Oil Bottles. WINDOW GLASS, of different sizes and qualities, for sale at low prices, for cash or approved paper at the usual credit, by

Thatcher & Thompson,

N W. corner Market & Second Streets.
dec 31—iftfhstutf

cal production. In 1909 it was licensed by the Owens Bottle Company to use the machine developed to manufacture druggists' wares. The following year the Whitney Glass Works obtained sole rights for machine production of oval-shape ammonia bottles and nonexclusive rights to general "prescription" wares. In 1912 when the Owens Bottle Company, retaining 51 percent of the stock, formed the Eastern Owens Bottle Company at Clarksburg, West Virginia, the Whitney Glass Works subscribed for 5 percent of the stock. In the same year when the Whitney Glass Works was in need of cash, the Owens Bottle Company loaned it $50,000 ($16,000 for accrued royalties and $34,000 cash) on its 6 percent second mortgage bonds. When George D. Whitney, president of Whitney Glass Works, died in February 1915, he had sizable personal notes outstanding. Rather than meet them by dumping his 1,954 shares of the Whitney Glass Works stock, the administrators of his estate turned to Owens for help. The Owens Bottle Company not only took up Whitney's notes but also advanced $50,000 in return for an option to buy Whitney's shares. Not long afterward, Owens exercised its option and thereby gained control. One result was the building of a new six-machine factory. The old one with seven machines was abandoned in 1919.) In the meantime, in 1918, Owens acquired all outstanding shares and then dissolved the Whitney Glass Works. A new million-dollar factory was built and operated until 1929, when the company entered into a merger with the Illinois Glass Corporation forming Owens-Illinois Glass Corporation.[68]

Like most factories specializing in bottles, that of the Whitneys apparently turned out vials, bottles, and druggists' ware of every description. In the 1860s, if not earlier, plain wine bottles and plain pocket flasks, such as GXV–26 and 27 in the Charts, were marked "WHITNEY GLASS WORKS" on the base. The marked flasks I have seen had screw-in glass stoppers patented by Samuel A. Whitney in 1861. Other marked articles were the handled flasks, like 6 in Ill. 48, made for Charles Wharton and inscribed on one side "WHARTON'S / WHISKEY / 1858 / CHESTNUT GROVE" and inside the base rim "WHITNEY GLASS WORKS, GLASSBORO N.J." A private mold having the name of a glassworks molded in the glass suggests that the glassworks made the mold for its customer. Possibly Whitneys made the Wharton handled flask like that shown in Ill. 56. There undoubtedly are dozens and dozens of bottles bearing the Whitneys' mark, but as yet wines, pocket flasks, and Wharton's flask are the only ones of which I have a record. However, a few advertisements and a "Prices Current" reveal the general nature of the output. In 1848 Whitney & Brothers headlined "Vials, Bottles, Jars & Demijohns," stated that all kinds of bottles would be made to order in private molds, and that orders would be taken for "any description of Black or Green Ware." The 1857 circular, of which (as previously mentioned) a copy is now in the Archives of The Corning Museum of Glass, claimed the works' wines, porters, Dutch gin bottles, demijohns, and carboys were "equal to the best made in Europe." And, of special interest to col-

lectors of wine and spirits bottles, particular attention was given to English wine bottle glass. From an 1862 "Prices Current," illustrated by Van Rensselaer, we learn that "druggists' ware" covered the following:

Common vials
Round prescriptions
Fluted prescriptions, long and short narrow mouth
Patent medicine and other vials
Oval vials and bottles
Paneled vials and bottles
Squares and oblong squares
Round castor oil, long neck
Concave, octagon, oval and fluted castor oils

Castor oil or lemon syrup
Cod liver oils
Magnesia
Packing bottles, common
Packing bottles, extra heavy
Acids and tinctures
Promiscuous Articles
Colognes (52 varieties)
Ink bottles (13 varieties)
Ink stands

Under glassware, with two or more items under each heading, were:

Jelly or Preserve Jars
Pepper sauce or Catsup Bottles
Worcestershire Sauce Bottles
Olive Oil Bottles
Pickle Jars
Olive Bottles
Caper Bottles

Mustard Bottles
Horse Radish Jars
Lemon Syrups
Flasks, plain and fancy Bottles
Specie Jars
Porter, Ale and Mineral Water Bottles
Snuff bottles and jars

Wine and liquor Bottles of "Every Description," included:

Wine Bottles, Dark Glass
Wine Bottles, Heavy and very superior
Jugs with Handles [presumably similar to 8 in Ill. 4a]

Demijohns
Rhine Wine Flask with handles [presumably similar to 1 in Ill. 48]
Champagne bottles
Carboys, finished with patent tools

Some, at least, of the pickle jars or bottles and sauce bottles were gothics similar to 1, 2, 11, and 12 in Ill. 74. Also listed were window, coach, and double-thick sheet glass from the Franklin Glass Works at Malaga.

By 1870, doubtless earlier, Whitney Brothers had joined the ranks of fruit jar manufacturers with their "Whitney AIR-TIGHT Fruit Jar." Apparently their jar could not compete with the popular Mason jar, and by 1878 the firm was making "Mason Fruit Jars."[69]

Several bottles well known to collectors of bitters bottles and Figured Bottles and Flasks were attributed to the Whitney Glass Works by Van Rensselaer and Knittle. I do not know the basis for the attribution, but it is reasonable to believe that Whitney's was one of the works in which the following were produced:

Indian Queen—for Brown's Celebrated Indian Herb Bitters, which were patented in February 1867; see 2 in Ill. 84.

Ear of Corn for National Bitters, patented 1867; like 4 in Ill. 84.

Fish for Doctor Fisch's bitters; similar to 3 in Ill. 50.

Wishart's Pine Tree Cordial, of which there are several varieties; similar to 7 in Ill. 49.

Log Cabin (tall) for Plantation Bitters, patented 1862 but apparently available in 1860.

Warners Safe Bitters

Tippecanoe

Jenny Lind calabashes inscribed "JENY.LIND." GI-102 and GI-103. ca. 1850/51.

Hunter and Fisherman calabash, GXIII-4, ca. 1850. The hunter is similar to one illustrating an advertisement by H. A. Duntze, gun maker, in the 1844/45 New Haven Directory.

Flora Temple (racehorse) handled flask, ca. 1860. GXIII-19, GXIII-21, GXIII-22, and GXIII-24.

Booz Bottles for E. C. Booz's Old Cabin Whiskey. Two-storied "cabin." 1860s-70s. GVII-3, GVII-4, and GVII-5.

23. HAMMONTON *Glassworks (ca. 1812–57).* HAMMONTON and WINSLOW *Glassworks (ca. 1831–85), Winslow, N.J.*[70]

Hammonton and Winslow are two more instances of communities growing up around a glassworks, and each was named for a son of William Coffin, Sr., one of the works' founders. According to long-accepted glassworks history, the Winslow glassworks was not built until 1831. However, Pepper states that William Coffin, Sr., acquired the Winslow property in 1829. If so, although she does not give the year in which the glassworks was built, the implication seems to be that it may have been before 1832, and either prior to 1831 or in that year. Since the Hammonton and the Winslow glassworks were largely Coffin and Hay family affairs, and the same molds for Figured Flasks may have been used in both works, it seems fitting to combine their brief historical sketches here.

In 1812, in Galloway Township, Gloucester County, William Coffin, Sr., built and operated a sawmill for John Coates. The site, about 13 miles from Coffin's hometown, Green Bank, was a lakeside in the midst of a heavily timbered tract of land. Apparently Coffin saw possibilities of utilizing the cleared land as well as the forest for expanding industry and creating a new community. In 1814 he invested in 1,598 surrounding acres, and later, in partnership with Jonathan Haines of the Gloucester Glass Works, started a window-glass manufactory. The date has been given as 1817 and as "1817 or 1820." If it was 1817 or in the next two years, they must have had plenty of capital and

great optimism, for those years were ones of depression. In any event, whichever year it was, or in between, the building of the glassworks doubtless followed or signaled Haines's departure from his Gloucester Glass Works and its acquisition by Samuel Clement, for whom the community was named Clementon. The partnership was not of long duration: Haines, selling his interest to Coffin, moved on around 1824 and founded Waterford. It would seem that for the next decade or so, William Coffin, Sr., ran the works alone, though it has been said that he took William, Jr., into partnership in 1823. However, in 1836 William, Sr.'s, son, Bodine Coffin, and son-in-law Andrew K. Hay either became managers or leased the glassworks, operating as Coffin & Hay. Two or four years later—Charles S. Boyer of the Camden Historical Society, who did the research on New Jersey glassworks for Stephen Van Rensselaer, gave the date as 1838; Adeline Pepper gives 1840—the Hammonton glassworks met the fate of so many of our early glasshouses: it burned to the ground. It was immediately rebuilt. In the meantime, Andrew K. Hay severed his connection with the works and became involved in the glassworks at Winslow. Presumably William Coffin, Sr., operated the rebuilt works until his death in 1844, when the business was taken over by two other sons, John Hammonton Coffin and Edwin Winslow Coffin. In 1851 Edwin sold his interest in Hammonton to his brother John. Business was poor in the last half of the 1850s, a period of tight money and of depression for many businesses, and John closed the factory in 1857.

The glassworks at Winslow apparently was primarily a bottle glassworks for close to two decades. It had been started between 1829 and 1831 by William Coffin, his son William, Jr., and Thomas Jefferson Pierce, with the firm name William Coffin, Jr. & Company. The site, not many miles from Hammonton, was a large timbered tract of land where an area was cleared for the glassworks and its attendant village, to which the middle name of Coffin's son Edwin Winslow was given. In 1833 the firm became Coffin & Pierce when William, Jr.'s, brother-in-law, Thomas Pierce, succeeded William, Sr., in the business. Around 1835 Pierce died, leaving William, Jr., to operate alone until he was joined by his brother-in-law, Andrew K. Hay, following the disastrous fire at Hammonton in 1838 or 1840. Sometime between then and 1847, Tristram Bowdle acquired an interest in the Winslow Glassworks, and the firm changed from Coffin & Hay to Coffin, Hay & Bowdle. Another change in ownership occurred in 1847, when William Coffin, Jr., sold his interest to his brother Edwin Winslow and John B. Hay, a nephew of Andrew K. Hay, and the firm of Hay, Bowdle & Company was formed. In 1851, a year after Bowdle's retirement, Edwin Winslow Coffin sold his interest in both the Hammonton and Winslow works, that in the latter to Andrew K. Hay. For the next 30 years Andrew K. and John B. Hay were its proprietors, operating as A. K. Hay & Company and producing window glass. After Andrew's death in 1881, his heirs and John B. Hay operated the works until John's retirement in 1884, when it was leased to Tillyer Brothers of Philadelphia. The end of May 1892 saw the end of the works: a disastrous fire consumed it and several nearby houses.

So far as I have learned, the only bottles that have been identified with the Hammonton Glassworks, and possibly later with Winslow, are the Figured Flasks in the following list. The inscription on the first four leaves no doubt that they originated at Hammonton and dates their advent at 1836–38. The other eight flasks, probably first produced in the same period, were attributed by Van Rensselaer, whose attribution is still generally accepted. It seems probable that molds for these flasks accompanied Andrew K. Hay when, after the fire in 1838, he left Hammonton for Winslow, and that they were used at Winslow during the next few years. (See Charts for line drawings of the flasks.)

GII–48. Eagle. *Reverse*: "COFFIN & JAY" in semicircle above American Flag, "HAMMONTON" below. Pint.

GII–49. Eagle. *Reverse*: "COFFIN & HAY" in semicircle above Stag, "HAMMONTON" below. Pint.

GII–50. Like GII–49 but half-pint. ca. 1836.

GII–51. Eagle. *Reverse*: Inscription like above. Pint.

GII–52. Eagle. *Reverse*: "FOR OUR" at lower left of American Flag, "COUNTRY" at lower right. Pint.

GII–53. Eagle. *Reverse*: Like GII–52. Pint.

GII–54. Eagle. *Reverse*: Like GII–52. Pint.

GII–55. Eagle. *Reverse*: Bunch of grapes. Quart.

GII–56. Eagle. *Reverse*: Bunch of Grapes. Half-pint.

GX–1. "GOOD GAME" below stag. *Reverse*: Willow tree. Pint.

GX–2. "GOOD" below stag, "GAME" at right. *Reverse*: Willow tree. Half-pint.

GX–3. Sheaf of rye. *Reverse*: Bunch of grapes. Half-pint.

24. WATERFORD GLASS WORKS, *Waterford, New Jersey (ca. 1822–1880)*[71]

As has been mentioned in connection with the Hammonton Glassworks, Jonathan Haines severed his association there with William Coffin, Sr., sometime between 1822 and 1824. Acquiring a partly cleared tract of wooded land not many miles away, he erected a glasshouse. The village that inevitably grew up around it he named Waterford, for the famous Irish glass center. When Haines died in 1828, Samuel Shreve, Thomas Evans, and Jacob Roberts became the proprietors. The exact dates of the ensuing ownerships are missing at present, but it is known that Roberts died, Joseph Porter purchased his interest, and the firm became Porter, Shreve & Company. Eventually Porter was able to buy all the stock. He then brought his sons into the business. The firm of Joseph Porter & Sons operated the works until the father's death in 1862, when one son,

William C. Porter, took over the management for a brief period. A year later apparently it was sold to Maurice Raleigh. Perhaps, like so many glassworks, that at Waterford was already experiencing financial difficulties due to the ill effects of the Civil War upon manufacturing. In any event, in 1863 it was forced to shut down. Raleigh revived the business and operated it as three glassworks under a single management—two for the production of window glass, one for bottles. At a later point, they were known as the DeWitt-Gayner Glass Works and, at the end, were run by Gaines Pardessus & Company for the production of lampshades. In 1880 they were abandoned, and in 1882 they burned.

Though little, aside from the ownerships, is known about the Waterford Glass Works, two events under Joseph Porter & Sons are said to have had far-reaching effects in the industry. According to Charles S. Boyer, who, while president of the Camden Historical Society, was a pioneer researcher into the history of New Jersey's glassworks, sometime before 1862 Joseph Porter instituted a weekly day of rest for his workers, shutting down the works on Sunday. During a blast it was still customary to blow glass the week-around so long as there was metal in the pots. Exactly how Porter arranged things to permit the holdover from Saturday night to Monday morning we are not told, but he did. The result was the spread of the practice to most other factories. Porter also showed his humanitarianism by increasing the pay of his employees so that "Waterford wages" became the talk of the glass world and led to wage rises in rival glassworks.

Even less is known about the specific products of the Waterford Glass Works than about its general history. Presumably window glass, bottles, and other hollow ware were blown intermittently in the early years. Later, as the works grew under Porter, the output consisted regularly of window glass, bottles, and flasks, including at least one Figured Flask. Though Stephen Van Rensselaer attributed to Waterford the quart TRAVELER'S COMPANION— Sheaf of Grain flask GXIV–1, Charles B. Gardner believed this flask probably was a product of the Westford Glass Works, Westford, Connecticut. There is, however, one flask, the attribution of which to Waterford has never been questioned: it is the quart Shield & Clasped Hands—Flying Eagle flask GXII–2, which is inscribed "WATERFORD" in an arc below a shallow arc of stars and above the shield with clasped hands—a design of the Civil War era. It has been recorded in aquamarine, light green, and light olive-yellow. Of 43 flasks in Group XII, it is the only one that can be associated with a particular glassworks. In 1927 Rhea Mansfield Knittle wrote: "The Waterford quart flasks are among the rarest American bottles." In 1941 it was rated common (150 or more specimens) by George S. McKearin and fellow collectors.

In the State of New York only one 18th-century glassworks survived into the 19th century—the Hamilton Glass Factory (see No. 11. Dowesborough . . . later the Albany Glasshouse . . .), and it failed about 1815. Though probably not a prime factor in its failure, loss of workmen to infant glassworks in the state, for which Elkanah Watson stated the works had been the nursery, had not helped. Of the 15 or more glassworks started between 1800 and 1830, nine were located near central New York lakes and the Mohawk River flowing from the center of the state across into the Hudson River near Troy. Towns and villages had been, and were, developing throughout the area as the postrevolutionary influx of settlers continued. Another factor in site selection doubtless was the plans for and eventual reality of the Erie Canal, the hyphen from Lake Erie to the Hudson providing continuous water transportation from the Great Lakes to New York Harbor. With three exceptions—the Bloomingdale Flint Glass Works (1820–40) on the fringe of New York City, the Brooklyn Flint Glass Works (1823–68), and the Mount Vernon Glass Works in Vernon—the works were window-glass manufactories. However, in more than one some vials and utilitarian containers may have been blown, as they were at the Rensselaer Glass Works, called Sandlake Glass Works by collectors (1806–53).[72] And amber slag found on the site of the Rensselaer Glass Works suggests that some bottles may have been produced in the late years of operation. So far as is known at present, the only works that specialized in bottles was the Mount Vernon Glass Works, and it was the only one in which Figured Flasks were blown in the 1800 to 1832 period.

25. MOUNT VERNON GLASS WORKS, *Vernon, New York, 1810–44, when works was moved to Mt. Pleasant, Saratoga, N.Y., 1844–ca. 1890*

On February 17, 1810, the New York State legislature passed an act incorporating, for 14 years, the Mount Vernon Glass Company of Vernon, in central New York, a few miles from Utica, Oneida Lake, and the Mohawk River. It was one of many spawned by the Embargo and Non-Intercourse Act that cut down, where not off, importations of glassware, and seemed to offer perfect golden opportunities to would-be investors in manufacturing. The incorporators were Abraham Van Eps, Benjamin Pierson, Daniel Pierson, Isaac Coe (the first agent), Benjamin Hubble, Oliver Lewis, William Root, Robert Richardson, Daniel Cook (also one of the incorporators of the neighboring Oneida Glass Company), and "others," all businessmen apparently with funds to invest. The stock was to consist of no more than 500 shares at $250 a share. The act provided also that the agent, superintendent, and all the workmen were exempted from jury duty. Their glassworks was built in time to be operating by September, but evi-

dently was far from an instant success. During the first seven years the stockholders had to meet assessments on all shares of their stock or forfeit them. There was a $10 assessment four times in 1811, twice in 1812, once in 1813; then $15 a share once in 1814; and $20 a share in the depression year of 1817. Insofar as newspaper notices revealed, the only dividends paid in the same period were in glass—$20 worth of bottles in June 1812 (see Ill. 11B) and $10 worth of glass in January 1821.[73]

The few advertisements for Mount Vernon glass that I have found indicate that, as in the case of many works, the products were sold wholesale and retail at the factory. They were handled also by local merchants and in Utica—at least some of the time. It is interesting to note that in 1811 not only merchants' wholesale custom was solicited but also that of "traders and pedlars." Perhaps many peddlers in the United States hawked glassware such as bottles of various kinds, tumblers, and the like, as hawkers had in England as early as the 15th century, but this is the only bit of evidence of glass being peddled in the United States that I have found as yet.[74]

It would appear that Mount Vernon's first seven years were lean ones and were not followed by seven fat ones. One of the company—Isaac Coe, the agent—was bankrupted in 1813, and one share of Mount Vernon Glass Company stock was part of his property auctioned for the benefit of his creditors. But Coe, insofar as newspaper evidence goes, was the only stockholder in such circumstances, and possibly he continued as agent of the glassworks. There is little evidence of activity beyond notices of stockholders' meetings and, already cited, assessments and dividends. On March 31, 1815, the state legislature passed an act allowing the stockholders to elect the company directors from among the stockholders, and on April 5, 1824, passed an act continuing in force the Acts of February 17, 1810, and March 31, 1815, until February 16, 1824. This is the latest item pertaining to the incorporated company that I have found before the Grangers entered the picture.[75]

Seemingly sometime after April 1824 and before February 1829, Charles Granger & Company acquired the Mount Vernon Glass Works. (Doubtless Charles's brother Oscar Granger, also an experienced glassman, was one of the company, as he was later.) My guess would be that the acquisition occurred in time for the late summer or early fall blast in 1824. Be that as it may, on March 11, 1829, the following notice dated February 23 appeared in the Boston *Columbian Centinel:*

GLASSWORKS FORSALE [*sic*] / The subscribers offer for sale or to rent, their GLASS ESTABLISHMENT, situate in Vernon, Oneida County, N. Y. 17 miles from Utica and 8 from the Canal [Erie] in a very healthy and flourishing part of the country.

The property consists of a Flint house and other necessary buildings attached, with a furnace ready for operation, a number of Pots, Tools and Moulds for Flint and Bottle Glass, a good ashery, one or two dwelling houses and about 5 acres of land. The property will be sold at a great bargain or, if desired, the subscriber will take a partner, and carry it on, provided a person of some capital and respectibility [*sic*] offers. The large and flourishing Villages in the western part of the State and near the western lakes, the vast trade carried on will at all times furnish a market for more glass than can be realized elsewhere. Wood is 75c per cord. If desired we will sell with it one or two hundred acres of valuable woodland / Charles Granger & Co. Vernon, 23d Feb. 1829.

There were no buyers, it seems. But one James E. Southworth, evidently a man of respectability and with capital, entered into partnership with Charles and Oscar Granger at some point between the 1829 notice and 1832, when data was being compiled for the 1833 Utica Directory in which Granger, Southworth & Company were listed as "manufacturers of flint glassware, phials & Bottles of all kinds."

The copartnership was of brief duration, being dissolved by mutual consent September 18, 1833. Operation of the glassworks was continued first by C. & O. Granger, then C. Granger & Company. Oscar apparently was again one of the company. In 1844, because of dwindling wood supply, the glassworks was moved to Mount Pleasant outside Saratoga, New York.[76]

The products of the Mount Vernon Glass Works were primarily bottles of all kinds blown from "the different kinds of BOTTLE GLASS," which were—if one accepts the company's claims—of a superior quality. The kinds of glass included "black," for which Mount Vernon's recipe is given in Part I, 3. Colors and Compositions. Probably this was the metal used for the "Porter, Cider and Beer Bottles

Bottle Glass.

THE *President & Directors* of the *Mount Vernon Glass Company*, give notice that they continue to manufacture all kinds of BOTTLE GLASS, of a superior quality, at their Factory in the town of Vernon, in the county of Oneida. Merchants, traders and pedlars, may be supplied, at *Wholesale*, on liberal terms, with any quantity of

Porter, Cider and Beer Bottles,
Of the usual size.

And common bottles from a half pint to four Gallons.

Orders addressd, and application made to DAVID PEIRSON, agent for the company, at the said factory, will be strictly attended to. WM. I. HOPKINS, *Sec'y.*
Vernon, April 6, 1811.   '21tf

11A. Advertisement of "Bottle Glass" products of the Mount Vernon Glass Company, Vernon, N.Y.; dated April 6, 1811, it appeared for over a year. Note the mention of *pedlars* as well as *merchants* and *traders*. (Utica, N.Y., *Columbian Gazette*, May 12, 1812.) *The New-York Historical Society, New York City*

THE stockholders in the *Mount Vernon Glass Company*, in Vernon, are hereby notified that they are required to pay to the Treasurer of said company, the sum of *Ten Dollars*, on each share by them respectively owned, on or before the fifteenth day of August next, or forfeit their shares and all previous payment thereon. They are further notified that on payment thereof, they will be entitled to receive a dividend of twenty dollars in bottles on each share. By order of the Directors. T. HART, *Treas.*
July 6, 1812.   88

BY virtue of an execution to me directed and delivered, I have seized and taken all the right and title of Amos Leavenworth in and to great lot no. 7, in Sadaqueada Patent in the town of Deerfield, with the appurtenances, which I shall expose to sale at public vendue on the 2d day of September next, at 2 o'clock p. m. at the house of L. Berry, innkeeper in Whitestown.
For James S. Kip, Sh'ff.
July 20, 1812.   8   J. B Pease.

NOTICE.

THE stockholders in the Mount Vernon Glass Company are hereby notified that they are requested to pay to the Treasurer of said company the sum of *Ten dollars* on each share of stock by them respectively owned, on or before the twentyfifth day of August next, or forfeit their shares and all previous payments thereon.

DIVIDEND.
A dividend of twenty dollars in bottles on each share will be delivered to the stockholders on payment of the above instalment. By order of the directors. T. *HART*,
Dated June 11, 1812—88   Treas.

District of New-York, ss:
WHEREAS a libel hath been filed in the

11B. The first of two 1812 notices of an installment due on shares of the Mount Vernon Glass Company, and of a $20 dividend in bottles on each share, to be delivered to each stockholder upon payment of the installments. This one is dated June 11. The second was dated July 6. (Utica, N.Y., *Columbian Gazette*, July 12, 1812.) *The New-York Historical Society, New York City*

of the usual size" advertised in 1811, and probably they were like, or closely similar to, the clear deep green bottle with "MOUNT VERNON M S W" seal, 6 in Ill. 45. As at least four other Mount Vernon seals have been recorded, it would appear that the custom of having personalized seals applied to wine and beverage bottles persisted in central New York. Black, green, and olive-amber glasses for bottles, however, were not the only kinds. Tumblers, stoppers, decanters, and other articles of tableware were blown from near colorless glass as early as the fall of 1811. At least a "composition of Best Green Glass" for such articles made at the Mount Vernon Glass Works was recorded and dated "Nov. 1811" in an anonymous glassman's notebook owned by The Corning Museum of Glass. It called for 120 lbs. of the best Vernon sand, 48 lbs. of pearl ash, 16 lbs. of lime, 19 lbs. salt, 1 oz. of arsenic, 1 oz. of antimony, and 1 oz. Magnesia, and 70 lbs. of broken glass (cullet). The glassman added: "This is a very pale green glass and could with the addition of 1 lb. of Arsenic become equal to flint glass." Actually, flint glass (lead glass) was added later to the Mount Vernon output, most likely after the nearby Seneca Glass Works, a flint-glass works, closed, which probably was after the War of 1812 ended in 1815, and before 1819.[77]

How long flint glass was produced I do not know, but I believe it was not made after the late 1820s, or when C. Granger & Company became proprietors. An 1843 advertisement by Horatio N. Walker, agent of the Mount Vernon glassworks, itemizes:

Square varnish bottles	Patent medicines: Liq-
Inks from ½ to 8 oz.	uid and Steers
White castor oil bottles,	opodeldoc
½ pt. pt. & qt.	Batemans [drops]
Linaments 2 & 3 oz.	Godfreys [elixir]
Black qt. & pt. bottles	Bristol oils
Flasks ½ pt. & pt.	Turlingtons [balsam][78]
Vials assorted ½ to 8 oz.	

That Figured Flasks were among the early half-pint and pint flasks was established long ago by the excavations of Harry Hall White, to whom all collectors and students of American glass are forever indebted. The Figured Flasks listed below were attributed to the Mount Vernon Glass Works on the basis of Mr. White's archaeological research, or by analogy to flasks so attributed:

GI–88. "LAFAYETTE" in semicircle above profile bust of Lafayette. *Reverse*: Masonic emblems. Pint. Colors: olive-amber; pale and dark olive-green. 1824.

GI–89. Similar to GI–88 but half-pint. Colors: olive-amber; clear deep green, pale green of yellow tone, deep olive-green; pale greenish yellow.

GI–89a. Inscription and bust like GI–89, laurel leaves below bust. *Reverse*: 13 6-pointed stars in arch over Masonic emblem like GI–89. Herringbone ribbing on ends. Half-pint. Colors: colorless with amethystine tint. Flint (lead) glass. ca. 1824–25. Kenneth M. Wilson's studies proved that either the mold for GI–89 was altered to GI–89a, or the pattern was used for both but elaborated to make GI–89a.

GI–89b. Like GI–89a but large scale. Pint. Colors: greenish aquamarine. ca. 1824–25. As in the case of GI–89 and GI–89a, Mr. Wilson found that either the mold for GI–88 was altered for GI–89b or the pattern was used for both but elaborated for GI–89b.

GVIII–11. Cornucopia—Urn. Half-pint. Colors: black (deep olive-green), dark olive-green.

GV–5. "SUCCESS TO THE RAILROAD" in horseshoe arch above horse and cart on rail lengthwise, each side. Pint. Colors: amber, golden amber, olive-amber; aquamarine; black (dark olive-green); dark olive-green, emerald-green, deep olive-green, dark yellow-green. Late 1820s. The mold for this flask was taken to the

Saratoga Mountain glassworks, where the works was moved from Vernon ca. 1844/45. It is not possible to tell which surviving flask was made where.

GVII–1. Log cabin bottle with "TIPPECANOE" in rectangular frame across bottle above door and windows. *Reverse*: Similar but with "NORTH BEND" in frame. Height 5½″. Pint plus. Colors: black (both dense olive-amber and olive-green). Harrison 1840 presidential campaign bottle.

GVII–2. Log Cabin with gabled roof and "TIPPE-CANOE" in narrow rectangular panel midway between top of door and edge of roof. Taller than GVII–1. Pint plus. Colors: black (dense olive-green). One example recorded. Harrison 1840 presidential campaign bottle.

GVIII–1. Sunburst each side. Pint decanter-flask. Colors: colorless; light green, deep bluish green, deep yellow-green. ca. 1817.

Harry Hall White found fragments of this flask in sufficient quantity at both Keene-Marlboro-Street and Vernon to warrant attribution of the flasks to both glassworks. If so, it seems likely to me that Henry Rowe Schoolcraft may have taken the mold for the flask to Vernon in 1817, when he returned there after failing to operate the Flint-glass Factory successfully at Keene.

As has been mentioned, by the mid-1840s the wood supply on land owned by or available to the Mount Vernon Glass Works was nearing complete depletion, and so Oscar Granger set out to look for a new location. The choice of a mountain site eight to ten miles from the village of Saratoga was not as unusual as it seems on the surface. Granger undoubtedly was familiar with the possibilities of the area, since his mother had come from Greenfield and he had been born at Moreau, Saratoga County, and the bottle needs of the active spring-water companies must have seemed to guarantee a certain and steady market for a glassworks in their vicinity. Having settled on the area, Granger, it would seem, decided that hauling ingredients for glass and other necessities up the mountain to the wood and potash was more practical than hauling the wood down to the glassworks. In any event, he built a sawmill first to process the wood for building the glassworks, dwellings for his family and workers, and a schoolhouse. Also, he had a plank road laid leading from the glassworks to the Saratoga road. In 1844, when all was ready, the Mount Vernon Glass Works was closed and the new one, called Saratoga Mountain Glass Works by collectors, opened. Tools, molds, workmen, families, even the plants from the cherished garden of Oscar Granger's wife, were transported to the tiny community called Mount Pleasant.[79]

In the beginning, apparently outside funds were needed and, for a few years, Walter S. Todd and John W. James were associated with Oscar Granger and his brother Charles' son, Henry C. Granger, in the firm of Granger, James & Company. All management and operation of the glassworks were under Oscar and Henry C. Before the mid-1850s, seemingly Todd and James withdrew from the firm, which became O. & H. Granger. In another decade it was Granger and Company, and it seems likely the company may have included Niles, another nephew of Oscar, and Oscar's two sons, Foster O. and Lyman F. Granger. It seems probable also that Niles, who was to obtain a patent on a glass furnace on August 4, 1868, succeeded to a managerial position when Henry C. died in May 1867. A little over three years later, September 1870, Oscar Granger died in his sixty-eighth year. It was about that time that the works was sold to spring-water companies and moved into Saratoga to an area christened Congressville. Niles Granger continued as manager of the new Congress and Empire Spring Company Glass Works, which operated into the 1890s.

Information is scanty, but it would appear that the Mountain glassworks, though not a large establishment, was successful and profitable. For instance, the 1855 state census reported the number of employees as 45 and the value of the yearly output as $25,000. In 1860, the national census reported 50 men employed and a yearly production worth $29,500. There seems no reason to believe the business did not continue to be profitable and to increase during the next 30 years, first at the Mountain works and later at Congressville. The principal products, of course, were bottles for the various Saratoga spring waters. Excavations made by Harry Hall White and, later, Fenton Keyes establish that, quite apart from unmarked hollow ware, bottles were blown in at least 31 private molds belonging to spring-water companies. (See Part III. Wine, Spirit, and Beverage Bottles: 6. Spring, Mineral, and Soda Water Bottles.) One of these is illustrated by 8 in Ill. 49, a deep shaded amber bottle with inscriptions "HIGH ROCK CONGRESS SPRING / 1767" in an arch above a large rock in low relief, below which is "C &W / SARATOGA, N.Y." Another is 11 in Ill. 45, a black (deep olive-green) glass bottle also typical of those used in bottling Saratoga spring waters. It is inscribed "C. W. Weston & Cº" on the shoulder, which dates it between 1848 and 1861, the years the firm owned the Empire Spring.

Mr. White's excavations established also that two of the Mount Vernon molds for Figured Flasks had been taken to the Mountain glassworks and used there, testifying to the almost perennial popularity of Railroad and Cornucopia–Urn designs. The flasks, illustrated by line drawings in the Charts, were

GIII–11. Cornucopia—Urn. Pint. Colors: black (deep olive-green), clear dark olive-green.

GV–5. "SUCCESS TO THE RAILROAD" in horseshoe arch above horse and cart on rail, lengthwise of flask. Pint. Colors: black (deep olive-green), dark olive-green.

During the first and critical years of the 19th century, at least 25 glassworks were operated at one time or another in New England, mainly in Mas-

sachusetts. Some, especially those of the war period, withered and died in a short time; some were moderately sized works running for around two or three decades; a few flourished half a century or more. Two were survivors from the late 18th century—the Boston Glass Manufactory for crown glass (see No. 12) and the Pitkin Glassworks in East Hartford, Connecticut (see No. 13), where bottles and flasks were blown. The majority of the new glassworks were started for the production of window glass, just prior to or during the War of 1812. Five of these war babies were located in the Berkshires, where superior sand for glassmaking had been discovered. In their brief lifetime, most of them, like the Franklin Glass Works (1812–16) in Warwick, produced some vials and other containers mainly for local consumption. Only seven of the works started were bottle manufactories—the Keene-Marlboro-Street Glassworks at Keene, New Hampshire (see No. 26); the short-lived Ludlow glassworks (1815–?) near Springfield, Massachusetts, the name of which was long ago given by collectors to bottles such as 4 and 5 in Ill. 46; the New-England Glass-Bottle Company (see No. 27) in Cambridge, Massachusetts; and four Connecticut glassworks—John Mather's Glassworks (No. 28), the Coventry Glass Works (No. 29), the Willington Glass Works (No. 30), and the Glastenbury Glass Works (1817–27 or 1833), where excavations revealed production of Pitkin-type flasks but not Figured Flasks.[80]

However, there was vial and flask production in some of Massachusetts' flint-glass works. It will be recalled that the Boston Crown Glass Company, proprietors of the Boston Glass Manufactory on Essex Street, not only built a cylinder-glass works at Chelmsford in 1802, but nine years later built another in South Boston that became known as the South Boston Flint Glass Works not long after flint-glass production was introduced successfully. Three others were eminently successful: the New England Glass Company (No. 27), Thomas Cains's Phoenix Glass Works (ca. 1820–May 1870) in South Boston, and the Boston & Sandwich Glass Works (1825–88), Sandwich. The first two, in addition to the South Boston Flint Glass Works, are thought to be possible sources of one or more of the heavy Masonic flasks GIV–5 through 14, heavy Sunbursts GVIII–3, 4, and 14 through 17, and Concentric Ring Eagles GII–76 and 76a. Though it has been said that some Figured Flasks were produced at Sandwich, I know of no proof. However, flasks of some sort were blown there, for "flasks" were entered several times in Deming Jarves's account book of 1825, now owned by the Henry Ford Museum. Possibly the Sandwich flasks were of the English type like 3 in Ill. 100 and blown-three-mold flasks such as 1 through 3 in Ill. 121.

26. KEENE-MARLBORO-STREET GLASSWORKS,
Keene, New Hampshire, 1815–41

By the summer or early fall of 1814, not long after the establishment of Keene's window-glass works, two of its 13 proprietors—Daniel Watson, a successful business-man, and young Timothy Twitchell, soon to become his son-in-law—were itching to start a flint-glass works. The continuing War of 1812 and consequent dearth of English fine glassware were strong inducements. Also, Keene seemed a likely spot for such an adventure inas-much as wood for fuel and potash, boxes and buildings, was plentiful and cheaper than in more urban areas; "good rock sand" was available not more than 60 miles away and probably nearer; within 12 easy miles of the village was the Connecticut River, providing water carriage leading to "all points of the United States and the world"; and through the village ran the Boston turnpike over which all travel to that city, some 80 miles distant, and to other eastern points had to pass. Too, about a half-mile from the village edge, Wat-son owned property, both suitable and available as a glass-house location, and abutting the pike. (The stretch of pike through the village later became Marlboro Street.) All that seemed lacking were glassmen and—above all—one of that rare breed of competent glassmen who was not only skilled in the various compositions of glass, mixing batch, melting it, and fabrication of the metal but also knowl-edgeable about construction of glasshouses, furnaces, and ovens: in fact, a superglassman. Such a man, at least by reputation, was not far away in the capacity of superinten-dent of the Vermont Glass Works at Salisbury—Henry Schoolcraft, who, at 17, had been superintendent of the Ontario Glass Works at Geneva, New York, in 1810 and 1811. As Lawrence Schoolcraft, Henry's father, was in Keene as superintendent of the New Hampshire Glass Works, Watson and Twitchell discussed their project with him, and since he agreed with them that it had good pros-pects, they chose him to approach Henry about joining them.[81]

It was late in November 1814 when Lawrence Schoolcraft wrote to his son about the flint-glass project, offering to further the plan if Henry was interested—and enjoining him to secrecy. Henry was interested; he was dissatisfied at the Vermont Glass Works, in part because the proprietors were behind in his $1,000 a year salary. Also, flint glass and its production, not window glass, were currently objects of his devoted research. In January 1815, after some correspondence with Timothy Twitchell, he went to Keene to meet with his prospective partners. A partnership was formed, doubtless with Daniel Watson putting up most of the needed capital. Many pertinent

matters were settled, including the type of glasshouse for which Henry Schoolcraft left a sketch when he returned to Vermont. From then on, the project moved with deliberate speed toward completion of the glassworks, which today is generally called the Keene-Marlboro-Street Glassworks, but during its first few years of existence was called the Flint Glass Factory, and known also as the South Glass-House. Apparently the buildings were completed by the late summer of 1815 and in operation by November. The glasshouse was an octagonal wooden structure, 42 feet at the base and rising 53 feet in cone formation, terminating in a spacious ventilator for the escape of smoke and other "gaseous bodies" from the brick seven-pot furnace within. Wings provided rooms for activities other than the actual fabrication of glass, such as pot making and batch mixing. In addition, there were "works" for cutting and polishing all kinds of glass. Also, according to an 1816 advertise-ment, there was a warehouse that served, too, as sales headquarters.[82]

Early in the spring of 1815, between March and mid-April, Henry Schoolcraft severed all connection with the Vermont Glass Works and went to Keene. It must have been between this event and the first blast in the new glasshouse that he made what may have been a momentous journey. According to his manuscript autobiography (writ-ten in the third person), for which I am indebted to Kay Fox of Keene for excerpts:

He visited the most celebrated works of this kind, erected by foreign skill, at South Boston, Cambridgeport [Cambridge] and other places in New England. Either in search of the best examples of success or suitable materials to be employed, he passed through all New England where the manufacture had been attempted, and crossing the Hudson River, at Rhinebeck, ascended the Catskill Mountains.

At South Boston he must have met and consulted Thomas Cains, who had persuaded the proprietors to let him build a furnace for the production of flint glass, whereby Cains became the father of lead-glass production in the eastern United States. Undoubtedly Schoolcraft visited the Bos-ton Porcelain and Glass Manufactory in Cambridge; in Connecticut, the bottle manufactories of the Pitkins, Thomas Mather, and the Coventry Glass Company; and in New York, possibly the window-glass houses of the Woodstock Glass Manufacturing Company and the Ulster Glass Factory, and surely the Hamilton Glass Factory near Albany, where he had first acquired knowledge of glass from his father when Lawrence was the superinten-dent. In fact, in October 1815, he was in Albany to buy cullet, doubtless from the glassworks if possible. Though he made no mention of seeking to lure competent glassmen away from their employers, or to jump contracts, for em-ployment by Twitchell & Schoolcraft, it seems axiomatic that such enticement was one of Schoolcraft's aims on that tour of the glassworks. At any rate, from somewhere, 16 workmen were secured with whom to begin glassmaking in November. Still, the ever-present need for skilled blowers is evident from a futile attempt to import German glassblowers.[83]

On August 10, 1815, about three months before the first glass was produced, a notice was published announcing the dissolution of the copartnership of Daniel Watson, Timothy Twitchell, and Henry R. Schoolcraft. At the same time the copartnership of Twitchell & Schoolcraft was announced. Among the conditions retroactive to February 1, 1815, was the stipulation that the partners were to share equally all expenses and any profits, and neither was to engage in any other occupation without the consent of his partner. Schoolcraft was to have charge of all work within the glasshouse, which included, of course, the composition and melting of flint and other glasses. Twitchell was to keep the books and be the firm's agent. In fact, he was to have charge of all "out door business," including purchase of materials. Their first (brief) advertisement was as follows:

GLASS
The public are informed that the Glass Ware Manufactory, which has been erected by the subscribers in this town is now in operation where they will constantly manufacture and make for Sale Flint Glass Tumblers and Decanters, and such other discriptions of Glass Ware as are generally manufactured at similar works.
Keene, Nov. 29, 1815
TWITCHELL & SCHOOLCRAFT.

The glass must have been of superior quality if Schoolcraft's description of it was anywhere near reality. In his manuscript autobiography he said of his "crystal": "The ware is in every respect perfect, clear, heavy, pure, limpid."[84] One could ask no more even of the finest English flint glass.

Nevertheless, business was not brisk. Customers did not flock to Twitchell & Schoolcraft's warehouse. Nor did orders flow in. And "foreign" orders were essential to success—a village of roughly 1,600 could hardly support a glassworks. By mid-January 1816, an attempt to increase sales was made by removing "their warehouse from their glass manufactory, to the *red House* [a store] one door north of SHIRTFELT'S Tavern." Wholesale and retail, their glassware was offered at very reduced prices, and then a liberal discount would be made on wholesale purchases. Also, in lieu of cash, most kinds of produce would be taken in payment. Still, sales continued to be poor and debts increased. By March 1816, Timothy Twitchell had had enough of glassmaking. In a notice dated March 30, 1816, Twitchell & Schoolcraft announced the dissolution of their copartnership. On the same day Henry R. Schoolcraft and Nathaniel Sprague, a bachelor of 26 and former agent for the New Hampshire Glass Works, announced they had formed a copartnership and had assumed the debts of the old firm. Also, they were to receive any monies owed to Twitchell & Schoolcraft.[85]

The fate of the new partnership was no rosier than that of the previous one, in large part because of the deadly influx of English flint glassware immediately following the war's end in December 1815. Nevertheless, Schoolcraft & Sprague optimistically continued efforts to root their flint-glass production. But that to do so was hopeless is implicit in the lack of demand—a discouraging state revealed, for instance, by a July 1816 letter they received from a Boston firm: "We cannot at present recommend your sending any glass here, as our market is completely overstocked with all kinds of glass & crockery ware, which makes it very low and dull sale." The month before this bad news arrived, Schoolcraft & Sprague had been given heartening encouragement by the state legislature, when it exempted the Flint Glass Factory from taxes for five years and exempted all workmen from military duty so long as they were actually working at the glass factory. The smallness of the works and its work force is apparent from the list in the Act of Exemption; besides the blowers, one master stoker, two common stokers (a glass furnace devoured wood voraciously), two wood dryers, one calciner, and one pot maker. In spite of their money and production problems, in October 1816 Schoolcraft & Sprague were advertising for apprentices—two or three 14-year-olds were wanted to learn the art of flint-glass blowing. Whether or not they conducted business at the Red House store, I have not learned. Probably they did not. At least, the only one advertising ware from the flint factory seems to have been Dan Hough (said by Van Rensselaer to have been an apothecary) who, in December 1816, added to his usual stock a large assortment of Schoolcraft & Sprague's flint glassware consisting of "Tumblers, Wines, Decanters, Pitchers, &c." Stating that the prices were lower than those on imported glass, he offered their glass wholesale and retail.[86]

Early in 1817, Schoolcraft & Sprague were forced by lack of funds and credit to admit to the failure of their project. Their indebtedness had mounted beyond even their optimistic hopes of ever meeting it. A large portion of their obligations was to Henry's father Lawrence and the prosperous Keene merchant Justus Perry. In December 1816, they had mortgaged their property to Perry for $300. That in January 1817 they still believed the business could be salvaged is indicated by their also pledging the property for $600 to Lawrence Schoolcraft, who, incidentally, had returned to Vernon after his two-year contract with the New Hampshire Glass Company expired. The $600 transfusion was not enough, and on February 3, 1817, Schoolcraft & Sprague published the notice that their copartnership had been dissolved by mutual consent. Sprague turned to teaching and later became an Episcopal minister. Schoolcraft went to the family home in Vernon, New York, and a few months afterward declared himself a bankrupt. His glass adventure had met an ignominious end, but a long, interesting, and noteworthy career lay ahead of him. He went west, and in 1820 the United States government appointed him geologist to an expedition in the Lake Superior Country. Three years later he was made Indian agent for that area, and—as is well known—he became an authority on the language and customs of the native Indians, one of whom he married.[87]

Evidently finding it impossible to collect the $300 owed him, Justus Perry foreclosed the mortgage on the glassworks and, having no need to worry himself about the depression, decided that glass manufacture would be another good egg in his business basket. Being a canny Yankee merchant and reading the glass signs of the times, he seems to have decided to concentrate on bottles, not flint-glass tableware. Consequently it was not surprising to find him advertising, about two weeks after Schoolcraft & Sprague dissolved, in the Hartford *Connecticut Courant* for "three first rate glass blowers for bottle work." (See Ill. 118.) Undoubtedly he chose the Hartford paper because, among those likely to read it, there would be glassblowers employed in the bottle glassworks in East Hartford, Coventry, West Willington, and Glastenbury, Connecticut. The decision to be a bottle producer is further borne out by his second advertisement appearing March 19, 1817, in the *New Hampshire Sentinel* announcing a "Complete assortment of GLASS BOTTLES" at wholesale at the Flint Glass Factory. No retail sales were made at the factory, and although the bottles were sold locally at Perry's store, the few advertisements over the next two years were aimed at a wholesale customer for various kinds of bottles. Further evidence of the change from flint glass to green glass, except possibly for special orders, is the statement in an editorial in the *New Hampshire Gazeteer,* reprinted in the *New Hampshire Sentinel* of August 23, 1817, stating that the Flint Glass Manufactory "is not now in operation except for the manufacture of bottles of various kinds." Moreover, Perry's 1818 advertisement for "800 bushels of ASHES of an extra quality made of hard wood" and later ones for house ashes suggest that the metal from which bottles and flasks were regularly blown was not of the first quality of green glass. All this, incidentally, casts doubt on the longtime attribution of colorless flint-glass decanters and other articles in the blown-three-mold geometric Sunburst patterns GIII–16 and GIII–19 to the Keene-Marlboro-Street Glassworks—unless, contrary to present dating, these sunburst patterns evolved as early as 1815–17. But that is another problem and does not involve the bottle-glass decanters in those patterns of which Harry Hall White found fragments in quantity on the factory site. Bottles probably could not have made a fortune for Perry during the depression years, but neither did they cause him to fail. His report in the 1820 census stated that the condition of the factory was "good" and it was "doing well." His capital he estimated to be $15,000 and the worth of the yearly production, $30,000.[88]

From 1822 until September 1835, when he retired from active participation in the operation of the glassworks, Perry had one or more members of his family in business with him. First, on September 14, 1822, taking his brother-in-law John V. Wood into the business, he formed the firm of Perry & Wood. Four years later, also in September, the firm was dissolved and Wood, having bought an interest in the window-glass factory, entered into the firm of Holman & Wood. At the same time Perry took his half-brother Sumner Wheeler into partnership, and formed Perry & Wheeler. Thus the pint and half-pint Sunburst flasks, GVIII–8, 9, and 10, initialed "P&W" could have been, and undoubtedly were, made by both Perry & Wood and Perry & Wheeler. Perhaps most of these flasks were blown between 1822 and 1830, though, of course, the molds might have been used after 1830, when the 21-year-old younger half-brother Quincy Wheeler was taken into partnership and the firm became Perry, Wheeler & Company.[89] This company's 1832 report to the federal government reveals that the work force had more than doubled in the 12 years since the 1820 report, but that the value of the glass produced was only a little over half the 1820 amount. In 1832, in other words, 30 men, 8 boys, and 6 women and girls produced $16,000 worth of glass, whereas in 1820 just 16 men, 4 boys, and 2 girls had produced $30,000 worth. Perhaps in 1831/32 Perry was reporting an off year. In any event, either the profits from prior years were sufficient to finance an expansion of the works or Perry put up more capital, for a new stone glasshouse was built in 1829. If the specifications given in Perry's 1828 advertisement for materials, as well as for erecting the building, were followed, the new factory was considerably larger than the old one and of different form: it was to be 100 feet long, 50 feet wide, and 16 feet high, with walls 2½ feet thick.[90]

In September 1835 the *New Hampshire Sentinel* carried the notice of the dissolution of Perry, Wheeler & Company. Sumner and Quincy Wheeler, as S. and Q. Wheeler, continued to operate the glassworks and run the store, in both of which Perry and other members of the family seem to have had an interest. In a very few years the firm was to suffer from the depression of the late 1830s, the sudden death of Quincy Wheeler in 1839, and—so a local historian asserted—from the Temperance movement's having drawn so many converts as to have an adverse effect on the bottle business. Perhaps it did locally; at least, Kay Fox found that by March of 1842 more than half of Keene's small population had taken the pledge. Be that as it may, by 1841 the businesses, especially the glassworks, were in great difficulty. Still, Joseph Foster, an English glassman who had been a master blower at the Keene-Marlboro-Street Glassworks for many years, believed it could be operated profitably. He formed a company for the purpose. However, Foster, like Henry Schoolcraft, was overconfident; the venture failed.

A notice in the *New Hampshire Sentinel* found by Carl Flowers indicates that Sumner Wheeler & Company also tried to resuscitate the glassworks. On June 15, 1848, a notice published of the dissolution of the copartnership of Sumner Wheeler and Almond Woods was followed by the statement: "The glass business will be continued as usual by Sumner Wheeler." But he was unsuccessful, and the works closed permanently about 1850.[91]

It would appear that under Henry Schoolcraft's management during the first year and a quarter of the Flint Glass Factory's existence, flint-glass tableware was the principal product. Decanters, wines, tumblers, and pitchers were the only articles specifically mentioned in advertisements, but "such other descriptions of Glass Ware as are generally manufactured at similar works" could be had for the ordering.[92] These, of course, do not concern us here, but the Figured Flasks—unfortunately not advertised as such—do. There can be no doubt that some of the heavy Masonic Flasks, GIV–1 through 14, which really are not pocket flasks but decanter flasks, were produced by Twitchell & Schoolcraft and Schoolcraft & Sprague, and probably in the first months of Justus Perry's operation of the works. Fragments of the type were unearthed on the factory site by Harry Hall White. Flask GIV–2 has the initials "HS", those of Henry Schoolcraft, and examples tested for lead content have proved to be blown from lead glass. Flask GIV–1 has the initials "I" and "P" joined by a bar in the center, for Justus Perry. It was the only one in the series to be rated as common and occurring in a wide range of colors when George S. McKearin compiled the Flasks Charts in 1941, two factors that would indicate a not inconsiderable production. These two flasks were blown in the same mold, first the "HS" flasks, then the "IP" for which the "HS" mold had been altered by filling in the "S" and forming a "P" by a loop to the right upright of the "H." Thus, the left upright of the "H" became an "I" (still used in the 19th century for "J") joined by a bar to the "P." This not unusual altering of a mold was suggested by Dr. Julian Toulouse and confirmed by Kenneth M. Wilson's comparative studies. Mr. Wilson found also that a second alteration occurred whereby the connecting bar was removed, leaving the two letters separated. As yet I know of only one flask, that in the collection of The Corning Museum of Glass, from the mold after the second alteration.

It should be expected that if Figured Flasks were to be blown at the Flint Glass Factory, there would be Masonic flasks among them. Henry Schoolcraft had become a Mason in 1814 while at the Vermont Glass Works; Justus Perry undoubtedly was one and probably participated in forming Keene's Royal Arch Chapter in 1816. In fact, any man of any account in New England was a Mason, so strong was the fraternity in society, business, and politics. It was natural too that closely similar flasks lacking an identifying mark or association with another glassworks were attributed by analogy to Keene. Thus collectors and students have accepted the attribution of the Masonic flasks GIV–1 through 14—that is, from 20 molds—to the Keene-Marlboro-Street Glassworks and of several others as possibly or probably Keene. Here I have parted company with the past, and in many instances have changed the old notations in the Charts under "Glass House" to New England. My main reason is that I believe there were altogether too many molds for a glassworks as small as the Flint Glass Factory, or for its size when operated by Justus Perry and the later firms. Also, it seems unreasonable that no other works produced so popular an item. Three or four molds in each size might possibly be needed by Perry, but surely neither he nor his predecessors needed 20. Most of

the flasks tested have shown a substantial lead content.

This raises, of course, the question of where these flasks, some of them blown from lead metal, were produced if not at Keene. I have no certain answers, only conjectures. One possibility—probability, I believe—is the Mount Vernon Glass Works, Vernon, New York, on the site of which Harry Hall White found fragments of the Sunburst GVIII–1, as he did also at Keene. (One wonders whether Henry Schoolcraft took the Sunburst mold with him when he returned to Vernon in 1817.) Two other strong probabilities are the South Boston Flint Glass Works and the New England Glass Company. Both advertised flasks and offered them on their price lists—unhappily, without describing them. All this leads to a pet and, at this point, untested theory. It will be remembered that before glassblowing started at the Flint Glass Factory, Henry Schoolcraft visited the South Boston Glass Works. I believe it is probable that among the articles introduced and produced by Thomas Cains, Schoolcraft found some of these heavy decanter-flask Masonics and also Sunbursts. I believe, too, it is probable that while in Boston he ordered the "HS" mold from the moldmaker who supplied Thomas Cains and also one for the Sunburst GVIII–1. Other works in which the heavy Masonics may have been blown, *if* their popularity was such it lasted into the 1820s, are Thomas Cains's own Phoenix Glass Works (ca. 1820–70) and the New-England Glass-Bottle Works.

As previously mentioned, it seems likely that Justus Perry made flint-glass Masonic flasks with his initials, perhaps on special order, in the early months of operating the Flint Glass Factory. But there is no doubt that his regular output was blown from ordinary bottle-glass. And the factory soon became known as the Bottle Factory. In only two of the advertisements found, one in May 1820 and the other in February 1831, was there mention of the kinds of bottles. In 1820, fluted flasks, blacking and snuff bottles, and inkstands were offered as well as "bottles"; in 1831, "Almost all kinds, shapes and sizes of *black* and *light green* bottles from *4 ounces* to *10 gallons.*"[93] (The italics are mine.) Possibly the fluted flasks were what today are called ribbed Pitkin-type, of which Harry Hall White found a convincing number of fragments. When Quincy Wheeler died intestate in 1839, an inventory of all property had to be made; according to the list sent to me by Kay Fox, the following were on hand:

Flasks, pint	82,800
half-pint	76,600
Junk bottles	3,168
Bottles, pint	3,168
half-pint	23,328
8 ounces	30,240
6 ounces	30,525
4 ounces	14,688
Snuff bottles	
½ pound	19,320
Blacking bottles, sq.	21,000

Ink Stands No. 1	10,080
No. 2	12,240
Mustards, green	
½ pound	3,312
Mustards, fancy green	3,168
—possibly GVIII–19?	
Bottles, 2 gallon	192
1 gallon	240
half gallon	432
quart	300
pint	480
Demijohns 2 gallon	1,500
1 gallon	13,010
half gallon	9,900
Jars, quart	600
Phials opedelin[sic]	5,760
8 ounces	864
6 ounces	6,480
4 ounces	7,632
2 ounces	4,032
1 ounces	2,448

Again Figured Flasks were not mentioned. However, there were marked Masonics and Sunbursts blown from green glass during the Perry regimes, and Harry Hall White's excavations also established a few unmarked flasks—a Washington–Jackson, Eagle–Cornucopia, Cornucopia–Urn, and two Railroads—as Keene products. The list below includes only those Figured Flasks still definitely attributed to the Keene-Marlboro-Street Glassworks. They are given in the order in which they were originally charted, not chronologically.

GI–31. "WASHINGTON" in arc above profile bust of Andrew Jackson in uniform. *Reverse*: "JACKSON" above profile bust of Andrew Jackson in uniform. Pint. Colors: amber, light and dark olive-amber; light and dark olive-green. Usually assigned to the 1824–28 period, but the researches and conclusions of Carl Flowers, Jr., historian and collector of Keene glass, have established to my satisfaction that 1832, the centennial of Washington's birth, was the probable occasion prompting production of GI–31. (See Part VIII, 4C, Adams and Jackson.)

GII–73. American Eagle–Cornucopia, tilted "X" at left. Pint. Colors: dark amber, golden amber, olive-amber; deep green, dark olive-green, yellow-green. ca. 1824.

GIII–7. Cornucopia–Urn. Half-pint. Colors: amber, golden amber, olive-amber; aquamarine; black (dark olive-green); clear green, light green, blue-green, light emerald-green, deep olive-green, deep yellow-green. ca. 1824.

GIV–1. Masonic decoration. *Reverse*: "E PLURIBUS UNUM" on ribbon above American Eagle, "IP" in beaded oval frame below eagle. Heavy decanter-flask. Pint. Colors: amethyst, pale amethystine; black (deep amethyst); pale blue, grayish blue, sapphire-blue, violet-blue; colorless; green, green of yellow tone, deep bluish green, light yellow-green; moonstone. If the "HS" mold was altered to "IP" with a bar by Schoolcraft & Sprague, to supply Justus Perry with flasks bearing his initials, the first might have been blown in 1816; but if Justus Perry himself had the change made, the first would be in 1817, probably soon after he took over in February of that year.

GIV–1a. Like GIV–1 but crossbar connecting "I" and "P" removed. Pint. Colors: clear green. ca. 1817–18?

GIV–2. Like GIV–1 but initials "HS" in frame. Pint. Colors: black (dark olive-amber); pale green, light green, deep green, emerald-green, olive-green. Late 1815.

GIV–17. Masonic Emblems. *Reverse*: "KEENE" in oval frame below American Eagle. Pint. Colors: amber, golden amber, olive-amber; aquamarine; pale green, olive-green, yellowish olive-green. 1820s.

GIV–18. Similar to GIV–17, but the "KEENE" in oval frame has no center crossbar on the three E's. Pint. Colors: amber, golden amber, olive-amber; dark olive-green. Probably 1820s.

GIV–19. Similar to GIV–18 but without trowel, skull, and beehive on obverse. Pint. Colors: amber, olive-amber; olive-green. Probably 1820s.

GIV–20. Like GIV–19 but 2 dots equidistant between sun and crossbones on obverse. Pint. Colors: amber, olive-amber, yellowish olive-amber. Probably 1820s.

GIV–24. Masonic emblems—American Eagle. Half-pint. Colors: golden amber, amber, olive-amber; aquamarine; black (dark olive-green); deep olive-green. Probably 1820s.

GV–3. "SUCCESS TO THE RAILROAD" in horseshoe arch over horse and cart on rail lengthwise. Pint. Colors: amber, golden amber, olive-amber; aquamarine; dark olive-green. ca. 1830.

GV–4. Similar to GV–3. Slight differences include lack of mane on horse. Pint. Colors: olive-amber; aquamarine; green, olive-green. Kay Fox suggested that plans for a Boston to Brattleboro railroad, with possibly a branch through Keene and Walpole, may have inspired these railroad flasks around 1830. Justus Perry was said to have been interested in the project, which was "the absorbing question of the time for the people of Keene and vicinity." The road did not materialize, and Keene had no railroad until 1848.

GVIII–1. Sunbursts each side. Heavy decanter-flask. Pint. Colors: colorless; light, medium, and deep green, deep bluish green, deep yellow-green, green shading to amber; moonstone. Late 1815.

GVIII–8. Sunburst each side; "KEEN" on oval center on

one side; "P&W" on other. Pint. Colors: golden amber, olive amber; dark olive-green. ca. 1822–30.

GVIII–9. Similar to GVIII–8 but "KEEN" goes from top to bottom of oval center. Half-pint. Colors: deep brilliant amber; aquamarine; pale green, dark olive-green. ca. 1822–30.

GVIII–10. Sunbursts and edges similar to GVIII–9 but shoulders square. Half-pint. Colors: brilliant amber, olive-amber; green tint, olive-green.

27. THE NEW ENGLAND GLASS COMPANY (1818–88) and NEW-ENGLAND GLASS-BOTTLE COMPANY (1827–45), *Cambridge, Massachusetts*

Early in 1818 the New England Glass Company was incorporated by a group of men that included Deming Jarves, who was the company's agent until he left in 1825 to found the Boston & Sandwich Glass Works. The previous November the group had bought the works built in 1814 on Lechemere Point, Cambridge, by the ill-fated Boston Porcelain & Glass Manufacturing Company. In a short time they had enlarged the plant and, before 1820, added a glass-cutting department. In fact, this works, the second successful flint-glass manufactory in the East, was shortly to be—and would remain—renowned for the high quality of its fine table and ornamental wares. The first real check to its prosperity came shortly after 1864, when William Leighton's experiments at the works of Hobbs, Brockunier & Company, Wheeling, West Virginia, resulted in a new formula for lime glass, cheaper to manufacture than lead glass but having nearly the same brilliance. To effect savings and meet competition, many glassworks quickly switched to the new glass. The New England Glass Company, however, did not lower its standards and cheapen its glassware. Its last 20 years were progressively troubled ones. Among the directors' problems were rising production costs and competition from the lime-glass products, especially from the Midwest.

In 1878, William L. Libbey, who had been agent for six years, leased the works but operated only one of the four furnaces. When William died in 1883, his son Edward D. Libbey, who had joined him in 1880, continued the business in spite of unsettling conditions, financial handicaps, and a plague of blowers' strikes. Libbey finally warned that if the fires had to be drawn again, they would never be relit. Nevertheless, another strike was called. And, in 1888, Mr. Libbey shut down the works and moved the business to Toledo, Ohio.[94]

Although the principal product of the New England Glass Company was fine glassware, it produced also a complete line of apothecaries' and chemical wares at least through the 1820s. Naturally, among the articles for druggists were the usual patent-medicine vials—British Oil, Peppermint, Turlington's, opodeldoc, Bateman's, and Godfrey's. And, during the first two decades of its existence, flasks were blown. The earliest evidence pertaining to flasks is an 1819 auction notice in which four packages of

"prest pocket bottles" were listed. (Since mechanical pressing had not yet been invented, *prest* in this instance doubtless meant blown-molded in a design.) The following year, nine packages of pint and half-pint "green" (presumably meaning the kind of metal, not the color) "Pocket Flasks" were advertised. In May 1829 the company sold to W. E. Mayhew in Baltimore many dozen black and green oval pint flasks,[95] which, it seems probable, were blown for it by the New-England Glass-Bottle Company. At least it is believed that, after the glass bottle company went into production in January 1827, the New England Glass Company had its orders for flasks, certainly ordinary flasks, filled by the new company. Beyond the probability that the 1819 flasks were blown-molded in a design, the brief items furnish no clue as to the category in which to place the flasks. In this instance "prest" might have been pattern-molded, blown-three-mold, or figured. The possibility of unmarked heavy Masonics, Sunbursts, and Concentric Ring Eagles (GII–76 and 76a) being blown at the New England Glass Company has already been mentioned. Two marked Masonic flasks are considered sufficient testimony to the fact that they were products of the New England Glass Company:

GIV–26. Masonic Emblems—American Eagle, "N.E.G." in oval frame. Half-pint.

GIV–27. Masonic Emblems—American Eagle, "NEG/C⁰" in oval frame. Pint.

Two others with initials are attributed to the New England Glass Company:

GII–77. Concentric Ring Eagle; eagle medallion— "N.G/C⁰" medallion in oval frame. Pint, plus.

GIV–15. Masonic Emblems—American Eagle, "N.G.C⁰" in oval frame. Pint.

Though it was an important source of black- and green-glass bottles of every description for about 19 years, known facts about the New-England Glass-Bottle Company and its operation are comparatively few. The company was incorporated, so Lura Woodside Watkins wrote, on February 15, 1826, "for the purpose of manufacturing black and green glass wares in the City of Boston and town of Cambridge." The incorporators were Deming Jarves and Edmund Monroe. Deming Jarves, it will be recalled, was one of the founders of the New England Glass Company and its agent until he left the concern to establish his Sandwich glassworks in 1825. Edmund Monroe, a wealthy man with investments in several business adventures, was also one of the founders of the New England Glass Company. Incidentally, when Jarves decided to incorporate his Sandwich business, Monroe was one of the group incorporating the Boston and Sandwich Glass Company, an event that occurred late in February 1826. And it was Monroe who owned the land on which the New-England Glass-Bottle Company was built, land he sold to the com-

Prices Current of Ware,

MANUFACTURED BY THE NEW-ENGLAND GLASS-BOTTLE COMPANY.......BOSTON.

Item	Size	Price Per Groce.		Item	Size	Price Per Groce.		Item	Size	Price Each.	
Porter Bottles, 1st quality	1 qt.	8	50	Soda Bottles, ...	½ pint	6	75	Jars, ...	1 gall.		25
" " 2d "	1 qt.	7	50	Mead Bottles, ...	½ pint	6	50	"	2 "		38
Wine Bottles, 1st "	1 qt.	8	50	Flask Bottles, ...	½ pint	6		"	3 "		45
" " 2d "	1 qt.	7	50	" "	1 pint	7	25	Bottles, Wickered, ...	1 qt.		20
Porter Bottles, 1st "	1 pint	7	50	" "	1 qt.	8	50	" "	2 qt.		30
" " 2d "	1 pint	7		Carboys,*	1 gall.		25 (Price each.)	" "	3 qt.		38
Wine Bottles, 1st "	1 pint	7	50	"	2 "		35	Demijohns, Wickered, ...	1 gall.		40
" " 2d "	1 pint	7		"	3 "		45	" "	2 "		60
Champagne Bottles, ...	1 qt.	10		"	4 "		56	" "	3 "		70
" "	1 pint	8		"	5 "		65	" "	4 "		75
Claret "	1 qt.	.9		"	6 "		75	" "	5 "		80
" "	1 pint	7	50	"	7 "		85	" "	6 "		90
Bottles, ...	full qt.	10		"	8 "		90	" "	7 "	1	
"	2 qt.	16		"	9 "		95	" "	8 "	1	10
Octagon Bottles, ...	½ pint	6		"	10 "	1		" "	9 "	1	20
" "	1 pint	8		"	11 "	1	10	" "	10 "	1	30
Blacking Bottles, ...	½ pint	6		"	12 "	1	20				
" "	1 pint	8		"	13 "	1	40				
Ink Bottles, ...	6&8 oz	6		"	14 "	1	50				
Mustard Bottles, ...	1 lb.	8		"	15 "	1	55				
" "	½ lb.	7		"	16 "	1	60				
Preserve Bottles, ...	1 pint	8		"	17 "	1	65				
" "	1 qt.	10		"	18 "	1	70				
" "	2 qt.	16		"	19 "	1	75				
Lavender Bottles, ...	1 pint	7	50	"	20 "	1	85				
Specie Bottles, ...	2 qt.	17		Bolt Heads, ...	1 "		35				
" "	1 qt.	10		Acid Bottles, ground stopped, ..	1 qt.		13				
Fruit Squares, ...	2 qt.	18		" " " "	2 qt.		20				
" "	1 qt.	11		" " " "	1 gall.		33				
Snuff Squares, ...	1 lb.	9		" " " "	2 "		50				
" "	½ lb.	7	50	" " " "	3 "		60				

* Now used almost exclusively by the manufacturing chemists in Massachusetts, and said by them to be superior to those of foreign manufacture. An extra charge of 25 cents is made for packing in tubs for use on all sizes under 10 gallons; for 10 gallons and over, 40 cents.

THE NEW-ENGLAND GLASS-BOTTLE COMPANY manufacture every description of Black and Green Ware, of a quality not excelled. All the above variety constantly on hand, to which continual additions are making.—Any articles usually manufactured at similar establishments are made to order, with all possible despatch.—Orders, (which may be sent to the Manufactory, East Cambridge, left at the Post Office, Boston, or at E. Munroe's, 57 State Street, where the agent may be seen daily, from 10 to 12 o'clock, A. M.) are respectfully solicited, and will meet with prompt attention.

Selling Agent in Boston, A. T. HALL, No. 99 Milk Street.

Boston, November 1, 1829.

RALPH SMITH, } Agent for the New-England Glass-Bottle Company, Boston.

12. New-England Glass-Bottle Company's prices current, November 1829. *Charles B. Gardner Collection, Wheaton Historical Village, Millville, N.J.*

pany for $4,350 on December 28, 1826.[96]

The glassworks went into production in January 1827 and apparently was a profitable venture up to the time of closing—for unknown reasons—in May 1845, when the original property was deeded to L. P. Grosvenor for $1,700. At the time, the president was Andrew T. Hall, one of the incorporators of the Boston and Sandwich Glass Company and one-time treasurer of the New England Glass Company.

Reports by the company to the New York City convention of the Friends of Domestic Industry in 1831 and to the United States government in 1832 provide information about the state of the works, the materials used, and the employees in those years. The capitalization was $50,000. The furnaces were fired with coal from Virginia. Ingredients for the glass appear to have been "wood ashes from families," "leached barilla from soap factories," marine salt, lime, and "sand from the seashore." One ton of iron a year was used, presumably for making glassmakers' tools and also molds. At least an excerpt from a bill of lading for nine hampers of glass bottles to Seth Low of New York City, sent to me by Kenneth M. Wilson, would seem to indicate the probable existence of a mold department: lemon syrup bottles were delayed "owing to a delay in the completion of the mould." Seth Low, by the way, apparently was the New York City agent of the company. The staff was not a very large one: an average of 40 men, 12 boys under 16 years of age, and 11 women and girls. Their total wages were around $20,000 a year. The annual production was estimated at 6,000 gross—864,000 bottles. A third of the output was sold in Massachusetts; two-thirds in Maine, Rhode Island, New York, Maryland, Virginia, Ohio, Kentucky, and Louisiana—a surprising number of states; and a few bottles in the West Indies.[97]

From the 1829 Prices Current, Ill. 12, and a few advertisements by the company's agents, we learn the kinds of bottles made at the New-England Glass-Bottle Company and the claims made for them. The earliest of the advertisements, one by Deming Jarves, the company's agent during the first year, offered "BLACK BOTTLES, &c. 50 groce *heavy* Porter Bottles, 100 do Wine Bottles, 50 do Pint Bottles, 20 do Oil Bottles, 160 do half-pint and pint Pocket Bottles" at factory prices, and stated that "*any article in the Black Glass line will be made to pattern . . . on favorable terms.*" (The italics are mine.) It is interesting to note that more of the pocket bottles were offered than of any other article. In the fall of 1827 William Muzzey, the Philadelphia agent for the new bottle manufactory and also agent of the New England Glass Company, advertised "heavy Porter and Wine Bottles, quarts and pints, Acid Bottles, Carboys, Flasks, Snuffs, Vials etc. etc." The heavy porter and wine bottles may have been like bottle 8 in Ill. 45, which has a depressed base and outer rim inscribed "NEW ENG. GLASS BOTTLE CO."—and may have been one of the first American-made bottles to be inscribed on the base, as were the patent English Bristol bottles of Henry Ricketts (see Ill. 54). In December 1827, the company's Hartford agent, Peter Morton, claimed the

junk and wine bottles of all kinds were "better than any foreign Bottles" and that the New-England Glass-Bottle Company's glass was of a quality "superior to any other black and green glass made in this Country." Early in 1829 Ralph Smith, who followed Jarves as agent, said that "all the variety of Black and Green Glass Ware, usually made at similar establishments and of a quality highly improved," was being manufactured.[98]

From a "Notice" by Thomas G. Fessenden in the *New England Farmer and Horticulture Journal,* 1831, sent to me by Kenneth M. Wilson, it would appear that strength was one feature of the improvement in the ware and its superiority to that of other glassworks. Mr. Fessenden wrote as follows:

This company went into operation in January 1827 . . . and the manufacture of glass bottles of every description has since been very successfully prosecuted . . . [it is] now manufacturing one hundred and fifty groce of bottles [21,600] per week, which far exceeds the amount made in the same time by any other factory in Europe or America. A hydraulic press for testing the strength of the bottles, has been obtained, which operates with perfect equality on every species of bottles submitted to its operation. A table is given of the comparative strength of English, Bristol and American, Boston [New-England Glass-Bottle Company] porter bottles, by which it is shown that the latter are altogether superior to the former. The same results were elicited in regard to the comparative strength of French claret and champagne bottles, and those for the same purpose of American manufacture. Let those concerned patronize the American product.

Unfortunately, with the exception of the marked bottle, 8 in Ill. 45, the products of this important bottle manufactory cannot be identified today. It seems logical to conclude that Figured Flasks were among the half-pint and pint "Pocket Bottles" and half-pint, pint, and quart flasks. Too, it seems logical to conclude that after January 1827 the New England Glass Company would have the flasks to fill its orders blown for it at the New-England Glass-Bottle Company. But there is no proof of either proposition.

28. JOHN MATHER'S GLASSWORKS, *East Hartford, Orford Parish, Connecticut, 1805 –ca. 1820, ca. 1830?*

For nearly half a century, to students of American glass, John Mather's glassworks has been no more than a statistic in the history of our glass industry. A local history of Hartford County, one followed by 20th-century students, stated simply that this Connecticut glassworks was a unit of a small settlement, Parker Village, created by John Mather in 1808. No individual pieces have ever been attributed to it, insofar as I know, as they have been to the contemporary Connecticut glassworks. No bottles or flasks have ever been identified with it. Yet, for at least a decade and a half, if not longer, this glassworks was an important source of bottles and flasks, a rival of the nearby Pitkin Glassworks and, later, the Coventry and the Willington Glass Works.

Though John Mather, his works, and his glass bottles are still obscure, they now have enough substance to cast a shadow. Evidence of his business activities in the Hartford area first came to my attention through his advertisements as a merchant from 1802 to 1804 and, in 1805, as owner of a "New Glass House." Apparently his general store in Hartford, conveniently located near the state's pulsing artery of trade, the Connecticut River, was well stocked not only with domestic goods but also with imports from out-of-state and overseas. He offered the usual items, such as molasses, wines, spirits, teas, spices, fruit, and tobacco, window glass (probably from the Boston Glass Manufactory), and ironware, crockery, and the more sophisticated Davenport earthenware from Liverpool, England; likewise unusual items such as reed poles from South Carolina "on terms pleasing to reed-makers." Also, as witnessed by eight hogsheads of brown sugar, products were taken on consignment. Gunpowder, too, was received from and delivered to vessels and boats on the river and, when desired, stored "at a third less than at the magazines," with a discount on large quantities. This last product was soon to be manufactured by John Mather himself.[99] All in all, it would appear that he was a prosperous Connecticut Yankee.

As did many of his Yankee competitors of that era, John Mather built on a general-store foundation, diversifying his business interests fairly rapidly.[100] In East Hartford, by purchase and lease, he acquired land that he developed into a small settlement around various mills and manufactories. This adventure apparently began in 1803. At least, his purchase on May 19, 1803, of "one piece of land with dwelling thereon" north of the "Paper Mill Road" is the first of which I have found record. The next acquisition was a 999-year lease at $5 annual rent. Although it appears this lease, granted by Nathaniel Hammond of Bolton, Connecticut, was not drawn until August 1803, and not recorded until November 14, the phrase "works belonging thereto which said Mather is now building" must indicate that his arrangements with Hammond were made and work started prior to August, possibly about the time of his May 19 purchase. Also granted to Mather was "the privilege of constructing a mill dam of any height across the Brook [running] through said land" and "as many mills, manufactories and stores of any kind" as his project necessitated or, as a similar lease from Jason Hammond, recorded March 24, 1804, stipulated, "as may be necessary for improving to profit and advantage, said mill seat. . . ." In addition, gravel could be taken, free of charge, from any part of the land for use in constructing the dam and buildings. Also, wood could be cut at the "price of fire-wood standing." Over some 15 years, the settlement spread northward from the Paper Mill Road as abutting lots of land were acquired by John Mather alone and in partnership with his brother Charles.[101]

And, of course, manufactories and dwellings multiplied too. How many of the mills and factories John Mather may have operated as sole proprietor or in partnerships, I do not know at this time. However, indentures and newspaper advertisements point to powder mills and the glassworks as two of his principal concerns. Ours, naturally, is the latter, and finding contemporary evidence of its existence was as exciting as a gold strike could be. The first evidence was the following advertisement:

WANTED to contract for the Cutting and splitting 750 cords of Wood to be done within 4 months. Apply to the New Glass House.

Also wanted 1000 bushels Wood-ASHES for which Cash will be paid.
East-Hartford, Aug. 16 1805[102]

In the light of local history, there could be little doubt the new glasshouse was John Mather's—the *old* one would be the Pitkins' (see No. 13. Pitkin Glassworks, East Hartford). Obviously the new glasshouse was in operation by the summer of 1805—not 1808, as has been recorded—though the advertisement gives no enlightenment as to just when it was built, its size or type of construction, or the exact date of the first melt. But the amount of wood to be processed would seem to indicate that, as one would expect, the furnaces were wood-burning. And the amount of wood ashes points to production of ordinary green or bottle glass.

Although it is known from later advertisements that bottles and flasks were the product of Mather's glassworks, Mather had hoped to produce window glass as well. However, John Mather was a merchant-entrepreneur, not a practical glassmaker; his glassmen were not versed in the art of window-glass making, and, so he wrote, "the secret" of that art was "entirely confined in this country to the knowledge of a few persons in the States of New York and Massachusetts." Since these two—the Albany Glass Works (see No. 11. Dowesborough Glassworks . . .) and the Boston Glass Works (see No. 12. Boston Glass Manufactory)—were profitably filling a fair portion of the country's window-glass needs (at least in the Northeast), Mather figured that, at the very least, a manufactory in Connecticut would capture the state's market for that commodity. Therefore, possibly starting in 1805, he experimented to determine the proper materials for window-glass metal and methods of "mixing, melting and working the same." Such was the expense that, though he believed the experiments fully successful, he found his funds insufficient for the introduction of window-glass production. Consequently, on May 15, 1806, he petitioned the General Assembly at Hartford to lend him "on good security a sum from the State Treasury not exceeding six thousand dollars for a period not exceeding five years, or some other way grant him relief." The "Prayer of the foregoing Petition [was] not granted."[103] This apparently was the epitaph to Mather's window-glass dream, though as late as September he seems to have borrowed $1,600 from his brother Charles for some purpose.[104]

Perhaps the assembly's rejection of Mather's seemingly attractive and reasonable proposal was to his advantage. Had he enlarged his glassmaking facilities during the summer and early fall, his losses and ensuing expenses would have been far greater when his glassworks was "consumed by fire" on the last Sunday in October 1806.[105] Hardly were the ashes cool before clearing away debris and rebuilding began. In less than three months—by January 17, 1807—Mather could announce to former customers and the general public that the new glasshouse had been reestablished and glass bottles were being produced.[106]

In part, at least, the necessary funds may have been lent by Charles Mather, for, in return for $2,400, John gave as security about 39 acres of land purchased May 10, 1806, in addition to that leased from Nathaniel and Jason Hammond in 1803. Included also were the buildings thereon, among them a powder mill and blacksmith shop with its tools and implements[107] (in which, doubtless, the irons and other tools for the glasshouse were made and repaired). This loan, the fire loss, and rebuilding perhaps account for John's taking his brother Charles as partner in various of his enterprises. In any event, from November 1809 through 1811, possibly 1813, the glassworks was operated by John and Charles Mather; so too were powder mills and an East Hartford general store.[108]

As yet, comparatively few advertisements have been found mentioning his bottles or pertaining to his works. But one among them must be quoted in full as a significant bit of our glass industry history, a commentary digesting in 119 words one source not only of Mather's personal business worries and troubles but also that of most early 19th-century glass manufacturers. It illuminates a chronic handicap, the paucity of skilled experienced craftsmen, and the not uncommon *laissez faire* practices to overcome and to counteract it. The advertisement ran as follows:

FIFTY DOLLARS REWARD.

WHEREAS there has been of late, at sundry times, in a clandestine manner, some person or persons unknown to us, supposed to be employed by a company at Vernon, state of New-York, to entice away the Glass-Makers, belonging to these Works, by making such offers as they have no intention to perform; and do us such an injury that we should be obliged to stop our Manufacture so to enable them to establish theirs. We do hereby offer the above reward to be paid to any one, who will discover to us the person or persons, so that a process may be served in this state, whereby he or they may be brought to justice.

JOHN & THOMAS MATHER.

East-Hartford, Dec. 30th, 1809.[109]

The Vernon company suspected by the Mathers of attempted piracy must have been the Oneida Glass Company, which established the first glassworks in central New York, a window-glass house supervised by Lawrence Schoolcraft, who, at odds with the management at Hamilton, near Albany, left that works to join the Vernon group.[110]

The lack of facts about the alleged attempts to raid the Mather staff tantalizes. However, if the works suffered actual injury, it apparently was not a crippling one. Though present data is scattered thinly over the years after 1809 and peters out early in the 1820s, it nonetheless points to continued operation for some years. Even in the deepening depression year of 1818, it was recorded that in the two glassworks (those established by the Pitkins and Mather) in East Hartford "vast quantities of bottles" were produced and sent "to various parts of the country."[111] So far, I have found no positive evidence Mather operated his glassworks after 1817, though land records show his continued activity in the early 1820s and after East Hartford became Manchester in the spring of 1823. Also, although there is at present no way of determining whether they were from the Pitkin or the Mather glassworks or both, "East Hartford bottles," in large quantities, were advertised by Hartford merchants through the spring of 1821.[112] Possibly their nonappearance later means that both the Pitkin and the Mather glassworks had not been able to withstand the pressure of the depression. In any event, it strongly suggests that John Mather was not producing glass bottles of any kind.

Even more tantalizing are the very few Mather advertisements mentioning bottles from his or other glassworks. On January 15, 1806, he advertised 100 crates of glass bottles that must have been imports. At least he stated frankly that they were "of a quality superior to any made at these or any other works in this country, being made very thick, handsomely finished and of the best glass."[113] However, a year later, he claimed his own bottles were "of an improved quality superior in strength and beauty, to any before made in this country."[114] The next reference to bottles was not until 1815. Then, among the various wares available at his East Hartford store, were 50 crates of glass bottles, 300 gin cases (square bottles in cases), 300 demijohns, and a few gross of junk bottles. (The last quite likely were similar to the bottle illustrating the advertisement in Ill. 58B.) Whether all these were his own products or imports, he does not say, but certainly they were types he did produce. In fact, as indicated by his February 10, 1817, advertisement, Ill. 115, demijohns were made in large quantities at the time, though apparently not steadily enough to warrant having a wickering department.[115]

The 1817 advertisement, Ill. 115, with its "figured pocket bottles," adds, I believe, a vital feature to the unfinished picture of American flasks. I had often wondered what their makers called the flasks with relief designs that are termed Masonic, Historical, and Pictorial by collectors. Now I believe that it probably was "Figured" and that John Mather must be included in the small group known, or thought, to have produced them before the 1820s. Unfortunately he did not say—doubtless he had no need to, insofar as prospective customers were concerned—what the figures were that were "suitable for the southern market." Only speculations can be offered, stemming from known designs of the pre-1820s— Sunbursts? Masonics? Eagles?

Another speculation arises from lack of proof as to how long Mather's glassworks was owned and operated by him after 1817. It may be that Joseph Merrow and James Bidwell, Jr., acquired it sometime after the mid-1820s. In 1820, Merrow & Bidwell, who also had been conducting various enterprises in East Hartford, apparently were so financially embarrassed that they expected to close their "considerable stock of goods, a Distillery, Powder Mills, Carding & Clothier's Work, Spinning Machines and . . . Real Estate."[116] Whether or not they found a buyer I have not learned, but they seem to have moved to Hartford and started a store in that city. In 1827, they were "soliciting a share of the public patronage" for the products of their "Hartford Glass Manufactory." As I have found no evidence of a glassworks actually within the city of Hartford, it may be that this was Mather's glassworks being resuscitated or recently taken over by Merrow & Bidwell. In any event, they were offering packages of "Black and Light Glass Ware, such as Bottles of nearly every description, Flasks, Jars, Canisters, Inkstands, Ink and Blacking bottles &c. &c."[117] It is not improbable that Figured Flasks were produced by them.

29. COVENTRY GLASS WORKS, *Coventry, Connecticut, 1813–49*

On January 14, 1813, seven men signed an agreement to erect a glass factory at Coventry, a post town 18 miles east of Hartford, Connecticut, on the Willimantic River. They were Captain Nathaniel Root (senior), Ebenezer Root, Nathaniel Root, Jr., and Joseph A. Norton of Coventry and Eli Evans, Thomas W. Bishop, and Uriah Andrews of East Hartford. Not one of the Coventry men was a glassmaker, but those from East Hartford, doubtless employed at either the Pitkin or Mather glassworks, were glassblowers who would manage the practical and technical side of the business. The glasshouse was to be built on an acre of ground owned by Captain Root, near the house of Nathaniel, Jr. The rental of the land was a token one of $1 a year. It was decided that there would be a capital stock of $10,000 divided into 32 shares, of which 16 were to go to Nathaniel Root, Sr., Ebenezer, and Nathaniel, Jr., 8 to Joseph Norton, and 8 to the three blowers. The blowers were to devote as much time to the actual manufacturing as the majority deemed necessary for their interest and the benefit of the company. In return, they were to receive $26 a month for actual labor and $45 a year for every year of actual labor, in addition to monthly wages for five woodmen (woodchoppers), all to be paid out of the company's joint funds. Any partner was also to be compensated for time and money he spent on company business. No contract was to be signed, made, or paid unless a majority of the company agreed to it. Each one voted in accordance with his number of shares. And of course an annual statement was to be made. If there was a loss after three years of operation, a partner might withdraw his interest after a 60-day notice. Finally, each partner was to take a loss or secure a profit according to his number of shares. On the original document a line is drawn through the name of Thomas W. Bishop, who, it would seem, had second thoughts about the proposition and withdrew before the project was actually launched.[118]

Exactly when the glasshouse was built and in operation is uncertain. However, an October 1814 receipt signed by Joseph Norton, Ebenezer Root, Uriah Andrews, and Eli Evans shows that on the twenty-ninth Nathaniel Root, Jr., paid in $500, "being in full for five shares put into the Glass Factory Company to *be* established. . . ." (The italics are mine.) Four days later, November 3, the same four men and Nathaniel Root, Sr., certified the appointment of Nathaniel Root, Jr., as agent of the Coventry Glass Factory Company until April 1, 1815. As agent, he was to have "sole management of all the concerns" of the company, to keep all accounts, make all sales, and pack all the glass. For all these services he was to receive $20 a month. These items suggest to me that the works was in operation by November 1814. That the landholdings were increased in February 1815 is evident from the fact that Nathaniel Root, Sr., sold the company two pieces of land for $50.[119]

What happened between February 1815 and October 1816 is a mystery. But on October 15, 1816, over three years after the initial agreement was signed, new copartnership papers, called the Glass Factory Company Constitution, were signed by Nathaniel Root, Sr., Ebenezer Root, Nathaniel Root, Jr., Joseph Norton, Eli Evans, and Uriah Andrews. The statement that they had "erected a Glass Works and other buildings and put same in operation" preceded the articles of the constitution. The capital was only a little over a third of that specified in the original agreement: $3,200 divided into 32 shares at $100 a share. Of these, ten each were to go to Ebenezer Root and Nathaniel Root, Jr., eight to Joseph Norton, four to the glassblowers Eli Evans and Uriah Andrews. The capital could be increased if desired, and each partner would contribute according to the number of his shares. Anyone failing to meet the required sum would be taxed with interest and, if necessary, his stock held to satisfy the debt. No shares were to be sold without first giving the company the opportunity to buy them "on as good terms as . . . to any other Persons." Of course, each partner was to share in profits or losses according to his stock. An agent was to be appointed to have sole management of all the factory concerns and to keep the accounts, which could be inspected at any time by the copartners. He also had the power to give receipts for shares and notes in the name of the Coventry Glass Factory Company. If the majority of the copartners, each voting in accordance with the number of his shares, deemed it desirable, the agent, who could not vote for himself, could be removed. As in the first agreement, there were special articles applying to the glassblower partners, Evans and Andrews. Agreeing to serve the factory for at least three years from May 1813, they were to spend as much time in the factory as appeared to be in the interest of the concern and to receive $45 a year for each year of actual labor in addition to $1 a day for work in the factory or, when blowing, the prices agreed upon for blowing the different kinds of glass. However, the blowers did not "have the liberty of Blowing all of one kind but an equal proportion of each."[120]

How long the "constitution" was in effect has not been established as yet. It is believed that Thomas Stebbins was operating the works in 1820, and that the Lafayette flasks marked "T.S." (see list at the end of this thumbnail sketch and Charts, Group I) were made by him, possibly late in 1824. Unless the second "S" in "S & S" on some Lafayette flasks was an error for "C," it would appear that Thomas Stebbins was joined briefly by another Stebbins, perhaps early in 1825. In any event, probably also in 1825, the firm became Stebbins & Chamberlin—Thomas Stebbins and Rufus B. Chamberlin—and it too produced a Lafayette flask. This firm also was short-lived, for the glassworks was taken over in 1828 by Gilbert Turner & Company.

Jesse A. Bairnard, whose sources of information "have been contemporary documents and records in town and state archives," has kindly given me data on this company. On October 31, 1828, Jasper Gilbert, John Turner, and Rufus B. Chamberlin, all of Coventry, and John Turner's brother Levi of Mansfield, forming Gilbert Turner & Company, became owners of both the Coventry and the Willington Glass Works. Five years later, Elisha Johnson, then of Willington, bought Levi Turner's interest. In 1835 another Willington man, Alvin B. Preston, acquired a one-eighth interest in the company. (Jasper Gilbert, John Turner, and, apparently, Alvin Preston were among the founders of the Ellenville Glass Works at Ellenville, New York, in 1836.) In the spring of 1848 Rufus B. Chamberlin became the majority owner of Gilbert, Turner and Company by buying up the interest of Johnson, Preston, and Jasper Gilbert. Thus, Chamberlin and John Turner were the sole owners and the old firm was dissolved.

Exactly how long Chamberlin and Turner continued to operate the Coventry Glass Works has not been established definitely. It has been said that lack of wood for fuel caused the closing of the glassworks in 1848.[121] However, one of the two account books of Gilbert, Turner & Company found by Kenneth M. Wilson in the Connecticut State Library was for the years 1846–50. This would seem to indicate that the works was in operation longer than has been thought. Still, the bottles and inks itemized in the accounts were sold in the years 1846 and 1847 and, if all sales were recorded, the numbers seem small for a prosperous glassworks. Thus it may be that, though production ceased in 1848, winding up of the firm's affairs continued for about a year.

Among the articles itemized were the following:

Porters, half-pt.	Inks, 2 oz, 8 oz, pt. and qt.
(and presumably, pt.)	Inkstands: old fashion
Wines	Large
"Clarretts"	H & B
Flasks, half-pt. and pt.	D & B
Snuff bottles, ½-lb. and lb.,	Pyramid
long half-lb.	fluted green
Blacking bottles, sq.	fluted
Octagon vials, flint, 8 oz.	
	Demijohns
Pres[?] vials, 2 oz.	Mold, made by H. B. Henry
Concaves, Light 1½[?]	

There was also a purchase of 50 bundles of willow,[122] which were to be paid for in bottles. The willows doubtless were to be used in covering demijohns.

Excavations made on the site of the Coventry Glass Works by Harry Hall White unearthed shards of many of the works' products. There were sufficient fragments to show that the ubiquitous chestnut bottles like 5 in Ill. 46 and 9 in Ill. 88 were blown there, also Pitkin-type flasks like 3 and 9 in Ill. 88. Other shards showed that the snuff bottles were the usual rectangular ones with chamfered and with fluted corners and square forms. The blacking bottles were the classic squares. Fragments were found also of Swaim's Panacea bottles like Ill. 83. Some of the inkstands were blown-three-mold in geometric patterns—GII–2, having a narrow band of large diamonds below a wider one of small diamond diapering; GII–16, having a band of vertical ribbing below one of diamond diapering; GII–18, having a band of diamond diapering between bands of vertical ribbing. There were five molds in all for these inkstands—one for GII–16, and two each for GII–2 and GII–8 for two sizes of stands in each pattern. Mr. White also established that Coventry was the source of several Figured Flasks.[123]

In the following list these flasks are indicated by "fragments." The Lafayette flasks are listed in the order I believe they appeared. The dates are the year or period in which I believe the flask may have been first blown.

GI–33. "WASHINGTON" above bust facing left. *Reverse*: "JACKSON" above bust facing left. Pint. Fragments. ca. 1832.

GI–34. "WASHINGTON" above bust facing right. *Reverse*: "Jackson" above bust facing left. Half-pint. Fragments. ca. 1832.

GI–34a. Like GI–34 but pint size. Attributed on basis of similarity to GI–34. ca. 1832.

GI–80. "LA FAYETTE" above bust, bar below bust and above "T.S." *Reverse*: "DEWITT CLINTON" with *D* reversed, above bust; below bust, "COVENTRY" in semicircle above "C-T". Pint. Fragments. Probably 1824.

GI–83. "LA FAYETTE" above bust, bar below bust and above "T.S" *Reverse*: Masonic emblems. Pint. Probably 1824.

GI–84. "LAFAYETTE" above bust, bar below bust and above "T.S." *Reverse*: Masonic emblems. Half-pint. Probably 1824.

GI–85. "LAFAYETTE" above bust; below bust, "COVENTRY" in semicircle above "C-T". *Reverse*: Arch of stars above oval frame with Liberty Cap on pole; "S&S" below frame. Pint. Fragments. ca. 1825.

GI–86. Similar to GI–85 but half-pint. ca. 1825.

GI–87. Similar to GI–86 but no stars on reverse. Half-pint. ca. 1825.

GI–87a. Similar to GI–87 but pint size. ca. 1825.

GI–81. "LA FAYETTE" above bust, "S & C" below bust. *Reverse*: "DE WITT CLINTON" above bust, "C-T" below bust. Half-pint. ca. 1825–26.

GI–81a. Like GI–81 except for two corrugations around flask at base instead of three. ca. 1825–26.

GI–82. Like GI–81 in design; no initials below bust of Lafayette. Half-pint. ca. 1825–26.

GII–70. Eagle lengthwise on each side. Pint. Fragments. Probably the 1820s.

GII–71. Like GII–70. Half-pint. Fragments. Probably the 1820s.

GIII–4. Cornucopia—Urn. Pint. Fragments. Probably 1820s.

GV–6. "SUCCESS" above and "TO THE RAILROAD" below Horse and Cart on rail, lengthwise, on each side. Pint. Fragments. Late 1820s–1830s.

GV–8. "SUCCESS TO THE RAILROAD" in deep arch above Horse and Cart on rail, lengthwise. *Reverse*: 17 stars and spread American eagle lengthwise. Pint. Fragments. Late 1820s–early 1830s.

GV–9. Like GV–8 but no inscription or stars. Pint. Fragments. Late 1820s–1830s.

GV–10. "RAILROAD" above and "LOWELL" below Horse and Cart on rail, lengthwise. *Reverse*: 13 stars and lengthwise spread eagle. Half-pint. Fragments. Probably 1829–32.

GVIII–3. Sunburst each side. Pint. Fragments. Probably 1820s.

GVIII–16. Sunburst each side. Half-pint. Fragments. Probably the 1820s. A few fragments from one of these flasks were found recently on the site of the Pitkin glassworks.

GVIII–18. Sunburst each side. Half-pint. Attributed. Probably 1820s.

In the 1941 charts in *American Glass*, two rare Masonic half-pint flasks were attributed to Coventry by George S. McKearin in consultation with other students and collectors. One was the half-pint so-called "Hour-Glass" Masonic GIV–29, which Van Rensselaer thought probably was a Coventry flask. The other, also a half-pint, was the so-called Crossed-Keys Masonic GIV–30, which Van Rensselaer said was attributed to "J.P.F."—that is, Joseph P. Foster, supposedly of the Pitkin glassworks.

30. WILLINGTON GLASS WORKS, *West Willington, Connecticut, 1815–72*

Another glassmaking venture late in the War of 1812 period was that undertaken at West Willington, a small Connecticut town a few miles northeast of Coventry and only 26 miles from Hartford. In 1814, a stock company was formed by John Turner, Ebenezer Root, and Frederick Rose—all presumably of Coventry—and Roderick Rose, Stephen Brigham, Jr., Elisha Brigham, and Spafford Brigham—all of nearby Mansfield. Abiel Johnson, Jr., is also said to have been one of the organizing group and, briefly, the works' first proprietor. Stephen Brigham, Jr.'s, association was also brief; he sold his interest for $500 in January 1815—to whom is not revealed by the meager information about the early years of the works, which in 1815 was producing bottles, competing with Pitkin, Mather, and Coventry (see 13, 28, and 29). It would appear that, excepting Abiel Johnson, Jr., and Stephen Brigham, Jr., the founders remained the owners until October 31, 1828, when Gilbert, Turner & Company acquired this glassworks and also the Coventry works. This company operated the Willington Glass Works until 1847.[124]

Actually, there are few other facts to cite or inferences to make about the first 32 years of the glassworks' existence. One infers that the Willington Glass Works was at least moderately successful. On the factual side, there is advertising evidence of out-of-town agents handling the output, which consisted of bottles, mainly "common black ware." If, as I believe, an advertisement sent to me by Kenneth M. Wilson relates to the Willington Glass Works, then Belden, Merriman & Company were the agents in New Haven, Connecticut, in 1816.[125] (Their appointment by John Turner suggests that he was in a position of some authority, perhaps the company agent.) In the late 1820s and early 1830s, probably before and after that period, William Monroe Muzzy was the agent in Philadelphia, where he also represented the New England Glass Company, the New England Crown Glass Company, and the New-England Glass-Bottle Company, all of Cambridge, Massachusetts, and the Boston and Sandwich Glass Company of Sandwich in the same state. A Hartford agent of the Willington Glass Works was Lee, Hopkins & Butler, who advertised "Willington porter bottles" in 1829.

Early in the spring of 1847 Gilbert, Turner & Company, which within about two years was to close down its Coventry Glass Works, sold the Willington Glass Works to a group of six men—Harvey Merrick, Elisha Carpenter, William M. Still, William and Francis Sheffer, and James MacFarlane. In April of that year they incorporated the Willington Glass Company. Their capitalization was $6,500 from 260 shares at $25 a share. The purpose of the corporation was "to manufacture and sell glass ware in all its various branches." The company was also to establish a store, handling "all the articles usually kept in a retail country store." It appears, however, that over two years were to elapse before the company went into production, and then its products were not glassware in general but bottles, as they had been from the beginning of operations in 1815. Presumably this was in October 1849, for Harry Hall White found no mention in Willington documents of glassmaking before August 15 and an undated plan to make glass in October. It appears, also, that 26 men were employed: eleven glassblowers, one batch mixer, one for "material barrow," one to fill the wood oven, three to tend the pot oven, one fireman, one "choreman," and seven bottle packers. In addition, there were three sets of boys to "carry off" (finished products to the leer) and one set to "break off" (moils from the blowpipes?).[126]

For nearly eight years the company prospered. Their wares apparently were sold mainly in the East through agents in large centers, who in turn supplied customers in their areas. But there were also large direct sales to manufacturers using containers of various sorts—for instance, ink bottles to Elisha Packard, Quincy, Massachusetts, and snuff bottles to Lorillard's, New York City. The latter, Mr. White tells us, were "marked 'L' in a square tilted in one corner." That the Willington products were well received and made in quantity is evident from the payment of a 20 percent dividend with interest in 1849, the first year of operation, and of dividends up to 40 percent in the ensuing seven years. It was indeed too good to last. The Willington Glass Company's prosperity came to an abrupt end in the panic of 1857. The company never recovered. Though it limped through another decade, its last years were mainly ones of phasing out the business and settling debts. The fires in the glassworks went out sometime before the last of the company's accounts were closed in January 1873.[127]

Although, so far as is known at present, no marked bottles or flasks were made at the Willington Glass Works prior to 1849, it seems safe to assume that the output consisted of the various types of bottles in demand during the works' first period, 1815 to 1847. The Belden, Merriman & Company advertisement of 1816, already referred to, offered "gallon, 2 quart, quart, pint and half-pint bottles, pint and half-pint flasks, and inkstands at factory prices plus cartage. It would not be surprising if the flasks were Pitkin type. The ubiquitous chestnut bottle of the late 18th to early 19th century was among the types blown there—such as 4 and 5 in Ill. 46. The collection of Charles B. Gardner included a fine, deep-green chestnut bottle that is well authenticated as Willington glass. It is 6½ inches in height and—a feature making it exceptional—bears an applied seal with the initials "S:B". Another possible Willington sealed bottle, also formerly in the Gardner Collection, is cylindrical with short neck and folded collar. It is olive-amber in color, and the seal bears the initials "P.B." above a small Masonic emblem. The porter bottles advertised in 1829 doubtless were similar to that illustrating James Butler's 1827 advertisement of Philadelphia bottled porter (Ill. 58B). In the second period, 1849 to 1872, Mr. White learned from account books, demijohns dominated the sales for a long time, with wines and flasks running second. Also, the following articles appeared in the account book from 1865 through 1872:

Eagle flasks, ½ pt., pt. & qt.	Gins (square)
Screw top flasks	Ales, pt.
Porters, ½ pt., pt. & qt.	Kissengers (?)
Schnapps	Wines, 5, 5½ & 6 (fractions of a gallon)

Wines, screw top	Minerals (S.H.S.) ½ pt.
Wines, swell neck	" , C & E (Congress & Empire Springs), pt.
Demijohns, ¼, ½, 1, 2, 3, 4, & 5 gal.	American Mineral Water Co., ½ pt. & pt.
Inks, 4, 6 & 8 oz., pt. & qt.	S & N Bitters
Oils, pt.	Booze bottle (GVI–3) (1865 & 1866)
Oval blacking (Lyons)	
Snuffs, oblong, lb. square, ½ lb. & lb.	

Mr. White's excavations unearthed aquamarine and amber fragments of gothic pickle bottles or jars like 2 in Ill. 73 in pattern and in quantities indicating production at Willington. There were also many fragments of wine bottles of Type 12, and like 12 in Ill. 46. These were marked "WILLINGTON GLASS WORKS" on the base rim.

The accounts yielded a little information about molds, too. "Entries showing exchange of molds and supplies between various near-by glasshouses indicate that molds would be used by one company during a price agreement or contract, and then passed on to another." A March 2, 1870, entry read "1 swell neck Qt bottle mold at Newburgh at Burrows Factory. Bartlett has agreed to get D. John [demijohn] Molds and this swell neck mold and send them here." A "swell neck bottle" was probably what some collectors call a lady's leg bottle, which incidentally was being produced in France in 1834 if not earlier.[128] Other entries mentioned the following molds and their costs:

Square gin mold, 1 qt.	$25
1 2 gal. iron mold, demijohn	$30
1 "6" wine	$25
1 swell neck mold	$25
1 long [cylindrical?] ½ gal. D. John mold	$25
1 long 1 gal. D. John mold	$25
1 long 2 gal. D. John mold	$25

Although it is not unlikely that unmarked Figured Flasks were blown at the Willington Glass Works, as yet the only certain Willington flasks are the five listed here, all believed to have been brought out probably in the 1850s.

GII–61. "LIBERTY" / Eagle and Wreath. *Reverse*: "WILLINGTON [in arc] / GLASS, CO / WEST WILLINGTON [in semicircle] CONN". Quart.

GII–62. Similar to GII–61 but comma after "WEST." Pint.

GII–63. Similar to GII–61 but no comma after "GLASS" and "Co" below "GLASS". Half-pint.

GII–64. Similar to GII–62. Pint.

GII–63a. Similar to GII–61. Half-pint.

In the Midwest, glassmaking was to put down deeper roots and spread beyond the Pittsburgh region during the years 1800 through 1832. The western market for domestic wares was to broaden as the population boomed, not only from the increase of

13. Advertisement by the proprietors of the Maysville Glass Works, Maysville, Ky., dated January 19, 1815. This presumably short-lived works was still in operation when the Englishman Adlard Welby visited the town in 1820. (Cincinnati, Ohio, *Liberty Hall and Cincinnati Gazette*, Apr. 8, 1815.) *Ohio Historical Society, Columbus, Ohio*

14. Advertisement by Hough, Rees & Co., proprietors of the Cincinnati Glass Works, which was established in 1815 by Anthony, Hough and Rees, Cincinnati, Ohio. (*Liberty Hall and Cincinnati Gazette*, Mar. 25, 1816.) *Ohio Historical Society, Columbus, Ohio*

15. Advertisement by the proprietors of the Zanesville Glass Works, Zanesville, Ohio, of white hollow ware and announcing plans to build a green-glass house for window glass and green hollow ware, dated January 4. (Cincinnati, Ohio, *Liberty Hall and Cincinnati Gazette*, Jan. 29, 1816.) *Ohio Historical Society, Columbus, Ohio*

native-born but from a stream of new settlers. Such was the growth that new states emerged—Ohio in 1803, the same year the Louisiana Purchase added thousands of acres to the United States' western territory; Indiana in 1816; Illinois in 1818; and Missouri in 1821. In the meantime, along the Gulf of Mexico, Louisiana joined the Union in 1812; Mississippi, in 1817; and Alabama, in 1819. The expanding need for window glass, bottles, and tableware was an invitation to would-be glass manufacturers. Though imported glass, including bottles, was handled by merchants in some, if not all, of the principal towns of the Midwest and South, the quantity was not so large as in the East, except perhaps at New Orleans. And eastern glassware was not a serious competitor even at the end of the period after the Erie Canal had facilitated and cheapened transportation. Thus, conditions were favorable for a healthy growth of glassmaking, and, as elsewhere, they gave rise to too many glassworks. As we have seen, General O'Hara's Pittsburgh Glass Works (see No. 16) and the New Geneva Glass Works (No. 17) were in operation when the new century opened. In the first three decades at least 33 more were started, mainly after the War of 1812, of which at least 19 operated after 1830. And six or seven more were started in the next two years.

The new midwestern glassworks were located in four states—Pennsylvania, Ohio, (West) Virginia, and Kentucky. In the Pittsburgh and the Monongahela area, between the city and New Geneva, there were 19 new ventures, of which 14 were in Pittsburgh and its immediate environs—Williamsport, Birmingham, and Temperanceville. And six of those were established for the production of flint glass. The others were bottle and window-glass houses. But even two of the famous flint-glass works—Bakewell's Pittsburgh Flint Glass Works and Robinson's Stourbridge Flint Glass Works—were to be among the makers of Figured Flasks. It should be noted also that Thomas Pears (nephew-in-law of Benjamin Bakewell) and the Bakewells, as Thomas Pears & Company, attempted to establish a black-glass bottle manufactory (see Ill. 16.). It was inspired perhaps by the black-bottle works Pears had seen in France in 1815 when he was trying to recruit French glassblowers. In any event, Pears returned to France in 1818 and, between June and September, succeeded in securing a staff—"4 blowers, 4 garcons, 2 gammains and a director"—for the new works erected on Water Street opposite the Bakewell manufactory. This venture apparently was the first specifically for the manufacture of the important black bottle. It failed, probably in 1819, the year

Black Porter & Claret Bottles.

THOMAS PEARS & CO. Pittsburgh, having obtained a complete set of workmen from Europe, have commenced the manufacture of Black Porter and claret bottles, of the same kind and quality as the imported; and offer for sale an extensive assortment of them, and of Hollow Ware, at the following reduced prices:

Porter and Claret Bottles, $18 per groce,
Gallon   do. $4 per dozen,
Half gallon do $2½ do.
Quart   do. $1½ do.
Pint Flasks, $1 do.

Orders addressed to *Thomas Pears & Co.* or *Bakewell, Page & Bakewell*, at Pittsburgh, will be executed with punctuality and dispatch. Samples may be seen by applying to

E. & J. N. ROBINS,
No. 3, Lower Market-st.
Cincinnati, March 2.   37 3m

16. Advertisement of black porter and claret bottles made by Thomas Pears & Co., Pittsburgh, Pa. Note that apparently the production of these particular bottles depended upon obtaining "a complete set of workmen from Europe." (Cincinnati, Ohio, *The Cincinnati Inquisitor and Advertiser*, June 15, 1819.) *The New-York Historical Society, New York City*

BIRMINGHAM Glass Works

THE Birmingham Glass-Works are in operation and will be conducted in future by the subscribers, under the firm of

Frederick Wendt & Co.

Any orders in our line will be thankfully received and punctually attended to.—The Glass manufactured here is equal if not superior to any manufactured in the western country.

Frederick Wendt,
Charles Imsen,
A. Sullivan.
Sept. 22d, 1826.

17. Advertisement announcing that the new firm of Frederick Wendt & Co. was operating the Birmingham Glass Works, Birmingham, Pittsburgh, Pa. (Pittsburgh, *The Statesman*, Oct. 14, 1826.) *Historical Society of Western Pennsylvania, Pittsburgh, Pa.*

operations began,[129] and doubtless—in part, at least—because of the current depression, though the bottle and window-glass manufacturers did not suffer so much as those producing flint glass.

In Ohio ten glassworks were built between 1814 and 1825. In connection with three, my information is so meager that it is little more than statistics: one started at Portage about 1821, where presumably bottles and other hollow ware were blown; one was built at Painesville about 1825; and the Zanesville White Flint Glass Manufactory operated ca. 1820 to 1822. Five operated for about a decade in the southern part of the state on the Ohio River, one at Cincinnati (Ill. 14) and one at Moscow, each producing window glass, bottles, and flasks; in the northeastern area, one at Mantua and two at Kent, each mainly bottles, flasks, and other hollow ware. Harry Hall White's excavations on the site of the Park, Edmunds and Park Kent glasshouse (1824–ca. 1834) established that blown-three-mold in the geometric pattern GII–6 was one of the products. In Ill. 122 a flask (7) and decanter (8) attributed to this glassworks are shown. Two of Zanesville's glassworks survived into the early 1850s. Though bottles, flasks, and articles of tableware blown from the same bottle-glass metal have been identified only with Zanesville, Mantua, and Kent, it is possible the same general types, excepting blown-three-mold at Kent, were blown in the other glassworks. Some were unadorned, but the majority apparently were pattern-molded in ribbings and, less frequently, in diamonds. Globular bottles such as those in Ill. 96 are associated especially with Ohio, Zanesville in particular. And present information indicates that in only three was a Figured Flask produced—Moscow, Zanesville, and Mantua.

In the narrow panhandle of (West) Virginia between Ohio and western Pennsylvania, three glassworks were established. One was built in Wellsburg (called Charlestown prior to 1819) in 1813 or by 1815. Of two erected in Wheeling, one was started in 1820 as a window-glass and hollow-ware

glasshouse (see No. 40); the other, in 1829 for the production of flint glass. All were to operate after 1829. Data on the Wellsburg glassworks are frustratingly limited and sometimes contradictory.[130] However, all sources agree that its leading spirit until his death in 1828 was Isaac Duval, an experienced glassman who is said to have been one of John Frederick Amelung's superintendents at the New Bremen Glassmanufactory, Maryland. Though Duval and his two partners, presumably also glassblowers, are said to have set out to manufacture—and succeeded in doing so—flint glass, *white* and *green* metal were also made. The works is of interest to bottle and flask collectors because there can be little, if any, doubt that midwestern types of pattern-molded hollow ware were blown there. In fact, possibly the "ten-diamond mold" so long and securely associated with Zanesville, Ohio (see flasks 4 and 10 in Ill. 97 and jug 3 in Ill. 99), was used at some time in the early years of the Duval works. In The Corning Museum of Glass is a small, brilliant, light-green "ten-diamond" dish that has a Duval history. It was acquired some 40 and more years ago by George S. McKearin, and its previous owner, an elderly woman, had inherited it with a family history of its having been purchased in 1818 and having been blown by a man named Duval in Wellsburg.

It should be noted that the earliest (April 1817) of the few advertisements pertaining to Wellsburg that I have seen did not mention flint, but white glass hollow ware, of which Jesse Reeder, the Cincinnati agent, had a large quantity for sale "at the Charlestown [Wellsburg] and Pittsburgh prices and freight." From an advertisement dated May 14, 1819, it appears that Isaac Duval & Company had ceased production the previous November—probably because of the depression—and in the spring of 1819 John J. Jacobs & Company had the works in blast, ready "to fill any orders in the WHITE FLINT & GREEN HOLLOW GLASS" line. The company's assurance of well-shaped ware of "correct size and each size uniformly the same" suggests bottles as well as other vessels. Also of interest is the offer to barter "for any articles of the product or manufacture of other parts of the country . . . particularly . . . of Kentucky, Ohio and Missouri." Wheeling was another outlet. Apparently Duval soon returned to the works and the production of flint glassware of high quality, perhaps after 1820 when, according to the census report of that year, the works operated "with great difficulty on account of bad sales." A June 1828 advertisement in connection with the Cincinnati Glass Cutting Manufactory announced the receipt of *"superior plain glass*, from the glassworks of Mr. I. Duval. . . ." As has been mentioned, Duval died in that year, and from then on the history of the works is still to be unraveled. It is thought that it closed in the late 1840s, and it seems likely "The Old Virginia Flint Glass Works" advertised for sale or rent in January 1847 by George N. Catts was the old Duval works.[131]

In Kentucky, at Maysville, was one short-lived glassworks that, unfortunately, has not been the object of intensive research as yet. The few facts I have about this only Kentucky glassworks before the 1840s derive from two newspaper advertisements and a traveler's comment. As in so many other cases, the works apparently was built toward the end of the War of 1812, but who the proprietors were I have not learned. However, it is evident from the January 1815 Maysville Glass Works advertisement (see Ill. 13) that they had appointed J. & J. Sumrall their agent, to whom all Cincinnati orders were to be given. They claimed too that their output of window glass and hollow ware was "of every size and description and of superior quality"—to be sold at

Pittsburgh prices. The second advertisement was the same in wording except that William Porter replaced the Sumralls as agent. It appeared early in February and ran through August 19, 1816. Though no later advertisements have been found as yet, the glassworks apparently was in operation in 1820. At least, Adlard Welby, an Englishman, mentioned a Maysville glassworks in his account of a visit to the town on his trip to the United States and the English settlement in Illinois.[132] Though the Maysville Glass Works operated only briefly, it merits note because it is most likely that among its hollow glass were pattern-molded bottles and flasks of midwestern type.

31. BAKEWELLS; THE PITTSBURGH FLINT GLASS WORKS, *Pittsburgh, Pennsylvania, 1808–82*[133]

Bakewells, as the Pittsburgh Flint Glass Works is informally called by collectors and students of American glass, was in many respects the most renowned of the early midwestern glassworks. Though, in a long life of nearly three-quarters of a century, its fame arose from its fine flint glassware, the first successfully produced in the United States, its history is briefly sketched here because Figured Flasks and green-glass containers—vials, bottles, flasks—also were produced.

The business was mainly a family affair of which, so present evidence indicates, Benjamin Bakewell was the head and the heart for almost 36 years. Bakewell had had no connection whatever with glassmaking, and had no knowledge of it, when he settled in Pittsburgh. His experience was far removed from manufacturing processes. At 14, he had been apprenticed to a haberdasher in Derby, England, where he was born in August 1767. At 21, after serving his apprenticeship, he found employment as a salesman in a London mercer's shop. In his twenty-fourth year, he opened a shop of his own, handling mainly French merchandise. When the French war severed his supply line, he, like many others, turned to the United States, and in 1794 moved his family to New York City. There he became an importer again. Four years later, with his brother William, he started a brewery in New Haven, Connecticut, a successful venture in which, it was said, the ale brewed was "quite equal to the celebrated product of Burton-on-Trent." Had it not been for a disastrous fire that consumed the brewery in 1804, Benjamin Bakewell might never have become a glass manufacturer, one whom Deming Jarves of the Sandwich Glass Works ranked above all others in the field of flint glass. Be that as it may, Bakewell returned to New York City and importing, only to be caught again in the net of a conflict. President Jefferson's embargoes, heavy bond, and special licenses were the final blows breaking many importers, including Benjamin Bakewell.

In September 1808, Benjamin Bakewell, the Englishman Benjamin Page (a good friend and New York importer who had managed to salvage his capital), and Thomas Kinder (representative of Robert Kinder & Company, an assignee of Bakewell) set out for Pittsburgh to survey business opportunities west of the Alleghenies. They went seeking a profitable business for Bakewell and, for the others, investment of idle capital. It did not take long to decide that the solution to their problems lay in the manufacture of glassware, especially flint glassware, and that the means was at hand in the glassworks built the previous summer by George Robinson and an English glassblower, Edward Ensell. Ensell, possibly Robinson too, had left employment in O'Hara's Pittsburgh Glass Works. Handicapped by insufficient capital as well as lack of the proper materials and—worse—knowledge of all the furnaces and various processes necessary to glassmaking, Robinson and Ensell had floundered. On August 21, 1808, they dissolved their partnership. Benjamin Bakewell and his partners, arriving soon afterward, rescued the project. The new firm was called Bakewell & Ensell, with Bakewell, experienced in administration and selling, as manager, and Ensell, the glassblower, as superintendent of the manufacturing. By mid-October they were advertising a limited range of glassware consisting of articles in daily use.

The next few years were critical ones indeed. Benjamin Bakewell almost immediately realized that Edward Ensell had overestimated his capacities as an all-round practical glassman. Consequently Bakewell found himself faced, at 41, with the considerable task of mastering the fundamentals of glass manufacture. Although this could not be accomplished overnight, he made enough headway in the six months between October 1808 and April 1809 to enlarge the firm's assortment of wares. After February 1809, when Ensell was "forced to withdraw," Bakewell had all the reins in his own hands. The firm became B. Bakewell & Company. About two years later, March 1811, Thomas Kinder, perhaps not having the same faith as Bakewell and Page in the prospects for developing a profitable business, or having become impatient with the rate of progress, withdrew the support of Robert Kinder & Company, leaving the field to Bakewell and Page. Yet Bakewell was able to build a second glasshouse by June of 1811; and, apparently realizing that the demand for their flint glassware was insufficient to carry the works, he informed the public that in addition to the usual flint glassware "articles of GREEN GLASS" could "now be offered at the usual prices"—presumably the current Pittsburgh prices.

On September 1, 1813, Bakewell & Page took into partnership Bakewell's son Thomas, a chemist who had already become an invaluable assistant, helping to solve many of the technical problems, and who was to succeed his father in the management of the concern. Except for about a year ending in December 1815, when Henry Bostwick, a Bakewell glassblower, had an interest in the works, the two Bakewells and Benjamin Page were the sole proprietors. Apparently they weathered the depres-

sion following the War of 1812 without too much financial discomfort. In fact, in some ways they may have profited. At least an advertisement in the August 20, 1817, issue of the St. Louis *Missouri Gazette* stated that Bakewell, Page & Bakewell "having engaged more workmen at lower wages . . . [were] enabled to reduce their prices of GLASSWARE." The firm was to attain a wide reputation for the quality of its fine wares, filling an order for drinking vessels from President Monroe and thereby becoming the first glass manufacturer in the country to supply domestic glassware for the White House. Its cut glass earned honorable mention and awards at exhibitions of the Franklin Institute of Philadelphia.

It was also in the period of this firm that John Palmer Bakewell was employed, and on September 9, 1825, he obtained the first patent in the United States for mechanically pressing glass, one for knobs. These were the beginning of Bakewells' pressed glass, which was to become an important line. On August 1, 1827, John Bakewell was taken into the partnership and an *s* was added to the second Bakewell in the name. In their 1832 report to the government, Bakewell, Page & Bakewells stated that the invested capital was then $100,000, none of which was borrowed, and that over the years the value of their yearly output had run from $20,000 to $100,000.[134]

Bakewell, Page & Bakewells was dissolved July 31, 1832, following Benjamin Page's retirement and, according to the family records, Bakewells & Company was formed the next day with Alexander M. Anderson as the "company." However, advertisements in the *Cincinnati Daily Gazette* testify to the firm's name being changed to Bakewells & Anderson by January 1833.[134a] On July 18, 1836, the *Daily Pittsburgh Gazette* carried the following announcement: "PITTSBURGH FLINT GLASS MANUFACTORY / This well known establishment will henceforth be conducted by Benjamin, Thomas & John P. Bakewell in conjunction with John Palmer Pears, under the firm of Bakewells & Company." John P. Pears was the first of the nephews of Benjamin Bakewell to be taken into the partnership. However, it was seven years later, with the retirement of John Palmer Bakewell in July 1843 (perhaps because of ill health; he died the following November) that the firm name was changed to Bakewell & Pears, which operated the glassworks until the death of Benjamin Bakewell in 1844. From August 1, 1844, until 1880 the title was Bakewell, Pears & Company, as sons, grandsons, nephews, and great-nephews entered and retired from the partnership. Not all these years were profitable ones. About 1840, toward the end of the depression after the Panic of 1837, the works was shut down for a while. In 1845 the factory burned to the ground, but a new and better one was immediately built. It seems probable that in the 1870s business was not so brisk as in the previous years, for in 1880 Bakewell, Pears & Bakewell Limited was formed; it dissolved the next year. The end of the famous Bakewells had come.

Of course, the concern here is not with Bakewells' fine

table and ornamental wares, but with their bottles and flasks, which naturally did not receive the same detailed attention in advertisements as did the finer products. In the first advertisement, that of Bakewell and Ensell in October 1808, phials and pocket bottles were offered as well as decanters, tumblers, cream jugs, sugar basins, and salts. Inasmuch as Bakewells did not expand their production to include green glass until 1811, it seems safe to conclude that prior to the spring of that year all their bottles and flasks were blown from flint glass or from white glass. A guess might be hazarded that the pocket flasks were pattern-molded in diamond and ribbed designs. Perhaps they were similar to 2 and 3 in Ill. 100. In 1811, the green-glass articles were pint, quart, half-gallon, and gallon jars and bottles, pint and half-pint flasks, patent medicine bottles, and quart and half-gallon square liquor bottles (case bottles). The patent medicines doubtless included the usual roster, among them Bateman's, Turlington's, Dalby's, Stoughton's, British oil, and opodeldoc. Some of the flasks probably were Pitkin type, similar to those in Ill. 89, and midwestern types, similar to those in Ills. 97 and 98. In 1821 E. Pearson of Cincinnati announced he had received from Bakewell, Page & Bakewell a quantity of well-assorted glassware; among the articles mentioned were porter, snuff, blacking, and mustard bottles and vials assorted. An 1824 advertisement ended with "Porter and Claret bottles, Vials &c &c" and one in 1837 with "a complete supply of vials, bottles, flasks etc."[135] Again, with the exception of three Figured Flasks, information about the bottles and flasks is limited to generic names. As in many similar circumstances, one can conclude only that Bakewells' products in any one period were the same types and forms as those of their competitors.

Although only three Figured Flasks are so marked as to prove them Bakewell items, it seems most probable that there were others—possibly one or more of the 13 Washington–Eagle pint midwestern flasks. All three are marked with the initials "B P & B," which stand for either Bakewell, Page & Bakewell or Bakewell, Page & Bakewells. I think there can be no doubt that the American System flask was brought out about 1824, in fact probably in that year, but I doubt that the Scroll flasks were originated before 1830. The dates given below are those of the probable year or period when the flask was first blown.

GIX–38. Scroll, "B P & B" replacing fleur-de-lis on one side. Bakewell, Page & Bakewells. 1830s.

GIX–39. Similar to GXI–38, but with circular base. Bakewell, Page & Bakewells. 1830s.

GX–20. "AMERICAN" in curve above and "SYSTEM" below steam riverboat. *Reverse*: "USE ME BUT DO NOT ABUSE ME" in arch over a sheaf of rye, "B.P & B" in oval frame below sheaf. Bakewell, Page & Bakewell. Recorded in colorless flint glass of lavender tinge. 1824.

32. BRIDGEPORT GLASS WORKS, *Bridgeport, Fayette County, Western Pennsylvania, ca. 1811–47*

At Bridgeport, a log-cabin village on the east side of the Monongahela below Pittsburgh, a glasshouse was said to have been erected in 1811, operating in October of that year. The late John Ramsey's researches revealed that the glasshouse was started by John Troth, Henry Minhart, Isaac Van Hook, and associates. Advertisements of Bridgeport Glass Works stock for sale in December 1815 and May 1816 indicate that, if not among the original associates, Jonah Cadwalader and Isaac Kimber had an interest in the project not long afterward. It seems probable that production, as it did in most works, fell off during the depression and lean years following the War of 1812. Anyway, the works was offered for sale in 1822 by the agent James Truman. Perhaps it was purchased then by Benedict Kimber, who, all known accounts state, bought the Bridgeport Glass Works about 1822. Kimber, so Mrs. Knittle wrote, was "said to have been one of the New Bremen (Maryland) glass-experts who had come to America from Germany with Amelung. . . ."[136]

The exact length of Benedict Kimber's proprietorship is not yet known. It has been placed at 1837, and also the 1840s, when he became interested in the Brownsville Glass Works. Possibly he retained a minority interest when the firm of N. & P. Swearer was formed. This may have been as early as 1824 if, as seems likely, "the last eight years" in N. & P. Swearer's April 18, 1832, report to the government referred to their own operation of the works. At least they knew nothing about the production prior to 1824. The answers to the questions on that questionnaire reveal that 27 men and boys were employed at the Bridgeport Glass Works in 1832, receiving in all about $7,300 a year, for which they worked 8 to 12 hours a day for 11 months of the year. The firm also stated they had no home market and their nearest one was 300 miles away. Specifically, they mentioned Louisville, Kentucky; Baltimore, Maryland; and Philadelphia, Pennsylvania. At the latter two, their glass had to compete with foreign imports. By 1837, the Swearer firm had given way to A & B Kimber—the "B" doubtless was Benedict. And, so far as I have been able to learn, this firm remained the owner until 1847, when apparently the works was closed.[137]

The principal product of the Bridgeport Glass Works was window glass. The annual output in 1826 was said to have been 4,000 boxes at $4 each. Six years later (1832) the production had increased by 500 boxes, but the price remained the same, and in that same year, $2,000 worth of hollow ware was also blown.[138] It seems possible "chestnut" flasks pattern-molded in ribbing and possibly diamonds, too, similar to 1 and 3 in Ill. 95, were blown in the early years. However, none has ever been attributed to Bridgeport. On the other hand, a rare Figured Flask is considered a Bridgeport product, specifically of Benedict Kimber. It is GI–13, having a bust of Washington in uniform below "WASHINGTON" on the obverse and, on the reverse, an American Eagle with thunderbolt and olive branch in talons, below sunrays radiating to a semicircle of 13 stars. The eagle is perched on an oval frame enclosing "B. K." Even if Benedict Kimber was not the owner of the works after 1824, the flask could still be his, brought out between 1822 and 1824.

33. NEW BOSTON GLASS WORKS,
Baker and Martin, Perryopolis,
Fayette County, Pennsylvania, ca. 1816–ca. 1837[139]

There is little information about the New Boston Glass Works built in the village of Perryopolis on the Youghiohenny River, which flows into the Monongahela. Pittsburgh was not very many miles away. The name suggests that the still-unknown men who built and owned the glasshouse may have emigrated to western Pennsylvania from the Boston area of Massachusetts. Possibly they were glassmen who had been on the staff of one of the glassworks in Boston or its vicinity. Possibly they had chosen Perryopolis as the site for a glasshouse because the area had an abundance of some raw material that was "of a peculiar and excellent quality for the manufacture of glass" and was shipped to some of the Pittsburgh glassworks. Exactly when this window-glass and bottle house was established is undetermined as yet. Three dates have been given—1816, 1823, and the first quarter of the 19th century. Certainly it was before 1820, for in February of that year 100 boxes of window glass were "seized and taken in execution as property of the Perryopolis green Glass Company at the suit of Taylor & Howland," and were advertised as in a sheriff's sale. The company survived the period of hard times. However, it would appear it was never a very large enterprise: in 1826 the total output consisted of 2,000 boxes of window glass and hollow ware valued at $8,000, and in 1832 the entire capital investment was reported as $4,500.[140]

At some point, if they were not the founders, Jonathan Baker and John F. Martin acquired the glassworks— probably by 1824 if, as is possible, the initials "B & M" on the extremely rare American System flask GX–20a stand for Baker and Martin. (For the design of the flask, see 3 and 4 in Ill. 125.) It would appear from their answers, made in April 1832 to the federal government questionnaire on manufactures, that by then the production of hollow ware of any kind had ceased or become insignificant, for they reported only window-glass manufacture—a yearly output of 4,000 boxes sold at $3.62½ a box. Since, as listed, their raw materials alone cost a yearly total of $7,450, their gross profit must have been well below $7,000, and that represented a decrease due to domestic competition. Their employees were 29 in number, of whom eight were blowers paid 85ᶜ for each 100 feet of glass blown, and two were glass cutters who, for cutting the sheets into panes, were paid $18 a box. All the other employees were paid by the month—$18 each to seven "hands"; $4 each to eight boys; $16 each to three coal diggers and one wagoner. The following year in an advertisement dated Perryopolis, Sep-

tember 4, 1833, Baker & Martin announced the dissolution of their partnership. Although the next bit of evidence of the glassworks is a listing of Baker, Stewart & Company in a Pittsburgh 1837 directory, it may be that Jonathan Baker joined with a Stewart and others after his partnership with John F. Martin was "dissolved by mutual consent."[141] If John Ramsey's findings are correct, the company did not survive the 1837 panic.

As I have said previously, it is possible that the American System flask GX–20a with initials "B & M" in the waves beneath the riverboat is a product of Baker & Martin. So too probably is the extremely rare General Jackson flask GI–67, which has on the reverse the initials "B & M" in the beaded oval frame beneath the American eagle.

34. WILLIAM IHMSEN, *Williamsport and Pittsburgh,*
Pennsylvania[142]

The Ihmsens (spelled also Impsen and Imsen), who were among Pittsburgh's foremost glassmen and manufacturers from the early to the late 19th century, stemmed from a line of Germans who had been glassmen for over two centuries. William was a son of Charles Ihmsen who, around 1795, emigrated to the United States. It is said that he went first to the New Bremen Glassmanufactory of John Frederick Amelung near Frederick, Maryland. In 1807 he moved west, settling in Pittsburgh, where he blew glass for more than one glass manufacturer and became partner in more than one firm of manufacturers. It is said also that he built a green-glass works of his own in 1814 in Birmingham.[143] It is probable that William and his brother Christian served their apprenticeship under their father, surely in one of the works in which he had an interest.

There is conflicting evidence as to exactly when William Ihmsen himself became the owner of a glassworks, one in Williamsport (later called Monongahela City), a small village on the Monongahela River about 20 miles above Pittsburgh, a location convenient to coal beds. However, it would appear from John Ramsey's research in the late 1930s that around 1820 Ihmsen built his Williamsport Glass Works for the production of bottles and flasks, and that in 1826 he leased a glassworks, which was under construction in 1814 and was operating in 1815. According to reports, 3,000 boxes of window glass were sold in 1826.[144] It seems a fair assumption that he had rented his second works for the production of that commodity.

In the 1830s William Ihmsen expanded his interests. By 1831 he had formed a copartnership with his brother Christian in still another glassworks. They had "erected a factory for the manufacture of Vials and Bottles" apparently in Pittsburgh, and maintained a warehouse on Third Street where they intended to keep "a very general supply of Window glass assorted and boxes of Hollow-ware for country merchants, vials of all descriptions, Porter, Castor Oil and all other Bottles." By 1833 William Ihmsen was also in partnership with William McCully, who had been apprenticed first at Bakewells' and from there moved on to

GLASS WARE.
W. & C. IHMSEN,
PITTSBURGH.

THE undersigned have formed a co-partnership in manufacturing of WINDOW & HOL LOW-WARE GLASS. They intend keeping a very general supply of Window Glass, assorted boxes of Hollow-Ware for country merchants, Vials of all descriptions, Porter, Castor Oil and all other Bottles. Having expressly erected a factory for the manufacture of Vials and Bottles, they wil warrant their Glass equal to the best eastern articles to be found in market. Orders promptly filled at their Warehouse on THIRD STREET, between Wood and Smithfield streets.

Western merchants are respectfully invited to call and examine for themselves.

WILLIAM IHMSEN,
CHRISTIAN IHMSEN.
October 5th, 1831—tf

18. Advertisement of glassware, including vials and bottles, made by W. & C. Ihmsen, Pittsburgh, Pa. Note that the advertisement is dated October 5, 1831. (Pittsburgh, *The Statesman*, Oct. 3, 1832.) *The New-York Historical Society, New York City*

"O'Hara's," the Pittsburgh Glass Works, becoming a journeyman by 1829. Though the advertisement of Ihmsen's and McCully's new vial factory gives a Wood Street, Pittsburgh, address, apparently the new works was in Williamsport "in conjunction with their window glass manufactory." They claimed, as was not unusual with most manufacturers, that they made "all sorts and sizes of vials and Bottles of a very superior quality" and stated that "sizes [would be] made to any given pattern exactly." It is interesting to note, too, that barter still persisted: scorched salts and pearl ash would be taken in exchange for glass.[144a] In 1840 when William Ihmsen died, if not before, the factories became part of William McCully & Company.

Although it seems unlikely that William Ihmsen—or William and his partners—produced only one Figured Flask, today there is proof of only one. That one, a rarity, is GII–10, charted in the Eagle group because of the American eagle on the side chosen as the obverse. In the oval frame on which the eagle perches is "GLASS" and above the eagle "W. IHMSEN, S", leaving no doubt as to the producer. On the reverse, as charted, is "AGRICULTURE" arching above a sheaf of grain, in turn above scattered farm implements—fork, rake, sickle, scythe, and plow. It is believed that William Ihmsen produced this flask in his Williamsport Glass Works in the mid- to late-1820s.

35. JOHN ROBINSON'S STOURBRIDGE FLINT GLASS WORKS, *Pittsburgh, Pennsylvania*

In 1823 John Robinson, a skilled glassman, built a flint-glass works, the fifth of its kind, in Pittsburgh near the corner of Ross and Second streets. Robinson was an Englishman said to have come to America from Stourbridge, where doubtless he learned his craft. Such was his pride in his "mother works" that he named his new glassworks the Stourbridge Flint Glass Factory.[145] That apparently he quickly met with success, and found a ready

market to the westward and probably close to home also, is suggested by the regular advertisements of his Cincinnati agents, Henry Bearpark and Lot Pugh, in 1824 and 1825. Of course he, like other manufacturers, claimed the quality of his "*Plain, Engraved and Fancy Cut* [wares] of every description" to be "equal if not superior to anything of the kind manufactured in the United States."[146] Jones reported in *Pittsburg in the Year 1826* that Robinson employed 18 glassblowers, decorators, and engravers whose yearly production was valued at $22,000—not a bad start for a three-year-old venture.

The next year—according to the United States Patent Index—following in the footsteps of John P. Bakewell of Bakewell & Company, Pittsburgh (1825), and Whitney and Robinson of the New England Glass Company, Cambridge, Massachusetts (1826), John Robinson obtained a patent for a process to press glass knobs. These seem to have initiated the pressing of other objects and to have been produced in large quantities: In June 1830 "300 setts of Patent Glass Knobs" were offered for sale at reduced prices.[147]

From the same June 19, 1830, advertisement we learn that John Robinson had taken a son into the business with him. Whether he was John, Jr., or Thomas is not stated, but one may perhaps assume it was John, Jr., who, it seems likely, was the elder son. Nor is the exact year known but, as the advertisement reveals, by the date of the advertisement J. Robinson & Son were opening a new shipment of glassware in their "Pittsburgh Glass Ware House" that they maintained on Fifth Street in Cincinnati. There their "large and extensive assortment of rich cut, plain, and pressed / FLINT GLASS WARE" was for sale on reasonable terms.[148] About three years later the readers of the *Cincinnati Daily Gazette* were informed that this Cincinnati enterprise was being closed in order to "attend more strictly" to their Pittsburgh glass manufacturing. Therefore the firm sought to settle all debts owed by or to them at once. Also, to dispose of the still extensive stock on hand, which was "suitable to this and neighboring markets," they were offering all glass at "the lowest possible terms for cash or approved paper." An agency to handle the Stourbridge Flint Glass Works' products was to be appointed, and by October 1833, if not sooner, Nathan Hastings, "late of Hastings & Knight," became the agent for J. Robinson & Son.[149] In the meantime, by 1832 the firm's capital had risen to $33,000, the employees to 36 men and boys, and the annual output to a value of $43,000.[150]

By October of 1834 John Robinson, Sr., was no longer in the firm running the Stourbridge Flint Glass Works; it was the business of his two sons, John, Jr., and Thomas—under the name J. & T. Robinson. It may be that the father had been forced to retire because of illness, as he died in 1835 or 1836. John Jr.'s, and Thomas's October 6 advertisement in the *Pittsburgh Gazette* announced that a new factory at Kensington had been built:

TO MERCHANTS GENERALLY / New Stourbridge Flint Glass Works / The subscribers respectfully inform the public that they are now manufacturing FLINT GLASSWARE in all its variety and are prepared to fill all orders with dispatch. They invite dealers to give them a trial and examine their assortment. They are disposed to sell low, and on accommodating terms / J. & T. ROBINSON

At some point between the fall of 1834 and the time when data for Harris's 1837 Pittsburgh Directory was compiled, the Robinsons took Alex M. Anderson into the firm. This Anderson probably was the same one who had lately been the Anderson of Bakewells & Anderson, and it seems likely the Jackson hard times had made it necessary for the Robinsons to seek further financing. Harris gives the factory location as "Kensington opposite the gas works"; also, the information that 65 hands were employed producing annually $90,000 worth of cut, pressed, and plain glassware. The next we hear of this important glassworks is that it closed in 1845.[151]

Although in not one of the advertisements of John Robinson, J. Robinson & Son, J. & T. Robinson, or Robinson, Anderson & Company that I have read has there been mention of bottles, to say nothing of Figured Flasks, no student or collector doubts for a moment that two extremely rare portrait flasks were produced by John Robinson and two, possibly three, scrolls by J. Robinson and Son. Moreover, the rare portrait flasks tested for lead content have proved to be lead glass. The molds for the portrait flasks have the initials "J.R" and were carved by Joshua Laird, a Pittsburgh moldmaker who was sufficiently proud of his achievements to sign them, as shows in the description below. These two probably date 1824–28. Of the two scroll flasks believed to be definitely brought out by J. Robinson & Son, one has the initials "J.R.& S"; the other, "J.R. & Son". The dating of the advertisements mentioned above has led to the dating of the flasks as between June 1830 and 1834. The flasks appear in the charts as follows:

GI–6. *Obverse:* "GENERAL WASHINGTON" arching above a bust of Washington in uniform. *Reverse:* Nine 6-pointed stars above an American eagle with laurel branch in beak, shield on breast, standing on beaded oval frame, thunderbolt in right talon and olive branch in left; "J.R." within frame; "LAIRD S.C. [sculpit] PITT" below frame. Pint. 1824–28. Very rare.

GI–66. *Obverse:* "GENERAL JACKSON" arching above bust of Andrew Jackson. *Reverse:* Eight 6-pointed stars and one 5-pointed above American eagle with laurel branch in beak, shield on breast, standing on beaded oval frame, thunderbolt in right talon and olive branch in left; "J.R." within frame; "LAIRD S.C. PITT" below frame. Pint. 1824–28. Extremely rare.

GIX–42. Scroll flask. *Obverse:* Large anchor within "scroll," a large "pearl" at each side of fluke. *Reverse:* Within scroll, large fleur-de-lis and "JR. & S"; large "pearl" above "J" and "S". Half-pint. ca. 1830-34. Rare.

GIX–43. Scroll flask. *Obverse:* Small fleur-de-lis with scroll; pearl at each side of upper "stem" of scroll and one at each side below bottom of scroll. *Reverse:* Scroll forming elaborate frame at bottom; "J R & SON" within frame; "pearls" as on GIX–42, with also one in each loop of bottom of frame. Pint. ca. 1830–34. Scarce.

GIX–41. Scroll flask, probably by J. Robinson and Son. Like GIX–42 but without "J R. & S". Half-pint. ca. 1830–34. Scarce.

36. BROWNSVILLE GLASS WORKS, JOHN TAYLOR & COMPANY, *Brownsville (Redstone), Fayette County, Western Pennsylvania, 1828–1900*

Brownsville in western Pennsylvania was a favorable location for business and manufacturing: southeast of Pittsburgh and very near Bridgeport, it was situated on the east bank of the Monongahela, and through it ran that vital east-west trade artery, the National Road. Students of American glass are indebted to Rhea Mansfield Knittle for such information as has been published concerning George Hogg, who, taking advantage of the situation, built the Brownsville Glass Works in 1828. Hogg was an Englishman. At 20 he left his job in an iron foundry and emigrated to America, arriving in 1804 at Brownsville, where an uncle was living. It would appear from Mrs. Knittle's account that, in the 24 years between his settling in Brownsville and building his glassworks, George Hogg, with his Uncle William,

gradually built up a mercantile and forwarding business in the middle West, until they owned fifteen agencies in Western Pennsylvania and Eastern Ohio towns. They also operated a fleet of Merchant Marine on Lake Erie, with yards at Sandusky and canal-boats along the Cuyahoga River. Glass from the works at Brownsville was in this manner widely distributed.[152]

However, not all the glass so distributed was produced by George Hogg—nor was all glass made by his successors so distributed. There were to be many changes of owners and lessees in the 72 years of the glassworks' operation. The first change occurred perhaps less than a year after Hogg launched his glass factory, when he leased the works to John Taylor & Company early in 1829 or late in 1828. If, as Mrs. Knittle states, he "retained supervision of furnace operations," it probably was for a brief period. A year or two later he sold the works to John Taylor and Edward Campbell. John Taylor & Company was short-lived, but there is nonetheless more information about the works under this firm than under any of the later ones. A newspaper advertisement dated May 8, 1829, shows that the company had appointed W. P. Jones of Cincinnati, Ohio, their agent. Perhaps there were agents also in other large midwestern communities; one would expect so. However, in their report to the federal government, dated

April 16, 1832, they stated that their glass was sold "princi-pally in the East, Baltimore and Philadelphia," where it met the competition of foreign glass. Their annual product was 4,500 boxes of window glass at $4 a box, totaling $18,000, and $2,000 worth of glassware—the same, inci-dentally, as that of their neighbor, the Bridgeport Glass Works. This production was achieved by 27 men and boys working 8 to 12 hours a day for 11 months of the year, for an average total of $7,250 a year.[153]

Perhaps it was shortly after making the 1832 report that John Taylor sold his interest to William R. Campbell, and the firm became briefly Edward Campbell & Company. Still later in the year Edward Campbell sold his interest to Robert Forsyth. Though Mrs. Knittle stated that Forsyth sold his stock back to Edward Campbell in 1834, R. For-syth & Company was listed in Harris's 1837 Western Directory. This may have been a carryover listing, for a John C. Gabler & Company, Brownsville glass manufac-turers, was also listed in the same directory. Moreover, it was said that in 1837 the Brownsville Glassworks was purchased by two glassblowers from the East, Gue and Gabler. Apparently they promptly failed in the 1837 panic. The glassworks, auctioned at sheriff's sale, was bought in by its original owner, George Hogg. Around two years later Burke, Sedgwick & Company became the pro-prietors, and were followed about 1843 by Benedict Kimber, who had left the Bridgeport Glass Works. When Kimber died of cholera, Haught, Schewere (or Swearer) & Company succeeded him. Various dates of this occurrence have been given—1846, 1848, and 1851. Apparently the new firm ran into financial difficulties, for Robert Rogers purchased the glassworks in 1855. From him, Haught, Schewere & Company leased the works for about eight years. Then F. & F. Schewere became the lessees for a brief period. A George Wells, who added an eight-pot furnace and made other improvements, owned the works from 1864 until 1873. In that depression year Schmertz & Quimby acquired it. Another eight years passed before the Brownsville Glass Works changed hands again. From 1887 to 1900 it was operated by a cooperative company.[154]

Apparently window glass, bottles, and flasks were the products of the glassworks throughout its long lifetime. Mrs. Knittle states that George Hogg started the works for the manufacture of green and black bottles. If so, when John Taylor and Company became the operators, window glass was added. This is evident from the May 1829 adver-tisement by W. P. Jones, the Cincinnati agent. Moreover, the blowing of window glass may have taken a lion's share of the working time: 16 different sizes, ranging from 7 by 8 to 15 by 18 panes, were given. Also advertised were porter bottles, gallon, half-gallon, quart, and pint bottles[155]—unmarked, presumably. But more exciting for collectors of Figured Flasks are two in the historical category attributed to John Taylor & Company because of the initials "J. T & Co." The characteristics of the flasks are those of the right period and the initials fit no other recorded glass manufacturer of the period. The two flasks, illustrated by line drawings in the Charts, are:

GI–62. "JOHN Q. ADAMS" arching above portrait bust. *Reverse*: 13 stars above American eagle perched on beaded oval frame, "J. T & C^O" below frame. Ex-tremely rare.

GI–64. "ANDREW JACKSON" arching above portrait bust, similar to GI–62.

In 1927 Mrs. Knittle wrote:

We know that Brownsville made a "Pike's Peak" bottle [Group XI], an "Eagle, reverse Eagle" [Group II] and "Union and Clasped Hands" [Group XII] and other standardized types of flasks during the period from 1850 to 1870. It will probably be several years before we can prop-erly place their varieties of well-known designs....[156] Now, a half-century later, we are no nearer being able to assign a specific Pike's Peak, Union & Clasped Hands, or Eagle-reverse-Eagle to the Brownsville Glass Works.

37. ZANESVILLE GLASS MANUFACTORY, *"White Glass Works," Zanesville, Ohio, 1815–51*[157]

In 1815 eight businessmen made plans for a glassworks in Zanesville, Ohio, a town incorporated on January 21 of the previous year. At first glance it might seem a foolhardy venture in so small an interior town—the population was only around 1,200. But Zanesville served as market town for a rich agricultural area in a county of 14,000. And, being on the Muskingum River that flowed into the Ohio, it was favorably situated for water transport of produce and wares to small and large markets, not only along the Ohio but to the south and west. Moreover, the National Road that was to pass through Zanesville would provide a better land route than the post road. All in all, Zanesville seemed a strategic location for a glassworks, and—in 1815—the effects of the post–War of 1812 depression had not yet reached the Midwest. It was on May 13 of that year that General Isaac Van Horn, his stepson David J. Marple, Samuel Sullivan (owner of a pottery), Samuel Herrick, Rees Cadwalleder, Dr. John Hamm, E. Buckingham, and Edmund Jones (who was superintendent of the works) signed articles of agreement incorporating the Zanesville Glass Manufacturing Company. The first article provided that the capital stock could amount to $50,000 in shares of $500 each, but that when $7,000 had been subscribed the company could proceed with the establishment of its glassworks—acquire a building site, erect the necessary buildings, and secure competent workmen and the neces-sary material for making glass.

Actually, though payment was not made until May 26, 1818, arrangements had been made to purchase (for $400) lots on the southwest corner of Market and 3rd streets, and not only had the glasshouse been erected there but it was in operation before May 13, 1815. On the previous day, the *Zanesville Express* carried the following:

The glass works lately erected in this town have commenced their operations. Glassware of superior quality is produced. To the friends of domestic manufactures and their thriving employment in this country this intelligence must afford satisfaction.

The intention was to produce white hollow-ware, neither window glass nor green-glass wares. And, apparently, during the first two years only white hollow-ware was blown. Hence the popular name the "White Glass Works." The ware was "pronounced by judges to be equal to any of the kind manufactured in the U. States"—or so a December 6, 1815, news item in Chillicothe's *The Weekly Recorder* reported under "Internal Improvements." The same item reported, as did also the advertisement in a January 4, 1816, Pittsburgh newspaper, that in the following spring the company would build additional facilities for the manufacture of window glass and green hollow-ware. Probably it was later in 1816 that actual work on the new building began, and although completion was said to be a matter of "small expense," the building was still unfinished by February 2, 1817, when the entire property was offered for sale. The green-glass works probably was in operation before the year was out.

The next five years were marked by changes in ownership. The first occurred in March 1817 when Stephen Smith (successor to Samuel Sullivan as president), Isaac Van Horn, Robert Fulton (successor to Rees Cadwalleder as trustee), David J. Marple, and Samuel Herrick were the five trustees (directors) required by Article 2 of the original agreement. On March 13, there was reorganization through a double transaction: the five trustees sold the land, works, and "all appurtenances, implements and tools . . . for the manufacture of glassware or in any wise appertaining to the same" to one John Campbell for $6,000. Campbell in turn at once deeded the property for $3,000 to Isaac Van Horn, Dr. John Hamm, Samuel Herrick, Jeffry Price, and Daniel Stilwell—the last two apparently were new members and trustees. Norris Schneider and Everett Greer, whose researches into the history of Zanesville's glassworks are the most recent, state that the purpose of the sales seems to have been "to allow Fulton and Smith to be compensated and retire." About two years and eight months later, November 4, 1819, Daniel Stilwell withdrew or lessened his interest by selling to Oliver Dubois and George Kinsey, who, on the tenth of the month, sold to the Reverend Joseph Shepard (Sheperd), Thomas Mark, and William Bingham. Perhaps they provided the financial backing for a group of glassmen, Edmunds, Bingham & Company, to start the short-lived Zanesville White Flint Glass Company. It seems probable that for this new adventure, launched by May 1820, the company rented the original "White Glass Works." It is interesting to note that in their announcement, dated May 2, and running in *Liberty Hall and Cincinnati Gazette* from May 31 through July 26, 1820, they offered to barter glass for red lead, pearl ashes, and saltpeter. It is unclear whether or not the owners operated the green-glass works during the period of 1820 to 1822 when a new company was formed.

In any event, it was in 1822 that the Reverend Joseph Shepard, who already owned an interest, James Crosby, and Charles Bostwick formed J. Shepard & Company and bought the glassworks, which they operated for about 16 years. A little more is known about Shepard and Crosby than about the other men who were at one time or another among the proprietors of the Zanesville Glass Works. The Reverend Shepard was an Englishman from Numealton, Warwickshire, who settled in Zanesville in 1812 at the age of 33. Since, according to church records, Shepard was entered as a deacon of the First Baptist Church, it may be that he was a "Reverend" by courtesy rather than by ordination. Though it is said he preached on Sundays, tombstones were his livelihood. He was 50 when he first became financially interested in the Zanesville Glass Works and 52 when J. Shepard & Company was formed. His ventures so prospered that, at his death in March 1852, he left $3,000 to each of his five children. James Crosby, nine years Shepard's junior, was also an Englishman, born in Westmorland County in 1777. In 1800 Crosby was sent from England to New York City as agent for the Phoenix Insurance Company. After war with England was declared in 1812, Crosby, with other enemy aliens, was sent out of the city to be interned in Orange County, New York. Apparently he returned to New York City when released and in 1817 moved to Zanesville, where he became a naturalized citizen of the United States. He, like Shepard, was interested in the affairs of his church, serving as warden of the Episcopal Church. He must have been interested in local politics and government too, for he was town recorder in 1823 and 1825 and city clerk from 1851 until 1857. The following year, in February, Crosby died.

In the meantime, the Zanesville Glass Works at Market and 3rd streets had had several proprietors and finally closed. In 1835, seven years after the firm of J. Shepard & Company had taken over the works, Charles Bostwick withdrew his interest, which presumably was taken up by Shepard and Crosby. Three years later Shepard retired, but until 1851 he retained his interest in the land on which the glassworks and its ancillary buildings were located. With the dissolution of the firm, Crosby had resolved to continue operations alone. In his December 21, 1838, announcement in the Zanesville *Aurora* he thanked customers for their past patronage and solicited its continuance. However, he closed down some time in 1839, most likely because the business was suffering from the current depression. The glassworks was idle until 1840, when it was purchased by Alfred Merrick, who, after producing hollow ware for about a year, sold it to Daniel Kinney in 1841. The next year, 1842, six skilled glassmen from Pittsburgh—George Washington Kearns, Thomas Reynolds, Joseph Burns, W. F. Spence, Samuel Turner, and George Wendt—formed Burns, Reynolds & Company and rented the "White Glass Works." The following enlightening advertisement appeared in the *Aurora* on August 22, 1844:

ZANESVILLE VIAL AND BOTTLE FACTORY.—The undersigned having leased the above

works, and made extensive repairs upon them are now manufacturing Vials, Bottles and Hollow ware generally. Being practical mechanics themselves making all their own ware, which, with the use of good materials will enable them to equal that of
PITTSBURG MANUFACTURE
They are provided with a good assortment of moulds among which are a number adapted to the Patent
    medicines most in repute
Glass ordered in individual moulds, supplied at the
    shortest notice
Merchants' and Druggists' bids filled to order upon as favorable terms as can be procured elsewhere.
Aug. 22, 1849—3m   BURNS, REYNOLDS & CO.

In the same year Reynolds and Wendt sold their interest, and about two years later, in 1846, Kearns and Burns also sold theirs. Then Arnold Lippitt entered the scene. Lippitt was a book publisher and partner in J. R. and A. Lippitt, wholesale and retail dealers in books, stationery, drugs, medicines, and dye stuffs. Lippitt, by the way, first made a brief attempt to become a glass manufacturer at the Sligo glassworks (see No. 38) in the 1830s, probably late in the decade. At the time he took over the Zanesville Glass Works on Market Street he had been operating the Sligo glassworks, a second time, for about two years.[158] He failed at Sligo in 1847, and in 1851 he closed down the Market Street works. It would appear that the "White Glass Works" (the name is used to embrace its green-glass offspring) was never reopened. Local competition may have been at least in part the cause.

Foremost among the midwestern bottles and flasks are those sometimes called Ohio-Stiegel because of their pattern-molded designs, fine metal and color, and attractive forms. And it seems more than likely that Ohio-Stiegel types and also Figured Flasks made up the 300 boxes of "Bottles and Flasks assorted sizes from the Zanesville Glass Works" that were advertised by Allison Owen of Cincinnati in July of 1831.[159] Though no documentary proof has been found, nor shards unearthed, I think no one doubts that the "White Glass Works" was the source of many of the finest of those pattern-molded containers—in particular, 24-rib swirl bottles with nearly spherical bodies like the amber ones, 1 through 4 and 6 in Ill. 96; 24-rib swirl "bee hive" bottles like the grayish blue 1 in Ill. 94; also 10-diamond jugs like the reddish amber 3 in Ill. 99, chestnut flasks like the light olive-green 2 in Ill. 98, and brownish ambers like 4 and 10 in Ill. 97. (See Part VI: 4. Midwestern Bottles, Flasks, and Jugs.) The brilliance of the metal probably derived from the exceptionally fine silica available to Zanesville's glass manufacturers. (There is evidence that local flint may have been used.[160]) The wide range of ambers, from "black" to golden, and greens from light to medium emerald in which J. Shepard & Company's Agriculture–Masonic and Eagle Figured Flask GIV–32 occurs would seem an indication of the colors in which the pattern-molded bottles and flasks may be found. These, it is believed, were made over a period of years, probably from around 1817 up through 1835 or 1840. At

least it would seem that pattern-molded bottles and perhaps flasks continued in strong favor longer west of the Alleghenies than east of them. In connection with the molds, it is important to note and keep in mind that the presence of 24 ribs in themselves—be they vertical, swirled, or broken swirl—on a bottle or flask does not constitute proof of Zanesville origin. Molds producing 24 ribs were used in several glassworks. As for the 10-diamond mold, possibly it was used at Isaac Duval's Wellsburg, (West) Virginia, glassworks before its use at the Zanesville Glass Works.

As for the category of Figured Flasks—doubtless not long after J. Shepard & Company was formed they brought out the previously mentioned pint flask GIV–32, charted in the Masonic Group because of the Masonic Arch and Pavement in the design on the obverse, as charted. As comparison of the line drawings in Group IV shows, there is a close similarity between the design of GIV–32 and Dr. Dyott's flask GIV–37, brought out in 1822 at his Kensington, Philadelphia, glassworks, and the obverse of his GIV–34 and GIV–35, ca. 1826–28. It will be noted that the arch is not so well rendered in the Zanesville flask; for instance, the stones in the arch above the pillars are loosely placed. The eagle design on the reverse of GIV–32 also is similar to that on Dyott's GIV–37. But GIV–32 has "ZANESVILLE" in arc at top of the sun rays; "OHIO" in beaded oval frame; and, in reverse arc below, "J. SHEPARD & CO." with the S reversed.

One other Figured Flask is thought to be a probable J. Shepard & Company product, namely the half-pint Eagle–Cornucopia, GII–18, with "ZANES" following the upper line of the beaded oval frame and "VILLE" the lower. The designs on obverse and reverse of this flask are closely similar to Dyott's half-pint GII–43, ca. 1826–28. It seems likely that the Zanesville flasks were inspired by Dyott's Kensington flasks.

38. MUSKINGUM GREEN GLASS WORKS, "Sligo Glass Works," Zanesville, Ohio. 1816–49.

In 1816 a glasshouse for the production of window glass and hollow ware was erected at the mouth of the Sligo Run where it emptied into the Muskingum River. The proprietors were Peter Mills & Company. None of the four founders was a practical glassman, but each had money to invest. In the early 1800s Peter Mills had bought furs in Canada and the Far West for John Jacob Astor. He had settled in Zanesville before or by 1810, the year he became a Freemason there. That he was active in local politics seems evident, for in 1814 he was elected a trustee of the town. He was also active in the Presbyterian Church and was its treasurer in 1815. Captain James Hampton, a Zanesville contractor, superintended the building of the glasshouse. James Taylor, a native of Virginia, was a Zanesville storekeeper; his store was a local outlet for the Company's glass. The fourth founder, Alexander Culbertson, Jr., had arrived in the town in 1808 when his father emigrated from Franklin County, Pennsylvania. Culbertson—like Taylor, he owned a store on Main Street—became manager of the Muskingum Green Glass Works, as it was called when Peter Mills & Company began production on June 20, 1816. Incidentally, Schneider and Green apparently found no record to confirm Mrs. Knittle's statement that the works was started by James Taylor and Alexander Culbertson and called the New Granite Glass Works.[161]

In a little over three decades of production, the Sligo glassworks was to have at least eleven different operators. The first, Peter Mills & Company, for some unknown reason (perhaps the long depression that was a period of casualties among our glassworks) dissolved in the early fall of 1819. The following announcement, quoted by Schneider and Green, appeared in the *Muskingum Messenger* on September 4 of that year:

Green Glass Manufactory. The subscriber would inform his friends and the public that he now makes and keeps constantly on hand at his manufactory, Zanesville, Ohio, window glass of all sizes and *hollow ware of every description*, superior to any ever made heretofore in the above manufactory; and equal to any glass that I have seen. All orders thankfully received and punctually attended to. Alex Culberton. [The italics are mine.]

In his business ventures Culbertson profited sufficiently to be able to leave an estate of $70,000 when he died suddenly in 1823. His widow then assumed an active role and operated the works until 1832.

In that year Thomas Murdock, one of the glassmen employed, and Joseph Cassel, son-in-law of the Culbertsons, took charge. After perhaps four or five years the works was operated as a bottle manufactory by Arnold Lippitt, who—as previously stated (see No. 37. Zanesville Glass Manufactory)—was a book publisher and, with J. R. Lippitt, maintained a Main Street store stocked with books, stationery, drugs, medicines, and dye stuffs. Though all the dates have not been learned, it is known that Lippitt was followed swiftly by the Murdock brothers, R. P. Robinson, S. B. Johnson & Company (a partnership of J. M. Kirkpatrick and S. B. Johnson), and, in March 1840, Kirkpatrick. About two months after Kirkpatrick announced, on March 19, that he had "taken the Manufactory" and that his "terms [could] be to suit the times" (depressed), S. B. Johnson advertised on May 2 that *he* had taken over the glassworks. As neither Kirkpatrick nor Robinson mentioned hollow ware in their announcements, it may be that no bottles were blown during their regimes. It would appear that under Robinson the Sligo Glass Works was in production about two and a half years, until the fall of 1842, when Arnold Lippitt again came on the scene. On November 9 he ran an announcement in the *Aurora* that, having just put the Sligo Glass Works into successful operation, he was prepared to take orders for window glass or hollow ware of a quality equal to that of Pittsburgh products. It is especially interesting to note the

continuation of barter at this late date: he wanted 30 tons of scorched salts, for which he would give window glass, hollow ware, groceries, and some cash.

Lippitt ran the Sligo Glass Works for about five years. In 1847, the year after he leased the Zanesville Glass Works (see No. 37) the Sligo was taken over by J. B. and S. L. Cochran, tobacconists on Main Street. According to a news item in the Zanesville *Courier* for September 27, 1849, the works had been "taken for a term of years." From the same item we learn also that the furnace contained eight pots and was "of the most approved construction, the escape of smoke being especially excellent." And at the time, the employees numbered about 20: "eight blowers, their attendants, two or three cutters [of window glass], five or six other hands, packing box makers, firemen and pot makers. . . ." In spite of their boast that their window glass defied comparison and excelled that manufactured in Pittsburgh, the Cochran brothers appear to have failed in 1849.

Although students do not doubt that pattern-molded bottles and flasks were blown in the Sligo Glass Works, and that a 24-rib mold was probably among those used, specific identification is not possible as yet. Not even such chancy evidence as family tradition has attributed any recorded pattern-molded hollow ware to Sligo. And inasmuch as there is no evidence of production of glass in artificial colors or in the varied ambers that are associated with Zanesville, the conclusion seems tenable that the hollow ware produced at Sligo was blown from window-glass metal and occurred in greens from aquamarine to medium green, as do the Figured Flasks marked "MURDOCK & CASSEL."

Two designs are known to have been used at the Sligo Glass Works when it was being operated by Thomas Murdock and Joseph Cassel. One is the Agricultural and Masonic–Eagle, GIV–33, like Zanesville Glass Works's GIV–32 but with "MURDOCK & CASSEL" below the oval frame instead of "J. SHEPARD & CO." (with reverse S). In fact, the Shepard mold appears to have been acquired by Murdock and Cassel. Studies by Kenneth M. Wilson and the late Crawford Wettlaufer determined that the Shepard mold GIV–32 was altered to make GIV–33—the "SHEPARD & CO." with reverse S was filled in and "MURDOCK & CASSEL" cut in the mold. The other design, that of GX–14 and GX–14a, really falls in the category of blown-three-mold. The geometric pattern consists of a wide band of vertical ribbing at bottom separated, by a single horizontal rib, from a narrow band of diagonal ribbing to the left. Above, the diagonal ribbing is, on the obverse, "MURDOCK [in arc] / & / CASSEL"; on the reverse, "ZANESVILLE [in arc] / OHIO." GX–14a differs from GX–14 in having larger lettering.

39. CINCINNATI GLASS WORKS, *Cincinnati, 1815–24?*, and MOSCOW GLASS WORKS, *Moscow, Ohio, 1823–ca. 1830*

The history of these two glassworks is largely skeletal;

its bones are mainly advertisements and notices in newspapers and the comments of a few travelers. The Cincinnati Glass Works was one of several started in the United States during the last year of the War of 1812, and one of the earliest in the Midwest outside of the Pittsburgh area. Like many others of the period, it was a short-lived venture, lasting a little less than a decade. It was also in a period in which would-be glass manufacturers still appealed to patriotism, national and local.

In April 1815, Christopher Anthony, Isaac Hough, and Lewis Rees informed the friends of "Western improvement and commercial independence" that their Cincinnati Glass Works was in operation producing glass of "a quality equal to any kind manufactured in the western country."[162] The glasshouse, so the traveler Elias Pym Fordham recorded, was located at the lower end of the city (that is southwestern) and on the Ohio River, a strategic manufacturing location with water carriage up and down the Ohio and its tributaries to interior and southern towns as well as those along the river. And, according to another traveler, Henry Bradshaw Fearon, it was "on a tolerably large scale." David Thomas, who visited Cincinnati in 1816, reported that "works for green glass have lately gone into operation but some articles produced are very imperfect."[163]

By April of 1816 the firm had become Hough, Rees & Company. Christopher Anthony apparently was no longer one of the firm, though notice that his one-third interest was to be sold at the glasshouse on May 3, 1816, was not published until March 31, 1817, nearly a year after Anthony's death. In August 1816, Hough, Rees & Company appointed James & Douglass, Cincinnati merchants, as agents for the sale of window glass and hollow ware, which suggests the possibility of their being members of the company. The window glass was said to be equal to that of (New) Geneva—that is, of the "Gallatin" glassworks—and assortments of hollow ware were put up in boxes for the convenience of country merchants. Their glass, the proprietors pledged, would not be inferior to any made in any glassworks in the Western Country."[164]

No evidence has been found as to who secured Christopher Anthony's interest in the Cincinnati Glass Works. Possibly it was acquired by Henry Teater or Lot Pugh or shared by them. Be that as it may, a little over three weeks after the sale was to occur, Henry Teater advertised that he had rented the glassworks from Hough, Rees & Company and that operations would begin as soon as the weather permitted. (It will be remembered that it was not customary for glassworks to be in blast the year round.) Teater's statement that he had "procured a set of COMPLETE WORKMEN" suggests that Hough, Rees & Company had suffered from the common plague of the period—shortage of skilled glassmen. Perhaps Teater's complete set were from Pittsburgh, where glass manufacturers were enduring a depression. Teater, too, made a plea to local self-interest: "Merchants and Gentlemen building will no doubt readily see the propriety of leaving their money immediately in their own neighborhood, as they will have reasonable ex-

pectation of getting it again in the course of trade." The following July, Teater appointed James & Douglass as his agents.[165]

Teater's tenancy was a short one; on February 25, 1818, Lot Pugh, a commission merchant, and Henry Teater announced that they had purchased the Cincinnati Glass Works, which would be operated by the firm of Pugh & Teater. They stated also that they were making "extensive arrangements to have them [the works] in operation as soon as possible." Apparently they ran into difficulties of which they left no record. At least, the next advertisement found was not until the end of June. Then Pugh & Teater, commission merchants as well as glass manufacturers, were "happy to state the manufacture of GLASS [had] commenced":

And the public will at once discover that this establishment is one in which this place is deeply interested; as it will manufacture from 30 to 40 thousand dollars worth of glass per annum, liberal patronage from the citizens is therefore respectfully solicited.[166]

It would appear that Pugh & Teater was not routed by the competition of Pittsburgh and New Geneva glass, which was sold in the Cincinnati market. They themselves sought no Pittsburgh or eastern markets, but they carried competition into their other rivals' territories. In October 1819 their "window glass of any sizes" and "hollow-ware to suit any orders" were advertised in the newspapers of Chillicothe and Vincennes, Ohio; St. Louis, Missouri; Louisville, Frankfort, Lexington, and Maysville, Kentucky; and Nashville, Tennessee. The current country-wide money problem was reflected in the proprietors' assurance that they would "not ask for anything better than Cincinnati Bank Paper in payment." However, by the spring of 1821 when Pugh & Teater stated they had rented the Cincinnati Glass Works, they headed a new advertisement of goods they had for sale or wished to buy: "*Encourage Domestic Manufactures.*" Also by then, they had had to resort to barter at their store, though cash would not be "refused" for the articles they handled and would be paid out for those wanted. The following year, in an advertisement of their various wares, Pugh & Teater stated the glassworks had been rented for "a term of years."[167] Provokingly, there was no clue whereby identification of the lessees could be made, unless they themselves had resold the works without publishing the fact and then rented from the new owners. The last bit of evidence I have of activity in the Cincinnati Glass Works is a September 1823 advertisement of Cincinnati window glass for sale by Adams & Smith, No. 4 Loring's Row, Front Street, that appeared as late as the January 1, 1824, issue of the *Cincinnati Gazette.* Quite likely the works had closed, for by then the Moscow Glass Works was in production.[168]

In fact, it is believed that the Moscow Glass Works of Pugh & Teater was completed by July of 1823, and it is known that it was in operation by October of that year. On January 25 of the previous year, Lot Pugh and Henry

Teater had acquired, for $10,000, a large tract of densely timbered land on the south side of Ray's Run near the village of Moscow above Cincinnati. Five days later they conveyed it to Lewis Whiteman in trust, and not until March 31, 1825, did full title pass to them. In the meantime they had built a large two-storied stone glasshouse and 12 log houses to accommodate their workmen at the glasshouse. The timber undoubtedly provided the logs for the houses and potash for the glass, as well as the "shyders" (two-foot lengths of wood) that were used along with Pittsburgh coal to fire the furnaces. The sand for the glass was obtained about nine miles above Cincinnati and floated down the Ohio River in flatboats to the company landing.[169]

Most of our scant information about the Moscow Glass Works and its proprietors derives from advertisements in the *Liberty Hall and Cincinnati Gazette*. The first of the few Pugh & Teater advertisements found so far, dated October 21, 1823, ran through June 15, 1824. In it they announced that the "GLASS! GLASS!" they were receiving from their new establishment at Moscow was being offered low for cash or in exchange for other merchandise in which they dealt. They were not their own sole agent, however; they had appointed Kilgour, Taylor & Company, also in Cincinnati, who accepted orders for glassware and kept an assortment of Moscow glass on hand. Also, during the year, boxes of Moscow window glass were sold by W. C. Rogers at "City Auction," along with Pittsburgh and Wellsburg window glass.[170]

Early in November 1824 Pugh & Teater rented the Moscow Glassworks to William Teater and Nathaniel (or William) Pepperd. The new firm of Pepperd & Teater appointed Henry Bearpark, a commission merchant, as their agent in Cincinnati. In his advertisement Bearpark candidly informed prospective customers that it was useless to say much about the quality of the glass, as it was "well known to stand deservedly high in the market, but it [might] not be improper to state that a very considerable improvement [had] recently taken place both in the quality and the packing." As Pepperd and Teater's agent, Bearpark was continually in the market for black salts and pot and pearl ashes used in making the glass. Lot Pugh and Henry Teater, however, were not long completely out of the Moscow Glass Works picture; sometime before Christmas 1824, they joined Bearpark in forming Pugh, Bearpark & Company. Like many of Lot Pugh's business associations, this one, too, apparently was short-lived—briefer than most, as the firm was dissolved May 21, 1825. Pugh continued the business alone and as agent for Pepperd & Teater until August, when, as the new 1825 blast started, the proprietors transferred the agency to William Hartshorne, a commission merchant at Warehouse No. 6, Commercial Row, Cincinnati. After that, information peters out with only brief advertisements of window glass for sale in the city[171] and the statements of local historians, according to whom Teater became sole proprietor and closed the works about 1830, after which the glasshouse was converted into a distillery.[172]

As in the case of its history, information about the products of the Moscow Glass Works has come mainly from advertisements in *Liberty Hall and Cincinnati Gazette*. From them it is evident that, as at the Cincinnati Glass Works, at the Moscow Glass Works the principal product was window glass, and as usual where that was made, the metal was used also for picture glasses and clock faces. But apparently bottles and flasks played a larger role at Moscow. More kinds were mentioned, and when the new 1825 blast started in August, bottle production was stressed. The firm's August 12, 1825, advertisement was headed "Moscow Window Glass / AND BOTTLE FURNACES in blast." From 1823 into 1825, hollow ware was detailed as gallon, half-gallon, and quart bottles, oil and porter bottles and flasks. The "wine" bottle of 1823 was replaced in subsequent advertisements by "claret," indicating an unexpected popularity of that French wine west of the mountains. Also mentioned in 1825 only were "jars and pitchers," which doubtless were not innovations but had been covered previously by the final "etc."[173] It is probable that this Moscow hollow ware was blown from both green- and amber-colored glass. At least Harry Hall White, writing to George S. McKearin in April 1941, after he had located and superficially examined the site of the Moscow Glass Works, stated: "From surface indications it is another 'country g. h.' making green and amber."

Not surprisingly, in light of the tremendous consumption of beer and porter and the consequent number of breweries and bottlers, porter bottles were a specialty given very particular attention. In 1824 Moscow's were said to be strong, heavy, and blown from *black* glass. Perhaps they were similar to the bottle shown in Ill. 58B and bottle 6 in Ill. 45. And they were "warranted equal, if not superior, to any ever manufactured in the western country." A year later Pepperd & Teater announced their intention to give particular attention to their season's production of porter bottles so that they would have a full stock to fill orders and contracts. At that time they considered their porters to be not only "equal, if not superior," to midwestern rivals but "a superior article equal in strength to the English bottles and at lower prices." Brewers and bottlers were invited to examine the Moscow porters and enter into contracts for them.[174]

As for the flasks, the probability is that at least some of those advertised from 1823 to 1825, like the Cincinnati flasks, were pattern-molded on a single gather of metal, similar to example 5 in Ill. 91, or on a double gather—the Pitkin type—similar to 5 in Ill. 89. But for collectors of Figured Flasks, historicals in particular, the most exciting advertisement was that of August 12, 1825. In that one, without emphasis, following "ribbed" came "Lafayette, Clay, and Jackson flasks."[175] This evidence of portrait flasks commemorating three of the people's heroes is as frustrating as it is thrilling to students of these flasks, for no Henry Clay or Andrew Jackson flask can be even tentatively attributed to Moscow and only one Lafayette is a possibility. That Lafayette flask is GI–93, which is discussed in detail in Part VIII: 4. Historical Flasks:

Lafayette and Dewitt Clinton. The ribbed flasks may have been either pattern molded and fashioned by free-blown techniques or blown in a full-size two-piece mold, as were the portrait flasks.

40. MANTUA GLASS WORKS, *Mantua Township, Portage County, Ohio, 1822–29*

The Mantua Glass Works was established by David Ladd and Jonathan Tinker, two Easterners who had emigrated during post–War of 1812 depression to Mantua Township in the Western Reserve, the northern part of Ohio that had once belonged to Connecticut. Though it operated only about seven years, the Mantua works became a famed midwestern glasshouse through the publication, in *The Magazine* ANTIQUES, of the results of Harry Hall White's researches and excavations of the factory site. To him, collectors and students are indebted for such facts as are known about David Ladd, Jonathan Tinker, and the Mantua Glass Works.[176]

It was in 1816 that David Ladd with his brother Jeduhan and their families arrived in Mantua Township, a location doubtless chosen because their brothers Daniel and Ezekiel were living there already. It was a rural, still almost frontier, community with three small villages—Mantua Corners, Mantua Station, and Mantua Center: not a likely site for a successful glassworks. To start making a living, Ladd, an enterprising Connecticut Yankee who had been a clerk in West Hartford, brought with him "a small supply of dry goods." In the fall of the following year he was able to build a double log cabin at Mantua Corners on land owned by his brother Ezekiel. A few months later, in the spring of 1818, Ladd purchased 20 cows, rented a pasture from William Skinner, and by summer was in the dairy business. In the fall, to dispose of his cheese, he built a boat to navigate the rivers but not too cumbersome for portage at the falls of the Cuyahoga and again at Wetmore's Mill en route to New Portage on the Tuscarawas River. This he accomplished by "splitting it [the canoe] lengthwise with a saw and widening it by putting in boards or planks so as to give it the wished for demension." From New Portage, Ladd went down the Tuscarawas into and down the Muskingum River until he found a good market for his cheese and the boat. The venture, it is said, was profitable.

Since the cheese-and-boat adventure had paid, David Ladd doubtless repeated his trip as long as he maintained his dairy. However, the next report of him was that in the summer of 1821 he built a large brick kiln—to the puzzlement of the community, as there was little demand for bricks. The mystery was solved in the fall when David Ladd began transforming the tannery built in 1812 by his brother Daniel into a glassworks. The work of conversion was entrusted to Oliver Lewis—joiner, carpenter, expert millwright, and bridge builder. Lewis had been one of the incorporators of the Mount Vernon Glass Company at Vernon, New York, and had emigrated to Mantua a few years before. Lewis's son-in-law Jonathan Tinker, an expert glassblower who doubtless had practiced his art at Mount Vernon, had also moved to Mantua. It was he who was in charge of the new Mantua Glass Works and its production. It seems not unlikely that Lewis and Tinker had sparked David Ladd's interest in starting the works. Be that as it may, Ladd's interest was short-lived: in 1823, he withdrew from the Mantua Glass Company, moved to Carthage not many miles away (Carthage and its near neighbor Franklin became Kent in 1832), and with new associates started another glassworks. Apparently there were several different investors in the Mantua Glass Works between the departure of David Ladd and the spring of 1829, when glassmaking ceased. The market for its hollow ware was too small.

The first contemporary evidence as to the nature of the glass blown at the Mantua Glass Works was found by Mr. White in *The Western Reserve Chronicle* for January 16, 1822: "The glass is said to be superior for its clearness." In the February 9 issue of the paper the editor wrote:

We have lately received as a present, from the proprietors of the Glass Works in Mantua, a very clear well-shaped decanter and elegant sweetmeat, as a specimen of their skill in the important manufacture in which they are engaged. Both of these articles are ample proofs of the ability of the enterprising and meritorious owners of this establishment to serve the public in their line of business . . .

Somehow "very clear" sounds to me as though the decanter was blown from colorless glass. If so, was it white glass or flint glass? Probably that question can never be answered categorically—but it was said that the Skinners and their associates, the first to take over after Ladd left, "manufactured a considerable amount of flint glass as well as common glass." Possibly some flint glass was made; if so, it probably was in small quantity, for the pieces attributed to Mantua and the hundreds of shards uncovered by Mr. White were non-lead glass.

Though bowls of various sizes, pitchers, sugar bowls, and druggists' and ink bottles were among the articles blown at Mantua, bottles, mainly globular or calabash shape, and chestnut pocket flasks appear to have been the principal products. Moreover, the shards indicated that unornamented ones were in the minority. The majority were pattern-molded. Most of them were patterned in 16-rib and 32-rib dip molds, and the ribbing was more often swirled or in broken swirl than left vertical. The aquamarine bottle 6 in Ill. 94 possibly is Mantua. Less frequently used than the rib molds was a 15-diamond small piece-mold, and then for flasks. The brilliant yellow-green flask 2 in Ill. 97 is an example attributed to the works; the brilliant aquamarine flask, 7 in Ill. 91, probably Mantua; and the light golden amber flask, 11 in Ill. 98, possibly Mantua. The Pitkin-type flask was another Mantua flask, and the golden amber flask 4 in Ill. 89 in 32 ribs is possibly an example. I hasten to add that all pieces patterned in 16 ribs or 32 ribs or 15 diamonds are *not, ipso facto*, Mantua: molds of the same number of ribs and diamonds were used in other glassworks—East and Midwest. Another mold used at Mantua to a limited extent was one for a blown-three-mold decanter in the geometric pattern GII–33—a band of diamond diapering between bands of vertical fluting, with a horizontal rib separating the bands.

So far as is now known, only one Figured Flask was blown at Mantua—the extremely rare Andrew Jackson–Masonic GI–70, of which Mr. White found aquamarine and amber fragments. The flask, in shape and edges similar to the Coventry Lafayette flasks, has the initials "J T" for Jonathan Tinker at top on the obverse, above "A. JACKSON" in semicircle above a profile bust that in no way resembles Jackson, and "OHIO" in a bottom panel. On the reverse are Masonic emblems, fitting companions to Jackson, who was as proud of being a Mason as the Masons were proud of him. The mold may have been taken to Mantua by Jonathan Tinker, and the bust may have been intended to represent another national figure. Although I have never seen the flask, I accept Mr. White's finding that:

The lettering A JACKSON evidently was not the original inscription cut in the mold. Either some patching was done, or some kind of alteration was made in the lettering, for traces of other letters unrelated to the present inscription are faintly perceptible.

41. VIRGINIA GREEN GLASS WORKS *of Knox & McKee, later the Fairview Glass Works of Wheat, Price & Co., East Wheeling, (W.) Virginia, 1820–ca. 1848*[177]

In 1820 George Carruthers, a glassblower formerly of Brownsville, Fayette County, Pennsylvania, enlisted two other glassmen, Peter Yarnell and Thomas McGiffen, in starting the first glassworks in Wheeling, (West) Virginia. Wheeling, a rapidly growing town with extensive trade up and down the Ohio River, seemed a likely place in which to manufacture glass, especially window glass and bottles, and so it eventually proved to be. On June 20, 1820, having borrowed $4,000 from George List, Jr., Carruthers paid for the five lots that he had rented as the site of the glassworks in East Wheeling. By mid-September he was able to announce that the works was in production and he could supply merchants and other customers with window glass and hollow ware of "every description." His optimistic expectations of orders from midwestern communities are evidenced by his instructions to editors of newspapers in Steubenville, Washington; Bellemont, Ohio; and Maysville, Kentucky, to run his advertisement, dated September 16, for three weeks.

However, customers did not beat a path to Carruthers's glasshouse, and in less than six months of operation he faced a financial crisis. Yarnell and McGiffen had pulled out of the venture and were succeeded by Pennell and

Gregg. During their brief interest in the works, the firm name became Pennell, Gregg and Carruthers. By March 1821 Carruthers was over his head in debt to nine restive creditors. Two were paid in glass—20 boxes of window glass. As security for the other debts Carruthers had to put up all his household belongings, even to the pots and kettles and "all cubboard ware"—that is, china, glass, silver spoons, and eight flasks. (The number of feather beds, dining tables, and Windsor chairs would seem to indicate that Mrs. Carruthers contributed to the family income by running a boarding and rooming house.) Also named as security were four tons of pots and clay, "purl" ashes, all glasshouse tools, an iron grinding mill, and bars of iron on hand. Even so, he was unable to pay off all his debts, and it was with difficulty that Carruthers kept the glassworks in operation, though his creditors apparently became patient. But in 1824 George List, Jr., from whom Carruthers had borrowed the money to purchase the site of the works, foreclosed. The glassworks was sold at public auction for $4,367 to Charles Knox and Redick McKee, who christened it the Virginia Green Glass Works. They retained Carruthers as superintendent, a position he held for about five years. Carruthers then apparently abandoned glassmaking: by August of 1830 he was advertising his Golden Ball Tavern in Wheeling.[178]

Knox and McKee, a firm formed in 1820 by Charles Knox, Redick McKee, and Noah Zane, not only had a grocery in Wheeling but also a prosperous widespread commission and forwarding business. Thus they did not lack for capital to finance glassmaking at the Virginia Green Glass Works or for contacts with potential customers east and west. In 1828 a New York City newspaper carried an item in which it was reported that Knox & McKee manufactured $24,000 worth of "superior window glass" annually and employed 30 hands. According to an undated letter written by Colonel McKee, 3,000 to 4,000 boxes of window glass in all sizes from 6 feet x 8 feet through 14 feet x 20 feet, were blown yearly and large quantities of green hollow ware, including gallon, half-gallon, and quart bottles, "innumerable" pints, oil and porter bottles.[179] Flasks were not mentioned—except for the eight in Carruthers's "cubboard"—and perhaps were not blown in quantity. Nevertheless some pattern-molded pocket bottles were more than likely produced and certainly three figured historical portrait flasks were made by Knox & McKee.

The three Figured Flasks are the extremely rare Andrew Jackson GI–69, the rare Lafayette GI–92, and the Henry Clay GI–130, of which only one example is known today and that was not recorded until 1970. The reverse of all three flasks is the same design, with the American eagle as the principal motif and "WHEELING" in a semicircle at top above the frame; on the edges, "KNOX &" at lower left of frame and "McKEE" at lower right—except there are no cannonballs on the Clay GI–130. On the obverse, within a Masonic arch is a small profile bust, identified on GI–69 by "ANDREW" at upper left of frame and "JACKSON" at upper right; on GI–92 by "GENERAL" at left along lower half of frame and "LAFAYETTE" at right; on GI–130, "HENRY" at upper left of frame and "CLAY" at upper right. The Clay bust varies slightly from the Jackson and Lafayette, which are the same. The sameness of GI–92 and GI–69 in all details of the design points to the possibility of a mold alteration besides that of GI–92 in which the lettering was filled in to change it into GI–93. (See the line drawings; for discussion, see Part VIII: 4. Historical Flasks.) The Henry Clay flask doubtless was brought out in 1824 or 1825, perhaps commemorating the passage of the 1824 tariff as well as the father of the American System. The Jackson flask probably was of the 1824–28 period. The Lafayette probably dates 1824/25, before or at the time of the general's visit to Wheeling. The Masonic arch was an appropriate symbol, since the three were ardent and notable Masons.

But to return to the glassworks: in 1830 Knox & McKee, having decided to give up the business of glass manufacturing, ran the following advertisement:

VIRGINIA GREEN GLASS WORKS
For sale or Rent
POSSESSION TO BE GIVEN THE FIRST OF
JULY NEXT

The subscriber, with a view of giving their exclusive attention to their mercantile pursuits, will sell the above valuable and lucrative property, with the buildings and lots adjacent or they will lease the same to a responsible individual or company for a term of years! The establishment is in complete repair, and from its location, possesses advantages and facilities for manufacturing and for sale, inferior to none and superior to most of the kind in the Western Country.

If the establishment is rented the leasee will be required to sustain the high reputation of the "brand". For terms apply (previous to the first of April) to McKEE, CLARKE & CO. Pittsburgh, or to KNOX & McKEE, Wheeling.
January 19—.[180]

On March 24, Ensell & Plunkett of Pittsburgh signed a three-year lease with Knox & McKee. The yearly rent was to be $900 payable quarterly and in best-quality window glass—100 boxes of 10 x 12 at $5 a box and 100 boxes of 7 x 9 at $4 a box. Ensell & Plunkett agreed also to purchase from Knox & McKee the following supplies: salt, potash, wood ash, sand, pot clay, straw, wood, boxes, and box boards. The right to build on the unimproved corner lot was reserved by Knox & McKee. This they did, erecting a flint-glass house before the expiration of the lease. Ensell & Plunkett did not renew their lease in 1833, or perhaps Knox & McKee had other ideas. In any event, Ensell & Plunkett built a glassworks in North Wheeling. And in July Knox & McKee sold a half interest in both the Virginia Green Glass Works and the neighboring new works to Jesse Wheat and John Price. The new firm was called Wheat, Price & Company and the name of the works was changed to the Fairview Glass Works.[181]

During the period in which Wheat, Price & Company

operated the works, they brought out two very rare figured historical portrait flasks, GI–115 and GI–116, on neither of which is the profile bust identified. However, it seems probable that the bust on GI–116 was intended to represent John Tyler. (See Part VIII: 4. Historical Flasks, Tyler.) On each the bust is framed by the inscription, reading from left to right, "WHEAT, PRICE & Cᴼ. WHEELING. VA." On the reverse is a glasshouse and "FAIR" at upper left, "VIEW" at upper right, and "WORKS" below the house.

On January 31, 1834, John and Craig Richie and George Wilson bought the Fairview Glass Works from Wheat, Price & Co. Wilson contributed the $27,000 purchase price and the Richies, the glass manufacturing know-how. The firm of Richie & Wilson was successful until the Panic of 1837, when the Merchants and Mechanics Bank, to which $30,000 was owed, had to step in. It was agreed that Richie & Wilson should continue to operate the window-glass works and that the flint-glass works should be rented. Francis Plunkett and Hall Miller, the lessees for about three years until they moved to South Wheeling, also operated the window-glass works after Richie & Wilson went bankrupt. The last operators of the glassworks were Evans & Andersons, who in 1845 leased the flint-glass works for the manufacture of vials and bottles. Though the lease was for five years, they ceased operations about 1848. About 1849 both glassworks were torn down and the land divided into building lots.[182]

42. MARYLAND GLASS WORKS, *John Lee Chapman, Baltimore, Maryland, 1850–62*

About 15 years after the Baltimore Flint Glass Works at Fell's Point closed and was dismantled, the second Fell's Point glasshouse was built on the northeast corner of Caroline and Lancaster streets by John Lee Chapman, who christened it the Maryland Glass Works. John Lee Chapman was a son of John Chapman, a druggist who was one of the proprietors of the Baltimore glassworks, so perhaps it was not surprising that his son became a druggist and a manufacturer of bottles. (A druggist's business, as I have remarked often, necessitated the use of innumerable glass containers of various sorts.) Moreover, John Lee Chapman became the son-in-law of George Chapman, who apparently had managed the Baltimore Flint Glass Works and also owned a glass store at 40 Charles Street. When his father-in-law died in 1845, John Lee Chapman—who, with his wife, had been appointed to administer the estate—devoted his time to the glass store and left the running of the druggist shop to his brother Jonathan.

It was on land previously owned by his father-in-law that John Lee built his own source of glassware. His Maryland Glass Works probably was built during 1847 or 1848 and certainly was in operation in 1849. The depression during the last years of the 1850s brought financial difficulties, as it did to so many of the country's glassworks. The Maryland Glass Works probably suffered also from John Lee's absorption in politics even though his brother Jonathan had been drawn away from the drug business to help manage the works. In fact, by 1860, the operation of the works was in his hands. Two years later when John Lee was elected Mayor of Baltimore, all production apparently ceased. In 1863, so Deverne A. Dressel found, the glassworks was abandoned and the land sold to become a foundry site.[183]

And so the second Fell's Point glassmaking venture passed into glass history leaving, so far as I have yet learned, only a small legacy of identifiable wares—a few Figured Flasks—and little specific knowledge of the nature and styles of its wares. Mr. Dressel found that in 1853 the directory listing mentioned flint as well as green glass and that, later, production was expanded to include window glass. The Maryland Glass Works did have one distinction shared with only a few United States glassworks: the glassware of J. L. Chapman, Baltimore, Maryland, was number 68 of the glass exhibits at the 1851 Crystal Palace in London, the first world's fair. From the catalog we learn that the composition of the glass was unusual: "The glass is made in uncovered pots without the use of lead or pearl ash and the founding is done by night in 12 hours." The Englishman "R E"—presumably familiar with glassmaking—added the following comment:

In the manufacture of glass lead and alkalis are employed as a flux to the other materials. This is considered to render their fusion more ready and complete. The glass in question is characterized, it is stated, by an absence of these ingredients, and under such circumstances the degree of heat necessary to their fusion must have been extremely intense to have effected it in the time stated.[184]

No award was given to the glass, and unfortunately I could find no listing of the articles in the exhibit.

At present, only the seven flasks listed below have been identified with John Lee Chapman's Maryland Glass Works. It should be noted that the sizes are those of pocket flasks; the shape, one that was introduced about 1850, and their designs, sufficiently popular to warrant four pint and three half-pint molds. Also note that one pint and two half-pints have no inscription identifying them with the Maryland Glass Works. However, because they have the same designs, though varying slightly in details, they were attributed to Chapman about a half century ago. I have charted them in Group XIII, Pictorial Flasks. I believe they were first produced about 1850 and probably blown throughout the lifetime of the glassworks.

GXIII–8. Sailor, above plain bar. *Reverse*: Banjo Player, above plain bar. Half-pint.

GXIII–9. Like above, but bar on reverse inscribed "BALT. MD." Half-pint.

GXIII–10. Like GXIII–8, but bar on reverse inscribed "CHAPMAN." Half-pint.

GXIII–11. Soldier, bar inscribed "BALT. MD." *Reverse*: Ballet Dancer, bar inscribed "CHAPMAN." Pint.

GXIII–12. Like above.

GXIII–13. Like above.

GXIII–14. Like above, but no inscription on bars.

43. SPRING GARDEN GLASS WORKS, *Baltimore, Maryland, 1851–56*

As in the case of the Baltimore Glass Works, I am indebted to Deverne A. Dressel, whose researches have checked, corrected where necessary, and expanded the historical data on the Spring Garden Glass Works. However, on two points all writers seem to have agreed: the glassworks was a cooperative adventure of glassblowers from the Baltimore Glass Works at Federal Hill (see No. 18), and as such it was short-lived—conceived in 1850 and failing in 1856. With the knowledge, and perhaps encouragement, of the proprietors of the Baltimore Glass Works, plans to build a separate glassworks for the manufacture of containers were made by Jacob Leigh, William Garton, David Lawson, William Swindell, and Frederick and Lewis Schaum—blowers in the Federal Hill bottle department. The two Schaums were sons of Lewis Schaum of Schaum, Reitz & Company, then operating the Federal Hill works. The new firm of F. Schaum & Company was assured success, so it seemed, by an agreement that Baker Brothers & Company should be sole agents for marketing the production.

Late in 1850 Swindell, Garton, and Leigh rented land on Eutaw Street on which to build the new glassworks. The lease was for ten years at an annual rental of $400, and John Boyd & Son—the lessors—were given a $1,700 mortgage to erect a glasshouse and ancillary buildings, which were to be worth at least $3,000. In February 1851 F. Schaum & Company arranged further with Boyd & Sons for a right of way to Ostent Street, and for their providing wharfage into the Patapsco River for landing wood by mid-July. Before the end of the year the new glassworks, called the Spring Garden Glass Works, was in operation.[185]

The early 1850s were years of general prosperity, and the Spring Garden Glass Works did well. Perhaps the majority of the firm came to feel that the sole agents ought to do better by them, or that they themselves were sufficiently well established to do as well and better by themselves. In any event, late in May of 1854 F. Schaum & Company announced that as of June 14 the agency of Baker Brothers & Company for the Spring Garden Glass Works would end, and all orders would be taken by the company at South Eutaw Street. Whatever the reasons for this step, it was not taken by unanimous agreement of the partners. William Swindell, presumably because of the decision to adopt direct selling, withdrew from the firm, and on May 27 the lease on the land held by Garton, Leigh, and Swindell was assigned to the remaining partners in F. Schaum & Company. Garton and Leigh as well as Swindell were paid $1,400 by the company, but they remained in the firm for the time being. The next to withdraw and receive payment for his interest in the glassworks was Lewis Schaum, on November 28. Both glassmen returned to the Baltimore Glass Works at Federal Hill, where—perhaps in part at least in retaliation for the broken sales agreement—bottle production was revived.

William Garton and Frederick Schaum also returned to Federal Hill when they withdrew from F. Schaum & Company in June of 1855. At that time a new firm was formed: Davis, Lawson & Company, in which Jacob Leigh, David Lawson, John W. Davis, and Edward G. Sturgeon were copartners. Only three months later it was dissolved and Sturgeon acquired all the assets, though "Captain" Edward G. Sturgeon and John Davis were listed as glass manufacturers in the Baltimore 1856/57 directory. However, Sturgeon was as unsuccessful as his predecessors, and on June 16, 1856, Baker Brothers & Company acquired all interest in the Spring Garden Glass Works. By 1859 it was to become the bottle department of the Baltimore Glass Works, and by 1863 it passed into glass history as the name of a factory. Henceforth the Eutaw Street works was to be called the Baltimore Glass Works, and when the Federal Street Works drew its final fires in the 1870s, the Eutaw Street works was the source of all glassware produced by the Baltimore Glass Works.[186]

The first firm name F. Schaum & Company suggests that Frederick Schaum may have been the leader of the group of glassmen. Possibly he was the most experienced of them in various aspects of glassmaking. Certainly if, as seems most probable, he was the F. Schaum of Baltimore who obtained a United States patent on a glass furnace in April 1854, it would appear that he was of an inventive turn of mind and his experience went far beyond that of blowing bottles.[187]

The products of the Spring Garden Glass Works were exclusively bottles, flasks, and other containers. In 1852 when Baker Brothers & Company advertised as sole agents of the "BALTIMORE, and also Spring Garden Glass Works" (note the lower case for the latter), the Spring Garden wares mentioned were "druggist vials, bottles, wine, porter and soda bottles, pickle jars, specie jars, tumblers, flasks. . . ." In August of 1854, advertising the wares available at their retail outlet at 47 Calvert Street and on order, F. Schaum & Company listed "Druggists Glassware, Porters, Ales, Ciders, Lemon Syrups, and Wine Bottles, half-pint, pint and quart Flasks, Pickling and Preserve Jars"—and, as was customary, stated "particular attention" was paid to "private moulds."[188]

Except for the few Figured Flasks, the products of the Spring Garden Glass Works are anonymous in the vast quantities of containers produced in the period, as are those of most other factories. It seems likely that some sorts of unmarked flasks were produced in addition to the four inscribed flasks included in Group XIII (Pictorial Flasks) and listed below. It should be noted that the anchor and inscribed pennants were popular devices of the period, and were used by the Baltimore Glass Works, the Isabella

Glass Works at New Brooklyn, New Jersey, and the Richmond Glass Works in Richmond, Virginia.

GXIII–58. Anchor, Pennants inscribed "SPRING GARDEN GLASS WORKS". *Reverse*: Log Cabin. Pint. 1851–56.

GXIII–59. Pint. Similar to above.

GXIII–60. Half-pint. Similar to above.

GXIII–61. Half-pint. Similar to above.

44. KENSINGTON VIAL AND BOTTLE WORKS,
Sheets & Duffy, Kensington, Philadelphia, Pennsylvania, 1845–ca. 1874

The Kensington Vial and Bottle Works, which operated a little over a quarter of a century, was another of the many works established by glassblowers. In this instance there apparently were only two—Daniel Sheets (spelled also Sheetz) and Hugh Duffy, both of whom had blown glass for Dr. Dyott. Both were witnesses for the defense at Dr. Dyott's trial for fraudulent bankruptcy in 1839. Both testified to the doctor's "good character." In his testimony, Daniel Sheets said he had known the doctor for 14 years and had worked for him for nine. Presumably Sheets was, therefore, an experienced glassblower, as Duffy doubtless was also. And since the works was in production until the great depression that started in 1873, it would appear that they also were capable glassmakers and managers. Their first listing in the Philadelphia City Directory was in 1846—Sheets & Duffy, glass works Dyottville. Their last was in 1873. An 1848 advertisement gave the location of their works as "upper yard, Dyottville, Kensington, Philadelphia." This suggests that Sheets & Duffy either took over one of the five Dyottville glasshouses or converted one of the Dyottville buildings into a glasshouse.[189]

The Kensington Vial and Bottle Works was just that—a bottle manufactory only. As the 1848 advertisement revealed they produced "*every description* of Vials, Bottles, Demijohns and Carboys" (the italics are mine). In other words, they made the same sorts of containers as did other bottle manufacturers. And like that of other manufacturers, their output is mainly anonymous. In fact, only one flask and one calabash bottle are known that were marked with their name. The flask is GXV–22, a quart flask having "SHEETS & DUFFY" in an arc above a horizontal "KENSINGTON". The period indicated by the shape and ends of the flask is the 1860s. It seems likely that someday the same flask in pint and half-pint sizes will "turn up." The calabash is GXIII–41, having a sheaf of grain with crossed rake and fork on one side and, on the other, "SHEETS & DUFFY" in a semicircle over an eight-petaled ornament.

GXIII–42, like GXIII–41 but without inscription, is attributed to Sheets & Duffy. Three other calabash bottles were attributed to this firm by Van Rensselaer: GXIII–44 and 45 (Van Rensselaer GVI–86; he did not differentiate the two) having a sheaf of grain with crossed rake and fork on obverse and eight-pointed star on the reverse; and GXIII–45 (Van Rensselaer GVI–116) having a similar design on the obverse and a tree in foliage on the reverse.

GLASSHOUSE SKETCHES Nos. 45 through 79
by Kenneth M. Wilson

45. BRIDGETON GLASS WORKS, *Bridgeton, N.J.* *1836 (or 1837?)–55*

Like so many other glasshouses, the Bridgeton Glass Works, as it is loosely termed today, underwent many changes of ownership and firm names. This factory, to which a number of Figured Flasks are attributed, was established in 1836 or 1837 by Nathaniel L. Stratton and John P. Buck as Stratton, Buck & Co. It was strategically located along the Cohansey River, which provided a convenient and inexpensive means for transporting needed raw materials to the factory and finished products to market. In addition to the factory, the owners possessed great tracts of land and operated a general store. In 1841 the works suffered a devastating fire, and when John Buck died the next year Stratton gave up glassmaking. The principal products of the factory during this period were bottles. The two portrait flasks GI–24 and GI–25, marked "Bridgeton" and "Bridgetown" respectively, were probably produced during this period, ca. 1836–41, as well as possibly later during the ownerships of Rosenbaum (ca. 1843–45) and the Bodines (1846–55).

It appears evident that a John G. Rosenbaum rebuilt the works sometime after the fire and operated them until 1846,[1] when they were bought by Joel Bodine & Sons. This was the same Bodine who, with his sons Joel F., John, and William E., had established the Washington Glass Works in Williamstown, Camden County, New Jersey, in 1839 for the manufacture of bottles and hollow ware. This works— its name became the Williamstown Glass Works in the early 1850s—continued in operation until about 1917, and Bodines continued to be members of the firm throughout much of its history.

Joel Bodine & Sons operated the works in Bridgeton until 1855, when it was sold to the firm of Maul, Hebrew & Co., which failed that same year. It was undoubtedly during the ten-year period of the Bodines' operation that all the flasks marked "Bridgeton" and "Bridgetown" (GI–24, GI–25, GI–111, GX–7), as well as those (GX–8, GX–8a, and GX–9) attributed by shape and design, were produced. Probably these flasks were so marked after the name of the town, rather than that of the glassworks, since the glassworks bore that name for only part of the time between 1856 and 1863. Joel Bodine apparently was not an easy man to work for. In a letter dated January 12, 1845, Thomas Stanger, glassblower, wrote to his brother John

Stanger in Glassboro, New Jersey, describing his employer, Schaum, owner of a bottle factory in Philadelphia:

Besides that I don't like Schaum at all and he dont like me. so we are even there, he is so crabbed, I expect he lost money on his window glass house . . . to give you an idea of his tigerlike disposition I will mention an incident that happened yesterday; one of the tenders about 10 years old, threw a stick of wood through the wheel of a wheel-barrow as another boy was wheeling it along, which so incensed his honor that he beat the little fellow so much that he is unable to work, almost every day we have an exhibition of the effect of his anger. Heffer says he is worse than Joel Bodine, and I think so too, so you need not wonder that I wish to get away.[2]

Potter and Bodine (General David Potter of Bridgeton and Francis I. Bodine of Philadelphia) bought the works at sheriff's sale (probably in late 1855 or early 1856) and operated it until 1863. It was during only this period that these works were sometimes called the Bridgeton Glass Works. That the firm also produced fruit jars is evident from one marked *Potter & Bodine Air Tight Fruit-Jar Philadelphia*. This jar was patented October 19, 1858. An advertisement of Potter and Bodine in the Philadelphia Directory of 1860 lists the following:

Private mould bottles and vials, wine bottles, bitters bottles, handled flasks, handled jugs, mineral water bottles, porter bottles, plain flasks, specie jars, tumblers, druggists glassware, pickle jars and Patent Hermetically Sealed Fruit Jars.[3]

In 1863 David Potter sold his interest in the firm to Francis and J. Nixon Bodine (sons of Samuel and nephews of Joel), who operated as J. and F. Bodine until 1867. By 1870 new owners took over and formed the Cohansey Glass Manufacturing Co. Among numerous other types of bottles and jars, this firm produced the Cohansey Fruit Jars.[4] In 1874 they showed "green and brown glass bottles, fruit jars, flasks, etc." at the Franklin Institute and received an honorable mention award for third place for their fruit jars.[5] In addition to bottles and hollow ware, the firm was also producing window glass by this time. In 1876 they received an award for cylinder glass, bottles, vials, and demijohns at the Centennial Exposition.[6] By 1899 the firm had been expanded to include two hollow-ware and three window-glass plants, and at its operating peak employed 500 men and boys; its property and stock were valued at a quarter of a million dollars, and its glass production amounted to $300,000 a year. Besides fruit jars, druggists' bottles, vials, beer and wine bottles, carboys, and bottles and also jars for acid, the firm specialized in doing private mold work. Many of these molds were produced by the noted firm of Charles Yokel, established in Philadelphia in 1855.

The following Figured Flasks are attributed to the "Bridgeton Glass Works":

GI-24. *Obverse*: "WASHINGTON" in arc above profile bust of Washington in uniform, facing left. *Reverse*: "BRIDGETON NEW JERSEY" in arc over profile bust said to be General Taylor, in uniform, facing left; there is a 5-pointed star between Bridgeton and New Jersey. Pint. Colors: amber, green, dark olive-amber ("black"), aquamarine, to almost colorless. Common ca. 1836-50.

GI-25. *Obverse*: "BRIDGETOWN NEW JERSEY" in arc over classical bust of Washington, facing right. *Reverse*: "BRIDGETOWN NEW JERSEY" in arc over classical bust, facing right, thought to be that of Henry Clay. Quart. Colors: dark olive-amber ("black"), sapphire-blue, aquamarine. Common. ca. 1836-50.

GI-111. *Obverse*: "NEW JERSEY BRIDGETON" in slight arcs to the left and right, respectively, of a profile bust, possibly Louis Kossuth, facing right. *Reverse*: Shallop, sailing to the left. Pint. Colors: clear light green, aquamarine. Scarce. ca. 1851-55 or a little longer.

GX-7. *Obverse*: Shallop, with pennant flying, sailing to the left. *Reverse*: "NEW JERSEY" and "BRIDGE-TOWN" in slight arcs on the left and right sides of the flask, respectively. Half-pint. Colors: dark olive-amber ("black"), pale aquamarine. Scarce. Probably ca. 1846-55.

GX-8. *Obverse*: Shallop, with pennant flying, sailing to the left. *Reverse*: Large fancy 8-pointed "star" or "daisy" with tiny 3-pointed motif or floral device between rays of the "star" or petals of the "daisy." Half-pint. Colors: clear deep green, aquamarine, sapphire-blue. Scarce. Probably ca. 1846-55.

GX-8a. *Obverse*: Shallop like that on GX-8a. *Reverse*: Large "star" or "daisy" as on GX-8 but on plain background as in GX-9. Half-pint. Color: aquamarine. Comparatively scarce. Probably ca. 1846-55.

GX-9. *Obverse*: Shallop, with pennant flying, sailing left; no water. *Reverse*: Large simple 8-pointed "star" or petaled ornament. Half-pint. Colors: clear yellow-green, clear green, aquamarine. Scarce. ca. 1846-55.

46. PENDLETON GLASS WORKS, MILLFORD GLASS WORKS. *ca. 1838-ca. 1860?*

As is true of so many glassworks, the history of the works in Millford, New Jersey, which operated under several names and managements, is, for the most part, shrouded in mystery. It was established as the Pendleton Glass Works about 1838 in what was then Pendleton, New Jersey, which became Millford (sometimes spelled Milford), by Mathias Simmerman and associates. Simmerman had been one of the founders of the Free Will Glassworks in Williamstown, New Jersey. Products of the Pendleton glasshouse were bottles and hollow ware, but none of them can now be identified.

Sometime before 1850, Lippincott, Wisham & Co. operated the works and sold their products through J(ohn) Huffsey & Co. of Philadelphia.[7] That J(ohn) Huffsey & Co. had a more direct relationship with, or were the new owners of, this factory, and also that its name had been changed to the Millford Glass Works,[8] were indicated by the following advertisement from *Philadelphia As It Is*, 1852:

> Atlantic and Millford Glass Works
> Crowleytown and Millford, Burlington, N.J.
>   J. Huffsey & Co.
> Manufacturers and Dealers in Every Description
>   of Druggist Glassware
> Office No. 50 North Fourth Street, above Arch,
>   Philadelphia

Glassware for druggists appears to have become an important part of the factory's production.

According to J. Edward Pfeiffer, John Huffsey was also the manager of these two glasshouses in that year.[9] That he was an experienced glassman is indicated by Philadelphia directories, which list him as a glassblower between 1843 and 1851 and as a glass dealer between 1852 and 1855. In 1855 he is listed as one of the firm of Huffsey and Myers, glass dealers at 50 North Fourth Street, Philadelphia. Samuel Huffsey, his brother, had opened this store on September 17, 1849, as a bottle broker and glasshouse supplier, and as agent for M. H. Myers of New York City. Samuel is listed in the Philadelphia directories for the years 1851 through 1857 as a glass dealer at the same address. Born in Port Elizabeth, New Jersey, in 1801, he began his glassblowing career there as a vial blower. Afterward, he worked in numerous factories in Philadelphia, including T. W. Dyott's Kensington Glass Works, and in Pittsburgh and New Jersey. His work and wanderings are well chronicled by Adeline Pepper in *The Glass Gaffers of New Jersey*. On May 31, 1856, while either or both of the Huffseys may have been the owners of the Millford Glass Works, it was sold at sheriff's sale to Joseph Iszard for $4,600. Samuel Iszard & Co. was formed and operated the works for a time, but the company failed and the factory closed sometime before 1860.

There has long been conjecture as to the source of two calabash bottles bearing likenesses of Jenny Lind and Louis Kossuth, each also marked with the name "S. Huffsey." Although I cannot be certain, it seems very likely that both these flasks, described as follows, were produced in the Millford Glass Works:

GI-99. *Obverse*: Three-quarter view of Jenny Lind turned to the left, wearing a plain broad collar called a bertha, almost encircled by a wreath of two branches, with the name "JENNY LIND" above in arc. *Reverse*: view of a glasshouse with "S. HUFFSEY" in straight line below, "GLASS" to the left, and "WORKS" to the right above. Quart. Colors: sapphire-blue, deep blue, green, olive-yellow, deep green-yellow, olive-green, and aquamarine. Common. ca. 1850-55.

Possibly the above was made later at the Isabella Glass Works, since J. E. Pfeiffer found that S. Huffsey sold a mold to Thomas W. Stanger of that firm on September 2, 1854; perhaps also produced at the Williamstown Glass Works, since T. W. Stanger loaned a Jenny Lind mold to Bodine and Thomas, proprietors of that glassworks, on May 26, 1870.

GI–112. *Obverse*: Frontal bust of Louis Kossuth wearing plumed hat, surrounded by two flags on each side and "LOUIS KOSSUTH" above. *Reverse*: Frigate sailing left on two rows of waves with "U.S. STEAM FRIG-ATE MISSISSIPPI S. HUFFSEY" in three lines be-low. On the upper arc of the casing of the wide wheel paddle is "S. HUFFSEY" and on the base: "PH. DOF-LEIN MOULD MAKER NTH.5^t, S^t. 84."Quart. Col-ors: black (dark olive-green), olive-green, emerald-green, yellow-green, and aquamarine. Comparatively scarce. ca. 1850–60.

Possibly: GI–101. *Obverse*: Three-quarter view of Jenny Lind, surrounded by wreath with "JENNY LIND" above, all as in GI–99. *Reverse:* Glasshouse like that on reverse of GI–99, with "MILLFORA G. WORK'S" in an arc above. Quart. Color: aquamarine. Comparatively scarce. ca. 1850–60.

47. BROOKLYN GLASS WORKS, ISABELLA GLASS WORKS, NEW BROOKLYN GLASS WORKS, *1831–76*

In 1831 John Marshall and his son-in-law, Frederick Stanger, began building a bottle glasshouse in what was then called Seven Causeways, which later became known as Brooklyn, and even later as Old Brooklyn. Frederick Stanger, a practical glassman of some considerable experi-ence, was in charge of building the furnace, since John Marshall was not a glassman. Unfortunately, Stanger died on May 14, 1831, at the age of 45. Nevertheless Marshall carried on, assisted by Thomas W. Stanger, Frederick's cousin, and the factory had its first "blast" in 1832. Later, in 1835, T. W. Stanger married Elizabeth Marshall Stanger, Frederick's widow, who was 15 years his senior.

The firm was known as Marshall and Stanger until Sep-tember 1839, when Marshall, then 71, withdrew. Several ownerships followed: Thomas W. Stanger; Stanger & Dot-terer; Thomas W. and F. Stanger with John Marshall Stanger as silent partner (the F. Stanger being *another* Frederick Stanger); then Thomas W. Stanger again. All these changes of ownership are documented in 13 glass-house ledgers starting in 1839 and running until 1884, in the possession of J. Edward Peiffer, who has generously shared this information.[10] The ledgers refer to glass pro-duction in both this glasshouse and the second one estab-lished nearby by T. W. Stanger.

According to these ledgers, a wide variety of vials of various sizes, medicine bottles such as opodeldocs, quart and pint castor oils, numerous other oil bottles, mustards,

and inks were produced by the firm; no Figured Flasks are listed. In 1840 appears the first notation for iron molds. In 1856 this factory and a gristmill owned by Thomas W. Stanger were destroyed by fire. In reporting the fire, the Woodbury *Constitution* noted the location as being Old Brooklyn. The glassworks was apparently rebuilt, for in the following year it was purchased at a sheriff's sale by C. B. Tice, who operated the factory until 1868.[11]

Possibly as early as 1848, but certainly by 1850, Thomas W. Stanger began building a new glasshouse containing a seven-pot furnace about a mile from the one in Brooklyn. This he called the Isabella Glass Works, after his daughter, and it is listed as such in the company's ledger for about two years. Later, it was called the New Brooklyn Glass Works to distinguish it from the original factory, sub-sequently called the "Old" Brooklyn Glass Works. The first known listing of this factory was July 20, 1850; glassblowing began there September 9 of that year.[12] Vi-als, bottles, and containers of the same types listed above were also made here. Of particular interest to flask collec-tors is an entry in the ledger dated September 2, 1854, noting the purchase of a Jenny Lind mold from Samuel Huffsey for $15, less $1.12. Also, the first order of Jenny Lind bottles, quart size, was for 32¼ doz., sold to Samuel Huffsey at $10.12. This *may* have been the same mold used to produce the Jenny Lind calabash bottle GI–99, attrib-uted to the Millford Glass Works.

In February 1857, possibly because of the depression, the factory was rented to Job Norcross and Isaac W. Bar-ton for $50 a month. F. W. Stanger remained as superin-tendent, but the venture lasted only until May 16, 1857. From 1858 until 1864 the factory was rented to Clayton B. Tice and Joseph Ayers. In the latter year it failed because of a strike. Sometime afterward the glasshouse was reac-tivated, possibly by Thomas W. Stanger, who may have had a continuing interest in it. On May 26, 1870, he loaned a Jenny Lind mold, possibly that for the calabash bottle GI–99, to Bodine & Thomas of the Williamstown Glass Works, indicating that this mold was still in use some 20 years after the arrival of the celebrated songstress in this country.

According to the ledger of 1876, owned by J. E. Pfeiffer, "the Japanese government sent one of their representa-tives to this factory to observe glass making there . . . [he] stayed about a year, observing, making sketches and draw-ings of the works and when he left he induced several of the blowers to accompany him back to Japan." A note dated December 11, 1876, states: "commenced blasting today." The last positive record of production appears in the ledger on December 25, 1876: "teams could not travel—compelled to pull fire." Perhaps these conditions influ-enced the glassblowers who went to Japan. On October 1, 1881, a quantity of potshells, molds, stand plates, and other equipment was sold to the Woodbury Glass Com-pany. David Frederick was paid $3 for carting the above potshells (about 1¼ tons) to Woodbury, New Jersey. There are notes, however, of selling bottles as late as 1884.

Thomas W. Stanger, who was born December 11, 1811,

lived in retirement until he died February 23, 1892. Appropriately, he is buried in Glassboro, New Jersey, where in 1780 an earlier generation of his family, former employees of Wistar, started the first glassworks in the young "United states." It is interesting to note in passing that from 1840 to 1853 an Elizabeth Parker was listed as a glassblower at one or both of these Brooklyn glasshouses.[13]

The following Figured Flasks, each bearing the name Isabella Glass Works, can be definitely attributed to this factory:

GXIII–55. *Obverse*: Anchor with pennants with "ISABELLA" in upper one, "GLASSWORKS" in lower. *Reverse*: Three-quarter view of a glasshouse with furnace chimney in center from which smoke issues, and small chimneys at three corners, Quart. Colors: aquamarine, pale yellow-green. Scarce. 1850—possibly 1860 or 1870.

GXIII–56. *Obverse*: Anchor with pennants, like GXIII–55. *Reverse*: Sheaf of grain on crossed rake and 3-tined fork. Pint. Colors: aquamarine, green. Rare. 1850–possibly 1860 or 1870.

GXIII–57. *Obverse*: Anchor entwined with rope attached to a pennant above and below the anchor, "ISABELLA" in the upper pennant, "GLASS-WORKS" in the lower. *Reverse*: Glasshouse with large furnace chimney at center and five small chimneys. Half-pint. Colors: aquamarine, deep green. Rare. 1850—possibly 1860 or 1870.

48. FISLERVILLE GLASS WORKS, *Fislerville (Clayton), N.J., 1850–ca. 1914*

In 1850 Jacob P. Fisler, Jr., and Benjamin Beckett established the Fislerville Glass Works in Fislerville (formerly Fislertown), New Jersey, which was renamed Clayton in 1867.[14] It was located along the east side of the Glassboro and Malaga Turnpike on 75 acres of wooded land. In addition to a small glasshouse and other necessary buildings for the manufacture of glass, there were also a store, a barn, and several dwelling houses. The firm name was Beckett and Fisler. Less than a year after its founding, Beckett withdrew and Edward Bacon bought into the firm, which became known as Fisler and Bacon. The company continued in this style until 1856, when Bacon was killed in a railroad accident in Burlington, New Jersey. Fisler then sold the business to John M. Moore, who first rented the factory and then purchased it.[15]

In April 1859 George C. Hewitt and Jeremiah D. Hogate joined the firm, which became known as John M. Moore & Co. Hewitt sold his interest in the business in 1863 to D. Wilson Moore, a brother of John M. Moore, and the name

of the firm was changed to Moore Brothers & Co. The next year Hogate sold his interest to the two Moore brothers, and the firm became known as Moore Brothers. The brothers conducted the business very successfully from 1864 until 1880. In that year Francis M. Pierce, Harry Steelman, and Charles S. Fisler were taken into the firm, which again became Moore Brothers & Co. Later that same year Fisler withdrew and the name once again became Moore Brothers.

The following advertisement, which appeared in *Philadelphia and Its Manufacturers* in 1867, notes some of the products of Moore Brothers:

FISLERVILLE GLASS WORKS,
Fislerville, Gloucester Co., N.J.
Office—33 South Front Street, Philadelphia.

MOORE BROTHERS,
Manufacturers of
Druggists' and Perfumers' Glassware;
Wine, Porter and Mineral Water Bottles;
Pickle, Preserve, Jelly, and Air-Tight Fruit Jars;
Syrup, Sauce, Caper and Olive Bottles,
Also, every description of Crockery Dealers' Glassware.

Manufacturers of
MOORE'S PATENT AIR-TIGHT FRUIT JARS.
Orders addressed as above will meet with prompt attention.

John M. Moore
P. Wilson Moore   Particular attention paid to Private Molds.

By 1883 the works covered about 20 acres and included four large factories for making bottles and a smaller one for making either bottles or stoppers. There were also a steam-operated sawmill and gristmill, elevated railroad tracks for delivering coal to storage bins, and a number of other ancillary buildings, including a large three-story store with offices attached. A railroad track ran through the entire yard, connecting with the West Jersey Railroad track. At this time the firm's capital investment was between $300,000 and $400,000, and about 500 hands were employed. The business, amounting to approximately $300,000 annually at this time, extended throughout the United States and much glass was imported as well. *The Industrial Directory of New Jersey* of 1912 listed Moore Brothers as employing 600 hands. The firm continued until shortly before World War I.[16]

Despite the firm's successful development and the production of many kinds of bottles and other containers, the following calabash bottle is the only one that can at this time be assigned to the Fislerville Glass Works:

GI–107. Calabash bottle. *Obverse*: Bust of Jenny Lind, three-quarter view to left, wearing a plain broad bertha with two short branches below and "JENNY LIND" in a ribbon above. *Reverse*: Glassworks with large furnace chimney in center, 8 smaller chimneys at corners, and "FISLERVILLE GLASS WORKS" in scrolled ribbon above. Quart, plus. Colors: clear amber, clear yellowish green, clear deep green, bluish green, and aquamarine. Common. 1850–1860 or later.

49. CROWLEYTOWN GLASS WORKS; ATLANTIC GLASS WORKS, *Crowleytown, New Jersey, 1851-66*

The Crowleytown Glass Works, situated on the Mullica River about two and a half miles below Botato (Pleasant Mills), was, according to earlier writers,[17] established in 1851 by Samuel Crowley. It was a bottle glasshouse containing an eight-pot furnace operated by 12 blowers. Crowley, who was not an experienced glassman but who had owned a quarter interest in the Greenbank Glass Works from some time in 1838 to 1840, is said to have operated the works for about a year, and then sold out to New York City interests. This new company employed John Huffsey as manager (see No. 46, Pendleton and Millford Glass Works). Its glasshouse was known as the Atlantic Glass Works, and its products were sold through J. Huffsey & Co. of 50 North Fourth Street, above Arch Street, Philadelphia. The Burling Brothers were said to have operated the factory in 1858/59.[18]

According to the more recent researches of J. Edward Pfeiffer, noted collector and researcher of New Jersey Glass, however, this history may not be entirely correct. Pfeiffer's research indicates that John Huffsey and his associates built the factory and Samuel Crowley, Jr., furnished the land.[19] Doubtless Crowley had an interest in the glasshouse and a contract for supplying lumber and carting. The first "blast" of the factory occurred in September 1851. An advertisement in *Philadelphia As It Is*, 1852 (see No. 46, Millford Glass Works), terms the glasshouse the Atlantic Glass Works, and notes J. Huffsey & Co.'s association with it as "manufacturers and dealers in every description of druggists' glassware." About 1858 or 1859, Clayton Parker, a glassblower there, is said to have blown the first Mason jar.

An indenture dated August 10, 1864, indicates that Samuel Crowley, Jr., head of the "Crowleyville" glass factory, rented the factory to David F. Felt of New York City.[20] (Crowleyville was the name of Crowleytown at the time the works was established; hence the spelling "Crowleyville" in this document.) Of additional interest is the fact that the indenture for the rental of the factory also included the use of the following molds: "one gallon pickle jar mould, one-half gallon do, one qt. do, one pt. do, three pepper sauce moulds (two pints and one quart), one wine mould, one mineral and one porter mould." The last "fire" or "blast" took place in 1866, after which the plant was apparently abandoned.

During the course of his researches, J. Edward Pfeiffer has also uncovered a number of fragments of Washington–Taylor flasks as well as a Franklin flask.[21] It is *possible* that these flasks of the type known to have been made at the Dyottville Glass Works in Kensington were also produced at Crowleytown. They are as follows:

GI–52. *Obverse*: Washington, profile bust facing to the left, no inscription. *Reverse*: Taylor portrait bust facing to the left, no inscription. Colors: olive-yellow, light olive-amber, citronlike "colorless." Fragments of the same citronlike-colored glass and slag also found on the site. Common. 1851–60.

GI–53. *Obverse*: Washington, portrait bust facing to the left, no inscription. *Reverse*: Taylor, portrait bust facing to the left, no inscription. Color: green. Comparatively scarce. 1851–60.

Other fragments, similar to flasks produced at Dyottville and in amber glass, were found but are not identifiable. It is possible that these may have been fragments from such flasks as GI–37, GI–40, GI–41, GI–43, and GI–47. An amber fragment of GI–97 bearing a portrait of Benjamin Franklin on each side but with no inscription was also found there. This is from a quart-size flask. Finding these fragments at the site of the Crowleytown Glass Works would seem to indicate that the flasks were indeed produced there—as a result of buying or borrowing the mold, or because the mold was made by the same maker who produced molds for Dyottsville. There is also the possibility that these fragments may have been cullet to be used in batches for the production of any kind of bottles.

50. BULLTOWN GLASS WORKS, *Bulltown, Burlington County, New Jersey, 1858–ca. 1870*

In 1858 Samuel Crowley, Jr., who had been associated with the Greenbank Glass Works in 1838/39, and also was one of the proprietors of the Crowleytown Glass Works (see No. 49), established the Bulltown Glass Works. The factory is reputed to have been the smallest in New Jersey, containing only a five-pot furnace. It was located in Bulltown (now Waldo) two and a half miles east of Crowley's Landing, about two miles from the Mullion River.[22] Adeline Pepper has published a plan of the property which indicates that it belonged to the Burlington, Atlantic, Cape May, and Philadelphia Glass Manufacturing Company.[23] The factory, a bottle glasshouse, operated until about 1870. In his research on New Jersey factories for Stephen Van Rensselaer, Charles S. Boyer of the Camden Historical Society found that remains of the furnace foundations and a part of a melting pot could be seen in the early 1920s, but today no remnants of the Bulltown factory remain. The site is now a cranberry bog.

The specific types of bottles produced at this factory are unknown, but it is said that some of the early Mason jars were produced there, after they had first been blown at the Crowleytown Glass Works. Fragments of flasks in the sheaf of wheat and star design were found at the site by J. Edward Pfeiffer.[24] A half-pint flask in the design was recovered from the foundation of a dismantled house at nearby Merrygold, said by the owners, on the basis of oldtimers' recollections, to have been made at Bulltown. These facts are indications that the following two flasks may *possibly* have been produced there:

GXIII–39. *Obverse*: Sheaf of grain tied about the middle, parted in the center at the top, set on a crossed rake and 2-tined fork. *Reverse*: 5-pointed star like that on GXIII–

38, but smaller. Pint. Colors: aquamarine, amber, emerald-green, and yellow-green. Scarce. 1860–70.

GXIII–40. *Obverse*: Sheaf of grain, short, with no tie, parted in the center at the top, set on a crossed rake and large 2-tined fork. *Reverse*: 5-pointed star like that of GXIII–38, but smaller. Half-pint. Colors: amber, aquamarine, green, and emerald-green. Scarce. 1860–70.

51. LOCKPORT GLASS WORKS, *Lockport, New York, 1843–80s?*

Lockport is located in Niagara County in western New York about 20 miles northeast of Buffalo. It had few settlers until after 1820, but in 1822 it was made the county seat and in 1823 it became the temporary headquarters for construction on the Erie Canal. A series of locks was built at Lockport to raise and lower the canalboats from one level to another, and this led naturally to the designation "lower town" and "upper town."

Lockport also had service on the Rochester, Lockport and Niagara Falls Railroad as early as 1834, and on the Buffalo and Lockport Railroad by 1852. The village was surrounded by forests, which provided wood for both fuel and potash; lime was available from nearby Williamsville in Erie County and sand from Verona in Oneida County. Thus, Lockport had abundant fuel and raw materials for glassmaking nearby and excellent transportation facilities for distributing the finished products to both local markets, such as the nearby port of Buffalo, and more distant points (including Canada). It was an ideal location for the establishment of a glasshouse.

Until recently, it has generally been accepted that the Lockport Glass Works was founded in 1840, but research by James D. Billota has disproved this[25]. His research indicates that a Mr. Twogood from Mount Morris, New York, established the works in the spring of 1843 in a rented building that formerly had been a soap and candle factory, located on the corner of Gooding and Grand streets in North Lockport. Twogood's works began the production of medicine bottles and vials in September of 1843,[26] but because of limited capital (estimated at between $10,000 and $25,000) he sold out to the partnership of William Parsons and Abijah H. Moss in September of 1844.[27] Neither was a practical glassman. Parsons was a dealer in groceries and dry goods; Moss, an attorney and at one time president of the National Exchange Bank of Lockport. Undoubtedly bottles and vials continued to be their chief business, but starting on September 23, 1844, under the heading "Lockport Glass Works," they advertised in the *Niagara Courier*: "The subscribers have enlarged and improved these works and are ready to fill orders for the various kinds of hollow glassware on liberal terms and on the shortest notice. Particular attention paid to private moulds."

Apparently Parsons and Moss also ran into financial difficulties, for in August of 1845 they sold the company to George W. Hildreth and Company.[28] This firm consisted of four prominent Lockport businessmen and civic leaders. In addition to Hildreth, who operated a small iron foundry and was also a manufacturer of agricultural implements, there were Silas H. Marks, owner of a dry goods and grocery store, member of the Canal Enlargement Committee of Lockport, and also a member of the board of directors of the National Exchange Bank of Lockport; William Keep, who was at one time president of the National Exchange Bank of Lockport and who was also a member of the Canal Enlargement Committee of Lockport, as well as chairman of the board of trustees for the village of Lockport; and A. T. Webber. The firm's advertisement in the *Niagara Courier* of August 27, 1845, noted: "druggists' ware and bottles to be manufactured. Factory refitted and repaired. New orders equal to the capacity of the works."

Under Hildreth's direction, the company began in the spring of 1846 to erect a new set of buildings on a two-acre lot in the northeastern section of the village known as "upper town." Its location was in the block of Green Street and Transit Road, facing Green Street, and bordered by Hawley and Grand streets. In late August of 1846, the firm began glassmaking operations at their new site, and on September 2, the *Niagara Courier* carried the following descriptive account of the new works:

It is now the most extensive in the state for the manufacture of hollow glassware, and the only one in Western New York. In the main building, just erected, is the large furnace containing pots for melting glass, and capable of supplying constantly 14 blowers. In the same building are the drying and tempering ovens. They are all very conveniently sited, to accommodate the workmen and are constructed in the most substantial manner.

The process for drying the wood is entirely original, and is a very great improvement on the plan in use elsewhere. It is done by means of a hot air furnace, and the wood, when dried, is transported to where it is sawed by a sleigh. Outside is a horse-powered saw, for sawing, and the amount consumed daily is about four cords. The packing, warehouse and office are in a separate building, 25 feet by 112 feet, where the wares are stored, orders supplied, and business transacted. The works give steady employment to about 40 men, and the wares produced here are of the first quality. As evidence of this, it is sufficient to state the proprietors have received extensive orders.

This was a large operation for western New York. Less than a week after the new factory opened, the main factory building was completely destroyed by fire caused by sparks from one of the drying ovens. The melting furnace and the annealing ovens were not materially damaged, however, and the glasshouse building was immediately rebuilt, resulting in no material delay in production.

Webber's interest in the company was possibly the largest. When he died in the fall of 1850, his heirs sold his interest to Francis Hitchins. Before entering the glass business, Hitchins, who had come from England in the 1830s, had worked as a contractor in the enlargement of the

LOCKPORT GLASS WORKS.

FRANCIS HITCHINS,

(SUCCESSOR TO HILDRETH & CO.,)

Manufacturer of

VIALS, BOTTLES

AND

HOLLOW WARE.

Common, Prescription, Patent Medicine, and all kinds of Vials;

Castor Oil, Packing, Heavy, Perfumery, Cologne, Hair, Acid, Mineral, and Soda Bottles;

Bell Glasses, Hyacinth Glasses, Lamp Globes, and Digesting Bottles.

N. B.—The Glass is carefully packed, and can be forwarded by water and railroad from the Factory; and is not liable to break from land carriage.

Vials, Bottles, &c., Made to Order.

Particular attention will be given to private moulds of every description.

MOULDS MADE & LETTERED IN THE BEST STYLE

And on the most reasonable terms.

PATENT FRUIT JAR.

It possesses superior advantages over every other Can or Jar heretofore brought to public notice for the preservation of Fruit for any period of time. It is made of Glass, and for strength and durability it stands unequalled in the country. Some of its peculiar and very important advantages we will not fail to mention:

First—The material of which it is composed is perfectly safe, and will not corrode and poison the Fruit, as is often the case when put up in tin and other poisonous substances.

Second—By being transparent, the condi-tion of the Fruit can be ascertained at pleasure; while they are so easily cleansed that they are as good as new for succeeding years. The shape of the neck, also, is such that the cork cannot be forced in by the atmospheric pressure on it, caused by the cooling and consequent contraction of the Fruit in the bottle. This is a very desirable quality and worthy of notice.

It is almost useless to state that the brief experience of a single season has demonstrated to thousands the superiority of this bottle in every respect, and that they are

CHEAPER

than any other bottle, jar, or can of merit ever brought before the public, and so CHEAP as to be within the reach of all.

All orders will receive prompt attention, addressed to

FRANCIS HITCHINS, Lockport, Niagara Co., N. Y.

19. Advertisement of Francis Hitchins for the Lockport Glass Works, which appeared in an unidentified newspaper in 1860. Presumably the buildings that made up the Lockport Glass Works are accurately depicted in the cut accompanying the advertisement. The wide variety of bottles and containers the firm produced are mentioned in the advertisement. The same cut appears on billheads of the firm, but with the addition below the illustration of the name "FRANCIS HITCHINS," to the left of which is an illustration of locomotives pulling several cars; to the right, a canalboat is being towed by three horses or mules. Below these additions is the explanation "Manufacturer of Phials, Bottles and Hollow Glass Ware, Lockport, N.Y." The inclusion of a locomotive and cars and the canalboat reveals Francis Hitchins's recognition of the importance of adequate transportation for carrying his products to markets. This factor aided the Lockport Glass Works in continuing in business for more than half a century. *Niagara County Historical Society, Lockport, N.Y.*

Erie Canal and also had a half-interest in a tannery. In June of 1851, Hitchins leased the glass factory from the remaining partners for a two-year period, at the end of which, in June 1853, he bought them out.[29] Under his ownership, the Lockport Glass Works produced its greatest variety of glass. This is borne out by an 1860 advertisement[30] that lists among other wares the following bottles (Ill. 19): "Common, Prescription, Patent Medicine, and all kinds of vials; Castor Oil, Packing, Heavy, Perfumery, Cologne, Hair, Acid, Mineral, and Soda Bottles." According to the same advertisement, the factory also produced "Bell Glasses, Hyacinth Glasses, Lamp Globes and Digesting Bottles," as well as "Vials, Bottles, etc., Made to order." Particular attention was given to "private moulds" of every description, and the firm boasted of "MOULDS MADE AND LETTERED IN THE BEST STYLE."

Though no mention is made of flasks, it was probably during this period, and possibly just before it, that the firm made the "quart" flask GI–60 bearing the classic bust of Washington with the words "LOCKPORT GLASS WORKS" in an arc above. On February 12, 1861, during Hitchins's proprietorship, the *Lockport Daily Advertiser & Democrat* published a lengthy article describing the "Works and Its Operations." It noted, in part:

On entering the spacious room in which the glass is melted we behold in the center of the area, a large conical looking stack of stone and mortar, or Chimney which is pierced in the lower part by a series of round holes glaring like fiery eye-balls: twelve round holes called "ring" holes about the diameter each of a good size full moon. These holes are on the same level and extend at equal distance around the circumference of the stack. Surrounding the latter also is an elevated platform, occupied by the glassblowers . . .

The largest demand for bottles came from the producers and distributors of patent medicines, bitters, beer, soda, and mineral waters. Some of these firms became nationally known, and required large quantities of bottles for their products. In 1833 Dr. George W. Merchant established his famous "Gargling Oil" laboratory at the "Old Stand, corner of Main and Cottage Streets near the 'Big Bridge,' Lockport, New York."[31] This medicine, which was to become world famous, also was known simply as "Lockport Gargling Oil." It was a guaranteed panacea, good for "man or beast" and everything in between. These bottles (Ill. 20) are found in aquamarine, emerald-green, and blue. The name "G. W. MERCHANT" was embossed on one side and "Gargling Oil/Lockport, N.Y." on the other. Dr. Merchant's Gargling Oil came in four sizes: the two-ounce bottle sold for 25 cents, the four-ounce one for 50 cents, the eight-ounce one for a dollar, and the ten-ounce size for $1.25. Probably the empty bottle cost Merchant as much as all his material, labor, and other expenses combined. The "Gargling Oil" contained 44 percent alcohol, with one grain of opium per fluid ounce. If the customer were truly ailing, undoubtedly he or she forgot all aches and pains after a few doses of Dr. Merchant's remedy. This firm

20. Two bottles for Dr. Merchant's Gargling Oil. *Left:* aqua, about 1870. *Right:* deep, clear green, inscribed "FROM THE/LABORATORY/OF W. MERCHANT/CHEMIST"; about 1855. *Collection of Owens-Illinois, Toledo, Ohio*

bought the largest number of bottles from the Lockport glasshouse. "In one year (1866), one million bottles were manufactured for the use of the company, mostly made at the glass works in this city."[32]

Another large user of bottles made at the Lockport Glass Works was the Oak Orchard Mineral Springs Company, later called the Oak Orchard Acid Springs. This company was formed by Isaac Colton and Thomas Olcott for the purpose of bottling spring water. They also operated the Oak Orchard Hotel, a popular resort from 1848 to 1860. The spring water, which contained—according to Professor Hadley of Geneva College—"free sulphuric acid," came from at least five springs located around Alabama Center, in Genesee County, each of which produced a different-tasting water. Various colored bottles were used to denote the water from these different springs. The bottles ranged in color from light to dark amber, light to dark blue, and emerald-green. They were marked on the base "Glass from F. Hitchins Factory, Lockport, New York" (Ill. 21) and embossed "Oak Orchard Acid Springs" around the shoulder of the bottle (Ill. 22). In 1849 Colton (a former president of the Lockport Bank in "lower town") and Olcott (a land speculator from Albany) used approximately 25,000 of these bottles made at the Lockport Glass Works.[33]

The Niagara Star Bitters Company, located on the corner of Lock and Ontario streets in Lockport, was another good customer of the glassworks. Operated by the

21. "Oak Orchard Acid Springs" bottle, embossed on the base "GLASS FROM F. HITCHINS. FACTORY. LOCKPORT NY." *The Corning Museum of Glass*

22. Bottle made in F. Hitchins Lockport Glass Works, marked on the shoulder "OAK ORCHARD ACID. SPRINGS". Dark olive-green bottle glass. Early 1860s. *The Corning Museum of Glass; acc. no. 64.4.47*

partnership of Fletcher, Hoag, and John W. Steele, it purchased between 72,000 and 75,000 bottles annually. In addition to this firm, which was probably the only large distiller of hard liquor located in Lockport, 15 brewers and distillers were listed in Niagara County in 1855.[34] The Lockport Glass Works made bottles for many of these local breweries (as well as later ones), including such firms as the Anton Ulrich Brewing Company, Christy & Jenney, Drapers Brewery, David Dye, Enright Brewery, John Gibson Brewery, Humphrey & Jenney, Chas. H. Kandt, Lockport Brewery & Malt House, Lockport Brewing Co., Lockport City Malt House, J. B. Naismith, Newtons Brewery, Ontario Malt House, J. H. Patterson Lockport Brewery, Steele & Hoag Malt House, Union Brewing Co., and Wendel Bros.[35] The majority of these bottles were originally made of aquamarine-colored glass—for example, those for the Ulrich, Richardson, Mayers, Naismith, Crandall, Lock City, and Jenney companies. The Hoag & Steele bottle was made in a medium to dark amber glass. After the Civil War, however, the glassworks made less green bottle glass and concentrated more on light aqua and "colorless" glass products. Soda and mineral water bottles were made by Lockport for the following Lockport firms: Cherry

Blossom Bottling Works, Connelly & Cushin, M. Crandall, Crogan & Meyers, Donnelly & McGlynn, George H. Downes, Lock City Bottling Works, Lockport Bottling Works, Mayer Wein, W. M. Mayers, and M. Richardson.[36]

By no means all Lockport Glass Works products were made for local use. For example, in 1846 the *Niagara Courier* noted that "heavy orders have been filled from various parts of the state and Canada," and on July 8, 1853, the *Lockport Daily Courier* stated:

The wares manufactured go principally to Canada, though a fair amount of orders came from New York and other large cities in this section of the country. The mineral water bottles manufactured here have a reputation excelling all other manufactures, and are sent to distant places throughout the country.

Francis Hitchins operated the Lockport Glass Works from 1850 until July 1866—the longest period under one ownership. The business was then purchased by some of the glassblowers, and on July 21, 1866, it was reincorporated for a 20-year period as the Lockport Glass Manufacturing Company, with capital stock valued at $15,000. The ownership was reorganized as a trusteeship. One hundred

23. Colorful lithograph advertising Dr. Merchant's Gargling Oil, dated 1852. *Collections of Greenfield Village and the Henry Ford Museum, Dearborn, Michigan* and fifty shares of stock valued at $100 per share were issued. John Shine, Robert Johnson, James Maroney, and Edward Batten each bought 10 shares; Michael Cahill and Patrick Glynn each owned 5 shares. The remaining 100 shares—the controlling interest—were bought by Joseph Batten.

The production of fruit jars was started at Lockport Glass Works about 1860 under Hitchins's ownership, as noted in his advertisement (Ill. 19). After 1866, under the Batten trusteeship, fruit jars became a very large part of the firm's production. In that year they advertised such wares as the " 'Hero' self-sealing fruit jar, black and ruby bottles, druggists green glassware and flasks. Private moulds made to order."[37]

On July 16, 1869, the trusteeship sold its interest to S. B. Rowley of Philadelphia, who owned there one of the largest glasshouses in the country. According to the *Lockport Daily Journal and Courier* of August 2, 1869: "The Lockport Glass Works is one of a chain of 13 factories, either owned or controlled for, by the owner of the 'Hero,' 'Gem,' and 'All Right' fruit jars. W. J. Smith is the agent in charge here." On July 13, 1870, about a year after Rowley acquired the firm, the *Lockport Daily Journal* noted:

The factory now has in its employ 115 hands, including women and boys, and turns out an average 6,000 jars daily. To judge still further of the enormous extent of its business, we may state that since the organization of the works in this city, nearly three million jars have been manufactured.

Another news report, in the *Lockport Daily Journal and Courier*, August 21, 1869, stated:

Mr. Smith was obliged to decline orders for 30,000 jars recently, for it would be in vain to attempt to fill them before the present season is over. Since the first of February, they have made and sent off about 435,000 of the "Gems" alone to several buyers from abroad.

Under the Rowley ownership, the works was enlarged and production facilities doubled. The *Lockport Daily Journal* of November 10, 1870, reported:

The manufacturing of glass is not suspended owing to the enlargement of the facilities. The former capacity of the factory is now being doubled. The stone walls are being extended on all sides, the furnace made proportionately large, three or four additional ovens for tempering the glass are being erected, and the pots which are placed in the furnace and in which the glass is made are four times their number, and three times larger than was used a few years ago.

In all, $30,000 worth of improvements were made, in addition to steam power to drive the grinding wheels, or mills, which were used by four men in grinding the rough edges from the mouths of the fruit jars. During Rowley's ownership, approximately 720 tons of sand, obtained from

Vineland, New Jersey, were used each year. The total ingredients consumed at that time averaged about 6,000 pounds daily or about one pound of raw material per jar produced. Also, as a result of the modernization and expansion under Rowley, the works began to use coal as fuel for the melting furnace, consuming about 160 tons per month.

Despite these improvements and the extended production, Rowley retained his ownership only until 1872, when he sold the business to Alonzo J. Mansfield of Lockport.[38] After suffering two fires in the early part of 1878, a large part of the factory was destroyed by fire later that year. Mansfield rebuilt it on an even more extensive scale. At that time the works employed between 75 and 100 hands, of whom 30 were boys and 15 girls, all under 18 years of age. According to Van Rensselaer, Mansfield was then doing business amounting to approximately $75,000 annually.[39] The firm continued in this style until 1904, when it was reorganized with Alonzo J. Mansfield as president, S. J. Clark as vice-president, and George Emerson as secretary-treasurer.[40]

During Mansfield's operation, the major part of the production continued to be fruit jars, the "Mansfield Mason" being the company's chief product, but other bottles were made as well. Among them, beginning in the 1880s, it is believed were bottles made for the hair restorer promoted by the famous seven Sutherland sisters from Cambria, in Niagara County, New York (Ill. 24).[41] The seven sisters, proclaimed to have the longest hair in the world (seven feet long and four inches thick), were billed as musical entertainment more on the merit of their remarkable floor-length hair than on their talent. Realizing this, their father had the brilliant idea of concocting a mixture of vegetable oils, alcohol, and a little rainwater and marketing it as "hair grower," to which his long-haired daughters could well testify. They traveled widely, advertising their product, which made a fortune for them. Although fruit jars constituted the largest share of the Lockport firm's production in its later years, other bottles and (in the 1870s) flasks continued to be made there.

The following flasks are known to have been made at Lockport or are, by association of design and style, believed to have been made there:

GI–60. *Obverse*: Washington, a classical bust facing left with "LOCKPORT GLASS WORKS" in arc above the bust. *Reverse*: Washington, classical bust facing left. Quart. Colors: aquamarine, deep blue, sapphire-blue, deep bluish green, and medium green. Scarce. Late 1840s and 1850s.

GI–61. Classical bust of Washington facing left on each side, no inscription. Quart. Colors: aquamarine, very dark yellow-green, clear deep green, dark olive-green (black), light sapphire-blue, light green, and emerald-green. Scarce. Late 1840s and 1850s.

GXIII–30. *Obverse*: "WILL YOU TAKE" in a shallow arc above "A DRINK" in a straight line below, above a

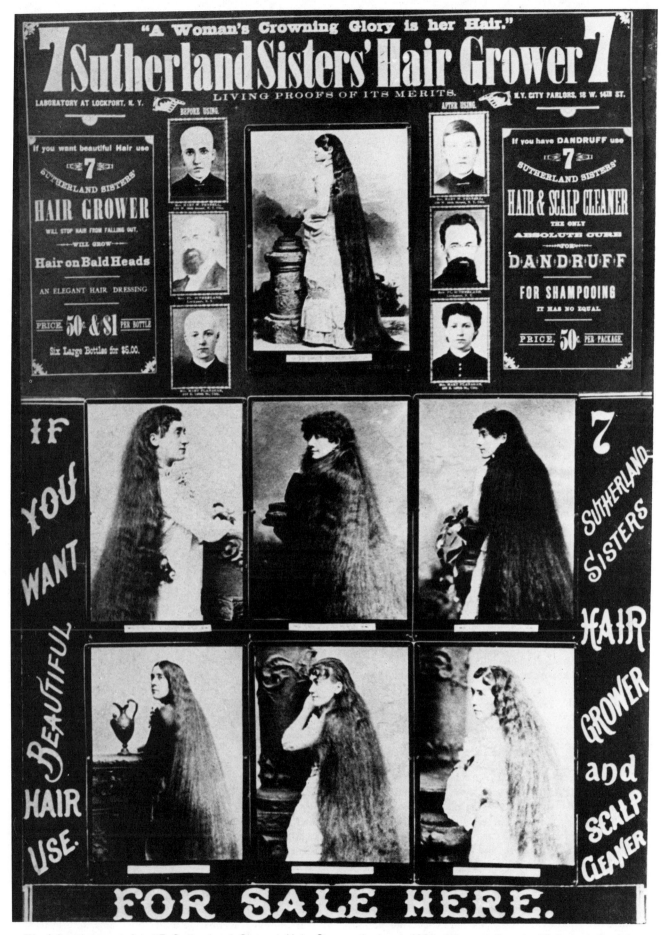

24. Advertisement for "7 Sutherland Sisters' Hair Grower," about 1890. *Niagara County Historical Society, Lockport, N.Y.*

geometric decorative or floral device. Below that, "WILL A" above a stylized duck over "SWIM?" *Reverse*: Plain. Half-pint. Colors: yellow-green and aqua. Probably ca. 1865–75.

GXIV–6. *Obverse*: "TRAVELER'S with the S smaller than the other letters, in a shallow arc above a stylized duck or goose with neck curved to left and head to left above small wing; the word "COMPANION" in a concave arc below. *Reverse*: "LOCKPORT" in a shallow arc above an 8-petal starlike flower, with large bead at the center. The words "GLASS" and "WORKS" in two straight lines below. Pint. Colors: aquamarine, blue-green, and yellow-green. Scarce. Probably late 1850s and 1860s.

52. LANCASTER GLASS WORKS, *Lancaster, New York, 1849–1904 or 1908*

On April 21, 1849, the *New York Tribune* carried the following brief announcement:

NEW GLASS WORKS. —Messrs. Reed, Allen, Cox and Co. of Pittsburgh have purchased a site and are erecting buildings for the manufacture of Glass in the village of Lancaster, near Buffalo. They will commence manufacturing about the 1st of August, This will be an important branch of business for Lancaster.[42]

This brief announcement notes rather precisely the inception of the Lancaster Glass Works, and corroborates statements by both Van Rensselaer[43] and Harry Hall White[44] that the firm was founded in Lancaster in 1849 by eight glassblowers from Pittsburgh. To date, Harry Hall White's researches, as presented in *Antiques*,[45] shed the most light on this factory and its operations. According to him, the glasshouse was located on Factory Street, later Court Street (on a three-acre site at what is now the corner of Lake Avenue and James Place). It seems to have had a very small furnace containing only five pots, each of which was not over two feet in diameter.

After an unknown period, a change occurred in the firm, apparently with some of the founders selling their shares in the business to Samuel S. Shinn, at which time the firm became Reed, Shinn & Company. In 1859, while the factory was being operated by this firm, a fire destroyed much of it, but it was rebuilt almost immediately and continued under control of the same firm until 1863. In that year, Dr. Frederick ("Frank") H. James purchased Shinn's interest, and carried on the business with N. B. Gatchell as James, Gatchell and Company. Following the Civil War, James and Gatchell bought the interests of their partners and continued the business under their own names.

Advertisements in the Directory of 1866[46] state the firm manufactured "glassware of every description, with a large supply on hand." Nevertheless, except for a limited number of offhand pieces—especially pitchers in the South Jersey style—the basic products of the factory seem to have been bottles and flasks, except for a certain period

during the Civil War, when telegraph insulators were made in large quantities. The limited number of workmen listed in the Directory of 1866 as employees of the Lancaster Glass Works would indicate the factory and its operations continued to be rather small at that time. Glassblowers listed were J. D. Fry, J. V. Voll, H. Kupper, B. Myers, and J. Springer; Sherman Remington was listed as a pot maker and Thomas Leary as machinist and moldmaker. Assuming that each glassblower headed one shop, and also that only those glassblowers listed in the Directory were working for the firm at that time, the factory seems to have had five shops, which is a rather small operation; as such, it is surprising to find a machinist and moldmaker as part of the staff. Therefore, it can be concluded that the principal products of this small factory were mold-blown glassware.

Dr. James purchased Gatchell's interest in the works about 1866, and the firm became known as the James Glass Works. From that time until 1861 when Dr. James retired, many of the bottles in the following list were produced:

Bottles

Hostetter's Bitters
Dr. Fisch's Bitters
Plantation Bitters
Warner's Tippecanoe
    Bitters
Earner's Safe Bitters
Wishart's Pine Tree
    Cordial
C. W. Merchant,
    Lockport, N.Y.
Clarissy's White Oil
    Linament
Shilo's Cough Cure
John Roach Bitters
Stimson and
    Hebblewhite Blacking
C. B. Woodworth,
    Rochester, N.Y.
    Many shapes: boots,
    slippers, etc.

Summerville Horse
    Medium, Buffalo,
    N.Y.
    (Shape of a horse's
    hoof)
Monitor Inks
Barrel-shaped bottles
    and Flora Temple

Flasks

Scroll
Traveller
Railroad with Eagle
Urn-Cornucopia
Clasped Hands
Shoo-fly
Picnic

According to White, these products were identified by Frank H. James, son of Dr. James, the former owner, and John G. Lumbrix, who began work in the factory in the fall of 1861, as having been made at the Lancaster factory. Some of these bottles and flasks were also made at other factories.

This glassworks probably also made beer, soda, mineral water, and—definitely—porter bottles. Examples of the porter bottle are known in light gray-blue glass, with a thick, deep, sloping collar and a small domed kick-up, inscribed "LANCASTER" in a shallow arc with "GLASS WORKS" below (3 in Color Plate XIV). On the reverse is "XX".

Following Dr. James's retirement, a group of workmen at the plant took it over and carried on the business as The Lancaster Cooperative Glass Works Limited (Ill. 25). The firm continued to operate under this name until at least

ESTABLISHED, 1849.

⊷ Lancaster Co-operative Glass Works. ⊷

(Successors to Frederick H. James.)

MANUFACTURERS OF GREEN, AMBER & FLINT GLASS.

Particular Attention Given to Private Molds.

HIGH PRESSURE BOTTLES A SPECIALTY.

Public Telephone, Times Office.　　　**Lancaster, Erie Co., N. Y.**

25. An 1895 advertisement of the Lancaster Co-operative Glass Works from the *Smith Directory. Buffalo and Erie County Historical Society, Buffalo, N.Y.*

1904[47] or, possibly, until 1908, according to Stephen Van Rensselaer.

The marked flasks in the following list can be definitely attributed to the Lancaster Glass Works; the others may be attributed to it by analogy of design:

GIII–16. *Obverse*: Cornucopia, filled with fruit and/or produce. *Reverse*: Urn filled with fruit and/or produce with "LANCASTER GLASS WORKS, N.Y." in arc above. Pint. Colors: light blue, peacock-green, emerald-green, violet-blue, clear amber, golden amber, sapphire-blue, light green, olive-green, and aquamarine. Common. Probably 1849 to about 1860.

GIII–13, by analogy of design. *Obverse*: Cornucopia. *Reverse*: Urn. Half-pint. Colors: very pale green, emerald-green, and aquamarine. Common. Probably about 1849 to about 1860.

GIII–15. *Obverse*: Cornucopia. *Reverse*: Urn. Half-pint. Colors: deep yellow-green, deep blue-green, and aquamarine. Common. Probably 1849 to about 1860.

GIII–17. *Obverse*: Cornucopia. *Reverse*: Urn. Pint. Colors: deep yellowish-green, emerald-green, pale green, aquamarine, deep bluish-green, pale yellow-green, clear deep amber: golden amber: red-amber, light bluish-green, medium green, deep olive-green, and deep yellow-green. Common. Probably 1849 to about 1860.

GIII–18. *Obverse*: Cornucopia. *Reverse*: Urn. Pint. Colors: deep yellowish green, deep brilliant green-yellow tone, red-amber, olive-amber, blue-green, deep emerald-green, and olive-green. Rare. Probably 1849 to about 1860.

GXIV–4. *Obverse*: "TRAVELER'S" inscribed in shallow arc above an 8-pointed "star" or ornament with petal-like points, with "COMPANION" in reverse arc below.

Reverse: "LANCASTER" in shallow arc above a star as on the obverse, "ERIE. CO., N.Y." in reverse arc below. Pint. Colors: amber (or olive-yellow), aquamarine, and blue-green. Scarce. Probably about 1860 to early 1870s.

GXIV–5. Like GXIV–4, but shorter in proportion to width. Height approximately 6¾ inches in contrast to GXIV–4 height: 7⅜–7½ inches. Pint. Colors: amber (?), aquamarine, blue-green, olive-yellow, and deep wine. Scarce except for deep wine, which is very rare. Probably about 1860 to early 1870s.

GXV–11. *Obverse*: Inscription: "LANCASTER GLASS-WORKS" in semicircle and "FULL PINT" in larger letters in a straight line starting under the "L" and ending at the "S." Plain. Pint. Color: aquamarine. Rare.

Flasks attributed to, and generally accepted as having been made at, the Lancaster Glass Works:

GV–1. *Obverse*: Simplified locomotive to left on rail with the inscription "SUCCESS TO THE RAILROAD" almost surrounding it. *Reverse*: Similar with slight variations. Pint. Colors: olive-yellow, light sapphire-blue, golden amber, deep amber, clear green, clear olive-green, aquamarine, colorless with pale yellow tint, cloudy yellowish or mustard-green—almost opaque. Comparatively scarce. Probably 1849 to about 1860.

GV–2. Variant of GV–1, but with different base. Pint. Color: clear dark olive-green. Rare. Probably 1849 to about 1860.

Flasks possibly made at the Lancaster Glass Works:

GIX–10. Scroll, with no inscription. Same on reverse. Pint. Colors: vibrant yellow-green, pale yellow-green, greenish blue, deep yellow-green, bluish green, brilliant yellowish olive, pale amethyst, and aquamarine. Common. Probably 1849 to about 1860.

GIX–11. Scroll, variant of GIX–10, but upper stars are irregular and there is a slight space between the sides of the upper pair of scrolls at the center. Reverse is like the obverse, but with variation in size of lower star. Pint. Colors: deep sapphire-blue, dark olive-green (black), emerald-green with bluish tone, and aquamarine. Common. Probably 1849 to about 1860.

GXIII–20. *Obverse*: Panel bearing racehorse standing on bar facing left with inscription "FLORA TEMPLE" in shallow reverse curve above. Below the panel is the inscription "HARNESS TROT 2.193/4" above "OCT. 15, 1859." *Reverse*: Plain. Quart (usually no handle). Colors: reddish amber, deep green, medium green, yellow-green. Common. Probably 1859 through 1860s.

GXIII–23. Flora Temple flask, like GXIII–20, but pint size and "Oct. 15, 1859" omitted. Colors: deep green, bluish green, and olive-green. Common. 1859 probably through 1860s.

53. ALBANY GLASS WORKS, *Albany, New York. ca. 1847–50*

The Albany Glass Works is known to have existed because of pint and half-pint flasks that bear its name. Unfortunately, very little else is known about this factory, and the fact that both flasks are in the style of the late 1830s and early 1840s, and that the following meager evidence indicates the factory operated for only a short time about the middle of the century, adds even more perplexity to the situation.

The first reference to this Albany glasshouse appears in the records of the Franklin Institute, Philadelphia, which indicate that the Albany Glass and Porcelain Company exhibited at its 17th Exhibition in 1847.[48] The next reference to the glasshouse appears in the Albany Directory for 1848/49.[49] In the "Mercantile Guide" portion of the directory, Dougherty & Cook are listed as "Manufacturers of Vials, Jars, Bottles &c. of every description, corner of Church & Schuyler-sts." In the main body of the directory, Dougherty & Cook also appear as "manufacturers of glass ware," and Daniel Dougherty is listed as a "glass blower" residing at 198 Green Street. This is the only year in which this firm or these listings appear; they do not occur in earlier or later directories. In the Albany Directory for 1849/50, on page 20, under the heading "Albany Mercantile Cards," is listed the "Albany Glass Works, corner of Church and Schuyler sts. Dan'l O. Ketchum, Agent."[50]

Daniel Ketchum is listed as residing at 41 Broad Street in the 1850/51 Albany Directory. There is no mention of him, however, as agent of the Albany Glass Works. He is also listed again at the same address in the directory for 1851/52.[51] This directory also lists Daniel Dougherty as a glassblower residing at 90 Schuyler Street. No mention is made of either Ketchum or Dougherty in the 1853 directory, but a "Glass Reflector Manufactory" is listed along with Thomas Owen at 51 Green Street.[52]

The only other possible reference to glassmaking in Albany during this era occurs in the 1847/48 and 1848/49 directories, both of which carry the enigmatic listing of a "Glass Works Square" at a location given as "121 Corner Broadway & Ferry Sts." This, however, was about six blocks from the corner of Church and Schuyler streets, where the Albany Glass Works was located, according to the 1849/50 directory.

In 1850, the Albany Glass Company received a diploma for glass water pipes exhibited at the Annual Fair of the American Institute of the City of New York.[53] On the basis of this scant information, it would appear that the Albany Glass Works or possibly its predecessor, the Albany Glass and Porcelain Company, was in operation from about 1847 through 1850 or 1851, and it was during this span of four or five years that the pint and half-pint flasks bearing the name "Albany Glass Works" were produced. This being the case, one must recognize that the styles and forms usually associated with an earlier era (i.e., in this case, the late 1820s and 1830s) may at times continue in use until a much later date. The same is true of the railroad and cornucopia flasks that are characteristic of the 1830s made at the Lancaster Glass Works, which did not begin operations until 1849.

The following flasks were produced at the Albany Glass Works:

GI–28. *Obverse*: Washington, small three-quarter view facing left, in uniform, surrounded by the inscription: "ALBANY GLASS WORKS" in a deep "horse-shoe" arch with the words "ALBANY, N.Y." in two lines below. *Reverse*: Full-rigged ship sailing to the right. Pint. Colors: light sapphire-blue, aquamarine, clear amber, dark amber, deep green, and clear olive-green. Comparatively scarce. ca. 1847–51.

GI–30. *Obverse*: Washington, shown in a small three-quarter view facing left, in uniform. *Reverse*: plain except for the inscription "ALBANY GLASS WORKS" in a deep "horse-shoe" arch following the contour of the flask with the letters "N Y" below. Half-pint. Colors: olive-yellow, deep green, clear amber, aquamarine. Comparatively scarce. ca. 1847–51,

54. NEWBURGH GLASS COMPANY, *Newburgh, New York, ca. 1866–ca. 1875*

Practically nothing is known about this glassworks, yet several bottles of black glass embossed on the base "NEWBURGH GLASS CO. PATD. FEB. 28, 1866" have been found,[54] as well as a few pint flasks bearing the same inscription with "NEWBURGH GLASS CO." in a circle on the upper half of the obverse and the balance on the lower half. The reverse of the flask is plain. Despite this, and the fact that E. Ruttenber's *History of New Windsor,* printed in 1912 by the *Newburgh Journal,* indicates a glass-house was established in Newburgh in 1867, the firm is listed in only one issue of the Newburgh Directory, that of 1872/73.[55] In that year there is an entry in the advertising section of the directory: "GLASS WORKS, Newburgh Glass Works, Burrows, Regan and Roche, Prop's, New Windsor." No entries regarding this company, nor these men, appeared in any of the directories either several years before or after these dates. Nor is the exact location of this factory known, but in an atlas of Orange County published in 1875, a map of New Windsor designates a parcel of land between the river and the Newburgh Turnpike (now called the River Road) as the "Glass Co.," suggesting the possibility that the factory might still have been in operation at that date.[56] If so, one can speculate that the factory was probably in operation for at least about ten years from 1866 (the patent date on the bottles and flasks) to 1875, if the information in the atlas was up to date.

Apparently the Newburgh Glass Works made some bottles for the Willington Glass Company of West Willington, Connecticut. Harry Hall White in his article in *Antiques*[57] about that factory, quotes from a day book of the factory kept by one of the proprietors, Harvey Merick: "1 swell neck Qt bottle mold now at Newburg at Burrows Factory. Bartlett has agreed to get D. John Molds and this swell neck mold and send them here." The entry is dated March 2, 1870. The swell-neck bottle may have been for beer, ale, or porter. It is not clear whether the "D. John Molds" were also at Newburgh, or were being returned from elsewhere, but undoubtedly demijohns of various sizes were part of the production of this factory.

GXV–15. *Obverse:* inscription, in a circle: "NEW-BURGH GLASS CO." in upper half, "PAT$\underline{d}$ FEB 28th 1866" in lower half of circle. *Reverse:* plain. Pint. Colors: olive-amber, amber. Scarce. ca. 1865–75.

GXV–15a. Like GXV–15. Half-pint. Color: amber. Rare. ca. 1865–75.

55. GRANITE GLASS WORKS, *Mill Village, Stoddard, New Hampshire, 1846–60*

The Granite Glass Company was formed in 1846 by Gilman Scripture, John M. Whiton, Jr., and Calvin Curtice. None seems to have had any practical glassmaking experience, but each was a man of some importance in the community and together they ran the village store. Scripture was a justice of the peace and selectman, and after their glassmaking venture failed, he retired to Nashua, where he was later elected mayor. Whiton was postmaster of Stoddard in 1852. Little is known of Curtice, except that he came to Stoddard from Windsor, New Hampshire, in 1847 and worked for the company as a contract shipper or distributing agent.

The glasshouse, which contained an eight-pot furnace, was located along the high bank of a small stream on the south side of the road to Antrim.[58] In the winter of 1847 it

burned down, but it was soon rebuilt and glassmaking was resumed. Though formed as the Granite Glass Company and usually known by that name, in 1849 it was listed in the *New England Mercantile Union Directory* as "C. Curtis & Co., black glass bottles."[59] During its nearly 15 years of operation, the Granite Glass Company produced the usual types of green and "black" glass bottles and containers typical of the era. It is interesting to note the numbers of these bottles an experienced blower could produce in a single day. George W. Foster seems to have been such a craftsman. He acquired his skills in South Stoddard's first glasshouse, that built in 1842 by his father, Joseph, in the area called The Box. When it was forced to close in 1850 and was taken over by Scripture, Whiton, and Curtice,[60] George with his older brother, Henry, entered the employ of the Granite Glass Company. Fortunately for glass historians, George kept a diary. In it he recorded having blown 532 quart wines one day and, another day, 250 quart brandies, and also that 138 one-gallon demijohns were blown daily.[61] Other products of the Granite Glass Works were snuff and blacking bottles, 16-sided and plain conical inks, ink bottles, medicine bottles, bitters, pickle, and spring water bottles, as well as preserve jars and half-pint Figured Flasks. Numerous fragments of all these types of bottles and containers have been found at the site of this factory by Lura Woodside Watkins, but apparently none of the quart and pink flasks like GII–80 and GII–81. The fact that she found also fragments of the same types of bottles and containers at the sites of the other Stoddard glasshouses indicates they were all producing essentially the same wares. In 1854, according to *Gould's History of Stoddard,* the firm was "making annually $25,000[62] worth of bottles of various sizes and descriptions."

The sand for this factory, as well as for other Stoddard factories, was procured from Center Pond and from sandpits near Munsonville and Antrim. For the inexperienced or careless, the pits could be hazardous: in March 1853, Henry Whitman, a young man of 17, working for the Granite Glass Company, was digging sand near Antrim and "incautiously dug under a bank when it suddenly caved in upon him, crushing him under its weight and killing him instantly."[63] According to James D. Cutter of Antrim, who had been a blower in the Granite Glass Works as well as at two other Stoddard glasshouses, the batch for bottle glass was made up of eight parts of local sand, twelve of ash, and two of salt. Most of the glass made in the Stoddard factories is full of bubbles, that of the Granite Glass Company especially so. Incidentally, as so often happens in glassblowers' families, James Cutter had followed his father, Xenophone, into the craft. Xenophone Cutter was a blower for the Granite Glass Company when it opened in 1846.

That the Granite Glass Works was in financial trouble within ten years is evident from George Foster's diary. On January 1, 1856, he wrote: "Whiton and Curtice owe me $186.19 besides note for $150.00, total my due $336.19." This was followed by: "Today is the first day of the year. I am blowing Qt. Wines, at the Granite Glass Works, Stoddard, N.H., John M. Whiton and Calvin Curtice proprietors . . . " It should be noted that no mention is made of Mr. Scripture, who is usually cited as one of the proprietors, and who therefore may have left the firm by that time. George also recorded that he made 290 quart wines that day. On January 8 he made 250 brandies and the same number again on January 14. On January 22 he recorded: "Made 460 Qt. Wines. Had to burn green wood in furnace most all day." On February 14, 1856 he wrote in his diary: "Whiton and Curtice sued and all their property attached by Sheriff Joshua Wyman. The Keene Ashuelot Bank put on first for $5000 and there were twelve or fourteen others. I am on for $500 or more which they owe me. The sheriff wanted me to work and blow glass out and he would see that we were all paid." The next day he recorded: "Made 532 Quart Wines for Sheriff Wyman. As soon as we was down, they cleaned out the furnace so as to heat it up again another fire."[64]

It is interesting to note that George Foster, having received an invitation from William McCully of Pittsburgh to work there, left for the McCully Glass Works on February 26, 1856; after returning to Stoddard in May, he was asked by Mr. Whiton on September 5, 1856, to blow at the Granite Glass Works when operations were resumed. He also received a similar offer from Mr. B. F. Messer, he recorded. On September 19 he wrote: ". . . also fixed set pots (6 of them) into their places in the furnace. We also set two pots from the pot oven in the afternoon . . ." September 22 he noted: "Today, we began to blow at the Granite Glass Works. I worked in my old place. The glass did not work very well today—was stiff. Made 236 Quart Wines." He continued to work there until November 8, 1856, when he wrote in his diary: "I worked pretty fast today—nine hours lacking 5 minutes. The furnace went out at 4 PM." On November 12 he settled with Curtice for $138.92; his total earnings for the seven weeks the factory was again in operation were $177.47.

On November 26 of that year an auction was held at which George W. Foster obtained 49 old cast-iron molds at $1 each. But this was not the company's entire supply of molds, for George Foster noted in his diary: "I supposed that I was buying all of the company's molds, but they deceived me."[65] It was George L. Curtis who bid in most of the factory equipment. Curtis, who was born in Windsor, New Hampshire, November 22, 1825, entered into partnership with B. F. Messer to carry on the business. In 1857 Messer sold his share of the partnership to Curtis, who continued to operate the Granite Glass Company until 1860, when it closed for good. In that year, also, Curtis sold two packing houses to Weeks and Gilson, who, with three other partners, had established the South Stoddard Glass Manufacturing Company in 1850 in "The Box" area. Presumably these warehouses in The Box were the ones that the firm of Scripture, Whiton, and Curtice had acquired in 1850 from Joseph Foster's assignee after his failure. Curtis continued to operate his store in Stoddard until 1872, when he moved to Nashua, New Hampshire, where he entered the wholesale and retail grocery business.

The following list of flasks is attributed to the Granite Glass Company because they bear its name, or are likely to have been made there because of similarity of their designs to those in marked flasks:

GII–80. *Obverse:* American eagle with head turned to left, with a large shield on breast having 7 vertical bars; above the eagle is a pennant inscribed "GRANITE"; below the eagle is a large oval frame containing the words "GLASS CO." in letters of unequal size. *Reverse:* like the obverse, but inscribed within the frame at the top "STODARD"; at the bottom "NH". Quart. Colors: clear amber, golden amber, olive-amber. Very rare. 1846–60.

GII–81. *Obverse:* similar to GII–80 but inscription below is "GLASS. CO." *Reverse:* same as obverse, but the inscription is "STODDARD" and the "N H" below is centered in the frame. Pint. Colors: light and dark brown-amber, olive-amber. Common. 1856–60.

GII–82. *Obverse:* like GII–81 but no inscription in the frame. *Reverse:* like GII–81, but letters of the inscription are smaller, with faint periods after "N" and "H". Pint. Colors: light amber, golden amber and olive-amber. Scarce. 1846–60. Attributed to a Stoddard, New Hampshire, factory, probably the Granite Glass Works, on the basis of the relationship of the design to GII–81.

GII–83. *Obverse:* similar to GII–81, but the bottom of the frame is about ⅜ inch from the base and there is no inscription. *Reverse:* like the obverse, but the bottom of the frame about ⅝ inch from the base. Pint. Colors: amber, olive-amber, light olive-green, light yellow-green. Common. 1846–60. Attributed to New England, possibly Granite Glass Works.

GII–84. *Obverse:* similar to GII–81; bottom of the frame about ¼ inch from base and there is no inscription. *Reverse:* like obverse. Pint. Colors: olive-amber and olive-greens. Common. 1846–60. Attributed to New England, possibly the Granite Glass Works.

GII–78. *Obverse:* as in GII–80 but no inscriptions and with minor variation. *Reverse:* like obverse. Quart. Colors: ambers, deep clear green, and olive-green. Common. Attributed to the Granite Glass Works, Stoddard, New Hampshire, by Van Rensselaer, apparently on the basis of its similarity to GII–80; however, the possibility of a common mold maker instead of a common source should be considered. 1846–60.

GII–79. *Obverse:* like GII–78, but the body of the flask is slightly longer and fractionally wider at the point of greatest width. *Reverse:* like obverse. Quart. Colors: shaded amber, olive-amber, and olive-green. Common. 1846–60. Attribution same as GII–78.

GXV–6. *Obverse:* plain, except for the inscription in three straight lines: "GRANITE/GLASS"/"Co." *Reverse:* plain except for inscription in two straight lines:

"STODDARD"/"N H". Quart. Color: deep reddish amber. Comparatively scarce. 1846–60.

GXV–7. *Obverse:* plain, except for inscription in three straight lines: "GRANITE"/"GLASS"/"CO". *Reverse:* plain except for inscription in two straight lines: "STODDARD"/"N H". Pint. Colors: brown-amber, olive-amber, red-amber, brilliant slightly golden amber. Common. 1846–60.

GXV–8. *Obverse:* like GXV–7, but the body is taller. *Reverse:* like reverse of GXV–7 but there is a variation in form and size of letters. Pint. Color: olive-amber. Common. 1846–60.

56. NEW LONDON GLASS WORKS, *New London, Connecticut, 1856–65+*

The New London Glass Company was organized on August 27, 1856, but little is known of its subsequent history or that of the other glass companies that operated in New London, Connecticut. The organizers of the original company were N. S. Perkins, Jr., president, and Lorenzo Hodsden, secretary and treasurer, both of whom were directors, along with Leonard S. Shaffer and Thomas W. Perkins. The capital stock of the company was $12,000, and so it was a relatively small operation.[66] It is not known exactly when the company began glassmaking. In the *New London Land Records*[67] an entry dated October 10, 1857 reads: "Perkins and Smith [sold or transferred] to the New London Glass Co., one tract of land 250 feet square, Smith, Goshen and Trumbull Streets, Fort Neck." This entry may refer to one of three things: the date of the legal transfer of land on which the glassworks had already been built (possibly the glassworks was then in operation); the date of the initial purchase of land for the factory, in which case manufacturing operations probably did not begin until late 1857 or even early 1858; or the date of the purchase of an additional plot of adjoining land by the company.

The 1857/58 Directory[68] named, in addition to the original founders of the company, Mr. Dexter of Howard Street and Mr. James Shaffer of Colt Street as glassworkers. The 1859/60 Directory[69] lists none of these men, but an advertisement in it for the New London Glass Company situated on Fort Neck lists Messrs. Warren and Co. as proprietors. To confuse matters, the New London Glass Works is listed in this directory at Shaw's Neck.[70]

On September 24, 1859, the *New London Land Records*[71] again record the sale of land in connection with a glassworks in New London: "Union Glass Works of Charles Prentis in the Fort Neck, Smith and Walbach Streets. 2 Tracts of land, 500 feet square." This transaction suggests that either Charles Prentis had purchased the property of the New London Glass Company from Messrs. Warren and Co. and sold it to the Union Glass Works, or that Prentis was selling land that he owned to a new glass firm and factory in that city, on land adjoining or almost adjoining that of the New London Glass Company. Thus, in 1859, there *may* have been two glass factories in

New London. Next to nothing is known about the operations or products of this company, but it did produce at least one flask (GXI–23) marked "UNION GLASS WORKS".

The next information about glassmaking in New London comes from the *New London Chronicle*, which reported on August 13, 1863, that "the glassworks near Fort Trumbull" that had been idle had been purchased and was to be "operated by William Barry and Nathan S. Fish." This firm, of which Fish was the manager, was called Thames Glass Works Co. On August 26, 1863, the *Morning Chronicle* noted:[72]

GETTING READY. Carpenters, Masons, Blacksmiths and other mechanics are busily employed in getting the Glass Works ready for operations. They are tearing down walls, altering the general arrangement of things, building new rooms, &c. The new proprietors of the establishment hope to be under full headway in about two months.

The *Norwich Weekly Courier* reported on December 22, 1864: "The Thames Glass Works Co. is manufacturing a large amount of light and dark green glass. The Co. has a first rate reputation." The 1865/66 Directory[73] lists as glassblowers Christopher Trainy, Carlos W. Foster, William Johnson, Peter Benard, William Brophy, Patrick McCardell, John Smith, John J. Squire, and Fred Bronneshalz, and as glassworkers: Jacob Felton, John Rockwell, Horatio R. Smith, and N. S. Fish, manager. Preserve jars were among the products of this factory, and on October 18, 1864, a patent was granted to the firm for a jar top. These quart jars, of aqua-colored glass, are embossed with the words: "PAT^D-OC^T—1864/March & Sep^{t}1865" in a circle enclosing, in a straight line, "J. J. SQUIRE." The company also produced pressed amber glass insulators for telegraph wires.

According to Van Rensselaer,[74] Nathan S. Fish and William Barry subsequently sold the property to Ellenville, New York, interests. In any event, in December 1865 the glass factory was taken over by a new firm and put in operation as the Fort Trumbull Glass Works. The officers of that company were D. S. Calhoun, president; N. Hendricks, secretary and treasurer; J. R. Gilbert, agent. H. G. Foster was also associated with the company. A stock certificate (Ill. 56) dated June 2, 1868, shows that Gilbert was then president of the company.

The following excerpts are from an account of a reporter's visit to this glasshouse published in the *New London Chronicle* on October 20, 1866:

Since the company have come into possession, they have put in new furnaces, enlarged the works and their capacity is nearly double what it was. They give employment to about eighty men and boys in the different departments . . . The factory is a wooden building ninety feet long by sixty one feet wide. In the building are the furnaces, ovens, pipes, etc., for melting and blowing the glass . . . Besides the other buildings there is a building which contains a room and implements for the manufacture of the clay pots

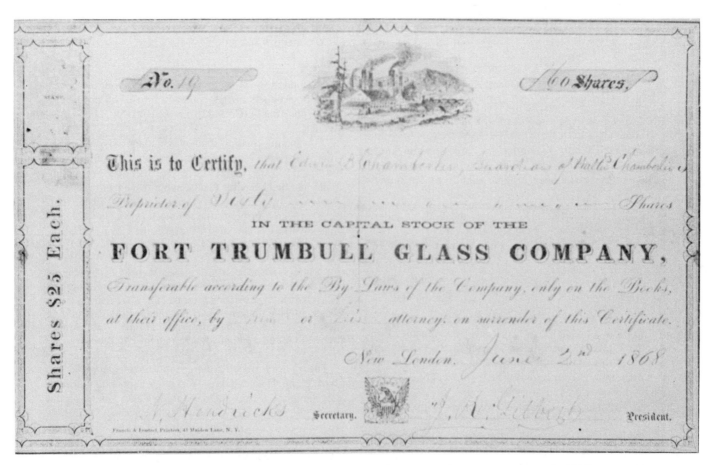

26. Stock certificate of the Fort Trumbull Glass Company, New London, Conn. Dated June 2, 1868, it bears the signature of J. R. Gilbert as president. Formerly in the collection of the late Charles B. Gardner. *Wheaton Historical Village, Millville, N.J.*

which hold the glass. There is also a blacksmith's shop, in which the iron work for the establishment is done. The pipes for blowing the glass are made in this shop . . . They cannot be kept in good order but a day or two and consequently there are a large number of pipes made in the space of a month. There is an engine connected with this establishment which supplies the necessary power.

The article also reported that about five tons of material a day were used, and that the company manufactured all kinds of green and amber bottleware, from small half-ounce vials to 15-gallon carboys. Specifically listed in the article were bottles for Perry Davis' Painkiller, Dr. Ford's Pectoral Syrup, Wilbor's Rheumatic Medicine, Ring's Ambrosia, Knowles' Hair Invigorater, and Hyatt's Life Balsam. In addition, they manufactured bottles for numerous other similar preparations.

The following advertisement, which appeared in the *Connecticut Business Directory* of 1866, sheds further light on the broader aspects of the production of this firm:

FORT TRUMBULL GLASS COMPANY,
New London, Connecticut,
MANUFACTURERS OF

GREEN AND AMBER GLASS,

Druggists' Ware, Fruit and Pickle Jars, Wines,
DEMIJOHNS, FLASKS, &C., &C.

Bottles made to Order in Private Moulds.

N. HENDRICKS, Secretary   J.R. GILBERT, Agent

Though no flasks are known bearing the Fort Trumbull Glass Works name, it is interesting to note that flasks are listed in the advertisement as well as "Bottles made to Order in Private Moulds." It is not beyond the realm of possibility that some flasks originated by their predecessors bearing the inscription "New London Glass Works" continued to be made by this firm.

A number of marked flasks, listed below, were produced by these several New London glass firms:

GII–66. *Obverse:* eagle above wreath (similar to that on Willington and Westford flasks) with seven 5-pointed stars above. *Reverse:* anchor with line attached, "NEW LONDON" in pennant above and "GLASS WORKS" in pennant below. Quart. Colors: copper-amber, golden amber, red-amber, yellow-amber, aquamarine, emerald-green, very pale. green. Rare. 1857–1859 or 1863.

GII–67. *Obverse:* eagle, head turned to the left, holding laurel wreath with nine 5-pointed stars above. *Reverse:* anchor with line attached, with "NEW LONDON" in pennant above and "GLASS WORKS" in pennant below. Half-pint. Colors: olive-yellow, clear deep green, pale yellow-green, olive-amber, pale green, aquamarine, pale yellow-green shading to amber, golden amber, emerald-green. Comparatively scarce. 1857–1859 or 1863.

GII-68. *Obverse:* eagle in flight, facing right, with seven 5-pointed stars above. *Reverse:* anchor with line attached, with "NEW LONDON" in pennant above and "GLASS WORKS" in pennant below. Pint. Colors: olive-yellow, clear golden amber, clear green, deep bluish green, pale yellow-green, olive-amber, clear green with yellow streaks, emerald-green, and olive-green. Comparatively scarce. 1857–1859 or 1863.

GXV-23. *Obverse:* "UNION GLASS WORKS" in arc above "NEW LONDON" (in straight line and of larger letters) "C$^{\underline{T}}$" (the C is a large capital, and the T is a small capital the top of which aligns with the top of the C; there is a line under the T). *Reverse:* plain. Pint. Color: aquamarine. Scarce. Probably September 1859–63.

57. WESTFORD GLASS WORKS, *Westford, Connecticut, 1857–73.*

As the Westford Glass Works at Westford, not far from West Willington, Connecticut, has not been the object of intensive research as yet, there is not much information about it or the men who owned and operated it. Apparently they were not a superstitious lot: 13 stockholders, putting up about $18,000 in capital, formed a company to manufacture bottles and built the Westford Glass Works in 1857.[75] Its certificate of incorporation as a joint stock company, dated March 21, 1857, lists the 13 stockholders and their holdings.[76] Thomas C. Cary is listed as president and director; John S. Dean, Dan Chaffee, and Edwin A. Buck are also listed as directors. James Richmond, one of the larger stockholders, became secretary of the company. By January 25, 1860, Palmer Convers had become president and T. C. Cary secretary and treasurer. According to the Vital Records of Ashford, Connecticut, on August 10, 1864, the company circumstances were recorded as follows:

Amount of Capital paid in	$18,000.00
Amount of Capital invested in real estate	10,925.00
Amount of Capital invested in personal estate	19,068.21
Notes Receivable	1,392.00
Accounts Receivable	4,475.44
	$53,860.44
Amount of Debts of said Company	$20,481.15
Notes Payable	6,346.15
	$26,827.30

These records also noted that there were 720 shares of stock outstanding, of which Edwin A. Buck owned 155, John S. Dean 156, and James Richmond 100. The company failed in 1865. Probate records[77] dated May 18, 1865, contain an inventory of the "estate of Westford Glass Co., assigned for the benefit of all their creditors." Real estate listed included a "Barn, Blacksmith's shop, Pot House,

Factory and packing house" as well as a farm of about 50 acres and a "House west of Church occupied by L.M. Neville," the whole valued at $5,500.

The factory produced a variety of the bottles, containers, and flasks then in demand, undoubtedly very much like those made at the nearby Willington Glass Works. This opinion is corroborated by the inventory noted above— from it, the size and scope of the company can be estimated. For example, 11 chairs and 10 marvers are listed, indicating there were probably 10 or 11 "shops." Since it is likely there were two or three men and a boy per shop, 30 to 40 glassmakers were doubtless involved in making the various bottles and jars produced there. The works were, therefore, about the size of the Willington Glass Works.

The following bottles and molds for bottles and flasks listed in the inventory will be of particular interest to bottle collectors: quart ink bottles at $6 per gross; demijohns of one-quarter gallon, one-half gallon, two-gallon, and five-gallon capacities, both handled and unhandled; molds for Schnapps bottles of pint and quart sizes; a mold for a half-pint ale bottle; two half-pint flask molds and a quart flask mold; a one-pint ink mold; a quart porter bottle mold; molds for wine bottles designated 5, 6, and 7 (probably indicating capacities of 1/5, 1/6, and 1/7 gallon), as well as one clay carboy mold; one two-gallon clay mold and two five-gallon clay molds; and a carboy finisher, probably a lip-forming tool.

Many of the demijohns were covered with wicker, as references to loose rattan ("Rattan, all on hand") and a reference to "one box stove in Willow Shop" and a willow cutter indicate. From these references, as well as that to "About 215 half gal. demijohns at Mrs. George Chapman to cover," it is apparent that many of the demijohns were covered with rattan or willow at the factory and others were "farmed out" to farms and houses in the neighborhood to be covered, then returned to the factory.

Among the preserve jars that can be definitely attributed to this factory, but that were also made at Willington and possibly in South Jersey factories as well, are the flat 10-sided wide-mouthed bottles with broadly rounded lips that are generally termed huckleberry bottles. A number of these bottles containing berries were found by the late Henry Knowlton, a long-time resident of Mansfield, Connecticut, and a collector and dealer in Connecticut glass. Several examples in the collection of Old Sturbridge Village, one still bearing sealing wax and its cork, were presented by a donor whose forebear went to the Westford factory to purchase them and used them for preserving blueberries.

Edwin Augustus Buck was one of the principal stockholders in the initial group, and it was he who had the largest interest in E. A. Buck & Company, which took over the glassworks later in 1865, after the failure of the original company. This firm also operated for about eight years. Apparently another of the depression victims, it ceased production in 1873, the year after the Willington Glass Works was closed. As in the case of the Willington Glass Works, though Westford made some aquamarine glass (a barrel of manganese valued at $10 and "1 cask Manganese in Bleach House, 22.50" listed in the 1865 inventory suggest the intent to decolorize their glass), its products were primarily olive-green, olive-amber, "black," and rich reddish or "blood" amber. Actually, the two works filled orders for each other on occasion. The tradition that this happened is borne out by December 2, 1869, entries in the Willington documents owned by the late Henry E. Knowlton of East Mansfield, Connecticut. One entry indicates the Willington Glass Company filled three orders for the "Pint Westford Flasks" at 75¢ a dozen![78]

As an examination of the line drawings of the Willington and Westford Eagle flasks GII–61 through GII–65 in the Charts, Part VIII, shows, though varying in detail the eagle sides are the same design. The other flasks bearing the Westford name fall in the Pictorial Group XIII, having a sheaf of grain on the obverse. In all, four Figured Flasks can be called Westford, as in the following list:

GII–65. *Obverse:* "LIBERTY" above the American eagle perched on wreath of "laurel" leaves. *Reverse:* "WESTFORD [in arc] GLASS/CO/WESTFORD [in arc]/CONN." Half pint. Colors: olive-amber, deep reddish amber, medium amber, pale green, and deep olive-green. Comparatively scarce.

GXIII–35. *Obverse:* Sheaf of grain, bound above middle, parted at center at top; rake and pitchfork crossed behind sheaf. *Reverse:* "WESTFORD GLASS CO. [in deep arc] WESTFORD/CONN." in two straight lines below. Pint. Colors: deep red-amber, amber, deep olive-green. Common.

GXIII–36. *Obverse:* Sheaf of grain, like GXIII–35, but sheaf a little wider, and a 5-pointed star is between the handles of the rake and fork. *Reverse:* inscription like GXIII–35, but letters in WESTFORD GLASS CO. slightly smaller. Pint. Color: olive-green. Comparatively scarce.

GXIII–37. Like GXIII–35, but smaller scale. Half-pint. Colors: amber, olive-amber, olive-green. Common.

58. CHRISTIAN IHMSEN AND SONS, *Pittsburgh, Pennsylvania*[79], *1836–68+*

For well over a quarter of a century Christian Ihmsen, glassman, brother of William and son of Charles Ihmsen, was one of the leading glass manufacturers of Pittsburgh. His career in the ownership end began after Charles Ihmsen's death in 1828, when Christian succeeded to his father's place in the firm of Sutton, Wendt & Company, which operated the Birmingham Glass Works. This works, consisting of two houses—one for the manufacture of window glass and the other for green glass—had been established in 1810 in Birmingham, then a new community a mile from Pittsburgh and on the opposite side of the Monongahela, by Edward Ensell, Frederick Wendt, and Charles Ihmsen, all blowers whose craft was first practiced in Pittsburgh in General O'Hara's Pittsburgh Glass Works

(see No. 16). Christian's next venture seems to have been in 1831, when he and his brother William formed a copartnership, presumably in the Williamsport window-glass works of William and in a newly erected "factory for the manufacture of Vials and Bottles." "Western merchants [were] respectfully invited" to call at the partners' Pittsburgh warehouse on Third Street to examine the wares, which were warranted equal to the best eastern articles on the market. Their output, like that of their competitors, included porter bottles.[80]

In or by 1836, Christian's interest in glass manufacture expanded to include the making of flint-glass wares—with T. T. Whitehead and one Phillips. I have yet to learn Phillips's first name or initials. He may have been one of Pittsburgh's Phillips glassmen or, as Whitehead probably was, a man with capital to invest. Be that as it may, the firm operated the Pennsylvania Flint Glass Works in Birmingham. But of particular interest in the history of our bottle industry was their works built for the production of black-glass wares: ". . . champagnes, clarets, wines, Porters, and other bottles, demijohns, carboys and Druggist wares generally." At the time, according to Harris's *Pittsburgh Business Directory* for 1837, this works was the only black-glass factory in the Midwest, and the prospects for its success were considered to be excellent. The owners could well boast of equaling English imports, at least insofar as fabrication was concerned, for, of about 35 hands, 15 were blowers "from the celebrated Black Bottle Factories of Bristol. . . ." The weekly production was about 12,000 bottles of various kinds, and the value of the yearly output was estimated at $60,000. Apparently, around 1840, the factory was taken over by C. Ihmsen & Company. And about the same time, certainly by 1846, the firm of Young, Ihmsen & Plunkett—William Young, Christian Ihmsen, and Francis Plunkett—became owners of the flint-glass works.[81] The firm was listed in Fahnstock's 1850 Directory but not in Thurston's 1867/68 Directory. Possibly, in the interim between directories, the works was acquired by C. Ihmsen & Sons, who were listed by Thurston under flint glass manufacturers.

Not only was Whitehead, Ihmsen & Phillips established in or by 1836, but Christian Ihmsen also formed C. Ihmsen & Company to operate his window glass and vial and bottle factories. Not surprisingly, the company maintained two warehouses, one in Birmingham and another in Pittsburgh on Third Street. It was reported in 1837 that the annual output (presumably for 1836) of window glass was 5,500 boxes of first-quality glass valued at $38,000. And in the vial factory 14 blowers, 8 assistants, and 10 other workmen accounted for 112,600 *gross* of vials ranging in sizes from a half dram to 16 ounces and 60 gross of flasks, oil bottles, and hollow ware.[82] If sales and production fell off following the 1837 panic and in the ensuing depression, apparently the fall was not crippling, as it was for some glass manufacturers. Insofar as Figured Flasks are concerned, again there is the situation that, though it seems improbable that only one was among the flasks undoubtedly blown in the years after the specific mention in 1837, only one *identifi-*

able with the company has been recorded as yet. That flask is the common pint Pike's Peak flask, GXI–29, having "FOR PIKE'S PEAK" (with reversed apostrophe) in an arc above the figure of a prospector and, in the frame below, "C:IHMSEN & CO/PITTSBURGH PA" and, on the reverse, an American eagle.

In 1860, about two years before his death in 1862, Christian Ihmsen took two of his sons, Charles T. and William, into the business, known henceforth as C. Ihmsen & Sons. (In 1855 Christian, Jr., had established the Ihmsen Glass Company, which by 1886 was the Ihmsen Glass Company Ltd.; it operated until 1895.) The McCreadys state that the sons, Charles and William, were not as capable as their father, and they failed. However, that catastrophe was not immediate, for the firm advertised in Thurston's 1867/68 Directory as "manufacturers of every variety of / Vials, Bottles and Window Glass / Black Porter, Wine and Claret Bottles, Demijohns / and mineral water bottles." Perhaps the firm failed during the long depression from 1873 to 1879. In any event, C. Ihmsen & Sons produced two pint Figured Flasks in the Shield and Clasped Hands design, Group XII. One, the scarce GXII–20, has "UNION" between the arc of stars and top of the shield on the obverse and, on the reverse, the flying eagle with shield and pennants. The lower pennant, where it crosses the shield, is marked "C I & Sons". The second, the comparatively scarce GXII–23, has "UNION" in the frame on the shield on the obverse and "C I & Sons" in the frame below the flying eagle on the reverse.

59. WM. McCULLY & CO., *Pittsburgh, Pennsylvania*

William McCully was born near Shane's Castle, County Antrim, Ireland, about 1800. He was brought to America as a young child by his parents, who settled in Chatiers township, near Pittsburgh. Shortly afterward his father died, and William received only the rudiments of an ordinary common-school education. He served his apprenticeship, and learned glassblowing, at the Bakewells factory located at the foot of Grant Street, which much later became the site of the B & O Railroad depot. From Bakewells, where apparently he blew only flint glass, he went as a journeyman glassblower to O'Hara's Pittsburgh Glass Works on the south side of the city, opposite the Point, where he learned to blow window glass.[83]

In 1830,[84] with Capt. John Hay, he erected a flint glass factory on Railroad Street at the foot of Nineteenth Street, Hay furnishing the greater part of the money, McCully the technical experience. After this works was flooded in 1832, McCully withdrew and Capt. Hay continued to operate it alone. In 1833 McCully built a bottle glasshouse at the corner of Sixteenth and Liberty streets for the production of green and black glass bottles. In 1834 he became interested with William Johnson in a window-glass factory at Monongahela City. Two years later, the firm of William McCully & Co. was founded. It consisted of William McCully and Frederick Lorenz, Sr., founder of the Sligo Glass Works about 1819. In 1838 Thomas Weightman

joined the firm. Subsequently, a dissolution of this partnership took place, and in 1851 McCully purchased from Lorenz the stone building known as the Sligo Glass Works. The next year McCully tore this building down and erected what was claimed to be the first brick glasshouse in Pittsburgh. The next was built in 1854. After the erection of this new factory, William McCully admitted his only son, John F., into the partnership, the firm name becoming William McCully & Co. In 1852 Mark W. Watson also became a member of the firm, and John N. King joined the concern as a partner in 1855. Both Watson and King were sons-in-law of McCully. When William McCully died in 1869, the business was successfully continued by Watson and King under the old firm name.[85]

William McCully was not only a successful glass manufacturer; he had other business interests as well. He served as a director on the boards of a number of institutions in the city and took a special interest in the Farmer's Deposit & Exchange Bank. He was apparently one of the leaders of the glass industry in Pittsburgh. Among other things, he was the first to build a seven-stone wheel oven for flattening window glass west of the Allegheny Mountains.

Starting from a comparatively small beginning, the company operated six different factories by 1879, employing a large number of workmen. The others were called the Pittsburgh, Phoenix, Sligo, Empire, and Mastodon glass factories. Two were situated on Carson Street on the south side of Pittsburgh, one on Liberty Street, one on Twenty-second Street, and two on Twenty-eighth Street. The offices of William McCully & Co. were located at 18 & 20 Wood Street, Pittsburgh. The firm continued in business until at least 1889. According to one source in 1879, "The extent of the operations are without doubt unsurpassed by any similar house in this country or Europe, while the products find a market all over the civilized world."[86] Window glass, white, green, and black glasswares, demijohns, fruit jars, and so on were produced in these factories, but little is known of the specific products. A wine bottle is recorded bearing on the flat base rim, around a small concave disk with nipple at the center: "W. McCully & Co." On the shoulder is the inscription: "Louis Webber" with "Louisville Ky." below. This bottle may possibly have been made at McCully's Phoenix Glass House.

One case of amber bottles marked "W McCULLY & CO/PITTSBURGH PA" on the bases and "PATENTED" on the shoulders was taken from a steamer that sank on April 1, 1865, on its maiden voyage up the Missouri, on its way to a mining area in Montana. Although the bottles are of a type morphologically associated with whiskey, their contents include only four percent alcohol by volume, and the identity of the liquid remains unknown. In addition to the bottles, four dozen panes of window glass from the cargo are also known to have been produced by the McCully firm.[87]

Among the workmen in McCully's factories was William M. Grace (apparently his nephew); after being employed as a glassblower for seven years, he took charge of one of

McCully's factories in 1844. From 1851 to 1860 he was with the McCully's Sligo Glass Works.[88] Another well-known glassblower who worked for a short period for McCully was George W. Foster, whose father, Joseph, had started the first glasshouse in Stoddard, New Hampshire, in 1842, the first of a five-generation line of glassmakers in America. According to George Foster's diary,[89] on January 29, 1856: "I got a letter from William McCully—Pittsburgh, Pa., to go blow for him." On February 26 of the same year he wrote: "Took stage to Philadelphia and Railroad to Pittsburgh, fare, $9.00, leaving at 9PM and arriving at 3PM on the 27th." He then noted that he started blowing at William McCully's wine bottle factory, of which a Mr. McClardy was manager.[90] His diary also indicates: ". . . the pots hold one hundred and twenty quart wine bottles." He recorded on March 14 that he made 39 dozen quart wines at 9 cents a dozen, further noting: "I have never made quart wines for less than 12½ᵉ per dozen, but the manufacturers are cutting down the price every year."

George's older brother, Henry, also worked for Mc-Cully, apparently as a "spare" or extra employee, serving as a replacement for workers who did not show up for work because of sickness or for some other reason. Seemingly dissatisfied with his lot, Henry left Pittsburgh on March 2, 1856, returning to Stoddard by railroad by way of Philadelphia, according to George's diary. George remained until May. On April 29 he wrote in his diary: "Made 28–9 dozen Quart Wines at 9½ᵉ per dozen." On May 17 his diary entry indicates that the McCully factory halted operations (probably for the customary seasonal shutdown). On May 22 he wrote that he settled with William McCully & Co., earning $187.68 while blowing there. He then returned to Stoddard, New Hampshire, by railroad by way of Philadelphia, New York, and Keene.

A sense of what the manufacturing city of Pittsburgh was like, with its numerous glasshouses and ironworks, is concisely but vividly conveyed in a letter of August 27, 1846, from Thomas Stanger, working in a bottle glasshouse in Pittsburgh, to his brother John M. Stanger in Glassboro, New Jersey.[91] Because of its descriptive quality, it is quoted in full:

Dear Brother

. . . I have no news of an interesting character to write you from here, there is no use of giving you an elaborate description of this place for you have already read a humdrum description of it and it is about what it is represented to be, there is one street about 1 mile long lined on both sides with quite respectable looking dwellings where the fashionable people of the city live, and about ¼ of the city is well-built though black-looking storehouses the rest is one mass of dirt and smoke completely filled up with furnaces, foundries, factories, mills etc. in almost endless succession, from which clouds of smoke are constantly ascending, there are no less that 19 Glass factories of different kinds within one mile of the centre of this city, and more iron furnaces than you ever heard tell of, the churches here are about as black outside as glass factories commonly are, the people here are pretty much of a

church-going people and do not appear to me to be half such barbarians as the[y] are generally represented in the east to be I have no fault to find with anything connected with myself except that I have to change orders so much, there is such a demand for glass out here, that in the summer every thing made of glass is sold, and when the fire begins a complete assortment is immediately wanted, by the way the Glass-factory at Lockport burned down a few days ago, it is to be immediately repaired, our Pots do not stand a great while before they wear out, our first setting were in only 4 weeks when they were all thrown out at one time and a new setting put in.

. . . I do not know how the weather has been with you, but out here it has been so intensely hot that it has been very uncomfortabl[e] blowing, but now it is a little cooler and I hope we shall have it better, one of McCully's blowers (a western man) has quit and gone to another factory to work, there is plenty of places here for vial blowers yet, and vial blowing is as good as bottle blowing out here, I have a single pit and make no more money than some of the vial blowers,

I am well at present except that I have a cold which is getting better all the rest of the eastern blowers out here are well and in good spirits. . . .

. . . Yours Affectionately
Thomas Stanger

The following flasks are attributed to William McCully & Co.:

GXI–12. *Obverse:* Prospector, stocky body with upper left arm not evident, wearing a low-crowned derby, a swallow-tailed coat, and tight trousers and carrying a pick-axe, with a pack in his left hand resting over his shoulder; he is walking to the left on a small round-ended oblong frame. *Reverse:* eagle, similar to GII–113 but facing toward the left, wings partly raised, spread downward and outward; extending from the beak is a wide pennant with "hook" end to the right in an arc above the eagle. Below the eagle is a large oval frame containing the inscription "W.MᶜC & Co/GLASS WORKS/PITTS. PA." Pint. Color: aquamarine. Rare.

GXI–16. *Obverse:* Prospector; like GXI–15, made by the Arsenal Glass Works of Pittsburgh. *Reverse:* like reverse of GXI–15 but with the inscription: "W.MᶜC & Co." (large), below which are the words "GLASS WORKS" and below that "PITTS•PA". Pint. Color: aquamarine. Rare.

GII–113. *Obverse:* eagle, head to left, with shield on breast with a wide pennant with a thin "hook" extending from the beak to the right in an arc above the eagle. Below the eagle is a large oval frame containing the inscription "PITTSBURGH" below which is "PA" and below that "MᶜC & Co." *Reverse:* like obverse but with variations in the wing of the eagle, and there is no inscription. Pint. Colors: amber, aquamarine, yellow-olive-green. Attributed to William McCully & Co. of Pittsburgh on basis of the inscription. Scarce.

60. SAMUEL MCKEE & CO.; PENNSYLVANIA GLASS WORKS, *Pittsburgh, Pennsylvania, 1834–86*

In 1834 Samuel and James McKee and James Salisbury erected a window-glass house and established the firm of McKee & Co. in Birmingham, Pittsburgh. Samuel, who was born in 1808, had learned cylinder-glass blowing as a boy. In 1836 Samuel, James, and Thomas McKee organized the Pennsylvania Glass Works located near 13th and Carson streets,[92] the firm name being S. McKee & Co.

According to Van Rensselaer,[93] the McKees had three glasshouses: the earliest along Sarah Street between Twelfth and South Thirteenth streets, one at 102 Second Street, and one at 23 Wood Street. One of these factories was devoted exclusively to the manufacture of bottles and flasks of all kinds and sizes; it became one of the largest in the country. In April of 1837 the window-glass house of S. McKee & Co. employed 40 men; it used 50,000 bushels of coal annually and manufactured 5,500 boxes of window glass annually with a value of $38,500. The glassworks was valued then at $10,000.[94]

In 1840 the firm built a new works.[95] Perhaps it is this third factory established by McKee to which Van Rensselaer refers. In 1860, upon the death of his brothers, Samuel McKee became sole proprietor of the business, and he remained so until his death in 1877, when he was succeeded by Daniel and C. J. McKee and A. C. Dravo, who were still proprietors in 1879.[96] In that year, the works owned by the firm covered more than four acres and consisted of two window-glass factories and one bottle-glass factory. In addition, there were a flattening house, cutting rooms, storehouse, blacksmith shop, engine rooms, pot room, and grinding mill. Apparently the best machinery and most effective laborsaving devices were used in these factories. An average of from 200 to 280 men and boys were employed at that time, whose total earnings were over $2,600 per week. Products of S. McKee & Company were sold throughout the whole United States.

In 1886 S. McKee & Co. was operating three furnaces for the manufacture of window glass and one for the manufacture of green glass.[97] The office of their green-glass works was located at 62 Water Street. This works, in which a wide variety of bottles of the period was produced, contained one seven-pot furnace.[98] The firm was still in business as S. McKee & Co. in 1888, despite the fact that Samuel McKee was deceased.[99]

Little is known of the bottles, flasks, and other containers produced by S. McKee & Co., but the marked flask below was made at that factory:

GIX–26. Scroll flask. *Obverse:* heart-shaped frame and scrolls with the inscription "S.M'KEE" in a straight line between the scrolls. In the upper part of the frame is a large 8-pointed star: a similar 8-pointed star is in the space above the frame. *Reverse:* similar to the obverse, but the upper star has 9 points and the name is omitted from the frame. Pint. Color: aquamarine. Extremely rare. Probably made ca. 1836–40.

61. A. & D. H. CHAMBERS, *Pittsburgh, Pennsylvania, 1841–88*

In 1841 Alexander Chambers, David H. Chambers, and John Agnew established a small factory for making green-glass wares in what was then the fifth ward of the city. The firm was called Chambers & Agnew. The latter soon withdrew, and a Mr. Anderson and Alexander & David H. Chambers formed a new copartnership named Anderson, Chambers & Co. They built a factory in Birmingham (south Pittsburgh) at the corner of South Sixth and Bingham streets. Their principal products were window glass and vials.

In 1843, after Anderson withdrew from the business, the firm became A. & D. H. Chambers.

The firm erected a new glassworks in 1852 at the corner of Sixth and Water streets, which was called the Pittsburgh Glass Works.[100] The following advertisement, which appeared in Thurston's Directory of 1867/68, gives us a generalized idea of the products of this firm:

Alex Chambers   Robert Riddle

Pittsburgh Glass Works

A. & D. H. Chambers,

Manufacturers of

Vials, Bottles, Window Glass,

Carboys and Demijohns

Nos. 117 Water & 154 Streets, Pittsburgh, Pa.

David Chambers died in 1862 while in Chicago, but the firm continued to operate under the same name, with Alexander Chambers as the guiding light. According to a trade card dated October 1866, Alexander Chambers and Robert Riddle were the proprietors. A similar trade card dated May 24, 1872, lists Alexander Chambers, Joseph A. Chambers, Robert Riddle, and Hartley Howard as proprietors of the firm. The location is given on both trade cards as 117 Water Street and 154 First Avenue in Pittsburgh. Hopkins's 1872 *Atlas of Pittsburgh* also lists (in the directory on page 5) A. & D. H. Chambers at 117 Water Street and 154 First Avenue.

When Alexander Chambers died in 1875, his son James A. Chambers succeeded him, and the business continued to operate as A. & D. H. Chambers at least through 1888.[101] It is listed in Thurston's 1886 *Pittsburgh Progress* as operating two factories containing two furnaces with a total of 12 pots. Despite the fact that it was in business for at least 45 years, little is known of the specific products of the firm.

Marked Union (Shield) and Clasped Hands flasks, as well as Pike's Peak flasks, are known to have been two of their products. The latter, which probably first came on the market about 1858 or 1859, were produced for more than a decade by A. & D. H. Chambers. Two price lists rescued in 1926 by Harry Hall White from the office rubbish of the Redwood Glass Works in Redwood, New York, confirm this.[102]

FLASKS
Pike's Peak and Union Patterns

½ pint, Eagle, new style, 6 doz. boxes . . . per gross, $7.20
1   "   "   "   6   "   "   9.60
Quart   "   "   6   "   "   12.00

. . . . per cent discount cash

Prices had risen considerably by 1872, as their price list of that year indicates, and a ¼-pint size had been added:

FLASKS
Plain, Pike's Peak, and Union Patterns

¼ pint . . . 6 dozen boxes, per gross, $10.00
½   "   . . . 6   "   "   12.00
1   "   . . . 6   "   "   16.00
Quart . . . 6   "   "   24.00

The following five marked flasks were produced at A. & D. H. Chambers during the 1860s and 1870s:

GXII–9. *Obverse:* shield and clasped hands with "OLD RYE" in an oval frame below, the shield partially surrounded by a short, heavy laurel branch on each side, 13 stars above the shield (one star above each end of the shield, 11 in a semicircle) above "UNION". *Reverse:* eagle flying to the right with a large plain shield on its breast and a plain pennant floating above. The long lower pennant is inscribed "A & D H C." and a narrow frame below is inscribed "PITTSBURGH". Quart. Colors: aquamarines and light yellow-green. Common. ca. 1865–75.

GXII–25. *Obverse:* shield and clasped hands above a small oval frame containing "OLD RYE" with 13 large stars above (one at each end of the shield and 11 in a semicircle) over "UNION". *Reverse:* eagle flying to the right with shield on its breast, with pennant flying above and diagonally across the shield containing the initials "A & D H C". The geometric frame below embossed "PITTSBURGH". Pint. Color: aquamarine. Scarce. ca. 1865–75.

GXII–26. *Obverse:* like GXII–25. *Reverse:* like reverse of GXII–25. Pint. Color: aquamarine. Comparatively scarce. ca. 1865–75.

GXII–27. *Obverse:* shield and clasped hands with oval panel inscribed "A.& D.H. C" with 13 stars above the shield and the word "UNION". *Reverse:* eagle flying to the right with shield on breast and pennant below that with a large frame inscribed "PITTSBURGH PA". Pint. Color: aquamarine. Comparatively scarce. ca. 1865–75.

GXIII–3. *Obverse:* girl riding old-fashioned bicycle to the left, in profile, with hair in a bun at the back, wearing a short hat, a short bodice, and skirt. *Reverse:* eagle to the right with shield on breast and from the beak a pennant flying above the eagle. Below the eagle in an oval frame

are the initials "A & D H.C". Pint. Colors: aquamarine and yellow-green. Scarce. 1870s.

62. CUNNINGHAM & CO., *Pittsburgh, Pennsylvania, 1845–1930*

In 1845 Wilson Cunningham, a 33-year-old practical glassman, joined with George Whitten Jackson to erect a bottle- and window-glass factory on Water Street in Pittsburgh. However, the glassworks did not get well under way until 1850, at which time cylinder glass, black bottle glass, flint glass, and druggists' glass were advertised. Cunningham and Jackson carried on a foundry also and dealt in grain as well as iron, steel, and glass until 1852. It would seem that after that year Jackson was no longer associated with Cunningham and the firm was composed of Wilson Cunningham, his brother Robert, and George Duncan. Such was the information gleaned by Rhea Mansfield Knittle in her researches.[103] It gives rise to some puzzlement, since an 1879/80 review of Pittsburgh businesses[104] and an 1889 history of Allegheny County indicate that, in 1849, Wilson Cunningham, his brother Robert (who was born in 1817), another brother (Dominick O.), and George Duncan formed the firm of W. Cunningham & Company and established the Pittsburgh City Glass Works. The solution may be that it was in 1849 Jackson withdrew from the glass partnership with Wilson Cunningham, who then formed W. Cunningham & Company, but that Jackson continued his partnership with Cunningham in the foundry and in their wholesale and/or retail business.

Perhaps the panic sparked by bank closings in the spring of 1857 and the ensuing depression caused financial problems for W. Cunningham & Company, necessitating bringing a new partner into the firm. Be that as it may, in 1857[105] Dominick Ihmsen, whose family had been associated with Pittsburgh glassmaking since 1797—first as employee and by 1810 founder of a glassworks—became a partner, and the firm name was changed to Cunningham and Ihmsen. In 1878, after 42 years of operation, Dominick Ihmsen sold his interest to the other partners. The new firm, Cunningham & Company, was formed by the Cunningham brothers (Wilson and Robert) and Wilson's son Dominick O. Two years later, in 1880, when Dominick O. Cunningham became sole owner of the business, he changed the name of the firm to D. O. Cunningham & Company.

This Dominick O. Cunningham was born in 1854 in Allegheny County, of which Pittsburgh is the industrial heart.[106] As would be expected, he was brought up in the glass business and became a thoroughly practical and experienced glassmaker. Nevertheless, glass was not his sole interest: he was a senior member of the large lumber firm of Schuette Company, a director of the City Insurance Company, and a member of the Chamber of Commerce; and like his father and uncles before him, he was an active civic leader. Glass, of course, was his primary concern. His firm's two extensive factories for the manufacture of window glass, bottles, and fruit jars were located between Twenty-second and Twenty-sixth streets on Jane Street on the south side of Pittsburgh, the buildings covering an area of two complete city blocks. In addition to an office at the factories, the company had another in the warehouse at 109 Water Street. Between 250 and 300 workmen were employed at weekly wages amounting to about $2,000. Its trade extended all over the United States from Canada to Mexico.

Dominick O. Cunningham died on March 26, 1911, but the firm continued in business until 1931.[107] At that time D. O. Cunningham & Company was taken over by All-Pak, which was also the successor to one of Cunningham's later rivals, the Allied Can and Container Company. The All-Pak firm, however, did not continue glassmaking; it was simply a distributing firm.

During its history, the Cunningham company produced all sorts of bottles, containers, and fruit jars. Some of the wine and/or spirits bottles are marked "CUNNINGHAM & IHMSEN" (see Part III, Section 2). And in 1961 workmen tearing down St. Joseph's Church on the south side of Pittsburgh discovered a dozen glass bottles marked on the base "D. O. C." They were identified by Mr. B. K. Simon, vice-president of All-Pak and a collector of bottles, as pop bottles made by D. O. Cunningham & Co. about 1900. These bottles also bore the name of William Padden Co., a South Side bottling house. Another bottle in Mr. Simon's collection, dating from about 1880, was embossed with the name "J. C. BUFFUM CO." and "PIONEER BOTTLER, ESTABLISHED 1845." Another bottle bearing the "D. O. C." mark dating from about 1900 bears the name "EDWARD F. McCAFFERTY"; he was also the operator of a soft-drink firm. A newer one in Simon's collection dating from about 1920 is marked "WILLIAM H. HOLMES CO."

"Cunningham" was one of the long-time leaders in producing beer bottles, and old ledgers show orders from breweries all over the Middle West. The last firm also supplied bottles for Poland Water from 1906 until its closing.[108] Besides wine and spirit bottles Cunningham & Ihmsen also marked fruit jars. One is marked on the side "CUNNINGHAM & IHMSEN" and dimly cut on the bottom is "1868"—which would be the first date of manufacture. It probably was produced between 1868 and 1879. It is of the type known as a "groove-ring wax sealer." A second preserve jar manufactured by one of the Cunningham firms is embossed "CUNNINGHAM'S & CO." This is also a "groove-ring wax sealer," similar to the one mentioned above, and is probably a continuation of the production of it. It, however, is from a different mold and bears the name on the bottom only. It must have been made sometime after 1878, since in that year the firm name was changed to Cunningham & Co. A later jar made by D. O. Cunningham Glass Co.—between 1882 and 1931—is also a "groove-ring wax sealer," made in green glass with "D O C" marked on the side.

The following flasks are attributed to Cunningham & Ihmsen:

GII–127. *Obverse:* small eagle, head to right with long neck; long shield on breast; three arrows in each talon. Below the eagle "C & I" is inscribed in a large oval frame. *Reverse:* similar to the obverse, but the left wing contains 11 ribs instead of nine, the right wing is shorter, and the shield is broader. Half-pint. Color: aquamarine. Cunningham & Ihmsen, Pittsburgh, Pennsylvania. Comparatively scarce. 1857–67.

GXV–5. *Obverse:* plain, except for the inscription "CUNNINGHAM & IHMSEN" in a semicircle with the word "GLASSMAKERS" in a straight line above the words "PITTSBURGH, PA" in another straight line below. *Reverse:* plain. Pint. Color: aquamarine. As inscribed (i.e., Cunningham & Ihmsen). Scarce. 1857–67.

The following flasks are attributed to Cunningham & Co.:

GII–142. *Obverse:* eagle flying to the right; pennant passing over the left wing, the lower part across the shield, forked and slanting downward; in pediment of monument below a sailing ship at the left a sheaf of wheat at the right; also a rifle above a large American flag with six stripes and 32 stars, flying to the left; the base of the frame is inscribed "CONTINENTAL"; at each side, rising from scrolls, is a laurel branch topped by an unfeathered large dove with olive branch in its beak. Just above the top of pediment are 13 tiny "stars," seven on the left and six at the right. *Reverse:* similar to GII–141, but the Indian is stockier and is wearing a headdress and short skirt; the dog is larger and near the Indian's right foot; a bird is perched on the top of the short leafless tree rising from right end of the frame. In the frame are the words "CUNNINGHAMS & Co." in a semicircle above an ornament with the words "PITTSBURGH. P". Quart. Colors: aquamarine, light cornflower blue, green, and olive-yellow. Scarce. 1875–86.

GII–110. *Obverse:* eagle, small head to left, long neck; shield on breast, narrow pennant extending from beak to the right in a shallow arc above the eagle; below the eagle is a large oval frame with the inscription "CUNNINGHAM" following the upper line of the frame, "PITTSBURGH" in a concave arc following the lower contour of the frame, and "&Co." in the center. *Reverse:* like obverse, but 14 fine ribs instead of 11 heavy ribs in the wing, and in the oval frame are the words "GLASS" and, below, "MANUFACTURERS" following the lower line of the frame. Quart. Color: aquamarine. Common. ca. 1875–86.

GII–111. *Obverse:* eagle with head to left, short wide pennant above; a large round-ended oblong frame below the eagle contains the inscription "CUNNINGHAM" following the upper line of the frame and

"PITTSBURG" following the lower line of the frame, with "& Co." in the center. *Reverse:* like the obverse, but 14 ribs in the right wing instead of 10 and 11 ribs in the left wing instead of 9. The frame below contains the inscription "GLASS" at the top and "MANUFAC-TURERS" at the bottom. Pint. Color: light blue. Common. ca. 1875–86.

GII–112. *Obverse:* eagle, head to the left, broad shield on breast, with wide pennant with short end from beak to right arc above the eagle. Below the eagle is a large oval frame with the inscription "CUNNINGHAM" following the upper line of the frame, "PITTSBURGH" following the lower line of the frame, and "& Co." in the center. *Reverse:* like the obverse, but 13 ribs in the right wing instead of 16 and 9 in the left instead of 11. Inscribed in the frame is "GLASS" at the top and "MAN-UFACTURER'S" at the bottom. Pint. Color: light yellow-green.

63. ADAMS & CO., *Pittsburgh, Pennsylvania, 1851–88 (and probably afterward)*

The old Stourbridge Flint Glass Works, established in 1823 by John Robinson, was taken over in 1851 by John Adams and a Mr. Macklin, who established Adams, Macklin & Co. as a flint glass manufactory. The glasshouse was located at the corner of Ross and Second streets.[109] According to late 19th-century authorities, John Adams is credited with developing a superior form of lime glass as a substitute for lead glass, which greatly reduced the manufacturing costs of glass tableware.[110] In 1860 a new glassworks was built on the south side of Pittsburgh, in an area known as Birmingham, at the corner of William and South Tenth streets. At about the same time, or in 1861, the firm became Adams & Company. The partnership consisted of John Adams, Godfried Miller, A. A. Adams, W. Adams, James Dalzell, and George F. Easton.[111] In 1864 the firm, listed as members of the Flint Glass Manufacturers Association, contributed $200 to Pittsburgh's Sanitary Fair.[112] Hopkins's 1872 *Atlas of Pittsburgh* lists the works at Tenth and William streets with an office and warehouse opposite the glassworks at 103 Tenth Street.[113]

It is not known just when this company—which was noted for its pressed- and blown-glass tableware that was shipped throughout the South and to the West—began producing green glassware, but they were certainly doing so by 1867, as the following advertisements from Thurston's Directory of 1867/68 indicates:[114]

Adams & Co.
Manufacturers of
Flint, Green and Amber glass,
Lamp Chimneys of every Variety, Style and Weight
Made to Order
Also Fruit Jars of the most approved kinds.
Office & Factory corner of McKee and William Streets, Birmingham
One Square from Passenger Cars.

In November 1886 John Adams, the senior partner, died, but the firm continued to operate as Adams & Company, being carried on by the surviving partners: George F. Easton, David E. Carle, Godfried Miller, August A. Adams, William Adams, and S. G. Vogeley.[115]

The following three Figured Flasks bearing the initials "A & CO." are attributed to Adams & Co. on the basis of the research by John Ramsay:

GXII–1. *Obverse:* shield and clasped hands with the word "UNION" above. *Reverse:* eagle, flying to the right with shield depending from the breast, with two pennants floating from its beak, the lower crossing the shield and bearing the initials "A. & CO." Quart. Colors: deep amber, aquamarine, and light yellow-green. Common. ca. 1865–75.

GXII–21. *Obverse:* shield and clasped hands similar to that on GXII–1 but of smaller scale. *Reverse:* eagle, flying to the right, similar to GXII–1 but smaller scale and the shield is plain. "A & CO." appears on the long section of the lower pennant. Pint. Colors: deep amber, shaded golden amber, aquamarine, and pale yellow-green. Common. ca. 1865–75.

GXII–22. *Obverse:* shield and clasped hands with the word "UNION" above, similar to GXII–1 but of smaller scale. *Reverse:* eagle flying to the right, like GXII–1 but smaller. The pennants are plain, except for "A. & CO." Pint. Colors: deep amber and light green. Common. ca. 1865–75.

64. E. WORMSER & CO., *Pittsburgh, Pennsylvania, 1854–1927*

In 1854 Wormser, Burgraff & Company established a green-glass house that was operated under the trade name of Pittsburgh Green Glass Company. The founders of the company were Ephraim Wormser and a Mr. Burgraff.[116] In the depression year 1857 the firm was joined by William Frank of Wm. Frank & Company. (William Frank was the brother-in-law of Ephraim Wormser, with whom he had a long business association.)[117] The name was then changed to E. Wormser & Company. The works of the Pittsburgh Green Glass Company was located on Twenty-second Street near Pennsylvania Avenue. Little is known of the products of the factory, but presumably they made the usual line of black- and green-glass bottles for all types of beverages, including beer, porter, and wine, as well as condiments and the like. A soda water bottle marked "E W & CO" is No. 3 in Ill. 49. Blown in a full-size mold, it also bears an eagle similar to that on flask GXII–14.

In 1858 William Frank and Ephraim Wormser jointly purchased property (about three acres or more) about four miles east of downtown Pittsburgh, on which they erected a new glassworks.[118] It was located between what was then Braddocks Field Plank Road and the Monongahela River. As the city developed, this location later came to be just east of the intersection of Second Avenue and Greenfield

Avenue, about one-quarter mile from the station of the Pittsburgh and Connellsville Railroad (later the Baltimore & Ohio Railroad). At one time the railway station was called Frankstown after William Frank; later it was known as the Laughlin Station. The new factory was called the Frankstown Glass Works. It is probable that the works built in 1854 was dismantled when this new works was built. Essentially, the partnership consisted of the two companies: the one that sold the Frank bottles was first known as Wm. Frank & Company, and afterward as Wm. Frank & Sons. (See historical sketch No. 65, Frankstown Glass Works.) The Wormser bottles were sold first by E. Wormser & Co.; in 1875 or 1876 by the Wormser Glass Company; then briefly by Wormser Glass Co. Ltd.; then, by 1884, again by the Wormser Glass Co. The Union Flasks GXIII–15 and 16 marked "E. Wormser & Co." were produced in the Frankstown glassworks, which was destroyed by fire in 1874.[119]

In 1864 Ephraim Wormser purchased a little more than five acres of land on Second Avenue near the railroad station, on a bluff overlooking the Monongahela River.[120] Two years later, Wormser deeded his part interest in the Frankstown Glass Works to William Frank.[121] In 1876 William Frank severed his business connections with Ephraim Wormser, and about the same time the firm name was changed to Wormser Glass Company.[122] Six years afterward, Ephraim Wormser deeded a portion of his residence property on the bluff above the Laughlin Railroad Station, which he had purchased in 1854, to Wormser & Co. Ltd.[123] A new glasshouse operated by this company was then built on the property. Apparently during the interim between 1876 when the Frankstown Glass Works burned and the building of the new glasshouse in 1882, Ephraim Wormser had his glassware made by others. According to the Pittsburgh Directory of 1884, the firm name reverted to Wormser Glass Company in that year. Following the death of Ephraim Wormser, the firm was carried on by his son Joseph. It continued in operation until about 1927, when the works was shut down and dismantled.

The following flasks are attributed to E. Wormser & Co.:

GXII–15. *Obverse:* large pointed shield enclosing clasped hands, below which is a series of vertical lines interrupted by an oval frame. The word "UNION" is in a slight arc above the shield; above this in a slight arc are 13 stars; there is a leafed branch on each side of the shield. *Reverse:* eagle in flight; ribbon from beak above and below passes through or behind the shield. There is also an olive branch below the shield. Below this, near the bottom of the flask, is a frame with incurved ends and points extending above and below the center, within which is the inscription "E. WORMSER & CO." The inscription is so crowded that the small "o" of "Co" is just outside the frame. Below this are "PITTSBURGH" and "PA" with a period below and between P and A almost in the bottom point, and below the letters "SB" in Pittsburgh. Quart. Colors: golden amber, aquamarine,

olive-yellow, light yellow-green, deep amber, and deep blue. Common. Probably ca. 1861–76.

GXII–16. *Obverse:* like GXII–15 but stars slightly smaller. *Reverse:* like GXII–15. Quart. Color: aquamarine. Common. Probably ca. 1861–76.

65. FRANKSTOWN GLASS WORKS, *Pittsburgh, Pennsylvania, 1858–74*

William Frank (1819–91) began operating William Frank & Co. as a wholesale and retail mercantile business in 1846, according to his memoirs written in 1889.[124] The Pittsburgh Directory of 1850 also records the firm in this fashion. In 1857 William Frank became a partner with his brother-in-law, Ephraim Wormser, in Wormser, Burgraff & Co., according to the Pittsburgh Directory of 1856/57, a company founded in 1854. (See No. 64. E. Wormser & Co., 1854–1927.)

In the following year, 1858, William Frank and Ephraim Wormser jointly purchased a little more than three acres of land about four miles east of downtown Pittsburgh, located between Braddocks Field Plank Road (now Second Avenue) and the Monongahela River.[125] This was about two-tenths of a mile east of the intersection of Second Avenue and Greenfield Avenue on the south side of Second Avenue. It was also about a quarter-mile from the station of the Pittsburgh and Connellsville Railroad, which later became the Baltimore and Ohio Railroad. The station (and the area around the glasshouse) was called Frankstown after Mr. William Frank, according to his memoirs. Still later it was called Laughlin Station. On this site William Frank and Ephraim Wormser built the Frankstown Glass Works. The name of the firm was Wm. Frank & Co.

In March 1866 Ephraim Wormser deeded his interest in the Frankstown Glass Works to William Frank, and the firm name was changed to "Wm. Frank & Sons."[126] It is interesting to note, however, that the first listing under this name occurs in the Pittsburgh Directory of 1870/71.

Hopkins's *Atlas of Pittsburgh*, 1872, lists "W. Frank & Sons, Frankstown Glass Works, Manufacturers of Vials, Bottles and Demijohns. Office and Warehouse, 92 and 94 First Avenue."[127] A letterhead of the firm dated Pittsburgh, May 1, 1874, indicates they were manufacturers of "Vials, Bottles and Fruit Jars."[128] In addition to producing the five marked Figured Flasks listed below, as well as some produced for E. Wormser & Co. (see No. 64), a wide variety of vials, bottles, and fruit jars typical of the period was part of their production.

As happened to so many glassworks, the Frankstown Glass Works was destroyed by fire in 1874, but it, unlike many others, was not rebuilt.[129] A few years later, the Pittsburgh Directory of 1876/77 still listed "WM. FRANK & SONS, AUCTRS, AND PROPS. FRANKSTOWN GLASS WORKS." In the same year, 1876, William Frank retired from both Wm. Frank & Sons and E. Wormser & Co. In his memoirs, Frank indicated he was associated with Wormser in this business for 19 years (probably 1857–

27A. Left: Bottle for DR. HENLEY'S CALIFORNIA IXL BITTERS. Right: Soda water bottle with embossed inscription "J.C. BUFFUM & CO in a slight arc, with "Pittsburgh, Pa." in a straight line below. **B.** The reverse near the base, bears the two initials "W.F."

76). After that year directories list him as "Wm. Frank & Sons, Wholesale Drygoods."[130]

The following bottles in the collection of Mr. James Frank, great-grandson of William Frank, are products of the Frankstown Glass Works, each bearing some variation of the company's mark:

DR. HENLEY'S CALIFORNIA IXL BITTERS (Ill. 27A). The reverse is plain; the base bears the mark, in a circle, "W. FRANK & SONS PITT." Blown in a mold of a medium aqua-colored glass, it is 12 inches high and 3¼ inches in diameter at the base. The lip, formed by being rewarmed after having been whetted off the blowpipe, is reinforced by a crude ring below its termination.

Soda bottle of medium aquamarine glass, blown in a mold and bearing the inscription "J. C. BUFFUM & Co." in a slight arc, with "PITTSBURGH PA." in a straight line below (Ill. 27A). On the reverse, near the base, are the initials "W.F." (Ill. 27B). The bottle is 6¾ inches high and 2½ inches in diameter at the base. J. C. Buffum was a large bottler in Pittsburgh in the second half of the 19th century. Other soda bottles bearing the Buffum name have been found bearing the initials of other glasshouses.

"Back bar" bottle, of deep amber glass blown in a mold, undecorated except for an embossed oval cartouche open at the top (Ill. 28). Within the cartouche is a white paper label lettered in gold "A.BRANDY" with red and black shading, and further embellished by geometric motifs in gold, red, and black, the whole surrounded by a gilt border. The paper label is covered and protected by a contoured piece of glass carefully fitted and cemented over it. On the bottom of the bottle is embossed "WM. FRANK & SONS. PITT." This bottle is 11½ inches high and 3½ inches in diameter at the base. It was undoubtedly originally used as a serving bottle, or "back bar" bottle, and was being so used in 1971 on a reproduction of the boat *Robert E. Lee River Queen* at St. Louis, when the vessel's furnishings were sold at auction to satisfy creditors, according to James Frank. It doubtless represents a typical, fairly inexpensive type of bar furniture of the post-Civil War era.

Spirits bottle, probably for wine or whiskey, of deep amber glass blown in a turn mold (Ill. 28, at right). The bottle is plain except for the deeply embossed inscription "WM. FRANK & SONS. PA." on the base (Ill. 29). About 10¾ inches high and 2½ inches in diameter at the base.

Medicine bottle or flask, mold blown of aquamarine glass, plain on both sides except for the embossed inscriptions "W. FRANK & SONS" on the obverse, and "PITTSBURGH" on the reverse. The reverse also bears a paper label "SPIRITS OF CAMPHOR" from a drugstore in what appears to be Charleston, West Vir-

29. Detail of the base of the bottle at the right in Ill. 28. The inscription reads "W.M. FRANK & SONS. PA."

28. *Left:* back bar bottle, gilded label, "A. BRANDY". *Right:* Spirits bottle, for wine or whiskey.

30. Four identified products of the Frankstown Glass Works. *Left to right:* Aqua ½-pint flask, for medicine or liquor, plain on both sides except for embossed inscriptions "W. FRANK & SONS" on the obverse and "PITTSBURGH" on the reverse. A paper label on the reverse indicates this flask was used to contain "SPIRITS OF CHAMPHOR." It has an internal screw thread to accept a threaded glass stopper, a closing device patented by Himan Frank, August 6, 1872. Bitters or medicine bottle, embossed on the base: "WM. FRANK & SONS" with the mirror image of "PITTS" in the center. Whiskey or spirits bottle, mold-blown, embossed on the base: "WM. FRANK & SONS." Height, 10¾". "Wax sealer" fruit jar of aqua glass marked on the base: "WM. FRANK & SONS, PITTS."

ginia (Ill. 30). The bottle is of half-pint capacity, 5⅞ inches high. Interesting features are the internal threads and glass screw cap that make up the closure. This form of threaded neck and closure was invented by Himan Frank of Pittsburgh, one of four sons of William Frank. Two patents were issued to him on August 6, 1872: No. 130208, spec. 89, accompanied by drawing number 30, relates to a "Bottle Stopper." Patent No. 130207, spec. 88, drawing number 30, is entitled "Tool for Forming Bottle Mouths." Incidentally, Himan Frank on the same date received patents for what were probably technological improvements in the glass melting furnace: a "Regenerative Furnace Valve" and a "Metallurgic Gas Furnace Valve."

Bottle blown in a square mold with slightly rounded corners, with a short neck and broad, sloping collar. This bottle of deep amber color was probably intended for bitters or some form of proprietary medicine. It is plain except for embossing on the base "WM FRANK & SONS" with a mirror image of "PITTS" in the center. It is 2⅝ inches in cross section and 9½ inches high (Ill. 30).

Whiskey or other spirits bottle (Ill. 30), probably; mold blown of dark amber glass, plain except for an oval cartouche open at the top like that on the bar bottle marked "BRANDY" shown in Ill. 28, and an applied ring around the long neck. On the base is the embossed inscription "WM. FRANK & SONS." Height 10¾ inches.

Plain fruit jar (Ill. 30), a "wax sealer" with a groove at the top of the lip to take a tin lid; blown in a mold. It is marked on the base "WM. FRANK & SONS, PITTS." and is 7 inches high.

Among other bottles that may have been made at the Frankstown Glass Works is a barrel-shaped amber bottle embossed "CHAPIN & GORE, CHICAGO" on one side and "SOUR MASH 1867" on the other. This attribution is postulated on the fact that the base is marked "H. FRANK'S PAT.–AUG. 1872." However, it should be noted that a bottle of the same form, with the same inscription and without the patent mark on the base—but marked on the base "HAWLEY GLASS WORKS HAWLEY PA."—was obviously produced by that firm. A half-pint amber flask with threaded mouth for a glass stopper bearing the embossed inscriptions "CHAPIN & GORE, CHICAGO" on one side and "SOUR MASH 1867" on the other side may also have been made by the Frankstown Glass Works. It is embossed on the base "H. FRANK PAT. AUG. 6th 1872."

The following marked Figured Flasks were made at the Frankstown Glass Works between 1866 and 1874 (Ill. 31):

GXII–32. *Obverse:* shield and clasped hands in frame with the oval frame embossed "W.F. & SONS" above and "UNION" above the shield. *Reverse:* flying eagle with pennant; plain, empty 6-pointed frame below. Half-pint. Color: aquamarine. Comparatively scarce.

GXII–38. *Obverse:* shield and clasped hands with a large oval frame below containing the inscription within its perimeter "WM. FRANK & SONS" and "PITTS" in the center bottom of the oval. *Reverse:* cannon facing left; American flag flying to the right, rising from a pyramid of cannonballs behind muzzle of the cannon. Quart. Colors: golden amber, aquamarine, light olive-green. Comparatively scarce.

GXII–38a. *Obverse:* like GXII–38, but with 19 tiny stars. *Reverse:* like GXII–38, but cannonballs are slightly smaller. Quart. Colors: greenish amber, deep sapphire-blue, yellow-green. Comparatively scarce.

GXII–39. *Obverse:* shield and clasped hands, similar to GXII–38 but smaller scale and the "UNION" larger in proportion to the rest of the design. *Reverse:* cannon and cannonballs, similar to GXII–38 but of smaller scale. Pint. Colors: shaded amber, golden amber, aquamarine, cornflower blue, and sapphire-blue. Comparatively scarce.

GXII–39a. *Obverse:* shield and clasped hands, closely similar to GXII–39, but in the lower field of the shield, the vertical bars are close to the sides, and there are 22 leaves on the left laurel branch and 28 on the right. *Reverse:* cannon and cannonballs, very similar to GXII–39 but with six small cannonballs in a triangle; the flag is narrower with 11 stars and 5 stripes. Pint. Colors: golden amber, red-amber, aquamarine. Comparatively scarce.

In addition to these pictorial flasks, the Frankstown Glass Works also produced half-pint and pint flasks of aqua and amber glass with internal screw threads and glass screw-threaded stoppers patented by Himan Frank, son of William, on August 6, 1872. These flasks were plain, except for the inscription "W. FRANK & SONS" on the obverse and "PITTSBURGH, PA." on the reverse. An example of the half-pint aqua flask with internal screw thread in the neck is shown with an aqua glass stopper in Ill. 31.

66. GEORGE A. BERRY & CO., *Pittsburgh, Pennsylvania, ca 1853–65*

In 1834 or 1835 George Kendall and Thomas Patten erected a glasshouse in Belle Vernon, located along the east bank of the Monongahela River, about 20 miles south of the present center of Pittsburgh, but they failed before any glass was manufactured. Their uncompleted factory was taken over in 1835 by William Eberhart, Sr., who made his first "blast" in February of 1836, which ended on the first of July. Window glass, bottles, and other hollow wares were his products.[131] Eberhart built a new glasshouse in Belle Vernon in 1841. Bottles, as well as cylinder glass, were blown in this factory. The financial stringency of 1853 crippled many of the glasshouses of the Monongahela–Ohio area, and long-term credits and renewals contributed to bankrupt Eberhart.

31. Four marked products of the Frankstown Glass Works. *Left to right:* Quart aqua flask. Shield and clasped hands on the obverse and marked "WM. FRANK & SONS". Flag and cannon on reverse. Height, 8⅝". Dark amber pint flask: flag and cannon on the obverse; the reverse is marked "Wm. Frank & Sons, Pitts." and shows a shield and clasped hands. Height, 7¾". Light amber pint bottle: plain on obverse except for "W. Frank & Sons"; plain on reverse except for "Pittsburgh, Pa." Bottle has patented internal screw thread in neck to receive a patented glass stopper with screw threads, shown at right. Half-pint aqua flask: eagle with shield on the obverse; shield and clasped hands and "W.F. & Sons" on the reverse. Height, 6⅛".

In either 1853 or 1855 George A. Berry of Pittsburgh took over the glasshouse and buildings erected by Eberhart in 1841.[132] Berry revived the business under the name of George A. Berry & Co. His partners were J. B. McKennon (or McKeen) and Samuel Vanhook. McKennon and Vanhook apparently soon withdrew from active management of the works, and became agents for the sale of window glass, bottles, flasks, and other glassware produced by the factory. Again, except for the marked flasks listed below, little is known about the individual products of the firm. Robert C. Schmertz & Co. purchased the factory in 1865 and specialized in producing glass for pictures, showcases, and storefronts. The works was then called the Duquesne Glass Works; the company had a warehouse in Pittsburgh at 97 and 99 First Street. According to Knittle, he is said to have been the first manufacturer to produce ground and frosted window glass for offices. By 1876 the firm had become R. C. Schmertz & Co.;[133] it was still operating in 1886. Hopkins lists Geo. A. Berry as located at 75 Water Street in Pittsburgh in 1872 but gives no indication of his business.[134]

The following flasks were produced by George A. Berry & Co.:

GII–98. *Obverse:* eagle, the small head to the left, with a narrow pennant from beak to the right, above the eagle; below is a large oval frame containing the inscription "GEO.A." at the top center and "BERRY & CO." at the bottom, following the contour of the frame. *Reverse:* like the obverse, but there are 9 ribs in the right wing and 6 in

the left, and the oval frame is empty. Quart. Color: aquamarine. Comparatively scarce. 1853 or 1855–65.

GII–98a. *Obverse:* similar to GII–98, but with only 8 widely spaced ribs in the right wing and only 6 in the left. *Reverse:* like the obverse, but with no inscription. Pint. Color: aquamarine. Common. 1853 or 1855–65.

GII–98b. *Obverse:* presumably similar to GII–98 and GII–98a. *Reverse:* presumably like the obverse, and with no inscription in the frame. Half-pint. Color: aquamarine. (We have never seen this flask; it is presumed to be scarce.) 1853 or 1855–65.

The following flask may have been a product of George A. Berry & Co. because of its close similarity to GII–98. It may, however, have been made by another manufacturer from a mold made by the same moldmaker who made the molds for Berry & Co.:

GII–99. *Obverse:* eagle like that in GII–98, but the frame below the eagle contains no inscription. *Reverse:* like the obverse. Quart. Color: amber. Common. This flask was probably made ca. 1850–65.

67. RAVENNA GLASS WORKS, *Ravenna, Ohio, ca. 1857–ca. 1880*

The history of glassmaking in Ravenna, Ohio, is like that of New London, Connecticut—obscure and very complicated. On the basis of documentary evidence, it seems likely that glassmaking began in Ravenna in 1857, but according to some local tradition it may have started as early as 1851. In that year, two coincidences occurred to Mr. Seth Day, owner of a general store and member of the Ravenna Board of Trade. One day after returning from Cleveland with supplies he had bought, he broke a large pane of window glass as he was unloading it. Very soon after this mishap, the Board of Trade received a letter from a glassmaker in the Pittsburgh area expressing interest in the possibility of starting a glassworks in Ravenna. Again, local tradition has it that Mr. Day agreed to pay expenses for the man to investigate Ravenna for such a venture. The "Seth Day Glass Co" is said to have resulted, since there was an abundance of wood and fine sand available in the area. It is said that this company was later reorganized as the "Ravenna Glass Works."[135]

Documentary evidence definitely establishes the founding of the Ravenna Glass Company in 1857. A deed dated August 19, 1857, records that Seth Day, Mary Day, Ebenezer Spaulding, Francis F. Spaulding, Samuel H. Terry, and Hellen M. Terry, for the sum of $500, sold to the Ravenna Glass Company .62 acre of land, "Being on which the Glass factory is building . . ." and ". . . being a part of Lot number Six in the S. Division of Lots in Ravenna . . ."[136] On September 3, 1857, the Ravenna Glass Company purchased from Benjamin G. Hopkins two acres of land, a part of Lot 31, adjoining their previously purchased land, for the sum of $500. This land was actually situated in the township of Franklin (now Kent). In the description of the boundaries of this two-acre plot, it is interesting to note: ". . . beginning at a Nick cut in the rock on the west bank of the Cuyahoga River and known as the South East Corner of the Glass House Lot . . ." It seems unlikely that this reference to the glasshouse lot can be to property purchased just two weeks previously; rather, the reference suggests that a glasshouse *had* occupied this site earlier, as noted above.[137]

The Ravenna Glass Company purchased a third piece of land containing 1.89 acres, as indicated by a deed dated September 8, 1857. It was acquired from Horace Y. Beebe and his wife and was part of Lot 60 in the south division of lots in Ravenna.[138]

These three purchases combined to provide the Ravenna Glass Company with approximately four acres of land. Whatever the good fortunes or prosperity of the company may have been, it was certainly accompanied by many adverse actions, as attested by a dozen or more suits or levies brought against the company for damages and debts. On February 27, 1858, William D. Durham received of Ebenezer Spaulding: ". . . One hundred dollars the amount of damage assessed in my favor for the land used and occupied as a road running north from the road leading from Ravenna to Franklin by the Glass Works to the turnpike and the West line [now Cleveland Road] of the corporation of the Village of Ravenna."[139] In an action brought by William Pittman against the Ravenna Glass Company on November 21, 1860, Sheriff Williams indicated that he had, on November 23, 1860, made a ". . . due

and diligent search" and that he found "no goods of the within named Glass Company whereon to levy."[140]

On March 16, 1861, the property of the Ravenna Glass Company was appraised for a sheriff's sale and valued at $4,175. The property was then advertised for sale at the courthouse in Ravenna on April 20, 1861. At that time it was "Struck off to John and George Forder" for the sum of $2,783.34.[141] Whether John and George Forder ever operated the works is not known. About a year later, on July 19, 1862, the property was again sold at sheriff's sale and was acquired by George Messenger for $2,400.[142]

By the spring of 1863 the company was apparently in serious financial shape. On April 13 of that year, the sheriff levied upon all the real and personal property of the Ravenna Glass Company.[143] In the document, a reference to a railway leading to the Ravenna Glass Works is noted, whereby it should have had good access to markets. Included in the description of property levied upon were ". . . furnaces, ovens, mill pots, moulds, machinery, stock fixtures necessary to be used in prosecuting the business of Manufacturing, Packing and Shipping glassware situated or appertaining to said furnaces. . . ." A note at the end of the levy indicates that the account was returned ". . . wholly unsatisfied for want of time to advertise. Sheriff's office, May 11, 1863, William F. Parsons, Sheriff."

The company was again levied against on May 28, 1863, when Warner & Loop brought suit against the Ravenna Glass Company in the amount of $1,904.80.[144] On the same day, Warner & Loop also brought suit for the amount of $2,254.57. Neither suit appears to have been settled. Ebenezer Spaulding seems to have continued to be involved as one of the principals of the company, since he is mentioned in a suit against the Ravenna Glass Company by Dennis C. Day on October 18, 1865.[145] Whatever may have transpired in the interim, the deed recorded September 15, 1869, indicates that the Ravenna Glass Company was then purchased by the Diamond Glass Works.[146]

According to Rhea Mansfield Knittle, the Ravenna Glass Company was incorporated in 1867 by F. W. Coffin, George Robinson, D. C. Coolman, H. H. Stevens, and J. B. Horton.[147] Also according to her, this firm adopted the trade name of the Diamond Glass Company, but according to the deed noted above, Mrs. Knittle was in error about the 1867 date. According to her, Stevens and Coffin withdrew in 1874, and in 1875 Robinson sold his interest. The company at that time produced both bottles and window glass, and made the double-strength windows for the Ohio building in the Philadelphia Centennial Exposition in 1876.

Except for a few marked flasks and one marked calabash bottle, not much is known about the production of the Ravenna Glass Company. According to Van Rensselaer, the sand used in the factory was hauled by wagons from Sandy Lake, about three miles southeast of Ravenna. He also states that Ira J. Strong of Kent, Ohio, 80 years old in about 1925, went to work in the shipping room of the Ravenna Glass Company in 1863, at 17 years of age. Strong said that he remembered packing ". . . Washington–

Taylor pint flasks, quart calabash bottles with crossed pitchfork and rake, reverse sheaf of rye, and Jenny Lind calabash bottles, Union flasks and others."[148]

The following marked flasks were made by the Ravenna Glass Company:

GII-37. *Obverse:* American eagle, head turned to the left, with 13 fairly large 5-pointed stars in a semicircle above the eagle. *Reverse:* anchor, and above it "RAVENNA" in a narrow curved frame. At the bottom of the flask in a curved frame is the word "COMPANY" and above the frame and just below the anchor, the word "GLASS". Pint. Colors: yellow, olive-yellow, light and deep olive-green, pale green, emerald-green, deep blue-green, clear green, olive-amber (black), clear deep amber, and aquamarine. Common. 1857–ca. 1869.

GXIV-2. *Obverse:* "TRAVELER'S" in an arc above, and "COMPANION" in a reverse arc below, with a starlike ornament composed of 8 small triangles around a plain circle about 9/16″ in diameter in the center. *Reverse:* star as on obverse with "RAVENNA" above and "GLASS Co" below. Quart. Colors: aquamarine, brown, and deep yellow-green. Comparatively scarce. 1857–69.

GXIV-3. *Obverse:* inscriptions as on GXIV-2, with similar star. *Reverse:* star, like obverse; inscription like reverse of GXIV-2. Pint. Colors: amber, aquamarine, and deep yellow-green. Comparatively scarce. ca. 1857–69.

GXV-17. *Obverse:* plain, except for the inscription in three straight lines: "RAVENNA/GLASS/WORKS". *Reverse:* plain. Pint. Color: golden amber. Scarce. ca. 1865.

The following flasks are attributed to Ravenna based upon characteristics related to the above:

GI-104. *Obverse:* Jenny Lind, three-quarter view turned to the left, within a large, almost encircling wreath, with the words "JENY LIND" in an arc above. *Reverse:* view of a glasshouse. Quart. Colors: sapphire-blue, cornflower-blue, clear light blue, bluish green, clear brilliant amber, yellow-green, pale green, medium and deep emerald-green, and aquamarine. Common. Probably 1857–ca. 1865.

GI-105. *Obverse:* three-quarter view of Jenny Lind facing left, very similar to GI-104. *Reverse:* glasshouse, again similar to GI-104. Quart. Colors: aquamarine and light green. Rare. 1857–ca. 1865.

GXI-47. *Obverse:* prospector, standing and facing right, with a short loose coat, short staff with pack and tools at end over right shoulder, with a cane in his left hand. Above is "FOR PIKE'S PEAK" in a semicircle. *Reverse:* hunter at left, shooting a stag at right, facing right and pitching forward onto knees. Quart. Colors: amber; clear, medium, and deep green. Comparatively scarce. Probably ca. 1860–70.

GXI-49. *Obverse:* prospector facing right; like GXI-47, but the cane is shorter. *Reverse:* hunter shooting a stag, as on GXI-47, but below the figures "E. KAUFFELD" in a straight line. Quart. Colors: colorless with a faint pinkish tint in the base. Extremely rare; only one specimen recorded. ca. 1860–70.

68. GEORGE W. KEARNS; ZANESVILLE, OHIO, GLASSHOUSES, *1842–1923 and later*

As in the case of so many other glassblowers and glasshouse proprietors, the career of George W. Kearns is a difficult and complicated one to trace. Kearns first appeared in Zanesville in 1842, arriving there from Pittsburgh along with six other practical glassblowers. On the payment of $500 each to James Crosby, these six men took over the White Glass Works, which had been established in 1815 and had been operated fairly successfully by several concerns until 1839. In the previous year, the Reverend Joseph Shepard had withdrawn from the firm, selling his shares to the last remaining partner, James Crosby, who failed and closed the works in 1839.

The new owners employed from 40 to 44 hands; bottles and flasks constituted the bulk of their output. Along with Kearns, the other owners were Joseph Burns, W. F. Spence, Thomas Reynolds, George Wendt, and Samuel Turner. After two years had passed, Turner and Spence sold their interests to Arnold Lippitt. Sometime between then and 1848, by which time the business had dwindled to practically nothing, George Kearns also sold his interest in the White Glass Works.

In 1849 Kearns, along with one of his former partners, Joseph Burns, and John W. Carter, built the first bottle glasshouse on the Putnam, or western, side of the Muskingum River. The factory was located at the corner of Muskingum Avenue and Harrison Street on the riverbank, where steamboats could conveniently land. Its volume of business was large and its location afforded it excellent shipping facilities. The firm name was Burns, Kearns & Co.[149]

In 1852 John (or Jehu) Carter, possibly a silent partner in Burns, Kearns & Co., took over the operational rights of this factory and operated it until 1877. Carter was born in Philadelphia on October 26, 1817, and came to Elizabethtown, Pennsylvania, when his mother married Joseph Dill Abel, a glassblower from whom Carter learned glassblowing. In 1840 Marcus Abel, Carter's uncle, moved to Zanesville to work in a glass factory there, and Carter followed, eventually marrying Sarah Woodruff, the daughter of Cornelius and Susan Woodruff. In 1856 the factory was bought by Cornelius Woodruff, Carter's father-in-law. The firm then became Carter & Woodruff, later becoming Carter & Gillespie and finally Carter and Carter.[150]

In 1870 this firm became the exclusive makers of Haines fruit jars, patented March 1, 1870. This jar was sealed with a tin lid similar to the tin lids used on the old stoneware fruit jars. Carter secured a patent for an improved cover and perfect joint on the Haines jar in 1875. Two years later the factory closed, and in 1882 it was sold to the Muskingum Fire Brick Company. Very little is known of the specific products of this company from its inception to its closing.

In the meantime, George W. Kearns had become involved with the flint glassworks originally built in 1852 by William C. Cassel and William Galigher (who is sometimes referred to as Gallagher).[151] This glassworks, located on First Street at the foot of Market Street, eventually developed into the large two-acre plant No. 1 of Hazel-Atlas Company, torn down in 1962. The Zanesville *City Times* of August 6, 1853, carried the following announcement regarding this enterprise:

The new Flint Glass Works at the foot of Market Street has had fires up for some days, tempering the vessels and furnaces, preparatory to commencing operations. Everything is being made ready in the most perfect and thorough manner for carrying on a large business in this establishment. The structure itself occupies a most favorable location, and the building has been planned to embrace every convenience. The moulds, too, are of the most modern and tasteful patterns, and the machinery throughout is the best in use anywhere.

Another newspaper, the *Courier,* wrote: ". . . Company expected to produce glass superior to the products of Wheeling and Pittsburgh and at prices cheaper than factories in those cities."[152]

By April 27, 1860, the firm had become G. W. Kearns & Co. In addition to George, the partnership included Noah Kearns and Joseph Burns, who may have been working for Cassel and Galigher. At first they rented the factory, but on September 2, 1856, they purchased it. On that day the *City Times* wrote:

A new firm has been organized to operate the works at the foot of Market Street. The firm is G. W. Kearns and Co. who immediately proceed to putting the works in order for the manufacture of bottles and vials, etx. The new firm took over the operating rights from Cassel & Galigher.

A few years later, according to Rhea Mansfield Knittle,[153] it was converted to a warehouse, but this may be in error, for Schneider & Greer[154]—in the *Sunday Times Signal,* Zanesville, Ohio, August 19, 1956—quote an advertisement showing that bottles were still being made at the factory on First Street at the foot of Market Street in 1868. Just when the factory ceased operations is not known, nor are the specific products of the factory, but they were undoubtedly producing the types of bottles and containers currently in demand throughout their years of operation.

George Kearns was involved in yet another glassworks in Zanesville. According to the 1860 directory, the firm of "Kearns, G. W. and Co." were "proprietors Zanesville Glass Works, West Side First between Main and Market."[155] Again, the company consisted of George Kearns, Noah Kearns, and Joseph Burns. On June 19, 1860, the *Courier* announced that the Zanesville Glass Works was

making fruit jars with lids held in place by a wire fastening, "so only a small quantity of cement is necessary." Prices of quart jars were $1.50 a dozen; of half-gallon jars, $2 per dozen.

In 1863, or perhaps 1865, a window-glass house was completed and operated by this firm. The window-glass house operated until about 1895. When Burns died, his heirs withdrew their interest and the two Kearns continued all the glassmaking operations alone. An advertisement in the 1868 directory indicates the broad scope of their operations: "Zanesville Glass Manufactories. G. W. Kearns & Co. Manufacturers of window glass, druggists' ware, fruit jars, demijohns, insulators and colored glass ware. Office and Factories First Street, near railroad depot, Zanesville, Ohio." The advertisement confirms the fact that the same firm was operating two glasshouses, one for making bottles on First Street at the foot of Market Street and the other on First Street at Main Street for making window glass.[156] By 1867 the firm name apparently had been changed to the Zanesville City Glassworks, for on December 19 of that year the *Signal* published a story about the "City Glass Works of Kearns & Co." It indicated that 60 men were employed making window glass and other ware, and that the products were shipped throughout the West. The following year Captain Joseph T. Gorsuch and F. H. Herdman formed a partnership with George W. and Noah Kearns for the operation of the glass manufactory at the foot of Market Street. In 1870 the factory at the foot of Main Street was still making window glass and that at the foot of Market Street producing bottles. In 1875 the company built a new "flint glass" plant on the site of what eventually became known as Hazel-Atlas Plant No. 1, as previously mentioned. On August 2, 1875, the *Courier* stated:

Fires have been kindled in the furnaces of the new large and extensive flint glassworks North First Street, and it is expected that in the course of a few days work will be commenced giving employment to a large number of persons. The bottle and window glasshouses belonging to Messrs. Kearns, Herdman and Gorsuch will resume operations about the first of September, with greatly increased force of hands.

A few days later it indicated ". . . All kinds of flint glass, bottles, lamp chimneys, etc. will be manufactured. One shop now making lamp chimneys, an entirely new branch in this city . . . all shops . . . ten will be in operation in a few days." Despite the fact that it was called a "flint glass" works, the nature of the articles being produced there strongly suggests that the glass was probably colorless lime glass.

In 1876 there is a reference to the Zanesville City Glass Works of Kearns, Herdman and Gorsuch selling window glass at $3.75 per box. George Washington Kearns withdrew from the firm in 1877 and built the "Dinky" plant on Luck Avenue. It was called the Dinky because it was smaller than the parent plant on Market Street. Ink bottles, medicine bottles, and flasks are said to have been produced there in the amount of about 45,000 bottles per year.

32. Contemporary illustration of George W. Kearns & Co. glasshouse in Zanesville, Ohio, from a broadside formerly in the collection of Charles B. Gardner. *Wheaton Historical Association, Millville, N. J.*

George Kearns died in 1906, and the Dinky plant closed two years later.[157]

Meantime, the firm from which Kearns withdrew continued its glass manufacturing in Zanesville. In 1878 the "Green Bottle House" made fruit jars exclusively, and the average production was "about 75 gross per day." On April 10, 1878, the *Courier* noted: "If you want to see a handsome specimen of fruit canning, call at Mershon's and see a three gallon fruit jar of pears. Kearns, Herdman and Gorsuch manufactured the jars—the Mason patent—and the fruit was put up by a New York house."[158] During 1879 the Glass Blowers Union compelled the blowers in the Kearns factory to agree to regulations that were not acceptable to the owners. Having large orders to fill, the company did nothing at the time, but when work was slack they discharged their window glass blowers and gatherers, and employed Charles D. Williams of Kent, Ohio, to go to

Belgium and employ 24 glassworkers from Charleroi. These men arrived in New York on December 18, 1875, where they were met by a Mr. Gray and Emile Borullt, foreman of the Belgians.

By 1880 the directory did not list the window glass factory but did list "Noah and James Kearns, Joseph T. Gorsuch and William T. Gray as proprietors of Kearns, Herdman and Gorsuch at the southeast corner of First and Main Streets." The firm continued to expand. On February 3, 1886, Kearns-Gorsuch Glass Company was incorporated with capital of $200,000. J. T. Gorsuch was president, W. T. Gray was vice-president, F. H. Herdman, secretary-treasurer, and Noah Kearns, superintendent. On November 6, 1887, the *Courier* described the plant as occupying two acres by the Muskingum River and the canal, and across the McIntire property of 132 square feet in the heart of the city. The company employed 275 men at that time and specialized in producing fruit jars.[159] On April 25, 1890, the *Courier* indicated that Kearns, Gorsuch Glass Company "own and control three factories in all, located in the heart of the city, and their entire plant covers five acres of ground."

In 1891 their window glass factory passed into the hands of the United Glass Company. It operated intermittently for two years thereafter, then closed. No window glass was produced after 1895. Since the United States Glass Company had given stock in exchange for the plant, Kearns-Gorsuch Glass Co. later surrendered the stock and took back the factory property. In 1902, about 30 years after it had been built, the First Street plant burned. Two years later, in 1904, a new plant was built north of the original First Street factory. In 1912 the Kearns-Gorsuch Bottle Company bought the Barnesville Bottle Company of Barnesville, and Ralph Gorsuch, the son of Capt. Joseph Gorsuch, was manager until it burned on March 3, 1921. Captain Gorsuch died in 1914, and his son Ralph became president of the company.

The *Times Signal* of January 29, 1920, announced the merger of the Hazel-Atlas Glass Company of Wheeling and the Kearns-Gorsuch Bottle Company. The merger was brought about by the keen competition following the invention and introduction of the automatic bottle-making machine. At that time the officers were as follows: president, Ralph Gorsuch; vice-president, W. M. Bateman; secretary, C. O. Stewart; manager of the Zanesville plant, E. J. Gorsuch. The Hazel-Atlas Company was the larger of the two merging companies. On January 8, 1923, the *Signal* announced the opening of the Hazel-Atlas Plant No. 2. "The big Kearn-Gorsuch Glass Plant on Ridge Avenue will open this morning at seven o'clock when the first shift will start to work . . ." About 200 men and women were employed on three shifts in this plant, making glass containers for food of all kinds. Their plant at Market Street then became Plant No. 1. It operated for 35 more years until, after a temporary suspension of activity in May 1958, it was permanently closed. This plant stood on the site of the original factory erected in 1852 by Cassel and Galigher. It was razed in 1966. By that time, two additional mergers had taken place. On September 15, 1956, Hazel-Atlas became a division of the Continental Can Company. This company closed the No. 1 Plant on November 1, 1958. On April 2, 1964, Continental Can Company sold the plant to the Brockway Glass Company of Brockway, Pennsylvania. This firm razed the No. 1 Plant and thereafter concentrated all its operations in the Ridge Avenue Plant.

The following flasks are attributed to the various glasshouses of G.W. Kearns & Co.:

GII–129. *Obverse:* eagle with large head turned to the right; below the eagle a large rectangular frame with in-curved corners containing the words "ZANES-VILLE." across the center of the flask and the word "OHIO" below, in line with the "VILLE." *Reverse:* similar to the obverse, but the eagle is larger, the olive branch is longer, and there is no inscription. Pint. Col-

ors: aquamarine and light green. Rare. Attributed to the Zanesville Glass Works, Market Street, Zanesville, Ohio, operated by G. W. Kearns & Co. 1852–63.

GXV–28. *Obverse:* plain except for the inscription, within an elliptical frame 2⅛ inches wide and 4¼ inches high, of the words "ZANESVILLE" at right, "GLASS WORKS" at left, and "CITY" in the center, all lengthwise. *Reverse:* plain. Pint. Colors: amber, aquamarine, and deep wine. Zanesville City Glass Works, Zanesville, Ohio, operated by George Kearns & Co. ca 1867–ca. 1875. Scarce.

The following flasks may have been produced in one of Kearns's Zanesville glasshouses:

GXI–44. *Obverse:* tall prospector with large head, the hair indicated by small dots and the eye by a large dot; the figure has thin arms, spindly legs, and wears a derby, a short loose coat flaring at the back, and tight trousers; his right hand holds a long-necked cylindrical bottle to his lips, and his left has a long cane; he is walking right on an irregular bar near the base of the flask. *Reverse:* eagle, small shield with five vertical bars, olive branch held in beak and curving upward to the left above the head as on GII–129. Below the eagle is a large rectangular frame with in-curved corners; no inscription. Pint. Colors: aquamarine, light and dark green, and yellow-green. Source unknown; possibly Zanesville, Ohio, or else blown in a mold made by the same moldmaker as the Zanesville eagle flask, GII–129. Scarce. ca. 1858–70.

GXI–45. *Obverse:* similar to GXI–44, but prospector has a larger head and stouter legs. *Reverse:* similar to GXI–44, but the left wing of the eagle is higher than the right and the shield smaller in proportion to the body. Frame below the eagle is also much smaller. Pint. Colors: aquamarine, green, and yellow-green. Scarce. ca. 1858–ca. 1870.

69. THE UNION GLASS WORKS; R. KNOWLES & CO., *Wheeling, (West) Virginia*

In 1849 R. Knowles & Co. was formed, and the Union Glass Works erected. The principals were Richard Knowles, a vial blower from England, three glassblowers—Cambern, Gorrell, and McGranahan—and Morgan Ott. Ott provided the capital; the other four were the practical glassmen. They purchased several lots at First and Mercer streets (now Twenty-fourth and Jacobs streets) and built their glassworks there. Its products were vials, bottles, and every description of druggists' glass. Cambern, Gorrell, and McGranahan withdrew in 1850, and A. E. Quarrier bought their interest, the name becoming Quarrier, Ott & Co. The firm did a large business. Its capital stock amounted to $40,000, it employed about 130 hands, and the annual output was valued at $125,000.[160]

An advertisement in the Wheeling Directory for 1851 stated:

Union Glass Works—Quarrier, Ott & Co., Manufacturers of Vials, Bottles, etc. corner of First & Mercer St. Center Wheeling. Common vials, Prescriptions, Green Glass Jars, Acid bottles, Mineral & Soda Bottles, Patent Medicine Vials, Ink Bottles, Druggist's Packing Jars, Flasks, cologne Bottles, etc.

Two of Richard Knowles's three sons, George and Richard, Jr., worked with him in the glasshouse, but his third son, Edward, refused. Apparently after Edward joined the Union Army during the Civil War, a break in family relations occurred that was never healed. Following the war, Richard and his two glassmaking sons moved to Glassport, Pennsylvania, after which the factory was sold to the Ohio Glass Company. That firm, which was managed by Peter Leighton, continued in business for many years producing window and plate glass. Eventually the property was sold and a car barn was built on the grounds by the local traction company.[161]

Despite extensive production over a number of years, only one marked flask remains as evidence of the Union Glass Works' production.

GIX–47. Scroll. *Obverse:* within the scroll medallion "R. KNOWLES & CO" on the left side (the "CO" in smaller capital letters than the balance of the inscription) and "Union Factory" on the right side. "SOUTH WHEELING" appears in circular form surrounding "VA" in the center of the medallion. There is a large 8-pointed star above. *Reverse:* a large conventional, modified fleur-de-lis ornament, with a large 8-pointed star above. Pint. Color: aquamarine. Extremely rare. 1849–50.

70. McCARTY & TORREYSON, *Wellsburg, formerly Charlestown, (West) Virginia*

Like that of so many other glasshouses, the history of the glasshouse operated as McCarty & Torreyson is obscure. Both these men appear to have been part of a group of Irish glassmen who migrated to this country and became associated with the glasshouse that had been established in 1813 by Isaac Duvall. It is possible that the firm may have merged with another called the Riverside Glass House. In any event, by 1842 McCarty and Torreyson apparently bought out the interest of the other members of the concern and thereafter produced a wide variety of bottles, including a number of Figured Flasks. Just how long the firm operated is not known, but it did produce at least three marked flasks, listed below, and because of their similarity to these three, other Jenny Lind flasks are attributed to the firm.

GIX–48. Scroll. *Obverse:* "M'CARTY & TORREYSON" in an arc above a star and the word "MANUFACTURERS" in a straight line above "WELLSBURG, V A." in

a concave arc. *Reverse:* sunburst. Color: light bluish green. Scarce. ca. 1842.

GIX–49. Scroll. Like GIX–48, but without star and ornament. Quart. Color: light green. Rare.

GIX–50. Scroll. Similar to GIX–49; the reverse is plain. Quart. Color: light bluish green. Rare.

Because the forms are so similar to those listed above (GIX–48, 49, and 50), flasks GI–108, 109, and 110, containing the bust of Jenny Lind, are also attributed to this factory.

71. THE KENTUCKY GLASS WORKS, *Louisville, Kentucky, ca. 1850–55; and* LOUISVILLE GLASS WORKS, *ca. 1855–73*

A search of Louisville newspapers and histories has established that, despite vague reports of a glasshouse there in 1814,[162] there was no glassworks in that city until 1850. But, according to *The History of Louisville . . .* by Ben Casseday, there was one glass-*cutting* works in Louisville by 1840, and a second was established in 1845. The latter was the firm of H. & T. Hunter, which apparently produced a wide variety of cut glass on blanks obtained from Pittsburgh.[163] Evidence of Hunter's glass-cutting activities is to be found almost continuously in the Louisville Directory from 1844 to 1870, but these directories list no glass factories through 1849.[164]

The first evidence of a glasshouse operating in Louisville is found in the *Seventh Federal Census for 1850*, which lists a glass factory there employing 50 workmen, 21 of whom are listed as glassblowers, which is a very high percentage of the total number of workmen. The specific date of the establishment of this factory is not known, but a listing in the 1850 census verifies that it was in operation in that year, and was *possibly* established in late 1849. The following advertisement, which (with its misspelling) appeared in the *Louisville Morning Courier,* August 12, 1850, furnishes a few more details about the factory and its founders:

KENTUCKY GLASS WORKS.

TAYLOR, STANGER, RAMSRY & CO., Manufacturers of Vials, Demijohns, Porter and other Bottles, of every description, are now in full operation and ready to receive orders, at their establishment on Clay, near Washington st., Louisville. Orders left at Cas eday & Hopkins' store, on Main, near Third street, will be promptly attended to.
Particular attention paid to private Moulds. au12 dly

The men listed in the firm name were probably James Taylor, John Stanger, and Joseph Ramsey, Jr., since their names are also listed in Louisville directories of the period and/or in subsequent advertisements of the firm. The following are listed in the directories as glassblowers: William Doyle, John Stanger, Gottleopold, Joseph Ramsey, Jr., Thomas Greiner, and Frederick Mowrey. Adam Bedenburg is listed as a pot maker and John Reilly and H. Adernechter as laborers. Probably most of these men migrated southward to Louisville from Pittsburgh, Wheeling, or one of the Ohio factories such as Zanesville, where they may have learned their trade.

As in the case of so many newly founded glasshouses, this fledgling enterprise soon found itself in difficulties, possibly for lack of sufficient capital or of capable administration. In any event, in November 1850, just a few months after the date of the advertisement quoted above, the original partnership was dissolved and the company reorganized. At that time George L. Douglass, a Louisville planter and presumably a man of wealth, joined the firm. The original factory name, Kentucky Glass Works, was retained, but the firm name was changed to Douglass and Taylor, suggesting a major investment on the part of Douglass. An advertisement by the new concern on November 28, 1850, notes the change in ownership, and also provides us with at least a limited knowledge of the products of the factory:[165]

KENTUCKY GLASS WORKS

Geo. L. Douglass and James Taylor having purchased the above works, have formed a partnership, under the name and style of Douglass and Taylor.

They have a good stock of ware on hand, and will fill promptly orders for all description of green and black glassware, consisting of fancy and plain vials of every description; Packing, Porter, Mineral and Wine Bottles, Pickle and other Jars, Flasks and Demijohns.
   Particular attention paid to private moulds.
   Orders by mail, or left at Casseday and Hopkins store on Main near Third Street or at the Works on Clay Street near Main will receive prompt attention.

The firm continued in business in this style, presumably prospering to a degree, until about 1855. An advertisement in the *Louisville Directory* for 1855/56[166] notes a change in the firm name to Douglass, Rutherford & Co. At the same time the factory was called the Louisville Glass Works. The works remained on Clay Street, near Main, but according to the advertisement in Ill. 33, its warehouse was then on the east side of Second Street, between Main and Market streets. The proprietors included—in addition to George Douglass—John Stanger and William Doyle (two of the glassblowers from the original firm) and two newcomers, William Douglass and Thomas Rutherford. The latter, apparently a relative of John M. Rutherford, then a member of the Exchange Banking Office, presumably added financial strength to the company.

In 1856 or 1857[167] Dr. John A. Krack, who later became prominent in Louisville business and civic circles, purchased a half-interest in the concern and served as its principal administrator until 1873. From 1856 or 1857 until 1865, the Louisville Glass Works was operated as Krack, Stanger & Co.[168] Krack, a native of Baltimore, had received his medical degree in Louisville in 1850; he owned and operated a drugstore on the northwest corner of

Shelby and Market streets from 1852 to 1857. Therefore he probably ordered apothecary wares and bottles from the local glassworks.[169] An advertisement of the firm in the 1859/60 Louisville Directory contains an interesting illustration of their works, Ill. 34, which remained at their original location; the company relocated their warehouse adjacent to the factory at the southeast corner of Clay and Franklin streets.

Advertisements during the following ten years, up to about 1869, suggest that this was probably the company's most prosperous period. In addition to flasks and bottles, a wide variety of other glassware was advertised, including coal-oil lamps, trimmings, and tumblers, as well as glassware for druggists, confectioners, and grocers. In 1865 the works also supplied all the insulators for the first telegraph and fire alarm system in Louisville.[170] By 1865 or 1866 the firm name had become J. A. Krack & Co. In *Williamson's Annual Directory of the City of Louisville, 1865 and 1866* the firm advertised: "J. A. Krack & Co., Louisville Glass Works, Manufacturers and dealers in window glass, vials and bottles, coal oil lamps and trimmings, tumblers, etc. Factories: cor. Clay and Franklin Sts. Salesrooms; on Main St. above 4th. (north side)."[171]

Sometime before 1869 John Stanger withdrew from the company, and in 1869 Krack was joined by Leander S. and William Reed; the firm name was changed to Krack & Reed & Co. In 1871 Dr. Krack withdrew, and the Reed brothers operated the company as L. S. Reed & Brother. Apparently from about 1869 onward the business began to fail. One of the Reeds left the company shortly after 1871 and joined Krack, who had been appointed as assistant city assessor. From 1874 to 1875 the Louisville Glass Works was located at Twenty-eighth and Montgomery streets.

In 1879 the address was High Street, between Twenty-seventh and Twenty-eighth streets. In 1880, while located at that address, the firm name was changed to Louisville Plate Glass Works, after it was purchased and operated by the DePauw American Plate Glass Works, across the river from Louisville in Albany, Indiana.[172]

No marked flasks are known from the operation of the Kentucky Glass Works, but between 1850 and 1852 it is probable that the 2½-quart eagle flask marked "FARLEY & TAYLOR, RICHMOND, KY." was made there, as well as an almost identical unmarked flask of the same capacity, both of which are described below. Farley and Taylor, merchants in the 1840s, operated a general store in Richmond, Kentucky, from 1850 to 1852, when their partnership was dissolved. These flasks were undoubtedly made to their order for the liquor they bottled and sold. Numerous flasks marked "LOUISVILLE GLASS WORKS" can be definitely ascribed to that firm, as well as a number of unmarked flasks that are closely related in design. They are listed below.

Kentucky Glass Works flasks:

GII–27: *Obverse:* eagle with wings outstretched, three arrows in right talon, olive branch in left talon, shield on

33. Advertisement for the Louisville Glass Works of Douglass, Rutherford & Co. from *The Louisville Directory and Annual Business Advertiser* for the years 1855/56. *The Magazine ANTIQUES*

34. Illustration of the Louisville, Ky., glassworks of Krack, Stanger & Co. The original is in the collection of the Louisville Public Library. *The Magazine ANTIQUES*

breast with curved ribbon above, and elongated, scalloped elliptical ornament below. *Reverse:* "FARLEY & TAYLOR" above "RICHMOND, KY."; otherwise plain. 2½ quart. Colors: cornflower-blue, light blue, colorless, light emerald-green, olive-green, and aquamarine. Probably made at the Kentucky Glass Works between 1850 and 1852. Extremely rare.

GII–26. *Obverse:* American eagle, head turned to left, with wings raised and outstretched, shield on breast, two arrows in right talon and ill-formed laurel leaf in the left; a curved ribbon containing 5 starlike ornaments extends from the beak of the eagle; below is a large, elongated stellar ornament. *Reverse:* the same as the obverse. Quart. Colors: emerald-green, olive-yellow, brilliant yellow-green, clear golden amber, deep amber, aquamarine and deep bluish green, and light blue. Common. Possibly made at the Kentucky Glass Works, ca. 1850–55.

GII–22. *Obverse:* eagle with wings outstretched, curved pennant containing the word "UNION" coming almost from the beak, the eagle's head turned to the left; below the eagle an oval frame contains a large, elongated, 8-pointed star. *Reverse:* a large lyre with two semicircular rows of 4-pointed stars above. Pint. Colors: brilliant green, light green, yellow-green, and deep aquamarine. Rare. Possibly made at the Kentucky Glass Works, ca. 1850–55.

GII–25. *Obverse:* eagle and ribbon, similar to GII–22, but instead of the word "UNION" there is random ribbing. *Reverse:* same as obverse. Pint. Colors: aquamarine, golden amber, moonstone, and olive-yellow. Scarce. Possibly made at the Kentucky Glass Works, Louisville, Ky., ca. 1850–55.

Flasks attributed to the Louisville Glass Works, ca. 1855–73:

GII–29. *Obverse:* eagle in small plain medallion surrounded by vertical ribbing. *Reverse:* plain vertical ribbing, no eagle or medallion. Pint. Colors: amethyst bordering on puce, aquamarine, colorless, pale yellow-green, and light green. Extremely rare.

GII–30. *Obverse:* eagle in a small round plain medallion surrounded by vertical ribs. *Reverse:* vertically ribbed, no medallion. Half-pint. Colors: yellowish olive-green, pale yellow-green, aquamarine, and medium blue. Very rare.

GII–31. *Obverse:* eagle in an irregular oval medallion surrounded by vertical ribbing. *Reverse:* same as obverse. Quart. Colors: emerald-green, medium green, aquamarine, very pale green, and clear deep green with a yellow tone. Comparatively scarce.

GII–32. Similar to GII–31, but of pint capacity. Colors: very pale green, yellowish olive-green, deep aquamarine, brilliant green, and colorless with green tinge. Rare.

The above four flasks are attributed to the Louisville (Kentucky) Glass Works on the basis of the following six flasks of similar design that *are* marked "LOUISVILLE KY. GLASS WORKS":

GII–33. *Obverse:* eagle in an oval medallion surrounded by vertical ribbing. *Reverse:* same as obverse, except the plain oval contains the words "LOUISVILLE" in a slight arc above "KY" with GLASS WORKS" in a concave arc below. Half-pint. Colors: deep golden amber, red-amber, olive-amber, dark amber, very pale green, deep green, blue-green, and aquamarine. Comparatively scarce.

GII–34. Similar to GII–33, but of pint capacity. Colors: deep olive-yellow, olive-green, light green, and aquamarine. Extremely rare.

GII–35. *Obverse:* eagle flying to the right in a large plain oval, surrounded by vertical ribbing, except for a plain 6-pointed scalloped panel below containing the words "LOUISVILLE KY" in a slight arc at the top and "GLASS WORKS" in a slight arc below. *Reverse:* like the obverse, but no design or inscription in the two plain panels. Quart. Colors: golden amber, deep amber, deep grass-green, deep emerald-green, blue-green, and aquamarine. Common.

GII–36. Similar to GII–35, but of pint capacity. Colors: olive-yellow, yellow-green, amber, olive-green, pale blue, and aquamarine. Common.

GII–114. *Obverse:* eagle with small head to the left and narrow pennant extending from the right in a shallow arc above, with a large oval frame below the eagle containing the inscription "LOUISVILLE" following the upper contour of the frame, with "KY" in the center at the bottom of the frame. *Reverse:* like the obverse, but with the inscription "GLASS" at the top of the oval frame and "WORKS" at the bottom center of the frame. Quart. Colors: aquamarine, green, and light yellow-green. Scarce.

GII–115. *Obverse* and *reverse:* similar to GII–114, but of pint capacity. Colors: aquamarine, light olive-amber, and light emerald-green. Scarce.

The following marked scroll flasks are also attributed to the Louisville Glass Works and were probably made between 1855 and about 1873:

GIX–6. *Obverse:* two large 6-pointed stars, heart-shaped scrolls with the inscription "LOUISVILLE KY" between the scrolls. *Reverse:* same as obverse, but "GLASS WORKS" appears in a straight line between the scrolls. Quart. Colors: light green with a yellow tone, olive-green, and aquamarine. Comparatively scarce.

GIX–7. *Obverse* and *reverse:* very similar to GIX–6, but the lower stars on both the obverse and the reverse are slightly smaller, and the lettering is slightly different.

The base of this flask also has two nipples on one side of the straight base mold mark. Quart. Colors: aquamarine and deep amber. Scarce.

GIX–8. *Obverse:* 8-pointed star at the center, with a smaller indistinct star above; heart-shaped scrolls contain the inscription "LOUISVILLE KY" in a straight line. *Reverse:* similar to obverse, but the inscription is "GLASS WORKS" in a straight line. Pint. Colors: light green, aquamarine, moonstone, yellow-green, and canary. Comparatively scarce.

GIX–9. *Obverse* and *reverse:* similar to GIX–8, except that the inscriptions "LOUISVILLE KY" and "GLASS WORKS" are smaller and are in curved lines. Pint. Colors: golden amber, reddish amber, citron, yellow-green, and aquamarine. Comparatively scarce.

72. KEYSTONE GLASS WORKS, *A. R. Samuels, Philadelphia, Pennsylvania, ca. 1866–ca. 1874*

Little is known about the Keystone Glass Works or Adam R. Smith, who apparently established it in time to be listed in the 1867 Philadelphia City Directory as a glass manufacturer. And that little comes from city directories, advertisements in them, and Freedly's *Philadelphia and Its Manufactures* (1867). From 1845 through 1859 a John Samuels was listed as "glassblower"; in 1860 he appeared as a dealer. From 1850 through 1860 Adam Samuel (no *s*) was listed as "glassblower," and in 1861 his widow was listed. The addresses of the two blowers indicate they were employed in one of the three factories then operating in Kensington—the Union Glass Works, the Dyottville Glass Works, or the Kensington Vial & Bottle Works of Sheets and Duffy. It seems probable that Adam R. Samuels was the son of either John or, with an *s* added to his surname, Adam.

Be that as it may, Adam R. Samuels first appeared in the City Directory of 1860 as a dealer in "lamps and sealing jars"; in 1862 he was listed as a dealer in "fruits" (presumably fruit jars). It may be that he had the agency for the fruit jars said to have been produced by a Mr. Heller in the Medford, New Jersey, glassworks. However, Adam R. Samuels has been identified by Van Rensselaer and Knittle as the Samuels of Yarnall and Samuels of Philadelphia, who in 1863 bought the Medford works into which so much money went for improvements that none was left for operating.[173] The following year Adam R. Samuels appeared as a merchant; in 1865 as a dealer in airtight stoppers; and in 1867 as a glass manufacturer—the Keystone Glass Works on the southeast corner of Howard and Oxford streets, Philadelphia. In 1874 this factory was being operated by William H. and John B. Samuels, who—it seems probable—were sons or nephews. That was its last listing.

Present evidence would seem to indicate that the mainstay of the Keystone Glass Works was the fruit jar. In 1867 five different "patent jars" were being manufactured: Franklin, Kline (1863), Mason, Haller (1860), and Willoughby's (1859).[174] Just which of the Mason jars of the period A. R. Samuels produced in his Keystone Glass Works cannot be stated with any certainty. Haller fruit jars are not listed by Dr. Julian Toulouse, doubtless because none appeared in the collections on which he drew for his book.[175] One wonders if "Haller" could have been "Heller," the man said to have turned the Medford, New Jersey, works into a fruit jar factory.

The Mason and Haller patented jars were not mentioned in an 1870 Keystone advertisement in the Philadelphia City Directory, but Samuels stated he was the "Proprietor of Willoughby's, Kline's and Franklin Fruit Jars." It seems possible that he had acquired the rights to these jars prior to that date. Dr. Toulouse lists a Willoughby's Stopple patented January 4, 1859, and says, "This sealing device was used in many jars during the 1860–70 period." It doubtless was the type on the Willoughby's produced by Samuels. According to Dr. Toulouse, A. R. Kline of Philadelphia patented a glass stopper with rubber seal that fit into the tapered neck of a handmade round jar with "pressed laid-on-ring in blue and blue green." He lists also a Franklin fruit jar of about 1865, with Mason shoulder seal on a handmade round jar with ground lip, occurring in blue-green and aquamarine. On the side an opensided circle is formed by the word "FRANKLIN" above and "FRUIT JAR" below. He suggests as a possible maker Gillinder's Franklin Flint Glass Company (1861–1930).[176] That company, however, was a producer of flint-glass tableware and fancy ornamental glass, not bottles and jars. In the light of Samuels's statement, it seems safe to say the jar described by Dr. Toulouse was a product of the Keystone Glass Works.

One calabash bottle in the Historical category has been recorded and attributed to the Keystone Glass Works because of the initials "A. R. S." on the eagle side. In the Charts it is GIV–42, which has on the reverse a flying eagle with shield and pennants, thunderbolt, and laurel spray above "A. R. S." and on the obverse 13 stars above, and laurel sprays flanking a large shield with clasped hands above a small square and compass, in turn above "UNION" in oval frame. Because of the square and compass, this calabash of the Civil War period and later was charted in the Masonic group IV. It is now known that the bottles probably commemorated the Junior Order of United American Mechanics, whose insignia was the square and compass and clasped hands within shield.

73. CLYDE GLASS WORKS, *Clyde, New York, ca. 1864–80*

In 1827 William S. De Zeng and James R. Rees formed the partnership of De Zeng & Rees, for the manufacture of glass in Clyde, a town favorably situated along the Erie Canal. De Zeng & Rees began operations and produced the first glass in the fall of 1828. The principal product of their factory was window glass, produced by the cylinder, or broad glass, method. The firm continued in business until the 1860s, producing window glass, with probably some bottles as by-products.

In 1864 a bottle glasshouse was built in Clyde by Orrin Southwick and Almon Woods, who operated as Southwick & Woods. Their products were hollow wares of all sorts, principally bottles, fruit jars, and the like. A short time later the firm became known as Southwick & Reed, the partners being Orrin Southwick and Charles W. Reed. About this time the window glass factory started in 1828 by De Zeng was combined with the bottle glasshouse under the name of Southwick, Reed & Co. The partners in this firm were William C. Ely, Dr. Linus Ely, Orrin Southwick, and—later—Charles W. Reed, John Schindler, and George H. Hoyt. One of the principal products of this factory was Mason jars made under the November 30, 1858, Mason patent.

On July 24, 1873, the factory burned, but it was immediately rebuilt. It was enlarged and repaired in 1878, and the old cornerstone replaced with a new one on August 10 of that year. Owners of the firm at that time were Charles W. Reed, George Hoyt, William C. Ely, and John Schindler. In 1880 Mr. Reed retired, and the firm became Ely, Son & Hoyt, Charles D. Ely having joined the firm. After William C. Ely died in 1886, another son also entered the business and the firm name became William C. Ely's Sons & Hoyt. The firm continued to operate under this style until 1895, when the manufacture of window glass was discontinued. Then it was incorporated as the Clyde Glass Works. Its first corporate directors were Charles D. Ely, George H. Hoyt, George H. Hoyt, Jr., G. R. Bacon, James R. Miller, William W. Ledd, and Frank H. Warren.

In that same year (1895), a tank system of glassmaking was placed in service, using fuel oil for heat, replacing the old clay melting pots. A continuous gas producer was installed in 1903, along with new glass melting tanks. Mason jars, of the revised style, were one of the chief products of the factory, which, when run at full capacity, gave employment to about 85 men, 45 boys, and 6 girls. The weekly payroll amounted to approximately $1,000. Some of the blowers received as much as $8 per day.

George O. Baker and William A. Hunt joined the firm, apparently in 1903. Unfortunately, the development of the automatic bottle-making machine, invented by Mike Owens, and the fact that the plant was not easily accessible to the railroad, spelled its doom. In July 1915 the firm suspended operations with 80 tons of glass still in its tanks. Although many efforts were made to revive the works, they all failed. The factory buildings were finally cleared away and a General Electric Plant was built on the site.[177] Today (1975), in Clyde, Parker Hannifin Company operates where once the old glassworks was located.

Morrison notes, in a revised edition of his *History of Clyde*, published in 1969: "A strike by the glass-blowers was settled in August 1862. Ten and twelve year old boys struck the bottleworks in October 1866." He also mentions that "glass puzzles and many walking canes were made by the workmen when time would permit."

A picture of the Clyde Glass Works on a postcard, which probably dates from about 1890, was secured by George S. McKearin along with four funnels of clear, aqua, and amber-colored glass said to have been made at the works. They came from a dealer, who had bought them from the niece of Mr. Bacon, at one time president of the Clyde Glass Works and its superintendent (according to this niece) from 1880 until—and probably including—1910, when he retired.

The following three marked flasks were produced at the Clyde Glass Works:

GXV–1. *Obverse:* "CLYDE GLASS WORKS" in a semicircle above "N.Y." in larger letters. *Reverse:* plain. Quart. Colors: amber, aquamarine, colorless, and green. Scarce. Probably 1864–ca. 1880.

GXV–2. *Obverse* and *reverse:* like GXV–1, but smaller. Pint. Color: amber. Scarce. 1864–ca. 1880.

GXV–3. *Obverse* and *reverse:* like GXV–1, but the letters are slender. Half-pint. Color: amber. Scarce. 1864–ca. 1880.

74. THE NEW GRANITE GLASS WORKS, *Mill Village, Stoddard, New Hampshire, 1861–71*

The New Granite Glass Works was the last glass factory to be established in Stoddard, though it was not the last to survive. This company was organized in 1860 or 1861 by George W. Foster, the son of Joseph Foster, who had established the first glasshouse in the area at "The Box" in South Stoddard in 1842. It was in operation at least by May 20, 1861, the date of the first entry in the original payroll book, still in possession of George Foster's grandson.[178] Of the six men who joined George in the venture, four were Fosters: Charles W., Joseph E., another Joseph, and William W. George managed the works; Charles and William were glassblowers. Their youngest brother, Joseph E., who was 14 years old in 1861, was responsible for making the wicker covers for carboys and demijohns. Henry Gilman Foster, George's older brother, is listed on the payroll only from October 7, 1861, through November 11, 1861. At sometime prior to his death in Manchester, New Hampshire, in 1863, Joseph, the father, also worked at the factory as a blower.

According to a letter and a business card (Ills. 35 and 36) still in the possession of a descendant,[179] the New Granite Glass Works made essentially the same products as the other Stoddard factories: wines, porters, flasks, snuffs, inks, schnapps, fruit jars, and cider and medicine bottles, as well as willow-covered demijohns of all sizes. In addition, the firm also advertised glass telegraph and lightning rod insulators (Ill. 36). It is interesting to speculate whether the telegraph insulators were mold-blown or pressed—if, indeed, any were ever made there, which seems doubtful. If any were made, it seems likely that at that date they would have been pressed—a new dimension in glassmaking in New Hampshire. Three distinct items produced at the New Granite Glass Works of particular interest to flask

New Granite Glass Works.

GEORGE W. FOSTER,

MANUFACTURER OF

BLACK GLASS BOTTLES, AND PRESERVE JARS,

OF EVERY DESCRIPTION,

Such as Wines, Porters, Flasks, Snuffs, Inks, Schnapps, Fruit
Jars, Cider and Medicine Bottles ; Also, Willow
Covered Demijohns, of all Sizes, &c. &c.

ALSO,

Glass Telegraph and Lightning Rod Insulators

Of any Pattern or Weight,

STODDARD, N. H.

N. B. Particular attention given to Private Moulds.

35. Trade card of George W. Foster at his New Granite Glass Works. A wide variety of glassware typical of green-glass bottle houses is advertised.

collectors are the so-called flag flasks, described below and in more detail in the Charts.

According to John M. Foster and Kay Fox,[180] in late 1862 George Foster left Stoddard to go to Boston to establish a bottle and demijohn distributing center there, taking up residence in nearby Roxbury. One of his activities was the establishment of a "Bottle and Demi-john Warehouse" in 1862 at 106 State Street. He later moved his operations to 14 Blackstone Street in Boston. About two years later he, and apparently his brothers, sold their interest in the New Granite Glass Works to Charles B. Barrett, a Boston liquor dealer who had been one of their best customers. Barrett, who was first listed in the Boston Directory in 1857, continued to be listed under the wine and liquor business until 1890, when he was recorded as an importer of German peat moss. George's brothers remained with the concern as glassblowers even after its change in ownership. Barrett continued to operate the New Granite Glass Works until 1871, when fire destroyed the factory.[181] It was never rebuilt. This was probably because of the growing demand by the public for "clear" bottles, which had never been made in Stoddard, apparently because it was uneconomical to purify the local raw materials, as would have been necessary to produce such glass. With the cessation of activities in the New Granite Glass Works, glass manufacturing came to an end in Mill Village. However, it continued until 1873 at the Weeks & Gilson factory in "The Box" in South Stoddard.

With the exception of the telegraph and lightning rod insulators advertised by George W. Foster (which may not have been actually made, since none has come to light to the best knowledge of the authors), the New Granite Glass Works produced much the same types of wares as were being made in the other Stoddard factories. A number of these are mentioned on Foster's business cards and in the letter he distributed to prospective customers dated Stoddard, N.H., June 1861. Similar wares are mentioned in the advertisement of C. B. Barrett (Ill. 37), many of which he undoubtedly used in his own liquor business, as attested by the following statement contained in his advertisement:

I am the only manufacturer in New England who sells his own wares, Therefore can give my customers the agent's commission. With my long experience, improvement and enlargement of my Factories I am now prepared to supply the trade with better ware, from my new and improved molds, at Less Price than any other house in the State.

The flasks listed below are attributed to the New Granite Glass Works:

GX–27. *Obverse:* large American flag to the right with nine stripes and thirteen stars. *Reverse:* inscription in a deep arch "NEW GRANITE GLASS WORKS" enclosing "STODDARD" in an arc above the letters "N.H." Pint. Colors: amber and olive-amber. Rare. 1861–71.

GX–28. *Obverse:* similar to number GX–27. *Reverse:* similar to GX–27. Half-pint. Colors: amber and olive-amber. Rare. 1861–71.

GX–29. *Obverse:* American flag bearing 16 stars and 13 bars on pole on the left. *Reverse:* inscription in a deep arch as in GX–27, "NEW GRANITE GLASS WORKS" enclosing in an irregular slight arc, "STODDARD" above the letters "N.H." Pint. Colors: clear amber and deep olive-green. Extremely rare. 1861–71.

75. ARSENAL GLASS WORKS, *Pittsburgh, Pennsylvania, 1865–69/70*

The only evidence known today that testifies to the existence of an Arsenal Glass Works in Pittsburgh is very tangible indeed: it consists of the molded inscription "ARSENAL GLASS WORKS/PITTS. PA" on three Pike's

NEW GRANITE GLASS WORKS.

STODDARD, N. H. June, 1861.

F. H. Palmer,

Dr. Sir

I would respectfully inform you, that I am fitting up the above named WORKS, for the Manufacture of BLACK GLASS BOTTLES, FRUIT JARS, and TELEGRAPH INSULATORS of every description,—

Such as Wine, Porter, Ink, Snuff, Schnapps, Cider and Medicine Bottles; ALSO, Willow Covered Demijohns,—Wholesale and Retail,

All of which I will guarantee shall be as good as any Glass Ware made in the United States, or any other Country.

I shall pay particular attention, also, to the Manufacture of GLASS TELEGRAPH and LIGHTNING ROD INSULATORS, and to those using INSULATORS, I would refer them to the Montreal Telegraph Company, at Montreal. C. E. for information as to the quality of those I manufactured at my Canada Glass Works, St. Johns, C. E.

The advantages which will be derived by purchasing from me, must be evident to every buyer of Glass, as I have been a Glass Bottle-Blower, and Manufacturer of Glass for nearly twenty years, and having a thorough practical knowledge of the business, so that I can manage my own establishment, which will enable me to sell Glass at prices somewhat less than you can purchase for, at other Manufactories,

I shall be in operation in August next, and will then be prepared to fill any orders which you may favor me with.

Trusting, Dear Sir, that you will give the above your favorable attention, and waiting the pleasure of your esteemed orders.

I am very respectfully yours.

GEORGE W. FOSTER.

36. Printed letter circulated by George W. Foster in June 1861, after his return to Stoddard, New Hampshire, from Canada; he founded the New Granite Glass Works in Stoddard.

38. Iron mold consisting of two pieces hinged at the base, for producing the "Iodine Spring Water" bottle made in the South Stoddard Glass Works. It is illustrated here to indicate the types of molds undoubtedly also used at the New Granite Glass Works and at other glass works in Stoddard. *Collection of Mr. Karl G. Upton*

37. Advertisement from the *Portland Directory* by C. B. Barrett, who purchased the New Granite Glass Works from George Foster, probably in part to assure himself, as a liquor dealer, of an ample supply of bottles.

Peak flasks: a quart, GXI–13; and two pints, GXI–14 and GXI–15, for each of which there was a mold. In his careful researches, the late L. Earl Dambach found no record of a glassworks so named; no advertisements by such a works; no listing in a city directory. Therefore he concluded— logically, it seems to me—that the name was given locally to a Pittsburgh glassworks operating near the United States Arsenal. And, it might be added, apparently adopted unofficially by the proprietors of the works, who used it in three of their flask molds.

Mr. Dambach kindly sent to us his bits of evidence gleaned from Thurston's Pittsburgh directories and Wood & Company's *Pittsburgh Business Almanac*. In Thurston for 1865/66, Charles Jeremy & Company were listed as "glass manufacturers" between Borough (Forty-first) and Chestnut (Forty-second) streets, a city block distance from the United States Arsenal (also called Allegheny Arsenal and Pittsburgh Arsenal) situated between Thirty-ninth and Fortieth streets. It would appear that one member of the company was George Heitzman, who was listed as a glassblower from 1863 through 1872 at least. From 1867 through 1869 the Wood & Company almanac listed "Jeremy, Heitsman & Co. Glassmanufactures," but the address given was Lafayette Alley, Lawrenceville (then and now [1962] the arsenal district). Perhaps there were offices or warehouses at one location and glassworks at the other; a second works seems unlikely. Last, Thurston's directory for 1869/70 indicates that Charles Jeremy was no longer active in glass manufacture but was listed as a real estate agent. Possibly he had disposed of his interest, or sold the factory, to W. F. Modes, who named it the Aetna Glass Works. Be that as it may, the Aetna Glass Works at "42nd St. Late Chestnut" was listed in the same 1869/70 Directory that carried also W. F. Modes's advertisement of bottles, demijohns, porter, ale, soda bottles, and also "Victor" and "Triumph" fruit jars. Inasmuch as this apparently is the only record of the Aetna Glass Works, it would appear that Mr. Modes, too, was unsuccessful.

It seems safe to conclude, at least tentatively, that the three recorded Pike's Peak flasks inscribed with the name Arsenal Glass Works were blown at the glassworks located near the Arsenal in Pittsburgh and brought out either by Charles Jeremy & Company or Jeremy, Heitzman & Co.

76. TIBBY BROTHERS GLASS WORKS, *1866–ca. 1904*

The first mention of a Tibby in Pittsburgh city directories appears in the 1863/64 one, in which John Tibby is listed as a glassblower living at Mulberry Alley and Carroll. In the next year, his address was Carroll near Kent, but the entry in the 1866/67 directory notes the address as at the corner of Canal and Mulberry Alley. It is possible that the previous reference to Carroll should have been Canal, since that is the old name for Eleventh Street in downtown Pittsburgh.[182] The directory of 1864/65 lists William Tibby as a glassblower living at 815 Penn Street, also a downtown address.

An 1870 Pittsburgh census includes a number of Tibbys, or Tibbeys, associated with either glass or flint glass manufacturing, all but one of them listed as having been born in Ireland. All are also listed with rather substantial personal and real estate holdings. It is interesting to note that, in the census, Tibby is spelled in three instances as Tibbey and in one as Tibby. James Tibbey, 40 years old, is listed with $8,000 of real estate and $18,000 as his personal estate, and with the occupation of glass manufacturing. Matthew Tibbey, 44, had no real estate but a personal estate valued at $3,500; his occupation was flint glass manufacturing. William Tibbey, 39, who was born in Pennsylvania, had no

Tibby Bros: Glassworks, Sharpsburg.

39. A watercolor titled *Tibby Bros. Glassworks, Sharpsburg, Pa.,* painted in Sharpsburg in 1880 by W. Heerlein. *Collections of Greenfield Village and the Henry Ford Museum, Dearborn, Michigan*

real estate but a $3,500 personal estate; his occupation is listed as glass manufacturing. John Tibby, 42, with real estate valued at $6,500 and a personal estate of $6,000, is listed as a flint glass manufacturer.[183]

According to Van Rensselaer,[184] Tibby Brothers was established in 1866, and operated two separate factories, one located at the corner of Twenty-second and Smallman streets in Pittsburgh; the second factory was in Sharpsburg. They are first listed in the Pittsburgh Directory of 1867/68 as manufacturers of flint-glass vials and the like, with offices at 90 Water Street and works at Lumber Street near Penn. The 1871/72 Directory lists the office address as 84 Water Street. In the 1872/73 Directory, James J., John, Matthew, and William were listed as "of Tibby Bros." According to the 1876/77 Directory, the office address was 13 Wood Street. The next directory available, 1884/85, describes the firm as "FLINT AND PRESCRIPTION GLASS WORKS, MAIN, O'HARA TWP."

Thurston, in his 1886 *Pittsburgh Progress. . . ,* lists Tibby Bros. Flint (Vial and Bottle or Druggists) Glass Works, with an office and firm in Sharpsburg, the firm operating two factories with two furnaces and a total of twenty pots.[185] The *1886 Atlas of the Vicinity of Pittsburgh and Allegheny* shows the Tibby Bros. Glass Works just east of Sharpsburg in O'Hara township, along the Allegheny River. The works consisted of five large frame buildings and a small one, located on a three-plus-acres site. This Tibby Bros. Glass Works appears in Ill. 39, as taken from a charming watercolor in the collection of Greenfield Village and the Henry Ford Museum, drawn by W. Heerlein and dated Sharpsburg, 1880.

Apparently Tibby Bros. prospered from the start. Contemporary accounts indicate that each of the four brothers was a practical glassman and a highly respected businessman of Allegheny County. The business consisted largely of flint prescription vials and bottles and druggist's wares. According to Van Rensselaer,[186] they employed a total of 175 hands in their two factories and by 1876 were producing ware annually in the amount of $200,000. Although the firm Tibby Bros. was no longer listed in the 1902/03 Directory, a biographical account of William C. Tibbey, published in 1904, states that he was secretary and general manager of Tibby Bros. in Sharpsburg.[187] He was the son of William Tibbey, one of the founders of Tibby Bros., born in Pittsburgh on April 24, 1866. According to this account, Tibby Bros. was still a flourishing concern, having a plant equipped with three furnaces, all in Sharpsburg, and employing about 250 men. It is not known just when the company went out of business, but presumably sometime early in the 20th century.

The following two marked flasks were products of Tibby Bros.:

GXIII–33. *Obverse:* sheaf of grain, very fine stalks, curving at the top to the right and left, bound about the middle. *Reverse:* plain. Pint. The base of this flask, in the form of a long oval depression, is marked "TIBBY BROs PITTS PA". Colorless. Rare. Probably 1866–ca. 1876.

GXIII–33a. *Obverse* and *reverse:* like GXIII–33. The base is also marked in the same way. Half-pint. Colorless. Rare. 1866–ca. 1876.

40. Letterhead of Tibby Brothers.

TIBBY BROTHERS,

MANUFACTURERS OF ALL KINDS OF

FLINT PRESCRIPTION VIALS, BOTTLES, FLASKS, ETC.,

Office and Works, SHARPSBURG, PA.

In a branch of industry which requires special training of a high order, technical knowledge and expert skill, the firm of Tibby Brothers has been accorded a very large measure of support as manufacturers. They enjoy a reputation and trade thoroughly national in extent and eminently creditable. They established their business originally in 1866, at Twenty-second Street, Pittsburg, with one furnace and six pots. In 1872 they built a ten pot furnace at Sharpsburg, Pa., and another of the same size in 1875, and a third in 1881. Their works now cover four acres of ground and give employment to two

CITRATE MAGNESIA.

MILK BOTTLE.

BEER BOTTLE.

MONOGRAM SQUARE.

GUYASUTA OVAL.

BOTTOM VIEW.

above requires the consumption of four hundred cars of coal, one hundred cars of sand, fifteen cars of lime, thirty-five cars of soda-ash, and ten cars of nitrate, making a total of material of eleven thousand tons, while the product amounts to three thousand tons, value $225,000. The labor for ten months amounts to $80,000. Catalogues and price-lists are furnished on application, and orders of whatever magnitude receive immediate and satisfactory attention. The co-partners John, William and Matthew Tibby, are among the most prominent and popular glassworkers in the country. The

hundred and thirty skilled workmen. The specialties of the firm include a vast variety of flint prescription vials, pickle and milk jars, catsups, beer, brandy and flasks, etc. Special attention is given to lettered ware of various kinds. The production of the firm is ably assisted by their four sons, J. R. W., J. S., J. K. M. and W. C. Tibby, in the management, thus insuring young blood in the management of affairs. Mail and telegraph address, P. O. Box 1022, Pittsburg, Pa.

41. An illustrated description of the Tibby Brothers firm that appeared in *Allegheny County, Pennsylvania; Illustrated*. . . . Pittsburgh, Pa. The Consolidated Illustrating Co., ca. 1896, p. 254. *Historical Society of Western Pennsylvania*

77. THE WHEELING GLASS WORKS, *North Wheeling, West Virginia, 1860–69*

George W. Robinson and his father, S. G. Robinson, purchased the debt-ridden firm of McAfee & Russell in 1860. This was the works originally built in 1848 by Thomas Sweeney, a Mr. Baker, and a Mr. Heburn in North Wheeling. It was sold in that same year to Tivis and Bankerd, of the Wheeling Glass Manufacturing Co., who manufactured window glass. Subsequently it passed through several other partnerships before the Robinsons bought it.[188]

The works was located at the foot of McLane Street, and a warehouse was maintained at 75 Main Street.[189] The Directory of 1867/68 lists George W. Robinson as "Manufacturer of Window Glass, Druggist Glassware, Fruit Jars, Flasks, Bottles." In the Directory for the following year, 1868/69, in which the firm was last listed, the description reads: "Manufacturers and dealers in window glass, green and black glass bottles, druggist's ware." The address was listed as 8 Main Street. Possibly the works was then idle for two years before the Franklin Glass Company bought it in 1872. In 1881 it became the Wheeling Window Glass Co. and apparently was devoted solely to making window glass. In the following years, the North Wheeling Glass Co. took over the factory and manufactured bottles. The name was changed in 1919 to the North Wheeling Glass Bottle Co.; the firm failed in 1925, when the bank foreclosed. The following year the Eastern Glass Co., Inc., operated the factory for a short time before it was finally abandoned.

The following three flasks are known to have been made at George W. Robinson's firm, the Wheeling Glass Works:

GXIII–26. *Obverse:* dog's head and neck in profile, with "GEO. W. ROBINSON" in an arc above an "N⁰8 Main Sᵀ" above "Wheeling W. Va." in straight lines. Pint. Color: aquamarine. Rare. 1868–69.

GXIII–26A. Like GXIII–26, but of quart capacity. Color: aquamarine. Rare. 1868–69.

GXV–18. *Obverse:* plain except for the inscription "GEO. W. ROBINSON" in an arc with "No. 75" in a straight line below and "Main St. W. Va." in a concave arc below that. *Reverse:* plain. Quart. Color: aquamarine. Rare. 1867–68.

GXV–19. Like GXV–18, but of pint capacity. Color: aquamarine. Rare. 1867–68.

GXV–20. Like GXV–18 and 19, but half-pint. Color: aquamarine. Rare. 1867–68.

78. INDIANAPOLIS GLASS WORKS CO., *Indianapolis, Indiana, ca. 1870–77*

Very little is known about this glassworks. Indianapolis City directories from 1870 to 1877 list the company as located at the corner of Kentucky Avenue and Sharps Street, along with the following names: V. Butsch, James Dickson, Fred Ballman, Charles Brinkman, Fred Ritzenger, and Joseph Deschler.[190] No listing for the factory occurs after 1877. The factory may have ceased operations in 1876, despite being listed in the 1877 Indianapolis City Directory. According to a letter from George Austin: "Indiana Historical Society says the plant was in operation from 1870 to 1876."[191]

The only other reference to this company known to me at the present is from W. R. Holloway's *Indianapolis. . . ,* published in 1870,[192] which says:

In 1869 a company of six German residents was formed to make glassware here. In the fall and winter their building was erected and furnace prepared, and they began blowing bottles, vials and fruit jars, with such entire success that they soon got an order from Philadelphia for $40,000 worth of fruit jars. The sand was brought at first from the Fall Creek Bluffs near Pendleton, and was a friable sandstone needing to be "stamped" to be used—but latterly river sand has been successfully used and is cheaper. During the past summer they have erected another blowing house and have just put up an extensive warehouse for the storing of their goods. The works cover nearly a half square on Kentucky Avenue and Merrill Street.

Why, after such a propitious start, this factory remained in business for only six or seven years is a mystery at this time. It is possible that the works burned and were never rebuilt. Fruit jars were apparently one of the company's major products, and they also probably produced the usual variety of bottles and vials currently in demand. Two plain flasks marked Indianapolis Glass Works indicate they produced flasks. These are described as follows:

GXV–9. *Obverse:* plain except for the inscription, in a deep arch: "INDIANAPOLISGLASSWORKS"—with no space between the words. *Reverse:* plain. Quart. Colors: aquamarine and strong green. Rare.

GXV–10. *Obverse:* plain except for the inscription, in a semicircle, "INDIANAPOLIS. GLASS WORKS" in small letters. *Reverse:* plain. Pint. Colors: aquamarine and light peacock-blue. Rare.

79. RICHMOND GLASS WORKS, *Richmond, Virginia, 1855–65*

The presence of an extremely rare pint flask bearing an anchor on the obverse with a pennant above and below containing the words "RICHMOND" and "GLASSWORKS" respectively (Ills. 43A and B)[193] has long raised the question as to the whereabouts and history of the factory in which it was made. It had been speculated that it might have been located in either Richmond, Virginia, or Richmond, Kentucky. As a result of the research and archaeological investigations (Ill. 42) of James Gergat,[194] this question has been settled. Mr. Gergat has found that there was not just one glasshouse in Richmond, Virginia, but two glasshouses operated by four firms.

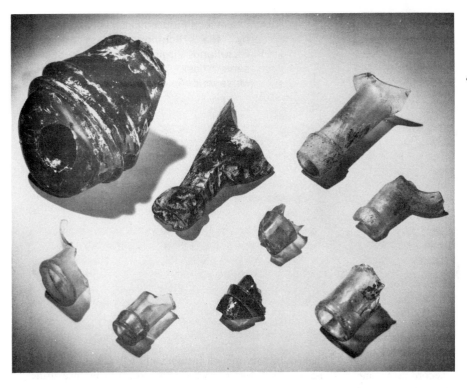

42. Fragments of bottle necks and rims and, in the upper left-hand corner, a portion of a telegraph insulator excavated at the site of the Richmond Glass Works or the Virginia Glass Works by James Gergat. The necks of two bottles at the lower-left and lower-right corners appear to be those of Figured Flasks like the one shown in 43 *A. & B.* Next to the insulator is a "blob-top" soda water bottle. The other sloping-collared bottles are probably for bitters or proprietary medicines. *Collection of Mr. James Gergat. Greenfield Village and the Henry Ford Museum, Dearborn, Michigan*

The first of these factories is of little interest to bottle collectors, since it was a crown glass factory, but it is mentioned here as of possible interest to glass collectors. The *Virginia Patriot* of February 6, 1817, carried the following announcement:

The Glass House of Samuel G. Adams, Esq. is now finished. This is intended for Crown glass. The building is of brick. It is expected that glass will be made next week; and it is hoped hereafter Boston glass will not be considered as the best made in the U. S.

Insurance policy No. 811 of the Mutual Assurance Society of Richmond, Virginia, dated March 29, 1817, contains a simple plan of the factory and its outbuildings; the entire property was insured for $8,500. The factory was a square building surrounded on four sides by attached wooden sheds. The main factory, of brick, had a shingled roof. Unfortunately, the dimensions are not given on the plan, but a domed structure indicated in the center of the square building is designated as a "furnace." A smaller building identified as a "Clay House" is nearby, as is Mr. Adams's dwelling house, which stood within 30 feet of the main building. Possibly Adams, like many other glassmaking entrepreneurs, encountered some difficulties in getting his factory started, for according to the *Virginia Patriot* of January 24, 1818, it was not until then that it began operations: "The Richmond Crown Glass Factory is now in operation—Orders for either Coach or Window Glass, will receive immediate attention. Samuel G. Adams." This advertisement appeared several times, the last on April 11, 1818.

On April 22 of that same year, Billings & Thomas, auctioneers, advertised in the *Virginia Patriot*:

Window Glass

160 Boxes	8 x 10
20 do	10 x 12
30 do	9 x 11
20 do	10 x 12 crown

on consignment from the manufactory; and for sale on liberal terms, by
        Billings & Thomas (auctioneers)

Joseph D. Weeks noted in his census of glassworks[195] that Deming Jarves, at that time agent for the New England Glass Company, and later founder of the Boston & Sandwich Glass Company, stated that a Dr. Adams of Richmond, Virginia,

made large offers of increased wages to the workmen of the Essex-Street Works [of the Boston Glassmanufactory], who were induced to abandon their places of work and violate their indentures. They succeeded in reaching Richmond to try their fortune under the auspices of the doctor. A few years' experience convinced them of the fallacy of increased pay, for, after very heavy losses, the works were abandoned and the workmen thrown out of employ.

The *Richmond Enquirer* of Tuesday, July 17, 1821, carried the obituary of Samuel G. Adams, noting that he had died on the previous Saturday night, and that he had been a local merchant and the brother of the mayor. Although

43A. Obverse of Figured Flask GXV-51 (made by the Richmond Glass Works, Richmond, Virginia). **B.** Reverse of the same flask. Height, 7½". *Virginia Museum of Fine Arts, Richmond*

started with great expectations, his firm apparently remained in business only a few years. According to one author,[196] writing about Richmond in February 1817, "the city was making rapid progress commercially and industrially. Among other things, an establishment for making crown glass and designed to break the dominance of Boston in the trade had just been built by Samuel G. Adams, brother of Dr. John Adams." According to another author writing about Richmond's industries,[197] Samuel G. Adams's factory was located on the north side of Broad Street between Twenty-second and Twenty-third streets.[198] "In 1855, years after Adams' death, a Dr. Gavinzel erected a large glass furnace and factory on Louisana Street in Rocketts and when this was destroyed by fire the following year different interests erected two other glass works which attained to considerable importance."[199] It is these factories that are of interest to bottle collectors.

Shortly before Dr. Gavinzel entered the glass manufactory business, several men who had recently immigrated to America attempted to establish a glass factory in Richmond. Perhaps the eldest member of the group, and undoubtedly the prime mover behind the venture, was Hendrick Thon, who was born about 1814 in Hanover, Germany.[200] On July 18, 1855, Thon entered into "Articles of Copartnership for the purpose of conducting the business of a Glass factory, in the manufacture of glass, and glassware, in the city of Richmond, under the name and style of Henry Thon & Company."[201] Thon's partners included Nicholas Beck, a native of Prussia, Nicklaus Frohlinger, a native of France, Mikel Duchateau, Ferdinand Storm, and Louis Kohlenberg. Some of these men had been residing at least temporarily in Baltimore and Philadelphia.[202] On July 27, 1855, the nine-day-old copartnership entered into an agreement with Hiram W. Tyler, Franklin Stearns, and John Thompson.[203] In ex-

change for four annual installments of $200 at 6 percent interest, the new firm received a parcel of land measuring 145 feet by 106 feet.

On November 20, 1855 came another development in the annals of the "Richmond Glass Works":[204] Frohlinger, Storm, and Duchateau decided to leave the partnership. The sum of $250 was returned to Storm, $620 to Duchateau, and $155 to Frohlinger. The reason for dissolution of the partnership is not known, but one possibility can be suggested. That same day, after the aforementioned settlement, an agreement was entered into between Thon and his two remaining partners and Dr. George Gavinzel, a local physician.[205] The very precise terms of this clearly established Gavinzel as sole proprietor of the manufactory, a change that may have been unacceptable to the three men and their wives, especially after the effort they must have expended in the venture. Certainly the fear or reality of financial overextension in an already shaky environment may have influenced their decision. Frohlinger returned to Baltimore.[206]

The new agreement stated that Thon, Kohlenberg, and Beck did not have the means to carry out the glassmaking effort independently, and consequently must sell out to Dr. Gavinzel, who agreed to pay $3,000 and assume the remainder of the debt to Tyler, Stearns, and Thompson. In return for a $1,500 repayment to Dr. Gavinzel, Thon, Kohlenberg, and Beck were given a five-year contract "to work as journeymen at their business of glass manufacturers . . . receiving for their labour the same rate per piece that may be from time to time paid by similar factories in the City of Baltimore, Maryland . . ." The foreman of the works would receive in addition $100 per year. At the expiration of the five-year term Dr. Gavinzel agreed to turn over a half interest in the grounds and buildings provided that any of his investment costs, including new construction and the initial $3,000, were compensated for by the company's profits. Gavinzel also provided for an annual audit, flood and fire insurance, and the right to close the business at any time.

On December 8, 1855, the *Richmond Dispatch* carried the following announcement:

The Glass Factory, in Rocketts, is now in operation, and turning out some as pretty specimens of blown glass as anyone need wish to see. When the works are completed, and all the machinery put under way, the sight will be an imposing one to those who have never before visited an establishment of the kind. We understood that the strength of the articles now manufactured have been thoroughly tested and proved equal to any others made in this country. When this fact is made known to the public, with the additional one that all kinds of glass ware will be made as good and as cheap as they can be had elsewhere, we predict that the Richmond glass foundry will be kept constantly employed in supplying orders from the every portion of the South.

The following announcement carried in the *Richmond Dispatch*, December 12, 1855, seems to underline their apparent intention to capture a large portion of the market for glass in the South:

Richmond Glass Works
George Gavinzel
Manufacturer, Corner of Main and Tyler Streets
Rocketts, Richmond, Va.
Has constantly on hand a large assortment and can furnish to order every article of white or green glass of any pattern or color required.

Jars, Demijohns	Porters, Lamp Glasses &c
Tumblers, pressed	Decanters, Minerals
do , plain	Madeira Wines, Rhine do
Lemon Syrups	Colognes, Flasks
Castor Oils	Vials of every description
	and Pickles of every variety

Moulds made to order and particular attention given to their faithful execution.

Of particular interest is the variety of bottles advertised, including flasks. Fortunately, here—for the first time—the name "Richmond Glass Works" appears specifically, and the location of the glassworks is specifically noted. However, this address may have been only that of the office, not the factory, which was often located some distance from a company office. Ten days later, on December 22, 1855, the *Richmond Dispatch* contained the following advertisement:

Wanted—immediately, at the Richmond Glass Works, several thousand bushels of clean white sand. Samples must be left at the office of the Glass Works, Rocketts.

As happened to so many glass factories, the Richmond Glass Works suffered a severe fire and was apparently destroyed, according to the February 4, 1856, issue of the *Richmond Dispatch*, which recorded the event as follows:

Yesterday morning the new glass factory in Rocketts,

owned by Dr. Gavinzel, was set on fire and completely destroyed. Dr. G estimated his loss at $13,000, upon which he was partially insured. On the building, the Virginia Fire and Marine Company of this city lose $2000. On the stock and fixtures, the National Company of Baltimore loses $3500, and another company in that city an equal amount.

The Glass factory had been in operation a short time only, and those who ought to have known, thought it would be a money making concern. We hope Dr. G may lose but little, and that he may find it to his interest to re-build at once and go ahead.

Three small frame buildings, near the factory, occupied by negroes, were burned at the same time. Loss $1500.

A bit of human interest, possibly as a result of the fire, was reported in the *Richmond Dispatch* on February 5, 1856:

Severe injury—Joseph Kolenburg was arraigned before the Mayor yesterday to answer the charge of assaulting and beating and breaking the collar bone of William Thon, but owing to the absence of the witness the examination was postponed until this morning.

Joseph Kolenburg and William Thon were evidently glassworkers (perhaps glassblowers) in the factory. Thon was undoubtedly related to Henry Thon of the original firm, Henry Thon & Co. Seemingly justice was sought and carried out much more quickly in the mid-19th century than today, for on the next day, February 6, 1856, the *Richmond Dispatch* carried the following story:

Violence not proved—Joseph Kolenburg was arraigned before the Mayor yesterday morning to answer the charge of violently assaulting and beating William Thon, and breaking his collar bone.

The evidence proved that Thon had attacked a smaller boy in the glass factory, last Wednesday, and had him by the hair of the head to beat him, seeing which the prisoner caught Thon and pulled him backwards, in doing so both of them fell, Thon breaking his collar bone. There being no malice proved, and no design to injure the complaint, the warrant was dismissed.

The next indication of what seems to have been the fate of the Richmond Glass Works was reported in the *Richmond Dispatch*, September 5, 1856:

The Glass Works, at Rocketts, is being rebuilt on a large scale, and when completed, will prove most attractive to those of our citizens who have never witnessed the operation of making tumblers, pitchers, bottles, bowls, jars, etc., out of raw material. We understand that Mr. Atlee expects to commence the manufacture of work in the course of two or three weeks, and that he then expects to be able to furnish the merchants of Virginia, North Carolina, and Tennessee with such glass ware as they may need, and at prices that cannot fail to ensure customers. If the South wishes to become independent, she must encourage her own people in mechanism and manufactures.

Perhaps from this account one can conjecture that Mr.

Atlee, the owner of the land on which the glasshouse was built, was the entrepreneur behind the development of the original factory, which he *may* have leased to Dr. Gavinzel and which, after the fire and subsequent failure of Gavinzel's operation, Atlee undertook to rescue by assuming direct ownership and the direction of the operation. If so, subsequent accounts indicate he was at least fairly successful in the venture. According to the *Richmond Dispatch* of September 16, 1856, the factory had been reactivated on the preceding day:

The Glass Works at Rocketts went into operation yesterday, and attracted a large number of visitors, who were extremely anxious to witness the modus operandi of making tumblers, decanters, and other glass ware. To those who have never seen anything of the sort, the process is a very novel one, and as the busses run within one hundred yards of the factory we presume that many of our citizens will visit the works in the course of the week.

Encouragement for the success of the reactivated glassworks was expressed in the following account in the *Richmond Dispatch* of December 20, 1856:

The Glass Works

Every new branch of manufactures introduced into this city is an addition to its wealth and capital, and a material contribution to the public benefit and advantage of the locality. The Glass Works erected below Rocketts may be considered an enterprise of this kind, and are therefore worthy all the support and encouragement that can be extended to them by the commercial community. Mr. Jacob S. Atlee, the proprietor, has embarked in the business with energy, and is conducting it with a zeal which shows that he is determined to merit success. He has a number of skillful workers in glass, and his establishment wears the appearance of great activity and industry. It is turning out a large amount of glass-ware, which seems to be of very excellent quality. The process of converting the sand into glass is quite interesting, and a person curious in mechanics, will find it a gratification to pass a short time in observing it. We hope the trade will rapidly take up the manufactures of Mr. Atlee and keep his works employed. It should be remembered that every dollars worth bought of him is so much capital kept at home.

The final sentence in the account reveals Southerners' growing awareness of the need to promote industry and self-sufficiency in the South.

The difficulties of tracing the history of glass factories and their products are well indicated by the following advertisement, which appeared in the *Richmond Dispatch* of April 2, 1857:

Virginia Glass Works - - The Proprietor of this establishment respectfully informs dealers and consumers of Glass Ware, that he is prepared to fill all orders that he may be favored with.

He will keep always on hand, and manufacture to order, every description of

Druggists Ware	Jars of all kinds
Mineral Water Bottles	Covered Demijohns
Porter and Wine do	Carboys, Tumblers, Flasks, &c.
Ink and Cologne do	Claret and Sweet Oil Bottles

Together with every variety of Glass Hollow Ware of the green work kind.

Particular attention will be given to private moulds.

Orders of the city handed to the drivers of Ernest's regular omnibus line will reach the factory in a few minutes, and receive prompt attention.

Jacob S. Atlee, Proprietor.

Note that, instead of referring to the Richmond Glass Works, the advertisement begins with the words "Virginia Glass Works." Though no address is given, Jacob S. Atlee is listed as proprietor, and the types of goods being manufactured are the same as those in the previous advertisement. Therefore, it is probably safe to assume that the name of this glassworks was being taken "with license" or that the factory name was being changed. It should be of interest to glass collectors to learn that the same advertisement appeared the next day, and through April 15, 1857, with the following addition: "Broken Glass—I will give a half cent per pound for all kinds of Broken Glass; for pure Flint 2 cents." Atlee's interest in flint-glass cullet raises the question whether this firm was also producing some flint glassware. The following announcement in the *Richmond Dispatch* of April 13, 1857, indicated what apparently was a *new* interest in the saving and selling of broken glass in Richmond:

The establishment of the glass works at Rocketts has opened a new traffic in this city—that of buying and selling broken glass—which is carried on extensively by a few persons. Some few years since, the idea of saving the pieces of a broken tumbler or window pane, never occurred to any of our citizens, who looked upon such rubbish as valueless and dangerous; but now the fragments are packed away as carefully as old rags, until the "broken glass merchant" comes along, pays the price and takes them off.

The extent of the Richmond Glass Works was noted in the *Richmond Inquirer* of October 3, 1857, which carried the following data from newspaper interviews at factory sites: "1 Glass Works 55 hands, $2000 (Value of Tools and Machinery), $15,000 (Value of Real Estate Occupied), $40,000 (Amount-Sales)." A respectable number of demijohns covered with wicker must have been manufactured by the company—almost every bottle glasshouse made them—for on October 14, 1857, the firm advertised in the *Richmond Dispatch*: "Wanted—10 Willow Workers to cover Demijohns. Constant employment for the year. Jacob S. Atlee." Atlee was undoubtedly an energetic entrepreneur; on January 23, 1858, the same paper printed a letter referring to the fact that Atlee's Manufactory was in successful operation and also noting that he had established a pottery factory in Virginia.

A wide variety of types of glass and bottles was apparently manufactured annually by this firm (called here the Virginia Glass Factory), according to the following advertisement:[207]

Extensive Sale of Glassware
at the Virginia Glass Factory, in
Rocketts—Will be sold, at public auction, at the Virginia
Glass Factory, in Rocketts, on Tuesday morning, the 23rd
instant, commencing at 10 o'clock, the largest stock of
Glassware ever offered in Virginia, embracing in part Jars,
Wine Bottles, Tumblers, Goblets, Flasks, &c., together
with an extensive assortment of Apothecary's ware; also, a
splendid variety of Preserve and Pickle Jars, Demijohns,
all sizes, &c.

The attention of country merchants and visitors attending the State inaugural, would find it to their advantage to
attend this sale, the stock being very extensive and desirable, suitable for the city and country trade.

Sale preemptory and without any reservation whatever.
Terms cash.

Larus & Shine
Auctioneers

On February 19, 1858, "An ACT to incorporate the
Virginia glass company at Port Mayo in the county of
Henrico" was passed by the General Assembly of Virginia.
The Act stated:

CHAP. 419.—An ACT to incorporate the Virginia glass
        company at Port Mayo in the county of
        Henrico.
        Passed February 19, 1858.

1. Be it inacted by the general assembly of Virginia, that
Jacob S. Atlee, Richard O. Haskins, Robert A. Mayo,
Jacob Leigh, Horatio Smith and such other persons as may
hereafter be associated with them, shall be and they are
hereby incorporated and made a body politic and corporate, under the name and style of The Virginia Glass Manufacturing Company, for the purpose of manufacturing
glass at Port Mayo in the county of Henrico; and the said
company are hereby invested with all the powers and
privileges conferred, and made subject to all the rules,
regulations and restrictions imposed by the fifty-sixth and
fifty-seventh chapters of the Code of Virginia, so far as the
same are not inconsistent with the provisions of this act.
2. The capital stock of the said company shall not be less
than twenty-five thousand dollars nor more than two
hundred thousand dollars, to be divided into shares of fifty
dollars each; and it shall be lawful for the said company to
purchase and hold lands at said Port Mayo in said county of
Henrico, not less than one acre nor more than one hundred
acres in quantity.
3. This act shall be in force from its passage, and shall be
subject to any alteration, modification or amendment, at
the pleasure of the general assembly.

Being called therein "The Virginia Glass Manufacturing
Company" formally established the name of the firm at this
time, as alluded to as early as April 2, 1857. This change
further serves to complicate the already confused picture
of glassmaking in Richmond. The *Richmond Dispatch* of
February 22, 1858, also confirmed a possible change in the
factory name by the following short advertisement: "Sale
of Glassware at the Virginia Glass factory in Rocketts. Sale
on Tuesday 23rd."

Jacob S. Atlee was involved in other matters as well.

One of the best-known citizens of Henrico County, he
served in numerous civic offices. He was, for example, a
justice, as the *Richmond Dispatch* of September 20, 1858,
indicated: "Justices Jacob S. Atlee and John O. Taylor
concurred with resolving a dueling dispute." In December
1859 he advertised: "I have constantly on hand a supply of
fresh burnt lime."[208] Accounts from the same paper on July
3, 1861, indicate that with the coming of the War Between
the States, other problems beset Jacob S. Atlee. On that
date he was accused of "Supposed Disloyalty"—charges
stemming from a pass issued by General Butler permitting
"Mr. Atlee and his vessel to pass Old Point." Three days
later, on July 6, the *Dispatch* reported that Jacob S. Atlee
was "Honorably Acquitted." The *Richmond Examiner* of
the same date stated that: "Mr. Atlee became involved in
these charges partly in his endeavor to . . . procure soda
ash and a particular kind of clay, essential to the manufacture of telegraph wire insulators. . . ." Subsequent reports
indicated falsely—but happily for Mr. Atlee—that he had
been caught, convicted as a spy, and hanged.

Records indicate that a number of the workers in this
factory were from Prussia. William Thon became a naturalized citizen on April 4, 1860.[209] According to county
records, he was listed as an alien, a native of Prussia, who
arrived in the United States before he was 18; he was 21
when he was naturalized, and had lived in the United
States at least five years and in the state of Virginia for at
least one year. This was the same Thon who, in 1855, had
his collarbone broken in the scuffle with Joseph Kolenburg, as noted above.

On October 6, 1863, after approximately seven or eight
years of operating the glass factory, Jacob S. Atlee transferred ownership of the works to William S. Morris. The
Richmond Glass Manufacturing Company was incorporated by Henrico County on October 30, 1863, and licensed
to manufacture glass, glassware, tile, and crockery ware,
and to commence production immediately. The company
continued its operations until the night of April 2, 1865,
when federal forces occupied the glass works and used it as
a stable. No glass was produced thereafter, and in 1868 the
factory burned to the ground.

Thus ended the life of the "Richmond Glass Works." The
only evidence of its products is that given in the foregoing
advertisements and announcements, and the facts that can
be deduced from the fragments excavated by Mr. Gergat,
some of which are shown in Ill. 42. The only recognized
surviving product of this factory is the following extremely
rare figured flask:

GXV–51. *Obverse:* large anchor with cable extending
    through to a ribbon-shaped frame above and below. In
    the upper frame is "RICHMOND" and in the lower
    frame: "GLASS WORKS." *Reverse:* view of a glass-
    house with a tall chimney in the center and two small
    chimneys at each end, with smoke issuing from all.
    Below at right is an upright barrel and at the left a similar
    barrel lying on its side. Pint. Colors: light green or deep
    aquamarine. Extremely rare; only three or four spec-
    imens are known. Probably 1855–65; possibly 1855–58.

44. BLACK-GLASS WINE AND SPIRITS BOTTLES: ENGLISH TYPES ca. 1630–50 through 1730

All were free-blown—shaped by blowing and manipulation with hand tools—with thick walls for strength and dark color to protect the wine from color loss, with everted plain lip and applied string-ring, below which was put the packthread "tying in" the cork. From about 1630–50 to 1680–85 a flangelike string-ring was laid on about a half-inch, sometimes nearer a quarter-inch, below the lip; from about 1680–85 into the early 1700s, a string-ring, flangelike or with sloping edge, usually about one-eighth inch below the lip. The necks of Type 1, ca. 1630–50—1665 and Type 1a, ca. 1650–65, were tall, about half again as long as the body's depth; of Type 2, ca. 1660—1685–90, short and from a deeper body. The bodies were narrow-based with small low kick-up. The neck of Type 3, ca. 1680–1715, was very short; of Type 4, ca. 1700–1730, short. The bodies were wide-based and squat with high kick-up, conical or domed. The body of Type 5, ca. 1715–20, shown in Ill. 52, was deeper and narrower with sides slightly slanting inward to a sloping shoulder, comparatively short neck, a high conical or domed kick-up. All six types are found with applied seals. Types 1 and 1a, conceivably, were blown at the Salem (Mass.) glasshouse. These and Type 2 could have been blown at New Amsterdam, though any bottles produced before 1664 doubtless were akin to the contemporary Continental thin-walled bottles rather than to the English. (Half-bottles and quarter-bottles like Nos. 3, 5, and 7 are quite rare.)

Nos. 2, 3, 5, and 8, formerly in the Charles B. Gardner Collection. Nos. 4, 7, and 9, The Corning Museum of Glass, and Nos. 1 and 6, The Henry Ford Museum, formerly in the George S. McKearin Collection.

1. Type 1 (ca. 1630–50—1665), olive-green, slightly iridescent; small globular body; shallow rounded kick-up. Found in a Rhode Island Indian grave. Capacity, 1 pt. 11 oz. Height, 8⅝". Greatest diameter, 5½".

2. Type 1a (ca. 1650–65), black (dark green); cuplike body; shallow conical kick-up. Found in a Rhode Island Indian grave. Capacity, 1½ pt. Height, about 8". Greatest diameter, 5⁵/₁₆".

3. Type 1a, half-bottle; black (dark green); asymmetrical body; shallow conical kick-up. Capacity, 14 oz. Height, 7½". Greatest diameter, 4½".

4. Type 2 (ca. 1660—1685–90), black (olive-green);

deep bowllike body; shallow conical kick-up. ca. 1680. Capacity, about 1 pt. Height, 6½". Greatest diameter, 5¾".

5. Type 4 (ca. 1700–1740), handled half-bottle; black (dark green); slightly tapering side to sloping shoulder; high conical kick-up. Capacity, about 14 oz. Closely similar to the flint-glass decanter-bottles of the early 18th century, illustrated by W. A. Thorpe in "Evolution of the Decanter."

6. Type 3 (ca. 1680–1730), black (dark olive-green); squat body; wide domed kick-up. Capacity, 2½ qt. Height, 7³/₁₆". Greatest diameter, 7⅞".

7. Type 3, quarter bottle; black (dark olive-amber); squat body; wide domed kick-up. Capacity, 10 oz. Height, 4½". Greatest diameter, 4⅜".

8. Type 3, black (dark green); squat body; domed wide kick-up; on shoulder, seal: "I W / 1695". Capacity, 1 qt. 2 oz. Height, 6¼". Greatest diameter, 6¹/₁₆".

9. Type 4 (ca. 1700–1740) black (dark olive amber); squat body; domed kick-up; on shoulder, seal: "N / Green / 1724". Capacity, 1 qt. 5 oz. Height, 6⅞". Greatest diameter, 6". Though this bottle, from Rhode Island, presumably was made for a member of the Rhode Island Green (or Greene) family, the supposition (*American Glass*, p. 426) that it was for the Revolutionary major general Nathanael Greene is untenable since he was born in 1742.

A similar, apparently "black glass," bottle, but with skillfully rounded neck-ring and smooth lip, depicted in a still life by Luis Menendez (1716–80), suggests production of heavy wine bottles in Spain, at least by the 1700s.

10. Olive amber; squat domed body, wide long neck tapering to flat string-ring; wide base with broad high kick-up. Capacity, 1 pt. 10 oz. Height, 7⅝". Greatest diameter, 5⅜".

This bottle is un-English in form and like No. 4, "debut du XVIIIe siècle," Planche T, in R. Chambon's "*L'Historie de la Verrerie en Belgique du IIe Siècle à Nos Jour.* It seems likely it came from the Belgian region of the Low Countries.

In William van Mieris's *The Apothecary Shop*, painted about the end of the 1600s, bottles of similar form were depicted on the shelves behind the apothecary and his customer (No. 7 Ill. 3).

Except for No. 3, these bottles show steps in the progression of cylindrical-bodied bottles. Nos. 1, 2, and 4, free-blown and thick-walled, were types probably produced at Wistarburgh, Germantown, New Windsor, and Newfoundland. The medium-walled Nos. 3, 5, 6, and 7 were molded for body form only; the shoulders and necks were formed by blowing and manipulation, a method instituted in Bristol, England, about 1750 but practiced to a limited extent in the 18th-century production of commercial bottles. The bases of 1 through 7 have pontil marks; the others do not. Nos. 8, 10, and 11 were blown in full-size molds having a body part and two-piece upper part, a type in use soon after 1800. Nos. 9 and 12 were blown in full-size two-piece molds, a type of mold used for a few patent medicine bottles after about 1754 but, so far as I know, not for flasks and bottles until the early 19th century.

Nos. 2 and 11, formerly in the George S. McKearin Collection; Nos. 3 through 6, 8 through 10, and 12, Corning Museum of Glass; Nos. 1 and 7, Henry Ford Museum.

1. Type 6, ca. 1730–60. Dark olive-green; wide sloping string-ring below beveled lip; high domed kick-up; seal: "W / Ludlow". Capacity, 1 qt. 13 oz. Height, 10". Greatest diameter, 6¹⁵/₁₆".
2. Type 6. Dark olive-green; flangelike string-ring below everted lip; high conical kick-up. Capacity, 13 oz. Height, 8½". Greatest diameter, 4¾".

   A bottle of this type was depicted in William Hogarth's *Beer Street,* 1751; a similar bottle in J.B.S. Chardin's (1699–1779) *Le Panier de Raisins.*
3. Olive-amber; 2 wide sides and, at each end, 3 narrow; beveled string-ring below everted lip; slightly depressed base, only a trace of pontil mark; seal: "W / Vassall / 1760". Capacity, 1 qt. 14 oz. Height, 11⅝". Diameter, at shoulder, 3³/₁₆" x 5". Similar bottles have been recorded with seals dated 1736, 1739, 1751, 1769, and 1785. Though primarily a Continental type, they were made in England to a limited extent, and probably in America.
4. Type 7, ca. 1745–50—1790. Olive-amber; heavy string-ring below beveled lip; high narrow domed kick-up; seal: "S / Colton / 1767". Made for Samuel Colton, "Marchant Colton," Tory of Longmeadow, Mass. Capacity, 1 qt. 7 oz. Height, 9⅜". Greatest diameter, at shoulder, 4¹¹/₁₆".
5. Type 9, ca. 1780–1810. Black (olive-green); beveled string-ring below plain lip; deep conical kick-up; seal: "Ch Ch / C.R. / 1810". Capacity, 1 pt. 15 oz. Height, about 10⅞". Greatest diameter, at base, 3½".

   Bottles so sealed were used for wine served to the College Dons at Christ Church Common Room, Oxford, England, and are believed to have belonged to the tavern keeper or wine merchant supplying the wine.
6. Type 10a, ca. 1810–25. Clear deep green; thick rounded string-ring below beveled lip; medium conical kick-up; seal: "Mᵗ VERNON / M S M / GLASS Cᴼ."; blown at the Mount Vernon Glass Works, Ver-

non, N.Y. Capacity, 1 pt. 11 oz. Height, about 9⅜". Diameter 3⅞".

   Other recorded seals bear the initials "J L," "J H," "T R C," and "W B." It seems likely the "PORTER, BEER and CIDER BOTTLES" advertised by the company in April 1811 were of this type.
7. Type 10, ca. 1810–1830. Dark olive-green, tooled sloping collar; wide domed kick-up; seal: "WINE / P. C. Bʀooᴋs / 1820". Capacity, 1 qt. about 4 oz. Height, about 10". Diameter, 4⅜".
8. Type 11a, ca. 1827–45. Black (olive-amber); lower part of neck formed in the mold; tooled sloping collar with lower bevel; depressed base with outer rim inscribed "NEW ENG. GLASS BOTTLE CO." (New-England Glass-Bottle Company, Cambridge, Mass.) Capacity, 1 pt. about 10 oz. Height, about 8⅝". Diameter, 4".

   Molded inscriptions on outer rim of base apparently were initiated by H. Ricketts & Co., Phoenix Glass Works, Bristol, England, between 1814 and 1821.
9. Type 12, ca. 1850–60—1880. Light olive-amber; neck formed in mold; deep sloping collar with lower bevel; nipple at center of smooth concave disk, inscribed on outer flat rim: "DYOTTVILLE GLASS WORKS PHILA". Capacity, 1 pt. about 14 oz. Height, 11½". Diameter, 3¼".
10. Type 11, ca. 1814–21—1853. Black (olive-green); sloping collar with lower bevel; large nipple at center of smooth concave disk, inscribed on outer flat rim "H. RICKETTS & CO GLASS WORKS BRISTOL"; on side, seal: "W. Leman / Chard / 1771". Capacity, 15 oz. Height 8⅜". Diameter, 2⅞".

    Presumably 1771 is the date Leman established his business in Chard, Somerset, England. The bottle could not have been blown before 1814 when the firm of H. Ricketts & Co. was formed, and not before 1821 unless the company's bottles were marked before Henry Ricketts obtained his patent. The company made bottles for American wine merchants also, among them black (olive-green) bottles with "PATENT" on the shoulder and, on one side, a seal with a bunch of grapes encircled by "BININGER. NEW YORK."
11. Type 11b, ca. 1840–70s. Black (olive-green); neck formed in mold; collar similar to No. 10; base: wide flat rim around concave disk with nipple at center; inscribed on shoulder "C W WESTON & C."; typical spring-water bottle, blown at the Saratoga "Mountain" glassworks, ca. 1848–61, the years the firm operated the Empire Spring. Capacity, 1 pt. 13 oz. Height, 9¾". Diameter, 4".
12. Type 12, ca. 1850–60—1880. Brilliant olive-green; slightly sloping collar with lower bevel; base: nipple at center of shallow dome, outer flat rim inscribed "WHITNEY GLASS WORKS". Capacity, 1 pt. about 14 oz. Height, 11¾". Diameter, about 3¼".

    The same form and inscription occur in bottles with the neck threaded inside for patented (1861) screw-in glass stoppers like that of flasks (GXV-15).

46. CHESTNUT BOTTLES and DEMIJOHNS, 18th–early 19th century

Top row. Bottles Nos. 1 through 5, fashioned in shapes typical of common utilitarian bottles of the period, were used for all kinds of liquids, including beverages, of course. For use of the traveler or the worker in the fields, often some sizes were covered with wicker or leather, occasionally with latticed straw-work like No. 5. Medium and large sizes were sometimes sealed for private individuals—as was No. 1 with a seal initialed "I B"—and for lodges or their members: No. 3 has a Masonic seal. Small sizes like No. 2 (also Nos. 3 through 7 in Ill. 47) perhaps were used mainly for medical preparations and also for essences and flavorings. Their scarcity suggests a more limited production than of larger sizes. Probably, too, most of the surviving small ones are 18th century. All have a pontil mark.

All formerly in the George S. McKearin Collection.

1. Brilliant clear green bubbly glass; heavy-walled, large irregularly ellipsoidal body, neck tapering to round-collared lip; broad kick-up. On the wide shoulder is a crude seal with scalloped inner edge around a depressed center with uneven initials "I B" seemingly formed by a fine thread trailed on rather than by stamping. Capacity, 2 qt. 6 oz. Height, 10⅝". Greatest diameters, 5⅜" by 6¼".

2. "Apothecary bottle"; light olive-green bubbly glass; thinly blown, ovoid body tapering into long neck, turned-over collar; tiny shallow conical kick-up. Capacity, 2 oz. Height, 3³/₁₆". Greatest diameter, about 1¹¹/₁₆".

3. Brilliant light olive-amber; medium-walled chestnut-shaped body, short neck tapering to irregular collar; medium wide and domed kick-up. On the shoulder is a Masonic seal with small linear emblems, including the Arch, Pavement, Square and Compass, Beehive, Key, and Coffin. Rare. Capacity, 1 gal. 6 oz. Height, about 12½".

4. Olive-amber; thinly blown, chestnut-shaped body, short neck, rolled-over collar; very slight kick-up. Attributed to Connecticut. Capacity, about 5 oz. Height, 4½". Greatest diameters, 2⅛" by 3".

5. Light olive-amber; thinly blown, fat chestnut-shaped body, short neck tapering to thick round collar; medium domed kick-up; latticed straw covering with four loops below the collar for strap or other means of carrying. Capacity, 2 qt. 3 oz. Height, about 9½". Greatest diameters, 5¼" by 6½".

Bottom row: Large bottles, usually wickered, for bottling and shipping liquids were first called demijohns and carboys in the mid-1700s and, presumably, were usually molded for body form. By the early 1800s, *demijohn* was applied mainly to wickered bottles of 1-quart to 5-gallon capacity, used primarily for bland liquids; *carboys* to bottles from 1 to 20 gallons, set in heavy wicker tubs, for acids and other chemical preparations. Hence No. 6, holding a little over 5 gallons, and No. 7 of quart size are called demijohns here. The ellipsoidal body-type evolved by the mid-1600s. It probably was that of "oval" bottles occasionally advertised in American newspapers from 1776 into the early 1800s—among them, oval quart bottles "fit for bottling beer, cider and other liquors for family use." (Philadelphia, *Pennsylvania Packet,* Apr. 13, 1789.) All formerly in the George S. McKearin Collection.

6. Oval demijohn; olive-green glass appearing deep blue at top of body and neck in reflected light; ellipsoidal body, long slightly tapering neck, wide flat ring laid on below plain lip; smooth slightly depressed base. Capacity, 5 gal. 1 qt. Height, 19¾". Greatest diameters, 9⅝" by 17½".

7. Oval demijohn; black glass (deep olive-green); thick-walled ellipsoidal body with unusually flattened sides, tapering neck, rounded string-ring laid on about ¼" below plain lip; low kick-up, pontil mark. Probably mid-19th century. Capacity, 1 qt. Height, 7¾". Greatest diameters, 3½" by 7⅝".

8. Black glass (deep olive-green); thick-walled ellipsoidal body narrower at base than shoulder and with flattened sides, tapering neck, flangelike string-ring laid on about ½" below everted plain lip; shallow kick-up, pontil mark. Probably first half of the 1800s. Capacity, 6 oz. Height, 4¾". Greatest diameters, 2½" by 3⅝".

Top row: Demijohns and small bottles show a variety of characteristic forms. The body shapes of Nos. 1 and 2 are less common than the globular and ovoids, and doubtless the gathers were blown into molds for body form. Miniature demijohns, as collectors call rare small bottles like Nos. 3 through 7, ranging from 1 to 4 or 5 ounces in capacity, perhaps were used mainly for medicinal preparations.

Nos. 1 through 7, formerly in the George S. McKearin Collection.

1. Black (deep olive-green); "cup body" having one side more curved than the other and the curved shoulder longer, long neck tapering from wide base to wide flat string-ring laid on below irregular plain lip; shallow wide concave base, no pontil mark. Capacity, 1 gal. 10 oz. Height, about 13¼". Greatest diameter, 8¹/₁₆".
2. Olive-green, bubbly glass; body with short straight sides spreading to long rounded shoulder, short cylindrical neck, narrow mouth, flanged lip; flat base, pontil mark. Probably early 19th century. Capacity, 4 oz. Height, 3⅜". Greatest diameter, 2⅛".

    Illustrated also in *American Glass,* No. 16 Plate 226.
3. Olive-amber; spherical body, short slightly tapering neck, wide thick flanged lip; very shallow concave base, slight pontil mark. Capacity, 3 qt. 7 oz. Height, about 10⅜". Greatest diameter, 7¾".
4. Light olive-amber, bubbly glass; irregular globular body, short cylindrical neck, flanged lip; slight kick-up, no pontil mark. Capacity, 1½ oz. Height, 2". Greatest diameter, 1⅜".
5. Black (deep olive-green), bubbly glass; thick-walled ovoid body, short neck tapering to narrow mouth, very heavy flanged lip flattened on top; slight kick-up, pontil mark. Capacity, 1¾ oz. Height, 2⅝". Greatest diameter, 1¾".

    Illustrated also in *American Glass,* No. 13 Plate 226.
6. Brilliant light olive-amber, bubbly glass; thin-walled well-formed globular body, short neck, wide mouth, turned-over collar; slightly concave base, no pontil mark. Capacity, 3¾ oz. Height, 3⅜". Greatest diameter, 2⁷/₁₆".
7. Dark olive-amber, bubbly glass; thick-walled large globular body, short neck tapering to narrow mouth, flanged lip; slight kick-up, slight pontil mark. Capacity, 4 oz. Height, 3½". Greatest diameter, 2⅜"

Bottom row: Square bottles, called also *Case, Rum* and *Gin.* Excepting No. 12, blown in a full-size two-piece mold in the late 1800s, all are 18th- to early 19th-century types molded for body form with sides arched at top so shoulder starts in a spandrillike area at the corners.

They show characteristic variations in slant of the sides, type of shoulder, and neck finish. The common name *case bottle* derives from square bottles being kept and shipped in cases holding from 6 to 24 bottles. Examples similar to No. 10, but usually with longer necks, were depicted in many 17th-century Dutch and Flemish paintings, one of which is shown by No. 2 in Ill. 4. Square bottles with sides slanting slightly outward to the shoulder evolved by 1700, if not earlier, and became the standard Dutch gin bottle.

All formerly in the George S. McKearin Collection. Nos. 10 and 11, The Corning Museum of Glass; No. 13, Collection of George B. Austin; No. 8, Collection of Richmond Morcom.

8. Dark olive-green; slender proportions; round-collared lip, varying in width; slight kick-up, pontil mark; on one shoulder, circular seal with initials for A. Van Hoboken & Co., Rotterdam, The Netherlands; type used by the firm from its founding in 1784 until about 1894. Capacity, 1 qt. 5 oz. Height, 11½". Diameter, at base 2¾"; at shoulder, 3¾".

    Illustrated also in *American Glass,* No. 4 Plate 223.
9. Dark olive-amber; everted lip; 8 molded radial ribs from center of medium kick-up, pontil mark; one from a case of 12 bottles. Capacity, about 1 qt. 8 oz. Height 9⅞". Diameter at base, about 2⅞"; at shoulder, 3½".

    Illustrated also in *American Glass,* No. 7 Plate 223.
10. Light olive-green, bluish on shoulder and neck; unusual in color and in near verticality of sides; wide-flanged lip; flat base, pontil mark. Probably 18th century. Capacity, 2 qts. 3 oz. Height 11". Diameter at base, about 3⅝"; at shoulder about 4".
11. Preserve jar; dark olive-amber; molded for body form like the bottles, short flat shoulder, wide mouth with irregular wide flanged lip; medium kick-up, traces of pontil mark. Probably early 19th century and American, possibly Connecticut. Capacity, 1½ qt. Height, 9⅝". Diameter at base, about 2⅝"; at shoulder about 3⅝".

    Illustrated also in *American Glass,* No. 5 Plate 223.
12. Gin bottle; clear olive-amber; blown in full-size two-piece mold; deep wide flat-collared lip; smooth concave disk at center base; inscribed on one side "J.J. MELCHERS / Wᶻ"; paper label in color: THE LARGEST / GIN / DISTILLERY / of / SCHIEDAM. . . . J.J. MELCHERS Wᶻ / SCHIEDAM / Registered." Late 19th century. Capacity, 4 oz. Height, 5⅜". Diameter at base, about 1⅛"; at shoulder, 1⅝".
13. Clear green; flanged lip; base slightly concave, pontil mark; rare size and color. Probably American. Capacity, ½ pt. Height, 4⅝". Diameter at base, 2"; at shoulder, 2¾".

Handled bottles and flasks apparently were not produced on a large scale until the mid-19th century, when they became a popular form, particularly for packaging spirits. The majority may have been the plain ones to which liquor manufacturers and dealers attached their labels, as on No. 1. Occasionally molded or applied seals, as on No. 9 here and Nos. 1 and 6 in III. 99, bore the brand name of the liquor distiller or merchant. Many distillers and merchants owned private (inscribed) molds, obtained from moldmakers or through a glassworks, which they sent to bottle manufacturers to have their orders filled. Nos. 6 through 9 are examples of bottles blown in full-size two-piece private molds. As yet no census has been taken of these interesting documents of the liquor industry; presumably there were hundreds of them, especially in the third quarter of the 19th century.

Nos. 2 through 5, 7, 8, and 10, formerly in the George S. McKearin Collection. Nos. 1, 6, and 9, formerly in the Collection of Gordon Bass.

Top row:

1. Red-amber; free-blown; chestnut shape, short cylindrical neck, flat ring laid on below plain lip; medium kick-up, pontil mark; applied small heavy "D" handle, turned-back tip. Original paper label: "OLD / WESTMORLAND RYE / WHISKEY / MOUNT PLEASANT / Westmorland Co. Pa. / Drink me pure, water me not/I am genuine from the Rye lot." Capacity, 1 pt. about 6 oz. Height, 7". Greatest diameters, 3⅝" by 5³⁄₁₆".

2. Olive-amber; free-blown; ovoid body, short cylindrical neck, wide flat sloping-collar; flat base rim, domed kick-up, pontil mark; applied semi-ear-shaped handle, turned-back end. Capacity, 1 pt. 3 oz. Height, 6⅛". Greatest diameter, 3".

3. Brilliant clear deep green; free-blown; chestnut shape, long wide neck, irregular turned-over collar; base, slightly depressed, pontil mark; applied crude angular handle. Attributed to South Jersey. Capacity, 14 oz. Height, 6³⁄₁₆". Greatest diameters, 2½" at base by 4½".

4. Deep amber; free-blown; flattened chestnut shape, slender cylindrical neck, flat ring laid on below plain lip; medium kick-up, pontil mark; applied slender semi-ear-shaped handle, curled end. Capacity, 15 oz. Height, 7⅜". Greatest diameters, 2⅜" at base by 5⅛".

Middle row:

5. Deep amber; free-blown; waisted body, flaring below waist to wide base and ovoid above, short neck, double round collar similar to flask neck finish No. 19; nearly flat base, pontil mark; applied loop handle with tooled "leaf" end. Capacity, 1 pt. 5 oz. Height, 8½". Diameter at base 5½"; above waist 3¾".

6. Black glass (deep shaded amber), long oblate body with flattened sides and rounded ends, sloping shoulder, cylindrical neck with long pouring lip; molded inscription on one side: "WHARTON'S / WHISKEY / 1850 / CHESTNUT GROVE"; inside outer base rim: "WHITNEY GLASS WORKS GLASSBORO

N J". ca. 1860. Similar in shape to the Flora Temple Flask GXIII–19. Capacity, 1½ pts. Height, about 10". Greatest diameters at shoulder, 2⅜" by 4½".

A flattened chestnut handled bottle formerly in Charles B. Gardner's collection has a molded seal inscribed "CHESTNUT GROVE WHISKEY C.W." and a paper label of Charles Wharton, Jr., dated Philadelphia, Sept. 9, 1858, with the testimony of James R. Chilton, M.D., analytical chemist, that the whiskey "is entirely free from Poisonous or Deliterious [sic] substances . . . is an unusually pure and fine-flavored quality of whiskey." Also, a firm of analytical chemists stated it contained no fusel oil.

7. Black (deep amber); straight sides spreading slightly to curve at sloping shoulder, short neck, deep sloping collar; molded inscription on side: "R. B. CUTTER / LOUISVILLE, KY"; base depressed; applied small "U" handle, curled end. Possibly the Louisville Glass Works, 1850s. Capacity, 1 pt. 9 oz. Height, 8⅝". Greatest diameter at shoulder, 3³⁄₁₆"; at base, 2¹³⁄₁₆".

A similar bottle was inscribed "R. B. CUTTER'S [in arc] / PURE / BOURBON [inverted arc]". In 1850 the Louisville Glass Works advertised "vials, demijohns, porter and other bottles of every description. Particular attention paid to private moulds". (Quoted by Van Rensselaer from the *Louisville Morning Courier*.)

Bottom row:

8. Shaded amber; ovoid body, short neck, deep flat collar similar to flask neck-finish No. 15; base rim, slightly depressed center, pontil mark; applied small loop handle with curled end; molded inscription on side: "BININGER'S / DAY DREAM / A. M. BININGER & CO / Nᴼ 19 BROAD Sᵀ N.Y." Firm listed in New York City directories at 19 Broad Street 1861–64. Capacity, 1 qt. 2 oz. Height, about 6⅛".

9. Amber, cylindrical body, sloping shoulder, short cylindrical neck, collared lip as on No. 5; flat wide base rim, large smooth concave center; molded inscription: "NO 19 BROAD Sᵀ" in straight line below "A. M. BININGER & CO." in arc, and above "NEW-YORK" in reversed arc; applied small "U" handle, curled end, attached below collar on neck and on shoulder. Original fancy colored paper label with floral border; at top right, blue ribbon inscribed "BININGER'S / BOUQUET GIN" and, above, lady at top of stairway greeting cavalier; on next to bottom riser of stairs, "Established 1778"; at bottom of label "A. M. BININGER & Cᴼ N Y Sole Proprietors". 1860s. Capacity 1 pt. 5 oz. Height, 7⅞". Diameter, 3⅜".

10. Deep amber; pattern-molded ribs; taper shape, short cylindrical neck, collared lip as on No. 5; nearly flat base; on side, a bottle ticket simulated by applied heavy thread around neck in "V" terminating at heavy ovoid seal impressed "THE / OLD MILL / WHITLOCK & Co."; applied heavy semi-ear-shaped handle with long crimped and turned-back end. Probably 3rd quarter of the 19th century. Capacity, 1½ pt. Height, 8½". Diameter at base, 4⅜".

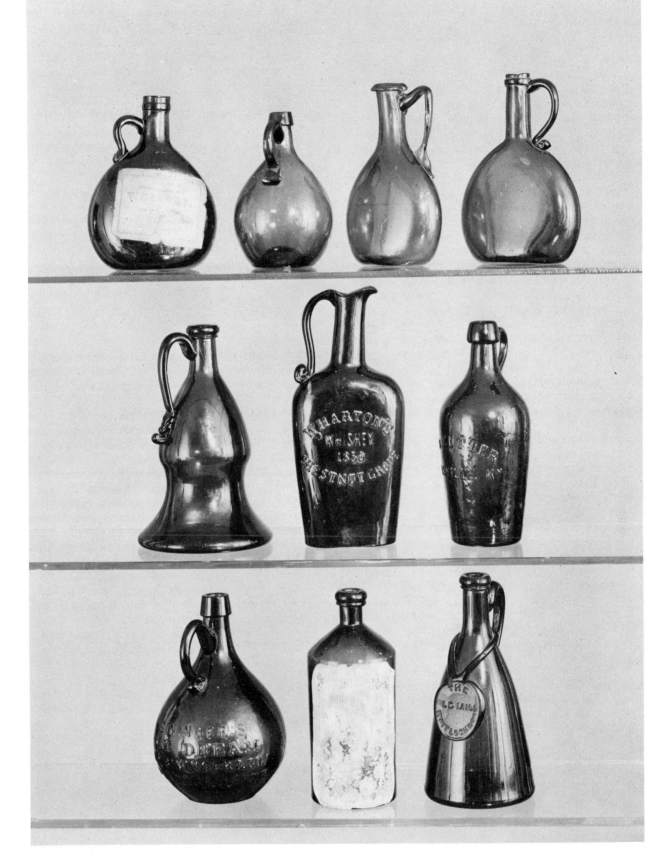

The bottles shown here were blown in full-size two-piece private molds.

All formerly in the George S. McKearin Collection. Nos. 1, 4, 5, and 8, Henry Ford Museum; No. 2, Collection of J. E. Pfeiffer; No. 9, formerly in the Charles B. Gardner Collection. No. 10, Collection of George Austin; No. 11, Collection of Gordon Bass.

Top row:

1. Deep bluish green; taper shape, thick wide round collar; smooth domed base, black oxide deposit from pontil; *obverse:* inscribed "UNION GLASS WORKS / PHIL^A" above building (New York City's Crystal Palace, first U.S. World's Fair, in low relief); *reverse:* inscribed "CRYSTAL PALACE [in arc] / PREMIUM / SODA WATER / W.EAGLE / NEW YORK". First made for William Eagle, ca. 1853/54 by Hartell & Lancaster, Union Glass Works, Kensington, Philadelphia. Capacity, 8 oz. Height, 7¼". Diameter at base, 2⅛".

2. Soda water bottle, emerald-green; cylindrical body, short sloping shoulder, short neck, thick wide round collar; domed base, black oxide deposit; on one side, rectangular panel with well-modeled American eagle, head to its left, wings raised and partly spread, tail to its left, olive branch in right talon, thunderbolt (3 arrows) in left. Possibly Crowleytown glassworks, N.J. ca. 1851–67. Capacity, 10 oz. Height, 7¹/₁₆". Diameter, 2⅛".

3. Soda water bottle, aquamarine; taper shape, thick wide round collar; smooth base; on one side: flying eagle and pennant inscribed "E W & Co"; below eagle, "WORKS" in rectangular frame with incurved corners. Attributed to E. Wormser & Co., Pittsburgh, Pa., ca. 1857–75, because of the inscription and close similarity to the eagle on GXII–14. Capacity, about 10 oz. Height, 7⅜". Diameter at base, 2⅛".

4. Soda water bottle, dull emerald-green; cylindrical body, long sloping shoulder, long neck, thick wide round collar; slightly concave base, dot at center; *obverse:* arc of sunrays above small eagle, head to its right, wings raised and partially spread, talons holding cord of shield with 3 horizontal bars above 8 vertical bars and flanked by crossed and draped American flags and, at bottom, branches of olive or laurel; *reverse:* inscribed "CH^S A. HUMBAGH & C^O / SAVANNAH [in arc] / GEO." Probably third quarter of the 19th century. Capacity, about 10 oz. Height, 7½". Diameter, 2⅛".

Middle row:

5. Clear deep green; cylindrical paneled body, high rounded shoulder, short neck, sloping wide collar; base, narrow depressed flat band around shallow dome, pontil mark; on 3 wide panels: (1) "SWAIM'S (2) PANACEA (3) PHILAD^A." Adopted in 1828 by William Swaim to combat counterfeiting of his Panacea; illustrated his advertisements and, as late as 1852, those of his successor, James Swaim, who adopted a new but similar bottle before 1874. Capacity, 1 pt. 6 oz. Height, 7⅝". Diameter, 4½".

6. Olive-amber; rectangular, chamfered corners, curved short shoulder, wide neck, narrow round collar; smooth base, shallow disk at center; inscribed lengthwise on sides: (1) "PHOENIX / BIT-

TERS (2) JOHN [in arc] / MOFFAT"; on ends: (1) NEW YORK (2) PRICE $1.00". Occurs also in aquamarine and olive-green. From one of 6 different molds used for these bitters between 1836 and 1867. Capacity, 8 oz. Height, 5¹/₁₆". Body, 1¾" by 2½".

7. Emerald-green; square, chamfered corners, curved short shoulder, long cylindrical neck, flat wide collar; smooth base, large concave disk at center; sides: (1) plain, (2) "PATENT" (in arc) above Pine Tree in low relief, "1859" below, (3) "L.Q.C.WISHART'S" (lengthwise), (4) "PINE / TREE / CORDIAL / PHIL^A". Possibly blown at the Lancaster Glass Works, Lancaster, N.Y., one of the known producers of Wishart's bottles. ca. 1861–73. Capacity, about 12 oz. Height, 7⅞". Body, 2¼" square.

8. Deep shaded amber; cylindrical body, curved shoulder, wide neck, wide flat collar above bevel; smooth base, 3 nipples across slightly concave center; on one side: large rock in low relief below inscription in arch "HIGH ROCK CONGRESS SPRING" and in curved line, "1767"; below rock "C & W / SARATOGA. N.Y." Blown at the Saratoga "Mountain" glassworks, ca. 1844–70. Capacity, 1 pt. about 2 oz. Height, 7¹/₁₆". Diameter, 3⅛".

Bottom row:

9. Bitters bottle, shaded brown-amber; square, chamfered corners, cylindrical neck, wide flat collar; smooth base, large concave disk; on 3 sides, 6 cannon facing alternately right and left; on fourth side, at top, tent surmounted by flagpole with flag flying to left; on shoulders, crossed sabers and, at each corner, cannon pointing toward neck. Probably of the Civil War period. Capacity, 1 pt. about 10 oz. Height, 10". Body, 3¼" square.

10. Pineapple bottle, deep amber; diamond diapered body, long neck with bulge above elongated diamonds and below cylindrical section, heavy round collar above narrow bevel; pontil mark; on one side: large diamond-shaped label panel interrupting the diamond diaper; original paper label: "The Best Tonic" above bust of woman, "BROWN'S IRON BITTERS" below. Occurs also in aquamarine. Mid-19th century. Capacity, about 1½ pts. Height, 9". Greatest diameter, about 4".

Two other molds for pineapple bottles had a smaller label panel, bounded by 2 instead of 3 diamonds. One was inscribed "W & C / N Y"; the other, "J C & Co".

11. Bitters bottle, shaded brown-amber; square, rounded corners, short cylindrical neck, wide flat sloping collar with flat ring at bottom; smooth base, square depression; sunken panels on sides and shoulders; (1) side: stylized eagle (no feathering) flying to left, long arrow in beak; shoulder: "PAT^D"; (2) side: lengthwise, "E. DEXTER LOVERIDGE / WAHOO BITTERS"; shoulder: "D W D", (3) side: plain; shoulder: "D W D", (4) side: like (2); shoulder: "XXX". Capacity, 1 pt. 10 oz. Height, 9⅞". Body, 2¹³/₁₆" square. In the specifications for the patent, No. 1837, granted Nov. 3, 1863, to E. D. Loveridge of Buffalo, N.Y., the design differs in the rendering of the eagle and in having "1863" on the shoulder above the plain panel.

Gemel bottles—twin bottles blown separately and fused together, with plain necks curved in opposite directions or, occasionally, parallel—were a common form for oil and vinegar. Those blown in bottle and window-glass houses as individual pieces for family and friends were usually thicker-walled and less carefully formed than commercial gemels. Gemel bottles in both categories were often decorated with applied and tooled ornamentations such as prunts and quilled and milled (rigaree) ribbons of glass. Perhaps the favorite decoration (see No. 2) was loopings of contrasting color, or colors, obtained by dragging into loops threads of glass applied around the unformed parison and imbedded by marvering.

Bellows bottles, similarly ornamented, were a popular form in the first half of the 19th century, produced commercially and also occasionally as individual pieces. The "Bellows bottles, small size" ($1.00 each) appearing among the Boston Glass Manufactory's flint glasswares (ca. 1813–16) presumably were a free-blown bellow's shape like No. 1. The "Bellows bottles" (50¢ a dozen; large, 62½¢) listed by the Williamstown Glass Works, ca. 1853/54, would have been blown-molded from bottle glass, perhaps as fancy bottles for cologne.

Saddle bottles, so called by collectors because such bottles were said to have been hung on the saddles of travelers on horseback, evolved by the 17th century at least, and probably were widely used in the 18th century. Like pocket bottles, they were usually given a protective covering such as leather or wicker and, of course, straps. They are seldom found in the United States, and whether they were blown in any of our early glasshouses is still a moot question. However, some may have been imported. Perhaps they were the "large Quart bottles, flat . . . " offered to Bostonians on Feb. 1, 1728 (Boston News Letter).

Illustrated also in American Glass: 1 by No. 1 Pl. 229, 6 and 7 by Nos. 3 and 4 Pl. 226; in Two Hundred Years of American Blown Glass: 4 by No. 1, Plate 103.

Nos. 1, 2, 5, and 7, formerly in the George S. McKearin Collection (No. 2, also ex-Collection of Dr. Henry Smith); No. 6, ex-Collection of Alexander Drake, pioneer collector of early 1900s; No. 3, Collection of Mrs. Donovan-Farrell; No. 4, The Corning Museum of Glass.

Top row:

1. Bellows bottle, South Jersey type; free-blown; fashioned in form of bellows, with applied and tooled decoration; flattened pear-shape body, long neck tapering to heavy round collar; colorless glass with opaque white and pale blue loopings on body and 4 wide white bands extending in slight spiral through collar; on each end: 2 applied colorless ribbons from applied plain wafer on base to double-ring collar at base of neck, quilled upper part and rigaree lower; on one side: applied dark blue button at center; on other side: vertical row of 3 colorless s-scrolled prunts and rigaree; on neck: spiral blue thread; rectangular blue handles. ca. 1815–40. Possibly New England Glass Co. Capacity, about 12 oz. Length, 10¼". Greatest width, 4⅛". Greatest depth, 2⁷/₁₆".

2. Gemel bottle, South Jersey type; aquamarine with opaque white loopings; long flattened ovoid bodies, one neck to right, other to left; applied, irregularly circular wafer on base, pontil mark. Attributed to South Jersey, first half of the 19th century. Capacity of one, about ½ pt; of other, a little over ½ pt. Height, 8¼". Greatest width of one, 3¾"; of other, 3½". Greatest depth of both together, 2⅝".

3. Gemel bottle; colorless with latticinio-like opaque white spiral threading; flattened ovoid bodies, one long neck to right, other to left; applied circular foot, polished base. Attributed to the New England Glass Co. ca. 1818–50. Capacity of one, about 7 oz; of other, about 8 oz. Height, 7⅝". Greatest widths, 4". Greatest depth of both together, 2". Diameter of foot, 1⅞".

4. Ornamental bottle, green, colorless trim; patterned in an 18-rib mold and expanded; flattened ovoid body tapering slightly from shoulder to applied circular crimped colorless foot, short neck, plain lip; decorated by 6, nearly equidistant, quilled colorless ribbons. Blown by Emil Larsen, Vineland, N.J., ca. 1932–36. Capacity, about 4 oz. Height, 8¼".

Bottom row:

5. Saddle bottle; bubbly iridescent light olive-amber glass; flattened circular body, long neck tapering to everted plain irregular lip; unstable base, slightly pushed up, pontil mark; spiral thread on neck, starting from a large blob on shoulder and ending in small node. Attributed to Spain, 17th–18th century. Capacity, about 1 pt. 6 oz. Length, 12½". Greatest width, 6⅝". Greatest depth, 1½".

6. Saddle bottle, rich clear green; thick-walled chestnut body, long neck wide and tapering to short shoulder below short narrow cylindrical section, wide thick flange; unstable base slightly pushed up, pontil mark; spiral thread (part missing) on long section of neck. Attributed to Persia, 17th–18th century. Capacity, about 1 pt. 14 oz. Length, 10½". Greatest width, 6¼". Greatest depth, 2⁹/₁₆".

7. Wine flask, olive-amber; type possibly used also as saddle bottle; flattened ovoid body with long slender neck, plain lip; smooth unstable rounded bottom. Provenance unknown. Attributed to the 18th century. Capacity, about 1½ pt. Length, 12⅜". Greatest width 6¼". Greatest depth, 2".

Among unusual rare American bottles and flasks are those decorated by glass applied to itself and tooled. On some the decoration that elevates the bottle from the ordinary is only a fancy collar, as on No. 1 or threading as on No. 6, or a contrasting collar like the opaque white on No. 8. On others, ornamentation is more elaborate: ribbons tooled into rigaree (milling) and quilling (crimping) as on Nos. 2 through 5 and 10; "leaf" tooling, as on No. 10; and rarely, "lily-pad." Lily-pad Type 1 adorns the powder horn, No. 9, itself a rare form in bottle glass. Spanish flasks of the 1600s—doubtless also later and elsewhere on the Continent—were decorated with rigaree, quilling, threading, and prunts. Colorless lead-glass English flasks were sometimes lavishly adorned, as shown by Nos. 1 and 3 of Ill. 121. Thus, there was a precedent for so decorating American bottles and flasks. However, the American green-glass survivors so adorned probably were not commercial products but individual pieces, fashioned by blowers as gifts or to embody a whimsical fancy like the little smelling bottle, No. 2.

Bottle No. 7, compartmented by tooling, is a Continental type, rarely blown in American glasshouses and possibly only as an individual piece. This may be the bottle described in Edwin Atlee Barber's account of the Coventry Glass Works and pieces owned by "the late Nathaniel Root, . . . a son of the first agent of the company": "a curiously shaped four-sided bottle with upper and lower compartments connected by five separate twisted tubes which allow free passage of the contents." The description fits No. 7, which was found over sixty years ago in that section of Connecticut and attributed to Coventry by the owner.

Nos. 1, 4 through 8, and 10, formerly in the George S. McKearin Collection. Nos. 2 and 3, Collection of Arthur Barris; No. 9, The Corning Museum of Glass.

Top row:

1. Olive-green; chunky flattened globular body (similar to that of some 18th-century pocket bottles), long tapering neck with medial crimped collar and flaring at top to applied flat string-ring of irregular width, plain lip; shallow kick-up, pontil mark. Probably 18th century. Capacity, 1¾ pt. Height, 7¼". Greatest diameters, about 3½" by 4½".

2. Whimsical smelling bottle, South Jersey type; pale green; manipulated to simulate human form; applied ribbon of glass crimped for "arms" and extending from "hips" to "feet" in rigaree; long neck spreading slightly to plain lip. Capacity, about 2 tsp. Length, 3⁷/₁₆". Illustrated also in *American Glass,* No. 2, Plate 241.

3. Smelling bottle, South Jersey type; pale green; body constricted to form upper spherical compartment and lower long ovoid, cylindrical neck, plain lip; applied circular foot, pontil mark; 4 ribbons starting from flattened blob on sphere, looped free to shoulder of ovoid and continuing in rigaree, spiraled and tapering, to foot. Capacity, ½ oz. Height, 2⁹/₁₆".

Diameter foot, about ¾". Illustrated also in *American Glass,* No. 24, Plate 240.

4. Flask, grayish light green; thick-walled, flattened ovoid, long cylindrical neck, plain lip; pontil mark; quilled ribbons on ends and middle of sides. On basis of its history and provenance, attributed to the New Geneva Glass Works, Pa., ca. 1798–1807. Capacity, about 2 oz. Height, 3¹¹/₁₆". Greatest diameters, about 1⁵/₁₆" by 2⅜".

5. Flask, light green; thick-walled, flattened circular form, wide cylindrical neck, plain lip; pontil mark; quilled ribbons on ends. Possibly South Jersey. Capacity, ½ pt. Height, about 4⅞". Greatest diameters, 1⅞" by 5⅛".

6. Bottle, light yellow-green of muted tone found mainly in 18th-century bottle glass; thick-walled globular body, long neck tapering to heavy turned-over collar; shallow kick-up, pontil mark; wide-spaced fine threading on body. Capacity, about 1 pt. Height, 7¹/₁₆". Greatest diameter, about 4¼".

Bottom row:

7. Pinch bottle, olive-green; walls pinched together forming 5 tubes—one at center, one at each of 4 corners—leading from small spherical upper compartment to lower rectangular; short cylindrical neck, flaring wide-flanged lip; flat base with crude quatrefoil indentation. Attributed to the Coventry Glass Works, Conn., ca. 1813–40. Capacity, ½ pt. Height, about 6⅛". Diameter at base, 3" by 3⁹/₁₆". Illustrated also in *American Glass,* No. 2, Plate 230.

8. Flask, deep amber with opaque-white lip; flattened chestnut shape, long neck flaring at lip; pontil mark. Capacity, about 5 oz. Height, about 4½". Greatest diameters, 1⅝" by 3".

9. Powder horn, black glass (deep olive-amber); long ovoid body tapering into curved neck with heavy scalloped collar about ½" below plain lip; on body, short layer of glass tooled into lily-pad Type 1 and button knob with pontil mark. Attributed to New York State, probably Mount Vernon Glass Works or the Saratoga "Mountain" works. ca. 1810–45. Length in straight line, 8¾". At least three others have been recorded—two of them undecorated aquamarine: one, blown at the Peterboro (N.Y.) glassworks early in the 19th century; the other at the Redwood Glass Works (N.Y.) after 1833. The third is of "colorless" glass with opaque white loopings.

10. Gemel bottle, dark olive-amber; flattened ovoid (large oval opening in diaphragm) tapering to an irregular applied gather lapping over the sides to form a crude foot; oval double mouth, plain lip; on edge of each section, quilled and rigaree ribbons; on sides, "leaf" tooled ribbon of irregular width. New England, possibly Keene-Marlboro-Street glassworks. Early 19th century. Capacity, about 1 pt. 2 oz. Height, 7½". Greatest diameters, 3½" by 4". Illustrated also in *American Glass,* No. 7 Plate 229.

Part III

WINE, SPIRITS, AND BEVERAGE BOTTLES

At one time or another in the course of their long history, glass bottles of green-glass metal have performed three main functions for wine, spirits, and other beverages: service to the drinker, transport to and storage for the seller and buyer, of which the last two seem to have been comparatively late practices. By the first century A.D. there were glass amphorae in the Roman world, presumably like their pottery prototypes used for transporting and storing the gifts of Bacchus and man's ingenious concoctions. By the middle of the first century, so Gwain McKinley pointed out in his paper "Collecting Roman Glass," presented to the London *Glass Circle*, Roman square bottles were used as packing bottles "for the transportation of liquids all over the Empire." It seems safe to say that from about 1 A.D., whenever and wherever glass bottles were made, some of them functioned as vessels from which wine, spirits, and other beverages were served. It will be recalled that Theophilus's "flask with a long neck," the bladder bottle, was a serving vessel, even drunk from, in the Middle Ages. Also, that decanterlike bottles were being fashioned for table use by the end of the 1400s. Other and less elegant bottles were used

likewise in castle and abbey, home and tavern, even before the Renaissance. Nevertheless, though comparatively speaking it can be said production of glass bottles was on the increase, their use for conveying potables to customer or to the tables of the well-to-do did not become *customary* anywhere on the Continent before the 15th century; in France, not until the 16th century, and in England even later.[1] However, by 1558 rosewater, "precious licoure," medicinal and sweet waters were being bottled in glass bottles, or at least glass bottles were advocated for that purpose in England as well as France.[2] Therefore it seems not impossible that bottles for serving "the lords wine" at Privy Council were sometimes glass ones, though whether they were ordinary bottle glass or the Continental-type decanterlike bottles or of other material the records do not reveal.[3]

Moreover, until about the last half of the 16th century, the use of glass bottles for alcoholic beverages was confined to a minority of the populace, and apparently no particular forms of bottles were specifically identified with such beverages, except perhaps more or less locally on the Continent for wine. In the illustrated catalog, 1550–55, from which Chambon, in his *L'Histoire de la Verrerie en Belgique*, showed some of the products of Colinet's Macquenoise Glassworks in Belgium, two forms were designated as *bouteille à vin*. One was a slender, nearly cylindrical bottle foreshadowing the standard wine bottles of three centuries later, and the other was a taper-shape bottle. Also illustrated was a square bottle with flat shoulder and straight cylindrical neck identified as *allemande*,[4] from which it may be assumed the square bottle was a German form adopted by Colinet. Perhaps even then square bottles were a favored shape for brandy and other spirits, as apparently they were from the 17th into the late 19th century.

Except for the Colinet types, I have found no evidence as yet that special types of glass bottles were called *wine bottles* before the 17th century, and apparently not until the late 18th and early 19th were certain bottles given the name of other potables. However, a late 16th-century bottle in the Barrelet Collection, Paris, France, which was excavated at the Abbey of Saint Basel in Champagne (a province famed for its wines), looks as though it should have been called a wine bottle. It has a rather wide-based onion-shaped body with a glass seal on the shoulder and a long slender neck with string-ring well below a plain lip.[5] This has a general resemblance to the earliest English (Type 1 in Ill. 52) and Belgian wine bottles of the next century. It was also in the 17th century that glass seals to denote ownership became fashionable. In any case, it is the English wine bottle, sealed and unsealed, and its development that have been most thoroughly studied and have the greatest interest for American collectors.

1
SEALED BOTTLES

"Sealed bottle" is a collector's term arising naturally from the presence of an applied seal on the shoulder or side of a wine bottle. Such a device presented no problem of craftsmanship or manufacture: it was an easily applied button of glass impressed with the armorial bearing, name, initials, or address of the customer for whom a bottle was blown; frequently it also included the date. Because the dates on sealed bottles have been the principal means of determining the period during which a particular type of bottle enjoyed popularity with the wine trade and its clients, and of tracing the evolution of the English wine bottle, a brief consideration of the practice seems in order before discussing the types of bottles themselves.

Since the seal to identify property and indicate ownership was a device employed almost from the dawn of history, it is not surprising it was applied to glass bottles. Perhaps the earliest recorded sealed bottle is the one in the Barrelet Collection mentioned above. The seal is impressed *Sigillum monasterii scanti Balali* and attributed to the 16th century. Obviously the use of glass seals to denote ownership occurred at least once in the glassworks where the monastery's bottles were blown—probably, Mr. Barrelet says, in the Argonne. This seal, however, is that of a monastery, not of an individual. Chambon refers to glass seals as a 17th-century English innovation, and indicates that the practice of applying a personalized glass seal was preceded, on the Continent in the late 16th century, by glass lozenges in which seals of wax were placed. A crested or initialed and dated glass seal was just the sort of conceit that might have been expected of Sir Kenelm Digby, who was credited with the invention of the English glass wine bottle by at least two contemporaries, but there seems to be no evidence that he ordered them put on his wine bottles.[6] It appears that the personalized seal was not adopted in England until midway in the century, and from then into the early 19th century the types 1 through 11 shown in Ill. 52 were often sealed. Ivor Noël Hume has established that bottles with seal impressed with the initials "R W" but no date were made for Ralph Wormeley, a Virginia colonist, apparently about 1650. The year 1650 was also that of the earliest recorded Continental dated personal sealed bottle: "Indocus Goethals 1650" was inscribed on the seal. The earliest recorded date on a seal found in England is 1652, but the seal is all that survived of the bottle. The date 1657 is the earliest recorded on the seal of an intact bottle. This bottle probably was from a King's Head Tavern, since the seal was impressed with the initials "R M P" and a King's Head.[7]

If the custom of having bottles sealed was affected first by the nobility—as well may be the case, inasmuch as such special-order bottles no doubt were luxury items—it was soon followed by tavern keepers, whose seals frequently included the symbol of the tavern. Though the custom was not general as yet, by the 1660s gentlemen as well as nobles were indulging themselves in sealed bottles. In 1663, Samuel Pepys, Civil Servant proud of being addressed as "Esquire," had the pleasure of seeing his "new bottles, made with my crest on them, filled with wine" at Mr. Rawlinson's, "five or six dozen of them." Sealed or not, the bottles served as decanters at the dining table, and gentlemen who, like Mr. Povey of Lincoln's Field Inn, had "pretty cellars" for convivial entertainment ranged their wine bottles in tempting display. By the 18th century, if not before, the sealing of bottles was widespread in England, doubtless on the Continent too. For the gentry and tavern keepers who could afford them, there was a certain prestige in personalized wine bottles; for the wine merchants, it was hoped, the seal with name assured the return of the bottles to the rightful owner for refilling and prevented their use by competitors. Sealed bottles were adopted also by wine shippers.[8] Not only bottles of the types illustrated by 1 through 11 of Ill. 52 were sealed, but also, occasionally, eight-sided bottles like 3 in Ill. 45, and square bottles like 3 in Ill. 46, both molded for body form. Likewise, chestnut bottles of medium, and sometimes large, sizes like 1 and 2 in Ill. 47 were sealed to a limited extent.

The custom, as previously noted, sailed across the Atlantic to the colonies, where—as proved by considerable archaeological evidence—tavern keepers, merchants, and well-to-do gentlemen had their wine bottles made for them in England. Wine bottle 8 of Ill. 4 with seal bearing "N / Green / 1724" must have been blown in England, for so far as is known at present no colonial glasshouse was operating in the 18th century until Caspar Wistar established his works at Wistarburgh in southern New Jersey in 1739. I, among others, believe some sealed bottles were produced at Wistarburgh in the years between 1739 and 1775. One of them may be the well-known wine bottle with seal impressed "W^m / Savery / 1752" that was made for William Savery, the famous Philadelphia cabinetmaker, and, according to family tradition, was used for his Madeira wine imported from the West Indies. He must have known his fellow citizen Caspar Wistar, and it would seem natural that, being a colonial craftsman himself, he would have had sufficient sympathy with Wistar's project

to express it in orders for his wine bottles, to say nothing of the fact that they doubtless would have been less expensive than sealed bottles made to order in England. This Savery bottle may be seen at the Philadelphia Museum of Art, where it is on loan exhibition. Also at least one seal, a crudely formed one, with the initials "N·S" has been found on the site of Wistarburgh.[9] However, it is impossible now to ascertain whether the seal was from a faulty bottle or one broken in the process of fabrication or merely part of cullet. And, of course, a single seal no more indicates origin than a single swallow does summer.

Another probable source of these bottles is the Glass House Company of New York, which *offered* to seal bottles for "all Gentlemen that wants Bottles of any size with their names on them" (Ill. 6A).[9a] Tradition credits the Glass House Company of New York with two now belonging to the Van Cortland Mansion, New York City. "Sidney Breese / 1765" is impressed on one seal, "F V C"—possibly for Frederick Van Cortland—on the other. Certainly it would be surprising if not one New York or Philadelphia gentleman patronized the struggling new home industry instead of ordering his bottles from England. Also, fragments of two seals have been excavated on the site of the Temple, New Hampshire, glassworks of Robert Hewes, 1780–early 1781. Part of one, found by John Gayton about 1950 near "a small furnace," has the letters "PLE" (presumably part of "Temple"). The other, found in 1963 by Richmond Morcom, is complete and on the back is part of the wall of the bottle to which it was affixed. It bears the inscription: "ROB. / HEWES / [probably] MANU / [possibly] 1781" in four lines. Still, I know of no 17th- or 18th-century sealed bottles that can be *unqualifiedly* attributed to a specific American glasshouse.

Though it is believed by many students that in the natural course of glass events some sealed bottles were made here, at present the earliest private sealed bottles recorded that are incontrovertibly American are those blown at the Mount Vernon Glass Works, Vernon, New York, ca. 1810–25. The seals, besides having initials, are impressed "M$_T$ Vernon" in a semicircle over the initials and "GLASS C^O" below, as shown by 6 in Ill. 45, which is clear deep green in color; the initials "M S W" are on its seal. A similar seal bearing "J H" that was found on the glassworks' site and a similar bottle with seal bearing "J L" are owned by John W. Norton of Cazenovia, New York. Two other seals are recorded that were excavated on the site: "T R C" appears on one and "W B" on the other; both are from olive-green bottles. "J L" are the only initials that have been identified. The "J L" bottle was one of a lot, original number unknown, made for Jan Lincklaen, agent in the Vernon district for the Holland Land Company. It was one of several from the original lot inherited by a granddaughter of Jan Lincklaen and given by her to Mr. Norton. Lincklaen, who was born in Amsterdam, Holland, on December 24, 1768, died at Cazenovia on February 9, 1822. The Mount Vernon Glass Company was incorporated in 1810.[10] Thus this bottle can be dated ca. 1810–22. Obviously, the sealed deep clear green and olive-green bottles were made from different batches of metal and hence probably at different times. Consequently it seems safe to conclude that the glassworks produced such special-order bottles from time to time in its early years, though the extreme rarity of the bottles points to limited orders.

It would seem that by the time the Mount Vernon bottles were sealed, the custom of having *private* bottles with or without a personalized seal was rarely practiced in the United States, nor probably in England either. The latest sealed wine bottle of which I have record at this time is an English imperial quart (40 oz.) Phoenix Glass Works bottle inscribed on the shoulder "PATENT" in one leaf of the mold and "IMPERIAL" in the other; and H.RICKETTS & CO. GLASS WORKS BRISTOL" on the flat outer rim of the base. On the side, about an inch below the "MP" of Imperial, is an applied seal bearing "J. / Head / 1825". Whether J. Head was a tavern keeper,

liquor dealer, or private individual is not known, but the last seems most unlikely. Present evidence indicates that, in the United States, the use of seals was resumed in the mid-19th century on bottles for dealers in, and makers of, spirits. Some of the seals were applied in the old way; most of them were molded. Two of these commercial bottles, called also jugs because of their applied handles, are illustrated by 1 (with molded seal) and 6 (with applied seal) in Ill. 94. Another with an applied seal is shown in Ill. 95.

Before proceeding to wine bottles in general, a personal observation regarding the style of lettering comes to mind, which may be of interest. With three 18th-century exceptions, on all the 17th- and 18th-century seals in the glass that I have seen in illustrations and photographs, or heard of, the first letter of a name was a capital and the others were in script. One exception is an English bottle, Type 5, in the collection of the late Melvin Billups. It is light in weight and olive-green in color, and "E / Herbert / 1721" appears on the seal. The other two are the Temple seals mentioned above, dating about 1780–81. These have large capital letters with serifs. On the other hand, except on a few Ricketts's patent bottles, the 19th-century seals that I have seen have capital letters, large or small. Though, possibly, the style of lettering would be a thin dating reed on which to lean, it would serve to indicate whether a sealed bottle with name but no date was likely to be pre- or post-1800.

2
ENGLISH WINE BOTTLES, CA.1630-50 to CA.1814-21 AND AMERICAN 19TH-CENTURY VARIANTS, CA. 1810 to 1850-60

Sealed or not sealed, the distinctive English glass wine bottles of the 17th and 18th centuries are of deep interest to many American bottle collectors and museums. The reasons are many-fold: they were used in American homes and taverns; they doubtless were copied in American glasshouses operating in their period; even though fashioned from ordinary green glass, they have for many of us the indefinable charm of free-blown glass in which function and form are

well married; they are tangible evidence of social customs, of commercial and industrial developments, and of the effects these factors exercised on form. From their beginnings between about 1630 and 1650, the English wine bottles went through several changes in shape before the emergence of the tall cylindrical wine bottles of the late 18th century and Henry Ricketts's bottle patented in 1821; and, in general, they were paralleled on the Continent.

52. "WINE and SPIRITS" BOTTLES SHOWING FORM DEVELOPMENTS FROM ABOUT 1630–50 TO ABOUT 1850–60

The evolution of the English wine bottle from free-blown, molded for body form, to full-size molded, is illustrated by Type 1 through Type 11, excepting 10a, 11, and 11b, which, with 12, are American versions of 19th-century cylindrical bottles. Color and dimensions given are those of only the specific bottle drawn.

1. Type 1, ca. 1630–50—1665; relatively small globular body, small kick-up; long neck, thin flangelike string-ring laid on, usually about ½", sometimes nearer ¼", below plain lip. See No. 1 in Ill. 44.

2. Type 1a, ca. 1650–65; relatively small cuplike body, sides spreading to slightly flattened shoulder, approaching Type 2 but with neck as long as or only slightly shorter than Type 1. See 2 and 3 in Ill. 45.

3. Type 2, ca. 1660—85–90; body slightly larger than Type 1 and 1a, cuplike and bowllike and taller, shallow kick-up; neck much shorter; flangelike string-ring laid on about ¼" below lip. See No. 4 in Ill. 44.

4. Type 3, ca. 1680–1730; squat broad body, rounded or conical kick-up, higher than on Types 1 and 2; short neck, wide at base and tapering; flangelike or slope-edged string-ring laid on about ⅛" below lip, which is usually everted. See 6 and 7 in Ill. 44.

5. Type 4, ca. 1700–40; similar to Type 3 but taller body, narrower base. Black (dark amber), appearing dark greenish blue in reflected light (when the light does not come directly through the bottle). This condition, occasionally found in early bottles, especially of olive-green and amber, is due to impure ingredients in the mixture.

6. Type 4a, ca. 1700–40; sides slanting slightly inward to flattened shoulder; higher kick-up. See Nos. 5 and 9 in Ill. 44.

7. Type 5, ca. 1715–40; taller body than Type 4; still broad but usually of less circumference than preceding types, sides slanting slightly inward to sloping or slightly flattened shoulder; wider and higher kick-up; neck longer in proportion to height of body; flangelike or slope-edged string-ring laid on about ⅛" below plain everted lip; step toward the cylindrical body, and approaching that evolved about 1730. Black (olive-green). Height 7¼". Widest diameter 6".

8. Type 6, ca. 1730–50; still taller body, "straight" sides, curving or sloping shoulder; very high kick-up in base; longer neck; flangelike, sloping or rounded string-ring laid on below plain everted, beveled or flat lip. See detail from William Hogarth's *Beer Street,* No. 8 in Ill. 4, and Nos. 1 and 2 in Ill. 45.

9. Type 7, ca. 1745–50–1779; taller, definitely cylindrical, and more slender body, flattened or rounded shoulder; occasionally shallow, usually wide and deep, kick-up in base; tall neck with flat, sloped or rounded string-ring immediately below plain flat or beveled lip. See No. 4 in Ill. 45. An example formerly in the collection of Charles B. Gardner bears a seal impressed "Danl / Iones / 1760"; a nearly flat base.

10. Type 8, ca. 1769–90; taller and much more slender body and neck than Type 7, but lips and string-rings of same types; very high narrow kick-up (3" in example illustrated). Black (olive-amber). Height 9½". Greatest diameter 4". In Plate 4, *Sealed Bot-*

tles, Lady Sheilah Ruggles-Brise illustrates one with seal impressed "Major / Grant / 1769".

11. Type 9, ca. 1780–1830; still taller and more slender body, short curved shoulder; neck shorter in proportion to body height; sloping string-ring just below sloping lip; high conical or medium-to-high domed kick-up; sometimes free-blown, usually molded for body shape, with shoulder and neck formed by manipulation. See No. 5 in Ill. 45.

12. Type 10, ca. 1810–30; cylindrical body with sloping curved shoulder, greater circumference than Type 9 and neck shorter in proportion to body height; sloping collar, with and without lower bevel, appearing for the first time about 1810; usually medium domed kick-up; sometimes free-blown, usually molded for body shape, and shoulder and neck formed by manipulation. See No. 7 in Ill. 45.

13. Type 10a, ca. 1810–25; similar to Type 10 in proportions, to Type 9 in shoulder; shallower kick-up; sometimes free-blown, mainly molded for body shape, and shoulder and neck formed by manipulation. See No. 6 in Ill. 45.

14. Type 11, ca. 1814–21—1853(?); cylindrical body, short rounded shoulder, straight-sided tapering neck, deep sloping collar with lower bevel; base with flat outer rim around concave disk with and without nipple at center, and no pontil mark; blown in full-size mold; introduced by H. Ricketts & Co., Phoenix Glass Works, Bristol, England; process of manufacture, patented by Henry Ricketts in 1821, included mold having a two-piece cover or upper part to form shoulder and lower neck, and body part with opening in bottom for a pricker-up to form center base. Deep olive-green; on side, seal: "Jn⁰ / Furse. / 1823"; marked on base rim: "H. RICKETTS & C⁰ GLASS WORKS BRISTOL"; "PATENT" on shoulder. 38 oz. Ht. 10½". Dia. 4".

(Not shown). Type 11a, ca. 1827–45; similar in shape, proportions, and neck finish to Type 10; base slightly depressed or with outer rim (plain or inscribed) around depressed center; blown in full-size piece molds—both two-piece and Ricketts's type have body part and two-piece upper part. See 8 in Ill. 45.

15. Type 11b, ca. 1840–70s; closely similar to Type 11, circumference of body a little greater in proportion to overall height; base with wide flat rim around concave disk, usually with nipple at center, no pontil mark; blown in same types of molds as Type 11a. See No. 11 in Ill. 45.

16. Type 12, ca. 1850–60—1880s(?); standard American wine bottle of the period; slender, tall, straight-sided cylindrical or with slight outward slant of sides; short curved shoulder; long neck; deep collars with lower bevel formed by a tool or in the mold itself; base with outer flat rim (plain or inscribed) around a smooth center—a dome section varying in depth and often with nipple or figure at center; formed in same types of molds as Type 11a. Olive-amber; outer rim of base inscribed "WEEKS & GILSON. SO. STODDARD. N.H." around low dome with dot at center. ca. 1853–73.

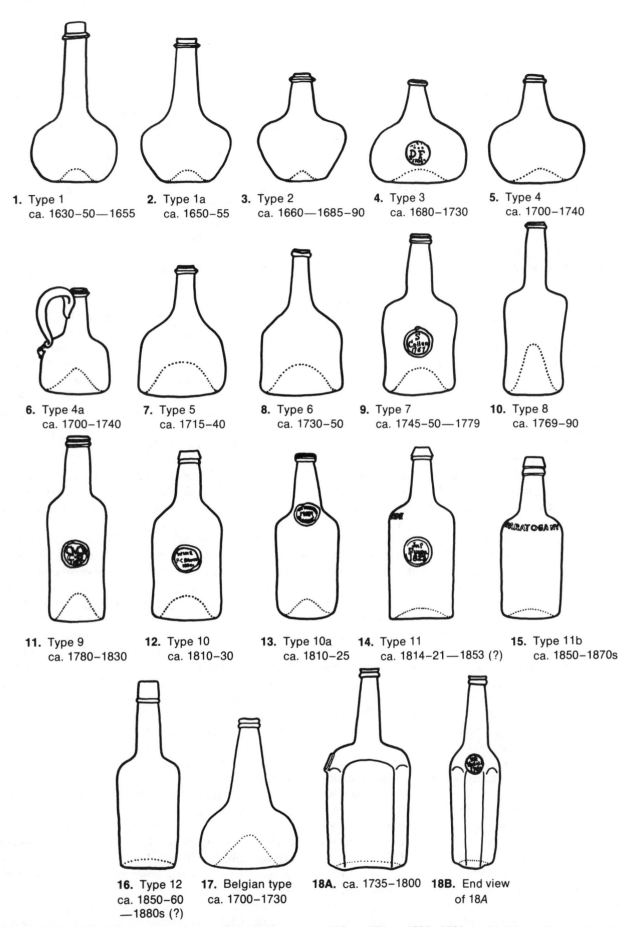

1. Type 1
ca. 1630–50—1655

2. Type 1a
ca. 1650–55

3. Type 2
ca. 1660—1685–90

4. Type 3
ca. 1680–1730

5. Type 4
ca. 1700–1740

6. Type 4a
ca. 1700–1740

7. Type 5
ca. 1715–40

8. Type 6
ca. 1730–50

9. Type 7
ca. 1745–50—1779

10. Type 8
ca. 1769–90

11. Type 9
ca. 1780–1830

12. Type 10
ca. 1810–30

13. Type 10a
ca. 1810–25

14. Type 11
ca. 1814–21—1853 (?)

15. Type 11b
ca. 1850–1870s

16. Type 12
ca. 1850–60
—1880s (?)

17. Belgian type
ca. 1700–1730

18A. ca. 1735–1800

18B. End view
of 18A

17. ca. 1700–1730; Belgian type of early 18th century, similar to the English Type 3, neck wider at base and longer in proportion to height of body; flat neck ring laid on below everted lip; very broad high kick-up, in some instances occupying most of body. Olive-amber. Height 7⅝". Widest diameter 5⅜".

18A and **B.** ca. 1735–1800; molded for polygonal body shape—two broad sides and, forming each end, three narrow sides; neck length varies in proportion to body height; string-ring laid on below lip; nearly flat base, no kick-up. See 3 in Ill. 45.

The English wine bottle was characterized by a sturdy functional form, thick-walled for strength and dark in color to protect the wine from loss of color. It was an innovation in glass bottles, English or Continental, and although called a wine bottle, it was used for spirits and other beverages. The credit for its invention was given to Sir Kenelm Digby by two glassmakers, Henry Holden and John Colinet, who stated in 1661 that they were making Sir Kenelm's wine bottles for him in 1632. This may be a bit of apocryphal English glass history, but, if true, it would not be the first instance of something new in glass having been a conception from outside the ranks of glassmen. Sir Kenelm seems to have had a compelling curiosity about things scientific, among them medicine and chemistry, which included glass. He had also a gourmet's attitude toward meat and drink. He acquired and contributed to a practical and sometimes empirical knowledge of the cookery, beverages, and medicine of his era. In his extensive collections of recipes his recommendations for the use of glass bottles reveal his appreciation of their peculiar desirability as containers.[11] Consequently it seems not improbable that he conceived the idea of a new wine bottle more practical than the somewhat thin-walled, lightweight, and light-colored bottles of his time, and as strong as the stoneware and stronger than the English delft wine bottles generally used for serving wines. If Sir Kenelm was not the inventor, probably Sir Robert Mansell or one of his glassmen was; for it would seem that Mansell & Company, which at the time enjoyed a near, if not complete, monopoly in English glassmaking, initiated the production of the new wine bottle and persuaded—if persuasion was needed—the London Company of Glass Sellers to adopt and push it. In any event, the subsequent growth and development of the English bottle industry are credited to the new wine bottle and the changing customs that it accompanied.[12]

The earliest wine bottle, Type 1 (1 in Ill. 52), was in vogue from sometime between about 1630 or 1650 to 1665, perhaps inspired by, but not imitating, the forms of serving vessels of other materials. It had a globular, sometimes nearly spherical, body, a small base and slight kick-up, a tall and comparatively wide neck—about half again as long as the body was high—tapering to a slightly everted lip, and a flangelike string-ring, which usually was laid on at least a half inch, but occasionally less, below the lip, as shown by 1 in Ill. 44. The string-ring was functional: the pack thread, and later wire, that held in the conical cork was tied under the ring. About 1650 a variant of Type 1 appeared having a cuplike body

with sides spreading to a flatter shoulder—Type 1a (2 in Ill. 52). Both Type 1 and its variant, Type 1a, went out of fashion about 1665, perhaps a social reaction "because so tall a neck was liable to be caught by loose sleeves." Whatever the reason, shortly after the Restoration a decided change occurred in the proportions: the neck became much shorter and the body became bowl- or cuplike and taller. The kick-up remained small and low, and the string-ring was usually nearer the lip than on its predecessors, as on 2 and 3 in Ill. 44. With slight variation, this form—Type 2 (3 in Ill. 52), of which 4 in Ill. 44 is an example—was characteristic of the period from about 1660 to 1685–90.[13]

As in the case of the later free-blown bottles, these wine bottles did not conform to an exact and uniform measure but were made in three general sizes: "quart," "half-bottle," and "quarter bottle." The "quart"—1 in Ill. 44—holds a pint and 11 ounces by our measure; the "half-bottle"—3 in Ill. 44—about 14 ounces. The half-bottle and quarter bottles, quite rare today, undoubtedly were less in demand. The collection of Charles B. Gardner included two of the rare quarter bottles: one, similar to 2 in Ill. 44 in shape, is 5¼ inches in height and 5 ounces in capacity; the other, similar to 3 in the same illustration, but more skillfully formed, 5⅝ inches in height and 7½ ounces in capacity.

These 17th-century English bottles were used in the colonies, though they were far from plentiful, probably in part because few of the small population could afford them. Bottles of Types 1 and 1a have been found in Indian graves in Rhode Island, among them 1 and 2 in Ill. 44, and in Connecticut. Because some of them were found in the graves of Indian kings, they are sometimes called King's bottles. Presumably the bottles came into the possession of the Indians through trade in which firewater was so potent a persuader in bargains to the colonists' advantage. Yet inasmuch as the colonial supply of glass bottles was scant, to say the least, in the period of the King's bottles, they seem an extravagant container to have been used regularly. Could it be that they were gifts to the kings—an extra commission, as it were? Also, fragments of bottles and whole bottles have been unearthed in the excavations at Jamestown. These can be proof only of the fact that some of the inhabitants owned English wine bottles, not of manufacture in either of Jamestown's ill-fated glasshouses, as has been conjectured at times: both houses were too early.[14]

However, if the creation of the English wine bottle antedates 1650, it is conceivable Type 1 was blown in the short-lived Salem, Massachusetts, glasshouse (ca. 1639–42 through 1645–61), and that both Types 1 and 1a were blown there if the works operated until 1661 or later, as well may have been the case. Also, though the possibility of production in the New Amsterdam and New Windsor (New York) glasshouses should be entertained, it seems more likely to me that any wine bottles blown there from about 1645 to the English occupation would have been akin to the thinner-walled Continental bottles of the period, having a more spherical and taller body and longer, more slender, and sharply tapering neck. On the other hand, if glassmaking continued after New Amsterdam became New York City in 1664—and there are indications that it did[15]—bottles of Type 2 may have been blown. Incidentally, that most of the Dutch homes in New Amsterdam were humble ones does not preclude the likelihood that the inhabitants possessed glass bottles, for Dutch paintings such as David Teniers's *Peasant Interior* (William Rockhill Nelson Gallery, Kansas City, Missouri) attest to their presence in the homes of the humble. The bottles are shown in detail 2 of Ill. 4.

Toward the end of the 17th century—the approximate dates have been given as ca. 1680 and ca. 1685—a radical change in proportions and shape occurred for which I have found no specific explanation. Presumably contributing factors were changing social customs and the efficacy of a base guaranteeing perfect equilibrium on the table. It may or may not be significant that the change came a few years after George Ravenscroft perfected his glass of lead and began producing lead-crystal bottles for table use. Among the articles named in his May 29, 1676, price list, still among the records of the London Company of Glass Sellers, were quart (16 ounces), pint (10 ounces), ½ pint (8 ounces), and ¼ pint (5 ounces) ribbed bottles and, in the same sizes, bottles that were "all over nipt diamond waies." It could not have been long before the lead-crystal bottles, colorless vessels in which the color of the newly popular port wine glowed and its beeswing could be detected, caused the banishment of the dark glass wine bottle from the gentleman's table to the wine cellar, the tavern, the club, and stag party. To quote Mr. Thorpe: "The wine-bottle only appeared on tables where good looks did not matter and a drunk-proof shape mattered a good deal."[16]

Whatever the cause, the body of the wine bottle became wide and squat with sides of a pronounced curve, sometimes as though a sphere had been squashed down, or rising in a gentle, shallow curve to a rather flattened shoulder—Types 3 and 4 (4 and

5 in Ill. 52). It had a high kick-up formed by pushing upward and inward the broad base of the bottle, thereby reducing the capacity promised by its profile. The neck became short, wide at its base, and tapering to an everted lip about one-eighth of an inch below which a flangelike or slope-edged string-ring was laid on. One reason the string-ring was laid on almost directly below the lip may have been that certainly by 1686, probably at least a decade earlier, cylindrical or slightly tapering corks set in flush with the top of the lip had been made possible by the invention of the corkscrew. Nevertheless, the string-ring, considered by some students to be mainly ornamental, was still as functional as before whenever a cork was tied in, or a cover tied over it, and it also strengthened the neck at a point of pressure.

About 1715, probably because of binning wine—of which more later—the ranks of the squat short-necked bottles were joined by Type 5 (7 in Ill. 52), having greater depth of body, sides slanting slightly inward to a sloping shoulder, and a longer neck—the first step in the evolution of the English cylindrical wine bottle. One wonders if this may not have been the type of the two glass bottles that Samuel Sewall gave to Mrs. Dorothy Dennison and, as he wrote to her on November 31, 1716/17, when he was terminating their friendship, were hers to keep along with the other small things he had given to her.

With minor variations, the general forms of Types 4, 4a, and 5 (illustrated by 4 through 6 in Ill. 52 and 5 through 9 in Ill. 44) persisted until about 1730 or 1740. Two of them with seals are shown by 8 and 9 in Ill. 44. The seal of 8, Type 3, bears the initials "I W" and the date 1695; that on the latter, a Type 4 variant, "N / Green / 1724". This one, illustrated also by 8 in Plate 220 of *American Glass*, came from Rhode Island with the history of having been handed down in the Green family (spelled with and without a final "e"). The supposition that the bottle might have been made for Nathanael Green, Major General in the Revolutionary War, is untenable since he was not born until 1742. Nor is it likely his father Nathanael, born in 1707, was ordering wine bottles at the age of fourteen. As previously mentioned, not even a remote possibility of colonial manufacture of this bottle or of Types 3 through 5 can be considered at present, for as yet there is no record of a colonial glasshouse operating in the period from about 1682 to 1739. However, as with Types 1 and 2, archaeological evidence proves that these bottles of the late 17th and early 18th centuries, sealed and unsealed, were owned by Virginians. They have been found also in other sections of the country. Some were in Indian graves, particularly in Alabama, and from this circumstance are frequently called Trade Bottles because, presumably filled with spirits, they were used in trading with the Indians. Bottles so used were not sealed, of course, and would have been among those imported by merchants. It is probable that wine bottles were imported for sale to merchants, grocers, and individuals before 1712, the first year in which I have found "empty bottles" advertised. They were among Bristol glassware offered in Boston. The next advertisement found, one for "large quart bottles," appeared in 1728.[17] Neither type nor form was indicated, but it seems a fair assumption that they were bottles of Types 4 and 5, or at least that the shipments included such wine bottles.

Early in the 18th century a wine bottle mutation occurred that was alien to the bottles of the time and quite out of the accepted line of evolution as established by writers and as is reflected in Ill. 52. It was a long cylindrical bottle, slender and free-blown, and may have followed very closely the introduction, around 1700, of port wine, the popularity of which continued to wax as that of claret waned. The appearance of this bottle in the wine bottle family is evidenced by a bottle listed by Lady Ruggles-Brise in *Sealed Bottles*. Possibly earlier ones have been listed of which I have not learned, but, in any event, the seal of this one bears "James Okes, 1735". Lady Ruggles-Brise believes that James Okes was a wine merchant, and refers to the bottle as "one of the earliest cylindrical port bottles which could have been binned in the modern way"—that is, on its side. In his "Bottle-Decanters and Bottles," John M. Bacon, while recording the fact that some writers consider long cylindrical bottles were blown for port from 1728, asks, "but were there any bottles for laying down port before that date?" In his opinion, "the fact that port was being drunk in this Country [England] soon after 1700 implies that it was laid down earlier than is generally supposed." Further, he expresses agreement with W. A. Thorpe's suggestion that 1700 is about the date of "straight-sided bottles for laying down port."[18] The opinions of these two eminent scholars in the field of English glass carry convincing weight. However, functional as this port bottle was, it apparently was not accepted by gentlemen and tavern keepers as *the* wine bottle par excellence for all beverages, though it probably was the commercial form adopted by wine merchants for aging port wine and for laying it down in customers' wine cellars. The consensus seems to be that the slender cylindrical form was not fully

realized until after the Bristol glasshouses began blowing their commercial bottles in molds for body form about 1750.[19] Still, that neither the commercial cylindrical form nor the method of molding was soon adopted in general is evident from the longevity of the free-blown Types 6, 7, and 8, Ill. 52.

Before discussing these types and pursuing the evolution of glass wine bottles further, a digression seems called for—a brief consideration of the early methods of stopping or, to use the current term, closing bottles, bottling wine and other potables, and binning them. The data—drawn from the literature on bottles, enlightening references in treatises on cooking, beverages, sweet waters, and medicinal preparations, and also artists' depictions of bottles—will perhaps serve as steppingstones to further knowledge of these facets of bottle usage. The methods are important and interesting to collectors and students of bottles, if only because they must have been influenced by and exerted influence upon the physical characteristics and features of glass bottles. Also, *their* evolution must have been among the causes and effects contributing to the development of bottle manufacturing and commerce in beverages. And, naturally, they must have been intimately important to the four- and eight-bottle men of "merrie" England and their American counterparts, who were no less merry.

In spite of the 20th-century American preference for screw caps and metal bottle caps, the material immediately associated with bottled liquid in the minds of bottle collectors is cork. However, several other materials preceded the *general* use of cork, and for a time these were used as well as cork. One of them was wax, which was usually then covered with leather or parchment. A French book translated into English in 1558 directed that "water to heale all wounds" was to be put into "a violl well stopped with syzed cloth" and that "a precious Licoure" be put into "violles or glasses stopped with waxe or bombase [raw cotton or cotton wool] and parchment over." Also, at least in some French centers of wine making, wool dipped in wax was used as a bottle stopper into the late 17th century—if Edward R. Emerson's information is correct regarding the method used at the monastery of St. Peter's, Hautvillers in the Champaigne district.[20]

Although the 15th- and 16th-century sources do not pertain to potables that normally were drawn off from cask, hogshead, or the like into serving vessels, it seems probable that the same materials and methods were sometimes used for wines and other beverages. In part, my belief stems from pictorial evidence. For instance, a glass bottle of wine (presumably) with a covering tied over the straight-sided mouth was depicted by Jaime Huguet (Spanish artist of the Catalan School) in *The Last Supper* in an altarpiece ordered in 1463 by the Guild of Tanners for the Capilla Mayor de San Augustin, Barcelona, and completed in 1486. I have not seen the original, but in a color reproduction the bottle appears to be blown from light greenish amber glass and to have a covering of whitish material. Perhaps the painter's intention was to represent parchment or sized cloth. About 50 years *earlier,* in the painting *St. Barbara Reading,* the Master of Flémalle (1375?–1444, Flemish School) depicted a footed decanterlike bottle of wine (?) stopped with what appears to be a spill of paper somewhat similar to those shown in the Details in Ill. 1 from Teniers's paintings of a 17th-century village doctor's "office" and an alchemist's laboratory. One assumes such spills were only temporary stoppers in serving bottles of wine or bottles of liquid about to be, or being, used.[21]

Details 1 and 2 illustrate types of 16th-century covering. In Detail 2 from a lay scene, *A Woman Playing the Clavichord,* attributed to the Flemish painter Jan Van Hemessen, close-fitting covers were depicted over the mouth and upper neck of two bottles partly full of a rosy liquid. Of course, it is impossible to tell whether the artist's models had a "stopper" of some sort pushed in flush with the lip. The coverings, apparently of cloth, show no folds above the cord and appear to be flat over the mouth. Judged by the rendering, the lips of the bottles were everted or finished with a narrow flange, but no string-ring was laid on the neck as on the new-type English wine bottles evolved between 1630 and 1650 that were stopped with tied-in corks. Also, the bodies taper gently into a short neck, whereas in the 15th- and 16th-century paintings I have studied, most of the many bottles and bottle decanters were depicted with straight-sided vertical necks, often with plain lips. Such a bottle, but evidently with everted or flanged lip, appears in Detail 1 from the *Holy Family* by Joos Van Cleve (ca. 1490–1540, Flemish School). Whether the covering, also reddish in color and tied over the mouth and neck, was intended to represent paper or cloth, I could not determine. Another early 16th-century illustration of closure is shown in *The Card Players* (National Museum, Washington, D.C.) by Lucas Van Leyden (1495–1555), the Dutch artist who may have fathered genre painting. On a recessed shelf in the background sits an olive-amber globular bottle with tapering neck and apparently plain lip above which rises a reddish "stopper" of undetermined material.

Just when western Europeans first fashioned cork into a bottle stopper is still to be determined with certainty. According to Pliny, writing in the 1st century A.D., though cork was used particularly as buoys on anchor ropes, it was used also for the soles of women's winter shoes and bungs for casks. The last suggests the possibility, if not the probability, it was likewise made into corks for glass and ceramic bottles and jars. If so, perhaps the practice and knowledge of this usage disappeared in the Dark Ages, and reappeared, as did so much else, about the time of the Renaissance. It seems likely bottle corks were being made for glass bottles toward the end of the 15th century. It is certain they were in the 16th, as shown by a 1530 reference called to my attention by Robert J. Charleston, Keeper of the Department of Ceramics of the Victoria and Albert Museum, London: "Stoppe the bottle with a corke." The earliest reference I myself have found was in the 1588 *Good Hous-wives Treasurie,* in a recipe for rose water, which, if the directions were faithfully followed, would "last two or three years." The "glasses" (common term for bottles) in which the rose water was to be kept were to be stopped with "wax or corke and some sercenet [probably sarsenet, a soft silky fabric] about the Corke or waxe and covered with leather or parchment."[22]

Although I have studied photographs of hundreds of paintings, and some paintings themselves, in which glass bottles, with and without stoppers or covering, were among the details, not until the 17th century did I find a bottle stopped with identifiable cork. Still, it seems probable that by the end of the 16th century, definitely by the early 17th, corks had become the *normal* stoppers of pottery and ordinary green-glass bottles from which potables were served or, in some cases, in which they were bottled for aging and storing. A significant Shakespearean reference occurs in Act III Scene II of *As You Like It* —late 16th–early 17th century. Rosalind, trying to discover the identity of her verse-making admirer, says to Celia, "I would thou could'st stammer, that thou might'st pour this concealed man out of thy mouth, as wine comes out of a narrow mouthed bottle; either too much at once, or none at all. I pr'y thee take the cork out of thy mouth, that I may drink thy tidings."

With one exception, only cork was mentioned in the various 17th-century writings I have read concerning the ways and means of home preparation of beverages, sweet waters, and medicinal waters. The exception was glass, and that after midcentury; glass stopples ground to fit were recommended in one of Sir Kenelm Digby's pre-1655 recipes and by "J. W. Worlidge, Gent." in his 1676 treatise of cider.[23] It must be remembered, however, that not only were most recipes well tested before appearing in print; many, with or without minor changes, were handed down from one generation to the next. Consequently, many of those published in the 1600s may well have been followed for years, even a century. Perhaps the earliest 17th-century reference to corks that I have read was in 1605 in one of the Star Chamber Accounts lent by Andre L. Simon for the Wine Trade's exhibition in London in 1933. One of the items was for 2s 6d due the butler, Edmund Tomlins, for "corks to stop bottles"; it was preceded by an item of 13s 4d for "bottles to bring the lords wine in." Others of the accounts indicate that from at least 1590 the lords' wine was served from bottles into which the wine, stored in the Star Chamber's wine cellar, was drawn off as required from hogsheads of claret, white wine, red wine, and sack consumed by the lords. Unfortunately the material of the bottles, even in a 1639 item for "sweet wine and bottles from the tavern," was not specified.[24] They very well may have been glass bottles, and those in 1639 just possibly like Type 1, Ill. 52.

The earliest 17th-century references to corks that I myself found in recipes were in Sir Hugh Plat's *Delightes for Ladies . . .* , edition of 1609 (probably also in the first edition, 1602), and Gervase Markham's *The English Hus-wife*, 1615. The same recipes are also the earliest I found for *bottling* beer and ale. In his "The True bottling of Beere," Sir Hugh directed that it be bottled when ten or twelve days old, "making your corks very fit for the bottles, and stop them close . . . ." His explanation of the waiting period before bottling seems quite significant:

The reason why bottle-ale is both so windie and muddie, thundering & smoking upon the opening of the bottle [is] because it is commonlie bottled the same day it is laid in the Cellar, whereby his yeast, being an exceeding windie substance, being also drawne with the ale not yet fined, doth incorporate with the drinke, and maketh it also verie windie, and this is all the lime and gun-powder wherewith bottle ale hath beene a long time so wrongfully charged.

This statement, in particular "commonlie bottled" and "a long time," suggests strongly that bottling homemade beer and ale was no innovation; if not, it must have been customary to some extent in the late 1500s, if not earlier. Markham was more explicit about "stopping close"—the corks in the bottles of

ale were to be "tied in with pack-thread."[25] Again, though there was no mention of the material of the bottles or the form of the corks, glass bottles may have been used. And whatever the nature of the bottles, the corks doubtless were conical, as they were for wine bottles and as presumably they were in the previous century, for easy extraction. If so, and if the bottles were glass, they probably had a stringring laid on the neck under which the pack thread could be tied securely. And the lip may have been everted, a feature probably facilitating withdrawal of the cork, as did its conical form, which was a necessity until the advent of a strong corkscrew and bottles strong enough to take a driven-in cork.

In several of the recipes collected and evolved between about 1625 (if he began his recording and experiments in his early twenties) and his death in 1665, Sir Kenelm Digby recommended that mead and metheglin be bottled in glass bottles and stopped "close with Cork tied in" and, in one instance, with "ground stopples of glass." It is interesting to note that regarding a meath (mead) made by a Mr. Webbe, Sir Kenelm said, "when it had wrought and is well settled (which may be in about two months or ten weeks), draw it into Glass-bottles." In another he recorded that on the morning of September 4, 1663, Mr. Webbe "Bottled up into Quart bottles the two lesser rundlets of this meath," which he then set in a cool cellar and said would be ready to drink in three weeks. Also when bottling Lady Vernon's white metheglin, the corks should be rubbed with "yest" (yeast), if not made in the spring with clove-gilly flowers among the flowers and spices.[26]

If it was customary to bottle and store beers, ales, and doubtless cider, meads, and metheglins in glass bottles before the mid-17th century, one wonders if it was true also of some wines, especially homemade wines. In fact, it is not impossible that Lady Powe's recipe for cowslip wine, which was to be bottled after standing "stopped close" in a large vessel of unspecified sort for three weeks or a month, may have been used and passed along for many years before being published in *The Receipt Book of Ann Blencowe* in 1694. But, as yet, I know of no specific reference that implies keeping or storing *wine* in glass bottles, and packaging it for transport, earlier than one sent to me by Mr. Charleston: In 1651 a Phineas Andrews sent by carrier "two doussen glasse bottles of the best Canary Dick Weeden hath" to his friend Henry Oxiden. Mr. Charleston points out that as "these bottles were to travel a long way," they must have been strong and "tough." In other words, they must not have been the fragile thin-walled bottles most characteristic of the period before the advent of the new wine-bottles. Samuel Pepys's diary gives an instance of storing wine in glass bottles. His five or six dozen sealed bottles purchased in 1663 may indicate a modest wine cellar in which wine was stored in bottles for a short time anyway, though he still kept tierces of claret and smaller containers of other wines.[27] In "Bottles Mainly Glass," Mr. Charleston noted that between 1671 and 1691 "the Earl of Bedford ordered an average of 58 dozen quart bottles each year." An "average" of 696 bottles filled with wine, or wine and other beverages, was not a small cellar, and it seems probable they were binned before the end of the period covered.

Though some potables, possibly including homemade wines, were bottled and stored in bottles, perhaps of glass, early in the 17th century, *binning* bottles is another matter altogether. It is generally believed that binning more or less coincided with the invention of a corkscrew strong enough to extract a driven-in cork, and resulted in part from the practicality of that useful gadget. With the advent of such a corkscrew, cylindrical corks could be inserted flush with the lip of the bottle, obviating the use of conical corks tied in with pack thread or wire. The new form of cork could be longer too, and certainly was by the early 18th century, if one can judge by the cork with a presumably early type of corkscrew piercing its center depicted in a self-portrait by the French painter Alexis Grimou (1678–1733). Smiling with lips and eyes in anticipation or gratification, he holds a filled wine glass in one hand and, with the other, grasps by its neck a black wine bottle. Until about 20 years ago, 1702 was the date of the earliest known reference to a corkscrew, one quoted by Mr. Bacon in 1939: "like the worm of a bottle-screw." Subsequently Lady Ruggles-Brise found a "cork-drawer," at 00-03-06 in the 1686 accounts of a Dr. Claver Morris, who seems to have maintained a cellar of a comforting size, since he bought also "12 dozen of quart-glass bottles" and "5 dozen of Corks" during the same year. That *cork-drawer* and *bottle-screw* were two names for a tool to extract corks is the only logical conclusion. The latter term, by the way, is the only one I have found in any 18th- or early 19th-century dictionaries. Though corkscrew occurred in early 18th-century writings, its adoption apparently was neither swift nor general, at least among lexicographers. In fact, from present evidence, it might be called a Victorian term. However, evidence that cork-drawers existed by 1681 was sent to me recently by Robert Charleston: N. Grew ended a description of "The WORME-STONE" with "Not much unlike a Steel Worme used for the drawing of *Corks* out of *Bottles*."[28]

Further researches probably will uncover a reference to an instrument for drawing corks before 1681, for Worlidge's *Treatise of Cider* carries binning back a decade for cider, if not for wine, and leads to the supposition that some sort of cork-drawers must have been in existence before 1676. The following passages from his Treatise are quoted at length, not only because of their evidence of storage and binning, even by *laying bottles on the side* at that time, but also their appreciation of the glass bottle's superiority as a container, and methods of closure:

Glass-bottles are preferr'd to Stone-bottles because that Stone-bottles are apt to leak, and are rough in the mouth, that they are not easily uncork'd; also they are more apt to taint than the other; neither are they transparent, that you may discern when they are foul, or clean: it being otherwise with the Glass-Bottles, whose defects are easily discern'd, and are of a more compact metal or substance, not wasting so many Corks.

To prevent the charge of which you may, with a Turn made for that purpose, grinde or fit Glass-stopples to each Bottle, so apt, that no Liquor or Spirit shall penetrate its closures; always observing to keep each Stopple to its Bottle: which is easily done, by securing it with a piece of Packthread, each Stopple having a Button on the top of it for that end. These Stopples are ground with the Powder of the Stone *Smyris*, sold at the Shops by the vulgar name of *Emery*, which with Oyl will exquisitely work the Glass to your pleasure.

The onely Objection against this way of Closure, is, That not giving passage for any Spirits, the Liquors are apt to force the Bottles; which in Bottles stopt with Cork rarely happens, the Cork being somewhat porous, part of the Spirits, though with difficulty, perspire.

* * * * * *

Great care is to be had in choosing good Corks, such good Liquor being absolutely spoiled through the onely defect of the Cork; therefore are Glass Stopples to be preferr'd, in case the accident of breaking the Bottles can be prevented.

If the Corks are steep'd in scalding water a while before you use them, they will comply better with the mouth of the Bottle, than if forc'd in dry: also the moisture of the Cork doth advantage it in detaining the Spirits.

Therefore is laying the Bottles sideways to be commended, not onely for preserving the Corks moist, but for that the Air that remains in the Bottle is on the side of the Bottle which it can neither expire, nor can new be admitted, the Liquor being against the Cork, which not so easily passeth through the Cork as the Air. *Some place their Bottles on a Frame with their noses downward* for that end: which is not to be so well approved of, by reason that if there be any least settling in the Bottle, you are sure to have it in the first Glass. [The italics are mine.]

Placing the Bottles on a Frame, as is usual, or on Shelves, is not so good as on the ground, by reason that the farther from the earth they stand, the more subject they are to the variation of Air, which is more rare in the upper part of a Cellar or other Room, than in the lower . . .

Settling Bottles in Sand is by many not onely made use of, but commended, although without cause, it not adding that coldness to the Bottles as is generally expected . . .

The placing of Bottles in Cisterns of Spring-water, either running or often changed, is without all Peradventure the best way to preserve *Cider* or any other Vinous Liquors. A conservatory made where a recruit of cool refrigerating Spring-water may conveniently be had, will so long preserve *Cider* until it be come to the strength even of Canary it self. Bottles let down into Wells of water . . . or little vaults on the sides of Wells near the bottom, may supply the defect of Spring-water in your Cellar . . .[29]

Except perhaps for his advice to lay bottles sideways, Mr. Worlidge obviously was writing about methods of storage already practiced. Therefore the conclusion seems inescapable that in some cellars before 1676 bottles of cider and "other Vinous Liquors" were binned upside down—that is, with "their noses downward" through a hole and shoulders resting on the shelf or frame. If cider was bottled and so binned *before* 1676, why not wine and spirits? In any event, whenever binning of wine started, it would appear that the bottles were binned upside down. Shelves with the necessary holes in them still exist in some cellars, and bottles have been found with traces of lees adhering to the inside of their shoulders. This method of binning would seem to be the practical one for the globular and squat wine bottles of the 17th and early 18th centuries, which would have presented difficulties in laying sideways as advocated by Worlidge. Binning on the side, to be completely practical, would seem to necessitate a somewhat cylindrical form of bottle, or a square one. What were Mr. Worlidge's bottles? It would seem that the evolution of the *dark thick-walled cylindrical wine bottle* did not begin until the early 18th century, and present evidence indicates that the method of binning on the side was neither the standard mode nor widespread much before the middle of the century.[30]

Binning, as well as packaging beverages in bottles for shipping, doubtless exerted influence on the form of wine bottles. And, from about 1730 onward, the progression in shape and proportions of the wine bottle was toward a standard cylindrical blown-molded wine bottle. It was neither abrupt nor uniform: one form did not go out immediately as another came in; they overlapped. Steps in that 18th-century evolution are illustrated by the line drawings of Types 6 through 10 (8 through 12 in Ill. 52) and by bottles 1, 2, 4, 5, and 6 in Ill. 45.

As mentioned before, the cylindrical port bottle probably came into being around or shortly after 1700, and the free-blown types 6, 7, and 8 embraced the long period from about 1730 to 1790. Their lips—except occasionally on Type 6, which often was everted—were usually flat or beveled, and the string-ring (flat, sloped or beveled, or rounded) was immediately below the lip. By about 1745 or 1750, as shown by 4 in Ill. 45 and Type 7, ca. 1745 or 1750–70 (9 in Ill. 52), the shoulder was normally short and flattened instead of being long, gently rounded or sloping as on Type 6 (ca. 1730–50), shown by 1 and 2 in Ill. 45; the body, though still of generous circumference, definitely cylindrical and taller; the kick-up, still wide and high. By 1769, if not earlier, a new form had evolved, having a still taller and more slender body, a neck tall in proportion to the body, and a high conical kick-up—Type 8 (ca. 1769–90), shown by 10 in Ill. 52. It is probable too that many were medium-walled instead of thick-walled. By about 1780, Type 9 (ca. 1780–1830), shown by 11 in Ill. 52, had become a standard wine bottle form, having a slender cylindrical body with gently curved short shoulder, a neck shorter in proportion to the body, and a lower kick-up. The body was shaped in a mold and the shoulder and neck by manipulation. By this time wine bottles were mainly commercial and, it would seem, less often made for private individuals.

The sealed bottle, 5 in Ill. 45, and 11 in Ill. 52, is an example of Type 9; it was used for the wine served to dons in Christchurch Common Room, Oxford, England. "Ch.Ch. / C.R. / 1801" is on its seal. Seals of Christchurch bottles dated 1771 and 1804 and a bottle ca. 1780 have been recorded also. It is believed that these bottles, and those for other colleges also, belonged not to the college but to the tavern keepers or wine merchants who supplied the dons' wine.[31] And it is interesting to note that before bottles of standardized capacity were produced, the bottles supplied by tavern keepers would have been filled at the tavern with prescribed measures of wine, "for it was illegal to sell wine other than by measure in days when the hand-manufactured bottles offered no guarantee of their uniform capacity."[32]

Bottles of all these types have been found in America. Inasmuch as the colonial population and prosperity had increased, probably many bottles of Types 6, 7, and 8 were both made to order in England for colonists and imported for sale to merchants, grocers, and individuals, and naturally in larger quantities than earlier types. The majority, if not all, of the seals and sealed bottles excavated at Williamsburg no doubt were special-order bottles made in England for their owners. The substantial number of plain bottles, presumably used in the Indian trade and excavated in Alabama by Dr. R. P. Burke of Montgomery, probably came from England. From about 1730 bottles, by far the majority of "quart" size, were advertised with increasing frequency in newspapers in ports of entry and in inland towns, and some must have been the English wine bottles. Also, by the 1740s at the latest, bottled wines were being imported. In 1744 two Charleston, South Carolina, merchants received shipments of wines in bottles: one, "Clarret and cherry wine from Scotland"; the other, "White and Red Port wine."[33] Of course whether the wine from Scotland was in wine bottles of Type 6 is in the realm of conjecture. And the port wine, if it was not bottled in England but came direct from Portugal, probably was in Continental bottles—at least one conjectures that bottled wines arriving from Portugal, France, Spain, and the Islands would naturally be in Continental bottles. Still, the majority of bottles, filled and empty, came from England.

Although most of the 18th-century English-type wine bottles found in this country probably were English products, from a chronological standpoint bottles of Types 6, 7, 8, and 9 *could* have been blown in American glasshouses and doubtless were, though not in large quantities excepting probably Type 9. Bottles of Types 6 and 7 could have been blown at Wistarburgh, at Germantown, and by the Glass House Company of New York. It has already been noted in connection with the sealed bottles that possibly the "Wm Savery" bottle dated 1752 was a Wistarburgh product and that the "Sidney Breese, 1765" and "F V C" bottles might have been made by the Glass House Company of New York. Type 8 could have been made at Wistarburgh and by Stiegel at Manheim, Pennsylvania. Type 9 could have been made at Glassboro, New Jersey, by the Pitkins in East Hartford, Connecticut, the Pittsburgh Glass Works and the New Geneva Glass Works in western

Pennsylvania—in fact by any glasshouse where bottles were produced in its period, ca. 1780–1830. Still, in spite of the fact that advertisements and other sources *prove* manufacture of bottles by these early houses, there are no *authenticated* examples of the black glass wine bottles—so far as I know—nor is there any *proof* the houses made bottles of these types. Nevertheless there is the strong probability, a belief held by many, that as in the case of other articles of glassware, the types produced in England and imported into the colonies were copied by American glassmakers, if only as special orders. As for the 19th century, it is almost axiomatic that from 1800 on, our American glasshouses in which bottles were the principal product produced wine, spirit, and beverage bottles of the various standard forms as they evolved. But here again, unless there is a seal identifiable with a particular glassworks, a mark, or the name of the works, it is virtually impossible at the present time to distinguish between domestic and imported bottles. And literally thousands were imported, at least through the first half of the 19th century.

Variations of cylindrical bottles appearing from about 1810 to 1850–60 are shown by bottles 6 through 12 in Ill. 45 and the line drawings of Types 10, 10a, 11, 11a, 11b, and 12 included in Ill. 52. Types 10 and 11 are English developments; the others, possibly American. With the exception of Type 12, which became an American standard wine and spirits bottle, it would seem that the others were general-purpose beverage bottles.

Types 10 and 10a were sometimes free-blown but mainly molded for body form with shoulder, neck, and lip formed by manipulation and tooling—a method, as stated above, used to a limited extent in the production of commercial cylindrical bottles in the last half of the 18th century. Usually the mark of the mold top is discernible at the top of the body where the shoulder starts, and sometimes the surface of the body is slightly pebbled, resembling hammered metal, as a result of the gather's having been blown in too cold a mold. The kick-up, either conical or domed, is shallower than on the earlier types. Bottle 7 in Ill. 45 and line drawing 12 in Ill. 52 illustrate Type 10, which came in about 1810 and went out about 1830. "WINE / P.C. BROOKS / 1820" is on its seal. The presence of the word *wine* suggests that the bottle was made for a wine merchant rather than a private individual. However, neither P. C. Brooks's occupation nor his location is known at present—nor whether the bottle is English or American. In any case, at present, I have no record of a later *dated* black-glass wine bottle molded for body form only. A distinctive feature of Type 10 is its sloping broad collar. It was believed until recently that this type of collar appeared about 1820 and thus established the earliest date of the bottle type as ca. 1820. Now the date of the sloping collar has been pushed back at least a decade by a seal dated "1810" on a Type 10 bottle from the collection of Charles B. Gardner. It still seems true, however, that this type of collar was not used *extensively* before the 1820s. With variations of depth and, also, with and without a lower bevel (string-ring), it became one of the common neck finishes on bottles and flasks of many kinds. The blown-three-mold flask, 6 in Ill. 122, ca. 1820, has a collar like that of the Brooks bottle.

Bottle 6 in Ill. 45 and line drawing 13 of Ill. 52 illustrate an American form that I have dubbed Type 10a. It, too, was molded for body form only, but it has a shorter, flatter shoulder than Type 10 and a slightly longer neck finished with a rounded string-ring below a plain lip. The color is clear deep green, one far less frequently encountered than the normal olive-greens and olive-ambers. As the seal shows, it was made at the Mount Vernon Glass Works for an individual whose initials were "M S W." Similar bottles probably were blown in other American glasshouses, and in the same period, which probably was about 1810 to 1830. I believe the bottle shows the form of the "PORTER, BEER and CIDER" bottles advertised by the Mount Vernon Glass Company in April 1811. And bottles of this type probably were among the dividend bottles—to the value of $20 on each share of stock—that in July of 1812 the directors authorized to be delivered to stockholders upon payment of the installment due on their stock.[34]

Types 11, 11a and b, and 12 were steps in the slow progress toward mechanical and mass production and the shrinkage of handwork. They were blown in full-size piece molds—time- and laborsaving devices ensuring uniformity of shape and capacity, but craft-cheaters. Instead of the old-fashioned kick-up, with few exceptions their bases had an outer rim, normally flat, around either a depressed base or concave disk or (on some of Type 12) a dome section. Frequently at the center of the base there was a nipple (called also *dot* and *bead*) and normally no rough pontil mark, though some had an oxide deposit from a bare pontil. Though a holding device of some sort apparently was used in England in the 1820s by H. Ricketts & Company at least, it was not until about the mid-1840s, possibly a bit later, that such tools, instead of the pontil or blowpipe, came into fairly general use in our large bottle glasshouses to

hold a bottle during the neck-finishing process. That finish was usually a sloping collar with lower bevel formed by a special tool for the purpose (Ill. 53A) and, by the late 19th century, formed in the mold itself in some factories.

Present evidence at hand indicates that Type 11, the first of these bottles and an important milestone in bottle production, was introduced between 1814 and 1821 by H. Ricketts & Company, proprietors of the Phoenix Glass Works, Bristol, England, and also that Henry Ricketts initiated the practice of molding the name of the glassworks or company and the address on the outer rim of the bottle base.[35] Perhaps even before 1814, starting from an English method of inserting the gather of molten glass into a mold of the exact size and shape of the body, and forming the neck "on the outside,"[36] Henry Ricketts was conducting the experiments that resulted in an almost revolutionary method and apparatus, for which he received his 14-year patent December 5, 1821.

Ricketts's invention consisted of

an improvement upon the construction of all molds heretofore used in the manufacture of bottles, an entirely new method in the construction and operative movements and appendages of such molds, particularly in reference . . . to making of bottles such as are used to contain wine, beer, porter, cyder, or other liquids.

He claimed further:

By this my sole Invention, the circumference and diameter of bottles are formed nearly cylindrical, and their height determined so as to contain in given quantities or proportions of wine or beer gallon measure, with a great degree of regularity or conformity to each other, and all the bottles so made by me after this method present a superior neatness of appearance and regularity of shape for convenient and safe stowage, which cannot by other means be so well attained.

The mold itself consisted of two parts—a cover or upper part in two pieces to form the shoulder and *part* of the neck, and a lower or body part that had a wide-open space in the bottom for the "mechanical" punty or pricker-up to form the center bottom of the bottle. The operation of the entire mechanism (Ill. 54) required use of the blower's two hands and feet. As described in the specifications, "The act of treading upon the mushroom-shaped cap of *M*, marked *O*, so raises the knocker-up *N* against the punty *S* under the mould as to produce the concavity usually

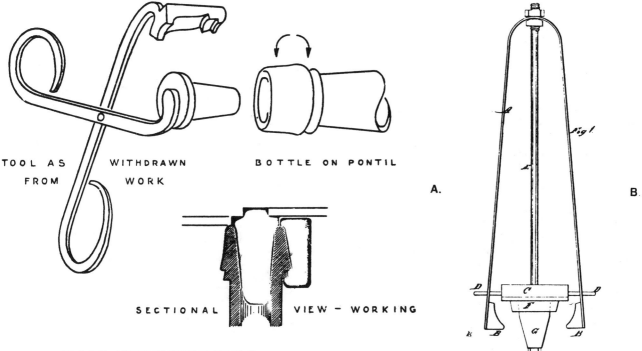

TOOL AS WITHDRAWN FROM WORK

BOTTLE ON PONTIL

SECTIONAL VIEW - WORKING

A.

B.

53. A & B. NECK-FINISHING TOOLS

A. The line drawings were developed from a description that appeared in the 7th edition (1842) of the *Encyclopaedia Britannica,* Vol. X, p. 579: "The finisher then warms the bottle at the furnace, and taking out a small quantity of metal on what is termed a ring iron, he turns it once round the mouth forming the ring seen at the mouth of bottles. He then employs the shears to give shape to the neck. One of the blades of the shears has a piece of brass in the center, tapered like a common cork, which forms the inside of the mouth, to the other blade is attached a piece of brass, used to form the ring." This did not appear in the 6th edition (1823), though

it is probable the method of forming collars was practiced in some glasshouses at that time.

B. From specifications for A. Stone's patent No. 15, 738, Sept. 23, 1856. The exact period in which neck-finishing tools evolved having metal springs with two jaws instead of one, to form collars, is undetermined. It doubtless was some time before Amosa Stone of Philadelphia patented his "improved tool," which was of simpler construction, as were many later ones. Like Stone's, "the interior of the jaws [was] made in such shape as to give the outside of the nozzle of the bottle or neck of the vessel formed the desired shape as it [was] rotated between the jaws in a plastic state . . . " U.S. Patent Office.

formed at the bottom of the bottle, and . . . effectually secures a symmetry of shape." By treading on the mushroom-shaped cap *R*, the arms of the cover or upper part of the mold were raised to close the two halves. Release of pressure on the cap *O* allowed the knocker-up to drop, disengaging the pricker-up; on cap E, allowed the weight of the arms to open the upper part of the mold. If desired—and Ricketts did—within the bottom of the mold could be placed a ring or washer upon the surface of which could be "engraven the address of the manufacturer, together with figures or marks indicating the size of the bottle." Also, according to the thickness or thinness of the ring, the body of the mold was "shortened or increased and the various sizes of the bottles produced."

The Ricketts bottles, many of which have survived from the quantities imported by Americans, are of course immediately identifiable by the name on the

base. All those I have seen have the inscription "H. RICKETTS & Cº GLASS WORKS BRISTOL"—as shown in the patent specification drawings; that was the usual legend until the firm became Powell & Ricketts in 1853. And, as in the case of all bottles blown in the type of mold described, a circular mold seam is usually discernible at the top of the body and opposing vertical seams on the shoulder and lower neck. Not all the bottles with the above inscription have a mark or figure at center base to designate size; some, like 10, Ill. 45, have a nipple at the center and the others are plain. The collar was tooled into a slope with lower bevel, and by 1840, doubtless much earlier, formed by a neck-finishing tool with one or two jaws, probably similar to those shown in Ill. 53A. At some point molds were introduced for bottles with a plain base rim and the inscription "H.R. BRISTOL" around a nipple at center of a conical kick-up, and with entire neck formed

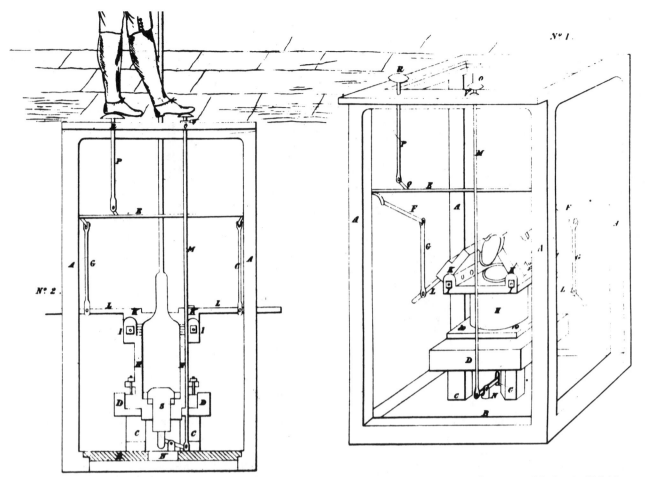

54. Plans Nos. 1 and 2 from Henry Ricketts's specifications for "An improvement in the Art or Method of Making or Manufacturing Glass Bottles" showing the frame for the mechanism "fixed in a pit formed in the floor." The frame—it could be of "iron, wood or other material"—could be "placed in any more convenient part of the glasshouse" if desired. In Plan No. 1, a perspective view of the mechanism, *H* designates the body-forming section of the mold and *K* the opened two-piece shoulder and lower neck section. The open center in the bottom of the mold is not visible. In Plan No. 2 a section of the mechanism is shown with a bottle being molded. The blower, having pressed the cap *O*, has raised the knocker-up *N* to force the punty *S* to form the "concavity usually formed at the bottom of the bottle," and by pressing on the cap *R*, has closed the pieces of the upper part. Patent No. 4623, Dec. 3, 1821. *British Patent Specifications* (printed in London 1857).

in the mold. The last feature would indicate a later type of mold than that described in the patent, and late 19th century if Mr. Hume's statement "completely machine made" included the collar,[37] since forming the collar in the mold evolved sometime after 1850—at least, in American bottle production. Also, the bottle was the *slender* cylindrical form like Type 12.

Both these types of Ricketts bottles have "PATENT" molded on the shoulder. Perhaps I should say they "normally" do, for "PATENT" does not appear on the black-glass bottle, 10 in Ill. 45, with a large nipple at center base and "W. Leman / Chard / 1771" impressed on a seal on the side. (According to Lady Ruggles-Brise, 1771, which could not have been the date of the bottle, is the probable date Leman established his business at Chard, Somerset, England.) Two explanations of the absence of "patent" seem

possible: the Leman bottles may have been blown before 1821 during the experimental stage of the improved method of manufacture, or "PATENT" was not cut in all the molds used in the mechanism. Certainly by 1822 it was the rule, even on special-order bottles. The collection of Charles B. Gardner included three sizes of bottles with the first base rim inscription that have applied and dated seals: (1) olive-green, 26 ounces, seal with "I.F./1822"; (2) deep olive-amber, 38 ounces, seal with "Jnº / Furse / 1823", shown by 13 in Ill. 52; (3) olive-green, 40 ounces, seal with "J./Head/1825" and "IMPERIAL" on shoulder opposite "PATENT". These bottles were obtained in the United States, but it has not been determined whether they were made for Englishmen, as seems most likely, or Americans, as may be possible. Special-order wine bottles with "PATENT" on the shoulder and the first inscription on the base rim were made at the Phoenix Glass Works for at least one American firm of tea and wine merchants—Biningers of New York City, whose business, according to labels found on bottles made for them, was established in 1778. The bottles, blown from black (dark olive-green) glass have on the side an applied seal with "BININGER.NEW YORK." encircling a bunch of grapes in low relief. These bottles are believed to be the earliest marked Bininger bottles that have been recorded. An example is illustrated by 2 in Plate 223 in *American Glass*.

The form of the bottle and the marking on the base were to be reflected in American wine and beverage bottles, but how much influence Ricketts's apparatus exerted upon American production is undetermined. As yet I have found no evidence that it was ever copied here, even after the expiration of his 14-year patent. If full-size molds were not in use for wine and other beverage bottles of this kind by the time of the patent, the influence must have been considerable. But it is probable that manually operated full-size molds having a body part and two-piece upper part had already been introduced in some American glassworks. Also, in the light of the steady importation of Ricketts's bottles of "Superior neatness" and "regularity of shape," it seems likely that more than one of our bottle manufacturers would have turned to the full-size two-piece mold, which likewise ensured uniformity of shape and capacity and had been used for at least one American patent medicine bottle by 1809 and Figured Flasks about 1814.[38] As for the marking, with one exception the recorded marked beverage bottles having the base type of, or similar to, the Ricketts bottles cannot be dated before the mid-1840s and later.

The exception is a type of bottle produced by the New-England Glass-Bottle Company of Cambridge (1827–45), Massachusetts, having the molded inscription "NEW ENG. GLASS BOTTLE CO." on the base, probably the first to be so inscribed in the United States. The inscription is not boldly molded on the rare example 8 in Ill. 45, which is black glass and might be classified as a junk bottle. It is a sturdy bottle, well suited to porter, beer, ale, and certainly cider, which, as an 18th-century writer observed, required "special precaution in the bottling, being more apt to fly, and burst the bottle than other liquors."[39] The similarity of the bottle in Rufus F. Phipps's 1822 advertisement of lemon syrup, Ill. 57, and in the 1827 advertisement of James Butler, proprietor of a Philadelphia Porter and Cider Vault, Ill. 58B, to the New-England Glass-Bottle Company's bottle offers pictorial evidence suggesting that the

nature of their contents varied widely. These bottles, which I have called Type 11a, seem to be transitional between Types 10 and 11, one reason I believe they were first made in the early years of the company's career. In shape and proportions they are similar to Type 10; to Type 11, in neck finish of flat sloping collar with lower bevel and base with rim around a depressed center—in this instance, a slightly rounded rather than flat or sloping rim. Also, they were blown in a mold having body part and upper part forming the shoulder and lower neck. Some bottles of similar type, but anonymous as to factory, were blown in full-size two-piece molds and have opposing vertical mold marks.

The American bottles I have called Type 11b (15 in Ill. 52) were made from about 1840 into the 1870s at least. Though the proportions of neck to body differ slightly, they are closely similar to Type 11 in shape. They were blown in molds having body part and two-piece upper part and, on the base, an outer rim around the center with and without a nipple or other device. The upper mold seams extend to the collar formed by a neck-finishing tool. These bottles may have been used by some bottlers for wine and spirits, as was assumed 30 years ago when they were included in that category in *American Glass*, but today it seems more probable that they usually held less ardent liquids, including spring water. In fact, the bottles like 11 in Ill. 45 inscribed "C.W.WESTON & Cᵒ SARATOGA N.Y." on the shoulder were used by the company to bottle the waters of the Empire Spring during its period of ownership, 1848–61. They are attributed to the Saratoga "Mountain" glassworks on the basis of fragments excavated by Harry Hall White and Fenton Keyes. The mold was a private one—that is, the property of the customer for whom the bottles were blown, and whose orders were not always filled by the same bottle manufacturer. Thomas W. Dyott's statement in an 1825 advertisement of Dyottville bottles that special attention was given to private molds was one made by most bottle manufacturers in the years to come.[40]

Type 12, a standard American wine and spirits bottle, from roughly about 1850 to 1860 through the 1880s at least, is illustrated by line drawing 14 in Ill. 52 and bottles 9 and 12 in Ill. 45. It was a slender straight-sided bottle, cylindrical or with sides slightly slanted to the short curved shoulder, and with long neck. It was blown in both types of full-size molds mentioned above. However, if the bottles examined can be assumed to represent a preference, the molds with body part and two-piece upper part were preferred. On some, the vertical mold seams occur only

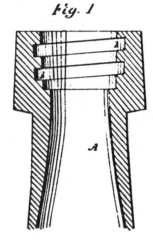

Fig. 1

S. A. Whitney,
Bottle Stopper.
N? 31,046.

Patented Jan. 1, 1861.

Fig. 2.

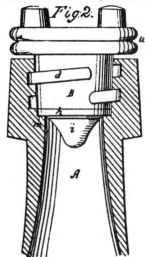

55. From Samuel A. Whitney's specifications for his "Bottle Stopper," patent No. 31046, Jan. 1, 1861. Fig. 1 shows the grooves in neck of the bottle. Fig. 2, on which *"h"* is a cork washer, shows the stopper in place. "The stopper is formed by pressing or casting the molten . . . glass in molds of the desired shape. . . . Although . . . applicable to a variety of bottles and jars, it is especially well adapted to and has been more especially designed for use in connection with mineral-water bottles, and such as contain effervescing wines, malt liquors, &c., the corks used in this class of bottles, if not lost, being generally so mutilated as to be unfit for second use when the bottles are refilled." (U.S. Patent Office.)

Flasks and wine bottles fitted with the patent stoppers were also produced at the Whitney Glass Works, Glassboro, N.J. (See GXV–26, in the Charts.)

on the shoulder; on others, they extend partway up the neck; on still others, to the collar. The base had a flat outer rim around a smooth depressed center that was a dome section varying in depth and often with a nipple, character, or numeral in the center. Generally the bottles were held in a snap or similar device during the neck-finishing process, so usually there is no pontil mark. Sometimes, as on other bottles of the midcentury, instead of a pontil scar in the glass there is a deposit of grainy blackish substance, occasionally reddish, on the surface glass of the base. This was a transfer to the glass, from the end of the pontil, of oxide caused by frequent reheating, and it occurred when a bare pontil was used—that is, when the end was not coated with molten glass before being attached to the bottom of the bottle. As explained in the note to the Jenny Lind calabash bottles following GI–107 in the Charts, the black color was caused by oxide from a pontil in a low state of oxidation or what is called a ferrous state; the red resulted when the black oxide turned (through oxidation) into ferric or red oxide. The neck, finished with a special tool for that purpose, was of the general type shown in Ill. 53A; normally it had a variant of the wide-

sloping and narrow-bevel collar shown by 9 and 12 in Ill. 45. Corks were the normal stoppers, but at the Whitney Glass Works some bottle necks were threaded inside for a screw-in glass stopper (Ill. 55).

Several of the bottles have been recorded that have the manufacturer's or glassworks' name on the base rim.[41] Unless otherwise stated, those in the following short list were blown in molds having a body part and two-piece top part:

1. "WEEKS & GILSON . SO.STODDARD. N.H." (line drawing No. 4 of Ill. 52). This factory, established about 1850 in South Stoddard, New Hampshire, was operated by the firm of Weeks & Gilson from about 1853 to 1873.

2a. "DYOTTVILLE GLASS WORKS PHILᴬ" (9 in Ill. 45): nipple at center of very shallow dome; blown in full-size two-piece mold.

 b. "DYOTTVILLE GLASS WORKS PHILᴬ":no mold seams visible on neck; sloping collar with unusually deep sharp bevel.

 c. "DYOTTVILLE GLASS WORKS PHILᴬ": mold seams from top part to collar.

d. "DYOTTVILLE GLASS WORKS PHIL<u>A</u>": at center base, small nipple in curve of figure "5"; "PATENT" on shoulder; no mold seams visible on neck.

e. "DYOTTVILLE GLASS WORKS PHIL^A": nipple at center of shallow dome of base and trace of black-oxide deposit showing pontil was used to hold bottle during the neck-finishing process; "PATENT" on shoulder; no mold seams visible on neck. One of these bottles in the collection of Charles B. Gardner was from a special order having on the side an applied seal with "CLASS / of / 1846 / w."

The earliest of the marked Dyottville wine bottles may have been produced by Benners, Smith & Campbell, the firm operating the works from 1846 to about 1853. By this period the Dyottville Glass Works no longer embraced the five originally comprising Thomas W. Dyott's Dyottville Glass Works, Kensington, Philadelphia, in 1833. According to Miss Julia L. Crawford of the Free Library of Philadelphia, the Dyottville Glass Works was listed to 1923 in the City Directories.

3a. "WHITNEY GLASS WORKS": (12 in Ill. 45), nipple at center of shallow dome of base.

b. Same inscription and base type as *a*; deep collar threaded *inside* for screw-in glass stopper patented in 1861 (Ill. 55) and used also in flasks like GXV–26 and 27.

c. Same inscription and base type as *a*; "PATENT" on shoulder; no mold seams visible on neck.

The Whitney Glass Works, consisting of the old Olive Glass Works started about 1780 and the Harmony Glass Works started in 1813, was controlled by the Whitney Brothers in 1839. In 1918 the Whitney Glass Works was taken over by the Owens Bottle Company.

4. "WILLINGTON GLASS WORKS": large nipple between two small ones across center of shallow dome of base; mold seams from top part to collar. The Willington Glass Works, West Willington, Connecticut, operated from 1815 until 1872. The presence of mold seams on the collar indicates manufacture in the late years of the factory.

5. "ELLENVILLE GLASS WORKS": "X" with a small bead at intersection of lines, in center of shallow dome of base; mold seams from top part on lower neck. The Ellenville Glass Works, Ellenville, New York, operated from 1836 into 1896.

6. "BUSHWICK GLASS WORKS": nipple at center of shallow dome of base; mold seam from top part to collar; "PATENT" on shoulder. This bottle probably was produced in the works established about 1865 in the Bushwick section of Brooklyn, New York, as a flint-glass works, which later became a bottle manufactory prospering into the 1890s.

7. "CUNNINGHAM & IHMSEN": concave disk on base; mold seams from top part to collar. The glassworks established on Water Street, Pittsburgh, Pennsylvania, in 1845, was operated from 1857 to the early 1880s by the firm of Cunningham & Ihmsen. One of these bottles formerly in the collection of Charles B. Gardner has its original paper label reading: "Bianco Port Wine / This wine we get direct from the Custom House / and can guarantee it a superior quality / Bottled by W. S. Beach / 676 Fifth Avenue, Cor. Moultrie St. / Pittsburgh Pa." Miss Dorothy English of the Carnegie Library, Pittsburgh, informed me that W. S. Beach, druggist, was listed in the City Directories at this address from 1877/78 through 1895.

8. "W. McCULLY & CO.": inside base rim has flat band around a small concave disk with nipple at center; mold seam from top part to collar; inscribed on shoulder, "LOUIS WEBER / LOUISVILLE KY." From about 1841 Wm. McCully & Company operated four glassworks for varied lengths of time. The firm name continued after the death of William McCully in 1859, into the late 1860s at least. Perhaps these bottles were produced in the Phoenix Glass Works, the one started in 1832 by William McCully for the manufacture of bottles and vials of all kinds.

9. "LYONS / MA:KER / BROS" on dome of base, not rim; mold seams of top part onto lower neck; narrow space between wide flat collar and narrow ring. This company has not been identified as yet.

Many more marked wine bottles were produced by works other than the few listed above. These few, however, would seem to indicate a widespread practice, over a long span of years, of so identifying a glassworks' products. Doubtless, too, as in the case of the Dyottville and Whitney glassworks, each manufacturer had several molds, perhaps in use at the same time and certainly used over a period of years.

3

OTHER 18TH-CENTURY AND COMMERCIAL WINE BOTTLES

At this point I must go back to two early wine bottle types included in the line drawings of forms shown in Ill. 52, and to bottles given the name of a particular wine. The two 18th-century wine bottle types that do not fit into the progression of English forms are illustrated by bottle 10 of Ill. 44 and line drawing 17 in Ill. 52, and bottle 3 of Ill. 45 and line drawings 18A & B in Ill. 52. The latter, 3 in Ill. 44, commands our attention because it was a type presumably blown in some American glasshouses; the former, 10 in Ill. 44, because it was described in *American Glass* as "a variant of the squatty type," assigned to the period ca. 1700–1730, and assumed to be an English variant of Type 3. Since the publication of R. Chambon's *L'Histoire de la Verrerie en Belgique du IIe Siècle à Nos Jour*, I believe that, in the case of 10, I have to change my mind about the provenance of bottles of this form and proportions, having a squat body but with neck longer and much wider at the base than English bottles of the period. It has also a very broad, deep kick-up, which on examples I have seen occupies most of the body. On Plate T, Mr. Chambon illustrates by line drawings the changes in Belgian wine bottle forms from the beginning of the 17th century to the end of the 18th. His 4 in Plate T is so closely similar to the bottle illustrated by 10 and line drawing 17 that there can be little question the latter is a Belgian bottle or, if the type was not limited to Belgium, Continental.

It should be noted that early in the period of this Belgian form, dark glass thick-walled wine bottles were introduced in Continental glassworks, at least in Belgium and France. Their adoption was occasioned by a new development in wines—namely, the French sparkling wines, which necessitated a stronger bottle than had been made in Continental glassworks. The English wine bottles obviously were well known on the Continent, for about 1713 Nizet of Liège went to England on the first of several visits for the purpose of learning how to make the glass that had the requisite resistance to the forces of the sparkling wines, and also to acquire knowledge of lead glass production.[42] So far as I have discovered, bottles like 10 in Ill. 44 are seldom found in the United States, and one speculates as to how they got here. American production cannot be the answer or

possibility, unless future research unearths a colonial glassworks operating in the 1700–1739 period. That leaves importation—full or empty. Importation of empty bottles for sale to the colonists was unlikely in the Atlantic English colonies, but possibly some wines bottled in them may have been brought directly from the Continent. That some might have entered through New Orleans is suggested by a bottle seemingly of this type (I have seen only a photograph) in the collection of Dr. R. P. Burke, Montgomery, Alabama. It was found in an Indian grave in that state.

The flattened octagonal bottle 3 and line drawings 18A & B may be Continental, English, or American. Bottles with octagonal molded bodies, either equal-sided or flattened with two broad sides and, at each end, three narrow ones, were favorite forms on the Continent but apparently had less appeal in England. Such wine bottles, according to Mr. Hume, are comparatively rare in England today, and small sizes for other purposes are rare. In American 18th-century glasshouses, where the glassmen were mainly from the Continent, polygonal bottles must have been blown. However, no matter how logical that assumption may be, only archaeological research can determine its validity. Insofar as date is concerned, wine bottle 3 in Ill. 44 with flattened octagonal body, long neck with string-ring immediately below an everted lip, and seal impressed "W / Vassal / 1760" could be American. Unhappily, who W. Vassal was, what his occupation, and where he lived are unknown. When *American Glass* was published in 1941, the period of this type of wine bottle was presumed to have been from about 1750 to 1770. Since then several more bottles with dated seals have been recorded, proving that octagonal wine bottles were being sealed as early as 1736 and as late as 1785. The collection of Charles B. Gardner included an example of similar proportions to 3 in Ill. 45, with seal bearing the name "JNᵒ Collings" and the date 1736. Another, but smaller bottle, with seal dated 1739, is illustrated on Plate XCV in the Catalogue of the Wine Trade Loan Exhibition at Vintners Hall, London, 1933. In Plate 2, *Sealed Bottles*, two are illustrated that have thicker and shorter bodies and shorter necks than W. Vassal's. Both are sealed: one, "Jnᵒ / Andrews /

222

1779"; the other, "A * T / 1785". The former, Lady Ruggles-Brise believes, may have been made for John Andrews (1736–1809), "an historical writer and pamphleteer" who lived at Kennington, Surrey.[43]

As has been stated in the section on bottle family names, in 18th-century advertisements, the names of two wines—champagne and claret—were given to bottles. In what features the champagne and claret bottles differed from the glass of 18th-century English wine bottles of Types 1 through 9 may only be speculated at present. Nevertheless a surmise seems justifiable that the "Champaign bottle," which appeared by 1757, was so dubbed because it did differ in some respects from other wine bottles, and probably originated in France, the home of that wine. One hint as to a difference lies in a 1757 advertisement offering Bostonians "full quart long neck'd Champain bottles in hampers." "Long neck'd" suggests that a longer neck than was customarily given to other wine bottles was a peculiarity of the champagne bottle. The source was not mentioned, but presumably the bottles came from England, even if they originated in France. *If* special bottles for bottling champagne were being blown in England at the time, it seems likely they were of the French type for that sparkling wine. Perhaps it may be assumed they were blown from stronger and more carefully prepared metal, a desideratum of which French bottlers and bottle manufacturers had been well aware since the advent of effervescing wines. As a mid-19th-century writer stated in connection with bottles for such wines, "it is necessary that the component parts be thoroughly mixed, when the mass is in a state of fusion; and that in every part the glass should be of equal thickness throughout that in every part the glass may be equally strong and able to resist the pressure of the fixed air confined within."[44] Another possibility is that, as in the early 19th century, the lip was plain and a narrow flat band laid on below, and the form slender, straight-sided, and tapering at top into the long neck. Although champagne bottles may have been produced in American glassworks before 1829, the earliest mention I have seen was in the 1829 Price List of the New-England Glass-Bottle Company (Ill. 18). It will be noted that the "Champagne bottles" were listed at $8.00 a gross for pints and $10.00 for quarts, whereas "Wine Bottles" of first and second quality were $7.50 and $7.00 a gross respectively. Obviously the champagnes were of better quality—or required more handwork.

Though perhaps the name *claret* was given to a particular sort of bottle for bottling that famous French still wine before 1779, it was in that year the term *claret bottle* was first found in advertisements: the Philadelphia firm of Harmon & Lewis advertised "Choice Claret in prime order for bottling" and offered "the highest price for empty Claret bottles." That the demand for claret bottles was greater than the supply, even late in the century, is suggested by a 1795 offer of the highest price for "EMPTY BOTTLES, of which preference will be given to claret bottles." Just before the turn of the century, if not earlier, claret bottles were being produced in the United States. As yet, the first known mention of American-made claret bottles was in an April 1798 advertisement of glassware produced by Christopher Trippel & Company, the firm then operating the "Old Glass Manufactory at Kensington" (the Philadelphia Glass Works). The following November 1798 (see Ill. 7A), claret bottles were among those advertised by Carpenter & Heston, proprietors of the New-Jersey Glass Manufactory.[45]

As would be expected, in the early 19th century *claret bottle* appeared fairly often in the advertisements, mainly of imports, and the bottles were imported in vast quantities. In 1801 alone, just one Philadelphia importer announced the arrival of a shipment of 10,000. Occasionally, later, the imported bottles were specified as French, German, or Bristol (English). I found American claret bottles listed in only a very few advertisements between 1800 and the 1830s. From about 1820, they appeared in a few of the price lists and records of glassworks available to me, though they undoubtedly were blown in several works. In the Midwest at Pittsburgh, Pennsylvania, in 1804, O'Hara & Craig were offering claret bottles produced in their Pittsburgh Glass Works. In 1819, Thomas Pears & Company headed the advertisement of their new bottle manufactory with "Black Porter & Claret Bottles," which, as the firm had "obtained a complete set of workmen from Europe [France]," were to be "of the same kind and quality as the imported." Like the black porter bottles, clarets were to sell for $18.00 a gross. Even Bakewell, Page & Bakewell, already so famous for their extraordinarily fine tableware, produced claret bottles in 1824, if not before. In the East, claret bottles must have been produced by Dyott—as glass factor he handled them in 1819—and other bottle manufacturers, but as yet I have not found the term in Eastern sources until 1829, when the New-England Glass-Bottle Company's price list (Ill. 18) of that year gave the current prices for quart claret bottles as $9.00 a gross and for pints, $7.00. It is interesting to note the drop of prices between 1819 and 1829, so indicative of increased American production and competition and also of tariff protection.[46]

None of the listings gave a clue as to exactly what "kind and quality" characterized the typical claret bottle. However, that the French claret bottle was the model and considered superior to any deviation from it, at least by some American manufacturers and their customers, may be inferred from Deming Jarves's 1831 advertisement of the New-England Glass-Bottle Company's claret bottles as "a correct imitation of the French." It certainly would be natural in any period for the current French claret bottle to constitute the norm for claret wine wherever it was made and/or bottled. Presumably, unlike bottles for effervescing wines, the French bottles for claret were thin-walled: in 1832 an Englishwoman, advising the frugal housewife to save bottles for bottling cider and beer, warned that "if they are thin French glass like claret bottles they will not answer."[47] Presumably too they were cylindrical bottles, but the only description of a claret bottle I know of is a

humorous one, sent to me by Kenneth M. Wilson, from "A Chapter on Bottles," which appeared in the Boston *Daily Evening Transcript* for September 17, 1831, and which confirms the conclusion that the classic claret bottle was a long-necked, tall thin bottle:

Now turn to that tall, lean, lank-looking long necked chap Monsieur Claret. Weak as the liquid he holds, a north wind must never breathe upon him; touch him gently or you will shiver him to atoms. He is one of your slender-built gentlemen, somewhat quakish, with falling shoulders and a very high crowned hat. . . .

Before closing my inconclusive comments on the bottles given the names of wines in the 18th century, I should mention again that Lady Ruggles-Brise referred to a free-blown cylindrical sealed bottle with the date "1739" as a "cylindrical Port bottle."[47a] Whether it was called port in its period I do not know, nor have I found port bottles advertised or mentioned in price lists or records.

4
SQUARE, OR CASE, AND SPIRITS BOTTLES

Square bottles, of which types are shown in Ill. 47, have generally been classified by collectors as "spirits" bottles. However, just as wine bottles served also as containers of spirits and other potables, so the contents of square bottles were not confined to spirits. They were used also in the laboratory of the alchemist and shop of the apothecary. And in the 18th century square bottles were used widely in packaging sweet and salad oils, usually shipped in cases [boxes with compartments, usually for each bottle] made for that purpose.[48] Nevertheless, they are being discussed briefly here under spirits bottles, for the long association still clings and it would seem that sometime before the 18th century certain of the ordinary green-glass commercial square bottles had become *standard forms* for spiritous liquors such as brandy, rum, and gin.

Although square bottles were produced in the Roman and Merovingian eras—probably in the Middle Ages too—their proportions were more squat than those of the squares that emerged in the 16th century, presumably in Germany. At least, as

has been cited, Colinet's 1550–55 catalog of the Macquenoise glassworks (Belgium) included a tall slender square, flat-shouldered bottle with short cylindrical neck and the legend *allemande;* squares were also produced in France. That in the 17th century similar square bottles became a common form has been recorded in many paintings by Dutch and Flemish, even Spanish, masters. In the Details from paintings—3, 6, and 9 of Ill. 3—are three short-necked squares that were included in the equipment of alchemists as well as being used for wines and spirits, and in Detail 2, Ill. 4, one with *very* short neck, which presumably was favored for potables. In England, also, such square bottles were used from the early 17th century. By the last quarter of the century, if not before, English green-glass squares were being produced in pint, quart, pottle (two-quart), three-pint, gallon, and double (two) gallon sizes. Also, they were blown "single" and "double." The singles would have been blown from a single gather of metal and probably were rather thin-walled; the doubles would have had a second gather upon the first, and consequently would have been thicker walled, darker in color, and stronger.[49] One supposes the doubles were probably produced by what has been called the German half-post method, in which the second gather terminated on the shoulder below the neck. It is possible but at present unprovable that square bottles were produced in the 17th century in the Salem, Massachusetts, glassworks (ca. 1639–43 through 1645–61). And it seems probable they were among the glassware of the mid-century works in New Amsterdam and New York.

Wherever they originated, square, or case, bottles were customarily blown in clay or perhaps sometimes wooden molds for body form into the 19th century, and their sides were usually arched at the top, with a gentle shoulder curve rising from a spandril-like area at the corners. Shoulder, neck, and lip were formed by manipulation and tooling—as were those of the Roman and Merovingian bottles. In the 17th century, and to a limited extent in the 18th, the common square bottles were generally thin-walled and blown from light olive-green to pale amber metal. Their width of base and shoulder was nearly the same, so the sides had but a very slight outward slant to the shoulder, and frequently—as are 10 and 13 of Ill. 47—were very lightly concave. Normally, on the 18th-century squares, the base was moderately to considerably narrower than the shoulder, with a consequent sharper slant of the sides, as on 1 in Ill. 47. The walls were thicker and the glass dark in color, more often than not appearing black. Though often fitted with a screw cap in the 17th century, the short to very short necks of the green-glass commoners were finished usually with either an everted or flanged lip. The short necks of the aristocrats of the family, usually blown from colorless or near colorless glass, were fitted with a metal mounting for a screw cap or given a flanged lip and stopper, and some were rectangular instead of square. Two 17th-century square bottles with screw caps are shown in Detail 3 in Ill. 4, from a painting by P. J. Quast (1604–47) of a brandy dealer and his wife—an elderly pair who look as though their profits were often reduced by their consumption of the commodity. Perhaps the moment chosen for this enlightening bit of genre was the start of their day, for the dark color of the bottles may have been due to their contents rather than their metal.

The square shape was a most convenient one for shipping in wooden cases; and the square or rectangular, for traveling cases and for liquor cases or cabinets kept handy in a gentleman's home. And these functions may have evolved in the 17th cen-

tury. To quote Mr. Hume, "it is reasonable to suppose that this may have been the kind of wine bottle that was kept in wicker or wooden 'sellers' in the early part of the century [in England]." It seems reasonable to suppose, too, that *square* was the form of the "2: larg greene glasses" for wine (glasses was a common term for bottles in 17th-century England) that, with their box, were entered as £0.4.0, September 3, 1669, in the Glass Sellers' bills at Woburn Abbey.[50] In his diary on August 13, 1688 (or 1689), Samuel Sewall noted the arrival of "1 Small case Liquors" and "1 Great Case Bottles (Liquors in comon)" in the cargo of the *America*. If *case* implied square bottles, as it certainly did in the 18th century, then liquor in cases of square bottles was being shipped, if only occasionally, to the colonies toward the end of the 17th century. There can be no doubt that the Geneva in cases of twelve bottles imported into Philadelphia in 1751[51] was in square bottles: for whatever other liquids they may have been used, apparently they had been the standard Dutch gin bottle for a century or more.

By the 18th century *case*, instead of *box* or *seller*, had become the common term for the shipping and home receptacles, and it led naturally to the common name *case bottle* for the square bottles shipped and kept in cases—both bottle-glass squares with very short necks and everted or flanged lip and squares of flint or other fine glass with metal caps or flanged lip and stopper. Contemporary writers and newspaper advertisements attest to the fact that case bottles were not uncommon in America by the early 18th century. One interesting reference reflecting customs and contents was made by Colonel William Byrd. The colonel recorded that in September 1728 "a wretched machine," "a clumsy vehicle," hired by Carolina gentlemen to carry their effects to Roanoke, "met with a very rude clogue, that broke a Case-Bottle of Cherry Brandy in so unlucky a Manner that not one precious Drop was saved." Case bottles, sometimes called *square case*, and cases of bottles were widely advertised from 1741 into the early 1800s. One shipment from Rotterdam announced on January 2, 1808, contained 1,000 cases with empty bottles.[52]

Sizes of cases and bottles were mentioned infrequently, but from those given it is evident that in the 18th century case bottles ranged from a pint to four gallons in capacity, and by the early 19th to five gallons.[52a] But since the majority of the green-glass survivors found today are from a pint to two quarts in capacity, it may be that these sizes predominated. Also, pint to gallon were the usual sizes for private cases. The sizes of the cases varied with the number of bottles and the uses for which they were intended. The cases mentioned in advertisements held 6, 7, 9, 12, 15, 16, or 24 bottles. However, six and seven appear to have been the usual number in traveling cases and fine ones for the home. Bottles of pint and quart sizes and also drinking vessels equipped the traveling case that frequently accompanied the gentleman on his journeys in the 18th and early 19th centuries. For travel and home, fine cases, many of mahogany, were usually fitted with glass-stoppered square or rectangular bottles of flint or of white glass—"fine polished," as one Baltimore merchant boasted.[53]

American cabinetmakers provided some of the cases that were normally included in the gentleman's dining room furniture, but probably even more were imported in the 18th century. George Washington, complaining about the cost (17 Guineas) of a case for Mount Vernon bought in London, wrote to Robert Carey & Company, on August 1, 1761:

Surely there must be some mistake, or as great an Imposition as ever was offered by a Tradesman. The case is a plain one and such as I could get in this Country (Where work of all kinds is very dear) of the same stuff and equally as neat for less than 4 Guineas. Is it possible that 16 gallon Bottles with ground stoppers can be cost 13 Guineas?

(It will be noted Washington's case held over twice the more usual number of bottles.) Not only elegant and plain cases with colorless and flint-glass bottles, but also simple cases with ordinary green-glass bottles, were frequently a part of the equipment of well-appointed homes in cities, towns, and on Southern plantations. Among the articles listed in a Virginia plantation sale in 1802 was "1 large Rum case with bottles" that had a capacity of 24 gallons in all.[54] The liquor case was also a necessary article when sea captains outfitted their vessels for voyages, and then it more often contained rum than any other liquor.

Kill-devil (the 17th-century nickname[55] of that ubiquitous and profitable American spirit rum) must have filled thousands of case bottles, as did gin, called also Geneva and Holland, which was customarily shipped and kept in case bottles. Hence, it was quite natural that by the 19th century, if not before, the names *rum bottle* and *gin bottle* were given to square case bottles blown from dark olive-green and olive-amber glass with sides rising in a moderate to pronounced outward slant. Two of these bottles are illustrated by 8 and 9 in Ill. 47. The vari-

ant, 8, with narrow base, sharp slant of sides, and wide shoulder, is associated particularly with gin, and presumably it replaced the more straight-sided square as the standard Dutch gin bottle sometime in the 18th century. That it satisfied Dutch distillers as a perfect gin bottle into the late 19th century, and for some markets into the mid-20th, is evident from the small bottle, 12 in Ill. 47, blown in a full-size piece mold. The label, which is the original one, reads "THE LARGEST / GIN / DISTILLERY / of/ SCHIEDAM. J.J. MELCHERS wz / SCHIE-DAM"; it indicates the filled bottle was intended for English-speaking markets. The distillery was established in 1841 and is still operating. In 1964 a letter from the firm informed me that bottles in $3/16$, $3/8$ (½ fifth), ½, ¾ (fifth), and 1 liter sizes were then still used, "although for very restricted areas, mainly in West-Africa, but with flat bottom"—that is, no disk. Just when bottles like 12, with deep, flat-collared lip and small, smooth concave disk in the base, were first made, and when they were replaced by the flat-bottomed one, are not known. Nor is it known when the label was first used. Mr. Melchers's 1964 letter said it was "still in use between the first and second world war and . . . still [is] for a single distinction as the analphabetic population in various African countries set a high value upon completely identical labels—they even count the letters." Incidentally, Schiedam gin was long known in the United States: Peter Morton of Hartford, Connecticut, advertised in the *American Mercury,* December 27, 1825, that he had 5 pipes of Holland gin, Swan's and Schiedam's brand, at his warehouse.

In the past, example 8 in Ill. 47, which has been rare in my experience and exceptional in being sealed, has been attributed to the late 18th or early 19th century, and assumed to be Continental. The initials on the applied seal were believed to be "A|H", though the right side of the "A" flares a little to meet the left of the "H" and form a narrow slanting "V". My inquiries over the years produced no information about the origin of this bottle until early in the winter of 1964, when Richmond Morcom informed me that he now owned gin bottle 8 and one like it, including the applied seal *but* blown in a full-size two-piece mold inscribed lengthwise "AVAN HOBOKEN & CO̱ / ROTTERDAM" on two sides. As he suggested, it seemed probable that the initials actually form "A V H" and stand for A. van Hoboken & Company, and the free-blown and un-inscribed 8, as well as the bottles with molded inscription, was made in the Netherlands. Consequently I wrote to Hoboken de Bie & Company, Rotterdam, enclosing a photograph of sealed bottle 8 from Ill. 47. Mr. Reuter, who kindly answered my queries, replied that "A. van Hoboken & Co. (A V H), the owner of our firm, Hoboken de Bie & Co. . . . established in 1784, are still going strong." However, the distillery is not so important today as are the banking and big business interests of the firm, and A. van Hoboken & Company's gin is no longer exported to the United States. Free-blown sealed bottles like 8, to which he referred as "hand blown," were used up to about 1888. They were followed by bottles blown in a mold with the name inscribed on two sides, and since 1923 these have been "made mechanically."

The Charles B. Gardner Collection included another example of molded and inscribed bottle that is of particular interest. It has paneled corners, a heavy, crude wide flange, and an applied seal on the shoulder with the initials "N I". Who "N I" was has not been learned, possibly a dispenser of A. van Hoboken & Company's gin. If gin bottles were sealed for distillers and dispensers of gin, it is not impossible that square case bottles were sealed for tavern keepers, perhaps even for private individuals. It may be of interest to note that in Sewall's play, *A Cure for the Spleen* (1775), the character Trim remarks to Fillup "If we come to gun-powder and cold iron, I'll be shot if you a'int found intrenched in your bar, behind a tier of case-bottles, loaded with good cherry slings."

Also rare is the jar, 11 in Ill. 47, so similar to 8 in shape. Since there is no evidence at present that jars of case, or gin bottle, form were ever imported or, for that matter, were ever a common commercial product, it seems safe to conclude that the few which have turned up were blown in an American glassworks where gin bottles were a regular product. Jar 11 may have been blown in one of the Connecticut glassworks. It is closely similar to one bought about 50 years ago by William Knowlton in Mansfield Depot, Connecticut, which was included in an illustration of Connecticut glass in Harry Hall White's article on the Willington Glass Works, West Willington, established in 1815.[56] A third is in the collection of New England glass at Old Sturbridge Village.

Whereas it is only a possibility that green-glass case bottles were produced in the 17th-century colonial glassworks at Salem, New Amsterdam, and New York, it is a certainty they were blown in 18th- and 19th-century works. And not all early American square case bottles were the green-glass commoners; flint and white glass aristocrats were produced also. There is definite evidence of the following producers of square or case bottles in the 18th and early 19th centuries:

1. Germantown glassworks, Massachusetts. Joseph Palmer advertised case bottles in 1755; square bottles from one to four quarts in 1760.

2. Wistarburgh, New Jersey. Milo Naeve of the Henry Francis du Pont Winterthur Museum informed me that among the bottles mentioned in Caspar Wistar's will in 1752 were "half gallon case Bottels." In 1765 "various kinds of bottle cases and other bottles from one gallon to half pint" were advertised by Richard Wistar. Also, half-gallon case bottles were among the bottles named in his 1769 advertisement.

3. Stiegel, Manheim, Pennsylvania. Among many entries of sales to the glassblowers themselves was one of a gallon case bottle to Martin Greiner, who blew mainly bottles and a small quantity of tableware in the period from October 1765 to April 1767. Three other sales of case bottles appeared (one of a dozen and two of a half-dozen) and one of six square bottles. Size was not given. It seems unlikely these sales represent Stiegel's total production of case bottles at Elizabeth Furnace and the first Manheim works.

4. Bakewell, Page & Bakewell, Pittsburgh. When the firm added green-glass wares to the output in 1811, half-gallon and gallon square liquor bottles were among the articles offered to the public.

5. Schuylkill Glass Works, Philadelphia. This works was producing and advertising case bottles in half-gallon and gallon sizes in 1813.

6. Philadelphia Glass Works. This sole American competitor of Stiegel's for the domestic market in flint glassware was making "white flint" case bottles in 1773. Probably green-glass ones were blown also.

7. New England Glass Company, Cambridge, Massachusetts. "Liquor sq[ares], stoppered the same as salt mouths" appeared in a price list about 1818.[57]

If these few works produced the green-glass and flint-glass case bottles so much in demand, surely others did also. But again the fact confronts us that at the present time there is no means of determining which of the bottles found here are American and which foreign.

It seems odd, but the second decade of the 19th century is the last in which *case* and *square* liquor bottles appeared in the many sources of information covered, which suggests that there may have been a change in both customs and merchandising in the second quarter of the century, excepting the typical "Dutch" gin bottle. Even in the 1850s the Whitney Glass Works, Glassboro, New Jersey, listed "Dutch Gin Bottles" among its products. In the same decade typical Dutch gin bottles with sharply outward-slanting sides were made for A. M. Bininger & Co. of New York City, perhaps at the Whitney Glass Works. The collection of Charles B. Gardner included a pint emerald-green example blown in a full-size two-piece mold, with lengthwise inscription "A.M.BININGER & Co / NEW YORK" on one side; it had a flanged lip. The original paper label proclaimed the one-time contents as superior Old London Rock Gin, imported and sold by Bininger & Co. at 329 Greenwich Street, where the firm was located from 1852 through 1857.

In the accounts of the Willington Glass Works a "1 QT. Square Gin Mold 25.00" was entered sometime between 1842 and 1872.[58] This mold, doubtless a full-size two-piece mold, probably had the usual outward-slanting sides but may have had vertical. And although it was most likely without design or lettering, that possibility cannot be entirely ignored since such square bottles were used, apparently to a limited extent, for ardent liquors. Among them is a figured and lettered bottle, probably of the late 1850s or 1860s, that falls in the pictorial category of Figured Bottles. On one side, in low relief, is a jockey mounted on a racing horse—suggestively racing toward the bottom of the bottle. On another side is the inscription "LONDON / JOCKEY"; "CLUB/ HOUSE / GIN" is on the third. The remaining side is plain for a label, presumably extolling the brand of gin as well as giving the dispenser's name. It was a sufficiently popular gin and gin bottle to have required at least three molds, each differing slightly in the arrangement of the lettering and rendering of the relief design, or so I was informed by Charles B. Gardner. His collection included them in light green, emerald-green, light and dark olive-green, and amber. The only example I have seen holds not quite a quart, has a deep sloping collar without lower bevel, and is olive-yellow in color. In this color, fragments in the design have been found on the site of the Crowleytown's Atlantic Glass Works, New Jersey, by J. E. Pfeiffer, though from which mold has not been determined.

Certain it is that from the 1850s into the late 19th century, many wine and liquor merchants and distillers adopted new packaging for some of their whis-kies and gins, including bottles and flasks with applied handle and sometimes a pouring lip—jugs, as they are usually called by collectors. The majority of them were blown in full-size piece molds, many of which were private molds with name of merchant, distiller, or liquor and sometimes an address as well. There was no one form type but a wide variety of shapes, some of which are shown in Ills. 48 and 99. Among them was the flattened chestnut shape, like flasks of an earlier period, but with longer neck, like that in Ill. 56. Two others are represented by 1 and 4 in Ill. 48. The former has its original paper label with the legend "OLD / WESTMORLAND RYE / WHISKEY / MOUNT PLEASANT / Westmorland Co. Pa. / [and the admonition] Drink me pure, water me not. / I am genuine from the Rye Lot." Some were of a contemporary flask form similar to the Flora Temple flask GXIII–19 but with long neck and pouring lip, like 6 in Ill. 48, which has the molded inscription "WHARTON'S / WHISKEY / 1850 / CHESTNUT GROVE" on one side and, on the outer rim of the base, "WHITNEY GLASSWORKS GLASSBORO N.J."

One bottle shape was the ovoid or piriform (reminiscent of the free-blown bottles, which it is said evolved in the 15th century) like 2 and 8 in Ill. 48. The latter is inscribed "BININGER'S / DAY DREAM / A. M. BININGER & CO. / № 19 Broad S N.Y." (Day Dream! I have not discovered to what beverage this enticing name was given by the famous wine and liquor merchants.) Another inscribed A. M. Bininger & Company bottle of the same period, ca. 1861–64, is 9 in Ill. 48. It has the original fanciful label announcing the contents as "BOUQUET GIN". As bottles, among the most interesting are those of taper shape, like fine decanters of an earlier period. Two of these that are pattern-molded in fine ribbing and then free-blown are 6 in Ill. 99 and 10 in Ill. 48. An applied seal impressed "STAR WHISKEY / NEW YORK / W. B. CROWELL JR" is on 6. (I found a W. B. Crowell listed only for 1862 in the City Directories examined.) On 10, the decanter motif was carried out by an applied simulated bottle ticket hung around the neck and impressed "THE / OLD MILL / WHIT-LOCK & CO." Bottle 1 in Ill. 99 is also ribbed and sealed—"J.F.T. & C⁰ PHILAD" in a circle—but it was formed, patterned, and sealed in a full-size two-piece mold. These are but a few of the many of which a census has not been taken as yet.

Before turning to other 18th- and 19th-century bottles made and used in America for beverages, it should be reemphasized that excepting perhaps the type of handled bottles and flasks cited above, the

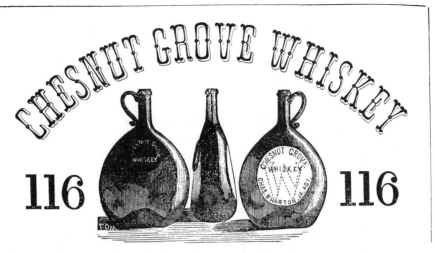

56. From an advertisement of Chestnut Grove Whiskey—"For Sale Retail by Druggists Everywhere"—for which Charles Wharton, Jr., was wholesale agent, 116 Walnut Street, Philadelphia, which appeared in Cohen's *Philadelphia City Directory, City Guide and Business Register for 1860*, p. 38, "Business Register." *The New-York Historical Society, New York City*

bottles discussed in the preceding pages were not used exclusively for wine and spirits, though long identified with them. It should also be pointed out that the Figured Bottles and Flasks to which Part VIII of this book is devoted were mainly containers of hard liquors. They are in a class all their own and deserve to be considered separately.

5
JUNK BOTTLES – ALE, BEER, PORTER, AND CIDER

Among the innumerable potables invented by man, perhaps none was more ubiquitous in 17th-, 18th-, and early 19th-century England and America, more refreshing to the palate or more gentle to the pocketbook, than cider and those three closely related beverages—ale, beer, and porter. And, incidentally, even in the early 19th century, they were not so relatively innocuous as they are today. In fact, if they did not stimulate so quickly as spirits, they did engender a spry exhilaration. They were consumed in nearly immeasurable quantities, on all sorts of occasions and at breakfast, dinner, supper, and between meals, particularly cider in the northern colonies. Such being the case, they had an important role in the domestic economy of many a household and were the source of a handsome income to many a brewer and cidermaker. Although—as has been mentioned in connection with binning and storage—ale, beer, and cider were bottled domestically in the 17th century, apparently not until the 18th century did commercial bottling in glass bottles become customary. By then, bottled English beer, ale, porter, and cider were being imported and sold by American merchants. One wonders whether imported bottles, or perhaps domestic junk bottles from Stiegel's Manheim glassworks, were used by the Lancaster, Pennsylvania, brewer whose "Brew'd Bottled Beer" was advertised in Philadelphia in 1767.[59] And, of course, some of the imported empty bottles must have been bought by American producers of cider and hop and malt drinks. By the late 18th century—if not before—these beverages were being bottled in the North for export, especially to the West Indies. In fact, they were considered one of the young United States' important export products.[60]

Bottles were indeed an economic necessity. Some of those used must have been produced in our 18th-century glassworks, as, of course, they were in many of our 19th-century bottle houses. However, the bottles were mainly imported in the 18th and the first quarter of the 19th centuries. Even so, the supply was limited—there were just not enough bottles of any kind made in America or imported to meet the growing and varied demands, and the pinch sharpened during and following the Revolution. Among many others in need of bottles, brewers and cidermakers resorted to offers of ready money for glass bottles—and at good and generous prices. It was not unusual to offer customers three and more shillings a dozen for bottles returned. In one instance, in 1797, a Hartford dealer charged 16s. 2d. for a dozen bottles of porter, but only 12s. if the bottles were returned. Also, empty bottles were taken in part payment for full ones. During the Revolution, customers sometimes even had to supply their own bottles. One Sam Hudson, who bottled cider in Philadelphia, announced in 1779: "Any persons possessed of bottles may have them filled at reasonable price, to whom, on notice he will send for the bottles."[61] It was not until after the depression following the War of 1812 that quantities of bottles adequate to the increasing demand were provided by imports and American bottle manufacturers.

Although many advertisements and other sources have shed light on the supply, sizes, and metal, they are mute on the matter of greatest concern to students and bottle collectors—namely, whether the types of bottles for cider, ale, beer, and porter differed from those for wine, spirits, and liquids generally. Lacking evidence to the contrary at present, most students believe they did not, at least before the 19th century. The various English-type wine bottles undoubtedly were used for home bottling and, by the time the cylindrical forms evolved, for commercial packaging. If late 18th-century flint-glass decanters were labeled "Ale" and "Beer" by engraving and enameling and flint-glass drinking vessels labeled "Cyder"—and they were—certainly these potables were not too humble for the black-glass wine bottles. The utilitarian globular and chestnut bottles must also have been used, particularly for home bottling. And oval quart bottles, possibly like 7 in Ill. 46, were advertised in 1789 in Philadelphia as "fit for the bottling of beer, cyder and other liquors for family use."[62] Not until the late 18th century did the terms *beer bottle, porter bottle,* and *junk bottle* (the American name for the green- and black-glass bottles for cider and the other beverages)[63] occur in the many advertisements I have read. Stiegel listed "junk bottles" in his 1769–70 Manheim glassworks' account book, but whether he used the name in the same sense is undetermined. Possibly he did. In any event, whether so naming the bottles meant that they differed in type from wine bottles of the period can only be conjectured. If they did, it may have been in greater circumference of body in proportion to height and length of neck, as seems to have been the case after about 1810.

As previously stated, I surmise with others that cylindrical bottles of Types 10a and 11a, ca. 1810–

45, like 6 and 8 in Ill. 45, were used for bottling cider and malt and hop beverages. The Mount Vernon bottle (6) I believe probably was the form of the porter, cider, and beer bottles announced in bold type in April 1811 by the Mount Vernon Glass Company and offered in any quantity at wholesale on liberal terms to merchants, traders, and peddlers. The black-glass bottle (8) may well be one of the New-England Glass-Bottle Company's first-quality porter bottles. At least, it seems likely that the company's second-quality porter bottles offered at $7.50 a gross in 1829 were green-glass and its first-quality at $8.50 a gross were black glass, the stronger metal, and also that they had been in production for two years since the company's porter bottles were on sale in Troy, New York, in 1827.[64] The Mount Vernon Glass Company advertisement made no mention of capacity, merely "of the usual sizes." The New-England Glass-Bottle Company's price list specified pint and quart. Judged by their appearance in many advertisements, these two were the "usual sizes" of bottles used for cider, porter, and its cousins, even for some years after half-pint porter bottles were introduced. The imported English bottles were usually "pint and quart" but occasionally included half-gallon, gallon, and imperial [gallon].[65] It should be added that, like wine bottles, these two types— 10a and 11a—were not dedicated to those beverages alone. They must have been used also for other potables such as mead and metheglin, spruce and birch beer, and also for syrups for flavoring and punch. The "Lemon Syrup" bottles in Ill. 57 and porter and cider bottle, Ill. 58B, are similar to 8 in Ill. 45, from the New-England Glass-Bottle Works.

The English porter bottles, as advertised from about 1800 on, were imported mainly from Bristol. It should also be noted that, about 1800, *porter bottle* became the term so much more frequently used than *beer bottle,* or such a phrase as "fit for beer and ale," it might be considered a generic name for bottles associated primarily with malt and hop beverages. From about 1821, the Bristol bottles apparently preferred above all others were Henry Ricketts & Company's patent porter bottles, as well as its wine bottles. (See Ill. 54 and section 2 on wine bottles.) Black-glass porter bottles were considered superior to the green, and green porters were rarely listed among the imports advertised. The black-glass porters, being better quality, were more expensive whether imported or domestic. For instance, under "Prices Current" in the *Daily Pittsburgh Gazette,* September 6, 1833, Pittsburgh green porters were $7.50 a gross whereas black porters were $12. Not

Wholesome Beverage.

Phipps' Real Lemon Syrup

FOR making Lemonade or Punch of an excellent quality and with the greatest despatch.— Sold wholesale and retail by the Manufacturer **RUFUS F. PHIPPS**, at his Store near the Square, Charlestown, (Mass.) Likewise, by Thompson & Pierce, No. 6, Market-square ; Stone & Crosby, corner of Charles and Cambridge-streets; John A. Lamson, No. 2, Boylston-square ; Wm. B. Bradford, 17, India-street ; John R. Bradford, 16, Dock-square ; James Shepherd, 57, Hanover-street, Boston, and by most Grocers of respectability in the State.　July 20

57. The bottle (similar to No. 8 in Ill. 45) illustrating Phipps's advertisement, which appeared in the Boston *Evening City Gazette,* Aug. 3, 1822, represents a common junk bottle used for all sorts of potables, including beer and also porter as shown by Ill. 58*B. American Antiquarian Society, Worcester, Massachusetts*

unnaturally, since the English porter bottles, black or green, were considered the most superior made anywhere, most American bottle-manufacturers aimed to equal them in quality and durability, and many claimed to do so. The following quotation from an advertisement by Pepperd & Teater in *Liberty Hall and Cincinnati Gazette* for August 12, 1825, reflects this objective and also the importance of breweries and bottles for them in the midwestern economy:

The public are specially notified that particular / attention will be paid to the manufacture of Por- / ter bottles, so as to be able the commencing / season to furnish a full stock of those of a superior quality. Brewers and bottlers generally / in the western country are invited to examine / the quality of the Moscow Porter bottles, and / enter into contracts, where they may depend / on a superior article, equal in strength to the / English bottles and at lower prices.

It is interesting to note that, according to a July 16, 1824, advertisement in the same paper, the Moscow

porter bottles were "strong, heavy, and black." Nevertheless, that some English porter bottles were present even in Cincinnati far from the eastern seaboard is evident in merchants' advertisements. For instance, in April 1830 "English porter bottles, received via New Orleans," were offered by one merchant. And on May 15, 1829, 12 gross of English porter bottles were offered.[66] However, 25 gross of undoubtedly domestic manufacture were also advertised on the same day in 1829.

As was pointed out at the beginning of this brief discussion of junk bottles, contemporary sources were mute as to the exact shape of bottles for cider, beer, ale, and porter. In fact, the only early reference to shape that I have found was just as tantalizing as its omission of all descriptive words. In the *New York Commercial Advertiser* of November 1, 1830, Masters & Markoe advertised "Bristol Patent quart and pint Porter Bottles / Do old shape pint bottles." At present one can only speculate about the shape of the *old* as compared to that of the *patent.* However, there is a bit of pictorial evidence, an illustration of an advertisement, which suggests that after 1800, but before 1815, a particular form of porter bottle did appear. A squat bottle, cylindrical with flattish shoulder, was depicted in Paul Reilly's 1815 advertisement of porter (Ill. 58A). The illustration may be more of a caricature than a portrait, but it undoubtedly approximated a form that had been evolved by then—especially for ale, beer, and porter. Perhaps it was brought out by Henry Ricketts & Company of Bristol about 1814, but whether it was the "old shape" mentioned in 1830 or the shape of the "patent" porters is conjectural. In any event, a somewhat squat bottle continued to be *a*, if not *the*, popular standard form into the late 19th century. By the midcentury such porter bottles, usually 8 to 12 ounces in size and blown from emerald-green or blue glass as well as from the usual black and green metal, were given thick, deep, and sloping or rounded collars like those of mineral and soda water bottles, and were often marked with one, two, or three *x*'s.

In the Charles B. Gardner collection was a cylindrical squat-bodied half-pint bottle similar to that in the 1815 advertisement—medium green in color, with thick rounded collar and a nipple at the center of a depressed base. On one side was the molded inscription "PHILADELPHIA [in semicircle] XXX / PORTER & ALE"; "HONESDALE / GLASS WORKS [in semicircle] /PA." appeared on the other. This bottle is attributed to the 1840–61 period of the Honesdale Glass Works at Traceyville (near Honesdale), Pennsylvania; the works was destroyed by fire

58A. Corked porter bottle and corkscrew illustrating advertisement by Paul Reilly, Philadelphia dealer, of bottled porter "suitable for any of the West India Markets." (Philadelphia, *Poulson's American Daily Advertiser,* Oct. 13, 1815.) *The New-York Historical Society, New York City*

PHILADELPHIA BOTTLED PORTER,
Of very superior quality, fit for immediate use, in any quantity, from a single bottle to a hogshead, may be had at
JAMES BUTLER'S,
PORTER AND CIDER VAULT,
No. 112 FULTON,
near the corner of Nassau-street.
Quarts, at $1 per dozen.
Sent to any part of the city free of expense.
Cash for Empty Bottles.
Shipping orders put up at the shortest notice.
je 13–1w

58B. Junk bottle from which a corkscrew is removing the cork with a "pop," illustrating advertisement of James Butler's New York Porter and Cider Vault, at which Philadelphia porter could be purchased by the bottle, by the dozen quarts at $1, and shipped. Note that city deliveries were free and, even in 1827, cash was being offered for empty bottles. (*New York Commercial Advertiser,* June 13, 1827.) *The New-York Historical Society, New York City*

in 1861 and not rebuilt until about 1871. Another of these porter bottles from the same collection is light gray-blue, with a thick deep sloping collar and small domed kick-up. On one side it is inscribed "LANCASTER [in shallow arc] / X / GLASS WORKS" and "X X" appears on the other.[67] This glassworks, established in Lancaster not far from Buffalo, New

York, operated from 1849 until about 1900. A third porter is deep rich green in color, has a deep sloping collar with lower bevel and a high dome kickup with black oxide deposit. On one side it is inscribed in small letters "DYOTTVILLE GLASS WORKS" [in deep arch] / PHILAD^A"; on the other, in large letters, "B.L.WINN." A fourth, also rich green in color, has a sloping collar rounded at bottom and a base with the circular inscription "DYOTTVILLE GLASS WORKS" in large letters inside the outer rounded rim. Both may be attributed to the 1844–60 period of the works.

In the collection of Warren C. Lane, another interesting porter bottle has a sloping instead of rounded shoulder and is emerald-green in color. It is inscribed on one side "W.EAGLE / CANAL $^{ST.}$ N.Y."; "PHILADELPHIA PORTER" on the other. In the New York City directories, William Eagle was first listed in 1845. His 1851/52 listing included "premium soda and mineral water, Philadelphia and London porter, XX and Scotch Ales, Champaign cider &c." From 1854 through 1885 his establishment was located at the corner of Varick and Canal streets. Thus this bottle would have been made no earlier than 1854.

Here again we have a situation in which, even though there is ample evidence that certain bottles (in this case, those for cider, ale, beer, and porter) were an important line of many bottle manufacturers, only those marked with the name of a works or firm can be positively identified with a particular glassworks. The porter bottles advertised in 1813 by the Schuylkill Glass Works, Philadelphia, in 1819 by Thomas Pears & Company and in 1823 by Bakewell, Page and Bakewell of Pittsburgh, and in 1815 by Pepperd & Teater of Moscow, Ohio, would not have been marked since, so far as is known at present, the practice had not been adopted as yet by American bottle manufacturers. Even Thomas W. Dyott, who in 1827 warranted the porter bottles blown in his Philadelphia and Kensington Glass Works to be "equal in strength to Bristol Bottles," apparently did not carry his emulation to the point of inscribing his bottles on the base,[68] but the New-England Glass-Bottle Company may have. However, the recorded *marked* bottles that definitely were used for porter were produced in the mid- to late 19th century. Nevertheless, they offer an interesting field of bottle collecting, especially since—as in the case of the handled spirits and the wine bottle with name of glass manufacturers, glassworks, and merchants—no complete census has been taken of the marked porter bottles.

6
SPRING, MINERAL, AND SODA
WATER BOTTLES

For two millennia or more man's faith in the medicinal properties of natural mineral waters elevated them to a position of importance and even fashion among his innumerable and often odd panaceas for assorted ills; in the 18th century, it led to the artificial production of mineral water and to soda water.[69] Though today most of us consider these beverages to be mainly pure and refreshing waters and diluters of ardent liquors, the medicinal aura still clings to many of them. Inevitably accommodations, which in many instances developed into fashionable spas for the ailing in search of a cure, grew up around many of the springs celebrated for their curative waters. Just as inevitably, as their fame spread, many waters were eventually bottled commercially—some from famous English and Continental springs even in the 17th century. By the end of the 18th, bottling of spring waters was common and important enough to be mentioned in the *Encyclopaedia Britannica*:

The virtues of Spaw, Pyremont, Scarborough and other waters depend on their being well bottled and corked, otherwise they lose their taste and smell. To preserve them, it is necessary the bottles be filled up to the mouth, that all air may be excluded . . . The cork is further secured with cement . . .

By 1786 Seltzer water from Kronthall and, by 1789, Pyrmont water from Hamlin, Germany, were imported by American merchants.[70]

But Americans were not dependent upon imported waters: America, too, had springs with recognized medicinal properties. In 1683 William Penn reported to the Society of Traders that "we have also mineral waters that operate in the same manner with Barnet and North-Hall [England]," and that there were others in Pennsylvania with "purging mineral waters . . . as good as Epsom."[71] Several, long used by the Indians, were "discovered" in the 18th century in various localities in the colonies and young states. Among them was one in Boston at which Jackson's Spaw was established in 1767; the waters were "recommended by the most Eminent Physicians for their efficacy in a great Variety of Disorders." They were bottled as well as drunk at the spring, and if one had a physician's certificate of inability to pay, a bottle of water was free; if not, the

charge was "1 copper for every quart bottle to carry away." Apparently the chronic bottle shortage of the period plagued Jackson, for persons sending for the water were requested to send the bottles to be filled. Springs only four miles from Philadelphia, at Harrowgate, had become a fashionable spa by 1788. There, besides lodging, entertainments, and "a good and plentiful table with Liquors of the best quality," three different mineral waters were served that had been analyzed and approved by the noted Dr. Rush and a Dr. Moyes of Philadelphia. Far away from any town or city were the more famed springs of Ballston and Saratoga. In 1811 J. B. Dunlop, a touring Scotsman, called Ballston the Cheltenham of the United States, which in summer attracted "all fashionables of the Union, some for pleasure & others in quest of health of which the water [was] considered a renovator." Both objectives, he found, could be well satisfied while staying at the Sans Souci, the most famous and commodious of all the inns. So renowned were the Saratoga waters—"emetic, cathartic and diuretic . . . good in scrofulous and rheumatic affections; likewise in venereal taints"—and their cures that not even the difficulties of transportation kept the little village from acquiring "the appearance of a place of fashion and extravagance" and becoming "the resort of the most polite and polished society" before the 1820s.[72] However, whether any spring waters besides Jackson's Spaw water were sold by the bottle before the early 19th century is not known at present. Nevertheless, since the water from that Boston spring was bottled, it seems likely waters of other springs in or near towns and cities were also, though not on a large scale.

Certain it is that early in the 19th century the celebrity of the Ballston springs and those at Saratoga about seven miles northwest of Ballston led naturally to a market for their bottled waters. However, it has not been determined exactly when these waters were first *bottled*, either at the springs for shipment to other localities or by apothecaries in other communities. That water from at least one of the Ballston springs was available to Albany citizens by 1809, if not earlier, is evidenced by General Peter Gansevoort's purchase of "six bottles Ballston water." Of Saratoga's waters, apparently that of the Congress Spring was the first obtainable by medicinal spring-water addicts away from the springs. In part perhaps this was so because, if J. B. Dunlop's observations in 1811 were correct, "one glass [would] operate as effectually and promptly as half a dozen of the others." In 1815 Joseph Wiswell of Troy, New York, advertised that he kept Saratoga Congress water constantly for sale but did not say whether or not it was bottled. If it was not being bottled in 1815, it definitely was by 1816 when it was advertised in Philadelphia by T. W. Dyott & Company. Thomas W. Dyott, M.D., known throughout the country for his patent medicines and famous today with bottle collectors as a manufacturer of Figured Flasks, made arrangements with Dr. Harmon G. Wynkoop of Albany to supply him with both Ballston and Saratoga spring waters. In 1819, Dr. Dyott stated that the Saratoga Congress water that he sold in boxes of one, two, or more dozen bottles was bottled and wired at the Spa.[73] Obviously commercial bottling had been instituted *at* the spring by 1819.

By then, if not before, perhaps Ballston waters were bottled at the springs and possibly those of springs in other parts of the country—for instance, the medicinal springs in Washington County about ten miles from Pittsburgh, where the waters had a fine reputation by 1788.[74] Be that as it may, if one can judge from newspaper advertisements, none equaled the popularity of Saratoga Congress water, at least in the East, and by the 1820s bottling the water was on its way to becoming a thriving industry. In 1827 in Hartford, Connecticut, alone, two establishments were handling large quantities bottled by Lynch & Clarke, owners of the Congress Spring. One, the Sign of the Good Samaritan, advertised in July of that year that "1 to 5000 Bottles of Congress Spring Water, put up at the Springs, in a 'superior manner *at the proper season when the water was most pure*', may be had at 21 cents a bottle, $2.25 per dozen, or $4.25 per box, containing 2 dozen . . ." Eventually the waters of most Saratoga springs were bottled. By 1878 the industry and market had reached such proportions that 75,000 to 100,000 bottles of water were sold each year by the Congress and Empire Spring Company, just one of several companies. And the waters were not only sold all over the United States but exported in considerable quantities to the British Provinces, Mexico, the West Indies, South America, Europe, and China.[75] Bottle collectors traveling in these places may one day have the thrill of finding Congress and Empire Spring bottles in local antique shops.

What were the spring water bottles like, and where

were they made? There seems to be no solid evidence of the type of bottle used by Dr. Wynkoop in bottling Saratoga water or in the early days at Ballston and other springs where water may have been bottled. However, it may be surmised they were olive-amber and olive-green cylindrical bottles, probably molded for body form, perhaps akin to the Mount Vernon bottle, 6 in Ill. 45, Type 10a, in pint and quart sizes, and normally with a thick deep flat collar usually with a lower bevel, which definitely was functional. Dyott's 1819 reference to "wired" not only indicated the current method of ensuring the cork against the forces of the waters but also a neck finish in the form of a heavy collar under which the wire could be secured. Wiring continued to be the standard practice in bottling spring waters. The Charles B. Gardner Collection included an emerald-green bottle with its original wiring intact, and such of the contents as had not evaporated over the years. The bottle was one of the thousands produced at the Saratoga Congressville glassworks in the 1870s in a private mold having on one side a large open block "C" within an arch formed by the inscription "CONGRESS & EMPIRE SPRING CO. / SARATOGA N.Y." and, on the other, "CONGRESS WATER". The wire crosses the cork, which is inserted flush with the lip and is "tied" in the crevice between the bottom of the deep flat collar and lower bevel. The wire used at that period was "manufactured expressly for the purpose from the first quality of copper, some 2,000 lbs. being used annually."[76]

But to return to the bottles used at Saratoga (also at Ballston) before the 1840s: where they were blown is a matter of speculation, but, from the standpoint of transportation, likely sources would have been T. W. Dyott's Kensington and, later, Dyottville works, South Jersey and Connecticut glasshouses, and perhaps the Mount Vernon Glass Works, especially after the completion of the Erie Canal in 1825. Wherever they were made, the earliest recorded bottles definitely known to have contained Saratoga spring water were blown in molds inscribed "LYNCH & CLARKE / NEW YORK". They were olive-amber and olive-green, with tall cylindrical body, very short shoulder, and neck with the type of collar mentioned above. The circumference of the body in proportion to height was slightly greater than that of the usual wine bottles of the same capacity, and the neck was much shorter.

The firm of Lynch & Clarke, mineral water dealers, was formed about 1811 by Thomas Lynch and Dr. John Clarke, who has been credited with the introduction of the first soda-water fountain in New York City. In 1823, doubtless acting for the firm, Dr. Clarke purchased the "spring farm" on which were located the Columbia Spring and the already long-famed Congress Spring, and commenced bottling Congress waters for exportation and sale. After Thomas Lynch died in 1833, John Clarke carried on alone until his death in 1846, when his heirs formed Clarke & Company. About 1852 William White acquired an interest in the company, and the firm became Clarke & White. After William White died in 1865, a group that incorporated as the Congress and Empire Spring Company bought the Congress Spring property and also the Empire Spring, the waters of which had been bottled since about 1848.[77] All of which neatly establishes the periods of the spring-water bottles inscribed with the various owners' names, with the possible exception of the terminal date of the Lynch & Clarke bottles and the beginning date of the John Clarke bottles. Presumably bottles bearing "LYNCH & CLARKE" were adopted when the firm began bottling their spring waters, or shortly afterward, but whether John Clarke continued to use bottles from the Lynch & Clarke mold for a time before having his own inscribed "JOHN CLARKE / NEW YORK" around the shoulder is not determined. The former procedure seems likely. At least, the recorded John Clarke bottles I know of were blown at the Saratoga Mountain glassworks ca. 1845–46.

In fact, the source of the majority of the bottles for the various Saratoga spring waters has been established only from about 1845, and also the types of bottles—except for those from Lynch & Clarke. For the types, we are indebted to the private molds inscribed with the names of springs, spring water companies, and the owners of the springs. The C. W. Weston & Co. bottle, 11 in Ill. 45 and Type 11b of Ill. 52, and the High Rock Congress Spring bottle, 8 in Ill. 49, are typical examples. (Incidentally, the date 1767 on the High Rock bottle signifies the first year in which the water of any Saratoga spring is *said* to have been drunk by a white man: Sir William Johnson, who was persuaded by his Indian friends to take the waters for a number of days, was cured of the gout and able to travel back to Schenectady on foot.[78] Whether the story is history or legend, I do not know.) The main source of bottle supply was the Saratoga Mountain glassworks a few miles from Saratoga and the later Congressville glassworks in the village. Plans for the works on Kayaderosseros Mountain (Mt. Pleasant) were afoot in 1843 when dwindling wood holdings forced the Mount Vernon

Glass Works to seek another location; the choice of the Saratoga neighborhood was influenced, in part at least, by the voracious demand for bottles at the springs. Within two or three years, wagonloads of bottles were descending the mountains on their way to the springs. According to the 1860 census, $29,500 worth of bottles was produced—not all, however, for the spring-water companies. Excavations conducted on the factory site by Harry Hall White and, later, by Fenton Keyes turned up many bottles blown in private molds; the colors were those natural to bottle glass—"black," olive-green, olive-ambers, and dark amber—and the principal sizes were "pints" and "quarts." The C. W. Weston & Co. bottle, 11 in Ill. 45, holds a pint and about 13 ounces and the shaded amber High Rock bottle, 8 in Ill. 49, a trifle over a pint. After the Mountain factory was abandoned about 1870 and the new works built near the springs in the Congressville section of Saratoga, the bottles produced were mainly in deep clear greens—emerald, bluish, and yellowish in tone—and half-pint sizes similar in form to the squat porter bottles were introduced.[79]

Though the Saratoga glassworks was so near at hand as to reduce transportation costs to the springs to a minimum, some of the bottles blown in private molds were produced elsewhere. In the account books of the Willington Glassworks, West Willington, Connecticut, Harry Hall White found an entry of May 3, 1866, for "1 Pt. C & E (Congress and Empire Spring) gross $10.00." Some of the bottles for the Star Spring Company and High Rock Congress Spring were produced at the South Stoddard Glass Works, New Hampshire. This works, nicknamed The Box because it was built in the area of the four crossroads that was so called, was started in 1850 by five men, of whom Luman Weeks and Frederick A. Gilson were to constitute the firm in 1853 and operate the works for 20 years. Just when, or how extensively, spring-water bottles were blown for the Star Spring Company and the High Rock Congress is undetermined, but that they were was established by the researches of Lura Woodside Watkins. In examining the factory site, she unearthed evidence of pint reddish amber bottles inscribed "STAR SPRING CO." above an open star, "SARATOGA / N.Y.", and of quart reddish amber bottles like 8 in Ill. 49: a shade of amber *not* produced at Saratoga. Van Rensselaer states that pint High Rock Spring bottles with the date 1767 were blown also from golden amber glass, and the variant without the date, from olive-green, and that Congress Spring bottles were another product of The Box.[80] Though of different colors, the bottles were, of course, the same type as those blown at Saratoga in the same period—that is, standard spring-water bottles blown in full-size molds, having a base with flat rim around a center without pontil mark.

Future research may reveal that other works also blew bottles for Saratoga spring-water companies: more varieties of bottles are recorded than those of which fragments have been unearthed on the glassworks site. Mr. Keyes listed 41 bottles from private molds with identifying molded inscriptions. They included the following for particular springs:

Saratoga A Spring Co.	S.A.W. (Saratoga Arondack Water)
Champion Spouting Spring	Congress Spring Water, 2 variants
Congress & Empire Spring Co., 5 variants	Eureka Spring
	Geyzer Spring, 2 variants
Excelsior Spring, 2 variants	High Rock Spring, 3 variants
Lincoln Spring	Pavilon Spring
Red Spring	Seltzer Spring, 2 variants
Star Spring, 3 variants	Triton Spouting Spring
Union Spring	Vicy Spouting Spring, 2 variants
Hathorn Spring, 2 variants	

Also listed, without inclusion of the spring name, were L. S. Carlsbad, Lynch & Clarke, John Clarke, Clarke & Co., Clarke & White, C. W. Weston & Co., and D. A. Knowlton. The various "Clarke" bottles were, as stated above, Congress Spring Water bottles. The C. W. Weston & Co. and D. A. Knowlton bottles were Empire Spring Water bottles. Because of the similarity of the water to that of the Congress Spring, this spring, first tubed in 1846, was called New Congress Spring until 1848, when it was bought from Henry S. Robinson by George W. Weston and Peckham H. Green. The new owners under the firm name of C. W. Weston & Company rechristened the spring Empire and embarked upon commercial bottling of its waters. In 1861 the Empire Spring was sold to D. A. Knowlton for $100,000; two years later Knowlton sold out to the Saratoga Empire Spring Company. In 1865, as previously stated, the Congress and Empire Spring Company acquired both properties.[81] And, from the 1870s, it would appear that bottles for the firm were produced in the Congressville glassworks.

Although the majority of the spring-water bottles recorded were for Saratoga waters, and blown in one or the other of the Saratoga glassworks, these were, of course, not the only ones. Van Rensselaer lists bottles for the Gettysburg Springs in Pennsylvania; the Missiquoi, Albergh, Middletown Healing, and Vermont Springs in Vermont; Buffalo Springs in Virginia; Richfield and Ballston Artesian Springs in New York; and Poland Springs, Maine. The last had an atypical bottle in the form of a bearded man, familiarly known to collectors of figure bottles as "Moses Striking the Rock." It is inscribed "PO-LAND WATER" and "H. RICKER & SON, PROPRIETORS". In the collection of the Glass Containers Manufacturers Institute, Inc., is a rare pint bottle made for the Washington Springs in Ballston. On one side is a portrait bust of George Washington within an arch-topped frame formed by the inscription "WASHINGTON SPRING CO / BALLSTON SPA / N.Y." It is a rich emerald-green in color and of the same form as the High Rock bottle, 8 in Ill. 49.

Two other New York State springs and the bottles for their waters have been called to my attention, and information about them kindly sent to me by Robert F. W. Meader, director of The Shaker Museum, Old Chatham, New York. One was the Quaker Springs near Schuylerville, not far from Saratoga. It would appear that Isaac W. Meade & Company bottled these waters in the 1870s and early 1880s. However, he called the waters "Old Saragota," the name by which it is said Schuylerville was called at one time. A "quart" bottle in Mr. Meader's collection is inscribed "OLD SARATOGA WATER / QUAKER SPRINGS / SARATOGA Co. N.Y. / I. W. MEADE"—from its photograph, it appears to be like the C. W. Weston & Co. bottle, Type 11b of Ill. 52. Its color is "a brilliant emerald green with a distinctly bluish cast," which suggests the Saratoga Congressville glassworks as its place of origin.

The other springs were the Lebanon Springs not far from the New York-Massachusetts line. Like most of America's other medicinal waters, the Lebanon's healthful virtues, absorbed both as a beverage and a bath, were long known to the native Indians and revealed by them to white men—in this instance, it is said, to "an arthritic Revolutionary Captain Hitchcock." Hitchcock was so benefited by using Lebanon Springs water that he bought the springs and the surrounding land in 1788 and made his home there. Commercial exploitation began with the small fee Captain Hitchcock charged for the use of his bath. Around 1790 the numbers seeking health or relief at the Springs had so increased that two hotels were built to accommodate them, "and in 1794 the nucleus of the later famous 'Columbia Hall' was erected, to be enlarged, extended and rebuilt many times." At some period in the mid- or late 19th century the proprietors introduced the practice of hanging a bottle of spring water on the doorknob of each room so it would be available when the guest arose. Individual bottles of the water were also provided at each meal. Mr. Meader's examples of these bottles appear to be late 19th-century types. Both are of pint capacity, of a distinctly green color and thick-walled with heavy, deep, rounded collar on the lip, the sort sometimes called today by the inelegant name "blob." The table model, 8¾ inches in height, is club shaped and has the numbers 2443 molded in the small flat base; the "hanging" model, 8¾ inches long overall, is amphoralike in shape, very pointed at the end—often called "torpedo" today.

Though not all the popular spring waters were bottled, inasmuch as more than 128 medicinal springs were attracting the ailing in 1873, and were given approving recognition by physicians, there must be many more spring-water bottles still to be recorded.[82]

Popular as the natural mineral-spring waters were, they were to meet stiff competition from soda water and other artificial mineral waters. (The term *mineral water* will be used for the artificial waters, as *spring water* has been for the natural mineral waters.) By the late 18th century soda water, which had been made in the laboratory in 1727, and mineral waters were being produced abroad. In America, by 1793, a "method of making an artificial water resembling that of Saratoga [the High Rock Spring] both in sensible qualities and medical virtue" had been discovered by Valentine Seaman, M.D., of New York City.[83] However, present evidence indicates that it was toward the end of the first decade of the 19th century that American manufacturers of soda and mineral waters first stimulated the American public's thirst for these palatable cures of its constipation, indigestion, and more stubborn and obscure ailments.

Thaddeus Sherman of New Haven, Connecticut, if not the first adventurer into this medicinal beverage field, was certainly in the vanguard. In 1808 he announced the establishment of his manufactory of mineral waters, which was to be conducted under the direction of Professor Silliman of Yale, thus presumably inspiring the confidence of New Havenites in his products. It can be assumed that the citizens of New Haven—of the United States, in fact—were not yet familiar with artificial beverages of this nature, for Mr. Sherman pointed out that, though little known in this country, soda water was "extensively used in Great Britain for the restoration of health and as an article of luxury." Moreover, although his establishment was competent to manufacture any kind of mineral water, for the present he intended to limit his experiment principally to soda and Ballston waters. The latter, he soon claimed, were "so nearly like the celebrated Springs of that name that they answer the same valuable purpose." Sherman's hope of success was not disappointed. Nor, if he had not been preceded, was he long alone in making the new beverages. Other manufacturers shortly appeared on the American scene, and soda and imitation Ballston water were soon followed by such others as Rochelle, Seltzer, and magnesia waters. Once accepted, they all achieved immense popularity, though none greater than that of soda water. From small individual enterprises serving a local community, the manufacture of soda and mineral waters developed to a commercial status even before the 1820s in some places. As early as 1818 the Old Established Mineral and Soda Fountain in Boston was putting up its waters "in bottles to suit Town, Country and West Indian markets."[84]

The production of these waters was accompanied by the introduction of "fountains" in many towns and cities. At first they were installed at the manufacturers and in the offices of doctors; very soon afterward in druggists', grocers', and confectioners' shops, and a little later in new "fountain" establishments often called Pavilions—the forerunner of the ice-cream parlor. Adlard Welby recorded in 1821 that, among the many houses open for the sale of soda water, some were fitted up with Parisian elegance. The beverages could be purchased not only at a fountain by the glass, drawn off brisk and sparkling for those who wished to drink them in perfection, but also by the bottle for home consumption that was sanctioned by fashion and the physician. Even if Welby's observation that "the first thing every American who can afford three pence takes on rising in the morning is a glass of soda water" is an exaggeration, it reflects the probability that the fountain sales of bottled waters must have been as profitable as by the glass.[85]

Also, it is interesting to note that by the time of Welby's visit to the United States, man's ingenuity in concocting beverages had extended to heightening the appeal of mineral waters as a refreshment as well as a medicinal drink: the soda, if not the ice-cream soda, had been invented by mixing syrups of various flavors, such as pineapple, strawberry, and raspberry, with the mineral waters, especially soda water and especially in hot weather. Flavored soda water may not have been bottled or sold at fountains by 1821, but it was certainly drunk at home and, within a decade, at fountains. Moreover, that by 1829 soda water sometimes invaded even the realms in which hard liquors reigned is suggested by a "To Let" advertisement of "one of the best stands in the City [Boston] for a Bar Room and Soda Establishment."[86] It probably is more than coincidence that the American passion for mineral and soda waters intensified as the burgeoning American Temperance Movement became more effective.

Whatever the stimuli, the manufacture of mineral and soda waters was destined to become a lucrative nationwide branch of the beverage industry. Inevitably, the demand for bottles led to their becoming an increasingly large and profitable line in several glassworks in various parts of the country. Naturally, however, bottles had been a necessity almost as soon as the public was first introduced to the beverages. And, once again, the types or type of bottle used before the evolution of special bottles about midcentury can only be conjectured. If only there were even a hint as to the physical characteristics of the (old) Kensington Glass Works' "Seltzer bottles" advertised in 1812, the Olive Glass Works' half-pint, pint, and quart "Seltzer bottles" that Dr. Dyott advertised in 1816, and Dyott's own Philadelphia and Kensington Glass Works' 3,000 dozen mineral water bottles in 1825[87]—36,000 mineral water bottles, produced by one manufacturer alone, and doubtless not the total production for the year! It may be argued that insofar as his bottles were concerned, Dyott and other bottle manufacturers as well made no distinction between natural mineral spring waters and artificial mineral waters, and ipso facto the same type of bottle served for both. In fact, I believe that was the case for many years. One form would have been that of the Lynch & Clarke Congress Spring Water bottles. That this general type was still used in midcentury is evident from two bottles from the Gardner Collection. One, olive-amber in color, has a sloping collar, a smooth shallow dome base, and is inscribed in two lines "HAN-BURY SMITH'S / MINERAL WATERS". Its capacity is about 18 ounces. The other, olive-green in color, has the same inscription and type of base, but a sloping collar with lower bevel and a capacity of eight ounces. Before the 1840s, I believe the sizes were mainly pint and quart. I say "mainly" because half-pint soda-water bottles *were* listed by the

New-England Glass-Bottle Company in 1829 (Ill. 18), and since there is no indication they were an innovation, it may be that soda and mineral water manufacturers had ordered this small size earlier.

Some students believe that new types of bottles for soda and mineral waters, perhaps designed by a manufacturer of the beverages as the most functional and distinctive, evolved about 1830; others, that they did not appear before the 1840s. The census-taking of soda- and mineral-water bottles is incomplete, and present evidence that I have is too limited to preclude the possibility that the types did not evolve before 1840, though most of the evidence does point to the later period. On the side of 1830 is the fact that the New-England Glass-Bottle Company did include "Soda Bottles" among several named for their intended contents; therefore it seems not unlikely that the bottles differed from those for other liquids in more than their half-pint capacity. For instance, they may have been even heavier-walled than spring-water bottles to withstand the pressure of their contents, and may have had thicker collars for the same reason. On the other hand, the recorded mineral and soda-water bottles are mainly those blown in private molds with the names of glassworks, manufacturers, and handlers of the beverages in the 1840s and later—with the exception of W. P. Blagrove, who appeared in the Brooklyn City Directories as a druggist as early as 1832. Moreover, the bottles I have seen that are not inscribed have midcentury base types. Usually, whether plain or inscribed, they have either a black-oxide deposit from the pontil or a smooth base. As I have pointed out previously, the black-oxide deposit occurred sometimes when a bare pontil was attached to the bottle to hold it during the neck-finishing process. The smooth base with neither a glass pontil scar nor oxide deposit resulted when the bottle was held in a holding device instead of being attached to the pontil. The exact date of the introduction of holders in American glassworks is undetermined, but it is usually said to have been about 1850. The mid- to late 1840s seems probable to me, though some such device may have been used in the 1820s in the production of Ricketts's patent bottles at the Phoenix Glass Works, Bristol, England.

Whenever they emerged, the soda- and mineral-water bottles that became, and for decades continued to be, standard types were *mainly* 8 to 14 ounces in capacity, with the half-pint size predominating—or at least surviving in larger numbers. In color, they were *mainly* aquamarines, greens, and blues, from soft grayish to sapphire to deep cobalt, although dark glasses—olive-ambers

CLARIDGE & RUDOLPH,
EAGLE GLASS WORKS,
Near Morris & Co.'s Machine Works, Kensington,
PHILADELPHIA,
Manufacturers of Druggists' Vials and Bottles; Ink and Cologne Bottles; Blue, Red and Green Mineral Water Bottles, and Porter Bottles of superior quality.

Particular attention paid to private moulds.

---

59. At present the only evidences of the Eagle Glass Works' existence are this advertisement and the factory's site in Kensington as shown on J. C. Sibley's 1849 map of Philadelphia. As yet no marked bottle from the Eagle Glass Works has been recorded. Nor has one of red glass. (From *O'Brien's Philadelphia Wholesale Business Directory and Circular, For the Year 1848*, p. 204.) *The New-York Historical Society, New York City*

and olive-greens—were still used for some customers' bottles, and occasionally puce. In 1848 the Eagle Glass Works of Kensington, Philadelphia, advertised red as well as blue and green mineral-water bottles (see Ill. 59), but I have yet to see or hear of a red one or one marked with the name of this works. Normally the bottles were thick-walled, as befitted containers destined to hold effervescing liquids. And regardless of their shape, they had a distinctive feature in common: a very deep thick collar, which seems out of proportion to its host but was definitely functional. The collar, either well rounded or slightly sloping, was formed by a special tool of a type similar to the two-jaw tool in Ill. 53A; as has been noted, this collar has been called blob by recent generations of bottle collectors. The bottles, usually slender, were of several typical shapes: taper; club, like a miniature Indian club or tenpin; cylindrical with short rounded or sloping shoulder, often with short panels around the lower body; hexagonal; octagonal; "egg," an ovate small bottle somewhat amphoralike with unstable base. Only the egg minerals were new in American beverage bottles. Eventually there were two types—one like the English prototype and often called cucumber by some collectors today; the other, slenderer and narrower at the rounded end and, as already mentioned, often called torpedo today.

At present, available evidence seems to indicate that the unstable ovate or egg minerals originated in England and were used there long before they were adopted by manufacturers of artificial mineral waters and produced by bottle manufacturers in the United States. Until 1974, most, if not all, students of "soda"-water bottles accepted the statements of Victor Wyatt in his 1965 "From Sand Core to Automation" published by the Glass Manufacturers' Federation of England—namely, that the "egg" mineral was designed and patented in 1814 by William Hamilton, a British manufacturer of soda and other artificial mineral waters. (The Hamilton bottle depicted had a very heavy, deep, nearly straight-sided collar.) According to Wyatt, the form did not "gain widespread popularity in England until about 1840," and was finally displaced completely by 1900 by a flat "egg" bottle introduced around 1870.[88] However, a February 1974 letter from Ed Spencer, collector and writer in York, England, explained that copies of Hamilton's patents indicate the egg mineral was not patented by Hamilton in 1814, but that an 1809 patent for a new method of making artificial mineral waters included in the specifications "a detailed description of the egg-shaped bottles to contain the liquid . . ." After receiving this information, I obtained from the Public Library in New York City a photocopy of Hamilton's 1814 patent specifications and later a copy of the accompanying drawings, which show a long slender bottle in position to be filled but without a collar. The patent, No. 3819, not only was for "Manufacture of Soda Water &c." but contained not a word about a bottle of any sort in the text. The reference librarian wrote me that no 1809 patent was found in the library records of British patents.

In the summer of 1974, Ms. Olive Talbot of London, England, solved the mystery of Hamilton and the egg minerals for me. Generously sharing her researches, she kindly gave permission to quote from her letters and her article, "The Evolution of Glass Bottles for Carbonated Drinks," which appeared in the 1974 number of *Post Medieval Archeology*:

William Hamilton of Dublin was granted Patent No. 3232 in 1809 for "A New Mode of Preparing Soda and other Mineral Waters, Spirituous, Acetous, Saccharine, and Aromatic Liquers, and Sundry Improvements relative thereto" . . . he includes the following reference to bottles:

"I generally use a glass or earthen bottle or jar of a long ovate form, for several reasons, viz, not having a square bottom to stand upon, it can only lie on its side, of course, no leakage of air can take place, the liquid matter being always in contact with the stopper. It can be much stronger than a bottle or jar of equal weight made in the usual form, and is therefore better adapted for packing, carriage etc. The neck of the bottle and mouth are sometimes formed that it may serve as a drinking glass if necessary. I commonly stop with cork, which, from the excessive pressure generally existing within the bottle, flies out on the detaining strings being cut; but sometimes I use glass or earthen stoppers, fitted conically in the usual way, or ground in across the neck. I also occasionally use stoppers of various ligneous matter, closing the pores with coatings of insoluble compounds." No drawing accompanied this specification, but Hamilton's later patent . . . 1814 . . . which makes no reference to bottles in the text, has accompanying drawings of his carbonating and filling apparatus with an ovate bottle attached . . . it is extremely probable that the egg shape for carbonated drinks was devised well before Hamilton's patent of 1809 . . .

Regarding the origin of the egg mineral, Ms. Talbot wrote:

If, as seems probable, the ovate shape was already in use for carbonated drinks before Hamilton's patent of 1809, it is unlikely that he could have secured exclusive rights to this shape. It seems preferable, therefore, to refer to it as the "egg" bottle rather than the "Hamilton" bottle.

There is a strong tradition in the mineral water trade that the egg bottle was first devised by Nicholas Paul rather than by William Hamilton, who often receives the credit . . . Dr. Gibbs . . . states that these bottles were devised by Nicholas Paul who was an expert mechanic and had learnt much about practical chemistry and the gases from the Swiss professors deSaussure and Pictet.

Ms. Talbot found also that Nicholas Paul had been a partner of Jacob Schweppe for a while. Although J. Schweppe & Co. certainly used the egg bottle in the company's early days, "possibly as early as the 1790's," she added: "Jacob Schweppe was definitely in London in the 1790's, but we can't *prove* at present that he used egg-shaped bottles then."

Present evidence indicates that in the United States the egg minerals were never called Hamilton's bottle, and not until sometime after 1840 was there even limited production here. In January 1845 Thomas Stanger of the famous South Jersey family of glassmen wrote from Philadelphia to his brother John in Glassboro, New Jersey:

Now I am trying to make egg minerals they are a very difficult bottle to make they are round like an egg at the bottom and are finished in a large heavy clumsy Dutch machine called a clamp, they must weigh a pound and they are so uncommonly particular with them I can make but very few of them in a day [at 14¢ a dozen!].[88a]

Many soda- and mineral-water bottles are plain, commanding attention only by their shape and color. The majority—and most sought after—are inscribed with names, as mentioned above. Perhaps most exciting are those with designs placing them in the pictorial and historical categories, like 1 in Ill. 49, on which the New York Crystal Palace of 1853/54 is depicted, and 2, 3, and 4 in Ill. 49 with an American eagle. These are included in the list below, to give a hint of the variety in the category and for the light they shed on the period of their manufacture.

1. W.P.BLAGROVE: Puce, about nine-ounce capacity; club shape with 12 alternating wide and narrow panels; sloping collar, which is neither as deep or thick as the norm; pontil mark on base; inscribed on wide panels: "BLAGROVE'S / SUPERIOR / AERATED / MINERAL / WATER / BROOKLYN". (Collection of Preston Bassett.)

   W. P. Blagrove, Mr. Bassett found, was a Brooklyn druggist, listed in the City Directories irregularly from 1832 through 1850. This very rare bottle, being 12-sided and having a pontil mark and unusual type of sloping collar, probably was one of the first of the new types for soda and mineral water. It may have been made for druggist Blagrove in the 1830s.

2. M.T.CRAWFORD: Light gray-blue, half-pint; cylindrical, with short rounded shoulder, thick sloping collar; base: dome, black oxide deposit; inscribed on one side "UNION GLASS WORKS PHILAD^A [in semicircle] / SUPERIOR / MINERAL WATER" [inverse semicircle]; on other side, "M.T.CRAWFORD / HARTFORD C^T". (Formerly in the collection of Charles B. Gardner.)

   Thompson Harlow of the Connecticut Historical Society informed me that Morrison T. Crawford appeared in the Hartford City Directories in 1847 as a cigar maker. In 1850 he had a bottling establishment and advertised: "Mineral or Soda Water, Philadelphia Porter and Ale, Champaign Cider. These liquors are of superior quality and will bear transportation to any part of the world in safety." Since after 1856/57 only his home was listed in the Directories, it would appear he retired from business. Therefore his bottles would date between 1850 and 1858.

   This Union Glass Works was located in the Kensington area of Philadelphia. From its inception in 1826 until 1844 it was one of the important sources of fine flint-glass wares. In 1847 it was reopened by Hartell & Lancaster, principally for the production of bottles of all kinds.[89] In 1858 or 1859 the firm became Hartell & Letchworth; the works were operated until about 1876.

3. J.& A. DEARBORN

(1) Gray-blue, half-pint; cylindrical body, rounded shoulder, thick rounded collar; base: shallow dome, black oxide deposit; inscribed on one side "J. & A. DEARBORN [in arc] / N.Y."; on other side "ALBANY GLASS WORKS [in semicircle] / D / NEW YORK [inverse semicircle]". (Formerly in the collection of Charles B. Gardner.)

This Albany Glass Works is an elusive one, still to be run to earth. But not so the Dearborns. John Dearborn's first listing in the City Directories—in 1842/3—included "root beer"; Alexander's—in 1844/5—included "coffee saloon." In 1847 Dearborn & Co. were operating the soda and mineral water manufactory established at 95 Third Avenue by Adam W. Rapp in 1843. The following year, 1848, the firm was listed as J. & A. Dearborn & Co., and by 1854 it had moved to 83 Third Avenue. In 1855/6 Alexander's listing was as "late soda water," and the firm was again Dearborn & Co., of which John was the Dearborn. From 1858/9 through 1867 both Alexander and John were listed with "soda water" but no firm name was given. Thus, it would appear that Alexander returned to the firm after a brief retirement, and it seems likely the name J. & A. Dearborn (no "Co.") was taken at that time. If so, the period of the bottles inscribed with this name may be ca. 1858–67.

(2) Gray-blue, half-pint; octagonal body, short sloping shoulder, thick sloping collar; sunken base, black oxide deposit; inscribed lengthwise

on four alternate panels: "UNION GLASS WORKS [with star at left of Union] / MINERAL WATERS / NEW YORK / J. & A. DEARBORN". (Formerly in the collection of Charles B. Gardner.)

(3) "Smokey cobalt blue," 8½ ounces; cylindrical, sloping short shoulder, thick sloping collar; base: dome, black oxide deposit; inscribed on one side "UNION GLASS WORKS PHILADA [in arc] / D / NEW YORK"; on other side "J & A. DEARBORN [in arc] / N.Y." It was produced by Hartell & Lancaster. See 2. (Collection of Merle D. Baasch.)

4. GEORGE EAGLE: Clear light green, half-pint; tall slender cylindrical form with short rounded shoulder, thick sloping collar; base: deep kick-up, pontil mark; molded in a geometrical pattern of three horizontal ribs above diagonal ribbing and diagonal panel inscribed "GEO. EAGLE". (Collection of Preston Bassett.)

Mr. Bassett found that George Eagle, a bottler of beverages in New York City, was listed in the Directories from 1840 to 1852/3, which nicely establishes the period of the bottle. However, in our opinion, it was used nearer to 1840 than 1850. It is a very rare bottle, differing from the soda-bottle norm in being rather thin-walled and in its geometric pattern. It is interesting to note that some glassblower used George Eagle's mold to pattern gathers that he fashioned into a pitcher and a mug. The pitcher, now in Mr. Bassett's collection, and the mug, now in that of the Henry Ford Museum, are illustrated in Plate 62, *American Glass*.

5. WILLIAM EAGLE

(1) Rich deep green, half-pint; cylindrical body, rounded shoulder, thick sloping collar; base: high dome, black oxide deposit; "W. EAGLE'S / SUPERIOR/ SODA & MINERAL/ WATER" inscribed on one side. (Collection of Preston Bassett.)

Mr. Bassett found William Eagle, "soda water," first listed in the New York City Directories in 1845 at the same address as George Eagle, presumably his father. By 1849 he had his own establishment and his listing included "Soda, Mineral Water, Porter and Ale." His last listing was in 1885. The bottle described above probably dates ca. 1849–60.

60. After nearly a quarter-century of flint-glass production, the Union Glass Works became primarily a bottle manufactory in 1847. *The New-York Historical Society, New York City*

(2) William Eagle—Crystal Palace: see 1 in Ill. 49. (Henry Ford Museum.)

This rare bottle must have been used first in 1853/4 when the first World's Fair in the United States was being held in New York City's Crystal Palace, a pocket edition of London's of 1851. William Eagle apparently sought to commemorate the event or, perhaps more likely, capitalize on it by christening his soda water "Crystal Palace Premium Soda Water."

(3) Light gray-blue, half-pint; cylindrical, short rounded shoulder, thick sloping collar; base: dome, black oxide deposit; inscribed on one side "UNION GLASS WORKS PHILAD^A [in semicircle] / SUPERIOR / MINERAL WATER" (in inverse semicircle); on the other side "W.EAGLE [in arc] / NEW YORK". (Formerly in the collection of Charles B. Gardner.)

It seems likely this bottle may have preceded Eagle's "Crystal Palace" bottle; if so, it would date between 1849 and 1854. It was produced by Hartell & Lancaster. See 2.

6. T.W.GILLETT

(1) Gray-blue, half-pint; straight-sided octagonal body with short sloping shoulder, thick sloping collar; smooth sunken base; inscribed lengthwise on two adjacent panels, "T.W.GILLETT / NEW HAVEN". (Formerly in the collection of Charles B. Gardner.)

(2) Blue, 12 ounces; octagonal, pontil mark on base; inscribed "T.W.GILLETT / NEWHAVEN"; a 6-pointed star on the panel opposite that with the inscription. (Listed by Van Rensselaer, p. 286.)

Miss Eileen O'Neil of the New Haven Free Public Library has informed me that Thomas W. Gillett, spelled also Gillette, was listed as a soda water manufacturer from 1850/1 through 1855/6.

7. J.W.HARRIS

(1) Gray-blue, half-pint; hexagonal with flat narrow band at base of neck; thick rounded collar; base: shallow dome, black oxide deposit; on one side: one panel inscribed lengthwise "J.W.HARRIS"; a star on panel to the left, opposite the "J"; on the other side: "NEW HAVEN" on the opposite panel. (Formerly in the collection of Charles B. Gardner.)

Miss O'Neil informed me that J. W. Harris was first listed in the City Directories in 1844/5 as "beer maker" and last listed in 1866/7 as "soda manufacturer." "Soda manufacturer" was

added to "beer" from 1852/3 through 1859/60; for the next two years only "mineral and soda water" were given. However, the omission of soda from the earliest listing does not necessarily mean Harris was not producing soda water at that time.

(2) Sapphire-blue, half-pint; same shape as *(1)*; shallow dome in base; on one side, on two adjacent panels, inscribed "J.W.HARRIS' / SODA WATER"; on other side, on opposite panel, "NEW HAVEN". (Formerly in the collection of Charles B. Gardner.)

8. J. & T. W. HARVEY: Clear green, half-pint; taper shape, thick round collar; base: dome with dot at center, black oxide deposit; on one side, large open block "H"; on other side, inscribed "J. & T. W. HARVEY [in arc] / NORWICH / CONN." (Formerly in the collection of Charles B. Gardner.)

Joseph and Irus Harvey were listed in the Norwich Directory in 1852. At some point between that year and 1866 the firm became I. W. Harvey & Co.

9. CH^S. A. HUMBAGH: see 4 in Ill. 49. (Henry Ford Museum.)

10. D. L. ORMSBY: Light gray-blue, half-pint; cylindrical body, sloping shoulder, thick round collar; inscribed on one side "D. L. ORMSBY / NEW YORK" and on the base "UNION GLASS WORKS PHILA."

Dorman L. Ormsby was first listed in the City Directories in 1840/1 as a brewer. In 1843/4 "root beer" was mentioned. By 1860 the firm was D. L. Ormsby & Son. Therefore this bottle presumably was first produced for Ormsby and used before 1860.

11. A. W. RAPP: Sapphire-blue, 10 ounces; cylindrical body, curved shoulder, thick sloping collar; base: deep dome, black oxide deposit; inscribed on one side, in small light letters, "DYOTTVILLE GLASS WORKS [in deep arch] / PHILAD^A" above "A.W.RAPP / NEW YORK" in large letters; on other side, "MINERAL WATERS" (arch) over large "R / THIS BOTTLE / IS NEVER SOLD".

Adam W. Rapp was first listed in the City Directories in 1843/44 at 95 Third Avenue, where he prepared soda and mineral water with a variety of syrups, put up "in Glass Bottles." The flavors listed in his advertisement in the Directory were sarsaparilla, lemon, ginger, "pine apple [sic]," wintergreen, orgeat, strawberry, raspberry, blackberry, peach, and vanilla. Two years later Alexander Dearborn, proprietor of a coffee saloon from 1844 through 1846, was a member of Adam W. Rapp & Co. In 1847 the firm was Dearborn & Co., succeeded in 1848 by J. & A. Dearborn & Co. (see 3). Adam W. Rapp disappears from the directories in 1848. It would seem, therefore, that his bottles were first used between 1843 and 1844, and possibly up until 1847.

Like the wine and porter bottles marked Dyottville Glass Works, these bottles also were not produced by Thomas W. Dyott, founder of the works. Following Dyott's bankruptcy in the fall of 1838 and his brother Michael's death on December 31, 1838, it is said that the works were idle until about 1842, when Henry Seybert rented one of the factories. In 1844 Henry B. Rapp was listed as agent of the Dyottville works. Possibly Henry B. was a relative of Adam W. Also in 1844 the firm of Benners, Smith and Campbell took over the works; it operated them until 1852, when the firm of H. B. & J. M. Benners was formed.[90]

12. J. TWEDDLE JR.: Clear green, half-pint; cylindrical body, rounded shoulder, thick sloping collar; base: low dome, black oxide deposit; inscribed on one side "J. TWEDDLE J^R'S [in arc] / CELEBRATED / SODA OR MINERA / WATERS"; on other side, "BARCLAY STREET [in arch] /41/L NEW YORK". The moldmaker could not get the *L* (final letter of mineral) in the same leaf (piece) of the mold as "MINERA" in the third line of the inscription.

By 1845/6 John Tweddle, Jr., apparently succeeded to the soda and mineral water business established by his father, who had first been listed in the City Directories 1843/4. The 1846/7 listing included "put up in glass bottles." This bottle must have been used between 1849/50 and 1856, the only years John Jr.'s address was given as 41 Barclay Street.

13. ALBANY GLASS WORKS: see 3, J.&A. DEARBORN.

14. DYOTTVILLE GLASS WORKS, PHILADELPHIA
(1) Emerald-green, half-pint; taper shape, thick rounded collar; base: dot at center of smooth conical kick-up; inscribed on one side "DYOTTVILLE GLASS WORKS [in deep semicircle] / PHILAD^A". (Formerly in the collection of Charles B. Gardner.)

(2) See 11, A. W. RAPP.

15. HAMILTON GLASS WORKS: Strong aquamarine, half-pint; taper shape, thick sloping collar; base: low conical kick-up with traces of black oxide deposit; inscribed on one side "HAMILTON GLASS WORKS [in deep arc] / N.Y." (Formerly in the collection of Charles B. Gardner.)

I have to confess ignorance of this glass factory, which I surmise operated in the last half of the 19th century.

16. LANCASTER GLASS WORKS: Gray-blue, half-pint; taper shape, thick sloping collar; base: high dome, black oxide deposit; inscribed on one side, "LANCASTER [in arc] / GLASS WORKS / N.Y."

The Lancaster Glass Works was established at Lancaster, New York, in 1849 by eight glassblowers from Pittsburgh, and was operated by various firms until the 1890s or into the first decade of the 20th century.[91]

17. UNION GLASS WORKS, location not given
(1) Sapphire-blue, half-pint; ten panels, 1¾ inches in height, around lower part of body, cylindrical above, short shoulder, thick round collar; base: smooth deep dome kick-up; on one side, well-modeled American eagle with head to right, wings spread, tail depending between spread legs, long pennant held in talons; on other side, inscribed "SUPERIOR / MINERAL / WATER / UNION GLASS WORKS".

(2) See 3, J.&A. DEARBORN.[92]

18. UNION GLASS WORKS, New London, Connecticut
(1) Clear green half-pint; taper shape, thick sloping collar; base: dome, black oxide deposit; inscribed on one side "UNION GLASS WORKS [in arc] / NEW LONDON C^T."[93]

These bottles were blown from a light yellow-green glass as well as medium emerald-green. The mold probably was one used at the Crowleytown Glassworks, New Jersey, ca. 1851–67. Mr. Pfeiffer found fragments of at least one of these bottles of a medium emerald-green color on the factory site.

(2) Brilliant sapphire-blue, half-pint; same form as the CH[S] Humbagh & Co. bottle, 4 in Ill. 49, and with same eagle, flag, and shield (very slight differences in size of stars and other details) on one side, but on the other inscribed lengthwise "SUPERIOR SODA WATER"; with a plain domed base.

The above list is very far from complete. On pages 282–87 of the 1926 edition of *Early American Bottles and Flasks,* Van Rensselaer lists 32 additional examples inscribed with names. For three of them, the dates of the manufacturers of the waters were found in city directories. All three were in the 1850s. There must be dozens and dozens of these soda- and mineral-water bottles still to be recorded. It should also be emphasized that although there can be no doubt, on present evidence, the described bottles were *standard* in the mid- to late 19th century for soda and mineral waters, they were not used exclusively for these beverages. They were used also in bottling soft drinks such as root beer and carbonated mead, and even medicines. The former Gardner Collection included a gray-blue half-pint cylindrical bottle with short rounded shoulder and thick round collar that is inscribed on one side "D[R] THORNTON/ LEWISBURG/P[A]" and, on the other, "COMPOUND / SYRUP OF / WILD CHERRY". All of which is a reminder that there were no hard and fast rules limiting the use of a particular type of bottle to particular contents or purposes.

7
SADDLE BOTTLES
OR LONG-NECKED FLASKS

The name *saddle bottle* for bottles like 5, 6, and 7 in Ill. 50 was collector-coined, so far as I have been able to learn. Although it may have occurred in early writings, it did not appear in the various primary sources covered. Nor did I find a name or reference that could be interpreted as a *saddle bottle,* or even canteen, of glass. *Saddle bottle* apparently derived from a seemingly logical assumption, or report of tradition, that travelers on horseback hung this type of bottle on their saddles. Certainly it was a practical shape for such a purpose. And certainly it would have been convenient so to place one's liquid comfort in the days when travel was more by horseback over the trails and the few primitive roads than in a "clumsey Vehicle."

Whatever its common name, the so-called saddle bottle apparently was a ubiquitous type of bottle (or flask), one that had evolved by the 17th century, probably long before. It was a free-blown bottle with flattened body; a long, usually slender, neck, with plain or collared lip—in fact, a long-necked flask, and in spite of its flattened instead of balloon body, it calls to mind Theophilus's directions for blowing flasks with a long neck. In general the walls of the bottle were medium to thin, inviting a coat of wicker, leather, or other material, which provided also the means for attaching straps for hanging or carrying the bottle. Without its osier covering, including han-

dles and loops for straps, the 17th-century bottle in the Detail from Jan Steen's *The Physician's Visit* (4 in Ill. 4) could be a "saddle bottle" in American collector's terminology. It may have contained Florence wine for the patient. Actually, the plain-lipped and osier- or straw-covered bottles appear to have been first used for bottling and shipping Italian wines. These doubtless inspired sensible imitation in many glassmaking communities. They did in England, where in 1709 Anne Trasker, who stated that "no other person exercise[d] the same trade in England," obtained a 14-year patent on "covering and caseing with flagg, rushes and straw flask glasses now used in England in imitation of those which came from Florence . . ."[94] In his *A Midnight Conversation* (1734) Hogarth depicted bottles of flattened shape (similar to 7 in Ill. 50) with wicker or straw covering, but neither handles nor loops. Some were on the floor, one was flat on the table, and the mantle was covered with them. Their number, exceeding that of the drunkenly merry gentlemen, suggests their contents had gone into the enormous punch bowl.

Although the plain-lipped bottles may have been primarily commercial wine containers, those with collared lip and sometimes applied decoration were surely canteens. Some are thick-walled like 6 in Ill. 50, which was formerly in the collection of Alexander Drake, one of the pioneer bottle collectors in the United States, and was attributed to Persia, 17th–18th century. It was blown from clear, rich green glass. Heavy threading (some missing now) decorates the unusually wide lower three-quarters of the long neck, and the short slender cylindrical upper part is finished with a wide-flanged lip. Example 5 in the same illustration, blown from bubbly light olive-amber glass, with spiral thread adorning its neck to a point well below a plain everted lip, was attributed to Spain, 17th–18th century. Though both have a shallow kick-up, neither will stand; they are unstable, like all others I have seen. Perhaps the more common type used as saddle bottles and canteens was like 7, with rounded unstable base, no ornamentation, plain lip, and a protective covering.

Whether example 7 in Ill. 50 is wine flask, saddle bottle, or canteen, it could be an American bottle.

However, American production of these bottles has long been questioned, in part because comparatively few have been found here. Still, in the light of their utility—for it is believed such bottles served as travelers' canteens filled with wine, or more likely spirits, sometimes even water—they would seem a natural output of any of the early glassworks producing bottles. Even if none were American-made, some doubtless were imported. It seems possible this bottle may have been the type of "large Quart Bottles flat . . ." sold by Nathaniel Cunningham at his "Dwelling House" and of "very good flat Quart Bottles" to be sold by Messiers Bill & Sewall at their warehouse on Dock Square, both in Boston in 1728.[95] It is also interesting to note that among the bottles excavated by Dr. R. P. Burke of Montgomery, in Alabama Indian graves antedating 1814, there was a "saddle bottle" similar to No. 7.

Part IV

UTILITARIAN BOTTLES AND COMMERCIAL CONTAINERS

1
UTILITARIAN BOTTLES, FREE BLOWN AND MOLDED FOR BODY FORM

In the 18th century glass bottles assumed an important economic role in Europe, and, as we have seen, their production in America was sending down feeble roots. By the start of the century, so successful had been their competition with containers made of other substances, especially for potables and medicinal preparations, that the word *bottle* had come to signify a *glass* bottle to most people. Both the commercial and domestic usage of bottles and jars increased steadily and—particularly from the midcentury on—so did the number of liquids, medicines, and other products put up and stored in glass containers. Consequently, production was greatly accelerated, of not only the important wine and spirits bottles but also other glass containers, both free-blown and molded for body form. In the main they were not new types and they persisted into the 19th century. A few were, or came to be, associated with the packaging of specific contents, but most of them were simply utilitarian containers used for many and diverse contents.[1] Not only the doctor and druggist, the housewife, and the producer and dispenser of beverages, oils, cosmetic and medicinal waters, but also the grocer, the confectioner, the

perfumer, and the snuff and mustard manufacturer were among the users of glass containers.

Unhappily few advertisements of bottled products mention or indicate the form of the bottle. Nor, in most instances, have glass manufacturers enlightened us as to the intended purpose of most types, so one has to tread the rough ground of inference and speculation. One thing, however, seems certain: the majority were the *common* bottles and jars of their periods, blown—as were the wine and spirit bottles—from green glass ranging in color from light amber, olive-amber, greens and olive-greens to black, and, occasionally in the early 19th century, aquamarine. Whatever their functions or names, in their variety of shape, size, and color they offer a particularly interesting field of collecting and, incidentally, a *relatively* inexpensive one. Several of the characteristic forms of these 18th- and early 19th-century containers, free-blown and also molded for body form, are shown in Ills. 46, 47, 72, and 75.

Probably the common free-blown bottles were the cheapest. A glance at any such group makes it apparent they were not blown to a pattern specifying dimensions for circumference and depth of body, shoulder form, or length and width of neck. And the blowers obviously followed no blueprint for shape or standard measure. The bottles were fashioned in a variety of shapes, some of which were almost timeless types. But although the *types* were mainly globular, ovoid, taper, cylindrical, and chestnut, with neck varying in length, width, and finish, the bodies of many—the majority that I have seen—were neither carefully nor symmetrically formed. Whether due to lack of skilled craftsmanship or the necessity to blow as many bottles as possible in the shortest time, many were to some degree asymmetrical or lopsided. Yet a sort of charm is inherent in these minor variations from a norm—in a bottle with one shoulder hunched and the other sloping, or its body more bellied on one side than on the other, as on 1 in Ill. 47 and 2 and 3 in Ill. 46. The bottles most frequently encountered by American collectors are the various globular ones that were made over a span of more than 100 years in most American glasshouses producing bottles—from the works of Wistar and Stiegel through to the mid-19th century—but few can be attributed to a particular glassworks. In sizes they range from about 2 inches to about 20 inches in height and in capacity from under an ounce to several gallons. The large sizes will be considered in section 3, Demijohns and Carboys, the names first applied to them about the mid-18th century.

Among the many bottles undefined as to intended function are the small globular and ovoid bottles holding from about one to four or five ounces, like those in Ills. 46 and 47. It is believed they were used by doctors and druggists for their simple and compound medicines. Possibly they were used also by country merchants and housewives for essences and medicinal and other liquid preparations. Their scarcity today suggests that they were not blown in the same quantities as larger ones. Also, to me, it seems probable that most of the survivors were blown in the 18th century: in the early 19th century, commercially at least, they would have been rendered obsolete by the more convenient and uniform types.

In small (but over four or five ounces) and medium sizes the predominant type seems to have been the "chestnut bottle," so called because the body, tapering at top into the neck and with slightly flattened sides, resembles the American chestnut. They are frequently referred to by dealers and collectors as "Ludlow bottles" because, in the early days of interest in American bottles, they were first attributed to a glassworks that operated about 1815 at Ludlow, Massachusetts, not far from Springfield. Who made

the attribution and on what basis, I do not know—presumably, examples found in the locality of Ludlow were attributed by local and family tradition to the "old glassworks" near home. And doubtless the type was blown there. However, "Ludlow" is a misleading name, like so many names arising from the association of a type of bottle or flask with a particular glassworks—an association based on the meager information available 50 and more years ago. Actually, the chestnut type was ubiquitous in the 18th and early 19th century.

These bottles probably were "all-purpose" insofar as their liquid contents were concerned, though perhaps they were used primarily for potables. Certainly bottle 5 in Ill. 46, with its original latticed straw covering, was filled with water, cider, or more ardent comforters for a traveler or worker in the fields. It may be that the "quart and 2 quart farmers' bottles" advertised (Ill. 7A) in 1799 by Carpenter & Heston, proprietors of the New-Jersey Glass Manufactory near Woodbury,[2] were of this or a similar type, and served as canteens or as containers for homemade wines, cider, malt and spruce beers, and vinegar. It could have been a chestnut bottle that the intrepid Madam Knight saw in an old man's cottage where she stopped when she was traveling on horseback from Boston to New York in 1704. She recorded: "This little Hutt was one of the wretchest I ever saw . . . Nar any furniture but a Bedd with a glass bottle hanging at ye head of it, an earthen cupp, a small pewter Bason, a block of wood instead of chair."[3] Glass bottles were scarce at that period, but obviously their possession was not limited to the affluent.

Medium-sized chestnut and globular bottles were sometimes dedicated to potables and sealed for private individuals who perhaps did not care to invest in the more fashionable wine bottles. Five of these, dated 1710, 1725, 1727, and 1730, are illustrated in Plate 3 in *Sealed Bottles*. Occasionally large bottles were sealed also. Two rare examples, presumably of later date and possibly American, are shown in Ill. 46. Example 1 at the top left holds a bit over two quarts and is unusual in its tall ellipsoidal form and in the type of seal, which has a scalloped inner edge and the initials "I B" formed by trailing on a fine thread of glass. The other, top center (3), is a Masonic bottle slightly over a gallon in capacity, which suggests it may have been blown for a Masonic Lodge rather than an individual Mason. It is chestnut shape and the seal bears small linear Masonic emblems, including the Arch and Pavement, Square and Compass, Beehive, Key and Coffin. Formerly in the collection of Charles B. Gardner was the only 19th-century

American sealed chestnut bottle as yet recorded: an olive-amber bottle about 6¼ inches in height, with an applied scalloped collar on the lip and a seal impressed "S : B" on the shoulder. It is attributed to the Willington Glass Works, which was established at West Willington, Connecticut, in 1815.

There were likewise free-blown cylindrical green-glass bottles of the mid-18th to early 19th century that may be classified as utilitarian, since, so far as is known today, they met a variety of commercial and household needs. They are not so numerous today as the globular types and chestnuts, perhaps because they were not produced in the same quantities. Those I have seen range in size from a few ounces to a quart or more. They vary widely in proportion of circumference to body height, and in shoulder form, length and width of neck, and lip finish. Some have wide mouths, approaching a jar in form. Examples of these cylindrical bottles are 7 in Ill. 75 and 9, 11, and 12 in Ill. 72. The tall slender bottle, No. 11, has a sloping turned-over lip, which seems to have developed in the late 18th century. This bottle has the appearance of a wide-mouth apothecary vial—perhaps it was used in a doctor's dispensary or an apothecary shop. Or it could have been in a housewife's medicine chest (essential in households well into the 19th century), or her chest for flavoring essences and seasonings. A plan for the latter chest with a list of recommended contents is shown in Ill. 61. The bottles for it would have been either square or cylindrical.

Bottles 9 and 12 of Ill. 72 also have large or wide mouths—9 is quite similar in form to the cylindrical wine bottles of the mid-18th century, and it has also the dome kick-up and flat string-ring of that period. There is no means of determining that it is American, but it could have been blown at Wistarburgh, New York, or Germantown. Because I have so far found only one 18th-century advertisement of imported wide-mouth bottles, and those of large size— namely, wide-mouth half-gallon and gallon pickle bottles[4]—I incline to an American attribution. (Admittedly that is flimsy evidence.) Bottle 12 is similar in body form, including the typical kick-up, to Type 9 (11 in Ill. 52), which evolved about 1780. It too could be American, late 18th to early 19th century.

The advertisement cited above and the directions for preserving given in cookery books leave slight doubt that wide-mouth bottles like 9 and 12 in Ill. 72, as well as other wide-mouth types, were used in many households to put up fruit preserves and various sorts of pickles, such as walnuts, mushrooms, beans, and cucumbers. After all, pickling and preserving were centuries old, and wide-mouth bottles

304   GRAVIES AND SAUCES.

1 Pickles.	14 Curry Powder (No. 455.)
2 Brandy.	15 Soy (No. 436.)
3 Curaçoa (No. 474.)	16 Lemon Juice.
4 Syrup (No. 475.)	17 Essence of Anchovy (No. 433.)
5 Salad Sauce (Nos. 372, and 453.)	18 Pepper.
	19 Cayenne (No. 405, or 405**.)
6 Pudding Catsup (No. 446.)	20 Soup-herb Powder (No. 459.)
7 Sauce Superlative, or double relish (No. 429.)	21 Ragout Powder (No. 457.)
8 Walnut Pickle.	22 Pea Powder (No. 458.)
9 Mushroom Catsup (No. 439.)	23 Zest (No. 255.)
10 Vinegar.	24 Essence of Celery (No. 409.)
11 Oil.	25 Sweet Herbs (No. 419.)
12 Mustard, see (Nos. 370, and 427.)	26 Lemon Peel (No. 408.)
	27 Eshallot Wine (No. 402.)
13 Salt, see (No. 371.)	28 Powdered Mint.

In a drawer under.

Half a dozen one ounce bottles.	Nutmeg grater.
Weights and scales.	Table and tea-spoon
A graduated glass measure, divided into tea and table spoons.	Knife and fork.
	A steel, and a
Corkscrew.	Small mortar.

1	5	13	21
	6	14	22
2	7	15	23
	8	16	24
3	9	17	25
	10	18	26
4	11	19	27
	12	20	28

N. B. The portable MAGAZINE OF TASTE alluded to in page 47, may be furnished with—a four-ounce bottle for Cogniac (No 471,)—a ditto for Curaçoa (No. 474,)—an ounce bottle for Essence of Anchovy (No. 433)—and one of like size for Cayenne Pepper (No. 404, or 405.)

61. Plan for a Housewife's Chest to be fitted with containers of the recommended seasonings, flavorings, sauces, and pickles. (From *The Cook's Oracle*, Boston, 1823, p. 304.) *The New-York Historical Society, New York City*

certainly were far from new to the English world in the 18th century, the period in which I first found specific mention of them. It is probable that the "glasses" used for preserves in the 16th century had a wide mouth. Also, it is interesting to note that although spirits perhaps preceded syrups in preserving fruits—and possibly brandied fruits were the sort most frequently carried by grocers and confectioners into the 1800s—syrups were used in the 1500s, probably much earlier. However, the earliest English recipes I have read were a few "found out by the practice of Thomas Dawson," and published by him prior to 1587. At least, his little book *The Good husvvifes Ievvell* was "Newly set forth with Additions" in that year. His preserved quinces, "Pear Plummes," and "Orenges" were cooked in syrup. Of the plums, he wrote ". . . let them stand in the vessel [brasse potte] all night and in the morning put them into your pot or glasse and couer them close." His oranges also were to stand all night, but upon the embers, before being put in "glasses or Gallie pottes"; but the quinces and their syrup were to be put piping hot into "a faire gallie pot [clean earthen pot]," not "in a glasse for it will breake." How the glasses and gallipots, which probably had wide mouths, were to be *covered close* Dawson did not explain.[5]

I have not learned just when experimenters with preserving evolved the method familiar to us as "canning"—that is, boiling the fruits in their glass containers set in water-filled vessels. Contrary to popular belief, this method was not a 19th-century innovation. In 1730 explicit directions were given by Charles Carter for preserving in glass bottles—directions that must have been followed in England for many years, if not a century, before being incorporated into a published work on cookery. In his recipe for gooseberries "to keep all year," Carter instructed that they be put in glass bottles, corked, boiled in the bottles, then set in a gentle oven. In the 1742 edition of her book, if not in the first in 1718, Mrs. Eales, "confectioner to King William and Queen Mary," specified a "large mouth'd bottle" that was to be set in a kettle of water up to the neck, taking care not to wet the cork, and heated over a slow fire until the gooseberries looked white. She added the admonition: "Set the bottle upon a cloth when it comes out of the Kettle because it is apt to break. When cold drive the corks hard and pitch them down." (Covering the cork with pitch was, of course, for the purpose of ensuring airtightness.) In 1751 the author of a book for country housewives gave much the same recipe for gooseberries and other fruits but specified quart bottles and corks "of the best Velvet Sort." The bottles were to remain in the kettle until cold, after which the corks should be covered with pitch or wax or a leather tied over them.[6]

Cookery books provide evidence of other uses of wide-mouth bottles. In preserving yeast, one method cited in the 1751 book mentioned above was to put it in "a Stone or Glass Bottle that has a wider mouth than common Bottles have." That homemade syrups to be used in potables such as punch or in various desserts and sauces were often put up in wide-mouth bottles is suggested by Frederic Nutt's 1790 directions to put bladders (tied down) over the corks of bottled orgeat syrup, likewise lemon, orange, and pineapple syrups. Wide-mouth bottles as well as jars undoubtedly were also among those in which herbs, spices, and flours, even dried vegetables, were kept

on hand to be used as needed. One popular seasoning that 17th-century cooks kept "in a viol-glasse close stopt" was "the Italian," a mixture of coarsely powdered coriander seeds, anniseed, fennel seeds, cloves, and cinnamon, with or without a little finely powdered winter savory.[7]

If used by housewives and their cooks for all these purposes, wide-mouth bottles must have been so used by the many confectioners and other shopkeepers selling pickles, preserves, and the like. The 18th-century advertisements I have read that offer preserves, jellies, syrups, et cetera for sale give ample evidence that there were many retailers of such delicacies, and I should expect that if there had been colonial newspapers in the 17th century, similar evidence might be found. However, this trade would probably be confined to the "cities" as, at present, it appears to have been in the 18th. For instance, to cite a few:

(1) in 1731 the Widow Bonyod informed Bostonians she had for sale at Cornhill "all sorts of Fruits in Preserves, jellys and surrups . . . all sorts of conserves . . ."

(2) in 1769 Peter Lorent, confectioner and distiller from London, after working in England, France, and Italy, had settled in Boston, where he would "preserve a great variety of Fruits and also make cordials and syrups . . ."

(3) in 1775, in Philadelphia, James and Patrick Wright, confectioners from Edinburgh, offered "Preserves in season . . . Jellies of all kinds . . ."

(4) in 1789 Crosby & Norris of Charleston, South Carolina, offered "Fruits in Brandy . . . Preserves in syrup."

(5) in 1794 at the New York sugar work manufactory of Joseph Delacroix, besides several kinds of bottled syrups, syrup of punch could be bought—a syrup that he claimed required "no other preparation than that of adding one fifth of the same to four times as much cold or warm water, which in an instant procures an excellent punch ready to use and superior to what is commonly made." Merchants and masters of vessels were advised they could be "supplied at all times with any quantity for retail or exportation . . ."[8]

Though the fabric and containers were rarely mentioned in the advertisements, it seems more likely than not that a large proportion were of glass.

When "canning" became a wholesale business in

the 19th century, wide-mouth bottles as well as jars—in fact, they were sometimes called jars—continued to be a favored type: cylindrical, square, or hexagonal in body form. The bottles illustrated under "BRANDY FRUITS &c" in the 1880 catalog of Whitall, Tatum and Company, Millville, New Jersey, were molded wide-mouth bottles of tall cylindrical form with sides tapering at top into a long wide neck; on the "Fancy French" variety the sides of the body spread to a short rounded shoulder below a very long neck with two decorative rings and a wide mouth. Several of the mid- to late 19th-century fancy commercial pickling and preserving bottles are shown in Ills. 73, 74, and 62. Starting probably in the 1840s, Victorian Gothic influenced the design of even such humble containers. This was especially true in some eastern glasshouses—for instance, Stoddard in New Hampshire; Westford and Willington in Connecticut; and several works in the South Jersey–Philadelphia area. The Gothic influence on some bottle designs continued at least through the 1880s. In general, the term *wide-mouth* as used in the 19th century seems to have applied mainly to druggists' ware.

In the same utilitarian category are 18th- to early 19th-century plain bottles that were molded for body form, with shoulder and neck being fashioned by manipulation and tooling. Each is an individual, its minor variations giving it a personality that, to my eyes, is absent from the later unpatterned commercial bottles blown in full-size molds—regiments of bottles of uniform shape. Square and rectangular with and without chamfered corners, hexagonal and octagonal, those molded for body form only, like the free-blown utilitarian bottles, offer fascinating variations in proportions, shoulder form, neck, and lip finish. In size they generally ran from about five ounces to about a quart in capacity. It is said that molded bottles of rectangular form with chamfered corners (octagonal to some collectors and students) are comparatively rare in England, and that many-sided bottles, such as the hexagonal and octagonal (equal sides), were not commonly produced there after the 17th century.[9] Therefore the likelihood is stronger that bottles of these types found in America were American-made.

A few typical bottles with molded bodies which represent types that could have been, and undoubtedly were, made in American glasshouses of their period are illustrated by 1 to 8 in Ill. 72. Wide-mouth bottles with molded body like 1 and 4 are far less frequently found today than the others. In fact, 4 is a quite rare variety of the rectangular with chamfered

62. Containers illustrating an advertisement of the products of Dayton & Benedict, 119 Beekman Street, New York City. Note the coverings, possibly bladders or parchment, tied over the wide-mouth bottles and the jar labeled "PRESERVES." The container labeled "PICKLES" shows a Gothic design similar to that of No. 5 in Ill. 73, and the square tapered bottle labeled "CATSUP" is similar to No. 1 in Ill. 74. The container at left rear with label depicting fruit is similar to the "Brandied Fruits" illustrated in the 1880 catalog of Whitall, Tatum & Co., Millville, N.J. (Advertisement from the New York City Directory, 1853/54.) *The New-York Historical Society, New York City*

corners. Because of its flangelike string-ring, short body with very wide sides, and very thick walls, I believe it was blown in the first half of the 18th century, surely before the third quarter. The tremendous amount of wear on its sides testifies that its survival was not due to lack of use. The black-glass bottle with sausagelike neck and narrow flat string-ring, 2 in Ill. 72, is similar to the sealed bottle, 3 in Ill. 45, that is dated 1760. It and the others with slender neck and narrow mouth certainly were mainly containers of liquids. Similar to 2 and 3 is a bottle illustrating a November 12, 1808, advertisement in the Hartford *Connecticut Courant* of Hopkins's "Cordial Purging Elixer," which is shown as a dark bottle with a white panel on the side inscribed "CORD / PURG / ELIX" (Ill. 63). Thus it would seem that medicinal panaceas were among the liquids that bottles of this type contained. In fact I would hazard the guess that, by the late 16th century at least, in England and on the Continent bottles similar to 2 and 3 and those in the middle row in Ill. 72—as well as free-blown types, of course—may have been used not only for liquid medical preparations but also for sweet waters, syrups, and juices such as those of lemon, orange, and lime.

For those whose curiosity goes beyond the glass vessel itself and its usages, "stopping" and "sealing" (that is, "closure") become an interesting aspect of

Valuable Family Medicines,

WHICH, in a ſhort time have attained ſuch teſtimonials of approbation, as perhaps, no other Medicines in the form of *Noſtrums* or *Patent Medicines* ever acquired; which evidence may be ſeen in the hands of meſt of the Phyſicians of eminence and Druggiſts in this State, and many other places, in form of a Circular Letter—being recommendations form a number of Phyſicians and gentlemen of the firſt reſpectability, the reſult of *experience*, who have favored the proprietor with their names, but are unwilling to ſee them in every newspaper they take up attached to an advertiſement.

63. Daniel Hopkins' Cordial Purging Elixir was "sent abroad in pint and half pint bottles handsomely labeled and sealed, with directions.—Price of pint bottles One Dollar and Twenty-five Cents, and of half pint do Seventy-five Cents, by retail ... " (Hartford, *Connecticut Courant*, Nov. 2, 1808.) *The New-York Historical Society, New York City*

all kinds of preserving. But information is incomplete and unorganized as yet. By and large, the early writers and translators into English of early books on cookery, potables, household economy, and medicine apparently assumed that cooks and housewives were familiar with contemporary practices (most of them undoubtedly were), and so were sparing of detailed instructions. Still, though our gleanings are meager, fortunately some writers occasionally did give directions for closure. Though I have discussed some of these in connection with potables (Part III. WINE, SPIRITS, AND BEVERAGE BOTTLES, 2. English Wine Bottles . . .), a few will be repeated here because they must have been common ones at the time, not restricted to bottling the specific contents for which the recipe was given, and also used in both narrow and wide-mouth bottles. Evidence that bombase (raw cotton or cotton wool) was formed into a stopper and the mouth of the bottle then covered with parchment or sized cloth appears in a mid-16th-century recipe for water to heal all wounds. Probably the bombase was often dipped in wax or rosin, as was wool for stoppers in France. In "How to Styll Rosewater that it may well keepe," a recipe published in 1588, the distilled rose water was to be put into "glasses" stopped "with wax or corke and some sercenet [probably sarcenet, a soft silky material] about the corke or waxe and

[covered] . . . with leather or parchment." (As mentioned previously, glasses or violles were terms sometimes designating glass containers specified in 16th-century and some 17th-century recipes, such as those for sweet waters and preserves.) By the 17th century directions called for the use of packthread to "tie in" the cork, a process that presumably meant passing the cord (later wire) over the top of the cork and tying it under the string-ring on the bottle neck. It seems most probable that liquid preparations such as rose water were usually bottled in narrow- rather than wide-mouth bottles. Incidentally, not the least of rose water's virtues was that of flavoring, and its potency and persistence are suggested by a warning given to frugal housewives in the early 1800s: "Bottles that have been used for rosewater should be used for nothing else; if scalded ever so much they will kileth spirit that is put in them."[10]

The great enemies of any bottled substance naturally subject to spoiling or deterioration—preserves, syrups, juices, sweet and medicinal waters, potables—were air and leakage. Hence the extra precaution of covering the cork with pitch or wax and/or tying a piece of leather, parchment, or a bladder over the cork and the top of the neck of the vessel. (These were applied also to jars.) Some recipes directed that the neck of the bottle be *dipped* in wax or pitch or as did the Scottish Mrs. Hannah Robertson, in rosin. Sometimes both a leather and a bladder were used. In 1790 Frederic Nutt recommended using both over corks for sealing apricots and other fruits in brandy, and six years later, so did Amelia Simmons in her recipe for bottling peas. It should be noted that although "Hog's Flair or Bladders" did not appear before the mid-18th century in the hundreds of recipes read,[11] their very nature would seem to suggest use in preserving even before leathers. Certainly they bear testimony to the persistence of culinary practices handed down through generations, for they were being used by housewives in some rural areas of the United States in the early 20th century, and still may be used.

The recipes of Amelia Simmons, "An American Orphan," command more than a passing glance because, in 1796, she compiled and published the first American cookbook. In her *American Cookery* "adapted to this Country and all Grades of Life," Amelia, like other authors of cookery books, borrowed freely from her predecessors, so one does not know whether her methods (given below) were indigenous or not. In any event, they reveal at least some of the American housewife's practices in the late 18th century and probably far, far earlier. The following recipe is of particular interest because it deals with a vegetable, not a fruit:

To keep Green Peas Till Christmas
Take young peas, shell them, put them in a cullender to drain, then lay a cloth four or five times double on a table, spread them on, dry them very well, and have your bottles ready, fill them, cover them with mutton suet fat when it is a little soft; fill the necks almost to the top, cork them, tie a bladder and a leather over them and set them in a dry cool place.

For "The American Citron" in syrup, she said to "put them into bottles with wide mouth, pour the surrup over them, and cover them with oil."[12] One would expect the bottle for the peas to be wide-mouth also. Possibly both were types that would be called jars. Be that as it may, there can be little doubt similar or the same methods were used in sealing jars.

2
JARS

Naturally jars belong in the utilitarian category. Perhaps, strictly speaking, the only glass vessels to which the name *jar* should be given are those with *very* wide mouth and *very* short neck or, like 6 in Ill. 75, virtually no neck at all. Nevertheless, *jar* was, and (as already pointed out) still is, applied often to bottles with a comparatively wide neck and wide mouth—square, like 9 in Ill. 74, and cylindrical. Consequently, inasmuch as advertisers were niggardly of descriptive adjectives, one cannot know whether their *jars*, full and empty, were a wide-mouth bottle form or vessels with very wide short neck and wide mouth. Actually, the term *jar* occurred most infrequently in the many 18th-century advertisements read. There were a few instances of oils, honey, olives, and raisins packaged in jars, but no clue to their form or to the material from which they were made.[13] In fact, as stated in Part I (2. Bottle Family Names), in our researches the first recorded mention of jars that were unquestionably glass was that of Stiegel's "Blue Flower Jars," and they are believed to have been vases. The second was in a 1777 advertisement of the wares of "the late Philadelphia Glass Works." And the next one was not until 1800, when the Pittsburgh Glass Works offered to Philadelphians and Pittsburghians pickle jars, which probably were of the same sizes as those quoted in 1810 to one Joseph Carson—namely, pint jars at 30 cents a dozen, quart at 40 cents, half-gallon at 60 cents, and gallon at 96 cents. Still, though the name may not have been applied to glass containers until about 1800, or infrequently applied, cylindrical and square vessels that I would call *jars* were being blown in the 17th century, if not before, as they had been in the first century A.D. In the homes of the

gentry, if not of the yeomanry, square vessels similar to those depicted in Details 3 and 6 of Ill. 3, from paintings by David Teniers the Younger, and cylindrical or "rounds" also undoubtedly sat on many pantry shelves, filled with meals, herbs, spices, pickles, and preserves. The *pickle glass* recommended in 1699 for keeping "Brown Buds and Pods" for "sallet" ingredients probably was a green-glass wide-mouth bottle or jar. Mr. Thorpe believed that the 10½ dozen "marmelet glasses" purchased for Woburn Abbey between June 12, 1678, and June 4, 1691, were "probably green glass jam jars of cylindrical or square shape."[14]

There can be no doubt that jars, though in fewer numbers than bottles, were among the products of our 18th- as well as 19th-century glasshouses. Nor can there be doubt that they were used by doctors and druggists for powdered ingredients for medicinal preparations; in the household as storage and preserving vessels; for commercial storage and packaging of flours, sweets, pickles, and preserves by individual confectioners and others dealing in such commodities. As early as 1748, New York City merchants were putting up pickled oysters in glass and earthen vessels for sale in the West Indies.[15] Presumably the glass vessels would have been jars or very wide-mouth bottles. So too would have been the "Pots for Pickles, Conserves, etc. of all sizes" made at the Germantown glassworks and offered by Joseph Palmer to Bostonians in 1760 (Ill. 5). The usual absence of jars among specified products may indicate they were not an important large line of hollow ware, but *not* necessarily that none were blown: the "&c" often ending advertisements could have included jars. In any event, they would have been mainly cylindrical and square forms, which were after all basically so completely functional they have never been abandoned. And in the early 19th century, when several American glassworks advertised jars,[16] the cylindrical would have been mainly free-blown and the squares, molded for body form as they had been in previous periods. They probably ranged in size from small apothecary jars like 12 in Ill. 75 to gallon sizes, with the larger sizes predominating.

In my opinion there is more than a chance that the 18th- and early 19th-century jars found here are of American fabrication. For one reason, imported products in jars that possibly, but far from certainly, were of glass were mentioned so infrequently in the advertisements. For another, except for the wide-mouth pickle bottles already cited, imported *jars* were offered for sale in none of the advertisements read. Attribution to a particular glassworks or area has rarely been possible, and then only in cases of free-blown jars handed down in families of glassblowers and their neighbors, with the history of having been blown in a local glassworks. Most of these "pedigreed" jars were blown in glassworks specializing in green-glass containers; some were blown in window-glass houses that made a small quantity of utilitarian hollow ware to meet local needs, or by blowers who fashioned them for friends and family. Naturally those from window-glass metal normally were in various shades of aquamarine; those from green glass, normally in the dark, natural bottle-glass colors. Though varying in size and proportions, they were mainly cylindrical in form with body or shoulder contracted below a flanged mouth, or with a very short wide neck finished with rolled-over collar or flange, which, of course, formed a perfect "anchor" for tying down a cork or a cover such as a bladder over the cork. Even after the advent of patented molded jars in the late 1850s, free-blown jars were occasionally blown in small glasshouses, and the old methods of closure also continued in use to some extent. The majority of these jars that I have seen were early to mid-19th century.

The early methods of closure, as already mentioned, undoubtedly were used also for jars. However, not surprisingly, the term *jar* did not appear in the many recipes studied until the end of the 18th century, though in a few references the vessels recommended might have been jars. The references also shed a bit more light on sealing vessels to prevent leakage and protect the contents from exposure to air. According to Mrs. Eales, confectioner to King William and Queen Mary, oil could be used in preserving fruit juices: "juice of Sevile oranges and lemons for Punch, sauces, Juleps and other purposes" could be preserved all year in "a deep glass vessel" if "well covered and sallad oil floated on top." (Naturally the oil preceded the covering.) The phrase "deep glass vessel" suggests the possibility of a jar (or wide-mouth bottle). Moreover, though the recipe appeared in her 1742 edition (doubtless in the two earlier ones also), it was one she probably followed or knew of in the 17th century, since William's reign ended in 1702. Mrs. Eales also used brandied papers—that is, pieces of paper cut to the size of the vessel's mouth and dipped in brandy, to place on top of jellies put up in pots (jars probably) or jelly glasses, a practice still followed by some housewives in the 20th century. Some compilers of cookery books felt corks were unnecessary for some, perhaps all, homemade pickles. Amelia Simmons recommended only a "bladder or leather" for cucumber pickles in jars (material not specified) and for pickled barberries in pots or glasses.[17] Such a method would hardly have sufficed for pickles transported and sold in stores.

As for most containers, it is not known exactly when the full-size piece mold was first used for jars, though probably the large bottle-glassworks adopted the method before 1830. Since Dyott had been using piece molds for patent medicine bottles and Figured Flasks, he may have used them also for his pickling and preserving jars advertised in 1822, which, two years later, he described as having straight and turned-over tops and running from a half-pint to a gallon in size.[18] By then, the demand for jars and wide-mouth bottles was on the increase because pickling, preserving, and the like by individual confectioners and others dealing in such products was about to be superseded by large-scale wholesale commercial "canning," which was started in France by Nicholas Appert, confectioner and chef. Inspired by a 12,000-franc prize offered to anyone who invented a method of preserving food for the French armies on campaign, Appert applied to meats and vegetables, as well as fruits, the century-old (at least) home method of filling bottles with fruit, with and without syrup, sealing them with cork, and boiling them. By 1809, after more than a decade of experimentation, he succeeded in canning over fifty different foods—not just "to be kept all year," as the cookery books boasted, but for many years. His example was soon followed in England and later in America.[19]

It has been said that in Boston about 1821 an

Englishman, William Underwood, pioneered the preserving industry in the United States. The first of his advertisements found as yet—Winifred Collins of the Massachusetts Historical Society sent me a transcript of it—appeared in the *Boston Daily Advertiser*, December 31, 1822; since it was on page one, unless that newspaper deviated from long-established custom the advertisement probably had appeared earlier on page three, possibly page two. In it, Underwood announced he had commenced manufacturing superfine mustard and also had for sale "essence of anchovies, Cavice, Harvey's Reading, Quinn and other rich sauces, walnut and mushroom catsup, picallilly and other pickles in jars and bottles, likewise India currie powder, lemon syrup, Borgona anchovies, &c &c." These were not surprising items to be sold in glass bottles and jars—most of them already had been in the 18th century—but Underwood was wholesaling. His products were being sold not only at the manufactory but "by the principal grocers in Boston," and orders were filled "for the East and West Indies, South America &c."[20]

Commercial preserving certainly must have intensified two problems—namely, uniformity of shape and capacity of containers, and the airtightness and commercial practicability of the customary methods of closure. Of course the solution to the problem of uniformity was the full-size piece mold, as it was in other fields of packaging products in glass. Simplification and reliability of closure were not so readily achieved. What methods of stopping and sealing were used by William Underwood I do not know. Perhaps, like housewives, he used one or more of the long-established methods, but more likely he followed that of Appert, which had been available in published form since 1810, or that of Durant or of Cooper in England. Of these three, Thomas Cooper's, evolved after a decade of experimentation, is the only one that I have read.

Because Cooper's "Art of Preserving" was published in Reading, Pennsylvania, in 1824,[21] and hence available to—and probably in some instances followed by—Americans, it seems pertinent to give some of the details here. Cooper used wide-necked (wide-mouth) glass bottles for liquids such as gravies, broths, juices of plants, fruits, and herbs, and glass jars for "solids and bulky substances" such as vegetables, poultry, fish, and meats. Since "the ordinary bottles had generally necks too small and ill made; . . . also too week to resist the blows of the bat [driving in the cork] and the action of fire [boiling in water]," he had bottles made especially for his use, "with wider necks, and those necks made with a projecting rim or ring on the interior surface, placed

below and resembling in form, the rim which is at the top of the exterior surface . . ." The inner rim served to compress the cork, driven in three-fourths of its length, thus strengthening its resistance to swelling or expansion of the contents that was caused by the heat. His jars with necks two, three, and four inches in diameter, like the bottles, were "furnished with a projecting rim, not only in order to strengthen the neck but also for receiving the iron wire destined to bind the corks"—as on the bottles. However, the width of the necks increased the difficulty of adequate corking because of the thinness of the necessary fine-quality corks and "ascending pores being against the grain." To overcome this obstacle, Cooper made stoppers: three or four pieces of cork "from twenty to twenty-four lines in length," placed in layers the way of the grain and with pores horizontal, were glued together with a special preparation that set in about a fortnight. Then the stoppers were cut to fit the mouth of the jars, and the whole outside covered with a luting—a paste made from powdered slaked quicklime mixed with a cheese from skimmed milk, which hardened rapidly and withstood the heat of boiling water. Since the stopper was too wide for "the wire to have any effect on it," he fastened a piece of cork, seven or eight lines high and 16 or 18 lines in diameter, in the center of the stopper, which enabled him "to make the wire take a proper hold . . . and give due strength and solidity to the stopper." Using a canvas or coarse linen bag for each bottle, instead of separating them by straw or hay in the boiler, Cooper then applied "the preserving principle, that is, *heat*." This, he said, was "the most easy part of the operation," and a day or even two weeks afterward he placed his bottles and jars on shelves in a cool and shady place, but if they were to be sent a great distance, he thought it worthwhile to pitch them.

Apparently closure remained a somewhat elaborate and lengthy process throughout the first half of the 19th century. In the 1850s, and later, many experiments were made to improve airtight and quick closure by means of various sorts of glass or metal covers, which normally were accompanied by a rubber washer. The majority of jars were made with a neck either threaded for glass or metal screw-cap or shaped for a glass cover to be held tight in place by a heavy wire fastening. Among other sorts was one with glass lugs that fit into slots in its glass cover. But none was more successful or, in the housewife's apparent estimation, more effective than the famous Mason jars, which for nearly three-quarters of a century bore the molded inscriptions "MASON'S / PATENT / Nov. 30th / 1858" or "MASON'S / IM-

PROVED" that followed a slightly later patented improvement. These inscriptions were perpetuated by many fruit-jar manufacturers after Mason's original jar and the eight improvements patented between 1858 and 1874 entered the public domain, enabling manufacturers to make as many as they pleased. Simply "MASON'S" and "MASON" were also used. Moreover, some manufacturers adopted compound names that included the confidence-inspiring "Mason's."[22] "MASON'S / KEYSTONE" was one such name. Dr. Julian H. Toulouse, in his *Collector's Manual–Fruit Jars*, lists some 290 jars with names that include "Mason's." In short, "Mason's" and "Mason" became generic names conveying an assurance of quality.

But to return to the originator: the research department of the former Glass Container Manufacturers Institute established the principal facts about John L. Mason of New York City and his jars. Their booklet "Mason Jar. Centennial—1858–1958" says that when Mason devised the mold for his new jar, he already held patents for "screw-caps or nozzles and caps for bottles, jars, etc." After patenting his jar with improved neck-threading for a metal screw-cap with "india rubber" washer, he took three partners, and they conducted a thriving business in New York City for several years producing the caps for the jars and marketing the jars. The first jars are said to have been blown for Mason in Crowleytown's Atlantic Glass Works, started by Samuel Crowley in 1851. However, this small New Jersey glassworks was not the only one in which jars were blown in molds according to Mason's specifications for Mason's firm while it was in business. In 1873, Mason left New York for New Brunswick, New Jersey, and soon afterward became associated with the Consolidated Fruit Jar Company, to which he assigned his rights in his first two patents. In 1875, shortly after the expiration of these two patents, Mason assigned his remaining rights in jar improvements to the company. As indicated already, during the last quarter of the 19th century Mason jars were produced in many factories specializing in containers.

In the meantime, Mason jars had not been without competitors; they had been preceded as well as followed by other patented fruit jars. Frequently the patent was obtained on a very slight, though presumably effective, improvement (or so it seems to me). For instance, in the specifications for the fruit jar patented in 1861 by John M. Whitall (Whitall, Tatum & Company, Millville, New Jersey), Mr. Whitall stated:

I am aware that it is not new to make a groove around the mouth of a jar, nor to secure the cover [glass] with a bent wire or hasp, and also that a packing ring [washer] of india rubber has been used between the cover and the jar; but I believe it is new to bevel the undersides of the cover, so as to make it press first and hardest on the inside corner of the packing ring when it is applied to the jar.[23]

Ideas for improving fruit jars were not limited to inventors like Mason or to glassmen like Whitall; they emanated from a surprising variety of sources, including—so Dr. Toulouse informed me—"a small town South Carolina woman and a 'Henry County,' Iowa, man who were probably users . . ." And the various sources were fertile producers of ideas for ideal jars: in his book Dr. Toulouse recorded around 1,150 varieties, and he believes more are still to be discovered.[24]

The majority appeared after 1880, their production stimulated perhaps by the increased usage in commercial packaging, which had not been extensive before 1880. In the same decade experiments with machinery for mechanical blowing were stimulated by Philip Arbogast's 1881 patent on a press-and-blow process, which he had been unable to implement with a practical machine. By 1892/93 others had devised successful machines in which wide-mouth jars could be produced. Thus fruit jars were in the vanguard of containers made by semiautomatic production. And by 1901 one or another of several semiautomatic processes accounted for the majority of fruit jars produced in the United States.[25] Not too long afterward, they were produced by fully automatic means.

3

DEMIJOHNS AND CARBOYS

It was about the middle of the 18th century that large bottles, normally wickered, for shipping and storage of liquids were first called demijohns and carboys by some manufacturers and merchants. They had long been blown and often were covered with leather or wicker, but probably in comparatively small numbers before their commercial use in shipping became prevalent. *Botae*—that is, bon-bonnes (demijohns)—were being blown in France by the beginning of the 14th century. If there, doubtless elsewhere too. Their capacity is not mentioned, but it seems probable they held at least one or two gallons, as did the green-glass gallon and double-gallon bottles listed by the London Company of Glass Sellers in 1677/78. And there is indication that even larger ones were blown in England before that time: Sir Kenelm Digby (ante 1669) recommended "a great double glass bottle that will hold two gallons or more" for his sack with clove gilly-flowers. By the mid-18th century imported bottles of four to twenty gallons were advertised occasionally in American newspapers, among them "wickered bottles that will hold up to 5 gallons."[26]

However, not all the bottles of large size used in America were imported; they were produced also in our American glasshouses. Bottles "up to 3 gallons and upward" were advertised by Thomas Lepper, "Store-Keeper to the Glass House Company," on Sir Peter Warren's dock, New York (Ill. 6A). And, though not in great quantity, three-gallon bottles were produced by Stiegel. Possibly bottles over a gallon in capacity were blown to order by most American manufacturers of bottles, but the gallon was the largest size in the regular output itemized in the few 18th-century advertisements known to me: bottles "equal to any imported," advertised in 1760 by Joseph Palmer, Germantown, included gallon size (Ill. 5); Richard Wistar, Wistarburgh, offered gallon bottles of "full measure" in 1769; "green glass bottles from pint to gallons," produced by John Frederick Amelung & Company, New Bremen, could be purchased in Baltimore in 1788; gallon bottles were among the "Home made glass bottles," almost certainly blown in the Pitkins' East Hartford glassworks, advertised in Hartford in 1794.[27] Possibly these large bottles were ordinary globulars or chestnuts; probably some were carefully fashioned demijohns or carboys blown in molds for body form. If so, it is a fair assumption that they were not advertised as *demijohns* or *carboys* because those names were still being used sporadically by both merchants and glass manufacturers, at least in America. Nevertheless, though *carboy* appeared in no advertisement of American-made large bottles in the period, the name *demijohn* appeared in two. In 1788 Robert Hewes, then superintendent of the Pitkins' works in East Hartford, announced to hoped-for Boston customers that "DIME'JOHNS, or any other large Bottles" could be obtained by leaving

one's name with Mr. William Cunningham near the Liberty Pole (Ill. 8A). In 1790 John Heefke, one of the partners in the De Neufville glassworks at Dowesborough near Albany (later the Albany Glass-House), advertised "A Parcel of Brown Wickered Demie Johns fit for shipping"[28]—also another bit of evidence that Americans were shipping liquids in glass bottles.

Differentiation between demijohn and carboy "in the glass" has always been puzzling. Seemingly there was none in the 18th century, or if there was any, I have yet to discover it. The names apparently were used interchangeably before the 19th century and, as remarked above, for large shipping and storage bottles usually covered with wicker. The earliest appearance I have found of the name *demijohn* was in a 1762 advertisement of arrack (a high-powered oriental spirit) in "demy johns"; of *carboy,* one of "wickered bottles or carboys from 1 quart to 7 gallons" in 1767. Incidentally, this was the only mention of carboys of less than a gallon. And the only advertisement of demijohns of over five gallons was one of eight- and nine-gallon demijohns for spirits of turpentine in 1792.[29] From about 1800 on, advertisements indicate that gradually both manufacturers and the public had made up their minds as to the special functions as containers, and the relative sizes, of bottles called *demijohn* and *carboy.*

With only two exceptions among the hundreds of advertisements read, demijohns contained noncorrosive and bland liquids such as spirits, wines, and other beverages, medicinal cordials, fruit juices, oils, honey, and toilet water. In a few instances, shortly before and after 1800, demijohns arrived from the Continent filled with sugarplums, lentils, pearl barley, juniper berries, or peas. This use doubtless was a convenience, to conserve shipping space and cut freight charges, rather than the customary way to contain such products. The normal sizes, as indicated by advertisements and price lists, were from one quart to five gallons, and the last occurred most frequently. The only 19th-century exception to the five-gallon limit that I have seen occurs in the 1829 price list of the New-England Glass-Bottle Company of Cambridge, Massachusetts (Ill. 18). This company, it will be noted, listed "wickered demijohns from 1 to 10 gallons"; in the company's terminology, covered bottles of one-, two-, and three-quart sizes were not demijohns but "bottles wickered." Incidentally, it is interesting to note that on Dyott's price list (Ill. 9C) of about 1825, prices were higher than those of the Cambridge works: Dyott's quart demijohns were $3.00 a dozen; half-gallon, $4.00; gallon, $6.00; 2-gallon, $9.00.[30]

Before 1825 carboys were neither so often advertised nor listed as were demijohns. Except in the 1767 advertisement cited above, they ranged from one to 20 gallons in capacity; six gallons and up were the common sizes. Normally carboys were set in "tubs," usually of heavy wicker, that were a more effective armor against breakage than the skin-fitting wicker coats of demijohns. They were sold by bottle manufacturers either with their tubs or, to customers supplying their own tubs, "naked." Presumably the tubs evolved in the late 18th century when the carboy became principally a container for such liquids as oil of vitriol, Aqua Fortis, muriatic acid and Nitre Fortis, varnishes, and ether.[31] In 1829 the New-England Glass-Bottle Company claimed that its carboys were "used almost exclusively by the manufacturing chemists in Massachusetts and were said by them to be superior to those of foreign manufacture." That carboys were usually larger and heavier than demijohns seems implicit in the freight charges for Hudson River transport in 1816; according to the *New York Evening Post* for March 16 of that year, the freight on carboys was 4s. each; that on demijohns was 2s. 6d. (only 1s. if empty).

Physically the majority of demijohns and carboys were "big bellied" globular or ovoid bottles, occasionally with slightly curved sides slanting outward to a flattened curved shoulder like 1 in Ill. 47. Toward the end of the 18th century "oval demijohns" appeared in advertisements.[32] They had been made long before, however, if they were similar to 6 in Ill. 46, which in turn is similar in shape to the leather-covered bottle shown in Detail 1, Ill. 4, from Jan Steen's 17th-century painting. About the middle of the 19th century, or a little later, the ranks of the common big-bellied bottles were joined by big cylindrical ones and those with tall bodies and outward slanting sides (Ill. 65). By the third quarter of the century the cylindrical form seems to have been favored for sizes up to three or four gallons. In shape and proportion, the 1876 demijohns shown in Ill. 66 are typical of the earlier ones but atypical in their covering, which had a layer of soft elastic tule reed under the wicker, "an improvement" patented by Carlton Newman of the San Francisco and Pacific Glass Works, San Francisco, California.[33] As befitted their functions, demijohns and carboys were sturdy bottles with substantial walls and generally blown from tough glass in the composition of which special care doubtless had been taken to ensure against the corrosive action of any contents, especially in the case of carboys. A mid-19th-century writer warned that "in bottles to contain acid care should be taken to combine chemically the alkali and the lime so as not to incur the risk of their being acted upon by the acid and subject to decomposition.[34]

After about 1810 or 1820 the common lip finish was a thick, deep, and flat sloping collar (see Ill. 64). Prior to that time demijohns and carboys usually had either a narrow flat collar or a heavy string-ring laid on below a plain lip, or sometimes—as in the case of large sizes such as 6 in Ill. 46 and 1 in Ill. 47—a rough lip, neither fire-polished nor tooled. As a rule, when the lip itself was not finished in any way on such large bottles, an accompanying feature was an unscarred base, which might be nearly flat or have a rather shallow kick-up. In other words, the string-ring was laid on before the bottle was cracked off (whetted off) the blowpipe, and since the neck orifice was not to be finished further, there was no need to attach a pontil to the base to hold the bottle during a neck-finishing process (or, in the case of small sizes, to use a holder after those tools were introduced). In glassblower's parlance, the bottle was not "stuck up." One assumes that this procedure must have been followed in the blowing of a "great bottle," the largest of which I have record, in the works of the New-England Glass-Bottle Company in 1829. For this event, given wide publicity in *Nile's Register*, William Cuming gathered the metal, which was handled by James Proudlock, to fashion a great bottle weighing 43 pounds and holding 31 gallons.[35] Whether the feat was done as a show of skill or to fill a special order, the reporter did not say. Nor did he mention a mold being used for body form. On the weight of the metal in a gather for late-19th-century large carboys, light is shed by an article in the *Salem [N.J.] Sunbeam*, July 9, 1959. The five-gallon carboys produced at the Gaynor Glass Works, established in New Jersey by John Gaynor in 1874, required 12 pounds of molten glass, and the 13-gallon size, 26 pounds. Both necessitated "considerable 'puffing'" by the blower!

Though perhaps, throughout the early 1800s, in some American glassworks sizes from a quart up to, or including, a gallon were often free-blown, it seems likely to me that the majority were molded for body form and size or blown in full-size piece molds. Although I know of no documentary evidence to support the supposition, I believe it likely that clay molds were used more generally than wooden or metal ones, especially for the larger demijohns and carboys. It seems certain that clay was a favored material for demijohn molds into the late 1800s, for, as Kenneth M. Wilson informed me, two five-gallon clay molds, a two-gallon clay mold, and one clay

BENNERS, SMITH & CAMPBELL,

Dyottville Glass　　　　　　　Works, Kens.

Vials, Bottles,　　　　　　**Demijohns &c.**

Office and Warehouse, 35½ South Front Street,

PHILADELPHIA,

Manufacturers of Carboys, Demijohns of all sizes, Wine, Porter, Soda and Mineral Water, Lemon Syrup and Ink Bottles, Jars, and Druggists' Bottle and Vials of every description.

All kinds of Bottles and Vials made to order in private moulds.

H. B. Benners.　　S. D. Smith.　　Quintin Campbell, Jr.

64. Typical big-bellied demijohn with wicker coat. *(O'Brien's Philadelphia Wholesale Business Directory and Circular, For the Year 1848, p. 203.) The New-York Historical Society, New York City*

CHESTER F. COLTON,

Druggist and Apothecary, has constantly on hand a full and complete assortment of Drugs, Medicines, and Chemicals, at wholesale and retail; also a choice selection of London and Paris Perfumery and Fancy articles.

Particular and undivided attention will be given to the preparation of Physicians' Prescriptions, at all hours.

☞Leeches constantly on hand, and applied.

C. NEWMAN'S IMPROVED ELASTIC DEMIJOHN. (Patented January 26th, 1875.) By referring to the engraving, in the foreground will be seen a bottle partially covered : *a* represents the glass, *b* the tule reed, and *c* the wicker work. It will be seen that the bottle is first covered with the tule reed—a soft elastic substance—forming a cushion, on which the rattan is woven. By this means the bottle is doubly protected, and made doubly valuable, from its immunity from breakage. Its advantages are so many and obvious, that it needs no argument to prove its merits. Those who use demijohns will see at once the superiority it possesses over all other covered bottles·

66. Demijohns with Carlton Newman's patented covering (January 26, 1875) of rattan woven over a coat of soft elastic tule reed; made at the San Francisco & Pacific Glass Works, established 1865, C. Newman & Co., Proprietors. *(San Francisco City Directory, 1876.) Courtesy of Don Reich*

65. Tall slender demijohn with outward slanting sides, wicker coat. *(Hartford [Conn.] New Directory and Guide Book, 1842, p. 104.) Connecticut Historical Society, Hartford, Conn.*

carboy-mold were among the inventory items in the Westford Glass Company's 1865 records. As in the case of Dr. Dyott's statement in his exposition that his molds were clay, the Westford inventory did not mention the type of mold, but it seems a safe assumption they were piece molds. Mold seams on some demijohns and carboys leave no question that some were blown in full-size two-piece molds and others in molds having a one-piece body part and two-piece shoulder and lower neck part, as did the bottles blown under Henry Ricketts's 1821 patent. Perhaps the latter type was introduced in American works producing these large shipping and storage bottles about the time the Proudlock great bottle was blown. However they were formed, apparently more care and skill was expended on demijohns and carboys than on common globular and chestnut bottles, and perhaps the early ones conformed more closely to standard measure of capacity.

It is evident from advertisements and price lists that, from the early years of the 19th century, demijohns and carboys steadily increased in importance as products of our bottle glassworks, east and west. Even so, that the demand was not satisfied seems implicit in the continued importation of demijohns, which were frequently advertised in Atlantic seaboard newspapers as arriving in lots of a thousand and more. Because of importation, because of widespread domestic production, and because—so far as I have been able to learn—the bottles were not marked with a manufacturer's or glassworks' name, it is virtually impossible to attribute an individual specimen to a particular glassworks. Nor does exact dating seem possible, though a broad general period may be determined by the method of fabrication and neck finish. Lastly,

since few old ones are found today with their original covering or in tubs, it is still a question as to which of the bottles—at least, those under six gallons—were demijohns and which carboys. Except for the evidence about the differences in size and usage established by advertisements and manufacturers' terminology, we are back at our starting point in the matter of differentiation. Today, depending on the collector's preference, demijohn and carboy are used interchangeably as they were in the 18th century. And, in most instances, puzzlement remains as to whether the big naked bottles originally wore a wicker coat or were set in a tub, whether they first contained a chemical preparation or a sweet water like lavender.

4
COMMERCIAL CONTAINERS

As applied in the following brief discussion, the term *commercial container* has been chosen to cover bottles that were given the name of their intended contents in 18th- and early 19th-century advertisements, a few account books, and price lists, and that were produced primarily for manufacturers of certain products, other than beverages, to be sold wholesale and retail.

(1) Snuff Bottles

Snuff is a preparation of tobacco graphically named for the method of taking it—snuffing it up one's nostrils. How it was first made when introduced into Europe in the 16th century I have not discovered, but in time the process became a long and complicated one. Several months of fermentation were required after the tobacco had been treated with a sauce composed of common salt, sometimes other salts, and aromatic substances for scent and flavor, such as essential oils of cinnamon, nutmeg, and lavender, and rose water and bergamot. At first the duly sauced and fermented leaves were made into tight spindle-form little bundles called carottes, which did not require containers such as glass bottles. When a pinch was wanted, the snuffer grated the ends of the carotte on a snuff rasp. This was doubtless the familiar form in 17th-century England,

where snuff taking was common and also very fashionable in the politest circles—in the colonies, too. By the 18th century, if not before, snuff was being manufactured in the more convenient forms of coarse or "bran," granulated, and finely powdered. By then snuff taking was an almost universal habit of both men and women. Lord Stanhope estimated that the time spent by "every professed, inveterate and incurable" addict's taking a pinch of snuff, then blowing and wiping his nose, amounted to 36½ days a year. And it was not taken for titillation only or to show off a precious snuffbox: it was also taken medicinally.[36]

It is said that Jean Nicot, French ambassador to Lisbon in 1561, took back to France American tobacco that, ground up and snuffed, cured Queen Catherine de'Medici of constant headaches by causing sneezes so powerful they cleared her sinuses.[37] Thus the medicinal use of snuff began long before medicated snuffs were invented by doctors and apothecaries. It was about the mid-18th century that Royal Patents were first granted for medicinal snuffs—*cephalic snuff*, these were most often called in the next century. They were primarily cures for catarrh and headaches, but one patentee claimed his snuff acted also as a dissolvent on the stomach and lungs, as an alterative on the blood and juices; another's was serviceable in "Disorders of the Hypocondriac [*sic*] and Melancholy kind." Even unmedicated snuff was said to be of service to the eyesight. Claims for American brands, in the 19th century at least, emphasized catarrh and headache. Little wonder that, by the 1840s, innumerable kinds and brands of snuff, medicated or unmedicated, were available to snuff takers and, it was said, new ones were invented daily.[38] Bottles were needed for them.

Just when bottling of the coarse to fine snuffs for retail sale began, I have not learned. It may have been about the turn of the 17th into the 18th century, definitely in the early 1700s. Scotch snuff, apparently the 18th-century favorite in America, may have been imported in bottles as well as in bladders before 1731, when John Scott, New York City merchant, offered "very good Scotch snuff in Bottles." By the midcentury, at least, snuff was being manufactured in the colonies, and its manufacturers were hampered by an insufficient supply of bottles—as were all who used bottles for their products. In Boston in 1756 one "Master-Workman, lately foreman to the famous Kippen of Glasgow," announced that the best snuff was to be had by the pound at the Dwelling House of Peter Barbour in Wing's Lane and that money or snuff would be given for bottles. The offer was repeated in 1757 in an advertisement that suggests his snuff had not been received with the same enthusiasm as the imported Scotch, for he included a plea for custom calculated to appeal to pocketbook and local patriotism: "Snuff upon Trial. AT LEAST as good and much cheaper than the foreign . . . It is therefore presumed that private interest, as well as REGARD FOR THE PUBLIC, will give it the preference to any that is imported from abroad . . ."[39]

This Boston snuff maker may have purchased snuff bottles, "equal to any imported," from Joseph Palmer's Germantown glassworks. Those in New York and Philadelphia could have obtained theirs from Wistarburgh before the Revolution, and some at least from Stiegel's Manheim Works, where 1,084 snuff bottles were blown in February of 1767 alone. In 1780 presumably the need for bottles prompted Thomas Leiper, Philadelphia tobacconist, to take over the Philadelphia Glass Works in Kensington. If this was the Pennsylvania works reported by Lord Sheffield in 1783, then snuff bottles undoubtedly were in its output. However, after the war Leiper apparently was not able to put—or keep—the works on its production feet: in 1788 he was ordering snuff bottles from the De Neufville works at Dowesborough, near Albany. Possibly he also patronized the New-Jersey Glass Manufactory, where snuff bottles must have been blown before they were advertised by Heston and Carpenter in 1799. Nichol-

son's glassworks on the Schuylkill was a logical source in 1795 and as long as the works produced bottles. And though Christopher Trippel & Company could not have operated the old Philadelphia, or Kensington, Glass Works more than about two years after apparently renting it from Leiper in 1798, surely Leiper would have bought their snuff bottles also.[40] Snuff bottles undoubtedly were blown in the Pitkins' East Hartford works in the 1790s, too.

To borrow again a phrase from early advertisers of glassware, it would be "too tedious to enumerate" all the 19th-century glasshouses, eastern and western, in which snuff bottles *probably* were blown. However, the few now known to have specifically advertised, or otherwise mentioned, snuff bottles testify to the fact that they were more widely produced than was believed even 20 years ago—and to the prevalence of the snuff habit. It is interesting to note that snuff bottles were being blown west of the Alleghenies in the Pittsburgh Glass Works of James O'Hara by 1805—if not earlier. Also, probably after 1811, when green-glass wares joined flint glassware, they were a line of Bakewell's Pittsburgh Flint Glass Works so famous for its fine flint and cut glass. One indication of the considerable demand by the 1820s was an advertisement of 6,000 dozen (72,000!) snuff bottles for sale by Thomas W. Dyott, one of several then producing them. Also, in 20 years, so had supply, demand, competition, and improved transportation worked to the benefit of the consumer that, whereas James O'Hara had charged James Morrison of Kentucky $1.00 a dozen for both pound and half-pound snuff bottles, Dyott was selling his at 50 cents a dozen for half-pound and 60 cents for pound. Just when "polite society" came to consider snuff taking a nasty habit in the poorest taste, so that the habit and consequent demand for bottles dwindled, I have not ascertained. In any event, Whitall Tatum & Company of Millville, New Jersey, were still producing pound and half-pound "Maccaba" and half-pound "Scotch" snuffs in the 1880s.[41]

As in the case of most bottles, the advertisements and price lists mentioned sizes, of which pound and half-pound were standard, but were uninformative regarding the forms of the glass containers for packaging snuff. There was one exception: in 1830 the New-England Glass-Bottle Company's "snuff squares" were offered for sale by their New York City agent Seth Low.[42] However, several bottles that were fortunately found with their original contents provide tangible evidence of the types *commonly* used for bottling snuff. From these it appears that, though perhaps the square was just one of several types, with wide or narrow mouth, it might be termed the classic form from the 18th through the 19th century. Example 11 in Ill. 75 is typical of the 18th century, probably carrying over into the early 19th. In the Henry Francis du Pont Winterthur Museum, a similar "pound" bottle (medium green, 2¾ inches square, 5½ inches in height) has most of its original label for "Lorillard's / MACCOBOY SNUFF" still intact, and the address—"No. 30 Chatham–Street . . . New-York"—dates the bottle between 1797 and 1818. Also in Ill. 75, No. 13 is attributed to the late 18th or early 19th century.

Though I did not find the term *jar* used in connection with snuff until about 1820, it is probable that very wide-mouth bottles or jars like 6 in Ill. 75 were used for snuff as well as other powdered substances. This seems quite likely, since in her *American Cookery* (1796) Amelia Simmons suggested that "to keep Damsons" they be put in "snuff bottles"—stopped tight, of course, so no air could get to them. Also, rectangular types like 1 and 6 of Ill. 72 are believed to have been used in the 18th century, and the latter definitely was used in the early 19th. Polygonal bottles like 10 in Ill. 75 were used likewise to some extent in the 18th and early 19th century. Possibly all these types were among the snuff and other bottles "of all patterns" advertised in 1798 by Christopher Trippel & Company.[43]

Through the early 19th century the square, rectangular, and polygonal bottles were probably blown mainly in clay molds for body form, the sides arching at the top and blending into the shoulder. Occasionally a simple device is found on the base, and it has been suggested that this may make it possible sometime to identify the bottles with specific glassworks, if sound archaeological excavations of available factory sites are conducted. For instance, one variety of square snuff that has been attributed to Connecticut—Coventry or Willington—on the basis of geographical distribution and family history has on the base two diagonal ribs to the right crossed by two to the left, placed asymmetrically. Gradually, perhaps starting in the 1820s, the molding for body form only was superseded by the use of full-size two-piece molds. A few had molded inscriptions, as has 15 in Ill. 75. This olive-amber rectangular bottle with deeply incurved corners was blown in a private mold (probably a metal one) with the lengthwise inscription "J.J.MAPES / 61 FRONT. STREET / N — YORK". It may be dated between 1824 and 1834/35, the years James J. Mapes, merchant, was listed in the city directories at this address. Listed as a

67. Rectangular bottle, in an 1817 advertisement of Dr. Waterhouse's Aromatic Snuff, which appeared in the Hartford, *Connecticut Courant*, Feb. 11, 1817. *The New-York Historical Society, New York City*

68. Square bottle in an 1824 advertisement of Dr. Waterhouse's Aromatic Snuff. (New York, *Commercial Advertiser*, Jan. 9, 1824.) *The New-York Historical Society, New York City*

"chemist," he was located at 28 Leonard Street in the 1835/36 directory. However, the majority of the surviving snuff bottles I have seen that were blown in full-size two-piece molds are not so early; they date from the last half of the century and had flat chamfered corners and smooth base following the contour of the body. Whatever the period or method of fabrication, the bottles were blown from green glass, with olive-greens, olive-ambers, and ambers the predominating colors.

To many collectors, among the most interesting of the snuff bottles are the 19th-century bottles with the original labels, which have a fascination all their own and establish the period of the bottles they embellish. Bottle 14 in Ill. 75, which was blown in a two-piece mold in rectangular form with chamfered corners, has the label for William C. Lemon's Maccaboy snuff, manufactured and sold at No. 4 Wall and 213 Duane streets, New York. Lemon was listed in the city directories at this address from 1846 to 1851. Peter Lorillard's label on an olive-green bottle of the same type as Lemon's is significant in its revelation that snuff makers as well as patent-medicine proprietors had their problems with imitators. It reads:

Caution: Purchasers are requested after having disposed of the contents of this bottle to tear off and deface the label on the outside in order to prevent unprincipaled [sic] persons from making use of the same to palm off a spurious and inferior snuff. Beware also of counterfeit labels. P. Lorillard.

The purchaser did not take the caution completely to heart—only a fraction of the label was defaced. Lorillard's delightful label depicts an Indian standing beside a tobacco barrel, holding in his hand a long-stemmed pipe that is issuing smoke; at the left is a tobacco plant. Inscribed above the barrel is "LORILLARD'S"; below is "MACCOBOY SNUFF / Manufactured and sold by / P . . . Lorillard, late / Peter & . . . Lorillard / 16 . . . Chambers Street, . . . [Ne]w-York." Peter Lorillard, successor to Peter and George Lorillard, was located at 16 Chambers and 69 Wooster streets from 1860 to 1865.

(2) Mustard Bottles

Since remote times mustard has been numbered among the members of the vegetable kingdom widely used for medicinal virtues and as a seasoning and condiment, to enhance the flavor of foods. In England by the 18th, if not the 17th, century the preferred form was flour (meal) made by grinding the mustard seed in a mill and sifting the flour; the condiment was prepared from this, as needed, by mixing it with vinegar or water and salt. Although there is evidence that some Englishmen knew mustard flour was being manufactured and sold in Venice in the early 17th century, it may be that in England and the colonies it was almost, if not entirely, "homemade" until the early 18th century. It is said that the sale of mustard flour dates from 1720, and that under the name of "Durham mustard" it quickly became popular after pleasing the taste of George I of England. If mustard flour was made in the colonies, it seems likely it was made by cooks, housewives, and the keepers of public houses until the mid-18th century. At least, 1755 was the first year in which I found evidence of an attempt to manufacture flour of mustard commercially. In that year the following advertisement appeared in the Philadelphia *Pennsylvania Journal*:

Whereas Benjamin Jackson, late of London, intended to carry on a mustard manufactory in this City but has been hitherto greatly disappointed he not being supplied with a proper quantity of mustard seed This is therefore to acquaint those who have any of them, or are inclineable to raise any, that they may have Forty Shillings per bushel, or in proportion for a smaller quantity, (which is 15 pence per quart) — The best time to sow it is in the fall.[44]

Some readers of his notice must have been so tempted by the forty shillings as to plant mustard, for Jackson seems to have been firmly established as a mustard manufacturer—a chocolate manufacturer, too—in 1757. Moreover, he was packaging his mustard in bottles. "Having lately imported vials from England," he was able to supply "merchants, Masters of vessels and others with any Quantity of Mustard by the Doz. or gross," which suggests the tentative conclusions that the bottles were on the small side and that the name *mustard* was not yet usual for a particular type of bottle. Though mustard had been imported in bottles at least by 1755, the term *mustard bottle* did not appear until 1758. A year later Wagstaffe & Hunt, competitors of Jackson, announced that, although it had been "the Practice in England to pack it [mustard] in Casks" (for shipping, presumably), those who "pack it in Bottles, and put their own Names on them, in Cities and Towns, which saves Freight, Land Carriage &c. and . . . [who are] inclined to settle a correspondence" with their firm could be supplied with the bottles and "instructions how to pack." Being in Philadelphia, not far from Wistarburgh, the firm may have had Wistar's glassworks in mind as a source of mustard bottles. It seems unlikely that Richard Wistar did not have mustard bottles for sale before he specifically advertised them in 1769.[45]

Evidence indicates Wistar was not the only glass manufacturer providing mustard bottles in the 18th century. Stiegel produced ordinary mustard bottles as well as flint-glass mustard pots for table service. In 1795 they were mentioned among the bottle products of Nicholson's Glass Factory, Philadelphia; in 1799, of the Kensington glassworks, Philadelphia, and of the New-Jersey Glass Manufactory. As a matter of fact, one can presume that some bottles used for mustard flour were blown in all our bottle-glass houses of the last half of the century. But even so, the supply often failed to meet the demand as mustard manufacturers multiplied in cities and towns. More than one offered "the best price for new and old mustard bottles" or "cash for seed and empty bottles."[46] Of whatever type, the mustard bottles would have been blown from green glass in its natural colors. And they would have been mainly pound and half-pound sizes, as were the snuff bottles; occasionally, quarter-pound. About the turn of the century quart sizes probably were produced, since they were being imported from England.[47]

In the advertisements of Wistar and the New-Jersey Glass Manufactory the isolation and pairing of "snuff and mustard bottles" lead to the tentative conclusion that the same form, or forms, served for both these powdered substances. Nicholson's 1795 mustard bottles were "square and round pound and half pound." Possibly there was a preference for square containers, blown in molds for body form, like the so-called snuff bottle and jar 6, 11, and 13 of Ill. 75, for packaging mustard as well as snuff in the 18th and early 19th century. The first reference I have so far found to form after 1795 was in 1808, when "London Mustard Squares" were advertised in New York City. Mustard squares were listed even by the Boston Glass Manufactory and the New England Glass Company, and the low price of $6.00 a gross as compared with the price of flint-glass articles would seem to indicate they were green-glass packaging bottles. But squares and rounds were not the only forms: there is pictorial evidence that rectangulars probably with, as well as without, chamfered corners were in use in the late 1750s. Benjamin Jackson illustrated the 1758 advertisement of his new mustard factory with a bottle (Ill. 69) similar, except for the corners, to the slender olive-amber bottle 1 in Ill. 72. The inference is inescapable that the type was associated with flour of mustard, and possibly it was called *mustard bottle* at the time. (Perhaps Jackson, after he was well established, obtained his bottles from Wistarburgh, the nearest of the three colonial glassworks in operation in his period.) Variants of this type, as well as squares with chamfered corners, continued in use in the 19th century if bottles of these types inscribed "LONDON" were mustard bottles, as is believed. That "London"

BENJAMIN JACKSON,

69. Rectangular bottle, a type used for various dry preparations, similar to No. 1 in Ill. 72. (Philadelphia, *Pennsylvania Gazette*, Aug. 10, 1758.) *The New-York Historical Society, New York City*

mustards were produced in American glassworks for what was apparently a popular brand of English mustard is evident from their appearance on Dyott's price list ca. 1825; in the 1839 account book of Marshall & Stanger, New Brooklyn glassworks; Solomon Stanger's "Blowers' Book" of 1848/49 at Glassboro; and the price list of the Williamstown Glass Works put out by the agent William Burger while located at 50 and 52 Cortlandt Street, New York, 1835–56. It is interesting to note that "London Mustards" were grouped with the patent medicine bottles on the Williamstown price list, which, judged by the other items, probably was issued ca. 1840–54.[48] Dyott's London Mustards, by the way, were $3.50 a gross, whereas his plain mustards were $3.25 a gross.

In the 19th century there were, of course, the same improvements in the method of producing mustard bottles as for others, an expansion of sizes and types of bottles. They were being blown in full-size piece molds that, as has been said before, could guarantee uniformity of shape and capacity. "Assorted sizes" were advertised in 1831; these, as in the 1880s, may have been two, three, four, six, eight, twelve, and sixteen ounces and quarts. At some undetermined point, possibly in the third quarter of the century, barrel-shaped bottles were introduced. Also, some individual mustard manufacturers had adopted the prevalent fashion of having distinctive bottles blown in their private molds, and apparently these bottles were more often aquamarine than the dark natural colors. An example, a rather charming figured and lettered one, is illustrated by 7 in Ill. 78. It is wide-mouthed and cylindrical, with long sprays of delicate oak leaves and acorns wreathing "FIENTZ/PHIL[A]" on one side and "MUSTARD FACTORY" on the other. As yet I have been unable to trace this firm, but the indicated location of the factory suggests that the bottles were blown in the Philadelphia–Baltimore–South Jersey area, since the nearer the source of supply to the customer, the lower the cost of transportation. As is so unfortunately true of most bottles unmarked by their manufacturers, origin is at present in the realm of conjecture and speculation. However, there can be no doubt mustard bottles were a product of many 19th-century glasshouses, and in quantity. Even in 1818 Dyott alone, as agent for the Olive and the Gloucester glassworks in New Jersey, advertised "5000 mustard bottles of superior quality [60,000 mustard bottles!]."[49]

(3) Blacking Bottles

Since blacking for leather goes back to the days of Rome, if not further into antiquity, private individuals and their servants must have performed the humble chore of blacking boots, harness, and other leather articles for many centuries. However, the earliest literary reference to shoe blacking in the various sources I consulted was in the 18th century. Doubtless some form of blacking was made for sale before then, but it was often made at home, especially in the country. Books on household economy contain a wide variety of recipes for its preparation. Mrs. Harrison, in her *Housekeeper's Pocket-Book and Compleat Family Cook*, first published in 1733, gave one of the simplest. It consisted merely of a sufficient amount of lampblack mixed with an egg, and obviously was made for the occasion, not to keep on hand. It was to be applied with a sponge, very thin, and rubbed with a hard brush when dry. And she added an admonition bootblacks today should heed: "Take care the shoes are first well cleaned with a hard Brush, otherwise they will not look near so beautiful." Such blacking would not have been bottled, but Mr. Roberts's (1828) best liquid blacking, which produced a brilliant jet black and was not in the least injurious to leather, definitely required a container, for it was made in quantity. It consisted of the best ivory black, sour beer or porter, molasses, sugar candy, gum arabic, and sweet oil. Roberts directed it should be kept "corked tight in a jar or what you chose to put it in," and glass bottles may have been among the containers chosen. Even as late as 1834 newspapers printed blacking recipes. One of them asserted that perhaps the best shoe blacking in the world was made from elderberries.[50] Of course blacking had become a commercial product long before the 1830s.

Probably by the mid-18th century blacking was first manufactured extensively for sale in stores, and then perhaps mainly in the form of blacking cakes. In the convenient form of liquid it was imported and possibly also made in the colonies by the 1760s. The earliest mention found was in 1764, when William Tweedy of Newport, Rhode Island, advertised "fine liquid shoe blacking, much in use for leather bottoms of chairs."[51] Still, it would appear from newspaper advertisements that until the 19th century commercial liquid blacking may have been less favored than the blacking cakes from which the purchaser prepared his own, and later was not so popular as paste blacking. However, whether the commercial product or homemade from a cake, liquid blacking necessitated containers, and glass bottles probably were preferred. Almost any of the cylindrical, square, rectangular, or polygonal bottles imported or blown in our 18th-century glasshouses would have been

suitable containers and must have been used. For instance, the four-ounce black-glass octagonal bottle, 1 in Ill. 75, might well have been used for blacking. Judged by early 19th-century blacking bottles, those used in the 18th century would have been mainly of small size.

The earliest appearance of the name *blacking bottle* and reference to American-made blacking bottles was in an 1813 advertisement of the Schuylkill Glass Works, Philadelphia. But surely they had been made before, and also made in other glassworks specializing in bottles. Of course no clue was given as to specific form. However, cylindrical and square forms of slender proportions appear to have been the standard 19th-century ones. Perhaps the squares predominated, for the majority of those recorded with an original label or molded inscription identifying them as blacking bottles are slender squares. Normally either form had an everted lip, like 3 in Ill. 75, or a short neck spread at the lip, like that of 4 in the same illustration. Like so many other commercial bottles, they were either free-blown or molded for body form through the early 19th century, and thereafter usually formed in full-size two-piece molds. By 1829, if not sooner, blacking bottles were equipped with swabs or sponges to apply the blacking; "6 groce of sponge blacking bottles" were advertised in Boston in that year. According to an 1833 report on United States manufacturers, 8,000 bottles were required for the liquid and sponge blacking produced by two blacking manufacturers in Boston, Massachusetts. Incidentally, the bottles, possibly from the New-England Glass-Bottle Company, cost 3 cents apiece, a cent more than tin canisters for paste blacking, which in value was ten times that of the liquid and sponge.[52]

Though, as indicated by manufacturers' price lists and surviving labeled bottles, blacking bottles were mainly four to six ounces in capacity, blacking was put up also in larger bottles. These, perhaps, were less often purchased by the man who blacked his own boots than by the bootblack who polished the boots of travelers on packet boats and of the patrons of public houses. Dyott listed half-pint blacking bottles about 1825, and the New-England Glass-Bottle Company, half-pint and pint in 1829. The prices, it is interesting to note, do not reflect beneficent effects of the Protective Tariff of 1828 for the consumer: Dyott sold his half-pint bottles at 50 cents a dozen; the New-England Glass-Bottle Company, its half-pint at $6.00 a gross and pint at $7.50. But dozen and gross quantities may reflect increased consumption. It probably was only a little over a decade later that round (cylindrical) blacking bottles from the Williamstown (N.J.) Glass Works were selling for $3.00 a gross (that is, 25 cents a dozen), 4 oz. squares at $3.00 a gross, and 6 oz. at $3.50.[53]

Blacking bottles 3 and 4 in Ill. 75 bear their original labels, which establish the period of these particular bottles. Cooley's bottle (3) must have been used between 1845, the year in which he entered his label according to Act of Congress, and 1859, the last in which he appeared in the Hartford, Connecticut, directories, where he was first listed as a druggist and apothecary in 1841. Bostwick's bottle (4) must have been used in 1832/33, for 1833 was the only year in which A. Bostwick was listed in the Albany city directories. Bostwick was content to warrant his black varnish for shoes, boots, and harness as "a First Rate Article," whereas Abial A. Cooley was more explicitly boastful. As shown on the label, Cooley's was his own "Elastic Water-Proof MILITARY BLACKING for rendering Leather impervious to Water and giving the surface an elegant polish, without destroying its soft, supple & elastic qualities." It would in no way crack or injure the finest leather. In fact, after repeated blacking, old leather would have the soft pliable texture of new. This bottle of Cooley's is the more interesting for having its original swab or sponge.

Possibly bottle 2 in the same illustration was also used for blacking before Cooley adopted his label in 1845. Blown from dark olive-amber glass, it is an interesting elliptical bottle with molded lengthwise inscription in three lines: "A.A. COOLEY / HARTFORD / CON." The other two were blown from dark olive-green glass. As a matter of fact, all the blacking bottles I have seen were in natural green-glass colors in shades of deep greens and ambers. There is no guessing as to which of the many glassworks of the 1830s produced the bottles used by Bostwick in Albany, but since Cooley was located in Hartford, quite likely his bottles were blown for him either at the Coventry or the Willington Glass Works.

The collection of Charles B. Gardner included another inscribed bottle that definitely was for blacking. It is the normal slender square, 4¾ inches in height, dark olive-green in color, with tall, wide cylindrical neck spreading slightly to a lip with narrow inside fold; on the base is a pontil mark. It has a molded inscription on each side: (1) "REAKIRT'S" (2) "PATENT / JAPAN" (3) "SPONGE" (4) "VARNISH". *Varnish* appears to have been a name for superior blacking, perhaps applied mainly to the special *Japan* variety. So far as I have discovered,

the name did not appear before the 1820s: half-pint blacking and half-pint varnish bottles were among those on Dyott's price list of about 1825.

(4) Ink Bottles

Ink and its containers, like blacking, have a long history, but ink to inscribe man's annals and records doubtless was a more ancient and certainly more vital invention than blacking. It was made in many colors by the ancients, and even sympathetic inks were known in the time of Ovid. Writing with ink, or by any other means, was of course in direct proportion to literacy and education. Moreover, in colonial America, though ink was a daily necessity to professional, business, and government men, private correspondence was far from brisk, for unless an accommodating traveler carried one's letters, a high charge had to be paid to the post rider. But, fortunately for researchers and historians, diaries were kept and books were written. Still, it is not surprising that references to ink and its sale are comparatively infrequent throughout the 18th century; not until the 19th could its use by the citizenry be called general. Nevertheless, ink for home use was manufactured commercially in the 17th and 18th centuries, and sold by printers, stationery and bookshop keepers, and druggists. It was also homemade. Many 18th- and early 19th-century books on the arts and sciences and home economy contained recipes for it. Robert Dossie, in 1764, gave recipes for black writing ink, likewise red, green, yellow, and secret (sympathetic ink that left no visible trace and had to be brought out by heat or vapor). The process of making ink was not a complicated one. A recipe recommended to young men in 1792 called for a quart of water, four ounces of gall, two of copperas, and two of gum arabic. Rainwater in which green peelings of walnuts and oak sawdust or small chips of oak had been macerated might be substituted for plain water to produce a still stronger and better ink.[54] Since ink was still rather expensive, such recipes probably were often followed.

However, commercial inks must have been available to the 17th-century colonists since, as mentioned above, ink was used daily in government and business, and diaries were kept and books written. And naturally the demand expanded with the country's growth and the increasing literacy of the population. Yet apparently until the late 18th or even early 19th century, liquid ink was not the most common commercial form, but rather wafers and powder from which the purchaser made his own ink by adding water. Cakes and sticks for the same purpose were 18th-century forms. Powder was the commonest of all, and was still advertised as late as 1826. The stick seems to have been an invention of one Ellis Hughs of East Cain Township, Chester County, Pennsylvania. At least he claimed it was "new invented," and preferable to ink powder, which spilled and was wasted in traveling and decayed with age.[55]

From an advertisement reading "Ink Powder and Ink," it can be inferred that liquid ink could be obtained by 1742 at the latest, by those who preferred and could afford it. The kinds of ink offered to the public were red, black, India, and Japan. There was also ink for marking fabrics, and by the time of the Revolution a method of stamping, instead of writing, on fabrics had been invented. In 1775 Nicholas Brooks of Philadelphia advertised

curious original presses for marking in a particular method with a liquid that will stand the severest washing and boiling, and is more regular and beautiful than the nicest needlework, as it cannot be picked out which is often the case when linen is marked in the formally usual but not disapproved of method . . .

This ink, called indelible, was named *durable* by the early 19th century; it was pointed out that using it to mark silk, linen, and cotton took a quarter of the time required to mark by needlework. And "durable inks," as the bottles for this indelible ink were called, were made in many of our glasshouses.[56]

When liquid ink was made by dissolving powder, cake, or a bit of stick in water, probably only sufficient was made at a time to fill the inkhorn, inkstand, pocket-ink or thumb bottle; but when made at home in larger quantity from any of the many recipes, or when commercial ink was sold, a larger container was required. It is likely that by the 18th century the usual container was a glass bottle whenever possible; even if more fragile than pottery and stoneware, glass showed the level of the contents. It also seems evident that, as today, the bottles of ink sold to private individuals were mainly small, containing only a half to four or five ounces. Advertisements of vials and phials of red and Japan ink suggest that in the 18th and early 19th century the bottles were of the various types of apothecary vials. For commercial houses, lawyers, and others using ink constantly and in quantity, it must have been put up in larger bottles — glass, pottery, or stoneware. Black writing ink in pint and quart bottles was advertised in the 1790s, and in 1821 John Stickney of Lexington, Ken-

tucky, announced receipt of a large quantity of writing ink, which was for sale by the pint, quart, or gallon.[57]

Some of the small and large bottles used in the 18th century must have been made in American glasshouses. However, no source I have read mentions American-made bottles for ink nor the term *ink bottle*. Although Stiegel advertised "inks of all sorts" in 1772, there is nothing to show whether bottles for commercial packaging were included. Since, with one exception, none of the many advertisements read mention imported *ink bottles* but many mention *inkstands, ink cups,* and *ink sockets,* probably Stiegel's "all sorts" fell *not* in the category of green-glass commercial bottles, but rather in that of pocket inks and desk receptacles for ink. The one exception was "green glass ink bottles" advertised by one George Ball in New York City in 1775. One 1788 advertisement of Thomas Tisdale, Hartford merchant, listed "round and square common inks," which may have been green-glass desk bottles, since they were "common," but it may be inferred they were not already filled with ink.[58] All in all, the present meager information suggests that the small and large bottles used by ink manufacturers for packaging were common utilitarian types of the time, which could have included square, polygonal, and cylindrical.

These basic forms appeared among ink containers of the 19th century, and like other bottles they were free-blown or molded for body form before the prevalent use of the full-size piece mold. Until midcentury the majority were blown from bottle glass in its natural colors. Soon afterward aquamarine became as common — and then predominated; blue glass was used also, though examples in this color are rare today. Bottle 7 in Ill. 75, a three-ounce olive-amber, is typical of the cylindrical ink bottles blown in full-size piece molds in sizes from three ounces to a quart. In Ill. 70 three typical bottles may be seen. They show the relative sizes — perhaps one-half pint, pint, and quart — and two types of neck finish of cylindrical bottles used at Hoover's Ink Manufactory, Philadelphia, in 1848. About the same time such bottles were often given a pouring lip, which facilitated the filling of individual ink containers.

Square, octagonal, and cylindrical bottles were sometimes blown in private molds with identifying inscriptions. For instance, 6 in Ill. 76, an octagonal aquamarine bottle, was inscribed lengthwise "HARRISON'S / COLUMBIAN / INK" on three contiguous sides. It has been recorded in sizes from about one ounce to a gallon in capacity, blown from

HOVER'S INK MANUFACTORY,

No. 87 North Third Street, Philadelphia.

JOSEPH E. HOVER, Manufacturer

70. Hoover's cylindrical ink bottles, showing three sizes and two types of neck finish, from *O'Brien's Philadelphia Wholesale Business Directory and Circular, For the Year 1848,* p. 229. *The New-York Historical Society, New York City*

both aquamarine and deep blue glass. Of several bottle forms in which Apollos W. Harrison packaged his black, blue, and red inks, it is the only one recorded in gallon size. Among Harrison's other bottles was the squat octagonal like 12 in the same illustration, inscribed on three contiguous sides "HARRISON'S / COLUMBIAN / I N K"; this has been found in clear greens as well as aquamarine. Possibly another was the little colorless log cabin (similar to 14 in Ill. 76) inscribed "HARRISON" on one side of the roof and "TIPPECANOE" on the other. This bottle immediately calls to mind the colorful, boisterous 1840 presidential campaign in which the log cabin and sobriquet Tippecanoe were so intimately and effectively linked with William Henry Harrison that the association persists to this day. Apollos Harrison must have had a vivid recollection of that campaign, and he may well have been inspired by having the same famous surname to order the Tippecanoe–Harrison log cabin bottles made for his ink. Be that as it may, the two types of octagonal bottles, if not the log cabin, may have been standard Columbian ink bottles throughout the thirty years or so Harrison manufactured inks. (In the Philadelphia city directories his first listing, 1847, was "Apollos W. Harrison, books, maps and ink." By 1877 only his residence address was given, so it may be assumed he had retired.) Of the virtues of his black ink, one of Harrison's labels said: "This ink flows more freely from the Pen, gives a stronger and more durable color and corrodes steel pens less than any other. It is the best quality for all purposes and particularly for use with Root's Penmanship." The address on the label was 8½ S. 7th Street, where he was located from 1847 through 1851.

An aquamarine cylindrical bottle, 4 in Ill. 76, which was lifted from the pedestrian class by the gadroon ribs on the shoulder, was inscribed "E.WATERS / TROY · N Y". This form, one of at least two for Waters' inks, apparently was produced in sizes from about an ounce to about a pint. The other known form, 3 in the same illustration, was an unusual hexagonal, rather onion-shaped, small bottle, an individual type perhaps designed by Elisha Waters himself and derived from the standard cones (plain pyramids). It was inscribed lengthwise "WATERS / INK / TROY. N.Y." on three contiguous sides, and has been recorded so far only in aquamarine in about 1½-ounce size. Elisha Waters, Jr., druggist, first listed in the Troy city directories of 1838/39, started his manufacture of black, blue, carmine, and indelible inks sometime before the spring of 1846. On April 16 of that year, in reply to Waters's inquiry about the quality of his black ink, Edgar A. Barbar and J. Carpenter of the Comptrollers Office, Albany, wrote that in their opinion his black ink was "equal to any other now in use," and added "It is free from sediment, flows freely and smoothly, and its color is clear and beautiful." As yet it is undetermined whether Elisha Waters (he dropped "Jr." before 1850) continued his ink manufactory— or sold out—after he turned from the wholesale and retail druggist business to the manufacture of paper boxes in 1862.[59]

Present evidence indicates it was in the 1840s that the trend started toward multiformity in small, standard and individual, ink bottles, particularly for home and school use. (By then, it seems, the slate and slate pencil were on their way to obsolescence.) Several of these are pictured in Ill. 76. Bottles 1, 2, and 8 through 12 were standard ink-bottle forms in which sometimes private molds were inscribed for an ink manufacturer, as in the case of 1, 9, 10, and 12. It has been said that the cones—conical bottles with sides tapering to a short cylindrical neck (plain pyramids)—were first introduced in 1840, and also the short-shouldered cones like 1, blown from green glass in its natural colors, including aquamarine. It probably was about the same time that the paneled pyramids (*fluted* in glass manufacturers' terminology, but today called simply *pyramids* by collectors), which have been recorded in aquamarine, ambers, greens, and—rarely—blue and amethyst, became popular. So too did squat bottles with paneled short sides. Some were octagonal like 12; others, 12-sided like 9 and 11. Those like 11 have been recorded in one- and two-ounce sizes only and are predominantly aquamarine in color, though occasionally green, including emerald. Unlike 9 (inscribed in two lines "BUTLER'S / CINCINNATI") and the Harrison bottle 12, none of those like 11 has been recorded that was blown in a private mold.[60]

Another standard commercial type, which perhaps did not evolve before the 1850s, was the fountain ink. Bottles of this type had very short straight sides, either plain or paneled, below a dome top with short cylindrical neck at the side. However, only half the side was paneled on 10, which was blown in a private mold inscribed "J / & / I / I / M" on the panels and "PAT^D OCT. 31st 1865" on the dome above. The patent probably was on the ink rather than the bottle, for the same type of bottle was made with the initials only, and presumably prior to the patent date. In any event, the original label on one of them indicates they were among the individual inks for schoolchildren. It reads "Moore's Excelsior School Writing Ink. Manufactured by J. & I. E. Moore, Warren, Mass." Fountain inks were still popular types to at least the turn of the century; the cone and pyramid into the early 20th century.[61]

Though predominating, the simple forms cited above were not the only ones for small ink bottles. The Victorian love of fancy and fanciful bottles spread to ink bottles, and apparently many ink manufacturers sought distinctive bottles to identify their brands by their packaging as well as by a molded inscription and paper labels. In general, the bottles were molded in the shape of objects rare to, or completely foreign to, glass as a material. A few examples are illustrated by 5, 6, 8, and 13 through 15 in Ill. 76. The "W. E. Bonney" barrel (13), which was produced in sizes up to and including a quart, and P. E. & Co. cask (15) are among the comparatively simple and believable representations. Except for the type of stabilizing support, the cask is like the design for the "Barrel" ink bottle (Ill. 71) that was patented by Alonzo French of Philadelphia in 1870. French claimed "the under-flat surface opposite the bung or neck" and extending beyond the sides was an improvement on L. N. Peirce's 1865 design, the rights to which French had acquired in 1869.[62] The little house (5), the building (8—a bank, as we know from the label), and locomotive (6) are among the more fanciful. The little house with touch of Victorian gothic in its doorway may have been used by more than one ink manufacturer: it has no inscription or initials. The bank building (inscribed on the roof, at right, "S.I. / COMP") was a natural for the Senate Ink Company's "Bank of England Writing Fluid," with sturdy bottle and name conveying an assurance

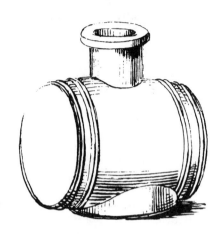

Fig. 1.

71. From design patent No. 3871, Mar. 1, 1870, for A. French's Barrel Bottle, an improvement on L. N. Pierce's 1865 design. (U. S. Patent Office.)

of reliability and sound worth. Logical, if not too practical, was a glass locomotive for an ink called "Locomotive Ink Fluid." All these, excepting possibly the W. E. Bonney barrel, may be attributed to the last third of the century. But where they, or the other types, were blown is an unanswered, possibly today unanswerable, question.

In fact, very rarely can a factory attribution be given to any ink bottle, and at present certainly not on the basis of physical characteristics. All in all, present data are both scarce and indefinite. Ink bottles were mentioned only rarely in the glass manufacturers' advertisements I have read, and then just as "inks." Nor on the price lists of glass manufacturers that I have seen were their inks described, though such terms as *carmine, durable,* and *mordant*[63] suggest the possibility of a special type for each of these kinds of ink. In the 1839 account book of Marshall & Stanger (New Brooklyn, New Jersey), J. E. Pfeiffer, who for some years has been digging extensively into the history of South Jersey glasshouses and their products, found entries of "Octagon red inks"; also durable and four- and six-ounce inks. As yet, this is the only reference associating a form with a particular kind of ink, and there is no evidence that octagon inks were peculiar to red ink. As a matter of fact, Harrison's octagon inks would indicate the contrary. In late account books of New Brooklyn, which was called the Isabella Glass Works after July 20, 1850,

Mr. Pfeiffer found also pyramid inks, 1849–64; cone, 1850–57; "Woods" (possibly like 1 in Ill. 76); and "Harrison," 1855–57—the last doubtless were made for Apollos W. Harrison, but "Harrison" gives no clue as to which of his bottles they were. Of the pyramids, Mr. Pfeiffer writes: "I can truthfully say the pyramid inks were made in all the Jersey Bottle Houses." They were likewise a product of the Stoddard glasshouses.

Actually, it is safe to say that ink bottles were blown in most glasshouses, east and west, specializing in bottles. But works not having their own moldmaking department obtained their molds from firms of moldmakers, and so—especially for standard ink bottles—the same forms were produced by many bottle manufacturers; also, ink manufacturers having their own private molds patronized more than one glassworks. Still, annoying as it may be to the collector not to be able to assign a factory origin to a particular specimen, for most of us this in no way detracts from the interest in ink bottles as bottles— they add a spice of variety to a bottle collection, and offer a fascinating and relatively inexpensive category for specialization.

These bottles illustrate virtually international types that undoubtedly were blown in many American glasshouses. The cylindrical bottles Nos. 9, 11, and 12 on the bottom row were free-blown. The others, Nos. 1 through 8 and 10, were blown-molded for body form in wooden or clay molds. The sides of the rectangular (with and without chamfered corners) and of the octagonal bottles arch at the top, blending into the shoulders. Around 1830, probably even earlier, bottles of the same body forms were blown in full-size two-piece molds, and aquamarine joined the natural dark bottle-glass colors. Nos. 1 and 4 and the cylindrical bottles were given wide mouths, a feature less often seen on bottles found today than the same forms with more slender necks and narrow mouths. Evidence as to the functions of early wide-mouth bottles is slight, but it suggests that flour of mustard, powdered preparations, and various kinds of pickles and preserves were numbered among their contents. Nos. 2, 3, 5, 7, 10, and 11, formerly in the George S. McKearin Collection. Nos. 1, 4, 6, 8, 9, and 12, The Corning Museum of Glass.

Top row:

1. Wide-mouth bottle, clear olive-amber; thick-walled, rectangular body, chamfered corners, short rounded shoulder, wide short neck flaring at mouth with round string-ring laid on about 1/8″ to 1/4″ below plain lip; smooth, slightly depressed base. Capacity, 14 oz. Height, 7¼″. Body, about 1¾″ by 3″ at base.

   Similar to the bottle illustrating a 1758 advertisement of Benjamin Jackson, Philadelphia mustard and chocolate maker from London, and, in body form, to those in details Nos. 4 and 8 of Ill. 3 from 17th-century paintings. Similar aquamarine and dark-colored bottles with flat and with incurved corners were blown in full-size piece molds in the 19th century.

2. Black (deep olive-green); medium-walled body similar to No. 1, curved shoulder bulging over wide sides, long slender sausage neck with narrow flat string-ring laid on about 1/8″ below narrow turned-over lip; slight depression on base. This 18th-century type was blown in several sizes, including wine bottles with and without seals affixed to the shoulder, like No. 3 of Ill. 47, dated 1760. Capacity, about 14 oz. Height, 9⅛″. Body, about 1¾″ by 3″ at base.

3. Brilliant clear olive-green; medium-walled body similar to No. 2, shoulder curved at one end and sloping at other, tapering neck, narrow sloping collar; base slightly depressed, trace of pontil mark. Capacity, about 12 oz. Height, 7⅞″. Body, about 1⅞″ by 2¾″ at base.

   Similar to bottle illustrating an 1808 advertisement of Hopkins' Cordial Purging Elixir, Ill. 63.

4. Wide-mouth bottle, black (deep olive-green); thick-walled, unusually squat body with wide sides, narrower ends, and chamfered corners, rounded shoulder (shorter at one end than other), wide neck tapering to flangelike string-ring laid on below plain lip. First half of the 18th century. Capacity, 1 pt. 9 oz. Height, 8″. Body, about 3″ by 4½″ at base.

Middle row:

5. Clear olive-green bubbly glass; thin-walled octagonal body, rounded shoulder, long neck, irregular everted lip; medium kick-up, slight pontil mark. Found in New England in 1924; possibly blown in an early Connecticut glassworks or at the Keene-Marlboro-Street Works, N.H. Capacity, about 9 oz. Height, 5¾″. Greatest diameter, about 2⅜″.

6. Light olive-green, bubbly glass; thin-walled, rectangular body, long shoulder sloping into wide neck tapering to flaring plain lip; base slightly depressed, pontil mark. Capacity, about 5 oz. Height, 4¾″. Body, 1¼″ by 2⅝″.

7. Dark olive-green, bubbly glass; medium-walled octagonal body, long rounded shoulder, short neck tapering and contracted slightly below heavy round string-ring laid on just below plain lip; high domed kick-up, pontil mark. Probably last half of the 18th century. Found in New England; possibly made at East Hartford, Connecticut, or Germantown, Massachusetts, glassworks.

8. Dark olive-amber, bubbly glass; octagonal body, long shoulder curving to wide neck tapering to heavy sloping collar; low domed kick-up, pontil mark. Capacity, about 1 pt. 2 oz. Height, 7″. Diameter, 3″.

Bottom row:

9. Wide-mouth bottle; deep olive-green; tall cylindrical body, short rounded shoulder, wide neck tapering to wide mouth with heavy flat string-ring laid on flaring plain lip; wide, medium-high domed kick-up, trace of pontil mark; closely similar to black glass wine bottles, ca. 1765–90. Capacity, 1 qt. 1 pt. Height, 9¼″. Diameter, 4⅞″.

10. Wide-mouth bottle, clear olive-green; cylindrical body, sloping shoulder, wide short cylindrical neck, sloping turned-over collar; slight kick-up, pontil mark. Probably first half 19th century. Capacity about 1 pt. 2 oz. Height, 6″. Diameter, 3⁵/₁₆″.

11. Wide-mouth bottle, clear olive-green; tall cylindrical body, curving shoulder, very short neck, sloping turned-over collar; nearly flat base, trace of pontil mark. Capacity, about 14 oz. Height, 7½″. Diameter, 2¼″.

12. Wide-mouth bottle, deep olive-green; tall cylindrical body, long sloping shoulder, short neck tapering slightly to turned-over collar; deep domed kick-up; body similar to wine bottle Type 9, ca.1790–1810. Capacity, 1 pt. 5 oz. Height, about 8⅞″. Diameter, about 3⅝″.

73. BLOWN-MOLDED WIDE-MOUTH PRESERVE and PICKLE BOTTLES ca. 1840–75.

Except for No. 1, blown in a mold having cylindrical body part and two-piece upper part for shoulder and neck, all were blown in full-size two-piece molds. Nos. 4, 5, 6, and 10 show variants of the Gothic bottles so popular from about 1840 throughout the late 19th century. No. 6 is the most elaborate of these bottles recorded as yet.

Nos. 1 through 5, formerly in the George S. McKearin Collection. No. 7, The Ohio Historical Society; Nos. 8 through 10, The Henry Ford Museum; No. 6, Collection of J. E. Pfeiffer.

Top row:

1. Black (deep olive-green); cylindrical body, 10 panels on curved shoulder tapering from rounded ends to short wide neck, deep galleried rim with half-round molding above straight sides; smooth base, large nipple at center of deep domed kick-up. Possibly blown at the Saratoga (N.Y.) Mountain glassworks. ca. 1844–70. Capacity, 2 qts. Height, 10¼".

2. Brown-amber, bubbly glass; long squared octofoil body with narrow lobe (rib) on each side and wide at corners, sloping plain shoulder, short wide cylindrical neck, rolled-over collar; smooth base, small deep dome kick-up. Attributed to New Granite Glass Works, Stoddard, N.H. ca. 1865–71. Capacity, 1 pt. 10 oz. Height, about 8". Diameter, 3".

3. Brown-amber; long cylindrical slender body tapering at top into long neck, 10 round-end panels starting 4¼" from base and tapering to about ¾" below mouth, round collar with lower bevel; smooth depressed base. Attributed by family history to the Willington Glass Works, West Willington, Conn. ca. 1840–70. One of a lot found about 1920 in the vicinity of the glassworks, a few of the bottles still containing blueberry preserves. Capacity, 1 pt. 15 oz. Height, 11¼". Diameter, 3".

4. Gothic, brown-amber; square body with narrow chamfered corners, sloping shoulder, round collar-rib at base of wide cylindrical neck, rolled-over round collar; base, deep domed kick-up, pontil mark; each side: sunken Gothic arch, ribbed pillars, "tulip" capital, ogival ribs on outer side of small palmette at point; inner frame, double ogival at top, small quatrefoil above pendant conventional ornament in center. Rare in color. Attributed to the Westford Glass Works, Westford, Conn. Mid-19th century. Capacity, 1½ pts. Height, 8⁵⁄₁₆". Body, about 3" sq.

5. Gothic, citron; square body, chamfered corners, tapering at top to round collar-rib at base of wide cylindrical neck, rolled-over collar; smooth base, wide domed kick-up; each side: sunken Gothic arch, plain pillars, "tulip" capital, at top, ogival ribs on outer side to large palmette at point; inner frame, double ogival at top, sunken quatrefoil in square diamond above pendant trefoil in center, ogival ribs at sides; inverted triangle below collar rib. Very rare in color. J. E. Pfeiffer found aquamarine fragments of similar design on sites of the Bulltown (ca. 1853–71) and Crowleytown (ca. 1851–67), N.J., glassworks. Capacity, 1 qt. 15 oz. Height, 11¹³⁄₁₆". Body, about 3⅜" sq.

Bottom row:

6. Gothic, brilliant green; square body, chamfered corners, long slightly double-ogee shoulder sloping to wide cylindrical neck, round collar; smooth base, nipple at center of dome kick-up; each side: elaborate Gothic arches; on body, formed by wide rib, finial at keystone, one plain for label, 3 filled with diamond lattice; on shoulder, arch top supported by spool-like capital, filled with honeycomb diaper, large trefoil ornament at point. J. E. Pfeiffer found aquamarine and light green fragments on the Crowleytown glassworks' site. Capacity, 2 qts. 5 oz. Height, 13⅞". Body, 4" sq.

7. Petal and Panel, light yellow-green; long body, 12-sided between 6 broad ogival petals bisected by vertical rib, at bottom and 6 inverted on rounded shoulder, wide cylindrical neck, narrow round collar; base, dome kick-up, pontil mark. Found in the Midwest and probably produced there. Possibly 2nd quarter of the 19th century. Capacity, 1 pt. 14 oz. Height, 8⅜". Greatest diameter, about 3½".

8. Clear green; at top and bottom of cylindrical body, chain of wide-spaced large beads between wide horizontal ribs, on sloping shoulder 16 long fan-flutes tapering to round collar-rib at base of short wide neck spreading slightly to narrow flange; medium dome kick-up, trace of pontil mark; inscribed on side, "W. D. SMITH" in arc above "N. Y." Blown in a private mold of William D. Smith, pickle and preserve manufacturer, listed in City Directories 1843–59. Capacity, 1 qt. 18 oz. Height, 11½". Greatest diameter, about 4½".

9. Clear green; square body, chamfered corners, sloping shoulder, two round collar-ribs at base of wide cylindrical neck, round collar; base, small narrow dome kick-up, pontil mark; on body: sides recessed and arched at top with scroll ornament; fancy leaf ornament on two opposite sides; plain side opposite one with lengthwise inscription "J. MC COLLICK & CO / NEW YORK." "Jane M'Collick, pickles," was first listed in the City Directories in 1848; from 1851 to 1865 as either "Jane M'Collick & Co." or "J. M'Collick, & Co." The 1860 listing included: "pickles, preserves, sauces, jellies, jams, catsups, syrups etc., hermetically sealed fruits, vegetable & pie fruits, and grated horse radish." Being in New York City, Jane McCollick and William D. Smith quite likely ordered their containers from one of the South Jersey bottle manufacturers. Capacity, 1 pt. Height, 8⅝". Body, 2¹⁄₁₆".

10. Gothic, aquamarine; hexagonal body, curved shoulder, wide collar-rib at base of short wide cylindrical neck, round collar; smooth base, concave disk; each side: sunken Gothic arch with ogival band below trefoil in ogival top, scalloped edge at bottom; on one panel, original paper label, "GERKINS / From / W. K. LEWIS & BROS / 93 / BROAD ST. / BOSTON / MASS. Manufacturers of Pickles, Pre / serves, Condensed Milk, Her / metically sealed articles etc." The listing appeared in the 1856–70 City Directories. Capacity, 3 qts. 7 oz. Height, 13⅛". Diameter, about 4⅞".

Excepting No. 9, molded for body form only, all were blown in full-size two-piece molds. Nos. 1 through 7 and 13, types generally called sauce or pepper sauce bottles, were used also for catsup, ketchup, juices, syrups, essences, even capers. Nos. 1, 3, and 11 through 13 show variants of the Gothic designs. J. E. Pfeiffer found fragments of bottles in the designs of Nos. 1, 8, 10, and 11 on the site of the Crowleytown glassworks (ca. 1851–67), N.J.

Nos. 1 through 7, 10, and 13, formerly in the George S. McKearin Collection. No. 5, Ohio Historical Society; No. 12, Henry Ford Museum; Nos. 8, 9, and 11, Collection of J. E. Pfeiffer.

Top row:

1. Gothic, aquamarine; square body, narrow chamfered corners, tapering to very slender plain neck, round collar with lower bevel; plain base, pontil mark; on sides: sunken plain Gothic arch below tapering panel with large trefoil below conventional ornament in relief. Capacity, 7 oz. Height, 9¼". Base, 1⅞" sq.

2. Gothic, clear green; hexagonal body tapering to long cylindrical neck, collar like No. 1; smooth base, sunken disk; on sides: sunken Gothic arch, beveled sides, narrow inner frame below tapering panel with trefoil ornament similar to No. 1 and, at top, stylized flower motif. Capacity, 7 oz. Height, 8⅞". Base, about 2" sq.

3. Gothic, aquamarine; rectangular body, narrow chamfered corners, sides rising in attenuated S-curve to cylindrical neck, collar like No. 1; smooth base, ringed concave oval; 3 sides: wide medial vertical rib from base to neck; 1 side: sunken Gothic arch (label panel). Capacity, about 6 oz. Height, 8½". Base, 1½" by 1⅝".

4. Gothic, aquamarine; quatrefoil body tapering to cylindrical neck, narrow flange; pontil mark; on sides: narrow sunken Gothic arch tapering sharply to point; on lobe corners, 3 short horizontal ribs alternating with large diamond on small rectangular convex panel and, at top, small hourglass-like motif. Occurs also in deep blue and in larger sizes. Capacity, 2½ oz. Height, 5⅝". Diameter of base, 1½" at sides; 1⅝" at lobes.

5. Aquamarine; quatrefoil body tapering to slender tapering neck, very narrow mouth with flat-topped everted lip; pontil mark; on 3 sides, 5 stars in vertical row; 1 side, plain; lobe corners, rope ribbed. Occurs also in 2 oz. size, with plain lip. The few recorded examples were found in Ohio, suggesting a probable midwestern origin. Capacity, 4 oz. Height, 7⅝". Base, 1½" sq.

Middle row:

6. Deep clear green; spirally ribbed long conical body, plain cylindrical neck, collar like No. 1; smooth depressed base inscribed in circle "S. & P. PAT APP FOR." Late 19th century. Capacity, 10 oz. Height, 8⅛". Diameter of base, about 2⅞".

7. Deep clear green; horizontally ribbed, hexagonal tapering body with plain Gothic label panel from base to 7th rib on one side, plain cylindrical neck, collar like No. 1; bottom rib inscribed, on 4 sides, "E R D / & C⁰ PAT^D / FEB 17 / 1887"; smooth base inscribed in circle "R DURKEE N.Y." Capacity, 6 oz. Height, 8". Diameter of base, 1¾".

8. Light green; short square body, chamfered corners, long wide neck with lower half a double-ogee 8-paneled bulge and upper, plain cylindrical, flat turned-over collar; base: bead at center of dome kick-up, pontil mark; on body, sunken bevel-edged Roman arches—3 latticed, 1 plain. Capacity, 6 oz. Height, 6⅜". Body, about 1¹³/₁₆" sq.

9. Wide-mouth bottle or jar, clear green; square body, chamfered corners, sides with rounded tops blending into sloping shoulder, short wide cylindrical neck, round turned-over collar; base: shallow dome kick-up, pontil mark. 18th–early 19th-century type. Attributed to Bulltown or Crowleytown by J. E. Pfeiffer. Capacity, 1 pt. 11 oz. Height, 7½". Body, 3" sq.

Bottom row:

10. Pale aquamarine; square body, chamfered corners, long shoulder sloping to collar-rib at base of short wide cylindrical neck, round turned-over collar; smooth base, shallow dome kick-up; on sides, leaf sprays framing top and bottom of sunken oval panel. Capacity, 1 qt. 8 oz. Height, 10⅞". Body, about 3¼" sq.

11. Gothic, emerald green; square body, chamfered corners, short shoulder sloping to collar-rib at base of wide neck spreading slightly at turned-over collar; smooth depressed base; on sides, sunken Gothic arch, plain inner frame, outer side ornamented at top by row of three scroll motifs and palmette at point. Capacity, 1 pt. about 6 oz. Height, about 9½". Body, 3" sq.

12. Gothic, deep emerald green; square body, chamfered corners, shoulder sloping to collar-rib at base of short wide cylindrical neck, round turned-over collar; smooth base, dot at center of dome kick-up; on sides, sunken double-frame Gothic arches; in point of inner frame bead-trefoil below intaglio quatrefoil in large diamond; top of outer frame flanked by three 2-lobed motifs and, at point, diamond between slender curved ribs; over one arch and corners, part of original label with American Eagle below "TAMARINDS" and above "Prepared by W. K. LEWIS & Co. . . . 6 BROAD STREET / BOSTON." Firm listed in Boston City Directories, 1840/41–42/43. Capacity, 14 oz. Height, 7⅜". Body, 2⅜" sq.

13. Gothic, clear light green; square body, chamfered corners, shoulder sloping sharply to collar-rib at base of long cylindrical neck, deep sloping collar with lower bevel; smooth base, large concave disk; on sides, sunken double-frame Gothic arch with ogival top; in point of inner frame, ornament like that of No. 12; on side of outer frame, ornaments like No. 11. Rare. Capacity, 1 pt. Height, 10½". Body, about 2⅝". sq.

These containers illustrate types of bottles and jars used over a long period for packaging such products as snuff, mustard, shoe blacking, medicinal powders, and inks. Nos. 7 and 12 are free-blown; Nos. 1, 6, 8, 10, 11, and 13, molded for body form with tops of sides rounded or arched and blending into shoulder; Nos. 2, 5, 9, 14, and 15, blown in full-size two-piece molds.

Illustrated also in *American Glass,* Plate 227: 2, 3, 4, 6, and 14 by Nos. 6, 8, 9, 1, and 2; 10 by No. 11 of Plate 228.

Nos. 1, 5, 7 through 13, 15, and 16, formerly in the George S. McKearin Collection. Nos. 2 and 3, Old Sturbridge Village; Nos. 4, 6, and 14, The Henry Ford Museum.

Top row:

1. Dark olive-green; octagonal body, short sloping shoulder, everted plain lip; plain base. 18th–early 19th century. Capacity, 4 oz. Height, 4¼". Diameter, 1¾".

2. Dark olive-amber; elliptical body, short sloping shoulder, cylindrical neck, plain lip; pontil mark; on one side, lengthwise inscription: "A A COOLEY / HARTFORD / CON." Probably Coventry or West Willington Glass Works. 1841–59. Capacity, 4 oz. Height, $4^{7}/_{16}$". Greatest width, 2¼". Greatest depth, $1^{5}/_{16}$".

3. Blacking bottle, olive-green; square body, flattened shoulder, cylindrical neck, everted plain lip; pontil mark; original sponge. Paper label on three sides: "[1] Cooley's Elastic Water-Proof / MILITARY BLACKING / For rendering Leather impervious to Water and / giving the surface an elegant polish, without / destroying its soft, supple & elastic qualities. [2] NOTICE / A few applications of this compound will convince the most / incredulous of its superiority over any other article in circu / lation for the same purpose and after repeated applications / for months, they will find their Boots, Shoes, Harness &c / possessing the soft, pliable texture of new ones, and it is in / no way liable to crack or injure the durability of the finest / leather. Entered according to the act of Congress 1845 / A.A. Cooley. [3] Direct . . . " Probably Coventry or West Willington Glass Works. 1845–59. Capacity, 4 oz. Height, $4^{9}/_{16}$". Body, about 2¼" sq.

4. Blacking bottle, dark olive-green; square body, chamfered corners, short sloping shoulder, wide neck spreading at plain lip; pontil mark. Paper label on three sides: "BLACK / VARNISH / FOR S[h]oes, Boots, Harness &c. / Manufactured and Sold WHOLESALE & RETAIL, / and Wa[r]ranted a First Rate Article / By / A. Bostwick. / Albany, N.Y. July 23, 1833." Capacity, 4 oz. Height, 4½". Body, 1½" sq.

5. Bottle, bubbly olive-amber glass; cylindrical body, long sloping shoulder, short neck flaring to plain lip; pontil mark. Early to late 19th century. Capacity, 5 oz. Height, about 4". Diameter, 2½".

Middle row:

6. Jar, bubbly olive-green glass; square body tapering at top to wide mouth, narrow flange; plain base, slightly concave center. Paper label: "POWDERED / JALAP / PREPARED & SOLD / by / Dʳ THOS RITTER / Nᴼ 104 CHERRY Sᵀ N.Y." ca. 1836. Capacity, about ½ lb. Height, 4¼". Body, about 2⅛" sq.

7. Bottle, bubbly light olive-amber glass; long cylindrical body, sloping shoulder, short neck, sloping turned-over collar; high domed kick-up, pontil mark. Late 18th–early 19th century. Capacity, 5 oz. Height, 4½". Diameter, 2¼".

8. Bottle, dark olive-green; square, wide chamfered corners, short shoulder, very short wide neck, plain lip; base, circular depression, trace of pontil mark. 18th–early 19th century. Capacity, 4 oz. Height, 3⅝". Body, 1¾" sq.

9. Ink bottle, dark olive-amber; cylindrical body, rounded shoulder, narrow neck, plain lip; shallow kick-up, pontil mark. 19th century. Capacity, about 3 oz. Height, 4½". Diameter 1⅝".

10. Bottle, deep olive-green; octagonal body, nearly flat shoulder, very short flaring neck, plain lip; shallow conical kick-up, pontil mark; still holds snuff. 18th–early 19th century. Capacity, ½ lb. Height, 4⅛". Diameter, 2⅞".

Bottom row:

11. Snuff bottle, emerald-green; square body, shoulder curving to narrow flanged mouth; trace of pontil mark. Probably 18th century. Capacity, 1 lb. Height, about 5¾". Body, 2⅞" sq.

12. Jar, light yellow-green; sides flattened giving roughly square shape, sloping at top to flanged mouth; tiny conical kick-up, pontil mark. Probably 18th century. Capacity, about ¾ oz. Height, 1½". Diameter, about 1".

13. Wide-mouth snuff bottle, dark olive-green; square body, short shoulder curving to flanged mouth; pontil mark. 18th–early 19th century. Capacity, ½ lb. Height, 4⅜". Body, about 2⅜" sq.

14. Snuff bottle, olive-green; rectangular body, chamfered corners, shoulders curving to narrow everted lip; pontil mark. Paper label: Indian standing at left, left hand on top of sign reading "MACCOBOY / SNUFF / MANUFACTURED / & SOLD BY / WM. C. LEMON / No. 4 WALL / & 213 DUANE·STS. / NEW YORK." 1846–51. Capacity, ½ lb. Height, 4¼". Body, 1⅝" by 2⁹/₁₆".

15. Bottle, olive-amber; rectangular body, incurved corners, nearly flat shoulder, narrow flaring lip; pontil mark; on one side, lengthwise inscription: "J J MAPES / 61 FRONT.ST / N. YORK". 1824–35. Capacity, ½ lb. Height, 4⅜". Body, 1⅞" by 2⅝".

16. Bottle, streaked puce; octagonal body, short flat shoulder, long wide neck, applied crude collar just below irregular rough lip; plain base. Attributed to Persia. 18th–early 19th century. Capacity, 8 oz. Height, 5½". Diameter, 2⅛".

76. INK BOTTLES, BLOWN IN FULL-SIZE TWO-PIECE MOLDS, mid–late 19th century
Collection of William E. Covill, Jr.

Top row:

1. Deep aquamarine; conical body, short rounded shoulder, cylindrical neck, tooled narrow collar; pontil mark; on label panel: "WOOD'S / BLACK . INK / PORTLAND." Occurs also in amber. Capacity, 1½ oz. Height, 2⅜". Diameter at base, 2¼".

   No Wood appears as ink manufacturer in Portland, Me., City Directories 1834 to 1875, but since druggists often made ink, perhaps the Wood of Nos. 1 and 2 was Nathan Wood, listed as druggist 1850/51, and by 1863 as "patent medicines" (see No. 15, III. 80).

2. Aquamarine; pyramid (octagonal cone), cylindrical neck, smooth lip with narrow inside fold; pontil mark; paper label: "WOOD'S / FINE BLACK / RECORD INK / PORTLAND." Without label, occurs also in amber, olive-amber, amethyst, blue, and olive-green. Capacity, 1½ oz. Height, 2⅜". Diameter at base, 2".

3. Aquamarine, hexagonal onion-shaped body, collar-rib at base of neck, tooled everted lip giving narrow-collar effect; pontil mark; inscribed lengthwise on 3 contiguous sides "WATERS / INK / TROY. N.Y." Made for Elisha Waters, wholesale and retail druggist and ink manufacturer. ca. 1846–62. Capacity, 1½ oz. Height, 2⅝". Diameter at base, 1¾".

4. Pale aquamarine; cylindrical body, 16 gadroon ribs on short sloping shoulder, short neck, applied collar with narrow straight sides below wide flange; trace of pontil mark; inscribed on side, "E. WATERS / TROY· N Y". Capacity, 1 oz. plus. Height, 2¼". Diameter, about 1⅜".

Second row:

5. Aquamarine; house with incurved roof, cylindrical neck, collared lip formed in the mold; smooth flat base. Late 19th century. Capacity, 2 oz. Height, 2⅞". Body, 1½" sq.

6. Aquamarine; locomotive, smokestack neck, rough lip; smooth base; inscribed on one side, "PAT. OCT. 1874" and, on the other, "TRADE MARK"; on front, paper label: "LOCKMAN'S [in semicircle] / LOCOMOTIVE / INK / FLUID." Capacity, about 1½ oz. Length, about 2⅛". Height at neck, 1⅞".

7. Deep aquamarine; octagonal body, short nearly flat shoulder, cylindrical neck, applied wide flange; pontil mark; inscribed lengthwise on three continuous sides "HARRISON'S / COLUMBIAN / INK". Occurs also in deep blue and in sizes ranging from 1 oz. to 1 gallon. Made for Apollos W. Harrison, Philadelphia. ca. 1847–77.

8. Aquamarine; bank building with mansard roof, cylindrical neck, collared lip formed in the mold; flat base rim around flat smooth rectangular center; on curve of roof (at right) inscribed in two lines "S.I. / COMP."; on rear label panel, paper label: "BANK OF ENGLAND / Writing Fluid, / MANU-FACTURED BY / THE SENATE INK CO. / PHILA-

DELPHIA." Occurs also in opaque white. Late 19th-early 20th century. Capacity, about 2 oz. Body, 1¼" by 1¾".

Third row:

9. Light olive-green; short 12-sided body, wide nearly flat shoulder, long cylindrical neck, lip tooled giving narrow-collar effect; narrow flat base rim around concave disk, pontil mark; inscribed (1 letter to each of 10 contiguous sides) in 2 lines, letters canting to the left: "BUTLERS INK / CINCINNATI." Capacity, 1½ oz. Height, 2½". Diameter, 2".

10. Aquamarine; fountain ink: short straight sides with 6 panels at back, and below dome top with short neck, at top front, rough lip; smooth flat base; inscribed on panels "J / & / I / E / M" and on dome above panels "PAT^D OCT 31st 1865". Made for J. & I. E. Moore, Warren, Mass. Without "PAT^D . . ." occurs in amber, blue, and greens. Capacity, about 1½ oz. Height, 1½". Diameter, 2⅛".

11. Aquamarine; 12-sided body, long curved shoulder, short cylindrical neck, narrow turned-over collar; pontil mark. Occurs also in greens, including emerald. Capacity, 1 oz. Height, 1¾". Diameter, 1¾".

12. Aquamarine; octagonal straight-sided body, long curved shoulder, short cylindrical neck spreading at lip and tooled giving narrow-collar effect; shallow conical kick-up, pontil mark; inscribed on three contiguous sides "[1] HARRISON'S [2] CO-LUMBIAN [3] I N K". Occurs also in greens. ca. 1847–77. Capacity, 2 oz. Height, about 2". Diameter, 2".

Fourth row:

13. Light aquamarine; barrel, horizontal ribs simulating hoops and broken on reverse by elliptical label-panel extending from shoulder to base, flat shoulder, cylindrical neck, lip tooled giving narrow-collar effect; curved base rim around slightly depressed center, pontil mark; inscribed in center obverse "W. E. BONNEY." Late, produced in sizes up to and including 1 quart. Capacity, 2 oz. Height, about 1⅝". Greatest diameter, about 1¹³/₁₆".

14. Colorless; log cabin, door and window on each long side, window at each end, short neck, round collar formed in the mold, rough lip; smooth flat base. Capacity, about 3 oz. Height, 2⅜". Body, 1⅞" by 2½".

   The earlier small colorless log cabin bottles (presumably for ink) inscribed "HARRISON" on one side of the roof and "TIPPECANOE" on the other may have been made for Apollos W. Harrison in the late 1840s.

15. Blue-aquamarine; cask, hoops at ends, on side and resting on 2 narrow rectangular supports, cylindrical neck, flange; smooth base; inscribed on one side "PETROLEUM [in semicircle] / P.E. & C^O"; on the other "WRITING / FLUID". Capacity, 2 oz. Height, 2⅜". Diameter, 1½".

77. APOTHECARY VIALS, PROBABLY from AMERICAN GLASSHOUSES

These vials illustrate a wide variety in forms and sizes of (unless otherwise indicated) 18th- to early 19th-century types, all with a pontil mark. Five bear original labels. Three of these have a druggist's name, which, however, does not necessarily date the bottles, since old vials were reused. In times of shortages, vials were sometimes taken in payment for medicine and purchased from housewives—apparently as late as the 1830s if they heeded Mrs. Child's advice to save vials and bottles, as "apothecaries and grocers would give something for them."

Nos. 1 through 4, 6 through 11, 13 through 17, and 19, formerly in the George S. McKearin Collection. Nos. 5, 12, and 18, Old Sturbridge Village.

Top row:

1. Light green; free-blown; cylindrical body (walls of varying thickness), short rounded shoulder, cylindrical neck, plain lip. Capacity, about 2/3 dram. Height, 1⅛". Diameter, about ¾".

2. Light olive-green; free-blown; slender cylindrical body, short curved shoulder, cylindrical neck, wide flange. Capacity, 2/3 dram. Height, 1⅝". Diameter, about ⅝".

3. Light yellow-green; possibly blown in clay mold; long cylindrical body, short curved shoulder, cylindrical neck, thick flange. Capacity, ½ oz. Height, 2⅜". Diameter, about ¾".

4. White (colorless, pale aquamarine in thick lower sides and bottom); free-blown; long cylindrical body, short sloping shoulder, cylindrical neck, everted lip. Capacity, ½ oz. Height, 2⅞". Diameter, about ¾".

5. Green tinge; possibly blown in clay mold for body form; thin-walled cylindrical body, sloping shoulder, cylindrical neck, flange; medium kick-up; paper label: "Oil of Pennyroyal" in ink; printed, "Prepared by / JOHN BRADDOCK / AT THE / People's Family Medicine Store / 306 North Main Street / HARTFORD, CONN." (1846–55/6 address). Capacity, 2 oz. Height, 2¾".

6. Aquamarine tint; possibly blown in clay mold for body form; thin-walled wide cylindrical body, long nearly flat shoulder, cylindrical neck, flange. Possibly mid-19th century. Capacity, 1 oz. Height, 2¼". Diameter, about 1⅛".

7. Aquamarine tint; blown in full-size two-piece mold; thin-walled wide 12-sided body and curved shoulder, long wide cylindrical neck, narrow flange. Possibly mid-19th century. Capacity, 1 oz. Height, 2". Diameter, about 1 3/16".

8. Light aquamarine; blown in full-size two-piece mold; thick-wall; sides sloping to wide mouth, round collar. First half of 19th century. Capacity, ¾ oz. Height, 1¼". Diameter at base, about 1".

Middle row:

9. Aquamarine; molded for body form; thin-walled 12-sided body, long sloping shoulder, narrow cylindrical neck, wide mouth, flange. First half of 19th century. Capacity, 2 oz. Height, 3¼". Diameter, 1⅜".

10. Aquamarine tint; possibly blown in clay mold for body form; thin-walled cylindrical body, short flat shoulder, wide short cylindrical neck, wide mouth, narrow flange. Capacity, 5 oz. Height, 4". Diameter, 1⅞".

11. Aquamarine; like No. 9 but larger; old, but probably not original, metal-topped cork. First half of 19th century. Capacity, 5 oz. Height, 4". Diameter, about 1⅞".

12. Light green (deep tone in thick base); possibly blown in clay mold for body form; long slender cylindrical body, very short sloping shoulder; cylindrical neck, wide flange; fitted with old cork. Paper label: "Oil WINTERGREEN / From / A. F. SHERMAN; / Druggist and Apothecary, / Dealer in Books and Stationary, Varnish, Spts. / Turpentine, Birdca / ges and Seed, Toys and / Toy Books, Confections, &c &c / LUDLOW, VT." Alvah F. Sherman, sole proprietor, 1857–66. Capacity, 1½ oz. Height, 4⅛". Diameter, ⅞".

13. Pale aquamarine; possibly blown in clay mold for body form; long slender cylindrical body, very short sloping shoulder, long neck, wide flange. Paper label: "PEPPERMINT". Capacity, about 1½ oz. Height, 4⅛". Diameter, about 13/16".

14. Clear bluish green; molded for body form; thick walls and base, large nipple inside at bottom of long slender square body, very short sloping shoulder, short neck, wide flange. Capacity, about 1 oz. Height, about 3⅜". Diameter, ¾".

Bottom row:

15. Deep yellow-green; free-blown; thick walls and base; small dome inside at bottom of long cylindrical body, short irregular shoulder, narrow cylindrical neck, wide flange. Capacity, 2 oz. Height, about 5". Diameter, about 1 5/16".

16. Light olive-amber; free-blown; tall taper shape, slight shoulder, short narrow cylindrical neck, wide flange. Capacity, 3½ oz. Height, 6". Diameter at base, about 1⅝".

17. Colorless; free-blown; long cylindrical body, long sloping shoulder, tapering neck, wide flange; wide high dome kick-up. Paper label: "Genuine Essence of / GOLDEN ROD". Capacity, 7 oz. Height, 6½". Diameter, about 1⅞".

18. Light green; free-blown; long cylindrical body, long sloping shoulder, long spreading neck, wide flange; high conical kick-up. Paper label: "TINCT. CAMPHOR. / PREPARED AND SOLD BY / COWLES & LEETE, / Successors to / Dr. NATHANIEL BOOTH, / *54 State Street,* NEW HAVEN CONN." 1850–58 address. Capacity, 6 oz. Height, about 6". Diameter, about 1⅞".

19. Clear green; molded for body form; square body, fluted corners, short rounding shoulder, short wide cylindrical neck, wide mouth, narrow flange. Capacity, 3½ oz. Height, 5⅛". Body, about 1¼" sq.

All were blown in full-size two-piece molds and, except for No. 12, have a pontil-marked plain base. Nos. 7 through 14 were blown in private molds for proprietary medicines. Nos. 2, 3, and 4 are rare whimseys, patterned in lettered molds for patent medicine vials.

Top row:

1. Aquamarine; long slender elliptical body, cylindrical neck, everted tooled lip. Paper label: at center, yellow lemon with green leaves and stem on white ground; green on yellow ground, "GOODWIN'S/ PURE / CONCENTRATED / EXTRACT OF LEMON/ FOR FLAVOURING PASTRIES/SAUCES AND JELLIES/ALSO A PLEASANT PERFUME." Mid- to late-19th century. Capacity, 2 oz. Height, 4$^{13}/_{16}$". Greatest width, 1½". Greatest depth, 1".

2. "Beaver" hat, clear green; high crown, narrow brim turned up on sides, down in front and back, narrow outside fold on rim; first letters of the molded inscription cut off, leaving, in three lines, lengthwise: " . . . GATES / . . . OYNE / . . . OIAL." Height, 1¾".

3. Hat, light green; very high crown, brim shape of No. 2, plain rim; inscribed: on one side, "LIQUID"; on other, "[OPO]DELDOC" (first letters cut off). Ht., 2".

4. "Quaker" hat, pale aquamarine; low crown, broad brim turned as on No. 2; on one side, lengthwise inscription in three lines: "BEPSC . . . / ANOD . . . / CORD . . . " (last letters cut off; second word, probably anodyne; third, cordial). Height, 1⅛".

5. Blue-aquamarine; long rectangular body, fluted corners, long cylindrical neck, narrow round collar; inscribed lengthwise on one side: "GENUINE ESSENCE": paper label on other side: "From FREDERICK KLETT & Co's / ESS. PEPPERMINT. / Drug & Chemical Warehouse, N.E. Cor. Callowhill / and Second Streets, Philad'a." 1843–58 address. Capacity, 1½ oz. Height, 4⅞". Body, ⅝" by 1⅛".

6. Aquamarine; 12-panel body, sides spreading to shoulder sloping into long cylindrical neck, tooled lip; type used mainly for colognes. Paper label: "ESSENCE OF WINTERGREEN / PREPARED BY/ S.E. FAY DRUGGIST / ATHOL DEPOT / MASS." Sereno E. Fay, sole proprietor, 1861 to 1865. Capacity, about 2 oz. Ht., 5⅛". Widest diameter, 1½".

Middle row:

7. Figured and lettered wide-mouth bottle, aquamarine; cylindrical body, sloping shoulder, short wide neck, turned-in lip; sprays of oak leaves and acorns enclosing "FIENTZ / PHIL^A" on one side and "MUSTARD FACTORY" on other. Possibly third quarter of 19th century. Capacity, about ½ lb. Height, 5$^1/_{16}$". Diameter, 2⅜".

8. Pale green; rectangular, chamfered corners, slightly curved shoulder, long cylindrical neck, narrow flange; inscribed lengthwise: on one side, "DR JAYNE'S INDIAN"; on other, "EXPECTORANT PHILAD^A" David Jayne, M.D., druggist, S. 3rd St., 1840–49. About 4 oz. Height, 5$^1/_{16}$". Body, 1⅜" by 1⅞".

9. Pale green; long cylindrical body, very short shoulder, long cylindrical neck, narrow flange; inscribed lengthwise: "DR JAYNE'S / CARMINATIVE / BAL-

SAM/PHILAD^A". 1840s. About 2½ oz. Ht., 4⅞". Dia.,1".

10. Pale green; rectangular, incurved corners, long rounding shoulder, cylindrical neck, narrow flange. Paper label: "CO[NCE]NTRAT[ED] COMPOUND/FLUID EXTRACT/of SARSAPARILLA/PREPARED AND SOLD, ONLY, AT THE/Chemical Warehouse, NEW-YORK/ *Comstock & Co.*/DIRECTIONS . . . ." Comstock & Co., 1841–48. 6 oz. Ht., 5½". Body, 1½" by 2$^3/_{16}$".

11. Figured and lettered, aquamarine; elliptical body, curved shoulder, long cylindrical neck, flat collar; inscribed on one side: "INDIAN" (in arc) above figure of Indian wearing feathered headdress (center left), "CLEMENS' " (arc, upper right of figure), "TONIC" (arc, upper left), "PREPARED" (arc, lower right), "BY" (arc, lower left), "GEO. W. HOUSE" (at bottom); on other side, paper label: "CLEMENS' / INDIAN TONIC, / Infallible cure for AGUE AND FEVER / Prepared and sold, wholesale & retail by GEO. W. HOUSE, Nashville Ten. Price, $1 per bottle. DIRECTIONS . . . " Original cork and part of sealing wax on top. Capacity, about 5 oz. Height, 5¾". Width, 2⅜". Greatest depth, 1⅝".

Bottom row:

12. Pale aquamarine; rectangular, chamfered corners, sunken panels, curved shoulder, long cylindrical neck, wide round collar above narrow one; *obverse:* bevel-edged sunken panel inscribed "DAVIS" above paper label depicting flying eagle between pennants with "Joy to the World" above scrolled leaves and flowers framing portrait medallion of Davis and flanked by Hygeia, goddess of medicine, with snake around her neck; cartouche with "PERRY DAVIS' / VEGETABLE / PAIN KILLER / Manufactured by PERRY DAVIS & SON / PROVIDENCE, R.I."; at bottom, Hope and an anchor between diagonally placed ovals with "50"; *reverse:* paper label: "$0.01" above Eagle with shield, and "Providence January 1st 1854 / For Value received We promise to pay / to the bearer ONE CENT on demand / at our office in the City of Providence / Perry Davis & Son."; ovals with "1" diagonally placed at corners. Possibly Fort Trumbull Glass Works, New London, Conn. ca. 1866. About 6½ oz. Height, 6⅝". Body, 1½" by 2¼".

13. Figured and lettered, aquamarine; elliptical body, flattened shoulder, wide cylindrical neck, narrow turned-in collar; *obverse:* arched frame inscribed "PREPARED BY [left] G.A. BUCKHOUT [top] MECHANICVLLE [right] SARATOGA CO. N.Y. [bottom]", framing standing horse below "DUTCH" and above "LINIMENT"; *reverse:* similar frame inscribed "THE ONLY GENUINE [left] LINIMENT [top] FOR THE HORSE [right] PRICE FIFTY CENTS [bottom]" framing rearing horse. Capacity, 14 oz. Height, 6¾". Width, 4". Depth, 1$^{15}/_{16}$".

14. Deep aquamarine; octagonal body, curved shoulder, short neck, wide flat collar; domed kick-up; inscribed lengthwise on alternate sides: "DR WISTARS / BALSAM OF / WILD CHERRY / JOHN E. PARK / CINCINNATI. O." ca. 1850s. Capacity, about 12 oz. Height, 6¼". Diameter, 2½".

15. Pale green; long cylindrical body, flat shoulder, cylindrical neck, narrow round collar. Paper label: "ATWOOD'S / GENUINE VEGETABLE PHYSICAL JAUNDICE / BITTERS . . . Aug. 15, 1863. Nathan Wood. BEWARE OF COUNTERFEITS AND IMITATIONS!" About 10 oz. Height, 6¾". Diameter, 2⅛".

Illustrated also in *American Glass:* 2 and 4 by Nos. 18 and 20 in Plate 242.

Nos. 1 through 5, 7 through 11, 14, and 15, formerly in the George S. McKearin Collection. Nos. 6, 12 and 15, Old Sturbridge Village; No. 14, The Ohio Historical Society.

My earliest record of the medicine chest—or box—is an advertisement in the *Boston News Letter,* July 16, 1711: "There is lately come from England a quantity of Druggs and Apothecary's Ware, done up some in large and others in small boxes, fit for Gentlemen's Families that live in the Country distant from Doctors and for small vessels that carry no Chyurgeons &c. Wherewith any person may be reasonably furnished by Edward Caine in Pudding-Lane, Boston." But the medicine chest had long been an indispensable part of a ship's equipment and also a normal household article. In fact, such chests, or their equivalent, were essential to those "distant from Doctors" whether on southern plantations, northern farms and estates, or in small, so often doctorless, communities. Even into the late 19th century druggists advertised "Family Medicine Chests" with directions for the use and preparation of medicines. Although chests or cabinets were normal equipment in a doctor's office, for the country doctors, so many of whom traveled on horseback from patient to patient in the countryside, there were saddle-bag medicine kits. The mahogany medicine chest No. 1 illustrates one of the more elegant, fitted with colorless, possibly lead glass, square bottles with ground stoppers, and mortar and pestle used in preparing the ingredients of medicines. More ordinary, less expensive, chests were fitted with green-glass bottles, square and cylindrical, stopped with corks; saddle bags, like No. 7, usually with ordinary cylindrical vials.

Patent and proprietary medicines inspired a new type of vial—namely, an inscribed bottle blown in a full-size piece mold. Nos. 2 through 6 illustrate two 18th-century forms for two famous English patent medicines. Nos. 2, 3, 5, and 6 show four variants of the form adopted in 1754 by Robert Turlington for his Balsam of Life "to prevent the villainy of some persons who buying up my empty bottles have basely and wickedly put therein a vile spurious counterfeit sort"—so far as we now know, the first of the inscribed patent medicine bottles. The type, varying only in the inscriptions, neck finish, and lengths of end planes, was used here and abroad throughout the Balsam's long lifetime of over 150 years. The four bottles illustrated, all attributed to the 19th century, probably were blown in American glassworks and used for American preparations of the Balsam. The form of No. 4, apparently adopted in the 1780s by the English apothecary Dalby for his Carminative, was used throughout the 19th century. As in the case of Turlington's Balsam and bottles, both Dalby's medicine and bottle were produced by Americans. All the bottles shown have a pontil mark on the base.

No. 1, Henry Francis duPont Winterthur Museum; Nos. 3, 4, and 5, formerly in the George S. McKearin Collection; 2 and 6, now in the Collection of Preston R. Bassett; No. 7, The New-York Historical Society.

1. Mahogany medicine chest with brass handle; free-blown colorless mortar and pestle; colorless square bottles blown in a mold for body form, fitted with glass stoppers. (In right center rack, original bottles replaced by two with pewter caps.) Attributed late 18th to early 19th century. Chest: Height, 12¾". Width, base molding at front, 9⅜". Depth, base molding at side, 8".
Large bottles: Overall height, 4⅜". Body, 1¾" by 2".
Medium bottles: Overall height, 3⅜". Body, 1⅛" by 1½".
Small bottles: Overall height, 3". Body, 1¹/₁₆" by 1⅛".
2. Pale green tint; narrow ends rising in 5 planes, flat sides, short flat shoulder, long cylindrical neck, flanged lip, inscribed: *obverse,* "THE / KINGS / PATENT"; *reverse,* "TUR / LING / TONS / BALSAM"; ends plain. Capacity, about ¾ oz. Height, 2½". Greatest width, 1¼".
3. Aquamarine; shape similar to No. 2, tooled plain lip; inscribed: *obverse,* "BY / THE / KINGS/ROYALL/ PATENT / GRANTED / TO"; *reverse,* "ROB^T/TURLI/ NGTON/ FOR HISI/NVENTED/BALSOM/OF LIFE"; one end, "LONDON"; other end, "IAN^Y 26 1754". Capacity, about 1 oz. Height, 2⅜". Greatest width, 1⁵/₁₆".
4. Aquamarine; body tapering to short shoulder, long neck spreading slightly to plain lip; inscribed lengthwise: *obverse,* "DALBYS"; *reverse,* "CAR-MINATIV". Capacity, about 2 oz. Height, 3⅞". Diameter at base, 1⁹/₁₆".
5. Aquamarine; shape similar to No. 2, long cylindrical neck, plain lip; inscribed in block letters: *obverse,* "BY / THE / KINGS / ROYAL / PATENT / GRANTED / TO"; *reverse,* "ROB^T / TURLI / NGTON / FOR HIS / INVENTED / BALSOM / OF LIFE"; one end, "LON-DON"; other end, "JAN. 28 1770". Capacity, about 1 oz. Height, 2½". Greatest width, 1⅜".
6. Aquamarine; shape similar to No. 2, curved shoulder, short cylindrical neck, flanged lip; inscribed: *obverse,* "BY / THE / KINGS / ROYALL / PATENT / GRANTED / TO"; *reverse,* "ROB^T / TURLI / NGTON / FOR HIS / INVENTED / BALSOM / OF LIFE"; one end, "LONDON"; other end, "JAN^Y 26 1754" with the "4" reversed. Capacity, about 1 oz. Height, 2⅜". Greatest width, 1⁵/₁₆".
7. Doctor's leather saddle-bag medicine kit, equipped with slender cylindrical green-glass vials with short curved shoulders, long cylindrical neck, three with flanged and two with plain lip. In bag: aquamarine; height, 5". Standing: at right, light green, height 3½"; at left, pale aquamarine, height 4". On sides: pale aquamarine, plain lip; heights, 3¼" and 3⅜".

The original owner of the saddle-bag kit was Dr. Myron Orton (1748–83), who practiced in Niagara County, New York, and also served in the local militia.

1

2   3

4

5   6

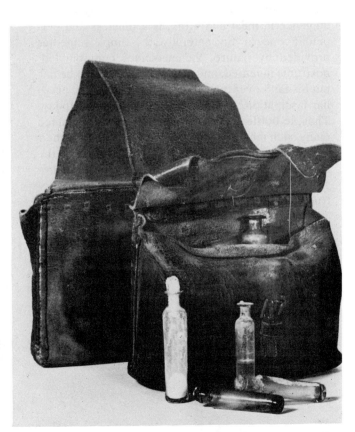

7

Part V

MEDICINE AND BITTERS BOTTLES

Man's preoccupation with all the ills to which his flesh is heir, along with those induced by overindulgence in meat and drink, is a timeless and perpetual concern. So, naturally, the simple remedies provided by nature, the medicines compounded, nostrums invented, and weird cures in which he has put his faith over the centuries have their own peculiar fascination, just as the miracle drugs do today. Thus, to bottle collectors, the bottles that contained many such medicines have a dimension beyond their interest as bottles: they are also documents in the history of medicine and quackery, and of man's search for health and well-being. This is particularly true of vials and bottles still bearing their original labels, the patent and proprietary medicines, and the bitters bottles, a few of which are shown in Ills. 49, 77, 78, 79, 84, and 85. Among the medicines represented are age-old simple medicines "prepared by nature alone" and compound medicines "owing to the industry of man," who variously mixed the simples together.[1] Some of these contents as well as the bottles themselves will be included in this brief discussion of vials and medicine bottles, which have been so important a product of glassmakers from the days of Rome to our own, and so necessary to the dispensers of medicines as well as to family and sea captains' medicine chests.

1

APOTHECARY VIALS

In America, apothecary vials were all too scarce in the 17th and early 18th centuries. So too, indeed, were apothecaries and doctors. And perhaps, more often than not, the doctor had to be his own apothecary and prepare his own medicines. The situation improved gradually in the 18th century—more doctors, more druggists, and more vials. Vials must have been imported in fairly substantial, if insufficient, numbers even before the mid-18th century, for references to them occur in early writings, druggists' account books, and notices of sales of druggists' equipment. Also obtainable were boxes, or chests, "fit for Gentlemen's Families that live in the Country distant from Doctors and for small vessels that carry no Chyrgeons &c."[2] However, in the newspaper advertisements I covered, there was no mention of *empty* vials for sale until 1747. From then on they appeared with fair frequency, sometimes offered by the crate or gross, even by the hogshead.[3]

Perhaps the majority of the imported vials were *common* ones blown from green glass made according to Robert Dossie's cheapest composition of green or common phial glass, or a similar one that would "be green but tolerable transparent." The *better* vials, of which many were imported, doubtless were white glass of "a kind betwixt the flint glass and the common bottle or green glass" that would "come very near to the crystal glass." The *best* of the imported vials were single or double flint, and were fitted with ground-glass stoppers, as are those shown in the medicine chest in Ill. 79; corks were good enough for white-glass and ordinary green-glass vials. Whatever their metal or form, the capacity of the vials was generally half an ounce to eight ounces.[4] Perhaps the predominant form was the cylindrical, free-blown or molded for body form, a type that was being produced in England in the 17th century.[5] Vials molded for body form probably were blown in molds similar to those still used generally for plain vials in American glasshouses in the 1830s, in some into the late 1850s—namely, "a mass of clay with a cylindrical hole in it of the proper diameter and depth."[6] There were also square vials, molded for body form, with and without chamfered corners, and taper-shape vials, like 16 and 19 in Ill. 77. Square or cylindrical, they were fashioned with either a narrow or wide mouth; the wide-mouth vials usually cost more, at least in the 19th century.[7]

Apothecary vials were blown in 18th-century American glasshouses also, but not perhaps until shortly before the Revolution. In this instance the now-familiar refrain "undoubtedly blown also at Wistarburgh, by the Glass-House Company of New York, and at Germantown" can be omitted: so far as present evidence indicates, vials were not included in their regular output, though that probably included small globular and chestnut bottles (like those in Ill. 47), which are believed to have been used for medicinal preparations. These were not, of course,

standard vials, and they could hardly have been preferred to the cylindrical, tapered, and square vials. One or all of these forms must have been the type or types blown in the last third of the century, but the few known advertisements of American glassmakers give no clue to either form or metal. "Phials of all sorts for Druggists" were advertised by Stiegel in 1772; "Phials of all sizes," in 1775 by the Philadelphia Glass Works, Stiegel's rival, which managed to survive his Manheim venture by a year or so. Vials were also made by Felix Farrell and George Bakeoven, who may have taken over the Philadelphia Glass Works in 1777, when they attempted to maintain a glass manufactory during the Revolution. And vials were among the bottles blown at the New Bremen Glassmanufactory when John Frederick Amelung was struggling to establish a manufactory of fine glassware. "Vials assorted from half ounce to 8 ounces" were a regular product of the New-Jersey Glass Manufactory under Carpenter & Heston, who rescued the works the Stanger Brothers had started about 1780.[8] The vials produced in these 18th-century glassworks probably were blown from both white glass and green glass, and the colors probably were greens of "tolerable transparency," aquamarines, and near colorless. A 1773 advertisement of "an assortment of home-made white flint glass among which are Apothecaries furniture . . ."[9] suggests that Stiegel and/or the Philadelphia Glass Works may have spared some of their precious lead-glass metal for apothecary vials.

Like other essential bottles, apothecary vials became a profitable line for many bottle manufacturers in the 19th century. However, if the testimony of Thomas W. Dyott, M.D., is reliable—and he certainly was in a position to judge—very early 19th-century vials were an inferior article compared with the English imports—at least those produced in the county of Philadelphia and in southern New Jersey were. Dr. Dyott asserted that the manufacturer's knowledge was theoretical and the workmen equally deficient. The metal also was inferior in quality and strength even though the vials were produced from the finest materials and by the most expensive process. Unhappily for us, he did not describe the process. Presumably he referred to mixing and melting the batch rather than fashioning the vials, since he complained also that the vials were not well formed. Moreover, they were too limited in quantity as well as quality until after the War of 1812.[10] Vial blowing, it seems, was an art requiring nicety of judgment and skill and one in which few glassblowers in the United States were proficient in the period Dyott mentioned. Later, apparently vial blowing became the specialty of many.

After the war and through the 1820s, if not longer, apothecary and essence vials were blown not only in bottle manufactories but also in such establishments for the production of fine flint glassware as the Boston Glass Manufactory's South Boston works, the New England Glass Company in Cambridge, Massachusetts, and Bakewells in Pittsburgh, Pennsylvania. Those from the Boston and Cambridge works probably were white glass, possibly flint too. Though some of the Bakewells' vials probably were of the better-quality metals, it seems likely that green-glass vials were blown when green-glass wares were added to their output in 1811. However, American producers felt the duties on imported vials were discouragingly low. Not until 1824 did Congress heed complaints. Then, and again in 1828 and 1832, specific and more protective duties were imposed instead of the blanket ad valorem duty. In 1824 a gross of apothecaries' vials of four ounces or less paid $1.00 and those over four ounces but not over eight, $1.25; in 1828, vials not over six ounces, $1.75; in 1832, vials of six ounces but not over 16, $2.75.[11]

Naturally the satisfactory functional vial forms of the 18th century persisted, with narrow- and wide-mouth cylindricals and squares predominating, but their ranks were joined by many-sided bottles such as 9 and 11 in Ill. 77. There were also tall slender rectangular vials, which became a standard type for essences. They were blown mainly in full-size two-piece molds, many with the molded inscription "GENUINE ESSENCE," as on 5 in Ill. 80. Presumably this type, with and without inscription, was that of the "Peppermints" and "Peppermint Essence" advertised and listed by glass manufacturers,[12] who possibly copied the type of vials used for John Juniper's essence of peppermint patented in England in 1762. The full-size piece mold, long used in England for some inscribed vials, was adopted for lettered vials not long after 1800 by one or more American manufacturers. Eventually it completely replaced free-blowing and molding for body form, though in some glasshouses these two methods of production continued into the late 19th century. And, in some, by the late 1850s molds in which the mouth or lip finish was mold-formed were in use (Ill. 82). As in the 18th century, the usual vial sizes were from one-half ounce and under, to eight ounces; occasionally, as much as 16 ounces. Though they were a line of many glassworks, vials are anonymous, for they are unmarked and standard types.

The vials shown in Ill. 77 illustrate the variety and sizes characteristic of the 18th into the mid-19th century, as well as both free-blown and blown-molded techniques. Most of them, I think, would not meet Dr. Dyott's requirements for vials, and the supposition that they are American does not seem hazardous. The cylindrical bottles 12, 13, and 15, it should be noted, are closely similar to those in the doctor's saddlebag medicine kit, Ill. 79. The medicine bags of town and city, as well as country, doctors were fitted out with cylindrical vials. Doubtless they were also used to hold the medicinal powders, pills, and liquids in well-fitted but unpretentious medicine chests, as squares were in elegant chests like the one shown in Ill. 79. That in some communities doctors, as well as druggists, prepared and serviced medicine chests is evident from an advertisement in *The Inquirer*, July 29, 1837, by Dr. Nelson Isham, practicing physician on Nantucket island: "New Medicine Chests put up for $40. Old ones replenished for $25. Warranted to give satisfaction."

Although used for any preparation doctors and druggists saw fit, the slender square, cylindrical, and taper vials 14, 15, and 16 are types associated specifically with three English patent medicines that were sold in the colonies by the mid-18th century, if not before: British Oil, Dr. Bateman's Pectoral Drops, and Godfrey's Cordial.[13] British Oil—or British Rock Oil, as it was also called in the 18th century[14]—was "a form of crude petroleum" said to be a cure of "Rheumatick and Scorbutick and other Cases"; it was packaged in tall slender square bottles. Dr. Bateman's Pectoral Drops, patented in 1726 as a "new Chymical Preparation and Medicine," was put up in tall slender cylindrical vials. These remarkable drops, incidentally, were claimed to exceed "all other medicines yet found out for the Rheumatism . . . useful in Affliction of the Stone and Gravel, Pains, Agues, Colds and all Ailments of the Breast," and it was recommended that they be taken in Mountain Wine, ale, posset, tea, or any other potent diuretic.[15] Godfrey's Cordial, which may date from the 1660s, had more than one claimant to the *genuine* preparation; it was put up in tall slender conical vials. All, of course, had distinctive printed paper wrappings, and the English vials for British Oil, if not the others, came with and without lettering. The same types of vials were still being used for the medicines in the early 20th century. These nostrums were prepared by some American druggists shortly after the Revolution, possibly earlier, since the war drastically curtailed importations. Doubtless they were put up, when possible, in the type of vial with which the public associated these English medicines. There is, however, no evidence as yet that American manufacturers produced vials called specifically British Oils, Bateman's, and Godfrey's before the War of 1812. But it is certain that, from that period on, many manufacturers produced them in both green and white glass.[16]

Vials 5, 12, 13, 17, and 18 in Ill. 77 still wear their original druggists' labels. In these instances, the vials probably were of the same period as the labels. However, it should be kept in mind that the date or period of a vial is not always necessarily that of its label, especially if it was used by dispensers in small communities or during periods of chronic bottle shortages: the vial could be older. In the 18th and early 19th centuries, druggists welcomed old empty vials. It was not unusual for them to inform purchasers of their medicines that "vials will at all times be received for cash." Even in the 1830s housewives were advised to save vials and bottles as "Apothecaries and grocers [who also stocked medicines and essences] will give something for them."[17]

Vial 5 was blown perhaps in a clay mold for body form and, since it has only a tinge of green, from near colorless glass. The proportion of its circumference to body height apparently was characteristic also of some cylindrical vials from the early to late 1800s. The label—it reads "Prepared by / JOHN BRADDOCK / AT THE / FAMILY MEDICINE STORE / 306 North Main Street / HARTFORD CONN."— places the use of the vial between 1846 and 1855/56, the years John Braddock was listed at this number in the city directories. "Pennyroyal" is written in ink at the top of the label, suggesting that John Braddock practiced Yankee thrift, saving the expense of individual labels for his family medicines by writing in the name of his preparations. His was but one of many "family medicine" stores: in most cities and towns they were a convenient source of innumerable simple, compound, and patent medicines, particularly for the scores addicted to the habit of self-dosing without benefit of a doctor's prescription. Perhaps too, as in the 18th century, the druggist would prepare medicines according to family recipes, of which nearly every housewife had a collection handed down from generation to generation.[18] Unquestionably many a housewife had such recipes for making oil or water of pennyroyal or for using the leaves in healing concoctions. If not, she doubtless owned one of the books containing or devoted to home remedies. But those prepared by a druggist certainly saved her time and trouble.

Pennyroyal is one of the medicinal herbs recorded prior to the 6th century by an unknown writer. In her *Herbs for the Medieval Households*, Margaret Freeman quotes this writer as saying, "If any endure nausea on shipboard, let him take the herb pulegium [pennyroyal] and wormwood, let him pound them together with oil and with vinegar and let him smear himself therewith frequently." In medieval days, besides being considered good for head and chest colds, pennyroyal was thought to be beneficial in such afflictions as "an itching boil," "disease of the belly," and "the cramp."[19] In his *English Hus-wife*, published in 1615, Gervase Markham recommended pennyroyal, either boiled in white wine or the juice itself, for the black jaundice. In the 18th and 19th centuries it was given to sufferers of simpler ills. Peter Kalm, visiting America in 1748, found that the herb grew plentifully "in dry places in the country" and was "reckoned a very wholesome drink as tea when a person got cold," since it promoted perspiration.[20] Miss Freeman states that it is still used as tea by "country folks" for cramps and colds. However, its greatest popularity seems to have been as a remedy for hysteria. As a water it was so employed, "sometimes with good effect"; as an essential oil it was more efficacious: only one to four or five drops were necessary. Pennyroyal was used also as an ingredient in compound medicines such as Mary Morris's Poppy Water for an "Asthma and Glister for the Wind," and in some patent medicines—for instance, Dalby's Carminative,[21] which apparently was then as necessary to family life as Castoria was, sixty or so years ago.

The light green and somewhat thick-walled vial 12 also may have been molded to form its slender cylindrical body. The label reads "OIL WINTERGREEN / From A. F. SHERMAN / DRUGGIST AND APOTHECARY / Dealer in Books and Stationery, Varnish, Spts / Turpentine, Birdcages and Seed, Toys and / Toy Books, Confections &c &c. / LUDLOW, VT." After selling medicines in northern New York, first traveling by shanks' mare and then by wagon, Alval F. Sherman studied the drug business with a doctor in Brandon, Vermont. In 1857 he bought a drugstore in Ludlow, and in 1866 took his brother into partnership. Therefore this vial could not have been used before 1857, and probably was not used after the new firm, "Sherman Bros.," was formed. Drugstores in the nature of an emporium were no more of a phenomenon in those days than in ours. As for wintergreen, it is another of nature's simples and, being astringent, it was given for diarrhea. However, its principal use seems to have been as an aromatic flavoring for confections and a mask for many medicines of disagreeable taste.[22]

Another bottle that contained a wintergreen preparation is an aquamarine example, 6 in Ill. 78. The label reads "ESSENCE OF WINTERGREEN PREPARED BY / S. E. FAY DRUGGIST / ATHOL DEPOT / MASS." Instead of a vial or essence vial, Mr. Fay used a 12-panel bottle of the type associated primarily with cologne and other sweet waters. These panel bottles (see 2 and 1 in Ills. 113 and 114) have been found mainly in artificial colors—greens, blues, and amethysts—in several sizes. They were produced probably from the 1830s into the late 19th century. Since the labeled bottle is ordinary aquamarine glass, it may be that bottles of this type in the cheaper metal were commonly used for essences. On the other hand, the presence of the label may merely be an indication that when standard vials were not at hand, druggists used any bottles suitable for their preparations. Presumably S. E. Fay was Sereno E. Fay who, after teaching school for a few years, established a grocery business in 1861 and in 1865 took his brother, Othello A. Fay, into partnership. Sereno E. retired in 1888.[23]

The pale aquamarine vial (13) is thin-walled and probably blown in a clay mold for its slender cylindrical body. Its label reads simply "PEPPERMINT"—which was another herb with an enviable reputation for its aromatic and cordial medicinal properties. It was prepared mainly as an essential oil or an essence or a distilled water. In one form or another it was widely used as a simple medicine and as "an ingredient in several officinal preparations."[24] As an essence it became a popular nostrum about 1762, the year John Juniper, English "Chymist and Apothecary," patented "A new Medicine called *Essence of Peppermint* which contain[ed] all the Virtue of that Plant." The essence was so simple to make that Juniper's patent could not have been very effective, especially as pirating of popular nostrums was customary, and Juniper's became *very* popular. Be that as it may, it was not long before Essence of Peppermint, English and American, was available to the American public, many of whom were willing to pay the higher price charged for the English than for the American preparations.[25] It was considered "A very excellent remedy for sickness and faintness at the Stomack, flatulence, cramps, vomiting &." Dosage doubtless varied, but one 19th-century firm of druggists and apothecaries recommended 30 to 50 drops in water or on sugar.[26] Peppermint was apparently a gentle medicine compared with many others, so it is not surprising that its

popularity was not eclipsed as nostrums multiplied in the 19th century. It was also a flavoring, and in the 20th century, one of its most unkind uses was to flavor castor oil.

Vial 17 was free-blown from colorless glass. It is undoubtedly a 19th-century vial but a type persisting from the 1700s well into the 1800s. Its label reads merely "Tincture of GOLDEN ROD." In the 20th century goldenrod has been libeled as a culprit in causing hay fever; in the 17th, 18th, and 19th centuries it was credited with remarkable medicinal properties. Essence of goldenrod was used in preparing a tincture that was a trusted 18th-century treatment for kidney stones. And it was not cheap: one James Rivington of Philadelphia sold his Tincture of Gold Rod at 9s. a bottle in 1762. The next year the Boston firm of Rivington & Miller claimed:

This medicine has been found very excellent in preventing the Gravel from concreting to Stone, and discharging it without Pain; it will bring away all gravel as fast as it is deposited in the Kidneys and never suffers it to lodge or form Stones again and it has been found by experience to excell Mrs. Stephan's and all other Medicines used in dissolving Stones.

Although John Monroe, in *American Botanist, and Family Physician*, published in 1824, did not mention kidney stones and gravel, he did state that decoctions of the herb goldenrod were "excellent in weakness and debility . . . and a preventive of consumptions and dropsies."[27] Small wonder goldenrod, growing wild and abundantly, was a home remedy as well as one prepared by druggists.

Vial 18 was free-blown from light green glass. Were it not for the label establishing the period in which it was used as 1850 to 1858, I should not have hesitated to assign "late 18th–early 19th century" to the vial on the basis of its physical characteristics. Its label reads "TINCT. CAMPHOR / PREPARED AND SOLD BY / COWLES & LEETE / Successors to / Dr. NATHANIEL BOOTH / 54 *State Street* / NEW HAVEN.CONN." Cowles & Leete succeeded Dr. Booth in 1850 and were listed at this address through 1858. Perhaps the vial was blown before 1850 if Dr. Booth had a good supply of vials on hand when Cowles & Leete acquired "the old established Drug Store," which, they stated, had been in successful operation since 1824.[28]

Camphor, prepared from juice extracted from the bark, roots, and leaves of the "camphire tree," is another old remedy credited with a variety of therapeutic values. Some of us will remember wearing camphor bags around the neck in winter to prevent colds; many, the use of the liquid preparation to dry up cold sores. By some 18th-century doctors its virtue was attributed only to its sedative property, and they considered it to be capable of doing as much harm as good. Nevertheless, even in the 19th century, it was considered effective "as a nervous stimulant in low forms of fever, also in diarrhea,

cholera and catarrh." And the tincture of camphor was a home remedy for headaches and nervous disturbances.[29] Camphor had also an astonishing use in summer: "A tablespoon full of the spirit of camphor, has been found an infallible remedy against the fatal effects of drinking cold water in warm weather . . . every housekeeper should be provided with a phial of it at this season of the year."[30]

2
PATENT AND PROPRIETARY MEDICINE BOTTLES

Another interesting category in the field of bottle collecting includes patent and proprietary medicine vials and bottles with labels, molded inscriptions, or, occasionally, figures such as the Indian on the Indian Tonic bottle, 11 in Ill. 78. Even more intimately than the apothecary vials, these are documents in the long history of medicines, particularly of 19th-century nostrums and panaceas. The name *patent* for both the containers and the medicines stems from the King's Royal Patents, first granted in the 17th century to inventors of medicinal remedies; it is applied commonly to the proprietary medicines and their containers as well. Actually, most Americans then entering this lucrative field of medicine seem to have preferred to be proprietors rather than patentees. It was a more profitable status because, since a copyright could be renewed every 20 years, the proprietor could perpetuate his exclusive rights in his medicine (insofar as law was concerned) by simply registering the name of his medicine and his label. A patent, by contrast, expired in 17 years, throwing the formula and name into the public domain.[31]

However, preparation of nostrums by Americans did not wait for the founding of the United States Patent Office or Registration by Act of Congress. As has been mentioned, by the time of the Revolution several popular English patent medicines were being made according to the English formulas, or to versions of them, by American doctors and druggists. The highly remunerative practice never waned. And many of these dispensers of medicines also dispensed their own cures, which they themselves had discovered or had acquired from others. But not until the 19th century did American nostrums flourish epidemically. All were packaged with distinctive identifying labels and wrappers; many of them were

put in vials and bottles blown in full-size piece molds with identifying inscriptions, mainly private molds, which seem to be innumerable.

Until recently, though a few late-18th-century advertisements suggested that blown-molded lettered bottles were in use for some patent medicines, there was no proof they were not introduced in the early 19th century. It has now been established that full-size piece molds were used for this purpose by the mid-18th century in at least one instance. In their paper "Old English Patent Medicines in America," George B. Griffenhagen and James Harvey Young illustrate the inscribed vial adopted by Robert Turlington for his Balsam of Life in 1754. Ten years earlier Turlington had obtained the King's Royal Patent for his balsam compounded of 27 ingredients. It was a miracle medicine, "A Friend of Nature, which it strengthens and corroborates when weak and declining, vivifies and enlivens the Spirits, mixes with the Juices and Fluids of the Body and gently infuses in its kindly Influence into those Parts that are most in Disorder." Inevitably Turlington soon had to combat imitators. Hence, he had new bottles made for him "to prevent the villany of some persons who buying up my empty bottles, have basely and wickedly put therein a vile spurious counterfeit sort."[32] As depicted, the bottle, with flange lip, was the same basic shape—except for a sloping foot in the drawing, and that probably was due to faulty perspective — as those illustrated in Ill. 79. It was inscribed "BY/THE/KINGS/ROYALL/PATENT/ GRANTED/TO" (on the obverse) and "ROB[T]/ TURLI / NGTON / FOR HIS / INVENTED / BALSAM / OF / LIFE" (on the reverse). Starting at the shoulder and ending on the long plane of one end, "LO / N / DON" was inscribed; starting on the long

80. Square vial. (Boston, *Evening Gazette,* Feb. 9, 1822.) *The New-York Historical Society, New York City*

81. Cylindrical vial. (*Utica Intelligencer,* Sept. 11, 1827.) *New York State Library, Albany, N.Y.*

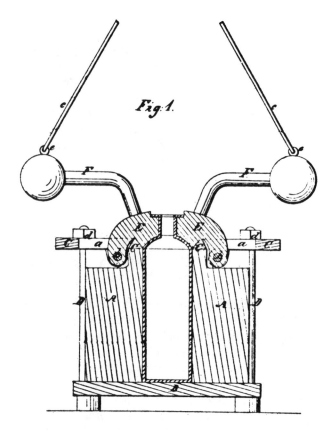

82. Fig. 1, from the specifications of Patent No. 22,091, Nov. 16, 1858, granted Samuel S. Shinn of Reed, Shinn & Co., Lancaster Glass Works, Lancaster, N.Y. "The mold shown is for blowing druggists' vials, but the same construction is applicable to molds for all kinds of bottles." "A" forming the sides of the bottle was a block of clay; other parts were of metal. "E E," opening for insertion of the gather and the withdrawal of the bottle, formed the shoulders, neck, and mouth (i.e., neck finish). *U.S. Patent Office*

plane and ending on the shoulder of other end was "JANU^Y /26 / 1754". Though varying in the length and sharpness of the planes and in inscription, the basic form of the Turlington vial was never changed during the balsam's long lifetime of over 150 years.

Though there is only a possibility that some Turlington vials were produced in the United States before the War of 1812, it is a certainty they were afterward. And they were far less expensive than those obtained in England during the period Dr. Thomas W. Dyott called the British Monopoly. Prior to the war, imported Turlingtons were $5.50 a gross; afterward, American copies could be bought (from 1815 through 1818) as low as $3.50 a gross; and in another 15 years those blown at Dyottville were only $1.00.[33] The four Turlingtons shown in Ill. 79 pre-

sumably are 19th-century vials and, I believe, American-made. With the exception of a late 19th- to early 20th-century Turlington vial of colorless glass and one colorless vial with molded date "JAN 28 1770" like 5 in Ill. 79, those I have seen were pale green or aquamarine in color. Also, those I have examined were from several different molds with inscriptions varying in size, form, and placement of the letters, and variations in the spelling of "royal," "invented," and "balsam" and in the abbreviation of January, in which the "u" of the original illustration was omitted, as shown in the following list:

1. ROYAL / INVENTED BALSOM / IANY
2. ROYAL / INVENTED BALSAM / JANY.
   (with and without date)

3. ROYAL / INVENTED BALSOM / *no* inscription on ends
4. ROYAL / INVENTED BALSOM . JAN 28 1770 (5 in Ill. 79)
5. ROYAL / INVENTED BALSAM / JAN. (no date discernible on the one examined)
6. ROYALL / INVENTED BALSOM / JAN^Y and "4" of date reversed (6 in Ill. 79)
7. ROYALL / NVENTED BALSOM /IAN^Y (3 in Ill. 79; the "I" is omitted)
8. ROYALL / VENTED BALSOM / JA^YN; smooth base with relief figures "82"; colorless; late 19th–early 20th century
9. ROYAL / IVENTE BALSOM / 72 YNAY (I am indebted to Preston Bassett for the full data on 4, 6, 8, and 9.)

One particularly interesting variety from still another mold—and comparatively rare in my experience—is shown by 2 in Ill. 79. It has only "THE / KINGS / PATENT" on the obverse and "TUR / LING / TONS / BALSAM" on the reverse. Many more than the molds noted must have been used in the balsam's long lifespan.

One would expect that so clever a device as Turlington's distinctive bottle would have started an immediate fashion in patent medicine bottles, but it seems to have had few followers among other 18th-century inventors of nostrums. Present evidence indicates that not until shortly after 1800 did an actual trend start toward lettered vials and bottles for proprietary and patent medicines. And, even then, many patentees and proprietors of medicines continued to rely on a particular form of plain vial with identifying label and wrapper. At the present time, it seems probable that the first American to adopt such a container and have his own private mold was Dr. Thomas W. Dyott, who so successfully introduced Dr. Robertson's medicines to the American public.[34]

Starting his family medicine venture in Philadelphia in 1805, Dr. Dyott quickly met with phenomenal success, due perhaps as much to the great number of agents he persuaded to handle his family medicines throughout the country as to his lavish advertising, which spread the extravagant claims for his medicines' curative powers. As mentioned above, his family medicines included Dr. Robertson's amazing nostrums. Particularly touted was the celebrated Stomatic Elixir of Health at $1.50 a bottle, which had been

proved by thousands who . . . experienced its beneficial effect to be the most valuable medicine ever offered to the public, for the cure of Coughs, Colds, Consumptions, the Whooping Cough, Asthma, pain in the Breast, Cramps, and Wind in the Stomack, removing Costiveness, Sickness at the Stomack, Head Ache, loss of Appetite, Indigestion &c.

It had proved also to be a certain remedy "for the Dysentery or Pox, Cholera Morbus, severe Griping and other diseases of the Bowels and Summer Complaint in Children." Another was his Vegetable and Nervous Cordial or Nature's Grand Restorative, also $1.50 a bottle, for immediate relief of "Pulmunary Complaints or disorder of the Breast and Lungs, even in the most advanced state." However, there were other nostrums on the market with similar claims, and it was perhaps competition that, by 1809, led Dr. Dyott to package his Dr. Robertson's medicines in lettered bottles. At the end of the roster of his medicines advertised in that year was the following warning: "Dr Robertson's Family Medicines are put up in square flint glass bottles American manufactured with these words impressed on the glass—'Dr Robertson's Family Medicines, prepared only by T. W. Dyott.' " There was an additional caution that "none are genuine without the signature of T. W. Dyott, M.D." on the wrapper.[35]

It is not surprising that so enterprising a businessman as Dr. Dyott adopted a lettered bottle for his medicines, nor that he failed to mention the name of the manufacturer of the bottles. But in the light of his subsequent remarks on American apothecary vials made before the War of 1812, it is a bit surprising he had them made in an American glassworks, even though they would be cheaper than if ordered in England. And it is downright aggrieving that the source of his square flint-glass bottles is a question in the maw of speculation and surmise. There is also the question as to whether the bottles were actually *flint* (that is, lead glass), or Dr. Dyott was using that quality-status term for white glass. A logical surmise is that the American bottles in which Dr. Dyott put up medicines at his Patent Medicine Warehouse were blown in one of the two nearby glassworks—namely, the Philadelphia Glass-House, on the Schuylkill, and the (old) Kensington Glass Works, in Kensington, Philadelphia. According to one who had been an intimate of Dr. Dyott, Dyott bought his blacking bottles at the latter works. If so, he may have had the first of his Dr. Robertson bottles made there. Later he doubtless obtained them from the Olive Glass Works, New Jersey, in which he acquired an interest in 1815.

The Philadelphia Glass-House and, later, the Kensington did plan to produce flint glass, and the former advertised in 1808 that "a person well qualified to manage a Flint Glass Manufactory [would] be treated on liberal terms."[36] But no evidence has as yet come to light establishing that either works succeeded in producing flint glass. The other glassworks were window- and bottle-glass houses laying no claim to flint glass production, so far as I have been able to discover. Therefore, until proof to the contrary is found, the safe assumption seems to be that Dr. Dyott's bottles were white glass, impressively called flint. Nevertheless, there is another possible source of bottles used by some western agents—for instance, J. P. & J. W. Skelton of Pittsburgh, Pennsylvania. If, as seems certain, the medicines were shipped to Pittsburgh in demijohns, the square flint-glass bottles were probably of local manufacture. In 1810 there were three glasshouses in Pittsburgh in which the bottles could have been blown from either flint or white metal: O'Hara's Pittsburgh Glass Works, the Pittsburgh Flint Glass Works of Benjamin Bakewell & Company, and George Robinson's small works.[37] Wherever blown, and whether they were white or flint glass, the term *flint glass* carries the implication of colorless bottles, for it would not have been applied to green-glass containers. The question of metal could be answered only by examination of one of the bottles, and no specimen fitting Dr. Dyott's description has been recorded.

However, it is proven that if Dr. Dyott actually used flint-glass or white-glass bottles at first, he abandoned them for green-glass rectangular ones with nearly flat shoulder, cylindrical neck, and flanged lip—and bearing the same, now-famous, inscription. Perhaps the change was to reduce the cost of packaging and boost the profits after Dr. Robertson's Family Medicines were so widely accepted by the ailing citizenry that they could compete successfully with the English and other nostrums. In any event, they must have been blown by the thousands, but so far only two specimens have been recorded. One was in the collection of the late Edgar Hoffman, and it disappeared in the mail in 1940 on its return trip to Mr. Hoffman after being photographed for illustration in *American Glass,* where it appears as 14 in Plate 242. A second, found in Ohio, is owned by Ralph Bond of Akron. However, Vernon L. McCord of Tallahassee, Florida, reports he has one that was dug up in New Orleans early in 1971. And in May 1971 James B. Kirk of Linwood, New Jersey, wrote that he had dug up one of Dr. Dyott's bottles in Corbin City (formerly North Tuckahoe) "about ten feet from the swamp that

fronts the Tuckahoe River." Since then Dorothy Maderias reported that one was unearthed several years ago during a "bottle dig" at West Dennis, Cape Cod, Massachusetts.

Just when these five-ounce bottles were adopted and how long they were used, I have not learned. Before 1815 they probably were blown at the old Kensington Glass Works, then for a few years at the Olive Glass Works. Dr. Dyott would certainly have made them for himself at the new Kensington Glass Works after he became proprietor about 1821, and later at his Dyottville Glass Factories until they closed in 1838 because of his bankruptcy. It will be recalled the Doctor returned to the drug business in 1841, and perhaps he purchased the bottles from the Dyottville Factory when it was reopened by Henry Seybert in 1842. Until his death in 1861 Dr. Dyott and his sons, John B. and Thomas, Jr., were in business together as druggists and commission merchants.[38]

Although this Dyott patent medicine bottle has a special interest because of Thomas W. Dyott's colorful career and because it is the earliest known to have been made for an American proprietor of medicines, it is but one of probably thousands in a field only partly gleaned. A catalog of even those now recorded in various collections would be impossible within the confines of these covers. Therefore, I shall content myself with comments on the few patent medicine bottles shown in Ills. 49, 78, and 79, and the preparations they contained. None can be attributed to a particular glassworks, but in most instances the period of use has been determined.

In Ill. 49, example 5 is a clear deep-green cylindrical bottle with three inscribed panels: "SWAIM'S" on one, "PANACEA" on another, "PHILAD^A" on the third. This proprietary medicine bottle is a document in the constant battle between the inventor of a nostrum and the pirates in the ocean of cures flooding the country in the 19th century. According to Professor James Harvey Young, Swaim's Panacea, invented by William Swaim in 1820, was "basically . . . a syrup of sarsaparilla"; a second ingredient was oil of wintergreen and a third was mercury, in the form of corrosive sublimate. The preparation quickly achieved fame as a "cure of Incipient Consumption, Scrofula, General Debility, White Swelling, Rheumatism, Diseases of the Liver and Skin, and all diseases arising from Impurities of the Blood, and the effects of Mercury." Swaim, too, quickly had imitators and detractors to combat. In spite of the fact that his Panacea had drawn "the most unqualified approbation from *Patients* and *Medical Practitioners of the highest respectability,*" Swaim alleged that some physicians had circulated false reports about this valuable medicine, reports that could originate only in envy or the mischievous effect of spurious imitations. One at least among the counterfeiters, J. Shinn of Frederick, Maryland, frankly and cannily announced in 1824 that he had "discovered the composition of Swaim's celebrated Panacea." Adding insult to injury, he reduced the price from $3.50 a bottle to $2.50, and $24 for a dozen. Moreover, he generously offered to supply his Panacea, compounded according to Swaim's formula, free to all charitable institutions in the United States and to the poor. Swaim counterattacked by reducing his price to $2.00 a bottle—because of "increasing demand"—and by changing his bottles so the public would instantly recognize the genuine Panacea at a glance.[39]

In fact, Swaim twice changed his packaging. The second time was about 1828, when he adopted the bottle that appears as 5 in Ill. 49. For added insurance the bottle (Ill. 83) was depicted in his advertisements, which announced:

To the Public—In consequence of the numerous frauds and impositions practiced in reference to my medicine I am again induced to change the form of the Bottles. In future the Panacea will be put in round bottles, fluted longitudinally, with the following words blown in the glass, "SWAIM'S PANACEA PHILAD[A]". These bottles are much stronger than those heretofore used, and will have but one lable, which covers the cork, with my own signature on it, so that the cork cannot be withdrawn without destroying the signature, without which none is genuine.

The label with signature was a necessary precaution, since Swaim's empty bottles might be acquired and used by counterfeiters, who were in no way discouraged by Swaim's protests and protective tactics. As late as 1852 his successor, James Swaim, still found it necessary to describe the bottle and to caution "Persons wishing to obtain the genuine SWAIM'S PANACEA" to beware of imposition and make sure the name was spelled correctly on both bottle and label, or they might be "imposed on by medicine in imitation of them by a person bearing a somewhat similar name, well calculated to deceive." However, "envy's pen dipped in gall," as William Swaim had prophesied, had been unable to tarnish the Panacea's reputation at home or abroad, so James Swaim was able to include in his advertisement a long list of approving physicians and eminent persons; among them were one J. Chipman, member of the Royal

PRICE TWO DOLLARS PER BOTTLE.

TO THE PUBLIC.

IN consequence of the numerous frauds and impositions practised in reference to my medicine, I am again induced to change the form of my BOTTLES. In future, the PANACEA will be put in round bottles, fluted longitudinally, with the following words blown in the glass, "*Swaim's Panacea, Philada,*" as represented above.

These bottles are much stronger than those heretofore used, and will have but one label, which covers the cork with my own signature on it, so that the cork cannot be drawn without destroying the signature, without which none is genuine. The medicine may consequently be known to be genuine when my signature is visible; *to counterfeit which will be punishable with forgery.*

83. Illustration from an 1828 advertisement of Swaim's Panacea, depicting the second bottle adopted by William Swaim in his efforts to prevent counterfeiting of his famed Panacea. (New York, *Commercial Advertiser,* Oct. 7, 1828.) *The New-York Historical Society, New York City*

College of Surgeons, London, Jose Eourenco de Luz, Professor of Surgery, Lisbon, and G. W. Irving, late Minister to Spain.[40]

Perhaps Swaim's bottles will be found one day in England, Portugal, and Spain—not only bottles like 5 in Ill. 49 but also the new bottles adopted by Swaim's Laboratory sometime between 1852 and 1876. The latter had a wide arched label panel in place of two or three of the "longitudinal flutes" and doubtless was still the official bottle in 1901, the last listing of Swaim's Laboratory in the Philadelphia city directories. The bottles undoubtedly were made for the Swaims by several bottle manufacturers. One would expect that the Philadelphia and South Jersey glassworks were the main sources. However, fragments of bottles used before 1852 were found by Harry Hall White on the site of the Coventry Glass Works, Coventry, Connecticut, apparently in sufficient numbers to warrant the conclusion they were made there.[41]

In Ill. 78, item 3 is a blower's whimsy, a hat, for which the gather of aquamarine glass was blown in a full-size two-piece mold with "LIQUID" cut in one piece and "OPODELDOC" in the other. In finishing the hat the letters "OPO" were cut off. The whimsy could have been blown in any one of the many works producing patent medicine vials. Though opodeldoc and lettered vials for it had been made long before the late 1820s, that period was the earliest in which I found "liquid" modifying "opodeldoc." On Dr. Dyott's price list, ca. 1825 (Ill. 9c), under vials were "opodeldoc," "ditto (small size)," and "Liquid opodeldoc," each at $3.50 a gross.

Opodeldoc was not the scientific name of a drug or one of Nature's simples but a 16th-century word coined for a variety of medicated plasters by the Swiss-German physician and alchemist Paracelsus. By the early 18th century, in Britain, it became the pharmaceutical name for a soap liniment. To this, about 1767, a Dr. Steer added ammonia and launched his proprietary *Steer's Opodeldoc* on its long and profitable career lasting over a century. Though it may have speedily and certainly cured the "bruises, sprains, burns, cuts, chilblains and headaches" of colonists, I have not found it advertised before 1788. However, it could not have been long before American preparations were on the druggists' shelves. In any event, there were several by the 1820s, and their proprietors railed against "a host of servile imitators (instigated by envy and self interest)." All seem to have agreed that this chemical embrocation was good in all cases of external injury, but they vied with one another in extending its usefulness to such specific conditions as frozen limbs, burns, scalds, weakness, and rickets.[42] Many frugal 19th-century housewives probably also made opodeldoc from recipes given in books on the useful arts and sciences, household economy, even in almanacs. Home preparations were recommended because this excellent family medicine, so easily made, deteriorated from heat, age, and exposure, and according to Mrs. Beeton in 1868, was "difficult to procure either pure or freshly made." Nevertheless, the homemade opodeldoc, like other domestic preparations, made no dent in the profits from packaged brands for "sprains, rheumatism, contraction of the tendons, and stiffness of joints."[43]

The official vial, presumably used from about 1767, for Dr. Steer's popular opodeldoc appears to have been of slender cylindrical form with cylindrical neck and plain lip, either with or without the inscription "OPODELDOC." After the War of 1812, and to the end of the century at least, these vials were produced by several American bottle and vial manufacturers. For many years even firms specializing in fine tableware, such as the South Boston branch of the Boston Glass Manufactory and the New England Glass Company, produced opodeldocs—*Best*, which would have been blown from fine colorless metal, and *Inferior*, which doubtless were blown from green glass. It is interesting to note that whereas in the depression year of 1817 the Boston Glass Manufactory's *best* were $6.00 a gross and the *inferior*, $4.50, in 1818 those of both firms were $8.00 and $6.00 respectively, and the best were as costly as the English had been during the "British Monopoly" before the war. But by 1830 the tariff of 1828 and greater domestic competition had caused a considerable reduction in price—for example, Dyottville opodeldocs were only $2.60 a gross.[44] It may have been only a few years before then that the vials with molded inscription "LIQUID" in addition to "OPODELDOC" and with flanged lip were first blown; they seem to have become standard for American preparations, which made no claim to having been compounded on Steer's formula. Also in the 19th century, at least one maker of opodeldoc had his own private mold. The collection of Charles B. Gardner included an amusing figured and lettered bottle of the third quarter of the century graphically illustrating the amazing effects of Lord's Opodeldoc. It is an oval aquamarine bottle with long neck and flat collar. On one side, an arch-top panel has the inscription "LORD'S" above and "OPODELDOC" below the figure of an ex-cripple—a man with crutch raised in his right hand, his left arm and leg gleefully raised, and the crutch thrown away below.

Vials 8 and 9, Ill. 78, were blown in private molds for Dr. David Jayne who, in 1839, was listed as M.D. and druggist in the Philadelphia city directories for the first time. However, it seems certain that Dr. Jayne had been practicing elsewhere before opening his Philadelphia office and his druggist business: he and some of his medicines already had a wide reputation in New England before 1840. In the spring of that year Charles G. Barnard offered his fellow citizens on Nantucket Island Dr. Jayne's Expectorant, Tonic Vermifuge for the expulsion of worms, and Dr. Jayne's Hair Tonic, all "prepared only by Dr. Jayne, 20 South Third Street, Philadelphia . . . Price $1." Also in 1840, the proprietor of the Hartford "Family Medicine Store" at the Sign of the Good Samaritan, E. W. Bull, stated: "From long personal acquaintance with Dr. Jayne, we know he is no quack and his medicines are not nostrums of the modern cry-up but the result of his long experience as a practicing physician and the expense of great labor." In 1845 the doctor started a yearly publication, "Jayne's Medical Almanac and Guide to Health," for free distribution to prospective users of his preparations. The 1850 Almanac claimed that 2,500,000 copies were distributed yearly. In 1846, with his sons, David W. and Eben C., Jayne formed "David Jayne & Sons, Proprietors of Jaynes Family medicine." "David Jayne & Sons, druggists" was listed in the directories at 84 Chestnut Street from 1851 until 1858. By then the Jayne preparations included, besides those mentioned above and below, Jayne's Specific for the Tape Worm; Jayne's Alterative (scrofula, goitre, cancer, diseases of the skin and bones); Jayne's Sanative Pills (alterative and purgative); Jayne's Ague Mixture; Jayne's Liniment or Counter Irritant (sprains, bruises, etc.); Jayne's Liquid Hair Dye and American Hair Dye (powder).[45]

From 1858 through 1887 the firm David Jayne & Sons was at 242 Chestnut Street, and variously listed as "druggists," "Druggists and Chemists," or "Patent Medicines." In the meantime Dr. David Jayne, the inventor of Jayne's preparations and founder of the firm, served as president of the Commonwealth Insurance Company of Philadelphia, 1860–66. When he died—apparently in 1866—it was said that he left a fortune of $3,000,000.[46] If, as reported, he was "as poor as he could be" when he prepared his first medicine, certainly his descendants, who carried on the firm and business, knew no want.

The pale-green rectangular bottle with chamfered corners (8) is inscribed lengthwise "DR D. JAYNE'S / INDIAN" on one side and "EXPECTORANT / PHILAD^A" on the other. *Expectorant* explains itself in purpose, but just what ingredients made it an *Indian* one is Dr. Jayne's medical secret. Dr. Jayne was neither the first nor the last 19th-century doctor, or quack, to call one of his medicines "Indian"; even if his cure was not based on an old Indian remedy, the name carried that implication. From colonial times, the Red Man had revealed his empirically acquired knowledge of botanical medicinal preparations to the White Man. Gabriel Thomas reported in 1698 that the Indians' knowledge and use of "many curious and excellent Physical Wild Herbs, Roots and Drugs" made them "as able Doctors and Surgeons as any in Europe, performing celebrated Cures there with and by the use of particular Plants only." The very name *Indian* came to inspire confidence in many medicines, so deep was the general public's respect for Indian medicinal concoctions, if little or

none for their discoverers. Jayne's Indian Expectorant was accepted as a cure for "coughs, colds, sore throat, asthma and all affections of the lungs."[47] Also pale green in color and blown in a full-size two-piece mold is example 9 in Ill. 78, a tall cylindrical vial inscribed lengthwise in four lines "DR JAYNE'S / CARMINATIVE / BALSAM / PHILAD^A". Dr. Jayne's carminative balsam was but one of many combining aromatic substances with carminative agents to relieve colic, griping, and flatulence.

Also in Ill. 76, example 10, a pale-green rectangular bottle with incurved corners, blown in a full-size two-piece mold, is a type often used for proprietary medicines, mainly in the period from about 1825 to 1850, and usually having a druggist's or proprietor's label rather than molded inscription. The original label on this bottle reads "CO[NCE]NTRAT[ED]COMPOUND / FLUID EXTRACT / of / SARSAPARILLA / PREPARED AND SOLD, ONLY AT THE/*Chemical Warehouse,* NEW-YORK/*Comstock & Co.*/DIRECTIONS FOR USING/Comstock's Sarsaparilla/For Adult—take two tea-spoonsfull, / Children—one tea-spoonfull, / Infants—half tea-spoonfull. / To be taken three times a day before eating / clear in a little water." Comstock & Company was listed in the city directories from 1841 through 1848, which fixes the period of the bottle and label nicely. In 1849 the firm became Comstock & Co. Brothers and found it necessary to add an extra label with "the facsimile signature of Dr. Lucius S. Comstock," inventor of the preparation, and to warn "Traders' not wishing to countenance piracies upon other's preparations" that none was genuine without that label.

In the 17th century sarsaparilla was considered an admirable blood purifier and, for over a century, a specific cure for syphilis. It was perhaps less often used as a simple medicine than as an ingredient in various medical concoctions such as diet drinks for the "cure of Venereal Disease," "the running Gout, and for all infections." After being eclipsed by newer cures during the late 18th and early 19th century, it caught the attention of American druggists and proprietors of family medicines in the 1820s, not as a *cure* for syphilis but as a sort of tonic. At the Sign of the Good Samaritan in Hartford, syrup of sarsaparilla, drawn with soda water, was recommended as a pleasant medicinal beverage correcting the "perspiratory functions of the skin and imparting tone and vigor to debilitated constitutions." By the 1830s compound syrups of sarsaparilla were on their way to becoming a popular nostrum. With touted curative powers that might have amazed even the 17th-century quacks, brand succeeded brand into the 20th century. Typical of the extravagant claims for its efficacy were those of Charles Marshall of Philadelphia:

For the Cure of Obstinate Eruptions of the Skin— Pimples or Pustules on the face—Biles which arise from an impure habit of body—Scaly Eruptions— Paines in the Bones—Chronic Rheumatism— Teeter—Scrofula or King's Evil—White Swelling—Syphilitic Symptoms, and all disorders arising from an impure state of the blood, produced either by long residence in a hot and unhealthy climate, the injudicious use of mercury &c.

Later "dropsy, Exposure or Imprudence in Life," and "Chronic Constitutional Disorders" joined the roster of ailments cured by Sand's sarsaparilla preparations.[48]

By the late 1840s Dr. Townsend's Sarsaparilla, a name familiar to many bottle collectors, was in the spotlight of quackery fame as the "Wonder & Blessing of the Age—The most extraordinary medicine in the World." None was genuine unless put in "*Square bottles* which contain a quart, and signed with the written signature of S. P. Townsend, and his name blown in the glass." If purchased from Dr. T. W. Dyott & Sons, the purchaser received the further benefit of a copy of Dr. Dyott's "Oracle of Health."[49] As in the case of so many of the bottles blown in private molds, not all those for Dr. Townsend's Sarsaparilla were blown in the same factory. "Townsend's" appeared in Solomon Stanger's Glassboro Blowers Book 1848/49. An 1848 record from Joseph Foster's Stoddard Glassworks, New Hampshire, shows that "square quart sarsaparilla bottles" with the molded inscription "Dr. Townsend's Sarsaparilla, Albany, N. Y." were made for Townsend for $9.00 a gross delivered in Albany. In 1866 Townsend's bottles were being produced by the Fort Trumbull Glass Works, New London, Connecticut.[50] Undoubtedly during the long popularity of Dr. Townsend's brand of sarsaparilla, they were made by many other bottle manufacturers as well.

The aquamarine elliptical or oval-bodied bottle, 11 in Ill. 78, is also one that was made for another of the many medicines supposedly of Indian origin. It was blown in a private mold having on the obverse a low-relief figure of an Indian (wearing a feathered headdress) and the inscription "INDIAN" (above the figure), "CLEMEN'S PREPARED" (at right), "TONIC BY" (at left) and "GEO. W. HOUSE" (at bottom). The original label on the reverse reads:

CLEMEN'S / INDIAN TONIC / Infallible cure for

AGUE AND FEVER / Prepared and sold, wholesale & retail by GEO. W. HOUSE, Nashville, Ten. Price $1 per bottle. DIRECTIONS / Those of very weak and delicate habits, will commence six hours before the CHILL or AGUE is expected to come on, and take a dose every hour—if a grown person—until they take all in the bottle. Youths and children should take ten doses. The stout and robust may commence, three hours before the Chill or Ague is expected, and take a dose every half hour—and this is the best method of taking it, nine cases in ten. Dose—For a grown person, a *large* table spoonful. From 9 to 14, two or three tea spoonsful. Good measure each dose. READ THE WRAPPER.

It was an expensive medicine if the directions were followed, for the bottle apparently held about five ounces. (The original cork and seal were not removed to measure its capacity.) Neither Clemen, by whose formula the Indian Tonic was made, nor George W. House, who packaged it in such quaint bottles, has been pinpointed as to period. Neither, according to information from the Nashville Public Library, is to be found in a Nashville directory.

In Ill. 78, example 12 is a type of blown-molded rectangular bottle new to the mid-19th century; it has chamfered corners and a sunken bevel-edged panel at the top of one side. This one was blown in a private mold for Perry Davis's Vegetable Painkiller, and the panel is inscribed "DAVIS". On each side is an original label, which is described in the caption. It is not known where Davis's bottles were blown before 1866, but in that year he gave an order for them to the Fort Trumbull Glass Works, New London, Connecticut.[51]

In December 1829 Perry Davis, a shoemaker in Taunton, Massachusetts, was nigh unto death from a deep-seated cold, which not only settled in his lungs but caused other distressing body disorders. All the remedies he took met stubborn resistance from his entrenched maladies. So, in hope *only* of relief, Davis made a preparation of his own from gums and plants, and it proved to be a *cure*. He named his miraculous medicine *Vegetable Painkiller* and, in 1845, registered it according to the Act of Congress. In the meantime he had moved to Providence, where his painkiller was manufactured until 1895, when the family business was transferred to New York City. The medicine proved indeed to be "A Joy to the World" as his 1854 label proclaimed. It became a household remedy throughout the United Kingdom as well as the United States. In fact, between missionaries carrying it to the "heathen" and sea captains including it in their medicine chests, its fame was worldwide. Under the label "LINIMENT (Painkiller Brand)" it was still being sold in the United States and Canada in 1958.[52] However, like other proprietors of nostrums, Perry Davis had to cope with imitations and name stealers. As a result he appealed to users of his painkiller to destroy the label as soon as the bottle was empty in order to prevent base competitors from procuring and using the labeled bottles for their spurious preparations. (Ethics in the nostrum field had not improved since the days of Robert Turlington.) Fortunately not all consumers of Vegetable Painkiller complied with his request, or the interesting label on 12 in Ill. 78 would not have survived. The label, with portrait of Davis, was engraved by Wellstood, Hank & Whiting, New York, and registered by Act of Congress in the year 1854.

Also in Ill. 78 is a deep aquamarine octagonal bottle (14) blown in a private mold of Dr. John D. Park of Cincinnati, Ohio, for Dr. Wistar's Balsam of Wild Cherry, which was basically a compound prepared from wild cherry bark and extract of tar. John D. Park, I was informed by William S. Keener of the Ohio Historical Society, first appeared in the Cincinnati city directories in 1843, as a partner of Benjamin Sanford and a dealer in medicines. In 1848 he was on his own, dispensing "patent medicines," and in 1853 he used the reassuring term family medicines. Sometime before 1881 he established the firm of John D. Park and Sons.

In 1851 Park advertised Wistar's Balsam "for the instant relief and Permanent Cure of Asthma, Consumption, Coughs, Colds, Hoarseness, Influenza, Bronchitis, Bleeding of the Lungs, Difficult Breathing, Liver Affections, Pain and Weakness of the Breast or Side, Disorders of the Lungs and Chest."[53] The probability is that Dr. Park, among others, made as well as sold the balsam, for in the east in the 1840s there were warnings that "none was genuine unless signed by L. Butts," for which all orders were to be sent to Seth E. Fowle, Boston, Massachusetts. Obviously, as usual, the nostrum's "curing many cases after the skill of the best physicians was unavailing" had led to imitations being palmed off on the suffering public by unprincipled counterfeiters.[54] One wonders whether the Dr. Caspar Wistar, whose office was first listed in the Philadelphia city directories for 1841, had inherited the formula for "Wistar's Balsam of Wild Cherry" from Dr. Caspar Wistar of Philadelphia, son of the founder of the Wistarburgh Glass Works. Be that as it may, this "Nature's Own Prescription" was said to be one of the oldest and most reliable remedies in the world, and like many others it drew forth recommendations from

physicians and unsolicited testimonials from its grateful users. Even the clergy. In 1864 the Reverend Francis Lobdell considered it a duty he owed to suffering humanity to testify to the virtues of this balsam for colds, coughs, or sore throat—or so an advertisement claimed. He commended it to his brethren in the ministry and to public speakers generally, and closed his "unsolicited" letter with the remark: "Perhaps the Balsam does not effect all persons alike, but it always removes my hoarseness, and fits me for the minister's hard working day—the Sabbath."[55]

In Ill. 79 the light green-aquamarine vial of taper shape (4) was blown in a full-size two-piece mold having "DALBYS" cut lengthwise in one piece and "CARMINATV" in the other. It is the same general type as the official vial for Godfrey's cordial, but shorter and less slender in proportions. Such a lettered vial apparently was adopted in the 1780s when Dalby, an English apothecary, first marketed his carminative, and it was used throughout the 19th century for American preparations of Dalby's Carminative. As in the case of vials for other English patent medicines, "Dalbys" were blown in American bottle and vial works after the War of 1812, if not before. And they were cheaper than the English. By 1815 they could be obtained for $3.50 a gross, whereas during the "British Monopoly" they were $5.50. Unlike Turlingtons, Opodeldocs, Batemans, and Godfrey's vials, Dalbys do not appear on the early price lists of the Boston Glass Manufactory and the New England Glass Company. The few recorded were blown from green glass, and they are listed under green glass in two catalogs of the 1880s. All of which suggests the probability that even the early Dalbys, English and American, were not blown from white glass but always from green glass.[56]

As for Dalby's Carminative itself, it was especially good for "all those fatal disorders in the Bowel's of infants," and was one of the eight popular English patent medicines that the Philadelphia College of Pharmacy admitted to its pharmacopoeia in 1824. Naturally it had, and continued to have, many imitators over the years and perhaps as many variations in formula as imitators. One mid-19th-century preparation of Dalby's Carminative must have had a pleasant flavor for children, though there is no record they cried for it. The formula called for two scruples of carbonate of magnesia, one drop of oil of peppermint, two of nutmeg, three of anniseed, thirty of "tinctor" of castor, fifteen of assafetida, fifteen of spirits of pennyroyal, thirty of compound tincture of cardanous, and two fluid ounces of peppermint water.[57]

3
BITTERS BOTTLES

Another division of the patent-medicine category is the bitters prepared from medicinal roots and herbs having a bitter, disagreeable taste, such as gentian root and hops. Though they yielded their virtue in both water and spirits, alcoholic potables—not strangely—were the preferred extractors as well as a vehicle when bitters were taken by drops. Their general effect was to constrict "the fibres of the Stomach and Intestines, to warm the habit, attenuate the bile and juices in the first passages and promote natural evacuation." They did good service also in "weakness of the Stomach, loss of appetite, indigestion and like disorders proceeding from laxity of the solids, or cold indisposition of the juices." In the 19th century when bitters-taking was to sweep the country, and competition with panaceas had to be met, the claims for their curative powers often extended beyond the digestive tract—as in the case of Moffat's Phoenix Bitters, to the liver and the blood, and for colds, fevers, and dropsy. However, the use of bitters for digestive disturbances seems to have been nearly timeless. It can be assumed they were often made at home by steeping roots and herbs in brandy or spirits for a few days; 17th- and 18th-century household books on medicine and cookery, also druggists' handbooks in the 19th century, contained recipes for making bitters and for using them in homemade remedies. They could be purchased, of course, from doctors and druggists. Also, in the 18th century at least, a dose of bitters would be served at ordinaries and taverns to any patron feeling the need "to qualify his humours," as did Philip Fithian when, stopping at a tavern en route to Virginia in 1774, he called for a gill of bitters followed by a dish of tea to cheer him.[58] By then bottled bitters had been available in American druggists' shops half a century or more, among them Stoughton's Bitters.

Perhaps the first preparation of bitters to be patented was that of the Englishman Richard Stoughton, and then after 20 years of curing English stomachaches. In 1712 he patented his bitters under the grand names of "Stoughton's Elixer Magnum Stomachii or the Great Cordial Elixir otherwise called the Stomatic Tincture of Bitter Drops." By taking 50 or 60 drops of this marvelous bitters "in Spring Water, Beer, Ale, Mum, Canary, White Wine with or without sugar, and a dram of brandy as often

as you please," one could cure any stomach ailment. When Stoughton's, as it was usually called instead of by one of its long official names, made its American debut about 1730, room was promptly made for it on shelves and in medicine chests, though it did not completely dislodge bitters prepared by local doctors and druggists. Eventually, however, it was found expedient to compare American bitters favorably with Stoughton's. For instance, the "excellent Bitters for sail [sic]" by R. McClure of Cincinnati, Ohio, in 1794 "were made agreeable to the London dispensatory, and equal if not superior to any made by Stoughton." Nevertheless, in spite of imitators and unrelenting competition, Stoughton's long maintained its reputation and its market, and the name survived on American bitters into the late 19th century.[59]

The form of the original bottle for Stoughton's bitters is not determined. It would seem that unlike some other English patent medicines, there was no standard form for Stoughton's. The Stoughton bitters bottle described by James H. Thompson in his book *Bitters Bottles* sounds mid- to late-19th century, and presumably was made for an American brand of Stoughton's. As described by Mr. Thompson, it was a round amber bottle with tapering body, domed shoulder, 5-inch-long bulged neck, square (that is, straight-sided) flanged lip, and flat base. Perhaps it was the type the Williamstown Glass Works listed ca. 1840 to 1854 as "Stoughton's" at $2.25 a gross. Whatever the form of the bottles, the bottling of the bitters was not always done by the maker only, but also by the dispenser. From the 1750s on, some colonial apothecaries who prepared Stoughton's Bitters put up the bitters in Stoughton vials imported from England.[60] On April 20, 1814, "1 BBL Bitters (Stoughton)" was advertised in the *Albany Register* by Barent C. Staats. It seems unlikely Staats was the only purchaser of Stoughton's by the barrel, a quantity that gives more than an inkling of the popularity of the brand.

Before bitters-taking became a daily habit of thousands of Americans in the last half of the 19th century, the various bitters were packaged *mainly* in standard medicine bottles, vials, and small utilitarian bottles. These were mainly cylindrical, rectangular with chamfered corners, and—in the 19th century—many-sided, and they were in various shades of amber, green, and aquamarine. In general, the liquid capacity of the containers was from about five to eight or ten ounces. An example of the rectangular ones with chamfered corners used for medicines and proprietary bitters is illustrated by 6 in Ill. 49. It was blown from olive-amber glass in the private mold for Phoenix Bitters, inscribed lengthwise on one side "PHŒNIX / BITTERS" and "JOHN [in arc] / MOFFAT" on the other; "NEW YORK" on one end and "PRICE $1.00" on the other. Besides aquamarine, olive-green, and olive-amber bottles from this mold, bottles from five other molds have been recorded. The main variations from the pictured example (6) are as follows:

1. Letters and figures more slender
2. Slightly taller bottle; "PRICE I DOLLAR"
3. "PRICE 1 DOLLAR"
4. "JNO̲ MOFFAT" and "PRICE $1"
5. Like 4 but letters much larger.

The bottles I have seen that were blown in these five molds had a pontil mark, whereas 6 in Ill. 49 has a smooth base with slightly depressed disk at center. It was not "stuck up" on a pontil but held in a holding device during the process of finishing the neck. Probably it was blown after 1850. Although most of the bottles were blown from green glass, the mold having "PRICE 1 DOLLAR" was used for colorless bottles and the one with "JNO̲ MOFFAT" in larger letters for rich amber. In the collection of Carlyn Ring there is a larger bottle (7 inches x 3¼ inches x 2⅛ inches) having "JOHN" in an arc above "MOFFAT" on one side; "PHOENIX/BITTERS" on the other side; "NEW YORK" on one end and "PRICE $2.00" on the other end.

Whichever of the six smaller molds was the first, it probably was adopted about 1836. In that year John Moffat, who had invented or acquired the rights to the bitters, was first listed in the New York City directories—as the proprietor of "Life Pills & Phoenix Bitters." By the time the 1839/40 directory was compiled, John had been succeeded by William B. Moffat, listed as maintaining a medical office for the sale of the pills and bitters. In 1863/64 William's widow was listed, and she apparently conducted the business through 1867. However, by 1860, if not earlier, Moffat's Phoenix Bitters for "Fever, Ague, Dyspepsia, Dropsy, and Piles" were enjoying a wide sale indeed, even if a Wheeling, (W) Virginia, dispenser's statement that they were "for sale by all druggists" was an exaggeration.[61]

The occasional use, after midcentury, of the typi-cal cylindrical medicine vials for some proprietary bitters is illustrated by 15 in Ill. 78. It is a pale green, tall cylindrical form with flat shoulder, cylindrical neck, and narrow round collar, and was blown in a full-size two-piece mold. The paper label reads:

ATWOOD'S GENUINE VEGETABLE
PHYSICAL JAUNDICE BITTERS
This is an effective cure for Jaundice, Headache, Dyspesia, Worms, Dizziness, Loss of Appetite, Colds and Fevers, and Darting Pains. It cleans the blood of humors, and moistens the skin, and is good for Liver Complaints, Strangury, Dropsey, Croup and Phthisic. DOSE for adult, from half a table spoon to half a wineglassful, according to the strength of the patient.
DIRECTIONS. For Bilious Difficulty, take enough to operate smartly as a cathartic, and follow taking a little morning and evening to clear the stomach of bile and regulate the bowels. For Fevers, to be taken in large doses once in four hours while it operates smartly as a physic; at the same time take a good sweat, and continue taking enough Bitters every morning to keep the bowels in good order. In Liver complaint, to be taken the same as in Dyspepsia, applying one of Atwoods Strengthening Plasters between the shoulders, and wherever the patient has most pain, which generally effects a cure in short time, if administered in season. It is safe in all cases and meets the approbation of all who have had an opportunity of using it.

Prepared by NATHAN WOOD, Sole Proprietor, 200 . . . Corner of Plum Street, Portland, Me. NOTICE. I hereby give notice to the public and those who use "Atwood's Bitters" that I have purchased of Dr. Atwood his entire right and interest in the medicine known as "Atwood's Genuine Vegetable Physical Jaundice Bitters", and that he has delivered to me the Original and genuine receipt for making this Medicine with instructions for compounding the same. The Public can rely upon every bottle of At-wood's Bitters, prepared by me, to be made of the choicest Roots, Gums and Barks, and that they contain no mineral or poisonous drug whatsoever.
After this date each bottle of Atwood's Bitters to be genuine must bear my signature.
Aug. 15, 1863. Nathan Wood.
BEWARE OF COUNTERFEITS AND IMITA-TIONS!
Sold by dealers in Medicine generally throughout the country.

On the reverse of the vial is a stamp dated "Nov. 24, 1864," indicating that this particular vial of Atwood's Bitters could not have been sold at an earlier date.

Cylindrical bottles like 16 in Ill. 78 were not the only ones used by Nathan Wood for Atwood's Bitters. Olive-amber bottles with sloping collar and of the same form as Moffat's Phoenix Bitters' bottles have been found with the same label as that on 16. Also a later bottle, like 16 in form but with straight-sided flat flange, was ammunition in the battle with counterfeiters: it was inscribed around the top of the shoulder "N. WOOD SOLE PROPRIETOR"; on outer rim of the base was "ATWOOD'S BITTERS" and across the center of the base, "GENUINE".

Prior to Wood's acquisition of Atwood's rights and formula, the bitters had been manufactured at Georgetown, Massachusetts. One, if not the only, bottle used by Atwood himself was aquamarine, 12-sided with sloping shoulder, short cylindrical neck and straight-sided flat flange, smooth depressed base with nipple at center, and molded inscription on six sides: (1) "ATWOOD'S" (2) "JAUNDICE" (3) "BITTERS" (4) "MOSES ATWOOD" (5) "GEORGETOWN." (6) "MASS." One of the Georgetown dispensers of the bitters used the same type of bottle, also inscribed but with "M.CARTER & SON" instead of "MOSES ATWOOD". The original label on one of the M. Carter bottles in the collection of Warren G. Lane gives the same list of disorders as Wood's label, but ends with "Manufactured by Moses Atwood, Georgetown, Mass."

From the 18th well into the 19th century bitters apparently were normally taken in comparatively small doses: a number of drops or a teaspoonful in a pleasant and usually stimulating vehicle. But toward the middle of the 19th century, a natural side effect of the accelerating Temperance Movement began to show itself in increased production and consumption of liquid medicines in which the principal liquid was wine, whiskey, brandy, or other spirit. In the case of bitters, doses were more and more often by the tablespoonful or wineglassful, and inevitably their popularity was on the upswing. It would seem that by 1850 most bitters were actually an alcoholic beverage disguised as medicine by bitter herbs, root, and barks, though still regarded only as medicine by unsuspecting bitters addicts. With free conscience, many a staunch Temperance man and woman innocently enjoyed a cocktail of bitters, not just before dinner but before breakfast and lunch as well. Such is the power of words and advertising that, for years, to the minds of even dedicated Temperance advocates, "Bitters" tacked onto "Bourbon Whiskey" not only removed the curse of intemperance but subtly changed the nature of the evil spirit. Not until late in the century did proprietors of bitters find it necessary to reassure their customers with statements from State assayers and chemists, such as that on the

wrapper for Quaker Bitters, 9 in Ill. 85: "This is not a beverage nor an intoxicating liquor but an official medicinal preparation, containing extracts of Roots and Herbs."

The pervasiveness of dosing one's self with bitters morning, noon, and night and the change in dosage were reflected in a spate of new brands of "medicinal" bitters and also in the capacity of the bottles, most of which became larger. With a few exceptions, such as the bottles for Phoenix Bitters and Atwood's Genuine Physical Jaundice Bitters discussed above, the liquid capacity of bitters bottles, although sometimes only a pint, was usually from 1½ pints to a little over a quart.

The mid-19th century brought also a wide variety of types of bottles for bitters, all blown in full-size piece molds. In fact, in numbers the recorded bitters bottles rival the Figured Flasks. Mr. Thompson listed 456, not counting variants of some particular bottles. In many instances only the name of the bitters was given, without a description of the bottles. Usually a molded inscription identified the bitters. Though ambers predominate in the bottle colors, in some varieties there are many shades of green, also occasionally brown, wine, amethyst, puce, and aquamarine. Since these are late bottles, they normally have no pontil mark, having been held in a snap or similar device during the neck-finishing process. From the bottles described by Mr. Thompson it is evident that although medicine-bottle types, such as the Quaker Bitters bottles 7, 8, and 9 in Ill. 85, in aquamarines, ambers, and greens persisted (he listed 56 rectangular), the tall slender square bottles, usually with chamfered or rounded corners, predominate. Slender barrel-shaped bottles are a close second. And there are around 21 varieties of so-called log cabins, of which 3 and 6 in Ill. 85 are rare examples. Though the buildings are two-storied, they are called log cabins because of the broad horizontal ribs simulating logs. The neck, or chimney, has a tool-formed deep flat collar. In his researches into patented cabin bottle designs, Arthur G. Peterson found that the first such design was patented February 18, 1862, by P. H. Drake of Binghamton, New York. Appropriately, it was used for Plantation Bitters.[62]

The slender barrel bottles, with and without molded inscription, have horizontal ribs simulating hoops that occur in varied groupings. Usually they have a thick flanged lip or deep flat collar, which was formed by a neck-finishing tool or, on very late bottles, in the mold itself. A typical barrel bottle is shown in Ill. 86. It was the standard bottle for

Greeley's Bourbon Whiskey Bitters, and with it is shown the salesman's wooden case, a rare item. The case is square, stained brown, with overhanging lid and a leather strap handle. On each of three sides is a full-size cutout of Greeley's Bottle in color. Rich olive-green in color, this bottle has heavy horizontal ribbing above and below a label-band, which is inscribed on one side "GREELEY'S BOURBON" in a semicircle above "BITTERS". In the space between the inscriptions is a 3-cent Internal Revenue proprietary stamp with a portrait bust of "G. Washington" on a green ground. On the other side is a Greeley's label in the form of three contiguous disks. That at the left reads: "These Bitters are prepared of PURE OLD BOURBON WHISKEY in combination with the active principle of many simple Alteratives & bitter Tonics. In case of Dyspepsia, Liver Complaints, Debility or Weakness of the System they are an excellent Remedy and are a certain preventative of Chills & Fever. A trial will establish their merits." The one in the center is inscribed "BOURBON WHISKEY BITTERS" in a semicircle above a girl holding a sheaf of rye at waist height; a large sheaf of rye lies on the ground at left and a path leads off toward mountains at right. The disk at right reads "A WINE GLASS FULL should be taken before each meal. Ladies and children should begin with a less quantity & increase. As an agreeable Stomactic these Bitters are unsurpassed. POLLARD & C⁰ BOSTON, MASS. Agents for the United States. Sold by Druggists & Grocers Everywhere."

According to Van Rensselaer, Pollard & Company was listed in Boston directories from 1869 to 1872, in which year the firm became Wood, Pollard & Company, which was listed until 1918; hence the name on the labels must have been changed. How long Greeley's Bitters were sold is not determined at this time, but certainly long after the new firm was formed. Greeley's bottles have been recorded in ambers, including a bright golden amber, deep wine, reddish amethyst, aquamarine, and light and dark smoky. On the late bottles, possibly first made in the 1880s, the lip flares about a quarter of an inch to the wide, thick flat flange and appears to have been formed in the mold.

The square bitters bottles usually have a tool-formed or, on late ones, mold-formed deep flat collar, narrow chamfered or rounded corners, straight or paneled sides and shoulder, and molded relief decoration, as well as inscriptions. Four variants are shown by 9 and 11 in Ill. 49 and 1 and 3 in Ill. 85. The clear amber Jackson's Stonewall Bitters (3) is rare.

The inscriptions on the panels of the unusual overhanging shoulder—(1) "QUILIN"; (2) "BROˢ & CO"; (3) "ST LOUIS"; (4) "MO"—indicate a private mold for that company, which, even if it was not the proprietor of the bitters, sold them. On three of the deep panels on the side, the low relief decoration represents a stone wall, above which (on one side) "JACKSON'S" is inscribed lengthwise; on the other two is a plain band.

Also rare are the brown-amber bottles 1 in Ill. 85 and 9 in Ill. 49, each with a small stylized eagle at the top of one panel. Mr. Gardner's wide experience led him to believe the American eagle, so popular a motif on Figured Flasks, appears on only a very few bitters bottles. At the top of the front panel of No. 1 are 13 small stars and a flying eagle; on the panels at left and right, inscribed lengthwise, "JOHN · W· STEELE'S / NIAGARA · STAR · BITTERS". On the small semicircular shoulder panels above the eagle and inscribed panels is a large star. In the one above the plain label-panel of the fourth side is the date "1864," presumably the year Steele marketed his bitters. More elaborate in design is 9 in Ill. 49, with chamfered corners and, on three sides, six cannons without carriage facing alternately left and right. At the top of the fourth side is a tent (an undetailed pyramid) surmounted by a flagpole and flying flag. On each side of the shoulder are crossed sabres and, at each corner, a cannon with muzzle toward the neck. The choice of motifs for decoration suggests that the bottle was adopted during the Civil War.

The shaded amber Wahoo Bitters bottle, 11 in Ill. 49, which has rounded corners and rectangular sunken panels on the sides and shoulders, is not a rarity, but at the top of one panel it has a small stylized eagle flying to the left with a long arrow in its beak. On the shoulder panel above the eagle is "PATᴰ". The panels at right and left are inscribed lengthwise "E. DEXTER LOVERIDGE / WAHOO BITTERS". "XXX" is on one shoulder and "D W D" on the other. "D W D" appears also on the shoulder panel above the plain label-panel of the fourth side. Some of the Wahoo Bitters bottles, it is said, were produced at the Lancaster Glass Works, a convenient source since Loveridge, sole manufacturer and proprietor of the bitters, was located in Buffalo, New York. It was on November 3, 1863, that he received a United States patent on the design for his bottles and registered labels. Views of the four sides, with labels on two, are shown in the design patent, No. 1837. Although the inscribed sides are like those of No. 11, there are differences in the other two sides. The label-panel side, shown in the patent specification as Fig. I, has the date "1863" on the shoulder instead of "D W D". The opposite side, shown as Fig. II, has a plain shoulder and a quite different eagle—a chubby bird standing on a bar, wings raised, head turned to its left and a ring in its beak. The revealing labels are printed on the panels of Figs. I and II, and I must confess the one filling the panel below the eagle especially fascinates me. It is a "PROCLAMA-TION" stating, in part:

I, E. Dexter Loveridge, of the United States of America, State of New York and City of Buffalo, do hereby declare to all People, of whatever Kingdom, Land, Name, Nation or Color, Bond or Free, that I will furnish my celebrated Wahoo Bitters for VALUE RECEIVED. ALL THAT HAVE must PAY, and to those that have NOT my charity will extend; for have it you must, in order to enjoy life, and to live to the age when the eye of hope looks from time to eternity, contemplating the glory yet to be revealed.

The Wahoo Bitters are entirely vegetable, being compounded of some twenty different roots and barks. This compound was procured in part, from the most eminent Indian Physicians known among our North Western Tribes; the balance from my own Botanical researches, and is a profound secret, making the best compound ever invented for the Preservation of Health. The Spirits used to preserve these Bitters, so that they will keep in any climate, is not an adulterated Alcohol, flavored with poisonous drugs, and claimed to be Foreign Importation but is a
PURE RYE WHISKEY!

One wonders whether the humanitarian Mr. Loveridge was ever called upon to extend his charity to any who could NOT pay. The label on the dated side is a handsome one with a powerful-looking Indian brave depicted below a four-line inscription reading "THE GREAT INDIAN BEVERAGE [in arc] / LOVERIDGE'S / CELEBRATED / Wahoo Bitters" (large letters in arc). The statement, in small type below the brave—"The Wahoo has always been valued by the Indians as possessing rare medicinal virtues. Scientific Analysis has proved it to be a Tonic, Laxative, Diuretic and Expectorant"—is followed by a short list of complaints it will cure or alleviate and the advice: "DRINK AS A BEVERAGE"!

Though classified today as bitters bottles, not all the typical square and slender barrel bottles associated with bitters were used solely for bitters; some were used for other patent medicines well fortified with liquor. For instance, a square bottle was adopted for Wishart's Pine Tree Cordial. Wishart's bottles were made in at least three sizes: 11 ounces, of which 7 in Ill. 49 is an emerald-green example; 16 ounces, and 25 ounces. All have a plain label-panel; a second is inscribed lengthwise "L.Q.C. WISHART'S"; a third, inscribed "PINE TREE / TAR CORDIAL / PHIL$^{\underline{A}}$". On the fourth side of the pint bottles is a pine tree in low relief with "TRADE" in a shallow arc above and "MARK" below. This bottle probably was not made before October 27, 1874, when, according to the United States Patent Records, H. R. Wishart registered a trademark. On the 11- and 25-ounce bottles the fourth side likewise has a pine tree in low relief with "PATENT" in a shallow arc above and the date "1859" below. Although only one mold has so far been determined for the 25-ounce bottle, there were at least three for the pint and five for the 11-ounce sizes. In no two molds were the pine trees identical. The color range is wide, including olive-, emerald-, bluish, clear deep, and yellow-greens and golden amber.

The Lancaster Glass Works, which was established in 1849 at Lancaster, near Buffalo, and operated until about 1908, is said to have been one source of bottles made for Pine Tree Cordial. Wherever made, presumably the first were produced in 1859 for Lucius Q. C. Wishart; and those without "TRADE MARK" were used through 1873, when apparently Lucius sold his interest in the cordial, or a new firm was formed for which H. R. Wishart (son?) patented the trademark. Lucius Q. C. Wishart had started business as a paint dealer and grocer in Philadelphia by 1856, but after patenting his Pine Tree Tar Cordial in 1859, he entered the field of patent medicines. From 1860 through 1873 his listings in the city directories included "patent medicine" or "druggist" or "physician." In 1874 he was a mere "salesman."[63]

The standard square bottle with chamfered corners was used also in packaging hard liquors in the same period as handled bottles and flasks like those in Ills. 48 and 99. At least they were by A. M. Bininger & Company of New York, as evidenced by two labeled bottles of about quart size that were in the collection of Charles B. Gardner. One has its original label for Old London Dock Gin, and is inscribed lengthwise on the other three sides: (1) "A.M. BININGER & CO / NO. 17 BROAD S$^{\underline{T}}$"; (2) "OLD LONDON DOCK"; (3) "GIN". In the city directories the firm was listed at this address from 1859 to 1861. The other wears its original label for Old Times Family Rye on one side and is inscribed lengthwise on the other three sides: (1) "BININGER'S OLD TIMES / FAMILY RYE"; (2) "DIS-

TILLED IN 1848"; (3) "A.M.BININGER & CO / NO 19 BROAD ST. N.Y." The firm was listed at this address from 1861 through 1864.

Also, as is not surprising in a period of fancy bottles, besides the simple forms—square, barrel, and log cabin—used for many brands of bitters, individual and distinctive bottles were designed for specific brands. One is the extremely rare Traveler's Bitters bottle, 5 in Ill. 79, which is of special interest to collectors of Figured Flasks, for on one side of its tall oblate body is a large figure of a man wearing a low-crowned hat, long coat, and tight trousers, with a cane in his right hand; he is strolling to the left— quite similar to the prospector on the Pike's Peak flasks, Group XI. Many of the bottles fall also in the category of Figure Bottles—for instance, the Berkshire Bitters bottle in the form of an ear of corn, 4 in Ill. 79; the figure of an "Indian Queen" for Brown's Celebrated Indian Herb Bitters patented 1867, 2 in Ill. 79; the bust of George Washington for Simon's Centennial Bitters, 2 in Ill. 79; and the fish for Dr. Fisch's Bitters patented by W. H. Hare in 1866 (3 in Ill. 79 is one of three varieties). Also representational is the Lighthouse bottle, 6 in Ill. 79, for Seaworth Bitters Company of Cape May, New Jersey, and the cannon for General Scott's Artillery Bitters, No. 1 in the same illustration. In the experience of Charles B. Gardner, this is the rarest of the known bitters bottles. It is interesting to note that A. M. Bininger & Company used the same cannon, but with larger star below the pennant, in the years 1861 to 1864, if not later, for its "Bininger Great Gun Gin." Gin, bitters, and bottles—all apparently were canny merchandising, calculated to appeal to Northern emotions and sympathies aroused by the Civil War.

Another attractive bottle usually included in the Bitters Bottle class is the "pineapple" bitters, 10 in Ill. 49, seemingly so called not from a brand of bitters but because it reminded someone of a pineapple. The body was molded in large diamond diapering broken by a large diamond-shaped label-panel; the long neck has a bulge above elongated diamonds and below a plain cylindrical section; the lip has a tool-formed deep, round collar above a narrow bevel; the base is plain but has a pontil mark. On the label-panel, the label (I believe it to be original) depicts a portrait bust of a young woman and is inscribed "THE BEST TONIC" above the bust and "BROWN'S IRON BITTERS" below. Occasionally bottles from this mold are found in aquamarine and olive-green. Three other molds had a smaller label-panel, bounded by two instead of three diamonds. In one the panel was plain; in one, inscribed "W & C/N.Y."; in the third, inscribed "J.C.& C$\underline{O}$". The mold with the small plain panel and that with "W & C / N.Y." were used on a few occasions, at least, to pattern gathers fashioned into other articles. The collection of Charles B. Gardner included a handsome handled chestnut flask of rich amber glass patterned in the "W & C" mold, and the Henry Ford Museum has a brilliant aquamarine sugar bowl with set-in cover patterned in the same mold. The cover has a plain applied knob finial; the bowl has an applied stem and circular foot. The Museum also has an amber handled jug, with wide neck and flaring rim, that was patterned in the mold with the small plain panel. Since only one of each of these articles has been recorded, the chances are 99.44 percent that they were individual pieces, not commercial products. Mr. Thompson states that the pineapple bitters bottles were used as containers of flavoring bitters,[64] and Mr. Gardner told me he surmised that they were bar decanters and not used for proprietary medicinal bitters. However, the label on No. 10 leads me to believe that, if for no other bitters, this variety of the pineapple bottles was adopted for Brown's Iron Bitters—especially good for women—as the "Indian Queen" was for Brown's Indian Herb Bitters.

The number of listed marked bitters bottles continues to increase as the census continues. Richard Watson, in his *Bitters Bottles* and *Supplement to Bitters Bottles*, has listed 520 marked ones and 232 "label only bitters."[65] Carlyn Ring, whose collection undoubtedly is the largest ever assembled, informed me that she has "over 700 with the word 'Bitters' molded in the glass."

84. FANCY BITTERS BOTTLES

These bottles illustrate a few of the fancy and distinctive bottles designed for different popular brands of bitters from the 1850s into the late 19th century. They were blown in full-size two-piece private molds.

Formerly in the Charles B. Gardner Collection.

Top row:

1. Cannon, shaded amber; plain unpolished lip; smooth base; *obverse:* inscribed in three lines below molding at top: "GENL SCOTTS [in arc] / NEW YORK / ARTILLERY BITTERS"; *reverse:* below molding, rippled pennant in arc above small star at center (showing through the glass in the illustration). Extremely rare. Capacity, 24 oz. Height, 12½". Diameter at base, 2⅝".

   The same cannon but with larger star below pennant was used by A. M. Bininger & Co. in the years 1861 to 1864, if not later, for Bininger's Great Gun Gin. It was inscribed below the molding "A. M. BININGER & CO [in arc] / 19 BROAD ST / N.Y."

2. Indian Queen, amber; plain lip; nipple at center of smooth base; shield at lower right, inscribed "BROWN'S / CELEBRATED / INDIAN HERB BITTERS"; on back, below robe, "PATENTED / FEB 11 / 1868." Comparatively scarce; occurring mainly in light golden to brown-amber, occasionally in colorless and olive-green. Capacity, 24 oz. Height, 12¼". Diameter of base, about 3¼".

   A variant of the so-called Indian Queen is inscribed on the back in slanting arc, below robe, "PATENTED / 1867". Possibly the mold so inscribed anticipated the actual granting of the patent. A similar figure, used as a whiskey bottle, holds the shield high in the left hand and against the body. On the shield is the inscription "MOHAWK WHISKEY" in a deep arc following the contour of the shield, and below, "PURE / RYE".

3. Fish, shaded amber; sloping collar; smooth base inscribed below one eye "W. H. WARE / PATENTED 1866" and, below other eye, "THE / FISH BITTERS" Capacity, 20 oz. Height, 11⅝". Diameters of base 2¼" by 3½".

   This is one of three fish bottles for Doctor Fisch's Bitters patented by W. H. Ware. One, probably the first, is inscribed "DOCTOR FISCH'S / BITTERS" and occurs commonly in ambers, rarely in clear light green, amethystine, and light olive.

Bottom row:

4. Ear of corn, golden amber; deep flat collar with rounded molding at bottom; smooth base; oval label panel above rectangular panel inscribed "NATIONAL / BITTERS". Comparatively scarce, occurring in ambers from golden to brown, and in aquamarine. Capacity, 21 oz. Height, 12⅜". Diameter of base, 2¾".

5. Amber; tall oblate body, four long slightly concave shoulder panels tapering into a long neck, deep sloping collar; large concave disk on base; *obverse:* figure of a bearded man wearing a low-crowned hat, long coat, and tight trousers, with cane in his right hand, strolling to the left—quite similar to the prospectors on the Pike's Peak flasks; *reverse:* on shoulder, "183A / 1870"; on left end, "TRAVELLERS"; on right end, "BITTERS". Extremely rare. Capacity, about 24 oz. Height, 10¼". Greatest width 3½". Greatest depth, 2½".

6. Lighthouse, shaded light amber; sloping deep collar; smooth depressed base; inscribed below small four-pane window "SEAWORTH [in deep arc] / BITTERS / CO / CAPE MAY / NEW JERSEY / U.S.A." on other side, four-panel door and two four-pane windows. Rare. Capacity, 14 oz. Height, 11½" Diameter at base, 2⅞".

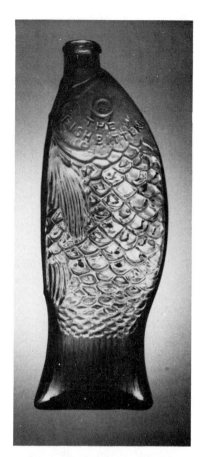

These bitters bottles were blown in full-size two-piece molds, and have no pontil mark on the base. Nos. 1 and 3 are rare bottles in two varieties of the square form with sunken panels; Nos. 4 and 6, of the Log Cabins. No. 2 is classified also as a figural (bottle). No. 5, a rectangular obelisk, is, so far as I know at present, peculiar to Carey's Grecian Bend Bitters. Nos. 7, 8, and 9 illustrate a standard late 19th-century type of bottle for many purposes, and one used for Quaker Bitters. Like many others, the proprietors of Quaker Bitters seem to have relied more on labels and wrappings than on the bottle itself to identify their panacean bitters.

Formerly in the Charles B. Gardner Collection.

Top row:

1. Brown-amber; square with sunken arc-topped panels on sides and small semicircular panels on shoulders, deep sloping collar with molding at bottom; large concave disk in base; sides: (1) 13 small stars above stylized eagle at top of side panel; (2) inscribed lengthwise: "JOHN · W · STEELE'S / NIAGARA · STAR · BITTERS"; (3) plain (label-panel); (4) like (2); shoulders: (1), (2), and (4), large star; (3) "1864". Rare. Capacity, 24 oz. Height, 10⅛". Body, 2¾" sq.

2. Golden amber; portrait bust of George Washington on wide circular base, short neck, round collar; inscribed on band at bottom of bust: front, below circular label-panel; "SIMONS CENTENNIAL BITTERS"; back, "TRADE MARK." Occurs also in deeper ambers and aquamarine. Capacity, 24 oz. Height, 9⅞". Diameter of base, 4⅛".

   Reproductions of this bottle, made in recent years, have a pontil mark on the base and the inscription is faint.

3. Clear amber; square with sunken panels on sides and tapering panels on overhanging shoulder with rounded corners; deep flat sloping collar; concave disk on base; sides: (1) "JACKSON'S" inscribed lengthwise above a stonewall; (2) plain band above stonewall; (3) plain label-panel; (4) like (2); shoulder panels inscribed: "[1] QUILIN [2] BROˢ & Co [3] ST. LOUIS [4] MO." Rare. Capacity, 20 oz. Height, 9½". Body, 2⅝" sq.

Middle row:

4. Log Cabin, amber; tall rectangular body, broad heavy horizontal ribs simulating a two-storied log cabin with steep gabled roof and tall chimney, deep sloping flat collar; front and back: tall plain door at left of single pane window, two similar windows in upper story; similar window in upper story of one end and plain sunken label-panel in other end; inscribed on roof: front, "HOLTZERMANN'S"; back, "PATENT / STOMACH / BITTERS". Capacity, 26 oz. Height, 9½". Body, 2⅞" by 3¼".

5. Puce, rectangular obelisk with rounded rope corners (attenuated diagonal "S" ribs), short neck, rounded collar; deep concave disk on base; on sides at top, three-pane Gothic window, frame ornamented by serpentine rib; on ends near top, oval frame ornamented by serpentine rib; on one side, well below window, inscribed: "CAREY'S / GRECIAN / BEND / BITTERS". Extremely rare. Capacity, 24 oz. Height, 9½". Body, 2¼" by 3¼".

6. Log Cabin, dark brown-amber (black in reflected light); tall rectangular body, broad horizontal ribs on sides and fine vertical on steep gabled roof, short chimney, very deep flat collar; on front, tall plain door at left of large 12-pane window and two 9-pane windows, two 9-pane windows in upper story; inscribed: front and back of roof "KELLY'S / OLD CABIN / BITTERS"; gable, "PATENTED" in shallow arc above "1863". Rare; occurs in ambers from light to brown. Capacity, 26 oz. Height, 9⅛". Body, 2⅝" by 3⅜".

Bottom row:

7. Aquamarine; rectangular with narrow chamfered corners and sunken panels, long neck, narrow flat straight-sided collar; on base, diagonal mold seam to large shallow disk; inscribed lengthwise: "Dᴿ FLINT'S" (one end); "QUAKER BITTERS" (back); "PROVIDENCE R.I." (other end); front, fancy paper label: "DR. H. S. FLINT & CO'S / CELEBRATED / QUAKER" above small cartouche depicting a Quaker holding a bottle in his left hand and cane in right, bushes at left, house at right; below cartouche "ROOT / AND [above] CHOICE / HERB / BITTERS / TRY THIS AND THOU SHALT / BE BENEFITTED!! / PATENTED 1872". Capacity, 21 oz. Height, 9⅜". Body, 2³⁄₁₆" by 3¼".

   This bottle apparently was preceded by one of the same type and size with "OLD DR. WARREN'S" inscribed on one end and "FLINT & CO. PROVI. R.I." on the other. Presumably H. S. Flint & Co. acquired the rights to Dr. Warren's Quaker Bitters and patented them in 1872, selling them at $1.00 a bottle.

8. Aquamarine; same form and size as No. 7 and with same inscription on the back; no inscriptions on ends, but slightly raised circles (where the letters would be) that may indicate the mold had been filled in to eliminate the inscriptions; on front, part of label or wrapper with new trademark—a large figure of a Quaker, similar to that of the label on No. 7, and below "TRADE MARK / DR. FLINT'S QUAKER BITTERS".

9. Aquamarine; same form and size as No. 7; the new-style wrapper, orange with black print, nearly intact; Quaker of trademark a little less long-faced and more portly than on No. 8; lengthwise at left, "NEW STYLE WRAPPER" and, at right, "ADOPTED JANUARY 1st 1882"—apparently by Cross & Clark, successors to H. S. Flint & Co.

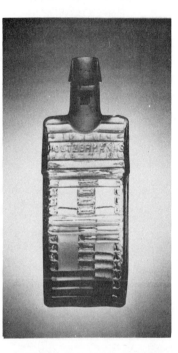  

The practice of giving bottles protective coats made of leather or woven from reeds, rushes, straw, or wicker is centuries old. A straw- or rush-covered carafe depicted in a "Nativity" by a 15th-century painter (Venetian school of Carlo Crivelli) is pictorial proof of protective covering by the 1400s. Probably "Florence bottles" so covered, used as containers for Italian wines and oils, inspired sensible imitation in many Continental glassmaking communities. By the 16th century large bottles, later called demijohns, were given leather and wicker coats. But apparently in England smaller bottles were not so covered until the early 18th century: In 1709 one Anne Trasker, stating "no other person exercises the same trade in England," obtained a patent on "covering and casing with flagg, rushes and straw flask glasses now used in England in imitation of those which come from Florence . . ." Naturally the practice extended to pocket bottles when they became a normal article of a gentleman's accoutrement. That rushes were still used in America in the third quarter of the 19th century is evident from the first flask shown here. Leather, of course, is still used. Nos. 1, 2, and 3 probably are unpatterned.

All formerly in the George S. McKearin Collection. Nos. 1 through 4, 6, and 7, The Ohio Historical Society; No. 5, The Henry Ford Museum.

1. Pocket bottle, aquamarine; long body, rounded ends and flat sides (the type glassmakers called *oval*), short cylindrical neck, plain lip, flat base, probably formed in a full-size two-piece mold; coat of woven rushes, loop for straps about an inch from base and (missing) at shoulder. 3rd quarter of the 19th century. Capacity, about 14 oz. Height, 6¾". Greatest width with coat, 3¹³/₁₆". Greatest depth, 2⁵/₁₆".

2. Pocket bottle, colorless of greenish tinge; free-blown; ovoid body tapering to small unstable base, short neck, plain lip; coat similar to No. 1; fitted with metal-topped cork. Late 18th–early 19th century. Capacity, about 4 oz. Height, 5¾". Greatest width with coat, 2⅝". Greatest depth, 1¹¹/₁₆".

3. Flask, aquamarine; blown in full-size two-piece mold for one of the Washington–Taylor flasks—whether GI–37, 39, 42, or 43 cannot be determined without removing the wicker covering—form No. 20; unusually long neck with collar No. 15; wicker coat, large loop handle of rope-twisted wicker. Dyottville Glass Works, Kensington, Philadelphia, ca. 1847–60. Capacity, 1 qt. 6 oz. Height, 9¾". Greatest width with coat, 5⅝". Greatest depth, 1⅜".

A GI–42 flask in the collection of George Austin has the same kind of covering. It is said the flasks were given an extra long neck when they were to be wickered.

4. Pocket bottle, colorless of aquamarine tint; free-blown; chestnut shape, neck spreading to plain lip; coat like No. 1. Late 18th–early 19th century. Capacity, about 5 oz. Height, 5⅛". Greatest width with coat, 3½". Greatest depth, 1⅞".

5 a & b. Salesman's sample case and bitters bottle. Case: square wooden box with hinged lid, stained brown; cut-out of labeled Greeley's Bourbon Bitters bottle on 3 sides; leather strap handle. Height, 10¾"; 4¼" sq. Bottle, rich olive-green; blown in full-size two-piece mold; slender barrel shape, short shoulder and neck, thick flat flange; smooth, slightly concave base; label band, between wide horizontal ribbing, inscribed on one side "GREELEY'S BOURBON" in semicircle above "BITTERS"; with original 3ᶜ INTERNAL REVENUE proprietary stamps with portrait bust of "G. Washington" on green ground; on plain side, 3 disk label: At left, "These Bitters / are prepared of / PURE OLD BOURBON WHISKEY / in combination with the active principle of many simple Alternatives & Bitter Tonics. In all cases / of Dyspepsia, Liver Complaints. / Debility or Weakness of the system / they are an excellent Remedy / and are a certain preventative /for Chills & Fever. / A TRIAL will establish their merits." At center, "BOURBON WHISKEY BITTERS" appears in semicircle above a girl holding a sheaf of rye, large sheaf on ground at right, path and landscape at left. At right, "A WINE GLASS FULL / should / be taken before each meal / Ladies & Children should begin with a less quantity & increase. / As an agreeable stomachic/ these Bitters are unsurpassed. POLLARD & Cᴼ BOSTON, MASS. Agents for the United States. / Sold by Druggists & Grocers / everywhere." These were typical claims arming the host of alcoholic bitters with respectability to meet the Temperance forces in the last half of the 19th century. ca. 1869–72. Occurs also in aquamarine, light and dark smoky, ambers golden to brown, amethyst, and deep wine. Capacity, 1 qt. 2 oz. Height, about 9¼". Greatest diameter, 3½".

6. Pocket bottle, aquamarine; free-blown; chestnut shape, cylindrical neck, plain lip; leather coat. Late 18th to early 19th century. Capacity, 3 oz. Height, 4¼". Greatest width, with coat, 3⁵/₁₆". Greatest depth, 1⅜".

7. Pocket bottle, brilliant olive-green; blown in full-size two-piece mold in Eagle–Anchor design GII–37; rare color; tooled leather coat. Ravenna Glass Works, Ravenna, O., ca. 1857–70. Capacity, 1 pt. 2 oz. Height, 7½". Greatest width with coat, 3¹/₁₆". Greatest depth, 2⅜".

Except for Nos. 2, 9, and 10 fashioned from single gathers of glass, these containers are Pitkin-type, blown by the "German" half-post method. A slightly inflated initial gather, the *post,* was dipped in the metal for a *half-post,* a layer not extending the full length of the post, but strengthening the container's walls. The double gather was inflated in a rib-mold to impress ribs on the half-post. For vertical ribs, the embryonic body was expanded to the desired size; for swirled, it was twisted to right or left. For broken-swirl, the initial vertical ribs were swirled, then the gather was again inflated in a rib-mold to impress vertical ribs upon the swirled, thus breaking their continuity. Very occasionally, the second ribbing was swirled in the opposite direction to the first.

For years all flasks of this type were attributed to the Pitkin Glassworks, East Hartford (Manchester, 1823) Conn., ca. 1788–1830, and proof has been found in the form of fragments that they were blown there. Pitkins probably were blown in many of our 18th to early 19th-century works producing bottles and flasks. "Pitkin" flask sources proven by excavations of glasshouse sites now include the Gloucester Glass Works, N.J., the Coventry Glass Works and the Glastenbury Glass Works, Conn., the Keene-Marlboro-Street Glassworks, N.H., and the Mantua Glass Works, O., as well as the Pitkin factory. And high incidence of certain Pitkin-type flasks in the Midwest points to works besides Mantua. Hence *Pitkin* has been stripped of its factory designation and invested with a generic one, with *type* appended for safe measure. In the category, flasks are numerous; jars and bottles, rare.

All the containers shown here are rare. In common, they have a shallow kick-up and a pontil mark obscuring the rib endings on the base.

Illustrated also in *American Glass;* 1 and 3 by Nos. 5 and 2 in Plate 47; 7 and 8 by Nos. 12 and 16 (measurements and rib number incorrect) of Plate 233; 9 by No. 3 in Plate 230. In *Two Hundred Years of American Blown Glass,* 3 by No. 4 in Plate 105; 1 by No. 6 in Plate 105.

Nos. 2, 4, 5, 6, and 10, formerly in the George S. McKearin Collection. Nos. 1 and 3, The Corning Museum of Glass; No. 7 (also ex-collection of Alexander Drake), The Henry Ford Museum.

1. Pitkin-type jar, clear olive-green; cylindrical body sloping at top to wide neck flaring to plain lip; 36-rib broken-swirl: first ribbing tight, swirled left; second, vertical, ending about ½″ below swirled. New England. Capacity, 15 oz. Height, 5½″. Greatest diameter, 3″.

2. Bottle, clear olive-green; 15 vertical ribs, slightly twisted to left at top of chunky flattened globular body and on lower part of long cylindrical neck, flat collar laid on around plain lip; ribs invisible on base, probably obliterated in fabrication; body shape similar to some Stiegel-type pocket bottles, typically 18th century but occasionally occurring in the early 19th. Provenance unknown. Capacity, 10 oz. Height,

5¼″. Greatest width, 3¾″. Greatest depth 2⅛″.

3. Pitkin-type wide-mouth bottle, dark olive-amber; unusual form: sides spreading slightly then tapering to narrow nearly flat shoulder, flaring neck, plain lip; 32-rib broken-swirl: first ribbing tight, swirled to right; second, vertical, ending less than ½″ below swirled. New England. Capacity, 14 oz. Height, 5″. Greatest diameter, 3⁵/₁₆″.

4. Pitkin-type flask, yellow-green of muted tone; 20 heavy vertical ribs fading out at bottom, probably from expansion and manipulation; body similar to No. 2, long neck spreading slightly above medial incised line to everted plain lip; large areas of wear on sides testify to much usage; the muted color, rare in 19th-century bottle glass, closely similar to the 18th-century fragment No. 5. Capacity, about 14 oz. Height, 5⅝″. Greatest width 3⅛″. Greatest depth, 2⅜″.

5. Fragment, part of a tooled knopped stem and of a vessel's bowl or foot, excavated on the Wistarburgh site over 40 years ago; yellow-green bottle glass with some iridescence and foreign matter, in color closely similar to Nos. 4 and 8.

6. Pitkin-type bottle, cloudy olive-green; wide-spaced 19-rib broken-swirl: first ribbing swirled to right; second, vertical; slightly flattened globular body, long plain neck spreading at plain lip. Provenance unknown. Capacity, about 6 oz. Height, about 4½″. Greatest width, 2¹⁵/₁₆″. Greatest depth, 2⅜″.

7. Pitkin-type flask, olive-green shading to deep amber (black) at top; 28 wide-spaced pronounced fine vertical ribs on chestnut-shaped body, below what appears to be an applied and flattened plain band from which fine close ribs extend nearly to plain lip of spreading neck; only recorded example with this most unusual treatment. Provenance unknown. Capacity, 1 pt. about 3 oz. Height, 6⁷/₁₆″. Greatest width, 4⅝″. Greatest depth, 2⅞″.

8. Pitkin-type flask, muted yellow-green, deep bluish bloom in base, shoulder, and neck; 26 ribs swirled to left; flattened ovoid body, cylindrical neck, applied irregular rounded flange—an unusual feature; color similar to Wistarburgh fragment No. 5. Provenance unknown. Probably late 18th century. Capacity, 1 pt. about 7 oz. Height, about 7¾″. Greatest width, 5½″. Greatest depth, about 2⁹/₁₆″.

9. "Powder-horn" flask; olive-amber; 28 unusually fine ribs; slender ovoid body tapering into curved neck, round collar (rare form) laid on about ¼″ below plain lip; wooden stopper possibly original. Attributed to New England, probably Connecticut, where it was found in a private home near Manchester, formerly East Hartford. Height, about 7⅝″.

10. Bottle, olive-green; 36 vertical ribs; chestnut shape so flattened on one side and curved on the other that it leans like Pisa's tower, very short neck tapering to round collar. Provenance unknown. Capacity, 1 pt. about 9 oz. Height, 7⅛″. Greatest width, 4⅞″. Greatest depth, 3⁵/₁₆″.

Comparative study of Pitkin-type flasks points to certain varieties as distinctively New England (Keene and Connecticut); others, as Midwest. In general the New England, of which Nos. 2 through 6, 9, 10, and 11 are typical, have combinations of the following features: colors—mainly clear olive-ambers and olive-greens of limited tonal range, occasionally clear green, very rarely amethyst; ribbing—fine, patterned usually in 32- and 36-rib molds, vertical, more often swirled or broken-swirl in which the vertical usually ends well below the swirled, sometimes ¾" or more; weight—comparatively light; shapes—most commonly, fat flattened and tapering ovoid, with the greatest depth (diameter between sides) near the base, often with a slight concavity on the sides a bit above the bottom of the flask.

In general, the midwestern Pitkin-type flasks, of which No. 1 and most of those in Ill. 89 are typical, have combinations of the following features: colors, normally more brilliant than New England's—mainly a wide range of greens, ambers from golden to brown-amber, occasionally aquamarine, very rarely violet-blue; ribbing—fine to heavy, patterned mainly in 16-, 20-, 24-, and 32-rib molds, occasionally 26-, 30-, 36-, and 44-rib molds, most frequently broken-swirl, with the termination of the vertical ending a little below the swirled, occasionally vertical or swirled; weight—heavy as compared with the New England; shapes—(1) flattened globular, often approaching circular, as in No. 1; greatest depth at shoulder or approximately the same from shoulder to bottom, (2) flattened ovoid with greatest depth about middle of body. Exceptions test the rule. Also, mavericks like Nos. 5 and 8 are unattributable on the basis of features alone. Wherever made, the sizes of Pitkin-type flasks are mainly half-pint and pint but include a few "miniatures" such as No. 7 and a few midwestern quarts like No. 10 in Ill. 89. Excepting Nos. 5 and 10, the pontil mark obscures the rib-termination on the base of the flasks opposite.

Illustrated also in *American Glass:* 3, 5, and 10 by Nos. 1, 5, and 13 of Plate 233; in *Two Hundred Years of American Blown Glass:* 7 by No. 5 of Plate 105.

Nos. 2, 3, 5, 6, and 8 through 11, formerly in the George S. McKearin Collection. No. 10, ex-collection of Louis Guerineau Myers; No. 4, Collection of George Austin; No. 7, The Corning Museum of Glass; No. 1, The Henry Ford Museum.

1. Flask, dark brown-amber; 36-rib broken swirl, vertical ending a little below the swirl to left; flattened circular body, short neck spreading to plain lip; medium kick-up. Midwestern. Early 19th century. Capacity, 1 pt: 3 oz. Height, 5¹⁵/₁₆". Greatest width, about 5¾". Greatest depth, 2⅛" at shoulder.

2. Flask, clear green; 36-rib broken swirl, vertical ending well below the swirl to left; fat ovoid body with slight concavity above base on sides, cylindrical neck, plain lip; medium kick-up. New England. Possibly Keene-Marlboro-Street Glassworks. Early 19th

century. Capacity, about 9 oz. Height, 5⅝". Greatest width, 3³/₁₆". Greatest depth, 2¹/₁₆" above base.

3. Bottle, olive-amber; 36-rib broken-swirl, vertical ending well below swirl to right; ovoid body, long neck, deep everted plain lip; unusually high kick-up. New England, probably Connecticut. Capacity, 8 oz. Height, 6¹/₁₆". Greatest width, 3³/₁₆". Greatest depth, 2" above base.

4. Bottle, olive-amber; 36-rib broken swirl, vertical ending well below swirl to right; very rare form: sugar-loaf body, long cylindrical neck, wide flanged lip; nearly flat base. New England. Capacity, about 6 oz. Height, 5½". Diameter at base, 2¾".

5. Flask, brilliant light amber; 32-rib broken-swirl, ribs from small plain center on base, vertical and swirled to about same point below half-post; unusual flattened broad pear-shape tapering sharply at top to long cylindrical neck, lip with turned-over collar—a rare feature; conical kick-up. Provenance unknown; color and collar suggest Midwest. Probably early 19th century. Capacity, 1 pt. plus. Height, 7". Greatest width, about 4½". Greatest depth, 2⅜" at base.

6. Flask, clear light olive-green; 36 fine ribs swirled to left; ovoid body, slightly indented below shoulder on sides, short neck, plain lip; shallow kick-up. New England. Capacity, about 8 oz. Height, 5⅛". Greatest width, 3¼". Greatest depth, 2⅛" at base.

7. Flask, olive-green; 32 fine ribs swirled to right; flattened ovoid body, short cylindrical neck, plain lip. New England. Capacity, about 5 oz. Height, 3½". Greatest width, 2½". Greatest depth, 1¾".

8. Flask, deep olive-green; 36-rib broken-swirl, heavy ribs swirled right and left, ending at about same point below top of half-post; tapering flattened ovoid body, cylindrical neck, everted plain lip. Provenance unknown. Capacity, about 14 oz. Height, 6⅜". Greatest width, 3⅞". Greatest depth, 2¼" at base.

9. Flask, clear deep olive-green; 32 fine ribs swirled to right; much flattened ovoid body, sides slightly concave between base and shoulder, cylindrical neck, plain lip. New England. Capacity, 1 pt. about 3 oz. Height, 7⁹/₁₆". Greatest width, 4¹¹/₁₆". Greatest depth, 2¹/₁₆" at base.

10. Flask, olive-amber; 32 vertical ribs from small plain center on base; pear-shaped body tapering sharply at top to long cylindrical neck, plain lip. Attributed to New England. Capacity, 1 pt. about 4 oz. Height, 6⅞". Greatest width, 4½". Greatest depth, 2½" at base.

11. Flask, olive-amber; 36-rib broken-swirl: fine swirl to right; vertical faint and extending only about halfway up body; flattened ovoid, ends very thin at center giving a roughly diamondlike cross section through middle of flask, ovoid above and below, wide neck spreading to plain lip. Capacity, 1 pt. Height, 7½". Greatest width, 4". Greatest depth, 2¹¹/₁₆" at base.

89. MIDWESTERN PITKIN-TYPE FLASKS, early 19th century

At the present time none of these midwest Pitkin-type flasks can be attributed definitely to a particular glassworks. The variety in color and ribbing and the diversity within the general forms characteristic of the Midwest point to the probability of several sources. Nos. 3 and 6 have a rare feature in their collars, which are similar to some of those on midwestern pattern-molded bottles, and have not been found on any New England "Pitkins." It should be noted that in the broken-swirl on Nos. 1, 2, and 8, the vertical ribs terminate well below the swirled, as on most of the New England types. The others have the midwestern characteristic of almost coincidental termination of the two ribbings. The pontil mark obscures the rib termination on the base of all but No. 12.

Illustrated also in *American Glass:* 6, 7, 8, and 10 by Nos. 11, 8, 10, and 17 in Plate 233; in *Two Hundred Years of American Blown Glass:* 1, 3, and 5 by Nos. 3, 2, and 1 in Plate 105.

Nos. 7, 11, and 12, formerly in the Collection of George S. McKearin. Nos. 1, 3, and 5, The Corning Museum of Glass; No. 10, The Henry Ford Museum; Nos. 8 and 9, Collection of the Ohio Historical Society; Nos. 2, 4, and 6, Collection of Henry G. Schiff.

Top row:

1. Brilliant deep green; 24-rib broken-swirl; wide-spaced vertical ribs, close swirled to right; flattened broad ovoid body tapering at short double-ogee shoulder, neck spreading slightly to tooled round-collar effect at plain lip. Capacity, 1 pt. about 2 oz. Height, 6½". Greatest width, 5⅛". Greatest depth, 2".
2. Light yellowish green; heavy 20-rib broken-swirl, swirled ribs to right; 18th-century chunky flattened globular high-shouldered body, long cylindrical neck, tooled line giving collar effect to plain lip. Possibly New Geneva Glass Works, ca. 1799–1815. Capacity, 10 oz. Height, 4¾". Greatest width, 4". Greatest depth, 2⁷/₁₆".
3. Brilliant yellowish green; 26-rib broken swirl, swirled ribs to right; flattened circular body, long cylindrical neck, flaring turned-over collar—rare feature; very rare size. Capacity, about 4 oz. Height, 3½". Greatest width, 2⅞". Greatest depth, 1⁹/₁₆".
4. Golden amber; 32-rib broken-swirl, swirled ribs to right; flattened ovoid body, short neck spreading slightly to plain lip. Possibly Mantua Glass Works, 1822–29. Capacity, 1 pt. about 4 oz. Height, 6⅞". Greatest width, 4⁹/₁₆". Greatest depth, 2⁵/₁₆".

Middle row:

5. Brilliant light emerald-green; 24-rib broken-swirl, swirled ribs to left; flattened ovoid body, slender neck spreading very slightly to plain lip. Capacity, 1 pt. about 4 oz. Height, 7⅜". Greatest width, 4⅜". Greatest depth, 2¼".
6. Deep red-amber; tight 44-rib broken-swirl, unusually flattened circular body, long cylindrical neck, turned-over collar; extremely rare in color; only recorded example patterned in a 44-rib mold. Found in Ohio. Capacity, 8 oz. Height, about 5¼". Greatest width, 4⁵/₁₆". Greatest depth, 1¾".
7. Deep yellow-green; heavy 16-rib broken-swirl; flattened ovoid body tapering to unusual short flat shoulder, long cylindrical neck, narrow flanged lip—rare feature. End of 18th to early 19th century. Capacity, little over 1 pt. Height, 6⅜". Greatest width, 4⅞". Greatest depth, 2⅜" at base.
8. Brilliant clear deep green of yellow tone; 16-rib broken-swirl, swirled ribs to right, heavy at top in thickness of half-post, nearly flat in lower body where wide-spaced vertical ribs stand out; flattened circular body, cylindrical neck, plain lip. Capacity, 1 pt. about 2 oz. Height, 6¼". Greatest width, 5". Greatest depth, about 2⅛" from shoulder to base.

Bottom row:

9. Brilliant light aquamarine; tight 30-rib broken-swirl, ribs from center base, swirled ribs to right; flattened broad ovoid body, short cylindrical neck, plain lip. Capacity, about 9 oz. Height, 5⁵/₁₆". Greatest width, 4³/₁₆". Greatest depth, 2¹/₁₆" at shoulder.
10. Light aquamarine; 32-rib broken-swirl, swirled ribs to right; flattened tapering ovoid body, narrow cylindrical neck, plain lip; extremely rare size. Capacity, 1 qt. about 5 oz. Height, 8". Greatest width, 5½". Greatest depth, 3" about center of body.
11. Bubbly aquamarine glass; 32 vertical ribs; flattened pear-shaped body, cylindrical neck, plain lip; nearly flat base. Capacity, 1 pt. Height, 6¼". Greatest width, 4¼". Greatest depth, 2¾" above base.
12. Blue aquamarine; tight swirl to left, patterned in 30-rib mold with ribs to large plain base; tapering flattened ovoid body with sides incurved above base, long neck spreading slightly to plain lip; plain base. Attributed to Midwest on basis of locality in which it was found. Capacity, 6 oz. Height, 5¹¹/₁₆". Greatest width, 2¹⁵/₁₆". Greatest depth, 1⅜" at base.

90. STIEGEL-TYPE BOTTLES, 18th and 20th centuries

"Pocket" bottles Nos. 1, 2, and 3 are representative of plain and pattern-molded vertically and swirl-ribbed types attributed to Stiegel. Though generally described as half-pints, their capacity is usually a few ounces over eight. Their 18th-century form was of Continental ancestry—chunky with greater depth in proportion to height and width than the generality of flasks—perhaps becoming old-fashioned even in Stiegel's period, though occurring sporadically in very early 19th-century midwestern bottles. The rarity of plain bottles like No. 2 suggests that fewer of these were produced than of ribbed and diamond bottles.

Though bottle No. 4 came from England, labeled an "18th-century Bristol field bottle," the half-post and non-lead metal point to the Continent. In the opinion of Dr. Robert J. Charleston of the Victoria and Albert Museum, London, the flask *is* Continental, probably German. In form and half-post it is akin to eastern Pitkin-type flasks. The pattern-molded *honeycomb* or *pearl diaper,* seldom found on American glass, is similar to the "diamonds" of 2 in Color Plate II.

Nos. 5 through 8 are 20th-century flasks. Quite different in form from all the others is No. 5, an imitation Stiegel bottle produced in and imported from Czechoslovakia about 1930. Emil J. Larsen blew the others. In 1887, at the age of ten, he emigrated from Sweden with his father, a glassblower, and he himself became a glassblower, working in many glassworks, including the famous Dorflinger works, White Mills, Pa., and the Durand Glass Works, Vineland, N.J. In 1932 he started his own furnace on his premises in Vineland, and from time to time for about ten years made a wide variety of blown glass. His flasks are mainly in ribbed and diamond patterns. In general they are ovoid, of generous depth, heavier than 18th-century bottles of similar measurements, and usually they have an abrupt neck shorter in proportion to the body height. Although the sizes range from a few ounces to about 1½ pints, "half-pints" and "pints" predominate. The colors are mainly amethysts and blues, rarely pure greens, purple, and red. Today these handsome flasks, representing a brief renaissance of Stiegel-type glass, are deemed collectible in their own right.

Nos. 1, 2, and 3, Collection of the late Melvin Billups; No. 6, Collection of George Austin; Nos. 4, 5, 7, and 8, formerly in the George S. McKearin collection.

Top row:

1. Deep rich amethyst; 20 pronounced vertical ribs from small plain center on base, and widely expanded on body; chunky flattened globular body, long neck, plain lip; pontil mark. Attributed to Stiegel, ca. 1770–74. Capacity, about 11 oz. Height,

5⅜". Greatest width, 3¹³/₁₆". Greatest depth, 2¹/₁₆" below center.

2. Clear amethyst; chunky slightly flattened globular body, long neck flaring at plain lip; pontil mark. Attributed to Stiegel, ca. 1770–74. Capacity, nearly 12 oz. Height, 5". Greatest width, 4½". Greatest depth, 3¹³/₁₆".

3. Light amethyst; 18 pronounced ribs swirled to right; fat ovoid body, long neck spreading to plain lip; pontil mark. Probably Stiegel, ca. 1770–74; found in Shippensburg–Chambersburg, Pa., area. Capacity, about 11 oz. Height, 5⅜". Greatest width, 3⅝". Greatest depth, 2⅝" at center.

Middle row:

4. Deep amethyst; blown by half-post method; patterned in irregular honeycomb diaper with 24 "cells" in horizontal row and described by fine ribs; slender flattened ovoid body, long wide neck spreading to plain lip; flat plain base with much wear, trace of pontil mark. Probably German. 18th century. Capacity, about 12 oz. Height, 6". Greatest width, 3⁷/₁₆". Greatest depth, 2⅝" at center.

5. Amethyst; blown in a full-size two-piece mold having 16 flutes below rows of diamonds; very flattened body with high curved shoulder, sides tapering to small flat elliptical plain base, long wide neck, plain lip; pontil mark. Czechoslovakia. ca. 1930. Capacity, about 8 oz. Height, 4⅞". Greatest width, 3¹³/₁₆". Greatest depth, 2⁵/₁₆", below shoulder. (Illustrated also in *American Glass,* No. 8 in Plate 232.)

6. Brilliant light red; patterned in a 12-diamond four-piece mold having a plain center in base; fat tapering ovoid body, neck with unusual flare to plain lip; pontil mark. Blown by Emil J. Larsen, Vineland, N.J., ca. 1932–42. Capacity, 1 pt. Height, 5¹³/₁₆". Greatest width, 4". Greatest depth, 3³/₁₆", below center.

Bottom row:

7. Deep amethyst; 18 pronounced ribs swirled to right and tooled flat on neck; fat ovoid body, slightly spreading neck, plain lip; pontil mark. Blown by Emil J. Larsen, Vineland, N.J., ca. 1932–42. Capacity, 1 pt. plus. Height, 6". Greatest width 4". Greatest depth, 2⅞", at center.

8. Deep reddish amethyst; 18-rib broken-swirl, ribs from plain center on base, swirled ribs to right, tooled flat on neck; tall flattened ovoid body tapering to short neck, plain lip; faint trace of pontil mark. Blown by Emil J. Larsen, Vineland, N.J., ca. 1932–42. Capacity, about 18 oz. Height, 6¼". Greatest width, 4½". Greatest depth, 3", below center.

91. PATTERN-MOLDED CONTAINERS, mainly early 19th century

With the exception of Nos. 4, 6, and 8, these containers are definitely early 19th-century midwestern examples. Bottles Nos. 1 and 9 and the extremely rare Pitkin-type jug, No. 11, have the popcorn-kernel broken swirl, very rare on containers other than flasks. In collectors' terminology, chestnut flasks like No. 5 holding over a pint but less than a quart are *grandmother* flasks; those like No. 10 holding a quart and more, *grandfather* flasks. Both occur more often in ambers than in aquamarines or very light greens. Fewer grandmother flasks are known than grandfather, which are quite scarce compared with the usual "half-pint" to "pint" pocket bottles. Also, no grandfather flasks have been recorded in reticulated designs. Flasks in an expanded diamond pattern are far less numerous than ribbed; they occur mainly in "half-pint" size, rarely in "pint." Those patterned in a 15-diamond mold, like No. 2, are rare; those in the "Zanesville" 10-diamond mold, like No. 3, are nearly common, though rare in some colors. The flattened ovoid or elliptical forms of Nos. 6, 7, and 8 were popular for pocket bottles in the 18th century. Those with everted lip like No. 6 are often called *nursing bottles;* such usage is uncertain. All have a pontil mark on the bottom.

Nos. 3, 4, 6, 7, 8, and 10, formerly in the George S. McKearin Collection. No. 5, The Henry Ford Museum; No. 11, Collection of the Ohio Historical Society; Nos. 1 (also ex-collection of Alfred B. Maclay), 2, and 9, Collection of Henry G. Schiff.

Top row:

1. Bottle, light green; 24-rib popcorn-kernel broken-swirl, first ribbing swirled to left, second slightly to right; rare taper shape, flanged lip; medium kick-up. Extremely rare in broken swirl. Attributed to Zanesville, O. Capacity, about 6 oz. Height, 6⅛". Greatest diameter, 2¼".

2. Flask, brilliant light green; patterned in small piece-mold having rows of 15 diamonds above 15 flutes; chestnut shape, short cylindrical neck, plain lip; shallow kick-up. Extremely rare. Capacity, about ½ pt. Height, about 4½". Greatest width, 3½". Greatest depth, 2⁵/₁₆". Illustrated also in *American Glass,* No. 13 Plate 235.

3. Flask, brilliant light green; patterned in small two-piece mold having rows of 10 diamonds or ogivals above 10 flutes; chestnut shape, wide cylindrical neck, narrow flanged lip (rare feature); nearly flat base. Attributed to Zanesville, O. Capacity, about ½ pt. Height, 5⅛". Greatest width, 3¾". Greatest depth, 2¹/₁₆" at base. Illustrated also in *American Glass,* No. 15 Plate 235.

4. Bottle, brilliant green-aquamarine; 20 ribs, swirled to right, faint at bottom; barrel-shaped body (rare form), cylindrical neck, everted plain lip; very shallow kick-up. Provenance unknown. Capacity, ½ pt. Height, 4⅛". Greatest diameter, 2¹³/₁₆".

Middle row:

5. Grandmother flask, aquamarine; 24-rib broken-swirl, fading at bottom, first ribbing swirled to right; chestnut shape, cylindrical neck spreading at plain lip; shallow kick-up. Rare size. Midwestern. Capacity, 1 pt. about 14 oz. Height, 7¾". Greatest width, about 5¼". Greatest depth, 3¼" just above base.

6. Pocket bottle, type often called *nursing bottle,* muted light yellow-green; patterned in small two-piece mold with rows of 12 diamonds starting at center base, expanded and elongated on body; flattened long elliptical body tapering at top to short neck, everted plain lip; small rounded base. Eastern, found in South Jersey. Probably late 18th century. Capacity, about 9 oz. Height, 6½". Greatest width, 3". Greatest depth, about 2¾".

7. Pocket bottle, brilliant light green; patterned in a 15-diamond mold; flattened long elliptical body, short neck spreading slightly to plain lip; tiny conical kick-up. Probably Mantua, O., 1822–29. Capacity, about 6 oz. Height, 6⅛". Greatest width, 2⅝". Greatest depth, 1⅝" at shoulder.

8. Pocket bottle, yellow-green; patterned in honeycomb diaper (14 cells in horizontal rows starting from center base) in small two-piece mold; long slender flattened ovoid body tapering at top to cylindrical neck, unusual sloping turned-over collar; tiny conical kick-up. Provenance unknown, possibly foreign. Late 18th–early 19th century. Capacity, 1 pt. about 3 oz. Height, 7⅛". Greatest width, 3¹³/₁₆". Greatest depth, 2⁵/₁₆" at bottom.

Bottom row:

9. Bottle, brilliant light green; 24-rib popcorn-kernel broken-swirl, one ribbing swirled to left, other to right; globular body, cylindrical neck, flat turned-over collar; medium kick-up. Extremely rare. Midwestern. Capacity, 1 qt. about 1 oz. Height, 7½". Greatest diameter, 5".

10. Grandfather flask, brilliant aquamarine; 24 ribs, swirled to right, converging at slightly off-center point on base; fat chestnut body, cylindrical neck, plain lip; shallow kick-up. Probably Zanesville, O. Rare size in aquamarine. Capacity, 1 qt. about 4 oz. Height, 7¾". Greatest width, 6⁵/₁₆". Greatest depth, 3⅝" at top.

11. Pitkin-type jug, blue-aquamarine; half-post terminating irregularly well below neck; 32-rib broken-swirl, first ribbing swirled to right; ovoid body, short cylindrical neck, heavy sloping collar applied around plain lip; applied circular foot; applied strap handle with medial rib and wide flat end with turned-back triangular tip. Extremely rare. Possibly Mantua, O., 1822–29. Capacity, 1 pt. about 13 oz. Height, 7⅛". Greatest diameter, 4¼".

Part VI

PATTERN–MOLDED BOTTLES, FLASKS, AND JUGS

When and where pattern molds were first used in America is undetermined. There is no doubt in the minds of most students that pattern-molded glass, including pocket bottles, was blown in Henry William Stiegel's Manheim glassworks (Pennsylvania, 1765–74). However, though it is probable the first colonial pattern-molded table glass was produced at Manheim, it is possible (I believe probable) that pattern-molded flasks and other containers were blown earlier at Wistarburgh and in other 18th-century glasshouses. They would be, of course, as European as were the men who blew them and whose apprentices followed the same technical and stylistic paths. Styles were tenacious; changes came slowly, and often the old appeared alongside the new. Not until after 1800, so far as has been learned, did distinctive American forms and treatments evolve, and then in midwestern glasshouses of the Pittsburgh–Monongahela region, the Wheeling–Wellsburg area in (West) Virginia, and in Ohio.

However, whether of Continental or midwestern type, whether eastern or midwestern, no category of American bottles and flasks gives more aesthetic satisfaction to the collector than the pattern-molded.

Even the uninitiated and casual viewer is not immune to their appealing individuality and fascinating colors, the charm and effectiveness of which are enhanced by the subtle lights and shades of the molded and expanded designs, even of simple vertical ribbing. To the collector's eye, each bottle, flask, or rare jug—containers all, in present-day parlance—is an individual, skillfully and, it often seems, lovingly fashioned but seldom, if ever, constrained within the exacting requirements of capacity and shape that were soon to be met by use of the full-size piece mold, which ensured standard measure and uniform shape. Although the role of the pattern mold was vital in "costuming" these containers by impressing a design in the glass, it was not the star role. That was played by craftsmanship, for in essence the containers were free-blown.

The method of fabricating pattern-molded glass that produced such pleasing results is familiar to most old-timers in the field. So, too, are the terms *pattern mold*, *pattern-molded*, *dip mold*, *small piece-mold*, and *part-size piece mold* commonly used in connection with the process. However, for the neophyte as well as the seasoned informed collector, knowledge of production methods adds that extra dollop of appreciation that understanding of techniques brings to the enjoyment of creations in any art or craft medium. Thus the terms require translation into meaningful language.

1
PATTERN MOLDS AND PATTERN MOLDING

The terms *pattern mold* and *pattern-molded* or *pattern molding* have been solidly rooted in the American glass antiquarians' special language for over 50 years. Apparently, as used by American glass collectors and students, they were not transplanted from the glassman's cant but were germinated by laymen to tersely designate certain types of molds in the glassman's equipment and their use in glassmaking. So far as I have been able to learn, *pattern mold*, which led logically to *pattern-molded* and *pattern molding*, first appeared in literature on American glass in Frederick William Hunter's *Stiegel Glass*, published in 1914, a time when collectors of American glass were few indeed. Hunter, in describing the process by which certain "Stiegel" wares were made, stated "the pieces [were] impressed in the early stages of the making with a design obtained from a small 'pattern-mold.' "[1] (Thereafter he dropped the quotes.) Thus, pattern mold means simply a mold for the purpose of impressing a design on an unformed gather of metal but not of producing the final shape of the gather. And the term *pattern-molded,* or *pattern molding,* designates the means by which the pattern on a finished article was obtained; it also indicates that shape was not the business of the mold but of the glassblower.

The process was simple and, unless the gather was exceptionally heavy or only slightly expanded, it produced characteristics peculiar to glass so patterned. The blower would insert the gather of metal into the mold, pushing it or, in some cases, blowing to inflate it against the patterned sides of the mold so that the pattern was impressed upon the receptive soft glass. Withdrawing the gather, he would proceed to fashion the desired article by blowing and manipulation—free-blowing. In the process, inevitably, the original impression was altered, in particular by expansion of the pattern on the body of the piece and, on small-necked vessels, by shrinkage below and on the neck. It is because the gather was expanded *after* molding and *during* the free-blowing

that the adjective *expanded* is so often used to modify the design—*expanded vertical ribbing*, *expanded diamond*, and so on. In examining pattern-molded open-top vessels such as bowls and pitchers, Hunter determined that this type of molding and the expansion produced a relationship between inner and outer surfaces different from that on pieces blown in full-size piece molds. Normally, pattern-molded pieces have exactly corresponding inner and outer contours. For example, a rib on the outside has a corresponding rib on the inside. On the other hand, pieces blown in full-size piece molds in which relief decoration as well as shape was obtained normally have concavo-convex surfaces—that is, a protuberance on the outside has a corresponding hollow on the inside, and vice versa. This relationship may not maintain if the gather used was *large* in relation to the size of the article fashioned, in which case the inner surface would be smooth and even, as it is on mechanically pressed glass, and the walls thick.

As stated in Part II, Section 1, "Ancestry of Bottles Used and Made in America," both types of molds were employed in the fabrication of Roman glass, but apparently they gradually fell into disuse in western Europe during the dissolution of the Empire and when the art of glass was marking time. Just when they again were revived as part of Western glassmen's equipment is uncertain. Gustav Pazurek has stated that in Germany "grooves and ribs impressed with wooden forms were popular even by the end of the Middle Ages." Certainly in the 15th century, if not sooner, some species of pattern molds were being used in Venice and elsewhere on the Continent. In England rib molds were used by the latter half of that century.[2] Inasmuch as the term of service of an individual wooden mold doubtless would have been comparatively short because of wear and the charring by hot plastic glass, more durable materials must soon have become normal. Perhaps even in the Middle Ages metal pattern molds were made. Copper and brass were definitely

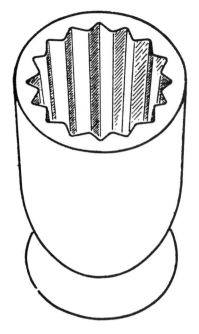
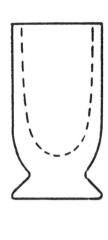

92. Dip mold, grooved to produce ribs, commonly called a rib mold; based on photographs and description of the 16-rib mold presumably used at the New Geneva Glass Works, formerly owned by Logan Ross, now in the Collection of The Corning Museum of Glass. Height 5″. Inside depth, 4½″.

used in the 1500s and 1600s in some European glassworks; also marble. "Several sorts of Iron Molds" were among the tools listed by C. Merritt as equipment used at English green-glass furnaces in the 17th century.[3] Presumably those used in American glasshouses were usually iron or brass.

Whatever the material of the so-called pattern molds, they were of two distinct types. One was a dip mold, such as that shown in Ill. 92, a seamless block or form hollowed at the center, with sides in a slight downward taper as shown in cross sections 2 and 3 of Ill. 93B. The name was appropriate, since the blower might be said to "dip" his gather in the mold, pressing or inflating it against the pattern and quickly withdrawing it. In such a one-piece mold, of course, a pattern could consist only of vertical elements in alternate intaglio and convex or flat surfaces. Otherwise the molded impression—one of diamonds or swirled ribs, for example—would have been distorted as the patterned gather was withdrawn from the mold. In other words, if a gather of glass was to be patterned in any design composed of, or including, crossed or curved lines *and* removed from the mold with the pattern intact, a mold that could be opened and shut was a necessity. Thus the piece mold was the second kind of pattern mold,

the kind used for diamonded or other reticulated and elaborate designs and sometimes—probably rarely—for vertical or, as in 3 of Ill. 93B, swirled ribs.

Over the centuries, the dip molds functioning as pattern molds have varied considerably in width and depth as well as grooving. So far as I know, the earliest representation of the dip mold appeared in Agricola's illustration of a 16th-century glasshouse interior (Ill. 2). Two shallow dip molds were shown, without doubt the sort used in the German forest glasshouse in Agricola's lifetime, which he probably also saw when he visited Italy, where they doubtless were used much earlier. One, it will be noted, was square with concave scalloped center; the other, circular with deep V-shaped grooves. Similar molds appeared in Blancourt's illustration of a 17th-century glasshouse interior so nearly identical with Agricola's as to suggest pirating. However, among the glassmaker's tools that Blancourt illustrated were two deep molds, one nearly cylindrical and the other triangular, without any pattern inside. It may be that grooved, deep dip molds were a later development: the plain dip mold 1 and ribbed mold 2 of Ill. 93B were taken from illustrations of tools used in a French *verrerie en bois* in the last third of the 18th century, if not earlier, in the production of drinking vessels and other utensils.[4] It would appear that in American 18th- and early 19th-century glasshouses, the deep dip mold was preferred to pattern the glass for ribbed and fluted bottles, flasks, and jugs, such as those shown in Ills. 51, 87 through 91, and 94 through 100.

Although it was the vertical grooves that produced ribs on the glass and the convex scallops that produced fluting, the molds have long been called rib molds, generally with a numerical prefix indicating the number of ribs impressed on the glass. One type, shown in Ill. 92, was based on a photograph and description of a 16-rib mold from the New Geneva Glass Works, New Geneva, Pennsylvania, formerly owned by Logan Ross, a descendant of one of the founders of the glassworks. Mr. Ross also inherited a 20-rib mold and a 16-diamond small piece-mold. (All three molds are now in the collection of The Corning Museum of Glass.) The 20-rib mold is a little wider and deeper than the 16-rib mold.[5] This fact led to the conclusion that, as might be expected, when spacing of the grooves was the same, the greater the number of ribs the larger the mold. Study of ribbed pieces has revealed also that individual rib molds varied in depth of grooving, spacing between intaglio and flat or convex surfaces, and

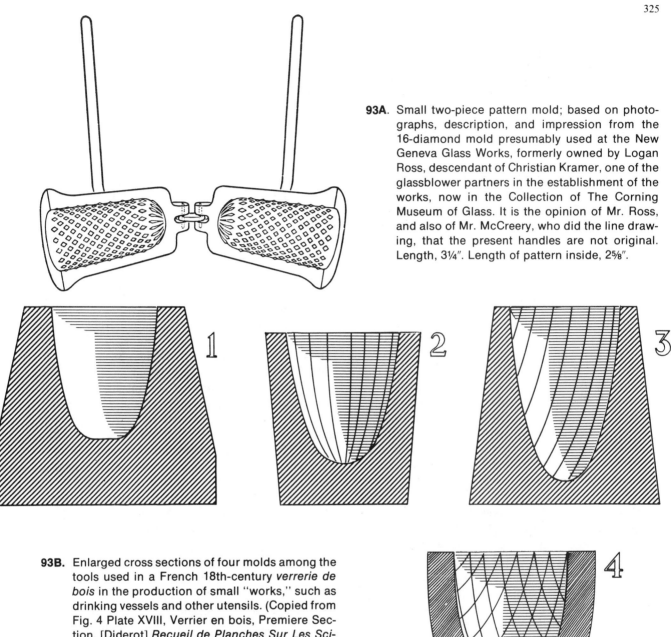

93A. Small two-piece pattern mold; based on photographs, description, and impression from the 16-diamond mold presumably used at the New Geneva Glass Works, formerly owned by Logan Ross, descendant of Christian Kramer, one of the glassblower partners in the establishment of the works, now in the Collection of The Corning Museum of Glass. It is the opinion of Mr. Ross, and also of Mr. McCreery, who did the line drawing, that the present handles are not original. Length, 3¼″. Length of pattern inside, 2⅝″.

93B. Enlarged cross sections of four molds among the tools used in a French 18th-century *verrerie de bois* in the production of small "works," such as drinking vessels and other utensils. (Copied from Fig. 4 Plate XVIII, Verrier en bois, Premiere Section, [Diderot] *Recueil de Planches Sur Les Sciences, Les Arts Liberaux et Les Arts Mechaniques,* Avec leur Explication, Paris, 1771.)

The caption for Fig. 4 says only that it consists of molds, grooved and plain, for blowing the "postes" (i.e., gathers of molten glass) and molding them. The scale of measurement given is in pouces and pieds and, as applied to the molds, translates into about 7″ in height and about 4¼″ to 5¼″ in top diameter. From the text, it is apparent that these molds were generally made of copper, whereas those for bottles such as "black" and other beverage bottles were of brass. The plain dip mold, identified here as No. 1, was a one-piece mold. The vertically ribbed mold, No. 2, probably was a two-piece mold, since the text refers only to No. 1 as a one-piece mold. However, that ribbed one-piece molds were used also is

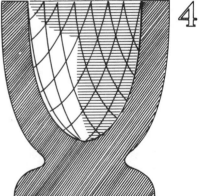

evident from the illustration of one in Plate XIX—a thin-walled truncated cone, fluted on the inside. The spirally ribbed and the diamond mold, Nos. 3 and 4, were two-piece molds, of which the shutting and closing device, presumably handles, was not drawn.

the termination of the ribs in the bottom of the mold. The spaces between grooves varied from pronounced to practically no space at all, with the inner surface in contiguous convex or concave scallops— the convex producing a flutelike pattern and the concave, a ribbed. In some molds the ribbing faded into a plain center at the bottom. In some, the ribs had rounded or pointed ends around a plain center. In others, they converged at the center, as in the New Geneva molds. In still others, the ribs ran to a small or large nipple or to a terminal ring. However, as anyone interested in discovering the characteristics of the mold in which a particular piece was patterned will find, it is often either difficult or impossible to determine positively the type of grooving in the mold—except perhaps for a glassmaker. In part this is because the end result of the original impression depended upon the degree of expansion in blowing and of manipulation in forming the vessel. Also, it is only occasionally possible to ascertain with certainty the termination of the ribbing in the bottom of the mold because, on most pieces, the pontil mark destroyed or concealed the evidence. And sometimes the ribbing at the bottom or on the base of a vessel was obliterated in the process of fabrication.

Whatever its number, size, spacing, or ending, as the ribbing came from the mold it was vertical, but it could be swirled and combined with swirled. Also, whatever the direction of the ribbing, the ribs were expanded on the body of the vessel and, in the course of fabrication, were drawn close together at the top of the body and on the neck, however far apart they may have been in the mold. From the surviving bottles, flasks, and jugs, it would seem that swirled ribbing was more popular than vertical, particularly in the Midwest. It was obtained by simply twisting or swirling the vertically ribbed gather of glass before and/or during the formation of the vessel. Still more attractive is the combination of vertical and swirled, christened *broken swirl* by collectors. After the first pattern molding, the ribs were swirled. Then the gather was again inserted into a mold and expanded to impress vertical ribs upon the swirled, thereby breaking their continuous line. Occasionally the second ribbing was swirled slightly in the direction opposite to the first. Usually the mold used for the second ribbing had the same number of ribs; in fact, usually the same mold was used, but occasionally a mold of a different number of ribs was used, as in the case of 10 in Ill. 94.

As I have mentioned previously, piece molds were a necessity for designs having any crossing or curving lines, and apparently several kinds of piece molds served as pattern molds. One resembled a small antique waffle-iron (Ill. 93A); it definitely was used in American glasshouses by the late 18th century. Another, as shown by cross sections in the French *Recueil de Planches sur les Sciences*, *Les Arts Liberaux et Les Arts Méchaniques* . . . (1771), was a sturdy mold (Ill. 93B Nos. 3 and 4), similar in forms, and presumably weight, to the one-piece dip molds and used in the French *verrerie en bois*. It should be noted that whatever device (probably handles) served to open and close the French molds was not included in the drawing. Since the only pictorial evidence I have found of this kind of ribbed and diamonded piece mold is French, the term *French* will be used to differentiate it from the small waffle-iron type. However, it seems unlikely that these French pattern molds were used in France only, and likely that some glassblowers in America were familiar with them. In studies of early 19th-century midwestern hollow ware made by Miles A. Smith, Earl Seigfred, and James H. Rose, two readily discernible mold seams were found on several pieces, all patterned in 24-rib piece molds. These pieces established the existence of three or four vertically ribbed (24 ribs) two-piece molds that were used in the Midwest.[6] My own studies have shown that a 14-rib and a 28-rib two-piece, vertically ribbed mold were used to pattern gathers for smelling bottles and that a 24-rib mold was used to pattern Mexican hollow ware of this century—including bottles closely resembling the midwestern globulars. The small number of these molds now known and the small number of recorded pieces patterned in them suggests limited use. Although the kind of pattern piece-mold used cannot be determined at present, it seems to me that the French is a definite possibility. One reason is that the French type was, apparently, more stable and substantial than the waffle-iron type.

However, when one considers the small "waffle-iron" piece mold, one finds sound evidence testifying to its use in American glasshouses. This type of pattern mold is still occasionally called a part-size mold (Hunter's term), but in general it has for many years been designated by the equally lay term *small piece-mold*—the example shown in Ill. 93A is only 3¼ inches in outside length. Both terms have been useful in distinguishing it from the full-size piece mold, the inner surface of which was the size and shape of a particular vessel. The two pieces, or leaves, of the small piece-mold were hinged together, and a handle for opening and closing the pieces was attached to each half, as on some old-fashioned waffle irons. The mold illustrated in Ill.

93A was based on a description, a photograph, and an impression from the 16-diamond mold sent to me by its former owner, Logan Ross. (For convenience, pattern molds in a diamond or ogival diaper pattern have been designated by "glass antiquarians" by the number of diamonds in a horizontal row.) Its history leaves no doubt that this particular small piece-mold was used at the New Geneva Glass Works, New Geneva and Greensburgh, Pennsylvania, and quite likely at New Bremen in Maryland. The late Harry Hall White found that similar molds were used in the early 20th century at the Mount Washington Glass Works of the Pairpoint Corporation, New Bedford, Massachusetts.[7] Hence it seems safe to assume the New Geneva mold was typical of the small piece-molds used, perhaps over a span of 150 years or more, in American glasshouses for reticulated and elaborate designs such as those of the bottles, flasks, and jug shown in Ills. 91 and 97 through 100—and perhaps for ribbed patterns too.

Although both small piece-molds and ribbed dip molds probably were part of the equipment in most early American glasshouses producing bottles and flasks, it would appear that the latter predominated. In addition to the extant 16-rib and 20-rib New Geneva molds, dip molds having 21 different numbers of ribs have been determined. But 23 was not the limit of the molds: variety in type of grooving and termination of the grooves in molds having the same number of ribs considerably extends the actual number of rib molds used at one time or another in various eastern and midwestern glassworks. Also, almost certainly, in many instances there was more than one mold having the same number of ribs *and* the same type of grooving and termination in the bottom of the mold. On the other hand, the number and variety of piece molds, even including the aforementioned ribbed piece molds, appears to have been limited. At present I have record of only 15 with reticulated patterns, two or three for the checkered diamond, one each for the Stiegel-type diamond-daisy and daisy-in-hexagon. Of these, all but the New Geneva 16-diamond mold were determined from examination of actual containers.

Few pattern molds, either ribbed dip molds or piece molds, have been identified, and there is no evidence those few were the exclusive property of the works. In some cases, tradition and the geographical area where pieces patterned in molds of certain rib and diamond (or ogival) count were discovered has led to association of the mold with a particular works or area; later, the same sort of evidence has connected the same number of ribs or diamonds with other works. Though Harry Hall White's excavations established that a 16-rib, a 32-rib, and a 15-diamond mold were used at the Mantua Glass Works, Mantua, Ohio, and a 20-rib mold at the nearby Kent glassworks, the fact remains that molds of the same units were used elsewhere. As mentioned above, 16-rib and 20-rib molds were used at New Geneva.[8] True, the ribs in the Mantua 16-rib mold ran to a terminal ring and, in the New Geneva 16-rib mold, converged at center bottom, but neither was unique in its terminal characteristics. Nevertheless, there has been an unfortunate tendency among collectors and dealers to attribute a piece of glass to a specific glassworks or area because it had the number of ribs or diamonds in molds associated with that glassworks or area.

There are many more reasons for shying away from rib or diamond count as the sole basis for attribution. Certainly not all molds became scrap iron as soon as the fires of a doomed glassworks were extinguished forever. It is a fair assumption that the molds of the short-lived Mantua Glass Works (1822–29) became part of another works' equipment, purchased for it or carried to it by one of the glassblowers. Like glassmen—and sometimes with them—molds traveled from one glassworks to another. Presumably when John Frederick Magnus Amelung, son of John Frederick Amelung, left the Baltimore glassworks to go to James O'Hara's Pittsburgh Glass Works, he took molds with him. At least O'Hara, writing to Amelung on July 30, 1805, said: "Should you think proper you are very right in procuring the molds, I wish you to have them complete."[9] Whereas "procuring" might indicate Amelung planned to have molds made in Baltimore for him, it seems more likely to me that he referred to molds he had for use in the shaky Baltimore glassworks between 1800 and 1805, and that the molds probably had been used previously at the New Bremen Glassmanufactory. It is frustrating that there is no evidence as to the kind of molds Amelung suggested he take to Pittsburgh, but O'Hara's "complete" suggests that pattern molds as well as molds for shaping wine and porter bottles were among them. It is probable, too, that the molds used at New Geneva were among the tools that the German glassblower-partners brought with them in 1797, and that they had been used at the New Bremen Glassmanufactory, where the blowers had practiced their art until the failure of John F. Amelung & Company in 1795. They may even have been part of the equipment brought from Germany by Amelung and his associates in 1784.[10]

Still another factor in the problem of molds is their

common source, for few works were equipped to produce their own molds. It seems likely that many molds used in the early midwestern glassworks were made in Pittsburgh foundries. In the East, foundries in or not far distant from coastal urban centers would have been possible sources. Last, it must be kept in mind that many pattern-molded 18th-century flasks, bottles, and articles of tableware had the same

number of ribs or diamonds as those blown in the 19th century, and some were foreign-made. Therefore it seems obvious that in *themselves* the number of diamonds in a horizontal row or of ribs cannot constitute a basis for attribution to a specific glassworks or period. In fact, a wise rule is: Do not attribute a piece to a glassworks on the basis of the number of ribs or diamonds *alone*.

2
PITKIN-TYPE BOTTLES AND FLASKS

An outstanding class of early American pattern-molded ribbed containers is the so-called *Pitkin type*, in which flasks are numerous; bottles, rare; jugs and jars, extremely rare. These containers, several of which are pictured in Ills. 87 through 89, were made by the so-called German half-post method and are of Continental ancestry. By this method, the initial gather of metal was first slightly inflated and then dipped into the metal for a half-post—that is, a second layer that did not cover the full length of the first gather or post; in collectors' language, *double dipped*. Half a century or more ago, someone ignorant of the half-post method explained the curious thickening that ended on the shoulder of a flask as evidence of an "inserted" neck. For years collectors fostered the misconception that the neck was inserted *after* the body was formed, and even today the term *inserted neck* crops up. Such an impractical feat of glassblowing was not practiced.

The half-post method must have evolved because the half-post gave the body an advantage over a single-gather vessel by thickening and thus strengthening the walls, increasing resistance to the inherent fragility of glass. By the latter half of the 1600s the method was used in European production of square or case bottles, if not other forms, and presumably was employed in making pocket bottles at some point in the 18th century, if not earlier. In the case of Pitkin-type bottles and flasks, the half-post was patterned in a rib mold *after* the second gather was made. There was one insertion in a mold if vertical or spiral ribbing was desired and a second if the broken-swirl was to be the final decoration. The method and rib molds undoubtedly were introduced by Continental glassblowers into more than one American glasshouse, perhaps first at Wistarburgh about 1740. Nevertheless, *all* flasks so made and

decorated were *Pitkins* to our pioneer bottle collectors.

The name was adopted in the period when knowledge of American glassworks and their products was limited to what was published in Barber's and Hunter's pioneer books on American glass, and to word-of-mouth news of collectors' discoveries of other glassworks. And, like the terms *Stiegel*, *Wistarburgh*, and *Ludlow*, *Pitkin* originally indicated a specific factory origin. This was inevitable, since apparently the first of the flasks known to collectors were attributed by family and local history to the Pitkins' East Hartford glassworks, at East Hartford, Connecticut. (East Hartford became Manchester in 1823.) Though, long ago, *Pitkin* was stripped of its factory significance and invested with a generic one, it still misleads newcomers to the field of bottle collecting, but it is too deeply rooted to be eradicated. Anyway, understood to designate a class, it is a handy convention and the addition of the word *type* dissociates the particularization. However, though *Pitkin-type* entered the vocabulary of glass terms some years ago, more often than not, in common usage, *type* is as silent as a cockney's *h*.

For many years American flasks of this type in olive-greens and olive-ambers, like 2 and 3, 6 and 7, and 9 through 11 in Ill. 88, were considered a product *only* of the Pitkin glassworks. This glassworks, built in 1783, enjoyed no success until around 1791, but local history says it operated until about 1830 when, having exhausted their wood lots, the owners faced a fuel problem beyond their financial solution.[11] Although various sorts of containers were the main product, no definite *proof* that Pitkin-type flasks were made at the Pitkin works is known at present, and no extensive excavation that might unearth such proof has been made on the glasshouse site. On the other hand, local and family histories insisting that "Pitkins" were blown at Keene, New Hampshire, were substantiated in the late 1920s. Harry Hall White's excavations and researches proved that olive-green and olive-amber Pitkin-type flasks with ribbing swirled to either right or left and in broken-swirl were produced at the Marlboro-Street glassworks started in Keene, New Hampshire, in 1815. Later, his digs at Coventry, Connecticut, a few miles from Hartford, revealed that the same types were produced at the Coventry Glass Works, which was started in 1813. Also, the majority of ribbed shards unearthed there were from flasks patterned in a 36-rib mold. Excavations on the Glastenbury glassworks' site in 1962 indicated still another source of Pitkin-type flasks. This works, unknown until about fifteen years ago, was likewise not far from Hartford, and according to the findings of Kenneth M. Wilson while curator of Old Sturbridge Village, apparently operated from the spring of 1816 into the late 1820s or perhaps as late as 1833.[12] Another probable (I feel, almost certain) Connecticut source was the East Hartford glassworks established by John Mather and operated from 1805 perhaps into the early 1830s. Possibly such flasks were among the bottles in the "100 Crates Glass Bottles of a quality superior to any made at these or any other works in the country being thick, handsomely finished and of the best glass . . . on hand at the New Glass House in East Hartford" and advertised by John Mather in January 1806.[13] One source outside New England was the Gloucester Glassworks at Clementon, New Jersey, which is said to have operated from around 1800 until about 1825. In the fall of 1962 and in 1963, Richmond Morcom unearthed fragments of many Pitkin-type flasks blown from aquamarine, olive-amber, and olive-green glass and patterned in vertical and in broken-swirl ribbing. Among the first fragments he found, I saw part of a neck and shoulder on which the ribbing termination was similar to that characteristic of New England varieties.

All this does not mean, however, that *no* Pitkin-type flasks were blown at the Pitkins' glassworks, in which the span of operation overlapped Keene's and Coventry's, Mather's and Glastenbury and Clementon. In fact, one reasonably assumes that they were, not only because of local and family tradition (by themselves alone, weak links in attribution) but also because, apparently, the type was common before the end of the 18th century. If not imported—and importation seems unlikely[14]—the pint and half-pint dram bottles advertised in Hartford's *American Mercury* on April 21, 1788, may have been Pitkin-

type blown in the nearby Pitkin works. So too may have been the half-pint drams advertised in the same paper on July 19, 1790, with the bait phrase "suitable to carry the comfort of life into the field." (As has been pointed out in *Bottle Family Names*, in the 18th and early 19th centuries *dram bottle* and *pocket bottle* were more common names than *flask* for an individual's private container ranging in size from a few ounces to a pint or a little more.)

But, as remarked above, not only the New England varieties were christened *Pitkin*: all ribbed flasks made by the half-post method, in whatever locality they might be found, were called *Pitkin*, and usually attributed by dealer and collector alike to the Pitkin glassworks. Thus the name embraced many that may have emanated from other eastern glassworks of the 1700s and very early 1800s, as well as the distinctively different "Pitkin-types" found west of the Allegheny Mountains. In some quarters even the idea of midwestern origin was resisted, as it long was for pressed lacy glass, until Harry Hall White unearthed evidence that both amber and aquamarine ribbed flasks had been made by the half-post method in the Mantua Glass Works, Ohio. Then geographical distribution and high incidence of the distinctive types found in the midwestern area were accepted as evidence of midwestern origin. Although Mantua is still the only proven source, it is now generally conceded that Pitkin-type flasks were blown in other and earlier midwestern glasshouses producing containers—as most of them did. In fact, it seems a safe assumption that probably nine out of ten Pitkin-type flasks found in midwestern homes were blown in a midwestern glassworks.

The tenth is reserved for an immigrant in the pocket or possession of a settler from the East: not surprisingly, eastern Pitkin-type flasks have been found in northern Ohio, brought by settlers, mainly Connecticut Yankees migrating to New Connecticut—The Western Reserve—so long a "province" of their state. But, insofar as is known at present, eastern bottle products were not shipped to western markets in the period these flasks were popular. Nor did midwestern bottle products actually invade eastern markets, though there is evidence of attempted raids on that of Philadelphia. For instance, O'Hara & Craig, then proprietors of the Pittsburgh Glass Works, advertised in Philadelphia newspapers from March 1800 to March 1801. The products offered included "Bottles of all kinds and of any quantity . . . together with pocket flasks . . . at least 25 percent lower than articles of the same quality brought from any of the seaports of the United

States."[15] At that time the 25 percent may have tempted bargain-minded Philadelphians, to whom wares even from other states were still considered "imports." Of course whether or not Pitkin-type flasks were among the pocket flasks is a matter of conjecture. They may have been. There is also the possibility the pocket flasks were unpatterned or pattern-molded and blown from a single gather of glass.

Starting from the shards unearthed at Coventry, Keene, and Mantua, and relying heavily on geographical distribution, comparative study of Pitkin-type flasks has established certain combinations of physical characteristics as indigenous to New England—that is, Keene–Connecticut—and others, to the Midwest: characteristics typically distinctive and differentiating certain varieties from one area, from those of the other. However, if Mrs. Knittle is correct in her statement that the head workmen at the Pitkin glassworks were from New Jersey,[16] then probably there were Pitkin-type flasks from early South Jersey houses like or closely similar to those from New England. Nevertheless, for the present I shall not broaden the area of these particular varieties to "eastern." New England "Pitkin-types" are shown by 2, 3, 6, 7, 9, 10, and 11 in Ill. 88.

Of New England "Pitkin-types," it may be said that, in general:

1. They are comparatively light in weight in spite of the half-post.

2. The predominating shape is ovoid, tapering to the top and normally flattened, so that it might be said to have wide sides and narrow ends. And usually the depth—that is, the diameter from front to back of the sides—is greatest near the bottom of the flask.

3. Often there is slight concavity on the sides a bit above the bottom of the flask. This feature may have been an unintentional idiosyncrasy given by a particular glassblower or characteristic of a particular glassworks.

4. The ribbing is fine, narrow, patterned mainly in 32-rib and 36-rib molds in which the grooves forming the ribs apparently were contiguous. Swirled and broken-swirl ribbing occurs far more frequently than vertical. In the broken-swirl, the second ribbing terminates, as a rule, well below the swirled, sometimes three-quarters of an inch or more, and the swirled ends below the top of the half-post. Occasionally the closeness of the two ribbings produces a popcorn kernel effect, and sometimes the second ribbing is swirled slightly from the perpendicular. With very few exceptions, the swirl of the broken-swirl was to the right on the many flasks examined.

5. The sizes are mainly from about a half-pint to about a pint, with pints outnumbering the smaller sizes, or at least surviving in greater number. A few have been recorded that hold about a quarter-pint and one, even less than a gill.

6. The normal color range is limited to shades of olive-green and olive-amber, although some are a deep clear green. Possibly these were blown at Keene. Considered in the light of the wide color range of early Keene sunburst and Masonic flasks (see Charts, Groups III and IV), this true green would not be unexpected in Keene Pitkin-types.

As of the moment, three amethyst Pitkin-type flasks of around half-pint capacity are known. Two are definitely New England in form. One of them (once owned by Charles B. Gardner), very brilliant in color, was patterned in a 32-rib mold, and the fine ribbing was swirled to the right. Its ovoid form is slightly concave on one side above the bottom of the flask. The second, whereabouts now unknown, is so deep an amethyst as to appear black in reflected light. Because of its similarity in color to a few "IP" (Justus Perry) Masonic flasks (GIV–1 in the Flasks Charts) blown at Keene-Marlboro-Street, and the fact that that factory produced Pitkin-type flasks, Keene origin seems not unlikely. The Gardner amethyst flask may also have been a Keene product. The ovoid body of the third amethyst Pitkin-type wears the broken-swirl, with swirl to the right. Unfortunately, it has been impossible to ascertain the number of ribs or the profile. From its photograph, it would appear to have no less than 24 ribs and probably at least 32, and its greatest depth appears nearer the center than the bottom of the flask. It is illustrated by No. 6 in Plate 233 of *American Glass,* described as "type unidentified," and recorded as in the Henry Francis du Pont Collection. Later, it was owned by Richard Loeb and was illustrated on page 17, No. 88, in the Parke-Bernet sale catalog of the Richard Loeb Collection, 1947. No mention is made of the half-post, which is clearly visible in the illustration. The catalog attribution to the Midwest apparently was made by the late Neil C. Gest, from whom it was acquired, but on what basis cannot now be ascertained. Judged by its photograph, it is not a typical midwestern Pitkin-type flask.

Midwestern Pitkin-type flasks are more varied than those of New England, possibly indicating wider-spread production beginning at a later date and perhaps less influence from the early Continental prototype. Of midwestern Pitkin-type flasks, it may be said in general that:

1. They are, as a rule, heavier than the New England, for more metal was used in their fabrication.

2. Their forms are of three general types. The predominating form, which in our experience never occurs in the New England flasks, is the wide, flattened globular, like 8 and 9 of Ill. 90, often approaching the circular, as does 1 in Ill. 88. Normally the greatest depth is at the shoulder, but in many instances the depth is approximately the same from top to bottom. A second, and only occasional, form has a bulbous body, a carryover of an 18th-century form similar to some Stiegel-type pocket bottles, as in the case of 2 in Ill. 89. The third form, shown by 4, 5, and 10 in the same illustration, is the flattened ovoid, but it will be noted that the taper at the top is more curved and less abrupt than that of most New England Pitkin-type, and the greatest depth, like the width, is usually about the middle of the body.

3. The ribbing was obtained in a greater variety of molds: primarily, 16-, 20-, 24-, and 32-rib molds; occasionally 26-, 30-, and 36-rib molds; rarely, a 44-rib mold; possibly, a 19-rib mold. In general, the ribbing is heavier than on the New England, frequently with heavy swirling toward the top of the half-post. Although the ribbing is vertical or swirled on many of the flasks, the broken swirl, often popcorn kernel, predominates. And, in the broken swirl with few exceptions, the terminations of the swirled and vertical ribbing on the half-post nearly coincide, or the vertical ends only a little below the swirled.

4. Again "pints" appear to have outnumbered flasks of less capacity—hardly surprising in an age when a single dram was little comfort. Rare indeed are those, like 3 in Ill. 89, holding less than six or eight ounces, and even rarer is one like 10 in the same illustration, of quart capacity, practically disqualifying it as a pocket bottle.

5. By and large, the metal of the midwestern Pitkin-type flasks is more brilliant than that of the eastern; the colors more vibrant and their spectrum wider. Rarely, if ever, is the glass of the same olive-green and olive-amber of New England flasks. The colors are chiefly *clear* greens in many shades, ambers from golden to brown tones, and aquamarine.

A midwestern bottle and a flask of about half-pint capacity have been recorded in a brilliant violet blue. The bottle, now in The Corning Museum of Glass, has an ovoid, almost barrel-shaped, body. The flask, in the Lorimer Collection in the Philadelphia Museum of Art, has the characteristic flattened globular form with greatest width and depth at the shoulder. Both were twice patterned in a 16-rib mold for the broken swirl; the first ribbing was swirled to the right. The bottle was found in a home in Ohio but unaccompanied by any tradition or history of origin. Where the Lorimer flask turned up is unrecorded.

As would be expected, not all Pitkin-type flasks fit neatly under either "New England" or "midwestern." There are many instances in which neither the New England nor the midwestern mantle fits a particular Pitkin-type flask—without doubtful alteration. Among the mavericks that intriguingly excite speculation are flasks like 5 and 8 in Ill. 88 and 4 and 9 in Ill. 87. Since there is now no record of where they were found, there is not even a geographical hint as to possible origin. Those in Ill. 88 have both New England and midwestern features. Also, the golden amber color of 5 would seem to preclude New England and to point westward, as does the collar and the termination of the ribbing on the half-post. The flasks in Ill. 87, I believe, may be 18th century, in part because they were blown from a dull, muted, yellowish green glass rarely seen in bottles made after the turn of the century. Moreover, 4, patterned in a 20-rib mold, was given the 18th-century chunky, flattened globular body similar to some of the Stiegel-type pocket bottles, in which Pitkin-type flasks are rarely found. It must be admitted, however, that flasks so very 18th century in feeling might have been blown in the *early* years of the 1800s in the Midwest, where the influence of 18th-century shapes and features lingered on in some commercial products longer than it seems to have in the East. The New Geneva Glass Works—both the first on George Creek just outside the village of New Geneva and the new, built in 1807, across the Monongahela in Greensburgh—and the Pittsburgh Glass Works seem probable producers of Pitkin-type flasks. Bottles were blown at both these glassworks just before 1800, and among the products of the Pittsburgh Glass Works advertised in 1800/1801 were "Pocket bottles."[17] Of more possible significance is the fact that, in the early years of both works, the glassblowers were from Germany or had been trained by Continental blowers.

As for possible eastern 18th-century sources of Pitkin-type flasks, there were several works besides the Pitkins' in which the strong—in fact, predominant—influence of Continental techniques, together with the functional sturdiness of the type of flask, may have led to their production, albeit perhaps in limited quantities. Of course these factors are neither evidence nor proof; still, they point to a probability. Some of these flasks have been attributed to Stiegel. Pitkin-type flasks would have been a "natural" for Stiegel, particularly before he was bewitched by English-style pattern-molded wares, and it is not unlikely that flasks handed down in families in the Pennsylvania section where his glass was sold may have been blown in his works. Some doubtless were similar to 4 of Ill. 90, with the chunky, slightly flattened globular or ovoid body like the amethyst bottles, such as the diamond-daisies, attributed to him. Also, broad and deep flattened globular—nearly circular—Pitkin-type flasks (and single-gather too), usually with 14 or 15 ribs, have been found in his market area and were attributed locally to Stiegel. In the collection of George Austin, an unusual example of this Pitkin-type, in a fine, clear, medium green of yellow cast, has 14 slightly swirled ribs forming flutes with curved tops just below the termination of the half-post. It holds about 15 ounces. Besides these two typically 18th-century forms, Pitkin-type flasks similar to ovoid midwesterns and clear green in color, including (according to Sam Laidacker) emerald and yellowish emerald-green, have been found in the Stiegel country and are believed by Mr. Laidacker to be Manheim products.

However, Stiegel's glasshouses were not the only likely producers of these sturdy flasks. Probably some Pitkin-type flasks of these forms were blown at the Philadelphia Glass Works, if not when rivaling Stiegel, then when operation was revived around 1800. "Moulds" were among the utensils mentioned in the deed of sale of the works by "Robert Towars et al" to Isaac Grey and the Elliots—John Sr., John Jr., and Samuel—on November 5, 1772. And in February 1775 "pocket bottles" were among the articles advertised by John Elliot & Company. Also, of course, there is Wistarburgh, a strong probability. It would not be unlikely that Pitkin-type flasks were, or were among, the "Six Dozen of Pocket Bottels" that, with window glass and other bottles, Caspar Wistar stipulated in his will (1752) should be turned over yearly by his son Richard to his younger son Caspar.[18] Other houses in which Pitkin-type flasks may have been blown before the Revolution were the Germantown glassworks in Massachusetts and the New Windsor and the Newfoundland glassworks in New York; after the war, the Dowesborough Glassworks (later Albany Glass House, the Hamilton Glass Factory) near Albany, New York, the New-Jersey Glass Manufactory started in South Jersey by the Stanger brothers just before the end of the war, and Amelung's New Bremen Glassmanufactory, Maryland. Probably, in the early 1800s, South Jersey houses other than the one at Clementon produced some Pitkin-type flasks. This is all "iffy," and doubtless unprovable one way or the other unless scientific excavations are conducted on the few sites that as yet have escaped the voracious appetite of towns and cities for land.

Although flasks comprised probably more than 90 percent of the Pitkin-type containers, a few jars and bottles and one jug have been recorded. And excepting a small bottle (6 in Ill. 87) and the jug (11 in Ill. 91), all I have seen are New England type. Three, each with broken swirl, are pictured in Ills. 87 and 88. The small jar, patterned in a 36-rib mold, was blown from clear olive-green glass; the unusual wide-mouth bottle, in a 32-rib mold, from dark olive-amber glass. Bottle 4 in Ill. 88 was also blown from olive-amber glass, but so deep as to be black in reflected light. Its body, patterned in a 36-rib mold, was given the so-called sugar-loaf shape rarely encountered in green-glass bottles of any period or even in white and flint glass decanters after the third quarter of the 18th century. The jug was blown from blue-aquamarine glass and patterned in broken-swirl obtained in a 32-rib mold. It was given a deep, well-formed ovoid body and—a rare feature—an applied circular foot. It was found in Ohio but without any history attached to it. Nevertheless, a midwestern attribution is indicated, and the locale, in conjunction with the 32 ribs and the color, tempts one to tentative attribution to the Mantua Glass Works. Containers such as jars, bottles, and the jug are so rare as to suggest they were individual pieces, or possibly special orders, rather than a regular commercial product, and also that they were fashioned by blowers in only a few glasshouses. On the other hand, flasks that were patterned in molds of many rib counts—14, 15, 16, 18, 19, 20, 24, 26, 28, 30, 32, 36, and 44—must have been a regular line in many glasshouses operating in the latter third of the 18th and in the early 19th centuries.

In conclusion, it must be confessed that there is no reliable evidence as to just when the production of Pitkin-type flasks ceased. My own belief is that they were a vanishing species in the East by the 1820s, unable to survive the environment of fashion created by the Figured Flasks, which began multiplying rapidly in that decade. In the Midwest, especially outside the Pittsburgh–Monongahela area, their extinction perhaps did not occur until the 1830s. However, no categorical statement can be made: these approximate periods marking the possible end of Pitkin-type flasks are conjectures. Still, it seems logical that in the natural course of glass events neither Pitkin types nor the single-gather pattern-molded chestnut and other flasks could long survive the competition of Figured Flasks such as the Masonics, Historicals, and Decoratives blown in the time- and laborsaving full-size two-piece molds, which ensured uniform shape and capacity as well as offering a new style of molded design—fresh with decorative, topical, and patriotic appeal.

3
STIEGEL-TYPE BOTTLES AND FLASKS

As already stated, pattern molding, long used in England and on the Continent, was perhaps first practiced in America at Wistarburgh, but its first extensive use apparently was by Stiegel's blowers. In the preceding section, mention has been made of the probable Stiegel production of Pitkin-type flasks made by the half-post method and ornamented by pattern-molded ribbings. In this section, the pattern-molded bottles and flasks to be discussed were blown from a single gather of metal, patterned in either rib molds or pattern piece-molds having simple diamond and more elaborate designs.

For many years after the publication of Hunter's *Stiegel Glass* in 1914, nearly every piece of glass falling into this category, whether bottle, flask, or article of tableware, was ipso facto attributed to Manheim, or rather to Stiegel; for it was the man and his kaleidoscopic career that roused the sympathy and fired the imagination of Hunter and his followers. *Stiegel* became, and remains, an American glass label with which to conjure up the status of desirability and of value in dollars and cents. However, as research into American glassworks and their products progressed and familiarity with foreign wares increased, the realization slowly crystallized not only that many of the pieces attributed to Stiegel were of probable English or Continental origin but also that the technique of pattern molding probably did not appear on the American glasshouse scene with Stiegel, nor did it disappear from the scene with the total eclipse of Stiegel as a glass manufacturer in 1774. It was practiced in many later houses, especially in the early 19th-century production of hollow ware in the Midwest. The corollary, naturally, was that not all "Stiegel" pattern-molded glass was or could have been blown in Stiegel's glassworks.

Thus, like several other names impregnated with specific attribution to manufacturer, glassworks, and period, *Stiegel* was exposed as a label carrying false claims insofar as the majority of pieces on which it was placed were concerned. Hence *Stiegel-type* was adopted long ago by student and informed collector. Nevertheless, in spite of 40 or more years of spreading adherence to *Stiegel-type*, one still hears and sees *Stiegel* applied with all its particularizing significance to pieces that either could not have been or only possibly could have been blown at Manheim. The newcomer to the field of glass collecting should beware of the unqualified term *Stiegel*. Today most of us use *Stiegel-type*, even for those pieces that may be attributed to Stiegel for one good reason or another.

It is certain, however, that bottles of various kinds were made by Henry William Stiegel. In fact, from the start of his adventure in glassmaking at Elizabeth Furnace in September 1763, until operations began in his second Manheim works in 1769, his principal products were window glass and bottles, including pocket bottles. During the blast from November 17, 1766, to April 30, 1767, a total of 1,068 pocket bottles was blown—all but 40 by three of Stiegel's five master blowers. And apparently pocket bottles were blown in even larger quantities after his ambition to produce flint-glass tableware was realized in the 1769 works, which he christened the American Flint Glass Factory. As late as February 1773, pocket bottles were in a long roster of wares itemized in an advertisement announcing the removal of Stiegel's New York "American Flint Glass Store" to the store of James and Arthur Jarvis. In Hunter's summary of the glassware listed from the beginning of 1769 to April 1770 as sold, out on consignment, or on hand in the Manheim store, two items of pocket bottles appear: one of 6,214 and one of 292. Of course, these figures may have included some of the pocket bottles blown in the 1767/68 blast and the fall of 1768, a period when the pinch of the general depression of colonial business and trade hurt cruelly. Nonetheless, they show an increased production over that of the fall of 1766 through the spring of 1767. The increase probably stemmed, in part at least, from Stiegel's courting a wider market after the Manheim flint-glass works was in production.[19]

Prior to the realization of his flint-glass ambition, Stiegel's output was sold mainly in Lancaster, Reading, York, and nearby towns and villages. The January 21, 1767, report to the Lords of Trade and Plantations stating that wares "of very ordinary variety" had no outlet "but to supply the small demand of the villages and farmers in the adjacent inland country" was close to the facts. But, by July of 1769, Stiegel was ready to change that doleful situation with his flint glass, examples of which were judged by the American Philosophical Society in 1771 to be "equal in beauty and quality to the generality of Flint Glass imported from England." Stiegel sanguinely expected to reap a harvest of prosperity from the righteous colonial anger sown by England's interfering Acts and Taxes, in the belief that indignant colonists would give preference to his glassware. Although his expectations were to be shattered by harsh personal and colonial economic and financial realities, Stiegel's market did expand, for a brief period, to include the import cities of Philadelphia, Baltimore, New York, and Boston.[20] And bottles, phials, and pocket bottles were among the articles sent to them.

Unhappily for us, "pocket bottles" and "pocket pints" (the latter occurring only a few times) sufficed for Stiegel's record requirements and advertisements. However, it is logical to conclude that, in the main, Stiegel's pocket bottles as well as his other bottles followed prevailing styles. Inevitably their forms and decoration would have been determined by 18th-century English and Continental bottles, probably through imports and certainly through the European glassblowers, who adhered to the techniques and styles in which they had been trained. All Stiegel's blowers were Germans in the 1763–69 period; afterward they were joined by English, Irish, and Italian craftsmen[21] seduced from England for the production of popular English-type wares. It is a fair assumption that the pocket bottles blown by the Germans at Elizabeth Furnace and the first Manheim glasshouse were "of ordinary variety" blown

from bottle glass in its natural colors and from window-glass metal that doubtless had a gray or greenish cast. Possibly some pocket bottles or flasks were decorated by engraving or enameling in the second Manheim works, the American Flint Glass Factory, where these methods were practiced, though I know of no authenticated examples. Certainly pattern-molded ones were blown from artificially colored metal, predominately amethyst, from the fall of 1769 into 1774. So far as I know at present, Amelung's New Bremen Glassmanufactory (1785–95) was the only other works from the start of Wistarburgh to the turn of the century in which extrinsically decorated and artificially colored glass was produced. On the other hand, it is a fair assumption that similar pocket bottles of ordinary variety, plain and pattern-molded, were blown in most if not all 18th-century glasshouses.

Among 18th-century type flasks or pocket bottles, some of which doubtless were produced by Stiegel as well as others, is the long, slender, flattened ovoid or elliptical—1 and 4 in Ill. 100 and 6, 7, and 8 in Ill. 91 are typical examples. This type, often given an everted lip, usually has an unstable base and ranges in capacity from about 7 to 16 ounces. And, as one would expect in the case of pattern-molded and blown flasks, no two have identical contours or measurements. In the early days of American bottle collecting, these flasks were thought to be nursing bottles. Whether they ever were filled with milk to feed the baby is a moot question today, but there is no doubt they served as pocket bottles filled with far less bland liquids. That the type was a characteristic 18th-century one has been established by archaeological evidence. For instance, fragments of several, patterned in three different rib molds, were among the pre-1800 shards excavated at the Sleepy Hollow Restoration, Philipse Manor, Philipsburg Lower Mills near Tarrytown, New York.

Plain and pattern-molded, such flasks doubtless were products of most of our late 18th- and very early 19th-century houses in which bottles were blown either as a main product or sideline. Their distribution was widespread. Of the many examples in the George S. McKearin Collection that were acquired from about 1919 into the early 1920s, more than a third came from New England homes; a few came from eastern New York, South Jersey, and eastern Pennsylvania. Only one or two—and they were acquired much later—came from the Midwest. Some pocket bottles of this type probably were imported occasionally by American merchants. I say "occasionally," for, as mentioned previously, the infrequent advertisements of dram bottles, pocket bottles, and pocket flasks suggest these articles were not imported in the same vast quantities as other bottles. However, possibly the long, slender, flattened pocket bottle was the type of the "flat half pint bottles" advertised in 1750, of the "flat half pint dram bottles" in 1768, and "green half pint dram bottles" in 1774—all offered in Boston newspapers.[22] Had prices only been quoted, they would have been a clue to whether *all* the flasks were green (bottle) glass or some were the aristocratic flint glass.

As yet, the survey of pocket bottles of this long, slender, flattened type has been far from comprehensive. Still, though *unpatterned* flasks of the same sizes, body forms, and limited color range have been recorded, it would appear that the majority were pattern-molded in either a ribbed or simple reticulated design such as diamond diaper. And diamond patterns evidently were less favored than the ribbed, perhaps because in using a ribbed dip mold the blower or journeyman did not need an assistant, whereas a boy or journeyman had to open and close the piece mold required for a diamond pattern. Three different diamond molds had been used to pattern a few of the many specimens studied. One, a 10-diamond mold, had ten diamonds in the horizontal rows above ten flutes at the bottom, the diamonds being formed by outlining ribs. Although the number of units is the same, this formation differs from that of the so-called Zanesville 10-diamond mold, which will be discussed under midwestern pattern-molded containers. A second mold was a 12-diamond and a third, a 15-diamond, and in each the diamonds seem to start at the center base of the mold. An example patterned in the 12-diamond mold is 6 of Ill. 91; one from the 15-diamond mold is 7 in the same illustration. Only colorless, or nearly so, pocket bottles have been recorded from the 10-diamond mold; light greens, including a muted yellow-green and a mere green tint, from the 12-diamond mold; and light greens from the 15-diamond mold. An example of the last, 7 in Ill. 91, was found in Ohio and attributed to the Mantua Glass Works, where—as proved by Harry Hall White's excavations—flasks of this form, as well as chestnuts, were patterned in a 15-diamond mold.

From the design point of view, the most interesting of these pocket bottles have a pattern consisting of alternate 16 long flutes pointed at each end and two rows of 16 diamonds. In the mold were at least three repeats of each, starting with the flutes. However, as was usual in the case of flasks patterned in diamond molds, the number and position of rows of the pattern varied on individual flasks, depending upon elongation in expansion and the amount of patterned gather used in forming the flask. Short flasks, such as the chestnuts, normally have fewer rows than the long-bodied ones. In this pattern, pocket bottles of the long flattened shape have been recorded in a smoky colorless glass, such as 1 in Ill. 100, and also in light green, including grayish and yellowish. Short flattened ovoids and chestnuts have been found in clear green, sea-green, and amber. Long or short, the flasks in this pattern are very scarce, if not rare.

The ribbed pocket bottles of the long flattened type were produced in far greater quantities than their more elaborate cousins, if one can judge from the survivors. They were patterned in dip molds of at least eight different numbers of ribs—12, 16, 17, 18, 19, 20, 22, and 24 ribs. And since, on most specimens examined, the usual pontil mark obscured or obliterated the termination of the ribs on the bottom, it was impossible to estimate how many molds of a given rib-count had the same type of termination in the mold or the same number of ribs. In any event, the variety in type and number of ribs indicates the existence of many molds and suggests their use in many glasshouses. Though there is no means at present of knowing whether the above-mentioned pre-1800 aquamarine and light muted green shards at Philipse Manor were parts of domestic or imported flasks, they are archaeological evidence that 16-rib, 20-rib, and 24-rib molds were used in the 1700s as well as the 1800s. The ribbing was vertical on the majority of the pocket bottles studied. Occasionally the ribbing was swirled, and in one instance, at least, the gather was twice patterned for the broken swirl like that on 2 in Ill. 100. This particular example was blown from brilliant colorless glass, probably in the early 19th century, and except for smelling bottles is the only one I have seen that was patterned in a 22-rib mold.

Colorless ribbed pocket bottles are exceptional and, unlike 2 in Ill. 100, usually have a gray or green tinge. Also, only a few have been found in the dark colors natural to bottle glass, and they were patterned in a 24-rib mold. The greatest variety of colors, and the only artificial colors, were in those patterned in 16-rib molds. In addition to the many aquamarines and light greens, these occur in sapphire-blue, amethyst, colorless, and colorless with opalescence at base, neck, and lip.

A variant of the long flattened ovoid pocket bottle had a very sharp taper in the lower half of the body to a tiny base, as on 3 in Ill. 100—shuttle-shape, in the English glass collector's glossary of terms. If ordinary bottle or window glass was ever used in their production, I have yet to see an example. All I have examined were blown from finer quality of metal than the more common varieties like 1 and 4 in Ill. 100, and the glass was brilliant colorless like 3, amethyst, or brilliant emerald-green in color. Some were patterned in an 8-rib mold. The ribbing usually was left vertical, sometimes swirled. Others were patterned in an 11-diamond mold having the design outlined in heavy ribs somewhat reminiscent of nipt-diamond-waies. In my experience, pocket bottles of this kind have not been found in any quantity in the United States.

The shuttle-shape was definitely an English one.[23] It has been thought the shape possibly occurred also in Continental pocket bottles but probably not in American. However, there is no solid evidence that such pocket bottles were not blown in any of our glasshouses. And, inasmuch as it was customary, from Stiegel's day on, to *copy* foreign styles, especially English, it seems likely this form of pocket bottle would have been blown here. *Where* is a matter of pure speculation at present. One possible source might have been Bakewell's in Pittsburgh, the first *successful* manufacturer of fine wares and flint glass in America. In October 1808, the firm—then Bakewell & Ensell—advertised pocket bottles along with decanters, tumblers, cream jugs, sugar basins, and salts. In the East, after persuading the Boston Crown Glass Company to allow him to produce fine glassware in a six-pot furnace in their South Boston works, Thomas Cains may have produced some pocket bottles. "Bottles" were among the wares advertised in February 1813. The New England Glass Company is another possibility, as pocket bottles were listed in the long roster of articles advertised in 1819.[24] Each of these establishments was English in its orientation, and most of the blowers were English or Irish. Apparently English influence on the styles of our early glass tableware far outweighed any other, so it is not unlikely the better grade of pocket bottles was affected also.

Another 18th- to early-19th-century type of pocket bottle, or flask, from about a half-pint to a pint in capacity, is the chestnut, so named by a pioneer collector to whom its shape seemed somewhat similar to an American chestnut. Of course, the body depth of the flasks is much less than that of bottles to which the name was also given and which are discussed under *Utilitarian Bottles*. Certainly some chestnut flasks would have been produced at Elizabeth Furnace and Manheim—and in other 18th-century glassworks—and, though sometimes as thin through as 19th-century chestnuts, they

tended to obesity. Also classified generally under chestnut flasks, though not truly chestnut in shape, are broad, flattened, but deep globulars nearly circular in contour. It is probable that many of these flasks found in Stiegel's market area, and handed down in families there, were blown in his works.

The majority of chestnut flasks are pattern-molded in either vertical or swirled ribs. In color, both plain and pattern-molded flasks are mainly light green of varied hue and tint, occasionally amber, rarely blue and amethyst. One interesting example in George Austin's collection was patterned in a 14-rib mold producing pronounced flattish vertical ribs that in expansion faded away toward the bottom of the flask. It was blown from a light sapphire-blue metal that appears identical with that of some fragments unearthed at Manheim. It holds about 14 ounces. Another, a flattened globular holding about 13 ounces and apparently patterned in the same mold, was blown from deep amber glass and the ribbing swirled to the right. In the Henry Francis du Pont Winterthur Museum are two Stiegel-type chestnuts—one medium and one fairly deep amethyst—patterned in a reticulated design formed by fine ribs similar to the small "diamonds" or honeycomb of 8 in Ill. 91. The latter has 14 "cells" in a horizontal row; the amethyst chestnuts, 20. And I have seen a few chestnuts in the diamond-daisy and small-diamonds-above-flutes patterns attributed to Stiegel. But the chestnut form in these two patterns is unorthodox, as it is also for the checkered-diamond in Color Plate II.

Like the chestnut flasks found in eastern Pennsylvania, those from other eastern areas were blown mainly from metal of light green tones. Some are unpatterned; a few are South Jersey-type with applied and tooled decoration, as in the case of 5 in Ill. 51; the majority are pattern-molded in ribs. The ribbing is either vertical or swirled, sometimes wide and contiguous and sometimes fine, giving a flute effect. The sizes are from about a half-pint to about a pint. I know of no identified example in the broken swirl.

Nevertheless, although there is always the possibility of importation, I believe most of the pattern-molded chestnut flasks found in the East were blown in an eastern glassworks. For instance, inasmuch as Pitkin-type flasks were products of the Keene-Marlboro-Street Glassworks, of Connecticut glassworks, and of Clementon in South Jersey, it is logical to assume that flasks blown from single gathers of metal were patterned in ribs also and fashioned in chestnut form, which, as has been

I. Spirits bottle with seal bearing the initials "RW", probably for Richard Wistar, son of the founder of the "Wistarburg" glassworks in Allowaystown, N.J. Probably made there between 1760 and 1776, and descended in the family to Miss Elizabeth Morris Wistar. Height, 9³/₁₆"; diameter of base, 4⁷/₁₆". From the Collection of Miss Wistar. *The Corning Museum of Glass*

II. Stiegel-type pattern-molded bottles, all blown from nonlead glass, 1770–95. The two bearing checkered diamond designs (1 and 3, left to right, amethyst and pale amethyst) were probably made at John Frederick Amelung's New Bremen Glassmanufactory, 1785–95, since numerous fragments of this pattern were found at the factory site during archaeological excavations there in 1962 and 1963 by The Corning Museum of Glass and the Smithsonian Institution. The others are attributed to Stiegel's American Flint Glass Manufactory, Manheim, Pa., ca. 1770–74. No. 2, a deep brilliant amethyst, is patterned in a diaper of large diamonds or ogivals; No. 4, of amethyst glass, bears lateral rows of small diamonds or ogivals above vertical flutes. No. 5, the amethyst daisy-in-hexagon design, is extremely rare; No. 6, the sapphire-blue diamond daisy, rare. These two designs have not yet been associated with any glass factory other than Stiegel's. No. 3, height, 6⅞". *Courtesy, The Henry Francis du Pont Winterthur Museum*

III. Common free-blown bottles, 1770–1830, probably from New England but of the type made in most bottle-glass houses in the colonies and elsewhere in America during that period. *Clockwise, from lower left:* large light green chestnut bottle; light olive-amber demijohn; olive-green square case (or gin) bottle; olive-amber decanter-bottle; *(center):* olive-amber chestnut bottle. *Collection of the Henry Ford Museum*

IV. Pitkin flasks and bottles, 1790–1830. *Clockwise from left:* **1.** Olive green with 38 broken-swirl ribs; height 6¾″. **2.** Midwestern, 1800–1830; deep amber with 36 broken-swirl ribs. **3.** Very rare bottle, probably New England, probably dating between 1810 and 1830, the body apparently blown in a mold for snuff bottles; medium olive-amber, with 37 broken-swirl ribs. **4.** New England, 1790–1830; olive-amber with 36 ribs swirled to the left. *Collection of the Henry Ford Museum*

V. Midwestern pattern-molded bottles and jugs, 1800–1835. *Clockwise from center left:* **1.** Globular bottle, amber, with 24 ribs swirled to right. **2.** Rare large globular bottle, light aqua, with 30 ribs swirled to left. Height, 11½″. **3.** Rare beehive-shape blue bottle with 24 ribs swirled to right, broken by 24 vertical ribs. **4.** Beehive-shape, aqua bottle with 24 ribs swirled to right, broken by 24 vertical ribs. It bears a paper label for "SPTS. CAMPHOR" and name of druggists McClellan & Pollock from Xenia, Ohio. (Gift of Preston R. Bassett.) **5.** Handled globular bottle or jug, deep amber, with 24 ribs. **6.** Taper-shape bottle, "citron," with 16 ribs slightly swirled to left. **7.** Handled globular bottle or jug, medium olive-green, with 24 ribs swirled to right. *Collection of the Henry Ford Museum*

VI. Midwestern pattern-molded pocket bottles or flasks, about 1800–1835. *Clockwise, from center left:* **1.** Rare small flask, deep olive-amber, with 18 vertical ribs. **2.** Grandfather flask, light golden amber, with 24 vertical ribs. **3.** Handled flask or jug, deep amber, with 24 ribs swirled slightly to right. **4.** Pocket bottle or flask, aqua, with 26 ribs swirled left. **5.** Pocket bottle or flask, pale "citron," with 20 vertical ribs. **6.** Pocket bottle or flask, very deep amber, with 10-diamond pattern, probably made in Zanesville, Ohio. *Center:* **7.** Pocket bottle or flask, "colorless," with 24 ribs swirled to left broken by 24 vertical ribs. *Collection of the Henry Ford Museum*

VII. Utility bottles and preserve jars made in various American window- and bottle-glass houses, 1790 to 1860. *Left to right, top row:* **1.** Large preserve jar, deep aqua, attributed to the Suncook Glass Works, Suncook, N.H., 1839–50. Height, 10¼″. **2.** Ink bottle, olive-amber, factory unknown; probably 1830–50. **3.** Preserve jar, olive-green, probably New England, 1830–50. *Middle row:* **4.** Preserve jar, pale blue, factory unknown, about 1860. **5.** Utility or preserve bottle, olive-green, probably New England, about 1830–40. **6.** Snuff bottle, deep olive-green, late 18th to early 19th century. **7.** Snuff bottle, olive-green, with original paper label: "POWDERED JALAP/PREPARED & SOLD/by/Dᴿ THOS RITTER/Nᴼ 104 CHERRY Sᵗ N.Y." Probably made in a New England or New York State bottle-glass house about 1836. Height, 4¼″. *Bottom row:* **8.** Utility bottle, dark amber, probably New England, about 1830–40. **9.** Shoe-blacking bottle with original label of A. Bostick, Albany, N.Y., dated July 23, 1833. Probably made in a New England or New York State bottle-glass house. **10.** Snuff bottle, olive-green, with original paper label of Wm. C. Lemon, No. 4 Wall and 213 Duane Sts, New York. Probably made in a New England or New York State bottle-glass house, 1846–51. Height 4¼″. *Collection of the Henry Ford Museum*

VIII. Blown-molded preserve, pickle, and condiment bottles made in various American bottle-glass houses between about 1840 and 1870. *Left to right, top row:* **1.** Pickle or preserve bottle, aqua, blown in the private mold of William D. Smith, pickle and preserve manufacturer, listed in New York City directories from 1843 to 1859. Probably made in a New Jersey factory. Height, 11½". **2.** "Pickle" bottle, deep aqua, with remains of original paper label with an American eagle below "TAMARINDS" and above "Prepared by W.K. LEWIS & Co. . . . 6 BROAD STREET/BOSTON." The firm is listed in Boston city directories 1840/41 and 1842/43. Probably from a Connecticut glasshouse. **3.** Pickle bottle, aqua, with original foil label marked "GERKINS" and "D.H. DAVIS/BOSTON . . ." Probably made in a Connecticut glasshouse about 1850. *Bottom row:* **4.** "Huckleberry" or "blueberry" bottle, deep reddish amber, attributed to the Willington or Westford Glass Works, 1840–70. **5.** Pepper, or other sauce, bottle, "colorless." Factory unknown; about 1850–70. **6.** Pepper sauce bottle, pale aqua. Factory unknown; about 1850–70. *Collection of the Henry Ford Museum*

IX. Smelling or pungent bottles. *Top row:* **1.** Seahorse, free-blown of "colorless" glass, with applied decoration. Possibly New England, 1813–30. **2.** Mold-blown, sapphire-blue glass, sunburst decorated. Probably New England, 1813–35. **3.** Mold-blown, emerald-green. Factory unknown; 1820–50. Height, 3⅛″. *Center right:* **4.** Mold-blown of opalescent glass, with original paper label "SUPERIOR/ PUNGENT"; also "WARRANTED" (reading sidewise). Probably made at the Boston & Sandwich Glass Works, 1850–88. *Bottom row:* **5.** Pattern-molded of deep cobalt-blue glass with 28 ribs swirled to right. Probably New England, 1813–30. **6.** Mold-blown, deep emerald-green glass, with sunburst decoration. Probably New England, 1813–35. **7.** Mold-blown pungent, opaque light blue glass. Possibly made at the Boston & Sandwich Glass Works, 1850–88. Nos. 1, 4, 7, *Collection of the Henry Ford Museum;* 2, 3, 5, 6, *Private collections*

X. Rare fancy cologne bottles, probably of American origin, produced—and popular—from about 1830 to the 1860s. *Collection of the Henry Ford Museum* (Nos. 2, 3, 5, 6, and 7, gifts of Mr. Preston R. Bassett)

XI. Decorative Figured Flasks, 1815–55. *Top row:* **1.** Sunburst, GVIII–2, "colorless." Keene (Marlboro Street) Glass Works, Keene, N.H., 1815–17. Height, 8″. **2.** Concentric Ring–Eagle, GII–76, light green. Possibly New England Glass Works, about 1820. **3.** Scroll, GIX–3, deep green. Midwestern, ca. 1850 to 1855. *Center:* **4.** Extremely rare Eagle–Flag, GII–52, opaque white. Coffin & Hay, Hammondton, N.J., ca. 1835–40. *Bottom row:* **5.** Masonic–Eagle, GIV–1, deep amethyst. Keene (Marlboro Street) Glass Works, Keene, N.H. 1817–ca. 1825. **6.** Eagle–Eagle, GII–24, aqua. Possibly Louisville (Kentucky) Glass Works, about 1855. **7.** "SUCCESS TO THE RAILROAD" GV–1, light sapphire-blue. Lancaster Glass Works, Lancaster, N.Y. 1850–55. *Collection of the Henry Ford Museum*

XII. Commemorative and decorative Figured Flasks, 1824–40. *Clockwise from lower left:* **1.** Lafayette–DeWitt Clinton, GI–80, olive-amber. Coventry Glass Works, Coventry, Conn. 1824–30. **2.** The American System, GX–21, yellow-green. Probably Bakewell, Page & Bakewell, Pittsburgh, about 1824. **3.** Jackson–Masonic, GI–69, light green with yellow tone. Knox & McKee, Wheeling,(W) Virginia, probably 1828. **4.** Old Cabin–Hard Cider, GX–22, aqua. Monongahela–Pittsburgh district, about 1839. **5.** Washington–Eagle, TWD, GI–14, light green. T. W. Dyott's Kensington Glass Works, Kensington, Philadelphia, 1826–30. *Center:* **6.** Jared Spencer, GX–24, olive-amber. Probably Pitkin Glass Works, East Hartford, Conn., about 1825. *Collection of The Corning Museum of Glass*

XIII. Decorative and commemorative Figured Flasks, 1830–70. *Clockwise, from center left:* **1.** Washington–Jackson, GI–32, olive-amber. Probably Keene (Marlboro Street) Glass Works, Keene, N.H. 1828–41. **2.** Baltimore Monument–Corn for the World, GVI–4, amber. Baltimore Glass Works, Baltimore, Md. 1846–50. **3.** Shield and Clasped Hands, GXII–5, yellow-green. Midwestern, 1860–70. **4.** Flag–New Granite Glass Works, GX–27, olive-green. New Granite Glass Works, Stoddard, N.H. 1865–71. **5.** "FOR PIKES PEAKE," GXI–53, very pale green. Midwestern; factory unknown. 1858–ca. 1865. **6.** Scroll, GIX–35, deep sapphire-blue. Midwestern; probably about 1850. *Center:* **7.** Jenny Lind, GI–109, light green. Attributed to M'Carty & Torreyson, Wellsburg, (W) Virginia, 1851–55. *Collection of The Corning Museum of Glass*

XIV. Soda and mineral water bottles, 1850–70. *Diagonal row at left, back to front:*
1. "CRYSTAL PALACE/PREMIUM/SODA WATER/W. EAGLE" bottle embossed on the obverse with the New York Crystal Palace. Deep bluish green. About 1853.
2. "SUPERIOR/MINERAL WATER/UNION GLASS WORKS"; probably Union Glass Works, Kensington, Philadelphia. Cobalt blue. About 1850. **3.** Soda water bottle, sapphire-blue, embossed "LANCASTER/GLASS WORKS/N.Y." 1850–60.
4. "Egg" mineral or soda water bottle, "colorless"; embossed "R.WHITE". Found in Canada; probably English, about 1860–80. *Diagonal row at right, back to front:*
5. Mineral spring water bottle, amber, embossed "MIDDLETON/HEALING/SPRINGS/GRAYS & CLARK/MIDDLETON SPRINGS VT." 1855–70. Height, 9⅝".
6. Mineral spring water bottle, dark amber, embossed "SHELDON SPRINGS/SHELDON/VERMONT". 1855–70. **7.** Congress & Empire Spring Co. mineral water bottle, dark green. Congressville Glass Works, Congressville, Saratoga Springs, N.Y. 1865–70. Nos. 1, 2, 3, 5, 6, and 7: *Collection of the Henry Ford Museum;* No. 4: *Private collection*

◄ XV. Mid- to late-19th-century whiskey bottles. *Clockwise, from left:* **1.** Pattern-molded handled bottle, yellowish amber, with seal marked "C.B. CROWELL JR STAR WHISKEY/NEW YORK". About 1850. **2.** Amber bottle with threaded glass stopper patented by Samuel Whitney, January 1861. Whitney Glass Works, Glassboro, N.J. 1861–70. **3.** Mold-blown whiskey bottle, deep reddish amber, embossed on the shoulder "CHAPIN & GORE CHICAGO" and on the body "SOUR MASH 1867". The bottle has a patented internal screw thread for a glass screw cap. It is embossed on the base "HAWLEY GLASS CO. HAWLEY PA." About 1870. **4.** Mold-blown bottle, deep amber, embossed below the applied handle "A.M. BININGER & CO." About 1865–70. **5.** Handled flask or jug, amber, with original paper label for "BININGER'S/ PIONEER BOURBON," entered according to an act of Congress in the year 1859 by Rufus Watles and L. C. Sauger in the clerk's office of the District Court of the Southern District of N.Y. 1859–70. *Collection of the Henry Ford Museum*

XVI. *(Left to right):* **1.** Scroll flask, reproduction like GIX–11; amber; manufacturer unknown, possibly Blenko Glass, West Virginia, about 1950–60. (See Ill. 152.) Also made in other colors including a deep ruby. *Collection of Miss Nancy Merrill.* **2.** Washington–Ship, GI–29, deep sapphire-blue, crude reproduction similar to GI–28, apparently blown in a plaster mold. Probably made in the 1930s by an unknown maker. *Collection of The Corning Museum of Glass.* **3.** Columbia–Eagle, a reproduction of GI–117a; blue. Made by the Historical Bottle Collectors Guild, Owens-Illinois, Toledo, Ohio (see Ill. 158). *Collection of Kenneth M. Wilson.* **4.** Success To The Railroad, reproduction of GV–5; aqua (also produced in olive-green or olive-amber). Made in Czechoslovakia in the early 1930s. *Collection of The Corning Museum of Glass.* **5.** Eagle–Flag, reproduction of GII–54; deep amber. Made by Clevenger Bros., Clayton, N.J. 1930s–1940s. *Collection of The Corning Museum of Glass.* **6.** Cornucopia-Urn, reproduction of GIII–4; green. The original was made at the Coventry Glass Works, Coventry, Conn. This reproduction (also made in a variety of vivid colors) was made by the Pairpoint Glass Works in Spain in 1961. (See Ill. 155.) *Collection of Kenneth M. Wilson.* **7.** Concentric-Ring Eagle flask, reproduction of GII–76; light green. Made by the Historical Bottle Collectors Guild, Owens-Illinois, Toledo, Ohio, 1972. (See Ill. 156.) *Collection of The Corning Museum of Glass*

XVII. *Top row, left to right:* Large case or gin bottle, green; probably English about 1790–1800. Spirits bottle, English, about 1650. Large globular bottle of golden amber glass pattern molded with 24 ribs swirled to the left; midwestern, 1815–35. "Black" glass (dark olive-amber) spirits bottle with seal bearing the words "WINE/P.C. BROOKS/1820"; probably English. Pickle jar, aquamarine glass; American, about 1840–65. Amber spirits bottle embossed on the base "WEEKS & GILSON, SO. STODDARD N.H."; made about 1865.

Bottom row, left to right: Rare "Amberina" colored pocket bottle, pattern molded with 24 vertical ribs; probably American, 1800–1820. Brilliant olive-yellow Figured Flask, GII–8, made in the Pittsburgh–Monongahela area, about 1830. Yellowish-green pocket bottle pattern-molded in a 10-diamond design; attributed to Zanesville, Ohio, 1815-35. Grandfather flask of deep reddish amber glass, with pattern molded broken-swirl design of 24 vertical ribs and 24 ribs swirled to the right. Aquamarine Scroll flask GIX-45; midwestern, about 1850. Blue soda water bottle made at Lancaster (N.Y.) Glass Works, 1849-60. Amethyst cologne bottle, possibly made at the Boston & Sandwich Glass Works, about 1860. (Photograph by Carl Malotka) *Collection of the Henry Ford Museum* stated, was one of the characteristic shapes well into the 1800s. However, the existence today of so few pattern-molded vessels—pitchers and bowls, for example—attributable to South Jersey glasshouses suggests only limited employment of pattern molds in that area. In fact, the so-called Stiegel tradition of pattern molding apparently was not perpetuated in eastern houses producing bottles and flasks in the early 1800s to the degree that it was in the midwestern. Had pattern molding prevailed, *many* household articles blown for friends or for local consumption surely would have been in the "Stiegel tradition," whereas—with very, very few exceptions— they are in the South Jersey tradition of freeblowing, unadorned or with decoration by glass applied to itself and tooled into many devices.[25] Consequently, though I do not doubt eastern production of pattern-molded chestnuts, and believe attribution to a specific glassworks is usually impossible or merely conjectural, it seems apparent that eastern production never compared in *quantity* with that of the midwestern houses of the same period.

Although Stiegel doubtless produced Pitkin-type and long, slender, flattened, ovoid pocket bottles and certainly made chestnuts, the 18th-century type of bottle particularly associated with his works is that illustrated in Color Plate II and by 1 through 3 in Ill. 90. These are chunky bottles with slightly flattened globular or ovoid body, deeper through in proportion to height and width than the general run of true pocket bottles of contemporaneous or later periods. The form is Continental, probably of South German derivation, and perhaps was becoming oldfashioned even by Stiegel's time. These bottles have been called *perfume bottles, toilet bottles,* and *pocket bottles.* The first two names do not appear in any Stiegel records or advertisements known to me; *pocket bottle* does. However, today, to many of us it seems unlikely bottles of this chunky form were used as pocket flasks. Doubtless they served as containers of a variety of liquids. Some I have seen had been used as camphor bottles, but in what period of their long lifetime is unknown. Be that as it may, I prefer to use just "bottle."

These Stiegel-type bottles have, of course, distinctive features other than form. Although they have always been called *half-pints*, they are more likely to hold 10 to 11 ounces. None, so far as I know, has been recorded that closely approaches a pint in capacity. Some were blown from ordinary bottle-glass metal and unpatterned, but the most familiar and desirable of them were blown from fine metal, usually in amethyst of various tones. Perhaps of all

glass attributed to Stiegel they have been more eagerly sought by collectors than any other article of possible Manheim origin. Rarely are they plain, unpatterned like 2 in Ill. 90; the majority are patternmolded and in more designs than any other early American bottles. The designs include both vertical and swirled ribbing, allover diamonds and ogivals, small diamonds-above-flutes, the diamond-daisy or daisy-in-square, and the daisy-in-hexagon. In Ill. 90, a characteristic vertically ribbed pocket bottle is illustrated by 1, patterned in a 20-rib mold, and the swirl-ribbed 3, patterned in an 18-rib mold. In Color Plate II an allover ogival is illustrated by 2; the small-diamonds-above-flutes, by 4; the diamonddaisy, by 6; and the daisy-in-hexagon, by 5.

Some of these designs may be Stiegel originals; others were not. The ribbed patterns seem to have been common wherever and whenever patternmolded glass was produced, occurring on flasks of many shapes, kinds, and colors of glass. And the simpler diamonds apparently were nearly as ubiquitous. The number of ribs, usually 16, 18, or 20, on these Stiegel-type bottles has neither time nor place significance, since molds of the same rib counts were used to pattern later American flasks and also foreign flasks. For instance, the sapphire-blue flask of tapering fat ovoid form, 5 in Ill. 97, which was patterned in an 18-rib mold, is Continental. It was found in Holland, and I believe it was blown there. On the other hand, many students today believe that the particular ogival variant, 2 in Color Plate II, was patterned in a Stiegel mold and also that the small-diamondsabove-flutes, the diamond-daisy, and daisy-inhexagon were originated by Stiegel.

The belief in Stiegel origin of these designs is tenaciously held in spite of the fact that no documentary or archaeological proof of the proposition has been found. Admittedly, the arguments for it are circumstantial. There are local and family traditions of Stiegel origin that, though an unsound basis in themselves alone, in this instance are consistent with the physical characteristics of the bottles. The forms and proportions are of the period, and the colors are evidenced by fragments unearthed by Frederick William Hunter's and John B. Kerfoot's "pick-andshovel" excavations on the glassworks' sites. More important, so far as I have been able to learn, no student or collector of foreign glass has ever seen or heard of an *exact* counterpart of these specific designs in any European glass, British or Continental. Nor, for that matter, has family or local tradition connected them with any other American glasshouse. Then too, in his ironworks, Stiegel had the means at hand to make his own molds. Lastly, and perhaps more essential, as his improvements in construction and types of iron stoves testify,[26] Stiegel had ingenuity and inventiveness that could have found another outlet in conceiving new pattern-molded designs for glass. After all, glass became an interest closer to his heart than iron stoves.

The two designs with "diamonds" are quite unlike each other. The overall ogival—usually called the 12-diamond, though the "diamonds" are not true diamonds—resembles nipt-diamond-waies, an ornamentation formed by nipping together applied threads of glass. The pattern, formed by fine ribs, consists of six broad petallike flutes on the bottom and twelve diamonds or ogivals in each horizontal row. The mold had at least nine rows of ogivals, but on individual bottles the ogivals are drawn into irregular ribs at the top of the body and on the lower neck, and the number of rows on some is less than nine, as the upper part of the patterned gather was cut off in fashioning the bottle or obliterated entirely in forming the neck. Also, in the small-diamonds-above-flutes, the so-called diamonds are not true diamonds; rather, they are more like the honeycomb seen on 4 in Ill. 90. But since the pattern has been described as diamonds-above-flutes for so long, I have not attempted to change its name. Formed by fine ribs, it consists of a diaper of 28 small concave diamonds in horizontal row above 28 slender long flutes that start from a plain center on the bottom of the bottle. As in the case of the 12-diamond or ogival, the number of rows varies on bottles, and for the same reasons; there were probably ten rows in the mold. In the collection of the late Melvin Billups were two examples unusual in size and shape. Instead of the normal chunky, flattened globular or ovoid, one is a chestnut, 6¼ inches in height, about 4⅜ inches in greatest width, and about 2⅝ inches in greatest depth. The other is a wide tapering ovoid with greatest depth, 2⁹/₁₆ inches, at the top. Its height is 5⅞ inches and greatest width is 4¹³/₁₆ inches. The bottles are rarer in these two patterns, if not so exciting in design, than those in diamond-daisy and daisy-in-hexagon.

In the opinion of most American glass collectors, the well-conceived diamond-daisy and daisy-in-hexagon stand at the apex of pattern-molded designs, and they are the most elaborate in American glass. They are close kin—one probably inspired the other. The daisy-in-hexagon (5 in Color Plate II) is far rarer than the diamond-daisy (6 in Color Plate II): only about eight or ten such daisy-in-hexagon bottles have been recorded, whereas at the present time some 40 or more diamond-daisies are estimated to be in private collections and museums. The daisy-in-hexagon design, described by fine ribs, consists of graduated flutes below three rows of six hexagons, each framing a flower with 12 concave petals and roundish center. As yet it has not been possible to determine accurately the number of flutes, for on the examples examined they are indistinct, sometimes to the point of nonexistence as a result of the expansion of the patterned gather. But it would appear that there are more than 30, probably 36.

The diamond-daisy design, also described by fine ribs, consists of 30 graduated flutes below three rows of five large diamonds, each framing a flower with 12 concave petals and roundish center. On the bottles in each pattern, the daisy motifs in the bottom row, being more expanded, are the largest and most uniform; in the second row the motifs are less expanded, smaller, and the angle at the top sharper; in the top row, having been pulled together in the process of fabrication, they become irregular ribbing below and on the lower neck. On some diamond-daisies the design is sharp and the describing fine ribs prominent. But on all daisy-in-hexagons I have seen, the pattern, even the ribs, was softened by the expansion of the gathers, as it is on 5 in Color Plate II. An interesting phenomenon is the effect of light upon the appearance of the pattern. In reflected light, the concavity of the petals, center of the daisy, and the flutes is apparent, but when light passes through the bottle—and likewise in photographs—these elements appear to be convex. This is also true of the small diamonds-above-flutes. Strange as it seems, neither of these patterns, nor the ogival and diamonds-above-flutes, seems to have been used in the production of Stiegel's tableware.

An intaglio diamond-daisy that most collectors and students, including myself, believed to be old and Stiegel-type, and called the "diamond daisy variant," became suspect 15 to 20 years ago of doubtful antiquity. It has the same number of diamond-daisies in horizontal row and of flutes as the diamond-daisy. However, the mold or molds may have had two rows of daisies instead of three, and the rendering of the design, though indistinct on a few pieces, was crisper and more precise and uniform. The motifs were not described by ribs formed by the type of grooving in the "Stiegel" diamond-daisy mold or other molds attributed to him. The diamonds are larger and the daisy more stylized and flowerlike, having longer, shallow, and more slender petals radiating from an oval center, with triangular spaces between their ends. Three examples in the McKearin Collection proved on spot test to be lead glass instead of the expected nonlead. This, however, did not seem suspicious since Stiegel produced flint glass.

This variant has been considered rarer than the diamond-daisy. And so it is—some five salts, two or three small jars, a bowl on a short standard, and perhaps no more than a dozen flasks appear to be all that are known in the design at present. The few flasks I have seen in the glass, or in photographs, had the Stiegel chunky form, a plain neck *sloping* to a narrow mouth and plain lip. They have been recorded in a light pinkish amethyst (as have the small jars). Another form, a tall flattened ovoid tapering at the top but with the same neck characteristic as the chunky, has been recorded in medium to deep amethyst. I have seen only two of the latter, and they have an abnormal pontil mark—namely, a lump of glass. Whether or not the flasks of the two forms were patterned in the same mold I was unable to determine when I had an opportunity to place one by the side of the other and examine them closely, for the pattern on the ovoid deep amethyst flask was attenuated and distorted in the process of fabrication. If they were not patterned in the same mold, then two similar molds were used.

In spite of my efforts to discover the facts of the matter, so far I have been unable to uncover any *proof* that this diamond-daisy variant—or intaglio—is a china egg planted in the Stiegel nest. Nevertheless, circumstantial evidence gathered from reports of opinions and conversations, coupled with the atypical character of the design and pieces, points to that conclusion. And in the opinion of a few dealers and students, but not all, the mold for the chunky diamond-daisy variant was made in the 20th century and its offspring were introduced into the American antiques market in the late 1920s or 1930s. However, the as-yet-unsubstantiated reports as to *where* the pieces were made do not agree. One places the locale as South Jersey; another, Czechoslovakia. Personally, I lean toward Czechoslovakia. Possibly the mold was sent to a customer who later had the ovoids blown in the South Jersey or Philadelphia area. Another report named Emil Larsen of Vineland, New Jersey, as the maker. However, in a letter of May 1962, Mr. Larsen informed me that he had not made the amethyst ovoid flask sent to him for inspection or any piece in the pattern. Nor did he know of any being made in South Jersey. If anyone has any positive proof, or actually *knows* where such a mold was made and used, I have yet to find that person—or he or she has been reluctant to divulge the information.

Although Stiegel is credited with being the first American glass manufacturer to make lead glass, it would appear that none of that choice metal was fashioned into bottles in the ogival, small-diamonds-above-flutes, diamond-daisy, or daisy-in-hexagon design. At least the specimens that have been tested for lead content have proved to be non-lead metal. However, the metal appears to be of good quality and brilliance. Also, apparently none of the ordinary bottle glass was used for bottles in these designs. As yet, the ogivals and small-diamonds-above-flutes have been recorded only in amethysts of varied depth of tone. The majority of the diamond-daisy and daisy-in-hexagon bottles are likewise in shades of amethyst. One of the former is so dark as to appear black in reflected light. One beautiful soft, light sapphire-blue diamond-daisy, 6 in Color Plate II, is known, and one deep reddish purple, which was formerly in the Alfred B. Maclay Collection. This one sapphire-blue bottle was found in Ohio about 50 years ago, innocent of any previous history. Presumably it had been among the prized possessions of a family moving into the western territory. At present, one colorless daisy-in-hexagon and one colorless diamond-daisy are in the Henry Francis du Pont Winterthur Museum. Two other colorless diamond-daisies are known. One is in a private collection; the other in the Henry Ford Museum. The latter came to light around 1930 in the cellar of a private home in my hometown, Hoosick Falls, New York, when a box of discarded bottles was lifted and the bottom fell out, spilling the contents onto the cellar floor. There, among Malto Yer-bine and patent medicine bottles, and still intact in spite of its hazardous tumble, was the first known colorless diamond-daisy—the only bottle of age and beauty in the lot! Nothing could be learned of its previous history. The extreme rarity of these bottles suggests that they were seldom blown from colorless glass or from blue.

To restate earlier observations, it is almost axiomatic that bottles of this type produced at Elizabeth Furnace and in the early years of the first Manheim works were blown only from green glass and, probably, from window-glass metal. Therefore, since the ogival, small-diamonds-above-flutes, diamond-daisy, and daisy-in-hexagon bottles have been found only in fine colorless or artificially colored metal, the conclusion seems tenable that they were not produced before the blast of 1769–70—late fall to spring.

Another 18th-century pattern-molded design generally classified as Stiegel-type is the so-called checkered-diamond illustrated by 1 and 3 in Color Plate II. It is an allover design—a diaper formed by a lattice enclosing in each diamond-shaped space four small concave "diamonds" or "petals." Apparently there were two molds in this diaper design—one having eight checkered-diamonds in each horizontal row and the other seven. There were at least six rows in the eight-checkered-diamond mold, but on the flasks the top row or rows appear as irregular ribs, having been pulled together in the fabrication of the flask. On the base, eight grooves produced pronounced ribs radiating from the center and forming a flowerlike design of flutes with rounded ends. As yet, only bottles have been recorded from an eight-checkered-diamond mold, and they are very rare. In the 18th-century chunky globular and ovoid shapes, one sapphire-blue and two or three amethyst are known at present. One of the amethysts, now in the Henry Ford Museum, was made by the German half-post method, and on spot test it proved to be nonlead—as doubtless are the others. In the tall broad flattened chestnut shape like 3 in Color Plate II, two pale amethyst, a few colorless of gray tone, and light green flasks have been recorded. Two of the last, similar in color and metal to some of the midwestern chestnut flasks, turned up in Ohio. The only one I have been able to measure for capacity holds about 18 ounces.

The seven-checkered-diamond mold may have had only five rows in the diaper. Apparently it was used primarily to pattern gathers for salts given a double-ogee bowl, ribbed knop, and applied plain circular foot. These occur in sapphire, deep and pale blue, purple, and colorless glass, and are rare. Unfortunately it has been impossible to determine the form of the ribbing on the base, since that part of the pattern appears as close ribs in the knop of the salt. The mold *possibly* was used to pattern the gathers for a few flasks. In the Henry Francis du Pont Winterthur Museum, there is a deep sapphire-blue flask that may have been patterned in the mold. It is a flattened chestnut shape, $5^1/16$ inches in height, $4\frac{1}{8}$ inches in greatest width, and (at lower body) $2^1/16$ inches in greatest depth. The pattern is so expanded on the lower half of the body as to be nearly nonexistent, and so pulled out of shape on the upper part that the motifs are distorted, though, with one exception, they appear to be the same type of diaper as that of the salts and of the flasks from the eight-checkered-diamond mold. One checkered-diamond seems to have a "hook" at top and bottom as on the flasks described below, but possibly this appearance resulted from the considerable elongation of the motif.

Also, on the bottom, fine ribs from the center form a seven-pointed starlike motif.

Unless expansion and size of gathers can alter a pattern-molded design more drastically than I have realized, there was another design with seven "checkered-diamonds" in horizontal rows. At first glance, it appears to be the same as the checkered-diamond diaper, but on close scrutiny it seems a distinctive relative with differences resulting from mold idiosyncrasies. The "checkered-diamonds" are really quatrefoils formed by pronounced ribs having a tiny hook at top and bottom and with concave center in each lobe. These quatrefoils, at least on three known bottles in the pattern, appear larger than the checkered-diamonds of the diaper pattern. They are also more widely spaced. And although the width of the surrounding space varies somewhat with the degree of expansion of the gather from which the flasks were blown, the general effect is not of a latticed diaper but of motifs isolated on a plain smooth field. On the bottom, fine ribs radiating from the center form a seven-pointed starlike decoration, as on the sapphire-blue flask described above.

All three of the bottles are colorless, and no two are exactly alike in shape or size. One, in the Henry Francis du Pont Winterthur Museum, is a Stiegel-type chunky ovoid, $5\frac{1}{4}$ inches in height, 4 inches in greatest width, and 2 inches in greatest depth. A second, formerly in the collection of Crawford Wettlaufer, has a Stiegel-type chunky globular body tapering slightly at top. It is 4 inches in greatest width, 2 inches in greatest depth, and only $4\frac{3}{4}$ inches in height. It was bought by Richard H. Wood many years ago in Virginia at an auction of the collection and stock of an "old time dealer" of Wilmington, Delaware. The third, part of the collection of the late Melvin Billups, was blown from an unusually heavy gather of metal, and consequently its flattened globular, approaching the circular, body is thicker walled than normal. It is 5 inches in height, 4 inches in greatest width, and $2\frac{1}{2}$ inches in greatest depth. On all three the motifs are very sharp, standing out more cleanly from top to bottom than do those I have seen in the checkered-diamond diaper. I believe that Winterthur's and Mr. Wettlaufer's bottles were undoubtedly patterned in the same mold, and probably Mr. Billups's also. Though the quatrefoils on his example are larger and more widely spaced than on the other two, the size of the gather and expansion may account for the difference.

Whether this quatrefoil pattern is an American original or not is an unanswerable question at this time, but there is no doubt the checkered-diamond diaper, once credited to Stiegel as the creator, is of German ancestry, used for bottles in the early South German glasshouses. In an article in *The Magazine* ANTIQUES, April 1932, Gustave Pazaurek illustrated an amber example, seemingly blown from a single gather of metal and given a flattened bulbous body with very short neck and collared lip.[27] For several years it has been thought that the design was used at Amelung's New Bremen Glassmanufactory, but the possibility of previous use by Stiegel lurks in the background. The checkered-diamond salts mentioned above have usually been found in localities nearer to New Bremen, closer to Frederick, Maryland, than to Manheim. An Amelung tradition clung to some of them. Also, a fragment of a dark-toned colorless checkered-diamond piece, presumably a flask, that was unearthed by Martin and Elizabeth Stohlman on the New Bremen Glassmanufactory site first contributed to the Amelung theory. Two more fragments—one colorless; the other, green—were unearthed during the 1962/63 archaeological excavations by The Corning Museum of Glass and the Smithsonian Institution under the direction of Ivor Noël Hume.[28] Since tools and equipment for the glassworks were brought from Germany, molds for one or both of the checkered-diamond diapers may have been among them. On the other hand, if one or both molds was—or were, if one is on the "con" side of the Stiegel theory—used at Manheim, later appearance at New Bremen can be simply accounted for: Amelung employed some of Stiegel's ex-craftsmen, who probably brought tools with them to New Bremen. It is assumed that the eight-checkered-diamond mold in which the light green chestnut flasks were patterned may have traveled westward, either with the New Bremen blowers who associated with Albert Gallatin & Company to start the New Geneva Glass Works or with Amelung's son Frederick Magnus, who was to take molds with him to O'Hara's Pittsburgh Glass Works.[29] Eventually the mold may have traveled on to an Ohio glasshouse where the light green flasks were blown—if the flasks themselves had not been taken to Ohio by migrant glassblowers or in household effects.

Before turning to the exciting midwestern bottles and flasks, Emil Larsen and his twentieth-century Stiegel-type flasks command our attention. Emil Larsen, the son of a glassblower, was born in Sweden in 1877. In 1887, when he was ten years old, he came to the United States with his father and soon began his career in glassmaking. He mastered the various phases of glassmaking and became one of our most skillful glassblowers, working and perfecting his craft in many glassworks. Among them were the famous Dorflinger glassworks at White Mills, Pennsylvania, the Pairpoint Glass Works in New Bedford, Massachusetts, and the Durand Glass Works in Vineland, New Jersey. In 1932 he gave up his regular employment at Durand and built a small furnace on his premises in Vineland. His operations were not continuous because, as he wrote to me in 1962, he "was called away to different places between times." In about ten years he closed down completely. For the next few years, before retiring to Florida, he traveled and trained glassmen in different factories. In his "own little factory," Emil Larsen made a wide variety of fine blown glass much of which is similar in forms and techniques to some of our late 18th-century and early 19th-century glass. For some, he turned to the South Jersey tradition of free-blowing and ornamentation by glass applied to itself and tooled. For some, especially flasks, he followed the Stiegel tradition of ribbed and diamond designs. Sometimes he combined the two traditions. From time to time in his career he acquired iron molds from defunct glassworks, about 30 in all. Among them were rib molds in "quite a variety of different ribs" and two "very old" four-piece diamond molds.[30]

Larsen's Stiegel-type flasks have distinctive characteristics, such as the following:

1. They are ovoid, of generous depth in proportion to height and width, and much heavier than 18th- and early 19th-century flasks of similar measurements.

2. The neck, as a rule, is shorter in proportion to height of body than that of earlier flasks, more precisely formed with more abrupt line of demarcation at its base, and the attentuated pattern is usually tooled quite flat.

3. The pontil mark is usually small and thin, sometimes a mere trace; occasionally it is a lump of glass.

4. The sizes run from a few ounces to about a pint and a half. And, as in the case of early flasks, "half-pints" and "pints" are the most numerous. Those well under 8 ounces or over 16 are rare.

5. The color range is wide, and beautiful—amethyst, mainly dark or reddish in tone; deep blue; rarely, deep pure greens and purple; very rarely, red.

Three of Larsen's Stiegel-type flasks are pictured in Ill. 90 (Nos. 6, 7, and 8). The rare brilliant light red (6) was patterned in a 12-diamond mold having a plain center in the bottom. As comparison of this flask with 2 in Color Plate II shows, the diamond design is quite different from that of the ogival (12-diamond) flasks attributed to Stiegel, which, it will be recalled, had broad petallike flutes on the bottom. The two deep reddish amethyst flasks, 7 and 8, in swirled and broken-swirl ribbing respectively, were patterned in an 18-rib mold producing pronounced heavy ribs.

Larsen's pieces were sold by him for just what they were: his own creations. Unfortunately, as flasks, and other pieces also, passed through more than one hand, many lost their Larsen identity and eventually landed in some collections as veritable Stiegel. However, today Larsen's flasks, representing a brief renaissance of Stiegel-type work, are deemed collectible in their own right.

4
MIDWESTERN PATTERN-MOLDED BOTTLES, FLASKS, AND JUGS

Not until the early 1920s were any students and collectors of American glass aware that extraordinarily beautiful pattern-molded glassware was blown in early 19th-century Ohio and other midwestern glasshouses of whose existence none had dreamed. Then, as local pickers and dealers began to canvass the area, more and more flasks, bottles, bowls, and articles of tableware, plain and in ribbed and diamond designs, were found west of the Alleghenies, mainly in Ohio and the adjoining territory. Obviously, being blown from single gathers of metal patterned either in rib dip-molds or pattern piece-molds and then fashioned by free-blowing, they were in the "Stiegel tradition," made by the "Stiegel technique." With the discovery of these wares, realization dawned that a whole new area of glassmaking in America had been uncovered, one in which not only the finest of the Stiegel tradition had been perpetuated but some distinctly American forms, colors, and an elaboration of the decorative technique had evolved. For many years the glass was dubbed Ohio Stiegel, not only because the pieces were pattern-molded and the majority attributed to Ohio but also in tribute to their craftsmanship and beauty. The consensus of collectors became, and still is, that at its finest this midwestern glass has never been excelled in America in attractiveness of forms, colors, and ribbed and diamond designs. In the main, the metal is nonlead bottle and window glass of a brilliancy beyond that of the eastern. The clear, often vibrant, colors are the rule, not the exception, and the wide spectrum, especially of greens and ambers, contains many nuances of tone that rarely—some of them, never—appear in products of eastern and foreign glasshouses.

Although a few were cognizant of midwestern glass, even they were unaware of the extent and importance of the early midwestern glass industry until the publication of Stephen Van Rensselaer's *Early American Bottles and Flasks* in 1926 and Rhea Mansfield Knittle's *Early American Glass* in 1927. It was with astonishment that collectors and dealers learned how many large and small midwestern, as well as eastern, glasshouses operated for a few years or decades in the first half of the 19th century. Still, though the possibility of several sources of Ohio and other pattern-molded glassware was implicit, only a few were explored. Even today, definite knowledge of where nonlead bottles and other hollow ware were blown is limited mainly to Zanesville, Mantua, and Kent glassworks in Ohio and the New Geneva Glass Works in Pennsylvania not far from Pittsburgh.

The New Geneva Glass Works on George Creek just outside the village of New Geneva was a window-glass house, but like most early window-glass houses, it produced bottles and hollow ware as a secondary line. The first blast was in January 1798. In 1807 a second house was erected across the Monongahela in Greensburgh, later called Greensboro, and although the George Creek furnace was abandoned shortly after production began at Greensburgh, the name New Geneva Glass works was retained. It is probable that the sole product after about 1830 was window glass. The character of some of the plain and pattern-molded hollow ware blown at the New Geneva Glass Works was determined from pieces handed down in the families of blowers and similar pieces found in the vicinity of the works. These "authenticated" pieces were blown from ordinary glass in a limited range of ambers and greens that do not have the brilliancy of metal or color, or variety of color tone, characteristic of most Ohio glass—presumably because of the difference in the ingredients of the metal. Nor were the gathers for the New Geneva pieces so expanded as to produce the thinness and delicacy of so many of the Ohio pieces. From pedigreed pieces, it is known that a 24-rib mold was used at the New Geneva Glass Works.[31] And, as previously mentioned, three New Geneva pattern molds are still in existence. The 16-rib dip mold is 5 inches in height. Its outside diameter at the top is 2¾ inches and at bottom, 3⅝ inches. Its inside diameter is 2¼ inches between the points of the ribs and 2½ inches at the grooves; inside depth is 4½ inches. The 20-rib dip mold is 5¾ inches in height. Its outside diameter is 3⅝ inches at the top and 3¾ inches at the bottom. Its inside diameter between the points of the ribs is 2¾ inches and between the grooves 3¼ inches. Its inside depth is 5¼ inches. In each, the ribs run to the center bottom. Ill. 92 is based on photographs and descriptions of these molds.

The New Geneva 16-diamond mold is the only known small piece-mold used in one or more of our early glasshouses. The same is true of the two rib-molds. It is quite likely that all three had been used at the New Bremen Glassmanufactory and taken to New Geneva by Christian Kramer, an Amelung blower, in whose family they have been handed down. Christian Kramer was one of the five German glassblowers from New Bremen who joined with Albert Gallatin & Company to start the New Geneva Glass Works. The molds were formerly owned by Logan Ross, a descendant of Kramer. The metal of the leaves of the diamond mold has not been positively determined, but Harry Hall White stated in his article "Pattern Molds and Pattern Molded Glass" (*The Magazine* ANTIQUES, August 1939) that the metal was brass or bronze. The handles (which Mr. Ross believes are not original) are iron, as are the link hinge and pin securing them. The outside diameter of each leaf is 1⅝ inches; the length, 3¼ inches. The inside diameter of the patterned surface is 1³/₁₆ inches; the inside length, 2⅝ inches. Because the description of the pattern given by Mr. White in his article, and repeated in *American Glass* (p. 121), seemed to contain a geometric anomaly, namely "17 diamonds in the bottom row and 16 diamonds in the top row," we asked Mr. Ross to check the mold. He sent us not only a complete description and photographs but also impressions from the mold. The pattern with leaves closed consists of 16 ribs about ⅜ inches long, tapering to the

center bottom of the mold. The grooves between the ribs blend into a horizontal groove from which latticed grooving rises and describes small relief diamonds. The grooves are about ¹/₁₆ of an inch wide. There are 16 diamonds in each of 16 horizontal rows and, of course, 8 diamonds in chain height. In each leaf, starting with the bottom row, alternate rows have 16 complete diamonds, and, at each end of the rows between, half-diamonds, which form full diamonds when the mold is closed. Ill. 93A was based on the impression, description, and photographs.

Zanesville's two early glassworks were started about the end of the War of 1812. The first, started by the Zanesville Glass Manufacturing Company for the production of "White hollow ware"—hence the local name The White Glass Works—was in operation by May of 1815. By the end of 1817, earlier plans to expand had materialized with the addition of a house "for the Manufacture of Window Glass and Green Hollow Ware of every description." The second Zanesville glass venture was the green-glass works established near Sligo Run in 1816 for the production of window glass and hollow ware. So bottles and other hollow ware were blown in both works.[32] But, although most students agree as to the colors and designs that are characteristic of pieces attributed to Zanesville, specific identification with either of the glassworks is still considered to be impossible, as is categorical attribution to Zanesville—or so some students believe. Thus, the glass associated with Zanesville is called simply Zanesville, though perhaps Zanesville-type should be used in connection with unpedigreed pieces since there is no proof that similar pieces were not blown elsewhere in the Midwest. In fact, at Mantua, Harry Hall White unearthed substantial numbers of fragments of plain and ribbed "calabash bottles [globulars] in deep amber shades hitherto attributed solely to Zanesville. . ." Also, it should be kept firmly in mind that neither the Zanesville Glass Works nor the Sligo was the first to produce green-glass bottles and flasks in Ohio or west of Pittsburgh: the short-lived Maysville Glass Works in Kentucky was in production by January 1815 and the Cincinnati Glass Works by April 1815.[33]

In the case of Zanesville, the character of its early plain and pattern-molded hollow wares was determined to the satisfaction of most students from a considerable body of evidence combining local tradition, point of discovery of a piece, and family history regarding it. Inherited pieces having a Zanesville history consistent with the design and physical glass characteristic of the period established a basis for tentative attribution of unpedigreed pieces found in the neighborhood and elsewhere in Ohio. From the accumulated evidence, it is generally agreed that Zanesville colors are predominantly ambers and greens in a wide spread of tones and hues; occasionally blues, mainly sapphire and cornflower; rarely moonstone. Miles A. Smith's studies led him to the conclusion that "Zanesville items do not show the variety of olive-ambers found in the Mantua and Kent areas." But one Zanesville color that is generally termed *olive-yellow* is, to many eyes, an amber hue of olive tone. Also, Mr. Smith found no amethyst pieces attributable to Zanesville. Nor has James H. Rose, long a student of midwestern glass and its distribution.[34] On the other hand, the George S. McKearin Collection included a well-authenticated large witch ball in a lovely light amethyst. Ribbings and, at least, one diamond or ogival design ornamented the pattern-molded pieces. Although more than one 24-rib mold undoubtedly was used to pattern Zanesville glass, at present there is *no evidence that a particular type of ribbing or termination in the bottom of the mold* was exclusive to Zanesville. It seems to me that molds of other counts must have been used also.

The only diamond mold as yet associated with Zanesville has distinctive characteristics, and is generally referred to as the Zanesville 10-diamond mold. Probably no longer extant, it is known only through the pieces patterned in the design of "large diamonds above flutes." At the meeting of the flutes and diamonds on several pieces, James H. Rose found a faint but definite horizontal mold seam.[35] Therefore, though designed to impress a pattern and not give form, the mold must have consisted of three pieces: a bottom piece with flutes and two upper pieces with diamonds. The formation of the diamonds reminds one of the early English nipt-diamond-waies in which applied vertical threads of glass were pinched together at four points into a diamondlike design. In fact, the possibility of their being nipt-diamond-waies was briefly considered before a comparative study of many specimens—table articles as well as flasks—proved a mold having identifying characteristics had been used. The diamonds are not true straight-sided diamonds but ogival in line. Nor are they of uniform size. They were described by narrow deep grooves, which produced pronounced ribs. And grooves formed the 10 ribs rising from the center bottom to the lower point of each diamond or ogival in the bottom row. The number of horizontal rows of diamonds is uncertain, since in fashioning a piece one or more rows at the top of the patterned gather

might be cut off. There are five rows, and at least one pulled into irregular ribs on the neck, on most flasks I have examined. The jug, 3 in Ill. 99, has eight rows, the top one of which was pulled into ribs. Miles A. Smith has well described the peculiarities of formation:

they are rounded at the corners, and in some cases the corners do not touch each other. Furthermore, at the point where the so-called diamonds merge into the vertical ribs, each of the lowest diamonds seems to wander into the merger with the appropriate rib in a different fashion. Several, but not all, of the diamonds have small loops of varying shapes at the bottom.[36]

The combined weight of colors and metal, local tradition, and reliable family histories of many flasks and a few sugar bowls, creamers, small bowls, and compotes tips the scales of probability toward conviction that the mold was used in Zanesville. However, use of the mold elsewhere is suggested by the history of a small shallow bowl fashioned from a gather of brilliant light green nonlead glass, which unmistakably was patterned in this mold. The bowl was acquired about 50 years ago from an elderly woman who had inherited it. She was quite unfamiliar with old glass and its makers but had been told that the bowl was purchased in 1818 and that it had been made by a man named Duval in Wellsburg, (W) Virginia. Perhaps family history was as unreliable in this instance as we all know it can be. Perhaps, quite innocently, identity had been transferred to this bowl from a piece that was blown in Duval's glassworks and bought in Wellsburg in 1818. Perhaps the bowl had been taken to Wellsburg by a migrant glassblower from Zanesville. At present, I know of no other 10-diamond piece, or any plain or pattern-molded piece, attributed to Duval. On the other hand, since surviving glass testifies to the demand for pattern-molded wares, they undoubtedly were produced in Duval's glassworks as well as elsewhere in the Midwest. Also, although his White Flint Glass Works was started in Charlestown (later called Wellsburg) in 1813 with the intention of producing fine flint ware, green-glass hollow ware was blown too, especially in the early years. Orders for "Green Hollow Glass" as well as "White Flint" were being solicited in May 1819 when John J. Jacobs & Company reopened the works, which had been closed since the previous November.[37] It seems to me that the history of the small bowl cannot be ignored. One previously suggested explanation is that there must have been two identical molds—but the many idiosyncrasies of this 10-diamond mold would seem to preclude *exact* duplication. Therefore, at present, I believe the small drop of Duval evidence might indicate the mold was taken from Wellsburg to one of the Zanesville houses, and so it does not dilute the Zanesville attribution.

In the case of Mantua and Kent, the same sort of evidence exists as for other early glassworks — namely, point of discovery, local tradition, family histories, and comparative study — but it is bolstered by revealing fragments unearthed on the factory sites by Harry Hall White. The output of the Mantua and Kent glassworks cannot have been tremendous, for they were small and short-lived. Nor can the demand for their wares have been widespread. In its seven years of operation, the Mantua Glass Works produced fine bottles, flasks, and other hollow ware, including articles for table use. Although it is said that "flint" as well as "common" glass was made, all authenticated pieces that have been tested were non-lead. But whatever the silica and other ingredients were, the "common" metal, as at Kent and Zanesville, was usually of uncommon quality. Not far from Mantua, in Kent (formed in 1863 from the two tiny adjoining villages of Carthage and Franklin Mills), there were two glasshouses: one started in 1823 and the other in 1824. Until around 1834, containers and some tableware were blown in each. Both Kent and Mantua glass was blown usually from brilliant metal that ran the gamut of ambers and greens associated with Ohio glass. A few pieces from each have been recorded in moonstone, a cloudy crystal probably intended to be colorless. There is at present no record of artificially colored Kent glass, but a few pedigreed Mantua pieces are a beautiful amethyst. Mr. White established that Mantua used a 15-diamond piece mold, a 16-rib mold with ribs running to a terminal ring at center bottom, and a 32-rib mold. At Kent he found a 20-rib mold was used.[38] The termination of the ribs in the bottom of the 32- and 20-rib molds is uncertain, so far as I have been able to learn. It seems unlikely that the molds determined from fragments were the only ones in the equipment of those two houses.

Before discussing midwestern bottles and flasks as a whole, the distribution of the commercial wares blown in the early glassworks merits attention, if only because a glassworks' markets indicate localities in which its products may "turn up" and where they mingled with and met the competition of wares from other glassworks. Inasmuch as certain designs, colors, and molds have been associated particularly with New Geneva, Zanesville, Mantua, and

Kent, their markets are of special interest and have been given more consideration in the past, but information about distribution is still very meager. Nevertheless, one generalization seems sound, at least at this stage of studies: the glassware sold outside the town in which they were produced (and its vincinity) went westward; the Allegheny Mountains, making transportation difficult and costly, were a barrier to successful competition with eastern glassworks in eastern markets. Of course, after the Erie Canal was opened, providing a water route all the way to New York City in 1825, that barrier was nearly leveled. Still, eastward traffic in glass was far from congested. Such information as I have at present about specific glassworks comes mainly from newspaper advertisements, a little documentary evidence, and conclusions drawn from the "find spots" of individual pieces. Naturally, or so one would assume, each works had a local market and supplied the community's glass needs in the kinds of wares produced. But this natural outlet was insufficient to support a viable enterprise: larger markets were a necessary nutriment, the lack of which doubtless explains the short life of many glassworks.

In New Geneva's case, light has been shed on the distribution of its early products by letters and accounts in the Gallatin Papers in the Manuscript Collection of the New-York Historical Society and by a few known advertisements in midwestern newspapers. New Geneva's nonlocal outlets were mainly Pittsburgh and the westward creeping markets in the towns along the Monongahela and Ohio rivers, to Kentucky and into southern Ohio. New Geneva window glass and hollow ware were sold, or consigned, both through agents and directly to town merchants and keepers of general stores, who in turn often sold by box or package to country storekeepers. In February 1806, the proprietor of the Sign of the Negro, a Pittsburgh glass and china shop, advised merchants descending the Ohio that he had a large assortment of superior-quality New Geneva window glass and hollow glass for sale at Pittsburgh prices. In March 1807 a notice that "hollow ware of the best quality" was being shipped from New Geneva appeared in *The Wheeling Repository*. In the Gallatin Papers is an August 1807 notation of glass at six Kentucky towns — Shelbyville, Georgetown, Frankfort, Lexington, Paris, and Maysville — and also at Cincinnati and Chillicothe in Ohio, at Pittsburgh, and at Wheeling. I believe that as more complete research in midwestern newspapers is done, advertisements probably will be found showing continued sale of New Geneva hollow ware in these areas until about 1830. However, the latest known advertisement, the second recorded by Josephine Jefferson, appeared in an 1826 issue of *The Wheeling Repository;* it announced a shipment of boxes of New Geneva hollow ware consisting of half-gallon, quart, and pint bottles, assorted.[39] Obviously, New Geneva bottles and flasks may be among those that are, and have been, found in the Pittsburgh-Monongahela region, the Wheeling area of West Virginia, northern Kentucky, and the southern part of Ohio. Families, among them perhaps those of glassmen or others associated with the New Geneva Glass Works, very likely took pieces of New Geneva glass with them. It should be kept in mind that any such pieces would perhaps have been blown from window-glass metal and certainly from green glass in its natural colors, but not from artificially colored glass such as blue and amethyst.

Geographically, the Zanesville glassworks were more advantageously located in Ohio than were Mantua and Kent, nearer faster developing parts of the state. Zanesville was a strategic site for commerce: it was on the navigable Muskingum River, emptying into the Ohio River, and as James H. Rose pointed out, on a main east-west land route, soon to become an extension of the National Road—now Route 40. Naturally Zanesville glass passed over these avenues of trade. Down the rivers and along the National Road, some wares, so Mr. Rose believed, went as far west as Indiana and to St. Louis, but fewer went eastward toward Wheeling. That section, of course, was already well supplied by the glassworks of Wheeling, Wellsburg, and the Pittsburgh and Monongahela area, including New Geneva. Mr. Rose found, too, that some Zanesville-type wares went north into the belt between the National Road and Route 30, and that a few, very few, pieces have been found as far north as Cleveland. The latter may have been among the household effects of new citizens rather than shop merchandise. The main Zanesville market, however, apparently was in the southwestern belt between the National Road and the Ohio River. It is interesting to note that, in searching Cincinnati newspapers for me, Mrs. Lee Adams found no advertisement of Zanesville glass after one in 1816 of white hollow ware and one in 1820 announcing white flint glass— until 1831. In July of that year Allison Owen announced arrival of 300 boxes of bottles and flasks of assorted sizes from the Zanesville Glass Works.[40]

In the case of Mantua and Kent, I know of no documentary evidence about where the wares were sold outside their immediate neighborhood. Today,

conclusions as to the main avenues of distribution still derive from the geographical distribution of the attributable pieces that have been found in private homes. On this point James H. Rose has given me the benefit of his conclusions from his experience of over 50 years. When Kent and Mantua glass traveled afield from the nearby communities, it seems to have penetrated *mainly* into the not-too-demanding, young, northeastern Ohio market—roughly the northeast quarter of the state. Even there it found a rival in Pittsburgh glass. Little seems to have gone south of what is now Route 30, from Pittsburgh through Canton and Mansfield and across the state. However, that some did is indicated by a statement made by Harry Hall White in a letter written over 40 years ago: he wrote that he knew "of 4 Ohio glasshouses that marketed their wares down the Tuscarawas River thru Zanesville." He commented also on the similarity of forms, pattern, and color from two of these to the so-called Zanesville products, adding "of this I have proof."[41] Unfortunately Mr. White did not identify the glasshouses, and—to the great loss of all students of American glass—he never found the time to publish the wealth of information gleaned by his meticulous research. However, I believe, it can be said with confidence that three of the houses were the two at Kent and the one at Mantua, all in villages on the Cuyahoga River, which flows into the Tuscarawas. At Zanesville and farther south and west, Mantua and Kent wares would have entered the stream of stiff competition. Surely their brief life-span is indicative of Mantua's and Kent's inability to survive competition with larger and more favorably situated works.

Clearly, no market belonged exclusively to any one glassworks. Therefore pieces found in or near any market area would not be ipso facto the product of only one, or two, glassworks. It is axiomatic that not all the bottles, flasks, or other wares found in the various areas where the products of New Geneva, Zanesville, Mantua, or Kent are known to have gone were necessarily from one of these houses. As has been stated time and again, glass from Pittsburgh itself and its environs, the largest glassmaking center in the Midwest, went into all sections west of the Alleghenies. And certainly wares from Wheeling and Wellsburg also traveled along the National Road and down the Ohio River. Then, too, glassware from Maysville in Kentucky and that blown at Cincinnati and Moscow in the southwest corner of Ohio joined the flow locally and possibly westward, briefly. The Maysville Glass Works, it will be recalled, was in complete operation by January 1815, producing window glass and hollow ware, and was still active when Adlard Welby visited the town in 1820. Hough, Rees & Company, proprietors of the Cincinnati Glass Works (established by Anthony, Hough, and Rees in 1815), advertised "Window Glass, Porter Bottles, Common Bottles, Flasks, Tumblers &c" in March 1816. (See Ills. 13 and 14.) Cincinnati was one center in which glass from many factories was sold and from which these wares, "packed to suit purchasers," went out to other communities and the countryside. Among the bits of evidence are the following advertisements, which are of interest to bottle collectors: Wm. C. Rogers, of the City Auction, No. 10 Lower Market Street, announced in October 1821 the receipt of "50 [boxes] of Pittsburgh & Brownsville Glass Ware" that included "Flasks, Mustard Bottles, &c" and would "be sold by the box or repacked to suit purchasers"; in December 1821, "150 boxes . . . comprising a complete assortment of nearly every description . . . " from the same two glassworks; in November 1823, "Pittsburgh, Wellsburg, and Moscow glassware." From May into July 1829, W. D. Jones advertised glass from "JOHN TAYLOR & CO'S. Glassworks, Brownsville, Pa.," including "Porter Bottles—Gallon, Half Gallon, Quart and Pint bottles . . . packed to suit purchasers."[42]

It is inconceivable to me that pattern molds were used to ornament gathers for bottles and flasks only by the midwestern quartet—New Geneva, Zanesville, Mantua, and Kent; but conceivable that such molds were part of the equipment of any midwestern glasshouse producing these essential containers. And, of course, circumstantial evidence testifies they were, especially in the Pittsburgh area. After all, manufacturers survive by providing merchandise of proven appeal, and—from the last third of the 18th century, at least—expanded ribbing and diamonds were among the standard decorations of pocket bottles, including chestnuts, and the occasional decoration of larger bottles. It is as improbable that this sort of decoration suffered obsolescence during the nearly 20-year period between the start of midwestern glassmaking in Pittsburgh in 1795 and that in (West) Virginia and Ohio, as it is that only the familiar quartet used it. More emphatically, the large number of different rib molds and the variety of diamond molds, the majority unidentified or unassociated with a particular glassworks, point to usage in several works and areas. And, it will be remembered, molds having the same number of ribs and diamonds were used in more than one glassworks. Moreover, since the early Ohio glasshouses—

probably Maysville, Kentucky, also—apparently were manned mainly by glassmen from the Pittsburgh area, pattern molding and some of the bottle and flask forms must have been introduced by them. The blowers, moving from one works to another as they did, may well have taken molds with them—as, presumably, J.F.M. Amelung did when he went from Baltimore to Pittsburgh in 1805, and as did Christian Kramer when he went from New Bremen to New Geneva in 1798. Certainly they did not leave behind their individual tricks of fashioning a bottle, of drawing out the neck and finishing the lip. Can any more probable conclusion be drawn than that bottles and flasks closely similar to some of those identified with New Geneva, Zanesville, Kent, and Mantua were blown elsewhere?

Unfortunately, actual proof of the validity of my conclusions seems unlikely. Although a few sites of possible midwestern sources of pattern-molded flasks and bottles are still (and others may be) available for excavations that might prove or disprove the production of such wares, their colors and other characteristics, there appears to be lack of both interest and funds to conduct scientific archaeological digs. On the other hand, invaluable archaeological evidence probably has been lost forever insofar as the glassworks located within, or in the environs of, Pittsburgh, Wheeling, and other urban centers are concerned: their sites have been absorbed by the cities and suburbs. However, because of the probable—most students believe, certain—widespread production of many types and forms, I use the regional term *midwestern glass*. Therefore, in discussing the general nature and characteristics of the bottles and flasks, I shall treat them mainly as a whole, regardless of individual glasshouses.

Not surprisingly in a region where whiskey had served as currency as well as a medicinal and titillating beverage, bottles predominate in midwestern pattern-molded glass. As a rule they are divided into three species: flasks, elliptical or ovate in cross section, with short neck, and, normally, plain lip; bottles, elliptical, ovate, or round in cross section, with long neck and, normally, collared lip; jugs—that is, handled bottles and flasks—with short to medium-long neck and, usually, collared lip. Characteristic bottles appear in Ills. 94, 95, and 96; flasks, in Ills. 91, 97, and 98; jugs, in Ill. 99. In my studies I have found that flasks constitute the largest group, though bottles run a close second. And jugs form the smallest group and are rare.

In describing these containers, it has been customary to designate their size, or capacity, by standard liquid measures. In reality, as was true of all free-blown bottles whose size of capacity was judged by the blower's eye, they so seldom conform to exact measure that few could have passed an Inspector of Weights and Measures, had there been one concerned. In the case of the flasks, though not all sizes have been found in all shapes, the overall range of capacity is from about an ounce to 1¾ quarts. Since they were primarily pocket bottles, those of about half-pint to a pint capacity far outnumber the others, and of these half-pints are in the majority. It seems likely the demand for those well under a half-pint or over a pint was not insistent. Those holding only an ounce or two may have been used as smelling bottles rather than for so unsatisfying an amount of liquor, or perhaps as toys. In any event the small ones, usually called *miniatures* by collectors, are extremely rare today. The "Grandmother" flasks, as those well over a pint but under a quart capacity have been dubbed, are scarce. Comparatively scarce too are the "Grandfather" flasks holding a quart or more. Flasks in ribbed patterns have been found in all sizes; those in diamond or ogival designs, from about half-pint to a pint. Of the pint ogivals, only a few have been recorded, and most of them were patterned in the Zanesville 10-diamond mold.

In spite of the fact that there were other forms, the midwestern flasks have long been grouped under the heading *chestnut flasks,* a name (as mentioned previously) derived from a general resemblance to a somewhat flattened American chestnut. Like all freeblown bottles, no two are *exactly* alike. But only occasionally did a blower produce a lopsided flask like 2 in Ill. 97; the majority of the many I have seen are exceedingly and exceptionally well fashioned and symmetrical. Whatever their basic type of shape, they vary in contour and in length and width of neck. The neck usually is finished with a plain lip, rarely with a narrow flange like that on 3 in Ill. 91 or a flaring lip as on 2 in Ill. 97. The bases may be flat, depressed slightly or with one of a variety of shallow kick-ups. Whatever the variation in line at the top or in the width, the greatest depth was normally toward the bottom of the flask. I have record of five basic shapes:

1. The flattened chestnut shape, which, it would appear, was given to the greatest number. Typical examples are 3 in Ill. 91; 2, 6, and 9 in Ill. 98; and 1, 4, and 10 in Ill. 97.
2. The wide "chestnut" approaching the circular in contour, with a bit of a taper at the top like the Grandfather flask, 10 in Ill. 98; and flasks 4, 5 and

7 in Ill. 98. In my experience this 19th-century variation of the Stiegel-type flask with near-circular body is peculiar to midwestern flasks, which also normally have less depth in proportion to height and width than those of the previous century.
3. The wide chestnut approaching the circular in contour, "fat" with high shoulder in a gentle curve, as on 7 in Ill. 97. This also, in my records, is peculiarly midwestern.
4. The flattened ovoid like 11 in Ill. 98 and 3 and 10 in Ill. 97.
5. Chunky, flattened globular similar to Steigel-type pocket bottles. Flasks of this form have been found only very occasionally. I believe they probably were blown in the first 10 or 15 years of glassmaking in the Midwest.

The features that, more than any others, set most midwestern apart from most eastern flasks are the brilliancy of the metal and the beauty of diversified colors enhanced by molded designs, which, breaking the even surface of the glass, create a fascinating play of light and shade. As one would expect, the colors natural to bottle glass predominate—that is, ambers and greens. But pure true ambers and greens probably were "artificial," intentionally produced by the use of metallic oxides, as were blues and amethysts. In any event, there are many green and amber shades, tones, and hues that are totally unlike those in the glass from which eastern bottles were blown, and that, as colors always do, defy adequate verbal description. Still, the ambers do run from a rare pale topaz through golden shades to a deep reddish and deep brown amber, sometimes so dark as to appear almost black in reflected light. Olive-ambers—that is, ambers of decided green tone—are less frequently seen than in eastern bottles. There is a profusion of greens: aquamarines, brilliant true green from light to dark, yellow-greens, sometimes a beautiful clear olive-green and olive-yellow. One of the most charming of the yellow-greens is a shade well-named *citron.* Aquamarines run from very pale to strong, usually greenish but sometimes bluish. Blues, which are comparatively rare, occur with a greenish tone, in a delicate cornflower hue, clear sapphire and cobalt, and very rarely a violet-blue and light blue tint. Amethyst is extremely rare. A few of these chestnut flasks have been found in amethystine and in colorless glass, sometimes streaked with amethyst. Also, the glass of a few, as yet associated only with the Ohio houses, is densely cloudy or milky somewhat resembling a polished moonstone, and hence called *moonstone*. It seems probable that the color, or condition, was not intentional, but rather due to faulty proportions of ingredients in the batch—perhaps the precipitation of some ingredient when a batch was melted, possibly lead in the attempt to make flint (lead) glass.

The molded patterns consist of ribbings and a few diamond designs. As on flasks from other areas and countries, the ribbing predominates—vertical, swirled to right or left, and broken swirl. The ribs were mainly contiguous, widely expanded as on the Grandfather flask, 10 in Ill. 98; pronounced and somewhat widely spaced as on 6 in the same illustration; fine ribbing from a mold with slightly convex spaces between grooves, producing in expansion a fluted effect, as on 1 of Ill. 97. The broken swirl displays considerable variety resulting from the type of ribs in the mold and the degree of expansion and manipulation in fashioning the flask. Three different broken-swirl effects are shown by 3, 7, and 9 in Ill. 97. The so-called popcorn kernel of 3 is similar to that of some of the Pitkin-type flasks. Sometimes the glass was so expanded that a delicate feathery effect was created, very much like an expanded diamond-on-the-diagonal. Some of the broken swirls—the last, for instance—seem almost distinctively American and midwestern. In fact, as I have said, in my experience of eastern glass the broken swirl occurs only on the Pitkin-type flasks blown by the half-post method, never on flasks or bottles blown from a single gather of metal.

As in the case of midwestern Pitkin-types, the number of ribs is more varied than on known eastern chestnuts. However, in my experience, the majority of ribbed flasks have 24 ribs. And from an examination of the few flasks on which the rib termination on the bottom was not obscured by the pontil mark, it is evident that at least three different types of 24-rib molds were used: one with ribs converging at center bottom; one with ribs running to a terminal ring; one with ribs fading into a plain center. Many flasks have been recorded that were patterned in 16-, 18-, and 20-rib molds; a few each in 14-, 15-, 17-, 19-, 26-, and 28-rib molds. Since bottles have been recorded with 12-, 13-, 30-, 31-, and 32-rib counts, one day doubtless flasks will be also. As stated previously, 16- and 32-rib molds were among those used at Mantua; a 20-rib mold at Kent; 24-rib molds at Zanesville; and 16-, 20-, and 24-rib molds at New Geneva. The incidence in the Pittsburgh–Monongahela area of flasks having 17, 18, and 19 ribs, as well as 16 and 20, points to molds of these counts having been used in some glassworks in that region. Also, it may be that a

glasshouse there used the two-piece 24-rib mold determined by Miles A. Smith from a study of several light green vertically ribbed flasks, a swirl-ribbed bowl, and several swirl-ribbed pitchers. The pitchers were found in the general neighborhood of Pittsburgh.[43] Lowell Innes informed me that 8-, 12-, and 15-rib molds were widely used for some Pittsburgh tableware, and he has found some examples from 14-, 18-, and 20-rib molds. Doubtless Pittsburgh flasks were patterned in them also.

There were few diamond molds and designs. Also, flasks with diamonds are far less numerous than those with ribs—except for the Zanesville 10-diamond "half-pint" chestnuts, which seem to be more common than broken-swirl. At present I know of midwestern flasks from molds of only five different diamond counts—that is, with the number in horizontal row 10, 15, 16, 18, or 20 diamonds. How many individual molds were made with these various numbers of diamonds is undetermined. Flasks patterned in 18- and 20-diamond molds are rare in my experience; those in 16- and 15-diamond molds, scarce; and those in the Zanesville 10-diamond mold, almost common, though rare in some colors and in the Grandmother size. The New Geneva 16-diamond mold and the Zanesville 10-diamond mold have already been discussed in detail. Although the New Geneva mold could have been closely duplicated, it seems practically impossible that the Zanesville mold ever had an *exact* counterpart. Lowell Innes believes that possibly a 16-diamond mold was used in one of the Pittsburgh glasshouses producing tableware. If so, the mold may have been used for flasks also, since most of the early houses specializing in table glass made green glass for bottles and flasks as well. As yet, neither an 18-diamond nor 20-diamond mold has been linked even loosely to a specific glassworks anywhere in the Midwest.

That in one anonymous works two different diamond molds were used is proved by a remarkable colorless sugar bowl with cover of amethystine tint. The cover was patterned in an 18-diamond mold, apparently an allover diamond design, not one having flutes below the diamond diaper, as does 2 in Ill. 91. The bowl was patterned in a distinctive 10-diamond mold having ten diamonds in horizontal row above ten panels. The pointed-arch tops of the panels are described by the lower half of the diamonds in the bottom row, and each panel is bisected by a fine vertical rib, which does not extend to the top of the arch. Though the only other piece I have seen that was patterned in this 10-diamond mold is a sugar bowl cover in deep yellowish green, appearing black in reflected light, I expect a flask will turn up someday. Both the cover and the covered sugar bowl were found near Carnot, Pennsylvania, on the Ohio River and only a few miles from Pittsburgh. Thus, that a Pittsburgh glasshouse was its place of origin seems not unlikely.[44] James H. Rose informed me that the Toledo Museum of Art has a blue broken-swirl (24-rib) sugar bowl with a cover patterned in this 10-diamond design.

The second largest group of midwestern containers is the bottle group. Generally midwestern bottles are thin-walled, astonishingly light in weight for their sizes, and, like the flasks, they do not conform to exact standard measures. They have been recorded in sizes from about two ounces to nearly six quarts, though not all sizes have been found in all shapes. To the best of my knowledge, the only bottles holding from four to about six quarts are the so-called Ohio swirl bottles—nearly spherical globulars like those in Ill. 96; and the only "miniatures," those holding six ounces or less, are globular. Brobdingnagian or Lilliputian, they are rare. Bottles of about a pint or two and three quarts are scarce. The vast majority are quarts—a few ounces under or over 32. It is said that bottles from about a quart to two quarts' capacity served as decanters in households and as bar bottles in public places. And apparently in some communities it was customary for storekeepers to have a bottle of whiskey handy for the refreshment of customers. At the store of Zenas Kent "the beverage was as free as water," and every visitor, whether dropping in for a chat or to make a purchase, was expected to "help himself." As a boy, his son Marvin (for whom Carthage and Franklin Mills were named Kent in 1863) was assigned the duty of keeping the whiskey bottle full.[45] Possibly that whiskey bottle had been patterned in the Kent 20-rib mold, or it may have been one of the Kent blown-three-mold bottles, of which 5 in Ill. 95 is an example.

Normally, it is assumed, the bottles were stopped with a cork, but the chances are not slight that some of the swirl bottles destined to serve as decanters or bar bottles were fitted with stoppers. When the two-quart swirl bottle, 3 in Ill. 96, was acquired, it had a stopper with short shank and flat button top. For some time, in spite of the fact that its amber color matched that in the collar of the bottle, where the glass was thickest, it was thought the stopper could not be original as there was no record that stoppers were made for these bottles. Later another, and smaller, swirl bottle with stopper of the same form turned up, and examination of the neck of each bottle

showed it had been beveled on the inside to accommodate a stopper.

Characteristic midwestern bottles are those in Ills. 94, 95, and 96, which show variations both within their basic shapes—inevitable in free-blown bottles—and in the typical neck finishes and bases. Almost without exception the neck is collared; the plain everted lip of 2 in Ill. 94 is an unusual treatment and, in my experience, one occurring only on the "miniatures." Sometimes the bases are only slightly depressed; normally they have a shallow to medium kick-up, which is domed or conical. On many specimens I have examined, the rib termination and the pontil mark are off-center, presumably because of the way the blower handled the gather. It has been suggested that this feature is found only on Zanesville bottles. That may be true. However, it may be that the bottles having it were fashioned by one blower, and he may have blown bottles in other glassworks. As for shapes, six main or basic types have been recorded:

1. The flattened chestnut-shaped flasklike body with long neck finished with an applied and tooled collar, of which 6 and 9 in Ill. 94 are examples. This shape is one I have rarely seen.

2. The slender cylindrical, usually with slightly incurved sides and with short shoulder sloping into a tapering neck with heavy collared lip, like 8 in Ill. 95, also rare. The shape and proportions, it will be noted, are similar to late 18th- and early 19th-century wine bottles.

3. The long ovoid or pear shape like 8 in Ill. 94 and 9 in Ill. 95, which have a deep, flat sloping collar formed by a special neck-finishing tool. (See Ill. 53.)

4. The common cylindrical types, more pedestrian in form than the foregoing, like 5 in Ill. 94 and 6 in Ill. 95, with long shoulder sloping into a comparatively short neck, which tapers to a heavy collared lip.

5. The beehive type, so-called because the body shape reminded someone of old-fashioned beehives. As shown by 1, 7, and 10 in Ill. 94, the sides are short, straight, or slightly curved; the shoulder, a long gentle curve to a tapering neck, which is usually short in proportion to the body height. As on the shapes mentioned above, a generous gather of metal was usually applied to the lip to form a heavy collar.

6. The globulars, which predominate, fall into two general groups: one with a taper at top into the neck, like 4 in Ills. 94 and 95; the other, nearly spherical like 2 to 6 in Ill. 96. Normally the globulars have a neck finish that, in collector's parlance, is called a turned-over collar, fairly deep and sloping as on 1 and 3 in Ill. 95, or narrow, straight-sided, and hugging the neck as on the swirl bottles 1 to 4 in Ill. 96. Bottles with nearly spherical bodies have rarely been found in eastern glass, and then they were unpatterned.

Another form, given apparently only to small bottles, is the taper shape with flanged lip like 1 in Ill. 91. The bottles of this decanter shape are scarce. Called *cruets* by midwestern dealers and collectors, they occur mainly in light greens. Their decoration seems to have been confined to ribbing, usually swirled. Mr. Rose informed me that there is considerable "find-spot evidence" that New Geneva as well as Zanesville produced cruets patterned in swirl ribbing. In the George S. McKearin Collection was one attributed to Mantua. It was a brilliant yellowish green patterned in a 16-rib mold, the ribbing swirled slightly to the left. The brilliant light green bottle, 1 in Ill. 91, attributed to Zanesville is one of two with popcorn kernel broken-swirl of which I have record at this time.

As in the flasks, the greatest charm of the bottles lies in their color and pattern-molded designs. In color, the same fascinating wide spectrum of aquamarines, greens, and ambers occurs. In blues, only a light cornflower and clear medium blue of gray tone have been recorded, and they are rare. The patterns are limited to ribbings — at least, so far as I know, no diamond designs have been reported. However, since a few, *very* few, "pint" 10-diamond jugs are known, bottles of small sizes might be expected, but those of a quart or more would seem most unlikely. If all diamond piece-molds used in midwestern houses were about the size of the New Geneva 16-diamond mold, it is doubtful if gathers sufficient to blow large bottles could have been patterned in them, and probably the workable gather that the molds would accommodate would have approached the "flying point" in the necessary expansion to blow even a quart bottle.

The ribbed patterns were vertical, swirled (more often to left than right), and broken swirl. The broken swirl is very rare on bottles, perhaps because of economy of time and effort in blowing bottles for more commercial purposes than the pocket bottles.

Molds of no less than 11 different rib counts were used — 12, 13, 16, 18, 19, 20, 24, 28, 30, 31, and 32. By far the preponderance of the bottles recorded have 24 ribs; those with other rib counts are scarce to rare. From a study of bottles on which the pontil mark does not mask the rib termination, it is apparent that 24-rib molds having at least five different types of termination were used in midwestern glassworks: ribs fading into a plain center; converging at center bottom; running to a terminal ring; running to a tiny nipple, and running to a large nipple, at center. The studies made by James H. Rose and Earl Siegfried also indicate that among the 24-rib molds, at least three were piece molds. Further evidence of the use of molds of different rib counts in a glassworks is embodied in 10 in Ill. 94. The gather was patterned first in a 24-rib mold and the ribbing swirled to the right, then patterned in a 19-rib mold for vertical ribs. As yet, I have no record of bottles patterned in a 14-, 15-, or 17-rib mold as I have for flasks, and except for the rib molds mentioned in connection with specific glassworks and the Pittsburgh glass field, none of the molds can be definitely identified with any works or area at this time.

The third group of pattern-molded containers consists of the ribbed and diamond jugs, or handled bottles, which I have found to be rare objects occurring mainly in midwestern glass, very rarely in eastern. Five are pictured — 2, 3, 4, 5, and 7 in Ill. 99. The only sizes that have been recorded are "pint" and "quart," usually a few ounces over the standard measure. Most of the known jugs are globular in form like 2, 3, and 4, but sometimes ovoid like 5, with short cylindrical neck, which is usually finished with a flat or sloping collar but occasionally with a flanged lip. Sometimes the applied handles are loop handles, as on 2, but more often they are strap handles, as on 3, 4, and 5. Normally the handles have crimped ends. A rarer form in my experience is a handled bottle like 7, with flattened, broad, chestnut flasklike body and tapering neck with applied ring below a plain lip, and with an applied small semi-ear-shaped handle. These occur in aquamarine and ambers. The colors of the globular and ovoid jugs are light to deep amber, greens, including the lovely citron shades, and aquamarine. On most of the recorded jugs, the pattern is swirled ribbing. On a few, the broken swirl occurs. All the ribbed jugs I have seen were patterned in a 24-rib mold. One of the rarest of the midwestern jugs is 3, which was patterned in the Zanesville 10-diamond mold and has seven horizontal rows of diamonds and one pulled into ribs at top.

Though not in the same category of American glass as the foregoing pattern-molded containers, the blown-three-mold globular bottles, usually attributed to Kent, are included here because they are typically midwestern in shape, and their geometric pattern, GII–6,[46] does not occur in any eastern blown-three-mold I have seen. These bottles received their pattern in a full-size piece mold, not a dip or small two-piece mold. Perhaps, before discussing them, a few words about blown-three-mold and its molds should be interpolated. Blown-three-mold is an artificial, and unsatisfactory, name for a body of glassware, mainly tableware, produced from about 1813 into the 1830s, in geometric, arch, and baroque patterns in full-size molds of two, three, or four pieces or leaves. Though a great many different vessels, including bowls, dishes, and other table articles, were fashioned, the basic full-size piece molds giving shape and pattern were made mainly for decanters, castor bottles, tumblers, and inkwells. Most other articles were, in essence, pattern-molded, for although the gathers were patterned in one of these basic molds, the objects were formed partly or entirely by free-blowing. Presumably the bottles in pattern GII–6, of which 5 in Ill. 95 is a rare example, were patterned in a mold for slender barrel-shaped decanter-bottles and fashioned into a globular form with long plain neck and collared lip. Even the shape of the GII–6 decanters, like 8 in Ill. 122, as they came from the mold was altered—widened at the base so that the bottom band of the pattern fell partly on the bottom of the decanter instead of being entirely on the side, as in the mold.

That a mold in pattern GII–6 was used at the Kent glassworks of Park, Edmunds & Park was established by the excavations of Mr. White. It had a band of 45 wide vertical ribs between bands of diamond diapering (3 diamonds in chain height, 27 around), a band of 15 gadroon ribs at top, a wide horizontal rib between the bands, and a plain base. Another mold having 46 vertical ribs has been determined, but *very* few pieces from it have been recorded. Actually, all the bottle-glass bowls and decanters, globular bottles, and flasks I have studied were patterned in the mold having 45 ribs. Its inner surface was shaped to form a slender barrel-shaped decanter-bottle. The majority of the globular bottles are about a quart in capacity and are usually aquamarine or light green in color, occasionally shades of yellow-green. Although there are many exceptions, in general the metal is not quite so brilliant as most other Kent, or Mantua and Zanesville, glass, and sometimes the color is cloudy. One of the exceptions is bottle 5 in Ill. 95. It is also the only one recorded as yet in amber—a brilliant, vibrant golden amber—and the only one of so large a size: three quarts and about eight ounces.

A few colorless lead-glass GII–6 decanter-bottles and pitchers are known, but I believe they cannot have been blown at Kent since there is no reliable evidence of lead-glass production there. I believe they originated in an earlier midwestern glassworks. And because of the general period of blown-three-mold popularity in such geometric patterns, it seems more likely the mold used for the Kent pieces was taken there from a house making lead glass, rather than the other way round. I conjecture that the GII–6 molds were used in a Wheeling, Wellsburg, or Pittsburgh glassworks. Long ago, tradition and place of discovery of a few pieces in this pattern pointed to the possibility of the mold of the Kent pieces—identical molds being unlikely—having been used at some time in a Wheeling glassworks. The lead-glass bottle-decanters give substance to the probability. Be that as it may, quite naturally pattern GII–6 is known to collectors as the Kent pattern.

Two light green flasks have been recorded in Kent GII–6 pattern. One is in the W. G. Russell Allen Collection in the Museum of Fine Arts in Boston. The other, 7 in Ill. 122, now in the Collection of the Ohio Historical Society, Columbus, came to George S. McKearin from Ohio. The flasks are closely similar in shape and color, but the one in the Allen Collection is more symmetrical and has a longer, wider neck. Although it has not been possible to bring the flasks together to compare for mold and pattern idiosyncrasies, when Kathryn Buhler was on the staff of the Museum of Fine Arts she compared a detailed description of 7 with the flask in the Allen Collection. It seems certain the two were patterned in the same mold, and that the mold was the one for a slender barrel-shaped decanter-bottle used at Kent. Also important to note is a colorless "glass of lead" Irish flask in this GII–6 pattern, which was illustrated in *Glass Notes,* No. 16, 1956, published by Arthur Churchill Ltd. and attributed by E. Barrington Haynes. The shape of the Irish flask is similar to that of 7, but more slender and much more tapering at the bottom. It raises the question of whether this particular geometric pattern, one of the few blown-three-mold patterns found in Irish glass, was copied in the Midwest. One cannot help speculating that a mold in the pattern or an object in the pattern may have come to the United States with a migrating glassman who settled in the Midwest after the War of 1812, and inspired the "Kent" mold. In any event, no colorless GII–6 flask has been found here as yet.

And blown-three-mold flasks, which are rare in any pattern, are even rarer in bottle-glass than in any other. The majority of those recorded were blown from flint (lead) glass in works producing tableware, as were the eastern flasks 1, 2, and 3 in Ill. 121 and 4 and 6 in Ill. 122. Like the Kent flasks, they were patterned in one of the basic molds before being shaped by blowing and manipulation. At present I know of only three instances in which molds to *shape* as well as *pattern* flasks have been determined. As yet, only flasks have been recorded from the molds, and they are rare flasks. One is illustrated by 9 in Ill. 122. It is a lovely yellow-green in color, and is illustrated also in *American Glass,* 2 in Plate 238. At that time, only one other specimen had been recorded, a colorless one. Recently I learned of another colorless and two aquamarine examples, making a total of five recorded at present.

Choice as the midwestern blown-three-mold containers are, for many of us they do not have so much personality as the less elaborate pattern-molded ribbed and diamond bottles, flasks, and jugs, which also provide the eye with a feast of color. In fact, in the opinion of most collectors, only some of the Stiegel-type pocket bottles equal or surpass the midwestern. Today, though the finest of the pocket bottles in the few patterns Stiegel may have originated still stand on the top rung of the collector's ladder of desirability, they are crowded a bit from the rung below by the midwestern containers.

94. MIDWESTERN PATTERN-MOLDED BOTTLES, Early to Mid-19th Century

The ribbed bottles shown here and in Ills. 96 and 95 illustrate the principal basic shapes, as well as the variety of neck finishes and of kick-up in the pontil-marked base, characteristic of midwestern bottles, and also the individuality of specimens in those shapes. Next to the near spherical (Ill. 96) and the globulars (No. 4 Ill. 95), the shapes most frequently encountered are the so-called beehive (Nos. 1, 5, 7, and 10 opposite) having short straight sides, long sloping and gently curved shoulder, and neck short in proportion to body height, and the short-sided cylindrical with long sloping shoulder (Nos. 6 and 7 Ill. 95). The long-necked flattened chestnut (Nos. 6 and 9) and the slender cylindrical with slightly incurved sides (No. 8 Ill. 95) are rare forms. The bottles in these three illustrations show also variety in vertical, swirled, and broken-swirl ribbing— the last, rarely found on these bottles. Also, besides at least three different 24-rib molds, molds of 12, 13, 16, 18, 19, 20, and 28 ribs were used to pattern the gathers from which the bottles were blown. No. 10 opposite is evidence that molds of different rib counts were used in the same glasshouse: the gather was first patterned in a 24-rib and then in a 19-rib mold.

Illustrated also in *American Glass:* No. 3 by 5 in Plate 235; Nos. 6, 7, and 9 by 8, 9, and 6 in Plate 236.

Nos. 4 (ex-Collection of Harry Hall White), 8, and 9, formerly in the George S. McKearin Collection. Nos. 2, 3, 5, 7, and 9, The Henry Ford Museum; Nos. 6 and 10, Collection of the Ohio Historical Society; No. 1, The Toledo Art Museum.

Top row:

1. Clear blue, gray tone; 24 ribs to right; beehive body, short neck, applied deep round collar on lip; off-center pontil mark, characteristic of some of the bottles attributed to Zanesville, O. Rare color, unusually dark in tone. Early 19th century. Capacity, 1 qt. about 5 oz. Height, about 8½". Greatest diameter, about 4¹¹/₁₆".

2. Pale yellow-green; 18 ribs swirled to right; globular body, tapering neck, everted plain lip; wide flat base with off-center pontil mark. Rare in size and lip. Early 19th century. Capacity, 6 oz. Height, 4¼". Greatest diameter, about 2⅞".

3. Aquamarine; broken-swirl: twice patterned in 20-rib mold, first ribbing swirled to left; melon-like body, unusually slender cylindrical neck, wide irregular flat collar on lip. Extremely rare. Early 19th century. Capacity, about 1 pt. Height, 5¹⁵/₁₆". Greatest diameter, about 3⅞".

4. Aquamarine; 24 wide vertical ribs; globular body, unusually wide cylindrical neck, turned-over collar on lip. Early 19th century. Capacity, 1 qt. about 2 oz. Height, 7½". Greatest diameter, about 4⅞".

Middle row:

5. Deep citron; 24 ribs in fine swirl to left on body and onto lower neck, either obliterated on base in process of fabrication or ribs in mold ran to large plain center; beehive body, short wide neck, flaring thick lip (unusual finish, formed from small applied gather). Early to mid-19th century. Capacity, 1 qt. about 26 oz. Height, 9⅜". Greatest diameter, about 4¾".

6. Light green; 16-rib broken-swirl: first ribbing swirled to right, second and vertical extending only part way up body; flattened chestnut-shaped body, long neck tapering to applied round collar on lip. Extremely rare. Possibly Mantua Glass Works, O., 1822–29. Capacity, 1 pt. about 13 oz. Height, 8¾". Greatest width, 5¼"; greatest depth, 3½".

7. Deep bluish aquamarine; 24-rib broken-swirl, first ribbing swirled to left; large beehive body, very short neck, round collar with lower bevel (similar to flask neck finish No. 19, Ill. 135), pontil mark slightly off-center on base. Rare in size; extremely rare in broken-swirl. Possibly Zanesville, O., late 1830s. Capacity, 2 qts. about 4 oz. Height, 9¼". Greatest diameter, about 5¾".

Bottom row:

8. Light blue-aquamarine; 24 ribs extending from center base and swirled slightly to left at top of body; long pear-shaped body, long neck tapering to deep flat collar (flask neck finish No. 15, Ill. 135). Probably ca. 1840. Capacity, 2 qts. about 10 oz. Height, 11¼". Greatest diameter, 5¾".

9. Light blue-aquamarine; 13 wide-spaced ribs, swirled slightly to right and drawn tight on neck; flattened chestnut-shaped body, neck tapering slightly to round collar on lip. Rare. Early 19th century. Capacity, 1 qt. about 4 oz. Height, 9¾". Greatest width, 5⅝"; greatest depth, 2⅞".

10. Light aquamarine; broken-swirl: first patterned in 24-rib mold, ribs swirled to right, then patterned in 19-rib mold for vertical ribs, widely expanded and only on sides; broad beehive body, very short neck tapering to round collar on lip. Extremely rare. Early 19th century. Capacity, 3 qts. about 12 oz. Height, 10⅜". Greatest diameter, about 6¾".

All bottles shown here were patterned in ribbed dip molds except the blown-three-mold No. 5, blown in a full-size piece mold. As determined by my analysis of 4,000 and more blown-three-mold pieces, the basic molds giving shape as well as pattern were made mainly for decanters, castor bottles, tumblers, and inkwells. In essence, the many other articles in the category were pattern-molded, for the gathers were patterned in one of the basic molds and the objects fashioned partly or entirely by free-blowing. The gather for this bottle was patterned in a mold for slender barrel-shaped decanter-bottles, in the so-called Kent pattern, GII–6, then expanded and given a globular body and long plain neck. Although the geographical area of discovery of a few bottle-glass pieces and two or three colorless lead-glass bottle-decanters points to the probable use of the mold in a Wheeling glassworks, or possibly in Wellsburg or Pittsburgh, its use at Kent, Ohio, ca. 1824–34 was determined by Harry Hall White's excavations on the site of the Kent glassworks of Park, Edmunds & Park. (Hence the term *Kent pattern*.) This has been further corroborated by more extensive excavations carried out by archaeologists from the Department of Anthropology of Case-Western University of Cleveland, Ohio, under the direction of Dr. David S. Brose. The site was relocated in the fall of 1965 by Duncan B. Wolcott, a knowledgeable collector of Midwestern glass, of Cuyahoga Falls, Ohio. Glass fragments and other artifacts excavated at the site are in the possession of the Western Reserve Historical Society. The remains of five of eleven furnace foundations that were found are now on exhibit at the Hale Farm and Village in Bath, Ohio. The excavations and relocation of the furnace remains were made possible by a grant from the Kettering Family Foundation and funds provided by the Western Reserve Historical Society.

In smaller sizes, several aquamarine and light green globular bottles and a few light yellow-green have been recorded in GII–6. No. 5 is the only amber one known at present, and the only one of so large a size. All have a small kick-up in the base and a pontil mark. Two other pieces in the pattern are shown in Ill. 122: a pocket bottle, No. 7, and decanter, No. 8.

Nos. 1 and 3 through 8, formerly in the George S. McKearin Collection (Nos.1, 6, and 7 also ex-Collection of Louis Guerineau Myers); No. 2, The Corning Museum of Glass; Nos. 9 and 10, The Henry Ford Museum; No. 8 (also ex-Collection of Alfred B. Maclay, and ex-Collection of W. T. Howe), Collection of Henry G. Schiff.

Top row:

1. Brilliant yellow-green; 12 vertical ribs widely expanded on melonlike body, pulled tight on long cylindrical neck; slightly sloping collar on lip; plain base. Rare in color and rib count. Early to mid-19th century. Attributed to Pittsburgh. Capacity, 1 qt. about 10 oz. Height, 8¼". Greatest diameter, 5". (Illustrated also in *American Glass,* No. 7 Plate 236.)
2. Yellow-green; 16 vertical ribs, widely expanded on melonlike body, fading on cylindrical neck; turned-over flat collar on lip. Extremely rare size. Early 19th century. Capacity, about 6 oz. Height, 3⅞". Greatest diameter, 3". (Illustrated also in *Two Hundred Years of American Blown Glass,* No. 4 Plate 107.)
3. Brilliant clear olive-green; 24 ribs, widely expanded on globular body, unusually long cylindrical neck, flat turned-over collar on lip. Rare in color. Early 19th century. Capacity, 1 qt. about 2 oz. Height, about 8". Greatest diameter, about 5".
4. Brilliant clear yellow-green; 24 fine ribs swirled to right on globular body and short neck tapering slightly to flat turned-over collar on lip. Early 19th century. Capacity, 1 qt. about 3 oz. Height, 7³/₁₆". Greatest diameter, about 5¼".

Middle row:

5. Blown-three-mold, brilliant golden amber; patterned in full-size three-piece decanter-bottle mold in the so-called Kent pattern (geometric pattern GII–6): band of 45 wide vertical ribs between bands of diamond-diapering (3 diamonds in height, 27 around), band of 15 gadroon ribs at top, wide horizontal rib between bands, plain base; globular body, plain cylindrical neck, collared lip. Only example recorded in amber and also of so large a size. Attributed to Park, Edmunds & Park, Kent, O., ca. 1824–34. Capacity, 3 pts. about 8 oz. Height, 8⅝". Greatest diameter, about 5¾".
6. Light olive-green; 24-rib broken-swirl, first ribbing swirled to left, showing on shoulder and neck to lip but lost on body through manipulation and expansion; second ribbing widely expanded vertical extending to top of sides; cylindrical body, long sloping shoulder, short tapering neck, applied wide angular collar on lip. Rare color. Early 19th century. Capacity, 1 qt. about 4 oz. Height, 8½". Greatest diameter, about 4½".
7. Brilliant olive-yellow (light amber of green tone); 24 ribs, swirled to left; slender beehive body, short plain cylindrical neck, applied deep angular collar on lip; off-center pontil mark. Very rare in color. Probably Zanesville, O. ca. 1820–40. Capacity, 1 qt. about 8 oz. Height, 9⅛". Greatest diameter, about 4⅞".

Bottom row:

8. Rich brown-amber; 24 fine vertical ribs; tall slender cylindrical body with sides slightly incurved between base and short sloping shoulder, neck tapering to applied angular collar on lip. Rare color in rare form. Early 19th century. Capacity, 1 pt. 8 oz. Height, 8⁷/₁₆". Greatest diameter, 4¹/₁₆".
9. Deep reddish amber; 24 ribs slightly swirled to left; taper shape, long neck, applied deep flat collar on lip (similar to flask neck finish No. 15); pontil mark off-center. Probably Zanesville, O. ca. 1840. Capacity, 3 pts. about 4 oz. Height, 10". Greatest diameter, about 5⅛".
10. Brilliant yellowish olive-amber; 24 fine ribs swirled to left on body, tight and vertical on neck, and extending from nipple at center base. Early 19th century. Capacity, 1 qt. about 4 oz. Height, about 8". Greatest diameter, about 5".

96. MIDWESTERN "OHIO" SWIRL BOTTLES, ca. 1815–40

In shape, proportions, and ribbed pattern, the so-called Ohio swirl bottles such as Nos. 1 through 4 and 6 are unlike any globular bottles identified with eastern glasshouses or—so far as is known at present—with contemporary foreign bottles, though similar plain bottles were depicted in 15th- to 17th- century paintings, and swirled ribbing decorated some English bottles of that period. These American swirl bottles are characterized by a generous globular, usually nearly spherical, body and, being thinly blown, are light in weight in relation to their size. The neck is slender, usually straight cylindrical but occasionally tapering slightly, and often short in proportion to body height. The lip on most recorded survivors is finished with a narrow flat turned-over collar—perhaps an individual blower's technique that became a style in one or more glasshouses. The base has a slight kick-up. In most instances a pontil mark obscures the type of rib termination on the bottom and, on many, both rib termination and pontil mark are off-center. These bottles have been recorded mainly in sizes from about a quart to nearly six quarts, and in brilliant colors—ambers of many tones, greens from green-aquamarine to olive, and yellow-greens, including citron. By far the largest percentage of the many examined were patterned in 24-rib molds. The ribbing is tight on the neck and, through expansion, fine on the body with tapering wide spaces between ribs in shallow fluting. Since the opening of the midwestern bottle fields in the early 1920s, these bottles patterned in 24-rib molds have been attributed to Zanesville, Ohio, ca. 1817–40. However, though no one doubts they were a regular product of Zanesville, the probability of their production in other contemporary midwestern houses is a certainty to many students. Blowers moved from one glasshouse to another; molds traveled too; and molds of 24 ribs were used in various houses. It is known one was used at the New Geneva Glass Works. Moreover, the study of individual bottles has proved the existence of several different 24-rib molds having different types of rib termination. Wherever blown, their numbers today are indicative of their popularity with midwestern customers; it is said that those from about a quart to two quarts in capacity were used as bar bottles and decanters.

Nos. 1 and 2, formerly in the George S. McKearin Collection. No. 3, The Henry Ford Museum; No. 5, Collection of Henry G. Schiff; Nos. 4 and 6, The Toledo Museum of Art.

Top row:

1. Greenish amber; 24 ribs to left; flat turned-over collar on lip. Capacity, 1 qt. about 3 oz. Height. 7¾". Greatest diameter, about 5¼".

   Although the ribs toward the center bottom are indefinite, there is a peculiar short rib across the center. At first glance it might seem to be part of a mold seam, indicating use of a two-piece mold, but the short rib is only about one inch long and, on the rest of the base and in the ribbing, there is no discernible evidence of use of a piece mold (ca. 1817–40).

2. Brilliant clear golden amber; 24 ribs to left, fading into plain center on bottom; flat turned-over collar on lip. Capacity, 1 qt. about 21 oz. Height, 7⅞". Greatest diameter, about 5¾".

3. Deep rich amber; 24 ribs to left, fading into plain center on bottom; flat turned-over collar on lip. Capacity, 2 qts. about 2 oz. Height, 8½". Greatest diameter, about 6¼".

   When acquired, this bottle had a stopper with short shank and flat button top and, in color, like that in the collar. That the stopper was original was discounted until another bottle with a stopper of the same shape was found, and close examination revealed that the inner neck of both was slightly beveled, apparently for fitting the stoppers.

Bottom row:

4. Golden amber; 24 ribs to left; flat turned-over collar on lip. Rare size. Capacity, 3 qts. about 4 oz. Height, 10". Greatest diameter, about 7½".

5. Deep amber; 16 vertical ribs; curved turned-over collar on lip. Extremely rare size. Capacity, about 5 oz. Height, 4⅛". Greatest diameter, 3".

6. Deep rich amber; 28 ribs to left; narrow slanting collar on lip. Extremely rare in size and rib count. Capacity, a little over 5¾ qts. Height, 12". Greatest diameter, about 9⅛".

97. PATTERN-MOLDED FLASKS, MAINLY MIDWESTERN, early 19th century

Of the flasks illustrated here, all but Nos. 5, 6, and 8 are definitely midwestern of the early 19th century. The ribbed patterns, of course, were impressed in dip molds; the diamond, in piece molds. Among the many fascinating variations in the midwestern broken-swirl, three are shown by Nos. 3, 7, and 9. The "chestnut" form of No. 7—fat, wide, and approaching the flattened circular in contour—seems to have been peculiar to the Midwest, possibly Ohio, and as yet has been found only with ribbed patterns. Flasks in vertical, swirled, and broken-swirl ribbing have been encountered far more frequently than those in diamond designs, such as Nos. 2, 4, and 10. Of the diamond designs, those patterned in 15- and 18-diamond molds are scarce. The majority still extant were patterned in the 10-diamond mold associated with Zanesville, Ohio, and in a design of diamonds or ogivals above flutes. And, though the ribbed flasks occur in many sizes, the diamond flasks are mainly "half-pint." Flask No. 10 of "pint" size is a rarity. All have a pontil mark.

Nos. 1, 4, 5, and 9, formerly in the George S. McKearin Collection; No. 6, ex-Collection of Alexander Drake; No. 3, The Corning Museum of Glass; Nos. 2, 8 (ex-Collection of Herbert D. Mason), and 10, The Henry Ford Museum; No. 7, Collection of Henry G. Schiff.

Top row:

1. Deep brownish amber; 24 ribs swirled to right; fat chestnut body, wide neck with tooled line below plain lip; flat base. Capacity, about 9 oz. Height, 4¾". Greatest width, 3¹³/₁₆". Greatest depth, 2⁵/₁₆" at base.
2. Brilliant yellow-green; patterned in 15-diamond mold; flattened chestnut body, cylindrical neck, unusual flaring plain lip; tiny conical kick-up. Extremely rare in color. Attributed to Mantua, O., 1822–29. Capacity, about 9 oz. Height, 5". Greatest width, 3¹³/₁₆". Greatest depth, 2¹/₁₆" at base.
3. Deep reddish amber, 24-rib popcorn-kernel broken-swirl, one ribbing swirled to right and other to left; slender flattened ovoid body, long neck spreading slightly to plain lip. Capacity, about 6 oz. Height, 5⅝". Greatest width, 3¹/₁₆". Greatest depth, 2". (Illustrated also in *American Glass,* No. 7 Plate 234; in *Two Hundred Years of American Blown Glass,* No. 5 Plate 106.)
4. Brownish amber; patterned in the "Zanesville" 10-diamond mold; flattened chestnut body, unusually thin at top, long cylindrical neck, plain lip; slightly depressed base. Attributed to Zanesville, O. Ca-

pacity, about 5 oz. Height, 5¼". Greatest width, 3¹³/₁₆". Greatest depth, 1¹¹/₁₆" at base.

Middle row:

5. Brilliant sapphire-blue; 18 pronounced vertical ribs on sides of body and lower neck; fat flattened ovoid body tapering sharply to long cylindrical neck, plain lip; plain flat base. Probably Continental, found in Holland. Late 18th century. Capacity, 1 pt. about 2 oz. Height, 6¾". Greatest width, 4¼". Greatest depth, 2¹³/₁₆" at base.
6. Brilliant sapphire-blue; 18-rib broken-swirl, first pronounced ribbing swirled very slightly to left and, second, vertical but swirled to right on neck; flattened chestnut body, long cylindrical neck, plain lip; slightly depressed base. Provenance uncertain, possibly foreign. Late 18th century. Capacity, about 1 pt. Height, about 6". Greatest width, 4". Greatest depth, 2⅜" at base.
7. Deep amber; 24-rib broken-swirl, first ribbing swirled to left; fat flattened globular body, slender cylindrical neck spreading at plain lip. Capacity, about 12 oz. Height 5". Greatest width, about 4". Greatest depth, about 2¼".

Bottom row:

8. Black (dark brown-amber); 25 wide-spaced fine sharp ribs, converging at center base; fat flattened chestnut body, irregular cylindrical neck, plain lip; shallow kick-up. Very rare in color and rib count. Possibly New England. Capacity, about 15 oz. Height, 6". Greatest width, 4½". Greatest depth, 2⅜" at about middle.
9. Grandmother flask, brilliant deep amber; 24-rib broken-swirl, first ribbing swirled slightly to left; tapering flattened ovoid body, long neck spreading slightly to plain lip. Extremely rare and unusual in type of broken-swirl, which, it should be noted, is similar to that of No. 6 in its near verticality. Capacity, 1 pt. about 5 oz. Height, 7¾". Greatest width, 5". Greatest depth, 2⅞" at bottom.
10. Brown-amber; patterned in "Zanesville" 10-diamond mold; flattened chestnut body, cylindrical neck, plain lip; shallow kick-up. Extremely rare in size and color. Attributed to Zanesville, O. Capacity, about 1 pt. Height, 6½". Greatest width, 4⅝". Greatest depth, 2½" at base.

Midwestern flasks in ribbed and diamond designs such as those shown here and in Ills. 91 and 97 were never excelled in America, or elsewhere, in brilliancy of metal and beauty of vibrant color, qualities enhanced because the flasks were blown from a single gather of metal, usually widely expanded, thus augmenting the play of light and shade. The colors are mainly ambers and greens, with more nuances of tone than in glass from other areas. The ambers ranged from pale topaz through golden shades to deep reddish and brown-amber, the last two sometimes so dark as to appear black in reflected light; the greens in profusion from pale to strong green-aquamarine, clear true greens from light to dark, many shades of yellow-green, including the well-named "citron," olive-greens, and olive-yellows. Blues are comparatively rare, occurring in pale tint, cornflower and violet hues, greenish, deep sapphire, and cobalt. Colorless, sometimes with amethyst streaks, amethystine, and moonstone are rare. Amethyst is extremely rare.

Though not all closely resemble the American chestnut in shape, the flasks have long been grouped under the heading chestnut flasks. Those illustrated demonstrate the individuality to be expected in free-blown flasks—conforming to general types of body form but varying in contour and in length and width of neck. Those like No. 4 and the grandfather flask, for instance, have a contour unlike any identified eastern flasks or any foreign flasks I have seen. Also shown is the range in sizes, only approximate to standard measures, from the rare one ounce of No. 8 to a quart and more of the grandfather, No. 10. All have a pontil mark.

Illustrated also in *American Glass:* 9 and 11, by Nos. 4 and 6 of Plate 235; in *Two Hundred Years of American Blown Glass:* 7 and 8 by Nos. 4 and 7 of Plate 106.

Nos. 1 through 4, formerly in the George S. McKearin Collection. Nos. 7, 8, and 9, The Corning Museum of Glass; Nos. 5 and 6 (also ex-Collection of Harry Hall White), The Henry Ford Museum; Nos. 10 and 11, Collection of Henry G. Schiff.

Top row:

1. Brilliant light citron; 20 ribs, starting from center base, swirled slightly to left on body, to right on neck; asymmetrical flattened globular body, unusually wide neck, plain lip; flat base, off-center tiny pontil mark. Rare. Capacity, 1 pt. about 6 oz. Height, 6¼". Greatest width, 5". Greatest depth, about 2¾".

2. Brilliant light olive-green; patterned in the "Zanesville" 10-diamond small two-piece mold; chestnut body, long neck, plain lip; flat base. Very rare in color. Attributed to Zanesville, O. Capacity, ½ pt. Height, 5⁷/₁₆". Greatest width, 3⅞". Greatest depth, 2" at base.

3. Grandmother flask, light yellow-citron; large bub-

bles in glass; 20 vertical ribs; unusual flattened pear shape tapering very sharply to spreading neck, plain lip; very shallow kick-up. Rare. Found in a private home in Ohio. Capacity, 1 pt. about 3 oz. Height, about 6¾". Greatest width, 4¾". Greatest depth, 2¹¹/₁₆" at base.

Middle row:

4. Brilliant golden amber; 24 vertical ribs; wide chestnut body, long unusual neck bulging below incised line giving collared effect to plain lip; base, slightly depressed. Capacity, ½ pt. Height, about 5". Greatest width, 3⅝". Greatest depth, 2⁵/₁₆" above base.

5. Deep brilliant amber; 18 pronounced vertical ribs, faint at bottom, heavy at top; wide chestnut body, very short neck spreading at irregular plain lip; tiny conical kick-up. Very rare size. Capacity, 4½ oz. Height, 3¹⁵/₁₆". Greatest width, 3⅛". Greatest depth, 1¹¹/₁₆" at base.

6. Amber of unusual orange tone; 16 sharp wide-spaced ribs converging at center bottom, swirled to right on body; exceptionally thin chestnut body, long slender neck spreading at plain lip; shallow conical kick-up. Capacity, about 13 oz. Height, 6½". Greatest width, 4⁹/₁₆". Greatest depth, 2⅛" at base.

7. Brilliant light amber; 16 vertical ribs; wide chestnut body, neck spreading at plain lip. Extremely rare in size. Capacity, 2 oz. Height, 3¹⁵/₁₆". Greatest width, 2½". Greatest depth, 1⅜":

8. Brilliant yellow-amber; 19 vertical ribs; flattened circular body, long cylindrical neck, plain lip; unstable base. Extremely rare size, probably used as a smelling bottle. Capacity, 1 oz. Height, about 3". Greatest width, 2³/₁₆". Greatest depth, 1⅛".

Bottom row:

9. Grandmother flask, golden amber; 16 rib broken-swirl, first ribbing swirled to right; chestnut shape, long neck spreading at plain lip. Capacity, 1 pt. Height, 6¾". Greatest width, 4¾". Greatest depth, 2¹¹/₃₂".

10. Grandfather flask, unusual amber of olive tone; 24 vertical ribs, widely expanded; wide chestnut body, long neck spreading to plain lip; nearly flat base. Capacity, 1 qt. about 8 oz. Height, 8½". Greatest width, 6⅞". Greatest depth, 3".

11. Light golden amber of hue termed golden yellow; patterned in 15-diamond mold and widely expanded; tapering flattened ovoid body, neck spreading slightly to plain lip; nearly flat base. Possibly Mantua, Ohio, 1822–29. Capacity, 1 pt. about 1 oz. Height, 6¾". Greatest width, 4¼". Greatest depth, 2½".

99. JUGS or HANDLED BOTTLES, 19th century

Two types of handled spirits bottles with seal of distiller or dispenser are illustrated by Nos. 1 and 6. No. 1 was blown in a full-size two-piece mold having 26 wide-spaced vertical ribs and seal. No. 6, with applied seal, was pattern-molded and fashioned by blowing and manipulation, as were the rare early 19th-century midwestern jugs, Nos. 2 through 5 and 7, which were patterned in 24-rib molds or, perhaps, the same mold. Because of the pontil mark it is impossible to determine whether the ribs faded to the center of the bottom of the mold, converged, or terminated at a nipple or ring. Nos. 2, 4, and 7 illustrate typical swirled ribbing; No. 5, the broken-swirl produced by twice patterning the gather from which the bottle was formed, the vertical ribs from the first insertion in the mold being swirled, those from the second cutting across the swirled. No. 3 was patterned in a small two-piece 10-diamond mold that has been identified with Zanesville, Ohio. Only a very small number of these midwestern globular and ovoid jugs have been recorded that were patterned in the same molds and blown from glass in the same colors as the bottles and flasks, particularly those attributed to Ohio. Of them, the 10-diamond are the rarest. The jugs occur in aquamarines, citrons, ambers, clear green, and yellow-greens. Even fewer of the flask-type bottles like No. 7 have been recorded, and only in aquamarine and ambers. All have pontil marks on the base.

Illustrated also in *American Glass*: 3, 4, and 5 by Nos. 1, 3, and 7 in Plate 237; in *Two Hundred Years of American Blown Glass*: 2, 3, 5 by Nos. 1, 3, and 2 in Plate 108.

Nos. 1 and 6, formerly in the George S. McKearin Collection. Nos. 2, 3, and 5, The Corning Museum of Glass; Nos. 4 and 7, The Henry Ford Museum.

Top row:

1. Brilliant amber; ovoid body with 26 wide-spaced vertical ribs extending from about ½″ above bottom to about ½″ below neck, and broken on side by circular seal bearing "J.F.T. & C⁰ PHILAD" in circle; cylindrical neck, double round-collared lip similar to flask neck-finish No. 19, Ill. 135; medium kick-up; applied loop handle with long tooled and turned-up end. Probably third quarter of the 19th century. Ca-

pacity, 1 pt. about 10 oz. Height, 7¼″. Greatest diameter, 4¾″.

2. Brilliant light amber; 24 ribs swirled to left; globular body, short cylindrical neck, flat turned-over collar on lip; applied handle with crimped and turned-back end. Capacity, 1 qt. about 2 oz. Height, 6⁵/₁₆″. Greatest diameter, 5¹/₁₆″.

Middle row:

3. Brilliant reddish amber; expanded diamond; globular body, short cylindrical neck, lip collared as on No. 2; applied broad heavily ribbed strap handle with crimped and turned-back end. Attributed to Zanesville, O., ca. 1815–35. Capacity, 1 pt. about 1 oz. Height, 5″. Greatest diameter, 4″.

4. Brilliant citron; 24 ribs swirled to right; globular body, short cylindrical neck with flaring turned-over collared lip; applied strap handle with flat valley between heavy ribs, crimped end. Capacity, 1 pt. 6 oz. Height, 5⅛″. Greatest diameter, 4½″.

5. Deep amber; 24 ribs in heavy broken-swirl; ovoid body, short cylindrical neck with narrow flanged lip; applied wide heavily ribbed handle with heavy crimped end. Capacity, 1 pt. about 7 oz. Height, 5⅜″. Greatest diameter, 4³/₁₆″.

Bottom row:

6. Dark brown-amber; 26 vertical ribs; conical body of tapered shape, short cylindrical neck with double round-collared lip pulled out and indented for pouring; applied seal on side impressed "STAR WHISKEY / NEW YORK / W.B.CROWELL Jᴿ·"; applied solid loop handle with "leaf" tooled and curled end. Probably 3rd quarter of the 19th century. Capacity, 1 qt. 2 oz. Height, 8¼″. Diameter at base, 4¹¹/₁₆″.

7. Brilliant amber; 24 ribs swirled to right and widely expanded; rare form: flattened chestnut shape, tapering neck with rounded ring laid on below plain lip; applied fat and tapering handle with crimped and turned-back end. Capacity, 1 qt. 4 oz. Height, 8¼″. Greatest diameters, 3³/₁₆″ by 6″.

These flasks were blown from colorless or near colorless glass, which apparently was seldom used for pattern-molded commoners like Nos. 1 through 5, though normal for more elegant pocket-bottles blown in houses producing fine glassware. Cut and engraved flasks doubtless were produced in several early American glasshouses, but their scarcity suggests that the American demand for such distinguished pocket bottles was limited in the 18th and early 19th century, and that many gentlemen as well as average citizens were content with plain and pattern-molded pocket bottles, with and without protective coats.

Pocket bottles Nos. 1, 2, and 4 are 18th-century types carrying over into the early 19th century; they occur more frequently in eastern areas than midwestern. Probably some of those found in the East were imports. Perhaps the imported "flat half-pint bottles" (*Boston News Letter,* June 25, 1750) and the "flat half-pint Dram bottles" (*Massachusetts Gazette,* April 21, 1768) were pattern-molded and of similar shapes. Pre-1800 fragments of bottles closely similar to No. 4 and patterned in 16-, 20-, and 24-rib molds have been excavated at Philipse Manor, near Tarrytown, N.Y. Bases among them had a small conical kick-up similar to those of Nos. 1 and 4, a type more frequently occurring on 18th- than 19th-century examples. Bottles such as Nos. 1 and 4 are often called *nursing bottles;* whether they were ever so used is a moot question. Although bottles like No. 3, sharply tapering to a tiny base, are typically English, it is likely some were blown in early American glasshouses where English fashion was dictator and British glassmen had joined the American ranks. All shown have a pontil mark.

Illustrated also in *American Glass:* 3 by No. 6 in Plate 230; 5 by No. 2 in Plate 79; 7 by Nos. 1 and 2 in Plate 37; in *Two Hundred Years of American Blown Glass:* 7 by Plate 104.

Nos. 1 through 4 and 6, formerly in the George S. McKearin Collection. No. 5, The Henry Ford Museum; No. 7, The Corning Museum of Glass.

1. Striated smoky glass; patterned in small two-piece mold, rare design of alternate rows of flutes (16) and diamonds (16 in two horizontal rows); long slender flattened ovoid body tapering to short neck spreading at plain lip. Late 18th to early 19th century. Capacity, about 9 oz. Height, 6⅞". Greatest width, 2¹/₁₆". Greatest depth, 1¾" near base.

   Occurs also in light gray-green, yellow-green, and clear light green. A very few green and amber chestnut flasks and green short flattened ovoids, patterned in the same or a similar mold, have been recorded.

2. Brilliant colorless glass; tight 22-rib broken-swirl; swirled ribs to left; long flattened ovoid body, cylindrical neck, plain lip. Probably early 19th century. Rare. Capacity, about 11 oz. Height, 7". Greatest width, 3¼". Greatest depth, 1¹⁵/₁₆" near center.

3. Brilliant colorless glass; patterned in small two-piece mold, diaper of concave diamonds (11 in horizontal row) above flutes, formed by heavy ribs; long

flattened ovoid body tapering sharply at bottom to tiny base, short neck, plain lip. Late 18th to early 19th century. Capacity, about 7 oz. Height, 6½". Greatest width, 3³/₁₆". Greatest depth 1½".

4. Bubbly colorless glass; 16 wide vertical ribs, long flattened ovoid body, short neck spreading slightly to plain lip, incised line about ³/₁₆" below lip giving effect of collar. 18th to early 19th century. Capacity, about 9 oz. Height, 6½". Greatest width, 2⅞". Greatest depth, 1⅞".

5. Pitkin-type, faint aquamarine tint; broken-swirl ribbing: first patterned in 32-rib mold, swirled to right; then patterned in 16-rib mold for vertical upon swirled; long ovoid body, long neck, plain lip; plain thick flat base. Rare. Early 19th century. Midwestern, possibly Mantua, O. Capacity, 1 pt. about 2 oz. Height, about 7½". Greatest width, 3⅞". Greatest depth, 2⅜".

6. Colorless glass of gray tinge; free-blown; thick-walled flattened ovoid body, long cylindrical neck, plain lip; flat base; wheel-cut decoration: honeycomb diaper on ends; on reverse (in place of waffled diamond), plain oval panel, probably for inscription, name, or cypher. Probably Irish, last half 19th century. Capacity, 1 pt. about 9 oz. Height, 8½". Greatest width, 4¾". Greatest depth, 2¾".

7. Colorless non-lead glass of faint smoky tone; free-blown; thick-walled, slightly flattened fat ovoid body, neck spreading to plain lip and ground inside at top probably to fit a glass stopper; thick flat base; engraved decoration—*obverse:* characteristic Amelung wreath composed of leaf sprays, daisylike flower, and wheat stalks enclosing *"F. Stenger"* in script above *1792; reverse:* circular medallion formed by two slender pinnate leaves joined at top and bottom by a four-petaled flower, enclosing a bottle, plow, trowel, and square in line down center. Amelung, New Bremen Glassmanufactory. 1792. Capacity, 1 pt. plus. Height, 6⅞". Greatest width, 3¹⁵/₁₆". Greatest depth, 2¾".

   This flask was acquired about 1920 by George S. McKearin from descendants of Francis Stanger and Elizabeth L. Campbell and—with it—their fracturwork marriage certificate dated March 11, 1803. A Francis Stanger was one of the Stanger brothers who, by the fall of 1781, completed the first Glassboro glassworks, the second in New Jersey. The name, prominent in American glassmaking from the late 1700s into the 1800s, was spelled with an "a" and "e" or two "e's". Thus it has been assumed that Francis of the flask and marriage certificate was Francis of the Glassboro works. Evidence of the origin of the flask lies in the dark cast and texture of the non-lead glass, the engraving technique, the style of decoration, and the formation of letters and figures, so like those on dated and inscribed Amelung pieces. Perhaps the emblems symbolized Stanger's craft, residence, and fraternity: the bottle for glassmaker; the plow for New Jersey (one being in the state's coat of arms); the trowel and square of a Freemason.

By the early 18th century apparently smelling bottles—or pungents, as they were also called later—were as necessary to ladies as the powder compact in the early 20th century. Those illustrated here show a variety of form and decoration and, unless otherwise stated, are attributed to the late 18th or early 19th century. All were free-blown except No. 6, and except for Nos. 6 and 7, all have a plain lip.

Collection of Arthur Barris.

Top row:

1. Colorless with imbedded opaque-white spiral ribbon; flattened ovoid; on ends applied colorless rigaree ribbon. Capacity, about ¾ dram. Height, 2⁷/₁₆". Greatest width, 1". Greatest depth, ½".

2. Seahorse, colorless, with imbedded opaque-white spiral thread; on ends, applied colorless quilled and rigaree ribbon. Possibly English. Capacity, under ⅔ dram. Height, 1¾". Greatest diameter, ⁹/₁₆".

3. Colorless, with imbedded bluish opaque-white nearly vertical threads; waisted body, flattened circular below spherical bulge; on ends, applied colorless ribbon: S-loop between quilled and rigaree. Attributed to England. Capacity, about ¾ dram. Height, 2⅛". Diameter of upper part, ¾"; of lower, ½" by 1".

4. Colorless; pattern-molded, 24 ribs swirled tightly to right; flattened ovoid tapering to sheared base. Probably American. Capacity, about ⅔ dram. Height, 1⅞". Greatest width, ⅞". Greatest depth, ½".

5. Colorless; thick-walled, wheel-cut, inverted pear shape; lip and oval base, polished; sides: gores of strawberry diamonds flanked by 2 triangular ribs (1 plain; 1 with serrated bevel); ends: long panel ribbed horizontally. Pittsburgh history. Early to mid-19th century. Capacity, about ½ oz. Height, 2⅛". Greatest width, 1⅝". Greatest depth, 1".

6. Colorless; pressed; four-sided, tapering sharply from narrow flat shoulder to small flat polished base, cylindrical neck threaded for metal screw cap; each side: printie block above twin notched ribs. Probably American. ca. 1880. Capacity, about ⅛ dram. Height, 2⅝". Diameter at top, ¾"; at end, about ¼".

Middle row:

7. Venetian-type latticinio, colorless with imbedded latticed and spiraled opaque-white ribbons; slender flattened inverted pear shape, unusually long neck, flanged lip. Probably American, late 19th century. Capacity, 1 oz. plus. Height, 4". Greatest width, 1⅝". Greatest depth, ¾".

8. Colorless; pattern-molded, 16 ribs swirled to right; slender ellipsoid body; base polished; on ends: applied vertical rigaree ribbon; on sides: applied ribbon: S-loop between quilling and rigaree. Height, about 3". Greatest width, including rigaree, 1¹/₁₆". Greatest depth, ⅝".

9. Colorless; corset-waisted, flattened ovoid above circular section, long neck with medial collarlike bulge; in thin wall between sections, a 1767 German or Dutch silver coin; on ends: applied ribbon: loops (at neck, missing right side) and rigaree; base formed by wafer turned back against sides; at center of ovoid section, waffled blue prunt. Probably Continental. Capacity, ½ oz. Height, 3¾". Greatest width, including rigaree, 1⁹/₁₆". Greatest depth, ½".

10. Colorless; long slender ovoid body; shallowly engraved, *obverse:* three pinnate leaves above and below "JR" in script; *reverse:* 3 long pinnate leaves, small stylized flower at top of center leaf; small glass stopper. Attributed to England. ca. 1765. Capacity, ½ oz. Height, with stopper, 3¾". Greatest width, 1⅛". Greatest depth, ⅝".

11. Colorless; thick-walled, long flat ovoid; shallowly engraved, *obverse:* "H L" in script below depending spray of three pinnate leaves and above two conventionalized fuchsialike flowers at end of leafed stem; *reverse:* two pinnate leaves above two 4-petaled flowers on long stems, and single leaves each side. Attributed to England. Capacity, 1 oz. Height, 4½". Greatest width, 1⅞". Greatest depth, ½".

Bottom row:

12. Seahorse, colorless; pattern-molded, 24 ribs swirled to right; on ends, applied wide ribbon: quilled above double loops and rigaree; at bottom, small wafer turned back against body on sides. Attributed to England. Capacity, ½ oz. Height, about 3¾". Greatest width, including quilling, 1¼". Greatest depth, ¾".

13. Seahorse, colorless; thick-walled; on ends, applied quilled ribbon and free-standing double S-loop from body to top of tail; shallow engraving, *obverse:* "T S N" below "sunflower" and above small bird perched in pinnate leaf; *reverse:* "1792" above flower on long stem with wide leaves each side, a pinnate leaf at right and left. Purchased in England. Capacity, ¾ oz. Height, about 4". Greatest width, including quilling, 1½". Greatest depth, ⅝".

14. Seahorse, colorless; on left end and tail, applied rigaree ribbons; right end above tail, leaf prunt; shallow engraving: *obverse,* in script lengthwise, "Cathⁿ Williams" between rows of dots flanking stylized 4-petaled flower at right and anchor at left; *reverse:* three conventionalized flowers forming trefoil at top of long stem with fine-leaf sprays above wide leaves. Perhaps a sailor's gift to his sweetheart. English or American. Capacity, ½ oz. Height, 3⅛". Greatest width, including ribbons, 1⁵/₁₆". Greatest depth, ¹³/₁₆".

15. Colorless; flattened ellipsoid; pattern-molded, 22 ribs swirled to right; on ends, applied quilled ribbons; on sides, serpentine heavy thread. Capacity, 1 oz. Height, 4⅛". Greatest width, including quilling, 1½". Greatest depth, ⁹/₁₆".

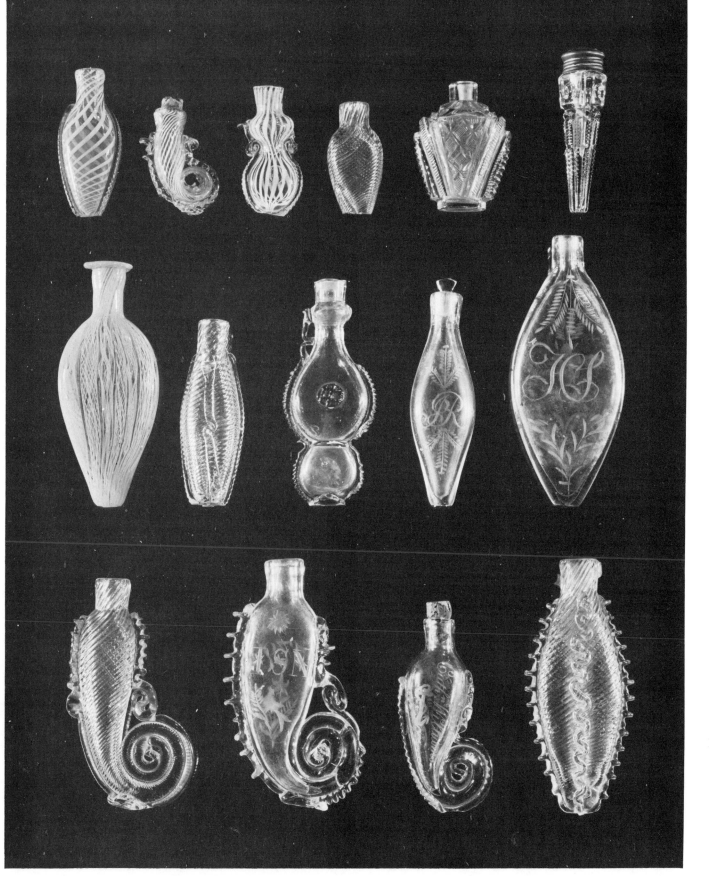

102. SMELLING BOTTLES, 18th–early 19th century

These free-blown smelling bottles illustrate types common to Great Britain and America. The middle and bottom rows depict the form dubbed *seahorse* by American collectors, with ovoid bodies, fat or lean, tapering to a curled tail that varies in the number of turns to the inner tip. The bodies are either plain or have imbedded threading of a contrasting color, or occasionally pattern-molded ribs, as on No. 8. Their characteristic decoration is glass of the same or a contrasting color applied in the form of ribbons and tooled. Perhaps the seahorse was the form of the "curious" smelling bottles advertised in the *Newport (R.I.) Mercury* on April 4, 1763, and of the New England Glass Company's "Dolphin pungents" selling for $1.20 a dozen in 1826. Smelling bottles Nos. 1, 2, and 3 on the top row are rare in form; Nos. 4 and 5, in color. All have a plain lip and were stopped with corks.

Illustrated also in *American Glass:* 3, 7, 8, 10, and 11 by Nos. 16, 13, 20, 21, and 17 in Plate 240.

All formerly in the George S. McKearin Collection. Collection of Arthur Barris.

Top row:

1. Brilliant green; flattened ovoid body tapering sharply to small rough base, wide collarlike bulge below slightly spreading neck; colorless quilled ribbons on ends; green scrolled heavy thread on sides. Capacity, about ½ oz. Height, about 3". Greatest width, including quilling, 1¾". Greatest depth, about ⅝".

2. Cobalt blue; small spherical body, very long neck with 2 wide collarlike medial bulges; on each "end," pair of colorless ribbons: crimped at collars, rigaree on body. Probably American. Capacity, about ¾ dram. Height, about 1⅞". Greatest diameter, 15/16".

3. Black (deep amethyst); crudely fashioned flattened globular body, long neck with wide medial collarlike bulge; on ends, black ribbons: quilled at collar, rigaree on body. Keene, N.H., history; probably an individual piece made by a blower in the Keene-Marlboro-Street glassworks, ca. 1815–20. Capacity, about ⅓ dram. Height, about 1⅞". Greatest width, including rigaree, 1¹/₁₆". Greatest depth, ⅝".

4. Olive-green; flattened ovoid tapering at bottom to small rough base. Possibly South Jersey. Capacity, about ¾ dram. Height, 2⅛". Greatest width, 1⅛". Greatest depth, ⅝".

5. Deep blue, imbedded greenish yellow loopings and slightly spiraled threads; very thick-walled; flattened ovoid tapering abruptly at bottom to tiny sheared base. Probably English. Capacity, ½ oz. Height, about 2½". Greatest width, 1⅜". Greatest depth, ⅝".

Middle row:

6. Seahorse, emerald-green; colorless quilled and cross-ribbed ribbons. Capacity, about ⅓ dram. Height, about 2". Greatest diameter, 9/16".

7. Seahorse, light gray-blue (violet tone in reflected light); rigaree of same color. Very rare in color. Capacity, about ⅔ dram. Height, about 2½". Greatest diameter, ⅝".

8. Seahorse, emerald-green; pattern-molded, 15 ribs swirled to right; emerald-green quilled and rigaree ribbons, double "S" loop between body and tail at left. Extremely rare. Capacity, about ⅔ dram. Height, 2⅝". Greatest diameter, 9/16".

9. Seahorse, dark emerald-green; colorless quilled and rigaree ribbons (originally probably a loop at left from quilling to rigaree on tail); each side, shallow engraving: (1) anchor on side above "H G" (?) and below conventionalized flower and pinnate leaves, (2) conventionalized spray with 3 flowers forming trefoil at top. Rare. Capacity, about ⅔ dram. Height, about 2¾". Greatest diameter, ¾".

10. Seahorse, clear amber; amber rigaree and looped ribbon at left and ribbed leaf at right. Very rare. Attributed to South Jersey. Capacity, about ¾ dram. Height, about 3". Greatest diameter, 13/16".

Bottom row:

11. Seahorse, colorless with imbedded spiraled opaque-white threads; quilled and rigaree blue ribbons; still filled with aromatic snuff. Rare size. Capacity, about ⅓ dram. Height, about 1½". Greatest diameter, ½".

12. Seahorse, colorless with imbedded twisted alternate opaque-white and light blue threads; twin narrow quilled and rigaree ribbons, not meeting at bottom; still filled with aromatic snuff. Capacity, about ¾ dram. Height, about 2⅝". Greatest diameter, 11/16".

13. Seahorse, light green; ribbons of same color, looped and quilled on left; pinched and leaf tooled on right. Very rare. South Jersey type. Capacity, about ½ oz. Height, 3½". Greatest diameter, ⅞".

14. Seahorse, colorless with imbedded opaque-white threading; colorless quilled and rigaree ribbons, overlapping at bottom. Unusually large size. Capacity, about 1 oz. Height, 4⅜". Greatest diameter, 1⅛".

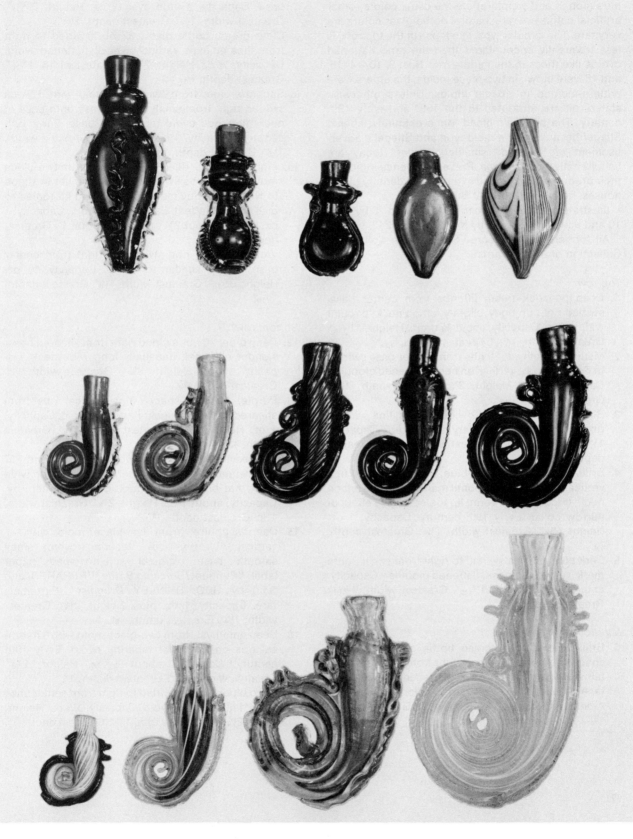

The ribbed smelling bottles shown here are types common to Great Britain and America. Colorless and blue (cobalt and sapphire) are the usual colors; other artificial colors are rare; natural bottle-glass colors are very rare. The circular type, like those in the top row, is less frequently encountered than the long flattened ovoids like those in the middle row. Nos. 9, 10, 14, 15, and 16 were blown in two-piece molds; the others were pattern-molded in rib dip molds. Unless otherwise stated, all are attributed to the 18th and early 19th century. The pattern-molded, once definitely labeled *Stiegel* because of the mold type and Stiegel's advertisement of "twisted" smelling bottles, today are usually called *Stiegel type*. Present evidence indicates their production continued in early 19th-century glasshouses, here if not in Great Britain.

Illustrated also in *American Glass:* 5 and 16 by Nos. 10 and 9 in Plate 240; 15 by No. 3 in Plate 242.

All formerly in the George S. McKearin Collection. Collection of Arthur Barris.

Top row:

1. Deep peacock-green; 20 ribs from center base, swirled right on body, slightly left on neck; circular wafer form. Capacity, about ¾ dram. Height, 1¹⁵/₁₆″. Greatest width, 1⁷/₁₆″. Greatest depth, ⁹/₁₆″.
2. Medium amethyst; 20 ribs from center base swirled to right on body, vertical on neck; flattened globular. Capacity, 1 oz. Height, 2″. Greatest width, 1⅝″. Greatest depth, ⁹/₁₆″.
3. Black (deep purple); 20 wide-spaced fine vertical ribs; flattened globular. Very rare in color. Capacity, 1½ oz. Height, 2¼″. Greatest width, 1¹³/₁₆″. Greatest depth, 1³/₁₆″.
4. Brilliant "electric" green-blue; 20 wide-spaced fine vertical ribs from small pontil mark, twisted to left on neck; circular wafer form; lip tooled to give effect of narrow collar. Early 19th century. Capacity, 1 oz. Height, 2¼″. Greatest width, 1¾″. Greatest depth, ⅞″.
5. Dark blue; 20 ribs swirled to right from small pontil mark, vertical on neck; flattened globular. Capacity, about ½ oz. Height, 1¹⁵/₁₆″. Greatest width, 1⁵/₁₆″. Greatest depth, ⅞″.

Middle row:

6. Brilliant clear olive-green bottle glass; 16 wide-spaced fine ribs swirled to right from sheared base, faint and vertical on neck; flattened ovoid, sharp taper at base. Extremely rare in color. Attributed to America. Capacity, 1 oz. Height, 3″. Greatest width, 1⁵/₁₆″. Greatest depth, ⅞″.

7. Brilliant emerald-green; 26 ribs swirled to right from base to lip; flattened ovoid, tapering at sheared base. Capacity, a little over ½ oz. Height, 2¹³/₁₆″. Greatest width, 1⅞″. Greatest depth, 1⅛″.
8. Clear green, bottle glass; 22 ribs swirled to right from sheared base, vertical on neck; flattened ovoid. Capacity, ½ oz. Height, 2⅜″. Greatest width, 1¹/₁₆″. Greatest depth, ⁹/₁₆″.
9. Sapphire-blue; from two-piece mold with 17 ribs swirled right from small smooth base onto base of neck; flattened ovoid tapering to base. Early 19th century. Capacity, 1 oz. Height, 3″. Greatest width, 1⅛″. Greatest depth, ¹⁵/₁₆″.
10. Light gray-blue, deep tone in base; from two-piece mold with 17 ribs swirled to right; similar in shape to No. 9 but body more rounded and lip tooled to give collared effect. Early 19th century. Capacity, 1 oz. Height, about 2¾″. Greatest width, 1″. Greatest depth, ⅞″.
11. Violet-blue; 22 ribs swirled to right from center base; shape similar to No. 9. Capacity, ½ oz. Height, 3¹/₁₆″. Greatest width, 1⅛″. Greatest depth, ¹³/₁₆″.

Bottom row:

12. Deep blue; 20 ribs swirled right from sheared base; slender elliptical, unusually long wide neck. Capacity, ½ oz. Height, 3¼″. Greatest width, 1″. Greatest depth, ¾″.
13. Purple; 12 wide-spaced fine vertical ribs from sheared base onto neck; flattened ovoid. Capacity, 1 oz. Height, 2¾″. Greatest width, 1⅛″. Greatest depth, ¾″.
14. Shaded amethyst; from two-piece mold with 17 ribs swirled to right; elliptical, unusually long wide neck; flat base, pontil mark. Early 19th century. Capacity, about 1 oz. Height, 2⅝″. Greatest width, 1⅛″. Greatest depth, ¹⁵/₁₆″.
15. Deep sapphire; from two-piece mold with 17 vertical ribs on body; tapering ovoid; small smooth base; original shield-shaped paper label: "Pungent/*Smelling Bottle*/PREPARED/ and Sold by / GEO. BRINLEY / *Druggist*". Extremely rare. Capacity, 1 oz. plus. Height, 2½″. Greatest width, 1¼″. Greatest depth, ⅞″.
16. Deep amethyst; from two-piece mold with 17 vertical ribs on body; fat tapering ovoid. Early 19th century. Capacity, about 1 oz. Height, 2⅝″. Greatest width, 1¼″. Greatest depth, 1″.
17. Deep blue; 24 ribs swirled to right from center base to lip; fat, tapering ovoid. Capacity, 1½ oz. Height, about 2¼″. Greatest width, 1⅜″. Greatest depth, 1″.

The rare figured smelling bottles in the top and middle rows were blown in full-size two-piece molds. Nos. 1 through 7 and 9 are attributed to the period ca. 1815 to 1830; Nos. 8 and 10 to mid-19th century. The late 18th- to early 19th-century Stiegel-type smelling bottles in the bottom row were patterned in rib molds and shaped by blowing and manipulation.

Illustrated also in *American Glass:* 2, 3, 6, and 7 by Nos. 9, 7, 14, and 18 in Plate 241; 12 by No. 5 in Plate 240; 14 by No. 6 in Plate 24.

All formerly in the George S. McKearin Collection. Nos. 1 through 14, Collection of Arthur Barris; No. 15, Collection of Henry G. Schiff.

Top row:

1. Scallop shell, aquamarine; fat shell body, wide long neck, inside fold. Capacity, about 3/4 dram. Height, 1 3/4″. Greatest width, 1 5/16″. Greatest depth, 13/16″.

2. Flower and petals, pale green; circular wafer body, long slender neck, wide flange; rough base; sides: (1) three slender petals with knoblike ends, (2) 8-petalled flower; ends: corrugated (11 short horizontal ribs in one leaf of mold; 10, in other). Capacity, 1/2 oz. Height, 2 1/4″. Greatest width, 1 3/4″. Greatest depth, 15/16″.

3. Pinwheel, aquamarine; circular wafer body, short neck, plain lip; rectangular base, pontil mark; sides: 5 ribs curving from large bead at center; ends: corrugated (7 ribs in each leaf of mold). Occurs in several colors. Capacity, 1 oz. Height, 2 1/4″. Greatest width, 1 13/16″. Greatest depth, 13/16″.

4. Concentric ring, pale green; circular wafer body, short neck, plain lip; pontil mark; sides: 4 rings, large bead at center; edges: beveled and corrugated (33 ribs in each leaf of mold); same design found on solid stoppers for flint-glass decanters and formed in a small two-piece mold with long handles. Occurs also in aquamarine, black (amethyst?), deep blue, emerald-green, and yellowish olive-green. Capacity, 1/2 oz. Height, 2 1/4″. Greatest width, 1 3/4″. Greatest depth, at bead, 15/16″.

5. Daisy, colorless; circular wafer body, short neck, plain lip; sides: alternate long (6 in all) and 2 short petals (6 pairs in all) from bead at center; ends: corrugated (20 ribs in each leaf). Occurs in various colors, including amethyst and bluish green. Capacity, about 3/4 dram. Height, 1 3/4″. Greatest width, 1 7/16″. Greatest depth, 3/4″.

Middle row:

6. Light greenish blue; flattened elliptical body, wide neck, plain lip; pontil mark; sides: (1) beaded frame, large 7-petal flower on leafed stem, 2 short pinnate leaves rising from small flower pot, (2) beaded frame, large pinnate leaf. Purchased from a descendant of John Ensell, Pittsburgh glassman, and, according to family history, blown by him. Capacity, 1 oz. Height, 2 11/16″. Greatest width, 1 3/8″. Greatest depth, 1″.

7. Colorless, green tint; flattened elliptical body, long neck, plain lip; small elliptical base; sides: conventional design of short scroll-ribs and beads; ends: corrugated (12 ribs in each leaf). Capacity, 1 oz. Height, 2 3/4″. Greatest width, 1 3/4″. Greatest depth, 7/8″.

8. Colorless; heart-shaped body, long neck, narrow flange; smooth base; sides: (1) graduated fan ribs below simple scrolls, (2) scroll ornament above plain area. Capacity, 1/2 oz. Height, 2 1/4″. Greatest width, 1 9/16″. Greatest depth, 3/4″.

9. Sunburst, pale blue; body, "shield shape" (ends: tapering curve to small base; long ogee shoulder, upper curve very narrow), wide neck, plain lip; pontil mark; sides: oval Sunburst; 12 heavy rays to bead at center; edges: beveled and beaded (7 each side, in each leaf of mold). Occurs in various colors including olive-green. Capacity, 1/2 oz. Height, 2 3/4″. Greatest width, 1 1/2″. Greatest depth, 9/16″.

10. Scroll, colorless; like No. 4 of Ill. 106 (GIX–40, Flask Charts) but neck threaded for metal screw cap; smooth base. Capacity, little over 1/2 oz. Height, 2 15/16″. Greatest width, 1 1/2″. Greatest depth, about 13/16″.

Bottom row:

11. Amethystine with amethyst streaks; 26 vertical ribs; ovoid, tapering to small sheared base. Capacity, about 1 oz. Height, about 3 3/8″. Greatest width, 1 3/16″. Greatest depth, 7/8″.

12. Fiery opalescent; 22 ribs swirled to right, wide-spaced on body; fat ovoid tapering to small base; pontil mark. Unusually large. Capacity, 1 1/2 oz. Height, 3 3/8″. Greatest width, 1 3/8″. Greatest depth, 1 1/8″.

13. Colorless; either 32 or 36 ribs swirled to right (too fine and expanded for accurate count); extremely flat ovoid, tapering sharply to small sheared base. English. Capacity, 1/2 oz. Height, 3 7/8″. Greatest width, 1 1/2″. Greatest depth, 1/2″.

14. Light wisteria; 22 ribs swirled right on body, nearly vertical on neck; fat ovoid tapering to small sheared base. Capacity, 1/2 oz. Height, 3 7/16″. Greatest width, 1 1/8″. Greatest depth, 11/16″.

15. Brilliant amber; 26 ribs, nearly vertical; ovoid tapering to small sheared base. Extremely rare in color. Capacity, 1/2 oz. Height, 3 1/8″.

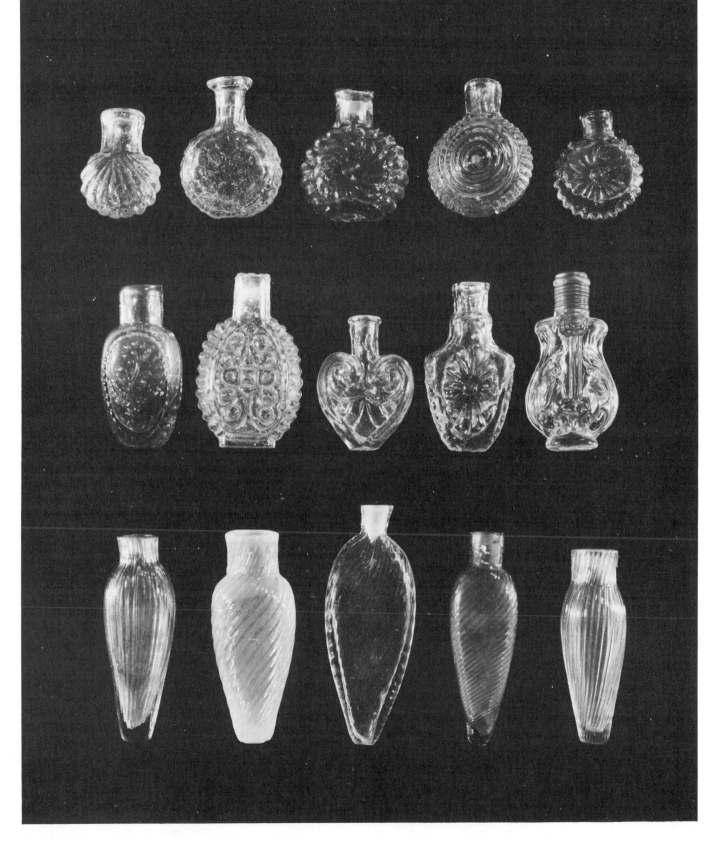

Except for No. 12, these rare figured smelling bottles are American examples of the fancy but not elegant varieties, some of which were produced in bottle houses. Except for the neck, the shape and pattern were obtained in a full-size two-piece mold. The sunbursts on Nos. 2, 4, 5, and 9—also on No. 9 of Ill. 104—are closely similar to some of those on the New England Sunburst flasks GVIII–1 through 16; that on No. 15, to the so-called stars on the Keene-Marlboro-Street Masonic flasks GIV–7. It seems likely that the smelling bottles are New England, some probably blown at Keene-Marlboro-Street works and some at the Coventry Glass Works, Conn. Some have a smooth base; others, a pontil mark, often so clean a scar that the bottom of the bottle appears to have been sheared off.

All formerly in the George S. McKearin Collection. Collection of Arthur Barris.

Top row:

1. Ribbed shield, light emerald-green; shield shape; pontil mark; sides: 13 beads (grouped: 1, 3, 1, 2, 6) above V-shaped ribbed panel (short central rib, 2 V-ribs); edges: beveled. Capacity, 1 oz. Height, about 2⅞″. Greatest width, 1⅝″.

2. Sunburst and diamond, emerald-green; shield shape; smooth base; sides: (1) 3 beads forming triangle above and below relief panel of 9 diamonds, circle of 6 beads with one at center and flanking panel at top; (2) bead ornament like (1) above and below relief oval sunburst of 12 triangular rays, 3 beads flanking sunburst at top; edges: beveled and beaded (11 small beads on each bevel). Capacity, 1 oz. Height, about 3¹/₁₆″. Greatest width, 1⅝″.

3. Sunburst, cobalt blue; circular wafer shape; pontil mark; sides: 24 rounded rays from small round concave center; edges: riblike mold seam. Capacity, about ¾ dram. Height, 1¾″. Greatest width, 1⅜″.

4. Sunburst, emerald-green; shield shape; pontil mark; sides: relief oval sunburst of 12 triangular rays from large bead at center; edges: beveled and beaded (9 beads graduated from large at top of each bevel to small at base). Occurs also in opalescent and olive-green. Capacity, about ¾ dram. Height, 2⅞″. Greatest width, 1½″.

5. Sunburst, deep amethyst; shield shape; flangelike bulge at base of neck; pontil mark; sides: relief oval sunburst of 12 triangular rays to center; edges: beveled and beaded (12 small beads on each bevel). Capacity, about ¾ oz. Height, 2¹³/₁₆″. Greatest width, 1½″.

Middle row:

6. Checkered-diamond and fan, sapphire-blue; flattened elliptical; sides: fan ribbing above and below checkered-diamond (9 beads in diamond), half-checkered-diamonds at sides; edges, including bottom: corrugated (26 ribs). Capacity, 1 oz. Height, about 2¾″. Greatest width, 1⅜″.

7. Diamond, emerald-green; flattened elliptical; pontil mark; sides: (1) relief diamond panel similar to No. 2; (2) relief oval sunburst similar to No. 2; sides: beveled. Capacity, about 1 oz. Height, 2⅝″. Greatest width, 1⁹/₁₆″.

8. Daisy, deep amethyst; like No. 5 in Ill. 104. Capacity, about ¾ oz. Height, 1⅞″. Greatest width, 1⅜″.

9. Sunburst, deep amethyst; shield shape; pontil mark; sides: relief oval sunburst of 12 triangular ribs to center; edges: beveled. Capacity, about ¾ oz. Height, about 2¹⁵/₁₆″. Greatest width, 1⁹/₁₆″.

10. Sunburst, deep blue; flattened elliptical; pontil mark; sides: unusual sunburst of 4 V's of 4 graduated triangular rays. Capacity, ½ oz. Height, 2⁹/₁₆″. Greatest width, 1⁵/₁₆″.

Bottom row:

11. Ribbed shield, cobalt blue; shield shape, long neck with wide medial collar-rib; pontil mark; sides: short center rib, 4 V ribs; edges: beveled. Capacity, ¾ oz. Height, about 3″. Greatest width, 1⁹/₁₆″.

12. Honeycomb, sapphire-blue; flattened pear shape tapering sharply at bottom; sides: (1) triangle of three small beads above honeycomb panel bordered at bottom by 6 small beads above plain area; (2) same beading but panel plain; edges: finely corrugated bevels (27 ribs at left; 24 at right). Purchased in England. Capacity, about ½ oz. Height, 2¾″. Greatest width, 1⅜″.

Also recorded is an opalescent example with traces of painted decoration and the inscription "WHEN THIS YOU SEE REMEMBER ME".

13. Concentric ring, olive-green bottle glass; like No. 4 in Ill. 104, but with 34 ribs in the corrugated beveled edges. Occurs also in black (possibly deep amethyst), and emerald-green. Capacity, ½ oz. Height, about 2¹/₁₆″. Greatest width, 1⅞″.

Bottles of the same form and design, except for a smaller bead at center, occur in deep amethyst.

14. Sunburst, peacock-blue; flattened elongated ovoid; sides: relief oval sunburst of 12 slender triangular rays from oval center; edges: beveled and beaded (20 small beads on 2 bevels; 19 on other 2). Capacity, ½ oz. Height, about 2¹⁵/₁₆″. Greatest width, 1¼″.

15. Sunburst, deep amethyst; elongated flattened diamond shape; pontil mark; sides: sunburst of 8 graduated triangular intaglio rays; edges: beveled and diagonally corrugated (about 20 fine ribs, each bevel, indistinct at bottom). Capacity, about ½ oz. Height, about 2¾″. Greatest width, 1⁵/₁₆″.

Part VII

SMELLING, SCENT, AND COLOGNE BOTTLES

by Kenneth M. Wilson

As the economy of the colonies improved, it encouraged a growing social life that required—even demanded, in some instances—certain fashionable accessories. Among them were smelling and scent bottles and snuff boxes. (The last need not concern us here.) Scent bottles, however, may have served a more serious purpose than fashion; in those predeodorant days, as in previous centuries, surely the fastidious appreciated a means of masking unpleasant odors. Smelling bottles too served a most useful purpose: when tight corseting was in vogue, a whiff from a smelling bottle would revive a lady from the vapors and fainting spells to which the severe lacing made her subject. So it was that, through a combination of fashion and necessity, smelling bottles (or pungent bottles, as they later came to be called) became almost as common in the 18th and 19th centuries as lipsticks are today. About 1750 an English critic of the smelling bottle vogue wrote:

The snuff box and smelling bottle are pretty trinkets in a ladies pocket, and are frequently necessary to supply a pause in conversation, and on some other occasions; but whatever virtues they are possessed of they are lost by too constant and familiar use, and

nothing can be more pernicious to the brain, or render one more ridiculous in company than to have either of them perpetually in one's hand.[1]

Though perhaps this critic's opinion may have embodied elements of truth, it carried little weight with the manufacturers and purveyors of the vast numbers and varieties of smelling bottles advertised throughout the 18th and 19th centuries. The contents of these bottles were varied: aromatic snuff, Eau de Luce for headaches,[2] various salts such as Delmahoys Burnt Salts,[3] Preston's Salt,[4] and Otto of Roses.[5] Thomas Tisdale of Hartford, Connecticut, summed it all up very nicely when he advertised in the August 18, 1788, *Connecticut Courant:* "Smelling bottles of various shapes—so absolutely necessary for little Misses in the approaching hot season."

The earliest reference to, presumably, smelling bottles of which I have knowledge appeared in the *Norwich Mercury* (England) on July 14, 1733: "Salt bottles double and single with cases."[6] In 1744 smelling bottles, possibly of glass or ceramic, set in silver with shagreen cases were offered to the ladies of Charleston, South Carolina.[7] By the mid-18th century, a wide variety of smelling bottles was being advertised in both England and the colonies. The *Birmingham Gazette* (England) of July 25, 1752, offered: "Cut smelling bottles of all colors." In the last half of the century, cut, gilt, and engraved smelling bottles of flint (lead) and opaque white glass, usually fitted like 10 in Ill. 101, were doubtless among those advertised as "elegant." Many of these 18th-century ones were originally contained in cases of shagreen, ivory, pierced bone, silver, or tortoiseshell. As time went on, the terminology used in referring to them changed, as it did with other types of accessories. The term *smelling bottle* continued to be used in the late-18th and into the mid-19th century, but by 1792 the term *pungent* (also variously spelled *pungeon, pungeant, pungeont*) was being used simultaneously. It became even more prevalent in the first quarter of the 19th century, and pungents continued to be advertised until late in that century. The John M. Maris & Co. catalog of 1889 illustrates more than a dozen cut-glass bottles with stoppers under the heading "PUNGENTS," followed by the statement: "We import a large line of Cut Pungents of Best Bohemian makes. We give a few styles below. Other styles in stock."

The widespread use of smelling bottles throughout the 18th century and most of the 19th as well is indicated by the selection of advertisements cited below. This almost universal advertising also suggests that smelling bottles were used by ladies in almost every economic level of society. Like other types of glass and bottles, the smelling bottles advertised for sale in the 18th century were, with some few exceptions, imported from England. Except as noted, very few were produced in America until the second decade of the 19th century. From then on, however, they became a regular part of the production of not only those glasshouses making fine flint glassware but also numerous bottle-glass houses that manufactured principally green- and black-glass bottles and containers.

On January 25, 1759, John Leacock, a goldsmith in Philadelphia, advertised "white and green smelling bottles, tip'd with silver, with or without shagreen cases." In Newport, Rhode Island, William and John Tweedy at the "GOLDEN EAGLE" offered for sale in the *Newport Mercury* of April 4, 1763: "Drugs . . . Medicine . . . Curious Smelling Bottles." Perhaps these were like 12 in Ill. 101. On May 2, 1768, Robert Bank of Philadelphia offered for sale in the *Pennsylvania Chronicle:* "a variety of Smelling bottles in cases, a few vials of elegant eau-de-luce." This substance (eau-de-luce) originated in France as competition to Hungary water, another toilet water, and was

advertised in England in 1754 as "imported from Paris and sold as a Volatile Essence for carrying in the pocket as a smelling bottle, stronger than many kinds of salts, more pungent than Lavender, Hungary or other odoriferous water." [8]

Two exceptions to importations in the 18th century were the smelling bottles produced by Henry William Stiegel at his Manheim glasshouses between 1769 and 1774, and those made at the Philadelphia Glass Works at least in 1775. Entries in Stiegel's Manheim account books from 1769 to April 1770 indicate 584 smelling bottles were on hand, on consignment, or sold. These may have been of several types, for on June 27, 1772, Stiegel advertised in Philadelphia's *Pennsylvania Gazette:* "enamelled smelling bottles, common smelling bottles, and twisted smelling bottles." The last were undoubtedly pattern-molded with fine ribbings, probably like those illustrated in Ill. 103, rows 2 and 3, and Ill. 104, row 3. One can speculate (and *only* speculate) that his common smelling bottles may have been like 4, in the top row of Ill. 102. The reference to "enamelled" smelling bottles immediately brings to mind the simple "peasant style" of enameling found on tumblers produced in this period, presumably by Stiegel, and certainly abroad, but the author knows of no enameled smelling bottle in this style. Since Stiegel's principal aim was to emulate the fashionable English style in an attempt to capture the colonial market for glass, one can but wonder whether he was attempting to imitate closely the often elegant opaque white and blue enameled or cut and enameled smelling bottles of English origin or pattern-molded (twisted) ones. Thus, as in the case of other Stiegel-type glass, we shall probably never be able to distinguish between those possibly made by Stiegel and those made in England.

John Elliott and Co., proprietors of the Philadelphia Glass Works, advertised in the February 27, 1775, *Pennsylvania Packet,* among a long list of flint glasswares: "proof bottles, pocket bottles . . . smelling bottles." There is no clue as to what type they were, but since this glassworks too was producing glass in the English style, the smelling bottles offered for sale were most likely pattern-molded and twisted, like those advertised by Stiegel, or possibly cut, since the firm offered some other cut glassware.

Asa and Daniel Hopkins, merchants in Hartford, Connecticut, advertised in the *American Mercury* of October 28, 1787, that, among other things, they had for sale "Rum, Sherry Wine . . . Smilling [*sic*] Bottles . . . also, MAXWELL'S SNUFF (much admired) in Bottles, and Bladders . . . " In Boston, Jonathan P.

Hall, druggist, offered in the *Independent Chronicle,* May 14, 1789: "a general assortment of Drugs & Medicine . . . Smelling-Bottles . . . " Also in Boston in the same year an auction was advertised in the *Massachusetts Centinel,* on October 7, offering "Elegant cut-glass smelling bottles, assorted . . . " On June 21, 1790, Thomas Tisdale, Hartford, Connecticut, advertised: "At the Pumpkin & Paddy JUST IMPORTED a large assortment of Double Flint and Tale Glass Goods, of a quality and figure superior to any heretofore imported into this state . . . consisting of . . . Smelling bottles different shapes." They were probably of English origin, since he added "also, a large assortment of Amsterdam Glass Tumblers and Mugs, some with covers, and from size of 5 pints to a gill, figured and plain." The assortment may have consisted of a number of the forms of the late 18th-century smelling bottles illustrated in Ills. 102 and 103.

The contents of 18th-century smelling bottles were usually salts; some bottles doubtless were also used to contain perfumes. The smelling salts varied, probably depending upon personal taste and the persuasiveness of local merchants. One formula consisted of crystals of ammonia scented with lavender or attar of roses. Hannah Kitchine of Boston apparently prided herself on her smelling salts, for she advertised on April 5, 1762, in the *Boston Gazette:* "Hannah Kitchine Makes a Smelling Mixture that will cure the Itch, or any sort of Breaking-out, there is several that pretends to make it, which know nothing about it. Inquire for her in Black-Horse Lane, at the Two Sugar Loaves."

The following two very similar formulas were apparently still popular for producing smelling salts in the early 19th century. The first is in Mrs. Mary Eston's *The Cook & Housekeeper's Complete and Universal Dictionary* published in 1822: "Reduce to powder an equal quantity of Salammoniac and quicklime separately, put two or three drops of the essence of bergamot into a small bottle, then add the other ingredients, and cork it close. A drop or two of ether will improve it." And in 1824, the *Arcana of Arts and Sciences*[9] advised: "To make smelling bottle PERFUMES &c take equal quantities of Salammonica and unslacked lime: pound them separately and mix them in a phial in which you have previously put three or four drops of essence of bergamot, and two or three of ether."

Nathaniel Smith, a powder and perfumery manufacturer in New York City, advertised in the *Daily Advertiser,* April 9, 1789, that he had for sale at the Sign of the Rose: "Smelling bottles and essence of bergamot, essence of lavender, do. of lemon, do. of orange, do. of chyme, with all kinds of perfume waters and various other articles."

A few words about these various ingredients may be in order here. The essences of lemon, orange, and chyme were used frequently in cooking. Bergamot and lavender were popular for preparing toilet or "sweet" waters, many of which were made by "ladies" at home; bergamot was also much in demand for preparing perfumes. In a letter written in 1775, one observer wrote: "At these shops two kinds are sold: essence of bergamot and . . . eau de jasmin de pourri . . . but the essence of bergamot is above all, as a single drop is sufficient to perfume a handkerchief and it ought to be, for it is very deer."[10]

Bergamot, an essential oil derived from the rind of the fruit of a species of citrus, is (according to Webster) a "curious variety of pear," or "a kind of orange having a pear-shaped fruit whose rind yields an essential oil much used in perfumery."[11]

It grows on small trees; the fruit and leaves are like the bitter orange. They are cultivated in the neighborhood of Reggio in Calabria, Italy, whence the entire supply of bergamot oil comes. After the extraction of the oil, it is allowed to rest until a greasy substance—bergamot—forms, after which it is bottled for use. The oil is a limpid, greenish-yellow fluid . . . having a powerful but pleasant citrine odor and an aromatic, bitterish taste. Its chief use is in perfumery and as a flavoring material in cookery.[12]

In the *Daily Advertiser* of January 5, 1795, Daniel Van Vorhis offered: "Smelling bottles with and without cases"—another indication that in many instances these small glass bottles were contained in some form of carrying case. The New York City *Diary* of November 20, 1792, advertised the "best sorts of plaited pungents and other similar bottles." This is the first utilization of the word *pungent* for smelling bottles known to me. Wilson & Prentiss of Hartford used the same term on April 4, 1796, when they offered for sale in the *Connecticut Courant:* "Drugs, Medicines . . . elegant GLASS FURNITURE, a great variety of pungent bottles . . . " William Seldon of Springfield, Massachusetts, apparently did not want to leave any question as to what he was offering when he noted in the *Federal Spy* on December 31, 1799: "Drugs, Medicines . . . Pungent smelling bottles" and "gilt and cut ditto."

The following price list from several English glass manufacturers, dated September 21, 1805, not only gives us an idea of the cost of these containers but describes several different types:

Smelling bottles and salt bottles, tale   2½d. each
    "   "   pinched   5d. each
    "   "   lapidary and
stoppers, small   4d. each
    "   "   oval,   "   5d. each
All above 2½ oz. 2 shillings per pound   6d. each
San Pareils [a term unknown to me] 2 s. per lb.
    6d. each

Following the Revolution, imports of smelling bottles of various types were received from countries other than England. An auction of French goods in Boston in 1813 included "crystal empty elegant smelling bottles."[13] An entry in the account book of Jeremiah Emlen, a Philadelphia druggist, notes on September 5, 1817: "Bought of North and Rogers one dozen Dutch smelling bottles .88."

It was just about at this time that the American firms making flint glass began to produce smelling bottles, or pungents, in quantity. Like other flint glassware produced here in the early 19th century, these smelling bottles undoubtedly were largely influenced by English ones in form and style. According to an entry in his account book on June 10, 1818, Jeremiah Emlen "Bought of Boston Glass Works groce Best pungents $15.00" and "1 groce Inferior twisted $7.50." The firm (actually, the South Boston Flint Glass Works, a subsidiary of the Boston Glass Manufactory) established by Thomas Cains, an Englishman from the Phoenix Glass Works in Bristol, began operating in December of 1812 or early in 1813. Two printed "Prices Current of South Boston Flint Glass Ware"—one dated August 20, 1818, the other August 26, 1819—are pasted in the back of Emlen's account book.[14] The 1818 one lists: "pungents, white [probably meaning colorless flint glass] $9.00 per gross. Ditto, fancy color best $16.00 per gross, ditto, richly cut——per dozen." There is no price per dozen for the richly cut pungents, indicating that it was dependent upon the style and extent of the cutting. In 1819 the following were listed:

Bottles, Smelling or pungents, Fancy
                                     $16.00 per gross
    "   "   "   "   Moulded and
                                      twisted
                                     $ 8.00 per gross

Again, it is quite likely that the twisted pungents or smelling bottles are like those shown in Ill. 103 and in the bottom row of Ill. 104. It is possible that some of the colored molded bottles in Ill. 105 represent the type of pungent or smelling bottles listed on the South Boston Flint Glass Ware Prices Current. They are also related to the Sunburst flasks produced in the New England area from about 1815 to 1825 or 1830.

Also pasted in the back of Emlen's account book is a printed price list entitled "Prices Current of Articles Manufactured by the New England Glass Company," which Emlen had dated by hand "September 1819." Included on this list are

Pungents, white [probably colorless flint glass]
                                    $9.00 per gross
    "   fancy col. best $16.00 per gross
    "   richly cut   _____ per dozen

Again, no price is listed for the cut pungents, indicating that the price would vary according to the design. In 1822 prices had dropped to $12.00 per gross for the South Boston Flint Glass Works fancy pungents. In that same year, they also offered for sale enameled pungents at $16.00 a gross.

Emlen purchased pungents or smelling bottles from other sources too. On March 26, 1823, he "Bot of Chever & Fales 24½ Doz. Dolphin Pungents @ 75¢, $18.06," or just a little over 6 cents each. It seems probable that these were like the dolphin pungents pictured in Ill. 102 in the bottom two rows, termed "seahorses" by collectors today.

Pungents were one of the first products made at the Boston and Sandwich Glass Works.[15] On July 16, 1825, twelve days after the factory began operating, John Snowden made "48 Best Pungeon" at 6 cents for a total of $2.88. On September 3, 1825, Michael Snowden made "100 Common Pungeants" at 5 cents each, for a total of $5.00. On November 26, 1825, Benjamin Haynes produced "420 Blue Common Pungeants" at 5 cents each, the same price as the common pungents made by Michael Snowden. On December 31, 1825, John Snowden made "290 Best Pungeants" at 8 cents each. Apparently these were more complicated than the best pungents he produced on July 16, since the latter are listed for only 6 cents each. On September 15, 1827, Benjamin Haynes made "110 Best pungeants," each apparently with "four pinches," at 8 cents each. In subsequent moves, other pungents with "four pinches" or three "pinchons" were produced at 8 cents each. This term, which also occurs occasionally in advertisements, is doubtless indicative of a type of decoration achieved by pincering hot glass applied to the surface of the vessel. The Boston and Sandwich Glass Works also produced dolphin pungents, as indicated by an entry of January 8, 1828, when John Doyle made "52 dolphin Tail Pungeants" at 6 cents each. The word "tail" here undoubtedly refers not to the tail of a dolphin but rather to an inferior quality of glass, the word sometimes being spelled as here, but most frequently as *tale*.

Other American firms are also known to have made pungents. *The Pittsburgh Gazetteer* of December 25, 1829, contained an advertisement for "cut and molded smelling bottles" made by Bakewell, Page & Bakewell. A merchant in New York City advertised in the *New York Gazette and General Advertiser* on November 10, 1837: "Pungeants and Smelling bottles, variety of green glass, among glass direct from the New England Glass Company and the Phoenix Manufactory." The Phoenix Manufactory referred to here was established in 1819 or 1820 by Thomas Cains after he gave up his lease on the South Boston Flint Glass Works. A price list of F. Plunket & Co's. Wheeling Flint Glass Works, dated December 12, 1837, listed "Pungeants assorted, per dozen, $1.00 to $1.37." In 1850 Henshaw and Edwards, of Boston, Prices Current, listed the following: "Pungeants, Mermaid, gross $8.50; Pungeants, empty elegant cut glass $2.50 per dozen." That same day Henshaw and Edwards, Boston, sent to G. Wardner, Windsor, Vermont, the following items:

Preston Salts, metal screw cap, small eyes, a neat article, $1.00 per doz

Parson's Pungeants, extra, French pattern $1.50 per dozen

Pungents, mermaid, gross $8.50

Pungents, small screw cap, gross $6.50

Pungents, Bottles, empty, elegant cut glass dozen $2.50

Phials for Otto Rose gilt dozen $1.12.

These items may be like those shown in Ill. 106, of various colors of glass, Nos. 7, 8, 9, 10, 12, 13, 15, and 18. If so, they were probably a new style at that time.

The price list of the Williamstown Glass Works, located in Camden County, New Jersey, dating from about 1853/54, lists under the heading FANCY PUNGEANTS the following: American Shield, American Eagle, Acorn, Cornucopia, Diamond, Dolphin, Grapes, Harp, Magnolia, Oak Leaf, Plain, Pine Apple, Rose, Strawberries and Urn. Each of these was priced at 50 cents a dozen, except for the Dolphin, which was 75 cents a dozen.[16]

As indicated above, smelling bottles (pungents) or

scent bottles continued to be advertised and used throughout the 19th century.

Like the scented smelling salts and their containers, perfumes, colognes, rose waters, and other concoctions of scent played a major role not only with ladies but also with gentlemen in the 18th century and (at least with the ladies) throughout the 19th century. One-gallon demijohns were frequently used as containers by dispensers and for shipping cologne and rose, Hungary, Florida, orange, and scented waters, a fact that suggests their prolific use. Smaller quantities of these waters and colognes were frequently put into square or long flat bottles, until "fancy" bottles came into vogue in America and France, probably in the late 1820s. Phials of various sizes were used for perfumes and other strong essences in even smaller quantities.

François Marie Farina's eau de cologne, first marketed in 1709,[17] was soon imitated in Europe and America, and the name was pirated, evidence of its popularity. Despite this, the marked absence of advertisements throughout much of the 18th century (at least until the last quarter of it) is in contrast to the great number of advertisements for smelling salts and smelling bottles during this same period. Nevertheless, the following advertisements indicate the prevalence of these scents. On December 3, 1763, Jonathan Arnwed advertised in the *Providence Gazette and Country Journal*: "All kinds of perfumery for Gentlemen and Ladies, such as distilled Lavender Water . . . " In 1765 Geradus Duyckinck advertised on August 15, in the *New York Gazette and Weekly Post Boy*, a wide variety of items for sale, including "perfumery, essences or oil of lavender, Burgamot, ambergrise," as well as "Cinnamon water double distill'd. Pepper and mint ditto. Hungary ditto. Lavender." Another merchant offered "orange flower water in pint bottles" for sale in 1768, and on January 27, 1794, James B. Clerie, merchant, in the *Diary* or *Evening Register* offered perfumes from Paris for sale, including "orange flower water a very pleasing smell." As previously stated, many of these essences and waters were used in cooking also. "A Valuable Sale of French Goods by Auction" advertised in the *Boston Columbian Centinel*, February 6, 1813, offered among many things: "14 cases containing a valuable assortment of Perfumery, viz. Eau de Cologne, Eau de Lavander double, Eau de Rose, Eau double en poison . . . "

By at least the fourth quarter of the 18th century a number of perfumery manufactories had been established in this country. As mentioned earlier, Nathaniel Smith, "Hair Powder and Perfumery

Manufacturer," was advertising his wares at the Sign of the Rose in New York City at least by 1789.[18] Undoubtedly some enterprising merchants also formulated their own colognes and sweet waters, as well as importing or purchasing them from such domestic establishments as Smith's. Perhaps some individuals did, too. The *American Housewife* of 1843[19] offered the following formula for making cologne water:

Turn a quart of alcohol gradually on two drachm of oil of rosemary, 2 drachm oil of lemon or orange flavor water; one drachm of lavender, 10 drops of cinnamon, 10 drops of cloves, a teaspoon of rosewater. Keep the whole stopped tight in a bottle. Shake it well. It will do to use as soon as made, but is much improved by age.

In view of the largely increased number of advertisements for cologne and sweet waters of all types in the second quarter of the 19th century, these preparations seem to have attained much greater popularity by then. In fact, the growing interest in various perfumes, colognes, and the like apparently soon became great enough to warrant a book on the subject for amateurs and "do-it-yourselfers." When Ponger's *The Art of Glass Blowing* was published in London in 1831, it carried an advertisement of *The Perfumer's Oracle* stating:

The object of this work is to present a comprehensive and practical account of the Preparation of PERFUMES & COSMETICS, according to the newest, most successful and most economical processes. It will be adopted either for Professional Persons or for Ladies who may wish to amuse themselves with this elegant branch of experimental science. Price 3s 8d.

An advertisement in Poulson's on May 18, 1827, of a public sale by Kuhn & French offered: "Fifteen hundred boxes cologne water in round and octagon bottles" for sale. During the previous week, this same firm had advertised at public sale: "COLOGNE WATER ONE HUNDRED DOZEN 1st quality Genuine Cologne Water in square bottles."[20] N. Prentiss, wholesale and retail perfumer in New York City, advertised on September 1, 1828: "American Cologne Water . . . ½ pt. bottles." L. W. Glenn of Philadelphia advertised in the *Daily Chronicle,* October 1, 1831: "Cologne Water etc. 200 Boxes superior cologne water in fancy bottles. Also cologne water in quart, pint and smaller bottles, and by the

gallon or less quantity." The following postscript to his advertisement indicates once again the apparent interest some women still must have had in concocting their own cologne: "Persons having favorite receipts for cologne water can have them compounded on the most reasonable terms." In the same newspaper there appeared, on October 7, 1831, a notice offering: "Cologne Water Jean Maria Farina . . . distillery from Cologne, Germany—original receipt . . . *only* in long flat bottles having J. M. Farina, J. F. M. blown on them."

Further interest in imported wares is evident from the "Good Samaritan," Isaac Bull of Hartford, who advertised in the *Connecticut Courant* November 4, 1833:

REAL GERMAN COLOGNE WATER. One Case (containing 40 Bxs.) of genuine Eau de Cologne, from the Manufactory of Francois Marie Farina le plus Ancien distillateur rue de Cloche No. 4711 vis a vis de la Poste aux Chevaux a Cologne. For Sale by the Box or single Bottle . . . at the sign of the GOOD SAMARITAN.

He also offered in the *Connecticut Courant* in the following year:

COLOGNE WATER. Warranted *equal* to any (except the German,) and by many preferred to that, put up in Bottles, of various sizes. Also, for sale by Demijohn, or small quantity, at less than half the price of the German. Prepared with care and uniformity and constantly for sale at the sign of the GOOD SAMARITAN.[21]

In 1835 Marshall C. Slocums offered in the *New York Commercial Advertiser:* "Farina Cologne Water, the true German in long bottles warranted." That the Farina cologne was held in high respect is evident from the following comment made about it by Miss Sedgwick in 1839:

The real thing, that would please us better than all the relics of Belgium, is the establishment of Eau de Cologne of the actual Jean Marie Farina, whose name and fame have penetrated as far as Napoleon's. No wonder that this distrust of all towns [?] should have elicited the perfumer [?] faculties. When someone said: "The Rhine washes Cologne!" it was pithily asked: "What washes the Rhine?"

Advertisements for rose water and other "sweet waters" and scents were also much more prevalent in the 19th century. Offered for sale were "15 demijohns of fresh rose water of a superior quality made from damask roses," at $1.00 a gallon in large or small quantities, at 29 Merchants Row, Boston.[22] On May 26, 1820, John Ashton & Co. advertised in the *New England Galaxy & Masonic Magazine:* "OTTO OF ROSES . . . HAVE rec'd per the ship Sally-Ann, direct from Smyrna, the Genuine Otto of Roses, in elegant gilt cut glass bottles—warranted as pure as was ever imported into this country—for sale as above by the dozen or single bottle."

In Troy, New York, Richard Gideons announced in *The Northern Budget* of December 3, 1822: "New establishment . . . Perfumery and Fancy Articles . . . Real Persian Otto of Roses in cut glass bottles." He also offered "Necklace bottles," which presumably were a small form of pungent or scent bottle to be worn around the neck, and seemed to have gained some degree of popularity at this time. A decade later, "COLOGNE, Lavender, & Florida Water, Cosmetic Wash Ball, Musk, Rose & Persian Otter, Rose Soap, Antique, Macassar and Bear's Oil" were offered for sale by J. Ingels of Utica, New York, in the *Utica Observer,* July 17, 1832. Henry P. Schawartz, a druggist in Allegheny, Pennsylvania, advertised "Florida Water" for sale in 1842.[23]

The above selection of advertisements indicates the widespread use of colognes, rose waters, and other scented waters, and strongly suggests their use was not restricted to large urban or cosmopolitan areas. Undoubtedly, too, their sale was not restricted to simply the upper classes of society.

I have noted here that various plain and common bottles—demijohns, quarts, pints, and so on—used for other purposes were also used to contain cologne, rose water, and other sweet waters. Some of the common bottles utilized by American manufacturers of these products were certainly imported ones that had been emptied of their original contents, particularly at the time when American glassworks could not meet the demand for bottles. But some undoubtedly were made in American glasshouses by the late 18th century, and certainly in the 19th century as American glassmaking developed. There are no references in Stiegel's account books specifically to cologne bottles, though some of the diamond daisy and daisy in hexagon pattern-molded bottles of rather bulbous cross section, as well as others of the same form, *may* have been used for this purpose. Certainly the amethyst ones, especially, were attractive enough to have been used by the ladies of the house on their "dressing" tables. Neither are cologne bottles specifically mentioned in any of Amelung's advertisements, but—again—a number

of his common or molded bottles, such as the checkered-diamond design, may have been used for this purpose. Both these manufacturers did make phials, some of which were doubtless used to contain perfume or essences. The same is true of the Philadelphia Glass Works, the Pitkin Works, and others such as the Gloucester Glass Works, in Clementon, New Jersey. Other early sources for such containers include, of course, Craig & O'Hara's Pittsburgh Flint Glass Works, Albert Gallatin's New Geneva Glass House, and Bakewells of Pittsburgh.

Another printed list pasted in the back of the account book of Jeremiah Emlen, the Philadelphia druggist, listed prices of flint glass for exportation, dated April 12, 1815, and signed at the bottom, "Thos. & Geo. Hawkes, Dudley" (England). Among many other items are the following bottles for perfumery manufacturers and merchants:

	s	d
Hungaries, green, per gross	20	6
Lavenders, small, " "	16	9
Lavenders, large, " "	37	9
Salt and smelling bottles, per gross	27	6

Among the earliest references known to me of bottles made in an American glasshouse specifically to contain a scented water is one to the Glastenbury Glass Factory Company. This factory operated in South Glastenbury, several miles southeast of Hartford, Connecticut, from 1816 to about 1827. On March 24, 1817, John Cunningham of New York City wrote to Ebenezer Goodale, Jr., one of the partners of the firm and its agent:

Sir having been informed that you carry on the glass Blowing business, and as I Shall want glass to a Considerable Amount if I can be Suited in quality and prices, the glass I shall want first is the Hungary Gile Bottles of a greenish colour if you Do not Know them by that name I can send you one for a Sample if you will inform me what the price will be and how many you think will go to the Pound I then can give you an Order.—I also Wish to know at what time I mite be sure of Having them Delivered Here.[24]

The "Prices Current of South Boston Flint Glass Ware" referred to above as being pasted in Jeremiah Emlen's account book is the earliest reference to American bottles made specifically for perfumery. Bottles relating to perfumes, essences, and colognes that appeared on the August 20, 1818, and the August 26, 1819, price lists include:[25]

			1818		1819	
			Prices	*Per*	*Prices*	*Per*
			$	gr.	$	gr.
Bottles	Perfumery		8	"	8	"
"	Lavender or Honey Water	½ oz			6	"
"	" " " "	1 oz	6	"		
"	" " " "	1½ oz	6	"	8	"
"	" " " "	2 oz	7	"		
"	" " " "	3 oz	8	"		
"	" " " "	4 oz	10	"	12	"
"	" " " "	6 oz	15	"		
"	Essence	½ oz	6	"		
"	"	1 oz	6	"		
"	"	2 oz	6	"		
"	"	3 oz	6	"		
"	"	6 oz	7	"		
"	Hungary or Cologne		6	"		

It appears that production of some bottles ceased, at least temporarily, in 1819, since they are unlisted. Undoubtedly, the output varied from year to year, but such bottles had been a part of the firm's production for at least several years, for their advertisement in the Boston *Columbian Centinel* of January 17, 1816, under "APOTHECARY SHOP LEDGER" noted, among other things, "Smelling and perfumery Bottles, Phials, common and essence."

A price list of articles manufactured by the New England Glass Company dated in writing September 1819 included the following bottles:[26]

			Dol.	Cts.	Per gross
Bottles	Perfumery		8		"
"	Lavender or Honey Water	1 oz.	6		"
"	" " " "	1½ oz	6		"
"	" " " "	2 oz.	7.50		"
"	" " " "	3 oz.	8		"
"	" " " "	4 oz.	10		"
"	" " " "	6 oz.	15		"

Also of interest to bottle collectors will be the following three entries, which appeared on the 1819 South Boston Flint Glass Works price list:

Flasks, Pocket or Hunting, green half pint per dozen	$1.00
Flasks, Pocket or Hunting, green one pint per dozen	$1.33
Flasks, Pocket or Hunting, green one quart per dozen	$2.00

and from the 1819 New England Glass Company's price list:

Flasks, pocket or hunting, 1 pint $3 doz.
      "   "   "   "   ½ pint $2   "

A comparison of the prices of these two firms shows the South Boston prices were higher for some perfumery items but lower than those of the New England Glass Company for flasks.

Entries in the "Sloar" book, which record the daily production of each of the shops in the Boston and Sandwich Glass Company from July 9, 1825, through December 1828, indicate consistent production of cologne bottles by that firm.[27] On December 17, 1825, John Doyle produced 236 Cologne Bottles at 3½ cents each. On June 17, 1826, he made 280 at 4 cents each. One week later Thomas Lloyd made 285 Cologne Bottles at 4 cents each. Again, on September 18, 1827, Thomas Lloyd produced 490 Cologne Bottles at 4 cents each. Whether the variation in price from 3½ cents to 4 cents each is indicative of a difference in the size of the bottle, or whether the price had simply increased a half-cent each in the intervening six months, is not known. Neither is the type of cologne bottle or the kind of glass from which it was made, colorless or colored, known from these records. One can speculate that they *may* be like the blown-three-mold toilet bottles GI–3, types 1 and 2; GI–7; and GI–9; but this seems unlikely, since entries in this book for molded wares are usually so noted.

T. W. Dyott, at his glassworks in Kensington, was another very large producer of bottles for cologne, rose water, and the like, especially from the late 1820s until his operations ended at Dyottville in 1838. He advertised cologne water bottles from 1818 onward, perfumery vials in 1825, and—though probably produced earlier—"fancy colognes" in 1831.[28] It was just about 1830 that "fancy" colognes became very popular both here and abroad, especially in France. In his tariff memorial of May 21, 1831, to members of Congress, Dr. Dyott referred specifically to "Fancy articles such as Cologne and Perfumery Bottles." One of Dyott's price lists, probably in use from 1824 to 1828, lists "cologne water vials @ $3.50/groce" and "cologne water vials (six-sided) @ $5.00/groce."[29] Dyott's 1825 advertisement offered 1,000 gross "Cologne Water Vials."

On August 8, 1829, N. Prentiss offered for sale in the *New York Commercial Advertiser,* "Cologne Water; in rich fancy bottles, of various qualities" at his

PERFUMERY MANUFACTORY. On November 9, 1839, he advertised in the same newspaper: "Cologne Bottles of the latest fashion and various colors and sizes for sale." On October 5, 1831, a merchant in Boston had advertised in the *Boston Daily Evening Transcript* "Fancy Lavender Bottles—from France," with the reminder that the fancy cologne bottles were very much in vogue and very popular abroad, as well as here. And in 1835 John Williams and Frederick Hollister of Utica, New York, offered among many other things both "genuine and imitation Cologne, in fancy bottles and of our own manufacture."[30]

The wide variety of these fancy forms is suggested by the following advertisement in the *New York Commercial Advertiser* of July 22, 1832:

Cologne water—Put up in a variety of bottles comprising about 30 different designs, 30 different kinds, viz. in pannell bottles nos. 1, 2, 3, 4, 5, 6, 7, Rivel in square toilet bottles, do in long bottles, Soyez in half pint bottles diamond pattern, Temple, Gothic, Lyre, Urn, Barrell, Octagon, Sexagon, Royal Lyre, Lafayette, Lady of the Lake, Statue of Napoleon, real genuine in long bottles . . . Snyder & Co., wholesale perfumers and importers, 30 Cedar Court.

This wide variety is further enumerated by Dyott in his January 16, 1835, "Prices Current" published in the *Democratic Herald;* it includes the long list of fancy colognes and pungents noted here:[31]

Long	Long Octagon
Hexagon	Castle
do large	Square Flower
Fluted	Column
Long Gothic	Flower-basket
Urn	Acorn
Lion	Cathedral
Dragon	do small
Lyre	do triangular
Fountain	Diamond
Round Flowered	Flower-pot large
Bellows	do middle
do large	do small
Barrel	Lily
do small	Panelled, 3, 4, 5, 7,
do large	10, 14 & 18 ounces
Hexagonal Barrel	

We cannot say for certain because we do not *know* specifically just where the bottles pictured in the following illustrations were made, but they do represent the subjects of a number of the colognes produced by Dyott: Ill. 107, Nos. 2 and 7, urn and gothic cathedral; Ill. 108, No. 7, bellows; Ill. 111, Nos. 1 and 5, lyre and lion; Ill. 112, No. 10, column; Ill. 113, Nos. 1 and 2, a fountain and panel bottle (12 sided). Some of these same designs were, of course, also being produced contemporaneously, and also later, by other glasshouses such as Joel Bodine's Williamstown Glasshouse in Camden County, New Jersey, and Stanger's factory in Glassboro, New Jersey, as indicated in the captions to some of these illustrations.

Without doubt, numerous other bottle glasshouses also made bottles for cologne and "sweet" waters. On May 1, 1847, according to the account book of Gilbert Turner & Co., operators of the Coventry Glass Works in Coventry, Connecticut, a merchant in New York City named Foreman, possibly an outlet or agent for the factory, was charged with the following:

14 gross Catherial [Cathedral] colognes 13/ 22.75

| 3 | " | Rose colognes | 20/ | 7.50 |
| 3 | " | 2 oz. colognes | 10/ | 6.00 |

In 1838/39, the Greenbank Glass Works in Burlington County, New Jersey, was producing medium, long, and plain cologne bottles.[32] The following fancy colognes were produced in Stanger's Glassboro glass factory, as indicated by a record in his Blower's Book for the blast of 1848/49[33]: cathedral, small diamond, flower basket, grape, lion, dahlia, rose, shell, star, temple, and tree. Again, a number of the bottles shown in Ills. 107 through 114 reflect the types produced at Stanger's glasshouse, if they are not necessarily the actual ones. In addition, of course, his glassworks also produced vials and bottles for essences of various types, including essence of roses.

According to a price list he published in 1853/54, William Burger, a wholesale druggist at Nos. 50 and 52 Courtland Street, New York City, was an agent for the Williamstown Glass Works. That factory produced the following fancy bottles for cologne and other perfumery, the price of each noted by the dozen: Acorn, 50 cents; Barrell, small 37½ cents, medium 50 cents, and large 75 cents; Cathedral, 62½ cents; Diamond, 62½ cents; Dragon, 75 cents; Flower Basket, 50 cents; Flower Pot, small 50 cents, medium 75 cents, large 87½ cents; Square Flower,

50 cents; Fluted, 50 cents; Harp, 62½ cents; Lion, 62½ cents; Lyre (no price); Panelled, 3 oz. 50 cents, 4 oz. 50 cents, 5 oz. 62½ cents, 10 oz. 87½ cents, 14 oz. $1.25, and 18 oz. $1.50; Rose, 44 cents; Urn, 62½ cents. Again, the types in general are suggested by those in Ills. 107 through 114.

Although "fancy" colognes of the type shown in these illustrations were primarily popular between 1830 and 1860, they continued to be produced in some forms until about the end of the 19th century. During the latter third of the century, a number of colognes and other scented waters were packaged and sold in novelty containers, such as hands, slippers, and statues. The Lancaster Glass Works in Lancaster, New York (Glasshouse Sketch No. 52), apparently produced many perfume and cologne containers for C. B. Woodworth of Rochester, New York, in the form of boots and slippers.[34]

Philip Doflein was a German who began his career as a moldmaker in Philadelphia in 1842. According to Edwin Atlee Barber, "one of his best portrait designs was a bust of General U. S. Grant made for a New York firm for the ornamentation of perfume bottles. This was done sometime between 1896 and 1900."[35]

During the last third of the 19th century, numerous "figural" bottles were manufactured to contain various products, but many of them were specifically intended for perfume or cologne. Their subject matter ranged from three-dimensional portrait busts of presidents to the female bust bottle patented by Chancey C. Woodworth on November 3, 1874, to Thomas P. Spencer's "crying baby bottle" (or, as he referred to it in his patent drawing, the "head of a crying child"), to novelty bottles such as the "Aquarium" perfume bottle, for which a patent was issued on September 3, 1889, to George W. Bean and Arauna M. and Stephen A. Vail as a perfume holder and stand. Other perfume bottles with novelty forms include a cigar-shaped bottle patented by Harry C. Powers on June 23, 1908, a revolver bottle that originally held perfume made by the Standard Perfume Works of New York City, patented by Emanuel W. Bloomingdale of New York City on November 6, 1888, and at least two varieties of "lantern" bottles made for the perfume trade, patented by Alfred P. Babcock on April 25, 1882, and August 18, 1891.[36]

In more recent years, a multitude of fancy bottles to contain perfume, colognes, and toilet waters have been placed on the market by a number of companies, but especially by the Avon Corporation. The latter are discussed in some detail in Cecil Munsey's *Collecting Bottles*, pp. 233–35, as well as in various articles in such contemporary magazines as *Old Bottle Magazine*. Though they are direct descendants of the early- and mid-19th-century fancy perfume and cologne bottles, because of their recent date and the fact that they have been discussed well elsewhere, they are not being considered in detail here.

The cologne bottles thus far discussed represent the containers in which the contents were packaged and delivered to the consumer. In many instances such containers, particularly those of "fancy" form, served a dual purpose as dispensers on milady's dressing table. By the 1840s and especially from 1850 onward, fancy bottles of a much finer quality were produced by numerous flint glass firms as containers and dispensers for perfumes and colognes. In the Seventeenth Exhibition of American Manufacturers, held at the Franklin Institute in Philadelphia, October 19–30, 1847, Hartell & Lancaster, operators of the Union Glass Works in Kensington, exhibited some of their wares. According to the catalog, their glassware

also presents something new. The articles, consisting chiefly of cologne and toilet water bottles,— opal, turquoise, enamelled, green chameleon, &c, were made in an open or hollow ware furnace, of bottle glass. Many of the tints are as rich as would be expected in flint glass, while the invoice price of the ware is so low that it must secure a constant demand. The hock, cologne and toilet bottles, of colored opaque body, are considered as deserving a First Premium.[37]

Cut-glass cologne bottles were produced even earlier. H. A. & E. G. Kelley advertised in the *Inquirer* of Nantucket on May 22, 1840: "Cut Glass Cologne Bottles. A few dozen new patterns just received."

Bohemian influence on American glass, especially in the manufacture of decorated wares, began to make itself felt quite dramatically about 1850, but it had been apparent from 1830 onward. This influence was primarily in the form of "cased and cut glass," but in many instances there were additional embellishments included in the decoration such as engraving, gilding, and enameling. Cased glass consists of an initial gather of colorless or colored glass, encased within one or more thin layers of other colored glasses, usually opaque but sometimes transparent, particularly red, whites, and blue. The art of casing, or "plating," glass was apparently not practiced here until about 1850, as the following quotation from an article in the *Brooklyn Evening Star* on May 28, 1851, indicates:

One of the most extensive and celebrated glass manufacturories in the United States is the "Brooklyn Flint Glass Works" located between Atlantic and State Streets, near the Atlantic Ferry.

Every description of staple and fancy Flint Glass Ware is made in this establishment. Plated or Bohemia Glass Ware is manufactured here in great perfection. *The art of plating glass has not been understood at all in America till quite recently, and if we mistake not, this is the only establishment in the country that manufactures it to any extent.* [Italics are the author's.]

A reporter's account from the *Boston Transcript* on June 16, 1852, about a visit to the New England Glass Works sheds further light on this Bohemian style, or "Americo-Bohemian glass."

We were repeatedly struck with the fact new to us that most of the exquisite richly colored and decorated glass ware which is so much admired under the name of "Bohemian Glass" is manufactured at these works. The variety and beauty of the articles manufactured there would scarcely be credited for one not a visitor; but we assure our readers that we saw many works that could not be surpassed in Bohemia or anywhere else in Europe. The various processes by which the different colors and the rich gilding are produced, we are not prepared to describe; but they are produced in these works in the utmost perfection . . .

The New England Glass Company exhibited a wide variety of wares at the New York Crystal Palace Exhibition in 1853.[38] Fully one-third of them were examples in the "Americo-Bohemian style." Among them were a number of toilet water or cologne bottles, such as: "Eleven plated and cut double-lip hock shape cologne; One square toilette, or cologne bottle, engraved; and One set plated, cut and gilded toilette water-bottle, tumbler, and stand."

The Boston and Sandwich Glass Company also produced a wide variety of cologne bottles, some cased and cut, and otherwise decorated in the Bohemian style, as well as many pressed-glass toilet bottles, which were also a major product of the New England Glass Company. Numerous other American makers of flint glass also produced such ware. A wide variety of pressed and also cut-glass cologne bottles of many forms were illustrated in the Whitall Tatum & Co. catalog of 1880. Pages 111 to 115 of the catalog of John M. Maris & Co., of Philadelphia, New York, and Chicago, issued in 1889, were devoted to fancy cologne bottles. The specific firms mentioned here were but a few of the numerous companies that manufactured and sold such bottles, but they serve nevertheless to indicate the widespread desire ladies of the day (as well as the night?) obviously had for these fancy bottles.

106. SMELLING BOTTLES, ca. 1820–90

Smelling bottles Nos. 1 through 5 were free-blown; the others, all American types, blown in full-size two-piece molds. Excavated fragments and bottles like Nos. 7, 8, and 9 indicate production by the Boston and Sandwich Glass Company, ca. 1850 to the late 19th century. Even if the designs originated at Sandwich, they doubtless were made elsewhere—pirating was customary. These and also Nos. 10, 11, and 12 through 19 doubtless occur in more colors than those of which we have a record.

Illustrated also in *American Glass:* 1, 3, 4, by Nos. 5, 30, and 24 in Plate 241; 11 by No. 10 in Plate 40.

All formerly in the George S. McKearin Collection. No. 11, The Corning Museum of Glass; the remainder, Collection of Arthur Barris.

Top row:

1. Cameo; frosted translucent blue tapering ovoid body with white casing cut in superbly modeled full flower, slender and broad leaves on obverse and bud with leaves on reverse; silver gilt mountings with hallmark (lion, anchor and [?]) between ''Gorham'' and ''Sterling.'' Possibly Thomas Webb & Sons, England. Late 19th century. Capacity, about 2 oz. Height, 3⅞''. Greatest width, 1⁹/₁₆''.
2. Frosted moonstone; white enamel sprays of pinnate leaves, daisies and small flowers with gilt centers; horn shape, short neck with metal mountings; small glass stopper, screw cap missing. Possibly American. ca. 1880. Capacity, about ⅔ dram. Length, about 3¾''. Greatest diameter ¹³/₁₆''.
3. Half blue-green glass with threaded neck and half cork-filled pewter forming elongated ''football'' capsule. Type produced at Sandwich in various colors, including golden amber. ca. 1850–88. Capacity, about ⅔ dram. Length, about 1¹³/₁₆''. Greatest diameter, ⁹/₁₆''.
4. Golden amber; wheel-cut, rectangular, rounding at shoulders, short neck, plain lip; sides: fan cutting above and below slender diamonded lozenge flanked by notching between cross-hatching; ends: corrugated by triangular ribs. Attributed to Ireland, ca. 1810. Capacity, ½ oz. Height, 2⅜''. Greatest width, 1¹/₁₆''. Greatest depth, ¹¹/₁₆''.
5. Cranberry; flattened body pinched to form 3 lobes below stepped neck, tooled lip. 19th century, last half. Capacity, ½ oz. Height, 2⅞''. Greatest width, ¹³/₁₆''. Greatest depth, ⁹/₁₆''.
6. Deep cranberry; flattened tear shape tapering to long neck with pewter mountings and screw cap; fine wicker coat. 19th century, last half. Capacity, about ¾ dram. Height, about 3½''. Greatest width, 1⅜''. Greatest depth, ⁹/₁₆''. Wickered smelling bottles were advertised as early as 1788 in the *Salem (Mass.) Mercury,* April 29.
7. Opaque white; slender polygon, short sides at top and bottom, elongated concave diamonds on wide sides; threaded neck; fancy metal cap with spray of roses on top. Occurs also in dark and light amethyst. Sandwich type, ca. 1850–88. Capacity, 1 oz. Height, 3¼''. Greatest width, 1¼''. Greatest depth, ¹³/₁₆''.

Middle row:

8. Marbleized green and white; waisted octagonal, wide side on front and back, 3 narrow sides between; threaded neck, ringed metal screw cap. Sandwich type, ca. 1850–88. Capacity, about ¾ oz. Height, 2½''. Greatest width, 1³/₁₆''. Greatest depth, ⅞''.
9. Deep sapphire-blue; similar to No. 8; plain cap. Paper label, ''MERRILL'S / OTTO of ROSE SMELLING SALTS''. Occurs also in light and emerald-green. Capacity, 1 oz. Height, 2⅝''. Greatest width, 1⅜''. Greatest depth, 1''.
10. Opaque-white; hexagonal (2 wide and 4 narrow sides) curving from deep base to wide collar-rib below threaded neck; plain cap. Sandwich type, ca. 1850–88. Capacity, about 1 oz. Height, 2⅜''. Greatest width, 1¼''. Greatest depth, ¹³/₁₆''.
11. Scroll, sapphire-blue; see Flask Charts, GIX–40. Very rare. Probably Midwestern. Mid-19th century. Capacity, 1 oz. Height, 2½''. Greatest width, 2⅝''.
12. Cobalt blue; double-waisted hexagonal; threaded neck, pewter cap. 19th century, last half. Capacity, about ½ oz. Height, 2½''. Greatest diameter, 1''.
13. Purple-blue; hexagonal, 2 wide flat sides front and back, 2 narrow on each end, rising in double-ogee curve from narrow sloping base; threaded neck, ringed pewter cap. Last half of 19th century. Capacity, about ¾ oz. Height, about 2⅛''. Greatest width, 1⅜''. Greatest depth, 1¹/₁₆''.

Bottom row:

14. Dark sapphire-blue; hexagonal, wide ogival panel front and back, 2 narrow ogival sides on each end; threaded neck, metal cap. Occurs also in light sapphire. Last half of 19th century, Capacity, 1 oz. Height, about 3³/₁₆''. Greatest width, 1¼''. Greatest depth, ¾''.
15. Violet-blue; slender rectangular with long neck, plain lip; geometric pattern: 3 bands of narrow vertical ribs separated by paired wide horizontal ribs, wide horizontal at top and bottom. ca. 1820–50. Capacity, about ¾ oz. Height, 3⅜''. Greatest width, ¹³/₁₆''. Greatest depth, ⅝''.
16. Dark amethyst like No. 7, including cap.
17. Light emerald-green; elliptical, rounding at base; threaded neck, ringed pewter cap; geometric pattern: alternate bands of fine vertical and horizontal ribbing, tapering ribs at top and bottom. Occurs also in sapphire-blue and colorless, and in olive-green bottle glass. ca. 1820–50. Capacity, about 1 oz. Height, about 3⅜''. Greatest width, 1⅛''. Greatest depth, ¹¹/₁₆''. (This was one of the examples of American glass exhibited in Germany in 1954 by the State Department.)
18. Deep amethyst, like No. 15.
19. Olive-green bottle glass; octagonal body, sides incurving above base and spreading to long sloping shoulder; threaded neck, cap like that of No. 7. Capacity, 1 oz. Height, about 3⅜''. Greatest width, 1¼''. Greatest depth, ¹⁵/₁₆''.

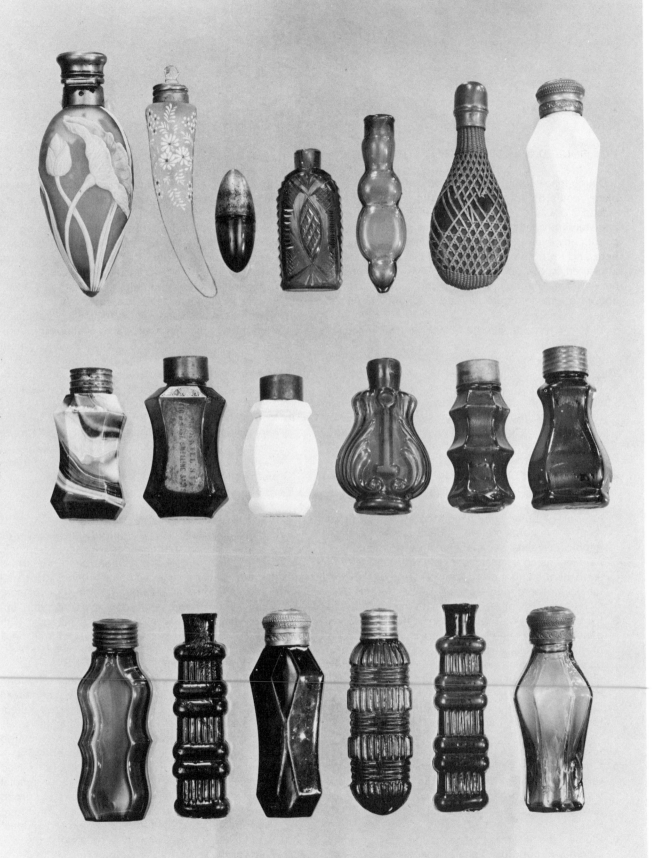

107. FIGURED COLOGNE BOTTLES, ca. 1830–60s

Dating fancy cologne bottles, blown in full-size two-piece molds for form and decoration, is necessarily elastic at present. Though advertisements indicate the first were introduced about 1830, few can be assigned confidently even to a particular decade. The majority here and in the next four illustrations are tentatively attributed to the period ca. 1830–60s. Those shown here are aquamarine in color, varying in depth of tone, and have rectangular bodies and a pontil mark on the base.

All formerly in the George S. McKearin Collection.

Top row:

1. Floral spray; incurved corners, raised panel on sides, long neck paneled below wide medial collar-rib, lip tooled into narrow collar; *obverse:* somewhat linear spray of flowers—tulip, rose, rosebuds and leaves; *reverse:* plain label-panel; ends: spray of leaves and berries. Capacity, 2 oz. Height, 5¹¹/₁₆″.
2. Urn; type of No. 1, body broad, no panels on neck, flatter collar-rib; *obverse:* linear leaf spray rising from short ribs at top of large urn with ribbed pedestal foot, globular body decorated by 4-petal ornament above horizontal rib, ribbed neck, large scroll handles; *reverse:* plain label-panel; ends: long pinnate leaf rising from slender vase with sloping foot, short stem, slender ovoid body bisected by horizontal rib, collared rim. Capacity, 3 oz. Height, 5⅛″. Occurs also in colorless glass with flanged lip.
3. Lyre; type of No. 1 but with narrow molding on panels; *obverse:* linear lyrelike ornament composed of simple scrolls, ovals and, at top, 5 long tears; *reverse:* panel like No. 6; ends: 5 pairs of gadroon ribs, single rib between top pair. Capacity, 2 oz. Height, 4⅞″.
4. Like No. 3 but with concentric gadroon ribs at bottom on each side. Capacity, 3 oz. Height 4⅞″.

Middle row:

5. Floral spray; type of No. 1 but with flanged lip; *obverse:* spray similar to No. 1 but more fully modeled; *reverse:* bead bordered label-panel; ends: spray of leaves and berries. Capacity, about 2 oz. Height, 5¹/₁₆″.
6. Plume; type of No. 1; *obverse:* tall plume formed by paired gadroon ribs, 3 short between top pair (see

No. 8, Ill. 111); *reverse:* panel bordered by chevron ribs to large oval bead at top, center, bottom, and sides; paper label, gold on white, "EAU DE" on scrolled ribbon above urn of flowers resting on panel with "COLOGNE"; ends: 5 pairs of gadroon ribs, single rib between top pair. Capacity, 3 oz. Height, 5⅞″.

7. Cathedral, Victorian gothic; deep paneled base, sloping shoulder, long neck, flange; *obverse:* 4 fine Y-like ribs in base panel, 2 columns each side rising from narrow plinth, simple capitals supporting ogival arch; between columns, panel with linear motif perhaps representing a cathedral; *reverse:* same but with latticed panel; ends: dot in each diamond of lattice. Occurs also in colorless glass. Capacity, about 3 oz. Height, about 5½″.
8. Madonna and Child, Victorian gothic; like No. 7 except dotted lattice on base-panels and the figure of the Madonna and child on obverse panel. Capacity, about 3 oz. Height, 5¹/₁₆″. Variant, same size, has plain lattice on ends and base panels.

Bottom row:

9. Hermes and vase; incurved corners and ends, wide globular section (flattened on sides), short neck, flange; sides of globular section: head of Hermes (Mercury) wearing winged helmet; each side, panel bordered by wide-spaced large beads; *obverse:* linear spray of wide-spaced "leaves" curving upward from central stem rising from tall vase with ribbed base, spool stem, ovoid body, ribbed neck spreading at rim, scroll handles; *reverse:* plain. Possibly French. Capacity, 6 oz. Height, 6¾″.
10. Type of No. 1 but body broad and neck very long with flanged lip; *obverse:* large conventionalized vase and flowers on rectangular raised and stepped panel; *reverse:* label-panel similar to No. 6, chevron ribs and oval beads smaller; ends: paired gadroon ribs. Capacity, 6 oz. Height, about 6⅞″.
11. Long slender body, incurved corners, raised panels on sides, neck paneled below medial collar-rib, narrow flange; *obverse:* paired gadroon ribs; *reverse:* palmette at top and bottom of long label-panel; ends: caduceus between stylized leaf and flower sprays. Capacity, 2 oz. Height, 6¼″.
12. View of the design on the end of No. 11.

Though classified by collectors as colognes, the bottles shown in Ills. 107 through 113 were used, of course, for all kinds of cosmetic liquids as well as cologne and toilet or "sweet" waters. A barrel cologne like No. 4 has its original label reading "ROSE / HAIR / OIL / Sweet Perfumes / W & W / Philadelphia."

All formerly in the George S. McKearin Collection. No. 2, Collection of Preston R. Bassett.

Top row:

1. Wickered round; aquamarine; basketry pattern on long cylindrical body and rounded shoulder, long tapering neck, flange; pontil mark. Capacity, about 3 oz. Height, 4⅝".

2. Wickered demijohn; pale aquamarine; basketry pattern on oval body, tooled lip; pontil mark; on obverse, large oval label-panel; applied U handle, unusual. Capacity, about 2½ oz. Height, about 2⅞".

   Similar bottles, up to half-pint size, have an arch rib simulating handles at ends on shoulder, and plain or round collar. A 3-ounce size has a smooth base with concave disk at center as on some flasks of the 1860s and later.

3. Wickered demijohn; pale green; similar to No. 2 but lip is plain; base, smooth. Capacity, about 1 oz. Height, about 1½".

4. Barrel shape; aquamarine; 3 wide horizontal ribs at top and bottom; tooled lip; smooth base; *obverse:* at center, large medallion of 3 alternate beads and stylized bellflower, 2 small panels at top and bottom; *reverse:* vertical serpentine rib (forming deep U) flanking large oval label-panel. Capacity, about 2 oz. Height, about 3".

   "Barrel" colognes (whether shape only or simulation of a barrel is not known) were advertised in 1832 (*New York Commercial Advertiser,* July 2); listed in Solomon Stanger's Blowers Book in 1852; listed by the Williamstown Glass Works ca. 1840–54—the last: small, 37½¢ a dozen; middle (presumably), 50¢; large, 75¢.

5. Potted Palm; aquamarine; cylindrical, plain shoulder, flanged lip; *obverse:* broad shallow urn with ribbed foot, diamond-diapered body and slender scroll handles, tall feathery palm; *reverse:* deep slender shield-shape label-panel; short vertical leaf sprays flanking point at top, long sprays at sides extending to shoulder from stems crossed below shield, short sprays curving at bottom to mold seam. Capacity, about 5 oz. Height, about 4¾".

Middle row:

6. Louis Kossuth, aquamarine; scroll bottle; tooled lip; pontil mark; *obverse:* 5-petal flower above portrait bust of Kossuth in uniform, inscribed below "L. KOSSUTH", within simple frame with knot at bottom, 3 leaf-ribs at waist; *reverse:* similar flower at top, scroll ornament at waist above large plain label-panel; wide short vertical ribs on sides of base. Very rare. Commemorating the Hungarian patriot's 1851 visit to the United States. Capacity, about 4 oz. Height, about 5¾".

7. Aquamarine; bellows shape, wide collar-rib below narrow on lower neck, collared lip; pontil mark; sides: wide vertical ribs on short bottom section of "bellows" and gadroon ribs on upper; on middle, wide-spaced short gadroon ribs from edge to rib enclosing, on obverse, small heart with 8-petal flower in each lobe and bisected by stem of tall spindly "palmette" and, on reverse, label-panel topped by short ribs; ends: plain. Capacity, about 5 oz. Height, about 6½".

8. Scrolled leaves and flowers, pale aquamarine; scroll shape, long neck, flange; pontil mark; *obverse:* upper zone, 5-petal flower similar to No. 6; lower, 6 trefoils circling small 8-petal flower (see No. 7, Ill. 111); *reverse:* similar, but label-panel in lower zone. Paper label: "EAU / DE / COLOGNE" in white on blue field. Capacity, about 4 oz. Height, about 5⅝".

Bottom row:

9. Arch and basket of flowers, light green; square, projecting plain base, chamfered corners; sides: 1, plain for label; 3 with basket of flowers under tall beaded Roman arch; at corners, columns with plain plinth, diagonally ribbed shaft, bead band; ogee shoulder, lightly scale-diapered; long neck, flange. Capacity, about 4 oz. Height, about 5⅜".

10. So-called Pocahontas, aquamarine; diamond-shaped, melon-rib knop at base of neck, flange; pontil mark; 2 sides: high relief figure of Indian (?) wearing 3-feather (?) headdress, tunic (abdomen bare), boots (?); left arm raised, triangle depending from hand; club (?) in right hand; left leg crossed in back of right, toe pointing downward; 2 sides: long vertical oval label-panel, fancy bowknot above, conventional ornament below, fine vertical ribs at corners. Capacity, about 5 oz. Height, 5".

11. Aquamarine; fancy six-sided form with 2 wide sides and 2 narrow on ends, long cylindrical neck, flange; pontil mark. Occurs also in colorless glass from a different mold. Capacity, about 4 oz. Height, 5".

12. Aquamarine; columnlike square body; graduated beads on chamfered corners to broad leaf at top; on 2 sides, sprays of leaves; on one, fine graduated curved spinelike ribs; on one, plain label-panel; fine collar-rib below large melon-ribbed knop; long neck, flat collar; base: sunburst of 11 triangular ribs. Occurs also in colorless glass. Late 19th century. Capacity, 2 oz. Height, 5¹³⁄₁₆".

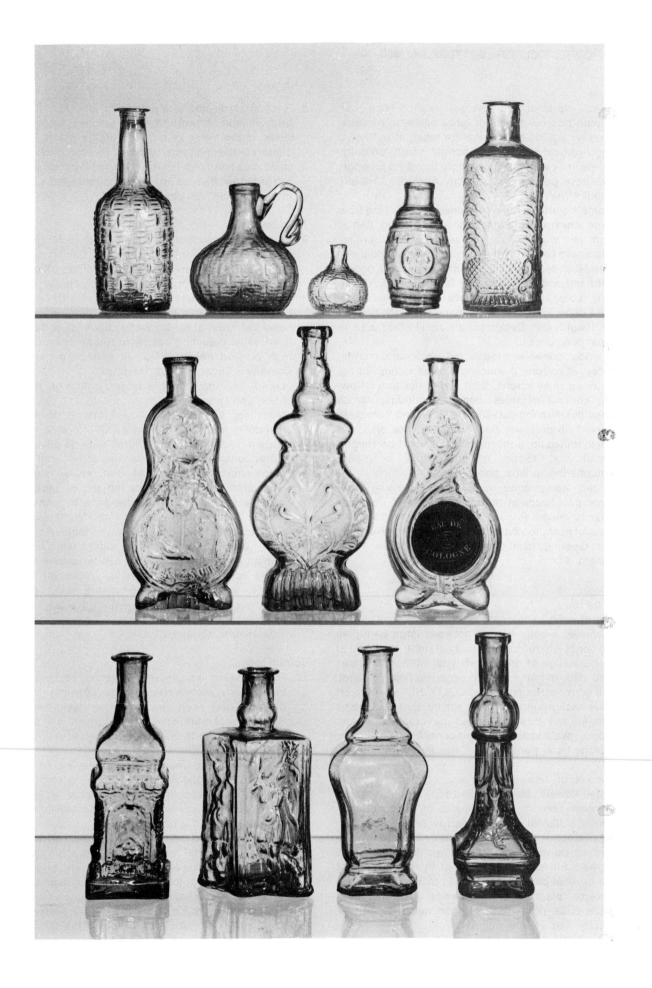

Top row:

1. Shell, aquamarine; *obverse:* scallop-edge cartouche ribs curving from large palmette to edge; *reverse:* scallop-edge panel for label; at bottom, 3 short vertical ribs between scrolls; scrolls on bulge below neck with plain lip; single broad rib on edge; oval base, pontil mark. Capacity, about 2 oz. Height, about 4^{11}/$_{16}$″.

2. Flame, colorless; *obverse:* ribbed flames rising from large chevron ornament; *reverse:* ribbed flames from two wide horizontal bars between "Scrolls" and above two short vertical ribs; relief shield panel with label depicting Diana, right arm raised, bow in left hand and fleeing deer at left. "[Ex] trait d'eau- / de [colog]ne" in point; ends: plain; collar rib at base of neck, flange; pontil mark. Capacity, about 1 oz. Height, 4^{1}/$_{8}$″. Design occurs also in 2-oz. size, in clear deep green.)

3. Rococo corset-waisted scroll, blue-aquamarine; sides: at bottom, 2 concentric rings within ¾ ring, between small scrolls, short leaf to beading following contour of sides; beads, continuing across shoulder, framing half-pinnate leaf rising from deep curved rib on lower body; diagonal ribs on lower neck; tooled lip; pontil mark. Capacity, 1 oz. Height, about 3½″. (Same design occurs in green-aquamarine, in 2-oz. size.)

4. Fluted, aquamarine; tapering flutes rising from large oval beads at bottom above sloping smooth base to melon-rib collar below narrow collar-rib at base of neck; tooled lip; flutes broken on reverse by flat tapering label-panel. Capacity, about 1 oz. Height, 4″.

Second row:

5. Floral spray, aquamarine; *reverse:* 2 small, long-stemmed 5-petal flowers between large pansylike flower at left, rose at top, daisy at right, small leaf at bottom edge of daisy, horizontal rib across stems and at top of frame with gilt-edged rectangular label, gilt scroll cartouche with "COLOGNE" in white on blue background; *obverse:* similar spray but stems longer and bound, flanked by crooked leaves; edges: oval beads; lower part of neck ribbed, flange; oblong base, pontil mark. Capacity, 1½ oz. Height, 4¾″.

6. Basket of flowers, colorless; *obverse:* bunched small flowers; basket, ribbed top, small diamonds on side; *reverse:* same but side of basket a label-panel; collar-rib at base of narrow neck, flange. Capacity, about ¼ oz. Height, 3^{5}/$_{16}$″.

7. Pot of flowers; colorless; sides: bunched small flowers and leaves (similar to No. 6); rectangular pot on obverse panel, motif formed of 3 fleur-de-lis; on reverse, plain label-panel; ends: leaf ornament; wide collar-rib at base of short neck, flange. Capacity, 1 oz. Height, about 4″.

8. Rococo scroll bottle, aquamarine; *obverse:* lower body, simple flower between scrolled leaves at sides; upper body, oval flower (heavy petals, oval center) between scrolls at sides; *reverse:* sides the same, bead and petal motif above label-panel, small beads below; flanged lip; flaring oblong base, pontil mark. Capacity, 1¾ oz. Height, 4¼″.

Third row:

9. Knight, Victorian Gothic, aquamarine; rectangular, sloping curved shoulder; long neck, flange, pontil mark; *obverse:* deep base, narrow ribbed panel; 2 columns rising from narrow plinth to capital supporting (on shoulder) ogival arch over 3 small ones; between columns: slender knight in armor; *reverse:* same but label-panel between columns; ends latticed; label depicting soldier in full-dress uniform, high plumed helmet, "Double extract / d'eau / de Cologne". Capacity, 1 oz. Height, 4″.

10. Like 9, but the knight is larger; lattice on ends, finer; and lip everted.

11. Musician, Victorian Gothic; colorless; *obverse:* mandolin player sitting under Gothic arch with large 4-petal flower in spandrel, rope-rib pillars at sides, concave diamonds flanking top of arch and below short scrolls, 3 ribs at point; *reverse:* similar large arch, over 2 trefoil-topped arches, pendant ornament in point, circular label-panel in spandrel; flange; pontil mark. Capacity, 1 oz. Height, 4¼″.

12. Aquamarine; elliptical, sloping shoulder, long neck, plain lip; pontil mark; sides: tall slender Roman arch within 3 rows of beads, narrow scalloped apron at bottom, below *(obverse)* fine scrolls, lower ending in 6-pointed star, upper elaborated by fine leaves, and *(reverse)* large sunflower above oval label-panel. Capacity, about 1 oz. Height, about 4¼″.

Bottom row:

13. Potted palm; aquamarine; sloping rectangular base; body with vertical ends between short diagonal ribs, short shoulder, long neck, narrow flange; pontil mark; *obverse:* tall "palm" with slender curving fronds, waffled pot; *reverse:* plain. Capacity, 2 oz. Height, 4^{1}/$_{16}$″.

14. Floral spray; aquamarine; rectangular, fluted corners, double ogee molding around panels, long neck with medial collar-rib, flange; *obverse:* spray of flowers and leaves; *reverse:* plain label-panel. Capacity, about 1½ oz. Height, 3^{7}/$_{8}$″.

15 & 16. Plume and column, aquamarine; *obverse:* fleur-de-lis capital, at top of ribbed shaft rising from diamond-diapered plinth and base; *reverse:* small quatrefoil at top of tall slender plume above shallow shield-shaped label-panel; small oblong base, pontil mark. No. 15 has flange; No. 16, tooled lip. Capacity, about 1½ oz. Height, 3^{15}/$_{16}$″.

All formerly in the George S. McKearin Collection.

Top row:

1. Swan and font; plain circular base, body in form of swan supporting wide cuplike ribbed font, ribbed shoulder with plain scalloped edge, narrow collar-rib at base of neck; flange; pontil mark. Capacity, 3 oz. Height, 5⅞″.

2. Arch and basket of flowers, hexagonal (2 wide, 4 narrow sides), chamfered corners; *body:* plain straight-sided base, inscribed on one side "M 182"; *corners:* column with plain rounded plinth, ribbed shaft, scroll capital; *sides:* beaded Roman arch, ribbed keystone; within one arch, label-panel; within 5, small basket of flowers; overhanging beaded molding; double-ogee shoulder: short plain lower curve; on long upper, scale-diaper panels tapering to narrow medial collar-rib of neck; flange; pontil mark. Capacity, about 3½ oz. Height, 4¾″.

3. Urn with dolphin base; hexagonal; straight-sided plain base, shallow step, 6-dolphin stem, ribbed urn with wide beaded band at top and ribs broken by label-panel on one side; ogee shoulder with ribbed upper curve; long neck, flange; pontil mark. Capacity, 4 oz. Height, 5⁷⁄₁₆″.

4. Victorian Gothic; triangular, chamfered corners; bottom panels and arches like "Knight," No. 10, Ill. 109; one side: label-panel; one side: profile figure of stout woman wearing head-to-foot veil; one side: figure of man wearing full-length cape; long neck, flange; pontil mark. Capacity, 3½ oz. Height, 5¹⁄₁₆″.

Middle row:

5. Sailing ship; flattened acorn shape; *obverse:* two-masted sailing ship, 5 rings on hull, arm and fluke of anchor curving upward at left; *reverse:* rope-framed oval label-panel above crossed stems of veined large oval leaves; arm and fluke of anchor curving from leaves to end of stems; between arm and stem, at left, the letter "O," at right, "T"; *edge:* medial ribs; trefoil motif on obverse and reverse of collar-rib at base of neck, flange; pontil mark. Capacity, about 2 oz. Height, 4¾″.

6. Column; triangular base: chamfered corners, incurved sides, one inscribed "D R" in script, claw feet on top at corners; body: convex sides, band short round-topped vertical ribs at bottom; diagonal ribs to bead, forming triangles with small stylized bellflower in points; corners: column, 5 stylized bellflowers on shaft, stepped capital; at top, band of alternate diamond and 2 oval beads, below wide scallop ribs; shoulder: diamond between tips of leaves in circlet ending at flattened collar-rib at base of neck; flange; pontil mark. Capacity, about 4 oz. Height, about 5½″.

7. Monument; square base; chamfered corners, letters "Q T" on right side, on left "501"; body: row of beading, sloping molding with alternate bead and trefoil motif; right and left side panels, unidentified motifs; *obverse:* linear motif resembling dollar sign below linear broad leaflike motif flanking tall door below small rectangular panel; *reverse:* label-panel; shoulder: leaf festoons on sides, eagle with spread wings and broad leaves at corners "holding" large plain sphere; leaf circlet at base of neck; flange; pontil mark. Capacity, 3½ oz. Height, 5″.

8. Elephant with rich trappings, trunk curled over basket of flowers, standing on rectangular base with incurved corners and vertical ribbing on 3 sides; long neck horizontally ribbed below medial collar-rib; flange; pontil mark. Capacity, about 2½ oz. Height, about 4¾″.

Bottom row:

9. Charlie Ross; scroll shape; smooth oval base; *obverse:* leaf-scroll medallion with waffled center in lower zone; full face portrait bust of boy and inscription "CHARLEY ROSS" in upper; *reverse:* same, but circular label-panel with bead molding in upper zone; leaf-ribbed knop at base of long neck, flat collar. Capacity, about 3 oz. Height, 5⅞″. ca. 1876.

   Charlie Ross, kidnapped July 1, 1875, was never found. Interest in the pursuit of his kidnappers and the trial of one of the three taken alive was countrywide.

10. Rococo, lyre or bellows shape; base: deep rectangular, long slender reverse S-ribs above plain molding and below rope molding; *obverse:* gadroon ribs flanking elaborate scrolled leaf and floral ornament with torchlike motif at center; narrow wide-spaced ribs at waist below graduated gadroon ribs; "D" in script at left corner on shoulder, "R" at right; *reverse:* same, but with 5 beads at top of label-panel; edges: medial rib at mold seam; ribbed collar-rib below plain one on lower neck; flange; pontil mark. Capacity, 5 oz. Height, 6¼″.

11. Memorial Hall, Philadelphia's World's Fair; elliptical base, arrowhead band; *obverse:* ogival honeycomb panel above oval frame with building and inscription "MEMORIAL . HALL. 1876"; below frame, broad shallow shield panel with palmette between scrolled slender leaves; *reverse:* same, but with oval label-panel; neck, 8 concave panels tapering downward to a point and below round collar-rib with diamond on obverse and reverse; flat collar; smooth base. Capacity, about 2½ oz. Height, 6½″.

12. Buddha; rectangular, plain base, chamfered corners; *obverse:* Buddha sitting under broad three-section arch with large beads at points and supported by twisted columns; *reverse:* similar columns, two-section arch with trefoil at point, label-panel above wide lattice band with dot at center of squares; "P D" on side of base; ends: arch and lattice; shoulder: 14 panels of scallop ribbing with large tear at bottom points; long neck, two bands of tapering broad ribs topped by collar-rib below plain section; flange; pontil mark. Capacity, 3 oz. Height, 6½″.

All formerly in the George S. McKearin Collection.

111. RARE COLORED FIGURED COLOGNE BOTTLES, ca. 1830–60s

All formerly in the George S. McKearin Collection; No. 5, ex-Collection Alexander Drake; Nos. 1, 3, 6, 8, and 9, ex-Collection of Preston R. Bassett, Collection of Henry Ford Museum.

Top row:

1. Lyre, translucent slightly opalescent "French" blue in reflected light, cold blue in direct; lyre or scroll shape; *obverse:* on side of base, 4 short curved ribs from deep curve of rib with scrolled ends; at sides, leaf spray in lower zone, in upper, spray of single leaves bordered by beading which extends across top at shoulder; at center, 4 long ribs between small hollow rectangles, with palmette at top and gadroon ribs at bottom; *reverse:* same, but label-panel in center; lower half of neck, a diagonally ribbed wide collar-rib; flange; pontil mark. Occurs also in aquamarine with flange and with turned-over collar; in colorless, with turned-over collar. Capacity, about 2 oz. Height, about 5″.

2. Paris' Pantheon, opalescent light "French" blue; classical building: square ribbed base, chamfered corners, ribs broken on label side by panel with letters "L V M"; on sides, columns at corners and between 3 recessed Roman arches; within arches, diamond-diapered panels, door in center one on obverse and label-panel in center one on reverse; below ornamental pediment, frieze inscribed "AUX GRAND HOMMES LA PATRIE RECONNAISANTE"; tall dome with circle of Roman arches, narrow ribbed band, circle of low arches, and, at top, vertical ribs dividing panels of graduated horizontal ribs; on lower half of long neck, short sunken panels between collar-ribs and large beads above top rib; flange; pontil mark. Probably French. Capacity, about 4 oz. Height, about 5⅝″.

   A colorless 6″ bottle in the same design but from a different mold is inscribed "MORRIS JOHNSON N——YORK".

3. Palmette and scrolled acanthus, cold blue; sloping rectangular base with coarse egg and dart in light relief from horizontal rib at top; *obverse:* scrolled acanthus leaves at sides, palmette in lower panel and latticing in upper; *reverse:* same but label-panel in upper zone; long neck, round-collar; pontil mark.

Occurs also in aquamarine bottle glass. Capacity, about 2 oz. Height, 5⅝″.

Middle row:

4. Knight, Victorian Gothic, light gray-blue; *obverse* and *reverse* like No. 9 and lattice of ends like No. 10 Ill. 109; long neck, everted lip; pontil mark. Capacity, 1 oz. Height, 4″.

   On a fourth mold, from which a heavy colorless bottle has been recorded, the design was more boldly and definitely modeled and had fine waffling on the ends.

5. Lion, light cold blue; broad rectangular, plain ends and slightly sloping shoulder, plain lip; pontil mark; *obverse:* leaf ornaments above and below framed panel with maned lion in profile and paw of right foreleg on ball (similar to the Bennington pottery lions); *reverse:* same leaf ornaments, label-panel. Capacity, about 4 oz. Height, 4¾″.

6. Lyre, clear amber; similar to No. 1 but modeling more linear; rays instead of palmette at circular and oval ends of strings. Capacity, 2 oz. Height, 4½″.

Bottom row:

7. Scrolled leaves and flowers, violet-blue; blown in the same mold as No. 8, Ill. 108; long neck, flange; pontil mark. Capacity, about 4 oz. Height, about 5⅝″.

8. Plume, cold blue; blown in the same mold as No. 6, Ill. 105; tooled round collar with narrow lower bevel, unusual neck finish on cologne bottles; pontil mark. Capacity, 6 oz. Height, 7″.

9. Violet-blue; deep oval base with 6 short vertical ribs on each side and scrolled ends of the ribs rising at edges of body to angular shoulder; center panel, scalloped flat molding enclosing 3 thin-stemmed flowers; sides of shoulder, sunburst below wide rib and between wide "fan" ends of rib, slender scrolls above rib; ends: plain; slight medial collar-rib on neck; tooled sloping flat collar. Capacity, 3½ oz. Height, 6⅜″.

   A variant having a bolder and sloping base with 6 small beads instead of vertical ribs on the sides and pronounced medial collar-rib on neck has been recorded in aquamarine.

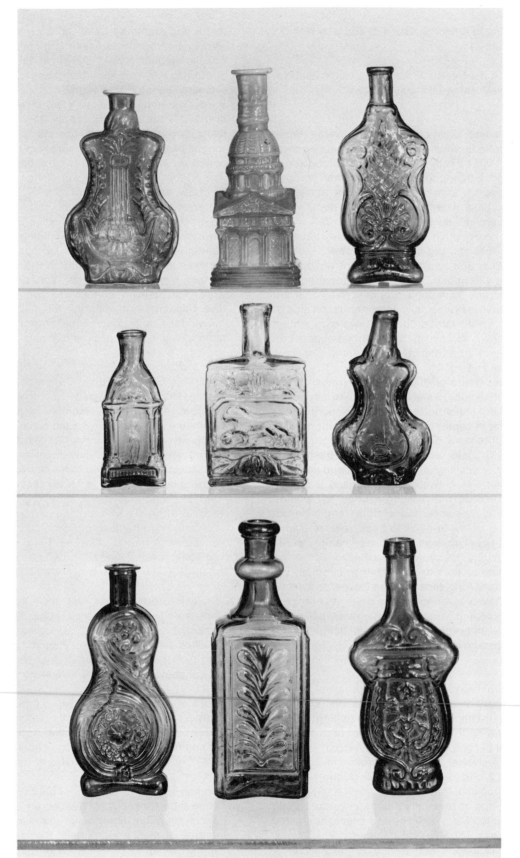

Illustrated also in *American Glass:* 6 and 9 by Nos. 13 and 16 of Plate 243.

All formerly in the George S. McKearin Collection. No. 6, now in The Corning Museum of Glass.

Top row:

1. Scrolled leaves; plain oblong base; *obverse:* bead, bar, and tulip between scrolled leaves below center panel with large beads at sides and in festoon above "H L"; above panel, trefoil between small scrolled leaves; *reverse:* same, but label-panel at center; scallops at base of neck; narrow flange; pontil mark. Capacity, about 1 oz. Height, 4″.

2. Scrolled heart; plain rectangular base; *obverse:* long S-scrolls starting from small flower, abutting below center and enclosing ornament of gadroon ribs to tiny V-ribbed "shield"; at center bottom, large bead and from outer side of scrolls, gadroon ribs continuing horizontally across ends; on side of shoulder, small scrolls curving inward to ribbed lozenge; *reverse:* same, but with label-panel in heart-shaped zone; flange; pontil mark. Capacity, about 2 oz. Height, 4″.

3. Pineapple: pedestal base with 2 rings below pineapplelike body; 3 small acanthuslike leaves and a small label-panel below diamond diapering with sunken dot at center of each diamond; short neck; flange; pontil mark. Capacity, 1½ oz. Height, 3³/₁₆″.

4. Flower and scale; *obverse:* large double-petaled flower above scale diaper; outer sides and ends; (at left) curved ribs between bars, scrolled leaf from lower bar to base, one rising from upper bar, ending in bulge on lower neck, and (at right) long leaf from base to bar below fine ribs to neck; *reverse:* same, but label-panel instead of flower; flange; pontil mark. Capacity, 1½ oz. Height, 3¹⁵/₁₆″.

5. Scrolled leaves; *obverse:* small bunch of grapes between tops of long wide scrolled leaves, and below scrolled leaves covering upper sides and ends; conventional motif at center bottom; *reverse:* same, but label-panel between leaves; narrow flange; pontil mark. Capacity, about 1½ oz. Height, 3⅞″.

Middle row:

6. Whimsey, patterned in a cologne-bottle mold; base: flaring, scalloped (8 ribs and 8 scallops with tiny trefoil alternating), topped by rope-ribbing; acorn-shape body with 4 panels: (1) compote of flowers, "D" at left of compote, "R" at right; (2) half "flower" between 4 slender horizontal scrolls, hook rib between top 2, dart between bottom 2; (3) short vertical spray of hooklike leaves above label-panel; (4) like (2); swirl ribs at base of wide neck; flange; pontil mark; applied fancy handles and amethyst crested birds. Height, 4⁹/₁₆″. Greatest diameter, 2⁵/₁₆″.

7. Vase; pedestal foot, long swirled ribs on side below lamb's tongue; ovoid body: 3 bands separated and topped by slender horizontal rib—(1) alternate pal-

mette and stemmed bead, (2) horizontal spray of slender half scrolls between large label-panel and circular medallion with "D R" in script, (3) meander or Roman key, on shoulder; flange; pontil mark. Capacity, about 1 oz. Height, 3″.

8. Vase; triangular pedestal: plain base, chamfered corners: 3 broad leaves topped by horizontal rib; ovoid body: fine vertical ribs rising from lamb's tongue band; long neck: spool lower half with horizontal rib between lamb's tongue bands, gadroon ribs on top of triangular knop; flange; pontil mark. Capacity, about 1 oz. Height, 3″.

9. Whimsey, patterned in cologne bottle mold; zigzag rib on side of circular base; hexagonal ovoid body contracted below rounded shoulder: 1 side, label-panel between leaf sprays; 5 sides, scrolled motif between leaf spray at top and inverted palmette at bottom; V-flutes on shoulder; collar-rib at base of wide neck, plain lip; pontil mark; applied fancy handles. Capacity, 4 oz. Height, 4½″.

Colorless and aquamarine colognes from the mold have a narrow neck and flange.

Bottom row:

10. Victorian Gothic column; 3 tiers of fancy Gothic arches: top, oval label-panel, 2 arches; middle and bottom, 4 arches; diamonded collar-rib below plain one on long neck; tooled collar; pontil mark. Capacity, about 3¾ oz. Height, about 9″.

11. Horn o' plenty; body: cylindrical between broad horizontal rib and round base, sharply tapering to neck above; on cylindrical body section, 2 "horns" with diamond-diaper disk above 3 graduated printies, 2 "horns" with bull's-eye above diamond diapering and flanking narrow Gothic label-panel; on taper, 4 bands of flutes; long neck; flange; smooth base. Label: "COLOGNE WATER / manufactured / by H. E. SWAN". Capacity, about 3 oz. Height, 6″.

12. Obelisk, broad vertical ribs down center of each side from base of cylindrical neck; narrow flange; smooth base. Label: pink roses, green leaves, gold foliated scrolls, Jenny Lind depicted as "Daughter of the Regiment," in cartouche, *Jenny Lind*" in script above "COLOGNE". Capacity, ½ pt. Height, 8¾″.

13. Rose spray; obelisk form with heavy rope-ribbed corners, tapering panels with sketchy rose spray on 3 sides, label-panel on other, cylindrical neck, tooled flat collar; smooth base. Label: "COLOGNE WATER" on scrolled ribbon. Capacity, 2 oz. Height, 6¼″.

14. Roman triumphal column; square plinth; unidentified motifs, except for helmet, on 3 sides, label-panel, on other; shaft: spiral band with low-relief figures of men and animals; thin square capital with 3 Roman arches on sides and supporting dimpled dome; collar-rib at base of short neck; flange; smooth base. Capacity, 4 oz. Height, 9″.

113. OPAQUE WHITE AND OPALESCENT COLOGNE BOTTLES

All formerly in the George S. McKearin Collection. No. 7, now in the Sterling Watlington Collection.

Top row:

1. Fountain, opaque white; deep straight-sided square base with chamfered corners, sunken label-panel on one side, on other sides, sunken panel with high-relief footed rectangular vessel (form of some pressed-glass salts of the 1830s) with incurved ends, short arch ribs on sides and gadroon rim; body, a classical architectural style: at corners, 3-sided block on shallow 3-sided base and fluted columns with fan-ribbed capitals; on sides, 4-petal flower with bead between petals, on recessed panel between corner blocks and, between corner columns, 2 fluted columns with fan-ribbed capitals flanking arched deep niche with small fountain, columns supporting beaded molding at bottom of narrow frieze with rectangular sunken panel below shallow pediment with sunburst; scale diaper on semidome at base of short neck; flanged lip; pontil mark. Capacity 4½ oz. Height, about 4½".

   A replica of a Paris fountain, this cologne may have been an import from France; one wonders whether the design could also have been that of the fountain colognes recorded in Solomon Stanger's Glassblowers Book of 1848/49 or of the fountain colognes on the 1840–54 price list of the Williamstown Glass Works, N.J.

2. Panel, opalescent; 12-sided; sides spreading to long shoulder sloping gently into long plain neck with flanged lip; flat smooth base. Probably 3rd quarter of 19th century. Occurs in amethyst and colorless. Capacity, 3 oz. Height, 4¾".

   The same design and shape recorded in 1½- to 2-oz. sizes (height, 4¼") in greens and deep blue; in about 9-oz. size (height, 7¹³/₁₆") in blues, greens, and aquamarines.

3. Ribbed, opaque white; 5 ribs each side and fine rib at each mold seam; sides of body tapering into long neck with flanged lip; smooth sunken base. Label: a gay mid-Victorian maid depicted above "CO-LOGNE". Probably 3rd quarter of 19th century. Capacity, 2 oz. Height, about 4¾".

4. Fountain, opalescent; variant of No. 1, slightly different in details—for instance, the 3-sided blocks are not so deep. Occurs also in aquamarine and colorless. Capacity, 4½ oz. Height, 4¾".

Bottom row:

5. Shell, opaque white of bluish tinge; *obverse:* fancy shell design with 12 short graduated arc-ribs be-tween curved ribs tapering from top into 12 broad ribs, in turn tapering to elliptical base; *reverse:* label-panel bordered by serpentine rib, with large fanglike rib on each inner curve and ending in an oxbow curve across base; heavy medial rib on ends; scroll ornament on each side of knop at base of short neck with flanged lip; polished base. Part of circular label: a mid-Victorian lady depicted above "...d'eau de cologne". Probably 2nd quarter of 19th century. Capacity, about 2 oz. Height, about 4⅞".

6. Opaque white; polygonal; 8 sides—2 wide, each flanked by 2 a little narrower, plus 2 narrow ends—short flare from base, long incurve on body with very short straight curve at top, sloping on shoulder into long neck with flanged lip; smooth base. Probably 3rd quarter of 19th century. Capacity, 2 oz. Height, 4⅞".

   Also recorded in the same design are amethyst and blue bottles of 2-oz. capacity from another mold having wider ends and slightly narrower sides.

7. Lion, opaque white, broad rectangular shape with plain ends, nearly flat shoulder, long neck, wide flange; pontil mark; *obverse:* heavy scroll ornaments above and below framed panel with large maned lion in profile and paw of right foreleg on ball; *reverse:* same, but label-panel is bolder in design than on No. 5 in Ill. 111. Capacity, 3½ oz. Height, 4½".

   This lion cologne and No. 5 of Ill. 111 I call variant 1 and 2. Molds were made for two others varying in details but of the same shape:

   Variant 3: *obverse:* small lion and panel as on No. 5 of Ill. 111, bead at flat corners of panel, scroll ornament similar to No. 7, above and below; *reverse:* more elaborate scroll ornament; *end:* paired gadroon ribs as on obverse of No. 11 in Ill. 107; recorded in aquamarine with long neck, tooled lip, pontil mark, 3½ oz. in capacity and 4½" in height.

   Variant 4: *obverse:* large high-relief lion similar to that on No. 7, bead at flat corners of panel, flatter scroll ornament than on No. 7 in narrower space above and below panel; *reverse:* more elaborate scroll ornament, like that of variant 3; wider plain ends as on No. 7; recorded in colorless glass with short neck, flanged lip, pontil mark, 4 oz. in capacity and 4" in height.

   Probably one or more of the 4 molds was used for the "Lion colognes" recorded in Solomon Stanger's Blowers Book 1848/49 and listed at 62½¢ a dozen by the Williamstown Glass Works, ca. 1840–54.

114. COLORED COLOGNE BOTTLES

If the descriptive word *paneled* was used in the 19th century, as it is today by collectors, to designate the types shown by Nos. 1, 5, and 8, then these types were in vogue in the 1830s and remained popular until late in the century. In 1832 Snyder & Company advertised paneled cologne bottles Nos. 1, 2, 3, 4, 5, 6, 7—the ounce size(?)—*(New York Commercial Advertiser,* July 2). The Williamstown Glass Works Price List ca. 1840–54 included paneled colognes: 3 & 4 oz., @ 50¢ a doz.; 5 oz., 62½¢; 7 oz. 75¢; 10 oz., 87½¢;14 oz., $1.25;18 oz., $1.50. Possibly ribbed bottles like No. 3 in Ill. 113 were called paneled also in the trade. Be that as it may, we believe that those paneled colognes, and the others having a smooth base with or without a pontil mark, fall mainly in the 3rd quarter of the century. Bottle No. 8 with label showing it was used for lavender water is also a long-lived type that must have been used for toilet waters in the early 19th century, probably before.

All formerly in the George S. McKearin Collection.

Top row:

1. Panel, peacock-green; 12-sided like No. 2, Ill. 113, but from a different mold. Capacity, 2 oz. Height, 4¼″.

2. Blown-three-mold, violet-blue; geometric pattern similar to GII–12: horizontal base-rib, band of vertical ribbing, band of diamond diapering between bands of 3 horizontal ribs, plain zone, single horizontal rib; taper shape, flanged lip; smooth base. Capacity, about 5 oz. Height, 6″.

3. Monument, deep sapphire; obelisk form, bricks simulated by hair-ribs, small block window in center of third row of bricks from top; *obverse:* rectangular raised-panel door at center bottom; short neck, flanged lip; smooth base with concave disk at center. Fancy label in color: "EAU DE / COLOGNE / SUPERFINE". Capacity, about 3 oz. Height, 5⁷/₁₆″.

The same design is recorded in opaque white and opalescent, with tooled round-collar, 4 oz. in capacity and 8¹/₁₆″ in height. Two other obelisk monument designs have bricks in low relief, a recessed door at bottom on obverse, short neck with narrow flanged lip. One with medium bricks occurs in moonstone and colorless, same size as No. 10; one with heavy bricks in colorless, same size as No. 10, and in deep blue, of 12-oz. capacity and 11¾″ in height. All doubtless were made in sizes from 3 to 12

and more ounces and in several colors.

4. Beaded flute, deep blue; taper form, long neck with everted lip; alternate plain and beaded flutes rising from round base to round collar-rib at base of neck; smooth base. Capacity, 3½ oz. Height, 6⁷/₁₆″.

Recorded also in colorless of about 2½ oz. capacity and 6″ in height; in puce of about 7 oz. capacity and 9¼″ in height.

5. Panel, bluish amethyst; 12-sided tapering form, flanged lip; smooth base, large concave disk. Capacity, 2 oz. Height, about 4¹³/₁₆″.

Recorded also in pale amethyst without disk in base; in 4-oz. size: in shades of amethyst and green, colorless and sapphire with and without disk in smooth base, occasionally with pontil mark; in 5-oz. size: in amethyst, opaque, light blue, clear green, and opalescent, disk in base; pints, in sapphire with flat collar on lip, disk in base. There are doubtless other sizes and a wide range of colors.

Bottom row:

6. Scale, deep puce; cylindrical body with 6 panels of 3 long scales, sloping shoulder, long neck tapering slightly to tooled round collar; kick-up in base, pontil mark. Capacity, about 4 oz. Height, about 5⅞″.

7. Paneled hourglass, light grayish blue; 8 broad panels tapering through waist and shoulder onto long neck with everted plain lip; pontil mark. Capacity, 5 oz. Height, about 5¾″.

Design recorded also in 2-oz. size, 4⅛″ to 4¾″ in height, in colorless, peacock-green, and aquamarine bottle glass.

8. Light sapphire-blue; taper shape, rolled lip; pontil mark; original paper label in color depicting peasant maid with goat within a rectangular frame with grapes and leaves, ribbon at bottom inscribed "EXTRAIT d'EAU DE LAVENDER". Capacity, 6 oz. Height, 6¾″.

Form recorded also in 2-oz. size in emerald-green, with smooth concave base; in 7-oz. size in red-amethyst and "French" blue, with kick-up in base and small pontil mark; in 12-oz. size in opalescent light blue, with kick-up and pontil mark; and in large size (16″ in height) in robin's-egg blue.

9. Panel, 12-sided long cylindrical body, rounding sloping shoulder, long cylindrical neck with narrow sloping tooled collar; kick-up in base, pontil mark. Capacity, 6 oz. Height, 6¼″.

Part VIII

FIGURED FLASKS AND CALABASH BOTTLES: DECORATIVE, MASONIC, HISTORICAL, PICTORIAL, AND LETTERED

1
BACKGROUND AND FABRICATION

On February 10, 1817, John Mather, proprietor of the bottle glassworks competing with the Pitkins' in East Hartford, Connecticut, advertised: "200 groce of figured Pocket Bottles, suitable for the southern market . . ." No clue appears as to the "figures" decorating those pocket bottles, nor to why those bottles were especially suitable for the southern market. Nor is there mention of the method of their fabrication. Nevertheless, considering the period and the pocket bottles probably being made in it, it seems highly probable that Mather's figured flasks were blown in full-size two-piece molds for both form and decoration, and that the designs may have included such motifs as the sunburst and possibly even the American eagle. In any event, for many years I have been aware of the deficiency of the long-used "historical" and "pictorial" as terms to embrace *all* the design categories represented by our 19th-century flasks and bottles with molded relief decoration falling in Groups I through XIV in the Charts. When I found John Mather's advertisement (Ill. 115) many years ago, it seemed to me that his term *figured* solved the problem. Consequently I have adopted it as a class name for the families of Decorative, Masonic, Historical, and Pictorial flasks and bottles.

It is generally conceded that no other category of American blown-molded glass is so rich in variety of design and that none so excelled in variety of color as Figured Flasks and Bottles. Though blown mainly from green glass in all nuances of its natural colors—ambers, from deep olive-amber to light amber; greens, from deep olive to light aquamarine—they were blown also from artificially colored metal—ambers, from golden to deep brown; greens, from sea to emerald; sometimes blues, from pale to deep cobalt; rarely amethyst, from reddish tone to brownish (puce); very rarely, deep purple; occasionally from colorless glass or glass meant to be so but tinged with pale blue, green, or amethyst. For some of the flasks blown in flint-glass works, lead metal was used.

The designs, in the main as American as Indian corn bread, have been classified as mentioned above, under four principal headings: Decorative and Masonic, which are small families; Historical and Pictorial, which are large families. Actually, many flasks could be transferred from one group to

115. Feb. 10, 1817 advertisement of bottles and flasks produced by John Mather in his glassworks in East Hartford (Manchester, after May 1823), Conn.; at present, this is the first-known mention of Pocket Bottles presumably in the category of Figured Flasks. (Hartford, *Connecticut Mirror*, Feb. 10, 1817.) *The New-York Historical Society, New York City*

another depending upon which design was chosen as the more important and, hence, as the obverse. For instance, inasmuch as the American eagle is the companion design on most of the Masonic flasks, these particular flasks are both Masonic and Historical. And it might be argued that all Masonic flasks should be classified as Historical because, for years, Masonry had so active a role in our politics, even leading to a national political party, the Anti-Masonic Party, in the 1840s. In fact, the majority of Figured Flasks do fall in the Historical group, especially those brought out prior to the midcentury. And it may be that some of those classified as Pictorial in GXIII will be traced eventually to an event or person of historical interest in the period of the flasks; some, such as the Flora Temple, were of topical interest.

Be that as it may, the Figured Flasks have a more opulent background of national tradition, historical and social significance, and topical interest than any other category of American glass. In the Historical family are found emblems and symbols of our national sovereignty, portraits of national heroes and designs associated with them and their deeds; portraits of presidential candidates, emblems and slogans of political campaigns; portraits of two captivating foreigners; emblems and designs, slogans and quotations, related to our economic life and hopes, to our defeats and victories in war. The majority were first brought out before 1850; many, reflections of the democratic trend of the times, in the 1820s and 1830s. Whether the designs were conceived by glassmakers or merchants, the makers of Figured Flasks created something entirely new in containers, pocket bottles in particular; but without a burgeoning market sensitive and alive to politics

and national pride, there probably would have been few Figured Flasks of historical and social significance. It could have been no mere coincidence that the designers of such flasks turned to men and events inspiring an ardent nationalism, or that the production of such flasks grew with the growing vital masses of the common people whose political voice was gaining the right to be heard in the mid-1820s, and soon would speak with authority.

The very existence of these Figured Flasks, today considered so important a category of American glass, was known to few students of American arts and crafts before 1900, when Edwin Atlee Barber of the Philadelphia Museum of Art listed 86 "historical" flasks in his slim volume *American Glassware*. During the next 20 years, flasks of this sort were to attract more than one of the small group of pioneer collectors of American glass. As usually happens under the stimulus of buyers' interest, the new demand was met and expanded by antiques dealers and pickers ferreting out more and more specimens from private homes. In turn, the research and recording by students—both collectors and dealers—were quickened. By 1921 and 1926 Stephen Van Rensselaer had listed hundreds of "historical" flasks in major designs and their variants in his *Early American Flasks and Bottles*, and thus stimulated a geometric progression in their popularity. In *American Glass* George S. McKearin charted 398 Figured Flasks and calabash bottles and six log cabin bottles from individual molds, all but a few of which first appeared before 1850. To these have now been added variants and designs found or reported since 1941 and falling in the original Groups I through X. Also, the Charts have been expanded by Groups XI through XV, in which are charted Figured Flasks appearing from about 1850 through the 1870s, and a few even later. Thus the charted Figured Flasks and Bottles from individual molds now number over 760. In Group XV only 33 flasks without decorative motif, but lettered with the name of the glassworks or customer for whom the flask was made, have been charted. Most of them were produced in, or after, the late 1850s. They are a type of advertising by merchant or dispenser and by glassworks. Perhaps cost was also a factor, since the simpler the mold, the less the cost. However, large as the number is, I am confident that the actual number of 19th-century Figured Flasks and Bottles in the Decorative, Masonic, Historical, Pictorial, and especially the Lettered families is still to be determined.

All these containers that I know of were blown in full-size two-piece metal molds, presumably mainly iron ones—by no other means of production then known could the size of any of the families have been so large, with gross upon gross of its members reproduced exactly. From a commercial point of view, bottle after bottle of uniform shape, size, and capacity, with or without ornamentation, certainly represented a vast improvement over free-blown pocket bottles and flasks, which, depending as they did upon the glassblowers' skill, judgment, and time expended, often had little more than token conformity to standards—though great charm of individuality. Moreover, the desirability of the full-size mold was enhanced by the numerical latitude of designs that could be cut in its leaves to produce relief decoration. Yet, it will be recalled, this type of mold for form and decoration, a favorite device of glassmakers in the Roman Empire, presumably disappeared from the Western glassman's equipment for centuries. Also, though the time of its reappearance is undetermined, and though by the Renaissance small ones were being used to form small parts such as decorative knops for the stems of vessels, apparently until the mid-18th century form was the only function of the full-size piece mold. Then, as observed in connection with medicine bottles, these molds began to be used also for lettering small patent medicine vials, of which Turlington's, similar in form to 2 and 6 of Ill. 79, was the first now on record. It seems strange, but, so far as I have ascertained, it is true that the possibilities of the full-size piece mold for ornamenting hollow ware were not utilized for nearly two millennia. At least, I have found no proof that one was used for decoration as well as to form a vessel until the early 19th century, certainly not in the United States. And present data indicate this impersonal and craft-cheating device was adopted for ornamenting fancy "whiskey" flasks between 1810 or 1812 and 1815.

After 1815 extensive mechanization of glassmaking was inevitable for many reasons, not the least of which was that though the War of 1812 had ended, the Industrial Revolution had not. Once the postwar depression lifted, industrialism reached out greedily for new areas. American glasshouses increased; population increased, and so too did the devotees of John Barleycorn. Actually, were it not for him and his less ardent companions among potables, our glass industry might not have been so rapidly rooted. The demand for bottles and pocket flasks, always insistent and insatiable, was nourishment for many large and small glasshouses in parts of New England, the Middle and Midwest states—from Keene, and later from Stoddard, New Hampshire, south through

southern Jersey and Philadelphia to Baltimore, Maryland; westward in New York State to Lockport and Lancaster by the 1840s, and from the Pittsburgh and Wheeling districts and Ohio to Louisville, Kentucky, by 1850. Thus, as the demand for flasks grew steadily, so too, as glassworks multiplied, did the competition for their markets. Consequently, as never before—and quite apart from the assurance of repetitive uniformity—the full-size piece mold was essential to the producers of flasks and bottles: it was a laborsaving and timesaving device permitting a degree of mass production. Moreover, once the fashion of relief decoration settled into a style, this type of mold with its infinite possibilities of design was indispensable. And it would seem that by the mid- or late 1820s the Figured Flask was destined to displace the lovely pattern-molded chestnuts and "Pitkins," and to be the typical American pocket flask for decades to come.

The great numbers of surviving Figured Flasks and Bottles brought out from about 1815 to late in the century are abundant evidence of their unstinted popular favor as containers with more than one generation of consumers. The number of molds, which has been determined from an examination of flasks, many with the same subject or motifs as the principal decoration, testifies to a keen competition between manufacturers of flasks and bottles. Study of the flasks has shown also that in some instances a mold was altered for some reason—for example, a change in a firm, as in the case of the Masonic flasks GIV–1 and GIV–2. (See 3. *Masonic Flasks*.) Though the majority of Figured Flasks cannot be attributed to a specific glassworks, inscriptions molded in the glass or shards excavated on factory sites, or both, have proved the production of closely similar flasks in several glassworks—for instance, the Railroad flasks (Group V) and the Eagles (Group II), the Pike's Peak (Group XI), and Shield and Clasped Hands (Group XII), and many others, as study of the Charts will show. In many instances the differences between two flasks in the same group are so slight that only by counting some repetitive detail, such as the beads on an edge or points of a "star," or by measuring seemingly identical motifs, can it be determined in which molds they were blown. These close similarities and the variants in the rendering of a particular motif or design, all of which add zest to collecting, doubtless point on the one hand to the pirating of designs of proven appeal—a hoary custom in countering a competitor's best-selling items—and also often to a source of molds common to several glassworks. Of course the design pirate might be the retailer of flasks or a liquor dealer; if so, he might order a mold direct from a moldmaker or through the glassworks from which he bought his flasks and bottles, unless the works was one of the few maintaining a moldmaking department equipped to produce such "fancy" molds.

Some glasshouses had a moldmaking department as an adjunct from their inception; in some, moldmaking departments were established when the output included molded glassware in quantities sufficient to make such an addition economical and profitable. By and large, it was the large glassworks specializing in bottles and flasks that included a mold department. Most glasshouses, especially in the early years of the Figured Flasks, operated on too small a scale to make such an adjunct economical; their molds were purchased from independent moldmakers.

Whether or not some moldmakers kept a stock of molds in currently popular designs, they certainly made them to order. Unfortunately, few moldmakers or firms including molds in their output have been identified, and of those who have been, the majority were in business in the mid- and late-19th century. One exception is Joshua Laird, who made glass molds in Pittsburgh, Pennsylvania, in the late 1820s and 1830s, though even in his case my data are still scarcer than the rare flasks surviving from his molds. He was not listed as a "glass mold maker" by Jones in 1826, but doubtless as early as 1828 he made molds for John Robinson, sole proprietor of the Stourbridge Flint Glass Works from 1823 to about 1830; certainly before June 1830, by which time the firm had become J. Robinson & Son, if—as no one really doubts—the mold for the Jackson–Eagle flask, GI–66, marked "J.R." and "LAIRD SC.PITT" was made for John Robinson. In December 1832 Laird obtained a United States patent on a glassblowing machine. In 1837 he was listed as "glass mold maker" in Harris's directory, but not in 1839.[1] Happily for students, he was sufficiently proud of his molds for Robinson's Washington–Eagle flask (GI–6) and Jackson–Eagle (GI–66) to include the inscription "LAIRD SC. [sculpsit] PITT." Because of the similarity to these two flasks in technique, and the feature of horizontal beading on the edges, which is typical of other early midwestern flasks in the portrait and eagle groups (GI–1 through 7, 9 through 12, 62 through 68, 76, and GII–1 through 9, 11 through 15 in the Charts), it is believed that most, if not all, of the molds for these flasks were made in Laird's shop for glassworks in the Pittsburgh–Monongahela area. Eventually it may be found that

during Laird's apparently short era there were other Pittsburgh workers in metal who also made molds for Figured Flasks. Certainly he was followed by others from whom molds were obtained by many of the glassworks in the area and doubtless farther afield.

In the East, I believe, molds for most New England glasshouses producing Figured Bottles were bought in Boston. One source perhaps was E. M. Bartholomew, moldmaker in South Boston, who may have supplied the Boston and Sandwich Glass Company's molds until 1828. At least in that year, after a year's apprenticeship, Hiram Dillaway was lured away from Bartholomew's shop by Deming Jarves to establish the glassworks' mold department. I believe also that the small houses in South Jersey, perhaps most of those located there, and the Kensington houses bought their molds in Philadelphia. However, the earliest Philadelphia moldmaker on record at present was Philip Dolfein, who made the mold for the Louis Kossuth–Frigate *Mississippi* calabash bottles (GI–112), probably early in 1851.[2] From all of which it is evident that the source of molds for glassmakers is a facet of the glass industry reflecting a need for thorough investigation.

In spite of recurrent alarms and rumors of "original" 19th-century molds being used in the 20th century to "reproduce" some of the popular Figured Bottles and Flasks, so far as investigations and inquiries have revealed, the only mold definitely known to have escaped the scrap heap and reworking is that for one of the Booz bottles (GVI), a mold owned by the Philadelphia Museum of Art and illustrated in Plate 262 in *American Glass*. For instance, Allie Clevenger has stated that he did not have the original 19th-century molds for the flasks he reproduced. This was confirmed by his widow, Mrs. Bowers, in an interview in April 1966, when she said, "The molds for all our wares were cut by a Millville man, now in his seventies, whose health no longer permits him to work."[3]

In any event, by the flasks the mold must be judged. It is evident from the flasks figured in them that the molds varied widely in quality of craftsmanship and of design. Of course most Figured Flasks, especially in the Historical and Pictorial groups, demanded more talent for sculpturing on the part of the metalworker and of drawing on the part of the designer than did one that was only lettered or bore a simple geometric design such as a sunburst. For this reason, at least in part, the molds embodying a degree of skill in these arts and in modeling were in the minority. In fact, in a large proportion of the molds in these two largest of the groups, the design was sketchy, sometimes little more than an incised drawing, but when it was molded in the glass the refractive property of glass often gave it the illusion of modeling and realism. It may be that deliberate advantage was taken of this glass characteristic, thus saving time and effort, particularly for most of the portrait flasks. Also, although the Taylor portrait profiles on GI–74 and 75, ca. 1850, are remarkable exceptions, it would appear that in most instances little effort was made to render a recognizable likeness; and in some, like the Taylor GI–77, none. Usually it sufficed to achieve a general resemblance to the subject, with appropriate costume and hairdo indicated, or accompanied by an associated symbol or phrase or name. Often only by the inscribed name or soubriquet could the subject be identified, or by a likeness to one so labeled.

In general, the earlier the flask, the more elaborately detailed and, relatively speaking, more skillfully drawn and sculptured the design. For instance, in the Historical category Dyott's Kensington molds and Laird's (though his portraits lean toward caricature) are superior, or so they seem to me. Their eagles (as a matter of fact, most early eagles) were vigorous detailed renderings compared with those on late flasks, excepting a few—for instance, the very eaglelike eagle on GII–138. However, not *all* early eagles were given such careful attention—for example, the eagles on the Masonic flasks GIV–1 through 27, though the Masonic emblems themselves were carefully executed and composed. Also, on the majority of the flasks that were brought out prior to the late 1840s in forms 11 through 15 and 17 through 19, the main design was on a rib-framed oval or semi-oval with decoration on the edges—that is, the area between the panel and medial mold seam on the end. On the eastern flasks the edge usually had a medial rib at the mold seam, sometimes two narrow ribs and one wide, and occasionally, in addition to the medial vertical rib, one or more ribs following the line of the panel. On the midwestern, the edges were usually either beaded or corrugated (short horizontal ribs). On early eastern flasks, and at least one midwestern (GI–70 Jackson–Masonic), having the designs on narrower and unpaneled sides with ends slanting slightly outward to a sloping, rounded or angled shoulder, the ends usually were corrugated or ribbed.

As midcentury approached, the trend toward a simpler style appeared. In *general*, though some flasks first brought out in the late 1840s and 1850s continued to have slightly convex sides and ends rising in a curve and rounding to base and shoulder,

the majority by 1850 were thinner through (front to back), and the norm became flat sides bearing the design and ends rising vertically or at an outward slant to a rounded shoulder. The shape of the attractive scroll flasks seems to have spanned both periods, and the calabash bottle was introduced about 1850, probably between 1845 and 1850. Excepting the Shield and Clasped Hands, Group XII, of the Civil War period, decoration was progressively simplified in the third quarter of the century. With the usual exceptions, such as the Pictorial GX–7 through 9 and 15 through 19, which presumably came out between about 1846 and 1850, the designs were on plain sides with only a fine vertical mold seam at the end or, less frequently, a medial vertical rib as on eastern eagle flasks such as GII–78. About the late 1860s many of the more practical, nearly flat-sided flasks were given a narrow paneled end or, as it is more frequently called, a "broad flat rib." One rib or panel was part of each leaf of the mold, which resulted in a diagonal mold seam on the base.

Of course the influence of current events of historical or topical interest on the subject of the relief decoration is obvious, but just what influenced flask shapes and the elimination of detailed edges is more obscure. Possibly a need to accelerate the obsolescence of old styles was felt in glass as in other wares. However, it seems likely that the increasing cost of molds contributed heavily to the new style and simplification in general. Also, the newer shapes were more practical for pocket and packaging. Perhaps, too, the extended use of the flask form for packaging liquor and other liquids accounted for the enormous increase in the production of "quart" flasks, and also of the calabash bottles. As a study of the Charts, or of a comprehensive collection, demonstrates, "pints" and "half-pints" (the normal sizes of pocket bottles) were usual before the 1840s. Though the early concentric-ring eagles GII–76 and 77 were charted in 1941 as having about a quart capacity, they actually hold only a few ounces over a pint. And the heavy Keene and New England-type Masonics such as GIV–1 and Sunbursts GVIII–1 and 2, which were charted as "pint" size, hold around 20 ounces. However, these flasks, all first produced before 1825 I believe, were decanter-flasks. At present the only quart flasks that one can be *positive* antedate 1840 are two of Dyott's: Franklin–Dyott GI–96 and Franklin GI–97. The inscription "KENSINGTON GLASS WORKS PHILADELPHIA" on GI–96 constitutes evidence that the flasks first appeared before Dyottville was formally established in 1833, even if Franklin flasks

**AMERICAN
GLASS WAREHOUSE,**
N. E. CORNER OF SECOND & RACE STREETS,
AND
No. 111, North Front Street.

THE subscriber respectfully informs his friends and the public, that his Glass Factories at Kensington, are now in full operation in manufacturing WINDOW GLASS, of a very superior quality, of all the various sizes in general use. Also, the following description of HOLLOW GLASS WARE, viz.:—Apothecaries Vials from ½ to 8 oz. Patent Medicine Vials of every description, Mustard, Cayenne Pepper, Olive, Anchovey, Sweet Oil, Seltzer and Cologne Water Bottles, Scotch, Rappee, and Maccabou Snuff do. Confectionary and Apothecaries Show do. Pickling and Preserving Jars, pint, quart, half gallon, gallon and two gallon Bottles, quarts, half gallon, gallon, and two gallon Demijohns, Oil Vitriol and Aqua Fortis Glass Stopper Bottles, Druggist's wide and narrow mouth Packing do. from half pint up to two gallons, American Eagle, ship Franklin, Agricultural and Masonic Pocket bottles, &c.

☞ Every description of hollow ware and large size Window Glass, made to order at the shortest notice, and on the most reasonable terms.

T. W. DYOTT,
Wholesale Druggist, &c.
N. E. corner of Second and Race streets.

N. B. From the particular attention which is paid in packing the Glass at the Kensington Factories, under the superintendance of Mr. John Hewson, in addition to which, it not having to undergo the risk of land carriage to the city, it is presumed that all glass will be delivered from the Warehouse, sound and in good order.

March 4   dtf

---

116. Thomas W. Dyott's advertisement, dated March 4 [1822], containing the earliest discovered mention of identifiable Figured Historical Flasks. Note that these flasks appear at the very end of a long list of "Hollow Glass Ware"; also, that Dyott's superintendent was John Hewson, presumably the Hewson of Hewson, Connell & Co., founders of the 19th-century Kensington Glass Works. Dyott's advertisement was still running in November 1822 in the *Aurora General Advertiser* of Philadelphia and illustrated by one box of window glass in the *United States Gazette and True American* in February 1823. *The New-York Historical Society, New York City*

413

GLASS WARE.
To Druggists, China Merchants, Country Storekeepers, and Dealers in Glass Ware.

20,000 gross Apothecaries' Vials,
15,000   do   Patent Medicine do.
  1000   do   Cologne Water do.
  1200   do   Mustard and Cayenne do.
  7000 dozen Quart Bottles,
  3000   do   half gallon do.
  3000   do   Washington & Eagle Pint Flasks
  3000   do   Lafayette and Eagle do   do
  3000   do   Dyott and Franklin   do   do
  2000   do   Ship Franklin & Agricul. do
  5000   do   assorted Eagles, &c.   do
  1000   do   Common Ribbed   do
  4000   do   Eagle, Cornucopia, &c. hf. pints,
  4500   do   Jars, assort'd, all sizes, [Bottles,
  5000   do   Druggists & Confectioners Show
  5000   do   Packing Bottles, assorted sizes,
  2000   do   Acid Bottles, gro. Stoppers,
  2000   do   Tincture Bottles, assorted sizes,
  3000   do   Mineral Water Bottles,
  6000   do   Snuff Bottles,
  5000 Demijohns, different sizes.

With a variety of other Glass Ware, all of which is manufactured at the Philadelphia and Kensington Factories, and in quality and workmanship is considered equal and in many of the articles superior to English manufacture. For sale by   T. W. DYOTT,
Corner of Second and Race Streets,
PHILADELPHIA.

---

117. This Dyott advertisement from an unidentified newspaper is identical in wording, through the address, with part of one that appeared at the end of a long list of Dyott's nostrums in the Philadelphia *United States Gazette,* Mar. 14, 1825, and in newspapers in other parts of the country. The one in the Philadelphia newspaper ended as follows: "Three or four first rate VIAL BLOWERS will meet with Constant Employment and Good Wages by applying as above. *.* Editors, throughout the United States, who advertise for T. W. Dyott by the year, will please insert the above until forbid. March 2—dtf". *The New-York Historical Society, New York City*

---

had not been advertised in 1824 and the "Dyott–Franklin" in 1825. It seems likely that the quart flasks GI–96 and GI–97 were among the "FLASKS, Fancy Quart" at 81½ cents a dozen, heading the group of Figured Flasks on Dyott's price list of about 1825.[4]

By whom the figured pocket bottle was conceived, in which of our glasshouses the first one was blown, and exactly how long before John Mather's 1817 advertisement may never be established. Even today, after so many years of research by various students, answers to these questions are still in the realm of conjecture. For many years the possibility has been entertained that the Pitkins's glassworks in East Hartford, Connecticut, was the first to produce this type of flask. There were several seemingly logical reasons for this tentative attribution, the strength of which has been diluted by more recent information: (1) Tradition attributed a few Figured Flasks to

the works. (2) Tradition also stated that a J. P. Foster, after serving as superintendent, "took over" the works or became "active manager" in 1810. Neither tradition has as yet been proven, but as has been said elsewhere in connection with Foster, "manager" seems the more likely status (see Sketch 13. *The Pitkin Glassworks*). (3) Two flasks, once believed to be among the earliest in the Figured category, undoubtedly were blown in a Connecticut bottle glassworks. One was GII–57, having on the obverse the American eagle above a frame with initials "J P F" and, below the frame, a tiny Masonic square and compass; on the reverse, a cornucopia and the inscription "CONN." The second was GX–24 with elaborate geometric decorative design and circular medallions on each side, one with the name "JARED SPENCER" and the other with "MANCHESTER CON." Because the initials "J P F" were presumed to stand for J. P. Foster, and because of closely similar design, GII–57 and GII–58 were considered "possibly" Pitkin, made in or soon after 1810; because Jared Spencer and the Pitkin glassworks were in Manchester, GX–24 and its close kin GX–25 and 26 were considered "probably" Pitkin.[5] Also, until recently, the Pitkin glassworks was the only Connecticut bottle-glass works known to have been operating before the Coventry Glass Works, which probably was not producing before 1814. Now it is known that in 1805 John Mather established a glassworks for bottles not far from the Pitkins's in *East Hartford*, the name of which was not changed to *Manchester* until *May 1823*, and it is probable Mather made Figured Flasks before his 1817 advertisement (Ill. 115). Consequently, it now seems as though Mather's works is as strong a probability as the Pitkins's. Moreover, Kenneth M. Wilson found documentary evidence that Jared Spencer purchased bottles from Mather, the Coventry, and the Willington Glass Works. Thus Coventry and Willington become possibilities, though I feel slight ones; none of the Figured Flasks at present identified with either by excavated shards or inscriptions is similar to the flasks in question.

Though the possibilities discussed above cannot be summarily discarded, today there is a trend toward the belief that the design of the first Figured Flasks probably was *one* among the pint Masonic Flasks GIV–1 through 12 and half-pint GIV–13 through 15, or perhaps the pint Sunbursts GVIII–1 through 8 and half-pints GVIII–14 through 18; and soon followed by the others among these. I personally lean toward a pint Masonic and a New England glassworks specializing, or hoping to specialize, in flint glass. Since, for many years, Masonic emblems had adorned vessels for potables—punch bowls, decanters, drinking glasses, flasks—and since even ordinary bottles bore Masonic seals, as on 3 in Ill. 46—blown-molded flasks with Masonic emblems in relief might be an innovation but not a revolutionary one. Also, many of these pint Masonics (Sunbursts too) were blown from lead glass, and their weight suggests they were intended to be decanter-flasks, related in function to the cut-glass decanter-flask 6 in Ill. 51. Many were far too heavy—some weighing nearly two pounds—for a well-dressed Freemason to carry in his pocket, but he might carry one in his saddlebag and keep one or more at his office or store, on the sideboard or in a liquor chest at home. Although these heavy Masonics—in fact, most from GIV–1 through 16—have long been attributed definitely or tentatively to the Keene Flint Glass Factory, usually called the Keene-Marlboro-Street

Glassworks, I have come to believe that possibly the first one was brought out before the establishment of the Keene works, and probably by Thomas Cains. Cains, it will be recalled, started the first successful eastern flint-glass furnace late in 1812 in the Boston Glass Manufactory's South Boston works, which soon was called the South Boston Flint Glass Works. And there he may have produced the first American tableware formed and/or patterned in a full-size piece mold. It seems possible, too, that Henry Rowe Schoolcraft may have seen heavy Masonics and Sunbursts when he visited the South Boston glassworks in the spring of 1816, before the Keene Flint Glass Works opened for the season.[6]

In any event it seems indisputable that, if not before, then by 1817 the Masonic flasks were being blown. At least it seems logical to conclude that the mold for the Masonic flask GIV–2 with initials "HS" (undoubtedly for Henry Rowe Schoolcraft) was used at the Flint Glass Factory on Marlboro Street, Keene, New Hampshire, between the summer of 1815 and February 1817. Certainly it was before 1818, for some of these flasks were among the objects recovered from the cargo of the *Caesar*, wrecked in May of that year. When the Schoolcraft and Sprague partnership dissolved in February 1817, a Keene merchant, Justus Perry, acquired the works. It must have been as soon as possible after he became owner of the Marlboro Street glassworks that he had the "HS" in the mold for GIV–2 changed to "I-P" for his own GIV–1 Masonic flasks. And later he had the horizontal of the "H" that joined "I" and "P" removed for his GIV–1a. Definite identification of the "HS" and "I-P" flasks with these two glass manufacturers and with Keene resulted from the excavations on the glasshouse site by Harry Hall White.[7] Others in this particular group of related Masonics were attributed to Keene by analogy—similarity in the emblems, in the rendering of the American eagle, in shape, colors, and—in many cases—unusual weight. Moreover, the geographical distribution of recorded specimens indicated a probable New England origin. The equally heavy Sunbursts, obvious kin of the heavy Masonics, were likewise attributed definitely or tentatively to Keene for the same reasons, and, in two instances, because Mr. White found shards at each site, to either Keene or the Mt. Vernon Glass Works.[8]

I feel no doubt that possibly one or two of the Masonics without initials and of the Sunbursts were products of the Keene-Marlboro-Street Glassworks, or that a Sunburst and possibly a Masonic were blown at the Mt. Vernon Glass Works; both works

118. Justus Perry's advertisement, dated Feb. 11, was inserted in a Hartford newspaper in hope of drawing blowers from one or more of the four glassworks operating near Hartford in 1817. Glass manufacturers seeking blowers and apprentices often advertised in newspapers published in the vicinity of competing glassworks. Perry had acquired the Flint Glass Factory (Marlboro Street, Keene) when Henry Rowe Schoolcraft and Nathaniel Sprague failed in 1817. (Hartford, *Connecticut Courant*, Feb. 18, 1817.) *The New-York Historical Society, New York City*

made flint glassware in their early years. I do doubt that *all* those attributed definitely or tentatively were from these two glasshouses. As the Keene-Marlboro-Street Glassworks' market was far from extensive, it seems impossible that 20 molds for Masonic and 19 molds for Sunburst flasks would have been needed, no matter how popular these items were with their customers. The same applies to the Mt. Vernon Glass Works, at Vernon in central New York, and also to other New England glassworks in the same period. Therefore I believe that the close similarity of the flasks in all design aspects indicates a common source of molds, probably in Boston, and for more than one New England glassworks. If this premise is accepted, then in which of the other works in the region were they blown? For the present at least, the Coventry Glass Works is ruled out, as are the Willington Glass Works and the Pitkins's, for the Figured Flasks identified definitely or tentatively with these works were quite alien to those under discussion. They were normal in weight for a pocket bottle, and they were blown from ordinary bottle glass (mainly olive-ambers and olive-greens) as, in my experience, were the individual pieces known to have been blown in these works. John Mather's East Hartford glassworks may have been one source, but as yet I know of no flask, bottle, or individual piece that has been even tentatively identified with his works. Thus we come back to the Boston area, where there were two glasshouses specializing in flint glassware but making green glass as well, in the probable period of these early

Masonics and Sunbursts.

One, as previously mentioned, was the South Boston Flint Glass Works of the Boston Glass Manufactory; the other, the New England Glass Company, which early in 1818 purchased the Cambridge furnace and property of the unfortunate Boston Porcelain and Glass Company, whose products, if any, are unknown. That any of these flasks was blown in the South Boston works, I hasten to state, is still only a probability. However, traveling bottles, nursing bottles, phials, and smelling and perfumery bottles were among the items enumerated by the proprietors in an 1816 advertisement. Also, early price lists included many patent medicine bottles, which would have been lettered in full-size two-piece molds, as well as vials and other apothecaries' ware, and under "Cut, Plain and Moulded Flint Glass Ware" in 1818, half-pint and pint pocket and hunting bottles were listed; in 1819, quarts in addition.[9]

In the case of the New England Glass Company, there is also evidence of probability. Pocket and hunting flasks of pint and half-pint sizes appeared under "Cut, Plain and Moulded Flint Glass Ware" on a price list of about 1818. Four packages of "prest Pocket flasks" were among the company's wares to be sold at auction by Jacob Peabody & Company in October 1819, and pint and half-pint green pocket flasks among those sold by Whitwell, Bond & Son in April 1820. And among glassware sent to a Baltimore merchant in April and May 1829 were dozens of pint oval black flasks at 3/ (50 cents) a dozen, and also in May, pint green oval flasks at 62½ cents a dozen[10]—the same price as the Historical flasks on Dyott's price list ca. 1825. All of which suggests that the company had—and supplied—a market for Figured Flasks. Since mechanically pressed glass was still some years away, there seems no doubt that "prest" meant blown-molded flasks with figuring of some sort—possibly geometric blown-three-mold and/or Figured Flasks. More important, the half-pint bottle-glass Masonic flask GIV–26 with initials "N E G" and the pint lead-glass GIV–27 with "N E G C⁰" in beaded oval frame below the American eagle are tangible evidence of the company's flasks. The consensus of most collectors and students has also been that the initials "N G C" on the heavy pint lead-glass Masonic GIV–15 and heavy lead-glass concentric-ring Eagle GII–77 (which must have functioned as a decanter) stood for the New England Glass Company. However, students of the company and its products were convinced that no Figured Flasks were actually blown at the Cambridge works. Therefore, in the Charts of 1941 Mr. McKearin accepted the tentative attributions of that time, saying that GIV–15 and GII–77 were "possibly Keene" and GIV–26 was "probably Keene." In connection with GIV–27, under Notes and Rarity he wrote:

Initials undoubtedly stand for New England Glass Co. but there has always been doubt as to just where this flask may have been made. Quite likely it may have been made at Keene, Marlboro St. for the New England Glass Co. Fragments found by White on site of Marlboro St. Works.

Lending weight to that presence of GIV–27 fragments was a letter from Mr. S. O. Richards, Jr., of the Libbey Glass Company, written in February 1928, which stated that during rush periods the New England Glass Company sometimes sent some of its molds to Keene for orders to be filled. That the molds were also used in the Cambridge works when there was no "rush" seems implicit in Mr. Richards's statement. However, if Keene filled New England Glass Company orders for GIV–27, it would have had to be before August 1817, by which time Perry had ceased manufacturing lead-glass wares and the New England Glass Company was not born![11] In any event, there is a spreading conviction that the New England Glass Company did produce Figured Flasks in its own works in the years prior to the establishment of the nearby New-England Glass-Bottle Company in 1827. After that, their orders for flasks and pocket bottles undoubtedly were filled by the Glass-Bottle Company — for instance, the oval black and green flasks sold to the Baltimore merchant in 1829.

Two other Masonic flasks thought possibly to be products of the Keene-Marlboro-Street Glassworks are the "1829" Masonics GIV–22 and GIV–23. Those tested contained a large enough percentage of lead to be considered flint glass, so the probability of Keene manufacture is almost nonexistent. Again, the Boston area seems the probable source — the New England Glass Company or the New-England Glass-Bottle Company. Whether future research in connection with Masonic and Sunburst flasks will show this thesis to be based on hard facts or the sands of conjecture, there can be no doubt that by 1822 Historical flasks were being advertised. In March of that year "American Eagle, ship Franklin, Agricultural and Masonic Pocket Bottles &c" (presumably the pint flasks GII–40 and 42 and GIV–37) were produced at the Kensington Glass Works and offered for sale by its proprietor Dr. T. W. Dyott, who — I believe today as I did 40 years ago — was in

the vanguard of producers of flasks in the Historical category. In fact, his March 1822 advertisement (Ill. 116) at present provides the earliest *provable* date for historical designs other than the American eagle, and is the first in which *any* of them can be identified. Nevertheless, one wonders if Dyott had not introduced them before that date, for in the advertisement these flasks were at the *tag end* of innumerable unnotable wares, not headlined, as one would expect of Dyott if they were a new article, a departure from the familiar in pocket bottles. Perhaps, however, it is solely because their advent seems to us a notable milestone that we feel so keen a merchandiser and lavish user of the newspaper medium as Dr. Dyott would have presented them with fanfare. After all, to keep both his glass and his medicines before the citizens, druggists, grocers, and other merchants of the United States, Dyott advertised in nearly every state of the Union. Thus, although there is little doubt today that the new style in containers was not originated by Dyott, his Figured Flasks may have been the medium of spreading it. Certainly by the mid-1820s, Figured Flasks of historical import, decorative design, and Masonic appeal were sufficiently popular throughout the country to induce their production in most, if not all, glassmaking centers.

Moreover, insofar as their cost was concerned, it probably put no strain on the budget of anyone who wanted a Figured Flask. If a Dyott price list of about 1825 is indicative of the general cost of Figured Flasks — as I believe it to be — they were not exorbitantly priced. Whether purchased by assorted patterns or single pattern, his pint flasks were listed at 62½ cents a dozen and the half-pint at 50 cents a dozen. These, of course, were wholesale prices; incidentally, they did not appear in the current newspaper advertisements (Ill. 117) itemizing most of the same flasks. (A notable exception was the "Lafayette and Washington" on the list; no example is known.) Still, with the wholesale cost of a single flask being a little over 5 cents and 4 cents, a pint flask probably retailed for no more than 10 cents and a half-pint for around 8 cents, or the equivalent in produce. Athenians of Athens, Georgia, who carried a Kensington pocket flask purchased from a local druggist or merchant who had responded to Dyott's 1826 advertisement,[12] to say nothing of Dr. Dyott himself, would be incredulous at the prices paid for these flasks in the 20th century. According to a friend who deals in flasks, "the average current [mid-1970s] values of good specimens" of the Kensington flasks listed below were then as follows:

Washington–Eagle, GI–16, aquamarine: $175
Lafayette–Eagle, GI–90, aquamarine: $275
      GI–91, aquamarine: $275
Franklin–Dyott, GI–94, brownish amber: $1,500
      GI–95, aquamarine: $275
Eagle–Ship *Franklin,* GII–42, aquamarine: $275
Eagle, GII–40, aquamarine: $150
Eagle–Cornucopia, GII–43, aquamarine: $325
Masonic & Agricultural–Ship *Franklin*, GIV–34,
    aquamarine: $275
      emerald-green: $550
Masonic & Agricultural–Eagle, GIV–37,
    aquamarine: $225

As these are not rare flasks, he believes the prices will not fluctuate much in the next few years.

Recent questions about the merchandising paths a Figured Flask followed on its way from the parent glassworks to a man's pocket led me to resurvey my research material for clues, and to come to several conclusions about this neglected phase of Figured Bottles and Flasks, *but* mainly those produced before about 1850. It would seem that they were *not* sold to the manufacturers of beverages. Though distillers shipped their liquors in demijohns as well as in wooden vessels such as barrels and casks, apparently they did not *bottle* them for sale in small quantities until the late 1850s. And I have found no advertisement or other evidence that early bottles and flasks were offered to distillers, or called to their attention. As for beer, ale, and porter, which were often bottled at the brewery, flasks were not the right shape for them. And whoever heard of a man filling a pocket flask with such brews anyway? Therefore it is necessary to look elsewhere for the manufacturers' outlets.

One such outlet, perhaps the most direct of several, was a wholesale (often retail also) department at a glassworks' warehouse or store at or near the works itself. Dr. Dyott's Philadelphia warehouse was one of the largest, if not the largest, of these. But smaller and earlier works maintained warehouses away from their works. After establishing the Flint Glass Works or South Glass House (Keene-Marlboro-Street Glassworks), Twitchell & Schoolcraft announced in the Keene *New Hampshire Sentinel* of January 20, 1816, the removal of such a warehouse from their works to "the *red House* one door north of SHIRTLEFF'S Tavern," and also that their glassware was obtainable, wholesale and retail, at reduced prices. A liberal discount was offered to those buying for resale, and most kinds of produce would be taken in payment. (In some coun-

LA FAYETTE FLASKS.
PINT Pocket Bottles, with the likeness of General La Fayette, and on the reverse, the United States Coat of Arms, are now blowing at the Kensington Glass Works, and for sale at the N E. corner of Second and Race streets, where orders will be received and executed at the shortest notice, by
sept 10—dtf   T. W. DYOTT.

119. Among the innumerable mementos marking General Lafayette's visit to the United States in 1824 were many pocket bottles bearing his "likeness." Dyott advertised his (GI–90 and 91) Sept. 10, 1824 in the *United States Gazette* of Philadelphia. *The New-York Historical Society, New York City*

try areas, even in a few cities, bartering produce of one kind or another for manufactured goods and wares seems to have been nearly as common a practice, into the 1830s at least, as it had been in the 18th century.) No doubt most Masons living in Keene and localities served by Keene merchants purchased an "H S" Masonic flask (GIV–2) at a reduced retail price at the "red House." However, by the end of December, Dan Hough who, according to Van Rensselaer, was an apothecary, advertised in the *Sentinel* that "in addition to his usual stock" he had Keene flint glassware at wholesale and retail. In the light of the then depressed economic conditions, it seems unlikely that he had bought the glassware; more probably he had taken it on consignment as unofficial, or official, agent of the glassworks.

In various cities and large towns from which merchandise flowed to smaller ones, an agent or factor offered another and undoubtedly necessary avenue of distribution. Although, after about 1830, he might be a factor representing several glass companies whose wares were to be seen in his establishment, the agent usually was a merchant, perhaps a wholesaler only but more likely one who specialized in china and glassware or had a general store stocked with nearly everything in demand, from fragile tableware to hardware, groceries to wines (imported) and liquors. In the large centers, such general stores more often than not were conducted for both wholesale and retail custom, at least into the 1830s. Sometimes a glass company advertised in its own name, designating its representative; sometimes the agent, or consignee, did so in his name. For instance, in November 1819 the New England Glass Company advertised in a Philadelphia (Pa.) newspaper that orders for their glassware would be taken by Cheerer & Fales of that city; in Hartford (Conn.), S. A. Thayer advertised in 1822 as agent of the New England Glass Company and referred to his place as the New-England Glass Store, though he carried also a general assortment of crockery and fine dinner sets. Perhaps he sold "NEGCᴼ" Masonic flasks (GIV–27) to individual retail customers as well as, by the gross, wholesale to other dealers, country merchants, and druggists. So, too, may have Peter Morton, Hartford importer and general merchant, who by 1825 was the company's agent and, in 1827, became agent for the New-England Glass-Bottle Company also.

At the western side of the country—if, as I believe, production of John Robinson's Washington–Eagle (GI–6) and Jackson–Eagle (GI–66) flasks continued after his firm became J. Robinson & Son—these Pittsburgh flasks doubtless were sold at the Cincinnati store maintained for a few years by the firm. In October, about ten months after this establishment was closed, Nathan Hastings of Cincinnati advertised an extensive assortment of Queensware, china, and glass, including "glassware of every description, from the manufactory of Messrs. Robinson & Son, Pittsburgh"—wholesale downstairs, retail upstairs. Surely at Hastings's more than one man went upstairs to buy a "JR.&S" half-pint (GIX–42) or a "JR&SON" pint (GIX–43) Scroll flask. Made nearer home and carried by Cincinnati merchants were the Moscow Figured Flasks (the Lafayette–Masonic GI–93 may have been one) first mentioned in August 1825, when Pepperd & Teater announced that their agent was William Hartshorn, whose warehouse was 6 Commercial Row, Cincinnati.[13]

In the main, whether buying direct at a glass company's store or warehouse or at those of an agent of the company, druggists and retail merchants seem to have been the wholesale customers. Also, at times, they might acquire American flasks—as well as all sorts of domestic and imported goods and wares—at one of many city auction houses. However, it seems that it may not have been until the slack period and depression following the War of 1812 that American glass manufacturers adopted the practice of sometimes consigning surplus stock on hand to the nearest city auctioneer. As has been mentioned previously, in October 1819 and April 1820, auctions of glassware from the New England Glass Works were conducted by Boston auctioneers; and among the packages of glass were some of flasks, which were specified in the spring sale as "pint and half pint green Pocket Flasks"—Masonics GIV–26 and GIV–27(?). In Cincinnati in 1828, one of the city auction firms advertised 300 dozen Lafayette flasks for sale, and another, 20 boxes of Lafayette flasks, unfortunately without naming their maker.[14] Possi-

bly the flasks were from the Moscow Glass Works, near Cincinnati.

Though perhaps the retail druggist and retail merchant purchased glassware most frequently through a middleman—auctioneer, agent, or wholesale dealer—they could send orders direct to the glassworks, and undoubtedly did. Glass companies sometimes invited them to do so, announcing their works in operation, perhaps listing some wares, and ending their advertisements in out-of-town newspapers with such statements as "Orders from a distance thankfully received and promptly executed." In my experience, most advertisements of this direct kind were those of manufacturers specializing in flint-glass tableware but producing also apothecary furniture and green-glass containers. Actually, at present, it would seem that Thomas W. Dyott was perhaps the only glass manufacturer specializing in the production of druggists' ware and all kinds of bottles and flasks who sought direct sales by advertising outside the principal focal centers for distribution by land and water to other areas—for instance, Boston, Hartford, and Philadelphia among those in the East; Pittsburgh and Cincinnati in the Midwest; Athens, Tennessee, and New Orleans in the South.

In a few advertisements, Dyott identified those whom he apparently considered his most likely customers and the principal dealers in his types of glassware in all sections of the country: for example, he directed the advertisement in Ill. 117 to "Druggists, China Merchants, Country Store-Keepers and Dealers in Glasswares." Identical with this advertisement, through Dyott's address, is the glass section ending an 1825 column-long advertisement, mainly of his nostrums, and concluding with the instruction to "Editors throughout the United States"—and there were many—who advertised for him by the year to continue "till forbid." The country store, incidentally, was a sort of miniature city general store, but perhaps carrying a wider variety of commodities such as dry goods and even patent medicines and some drugs in addition to the usual groceries, teas and spices, liquor, table and household wares, hardware, and so on. Among the "Dealers in Glassware," as anyone researching widely in early newspapers must realize, would have been those town and city merchants offering a general stock to meet local demand, and also grocers, as some merchants styled themselves in this period even when far from all their stock could be classed as groceries. Moreover, druggists, grocers, city merchants, and country storekeepers were perhaps the principal retailers of wines and liquor in the period of the early flasks, and beyond. Be it noted that Chestnut Grove Whiskey (see Ill. 56) advertised in 1860 by the Philadelphia wholesale agent, Charles Wharton, Jr., was "FOR SALE RETAIL BY DRUGGISTS EVERYWHERE." No other retail source was mentioned. What could be more natural than that Figured Flasks should be sold by the retailers of the liquids to fill them? Hence I conclude that probably a villager or farmer would be most likely to find a Figured Flask at the nearest druggist's store or country store, and doubtless to have it filled there if he wished. An urbanite, too, probably would go to a local druggist or a "Family Medicine Store" like Bull's Sign of the Good Samaritan in Hartford, or to a grocer or general store, where he could also purchase contents for his flask. However, though a Philadelphian undoubtedly could take his pick of Dyott's Kensington flasks at the "N.E. Corner" of Second and Race streets (see Ill. 9A), he probably could not get it filled there. At least, present evidence indicates that, though prior to 1822 hard liquors were taken in barter, unlike most druggists Dyott apparently did not continue to carry liquors, possibly because he believed in Temperance.

My conclusions as to the retailers who bought the early Figured Flasks from a glassworks or its agents or a wholesale dealer are bolstered by two Figured Flasks, two Figured Bottles, and a glass manufacturer's shipping box. These are also tangible evidence that the same classes of retailers bought the later flasks. Sam Laidacker informed me that some years ago—1944, in fact—he acquired from an old drugstore in Hannibal, Missouri, a number of common half-pint Shield and Clasped Hands flasks, and—more important than their being found in an old drugstore—they were in their shipping box, which was marked "Wm. McCully & Co., Glass Manufacturer, Pittsburgh, Pa. U 6 doz. half-pints." Presumably the "U" stood for "UNION", which was in an oval frame on the obverse of the flask. The obverse and reverse designs were the same as those of GXII–34 and 35, but the base type was not recorded, inasmuch as such differentiations were not made by students at the time Mr. Laidacker bought the flasks.

Of the four inscribed containers, the earliest probably was the extremely rare 2½-quart Eagle flask GII–27 inscribed on the reverse "FARLEY & TAYLOR / RICHMOND. KY." According to Van Rensselaer, Farley & Taylor moved from Louisville to Richmond in the 1840s, though whether as a business firm or individuals is unclear, and from 1850 to 1852 owned a "general merchandise store." The flask

itself and the related unmarked smaller sizes seem earlier than 1850, but possibly of the late 1840s. It seems probable that Farley & Taylor used the smaller sizes of this attractive eagle flask as well as their own large size. The two bottles GXIII–25 and GXIII–21 were pints, blown in private molds and inscribed on one side "GENTRY, SHOTE & CO / NEW YORK"; on the other side of GXIII–25 was a small horse in low relief and, on GXV–21, "GOOD / SAMARITAN / BRANDY". Gentry, Shote & Company were grocers at 121 Front Street, and their only listing in the city directories indicates the bottles probably were made for them in 1857 or early in 1858.[15] The second flask also was blown in a grocer's private mold. It is GXV–24, inscribed "GROCER" above "CONN" within a circle formed by "S.A.WHEATON PHOENIXVILLE". I have not learned the dates of S. A. Wheaton's grocery, but the form of the flask points to the early 1860s or early 1870s. Doubtless there are far more such flasks unknown to us at this time or bearing inscriptions that have not been identified with a particular retailer.

I do not mean the preceding discussion to imply that the wines and spirits sold by druggists and storekeepers were no longer packaged in the typical wine and spirit bottles of the period, for they certainly, and usually, were. Nor do I mean there were no other establishments in which wines and liquors could be purchased, for there certainly were. Among them were "Wine Cellars" and "Wine & Liquor Stores." My evidence (too limited as yet for definite conclusions) suggests that before midcentury these were (1) usually wholesale and retail businesses; (2) found in the large trading centers, particularly in the seaboard port cities; and (3) owned by merchants who were usually importers as well as dealers in the products of American distilleries. Present information indicates also that when wines and liquors were sold by the bottle, only the imported and domestic wine and spirit bottles of the period, and demijohns too, were used. For instance, the "Madeira in bottles, from 1807" and "Old Sherry Wine in Bottles" probably were bottled in Europe, as was much of the imported wine, but the wines and liquors from the firm's "general assortment" in the "3000 demijohns, from half to six gallons" may well have been bottled by the firm—and in American-made bottles.[16] Be that as it may, I have found not even a hint that "wine merchants" purchased any of the early flasks. Moreover, their not being named in the many Dyott advertisements I have read seems a significant omission.

However, in the early 1850s at least one wine and

liquor merchant had a pint Figured Flask made for him. The proof is embodied in the Dyottville-type flask GI–78 having the profile bust of General Zachary Taylor on one side and, on the reverse, the inscription "ROB^T RAMSAY / WINE & / LIQUOR MERCH^T / 281 8th AVENUE / N.Y." (see line drawing in the Charts, Group I). Flasks from this private mold are still extremely rare, as they were when Chart Groups I through X were first published in 1941. Perhaps this rarity stems from the fact that Ramsay apparently was in business in New York for only a brief period. Carolyn Scoon of the New-York Historical Society, who checked city directories for me, found him listed in just two, those of 1852/3 and 1853/4, and at 16 Roosevelt Street. The discrepancy in address raises several questions unanswerable at present. Perhaps the most likely explanation is that Ramsay ordered the flasks before he was actually in business and when he expected to be located at 281 8th Avenue. The fact that only this one flask made for a wine and liquor merchant has been recorded in over a half-century of flask collecting would seem to indicate it was not the practice in the wine and liquor trade to have private molds in Figured Flask designs. But it cannot be argued that therefore wine and liquor merchants of the 1850s and later did not adopt the use of such flasks without identifying inscriptions.

The same conclusions are drawn from three flasks that testify at least one saloon keeper and one firm of wholesale dealers and distillers had Figured Flasks blown in private molds. The flask blown for the saloon keeper is GXIII–89, which is illustrated by line drawing in the Charts, Pictorial Group XIII, and by 1 and 3 of Ill. 123. On the obverse, it should be noted, is a small man similar to the prospector on the Pike's Peak flasks, walking to left, with a bottle in one hand,

and also the interesting inscription "ROUGH / & / READY"—General Taylor's famous soubriquet—"HEASLEY'S". On the reverse "EASLEY'S / SALOON / HUNTSVILLE" is the identifying inscription. Mr. Doy McCall, the fortunate owner of the only recorded specimen of this flask, informed me that it was made for Hugh Easley, a saloon keeper in Huntsville, Alabama, some time before the Civil War. The other two flasks are the quart and pint Eagle flasks GII–134 and 134a in Group II (see Charts). Each is inscribed "D.KIRKPATRICK & CO / CHATTANOOGA / TENN". D. Kirkpatrick & Company were wholesale liquor dealers and, according to the 1871/2 Chattanooga Directory, proprietors of the Globe Distillery. It is believed that they were in business from shortly after the Civil War to the 1880s at least. Until 1965, when Richard H. Wood reported to me his acquisition of *the* pint GII–134a, the only known flasks in this Eagle design were the two examples of the quart GII–134. The probability is that the D. Kirkpatrick flasks were first blown for the company in the late 1860s or 1870. The Easley flasks may have been ordered around 1860.

Although the great majority of the Figured Flasks can be attributed to neither glassmaker nor dealer nor individual owner, the great variety and longevity of the designs and the continued infusion of new ones over the years attest to the wide and enduring appeal of this style in blown-molded flasks. Perhaps this stemmed not only from the significance or novelty of their designs but possibly also from their being a form of American art, though unrecognized as such in their day. Folk art has been suggested. However, they carried no tradition in designs, and they were a mass-produced commercial product. But certainly they were an expression of *popular art* in American glass.

2
DECORATIVE FLASKS

Of the four main categories of Figured Flasks, the Decorative is the leanest in variety, consisting chiefly of Sunbursts, Cornucopias and Urns of Produce, the so-called Scroll flasks, and the rare geometric designs.

A. Sunbursts

The sunburst is one of the most ancient of decorative motifs; even in prehistoric times it may have symbolized the life- and light-giving sun. However,

long before it appeared on American Figured Flasks (sometime between 1812 and 1815), it had become a purely decorative motif in arts and crafts and architectural ornamentation. That some of the sunburst flasks, Group VIII, undoubtedly were contemporary with the early Masonics, Group IV, if not preceding them, has been mentioned more than once. Several versions of this motif appear on flasks and other bottles. Besides those charted in Group VIII, a few appear on flasks in other groups: a pinwheel-like sunburst on the reverse of the midwestern Eagle flask GII–7; and circular sunbursts on the McCarty and Torreyson "Scroll" flasks (GIX–48, 49, and 50 made at Wellsburg, (West) Virginia, ca. 1830–50[?]. Some collectors feel that the so-called stars in frames below the eagle on Masonic flasks GIV–5 through 8, 12, 13, and 14 could as well have been called sunbursts. In fact, these last are very similar to the small oval sunburst placed lengthwise on the otherwise ribbed flasks GVIII–29 and 30. As sole motif, a large sunburst placed lengthwise graces each side of at least 35 flasks from different molds and one widemouth flask or jar—six more than the original 30 in the original Group VIII of the 1941 charts.

The majority of Sunburst flasks are attributed to the New England area, but it would be strange if not one was produced in Middle States bottle houses (other than the Mount Vernon Glass Works, Vernon, New York), or none in addition to those mentioned above in the Midwest. As a matter of fact, of the flasks charted in Group VIII only three can be given an unqualified factory attribution. The pint Sunbursts GVIII–8 and 9 inscribed "KEEN" and "NEEK" respectively and the half-pint inscribed "KEENE" obviously present no problem as to origin. Further, the initials "P & W" standing for either Perry & Wood or Perry & Wheeler establish approximately the period in which the flasks were first produced: (Justus) Perry & (John V.) Wood, 1822–28; (Justus) Perry & (Sumner) Wheeler, 1828–30. As I have said before, instead of the "Probably Keene" 1941 attribution of the heavy Sunbursts so similar to GVIII–1, I now lean to the geographical "New England" in most instances because, as previously stated, (1) it is unlikely so small a works required so many molds for a design, (2) a common moldmaker probably supplied more than one house in his area, and (3) I believe it is probable that at least some of the flint-glass decanter-flasks were produced at both the South Boston Flint Glass Works and the New England Glass Company, Cambridge. Also, because of shards found on the site of the Pitkin glassworks, that source has to be entertained as a possibility for Sunburst flasks GVII–5, 5a, and 7. The Coventry flasks and the marked Keene flasks also are ordinary bottle glass.

One of the most interesting Sunbursts is GVIII–24, not because of its design but because an individual olive-amber specimen gives evidence of its function. This particular flask wears a black leather jacket with loops on the edge for a cord or strap, and on one side of the jacket are the initials "P I" painted in yellow, possibly standing for Pennsylvania Infan-

try. This appears to be proof that flasks of this type were used as canteens—given protective coats and slung over the shoulder or hung on a saddle. If the interpretation of the initials is correct, the flask may have been from the South Jersey–Philadelphia–Baltimore area or the Pittsburgh–Wheeling–Wellsburg area.

B. Cornucopia and Urn of Produce

Like the sunburst, the cornucopia brimming with flowers or produce or both is an ancient motif, but one still symbolizing prosperity and plenty. According to one myth, Zeus (Jupiter), saved from his cannibalistic father Cronus and placed in the care of the Cretan King Melissius' daughters, was suckled by a goat. Breaking off one of the goat's horns, Zeus endowed it with the power of becoming filled with whatever its owner wished, and gave it to his nurses. According to another, as told to Theseus by the river god Achelous, when the god took on the form of a bull in his combat with Hercules, Hercules

grasped my neck with his arm and dragging my head down to the ground, overthrew me on the sand. Nor was this enough. His ruthless hand rent my horn from my head. The Naiades took it, consecrated it and filled it with fragrant flowers. Plenty adopted my horn and made it her own, and called it cornucopia.[17]

In the iconography of our early nationalism, Plenty and her most constant companion Liberty were symbols of two fundamental benefits the country offered to its inhabitants; they were represented by Grecian figures familiar to nearly everyone. In that period of widespread classical education, Plenty needed no interpretation—her overflowing cornucopia alone was a sufficient reminder of the young country's good prospects. Whether its user thought of it as purely decorative or a meaningful symbol, the cornucopia was a favorite motif in arts and crafts, at least through the first half of the 19th century.

Figured Flasks were no exception; several bear Plenty's brimming cornucopia. The Cornucopia–Urn flasks on which the cornucopia was chosen as the obverse are charted in Group III—18 in the original charts, two now added thereto. The cornucopia appears also as the reverse of 23 flasks, all in the Eagle Group. Of these, 11 are presumably eastern; 12, midwestern. And on six of the midwestern (GII–11, 11a, 12, 13, and 14, and GII–69), all half-pints, the cornucopia is inverted, spilling its plenty toward the bottom of the flask—symbolic, no doubt, of the contents running down the owner's gullet. In the main the inverted cornucopias are less fully developed than the others, with the exception of the even more sketchily rendered cornucopias on the later eastern varieties, those blown after 1849 at the Lancaster Glass Works near Buffalo, New York: GIII–13 through 18. The only Cornucopia flasks in the Group not having the Urn on the reverse are GIII–1, a midwestern inverted cornucopia with an interesting geometric design, including a six-pointed star, on the reverse, and GIII–2 and 3 having the cornucopia on each side. The Urn of Produce was another motif frequently used in the period of the flasks.

All the flasks on which the cornucopia appears, excepting the Lancaster varieties, are believed to have been first brought out in the 1820s and 1830s. Again, comparatively few can be definitely attributed to specific glasshouses or glassmakers. Of the eastern Cornucopias, an indisputable attribution is that of the Eagle flask GII–43 to Dyott's Kensington Glass Works, for it is so inscribed, falling in the 1822–32 decade. Also, there is no question as to the origin of GIII–16, since it is inscribed "LANCASTER GLASS WORKS N.Y." The half-pint flasks GIII–13 through 15 and the pints GIII–17 and 18 have the same style of cornucopia and urn, and so are attributed to Lancaster by design analogy. In this instance, I believe the flasks sufficiently popular and the works both large and prosperous enough so that six molds would not seem too many, though the possibility of more than one glassworks and a common moldmaker cannot be discarded. As stated more than once previously, the "J.P.F." Eagle–Cornucopia flask GII–57 and the GII–58 seem undoubtedly Connecticut, either Pitkin or Mather. Of those in Group III itself, GIII–4 is attributed to Coventry, GIII–7 to Keene-Marlboro-Street or Coventry, GIII–11 to the Mt. Vernon Glass Works and its continuation, the Saratoga Mountain Glass Works, after 1844—all on the basis of Harry Hall White's excavations of shards of these flasks on the glasshouse sites. Of the midwestern flasks with cornucopias on the reverse, one, the half-pint GII–15, is marked with the initials "F L"—presumably for Frederick Lorenz, who probably produced the flask in the late 1820s or early 1830s in the Pittsburgh Glass Works established by O'Hara & Craig. Another, GII–18, is inscribed "Zanesville" and probably was a product of J. Shephard & Co., Zanesville, Ohio, in the same period. Finally, the mold for GII–6 having almost the finest of the cornucopias—at least, not surpassed—is attributed to Joshua Laird and probably was made for a Pittsburgh glassman.

C. Scroll Flasks

For many years the flasks charted under the design classification Scroll were called violin flasks, pre-sumably because to the eye of a now-unknown collector or dealer their shape resembled the body of a violin. Later the term Scroll was generally adopted, perhaps because amber bottles existed that were actual representations of a violin. The Scroll flasks, with ends rising in an attenuated double ogee curve, are also characterized mainly by baroque ribs following the contour of all or part of the ends, small scroll ribs, small stars, and petaled ornaments. A few half-pints, namely GIX–32 through 41, have a fat little "fleur-de-lis" rising from a pair of small scrolls, and of these half-pints, two have an anchor, emblem of Hope, on the obverse. Also, they vary from the general rule in having not three baroque ribs enclosing the motifs, but a frame formed by a rib of medium width following the contour of the side and end. The rare Scroll flasks made by John Robinson and Son at the Stourbridge Flint Glass Works, Pittsburgh, Pennsylvania, half-pint GIX–42 and pint GIX–43, also have the fleur-de-lis, as does the similar GIX–44. The most elaborate, and perhaps the handsomest, in the group are GIX–45 and 46, more nearly violin-shaped. Another attractive deviation from the norm, not only in decoration but also in extreme thinness, is GIX–52, illustrated by 2 in Ill. 124. This rarest of all Scroll flasks—the only specimen recorded as yet—is a flask coveted by George S. McKearin for almost two decades before his patience was rewarded by its presence in his collection. Next to GIX–52 in rarity and quite different in character from all the others is the "Scroll" flask GIX–51; even in body it is only a far-distant cousin of the common herd of Scrolls. This flask, selected in 1941 for one of the most desirable flasks (Group A, 25), has on each side a flower and beads in the upper zone and, in the lower, a scrolled heart medallion flanked by horizontally placed slender oval ornaments.

The number of survivors and variants, and the wide range of colors of several, offer ample testimony to the popularity of the Scroll flasks. Of 53 flasks listed in group IX in the original charts—actually 54, since two molds for GIX–10 were recorded—51 are true Scrolls. New Scrolls or variants have been reported by many collectors, including Dr. Michael B. Krassner, the late Earl S. Dambach, Dan Meek, and Fred R. Salisbury. Mr. Salisbury, who has one of the most comprehensive collections of Scrolls (if not *the* most complete), has not only contributed to the variants but has generously charted the new ones and updated the 1941 Scroll chart for this book. Thus the total number now stands at 75! They must have been produced in many glasshouses and probably over three decades or more. Though identity of only a few makers has been determined, these few suffice to indicate that Scroll

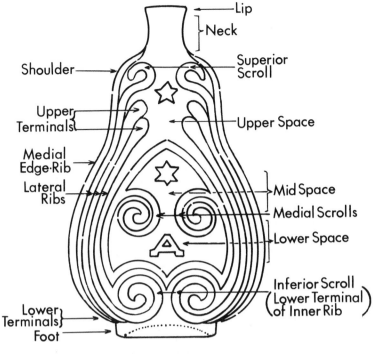

Scroll Nomenclature

120. Scroll nomenclature by Fred Salisbury. Drawing by Frederick H. Smith.

flasks were a favorite form from around 1830 through the 1850s at least. These makers, known from marked flasks, are as follows:

1. The half-pint Scrolls, GIX–38 and 39, have the molded initials "B P & B"—that is, Bakewell, Page & Bakewell or Bakewell, Page and Bakewells. If the former, the flasks *could* have been brought out any time from September 1813 to July 31, 1827, the span of the firm; if the latter, some time between August 1, 1827, and July 31, 1832, when Benjamin Page withdrew from the firm. Between 1827 and 1832 is the likely period, I believe.

2. The Robinson Scrolls—GIX–42 marked "J R & S", GIX–43 marked "J R & SON", and probably GIX–44 also—must have been brought out between June 1830 and about August 1834; in any event, before the firm became T. & J. Robinson in October of the latter year.

3. Flask GIX–26 marked "S.M'KEE" may have appeared in 1836 when the firm of S. McKee & Co. was formed, or within the next few years.

4. Scroll GIX–47 is inscribed on one side "R. KNOWLES & CO UNION FACTORY / SOUTH WHEELING / VA"—which dates it no earlier than 1849, when the firm began operation.

5. The latest marked Scrolls are those from GIX–6 through GIX–10 inscribed "LOUISVILLE KY" on one side and "GLASSWORKS" on the other, which would place their production no earlier than the mid-1850s.

6. The pint "Scroll" GIX–48 and two quarts GIX–49 and 50 are inscribed "M'CARTY & TORREYSON / MANUFACTURERS / WELLS / BURG VA". The exact dates of this firm, which apparently operated the glassworks established by Isaac Duval (the first in the town) about 1815, have not been determined. But it is believed the firm may have taken over the works in the early 1840s.[18] As clearly shown by the line drawing in the Charts, these flasks are Scrolls only by a stretch of the imagination: they do not have the heavy ribs and other characteristic ornamentation but have paneled or beveled edges and, on the reverse, a large sunburst.

It will be noted too that all the Scrolls listed above were products of midwestern glassmakers, which suggests exclusive manufacture in the Midwest, if one classes the Lancaster Glass Works near Buffalo as midwestern. Actually, belief that Scrolls were produced at Lancaster rests on two men's recollections of seeing Scroll molds in the storage room at Lancaster,[19] and the similarity in the keyed and numbered base of Scroll flask GIX–20 and that of the Railroad Engine flask GV–2. It seems unlikely that, had many been made in eastern glasshouses, not one would have had its own inscribed mold. Thus it appears at present that GIX–28, which is perhaps the most interesting of the marked Scrolls—certainly so from a historical standpoint—is midwestern. Marked "ROUGH" on the obverse and "READY" on the reverse, it was, of course, a memento of General Zachary Taylor. Though the soubriquet had been earned years before, the flask probably was produced first during his exploits in the Mexican War or during the 1848 presidential campaign—that is, during the three years from 1846 through 1848.

Last, it should be emphasized that the Scrolls differ from the other charted flasks in their range of sizes. The majority, as one would expect, are pints and half-pints, and there is a considerable number of quarts, which probably were added to the output in the 1840s, possibly late 1830s. The rare 2½-quart Scrolls, GIX–29 and 29a, have only two counterparts in size: the 2½-quart American Eagle flasks GII–27 and 28. Sizes as yet unique to the Scroll group are the miniature GIX–40, 2½ inches in height, and the giant gallon flasks GIX–30 and GIX–30a.

Blown-three-mold flasks, rarities in this category of American glass, have been recorded in ten Geometric patterns, of which eight were known when Blown-three-mold patterns were illustrated in *American Glass* in 1941.* Three geometric patterns—GII–18, GII–24, and GIII–23 (or –24)—are illustrated here in the top row. Four others—GI–3 Type 2, GI–22, GII–6, and GII–16—are shown in Ill. 122. Flasks occur also in patterns GII–7 and in GIII–6, which has a sunburst with radii to the focus. GII–7 differs from GII–6 in having flutes instead of gadroon ribs at the top. Excepting GI–22, the flasks were *patterned* in the full-size piece-molds made for other articles, then expanded and shaped by free-blowing. Flasks like those in this illustration, No. 4 of Ill. 122, and those in GIII–6 were blown from lead glass, in glassworks producing mainly tableware. Their scarcity suggests they may not have been a regular commercial product but either special orders or individual pieces made for friends or the blower's own use.

Illustrated also in *American Glass:* 4 and 6 by Nos. 12 and 11 of plate 239.

Nos. 1 and 2 (ex-Collection of Richard Loeb), The Hiram Norcross Collection; No. 3 (formerly in the George S. McKearin Collection), The Corning Museum of Glass.

Top row:

1. Colorless of greenish tinge; chestnut shape; possibly patterned in a GIII–23 mold, probably in a GIII–24, and the top band obliterated in fashioning the neck, for the pattern units indicate a GIII–24 half-pint decanter mold unlike any determined in GIII–23: 51 vertical ribs; sunburst-in-square with 20 radii and 2 chevron ribs in triangles; diamond diapering (3 in chain height, 36 around); 36 diagonal ribs to right; horizontal rib between bands; rayed (55 ribs) base, Type IV; rare size. Capacity, just under 16 oz. Height, about 4⅝". Greatest width, 4⁵/₁₆". Greatest depth, 2¹¹/₁₆".

2. Colorless; chestnut shape; pattern GII–18: 60 vertical ribs; diamond diapering (3 in chain height, 30 around, irregular at one mold seam); 60 vertical ribs (2 merging at one mold seam); horizontal rib between bands; 17 diamond indentations on base, drawn up on side of flask at bottom. One of 5 or 6

*Blown-three-mold geometric patterns are illustrated on pp. 247-57 in *American Glass.*

recorded. Capacity, about 9 oz. Height, 5⅛". Greatest width, 3⅝". Greatest depth, 2".

3. Colorless; chestnut shape; patterned in GII–24 half-pint decanter mold: 63 vertical ribs (2 filletlike at one mold seam); 63 diagonal ribs to right (1 nearly vertical at one mold seam); diamonds (29 around, those at mold seams smaller); 59 vertical ribs; diamonds as below; 50 or 51 diagonal ribs to left (2 seem to merge at one mold seam, one nearly vertical at another); 57 vertical ribs (1 very short, flanked by a slight diagonal at one mold seam); horizontal rib between bands; base: 55 rays to center obscured by pontil mark. One other colorless has been recorded and one light blue. Capacity, 10 oz. Height, 4¾". Greatest width, 3⅝". Greatest depth, 2¼".

Bottom row:

4. Strong aquamarine; blown in a full-size two-piece mold; sharply tapering, flattened ovoid body, plain neck and lip, flat base, pontil mark; conventionalized design: graduated short vertical ribs at bottom below inverted heart-shaped area with slender gadroon ribs rising from medial vertical rib and between floral chain. Provenance unknown. Probably 2nd quarter 19th century. Capacity, 10 oz. Height, 6⅛". Greatest width, 5". Greatest depth, 1⅞".

5. Pocket or "nursing" bottle, colorless; blown by the half-post method and pattern-molded in honeycomb diaper (32 cells in horizontal row, 9 in chain height) extending from bottom of body to about ⅜" below top of half-post; long tapering pear shape, flattened on one side, short neck, plain lip; small pontil mark. Continental, probably German. 18th century. Capacity, about 8 oz. Height, 6". Greatest width, 3⅛". Greatest depth, 2¹/₁₆".

6. Handled flask, colorless; blown by half-post method; patterned in three-piece mold: fine vertical ribs below wide band of 12 vertical panels—(1) oval beads above and below circular medallion with 8-petaled motif, (2) wide leaf spray, (3) pinnate leaf, (4) twin scallop ribbing, (5) twin pinnate leaf above and below medallion like (1); (6) diamond diapering, (7) repeat of (3); (8) chain with oval bead in each link, (9) repeat of (5); (10) petals tapering to medial rib, (11) horizontal ribs, (12) herringbone ribbing; chestnut shape, very long neck, plain lip; pontil mark; applied loop handle with long plain end. Attributed to the Austrian Tyrol. 19th century. Capacity, about 1 pt. Height, 6⅜". Greatest width, 4⅝". Greatest depth, 2¼".

Flasks Nos. 1, 2, 3, and 9, and the "toilet bottle," No. 5, were shaped as well as patterned in full-size piece molds. The gathers for Nos. 3, 6, and 7 were patterned in such a mold and then formed by free-blowing.

Illustrated also in *American Glass:* 3, 4, and 9 by Nos. 7, 4, and 2 in Plate 238.

Nos. 1 through 5 and 9, formerly in the George S. McKearin Collection. No. 6 (also ex-Collection of George Frelinhuysen), Collection of the late Melvin Billups; No. 8, The Henry Ford Museum; No. 7, Collection of the Ohio Historical Society.

Top row:

1. Flask, light olive-green, from a two-piece mold; slender flat ovoid, beveled ends and tapering to small plain flat oval base, plain neck and lip; pontil mark; *obverse:* oval frame enclosing 13 4-petal ornaments—"stars" (single row of 2 both above and below 3 rows of 3); grapevine along bevel; *reverse:* diamond-latticed panel; 19 beads along bevel. Capacity, 12 oz. Height, 7⅛". Greatest width, 2⅞". Greatest depth, 2⅛" at shoulder. Base, 1⁹⁄₁₆" by 1¾". The pattern, on a smaller scale and with 17 beads on the beveled side of the reverse, occurs also in half-pint flattened elliptical flasks recorded in emerald green and colorless of smoky tone.

2. Flask, olive-amber, probably from a two-piece mold (no mold seam discernible); shield-shape tapering at ends from plain flat shoulder to small plain circular base, very short neck, plain lip; on body: 32 pronounced vertical ribs; only recorded example. Found in Connecticut about 1920; probably New England. Capacity, 8 oz. Height, 4⅞". Greatest width, 3¼". Greatest depth, 1⅞" at shoulder. Diameter of base, 1⅛".

3. Flask, clear olive-green, probably from a two-piece mold (no mold seam discernible); ovoid body tapering at ends from plain rounded shoulder to small plain oval base, long neck, everted plain lip. Rare. Probably New England. Capacity, about 13 oz. Height, 7¾". Greatest width, 3½". Greatest depth, 2" at shoulders. Base, ¹⁵⁄₁₆" by 1¼".

Middle row:

4. Blown-three-mold flask, pale yellow-green, pale amethyst streak following ribbing to left; patterned in the GI–3 Type II (32 spiral ribs, plain base) three-piece mold for toilet bottles (see *American Glass,* p. 247), expanded and shaped by manipulation into a fat chestnut shape with short neck spreading to plain lip; pontil mark. After 60 years, still unique in my experience. Capacity, 1 pt. about 9 oz. Greatest width, 5⅛". Greatest depth, 3¹⁄₁₆".

5. Toilet bottle, light yellow-green, from three-piece mold in the same pattern as No. 4 but having 20 swirled ribs; taper shape, flanged lip; pontil mark; very rare in color. Capacity, 10 oz. Height, 6". Greatest diameter, 3¹⁄₁₆".

6. Blown-three-mold flask, brilliant clear green; made by the half-post method, patterned in a two-piece mold in GII–16 (band of 36 vertical ribs, of diamond diapering—4 in chain height, 22 around—single horizontal rib between bands and at top) with plain base pulled up onto the body of the flask; flattened broad globular body, long neck, applied wide heavy sloping collar; shallow kick-up, pontil mark. Only recorded example. Capacity, about 13 oz. Height, about 5⅝". Greatest width, 5¼". Greatest depth, 2¼".

Bottom row:

7. Blown-three-mold flask; brilliant clear green, patterned in GII–6 three-piece mold (see *American Glass,* p. 250) for slender barrel-shape decanter-bottle having 45 vertical ribs (one very narrow at one mold seam) between bands of diamond diapering (3 in chain height, 27 around, irregular at one mold seam), 15 gadroon ribs at top, broad horizontal rib between bands, plain base; flattened ovoid body, short neck spreading to plain lip. One of two recorded in clear green, the other in the W. G. Russell Allen Collection, Museum of Fine Arts, Boston. Attributed to Park, Edmunds & Park, Kent, Ohio, ca. 1824–34. Capacity, 1 pt. about 3 oz. Height, 7½". Greatest width, 4¼". Greatest depth, 2¼".

A GII–6 (units in bands, not known) "Irish flask, glass of lead" of more slender and tapering form was illustrated in *Glass Notes* No. 16, 1956, published by Arthur Churchill Ltd. As the exact pattern does not occur in eastern blown-three-mold glass, probably it was a treasured piece, or perhaps a mold in GII–6 was brought to the United States by a glassman migrating to the Midwest after the War of 1812. Midwestern production in GII–6 was proved by Harry Hall White's excavations of fragments in sufficient numbers to establish its use at Kent, Ohio. Also, a few pieces of GII–6 have been attributed to the Wheeling area.

8. Kent blown-three-mold decanter, brilliant clear green, patterned in the same GII–6 mold as No. 7, but given a sugarloaf body, long tapering neck, flanged lip; pontil mark; original stopper, formed in a pinch tool: circular wafer with vertical ribs on one side and horizontal on the other giving a waffle effect; shape and stopper characteristic of decanters produced at the Kent glasshouse of Park, Edmunds & Park, ca. 1824–34. Capacity, about 1 pt. Height, with stopper, 7⅜".

9. Blown-three-mold flask, yellow-green, from four-piece mold in GI–22 pattern (*American Glass,* p. 248) having band of 54 vertical ribs, one of 59 diagonal ribs, one of 58 tapering ribs, and a horizontal rib between bands; as formed in the mold: flattened sides, ends, below curved shoulder, tapering slightly to flat elliptical base; short neck with infolded lip; pontil mark. Another has been recorded in aquamarine; two, in colorless. Capacity, 1 pt. Height, 7⅜". Greatest width, 4⁵⁄₁₆". Greatest depth, 2¹³⁄₁₆" below shoulder.

Figured Flasks 1, 2, and 3 could hardly have been pocket bottles: they are quart size. Besides its rarity, the Easley Saloon flask, Nos. 1 and 3, inscribed with General Zachary Taylor's soubriquet "Rough & Ready"—fitting also some hard liquors—is important as proof that by midcentury Figured Flasks were indeed used in saloons as well as for packaging and toting. Flask No. 2 (GIV–4a) is a hitherto unlisted variety of the Baltimore Glass Works' Washington Monument–Corn for the World "quarts." The cornerstone of this monument, the first memorializing the Father of His Country, was laid in 1815. Though financed mainly by Maryland, a lottery that was advertised far and wide in 1815 gave patriotic citizens the opportunity to contribute to the completion of the monument. But not until 1829 was its crowning glory, the statue of Washington, placed at the top. Although the monument itself had more local than national import, in the 1840s the ear of corn and inscription "CORN FOR THE WORLD" reflected national aspirations—a particularly appropriate symbol and slogan for Baltimore flasks, for vast quantities of corn and cornmeal were shipped from Fells Point to foreign markets.

The variety of ribbed flasks blown in full-size piece molds apparently was limited and, except for the type of No. 9, and probably those mentioned in connection with No. 3 of Ill. 123, those I have seen were of shapes that did not evolve until around 1850. Pint ribbed flasks like the eagle-medallion flask GII–31 in the Charts, but without the eagle in oval frame—were doubtless blown in the same range of colors as GII–31, but I have seen only yellow-green. The ribbed flasks and the waffle flask illustrated here in the middle and bottom rows seem to be comparatively scarce, or else the simplicity of their designs has failed to excite enough collectors to bring them out of attics and cupboards. Yet they are attractive flasks, and like the figured ones were blown in full-size two-piece molds.

Nos. 1 and 3 (obverse and reverse), the collection of Doy L. McCall. Nos. 2 and 6 through 9, formerly in the George S. McKearin Collection. No. 2, The Corning Museum of Glass.

Top row:

1 & 3. GXIII–85, quart, aquamarine; unusual body form, reminiscent of that of the Columbia flask GI–120. *Obverse:* large figure of a man wearing shirt or short jacket and full trousers; walking left, right forearm held out below waistline and bottle in hand. Inscription: "ROUGH" (lengthwise close to right hand) "&" (above head) "READY" (lengthwise near edge and in line with back of head and body); below feet, "H. EASLEY'S". *Reverse:*

inscription: "EASLEY'S" above large hand pointing downward to "SALOON" above "HUNTSVILLE". The only recorded example and made, Mr. McCall discovered, for Hugh Easley, who ran a saloon in Huntsville, Alabama, some time before the Civil War. The rendering of the figure is akin to that of the prospectors on the Pike's Peak flasks, first produced during the 1859 Pike's Peak gold rush.

2. GVI–4a, quart, yellow-green; designs on large oval panels. *Obverse:* Washington monument (less detailed than on GVI–4), statue a mere spike. *Reverse:* inscription "CORN FOR THE WORLD" in deep semicircle above a large ear of corn. Extremely rare variety without the inscription "BALTIMORE" on the obverse. Attributed to the Baltimore Glass Works. ca. 1840s.

Middle row:

4. Pint, strong aquamarine; each side: alternate ribs and flutes, graduated in height from 4″ at edge to 5¹/₁₆″ at center, interrupted above base by relief panel with slightly incurved ends and ogival top and bottom (length, 1¾″; height at points, 1⅛″); tool-formed round collar below plain lip; shape similar to form 25; base, Type 10.

5. Half-pint, pale blue; each side: graduated broad ribs; plain neck; base Type 5, Ill. 136. Recorded also in aquamarine and cool light blue, with collar like No. 5; pint size in aquamarine, collar like No. 5 and base Type 1, Ill. 136.

6. Half-pint, aquamarine; closely similar to No. 4 in ribs and flutes, panel with shallow ogival sides and ends with center points (length at points, 1⅝″; height at points, about ⅞″); plain base, pontil mark.

Bottom row:

7. Half-pint, aquamarine; fine vertical ribbing; form 32 having wide flat band on ends; double round collar; base Type 24, Ill. 136. Recorded also in amber; pint size, with plain smooth base, in golden amber.

8. Half-pint, light yellow-green; edges corrugated and square relief diaper on sides; thick-walled, flat sides, ends curving to broad flat elliptical plain base, pontil mark. Possibly 1830s to 1840s. Recorded also in colorless glass, strong blue-aquamarine, and deep sapphire; pint size in deep blue, clear green, and black (purple).

9. Half-pint, light blue; each side: on oval panel with rib molding, 16 fine vertical ribs; heavy medial rib on ends; form 11, plain neck; plain base, pontil mark. It is believed that these flasks are the type of Kensington "Common Ribbed" pocket bottles advertised by Dyott in 1824.

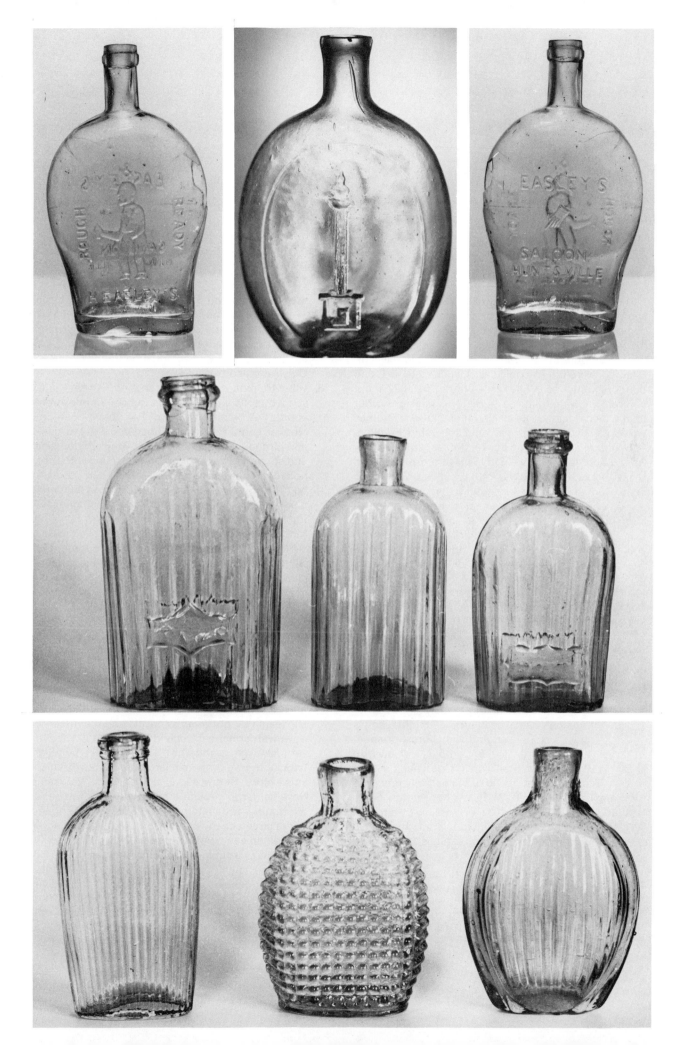

124. FIGURED FLASKS, ca. 1815–45

The American Figured Flasks, blown in full-size two-piece molds for relief designs, appear to have come into being between about 1810 or 1812 and 1815. It is believed that the first of these flasks falling into the main categories of Decorative, Masonic, Historical, and Pictorial, were the Masonic flasks, such as GIV–1, and Sunbursts, such as GVIII–1 (see Charts). By 1822, if not before, they were followed by Historical designs other than the American eagle. In March of that year Thomas W. Dyott advertised "American Eagle, ship Franklin, Agricultural and Masonic pocket bottles" (presumably GII–40 and 42 and GIV–35) blown at the Kensington Glass Works, Philadelphia. Perhaps it was Dyott who conceived the idea of expanding the decoration of pocket bottles with designs of national and local patriotic and topical appeal. In any event, such flasks became a typical American container for hard liquor and sometimes less ardent potable liquids. Of the four flasks illustrated here, Nos. 1, 3 and 4 fall in the Historical group; No. 2, in the Decorative.

All formerly in the George S. McKearin Collection. Nos. 1, 2, and 3, The Corning Museum of Glass; No. 4, The Henry Ford Museum.

Top row:

1. GI–16a, pint, colorless glass; designs on oval panels with rib molding. *Obverse:* inscription "GENERAL WASHINGTON." in arch above portrait bust of Washington in uniform, three-quarter view. *Reverse:* American Eagle, head turned to right (eagle's left); wings partly raised and right foreshortened, large shield on breast; thunderbolt (3 arrows) in right talon and olive branch in left; perched on large oval frame with inner band of beads. Only recorded example. Made by T. W. Dyott, Kensington Glass Works, ca. 1822–24 to 1832, or possibly by a manufacturer who obtained molds from the same moldmaker as did Dyott before establishing his own mold department at Dyottville.

Middle row:

2. GIX–52, pint Scroll flask, strong aquamarine; on each side: 3 scroll ribs following contour of ends, narrow middle and wide inner ribs forming frame with bluntly pointed tops, enclosing center design of scroll ribs around large palmette in lower part and, in upper, leaf and bladelike ribs with conical depression at center. Most elaborate of the Scroll flasks. Probably midwestern, made in the late 1830s. Only recorded example.

3. GII–144, pint, green; on each side: 9 heavy widespaced vertical ribs, the 3 at the center interrupted about 1¾" below neck and 1⅛" above base by a circular eagle medallion. Small eagle, head raised and turned to left (eagle's right); wings partly raised and spread downward; on breast, shield with broad horizontal bar above 4 short vertical bars; thunderbolt (3 arrows) in left talon and olive branch in right; medial vertical rib at mold seam on each end. New England, possibly Keene-Marlboro-Street, New Hampshire. ca. 1815–17.

Flasks of the same form and type of ribbing but without medallion have been recorded: pints in clear green, light and dark olive-green, and moonstone; half-pints in aquamarine, green, and amethyst.

Bottom row:

4. Pint, brilliant golden amber; the gather first patterned in a 16-rib dip mold before expansion in the full-size two-piece mold for the Eagle–Sunburst flask GII–7 with designs on oval panels with rib molding. *Obverse:* American eagle, head turned to left (eagle's right); wings partly raised and spread downward; on breast, shield with plain field above 5 vertical bars; thunderbolt (3 arrows) in large left talon and olive branch in large right. Above eagle, 6 small stars. Below eagle, tiny beaded oval frame. *Reverse:* large circular sunburst with 32 rays, each alternating ray tapering to heavy rounded end. Large circular beads between frame and medial vertical rib on each end, a characteristic of some of the early flasks from the Pittsburgh–Monongahela district. Very few Figured Flasks have been recorded with their designs superimposed on expanded vertical ribs, and this is the only one of the rare GII–7 flasks known at present. Midwestern, Pittsburgh–Monongahela district. Probably ca. 1820–35.

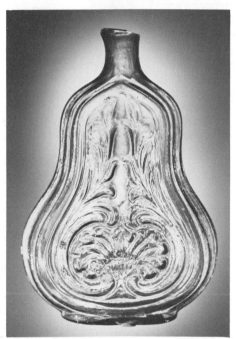

Hero of two revolutionary struggles, American and French, Lafayette occupied a special niche in American hearts. His heralded visit to the United States was eagerly awaited; his countrywide tour, August 1824 to September 1825, was triumphal; and it was signalized also for the citizenry by mementos in all sorts of fabrics and forms. Among practical items were 20 different pocket bottles. Rare examples are Nos. 1 and 4 with Masonic design on the reverse. (Freemasonry was proud of its famous member.)

Besides reverse designs on Lafayette and Andrew Jackson flasks, at least 51 molds were made for Masonic flasks, mainly between 1815 and 1830. Their decline is generally attributed to Masonry's becoming politically suspect: anti-Masonic feeling (flaring since 1826, when, allegedly, western New York Masons kidnapped and murdered William Morgan who planned to publish his order's secrets) crystallized into a political party about 1830. Possibly the Temperance Movement had an effect too. Flask No. 2 is an extremely rare one.

No. 3 is one of two Kensington flasks with the "ship Franklin" and "Agricultural and Masonic" designs, first advertised in 1822. On the obverse are "Farmers Arms" within a Masonic arch, pillars and pavement, appealing to agricultural and trade interests and to Masons; on the reverse, the ship *Franklin,* an appeal to patriotism and commerce. The *Franklin*—74, launched at Philadelphia in 1815, made flagship of our Pacific fleet in 1821, was "looking after the interests of American merchants in Chili and Peru" in 1822. The battle cry "FREE TRADE AND SAILORS RIGHTS," adopted by the Free Traders in the 1820s heightened the trade appeal of No. 3.

Flask No. 5 reflects several facets of midwestern interests. The sheaf of rye symbolized agriculture and hard liquor, with temperance advised in "USE ME BUT DO NOT ABUSE ME." The steamboat of the type plying rivers and lakes symbolized that advanced means of transportation, speeding exchange of produce and wares. Henry Clay's phrase "The American System" succinctly advocated internal improvements and protective tariff, both critically important to Pittsburgh as the leading western manufacturing and trade center and ardently advocated by Henry Baldwin, Pittsburgh's congressman. In August 1824, at a banquet given for him by Pittsburgh's leading manufacturers after passage of the protective tariff, he attributed the final victory largely to Clay, offering a toast "To Henry Clay and The American System." To Pittsburghers, Baldwin was the hero, especially to glassmakers who at last were adequately protected. While the first flasks might have been blown any time between 1818 and 1824, probably 1824 was the year.

Nos. 1, 2 and 5 (ex-Collection of George S. McKearin), The Corning Museum of Glass; No. 3, The Garvan Collection, Yale University Art Gallery; No. 4, ex-Collection of Edwin Lefevre (present owner unknown).

1. GI–89a, half pint, colorless lead glass of pale amethyst tint. *Obverse:* small bust of Lafayette, facing right, partially enclosed by semiwreath of laurel branches crossing below bust; above, inscription in deep semicircle, "LAFAYETTE". *Reverse:* arch of 13 large 6-pointed stars enclosing Masonic arch, pillars and pavement; below keystone, a triangle; between pillars, square and compass on open book. Fine herringbone ribbing on edges. Glasshouse not definitely known but bust and emblems so closely similar to the Mt. Vernon Glass Works' Lafayettes that, since Mt. Vernon made both flint (lead) and bottle glass, it seems the probable source. ca. 1824. Only recorded example.

2. GIV–13a, half-pint, black (dark olive-amber). *Obverse:* Masonic arch, pillars and pavement (29 bricks); below keystone, large all-seeing eye; between pillars, square and compass on open book above radiant triangle enclosing letter "G"; outside left pillar, trowel above skull and crossbones and, of arch, blazing sun; outside right pillar, Jacob's Ladder ascending to "Cloudy Canopy" or "Star Decked Heaven" represented by radiant quarter moon between stars at right of arch; below pavement, "Pascal Lamb" at left, Ark of the Covenant at right. *Reverse:* American eagle, head turned to left (eagle's right); wings raised and partly spread downward; small shield on breast; thunderbolt (3 arrows) in left talon, olive branch in right. Above eagle, rippled pennant. Below eagle, 7-pointed star in beaded oval frame. Sloping collar with lower bevel, a rare feature. Only recorded example. Probably New England. ca. 1815–30.

3. GIV–34, pint, deep green, which a Kensington glassblower had fun turning into a turtle by applying broad legs and feet and, down the back, a crimped ribbon ending in a long slender tail. Designs on oval panels with rib molding. *Obverse:* Masonic arch, pillars and pavement framing "Farmers' Arms"— sheaf of rye, pitchfork, shovel, rake, sickle, axe, and scythe. Below pavement, scroll ornament. Between frame and medial rib on ends, inscription "KENSINGTON GLASS WORKS PHILADELPHIA". *Reverse:* full-rigged frigate sailing to right, American flag at stern; waves beneath frigate and inscription "FRANKLIN". Between frame and medial rib on end, inscription "FREE TRADE AND SAILORS RIGHTS". Unique whimsey. ca. 1822–32.

4. GI–88, pint, dark olive-green; gather patterned in a rib dip mold before expansion in the mold for GI–88. *Obverse:* bust of Lafayette, facing right; above in semicircle, inscription "LAFAYETTE". *Reverse:* Masonic arch, pillars and pavement; below keystone, a triangle; between pillars, square and compass on open book. Very rare. Mount Vernon Glass Works. ca. 1824.

5. GX–21, pint, brilliant olive-yellow. *Obverse:* paddle-wheel steamboat steaming to right through rippled water, long narrow flag flying to left from bow, American flag from mast back of smokestack; inscription, in curving line, "THE AMERICAN [above boat] SYSTEM" (below water). *Reverse:* arch of 27 small beads over sheaf of rye within inscription "USE ME BUT DO NOT ABUSE ME"; below sheaf, narrow oblong frame. *Ends:* short herringbone ribbing. One of 15 or 20 known examples, attributed to the Pittsburgh-Monongahela district, ca. 1824. Two other molds were made, each with initials in the oblong frame: one with "B.P & B"—Bakewell, Page and Bakewell; the other with "B & M", presumably—Baker & Martin, Perryopolis, Pa.

1

2

3

4

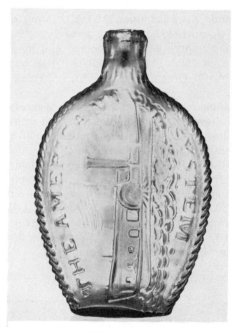

5

126. FIGURED WHIMSEYS AND HANDLED BOTTLES, 19th century

Apparently it was a rare occasion on which a blower used a bottle or flask mold to pattern a gather that he fashioned into another article, for example the jars, Nos. 1 and 3, and pitcher, No. 2. Such choice pieces are generally called *whimseys,* since there is no evidence at present that they were a commercial product but rather the whim or fancy of the blower, albeit often a practical one. Though handled bottles and flasks seem to have become a standard type for spiritous liquors in the third quarter of the century, very few of them were figured as are Nos. 4, 5, and 6, which fall in the Pictorial Group XIII. The rarity of No. 4 with pouring lip suggests it possibly was not a stock item as were Nos. 5 and 6. All were patterned in full-size two-piece molds.

Illustrated also in *American Glass:* 2, 3, and 4 by Nos. 6, 11, 9 and 10 Plate 252.

Nos. 1 (ex-Collection of Alfred B. Maclay), 2 (ex-Collection of Jacob Paxson Temple), and 4, formerly in the George S. McKearin Collection. No. 3, The Henry Ford Museum.

Top row:

1. Jar, dark olive-amber; patterned in the full-size two-piece mold for the common pint Eagle–Cornucopia flask GII–72; cylindrical body, plain short wide cylindrical neck, plain lip; pontil mark. Only recorded example. Possibly blown at the Keene-Marlboro-Street Glassworks, Keene, N.H. ca. 1820–50. Capacity, 1 pt. about 5 oz. Height, 6⅛". Greatest diameter, 3⅝". Diameter of neck, 2⁹⁄₁₆".

2. Pitcher, clear sapphire-blue; patterned in the full-size two-piece mold for the Sheaf of Grain—Tree calabash bottle GXIII–46; ovoid body, wide cylindrical neck flaring slightly at top to plain rim with tiny lip; applied wide two-rib handle with curled back end; base Type 30 (III. 136), pontil mark; *obverse:* sheaf of grain, crossed rake and pitchfork; *reverse:* tree in foliage, upper part diffused in expanding for neck. Only recorded example. ca. 1850s. Capacity, 1 qt. about 10 oz. Height, 7⅛". Greatest width, 5⅞". Greatest depth, 4⁵⁄₁₆".

3. Jar, olive-amber; patterned in the full-size two-piece mold for the common pint Cornucopia–Urn flask GIII–4; ovoid body, short spreading neck, plain lip; pontil mark. Coventry Glass Works, Coventry, Conn. ca. 1820–50. Only recorded example. Capacity, 1 pt. about 5 oz. Height, about 6¼". Greatest diameter, 4¼".

Bottom row:

4. Flask-jug, light amber of olive tone; blown in the mold for the comparatively scarce Horseman–Hound flask GXIII–17 having racing horseman on obverse and hound on reverse; tall elliptical body, rounded shoulder, long cylindrical neck, plain pouring lip; applied loop handle with crimped end attached on shoulder; pontil mark. Probably 1850s. Capacity, 1 pt. Height, 8⅛". Greatest width, 3¾". Greatest depth, 2¼".

5. GXIII–45, handled calabash bottle, bubbly glass, shaded amber; *obverse:* sheaf of grain, crossed rake and pitchfork; *reverse:* 8-pointed star; 6 broad vertical ribs on ends; neck scalloped at base, tapering to flat collar laid-on below plain lip; base Type 28; heavy applied handle with thumbpiece and long crimped end. ca. 1850s–1860s. Capacity, 1 qt. about 2 oz. Height, 9". Greatest width, 5⁵⁄₁₆". Greatest depth, 4⅛".

6. GXIII–24, handled flask, pint, shaded puce; *obverse:* relief panel, beveled top and sides, hanging from triangular rib with tassel in apex, inscribed "FLORA TEMPLE" above figure of horse; below panel, inscription "HARNESS TROT 2.19"; *reverse:* plain; shape, No. 27, Form Groups; round collar laid-on below plain lip. As the famous time was made on Oct. 15, 1859, the first of the Flora Temple flasks probably came out the end of the year or early in 1860. Capacity, 14 oz. Height, 8⅜". Greatest width, 4⁷⁄₁₆". Greatest depth, 2" at top of frame.

D. Fancy Geometric

Though the three flasks GX–24, 25, and 26 are charted and illustrated in the Miscellaneous Group X, that classification is no reflection of their importance and interest. Except for the corrugated (horizontally ribbed) edges, which seem almost an earmark of many early New England flasks, their designs are utterly unrelated to those of any other charted flasks, except the reverse of the Inverted Cornucopia GIII–1. Each has three zones of design or pattern: the upper with a large circular medallion; the middle with graduated curved ribs rising to form, with the bottom of the medallion, a shield-shaped area; and the third and lowest, filled with diamond diapering. The medallion on GX–24 has "JARED SPENCER" in an incomplete circle around two concentric convex rings with convex center; in the "shield" is a sunburst with concave center depending from three loops along the bottom of the medallion and three sunken diamonds in the center of the curved ribs. The reverse is the same except for the inscription "MANCHESTER CON." On GX–25, the medallion has concentric rings (two narrow between two wide) with four concave petals at center;

in the shield is a small disk depending from three three-pointed ornaments along the bottom of the medallion. On GX–26 the medallion has a relief decoration of eight petals, each rising from the space between large pearls, eight in all, enclosing a concave center; the shield is like GX–25.

At this point I have to repeat my previous comments on the dating and attribution of these flasks, which were once thought to be perhaps the earliest of the Figured Pocket Bottles and listed as "probably Pitkin." It is possible, perhaps probable, that GX–25 and GX–26 antedated GX–24, the Jared Spencer, Manchester, Connecticut, flask, which would place them before 1823. Since Manchester was not formed until May 1823, the Jared Spencer flask cannot be dated earlier. As for the tentative (definite, according to some) Pitkin attribution—at the time it was made, John Mather's East Hartford glassworks and his manufacture of "figured pocket bottles" were unknown. Now, as I have said, Mather is an equally tenable probability, especially since, as Kenneth Wilson discovered, Jared Spencer purchased bottles from Mather as well as from the Coventry and the Willington Glass Works, whereas no record of a purchase from the Pitkin works has been found as yet.

3

MASONIC FLASKS

As has been emphasized already, it would be in the natural course of glass and Masonic events for Figured Flasks to be blown for Masons. In fact, it is because Masonic vessels—sealed bottles and engraved decanters, punch bowls of different materials, and drinking vessels from firing glasses to huge ceremonial goblets—had long been made that I believe Masonic decanter-flasks like GIV–1 through 12 were probably the firstborn of the large family of Figured Flasks, and the first of those decorated with relief decoration, though the possibility of their being heralded by Sunbursts cannot be ignored. At present, 51 flasks of Masonic significance appear in Group IV of the Charts, most of them illustrated by line drawings (there were 42 in Group IV of the original charts). There are in addition eight portrait flasks in Group I and one eagle flask in Group II that bear a Masonic emblem. It will be noted in referring to the charts that this count includes the last five in

Group IV in the original Charts—namely: GIV–38 through 42, which have on the obverse the word "UNION" and a shield with clasped hands in the upper field, a square and compass in the lower. As noted in 1941, these had always been listed as Masonic because of the belief that the square and compass of Freemasonry had been combined during the Civil War period with the patriotic appeal of "Union," shield, and peaceful handclasp. However, even before publication of the charts in *American Glass*, the connection of these five with Masonry had been questioned by John H. R. Arms, secretary of the United Engineering Trustees, Inc., who pointed out the existence—prior to and after the Civil War—of a society called the Jr. O.U.A.M. (Junior Order of United Mechanics) whose insignia was a square and compass and clasped hands within a shield. This has been further confirmed, and I am now convinced the four flasks and the calabash bottle bearing the insignia commemorate this society.

Naturally there were several combinations of Masonic emblems on the obverse and of various reverse designs among the Masonic flasks, but—since Freemasonry was so important politically and socially—not perhaps so many as might be expected, especially in the portrait group, where so many of the subjects were prominent Masons. Of the flasks in the original Group IV, 28 and all those discovered since then have an elaborate display of emblems within and outside the dominating arch and pavement. Among these are the heavy, often lead glass, decanter-flasks, which have the United States coat of arms on the reverse above an oval frame with initials or ornament. An eagle below a pennant, also inspired by our coat of arms, appears on 11 others. In general, the eagles are rather settled conservative birds compared, for instance, to the eagle on the reverse of Dyott's Kensington flask GIV–37, ca. 1822. Also, on the obverse of this flask, none of the small emblems is used, just the arch and pavement enclosing Farmers' Arms—scythe, rake, and fork and a sheaf of grain. Five other flasks have the combined symbols of Masonry and Agriculture. Two of these, GIV–34 and 35, brought out by Dyott at Kensington ca. 1825, and another, the midwestern GIV–36 (which appears to be from a Laird mold), have the frigate *Franklin* on the reverse. Three other midwesterns on which the spade is included in the Farmers' Arms have, on the reverse, the American eagle—GIV–31, a quiescent bird beneath 13 stars; GIV–32 and 33, spirited eagles similar to Dyott's. Both GIV–32 and 33 are Zanesville, Ohio, flasks, and one can but conclude the molds were from the same moldmaker. The former is inscribed "ZANESVILLE / OHIO. SHEPARD" and could have been brought out any time after 1822 and before 1838; the latter, "MURDOCK & CASSEL", probably about 1832.[20]

Only four flasks in Group IV have Masonic emblems on both sides, GIV–28, 28a, 29, and 30, all half-pints. As the line drawings show, GIV–28 and GIV–28a have many emblems inside and outside of a more decorative arch and pavement than occur on other Masonic flasks—the pavement being finely tesselated, the shafts of the columns fluted, the arch ribbed. The edges too are distinctive, having tiny beads in rows and diamond formation. Though Harry Hall White found a sufficient number of fragments of GIV–28 to make him consider the possibility that the flasks emanated from the Ontario Glass Works on Lake Seneca, about three miles from Geneva, New York, Jasena Rappleye Foley's

exhaustive researches have established that in the period of these flasks the commercial product of this glassworks was cylinder window glass "exclusively."[21] The other two flasks, both of which have been attributed to Coventry, Connecticut, are so different as to stand out like beacons, for there are few emblems and they are boldly drawn; also, the edges are corrugated like those on other early Connecticut flasks in the natural bottle-glass colors. One, GIV–29, has on each side a large five-pointed star above the hourglass, below the crescent moon surrounded by seven stars, and between pillars. The other, GIV–30, has a large five-pointed star above crossed keys on one side and the square and compass on the other; it is usually referred to as the crossed keys. These are listed as extremely rare (1 to 10 recorded) and very rare (10 to 20 recorded) respectively. As a matter of fact, the majority of the Masonics range in estimated rarity from scarce to rare; only eight in Masonic Group IV and the portraits with Masonic emblems fall into the common or very common categories—that is, 75 to 150, or over 150, specimens known.

In the portrait group, Masonic emblems appear with portraits of two heroes notable to a large proportion of Americans: Andrew Jackson and General Lafayette. The flasks are very to extremely rare, so it may be they were made specially for certain Masonic lodges. Freemasonry was as proud of these two famous members as they were of being Masons. Probably the glassmakers, who either capitalized on this pride or were asked to produce the flasks, were Masons themselves. There are but two Jackson–Masonic flasks, both midwestern. One, GI–69, was produced by Knox & McKee at their Virginia Green Glass Works, Wheeling, (West) Virginia, probably in 1828, certainly before 1830 when the firm and name of the glassworks were changed. The other, GI–70, was blown at the Mantua Glass Works, Ohio, between 1824 (probably) and 1829 when the works closed.

On the Knox & McKee Jackson, the evidence of Masonry is the arch with triangular keystone framing the bust, the intended identity of which would be a mystery were it not for the inscribed name. This applies also to the firm's Lafayette GI–92, and to the Lafayette GI–93 lacking a maker's name but possibly produced by Pepperd & Teater in their Moscow, Ohio, glassworks. As comparison of the line drawings in the Charts shows, the Jackson–Masonic GI–69 and two Lafayette–Masonics GI–92 and 93 differ only in their inscriptions. (See General Lafayette in 4. *Historical Flasks*, section *B*.) On the reverse of the Mantua Jackson, ca. 1824–28, are many Masonic emblems as well as the arch and pavement, as on most of the eastern Masonics—not surprisingly, since Ladd's associate Jonathan Tinker went to Mantua from Vernon, New York.[22] Among the portrait flasks these four—GI–69, 70, 92, and 93—are the only ones recorded with Masonic emblems that are unquestionably midwestern. All the others are eastern: GI–80 through GI–87, Coventry, Connecticut, brought out by Thomas Stebbins probably in 1824 and made also by the later firms of Stebbins & Chamberlin and Stebbins & Stebbins; GI–88 and GI–89, GI–89a, and GI–89b, at the Mount Vernon Glass Works, Vernon, New York. Only one specimen each is known at present of GI–89a, a long-coveted half-pint lead-glass flask acquired finally by George S. McKearin at the auction of the flask collection of George Horace Lorimer, and GI–89b, a pint aquamarine. These two and the Mantua Jackson, of which one perfect and one imperfect specimen are recorded, are as yet the rarest of the Jackson- and Lafayette–Masonic flasks—in fact, of any flasks with Masonic emblems.

Aside from the four midwestern flasks having the Masonic emblems secondary to a famous Mason's portrait bust, and the midwestern GIV–31, 32, 33, and 36 having the arch and pavement enclosing Farmers' Arms, the flasks of Masonic significance, Group IV, emanated from eastern glasshouses. There Dyott's Masonic–Agricultural—Ship *Franklin* seems to have been the only one in the Baltimore—Philadelphia—South Jersey area. In New York, the Mount Vernon Glass Works, Vernon, produced its Lafayette–Masonics and possibly some like GIV–3 or one of its close kin, but by far the majority are attributed to New England. One might expect New England and New York to have been the main source, since this area was the special stronghold of Masonry, so long socially prominent and, until about 1830, politically important nearly everywhere in the United States. Moreover, archeological evidence has identified flasks with three houses in this area—Mt. Vernon in New York, Coventry in Connecticut, and Keene-Marlboro-Street in New Hampshire, operating by 1810, 1814, and 1815 respectively.

And of that majority, indisputably some were produced in the Flint Glass Works or, as it is identified today, the Keene-Marlboro-Street works—namely, the decanter-flasks in the wide range of colors, many of lead glass, bearing the initials "HS" and "IP" (the two letters joined). Surely "HS" on GIV–2 can stand only for Henry Schoolcraft, one of the founders of the glassworks, and the comparatively scarce

flasks must have been blown between the fall of 1815 and February 1817, the short span in which Schoolcraft and his different partners operated the Flint Glass Factory. As mentioned previously, examples of this flask were recovered from the wreck of the *Caesar*, which struck a coral head in May 1818.[23] Flasks GIV–1 and GIV–1a have the initials of Justus Perry, the Keene merchant who evidently foreclosed a mortgage on the works in February 1817 and who ran them alone until 1822, when John V. Wood became his partner. The GIV–1 flasks are of particular interest, for if Schoolcraft did not have the "HS" Masonic mold altered to make flasks for Justus Perry, then one of Perry's early acts as owner of the glassworks was to have the initials in the mold for the "HS" flasks changed to a joined "IP." Though the sameness of the flasks in all respects except the initials has always been obvious, the probability of an altered mold, so far as I know, was never considered by anyone before the late Dr. Julian H. Toulouse, retired chief engineer of the Owens-Illinois Glass Company, who included study of marks on bottles and flasks among his many activities. A study of the line drawings in Group IV, *American Glass*, suggested to him that the peculiarities of the placement and initials in the mold for GIV–1 ("I" instead of a true "J," joined by a bar to "P") probably resulted when the "S" in the mold for GIV–2 was filled in and a "P" formed by a loop on the right leg of the "H." In the spring of 1966 Dr. Toulouse asked me to test his theory by an examination of the two flasks. As I was unable to do so I turned, as I usually do with such problems, to Kenneth M. Wilson, then Assistant Director and Curator of The Corning Museum of Glass, who determined that Dr. Toulouse's diagnosis was correct. Subsequently, as Richard H. Wood discovered, the bar of the "H" was removed from the mold to make the flask GIV–1a. The few samples of Justus Perry's GIV–1 Masonic flask that have been tested proved to be lead glass. As has been mentioned in another connection, Perry had stopped production of lead glass by August 1817. Therefore any lead-glass flasks were blown before that date, unless Perry made lead glass occasionally for special orders. The bottle-glass Masonics GIV–17 inscribed "KEENE" and GIV–18 through 20a marked "KEENE" *without* a middle bar on the E's probably were blown throughout the period from about 1818 to 1830.

The other marked Masonic flasks in the Group are the extremely rare "NEG" GIV–15 and comparatively scarce "NEGC⁰" GIV–27. Again, tested examples proved to be lead glass. The difference in rarity suggests that the heavy GIV–15 was produced in far more limited quantities than the much lighter weight GIV–27. Too, it probably antedates GIV–27. The initials are those of the New England Glass Company. And it is believed by students today that these flasks really were first produced *by* that company, not *for* it by the Keene-Marlboro-Street Glassworks. However, some of the GIV–15 flasks may have been blown at Keene after 1818, since the New England Glass Company is said to have sent molds to Keene to expedite filling orders when it was overly busy. And probably any orders received after the establishment of the New-England Glass-Bottle Company in 1827 were filled at that new and nearby factory, which was related through its owners but was a separate entity. Also, the probability seems to me very strong that some of the unmarked Masonic decanter-flasks were products of the New England Glass Company, of the South Boston Flint Glass Works, and of Thomas Cains's Phoenix Glass Works in South Boston.

Likewise of special interest are flasks GIV–22 and GIV–23 with eagle above an oval frame with "1829" on the reverse, since they are dated and also may have brought down the curtain on Masonic flasks. They are rare flasks, and those tested are lead glass. Their geographical distribution points to New England as their source, and their lead content suggests the Boston area. Considering these points and the 1829 date, I believe they were products of Thomas Cains's Phoenix Glass Works or the New-England Glass-Bottle Company.

Finally, there is a flask having on the obverse a large six-pointed star on which is a large eye, and below the star, the letters "A D"; on the reverse is a similar star on which is a raised arm with fist clenching an object, above an unidentified emblem; the letters "G R J A" are beneath the star. It has long been a well-known flask, listed by Van Rensselaer as No. 1, Group VI, and in his description he referred to the "Masonic arm and emblem." But the flask was not included in his Masonic group. Nor was it in *American Glass,* as no satisfactory information as to the significance of all the insignia had been obtained. The flask is now included as GIV–42, on the strength of information generously given to me by the late L. Earl Dambach. Mr. Dambach's researches seem to establish that the "G R J A" stands for the Masonic Lodge "Grand Royal Jerusalem Arch" and the "A D" for "Alexander Delta Arch." Of the emblems, he wrote:

the Star of David . . . [is] composed of two equilateral triangles, one pointing upward toward heaven and the other pointing to the nether region . . . symbolically [showing] the contrast between good and evil, light and darkness and between knowledge and superstition. The all-seeing eye of God raised toward heaven is constantly looking after us. The arm holds the compass, an instrument of operative masons which has masonic significance. The light shines through the darkness and eliminates superstition.

As yet this flask, probably of the 1840s and later, is the only flask definitely first made after 1830 that is classified as Masonic.

In any event the large, if not vast, production of Masonic flasks lasted nearly three decades. About 1830 production seems to have ceased abruptly. Perhaps growing "respectability" brought on by the spreading Temperance epidemic contributed to the decline of whiskey flasks flaunting Masonic emblems, but the fall is definitely and strongly associated with the famous—in fact, notorious—Morgan episode in 1826, which sparked the smoldering anti-Masonic crusade and party, which in turn was to be a potent factor in state, congressional, and presidential elections: Masonry may still have been socially desirable among the "better sort," but politically it was suspect.

William Morgan, a stonemason in Batavia and a member of the Masonic Royal Arch chapter at Le Roy, New York, apparently was not in good standing with fellow members of the fraternity. His signature to a petition for the institution of a chapter at Batavia was objectionable to them because, if the charter were granted, he would be a charter member. Consequently, unknown to him, a second petition was made without his signature. Morgan, chagrined and angered by this exclusion from membership, sought vengeance, not only on his fellow townsmen who were members of the chapter, but on the whole Masonic fraternity. He entered into a contract with one David C. Miller, newspaper publisher at Batavia, to write a book revealing the secrets of Freemasonry. Although there was nothing in the tenets or principles of Masonry that needed to be hidden, certain hotheads among the local Masons vowed that the book should never appear. Consequently tremendous local feeling and a bitter fight involving Morgan and Miller developed, finally culminating on the night of September 12, 1826, in the kidnapping and disappearance of Morgan. It is said that he was driven in a closed carriage to Lewiston, Niagara County, and thence to unoccupied Fort Niagara, and there put into the stone magazine. From this point all trace of him disappeared; to this day his actual fate has never been revealed. As weeks and months went by, public excitement was so fired that mass meetings passed resolutions that all secret fraternities, Masons more than any, were a menace to freedom and the enforcement of law and order, that no Mason should be supported for public office, and that all newspapers which did not publish full reports of Morgan meetings should be boycotted. As the futile search for Morgan or his body continued, the tide of public feeling rose higher and higher and the anti-Masonry sentiment grew and spread throughout the whole state. Petitions were filed with the state legislature, and Governor Clinton issued a proclamation offering a reward of $1,000 for the discovery of Morgan and $2,000 for the discovery of his murderers.

By 1828 fuel was added to the flames by Miller's publication of the *Illustrations of Masonry by One of the Fraternity who had devoted Thirty Years to the Subject* and the *Narrative of the Facts and Circumstances relating to the Kidnapping and Presumed Murder of William Morgan,* put out by the Lewiston committee appointed for that purpose at one of the

many public meetings. In the local elections that followed, approximately 17,000 votes were cast for the anti-Masons; and the agitation, taking a frankly political turn, culminated in a local anti-Mason party. An anti-Mason convention was held at Utica in August at which candidates for Governor and Lieutenant-Governor were nominated and a committee appointed to call future conventions if necessary. Francis Granger, who was nominated for Governor, declined the nomination. So a second convention of anti-Masons was held in Le Roy, Morgan's hometown, at which Solomon Southwick was nominated. He polled more than 30,000 votes! Up to this time the anti-Masons had attracted little attention outside New York State, but now the agitation extended to Vermont, thence through New England, and soon spread throughout the entire United States. Thus was born the anti-Masonic party, which well into the 1840s was an active factor in both local and national elections.[24]

4
HISTORICAL FLASKS

For nearly 70 years all our Figured Flasks were classified as "historical," and so a large proportion of them are. To those who collect and study them, they are tangible vignettes of American history. But they were nothing so curious and impersonal to those who made and used them. Nor were they mere fancy containers for potables. Their designs gave them a significance in themselves, made them reminders of "unforgettable" men and events, made them visual stimuli to exuberant patriotism and pride in the nation and its heroes, even sparking the fierce political emotions so easily roused in every "true born American." The majority of these designs were brought out between 1822 and 1850—the period when the conservative democracy of the age of Hamilton withered and the radical democracy of the age of Jackson flowered; the period when a new and weak nation became strong enough to warn off would-be interferers in the national liberation movements to her south, though rationalizing her own interference and first battles fought on foreign soil—and all in spite of a slowly growing cancer of disunity over

slavery. It was a period when the average citizen, the common man, agreed with Mrs. Trollope's Cincinnati milkman that looking after the affairs of his country was a moral obligation, and a road in poor repair or a broken fence signified little compared "to knowing that the men we have been pleased to send up to Congress speaks handsome and straight as we chooses they should."[25] It was a period when the average citizen, the common man, did not view the symbols and emblems of his country with the usual complacency of today: he thrilled to them. He was not yet self-conscious about his ardent patriotism: he enjoyed wholeheartedly the speeches, toasts, poems, and songs lauding his America, her heroes, and her emblems, and not just on the Fourth of July. And so, of course, the Historical Flasks appealed to him.

The following groupings of these flasks are mainly a convenience, for many could fit as well into another group since they are adorned with more than one significant design or distinctive motif.

A. Emblems and Symbols
of the United States

THE AMERICAN EAGLE

Since antiquity the eagle, traditionally a bird symbolizing strength, power, and sovereignty, has been widely used as an emblem of state and, consequently, as a decorative motif in the arts and crafts of many nations. The young United States chose the American bald eagle as her emblem. Stylized, with shield or escutcheon on his breast, an olive branch (symbol of peace) in his right talon, and a bundle of 13 arrows (thunderbolt, symbol of power) in his left talon, he became the principal device of the Great Seal of the United States, adopted in 1782 before independence was indisputably won. Naturally the American eagle soon began its endless career as a decorative motif in or on nearly every conceivable fabric from granite to glass, put to nearly every conceivable use from architectural ornament to ornamental letterhead. Moreover, for over a century from the day of its adoption, the American eagle was beyond a doubt one of the most overworked national symbols or emblems ever employed to lend sanction and prestige to a firm, a business, an industry, or a bit of merchandise. It is hardly likely its aegis was spread to Figured Flasks from purely patriotic sentiments.

Be that as it may, the American eagle was chosen to decorate more flasks than was any other single motif in the entire repertory of flask designers. In all, individual molds for at least 323 charted flasks embossed him on pocket bottles and flasks. The majority were pocket-bottle size—that is, pint and half-pint—even after quarts became a standard product in the late 1840s. Of the total number, 159 flasks have been classified as *Eagle flasks*—that is, whether complemented by or complementing another device, the side with the eagle has been designated as the obverse of the flask. In 1941, in the original charts published in *American Glass*, 77 flasks were charted in the Eagle group, Group II. Presently, 84 flasks have been added—9 variants of flasks in the original group and 75 flasks produced from the late 1840s on. On a minority, as study of the Charts will show, the eagle was the only decorative motif, either on one side only or on both. Of those first produced in the early years, only three have no other motif or inscription: namely, the rare and choice GII–76, GII–76a, and GII–144; none boasts a well-drawn eagle, and the first and third have a small eagle medallion. Twelve have an eagle on obverse and reverse. On the

other hand, for some as yet purely speculative reasons, five times as many of the flasks first produced in the late 1840s and following years have only eagles. A calabash of the 1870s and 19 flasks have just one eagle (six in medallion), and 62 have an eagle on each side. In the 1920s the latter were oddly dubbed double eagles, and they are usually so called today.

Just under half the flasks now in Group II have a design other than an eagle on the other side—cornucopia, tree, bunch of grapes, anchor, stag, American flag, the frigate *Franklin*—but the eagle side was selected as the obverse or designating side. Today it seems to me likely that in some instances the eagle on the flask was the less important motif in the mind of the designer and vendor of them. For instance, that the frigate *Franklin* on GII–42 was the more significant feature to Dyott seems evident from his listing of "ship Franklin" pocket bottles (Ill. 117). Also, it would appear that it was the cornucopia rather than the eagle that was expected to attract buyers' attention to GII–43 (Ill. 117). However, a large number of the flasks having the American eagle on one side and another design on the other have been charted in other groups, the eagle being the reverse or secondary side—42 in Group I (Portrait flasks), 41 in Group IV (Masonic flasks), 6 in Group V (Railroad flasks), 40 in Group XI (Pike's Peak flasks), and 36 in Group XII (Shield and Clasped Hands flasks).

Comparison of the line drawings of American eagles in the Charts indicates varied renderings of this national symbol—from skillful to clumsy, detailed to simple, quiescent to vigorous, dovelike to ferocious. But there were very few *styles* of eagle. Dyott specifically mentioned the "United States Coat of Arms" in his 1824 advertisement of Lafayette pocket bottles (Ill. 119), and in general, like Dyott's, other flask eagles—particularly those created before midcentury—were intended to represent the country's seal. As on the Great Seal, he grasped an olive branch in his right talon and a thunderbolt (3 to 5 arrows, not 13) in his left, but sometimes the order was reversed and power took precedence over peace, doubtless by error, not intention. On many of the early flasks, both from eastern glassworks (including Dyott's) and from the Pittsburgh–Monongahela district, the sunrays fanned out above the eagle's head, calling to mind the assertion in the popular song that Columbia's Eagle "encircled with a flood of light" would always "supremely rise to lead her to victory in fight and bear her glory to the skies."[26] As yet, only Dyott's

Lafayette–Eagle (GI–90) and his two Washington–Eagle flasks (GI–14 and, if it exists, GI–15 in the Portrait Group) have been recorded with the inscription "E PLURIBUS UNUM" above the sunrays, but on many flasks stars of the skies were added, usually forming an arc or arch above the eagle or above the sunrays if they were present. A pennant, with each end forked, was placed above the "Coat of Arms" eagle—a somewhat stolid bird—on the reverse of most of the early New England Masonic flasks (Group IV), and the pennant on two was inscribed "E PLURIBUS UNUM"—the joined "IP" (Justus Perry) and "HS" (Henry Schoolcraft) Keene Masonics GIV–1 and GIV–2. Similar use of the pennant, but with one end forked or rounded and the other held in the eagle's beak, recurred on the numerous later and sketchily drawn "double eagles" from Stoddard and New England, Louisville, and the Pittsburgh area, and on the reverse of most Pike's Peak flasks (Group XI).

Actually, however, on comparatively few flasks was the eagle's pose at all similar to that on the Great Seal, not even on Dyott's flasks. It may be that the official eagle seemed too stylized to convey the vitality and both combative and protective spirit associated with him. But perhaps it is more likely that when designers and moldmakers needed models, they turned to sources offering more attractive and somewhat more realistic eagles. In fact, the similarity of many flask eagles to eagles illustrating contemporary newspaper advertisements and broadsides or embellishing business letterheads, and especially to the eagles on the gold and silver coins of the United States, suggests these media served as moldmakers' models before the 1850s. For instance, among many parallels that could be drawn, Dyott's eagle on the Lafayette–Eagle flask GI–90 is quite like the one on a 25-cent piece minted in 1821, and the eagles on the midwestern flasks GII–22 through GII–25, probably first produced in the mid- to late-1840s, are closely similar to the one on the half-eagle coin of 1834.

Naturally there were a few highly individual renderings—for instance, the eagle on GII–20 and the so-called pantaloon eagle on GII–75—but no radical style changes in eagle depiction occurred until midcentury. By then the flying eagle became popular. He was depicted with wings spread in flight, the shield on or at the lower edge of his breast, with or without olive branch and thunderbolt, and with long pennant held in beak and streaming back above him and downward below him. On flasks, this eagle appeared in oval medallions on two (GII–35 and GII–36) produced by the Louisville Glass Works, possibly as early as 1855. However, the flying eagle was used mainly on the reverse of the Shield and Clasped Hands flasks, Group XII, of the Civil War period and later. A similar treatment was used for the eagle on two Dyottville flasks, GII–38 and GII–39, of the late 1840s or early 1850s, *not* produced by T. W. Dyott but probably by Benners, Smith & Campbell or H. B. & J. M. Benners. The eagle was not yet in flight, but taking off from a mound of earth with the shield presumably grasped by his talons; in his beak was a long wide pennant, which had not yet been blown out above and below him.

Finally, note should be made also of a small attractive group of the 1850s: GII–61 through GII–67. These were produced in the Connecticut glassworks at West Willington, Westford, and New London. On all there is an alert eagle, with small crest, shield on breast, perched on an oval wreath of laurel leaves. On the obverse of five, "LIBERTY" was inscribed in a shallow arc above the eagle's head; on two, an arc of stars appears above the eagle. Also, on the reverse of these two is an anchor with a pennant above inscribed "NEW LONDON" and one below with "GLASSWORKS". Attribution is certain because the name and location of the glassworks were inscribed on the reverse of each flask. The close similarity in design and treatment of the obverse of these flasks suggests that one moldmaker supplied the three glassworks with the molds, and likewise points to the appeal of the design to the glassworks' customers.

From all the eagle flasks in Group II in 1941, George S. McKearin chose eight for Group A and ten for Group B of the Most Desirable Flasks, and seven for Rare Flasks, Group C. (See 8. *Most Desirable Flasks*.) A few further comments regarding five of these seem called for here. It should be emphasized that the two canteenlike flasks, GII–76 and GII–77, which are 12 and 13 in Group A, and the lately discovered GII–76a were not flasks in the ordinary sense. Their very weight, form, and breadth precluded use as pocket bottles and suggests they functioned as decanters. For decades the flasks with the initial "NGCᴼ" have been attributed to the New England Glass Company, and it has been argued that the absence of an "E" following the "N" was due to the exigences of space. Although the belief that the unmarked GII–76 may have been a Keene-Marlboro-Street product cannot be completely discarded, to some students (including myself) it seems as probable, if not more likely, both unmarked were blown in the Boston area. The South Boston Flint

Glass Works and Thomas Cains's Phoenix Glass Works are strong probabilities.

Another rare eagle flask is GII–19 (22 in Group B). On the obverse is a large but undetailed eagle flying to left, bearing in its talons two flags; on the reverse is a bit of morning glory vine with full-blown flower and leaves. This flask is of interest not only because of its designs but because it has a counterpart in pottery with brown Rockingham glaze and also with tan glaze. Both the glass and pottery flasks are attributed to the Midwest and believed to have been first produced in the late 1840s or early 1850s. Though presumably one of the flags was intended to represent the Stars and Stripes, it is impossible to identify either one. Nor have I been able to associate this representation with any historical event as yet, but it is tempting to conjecture that allusion to the Mexican War and annexation of Texas may have been intended.

Another of the significant flasks is also of midwestern origin, attributed to an unknown glasshouse in the Pittsburgh–Monongahela district because of the form and design of the flask itself, especially the beaded edge. It is the pint GII–9 (29 in Group A), particularly noteworthy because of the design on the reverse, a flying eagle with serpent in its beak. For millennia, even before the recording of Eve's temptation, the serpent has been a symbol of evil and corruption. According to one 18th-century book on emblems, "A SERPENT concealed in the grass is an apt emblem of fraud and vice."[27] And in the same handy guide for political parties and other organizations, the role of the eagle with the serpent was represented in emblems. An eagle worrying a serpent on the ground or flying off with one in its beak was nothing new in symbolism to American politicians or citizens in the period of Figured Flasks — there can be little doubt that its use on this flask had political significance. Stephen Van Rensselaer, in 1926, first associated it with William Henry Harrison's 1840 presidential campaign, calling attention to the propaganda of the American Ticket,[28] in which — beneath the inscription "*The Eagle of Liberty* / Strangling the Serpent / of *CORRUPTION*" — a large and purposeful eagle, its powerful wings spread outward and downward, was perched on a cactus and held in its beak a large serpent with neck and fanged head curved up and over the eagle's head. Below the cactus was the inscription "True American Ticket / For President / WM. HENRY HARRISON." However, as is now known, the theme of the eagle wrestling with the serpent of corruption also characterized the 1836

presidential campaign, and was dramatized by political lithographic cartoons in which Harrison was the indispensable powerful American eagle. Harrison adherents campaigned with sufficient vigor, particularly in the Midwest, to bring him in second in that presidential race. But not only is there the campaign evidence pointing to 1836 as a fitting time for the flask (GII–9) but also the form and design of the flask itself and of the eagle on the obverse are those of flasks earlier than 1840. Although this does not preclude the possibility, even probability, of such a flask's being a bit of 1840 propaganda, it seems even more likely to me that it was of the 1836 campaign. However, perhaps to be on the properly cautious side, the flask should be dated 1836–40.

The last of the five flasks is another midwestern creation, and of the Civil War period: GII–140. It is 9 in Rare Flasks, Group C. There is nothing unusual about the eagle on the obverse; it is the familiar and not too well drawn flying eagle with shield, olive branch, thunderbolt, and streaming pennants. But on the reverse is a creature new in American life, a draftee. He is depicted as a small man with large head; in his long swallow-tailed coat and tight trousers he is similar to some of the prospectors on Pike's Peak flasks (Group XI). He carries a portmanteau in his left hand; his right arm with opened hand stretches out before him as he walks toward a Springfield rifle pointed at his midriff. From his lips issues an S-curved pennant inscribed "DRAFTED". This bit of Americana in glass can logically be dated as 1862/3. In the summer of 1862, when the Union Army was desperate for new troops, all the bounties offered to recruits, all the patriotic propaganda and resolutions, all the meetings to arouse war fervor, failed in their purpose. The needed recruits just did not volunteer. As a result, on August 4, Secretary of War Stanton announced that 300,000 militiamen would be drafted to serve nine months. Men of draft age at once hurried to file exemption claims, and thousands of others began an exodus to Canada and Europe. The government soon had to forbid eligible men to leave the country. A brisk business in buying substitutes also flourished. Everywhere the draft was sharply resented and doggedly resisted. On the day they were to leave for camp, the drafted men of Bucyrus, Ohio, "marched to the town square and gave three cheers for 'the Constitution as it is, and the Union as it was.'" The failure of the 1862 draft caused Congress to pass the Conscription Act, the first federal draft law, in March 1863, making every man from 20 to 45 subject to call. It was made no more palatable by the many conditions for exemption, the acceptance of substitutes, and the fact that a man could buy himself off for $300, which the government could use to buy a substitute! Opposition erupted from every part of the Union, erupted in violent riots, fighting as bitter as that between men on the battlefield.[29] Though the violence was quelled, opposition never was. The Draftee flask is a memento, a reminder, of an awful period in our history.

Comparatively few of the flasks in the Eagle Group have been positively identified with a particular glassworks or attributed to one on the basis of close similarity of design to an inscribed flask. The list of marked flasks given below is not chronological, but by number in the order in which they were charted. The dates given are those of the year or period in which I believe the flasks were first produced.

1. GII–10. Eagle, "W. IHMSEN"—Agriculture. Pint. 19 of Group B, Most Desirable Flasks. Attributed to William Ihmsen's Williamsport glassworks, Pittsburgh, Pa., late 1820s–early 1830s.

2. GII–15. Eagle, "F.L."—Cornucopia. Half-pint. 20 in Group B, Most Desirable Flasks. Attributed to Frederick Lorenz, probably the Pittsburgh Glass Works, 1820s–1830s.

3. GII–18. Eagle, "ZANESVILLE"—Cornucopia. Half-pint. Probably J. Shepard & Co., Zanesville Glass Works, Zanesville, O., ca. 1832–38.

4. GII–33. Eagle (medallion breaking vertical ribs)—"LOUISVILLE / KY / GLASS-WORKS" (medallion breaking vertical ribs). Half-pint. ca. 1855.

5. GII–34. Like GII–33. Pint. ca. 1855.

6. GII–35. Flying eagle, "LOUISVILLE KY / GLASS WORKS" (each in medallion breaking vertical ribbing)—vertical ribbing. Quart. ca. 1855–60.

7. GII–36. Like GII–35. Pint. ca. 1855–60.

8. GII–37. Eagle—Anchor, "RAVENNA / GLASS / COMPANY". Pint. Ravenna Glass Works, Ravenna, O. 1860s.

9. GII–38. Eagle (with pennant and shield, taking off from mound of earth)—"DYOTTVILLE GLASS WORKS (in arch) / PHILADA". Slightly over a pint. Benners, Smith & Campbell

or H. B. & J. M. Benners, Dyottville, Kensington, Philadelphia, Pa. ca. 1846–59.

10. GII–39. Like GII–38 but reverse plain and capacity slightly under a pint.

11. GII–42. Eagle, "T.W.D"—Frigate, "FRANK-LIN". Pint. Thomas W. Dyott, Kensington Glass Works, Kensington, Philadelphia, Pa. ca. 1822.

12. GII–43. Eagle, "T.W.D", and on edges "E. PLURIBUS UNUM / ONE OF MANY"—Cornucopia, and on edges, "KENSINGTON GLASS WORKS / PHILADELPHIA". Half-pint. 1824.

13. GII–61. Eagle and wreath, "LIBERTY"—"WILLINGTON / GLASS, Co / WEST WILLINGTON / CONN". Quart. Probably 1850s.

14. GII–62. Eagle and wreath, "LIBERTY"—"WILLINGTON / GLASS, Co / WEST, WILLINGTON / CONN". Pint.

15. GII–63. Eagle and Wreath, "LIBERTY"—"WILLINGTON / GLASS, Co / WEST WILLINGTON / CONN." Half-pint.

16. GII–64. Eagle and wreath, "LIBERTY"—"WILLINGTON / GLASS, Co / WEST WILLINGTON / CONN." Pint.

17. GII–65. Eagle and wreath, "LIBERTY"—"WESTFORD / GLASS / Co / WESTFORD / CONN". Half-pint. Probably 1850s.

18. GII–66. Eagle, stars, and wreath—Anchor and inscribed pennants, "NEW LONDON" "GLASSWORKS". Quart. New London, Conn. 1857–59 or –63.

19. GII–67. Eagle, stars, and wreath—Anchor and inscribed pennants, "NEW LONDON" "GLASS WORKS". Half-pint. 1857–59 or –63.

20. GII–68. Flying eagle below arc of stars—Anchor, inscribed pennants, "NEW LONDON" "GLASS WORKS". Pint. 1857–59 or –63.

21. GII–48. Eagle—American Flag, "COFFIN & HAY / HAMMONTON". Quart. Bodine Coffin and Andrew K. Kay, Hammonton, N. J. ca. 1836.

22. GII–49. Eagle—Stag, "COFFIN & HAY / HAMMONTON". Pint. ca. 1836.

23. GII–50. Like GII–49. Half-pint. ca. 1836.

24. GII–51. Like GII–49 but stag omitted on reverse. ca. 1836.

25. GII–80. Eagle, "GRANITE." "GLASS CO" —Eagle, "STODARD / N H". Quart. Granite Glass Works, Stoddard, N.H. 1846–60.

26. GII–81. Eagle, "GRANITE." "GLASS.CO" —Eagle, "STODDARD / N H". Pint. 1846–60.

27. GII–82. Eagle—Eagle, "STODDARD / N.H.". Pint. Probably Granite Glass Works, Stoddard, N.H. 1846–60.

28. GII–98. Eagle, "GEO. A BERRY & CO."— Eagle. Quart. Glassworks of Geo. A. Berry & Co., Belle Vernon, Pa. ca. 1853–65.

29. GII–98a. Like GII–98. Pint. ca. 1853–65.

30. GII–98b. Listed by Van Rensselaer; presumably like GII–98a but half-pint size. Flask never seen by me.

31. GII–110. Eagle, "CUNNINGHAM & CO / PITTSBURGH"—Eagle, "GLASS / MANUFACTURERS". Quart. Mid–1870s(?).

32. GII–111. Similar to GII–110, same inscription. Pint. ca. 1853–65.

33. GII–112. Similar to GII–110, same inscription. Pint. ca. 1853–65.

34. GII–114. Eagle, "LOUISVILLE / KY"— Eagle, "GLASS / WORKS". Quart. Probably 1860s.

35. GII–115. Similar to GII–114, same inscription. Pint. Probably 1860s.

36. GII–127. Eagle, "C & I"—Eagle. Half-pint. Attributed to Cunningham & Ihmsen, Pittsburgh, Pa. ca. 1857–67.

37. GII–129. Eagle, "ZANESVILLE / OHIO"— Eagle. Pint. Probably Zanesville Glass Works, Market Street, operated by G. W. Kearns & Co. ca. 1860.

38. GII–142. Flying Eagle above monument, "CONTINENTIAL" [sic]—Indian shooting at bird, "CUNNINGHAMS & CO. / PITTSBURGH. PA." Quart. Glassworks of Cunninghams & Co., Pittsburgh, Pa. Mid –1870s(?).

THE NATIONAL FLAG OF THE UNITED STATES

People and their armies need a banner, a flag under which to rally and fight, and although the Americans had flags, they did not have an embracing national flag until June of 1777, when the Continental Congress adopted the Stars and Stripes.[30] Though the exact origin of the design is still a moot question, for generations nearly every American has been told— and has remembered from childhood—that Betsy Ross of Philadelphia made the first flag with 13 stripes and 13 stars on a blue field. Moreover, according to the traditional account, she made it for George Washington from his own design, which doubtless was inspired by the stars and stripes on the shield of his family's coat of arms. Whatever the facts may be, it was not until April 1818 that Congress limited the number of stripes to thirteen and decreed that there should be a star for each state in the Union.[31] Though the history of their flag doubtless interested Americans, it did not move and thrill so many as apparently did Draker's enduring poetic

When freedom from her mountain height
Unfurl'd her standards to the air
She tore the azure robe of night
And set the stars of glory there.

She mingled with it gorgeous dyes
The milky baldric of the skies,
And striped its pure celestial white
With streakings of the morning light.

Then from his mansion in the sun,
She called her eagle bearer down
And gave into his mighty hand
The symbol of her chosen land.[32]

★ ★ ★

Great as was its appeal as "our flag," an outward and visible sign of a deep patriotism, the Stars and Stripes was not so widely and generally employed as a decorative motif as was the American eagle. Perhaps, in part, this was because, from the point of view of decoration only, its simple geometry and its dependence on color did not recommend its use in many media or in the arts and crafts today known as the decorative arts. In any event, the American flag was used as a motif on few of our Figured Flasks.

As the only motif, the flag was chosen for one side of seven of the charted flasks. Only four of these were produced prior to 1850: GII–48 and GII–52, 53, and 54, charted in Group II, with a spirited American eagle as obverse and the American flag as reverse. On each the flag is depicted billowing gracefully in a swirl around its pole. On the quart GII–48, it is accompanied by the identifying inscription "COFFIN & HAY / HAMMONTON". The American eagle on the obverse is quite similar to the one on Dyott's Washington–Eagle and Lafayette–Eagle flasks, thus suggesting that the molds for all of them may have come from the same moldmaker, doubtless located in Philadelphia. This Coffin & Hay flask is believed to have been produced first ca. 1836 to 1838, the years Bodine Coffin and Andrew Hay operated the Hammonton, New Jersey, glassworks. On the other three flasks, the American flag was accompanied appropriately by the inscribed sentiment "FOR OUR COUNTRY". As the line drawings in the Charts show, each has a different version of the eagle with shield and semiwreath of laurel leaves. Nevertheless, because the flag on all three is in the same style as that on the Coffin & Hay quart, these pint flasks have always been considered products of the Hammonton glassworks. Today, however, it seems preferable to say "attributed to," though perhaps there really is little doubt as to origin and certainly none as to all four being produced in the same period. The three remaining flasks having the flag alone on one side—the half-pint GX–28 and pints GX–27 and GX–29—were brought out after the Civil War. Each is inscribed on the reverse with the glassworks' name and location: NEW GRANITE GLASS WORKS / STODDARD / N.H." (a factory established at Mill Village, Stoddard, in 1865 and operating into 1871).

The American flag was also used as part of a design on one side of at least eight flasks in designs brought out between 1840 and 1875. The earliest, and now rarest, was the Hard Cider flask, GX–22, on the reverse of which the American flag waves between an arc of stars and the inscription "HARD CIDER"; the latter appears above a barrel for that beverage of the poor man. The flagpole rises between the handles of the North Bend Farmer's plow at left front of the barrel. The flask, of course, was one of the innumerable propaganda items of the Harrison–Tyler forces in the 1840 presidential campaign—of which more later, in connection with the Harrison portrait flask. In point of time the flag was next used about 1851 on the Louis Kossuth–Frigate *Mississippi* calabash bottle. The portrait bust of the Hungarian patriot rises between crossed flags—the American flag at Kossuth's right and an unidentifiable one at his left. On the charted flasks the flag did not occur again as a design element until the end of the Civil War period. In Group XII, Shield and Clasped Hands flasks, on the reverse of five (GXII–38 through GXII–40) are a cannon and an American flag, the pole of which rises

from a pyramid of cannonballs. Of these flasks one, GXII–40, produced by "F.A.& Co"—presumably Fahnstock, Albree Company, Pittsburgh, Pennsylvania—in the 1860s, has a large flag with 13 stars. The other four, products of Wm. Frank & Sons, Frankstown, Pittsburgh, have smaller flags with fewer stars.

The last of the charted flasks having the flag as an important design motif was brought out by Cunningham & Company, also of Pittsburgh, presumably about 1875. On the reverse of this flask, GII–142, is an elaborate design and the inscribed word "CONTINENTIAL"—apparently *continental* misspelled—which has not as yet been satisfactorily interpreted. Besides the small American flag and small American eagle symbolizing the United States, there are a small ship and two sheaves of grain to represent her commerce and the agricultural products vital to her health and economy; on the obverse the Shield and Clasped Hands stands for the Union of the States. All of which leads at present only to speculation. Was the design symbolic of a country and its economy that was "continental" in scope, stretching from the shore of the Atlantic to the shore of the Pacific? Could the flask have been an 1876 Centennial item celebrating the geographical and economic expansion the country had attained in one hundred years?

FREEDOM'S STAR

In the minds of most Americans, stars are associated with the United States as naturally as is the American bald eagle. It is an association cemented by nearly 200 years of graphic symbolism and patriotic oratory, poetry, and song. But, in the main, the association is less with the whole country than with its parts—13 stars for the 13 original states; the flag's blue field of stars, of which, since 1818, there has been one for each of the states. For most Americans today, possibly since the Mexican War over a century ago, the association of a single large star has been with Texas, the "Lone Star State." Yet it would seem that from the early 19th century a single large star conveyed the concept of the "American Star," or "Freedom's Star," as one of our early patriotic songs was titled. And it is significant to note that one side of the United States silver 3-cent pieces minted from 1851 through 1872 bore a large six-pointed star with a small shield at its center, and the star was encircled by the legend "UNITED STATES OF AMERICA" and the date.[33]

In the decoration of Figured Flasks, small to tiny stars were often an element in the designs on the early eagle flasks and on the eagle-reverses of many portrait flasks, including all the Columbia; they were symbolic of the States of the Union. Though, as mentioned in connection with the American eagle, the stars often were 13 in number, as on the Great Seal of the United States, the number did vary usually from 6 to 14, depending upon the exigencies of space and design. However, on flask GII–47, only three rather large stars were placed above the handsome boldly drawn bird. These particular stars were given four points, whereas stars usually had either five or six points. In most instances the stars, emphasizing the historical significance though a secondary element of the overall design, formed an arc or arch above the main motif. For example, the 11 stars on the Lafayette flask GI–85 and 9 on GI–86 were graduated and arched over a frame enclosing the French Liberty Cap. As examination of the line drawings in the Charts shows, there were also a few other arrangements of stars—in double arcs as on GI–22, in pyramids as on GI–55, or on a pennant as on GII–26, where, incidentally, they are four-pointed. It will be noted also that on all the Shield and Clasped Hands flasks, Group XII, stars, usually 13 in number, were placed above the shield—11 in an arc and two, detached from their fellows, placed one at each end of the shield.

A single star was used as the sole motif on one side of 12 charted flasks, the first of which, I believe, appeared in the mid-1840s and the last possibly as late as the 1890s. Three of the stars were modest in size and rather high in relief. This type was used on the reverse of the quart, pint, and half-pint flasks, GXIII–38 through 40, having a sheaf of grain and crossed rake and pitchfork on the obverse and probably brought out in the 1850s. On the quart sheaf-of-grain flasks GXIII–44 and GXIII–45, an eight-pointed star was used. A flat star in low relief ornamented the obverse of flask GXIII–83, which was inscribed "RAVENNA GLASS WORKS" on the reverse. This is the only one of the "star" flasks definitely attributable to a specific glassworks; it probably was first made about 1857–69. On the obverse of GXIII–82 through 82c, skeletal stars were described by a fine outlining rib and were larger than the stars in relief. Whether or not the stars on these flasks in Group XIII were chosen as a patriotic symbol or merely an attractive decorative motif, I do not know; my guess would be that the intention was ornamentation.

On the other hand, there certainly was historical significance, probably both patriotic (depending upon one's point of view) and political, in the presence of the large star on the pint flask GX–10 and half-pint GX–11 with "LIBERTY" inscribed on the obverse above a large sheaf of grain. The star is different from any of the others recorded—larger, its five points outlined by fine twin ribs, and with a ringed dot at its center. Though possibly a few months or years younger, the flask itself is the same in form and treatment as the Dyottville-type Washington–Taylors, such as GI–37, which were first produced in 1847 or possibly early in 1848, and also like the Corn-for-the-World—Washington-Monument flasks blown at the Baltimore Glass Works, probably in the mid-1840s. This similarity places the Star–Sheaf-of-grain flasks in the same general period. Van Rensselaer attributed the half-pint, which he listed as GVI–82, to Dyottville; others, including George S. McKearin, believed both flasks were probably blown at the Baltimore Glass Works. It seems safe to say they undoubtedly were produced in a glassworks in the Baltimore–Philadelphia–South Jersey area.

Though the designer may have had in mind Freedom's Star, he may have intended a far more immediate and political significance—namely, the Texas situation, which had been agitating the country for some years. In the emotion-charged debate about Texas and Mexico, President Tyler was "the champion of the Annexation of Texas." Therefore, in 1844, his nomination for reelection was important to, and sought by, politicians and citizens eager for the "Reannexation of Texas," as they euphemistically labeled their expansionistic plans. In more than one city and town, "Texas meetings" were held at which a flag with the legend "Tyler & Texas" was hung near the presiding officer's chair. When the 1844 party convention was in session, a "Tyler & Texas" body of delegates met separately "for the sole purpose of nominating John Tyler," and "each wore on his coat a large gilt button adorned with a single star . . ."[34] It seems to me probable that the star on the two flasks represents the Lone Star of Texas. It may be that the flask was brought out in 1844 in response to "Tyler & Texas," and if not then, within the next two years, if my conclusions as to its meaning are correct.

COLUMBIA AND LIBERTY

What could be more fitting than that England's 13 colonies along the Atlantic seaboard should be given a feminine form of the name of America's discoverer? It may have happened when realization of a common cause and danger forged the first weak link in a chain of union during the French and Indian War. Perhaps inspired by the failure at Fort Duquesne and the death of Braddock, a long patriotic poem appeared in 1755. Among the lines were

And British *ARMS, our recent Loss repair:*
With Patriot Warmth, avenge thy Monarch's Name:
. . . .
And we no more, enlarge the Galic *Pride:*
May Science joy, beneath thy ruling Powers,
And Commerce flourish, on Columba's *Shore.*

Though perhaps occasionally used by versifiers in the ensuing years, *Columba* did not become a popular name for the group of colonies: they had, after all, no sense of oneness. However, during the early years of the Revolution it must have become familiar to many theatergoers and the readers of some newspapers, and Timothy Dwight of Connecticut may well have been among them. For instance, one writer, the creator of a new epilogue to the drama *Cato,* proclaimed Washington as "Thy scourge, O Britain! and Columba's boast!" Another, whose poem was published in Boston's *Continental Journal* in 1777, described Howe's men as "Appal'd [to] view Columba's Sons."[35] Later in the same year, Timothy Dwight coined the more euphonious *Columbia*; otherwise *Columba* might have been adopted throughout the country. It was while chaplain of a brigade of Connecticut volunteers that Dwight christened the United States *Columbia* in an exuberant song that is said to have become an inspiration to the troops of Washington's army and is believed to have been circulated among the soldiers in broadside form.[36] As Columbia was used more and more often in patriotic song and verse, toast and oration, it was accepted by the citizenry. Shortly after, if not by, the turn of the century, everyone north and south, east and west, was familiar with the newborn country's name and before long with its personification.

That Columbia should eventually become identified with Liberty and her personification as the Goddess of Liberty seems inevitable. Inevitably, too, there were to be variations in the representations of the Goddess of Liberty. The earliest, which probably stemmed from that of Britannia, occurred at least once before the Revolution. About 1774 one of our early cartoons was inspired by the colonists' reaction to the drama created by England's tea tax, the roles of the East India Company, loyalist merchants and citizens, and the Sons of Liberty. It was entitled "LIBERTY TRIUMPHANT: or the Downfall of OPPRESSION." In its upper-left corner "*Britannia*" was depicted in contemporary dress, seated with the British shield at her right side and a spear held by her right hand. In the upper-right corner was a closely similar figure, "*The Goddess of Liberty addressing herself to Fame and pointing to her Sons* [of Liberty]" garbed as Indians.

The British shield was at the left side of this figure, and the spear was replaced at her right by a pole topped with a "sugar loaf" Liberty Cap. After 1796 probably the most widely known Liberty was the engraving from the painting by Edward Savage, "*Liberty in the form of the Goddess of Youth; giving support to the Bald Eagle.*" The goddess Hebe was, of course, in classical robe, and among the details in Savage's picture were the American flag and the Liberty Cap.[37]

Henceforth, whatever the other features and details might be, the most familiar Liberty was a young lady with long wavy hair, standing erect, wearing a classical robe and sometimes the Liberty Cap also, but usually she held in one hand a staff at the end of which was a Liberty Cap, her distinguishing insignia. This was a Phrygian cap or Roman pilleus, close fitting and soft in "the form of a sugar loaf, broad at the bottom and ending in a cone." It became "the badge of freedom" among the Romans, who gave it—along with permission to wear it in public—to a slave when he was made a free man.[38] When the French Revolutionaries adopted it as their "badge of freedom," it assumed even more poignant significance for many Americans, especially the Republicans, "Jacobites," as the Federalists called them. It is probable that in America of the 1790s and early 1800s it was thought of as the French Liberty Cap. And it is not surprising that many American representations of Liberty were very close to the French, but then the United States *was* Liberty and Frenchmen had helped to make her so.

Other early depictions, which were perhaps the first to reach most Americans, appeared on the coinage of the United States. Only the head or bust of Liberty was shown from 1793 to about 1837. The earliest of these coins were the 1793 half-cent and large cent, copper coins on which the Liberty Cap was at the end of a short staff behind the goddess's head. From 1796 through 1807, the bust of Liberty wearing a large Liberty Cap appeared on the obverse of quarter eagles and eagles (our $2.50 and $5.00 gold pieces), though on lesser coins the cap disappeared after 1797 and was replaced on some by a band with "LIBERTY" inscribed on it. From 1807 to the end of the 1830s a seemingly more mature Liberty appeared wearing a *round* cap, as numismatists call the closer fitting cap with soft folds; this had "LIBERTY" inscribed on a band. Inasmuch as this version was used on all copper, silver (except the dollar), and gold coins of current denominations, it was doubtless the one most familiar to people everywhere in the country. It is not unlikely that some of these coins served as models for flask designers and moldmakers, for the caps worn by the Columbias on Historical Flasks are closely similar to the *round* caps of these coins.[39]

Profile busts of Columbia, each differing from the others somewhat in the delineation of features and details, graced six Historical Flasks, GI–117 through 122. Though no inscription identified this personification, certainly no American of the period needed to be told that the Grecian lady wearing a Liberty Cap symbolized his "America destined by Heaven to be the seat of Happiness and Freedom." On the reverse of each flask was a handsome, strong American eagle worthy of her trust, and as examination of the line drawings in the charts will show, though of the same type, each differed from the others in rendering. It will be noted also that the form for the four Columbia flasks GI–117 through 120 was different from that of other charted flasks, whereas GI–121 and 122 were closely similar in shape to Form 12 but fatter, having more depth from obverse to reverse. Not long ago Kenneth M. Wilson determined, by comparison and measurements of the Columbia flasks GI–117 and GI–119, that the mold for GI–117 had been altered by chiseling metal away from each curved panel to a depth nearly sufficient to eliminate "KENSINGTON" from the obverse and "UNION" from the reverse, so that the mold produced GI–119. Traces of the letters remain but are difficult to detect—for instance, the lower end of the "K."

None of these flasks can be classified as common even today. The very rare GI–118—the Columbia with the roundest of the caps and inscribed "UNION Co." "KENSINGTON"—and the extremely rare GI–122 were among the flasks chosen by George S. McKearin for Group B of the Most Desirable Flasks (39 and 40); the extremely rare GI–119 and 120 were chosen for Group A (33 and 34). Though flask GI–117, with the same inscriptions as GI–118, and flask GI–121 were classified as comparatively scarce, they are extremely rare in some colors—for instance, GI–117 in sapphire-blue and GI–121 in deep sapphire (reported by Sam Laidacker) and peacock-blue. In the latter color, only two flasks, each with a rolled-over collar, have been recorded as yet. One is imperfect; the other, which disappeared mysteriously from the George S. McKearin Collection in 1961, is perfect—or was when last seen by me.

Little is known of the exact origins of these six flasks. So far the initials "B & W" on the reverse of GI–121 have not been identified. Nor have the "ASHTON" on the obverse and "HOUGH" on the reverse of GI–120. On GI–117 and 118, because Columbia seemed the more distinguishing motif, the side with her bust and inscribed "KENSINGTON" was chosen as the obverse and the eagle side with "UNION Co." as the reverse. Thus the inscription as customarily read from obverse to reverse became *Kensington Union Co.* and was so recorded under GLASS HOUSE in the original charts of 1941. But, as has been mentioned elsewhere, I know of no works having that title or even so called. I believe that the correct reading should be *Union Glass Co., Kensington,* and that the glassworks may have been located at Kensington, Philadelphia, Pennsylvania. The question then arises as to which of the Union Glass Companies operated the works in which the flasks were produced, and when. The physical characteristics and conception of the motifs seem too early for 1847, when Kensington's first Union Glass Works was revived by Hartell & Lancaster, primarily for the production of bottles and flasks. However, although I have no evidence that Figured Flasks were made in the works during the period from 1826 into 1844, when that Union Glass Company was an important producer of fine flint glassware, it seems not unlikely some Figured Flasks may have been blown, especially since more than a few flint-glass manufacturers used lead metal for such flasks and even added green-glass wares to their products. It should be added that exhaustive research into the history and output of this glassworks, an outstanding one of its period, has not been made as yet.

We turn again now to the representation of Liberty or Columbia, and to the last of the flasks to be considered under this heading. Besides the early version of a seated Liberty in the cartoon mentioned above, there was another later but still 18th-century portrait presenting her as a seated Grecian or Roman lady, and probably suggested by the emblematic Britannia on English coins that would have been circulated in America from the colonial period into the 19th century. Moreover, 1785 English-made patterns for United States gold, silver, and copper coins had the seated classical figure holding scales in her left hand and a staff with a Liberty Cap at the end in her right, and bore the inscription "IMMUNE COLUMBIA". Similar but less elaborate depictions occurred on one-cent copper coins of several states before 1788. Among them were New Jersey's large one-cent piece of 1786, which was very closely similar to the English pattern, including the inscription, and New York's 1787 large cent inscribed "LIBERTY". In United States coinage the seated Liberty or Columbia appeared first on silver dollars of 1836.[40] Still other related versions were used in other media. Hence there was ample precedent for the pose and regalia of the symbolical female figure (not perhaps for her costume) on the obverse of the extremely rare Liberty flask GX–23. If there were any doubt as to her identity, the designer dispelled it by the sunrays from her odd headdress to a band with "LIBERTY" inscribed. Where this flask originated has not been determined. Nor has its period been learned, though the use of the Log Cabin and "LIBERTY" on the reverse suggest the 1840 Harrison presidential campaign.

B. Heroes and Celebrities

No flasks in the historical category capture one's interest more quickly than the portrait flasks in Group I, or exert more fascination, if only because of the novelty of embellishing common liquor flasks with the names and features of a nation's statesmen, heroes, and famous persons. Between about 1824 and 1936, mainly in the first 30 years of the long span, at least 21 individuals—20 men and one woman— were portrayed in the flask and bottle Hall of Fame. Of these, the profile bust on GI–115 has still to be identified, and a few others still fall in the realm of possibility or probability. The majority have been identified with certainty by an inscription, soubriquet, or likeness to a bust so labeled. Few, as I have said previously, could be identified definitely from the actual bust. Approximately half these flasks were brought out during presidential campaigns, presenting a favored candidate to the drinking public. The others memorialized heroes and notables famous from one end of the country to the other. They were not all Americans: five were foreigners—four, if one thinks of Lafayette as an adopted son of the United States, as most Americans did.

GEORGE WASHINGTON

If distinguished Americans were to be immortalized by a common glass container made primarily for hard liquor, George Washington, commander in chief of the Revolutionary Armies liberating the new nation from the old and first president of that new nation, was an inevitable choice. Washington himself probably would not have felt honored but would have considered the presumption a vulgar shaft wounding his dignity. Nor is it likely he would have been flattered by the coupling of his portrait bust with that of Andrew Jackson, suc-

cessful military hero or not. It is also unlikely that he would have been pleased by the implication of equality as presidential timber between himself, a patrician, and this republican champion of the common man, as undoubtedly was the propaganda intent in the Keene-Marlboro-Street and Coventry flasks. Be that as it may, the portrait bust of Washington has been recorded on 72 charted flasks. His likeness has been found on more flasks than that of any other personage and, by the 1820s, it was one appealing to nearly every American regardless of political party. Few remembered the old charge against him of monarchistic tendencies, one of many fostered by the Republicans. Two quite different aspects of Washington were emphasized: Washington the soldier on early flasks and one calabash of about 1850; Washington the statesman on the flasks and one calabash after about 1840, excepting perhaps GI–21.

On 32 flasks first offered for sale before 1840 Washington was depicted in uniform, thus commemorating his services to his country as a soldier—*Great Washington* whose warrior's breast was fired by Fair Freedom when "His bleeding country rous'd his soul."[41] Of these flasks, 14, all of pint size, were produced in midwestern glasshouses that probably were located in the Pittsburgh–Monongahela district. As yet these, believed to have been first made before 1830, are the only known midwestern flasks portraying Washington. The busts presented a three-quarter view, and as the line drawings show, each one differed from the others— doubtless an indication that no one portrait of Washington served as the model. Quite appropriately the American eagle was chosen as the motif for the other side of the flask. And, although the vigorous vital eagles had a general resemblance, each differed from the others in treatment and details, as the busts did. Nevertheless, it is thought that the molds, at least for the flasks with beaded edge, were the work of one moldmaker, Joshua Laird of Pittsburgh, who cut "LAIRD. SC.PITT." in his molds for the "J.R." Washingtons GI–6 and 6a. Inscription gave identity to all but two of the busts: "GENERAL WASHINGTON" on seven; simply "WASHINGTON" on one; more individual and intimate inscriptions on four other flasks, and only on these midwestern varieties—namely, "G.GEO' WASHINGTON" on the "F.L" flask GI–7; "G.G.WASHINGTON" on the "F.L." flask GI–8 and the unmarked GI–9; "G.WASHINGTON" on the unmarked GI–10. The last was perhaps the most common of Washington's signatures on military orders and reports as president, at least as they were printed in the newspapers, and it also appeared on internal revenue stamps. None of these flasks is common, and at present I know of only two complete sets of the 13 originally charted: one in the collection of The Corning Museum of Glass and the other in a private collection.

Flasks depicting Washington the soldier were produced in eastern glassworks also in the 1820s and 1830s; they included two varieties in half-pint size. On five New England flasks, five Baltimore (Maryland), and one Bridgeton (New Jersey), the bust was drawn in profile, and above it on all but one was the inscription "WASHINGTON" in a deep arc. On the reverse of the New England flasks "JACKSON" appears above a profile bust of Andrew Jackson in uniform. Fragments excavated on the factory sites by Harry Hall White furnished the basis for unqualified attribution of the pint GI–31 to the Keene-Marlboro-Street glassworks, Keene, New Hampshire, and of the pint GI–33 and half-pint GI–34 to the Coventry Glass Works, Coventry, Connecticut.[42] The rare pint GI–34a, unknown until 1965, when it was reported to me by Neil D. Sayles, has been attributed to Coventry on the basis of its close similarity to the half-pint GI–34. It will be noted that Washington faces right instead of left on these two. On the Baltimore pint flasks, only one bust was not identified by an inscription—namely, that on GI–20, on which "FELLS" was inscribed above Washington's bust and "POINT" below it on the obverse. On the reverse, the Washington Monument was depicted as it stood before the statue of George Washington was placed at its tip in 1829. No motif could have been a more appropriate one on a Washington flask produced in a Baltimore glassworks than this first monument to his memory. For many years this flask has been attributed to the Baltimore Glass Works, but today I believe there is a possibility that it was first produced in the Baltimore Flint Glass Works at Fells Point. "BALTIMORE GLASS WORKS" was inscribed on the other four flasks, GI–17 through 19. Though the bust on GI–17 and 17a and that on GI–18 and 19 are quite dissimilar, the intended portrayal of Washington was proclaimed by the inscription "WASHINGTON". Baltimore's Battle Monument was chosen for the reverse of GI–18 and 19; an unlabeled profile bust of a military man for that of GI–17 and 17a. A similar bust was portrayed on the reverse of the marked Bridgeton flask GI–24, but the bust of Washington below the inscription "WASHINGTON" on the obverse is quite unlike any of the Baltimore versions. For 40 or 50 years the unlabeled military hero has

been recorded as General Zachary Taylor, though quite unlike the other Taylor flask portraits in features and uniform—of which more later.

The remaining eastern flasks in the "soldier group" had a three-quarter bust, as did the midwestern. Two of them, the pint GI–28 and half-pint GI–30, are one of the unsolved puzzles in the history of Figured Flasks. It seems to me that, though described as "Washington" in uniform, the gentleman is in mufti and may not have been intended to represent Washington. The inscription on each established its origin as the Albany Glass Works, Albany, New York. Though a few bits of evidence indicate operation from about 1847 to 1850 or 1851, the history of this 19th-century works is still nebulous. On the other hand, the pint GI–14 was located as to maker and glassworks by the initials "T.W.D" and inscription "KENSINGTON GLASS WORKS PHILADELPHIA" (edge of reverse). The pint GI–16 was identified by the initials "T.W.D"; the as-yet unique specimen GI–16a (1 in Ill. 124) was attributed by analogy from its close resemblance to GI–16. On these Kensington Glass Works flasks brought out by Thomas W. Dyott, the inscription "GENERAL WASHINGTON" was arched above the bust, and a proud American eagle was placed on the reverse, as on the midwestern Washingtons. In fact, the rather close kinship in type and rendering between the midwestern flasks and those of Dyott arouses speculation as to whether Dyott's may have inspired the others. Possibly Jacob Slough (see Ill. 9A) transported Figured Flasks to Pittsburgh as well as demijohns of medicines and carboys of chemicals. In any event, perhaps in the fall of 1823 or spring of 1824, certainly by fall of 1824 (see Ill. 119), Dyott had added portraits to his line of Figured Flasks, the Washington GI–16 among them. In October 1824, he advertised "Washington, La Fayette, Franklin, Ship Franklin, Agricultural and Masonic, Cornucopia, American eagle and common ribbed Pocket Flasks" among the products of the "Philadelphia and Kensington Vial and Bottle Factories."[43] In March of the following spring he listed "Washington and Eagle Pint Flasks"—*3,000 dozen* of them. (See Ill. 117.)

Dyott's Washington charted as GI–14 demands special attention: for many collectors it is the most interesting of all Washington flasks and in some respects the most historically significant. It commemorated a historic event of 1826. In that year, on the Fourth of July, death came to two of America's greatest sons and patriots—John Adams, the second president of the United States, and Thomas Jefferson, the third. It was also the 50th anniversary of the adoption of the Declaration of Independence by the Continental Congress. These two men—Jefferson, who wrote the Declaration, and Adams, who, as Jefferson said, "was the colossus of the stirring debate" leading a reluctant Congress to vote its adoption by a majority of only one—eventually formed a friendship that endured until they died, in spite of their leadership of bitterly opposing political parties and ideologies, the Federalist and the Republican. The coincidence of their dying within a few hours of each other on the same day and, of all days, the golden anniversary of the adoption of the Declaration that was the very foundation of American democracy, was a singularly moving occurrence, stirring the hearts and imaginations of all Americans whatever their political credos. It was no seven-day wonder: a year later at a public dinner, one of the toasts was to "John Adams and Thomas Jefferson—Embalmed in the hearts of 12,000,000 freemen—the temple erected to their memories will be more glorious than the pyramids, and as eternal as their own imperishable virtues." Thomas W. Dyott was quick to signalize the event by taking the mold for his Washington–Eagle flask (charted as GI–16) and having "E PLURIBUS UNUM" cut above the sunrays radiating from the eagle's head and, on the edge of the obverse, the inscription "ADAMS & JEFFERSON JULY 4 A.D. 1776". At the same time "KENSINGTON GLASS WORKS PHILADELPHIA" was cut in the edge of the reverse. As close examination revealed, all details of the two flasks GI–16 and GI–14 appeared to be identical except for the additional inscriptions. Moreover, the letters of E. Pluribus Unum that were to be on the commemorative flasks were superimposed on the tips of the sunrays above the eagle in the original mold. This flask must have been a very popular item, for it is common today except in some colors—for example, deep sapphire-blue, of which only three or four specimens have been recorded.

The statesmanlike classical bust of Washington as "The Father of His Country" appeared about 1850 on one calabash bottle with tree in leaf and, mainly after 1840, on flasks, with the probable exception of GI–21, 22, 23, and 25. The flasks were of three designs: one, as shown by GI–21, having a heavy rib at the mold seam on each end, the designs on a large oval panel framed by a heavy rib, was recorded in quart size only; the second, the Dyottville-type shown by GI–37, had ends tapering less toward the base than on GI–21, plain edges, and designs on unframed oval panels; the third was similar to the Dyott type but without panel and thicker through.

On the first type, GI–21, "FELLS" was inscribed above and "POINT" below the bust of Washington, and on the obverse, "BALT^O" below the Washington Monument in its unfinished state. Since the statue of Washington was not placed atop the shaft until the fall of 1829, this flask doubtless was first produced prior to that event. Two others, GI–22 and 23, were inscribed "BALTIMORE GLASS WORKS" (the double "S" of glass was reversed on GI–22), and each has on one side a classical profile bust now believed to represent Henry Clay. Their shape is so similar to the Fells Point quart that it seems most probable they were first produced about the same time, possibly early in 1832 and to celebrate Washington's centennial and Henry Clay's presidential nomination by the National Republican Party at its Baltimore convention, December 1831. Also similar is the quart Washington–"Clay" GI–25, having "BRIDGETOWNNEWJERSEY" (*sic*) in deep arch over each bust, but since the factory dates from 1836 or 1837, it could not have been blown earlier and perhaps it was not blown until the time of the 1842 presidential campaign. Stars and a large American eagle were on the reverse of GI–26, its three variants, and 27. These have no identifying inscription and are believed to have been produced in either the Baltimore Glass Works or the Bridgeton Glass Works, or some in each works. Only two flasks, the quarts GI–60 and 61, have been recorded in this third design, that without panel on the sides. One had the classical bust of Washington on each side and "LOCKPORT GLASS WORKS" in an arch over the bust on the obverse; the other, attributed to Lockport, had no inscription and one undecorated side.

The largest group, 28 in all, was that of the Dyottville, or rather Dyottville-type, flasks made in quart, pint, and half-pint sizes: GI–37 through GI–59 in the Charts. The reverse was plain on GI–47 and GI–48. A sheaf of grain was depicted on the reverse of GI–59, and a different type of sheaf with crossed rake and fork on GI–57 and GI–58. The sheaf on GI–59 was similar to that on Pictorial Flask GXIII–48 of the Baltimore Glass Works; the sheaf, rake, and fork on GI–57 and GI–58 to those on Pictorial Flask GXIII–34 produced by the Mechanic Glass Works, Philadelphia, and also to those on the half-pint flask GXIII–49 and the calabash bottle GXIII–52, both products of the Baltimore Glass Works. The remaining 23 Dyottville-type Washington flasks had the profile bust of General Zachary Taylor in uniform on the reverse. Two of these, the quart GI–37 and pint GI–38, were inscribed "DYOTTVILLE GLASS WORKS PHILA.A". Although these were the only two in the entire Dyottville-type series that were identified with Dyottville by inscription, no one doubts that several of the others may have been Dyottville products. Since GI–37 and GI–38 had Taylor's famous "General Taylor Never Surrenders" inscribed, it seems probable that Dyottville produced the flasks inscribed with two other Taylorisms: "A Little More Grape Captain Bragg" and "I Have Endeavored To Do My Duty". Among the Washington-Taylor quarts made at, or attributed to, Dyottville, some GI–42 flasks, and possibly GI–37, 39, and 43 also, were wickered, and those destined to be so covered were given a longer neck than others. One of these flasks with wicker jacket and twisted handle is 3 in Ill. 79.

Use of the term "Dyotteville-type" today instead of attributing *all* GI–37 through GI–59 flasks definitely to the Dyottville Glass Works, as has been done heretofore, was suggested by the fact that only two of the entire group were inscribed with the Dyottville name. In addition, popular as these Washington–Taylors undoubtedly were, even many years after the first one appeared in 1847 or 1848, it seems unlikely that so many quart, pint, and half-pint molds would have been needed by a single works to meet its demand. And Sam Laidacker has found reasons to believe the Lockport Glass Works made GI–47 and GI–48 (which have "THE FATHER OF HIS COUNTRY" arching over the bust of Washington and have a plain reverse) and also the Washington–Taylor GI–51 without any inscription. In New Jersey, J. E. Pfeiffer has unearthed evidence suggesting that at least some of the flasks were blown in the Crowleytown glassworks, which was established in 1851. He found fragments of GI–52 in citron and GI–55 in green, both matching colors, and apparently metal also, of other types of bottles produced in the glassworks. Moreover, it is not unlikely that some were produced in other South Jersey glassworks, or in a Philadelphia works other than Dyottville, or in one of the Baltimore glassworks. None of these flasks, it will be remembered, was produced by Dyott. His connection, and that of his brother Michael, with glassmaking and Dyottville had been severed several years before any of the flasks was brought out in 1847 or 1848 by Benners, Smith & Campbell, then owners of the Dyottville Glass Works.

Of the many titles given to George Washington and soubriquets by which he was called—the American Fabius, the Cincinnatus of the West, the Farmer President, among them[44]—"The Father of His Country" was the only one to appear on whiskey flasks, and only on the Dyottville-type. In part, it doubtless was chosen because "The Father of His Country" was the most familiar to the most people in the mid-19th century, as it is to Americans today. One wonders why this title was not used, nor his statesmanship symbolized, on the earlier flasks. It would seem that the earliest known expression of the sentiment in this title was in 1779, in a Pennsylvania-German almanac, as "Des Landes Vater."[45] A decade later, when Washington was inaugurated our first president on April 30, 1789, he was called The Father of His Country in a few newspaper accounts of "This great occasion which arrested the public attention beyond the power of description. . . ." But the ode sung at many inaugural celebrations, in later years as well, was the "Ode to Columbia's Favorite Son." Another decade later, "The Father of His Country" was more widely used, this time in funeral eulogies, odes, and editorials delivered and written from the time of his death in December 1799 into the early months of 1800. In 1814, for many Baltimoreans and other Marylanders he was the Father of His Country, for a monument was planned to commemorate Washington "The Father of His Country" and a lottery conducted and widely advertised to raise part of the necessary funds.[46]

Still, the emphasis was primarily on his military stature and services, and continued to be well into the 1800s. Even to fellow Masons, apparently he was first of all the *General* and the *Chief*. Whether he was a greater general or statesman was debated in many circles. William Lynn, in the funeral eulogy he delivered before the Society of the Cincinnati of New York on Washington's birthday in 1800, stated that this controversy could be settled only by admitting he was "first in war and first in peace."[47] The Republicans of the time, and for many years to come, might admit his generalship, but they certainly questioned both his statesmanship and so complete a credit for the nation as "The Father of His Country" implied. Too, Americans generally were familiar with the figure of Washington as a general or a gentleman, not as a statesman in a toga. All in all, even through the 1830s, the majority seem to have thought of Washington most often as Columbia's defender on the field of battle, as her "matchless son"[48] rather than her father. Therein, perhaps, lies part of the explanation of the General on the early flasks.

The Washington flasks that have been identified with a glassworks or manufacturer by initials and/or name of the glassworks are listed below. The date or period given is that at which the flask is believed to have first appeared.

1. GI–6. "GENERAL WASHINGTON."—Eagle, "J.R." "LAIRD.SC. PITT." Pint. 23 in Group B, Most Desirable Flasks. Mold by Joshua Laird, Pittsburgh, Pa. Flask by John Robinson, Stourbridge Flint Glass Works, Pittsburgh, Pa. ca. 1824–30.

2. GI–6a. Variant of GI–6. See above.

3. GI–7. "G.GEO'WASHINGTON."—Eagle, "F.L". Pint. 16 in Group B, Most Desirable Flasks. Frederick Lorenz, Pittsburgh, Pa. ca. 1824–30.

4. GI–8. "G.G.WASHINGTON"—Eagle, "F.L." Pint. 20 in Group A, Most Desirable Flasks. Frederick Lorenz.

5. GI–13. "WASHINGTON."—Eagle, "B.K." Pint. 21 in Group A, Most Desirable Flasks. Attributed to Benedict Kimber, Bridgeport, Pa. ca. 1824.

6. GI–14. "GENERAL WASHINGTON"; (on edge) "ADAMS & JEFFERSON JULY 4 A.D. 1776"—Eagle, "E PLURIBUS UNUM"; "T.W.D"; (on edge) "KENSINGTON GLASS WORKS PHILADELPHIA". Thomas W. Dyott, Kensington Glass Works, Philadelphia, Pa. 1826. Inscriptions on edges and "E Pluribus Unum" cut in mold for GI–16 at the time Adams and Jefferson died.

7. GI–15. "GENERAL WASHINGTON"—Eagle, "T.W.D." Pint. Listed by Van Rensselaer as No. 2 DI, GV. So far as I have been able to learn, no one can verify the existence of this flask.

8. GI–16. "GENERAL WASHINGTON"—Eagle, "T.W.D." Mold of 1824, or possibly late 1823, altered to create GI–14. See 6 above.

9. & 10. GI–17 and GI–17a. "WASHINGTON"—Taylor(?), "BALTIMORE GLASS WORKS". Pint. As inscribed. Possibly brought out by the Baltimore Flint Glass Works ca. 1829–34.

11. & 12. GI–18 and GI–19. "WASHINGTON"—Battle Monument, "BALTIMORE GLASS WORKS". Pint. As inscribed. Probably late 1830s.

13. GI–20. Washington, "FELLS" "POINT"—Washington Monument, "BALT⁰". Pint. Balti-more, Md. Attributed to the Baltimore Glass Works. Possibly first brought out by the Baltimore Flint Glass Works ca. 1828–29.

14. GI–21. Washington, "FELLS" "POINT"—Washington Monument, "Balto". Quart. See 13 above.

15. GI–22. Washington, "BALTIMORE x GLASS.WORKS." (the double "S" reversed)—Henry Clay. Quart. As inscribed. Perhaps late in 1831.

16. GI–23. Washington—Henry Clay, "BALTIMORE x GLASS.WORKS." Quart. As inscribed. Perhaps late in 1831.

17. GI–24. "WASHINGTON"—Taylor (?), "BRIDGETON NEW JERSEY". Pint. Bridgeton Glass Works. Probably late 1830s.

18. GI–25. Washington—Henry Clay; "BRIDGE-TOWN NEW JERSEY", each side. Quart. Bridgeton Glass Works. Attributed to the early 1840s.

19. GI–28. Washington, "ALBANY GLASS WORKS / ALBANY / N Y"—Sailing Ship. Pint. As inscribed. Date?

20. GI–30. Washington—"ALBANY GLASS WORKS / N Y". Half-pint. See 19 above.

21. GI–37. Washington, "THE FATHER OF HIS COUNTRY"—Taylor, "GENERAL TAYLOR NEVER SURRENDERS", "DYOTTVILLE GLASS WORKS PHILA.ᴬ". Quart. As inscribed. First produced 1847 or early 1848 when works was operated by Benners, Smith and Campbell.

22. GI–38. Pint like GI–37. See 21 above.

23. GI–60. Washington, each side; "LOCKPORT GLASS WORKS" on obverse. Quart. Lockport Glass Works, Lockport, N.Y. 1840s.

BENJAMIN FRANKLIN AND THOMAS W. DYOTT

Thro every future age,
 Whils't history holds her pen,
She'll rank our honor'd sons
 Who've earned immortal fame,
Shall next to Washington's
 Record Great Franklin's name.

This stanza from an ode "On the death of Dr. Franklin"[49] was prophetic; in fact, in some respects,

Franklin's name precedes Washington's. Of all the extraordinary men who contributed to the independence of the colonies and founding of the United States, Benjamin Franklin seems to have had more talents and achieved deserved international fame in more fields than any other American-born patriot. Moreover, his life and career were proof to future generations that America offered *opportunity* to every man strong and capable enough to seize it: starting as a printer's devil, he became preeminent as an American publisher, writer, scientist, statesman, and philosopher. His luster was not tarnished by politics nor dimmed by the passage of time. At Fourth of July celebrations long after he died in 1790, he was often one of the notables toasted by men in many walks of life. At Troy, New York, in 1825, Charles MacArthur, speaking for the Association of Apprentices, included Franklin with Columbus, Hadley, and Fulton as a "Genius of Art." (At that time *art*, as used by MacArthur, who himself started as a printer's devil, meant the mechanical arts, which of course included printing.) Celebrations of Franklin's birthday continued for nearly half a century after his death—at any rate, newspapers published accounts of Franklin Birthday Suppers as late as 1834.[50] Perhaps by then a portrait of Benjamin Franklin had become not so much a reminder of Franklin the statesman as of Poor Richard and his maxims or the kite, key, and lightning. Everyone who went to school knew about them—and readers of newspapers frequently found quotations from Franklin's writings and remarks attributed to him.

Philadelphia had been the hub of Franklin's career, and Philadelphians naturally had a special pride in him. Almost as soon as Thomas W. Dyott immigrated to Philadelphia about 1805, he must have become aware that her most celebrated son was Franklin. Hence Franklin must have seemed an ideal subject to Dyott when he decided to mold portraits of patriots, and of himself, in his flasks—even though he apparently disagreed with the odist as to Franklin's position in the record: Dyott's 1824 advertisement ranked Washington first, Lafayette second, and Franklin third.[51] Moreover, in 1825, Dyott's own name took precedence over Franklin's: "3000 dozen Dyott and Franklin do do [pint flasks]" were among those advertised. (See Ill. 117.) In all, he produced three marked "Dyott and Franklin" flasks—pints GI–94 and GI–95 and the quart GI–96—having on one side his own portrait bust below the inscription "THOMAS L. DYOTT, M.D." and, on the other side, the inscription "BENJAMIN FRANKLIN" arching over the head of Franklin's bust. The edges

of GI–95 had no inscription. There can be little doubt that, as I have believed, pint GI–95 probably was the one advertised in 1824 and that it was followed probably late in 1825, or early in 1826, by GI–94 having the inscription "WHERE LIBERTY DWELLS THERE IS MY COUNTRY" on the edge of the Franklin side (obverse in the Charts) and "KENSINGTON GLASS WORKS PHILADELPHIA" on the edge of the Dyott side (reverse in the Charts).

Kenneth Wilson's examination of these flasks determined that the mold for GI–95 was altered by adding the edge inscriptions, to produce GI–94. The sentiment about liberty and country, long associated with Franklin, supposedly was expressed by him in a letter written from France in 1785. It became a quotation familiar to many Americans, cropping up in speeches and occasionally in print as a headline or introduction to patriotic effusions into the early 19th century. On the edge of the Franklin side of quart flask GI–96 another quotation associated with Franklin was inscribed—"ERIPUIT COELO FULMEN. SCEPTRUMQUE TURANNIS." Seeing this Latin sentence inscribed in his quart flask, the average man of the 1820s and 1830s was far more likely to translate it without difficulty into "He snatched the lightning from heaven and the sceptre from tyrants" than nearly anyone would today when a classical education is no longer a must. But probably he did not know that it was written in 1778 by a French statesman and economist, Anne Robert Jacques Turget, as the inscription for Houdon's bust of Franklin.[52] It may well be that this bust or an engraving derived from it served as the model for the portrait on Dyott's flasks.

Besides Dyott's three marked Franklin flasks, another eastern quart has always been believed to be a Dyott product. This handsome flask, GI–97, had the portrait bust of Franklin on each side but was innocent of any identifying inscription. Its attribution to Dyott's Kensington Glass Works derived from the fact that the bust of Franklin appeared to be exactly like that on the marked Franklin-Dyott quart GI–96. Now the validity of the attribution is strengthened, if not confirmed, by Kenneth Wilson's comparative study of the two flasks. He concluded that:

The same *pattern* was apparently used to make the mold for each side of GI–97. Either the same *pattern* was also used to make the Franklin side of GI–96, with added inscription, or, half of the same mold used to make GI–97 was used and the inscription ["ERIPUIT COELO FULMEN. SCEPTRUMQUE TURANNIS."] around the edge and the words "Benjamin Franklin" were added to it.

Inasmuch as this Franklin flask, classified as rare, has been found far less often than the others, perhaps one half of its mold was altered by cutting in the inscription for GI–96.

In the Midwest just one Franklin flask was produced, the pint GI–98, which was chosen by George S. McKearin for Group B, Most Desirable Flasks (No. 27). On the obverse, as charted, the inscription "BENJAMIN FRANKLIN" arched over the head of Franklin's portrait bust, which is similar to that on GI–94 and GI–95, but it will be noted in the Chart line drawings that Franklin was given a bald pate. The bust on the reverse, although varying in details, is recognizable as Thomas W. Dyott from its close resemblance to his bust on GI–94. Dyott's name was displaced by the inscription "WHEELING GLASS WORKS". That Dyott's flasks probably served as the model for the Wheeling flask is suggested by the similarity in the drawing of the subject and the fact that Dyott's wares, probably including his flasks, were not unknown in Wheeling. I believe this flask was brought out first in the 1830s, possibly by Ensell and Plunkett between 1830 and 1833 during their rental of the works established by Knox & McKee, who had called it the Virginia Green Glass Works. Still, it must be noted that Josephine Jefferson, in her very thorough and extensive research into the history of glassworks and the firms operating them in Wheeling and its environs, found no definite evidence as to the factory or firm producing this flask.[53] Since it is extremely rare today, whoever made it apparently did not produce it in vast quantities.

So far as I know, Thomas W. Dyott was the only glass manufacturer immortalized in glass by more than initials. He certainly did not qualify as a military hero, diplomat, or politician, but his name must have been a household word wherever his medicines were taken. Today collectors and students, grateful for his exciting flasks and the color he brought to the history of American glass, smile gently at his self-flattery in placing his own image with that of Benjamin Franklin. But I wonder if he really believed himself as famous or as well, if not better, known to the hundreds and hundreds of Americans throughout the country who read the daily or weekly Dyott advertisements in their newspapers and obtained Dyott nostrums from their local druggists, and to all who would purchase his flasks. One wonders, too, if he was aware of Dr. Franklin's celebrated improvement on musical glasses: the "Glassychord," which "formed them [musical glasses] into a compleat instrument to accompany the Voice; capable of thorough Bass, and never out of Tune . . ."—or so

the *Bristol Journal* of England reported in 1762.[54] Anyway, both men belong in a glass collector's Hall of Fame, and Dyott did much to create it.

GENERAL LAFAYETTE AND DE WITT CLINTON

Among the living personages commemorated on figured pocket flasks were DeWitt Clinton and the renowned Lafayette—Marie Joseph Paul Yves Roch Gilbert du Motier Marquise de Lafayette, to give him all his names. A special niche was reserved for Lafayette in the heart of nearly every citizen of the United States. To Americans, he was a national hero of two struggles for Liberty: the American and the French, and the more honored because, too humane and moderate for the French Terrorists, he escaped into exile and, in the cause of true liberty, suffered imprisonment by a foreign ruler. To Americans, he was not a foreigner but a fellow citizen; not the Marquis de Lafayette but General Lafayette of the American Revolutionary Armies, wounded at Brandywine, fast friend of his Commander in Chief, George Washington; not a renegade aristocrat and traitor to his class (as he still is to some Frenchmen), but an unpretentious democratic gentleman. A revisit to the United States by this distinguished and beloved man in 1824 was an event that had long been heralded and was eagerly awaited. Preparations for unstinted celebrations, banquets, and parades were under way well before he left France (in the little ship *Cadmus*) bound for New York City. Between August 1824 and September 1825 he was to have a triumphal tour of the country. His visit was an unforgettable event and an honor for cities and towns in every state in the Union; they vied with one another to pay him homage. It was an occasion their citizens marked by naming nearly everything in creation, and created, for him—streets and ships, theaters and towns, businesses and babies. (His tiny namesakes could be given "infant kid boots with the General's likeness stamped on them."[55]) As might be expected, alert merchants and manufacturers capitalized on Lafayette's popularity by quickly putting on the market mementos in all sorts of fabrics and forms, many of which were in production months before he even left France. Among the innumerable things his portrait adorned were, of course, ceremonial badges and buttons to be worn at celebrations in his honor; and, besides baby shoes, among the commercial products were parasols, furnaces, and glass pocket flasks. Eight of the 18 recorded flasks had Masonic decoration on the reverse.

Lafayette was indeed "The Nation's Guest," receiving such civil, military, and Masonic honors as have been accorded to few men—and the Freemasons regarded him as their special guest. Few people today, other than Masons, are aware of his connection with Freemasonry, for historians in general have touched lightly upon or omitted any reference to it. However, it was his prominence in Masonry, as well as the Masons' pride in him, that explains his being feted by Masonic Lodges everywhere on his tour of the States and accounts also for the Masonic decoration in conjunction with his portrait on Figured Flasks. Various state Grand Lodges made him an honorary member. The highest honors and degrees of the fraternity were also conferred on him, including—so Masons quite generally have believed—the 33rd degree (Freemasonry's highest) and the Knights Templar's degree. Lafayette took part as a Mason in events other than Masonic meetings and banquets, too. One of the prized possessions of the Grand Lodge of Massachusetts is the apron worn by Lafayette when he participated in laying the cornerstone of Bunker Hill Monument at Boston, June 17, 1825.

Masonic historians have disagreed regarding some of the degrees conferred upon Lafayette during this 1824/25 visit and even regarding his induction into the fraternity, a matter that will be of interest to those bottle collectors who are Masons. Although his induction into the 33rd degree and the legitimacy of the body conferring the degree upon him have been questioned, the records of various Masonic bodies in France indicate that he was so recognized. There has also been question as to whether the Knights Templar's degree was conferred on him by Columbian Commandery or by Morton Encampment No. 4. It has been recorded, too, that he received the order of Knighthood in Columbian Encampment, but that Morton Encampment (organized the previous year) had met with Columbian the afternoon when the distinguished Frenchman and Mason was thus honored.[56] Some Masonic historians have advanced the theory that during our Revolutionary War Lafayette was initiated into a "Military Lodge" at Valley Forge, and that Washington, the Commander in Chief, was in the Chair at the time of Lafayette's initiation. Others have stated that he was made a Mason at a celebration of the Feast of St. John held by the American Union Lodge in Morristown, New Jersey, on St. John's Day, December 27, 1779. They maintain also that Washington was in the Master's Chair and that the regalia of St. John's Lodge No. 1 of New Jersey was

used. This second theory is refuted by the fact that Lafayette, granted a furlough by the Continental Congress, had sailed from Boston for France in the frigate *Alliance* on January 11, 1779, and did not return to America until April 6, 1780. As a matter of fact, available evidence is against the theory that Lafayette became a Mason in America. Although official proof as to the date or scene of his entrance into the craft actually has never been discovered, the predominating evidence indicates that he had become a member of the Masonic Fraternity of France prior to coming to America.[57] He was then only in his twentieth year, but his youth would not have been a bar to admission to the fraternity.

Of the eight recorded flasks decorated with Masonic emblems and the portrait of Lafayette, two (charted as GI–92 and 93) were midwestern and were, moreover, the only Lafayette flasks identified with the Midwest. Both are rare flasks; one, GI–92, was chosen by George S. McKearin for Group B, Most Desirable Flasks (No. 26). On the obverse of each was an oval frame with Masonic pillars and arch over the profile bust of a man in military uniform; below the bust was an elaborated fleur-de-lis. On the edge, between the panel and medial rib at the mold seam, was inscribed "GEИᴸ LA" (at left of panel) and "FAYETTE" (at right of panel) identifying the portrait—incidentally, the only means of doing so. The placing of each word was somewhat unusual—roughly, in the lower two-thirds of each edge, following the curve of the panel (see line drawing in Charts). On the reverse of each was an oval frame with seven large stars above an American eagle so large that the bird looks cramped by the frame, which, it should be noted, was more flattened on the left than on the right side. Comparative study of these two flasks revealed that they apparently differed only in that one, GI–92, was inscribed "KNOX & McKEE WHEELING" on the edge of the eagle side with "KNOX &" at lower left of panel, "WHEELING" following the curve of the panel at top, and "McKEE" at lower right of panel. Consequently, for years they were both attributed to the Virginia Green Glass Works of Knox & McKee, Wheeling, (W.) Virginia, and, of course, were assumed to have been first made late in 1824 or early in 1825.

Then, about 1940, Rhea Mansfield Knittle discovered that an Ohio firm of bottle producers put out a Lafayette flask at the time of his visit. She reported finding a June 1824 advertisement of glassware, including "ribbed Lafayette, Clay and Jackson flasks . . ." produced by "Pugh & Teater" (actually,

Pepperd—not Pugh) in their small glassworks at Moscow, not far from Cincinnati, Ohio. "Ribbed" modifying "Lafayette . . . flasks" has caused some speculation.[58] The probability is that in setting the advertisement in type, the printer forgot to put a comma after "ribbed" and, as in the case of one of Dyott's designs in the same period, the meaning was "vertically ribbed flasks." Be that as it may, the advertisement and the likeness of the two known flasks GI–92 and GI–93 led Mrs. Knittle to two theories regarding Lafayette flask GI–93 without the inscription on the eagle side. First, she concluded that the GI–93 Lafayette probably was the Moscow flask. To most students, this seemed well founded, especially since the GI–92 and GI–93 flasks were, and still are, the *only* recorded midwestern Lafayette flasks, and *only two* glassworks in the Midwest had been established as sources of Lafayette flasks— namely, the Virginia Green Glass Works of Knox & McKee at Wheeling and the Moscow Glass Works, supposedly when it was being operated by Pepperd & Teater. Therefore Moscow has been accepted generally as the probable source of GI–93. It has since been learned that the Moscow flasks *were not advertised in 1824 but in August 1825*, and by Pepperd & Teater. However, this fact does not in itself invalidate her theories.[59]

Mrs. Knittle's second theory was that the un-marked GI–93 was produced *first* and that the maker of the mold later adapted it for the Wheeling firm by cutting in the inscription "KNOX & McKEE WHEELING".[60] This too seemed well reasoned, as the two flasks seemed identical in every detail except for the inscription on the reverse edge of GI–92, and cutting the inscription in the plain surface of the mold would have been a simple operation. But now it seems that, though there doubtless was an alteration, it was not that of cutting an inscription in the plain surface between the oval panel and the medial rib at the mold seam. And it seems too that an alteration possibly may have been made to produce the Knox & McKee Jackson–Masonic flask GI–69.

While assembling data for this section on Lafayette flasks, my comparative study of the line drawings of the two Lafayette flasks under discussion and the Jackson revealed no discernible difference between the obverse and reverse designs of the three flasks, only differing inscriptions. Also, whereas the letters of "GEN͟L LA / FAYETTE" were closely and evenly spaced along approximately the lower two-thirds of the frame, those of "AN-DREW / JACKSON" were more widely spaced, with *Andrew* at left along approximately the upper two-thirds of the frame and *Jackson* at right, starting a little below the top of the frame and ending about opposite the space between the base of the right pillar and small scroll of the fleur-de-lis ornament. This placement of the words struck me as peculiar and unnatural and, together with the designs seeming more alike than two peas, led me to the tentative conclusion that perhaps "GEN͟L LA / FAYETTE" had been eliminated and "ANDREW / JACKSON" added. No longer having the actual flasks to study, I asked Kenneth Wilson to investigate the possible mold changes by examining these flasks in the collection of The Corning Museum of Glass. This he kindly did. In his examination for possible inscription changes on the portrait side of these flasks, Mr. Wilson found that the surface of Corning's Jackson GI–69 was "so rough in general" as to complicate the search for any previous lettering, and that "the surface irregularities" of the plain edge above the Lafayette inscriptions on GI–92 and GI–93 were so vague as to preclude any opinion about them. On the other hand, his examination of GI–92 and GI–93, which included impressions for comparison, established that in the case of GI–92 "WHEELING" and, presumably, "KNOX & McKEE" had been *eliminated,* thus making a plain surface for the GI–93 flasks—the exact opposite procedure of that hitherto believed to have been followed. Hence, the Knox & McKee flasks doubtless were produced in 1824 and early in 1825.

This led naturally to questions as to when and how long the mold for GI–92 was used at Wheeling and when and how long that for the GI–93 was used at Moscow *if* the GI–93 flasks were the Moscow Lafayettes. As yet, these questions cannot be resolved by definite answers. There are several conceivable answers, and into each must be integrated a few other factors, bits of evidence raising more questions than they answer. One is that it was not in a June 1824 advertisement, as Mrs. Knittle reported, but in an August 12, 1825, advertisement of glassware to be on hand September 1 that Pepperd & Teater specifically mentioned Lafayette, Clay, and Jackson flasks. Earlier advertisements of Moscow products listed flasks without any reference to the kind. All this suggests that Pepperd & Teater probably did not have molds for any of the three Figured Flasks before the August blast but acquired them (or expected to do so) in time to put the flasks on the market in September. Also, that the firm may have obtained only the Lafayette mold, presumably GI–93, is suggested by the facts that (1) as yet no Jackson flask and no Clay flask have been recorded that are attributable, even tentatively, to Moscow and (2) GI–93 is as yet the only one of the known Lafayette flasks that is a possible Moscow product. The most puzzling question about Moscow's Lafayette flasks is the date of their advertisement. Whereas Clay flasks would have been timely any year from the 1820s through the 1840s, and Jackson flasks from 1824 certainly through 1832, it seems odd that a midwestern glassworks would *start* producing Lafayette flasks at the very end of Lafayette's visit to the United States. He left in September 1825.

Other tantalizing evidence of Lafayette flasks was found in 1828 advertisements in the *Cincinnati Daily Gazette*. Mrs. Knittle reported finding a January 1828 advertisement of 300 dozen Lafayette flasks "just received and for sale" by W. C. Rogers & Werth, and an April advertisement that mentioned the same number, "just received" by John Stinson & Company.[61] She concluded (1) that these 3,600 flasks were GI–93 flasks and Moscow products, which William Hartshorn, Cincinnati agent of Pepperd & Teater, had been unable to sell, (2) that the 300 dozen advertised by John Stinson & Company was the same 300 dozen offered by W. C. Rogers & Werth, and (3) that the 300 dozen was the stock on hand when the Moscow Glass Works closed, as she thought, by January 1, 1828.

In checking these advertisements for me, Mrs. Lee Adams found that both firms were Cincinnati auctioneers and that, from February 1 through 8, 1828, John Stinson & Company advertised "20 boxes LaFayette flasks / Terms 3 and 4 months." Also, the W. C. Rogers & Werth advertisement ran only a few days—through January 26—which suggests the flasks were either sold, or returned to the agent or manufacturer, by or shortly after the last appearance of the advertisement. On the other hand, the April advertisement of John Stinson & Company ran nearly two months—April 29 through June 24, 1828. Almost certainly these Lafayette flasks were products of a midwestern glassworks. Though the *possibility* they were from Wheeling cannot be completely ruled out, it seems to us more than likely Mrs. Knittle's conclusion that they were GI–93 flasks from Moscow was correct. If so, then the GI–93 mold probably was in use at the Moscow Glass Works late in 1827 or early in 1828, at least in the early months of that year. According to local history, Teater closed the works around 1830, and possibly the Lafayette flasks were in stock at the time of closing. Therefore, whether or not the Lafayettes advertised in April were the same lot as those offered in February, they may have been the last produced at Moscow.

After considering a variety of possibilities suggested by the present evidence, circumstantial and fac-

tual, I have reduced them to the two that seem to me the most likely. *But these are still conjectures*. One is based on the assumptions that (1) an original *mold*, that for GI–92, was altered for GI–93 and (2) the designs and inscriptions had been cut in a cast blank, as it is believed the best and most detailed molds for early flasks were. Starting from this point, the first part of the theory would be that (*a*) the mold for GI–92 was made for Knox & McKee, and used at the Virginia Green Glass Works, sometime in 1824. It would not be surprising if this had occurred early in the year, since—as mentioned previously—many Lafayette items were in production long before August when he arrived in the United States. (*b*) Whenever they were blown, the present rarity of these Lafayette flasks inscribed "KNOX & McKEE WHEELING" (only 20 to 25 specimens recorded so far) suggests limited production. Whether it was large or small, a supply of the GI–92 Lafayette flasks was blown in anticipation of sales during Lafayette's visit to the United States and to midwestern cities, including Wheeling. (*c*) At some time afterward, presumably in accord with an agreement between Knox & McKee and another firm, the mold was sent back to its maker to have the inscription filled in so that subsequently flasks blown in it were anonymous as to glassworks; or, possibly, the alteration was made in one of the glassworks.

The second part of the theory is that (*a*)*if* the mold was altered for Pepperd & Teater, arrangements must have been made before the firm's August 12, 1825, advertisement appeared, and the mold must have been delivered at the Moscow Glass Works in time for GI–93 Lafayettes to be on hand September 1. (*b*) If the Lafayette flasks advertised in January and April 1828 were the same lot of GI–93 blown in the Moscow Glass Works, the mold was still in Pepperd & Teater's possession probably late in 1827; or if the 300 dozen offered in April was a new lot of GI–93 from Moscow, Pepperd & Teater may have been using the mold in the spring of 1828. (*c*) On the other hand, if the mold had been reacquired by Knox & McKee some time before January 1828, these Lafayette flasks, probably GI–93, would have been blown in the Virginia Green Glass Works at Wheeling. Extending the theory to include GI–69, I might add that, possibly, when the mold was reacquired by Knox & McKee, it may have been altered for the firm's Jackson–Masonic flask GI–69 by filling in "GEN LA/ FAYETTE" and cutting in "ANDREW / JACKSON" on the obverse and, on the reverse, recutting "KNOX & McKEE WHEELING" where it had been filled in. According to this theory, the Jackson–Masonic GI–69 almost certainly would have been brought out in 1828. By then the popularity of the Lafayette flasks in the Midwest apparently was withering and that of Jackson flasks had definitely reached full bloom, both East and West. The 1828 presidential campaign, which actually started in 1824, was breeding various kinds of Jacksoniana, including Figured Flasks.

The second possibility was suggested by Kenneth Wilson—namely, that two metal molds were made from a *carved wooden pattern* for GI–92, and the inscription "KNOX & McKEE WHEELING" was filled in on one. This presupposes that the entire mold was cast—that is, a sand mold was made for each leaf of the metal mold (one for the obverse and one for the reverse) from a carved pattern, and each leaf with design and inscription was cast in this sand mold. By this theory: (1) having cast the GI–92 mold, the moldmaker cast a second metal mold in GI–92 in which the inscription on the eagle side of it was filled in either at the foundry or at one of the two glassworks; or (2), at the foundry, after the metal mold for GI–92 was cast, the moldmaker possibly may have tried *either* to eliminate the inscription from the sand mold by filling it in before casting the metal mold *or* to remove the words from the wooden pattern used to make the sand mold. The latter process, according to Mr. Wilson, would have been much the easier and a "much better job would have resulted." However, although alteration of the sand mold or of the wooden pattern may be possibilities to consider, it seems more likely the inscription in the metal mold was filled in. Whatever method was followed, the removal of the inscription was incomplete and, as Mr. Wilson's studies revealed, part of the word WHEELING is discernible still on the GI–93 flasks.

The established facts, and those postulated, fit easily into the theory, or possibility, that the method of moldmaking by casting and carving was used and that two metal molds were made—one for GI–92 without inscription and one for GI–93 with inscription eliminated. Moreover, the problems inherent in the theory of one mold in *two* or *three* guises, as it were, do not arise in the theory of two cast metal molds. The firm, probably Peppered & Teater, owning the mold for GI–93 could use it as often and as long as there was a market for its Lafayette flasks. The same would be true of Knox & McKee, for whom GI–92 was made. Also, if Knox & McKee had its GI–92 altered for its Jackson GI–69, the operation could have been performed at any chosen time after production of Lafayette flasks ceased.

The other 16 Lafayette flasks, four of which were found at different times after 1941, were products of eastern glasshouses. With perhaps two possible exceptions, they were brought out by one or the other of only three works: T. W. Dyott's Kensington Glass Works in Philadelphia; the Mount Vernon Glass Works, Vernon, New York; and the Coventry Glass Works, Coventry, Connecticut.

Only 37 days after Lafayette landed at Castle Garden, New York City, Dr. Dyott was advertising a special Lafayette pint pocket bottle (see Ill. 119). Lafayette was depicted as the General in uniform, in three-quarter view, and by a bust that showed at least a feeble attempt at portraiture. On the reverse was a fine American eagle that Dyott advertised as "the United States Coat of Arms," though (as on other Dyott flasks) the pose was not that of the eagle on the Great Seal. Actually, Dyott brought out two Lafayette flasks. One, GI–91, had "GENERAL LA FAYETTE" arching over Lafayette's head; the initials "T.W.D." were in the oval frame that served as the eagle's perch. The other, GI–90, was the same but in addition had "E. PLURIBUS UNUM" in an arc at the tips of the sunrays radiating from the eagle's head, "KENSINGTON GLASS WORKS PHILADELPHIA" on the reverse edges, and "RE-PUBLICAN GRATITUDE" on the edges of the Lafayette side. There can be little doubt that GI–91 *without* the edge inscriptions and the "E. PLURIBUS UNUM" was the one advertised in September 1824 (see Ill. 105) and that the mold for GI–91 was elaborated soon afterward by the additional inscriptions to produce GI–90. Incidentally, I believe it most probable that T. W. Dyott's designs were hand-carved in his molds or refined by carving after being cast. Two reasons for the change might have been that, as other Lafayette flasks appeared in the market, Dyott sought to make his own more pointed by the expression of gratitude, and he wanted to leave no doubt as to the originator of the flask. Dyott was a canny merchandiser. Also, in general, steps from the simple toward the elaborate seem a more natural progression than simplification of the more elaborate. A bit of extra weight may be added to the pro of my conjecture by the fact that, whereas the GI–90 flask with all the inscriptions is only comparatively scarce, the plainer GI–91 is rare today.

The remaining flasks have a profile bust depicting Lafayette not as a young soldier but as a mature man in civilian clothes, and the rendering is more of a silhouette than a portrait, recognizable only because "LAFAYETTE" is inscribed above the bust. Of these varieties, the Mount Vernon Glass Works was the source of two, the very rare GI–88 and 89 (4 and

5 in Group B, Most Desirable Flasks), and the almost certain source of two others, the extremely rare GI–89a and 89b. On all four the bust below the identifying "LAFAYETTE" was the same in conception and closely similar in rendering to those on the Coventry Glass Works Lafayette flasks GI–80 through 84, suggesting the same moldmaker may have supplied the molds to both glassworks. On the reverse of the Mount Vernon pint GI–88 and half-pint GI–89 were Masonic pillars, arch with keystone and pavement enclosing the triangle, above the square and compass on open book. Unlike all the other Lafayette flasks, these two have smooth edges except for a single narrow vertical rib at the mold seam. The attribution of the flasks to the Mount Vernon Glass Works was made on the basis of fragments excavated on the factory site by Harry Hall White.

So far, only one specimen each of the half-pint GI–89a and pint GI–89b has been discovered. Though of different size, the design and decoration of both was the same, pointing to the near certainty of a single source, which I believe probably was Mount Vernon, and one moldmaker. Moreover, the bust of Lafayette and inscription on the half-pint GI–89a were like those on the half-pint GI–89, and on the pint GI–89b were like those on the pint GI–88; but on GI–89a and GI–89b a semiwreath of laurel leaves completed the framing of the portrait. Also, on the reverse, the Masonic decoration on GI–89a (except for 18 bricks in the pavement instead of 13 and a narrow bar) was like that of GI–89, and on GI–89b like that on GI–88, but 13 large six-pointed stars, graduated in size, arched over the Masonic emblems. The edges of each were given a feature found as yet on no other Figured Flask in any category—namely, fine diagonal ribs on each edge meeting at the mold seam, thus forming a herringbone. Kenneth M. Wilson's comparative examination of the two half-pints and two pints established that "Either the same *mold* for GI–89 was elaborated to make GI–89a, or the same *pattern* was used for both but elaborated to make GI–89a" —including cutting the narrow bar in the GI–89 pavement to form an innermost row of five bricks. And the same applies to the molds for GI–88 and GI–89b. (For comparison of GI–89 and 89a and of GI–88 and 89b, see line drawings in the Charts and 1 in Ill. 125.) The half-pint GI–89a, illustrated also in *Two Hundred Years of American Blown Glass* by 1 in Plate 110, had been in the George Horace Lorimer Collection before being acquired for the McKearin Collection; it is now at the Corning Museum of Glass, as is the pint GI–89b. The half-pint was blown

from colorless lead glass—another feature bolstering the probability of the Mount Vernon Glass Works as the source. In what section of the country it and GI–89b were found, I do not know.

The majority of the Lafayette flasks were blown at the Coventry Glass Works, the first of them doubtless late in 1824 or very early in 1825. Masonic decoration was on the reverse of two, the pint GI–83 and half-pint GI–84 (2 and 3 in Group B, the Most Desirable Flasks). The decoration consisted of the pillars, arch with keystone, and pavement enclosing the triangle, and the square and compass on open book similar to those on the Mount Vernon Lafayette–Masonics, but in addition, on GI–83, the blazing sun was at the left and the quarter moon at the right of the arch, and on GI–84, a six-pointed star at right and left of the arch and a 12-pointed star below the pavement. Possibly these and GI–80 were the first of the Coventry Lafayette flasks, for the initials "T S" were inscribed below a bar, which in turn was below the bust of Lafayette. The initials were those of Thomas Stebbins, who was operating the Coventry Glass Works in the early 1820s. On the reverse of the pint GI–80 was a profile bust identified by "DE WITT CLINTON" (the "D" reversed) and a large "C–T" below the bust. The three half-pint flasks GI–81, 81a, and 82 have the same inscriptions—but with the "D" placed properly, the initials "C–T", and a similar bust with ears shown, as they were not on the Lafayette profiles. The obverse of GI–82 varied from the pint GI–80 in having no initials below the bust of Lafayette, and GI–81 and 81a varied in having the initials "S & C" (standing for Stebbins & Chamberlain, or Chamberlin), successors to Thomas Stebbins. All six flasks—that is, the two Lafayette–Masonic and four Lafayette–DeWitt Clinton—had the short horizontal ribs or corrugations on the edges, a feature characteristic of the early flasks made at or attributed to Coventry.

The four Lafayette–Liberty Cap flasks, GI–85 through 87a, were also Coventry products. The pint and half-pint GI–85 and 86 apparently were made in larger quantities than the pint and half-pint GI–87a and 87: the former are comparatively scarce today, whereas the latter are extremely rare. In fact, there are still only three or four known specimens of the half-pint GI–87 (1 in Group B, Most Desirable Flasks) and only one or two of the pint GI–87a reported by Charles B. Gardner. The edges of all were finely ribbed vertically, instead of corrugated. The obverse of each was inscribed "COVENTRY / C T" (the "N" omitted on GI–85) below the bust, and each bust was slightly different from the others.

The obverses also differed from the other Coventry Lafayette flasks in that the name "LAFAYETTE" formed a deeper and closer semicircle over the bust, which was given a less egg-shaped head and showed less of the coat. On the reverse of each flask was the Phrygian or, as most Americans called it, the French Liberty Cap on a short staff within an oval frame, but on the pint GI–85 and half-pint GI–86 were large six-pointed stars graduated in size, in a deep semicircle over the frame. Beneath the frame, each was inscribed "S & S"—for Stebbins & Stebbins. Although the exact span of operation of the Coventry Glass Works by Thomas Stebbins, Stebbins & Chamberlain, and Stebbins & Stebbins has not been determined, Stebbins & Stebbins was formed sometime before 1830.

It would seem that the Lafayette–Liberty Cap flasks were brought out *after* Lafayette's 1824/25 visit to the United States. There would have been nothing strange in such an occurrence, especially in the eastern part of the country: Lafayette and his activities, even uneventful ones, continued to be news right up to his death in 1834. As the *Utica N.Y. Intelligencer* of August 8, 1826, nearly a year after Lafayette left the country, stated: "Everything relating to Lafayette is interesting to the American reader." Among the many such news items I have read was one in the American press reporting that Lafayette and his son gave and received many toasts at the 1826 July Fourth celebration by Americans in Paris. Two events in 1829 possibly increased the sale of Lafayette flasks. Many Americans were proud and touched when it became known that Lafayette had directed his agent in New York City to obtain and send to France "earth from Bunker Hill to be placed over his body at his decease." (It was taken from the spot on which General Warren was supposed to have fallen.) Shortly afterward, they were even more moved by the "Generosity of Lafayette" when it was revealed that he had ordered United States lands granted to him by a grateful Congress to be sold and the proceeds used to discharge ex-President Monroe's debts, though "Mr. Monroe refused to permit it."[62] Americans tended, for well over a century, to utterly ignore ex-presidents and their problems once a president had served his purpose.

From time to time neophyte flask collectors and an occasional captive visitor from outside the flask fraternity have asked me why DeWitt Clinton was commemorated on historical flasks and in conjunction with Lafayette. The two men were not associated together with any great event, and they had not met before Lafayette's American visit, though it is

said they had corresponded. True, they were both ardent and prominent Masons, but the immediate reason for the Lafayette–DeWitt Clinton flasks undoubtedly was that Lafayette's 1824/25 stay in the United States coincided with the approaching completion of "Clinton's Ditch" from Lake Erie to the Hudson River. Although Clinton had been a widely known, active figure in the political life of the United States since 1790, especially of New York, his native state, his stature was not that of a hero except to the advocates of internal improvements in transportation, and to them it was colossal. Merchants, manufacturers, farmers, and others already profiting as section after section of the Erie Canal opened, presaging greater benefits to come, considered Clinton a champion of commerce and industry nearly, if not wholly, equal to Henry Clay. Months before the entire canal was opened, a pair of superb silver vases, 24 inches tall and copied from one found in the ruins of the Villa of Hadrian, was presented to Governor Clinton "by the Merchants of Pearl-Street, in the city of New-York, in testimony of their gratitude and respect for his public service."[63]

In a very real sense, the Erie Canal was DeWitt Clinton's creation. He conceived the plan and, failing to get it adopted by the Federal Goverment, persuaded the State of New York to undertake the project. As head of the Canal Commission, he was indefatigable in working for its development, most effectively while governor of the state, 1817–23. Unfortunately he was at political loggerheads with powerful opponents—particularly the "Albany Regency" headed by Martin Van Buren. As a result, he decided not to run again for governor and, in 1824, the "Regency" lost no time in humiliating him by securing his dismissal from the Board of the Canal, of which he was president. The act, so purely partisan, proved to be a political boomerang: an indignant public supported his candidacy in 1824, and in 1825 he was again governor, elected by an overwhelming and vindicating majority. In October his cup of satisfaction must have been filled to overflowing: as *governor* he could savor the fervid excitement when Lake Erie's waters ran into his "Ditch" at Buffalo and the gay fleet of canalboats made its triumphant voyage across the state, down the Hudson River to Sandy Hook, where he emptied two kegs of Lake Erie water into New York Bay. He was the lion of the celebrations and fabulous ceremonies in New York City.[64]

The grand opening of the canal was the culmination of months of being lionized. In June 1825, at a dinner given for Clinton in Philadelphia, Judge Peters offered a toast that expressed the general opinion and evoked "3 cheers, standing": "DE WITT CLINTON the FATHER of the most distinguished Public Improvement—The gratitude of our nation should be his merited reward." Later in the summer, on the invitation of the Ohio sponsors of internal improvements, Governor Clinton participated in the ceremonies marking the beginning of the Ohio Canal. Henry Clay was a guest also, and in the report of "each eating a public dinner in honor of the other," it was said that Clinton seemed "to wear the longer plume." Clinton could but be flattered by being ranked thus ahead of Clay, who was known the country over as "the Father of the American System"—that is, the policy of protective tariffs and internal improvements in transportation. Clinton's entire tour of Ohio was marked by unstinted hospitality and homage, nearly, if not quite, rivaling that accorded Lafayette. (At least one Ohioan, in fact, declared he would travel as far to see DeWitt Clinton as to see Lafayette.) From Ohio, Clinton went to Pittsburgh, where his reception was equally enthusiastic: a 24-gun salute greeted his arrival; a sumptuous public dinner was given in his honor; the Masons gave a supper for him worthy of a past Grand Commander, which he was; a "beautiful Steam Boat" was christened *The Clinton* and launched in his presence. One of the toasts at the public dinner summed up the midwestern feeling for him—much of the eastern, too: "He has won his country brilliant victories over time and space. Well does he deserve the triumphant honors which justice and gratitude have decreed."[65]

MAJOR SAMUEL RINGGOLD

Major Samuel Ringgold was the first American officer to be fatally wounded in the Mexican War, and his death was the more dramatic because he received the wound while leading his corps of Flying Artillery in its first engagement and in the first battle of the war. Until then he was known to comparatively few Americans outside the Army, federal officials concerned with the military, and, of course, his personal circle of friends and acquaintances. Still, he had had a fruitful and notable career in the 46 years since his birth in Washington County, Maryland, in 1800. Entering West Point when only 14, he graduated at the head of his class and won the highest honors awarded by the academy. The three years as aide to General Winfield Scott, which began his military life, were followed by a variety of broadening duties. At one time he was assigned to Ordnance at the important New York Post and, so it was said,

brought to this duty "not only great skill as an officer but superior inventive genius" that resulted in improvements on the "percussion cannon lock" and in devising "the military saddle now [1847] in general use in the army for dragoons and artillery." Between 1836 and 1838, as Captain of the 3rd Artillery, he was actively engaged in the Seminole War, and for his valiant services in the Florida campaign he was brevetted major.[66]

When the government decided to introduce the use of a flying artillery such as had proved so formidable in European wars, Ringgold was one appointed to organize a corps. Its first American trial, at Palo Alto on May 8, 1846, contributed immeasurably to the victory when Taylor's untried forces of about 2,300 faced Aristas's vastly superior forces, said to number 5,000 to 7,000 men. In the ensuing battle, Ringgold proved not only the ghastly effectiveness of the flying artillery he had developed but also his dedication to his men and his duty. "He pointed the guns with his own hands" while the supporting infantry at his rear "cheered rapturously the brilliant movements and destructive execution." Nor did he pause "until shot through the thighs by a cannon ball passing from right to left, carrying with it a large mass of muscle and integuments, and tearing off the front of the saddle and withers of the noble charger he rode." As he fell slowly from his horse, one of his lieutenants rushed to him, calling for a caisson to carry him to the rear. Ringgold protested: "Never mind. Go ahead with your men; all are wanted in front." After cautioning that care be taken to secure an empty caisson, since all ammunition might be needed, he finally consented to be taken from the field of battle. Three days later he died and was buried at Point Isabel with the honors of war.[67]

As the news of Taylor's glorious victory over vastly superior forces spread throughout the country, burnishing American pride and thrilling even those who were against a war with Mexico, reports of Ringgold's exploits and heroism at Palo Alto reached from metropolis to village. Immediately a committee was appointed in Baltimore to bring Ringgold's body back to Maryland from Point Isabel. One of Ringgold's teamsters, Sergeant Kelly, begged and received permission to accompany his commander's body to its final resting place. (This devoted sergeant had lost an arm in the battle.) At stopovers along the route on the long journey home, homage was paid to the dead hero of Palo Alto. Arriving in Washington by the southern mail line on December 16, 1846, they were met by a reception committee and a detachment of army volunteers as well as a large number of citizens, and the casket was escorted by a guard of honor to Jackson Hall, where it remained overnight. The next day, just over seven months after his death, Ringgold's body arrived in Baltimore. There it lay in state in the Merchants Exchange and was visited by thousands of men, women, and children of all ages until December 22, the day of the impressive funeral and procession such as are accorded to presidents. All business was suspended. Bells tolled. Flags were at half mast. Civil and military officials of the United States, of Maryland, and of Baltimore, a "splendid military cavalcade" formed by Corps of Volunteers "in full uniform" from many Maryland counties, from Baltimore, from Delaware, and from Philadelphia, all marched in the procession, accompanied by perhaps a dozen bands with muffled drums playing the death march.[68]

As apparently is normal when a national hero dies a dramatic death, the sincere mourning of many, the gushing sentiment of others, and the macabre interest of many more form a rich source of commercial profit. Ringgold's gallantry and the circumstances of his death were such a lode: he was soon commemorated by mementos that were bought and cherished by many Americans. Probably the first among them were the engravings and lithographs. One lithograph was advertised as early as June 3, 1846, less than a month after the victory at Palo Alto, and was available early in August. It was a full-length portrait "from a drawing on stone" by the eminent artist Persico, who derived his portrait "from an approved oil painting in the possession of the family of the deceased."[69] In another, published by J. Baillie, the major is mounted on his noble charger. Not surprisingly, the most popular seem to have been those with such titles as "The Fall of Ringgold" and "The Death of Major Ringgold" depicting the gruesome scene with the wounded man. Perhaps the most familiar today is that by Nathaniel Currier in which the bleeding Ringgold is supported by two of his officers and the bleeding charger lies on its back. Glass was also a medium of commemorative portraits: pressed glass cup plates inscribed "RINGGOLD / PALO ALTO" and blown-molded whiskey flasks, which probably were rushed to market as soon after May 11 as the molds could be made—sometime in 1846, I believe.

Flasks GI–71 and 72 have a profile bust and the inscription "MAJOR / RINGGOLD" on one side; on the other (charted as the obverse), is a profile bust of General Taylor and the inscription "ROUGH AND READY". These two pint flasks, each blown in exceptionally fine molds with well-cut design, presumably were produced in Baltimore, Van Rensselaer

attributed them to the Baltimore Glass Works. It certainly was most fitting that the portrait of a notable son of Maryland and hero of Palo Alto shared a place of honor with Rough and Ready Taylor under whom he served. The difference between the flasks was in the edges, those of GI–72 being smooth and those of GI–71 ribbed. Both flasks are common today, indicating that they probably were quite popular items, far more so than the Ringgold cup plates, which are now very rare. Strangely, GI–71 with the ribbed edge has been recorded in many colors, some rarely seen today, whereas GI–72 with the smooth edge has so far been recorded only in aquamarine and amethyst tint. Possibly the answer is a mold alteration. If so, inasmuch as GI–72 occurs only in aquamarine and amethyst tint (due probably to an excess of oxide of manganese or magnesium in the batch), I think it likely three ribs were cut in the GI–72 mold to make the mold for GI–71.

A third pint Taylor–Ringgold flask (Ill. 127), discovered in 1975 by Jack Whistance, has been charted as GI–131. In the argot of the antiques world, it was a "sleeper": it had been in the Charles B. Gardner Collection for over 35 years without being recognized by collectors or dealers as anything more exciting than a rare and unusual color in Taylor–Ringgold flasks. Comparing it with GI–71 and GI–72, Mr. Whistance saw an unrecorded variety from a third Taylor–Ringgold mold. This flask has the three vertical ribs on the ends or edges, as does GI–71, but does not have the slight incurve just above the base, as on both GI–71 and 72, and it is slightly larger overall. On the obverse the Taylor bust is more elongated than the one on the other two. The Ringgold bust is also longer, and the placing of the letters is quite different. The "J" of "MAJOR" is directly above the center of Ringgold's head, instead of to the left; the "R" of "RINGGOLD" is higher on the left—about in line with the left end of the bust—and the "D" is a bit lower on the right. Where and by whom GI–131 was produced is unknown at present. It seems to me unlikely that, popular as the Ringgold flasks GI–71 and 72 were (both listed "common"), the Baltimore Glass Works to which they were attributed would have had another mold. On the other hand, because of the three-rib edge in particular, it does seem likely that flask GI–71 may have been the model for the GI–131 mold.

When an editor of a Philadelphia newspaper, one of many eulogizing Ringgold in May of 1846, wrote "His memory will be gratefully cherished so long as honor has a votary, freedom a hero, or his country a name,"[70] he little dreamed that, except for a few

127A. Reverse of a pint aquamarine Taylor–Ringgold flask, GI–71. The Taylor-Ringgold flask GI–71, and also GI–72, attributed to the Baltimore (Md.) Glass Works commemorated General Zachary Taylor's victory over the Mexican forces in the battle of Palo Alto on May 8, 1846, and, in particular, Major Samuel Ringgold, Baltimore's Mexican War Hero, the first American officer to be fatally wounded in a battle fought on foreign soil. Undoubtedly the commemorative flasks were produced shortly after his death. (Photo by Raymond F. Errett) *The Corning Museum of Glass*

B. Reverse of a pint aquamarine Taylor–Ringgold flask, GI–131, similar to GI–71 but without the incurve on the ends above the base; with a slightly longer bust and slightly different placement of letters. This flask, as yet the only recorded specimen and for many years in the Collection of Charles B. Gardner, was identified as an unlisted variant by Jack Whistance in 1975. Because it seems unlikely that a third mold for Taylor–Ringgold flasks would have been needed at the Baltimore Glass Works the flask has been charted under Glasshouse as "unknown." However, it seems that a GI–71 flask may have served as the model for the mold. (Photo by Bruce Whistance) *Jack Whistance*

historians, it would be collectors and students of such tangible mementos as these flasks who would keep Major Ringgold's memory green. It seems safe to say he is as unknown now to the majority of Americans as the Unknown Soldiers in Arlington Cemetery.

JENNY LIND[71]

Two foreigners, one who took the country by storm and one who caused a storm in the country, were immortalized in popular glass bottles and flasks: Jenny Lind, the Swedish Nightingale, and Louis Kossuth, the fiery Hungarian revolutionary and patriot.

To those Americans who had been abroad in the late 1840s, especially to England, the marvel of Jenny Lind—her voice, her personality, her piety,

her charities—was inescapable. And to Americans who read items on European musical events and foreign news published in their own metropolitan newspapers, she was far from unknown. For at least four years before she signed the famous concert contract with P. T. Barnum, American editors published items reporting her generosity and her triumphs in opera and concert. In 1846, one such item, headlined "JENNY LIND IN VIENNA," proclaimed that her tones were like flames. Two years later when she was captivating England, Henry Colman observed in one of his letters from London:

Parts of her singing, or rather the singing of certain parts I have heard better executed by others; but, as a whole, I have never heard her equal, or scarcely any one comparable to her. I have never known such extraordinary compass of voice, such facility of execution, such flexibility, such beauty and melody of articulation and account . . . .

That year, 1848, bewitched Londoners were willingly, eagerly, paying the equivalent of $15 and $20 a seat to hear Jenny Lind sing, so Mr. Colman reported[72]—a considerable sum in buying power in those days; the dollar equivalent of 75 and 100 years later would have more than pleased the famous Scandinavian sopranos of our century, Kirsten Flagstad and Birgit Nilsson.

However, to the generality of Americans, Jenny Lind was not even a familiar name and, moreover, their level of music appreciation was nearer the minstrel show and the village church choir than the opera and oratorio. Yet it was for this general public, not the select sophisticates, that Jenny Lind had to be made an irresistible attraction if P. T. Barnum was to win his gamble. For Barnum had gambled as never before when he authorized the contract wherein Jenny Lind agreed to make no less than two appearances a week, giving a total of 150 concerts or oratorios within a year and a half in American cities and in Havana, Cuba, for a fee of $1,000 a performance, and in addition, after 75 concerts, one-fifth of the net profits if Barnum had already cleared $75,000, or to a revision of the contract if, after 50 concerts, the net returns did not meet expectations. Barnum accepted Jenny Lind's stipulations that, after the first two concerts in any city, she could give concerts for charity (she gave her voice, but Barnum paid all expenses) and that she would never be required to sing in an opera, the singing of which had long plagued her conscience since, to her, opera and the theater were immoral. Barnum also agreed to pay $25,000 to her musical director and $12,000 to a baritone of her choice, who was to take part in the concerts and oratorios; to provide Jenny Lind with a maid, a male servant, carriage, and horses with their attendants in every city, and to pay all traveling expenses of not only herself but also her companion and mentor Josephine Ahmansson and her secretary. As guarantee, he deposited with Baring Brothers in London the $187,500 in government bonds of the United States that he had scratched to raise. So Barnum definitely *had* to sell Jenny Lind to Americans, not primarily as a world-renowned diva of the operatic and concert stage but as a world-renowned "public attraction."

This feat had to be performed in only about six months. Barnum, self-styled "Prince of Humbug" and dubbed "Prince of Showmen" by posterity, lost no time applying to the problem his uncanny skills in promotion and publicity. Americans from one end of the country to the other were soon filled with an avid desire and curiosity to hear and, even more, see Jenny Lind. And they were in that condition long before August when she sailed from England in the "Jenny Lind Boat," as the *Atlantic* was called because so many Americans about to return home sought to have the status of traveling companion to Jenny Lind. Probably few American newspapers failed to carry news items from England or were not seeded with Barnum's releases and quotable statements. Perhaps, even more than her voice, her personality and charities were stressed for the benefit of the "masses," to use Barnum's word for the special public he wooed. According to one of his statements:

Since her *début* in England, she has given to the poor from her own private purse more than the whole amount which I have engaged to pay her, and the proceeds of concerts for charitable purposes in Great Britain, where she has sung gratuitously, have realized more than ten times that amount.[72a]

It was made known, too, that the reason Jenny Lind had accepted Barnum's bid—the highest of several—was that she wished to establish a hospital for the poor children of Stockholm, a project beyond the scope of her present means, which, however, were more than sufficient for her own needs. To give reality to all the praiseful words, Barnum circulated a portrait of Jenny Lind, familiarizing the people with her lovely person.

The result of Barnum's perspicacity in publicity was such that not only was the day of Jenny Lind's arrival a gala one, with a throng of over 30,000 at the pier to welcome her, but all New York seemed to go into a prolonged near-frenzy. The uncurbed enthusiasm, even before she had sung a note, so convinced Jenny Lind—Barnum too—of assured success that she obtained a favorable revision of her contract whereby, starting from the very first concert, she would receive one-half the net profits as well as her $1,000 fee, and either she or Barnum could terminate the contract after 100 concerts. Moreover, with Barnum's consent, she announced that she would give to charities $10,000, her share of the expected profits, from her first concert. The tickets for that concert, which was to be in Castle Garden, were auctioned—and the first ticket went for $225 to Genin the Hatter, whose store was next door to Barnum's American Museum and who derived almost instant fame and profits from the ensuing country-wide publicity. The $17,869 from the auction was an unprecedented figure for a single concert, but as the anticipated $20,000 was not cleared, Jenny Lind's share was only $8,500. Barnum contributed the $1,500 necessary to meet her promised $10,000. This act of generosity—but also one doubtless calculated to preserve the Jenny Lind image as created—was unpublicized. Nor did Jenny Lind herself reveal his share in her gift to New York charities. After all, her piety and generosity did not deprive her of a "business sense" or an appreciation of the importance of her public as well as personal image. Reading her life story, one tends to wonder if perhaps the love of humanity fathering her great charities was tinged by a fear of God.

Jenny Lind rode easily from wave to wave of popularity, prosperity, and generosity so long as she traveled under Barnum's aegis. From New York she went to Boston and Philadelphia, and back to New York again, on to Washington (where President Fillmore called); then to Havana for four scheduled concerts; thence to New Orleans, Natchez, Memphis, Nashville, and Cincinnati, before returning to New York and Philadelphia—all in nine months. During these months, so Barnum's biographer M. R. Werner found, Jenny Lind was better known and discussed "as Florence Nightingale than as the Swedish Nightingale." When she reappeared in New York after her conquest of the West, *The Republic* for June 1851 reported:

This lovely child [she was in her thirty-first year] of mercy and of song is again amongst us, after having made a tour of the Southern and Western States scattering charity and melody, like flowers along her path. The enthusiasm that greeted her on her first arrival has been tempered down to calm and deep-seated admiration of her virtues and genius . . . her concerts have been numerously attended and rapturously received.[73]

But now, too, discordant notes were increasingly breaking into the harmony between Barnum and Jenny Lind and those accompanying her, partly struck by her pianist Otto Goldschmidt, whose influence upon her was growing. As a result, after the ninety-third concert Jenny Lind broke the contract, refunding $32,000 to Barnum but even so netting $176,675.09. The break proved shattering to her publicity and to her concert receipts. Perhaps, in part, her appearance as Madame Otto Goldschmidt accelerated the dwindling of her audience and the returns from the few concerts she gave after her marriage to her pianist early in 1852. Be that as it may, the once ecstatic New York newspapers estimated that receipts from her farewell concert on May 22, 1852,

were only $7,000. And when she sailed for England only about 2,000 people gathered to wave her off, in contrast to the 30,000 who had hailed her arrival, though *The Republic* did say that she left "as she came among us, with flying colors and spotless reputation."[74]

But if Jenny Lind's attraction waned, that of the innumerable things named for her or decorated with her portrait did not. From the time of her landing and for years after her retirement in England, Jenny Lind things were echoes keeping alive the memories of her visit. As Barnum recorded, "Songs, quadrilles and polkas were dedicated to her, and poets sung her praises," and there were "Jenny Lind shawls, mantillas, robes, sofas, pianos—in fact everything was Jenny Lind." Even on faraway Nantucket Island, Jenny Lind rubber boots could be obtained at the Ladies Exchange.[75] Her devotees throughout the country could hang on their walls a portrait of her chosen from several lithographs. And her image was not limited to the graphic arts; it formed many odd functions—from a cast-iron caryatid supporting the board on which the family wash was ironed, to adorning glass whiskey bottles and flasks, of which I feel sure she disapproved, if she knew about them. Her portrait bust appeared on three flasks in the Midwest and on ten calabash bottles, mainly eastern, some of which were still being blown in the 1870s.

Of the three Jenny Lind flasks, one, GI–108, was a pint, which is scarce today, and two, GI–109 and 110, were quarts, which are now rare. The attribution of these flasks to the Midwest arose mainly from the geographical distribution of the recorded specimens and the specific attribution to McCarty & Torreyson of Wellsburg, (W.) Virginia, from Van Rensselaer's 1926 statement that they "probably" were produced by this firm, which presumably was operating the old Duval glassworks in the Jenny Lind period. The basis of the attribution seems to have rested solely on the similarity in form of the Jenny Lind flasks to flasks GIX–48 and GIX–49 in the Scroll Group, inscribed "M'CARTY & TORREYSON / MANUFACTURERS / WELLSBURG, VA." Except for a light green reported by Sam Laidacker, these flasks have so far been recorded only in aquamarine. As will be noted by a study of the line drawings in the Charts, the flasks, unlike the calabash Jenny Linds, bore no identifying name. But the bust was so closely similar to those on the calabash bottles as to be unmistakably intended to represent the famous singer, and—as on most of the bottles—she wore a plain bertha with brooch at the throat. Though on the flasks no laurel wreath symbolized her triumphs as on the bottles, there was, perhaps even more appropriately, a lyre in the lower section below her portrait.

Of the ten calabash bottles, nine—GI–99 through GI–106—are so closely similar in the depiction of Jenny Lind, and of the glassworks on the reverse of seven (all but GI–100 and 106), as to suggest, if not a single moldmaker, more than one mold by one moldmaker, and pirating. Though each portrait varied slightly from the others, Jenny was shown with a long oval face, her hair way down over her ears with a suggestion of a bun low in back; wearing a plain bertha, except on GI–102 and 103, pinned with a brooch; and framed in a laurel wreath of two branches with the tips not quite meeting at the top. On the reverse, the two-storied glassworks with shrubs at left and tree at right were more like many-chimneyed dwellings than the familiar glass factory. It will be observed also that, aside from any inscriptions and designs, the bodies of GI–99 through GI–101 were smooth, whereas those of GI–102 through GI–106 were ribbed except for the design panels; all had "fluted" necks. Only GI–99a, of which just one specimen has been recorded as yet, was without an identifying name. On the others, "JENNY / LIND" was inscribed on GI–99, GI–100 ("KOSSUTH" above a profile bust of Louis Kossuth on the reverse), GI–101, and the extremely rare ribbed GI–106 (tree in foliage on reverse), and "JENY / LIND" was on GI–102 through GI–105.

The tenth calabash, GI–107, inscribed on the reverse "FISLERVILLE / GLASS WORKS" in banners curving to form a broken arch above a typical glass factory of the period, had a quite different representation of Jenny below "JENNY LIND" in a faintly outlined frame and above two short sprays of laurel. Her face was fuller and not as long as on the other calabash bottles; her hair, though fashionably covering her ears, was puffed out, not drawn down and looking like hound's ears. On the Fislerville calabash, Jenny wore a décolleté gown instead of one with sedate bertha. Perhaps the designer, in showing her in an off-the-shoulder gown, had in mind Jenny Lind's role as the concert singer, the Swedish Nightingale, whereas the designer of the more modest gown was thinking of her role as a pious, charitable "Florence Nightingale," to borrow Mr. Werner's term. In this connection it is interesting to note that in one news item reporting Jenny Lind Goldschmidt's last concert, she was described as "dressed more richly than usual, as if desirous to pay the utmost respect to her hearers in the least important particular."[75a] The Fislerville calabash differed

also in having the edges of the body fluted and the bottom of the neck scalloped, as did some of the pictorial calabash bottles in Group XIII—for instance, the Hunter and Fisher bottles GXIII–5 and 6.

All but two of the calabash Jenny Linds have been attributed definitely or tentatively to specific glasshouses. Two might be said to attribute themselves, since a glasshouse name was inscribed on the reverse—the Fislerville mentioned above and GI–101 inscribed "MILLFORA. G. WORK'S" (of which more later). The attributions, made by both Van Rensselaer and Knittle, of the other Jenny Linds known in 1926[76] are still accepted, except in the case of GI–99; they were as follows:

1. GI–99. "JENNY LIND"—"GLASS / WORK'S / S.HUFFSEY". Attributed to Samuel Huffsey as manufacturer. This attribution was believed to be correct until comparatively recent years. Though Samuel Huffsey may have had a financial interest in a glassworks in the period of the Jenny Lind bottles, he was not the owner of one. He was, however, an agent for manufacturers of glassware, and also supplied them with molds. Therefore it seems apparent these bottles marked with his name were made to be sold by him, and doubtless blown in a mold supplied by him. That the glassworks in which they were blown was in New Jersey is most likely. And I was informed by J. E. Pfeiffer, who for some years has been contributing new evidence regarding New Jersey factories by his invaluable research in old glasshouse records, account books, and other primary sources, that Thomas Stanger of the New Brooklyn Glass Works and the Isabella Glass Works purchased a Jenny Lind mold from Samuel Huffsey. Although he has found no definite proof as yet, Mr. Pfeiffer believes that possibly the GI–99 S. Huffsey Jenny Linds may have been blown in the Isabella Glass Works. I believe it not unlikely that the extremely rare GI–99a, which has no inscriptions, was also a Jersey product, possibly from the same glassworks. Possibly its mold was altered for GI–99 by cutting in that bottle's inscriptions.

2. GI–101. "JENNY / LIND"—"MILLFORA. G. WORK'S". Inasmuch as there was no known record of a glassworks called Millfora (nor is there today), Van Rensselaer concluded that the moldmaker had misspelled "Millford," as did Edwin Atlee Barber before him, and attributed this bottle to the Millford Glass Works at Millford,

New Jersey. I know of no reason to doubt the attribution. Also, the apostrophe between "K" and "S" of "Works" in the inscription, as on GI–99, suggests that the same moldmaker made both molds and that they were supplied to the glassworks by Samuel Huffsey.

3. GI–102. "JENY /LIND", bertha with embroidered edge—"GLASS" / 6-pointed star / "FACTORY". Attributed to the Whitney Glass Works, Glassboro, N.J.

4. GI–103. "JENY / LIND", 2-tier bertha with embroidered edges—no inscription on reverse. Attributed to the Whitney Glass Works, Glassboro, N.J.

5. GI–104. "JENY / LIND"—no inscription on reverse. Attributed to the Ravenna Glass Works, Ravenna, O. The high incidence of this common variety in the general area of Ravenna and not elsewhere led to general acceptance of this attribution made by both Van Rensselaer and Knittle. Local tradition of Ravenna origin contributed also to their attribution. Although at the present time there is no definite evidence that a glassworks was operating in Ravenna before 1857, the long-lived popularity of Jenny Lind commemorative items suggests that it is not impossible these Jenny Lind calabash bottles were made there long after her American visit. One wonders if perhaps the mold had been acquired from a glassworks that had been supplying the region with these bottles and had discontinued their production. The continued production of Jenny Lind calabash bottles even into the 1870s is evidenced by J. E. Pfeiffer's research in original glasshouse records, where he found that in 1870 the Jenny Lind mold of the New Brooklyn Glass Works was borrowed by Bodine & Thomas, the firm then operating the Williamstown Glass Works, Williamstown, N.J. The similar GI–105 "Jeny Lind" bottle was attributed tentatively to the Ravenna Glass Works by George S. McKearin.

The ribbed GI–106 with tree in foliage on the reverse was not known until some years after the publication of Van Rensselaer's *Early American Bottles and Flasks* and Knittle's *Early American Glass*. I have no clue to its source, but it seems likely it was an eastern product, as, apparently, were the majority of the Jenny Lind calabash bottles. The remaining bottle, GI–100, portraying the much-publicized foreigners, Jenny Lind and Louis Kossuth, was thought by Van Rensselaer to have been produced by Samuel Huffsey, for whom the mold was made by Phillip Dolflein. At least, in an interview in 1900, Dolflein, a German who began his career as a moldmaker in Philadelphia in 1842, stated that he had made the Lind–Kossuth mold for Samuel Huffsey.[77] Though, as has been mentioned previously, Huffsey was not classed as a glass manufacturer but a glass factor at the time of the Kossuth bottles, he may well have ordered this mold for use in one of the South Jersey glassworks whose products he handled.

LOUIS KOSSUTH, HUNGARIAN PATRIOT[78]

Although, prior to 1848, even the name of Louis Kossuth probably was unfamiliar to Americans in general, he was no stranger to the large "German" segments of the population, augmented in the 1840s by thousands more fleeing to religious and political freedom in the United States.[79] Doubtless the adults had followed avidly, and told their children, the details of Kossuth's career from his appointment at only 25 to the 1825 Hungarian Parliament, through his expanding liberal activities, his arrest for high treason in 1837, and four years' imprisonment, to his emergence as the popular leader wresting bits of local and commercial independence from Austria. The eyes of governments watched him also, including those of the United States. By 1848, he was being cursed by European rulers and hailed by their peoples as the inspiriting force of their revolutionary movements, and his status in Hungary became almost that of a dictator—but a benevolent dictator, for the people's good only, not his own aggrandizement. Not surprisingly, again Kossuth was declared a traitor, this time by the new emperor of Austria and king of Hungary, Francis Joseph, himself the product of a brief Vienna revolution. Refusing mediation offers made by the American minister at Kossuth's request, Francis Joseph resorted to arms in January 1849. The Austrians were defeated; independence was declared; Kossuth became governor. This triumph of Liberty was but a skyrocket: the czar intervened in Hungary, as did the Kremlin a little over a century later. By fall, Hungarian liberty was crushed with the aiding forces of the czar, who, Kossuth wrote later, "boasts that his mission is to be the scourge of all nations striving for Liberty . . ."[80] (The nature of "The Bear that walks like a man" did not change with a change in ideology.) Thousands, taken prisoner by the Russians, were given to Austria for punishment by death. Hundreds fled the country to take refuge in England, the United States, and Turkey. Louis Kossuth and his family were among those escaping to Bosnia, Serbia, then a province of the Ottoman Empire. There, the sultan and England agreed they should be interned until the fall of 1850.

In the meantime, what only Barnum's contrived publicity had done to prepare "the masses" for Jenny Lind's arrival in the United States, foreign and domestic news was doing, and continued to do, spontaneously for Louis Kossuth, inflaming Americans' inextinguishable interest in, and sympathy with, republican movements and their leaders. To Americans as to Hungarians, Kossuth became a hero, an intrepid David facing too many Goliaths. News of the brutal extinction of independent Hungary and Kossuth's exile yoked burning indignation to Americans' fervent sympathy. Congress, they said, should grant public lands, free, to all Hungarian refugees; Kossuth's liberation should be secured and asylum in the United States offered to him. These demands for action were but two of many loudly voiced throughout the country and echoed in state and national legislatures, and, of course, as widely reported by the press. Lest they lead to serious deeds, our secretary of state did try to obtain the release of Kossuth and his companions in the spring of 1850. The sultan's refusal served Kossuth's cause, insuring continuance of the vast pro-Hungarian chorus and antiphonal anti-Austrian–anti-Russian chants during the ensuing months of frustration. Finally, acting on a Congressional resolution, President Fillmore got the sultan's agreement to liberation of the Kossuth group and to their being brought to the United States by an American naval vessel. Already well over 100,000 refugees from Germany, Austria, and Hungary had been given asylum in the United States, and the *official* attitude of our Federal Government was that Kossuth was being offered political asylum. This, of course, was not what Kossuth wanted, and it was a condition he hoped to change. "M. Kossuth," so a correspondent to the *New York Herald* wrote on September 15, 1851, from Constantinople, "has accepted the generous offer of the Senate and together with the greater part of the refugees will embark in the *Mississippi* for New York."[81] Though Kossuth himself left the party and vessel at Gibraltar to proceed to England, where he was as eagerly awaited as in America, the U.S. Frigate *Mississippi* was to be forever associated with Louis Kossuth in the public mind, and commemorated by the calabash bottle GI–112. Kossuth's family and other members of the refugee party landed at New York

City on October 15, 1851.

Portraits and descriptions of Kossuth preceded him, satisfying in part the interested curiosity of Americans. The following description, which appeared in Nantucket's *The Inquirer* on November 14, 1851, is how one observer saw him:

PERSONAL APPEARANCE of Kossuth—He stands about 5 feet 8 inches in height, has a slight and apparently not strongly knit frame, and is a little round shouldered. His face is oval; a pair of bluish gray eyes, which some-how remind me of O'Connell [Irish patriot] in expression, well set beneath a full and arched brow, gave an animated and intelligent look to his countenance. His forehead, high and broad, is deeply wrinkled, and time has just begun to grizzle a head of straight dark hair and to leave a bald spot behind. He has not got the true Hungarian nose, but it is a fair, well-formed feature such as a French passport would describe as Moyen [average]; a thick moustache nearly covers his mouth except when he speaks or smiles, and unites the beard and whiskers in full flock of dark hair, falling down from his chin. The portraits are singularly unlike him in person or expression. Whether from his recent captivity or from constitutional causes there is somehow an air of lassitude in his look, to which the fatigues of the voyage [to England] not improbably contributed.

Altogether he gives one the idea of a man of thought rather than action; there is a speculative air in his face, mingled with some degree of melancholy which would mark him for a visionary or theoretical enthusiast rather than a great leader or soldier . . . he is simply dressed, dark green frock coat with a little silk braid at the back and edges . . . a common low crowned square felt hat . . .

Plumes were not mentioned, but two adorned his hat as it was shown in portraits in magazines, on Hungarian bond issues, and in glass—that is, the calabash bottle GI–112. The New York hatter, Genin, was to profit well from starting a fad in Kossuth hats, which large numbers of male admirers wore as a token of their support of Kossuth. Nor was the fad confined to New York—in Nantucket, as early as March 15, 1852, "another lot of Gent's and Boy's / Kossuth Hats" was advertised for sale by the haberdasher next door to the post office. One instance of "the KOSSUTH FEVER" was reported by a Bostonian, perhaps with tongue in cheek:

an honest, broad cheeked teamster, who in lack of a Kossuth feather, had struck a codfish in his cap, tail up, with a cracker attached to the side by way of a cockade—It was the best he could do to manifest in his humble way his zeal in behalf of the intervention doctrine.[82]

Not since the visit of Lafayette in 1824/25 had the arrival of a foreigner been so eagerly awaited, nearly countrywide. Nor had so royal and enthusiastic a welcome been given as that which greeted Kossuth. When, in the early hours of December 5, 1851, he landed from the W.W. Mail Steamer *Humbolt* at Staten Island Quarantine Ground, he was hailed by a large crowd of admirers, who had stayed up late to see him. Late (or, rather, early) as the hour was, a 21-gun salute was fired as he accompanied Dr. Doane, of the Quarantine, to the Doane home to spend the rest of the night. With day came the first of many receptions, parades, and banquets that were to be held in his honor as he traveled through the country seeking funds and support to retake his homeland. Most spectacular was his welcome next day, December 6, to New York City, where he stayed over a fortnight while going also to nearby cities and towns to plead his cause. His hopes of success in obtaining intervention by the United States against Austria and Russia were raised by the fervent responses to his eloquently preached doctrine that, "as the only living Republic and example of man's capabilities of self government," we had the moral duty and responsibility to intervene actively wherever the self-determination of a would-be republic such as Hungary was denied to national groups by any European state. Not since Citizen Genêt had any foreigner so tried to influence our foreign policy.

Kossuth must have hoped that "Washington" was lending a sympathetic ear. It was, though not as he wished. He was received, not as the governor of beleaguered Hungary but as an individual and a refugee. Our government and officials were careful to avoid giving any political interpretation to Kossuth's visit or to their reception of him. When he was received by President Fillmore, he delivered his prepared speech. The president replied briefly, expressing his happiness at welcoming Kossuth "to the land of freedom" and congratulating him on his release "from long confinement in Turkey." Then, according to newspaper reports, the president went on:

As an individual I sympathize deeply with you and your brave struggle for independence and freedom of your native land. The American people can never be indifferent to such a contest; but our policy as a nation in this respect has been uniform, from the commencement of our government—should your country be restored to independence and freedom, I should then wish you . . . a restoration to your native land; but should that never happen, I can only repeat my welcome to you and your companions here, and pray that God's blessings may rest upon you wherever your lot may be cast.

Kossuth's next disappointment came the following Monday, January 5, 1852, when the welcoming committee of senators informed him that he was not expected to address the Senate. Instead, the Senate adjourned so all could meet him. However, the congressional dinner in his honor with its toasts and speeches gave him the opportunity to plead his cause and draw a picture of the widespread calamity resulting from Russia's uncontested intervention in Hungary. In an interview with the secretary of the interior he "declared that the opposition which he met at the hands of Congress and the Executive convinced him that his mission to this country had completely failed [and that] he felt deeply disappointed at the reception he had met with at Washington." Nor could he draw any comfort from his interview with Henry Clay. The newspapers reported Clay's dramatic statement: "A dying man, I oppose your doctrine of intervention."[83]

It was a disappointed but undaunted Kossuth who left Washington to begin his fund-raising tour on which he continued also his call for more active aid by the United States. He headed west and south. Harrisburg, Pittsburgh, Cleveland, Louisville, St. Louis, and New Orleans were among the places where he was seen and heard. Except in lukewarm New Orleans, apparently he was received with open heart and hands, especially by the Friends of Hungary, a group working to raise cash contributions and sell bonds for a Hungarian loan. Incidentally, groups other than the Friends of Hungary, and in places unvisited by Kossuth, were raising money, as one editor put it, to "render some little service to the sacred cause of Hungarian liberty": the Dramatic Club of Nantucket contributed the proceeds of two performances to the cause, nearly $150. Of course, not all citizens were Kossuth admirers and supporters. In Cincinnati where, it was estimated, 30,000 gathered to hear him speak, the dissidents' point of view appeared in the *Cincinnati Gazette* and was reprinted as far east as Nantucket:

a large number of our citizens have had nothing to do with the matter, and a large number who have *attended* have done so only out of curiousity [*sic*]. A large amount, if not the larger, of contributors, have been those who paid merely for a convenient chance to see and hear the man as to whom so much has been said.[84]

By the end of April Kossuth was charming the sympathetic people of Massachusetts at Northampton, Springfield, and Boston and its environs, including Lexington, Concord, Salem, and Lowell. And again he was feted by town and state officials. But, though it was estimated that, before going on to Albany and Buffalo, he had received $27,000 from Hungarian bonds and other contributions, the people in general were not so eager and inflamed by the Hungarian and his cause. By mid-June it was reported, "the great Hungarian is now living privately at the Irving House, New York City, but in a few days leaves for England, there to wait and prepare for the beginning of the Great European revolution." Though in all around $100,000 had been raised for the cause, Kossuth had failed to budge the United States from its nonintervention policy. Secretary of State Daniel Webster must have heaved a great sigh of relief when the news of Kossuth's July 14, 1852, departure reached him. Like Jenny Lind's, his leaving was not accompanied by fanfare and regret.

Besides the fine calabash GI–112 with portrait bust of Kossuth in uniform and wearing a plumed hat as in his portrait in *The International Magazine of Literature, Art, and Science* (January 1, 1852) and also on the Hungarian bonds, there were two other calabash bottles and a pint flask. The calabash GI–100 having a bust of Jenny Lind on one side has already been mentioned. The other, GI–113, has a similar "likeness" of Kossuth and a tree in foliage on the reverse. This flask, blown in the Bridgeton Glass Works, New Jersey, also has a profile bust, one with more profuse beard than on GI–100 and GI–113. The model could have been the daguerreotype by Claudat of London.

SCOTT AND BYRON

Just when and by whom it was determined that the profile busts on the half-pint flask GI–114 represented Sir Walter Scott and Lord Byron, I do not know. But the classic bust facing right was identified as Scott and the one with the open-collared shirt and facing left, as Byron, some years before Van Rensselaer published his *Early American Bottles and Flasks* in 1926. Certainly there would be nothing odd in the choice of this Scottish master of the historical novel and English poet to be memorialized by American glass pocket-flasks, or in the appeal of such flasks to the American public: the works of both were widely and avidly read in the United States into the early 20th century at least. (Older generations of bottle collectors surely will remember Scott's *Ivanhoe* as required reading in public schools.) Byron was more than a popular writer: he was a

defender of liberty, a supporter of the Greeks in their struggles against the Ottoman Empire, and his death in 1824 was the more tragic because he was young. That the designer of the flask did not underestimate the attraction of the design seems evidenced by the fact that the so-called Byron–Scott flasks are still common today. They occur mainly in natural bottle-glass colors—olive-greens (sometimes so deep as to be black in reflected light), olive-ambers, ambers, and, according to Sam Laidacker, emerald-green. Apparently they were produced in a New England glassworks—Van Rensselaer said "attributed to" Keene; that is, the glassworks on Marlboro Street, Keene, New Hampshire. Accepting the identification, one would be inclined to date the first appearance of the flask as 1824/25, after Byron's death, or 1832/33, after Scott's. Perhaps the latter date is the more likely.

THE BATTLE AND THE WASHINGTON MONUMENTS, BALTIMORE, MARYLAND

For many years the flasks in Group VI, attributed to the Baltimore Glass Works, were called simply Baltimore monument; they were so charted in 1941. "The Monument" was said to commemorate the September 12-14 battle of North Point. Van Rensselaer's designation of over 50 years ago was more or less blindly accepted by collectors and writers. The obvious disparity in the representation of "the monument," if noticed at all, was attributed to a designer's lack of observation or a moldmaker's carelessness. That there were two quite different monuments was pointed out in 1953 in *The Story of American Historical Flasks*. But I find the error still persists, so I shall emphasize again the differences between the two monuments, though truth, it seems, is a weak eradicator of error.

The monument first to be planned and last to be finished was the Washington Monument—Ill. 113, the first erected to George Washington's memory. Plans for it were being made in 1809, but they had to be shelved because of the difficult times followed by the War of 1812. The state was to provide much of the money, but recourse was had also in 1813/14 to a nationally advertised lottery in which whole tickets were $10.50, halves $5.50, and quarters $3.75. At last, in 1815, the cornerstone was laid—appropriately on July 4. Placed in the cornerstone were "a copper plate and sealed glass bottle, containing a likeness of Washington, his valedictory address, the several newspapers printed in this city, and the dif-

128. Washington Monument, Baltimore, Maryland. The cornerstone for the first monument erected in memory of George Washington was laid on July 4, 1815. The 16-foot statue of Washington completing the monument was placed on its pedestal in November 1829.

Drawn by William Bartlett, engraved by D. Thompson. *American Scenery from drawings by W. H. Bartlett.* By N. P. Willis, Esq., London 1840. *New York Public Library*

ferent coins of the United States." The marble monument, which—it is said—set a style for similar American and European monuments, was "the first of an architectural kind" to be attempted. The tall plain column rose from a large square base to a simple capital supporting the pedestal for the figure of George Washington. It was not until 1829 that the 16-foot marble statue carved by the Italian sculptor Henrico Cancici was placed upon its pedestal, increasing the height of the monument to 204 feet. According to a contemporary account:

the attitude given to this figure represents the great man in the act of resigning his commission, and the authority with which he had been invested by his country, again into the hands of the people, having accomplished the great object of his appointment, the freedom and independence of the Union.[85]

The Washington Monument ornaments nine flasks, on four without and five with the figure of Washington in place. Only one of those lacking the statue was charted in Group VI: the half-pint GVI–2 with "FELLS" above a fisherman's or oysterman's shallop and "POINT" below, on the reverse. (The shallop was a familiar vessel in Chesapeake waters.) The other three are charted as the reverse of portrait flasks: the pint GI–20 and quart GI–21 with "FELLS" above the bust and "POINT" below, and the pint GI–73 with "FELLS POINT" in arc above the monument. All four, it will be noted, have in common the inscription "FELLS POINT" (the famous shipping area of Baltimore) as well as the statueless monument. Also, all four have forms, including a framed oval panel, that are characteristic of the 1820s and early 1830s. These features contribute to my theory that the four flasks were first brought out before the statue of Washington was placed on its pedestal in November 1829, and possibly by the short-lived Baltimore Flint Glass Works located at Fells Point, whose molds may have been acquired by the Baltimore Glass Works. I believe also that the military gentleman on GI–73 was not intended originally to represent Zachary Taylor, that the mold originally had no identifying inscription, and that "GEN^L TAYLOR" was cut in the mold during the Mexican War, in which Taylor became a popular hero. The most likely time would seem to be after the battle of Buena Vista in February 1847. (For additional discussion, see Historical Sketch No. 18. Baltimore Glass Works.)

All five flasks—three quarts, one pint, and one half-pint—with the complete Washington Monument on the obverse have, on the reverse, "CORN FOR THE WORLD" arching above an upright ear of corn. Four of the five have "BALTIMORE" in an arc beneath the monument. The one without the inscription, unknown in 1941, is pictured as 2 in Ill. 123. Corn for the world and an ear of corn were a slogan and symbol natural to Baltimore and appropriate on a Baltimore flask, for the city's prosperity depended in no small part on the shipment of corn and grains. There is, however, a possibility that those flasks whose forms alone place them in the mid- to late-1840s were associated with repeal of England's Corn Laws. These laws, first passed in 1815 to curtail imports, had had an adverse effect on agricultural exports from America. Baltimore had a vital interest in, and was vitally affected by, these laws. Baltimore newspaper reports testify to the deep concern of Americans at the attempts to repeal these laws. One, on May 23, 1846, when news that

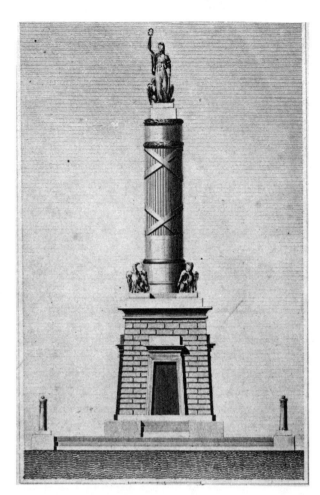

129. Battle Monument, Baltimore, Maryland. This monument was erected to commemorate Baltimore's defenders who died on September 12 and 13, 1814, in the Battle of North Point and the bombardment of Fort McHenry. From *The Casket*, S. C. Atkinson publisher, Philadelphia 1828. *New York Public Library*

the bill had not yet been passed by Parliament, ended: "Corn trade consequently remains in a very unsatisfactory state."[86] The satisfaction over the repeal of English Corn Laws in 1846 may have inspired the Corn-for-the-World flasks.

Baltimore's other monument, known as the Battle Monument (Ill. 129), was of local rather than national interest and did not command the widespread attention that the Washington Monument did. The Battle Monument was raised in commemoration of Baltimore's defenders who fell September 12, 1814, in the Battle of North Point and, the next day, in the bombardment of Fort McHenry. The funds for it were raised by a general and voluntary subscription. The cornerstone was laid with fanfare on September 12, 1815, the anniversary of the British attack and the death of "brave citizens" in battle. More elaborate than the Washington Monument, it had a square base in Egyptian style, with rusticated sides of 18 courses, a course for each state in the Union in 1814. At each

of the four corners at the top of the cornice was a large griffin. From this base rose a marble shaft resembling a Roman fasces with its fillets bearing the names of those killed in the battle and bombardment. The monument is climaxed by a heroic figure of Victory raising high a laurel crown in her right hand and holding a rudder in her left. This monument was completed in 1825.[87]

The Battle Monument is found on four flasks — GVI–1 and GVI–1a, GVI–3, and GI–18. The earliest, GI–18, has "WASHINGTON" in a semicircle above the profile bust of Washington in uniform, and on the reverse "BALTIMORE GLASS WORKS" in a horseshoe arch framing most of the monument. This flask is of the 1820–1830 period. The other three are of the 1840s. The two half-pints — GVI–1a, unknown in 1941, and GVI–1 — have a vine and grapes framing the Taylorism "A LITTLE MORE GRAPE CAPT BRAG" (see C. Presidential Candidates, Zachary Taylor), which dates them ca. 1847. The fourth, a pint, GVI–3, has "BALTIMORE" in an arc above the Battle Monument and "LIBERTY / & / UNION" on the reverse. This phrase[88] survived as a slogan from Daniel Webster's 1830 speech replying to Robert Y. Hayne's contentions that South Carolina, annoyed by the 1828 tariff act, had a right to nullify a federal law. Politicians in all camps shouted "Liberty & Union" in more than one campaign. Considering the speech applicable to the times, Nantucket's *The Inquirer* reprinted it in the summer of 1840. Webster's final purple prose was:

Let their [his eyes] last feeble and lingering glance rather behold the gorgeous ensign of the Republic, now known and honored throughout the earth, still full high advanced, its arms and trophies streaming in their original luster, not a stripe erased or polluted, not a single star obscured — bearing for its motto no such miserable interrogatory as *What is all this worth?*" nor those other words of delusion and folly, *Liberty first*, and *Union afterward*; but everywhere spread all over, in characters of living light, blazing on all its ample folds, as they float over the sea and over the land, and in every wind under the whole heavens, that other sentiment, dear to every true American heart.[89]

C. Presidential Candidates: *Their Portraits, Emblems, and Slogans*

For the United States, the second quarter of the 19th century was one of revolution in industry, in transportation, in commerce, and in politics. By the mid-1820s the age of Jackson was crossing the threshold, about to come in, and that of Hamilton was going out. The Herculean struggle between "conservative" and "radical" democracy was not only between politicians but between vociferous citizens as well. And the newspapers kept everyone alert on both sides. But there was more: what radios do today, bringing speeches, commentaries, and slogans to the ears of the public, was then done by popular political songs underlining the issues and characterizing the candidates for office. In addition, what television does today to bring the man and his platform before the eyes of the people was done then by a flood of broadsides and—especially after 1828—by cartoons and caricatures. It was possibly in 1824, certainly by 1828, that song and graphic political propaganda were joined by the figured whiskey flask. Liquor was far from an innovation as a vote getter, but its container was, and as such it was popular through the 1848 Taylor–Tyler presidential campaign. After a lapse of about 36 years, portrait flasks appeared again as campaign ammunition from 1884 to about 1900. Since that time a few commemorative portrait flasks have been produced, most of them in recent years. It is interesting to note that in 1956 there was what the *New York Herald Tribune* called a Tempest in a Whiskey Bottle. When a distiller hoped to designate his whiskey bottles as souvenirs of President Eisenhower's inaugural in 1956, his plan was objected to by the National Temperance League. At least the head of the league criticized Ohio's State Liquor Director for granting permission.[90] The protests must have caused the director second thoughts. So far as I know no such bottles were made.

JOHN QUINCY ADAMS AND ANDREW JACKSON, *6th and 7th Presidents*[91]

John Quincy Adams and Andrew Jackson are linked here because it is believed that flasks bearing their portraits were a part of the bitter contest between them and their adherents, for the presidency of the United States, that started in 1824 and increased in intensity through 1828.

John Q. Adams—defeater of Andrew Jackson in 1824, defeated by Jackson in 1828—was well suited by experience to head the country, at least insofar as foreign relations were concerned. Educated in Europe and at Harvard, schooled in diplomacy as secretary to two ambassadors, as minister to several European countries, and as President Monroe's secretary of state, he was perhaps the most able, active statesman of his time. All his learning and experience were filtered through a high and shrewd intelligence. Son of John Adams, our second president, John Q. came from a long-rooted and highly pedigreed New England family with a tradition of politics behind him. He was austere by nature, inflexibly honest in political dealings, a withdrawn formal man without a scintilla of appeal to the average man. Still, in the government and by many outside it, Adams was considered to be heir apparent to President Monroe. He thought so himself.

On the other hand, Jackson, son of a poor Scotch-Irish farmer in South Carolina, was a first-generation American. Jackson's qualifications for the presidency, by comparison with Adams's, seem far lower but more suited nationally to the temper of the times. He was a plantation and store owner, a lawyer who had a hand in writing the constitution for the new state of Tennessee when it was formed in 1796 from the western portion of North Carolina. He had served his state in Congress briefly in 1796, first as representative of the new state, then as senator in 1797/98, and for six years, 1798 to 1804, as judge on Tennessee's supreme court. Though he had fought against the Indians, not until the War of 1812 did he attain national stature. He was already a hero of the people when he was ordered to Florida, where he exceeded his authority in the campaign against the Seminole Indians. Though criticized in Congress, insofar as the people were concerned his successes further burnished the name and reputation of Old Hickory. Soon after his return to Tennessee he was elected United States senator. By then, many politicians were already thinking of him as presidential timber.

As the 1824 presidential campaign loomed, the Federalists were an emasculated party and the Republicans were splintered by sectional interests. By election day a peculiar situation had developed. One party of four factions was left in the field, and with four candidates: John Adams, who had been nominated by the Massachusetts legislature early in 1824, was the favorite son from New England; Andrew Jackson, whose camp felt sure of the West and South; Henry Clay, who hoped to capture western as well as eastern votes; and William H. Crawford, who looked hopefully to New York and the South. When the electoral votes were counted, Jackson led with 99, Adams had 84, Crawford 41, and Clay only 37. Since no one had a majority, the election went to the House of Representatives. There Clay, himself out of the running, threw his support and supporters to Adams, ensuring Adams's election. The Jackson faction reacted viciously with charges that the will of the people had been thwarted and the "Jackson" press was vehement in its accusations. Said one: "Expired at Washington on the ninth of February, of poison administered by the assassin hands of John Quincy Adams, the usurper, and Henry Clay, the virtue, liberty and independence of the United States."[92] The ungentlemanly campaign for the 1828 election was under way even before the inauguration of Adams in 1825.

Almost immediately Jackson and his followers had another and stronger peg on which to hang their campaign banners. By appointing Henry Clay his secretary of state, Adams appeared to turn the smoke of rumor into the fire of fact, for it had been said that, in exchange for Clay's support, Adams promised that Cabinet post to him if he himself was elected. The Jackson forces and the press promptly made "Bargain and Corruption" into a battle cry, and an effective one. Forgotten was the fact that John Quincy Adams had consistently taken General Jackson's side when Jackson's military conduct in Florida had been heatedly discussed and censured in Congress and Cabinet. Jackson fully believed the canard, and never forgave Adams for the alleged bargain. Jackson forces mustered their numbers and formed a political party, the Democratic Party. Although the new party had eager adherents, former supporters of Jackson, its strength was in the West. Jackson was a fellow westerner and, further endearing him to midwesterners, he was an advocate of more land for settlers and of moving the frustrating Indians farther west. He *was* a man of the people and was presented to them as a champion of the common man. As an advocate of wider suffrage and economic democracy, he became dear to many easterners, too, especially the immigrant laborers. By 1828 Hickory Clubs had been formed. Their members paraded and sang political songs boosting their candidate. There were equal demonstrations against John Q. Adams, who was thickly painted with the political brush as a snobbish and frigid aristocrat, a lover of kings and the trappings of monarchy, actually an advocate of return to a monarchy, a man of entrenched privileges. What little attraction John Q. Adams had for John Q. Public was minuscule by 1828. Jackson won easily, becoming our 8th president. In 1832 he won again, even more overwhelmingly, over Henry Clay.

The relative popularity of Adams and Jackson is reflected in the existence of at least 12 Jackson flasks and only one Adams. That one is flask GI–62 having "JOHN Q. ADAMS" in a deep semicircle above his portrait bust and, on the reverse, the American eagle, 13 stars, and "J.T. & C " below a beaded oval frame. Strangely, in the light of almost wholehearted western support of Jackson and equally almost wholehearted nonsupport of Adams, this flask was blown in a midwestern glasshouse, testifying to the existence of at least one Adams adherent in the Midwest or, since there is a companion Jackson J. T. & Company flask, at least a neutral. The firm probably was John Taylor & Company, operators of a small glasshouse in Brownsville, Pennsylvania, not far from Pittsburgh and New Geneva. If this tentative attribution is correct, the flask doubtless was brought out about 1828, as the firm is said to have owned the glasshouse from about 1828 into perhaps the early 1840s.

Of the flasks bearing Jackson's name, all but one (GI–70) depict Jackson in uniform. Seven—GI–64 through GI–70—were produced in midwestern glasshouses and five—GI–31 through GI–34a—in New England works. Midwestern flasks GI–64 through GI–68 are closely related by the type of large-beaded edges, the style, and treatment in depicting Jackson and, on the first four, by the style and treatment of the American eagle, stars, and beaded oval frame. The fifth has an elaborate flower, leaf, and acorn medallion on the reverse. In fact, so related are these flasks as to indicate the probability of one and the same moldmaker. "LAIRD. SC. [Sculpsit] Pitt." is below the beaded frame on the reverse of GI–66, a clue pointing to the Pittsburgh moldmaker Joshua Laird as the sculptor of the molds of all five flasks. In the oval frame of GI–66 are the initials "J.R."—undoubtedly those of John Robinson, proprietor of the Stourbridge Glass Works, Pittsburgh. Two others of the group have initials leading to attribution of probability. On GI–65 "J.T. & C°" appears beneath the beaded oval frame, as on the reverse of the Adams flask, and presumably stands for John Taylor & Company of Brownsville, Pennsylvania. On GI–67 the initials "B & M." are within the beaded oval frame; presumably they stand for Baker and Martin of the Perryopolis glassworks. Though the two unmarked and the Robinson flasks possibly date earlier than 1828, the "J. T. & C°" and "B & M." flasks probably were about 1828. All five have the inscription "GENERAL JACKSON" and a three-quarter view of the bust of Jackson in uniform. Jackson's hair, in front, is standing on end, doubtless in horror over the supposed Adams–Clay perfidy. His hair *was* conspicuous. On his way to his inauguration in 1829 he stopped off at several "cities," among them Cincinnati, where Mrs. Trollope was one of the throng witnessing his arrival. She wrote, "He wore his grey hair carelessly, but not ungracefully arranged, and spite of his harsh gaunt features, he looks like a gentleman and a soldier."[93] Praise indeed from the acid tongue of Mrs. Trollope.

The two remaining flasks GI–69 and GI–70 have small profile busts that bear no resemblance, even by caricature, to Andrew Jackson, but the inscriptions so identify them. As the line drawings show, Knox & McKee of Wheeling, (W.) Virginia, brought out GI–69, which appears to be identical with GI–92, except that GI–92 is inscribed "GENERAL LAFAYETTE," whereas "ANDREW JACKSON" is inscribed on GI–69. The possibility—I believe, probability—exists that here is another instance of mold alteration, that the inscription on GI–92 was filled in and that of GI–69 cut in about 1828; or, since GI–69 is extremely rare whereas GI–92 is only rare, the other way around in about 1824. (For discussion, see B. Lafayette and DeWitt Clinton.) The extremely rare flask GI–70 was proved by Harry Hall White's excavations to have been blown at the Mantua Glass Works, Mantua, Ohio. It has the initials "J T" (Jonathan Tinker) above "A JACKSON" in an arc above the small profile bust and "OHIO" in a panel at bottom. On the reverse are numerous Masonic emblems. Jonathan Tinker, an associate of David Ladd in starting the Mantua Glass Works, was a glassblower who had emigrated from Vernon, New York. Ladd too was an easterner, from Connecticut. So it is hardly a coincidence that this flask resembles the Mount Vernon Lafayette in form and has corrugated edges as do so many Connecticut flasks.

Students and collectors have believed these New England flasks were probably first produced in the 1824–28 period. However, Carl Flowers, historian and collector of Keene (New Hampshire) glass, has concluded—a very sound conclusion, I believe— that the Keene and Coventry Washington–Jackson flasks were primarily in celebration of George Washington's one hundredth birthday, February 22, 1832, and only secondarily as election propaganda for Jackson's 1832 presidential campaign. His researches, including extensive reading of newspaper accounts of the ambitious plans for Washington's Centennial and of the politics of the era, revealed far more excitement generated in the majority of Americans, especially New Englanders, about the Centennial than about Jackson's possible (and eventual) reelection. Although Jackson's popularity had apparently not increased among the influential and "upper-class" New Englanders, it had among the country people and labor—*but* not significantly

enough to win more than two states for him in 1832. Consequently, it would seem that although a flask depicting General and President Jackson would appeal to many more buyers of inexpensive liquor flasks than in 1828, that appeal would not be extensive. On the other hand, Washington's portrait doubtless would make Jackson acceptable, or tolerated, by all potential users of the flasks. It seems most probable that these Keene and Coventry flasks were produced in time for Washington's birthday, and possibly that the production started in 1831.

The New England Jacksons, four pints and one half-pint, have "JACKSON" in an arc above the profile bust (charted as the reverse) and, on the obverse, "WASHINGTON" in an arc above the profile bust of Washington in uniform. As established by fragments excavated in quantity on the factory site by Harry Hall White, GI–31 is a Keene-Marlboro-Street flask. I have designated GI–32 as "Eastern, probably New England," instead of "Probably Keene-Marlboro-Street." The remaining three, GI–33 through GI–34a, were attributed to the Coventry Glass Works on the basis of fragments found by Mr. White and, in the case of the pint GI–34a, by analogy to the half-pint GI–34. The GI–34a was unknown in 1941 when the original charts were compiled.

According to a theory I hold, two other eastern flasks may have been Jackson flasks and one probably was originally a Jackson flask. The two are the Baltimore Glass Works' GI–17 and the Bridgeton (N.J.) Glass Works' GI–24. Each has a bust of Washington in uniform on the obverse (as charted) and, on the reverse, a military gentleman not identified by inscription but designated as Taylor by Van Rensselaer. The obviously wide differences between this depiction of a military officer and those of General Taylor were noted long ago but were accounted for as representing a younger Taylor than the general in 1847/48. Too, the flasks themselves indicate an earlier period—1820s–1830s. Since I found nothing in Taylor's career to warrant a flask before the Mexican War; since the flasks are an early type; since the hair more closely resembles that of Jackson as rendered on the Coventry and Keene-Marlboro-Street flasks GI–31 through GI–34a; and since it seems unlikely Baltimore and Bridgeton did not produce Jackson flasks, I believe these two were intended for Jackson. The third flask is GI–73. As mentioned in connection with the Baltimore Glass Works and the statueless Washington Monument flasks, I believe it probable that GI–73 was first blown about 1828 and the inscription "GEN TAYLOR" cut in the mold during the Mexican War, and that the military gentleman perhaps was intended to represent Jackson.

WILLIAM HENRY HARRISON,
9th President, 1841[94]

Perhaps the most tumultuous presidential campaign, the one in which the *people* were most profoundly involved, was the 1840 Log Cabin and Hard Cider campaign that put General William Henry Harrison and, after Harrison's untimely death, John Tyler, in the White House. The Whigs had been confronted by two leading aspirants for the nomination—Henry Clay and William Henry Harrison—and at a time when they desperately needed as noncontroversial a man as possible, a man with deep and emotional appeal to the citizenry and a mollifier of all the party factions. Clay was not such a man: he would spark opposition from the Abolitionists; as a good Mason, he would antagonize former members of the anti-Masonic party; and as the father of the "American System" of high tariff and internal improvements, he was likely to alienate southern votes. Old Tippecanoe, on the other hand, was a "safe" man. Run by the new Whig party in 1836 as a dark horse unhobbled by any embarrassing opinions or pronouncements on ticklish issues, Harrison had received an astonishing number of votes and had run second in the race. And so he was chosen, and ordered to keep his opinions to himself.

Moreover, the Whigs provided no platform for Harrison and Tyler to stand on or for the opposition to hack at. But they prophesied that sound currency, high wages, and general prosperity would follow in the wake of Harrison's election—"two dollars a day and roast beef." Before the dilemma arising from the real issues could become crucial, the Democratic press and leaders gratuituously provided the Whigs with a solution by their aspersive and derisive comments on the honored patriot and former governor of the Indiana Territory, a military hero of the Indian and 1812 wars, victor in the battles of Tippecanoe and North Bend. Their slurs and sneers enabled the Whigs to present Harrison as a frontiersman, a farmer poor in worldly goods, living in a log cabin, and wresting a living from a reluctant soil by his own efforts, whereas in fact he was a member of an old Virginia plantation family, was born in a mansion, and lived in one near North Bend. He was presented as a drinker of the poor man's favorite beverage, hard cider, not luxury wines and champagne like his aristocratic opponent Martin Van Buren. Van Buren might be the "Little Magician" of politics and the

political "Fox of Kinderhook," but Harrison was "the Cincinnatus of the West" dropping his plow in the furrow to save his people from the corruption of the Democrats and eastern aristocrats. So effective was the false picture that, so a Washington correspondent of the *New York Evening Post* wrote—with tongue in cheek one would guess:

Gen. Harison's [*sic*] poverty has wakened the sympathy of the ladies of this District, and they are now at work getting up a subscription to supply the "war-worn hero" with a suit of clothes. If you have any old shoes, old boots, old hats, or old stockings, send them on and they will be forwarded to the "Hero of North Bend".[95]

But the tone of the clever Whig campaign had first been set, unintentionally, by remarks credited to a Clay supporter and given publicity in the *Baltimore Republican*: "Give him a barrel of hard cider and settle a pension of $2000. a year on him and my word for it he will sit for the remainder of his days in his log cabin by the side of a 'sea-coal' fire and study moral philosophy."[96] This gave immediate rise to the "Log Cabin and Hard Cider" candidate and campaign. Almost overnight log cabins sprang up on corners, greens, and squares throughout the country—headquarters of Whigs and Tippecanoe clubs, with latchstring always out symbolizing Harrison's open hospitality and democratic ways. The log cabin, so readers of Nantucket's *The Inquirer*, on August 15, 1840, learned, typified "economy and retrenchment . . . moderation in Government expenditures . . . simplicity and Republican living on the part of the President . . . no aping of royalty in luxury or prodigality." It was "an emblem of humility . . . intended to call back Officers of Government to early American manners." Hard Cider meant "no foreign drink . . . none of those costly wines . . . no deluging the President's house with expensive champagne." It meant also "the least expensive of all common drinks." Taken in moderation, it was a beverage "that has no captivation or temptation about it." It was a "rebuke upon the immense consumption of foreign seductive wine commonly drunk in the White House." "In a word," hard cider meant, "cheap and moderate living—frugality—prosperity—plainness" —and initiated *temperance in drink* in high places."

Outside the door of the log cabins a barrel labeled Hard Cider was kept, and it is said that the beverage was served generously to stimulate the voters' thirst for "Harrison and Reform." Naturally the Democrats attempted to make capital out of such intemperance and to alienate responsible citizens and temperance groups from Harrison. One of the Democratic handbills (now in the collection of the New-York Historical Society) gave an "Authentic view" of a barroom in the Log Cabin headquarters of a Tippecanoe Club on Broadway in New York City. It was equipped with decanters, bottles and glasses, and handbills. One of the last offered old familiar drinks and new ones — "Hard Cider, Egg Nog, Irish Whiskey, Tyler Punch, Harrison Juleps, North Bend Sherry Cobbler, and Tip & Ty, 'try it boys.' " From and to the Log Cabin came torchlight parades with banners bearing the slogans "Tippecanoe and Tyler Too," "The American Ticket," "Harrison and Reform."

Emblems and symbols of Harrison were embodied in many fabrics — tangible propaganda that was purchased by supporters and given often to hoped-for supporters. There were Harrison letter paper and mezzotints, Harrison and Tippecanoe handkerchiefs, and Harrison buttons. Harrison music: "Songs, marches and quicksteps ornamented with . . . portraits. Battle scenes; engravings of Log Cabins &tc . . ."—Harrison glass cup-plates and, of course, Harrison flasks. Two of the flasks, GI–63 and GX–22, and the two Log Cabin bottles GVII–1 and 2 are mementos of Harrison's 1840 campaign. (A third flask, GII–9 in the eagle group, is believed to be a campaign flask.) The bottles are miniature log cabins and are extremely rare. One, GVII–1, has "NORTH BEND" on a panel across the cabin above the door and the windows and "TIPPECANOE" on a like panel on the opposite side, thus commemorating Harrison's two outstanding military victories. The other Log Cabin, GVII–2, has "TIPPECANOE" on a narrow panel halfway between the top of the door and the edge of the steep gabled roof. They were brought out by the Mount Vernon Glass Works, Vernon, New York. The flasks are midwestern. Because of their general characteristics, including their beaded edges, they are attributed to the "Monongehela and early Pittsburgh districts." Only one, GI–63, bears a "likeness" of Harrison. It has "W.M H. HARRISON" in semicircle above the head of Harrison in a uniform having three rows of laurel leaves across his breast—the only symbol of his military victories. On the reverse is a log cabin with long American flag flying from a short pole at right ridge. In the foreground at left is a plow—symbol of the Farmer of North Bend and Cincinnatus of the West, and at right, a barrel—unmarked, but then no one needed to be told its content was hard cider. The other flask leaves no possible doubt as to the barrel's content; the barrel, with a plow, long flag, and stars, ornaments the reverse of GX–22, and the inscription "HARD CIDER" appears in an arc above the barrel.

The third flask (GII–9), also midwestern, is believed to be a Harrison campaign flask. But I believe, in part because the characteristics of the flask are those of flasks earlier than 1840, it is probable that this flask was blown at the time of the 1836 campaign. On one side is a typical flask eagle and, on the reverse, an eagle in flight with snake in its beak. The 1840 symbol on the True American Ticket for Harrison and Tyler was an eagle perched on top of a cactus, with a snake in its beak: "The Eagle of Liberty Strangling the Serpent of Corruption." On the other hand, an 1836 cartoon bearing the legend "High Places in Gov't like Steep Rocks only accessible to Eagles and Reptiles" shows the pool of corruption, Van Buren as a serpent in that pool over which hovers the Eagle, Harrison.

JOHN TYLER,
10th President, April 1841 – 45[97]

John Tyler, Harrison's vice-president, catapulted into the presidency by President William Henry Harrison's death only a month after inauguration, may have been commemorated by a Figured Flask blown at the Fairview Glass Works of Wheat Price & Company, Wheeling, (W.) Virginia, but, if so, it was not during the 1840 campaign or his presidency. He was definitely "Tyler Too" in the campaign, not a popular figure with the public, and as president his stand on such issues as a national bank and protective tariff alienated the Whig party and the North. Unlike the prophets, however, he was held in great honor in his home state of Virginia, where he had served as governor and twice as a member of the House of Delegates, as well as representing Virginia in the United States House of Representatives and Senate. The deed that may have inspired the flask GI–116 was his courageous vote against the Force Act of 1833. This act, arising from South Carolina's efforts to nullify the 1832 protective tariff acts, authorized sending federal forces into the state to collect the tariff. Tyler, opponent of the act, was prominent in the debate on it. When it came to a vote, other senators opposing the act walked out of the Senate chamber, leaving Tyler the only senator to cast a no vote. The wholehearted approval of Tyler's constituents and their pride in his courage were such that later they publicly expressed their appreciation by a banquet in his honor. Since the profile portrait on the flask is similar to some portraits of Tyler, especially the long hair in back and the beaklike nose, it seems a fair possibility that the flask, made in (W.) Virginia, is contemporaneous with the dinner and that the bust, unnamed for identification, was intended to represent Tyler. Be that as it may, the shape of the flask and its general design place it in the 1820–30 period. Wheat, Price & Company took over the Virginia Green Glass Works of Knox & McKee, Wheeling, (W.) Virginia, in 1833 and called it the Fairview Glass Works. They operated only a year. Thus, it seems safe to conclude that flasks GI–115 and GI–116 were first blown during 1833.

HENRY CLAY,
the Perennial Candidate[98]

Any time from the 1820s through 1844, Figured Flasks bearing a portrait of Henry Clay of Kentucky would have been timely. He had been in the forefront of national affairs almost from the year he first entered Congress, 1806, and active in foreign affairs even when he was not serving as John Quincy Adams's secretary of state. Seeking war with England, he was the leader of the young War Hawks "whose voice aroused our martial thunder"/"when foreign foes our rights denied"; whose voice, early in the war, gave rise to the ringing slogan "Free Trade and Sailors Rights." However, his high hopes of our acquiring Canada and of signing a peace treaty in Halifax were blasted; instead, he was one of the peace commissioners sent to Ghent to conclude the War of 1812.

Clay's belief in the power of compromise to achieve peaceful solutions of national problems resulted in his being called the Great Pacificator—in particular, through his role in securing passage of the Missouri Compromise whereby Missouri entered the Union as a slave state and Maine as a nonslave state. He earned this title, as well as the less honored "The Great Compromiser," time and again in the next 30 years. Early in his career, Clay had also adopted the cause of internal improvements through government aid, to facilitate transportation and draw the commerce of the country together; he championed, too, the protective tariff as a comfort and aid to infant industries, their owners, and mechanics. Thus, he was the "Father of the American System." He was also *for* a national bank and *against* slavery.

Actually, Henry Clay was so positive a figure in the battle of divisive issues that he seems to have been too controversial to win the coveted presidency. The brand "Bargain and Corruption"— already mentioned in connection with John Quincy Adams and the 1824–28 campaign—dogged him

throughout his ceaseless efforts to become president. He lost in 1824, having only 37 electoral votes, and again as Whig candidate against Jackson in 1832, having only 49. In 1836 and 1840, when his supporters seemed numerous, the Whigs passed over him in favor of a nonpolitical candidate uncommitted on issues—William Henry Harrison. He was the nominee in 1844, when Whig propaganda hailed him as "Harry the Star of the West," "The Honest and True." One of the campaign songs boosted Clay as

The industrious workmen's constant friend
He would exalt his low condition,
Protect his labor and defend
Him 'gainst all foreign competition.

Clay seemed to have more than a fair chance of defeating the Democratic candidate, James K. Polk, but then he refused to declare himself on the thorny issue of the annexation of Texas, thereby losing the antislavery northern votes and proslavery southern ones. He was defeated in a campaign in which fraud was brazenly and generally practiced, and in it the Democrats were the chief offenders. In spite of all this, but for the results in New York, which proved the pivotal state, Henry Clay would have realized his main ambition and become president of the United States.

One would expect that, over the years from 1824 through at least 1844, the portrait of Henry Clay would appear on many flasks. Yet, until the summer of 1970, the only flasks definitely known to have been associated with Clay had never been found or, if found, not identified. They are the flasks advertised in the summer of 1825 by Pepperd & Teater, owners of the Moscow Glass Works, Moscow, Ohio.[99] Now a flask (GI–130) inscribed "HENRY CLAY" has been discovered and acquired by Robert H. Wise—the most exciting event in the flask world in over a decade. The obverse is closely similar to the Jackson GI–69 and Lafayettes GI–92 and 93, but the head of the profile bust is a little narrower and longer and the bottom of the bust curves upward. "HENRY" is at upper left and "CLAY" at upper right of the panel. Except for the absence of the cannonballs below the olive branch at left, the reverse is like that of GI–69 and 92, including the inscriptions "WHEELING" and "KNOX & McKEE". In the light of the GI–92 and GI–93 relationship (see Lafayette and De Witt Clinton), one can but wonder whether Knox & McKee may have brought out their Henry Clay flasks in 1824 after the passage of the 1824 tariff, our first protective one, or

130. HENRY CLAY FLASK BLOWN AT THE VIRGINIA GREEN GLASS WORKS, WHEELING, (W) VIRGINIA. ca. 1824

This brilliant emerald-green flask (GI–130) is the only recorded flask inscribed "HENRY CLAY". The oval frame encloses a small profile bust within a Masonic arch above and a large fleur-de-lis at bottom. "HENRY" appears at upper left of frame and "CLAY" at right. On the reverse a similar frame encloses stars at top above an American eagle with head turned to left, shield on breast, and wings raised, the left one foreshortened. A thunderbolt of two arrows is held in the left talon and a large olive branch in the right. "WHEELING" appears in a semicircle outside top of frame, "KNOX" at lower left, and "& M^CKEE" at lower right.

The flask is like Knox & McKee's Jackson flask GI–69 and Lafayette flask GI–92, except for a few details. Whereas the two soldiers are in uniform, Henry Clay is in civilian dress. Also, the bottom of Clay's bust curves downward instead of upward as on GI–69 and GI–92. On the reverse of the Clay flask the cannonballs below the olive branch on GI–69 and GI–92 have been omitted. *Collection of Robert H. Wise*

possibly in the summer of 1825, when Henry Clay and DeWitt Clinton participated as honored guests in the ceremonies marking the beginning of the Ohio Canal. Whatever the specific occasion, if any, the flasks doubtless were in honor of the Father of the

American System, the goals of which were protective tariffs and internal improvements.

However, there are three portrait flasks of quart size—GI–22, 23, and 25—that, in 1926, Van Rensselaer called Taylor without giving his reasons for the designation, but that are now believed to be Clay flasks. These three have a bust of Clay on one side and one of George Washington on the other, both classical, a favorable comparison of the statesmanship of the two and one that doubtless would have been more palatable to Washington than the Jackson–Washington coupling. Unfortunately, no inscription names either portrait. Still, as comparison of the Chart line drawings shows, the presumed Clay portraits do resemble depictions of Clay, whereas they are utterly unlike any of Taylor, including those on Taylor flasks. Moreover, Taylor is always in uniform on the flasks. Two of the flasks were products of the Baltimore Glass Works, Baltimore, Maryland. One, GI–22, is inscribed "BALTIMORE GLASS WORKS" with reverse S's on the Washington side; the second, GI–23, "BALTIMORE GLASS WORKS" on the Clay side. The third flask, GI–25, is inscribed "BRIDGE-TOWNGLASSWORKS" in an arch above the portrait on both sides. Insofar as the Baltimore Glass Works is concerned, it could have brought out its Clay flasks anytime during Clay's career. Their similarity in shape to that of GI–21, having "FELLS" above a classical bust of Washington on one side and the Washington Monument without the statue of Washington on the other, suggests that GI–22 and 23 were first produced about the same time as GI–21. Inasmuch as the statue of Washington was not in place until the fall of 1829, it is believed GI–21 was brought out prior to that date. Still, perhaps three years later, Clay flasks were produced to celebrate Washington's hundredth birthday and Clay's candidacy for the presidency, and probably enjoyed many years of popularity. The Bridgeton or Bridgetown Glass Works, New Jersey, was not established until 1836 or 1837. It seems likely its Clay flask was first blown either in 1842, when manufacturers and their mechanics were celebrating the passage of the new protective tariff, or in 1844 when the Father of the American System was the Whig presidential candidate.

ZACHARY TAYLOR,
12th President, 1849–50

Zachary Taylor, the third of Richard and Mary Taylor's eight children, was born November 24,

1784. In 1788 Richard moved his family to Kentucky, settling near what is now Louisville. Schooling for his brood was a problem solved by engaging a tutor, one Elisha Ayres, a Yankee. Zachary grew up working with his father on the farm and with no idea of an army career. He expected and intended to be a farmer. Then, in May 1808, President Jefferson gave him a first lieutenant's commission. A year and a half later, as a captain, he went to the Northwest Territory to serve under General William Henry Harrison, against the Indians and, then, the English in the War of 1812. He was brevetted a major for his successful defense of Fort Harrison. With the return of peace and reverting to a captaincy again, Taylor resigned and went home to the farm "to make a crop of corn." However, in May 1826, he returned to the Army, for President Madison made him a major of the Third Infantry. Five years later, at 47, Taylor achieved the rank of lieutenant colonel. Though he saw some service in the Southwest, mainly Baton Rouge, Louisiana, he was assigned most of the time to the Northwest Territory, until the spring of 1832. Then Taylor, now a full colonel, was sent to Florida, where the Seminole War was going badly. Early in 1837 he was brevetted brigadier general for his distinguished service in the battle of Kissimmee (Okeechobee), a promotion apparently unnoticed outside military and government circles. Two hard unsatisfactory years followed. Taylor, growing progressively more dissatisfied, asked to be relieved of his command. After his request was granted in April 1840, he went to Fort Jesup, Louisiana, and soon afterward bought a plantation.[100]

Such was Taylor's inconspicuous career before the Mexican War. It had not been a career to make headlines across the country and to inspire Taylor flasks. The general public, certainly the majority of the electorate, knew little or nothing about General Taylor in July 1845 when he was sent to Corpus Christi in command of American troops. The Mexican War was to change all that. Our first war on foreign soil and one arising from the controversial annexation of Texas, it commanded public attention. Even before the battle of Palo Alto on May 8, 1846, in which Major Ringgold was fatally wounded (see Major Samuel Ringgold), anyone who read the newspapers, and most Americans did, could not escape news of Taylor and his forces. Among the other things they were told about Taylor was that "the principle of duty . . . seems to constitute the ruling principle of his conduct as it forms the basis of that composed self-reliance which never deserts him."[101] After the Battle of Buena Vista in February 1847 he

was a national hero. Faced with the numerically far superior forces of the Mexican General Santa Anna, he still had the courage and confidence to decline the Mexican's demand that he surrender. Next day Taylor's forces inflicted a humiliating defeat upon the enemy. From Taylor's brief but courteous letter to Santa Anna, press and politicians distilled the Taylorism "General Taylor Never Surrenders."

Almost immediately Taylor's friends and admirers were hailing him as our next president. And, as early as April 1847, the Whigs were holding meetings to nominate him. The crescendo of clamor for Taylor to be the Whigs' man continued until the party chose him. Like William Henry Harrison, he was an ideal candidate for a party wishing to sidestep definite planks in a platform on real issues, especially slavery. When approached, Taylor candidly confessed "that he knew very little about the questions which had been distracting the country for years past . . ." His political slate was clean. Moreover, even before the actual nomination, he had stated emphatically:

In no case can I permit myself to be the candidate of any party, or yield to party schemes . . . Should I ever occupy the White House, it must be by the spontaneous move of the people, and by no act of mine, so that I could [come] into the office untrammeled and be the chief magistrate of the nation and not of a party.

Nevertheless the Whigs argued that inasmuch as Taylor was a southerner and a slave owner (it was said he owned 300 slaves), the vote of the South would go to him and that, in the North, these facts would be counteracted by his role in the Mexican War. They nominated him in June. However, Taylor and many who voted for him were convinced he had been "drafted" in accordance with the wish of the people. And this belief prevailed even though there were nominees of five parties—Whig, Democratic, Free-Soil, Liberty (*Abolition*), and American (native American)—in the field and even though his majority in the election was not much over 140,000 votes.[102]

A little over a year after taking office, Taylor died. On July 4, 1850, after the laying of the cornerstone of the Washington Monument and attending the dinner in celebration of the anniversary of the country's birth, he was taken violently ill and soon died of Cholera Morbus.[103] Though no monument was erected to his memory, nor was even his name inscribed on his vault in the small family cemetery, his memory was kept green for many by the Taylor flasks.

Some 37 Figured Flasks have been identified with Zachary Taylor, all but two products of eastern glassworks in the Baltimore, Philadelphia, and South Jersey area, and all but three of them related to the Mexican War and the 1848 presidential campaign. Two of the three are GI–17 and GI–24 of an earlier period, having the bust of Washington in uniform on one side and on the other a military officer unidentified by inscription but called Taylor by Van Rensselaer, an identification accepted by collectors and students alike. The utter unlikeness of the two portrayals to those accompanied by an identifying inscription did not go unnoticed, but was explained as the depiction of a younger Taylor in an earlier period of his career. However, as we have seen, there was no event giving Taylor the stature to inspire a flask before the Mexican War. As I have argued in the sketch of Andrew Jackson, I believe the two flasks were intended to represent Jackson and were probably first blown around 1828. The third flask also appears to be earlier than 1847/48. It is GI–73 with the profile bust of a considerably younger officer wearing an earlier type of uniform, but with "GEN^L TAYLOR" in an arc above the bust. On the reverse are "FELLS POINT" and "BALT^O" and Baltimore's Washington Monument *without the statue of Washington*, pointing, I believe, to the flask's having been first produced about 1828. (See The Battle and the Washington Monuments, Baltimore, Maryland.) My theory is that the inscription "GEN^L TAYLOR" probably was cut in the earlier mold after the battle of Buena Vista in 1847. Also, one of the midwestern flasks, the extremely rare GI–76, depicts a younger officer than the rugged 63-year-old Taylor in 1847. Again, I believe it possible that the bust originally was intended to represent some other personage, and "ROUGH AND READY" was cut in the mold late in 1847 or early in 1848.

Besides GI–76, six other flasks bear Taylor's soubriquet "Rough and Ready." One is the extremely rare GI–77 with 13 stars, an eagle, and "MASTERSON" on the reverse, one of the quart flasks associated with Taylor. Only the nickname identifies it with Taylor: the poorly drawn bust depicts an utterly bald man wearing what appears to be a turtleneck shirt. The rarest in this small group is GXIII–89, owned by Doy McCall of Huntsville, Alabama. As the line drawing shows, "ROUGH" is at the right of a man holding a bottle in his outstretched right hand, "&" is above his head, and "READY" is at his back. Below the figure—a customer of the saloon apparently—is "H.EASLY'S"

and, on the reverse, "EASLEY·S" above a hand pointing down to "SALOON" above "HUNTSVILLE." Mr. McCall informed me that this quart flask was made for Hugh Easley, who ran a saloon in Huntsville before the Civil War.

The commonest flasks in the group are GI–71 and GI–72, having the bust of Major Ringgold on the reverse.* The difference between them is that GI–71 has ribbed edges and GI–72 smooth ones. It seems likely they were first brought out in 1846 following the death of Major Ringgold (see Major Samuel Ringgold). These two are attributed to the Baltimore Glass Works, as are the rare flasks GI–74 and GI–75, which also differ in that one has ribbed and the other smooth edges. The portrait bust of Taylor obviously was an attempt to present a genuine likeness of the man. On the reverse is "CORN FOR THE WORLD" arching above a cornstalk. This slogan, it will be recalled, was a boast and a boost for Baltimore's commerce in corn and grain exports.

Though Taylor was also called Old Zach and Old Buena Vista, it was "Rough and Ready" that became familiar in nearly every household during the Mexican War and the 1848 presidential campaign. Apparently it was during the Florida war that Taylor's troops began calling him Rough and Ready. According to George E. Shankle's *American Nicknames*, it was inspired by Taylor's custom of wearing "plain serviceable clothes," his dislike of "military show and ceremony," which he discouraged in his men, and his tireless efforts to so discipline them that they would "always be ready to well acquit themselves in any battle." In the *Rough and Ready Songster*, presumably published for the 1848 campaign, a verse gave a soldier's view:

> *"I knew him first," the soldier said,*
> *"Among the Everglades,*
> *When we gave the savage redskins*
> *Our bayonets and our blades.*
> *I think I hear his cheerful voice,*
> *–!On Column! Steady Steady*
> *So hard and so prompt was he*
> *We called him Rough and Ready."* [104]

The majority (22) of the flasks with a Taylor "portrait" are of the Dyottville type; with one exception, these have been charted with the bust of Washington as the obverse and that of Taylor as the reverse. The exception is GI–78 having the familiar type of Taylor bust on the obverse and, on the

*Since this was written, Jack Whistance has discovered a third Taylor-Ringgold flask charted as GI–131. See also text on Ringgold.

reverse—dating it as probably 1852–54—"ROB[T] RAMSAY / WINE & / LIQUOR MERCH[T] / 281 8th AVENUE / N. Y." Seven other Dyottville-type flasks have no other means of identification than the bust itself. That, however, is sufficient because of the similarity to those having an identifying inscription. The title "GEN. Z. TAYLOR" was molded in a quart and a pint flask; "G. Z. TAYLOR" on a pint. Eight, GI–37 through GI–41 (two quarts, a pint, and five half-pints), have "GEN. TAYLOR NEVER SURRENDERS"—perhaps the most popular of Taylorisms. The quart GI–43 and pint GI–44 have "I HAVE ENDEAVORED TO DO MY DUTY"—the Taylorism evolved from the general's remarks at a New Orleans dinner in his honor in 1847, at which he said that though he did not "accomplish as much" as he desired, he always "endeavored to perform [his] duty." A third remark—"A little more grape, Capt Bragg"—was used for only one Dyottville-type portrait flask, GI–42. However, enwreathed by a grapevine, it appears on two half-pints having Baltimore's Battle Monument on the obverse and also on two pints and a half-pint having "GENERAL TAYLOR NEVER SURRENDERS" and a cannon and cannonballs on the other side. Taylor's remark was to Captain Bragg during the battle of Buena Vista, and its effect was so "completely [to] inspirit him and his men, that they fired with redoubled vigor," contributing to the spectacular victory.[105]

The term Dyottville-type has been used because, as I have stated before, I do not believe that so many molds would have been needed at Dyottville even for so popular an item as the Washington–Taylor flasks appear to have been, and also because there is evidence of at least one other glassworks having produced the type. That was the one at Crowleytown, New Jersey, on the site of which J. E. Pfeiffer unearthed fragments of GI–52 and GI–53. And the fragments were of the same colors as those of other bottles, and appeared to be of the same metal. Actually, only two flasks—the quart GI–37 and pint GI–38—are inscribed "DYOTTVILLE GLASS WORKS PHILAD.[A]" However, of course, more than those two must have been brought out by Benners, Smith & Campbell, proprietors of the Dyottville Glass Works (1844–52). One, probably two, of the half-pint "General Taylor Never Surrenders" were Dyottville products. Also, the use of that Taylorism at Dyottville suggests use of the other two—"I have endeavored to do my duty" and "A little more grape Capt. Bragg." Perhaps the close similarity of the Dyottville-type flasks points to one moldmaker rather than one glass manufacturer.

ULYSSES S. GRANT,
18th President, 1869–77[106]

Ulysses S. Grant, a native of the Buckeye state, Ohio, was born in April 1822 in Point Pleasant, the first of Hannah and Jesse R. Grant's six children. The following year Jesse Grant, a tanner, moved to a farm in Georgetown not far from the Ohio River in the southwestern part of the state. There Ulysses grew up, working on the farm in the summer and attending school in the winter. In 1839, at 17, he received an appointment to West Point, and he was graduated in 1843, a lieutenant, undistinguished except for his excellent horsemanship. Although he had been an unwilling cadet, he acquitted himself well in the field during the Mexican War, in which he served first in General Taylor's forces and later in General Winfield Scott's army. In fact, for his conduct at Chapultepec in 1847 he was brevetted captain. In June 1848, when his regiment was ordered to leave Mexico City for Mississippi, he sought and obtained a leave of absence to return home to marry "his girl," Julia T. Dent. His tours of duty during the next six years were at outlying posts. The last was at Fort Humbolt, California, a "hardship" tour, as he was unable to have his family with him and "took to the bottle." By the spring of 1854 he was faced with the choice of resigning or facing charges, and so he submitted his resignation, to become effective July 31. Although during the ensuing years before the Civil War his efforts to make a living provided only a rather meager one, he did gain control of himself.

Shortly after the outbreak of war in 1861 Grant reenlisted and, with the rank of colonel, received command of the Cairo, Illinois, forces. His capture of Fort Donelson in February 1862 from the southern general Buckner was a brilliant victory, the first of which the Union Armies and victory-starved North could boast. Buckner had proposed an armistice. Grant had replied: "No terms except unconditional and immediate surrender can be accepted. I propose to move immediately upon your works." Henceforth he was known in the North as "Unconditional Surrender Grant." He won also a commission as major general and went on to further victories and command of the western army. In the meantime, the Union forces in the East continued to be outgeneraled; and in March 1864, Lincoln made Grant a lieutenant general and placed him in command of all the northern forces. Though another year of fighting followed, Grant finally succeeded in defeating General Robert E. Lee, receiving Lee's surrender on April 9, 1865, at Appomattox Court House.

The war was ended. Ulysses S. Grant emerged a brilliant general, a national hero, "the foremost citizen of the Republic," one whom, as the 1868 elections neared, leaders of both the Republicans and Democrats thought to be valuable presidential timber. Grant accepted the unanimous nomination of the Republicans. He was easily elected and was reelected in 1872. However, his administration was an unfortunate, a tragic, one for him, riddled with graft and corruption. Although Grant himself was personally honest and profited not at all from the scandalous operations, he had, as James Truslow Adams said, "a singular incapacity for choosing the right man for the wrong office, and then was so obstinate in his loyalty to the wrong ones, that the situation created was almost worse than if he had been a less honest and abler man."[107] He left the White House in March 1877 a poorer man than he had entered it, poorer in reputation and poorer in pocketbook. Before his death at Mount McGregor, New York, on July 23, 1885, he wrote his *Personal Memoirs*, in part at least in the hope that the proceeds would provide for his family.

A Grant flask would not be surprising, and for the past 45 years at least, the profile head on the rare pint flask GI–79 has been generally accepted as that of Ulysses S. Grant. According to information given to George S. McKearin by Stephen Van Rensselaer in the 1920s, the head was so identified by an old Pittsburgh flask-blower. If that identification is correct, flask GI–79 and also the rarer GI–79a without "UNION" on the reverse probably were first produced after one of his victories over the South during his service in the western arm of the Union Armies or after his final victory over Lee ending the Civil War in April 1865. That being the case, the wreath can be interpreted as a symbol of victory. On the reverse, it should be noticed, is the flying eagle design like that on the "Union" flasks—that is, those with Shield and Clasped Hands, Group XII, of the Civil War period and later.

GROVER STEPHEN CLEVELAND, *22nd President, 1885–89; 24th President, 1893–97*[108]

Grover Cleveland was born in 1837 in New Jersey, the fifth of nine children of a Presbyterian minister, Richard Fallen Cleveland, and his wife Ann. When Grover was four, the family moved to New York State, where his father was called first to Fayetteville and, in 1850, to Clinton. Attaining a fair education in these towns, he planned to go to Hamilton College, but when his father died in 1853, he abandoned col-

lege plans in order to support his mother and five of the children who were still dependent. First, he taught in the New York Institution for the Blind in New York City; in 1855, however, he decided on the law as a career, and after serving as clerk in a Buffalo law firm, he was admitted to the bar in 1859—a self-made man who was to become what many consider a *rara avis*, an honest politician. Cleveland did not serve in the Union Army during the Civil War: being the only son in a position to contribute to his mother's support, he hired a substitute, as was legal and a common practice. This fact was to become an ineffectual political weapon nearly a quarter of a century later in the 1884 presidential election.

Cleveland's political career as a Democrat began with the humble office of ward supervisor in Buffalo in 1862; in 1881, running as a "reform candidate," he was elected mayor of Buffalo. His conduct in office (always putting public interest before that of party; his integrity and honesty) won him the goodwill of the people and ill will of the political bosses—Tammany Hall, in particular. Nevertheless, he was elected governor of New York in 1882 and, in 1884, after the country had had 24 years of Republican rule, president of the United States on reform platforms. Unfortunately, Cleveland did not have sufficient support to implement the most controversial of his measures, the very proposal of which alienated interested pressure groups and *their* supporters in Congress. And his veto of some bills cost him dearly—for example, of the pension bills, which lost veterans' support as well as that of politicians worrying about the veterans' votes. Thwarted by the powerful opposition of the Republicans and industry, Cleveland failed to secure a reduction in the high protective tariff, which had been and still was a source of a large part of the many-million Treasury surplus, at the same time keeping consumer prices high and competition in the marketplace low. Likewise, with the Democrats and even many Republicans advocating cheap money and free coinage of silver, Cleveland—a believer in "hard money" and the gold standard—was unable to persuade Congress to his views. Civil Service reforms too were anathema to party bosses, and to most congressmen, who relished the spoils system. However, Cleveland had two outstanding successes. The first president interested in conservation, he rescued some 89,000,000 acres of usurped public land and in so doing aroused the enmity of railroad tycoons, cattlemen, and others who were profiting by the nation's loss. And, in 1887, he secured passage of an Interstate Commerce Act prohibiting many of the unfair practices and privileges of big business at the expense of small business. Incidentally, in 1886, he did one thing no other president has done: a bachelor president, he married while in the White House.

Perhaps because Cleveland's probity was unassailable, he was renominated in 1888 in spite of considerable opposition. Many Americans agreed with the following tribute by a Maryland admirer:

When like Diogenes of old,
The people ruled by power of gold
Cried out aloud on every hand,
"Oh! God, for a true and honest man!"
They found in you what they had sought,
A man too honest to be bought.

And by the magic power of gold
Our ruling men were bought and sold,
'Twas then you took your noble stand
To weed corruption from the land;
To bravely face the coming storm,
And introduce all true reform. [109]

Unfortunately, politicians and the businessmen who financed their campaigns seemed to care not a fig for government reform, and it threatened their party and vested interests. Cleveland lost the election to Benjamin Harrison, the Republican nominee, in 1888. But he won the popular vote by 100,000 votes. It is said he gladly returned to private life and started a law practice in New York City.

However, Cleveland was a private citizen for only one presidential term: in 1892 he was nominated again by the Democrats, not so much because the politicians wanted him as from popular demand. To placate those in the party who advocated a bimetal currency—gold and silver—the vice-presidential nominee chosen was Adlai Ewing Stevenson, a silverite and Illinois lawyer active in local and national politics since 1860, assistant postmaster general during Cleveland's first administration. The election was an overwhelming success for the Democratic ticket.

From the Harrison administration Cleveland inherited economic and financial conditions that turned into a panic brought on mainly by the Sherman Silver Act of 1890, which required the United States Treasury to buy and coin yearly nearly the entire production of the silver mines. Also, imports exceeded exports, practically the first adverse balance of trade since the Civil War. Cleveland's first step was to call a special session of Congress to repeal the disastrous silver act; the repeal was achieved through Republican support. Then, in 1890, he succeeded in stabilizing the government's finances through an arrange-

ment with J. P. Morgan, which proved to be justified although it outraged a large proportion of the public. In fact, nearly every act of Cleveland's alienated some group. As James Truslow Adams put it, "Cleveland by his strength and honesty, had antagonized almost every interest and prejudice of his followers and opponents." [110] He retired to Princeton, New Jersey, where he died in 1908.

There appear to have been at least three quite different Cleveland flasks and a figured bottle, but I have charted only the two flasks that I have seen, GI–123 and GI–123a. The former, a pint size, is a flattened flask with wide plain flat ends, a form that was introduced probably in the 1860s. On the obverse is a large circular medallion with portrait that, though unidentified by inscription, is obviously that of Grover Cleveland. In the concave disk on the smooth base is "A C Co", a company not as yet identified. This flask, I believe, was brought out in the 1884 presidential campaign, whereas the design of GI–123a was unmistakably of the 1892 campaign. The second design occurs in pint (GI–123a) and half-pint (GI–124) sizes. The flask is an elliptical barrel, flattened on one side where a long rectangular panel displaces well-rounded staves and hoops. On the panel "Our Choice" appears above facing portrait heads, below which is "Cleve & Steve /NOVEMBER 8th 92/MARCH 4th 93". On the reverse between the triads of hoops is a crowing cock in high relief. Van Rensselaer lists another Cleveland flask and a figured bottle, as follows, in his Group I:

16. Bust on circular panel, "Cleveland" to left of bust in semi-circle. Reverse: Bust of Hendricks on similar panel, "Hendricks" to right of bust. Pint—clear glass, flanged dcm [double collared mouth]. On oval (1 inch x 1½ inch) bottom "J. R. Hartigan's Patent—Pitts."(U)

18. In form of Bust of Cleveland. Round base marked "Cleveland". About ¾ quart—frosted clear glass. cm [collared mouth].(U)

WILLIAM McKINLEY, *25th President, 1897–1901* [111]

William McKinley, seventh of the nine children of William and Nancy McKinley, was born in Niles, Ohio, on January 29, 1843. Although the living made by his father was a meager one, William went to an academy and then entered Allegheny College in Pennsylvania. Because of illness, he went home at the end of his first term and, because of family finances, he was unable to continue his college education. After the Civil War, in which he was a volunteer and was brevetted major, he studied in a law office and attended the law school in Albany, New York. Admitted to the bar in 1869, he returned to Ohio to practice law in Canton and soon entered politics. In 1876 he was elected to Congress, and he served in the House of Representatives from 1877 to 1891.

A good Republican, McKinley championed high protective tariffs, and as chairman of the Ways and Means Committee, he was the chief architect of the 1890 tariff act, which imposed the highest duties ever on imports. Among the provisions was one requiring that such ware as china and glass be marked or labeled with a nonremovable name of the country or firm of origin—for example, "ENGLAND" was impressed on the bottom of English earthenware; "Dresden" was inscribed under the glaze on the German porcelain; and "BACCARAT," in tiny letters, was on pressed glass from that French factory. (The provision for that sort of marking was rescinded over a decade ago, and thereafter only removable labels were required.) With the 1890 swing back to Cleveland and the Democrats, McKinley was not reelected to Congress, but the following year he became governor of Ohio and served two terms in that office.

In 1896 the Republicans nominated William McKinley for the presidency, with Garrett A. Hobart, a New Jersey lawyer who had served in the state legislature, as running mate. Two Republican campaign slogans—"Sound Money and Protection" and "In Gold We Trust"—appeared soon on the McKinley coin flask GI–125; the first was in a semicircle above the portrait bust of McKinley, with "M^c KINLEY & HOBART" below; the latter, in an arc above a bee, with "1896" below. Like many Republicans, McKinley had been a silverite but had converted to the gold standard when it became the main plank in the Republican party platform. Although the pledge to a gold standard was not implemented until the spring of 1900, that of protection was kept in the 1897 tariff, raising duties to the highest level ever reached. The following year came McKinley's second, and somewhat reluctant, conversion to imperialism. Ostensibly—and as far as the public was concerned—the Spanish-American War finally triggered by the blowing up of our ship, the *Maine*, in Havana Harbor, was to liberate the Cuban people to establish their own democratic government. However, as the history of the Spanish-American War has unfolded, it indicates that the intention of a powerful coterie, including Senator Lodge and Theodore Roosevelt, was to acquire Spanish territory. In less than a year Cuba was liber-

ated, Puerto Rico occupied, and Manila, capital of the Philippines, had fallen to Admiral Dewey. Defeated Spain ceded Puerto Rico and Guam to the United States and accepted $20,000,000 for the Philippine Islands. In the meantime Hawaii had been annexed as a territory.

In 1900 William McKinley was again the presidential nominee of the Republicans, with Theodore Roosevelt, then governor of New York and a thorn in the sides of Tammany and big business, "kicked upstairs" as vice-presidential candidate. By the time McKinley, so long an opponent of free trade and a fervent believer in high protective tariff, entered upon his second term, he had experienced another conversion, or at least partial one, as a result of new insight into the importance of foreign trade and reciprocity given him largely by Jeremiah W. Jenks, a noted political economist at Cornell University. Opposed in Congress, he appealed to the people, who saw common sense in such statements as that we could not "forever sell everything and buy little or nothing." At a reception on September 6, 1901, the day after his much-applauded speech at the Buffalo Pan-American Exposition, President McKinley was shot in the stomach by a madman in the reception line. Though the surgeons who operated almost immediately fully expected him to recover, he died on September 14.

Besides the half-pint flask, GI–125, in the form of a coin mentioned above, two other McKinley flasks are recorded by Van Rensselaer, but I have never seen either one. They are in Van Rensselaer's Group I:

86. Bust of McKinley facing to the right, surrounded by Stars and above: "Gold Standard No Split Dollars". Underneath, "McKinley". Reverse: Bust of Hobart facing to the front, surrounded by stars. Above "Prosperity Protection"; underneath "Hobart". Circular (3½ inches), with oblong base. About ¼ pint—clear glass. Threaded mouth.(U)

87. "Genuine Distilled Protection". Bust of McKinley facing to front, below "McKinley". "For Sound Money Only". Reverse: Bust of Hobart in oval, below "Hobart". Pint clear glass. f.m. [flanged mouth]. Base lettered "Trade Mark Regd. Pat. Ap. For."(U)

WILLIAM JENNINGS BRYAN,
Democratic presidential candidate 1896, 1900, and 1908[112]

William Jennings Bryan was born in Salem, Illinois, March 19, 1860. He received a good preparatory education and then graduated from Illinois College in 1881 and two years later from Union College of Law. After practicing in Jacksonville in his home state, he moved to Lincoln, Nebraska, in 1887. It was there he became interested in politics, and from 1891 to 1895, as a Democratic representative, he served his state in Congress, where his gift for oratory soon made him famous throughout the country. Bryan was staunchly prosilver and antiprotection. In 1892 he made his first great speech in Congress, one against the protective tariff, and in 1893 his second, one in support of the silver act, which President Cleveland succeeded in having repealed. But his eloquent plea for silver won him the adherence of millions who, erroneously, saw in the free coinage of silver salvation from their financial woes. Though he lost his bid for a seat in the Senate in 1894—in fact, though he lost all his subsequent election campaigns—he remained the recognized leader of the Democratic party for the ensuing 30 years. In 1913 and 1914 he was Woodrow Wilson's secretary of state. His last and most spectacular public appearance was in Tennessee in 1925 as prosecutor in the famous trial of John T. Scopes, in which Clarence Darrow defended the young public-school teacher who had dared to teach Darwin's theory of evolution in defiance of the state law prohibiting such teaching. Bryan, the fundamentalist, won. At the end of the trial he became ill and died at Dayton, Tennessee.

The one Bryan flask of which I know, GI–126, like the McKinley flask GI–125, was in the form of a United States coin and of the same 1896 presidential campaign. On the obverse is the portrait bust of Bryan encircled by the Democratic slogan "IN SILVER WE TRUST" at the top, with stars at the sides and "BRYAN 1896 SEWALL" at bottom. At the center of the reverse is a handsome eagle with upraised, partially spread wings and with thunderbolt and olive branch in its talons, within a semiwreath of laurel. In a semicircle at the top outer edge is "UNITED DEMOCRATIC TICKET"; between the eagle's wing tips "WE SHALL VOTE" and, at bottom edge, 16 to 1; midway between the "U" and "16" and "T" and "1" is a large star. The 16 to 1 was to be the ratio of silver to gold should the party succeed.

FRANKLIN DELANO ROOSEVELT,
32nd President and first to be elected to four terms, 1933–45[113]

Franklin Delano Roosevelt, only son of James and Sara Roosevelt, was born on the family estate at Hyde Park, New York, January 30, 1882. To use a familiar cliché, he was "born with a silver spoon in his mouth." From his third year on, part of his year was spent in Europe; he had a tutor until he went to Groton at 14; and in 1900 he entered Harvard, where in his senior year he edited the Harvard *Crimson*. A year after graduating he married Anna Eleanor Roosevelt, niece of his fifth cousin Theodore Roosevelt, whom he admired and who urged that young men of substance go into public service. Perhaps because of this influence—and to prepare for such a career—Franklin Roosevelt entered Columbia Law School. Though he passed his bar examination he did not bother to take his degree: he was not ready for a career; social life, sailing, and riding to the hounds still had more appeal.

It was in 1910, when he was 28, that he entered politics on the state level as a Democrat, running for and winning a seat in the Senate, one to which he was reelected. In the Senate, starting as a champion of the upstate farmers, he was converted to the entire program of progressive reform. He served until March 1913, when Woodrow Wilson appointed him assistant secretary of the navy, a position he held for seven years during which he endeavored to reform the navy yards and, through the civilian employees, gained valuable experience negotiating with their labor unions. Then in August 1921 he was stricken with infantile paralysis, which left him paralyzed from the waist down. As is well known, he faced his affliction with indomitable courage and will. And, though off the political stage, he worked from the wings until 1928, when he was elected governor of New York for the first of two terms.

In 1932 Franklin Roosevelt, democratic scion of an old and wealthy patrician family, became the presidential candidate of the Democratic party—and at a time when a strong leader and reformer were desperately needed. The country's economy was near paralysis—the majority of the banks were closed; industrial production was less than half that of 1929; the unemployed numbered more than 13,000,000; and the farmers were in a state of despair. In his campaigning Roosevelt promised a New Deal, including aid to the farmer, federal development of electric power, and "policing irresponsible economic power," in which the controller held a public trust as well as a private one. Having told the people that "the only thing to fear is fear itself," he proceeded fearlessly to deal with the country's problems, helped by a sympathetic Congress or, at least, carrying the majority of Congress with him. First he stopped the continuing runs on banks by closing all of them until Congress could enact a measure permitting sound ones to reopen. A special session of

Congress was called, and in the first few months— the 100 days, it was termed—Congress quickly implemented several of the administration's revolutionary measures: the Reconstruction Finance Administration to aid business; the Federal Deposit Insurance Corporation to protect bank depositors; the Federal Emergency Relief Administration to provide funds for state relief agencies; the Civilian Conservation Corps to put young men to work on reforestation and flood control. Also established were the Farm Credit Administration; the Home Owner's Loan Corporation; Agricultural Adjustment Administration (later revised to the present act); the National Industrial Recovery Act; the Tennessee Valley Authority, and—likewise in 1933— the Securities and Exchange Commission. In June, Roosevelt instituted a managed currency, tripling the value of silver and devaluing the dollar. Six months later the gold content of the dollar was fixed at 59.06 percent of its former value. All strong medicine but beneficial to the patient at the time. The drastic measures of Roosevelt's first term, however, were not over: 1935 brought three more, alienating further the country's conservatives and increasing Roosevelt's hold on most of the people. They were the Social Security Act; the W.P.A. (Works Progress Administration), of which the Art Program was a part; and the National Labor Relations Board, better known as the Wagner Act, which was challenged but upheld by the Supreme Court. As the 1936 election approached, the country had been responding to the infusion of hope, aid, and reform; there was no doubt as to the Democratic nominee. Franklin Roosevelt was easily reelected.

The succeeding years were to have their crises as well as developments in foreign affairs, to say nothing of World War II. The fall of 1937 brought a sharp recession, which was promptly met by extensive government spending on soil conservation and public works. The groundwork for an alliance soon to come had been laid when Roosevelt recognized Russia in 1933. Also, the South American Good Neighbor Policy brought forth agreements on collective security and mutual defense. When war developed in Europe, Roosevelt persuaded Congress to revise the Neutrality Act. Thus, when Franklin Roosevelt was reelected to an unprecedented third term, the stage was set for the Lend Lease Act enabling the government to assist Great Britain and her allies with war materiel, which in turn meant more production and employment. When the Japanese bombed Pearl Harbor in Hawaii on December 7, 1941, our war production almost matched the combined output of Germany and Japan (and was soon to outstrip theirs). Four hours after the disastrous news arrived, Congress declared war. Four days later, Germany and Italy declared war on the United States.

War had not been unexpected, at least by the government and the well informed. In August, Roosevelt and Churchill had already conferred on a battleship in Canadian waters and had formulated the ambitious and idealistic "Atlantic Charter to provide national self-determination, greater economic opportunities, freedom from fear and want, freedom of the seas and disarmament." In January 1942 the aims of the charter were incorporated in the Declaration of United Nations made by the Allies and signed by 46 nations. In January 1943 it was Roosevelt who stated that the Allies would accept only unconditional surrender of the Axis. Though in failing health, Roosevelt—to the astonishment of many—was nominated by the Democrats for a fourth term and, perhaps in a large measure because so many felt there should not be a change in the midst of a war, he overwhelmingly defeated the Republican candidate, Thomas E. Dewey. Roosevelt was not to see the end of the war nor the formation of the United Nations he had so ardently advocated. While at Warm Springs, Georgia, for a rest, he died on April 12, 1945. Germany and Italy had been utterly defeated in 1944, but it was left to Harry Truman to order the atom bombs dropped on Japan later in 1945, ending her resistance.

Commemoration of Franklin Delano Roosevelt in a glass bottle was the idea of an individual citizen, not a glass manufacturer or political party. The calabash bottle GI–129 (it has a portrait bust of Roosevelt above the United States coat of arms on the obverse, and on the reverse "T V A" / a fist clenching a bolt of lightning / "the Norris dam / 1936") was designed by Dr. James S. Hall of Clinton, Tennessee. Referring to it as "the T.V.A. Commemorative bottle," Dr. Hall informed me that he had the bottles, a limited edition of 816, made by the T. C. Wheaton Company, Millville, New Jersey, and that the "order was completed in the Fall of 1936." As Dr. Hall was uncertain just where the mold for the bottle was made, he wrote to T. C. Wheaton Company and was assured that it had been made in their plant.[114]

D. Shield ("Union") and Clasped Hands

During the 1860s a new flask design, inspired apparently by the awful struggle to preserve the Union, became immensely popular, and its popularity continued into the 1870s. Though varying considerably in details and sometimes in general treatment, the design consists of a large shield having in the upper field not stars but short horizontal bars to a large frame shaped somewhat like a broad-waisted figure eight, within which are clasped hands, presumably clasped in union and friendship. Flanking the shield, on each side, is a long slender branch of pinnate leaves, perhaps intended to represent the olive branch of peace. Above the shield, with five exceptions, are 13 stars (11 in a long arc and one at each corner of the shield). The exceptions are GXII–9, 17, and 29 with 11 stars, GXII–38 with 14 stars, and GXII–38a with 19 tiny stars. And, with four exceptions (GXII–2, 6, 18, and 31), the word "UNION" lies between the stars and the top of the shield. The flasks with this design have been charted as Group XII, Shield and Clasped Hands, generally referred to as Union and Clasped Hands. In 1941, when *American Glass* was published, George S. McKearin hazarded the guess that probably there were 100 to 150 varieties. However, those I examined in his and other collections yielded only 51 from different molds. Of these, four were charted by Mr. McKearin as GIV–37, 38, 39, and 40.

On the reverse of the majority is a flying eagle with breast touching the top of a shield (presumably held in his talons). In his beak he holds the ends of a long double pennant, the upper half flying out above him and the lower flying down across the shield. On seven of the flasks no olive branch or thunderbolt extends from the lower sides of the shield. On four, there is the thunderbolt but no olive branch; on four, an olive branch but no thunderbolt. All the others have both thunderbolt and olive branch. Beneath the shield, near the bottom of the flask, is an ornamental frame. One rare quart flask, GXII–37, has "UNION," the clasped hands, and the shield on each side. One half-pint, GXII–36, has a frame (empty) and wreath like that on the "Grant" flask GI–79, a flask of the same form-type and with the flying eagle and "UNION" on the other side. A small group, eight flasks, are more intimately associated with war by the cannon, cannonballs, and flag on the reverse.

Undoubtedly the design for this group of flasks originated in the Midwest, quite probably in Pittsburgh. This is not surprising since, in the western areas—that is, west of the Alleghenies and north of Arkansas, Tennessee, and Virginia—most citizens felt as strongly about the Union as did Lincoln. They wholeheartedly supported his declaration that *the Union* was the issue of the Civil War, whereas in most of the North's eastern states abolition was

placed before preservation of the Union. Only one of the flasks is believed to have been produced by an eastern glassworks: GXII–2, attributed to the Waterford Glass Works, Waterford, New Jersey, because "WATERFORD" lies between the arc of stars and the top of the shield. All the others are attributed to the Midwest. Initials and firm names indicate that at least eight Pittsburgh firms were producers of Shield and Clasped Hands flasks. The quart GXII–1 and two pints, GXII–21 and 22, have "A & CO" on the pennant across the shield on the reverse, and Van Rensselaer's conclusion that the marking stood for Adams & Company has been supported by the researches of John Ramsay of Pittsburgh. Attributed to Lorenz & Wightman are a quart and a pint, GXII–4 and 18, with "L & W" in the oval depression on the base. Alexander and David H. Chambers used at least four molds in their production of these flasks. A quart and two pint flasks, GXII–9, 25, and 26, have "OLD RYE" in the oval frame below the shield on the obverse, "A & DHC" on the pennant across the shield on the reverse, and "PITTSBURGH" in the ornamental frame below. Another pint, GXII–27, has "A & D.H.C" in the frame in the lower part of the shield with clasped hands.

"E. WORMSER & C" ("o" outside frame) /"PITTSBURGH/PA" appears in the ornamental frame on the reverse of two different quart flasks, GXII–15 and 16. "CI & Sons" identifies two pint flasks, GXII–20 and 23, as products of C. Ihmsen & Sons (Christian Ihmsen and his sons Charles T. and William). William Frank & Sons put out six Shield and Clasped Hands flasks. One, a half-pint, GXII–32, has "W. F & / SONS" in the oval lower frame in the shield and the eagle motif on the reverse. The other five—three quarts, GXII–37, 38, and 38a, and two pints, GXII–39 and 39a—have "W^{M} FRANK & SONS /PITTS" in lower frame on obverse and, on the reverse, a cannon, cannonballs, and American flag. The same motifs appear on the reverse of two pints, GXII–40 and 42, and a half-pint, GXII–42a, produced by Fahnstock Albree & Company. "F A & Co" is in the lower frame of the shield. One marking, "L. F & CO" in oval frame in lower part of the shield on two quart flasks, GXII–13 and 14, and one pint, GXII–19, has yet to be identified.

Of the many Shield and Clasped Hands flasks that are without any physical clues as to manufacture, one of two, GXII–34 and 35, was a product of W^{m} McCully & Company also of Pittsburgh. I say one of two because at the time of discovery no differentiation between molds had been made. Anyway, in 1944 Sam Laidacker acquired a number of GXII–34 or 35 flasks from an old drugstore in Hannibal, Missouri. The flasks were in their original shipping box marked

"Wm McCully & Co. Glass Manufacturers, Pittsburgh, Pa. U 6 doz half pint."

5
AGRICULTURE, COMMERCE, AND TRANSPORTATION

Designers of Figured Flasks found significant decorative material among motifs that related directly or indirectly to the interwoven strands of our economic and social life, such as agriculture, commerce, "Free Trade," "The American System," transportation, and even temperance. The grapevine and grapes enwreathe "A LITTLE MORE GRAPE CAP^T BRAG" on the reverse of the Baltimore Battle Monument flask GVI–1. And the same design and inscription, but with the captain's name correctly spelled, appear on the reverse of the three "GENERAL TAYLOR NEVER SURRENDERS" and cannon flasks, GX–4 through GX–6. A bunch of grapes adorns the reverse of the two eagle flasks GII–55 and 56, thought to have been produced by Coffin & Hay, Hammonton, New Jersey, in the late 1830s. Two late flasks, GXIII–77 and 78, probably of the 1870s or 1880s, have a medallion with a bunch of grapes and large grape leaf. Vine and grapes, of course, symbolized wine and, by extension, alcoholic beverages. The ear of corn appearing on the reverse of Baltimore's Washington Monument flasks, GVI–4 through GVI–6 and GVI–4a, and the cornstalk on the two Zachary Taylor flasks GI–74 and 75, all with the slogan "Corn for the World," have been mentioned in 4B, Battle and Washington Monuments, and 4C, Zachary Taylor. The motif and slogan, as previously mentioned, were peculiarly appropriate to Baltimore flasks. Actually, motifs pertaining to agriculture seem to be in the majority and, of the flasks so decorated, only eight have been recorded that fell in the 1820s–1830s period. One rarity, GII–10, was charted in Group II because the side having "W.IHMSEN'S", "GLASS", and an American eagle was chosen as the obverse. On the reverse, "AGRICULTURE" arches above a sheaf of grain, below which are scattered farm implements—fork, rake, sickle, scythe, and plow. This pint flask is attributed to William Ihmsen's Williamsport glassworks and probably was first produced by him in the mid- to late-1820s.

Seven pint flasks of the early period, GIV–31

through GIV–37, having the Farmers' Arms (sheaf of grain with five or six farm tools) were charted in 1941 in Group IV because the arms were framed by the Masonic arch and pavement. On the reverse of four was the American eagle: GIV–31, having the beaded edges typical of the early Pittsburgh-Monongahela area, and an American eagle, facing left and in rendering similar to that of the United States coat of arms, probably mid- to late-1820s; GIV–32, having bead edges, and "ZANESVILLE", "OHIO", "J.SHEPARD" (with reversed S), a large eagle facing right, wings partly raised with right foreshortened, mid- to late-1820s; GIV–33, similar in design to GIV–32, but with "MURDOCK&CASSEL" below the oval frame; GIV–37, having a vertical rib on the edges at mold seam, a large American eagle facing right, wings slightly raised with right foreshortened, and in oval frame, initials "T.W.D." for Thomas W. Dyott of the Kensington Glass Works, Philadelphia—undoubtedly Dyott's "Agricultural and Masonic" flask advertised in 1822. The remaining three with Farmers' Arms and Masonic arch and pavement have the ship *Franklin* on the reverse: GIV–36, having a beaded edge of the early Pittsburgh-Monongahela type, probably mid- to late-1820s; GIV–35, doubtless Dyott's "Ship *Franklin* and Agriculture" of 1825; GIV–34, the mold for GIV–35 with "KENSINGTON GLASS WORKS PHILADELPHIA" added to the edges on the "Agriculture and Masonic" side and "FREE TRADE AND SAILORS RIGHTS" added to those of the "ship *Franklin*" side. "Free Trade and Sailors Rights," the slogan so effectively arousing anger in some quarters and securing support for the War of 1812, became a political and economic weapon in the 1820s and 1830s, rallying adherents to the still powerful antitariff forces. And the 74-gun frigate *Franklin* was an appropriate symbol to accompany the slogan. Though launched in 1815, too late for the war, she was "destined to become a bulwark of neutrality of freedom, of commerce and republican greatness . . ." In 1822 when Dyott first advertised his "ship

Franklin" flask (GII–42, with eagle on obverse), she was "on the coast of Chili in the Pacific Ocean, looking after the interests of the American merchants in Chili and Peru."[115]

From the late 1840s probably through the 1870s a sheaf of grain, usually with rake and fork crossed behind it, was a popular flask motif. Perhaps it was only coincidence that the popularity of this motif continued in the 1860s and 1870s when, following the 1862 Homestead Act, immigration from northern Europe, and the migration of easterners to the land west of the Mississippi, grain production burgeoned in that vast area—a rival to King Cotton after production of cotton returned to normal in the South following the war. Anyway, this motif could remind the owner of such a flask not only of American agriculture, so important in foreign trade, but also— especially when the motif was taken for a sheaf of rye—of our whiskey, so important in our national economy and such a bedevilment to the growing numbers of temperance people. The motif appeared in at least 31 flasks—quarts, pints, and half-pints. Only five decorated with a sheaf were charted in 1941, and they were of the Dyottville-type. On three, the sheaf is on the reverse and a classical bust of George Washington on the obverse. As charted, the other two—the rare pint and extremely rare half-pint GX–10 and 11—have "LIBERTY" in an arc above a "sheaf of rye" and, on the reverse, a large star (see 4A, Freedom's Star). As yet, only two midwestern flasks have been recorded having a sheaf of grain, GXIII–33 and GXIII–33a, brought out by Tibby Brothers of Pittsburgh or Sharpsburg, Pennsylvania, possibly in the 1870s. The remaining flasks having a sheaf of grain on the obverse as charted were products of eastern glassworks—the Westford Glass Works, Westford, Connecticut (1857–73); probably that at Bulltown, New Jersey, 1850s; Sheets & Duffy, Dyottville Upper Yard, Kensington, Philadelphia (1845–ca.1874), and the mystery works, the Mechanic Glass Works, Philadelphia. Charted as the reverse, the motif appears on five Anchor and Pennant flasks of the Baltimore Glass Works, probably in the 1850s–1860s, and one from the Isabella Glass Works, New Brooklyn, New Jersey, in the 1850s. It also is on the reverse of a "TRAVELERS COMPANION" pint flask (XIV–1) attributed to the Waterford Glass Works, New Jersey, by Van Rensselaer but thought by Charles B. Gardner to be a Westford product.

The anchor has long been a symbol of hope, but perhaps to the designers of flasks it symbolized mainly ships and shipping or was merely an attrac-

tive decorative motif. In any event, a large anchor with pennant above and below carrying the name of a glassworks ornamented at least 19 flasks of quart, pint, and half-pint sizes. An anchor alone was used for 12 late flasks (GXIII–63 through GXIII–74) having a plain reverse. The last of these is marked on the base "MADE BY / E. PACHAM & Co / BALTIMORE.MD"—nothing else has so far been learned about this manufacturer. Four of the "Anchor and Pennant" flasks having an American eagle on one side were charted in 1941 in the Eagle group: GII–37 of the Ravenna Glass Company, Ravenna, Ohio, late 1850s; and three (GII–66 through GII–68) of the New London Glass Works, New London, Connecticut, 1856–59. As the Chart drawings show, on GII–66 and 67 the obverse has an arc of stars above the American eagle perched on a wreath, the same design as on the eagle flasks of the Willington Glass Company and the Westford Glass Works, Connecticut. On the third New London flask the eagle is flying and is without shield, arrows, or olive branch. Of the Anchor and Pennant flasks produced in the Baltimore Glass Works, Baltimore, Maryland, six have been mentioned already in connection with the sheaf of grain motif; the other two, GXIII–54 and 55, probably were associated with the devastating Baltimore fire of 1850, in which two warehouses of the Baltimore Glass Works were destroyed. On the reverse is the phoenix, a sacred bird of the Egyptians that, according to one legend, at the end of its long life burns to ashes on the temple altar and rises again from the ashes as a young phoenix, feathering on the next day, and on the following, with pinions full grown, salutes the priest and flies away.[116] Beneath the phoenix is "RESURGAM" (I shall rise again). Thus the design can be interpreted to symbolize the city rising again from its ashes. Another Baltimore works, the Spring Garden Glass Works (1851–56), also used the Anchor and Pennant design. Its four flasks, GXIII–58 through GXIII–61, have a log cabin on the reverse. Likewise in the 1850s, the Isabella Glass Works put out three Anchor and Pennant flasks, two (GXIII–55 and GXII–57) with a glasshouse on the reverse and one (GXIII–56), as already mentioned, with sheaf of grain and crossed rake and fork.

Ships and small sailboats as well as anchors were chosen as motifs for a few flasks. The two United States naval vessels, the frigate *Franklin 74* and the United States steam frigate *Mississippi,* have already been mentioned in connection with the Farmers' Arms of the 1820s and early 1830s and Louis Kossuth, 1851 or 1852. On the reverse of the Albany

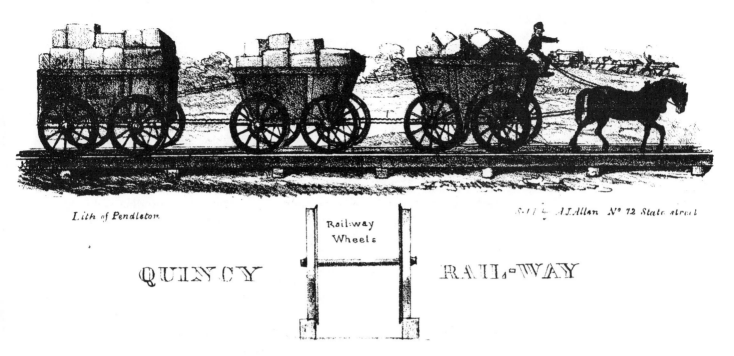

Railway Wheels

S.11 by A.J.Allen Nº 72 State street

QUINCY RAIL-WAY

131. David C. Johnston's lithograph of the "Granite Railway" at Quincy, Massachusetts. The railway, which opened October 7, 1826, was the first in the United States. Horse-drawn carts carried the granite block for the Bunker Hill Monument 2¾ to 3 miles from the quarry to Neponset River. *The American Antiquarian Society, Worcester, Massachusetts*

Glass Works' Washington flask GI–28 is an unidentified full-rigged sailing vessel. It will be recalled that very little has yet been discovered regarding this Albany Glass Works beyond the fact that it was operating in 1847 and, in 1850, received an award from the American Institute, for glass pipes. A group of seven flasks have a sloop or shallop like those used by the oystermen and fishermen of Chesapeake Bay and New Jersey waters. Six of the flasks are half-pint. One, GXI–2, has on the obverse the Baltimore Washington monument without the statue at the top and, on the reverse, "FELLS" above a shallop and "POINT" below, suggesting the flask was first blown in the late 1820s, whereas the other half-pints, GX–7 through GX–9, GX–8a, and GX–9a, may be as late as the 1840s. Flask GX–7 was a product of the Bridgeton Glass Works, Bridgeton, New Jersey. The one pint flask, the Louis Kossuth GI–111, also was brought out by the Bridgeton Glass Works, 1851 or 1852. Likewise, the unmarked flasks probably came from the Baltimore–Philadelphia–South Jersey area.

An exciting development in transportation also inspired flask designs: the railroad or railway, both the horse-and-cart type and the steam locomotive. The first American railway, a horse-and-cart, was the three-mile-long Quincy or Granite Railway chartered in 1825. (See Ill. 132.) On October 7, 1826, it began to carry granite blocks for Bunker Hill Mon-

ument near Boston, from the quarry to the wharf on the Neponset River en route to the site of the monument. In the next six years, at least 185 state and private companies projected plans for new railroads or incorporated or actually built roads. In 1827 the legislatures of Maryland, Virginia, and Pennsylvania incorporated the Baltimore and Ohio Railroad Company; the Baltimore and Ohio road was to connect Baltimore and Pittsburgh, in hopes of winning back commerce lost to the Erie Canal. The next longest planned was to be only 76 miles.[117] Newspapers gave full coverage to this marvelous new means of transportation, artists drew pictures of railroad cars and engines, and railroad companies issued descriptive broadsides with and without illustrations. Although perhaps the railway fever of the general public was at its peak by the 1840s, the extension of the lines was to continue for decades.

It is no wonder that railroad flasks, first appearing about 1830, and the slogan "Success to the Railroad" were timely for years—of the 14 railroad flasks charted, the slogan appears in seven. Two having a steam locomotive on each side have been attributed to the Lancaster Glass Works, Lancaster, New York (see note to GV–2); they may have celebrated the arrival of the New York Central in 1852. Five have the slogan and horse-and-cart on each side. The excavations of Harry Hall White on factory sites established Marlboro-Street-Glassworks, Keene, New

Hampshire, as the source of two, GV–3 and GV–4; Mount Vernon Glass Works, Vernon, New York, and in the late 1840s its successor, Saratoga Mountain Glass Works, as the source of GV–5; Coventry Glass Works, Coventry, Connecticut, as that of GV–6. Also Coventry products were the pint flasks GV–8 and GV–9 having the horse and cart on the obverse and, on the reverse, a handsome spread eagle and 17 stars in rather high relief as compared with others. Another Coventry flask is GV–10, the only half-pint in the group; it has "RAILROAD" at left above the horse and cart (a quite different cart, as the line drawings show), which face right instead of left, and "LOWELL" below the rail. On the reverse are an eagle similar to that on GV–8 and GV–9 and 13 stars. This was the only flask definitely associated with a specific railroad. The 25-mile Boston and Lowell road was first projected in 1829 and in 1830 stock was offered for sale. In 1832 the "work was now active," but some months were to elapse before this road was in use.[118] Therefore it seems likely the flask was brought out in one of these years, perhaps as propaganda or in celebration.

The rarest of the Railroad flasks, also one of the rarest Historical flasks, is GV–12, a colorless flask having an early type of locomotive on the obverse and a symbolical figure, apparently of Plenty, on the reverse. There is also, according to Van Rensselaer, "SUCCESS TO THE RAILROAD" on "somewhat flattened sides." The inscription does not appear in the line drawing in the Charts, as it did not show in the photograph in his book from which the line drawing was made. Mr. Van Rensselaer's theory was that the flask—he attributed it to the Baltimore Glass Works—may have been made to commemorate the completion of the Camden and Amboy Railroad in 1831, as that road is said to have put into service the first steam locomotive used in this country. My own feeling is that the flask may have commemorated the introduction of steam power in July 1831 by the young Baltimore and Ohio Railroad, a road of national as well as local interest.[119] On the other hand, Deverne A. Dressel, whose researches into Baltimore's glassworks have been extensive and in depth, believes the flask may have been inspired by the locally very important New Castle and Frenchtown Railroad, a connecting link in Baltimore–Philadelphia trade. (See No. 18. Baltimore Glass Works.)

One flask in Group XIV in the Charts (the Traveler's Companion flasks) is related to the railroad by the inscription on the reverse: "RAILROAD" in large letters in an arc above "GUIDE" in a straight line and smaller letters—an appropriate companion to "TRAVELER'S COMPANION" on the obverse. This rare half-pint flask, found in aquamarine and pale yellow-green, was one of the later flasks chosen by George S. McKearin for Group C of Most Desirable Flasks. It may have been brought out around 1850.

The American System flasks, high among the rarest and most sought-after flasks in the Historical group, were a midwestern product of the Pittsburgh-Monongahela area. In all, three molds have been identified: one for GX–21, having no factory identification, from which 15 to 20 flasks are known; a second for GX–20, having the initials B.P.& B (Bakewell, Page & Bakewell) in a frame at bottom of the reverse, from which one flask (colorless lead glass of violet tinge) has been recorded; and a third, for GX–20a having the initials "B&M" (possibly Baker & Martin, Perryopolis, Pennsylvania) in the waves on the obverse, from which only one specimen is known. Several facets of our economy were represented by the motifs and inscriptions of this design. On the reverse was a sheaf of rye, symbolizing agriculture and the hard liquor that had always had so large a role in our economy, especially in the Midwest, and presumably would be the temporary contents of the flask. But, at the same time, the inscription "USE ME BUT DO NOT ABUSE ME" was an appeal to temperance, the force of which was waxing. On the obverse was a steamboat of the type plying American rivers and lakes, symbolizing the comparatively recent innovation in water transportation that had revolutionized travel and trade and their cost. The appropriate "THE AMERICAN SYSTEM"—three well-recognized words—advocated internal improvements (highways and waterways), and high tariffs to protect domestic industry, as well as support of Henry Clay and his cohorts in the fight for all the words implied. "The American System" was as inextricably associated with Clay as was "The Great Compromiser"; apparently it was coined by him during the congressional battle of protective tariff vs. free trade, which culminated in the passage of the 1824 protective tariff. Henry Baldwin, a young congressman from Pittsburgh, who was Clay's leader in the fight in the House of Representatives, received wide recognition of his successful efforts, first in 1820 when he was "complimented with a public dinner in Philadelphia . . . for his zeal and ability as advocate of domestic manufacturers." A riverboat had been named for him by the summer of 1824, and after the triumph of protective tariff, Pittsburgh manufacturers, including Benjamin Bakewell, who was chairman of the committee, gave a banquet in Baldwin's honor, in appreciation for his successful efforts on Pittsburgh's behalf. Quite realistically Baldwin attributed the success of the Protectionists to Clay's persistent, untiring efforts, and proposed a toast to "Henry Clay and the American System."[120]

It is scarcely surprising that the American System design originated in Pittsburgh. And although it could have materialized earlier, the general belief is that the first flask appeared in celebration of the 1824 tariff. Moreover, the first may have been the B. P. & B—and at the time of that August dinner for Henry Baldwin.

6

SPORTS

Today it seems a little surprising that not more American Figured Flasks were inspired by sports. But sports were not so diversified in the era of the flasks as they became later, and Figured Flasks apparently required a broader basis of appeal than sports motifs would have provided. Moreover, the average—the common—man of the period had little leisure in his everyday life to spend on participation in sports, even as a spectator. He usually worked six days a week, 10 to 12 hours a day; and there was no radio or television to bring sports into his home. Of course, however, there were hunting and fishing—sport for some lucky men, livelihood for others. And for certain of the "better sort" there were "riding to hounds" and racing.

Of the 20 or so flasks that can be related to sports, most were brought out from around 1850 into the 1870s. Only four of the flasks charted in 1941 might be said to fall in such a category. They are two eagle flasks, GII–49 and GII–50, having on the reverse "COFFIN & HAY HAMMONTON" (dating them as 1836–38) and a stag, and two, GX–1 and GX–2, having "GOOD GAME" and a stag on the obverse and a weeping willow on the reverse. It was probably in the late 1840s or early 1850s that the three calabash "Hunting and Fishing" bottles GXIII–4 through GXIII–6 were first produced. On one side of all, a hunter wearing a tall hat is shooting at two birds in flight; on the other side, a fisherman, also wearing a tall hat, is holding up a fish he has just caught. The common one, GXIII–4, having the hunter and also two "bird" dogs instead of one, has always been attributed to the Whitney Glass Works, Glassboro, New Jersey. On GXIII–5, a scarce bottle, both the hunter and fisherman are at the left and a tall tree is at the right on the fisherman side. On GXIII–6, a rare bottle, the hunter is at the left and fisherman at the

right. The designs differ in other details, as comparison of the line drawings in the Charts show. Whether or not gentlemen hunters wore high-crowned, perhaps beaver, hats when hunting I do not know, but they were so depicted in advertisements of the 1840s—for instance, that of H. A. Duntze, gun maker, of New Haven, Connecticut, whose advertisement of a "general assortment of Sports men's articles including Double and Single Barrelled *Guns*, *Rifles*, Pocket, Side, Belt and Holsters *Pistols*" appeared in the 1844/5 New Haven [Conn.] directory. However, the hunter, a more cleanly modeled figure, on the rare pint flask GXIII–7 appears to be wearing a cap. On the reverse are two running "bird" dogs. This flask was attributed by Van Rensselaer to the New London Glass Works, which would date it in the 1856–59 period.

The sport of kings was commemorated by the Flora Temple flasks and possibly by the slender horse on the rare bottle made about 1858 for Gentry, Shote & Company, New York City grocers. The bay mare Flora Temple was well known throughout the country, even outside racing circles. In 1853 she brought the existing 1845 record of 2 minutes 29½ seconds down to 2 minutes 27 seconds. The eagerness of the public to see her and other famous trotters led, in 1857, to a visit by Flora Temple and Lancet (another racer) to Elmira, New York; Springfield, Massachusetts; and Hartford, Connecticut, where they raced for a share of the gate receipts and a purse. Later Flora Temple raced against local horses at Chicago, Illinois; Detroit and Kalamazoo, Michigan; Sondersby (?), Adrian (?), and St. Louis, Missouri—all of which served to further popularize harness racing. On October 19, 1859, she broke her own record, a widely reported event. "In the great trotting match for the citizens purse of $2,000, she won all three heats—time 2 32 1-2, 2 22 1-2, and 2 19 3-4, the last named being, of course, the quickest time ever recorded."[121]

The event gave rise to the Flora Temple flasks, for which six different molds have been recorded: two for the quart flasks GXIII–19 and GXIII–20, and four for pints, GXIII–21 through GXIII–24; they were unlike other flasks in shape, as shown by 6 in Ill. 126. All depict the horse below "FLORA TEMPLE" and above "HARNESS TROT 2.19¾/ Oct. 19, 1859". Since all Flora Temples are rated as "common," it would appear that they were a very popular design made in large quantities. Van Rensselaer, who did not list by molds, lists three Flora Temple bottles and states that Flora Temple flasks were produced by both the Whitney Glass Works, Glassboro, New Jersey, and the Lancaster Glass Works at Lancaster in western New York. In connection with the latter, a 73-year-old glassblower named Lambricks, who had worked in several glass factories, told Mr. Van Rensselaer that Flora Temples in green and amber were blown at Lancaster.[122] Although no definite attribution can be made, it seems possible that flasks from four of the molds were products of the Whitney Glass Works, namely the handled quart GXIII–19, the two pints with handle GXIII–21 and 22, and the pint GXIII–24 that is found both with and without a handle. The handles, of course, were applied to the molded flask. Possibly the quart and pint without handles, GXIII–20 and 23, were Lancaster products.

Two flasks, GXIII–17 and 18, depict a horseman on the obverse and a "hound" on the reverse. Perhaps they pertain to the hunt rather than racing.

Though the rider on GXIII–17 is astride a running horse, his position is not that of a jockey in such a situation. The rider on GXIII–18 has lost his cap as he strives to curb a runaway horse.

In the 1870s Americans, men and women, took to a new sport: bicycling. And it led to three pint flasks decorated with a girl riding on a bicycle of the earliest type, one that appeared about 1870. Though varying in detail, the depictions of the rider and bicycle are all closely similar, but the design on one flask, GXIII–2, is much smaller than on the other two, GXIII–1 and GXIII–3. And whereas the reverse of GXIII–1 and 2 is plain, that of GXIII–3 has a crudely drawn eagle with shield on lower breast, a thunderbolt in its talons, and the end of a pennant in its beak. Below the eagle, in an oval frame, are the initials "A. & DHC"—Alexander and David H. Chambers, proprietors of the Pittsburgh Glass Works (1843–86+). The other two, which incidentally are of a later shape having a broad flat end, have a pennant issuing from the girl's lips that bears the phrase "NOT FOR JOE". This phrase was from a popular comic song of the 1870s composed by an Englishman, Arthur Lloyd, and sung by him in the 1870 equivalent of the music hall. That the song became popular in America seems evident from its catchphrase being used in the decoration of a whiskey flask. The song was five stanzas long with spoken interpolations; the chorus ran:

> "Not for Joe," "Not for Joe,"
> If he know it,
> Not for Joseph;
> No, No, No "Not for Joe"
> Not for Joseph, oh dear no."

7

PIKE'S PEAK FLASKS

Pike's Peak or Bust—that phrase became the slogan of the 1858/59 rush to the "Kansas-Nebraska" gold fields, a slogan that was to appear often on the covered wagons of prospectors and to become a bit of American slang.[123] Actually, as pointed out in an early 1859 handbook, "Pike's Peak Gold [was] a Myth"; the nearest place to Pike's Peak at which gold to justify working had been found was Cherry Creek, 80 miles away.[124] The Peak, however, being fairly

well known, was a natural point of orientation for midwesterners and easterners ignorant of the general region.

It all began in the spring of 1858 when a group of white men and Cherokee Indians set out to prospect in the area of Pike's Peak, in hope of finding true the tales of Indians and travelers that there was "gold in them thar hills." The news of the venture was quickly followed by the formation of two companies to prospect the whole region along the Platte River. Soon the wildfire rumor of a great gold strike was spreading, gaining richness as it traveled eastward to the Atlantic. Conditions were exactly right for such a rumor to start an epidemic of gold fever: the country was still prostrate after another of its periodic depressions from overexpansion and overspeculation—"the great revulsion" of 1857. Swarms of unemployed workmen, bankrupt businessmen, and poor farmers, as well as adventurers who preferred finding to working for gold, had nothing to lose and everything to gain by following rumor's rainbow to Pike's Peak, and they did so during the many months of excitement. And so they came by the thousands, apparently mainly from western states— prospectors traveling in groups or singly, with ox-drawn covered wagons, with hand-carts, with wheelbarrows, with tool-laden donkeys, a bundle of personal effects over their shoulders.

"Hurrah for Pike's Peak—EXCITEMENT STILL INCREASING" proclaimed the *Allen County Democrat* of Lima, Ohio, on January 5, 1859, headlining excerpts from newspapers of more westerly towns, nearer the scene of action. The excitement emanated from not only those expecting to dig wealth out of gold pockets but also those expecting to dig it out of the prospectors'—"the emigrants' "—pockets. Leavenworth, St. Louis, Omaha, and St. Joseph were among the places whence the prospectors began the final lap of their journey to the gold fields with such equipment as they could afford. Local citizens had been quick to rush into the business of outfitting prospectors, and through word of mouth and their newspapers they continued to foster the illusion of limitless wealth to be had for the swing of the pick or thrust of the shovel. Nearly everything anyone had for sale was advertised as something essential to the prospector—"India Rubber Goods," designed especially for the journey across the plain; "Colt Revolvers"; "1000 yoke Work Oxen"; Lidiard's Morning Call, "the best Cocktail in the World and also a tonic," "especially valuable to a settler in the new country . . . preventing fever and ague . . . correcting the evils consequent on a change of water."[125] The western newspapers also printed maps to guide the prospector.

But more important were the handbooks that began appearing early in 1859. They too had maps, and they added advice on the various routes and means of travel from the East, described the terrain, and not only provided lists of the necessary tools, mining and camping equipment, and provisions, but

also gave the "cards" of outfitters. For tools, Colonel Gilpin of Independence, Missouri, recommended eight picks, four shovels, four axes, nine gold pans, one pit saw, two chisels, two augers, one saw, one frower, and one drawing knife. A large proportion of prospectors, perhaps the majority, were ill equipped, having limited resources other than brawn to invest. Parker and Huyett stated in their handbook that "Persons have left for the mines this spring [1859] on foot, taking in handcarts an outfit which did not cost over $20 per man; and the wheel-barrow man has gone with still less . . ." However, their recommended outfit for four men for six months called for the considerable capital investment of $754.89 to $764.89 ($54.50 less if luxuries were omitted). Of this, $305 was for the "TEAM"— three yoke of oxen, covered wagon with wooden axletree, wagon cover, chains, yokes, and so on. Provisions—19 items, including staples such as flour and sugar, coffee and tea, also dried fruits, even pickles, kegs of water, vinegar, and molasses, soap and candles—came to $183.50. Under hardware 31 items were listed amounting to $52.85; these included mining tools, cooking and eating utensils, rope, nails, and matches. Clothing and blankets came to $102.25. Under India-rubber goods were listed 15 items, among them pails, flasks, canteens, and cups; the cost ran from $66.89 to $76.89, inasmuch as such coats, pantaloons, overalls (all black vulcanized), and camp blankets varied in price. Six items of luxuries came to the aforementioned $54.50. Besides pipes and smoking and chewing tobacco, there was a half-barrel of bourbon whiskey at $20.00—less than the cost of a gallon of good bourbon today. To me, the most interesting items were 12 *cans* of Maltby's best oysters and 4 *cans* of fresh peaches. No figure was given for "GUNS, PISTOLS etc" because the price depended upon the quality, but the "cards" of dealers prepared to supply the demand at reasonable prices were given.[126]

These handbooks reported, too, on past and present discoveries of gold veins and on a prospector's prospects of acquiring the precious metal. In general, they erred on the optimistic side. Even in late 1858 reports that the fields were no Eldorado were already filtering back through word of mouth and the press. Often prospectors on the way to the mining sites met disillusioned prospectors returning home, some of them destitute and foodless. "The *St. Louis Democrat*, quoted by the *New York Tribune*, May 13, 1859" reported that 20,000 such men on their way home "threatened to burn Omaha, Leavenworth and St. Joseph because of the fraud practiced on them by the people of those outfitting towns."[127] Nevertheless, the stream to Pike's Peak continued to flow. In fact, many would-be prospectors who heard or read that such lodes as existed were far from rich, some even barren, believed that tales minimizing the strikes and ballooning the difficulties sprang from greed—that those who had already amassed wealth wanted to keep it for themselves. However, the conflicting testimony soon led to on-the-spot inspection by the eastern press. By the spring of 1859 *Frank Leslie's Illustrated Newspaper*, shortly followed by *Harper's Weekly*, sent its own artist-correspondent to record in picture and word the facts of the second gold-rush phenomenon in a decade. The correspondents of both publications sent back sketches from the scene—graphic records of bundle emigrants, of those with a handcart or wheelbarrow, of wagon parties, and of camping scenes along the route. In August *Harper's* correspondent reported that in the past ten days he had met "thousands of deluded and suffering gold-seekers retracing their steps to the quiet farms of the west," many of them "in a starving condition, barefooted, ragged and penniless."[128] But Horace Greeley of the *New York Tribune*, who had decided to investigate the contradictory evidence in person, wrote from Denver in June, "It is my strong belief that gold is scarcely less abundant in the Rocky Mountains than in California, though it seems for many reasons, far less accessible." Were the inspected areas well salted for Greeley's benefit? Skeptics suspected they had been. There was gold, but not enough for thousands. Henry Villard reported in his handbook that of 40,000 gold seekers only 2,000 were successful, and he did not record the extent of that success. In any event, the fever had subsided by the end of 1859.

One of the byproducts of the Pike's Peak gold rush was a sizable group of pictorial flasks, the first of which may have been blown late in 1858 or early in 1859 and the last probably some time in the 1870s. At least, Harry Hall White found that as late as 1872 A. & D. H. Chambers of Pittsburgh were making Pike's Peak flasks, and also Union flasks, which doubtless were our Union and Clasped Hands.[129] In all, 55 varieties of Pike's Peak, or prospector, flasks have been recorded—13 quarts, 29 pints, and 13 half-pints. One of the pint flasks was charted in 1941 in Group II, the eagles. This flask, GII–21, differs quite a bit from the other 54. The eagle, on the obverse as charted, is clearly intended to represent the United States' coat of arms. A star is at each side of the eagle's neck and an arc of 11 stars above him. Below the eagle is "MY COUNTRY" in an inverse arc. On

the reverse is "FOR PIKES PEAK" in a semicircle above the figure of a bundle prospector who wears a frock coat, tight trousers, and boots, but whose bundle does not contain any mining tools. The bundle prospector on the *obverse* of the other 54 flasks, which are charted in Group XI, is a sketchily drawn figure clad in tight trousers and coat with either short or long tail, wearing either a derby hat or a cap, and holding over one shoulder a staff with bundle or pack at one end from which the heads of one, two, or three mining tools protrude; and, except on nine flasks on which the prospector has only one arm, he has a cane in the other hand as (excepting on the prospector-hunter group) he "walks" to left or right on a round-ended rectangular frame. On some, he is a somewhat plodding man; on others, he walks purposefully, and on a few he is jaunty, as the line drawings show. On the reverse of the majority is a crudely rendered eagle with head turned to right or left, wings partly raised, shield usually below breast, a thunderbolt or, in a few instances, two in its talons. The beak holds the end of a narrow pennant that extends in a curve above the eagle's head. Such is the eagle of 35 flasks (GXI–7 through GXI–37 and GXI–40 through GXI–43). On the reverse of GXI–44 and 45 is a large eagle with head turned to right, partly raised wings spreading outward and downward, shield on breast, thunderbolt (3 feathered arrows) in its talons, and an olive branch held in its beak. On the reverse of two others (GXI–38 and 39) is the familiar flying eagle found on most of the Shield and Clasped Hands flasks. Below the eagle is a frame. One flask has a prospector on each side, and six have a plain reverse. The eight flasks having a hunter shooting a deer on the reverse are rectangular rather than the usual elliptical in cross section. These vary also from the norm in that there is no frame on either side.

Only 14 of the entire Group XI have a molded inscription or lettering other than "FOR PIKE'S PEAK" or "PIKES PEAK". Three, the quart GXI–8, pint GXI–9, and half-pint GXI–10, have "OLD RYE" in the frame on which the prospector walks and "PITTSBURGH PA" in that below the eagle. "Old rye" would seem to leave no doubt that the flasks were for hard liquor and probably used to package whiskey for retail sale. The name of a glass manufacturer occurs on only six flasks, and then in the frame on the reverse. Two rare pint flasks, GXI–12 and GXI–16, have "W. McC & Co / GLASS WORKS / PITTS.PA."; the scarce quart, pint, and half-pint flasks GXI–13 through GXI–15 have "ARSENAL GLASS WORKS / PITTS PA", which dates them from 1867 about through 1869/70; the common

A

B

132. "Miner" flask, GXIII–93, Imperial quart, strong aquamarine, extraordinarily thick walls. Though similar in shape to Pike's Peak flasks (Group XI), it is much taller in proportion to width. On the obverse (**A**), the tall miner, with a pickaxe held over his right shoulder, wears a short jacket, short pants ending above his knees, and "boots" with wide turned-over tops ending below his knees— clothing quite different from that of the prospectors on the Pike's Peak flasks and unlike any

known to have been worn by workers in any U.S. mines. On the reverse (**B**) is a linear depiction of a mine building and rigging of two wheels, cables, and a bucket in which workers were lowered into the mine and the mined product brought to the surface. Educated guesses of the mineralogists consulted are that the mine probably was a gold mine, or possibly a salt mine, and most likely in central Europe. These guesses, all the physical characteristics of the flask itself, and the miner's clothing have led collectors who have studied the flask to the considered opinion that it was not produced in the United States, but perhaps in Canada or possibly Great Britain, for a European customer, and in about 1900. (Photo by Bruce Whistance) *Collection of George B. Austin*

pint flask GXI–29 has "C. IHMSEN & Co / PITTSBURGH PA". Another pint, the scarce GXI–38, poses what is probably an unanswerable question: what letter was reamed out to form the block with "& Co." in the frame on the reverse? The comparatively scarce half-pint GXI–39 is also a puzzle, for in the reverse frame is "F & Co" with space enough between the F and the ampersand for a letter, suggesting an omission by the moldmaker. Possibly it was an "A." This is suggested as a possibility because the flask is the same form and has the same base type (Type 2, with small nipple at center of a shallow disk) as the Shield and Clasped Hands GXII–42 marked "F A & Co"—presumably Fahnstock, Albree & Company of Pittsburgh.

Also among the flasks that have always been puzzles are the quart, pint, and half-pint flasks GXI–34 through GXI–36 having the word "CEREDO" in the oval frame below the eagle. Since Ceredo is the name of a small West Virginia village of about 1,200 popu-

lation, students have for years considered the possibility that the flasks were made there for a merchant or a saloon keeper. However, in spite of many efforts to unearth information that might link the flasks with Ceredo, none was found until a few years ago. Lowell Innes has informed me that a possible connection was found by the late Earl Dambach of Pittsburgh. In a 1959 unpublished paper, "History of Ceredo and Kenove" by C. W. Thompson, in the Huntington Public Library, West Virginia, Mr. Dambach found the statement that the town of Ceredo had a salt works, a large grist mill, a match factory, a carriage factory, and a glass factory. Apparently Mr. Thompson, the author, did not give the dates when the glassworks operated. But, as Mr. Innes wrote, "This is circumstantial evidence that the lone marked Pikes Peak was made there, but it must serve until better explanation is given." Personally I feel the probability is very strong.

Another noteworthy Pike's Peak is the quart flask GXI–49 having "E.KAUFFIELD" in a straight line below the hunter. This is the rarest Pike's Peak in the entire group. Only one specimen has been recorded as yet, that formerly in the Charles B. Gardner Collection.*

*Since this section was written, another rarity in Pike's Peak flasks was reported by George Austin. It is charted as GXI–47a and has a previously unrecorded capacity of 27 ounces.

8
THE MOST DESIRABLE FLASKS,
GROUPS A AND B,
AND RARE FLASKS, GROUP C

Following is a condensation of the list of most desirable flasks prepared in 1941 by George S. McKearin for *American Glass*. After the passage of nearly 40 years, it was only natural to wonder whether it ought to be revised by deletion or addition. Several collectors and dealers were consulted, and with one exception they agreed that the listing of flasks should remain as it was. In part, this consensus was based on the fact that the choice of flasks for Groups A, B, and C was Mr. McKearin's own very personal choice, one regarded as of lasting interest because of his decades of studying and collecting the then-so-called historical and pictorial flasks and his comprehensive knowledge of them. Also, although each person consulted might have made a change here or there according to his own personal choice, there was general agreement with the listings.

Therefore, in the interests of conservation and economy, Mr. McKearin's list is presented here in condensed form, and the reader is referred to *American Glass*, pp. 489–511, for more detailed descriptions of these flasks, and Mr. McKearin's original notes about some of them. This condensed list also contains bracketed notes giving additional information and comments on some glassworks, dates, attributions, and colors. The colors are those seen by Mr. McKearin and myself since 1941 or reported to us by collectors and dealers since that time (the name of the reporter is given in parentheses). It is possible that in instances where closely similar colors have been reported, the same color may have been designated by more than one term. In any event, where several new colors are listed, the probability is that they increase the number of specimens known to, or estimated by, Mr. McKearin in 1941, and thus may affect the degree of rarity.

To return to the matter of demoting a flask or promoting one into a Group: Had my father, George S. McKearin, lived and been able to collaborate in writing this book as we planned, I doubt that he would have removed even one flask from any of the Groups, except possibly Group C. However, judging by his feeling for certain flasks unknown to him until

after the publication of *American Glass,* I believe he would have added at least four to Group A. They are the following, of which only one specimen is recorded at this time: GI–130, the only known example of Henry Clay flasks, produced by Knox & McKee, Wheeling, (W.) Virginia, shown in Ill. 130; GIX–52, to my eyes the handsomest flask in the Scroll Group, pictured as 2 in Ill. 124; GI–89a, the Lafayette–Masonic flask with herringbone edge, attributed to the Mount Vernon Glass Works, Vernon, New York, 1 in Ill. 125; and GII–144, the unusual flask with wide-spaced fine ribs broken by an eagle medallion, possibly produced at the Keene-Marlboro-Street Glassworks, Keene, New Hampshire, and shown here as example 3 of Ill. 124.

In Group C, some flasks have, in brackets, a different and lesser degree of rarity from that assigned to them in 1941. This was supplied by either Charles B. Gardner or Sam Laidacker or both. Each of these flask-wise students kindly gave his opinion of each flask in Groups XI through XV in regard to its degree of, or lack of, rarity. Also, it should be noted that in instances where the base is described simply as "smooth," the base type as charted has been given in brackets. It is only in comparatively recent years that mold seams and other features on the base of the later flasks have been noted and given serious attention.

In summary, then, the section that follows here is essentially a condensation of that which appeared in *American Glass*, with the additions noted above. For the sake of appearance and convenience, however, I have not treated it as a quotation, in order to avoid the problem of quotes with quotes—within quotes.

"What is the rarest early American historical flask known?" The answer? Frankly, we have none. If you apply the term "rarest" literally, any one of 10 or 15 flasks of which only one specimen is known might claim first place or the right to share it. Let us change the phrasing of our query and make it, "What is the most desirable early American historical flask?" That is different, but still practically impossible to answer with respect to any one flask.

On numerous occasions it has been suggested that we prepare a list of 10 or 15 flasks which from our own knowledge and experience we consider the most desirable. Before we had hardly begun to consider candidates for such a list we realized we could never limit it to that number. As a result, the number quickly grew to 42, and even then we were confronted with further candidates whose claim to recognition seemed equally strong. Therefore, to our list of 42, we have added an additional group of 40 flasks, most of which—although not quite so rare as those included in the first group—possess the same qualifications necessary to entitle them to rank among the "most desirable."

First of all, we must decide just what we mean by "most desirable" and what are the qualifications. Rarity is, of course, important but is only one of several elements which may cause a flask to be eagerly sought by every collector. Rarity alone cannot be the determining factor. We call to mind several flasks of which only a single specimen is known which we have not considered including in the list, for they have scarcely any appeal aside from rarity.

Let us enumerate qualifications which, in our opinion, entitle a flask to a place in the group:

First, rarity. We place this first because, after all, each flask, in addition to any or all other qualifications, must be "rare."

Second, beauty or attractiveness. It must appeal to the esthetic sense in form or decorative design.

Third, historical or other special significance. The design must have some appeal from the standpoint of historical, political, or popular interest.

Any flask to be included in the list must possess either the second or third or both qualifications, as well as that of rarity.

It is to be noted that *we have intentionally omitted color as one of the qualifications*. Although color may add greatly to the beauty and rarity of a particular flask, we are dealing in the list with "variety".

The numbers in the list are given only for the purpose of listing, not as ranking. The Group number and the name is given for each flask, as well as the number or approximate number of specimens of which we have knowledge, the colors in which we know it exists, and, where known, the name of the glassworks in which each of the flasks was made or the area of its probable origin.

DEGREE OF RARITY

Collectors of Historical Flasks are naturally interested in the comparative rarity of their specimens.

With this in mind, we have adopted a scale of terms based on the approximate number of specimens known to us at present, to use in connection with the flasks listed as most desirable and also in the flask chart. The scale is as follows:

Extremely rare . . . . .1–10 specimens
Very rare . . . . .10–20 specimens
Rare . . . . .20–35 specimens
Scarce . . . . .35–75 specimens
Comparatively scarce . . . . .75–150 specimens
Common to very common 150–more specimens

This scale of rarity refers only to the flask itself irrespective of the color. Many flasks classified as "scarce" or "common" are very rare in certain colors. Others designated as "rare" may be extremely rare in some color other than light green or aquamarine, and a flask listed as "common" may be very rare to extremely rare in blue or amethyst. In conclusion, the degree of rarity is necessarily flexible and the status of a flask may change at any time due to the discovery of additional specimens.

MOST DESIRABLE FLASKS—GROUP A

1. GII–59. Eagle–"Charter Oak" Tree; "LIBERTY". Pint. Peacock-blue, clear [colorless].
   Extremely rare; only two specimens. The flask of similar design in half-pint size is not rare.

2. GX–24. "JARED SPENCER"–"MANCHESTER. CON." Pint. Clear amber. [Olive-amber, deep golden amber (McKearin).] Extremely rare, about six to eight specimens.

3. GX–25. Deep olive-green. [Medium olive-green (Laidacker).] Similar to 2 but no inscriptions.
   Extremely rare, only three or four specimens.

4. GX–26. Pint. Similar to 2 and 3. Light amber. [Light olive-amber (Laidacker).]
   Extremely rare, three or four specimens.
   NOTE: These flasks, 2, 3, and 4, are attributed to the Pitkin Glass Works, Manchester, Conn. The identity of Jared Spencer has so far eluded us. [Since 1941 it has been learned that a second glassworks made bottles and flasks in East Hartford, which became *Manchester* in May 1823, and competed with the Pitkin glassworks. Therefore, the source of these flasks may be either the Pitkin works or John Mather's. The "official" name of the Pitkin, and of the Mather works, has not been discovered as yet. Jared Spencer was a resident of the town.]

5. GII–57.   Eagle;   "J.P.F."–Cornucopia; "CONN." Light amber; olive-green.

Extremely rare, only three specimens. Possibly Pitkin Glass Works.

NOTE: for additional information, see *American Glass*, p. 491.

6. GII–58. Eagle–Cornucopia. Clear light amber. [Olive-amber (McKearin).]

Extremely rare, only five or six specimens. Possibly Pitkin or Coventry.

NOTE: for additional information, see *American Glass*, pp. 491–92.

7. GIV–29. Masonic emblem. Reverse, same. Half-pint. Clear light amber; deep olive-green.

Extremely rare, about six specimens. Attributed to Coventry.

8. GIV–30. Star; Crossed Keys–Masonic Compass and Square. Clear light olive-amber. Half-pint.

Extremely rare, about six specimens. Attributed to Coventry.

9. GIV–22. Masonic Arch–Eagle; "1829". Clear glass with faint amethyst tint. [Colorless (Gardner).] Pint.

Extremely rare, four or five specimens.

10. GIV–23. Masonic Arch–Eagle; "1829". Half-pint. Clear [colorless] glass with faint amethyst tint. [Blown from lead glass.]

Extremely rare, only one specimen known.

NOTE: It is not definitely known where these two flasks, 9 and 10, were made. In general characteristics 9 conforms closely to the Masonic flasks marked "KEENE" in oval frame below the eagle, except in the matter of color. This also applies to the half-pint flask, 10, which conforms closely to the half-pint Keene Masonic flask with plain oval frame. See Masonic Group IV, 17 and 24 in chart. Clear [colorless] glass was also made at Keene and it is quite probable that these "1829" Masonic flasks were Keene products. [Definitely New England but probably not Keene unless, on occasion, Perry made a batch of lead glass to fill a special order. Today some students, including myself, believe that these flasks were blown in one of the South Boston glassworks, quite likely that of Thomas Cains. The presence of fragments on the Keene site remains a mystery. Possibly they were from a flask discarded by a workman or possibly part of cullet.]

11. GIV–15. Masonic–Eagle; "N.G.C°" Pale green; olive-amber. [Light yellow-green; olive-amber upper part and olive-green lower (McKearin).]

Extremely rare, only four specimens.

NOTE: It is not definitely known for what the initials "N.G.C°" stand. It is quite possible the flask was made at the Keene (Marlboro St.) Glass Works. [Students and collectors now lean toward attribution to the New England Glass Co., Cambridge, Mass. Examples tested for lead content proved to be flint glass—that is, lead glass.]

12. GII–76. About quart size. "Concentric Ring Eagle." Clear deep green; clear green, yellowish tone. [Emerald-green (McKearin).]

Very rare, about 12 to 15 specimens.

NOTE: [Examples tested for lead content proved to be lead glass.]

13. GII–77. "Concentric Ring Eagle"–"NGC°" About quart size. Clear light yellow-green; peacock-blue. [Medium yellow-green (McKearin).]

Extremely rare, only three or four specimens known.

NOTE: [Tested examples of this unmarked Concentric Ring Eagle canteen-flask proved to be lead glass. It is still believed the flask may possibly have been blown at the Keene-Marlboro-Street glassworks, 1815–17, though the South Boston Flint Glass Works or Thomas Cains's Phoenix Glass Works are considered strong possibilities.]

14. GIII–3. Cornucopia. Reverse, same. Pale green; dark olive-green. One and one-half pints.

Extremely rare, only two specimens. Possibly Keene.

NOTE: for additional information, see *American Glass*, p. 493.

15. GII–75. Eagle–Cornucopia. Pint. Green; olive-amber; pale yellow-green. [Olive-green (McKearin).]

Extremely rare, about six to eight specimens. Possibly Keene.

NOTE: for additional information, see *American Glass*, p. 493.

16. GI–70.   Jackson–Masonic   Arch.   Pint. Aquamarine. [Light green (McKearin) found after 1941.]

Extremely rare, only two specimens known. Mantua Glass Works, Mantua, Ohio.

NOTE: for additional information, see *American Glass*, p. 494.

17. GX–20. Steamboat; "THE AMERICAN SYSTEM"—Sheaf of Rye; "USE ME BUT DO NOT ABUSE ME". Pint. Clear [colorless], shading to pale violet.

Extremely rare, only one or two specimens. Bakewell, Page & Bakewell.

18. GX–21. American System flask. Pint. Brilliant olive-yellow; deep olive-green (black); clear green. [Green-aquamarine (Gardner); bluish green (McKearin).]

Very rare, ten to fifteen specimens.

NOTE: [Since 1941 another variety has been recorded, one having the initials "B & M"— probably Baker & Martin who, prior to 1832, acquired the glassworks started in Perryopolis, Pennsylvania, about 1816. There can be little doubt all three molds were made by the same moldmaker, and it is likely the one without initials was made for a third, and unidentified, glassworks.]

19. GI–62. John Q. Adams–Eagle; "JT & Co." Pint. Aquamarine.

Extremely rare, only four to six specimens. Attributed to John Taylor & Co., Brownsville, Pa.

NOTE: for additional information, see *American Glass*, p. 495.

20. GI–8. G.G. Washington–Eagle; "F.L." Pint. Clear light green. [Light yellow-green (Gardner); bluish aquamarine, colorless, and moonstone (Laidacker).]

Extremely rare, about five specimens. Frederick Lorenz, Pittsburgh district.

NOTE: for additional information, see *American Glass*, p. 495.

21. GI–13. Washington–Eagle; "B.K." Pint. Light green. [Pale emerald-green (Laidacker).]

Extremely rare, five or six specimens. Attributed to glass house of Benedict Kimber, Monongahela district.

NOTE: for additional information, see *American Glass*, pp. 495–96.

22. GI–12. Washington–Eagle. Pint. Cornflower-blue; light green; sapphire-blue.

Extremely rare, only four to five specimens. Monongahela and early Pittsburgh district.

23. GI–6. General Washington–Eagle; "J.R."; "LAIRD. SC. PITT." Pint. Clear [colorless]; clear [colorless] with amethyst tint; light green.

Very rare, ten to 15 specimens. Attributed to John Robinson, Pittsburgh. (Ca. 1824–1830.)

24. GI–66. General Jackson. Reverse, same as 23. Pint. Olive-yellow; aquamarine; clear [colorless] glass with amethyst tint. [Yellow-green (McKearin).]

Extremely rare, six to ten specimens. Attributed to John Robinson, Pittsburgh. (Ca. 1824–1830.)

NOTE: [In June 1830 the firm became John Robinson & Son; in August 1834, T. & J. Robinson. However, a pressed glass plate made by the firm is marked "J & T Robinson . . ."]

25. GI–76. General Taylor; "ROUGH & READY."–Eagle. Pint. Light yellowish green, aquamarine.

Rare, six to ten specimens. Monongahela and early Pittsburgh district.

NOTE: [The last paragraph of Mr. McKearin's note about Taylor on p. 497 of *American Glass* is revised here in the light of more recent research, which invalidates many of the original statements: Zachary Taylor, or "Old Rough and Ready," as his troops affectionately called him, was not, as was once thought, a sufficiently popular hero to rate a flask in the earlier years of his career. It is true that his ties with the Midwest were strong—he spent his boyhood and youth amid the stirring frontier scenes of early Kentucky, not far from the Monongahela–Pittsburgh district. He served with distinction in the War of 1812, and was breveted Major for his gallant defense of Fort Harrison, a stockade in central Indiana, against the Indians. Then followed a period of retirement until in 1832, as a colonel, he took part in the Black Hawk War. In 1837 he was sent to Florida where, in December, he won the battle of Okeechobee and was breveted Brigadier General. His soubriquet "Old Rough and Ready" may easily have been given him during his campaigns against the Indians. Therefore it did not seem farfetched for Mr. McKearin to conclude that this Taylor flask was made during the 1835–42 period, before Taylor became a national hero but after he had undoubtedly acquired in his own section of the country outstanding prominence and popularity because of his conduct in the Indian Wars. Now, however, it appears that his exploits did *not* create a great popular stir in the Midwest before the Mexican War. My conclusion is that the uniformed gentleman on this flask was not originally intended to honor Taylor, and that the mold was kept from an earlier period, and the inscription cut in it sometime between 1846 and 1848. The uniform cannot be identified, but it is more similar to those of the midwestern Washingtons than to the uniform of the late 1840s. Perhaps the portrait was supposed to represent General Lafayette originally.]

26. GI–77. "ROUGH AND READY"; Taylor [?]– Eagle. Clear deep green; aquamarine. [Pale green (Laidacker).]

Rare, 10 to 12 specimens. Monongahela and early Pittsburgh district.

NOTE: Here again is another Taylor flask that in stylization and the horizontally corrugated edges seems of an earlier period than 1847-50.

27. GI–98 Franklin–Dyott; "WHEELING GLASS WORKS". Pint. Clear light green, deep green. [Yellow-green (McKearin).]

Extremely rare, only five specimens.

NOTE: for additional information, see *American Glass*, p. 497.

28. GI–69. "ANDREW JACKSON"–Eagle; "KNOX & McKEE WHEELING". Light green of yellow tone; very pale green.

Extremely rare, only two specimens. Knox & McKee, Wheeling (W.) Va., [Virginia Green Glass Works. Ca. 1824–34.]

NOTE: [Josephine Jefferson (*Wheeling Glass*, 1947) established the date of the Knox & McKee operation of this glassworks as 1824 to 1834, and that during their operation the works was called the Virginia Green Glass Works.]

29. GII–9. Eagle–Eagle in Flight. Pint. Pale yellowish green; clear green; clear [colorless] with amethyst tint. [Colorless with blue tint, light yellow-green (McKearin).]

Very rare, about ten specimens. Monongahela-Pittsburgh area.

NOTE: Van Rensselaer, in describing this flask, No. 29, above, in his *Early American Bottles and Flasks*, refers to a cut in Gregory and Ginteau's *History and Geography of Ohio*, showing a similar eagle with serpent and inscription:

"True American Ticket
For President
Wm. Henry Harrison."

and above and below this, the slogan:

"Eagle of Liberty strangling
the Serpent of CORRUPTION"

Mr. McKearin felt this tied this flask in with the Harrison campaign. [In pose and rendering, the eagle on the flask is quite unlike the one illustrating the Ticket. I believe the flask probably was brought out during the 1836 campaign, not the 1840.]

30. GI–63. W<u>M</u> H. HARRISON–Log Cabin. Pint. Aquamarine.

Extremely rare, four specimens. Monongahela and early Pittsburgh district.

NOTE: for additional information, see *American Glass*, pp. 498–99.

31. GX–22. Log Cabin–"HARD CIDER"; Barrel. Pale greenish blue of peacock tone; aquamarine. [Strong blue-aquamarine (Austin); light blue (Laidacker).]

Extremely rare, about eight to ten specimens. Monongahela and early Pittsburgh district.

NOTE: for additional information, see *American Glass*, p. 499.

32. GX–23. Liberty–Log Cabin. Pint. Pale bluish green.

Extremely rare, only one specimen known.

NOTE: for additional information, see *American Glass*, p. 499.

33. GI–119. Columbia–Eagle. Pint. Four cobalt-blue, one moss-green shading to amber at neck [and one colorless (Summerville)].

Extremely rare, about six specimens known. [Probably Union Co., Kensington, Philadelphia.]

34. GI–120. Columbia; "ASHTON"–Eagle; "HOUGH &". Pint. Aquamarine.

Extremely rare, only one or two specimens. [Probably Union Co., Kensington, Philadelphia.]

35. GIX–51. Scroll; heart and flower–Reverse: Same. Quart. Light green. [Aquamarine (Laidacker).]

Extremely rare, about six to eight specimens.

Midwestern, but particular glasshouse not known.

36. GV–12. Locomotive–Symbolical Figure. Pint. Clear [colorless].

Extremely rare, only one specimen known. Attributed by Van Rensselaer to Baltimore Glass Works.

NOTE: [Now believed the flask probably celebrated the Baltimore and Ohio Railroad or the Newcastle and Frenchtown Railroad. (See Historical Sketch 18. Baltimore Glass Works, and—in Part VIII—4. Historical Flasks.)]

37. GX–29. U.S. Flag–"NEW GRANITE GLASS WORKS". Half-pint. Clear amber, deep olive-green.

Extremely rare, only two or three specimens. New Granite Glass Works, Stoddard, N.H.

NOTE: for additional information, see *American Glass*, p. 500.

38. GII–27. Eagle–"FARLEY & TAYLOR". Two and one-half quart. Aquamarine. [A second, one in deep amber, was in the Crawford Wettlaufer Collection.]

Extremely rare, only one specimen. Glasshouse not definitely known but it has been attributed to the Louisville, Kentucky, Glass Works. Farley and Taylor were probably liquor dealers or distributors.

39. GII–28. Identical with 38 except that reverse is plain. Aquamarine.

Extremely rare, three specimens known, a specimen in amber with damaged neck has been reported.

40. GVII–1. Log Cabin; "TIPPECANOE"– Reverse same, but "NORTH BEND." Pint plus. Dark olive-amber (black); deep olive-green (black).

Extremely rare, six to ten specimens. Attributed to Mount Vernon Glass Works.

41. GVII–2. Log Cabin; "TIPPECANOE."– Reverse: Same. Pint plus. Dark olive-green (black).

Extremely rare, one specimen known. Attributed to Mount Vernon Glass Works, Vernon, N.Y.

42. GI–106. Calabash; "JENNY LIND"–Tree. Quart. Aquamarine. [Emerald-green (Laidacker).]

Extremely rare, only one specimen definitely

known, although two others, one in green and one in amethyst, have been reported but not verified. [Perhaps the one reported by Laidacker is the green one of which Mr. McKearin heard.]

MOST DESIRABLE FLASKS—GROUP B

1. GI–87. LaFayette–Liberty Cap. Olive-amber.

Extremely rare; three to four specimens. Coventry Glass Works, Coventry, Conn.

NOTE: The similar half-pint flask with stars over oval frame enclosing Liberty cap is not rare.

2. GI–83. "LA FAYETTE"–Masonic Arch. Pint. Light amber. [Olive-amber, olive-green (Gardner).]

Very rare, about ten specimens. Coventry Glass Works, Coventry, Conn.

3. GI–84. "LA FAYETTE"–Masonic Arch. Half-pint. Deep olive-green; olive-amber. [Light olive-green (Gardner).]

Extremely rare, six to ten specimens. Coventry Glass Works, Coventry, Conn.

4. GI–88. "LA FAYETTE"–Masonic Arch. Pint. Pale olive-green; olive-amber.

Very rare, 15 to 20 specimens. Mount Vernon Glass Works, Vernon, N.Y.

5. GI–89. "LA FAYETTE"–Masonic Arch. Half-pint. Pale green of yellowish tone; clear deep green; deep olive-green; olive-amber; pale greenish yellow.

Very rare. 15 to 20 specimens. Mount Vernon Glass Works, Vernon, N.Y.

6. GIV–16. Masonic Arch–Eagle. Pint. Dark olive-green (black); very pale green; strong aquamarine. [Dark olive-green, clear green (McKearin); deep emerald-green (Laidacker).]

Extremely rare, six to ten specimens. Glasshouse not definitely known, but a strong probability that it was Keene, Marlboro St., Glassworks.

NOTE: for additional information, see *American Glass*, p. 502.

7. GX–27. Flag–"NEW GRANITE GLASS WORKS". Pint. Amber; olive-amber. [Olive-green (Laidacker).]

Very rare, 15 to 20 specimens. New Granite Glass Works.

8. GX–28. Flag–"NEW GRANITE GLASS

WORKS". Half-pint. Amber. [Deep olive-green (McKearin).]

Very rare, ten to fifteen specimens.

9. GII–7. Eagle–Sunburst. Pint. Light green; pale yellow-green; olive-yellow; clear amber; emerald-green; dark olive-amber (black). [Colorless, deep green, dark yellowish olive-green (McKearin); deep emerald-green, golden amber, light blue (Laidacker).]

Rare, about 20 to 25 specimens.

10. GII–8. Eagle–Scroll Medallion. Pint. Brilliant olive-yellow; clear [colorless] with pale violet tint. [Reddish amber (McKearin); light emerald-green, pale yellow-green, pale lavender, pale yellow (Laidacker).]

Very rare, ten to fifteen specimens. Monongahela or early Pittsburgh district.

11. GIV–31. Masonic "Farmers Arms"–Eagle. Pint. Clear yellowish green; light green.

Very rare, eight to ten specimens. Monongahela and early Pittsburgh district, particular glasshouse not known.

NOTE: for additional information, see *American Glass*, pp. 502–3.

12. GI–3. "GENERAL WASHINGTON"–Eagle. Pint. Deep golden amber; olive-yellow; aquamarine.

Extremely rare, eight to ten specimens. Monongahela and early Pittsburgh district.

13. GI–4. "GENERAL WASHINGTON"–Eagle. Pint. Aquamarine. [Light green (Laidacker).]

Extremely rare, five or six specimens. Monongahela and early Pittsburgh district.

14. GI–5. Same as 13 except unusual edge showing three vertical rows of horizontal beading. Yellowish green shading to olive-green in lower portion of flask.

Extremely rare, only one or two specimens known. Monongahela and early Pittsburgh district.

15. GI–11. Washington–Eagle. Pint. Clear green; aquamarine. [Light green (Laidacker); cornflower-blue, sapphire blue (McKearin).]

Rare. 20 to 25 specimens. Monongahela and early Pittsburgh district.

16. GI–7. "G. GEO. WASHINGTON."–Eagle; "F.L". Pint. Light green. [Olive-amber (Austin); aquamarine (McKearin).]

Rare, 20 to 25 specimens. Frederick Lorenz, Pittsburgh district.

17. GI–68. "GENERAL. JACKSON."–Floral Medallion. Pint. Deep olive-yellow; aquamarine; brilliant light green. [Light bluish green (McKearin).]

Very rare, 15 to 20 specimens. Monongahela and early Pittsburgh district.

18. GI–67. "GENERAL JACKSON"–Eagle; "B & M." Pint. Light green; clear [colorless] with amethyst or lavender tint. [Colorless (Laidacker).]

Very rare, four to six specimens. [Probably Baker & Martin, Perryopolis, Pa. See 18, Group A.]

19. GII–10. "W. IHMSEN'S."; Eagle–"AGRICULTURE". Pint. Clear brilliant green; aquamarine. [Light green (Dambach).]

Rare, 20 to 25 specimens. W. Ihmsen, Williamsport Glass Works, Pittsburgh district.

NOTE: for additional information, see *American Glass*, p. 504.

20. GII–15. Eagle; "F.L."–Cornucopia. Half-pint. Clear [colorless]; aquamarine. [Pale green (Laidacker).]

Extremely rare, six to ten specimens. Attributed to glassworks of Frederick Lorenz, Pittsburgh.

21. GII–20. Eagle–Reverse: Same. Pint. Aquamarine. [Emerald-green (Laidacker).]

Extremely rare, two or three specimens. Midwestern, glasshouse not definitely known.

22. GII–19. Eagle–Morning Glory and Vine. Pint. Aquamarine. [Pale green, light emerald-green (Laidacker); light green (McKearin).]

Rare, 20 to 25 specimens. Midwestern, glasshouse not definitely known.

NOTE: for additional information, see *American Glass*, p. 504.

23. GIII–1. Inverted Cornucopia–"Star" Medallion. Half-pint. Deep shaded amber; light green; pale olive-yellow; clear yellow-green. [Red-amber (Laidacker).]

Very rare, ten to fifteen specimens. Midwestern, glasshouse not definitely known.

24. GI–115. Portrait; "WHEAT PRICE & CO WHEELING' VA."–Glasshouse; "FAIR-VIEW WORKS". Pint. Brilliant yellowish olive-green; light bluish green. [Yellow-green, clear medium green (McKearin).]

Very rare, about ten to twelve specimens.

Fairview [Glass] Works, Wheat, Price & Co., Wheeling, Va. [ca. 1832–39].

25. GI–116. Similar to 24. Pint. Yellowish green. [Bluish green (Dambach).]

Extremely rare, about six to eight specimens.

NOTE: The factory [Virginia Green Glass Works] of Knox & McKee was at one period operated under the firm name of Wheat, Price & Co. [as the Fairview Glass Works, ca. 1832–39].

26. GI–92. "GEN^{L} LA FAYETTE"–Eagle; "KNOX & M^{C} KEE WHEELING". Pint. Light green, yellow tone; clear [colorless] glass, pale amethyst tint. [Moonstone (McKearin); emerald-green, blue aquamarine (Laidacker).]

Rare, 20 to 25 specimens. Works of Knox & McKee, Wheeling, Va. (now West Va.).

27. GIX–47. Scroll; "R KNOWLES & CO . . ." –Fleur-de-lis. Pint. Aquamarine.

Extremely rare, about five specimens.

28. GIX–28. Scroll; "ROUGH"–"& READY". Pint. Aquamarine.

Extremely rare, only one specimen known. Probably Pittsburgh district.

29. GX–31. Sheaf of Rye, Rake and Scythe–Horse. Slightly less than pint. Dark brownish amber.

Extremely rare, only one specimen known.

30. GII–29. Vertically ribbed with Eagle medallion–Reverse: Same. Pint. Amethyst, bordering on puce; light green. [Aquamarine, pale yellow-green (McKearin); colorless (Lane).]

Extremely rare, five to ten specimens.

31. GII–30. Similar to 30. Half-pint. Yellowish olive-green; aquamarine; pale yellow-green.

Very rare, eight to ten specimens. Attributed to the Louisville, Ky., Glass Works, ca. 1855.

NOTE: for additional information, see *American Glass*, p. 505.

32. GII–22. Eagle–Lyre. Pint. Deep aquamarine. [Light emerald-green, brilliant green (Laidacker); yellow-green (McKearin); light green (Wood).]

Very rare, ten to fifteen specimens.

33. GII–23. Eagle–Floral Medallion. Pint. Deep aquamarine. [Light blue (Laidacker).]

Very rare, ten to fifteen specimens. [Probably the Kentucky Glass Works, ca. 1849.]

NOTE: for additional information, see *American Glass*, p. 506.

34. GI–74. "ZACHARY TAYLOR"–"CORN FOR THE WORLD". Pint. Light amber shading to puce; clear dark olive-green; aquamarine; dark amethyst; clear golden amber; cornflower-blue. [Deep yellow-green (Laidacker); pale and light green (Dambach).]

Very rare, 15 to 20 specimens. Attributed to Baltimore Glass Works [ca. 1850].

NOTE: for additional information, see *American Glass*, p. 506.

35. GX–4. Cannon; "GEN^{L} . TAYLOR NEVER SURRENDERS"–A LITTLE MORE GRAPE CAP^{T} BRAGG". Deep amethyst; olive-green; puce; deep green; aquamarine. [Golden amber, deep amber (Dambach); red-amber, deep emerald-green, deep yellow-green (Laidacker).]

Rare, 20 to 25 specimens. Attributed to Baltimore Glass Works.

NOTE: This flask occurs also with smooth edges.

36. GI–22. Washington; "BALTIMORE X GLASS WORKS" (S's reversed in both "GLASS" and "WORKS")–Taylor [?]. Quart. Aquamarine. [Brilliant clear green (Dambach); olive-yellow (McKearin).]

Rare, probably 25 to 30 specimens. Attributed to the Baltimore Glass Works, Baltimore, Md.

37. GI–23. Washington–Taylor [?]; "BALTIMORE X GLASS. WORKS." (The R in works is omitted.) Quart. Deep puce; deep amethyst; clear yellow-amber; honey; light olive-green; aquamarine. [Yellow-green (Laidacker); light yellow-green (Gardner).]

Rare, probably 25 to 30 specimens. Attributed to Baltimore Glass Works, Baltimore, Md.

38. GVI–3. Baltimore Monument–"LIBERTY & UNION". Dark olive-yellow; aquamarine, dark wine; deep amethyst; brilliant olive-green. [Medium amber (McKearin); reddish amethyst, golden amber (Laidacker).]

Very rare, 10 to 15 specimens.

39. GI–118. Columbia; "KENSINGTON"–Eagle; "UNION.CO". Half-pint. Yellow-green; clear [colorless], shading to purple; clear, shading to blue; clear amethystine; aquamarine. [Pale yellow-green (Dambach); very pale green tint, yellow-green tint (Gardner); blue-green, pale lilac (Laidacker); cobalt, green (Quigley Collection).]

Very rare, 15 to 20 specimens. Probably Union Co., Kensington, Philadelphia. [See bracketed note to No. 40.]

40. GI–122.   Columbia–Eagle.   Pint.   Clear [colorless].

Extremely rare, only three or four specimens. Glasshouse not definitely known but may be Kensington Union Co.

NOTE: [Union Co., Kensington, Philadelphia. Because Columbia seemed the more distinguishing motif, the side with her portrait bust was chosen by collectors as the obverse. Hence, reading first the obverse and then the reverse, the inscription becomes "Kensington Union Co." However, no glassworks is known at present that had that official title or was so called. The correct reading doubtless is Union Co. Kensington—that is, Union Co., probably in Kensington, Philadelphia.]

SUPPLEMENTAL GROUP OF RARE FLASKS—GROUP C

In the remarks preceding the lists, A and B, of the 82 historical flasks which we consider the most desirable, we stated that rarity alone could not be the determining factor as to desirability, and pointed out that there are several flasks of which only a single specimen is known which were not included in either list. We are, however, as a matter of further interest to bottle collectors, including a supplemental list, Group C, of flasks which, from the standpoint of rarity alone are on a par with many of those included in the two preceding lists. These flasks, made after 1850 and not included in the charted Groups I–X, represent a later phase in flask and bottle design. Many of the flasks of this period were decorated with genre subjects, the treatment of which seems to reflect the contemporary influence of cartoons and popular illustrations, catch phrases, and so on. The forms, in most instances like 23, 28, 30 or 32, are not in themselves as attractive as earlier forms. Generally speaking the flasks and bottles of this period definitely reflect more standardization in shape and decoration which is characteristic of the gradual mechanization of bottle making. This may be one reason why the flasks in Group C never have had the same appeal as many of practically the same degree of rarity shown in Groups A and B; nor do they, comparatively speaking, command a price commensurate with their rarity. [These flasks are now charted in Groups XI to XIV.]

1. GXIV–6. "TRAVELER'S COMPANION"– "LOCKPORT GLASS WORKS". Pint. Deep blue-green; yellow-green; aquamarine.

Rare. [Scarce].

2. GXIV–5. "TRAVELER'S COMPANION."– "LANCASTER ERIE CO., N.Y". Pint. Olive-yellow; deep bluish green, aquamarine.

Rare. [Scarce.] Lancaster Glass Works, New York.

3. GXIII–62. Anchor; "RICHMOND GLASS WORKS"–Glasshouse. Pint. Light green.

Extremely rare, only two or three specimens known.

4. GXIII–7. Hunter–Two Dogs. Pint. Olive-yellow; pale green. [Light green (McKearin).]

Extremely rare. [Rare.]

5. GXI–45. Prospector–Eagle. Pint. Olive-yellow; aquamarine. [Yellow-green, green (McKearin).]

Very rare. [Scarce.]

6. GXI–44. Similar to 5. Quart. Light green.

Very rare. [Scarce.]

7. GXI–53.   Prospector;   "FOR   PIKE'S PEAKE"–Prospector; deer. Pint. Very pale green; aquamarine.

Extremely rare. [Rare.] Only three or four specimens known.

NOTE: for additional information, see *American Glass*, p. 508.

8. GXI–54. Prospector; "FOR PIKE'S PEAK"– Prospector;   "FOR   PIKE'S   PEAK". Aquamarine.

Extremely rare.

NOTE: for additional information, see *American Glass*, p. 508.

9. GII–140. Man Walking; "DRAFTED"–Eagle. Aquamarine.

Extremely rare.

10. GII–129. Eagle; "ZANESVILLE, OHIO". Pint. Aquamarine. [Light green (McKearin).]

Rare.

11. GXIII–32. Sheaf of Rye–Reverse: Similar. Pint. Aquamarine.

Rare. [Scarce.]

12. GXIII–31. Sheaf of Rye–Plain. Pint. Light Green.

Very rare. [Rare.]

13. GXIII–34.   Sheaf   of   Rye–"MECHANIC GLASS   WORKS   PHILADᴬ".   Quart. Aquamarine.

Rare [Scarce.]

14. GII–134. Eagle; "D. KIRKPATRICK & CO"– Plain. Quart. Aquamarine.

Extremely rare. Only two specimens known. [In 1965 Richard Wood reported a pint size.]
NOTE: for additional information, see *American Glass*, p. 509.

15. GII–141. Indian–Eagle. Quart. Aquamarine.
Very rare.

15a. GII–142. Indian; "CUNNINGHAMS & CO"–Eagle; "CONTINENTIAL." Quart. Clear light blue; olive-yellow; aquamarine. [Green, light cornflower-blue (McKearin).]
NOTE: for additional information, see *American Glass*, p. 509.

16. GXV–23. "UNION GLASS WORKS NEW LONDON C^T" Plain. Pint. Pale green; olive amber [Olive-green (McKearin).]
Rare. [Scarce.] Union Glass Works, New London, Connecticut.

17. GXIV–9. "TRAVELER'S COMPANION"–"RAILROAD GUIDE". Half-pint. Yellow-green; aquamarine.
Very rare. [Rare.]

18. GXIV–8. "TRAVELER'S COMPANION"–Plain. Half-pint. Aquamarine. [Light green (McKearin).]
Rare. Not listed by Van Rensselaer.

19. GXIII–30. Swimming Duck; "WILL YOU TAKE A DRINK . . ."–Plain. Half-pint. Pale yellow-green; aquamarine. [Light green (McKearin).]
Very rare in half-pint size.

20. GXIII–18. Jockey–Running Hound. Half-pint. Olive-yellow; dark amber; deep claret; aquamarine. [Pale yellow-green (McKearin).]
Rare [Scarce.]

21. GII–128. Eagle–Eagle. Half-pint. Light sapphire-blue; aquamarine.
Rare.

22. GXII–37. Shield; Clasped Hands; "UNION"–

Reverse: Same. Quart. Pale blue; olive-yellow; aquamarine.
Rare.

23. GII–116. Eagle–Eagle. Quart. Deep amber; aquamarine.
Very rare. [Scarce.]

24. GII–131. Eagle–Plain. Quart. Clear yellowish olive-green; aquamarine. [Yellow-green (McKearin).]
Rare.

25. GII–135. Eagle Medallion–Plain. Quart. Pale green. [Yellow-green (McKearin).]
Very rare. [Common today, according to Laidacker.]

26. GII–80. Eagle; "GRANITE. GLASS CO"–Eagle; "STODARD N H". Quart. Clear amber; olive-amber. [Golden-amber (McKearin).]
Very rare. Granite Glass Co., Stoddard, N.H.
NOTE: for additional information, see *American Glass*, p. 510.

27. GXV–6. "GRANITE GLASS CO"–"STODDARD N H". Quart. Deep reddish amber.
Very rare in quart size. [Comparatively scarce.] Granite Glass Co., Stoddard, N.H.

28. GXI–49. Prospector; "FOR PIKE'S PEAK"–Hunter; "E. KAUFFELD". Quart. Clear [colorless] with faint pinkish tone in base.
Extremely rare. Only one specimen known. Collection of Charles B. Gardner.

29. GXIII–1. Girl on Bicycle; "NOT FOR JOE"–Plain. Pint. Dark amber; aquamarine. [Shaded amber (McKearin).]
Rare.
NOTE: for additional information, see *American Glass*, p. 511.

30. GX–30. Trapper; "THE GREAT WESTERN"–Buck. Pint. Aquamarine.
Rare.

9
COLORS

At this point I digress to a brief discussion of colors and their nomenclature, for they are important aspects of glass and its description. And in no category of American glass is there more diversity of color and confusion of names than in that of Figured Flasks. As previously stated, the natural colors of glass range from light to deep green, from light amber to deep reddish and brownish amber, varying according to the natural oxides in the ingredients—the sand, the wood ashes or potash. All other colors and their hues, shades, and tints are artificially produced by means of metallic oxides. Natural or artificial colors may contribute not only to the distinguished esthetic value of a flask or bottle but also to its monetary value, for often color is an important, even the deciding, feature in the rarity of Figured Flasks and Bottles. A flask very common in aquamarine may be scarce or rare in olive-amber or olive-green, or vice versa. Many flasks that were usually blown from aquamarine or olive-green or olive-amber or amber bottle glass are comparatively rare in any other colors. Any of these flasks in amethysts or blues is scarce and frequently extremely rare. For all these reasons, collectors always are interested in which colors the various flasks may be found. Colors are, therefore, an indispensable feature in a complete description of a flask or bottle, and so the Charts (Groups I to XV) list the colors in which each flask is known to have been found. But like others attempting to name a color so that it can be visualized by someone else, glass collectors have been plagued by the lack of an accepted standard for glass and a chart of its colors.

There always has been, and probably will continue to be, great confusion in color nomenclature. In his book *Color Standards and Color Nomenclature*, published in 1912, when he was curator of birds at the United States National Museum, Robert Ridgway aimed at "the standardization of colors and color names." Toward that end he included 53 plates showing 1,115 named colors. This series of plates probably could be used as a color chart for the wide range of colors in which we encounter glass *if* it were available to the thousands of glass collectors and adopted by consensus. But that is impractical. However, in connection with terms, Dr. Ridgway quoted Mr. Milton Bradley's exposition of color terms, which can be of great value to all dealers and collectors in understanding colors, their terms, and application. The passage, quoted from an educational pamphlet by Mr. Bradley, reads:

The list of words now employed to express qualities or degrees of color is very small, in fact a half dozen comprise the more common terms, and these are pressed into service on all occasions, and in such varied relations that they not only fail to express anything definite but constantly contradict themselves . . . Tint, Hue, and Shade are employed so loosely by the public generally, even by those people who claim to use English correctly, that neither word has a very definite meaning, although each is capable of being as accurately used as any other word in our everyday vocabulary . . .

Color.—The term of widest application, being the only one which can be used to cover the entire range of chromatic manifestation; that is to say, the spectrum colors (together with those between violet and red, not shown in the spectrum) with all their innumerable variations of luminosity, mixture, etc. In a more restricted sense, applied to the six distinct spectrum colors (red, orange, yellow, green, blue, and violet), which are sometimes distinguished as fundamental colors or spectrum colors.

Hue.—While often used interchangeably or synonymously with color, the term hue is more properly restricted by special application to those lying between any contiguous pair of spectrum colors (also between violet and purple and between purple and red); as an orange hue (not shade or tint, as so often incorrectly said) of red; a yellow hue of orange; a greenish hue of yellow, a bluish hue of green; a violet hue of blue, etc.

Tint.—Any color (pure or broken) weakened by high illumination or (in the case of pigments) by admixture of white, or (in case of dyes or washes) by excess of aqueous or other liquid medium; as, a deep, medium, light, pale or delicate (pallid) tint of red. The term cannot correctly be used in any other sense.

Shade.—Any color (pure or broken) darkened by shadow or (in the case of pigments) by admixture of black; exactly the opposite of tint; as a medium, dark, or very dark (dusky) shade of red.

Tone.—"Each step in a color scale is a tone of that color." The term tone cannot, however, be properly applied to a step in the spectrum scale, in which each contiguous pair of the six distinct spectrum or "fundamental" colors are connected by hues. Hence tone is exclusively applicable to the steps in a scale of a single color or hue, comprising the full color (in the center) and graduated tints and shades leading off therefrom in opposite directions; or of neutral gray similarly graduated in tone from the darkest shade to the palest tint.

It may help in remembering these meanings if one thinks of *color* as forming a square upon which the *spectrum colors* and their *hues* are a medial horizontal diameter from which their *tints* rise in an upward vertical scale and their *shades* descend in a downward vertical scale, and, in the vertical scale of each color and hue, each *tone* is a step.

But to return to our immediate problem: Since no standardized charts are available to all of us, and as yet no practical method has been found for charting the colors of glass, the names of the colors listed in the Charts are mainly those now in general use, though not always consistently, by collectors and dealers. Excepting the initialed colors added to Groups I through X, supplied by others from flasks I have not seen, the colors in those groups are those of the flasks from my father's collection and of others made available for study. Of course it must be remembered that the names chosen designate the colors as I interpret the names and as I *saw* the colors in *natural daylight* — with the flask by itself, away from its fellow specimens. The light in which the designation of a color is determined is a prime factor because hue and tone vary with the degree and kind of light, and isolation of the flask is important because, when it is in a group, the color of a flask may be subtly affected by that of its companions and by other surroundings. Moreover, in many instances the color of a given flask would appear to others as a tone (step) in the color scale different from that designated by me. As most of us have learned by experience, it is a physical fact that rarely do any two pairs of eyes see any color or hue, tint or shade, in exactly the same tone. If you doubt this, listen sometime to two collectors, particularly of Figured Flasks, discussing the colors of specimens in their collections.

Also, many of the terms in popular use, it will be noted, do not coincide with any to be found in a scientific color chart. Many are based on analogy. For example, peacock-blue, jade-green, canary-yellow, cornflower-blue, puce, and so on — these are names associated with familiar physical objects such as gems, flowers, and living creatures. Puce, for instance, is the French name for the flea, and the color called puce is similar to the natural color of the flea. This naturally adds to the confusion of communication regarding color, especially since the same color may inspire different analogous names in different viewers. The problem is further complicated by differing color vocabularies, coupled with a different registering of color. Purple, violet-blue, or wine may be, and have been, called amethyst. The same blue may be cobalt to one and sapphire to another. Any one of a half dozen or more shades of green may be termed olive-green. Nevertheless, I do not feel listing colors in the Charts to be a futile gesture; rather, I hope it will be of interest and help to flask and bottle collectors, furnishing some information and providing a guide to the range and sort of colors in which each Figured Flask and Bottle has been recorded.

To that end, here are a few brief notes on some of the collectors' common color designations that may be helpful to the mind's eye, or at least to an understanding of the state of confusion:

1. *Aquamarine*, a color name that has been adopted by standard use and is by far the commonest color encountered in flasks, customarily has been applied to very light greens ranging from pale tints to decidedly bluish tones. Actually, it is constantly used interchangeably with "light green," which itself occurs in various tints and tones. Often, an aquamarine considered close to, but not quite, "light green," is called "green-aquamarine" or "strong aquamarine." When a blue tone is pronounced, it may be called "blue" or "bluish" aquamarine.

2. *Amber* has a wide range — from golden amber to dark reddish and brownish amber.

3. *Olive-amber* and *olive-green*, light to dark, natural colors of bottle glass and second to aquamarine in frequency of occurrence in Figured Flasks, call upon nature for a color term, the greens of olives, to designate the modification of amber and green hues. Thus when brownish amber is decidedly olive in tone, it is called olive-amber; when the olive takes over all but a trace of the amber, the color is called olive-green. The distinction is quite apparent when an olive-amber and an olive-green flask are held to natural light — in artificial light the color values may be reversed! Deep olive-green shows no trace of amber.

4. *Black* is used in instances in which the color of a flask appears to be almost, or entirely, black in reflected light. Actually, the color is usually dense amber or olive-amber or olive-green, or, occasionally, dense amethyst.

5. *Citron* is an apt color name, first used, I believe, by Rhea Mansfield Knittle (*Early American Glass*, 1926) to describe some of the midwestern, especially Ohio, glass of a brilliant greenish yellow color (according to some) or a brilliant tint of olive-amber with yellow tone (according to others). However described, it reminds one of a thin slice of candied citron with a bright sun shining through it.

6. *Greens* range in the horizontal and vertical scales as widely as, if not wider than, ambers. A great many are varying steps of yellow in tone; some, in blue — among the latter, peacock-green. It seems as though more analogous terms have been coined to fit hues of green than of any other color — emerald-green, sea-green, sage-green, apple-green, grass-green, and so on. Some collectors avoid emerald-green and sea-green for clear pure greens and instead designate them as medium and deep or dark.

7. *Olive-yellow* is a name often used for colors that give the general impression of a light yellow decidedly olive in tone.

8. *Blues*, perhaps the most frequently encountered artificial color in early flasks, range from pale clear to deep cobalt. Sapphire-blues of varied tones seem to predominate. Deep sapphire-blue and cobalt are sometimes used interchangeably.

9. *Amethysts* run from light tints to deep shades, but in a more limited scale than blue. Sometimes they are reddish, even bordering on *wine*, and sometimes brownish bordering on *puce*.

10. *Amethystine* is the name for colorless glass with amethyst tint. This tint usually arises from a bit too much manganese added to the batch, to eradicate the natural colors, that would result if a decolorizer were not added to the basic ingredients.

11. *Colorless* is the term used in Chart Groups XI through XV, as *clear* was in the original Groups I through X, to designate glass that is without, or meant to be without, any trace of color. *Clear* in the sense of colorless has been abandoned mainly because of its other customary meaning in reference to

glass—that is, to modify a color, as in "clear green" and "clear blue," thereby characterizing it as clean and bright, free of any dullness or cloudiness. Often, however, colorless flasks do show a tinge of color—green, blue, or amethyst usually—in certain lights and where the glass is thickest, as in the base.

12. *Moonstone* is the term for a translucent grayish milky condition resembling a polished moonstone. This is rarely encountered in flasks. At present it is believed to be an accidental "color" insofar as Figured Flasks are concerned, probably due to a miscalculation in the proportions of ingredients or to faulty melting of a batch intended to be colorless. This sometimes occurred when the inexperienced tried to make lead glass.

10
FORM GROUPS, NECK FINISHES, AND BASES

BOTTLE FORM OR SHAPE GROUPS

Edwin Atlee Barber, who for many years was Curator and Secretary of the Pennsylvania Museum and School of Industrial Art, Philadelphia, was one of the late 19th-century pioneer collectors of bottles and flasks in the United States. His small book, *American Glassware Old and New*, which he termed "A Sketch of the Glass Industry in the United States and Manual for Collectors of Historical Bottles," was published in 1900. It was, I believe, the first book on American glass published for collectors. In it, as I have stated previously, he listed a total of 86 varieties of American "historical" flasks and bottles, apparently all that were known to collectors at that date.

Taking the form or shape as a basis, he divided the bottles into six types designated I to VI. Today, several hundred varieties of these flasks and bottles are known to collectors, and there are many more distinct variations in shape and form. For the guidance of collectors and as one basis of classification, for shape only, Barber's idea seems worthy of elaboration. Therefore, from a study of actual specimens that were in the McKearin collection representing more than 95 percent* of all recorded varieties of

*In this revision of material from *American Glass* the numbering and groups of forms remain as drawn up by Mr. McKearin in 1941 without regard as to when individual forms probably were first produced.

Figured Flasks and Bottles, shown here is a group of line drawings (Ills. 133 and 134) consisting of 40 examples classified as to shape but including variations in type of edge. It must be understood, however, that there are many other slight variations (in some cases the difference in specimens shown is not pronounced), but this group will, it is hoped, enable collectors to assign specimens to one of the designated form or shape groups listed. (Pages 514-15.)

Note: The number refers to the shape or form. The size, color, or any descriptive details refer to the particular flasks used as model for the line drawing, and date to when the flask probably was first produced. In most instances other designs occur in the form, and may have been brought out before or after the flask illustrated. The dates for each Form Group represent the period within which the form probably was first introduced.

FORM GROUP I. Circa 1815–30
The horizontally corrugated (ribbed) edges are a characteristic of many flasks in this group of New England Figured Flasks.
1. Sloping shoulders: Pint. Amber. The famous "Jared Spencer" flask, attributed to Connecticut, probably either the Pitkin glassworks or that of John Mather, Manchester (formerly East Hartford), Conn. ca. 1823. Chart GX–24.

2. High shoulders, rounding just below neck: Pint. Olive-amber. Marked "KEEN" in oval in sunburst on

obverse and "P & W" (Perry & Wood, 1822–28 or Perry & Wheeler, 1828–30) in oval on reverse. Keene-Marlboro-Street glassworks, Keene, N.H. Chart GVIII–8.

3. High shoulders, more sharply angled than 2 and squared at base of neck: Pint. Brilliant green. Sunburst. Chart GVIII–1. ca. 1815. Type believed to have been made at Keene and probably, as indicated by the excavations by Harry Hall White, at the Mount Vernon Glass Works, Vernon, New York.

4. Rounding at shoulders, sloping on curve to neck. Barber Type I: Pint. Olive-amber. Chart GI–83. ca. 1824. Typical of flasks made at the Coventry Glass Works, Conn., in pint and half-pint sizes.

5. Similar to 4 but with vertically ribbed edges: Pint. Olive-amber. On reverse, initials "S & S" standing for Stebbins & Stebbins, Coventry Glass Works, Conn. Made in pint and half-pint sizes. ca. 1825. Chart GI–85.

6. Similar to 4 but with vertically ribbed edges and single medial vertical rib: Pint. Pale olive-green. Mount Vernon Glass Works, Vernon, New York. Made in pint and half-pint sizes. ca. 1825. Chart GI–88.

7. Similar to 4, 5, and 6 but narrower and with less pronounced flare at shoulders. Finer corrugations than 1 to 4 inclusive: Pint. Dark olive-green. Chart GIV–16.

8. Similar to 4 but broader at shoulders; edges vertically ribbed. Barber Type V: Pint. Yellow-green. Chart GIV–4. Typical of the heavy Masonic flasks attributed to New England, especially the Keene-Marlboro-Street glassworks, Keene, N.H. ca. 1815.

FORM GROUP II. Circa 1816–30
9. Edges rounding to shoulders, lower quarter sloping to narrow base; single broad vertical rib on edges: Pint. Pale aquamarine. Chart GI–117. Form found principally in Kensington, "Union.Co.", pint and half-pint flasks.

FORM GROUP III. Circa 1816–30
10. Flattened circular "canteen" flask; edges and sides with heavy concentric ribbing around central medallion: Approximately 1½ pints. Brilliant green. New England. Probably the New England Glass Works, Cambridge, Mass. ca. 1818. Chart GII–76.

FORM GROUP IV. Circa 1822–40
11. Edges rounding to base and shoulder, more curving than Group I; vertical ribs (one to three)* on edges. Occurs in quart, pint, and half-pint sizes. Barber Type

*Though the ribbing, as shown in the line drawing, is described in the charts as three vertical ribs on the edge, actually there is one medial vertical rib and a sort of horseshoe rib framing the design.

II: Pint. Olive-green. Chart GV–8, probably first brought out ca. 1826–28. Some variants of the railroad and other flasks of this form were made into the 1850s at least.

11. Quart. Deep green. One of Dyott's Kensington Glass Works' flasks probably first produced between 1822 and 1837. Chart GI–96.

12. Similar to 11 but with beaded edges and medial rib. Occurs in pint and half-pint sizes. Typical of the Monongahela and early Pittsburgh district: Pint. Clear green. Chart GI–65.

13. Similar to 11 but broader, flatter, and with fine vertical ribbing on sloping edge and from design to heavy medial vertical rib. Eastern: Pint. Olive-green. Chart GII–53. 1830s.

14. Similar to 13 but plump, broad with edges incurving slightly above base and with fine vertical ribs on edge. Eastern. Occurs in quart, pint, and half-pint sizes: Quart. Amber. Chart GII–55. ca. 1840.

15. Broad and rather flat; curving edges rounding to shoulder in incurving slope to base; herringbone ribbing on edges. Midwestern: Pint. Olive-yellow. Chart GX–21. ca. 1824.

16. Similar to 15 but taller and more slender in proportions; edges with horizontal ribbing from framing rib to narrow medial vertical rib. Midwestern: Quart. Dark green. Chart GI–77. ca. 1836–40(?).

17. Similar to 15 but narrower at shoulder and with large beading between framing rib and heavy medial vertical rib. Occurs in pint and half-pint. Midwestern: Pint. Pale yellow-green. Chart GII–7.

FORM GROUP V. Circa 1840–60
18. Similar to 11 but sides very flat; wide curving edges with narrow medial vertical rib. Occurs in pints and half-pints: Pint. Deep bluish green. Chart GIII–16. Lancaster Glass Works, Lancaster, N.Y. ca. 1849.

19. Similar to 18 but edges horizontally ribbed to heavy medial vertical rib. Occurs in two-quart-plus, quart, and pint sizes. Midwestern: Pint. Dark amber (black glass). Chart GII–24.

20. Sides rather flat; design on oval panel; smooth edges. Barber Type III. Occurs in quart, pint, and half-pint sizes: Pint. Yellow-green. Dyottville type. First produced 1847 or 1848. Chart GI–45.

20. Quart. Clear green. Dyottville Glass Works, Kensington, Philadelphia, probably brought out by Benners, Smith & Benners in 1847 or 1848.

FORM GROUP VI. Circa 1845–65
21. Long slender thin body with flat sides; smooth edges curving gently to narrow shoulders: "Pint." Amethyst. Dyottville Glass Works, Kensington, Philadel-

133. FORM GROUPS

134. FORM GROUPS

phia, probably brought out by Benners, Smith & Benners, ca. 1846–53.

22. Long slender body with smooth edges curving sharply to high shoulder. Occurs in quart, pint, and half-pint sizes: Quart. Clear green. New London Glass Works, New London, Conn. ca. 1857. Chart GII–66.

23. Similar to 22 but shoulder gently rounded and not so high. Occurs in quart, pint, and half-pint sizes: Pint. Olive-yellow. New London Glass Works, New London, Conn. ca. 1857. Chart GII–68.

24. Broad flat sides with smooth edges curving to rounded shoulder. Occurs in pint and half-pint sizes: Pint. Clear deep olive-green. Ravenna Glass Works, Ravenna, O. ca. 1860. Chart GXIV–3.

25. Vertically ribbed broad body with tapering edges rounding at shoulders. Occurs in quart, pint, and half-pint. Midwestern: Quart. Emerald-green. Louisville Glass Works, Louisville, Ky. ca. 1855. Chart GII–31.

25. Half-pint. Yellowish olive-green. Louisville Glass Works. Chart GII–30.

26. Similar to 20 but with sharper edges and rounding to high shoulder. Occurs in pint and half-pint. Midwestern: Half-pint. Olive-amber. Louisville Glass Works. ca. 1855. Chart GII–33.

27. Long body, flat sides, smooth edges curving gradually to base and long sloping shoulder. Occurs in quart and pint sizes with and without applied handle: Quart. Puce. First produced 1859 or 1860. Chart GXIII–19.

FORM GROUP VII. Circa 1860–75

28. Broad body, straight tapering smooth edges, long rounded shoulder. Occurs in quart, pint, and half-pint sizes. Types produced extensively in Pittsburgh glasshouses: Quart. Light amber. W^M Frank & Sons, Frankstown Glass Works, Pittsburgh, Pa. ca. 1866. The line drawing should show 13 stars and "SONS" instead of "SON". Chart GXII–38.

29. Long body, edges spreading slightly to long curving shoulder; smooth edged with and without medial vertical rib. Barber Type VI. Occurs in quart, pint, and half-pint: Pint. Clear deep olive-green. Pittsburgh, Pa. Chart GII–108.

30. Similar to 29, smooth edge. Occurs in quart, pint, and half-pint sizes. Characteristic of Pike's Peak flasks, Group XI. First produced ca. 1859 or 1860: Half-pint. Aquamarine. Midwestern. Chart GXI–27.

31. Long rather narrow body, rounding shoulder, straight smooth edge. Occurs in quart and pint sizes: Pint. Aquamarine. Zanesville, O. Chart GII–129.

31. Quart. Aquamarine. Pike's Peak flask. Chart GXI–44.

32. Fairly flat, smooth edges rounding at shoulder and with medial broad flat rib or narrow panel. Occurs in pints and half-pints: Pint. Aquamarine. Probably first produced in the late 1860s. Chart GX–30.

FORM GROUP VIII. Circa 1845–70

33. So-called "fiddle" shape, panel sides and edges terminating in 10-sided base. Occurs in quart and pint sizes. Midwestern: Pint. Aquamarine. Attributed to M'Carty & Torreyson, Wellsburg, W. Va. ca. 1850. Chart GI–108.

34. So-called "fiddle" shape, sides rounding to broad medial end rib; circular foot: Quart. Aquamarine. Midwestern. Chart GIX–51.

35. So-called violin shape, corset waisted. Occurs in quart, pint, and half-pint sizes: Pint. Aquamarine. Chart GIX–45.

Note: Actually, corset-waisted scroll flasks, GIX–43 (with longer curve between the upper section and lower), were produced by John Robinson & Son, Stourbridge Flint Glass Works, Pittsburgh, Pa., ca. 1831–34, and possibly also in the same period, GIX–44. It is probable that the unmarked mold was used for some time after the closing of the Robinson works in 1845.

36. So-called violin shape with heavy medial end rib in slight ogee curve to curved shoulder. Occurs in two-quart-plus, quart, pint, and half-pint sizes: Pint. Colorless glass. Chart GIX–14.

Note: This shape also was first produced before 1845, at least in half-pint size. The half-pints were made with initials "B.P.&B." standing for Bakewell, Page & Bakewell or, more probable, Bakewell, Page and Bakewells. If the latter, they were first produced in the period 1827–32.

37. So-called violin shape with heavy medial end rib in ogee curve to slightly squared shoulder: Half-pint. Deep green. Chart GIX–42.

FORM GROUP IX. Circa 1850–75

38. Calabash shape, edges fluted vertically. Barber Type IV: Quart. Yellow-green. Chart GI–112.

39. Calabash shape, smooth edges, shallow flutes on long neck: Quart. Olive-yellow. Chart GI–99.

40. Calabash shape, with heavy ribs on body except for design area; neck shallowly fluted: Quart. Sapphire-blue. Chart GI–104.

41. Calabash shape, edges with heavy vertical ribs. Oc-

curs with and without handle: Quart. Dark amber. Chart GXIII–45.

NECK FINISHES (*See pages 518 & 519.*)

The line drawings in Ill. 135, numbered from 1 through 20, show the various types of neck finish given to Figured Flasks and Bottles. The designation of the flask underneath each number indicates the particular variety from which the line drawing was made. It should be noted also that many collectors have used the term "sheared lip" for the plain lip. Actually, the general practice in producing flasks was to fire-polish (i.e., reheat the lip) after cracking off the flask from the blowpipe. Although it would have been possible for a skilled gaffer to use his shears to even the lip, it would hardly have been practical from a cost point of view for flasks selling at only a few cents each—except possibly the heavy and early Masonics and Sunbursts, which were more decanter-flasks than ordinary pocket, bar, or retail containers.

BASE TYPES (last half of the 19th century)
(*See page 520.*)

Distinctive basal characteristics of Figured Flasks and Bottles resulted mainly from (1) the type of mold used and (2) the tool used to hold the vessel during the neck finishing and the procedure in attaching the tool to the bottom of the vessel.

Prior to about 1850, flask bases normally had an end-to-end bisecting mold seam because half the mold-base was an integral part of each of the pieces or leaves of a full-size two-piece mold. They had also a pontil mark where the punty (pontil) had been attached to the bottom of the flask. The mark or scar left upon removal of the pontil was (1) a rough glass scar when the pontil end had been dipped in the pot of metal to tip it with glass, (2) a shallowly pitted, somewhat grainy-looking circular mark when the glass-tipped pontil was lightly sand-coated, or (3) a ring of glass from the moile (glass left on blowpipe when the vessel was separated from it) when the blowpipe was used as a pontil. Often when a bare pontil was used, a grainy black—occasionally red—deposit was made on the base. According to Frederick Carder, founder of the Steuben Glass Works, this black oxide, or red oxide, was a deposit from the "punty (pontil) resulting from the degree of heating and use without coating the end of the pontil with glass."

The exact date is not known on which holding devices such as the "cup" and "snap case" evolved to hold a vessel during the finishing, thus avoiding a pontil mark and leaving a "smooth base." It seems probable that such a device was introduced into United States glasshouses in the mid- to late-40s. Holding devices, however, did not completely displace the pontil, and the use of both kinds of tools in a glassworks was not unusual. It should be noted that in the original charts that appeared in *American Glass* in 1941, the only flasks recorded with "smooth" bases are flasks in designs first produced in 1847/48 Dyottville-type Washington–Taylors and about 1850/51.

Apparently from about 1850 or the late 1840s on, there was more diversity in the construction of mold bases. One type of "keyed" base is shown by the line drawing for GIX–10. Others are illustrated here in which end-to-end lines show the mold seam. In some the base seam terminates at the edge of a concave center. Those having a central concave disk had a low circular post at the center of the base plate. Sometimes, as in the case of Type 4, a small central cavity on top of the post formed a nipple at the center of the concave disk on the bottom of the flask. A more elaborate ornament was the "star" of Type 14.

The 32 base types shown were found on flasks produced at various periods between about 1850 and 1890. They do not represent all the types that may have been adopted by moldmakers or manufacturers of flasks and bottles. A few variations are noted in the Charts—for instance, the type *without* a nipple at the center (GII–89), and it is probable others exist that are unknown to me. Also, it must be kept in mind that:

(1) each line drawing is of an individual flask base;

(2) each line drawing represents a type found not only in the flasks blown in the same mold as the flask that served as model for the drawing, but also on flasks of other sizes and of other designs;

(3) minor variations may occur in each type. For instance, the length of the diameter and depth of the curve in the seam, the length of the straight seam to the curve or center disk, and the diameter, depth, and curvature of the concave disk.

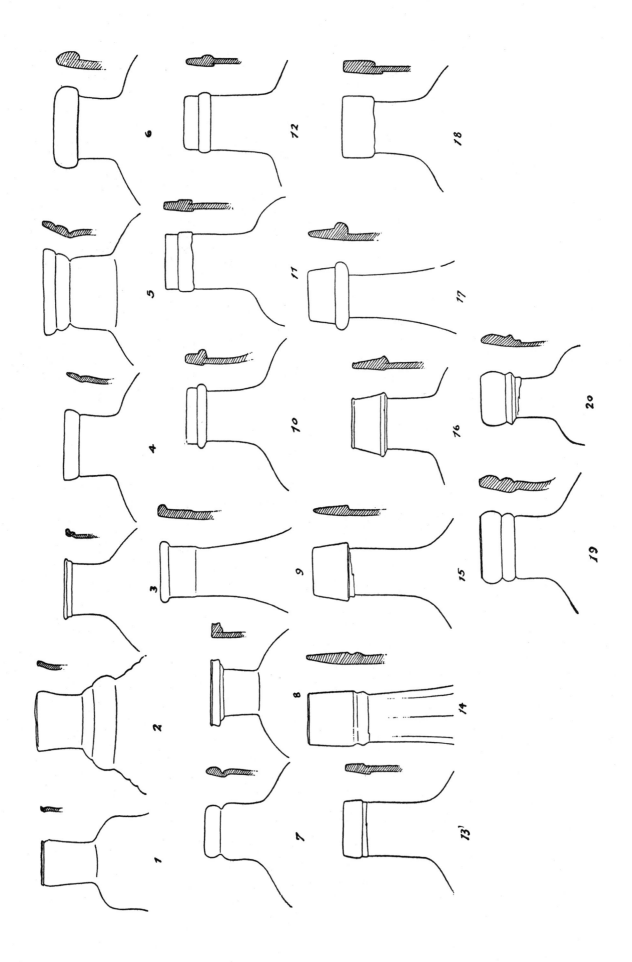

135. NECK FINISHES

1. Plain lip, with rough edge due to little or no fire polishing. Half-pint scroll flask, GIX–34.

2. Plain lip, smooth, fire-polished, "Jared Spencer" flask, GX–24.

3. Tooled, folded, or welted lip, slightly flanged and infolded, an unusual treatment on flasks. Pint. Zanesville Masonic–Eagle flask, GIV–32.

4. Tooled round collar, characteristic of heavy Keene Masonics. "J.K.B." flask, GIV–4.

5. Tooled "double" round collar. Masonic flask, Eagle above oval frame with large "star," GIV–6

6. Tooled rounded rolled-over collar. Masonic "J. K. B." flask, GIV–3.

7. Tooled and pinched in; very unusual treatment. Pint. Lafayette–Masonic flask, Mount Vernon Glass Works, GI–88

8. Tooled, flanged lip with flat top and squared edges. Half-pint. Washington "Albany Glass Works" flask, GI–30.

9. Tooled, rounded above ¾" flat band. Quart. Blue calabash (bottle), Washington–Tree, GI–35.

10. Tooled, narrow ring below thickened plain lip. Pint flask. Horseman on galloping horse, GXIII–13.

11. Tooled, flat ring below thickened plain lip. Quart. Scroll flask, GIX–3.

12. Tooled, broad rounded ring below thickened plain lip. Quart. Pike's Peak flask, Prospector each side, GXI–1.

13. Tooled, narrow beveled fillet below thickened plain lip. Quart. Washington Monument–Corn for the World flask, GVI–4.

14. Tooled, broad sloping collar above beveled ring. Quart. Calabash (bottle), Kossuth–Tree, GI–113.

15. Tooled, plain broad sloping collar. Quart. Washington–Taylor flask, Dyottville Glass Works type, GI–42.

16. Tooled, broad sloping collar with beveled edges at top and bottom. Quart flask. "TRAVELER'S COMPANION"–Sheaf of Grain, GXIV–1.

17. Tooled, broad flat collar sloping to heavy rounded ring. Quart. Calabash (bottle), Washington–Tree, GI–35.

18. Tooled, broad flat vertical collar, with and without uneven lower edge. Quart. Washington–Taylor flask, Dyottville Glass Works, GI–37.

19. Tooled, double rounded collar, upper deeper than lower; neck slightly pinched at base of collar. Quart. Washington flask, Lockport Glass Works, GI–61.

20. Tooled, broad round collar with lower bevel. Half-pint. Scroll flask, GIX–33.

20a (*not shown*). Like 20, but with narrow round above lower bevel.

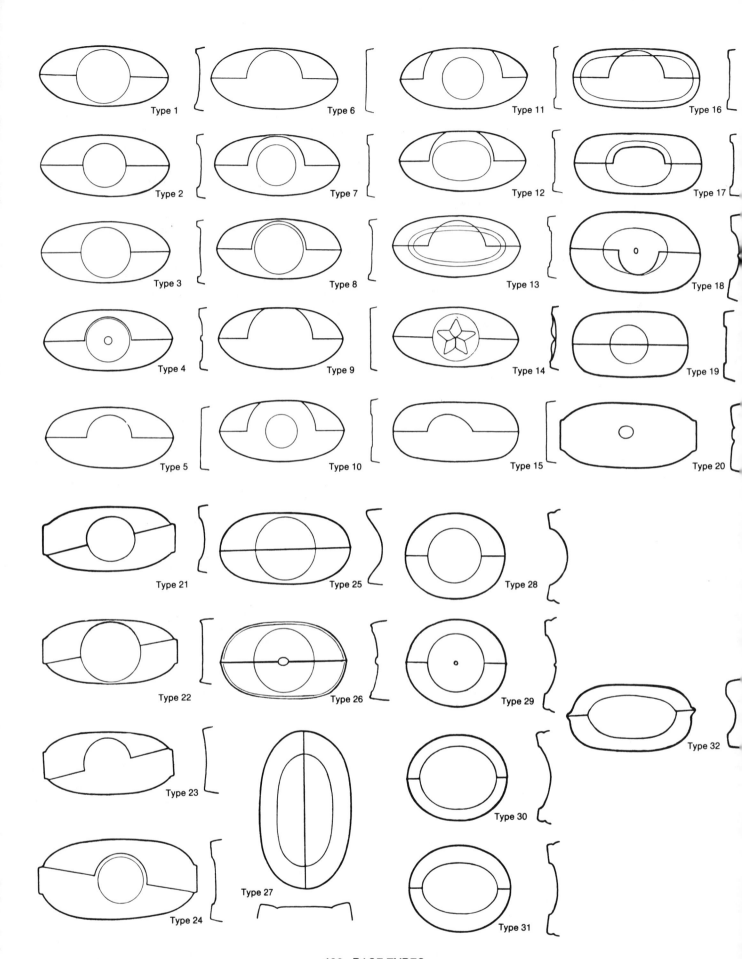

136. BASE TYPES

11
FIGURED FLASKS CHARTS

NOTE: Throughout these charts, colors not seen by me are designated by the informant's color terms, and each color is followed by the initials of the person reporting the color.

G.A. — George Austin
E.D. — L. Earl Dambach
C.G. — Charles B. Gardner

M.B.K. — Dr. Michael B. Krassner
S.L. — Sam Laidacker
W.L. — Warren Lane

D.M. — Dan Meek
F.S. — Fred Salisbury
O.S. — Orin Summerville

C.V. — Charles Vuono
C.W. — Crawford Wettlaufer
R.W. — Richard H. Wood

GROUP I—PORTRAIT FLASKS—WASHINGTON
Early Monongahela and Pittsburgh Districts and Early Kensington

OBVERSE	REVERSE	SIZE, FORM[1]	EDGES	NECK, BASE	COLORS	GLASSHOUSE	NOTES,[2] RARITY
GI–1. Washington. Large three-quarter view in uniform, facing left. "GENERAL WASHINGTON." in semicircle above bust.	American Eagle, head turned to right. Shield with 7 bars on breast; wings partly raised and right foreshortened. Thunderbolt (3 arrows) in its right talons, olive branch in left. Laurel branch in eagle's beak. nine 5-pointed stars in semicircle above eagle. Eagle stands on oval frame with inner band of 18 fairly large pearls. Only 2 leaves of the olive branch in left talons show clearly and the terminal leaf shows faintly on outer edge of wing.	Pint 12	Horizontal beading with vertical medial rib	Plain lip Pontil mark[3]	Deep green, bluish tone Deep green, yellowish tone Aquamarine Milky white Medium green (C.G.)	Unknown	Probably V. R. No. 5 D1; GV Scarce
GI–2. Washington. Varies slightly from No. 1. "GENERAL WASHINGTON." in semicircle above bust. Slight variation from No. 1 in size and arrangement of lettering.	American Eagle, head turned to right. Shield with 7 bars on breast; wings partly raised and right foreshortened. Thunderbolt (4 arrows) in its right talons, large olive branch showing all details in left. No stars above eagle. Eagle stands on oval frame, broken at top, with inner band of 25 tiny pearls.	Pint 12	Horizontal beading with vertical medial rib	Plain lip Pontil mark	Aquamarine Green, light Green, medium (R. W.)	Unknown	Probably V. R. No. 4 D1; GV Scarce
GI–3. Washington. Similar to No. 1 except uniform without epaulets. "GENERAL WASHINGTON" in semicircle above bust. Variation in lettering from Nos. 1 and 2. "N" in "General" reversed.	American Eagle, head turned to right. Narrower shield with 7 bars on breast; wings partly raised and right foreshortened. Short thunderbolt (3 short arrows) in its right talons, no olive branch in left. No stars above eagle. Eagle stands on oval frame, broken at top, with inner band of 12 fairly large pearls. Olive branches on either side of lower portion of panel.	Pint 12	Horizontal beading with vertical medial rib	Plain lip Pontil mark	Olive-yellow Deep golden amber Aquamarine Green, light (S.L.)	Unknown	Not listed by Van Rensselaer. NOTE: This flask is flatter than others in this group. Extremely rare

[1]Unless otherwise stated, the design on each side of all flasks in the Portrait Group is on an oval panel.

[2]The number given in the last column such as V. R. No. 1. D1; GII refers to Stephen Van Rensselaer's *Check List of Early American Bottles and Flasks.*

[3]Wherever only "Pontil mark" or "Plain" is given for base, there is a straight mold seam from end to end. The end of the pontil (punty rod) usually was dipped in molten glass before being attached to the base of the flask; to hold the flask during the neck finishing. As a result, when the flask was removed from the pontil, a small rough residue of glass remained on the base; this has been called a rough pontil-mark or pontil mark. In the past few years some collectors have called it a pontil scar. The older term, "pontil mark," was used by George S. McKearin in 1941 in *American Glass.*

GI-4. Washington. Similar to No. 1. Row of 9 short vertical ribs beneath bust. "GENERAL WASHINGTON." Similar to No. 1

American Eagle, head turned to right. Shield with 10 bars on breast; wings partly raised and right foreshortened. Thunderbolt (3 arrows) in its right talons, olive branch of different shape in left. Sunrays above eagle's head surmounted by nine 6-pointed stars. Eagle stands on oval frame broken at top with inner band of 13 fairly large pearls. Two crossed curving lines in center of frame. Five short and 2 long converging vertical ribs at bottom of flask.

Pint 12

Horizontal beading with vertical medial rib

Plain lip Pontil mark

Aquamarine Green, light (S.L.)

Unknown

Not listed by Van Rensselaer Extremely rare

GI-5. Washington. Same as No. 4 with similar inscription

Same as No. 4

Pint 12

Three rows of horizontal beading

Plain lip Pontil mark

Yellow-green. color deeper at base

Unknown

Not listed by Van Rensselaer. NOTE: We do not know of any other type of flask with beaded edges having this triple row. Extremely rare

GI-1 GI-2 GI-3 GI-4 GI-5

GROUP I—PORTRAIT FLASKS—WASHINGTON—Continued

OBVERSE	REVERSE	SIZE, FORM	EDGES	NECK, BASE	COLORS	GLASSHOUSE	NOTES, RARITY
GI–6. Washington. Similar to No. 1. "GENERAL WASHINGTON." Similar to No. 1	American Eagle, head turned to right. Shield with 7 bars on breast; wings partly raised and right foreshortened. Laurel branch in beak. Thunderbolt (3 arrows) in its right talons, olive branch in left. Nine 6-pointed stars above eagle. Eagle stands on oval frame with inner band of 16 fairly large pearls. "J. R." in oval frame beneath eagle. "LAIRD. SC. PITT" beneath oval frame.	Pint 12	Horizontal beading with vertical medial rib	Plain lip Pontil mark	Clear with amethyst tint Strong aquamarine Aquamarine, bluish (S.L.) Colorless (S.L.) Green, light (R.W.) Yellow-green, light (C.G.) Moonstone (S.L.)	John Robinson's Sturbridge Flint Glassworks, Pittsburgh, Pa. Mold by Joshua Laird, Pittsburgh moldmaker.	V. R. No. 10 D1; GV Very rare
GI–6a. Bust of Washington and inscription like GI–6.	Inscription and "J.R." as on GI–6. Eagle with shield, laurel branch in beak, thunderbolt and olive branch as on GI–1.	Pint 11	Same as GI–6	Plain lip Pontil mark	Colorless, smoky tinge	Same as above	Only specimen recorded. Reported by Kenneth R. Lewis.
GI–7. Washington. Similar to No. 1. "G. GEO. WASHINGTON." in semicircle above bust.	American Eagle, head turned to right. No shield on breast; wings partly raised and right foreshortened. Thunderbolt (3 arrows) in its right talons, large olive branch in left. Twelve small 8-pointed stars above eagle. Eagle stands on smaller oval frame, broken at top, with inner band of 17 small pearls. Below frame 2 olive branches tied together and extending on either side to top line of frame "F. L" in oval frame beneath eagle.	Pint 12	Horizontally beaded with vertical medial rib	Plain lip Pontil mark	Aquamarine Olive-amber (C.G.) Green, light (S.L.)	Frederick Lorenz, Pittsburgh	V. R. No. 8 D1; GV Rare
GI–8. Washington, three-quarter view in uniform, facing right; fuller faced and different arrangement of hair from others. "G. G. WASHINGTON" in semicircle above bust, letters large and widely spaced.	American Eagle, head larger and turned to left. Narrower shield with 7 bars on breast; wings partly raised Thunderbolt (3 arrows) in its left talons. Eagle stands on oval frame with inner band of 30 tiny pearls. "Pittsburgh" in semicircle above eagle. "F. L." in oval frame beneath eagle.	Pint 11	Vertically ribbed, 3	Plain lip Pontil mark	Clear light green	Frederick Lorenz, Pittsburgh	V. R. No. 9 D1; GV Extremely rare
GI–9. Washington. Similar to No. 2. "G. G. WASHINGTON" in semicircle above bust. Letters "G. G." widely spaced.	American Eagle, head turned to right. No shield on breast; wings partly raised and right foreshortened. Thunderbolt (3 arrows) in its right talons, small olive branch in left. Nine stars above eagle. Eagle stands on oval frame broken at top, with inner band of 10 fairly large pearls. Details of stars indistinct but apparently circular in shape with 12 points.	Pint 12	Horizontal beading with vertical medial rib	Plain lip Pontil mark	Dark olive-amber (black) Aquamarine Green, light (S.L.) Green, medium (C.G.) Yellow-green, light	Unknown	V. R. No. 7 D1; GV Rare

GI–10. Washington. Similar to No. 9. "G. WASHINGTON." in semicircle above bust.	American Eagle. Similar to No. 9. Smaller thunderbolt (3 short arrows) in right talons, different small olive branch in left. Eleven small stars above eagle and 1 at left of right wing similar to stars on No. 9. Eagle stands on oval frame with inner band of 15 small pearls.	Pint 12	Horizontal beading with vertical medial rib	Plain lip Pontil mark	Aquamarine Olive-amber Blue, light (S.L.) Green, light Green, medium (M.B.K.) Green, clear (R.W.) Olive-yellow	Unknown	V. R. No. 7 D1; GV Scarce
GI–11. Washington. Similar to No. 1. Branches, probably intended for olive, encircling bust.	American Eagle, head turned to right and body curving; wings partly raised in different position than any preceding flasks. Thunderbolt (3 arrows) in its right talons, olive branch in left, branch extending through lower tip of wing and leaves appearing at right of wing. Sunrays above eagle's head and 13 small stars at termination of rays. No oval frame.	Pint 12	Horizontal beading with vertical medial rib	Plain lip Pontil mark	Clear green Aquamarine Cornflower-blue Sapphire-blue Green, light (S.L.)	Unknown	V. R. No. 11 D1; GV Rare

NOTE: As to whether the branches are intended for olive or laurel is a matter of conjecture as the treatment itself is not distinctive. This likewise applies to branches under the eagle in No. 3 and No. 4. However, we are inclined to call the branches surrounding Washington's bust, olive branches (for peace) in view of the well-known slogan, "First in War, First in Peace and First in the hearts of his Countrymen," as applied to our first President. Also on No. 3 the olive branch which traditionally appears in either the right or the left talon is missing and therefore it is quite likely the branches below the eagle are olive branches. The branches on No. 7 are quite similar in treatment to those on No. 3.

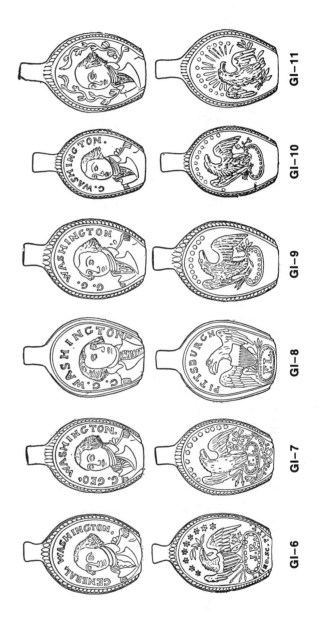

GI–11 GI–10 GI–9 GI–8 GI–7 GI–6

GROUP I—PORTRAIT FLASKS—WASHINGTON—*Continued*

OBVERSE	REVERSE	SIZE, FORM	EDGES	NECK, BASE	COLORS	GLASSHOUSE	NOTES, RARITY
GI–12. Three-quarter view, facing right; longer face than that of preceding; no epaulets on uniform.	American Eagle, head turned to right. Broader shield with 8 bars; wings quite different, right broader and left extended at right angles to body. Thunderbolt (3 arrows) in eagle's right talons and in the left talons 2 arrows and a shaft from one held in the right. No stars above eagle and no oval frame beneath.	Pint 12	Horizontal beading with vertical medial rib	Plain lip Pontil mark	Cornflower-blue Sapphire-blue Light green	Unknown	V. R. No. 118 G I. Note: While this is listed by Van Rensselaer as bust of Taylor, it is quite evidently Washington. Extremely rare
GI–13. Washington, three-quarter view, different uniform from any preceding. "WASHINGTON." in semicircle above bust.	American Eagle, head turned to left. Narrow pointed shield with 6 bars on breast; wings partly raised and left foreshortened. Thunderbolt (4 arrows) in left talons, small olive branch in right. Sunrays above eagle, thirteen 5-pointed stars surmounting rays. Eagle stands on oval frame with inner band of tiny pearl beading. "B. K." in oval frame below eagle.	Pint 11	Vertical ribbing	Plain lip Pontil mark	Pale yellow-green Emerald-green, light (S.L.)	Attributed to Benedict Kimber probably at his Bridgeport, Pa., Glass Works	Not listed by Van Rensselaer Extremely rare
GI–14. Washington. Three-quarter view in uniform. Similar to No. 1. "GENERAL WASHINGTON." in semicircle above bust.	American Eagle, head turned to right. Shield with 7 bars on breast, wings partly raised and right foreshortened. Thunderbolt (5 arrows) in its right talons, large olive branch in left. Sunrays above eagle's head. Eagle stands on oval frame with inner band of 28 small pearls. "E PLURIBUS UNUM" in semicircle above sunrays. In oval frame "T.W.D."	Pint 11	Vertically ribbed and with inscription "Adams & Jefferson July 4. A.D. 1776" "Kensington Glassworks Philadelphia." Three small stars after 1776	Plain lip Pontil mark	Deep sapphire-blue Deep green Dark amber Deep green, yellowish tone Aquamarine Brilliant golden yellow Emerald green, clear Red-amber (S.L.) Green, pale (M.B.K.) Emerald-green (S.L.)	Kensington Glass Works, Philadelphia	V. R. No. 1 D1; GV Common
GI–15. Washington. Same as No. 14	Same as No. 14	Pint 11	Same as No. 14 but inscription omitted	Plain lip Pontil mark	Aquamarine	Kensington Glass Works, Philadelphia	V. R No. 2 D1; GV NOTE: We have included this flask inasmuch as it is listed by Van Rensselaer. We do not have a specimen in our collection nor have we have been able to locate one in any other of several large collections. It is possible this variation does exist and if so it is an extremely rare flask.
GI–16. Washington. Same as No. 14	Same as No. 14 except "E. PLURIBUS UNUM" omitted	Pint 11	Same as No. 15. No inscription	Plain lip Pontil mark	Aquamarine Very pale aquamarine	Kensington Glass Works, Philadelphia	V. R. No. 3 D1; GV Comparatively scarce

No.	Obverse	Reverse	Size	Base	Lip/Pontil	Color	Glass Works	Rarity
GI–16a. Bust of Washington similar to GI–14, 15, and 16; ribs on epaulets and hair more distinct. Letters slightly thinner and period after "WASHINGTON." *See No. 1, Ill. 124.*	Similar to GI–16. No sunrays. Eagle's beak open, 3 arrows in left talon; olive branch between right talon and wing; no pearl between branch and eagle's leg. Thirty-two tiny pearls in oval frame. No inscription or "T.W.D."		Pint 11	Same as GI–16	Plain lip Pontil mark	Colorless	Probably Kensington Glass Works; possibly another obtaining molds from same moldmaker	Extremely rare. Only one specimen recorded 1965.
GI–17. Washington, profile facing left; long queue. Uniform with epaulet. "WASHINGTON" in semicircle above bust.	Taylor, profile facing left, uniform with high collar and epaulet. "BALTIMORE GLASs WORKs." in semicircle above bust.		Pint 11	Vertically ribbed 3, with heavy medial rib	Plain lip Pontil mark	Puce Pale yellowish green Golden yellow Aquamarine Yellow-amber (S.L.) Amethyst, pale pinkish (C.G.) Green, pale (S.L.) Green, deep (S.L.) [Emerald-green (R.W.) Olive-green (M.B.K.) Yellow-green (R.W.) Olive-yellow Wine (E.D.)]	Baltimore Glass Works	V. R. No. 8 D3; GV Comparatively scarce
GI–17a. Bust of Washington and inscription like GI–17.	Bust of Taylor and inscription like GI–17.		Pint 11	Smooth	Plain lip. Pontil mark	Aquamarine	Baltimore Glass Works	Very rare
GI–18. Washington, profile facing left. Roman nose. Different arrangement of hair, long queue; uniform with epaulet. "WASHINGTON." in semicircle above bust.	Battle Monument, Baltimore. "BALTIMORE GLASS WORKS" in semicircle around monument.		Pint 11	Vertically ribbed 3, with heavy medial rib	Plain lip Pontil mark	Cornflower-blue Aquamarine Medium blue Light green Olive-amber (S.L.) Sapphire-blue, medium (S.L.) Green, deep (E.D.) Emerald-green, deep (S.L.)	Baltimore Glass Works	V. R. No. 7 D3; GV Scarce

GI–12 GI–13 GI–14 GI–14 GI–17 GI–18

OBVERSE	REVERSE	SIZE, FORM	EDGES	NECK, BASE	COLORS	GLASSHOUSE	NOTES, RARITY
GI–19. Similar to No. 18	Similar to No. 18 but small period or pitmark after GLASS.	Pint 11	Smooth	Plain lip Pontil mark	Deep amethyst Clear green Medium blue Puce Aquamarine Amber, deep	Baltimore Glass Works	Not listed by Van Rensselaer Scarce
GI–20. Washington, profile similar to No. 17. "FELLS" above bust; "POINT" below bust.	Washington Monument without statue, Baltimore. "BALTᵒ" below monument.	Pint 11	Same as No. 1	Plain lip Pontil mark	Sapphire-blue Amethyst Wine Aquamarine Pale amethyst Brilliant honey Amber Vaseline Amber, pale streaked [Olive-amber, light smoky (E.D.) Cornflower-blue (R.W.) Colorless (R.W.) Yellow-green (S.L.) Puce (C.G.)]	Baltimore Glass Works	V. R. No. 9 D3; GV Comparatively scarce
GI–21. Washington, classical bust, profile with queue facing right. "FELLS" above bust; "POINT" below bust.	Washington Monument without statue, Baltimore. "BALTᵒ" below monument.	Quart 11	Heavy vertical medial rib with 2 narrow ribs forming outer edge of each panel	Plain lip Pontil mark	Deep olive-yellow Clear glass Sapphire-blue Aquamarine Olive-amber Amethyst, light Blue, light Colorless, amethystine tint (E.D.) Colorless, smoky Green, pale (M.B.K.) Green, light	Baltimore Glass Works	V. R. No. 3 D3; GV Comparatively scarce
GI–22. Washington, classical bust similar to No. 21. "BALTIMORE X GLASS. WORKS." The "S's" are reversed.	Classical bust facing right. NOTE: There is some doubt as to whom this bust is intended to portray. It has been generally listed as Taylor. However there is a strong possibility it may be intended for Henry Clay.	Quart 11	Vertically ribbed 3, with heavy medial rib	Plain lip Pontil mark	Aquamarine Green, medium (E.D.) Olive-yellow	Baltimore Glass Works	V. R. No. 10 D3; GV Rare
GI–23. Washington. Similar to No. 22. No inscription above bust of Washington.	Classical bust facing right, similar to No. 22 except hair different. "BALTIMORE X GLASS. WOKS." The "r" in works is omitted.	Quart 11	Heavy vertical medial rib with narrow rib each side and 2 narrow ribs forming outer edge of each panel.	Plain lip Pontil mark	Deep puce Aquamarine Deep amethyst Clear yellow Amber Honey Light olive green Green, light Yellow-green, light (C.G.) Yellow-green, medium (S.L.)	Baltimore Glass Works	V. R. No. 11 D3; GV Rare

NOTE: Van Rensselaer lists his No. 4 D3; GV similar flask without the inscriptions. We are not certain whether this flask exists. It may have been listed from a flask blown in a worn mold so that the inscriptions were very faint or obscure.

GI-24. Washington. Similar to No. 17 "WASHINGTON." in semicircle above bust. | Taylor. Similar to No. 17. "BRIDGETON ★ NEW JERSEY". | Pint 11 | Vertically ribbed 3, with heavy medial rib | Plain lip Pontil mark | Amber / Green / Dark olive-amber (black) / Aquamarine / Golden amber (S.L.) / Black (deep amber) (R.W.) / Sapphire-blue (S.L.) / Olive-green, deep (S.L.) — Yellowish olive-green (R.W.) / Peacock-green (R.W.) / Yellow-green, pale (C.G.) / Yellow-green, medium (R.W.) | Bridgeton Glass Works | V. R. No. 6 D3; GV Common

GI-25. Washington. Classical profile similar to No. 22. "BRIDGETOWN NEW JERSEY" above bust. | Classical bust similar to No. 22. "BRIDGETOWN NEW JERSEY" above bust. | Quart 11 | Same as No. 23. | Plain lip Pontil mark | Dark olive-amber (black) / Sapphire-blue / Aquamarine / Black (deep amber) (M.B.K.) / Green, clear (M.B.K.) — Green, light (S.L.) / Emerald-green (S.L.) / Yellow-green / Wine, deep (M. Knapp. Jr.) | Bridgeton Glass Works | V. R. No. 5 D3; GV Common

GI-26. Washington. Classical profile with queue, facing left. | Large American Eagle, head turned to right. Shield with 8 vertical and 2 horizontal bars on breast; wings partly raised and right foreshortened. Thunderbolt (3 arrows) in its right talons, olive branch in left. Seven 5-pointed stars above eagle and 5 below. | Quart 11 | Heavy vertical medial rib with narrow rib each side and 2 narrow ribs forming outer edge of each panel | Plain lip Pontil mark | Clear glass with faint amethyst tint / Clear dark amber / Blue / Aquamarine / Pale honey / Emerald-green / Honey-amber / Amethyst / Blue, translucent / Blue, sapphire shading to purple-blue (M.B.K.) / Green, pale (E.D.) / Green, medium / Olive-green / Yellow-green | Unknown, possibly Baltimore or Bridgeton Glass Works | V. R. No. 1 D3; GV Common

GI-20 GI-21 GI-22 GI-23 GI-24 GI-25 GI-26

GROUP I—PORTRAIT FLASKS—WASHINGTON—Continued

OBVERSE	REVERSE	SIZE, FORM	EDGES	NECK, BASE	COLORS	GLASSHOUSE	NOTES, RARITY
GI–26a. Bust of Washington similar to GI–26. Head slightly smaller, nose and lips slightly shorter, oval of eye larger; around queue, narrow ribbon with large off-center loop.	Eagle and stars similar to GI–26. Nine instead of 8 bars on shield. Stars slightly larger, sharper points and closer to eagle.	Quart. Similar to 11, shoulder more sloping, body broader	Same as GI–26	Plain lip Keyed like GIX–10.	Aquamarine	Probably Baltimore, Philadelphia or South Jersey area	Scarce
GI–26b. Bust of Washington similar to GI–26 and 26a. Head slightly smaller and shoulders narrower; longer nose; queue ribbon like GI–26a.	Eagle and stars similar to GI–26 and 26a. Head very slightly smaller. Nine vertical bars on shield. Stars larger and more sharply pointed.	Quart. Similar to GI–26a	Same as GI–26 *(at widest point.)*	Plain lip Pontil mark; flat outer rim	Aquamarine Green (light)	Same as above	Scarce
GI–26c. Bust of Washington similar to GI–26, 26a and 26b. Head slightly smaller and shoulders narrower than GI–26a and b; nose slightly less hooked; longer lips; queue ribbon, large and smooth over queue.	Eagle and stars similar to GI–26, 26a and 26b. Nine vertical bars on shield. Stars smaller than on GI–26, 26a, and 26b.	Quart. Similar to GI–26a	Same as GI–26	Plain lip Pontil mark	Amethystine tint Blue, Deep [?] Amethyst [?]	Same as above	Rare
GI–27. Washington. Similar to No. 26	Similar to No. 26	Quart 11	Smooth	Plain lip Pontil mark	Aquamarine Deep green Green, medium Olive-yellow	Same as No. 26	V. R. No. 2 D3; GV Comparatively scarce
GI–28. Washington, small three-quarter view facing left. "ALBANY GLASS WORKS." in semicircle around bust. Below bust in two lines "ALBANY N Y".	Full-rigged ship sailing to right.	Pint 11	Vertically ribbed 3, with heavy medial rib	Plain lip Double rounded collar Broad sloping collar Pontil mark	Light sapphire-blue Aquamarine Clear amber Dark amber Deep green Clear olive-green Olive-amber (W.L.) Red-amber (S.L.) Aquamarine (W.L.) Blue, pale (S.L.) Cobalt-blue, medium (S.L.) Cornflower-blue (M. Knapp, Jr.)	Albany Glass Works, Albany, N.Y.	V. R. No. 1 D4; GV Comparatively scarce

NOTE: The amethyst and deep blue that have been recorded appear to have been blown in the same mold as the colorless or amethystine tint, but their age has been questioned. The blue has a neck and top shoulder line similar to some of the Clevenger reproductions of GII–55. The amethyst has a pristine sharpness of design and a line at juncture of neck and shoulder uncharacteristic of 19th-century flasks. Still, as yet, we have been unable to trace these two flasks to a 20th-century source.

Box (GI–28 colors): Green, yellow tone (C.G.) Blue-green (R. W.) Emerald-green (S.L.) Yellow (M. Knapp, Jr.)

GI–29. Similar to No. 28 but design crude and details not as distinct. Apparently blown in a plaster mold. A vertical seam mark shows on the obverse. The "N" in "ALBANY" in the inscription around bust and the "N" in "N Y" are reversed. These flasks come in a deep sapphire-blue and a very unusual shade of deep yellow-green.   Rare

		Size	Ribbing	Lip / Collar	Color	Manufacturer	Rarity
GI–30. Washington, small three-quarter view facing left.	"ALBANY GLASS WORKS N Y" in elliptical formation.	Half-pint 11	Vertically ribbed 3, with heavy medial rib	Plain lip Double rounded collar Flat topped collar Pontil mark	Olive-yellow Deep green Clear amber Aquamarine Golden amber Green, medium Green, pale (S.L.) Yellow-green, light (S.L.)	Albany Glass Works, Albany, N.Y.	V. R. No. 2 D4; GV Comparatively scarce
GI–31. Washington, profile facing left, in uniform. "WASHINGTON." in semicircle above bust.	Jackson profile facing left, in uniform. "JACKSON." in semicircle above bust.	Pint 11	Vertically ribbed 3, with heavy medial rib	Plain lip Pontil mark	Dark olive-green Olive-amber Amber Olive-amber, light (S.L.) Olive-green, light (S.L.)	Keene-Marlboro-St.	V. R. No. 3 D4; GV Common
GI–32. Washington. Similar to No. 31 except bars on lapel of coat missing.	Jackson. Similar to No. 31 except bars on lapel of coat missing.	Pint 11	Same as No. 31	Plain lip Pontil mark	Strong aquamarine Amber Dark olive-green Olive-amber Green, light Emerald-green, pale (S.L.)	Eastern, probably New England	V. R. No. 4 D4; GV Comparatively scarce
GI–33. Washington. Similar to No. 31. "WASHINGTON." in semicircle above bust, letters smaller.	Jackson. Similar to No. 31. The bars on lapel of coat missing on each bust. "JACKSON." in semicircle above bust, letters smaller.	Pint 11	Same as No. 31	Plain lip Pontil mark	Dark olive-green Amber Olive-amber	Coventry, Conn., Glass Works	V. R. No. 6 D4; GV Comparatively scarce
GI–34. Washington, profile facing right with long queue in uniform. "WASHINGTON." above bust.	Jackson profile facing left, in uniform. "JACKSON." in semicircle above bust.	Half-pint 11	Same as No. 31	Plain lip Pontil mark Broad sloping collar (No. 15)	Olive-amber Amber Dark olive-green	Coventry, Conn., Glass Works	V. R. No. 7 D4; GV Common

GI–28   GI–30   GI–31   GI–32   GI–33   GI–34

GROUP I—PORTRAIT FLASKS—WASHINGTON—*Continued*

OBVERSE	REVERSE	SIZE, FORM	EDGES	NECK, BASE	COLORS	GLASSHOUSE	NOTES, RARITY
GI–34a. As on GI–34: inscription "WASHINGTON" in semicircle above profile bust of Washington in uniform, facing right.	"JACKSON" in deep arc above profile bust of Jackson in uniform facing left.	Pint 11	Like GI–34 but medial rib fading into mold seam	Plain lip Pontil mark	Amber, medium	Probably Coventry, Conn. See GI–34.	Reported by Neil A. Sayles. Only recorded example
GI–35. Washington not on oval panel; three-quarter view facing left, with queue, in uniform.	Large tree in foliage with 9 buds, with indented edges.	Quart 33 (Calabash)	Vertical fluting	Rounded tooled lip Broad sloping collar (No. 15) Pontil mark Smooth (Snap case)	Sapphire shading to purple-blue Sapphire-blue Aquamarine	Unknown	V. R. No. 8 D4; GV Common
GI–36. Washington not on oval panel; small classical profile bust with queue, facing left.	Large tree in foliage varying in details from No. 35.	Quart 33 (Calabash)	Vertical fluting	Broad sloping collar terminating in ring Pontil mark Narrow round collar, lower bevel (20a)	Aquamarine	Unknown	V. R. No. 10 D4; GV Scarce

Type produced by Dyottville Glass Works, Philadelphia, and Lockport Glass Works, Lockport, N.Y.

NOTE: The Dyottville-type flasks in all sizes occur with plain lip, double rounded collar, single rounded collar, and broad sloping collar. The base also occurs with pontil mark; with outer mold rim and depressed center with pontil mark; also smooth base, where snap case was used to hold bottle while finishing.

OBVERSE	REVERSE	SIZE, FORM	EDGES	NECK, BASE	COLORS	GLASSHOUSE	NOTES, RARITY
GI–37. Washington, classical profile bust with queue, facing left; broad band of toga showing. Above Washington "THE FATHER OF HIS COUNTRY"	Taylor profile bust in uniform, four buttons on coat, facing left. Above Taylor "GEN. TAYLOR NEVER SURRENDERS". Above panel "DYOTTVILLE GLASS WORKS PHILAD.ᴬ"	Quart 20	Smooth	See note for all flasks. Wide flat collar	Amethyst Clear green Olive-yellow Pale shaded amber Yellow-green Aquamarine Deep wine or claret Sage-green Light sapphire-blue Pale yellow-green Olive-amber Clear golden amber Sapphire-blue violet tone Amber, medium (S.L.) Honey-amber (R. W.) Cornflower-blue (C.G.) Sapphire-blue, medium (E.D.) Blue, violet tone (C.G.) Emerald-green (R. W.) Puce, medium (S.L.) Puce, deep	Dyottville Glass Works, Philadelphia	V. R. No. 1 D2; GV Common

GI–38. Washington. Similar to No. 37 but queue tied with 3 ribbons; narrow band of toga showing.	Taylor. Similar to No. 37 but 5 buttons on coat.	Smooth	Narrow flat collar	Pint 20	Olive-yellow Clear green Dark olive-green Deep amber (black) Aquamarine Olive-amber Cornflower-blue Deep amethyst (black) — Blue, pale (S.L.) Emerald-green, brilliant (R.W.) Emerald-green, medium (S.L.) Puce Wine	Same	V. R. No. 2 D2; GV Common
GI–39. Washington. Same as No. 37	Same as No. 37 but "DYOTTVILLE GLASS WORKS PHILAD.A" omitted.	Smooth		Quart 20	Amethyst Clear green Deep yellow-green Aquamarine Deep green Pale violet-blue Dark olive-yellow Golden amber (S.L.) Olive-amber, deep Blue, light (S.L.) — Blue, medium (S.L.) Green, light Emerald-green (R.W.) Blue-green, deep Peacock-green (R.W.) Olive-green (S.L.) Wine (S.L.)	Same	V. R. No. 3 D2; GV Common
GI–39a. Bust of Washington and inscription similar to GI–39.	Bust of Taylor and inscription like GI–39 but no buttons on Taylor's uniform.	Smooth		Quart 20	Yellow-green	Possibly Dyottville Glass Works, Philadelphia	Reported by Richard Wood, 1968 Very rare

GI–35   GI–36   GI–37   GI–38

GROUP I—PORTRAIT FLASKS—WASHINGTON—*Continued*

OBVERSE	REVERSE	SIZE, FORM	EDGES	NECK, BASE	COLORS	GLASSHOUSE	NOTES, RARITY
GI–40. Washington. Same as No. 37.	Taylor. Same as No. 38. Inscription same as No. 37 except "DYOTT-VILLE GLASS WORKS PHILAD.A" omitted.	Pint 20	Smooth		Amethyst Light green Aquamarine Sapphire-blue Olive-yellow Yellowish olive-green Dark moss-green Deep green	Dyottville Glass Works type	V. R. No. 4 D ; GV Common
GI–40a. Similar to No. 40 but no period after GEN and letters of inscription on each side slightly smaller (more finely cut). Four buttons on Taylor's coat.				Yellow-amber (S.L.) Blue, deep (S.L.) Emerald-green, medium (S.L.) Olive-green (S.L.) Yellow-green	Golden amber (G.A.) Aquamarine Blue, deep (E.D.) Green, yellow tone (E.D.) Olive-green		
GI–40b. Similar to No. 40 except GENL instead of Gen. Letters of inscriptions vary slightly from Nos. 40 and 40a. Four buttons on Taylor's coat, with wide space between third and lowest button.					Blue, pale Cobalt-blue Olive-green, deep Yellow-green, pale (E.D.)		
GI–40c. Similar to GI–40; bust of Washington in slightly higher relief, queue tighter. Same inscription as on GI–40, in narrower arch with "T" of "THE" opposite throat and "Y" of "COUNTRY" at lower ribbon of queue.	Similar to GI–40; bust of Taylor in slightly higher relief, hair indicated by "pebbling," 5 buttons on coat. Same inscription nearly oval, with "G" of "GEN" opposite second button from bottom and "ERS" of "SURREN-DERS" below epaulets; arc of 28 tiny beads below bust from "G" to "S."	Pint 20	Smooth	Plain Pontil mark	Aquamarine Green (medium)	Possibly Dyottville Glass Works, Philadel-phia	Rare
GI–41. Washington. Similar to No. 38, but neck slightly longer and face slightly raised. Inscription same as on No. 37.	Taylor same as No. 38 but 4 buttons on coat. Inscription same as on No. 40.	Half-pint 20	Smooth		Aquamarine Blue, light opalish (R. W.) Olive-green, deep Yellow-green (S.L.)	Same	V. R. No. 4 D2; GV Common
GI–42. Washington. Similar to No. 37. Inscription same	Taylor. Similar to No. 37. In semicircle "A LITTLE MORE GRAPE CAPTAIN BRAGG".	Quart 20	Smooth	Sapphire-blue, deep Sapphire-blue, white streaks Emerald-green, light (S.L.) Peacock-green (M.B.K.)	Amethyst, light tone Clear green Aquamarine Yellow-green with pale amber streaks Clear Alabaster (S.L.) Blue, deep (S.L.) Peacock-blue (M.B.K.)	Same	V. R. No. 15 D2; GV Common This flask is also found with long (2½") neck and sloping collar fitted into straw woven case.

ID	Description	Size	Base	Obverse/Reverse	Colors	Reference
GI-43	Taylor. Similar to No. 37. "I HAVE ENDEAVOUR,D TO DO MY DUTY".	Quart 20	Smooth	Same	Puce; Olive-yellow; Pale yellow-green; Aquamarine; Brown-amber (C.G.); Red-amethyst, light (S.L.); Aquamarine, milky, almost translucent — Green, light; Green, medium; Yellow-green, light (S.L.); Olive-yellow, deep (S.L.)	V. R. No. 12 D2; GV Common
G-44	Taylor. Similar to No. 38 except 4 buttons on coat. "I HAVE ENDEAVOUR,D TO DO MY DUTY".	Pint 20	Smooth	Same	Sapphire-blue; Golden yellow; Aquamarine; Golden amber, deep (S.L.); Amber, greenish (E.D.); Blue, gray tone; Blue, medium deep (S.L.) — Blue, cobalt (C.V.); Green, deep; Olive-green, yellowish (S.L.); Yellow-green (G.A.); Olive-yellow	V. R. No. 14 D2; GV Common
GI-45	Taylor. Similar to No. 37. No inscription	Quart 20	Smooth	Same	Pale yellow-green; Aquamarine	V. R. No. 16 D2; GV Very rare
GI-46	Taylor. In uniform—head different, elongated. "GEN. Z. TAYLOR" above bust.	Quart 20	Smooth	Dyottville Glass Works type	Dark amber (black); Aquamarine; Opalescent aquamarine (S.L.); Green, light; Emerald-green, pale (S.L.); Emerald-green (R.W.) — See note for all flasks	V. R. No. 9 D2; GV Common

GI-40c GI-41 GI-42 GI-43 GI-44 GI-45 GI-46

GI-43. Washington. Similar to No. 37. Inscription same

G-44. Washington. Similar to No. 38. Inscription same

GI-45. Washington. Same as No. 37

GI-46. Washington. Similar to No. 37. Inscription same

OBVERSE	REVERSE	SIZE, FORM	EDGES	NECK, BASE	COLORS	GLASSHOUSE	NOTES, RARITY
GI–47. Washington. Similar to No. 38 but queue tied with 3 ribbons; different arrangement from that in No. 38.	Plain	Quart 20	Smooth	Emerald-green, light (S.L.) Emerald-green, deep (S.L.)	Clear deep green Aquamarine Golden amber, light Blue, medium (C.G.) Blue, greenish (E.D.)	Same	V. R. No. 18 D2; GV Common
GI–48. Washington. Similar to No. 38 but forehead slopes back; queue tied with 3 ribbons, arrangement of ribbons different from that on either No. 38 or No. 47.	Plain	Pint 20	Smooth	Flat ring below plain lip (No. 11) Peacock-green (R.W.) Olive-yellow	Dark olive-green Aquamarine Deep green Blue, pale Blue, light (C.V.) Green, light (G.A.) Green, medium Emerald-green (S.L.)	Same	V. R. No. 17 D2; GV Common
GI–49. Washington. Similar to No. 38. "WASHINGTON" in semicircle above bust.	Taylor. Similar to No. 38, bust slightly narrower. "GEN. Z. TAYLOR" in semicircle above bust.	Pint 20	Smooth		Aquamarine Green, light bluish Gray-blue	Same	V. R. No. 10 D2; GV Common
GI–50. Washington. Similar to No. 38. "WASHINGTON" in semicircle below bust.	Taylor. Similar to No. 49. "G.Z. TAYLOR" in semicircle below bust.	Pint 20	Smooth	Green, light (R.W.)	Green, clear Aquamarine Pale blue Colorless Green, deep (S.L.)	Same	V. R. No. 11 D2; GV Common
GI–51. Washington. Similar to No. 37. No inscription on either side	Taylor. Similar to No. 37	Quart 20	Smooth	Golden amber (S.L.) Amethyst, deep (G.A.) Citron Green, pale Emerald-green, light (S.L.) Yellow-green (R.W.)	Aquamarine Cornflower-blue Dark amber (black) Yellow-green Pale sapphire-blue Pale yellow-green Dark green Amber, pale Amber, pale and murky with amethyst streaks (E.D.)	Same	V. R. No. 8 D2; GV Common
GI–52. Washington. Similar to No. 38. No inscription	Taylor. Similar to No. 38 except 4 buttons on coat. No inscription	Pint 20	Smooth	Flat ring below plain lip (No. 11) Yellow-green, medium Yellow-green, deep (E.D.)	Dark amber (black) Clear yellow-amber Pale yellow-green Clear amber Aquamarine Dark green, yellow tone	Same	V. R. No. 5 D2; GV Common

536

GI-53. Washington. Similar to No. 41. No inscription

Taylor. Similar to No. 41, but difference in spacing of buttons. No inscription

Half-pint 20

Smooth

Round ring below plain lip (No. 10)

Aquamarine
Clear olive-green
Amber, light (C.G.)

Same

V. R. No. 5 D2; GV Comparatively scarce

GI-54. Washington. Similar to No. 37 but without queue. No inscription

Taylor. Similar to No. 37. No inscription

Quart 20

Smooth

Broad sloping collar, terminating in round ring (No. 17)
Broad sloping collar (No. 15)

Pale amber
Aquamarine
Sapphire-blue
Light bluish green
Deep wine
Dark yellow-green
Deep amethyst
Pale yellow-green
Deep green, yellow low tone
Olive-yellow
Pale yellow-amber
Amber, deep (M.B.K.)
Olive-amber, yellowish (R.W.)
Teal-blue (M.B.K.)
Green, deep (C.G.)

Emerald-green, deep (S.L.)
Olive-green
Yellow-green, light (C.G.)
Yellow-green, deep (C.G.)
Olive-yellow (E.D.)

Same

V. R. No. 6 D2; GV Common

GI-55. Washington. Similar to No. 38 but very short queue, toga plain. No inscription

Taylor. Similar to No. 38 but 4 buttons on coat and decoration beneath chin missing. No inscription

Pint 20

Smooth

Deep yellow-amber
Aquamarine
Deep amber
Amber, medium
Yellow-amber
Green, light (R.W.)
Green, medium (R.W.)
Green, deep (C.G.)
Emerald-green (E.D.)
Yellow-green, pale (S.L.)
Olive-yellow (deep) (C.V.)

Same

V. R. No. 6 D2; GV Common

GI-47   GI-48   GI-49   GI-50   GI-51   GI-52   GI-53   GI-54   GI-55

537

GROUP I—PORTRAIT FLASKS—WASHINGTON—*Continued*

	OBVERSE	REVERSE	SIZE, FORM	EDGES	NECK, BASE	COLORS	GLASSHOUSE	NOTES, RARITY
GI–55a.	Bust of Washington like GI–55. No inscription	Bust of Taylor like GI–54. No inscription	Pint 20	Smooth	Sloping collar Smooth	Emerald-green (light)	Same	Reported by Dr. Michael Krassner Rare
GI–55b.	Bust of Washington like GI–55. No inscription	Bust of Taylor like GI–56. No inscription	Pint 20	Smooth	Plain Smooth	Aquamarine	Same	Reported by Matthew G. Knapp. Jr. Rare
GI–55c.	Bust of Washington like GI–55.	Bust of Taylor similar to GI–56, with tie.	Pint 20	Smooth	Like GI–55	Green, medium	Same	Reported by Richard Wood Very rare

NOTE: The large number of molds for the 25 varieties of the so-called Dyottville Washington flasks GI–37 through GI–59 suggests that some of the flasks were produced elsewhere, and possibly the molds obtained from one moldmaker. In the opinion of Sam Laidacker GI–47, 48, and 51 may be Lockport Glass Works products. J. E. Pfeiffer has found fragments of GI–52 in citron and of flasks like, or similar, to GI–55 in green on the site of the Crowleytown Glass Works (1851–66), Crowleytown, N.J. The fragments were not found in the "cullet area," and the colors are those of bottles produced in the works. Possibly Crowleytown acquired Dyottville molds or had the Dyottville style copied.

	OBVERSE	REVERSE	SIZE, FORM	EDGES	NECK, BASE	COLORS	GLASSHOUSE	NOTES, RARITY
GI–56.	Washington slightly different, no queue, no trace of toga. No inscription	Taylor. Similar to No. 41 except 5 buttons on coat and decoration on collar different. No inscription	Half-pint 20	Smooth		Golden amber Olive-yellow Aquamarine Green, clear Yellow-green, light (G.A.)	Same	Not listed by Van Rensselaer Comparatively scarce
GI–57.	Washington classical bust different from No. 37, no queue. No inscription	Sheaf of rye on crossed rake and pitchfork. No inscription	Quart 20	Smooth	Olive-green (C.G.)	Aquamarine Black (deep amber) Emerald-green (S.L.) Yellow-green, deep	Same	V. R. No. 121 D2; GV Common
GI–58.	Washington. Similar to No. 57 but toga plain. No inscription	Sheaf of rye on rake and pitchfork. No inscription	Pint 20	Smooth	See note for all flasks	Aquamarine	Dyottville Glass Works type	V. R. No. 122 D2; GV Common
GI–59.	Washington. Similar to No. 56. No inscription	Double-headed sheaf of rye; rake and pitchfork omitted. No inscription	Half-pint 20	Smooth	Cobalt-blue (Robert Mebane)	Aquamarine Sapphire-blue, deep (S.L.) Yellow-green, deep Olive-green (C.G.)	Same	V. R. No. 123 D2; GV Comparatively scarce

NOTE: Van Rensselaer lists bust on each of these last three flasks as Taylor and in a note in his check list, page 57, states, "These three flasks have always been called 'TAYLOR & SHEAF' flasks so we put them under this classification although there is some question as to the identity of the gentleman shown." There is not any question but that the bust on No. 59 is that of Washington and it is a fair assumption that the busts on No. 5, 57 and 58 are meant for Washington.

GI-60. Washington. Similar to No. 37 but varying slightly in details. "LOCKPORT GLASS WORKS" above bust.

Similar but variation in details of bust, the nose not as aquiline. No inscription

Quart 20

Smooth

Lockport Glass Works

Aquamarine
Deep blue
Sapphire-blue
Bluish-green, deep (E.D.)
Green, medium (M.B.K.)
Yellow-green (C.G.)

V. R. No. 19 D2; GV
Scarce

GI-61. Same as No. 60. No inscription on either side

Same as No. 60

Quart 20

Smooth

Lockport Glass Works

Aquamarine
Very dark yellow-green
Clear deep green
Dark olive-green (black)

Sapphire-blue, light (C.G.)
Green, light
Emerald-green

V. R. No. 20 D2; GV
Scarce

NOTE: On the Dyottville Washington flasks GI-37, 39, 42, 46, 47, 51 and the Lockport flasks GI-60 and 61, the toga of the bust shows the small round fibula used by the Romans to fasten it at the shoulder.

GROUP I—PORTRAIT FLASKS—ADAMS, HARRISON, JACKSON, and TAYLOR

GI-62. Adams, John Quincy; three-quarter view facing left. "JOHN Q. ADAMS" in semicircle above bust.

American Eagle, head turned to right. Shield with 7 bars on breast; wings partly raised and right foreshortened. Thunderbolt (3 arrows) in its right talons, large olive branch in left. Thirteen small 5-pointed stars above eagle. Eagle stands on oval frame with inner band of 16 pearls. "J. T & C⁰" below the oval frame.

Pint 12

Horizontal beading with vertical medial rib

Plain lip
Pontil mark

Aquamarine

Attributed to John Taylor & Co., Brownsville, Pa.

V. R. No 1 GI
Extremely rare

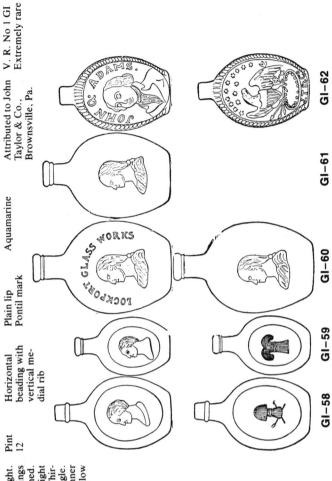

GI-56   GI-57

GI-58   GI-59

GI-60

GI-61

GI-62

GROUP I—PORTRAIT FLASKS—ADAMS, HARRISON, JACKSON, *and* TAYLOR—*Continued*

OBVERSE	REVERSE	SIZE, FORM	EDGES	NECK, BASE	COLORS	GLASSHOUSE	NOTES, RARITY
GI-63. Harrison, full three-quarter view facing left in elaborate uniform showing triple row of laurel branches on breast. "Wᴹ. H. HARRISON" in semicircle above bust.	Log Cabin, tall door with latch-string, window with 4 panes at right. Chimney on roof is capped and on peak at right. United States flag with 8 stars, on staff, flag blowing to left over roof. Below cabin large plow at left and cider barrel at right.	Pint 12	Same as No. 62	Plain lip Pontil mark	Aquamarine	Monongahela and early Pittsburgh District. Glasshouse not definitely known	V. R. No. 4 GI Extremely rare
GI-64. Jackson, three-quarter view facing left in uniform. "GENERAL JACKSON" in semicircle above bust.	American Eagle, head turned to right. Shield with 7 bars on breast, wings partly raised and right foreshortened. Thunderbolt (3 arrows) in its right talons, olive branch in left. Laurel branch in eagle's beak. Nine 6-pointed stars above eagle. Eagle stands on oval frame with inner band of 16 large pearls.	Pint 12	Horizontal beading with vertical medial rib	Plain lip Pontil mark Saucer lip	Aquamarine Green, light	Monongahela and early Pittsburgh Districts. Probably John Robinson	V. R. No. 51 GI Scarce
GI-65. Jackson, three-quarter view, facing left, in uniform. Bust and uniform differ from No. 64. "GENERAL JACKSON" in semicircle above bust.	American Eagle. Similar to No. 62. Thirteen 6-pointed stars above eagle. Eagle stands on oval frame with inner band of 17 large pearls. "J.T & C°" below oval frame.	Pint 12	Same as No. 64	Plain lip Pontil mark	Clear green bluish tone Aquamarine Yellow-amber (S.L.) Green, light Green, medium (M.B.K.) Emerald-green (S.L.)	Attributed to James Taylor & Co., Brownsville, Pa.	V. R. No. 50 GI Scarce
GI-66. Jackson. Similar to No. 64. "GENERAL JACKSON." in semicircle above bust.	American Eagle. Similar to No. 64. "J. R." in oval frame below eagle. "LAIRD. SC. PITT." in semicircle below oval frame.	Pint 12	Same as No. 64	Plain lip Pontil mark	Olive-yellow Clear glass with amethyst tint Yellow-green	John Robinson, Pittsburgh. Pa.	Not listed by Van Rensselaer Extremely rare
GI-67. Jackson, three-quarter view, facing left, in uniform, "wind-blown hair." "GENERAL JACKSON." in semicircle above bust. (Drawing by courtesy of Ernest W. Young)	American Eagle, head turned to right; wings partly raised and right foreshortened. Shield with 7 vertical bars on breast. Thunderbolt (3 arrows) in eagle's right talons, olive branch in left. Laurel spray in eagle's beak. Eight 6-pointed and one, the fourth from the right, 5-pointed stars above eagle. Eagle stands on oval frame with inner band of 16 large pearls. In oval frame below eagle, "B & M."	Pint 12	Horizontally beaded with vertical medial rib	Plain lip Pontil mark	Clear, amethyst tint Colorless	Monongahela and early Pittsburgh Districts. Probably Baker & Martin, Perryopolis, Pa.	Not listed by Van Rensselaer Extremely rare
GI-68. Jackson, three-quarter view, facing left, in uniform. "GENERAL. JACKSON." in semicircle above bust.	Conventionalized flowers, leaves and acorns forming large medallion covering entire panel. No inscription	Pint 12	Same as No. 67	Plain lip Pontil mark	Deep olive-yellow Brilliant light green Aquamarine Bluish green, light	Monongahela and early Pittsburgh Districts	V. R. No. 52 GI Very rare

GI–69. Jackson on narrow oval panel, small profile, facing right. Bust within Masonic Arch. and modified fleur-de-lis beneath bust and below arch and pillars. "ANDREW JACKSON." in semicircle around upper part of panel.

American Eagle, head turned to left. Shield with 7 bars on breast; wings partly raised and left foreshortened. Thunderbolt (2 arrows) in left talons, large olive branch in right. Seven 5-pointed stars above eagle. Below olive branch 6 cannonballs. "WHEELING." in semicircle above upper part of panel. "KNOX & McKEE" in semicircle around lower part of panel.

Smooth

Plain lip
Pontil mark

Light green, yellow tone
Very pale green

Knox & McKee, Wheeling, (W.) Va.

V. R. No. 54 GI
Extremely rare

Pint
11

GI–70. Jackson small profile, facing right. "J T" at top and "A JACKSON" in semicircle above bust. At base of flask "OHIO" in narrow frame. (Drawing by courtesy of Harry Hall White and *The Magazine* AN-TIQUES.)

Masonic Emblems. In the center Mosaic pavement with column at right and left, surmounted by archway with keystone. Within columns letter "G" above open book with square and compasses. Above arch radiant all-seeing eye. At left of archway blazing sun and beneath that the trowel, setting maul and naked heart. At right of archway quarter moon and stars. Beneath that appears the triangular form of the 7 lighted tapers, with the beehive beneath. Below pavement, crossbones and coffin with spade at right and sprig of acacia at left. For other Jackson flasks, see Nos. 31, 32, 33, 34.—Washington Group I.

Corrugated horizontally

Plain lip
Pontil mark

Aquamarine Green, light

Mantua Glass Works, Mantua, Ohio

Not listed by Van Rensselaer
Extremely rare

Pint
4

GI–63 GI–64 GI–65 GI–66 GI–67 GI–68 GI–69 GI–70

GROUP I—PORTRAIT FLASKS—ADAMS, HARRISON, JACKSON, *and* TAYLOR—*Continued*

OBVERSE	REVERSE	SIZE, FORM	EDGES	NECK, BASE	COLORS	GLASSHOUSE	NOTES, RARITY
GI–71. Taylor, small profile facing left in uniform. "ROUGH AND READY" in semicircle beneath bust.	Ringgold, small profile facing left, in identical uniform. "MAJOR" in semicircle above bust. "RING-GOLD" in semicircle beneath bust.	Pint 11	Heavy vertical ribbing (3)	Plain lip, Pontil mark *[box:]* Emerald-green, medium (S.L.), Emerald-green, deep (S.L.), Yellow-green, light translucent (C.V.)	Amethyst, Green, Pale blue, Aquamarine, Translucent pale jade, Clear, Clear with Amethyst tint, Colorless, blue tint, Bluish green, deep	Attributed by Van Rensselaer to Baltimore Glass Works	V. R. No. 99 GI Common
GI–72. Taylor. Same as No. 71	Same as No. 71	Pint 11	Smooth	Plain lip, Pontil mark	Aquamarine, Amethystine tint (S.L.)	Same as No. 71	V. R. No. 100 GI Common
GI–73. Taylor, profile facing left, in uniform. "GENL TAYLOR." in semicircle above bust.	Washington Monument without statue, Baltimore. "FELLS POINT" in semicircle above monument. "BALTo" in straight line beneath monument.	Pint 11	Vertically ribbed 3, with heavy medial rib	Plain lip, Pontil mark *[box:]* Green, brilliant (S.L.), Green, pale yellowish (M. Knapp. Jr.), Wine, deep (S.L.)	Amethyst, Aquamarine, Pale amethyst, Olive-yellow, Sapphire-blue, Deep yellowish green, Pale green, Pale greenish yellow, Grass-green (E.D.)	Baltimore, probably glassworks on Fells Point	V. R. No. 115 GI Common. Van Rensselaer also lists No. 116 G. I. a variation in this flask with Fells above the bust and Point beneath. This is found on the similar Washington-Baltimore flask, but we have never seen it on the Taylor flask.
GI–74. Taylor, profile facing right, entirely different bust in uniform. "ZACHARY TAYLOR" in semicircle above bust. "ROUGH & READY" in semicircle beneath bust.	Tall corn stalk. "CORN FOR THE WORLD" in semicircle above cornstalk.	Pint 11	Vertically ribbed 3, with heavy medial rib	Plain lip, Pontil mark *[box:]* Green, pale (E.D.), Green, light (E.D.), Yellow-green (S.L.)	Puce, Clear dark olive green, Amethyst, Cornflower-blue, Clear golden amber, Aquamarine	Baltimore Glass Works	V. R. No. 120 GI Very rare
GI–75. Taylor. Same as No. 74	Tall cornstalk different from No. 74. Inscription same as No. 74 but letters slightly different.	Pint 11	Smooth	Plain lip, Pontil mark	Clear dark olive-green, Aquamarine, Green, medium (E.D.)	Same as No. 74	Not listed by Van Rensselaer Rare
GI–76. Taylor, three-quarter view facing left, head elongated, in uniform. "ROUGH & READY." in semicircle above bust.	American Eagle, head turned to right. Shield with 5 bars on breast; wings partly raised and right foreshortened. Thunderbolt (3 arrows) in right talons. Ten large 5-pointed stars in semicircle above eagle. Eagle stands on oval frame with inner band of 19 medium-size pearls. Short diagonal ribbing beneath frame.	Pint 12	Horizontal beading, no medial rib	Plain lip, Pontil mark	Clear light green, yellow tone, Aquamarine, Green, light (S.L.)	Monongahela and early Pittsburgh District. Glasshouse unknown	V. R. No. 117 GI Extremely rare

GI-77. Taylor, three-quarter view facing right, in uniform. Bust entirely different from any other Taylor flask. Hair very fine so that head appears almost bald. Large 8-pointed star below bust. "ROUGH AND READY" in semicircle above bust.

American Eagle, head turned to left. Shield with 8 vertical and 3 horizontal bars on breast; wings partly raised and neither foreshortened, feathers appear very fine. Thunderbolt (3 arrows) in left talons, olive branch in right; branch consists of 3 leaves, the lower 2 in form of loops. Thirteen fairly large 5-pointed stars grouped above eagle. "MASTERSON" in semicircle above stars.	Quart 16	Horizontally corrugated with vertical medial rib	Plain lip Pontil mark	Deep green Aquamarine Green, pale (S.L.) Green, medium	Midwestern. Glasshouse unknown	V. R. No. 119 GI Very rare

GI-78. Taylor, profile facing left, in uniform. Bust similar to that on Dyottville Washington and Taylor flask No. 44. Four buttons on coat. For other Taylor flasks—See Nos. 17, 24, 37 through 46 and 49 through 56 in Washington Group I.

"ROBt RAMSAY WINE & LIQUOR MERCHt 281—8th AVENUE N. Y."	Pint 20	Smooth	Plain lip Pontil mark	Aquamarine	Attributed to Dyottville Glass Works	V. R. No. 9 GI Extremely rare

GI-79. Grant, very small profile bust, facing left. Laurel wreath tied with bow knotted ribbon at bottom and enclosing small scrolled medallion which contains the bust.
NOTE: Van Rensselaer lists this bust as Grant, basing the attribution on a letter from a Pittsburgh glassblower saying it was intended for Grant.

American Eagle, head facing right and wings raised about parallel with body. Eagle rests on shield with tiny stars but no bars. Thunderbolt (4 arrows) and olive branch protrude from either side of shield just above lower point. In eagle's beak long plain ribbon extending over and parallel with body and through shield beneath. Below, near base of flask, oval frame pointed at top and bottom. "UNION" in oval frame.	Pint 28	Smooth	Plain lip with laid on ring Smooth, circular depression at center	Aquamarine Amber Green, medium (R.W.) Green, light (S.L.) Yellow-green, pale (C.G.)	Unknown, probably Pittsburgh district	V. R. No. 46 GI Rare

GI-79a. Bust of "Grant" like GI-79.

Eagle and frame like GI-79 but no "UNION" in oval frame.	Pint 28	Smooth	Flat ring below plain lip Smooth, oblong depression at center	Aquamarine	Probably midwestern	Rare

GI-71   GI-73   GI-74   GI-75   GI-76   GI-77   GI-78   GI-79

GROUP I—PORTRAIT FLASKS—LAFAYETTE

OBVERSE	REVERSE	SIZE, FORM	EDGES	NECK, BASE	COLORS	GLASSHOUSE	NOTES, RARITY
GI–80. Lafayette, small profile facing right. "LA FAYETTE" in semicircle above bust. Beneath bust horizontal bar and below "T.S."	De Witt Clinton, small profile facing right. "DE WITT CLINTON" in semicircle above bust. "D" reversed. Beneath in semicircle. "COVENTRY" and below "C–T"	Pint 4	Corrugated horizontally, corrugations extend around flask at base and juncture of neck and body	Plain lip Pontil mark	Olive-amber Golden-amber (S.L.) Olive-green (E.D.)	Coventry, Conn. Thos. Stebbins	V. R. No. 57 GI Scarce
GI–81. Lafayette. Similar to No. 80. "LA FAYETTE" in semicircle above bust. Beneath bust "S & C" horizontal bar missing.	De Witt Clinton. Similar to No. 80. In semicircle above bust "DEWITT CLINTON" and beneath bust "C–T"	Half-pint 4	Same as No. 80 except 3 corrugations extend around flask at base instead of 2 as in No. 80	Plain lip Pontil mark	Deep olive-green Amber Pale olive-green Olive-amber Emerald-green (S.L.) Olive-green, medium (E.D.)	Coventry, Conn. Stebbins and Chamberlain	V. R. No. 58 GI Scarce
GI–81a. Bust of Lafayette, inscription and initials like GI–81.	Bust of DeWitt Clinton, inscription and initials like GI–81.	Half-pint 4	Like GI–81, except for 2 corrugations extending around flask at base instead of 3	Plain lip Pontil mark	Emerald-green Olive-green	Stebbins & Chamberlain, Coventry Glass Works, Coventry, Conn.	Very rare
GI–82. Similar to No. 80. "LA FAYETTE" in semicircle above bust. No letters beneath.	Same as No. 81	Half-pint slightly smaller than No. 81 4	Same as No. 81 except 2 corrugations extend around flask at juncture of neck and body	Plain lip Pontil mark	Clear light green (rare) Deep olive-green Olive-amber Amber	Coventry, Conn.	Not listed by Van Rensselaer Rare
GI–83. Lafayette, small profile facing right. "LA FAYETTE" in semicircle above bust. Beneath bust horizontal bar above letters "T. S."	Masonic Decoration—From mosaic pavement rise 2 columns surmounted by archway with keystone in center; beneath keystone, triangle, and between columns open book with square and compasses. Above arch at left blazing sun, and at right quarter moon. Thirty-two bricks in pavement.	Pint 4	Same as No. 80	Plain lip Pontil mark	Amber Olive-amber Olive-green (C.G.)	Coventry, Conn. Thos. Stebbins	NOTE: There is evidently a misprint in Van Rensselaer's list inasmuch as the description of his No. 62 (our No. 85) includes the reverse of this Masonic flask. Very rare.
GI–84. Lafayette, small profile facing right. Same as No. 83 except horizontal bar above "T. S." has short vertical ends.	Similar to No. 83 but 17 bricks in pavement. Above arch at left and at right large 6-pointed star. Below pavement large 12-pointed star.	Half-pint 4	Same as No. 80 except corrugations do not extend around flask at juncture of neck and body and only single corrugation extending around base	Plain lip Pontil mark	Deep olive-green Olive-amber Olive-green, light (C.G.)	Coventry, Conn. Thos. Stebbins	V. R. No. 59 GI Extremely rare

	Obverse description	Reverse description	Size	Ribbing	Lip	Color	Maker / Location	Notes
GI-85.	Lafayette, profile facing right. "LA FAYETTE." in semicircle above bust. Below "COVENTRY" in semicircle above "C–T". "N" omitted.	Oval frame enclosing French Liberty Cap on pole and semicircle of eleven 5-pointed stars above frame. Below frame "S & S".	Pint 5	Finely ribbed vertically. Two horizontal ribs at base which extend around flask	Plain lip Pontil mark	Pale aquamarine Amber Olive-amber	Coventry, Conn. Stebbins & Stebbins	V. R. No. 62 GI Comparatively scarce
GI-86.	Lafayette profile facing right. Similar to No. 85 except "COVENTRY" is spelled correctly with "N".	Same as No. 85 except 9 stars instead of 11.	Half-pint 5	Finely ribbed vertically 5 ribs	Plain lip Pontil mark	Olive-amber Amber Aquamarine Green, olive tone	Same as No. 85	V. R. No. 64 GI Comparatively scarce
GI-87.	Lafayette profile facing right. Inscription same as No. 86	Same as No. 86 but no stars.	Half-pint 5	Only 3 vertical ribs close together	Plain lip Pontil mark	Olive-amber	Same as No. 85	V. R. No. 65 GI Extremely rare
GI-87a.	Bust of Lafayette like GI-87; same inscription but "COVENTRY/C–T" as on GI-85 and about 1" above base.	Liberty Cap in frame; initials "S & S" more slender than on GI-87 and less heavy. No stars.	Pint 5	Same as GI-87	Plain lip Pontil mark	Olive-amber (light)	Stebbins & Stebbins, Coventry Glass Works, Coventry, Conn.	Only 1 specimen recorded (1966)
GI-88.	Lafayette profile facing right. "LA FAY-ETTE" in semicircle above bust.	Masonic decoration from mosaic pavement rise 2 columns surmounted by archway with keystone in center; beneath keystone triangle and between columns open book with square and compasses. Thirty-four bricks in pavement. No emblems outside arch.	Pint 6	Smooth with single narrow vertical rib	Plain lip Pontil mark	Pale olive-green Olive-amber Olive-green, deep	Mt. Vernon Glass Works, Vernon, N.Y.	V. R. No. 61 GI Very rare

NOTE: Van Rensselaer also lists No. 63, a similar pint flask with spelling "COVENTRY". This is apparently an error as the illustration of his No. 63 shows the spelling "COVETRY". We have never seen nor do we know of a pint flask with the correct spelling.

GI-80   GI-81   GI-82   GI-83   GI-84   GI-85   GI-86   GI-87   GI-88

GROUP I—PORTRAIT FLASKS—LAFAYETTE—*Continued*

	OBVERSE	REVERSE	SIZE, FORM	EDGES	NECK, BASE	COLORS	GLASSHOUSE	NOTES, RARITY
GI-89.	Lafayette. Similar to No. 88	Similar to No. 88 except 17 bricks in pavement and narrow bar as an innermost row.	Half-pint 6	Same as No. 88	Plain lip Pontil mark	Pale green, yellow tone Deep olive-green Clear deep green Olive-amber Pale greenish yellow	Mt. Vernon Glass Works, Vernon, N.Y.	V. R. No. 60 GI Very rare
GI-89a.	Bust of Lafayette like GI-89; semiwreath of laurel leaves from "L," below bust, to "E" at right; center leaf at top end of each branch, 5 leaves each side. Same inscription as GI-89. *See No. 1, Ill. 125.*	Thirteen 6-pointed stars forming arch over Masonic design like GI-89.	Half-pint 6	Herringbone ribbing: graduated diagonal ribs to wide center rib: obv. 41 right, 41 or 40 left; rev. 33 right, 41 left.	Plain lip Pontil mark	Colorless with amethystine tint	Probably Mt. Vernon Glass Works, Vernon, N.Y., or works obtaining molds from the same moldmakers as Mt. Vernon	Extremely rare. Only 1 specimen recorded (1965), and that was lead glass
GI-89b.	Like GI-89a, but bust of Lafayette like GI-88, larger scale. Semiwreath: center leaf at top of each branch; 7 leaves, each side.	Like GI-89a but scale larger; 34 bricks in pavement.	Pint 6	Same as GI-89a but diagonal ribs on obv. 45 at right, 35 at left; rev. 47 at right, 39 at left	Plain lip Pontil mark	Aquamarine (greenish)	Same as above	Extremely rare. Only 1 specimen recorded (1966).
GI-90.	Lafayette, large bust in uniform, nearly full face. "GENERAL LA FAYETTE" above bust.	American Eagle, head turned to left. Shield with 8 vertical bars on breast, wings partly raised. Thunderbolt (4 arrows) in left talons, olive branch in right. Eagle stands on oval frame with inner band of 21 medium-size pearls. Above eagle sunrays and "E. PLURIBUS UNUM" above rays. "T. W. D" in oval frame below eagle. On edges—"REPUBLICAN GRATITUDE" "KENSINGTON GLASS WORKS PHILADELPHIA"	Pint 11	Heavy vertical medial rib	Plain lip Pontil mark	Aquamarine Green, pale Emerald-green, light (S.L.)	Kensington Glass Works, Philadelphia, Pa.	V. R. No. 68 GI Comparatively scarce
GI-91.	Lafayette. Same as No. 90 on edges of obverse or reverse.	Same as No. 90 except "E. PLURIBUS UNUM" is omitted.	Pint 11	Heavy vertical medial rib	Plain lip Pontil mark	Aquamarine	Kensington Glass Works	V. R. No. 69 GI Comparatively scarce
GI-92.	Lafayette. Small profile in uniform facing right. Bust is within Masonic Arch and Pillars and modified fleur-de-lis below. "GENL LA FAYETTE" in semicircle around lower part of panel. The "N" is reversed.	American Eagle, head turned to left. Shield with 7 vertical bars on breast; wings partly raised and left foreshortened. Thunderbolt (2 arrows) in left talons, large olive branch in right. Six cannonballs below olive branch. Above eagle seven 5-pointed stars. "WHEELING" in semicircle above upper part of panel and "KNOX & McKEE" in semicircle around lower part of panel.	Pint 11a	Smooth	Plain lip Pontil mark	Clear glass Clear green Blue-aquamarine (S.L.) Emerald-green, light (S.L.) Moonstone	Knox & McKee, Wheeling, (W.) Va.	V. R. No. 66 GI Rare

BENJAMIN FRANKLIN

Number / Description	Inscription	Size	Base / Edge	Lip	Colors	Manufacturer	Reference
GI–93. Lafayette. Same as No. 92.	"WHEELING" and "KNOX & McKEE" omitted on the reverse.	Pint 11a	Smooth	Plain lip Pontil mark	Clear green, Green, light (S.L.), Blue-green (S.L.), Green, emerald, deep (M.B.K.)	Possibly Pugh & Teater, Moscow, Ohio. Previously attributed to Knox & McKee	V. R. No. 67 GI NOTE: Van Rensselaer lists this with cannonballs omitted, but all specimens we have seen show them. Rare
GI–94. Franklin, large three-quarter profile facing right. "BENJAMIN FRANKLIN" in semicircle above bust.	Thomas W. Dyott, large three-quarter profile facing right. "T. W. DYOTT, M.D." in semicircle above bust. On edges "WHERE LIBERTY DWELLS THERE IS MY COUNTRY" "KENSINGTON GLASS WORKS PHILADELPHIA"	Pint 11	Vertical ribs 3, heavy medial rib	Plain lip Pontil mark	Dark brownish amber, Aquamarine, Red-amber (S.L.), Green, clear (R.W.), Green, light, Emerald-green, light (S.L.), Yellow-green, light	Kensington Glass Works, Phila.	V. R. No. 38 GI Comparatively scarce
GI–95. Franklin, same as No. 94. Inscription same as No. 94	Dyott, same as No. 94. No inscription on edges	Pint 11	Same as No. 94	Plain lip Pontil mark	Aquamarine, Green, light (S.L.)	Same as No. 94	V. R. No. 39 GI Comparatively scarce
GI–96. Franklin, large three-quarter profile similar to No. 94	Dyott. Similar to No. 94. Inscription same as No. 94. On edges "ERIPUIT COELO FULMEN. SCEPTRUMQUE TYRANNIS" "KENSINGTON GLASS WORKS, PHILADELPHIA". Translated freely the inscription is "He snatches from the sky the thunderbolt, and the sceptre from tyrants."	Quart 11	Vertical ribbing different from pint	Plain lip Pontil mark	Deep green, Aquamarine, Amethyst, Clear with faint amethyst tint, Colorless, aquamarine tint (W.L.), Emerald-green, deep (S.L.)	Same as No. 94	V. R. No. 36 GI Comparatively scarce

GI–89   GI–90   GI–92

GI–94   GI–96

547

GROUP I—PORTRAIT FLASKS—LAFAYETTE—Continued

OBVERSE	REVERSE	EDGES	SIZE, FORM	NECK, BASE	COLORS	GLASSHOUSE	NOTES, RARITY
GI-97. Franklin, large three-quarter profile same as No. 96. No inscription	Franklin, same as obverse	Same as No. 96	Quart 11	Plain lip Pontil mark	Emerald-green Aquamarine Light yellow green Amber, deep Amethyst (S.L.)	Same as No. 94	V. R. No. 37 GI Scarce
GI-98. Franklin, three-quarter profile similar to No. 94. "BENJAMIN FRANKLIN" in semicircle above bust.	Dyott, three-quarter profile similar to No. 94 except head slightly smaller and slight variation in details of coat and tie. "WHEELING GLASS WORK'S" in semicircle above bust. The "S" after work is small and quite faint.	Vertically ribbed, 3, heavy medial rib	Pint 11	Plain lip Pontil mark	Clear light green Deep green Amber (S.L.) Emerald-green, deep (S.L.) Yellow-green	Wheeling Glass Works, Wheeling, (W.) Va.	V. R. No. 40 GI Extremely rare

GROUP I—JENNY LIND BOTTLES

OBVERSE	REVERSE	EDGES	SIZE, FORM	NECK, BASE	COLORS	GLASSHOUSE	NOTES, RARITY
GI-99. Jenny Lind, three-quarter view, turned to left, wearing broad plain collar or bertha. Large wreath encircling bust and above inscription "JENNY LIND". NOTE: Webster's Dictionary defines "bertha" as "a woman's shoulder cape or a decoration for bodice in imitation of short cape."	View of glasshouse with smoke issuing from chimney and with plain roof. At right of house tall tree; at left a bush or shrub. Above, inscription "GLASS WORK'S" below house "S. HUFFSEY".	Smooth	Quart 39 Calabash	Broad sloping collar Pontil mark *[boxed: Emerald-green, medium (E.D.) Emerald-green, deep (S.L.) Peacock-green (R.W.)]*	Sapphire-blue Deep blue-green Olive-yellow Deep green-yellow tone Light yellow-green Olive-green Aquamarine Amber, light (C.G.) Amber, dark (C.G.)	Made for Samuel Huffsey, Philadelphia, probably at the Isabella Glass Works, New Brooklyn, N.J. (J. E. Pfeiffer)	V. R. No. 75 GI Common
GI-99a. Bust of Jenny Lind and wreath like GI-99. No inscription	Glasshouse and inscription like GI-99.	Smooth	Quart 39	Broad sloping collar (No. 15). Type 28, pontil mark.	Aquamarine	Made for Samuel Huffsey, Philadelphia; probably a South Jersey works; possibly Isabella Glass Works	One specimen known (1965).
GI-100. Jenny Lind, three-quarter view, turned to left, wearing broad plain bertha. Large wreath encircling bust and above inscription "JENNY LIND". Bust and wreath varies slightly from No. 99.	Profile bust of Kossuth facing right. Above "KOSSUTH".	Smooth	Quart 39 Calabash	Broad sloping collar Pontil mark	Aquamarine Green, medium (G.A.)		V. R. No. 72 GI Comparatively scarce
GI-101. Jenny Lind, three-quarter view, turned to left, wearing broad plain bertha. Large wreath encircling bust and above inscription "JENNY LIND". Bust, wreath and position of inscription same as No. 99.	View of glasshouse similar to No. 99 and above "MILLFORA.G. WORK'S".	Smooth	Quart 39 Calabash	Broad sloping collar Pontil mark	Aquamarine Green, light (S.L.)	Unknown	V. R. No. 74 GI Comparatively scarce

NOTE: There seems to have been some doubt as to location of the factory making this bottle. Lippin-Barber, in *American Glassware* states: "I have not been able to locate these works. It is possible that the name may have been intended for 'Milford'." In Van Rensselaer's second book on bottles and flasks—the chapter dealing with New Jersey glasshouses—this bottle is attributed to "Millford Glass Works." The statement is made that in 1850 the plant was operated by "Lippincott, Wisham and Company." This would be the period in which the bottle was undoubtedly made.

	V. R. No.	Attribution	Color	Collar	Ribbing	Capacity
GI-102. Jenny Lind, three-quarter view, turned to left, wearing broad bertha with single band of decoration. Large wreath encircling bust and above "JENY. LIND".	V. R. No. 76 GI Comparatively scarce	Whitney, Glassboro, N.J.	Clear brilliant green / Aquamarine / Emerald-green (S.L.)	Broad sloping collar / Pontil mark	Heavy vertical ribbing, 11 ribs	Quart 40 / Calabash
View of glasshouse, smoke issuing from chimney and roof divided into squares. At right of house tall tree, at left small bush on shrub. Above house inscription "GLASS FACTORY." Large 6-pointed star just above and with lower point between the words "GLASS" and "FACTORY."						
GI-103. Jenny Lind, three-quarter view, turned to left, wearing broad decorated bertha. Large wreath encircling bust and above inscription "JENY. LIND".	V. R. No. 77 GI Comparatively scarce	Whitney, Glassboro, N.J.	Cornflower-blue / Aquamarine / Blue, light (S.L.)	Broad sloping collar / Pontil mark	Heavy vertical ribbing, 11 ribs	Quart 40 / Calabash
View of glasshouse, smoke issuing from chimney and roof divided in squares. At right of house tall tree, at left small bush or shrub.						
GI-104. Jenny Lind, three-quarter view turned to left, wearing broad plain bertha. Large wreath encircling bust and above inscription "JENY LIND". Bust slightly longer and narrower at shoulders; wreath varies slightly from Nos. 102 and 103. No period between "JENY" and "LIND".	V. R. No. 78 GI Common	Attributed to Ravenna Glassworks, Ravenna, Ohio	Sapphire-blue / Clear light blue / Bluish green / Clear brilliant amber / Yellow-green / Pale green / Aquamarine / Cornflower-blue (G.A.) [Emerald-green, medium (S.L.) / Emerald-green, deep (S.L.)]	Rounded collar / Pontil mark	Heavy vertical ribbing, 11 ribs	Quart 40 / Calabash
View of glasshouse similar to Nos. 102 and 103 but with plain roof, and no line of division in doors. Also variation in the tall tree at right and shrub at left.						
GI-105. Jenny Lind, three-quarter view turned to left, wearing broad plain bertha. Large wreath encircling bust, above inscription "JENY LIND". No period between "JENY" and "LIND". The bust is slightly longer than on No. 104, arrangement of hair different and there is a difference in the size of the bertha. There is also a variation in the wreath.	Not listed by Van Rensselaer Rare	Probably Ravenna, as the general characteristics are similar to the Jenny Lind bottles attributed to Ravenna	Aquamarine / Green, light (S.L.)	Rounded collar but not as large as in No. 104 / Pontil with disk	Heavy vertical ribbing, 11 ribs	Quart 40 / Calabash
View of glasshouse which shows variation in design from that on No. 104. The chimneys are quite different and taller and the smoke from the tall central chimney goes almost straight upward instead of turning downward as in all other Jenny Lind bottles with view of glasshouse. The tall tree at right and small shrub at left are also different.						

GI-98 GI-99 GI-100

GI-101 GI-102 GI-103 GI-104 GI-105

NOTES, RARITY	GLASSHOUSE	COLORS	NECK, BASE	EDGES	SIZE, FORM	REVERSE	OBVERSE
Not listed by Van Rensselaer Extremely rare	Unknown	Aquamarine Emerald-green (S.L.)	Broad sloping collar Pontil mark	Heavy vertical ribbing, 11 ribs	Quart 40 Calabash	Large tree in foliage with clusters of small fruit, globular in shape. Beneath tree at left, 7 similar fallen fruits and 5 at right.	**GI-106.** Jenny Lind, three-quarter view turned to left and wearing broad plain bertha. Large wreath encircling bust and above inscription "JENNY LIND" which is angled instead of rounded.
V. R. No. 73 GI Common	Fislerville Glass Works, Fislerville, N.J. The name Fislerville was changed in 1867 to Clayton.	Clear amber Clear yellowish green Clear deep green Bluish green Aquamarine	Broad sloping collar Smooth with circular depression. Also pontil mark	Vertically fluted edges	Quart 38 Calabash	View of glasshouse entirely different from that on any other Jenny Lind calabash bottles. Smoke from chimney blows to left instead of right. Beneath glasshouse is a row of barrels, kegs, and boxes with faintly outlined decorative flourishes beneath. Above glasshouse inscription "FISLERVILLE GLASS WORKS" with faintly outlined ribbon shaped frames following the curve of the inscription.	**GI-107.** Jenny Lind, three-quarter view, turned to left, wearing broad plain bertha. The bust is not within a wreath and is quite different from that on any other Jenny Lind calabash bottles. Arrangement of hair different, neck more slender and lower cut bodice. At lower edge of bust, very fine scalloping, and small wreath below. Above bust inscription "JENNY LIND" within faintly outlined frame following the curve of the inscription.

NOTE: It is customary to speak of the Jenny Lind Calabash bottles as of quart size. As a matter of fact, all varieties hold considerably more than a quart. There is probably some slight variation in capacity between these bottles of the same variety but the following measures taken from examples in our own collection may be interesting. It is to be noted that in each case dry measure is used, measuring capacity of the bottle to a point about half the length of the long neck:

No. 99—Jenny Lind, Huffsey bottle, 3 full pints.
No. 100—Jenny Lind, Kossuth, a trifle less than 3 pints.
No. 101—Jenny Lind, Millfora, a trifle less than 3 pints.
No. 102—Jenny Lind with star, a trifle less than 3 pints.
No. 103—Jenny Lind, Whitney Glass Works, full 3 pints.
No. 104—Jenny Lind, Ravenna type, a trifle less than 3 pints.
No. 105—Variant of No. 104, a trifle less than 3 pints.
No. 106—Jenny Lind with tree, a trifle less than 3 pints.
No. 107—Fislerville, quart and an eighth.
No. 107A—Counterfeit of Fislerville type, exactly 1 quart.

Nos. 99, 100, and 101 are characterized by the smooth edges. Nos. 102, 103, 104, 105, and 106 have heavy vertical ribbing on the edges and similar short ribbing below the design on each side. They all have long octagonally paneled necks and, with the exception of the Fislerville, a collar which preserves the octagonal effect at juncture of neck and body. On the Fislerville bottle the edges have vertical fluting and the neck terminates in deep scalloping.

The necks of Nos. 99, 100, 101, and 106 are longer than on the other varieties, the height of the first 3 being from $10\frac{1}{4}$ to $10\frac{7}{8}$ inches. The Fislerville and Ravennas are the shortest, ranging from $9\frac{1}{4}$ to $9\frac{1}{2}$ inches in height. The bases usually have pontil marks, sometimes quite deeply hollowed. The Fislerville bottles frequently have a smooth base with circular depression at center and no pontil mark as snap case was used to hold the bottle. On the base of the Ravenna bottles, black or reddish coloration is frequently present due to the method of heating punty irons and using them without dipping the end of the punty into glass. The cause of the black color was due to the oxide from the punty rod being in a low state of oxidation or what is called ferrous state. Where a red coloration is present then the black oxide has turned through oxidation into the ferric or red oxide.

NOTES, RARITY	GLASSHOUSE	COLORS	NECK, BASE	EDGES	SIZE, FORM	REVERSE	OBVERSE
V. R. No. 79 GI Scarce	Attributed to M'Carty & Torreyson, Wellsburg, W. Va.	Aquamarine Green-aquamarine, strong (E.D.)	Plain lip Pontil mark	Paneled vertically	Pint 33	Same as obverse	**GI-108.** Jenny Lind, three-quarter view, turned to left, wearing broad plain bertha. Beneath large Lyre with 3 strings. Each side of flask forms a large panel slightly recessed at the top, and following the shape of the flask which narrows at base and contracts with the narrow vertical panels on edges to form a flaring 10-sided scalloped base or foot.
Not listed by Van Rensselaer in quart size Rare	Same as No. 108	Aquamarine Green, light (S.L.)	Plain lip Pontil mark	Paneled vertically	Quart 33	Same as obverse	**GI-109.** Similar to No. 108.
V. R. No. 80 GI Rare	Same as No. 108	Aquamarine	Plain lip Pontil mark	Paneled vertically	Quart 33	Same as obverse	**GI-110.** Bust and Lyre similar to No. 109. Beneath bust a row of loop shaped ornaments and on the vertically paneled edge directly adjoining each side is a vinelike ornamentation running the length of the panel.

NOTE: Rhea Mansfield Knittle in her *Early American Glass* gives the name as M'Carty & Torreyson. Van Rensselaer lists it as McCarthy & Torreyson. On the marked flasks, scroll group IX Nos. 48, 49, 50 which are similar in shape to the above three Jenny Lind bottles the name reads M'Carty & Torreyson.

GI–107a. Counterfeit Fislerville bottle.
NOTE: 107A Counterfeit Fislerville bottle, quart. The accompanying line drawing shows the counterfeit of the Fislerville Jenny Lind bottle. These first appeared in the late 1920s or early 1930s. It is a relatively poor imitation. There is a decided difference between these and the originals. There is a slight variation in the letters of the inscription on each side. The bust is quite different. On the reproduction, the bust is broader being about 4.6 millimeters as compared with 4.2 just above the top ends of the bertha. The chin has a decidedly pointed effect and the bertha is much narrower. The wreath beneath the bust is also quite different. There is a decided variation in the lower door and the windows of the glasshouse, which are much larger in the counterfeit; also the barrels and kegs beneath the glasshouse are entirely different and the decorative flourishes beneath are missing. The reproductions originally appeared in aquamarine color. A few years later specimens in amethyst, blue, emerald green, and amberina appeared on the market.

OTHER PORTRAITS

GI–111. Kossuth, small profile with heavy beard, facing right. "BRIDGETON." At right of bust in semicircle and "NEW JERSEY" at left.

GI–112. Kossuth, full-faced bust in uniform with high hat and plume. Bust rests between furled flags, two on either side, lower left flag showing seven 5-pointed stars. "LOUIS KOSSUTH" in semicircle above bust.

Sloop sailing left with flying pennant.	Pint 11	Vertical ribs 3, heavy medial rib	Plain lip Pontil mark	Clear green Aquamarine Emerald-green, light (S.L.)	Bridgeton Glass Works, Bridgeton, N.J.	V. R. No. 104 GI Scarce
Large frigate sailing left, flags flying, large wheel on side of vessel and water beneath. Beneath water in three lines. "U.S. STEAM FRIGATE MISSISSIPPI S. HUFFSEY" On upper arc of wheel on frigate "S. HUFFSEY" and beneath markings possibly intended for letters too indistinct to be determined on any specimens we have examined. On base "PH. DOFLEIN MOULD MAKER NTH.5! St 84."	Quart 38 Calabash	Fluted edges 4	Sloping collar Pontil mark	Dark olive-green (black) Emerald-green Yellow-green Aquamarine Golden amber, light (S.L.) Golden amber, deep (S.L.) Amber, brilliant Amber, greenish tone, light Amber, dark (C.G.)	Made for Samuel Huffsey, Philadelphia, probably in a New Jersey glassworks. (J. E. Pfeiffer)	V. R. No. 56 GI Comparatively scarce

GI–106   GI–107   GI–107a   GI–108   GI–109   GI–110   GI–111   GI–112   GI–112 BASE

GROUP I—OTHER PORTRAITS—*Continued*

OBVERSE	REVERSE	SIZE, FORM	EDGES	NECK, BASE	COLORS	GLASSHOUSE	NOTES, RARITY
GI-112a. Bust of Kossuth, flags, and inscription like GI-112.	Frigate *Mississippi* like GI-112; "S. HUFFSEY" *not* in inscription; periods after "U.S." very faint.	Quart 39	Same as GI-112	Broad sloping collar (No. 15) Type 30; inscription like GI-112 Pontil mark	Aquamarine Colorless with aquamarine tint	Unknown. Mold by Doflein, Philadelphia, Pa.	Possibly the original mold and "S. HUFFSEY" added for GI-112. Extremely rare. Two specimens recorded (1965).
GI-113. Kossuth, small profile bust facing right, military collar showing. "KOSSUTH" in slight curve above bust. NOTE: For other Kossuth bottles see Jenny Lind Bottle in Group I—No. 100.	Tall tree in foliage.	Quart 39 Calabash	Smooth	Sloping collar with beveled ring Pontil mark Smooth with deep depression	Olive-yellow Aquamarine Yellowish green Brown-amber (C.G.) Blue-green (G.A.) Green, medium (R.W.) Green, light (R.W.)	Unknown	V. R. No. 55 GI Common
GI-114. Draped bust in classical mode facing right.	Draped bust in classical mode facing left. That facing right has been called Byron and the one facing right Scott, but we do not know the basis for this attribution.	Half-pint 11	Vertical ribs 3, heavy medial rib	Plain lip Pontil mark — Emerald-green (S.L.)	Olive-green Olive-amber Amber Black (deep olive-amber) Black (deep olive-green)	Unknown	V. R. No. 17 GVI Common
GI-115. Unidentified bust facing right. "WHEAT, PRICE & CO, WHEELING, VA." around bust, "N" in WHEELING reversed.	View of glasshouse with tall chimney from which smoke is issuing. "FAIR VIEW" at top. "WORKS" beneath glasshouse.	Pint 16	Horizontally corrugated with vertical medial rib	Plain lip Pontil mark	Brilliant olive-yellow Light bluish green Green, medium Yellow-green	Wheat, Price & Co. Wheeling, (W.) Va.	V. R. No. 124 GVI Very rare
GI-116. Unidentified bust, features and bushy hair, entirely different from No. 115. Inscription same	Similar to No. 115. Same inscription.	Pint 16	Same as No. 115	Plain lip Pontil mark	Yellowish green Bluish green	Wheat, Price & Co. Wheeling, (W.) Va.	Not listed by Van Rensselaer Very rare
GI-117. Columbia with Liberty Cap facing left. "KENSINGTON" in narrow curved frame below oval panel containing bust. Thirteen small 6-pointed stars surrounding bust, 10 short graduated vertical ribs at bottom of flask.	Large American Eagle, head turned to right. Shield with 10 vertical and 2 horizontal bars on breast, wings partly raised and right foreshortened. Thunderbolt (3 arrows) with feathered ends showing in its right talons, olive branch in left. Ten short graduated vertical ribs at bottom of flask. "UNION. C$\underline{\underline{o}}$". in narrow curved frame below oval panel containing eagle.	Pint 9	Single broad vertical rib	Plain lip Pontil mark	Aquamarine Sapphire-blue, deep (S.L.)	Kensington, Union Co.	V. R. No. 21 GI Comparatively scarce
GI-117a. Similar to No. 117 but flask a little smaller	Similar to No. 117	12 oz. 9	Single broad vertical rib	Like No. 117	Blue (deep)	Kensington, Union Co.	Reported by L. A. McCullough of Owens-Illinois. Collection of the Toledo Art Museum. Unique, as of 1976

GI–118. Columbia with Liberty Cap facing left. Features and arrangement of hair differing slightly from No. 117. "KENSINGTON" in narrow curved frame below oval panel containing bust. Thirteen small 6-pointed stars surrounding bust. 10 short graduated vertical ribs at bottom of flask.

Large American Eagle, head turned to left. Shield with 10 vertical and 3 horizontal bars on breast; wings partly raised and left foreshortened. Thunderbolt (3 arrows) in its left talons, large olive branch in right. Ten short graduated vertical ribs at bottom of flask. "UNION. C⁰." in narrow curved frame below oval panel containing eagle.

Half-pint
9

Single broad vertical rib
Smooth

Tooled lip
Plain lip
Pontil mark

Yellow-green
Aquamarine
Clear shading to purple
Clear shading to blue
Clear amethystine
Clear
Cobalt-blue
Green, clear
Green, pale (S.L.)
Green, tinge (C.G.)

> Yellow-green, tinge (C.G.)
> Yellow-green, pale (E.D.)
> Lilac, pale (S.L.)

Kensington, Union Co.

V. R. No. 24 GI
Very rare

GI–119. Columbia with Liberty Cap facing left. Thirteen small 6-pointed stars surrounding bust. 10 short graduated vertical ribs at bottom of flask. No inscription

Similar to No. 117. No inscription

Pint
9

Single broad vertical rib

Plain lip
Pontil mark

Cobalt-blue
Moss-green, shading to amber at neck
Colorless (O.S.)

Probably Kensington, Union Co.

V. R. No. 23 GI
Extremely rare

GI–120. Columbia with Liberty Cap facing left. Bust, Liberty Cap and arrangement of hair quite different from Nos. 117 and 118. "ASHTON" in narrow curved frame below oval panel containing bust. Thirteen larger 6-pointed stars surrounding bust. 10 short graduated vertical ribs at bottom of flask.

American Eagle, head turned to right similar to No. 117 except thunderbolt and olive branch differing slightly. Ten short graduated vertical ribs at bottom of flask. "HOUGH &" in narrow curved frame below oval panel containing eagle.

Pint
9

Single broad vertical rib

Plain lip
Pontil mark

Aquamarine

Probably Kensington, Union Co.

V. R. No. 22 GI
Extremely rare

GI–113   GI–114   GI–115   GI–116   GI–117   GI–118   GI–119   GI–120

GROUP I—OTHER PORTRAITS—*Continued*

OBVERSE	REVERSE	SIZE, FORM	EDGES	NECK, BASE	COLORS	GLASSHOUSE	NOTES, RARITY
GI–121. Columbia with Liberty Cap facing left. Similar to No. 117. Thirteen small 6-pointed stars in semicircle above bust.	Large American Eagle similar to No. 117 except 9 vertical bars on shield instead of I0. "B & W'" in script beneath eagle.	Pint Similar to 12	Vertical ribs 3, medial rib heavy	Plain lip Pontil mark Rolled-over sloping collar	Olive-yellow Pale yellow-green Aquamarine Peacock-blue (Two specimens known, each with rolled-over collar. One imperfect. Perfect one disappeared from the McKearin Collection in 1960.) Sapphire-blue, deep (S.L.) Emerald-green, pale (S.L.)	Unknown	V. R. No. 19 GI Comparatively scarce
GI–122. Columbia with Liberty Cap facing left. Similar to No. 121. Thirteen small 6-pointed stars in semicircle above bust.	Large American Eagle, head turned to right similar to No. 121, 9 vertical bars on shield. No inscription	Pint Similar to 12	Same as No. 121	Plain lip Pontil mark	Clear	Unknown	V. R. No. 20 GI Extremely rare

NOTE: On each of the above 6 Columbia flasks, the drapery on the bust shows the small round fibula which varies in detail on the different flasks.

For Portraits in Group I of—
De Witt Clinton—See Nos. 80, 81, 82—Lafayette Flasks.
Major Ringgold—See Nos. 71, 72—Taylor Flasks.
Thomas W. Dyott—See Nos. 94, 95, 96, 98—Benjamin Franklin.
Henry Clay—See Nos. 22, 23, 25—Washington and comments.
John Tyler—See No. 116 and comments.

NOTE: Re GI–117 and GI–119, Columbia–Eagle flasks; from comparison and measurements by Kenneth M. Wilson: "Conclusion: Both flasks were blown in the same mold; the name Kensington Union Co. was removed from the mold, apparently by chiseling metal away from each curved panel to a depth sufficient to eliminate the legend. Traces of them still remain, but are difficult to detect, e.g., lower end of "K" where it touches the oval surrounding Columbia."

NOTE: Van Rensselaer in describing his No. 20 states no stars. However, while stars are faint they definitely appear in each of the few specimens of this flask known to us, including the one from which Van Rensselaer's listing was taken.

OBVERSE	REVERSE	SIZE, FORM	EDGES	NECK, BASE	COLORS	GLASSHOUSE	NOTES, RARITY
GI–123. Portrait medallion: Grover Cleveland, large head, nearly three-quarter view, facing left; collar, bow tie, part of coat lapels and shirt.	Plain	Pint 32	Wide flat band	Double round collar Smooth; "A. C. CO." in concave disk	Blue-aquamarine	Unknown	Probably brought out during the 1884 presidential campaigns Scarce
GI–123a. Profile bust of Grover Cleveland, at left, facing one of Adlai E. Stevenson, on long rectangular panel with narrow molding. Above busts: linear ornament and inscription "OUR CHOICE" in arc. Below busts: linear ornament and inscription in 3 lines, "CLEVE & STEVE/NOVEMBER 8th 92/MARCH 4th 93."	Crowing cock, facing left, in high relief, on barrel staves (broad ribs) between triads of hoops (ribs); single hoop (rib) about ½" below shoulder and above base.	Pint Elliptical with flat side on obverse	Continuation of staves and hoops	Narrow round collar, lower bevel (20a) Smooth; concave disk at center	Aquamarine, (greenish) Colorless	Unknown	V. R. No. 17 GI Scarce

GI–124. Same design as GI–123a, on smaller scale; bust differs in rendering, longer faces, more hair. Same inscriptions

GI–125. "COIN" panel with milled edge, profile bust of William McKinley, encircled by inscription; "SOUND MONEY AND PROTECTION" separated by 5-pointed star, at each end, from "McKINLEY & HOBART" at bottom.

GI–126. "COIN" panel with milled edge, bust of William Jennings Bryan, three-quarter view, encircled by inscription "IN SILVER WE TRUST" separated by five 5-pointed stars, at each end, from "BRYAN 1896 SEWALL" at bottom.

Same design as GI–123a, cock smaller, facing right.	Same as GI–123a	Half-pint Same as GI–123a	Flat sloping collar, lower bevel Same as GI–123a	Amber (light shaded) Amethystine	Unknown	Not listed by Van Rensselaer In his Group I, Nos. 16 & 18 are Cleveland flasks not charted here nor seen by us. Scarce

Inscription: "IN GOLD WE TRUST" in arc at top above large honey bee in center; "1896" at bottom.	Milled	Half-pint U.S. coin; small elliptical base	Narrow round collar, lower bevel (20a) Smooth	Amber (shaded) Colorless	Unknown	V. R. GI–85. In his Group I he lists 2 McKinley flasks not charted here nor seen by us. Scarce

American eagle in center, wings spread and raised, olive branch and thunderbolt (3 arrows) in talons; within laurel wreath terminating below wing tips. Inscriptions: "WE SHALL VOTE" (small letters), above head and between wings; in semicircle, (left below wing) "UNITED", "DEMOCRATIC" (above eagle; between wing tips); "TICKET" (right, below wing); (at bottom, below wreath) "16 to 1". 5-pointed star at each side, midway between inscription and numerals.	Milled	Half-pint Silver dollar, small elliptical base	Narrow round collar, lower bevel (20a) Smooth	Amber (shaded) Colorless	Unknown	V. R. GI–6 Scarce

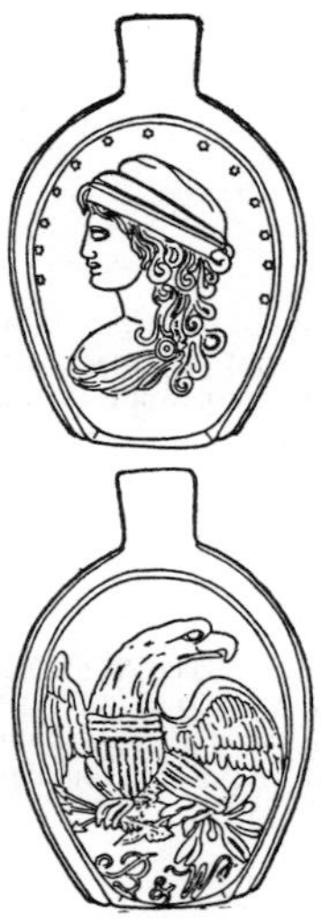

GI–121

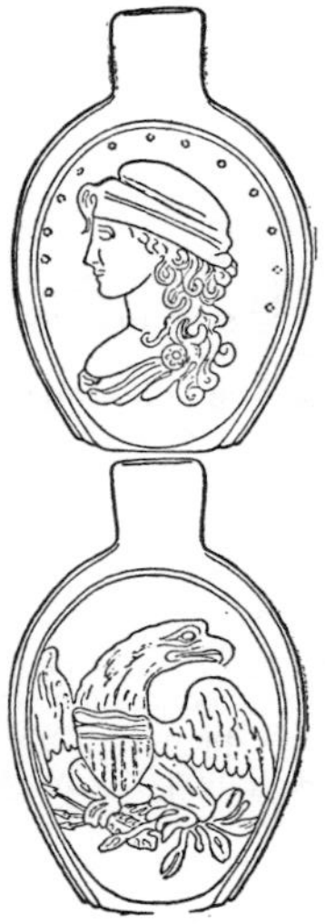

GI–122

GI–123

GI–123a

REV.

OBV.

CROSS SECT.

GI–124

DETAIL OF REV.

GI–125

GI–126

OBVERSE	REVERSE	SIZE, FORM	EDGES	NECK, BASE	COLORS	GLASSHOUSE	NOTES, RARITY
GI-127. Christopher Columbus, front-view bust, holding globe in hands, on oval panel with wide plain molding within wide frame of 6 rows of honeycomb diaper. Inscription: "COLUMBUS" in arc below bust.	Plain oval label-panel within frame like obverse.	Half-pint Flat oval, small elliptical base	Narrow, smooth between honeycomb extending from obverse and reverse	Melon-ribbed bulge between narrow collar at base of neck and threaded top with plain lip Smooth	Colorless	Unknown	V. R. GVI-9 Scarce
GI-128. Christopher Columbus, bust, nearly full face, wearing broad ripple-brimmed hat. Inscriptions: "COLUMBIAN EXPOSITION" in semicircle above bust; below bust, in 2 lines: "1893/A.E.M. BROS. & CO."	Inscription in 4 lines: "PENNSYL-VANIA (in arc)/PURE RYE/BAKER/WHISKEY (inverted arc)."	Pint Broad thin flattened body, ends curving at shoulder and bottom, ovoid base	Smooth	Variant of 19 Smooth	Amber	Unidentified	Scarce
GI-129. Franklin Roosevelt, full-face bust above American Eagle with large, crested head to right; spread wings raised upward, shield (4 bars) on breast, short, spread tail, widespread legs, thunderbolt (5 feathered arrows) in left talon, olive branch in right; in beak, end of pennant inscribed "E. PLURIBUS UNUM". At bottom left, "19"; at right, "36". Panel bordered by tapering ribs.	"TVA" at top above large hand clenching "lightning" (electricity); at lower center T.V.A. dam; 1936 at bottom. Panel bordered by tapering ribs.	Quart 39	Ribbed (9 ribs in all from panel to panel)	No. 15; 8 flat panels extending upward for about 2½" from collar-rib at base of neck Circular; broad flat rim	Aquamarine, (pale) around concave center with large eyelike motif at center	T.C. Wheaton Co. Millville, N.J.; special order for James S. Hall, M.D.	Commemorating the Tennessee Valley Authority. Designed by James S. Hall, M.D., bottle collector of Clinton, Tenn. Dr. Hall's order for 816 of the bottles was completed in the fall of 1936.
GI-130. Similar to GI-69 and GI-92, but head slightly narrower and longer; "HENRY" at upper left and "CLAY" at upper right of panel.	Similar to GI-69 & GI-92 but no cannonballs below olive branch "WHEELING" in semicircle above panel. "KNOX &" at lower left and "M'KEE" at lower right of panel.	Pint 11	Smooth	Plain lip Pontil mark	Emerald-green, rich	Knox & McKee, Virginia Green Glass Works, Wheeling. [W] Va.	Only known specimen owned by Robert H. Wise
GI-131. Taylor, small profile facing left; in uniform. Similar to GI-71 but bust more elongated. "ROUGH AND READY" in semiellipse below bust.	Ringgold, small profile facing left, in uniform similar to Taylor's. Similar to GI-71 but bust more elongated. "MAJOR" in semicircle above but with the "J" directly above center top of Ringgold's head instead of slightly to right of center as on GI-71. "RINGGOLD" in semicircle below bust, with the "R" a little higher on the left than on GI-71.	Pint 11 (No incurve near base as in GI-71. Entire flask larger.)	Heavy vertical ribbing (3)	Plain lip Pontil mark	Lavender-gray; translucent	Not known	Unique as of 1975. Discovered by Jack Whistance.

GROUP II—AMERICAN EAGLE FLASKS

Midwestern Area, including Monongahela and Early Pittsburgh district, Ohio, Kentucky, and Virginia (part now West Virginia)

NOTE: GII–1a, 4a, 11a, 15a, 17a, 32a, 63a, 72a & b, 73a, and 76a are charted as variants; they did not appear in Group II of *American Glass*, as they were unknown in 1941 and not listed by Van Rensselaer. Flasks from GII–78 on came out mainly ca. 1850 to 1875. As in *American Glass*, the direction of the eagle's head on these is given as the viewer sees it, but the description of the eagle's wings, etc., is from the eagle's own right and left. On GII–78 through 115, wing feathers are indicated by ribs, but head, neck, and body are not feathered, except slightly on GII–92. The vertical mold seam on the center edge of flasks with "smooth" edges is sometimes pronounced enough to be called a fine vertical rib, but it does not represent a decorative element in the mold. Unless otherwise indicated, flasks in all groups have a mold seam across the base.

GII–1. Designs on oval panels. American Eagle, head turned to right; wings partly raised and right foreshortened. Large shield with 6 bars on breast, tail feathers show below shield at right; thunderbolt (3 arrows) in its right talons. Eagle stands on oval frame with inner band of tiny pearl beads, 28 in number. Above eagle 10 small 5-pointed stars in semicircular formation and 1 faint star just beneath making 11 in all. At right of eagle's left wing is tiny circular dot. Just below oval frame short diagonal ribbing to left and right.

Similar to obverse except stars appear slightly larger.

Pint
12

Horizontally beaded with narrow vertical medial rib

Plain lip
Pontil mark

Yellowish olive-green
Dark olive-green
Light yellow-green
Aquamarine
Blue, pale (S.L.)
Green, aquamarine (E.D.)
Green, bluish (S.L.)
Green, medium (R.W.)
Olive-green, yellowish, light
Olive-green, yellowish, deep

Monongahela and Early Pittsburgh district, particular glasshouse unknown

V. R. No. 9 D1; GII Scarce

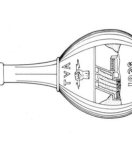

GI–127 OBV.

GI–128

GI–129

GII–1

SIDE

GROUP II—AMERICAN EAGLE FLASKS—*Continued*

OBVERSE	REVERSE	SIZE, FORM	EDGES	NECK, BASE	COLORS	GLASSHOUSE	NOTES, RARITY
GII–1a. Similar to GII–1; eagle's beak slightly wider open; second and third stars, 6-pointed; no dot (faint star) below stars at eagle's left.	Similar to GII–1	Pint 12	Same as GII–1	Plain lip Pontil mark	Golden amber	Monongahela and Early Pittsburgh district	Reported by J. Robert Rodgers. Extremely rare
GII–2. Similar to No. 1 except tail feathers do not show below shield at right, oval frame with inner band of larger pearl beads, 16 in number. Above eagle 10 stars.	Similar to obverse except only 9 stars above eagle, instead of 10.	Pint 12	Horizontally beaded with narrow vertical medial rib	Plain lip Pontil mark	Pale yellow-green Aquamarine Green-aquamarine (E.D.) Blue-green (S.L.)	Same as No. 1	V. R. No. 10 D1; GII Scarce
GII–3. Similar to No. 2 except nine 6-pointed stars above eagle, and olive branch which shows faintly in eagle's beak shows faintly. Laurel branch in eagle's left talons. In the oval frame beneath eagle is a vertical ornament which may be an accidental mark in the mold.	Similar to obverse except 8 of the stars are 5-pointed and one, the center star, is 6-pointed.	Pint 12	Same as No. 1	Plain lip Pontil mark	Aquamarine Deep golden yellow Green, medium (M.B.K.)	Same as No. 1	May be V. R. No. 7 D1; GII Rare
GII–4. Similar to No. 3 except 10 larger 6-pointed stars above eagle. Oval frame slightly narrower and inner band consists of 13 large pearls. No laurel branch in eagle's beak.	Similar to obverse	Pint 12	Same as No. 1	Plain lip Pontil mark	Pale yellowish green Aquamarine (C.G.) Green, pale (S.L.)	Same as No. 1	Not listed by Van Rensselaer Rare
GII–4a. Similar to GII–4; first star at left 7-pointed instead of 6-pointed.	Similar to GII–4; eighth star from left 6-pointed; others, 5-pointed.	Pint 12	Same as GII–4	Plain lip Pontil mark	Green (light)	Same as above	Same as above
GII–5. Similar to No. 1 except 11 large pearls above eagle and in line with the pearls at left a tiny circular dot just above the top of right wing of the eagle.	Similar to obverse, Eagle's tail feathers showing below shield at right, 10 large pearls in semicircle above eagle.	Pint 12	Horizontally beaded with narrow vertical medial rib	Plain lip Pontil mark	Deep yellow-green with olive tint	Same as No. 1	Not listed by Van Rensselaer Very rare
GII–6. American Eagle similar to No. 1 but instead of small stars, 9 medium-sized pearls in high relief, in semicircular formation and 1 rather faint irregular star immediately below fourth pearl from left.	Large cornucopia coiled to left and filled with produce.	Pint 12	Same as No. 1	Plain lip Pontil mark	Aquamarine Green, light (S.L.) Emerald-green, deep (S.L.)	Same as No. 1	V. R. No. 13. GIII Comparatively scarce

NOTE: There is a similarity in the beaded edges and the eagle design between these 6 flasks, GII–1 through 6, and the Washington Eagle flasks GI–1 through 9, the Adams flask GI–62, Jackson flasks GI–64 through 67, and the Taylor "Rough & Ready" flask GI–76. The designs may have been cut by the same moldmaker.

558

GII–7. Designs on oval panels. American Eagle, head turned to left; shield with 5 vertical bars on breast; wings partly raised. Thunderbolt (3 arrows) in eagle's left talons, small olive branch in right. Six small stars above eagle. Below eagle tiny oval frame.

Pint 17

Large circular sunburst with 32 rays, each alternating ray tapering to heavy rounded end.

Plain lip
Pontil mark

Emerald-green
Pale yellow-green
Light green
Dark olive-amber (black)
Olive-yellow
Clear amber
Golden amber (S.L.)
Blue, light (S.L.)
Green, deep

> Emerald-green, deep (S.L.)
> Olive-green, yellowish, light
> Olive-green, yellowish, dark

Large circular beading with heavy vertical medial rib

Same as No. 1

V. R. No. 2 D6; GIII
Rare

GII–8. Design on large oval panel. American Eagle, head turned to left; shield with 5 vertical and 1 horizontal bar on breast; wings partly raised. Feathers on eagle very fine and above shield are indicated by tiny dots. Thunderbolt (3 arrows) in eagle's left talons, small olive branch in right. Fourteen small stars (circular with indented points) above eagle in semicircular row of 11 and 3 above that at center. Below eagle tiny oval frame, faintly beaded, containing narrow rib in center.

Pint 17

Large scroll medallion covering entire panel and in center upright branch with 11 leaves — possibly intended as olive branch. Large convex pearl ornament at top of panel.

Plain lip
Pontil mark

Brilliant olive-yellow
Clear with pale violet tint
Moonstone
Reddish amber (S.L.)
Emerald-green, light (S.L.)

> Yellow-green, pale (S.L.)
> Lavender, pale (S.L.)
> Yellow, pale (S.L.)

Same as above

Same as No. 1

V. R. No. 1 D6; GII
Very rare

GII–9. Designs on large oval panels. American Eagle, head turned to left; shield with 5 vertical and 1 horizontal bars on breast; wings partly raised. Feathers on eagle very fine and on upper part of wings and above shield indicated by tiny dots. Thunderbolt (3 arrows) in eagle's left talons and small olive branch in right. Six tiny stars above eagle. Below eagle tiny oval frame.

Pint 17

American Eagle in flight, head down and turned to left. Grasped in eagle's beak is a serpent with its neck and head in loop below and remainder of body curled upward, over eagle, across left wing and straight down.

Plain lip
Pontil mark

Pale yellowish green
Clear green
Clear with amethyst tint
Colorless, blue tint

Large circular beading with heavy vertical medial rib

Monongahela and Early Pittsburgh district, particular glasshouse unknown

V. R. No. 14 D2; GII
Very rare

GII–10. Designs on oval panels. Large American Eagle, head turned to left; shield with 6 vertical bars on breast; wings partly raised and left foreshortened. Thunderbolt (3 arrows) in its right talons, olive branch in left. Eagle stands on oval frame containing the word "GLASS". Above eagle in semicircle "W. IHMSEN'S."

Pint 11

Large Sheaf of Rye and directly beneath crossed pitchfork and rake. At left of fork, sickle and beneath at left scythe and at right plow. In semicircle above sheaf "AGRICULTURE".

Plain lip
Pontil mark

Aquamarine
Clear brilliant green
Green, pale (E.D.)
Green, light

Vertically ribbed

W. Ihmsen, Williamsport Glass Works

V. R. No. 82. GI
Rare

GII–2 GII–3 GII–4 GII–5 GII–6 GII–7 GII–8 GII–9 GII–10

GROUP II—AMERICAN EAGLE FLASKS—*Continued*

OBVERSE	REVERSE	SIZE, FORM	EDGES	NECK, BASE	COLORS	GLASSHOUSE	NOTES, RARITY
GII–11. Designs on oval panels. American Eagle, head turned to left; abnormally large beak; wings partly raised and left foreshortened. No shield on breast. Thunderbolt (3 arrows) in left talons, olive branch in right. The stem of the branch extends down into the oval frame. Eagle stands on oval frame with inner band of 18 tiny stars in semicircle above eagle.	Inverted cornucopia, coiled to left and filled with produce. Cornucopia has 12 ribs.	Half-pint 12	Horizontally beaded with vertical medial rib	Plain lip Pontil mark / Olive-green (R.W.) Green, light (R.W.)	Deep amber Olive-yellow Aquamarine Clear, faint amethyst tone Yellow-green Golden amber, deep (S.L.) Emerald-green, light (S.L.)	Monongahela and Early Pittsburgh district, particular glasshouse unknown	V. R. No. 18 GIII Scarce
GII–11a. Similar to GII–11.	Similar to GII–11	Half-pint 12	Fine mold seam between horizontal beading; beads about 1/16" longer than on GI–11	Plain lip Keyed as on GIX–10; pontil mark	Yellow-green	Same as above	Reported by Richard H. Wood Extremely rare
GII–12. Designs on oval panels. Similar to No. 11 but letters "W.C" in oval frame below eagle.	Similar to No. 11 but slight variation in produce.	Half-pint 12	Horizontally beaded with vertical medial rib	Plain lip Pontil mark	Aquamarine Pale golden amber	Monongahela and Early Pittsburgh district, particular glasshouse unknown	V. R. No. 20. GIII Very rare
GII–13. American Eagle, head turned to left; abnormally large beak; wings partly raised and left slightly foreshortened. No shield on breast. Arrangement of feathers and tail entirely different from No. 11. Thunderbolt (4 arrows) in its right talons, olive branch in left. Eagle above an oval frame broken at base of flask and containing inner band of 10 large pearls. In large semicircle surrounding eagle are 18 stars, circular shape with indented points.	Broader inverted cornucopia, coiled to left and filled with produce. Cornucopia has seven ribs. Produce quite different from No. 11.	Half-pint 12	Same as above	Plain lip Pontil mark	Aquamarine Green, pale (S.L.) Green, medium (R. Wise)	Same as above	V. R. No. 19. GIII Very rare
GII–14. Designs on oval panels. Similar to No. 11 except no inner band of pearl beading in oval frame.	Inverted cornucopia, coiled to left, similar to No. 11 except variation in produce.	Half-pint Similar to F. 12	Smooth	Plain lip Pontil mark / Emerald-green, light (S.L.)	Olive-yellow Bluish aquamarine Green, light (E.D.)	Same as above	Not listed by Van Rensselaer Very rare
GII–15. Designs on oval panels. American Eagle, head erect and turned left; wings partly raised and right foreshortened. Large shield with 7 vertical bars on breast. Thunderbolt (4 arrows) in its right talons, large olive branch in left. Scattered sunrays surround eagle's head. Eagle stands on oval frame with inner band of 25 tiny pearls, and containing letters "F.L."	Cornucopia filled with produce, narrow body coiled to left.	Half-pint 11	Vertically ribbed	Plain lip Pontil mark	Clear Aquamarine Green, pale (S.L.)	Monongahela and Early Pittsburgh district, Frederick Lorenz	V. R. No. 24. GIII Very rare
GII–15a. Similar to GII–15; eagle's neck shaggy; 3 leaves at bottom and 2 at middle on left side of olive branch. right side as on GII–15; ribs below frame as on GII–16.	Cornucopia similar to GII–15; end more symmetrically curled and tip more rounded; ribs at bottom as on GII–16.	Half-pint 11	Same as GII–15	Plain lip End-to-end wide groove; pontil mark	Aquamarine (bluish)	Unknown: probably midwestern, possibly Pittsburgh	Reported by L. Earl Dambach Extremely rare

GII–16. Designs on oval panels. American Eagle, similar to No. 15 except oval frame has inner band of 17 larger pearls. Just below oval frame short diagonal ribbing to left and right.

GII–17. Designs on oval panels. American Eagle similar to No. 16 except leaves on lower right of olive branch different. Oval frame has inner band of 26 tiny pearls.

GII-17a. Similar to GII–17; no heads on upper 2 arrows.

GII–18. Designs on oval panels. Large American Eagle, head erect and turned to right; wings partly raised and right foreshortened. Large shield with 5 vertical bars on breast. Thunderbolt (4 arrows) in its right talons, large olive branch in left. Scattered sunrays surround eagle's head. Eagle stands on oval frame with inner band of beading not distinctly separated from line of frame. Within frame "ZANES VILLE"

The inscription is usually rather indistinct.

Catalog	Size	Form	Lip / Pontil	Colors	Glasshouse	Notes
GII–16	Half-pint 11	Vertically ribbed (3)	Plain lip, Pontil mark	Sapphire-blue; Aquamarine; Dark olive-green (black); Amber, golden, light; Amber, golden, deep; Blue-aquamarine (E.D.) / Gray-blue, Blue-green (M.B.K.)	Monongahela and Early Pittsburgh district, particular glasshouse unknown	Probably V. R. No. 16. GIII Rare
GII–17	Half-pint 11	Vertically ribbed (3)	Plain lip, Pontil mark	Aquamarine; Colorless; Green, light (R.W.); Emerald-green, light (S.L.)	Same as above	Not listed by Van Rensselaer Scarce
GII-17a	Half-pint 11	Same as GII–17	Plain lip, Smooth	Aquamarine	Same as above	Rare
GII–18	Half-pint 11	Vertically ribbed (3)	Plain lip, Pontil mark	Yellowish olive-green; Aquamarine; Dark amber; Brilliant yellow-green; Clear amber; Amber, golden (S.L.); Amber, deep (S.L.); Amber, red (S.L.); Green, light (S.L.); Green, medium (R.W.); Emerald-green (M.B.K.)	Probably J. Shepard & Co., Zanesville, Ohio	Not listed by Van Rensselaer Rare

GII–11 GII–12 GII–13 GII–14 GII–15 GII–15a GII–16

GII–17 GII–18

GROUP II—AMERICAN EAGLE FLASKS—*Continued*

OBVERSE	REVERSE	SIZE, FORM	EDGES	NECK, BASE	COLORS	GLASSHOUSE	NOTES, RARITY
GII–19. Designs on large oval panel. American Eagle, facing left; wings raised over and parallel with body, and standing on 2 furled flags.	Morning Glory and Vine. Gadrooning at base of neck on each side.	Pint Similar to F. 18	Heavy vertical medial rib	Plain lip Pontil mark	Aquamarine Blue-aquamarine Green, pale (S.L.) Green, light (S.L.) Emerald-green, light (S.L.)	Midwestern, glasshouse unknown	V. R. No. 6 D6; GII Rare Pottery flasks in similar size and design are known.
GII–20. Designs on large oval panels. Eagle of unusual appearance and seemingly standing erect in a swing. Its wings are comparatively short and partly raised at right angles to the body which is perfectly smooth without any portrayal of feathers. Neck very plump and sharply arched with head pointing right.	Same as obverse	Pint Similar to F. 18	Narrow vertical medial rib	Plain lip Pontil mark	Aquamarine Green, light Emerald-green (S.L.)	Midwestern glasshouse unknown	V. R. No. 15 D2; GII Extremely rare
GII–21. American Eagle, head erect and turned to right; wings partly raised. Large shield with 6 vertical bars and 17 tiny stars on breast. Tail feathers extend straight down below shield and thunderbolt (3 arrows) in its right talons, olive branch in left. Eleven small 5-pointed stars in semicircle above eagle and 2 additional stars, 1 on either side of eagle. Below eagle "MY COUNTRY" inscription slightly curved.	Figure of prospector, staff in left hand, pack over right shoulder, walking to left. Above in semicircle "FOR PIKES PEAK".	Pint 30	Smooth	Plain with laid-on ring Smooth with circular depression Double round collar Double angular collar	Emerald-green Aquamarine Green, light Olive-green Yellow-green (E.D.)	Probably Pittsburgh, particular glasshouse unknown	V. R. No. 24 GVII Comparatively scarce NOTE: Although this flask is usually included in the Pike's Peak group, the pose of the eagle and the disposition of the thunderbolt and olive branch more closely resembles that of the eagle on the great Seal of the United States than most of the eagle flasks, therefore we have included this in the eagle group.
GII–22. Designs on oval panels. American Eagle, head turned to left; wings raised and spread. Shield with 7 bars on breast. Extending from eagle's beak, ribbon in semicircle over head and containing word "UNION" between 2 small pearls. Above in 2 semicircular rows fourteen 4-pointed stars. Thunderbolt (3 arrows) in eagle's left talons, olive branch in right. Oval frame beneath containing large elongated 8-pointed star.	Large lyre and above in 2 semicircular rows fourteen 4-pointed stars.	Pint 19	Corrugated horizontally with vertical medial rib	Plain lip Pontil mark	Deep aquamarine Green, brilliant (S.L.) Green, light (R.W.) Emerald-green, light (S.L.) Yellow-green	Possibly Kentucky Glass Works, Louisville, Ky.	V. R. No. 5 D1; GII Rare
GII–23. Designs on oval panels. American Eagle similar to No. 22 but ribbon contains random ribbing instead of inscription. Similar oval frame with elongated 8-pointed star below eagle, and similar 14 stars above eagle.	Large conventionalized floral medallion and below oval frame containing elongated 8-pointed star.	Pint 19	Corrugated horizontally with vertical medial rib	Plain lip Pontil mark	Deep aquamarine Blue, light (S.L.)	Midwestern, possibly Kentucky Glass Works, Louisville, Ky.	Van Rensselaer No. 4 D1; GII Rare
GII–24. Designs on oval panels. Similar to No. 23. NOTE: In this particular flask the decoration in the ribbon over the eagle at 1 point forms a distinct "U."	Same as obverse	Pint 19	Corrugated horizontally with vertical medial rib	Plain lip Pontil mark	Sapphire-blue Yellow-green Deep amber Moonstone Dark amber (black) Clear Deep olive-yellow Aquamarine Clear green Blue, light (S.L.) [Cornflower-blue (R.W.) Colorless Emerald-green, light (S.L.) Olive-green (G.A.)]	Midwestern, possibly Kentucky Glass Works, Louisville, Ky.	Van Rensselaer No. 3 D1; GII Common

GII–25. Similar to No. 24 except that "U" is lacking in ribbon and point of ribbon varies in sharpness.

Same as obverse

Corrugated horizontally with vertical medial rib

Pint
19

Plain lip
Pontil mark

Aquamarine
Golden amber (S.L.)
Moonstone (S.L.)
Olive-yellow (S.L.)

Midwestern, possibly Kentucky Glass Works, Louisville, Ky.

Not listed by Van Rensselaer
Scarce

GII–26. Designs on oval panels. Large American Eagle, head turned to left; wings raised and spread. Shield with 5 vertical bars on breast. Thunderbolt (2 arrows) in right talons, olive branch in left. Ribbon with 5 small stars held in eagle's beak and extending to right above. Below eagle large stellar motif.

Same as obverse

Corrugated horizontally with vertical medial rib

Quart
19

Plain lip
Pontil mark

Emerald-green
Olive-yellow
Brilliant yellow-green
Clear golden amber
Deep amber
Aquamarine
Deep bluish green
Peacock-blue (R. W.)
Blue, pale (R. W.)
Emerald-green, light (S.L.)

Emerald-green, deep (S.L.)
Peacock-green (R. W.)
Olive-green (R. W.)
Yellow-green (S.L.)
Moonstone (S.L.)

Midwestern, possibly Kentucky Glass Works, Louisville, Ky.

Van Rensselaer No. 1 D1; GII Common

GII–27. Large American Eagle, head turned to left; shield with 7 bars on breast; wings widespread and raised slightly. Thunderbolt (3 arrows) in eagle's right talons and long olive branch in left. Large pointed elliptical ornament with 16 segments and small convex center below eagle.

Across center inscription in two lines "FARLEY & TAYLOR RICHMOND. KY".

Corrugated horizontally with vertical medial rib

2½ Quarts
19

Plain lip
Pontil mark

Aquamarine
Amber, deep (C. W.)

Midwestern, possibly Kentucky Glass Works, Louisville, Ky. Made for Farley & Taylor, Richmond, Ky.

V. R. No. 6 D1; GII Extremely rare

GII-19   GII-20   GII-21   GII-22   GII-23   GII-24   GII-25   GII-26   GII-27

GROUP II—AMERICAN EAGLE FLASKS—Continued

OBVERSE	REVERSE	SIZE, FORM	EDGES	NECK, BASE	COLORS	GLASSHOUSE	NOTES, RARITY
GII–28. Similar to No. 27	Plain	2½ Quarts 19	Same as No. 27	Plain lip Pontil mark	Aquamarine	Same as No. 27	V. R. No. 2 D1, GII Extremely rare
GII–29. Entire flask vertically ribbed except for small circular raised medallion about the size of a silver dollar on each side. The medallion carries a small American Eagle standing on narrow base; wings partly raised and head turned back to left.	Same as obverse	Pint 25	Vertically ribbed	Plain lip Pontil mark / Yellow-green, pale	Amethyst, bordering on puce. Light green Aquamarine Colorless (W.L.)	Attributed to Louisville Glass Works, Louisville, Ky.	Not listed by Van Rensselaer Extremely rare
GII–30. Similar to No. 29	Same as obverse	Half-pint 25	Vertically ribbed	Plain lip Pontil mark	Yellowish olive-green Aquamarine Pale yellow-green Blue, medium (Henry Ford Museum)	Same as No. 29	Not listed by Van Rensselaer Very rare
GII–31. Large oval medallion with upper and lower edges indented and containing American Eagle, head turned to left. Shield with 5 bars on breast; wings raised and spread. Thunderbolt (3 arrows) in left talons, olive branch in right.	Same as obverse. Entire flask except heavy vertical ribbing.	Quart 25	Vertically ribbed	Plain lip Double collared Pontil mark	Emerald-green Aquamarine Very pale green Clear deep green, yellow tone Green, medium (R.W.)	Louisville, Kentucky, Glass Works	V. R. No. 2 D3; GII. Listed in pint size Comparatively scarce
GII–32. Similar to No. 31	Similar to No. 31	Pint 25	Vertically ribbed	Plain lip Pontil mark / Green, brilliant (S.L.)	Very pale green Yellowish olive-green Aquamarine, deep Colorless, green tinge (E.D.)	Same as No. 31	V. R. No. 2 D3; GII Rare
GII–32a. Eagle medallion like GII–32 but with 3 small circular slightly concave depressions: 1 above eagle's head, 1 below left wing, 1 slightly lower below right wing.	Like GII–32	Pint 25	Vertically ribbed	Plain lip Pontil mark	Yellow-green	Attributed to Louisville Glass Works, Louisville, Ky.	Reported by Charles Vuono, 1967 Extremely rare
GII–33. Oval panel containing American Eagle, head turned to left; wing slightly raised and spread; shield on breast. Thunderbolt (1 arrow) in left talons, olive branch in right. Above eagle 5 stars.	Oval medallion with inscription in oval formation: "LOUISVILLE GLASS WORKS" and enclosing "KY". Entire flask except medallions covered with heavy vertical ribbing.	Half-pint 26	Vertically ribbed	Rounded collar Plain with laid on ring Smooth	Olive-amber Dark amber Very pale green Deep green Aquamarine Golden amber, deep (R.W.) Red-amber (S.L.) Blue-green (C.G.)	Louisville, Kentucky, Glass Works	V. R. No. 3 D3; GII Comparatively scarce
GII–34. Similar to No. 33 except 13 stars over eagle	Similar to No. 33	Pint 26	Vertically ribbed	Plain lip with applied ring below. Pontil with discoloration	Deep olive-yellow Aquamarine (S.L.) Green, light (G.A.) Olive-green, yellowish	Same as No. 33	Not listed by Van Rensselaer Extremely rare

564

GII–35. Large oval panel, top and bottom indented, containing American Eagle, facing right, wings raised above and parallel to body. Eagle rests on shield with 5 vertical bars. In eagle's beak narrow ribbon extending upward and above eagle and below through shield. Thunderbolt (4 arrows) protrudes from left side of shield just below ribbon. On lower part of flask rectangular panel with inscription "LOUISVILLE KY GLASS WORKS"

GII–36. Similar to No. 35 but shield without bars and grouping of arrows forming thunderbolt different.

GII–37. American Eagle, head turned to left; wings partly raised; shield with 6 vertical bars on breast. Thunderbolt (3 arrows) in eagle's left talons, olive branch in right. Thirteen fairly large 5-pointed stars in semicircle above eagle.

No.	Reverse	Lip	Size	Colors	Glass Works	Reference
GII–35	Angular vertical ribbing	Plain with laid on ring / Smooth	Quart 25	Golden yellow / Deep amber / Deep grass-green / Aquamarine / Blue-green (E.D.) / Emerald-green (S.L.)	Louisville, Kentucky, Glass Works	V. R. No. 4 D3; GII Common
GII–36	Vertical ribbing	Plain with laid on ring / Smooth	Pint 25	Olive-yellow / Yellow-green / Aquamarine / Amber / Blue, pale (S.L.) / Olive-green (S.L.) / Peacock-green (R.W.)	Same as No. 35	V. R. No. 4 D3; GII Common
GII–37	Smooth	Plain lip / Plain with laid on ring / Rounded double collar / Smooth / Smooth with disk	Pint 30	Olive-yellow / Deep blue-green / Clear green / Olive-amber (black) / Clear deep amber / Aquamarine / Green, pale (S.L.) / Emerald-green / Olive-green, light / Olive-green, deep	Ravenna Glass Co., Ravenna, Ohio	V. R. No. 73. GVI Common

GII–29   GII–30   GII–31   GII–33   GII–35   GII–36   GII–37

565

GROUP II—AMERICAN EAGLE FLASKS—Continued

New Jersey, Maryland, and Pennsylvania (excluding Monongahela and Early Pittsburgh district)

OBVERSE	REVERSE	SIZE, FORM	EDGES	NECK, BASE	COLORS	GLASSHOUSE	NOTES, RARITY
GII–38. American Eagle, facing to right; wings partly raised over body and poised on rocky formation which supports in center American shield below the eagle. In eagle's beak is grasped a ribbon extending backward across its body and with inscription "E PLURIBUS UNUM". Shield has 6 broad vertical bars and tiny stars which are faint.	Inscription in semicircle "DYOTTVILLE GLASS WORK'S" and below in slightly curved line "PHILADA".	Pint + 21	Smooth	Plain lip Smooth	Amethyst Puce Olive-yellow Aquamarine	Dyottville Glass Works, Philadelphia	V. R. No. 5 D7; GII Comparatively scarce
GII–39. Similar to No. 38 except ribbon does not show inscription. Formation of rocks different and shield has 7 small stars.	Plain	Pint minus 21	Smooth	Plain lip with laid on ring Smooth	Deep yellow-green Aquamarine Puce (G.A.)	Probably Dyottville Glass Works, Philadelphia	Not listed by Van Rensselaer Comparatively scarce
GII–40. Designs on oval panels. American Eagle, head turned to left; wings partly raised and left foreshortened. Large shield with 8 vertical bars on breast. Thunderbolt (4 arrows) in eagle's left talons, large olive branch in right. Sunrays (23 rays) surround eagle's head. Eagle stands on oval frame which is not broken at top, with inner band of 20 tiny pearls. A horizontal bar connects eagle's talons.	Same as obverse	Pint 11	Vertically ribbed (3)	Plain lip Occasionally with sloping collar Also double collared Pontil mark	Golden amber Dark amber Emerald-green Aquamarine Green, Medium Yellow-green (S.L.) Lemon-yellow, deep (DeVere Card)	Kensington Glass Works, Philadelphia	V. R. No. 7 D2; GII Common
GII–41. Designs on oval panels. American Eagle similar to No. 40 but head slightly larger and 26 sunrays. Ten vertical bars on shield. Oval frame does not show at top.	Large tree in foliage.	Pint 11	Vertically ribbed	Plain lip Pontil mark	Aquamarine Pale green	Kensington Glass Works, Philadelphia	V. R. No. 119. GVI Common
GII–42. Designs on oval panels. American Eagle, similar to No. 41 except 25 rays, slightly longer. Eight vertical bars on shield. End of olive branch extends into oval frame with inner band of 23 small pearls and contains letters "T.W.D". in oval frame beneath eagle.	Full rigged frigate sailing to right, American flag at rear; waves beneath frigate, and in semicircle beneath "FRANKLIN".	Pint 11	Vertically ribbed (3)	Plain lip Pontil mark	Pale green Brown–amber Aquamarine (E.D.) Yellow-green, pale	Kensington Glass Works, Philadelphia	V. R. No. 108. GI Comparatively scarce
GII–43. Designs on oval panels. American Eagle head erect and turned to right; large shield with 6 bars on breast. Thunderbolt (4 arrows) in its right talons, large olive branch in left. Scattered sunrays around eagle's head. Eagle stands on oval frame with inner band of 25 small pearls and containing letters "T.W.D".	Cornucopia filled with produce, narrow tip coiled to left.	Half-pint 11	Vertically ribbed (3) and with inscription "E PLURIBUS UNUM" "ONE OF MANY" "KENSINGTON GLASS WORKS PHILA-DELPHIA"	Plain lip Pontil mark	Aquamarine	Kensington Glass Works, Philadelphia	V. R. No. 14. GIII Scarce
GII–44. Similar to No. 43.	Similar to No. 43.	Half-pint 11	Vertically ribbed but without any inscription	Plain lip Pontil mark	Pale green Aquamarine (C.G.)	Same as No. 43	Not listed by Van Rensselaer Scarce

GII–45. Designs on oval panels. American Eagle, similar to No. 43 but no sunrays around eagle's head and olive branch slightly different. Oval frame beneath eagle without inner band of pearls.

GII–46. Designs on oval panels. Small American Eagle, head turned to right, body and wings in parallel position diagonally. Small shield with 4 vertical bars and 3 stars diagonally across lower part of eagle's body. Only eagle's right leg showing and large olive branch in talons.

GII–47. Designs on oval panels. Large American Eagle, head turned to right; wings partly raised and neither foreshortened. No shield on breast. Thunderbolt (3 arrows) in left talons, large olive branch in right. Three large 4-pointed stars above eagle.

GII–48. Designs on oval panels. Large American Eagle, head turned to right; wings partly raised and right foreshortened. Large shield with 7 vertical and 4 horizontal bars on breast. Thunderbolt (6 arrows) in eagle's right talons, large olive branch in left. Fine sunrays surround eagle's head. Eagle stands on plain double line oval frame.

Cornucopia filled with produce, tip coiled to left and terminating in floral motif. Produce differs from Nos. 43 and 44.	Half-pint	Vertically ribbed (3)	Plain lip Pontil mark	Greenish blue Aquamarine Sapphire-blue, light (S.L.) Blue, medium (M.B.K.)	Unknown	V. R. No. 15. GIII Scarce
Cornucopia filled with produce, tip coiled to left similar to that on Nos. 43 and 44.	Half-pint	Vertically ribbed (3)	Plain lip Pontil mark	Aquamarine	Unknown	V. R. No. 28 GIII Scarce NOTE: Dangerous imitations of this flask, some of them in colors, have been made.
Large tree in foliage.	Quart	Vertically ribbed, heavy medial rib	Plain lip Pontil mark	Aquamarine Deep green Emerald-green, medium (S.L.)	Unknown, possibly Coffin & Hay	V. R. No. 118 GVI Rare
Large United States Flag with 19 stars furled on standard. Above in semicircle "COFFIN & HAY." Below flag in semicircle "HAMMONTON"	Quart	Vertically ribbed, heavy medial rib	Plain lip Pontil mark	Sapphire-blue Dark amber Emerald green Citron Deep green Aquamarine Olive-yellow	Coffin & Hay, Hammonton, N.J.	V. R. No. 28 GI Common

GII–38   GII–39   GII–40   GII–41   GII–42   GII–43   GII–45   GII–46   GII–47   GII–48

GROUP II—AMERICAN EAGLE FLASKS—*Continued*

OBVERSE	REVERSE	SIZE, FORM	EDGES	NECK, BASE	COLORS	GLASSHOUSE	NOTES, RARITY
GII–49. Designs on oval panels. American Eagle, head turned to right; wings partly raised and right slightly foreshortened. Shield with 7 vertical and 3 horizontal bars on eagle's breast. Thunderbolt (6 arrows) in eagle's right talons, large olive branch in left. Very fine sunrays around eagle's head. Eagle stands on oval frame with very fine inner beading.	Stag with antlers, standing erect and facing to left. Above in semicircle "COFFIN & HAY." Beneath in semicircle "HAMMONTON"	Pint 11	Vertically ribbed, heavy medial rib	Plain lip Pontil mark	Dark amber (black) Aquamarine Pale yellow-green	Coffin & Hay, Hammonton, N.J.	V. R. No. 109 GI Scarce
GII–50. Designs on oval panels. Similar to No. 49 except slight difference in olive branch.	Similar to No. 49 except slight difference in grass beneath stag's feet, and no period after Hay.*	Half-pint 11	Same as above	Plain lip Pontil mark	Clear Deep bluish green Aquamarine Amber, deep (S.L.) Amethyst, pale (S.L.) Green, pale Emerald-green, pale (S.L.)	Same as above	V. R. No. 109 GI Scarce
				Emerald-green, deep (S.L.)			

*No period appeared after "Hay" on the flask which was drawn. Possibly it failed to take in the molding, for several flasks having the period were reported in 1963. Unfortunately, comparison for other possible mold differences could not be made.

OBVERSE	REVERSE	SIZE, FORM	EDGES	NECK, BASE	COLORS	GLASSHOUSE	NOTES, RARITY
GII–51. Designs on oval panels. American Eagle similar to No. 49	Similar to No. 49 except stag omitted	Pint 11	Vertically ribbed, heavy medial rib	Plain lip Pontil mark	Pale green Aquamarine	Coffin & Hay, Hammonton, N.J.	V. R. No. 25 GI Very rare
GII–52. Designs on oval panels. American Eagle, head, shoulders and wings only; resting on large shield. Eagle's head turned to left; wings partly raised and dropping parallel with each side of shield. Shield with 7 wide vertical bars and very narrow horizontal bars above. Beneath shield crossed olive and palm branches.	United States Flag with 13 small stars furled on tall standard. At left of lower part of flag "FOR OUR" and at right "COUNTRY".	Pint 14	Broad vertical ribbing	Plain lip Pontil mark	Golden amber Clear amber Pale green Aquamarine Milk-white	Attributed to Coffin & Hay, Hammonton, N.J.	V. R. No. 35 GI Common
GII–53. Designs on oval panels. American Eagle, head erect and turned to right; wings partly raised. Eagle stands on shield containing 9 narrow vertical bars and 3 wider horizontal bars. The vertical bars are grouped 3 in the center, 2 each on either side and single bar at each border of shield. Sunrays surround eagle's head and tips of wings extend downward parallel with upper part of shield. Below shield extending upward on either side olive and palm branches tied at center.	United States Flag with 20 small stars, furled on standard. In semicircle below flag "FOR OUR COUNTRY."	Pint 13	Fine vertical ribbing sloping to heavy medial rib, wide flat appearance	Plain lip Pontil mark	Clear olive-green Aquamarine	Attributed to Coffin & Hay, Hammonton, N.J.	V. R. No. 33 GI Comparatively scarce
GII–54. Designs on oval panels. American Eagle, head erect and turned to left, body inclined in same direction; wings partly raised. Eagle stands on shield with 6 broad vertical bars. Sunrays surround eagle's head and tips of wings drop down parallel to upper sides of shield. Below shield and extending upward on either side tied olive and palm branches.	United States Flag with 20 stars, furled on standard. Below flag in semicircle "FOR OUR COUNTRY."	Pint 13	Fine vertical ribbing	Plain lip Pontil mark	Olive-amber Aquamarine Pale olive-green	Same as above	V. R. No. 34 GI Comparatively scarce

GII–55. Designs on oval panels. American Eagle, head turned to left; wings partly raised. Shield with vertical and horizontal bars on breast. Thunderbolt (3 arrows) in right talons, olive branch in left. Above eagle thirteen 5-pointed stars.	Large bunch of grapes and smaller bunch at right depending from stem with 2 large leaves.	Quart 14	Fine vertical ribbing	Plain lip Pontil mark	Clear deep amber Aquamarine Deep green Amber, reddish (C.G.) Golden amber (R.W.) Green, clear medium Blue-green (S.L.) Yellow-green (C.G.)	Unknown, possibly Coffin & Hay	V. R. No. 44 GI Common
GII–56. Designs on oval panels. American Eagle, head, shoulders and wings only showing and resting on large shield with 5 broad vertical bars and 6 narrow horizontal bars. Eagle's head turned to left and wings extend downward parallel to sides of shield. Above 13 small 5-pointed stars. Below shield olive and palm branches knotted and extending upward on each side of lower part of shield.	Large single bunch of grapes depending from stem with three leaves.	Half-pint 14	Fine vertical ribbing	Plain lip Pontil mark	Aquamarine Deep green Amber (G.A.) Golden amber (S.L.) Olive-yellow (upper ⅔) and amber (lower ⅓)	Attributed to Coffin & Hay, Hammonton, N.J.	V. R. No. 43 GI Rare

New York and New England States

GII–57. American Eagle, head held erect and turned to right; shield with 6 narrow bars on breast; wings partly raised. Thunderbolt (4 arrows) in eagle's right talons, large olive branch in left. Thirteen small 5-pointed stars above eagle. Eagle stands on oval frame containing letters "J.P.F." Tassellike ornaments hand from upper line of frame, lower part of frame is extended and looped to form a medallion containing square and compasses and other ornamentation.	Large cornucopia coiled to left and filled with produce. Beneath, curved line with looped and scroll ends enclosing "CONN." Beneath line at each end of the scroll are 2 tiny ornaments.	Pint 4	Corrugated horizontally, corrugations extend around flask at base and juncture of neck and body	Plain lip Pontil mark	Light amber Olive-green	Possibly Pitkin Glass Works, East Hartford, Conn.	V. R. No. 22 GIII Extremely rare

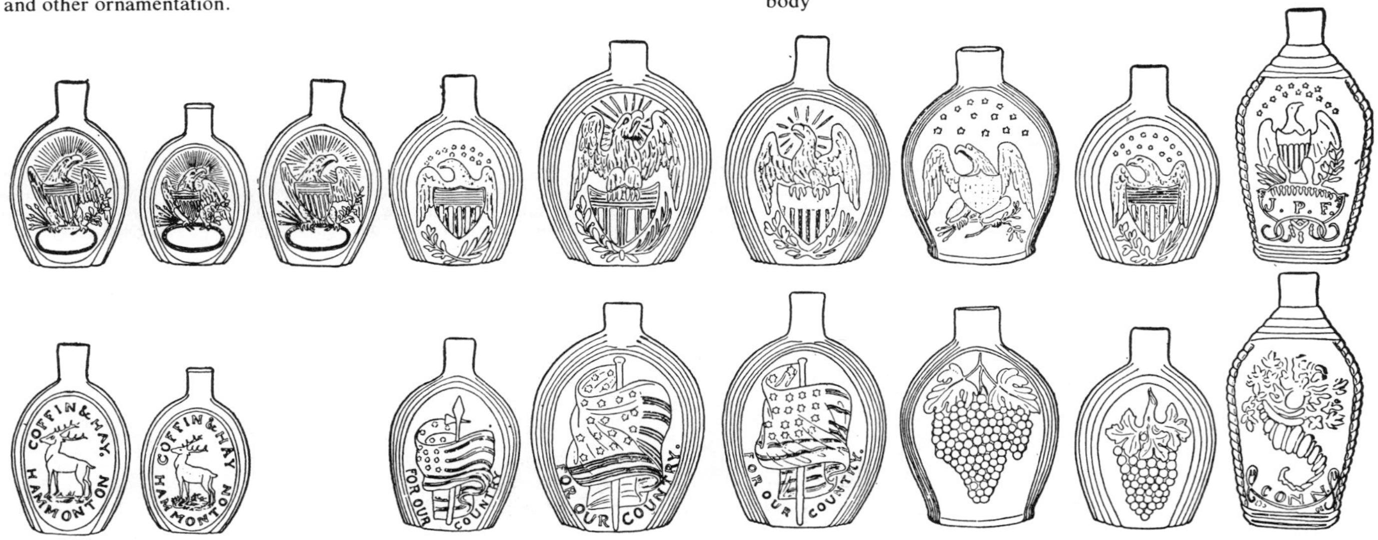

GII–49 GII–50 GII–51 GII–52 GII–53 GII–54 GII–55 GII–56 GII–57

GROUP II—AMERICAN EAGLE FLASKS—Continued

OBVERSE	REVERSE	SIZE, FORM	EDGES	NECK, BASE	COLORS	GLASSHOUSE	NOTES, RARITY
GII–58. American Eagle, rather crudely depicted, head held erect and turned to right. Shield with 6 bars on breast; wings partly raised, legs bent at right angles. Thunderbolt (3 arrows) in eagle's right talons, large olive branch in left. Lower part of branch extends below tail which is straight downward from point of shield. Above eagle 13 small 5-pointed stars.	Large cornucopia coiled to left and filled with produce.	Half-pint 4	Same as above	Plain lip Pontil mark	Clear light amber Olive-amber	Same as above	V. R. No. 26 GIII Extremely rare
GII–59. Large American Eagle, head turned to left; large shield with 7 vertical bars on breast; wings partly raised. Eagle is grasping large olive branch in talons.	Tall tree in foliage, generally referred to as "Charter Oak." Above the tree, frame with scrolled ends containing word "LIBERTY".	Pint Similar to 17, Ill. 133	Heavy vertical medial rib and heavy circular beading on either side forming oval panel which carries the design	Plain lip Pontil mark	Peacock-blue Clear	Unknown	Not listed by Van Rensselaer Extremely rare
GII–60. Designs on oval panels. Similar to No. 59.	Similar to No. 59	Half-pint Similar to 17, Ill. 133	Same as No. 59	Plain lip Pontil mark	Pale blue Golden yellow Deep sapphire-blue Yellow-green Clear green Clear amber Dark amber (black) Aquamarine Clear Golden amber (S.L.) Red-amber (E.D.) [box: Blue, pale (S.L.); Blue, greenish (S.L.); Peacock-blue (S.L.); Green, light (R.W.); Emerald-green (S.L.); Olive-green (S.L.)]	Unknown	V. R. No. 11 D7; GII Comparatively scarce
GII–61. Large American Eagle, head turned to left; wings partly raised and left foreshortened. Large shield with 6 bars on eagle's breast. Eagle stands on wreath of laurel branches. Above eagle in slightly curved line "LIBERTY".	Inscription in 4 lines, the first and third curved "WILLINGTON GLASS, Cº WEST WILLINGTON CONN"	Quart 22	Smooth	Plain lip Rounded collar Broad sloping collar Smooth	Clear deep green Dark olive-green Olive-amber Reddish amber, sometimes called blood amber Amber Emerald-green (S.L.)	Willington Glass Works, West Willington, Conn.	V. R. No. 129 GI (listed in half-pint) Common
GII–62. Similar to No. 61.	Inscription similar to No. 61 except comma after "WEST".	Pint 23	Smooth	Plain lip Rounded collar Broad sloping collar Smooth Pontil mark	Clear deep green Dark olive-green Olive-amber Reddish amber Emerald-green	Same as No. 61	V. R. No. 129 GI (listed in half-pint) Common

Description	Inscription	Capacity	Base	Lip/Collar	Color	Factory	Notes
GII–63. Similar to No. 62 except slight difference in eagle's legs and the laurel wreath.	Inscription in 5 lines the first and third curved "WILLINGTON GLASS Co WEST WILLINGTON CONN".	Half-pint 23	Smooth	Double rounded collar Smooth Pontil mark Plain lip	Clear deep green Amber Olive-amber Blue-green (S.L.) Emerald-green Olive-green	Same as No. 61	V. R. No. 129 GI Comparatively scarce
GII–63a. Similar to GII–63; eagle's legs less distinctly feathered, wings slightly shorter and tips nearer wreath with slightly larger leaves.	Same inscription as GII–63, variations in size of letters, "A" conspicuously smaller.	Half-pint 23	Smooth	Plain lip; double round collar Smooth	Olive-amber	Willington Glass Works, West Willington, Conn.	Comparatively scarce
GII–64. American Eagle similar to No. 62 but slightly smaller and body not slightly angled. Laurel wreath also slightly different.	Inscription similar to No. 62 but some of the letters slightly different, and comma after glass smaller.	Pint 23	Smooth	Plain lip Pontil mark Broad sloping collar (No. 15) Narrow round collar, lower bevel (20a)	Olive-amber Olive-green Amber Green, bluish, deep (C.G.) Emerald-green	Same as No. 61	V. R. No. 130 GI Comparatively scarce
GII–65. American Eagle practically identical to that on No. 63.	Inscription in 5 lines the first and third curved "WESTFORD GLASS Co WESTFORD CONN".	Half-pint 23	Smooth	Plain lip Pontil mark Broad sloping collar (No. 15) Narrow round collar, lower bevel (20a)	Deep reddish amber Olive-amber Amber, medium Green, pale Olive-green, deep (S.L.)	Westford Glass Works, Westford, Conn.	V. R. No. 125 GI Comparatively scarce Van Rensselaer lists this flask as also occurring in pint and quart sizes. We have never seen it in these sizes and it may be a misprint referring to his No. 129 which does occur in pint and quart sizes, our Nos. 61 and 62.

GII–58 GII–59 GII–60 GII–61 GII–62 GII–63 GII–64 GII–65

GROUP II—AMERICAN EAGLE FLASKS—*Continued*

OBVERSE	REVERSE	SIZE, FORM	EDGES	NECK, BASE	COLORS	GLASSHOUSE	NOTES, RARITY
GII–66. American Eagle, head turned to left, wings partly raised and left slightly foreshortened. Large shield with 6 bars on eagle's breast. Eagle stands on large laurel wreath. Above eagle seven 5-pointed stars.	Large anchor, in diagonal position across flask. Above anchor ribbon frame with inscription "NEW LONDON". Below anchor similar frame with inscription "GLASS WORKS".	Quart 21	Smooth	Plain lip Pontil mark Plain — Aquamarine (S.L.) Emerald-green, light	Clear deep green Very pale green Copper-amber (C.G.) Golden-amber (C.G.) Red-amber (C.G.) Yellow-amber (S.L.)	New London Glass Works. New London. Conn.	V. R. No. 3 GVI (listed in half-pint) Rare
GII–67. American Eagle similar to No. 66 except slight variation in the laurel wreath and nine 5-pointed stars above eagle.	Similar to No. 66 except end of rope of anchor turns to right below anchor instead of to left.	Half-pint 22	Smooth	Plain lip Double rounded collar Smooth Pontil mark Narrow flat collar Flat ring below plain lip (No. 11)	Olive-yellow Clear deep green Pale yellow-green Olive-amber Pale green Aquamarine Pale yellow-green shading to amber Golden amber (C.G.) Emerald-green	New London Glass Works	V. R. No. 3 GVI Comparatively scarce
GII–68. American Eagle in flight, head and body downward and head turned to right. Above eagle seven 5-pointed stars.	Similar to No. 67 except slight variation in position of letters in frames and in the lines of the lower frame.	Pint 22	Smooth	Plain lip Rounded double collar Smooth Pontil mark Plain — Olive-green (E.D.)	Olive-yellow Clear golden amber Clear green Deep bluish green Pale yellow-green Olive-amber Clear green with yellow streaks Emerald-green (S.L.)	New London Glass Works	V. R. No. 2 GVI Comparatively scarce
GII–69. Designs on oval panels banded at top and sides by beading parallel to that on edges. American Eagle with abnormally large beak, head erect and turned to left; wings partly raised and left foreshortened. Thunderbolt (3 arrows) in eagle's left talons, olive branch in right. The eagle itself is similar to that on No. 13. Short diagonal ribbing at base of flask.	Inverted cornucopia, coiled to left, filled with produce. Cornucopia has 12 ribs and is more slender in form than that on Nos. 11, 12, 13 and 14. The short diagonal ribbing is lacking at base.	Half-pint 12	Horizontally beaded with vertical medial rib	Plain lip Pontil mark — Emerald-green, medium light (S.L.) Lavender, pale (S.L.) Moonstone	Yellow-green Clear green Clear Aquamarine, deep (C.G.) Colorless, amethyst tint Green, light (S.L.)	Unknown	V. R. No. 17 GIII. Scarce

NOTE: While this flask is similar in its general characteristics to Nos. 11, 12, 13 and 14, we think it is an Eastern flask as it was well known among collectors before any other varieties turned up in the middle Western area. The cornucopia and the beading on the edges of the panels are identical with GIII–1. Of course, there is a possibility that it may have been blown in the Pittsburgh district.

OBVERSE	REVERSE	SIZE, FORM	EDGES	NECK, BASE	COLORS	GLASSHOUSE	NOTES, RARITY
GII–70. Designs on oval panels. Large American Eagle lengthwise, head turned to left; wings partly raised and spread. Shield with 7 vertical and 2 horizontal bars on breast. Thunderbolt (3 arrows) in eagle's left talons, olive branch in right. Designs in very high relief.	Same as obverse	Pint 11	Vertically ribbed (3)	Plain lip Pontil mark	Dark amber Olive-amber Dark olive-green	Coventry, Conn. Glass Works	V. R. No. 6 D7. GII Common

GII–71. Designs on oval panels. American Eagle similar to No. 70 except wings raised to slightly higher angle.	Same as obverse	Half-pint 11	Vertically ribbed (3)	Plain lip Pontil mark	Clear yellow-green Olive-yellow Olive-amber Olive-green Yellow-green (pale) shading to light amber in neck (C.G.) Green (G.A.)	Coventry, Conn. Glass Works	V. R. No. 7. D7. GII Common
GII–72. Designs on oval panels. American Eagle, head turned to right; wings partly raised. Shield with 5 vertical bars on breast. Thunderbolt (3 arrows) in eagle's right talons, olive branch in left. Eagle stands on rocky formation.	Large cornucopia coiled to left and filled with produce.	Pint 11	Vertically ribbed (3)	Plain lip Pontil mark	Aquamarine Clear golden amber Dark amber Olive-amber Dark olive-green	Unknown, possibly Keene-Marlboro-St.	V. R. No. 9 GIII Common
GII–72a. Similar to GII–72	Cornucopia similar to GII–73 but more slender and tail more curved; "X" not tilted in line with curve of cornucopia but straight in line with base.	Pint 11	Same as GII–72	Plain lip Pontil mark	Olive-amber	Unknown, probably Eastern.	Rare
GII–72b. Similar to GII–72	Similar to GII–73; tip of right leg of tilted "X" about 1½″ from base.	Pint 11	Same as GII–72	Plain lip Keyed base like GIX–10	Emerald-green	Same as above	Reported by DeVere A. Card Rare
GII–73. Designs on oval panels. American Eagle similar to No. 72, shield shows also 2 horizontal bars and the top almost straight instead of definitely scalloped as in No. 72.	Cornucopia similar to No. 72 but differing slightly in minor details and with an "X" at left of cornucopia.	Pint 11	Vertically ribbed (3)	Plain lip Rough ring from blowpipe used as pontil	Yellow-green Olive-amber Clear golden amber Dark amber Dark olive-green Green, deep	Keene-Marlboro-St.	Van Rensselaer does not list this flask with the same ribbed edge and heavy vertical medial rib as No. 72. He does list No. 11 GIII flask of similar design but apparently with smooth edges, our No. 74. Comparatively scarce

GII–66   GII–67   GII–68   GII–69   GII–70   GII–71   GII–72   GII–73

573

OBVERSE	REVERSE	SIZE, FORM	EDGES	NECK, BASE	COLORS	GLASSHOUSE	NOTES, RARITY
GII–73a. Like GII–73 except for base and color.	Like GI–73	Pint 11	Same as GII–73	Plain lip Keyed base	Aquamarine	Same as above	Same as above
GII–74. American Eagle similar to No. 73.	Cornucopia similar to No. 73	Pint 11	Smooth	Plain lip Pontil mark	Yellow-green Aquamarine Amber, dark (M. Knapp, Jr.) Blue-green (R. W.)	New England, works unknown	V. R. No. 11 GIII Common
GII–75. Large American Eagle, head turned to right. Large shield with 3 vertical bars on breast; wings partly raised. Full front view of eagle's legs and feathers abnormally ruffled giving balloonlike effect. Eagle is standing on plain semispherical rock.	Large cornucopia coiled to left and filled with produce.	Pint 11	Vertically ribbed	Plain lip Pontil mark	Green Olive-amber Pale yellow-green Olive-green	New England, works unknown.	V. R. No. 27 GIII Extremely rare
GII–76. "Concentric Ring Eagle." Circular shaped. The entire flask covered with heavy concentric ribbing except for oval medallion in center which carries the design on each side. Rather crude American Eagle, head turned to right; wings partly raised and left fore-shortened. The eagle's tail curves sharply to the right and the legs extending downward appear to grasp a crude olive branch in the talons.	Same as obverse. Extremely heavy glass; these flasks sometimes weigh as much as two pounds or more.	Quart (about) 12	Vertically ribbed	Plain tip Pontil mark	Clear deep green Clear green-yellowish tone Emerald-green (S.L.)	New England, possibly South Boston Flint Glass Works, Thomas Cains's Phoenix Glass Works, or the New England Glass Co.	Not listed by Van Rensselaer Very rare
GII–76a. "Concentric ring eagle"; eagle smaller than that of GII–76, with thinner neck, fatter left wing as it tapers toward the tip, and with smaller curl at tip of right wing.	Similar to obverse	Pint & about 2 ozs. 10, thinner through GII–76	Vertical mold seam	Plain lip Pontil mark	Deep greenish yellow	Probably New England Glass Works	Reported 1968 by Charles Vuono Extremely rare Only one known
GII–77. "Concentric Ring Eagle" same as No. 76.	Instead of eagle in medallion, letters "NG Co" in 2 lines.	Quart (about) 12	Vertically ribbed	Plain lip Pontil mark	Clear light yellow-green Peacock blue-green Yellow-green	Attributed to the New England Glass Works	V. R. No. 5 D3; GII Extremely rare
GII–78. American Eagle: large head to left, pronounced beak and eye; short neck; wings (lower two-thirds "feathered" by 4 vertical ribs) raised and spread slightly downward parallel with body; on breast, large shield with 7 vertical bars; stout tapering legs; olive branch in right talon, thunderbolt (3 arrows) in left. Above eagle: wide arced pennant with flaring forked ends. Below eagle: large oval frame of wide molding.	Like obverse	Quart 29	Vertical rib, about ⅜" wide	Plain lip Pontil mark	Ambers Green (deep clear) Olive-green	Attributed to the Granite Glass Works, Stoddard, N.H., by Van Rensselaer	V. R. GII–DII–4 does not differentiate between our GII–78 and 79 in body size. Attribution apparently based on similarity to our GII–80. But possibility of common moldmaker for more than one works should be considered. Common
GII–79. Like GII–78, but body of flask slightly longer and fractionally wider at point of greatest width.	Like obverse	Quart 29	Same as GII–78	Same as GII–78	Amber (shaded) Olive-amber Olive-green	Same as above	See Note GII–78 Common

GII–80. Like GII–78, but inscribed within frame: at top, "GRANITE." (period blends into molding at right end); at bottom, "GLASS CO.," in letters of unequal size.

GII–81. Similar to GII–80; inscription: "GRANITE."/"GLASS. CO."

GII–82. Like GII–81 but no inscription in frame.

GII–83. Similar to GII–81; bottom of frame about ⅜" from base; no inscription.

GII–84. Similar to GII–81; bottom of frame about ¼" from base; no inscription.

GII–85. Similar to GII–81; bottom of frame about ⅝" from base; no inscription. Body of flask slightly longer than GII–81.

GII–86. Similar to flasks GII–80–85 but scaled to smaller size of flask; 6 bars on shield; vertical ribs in wings extending halfway up; fish-tail ends of pennant more deeply forked.

GII–86a. Like GII–86.

GII–87. Like GII–86 but with 4-pointed "star" at center left in frame.

No.	Reverse	Size	Edge	Lip	Color	Manufacturer	Notes
GII–80	Like obverse but inscribed within frame: at top, "STODDARD"; at bottom, "NH".	Quart 29	Same as GII–78	Plain lip; Keyed, similar to GIX–10	Amber (clear); Golden-amber; Olive-amber	Granite Glass Works, Stoddard, N.H.	V. R. GII–DII–2. No. 26 rare flasks Group C; Very rare
GII–81	Like obverse but inscription: "STODDARD"/"NH" centered in frame.	Pint 29	Narrow vertical rib	Plain lip; Pontil mark	Brown-amber (light & dark); Olive-amber	Same as above	V. R. GII–DII–1. Common
GII–82	Like GII–81 but letters of inscription smaller; faint periods after "N" & "H".	Pint 29	Same as GII–81	Plain lip; Pontil mark	Amber (light); Golden-amber; Olive-amber	Stoddard, N.H., probably Granite Glass Works	V. R. GII–DII–3. Scarce
GII–83	Like obverse but bottom of frame about ⅝" from base.	Pint 29	Same as GII–81	Plain lip; rarely, round collar. Keyed, similar to GIX–10	Ambers; Olive-amber; Olive-green, (light); Yellow-green (light)	New England, possibly Granite Glass Works	V. R. GII–DII–4; See Note GII–78 above; Common
GII–84	Like obverse	Pint 29	Medium wide vertical rib	Plain lip; With & without pontil mark; no mold seam	Olive-ambers; Olive-greens	Same as GII–83	See Note GII–78 above; Common
GII–85	Like obverse	Pint 29	Same as GII–84	Plain lip; Pontil mark	Olive-green (dark)	Same as GII–83	See Note GII–78; Comparatively scarce
GII–86	Like obverse	Half-pint 29	Narrow vertical rib	Plain lip; Keyed like GIX–10; pontil mark	Amber (light); Golden amber; Olive-amber; Olive-green	Same as GII–83	See Note GII–78; Common
GII–86a	Like obverse	Half-pint 29	Same as GII–86	Plain lip; Pontil mark	Amber; Olive-green	Same as GII–83	See Note GII–78; Common
GII–87	Like GII–86	Half-pint 29	Same as GII–86	Plain lip; Pontil mark	Green (deep); Olive-amber; Olive-green	Same as GII–83	See Note GII–78; Common

GII–75   GII–76   GII–77   GII–78   GII–81   GII–86   GII–87

FRAME & "X"

REV.

GROUP II—AMERICAN EAGLE FLASKS—*Continued*

OBVERSE	REVERSE	SIZE, FORM	EDGES	NECK, BASE	COLORS	GLASSHOUSE	NOTES, RARITY
GII–88. Like GII–86 but with large bead ($^3/_{16}$″ plus in diameter), a little below center, in frame.	Like obverse but bead $^1/_8$″ plus in diameter, little to right of center, in frame.	Half-pint 29	Same as GII–86	Plain lip Pontil mark	Ambers Olive-ambers Olive-greens	Same as GII–83	See Note GII–78 Common
GII–89. Eagle similar to GII–83 but wings smooth and other details less sharp. bottom of shield nearly flat instead of pointed; forked ends of pennant faint. Oval frame as on GII–83.	Like obverse	Pint 29	Heavy vertical rib	Angular collar; narrow flat collar with lower bevel. Type 4, without nipple at center	Amber (dark) Aquamarine (bluish) Yellow-green (deep)	Unknown, possibly midwestern	Common
GII–90. Large eagle: small undetailed head to right with beak near top of wing; wings (9 diagonal ribs in right; 10 in left) with scalloped inner edge. partly raised and spread downward. left at slight angle on breast; shield with wide medial rib within "V" rib; straight legs. wide-spread; thunderbolt (3 blunt-ended arrows) in each talon; plain narrow pennant from beak in arc to left above eagle. Below eagle: large oval frame (wide molding) about $1^{15}/_{16}$″ x $2^3/_4$″.	Similar to obverse. Eagle slightly smaller, head held higher; 8 ribs in wings. Arrows more separated. Pennant a bit shorter and wider. Frame $1^7/_8$″ x $3^{13}/_{16}$″.	Quart 29	Smooth	No. 10. Type 1. in center in circle: "KH & Co. ZO".	Green (pale)	Attributed to midwest; possibly Zanesville, Ohio	Rare NOTE: In all instances in which "thunderbolt (3 arrows) in each talon" occurs, only heads appear; and part of shaft appear; they are described occasionally as "arrows with heads at each end."
GII–91. Similar to GII–90. Eagle's head to left and shorter; wings (10 ribs in right; 9 in left) wider spread from body; arrows heavier and with pointed heads; pennant to left. Very large frame, $2^1/_8$″ x $3^1/_{16}$″.	Like obverse except 10 ribs in each wing.	Quart 29	Smooth	No. 10 Type 1	Aquamarine Blue (light) Cornflower-blue Yellow-green	Unknown, presumed to be midwestern, probably Pittsburgh area	Common
GII–92. Eagle: head to left, pronounced beak and eye; wings with fine curved diagonal ribs (ends forming broken inner line), partly raised and spread downward. left parallel with body and right at wide angle; slight feathering on neck and on body, beyond shield on breast; 6 vertical bars on shield; thunderbolt (3 arrows, feathered ends in right talon) in talons. Wide plain pennant from beak in arc to right above eagle. slender forked end. Below eagle: large oval frame (wide molding thinning at bottom left) about $1^1/_2$″ x $2^9/_{16}$″.	Like obverse	Pint 29	Smooth	Nos. 11 & 12 Similar to Type 13, curve of mold seam within oval	Aquamarine Blue (pale) Emerald-green (light)	See GII–91	Scarce
GII–93. Small eagle: head to left; wings (15 ribs in right, 12 in left) partly raised and spread downward with wider angle at right: on breast, shield with 8 vertical bars; thunderbolt (3 crude arrows) in talons. Wide pennant from beak to right in shallow arc above eagle. Below eagle: large rounded-ended oblong frame (wide molding) about $1^3/_8$″ x $2^1/_4$″.	Like obverse except 2 arrows in left talon; small star at right nearly opposite top of wing and about $^1/_2$″ from mold seam on edge. Oval frame, about $2^1/_2$″ x $2^9/_{16}$″.	Pint 29	Smooth; small bead blending into mold seam about $1^1/_4$″ from base	Nos. 10 & 11 Type 2	Amber (dark) Brown-amber Aquamarine Yellowish green	See GII–91	Similar to V. R. GII–DII–9 Common
GII–94. Like GII–93 but seemingly 14 ribs in right wing; 12 in left. Frame, $1^3/_8$″ x $2^5/_{16}$″.	Like obverse but seemingly 12 ribs in each wing. Frame, $1^1/_2$″ x $2^9/_{16}$″.	Pint 29	Smooth	No. 10 Type 2	Aquamarine Cornflower-blue (light)	See GII–91	V. R. GII–DII–9 Common

	Obverse	Reverse	Capacity	Edges	Neck	Colors	Manufacturer	References & Rarity
GII–95. Small eagle, similar to GII–109, head to right, long neck; wings with 4 short diagonal ribs of which ends form inner side; raised high and spread slightly, downward and outward; 3 vertical bars on breast; long thunderbolt (3 crude arrows) in talons. Long narrow pennant from beak to left in arc above eagle. Below eagle: large oval frame (wide molding) about 1⁵/₁₆″ x 1¾″.	Like obverse	Half-pint 29	Fine vertical rib (mold seam)	Round collar (60) Type 5	Aquamarine (bluish) Green (light) Yellow-green	See GII–91	V. R. GII–DII–13 Common
GII–96. Similar to GII–95; finer ribs in wings, only 3 in left wing.	Like obverse	Half-pint 30	Fine vertical rib (mold seam)	Nos. 11 & 12 Type 5	Ambers (light and dark)	See GII–91	Similar V. R. GII–DII–13 Common
GII–97. Similar to GII–96; frame heavier.	Like obverse	Half-pint 29	Narrow vertical rib	Plain lip Type 5	Aquamarine (greenish) Yellow-green (pale)	See GII–91	See GII–91 Common
GII–98. Eagle: small head to left; wings with 10 wide-spaced ribs in right, and 9 in left, partly raised and spread downward at narrow angle to body (wider on eagle's right); on breast, shield with 5 vertical bars; short wide-spread legs; thunderbolt (3 arrows) in each talon. Narrow pennant from beak to right above eagle and with short, thin, upcurving end. Below eagle: large oval frame (wide molding) about 2⅛″ x 3¹/₁₆″, enclosing inscription "GEO. A. (at top center) BERRY & CO." (at bottom following contour of frame).	Like obverse but 9 ribs in right wing, 6 in left; plain frame, about 2⅛″ x 3¹/₁₆″.	Quart 29	Smooth	No. 11 Type 8	Aquamarine	George A. Berry & Co., Pittsburgh, Pa.	Size not listed by Van Rensselaer Comparatively scarce
GII–98a. Similar to GII–98; 8 wide-spread ribs in right wing, 6 in left; frame (very wide molding) about 1⅝″ x 2½″.	Like obverse but plain frame	Pint 29	Smooth	No. 11 Type 8	Aquamarine	Same as GII–98	V. R. GII–DIV–3 Common
GII–98b. Presumably similar to GII–98 and 98a.	Like obverse, presumably, and no inscription in frame.	Half-pint 29	Smooth		Aquamarine	Same as GII–98	V. R. GII–DIV–4. We have never seen this flask. Scarce
GII–99. Eagle like GII–98; frame about 2⅛″ x 3⅛″, no inscription.	Like obverse	Quart 30	Smooth	No. 12 Type 8	Amber	Possibly George A. Berry & Co. or mold from maker of Berry molds	Common
GII–100. Eagle (closely similar to GII–101): small head to left; wings with 16 fine ribs, partly raised and spread downward and outward, inner line rippled; on breast, shield with 5 short vertical bars, no definite bottom line; short wide-spread legs; thunderbolt (3 arrows) in each talon. Pennant from beak to right above eagle, short thin end. Below eagle: large oval frame (wide molding), 2⅛″ x 3¹/₁₆″.	Like obverse but 1 or 2 fewer bars in wings.	Quart 30	Smooth	No. 11. Mold seam like Type 12; nipple at center of shallow disk center in oblong depression	Aquamarines Olive-green (light yellowish)	Unknown, probably midwestern	Common

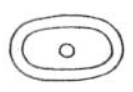

GII–88 FRAME OBV.

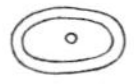

GII–88 FRAME REV.

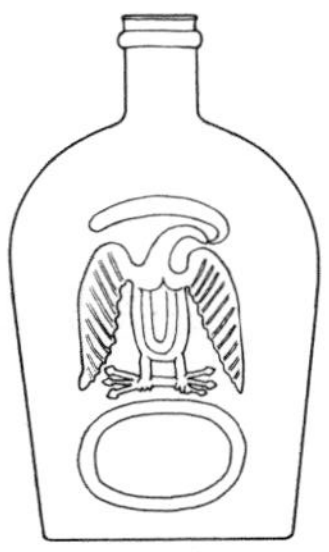

GII–90 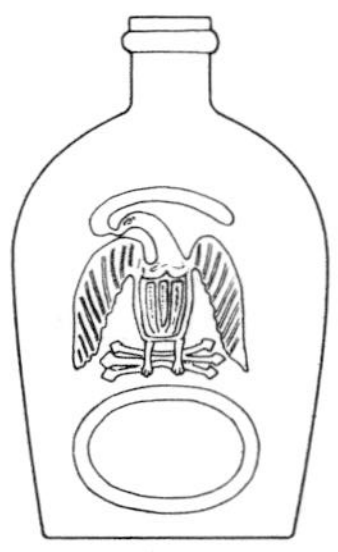 GII–91 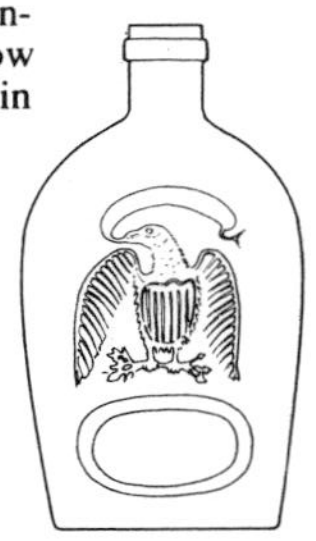 GII–92  GII–93 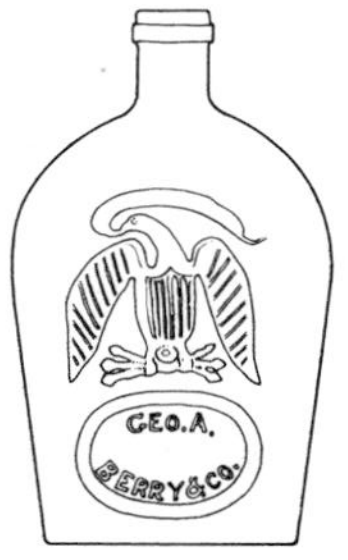 GII–98

GROUP II—AMERICAN EAGLE FLASKS—*Continued*

578

OBVERSE	REVERSE	SIZE, FORM	EDGES	NECK, BASE	COLORS	GLASSHOUSE	NOTES, RARITY
GII–101. Eagle: small head to left; long neck; wings with 13 fine ribs in right and 11 in left, rippled inner edge, partly raised and spread outward and downward; on breast, shield with 5 short bars, no bottom line; short wide-spread legs; thunderbolt (3 arrows) in each talon. Narrow pennant with short thin end, from beak to right in shallow arc above eagle. Below eagle: large oval frame (wide molding) about 2⅛″ x 3″, with inscription in large letters: "PITTSBURGH" (starting at center left and following close to frame to center right end) "PA" ("A" a little lower than "P").	Like obverse but 9 ribs in left wing. Plain frame about 2⅛″ x 3⅛″.	Quart 29	Narrow vertical rib ending about 1″ above base	No. 10 Type 9, but curves shallow	Ambers Olive-green (light yellowish)	Unknown; Pittsburgh area	Common
GII–102. Similar to GII–101; 12 fine wide-spaced ribs in wings. Frame about 2¹/₁₆″ x 3″; inscription: "PITTSBURGH" (about ¼″ below top of frame, starting at upper left and following line of frame to lower right) "PA" (at center, in line with "S" and "B"; "A" above half of "H", as on GI–105.	Like obverse but 14 ribs in right wing, 12 [?] in left; plain frame; end of pennant blunt.	Quart 29	Same as GII–101	Nos. 11 & 12 Type 9, but curves shallow	Aquamarine (bluish) Golden amber	Pittsburgh area	Common
GII–103. Similar to GII–101. Undetailed head; 11 wide-spaced ribs in wings. Narrow pennant with blunt end. Frame about 2⅛″ x 2¹/₁₆″; inscription in medium-size letters: about ⅛″ from top of frame. "PITTSBURGH" (starting left and above center following line of frame to right end above center) "PA" (at lower center in line with "SB").	Like obverse but plain frame about 2⅛″ x 3″.	Quart 29	Narrow vertical rib	Nos. 11 & 20a Type 6	Amber Cornflower blue (dark) Olive-green	Pittsburgh area	Common
GII–104. Similar to GII–103. Wings without ribs. Frame about 2³/₁₆″ x 3″; inscription: about ¼″ below top of frame, "PITTSBURGH" (starting center left end, following line of frame to center right end) "PA" (lower center, tops of letters in line with bottom of "P" and "H").	Like obverse but plain frame	Quart 29	Narrow vertical rib	No. 11 Type 9	Black (deep olive-green) Olive-green	Pittsburgh area	Common
GII–105. Similar to GII–101. Large head and beak, long eye; 13 ribs in right wing, 10 in left; 4 long bars and 1 short on breast. Pennant wide with short tapering end. Frame about 1⁹/₁₆″ x 2½″; inscription: about ⅛″ below top of frame, "PITTSBURGH" (starting at upper left end, following line of frame to lower right end) "PA" (at center in line with "S" and "B", "A" above half of "H").	Like obverse but bars on shield about same length; plain frame.	Pint 29	Narrow vertical rib	Nos. 10, 11 & 12 Type 9	Aquamarines Amber (light) Golden amber Olive-green Yellowish green	Pittsburgh area	Common
GII–106. Similar to GII–101. Small undetailed head; right wing; 9 ribs to rippled inner side; left, 10 ribs with round ends free on inner side; 6 bars on breast; feathered ends of 3 arrows in right talon. Frame about 1⁹/₁₆″ x 2½″; inscription: about ⅛″ below frame "PITTSBURGH" (starting center left end, following line of frame to right above center) "PA" (below center, tops of letters in line with leg of "P" of Pittsburgh).	Like obverse but 11 ribs in right wing, 10 in left; plain frame.	Pint 29	Narrow vertical rib	Nos. 10, 11, & 20a Type 5	Amber (shaded) Olive-amber Red-amber Aquamarine Black (deep olive-green)	Pittsburgh area	V. R. GII–DII–No. 17 Common
GII–107. Eagle like GII–106 but 10 ribs in right and 7 in left wing. Frame of medium-wide molding; inscription in very small letters, placed like GII–106 but "PA" slightly left below center.	Similar to obverse but 8 ribs in right wing, 7 in left, plain frame.	Pint 29	Narrow vertical rib	No. 11 Type 5	Black (deep olive-green)	Pittsburgh area	Comparatively scarce

GII–108. Eagle: undetailed head to left; wings with 4 (?) fine wide-spaced and nearly vertical ribs; on breast broad shield with 6 very narrow vertical bars; very short wide-spread legs; thunderbolt (3 arrows) in talons, feathered ends in right. Below eagle: large oval frame (wide molding) about 1⅝" x 2⁹/₁₆"; inscription "PITTSBURGH PA" placed as on GII–104. (See Form Groups No. 29.)

GII–109. Small eagle: head to right; wings with 4 wide ribs of which ends form inner side, raised high and spread downward and outward; "shield;" 4 vertical bars on breast; slender straight legs; long thunderbolt (3 crude arrows) in talons. Long narrow pennant, from beak to left in shallow arc above eagle. Below eagle: large oval frame (wide molding) about 1⁵/₁₆" x 1¾"; inscription: "PITTSBURGH" (starting at center left end, following line of frame to above center right end) "PA" (center; larger letters).

GII–110. Eagle: small head to left, long neck; wings with 11 heavy ribs in right, 9 in left and rippled inner edge, partly raised, spread downward and outward; on breast: shield with 5 vertical bars, no bottom line; short wide-spread legs; thunderbolt (3 arrows) in each talon. Narrow pennant with short thin end, from beak to right in shallow arc above eagle. Below eagle: large oval frame (wide molding) 2⅛" x 3¹/₁₆" with inscription: "CUNNINGHAM" (following upper line of frame) "& CO" (in center) "PITTSBURGH" (following lower line of frame).

GII–111. Eagle: long body, short thick neck and head to left, sunken eye; wings with 10 ribs in right and 9 in left, raised high, spread downward and outward; on breast, long slender shield with 7 vertical bars, no bottom line; thunderbolt (3 arrows) in talons, feathered ends in right. Short wide pennant with pointed end, from beak to right in shallow arc above eagle. Below eagle: large round-ended oblong frame (wide molding) about 1⅝" x 2⁹/₁₆"; inscription: following line of frame, "CUNNINGHAM" (upper) "PITTSBURGH" (lower), "& CO" (in center).

No.	Reverse	Size	Rib	Type	Color	Maker / Location	Rarity
GII–108	Like obverse but plain frame	Pint 29	Narrow vertical rib	Nos. 11 & 12. Similar to Type 5 but very short straight ends, curve shallow, long & close to side of base	Aquamarine Emerald-green Olive-green	Pittsburgh area	Common
GII–109	Like obverse but plain frame	Half-pint 29	Narrow vertical rib	Nos. 11, 19, & 20a Type 5	Aquamarines Emerald-green (dark)	Pittsburgh area	Probably V. R. GII–DII–16 Common
GII–110	Like obverse but 14 fine ribs in wings; inscription: "GLASS" (at top) "MANUFACTURERS" (at bottom, starting center left, following line of frame to center right); frame about 2⅛" x 3⅛".	Quart 29	Narrow vertical rib	No. 11 Type 9, but curve shallow	Aquamarine	Cunningham & Co. Pittsburgh, Pa.	Common
GII–111	Like obverse but 14 ribs in right wing, 11 in left; inscription like GII–110.	Pint 29	Fine vertical rib	No. 11 Type 5	Aquamarine Blue (light)	Same as above	V. R. GII–DII–7 Common

GII–101 GII–103 GII–105 GII–106 GII–109 GII–111

GROUP II—AMERICAN EAGLE FLASKS—*Continued*

OBVERSE	REVERSE	SIZE, FORM	EDGES	NECK, BASE	COLORS	GLASSHOUSE	NOTES, RARITY
GII–112. Eagle: head to left; wings with 16 ribs in right and 11 in left, rippled inner side; partly raised and spread (left) downward, (right) outward; on breast, broad shield with 5 vertical bars, no bottom line; very short legs; thunderbolt (3 arrows) in large talons, feathered ends in right. Wide pennant with short end from beak to right in arc above eagle. Below eagle: large oval frame (wide molding) about 2⅝" x 2⅝"; inscription: set in about ¼" and following line of frame, "CUNNINGHAM" (upper) "PITTSBURGH" (lower). "& CO" (in center).	Like obverse but 13 ribs in right and 9 in left wing; inscription like GII–110.	Pint 29	Narrow vertical rib	No. 11 Type 9, but shallow curves	Yellow-green (light)	Same as above	Comparatively scarce
GII–113. Eagle: head to left; 9 ribs in right wing, wide ends forming inner side, partly raised and spread (left) downward, (right) outward and downward; 5 vertical bars on breast; short thin legs; thunderbolt (3 arrows) in talons, feathered ends in right. Wide pennant with thin "hook" end from beak to right in arc above eagle. Below eagle: large oval frame (wide molding) about $1\frac{9}{16}$" x 2½"; inscription: "PITTSBURGH" (starting center left, following line of frame to right above center end) "PA" (in center) "M^{C}C & CO" (at bottom following line of frame).	Like obverse but 8 ribs in right wing; no inscription.	Pint 30	Smooth	No. 11 Type 1	Amber Aquamarine Yellow-olive-green	Attributed to Wm McCully & Co., Pittsburgh, Pa.	Scarce
GII–114. Eagle: small head to left, long neck; wings with 15 ribs in right and 17 in left, rippled inner right side, partly raised and spread downward and outward; on breast, shield with 5 vertical bars, no bottom line; very short thick legs; thunderbolt (3 arrows) in each large talon. Narrow blunt-ended pennant from beak to right in shallow arc above head. Below eagle: larger oval frame (wide molding) about $2\frac{3}{16}$" x $3\frac{1}{16}$"; inscription: "LOUISVILLE" (starting at center left end, following line of frame, to right end above center) "KY" (at center bottom).	Like obverse but 20 ribs in left wing; inscription: "GLASS" (at top) "WORKS" (at bottom center, following line of frame).	Quart 29	Narrow vertical rib	Similar to Nos. 6 & 20a Type 11	Aquamarine Green Yellow-green (light)	Louisville Glass Works, Louisville, Ky.	V. R. GII–DII–4 Scarce
GII–115. Eagle: small head and large beak, to left; wings with 9 ribs in right and 8 in left, ends forming inner side, partly raised and spread downward and (right) outward; 5 vertical bars on breast; short legs; thunderbolt (3 crude arrows) in talons. Wide pennant with short "hook" end, from back to right in shallow arc above eagle. Frame and inscription like GII–114, "LOUISVILLE" starting center left end, ending center right.	Like obverse but 11 ribs in right and 9 in left wing; inscription as on GII–114, but letters of "GLASS" slightly smaller than those of "WORKS."	Pint 29	Narrow vertical rib	Nos. 6a & 11 Type 5	Aquamarine Olive-amber (light) Emerald-green (light)	Louisville Glass Works, Louisville, Ky.	V. R. GII–DII–4 Scarce
GII–116. Large eagle: large head with large eye and small beak, to left; feathering of neck, breast and wings by short irregular ribs; wings slightly raised, spread outward and downward; below breast, long shield with 5½ vertical bars, ogee sides, rounded base; wide-spaced thin legs; thunderbolt (3 arrows) in claws of each talon. From beak, string of wide slightly rippled pennant in shallow reverse-S curve to right above eagle. Below eagle: long narrow round-ended oblong frame, about $1\frac{5}{16}$" x $3\frac{7}{16}$".	Similar to obverse; eagle slenderer; shield narrower, with 5 bars; pennant longer with forked end lower; frame, about 1¼" x $3\frac{5}{16}$".	Quart Similar to 22, Ill. 134	Smooth	No. 11 Type 1	Amber (dark) Aquamarine	Unknown	Scarce

GII-117. Similar to GII-116; frame, about 1 1/16" x 2¾".

GII-118. Eagle: large head with hooked beak and large concave almond-shaped eye, to left; neck and upper breast feathered by short ribs; wings with 9 ribs in right and 9½ in left (ends forming inner side), raised slightly and spread downward parallel to body; large well-defined shield. 3 stars in top panel above 3 wide-spaced vertical bars; heavy splayed legs; ovoid ball between talons, each with 3 claws holding thunderbolt (3 arrows). From beak, pennant with forked end, curving from below beak upward, then slightly downward to right above eagle.

GII-119. Similar to GII-118; 9 ribs in right and 11 in left wing; legs longer, straighter, and thinner.

GII-120. Small eagle: long body feathered by pebbling; small head to left; wings partly spread downward and outward, right slightly raised; long narrow shield with 5 vertical bars and rounded at bottom; straight thin legs; thunderbolt (3 arrows) in each talon. Very long narrow pennant with slightly forked end, curving upward from beak to right high above eagle. Below eagle and near base: long narrow round-ended frame (narrow molding) about 15/16" x 2¼".

GII-121. Eagle similar to GII-120; feathered by pebbling; large head with large curved beak and prominent eye, to left; wide neck; wings, right higher than left, partly spread downward parallel to body; long shield with 6 vertical bars, no bottom line; straight thin legs; thunderbolt (3 arrows) in each talon. Very narrow pennant with forked end curving upward from beak to right high above eagle and just beyond left wing. Below eagle and near base: long round-ended oblong frame, about 1⅛" x 2⅝".

No.	Reverse	Form	Edge	Mold	Color	Glasshouse	Remarks
GII-117	Similar to obverse; shield "waisted" at top; pennant longer.	Pint — Similar to 22, Ill. 134	Smooth	No. 11 Type 1	Aquamarine	Unknown	Comparatively scarce
GII-118	Similar to obverse; 10 ribs in right and 9 in left wing.	Pint 30	Smooth	Nos. 10 & 11 Type 1	Aquamarines, Brown amber, Olive-amber, Sapphire-blue (light), Green (light), Olive-green (light), Yellow-green (light)	Unknown	Possibly V. R. GII-DVII-3 Comparatively scarce
GII-119	Like obverse	Half-pint 30	Smooth	No. 10 Type 1	Aquamarines	Unknown	Scarce
GII-120	Similar to obverse; eagle's head more domed; 6½ bars on shield; pennant curved higher above eagle; frame about 15/16" x 2 3/16".	Pint 30	Smooth	No. 11 Type 11	Aquamarine	Unknown	Rare
GII-121	Similar to obverse; eagle shorter; shield longer in proportion to width; frame about 1⅛" x 2¾".	Quart 30	Smooth	No. 12 Type 1	Golden amber	Unknown	Rare

Figure labels: GII-112, GII-113, GII-114, GII-115, GII-116, GII-118, GII-119, GII-120, GII-121

581

GROUP II—AMERICAN EAGLE FLASKS—*Continued*

OBVERSE	REVERSE	SIZE, FORM	EDGES	NECK, BASE	COLORS	GLASSHOUSE	NOTES, RARITY
GII–122. Eagle similar to GII–120 but eye prominent, head larger and neck small in proportion to body; talons more defined. Frame about ¾″ x 1 13/16″.	Like obverse but end of pennant more deeply forked; frame about 1 13/16″.	Half-pint 30	Smooth	No. 11 Type 1	Aquamarine (pale)	Unknown	Comparatively scarce
GII–123. Eagle: feathered by short vertical ribs; large head to left; chunky neck, long body; wings spread downward close to body, tips only slightly curved; below breast, small shield with 3 vertical bars, no bottom line; very short straight legs; thunderbolt (3 crude arrows) in each talon. Wide pennant with forked end, curving upward from beak in deep arc to right above eagle. Below eagle: small round-ended oblong frame (narrow molding) about 5/16″ x 1¼″.	Similar to obverse but eagle's head flatter and neck chunkier; pennant shorter.	Half-pint 30	Smooth	No. 11 Type 1	Aquamarine (light)	Unknown	Comparatively scarce
GII–124. Eagle: feathered by short ribs; large head with large eye and beak, to left; chunky neck; wings partly raised and spread downward parallel to body; below breast, broad shield with 5 bars, no bottom line; very short straight legs; thunderbolt (3 crude arrows) in talons. In beak, string end of long wide pennant with deeply forked end to right in reverse-S curve above eagle. Below eagle: long rounded oblong frame (wide molding) about ⅝″ x 1⅞″.	Similar to obverse but eagle's head domed; frame about 11/16″ x 1⅞″.	Half-pint 29	Smooth	No. 11 Similar Type 1, center deeper and ovoid	Brown-amber	Unknown	Comparatively scarce
GII–125. Small eagle: head with large beak, to left; head, chunky neck and breast slightly pebbled; wings with 7 ribs in right and 5 in left, partly raised and spread downward close to body; below breast, wide shield with 4 vertical bars, no bottom line; short straight thin legs; thunderbolt (3 crude arrows) in talons. Wide short pennant with small point at end, from beak in shallow arc to right above eagle. Below eagle: large oblong frame (wide molding) about 1 1/16″ x 1⅝″.	Similar to obverse but eagle's head flatter; end of pennant more tapered and without point. Frame 1⅛″ x 1½″.	Half-pint 30	Smooth	No. 11 Type 5	Aquamarines	Unknown	Scarce
GII–126. Very small eagle: feathered by fine pebbling; head with large beak, to left; wide neck; wings partly raised and spread downward away from but nearly parallel to body; below breast, long shield with 5 vertical bars; short straight thin legs; talons grasping long slender stick, forked at left end. Wide faintly rippled pennant pointed at bottom of end, from beak, in shallow arc to right above eagle. Stick on which eagle perches, resting on top of leaves of large laurel wreath with stems crossed below long ribbon across bottom of wreath and with long forked ends hanging down toward base.	Similar to obverse but eagle's head shorter and less flat; pennant slightly wider and shorter.	Half-pint 30	Smooth	No. 10 Type 5	Amber (shaded) Golden amber Amethyst Aquamarine Blue (pale) Cornflower-blue Colorless Olive-amber (light) Puce	Unknown	V. R. GII–DII–4. Necks of amethyst, colorless & puce shorter than others Comparatively scarce
GII–127. Small eagle: head to right; long neck; wings comblike (9 ribs, sharp ends forming inner side), raised and spread downward parallel to body and tips curved inward; on breast, long shield with shallow curved V-top, 5 vertical bars, no bottom line; thin tapered legs; thunderbolt (3 arrows) in each talon. Below eagle: large oval frame (narrow molding) about 2 5/16″ x 2⅝″, with inscription "C & I".	Similar to obverse but 11 ribs in left wing, right wing shorter; shield broader.	Half-pint 29	Smooth	Narrow flat Similar to Type 7 but small concave dot at center of slightly dished disk	Aquamarine	Cunningham & Ihmsen, Pittsburgh, Pa.	V. R. GII–DVII–6 Comparatively scarce

No.	Edge	Capacity	Neck / Base	Color	Manufacturer	Reverse	References
GII–128	Smooth	Half-pint 30	Nos. 11 & 12, Type 7	Aquamarine; Sapphire (light)	Unknown	Similar to obverse but eagle slightly smaller, right instead of left wing lower and at wider angle to body; one end of frame in line with tip of right wing.	V. R. GII–DII–16; Rare flasks, Group C, No. 21; Rare
GII–129	Smooth	Pint 31	No. 10; Flat outer rim; mold seam, Type 5	Aquamarine; Green (light)	Probably the Zanesville Glass Works, of G. W. Kearns & Co., Market Street, Zanesville, Ohio.	Similar to obverse but eagle larger, olive branch longer; no inscription.	V. R. GII–DII–6; Rare flasks, Group C, No. 10; Form Group 31; Rare
GII–130	Smooth	Pint 30	No. 11; Similar to Type 7 but small, usually faint, flat dot at center of disk	Aquamarines	Unknown	Like obverse but eagle's head a little smaller; 7 bars in shield.	V. R. GII–DII–11; Scarce
GII–131	Smooth	Quart 30	No. 11, Type 1	Aquamarine; Olive-green; Yellow-green (light)	Unknown, probably midwestern	Plain	V. R. GII–DII–2; Rare flasks, Group C, No. 24; Rare
GII–132	Smooth	Pint 30	No. 11, Type 1	Aquamarine (pale)	Unknown, probably midwestern	Plain	Scarce

GII–128. Eagle: feathered by short ribs; large head with thin hooked beak and large eye, to right; wings raised and spread downward, left at angle to body; very short straight legs; thunderbolt (3 arrows) in each talon. Short wide slightly rippled pennant with forked end, from beak to left above eagle. Below eagle: long round-ended oblong frame (narrow molding) about $1\frac{1}{16}$" x $1\frac{3}{4}$"; one end in line with tip of left wing.

GII–129. Eagle: feathered by short ribs; large head with long hooked beak and large eye, to right; chunky neck and body; wings partly raised and spread downward and outward; on breast, tiny shield with 5 faint vertical bars; very short legs; thunderbolt (3 arrows) in each talon. Olive branch held in beak, curving upward and to left above head. Eagle placed left of center of side of flask. Below eagle: large rectangular frame with incurved corners (narrow molding); inscription: "ZANESVILLE," (across center; comma just below final "e") "OHIO" (below, in line with "VILLE").

GII–130. Eagle: small crested head with large hooked beak and large eye, to right; feathered by short ribs, ends on wings forming inner side; wide short neck; wings raised and spread downward, left at wide angle to body; on breast, large shield with dotted top panel above 6 vertical bars; long tail (5 ribs) below shield; wide-spread straight legs (at angle from end bars of shield); long thunderbolt (3 arrows with feathered ends) in right talon, short olive branch in left. In beak string of short pennant with forked end, to left above head and right wing. Below eagle: oval frame (medium-wide molding) about $1\frac{3}{8}$" x $2\frac{5}{16}$".

GII–131. Eagle: long head with small hooked beak, to right; feathering by short ribs; chunky neck; wings partly raised and spread downward nearly parallel with body; below breast, broad shield with 5 wide-spaced vertical bars, no bottom line; short legs; thunderbolt (3 arrows) in each talon. Long slightly rippled pennant of 2 parts: first with blunt end, from beak to left in shallow S-curve above eagle; second with forked end, from blunted end of first, curving down to left above wing. Below eagle: long round-ended oblong frame (narrow molding) about $\frac{15}{16}$" x 3".

GII–132. Similar to GII–130 but head with long hooked beak and small eye; long narrow oval frame (narrow molding) about 1" x $2\frac{3}{8}$".

GII–123 GII–124 GII–125 GII–126 GII–127 GII–128 GII–130 GII–131

583

GROUP II—AMERICAN EAGLE FLASKS—*Continued*

OBVERSE	REVERSE	SIZE, FORM	EDGES	NECK, BASE	COLORS	GLASSHOUSE	NOTES, RARITY
GII–133. Eagle: small head with curved beak and small eye, to right; feathered by pebbling; wings raised and spread downward, right at angle to body; below breast, shield with 3 stars in panel above 3 wide-spaced vertical bars (similar to GII–119); long straight splayed legs; thunderbolt (3 arrows) in each talon; narrow pennant with forked end, from beak to left above eagle. Below eagle: large oval frame (wide molding).	Plain	Pint 30	Smooth	No. 11 Type 1	Aquamarine	Unknown	Scarce
GII–134. Eagle: head with long beak and large eye, to right; body and wings feathered by large pebbling; short narrow neck and "legs" by fine pebbling; long slender body with wide "legs" and broad tail of 8 ribs spread downward below poorly defined talons; wings partly raised and spread downward parallel with body; tiny olive branch in beak. Inscription above eagle, "D. KIRKPATRICK & CO" in semicircle and below in arc, "CHATTANOOGA above "TENN" in straight line.	Plain	Pint 29	Smooth	No. 10 Type 1	Aquamarine	Unknown; midwestern	**Made for D. Kirkpatrick & Co.**, Chattanooga, Tenn., wholesale liquor dealers, proprietors of the Globe Distillery ca. 1865–80. Rare flasks, Group C, No. 14. Only 2 specimens recorded (1965)
GII–134a. Similar to GII–134 but with pronounced oval pebbling on body and without indication of legs, 8 tail feathers from body.	Plain	Pint 29	Smooth	No. 10 Type 1	Aquamarine (greenish)	Unknown; midwestern	See Note GII–134. Reported by Richard H. Wood, 1965. Only example recorded
GII–135. Eagle medallion: small eagle on slightly sunken panel about $3^{1}/_{16}$" in diameter; feathered on body, legs and upper wings by fine pebbling, on lower wings by fine ribs with ends forming outer edge; head, with large eye and long open beak, and body turned slightly to left; long wings spread and raised high as though taking off; heavy legs; small "olive branch" in each talon.	Plain	Quart Variant 32	Wide flat band (about ¾" wide)	Double round collar (upper wider than lower), narrow space between Type 21 but with "11P" in center	Green (pale)	Unknown	Rare flasks, Group C, No. 25, as "very rare" (1941) Sam Laidacker said common in 1962
GII–136. Eagle medallion: large well-drawn eagle in profile, facing left and perched on heavy curved bar; raised head with prominent eye and hooked beak; feathered by dashlike ribs; wings raised high and partly spread above body; shoulder and end of left wing shown; long thick legs; large talons grasping bar.	Plain	Quart Variant 32; end bands tapering on shoulders to neck	Wide flat band	Round collar, slight bevel below (20a) Type 21 but disk and mold seams faint; inscription at center: "LC&R"	Colorless	Unknown	Common
GII–137. Like GII–136 but not so well defined	Plain	Pint Like GII–136	Wide flat band	Like GII–136 Type 21 but disk and mold seam faint	Colorless	Unknown	Common
GII–137a. Like GII–136 but not so well defined	Plain	Half-pint Like GII–136	Wide flat band	Like GII–136 Like GII–137	Colorless	Unknown	Comparatively scarce

584

Description		Size	Base	Neck / Collar	Color	Glassworks	Rarity
GII–138. Eagle taking off from uneven ground, to right; feathering by short ribs; wings wide-spread above body; well-defined head with large eye and open hooked beak; long body with short tail, feathered legs, open talons. (One of the finest and most spirited stylizations of the American Eagle in figured flasks.)	Plain	Half-pint 29	Smooth	Double round collar Smooth, slightly dished	Amber (shaded)	Unknown	Scarce
GII–139. Small eagle: large head with large eye, to left; linear outline of head, neck, and outer side of wings; wings raised and spread downward close to body; neck and upper part of wings pebbled. 5 short ribs on lower wide bar above 5 short vertical bars; ribbed wide tail; single olive branch in right talon, thunderbolt (3 arrows) in left.	Plain	Half-pint Similar to 23, Ill. 134	Smooth	Very short neck Deep round collar; narrow round, lower bevel (20a) Type 1	Amber Blue (dark)	Unknown	V. R. GII–DII–1 Example with 1865 patent stopper reported Common
GII–140. Eagle (similar to those on reverse of Clasped-Hands flasks GXII): flying to right; plain head with long eye and thin hooked beak; feathering of body and wings by short ribs; right wing parallel to body and left above and beyond head; long tail of graduated ribs curved downward; shield with top line on breast, tilted to right below eagle. no bars but stars indicated in upper field by pebbling; long olive branch downward to left from side of shield and thunderbolt (4 arrows) to right. Two pennants, each of long plain blunt-ended section and a short slightly rippled fork-ended one, from beak in S-curve to left: upper—across tip of and along top edge of left wing and above most of right wing; lower—across shield below "stars," forked section in deep upcurve toward end of tail. Below eagle: round-ended frame. top and bottom curved to point at center, about 1⅝" x 2³⁄₁₆". Draftee walking left on uneven ground: small figure. large head. wearing long swallow-tailed coat with tails flying backward. tight trousers; carrying portmanteau in left hand; right arm extended from shoulder, hand open; shallow S-curved pennant at end of line issuing from man's lips and inscribed "DRAFTED". "Springfield" rifle with bayonet pointed at draftee's midriff. Below figure, broad shallow shield-shaped frame.		Pint 28	Smooth	No. 10 Mold seam similar to Type 6 but curve shallower; round-ended oblong depression at center	Aquamarine	Not definitely known Attributed by Van Rensselaer to Zanesville. Ohio	V. R. GVI–25. Rare flasks. Group C. No. 9. Inspired doubtless by The Federal Draft Act. Mar. 1863 Extremely rare
GII–140a. Like GII–140	Like GII–140	Pint 28	Smooth	No. 10 Short straight mold seam to round-ended depression with oval nipple off-center	Aquamarine	Unknown	Extremely rare

GII–134 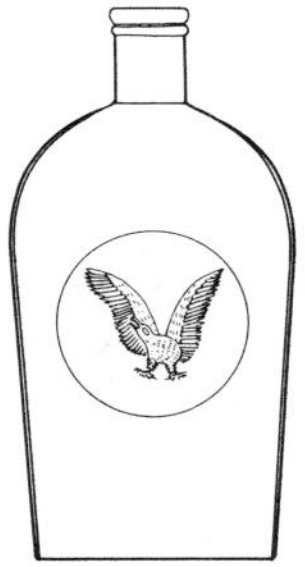 GII–135  GII–136  GII–138  GII–139 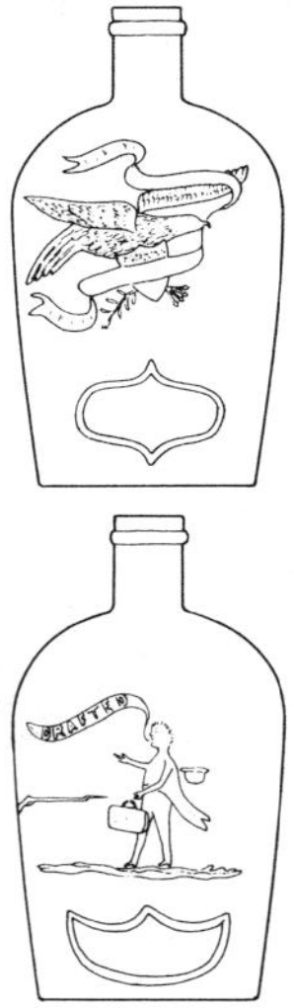 GII–140

585

GROUP II—AMERICAN EAGLE FLASKS—*Continued*

OBVERSE	REVERSE	SIZE, FORM	EDGES	NECK, BASE	COLORS	GLASSHOUSE	NOTES, RARITY
GII–141. Eagle flying to right: head with oval eye and small hooked beak; neck, body, and wings feathered by pebbling; right wing raised parallel to body and left above head to right; broad tail of 5 ribs slanting downward; tapered legs; 2 pennants from line in beak. in long shallow curves, thin at center, forked ends: upper line behind left wing. pennant to left above eagle; lower, below eagle, top end of first section seemingly held in talons. Below lower pennant: panel in style of architectural monument: semicircular pediment with simple scroll ornament flanking oval, supported by gallery of 22 narrow ribs; below ribs. large panel with sides incurved to point at center bearing a flag with 6 stripes (ribs) ending in points; base: narrow frame with ends in curve slanting to scrolls from which rise a slender curved rib topped by small bird, possibly dove, about to fly to right.	Indian wearing tunic and crown, facing left and shooting arrow at small bird in flight. Small dog behind Indian and in front of stylized tree. tall and leafless. Dog standing on and Indian's foot slightly above large rectangular frame of very narrow molding; side incurved to center points. with small scroll at each corner; at center, 4 oval petals with pearl at center.	Quart 28	Smooth	No. 12 Type 1	Aquamarine	Unknown: possibly Pittsburgh area. possibly Cunningham & Co.	V. R. GI–49 Rare flasks. Group C. No. 15 Very rare
GII–142. Design similar to GII–141 but more elaborate. Eagle more carefully formed; head with large eye and long hooked beak; feathered by ribbing; talons grasping top of plain shield. Upper pennant shorter and passing over left wing; lower across shield, forked end slanting downward; end of shield cut off by monument. In pediment of monument: central column, sailing ship at left and sheaves of grain at right; gallery, with top and base projecting at ends. of 13 arches; panel narrower at base and deeper curves on sides; rifle above large American flag with 6 stripes and 32 stars, flying to left; base frame inscribed "CONTINENTIAL"; at each side, rising from scrolls, laurel branch topped by unfeathered large dove with olive branch in beak. Just above top of pediment, 13 tiny "stars," 7 at left and 6 at right.	Design similar to GII–141, but Indian stockier, wearing headdress and short skirt; dog larger and nearer Indian's right foot; bird perched on top of short leafless tree rising from right end of frame. In frame. "CUNNINGHAMS & CO" (in semicircle above ornament and from below center left end to below center right) "PITTSBURGH, PA." across bottom.	Quart 28	Smooth	No. 12 Type 16 but end of flask not so rounded	Aquamarine Cornflower-blue (light) Green Olive-yellow	Cunningham's & Co., Pittsburgh, Pa.	V. R. GI–48 Scarce
GII–143. Flying eagle similar to GIV–42 and GXII–43; tail shorter and wider; feathering on body and right wing by fewer and longer dashes; left wing detached from body and tip blending into long section of upper pennant, lower pennant curving from beak down across large plain shield which is nearly at right angles to body; olive branch from left of shield below pennant, thunderbolt (3 arrows) from right.	Plain	Quart 38 (calabash)	4 vertical flutes	No. 15 Type 28, ends fluted	Aquamarine Grass-green Emerald-green	Unknown	V. R. GII–DII–10 Common
GII–144. *See No. 3, Ill. 124.* Nine heavy wide-spaced vertical ribs; 3 at center interrupted about 1¾" below neck and 1⅛" above base by circular eagle-medallion about 2½" in diameter and with molding the width of ribs. Small eagle: pebbled feathering; head raised, to left; long neck; chunky wings raised and partly spread downward; broad short body; on breast, shield with broad horizontal bar above 4 short vertical bars; thunderbolt (3 arrows) in left talon, olive branch in right. (Rib count does not include rib at mold seam on end.)	Vertical ribs	Pint Flattened irregular oblong, tapering slightly at bottom; high nearly flat shoulder	Vertical rib	Plain lip Pontil mark	Green	Possibly the Keene-Marlboro-Street Glassworks, Keene, N.H.	Eagle similar to GII–29 Only 1 specimen recorded (1965)

For American eagles in other groups, see the following:
GI–1 through 16a, GI–26 and 27, GI–62, GI–64 through 67, GI–69, GI–76 and 77, GI–79 and 79a, GI–90 through 92, GI–117 through 122, GI–126.
GIV–1 through 27, GIV–31 through 33, GIV–37 through 42.
GV–8 through 11.
GIX–7 through 45.
GXII–1 through 35, GXII–43.
GXIII–3.

GROUP III—CORNUCOPIA FLASKS

No.	Obverse	Reverse	Size	Edge	Neck / Lip	Colors	Attribution	Rarity
GIII–1. Designs on oval panels banded at top and sides by beading similar to that on edges. Inverted cornucopia, coiled to left and filled with produce.	Large circular beaded medallion containing large geometric star-shaped design with 6 ribbed points and in center circle small 8-petaled rosette. Beneath medallion modified symmetrical palm motif rising from pointed oval with hatching.	Half-pint Similar to 12, Ill. 133	Horizontal beading	Plain lip Pontil mark	Deep shaded amber / Pale olive-yellow / Clear yellow-green / Light green / Red-amber (S.L.)	Midwestern; glasshouse not definitely known	V. R. No. 21 GIII Very rare
GIII–2. Designs on oval panels. Cornucopia, narrow body coiled to left and filled with produce. NOTE: The cornucopia in this flask is similar to that on GII–43, Eagle and Cornucopia, Kensington Glass Works.	Same as obverse	Half-pint 11	Vertically ribbed 3, heavy medial rib	Plain lip Pontil mark Broad sloping collar (No. 15)	Deep bluish green / Clear brilliant amber / Aquamarine	Attributed to Kensington Glass Works, Philadelphia, Pa.	V. R. No. 23 GIII Comparatively scarce
GIII–3. Large cornucopia coiled to left and filled with produce. "X" at left of cornucopia. Collection of Clifton Blake.	Same as obverse	One and a half pints 11	Smooth with narrow vertical medial rib	Plain lip Pontil mark	Pale green / Dark olive-green	Unknown, possibly Keene-Marlboro-St.	V. R. No. 25 GIII Extremely rare

GII–141   GII–142   GII–143   GIII–1   GIII–2   GIII–3

GROUP III—CORNUCOPIA FLASKS—*Continued*

OBVERSE	REVERSE	SIZE, FORM	EDGES	NECK, BASE	COLORS	GLASSHOUSE	NOTES, RARITY
GIII–4. Designs on oval panels. Large cornucopia, coiled to left and turned in; filled with produce.	Large urn with 5 heavy vertical bars, filled with produce.	Pint 11	Vertically ribbed 3, heavy medial rib	Plain lip Pontil mark — [Green, light (R.W.); Emerald-green (S.L.)]	Clear green, yellowish tone; Aquamarine; Yellow-green; Olive-amber; Deep amber; Deep olive-green; Green, pale (R.W.)	Coventry, Conn., Glass Works	V. R. No. 1 GIII Common. Also listed in half-pint size. We have never seen a specimen of this flask.
GIII–5. Designs on oval panels similar to No. 4.	Similar to No. 4 but there is a distinct circular depression extending across the center rib and cutting into the edges of each adjoining rib.	Pint 11	Vertically ribbed 3, heavy medial rib	Plain lip Pontil mark	Olive-amber; Olive-green	Unknown	Not listed by Van Rensselaer Scarce
GIII–6. Designs on oval panels. Similar to No. 4 except slight variations in the produce in cornucopia. On each side tiny individual dots are used to accent the modeling of the design. NOTE: This bottle is very much later than the period of the historical flasks. It was probably made ca. 1900 to 1915, copying the mold of No. 4, not as a fake but for some special purpose as containers for perfume. We have seen specimens decorated by painting and fitted with fancy stopper. However, they are relatively rare.	Similar to No. 4 except slight variation in produce in urn.	Pint 3	Vertically ribbed 3, heavy medial rib	Plain lip Smooth	Reddish amber	Unknown	Not listed by Van Rensselaer Rare
GIII–7. Designs on oval panels. Cornucopia, coiled to left and filled with produce.	Urn with 6 bars and filled with produce.	Half-pint 11	Vertically ribbed 3, heavy medial rib	Plain lip Pontil mark — [Blue-aquamarine (S.L.); Green, medium; Green, deep (M. Knapp, Jr.); Blue-green (R.W.); Emerald-green (S.L.)]	Deep yellow-green; Light green; Aquamarine; Clear deep olive-green; Dark olive-green (black); Olive-amber; Amber; Golden amber (S.L.)	Keene-Marlboro-St., Keene, N.H.; also Coventry, Conn., Glass Works	V. R. No. 2 GIII Common
GIII–8. Designs on oval panels. Cornucopia, similar to No. 7 but large pearl at left.	Similar to No. 7	Half-pint 11	Same as No. 7	Plain lip Pontil mark — [Green, deep (R.W.)]	Golden amber; Olive-amber; Aquamarine (C.G.); Green, yellowish, light (C.G.)	Unknown	V. R. No. 3 GIII Common
GIII–8a. Like GIII–8 but pearl circular instead of oval, and nearer cornucopia.	Like GIII–8	Half-pint 11	3 vertical ribs heavy medial	Plain lip Pontil mark	Olive-amber	Unknown	Comparatively scarce
GIII–9. Designs on oval panels. Cornucopia similar to No. 7.	Similar to No. 7	Half-pint 11	Smooth without medial rib, only fine mold seam	Plain lip Pontil mark	Brilliant yellow-green; Pale green; Green, medium	Unknown	Not listed by Van Rensselaer Common

No.	Description	Secondary description	Size	Ribbing	Lip / Pontil	Colors	Location	Reference / Rarity
GIII–10. Similar to No. 7 except compound leaf on slender stem protrudes from left side of cornucopia.	Similar to No. 7		Half-pint 11	Vertically ribbed 3, heavy medial rib	Plain lip. Pontil mark	Light golden amber, Olive-amber, Dark olive-green, Green, clear medium (M.B.K.)	Unknown	V. R. No. 4 GIII. Common
GIII–11. Designs on oval panels. Similar to No. 7	Similar to No. 7 but there is a slight widening between the 2 center ribs forming what appears to be a slightly depressed circular spot.		Half-pint 11	Vertically ribbed 3, heavy medial rib	Plain lip. Very rarely with broad sloping collar; have seen only one specimen. Pontil mark	Clear dark olive-green, Deep olive-green (black), Green, medium, Blue-green	Saratoga (Mt. Pleasant) and Mt. Vernon, New York, Glass House	Not listed by Van Rensselaer. Common
GIII–12. Designs on oval panels. Cornucopia entirely different in form, sides not enclosed by line, giving a broken effect; coiled to right. Produce also entirely different.	Urn entirely different in form and with 7 vertical bars. Produce also different.		Half-pint 11	Vertically ribbed 3, medial rib heavier	Plain lip. Pontil mark	Amber, Olive-amber, Deep olive-green, Golden amber (M. Knapp, Jr.)	Unknown	V. R. No. 5 GIII. Comparatively scarce
GIII–13. Designs on oval panels. Slightly larger flask than Nos. 7 through 12. Cornucopia coiled slightly to right and filled with produce. In general appearance somewhat similar to No. 12 but details of fruit and ribbing of cornucopia different.	Urn filled with produce. The general form of the urn is similar to that on No. 7 but it is more slender and has seven bars instead of six. Produce in urn quite different and fewer pieces.		Half-pint 18	Vertically ribbed 3, with heavy medial rib	Plain lip. Pontil mark	Very pale green, Emerald-green, Aquamarine, Golden amber (R. W.), Olive-amber (C. G.), Olive-green	Lancaster, N. Y., Glass Works	V. R. No. 8 GIII. Common

NOTE: This circular depressed spot is characteristic of fragments of these flasks excavated on the sites of the Saratoga (Mt. Pleasant) and Mt. Vernon Glass Works by Harry Hall White. It is not found in fragments of similar half-pint cornucopia flasks excavated by him on the site of the Keene-Marlboro-St. Factory.

GIII–4   GIII–5   GIII–6   GIII–7   GIII–8   GIII–11   GIII–12   GIII–13

GROUP III—CORNUCOPIA FLASKS—*Continued*

OBVERSE	REVERSE	SIZE, FORM	EDGES	NECK, BASE	COLORS	GLASSHOUSE	NOTES, RARITY
GIII–14. Designs on oval panels. Similar to No. 13, but variation in size and distribution of produce.	Similar to No. 13 but slight variations in details of produce. Also handle does not touch side of urn, and there is a slight variation in the 2 center members in the base of the urn.	Half-pint 18	Vertically ribbed 3, narrow medial rib	Plain lip Pontil mark	Emerald-green Aquamarine	Lancaster, N.Y., Glass Works	Not listed by Van Rensselaer Comparatively scarce
GIII–14a. Like GIII–14	Like GIII–14 but with about dime-size circular depression in upper part of basket.	Half-pint 18	3 vertical ribs heavy medial	Plain lip Pontil mark	Bluish green. (deep)	Lancaster, N.Y., Glass Works	Reported by Charles Vuono
GIII–15. Similar to No. 14 but variation in produce and coil at end of cornucopia lacking.	Similar to No. 14 but variation in produce, part of which is very indistinct and ribs on bowl of urn entirely fade at juncture with stem. Handle of urn at right similar to No. 14 and not touching side of urn.	Half-pint 18	Vertically ribbed 3, narrow medial rib	Plain lip Pontil mark	Deep yellow-green Deep blue-green Aquamarine Blue, grayish	Lancaster, N.Y., Glass Works	Not listed by Van Rensselaer Common

NOTE: The three flasks Nos. 13, 14, and 15 show an unusual feature in that the panel carrying the design is sunken.

OBVERSE	REVERSE	SIZE, FORM	EDGES	NECK, BASE	COLORS	GLASSHOUSE	NOTES, RARITY
GIII–16. Designs on oval panels. Large cornucopia formed of horizontal bars not joined together or enclosed by line, giving a complete broken effect and coiled to right. Large heavy pearl just inside the curl of the lip. Cornucopia filled with produce loosely arranged.	Large urn with 5 bars similar to that on No. 4; filled with produce loosely arranged and different from No. 4. In semicircle above produce "LANCASTER.GLASS WORKS, N.Y." The period after the N is diamond-shaped. NOTE: A small oval ornament connects the outer right bar in the urn with the top frame of the urn. This does not appear on the other 2 pint flasks Nos. 17 and 18 that do not have the inscription.	Pint 18	Vertically ribbed 3, heavy medial rib	Plain lip Pontil mark Pontil with disk	Light blue Peacock-green Emerald-green Violet-blue Clear amber Aquamarine Golden amber (S.L.) Sapphire-blue (S.L.) Green, light (E.D.) Olive-green (C.G.)	Lancaster, N.Y., Glass Works	V. R. No. 6 GIII Common
GIII–17. Similar to No. 16 but variations in details of both produce and cornucopia.	Similar to No. 16 but variations in details of produce and urn and no inscription.	Pint 18	Same as No. 16	Plain lip Double rounded collar Pontil mark Narrow round collar [Green, medium Olive-green, deep Peacock-green (R.W.) Yellow-green]	Deep yellowish green Emerald-green Pale green Aquamarine Deep bluish green Pale yellow-green Clear deep amber Golden amber (S.L.) Red-amber (S.L.) Green, bluish, light	Lancaster, N.Y., Glass Works	V. R. No. 7 GIII Common
GIII–18. Similar to No. 16 but variations in details of produce and cornucopia. Also varies from No. 17.	Urn similar to No. 16 but bar forming continuation of handles is broken at top and turns down to join ribs of the urn. Produce in urn entirely different and shows leaves at top similar to No. 4.	Pint 18	Same as No. 16	Plain lip Pontil mark [Blue-green (S.L.) Emerald-green, deep (S.L.) Olive-green (R.W.)]	Deep yellowish green Deep brilliant green-yellow tone Olive-amber (S.L.) Red-amber (S.L.)	Lancaster, N.Y., Glass Works	Not listed by Van Rensselaer Rare

GROUP IV—MASONIC FLASKS

GIV-1. Masonic Decoration—From a mosaic pavement rise 2 columns surmounted by archway with Keystone in center; beneath Keystone radiant all-seeing eye and between columns radiant triangle enclosing the letter "G" and above it open book with square and compasses. At left of column, trowel with skull and crossbones beneath. At right of column is Jacob's Ladder ascending to "Cloudy Canopy" or "Star Decked Heaven," represented by radiant quarter moon surrounded by 7 stars at right of archway. At left of archway blazing sun. Beneath pavement at right beehive and at left crossed level and plumb line. Thirty-four bricks in pavement.

NOTE: On many of the flasks showing the Masonic Archway and Mosaic Pavement it is sometimes difficult to count accurately the number of bricks in the pavement. On many specimens 2 bricks show faintly at or in the base of each column and are included in the count. This is usually the case in connection with the Lafayette Masonic flasks made at Coventry, Connecticut, and Mount Vernon, New York, glass works.

GIV-1a. Like GIV-1.

GIV-2. Same as No. 1.

NOTE: It was learned in 1966 that GIV-2 was produced before GIV-1. The initials "HS" in the GIV-2 mold were changed to "EP". See text on Masonic flasks.

	Reverse	Size	Ribbing	Lip	Color	Factory	Rarity
GIV-1	American Eagle, head turned to left; shield with vertical and horizontal bars on breast; wings partly raised and left foreshortened. Thunderbolt (3 arrows) in its left talons, olive branch in right. Above eagle ribbon with inscription "E PLURIBUS UNUM" (letters frequently indistinct). Beneath eagle oval frame with letters "IP" joined together (old-fashioned J). The initials stand for Justus Perry.	Pint 8	Vertically ribbed (5)	Usually tooled; occasionally with plain lip, rarely with crude collared lip. Pontil mark	Amethyst, Deep amethyst (black), Clear green, Clear green, yellowish tone, Deep bluish green, Light yellow-green, Violet-blue, Clear, almost crystal, Pale amethystine moonstone, Dark olive-green (black), Blue, grayish, Blue, pale (M. Knight, Jr.) [boxed: Sapphire-blue, Green, deep]	Keene-Marlboro-Street Glass Works, Keene, N.H.	V. R. No. 18 D1; GIV Common
GIV-1a	Like GIV-1. Initials not joined—"IP" for Justus Perry—the bar joining the I and P in GIV-1 removed from the mold.	Pint 8	5 vertical ribs	Plain lip. Pontil mark	Green (clear)	Keene-Marlboro-Street Glass Works, Keene, N.H.	Rare
GIV-2	Same as No. 1 except oval frame with letters "H S." The initials stand for Henry Schoolcraft.	Pint 8	Vertically ribbed (5)	Usually tooled; occasionally with plain lip, rarely with crude collared lip. Pontil mark	Clear deep green, Light green, Dark olive-amber (black), Very pale green, Emerald-green (S.L.), Olive-green, Yellow-green (S.L.)	Same as No. 1	V. R. No. 20 D1; GIV Comparatively scarce

NOTE: The oval frames beneath eagle and containing the letters on Nos. 1 and 2 are usually referred to as beaded. Actually the frame is comprised of a classic laurel wreath, the 2 ribbons tied at center below the letters. On many of these flasks the oval frame appears to be perfectly smooth and also on some specimens the ribbon above eagle appears to be smooth. This is due to a cold mold or defective blowing. Van Rensselaer's No. 19 Div. I GIV is one of these flasks probably blown from a cold mold.

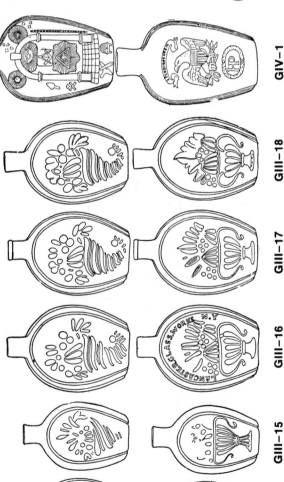

GIII-14 GIII-15 GIII-16 GIII-17 GIII-18 GIV-1 GIV-2

GROUP IV—MASONIC FLASKS—*Continued*

OBVERSE	REVERSE	SIZE, FORM	EDGES	NECK, BASE	COLORS	GLASSHOUSE	NOTES, RARITY
GIV–3. Similar to Nos. 1 and 2 except 31 bricks forming pavement and stars in "Cloudy Canopy" round without points; also slight variation in details of some of the emblems.	Similar to Nos. 1 and 2 except 12 tiny dots (3 rows) representing stars on upper part of shield instead of horizontal bars. Ribbon with heavy crimping (9 segments or folds in crimping) which resembles heavy beading and does not contain inscription. Large beaded oval frame containing letters "J.K It is not known for whom or what B." these initials stand. Some wag has suggested John K. Barleycorn.	Pint 18	Vertically ribbed (5)	Usually tooled; occasionally plain lip, rarely with heavy collared lip Pontil mark ___ Gray-blue Peacock-blue (S.L.) Olive-green between amber at top and base Lavender, pale (S.L.) Puce (S.L.)	Deep sapphire-blue Greenish blue Puce Clear with bluish tint Clear light green Clear bluish green Deep yellow-green Clear yellow-green with amber tones Clear olive-green with amber tones Peacock-green Clear Black (amber), light streaks near shoulder	Same as No. 1	V. R. No. 15 D1; GIV Comparatively scarce
GIV–4. Same as No. 3 but rays surrounding triangle slightly different in formation; also radiant sun not quite as large.	Similar to No. 3 except ribbon over eagle has more segments in crimping and apparently with regularized pattern of indentation which might suggest lettering. Letters "J.K. in oval B." frame slightly smaller and not as heavy.	Pint 8	Vertically ribbed (5)	Tooled Pontil mark ___ Olive-green Yellow-green, light	Cornflower-blue Peacock-green Clear light green Deep yellow-green Black (deep amethyst) Colorless, smoky from pennant to lip (E.D.)	Same as No. 1	V. R. No. 16 D1; GIV Less frequently encountered than No. 3 Comparatively scarce
GIV–5. Similar to No. 3 except 28 bricks forming pavement and slight variation in some of the emblems, especially fewer rays surround radiant triangle. all-seeing eye, sun, and quarter moon. Instead of 7 only 6 stars, round without definite points, surround quarter moon.	Similar to No.3 except the large beaded oval frame contains a large 8-pointed star. Size of star varies slightly in specimens. Shield on eagle's breast has only 8 tiny dots in 2 rows representing stars.	Pint 8	Vertically ribbed (5)	Tooled Plain lip Occasional specimens with wider mouth than normal Round rolled-over collar (No. 6), wide mouth Pontil mark	Amethyst and clear in striations, the over-all effect being of brilliant amethyst Clear light green Deep green-yellow tone Clear yellow-green ___ Clear, almost crystal Green, medium Green, deep	New England, works unknown	V. R. No. 11 D1; GIV Comparatively scarce
GIV–6. Same as No. 5	Similar to No. 5 except ribbon and oval frame appear smooth and not beaded which is probably due to cold mold or defective blowing.	Pint 8	Vertically ribbed (5)	Tooled Occasionally found with wider mouth than normal Narrow round ring below plain lip ___ Pontil mark	Clear light green Green, deep (E.D.) Yellow-green (S.L.)	New England, works unknown	V. R. No. 10 D1; GIV Comparatively scarce

592

Designation	Description	Capacity	Ribbing	Lip / Pontil	Color	Origin	Notes
GIV-7. Similar to No. 5 with slight variation in rays of radiant all-seeing eye; skull and crossbones slightly smaller.	Similar to No. 5 except shield has 12 dots, 3 rows of 4 each representing stars instead of 2 rows. Star in oval frame beneath eagle slightly smaller.	Pint 8	Vertically ribbed (5)	Tooled Pontil mark	Deep bluish green Colorless, amethyst-streaked Blue-green (G.A.) Green, light (S.L.) Green, medium (S.L.) *[Emerald-green, medium (S.L.) Yellow-green]*	New England, works unknown	Probably included as Van Rensselaer's No. 11 D1; GIV Comparatively scarce
GIV-7a. Like GIV-7	Like GIV-7 but pennant with open center, star tipped to left in beaded oval which has elongated bead like GIV-10.	Pint 8	5 vertical ribs	Plain lip Pontil mark	Yellow-green	New England, works unknown	Reported by Charles B. Gardner, 1968 Extremely rare
GIV-8. Similar to No. 7	Similar to No. 7 except star in oval frame beneath eagle slightly different in form.	Pint 8	Vertically ribbed (5)	Tooled Pontil mark	Deep bluish green Colorless (G.A.) Green, amber streaks Green, striations in varied shades	New England, works unknown	Probably included as Van Rensselaer's No. 11 D1; GIV Comparatively scarce
GIV-8a. Similar to GIV-7 and 8 but Paschal Lamb at lower left instead of Level and Plumb line.	Like GIV-8	Pint 8	5 vertical ribs	Plain lip Pontil mark	Colorless	New England, works unknown	Extremely rare
GIV-9. Similar to Nos. 7 and 8	Similar to Nos. 7 and 8 except star in oval frame is smaller; beading on some specimens shows only faintly on oval frame.	Pint 8	Vertically ribbed (5)	Tooled Plain lip Double flat collar Pontil mark	Light yellow-green Clear light green Emerald-green (S.L.) Olive-green	New England, works unknown	Probably Van Rensselaer's No. 14 D1; GIV but we have never seen the flask with a bar instead of ribbon over eagle's head. Scarce
GIV-10. Similar to No. 7	Similar to No. 7 except ribbon appears to have a vertical depression or dividing line in center. In the beading of oval frame 1 bead at lower right is elongated and extends downward well outside frame. The 8-pointed star within frame is smaller and very irregular.	Pint 8	Vertically ribbed (5)	Tooled Plain lip Pontil mark	Yellow-green Clear light green Clear light green, yellowish tone Emerald-green, light (S.L.) Green, bluish (E.D.)	New England, works unknown	Probably Van Rensselaer's No. 12 D1; GIV His No. 13 is apparently simply a No. 12 with shorter neck and tooled mouth. Scarce

GIV-8 GIV-9 GIV-10 GIV-7 GIV-5 GIV-3 GIV-4

GROUP IV—MASONIC FLASKS—Continued

OBVERSE	REVERSE	SIZE, FORM	EDGES	NECK, BASE	COLORS	GLASSHOUSE	NOTES, RARITY
GIV–10a. Similar to GIV–10	Similar to GIV–10 but star (more accurately 8-petaled flower) turned so the twin long petals fall at lower left in beaded frame. One bead at lower right elongated.	Pint 8	5 vertical ribs	No. 4 (tooled) Pontil mark	Yellow-green	Same as above	Scarce
GIV–10b. Similar to GIV–10	Similar to GIV–10 but with large 8-petaled flower (4 long and 4 short petals in alternate pairs) in beaded frame. One bead at lower right elongated as on GIV–10a.	Pint 8	5 vertical ribs	No. 4 (tooled) Pontil mark	Green (clear)	Same as above	Scarce
GIV–11. Similar to GIV–7	Similar to No. 10 except ornament in oval frame has lost any resemblance to a star and is more like a crudely formed small leaf. Van Rensselaer refers to it as like "head of a key."	Pint 8	Vertically ribbed	Tooled Plain lip Pontil mark	Clear with amethystine tone Clear light green Olive-yellow	New England, works unknown	V. R. No. 17 D1; GIV Rare
GIV–12 Same as No. 7	Similar to No. 7 except in the center of oval frame a small circle with slightly concave center.	Pint 8	Vertically ribbed	Tooled Pontil mark	Deep bluish green Emerald-green, deep (S.L.)	New England, works unknown	Not listed by Van Rensselaer Very rare
GIV–13. Similar to No. 3 except 28 bricks in pavement and symbol at right below pavement is the Ark of the Covenant and at left small animal, probably the Paschal Lamb. Rays surrounding blazing sun and radiant quarter moon fewer in number. Also radiant all-seeing eye slightly different in formation.	Similar to No. 3 except star in oval frame similar to that on No. 9.	Pint 8	Vertically ribbed	Tooled Pontil mark	Clear light green Yellow-green	New England, works unknown	Not listed by Van Rensselaer Rare
GIV–13a. Similar to GIV–13 but 29 bricks in pavement; design ending about 1¼" above base of flask. See No. 2, Ill. 125.	Similar to GIV–13 but arc of pennant shallower; head and neck of eagle slender; sharply beaded flatter oval frame with elongated 7-pointed star, bottom of frame 1¾" above base of flask.	Half-pint 8 Ends rounding below short shoulder then to tapering base	Smooth	Wide sloping collar, lower bevel Pontil mark	Black (dark olive-green)	Unknown	Extremely rare Only 1 specimen recorded (1965)
GIV–14. Similar to No. 13 except 33 bricks forming pavement.	Similar to No. 13 except beaded oval frame below eagle contains large 8-pointed star similar to that on No. 5.	Half-pint 8	Vertically ribbed	Tooled Plain lip Pontil mark	Deep bluish green Pale yellowish green Brilliant yellow-green Green, light	New England, works unknown	V. R. No. 9 D1; GIV Rare
GIV–15. Similar to No. 1 except with certain variations in the emblems, the most noticeable being the spread of the rays and blazing sun which are larger. The beehive rests on a longer table showing all 4 legs. Only 32 bricks in pavement. Crossed level and plumb line are different. NOTE: In No. 1 with letters "H S" and No. 2 with letters "I P" the rays surrounding triangle continue through the frame, filling the inner surface of the triangle and letter G. On all others up to and including No. 15, the inner surface is plain.	American Eagle entirely different from Nos. 1–14, head facing left, more slender body, no shield on breast. Thunderbolt (3 arrows) in its left talons, olive branch in right. Ribbon over eagle's head with crimping in a typical fold pattern. Beneath eagle large oval frame composed of 39 small pearls and containing inscription "N.G.Cº".	Pint 8	Vertically ribbed	Tooled Pontil mark	Pale green Olive-amber Olive-amber (upper part of flask) & olive-green (lower part) Yellow-green, light	Attributed to the New England Glass Co.	V. R. No. 3 D2; GIV Extremely rare

	American Eagle / Reverse	Capacity	Body	Lip	Color	Origin	Rarity
GIV–16. Masonic arch, pillars and pavement, 22 bricks forming pavement. Within arch at top radiant all-seeing eye and beneath square and compasses and below that radiant triangle, the rays extremely fine. There does not appear to be letter G in triangle. No emblems above and at sides of arch and pillars. Beneath pavement at right, beehive.	American Eagle, head turned to left; wings partly raised. Long pointed shield with bars and tiny dots representing stars on eagle's breast. Thunderbolt (3 arrows) in its left talons, olive branch in right. Plain ribbon above eagle's head; plain oval frame beneath eagle.	Pint 7	Fine horizontal corrugations, 2 corrugations extend around flask at juncture of neck and shoulders	Plain lip Broad sloping collar Pontil mark	Dark olive-amber (black) Very pale green Aquamarine Green, medium Emerald-green (S.L.) Olive-green (E.D.)	New England, possibly one of the Connecticut works	V. R. No. 21 D1; GIV Very rare

NOTE: The flasks Nos. 1 to 16 inclusive are usually very heavy glass, pint specimens sometimes weighing as much as 2 pounds.

	American Eagle / Reverse	Capacity	Body	Lip	Color	Origin	Rarity
GIV–17. Masonic Decoration—From a mosaic pavement rise 2 columns surmounted by archway with Keystone in center; beneath keystone radiant all-seeing eye and between columns radiant triangle without letter G, and above it open book with square and compasses. At left of archway blazing sun and below at left of column trowel and skull and crossbones. At right of archway quarter moon and 5 small stars. Just beneath the stars comet, tail not showing. Beneath pavement at right, beehive. Twenty-two bricks in pavement.	American Eagle, head turned to left; wings partly raised. Shield with bars and small stars on breast. Thunderbolt (3 arrows) in its left talons, olive branch in right. Above eagle plain ribbon. Below eagle oval frame with word "KEENE".	Pint Similar to 8, Ill. 133	Smooth with single vertical rib	Plain lip Pontil mark	Pale green Amber Olive-amber Olive-green Light yellowish olive-green Golden amber (S.L.) Aquamarine	Keene-Marlboro-Street Glassworks, Keene, N.H.	V. R. No. 2 D1, GIV Common
GIV–18. Masonic Arch, pillars and pavement. Similar to No. 17, except 6 stars surrounding quarter moon and without comet at right of pillars.	American Eagle similar to No. 15. Plain oval frame contains inscription "KCCNC". NOTE: The spelling of Keene as above is probably due to careless mold work.	Pint Similar to 8, Ill. 133	Smooth with single vertical rib	Plain lip Pontil mark	Amber Olive-amber Dark olive-green Golden amber (S.L.)	Same as GIV–17	V. R. No. 1 D1; GIV Common NOTE: On many of these flasks some of the bricks do not show plainly so that they appear to be only 12 in number.
GIV–19. Similar to No. 18 except trowel and skull do not show at left of pillars and at right of archway quarter moon does not show. Also beehive beneath pavement is missing.	Similar to No. 18. Same inscription "KCCNC" in oval frame.	Pint Similar to 8, Ill. 133	Smooth with single vertical rib	Plain lip Pontil mark	Amber Olive-amber Olive-green (E.D.)	Same as GIV–17	Not listed by Van Rensselaer but he does list No. 4 D1; GIV, similar flask but with "KEENE" in oval. Common

GIV-11 GIV-12 GIV-13 GIV-14 GIV-15 GIV-16 GIV-17 GIV-18

GROUP IV—MASONIC FLASKS—*Continued*

OBVERSE	REVERSE	SIZE, FORM	EDGES	NECK, BASE	COLORS	GLASSHOUSE	NOTES, RARITY
GIV–20. Similar to No. 19 except 2 pearl-shaped dots equidistant between sun and crossbones	Similar to No. 18 except 2 small dots at right of eagle. "KCCNC" in oval frame.	Pint Similar to 8, Ill. 133	Smooth with single vertical rib	Plain lip Pontil mark	Amber Yellowish olive-amber Olive-amber (C.G.)	Same as GIV–17	V. R. No. 5 D1; GIV Comparatively scarce
GIV–20a. Similar to GIV–20.	Similar to GIV–20 but, above eagle, faint dots in curve from left, short rib between 2 dots. Rib possibly meant to be a cane.	Pint Similar to 8, Ill. 133	Narrow vertical rib	Plain lip Pontil mark	Olive-amber	Same as GIV–17	Reported by Charles B. Gardner Rare
GIV–21. Similar to No. 17 except 7 stars instead of 5; triangle and open book with square and compasses smaller; trowel and skull and crossbones smaller. Immediately below crossbones is a scythe pointing to right. Comet with tail shows at right of right column.	Similar to No. 17 except oval frame plain	Pint Similar to 8, Ill. 133	Smooth with single vertical rib	Plain lip Pontil mark	Olive-green Olive-amber Amber	Same as GIV–17	V. R. No. 3 D1; GIV Comparatively scarce NOTE: The stars on this flask are very tiny and rather indistinct.
GIV–22. Similar to No. 17 except bricks forming pavement are smaller and 28 in number. Square and compasses within pillars smaller. Blazing sun smaller and what appears to be spade instead of trowel at left of column and skull rests on end of one of the crossbones. Also seven 5-pointed stars surround quarter moon instead of 5 and moon points upward to right instead of to the left. At right of pillar small emblem which may be intended for comet.	American Eagle similar to No. 17 except shield on breast smaller with horizontal and vertical bars instead of stars. Plain ribbon above eagle. Large oval frame containing date "1829" below eagle.	Pint Similar to 8, Ill. 133	Single narrow vertical rib	Plain, infolded lip Pontil mark	Clear glass with faint amethyst tint Colorless	New England, possibly Thomas Cains's Phoenix works and/or the New-England Glass-Bottle Co.	V. R. No. 8 D2; GIV Extremely rare
GIV–23. Masonic Decoration—From a mosaic pavement of 22 bricks rise 2 columns surmounted by archway with Keystone in center. Below Keystone allseeing eye and between columns radiant triangle without letter G. Above triangle open book with square and compasses. At left of archway blazing sun, at right quarter moon and 7 tiny stars. *(Courtesy of Toledo Museum of Art)*	American Eagle, head turned to right; wings partly raised. Eagle grasps large balls in talons. Above eagle plain ribbon. Below eagle oval frame containing date "1829".	Half-pint Similar to 8, Ill. 133	Smooth with single vertical medial rib	Tooled Pontil mark	Clear	New England, possibly Thomas Cains's Phoenix works and/or the New-England Glass-Bottle Co.	Not listed by Van Rensselaer Extremely rare
GIV–24. Pavement, columns, and archway similar to No. 23. Emblems within columns and archway differ slightly. Blazing sun at left of column. The crescent moon and stars are smaller, and the moon turns downward to right instead of upward to left. Comet at right of column.	Similar to No. 23 except oval frame beneath eagle plain.	Half-pint Similar to 8, Ill. 133	Smooth with single medial rib	Plain lip Pontil mark	Deep olive-green Amber Olive-amber Aquamarine Black (deep olive-green) Golden amber (S.L.)	Attributed to Keene-Marlborough Street	V. R. No. 8 D1; GIV Common NOTE: Specimens are found in which apparently the emblems at left of pillar and the triangle within pillar are missing. This is probably due to a cold mold or defective blowing.

596

GIV-25. Similar to No. 24 but no trace of Masonic emblems on either side of arch and pillars.

	Reverse	Lip	Mold	Capacity	Color	Where made	Rarity / Reference
GIV-25	Similar to No. 24 but details of eagle are different. The body is slightly larger, treatment of wings different and the large balls missing from eagle's talons. The shape and size of the oval frame beneath eagle also slightly different.	Plain lip Pontil mark	Smooth with vertical medial rib	Half-pint Similar to 8, Ill. 133	Aquamarine Clear light amber	Probably Keene-Marlboro-Street	Not listed by Van Rensselaer Rare

NOTE: We have seen only 2 specimens of this flask and each one is slightly different from No. 24 in that the body is much thicker through, especially in the upper portion and at the shoulders.

	Reverse	Lip	Mold	Capacity	Color	Where made	Rarity / Reference
GIV-26	Similar to No. 24 except oval frame contains letters "NEG".	Plain lip Pontil mark	Vertically ribbed, heavy medial rib and two smaller ribs	Half-pint Similar to 8, Ill. 133	Olive-green Black (deep olive-green) Olive-amber Green, clear (R. W.)	New England; probably New England Glass Co. or, if produced after 1827, New England Glass-Bottle Co., Cambridge, Mass. See note to GIV-27.	Not listed by Van Rensselaer Very rare Whether the new flasks reported with feathered breast and plain frame are a variant or the lack of feathers on those like the drawing was due to faulty molding is undetermined.

GIV-26. Similar to No. 24 except triangle is larger. Quarter moon faces upward to right and shape of stars is different. Below stars comet with circular head instead of oval. Also scythe pointing left beneath crossbones. Directly beneath triangle tiny emblem which may be plummet, but inverted.

	Reverse	Lip	Mold	Capacity	Color	Where made	Rarity / Reference
GIV-27	American Eagle, head turned to left; shield with vertical bars and small dots representing stars on breast; wings partly raised and right foreshortened. Thunderbolt (3 arrows) in eagle's left talons, olive branch in right. Plain ribbon above eagle. Beneath eagle oval frame with heavy beading and containing letters "NEG CO". On nearly every specimen the "O" is so faint as to be practically indiscernible. Specimens are also encountered where there is scarcely a trace of any of the letters.	Tooled Plain lip Pontil mark	Vertically ribbed, 5	Pint 8	Pale blue Brilliant yellow-green Dark olive-amber Pale green Aquamarine, decidedly bluish Aquamarine (E.D.) Colorless Colorless, lavender tint (S.L.) Green, yellow tone Olive-green (S.L.)	Probably New England Glass Co. and, if produced after 1826, New England Glass-Bottle Co.	V. R. No. 1 D2; GIV., also No. 2 (plain oval) Comparatively scarce In 1940, lacking evidence of flask production by N.E.G. Co., and with White's find of GIV-27 fragments on the Keene-Marlboro-Street site, it seemed likely Keene blew GIV-26 & 27 for N.E.G. Co. However, the company's pressed lion lamp bases have the same initials and "prest pocket flasks" (unidentified but believed to be blown in a figured piece mold) were advertised in 1819. After N-E-G-B. Co. started, orders probably were filled there.

GIV-27. Masonic Decoration—From a mosaic pavement rise 2 columns surmounted by archway with Keystone in center. Beneath Keystone radiant all-seeing eye and between columns radiant triangle enclosing the letter "G" and above it open book with square and compasses. At left of archway blazing sun and beneath at left of column trowel, skull and crossbones and scythe. Scythe points to right. At right of archway crescent moon surrounded by 7 small stars and beneath, comet with tail. Below pavement at right, beehive.

GIV-21 GIV-22 GIV-23 GIV-24 GIV-25 GIV-26 GIV-27

GROUP IV—MASONIC FLASKS—*Continued*

OBVERSE	REVERSE	SIZE, FORM	EDGES	NECK, BASE	COLORS	GLASSHOUSE	NOTES, RARITY
GIV-28. Masonic Decoration—From a finely tessellated mosaic pavement rise 2 columns surmounted by archway with Keystone at center. Beneath Keystone radiant all-seeing eye and between columns radiant triangle containing very large letter "G" which touches sides of triangle. Above open book with square and compasses, the edges of book touching rays of the eye and triangle. The columns show fine vertical ribbing. At left of archway blazing sun and at left of column compasses and quadrant (sign of past-master). At right of archway radiant quarter moon and at right of column 2 small emblems which may be intended for comet and crossbones. Beneath pavement at right beehive and at left coffin.	Similar Masonic Decoration except between the pillars level and plumb line, instead of book with square and compasses. At right of pillars radiant triangle ascending to "Star Decked Heaven"; at left of pillars trowel and crossbones. Beneath pavement, bee-hive at right, crossed level and plumb line at left.	Half-pint Similar to 7, Ill. 133	Covered with a vertical row of tiny dots each side of the mold seam and similar dots form a definite pattern on either side of the Masonic emblems	Plain lip Pontil mark	Clear green Deep yellowish green Green; bluish Peacock-green (R.W.)	Unknown	V. R. No. 7 D2; GIV Scarce
GIV-28a. Similar to GIV-28 but plain unfluted columns, plinths slightly narrower and taller; slightly smaller bricks in pavement; dots above radiant quarter moon at right, in circle around dot at center.	Similar to GIV-28 but columns, plinths, bricks, and dots above radiant quarter moon as on obverse.	Half-pint Similar to GIV-28 but broader through shoulder	Like GIV-28 but dots slightly smaller	Plain lip & in-folded lip Pontil mark	Green (light)	Unknown	Rare
GIV-29. Masonic Emblems consisting of large 5-pointed star between pillars; above star crescent moon surrounded by 7 equally spaced 5-pointed stars. Below star hourglass. Face clearly depicted in crescent moon.	Same as obverse	Half-pint 4	Finely corrugated horizontally	Plain lip Pontil mark	Clear light amber Deep olive-green Golden amber (S.L.) Olive-green (G.A.)	Attributed to Coventry, Conn., Glass Works	V. R. No. 40 GVI Extremely rare
GIV-30. Large 5-pointed star with convex center. Beneath star large crossed keys.	Large square and compasses enclosing large letter "G" which is reversed. There are definite markings on the compasses probably intended to represent the calibration.	Half-pint 4	Corrugated horizontally, corrugations extend around flask at base and at juncture of neck and body.	Plain lip Pontil mark	Clear light olive green Clear amber Golden amber (S.L.) Olive-amber	Attributed to Coventry, Conn., Glass Works	V. R. No. 23 GVI Very rare
GIV-31. Masonic pavement columns and archway with Keystone in center. Eighteen bricks in pavement rounded in form. Within archway "Farmer's Arms" sheaf of rye, pitchfork, shovel, sickle, rake, axe and scythe. Sheaf of rye points to left. Beneath pavement scroll ornament.	Crude American Eagle, head turned to left. Large shield with 8 vertical and 2 horizontal bars on breast; wings partly raised, legs raised. Thunderbolt (2 arrows) in left talons, olive branch in right. Eagle's tail rests on small oval frame with inner band of minute pearl beading and containing 4-petaled ornament. Thirteen 5-pointed stars above eagle. Designs on oval panels.	Pint 17	Large pearl beading with heavy vertical medial rib	Plain lip Pontil mark	Clear yellowish green Light green	Monongahela and Early Pittsburgh district, particular glasshouse not known	Not listed by Van Rensselaer Extremely rare

GIV-32. Masonic arch, pillars and pavement, 22 widely spaced bricks. Within arch "Farmer's Arms," sheaf of rye, pitchfork, shovel, rake, sickle, axe and scythe. Sheaf of rye, points to right instead of left. Beneath pavement elaborate scroll ornament.

American Eagle, head turned to right; shield with 7 vertical bars on breast; wings partly raised, right foreshortened. Thunderbolt (5 arrows) in its right talons, olive branch in left. Eagle stands on oval frame with inner band of 26 small pearls and containing word "OHIO". Sunrays surround eagle's head and above rays in semicircle "ZANESVILLE." In semicircle beneath oval frame "J. SHEPARD & CO." The "S" is reversed.

GIV-33. Similar to No. 32.

Similar to No. 32 except inscription below oval frame "MURDOCK & CASSEL".

GIV-34. Similar to No. 32 except stones forming arch slightly larger and flatter.

Full rigged frigate sailing to right, American flag at rear; waves beneath frigate and in semicircle beneath "FRANKLIN."

Pint 11	Vertically ribbed	Plain lip / Flanged lip / Pontil mark	Olive-yellow / Aquamarine / Golden yellow / Golden amber / Deep amber / Deep brownish amber (black) shaded (E.D.) / Amber, shaded (E.D.) / Amber, reddish (S.L.) / Green, light (R.W.) / Green, medium (R.W.) / Blue-green, light (C.G.) / Emerald-green (S.L.)	"White Glass Works", Zanesville, Ohio. Proprietorship of J. Shepard & Co.	V. R. No. 4 D2; GIV Common
Pint 11	Vertically ribbed	Plain lip / Pontil mark	Clear deep bluish green / Green, medium / Emerald-green (G.A.)	Murdock & Cassell, Zanesville, Ohio	V. R. No. 5 D2; GIV Extremely rare
Pint 8	Vertically ribbed and inscription "FREE TRADE AND SAILORS RIGHTS" "KENSINGTON GLASS WORKS PHILADELPHIA"	Plain lip / Pontil mark	Emerald-green, yellowish tone / Pale green / Deep amber / Aquamarine / Citron (S.L.) / Yellow-green (S.L.)	Kensington Glass Works, Philadelphia	V. R. No. 106 GI Common

GIV-28 GIV-28a GIV-29 GIV-30 GIV-31 GIV-32 GIV-34

GROUP IV—MASONIC FLASKS—*Continued*

OBVERSE	REVERSE	SIZE, FORM	EDGES	NECK, BASE	COLORS	GLASSHOUSE	NOTES, RARITY
GIV–35. Similar to No. 34	Similar to No. 34	Pint 8	Vertically ribbed—no inscription on edges	Plain lip Pontil mark	Pale green Aquamarine Yellow-green, light	Kensington Glass Works, Philadelphia	Not listed by Van Rensselaer Scarce
GIV–36. Similar to No. 34 except 18 bricks in pavement, and sickle is missing in "Farmer's Arms." Also slight difference in detail of base of sheaf and in scroll ornament below pavement.	Similar to No. 34 except letters in "FRANKLIN" slightly larger and no period. Slight variation in some details of ship.	Pint 12	Horizontally beaded with medial rib	Plain lip Pontil mark	Clear yellowish green Aquamarine Green, light (C.G.)	Monongahela and Early Pittsburgh district	V. R. No. 107 GI Rare
GIV–37. Similar to No. 34	American Eagle, head turned to right; shield with 7 bars on breast; wings partly raised and right foreshortened. Thunderbolt (5 arrows) in its right talons and large olive branch in left. Sunrays above eagle's head. Eagle stands on oval frame with inner band of 27 tiny pearl beads and containing initials "T.W.D."	Pint 11	Vertically ribbed	Plain lip Pontil mark	Pale yellow Aquamarine Pale green with translucent milky white striations, probably accidental	Kensington Glass Works, Philadelphia	V. R. No. 4 D3; GIV Common
GIV–38. Large Shield containing at top scalloped frame with clasped hands; above and at sides of frame square and compasses surrounded by 5 small 6-pointed stars; on either side of shield olive branch showing berries.	American Eagle, head turned to right, wings raised above and parallel with body. Eagle perched on shield with 9 vertical bars and 5 small stars. Thunderbolt (4 arrows) and olive branch protrude on either side of lower point of shield. In eagle's beak long narrow ribbons which extend in parallel line over eagle and below eagle through shield. Beneath on lower part of flask long plain oval frame pointed at top and bottom.	Quart 28	Smooth	Rounded collared lip Plain lip with applied ring Smooth Circular depression at center	Deep brilliant amber Aquamarine Red-amber (S.L.)	Pittsburgh district	Not listed by Van Rensselaer Very common
GIV–39. Similar to No. 38 except stars are 5-pointed; square and compasses slightly smaller; olive branch slightly different, does not show berries.	In general appearance similar to No. 38 but variation in detail of eagle's plumage. The shield plain and laurel branch extends from ribbon at left of shield. In oval frame letters "H & S"	Quart 28	Smooth	Flat collar Pontil mark	Aquamarine Green, light Yellow-green	Pittsburgh district	Not listed by Van Rensselaer in quart size but similar to No. 8 D4; GII Very common
GIV–40. Similar to No. 39 except 6 small 5-pointed stars surround square and compasses	Similar to No. 39 except olive branch protrudes from left side of shield and thunderbolt protrudes from ribbon just right of shield.	Pint 28	Smooth	Flat collar Pontil mark	Aquamarine	Pittsburgh district	V. R. No. 8 D4; GII Very common
GIV–41. Similar to No. 39 except slight variation in olive branches	Similar to No. 39	Half-pint 28	Smooth	Plain lip Pontil mark	Aquamarine	Pittsburgh district	Not listed in half-pint size by Van Rensselaer Common

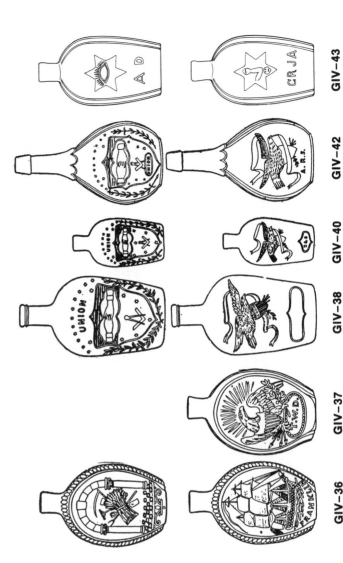

GIV-36 GIV-37 GIV-38 GIV-40 GIV-42 GIV-43

GIV-42. Large Shield containing large scalloped frame with clasped hands; vertical ribbing above frame and within shield. Beneath frame square and compasses and 3 tiny 5-pointed stars at either side. Directly below square and compasses small oval frame with word "UNION". Above shield 13 small 5-pointed stars; on either side of shield laurel branch.

NOTE: Flasks 38 through 42 have been listed previously as Masonic flasks because the square and compass were believed to have been added, for interest of Masons, to the patriotic "Union," shield and clasped hands of the Civil War period. Now, however, there seems no doubt that these flasks and the calabash bear the insignia of the Junior Order of United American Mechanics, whose insignia was a square and compass and clasped hands within a shield.

For other Masonic Flasks—see GI-69, 70, 83, 84, 88, 89, 92, 93. See also GII-57. This flask carries as part of the decoration the Masonic square and compasses.

GIV-43. Tall arch panel, slender horseshoe shaped; slightly above center, all-seeing eye of God with lashes on upper lid, on 6-pointed star presumably the Star of David. Below star: initials "AD", presumably for Alexander Delta Arch.

American Eagle, head turned to right; wings raised above and parallel with body. Eagle rests on plain shield. Thunderbolt (4 arrows) and olive branch protrude from lower part of shield just above the point. Beneath, letters "A.R.S." Eagle holds long plain ribbon in its beak, the ribbon extending above and parallel with eagle and through shield below.

Panel and 6-pointed star like obverse but, on star, arm bent at elbow, forearm raised vertically, compass[?] in hand: on bottom point of star, unidentified emblem. Below star: initials "GRJA", presumably for Grand Royal Jerusalem Arch.

Quart 38 Calabash	Fluted	Broad sloping collar Pontil mark	Aquamarine Pale yellow-green	A. R. Samuels, Philadelphia, Pa.	V. R. No. 1 D3; GIV Very common
Pint 29	Heavy vertical rib	Plain lip With and without pontil mark	Ambers Olive-ambers Olive-greens	Unknown. Attributed to Stoddard, N.H., by Van Rensselaer	Data on emblems and initials from L. Earl Dambach Common

---

NOTE: The only Masonic flasks we have seen which include the scythe among the Masonic emblems are Nos. 21, 26 and 27. The scythe always occurs in conjunction with the skull and crossbones or the coffin. On practically all of the Masonic flasks, the quarter moon forming part of the "Cloudy Canopy" or "Star Decked Heaven" faces upward to the left, but on the half-pint No. 24, attributed to Keene, the quarter moon faces downward on a similar flask marked "NEG," the quarter moon faces upward to the right. Also on pint flask No. 22 marked "1829" in oval frame, the quarter moon faces upward to right. The comet is found on only four flasks, Nos. 21, 24, 26, and 27. The rare Mantua Jackson Masonic flask, No. 70 in the Portrait Group I, is distinctive in that it shows 4 emblems not found on any other Masonic flask, namely the 7 lighted tapers in triangular form, the sprig of acacia, setting maul and naked heart. This flask also shows a spade and coffin. The only other Masonic flask showing the spade is the pint "1829," No. 22, and the coffin is found only on one other Masonic flask No. 28. No. 28 is the only Masonic flask showing the Ark of the Covenant and the Paschal Lamb. The half-pint No. 13 is the only Masonic flask showing the Ark of the Covenant and the Paschal Lamb. The hourglass is found on only No. 29 and the crossed keys on No. 30.

GROUP V — RAILROAD FLASKS

OBVERSE	REVERSE	SIZE, FORM	EDGES	NECK, BASE	COLORS	GLASSHOUSE	NOTES, RARITY
GV–1. Designs on oval panels. Early crude locomotive to left on rail. Inscription "SUCCESS TO THE RAILROAD" reading in semicircle from bottom of panel around locomotive to the bottom of the other side of panel.	Similar to obverse but the line connecting the tender with rear wheel shows a slight break and the "E" in "SUCCESS" carries a convex dot attached to the upper bar.	Pint 11	Vertically ribbed 3, heavy medial rib	Plain lip Pontil mark NOTE: On the base are shown 2 partial figures "5" in reverse, widely spaced. Other varieties without numerals have a straight mold line.	Olive-yellow Light sapphire-blue Golden amber Deep amber Clear green Clear olive-green Aquamarine Clear with pale yellow tint Olive-amber Cloudy yellowish or mustard green, almost opaque Grey-blue Blue, pale greenish Sapphire-blue, medium (S.L.) Emerald-green (S.L.) Yellow-green Yellow-opaque (S.L.)	Lancaster, N.Y. Glass Works	V. R. No. 83 GI Comparatively scarce
GV–2. Design on oval panels similar to No. 1	Similar to No. 1	Pint 11	Same as No. 1	Plain lip Pontil mark	Clear dark olive-green Golden amber Aquamarine (S.L.) Green, medium	Lancaster, N.Y. Glass Works	V. R. No. 84 GI Rare
GV–3. Designs on oval panels. Horse pulling cart to left on rail, cart filled with kegs. The side of the cart is subdivided into 6 quadrangular panels containing a pattern of ribs radiating from a central dot; only a portion of a panel appears over each wheel. Inscription in large letters "SUCCESS TO THE RAILROAD" reading in semicircle from bottom of panel around horse and cart to bottom of other side of panel. The "O" in "TO" is in the angle of the rail and tie. The letters "AIL" and "AD" in "RAILROAD" are connected at bottom. There are 8 spokes in the wheels of the cart. The end of rail at right is angled.	Similar to obverse but the "O" in "TO" is at the end of the rail. The "RA" in "RAILROAD" are connected at bottom. The "IL" are in a different position and there is a slight difference in some of the letters. Wheels of cart have 8 spokes. End of rail at right is a straight line. On both the obverse and the reverse the mane shows very definitely on the neck of the horse, in the form of fine vertical lines.	Pint 11	Same as No. 1	Plain lip Pontil mark	Aquamarine Clear golden amber Olive-amber Dark olive-green Amber, brilliant	Keene-Marlboro-Street	V. R. No. 92 GI Common

NOTE: These railroad locomotive flasks offer an interesting study in the mold variation between flasks carrying identical designs and inscriptions in the panels. Though Harry Hall White was unable to find fragments during his search on the site of the Lancaster Glass Co., attribution of these railroad locomotive flasks to this glasshouse has been generally accepted. The mold variation between Nos. 1 and 2 is explained at left. A third variation, the design and lettering identical, has a base with straight line mold mark in center, in contrast with keyed mold mark in base drawings 1 and 2, and the numerals as shown on the base are completely lacking in this variety. The Lancaster Glass Works is also credited with having made violin or scroll flasks in pint size. In this connection it is interesting to note that similar keyed bases and partial numerals are found on bases of Scroll flasks Nos. 10, 11, and 20, the latter showing "4 × 4" in reverse, but with a slight variation from similar numerals on railroad engine flask No. 2. The significance of these numerals is not definitely known but as they would read correctly in the mold instead of reverse as on the flask, it is probable they were for mold identification in the factory.

NOTE: Although the design and lettering on corresponding sides of this flask seem identical with that on No. 1, it was blown in a different mold. On the base of No. 2, at one edge is "4 × 4" reversed; at opposite edge what appears to be "200" reversed; the bottoms of the figures are cut off by the outer edge of the base. Also, the medial rib is narrower and lacks the angular break at the base that is present in No. 1.

GV-3a. Like GV-3 but no mane on horse; lettering in lower relief.

GV-4. Similar to No. 3, lettering nearly identical in form and placement but showing a lighter cutting in the mold. (The mane does not show on neck of horse.) The bottom of wagon box runs parallel with the horizontal wheel spokes forming double lines through the wheels. The "A" in "RAIL" is not connected at the bottom with the "T" as in No. 3 and the "A" and "D" of "ROAD" are not connected. (*Collection of Harry Hall White*)

GV-5. Designs on oval panels. Similar to No. 3 but letters slightly smaller. None of the letters in "RAILROAD" are connected at bottom. The "O" in "TO" is opposite the angle of rail and tie. End of rail is angled. NOTE: It is this variety of the Railroad Horse and Cart flask which was reproduced many years ago. There are slight differences in the mold used for the reproduction, the distinctive variation being that the horse's mane shows distinctly, the hairs being perpendicular.

GV-6. Designs on oval panels. Similar to No. 5, but lettering slightly smaller and inscription runs in reverse direction, "SUCCESS" being above the horse and cart and "TO THE RAILROAD" below. The wheels of the cart have 12 spokes and the bottom line of the wagon box runs parallel with the horizontal wheel spokes, forming double lines through the wheels same as in No. 4.

GV-7. Designs on oval panels. Similar to No. 5, but no inscription.

No.	Reverse	Ribs	Size	Lip	Color	Glasshouse	Notes
GV-3a	Like GV-3 but no mane on horse; lettering in lower relief.	3 vertical ribs (heavy medial)	Pint 11	Plain lip; Pontil mark	Olive-green	Unknown	Reported by Sterling Watlington. Scarce
GV-4	Similar to No. 3 but with same difference in bottom of wagon box and wheels and mane lacking on neck of horse.	Same as No. 1	Pint 11	Plain lip; Pontil mark	Aquamarine; Olive-amber; Green, medium (R.W.); Olive-green	Keene-Marlboro-Street	Not listed by Van Rensselaer. Rare
GV-5	Similar to obverse but the "O" in "TO" is opposite the tie and end of rail is in a straight line.	Same as No. 1	Pint 11	Plain lip; Broad sloping collar; Pontil mark	Clear deep olive-green; Dark olive-green (black); Olive-amber; Amber; Golden amber (S.L.); Aquamarine; Green, deep; Emerald-green (S.L.); Yellow-green, deep	Mt. Vernon, N.Y. and Saratoga (Mt. Pleasant)	V. R. No. 94 GI. NOTE: The line drawing shows a broad sloping collar which is a very unusual neck finish in the early flasks. Common
GV-6	Similar to obverse but the "THE" is opposite the angle of the tie.	Same as No. 1	Pint 11	Plain lip; Pontil mark	Clear amber; Olive-amber; Olive-green; Golden amber (S.L.)	Coventry, Conn.	V. R. No. 95 GI. Common
GV-7	Same as obverse, no inscription.	Same as No. 1	Pint 11	Plain lip; Pontil mark; Round collar; smooth base (C. W. Fenton)	Olive-green; Olive-amber	NOTE: We do not have any definite evidence as to glasshouse where this variety was made. The angles of the wagon spokes are almost identical with those in No. 5 and the horizontal barrel in the cart shows a perfectly smooth surface, which seems to be a characteristic of No. 5. It is a fair guess that this variety may have been made at either Mt. Vernon or Saratoga (Mt. Pleasant) glasshouses or at both.	V. R. No. 96 GI. Rare

GV-1   GV-2   GV-3   GV-4   GV-5   GV-6   GV-7

GROUP V—RAILROAD FLASKS—*Continued*

604

OBVERSE	REVERSE	SIZE, FORM	EDGES	NECK, BASE	COLORS	GLASSHOUSE	NOTES, RARITY
GV–7a. Similar to GV–7 but single rail with no ridge; 2 hoops on second keg from left, plain panels on cart.	Eagle similar to GII–70	Pint 11	3 vertical ribs (heavy medial)	Plain lip Pontil mark	Olive-green	Unknown	Rare
GV–8. Designs on oval panels. Horse and cart on rail with inscription "SUCCESS TO THE RAILROAD". Similar to No. 3, but the letters are more delicate in modeling and slightly smaller. The placement of the inscription relative to the horse and cart is different. Also the panels in wagon box are plain.	Large American Eagle lengthwise, head turned to left; wings partly raised and spread. Shield with 7 vertical and 2 horizontal bars on breast. Thunderbolt (3 arrows) in eagle's left talons, olive branch in right. Eagle in high relief. Seventeen large 5-pointed stars surround eagle.	Pint 11	Vertically ribbed 3, heavy medial rib	Plain lip Pontil mark	Olive-amber Amber Olive-green Golden amber (S.L.)	Coventry, Conn.	V. R. No. 90 GI Common
GV–9. Similar to No. 8 but no inscription	Similar to No. 8 but no stars	Pint 11	Same as No. 8	Plain lip Pontil mark	Olive-amber Amber Dark olive-green Golden amber (S.L.)	Coventry, Conn.	V. R. No. 91 GI Common
GV–10. Designs on oval panels. Horse drawing long cart on rail to right, cart filled with barrels and boxes. Below rail "LOWELL" and above "RAILROAD".	American Eagle, similar to that on No. 8 but 13 large 5-pointed stars surround eagle.	Half-pint 11	Vertically ribbed 3, heavy medial rib	Plain lip Pontil mark	Clear olive-green Light amber Olive-amber Emerald-green (S.L.)	Coventry, Conn.	V. R. No. 97 GI Common
GV–11. Designs on oval panels. Similar to No. 10 but impression of eagle over horse and inscription. Probably accidental or an individual item	Similar to No. 10	Half-pint 11	Same as No. 10	Plain lip Pontil mark	Olive-amber	Coventry, Conn.	Not listed by Van Rensselaer Rare
GV–12. Very early type of locomotive on rail to left. Figure of man in front of tender which appears to be filled with wood in front and barrels in rear.	Symbolical female winged figure facing left wearing high headdress and holding slender inverted cornucopia before her.	Pint Similar to 11, Ill. 133, but narrower at base	Vertically ribbed	Plain lip Pontil mark	Clear	Attributed by Van Rensselaer to Baltimore Glass Works	V. R. No. 82 GI Extremely rare

NOTE: On the somewhat flattened edges inscription "SUCCESS TO THE RAILROAD". The line drawing and data with respect to this flask is taken from Van Rensselaer's book, "Early American Bottles & Flasks." This inscription on edges is missing from the line drawing as it does not show in the photograph in his book.

NOTE: The definite attribution of most of these Railroad, Horse and Cart flasks has been made possible through excavations by Harry Hall White on the sites of the Marlboro Street Glass Works, Keene, New Hampshire; the Coventry, Connecticut, Glass Works and the glasshouses of Oscar Granger at Mount Vernon, New York, and Mount Pleasant near Saratoga, New York. In an article by Mr. White in the October, 1940 issue of the magazine *Antiques*, the flasks definitely proven to have been made at the above-mentioned glasshouses are illustrated and described. The Keene examples in aquamarine are referred to only with respect to our No. 4 (Fig. 6 in Mr. White's article). However, our No. 3 also occurs in aquamarine, but there is a very slight difference in the mold from the specimen illustrated by line drawing of No. 3. The variation occurs on the reverse and consists of a defect in modeling of the rear wheel of the cart which shows a small knob or lump above and to the right of the center of the axle. The probability is that an additional mold was made by taking an impression of No. 3 in a sand mold from which a plaster of Paris model was cast and a new cast-iron mold formed from this model. The difference is so slight that we have not listed it as a separate variety.

GROUP VI—BALTIMORE MONUMENT FLASKS

GVI–1. Designs on oval panels. Baltimore Monument. The entrance door is without step railing.

GVI–1a. Battle monument like GVI–1

GVI–2. Designs on oval panels. Baltimore Monument and beneath "BALTº". The entrance door is recessed and without step railing.

GVI–3. Designs on circular panels. Baltimore Monument and above in semicircle "BALTIMORE". The entrance door is without step railing.

Vine and grapes form a semicircular frame containing inscription "A LITTLE MORE GRAPE CAPI BRAG". Only one 'G' in "BRAGG". NOTE: It is interesting to note that on flask with similar design on the reverse No. 4 GX, the spelling "BRAGG" is correct with two "G'S." The arrangement of the vines and grapes is different and permitted the insertion of the final "G" without interfering with the encircling vine.	Half-pint 11	Smooth, no medial rib	Plain lip Pontil mark	Deep puce Pale aquamarine Amber, bright, medium (De-Vere Card) Green, medium (C.G.) Olive-green, light Olive-green, medium (E.D.) Wine	Baltimore Glass Works	V. R. No. 9 GI Scarce
Vine and grapes, inscription "A LITTLE MORE GRAPE CAPT BRAG" like GV-1.	Half-pint 11	Vertically ribbed (3, heavy medial)	Plain lip Pontil mark	Aquamarine	Baltimore Glass Works, Baltimore, Md.	Scarce
Small sloop with pennant flying sailing to right; above "FELLS", below "POINT".	Half-pint 11	Vertically ribbed 3, heavy medial rib	Plain lip Pontil mark	Pale yellow-green Pale aquamarine Aquamarine Amethyst, deep (M.B.K.) Olive-green, light Yellow-green (C.G.)	Baltimore Glass Works	V. R. No. 105 GI Comparatively scarce
				Puce, light (G.A.) Puce, deep (G.A.) Wine (C.G.)		
"LIBERTY & UNION"	Pint 20	Smooth, no medial rib	Plain lip Tooled lip Pontil mark	Dark olive-yellow Aquamarine Deep wine Deep amethyst Brilliant light olive-green Amber, medium Golden amber (S.L.) Amethyst, reddish (S.L.)	Baltimore Glass Works	V. R. No. 3 GI Very rare

GV–8   GV–10   GV–11   GV–12   GVI–1   GVI–2   GVI–3

606

OBVERSE	REVERSE	SIZE, FORM	EDGES	NECK, BASE	COLORS	GLASSHOUSE	NOTES, RARITY
GVI-4. Designs on large oval panels. Washington Monument with statue at top, and below "BALTIMORE". The step railing of the entrance door faces to left.	Large ear of corn in high relief. Above in semicircle "CORN FOR THE WORLD".	Quart 20	Smooth, no medial rib	Rounded collar; Narrow flat collar; Narrow bevelled fillet; Smooth; Round ring below plain lip (No. 10)	Purple; Peacock-blue; Pale blue; Deep amber; Golden amber; Olive-yellow; Puce; Clear yellowish olive-green; Aquamarine; Amber, shaded (C.G.); Red-amber (S.L.); Brown, smoky (W.L.); Blue, cold (W.L.); Cornflower-blue (G.A.); Sapphire-blue, light (E.D.); Citron (S.L.); Green, pale; Green, medium (C.G.); Violet (S.L.)	Baltimore Glass Works	V. R. No. 4 GI Listed only in quart size Common
GVI-4a. Washington Monument on large oval panel: at top of shaft, tier of 3 plain round elements graduated in size and statue represented by a spike; no ornamentation around base of shaft; no projections at bottom of plinthlike base; no hand nail on step of entrance at left. No inscription. *See No. 2, Ill. 123 also.*	Similar to GVI-4 but central ear of corn taller and narrower; curved ends of side leaves shorter, that of upper left nearly blending with leg of "R" in "Corn". First letter of "CORN" and last letter of "WORLD" below and farther from top of lower leaves.	Quart 20	Smooth	Plain lip; Smooth	Smoky colorless; Yellow-green	Baltimore Glass Works, Baltimore, Md.	Extremely rare
GVI-5. Similar to No. 4 but monument is different; base is larger and step railing of the door faces right instead of left. The letters in "BALTIMORE" are smaller.	Similar to No. 4 but ear of corn and top of stalk smaller. Letters in inscription also smaller. Design not in such high relief as in No. 4.	Quart 20	Smooth	Plain lip; Pontil mark	Yellowish olive-green; Olive-amber (C.G.); Aquamarine (E.D.); Yellow-green	Baltimore Glass Works	Not listed by Van Rensselaer Rare
GVI-6. Designs on oval panels. Similar to No. 5, the step railing of entrance door facing right.	Similar to No. 4 and in high relief	Pint 20	Smooth	Plain lip; Pontil mark; [Colorless (M. Knapp, Jr.)]	Pale aquamarine; Amber, light (C.G.); Amber, shaded (C.G.); Amber, deep (C.G.)	Baltimore Glass Works	V. R. No. 4 GI Scarce
GVI-7. Similar to No. 6 NOTE: Strange to say, it is only on this half-pint that the steps show between the entrance rails.	Similar to No. 6	Half-pint 20	Smooth	Plain lip; Pontil mark; [Olive-green; Wine, deep]	Deep olive-yellow; Dark olive-amber; Clear green; Pale aquamarine; Emerald-green (S.L.)	Baltimore Glass Works	V. R. No. 4 GI Scarce

For other Baltimore Monuments, see GI-18, 19, and GVI-1a; Washington Monuments, GI-20, 21, 73, and GVI-4a.

GROUP VII—CABIN BOTTLES

The cabin group includes only bottles in the form of a cabin.

OBVERSE	REVERSE	SIZE, FORM	ENDS AND ROOF	NECK, BASE	COLORS	GLASSHOUSE	NOTES, RARITY
GVII–1. In form of Log Cabin with hipped roof. Door at center with latch string at left and window either side. Cider barrel beneath window at right. Above door extending across bottle rectangular frame containing the word "TIPPECANOE".	Similar to obverse except inscription "NORTH BEND".	Pint plus	On each side of roof 8 graduated vertical ribs and 8 on the ends of roof. On each end of flask 11 heavy horizontal ribs representing the logs. Height to lower line of roof 2¾". Height of bottle to top of lip 5½". Width 3¾". Breadth 2¹¹/₁₆".	Broad sloping collar Pontil mark	Dark olive-amber (black) Deep olive-green (black)	Mt. Vernon Glass Works, Vernon, N.Y.	V. R. No. 81 GI Extremely rare
GVII–2. In form of Log Cabin with gable roof. Bottle taller and almost square in width and breadth. Door slightly different from No. 1 and latch string at right. Three horizontal ribs representing logs above and below rectangular frame carrying inscription "TIPPECANOE." (Collection of Edwin Lefevre.)	Similar to obverse ("TIPPECANOE" on both sides).	Pint plus	On each side of roof 9 heavy vertical ribs and on each end 27 ribs representing the logs.	Rounded collar Pontil mark	Dark olive-green (black)	Same as above	Not listed by Van Rensselaer Extremely rare

NOTE: This is one of the rarest historical bottles known. So far only two recorded specimens have been found. It probably preceded slightly in the Harrison Campaign the other "Tippecanoe" bottle No. 1. This conclusion is based on the fact that only the Battle of Tippecanoe is referred to while on the other bottle Tippecanoe and North Bend appear, which is in keeping with the slogan "Tippecanoe and North Bend" which developed as the Harrison Campaign progressed.

OBVERSE	REVERSE	SIZE, FORM	ENDS AND ROOF	NECK, BASE	COLORS	GLASSHOUSE	NOTES, RARITY
GVII–3. In form of Cabin with gable roof. Tall door with latch; window with 4 panes at right. Over door small 4-paned window and similar window above the large window.	Plain	Quart (about)	On one end inscription "E. G. BOOZ'S OLD CABIN WHISKEY." On other end inscription "120 WALNUT S⸆ PHILADELPHIA." Roof over obverse, inscription "E. G. BOOZ'S OLD CABIN WHISKEY." Reverse roof. "1840". That part of roof on each side which does not contain the inscription is marked off by squares. A variant GVII–3a like GVII–3 but with 2 dots under "ST" as on GVII–5 has been reported by Charles B. Gardner and Dr. Michael B. Krassner.	Broad sloping collar Smooth with circular depression	Golden amber Dark amber Red-amber (S.L.) Deep green Green, pale (S.L.)	Whitney Glass Works, Glassboro, N.J.	V. R. No. 14 GVI Comparatively scarce

GVI–4 GVI–4a GVI–5 GVI–6 GVI–7 GVII–1 GVII–2 GVII–3

GROUP VII—CABIN BOTTLES—Continued

GVII–4. Similar to No. 3	Quart (about)	Similar inscriptions on ends and roof. Roof similar except ridge beveled at ends.	Broad sloping collar Smooth with circular depression	Deep amber Olive-green, deep (S.L.)	Whitney Glass Works, Glassboro, N.J.	V. R. No. 15 GVI Comparatively scarce
GVII–5. Similar to No. 4	Quart (about)	Similar to No. 4. Two periods beneath the "T" in "120 WALNUT ST."	Very short neck with large rounded collar Smooth with circular depression	Pale green Aquamarine (S.L.)	Whitney Glass Works, Glassboro, N.J.	V. R. No. 16 GVI Very rare
GVII–6. Similar to No. 4	Quart (about)	Plain	On one end "JACOB S CABIN TONIC BITTERS". On the other end "LABORATORY PHILADELPHIA". On front of roof "JACOB S CABIN TONIC BITTERS". On reverse of roof no inscription. Roof blocked into squares on each side except space where inscription occurs. Beveled ends.	Slightly longer neck and tooled lip Pontil mark	Clear	Probably Whitney Glass Works, Glassboro, N.J.	Very rare

NOTE: These "Booz" bottles were produced at Whitney Glass Works, Glassboro, N.J. For many years they were supposed to have been made in 1840 at the time of the William Henry Harrison Presidential Campaign. The date 1840 on the roof is doubtless responsible for this misconception. The shape and details of the bottle do not in the least resemble the log cabin of the Harrison Campaign. Rather it is an ordinary small 2-story house with shingle roof and plain (not log) walls. All one needs to do is to compare it with a true Harrison Campaign Log Cabin bottle like No. 1. Actually, as pointed out by I. Hazleton Mirkil in the magazine *Antiques*, November, 1926, E. G. Booz was not located at 120 Walnut Street until 1860. Prior to that, he was listed in Philadelphia Directories as Edmund G. Booz, "importer and dealer in wines, brandies and liquors," 54 South Front Street. From 1860 to 1870, he was listed in similar business at 120 Walnut St. He died in 1870. The date 1840 on the bottle probably refers to the age of the Old Cabin Whiskey which it contained. There has been a popular impression that the word "booze" originated with or was derived from this bottle. This is entirely erroneous. The word is the usual and accepted form of bouse, and was used as early as the 17th century. The bottle, however, may have revived and popularized its use. While not rare, it is a bottle which has always been in great demand among collectors and therefore commanded a good price. About 1931 a very good reproduction of the variety with straight roof ridge was made, but the lettering differs slightly in size and a distinguishing characteristic is the omission of the period after the word "WHISKEY" on one end. By the end of that decade the reproductions appeared in fancy colors such as sapphire-blue and emerald-green. The bottle illustrated, No. 4, is of particular interest because of the metal cork the patent stopper which has on the bottom of the metal cork the inscription "PATENTED". "REISD JUN. 5 1871" "JAN 5 1875" with a large 3 in the center.

GROUP VIII—SUNBURST FLASKS

OBVERSE	REVERSE	SIZE, FORM	EDGES	NECK, BASE	COLORS	GLASSHOUSE	NOTES, RARITY
GVIII–1. Large Elliptical Sunburst (about 5″ × 2⅞″), 24 triangular sectioned rays, flattened at ends, forming closed ellipse. The effect is that of a raised panel. At center of sunburst 2 concentric rings with dot in center.	Like obverse	Pint 3	Horizontally corrugated. Corrugations extend around flask at the base and around upper part between neck and squared and concave shoulders.	Plain lip Pontil mark	Clear Deep yellow-green Light green Deep bluish green Emerald-green (R. W.) Green, shading to amber (C.G.) Green, medium Green, deep Yellow-green, light (S.L.) Moonstone, green tinge Topaz (S.L.)	Attributed to Keene-Marlboro-Street. Also Mt. Vernon Glass Co., Vernon, N.Y.	V. R. No. 15 GXXIV Comparatively scarce
GVIII–2. Similar to No. 1 but without concentric rings at center of sunburst.	Like obverse	Pint 3	Similar to GVIII–1; shorter ribs on one side than on other	Plain lip Pontil mark	Deep yellow grass-green Clear Clear green Green, deep	New England	V. R. No. 17 GXXIV Comparatively scarce
GVIII–3. Large Elliptical Sunburst (about 4¼″ × 2½″), 24 rounded rays rounding downward to surface of flask and forming scalloped ellipse.	Like obverse	Pint 3	Similar to No. 1	Plain lip Pontil mark	Olive-amber Clear amber Golden amber (S.L.) Emerald-green (S.L.) Olive-green (C.G.)	Coventry, Conn.	V. R. No. 19 GXXIV Scarce NOTE: This flask is very similar to Nos. 1 and 2 in shape but is somewhat smaller and usually found in olive amber and lighter in weight.

GVII–4   GVII–5   GVII–6

GVII–4 DET.

GVIII–1   GVIII–2   GVIII–3

GROUP VIII—SUNBURST FLASKS—*Continued*

OBVERSE	REVERSE	SIZE, FORM	EDGES	NECK, BASE	COLORS	GLASSHOUSE	NOTES, RARITY
GVIII–4. Similar to No. 3 but with petal-shaped ornament at center of sunburst. (Formerly Collection of Charles B. Gardner)	Like obverse	Pint 3	Similar to No. 1	Plain lip Pontil mark	Clear Green, pale	Unknown, may be Keene-Marlboro-Street or Mt. Vernon	Not listed by Van Rensselaer Extremely rare
GVIII–5. Sunburst similar to No. 3	Similar	Pint Similar to 1, Ill. 133	Similar to Nos. 1, 2, 3, and 4 but shoulders not so sharply angled and squared	Plain lip Pontil mark	Clear deep green Clear amber Deep olive-green Olive-amber Blue-green, pale (M. Knapp, Jr.) Emerald-green (S.L.)	Possibly Pitkin Glassworks, East Hartford, which became Manchester in 1823, Conn.	V. R. No. 14GXXIV Common
GVIII–5a. Sunburst similar to No. 3.—24 rays but at center 2 dotted concentric rings enclosing medium-size dot.	Like obverse	Pint 3	Similar to No. 5	Plain lip Pontil mark	Golden olive-amber Golden amber (S.L.) Olive-amber (E.D.)	Possibly Pitkin Glassworks, East Hartford, which became Manchester in 1823, Conn.	Not listed by Van Rensselaer Extremely rare
GVIII–6. Sunburst similar to No. 5. In addition 5 small pearl-shaped dots spaced in semicircle above sunburst, and beneath sunburst similar dot at left and at right. (Formerly Collection of Charles B. Gardner)	Like obverse	Pint Similar to 1, Ill. 133	Same	Plain lip Pontil mark	Clear olive-amber Emerald-green (S.L.)	Probably Keene-Marlboro-Street	Not listed by Van Rensselaer Extremely rare
GVIII–7. Sunburst similar to No. 5 but slightly larger. Rays do not come to a focal point, but at center is a slightly concave circle. At right and left of sunburst is a similar concave circle.	Similar to obverse but circle at center of sunburst not as pronounced, and circles at right and left missing.	Pint Similar to 1, Ill. 133	Similar to No. 5	Plain lip Pontil mark	Olive-amber	Possibly Pitkin Glassworks, East Hartford, which became Manchester in 1823, Conn.	Not listed by Van Rensselaer Extremely rare
GVIII–8. Sunburst similar to Nos. 1 and 2 except 28 rays and not as long, being about 4¼″ × 2⅝″; raised oval center with word "KEEN"	Same except "P & W" in oval	Pint 2	Horizontally corrugated; corrugations extend around flask at base and around upper part between neck and shoulder.	Plain lip Broad sloping collar Pontil mark	Dark olive-green Olive-amber Golden amber (S.L.)	Keene-Marlboro-Street P. & W. probably stands for Perry and Wood and also Perry and Wheeler	V. R. No. 8 GXXIV Also No. 16 Common
GVIII–9. Sunburst similar to No. 8 but 29 rays and word KEEN in reverse. Position reading from top to bottom of oval.	Same as No. 8 except 29 rays in sunburst	Half-pint Similar to 2, Ill. 133, but without bulge between neck and shoulders	Horizontal corrugations but do not extend around flask at top and bottom	Plain lip Broad sloping collar Rounded heavy collar Pontil mark	Pale green Deep brilliant amber Dark olive-green Olive-amber Golden amber (S.L.) Aquamarine (C.G.)	Keene-Marlboro-Street	V. R. No. 9 GXXIV Also No. 10 Common

Catalog entry	Reverse	Size/Shape	Shoulder/Body	Lip/Pontil	Color	Attribution	Rarity
GVIII–10. Same as No. 9	Like obverse	Half-pint Similar to GVIII–9	Same as No. 9 but shoulders more squared	Plain lip Pontil mark	Clear brilliant amber Olive-amber (E.D.) Green, tint (S.L.) Olive-green (C.G.)	Same	V. R. No. 13 GXXIV Rare
GVIII–11. Sunburst 29 rays, similar to Nos. 9 and 10 but plain oval at center.	Like obverse	Half-pint Similar to GVIII–9 and 10	Same as Nos. 9 and 10	Broad sloping collar Pontil mark	Deep green, yellow tone Emerald-green (S.L.)	Keene-Marlboro-Street	V. R. No. 18 GXXIV Common
GVIII–12. Sunburst 28 rays, similar to No. 8 but plain oval at center. (Formerly Collection Charles B. Gardner)	Like obverse	Pint 2	Same as No. 9	Plain lip Pontil mark	Clear bluish green Green, light Green, medium Olive-green	New England	Not listed by Van Rensselaer Extremely rare
GVIII–13. Sunburst similar in shape to Nos. 9, 10, and 11, but 26 rays at center two concentric rings enclosing dot. (Collection of Edwin Lefevre.)	Like obverse	Half-pint Similar to GVIII–9	Horizontally corrugated; corrugations extend around flask at juncture of neck and body	Broad sloping collar Pontil mark	Olive-amber Colorless Olive-green, deep (C.G.) Pale aquamarine (Helen C. Hickman)	New England	Not listed by Van Rensselaer Extremely rare
GVIII–14. Similar to No. 1 but 21 rays and single ring with dot at center	Like obverse	Half-pint Similar to 2, Ill. 133, but without bulge between neck and shoulders; tapers sharply to base	Horizontally corrugated, corrugations extend around flask at base, not at top; shoulders rounded and not squared	Tooled lip Plain lip Pontil mark	Brilliant clear deep green Brilliant yellow-green with olive tone	Probably Keene-Marlboro-Street	Not listed by Van Rensselaer Scarce

GVIII–4 GVIII–5 GVIII–6 GVIII–7 GVIII–8 GVIII–9 GVIII–10 GVIII–11 GVIII–12 GVIII–13 GVIII–14

GROUP VIII—SUNBURST FLASKS—*Continued*

OBVERSE	REVERSE	SIZE, FORM	EDGES	NECK, BASE	COLORS	GLASSHOUSE	NOTES, RARITY
GVIII–14a. Similar to GVIII–14 but sunburst, ring, and dot a little smaller.	Like obverse	Half-pint Like GVIII–14	Like GVIII–14 but instead of 20 corrugations and one at base	Plain lip Pontil mark	Green (deep bluish)	New England, not definitely known	Rare
GVIII–14b. Like GVIII–14 but 24 rounded rays to ring and dot center.	Like obverse	Pint Like GVIII–5	Like GVIII–14	Plain lip Pontil mark	Olive-amber	Same as above	Reported by Charles Vuono Rare
GVIII–15. Sunburst 21 rays. Similar to No. 14 but without ring and dot at center.	Like obverse	Half-pint Similar to GVIII–14	Same as No. 14	Plain lip Tooled lip Pontil mark	Blue Peacock-green Pale light green Clear light green Olive-amber, light (S.L.)	Probably Keene-Marlboro-Street	Not listed by Van Rensselaer Comparatively scarce
GVIII–15a. Similar to GVIII–15, 21 rays converging at center.	Like obverse	Half-pint Like GVIII–15	Like GVIII–15 but 19 corrugations, one at base	Plain lip Pontil mark	Olive-green	New England, not definitely known	Rare
GVIII–16. Similar to No. 15, 21 rays, but flask smaller	Like obverse	Half-pint Similar to 4, Ill. 133	Similar to Nos. 14 and 15 but only single corrugation extends around flask at base	Plain lip Pontil mark	Deep yellowish olive-green Clear deep olive-amber Clear deep olive-green Olive-amber (C.G.)	Coventry, Conn.	V. R. No. 12 GXXIV Comparatively scarce
GVIII–16a. Like GVIII–16	Like obverse	Half-pint Similar to GVIII–16 but squared shoulders	Like GVIII–16	Plain lip Pontil mark	Olive-green	New England, not definitely known	Rare
GVIII–16b. Like GVIII–16	Like obverse	Half-pint Like GVIII–16	Nineteen corrugations, no rib around base	Plain lip Pontil mark	Olive-green	Same as above	Reported by Charles Vuono Rare
GVIII–17. Similar to No. 16 but slightly longer and narrower; rays more rounded and not showing such pronounced triangular ends. Small concave oval at center of sunburst. (Collection of Edwin Lefevre.)	Like obverse	Half-pint 4	Corrugated horizontally	Plain lip Pontil mark	Clear Olive-amber (C.G.)	Probably Keene-Marlboro-Street	Not listed by Van Rensselaer Extremely rare

Obverse	Reverse	Neck/Base	Size	Lip/Pontil	Color	Where made	References / Notes
GVIII–18. Sunburst, 24 rays, similar to Nos. 3, 4, 5, and 6 but ends of rays more pointed.	Like obverse	Corrugated horizontally; corrugations extending around flask at base and also between neck and shoulder	Half-pint 4	Plain lip Pontil mark	Clear deep olive-green Clear amber Green, light Emerald-green, deep (S.L.) Olive-amber (Helen C. Hickman)	Coventry, Conn.	V. R. No. 11 GXXIV Comparatively scarce
GVIII–19. Sunburst similar to No. 3 but smaller and with concave circle or depression at center. Sunburst is about 3⅞" × 2⅜". NOTE: Sunburst Flasks Nos. 1, 2, 4, 14, 15, and 17 are brilliant very heavy glass similar to the metal found in the heavy Keene Masonic Flasks.	Like obverse	Horizontally corrugated	Height— 7" Body— 3⅞" × 3⁵/₁₆" Rectangular	Plain lip Pontil mark	Deep olive-green Red-amber (S.L.) Aquamarine (S.L.) Olive-green (S.L.) Puce	Keene-Marlboro-Street	V. R. No. 1 on Plate 96 GXVII Extremely rare NOTE: Although this is more of a snuff bottle or small jar than a flask, we include it because of its manifest similarity to the sunburst flasks made at Keene-Marlboro-Street
GVIII–20. Large oval sunburst. 36 rather slender rays tapering to rounded ends turned downward to surface of flask and forming scalloped ellipse. At center of sunburst 5 small oval-shaped ornaments in oval formation with one in center.	Similar but variation in size of petaled ornaments at center.	Vertically ribbed 3, with heavy medial rib	Pint Similar to 18, Ill. 133	Plain lip Pontil mark	Yellow olive-green Deep golden amber Pale green Olive-amber (black)	Unknown; Van Rensselaer attributes it to Baltimore	V. R. No. 1 GXXIV Comparatively scarce
GVIII–21. Similar to No. 20, 36 rays	Like obverse	Same as No. 20	Pint Similar to 18, Ill. 133, but tapers sharply to base	Plain lip Pontil mark	Pale green Colorless, amethystine tinge	Unknown	Not listed by Van Rensselaer but probably a variation of his No. 1 GXXIV Scarce
GVIII–22. Large oval sunburst, 36 rays similar to No. 20. (Collection of Edwin Lefevre.)	Like obverse	Rounded and smooth without medial rib	Pint Similar to 18, Ill. 133	Plain lip Pontil mark	Moonstone Green, pale Olive-green, pale (C.G.) Puce, deep Citron (C.G.)	Unknown	Probably V. R. No. 2 GXXIV Scarce NOTE: This has also been listed by Van Rensselaer in half-pint size, but if this variety without medial rib does occur in half-pint size, it probably has 28 rays as in No. 24.

GVIII–15 GVIII–16 GVIII–17 GVIII–18 GVIII–19 GVIII–20 GVIII–20 GVIII–21 GVIII–22

613

GROUP VIII—SUNBURST FLASKS—*Continued*

OBVERSE	REVERSE	SIZE, FORM	EDGES	NECK, BASE	COLORS	GLASSHOUSE	NOTES, RARITY
GVIII—23. Large oval sunburst, 36 rays, similar to Nos. 20, 21, and 22.	Like obverse	Pint Similar to 18, Ill. 133, but tapers sharply to narrow base	Smooth and sharply angled; no medial rib	Plain lip Pontil mark	Puce Olive-yellow Bronze-amber (C.G.)	Unknown	Not listed by Van Rensselaer but probably a variation of his No. 2 GXXIV Scarce
GVIII—24. Oval sunburst similar to No. 20 but with 28 rays and ornaments at center slightly different.	Similar but size of ornaments vary slightly	Half-pint Similar to 18, Ill. 133	Vertically ribbed with heavy medial rib	Plain lip Pontil mark [Aquamarine, pale (G.A.)]	Pale green Dark amber (black) Olive-amber (C.G.)	Unknown	Not listed by Van Rensselaer Comparatively scarce
GVIII—25. Oval sunburst similar to Nos. 20 and 21 but 24 rays and ornaments at center broader and giving effect of 5-petaled flower.	Like obverse	Half-pint Similar to 18, Ill. 133	Vertically ribbed 5	Plain lip Pontil mark [Green, deep (S.L.) Olive-green (S.L.) Puce (G.A.) Wine (C.G.)]	Yellowish olive-green Pale green Bronze-amber Amethyst, deep (S.L.) Aquamarine (E.D.) Green, light (R.W.)	Unknown	V. R. No. 3 GXXIV Comparatively scarce
GVIII—26. Large elliptical sunburst covering entire side of flask; 16 rays. The rays converge to a definite point at center.	Like obverse	Pint Similar to 17, Ill. 133, but elongated	Horizontally corrugated; herringbone formation; corrugations extend around flask just below neck.	Plain lip Pontil mark [Green, light bluish (G.A.) Olive-green, light (S.L.) Olive-green, medium (S.L.) Yellow-green, deep (S.L.)]	Dark olive-green (black) Deep aquamarine Clear deep green Light yellowish green Pale green Aquamarine, pale Colorless (C.G.) Colorless, green tinge (E.D.)	Unknown	Not listed in pint size by Van Rensselaer Comparatively scarce
GVIII—27. Similar to No. 26, 16 rays covering entire flask.	Like obverse	Half-pint Similar to 17, Ill. 133, but elongated	Same as No. 26	Plain lip Occasionally with rolled over collar Pontil mark [Yellow-green, deep (S.L.)]	Deep green, yellowish tone Clear with faint greenish tint Pale green Aquamarine (E.D.) Colorless (S.L.) Olive-green (C.G.)	Unknown	V. R. No. 5 GXXIV Also No. 7 which is apparently identical in design and edges Comparatively scarce
GVIII—28. Large elliptical sunburst, similar to No. 27.	Like obverse	Half-pint Similar to 17, Ill. 133	Vertically ribbed	Tooled lip Plain lip Pontil mark	Yellow-green Clear Aquamarine Green, deep (S.L.) Blue-green	Unknown	V. R. No. 6 GXXIV Comparatively scarce

GVIII-29. Elongated sunburst with 12 rays in small sunken oval panel. Band of tiny ornaments around inner edge of panel. Entire flask except panel covered with heavy narrow wide-spaced vertical ribbing, 18 ribs.

GVIII-30. Same as No. 29 in all particulars except no trace of band of tiny ornaments around inner edge of oval panel.

For other Sunbursts, see GII-7 and GIX-48 and 49.

NOTE: Harry Hall White, in his excavations on the site of the Keene-Marlboro-Street Glass Works, found fragments of various types of sunburst flasks. At Keene he excavated fragments of the marked varieties and of one other variety.[1] At Coventry, fragments of what appear to be our Nos. 3 and 16 were found.[2] These were all in the olive-amber and olive-green bottle glass. At Mount Vernon he found sunburst fragments in very heavy deep aquamarine, almost green.[3]

It is possible that some sunburst flasks of similar design, in olive-amber and olive-green glass, were made at both Keene and Coventry. We feel that most varieties of the very heavy sunburst flasks which occur in various shades of green, including aquamarine, very rarely blue and frequently in clear flint, were made at Keene. They coincide closely in weight and colors with the heavy Masonic marked in the oval beneath the eagle, "JP" (Justus Perry), "HS" (Henry Schoolcraft), and "JKB", which we think were made at Keene. Some of these heavy sunbursts in clear glass, aquamarine and clear strong green may also have been made at Mount Vernon. In the absence of absolute evidence such as has been furnished by Mr. White's excavations, it is necessarily a matter of conjecture as to the glasshouses that actually produced many of the flasks, which, of course, applies not only to the sunbursts but to many other flasks.

NOTE: Flasks like No. 24 have been found with a leather covering and with leather loops on the edge through which cord was passed so that the flask could be carried as a canteen. One of these flasks has a black leather casing with the letters "P I" in yellow on one side. Possibly the letters stand for Pennsylvania Infantry.

¹*Antiques Magazine*, June, 1927.
²Correspondence with Mr. White, 1927.
²Correspondence with Mr. White, also *Antiques Magazine*, November, 1940.
³*Antiques Magazine*, November, 1929.

OBVERSE	REVERSE	STAR POINT	SIZE, FORM	EDGES	NECK, BASE	COLORS	GLASSHOUSE	NOTES, RARITY
	Like obverse		Three-quarter pint. Similar to 7, Ill. 133, except edge	Vertical ribbing same as covering flask	Plain lip. Occasionally tooled with rolled collar. Pontil mark	Olive-yellow; Deep bluish green; Clear; Clear green; Pale bluish aquamarine; Amber, deep (S.L.); Olive-amber; Sapphire-blue (S.L.); Yellow-green (S.L.)	Unknown	V. R. No. 4 GXXIV. Comparatively scarce
						Clear green; Green, light (S.L.)	Unknown	Not listed by Van Rensselaer. Very rare

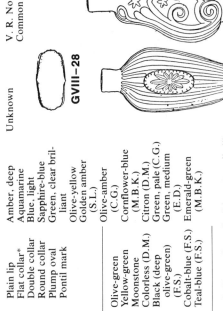
GVIII-28
GVIII-29
GIX-1

GROUP IX—SCROLL FLASKS—"VIOLIN OR SCROLL"

The chart of Scroll Flasks, Group IX in *American Glass*, was revised by Fred R. Salisbury and Helen McKearin and updated by the addition of flasks unrecorded in 1941.

OBVERSE	REVERSE	STAR POINT	SIZE, FORM	EDGES	NECK, BASE	COLORS	GLASSHOUSE	NOTES, RARITY
	Same as obverse	$\frac{6}{6}$ $\frac{6}{6}$	Quart 36	Vertical medial rib	Plain lip; Flat collar*; Double collar; Round collar; Plump oval; Pontil mark	Amber, deep; Aquamarine; Blue, light; Sapphire-blue; Green, clear brilliant; Olive-yellow; Golden amber (S.L.); Olive-amber (C.G.); Olive-green; Yellow-green; Moonstone; Colorless (D.M.); Black (deep olive-green) (F.S.); Cobalt-blue (F.S.); Teal-blue (F.S.); Cornflower-blue (M.B.K.); Citron (D.M.); Green, pale (C.G.); Green, medium (E.D.); Emerald-green (M.B.K.)	Unknown	V. R. No. 7 GXX. Common

NOTE: For Scroll nomenclature, see Ill. 120.
GIX-1. Large inverted heart-shaped frame formed by medial and inferior scrolls and containing large star with 6-fingerlike points. Similar 6-pointed star in space above frame.

*NOTE: A "flat collar" is an "applied" or "laid on" flat ring below a plain lip.

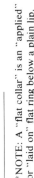

CROSS SECTIONS

GVIII-22 | GVIII-23 GVIII-23 | GVIII-24 | GVIII-24 | GVIII-25 | GVIII-26 | GVIII-27

OBVERSE	REVERSE	STAR POINT	SIZE, FORM	EDGES	NECK, BASE	COLORS	GLASSHOUSE	NOTES, RARITY
GIX–2. Scrolls and frame similar to No. 1 but medial scrolls larger; lower star, medium size, with 6 gothic-arch points.	Same as obverse	$\frac{6}{6}$	Quart 36	Vertical medial rib	Plain lip Plump oval Double round collar (M.B.K.) Pontil mark	Aquamarine Amber, golden Sapphire-blue Moonstone with pinkish tint Amber, deep (D.M.) Olive-amber (S.L.) Amethyst-pink (D.M.) Black (deep olive-green) Blue, light (C.G.) Blue, deep cobalt (M.B.K.) Blue, deep violet tone (C.G.) Apple-green (M.B.K.) Emerald-green (D.M.) Green, brilliant clear (F.S.) Olive-green (R.W) Yellow-green (D.M.) Moonstone, grayish Olive-yellow (M.B.K.)	Unknown	Not listed by Van Rensselaer Common
GIX–2a. Scrolls and frame similar to No. 2. Large upper and medium lower star—each with 6 sharp tapering points.	Same as obverse	$\frac{6}{6}$	Quart 36	Vertical medial rib	Plain lip Plump oval Double round collar Pontil mark	Yellow-green Blue, pale Green, light	Unknown	Not listed by Van Rensselaer Comparatively scarce
GIX–2b. Scroll and frame similar to No. 2. Medium lower star with 6 gothic-arch points; very large upper star with 8 clublike points.	Same as obverse of GIX–2	$\frac{8}{6}$	Quart 36	Vertical medial rib	Plain lip Misshapen oval Pontil mark	Aquamarine	Unknown	Rare
GIX–2c. Scrolls and frame similar to No. 2. Medial scrolls encircle teardrops at shoulders. Stars much smaller than on other quart scrolls. Slim tapering points. Upper star 6-point and lower 7-point.	Similar to No. 2 but both stars with 6 points.	$\frac{6}{7}$	Quart 36	Vertical medial rib	Plain lip Plump oval Pontil mark	Aquamarine Cornflower-blue	Unknown	Reported by Dr. M. B. Krassner Rare
GIX–2d. Scrolls and frame similar to No. 2, ⅝" raised round medallion between and overlapping the 2 medial scrolls, and slightly off-center to right.	Similar to obverse; concave medallion overlapping part of left scroll.	$\frac{6}{6}$	Quart 36	Vertical medial rib	Flat collar Plain oval Oxide deposit	Aquamarine	Unknown	Collection of Fred Salisbury Rare
GIX–2e. Scrolls and frame similar to No. 2; large 6-petaled flowerlike ornament instead of stars.	Same as obverse	$\frac{6}{6}$	Quart 36	Vertical medial rib	Plain lip Plump oval Pontil mark	Aquamarine	Unknown	Reported by Dr. M. B. Krassner Rare
GIX–2f. Similar to No. 2 in design, height, and width but with greater depth front to back.	Same as obverse	$\frac{6}{6}$	Quart plus (35 oz. to base of neck) 36	Vertical medial rib	Plain lip Plump oval, similar to Type 5 Pontil mark	Aquamarine	Unknown	Probably extremely rare

Description	Obverse	Fractions	Capacity	Rib	Lip / Mark	Color	Glassworks	Notes
GIX–2g. Scrolls, frame, and stars like No. 2e; height, width, and depth (front to back), same as No. 2f.	Like obverse but both small stars 6-pointed.	6/7 6/6	Quart plus 36	Vertical medial rib	Plain lip, Plump oval, Pontil mark	Aquamarine, deep Sapphire-blue (M.B.K.)	Unknown	Not previously recorded Rare
GIX–3. Scrolls and frame similar to No. 1 but scrolls less heavy and stars medium size with 6 tapered blunt points. Lower star slightly mis-shapen.	Same as obverse	6/6 6/6	Quart 36	Vertical medial rib	Plain lip, Flat collar, Pointed oval, Pontil mark	Aquamarine, Black (dark olive-amber), Violet-blue, Clear green, yellowish tone, Yellow-green, very dark, Amber, deep, Brown-amber, Golden amber (M.B.K.), Red-amber (M.B.K.), Cornflower-blue (M.B.K.)	Unknown	Not listed by Van Rensselaer Common
						Sapphire-blue (D.M.), Citron (M.B.K.), Emerald-green (M.B.K.), Olive-green, yellowish (S.L.), Sea-green (D.M.), Olive-yellow (F.S.)		
GIX–4. Scrolls and frame similar to No. 1; stars chunkier, points asymmetrical; upper star smaller than lower.	Same as obverse	6/6 6/6	Quart 36	Vertical medial rib	Plain lip (M.B.K.), Flat collar, Plump oval, Pontil mark	Yellow-green, clear Aquamarine (M.B.K.), Sage-green (D.M.), Sea-green (D.M.), Black (deep brown) (C.G.), Amber (F.S.)	Unknown	Not listed by Van Rensselaer Comparatively scarce
GIX–5. Scrolls, frame, and sharp 6-point stars similar to No. 2a; lower star much larger than upper.	Same as obverse	6/6 6/6	Quart 36	Vertical medial rib	Plain lip, Pointed oval with 4 small heavy dots, Pontil mark	Aquamarine (F.S.), Green, bluish medium (M.B.K.), Emerald-green (M.B.K.)	Unknown	Not listed by Van Rensselaer Scarce
GIX–6. Scrolls and frame similar to No. 2; large 6-pointed stars similar to No. 1, upper larger than lower. Between scrolls, in straight line, "LOUISVILLE KY", the "E" flowing into scroll above it.	Same as obverse except straight "GLASSWORKS" in straight line	6/6 6/6	Quart 36	Vertical medial rib	Plain lip, Plump oval, Pontil mark, Oxide deposits	Green, light, yellow tone Aquamarine Citron (M.B.K.), Emerald-green, light (M.B.K.), Olive-yellow (S.L.)	Louisville Glass Works, Louisville, Ky.	V. R. No. 14 GXX Comparatively scarce

GIX-2   GIX-2a   GIX-3   GIX-4   GIX-5   GIX-5 BASE   GIX-6   OBV. GIX-6   GIX-6

GROUP IX—SCROLL FLASKS—"VIOLIN OR SCROLL"—Continued

OBVERSE	REVERSE	STAR POINT	SIZE, FORM	EDGES	NECK, BASE	COLORS	GLASSHOUSE	NOTES, RARITY
GIX–7. Scrolls and frame similar to No. 6. Slightly smaller stars (lower smaller than upper); letters in inscription somewhat larger and of slightly different formation.	Like obverse of No. 6 except for different formation of letters	6/6	Quart 36	Vertical medial rib	Plain lip, Plump oval, with 2 large dots, Pontil mark, Oxide deposit	Amber, deep; Aquamarine; Olive-yellow (D.M.)	Louisville Glass Works, Louisville, Ky.	Not listed by Van Rensselaer Scarce
GIX–8. Large inverted heart-shaped frame formed by medial and inferior scrolls, medium 8-pointed star above medial scrolls and, in space below, "LOUISVILLE" in straight line. Smaller 8-pointed star in space above frame.	Same as obverse except for "GLASS WORKS" below medial scrolls.	8/8	Pint 36	Vertical medial rib	Plain lip, Long oval, Oxide deposit	Aquamarine; Canary; Green, light; Yellow-green (S.L.); Moonstone (S.L.)	Louisville Glass Works, Louisville, Ky.	V. R. No. 14 GXX Comparatively scarce
GIX–9. Same as No. 8 except letters smaller and inscription in curved line.	Same as No. 8 except letters smaller and inscription in curved line.	8/8	Pint 36	Vertical medial rib	Plain lip, Ring below plain lip (D. Meek), Long oval, Oxide deposit	Golden amber; Aquamarine; Amber, dark (M.B.K.); Amber, reddish; Citron (G.M.); Yellow-green (D.M.); Olive-yellow (D.M.)	Louisville Glass Works, Louisville, Ky.	V. R. No. 13 GXX Comparatively scarce
GIX–10. Scrolls and frame similar to No. 8; medial scrolls nearly touch. Two medium 8-pointed stars, upper slightly smaller than lower.	Same as obverse	8/8	Pint 36	Vertical medial rib	Plain lip, Round collar (M.B.K.), Long oval; figures "5x5," reversed, Oxide deposit	Amethyst, pale; Aquamarine; Greenish blue; Bluish green; Yellow-green, vibrant; Yellow-green, pale, and opalescent shoulders and neck; Yellow-green, deep; Olive, brilliant yellowish; Amethyst, deep (black) (M.B.K.); Amethystine (M.B.K.); Brown-amber (C.G.); Golden amber (S.L.); Red-amber (S.L.); Yellow-amber (D.M.); Cobalt-blue (M.B.K.)	Possibly Lancaster Glass Works, Lancaster, N.Y. (see note)	V. R. No. 8 GXX Common

Emerald-green, medium (M.B.K.)
Emerald-green, deep (M.B.K.)
Kelly-green, deep (M.B.K.)
Yellow-green, pale (C.G.)
Moonstone
Moonstone, deep & very milky (M.B.K.)
Yellow, light greenish (D.M.)
Red-violet (F.S.)
Sapphire-blue (M.B.K.)
Colorless (M.B.K.)
Green, light, with amber bands (M.B.K.)
Lime to smoky topaz to chocolate brown at neck (F.S.)
Golden amber (Helen C. Hickman)
Cornflower-blue (Helen C. Hickman)
Green, medium (C.G.)

NOTE: Besides the mold for this particular No. 10 flask with 2 reversed fives on its keyed base, several other glasshouses used molds producing very similar flasks with upper and mid 8-pointed stars of various sizes. Some of the molds produced a simple straight mold seam on the base. Some molds had keyed bases, with or without numerals or with partial numerals. No attempt has been made to chart as distinct varieties the flasks from molds with their differing base types or minor star variations. Possibly one, or more than one, of the molds with keyed base was used in the Lancaster (N.Y.) Glass Works, as the bases are similar to bases of some of the Railroad flasks attributed to Lancaster.

618

Description	Reverse	Mold no.	Size	Rib	Lip / Pontil	Color	Value	Rarity
GIX–10a. Scrolls and frame similar to No. 8. Medium 8-pointed star in mid space; slightly smaller 8-pointed star in upper space.	Similar to obverse; 7-pointed upper star.	8/8 8/7	Pint 36	Vertical medial rib	Plain lip; Long oval; Pontil mark; Oxide deposit	Aquamarine; Sage-green; Yellow-green	Unknown	Comparatively scarce
GIX–10b. Scrolls and frame similar to No. 8. Medium 6-pointed lower star; smaller 6-pointed upper star.	Same as obverse	6/6 6/6	Pint 36	Vertical medial rib	Plain lip; Wide heavy flat collar; Type 5; Oxide deposit	Aquamarine; Olive-amber (F.S.); Emerald-green (F.S.); Yellow-green (M.B.K.); Olive-yellow (M.B.K.)	Unknown	Comparatively scarce
GIX–10c. Scrolls and frame similar to No. 8, but smaller 6-pointed stars of equal size.	Same as obverse	6/6 6/6	Pint 36	Vertical medial rib	Plain lip; Long oval; Pontil mark	Amber, brilliant; Golden amber (M.B.K.); Blue-green (F.S.); Emerald-green, deep	Unknown	Comparatively scarce
GIX–10d. Scrolls and frame similar to No. 8. Medium 8-pointed lower star; smaller 9-pointed upper star.	Same as obverse	9/8 8/7	Pint 36	Vertical medial rib	Plain lip; Long oval; Pontil mark	Aquamarine; Citron	Unknown	Lorimer Collection, according to Fred Salisbury Rare
GIX–10e. Scrolls and frame like No. 8 with medium 8-pointed lower star and slightly smaller 8-pointed upper star as in No. 10a.	Like obverse but upper star has 9 points.	8/8 9/8	Pint 36		Plain lip; Plump oval; type 32; Pontil mark	Emerald-green	Unknown	Not listed by Van Rensselaer Probably rare
GIX–11. Scrolls and frame similar to No. 8 but with well-defined space between scrolls at center. Lower star like No. 10. Upper star, much smaller and ill-defined.	Similar to obverse	8/8 8/8	Pint 36	Vertical medial rib	Plain lip; Flat collar; Plump oval; Pontil mark; Oxide deposit	Aquamarine; Black (dark olive-green); Sapphire-blue, deep; Emerald-green, bluish tone; Amber, light (S.L.); Amber, deep (D.M.); Golden amber (DeVere Card); Cobalt-blue (D.M.); Citron (D.M.); Green, tint (S.L.); Olive-green, deep; Sage-green (D.M.); Yellow-green (D.M.); Pink (D.M.); Purple (D.M.); Apple-green (M.B.K.); Moonstone (M.B.K.)	Unknown	V. R. No. 9 GXX Common

GIX–7 BASE GIX–7 GIX–7 GIX–8 GIX–9 GIX–9 GIX–10 BASE GIX–10 VAR. GIX–10 GIX–11

OBVERSE	REVERSE	STAR POINT	SIZE, FORM	EDGES	NECK, BASE	COLORS	GLASSHOUSE	NOTES, RARITY
GIX–11a. Scrolls and frame similar to No. 8. Medium 8-pointed stars.	Same as obverse	8 8 / 8	Pint 36	Vertical medial rib, unusually wide and curved at base	Plain lip; Rounded ring collar; Plump oval; Pontil mark	Amber, clear brilliant; Golden amber; Aquamarine; Cornflower-blue, light; Cornflower-blue, pale; Olive-yellow; Olive-amber; Cobalt-blue (M.B.K.); Blue, deep (black) (M.B.K.); [Peacock-blue (M. Knapp. Jr.); Emerald-green, deep (M.B.K.); Olive-green (M.B.K.)]	Unknown	Not listed by Van Rensselaer. Common
GIX–12. Scrolls and frame similar to No. 8. Medium 7-pointed stars.	Same as obverse	7 7 / 7	Pint 36	Vertical medial rib	Plain lip; Long oval; Pontil mark	Black (dark olive-green); Apple-green (D.M.); Blue-green (C.G.); Emerald-green (S.L.)	Unknown	V. R. No. 10 GXX. Comparatively scarce
GIX–12a. Scrolls and frame similar to No. 12. Medium stars: lower, 8-pointed; upper, 6-pointed.	Similar to obverse; both stars 8-pointed.	6 8 / 8	Pint 36	Vertical medial rib	Plain lip; Oval; Pontil mark	Aquamarine; Cobalt-blue	Unknown	Rare
GIX–13. Scrolls and frame similar to No. 8. Medium 7-pointed stars.	Same as obverse	7 7 / 7	Pint 36	Vertical medial rib	Plain lip; Deep collar with lower bevel; Double round collar (M.B.K.); Long oval; Pontil mark; Rough ring; Oxide deposit	Emerald-green, deep, yellow tone; Amber (S.L.); Golden amber (C.G.); Aquamarine, strong; Green, light (M.B.K.); Yellow-green	Unknown	Not listed by Van Rensselaer. Comparatively scarce
GIX–14. Scrolls and frame similar to No. 8. Larger stars; lower, 7-pointed; upper, 6-pointed.	Same as obverse	6 6 / 7	Pint 36	Vertical medial rib	Plain lip; Flat collar; Plump oval; Pontil mark	Colorless, gray tone; Green, yellow tone; Olive-green, brilliant, light; Olive-green, brilliant, yellowish; Olive-yellow, deep; Amber (D.M.); Golden amber; Olive-amber, light (D.M.); Olive-amber, deep (M.B.K.); [Aquamarine (S.L.); Turquoise-blue (M.B.K.); Citron (D.M.); Green, tint (S.L.); Apple-green (M.B.K.); Emerald-green (S.L.)]; [Green, yellow tone, light; Green, yellow tone, deep; Peacock-green (M.B.K.); Yellow-green, deep (Helen C. Hickman)]	Unknown	Not listed by Van Rensselaer. Comparatively scarce

Mold	Obverse	Reverse		Capacity (oz.)	Rib	Lip / Form	Colors	Maker	Rarity
GIX–15.	Scrolls and frame similar to No. 8. Medium stars. Lower star, 8-pointed; upper, 7-pointed.	Similar to obverse. Small 5-pointed lower star; slightly larger 6-pointed upper star.	$\frac{7}{8}$ $\frac{6}{5}$	Pint 36	Vertical medial rib	Plain lip / Long oval / Pontil mark	Moonstone, Aquamarine (M.B.K.), Colorless (M.B.K.), Golden amber (S.L.), Olive-amber (S.L.), Sapphire-blue (C.G.), Emerald-green, medium (S.L.) — Emerald-green, deep (S.L.), Yellow-green (D.M.), Citron (M.B.K.), Canary (F.S.)	Unknown	Not listed by Van Rensselaer. Very rare
GIX–16.	Scrolls and frame similar to No. 8. Left inferior scroll very heavy, crowding right. Two small 5-pointed stars; upper star may show pinpoint suggestion of sixth point.	Similar to obverse, but upper star has 6 bold uniform points and inferior scrolls are of equal proportions.	$\frac{5}{5}$ $\frac{6}{5}$	Pint 36	Vertical medial rib	Plain lip / Round collar / Long oval / Pontil mark	Cornflower-blue, Olive-amber (S.L.), Aquamarine (M.B.K.), Sapphire-blue (S.L.), Cornflower-blue, pale (M.B.K.), Colorless, gray tone (D.M.) — Colorless, green tinge, Gray (M.B.K.), Yellow-green (Blaske)	Unknown	Not listed by Van Rensselaer Rare
GIX–16a.	Scrolls and frame similar to No. 8 but shoulders narrower and more tapering. Two medium 5-pointed stars with sharp tapering points.	Same as obverse	$\frac{5}{5}$ $\frac{5}{5}$	Pint 36	Vertical medial rib	Plain lip / Plump oval / Pontil mark	Aquamarine	Unknown	Rare
GIX–17.	Scrolls and frame similar to No. 8. Star without definite points.	Same as obverse	$\frac{0}{0}$ $\frac{0}{0}$	Pint 36	Vertical medial rib	Plain lip / Long oval / Pontil mark	Aquamarine (F.S.), Amber (D.M.), Cornflower-blue (M.B.K.), Emerald-green, medium (S.L.), Green, medium (M.B.K.), Olive-green, Olive-yellow, Black (deep olive-amber) (M.B.K.), Yellow-green (Helen C. Hickman)	Unknown	Common

NOTE: The absence of clearly defined star points could be due to a worn mold or a skimpy gather insufficient to provide a clear-cut rendering. The GIX–17 classification may provide a home for the several pint scrolls having small high-domed stars which were deprived of their true form due to haste or carelessness in production.

GIX–12   GIX–13   GIX–14   GIX–15   GIX–16   GIX–17

GROUP IX—SCROLL FLASKS—"VIOLIN OR SCROLL"—Continued

OBVERSE	REVERSE	STAR POINT	SIZE, FORM	EDGES	NECK, BASE	COLORS	GLASSHOUSE	NOTES, RARITY
GIX–17a. Scrolls and frame No. 8. Two small starlike ornaments. Between and overlapping medial scrolls, a ⅝" convex medallion. slightly off-center to the left. Left superior scroll rising high on neck.	Similar to obverse. No medallion. Very small 5-pointed star over left inferior scroll.	0 0 / 0	Pint 36	Vertical medial rib	Plain lip Long oval Oxide deposit	Aquamarine	Unknown	Probably very rare
GIX–18. Scrolls and frame similar to No. 8. Above medial scrolls, "Star" with scalloped edge. No star in upper space. Large bead (7/16" in diameter) on neck, ¼" above lower neck line.	Similar to obverse. No bead on neck.	0 0 / 0	Pint 36	Vertical medial rib	Plain lip Plump pointed oval Pontil mark	Sapphire-blue deep Aquamarine (M.B.K.) Sapphire-blue (D.M.) Yellow-green (D.M.)	Unknown	Not listed by Van Rensselaer Scarce
GIX–19. Similar to No. 18 but flask definitely smaller.	Same as obverse	0 0 / 0	Slightly less than pint 36	Vertical medial rib	Plain lip Pontil mark	Yellowish-green, pale Aquamarine (D.M.) Amber (D.M.) Sapphire-blue (D.M.)	Unknown	Not listed by Van Rensselaer Rare

NOTE: The 2 distinguishing features—absence of well-formed stars and "definitely smaller" (slightly less than pint)—observed when Mr. McKearin's charts were first published in 1941, have proved over the years to be unreliable criteria by which to establish a clear-cut identification. More recently, when a comprehensive check was made of the measured capacity of examples of all classifications of pint scrolls, it was found that their capacity, as measured to the base of the neck, varied from 12½ to 17¼ ounces. Viewed head-on, some of the flasks were definitely taller and broader than others, yet of lesser capacity because of less thickness as measured between the flat obverse and reverse surfaces. In a random selection of these variations, it is likely that indistinct or poorly blown examples from several of the "slightly less than pint" scrolls will wind up being classified as No. 19. The question, therefore, arises as to whether or not there is, in fact, a true No. 19—the product of an individual mold.

OBVERSE	REVERSE	STAR POINT	SIZE, FORM	EDGES	NECK, BASE	COLORS	GLASSHOUSE	NOTES, RARITY
GIX–20. Scrolls and frame similar to No. 8. Very large 6-petaled flower in lower space; large star with 8 tapering points in upper space. In upper space, large oval ornament, frequently appearing sunken or collapsed.	Same as obverse		Pint 36	Vertical medial rib	Plain lip Long oval Pontil mark Oxide deposit Keyed base Keyed base with 4x4 in reverse	Yellow-green, brilliant Amber (D.M.) Amber, golden (M.B.K.) Aquamarine (C.G.) Citron (M.B.K.) Green, clear (S.L.) — Aquamarine (F.S.) Amber (F.S.) — [boxed: Sapphire-blue (M.B.K.)]	Possibly Lancaster Glass Works, Lancaster, N.Y.	Not listed by Van Rensselaer Scarce

NOTE: It seems likely that the mold with plain keyed base was altered by cutting in the (reversed) "4x4".

OBVERSE	REVERSE	STAR POINT	SIZE, FORM	EDGES	NECK, BASE	COLORS	GLASSHOUSE	NOTES, RARITY
GIX–21. Scrolls and frame similar to No. 8. Faint oval in mid and lower spaces. Small 5-point star in upper space.	Similar to obverse but 5-pointed small star in upper and mid spaces. Faint oval in lower space.	5 5 / 0 0	Pint 36	Vertical medial rib	Plain lip Plump oval Type 31	Aquamarine	Unknown	Not listed by Van Rensselaer Rare
GIX–22. Scrolls and frame similar to No. 8. Small 5-pointed star in upper space. Medium 5-pointed stars in mid and lower spaces.	Same as obverse	5 5 5 / 5 5 5	Pint 36	Vertical medial rib	Plain lip Plump oval Pontil mark	Aquamarine	Unknown	Not listed by Van Rensselaer Very rare
GIX–23. Scrolls and frame similar to No. 8. Four stars: medium 8-pointed star in upper space; small 6-pointed star in mid space; small 4-pointed star above each inferior scroll in lower space.	Same as obverse	8 8 / 6 6 / 4 4	Pint 36	Vertical medial rib	Plain lip Long oval Pontil mark	Green, clear light Emerald-green, light Aquamarine, strong	Unknown	Not listed by Van Rensselaer Extremely rare

GIX-24. Scrolls and frame similar to No. 8. Letter "A" in lower space and upper space—probably intended to be stars.

GIX-25. Scrolls and frame similar to No. 8. Letter "e" in lower space. Raised dots in mid space and upper space similar to No. 24.

GIX-26. Scrolls and frame similar to No. 8. Inscription "S. M'KEE." in lower space. Large star with 8 tapering points in mid space. In upper space large less well-formed 8-pointed star.

GIX-27. Same as No. 26 except for a slightly sunken blank rectangle replacing all of the "S. M'KEE." but the final period.

NOTE: The presence of a period at the end of the blank rectangle on No. 27 leaves little or no doubt that the McKee mold for No. 26 was altered by removal of "S. M'Kee". In that case it may be that the altered mold for No. 27 was acquired by another glassworks.

GIX-28. Scrolls and frame similar to No. 8. "ROUGH" in lower space. Medium 8-pointed star in mid space.

GIX-29. Scroll patterning similar to but somewhat more elaborate than No. 1 (quart). Large compact 8-pointed star in mid space; similar star in upper space.

No.	Reverse	Dimensions	Capacity	Base	Lip / Pontil	Color	Maker	Notes
GIX-24	Similar to obverse. Faint oval in lower space.	$\frac{8}{8}$ $\frac{9}{8}$	Pint 36	Vertical medial rib	Plain lip / Long oval / Pontil mark	Aquamarine / Blue-green (M.B.K.) / Jade-green (D.M.) / Yellow-green (D.M.)	Unknown	Not listed by Van Rensselaer Rare
GIX-25	Similar to obverse but no letter in lower space.		Pint 36	Vertical medial rib	Plain lip / Ring below plain lip (D. Meek) / Flat ring, applied (M.B.K.) / Round collar (M.B.K.) / Long oval / Pontil mark	Aquamarine / Canary / Aquamarine, deep (C.G.) / Turquoise-blue (M.B.K.) / Green, light with amber streaks (M.B.K.) / Emerald-green, light (S.L.) — [boxed: Peacock-green (M.B.K.) / Yellow-green (C.G.)]	Unknown	V. R. No. 11 GXX Comparatively scarce
GIX-26	Similar to obverse. Exceptionally large stars and upper with 9 points. No inscription	$\frac{8}{8}$ $\frac{9}{8}$	Pint 36	Vertical medial rib	Plain lip / Plump oval / Pontil mark	Aquamarine / Green, pale (M.B.K.)	S. McKee & Co., Pittsburgh, Pa.	Not listed by Van Rensselaer Extremely rare
GIX-27	Same as No. 26	$\frac{8}{8}$ $\frac{9}{8}$	Pint 36	Vertical medial rib	Plain lip / Plump oval / Pontil mark	Green, pale yellowish	Possibly S. McKee & Co., Pittsburgh, Pa.	Not listed by Van Rensselaer Extremely rare
GIX-28	Same as obverse except for "& READY"	$\frac{0}{8}$ $\frac{0}{8}$	Pint 36	Vertical medial rib	Plain lip / Oval / Pontil mark	Aquamarine	Unknown	Not listed by Van Rensselaer Extremely rare
GIX-29	Same as obverse	$\frac{8}{8}$ $\frac{8}{8}$	Slightly over 2 quarts 36	Vertical medial rib	Plain lip / Long plump oval / Pontil mark / Oxide deposit	Aquamarine	Unknown	V. R. No. 19 GXX Rare

GIX-20 GIX-21 GIX-22 GIX-23 GIX-24 GIX-25 GIX-26 GIX-27 GIX-28 GIX-28 GIX-29

GIX-20 BASE

GROUP IX—SCROLL FLASKS—"VIOLIN OR SCROLL"—Continued

OBVERSE	REVERSE	STAR POINT	SIZE, FORM	EDGES	NECK, BASE	COLORS	GLASSHOUSE	NOTES, RARITY
GIX–29a. Simplified scroll design, similar to pint No. 47, flanking very large fleur-de-lis on either side of which is a large pearl.	Similar to obverse; no pearls		2¼ qts 36	Vertical medial rib	Plain lip / Plump oval / Polished	Aquamarine, pale / Colorless "crystal clear"	Unknown	Extremely rare
GIX–30. Five slender ribs, graduated in length, each side of a large inverted heart-shaped frame with simplified scrolls and without stars or other ornamentation.	Same as obverse		Gallon 36	Vertical medial rib	Plain lip / Plump oval / Polished	Colorless / Sea-green, light (F.S.) / Aquamarine, pale (F.S.)	Unknown	Collection of Dan Meek / Not listed by Van Rensselaer / Extremely rare
GIX–30a. Large frame formed by 2 inner ribs, scrolled at top and bottom and containing large conventionalized fleur-de-lis. The space between heavy solid medial edge-rib and inner scrolled rib, deeply valleyed from about 1½" above base to waist. Five large pearls: 2 in shoulder space; 1 above each of the upper scrolls; 1 each side of fleur-de-lis; 1 at bottom, centered below point at which lower scrolls nearly touch.	Similar to obverse but with a heavy short rib with 2 nodelike swellings, between medial and inner ribs, and without pearls within frame.		Gallon 35	Vertical medial rib	Plain lip / Plump oval / Polished	Strong green / Aquamarine	Unknown	Reported by George Austin / Extremely rare / One example recorded

NOTE: The fact that the rough pontil mark on known examples of Nos. 29a and 30a were ground off and the area polished suggests that these flasks were not produced in a bottle glassworks but one in which tableware was the specialty, requiring grinding and polishing equipment—such glassworks as the Bakewells' or the Robinsons' in Pittsburgh. Pa.

OBVERSE	REVERSE	STAR POINT	SIZE, FORM	EDGES	NECK, BASE	COLORS	GLASSHOUSE	NOTES, RARITY
GIX–31. Scrolls and frame similar to No. 8 but on reduced scale. Small star with 6 points in mid space; large star with 6 fingerlike points in upper space.	Same as obverse	6 / 6 / 0	Half-pint 36	Vertical medial rib	Plain lip / Narrow flat collar, applied / Pointed oval / Pontil mark	Aquamarine / Yellow-green, clear / Golden amber (S.L.)	Unknown	V. R. No. 6, GXX / Common
GIX–32. Large fleur-de-lis flanked by 3 ribs graduated in length. Inner and middle rib with club-shaped terminals. Outer ribs more slender and scrolled on shoulder. Small star with 6 fingerlike points.	Similar to obverse; star more angular and 5-pointed.	6 / 5 / 0	Half-pint 36	Vertical medial rib	Plain lip / Flat collar / Plump oval / Pontil mark / Oxide deposit / Rough ring	Yellow-green brilliant / Aquamarine (F.S.) / Golden-amber (S.L.) / Sapphire-blue (S.L.)	Unknown	Not listed by Van Rensselaer / Scarce
GIX–33. Scrolls and fleur-de-lis similar to No. 32 but small star 5-pointed.	Same as obverse	5 / 5 / 0	Half-pint 36	Vertical medial rib	Plain lip / No. 20 (deep rounded collar with lower bevel) / Plump oval / Pontil mark / Oxide deposit / Rough ring	Aquamarine / Cornflower-blue / Red-amber (S.L.) / Sapphire-blue, medium (S.L.) / Yellow-green (M.B.K.) / Blue-green (F.S.)	Unknown	Not listed by Van Rensselaer / Common
GIX–33a. Scrolls and fleur-de-lis similar to No. 32. Small 6-pointed star in upper space.	Same as obverse	6 / 6 / 0	Half-pint 36	Vertical medial rib	Plain lip / Plump oval / Pontil mark	Aquamarine, cloudy	Unknown	Not listed by Van Rensselaer / Extremely rare

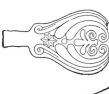

	Reverse	Edge	Size		Neck and Mouth	Colors	Base	Remarks
GIX–34. Scrolls and fleur-de-lis similar to No. 32. In upper space, very large 8-pointed star with lower point extending into space between upper terminals. Directly below, a large pearl.	Same as obverse	Vertical medial rib	Half-pint 36	8/0 0	Plain lip Flat collar Long, pointed oval Pontil mark	Amber, deep golden / Aquamarine / Bluish green / Colorless / Amber / Olive-amber (M.B.K.) / Sapphire-blue (M.B.K.) / Colorless, pink tint (M.B.K.) / Citron (G. May) / Green, brilliant (D.M.) Emerald-green, deep (S.L.) / Olive-green, yellowish (D.M.) / Olive-yellow (M.B.K.) / Olive-green (F.S.) / Red-amber (Helen C. Hickman)	Unknown	Possibly V. R. No. 1 GXX Comparatively scarce
GIX–34a. Scrolls and fleur-de-lis similar to No. 32. Eight-pointed star. Similar to No. 34 but more compact and slightly smaller and pearl medium size.	Similar to obverse; very small pearl.	Vertical medial rib	Half-pint 36	8/0 0	Plain lip Plump oval Pontil mark	Yellow-green	Unknown	Scarce
GIX–35. Scrolls and fleur-de-lis similar to No. 32. Medium-size 8-pointed star in upper space. Below, a medium-size oval ornament.	Same as obverse	Vertical medial rib	Half-pint 36	8/0 0	Plain lip Plump oval Pontil mark	Sapphire-blue, deep / Amethystine (M.B.K.) / Aquamarine, with white flecks (M.B.K.) / Golden amber (M.B.K.) / Turquoise-blue (M.B.K.) Colorless (M.B.K.) / Green, light (M.B.K.) / Emerald-green, medium (M.B.K.) / Yellow-green	Unknown	Not listed by Van Rensselaer Rare
GIX–36. Scrolls and fleur-de-lis similar to No. 32. Medium-size 8-pointed star similar to No. 35. Below, medium-size pearl.	Same as obverse	Vertical medial rib	Half-pint 36	8/0 0	Plain lip Plump, pointed oval Pontil mark	Aquamarine / Golden amber (M.B.K.) / Colorless (D.M.) / Sapphire-blue / Green, light (D.M.) / Emerald-green (D.M.)	Unknown	V. R. No. 4 GXX

NOTE: Since this flask was charted in 1941, several pearl ornamented half-pint Scrolls have been observed to have *oval* instead of round ornaments. In each case the flask appears to have been *stretched* during removal from the mold—or immediately afterward—thereby distorting the pearl as well as other relief details. The blue No. 35 at The Corning Museum of Glass, formerly in the McKearin Collection and the source of the charted description, seems to be such a flask with its "pearl" decidedly distorted to an oval by accident, not by a true mold impression. Since in all other features this particular flask is like No. 36 it seems probable No. 35 was blown in the mold for No. 36.

NOTE: Besides the mold for this flask, two others have been identified having approximately the same star and pearl characteristics, but each of the three varies slightly in the confirmation of the fleur-de-lis and quite noticeably in the shapes of the oval base.

Moonstone (F.S.)
Puce (M.B.K.)

GIX-30   GIX-31   GIX-32   GIX-33   GIX-34

GROUP IX—SCROLL FLASKS—"VIOLIN OR SCROLL"—*Continued*

OBVERSE	REVERSE	STAR POINT	SIZE, FORM	EDGES	NECK, BASE	COLORS	GLASSHOUSE	NOTES, RARITY
GIX–37. Scrolls and fleur-de-lis similar to No. 32. Medium-size 8-pointed star. Below, tiny pearl.	Same as obverse	$\frac{8}{0}$ $\frac{8}{0}$	Half-pint 36	Vertical medial rib	Plain lip Plump pointed oval Pontil mark	Black (dark olive-green) Red-amber, deep (S.L.) Golden amber (M.B.K.) Aquamarine Blue-green (C.G.) Emerald-green (Helen C. Hickman)	Unknown	V. R. No. 5 GXX Comparatively scarce
						Sage-green, deep (M.B.K.) Yellow-green		
GIX–37a. Scrolls and fleur-de-lis similar to No. 32. Medium-size 8-pointed star similar to No. 37. No pearl.	Same as obverse	$\frac{8}{0}$ $\frac{8}{0}$	Half-pint 36	Vertical medial rib	Plain lip Plump oval Pontil mark	Amber	Unknown	Scarce
GIX–38. Scroll ribs and fleur-de-lis similar to No. 32. Medium 8-petaled flower at top and large pearl below.	Similar to obverse. Fleur-de-lis replaced by scroll frame with "BP & B" and large pearl above medial scrolls and between terminals.		Half-pint 36	Vertical medial rib	Plain lip Pointed oval Pontil mark	Aquamarine Green, light Green, yellowish (R. Wise) Yellow-green (G.A.)	Bakewell, Page, & Bakewell, Pittsburgh, Pa.	V. R. No. 2 GXX Scarce
GIX–38a. Same as No. 38	Same as obverse		Half-pint 36	Vertical medial rib	Plain lip Mismatched oval Pontil mark	Amber Sapphire-blue Citron	Possibly Bakewell, Page & Bakewell, Pittsburgh, Pa.	Scarce

NOTE: The base, a mismatched oval, would seem to indicate that a half from *two* molds had been joined.

OBVERSE	REVERSE	STAR POINT	SIZE, FORM	EDGES	NECK, BASE	COLORS	GLASSHOUSE	NOTES, RARITY
GIX–38b. Similar to No. 38. Nine-petaled instead of 8-petaled flower at top. Pearl small as on No. 36. Shorter and more corset-waisted than other half-pints.	Same as obverse		Half-pint 36	Vertical medial rib	Plain lip Plump oval Pontil mark	Milky aquamarine	Unknown	Rare
GIX–39. Same as No. 38	Same as No. 38		Half-pint 36	Vertical medial rib	Plain lip Ring below plain lip (D. Meek) Precise circle Pontil mark	Aquamarine Lapis-lazuli blue Sapphire-blue, deep Moonstone, greenish Yellow-green, brilliant Amber (D.M.) Red-amber, deep (S.L.) Cobalt-blue (D.M.)	Bakewell, Page, & Bakewell, Pittsburgh, Pa.	V. R. No. 3 GXX Scarce
						Colorless (E.D.) Green, deep (G.A.) Green, light, with amber bands (M.B.K.)		
GIX–40. Miniature scroll flask. Four graduated fingerlike ribs following pear-shaped contour of flask; the innermost scroll at base. In center space, colonnette with rectangular plinth and concave disk capital.	Same as obverse		2½" tall 1½" greatest width 36	Vertical medial rib	Plain lip Oval Pontil mark	Sapphire-blue, deep Colorless	Unknown	Not listed by Van Rensselaer Extremely rare

GIX–37

GIX–38 GIX–38

GIX–39 BASE

GIX–39

GIX-41. Two ribs flanking pear-shaped frame, scrolled at base and enclosing large anchor, large pearl above and below each fluke.

GIX-42. Similar to No. 41 (Courtesy of Leslie Laughlin)

NOTE: All of the half-pints have oval bases except No. 39, which has a circular base.

GIX-43. So-called corset-waisted scroll flask. Large frame formed by ribs, scrolled at the top and looped at the bottom in an ogival effect and with parallel inner frame terminating at top in long oval finial and containing a large pearl above "JR & SON". Large pearl below each curved line at bottom of inner frame. Two large pearls below scrolls at top of outer frame. Long oval ornament within each loop at bottom of frame. Five-petaled motif below each end of frame at base.

GIX-44. Similar to No. 43. No inscription

GIX-45. Elaborate scroll decoration forming conventionalized acanthus leaves. Four-petaled flower at top; diamond at center; leaf motif at base.

GIX-46. Elaborate scroll design. Outer scrolls forming conventionalized acanthus leaves enclosing panel containing scrollwork with diamond at center and surmounted by 4-petaled motif. Three-lobed leaf finial between top scrolls.

No.	Reverse	Size	Edge	Lip / Base	Color	Maker	Rarity
GIX-41	Ribs and frame similar to obverse. Fleur-de-lis in upper portion of frame; large pearl below at right and left.	Half-pint 34	Vertical medial rib	Plain lip; Plump oval; Pontil mark	Aquamarine; Green, deep; Yellow-green; Green, light (S.L.)	Probably John Robinson & Son, Pittsburgh, Pa.	V. R. No. 12 GXX; Scarce
GIX-42	Similar to No. 41. "JR.&S" in slight arc between pearls and scrolls.	Half-pint 34	Vertical medial rib	Plain lip; Plump oval; Pontil mark	Amber, golden; Amethyst, deep; Aquamarine; Colorless; Lavender, light (M.B.K.); Yellow-green (S.L.)	John Robinson & Son, Pittsburgh, Pa.	Not listed by Van Rensselaer; Rare
GIX-43	Large outer frame, scrolled at top and bottom, containing fleur-de-lis. Two large pearls either side below top scrolls as on obverse and similar 8-petaled motifs at bottom. Crescent-shaped ornament connecting scrolls at center bottom of frame.	Pint 35	Vertical medial rib	Plain lip; Oval; Pontil mark	Amethyst; Black (deep amethyst); Aquamarine; Lavender (M.B.K.); Green, brilliant (S.L.)	John Robinson & Son, Pittsburgh, Pa.	V. R. No. 15 GXX; Scarce
GIX-44	Similar to No. 43	Pint 35	Vertical medial rib	Plain lip; Long oval; Pontil mark	Aquamarine; Green, light (S.L.); Green, deep (S.L.); Olive-yellow, light	Unknown. Probably Pittsburgh district	Not listed by Van Rensselaer; Very rare
GIX-45	Same as obverse	Pint 35	Vertical medial rib	Plain lip; Slim long oval; Pontil mark; Rough ring	Aquamarine; Green (D.M.); Emerald-green, light (S.L.); Yellow-green, light	Probably Pittsburgh district	V. R. No. 16 GXX; Scarce
GIX-46	Same as obverse	Quart 35	Vertical medial rib	Plain lip; Plump oval; Pontil mark	Aquamarine; Green (D.M.); Green, light (S.L.); Emerald-green, deep (M.B.K.)	Probably Pittsburgh district	V. R. No. 17 GXX; Scarce

GIX-40 GIX-41 GIX-41 GIX-42 GIX-42 GIX-43 GIX-43 GIX-44 GIX-45 GIX-46

GROUP IX—SCROLL FLASKS—"VIOLIN OR SCROLL"—*Continued*

OBVERSE	REVERSE	STAR POINT	SIZE, FORM	EDGES	NECK, BASE	COLORS	GLASSHOUSE	NOTES, RARITY
GIX–47. Ribs similar to No. 40 but proportionately enlarged. In center between inner ribs (scrolled at bottom) inscription: "R KNOWLES & CO" (following rib at left) "UNION FACTORY" (following rib at right) "SOUTH WHEELING" in circle around "VA". Large 8-pointed star in upper space.	Similar to obverse but large conventionalized fleur-de-lis between inner ribs.		Pint 36	Vertical medial rib	Plain lip Pointed oval Pontil mark	Aquamarine Green, light	R. Knowles & Co., South Wheeling, Va.	V. R. No. 18 GXX Extremely rare
GIX–48. "M'CARTY & TORREYSON" in semicircle above "MANUFACTURERS" in straight line. Below, in semicircle, "WELLSBURG, VA." Above "MANUFACTURERS", 8-pointed star containing a small 5-pointed star, and, below "MANUFACTURERS", conventional ornaments.	In circular frame, large sunburst with 24 rays from concentric rings at center.		Pint 33	Panel terminating at base	Plain lip Flat distorted octagon with diagonal mold seam Pontil mark	Green, light, bluish Aquamarine (S.L.) Emerald-green, deep	McCarty & Torreyson, Wellsburg, Va.	V. R. No. 58 GVI Scarce
GIX–49. Similar to No. 48. Same inscription but without star and conventional ornament	Similar to No. 48. Thirty-two rays in sunburst.		Quart 33	Same as above	Plain lip Like No. 48	Green, light Aquamarine (S.L.)	McCarty & Torreyson, Wellsburg, Va.	V. R. No. 58 GVI Rare
GIX–50. Similar to No. 49	Plain		Quart 33	Same as above	Plain lip Like No. 48	Green, light bluish Green, light	McCarty & Torreyson, Wellsburg, Va.	V. R. No. 59 GVI Rare

NOTE: Though these 3 flasks, GIX–48, 49, and 50 are not, strictly speaking, scroll flasks, many collectors have included them in the scroll group.

OBVERSE	REVERSE	STAR POINT	SIZE, FORM	EDGES	NECK, BASE	COLORS	GLASSHOUSE	NOTES, RARITY
GIX–51. Bisected by heavy horizontal rib. In upper part, 5 large pearls in semicircle above large 5-petaled flower. In lower part, 4 elongated ovals each side of large heart medallion.	Same as obverse		Quart 34	Vertical medial rib	Plain lip Plump oval with footlike base Pontil mark	Green, light Aquamarine (S.L.)	Midwestern	Very rare

NOTE: See also Jenny Linds. GI. Nos. 108, 109, and 110, which are included in the Scroll Group by many collectors.

OBVERSE	REVERSE	STAR POINT	SIZE, FORM	EDGES	NECK, BASE	COLORS	GLASSHOUSE	NOTES, RARITY
GIX–52. Three ribs follow pear-shaped contour of flask; inner 2 forming frame with blunt-pointed top. In lower center, large palmette flanked by scrolls that rise and unfold as acanthus leaves. Surrounding conical center of upper zone.	Same as obverse		Pint Similar to 34	Vertical medial rib	Plain lip Slim long oval Keyed like No. 10 Pontil mark	Green, light	Unknown	Extremely rare One specimen known in 1976

GROUP X—MISCELLANEOUS FLASKS

OBVERSE	REVERSE	SIZE, FORM	EDGES	NECK, BASE	COLORS	GLASSHOUSE	NOTES, RARITY
GX–1. Designs on oval panels. Stag with long antlers facing right. Beneath stag inscription "GOOD GAME" in 2 lines.	Weeping willow tree.	Pint 14	Fine vertical ribbing sloping to heavy medial rib	Plain lip Pontil mark	Aquamarine Green, light	Probably Coffin & Hay, Hammonton, N.J.	V. R. No. 110 GI Comparatively scarce
GX–2. Designs on oval panels. Stag with large antlers facing right. Beneath "GOOD" and "GAME" at right of stag.	Weeping willow tree.	Half-pint 14	Same as No. 1	Plain lip Pontil mark	Aquamarine	Same as No. 1	Not listed by Van Rensselaer in half-pint Scarce

GX-3. Designs on oval panels. Large sheaf of rye.

GX-4. Cannon mounted on 2-wheel carriage facing right; 15 cannonballs at left of wheel in foreground, rammer and swab beneath. A rammer leans against cannon in front of right wheel. There is a small building at right below cannon's muzzle. In semicircle around cannon
"GENL TAYLOR NEVER SURRENDERS".

GX-5. Similar to No. 4

GX-6. Design on oval panel. Similar to No. 4 but rammers and swab and small building missing.

GX-7. Designs on oval panels. Sloop with pennant flying sailing to left. Modeling representing water beneath boat.

Reverse design	Size	Ribbing	Lip/Pontil	Color	Attribution	Reference
Large bunch of grapes depending from stem with 3 large leaves.	Half-pint 14	Same as No. 1	Plain lip, Pontil mark, Broad sloping collar (No. 15)	Aquamarine Green, medium (C.G.) Olive-green	Same as No. 1	V. R. No. 42 GI Scarce
Vine and grapes form a semicircular frame containing inscription "A LITTLE MORE GRAPE CAPt BRAGG".	Pint 11	Vertically ribbed with heavy medial rib	Plain lip, Pontil mark [Red-amber (S.L.), Emerald-green, deep (S.L.), Yellow-green, deep (S.L.)]	Aquamarine Olive-green Deep green Deep amethyst Puce Amber, deep (R.W.) Golden amber (R.W.)	Attributed to Baltimore Glass Works	V. R. No. 7 GI Comparatively scarce
Similar to No. 4	Pint 11	Smooth, no medial rib	Plain lip, Pontil mark	Clear olive-green Green, deep (E.D.) Olive-yellow	Same as No. 4	Not listed by Van Rensselaer Comparatively scarce
Similar to No. 4 but arrangement of vine and grapes different.	Half-pint 11	Vertically ribbed with medial rib	Plain lip, Pontil mark	Yellow-green Golden amber Aquamarine Colorless (S.L.) Emerald-green, light (S.L.)	Same as No. 4	V. R. No. 8 GI Comparatively scarce
Inscription running lengthwise parallel to panel "BRIDGETOWN" on right from top to bottom. "NEW JERSEY" on left from bottom to top.	Half-pint 11	Vertically ribbed 3, with heavy medial rib	Plain lip, Pontil mark	Dark olive-amber (black) Pale aquamarine	Probably Joel Bodine & Sons, Bridgetown, N.J.	V. R. No. 103 GI Scarce

GIX-47   GIX-48   GIX-49   GIX-51   GX-1   GX-2   GX-3   GX-4   GX-6   GX-7

GROUP X—MISCELLANEOUS FLASKS—*Continued*

OBVERSE	REVERSE	SIZE, FORM	EDGES	NECK, BASE	COLORS	GLASSHOUSE	NOTES, RARITY
GX–8. Designs on oval panels. Sloop with pennant flying sailing to left. Similar to No. 7.	Large 8-pointed star with tiny 3-pointed ornament or possibly floral device between rays of star.	Half-pint 11	Same as No. 7.	Plain lip Pontil mark	Clear deep green Aquamarine Sapphire blue	Same as No. 7	V. R. No. 101 GI Comparatively scarce
GX–8a. Sailboat like GX–8 on panel like GX–9.	Large "star" like GX–8 on panel like GX–9.	Half-pint 11	Smooth	Plain lip Pontil mark	Aquamarine	Possibly Joel Bodine & Sons, Bridgetown, N.J.	Comparatively scarce
GX–9. Similar to No. 8 but with no waves showing beneath boat.	Similar 8-pointed star but without ornaments between rays.	Half-pint 11	Smooth	Plain lip Pontil mark	Clear yellow-green Clear green Aquamarine Green, light	Same as No. 7	V. R. No. 102 GI Comparatively scarce
GX–9a. Sailboat like GX–9	Large "star" like GX–8 but with "tulips" between "rays."	Half-pint 11	Smooth	Plain lip Pontil mark	Aquamarine	Same as above	Reported by Sam Laidacker Comparatively scarce
GX–10. Designs on circular panels. Large double-headed sheaf of rye tied with knob at center. "LIBERTY" above in semicircle.	Large 5-pointed star with concave circle at center containing small pearl.	Pint 20	Smooth	Plain lip Pontil mark	Aquamarine	Probably Baltimore Glass Works	V. R. No. 82 GVI, listed only in half-pint Rare
GX–11. Similar to No. 10 but slight difference in formation of sheaf.	Similar to No. 10	Half-pint 20	Smooth	Plain lip Pontil mark	Aquamarine	Probably Baltimore Glass Works	V. R. No. 82 GVI Rare
GX–12. Stout man wearing derby holding cane behind his back, bending forward and apparently engaged in argument with man also wearing derby and with long tailcoat, crouching, hands resting on upright umbrella; probably a caricature.	Grotesque head with large full face and elaborate headdress, chin resting on arm with index finger pointing down. At left of elbow 5 diagonal bars.	About half-pint Similar to 11, Ill. 133, but more slender	Smooth	Plain lip Pontil mark	Very pale green, yellowish tone Golden yellow Amber (S.L.) Black (deep olive-amber) Sapphire-blue Colorless (G.A.)	Unknown	V. R. No. 51 GVI Very rare NOTE: The specimen in golden yellow is probably unique in that it also shows design of expanded vertical ribbing, the gather having first been put into a small mold vertically ribbed and then expanded as the gather was blown into the 2-piece mold.
GX–13. Similar to No. 12. Designs on circular panels and entire flask except panels decorated by heavy swirled ribbing.	Similar to No. 12	Quarter-pint ovoid		Plain lip Pontil mark	Clear, slightly translucent	Unknown	Very rare Not listed by Van Rensselaer. NOTE: There is a possibility that Nos. 12 and 13 may be continental.

Flask	Obverse Description	Reverse Description	Size	Surface	Lip/Neck	Color	Maker	Reference / Rarity
GX-14.	Designs on oval panels. Inscription "MURDOCK & CASSEL" in 3 lines, the first curved and third straight. Beneath, rectangular band of heavy diagonal ribbing and below that a wider band of heavy vertical ribs extending to base of flask and with rounded tops.	Inscription "ZANESVILLE" in semicircle enclosing "OHIO" in straight line. Below ribbing similar to that on obverse.	Pint 11	Vertically ribbed with narrow medial rib	Plain lip / Pontil mark	Light green / Green, deep (M.B.K.)	Murdock & Cassel, Zanesville, Ohio	V. R. No. 62 GVI / Rare
GX-14a.	Like GX-14 but letters of "MURDOCK & CASSEL" larger; flask a little wider.	Like GX-14, but letters of "ZANES-VILLE OHIO" larger.	Pint 11	Vertically ribbed with narrow medial rib	Plain lip / Pontil mark	Green (light)	Murdock & Cassel, Zanesville. Ohio	Rare
GX-15.	Designs on oval panels. Large tree in foliage, bird perched on branch at right. Above panel in curved line "SUMMER".	Large bare tree, bird perched on branch at left. Above panel in curved line "WINTER".	Pint 20	Smooth	Plain lip / Double rounded collar / Pontil mark / Smooth	Dark puce (black) / Olive-yellow / Aquamarine / Yellow / Clear yellow-green / Amethyst, dense (S.L.) / Black (deep wine) (C.G.)	Unknown	V. R. No. 112 GVI / Common
GX-16.	Designs not on panels. Large tree in foliage similar to No. 15 but branches and foliage different. No bird in tree.	Bare tree, arrangement of branches different, bird perched on branch at left. No inscription	Half-pint 20	Smooth with large medial rib	Double rounded collar / Smooth	Aquamarine, both bluish and decided greenish tones / Yellow-amber (S.L.) / Olive-yellow	Unknown	V. R. No. 113 GVI / Comparatively scarce
GX-17.	Designs on oval panels. Large tree in full foliage. Bird omitted and no inscription.	Same as obverse	Pint 20	Smooth	Plain lip / Pontil mark	Sapphire-blue / Olive-yellow / Aquamarine / Clear deep amber / Yellow-amber (S.L.) / Blue, deep (S.L.)	Unknown	V. R. No. 114 GVI / Comparatively scarce

GX-8 GX-9 GX-10 GX-11 GX-12 GX-13 GX-14 GX-15 GX-16 GX-17

OBVERSE	REVERSE	SIZE, FORM	EDGES	NECK, BASE	COLORS	GLASSHOUSE	NOTES, RARITY
GX–18. Designs not on panels. Tree in full foliage with 15 large "buds" with indented edges.	Tree in full foliage but without buds; bird perched on branch at left.	Quart Similar to 20. Ill. 133. but edges more sloping	Smooth. no medial rib	Plain lip Double rounded collar Broad sloping collar Pontil mark Blue. pale (S.L.) Blue-green (S.L.) Wine. shaded	Amethyst Sapphire-blue Aquamarine Pale yellow-green Emerald-green Deep green Light green Golden amber (S.L.) Red-amethyst (S.L.)	Unknown	V. R. No. 111 GVI Common
GX–19. Designs not on panels. Tree in full foliage without buds.	Bare tree, bird perched on branch at left.	Quart Similar to 20. Ill. 133. but edges more sloping	Smooth with heavy medial rib	Plain lip Double rounded collar Pontil mark Emerald-green (S.L.) Yellow-green Lemon-yellow. pale (DeVere Card)	Dark amber (black) Aquamarine Canary Golden amber (S.L.) Amber. medium Black (deep amethyst) (G.A.) Blue. pale Citron (R. W.)	Unknown	Probably V. R. No. 115 GVI Common
GX–20. Early steamboat with paddle wheel. steaming to right. Long narrow flag streaming to left from bow and large American flag. stars and stripes flying from mast back of smokestack. Above boat in curving line "THE AMERICAN" and beneath the water through which the boat is steaming. the word "SYSTEM."	Large upright Sheaf of Rye encircled by inscription "USE ME BUT DO NOT ABUSE ME". Also encircling the sheaf and between it and the inscription 27 small dots or pearls. possibly intended to represent stars. Beneath sheaf narrow rectangular frame with curved ends and containing inscription "B. P & B".	Pint 15	Herringbone ribbing. no medial rib	Plain lip Pontil mark	Clear shading to pale violet	Bakewell. Page & Bakewell. Pittsburgh	Not listed by Van Rensselaer Extremely rare
GX–20a. American System similar to GX–20	Similar to GX–20 but initials "B & M" in frame.	Pint 15	Herringbone ribbing. no medial vertical rib	Plain lip Pontil mark	Green-aquamarine	Possibly Baker & Martin. Perryopolis. Pa.	Extremely rare (One specimen recorded, 1965)
GX–21. Similar in general appearance to No. 20 except that bow of boat is different. also wave motion different and the waves extend to the base of flask.	Similar to No. 20 except frame beneath the sheaf of rye does not contain letters B. P & B. and does not touch bottom of sheaf.	Pint 15	Same as No. 20	Plain lip Pontil mark	Brilliant olive-yellow Deep olive-green (black) Clear green Green-aquamarine (C.G.) Blue. greenish	Probably same as No. 20	V. R. No. 114 GI Rare

Pint 12	Horizontally beaded with vertical medial rib	Plain lip Pontil mark	Pale greenish blue, of peacock tone. Aquamarine Blue-aquamarine, strong (C.G.) Blue, light (S.L.)	Unknown Monongahela and Early Pittsburgh district	V. R. No. 30 GI Extremely rare
Pint Flattened oval shape tapering to small oval base	Smooth	Double rounded collar Pontil mark	Pale bluish green	Unknown	V. R. No. 70 GI Extremely rare
Pint 1	Corrugated horizontally, corrugations extend around flask at base and juncture of neck and body	Plain lip Pontil mark	Clear amber Golden amber, deep (S.L.) Olive-amber	Probably Pitkin Glassworks or John Mather's, East Hartford, which became Manchester in 1823, Conn.	V. R. No. 96 GVI Extremely rare

GX–22. Designs on large oval panels. Log Cabin with door at right and single window with 4 panes adjoining door at left. Chimney on left end of gable roof. Above cabin in partial semicircle 9 small 5-pointed stars. Beneath cabin in semicircle rail fence with gate at center.

American Flag at left on tall standard blowing in breeze to right. In the flag bars show plainly and there are tiny dots representing stars. Surmounting flag in partial semicircle 9 small 5-pointed stars and a similar tenth star fall in the field of the flag. Beneath flag in semicircle "HARD CIDER" and large cider barrel beneath. Below barrel at left a large plow. Stalks of grain rise from base of flask at right to a point level with center of barrel; at left there are 2 stalks of grain beneath the handles of the plow.

GX–23. Standing female figure representing Liberty supporting shield in her right hand holding a staff topped by Liberty Cap. At her left a form suggestive of an urn or pitcher. The figure wears a blouse with puffed sleeves and the United States flag is superimposed on the skirt. She wears a shepherdess-type hat and sunrays proceed from the head interrupted by a semicircular ribbon containing the word "LIBERTY". At her right is the letter "U" and below an 8-pointed star; and at her left the letter "S" and below similar 8-pointed star. The shield is decorated with 6 alternating and depressed vertical bars; the top band of shield bears the word "LIBERTY". The figure in pose and the position of staff is reminiscent of the classic conception of the shepherdess. (Courtesy Toledo Museum of Art)

At lower left part of flask Log Cabin with smoke issuing from the chimney and a small cone-shaped tree at extreme left. At the right is a pump facing a tall bare tree with a segment of rail fence extending from tree at extreme right. At base of tree is what appears to be a dipper. Beneath and connecting with this design is a rectangular frame containing the word "LIBERTY!" Upper part of reverse plain.

GX–24. Large medallion with inscription "JARED SPENCER." Enclosing 2 convex rings with concave center. Below a shield-shaped area containing pendant sunburst with concave center and loop at either side above. Flanking shield are converging ribs with sunken diamonds (3) between. Heavy diamond diapering covers lower part of flask.

Same as obverse except inscription "MANCHESTER. CON."

GX-18 GX-19 GX-20 GX-21 GX-22 GX-23 GX-24

GROUP X—MISCELLANEOUS FLASKS—*Continued*

OBVERSE	REVERSE	SIZE, FORM	EDGES	NECK, BASE	COLORS	GLASSHOUSE	NOTES, RARITY
GX–25. Similar to No. 24 but no inscription in medallion, which carries a heavy ring between 2 narrow rings, the inner depressed, and heavy ring at center with 4 petal depressions. The shield-shaped area beneath medallion carries a simpler pendant with narrow 3-pointed ornament above at either side. Converging ribs at sides of shield without the indented diamonds. Similar heavy diamond diapering on lower part of flask.	Same as obverse	Pint 1	Same as No. 24	Plain lip Pontil mark	Deep olive-green	Same as above	V. R. No. 97 GVI Extremely rare
GX–26. Similar to Nos. 24 and 25. Medallion ornament in relief by a circle of 8 large pearls enclosing convex disk. Outer zone of medallion contains 8 pointed petals alternating with pearls. Beneath medallion, the similar shield-shaped area contains a convex circular pendant with loop ornament above at either side. Converging ribs on either side of shield and diamond diapering below.	Same as obverse	Pint 1	Same as Nos. 24 and 25	Plain lip Pontil mark	Light amber Olive-amber, light (S.L.) Olive-amber, medium (S.L.)	Same as above	V. R. No. 98 GVI Extremely rare
GX–27. Large American Flag to right. 9 stripes and 13 stars.	Inscription in semicircle "NEW GRANITE GLASS WORKS" and enclosing "STODDARD" in an arc and beaneath "N. H."	Pint Similar to 8, Ill. 133	Smooth, with heavy vertical medial rib	Plain lip Pontil mark	Amber Olive-amber Olive-green (S.L.)	New Granite Glass Works, Mill Village, Stoddard, N.H.	V. R. No. 31 GI Rare
GX–28. Similar to No. 27	Similar to No. 27	Half-pint Similar to 8, Ill. 133	Smooth with narrow vertical medial rib	Plain lip Pontil mark	Amber Olive-amber Olive-green, deep	Same as No. 27	V. R. No. 31 GI Rare
GX–29. United States Flag with 16 stars and 13 bars on pole to left.	Inscription "NEW GRANITE GLASS WORKS" in three-quarter circle and enclosing "STODDARD" in an arc with "N. H." beneath.	Half-pint Similar to 8, Ill. 133	Smooth with narrow vertical medial rib	Plain lip Pontil mark	Clear amber Deep olive-green	New Granite Glass Works, Mill Village, Stoddard, N.H.	V. R. No. 32 GI Extremely rare
GX–30. Full-faced figure of trapper with beard dressed in buckskin suit and wearing broad-rimmed hat; knife in belt at waist and rifle, with butt resting on ground, held in left hand. Above inscription "THE GREAT WESTERN".	Buck with large antlers, body to left, head turned sharply back and giving effect of facing front.	Pint 32	Broad and flat	Plain lip with laid on ring below Smooth with circular depression and letter "C" at center	Aquamarine	Probably mid-western	V. R. No. 30 GVI Rare
GX–31. Upright sheaf of rye against 2 similar crossed sheaves with crossed rake and scythe. (Courtesy of Dr. Charles Osgood.)	Heavy horizontal bar supporting figure of standing horse.	Slightly less than pint Flattened circular shape	Vertically ribbed, 5	Plain lip Pontil mark	Dark brownish amber	Unknown	Not listed by Van Rensselaer Extremely rare

OBVERSE	REVERSE	SIZE, FORM	NECK, BASE	COLORS	GLASSHOUSE	NOTES, RARITY
GX-32. Linear rendering of ship with full sails; presumably representing Columbus's *Santa Maria*. Below waves, dates "1492-1892".	Inscription: "*Columbian Jubilee*" in script in diagonal line.	Pint Shoo fly (see drawing of GXIII-75)	Deep straight collar, lower bevel Smooth, with letter "D" at center	Colorless	Unknown	Comparatively scarce
GX-33. Circular depression below neck and above waffled body with cow at center.	Large sheaf of grain	¼ pint Ovoid, tapering at top into neck	Plain lip Pontil mark	Aquamarine Olive-green Yellow-green	Unknown	Reported by George Austin Listed by Van Rensselaer as GVI-22. ½ pt. However. 3 collectors report having seen only the ¼ pt. size.

GROUP XI—PIKE'S PEAK FLASKS—1859–1870s

Attributed to midwestern glasshouses. Smooth edges; medial fine mold seam on ends.
See also GII-21

OBVERSE	REVERSE	SIZE, FORM	NECK, BASE	COLORS	GLASSHOUSE	NOTES, RARITY
GXI-1. Prospector: large long head, long hair; wearing derby, wrinkled short-tailed coat and trousers; staff with pack (2 tools showing) at end, held by left hand and resting on left shoulder; cane in right hand; walking left on long round-ended oblong frame (narrow molding) about 1" x 3". Above prospector: in arc and medium-size letters, "FOR PIKE'S PEAK".	Plain	Quart 29	No. 12 Type 1 but center slightly oval	Aquamarines	Unknown	Scarce
GXI-2. Prospector: long head and hair; wearing hat with high narrow-domed crown; short-tailed coat and slightly wrinkled tight trousers; staff with pack (2 tools showing at end, held by left hand and resting on left shoulder; *no right arm*; walking left, feet not quite touching top of long round-ended frame (medium molding) about $1^{11}/_{16}$" x $2^{11}/_{16}$". Above prospector: in arc, "FOR PIKE'S PEAK".	Plain	Pint 29	No. 11 Type 6	Aquamarine Green (light)	Unknown	Similar to White A19V2 (White numbers, *Antiques*, Aug. & Oct. 1932). H. H. White apparently used the term "plain base," as do many, to mean "no pontil mark," and did not differentiate be- tween the various types of mold seams and centers on the bases. One of 6 on which the prospector has no right arm. Scarce
GXI-3. Like GXI-2 but 3 tools extending from pack; frame about 1⅛" x 2¾".	Plain	Pint 29	No. 11 Type 6	Aquamarine	Unknown	White A19V2 Scarce

GX-25 GX-26 GX-27 GX-28 GX-30 GX-31 GX-32 GXI-1 GXI-2

GROUP XI—PIKE'S PEAK FLASKS—*Continued*

OBVERSE	REVERSE	SIZE, FORM	NECK, BASE	COLORS	GLASSHOUSE	NOTES, RARITY
GXI–4. Prospector: slender; long head and long hair; wearing high-crowned hat, tailless coat with 2 pockets, tight trousers; staff with pack (2 tools showing) at end, held by left hand and resting on left shoulder; crooked cane in right hand; walking left on round-ended oblong frame (medium molding) about $^{13}/_{16}$″ x 2½″. Above prospector: in deep arc and medium-sized letters, "FOR PIKE'S PEAK," wide space between "R" and "P"; narrow between "S" and "P"; more space between "A" and "K" than between other letters in the words.	Plain	Pint 29	No. 6 Type 8	Aquamarine, greenish	Unknown	White A19V31 Reported in quart size also
GXI–5. Prospector: stocky; long head and hair; wearing small high-crowned derby, very short-tailed coat and tight trousers; staff with pack (2 tools showing) at end, held by left hand and resting on left shoulder; cane in right hand; facing left, standing on round-ended oblong frame (median molding) about 7/8″ x 2″. Above prospector: in arc and medium letters, "FOR PIKES PEAK".	Plain	Half-pint 29	No. 11 Type 5 mold seam, one end of curve just inside shallow disk	Aquamarines	Unknown	White A19V1 (GXI–5 or 6 or both), frequently found in Ohio V. R. GVII–12 Scarce
GXI–6. Like GXI–5 but frame about 7/8″ x 2$^{15}/_{16}$″, with one end rounded and other rounded at corners.	Plain	Half-pint 29	No. 11 Type 3	Aquamarines	Unknown	See above Common
GXI–7. Prospector: large long head, large eye, small ear; wearing high-crowned derby, swallow-tail coat, tight trousers; thin legs bent at knees; pickaxe with pack (2 other tools showing) in front of axhead; held by left hand and resting on left shoulder; long cane in right hand; walking left on left end of oblong frame (wide molding) about 1¼″ x 2½″. Above prospector: in arc, "PIKES PEAK".	Eagle: small head to left; long neck; wings with 10 ribs in right and 9 in left, partly raised, spread downward and outward; on breast, sunken shield with 6 vertical bars, no bottom line; thunderbolt (3 arrows) in each talon.* From beak, narrow pennant with point at end, to right above eagle. Below eagle: large oval frame (wide molding) about 2⅛″ x 3″. Eagle similar to Louisville, Ky., eagle GII–11.	Quart 30	No. 10 Type 7	Aquamarine	Unknown; attributed to Pittsburgh	White A19V17 V. R. GVII–17 (?) Common
GXI–8. Prospector similar to GXI–7, very slightly larger figure, longer head and bigger hat, feet blending into molding of frame. In frame "OLD RYE". Above prospector: in semicircle, "FOR PIKE'S PEAK".	Eagle: head to left; long neck; wings with 10 wide-spaced ribs in left and 14 fine in right, partly raised, spread downward and outward; on breast, sunken shield with 5 vertical bars, no bottom line; thunderbolt (3 arrows) in each talon. From beak, narrow pennant with point at end, to right above eagle. Below eagle: large oval frame (wide molding) about 2$^{3}/_{16}$″ x 3$^{3}/_{16}$″; inscription: "PITTSBURGH PA" starting at lower left end, following upper line of frame to center right end.	Quart 30	No. 11 Type 10	Aquamarine Blue (deep)	Unknown, Pittsburgh, Pa.	White A19V7 Common
GXI–9. Similar to GXI–8; Prospector without eye or ear, placed a little nearer left end of frame. Frame about 7/8″ x 2⅛″; inscriptions like GXI–8.	Eagle similar to GXI–8 but with heavy beak, short straight neck; 7 bars on shield; straight legs; thunderbolt (2 arrows) in left talon and crude olive branch in right. Frame about 1⅝″ x 2$^{9}/_{16}$″; "PITTSBURGH PA" starting at center left end, following upper line of frame around right end.	Pint 30	Nos. 10 & 11 Type 11	Aquamarine Yellow-green	Unknown, Pittsburgh, Pa.	White A19V7 Common

*NOTE: In all instances in which "thunderbolt (3 arrows) in each talon" occurs, only heads of arrows and part of shafts appear; sometimes described as "arrows with heads at each end."

636

GXI–10. Similar to GXI–8. Prospector with large broad head, no neck; left foot about center of frame and cane near end; coattail not forked; 1 tool in pack. Frame, oblong, rounded corners, about $^{11}/_{16}$″ x 1$^{11}/_{16}$″. Above prospector: in deep arc, "FOR PIKE'S PEAK".

GXI–11. Prospector similar to GXI–7, crown of hat rounder; pickaxe with pack (1 other tool showing), held in right hand and resting on left shoulder; long cane in left hand; walking left on round-ended oblong frame (wide molding) about $^{15}/_{16}$″ x 2″. No inscription

GXI–12. Prospector: large head and eye, no ear; stocky body with left upper arm missing; wearing low-crowned derby, swallow-tailed coat and tight trousers (no line of demarcation between coat and trousers); pickaxe with pack (1 other tool showing) held in left hand, resting on left shoulder; walking left on small round-ended oblong frame (wide molding) about $^{7}/_{8}$″ x 2$^{1}/_{8}$″. No inscription

GXI–10. Similar to GXI–8. Eagle with small head, thick neck, to right; 5 ribs in right wing and 4 in left; 5 bars on small shield; thunderbolt very crudely drawn. Frame, with molding wider at top than bottom, about 1$^{3}/_{8}$″ x 1¾″; "PITTSBURGH" starting lower left end, following line of frame to about center right end, "PA" at center bottom.

GXI–11. Eagle similar to GXI–9, large eye; 12 ribs in right wing, 10 in left; 6 bars on broad shield; crude thunderbolt or olive branch. Large oval frame (wide molding) about 1$^{9}/_{16}$″ x 2½″. At right of left wing, irregular short bar about in line with space between top second and third ribs of wing.

GXI–12. Eagle similar to GII–113; large head, with eye, to left; wings with 7 wide-spaced ribs in right and 6 in left, partly raised, spread downward and outward; on breast, small shield with 5 vertical bars; thunderbolt (3 feathered arrows) in ball-like talons, small dot between arrowheads. From beak, wide pennant with hook end, to right in arc above eagle. Below eagle: large oval frame (wide molding) about 1⅞″ x 2$^{9}/_{16}$″; inscription: "W. McC & CO (following top line of frame) GLASS WORKS (across center) PITTS. PA." (following bottom line).

Half-pint 30	Nos. 10 & 11 Type 5	Aquamarines Yellow-green (pale)	Unknown, Pittsburgh, Pa.	White A19V28 V. R. GVII–20 Common
Pint 30	Nos. 10 & 11 Type 8, concave dot at center	Aquamarines Emerald-green (dark)	Unknown	White A19V20 V. R. GVII–21 Common
Pint 30	No. 10 Type 7, but dot (?) at center of shallow depression	Aquamarine	Wm. McCully & Co., Pittsburgh, Pa.	Rare

GXI–7 GXI–8 GXI–9 GXI–10 GXI–11 GXI–12

GROUP XI—PIKE'S PEAK FLASKS—*Continued*

OBVERSE	REVERSE	SIZE, FORM	NECK, BASE	COLORS	GLASSHOUSE	NOTES, RARITY
GXI-13. Prospector: large long head, large eye; barrel-chested, legs bent at knees; wearing derby hat with brim curved on sides, swallow-tailed coat, tight trousers; short staff with large pack (3 tools showing) at end, held in left hand and resting on left shoulder; cane in right hand; walking left on, and cane near, end of oblong frame (medium molding) about 1¼″ x 2½″. No left upper arm. No inscription	Eagle similar to GXI–11, slightly larger; 10 ribs in right wing, 8 in left; 5 bars on shield; 3 arrows of thunderbolt feathered, feathered ends in left talon; pennant a little wider and with longer end. Frame about 2¹/₁₆″ x 3¹/₁₆″; inscription: "ARSENAL" (following top line of frame) "GLASS WORKS" (across center) "PITTS. PA." (following bottom line)	Quart 30	No. 11 Type 9	Amber Aquamarine Olive-yellow	Arsenal Glass Works, Pittsburgh, Pa.	White A19V19 Scarce
GXI-14. Prospector like GXI–12. Frame about ⅞″ x 2¹/₁₆″. No inscription	Like GXI–12, but 7 ribs in right wing and 6 in left; frame about 1⁹/₁₆″ x 2⁹/₁₆″ with inscription "ARSENAL GLASS WORKS PITTS. PA." placed as on GXI–13.	Pint 30	Nos. 10 & 11 Type 7, but concave dot at center of shallow depression	Amber Olive-green, yellowish	Same as above	Scarce
GXI-15. Prospector: large broad head, large eye, stocky body, knees bent; wearing flat-crowned and narrow-brimmed hat, short coat with long tail, tight trousers; short pickaxe with pack and 2 other tools, held by left hand and resting on left shoulder; long cane in right hand; striding left on long narrow round-ended oblong frame (very narrow molding) about ¾″ x 2⁵/₁₆″. No inscription. Tiny bead in mold seam about 3″ from base, at rear of prospector.	Eagle: small head with large beak and round eye, to left; wings with 10 ribs in right and 11 in left, partly raised, spread downward and outward; on breast, small shield with 5 vertical bars; small thunderbolt (3 feathered arrows) in talons, feathered ends at right. Below eagle: large oval frame (wide molding) about 1⁹/₁₆″ x 2¼″; inscription "ARSENAL (close to top of frame) GLASS WORKS (a bit below center) PITTS. PA" (close to bottom).	Pint 30	No. 11 Type 6, with small off-center circular depression	Aquamarine Emerald-green Olive-green Yellow-green	Same as above	V. R. GVII–23 (?) Scarce
GXI-16. Like GXI–15	Like GXI–15 but inscription: "WMcC & Co" (at top) "." (large period) above space between "GLASS" and "WORKS" (across center), "PITTS.PA" (at bottom).	Pint 30	No. 11 Type 6, with small off-center depression	Aquamarine	Wm. McCully & Co., Pittsburgh, Pa.	White A19V32 Rare
GXI-17. Prospector: slender; small head, large eye and ear; wearing flat-crowned derby, tight coat with long tail, and buttons down front; skin-tight trousers; long staff with pack and 3 tools at end, held in right hand and resting on right shoulder; long cane in left hand; walking left on long narrow round-ended oblong frame, about ⅝″ x 2¼″. Small nodule at left between edge and upper end of frame. No inscription	Eagle similar to GXI–11, 12 ribs in each wing; pennant wider and more curved at end; frame about 1⅝″ x 2½″.	Pint 30	No. 10 Type 5	Aquamarine Blue (light) Green (light)	Unknown	White A19V21 Scarce
GXI-18. Prospector similar to GXI–17 but with large head, stocky body; small hat with brim curved up on sides. Frame about ⁹/₁₆″ x 2⅞″. At left of frame, 2 large nodules, 1 opposite end and 1 slightly above. No inscription	Eagle similar to GXI–10; 7 ribs in right wing and 5 in left; long tapering legs; thunderbolt, 3 crude arrows; frame about 1⁵/₁₆″ x 1³/₁₆″.	Half-pint 30	No. 12 Type 5; with tiny nipple at center	Aquamarine	Unknown	White A19V22 V. R. GVII–5 (?) Scarce
GXI-19. Prospector: short, very large head with prominent eye and ear, short thick neck, barrel-chested and pot-bellied, stocky legs; wearing hat with curved crown and wide brim, no line to show end of coat, long coattail starting at upper arm; staff with pack (3 tools showing, held in right hand and resting on right shoulder; long cane in left hand; trudging left on long narrow round-ended oblong frame (very narrow molding) about ⁹/₁₆″ x 1¹⁵/₁₆″. No inscription	Eagle: head with small eye and beak, to right; wings with 7 ribs in right and 8 in left, partly raised, spread downward and outward; on breast, small heart-shaped shield with 5 vertical bars; thunderbolt (3 crude arrows) in talons; thick tapered legs; From beak, long blunt-ended pennant, to left in semicircle above eagle. Below eagle: large oval frame (wide molding) about 1⁵/₁₆″ x 1¹⁵/₁₆″.	Half-pint 30	No. 18 Type 13	Green (light)	Unknown	V. R. GVII–2 Comparatively scarce

GXI-20. Prospector: stocky; large head with prominent features; wearing small visored cap, short coat with short tail; staff with pack and 2 tools at end, held in left hand and resting on left shoulder; cane in right hand; walking left on long narrow rounded-ended oblong frame (narrow molding) about ⁹/₁₆″ x 1¾″. Above prospector: in slight arc, "PIKE'S PEAK".

Eagle, pose like GXI-19: small beak; 4 ribs in right wing and 5 in left; 5 bars on broad breast; thick tapered legs; thunderbolt (3 feathered arrows; heads to right) in talons. Below eagle; nearly circular frame (wide molding) about 1⅜″ x 1¹¹/₁₆″.

| | Half-pint 30 | No. 11 Type 1 | Aquamarine | Unknown | White A19V18 Scarce |

GXI-21. Prospector: long head, hair by dots, long neck, stocky body, thin legs; wearing cap with very short visor, long-tailed coat and tight trousers (no line between coat and trousers); pickaxe with pack (1 tool showing) at end, held in left hand and apparently resting on undrawn right shoulder; staff in right hand; walking left on round-ended oblong frame (wide molding) about 1″ x 2⅜″. Above prospector: in wide arc and large letters, "FOR PIKE'S PEAK", apostrophe reversed.

Eagle: small head with large thick beak, to left; narrow wings with 14 ribs in right and 12 in left, partly raised, spread downward nearly parallel to body; on breast, shield with 5 bars, no bottom line; slender legs; thunderbolt (3 arrows) in talons. From beak, long narrow pennant with forked end, to right in shallow S-curve above eagle. Below eagle: round-ended oblong frame (wide molding), slightly narrower at right end, about 1⅜″ x 2¾″.

| | Pint 30 | Nos. 10 & 11 Types 1, 3, & 5 | Aquamarine | Unknown | White A19V25; base type not given; plentiful in Ohio Common |

GXI-22. Prospector: short and stocky; large long head with long hair; wearing a small derby, short coat with short tail, tight trousers; short staff with pack (3 tools showing) held by left hand and resting on left shoulder; no right arm; standing on center of long round-ended oblong frame (narrow molding) about 1¹/₁₆″ x 2¹¹/₁₆″. Above prospector: in shallow arc "FOR PIKE'S PEAK", apostrophe reversed.

Eagle (similar to GII-131): feathered by short ribs; head with round eye and hooked beak, to right; wings raised and spread downward parallel to body; on lower breast, shield with 4 wide-spaced vertical bars; short legs; thunderbolt (3 arrows) in each large talon. From beak, wide rippled pennant with deeply forked end, in very shallow S-curve to right above eagle. Below eagle: long round-ended oblong frame (narrow molding) about ⅞″ x 3⁷/₁₆″.

| | Pint Similar to 31 | Nos. 10 & 11 Types 2 & 8 | Amber Aquamarine | Unknown | White A19V10 Comparatively scarce |

GXI-23. Prospector; similar to GXI-22; neck wider; lower and more curved crown on derby, coat with broad swallow-tail; walking left on smaller frame, about ¹¹/₁₆″ x 1¹/₁₆″. Above prospector: in arc and large letters, "FOR PIKE'S PEAK" with "E, A and K" run together at bottom. apostrophe reversed.

Eagle similar to GXI-22, 5 fine wide-spaced bars on shield. Below eagle: large round-ended oblong frame (wide molding) about ¾″ x 1¹¹/₁₆″.

| | Half-pint 30 | No. 11 Type 8, but center depression oval | Aquamarine Yellow-green (light) | Unknown | Scarce |

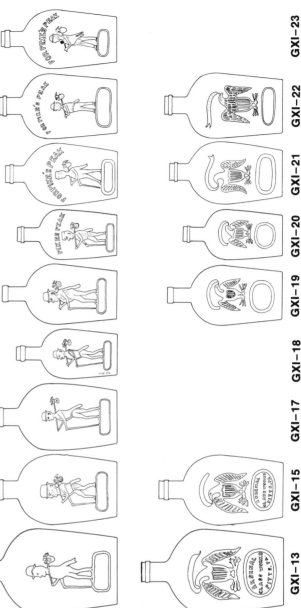

GXI-13 GXI-15 GXI-17 GXI-18 GXI-19 GXI-20 GXI-21 GXI-22 GXI-23

GROUP XI—PIKE'S PEAK FLASKS—*Continued*

OBVERSE	REVERSE	SIZE, FORM	NECK, BASE	COLORS	GLASSHOUSE	NOTES, RARITY
GXI–24. Prospector: short, stocky; large head with long pointed chin; wearing low large-crowned derby, short coat with broad short tail, tight trousers; staff with pack (2 tools showing) at end, held in left hand and resting on left shoulder; no right arm; standing on long narrow irregular frame (wide molding) about 1 1/16" to 1 3/16" x 3". Above prospector: in long shallow arc and small letters, "FOR PIKE'S PEAK", apostrophe reversed.	Eagle similar to GXI–22, but pennant narrower. Frame 1⅛" x 3⅛".	Quart 30	Nos. 11 & 12 Type 1	Amber (deep) Blue (light grayish) Green (yellowish)	Unknown	White A19V9 Comparatively scarce
GXI–25. Prospector: small; small head with large eye, short body, long legs; wearing visored cap, long tailed coat, tight trousers; staff with pack (3 tools showing) at end, held in left hand and resting on right shoulder; cane in right hand; walking left. Slightly below prospector: round-ended oblong frame (narrow molding) about 1" x 2⅜". Above prospector: in arc, close to head, and in very large letters, "FOR PIKE'S PEAK".	Eagle; feathered by oval dots; head with large oval eye and hook beak, to left, chunky neck; large wings partly raised and spread downward parallel to body; on lower breast, long slender shield with 4 vertical bars, no bottom line; slender tapering legs; slender thunderbolt (3 arrows) in each talon. From beak, long slender pennant with forked end, to right in long question-mark curve above eagle. Below eagle: round-ended oblong frame (narrow molding) about 1" x 2 5/16".	Pint 30	No. 11 Type 8, concave dot at center	Aquamarine	Unknown, probably Pittsburgh, Pa.	White A19V30 Comparatively scarce
GXI–26. Like GXI–25. Frame ¾" x 1⅞".	Like GXI–25	Half-pint 30	No. 11 Type 2	Aquamarine	Unknown, probably Pittsburgh, Pa.	Rare
GXI–27. Prospector: small, slender; small head, short body, long legs; wearing small visored cap; short coat with short tail, tight trousers; staff with pack (3 tools showing) at end, held in left hand resting on left shoulder; cane in right hand; walking left on large round-ended oblong frame (wide molding) about 1 1/16" x 2 9/16". Above prospector: in semicircle "FOR PIKE'S PEAK", very large letters, apostrophe reversed. (See Form Groups No. 30.)	Eagle: small; feathering irregular; small head with large beak, to left; chunky neck; narrow wings, partly raised, spread downward parallel to body; on breast, long narrow shield with 3½ vertical bars, no bottom line; long thin legs; thunderbolt (3 arrows) in each large talon with claws defined. Very long narrow pennant with forked end, from beak to right in shallow S-curve above eagle. Below eagle: large round-ended oblong frame (wide molding) about 1¼" x 2¼", deeper curve on left than right end.	Pint 30	No. 11 Short straight mold seam to large oval disk	Aquamarine	Same as above	White's A19V4 is either GXI–27 or 28 Common
GXI–28. Similar to GXI–27. Frame, 1⅛" x 2½".	Similar to GXI–27. Frame, 1¼" x 2 5/16".	Pint 30	No. 11 Short straight mold seams to round-ended oblong dished center about 2⅜" long	Amber Aquamarine	Same as above	See note above Common
GXI–29. Similar to GXI–27. Frame about 1⅛" x 2½".	Similar to GXI–27. Frame with inscription; "C. IHMSEN & CO (following top line of frame) PITTSBURGH PA" (following bottom line of frame).	Pint 30	No. 11 Type 2 but with small nipple at center	Aquamarine (pale)	C. Ihmsen & Co., Pittsburgh, Pa.	Common
GXI–30. Prospector: tall; long narrow head, thin neck, thick body and legs; wearing small peaked cap with visor, short-tailed coat and tight trousers; right leg incurved at knee, left straight; staff with pack (3 tools showing) at end, held by left hand and resting on left shoulder; long cane in right hand; walking jauntily left on long round-ended oblong frame (wide molding) about 1⅛" x 3 1/16". Above prospector: in deep arc and large letters, "FOR PIKE'S PEAK", apostrophe reversed.	Eagle: feathering by oval dots; small head with large beak, to left; wings partly raised, spread downward parallel to body; on breast, long wide shield with 5 vertical bars, no bottom line; short wide-spread legs; thunderbolt (3 arrows) in each talon. From beak, long pennant with wide forked end, to right in S-curve above eagle. Below eagle: large oblong frame (wide molding) with curved ends, about 1 7/16" x 3 3/16".	Quart 30	No. 11 Type 7	Aquamarines	Unknown	White A19V29 V. R. VII–1 Common

GXI–31. Similar to GXI–30 but pickaxe instead of staff over shoulder, 1 tool in pack. Frame 1⁵/₁₆″ x 1⁷/₁₆″.

	Capacity & Mold	Color	Rarity	
	Pint 30 · No. 11 Type 2	Aquamarine	Common	Unknown

GXI–32. Similar to GXI–30. Frame about ¾″ x 1⁹/₁₆″.

	Capacity & Mold	Color	Rarity	
	Half-pint 30 · Plain lip & No. 10 Type 5 mold seam, curve falling within circular depression	Aquamarine; Emerald-green (light)	Common	Unknown

GXI–33. Similar to GXI–30, bottom line of pack in line with "K" of "PEAK." Frame about ⅞″ x 1⅝″.

	Capacity & Mold	Color	Rarity	
	Half-pint 30 · No. 11 Type 5	Aquamarine	Common	Unknown

GXI–34. Similar to GXI–30. Prospector shorter, small head with small eye, thicker body, right leg incurved above knee. Frame, long oval, about 1⁵/₁₆″ x 2¹⁵/₁₆″, placed nearly at base of flask.

Eagle: feathering by sunken dots; head with large eye, hooked beak, held high, to left; wings partly raised and spread downward parallel to body; on breast, long narrow shield with 5½ vertical bars; heavy thunderbolt (3 arrows) in each large talon. From beak, long narrow pennant with forked end, to right in reverse S-curve high above eagle. Below eagle: large round-ended frame, narrower at left end than right, about 1⅜″ x 2⅞″; inscribed "CEREDO", near top line of frame. Frame centered on side of flask; eagle, off-center to left.

	Capacity & Mold	Color	Rarity	
	Quart 30 · Nos. 10 & 11 Type 11	Amber; Aquamarine; Bluish green (light); Emerald-green; Olive-green (light); Yellowish green	White A19V6 V. R. GVII–25; description states "also pint and half pint" Comparatively scarce	Unknown

GXI–35. Similar to GXI–34. Smaller scale. Molding of frame much narrower, ends less rounded and "CEREDO" nearer top.

GXI–35. Similar to GXI–34. Smaller scale. Frame about 1⅜″ x 2⁹/₁₆″.

	Capacity & Mold	Color	Rarity	
	Pint 30 · Nos. 10 & 11 Type 2	Ambers; Aquamarines; Green (light); Yellowish green	Comparatively scarce	Unknown, presumably same as GXI–34

GXI–24 GXI–25 GXI–27 GXI–30 GXI–34

GROUP XI—PIKE'S PEAK FLASKS—*Continued*

OBVERSE	REVERSE	SIZE, FORM	NECK, BASE	COLORS	GLASSHOUSE	NOTES, RARITY
GXI–36. Similar to GXI–34, smaller scale. Frame, about 3/4" x 1 9/16".	Similar to GXI–34. Smaller scale. Frame, 3/4" x 1 3/4".	Half-pint 30	No. 11 & narrow round, lower bevel (20A) Type 10, but center oval	Aquamarine	Unknown, presumably same as GXI–34	V. R. GVII–26 Comparatively scarce
GXI–37. Prospector: short, stocky; long head with small eye and long hair; wearing hat with small sugar-loaf crown, short coat with long tail, trousers; staff with pack (3 tools showing) at end, held in left hand at greater angle than usual to body, and resting on left shoulder; no right arm; walking left on long round-ended oblong frame (medium molding), narrower at left than at right end, about 1" x 2 7/16". High above prospector: in deep arc, "FOR PIKE'S PEAK".	Eagle: feathered by short ribs; small head with large hooked beak, to left; chunky neck; wings partly raised, spread downward parallel to body; on lower breast, shield with wide band of "star" (stippling) above 5 vertical bars (1 at each side, 3 in center); small thunderbolt (3 arrows) in each talon. From beak, long wide pennant with forked end, to right in reverse S-curve above eagle. Below eagle: long narrow round-ended oblong frame (medium molding) about 7/8" x 2 7/16".	Pint 30	No. 11 Type 1	Aquamarines	Unknown	Variant of V. R. GVIII–8 (?) Comparatively scarce
GXI–38. Prospector similar to GXI–34; smaller, slightly pot-bellied, stocky legs. Frame (medium molding) about 15/16" x 1 13/16". Above prospector: in arc, "FOR PIKE'S PEAK", apostrophe reversed.	Eagle: flying to right; right wing and body feathered by short ribs, left wing by long ribs, tail by downcurved ribs; head with prominent eye and long hooked beak; right wing spread above body to left, left wing above and beyond head to right; talons (not shown) presumably holding large shield, tilted to left, plain field at top, 5 graduated vertical bars below pennant crossing shield; long olive branch from lower left of shield to left behind and beyond end of pennant, thunderbolt (5 small arrows) to right. From beak, 2 long rippled pennants with wide deeply forked ends, upper across and along part of left wing to left in shallow double-S curve, lower across shield and olive branch to left in double reverse-S curve. Below eagle: oblong frame with incurved ends and shallow ogival top and bottom, about 1 1/16" (at center points) x 1 5/8" (at center ends). In frame small rectangular block and "& Co".	Half-pint 30	Nos. 10 & 11 Type 2	Aquamarines	Unknown	White A19V27 V. R. GVII–29, pt. White opined that the block in the frame resulted from cutting out initials originally in the mold. Scarce
GXI–39. Like GXI–38. Frame about 15/16" x 1 7/8".	Like GXI–38 but instead of block in frame the initials "F" and "&", wide space between "F" and "&", suggesting an initial was omitted, possibly "A". Flask, same form and with same base type as GXII–42 which is inscribed "FA & Co".	Half-pint 30	No. 11 Type 2, with small nipple at center of shallow disk	Colorless Yellowish green (deep)	Unknown, probably Pittsburgh, Pa., possibly Fahnestock, Albree & Co.	According to Van Rensselaer "FA & Co" stands for Fahnestock, Albree & Co. Comparatively scarce
GXI–40. Prospector: very large head with prominent features, short neck, barrel body, slender legs; wearing high-crowned derby; short coat with buttons down front, skin-tight trousers; staff with pack (3 tools showing) at end, held in right hand and resting on right shoulder; long cane in left hand; striding right on long narrow round-ended oblong frame (narrow molding), about 13/16" x 3 3/8". No inscription	Similar to GXI–9; 12 ribs in right wing, 11 in left, frame slightly narrower. No inscription	Quart 30	Plain lip Nos. 11 & 18 Type 5 mold seam, curve falling within deep circular depression	Golden amber Olive-amber Aquamarine	Unknown	White A19V23 Comparatively scarce

GXI-41. Prospector: short stocky figure; small long head; wearing short coat with short tail; pickaxe with pack at end, held by right hand and resting on right shoulder; cane in left hand; walking right of center on long narrow round-ended oblong frame (wide molding) about ⅞" x 2¾". Side of flask slightly concave in area of figure. Above prospector: in shallow arc, "FOR PIKE'S PEAK", bottom of "E" merges with "S". Rectangular area around and above head said to be due to alteration in mold to change head.

GXI-42. Like GXI-41, but very large head with large ear, eye, and beaked nose, long chin, and visored cap.

GXI-43. Prospector: short, stocky, thin arms, small long head with long nose; wearing visored cap, short coat with broad short flaring tail, trousers; short staff with pack (head of pickaxe showing between 2 [?] other tools) at end, held by right hand and resting on right shoulder; cane in left hand; walking right on long round-ended oblong frame (wide molding) about 1⅛" x 2½". Above prospector: in deep arc, "FOR PIKE'S PEAK", apostrophe reversed.

GXI-44. Prospector: tall; large head with hair indicated by small dots, eye by large dot; thin arms, spindly legs; wearing derby, short loose coat flaring at back, tight trousers; right hand holding a long-necked cylindrical bottle to lips; long cane in left hand; walking right on irregular bar near base of flask. See Form Groups, No. 31

Reverse (Eagle)	Size	Edges / Molds	Color	Origin	Remarks
Eagle: head with slender beak, to left; long neck and body; short wings with 9 ribs in right and 8 in left, partly raised, spread downward and outward; on lower breast, long shield with ogee left side, no bottom line and 3 vertical bars; thin splayed legs; thunderbolt (3 arrows) in each talon. Long pennant with wide slightly forked end, from beak to right in long reverse-S-curve high above eagle. Below eagle: large round-ended oblong frame (wide molding) about 1 7/16" x 2¾".	Pint 30	Nos. 11 & 12 Type 8, dot at center	Aquamarine	Unknown	White says A19V15 [GXI-41] and A19V14 [GXI-42] are from the same mold; one before, the other after alteration of the mold. However those we have seen have different bases. Scarce
Like GXI-41	Pint 30	No. 11 Type 1	Aquamarine	Unknown	White A19V14 Rare
Eagle similar to GXI-30, feathering by short ribs; 3 vertical bars on shield; thin legs; no pennant. Below eagle: long rounded oblong frame, about 1 1/16" x 2 9/16".	Pint 30	No. 11 Type 1	Aquamarine	Unknown, midwestern	Comparatively scarce
Eagle: small head with round eye and long beak, to right; long curved neck feathered by dots and wings and body by short ribs; wings partly raised, spread downward and outward; on breast, small shield with 5 vertical bars; heavy short splayed legs; long thunderbolt (3 feathered arrows) in long well-defined talons; olive branch held in beak and curving upward to left above head as on GII-129. Below eagle: large rectangular frame with incurved corners (narrow molding) about 2 7/16" x 2 13/16".	Pint 31	Plain lip & No. 11 Type 16, with and without black-oxide deposit from pontil	Aquamarines Green (light) Green (dark) Yellow-green	Unknown, possibly Zanesville, Ohio, or mold by same moldmaker as of Zanesville eagle flask GII-129.	GXI-44 or 45: White A19V24 & V. R. GVII-27 Scarce Rare Flasks, Group C, No. 6

GXI-37 GXI-38 GXI-40 GXI-41 GXI-42 GXI-43 GXI-44

GROUP XI—PIKE'S PEAK FLASKS—Continued

OBVERSE	REVERSE	SIZE, FORM	NECK, BASE	COLORS	GLASSHOUSE	NOTES, RARITY
GXI-45. Similar to GXI-44 but with larger head and stouter legs.	Similar to GXI-44 but left wing higher than right and shield smaller in proportion to body. Frame (very narrow molding) about 1¼" x 2¾".	Pint 31	Round collar Long mold seams from ends to small shallow disk at center of long round-ended oblong depression; with and without pontil mark	Aquamarines Green Yellow-green	See above	See note above Scarce Rare Flasks, Group C, No. 5
GXI-46. Prospector: short, stocky, with tiny hands and feet, large head; wearing hat with small flat crown and downturned (front & back) brim, short loose flaring coat, full trousers; short staff with large pack (2 tools showing) at end, held by right hand and resting on right shoulder; cane in left hand; straight-necked cylindrical bottle hanging from strap, below right arm; walking right. Above prospector: in arc and large letters, "FOR PIKE'S PEAK".	Hunter, at left, shooting stag at right; short, stocky, with tiny hands and feet and large long head; wearing Pilgrim-type hat, short loose coat, full trousers; straight-necked cylindrical bottle hanging from strap, below right arm, holding, slightly above shoulder height, gun from which smoke rises. Stag, facing right, pitching forward onto knees.	"Qt" (28 oz.) Similar to 31; round-ended oblong in cross section	No. 12 Slightly convex ellipse in center; on prospector side of mold between edge and ellipse, 3 small disks, 1 near each end, 1 at center	Aquamarine (pale)	Unknown	White A19V33 Scarce
GXI-47. Prospector standing and facing right; short; long hair; wearing flat-crowned and narrow-brimmed hat, short loose coat, tight trousers; short staff with pack and tools at end, held in right hand and resting on right shoulder; cane in left hand; straight-necked cylindrical bottle hanging from strap, below right arm. Above prospector: in semicircle and large letters, "FOR PIKE'S PEAK". Similar to GXI-49	Hunter, at left, shooting stag at right: short, stocky, with large head and long hair; wearing large hat with slanting flat crown and wide brim, short loose coat, tight trousers; straight-necked cylindrical bottle hanging from strap, below right arm; smoke rising from gun held to right shoulder; left leg straight and right bent at knee. Stag, facing right and pitching forward onto knees.	Quart 22; round-ended oblong in cross section	No. 11 Straight mold beams to long oval, deep with small disk at one end, shallow at other	Amber Green (clear) Green (medium) Green (deep)	Unknown, possibly The Ravenna Glass Works, Ravenna, Ohio	White's A19V13, either GXI-47 or 48 Comparatively scarce
GXI-47a. Similar to GXI-47. "FOR PIKE'S PEAK" in large letters in shallow arc above prospector. Smaller figure, less sharply defined; smaller hat with slightly higher crown; jacket body almost cone-shaped; legs stockier.	Hunter shooting, similar to GXI-47. Figure slightly smaller and less sharply defined; hat with high instead of flat crown; left leg bent and farther back from right. Small shallow circular depression in front of right foot.	27 oz. 22; round-ended oblong in cross section	No. 11 "Smooth" base, slightly dished ellipse at center; small depression (like that on reverse) near each end on obverse piece of mold	Aquamarine, light	Unknown	Reported by George Austin in 1976. Small circular depressions probably were *not* in the mold but were caused by the device holding the flask during neck finishing. Only 28-oz. size recorded so far.
GXI-48. Like GXI-47	Like GXI-47	Quart Same as above	No. 11 Similar to Type 16, but oblong depression small and at center, upper half within curve of mold seam	Aquamarine	Unknown	See note above Comparatively scarce

No.	Size	Mold	Color	Maker	Rarity / Notes
GXI-49	Quart; Same as above	No. 14 Straight mold seam across oval depression at center	Colorless (faint pinkish cast in base)	Unknown	Group C, Rare Flasks, No. 28. One specimen recorded
GXI-50	Pint; Same as above	Nos. 11 & 12 Type 1, but oval disk	Ambers Aquamarine Olive-yellow	Unknown Possibly Ravenna Glass Works, Ravenna, Ohio	GXI-50 or 51, V. R. GVIII-9 Common
GXI-51	Pint; Same as above	Nos. 11 & 12 Type 1 mold seam and disk	Aquamarine Olive-green	Same as above	White A19V12; says ½ pt. occurs also with same base V. R. GVIII-10 Common
GXI-52	Half-pint; Same as above	No. 11 Triangular ring Type 17	Aquamarine	Unknown	V. R. GVII-10; either GXI-52 or half-pint with base like GXI-51 Comparatively scarce
GXI-53	Pint; Same as above	No. 11 Type 15	Colorless (greenish tinge)	Unknown	White A19V11 Rare flasks, Group C, No. 7 Extremely rare, only 3 or 4 specimens recorded
GXI-54	Quart 31	No. 10 Type 2	Aquamarine	Unknown	White A19V5 Rare Flasks, Group C, No. 8 Extremely rare

GXI-49. Like GXI-47 but below figures, in straight line, "E. KAUFFELD". See Form Groups, No. 28.

GXI-50. Similar to GXI-47 but prospector walking; back a little more rounded; head a little forward; pack over left shoulder.

GXI-51. Similar to GXI-50; slightly smaller figure.

GXI-52. Prospector: small, stocky, with thin arms and long large head; wearing hat with flat crown and narrow brim; short loose coat and full trousers; long staff with 2 packs (shovel in first; 2 tools in second) at end, held by right hand and resting on left shoulder; cane in left hand; straight-necked cylindrical bottle (no strap) hanging below right arm; walking right. Above prospector: in semicircle and large letters, "FOR PIKE'S PEAK"

GXI-53. Prospector: short, stocky with large long head and thin arms (both forearms from left upper arm); wearing hat with large flat crown and narrow brim, voluminous short coat, tight trousers; short staff with large pack (pickaxe, another tool and handles of 2 showing) at end, held in left hand and resting on left shoulder; walking left. Above prospector: in deep arch and large letters, "FOR PIKE'S PEAKE"

GXI-54. Prospector: tall, thick-set; wearing small hat high flat crown and narrow brim, short coat with broad swallow-tail; full trousers apparently tucked into boots of about knee-length; long staff with pack (3 tools showing) at end, held by right hand and resting on left shoulder; crooked cane in left hand; walking right on irregular bar. Above prospector: in shallow arc, "FOR PIKE'S PEAK".

Reverse descriptions:

GXI-52. Hunter, at left, shooting stag at right. Small, with large head; wearing large hat with flat crown and narrow brim; long loose coat, tight trousers; holding at right shoulder, gun from which smoke rises; no bottle hanging at side. Large stag facing right, pitching forward onto knees.

GXI-53. Hunter, at right, shooting stag at left. Small, with long head, thin arms (right forearm from upper left arm); wearing small hat with flat crown and wide brim, short loose coat, tight trousers; holding (at about eye-level and slanting downward) gun from which smoke rises. Stag similar to GXI-46, facing left and pitching forward onto knees.

GXI-54. Similar to obverse but prospector smaller, more slender, and jaunty. Coattails shorter

GXI-46   GXI-52   GXI-53    GXI-54

GROUP XII—SHIELD and CLASPED HANDS FLASKS—ca. 1861–1870s

Edges smooth; medial fine vertical mold seam

OBVERSE	REVERSE	SIZE, FORM	NECK, BASE	COLORS	GLASSHOUSE	NOTES, RARITY
GXII–1. Large shield: narrow molding, shallow ogival top, ogival sides with point at meeting of upper and lower fields, then curving sharply to point at bottom; upper field: narrow horizontal bars to long (3¹/₁₆″) frame with rounded ends and top and bottom in shallow ogee curve, cuff and part of sleeve at ends; lower field; 7 broad flat bars of graduated lengths, broken by round-ended oblong frame (narrow molding about ⅞″ x 2¼″). Each side of shield: slender laurel branch. Above shield: 13 stars; 1 near each end of shield, 11 on right. In shallow arc above "UNION" in large letters, and with "I" slightly left of top point of shield.	Flying eagle, to right: feathering of neck, body, and wings by short ribs; tail 5 long curved ribs; head with prominent eye and slender hooked beak; wings raised in flight, right parallel with body, left above and beyond head; broad tail curved downward. Depending from breast and tilted to right, large shield with ogival top, sides curving to a point at bottom, stars indicated by irregular surface in field above 9 vertical bars; olive branch to left from lower side and thunderbolt (3 arrows) to right. From beak: 2 slightly rippled pennants with forked end; upper—flying in long shallow S-curve across tip of left wing and above eagle to left; lower—in deep S-curve, across shield diagonally above tip, below eagle to left; on long curve "A & CO" ("A" at left of shield). Below eagle: round-ended frame with shallow ogival top and bottom (narrow molding) about 3¹¹/₁₆″ long.	Quart 30	Nos. 10 & 11; angular collar, lower bevel Type 12	Amber (deep) Aquamarine Yellow-green (light)	Attributed by Van Rensselaer to Adams & Co., Pittsburgh, Pa.	V. R. GII–DIV–1 Common
GXII–2. Similar to GXII–1. No short horizontal bars below frame with clasped hands. Small oval frame, about ¹⁵/₁₆″ x 1¹⁵/₁₆″, in lower field of shield. Twenty leaves on left and 21 on right laurel branch. Above shield: 13 stars; 1 large near each end and 11 smaller in shallow arc above "WATERFORD" in arc.	Similar to GXII–1. Two rows of short ribs in left wing; body more slender and head more domed. Twelve stars in top field of shield; 8 narrow vertical bars in lower. Plain pennants. Frame about 3⁹/₁₆″ long.	Quart 30	No. 18 Type 1	Aquamarine Green (light) Olive-yellow (light)	Attributed to the Waterford Glass Works, N.J.	V. R. GII–124. Only Shield and Clasped-Hands flask attributed to an eastern glassworks Common
GXII–3. Similar to GXII–1. Shield longer and narrower, bottom point at base of side; very large clasped hands, frame about 2″ x 3⅞″; in lower field—5 groups of 3 narrow vertical bars (long in end groups), oblong frame (more rounded at one end than other) about ⅞″ x 2″, 3 groups of 3 narrow vertical bars below frame. Left laurel branch (19 leaves) extending to shoulder of shield; right (20 leaves) above shoulder. Thirteen stars; sixth in arc, nearly in line with space between "I" and "O" of "UNION".	Similar to GXII–1. Eagle chunkier, larger head with long downcurved beak; 2 rows of short ribs in left wing; 4 ribs in tail. Shield larger, sides more curved; plain upper field; 3 wide flat bars below crossing pennant. Five arrows in thunderbolt. Pennants rippled and shorter. Below eagle: round-ended oblong frame (narrow molding) about 1¹³/₁₆″ x 3″.	Quart 30	No. 11 Similar to Type 12, but curve of mold seam complete and shallower	Green Yellow-green (light)	Midwestern	Common
GXII–4. Similar to GXII–3. Bottom point of shield ¹/₁₆″ from base; clasped-hands frame about 1⅝″ x 2⅞″; oblong frame in lower field about 1³/₁₆″ x 2¹/₁₆″. Arc of stars shorter. Twenty-four leaves on left, 20 on right laurel branch.	Similar to GXII–1. Eagle chunkier, beak longer, both ends of wing-ribs forming edges; 4 ribs in tail. Shield plain. Ends of pennants more deeply curved, extending higher above and lower below eagle. Frame about 1¹/₁₆″ x 3″.	Quart 30	No. 11 Like above, but with "L&W" in oval depression	Golden amber Aquamarine	Attributed to Lorenz & Wightman, Pittsburgh, Pa.	Common
GXII–5. Like GXII–4, but arc of stars wider and shallower	Like GXII–4	Quart 30	No. 11 Type 1	Yellow-green	Midwestern	Common

GXII–6. Similar to GXII–3. Shield with deeper curves to center point at top and to bottom point about 1/16″ from base; clasped-hands frame about 1½″ x 2⅞″; 5 groups of 3 vertical bars more closely spaced above and below frame (about ⅞″ x 2⁵/₁₆″) leaving plain field at sides. Laurel branches, heavier, longer, and less curved, with stems farther from shield at bottom, 20 "veined" leaves on left, 19 on right. Eleven small stars in arc, star above each end larger. No inscription

GXII–7. Similar to GXII–3. Shield slightly wider and shorter, ending about ⅛″ above base; clasped-hands frame about 1⁹/₁₆″ x 3⅜″; oblong frame about ⅞″ x 2⅜″, inscribed off-center to left "NO. 2." "UNION" nearer top of shield and "I" in line with point. Stars smaller and lower on right end of arc. Twenty leaves (some "veined") on left laurel branch, 24 (some "veined") on right.

GXII–7a. V. R. GIIDV. No. 7 with "No. 2.", probably similar to GXII–7

GXII–8. Similar to GXII–3. Shield slightly shorter, wider and flatter top; bars differ in length and placement, end groups of vertical bars start above instead of below clasped-hands frame; clasped hands smaller and frame about 1⁷/₁₆″ x 3″; oval frame about 1⁵/₁₆″ x 2³/₁₆″. Smaller stars, arc shorter. "UNION" in large letters, midway between stars and shield, point of shield just to right of "I". Twenty-one leaves on left laurel branch, 26 on right.

Rarity	Locality	Color	Mouth	Size/Type
Common	Midwestern	Golden amber (light)	Flat collar, narrow beveled edge Type 1	Quart 29 (no rib on end)
V. R. GII-DV-1 Common	Attributed to Pittsburgh, Pa.	Amber (deep) Aquamarine Yellow-green	Nos. 11 & 19 but top angular Type 12	Quart 30
I have not seen this flask Common	Same as above	Amber	V. R. "Ringed mouth"; (probably No. 11)	Pint
Common	Midwestern	Blue (light) Yellow-green	No. 11 Type 8	Quart 30

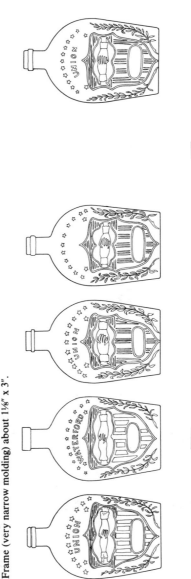

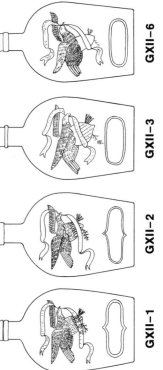

GXII–1 GXII–2 GXII–3 GXII–6 GXII–8

GXII–1 GXII–2 GXII–3 GXII–6 GXII–7

GROUP XII—SHIELD and CLASPED HANDS FLASKS—*Continued*

Edges smooth; medial fine vertical mold seam

OBVERSE	REVERSE	SIZE, FORM	NECK, BASE	COLORS	GLASSHOUSE	NOTES, RARITY
GXII-9. Similar to GXII-3. Small shield with deep sharp points at top and bottom, deeper curves on sides; large clasped hands, cuffs, no part of sleeves, in frame about 1$^{9}/_{16}$″ x 2$^{9}/_{16}$″ oval frame (about $^{11}/_{16}$″ x 1⅞″) with "OLD RYE". Short, heavy laurel branches in double ogee to top ends of shield; 17 leaves on left, 20 on right. Large stars, one above each end of shield, 11 in semicircle just above "UNION" in large letters, sixth in line with "I"	Similar to GXII-1. Eagle's wings curving upward, left short. Large plain shield only slightly tilted to right. Upper pennant curving upward beyond tip of left wing, forked end curving downward instead of upward; long lower pennant inscribed "A&DHC." at crossing center of shield. No olive branch or thunderbolt. Frame (narrow molding) with points at center top and bottom; inverted points at ends, about 1½″ x 2⅞″ overall; inscribed "PITTSBURGH".	Quart 22	No. 11 Type 2, but shallow center	Aquamarine Yellow-green (light)	A.&D.H. Chambers, Pittsburgh, Pa.	Common
GXII-10. Similar to GXII-3. Shield narrower through lower field, horizontal bars above and at upper sides of large frame (about 1⅞″ x 3″) with smaller clasped hands, left group of vertical bars from end curve of frame, single short bar from right end curve; oval frame about ¾″ x 1$^{15}/_{16}$″. Laurel branches (19 leaves on left, 22 on right) in double-ogee, left extending beyond top corner of shield and lower part of star. Thirteen large stars; 11 in deep semicircle with end ones close to top leaf of branch; one above, and nearly touching, ends of shield. "UNION" in large fancy letters, midway between 5 center stars and point of shield.	Similar to GXII-1. Small eagle, feathering of neck, body, and left wing rather pebbled, right wing by short ribs, tail of 5 graduated curved ribs; small head with long hooked beak; wings raised high. Large shield depending from breast at nearly right angle to eagle and top at right extending beyond breast, indication of horizontal bars above pennant and vertical bars below; long olive branch curving to left, thunderbolt (6 arrows) to right. Narrow pennants with wide deeply forked ends; upper curving upward across middle of left wing; lower, downward across shield above center and curved downward close to olive branch. Large frame (narrow molding) with deep ogival top and bottom, incurved ends, about 1$^{9}/_{16}$″ at points x 3$^{3}/_{16}$″ at corners.	Quart 30	Nos. 11 & 12 Type 12	Aquamarine Blue-green Olive-green	Midwestern	Common
GXII-11. Similar to GXII-3. Shield long and slender, upper curve of sides short and deep, lower long and shallow; narrow horizontal bars above and at upper sides of large frame (about 1⅞″ x 2$^{11}/_{16}$″) with small clasped hands; long oval frame about ⅞″ x 2⅛″. Most leaves of laurel branches "veined," 18 on left, 20 on right. Eleven stars in semicircle slightly smaller than stars near top ends of shield. "UNION" in small letters, sixth star in line with "I".	Similar to GXII-1. Eagle with raised head, heavy hooked beak, slenderer body and short downcurved tail, feathered by short ribs; narrow wings raised high, right feathered by pebbling, left comblike. Large plain shield, low on breast, 4 short olive branches at lower left, 1 at right. Long narrow pennants, upper across middle of left wing, lower across shield and with forked end curved downward. Frame similar to GXII-10, with deeper top and bottom curves, about 1⅛″ at points and $^{7}/_{16}$″ at curves, x 3¼″ at corners.	Quart 30	No. 12 Type 2	Aquamarine Green (light) Yellow-green	Midwestern	Common
GXII-12. Similar to GXII-3. Shield long and slender, upper curve of sides deep, lower long and shallow to blunt point about $^{5}/_{16}$″ from base; 3 groups of horizontal bars above and at upper sides of large frame (about 1⅝″ x 2⅜″) with very large clasped hands, cuffs but no part of sleeves; short vertical bar, at each side point flanking 5 groups of 3 bars, left group of 3 below frame and slanting left, oval frame (narrower at left end) about 1″ x 2¼″. Spindly laurel branches, 22 slender leaves on left, 24 on right. Stars, small, are long and shallow. "UNION" in large letters, sixth star and point of shield in line with "I".	Similar to GXII-1. Small chunky eagle, feathering of neck, body, and wings by pebbling, short broad tail by curved ribs graduated in length, head with no eye and snoutlike beak; wings raised high, tops straight and nearly in line; top of sturdy legs above shield. Large shield, top point between legs, 11 fine bars above pennant, 9 below; thunderbolt (3 arrows with feathered ends to left and heads to right). Pennants with wide deeply forked ends, upper across middle of left wing, lower across shield above middle and end curved downward. Frame similar to GXII-10, about 1$^{11}/_{16}$″ at points x 3$^{5}/_{16}$″ at corner points.	Quart 28	No. 12 Type 14	Aquamarine	Midwestern	Common

GXII–13. Similar to GXII–3. Long shield with high wide point at top, point at bottom about ⁷/₁₆" from base, long deep upper curve on sides; 3 groups of horizontal bars above and at upper sides of wide frame (about 1¹¹/₁₆" x 2⁷/₁₆") with large clasped hands, short cuffs, and vestige of sleeves; 5 groups of short vertical bars to top of round-ended oblong panel with "L.F. & CO". 3 groups of 3 vertical bars below. Spindly laurel branches, 22 leaves on left, 24 on right. Thirteen tiny stars; 1 near each end of shield (placed higher and farther in than on flasks GXII–12), 11 in semicircle with those at ends near top leaves of branches. "UNION" in large letter with serifs, just below stars; "I" slightly left of sixth star and point of shield.

GXII–14. Like GXII–13.

GXII–15. Similar to GXII–3. Shield with high wide point at top, more tapered lower field than foregoing, bottom point about ½" from base; horizontal bars above and at upper side of wide frame (about 1³/₁₆" x 2⅝") with very large clasped hands, cuff, no part of sleeves; short bar at point of sides, right group of 3 diagonal bars to side. 1st of left group to side others to top of small oval frame (about ¹³/₁₆" x 1⅞"); 1st and 3rd groups of 3 vertical bars slightly diagonal from bottom of frame to sides and middle group slightly right of center. Spindly laurel branches, 30 leaves (2 vestigial) on left, 32 on right, stems joined at "star" below point of shield. Small stars. "UNION" (letters with serifs), "I" in line with 6th star, point of shield with right end of "I".

Quart 30	Nos. 11 & 12 Type 1	Amber Aquamarine	Unidentified, Pittsburgh, Pa.	Comparatively scarce. The period after "L" is so faint on some specimens it is difficult to find or is missing.
Quart 30	Nos. 12 & 17 Similar to Type 12, but curve of mold seam shallower and complete	Aquamarine Olive-yellow	Same as above	Comparatively scarce
Quart 30	Nos. 6 & 11 Mold seam, like Type 16, through oval depression about 3¼" long.	Amber, golden Aquamarine Olive-yellow Yellow-green (light)	Made for E. Wormser & Co., Pittsburgh, Pa., at Frankstown Glass Works (started 1859 by Wm Frank and E. Wormser)	V. R. GII–DIV–14 Common

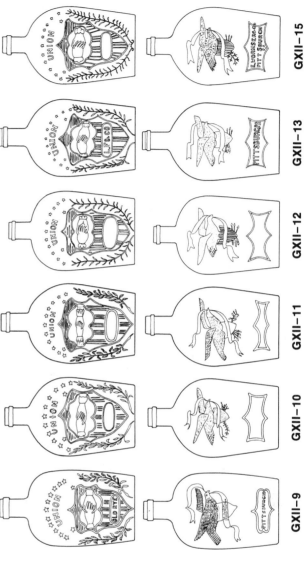

GXII–9 GXII–10 GXII–11 GXII–12 GXII–13 GXII–15

GROUP XII—SHIELD and CLASPED HANDS FLASKS—*Continued*

Edges smooth; medial fine vertical mold seam

OBVERSE	REVERSE	SIZE, FORM	NECK, BASE	COLORS	GLASSHOUSE	NOTES, RARITY
GXII–16. Like GXII–15 but stars slightly smaller	Like GXII–15	Quart 30	No. 19 Type 5	Amber, greenish Aquamarine	Same as above	Common
GXII–17. Similar to GXII–3. Long narrow shield, high point at top, short upper curve on side, long lower to point at base; 3 groups of horizontal bars above and below frame (about $1\frac{1}{4}$″ x $2\frac{5}{16}$″) with clasped hands, cuffs, no part of sleeves; 5 groups of long vertical bars (2 in left, 2 long and 1 short in right, 3 in others) to oval frame (about $\frac{3}{4}$″ x $1\frac{5}{8}$″), 3 groups of 3 short bars below frame. Eighteen leaves on left laurel branch, 22 on right, stems at base. Eleven large stars in wide shallow arc, no star at ends of shield. "UNION" in large wide-spaced letters, "T" in line with sixth star and point of shield.	Closely similar to GXII–6. Eagle's head smaller, with large eye and short hooked beak. Shield tilted more to right, 3 olive branches from lower left side; no thunderbolt. Rippled pennants wide; upper flatter with less curved end; lower hanging downward, across shield near tip and with end close to frame. Frame about $\frac{15}{16}$″ x $2\frac{1}{2}$″.	Pint 28	No. 12 Type 8	Aquamarine	Midwestern	Common
GXII–18. Similar to GXII–17. Long narrow shield, bottom point about $\frac{1}{16}$″ from base; horizontal bars above and at sides of frame (about $1\frac{1}{4}$″ x $2\frac{1}{8}$″) with clasped hands, cuffs, part of sleeves; 5 groups of 3 vertical bars (in left 1 tiny and 1 short, in right 1 tiny, others long) to round-ended oblong frame (about $\frac{3}{4}$″ x $1\frac{3}{4}$″), 3 groups of 3 short bars below frame. Twenty-one leaves on each laurel branch. Thirteen large stars; 1 near each end of shield; 11 in arc. No inscription	Similar to GXII–1. Chunky eagle, large head with large hooked beak, no eye; left wing almost rectangular, very short broad tail (5 curved ribs). Large plain shield; no olive branch or thunderbolt. Long plain pennants; upper across end of left wing, forked end flying upward; lower across center of shield, forked end deeply curved and close to frame. Round-ended oblong frame about $\frac{11}{16}$″ x $2\frac{1}{4}$″.	Pint 28	No. 11 Type 1, disk inscribed "L&W"	Aquamarine	Lorenz & Wightman, Pittsburgh, Pa.	V. R. GII–DIV–9 Common
GXII–19. Similar to GXII–1. Short broad shield, horizontal bars above and at upper sides of frame (about $1\frac{1}{4}$″ x $2\frac{9}{16}$″) with clasped hands, cuffs, and part of sleeves; 9 heavy widely spaced vertical bars (about $\frac{5}{8}$″ x $1\frac{1}{2}$″) inscribed "LF&CO", 5 bars below frame. Seventeen leaves on each laurel branch. Star nearly touching shield near each end; 11 in semicircle, larger except for first at left. "UNION" in small letters with serifs.	Similar to GXII–17. Eagle's head small. Plain shield. No olive branch or thunderbolt. Frame, about $\frac{13}{16}$″ x $2\frac{1}{4}$″, inscribed "PITTS-BURGH.PA".	Pint 28	Nos. 11 & 12 Type 6	Amber (shaded) Aquamarine	Unidentified, Pittsburgh. Pa.	Comparatively scarce
GXII–20. Similar to GXII–3. Short broad shield, 5 horizontal bars above and at sides of frame (about $1\frac{1}{4}$″ x $2\frac{1}{2}$″) with clasped hands, cuffs, part of narrow sleeves; below at sides, short vertical bars and, to frame, 5 groups of 3; 3 groups of 3 bars below frame; narrow round-ended frame with ogival top and bottom, about $\frac{3}{4}$″ x $1\frac{5}{8}$″. Eighteen leaves on left laurel branch, 16 on right. Very large stars; tiny dot at lower left of star near top left end of shield; star at right end, a little larger; 11 in semicircle. "UNION" in small closely placed letters midway between stars and top of shield; "T" in line with point.	Similar to GXII–1. Small slender eagle, fine feathering on neck, body, and right wing, long comblike left wing, 4 long downcurving tail ribs, large head with large eye and hooked beak. Large shield, pebbling above crossing pennant, 7 fine vertical bars below; spindly olive branch from lower left, thunderbolt (5 arrows as on GXII–3) from right. Wide plain pennants with sections about equal in length; upper, across left wing and most of its upper edge; lower, across shield above middle and inscribed "CI & SONS". Long frame with ogival top and bottom, inverted points at ends, about $1\frac{3}{8}$″ at points x $2\frac{1}{2}$″.	Pint 28	Nos. 10 & 11 Short straight mold seam to oblong depression	Amber (deep) Brown-amber Golden-amber Yellow-green	C. Ihmsen & Sons (Christian and sons Charles T. and William), Pittsburgh. Pa.	Scarce
GXII–21. Similar to GXII–1, smaller scale. Clasped-hands frame about $1\frac{5}{16}$″ x $2\frac{5}{8}$″; 5 groups of 3 vertical bars above oblong panel (about $\frac{5}{8}$″ x $1\frac{11}{16}$″) and 3 below. Nineteen leaves on left laurel branch, 21 on right. Stars large; arc of 11 deeper.	Similar to GXII–1, smaller scale. Shield plain, olive branch less spindly. "A & CO" in long section of lower pennant not so far to the left. Frame, very narrow molding, about $1\frac{1}{4}$″ at points by $2\frac{3}{8}$″.	Pint 30	No. 12 Similar to Type 12, but curve of seam shallower and completed, small nipple at center of depression	Amber (deep) Golden amber (shaded) Aquamarine Yellow-green (pale)	Attributed by Van Rensselaer to Adams & Co., Pittsburgh. Pa.	Common

No.	Size	Mold	Color	Origin	Rarity
GXII-22	Pint 30	No. 11 Same as above	Amber (deep) Green (light)	Same as above	V. R. GII–DIV–1 Common
GXII-23	Pint 29	No. 12 and flat ring below short section curving at top to narrower mouth Type 5	Aquamarine Yellow-green (light)	C. Ihmsen & Sons, Pittsburgh, Pa.	V. R. GII–DIV–5 Comparatively scarce
GXII-24	Pint 29	No. 11 Type 8	Aquamarine	Midwestern	Common
GXII-25	Pint 29	No. 12 Short straight mold seam to oblong depression with small nipple at center	Aquamarine	A. & D.H. Chambers, Pittsburgh, Pa.	Comparatively scarce

Similar to GXII–1, smaller scale; clasped-hands frame about 1 1/16" x 3 9/16"; 9 wide graduated bars above oval frame, 7 below. Twenty leaves on left laurel branch; 18 on right. Medium-size stars, "T" of "UNION" in line with top point of shield.

Eagle, flying right, short plump; feathering of body and wings by short wide-spaced ribs; left wing, comblike with parallel short ribs; tail, 4 long pointed ribs curved slightly downward; large head with large eye and long hooked beak. Large plain shield tilted to right. Wide plain pennants; upper, short, across end of left wing, and long, close to left wing, to forked end curving upward; lower, long section in curve across shield below middle, shorter with forked end and deeply curved upward. Round-ended frame with ogival top and bottom, about 1 3/16" x 2", inscribed "CI & SONS".

Similar to GXII–23. No inscription in frame

Similar to GXII–1. Small eagle, heavy feathering by short ribs; left wing, comblike; tail, 4 long graduated ribs; small head with small eye, long hooked beak; wings raised high, tail downward. Large shield, tilted to left, left corner and point on breast; fine horizontal bars above crossing pennant and fine vertical below. Spindly olive branch from lower left, thunderbolt (5 arrows) to right. Upper pennant with forked end and rippled, flying high above eagle; lower with longer section diagonally across shield and inscribed "A & D H C" ("A" and "C" falling just beyond sides of shield), short forked end parallel with tail. Frame (like GXII–11) with deep ogival top and bottom and incurved ends, about 15/16" at points x 2 1/4" at corner points, inscribed "PITTSBURGH".

GXII–22. Similar to GXII–1, smaller scale; clasped-hands frame about 1 1/16" x 3 9/16"; 9 wide graduated bars above oval frame, 7 below. Twenty leaves on left laurel branch; 18 on right. Medium-size stars, "T" of "UNION" in line with top point of shield.

GXII–23. Long broad shield, high top point; narrow upper field with shallowly incurved sides, 2 short wide-spaced bars below point, 3 above each end of frame with large clasped hands, cuffs, and parts of sleeves, 2 bars below each end of frame; lower field: 14 heavy vertical bars above round-ended frame inscribed "UNION", 11 below. Laurel branches at sides and curved below shield at bottom. 17 "veined" leaves on left, 16 on right. Thirteen large stars; 1 near and close to each top end of shield; 11 in deep arc, those at ends slightly smaller and close to top leaves of branches.

GXII–24. Similar to GXII–23. "UNION" below stars, point of shield in line with space between "N" and "I". Dot above 2 horizontal bars at lower end of clasped-hands frame; no inscription in oblong frame; instead of 11 bars below frame, 9 bars and dot at each end. Nineteen "veined" leaves on left laurel branch, 20 on right.

GXII–25. Similar to GXII–3. Large shield, horizontal short bars above and at upper and lower sides of large frame (about 1 1/2" x 1 9/16") with clasped hands, cuffs, and part of sleeves; 5 groups of 3 vertical bars above small oval frame (about 3/4" x 1 11/16") inscribed "OLD RYE", 3 groups of 3 bars below frame. Top leaf of laurel branches below top corners of shield, 16 leaves on left branch. 14 on right. Stars large; 1 at each top end of shield, larger than 11 in semicircle. "UNION", in very large fancy letters, nearer shield than stars; point of shield in line with "I".

GXII–18 GXII–19 GXII–20 GXII–23 GXII–25

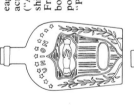

GXII–17

GROUP XII—SHIELD and CLASPED HANDS FLASKS—*Continued*

Edges smooth; medial fine vertical mold seam

OBVERSE	REVERSE	SIZE, FORM	NECK, BASE	COLORS	GLASSHOUSE	NOTES, RARITY
GXII–26. Like GXII–25.	Like GXII–25	Pint 29	No. 11 Type 5	Aquamarine	Same as above	Comparatively scarce
GXII–27. Similar to GXII–3. Short broad shield, very slight curves at top to high point at center; side points extending beyond top of shield; 3 horizontal bars at sides and at point above large frame and part of sleeves; short cuffs (3 lobes), and part of sleeves; 3 short vertical bars at side points, 5 groups of 3 short vertical bars above oval panel inscribed "A&D.H.C", 3 groups of 3 short bars below. Short laurel branches, 16 small leaves on left, 17 on right, stems nearly meeting at base. Thirteen small stars; 1 above and about midway between top point of shield and each end; 11 in deep arch, sixth dropped a little in line with space between "N" and "I" of "UNION" in large letters with serifs.	Eagle flying right: chunky, slight feathering of body and right wing; left wing with comblike top side; tail, 5 graduated ribs curved slightly downward; small head with large hooked beak. Large plain shield, point not quite touching breast; thunderbolt (3 arrows) from left below middle, large spindly olive branch from right. Long narrow pennants with deeply forked ends; upper diagonally across left wing at about middle, second section in straight line above right wing; lower, long section diagonal to side of shield, then straight across shield, second (short) section diagonally downward. Large frame (like GXII–11) with deep ogival top and bottom, incurved ends, inscribed "PITTSBURGH PA".	Pint 29	No. 11 Type 4	Aquamarine	Same as above	V. R. GII–DIV–2 (?) Comparatively scarce
GXII–28. Similar to GXII–15 and 29. Long narrow shield, very narrow molding, bottom point about ³⁄₈″ above base; upper field: 4 fine horizontal bars below point, 4 at corners above large frame (about 1¹³⁄₁₆″ x 2⅜″) with small clasped hands, ruffled cuffs, part of sleeves forming ends of frame; lower field: 3 groups of fine vertical bars (5 at left center, 4 at right) above and 3 groups of 3 below long frame with ogival top and bottom and incurved ends (about ¹⁵⁄₁₆″ at points x 1⁹⁄₁₆″ at corner points). Spindly laurel branches; 12 leaves on left, 11 on right, stems about ½″ apart at base. Thirteen very small stars; 1 at each end and about midway between top of shield and third star from each end of arc of 11. "UNION" in large letters, "I" nearly in line with point of shield.	Closely similar to GXII–15. Short section of lower pennant, narrow; 10 short vertical bars on shield above crossing pennant, 9 below. Frame, same type but shorter and wider in proportion.	Pint 30	Similar to No. 12, section above ring longer, rounded at lip Type 1	Reddish amber (deep) Aquamarine	Midwestern	Comparatively scarce
GXII–29. Similar to GXII–15. Long narrow shield, 3 horizontal bars at point, 2 from each corner to upper side of frame (about ¹⁵⁄₁₆″ x 1½″) with large clasped hands, short cuffs; below frame, 4 groups of 3 long narrow bars at ends diagonal to sides; 2 groups to oval frame (about ½″ x ¹⁵⁄₁₆″), 3 groups from bottom of frame. Eleven laurel branches; 21 leaves on left, 20 on right. Eleven 4-pointed small stars, varying in size; 1, tiny, nearly touching each top end of shield; 9 in arch, last at right nearly touching top leaf of laurel. "UNION" in large letters, "U" close to third star, "N" to seventh in arch.	Similar to GXII–15. Chunky eagle; neck, body, and wings feathered by pebbling, 5 long curved ribs in broad tail; thick neck, small head. Broad short shield, left end and point touching breast, 9 vertical bars above crossing pennant, 7 below, spindly long olive branch from lower left side, thunderbolt (3 wide-spaced arrows) from right. Upper pennant: first section tapering and across left wing to left, second section wide and parallel with right wing; lower pennant: long narrow first section curving down to side of shield and across center, short wide end parallel with olive branch. No frame	Half-pint 30	Nos. 10 & 11 Similar to Type 8, straight part of seam shorter; curved, longer and shallower	Ambers Aquamarine	Midwestern	V. R. GII–DIV–6 Common
GXII–30. Similar to GXII–19. Large shield; horizontal bar above frame (about 1″ x 1¹³⁄₁₆″) with clasped hands, cuffs; 5 flat vertical bars above oval frame (about ⁹⁄₁₆″ x 1¼″), 3 below. Sixteen "veined" leaves on each laurel branch. Thirteen large stars. "UNION", in large letters, close to top of shield; "I" nearly touching point.	Eagle closely similar to GXII–29. Stars indicated by irregular surface on shield above crossing pennant, no olive branch or thunderbolt. Pennants, slightly rippled, long sections wider. Below shield, round-ended oblong frame, tilted up at left end, about ¾″ x 1¾″.	Half-pint 30	No. 11 Similar to Type 8, but concave center ovoid	Aquamarine	Midwestern	Comparatively scarce

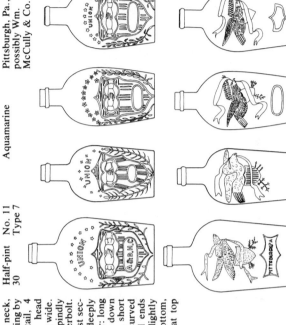

	GXII–31	GXII–32	GXII–33	GXII–34
Rarity	Common	V. R. GII–DIV–13 Comparatively scarce	Common	In 1944 Sam Laidacker acquired a number of GXII–34 or of GXII–35 from an old drugstore in Hannibal, Mo. They were in their original shipping box marked "Wm. McCully & Co., Glass Manufacturer, Pittsburgh, Pa. U. 6 doz. half-pints." Common
Origin	Midwestern	Wm. Frank & Sons, Pittsburgh, Pa., Frankstown Glass Works	Midwestern	Pittsburgh, Pa., possibly Wm. McCully & Co.
Color	Aquamarine, Golden amber, Yellow-green (light)	Aquamarine	Amber, Aquamarine, Yellow-green (light)	Aquamarine
Capacity	Half-pint 30	Half-pint 30	Half-pint 30	Half-pint 30
Neck	No. 11 Type 5	No. 11 Type 1	Round collar just below plain lip Type 5	No. 11 Type 7

Eagle descriptions

Eagle similar to GXII–3, smaller scale. Head raised. Plain shield, long spindly olive branch, from left downward, thunderbolt (4 arrows) from right. Wide long plain pennants with forked ends; upper, across end of left wing, forked section deeply curved upward; lower, forked section deeply curved down across shield, forked section deeply curved upward. Round-ended oblong frame about ⅝" x 2⁹/₁₆".

Similar to GXII–15. Top line of eagle's wings curved. Shield very large in proportion to bird, pebbled instead of barred; thunderbolt (3 arrows) from left lower side and olive branch from right. Upper pennant longer than lower and forked section narrower. Frame about 1" at points x 2¹¹/₁₆" at corner points.

Eagle flying right; rippled ribs feathering neck, body and right wing, left wing comblike; tail 4 graduated diagonal ribs; head with large eye and long hooked beak, wings raised high. Plain shield, tilted to right, from breast, no olive branch or thunderbolt. Long pennants: 2 sections of upper, about same length, first across and diagonally above left wing, second with forked end curving upward above right wing; lower: long first section diagonally downward across shield, short second section in deep upward curve, narrower forked end. Wide shallow shield-shaped frame (wide molding) about 1" at center points, width 1⅜".

Small eagle flying right; feathering of neck, left wing by short ribs; left wing by 2 rows with upper edge comblike; tail, 4 straight slightly diagonal ribs; large head raised, large eye, hooked beak; left wing wide. Plain shield, tilted to right from breast, spindly olive branch from lower left, no thunderbolt. Pennants long and wide; upper: long first section across end of left wing, short deeply forked second section curving up; lower: long first section, slightly rippled, curving down across shield and close to olive branch, short deeply forked second section deeply curved upward and near top of frame; forked ends near left edge of flask. Fancy frame, slightly convex top, more deeply curved bottom, deeply indented ogee ends; 1" x 1⅞" at top corners, 2" at bottom.

GXII–31. Similar to GXII–18. Slender shield, horizontal bars above frame (about ⅞" x 1¾") with clasped hands, cuffs, part of sleeves, bars below ends of frame; 3 long vertical bars to round-ended oblong frame (about ⅝" x 1⅜") and, below frame, 2 dots at each end, 3 short vertical bars in center. Long laurel branches; 16 leaves on left, 19 on right. Very large stars with each segment defined; 1 nearly touching top of shield near right end. 1 at left end placed higher; 11 in wide arch, end stars nearly touching top leaf of laurel. No "UNION"

GXII–32. Similar to GXII–15. Slender shield: 2 short bars at left and right, 3 in center above large frame (about ⅞" x 1⁷/₁₆") with clasped hands, cuffs; 3 groups of 3 fine vertical bars above and below large oval frame (about ⅞" x 1¼") inscribed "W.F.&" above "SONS". Spindly laurel branches, 24 leaves on left, 26 on right. Thirteen stars; 1 near top of shield well in from each corner; 11 in deep semicircle. "UNION" in small thin letters, close to stars, leaving wide plain field to point of shield.

GXII–33. Similar to GXII–3, small scale. Broad shield, short horizontal bars at left and right, 2 in center above, and at left and right below, large frame (about 1" x 2") with clasped hands, cuffs, part of sleeves; lower field: dot and single long bar ending about ¹¹/₁₆ x 1½"), 3 groups of 3 vertical bars above and below frame. Eighteen leaves on left laurel branch, 19 on right. Small stars. "UNION" in small letters, close to star, "I" slightly left of point of shield.

GXII–34. Similar to GXII–33, shield about ⅛" narrower at base, about ⅛" narrower at top; clasped-hands frame about ¹⁵/₁₆" x 1¹³/₁₆"; 3 groups of 3 vertical bars above and below oblong frame (about ⁹/₁₆" x 1⁵/₁₆"). Seventeen leaves on left laurel branch, 16 on right. Large stars. Letters of "UNION" wide-spread.

GROUP XII—SHIELD and CLASPED HANDS FLASKS—*Continued*

Edges smooth; medial fine vertical mold seam

OBVERSE	REVERSE	SIZE, FORM	NECK, BASE	COLORS	GLASSHOUSE	NOTES, RARITY
GXII–35. Like GXII–34	Like GXII–34	Half-pint 30	No. 11 & wide flat ring Similar to Type 2. disk more ovoid, small nipple at center	Aquamarine	Same as above	See note above Common
GXII–36. Similar to GXII–3. Long narrow shield, bottom point at base; upper field: no horizontal bars above or at sides of frame with clasped hands, cuffs and part of sleeves, 2 short bars below ends; lower field: 9 long vertical bars above narrow round-ended frame (about 7/16″ x 1⅛″), 7 short vertical bars below frame, those at ends short dashes. Sixteen leaves on left laurel branch, 17 on right; right longer, extending to end star of arc and about in line with top point of shield. Thirteen very large stars; one above and near each top corner of shield; 11 in shallow arc. "UNION" in wide-spaced letters close to stars; "I" in line with point of shield.	Tall narrow oval frame (very narrow molding) with short vertical rib at center top; bottom and sides, long scroll rib between; frame within open-top laurel wreath of 3 rows of "veined" leaves; at bottom, long bow with 3 knots between loops and long forked ends hanging down from loops and curving slightly outward.	Half-pint 30	No. 11 Type 7	Aquamarine	Midwestern	V. R. GVI–121 Common
GXII–37. Similar to GXII–10, bolder relief than others in group. Shield formed by wider molding; horizontal bars above frame (about 1¾″ x 3″) with clasped hands, cuffs, part of sleeves, short bars below ends; lower field: 2 short vertical bars each side, group of 4 bars between 2 groups of 3 above oval frame (about 1³/₁₆″ x 1¹⁵/₁₆″), 3 groups of 3 below frame and dashlike at ends. Twenty-two leaves on left laurel branch, 23 on right. Large stars, deep semicircle. "UNION" in large letters with serifs, a little nearer top of shield than stars.	Similar to obverse; short vertical bars instead of horizontal below ends of clasped-hand frame; fourth and fifth groups of vertical bars long, placed farther to left and right and extending beyond ends of oval frame.	Quart 30	No. 11 Type 12	Aquamarine Cornflower-blue (light) Olive-yellow	Midwestern	V. R. GVI–123 Rare Flasks, Group C. No. 22 Rare
GXII–38. Shield, long, narrow, with very deep curves in ogival top to high point and high narrow corners; short horizontal ribs at corners; large frame (about 1¹/₁₆″ x 1⁷/₁₆″) with very large clasped hands, cuffs; lower field: short dashlike vertical bar at each end of 16 fine short bars above large oval frame (about 1⅜″ x 2³/₁₆″) with inscription (from left bottom to right) "W? FRANK & SONS" (center bottom) "PITTS·"; 9 fine bars below frame. Spindly laurel branches; 30 leaves on left, 31 on right, 13 small stars; 1 at each end above corners and about in line with point of shield; 11 in wide shallow arc. "UNION" in large letters, close to stars; sixth in line with "I" (28 Form Groups).	Cannon, facing left; 6 spokes in wheels of gun carriage, 4 diagonal bars across "tongue." American flag flying to right on pole rising behind muzzle of cannon from pyramid of 10 cannonballs (4, 3, 2, 1), center one in second row and that at top blended with pole; 6 stripes in flag, stars indicated by pebbled surface; 2 ropes, with tasseled ends, at top left at angle to pole. Carriage, cannonballs and pole resting on slender horizontal bar.	Quart 28	No. 11 Type 2	Golden amber Aquamarine Olive-green (light)	William Frank & Sons, Pittsburgh, Pa., Frankstown Glass Works	Probably V. R. GI–13 Comparatively scarce
GXII—38a. Like GXII–38 but cannonballs slightly smaller.	Like GXII–38 but 19 tiny stars.	Quart 28	No. 11 Type 8	Greenish amber Sapphire-blue (deep) Yellow-green	Same as above	Comparatively scarce
GXII–39. Similar to GXII–38 but smaller scale, and letters of "UNION" larger in proportion to rest of design; top of shield not so deeply curved; frame with clasped hands, cuffs and vestige of sleeves, about 1¼″ x 2³/₁₆″; lower field: no dashlike vertical bars at sides and none below large oval frame inscribed "W? FRANK & SONS" (from left bottom to right) "PITTS". Twenty-seven leaves on left laurel branch, 23 on right. Fourteen stars, 12 in arc.	Similar to GXII–38 but smaller scale; 5 spokes in one wheel, 4 in the other; 3 diagonal bars to ribs framing edge of "tongue"; outside wheel not touching horizontal bar. Six cannonballs (3, 2, 1) in pyramid; flagpole showing between the 2 in second row. Flag with 12 tiny stars, 6 stripes.	Pint 28	Nos. 11 & 12 Type 1	Amber (shaded) Golden amber Aquamarine Cornflower-blue Sapphire-blue	Same as above	Comparatively scarce

654

Description	Size	Mold	Color	Maker	Rarity
GXII–39a. Closely similar to GXII–39; in lower field of shield, vertical bars close to sides. Twenty-two leaves on left laurel branch. 28 on right.	Pint 28	No. 11 Similar Type 4. very shallow depression	Golden amber / Red-amber / Aquamarine	Same as above	Comparatively scarce
GXII–40. Similar to GXII–3. Broad short shield; short horizontal bars above top and below ends of large frame (about 1⅜" x 2⅝") with large clasped hands, cuffs, and part of sleeves; lower field: 5 groups of 3 vertical bars (3 groups very short above oval frame (about 1³⁄₁₆" x 1⁹⁄₁₆") inscribed "FA&Co". 3 groups below frame and 1 group long at each end). Thirteen leaves on left laurel branch. 18 on right. Thirteen large stars. 1 above and near top ends of shield; 11 in deep semicircle. "UNION" in small fancy letters (like GXII–10 and 25) placed nearer top of shield than stars; "I" a bit left of shield's point.	Pint 30	No. 11; similar to 12, very narrow; Similar to Type 8, curve of mold seam flatter	Golden amber / Olive-amber / Yellow-amber (C. V.) / Blue (light)	Fahnestock. Albree & Co.. Pittsburgh. Pa.	V. R. GI–10 Common
GXII–41. Broad shield, narrow molding; thin horizontal bars above top and 2 short below ends of large frame (about 1⅛" x 2⅝") with clasped hands, cuffs, and part of sleeve on left; lower field: 4 groups of 3 vertical thin bars above and 3 below oval frame (about ⅞" x 1⅞"). Nineteen leaves on left laurel branch. "I" a bit left of shield's point.	Pint 28	Nos. 6, 11 & similar to No. 12. but section ring longer and rounded at lip Type 1	Amber (deep shaded) / Red-amber / Aquamarine / Yellow-green (light)	Midwestern	Possibly V. R. GI–12 Common
GXII–42. Closely similar to GXII–40, smaller scale. Inscription "F A & Co" close to end following top of frame; no vertical bars at left below frame. Seventeen leaves on each laurel branch. "UNION" in plain letters, placed nearer stars than shield. "I" a bit left of shield's point.	Half-pint 30	No. 11 Type 4	Aquamarine	Fahnestock. Albree & Co.. Pittsburgh. Pa.	V. R. GI–11 Scarce
GXII–42a. Like GXII–42	Half-pint 30	No. 11 Straight mold seam	Amber (dark)	Same as above	Scarce

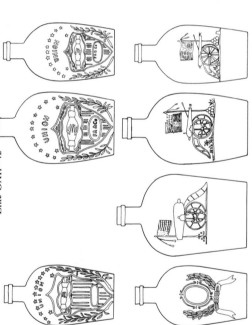

GXII–36   GXII–38   GXII–40   GXII–42

GROUP XII—SHIELD and CLASPED HANDS FLASKS—Continued

Edges smooth; medial fine vertical mold seam

OBVERSE	REVERSE	SIZE, FORM	NECK, BASE	COLORS	GLASSHOUSE	NOTES, RARITY
GXII–43. Similar to GIV–42. Short broad shield, fine horizontal bars in upper field above frame with clasped hands, cuffs, and part of sleeves; lower field: wide rounded ribs (14) above and (7) below round-ended oblong frame (about 1¹/₁₆″ x 2¹/₁₆″) inscribed "UNION" in wide-spaced letters. Nineteen leaves on left laurel branch, 20 on right; some solid, some "veined." Thirteen stars; 1 above and 4 in from each top corner of shield; 11 in shallow arc.	Similar to GIV–42. Large eagle flying to right; feathering by short ribs on neck, body, and right wing, left wing comblike, tail 5 long downcurving ribs; small head with large eye and short beak; wings raised. From breast, large plain shield tilted to right; long olive branch from left side, thunderbolt (4 arrows) from right. Long narrow pennants with forked ends; upper: across left wing near tip, flying to left, deep curve of short section close to top of right wing; lower in curve across shield, short section in very deep curve upward. No initials	Quart 38, calabash with wide vertically fluted edges	Round collar, lower beveling Type 31	Brown-amber Aquamarine Citron Green, yellowish Yellow-green (light)	Unknown Possibly A. R. Samuels, Philadelphia, Pa.	Very common

GROUP XIII—PICTORIAL FLASKS—Mainly ca. 1850–1880

OBVERSE	REVERSE	SIZE, FORM	EDGES	NECK, BASE	COLORS	GLASSHOUSE	NOTES, RARITY
GXIII–1. Girl riding old-fashioned bicycle to left, in profile. Girl with small head, large puffs of hair left and right; wearing long tight bodice, long full skirt, sash with large bow and long ends flying out in back; left foot on pedal of large front wheel; guard over small rear wheel; wheels on irregular bar. From lips, long forkended pennant, flying in question-mark curve above head and to right and inscribed "NOT FOR JOE" (title of popular song of 1870s).	Plain	Pint 32	Broad flat band	No. 10 Type 21	Amber (dark) Amber (shaded) Aquamarine	Unknown	Rare flasks, Group C, No. 29 Rare
GXIII–2. Similar to GXIII–1 but much smaller scale. No puffs of hair. Above front wheel, guard with end curved upward; no guard above rear wheel. Pennant longer in proportion to figure and in reverse S-curve.	Plain	Pint 32	Flat band, narrower than that of GXIII–1	Nos. 10 & 11 Type 22	Amber Aquamarine Cornflower-blue (light)	Unknown	V. R. GVI–63 Scarce
GXIII–3. Similar to GXIII–1. Girl with hair in bun at back; wearing small hat, short bodice, full skirt. Scroll guard over front wheel, straight guard over rear wheel, no pennant.	Eagle: feathering by short ribs; inner side of wings serrated; plain head with large eye and short hooked beak, to right; on breast, long shield with 3 wide vertical bars, rounded at bottom; short straight legs; thunderbolt (3 arrows) in talon. From beak, slightly rippled pennant in attenuated S-curve to left above eagle. Below eagle, oval frame inscribed, slightly to left of and below center, "A & DH.C".	Pint 29	Smooth	No. 12 Type 2	Aquamarine Yellow-green	A. & D.H. Chambers, Pittsburgh, Pa.	V. R. GVI–13 Scarce
GXIII–4. Hunter, facing left, standing on small hillock; wearing flat-top stovepipe hat, short coat, full trousers; game bag hanging at left side; arms raised, firing gun at two ducks flying upward at left. Large puff of smoke from muzzle, high above 2 bird dogs running to left toward section of rail fence.	Fisherman facing front, standing on shore near a large rock; wearing round-top stovepipe hat, V-neck jacket, full trousers. Fishing rod held in left hand, end resting on ground between feet (not shown from hand to shoulder); line in hairpin arch above hat and to right hand holding a large fish. Creel below left arm. Left background, mill with bushes at left and small tree at right.	Quart 38 (calabash)	4 wide, shallow flutes	No. 15, listed by Van Rensselaer. Plain lip. 8 scallops at base of neck Type 29; 2 small disks on fisherman side of mold	Ambers (golden to reddish) Aquamarine (bluish) Greens (light to deep) Wine	Attributed to Whitney Glass Works, Glassboro, N.J.	V. R. GVI–45 Common

GXIII–5. Hunter, facing right, standing on ground; wearing tall hat with nearly conical crown, short tight coat, tight trousers, hunting boots; arms raised high, firing at 2 small birds flying upward at right side. Long puff of smoke from muzzle. Bird dog just ahead of hunter, running to right toward bush and section of rail fence.	Fisherman, facing front, standing on low bank, wearing high flat-crowned hat, longer coat than GXIII–4 & 6, tight trousers; creel at right side. Fishing rod held in left hand (as on GXIII–4), line in hairpin arch above hat to small fish in left hand. Rock and rail fence at left end of shore; mill in right background; large tree on shore at right.	Quart 41 (calabash, no handle)	5 vertical ribs	Nos. 9 & 15, 8 scallops at base of neck Type 31	Aquamarine	Unknown	V. R. GVI–46 Scarce
GXIII–6. Hunter, facing right, standing on rough ground, legs wide-spread; wearing wide-brimmed hat with high peaked crown, short coat, trousers, hunting boots; arms raised, firing gun straight ahead at 2 birds in flight at right; large puff of smoke from muzzle. Small dog just ahead of hunter, running to right toward bush and rail fence.	Fisherman facing nearly front, standing on low bank; garb similar to hunter's; creel at left side. Rod held in left hand, as on GXIII–4, but curving to left above head, line with fish on end, hanging to left, caught in right hand well above fish. Rock and bush on left bank.	Quart 38 (calabash)	4 wide shallow flutes	Narrow round collar, lower bevel (20a) Type 28	Aquamarines Amber Olive-green	Unknown	V. R. GVI–47 Rare
GXIII–7. Hunter facing front standing on rough ground; wearing cap, long tight-waisted coat, full trousers, hunting boots; left arm bent at elbow; holding gun by both hands, at angle in front of body, barrel across left arm to right; small game bag at right hip, suspended by strap over left shoulder. Grass or reeds at left; bow end of skiff and reeds at right.	Two pointers running left over rough grassy ground.	Pint 23	Smooth	Similar to No. 19, narrower With and without pontil mark	Aquamarine Green Olive-yellow	Attributed to New London by Van Rensselaer	V. R. GVI–43 Rare
GXIII–8. Sailor, three-quarter face, arms akimbo, dancing hornpipe on 8-board hatch cover; wearing small hat, short-sleeved V-neck blouse with collar up against right cheek and neck scarf flying at right, tight sailor pants. About ⅜" below hatch cover, long rectangular bevel-edged bar, about ½" x 2⅜".	Banjo player, broad full face, sitting on long bench, playing banjo; wearing V-necked blouse, full trousers with narrow cuffs. Bucket at right of feet, pitcher at left. About ½" below, bar like that on obverse, about ½" x 2½".	Half-pint 24	Smooth	Plain lip; similar to No. 19 but narrower Tiny nipple at center; pontil mark	Amber Golden amber Olive-amber Aquamarine Olive-green Yellow-tone green	Attributed to the Maryland Glass Works of J. L. Chapman, Baltimore, Md.	V. R. GVI–75 Comparatively scarce

GXIII–1 GXIII–2 GXIII–3 GXIII–4 GXIII–5 GXIII–6 GXIII–7 GXIII–8

GROUP XIII—PICTORIAL FLASKS—Mainly ca. 1850–1880—Continued

OBVERSE	REVERSE	SIZE, FORM	EDGES	NECK, BASE	COLORS	GLASSHOUSE	NOTES, RARITY
GXIII–9. Similar to GXIII–8, figure larger and in higher relief, scarf wider. Bar narrower and less deep than GXIII–8 and 10.	Similar to GXIII–8, figure larger and in higher relief. Bar about 2¹¹/₁₆″ long. Flask wider. Bar inscribed "BALT. MD."	Half-pint 24, but shoulder more sloping	Smooth	Similar to No. 19, narrower Plain	Aquamarine	Same as above	Scarce
GXIII–10. Like GXIII–9. Flask slightly longer than GXIII–8 and 9.	Like GXIII–8 but bar inscribed "CHAPMAN".	Half-pint 24	Smooth	Plain lip Pontil mark	Aquamarine Olive-green	Chapman's Maryland Glass Works	Comparatively scarce
GXIII–11. Soldier facing front, standing on patch of ground; wearing spiked helmet, uniform with epaulets; with left hand holding rifle, with bayonet, at angle across body to right above shoulder; right extended above drum on ground. About ⅝″ below soldier, bevel-edged narrow rectangular bar (about ½″ x 2⅜″) inscribed "BALT. MD."	Ballet dancer, posed on patch of ground, holding tambourine (?) in hands about level with face, left foot turned sideways, right pointing downward; wearing ruffled ballet skirt, wide sash with forked ends flying out at back. About ⅝″ below dancer, bar like that on obverse but inscribed "CHAPMAN."	Pint 23	Smooth	Plain lip & No. 11 Short straight mold seams to larve oval depression, with and without pontil mark	Amber Aquamarine Green (deep) Yellow-green (pale)	Same as above	V. R. GVI-88 (covers GXIII–11, 12 & 13) Common
GXIII–12. Like GXIII–11. Bar placed slightly lower, slightly shorter.	Like GXIII–11. Bar, slightly shorter, placed slightly lower.	Pint 23	Smooth	No. 11 Type 18	Olive-amber Blue-green	Same as above	Common
GXIII–13. Like GXIII–12.	Like GXIII–12	Pint 23	Smooth	Nos. 11 & 12 Type 2, nipple at center of disk	Olive-amber Olive-green (medium & deep)	Same as above	Common
GXIII–14. Like GXIII–11, soldier's right hand smaller. Bar with "BALT. MD." about 2⁵/₁₆″ long.	Like GXIII–11. Bar without inscription, about ⁵/₁₆″ below dancer and about 2⁵/₁₆″ long.	Pint 23	Smooth	Plain lip On soldier side, wide deep groove parallel with straight mold seam Pontil mark	Aquamarine	Attributed to Chapman's Maryland Glass Works, Baltimore, Md.	V. R. GVI-87, obv. "bar inscribed BALTIMORE, MD." probably an error Common
GXIII–15. U.S. Army officer, wearing full-dress uniform of 1851–58 period; facing slightly left, standing at attention, long rifle, with bayonet, held vertically by left hand.	Large daisy with 11 slender double petals radiating from disk with large pearl at center.	Quart 38 (calabash)	4 wide vertical flutes	No. 15 8 scallops at base of neck Type 28, with and without black-oxide deposit from pontil	Amber, deep (C.V.) Aquamarine Green (light) Bluish green Emerald-green (light)	Unknown	V. R. GVI-89 Comparatively scarce
GXIII–16. U.S. Army dragoon in full-dress uniform of period 1851–58, mounted on high-stepping steed, riding right; blanket roll behind saddle; saber held erect in left hand with point near top of cap.	Large hound, walking right.	Quart Variant 29 (high-shouldered)	Smooth	Plain lip; angular collar; Nos. 10 & 11 With and without pontil mark	Amber Golden amber Red-amber Aquamarine Citron Green (light & medium) Emerald-green Olive-green (light)	Unknown	V. R. GVI-35 Comparatively scarce

GXIII–17. Horseman wearing cap, short tight coat with tail flying out at back, riding breeches; riding bareback. Horse with mane and tail flying, running right.

GXIII–18. Horseman wearing short tight coat with tail flying out at back, riding breeches and boots; leaning back off to left; leaning back and pulling reins to curb horse running right; mane and tail flying.

GXIII–19. Flora Temple: triangular cord with 2 tasseled ends, hanging from apex, supporting panel in relief, with beveled top and sides with taper to blend at bottom into body of flask. On panel, in low relief, inscription "FLORA TEMPLE" in shallow S-curve above racehorse standing on bar and facing left. Below panel: inscription "HARNESS TROT 2.19 3/4" above "Oct. 15. 1859." See 17. Form Groups.

GXIII–20. Design and inscriptions like GXIII–19. Flask slightly wider and thicker. No handle, but large oval bead on shoulder at point where end of handle was attached on GXIII–19.

GXIII–21. Flora Temple: like GXIII–19 but smaller scale and "Oct. 15. 1859" omitted.

Hound similar to GXIII–16 but tail raised at angle to body; walking right.	Pint 23	Smooth	Plain lip; narrow round collar, lower bevel (20a); No. 10 With and without pontil mark	Amber (shaded) Aquamarine Olive-green (light) Yellow-green Puce (light & dark)	Unknown	V. R. GVI–34; GVI–36 with handle. rare. See No. 4. Ill. 126 Comparatively scarce
Hound running right.	Half-pint 23	Smooth	Plain lip; narrow round collar, lower bevel (20a). Narrow outer rim; with and without pontil mark	Amber (dark) Aquamarine Yellow-green (pale) Olive-yellow Wine (deep)	Unknown	Rare Flasks, Group C. No. 20 Scarce
Plain	Quart 27	Smooth; handle attached at lower neck and shoulder	Nos. 10 & 20; wide flat collar with lower bevel Flat outer rim; flat rectangular center with cut corners	Amber (light to dark) Puce Wine (clear & murky)	Attributed to Whitney Glass Works, Glassboro, N.J.	V. R. GVI–16 Common
Plain	Quart 27 No handle	Smooth; large oval bead on right shoulder	Nos. 10 & 11 Same as GXIII–19	Reddish amber Green (deep) Yellow-green	Possibly Lancaster Glass Works, Lancaster, N.Y.	V. R. GXVI–16 Probably occurs with handle Common
Plain	Pint 27	Smooth; small handle	Narrow round collar, lower bevel (20a) Like GXIII–19, but mold seam nearer plain side	Red-amber (deep) Olive-green	Attributed to Whitney Glass Works, Glassboro, N.J.	V. R. GXVI–14 (?) Common

GXIII–12   GXIII–15   GXIII–16   GXIII–17   GXIII–18

GROUP XIII—PICTORIAL FLASKS—Mainly ca. 1850–1880—*Continued*

OBVERSE	REVERSE	SIZE, FORM	EDGES	NECK, BASE	COLORS	GLASSHOUSE	NOTES, RARITY
GXIII–22. Flora Temple: like GXIII–21.	Plain	Pint 27	Smooth; small handle	Nos. 10 & 12 Like GXIII–19, but center deep	Puce Wine	Same as above.	V. R. GXVI–24 (?) Common
GXIII–23. Flora Temple: like GXIII–21 but no handle, overlapping beads at points where upper and lower ends of handle would have been attached.	Plain	Pint 27, no handle	Smooth; beads at lower neck and shoulder	Nos. 10 & 12 Like GXIII–21	Green (deep) Bluish green Olive-green	Possibly Lancaster Glass Works, Lancaster, N.Y.	V. R. GXVI–15 Common
GXIII–24. Flora Temple: like GXIII–23. Flask slightly wider and thicker. Occurs with and without handle.	Plain	Pint 27	Like GXIII–23 & with handle	Nos. 10 & 12 Mold seam nearer plain side; no defined depression	Olive-amber (dark) Reddish amber	Attributed to Whitney Glass Works, Glassboro, N.J.	V. R. GXVI–14 (?) See No. 6 Ill. 126 Common
GXIII–25. Horse in high relief, slight modeling; braided (?) mane, long slightly arched full tail, left forefoot raised.	Inscription in large letters "GENTRY, SHOTE & Co" in semicircle, "NEW YORK" in straight line. ("Gentry, Shote & Co. grocers, 121 Front Street" was found in only one New York City Directory, that published May 1, 1858.)	Pint Globular, wide base, sloping shoulder; cylindrical neck	Smooth	No. 12 Type 28	Olive-amber Black (olive-green)	Unknown	V. R. GVI–28 Rare
GXIII–26. Dog's head and neck in profile. Above head, inscription (in arc, lower at left end than right) "GEO. W. ROBINSON."; below head "No 8 MAIN ST"; above "WHEELING, W.VA." in straight lines.	Plain	Pint 32	Broad, flat, slightly beveled at sides	No. 11 Smooth, slightly sunken	Aquamarine	Wheeling, W. Va., glasshouse at foot of McLure St., operated by Geo. W. Robinson	Robinson's business address 1867–69 was 8 Main St. (Virginia Ebeling, Ohio County Public Library) Rare
GXIII–26a. Like GXIII–26	Plain	Quart 32	Same as GXIII–26	No. 11 Type 24	Aquamarine	Same as above	See above
GXIII–27. Duck and inscriptions: "WILL YOU TAKE" in shallow arc above "A DRINK?", elongated conventional ornament, "WILL A" above large duck swimming left in water with reeds at each end, "SWIM?" below water.	Plain	Quart 32	Broad flat band	No. 11 Type 21	Aquamarine Yellow-green (light)	Attributed to the Lockport Glass Works, Lockport, N.Y.	Scarce
GXIII–28. Duck and inscriptions like GXIII–27 but smaller scale.	Plain	Pint 32	Broad flat band	No. 11 Type 22	Green (light)	Same as above	V. R. GVI–105 Scarce
GXIII–29. Duck and inscriptions similar to GXIII–28; duck with large eye with dot at center, breast feathered by dots. Letters of inscription smaller.	Plain	Pint 32	Broad flat band	No. 11; wide round collar below edge of lip, lower bevel Smooth, with dished oval center	Green (pale)	Unknown	Scarce Appears to be later than GXIII–27 & 28

Obverse	Reverse	Size	Edge	Base / Neck	Color	Glassworks	Rarity
GXIII–29a. Like GXIII–29 but smaller scale.	Plain	Half-pint 32	Broad flat band	No. 14 Smooth with small deep circular center	Strong aquamarine	Unknown	Reported by George Austin Extremely rare
GXIII–30. Like GXIII–27 but smaller scale.	Plain	Half-pint 32	Broad flat band	No. 11 & angular ring Type 24	Aquamarine Green (light) Yellow-green (pale)	Attributed to Lockport Glass Works, Lockport, N.Y.	Rare flasks, Group C, No. 19 Very rare
GXIII–31. Sheaf of grain: tall; 9 stalks (ribs) below binding, 11 spreading out above and with long broad spikelets; binding with fancy bow (3 ovals) at each side of sheaf. Below grain, large oval frame (narrow molding) about 1⅜" x 2¼".	Plain	Pint 28	Smooth	No. 11 Type 2	Aquamarine	Unknown	Rare flasks, Group C, No. 12 Rare
GXIII–32. Sheaf of grain: tall slender; 9 stalks below binding and curved outward. 12 fanning out above and with long spikelets; ends of binding looped in front.	Like obverse but 10 stalks above binding.	Pint 30	Smooth	No. 11 Type 1	Aquamarine	Unknown	Rare flasks, Group C, No. 11 Comparatively scarce
GXIII–33. Sheaf of grain: tall; very fine stalks, curving at top to right and left of central part; binding above middle, end hanging to right.	Plain	Pint 29	Smooth	No. 18 Long oval depression inscribed "TIBBY BROS PITTS PA"	Colorless	Tibby Bros. Pittsburgh or Sharpsburgh, Pa., works	Rare
GXIII–33a. Like GXIII–33.	Plain	Half-pint 29	Smooth	Same as above	Colorless	Same as above	Rare
GXIII–34. Sheaf of grain: large; fine stalks, curving outward below binding and in deep umbrellalike formation above; end of binding to right. Rake and pitchfork crossed behind sheaf; 2-tined fork from right to left; rake with 1 tooth at left and 3 at right, from left to right.	Inscribed "MECHANIC GLASS WORKS" (in arc) "PHILADA" (in straight line).	Quart Variant 28 (high shouldered)	Smooth	Plain lip Type 27 Pontil mark	Aquamarine Blue (light)	As inscribed	V. R. GVI–57. Rare flasks, Group C, No. 13 Scarce

GXIII–26 GXIII–27 GXIII–31 GXIII–32 GXIII–33 GXIII–34

GXIII–34

661

GROUP XIII—PICTORIAL FLASKS—Mainly ca. 1850–1880—*Continued*

OBVERSE	REVERSE	SIZE, FORM	EDGES	NECK, BASE	COLORS	GLASSHOUSE	NOTES, RARITY
GXIII–35. Sheaf of grain: tall; fine stalks, bound above middle; curving to left and right of center part at top. Rake and pitchfork crossed behind sheaf; small 2-tined fork, right to left; rake, left to right.	Inscribed "WESTFORD GLASS CO" in deep arcs "WESTFORD" above "CONN" in straight line.	Pint 22	Smooth	Plain lip & No. 20a Plain	Red-amber (deep) Olive-green (deep)	As inscribed	Common
GXIII–36. Similar to GXIII–35; sheaf a little wider at top; tines of fork long and more curved. Five-pointed star centered between handles of rake and fork, about 1/4" below sheaf.	Like GXIII–35, letters slightly smaller.	Pint 22	Smooth	No. 20 Plain	Olive-green	As inscribed	Comparatively scarce
GXIII–37 Like GXIII–35 but smaller scale.	Like GXIII–35 but smaller scale.	Half-pint 22	Smooth	Plain lip & No. 20 Plain	Amber Olive-amber Olive-green	As inscribed	Common
GXIII–38. Sheaf of grain: large, shorter, and wider in proportion than foregoing; coarse stalks, tied at middle; flaring at bottom; at top, curving to right and left of center part, above binding. Rake and pitchfork crossed behind sheaf, 3-tined fork from right to left, 4-toothed rake from left to right, heavier than on foregoing.	Star, 5-pointed, large and in high relief.	Quart Variant 28 (high shouldered)	Smooth	No. 19 & narrow round collar just below lip and with lower bevel Plain	Amber (C.V.) Grayish blue Emerald-green (deep)	Unknown	V. R. Sheaf & star GVI–76, qt., pt., & 1/2-pt. No distinction between designs and no form given Scarce
GXIII–39. Sheaf of grain: tall, slender; medium stalks, tied above middle, spreading slightly at bottom. Rake and pitchfork similar to GXIII–38, but fork 2-tined and handles touching center bottom of sheaf.	Star similar to GXIII–38 but smaller.	Pint 23	Smooth	No. 19; plain lip; narrow round collar just below lip and with lower bevel With and without pontil mark	Amber Aquamarine Emerald-green Yellow-green	Unknown; possibly Bulltown, N.J.	Scarce
GXIII–40. Sheaf of grain: short, broad; medium stalks spreading at bottom and curving to right and left of long center part at top. Large heavy rake and pitchfork; handles crossing at center bottom of sheaf and passing behind sheaf at wide angle; fork with 2 long tines, from right to left; rake with 1 tooth at left and 2 at right, from left to right.	Star similar to GXIII–38 but smaller.	Half-pint 24	Smooth	Plain lip; narrow round collar, lower bevel (20a) Plain, smooth	Amber Olive-amber Aquamarine Green Emerald-green	Attributed to Bulltown, N.J.	Fragments excavated on factory site by J. E. Pfeiffer Scarce
GXIII–41. Sheaf of grain: tall, slender; fine stalks, tied above middle, flaring at bottom, curving at top to right and left of "V" center. Rake and pitchfork crossing behind sheaf, handles touching at bottom of sheaf; 5-toothed rake from right to left; small 2-tined fork from left to right. Top of sheaf within ogival formed by 2 laurel branches curving down from small ring.	Inscribed "SHEETS & DUFFY" in semicircle above 8-petal ornament.	Quart 41 (calabash, no handle)	4 wide vertical flutes	No. 15 Scallops at base of neck Type 29	Aquamarine Blue (light)	Sheets & Duffy, Upper Yard, Dyottville, Kensington, Philadelphia, Pa.	V. R. GVI–84 Scarce
GXIII–42. Like GXIII–41 but fractional variations in size of motifs.	Ornament like GXIII–41, no inscription	Quart 41 (calabash, no handle)	Same as above	No. 15 Scallops at base of neck Type 29	Aquamarine Yellow-green (light)	Attributed to Sheets & Duffy. See above	V. R. GVI–85 Common

Design / Band	Ribs / Handle	Size	Neck / Lip	Color	Attribution	Rarity	Reference
Faint semicircular band, about ½" wide, with 7 wide-spaced faint small disks, above ornament like GXIII–41.	Same as above	Quart 41 (calabash, no handle)	Similar to No. 14, no lower bevel Scallops at base of neck Type 28	Aquamarine (pale)	Unknown	Common	
8-pointed star.	6 broad vertical ribs, center tending to blend at mold seam.	Quart 41 (calabash, no handle)	Nos. 11 & 20 Type 28	Ambers (medium & dark) Brown-amber Green	Attributed to Sheets & Duffy by Van Rensselaer	Common	V. R. GVI–86
Like GXIII–44	Same as above Handle: Semi-ear-shaped, crimped end; loop with top thumbpiece	Quart 41	No. 11 Type 28, with and without pontil mark; with and without black-oxide deposit from pontil.	Amber Brown-amber	Same as above	Common	V. R. GVI–86
Large tree in foliage, smooth trunk, triangular base.	4 wide vertical flutes	Quart 41 (calabash, no handle)	Double round collar, narrow bottom edge 8 scallops at base of neck Type 30	Aquamarine Sapphire-blue Wine (dark)	Attributed to Sheets & Duffy by Van Rensselaer	Common	V. R. GVI–116
Similar to GXIII–46, bark of tree indicated, small triangle of roots. Bird at top. to right.	Same as above	Quart 38 (calabash)	Double round collar: upper either wide or narrow, lower very narrow Type 29	Aquamarine Green (deep)	Unknown	Common	V. R. GVI–117

GXIII–35 GXIII–38 GXIII–39 GXIII–40

GXIII–41 GXIII–46 GXIII–47

GXIII–44 STAR ON REV.

GXIII–43. Similar to GXIII–41

GXIII–44. Sheaf of grain: high relief; tall; medium stalks, tied above center, deep umbrellalike formation above binding. Rake and pitchfork crossing behind sheaf; 2-tined fork from right to left; rake, left to right.

GXIII–45. Like GXIII–44 (No. 41 Form Groups)

GXIII–46. Sheaf of grain: large, tall; fine stalks, tied with wide binding above center; curving right and left at top with short center part. Rake and pitchfork with ends of handles crossing below center of sheaf, passing behind ends of sheaf; small 2-tined fork from left to right; rake with long bar and small teeth, from right to left.

GXIII—47. Sheaf of grain: tall, slender; fine stalks, tied high above middle; spreading at bottom, curving to right and left at top with deep V-part. Long rake and fork crossing behind sheaf; 2-tined fork from right to left; rake with long bar and small teeth, from left to right; tines and bar nearer top ends of sheaf than on foregoing, except GXIII–40.

GROUP XIII—PICTORIAL FLASKS—Mainly ca. 1850–1880—Continued

OBVERSE	REVERSE	SIZE, FORM	EDGES	NECK, BASE	COLORS	GLASSHOUSE	NOTES, RARITY
GXIII–48. Anchor and fork-ended pennants: upper pennant flying right above and from ring at top of large anchor (diagonally to right); cable attached to bottom left of ring, running in serpentine curve from left to right behind stock. shank and arm of anchor to lower pennant flying in shallow S-curve to left. On upper pennant "BALTIMORE" and small scroll; on lower, "GLASS WORKS" and small scroll.	Sheaf of grain: tall, slender, fine stalks, tied above middle, slightly spread at bottom, in long curves to right and left at top with center part. Rake and pitchfork crossed behind stock. shank and pitchfork flying in shallow sheaf, long handles below; narrow 2-tined fork, from right to left; rake with 1 long tooth left of handle and 3 right, from left to right.	Quart Variant 29 (high-shouldered)	Smooth	Plain lip; flat collar; round collar, lower bevel (20a) With and without pontil mark	Amber Golden amber (shaded) Aquamarine Peacock-blue Emerald-green Wine (deep)	As inscribed	V. R. shows qt. Plate 57 Comparatively scarce
GXIII–48a. Similar to GXIII–48	Similar to GXIII–48	Pint ?	Smooth	? ?	?	As inscribed	V. R. GVI-9. We have never seen this flask
GXIII–49. Anchor and Pennants similar to GXIII–48; no small scroll on either pennant; top pennant flatter. "GLASS WORKS" fills bottom pennant.	Sheaf of grain: short, coarse stalks tied at center with wide binding, top in umbrellalike formation. Short rake and fork crossing behind sheaf; 2-tined fork. right to left; rake, with 1 tooth at left and 3 at right of handle, from left to right.	Half-pint 24	Smooth	Similar to No. 10 Round collar, lower bevel (20a) Type 1, small disk	Amber (light) Olive-amber	As inscribed	V. R. GVI-8 Scarce
GXIII–50. Similar to GXIII–49; top pennant slightly more curved; flukes of anchor a little smaller.	Similar to GXIII–49; binding narrower and longer.	Half-pint 24	Smooth	Plain lip; narrow flat collar Tiny nipple at center of mold seam; pontil mark	Aquamarine	As inscribed	V. R. GVI-8, qt. Plate 57 Scarce
GXIII–51. Similar to GXIII–49; top pennant slightly more curved.	Similar to GXIII–49; sheaf a little more slender and taller; binding narrower and end longer; 2 teeth at left end of rake.	Half-pint 24	Smooth	Plain lip "Ringed mouth" (V.R.) Pontil mark	Aquamarine Olive-amber (light)	As inscribed	V. R. GVI-8, qt. Scarce
GXIII–52. Similar to GXIII–48; pennants wider and anchor smaller.	Sheaf of grain: tall, slender; fine stalks, tied above middle; wide umbrellalike formation at top. Small 2-tined fork and rake crossing behind sheaf; handles at ends of sheaf.	Quart 41 (calabash, no handle)	4 wide vertical flutes	Round collar, lower bevel (20a) Type 28	Aquamarine Blue (medium) Cornflower-blue	As inscribed	Scarce
GXIII–53. Similar to GXIII–48; pennants shorter and more deeply curved. end of lower curved down instead of up, no small scroll ornament at ends of inscriptions—"BALTIMORE" and "GLASS WORKS"; curves of cable less deep.	Phoenix rising from flames: crested head to right, beak open and tongue sticking out, breast broad (graduated ribs), feathered wings spread and raised parallel with head; radiating flames bordering wings and in arc, above head, between wing tips. Below Phoenix long rectangular panel inscribed "RESURGAM" (I will arise again).	Pint 23	Smooth	Plain lip; narrow flat collar With and without pontil mark	Amber Brown-amber Aquamarine Olive-green Yellow-green (deep)	As inscribed	V. R. GVI-11 (?) Common

GXIII–54. Similar to GXIII–53; anchor more slender, stock narrower.

GXIII–55. Similar to GXIII–48; wider pennants, no scrolls; upper inscribed "ISABELLA"; lower, "GLASSWORKS". Anchor longer and lighter; end curved; arms short; flukes, large.

GXIII–56. Like GXIII–55.

GXIII–57. Similar to GXIII–48 but heavier design; flukes of anchor pear-shaped and solid.

No.	Reverse description	Size	Base	Lip / Collar	Color	Made at / Inscribed	Reference
	Similar to GXIII–53, pennants wider, anchor more slender, stock narrower. Flames of same length, in arc. Below Phoenix, rectangular frame (very narrow molding) inscribed "RESURGAM".	Pint 23	Smooth	Round collar, lower bevel (20a); flat ring below narrow angular collar Type 4 but no nipple at center	Amber Golden amber Yellow-green	As inscribed	V. R. GVI–11 (?) Common
	Glasshouse: three-quarter view; gabled roof; at center of roof, furnace chimney from which smoke issues; small chimney at each of the 3 corners; in front, 2 small 4-paned windows above wide door flanked by 2 large 4-paned windows; along left side, narrow section with sloping roof, front half enclosed and with single-paned window on front and side and with chimney at corner, rear half (open?) with 2 arches. Tree at left rear.	Quart Variant 29	Smooth	Plain lip Small nipple at center of mold seam; with and without pontil mark	Aquamarine Yellow-green (pale)	Isabella Glass Works (as inscribed), New Brooklyn, N.J.	V. R. GVI–49 Scarce
	Sheaf of grain: large; fine stalks tied at middle, spreading at bottom, in deep curves to right and left at top with deep center part. Small rake and 3-tined fork with long handles passing behind sheaf close to ends and touching at center bottom; fork from right to left, rake from left to right.	Pint 24	Smooth	Plain lip Double round collar Same as GXIII–55	Aquamarine Green	Same as above	V. R. GVI–50 Rare
	Glasshouse in higher relief than GXIII–55; long and short roof with large furnace chimney at center, small chimney at right end, 4 on long side (2 about halfway down at front and rear, 1 at left corner, 1 in from right corner); in front, shutter and 2 windows below gable, tall narrow door between large windows with shutters thrown back and small 4-paned window and shutter near left end; on side, tall narrow door between 4-paned windows and shutters.	Half-pint 24	Smooth	Plain lip Same as GXIII–55	Aquamarine Green (deep)	Same as above	V. R. GVI–48 Rare

GXIII–48   GXIII–49   GXIII–52   GXIII–53   GXIII–54   GXIII–55   GXIII–56   GXIII–57

GROUP XIII—PICTORIAL FLASKS—Mainly ca. 1850–1880—Continued

OBVERSE	REVERSE	SIZE, FORM	EDGES	NECK, BASE	COLORS	GLASSHOUSE	NOTES, RARITY
GXIII–58. Similar to GXIII–48. Pennants in deeper curves, no small scroll ornaments; upper inscribed "SPRING GARDEN"; lower, "GLASSWORKS".	Log cabin: three-quarter view, facing right; door at right front, small 4-pane window at left; on end, similar windows in gable directly below a short chimney from which smoke issues; at other end of roof, short pole with 2 cross-arms (looks like a TV antenna). At right of cabin, tall leafless tree with bird perched on short branch at right; at left end of cabin, short tree. Between trees and in front of cabin, short irregular ribs forming semicircle of ground.	Pint 23	Smooth	No. 11; narrow flat collar; round collar, lower bevel (20a) Type 1	Aquamarine Blue (deep, cold) Olive-green (light) Yellow-green (light) Wine Olive-amber Olive-yellow	Spring Garden Glass Works (as inscribed), Baltimore, Md.	V. R. GVI–101 (?) Common
GXIII–59. Like GXIII–58 but anchor a little lighter and with short bar just below ring.	Like GXIII–58 but cabin fractionally smaller and ground pebbly instead of short ribs.	Pint 23	Smooth	Plain lip Similar to Type 1 but mold seam continues, and small nipple at center	Aquamarine	Same as above	V. R. GVI–101 (?) Common
GXIII–60. Like GXIII–58. Below lower pennant, narrow rectangular panel, rather high relief, about 2¼" long.	Similar to GXIII–58; roof of wide boards, narrow logs and tiny window in gable, wide below and, on front, door frame and no knob. No smoke from chimney. Tall leafless tree at right. Pebbly ground between cabin and narrow panel like that on obverse.	Half-pint 24	Smooth	Plain lip & No. 16 Small nipple at center of mold seam; with and without pontil mark	Amber (shaded) Aquamarine	Same as above	V. R. GVI–101 (?) Common
GXIII–61. Like GXIII–60.	Like GXIII–60	Half-pint 24	Smooth	Round collar, lower bevel (20a) Type 1	Amber (shaded) Olive-green (light)	Same as above	Common
GXIII–62. Similar to GXIII–48; no small scroll on pennants; cable from right to left instead of left to right; upper pennant inscribed "RICHMOND"; lower, "GLASSWORKS".	Glasshouse: low hip roof, tall furnace-chimney in center, 4 short chimneys (2 at back; 1 at each front corner), smoke issuing from chimneys; 2 small single-pane "dormer" windows; high arch-top 4-panel door, large 4-paned window at left of door and one at far right; line at right of dormer possibly to indicate division in glasshouse and lehr at right side. Below glasshouse at left, barrel on its side; at far right, barrel on end.	Pint 23	Smooth	Plain Small nipple at center of mold seam	Green (light)	Richmond Glass Works, Richmond, Va.	V. R. GVI–4 Rare Flasks, Group C, No. 3 Extremely rare
GXIII–63. Large heavy anchor on slight diagonal; cable running in long deep S-curve from large ring at top, to right behind thick stock and shank, extending in curve beyond short arms with large flukes. (Similar to GXIII–66.)	Plain	Quart Variant 32, taller in proportion to width, sides nearer vertical	Wide flat band	Round collar, lower bevel (20a) Type 22	Aquamarine (pale)	Unknown	The anchor flasks GXIII–63 through GXIII–74 attributed to last quarter of the 19th century

No. / Design	Edges	Size	Bands	Neck / Collar	Color	Locality	Rarity
GXIII–64. Similar to GXIII–63 but cable and anchor thin.	Plain	Quart Like above	Wide flat band	Narrow round collar, narrow ring Type 22	Golden amber	Unknown	Common
GXIII–65. Similar to GXIII–63	Plain	Pint Like above	Wide flat band	Round collar, lower bevel (20a) Type 22 (?)	Aquamarine	Unknown	V. R. GVI– (We have not seen this flask.) Common
GXIII–66. Large heavy anchor across side; cable, top end curving from left through large ring, running in long deep S-curve behind thick stock and heavy shank, short end curved parallel to bottom with short arms and large flukes.	Plain	Half-pint Like above	Wide flat band	Round collar, lower bevel (20a) Type 22	Aquamarine (pale)	Unknown	Common
GXIII–67. Similar to GXIII–66 but cable ending above right arm.	Plain	Half-pint Like above	Wide flat band	Round collar, lower bevel (20a) Type 21, letter "S" in disk	Amber (shaded)	Unknown	Common
GXIII–68. Linear anchor across side; slender cable running from top right, in S-curve behind slender stock and shank, extending in slight curve beyond center of thin arms.	Plain	Half-pint Like above	Wide flat band	Round collar, lower bevel (20a) Smooth with shallow disk	Amber (shaded)	Unknown	V. R. GVI–6 (We have not seen this flask.) Common
GXIII–69. "Anchor in depressed circular panel; flukes to left." V. R. GVI–6.	Plain	Half-pint ?	?	Collared mouth (V. R.) Type?; inscribed "AGCo"	Amber	Unknown	V. R. GVI–6 (We have not seen this flask.) Common
GXIII–70. Large anchor across side; cable from left through large ring, running in S-curve (lower triangular) behind heavy stock (tapered at ends) and slender shank, long forked end extending beyond small arm, small flukes with long spikelike ends.	Tall narrow arch-top panel	Pint (?)	Wide flat band	Narrow round collar, narrow ring Type?	?	Unknown	We have not seen this flask. Taken from H.H. White's photograph A6V7 Common
GXIII–71. Large anchor tilted slightly to right; chain from right of large ring, running in S-curve, behind end of heavy stock (tapered at ends) and shank, close to left side of shank, 3 links extending beyond right arm; large arrowhead flukes.	Plain	Half-pint Variant 32 taller in proportion to width; sides nearer vertical	Wide flat band	Narrow round collar, slight lower bevel Slender oblong depression	Colorless	Unknown	Comparatively scarce

GXIII–58 GXIII–60 GXIII–62 GXIII–64 GXIII–66

GROUP XIII—PICTORIAL FLASKS—Mainly ca. 1850–1880—*Continued*

OBVERSE	REVERSE	SIZE, FORM	EDGES	NECK, BASE	COLORS	GLASSHOUSE	NOTES, RARITY
GXIII–72. Large anchor on arched panel, tilted slightly to left and placed high on side of flask, formed by fine outlining rib; cable from right of 3 rings, running behind heavy stock (rounded ends with bars) and wide shank to left, then across shank to beginning of right arm; short arms with large flukes.	Plain	Pint Shoo-fly (see line drawing GXIII–75)	Wide bevel each side to mold seam	Narrow round collar, lower bevel (20a) Smooth, with "2" in relief	Aquamarine	Unknown	Comparatively scarce
GXIII–73. Anchor medallion: Large anchor, tilted to left; cable from left of large oblong ring, across heavy stock, behind tapering shaft near stock, then across stock above short arms with large flukes.	Plain	Quart 23	Smooth	Narrow round collar, lower bevel (20a) Smooth, large concave disk inscribed "A.G.Co."	Golden amber	Unidentified	Comparatively scarce
GXIII–74. Small circular panel with small upright anchor with oval ring, short heavy stock, slender straight shaft to point below long arms with small arrowhead flukes.	Inscription: "REGISTERED" above dot between 2 long dashes and "FULL QUART."	Quart Variant 32, taller in proportion to width; sides nearer vertical	Wide flat band	Narrow round collar, lower bevel (20a) Inscribed in 3 lines: "MADE BY/E PACKHAM & Co/BALTIMORE MD."	Golden amber	As inscribed on base	Comparatively scarce
GXIII–75. Key, large, at center, parallel with sides.	Plain	Pint Shoo-fly (see drawing of obv.)	Wide bevel each side to mold seam	Narrow round collar, lower bevel, ring below Similar to Type 1; small nipple at center	Aquamarine	Unknown	V. R. GVI–53 Common
GXIII–76. The Oak: slightly sunken circular medallion with spreading leafless tree; at lower side, left of trunk, "THE" in large letters and at right, "OAK".	Plain	Pint Variant 32, taller in proportion to width; sides nearer vertical	Wide flat band	Double round collar Smooth with disk at center inscribed "F"	Amber (light, shaded)	Unknown	Scarce
GXIII–76a. The Oak like GXIII–76	Plain	Quart Like above	Wide flat band	Both neck and base like GXIII–75	Brilliant amber	Unknown	Reported by George Austin Extremely rare
GXIII–77. Bunch of Grapes: slightly sunken oval medallion with large grape leaves at top flanking slender stem of large bunch of grapes, 2 tendrils curling away from left lower side of grapes and 1 from right.	Plain	Pint Like above	Wide flat band	Threaded for cap Type 21	Amber (olive tone) Amber, medium	Unknown	V. R. GVI–29 Comparatively scarce

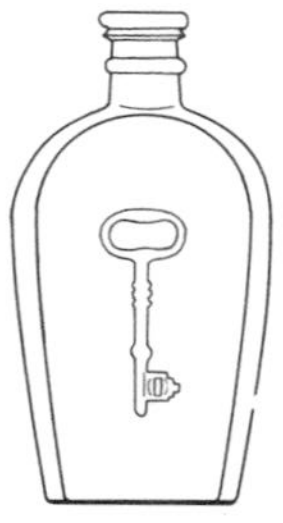

GXIII–75

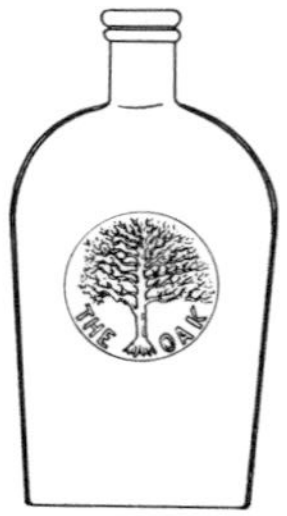

GXIII–76

Description	Reverse	Size/Type	Base	Neck/Collar	Color	Maker	Rarity
GXIII–78. Similar to GXIII–77 but 2 tendrils at right, 1 at left.	Plain	Half-pint Like above	Wide flat band	Threaded for cap Type 21	Amber	Unknown	Comparatively scarce
GXIII–79. Safe: slightly sunken circular medallion with safe (linear) in three-quarter view, tall, rectangular; 3 circular feet with dot at center, scrolls above and below dial and handle on front.	Plain	Pint Like above	Wide flat band	Round collar, lower bevel (20a) Type 21	Aquamarine (pale)	Unknown	V. R. GVI–74 (?) Comparatively scarce
GXIII–80. Like GXIII–79	Plain	Half-pint Like above	Wide flat band	Round collar, lower bevel (20a) Type 21	Aquamarine (pale)	Unknown	Comparatively scarce
GXIII–81. Wreath: ovoid; pinnate leaves crossing at top; stems crossing at bottom.	Plain	Pint Shoofly (see line drawing GXIII–75)	Wide flat band	Threaded for cap Type 1	Amber (olive tone)	Unknown	Comparatively scarce
GXIII–82. Star: 5-pointed, in outline by fine ribs.	Plain	Half-pint Type 23	Smooth	Threaded for cap Short straight seams to flat ring around disk	Amber	Unknown	Comparatively scarce
GXIII–82a. "Skeletal Star," like GXIII–82	Plain	Half-pint Probably 23 (?)	Smooth	"RM" (ringed mouth) ?	Amber	Unknown	V. R. GVI–104 (We have not seen this flask.) Comparatively scarce
GXIII–82b. "Skeletal Star," similar to GXIII–82	Plain	Half-pint Flat circular with oval base	Smooth	"CM" (collared mouth) ?	Colorless	Unknown	V. R. GVI–102 (We have not seen this flask.) Comparatively scarce
GXIII–82c. Star	Plain	Half-pint Probably 23 (?)	Smooth	"RM" (ringed mouth) ?	Amber	Attributed to Stoddard by Van Rensselaer	V. R. GVI–103, pint-size also (We have not seen these flasks.) Comparatively scarce
GXIII–83. Star: 5-pointed, flat, low relief.	Inscription, in poorly drawn letters: "RAVENNA" in arc above "GLASS" (large letters) above "WORKS" (widely spaced letters) in straight lines.	Pint 23	Smooth	No. 12 Pontil mark	Amber (shaded)	Ravenna Glass Works, Ravenna, Ohio	Comparatively scarce

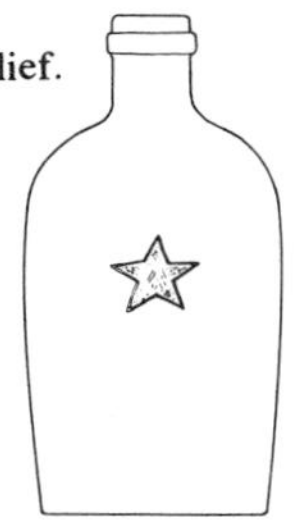

GXIII–83

GXIII–83

OBVERSE	REVERSE	SIZE, FORM	EDGES	NECK, BASE	COLORS	GLASSHOUSE	NOTES, RARITY
GXIII–84. Laurel wreath with open top, stems crossing at bottom, 20 leaves on each branch. Within wreath: liquor cask lying on its side, at left; 6 staves between 2 hoops and 3 at end; in middle 7 staves, bung at center; at right, 7 staves between 2 hoops and 3 at end.	Plain	Pint Broad, thin flattened body, sides curving at shoulder and bottom, ovoid base (See GI–128)	Smooth	Angular collar, lower bevel Smooth	Aquamarine Yellow-green	Unknown	V. R. GVI–12 says "probably Chapman" but form suggests 1880s–1890s Comparatively scarce
GXIII–85. Clock dial, 3¼" in diameter; linear Roman numerals; hands pointing about 10 of 5. Lattice of fine ribs between face and edge.	Sunburst of fine rays from smooth center. Lattice as on obverse.	Pint Like GXIII–84	Wide beveled rib	Angular collar, lower bevel Smooth	Colorless	Unknown	Probably 1880s–1890s Comparatively scarce
GXIII–86. Clock dial, 2⁵⁄₁₆" in diameter; linear Roman numerals; hands pointing to 12 minutes after 7; inscription, from X to II. "REGULATOR".	Plain	Half-pint Like GXIII–84	Smooth	Double round collar Smooth	Colorless	Unknown	Probably 1880s–1890s Comparatively scarce
GXIII–87. Clock dial, 4¼" in diameter; large Roman numerals; hands pointing to 11 o'clock; inscribed "BININGER'S" above numerals at top from end of X to beginning of II, "REGULATOR" at bottom from V of VIII to V of IV; at left, outside dial, "19 BROAD STᵀ"; at right "NEW YORK."	Plain	Pint Circular with oblong base	Smooth, curved	Double round collar Smooth	Golden amber	Unknown	V. R. GX–22 Address of firm 1861–63 Comparatively scarce
GXIII–88. Merry Christmas. Rectangular panel: girl wearing hat, sleeveless gown with tight bodice and three-quarter length skirt, half sitting on wine barrel, left hand on outer edge of barrel, right raised high and holding a wineglass. At top, inscribed in script, on diagonal line, "Merry Christmas"; at bottom, in block letters, "AND A" in straight line, "HAPPY NEW YEAR" in diagonal line.	Like GI–123. Crowing cock facing left on barrel staves between triad of hoops, single hoop about ½" below shoulder and above base.	Pint Elliptical with flattened side on obverse	Continuation of staves and hoops	Round collar, lower bevel (20a) Smooth with concave disk at center	Colorless (green tint in base)	Unknown	Probably 1890s Scarce
GXIII–89. Man: stocky figure; wearing shirt or short jacket, full trousers; walking left, right forearm held out below waistline, bottle in hand. Inscribed "ROUGH" (lengthwise, close to right hand), "&" (above head), "READY" (lengthwise and in line with back of head and body), "H.EASLEY'S" (below feet).	Inscribed "EASLEY'S" above hand pointing down to "SALOON" above "HUNTSVILLE".	Quart At ends long curve from neck down about ⅔ of body (greatest width 5½"), then nearly vertical to base (3¾" wide)	Smooth	No. 11 Mold seam to large deep oblong depression	Aquamarine	Unknown	Coll. Doy McCall Made for Hugh Easley, saloon keeper in Huntsville some time before the Civil War. (Information from Mr. McCall.) Only example recorded

GROUP XIV—TRAVELER'S COMPANION
Smooth edges with vertical mold seam

	OBVERSE	REVERSE		SIZE, FORM	NECK, BASE	COLORS	GLASSHOUSE	NOTES, RARITY
GXIII–90.	"C.C. GOODALE" in shallow arc above poorly drawn deer in low relief. "ROCHESTER" in reverse arc below deer.	Plain	Smooth	Half-pint 22	Similar to No. 15, formed in the mold Type 2	Amber	Possibly Rochester Glass Works, Rochester, N.Y. for C. C. Goodale of Rochester, N.Y.	Reported by George Austin Private mold Rare
GXIII–91a.	On lower part of waffled body, figure of a cow; small circular depression on upper body.	On lower part of waffled body, large sheaf of grain, crossed pitchfork and rake.	Smooth	Quarter-pint Ovoid	Plain lip Pontil mark	Aquamarine Olive-green Yellow-green Blue (shade?)	Unknown	Reported by George Austin. V. R. No. 22, GVI, listed as half-pint, yellow-green Extremely rare: 4 known in olive-green, 3 obtained in N.H.
GXIV–1.	"TRAVELER'S" inscribed in arc above, and "COMPANION" in reverse arc below; star ornament formed by circle of 8 small triangles around plain center about 11/16″ in diameter. Note squared "C" and "O", "N" with short bar at top left and leg of "R" with "knee."	Sheaf of grain: tall; lightly indicated stalks, tied at center, flaring at bottom; above binding flaring right and left of center V-part at top. Rake and pitchfork crossed behind sheaf; large 3-tined fork from right to left; rake with 4 teeth, from left to right.		Quart Similar to 22, body oblong in cross section	No. 16 Type 19	Brown-amber Reddish amber Olive-amber	Attributed by Van Rensselaer to Waterford Glass Works, N.J.; by Charles B. Gardner believed to be Westford Glass Works, Conn.	V. R. GVI–107 Common
GXIV–2.	Similar to GXIV–1 but letters, except "S", larger and all of same type. "A" in "COMPANION" has no crossbar. Eight-pointed star same type but with center about 9/16″ in diameter.	Star like obverse; inscription: "RAVENNA" above star and "GLASS CO" below.		Quart Similar to 23, body narrow oblong in cross section	No. 11 With and without black-oxide deposit from pontil	Aquamarine Brown Yellow-green (deep)	Ravenna Glass Works, Ravenna, Ohio	Comparatively scarce

GXIV–1 GXIV–1 GXIII–89 GXIII–89

TRAVELER'S COMPANION

EASLEY'S SALOON HUNTSVILLE

HEALSLEY'S ROUGH & READY

GROUP XIV—TRAVELER'S COMPANION—*Continued*

Smooth edges with vertical mold seam

OBVERSE	REVERSE	SIZE, FORM	NECK, BASE	COLORS	GLASSHOUSE	NOTES, RARITY
GXIV–3. Inscription like GXIV–2; points of star longer and more slender, center smaller	Star like obverse; inscription like GXIV–2. (See 24 Form Groups)	Pint 24	No. 17; round collar, lower bevel (20a); angular collar, lower bevel Type 1	Amber Aquamarine Yellow-green (deep)	Same as above	Comparatively scarce
GXIV–4. "TRAVELER'S" inscribed in shallow arc above, and "COMPANION" in reverse arc below. Eight-pointed star ornament formed by petallike points around center about ⅜" in diameter.	Star like obverse: above star, in shallow arc, "LANCASTER"; below, in shallow reverse arc, "ERIE. CO., N.Y."	Pint 24, but taller in proportion to width (height 7⅜")	Double round collar, just below lip Plain	Amber (?) Aquamarine	Lancaster Glass Works, Lancaster, N.Y.	V. R. GVI–109, amber, either GXIV–4 or 5 Scarce
GXIV–5. Like GXIV–4	Like GXIV–4	Pint 24 (height 6¾")	No. 11; round collar, lower bevel (20a); just below lip, round collar, lower bevel Plain	Amber (?) Aquamarine Blue-green Olive-yellow Wine	Same as above	See above Rare flasks, Group C, No. 2 Scarce Wine color reported by C. Vuono
GXIV–6. "TRAVELER'S" inscribed in shallow arc above, and "COMPANION" in reverse arc below, a large stylized duck with neck curved to left and head to left above shoulder of small wing.	Eight-petal starlike flower with large bead at center. Inscription: above flower, "LOCKPORT" in shallow arc and, below, "GLASS" above "WORKS", in straight lines.	Pint 24	Round collar, round collar, lower bevel—both just below lip Smooth, slight disk at center, with and without pontil mark	Aquamarine Blue-green Yellow-green	Lockport Glass Works, Lockport, N.Y.	V. R. GVI–110 Rare flask, Group C, No. 1 Scarce
GXIV–7. Inscription like GXIV–6	8-pointed star	Half-pint 24	Plain lip Plain, with and without black-oxide deposit from pontil	Amber Aquamarine Olive-yellow Yellow-amber (G.A.)	Unknown	V. R. GVI–108 (?) Scarce
GXIV–8. Similar to GXIV–7 but inscription in deep arcs, smaller letters and "S" same size as others.	Plain	Half-pint 24	Plain lip; angular collar above round Flat outer rim; with and without pontil mark	Aquamarine (pale) Green (light)	Unknown	Rare flasks, Group C, No. 18 Rare
GXIV–9. Inscription: "TRAVELER'S" in large letters and in semicircle; "COMPANION" in slightly smaller letters and in straight line.	Inscription: "RAILROAD" in arc and in large letters; "GUIDE" in smaller letters and in straight line.	Half-pint 24	Plain lip Plain, with and without pontil mark	Aquamarine (pale) Yellow-green (pale)	Unknown	V. R. GVI–106 Rare flasks, Group C, No. 17 Rare

GROUP XV—LETTERED—Mainly Glassworks

OBVERSE	REVERSE	SIZE, FORM	EDGES	NECK, BASE	COLORS	GLASSHOUSE	NOTES, RARITY
GXV–1. Inscription: "CLYDE GLASS WORKS" in semicircle above "N.Y.", in large letters.	Plain	Quart 22	Smooth	No. 17 Type 1	Amber Aquamarine Colorless Green	As inscribed. Attributed to the bottle factory established by Southwick & Woods, Clyde, N.Y., 1864	V. R. GXV–11, green Scarce
GXV–2. Like GXV–1	Plain	Pint 22	Smooth	Double round collar Type 2, small nipple at center	Amber	Same as above	V. R. GXV–11, amber Scarce
GXV–3. Like GXV–1 but letters slender	Plain	Half-pint 22	Smooth	Double round collar Type 2	Amber	Same as above	Scarce
GXV–4. Inscription: "CHEATHAM & KINNEY" in arc; in straight lines, "NASHVILLE" above "TENN—", "T" in line with "T" of Nashville and "—" in line with "Y" of Kinney.	Plain	Pint 32	Wide flat band	No. 11 Narrow outer rim, mold seam like Type 23, large disk at center	Aquamarine	Midwestern	Private mold. Firm listed in City Directories 1871-78 Rare
GXV–5. Inscription: "CUNNINGHAM & IHMSEN" in semicircle and, in straight lines, "GLASS MAKERS" above "PITTSBURGH.PA".	Plain	Pint 32	Wide flat band	No. 11 Type 23	Aquamarine	As inscribed	Scarce
GXV–6. Inscription, in 3 straight lines: "GRANITE/GLASS/C.O"; "G" and second "S" of glass smaller than other letters, with which their tops are aligned; "O" of CO smaller than "C" but not "lower case," period and bottom of "O" below bottom of "C".	Inscription, in 2 straight lines: "STODDARD"/"NH".	Quart 23	Smooth	Round collar, lower bevel (20a) Smooth; long oval depression	Reddish amber (deep)	As inscribed	V. R. GV–18 Rare flasks, Group C, No. 27 Comparatively scarce

GXV–6 — GRANITE GLASS C.o / STODDARD N H

GXIV–9 — TRAVELER'S COMPANION / RAILROAD GUIDE

GXIV–7

GXIV–6 — TRAVELER'S COMPANION / LOCKPORT GLASS WORKS

GXIV–4 — LANCASTER N.Y. ERIE.CO.

GROUP XV—LETTERED—Mainly Glassworks—Continued

OBVERSE	REVERSE	SIZE, FORM	EDGES	NECK, BASE	COLORS	GLASSHOUSE	NOTES, RARITY
GXV-7. Inscription, in 3 straight lines: "GRANITE"/"GLASS"/"CO", letters large and in alignment, no period after "C" as on GXV-6.	Inscription like GXV-6	Pint 23, short & wide	Smooth	Plain lip; round collar, lower bevel (20a) Smooth; small oval depression, with and without pontil mark	Brown-amber Olive-amber Red-amber	As inscribed	V. R. GV-18 (does not differentiate between pints—our GXV-7 & 8) Common
GXV-8. Like GXV-7 but body taller	Like GXV-7 but variations in form and size of letters	Pint 23	Smooth	Plain lip Plain	Olive-amber	As inscribed	See above Common
GXV-9. Inscription in deep arch: "INDIANAPOLISGLASSWORKS", no space between words.	Plain	Quart 30	Smooth	No. 10 Type 2	Aquamarine Green, strong (G.A.)	Indianapolis Glass Works (as inscribed), Indianapolis, Ind.	Rare
GXV-10. Inscription in semicircle: "INDIANAPOLIS.GLASS.WORKS", small letters.	Plain	Pint 32	Wide flat band	No. 10; ribbed ring Type 23	Aquamarine Peacock-blue (light)	Same as above	Rare
GXV-11. Inscription: "LANCASTER GLASS-WORKS" (in semicircle) "FULL PINT" (larger letters, in straight line starting under "L" and ending at "S").	Plain	Pint 30	Smooth	No. 18 Very short mold seam at each end to large smooth shallow oval	Aquamarine	Lancaster Glass Works (as inscribed), Lancaster, N.Y.	Rare
GXV-12. Inscription: "LOUISVILLE. K.Y." (Small letters in arc: "L" lower than "Y" and about ½" above "G" of glassworks) "GLASS WORKS" (straight line; larger letters). Nodule above "A", 2 smaller ones near right edge, apparently from small depressions in the mold.	Plain	Quart 32	Wide flat band	Plain No. 11 Type 24	Aquamarine	Louisville Glass Works (as inscribed), Louisville, Ky.	V. R. GV-32 Comparatively scarce
GXV-13. Inscription, in circle, ¾" above base: "LOUISVILLE·KY (upper half) GLASS WORKS" (lower half); period between "E" and "K" about opposite center arm of "E".	Plain	Pint 32	Wide flat band	No. 11 Type 24	Amber Aquamarine	Same as above	V. R. GXV-33 Comparatively scarce
GXV-14. Like GXV-13 but period after "LOUISVILLE" just at top of lower arm of "E" and a period between "GLASS and "WORKS".	Plain	Half-pint 32	Wide flat band	No. 11 Type 24	Aquamarine	Same as above	Comparatively scarce
GXV-15. Inscription, in circle: "NEWBURGH GLASS CO" (upper half), PATD FEB 27th 1866" (lower half).	Plain	Pint 22	Smooth	No. 11 Type 1	Olive-amber	Newburgh Glass Works, Newburgh, N.Y.	Scarce
GXV-16. Inscription, in shallow arc below shoulder: "PATENT". Small bead centered between shoulder, base and edges.	Plain	Pint 22	Smooth	No. 19 Type 26	Olive-amber Amber (C.G.)	Attributed to Stoddard, N.H. by Van Rensselaer.	V. R. GXV-38 Common

GXV–17. Inscription in 3 straight lines: "RAVENNA/GLASS/WORKS"; similar to GXIII–79 but letters thinner and smaller.	Plain	Pint 23	Smooth	No. 11 Plain	Golden amber (olive tone)	Ravenna Glass Works, Ravenna, Ohio	V. R. GVI–70 Scarce
GXV–18. Inscription: "GEO. W. ROBINSON (in arc)/No 75 (in straight line)/MAIN ST W. V.A" (in reverse arc).	Plain	Quart 32	Wide flat band	No. 11 Type 22 with ovoid disk; diagonal seam from lower left to right	Aquamarine	Wheeling, W. Va., glasshouse at foot of McLure St., operated by G. W. Robinson.	Warehouse address, 75 Main St., 1867–68 See Note to GXIII–26 Rare
GXV–19. Like GXV–18	Plain	Pint 32	Wide flat band	No. 11 Type 21 with ovoid disk; diagonal seam from lower left to right	Aquamarine	Same as above	See above Rare
GXV–20. V. R. GXV–41, same inscription as on GXV–18 above; placement not given.	Plain	Half-pint ?	Probably same as GXV–18	No. 11 ?	Aquamarine	Same as above	We have not seen this flask Rare
GXV–21. Inscription: "GENTRY, SHOTE & Co" (in semicircle) "NEW YORK" (in straight line). Letters more slender than on reverse of GXIII–25; more space between end of semicircle and straight line of inscription.	Inscription in 3 lines: SAMARITAN/BRANDY". "GOOD/"	Pint Globular, wide base, sloping shoulder, cylindrical neck	Smooth	No. 12 Type 28	Black (olive-green)	Unknown	ca. 1858 Private mold Rare
GXV–22. Inscription: "SHEETS & DUFFY" (in shallow arc), "KENSINGTON" (in larger letters and straight line); "K" and "N" just below ends of "S" and "Y".	Plain	Quart 32	Wide flat band	No. 11 Type 21	Aquamarine	Sheets & Duffy, Upper Yard Dyottville, Kensington, Philadelphia, Pa.	Probably occurs in pint and half-pint also Scarce

GXV–7   GXV–8   GXV–9   GXV–10   GXV–11   GXV–12   GXV–13   GXV–16   GXV–22

GROUP XV—LETTERED—Mainly Glassworks—Continued

OBVERSE	REVERSE	SIZE, FORM	EDGES	NECK, BASE	COLORS	GLASSHOUSE	NOTES, RARITY
GXV–23. Inscription: "UNION GLASS WORKS." (in arc) "NEW LONDON" (straight line and larger letters) above "CT"; large "C" and small "T" below "LO" of London.	Plain	Pint 22	Smooth	Round collar, lower bevel (20a) Smooth, with narrow outer rim	Olive-amber Aquamarine (pale) Olive-green	Union Glass Works, New London, Conn.	V. R. GXV–48 Rare flasks, Group C, No. 16 Rare
GXV–24. Circular frame. 2⁹/₁₆" in diameter, with flat molding, around inscription: "GROCER" across center of circle formed by "S.A. WHEATON PHOENIXVILLE"; below grocer, in larger letters, "CONN"	Plain	Pint 32	Wide flat band	Round collar, lower bevel (20a) Type 21	Aquamarine (pale)	Unknown	Private mold Scarce
GXV–25. Large oval frame with narrow molding, 2¹³/₁₆" in width and 3¹³/₁₆" in height. Inscription: "WHEELING" just within molding, following contour from upper left to right, ending with "G" lower than "W"; "VA" in straight line, "A" opposite "G".	Similar frame; at top, just within molding "OLD RYE".	Pint 29	Single heavy rib	No. 12 Type 32	Yellowish green (light & dark) Olive-green	Attributed by Van Rensselaer to the Union Glass Works of Quarrier. Ott & Co., Wheeling. [W] Va.	V. R. GXV–53 As West Virginia entered the Union June, 1863, this flask was first made before that date, probably between 1850 and 1863.
GXV–26. Plain	Plain	Half-pint 23	Smooth	Similar to No. 9, threaded inside for patent stopper Type 2; inscribed "WHITNEY" in one leaf of mold, "GLASS WORKS" in other	Brown-amber	Whitney Glass Works, Glassboro, N.J.	Stopper with milled edge, small deep hole at center top between high nipples, inscribed "PAT" on one side (between nipples) and "JAN" above "1861" on other side Rare
GXV–27. Plain	Plain	Pint 32	Smooth	Double round collar; threaded inside Like GXV–26	Olive-amber (light)	Same as above	See above Rare
GXV–28. Elliptical frame, 2⅛" in width and 4¼" in height, very narrow outer and inner molding forming wide band inscribed "ZANESVILLE" at right, "GLASS WORKS" at left, and, in center, "CITY" lengthwise.	Plain	Pint 32	Wide flat band	No. 10 Type 20	Amber Aquamarine Wine (deep)	Zanesville City Glass Works, Zanesville, Ohio	V. R. GXV–58, either our GXV–28 or 29. Scarce

GXV-29. Like GXV-28 but frame about 1/16" longer and narrower; flask taller and narrower than GXV-28.

GXV-30. Inscription in 5 lines: "BININGER'S (in arc)/ TRAVELER'S GUIDE (in curve)/A. M. BININGER & Co (in straight line)/No. 19 BROAD ST. N.Y." (reverse arc).

GXV-31. Inscription in 3 lines: "C.C.G./FULL PINT/ROCHESTER N Y" (in reverse arc).

GXV-32. Inscription in 6 lines: "HENRY LUTHER" (in shallow arc) "WINES" (in shallow arc)/&/ (in 3 straight lines) "LIQUOR/AMSTERDAM/N.Y."

GXV-33. Inscription forming a wide circle: "L.K. & CO. SYRACUSE N.Y."

GXV-34. "Seal", slightly depressed circle in diameter with "JHB"

Plain	Wide flat band	Pint 32	No. 10 Type 24	Yellow-green (citron)	Same as above	See above Scarce
Plain	Smooth	Half-pint Flat pear-shape	Double round collar Plain, unstable	Golden amber	Unknown	V. R. GX-20 1861-63 address Private mold Scarce
Plain	Smooth	Pint Similar to No. 22	Similar to No. 15, but formed in the mold Plain	Amber Aquamarine Blue	Possibly Rochester Glass Works, Rochester, N.Y.	Reported by George Austin Private mold Rare
Plain	Smooth	Pint No. 23	No. 20a Type 1	Aquamarine	Attributed by George Austin to the Clyde Glass Works, Clyde, N.Y.	Reported by George Austin Private mold Rare
Plain	Wide flat band	Half-pint Similar to No. 23 but with flat band on edges	No. 20 Plain	Amber	Unknown	Reported by George Austin Private mold Rare
Plain	Broad flat band	Quart 32	Tooled (similar to 20 but rounded collar narrow) 22	Strong aquamarine	Unknown	Reported by George Austin Very rare

GXV-23

GXV-24

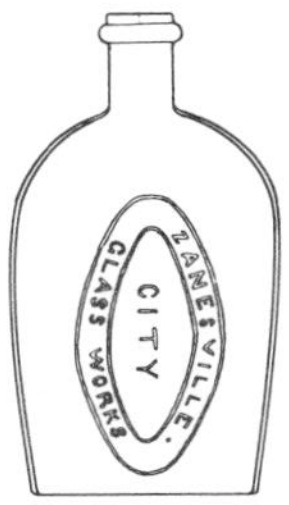

GXV-25

GXV-26 BASE

GXV-28

Part IX

20TH-CENTURY FIGURED BOTTLES AND FLASKS

by Kenneth M. Wilson

As in any field of collecting, when the supply of objects of adequate interest begins to dry up, ways are always found by enterprising (and unfortunately, in a few instances, unscrupulous) persons or companies to fill that demand. Reproduction of antiques has long been a profitable business, and when well done and presented honestly and forthrightly, these substitutes serve a very worthwhile purpose. Flasks and bottles are no exceptions: reproductions (only a few deliberately made to deceive) have been made at least since the 1920s. Some of them are extremely well made and, unless adequately marked, as are those made by the Owens-Illinois Historical Bottle Collectors Guild, may cause problems of identification for collectors now and, especially, in the future. Others, basically made as souvenirs or simply as "something colorful to put in the window," are such casual copies of early originals as to result in absolutely no possibility of confusing them with the old, except perhaps by the most eager, uninformed neophyte. The flasks offered for sale in such prolific numbers in gift shops throughout the country— some made by such firms as the Clevenger Brothers and some made abroad (a recognition of the great market for such objects)—are examples of this type

of reproduction. Many of these are wholly machine made and are purely decorative, even though based upon the specific forms and designs of the original old ones.

In addition to the reproductions, two other categories of 20th-century Figured Flasks and Bottles have become important to the collector and dealer. One is comprised of the commemoratives. The other may be called adaptations, although they are actually variations on the theme of Figured Flasks. (The term *variation* and *variant* are generally used in connection with original 19th-century flasks.) Adaptations may be described as those flasks and bottles that were inspired by earlier ones, those for which the form and relief design, usually including an inscription or, in many instances, a part of the original design, have been used. There is rarely, if ever, any doubt that these flasks are 20th-century products. Commemorative bottles and flasks inspired by 19th-century prototypes have been produced in ever-increasing numbers since World War II. All manner of events have been memorialized by them. A catalog of representative types of each of these categories follows.

1
COMMERCIAL REPRODUCTIONS OF CHARTED FLASKS AND BOTTLES

The term *commercial* is used here to differentiate between intended copies of 19th-century flasks, produced to be sold in shops, and special reproductions, such as those of the Historical Bottle Collectors Guild.

1. Flask GI–26. Washington–Eagle. Quart. *Obverse:* classical profile bust of Washington facing left (Ill. 137A). *Reverse:* American eagle with wings spread and beak turned to the right, with seven stars above and five below (Ill. 137B). The rectangular base is slightly hollow with rounded ends, and is smooth except for a scarred pontil mark. The glass is of good quality with a few bubbles and striations. Probably it was made in Czechoslovakia in the 1930s. Except for the fact that the neck was formed in the mold and a vertical mold seam is slightly evident up to within 1/16 inch of the mouth, which (like the original) is plain, having been finished by being reheated and tooled, the reproduction is a quite faithful copy of the common GI–26. This flask was made of bright cobalt-blue glass, as well as in other colors. Height, 8 inches.

2. Flask GI–28. Washington–Albany Glass Works. Pint. *Obverse:* bust of Washington facing left, "ALBANY GLASS WORKS" in an arch above and "ALBANY/NY" below in two straight lines (Ill. 138A). *Reverse:* ship sailing to the left (Ill. 138B). These crudely formed reproductions were made in amber and light blue glass, and possibly other colors as well. The neck was partially formed in the mold and completed by tooling. Though very similar in many respects to the comparatively scarce original GI–28, this reproduction differs in the style of lettering, which is sans serif, whereas there are serifs on the letters of the original. Its origin is unknown. Probably it was made in the 1930s in the United States.

3. Flask GI–29. Washington–Sailing Ship. Pint. *Obverse:* similar to GI–28, but the design is crude and the details indistinct, Washington being portrayed in uniform in a small three-quarter view facing left, with the inscription "ALBANY GLASS WORKS" surrounding the bust, with "ALBANY" in one line below and "N Y" below that. The "N" in "ALBANY" in the inscription and the "N" in "N Y" are reversed. A vertical seam mark shows the edge of the obverse. *Reverse:* ship sailing to the right, as on GI–28. These rare flasks apparently were produced in only a small quantity and may have been blown in a plaster mold. (See GI–29 in the Charts.) According to Charles B. Gardner, this theory is supported by remarks of Allie Clevenger, of Clevenger Brothers in Clayton, New Jersey, who produced a number of reproduction flasks and bottles as well as glass objects in the South Jersey style. Clevenger expressed the opinion that this reproduction may have been blown in a plaster mold, as well as the reproductions of flasks similar to GII–55 and GI–59. This reproduction of the GI–29 Washington–Sailing Ship was made in the 1930s and is recorded in both deep sapphire-blue glass and a very unusual shade of deep yellow-green. A sapphire-blue one is in the collection of The Corning Museum of Glass (accession no. 60.4.32).

4. Flask GI–37. Washington–Taylor. Quart. *Obverse:* classical bust of Washington facing left, with the "FATHER OF HIS COUNTRY" in an arc above (Ill. 139A). *Reverse:* bust of General Taylor with the inscription "GEN. TAYLOR NEVER SURRENDERS" above and partially surrounding the bust, and the inscription "DYOTTVILLE GLASS WORKS PHILAD.ᴬ" above and outside the oval panel with the inscription and bust of Taylor in low relief (139B). Made by the Clevenger Brothers Glass Works, Clayton, New Jersey, prior to 1960 and possibly as early as the late 1930s. It occurs in amethyst, teal blue, and other colors. The original GI–37 is one of the common Washington–Taylor flasks.

5. Flask GI–50. Washington–Taylor. Pint. *Obverse:* classical portrait bust of Washington facing left, with the word "WASHINGTON" in a concave arc below (Ill. 140). *Reverse:* the bust of General Taylor in uniform, facing left, the inscription "G.Z.TAYLOR" in a concave arc be-

137. Reproduction of the Washington-Eagle quart flask (GI–26). *A.* Obverse. *B.* Reverse. *Private collection*

A   B

138. Reproduction of the Washington–Albany Glass Works flask, GI–28; pint. *A.* Obverse. *B.* Reverse. *Collection of George O. Bird*

A   B

139. Washington–Taylor quart flask (GI–37) as reproduced by Clevenger Brothers Glass Works, Clayton, N.J. *A.* Obverse. *B.* Reverse. *Collection of Kenneth M. Wilson*

A   B

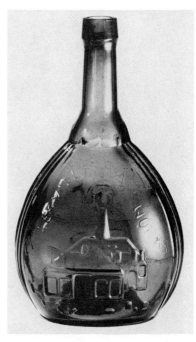

A

B

141. Jenny Lind calabash bottle, GI–107A; quart. This reproduction was made in Czechoslovakia. *A.* Obverse. *B.* Reverse. *The Corning Museum of Glass*

140. Obverse of a reproduction of the Washington–Taylor pint flask, GI–50. *Private collection*

low. The quality of the glass is poor to fair and the surface texture is rather rough, as if blown in a cold mold. The image is faint, except for the inscription. In general, this is a poor copy of the common GI–50; it is recorded in aquamarine only. Origin is unknown, but possibly Clevenger Brothers Glass Works in Clayton, New Jersey; probably produced from the 1950s onward.

6. Calabash bottle, GI–107A. Jenny Lind. Quart. Aquamarine. *Obverse:* three-quarter profile bust of Jenny Lind facing slightly to the left, with two laurel branches below and the words "JENNY LIND" in an arc above (Ill. 141A). *Reverse:* view of the glasshouse with a large conical chimney extending from the center of the roof, with seven other chimneys around the edges. The words "FISLERVILLE GLASS WORKS" appear in a reverse-curved arc above (Ill. 141B). As shown by the line drawings in the Charts, it closely resembles the common GI–107, but the neck does not taper quite like that of the original, and there are minor differences in the wreath and the base. This is listed by George S. McKearin as GI–107A, as a counterfeit imitating GI–107. Another distinguishing factor of

the fake is that it holds exactly one quart; the original holds more. This reproduction was made in Haida, Czechoslovakia, in the early or mid-1930s.

7. Flask. Eagle–Cornucopia (Ill. 142). Half-pint. Possibly this was intended to represent the rare GII–16 or scarce GII–17, but if so it is a very remote copy of either. It is crudely blown of light grayish blue glass with a slightly concave, pointed oval base with rough pontil mark about an inch in diameter. The neck was formed in a mold, reheated, and finished by hand. The glass is of fair quality, with a pebbly textured surface that may have been caused by use of a somewhat cold mold. Maker and date are unknown. The character and poor quality of this flask make it reminiscent of the crude reproductions of the Albany Glass Works' Washington–ship half-pint flask, GI–29. However, that reproduction may have been blown in a plaster of Paris mold taken from an original flask, whereas this was not. 5¼ inches high.

8. Flask GII–46. Eagle–Cornucopia. Half-pint. Amethyst. *Obverse:* small eagle leaning toward the left, but with head turned to the right. *Reverse:* cornucopia. Made at Clevenger Brothers Glass Works in Clayton, New Jersey, in the 1950s and probably earlier. It has a plain tooled neck and lip; the quality of the glass is poor, rather rough and bubbly. The original scarce

142. Reproduction of Eagle–Cornucopia half-pint flask, but by no means an accurate copy of either GII–16 or GII–17. Maker and date are unknown. *Private collection*

GII–46 has been recorded only in aquamarine glass. The reproductions were made in various colors.

9. Flask GII–54. Eagle–Flag. Pint. Amethyst. *Obverse:* eagle perched on shield, without vertical stripes as on the original, with olive branches below, as on the original (Ill. 143A). *Reverse:* unfurled flag on pole, with the inscription "FOR OUR COUNTRY" in a concave arc below (Ill. 143B). The quality of the glass is poor to fair, with roughly textured pebbly surface. Made by Clevenger Brothers Glass Works in Clayton, New Jersey, prior to 1960. A comparison with an original shows that the base of the original has a keyed mold mark, whereas the Clevenger reproduction has either a smooth base or a smooth base with a circular depression in it—evidence that reproductions of this flask were produced in two 20th-century molds. The depression, simulating a pontil mark, is characteristic of many of the reproduction flasks produced by Clevenger Brothers. In addition, the Clevenger eagle is less detailed than that of the comparatively scarce original GII–54.

10. Flask GII–55. Eagle–Bunch of Grapes. Quart. *Obverse:* large eagle, with head turned to left and wings partly raised; triangle of 13 stars above eagle (Ill. 144A). *Reverse:* large bunch of grapes below arch formed by the inscription

A   **B**

143A. Obverse of Eagle–Flag pint flask, GII–54. **B.** Reverse of the same flask. This reproduction was made by Clevenger Brothers of Clayton, N.J. *Private collection*

"CLEVENGER BROS. GLASS WKS CLAYTON, N. J." (Ill. 144B). The glass has a rather rough texture and is of poor quality. Probably this reproduction was brought out in about the 1950s; it is still being produced in various colors, including yellow-amber and light green. Another reproduction that, like the original GII–55, has no inscription on the reverse possibly was also a Clevenger Brothers' product from around the 1930s to 1950s. The glass is very poor in quality, full of bubbles and with a surface that, intentionally, was roughly textured. It is probable that a plaster mold was used.

11. Flask, GIV–1. Masonic–Eagle. Pint. *Obverse:* Masonic arch and symbols (Ill. 145A). *Reverse:* eagle, facing left, with outstretched wings and a ribbon above inscribed "E PLURIBUS UNUM", all above an oval wreath containing the letters "JP", the lower loop of the "P" extending leftward to the right side of the upright of the letter "J" (Ill. 145B). This flask, intended as a reproduction of the common GIV–1 (see Charts), differs from it in various ways but nevertheless is a well-made attractive flask. It differs from the original in the following respects: (1) the character of the eagle is entirely different, and the right side of the eagle's head and beak are of different contours; (2) the letter "J" replaces the "I" in the original, which represents a "J" for Justus; (3) the letters "JP" are centered within the wreath. In the original, the "IP" representing the initials of Justus Perry are off-center (to the left) because, as the late Dr. Julian H. Toulouse pointed out, the mold's original letters—"HS" for Henry Schoolcraft— were changed to "IP" for Justus Perry, who took over the glassworks on Marlboro Street, Keene,

682

A

B

144. Reproduction of quart flask GII–55, Eagle–Bunch of Grapes. *A.* Obverse. *B.* Reverse, which bears the inscription "Clevenger Bros Glass Wks Clayton N.J." *Private collection*

A

B

145A. Obverse of pint Masonic–Eagle flask GIV–1, as reproduced by an Italian glass factory for the Old Sturbridge Village gift shop. *The Corning Museum of Glass.* **B.** Reverse of same.

A

B

146. Reproduction, by an unknown maker, of the quart calabash bottle GIV–42, Union and Clasped Hands–Eagle. *A.* Obverse. *B.* Reverse. *Private collection*

reproduction, commissioned by Old Sturbridge Village for sale in its museum and gift shop in 1964, was produced by a glass factory in Italy; it is still being made.

12. Calabash bottle, GIV–42. Union and Clasped Hands–Eagle. Quart. *Obverse* (Ill. 146A): shield framing clasped hands above a compass and square, below which is "UNION" (very lightly) in a small oval frame; 13 stars above shield—11 in a wide arc and, in the space between arc and top of shield, a single star about in line with the third star from each end; a laurel branch at each side of shield. *Reverse* (Ill. 146B): eagle flying to the right, with pennants above and below, similar to the original but *without* the letters "A.R.S." below. The broad sloping collar, about one inch long, appears to have been laid on after the bottle was molded. The bottom is smooth with a rather deep circular depression about 2 inches in diameter in the base. The surface of the sides and the background of the body of the bottle are purposely textured with a slight pebbly effect, in contrast to the smooth surface of the original. The maker is unknown. The date is uncertain, but probably the 1960s, though an earlier period is not impossible. Height 9⅛ inches.

13. Flask. Railroad. *Obverse and reverse:* "SUCCESS TO THE RAILROAD" in horseshoe arch over horse-drawn cart of barrels, on rails. Pint. Similar to the rare Keene, N.H., flask GV–4. The neck was formed in the mold and finished by tooling after reheating. The base is slightly concave, either smooth or with lightly rough pontil

N.H., when Schoolcraft and his partner failed in 1817. In converting the letters to "IP," the left leg of the "H" became "I," representing the "J" in Justus; the bar of the "H" was not removed, and so the "I" in the original is attached to the "P," and the "P" was formed by converting the "S" The alteration left a rather wide space within the righthand portion of the oval on the original. The neck and the lip of the reproductions are plain, tooled; the slightly indented base is plain and sometimes has no pontil mark; on others the words "OLD STURBRIDGE VILLAGE" appear around the contour of the slightly hollow oval base. The original was produced in numerous colors (see GIV–1 in the Charts); the reproduction, in medium light bluish green, pale yellowish amber, and possibly other colors. The

147. Reproduction of "SUCCESS TO THE RAILROAD" pint flask, similar to the rare GV–4. Obverse and reverse are the same. *Private collection*

148. Another reproduction "SUCCESS TO THE RAILROAD" flask, similar to GV–3 and GV–5. *Private collection*

mark. The chief distinctions between this reproduction and the Keene GV–4 are a much more slender horse and lighter, finer lettering than on the original. The reproduction was produced in aquamarine and a very pale electric blue glass by an unknown maker prior to 1950 and possibly as early as the 1930s. The owner of the aquamarine example (Ill. 147) acquired it in 1951. The quality of the glass in the reproductions varies from rather poor, full of bubbles and striations, to a rather good quality with very few bubbles.

14. Flask. Railroad. "SUCCESS TO THE RAILROAD" in horseshoe arch over horse-drawn cart of barrels, on rails. Pint. Similar to the common GV–3 and GV–5, and also closely similar to the reproduction of GV–5 made in Czechoslovakia in the late 1920s (Ill. 149). The neck was formed in the mold, reheated, tooled, and flared out. The base is slightly concave with a straight mold seam and a rough pontil mark about ⅝ inch in diameter at center. The glass of the flask in Ill. 148 has a slight yellowish green tone, unlike any color of the Czechoslovakian reproductions. It probably was produced as early as the 1950s, if not earlier. The impression on this particular flask is fairly good except for the word "THE" in "SUCCESS TO THE RAILROAD". There are several obvious differences between this reproduction Railroad flask

and the previous one, No. 13. The letters are taller and a little narrower than on No. 13; the horse on No. 13 is much more slender and has thinner legs and an almost nonexistent mane. The mane on No. 14 is faintly comblike, though far from as boldly defined as the "sawtooths" on the Czechoslovakian reproduction No. 15. In addition, whereas the wheels of the railroad cart and its load of packages, or barrels, are ill formed on No. 13, they are well formed in sharper relief on No. 14 and also on the Czechoslovakian No. 15. In general, the details on No. 14 and No. 15 are closely similar to those on the original railroad flasks GV–3, 4, and 5 (see line drawings in the Charts).

15. Flask, GV–5. Railroad. *Obverse and reverse* like preceding flask in design. Pint. This reproduction of the common GV–5, the Railroad flask produced at Mount Vernon Glass Works and later at the "Saratoga mountain works" in New York, was the first copy of a railroad flask, probably the first reproduction of a Figured Flask; it was brought out in the late 1920s, by which time collecting bottles and such flasks had become of great interest to collectors of and dealers in American glass. It is an excellent copy, differing in only minor respects from its prototype. As comparison of Illustration 149 with the line drawing in the Charts shows, the chief and telltale differences from the original are in the

A   B

149. The example pictured here was the first copy of a Railroad flask to be made and probably the first reproduction of a Figured Flask. It closely resembles GV–5, differing only in minor respects. It was almost certainly made in Czechoslovakia. *A.* Obverse. *B.* Reverse. *Collection of Edward Pfeiffer*

curve of the horse's neck and in the mane, which has sharply defined sawteeth that serve as a quick identification feature, once one is aware of the variation. According to information given to Helen McKearin at the Period Art Shop in New York City soon after the flasks appeared on the market, this GV–5 reproduction was made in Czechoslovakia *for the shop* and the mold cost *$400.* On the other hand, according to Ruth Webb Lee writing in 1936, the importer of these flasks indicated that the mold cost $200 to make. The original flasks were recorded in 1971 in clear deep olive-green, olive-amber, and "black." Since then they have been recorded by Sam Laidacker in golden amber, aquamarine, deep green, emerald green, and yellow green. The reproductions were produced first in olive-green, olive-amber, and "black"; later, in other colors. Unfortunately, when they were brought out, some were peddled to antiques dealers in whose shops they were sold as originals until their spuriousness was realized and the telltale characteristic became familiar to collectors and dealers.

16. There is another "SUCCESS TO THE RAILROAD" reproduction that is such a poor imitation of GV–5 that it could not fool anyone. This flask, produced in numerous colors, was made in the Clevenger Brothers Glass Works in Clayton, New Jersey, by the 1950s if not before. The glass is of poor quality; the neck is plain; the base also is plain except for a hollow circle, which presumably is meant to simulate a pontil mark. These flasks are still being produced today.

150. Reproduction of the Sunburst GVIII–2. Obverse and reverse are the same. *Private collection*

17. Flask, GVIII–2. Sunburst. *Obverse and reverse* the same (Ill. 150). Pint. The neck was formed in the mold except for the last ⅛ inch, but this is barely perceptible. The base is very slightly concave, plain except for a slightly rough ½- or ⅝-inch-diameter pontil mark. This is a well-made reproduction, but it can be distinguished from the original because it is much lighter in weight and density. According to Charles B. Gardner, these flasks were made in Mexico for H. A. Mack of Boston, who imported and sold them. Though the exact date of production is not known, it was probably in the 1930s. The colors were light greenish blue, deep blue, and amethyst, possibly also aquamarine and the darker colored, deep blue glass.

18. Scroll flask GIX–10 (Ill. 151). Blown of very bubbly glass, yellowish green in color. Probably it was produced in other colors too. The base is slightly concave, and smooth except for the initials "CB," probably for Clevenger Brothers. These reproductions of the common GIX–10 usually appear with a slightly everted lip and probably were made at Clevenger Brothers Glass Works in Clayton, New Jersey, in the 1950s and 1960s. They are still being made today.

19. Scroll flask GIX–11 (Ill. 152). Pint. This reproduction was blown from a good quality of glass in light golden amber, cobalt-blue, amethyst, deep ruby, and possibly other colors. The neck was

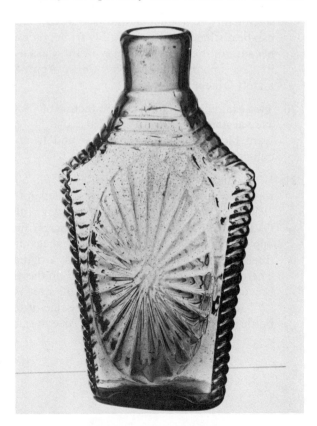

151. Scroll flask GIX–10, probably reproduced by Clevenger Brothers in the 1950s and 1960s. *Private collection*

152. Reproduction of pint Scroll flask GIX–11. *Collection of Miss Nancy Merrill*

formed in the mold up to within ⅛ inch of the lip, which was then reheated and finished by tooling. The oval-rectangular base is slightly concave, and smooth except for a slightly rough pontil mark about ⅝ inch in diameter. This reproduction of the common GIX–11 was produced at least as early as the 1950s, possibly by Blenko Glass Works in Milton, West Virginia. It is a fine-quality reproduction and unmarked, but it can be distinguished most readily from originals because of the superior quality of the glass and its very smooth, almost glossy finish. Approximately 7 inches high.

20. Two examples of another reproduction of GIX–11, varying only slightly from the one above, were blown from pale amethyst and from a cobalt-blue glass.

21. E. G. Booz's Old Cabin Bottle (Ill. 153). This reproduction—or "fake," as it was called in the 1930s—of the comparatively scarce Booz bottle GVII–3 with a straight roof (see Charts) first appeared in 1931. Several minor variances distinguish the reproduction from the original. There are two periods under the "T" in the abbreviation for "street" and no period after the "Y" following whiskey on the right side of the bottle as one looks at the obverse. Also missing

on the reproduction is the period following the word "WHISKEY" on the original's sloping roof. In addition, the letters in general differ slightly from those on the original. On the reproduction, a diagonal mold seam runs from opposite corners to a smooth circular depression about 2 inches in diameter at the center, whereas the base of the original has no seam. However, the neck is finished with a broad sloping collar laid on by hand, as on the original. This reproduction was made at Clevenger Brothers Glass Works in Clayton, New Jersey. Originally reproduced only in amber glass, by about 1940 it was also being made in other colors such as sapphire-blue and emerald-green. Several other reproductions of this bottle have been produced by other firms since 1931.

22. E. G. Booz's Old Cabin Bottle (Ill. 154), reproduction of the comparatively scarce GVII–4, with triangular cuts at the gable ends. These cuts are considerably larger than on the original, so that the lower edges extend through the second row of shingles, instead of just through the first, as on the original. In addition, the numerals in the date "1840" and the parentheses around the date on the reverse of the sloping roof are smaller than on the original and do not blend into the

686

153. Reproduction made at Clevenger Brothers Glass Works of E. G. Booz's Old Cabin Whiskey bottle, GVII–3. *Collection of the Henry Ford Museum*

154. Another reproduction of an E. G. Booz's Old Cabin Whiskey bottle, GVII–4. *Collection of George O. Bird*

line of shingles, either above or below. Just as the numerals in "1840" are smaller, so is the name "E. G. BOOZ'S" on the obverse side of the roof. Also, the apostrophe is considerably smaller than on the original. The curve of the hasp, or latch, on the door of the reproduction is much more attenuated and more finely ribbed than on the original. Finally, there is no period after the word "WHISKEY" on the right side of the bottle. As in the original, the base of the reproduction is plain except for a 2-inch circular depression in the center. The broad sloping collar was laid on by hand, as on the original. This reproduction was also made by the Clevenger Brothers Glass Works, and has been in production for many years. Several other varieties of reproductions of the very popular "Booz bottle" also exist, and are commonly sold in gift shops today. Among them is a rather poor, blue glass reproduction of the very rare Booz bottle GVII–5. It has a ¾ quart capacity. Its origin is unknown, as is its date, probably later than the others. Unfortunately, when the first reproductions were made in the early 1930s, they appeared in numerous antiques shops, and in many

instances were purchased by unknowing collectors, and dealers too, as originals.

23. Flask. GIII–4, Cornucopia and Urn. *Obverse:* upright cornucopia, with the lower end extending toward the left (Ill. 155A). *Reverse:* urn containing a melon and several varieties of fruit (Ill. 155B). This quite faithful representation of the common original GIII–4 was produced in 1959 by the Pairpoint Glass Works during the ownership of Robert Bryden and blown in a leased

155. Pairpoint Glass Works had this reproduction of the Cornucopia–Urn flask GIII–4 made in 1959 at a glasshouse in Spain. A. Obverse. B. Reverse. *Collection of Kenneth M. Wilson*

A   B

glasshouse in Spain. It was blown by hand (that is, by a glassblower) in a full-size two-piece mold, of which the obverse (cornucopia) section had been originally half of the mold used to produce the Old Sturbridge Village–Cornucopia flask designed as an adaptation of the original Cornucopia–Urn flask GIII–4 made in Coventry, Connecticut. The Pairpoint reproduction has a capacity of approximately one pint and is 6¾ inches in height. The plain, slightly concave base has the characteristic rough pontil mark left when a flask is stuck up (attached to a pontil) to hold it while the blower finishes the neck, which is not formed in the mold, and its lip by reheating and tooling. The example illustrated is a light greenish yellow, one of a variety of colors in which these flasks were produced. Except for the fine quality of the glass in the reproductions, and their consequent glossy surface, they could pass easily as originals.

2
REPRODUCTIONS BY THE HISTORICAL BOTTLE COLLECTORS GUILD

Probably the four most accurately and carefully reproduced flasks were made by the Historical Bottle Collectors Guild, an affiliate of Owens-Illinois, Inc. The program to accurately reproduce well-identified, limited editions of early American flasks and bottles was conceived in late 1971 or early 1972 by the Glass Containers Division, Venture Operations, of Owens-Illinois, under the direction of Phillip Williams, assisted by S. A. Smith. The late Charles B. Gardner, Cecil Munsey, the late Dr. Julian H. Toulouse, and the author were asked to form the advisory board to offer guidance. After much study and consideration, the Guild decided to issue the reproductions in strictly limited editions of 3,500 and to impress on the base of each bottle and flask the logo of Owens-Illinois—an "I" within an "O"—and also the serial, or registration, number and year of the issue. Each, with a small identification folder describing its history and origin, was to be packaged in a cloth bag and sell for $27.50. Then the Guild decided to develop a program of reproductions in sets of four. Each set would be available at $100 instead of $110, on prepublication order, as it were, by those who had become members of the Guild. Membership, available for only $2.50, entitled subscribers to advance information about future sets and also "Guild Markings," the Guild publication, of which actually there was only one issue.

After further careful consideration and much deliberation, two flasks and two bottles were selected to be reproduced for the first set: the Concentric Ring–Eagle "canteen" flask, GII–76; the Jacob's Cabin Tonic Bitters bottle, GVII–6; the Columbia–Eagle flask, GI–117A (GII–76, GVII–6, and GI–117A; see Charts), and the Star Whiskey bottle listed by Van Rensselaer as 7616. L. A. McCullough, replacing Mr. Smith as director of the Historical Bottle Collectors Guild, guided the first reproduction—the Concentric Ring–Eagle "canteen" flask (Ill. 156)—to fruition. The flasks were blown by Owens-Illinois glassblowers in the firm's Development Center in Toledo. However, instead of the proposed 3,500 edition, a total of only 675 was produced, of which 640 have a serial number on the base. Artist's proofs, numbered AP-1 through AP-15, are on 15 that were given to various people associated with the program, including members of the advisory board. The remaining 20 flasks, marked B-1 through B-20, were presented to members of the Board of Directors of Owens-Illinois and other special individuals.

The mold for the flask was made by Owens-Illinois workmen from the original Concentric Ring–Eagle flask GII–76 then in the collection of Charles B. Gardner. Like the original, the reproduction was stuck up with a pontil, cracked off the blowpipe, and its neck and lip finished by tooling and fire-polishing. It is probably the most accurately reproduced flask ever made, almost exactly conforming in its size, shape, detail of low relief design, color, and even weight to the original. Except for its somewhat more glossy surface, the light green glass containing a limited number of bubbles is almost undetectable from the original. In fact, it appears to differ from the original only in that the pontil-marked base is slightly indented and well identified by the firmly impressed OI symbol ("I" within an "O") and the date 1973. Also, each flask is marked in diamond point with a serial, or registration, number. These markings were

156. Concentric Ring–Eagle canteen flask, GII–76, reproduced by the Historical Bottle Collectors Guild. *Collection of Kenneth M. Wilson*

adopted to ensure that none of these faithful reproductions would ever enter the market to be sold as antiques. As an additional means by which collectors can identify the reproduction, the Guild had the flask reproduced in soda-lime glass instead of lead glass as the original had been. Thus, the collector can distinguish the reproduction from the original by means of the fluorescence under ultraviolet light.

The second offering of the Guild was a reproduction of the Jacob's Cabin Tonic Bitters bottle (Ill. 157): GVII–6 in the McKearin Charts and No. 191 in Watson's book, *Bitters Bottles*. Again, except for two minor points, this is a very accurate copy of the original that was in the collection of Charles B. Gardner. One variation from the original lies in the formation of the lip: on the reproduction it was formed in the mold; on the original, the lip was a laid-on flat ring. The other is the omission or faintness of the apostrophe between the "b" and "s" in "Jacob's" on the reproduction, both on the roof and on the side. A total of 792 of these bottles was produced. Of these, 750 have regular serial numbers; 15 have the AP–1 through AP–15 (artist's proofs); and 20 presentation bottles were marked B-1 through B-20. They were marked within a concave circle with a large OI symbol and "1974" in large figures, deeply impressed in the glass. Also, the base has a rough pontil mark about ⅝ inch in diameter. To provide collectors with an additional sure means of identifying the reproduction of the Jacob's Cabin Tonic Bit-

ters bottle, the Guild had a rare earth (samarium oxide) added to the batch. As a result, unlike the original, the reproduction fluoresces a distinct orange when exposed to ultraviolet light.

The third reproduction in this series was the Columbia–Eagle flask (Ill. 158A & B) carefully copied from the original in the collection of the Toledo Museum of Art. This rare flask, of slightly less capacity than the comparatively scarce GI–117, has been charted in Group I, portrait flasks, as a variant, GI–117A. The reproduction was made of cobalt-blue glass and is a faithful copy of the original. However, it has a narrow rolled lip formed in the mold simulating the tooled one of the original, but it was rewarmed and tooled after the flask was stuck up and cracked off the blowpipe. Also, the base has a rough pontil mark, but this differs from the original in being slightly concave, deeply impressed with the OI symbol and the date 1974, and a diamond point- or rotary-engraved serial number. A total of 707 of these Columbia–Eagle flasks was produced. Of these, 672 bear the usual "B" serial number, 1

157. Reproduction of the Jacob's Cabin Tonic Bitters bottle (GII–6) issued by the Historical Bottle Collectors Guild. *Collection of Kenneth M. Wilson*

158A. Obverse of the variant Columbia–Eagle flask GI–117A, the third offering in the reproduction series of the Historical Bottle Collectors Guild. **B.** Reverse of same. *Collection of Kenneth M. Wilson*

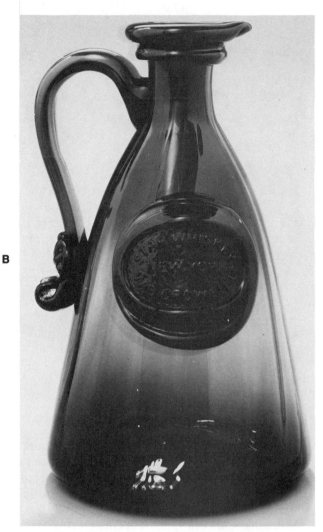

159. Reproduction of the Star Whiskey bottle issued by the Historical Bottle Collectors Guild. *Collection of Kenneth M. Wilson*

through 20, for presentation pieces. These flasks were blown in Toledo, at the firm's Development Center, by Owens-Illinois glassblowers. In addition to the identification marks noted, the Guild had this flask made of a soda-lime glass instead of the lead-oxide glass used for the original, so that the fluorescence under ultraviolet light would be another means of differentiating the reproduction from the original.

The fourth and final reproduction offered by the Guild was the Star Whiskey bottle (Ill. 159) produced in a mold made from an original bottle in the Charles B. Gardner collection. Although this reproduction is well formed, and every effort was made to achieve an accurate facsimile of the original, today's glassblowers had great difficulty in faithfully duplicating the lip, seal, and the swirl of the pattern-molded body of the bottle. Because the lip is heavier and thicker, and the seal is more rounded and larger, than on the original, a knowledgeable collector can detect the reproduction from the original. In addition, of course, the Guild had the bottle marked on the base; this time the logo, represented by the individual letters "O" and "I" above the date 1974, is within a circle about an inch in diameter. The slightly rough and slightly concave base has a rough pontil mark about 1⅛ to 1¼ inches in diameter. The engraved serial number, or artist's proof or presentation number, is also present. In addition, each specimen bears a gold rectangular label with the printed "OI" ("I" within an "O") symbol within a rectangle above a straight line and the word "Durobor" and, below the "OI" rectangle, "Made in Belgium." As the label indicates, the bottle was made by Owens-Illinois workmen in their Durobor plant in Belgium. It is

160. Reproduction of "A. Yoerger & Br." soda water bottle, made by Owens-Illinois. *Collection of Kenneth M. Wilson*

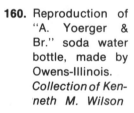

blown of a deep reddish amber glass containing a number of bubbles, and like the original is pattern molded. However, its almost vertical ribs are seen only in transmitted light but neither felt nor seen in reflected light. A total of only 558 of these Star Whiskey bottles was produced. Of these, 521 bear serial numbers, but the collector should be aware that, since these numbers are not consecutive because some collectors purchased sets with matched serial numbers, and on earlier editions some of these were higher than 521, the actual serial number on some runs into the 600s and 700s. There were 15 artist's proofs and 22 presentation pieces, all marked as were the other Guild reproduction flasks and bottles.

Partly because of the high expenses encountered in making such faithful reproductions, partly because of the difficulties in hand finishing encountered in the Star Whiskey bottle, but primarily because of the recession that began in 1974, the Historical Bottle Collectors Guild discontinued its program in 1974 after completion of only one set of two flasks and two bottles. Because of their quality, their limited edition, and the fact that the originals are so rare as to be virtually unavailable, these four reproductions will undoubtedly become "collector's

items"—probably within the near future.

Though not a Guild bottle or in the same category, another reproduction bottle made by Owens-Illinois is of interest to collectors of mineral water bottles. It is a soda water bottle bearing the name "A. YOERGER & BR./ ALTON ILL" (Ill. 160). The original was manufactured by the Illinois Glass Company at its first small glasshouse on Belle Street in Alton, Illinois. The reproduction was blown at the Owens-Illinois Development Center in Toledo, Ohio, in a mold made at the company's Alton Central Mold Shop, to commemorate the 100th anniversary of the founding of the Illinois Glass Company in 1873 by William Elliot Smith and Edward Levis. The Illinois Glass Company merged with the Owens Bottle Company in 1929 to form Owens-Illinois. This aquamarine bottle was blown in a mold by a glassblower, not a machine. It has a pontil mark, and the lip—though formed in the mold as a heavy, rounded, deep collar called a blob—was reheated and tooled also. In its mold-form "blob top," the reproduction differs from the original, which had an applied and tooled "blob." Only 600 of these bottles were made, for distribution to company executives and associates. Height of bottle, 7⅝ inches.

3
ADAPTATIONS

Within recent years, numerous Figured Flasks and Bottles have been made that cannot properly be described as either reproductions or commemoratives. Although 19th-century Figured Flasks, historicals in particular, clearly inspired their designs, these flasks and bottles vary from the originals to such an extent that they should not be called reproductions. Therefore, they are considered here as "adaptations." A catalog of a representative selection of these 20th-century adaptations of Figured Flasks follows:

1. Washington–Taylor (Ill. 161). Quart. Light amber. Adaptation of the common quart GI–37. *Obverse:* Classical bust of Washington facing left, and below "THE FATHER OF HIS COUNTRY" in horseshoe arch, similar to GI–37. *Reverse:* Bust of Zachary Taylor in uniform facing left, and below "GEN. TAYLOR NEVER SURRENDERS" in deep arch; similar to GI–37. Above the oval panel with bust of Taylor and

inscription in low relief: "EMPIRE GLASS WORKS" instead of "DYOTTVILLE GLASS WORKS PHILAD.ᴬ" as in GI–37. The back-

161. Made-in-Italy adaptation of the common quart Washington–Taylor flask, GI–37. *A.* Obverse. *B.* Reverse. *Collection of Kenneth M. Wilson*

A
B

A **B**

162. Adaptation of a quart Washington flask. Obverse and reverse are the same. *Private collection*

163. An adaptation derived from the pint Harrison–Log Cabin flask GI–63. *Private collection*

164A. Obverse of an adaptation of the rare Columbia–Eagle flask GI–122. **B.** Reverse of the same. The eagle is more like the one on GII–1. *Private collection*

ground is roughly textured, possibly to simulate age. The broad sloping collar, formed in the mold, is a simulation of an applied one that is typical of mid-19th-century flasks of this form. The Empire Glass Works apparently is a mythical one. This machine-made flask was purchased in a Nantucket, Massachusetts, gift shop in the fall of 1975. According to its paper label, it was made in Italy.

2. Washington (Ill. 162). Quart. *Obverse and reverse:* classical bust of Washington facing left, similar to the portrait bust on the obverse of the common GI–37 (see Charts) but with an unusually long, sharp nose; in arc above bust, "THE FATHER OF HIS COUNTRY" in letters like those on the common GI–47 (see Charts). The base has no pontil mark and is slightly concave, with edges ground flat. The sloping collar, about ⅝ inch long, was applied. The flask, blown from a good-quality glass and having an intentionally textured background surface, was produced in light blue, teal blue, a grayish blue, and possibly other colors. Probably it was made as early as the 1950s by the Clevenger Glass Works in Clayton, New Jersey; it still may be in production.

3. Harrison–Log Cabin (Ill. 163), derived from GI–63 (see Charts). Pint. *Obverse:* portrait bust of William Henry Harrison facing three-quarters left; "WILLIAM H. HARRISON" arching above bust. *Reverse:* log cabin with a flag at right end of ridgepole and floating to the left; a plow and a barrel below the cabin and above the date

"1841." The charted flask GI–63 has no date on the obverse. The neck of the adaptation was formed in the mold and finished by tooling. The base is slightly concave with an indentation near the center simulating a pontil mark. The flask illustrated is light, almost electric, blue in color. Its form is more characteristic of the 1860–70 era than of the 1840 period, when the original Harrison–Log Cabin flask was produced in the Monongahela–Pittsburgh area. The adaptation may have been produced by Clevenger Brothers.

4. Columbia–Eagle (Ill. 164). *Obverse:* bust of Columbia facing left and below arch of 13 small stars; apparently derived from the rare GI–122 (see Charts) and "LIBERTY" added below the bust. *Reverse:* American eagle, possibly derived from the scarce midwestern GII–1 (see Charts); starting above eagle's raised right wing and following line of panel to left, 10 relief dots instead of small stars as on GII–1; between dots and eagle, a five-pointed star below fourth dot at left of center—another deviation from GII–1. Shape is more characteristic of the 1860–70 period than of the 1820s and 1830s. This flask, with neck and lip finished by reheating and tooling, and plain base, was not machine-made but blown in the mold by a glassblower. Probably it was brought out in the late 1960s and early 1970s. The maker is unknown.

5. American Eagle–Ship *Franklin* (Ill. 165). Quart. Adapted from Dr. Dyott's Kensington Glass Works flask GII–42 (see Charts). *Obverse:* eagle

A   **B**

A   **B**

165. This quart American Eagle–Ship *Franklin* adaptation was derived from Dr. Dyott's GII–42 pint flask. It was produced as a container for Lestoil. **A**. Obverse. **B**. Reverse. *Collection of George O. Bird*

166. Adaptation of Concentric Ring–Eagle flask. **A**. Obverse. **B**. Reverse. On the original, GII–76, obverse and reverse were the same. The reverse of the adaptation shown here has a textured-surface medallion within the rings. *Henry Ford Museum photograph; Private collection*

above oval framing initials "T.W.D." *Reverse:* the ship *Franklin* sailing to right and above "FRANKLIN" in a concave arc. *Shape:* similar to Form 23, narrower in proportion to width and much less ovoid than the Form 11 of GII–42. *Base:* plain, marked with figure "7." *Neck:* rolled collar instead of plain like that of GII–42. This adaptation was produced in the late 1960s for the Lestoil Company of Holyoke, Massachusetts, as a container of Lestoil. Its capacity is 12 fluid ounces. Besides the light blue glass of the flask illustrated, it was produced in blue, amethyst, and colorless. In addition to this flask and, at the same time, three others including depictions of Columbia in the design were produced to contain Lestoil.

6. Concentric Ring–Eagle decanter-flask (Ill. 166), adapted from GII–76 (see Charts). *Obverse:* eagle, with wings spread, head facing right, on medallion within heavy concentric rings. *Reverse:* plain medallion with textured surface, within heavy concentric rings. Fitted with a hollow spherical stopper. This adaptation, which is approximately 8⅜ inches in maximum width, 8¾ inches in height without stopper, and 12¼ inches with stopper, is considerably larger than the original. According to report, it was made for a California winery as a container for wine. The author has seen it in two colors: a light transparent blue and a golden amber. Apparently it was produced in the early 1960s by an as-yet-unknown maker. Because of its size and its colors, which are unlike any in which the original

has been recorded, it cannot be mistaken for an example of the early 19th-century flask. Regardless of its age, it is a handsome flask.

7. Eagle–American Flag (Ill. 167). Quarter-pint. Topaz. Probably inspired by the quart Coffin & Hay GII–48 (see Charts). *Obverse:* eagle similar to that on GII–48, but with no sunrays surrounding its head. *Reverse:* flag, unfurled instead of furled, as on GII–48. The neck, instead of being plain, is threaded to accept a metal screw-cap.

The following three machine-made flasks, fitted with a spherical stopper, were made during the 1960s, probably as containers for spirits. Unlike the

167. This quarter-pint Eagle–American Flag flask was probably inspired by the quart GII–48 of Coffin & Hay (see Charts). Among other differences from the original, the neck of the adaptation is threaded for a screw cap. *Private collection*

168. Obverse of the Eagle–Cannon flask pictured here may well have been derived from one of the Willington Glass Works flasks (GII–61 through 64). *Private collection*

169. Obverse of an adaptation of a Sunburst–Clasped Hands flask, possibly GVIII–1, though the clasped hands on the reverse may have been inspired by one of the flasks in Group XII. *Private collection*

170. Cornucopia–Sheaf of Grain flask, an adaptation. *Private collection*

adaptations already listed, the designs of these three are composites of features of more than one 19th-century flask. Also, there is a slight variation in their forms.

8. Eagle–Cannon (Ill. 168). "Fifth" capacity. Lime green. *Obverse:* large eagle with raised and widespread wings, above a large poinsettia-like flower; in short arc above eagle, "LIBERTY"; possibly derived from one of the Willington Glass Works flasks (GII–61 through 64) or that of the Westford Glass Works (GII–65) having "LIBERTY" above a somewhat similar eagle that stands on a laurel wreath, not a flower. *Reverse:* cannon, possibly derived from one of the Union–Clasped Hands flasks of the Civil War period.

9. Sunburst–Clasped Hands (Ill. 169). "Fifth" capacity. Aquamarine. *Obverse:* large oval sunburst with ring around the dot at center; similar to the sunburst on GVIII–1 that has two rings around the center dot, instead of one as on this flask. *Reverse:* probably inspired by the framed clasped hands in upper zone of shield on the obverse of the calabash bottle GIV–42, or one of the Shield and Clasped Hands flasks, ca. 1861–70s, in Group XII (see Charts).

10. Cornucopia–Sheaf of Grain (Ill. 170). "Fifth" capacity Topaz. *Obverse:* "HORN OF PLENTY" in two curved lines above a large cornucopia filled with "fruit and vegetables," end curled to left; possibly derived from the cornucopia on GIII–5 or 6. *Reverse:* Sheaf of grain.

11. Ship *Franklin*–Anchor (Ill. 171). Pint. Yellowish green. *Obverse:* ship *Franklin* sailing to the right, above "FRANKLIN" in concave arc; presumably derived from either Dr. Dyott's common Kensington Glass Works' Agriculture & Masonic–Ship *Franklin* flask GIV–34 or the rare midwestern flask GIV–36 (see Charts). *Reverse:* anchor; "LIBERTY" on a pennant above and "AND UNION" on a pennant below anchor; presumably derived from the comparatively scarce New London Glass Works flask GII–68. At the center of the slightly concave base is an irregular indentation, presumably simulating a pontil mark. This adaptation does not conform in shape to Dr. Dyott's GIV–34 or 36 of the 1820s but is similar to the New London GII–68 of the 1860s.

12. Cornucopia–Grasshopper (Ill. 172). Pint. Opalescent white or opal. *Obverse:* cornucopia, very close representation of that on GIII–4 produced in the 1830s by the Coventry Glass Works,

694

A   B

171. Ship *Franklin*–Anchor flask, an adaptation. The obverse (**A**) with the ship is presumably derived from Dr. Dyott's GIV–34 or the midwestern GIV–36. The reverse (**B**) may well have been inspired by the New London Glass Works' GII–68. *Private collection*

A   B

173. This small (about ¼ pint) flask is an adaptation of the Sunburst pattern. **A**. The obverse is inscribed "Mother's Day Greetings." The similar sunburst on the reverse is centered with a cinquefoil. Made by the Imperial Glass Company and bearing their mark, the little flask may have been intended for a toilet water bottle. *Private collection*

A   B

172. Cornucopia–Grasshopper flask, an adaptation. **A**. The cornucopia on the obverse closely resembles the one on GIII–4. **B**. Reverse bears a grasshopper motif and the inscription "OLD STURBRIDGE VILLAGE"; this flask was especially made in Spain by the Pairpoint Glass Works for the museum gift shop at Sturbridge. *Collection of Kenneth M. Wilson*

Coventry, Connecticut. *Reverse:* grasshopper, lengthwise, surrounded by "OLD STUR-BRIDGE VILLAGE". While chief curator of Old Sturbridge Village, the author designed this flask as a stock item for the Old Sturbridge Village Museum Shop and "Horn of Plenty" Gift Shop, in both of which only accurate reproductions or objects closely related to the originals are sold. The cornucopia is appropriate to the latter. The grasshopper is particularly appropriate to the Old Sturbridge Village Museum Shop inasmuch as that insect is the symbol of the Village, chosen because, to the ancient Greeks,

it symbolized "sprung from the soil." And it is a peculiarly fitting symbol for, in a sense, the Village, a re-creation of the past, itself sprang from the soil. The flasks were produced for the Village by the Pairpoint Glass Company in a glasshouse it leased in Spain. Since they were blown in a mold and "stuck up" with a pontil, the neck, though partially formed in a mold, was finished by reheating and tooling. Also, the slightly concave base has a rough pontil mark. Though they were produced in numerous colors, including various shades of green, light blue, and aquamarine, very few were opalescent white—or opal—like the flask illustrated.

13. Mother's Day flask (Ill. 173). About ¼ pint. Light greenish yellow. *Obverse:* sunburst of ovoid shape narrower at base than top and inscribed "MOTHER'S DAY GREETINGS" in three lines. *Reverse:* similar sunburst with scalloped border and, at center, a cinquefoil. This flask, a product of the Imperial Glass Company, was machine-made, and its rectangular base bears the company's mark: an "I" superimposed on a "G." The neck was ground to fit a stopper, which is missing from this example. The flask, 4¾ inches in height without its stopper, probably was intended to serve as a toilet bottle. It probably was produced in the 1930s.

14. Scroll flask (Ill. 174). Quarter-pint. Vaseline (greenish yellow). Obverse and reverse, the same. Form and scroll design probably derived from the scarce pint GIX–45. Machine-made; neck ground to fit a stopper. Probably it was made sometime during the 1930–50 period and

174. In form and design, this ¼-pint Scroll flask may have been inspired by GIX–45, though the various design details have been considerably adapted. *Private collection*

175. The Shield and Clasped Hands flask shown here is adapted from the old ones charted in Group XII. The reverse is plain. *Private collection*

176. Bottle used by the J. W. Dant Distillery Company for their Kentucky Bourbon Whisky bears the long-popular old flask motif: an eagle with a shield on its breast. *Collection of Kenneth M. Wilson*

used as a perfume or cologne bottle. Its origin is unknown.

15. Shield and Clasped Hands (Ill. 175). Quart. Very pale greenish blue. *Obverse:* in space between arc of 11 stars and top of a large shield is "UNION"; a large star above each end of shield; framed clasped hands in upper zone of shield; at each side, a long laurel branch. *Reverse:* plain.

The design was derived from the flasks charted in Group XII, which were produced during and after our "War Between the States." The flask was machine-blown in a two-piece mold forming the body with plain, slightly concave base and the neck up to within ½ inch of the lip, which was formed in a separate mold part. The flask was probably made in the 1960s and, according to the store from which it was purchased, in Italy.

4

20TH-CENTURY
COMMEMORATIVE FLASKS

If further evidence is needed to substantiate the claim that old bottles and flasks form one of the main hobby interests of Americans, then certainly the large number of flasks and bottles produced in the 20th century in the manner of earlier, 19th-century ones, to commemorate national and historical figures or events or celebrate anniversaries, provides that evidence. Unlike the reproductions just discussed, these commemorative pieces are not exact copies of earlier containers, but they are often based

upon the forms and designs of the earlier ones and are certainly closely related in spirit and expression.

There are many precedents to serve as inspiration for the production of 20th-century commemorative flasks and bottles. Among them are flasks commemorating such heroes as Franklin, who died in 1780 (GI–95), and Washington (d. 1799) (GI–16), which were produced and advertised by T. W. Dyott as early as 1824. Other flasks bearing likenesses of Washington were made in numerous glasshouses

A   **B**

177. The Columbian Exposition of 1892/93 was commemorated by several flasks. The dates "1492–1892" on the obverse (**A**) of this example indicate the occasion: the 400th anniversary of Columbus's discovery of America. The obverse (**B**) is inscribed "Columbian Jubilee." (See GX–32 in the charts.) *The Corning Museum of Glass*

A   **B**

178. This flask is another commemorative of the Columbian Exposition. The obverse (**A**) shows a nearly full-face portrait of Columbus with the inscription "COLUMBIAN EXPOSITION" above it, and the date 1893 and "A.E.M. BROS. & CO." below. **B**. The reverse is marked, in four lines, "PENNSYLVANIA / PURE RYE / BAKER / WHISKEY". (See GI–128 in the Charts.) *The Corning Museum of Glass*

from the 1820s through the 1850s. Often, as in the case of the Washington–Taylor flasks (i.e., GI–37 through GI–56), these suggest the qualities of the contemporary political aspirant (e.g., Taylor) by association with the Father of His Country. In addition, pint and half-pint flasks portraying Lafayette & DeWitt Clinton (GI–80 through GI–82) were made in 1824/25 and afterward to commemorate Lafayette's triumphal second visit to America and Clinton's completion of the Erie Canal. The numerous Pike's Peak flasks commemorating the discovery of gold in that area and the three flasks (GI–127, GI–128, and GX–32) produced at the time of the Columbian Exposition, 1892/93, celebrating the 400th anniversary of Columbus's discovery of America in 1492, are additional examples of 19th-century commemorative flasks.

Aware that interest in the nation's early history had continued to grow steadily ever since World War II, manufacturers of glass containers—both large and small—hastened to "get on the bandwagon"—that is, to create historically associated products that would please this history-oriented segment of the population. Among the earliest of these 20th-century commemorative flasks and bottles were the Washington-Tree calabash bottle (Ill. 179) made by Owens-Illinois in 1932 and the Roosevelt-TVA calabash bottle (GI–129 in the Charts; Ill. 181) produced in 1936 by Wheaton to commemorate the building of the Norris Dam, the TVA's rural electrification program, and President

Roosevelt, who was chiefly responsible for it.

During the past 20 years the production of commemorative flasks and bottles has so proliferated that today we can almost be assured any major event will be memorialized by a Figured Flask or Bottle appropriate to the occasion. Witness the many bottle clubs that have had commemorative bottles designed and produced for their members, and the historical societies and like organizations that have honored historic events. Numerous distilleries, food processors, and other manufacturers have also utilized commemorative flasks and bottles, choosing subjects associated with major personages or events of the past or present and designs based upon or inspired by prototypes of Figured Flasks produced in the 19th century. Among the companies to do this, several stand out: the J. W. Dant Distillery Company, James B. Beam Distilling Company, and General Foods (to name just three). Certain glass manufacturers, such as T. C. Wheaton Glass Company of Millville, New Jersey, and Clevenger Brothers of Clayton, New Jersey, have also recognized the broad interest in and demand for decorated figured flasks and bottles and have initiated various series of commemorative containers—strictly as decorative objects—that have found a ready market.

Cataloged and illustrated here is a representative selection of 20th-century commemorative flasks and bottles. They vary greatly in their quality, both in design and execution, and most cannot compare to the best of the early 19th-century flasks. Some were

698

made by hand, but many were not. Those made on automatic bottle-making machines lack the individuality of the early flasks. Nevertheless, all of them represent an opportunity for the collector of the future—undoubtedly, in time, some of these flasks and bottles will be just as much sought after as 19th-century Figured Flasks are today. And like the earlier ones, these 20th-century commemoratives also reflect historical, political, social, and cultural events that are of interest to a wide segment of the population.

Early 20th-Century Commemoratives

1. Among the earliest commemorative bottles of the 20th century is a Washington–Tree calabash bottle (Ill. 179) of colorless glass, with probably a pint, or perhaps a pint and a half, capacity. *Obverse:* a classical bust of Washington facing left. *Reverse:* a flowering tree with two panels below each containing the dates 1732 and 1932. This bottle was machine-made by Owens-Illinois, Inc., at the time of the bicentennial of the birth of Washington. The base is a slightly concave oval bearing the Owens-Illinois symbol: an "O" with an "I" inside, within an elongated diamond. To the left is the numeral "2"; below is the numeral "1"; to the right is "2." This bottle was originally used as a container for vinegar. Height 7⅞ inches.

2. Washington–Eagle flask (Ill. 180), a colorless quart flask made on an automatic bottle-making machine by Owens-Illinois at their Alton, Illinois, plant in 1932, to commemorate the 200th anniversary of Washington's birth. It served as a vinegar container, but the manufacturer's records do not indicate for whom it was made or how many were produced. Adolf Harste of Owens-Illinois's Design and Development Department in Toledo designed it. It is not a reproduction in either form or decoration, but it was certainly inspired by early-19th-century Figured Flasks. The likeness of Washington is similar to that on the obverse of the quart Washington–Taylor GI–51 produced at Dyottville about 1850; the eagle closely resembles the one on the reverse of the Columbia–Eagle pint flask GI–117, attributed to the Union Glass Works in Kensington, probably about 1820–30, but here it was reduced in size to leave room above for a paper label reading: "Buy Centennial Vinegar." Strangely, only twelve (rather than the

A   **B**

179. The Washington–Tree calabash bottle was among the earliest of the 20th-century commemoratives. **A.** The obverse bears a classic bust of Washington. **B.** On the reverse, under a flowering tree, two panels bear the dates 1732 and 1932, indicating the bicentennial of Washington's birth. *Private collection*

A   **B**

180. Commemorative Washington–Eagle flask, honoring the 200th anniversary of Washington's birth. **A.** The likeness of Washington on the obverse resembles the one on the quart Washington–Taylor, GI–51. **B.** The eagle on the reverse resembles the one on GI–117. Above it, space was left to accommodate a paper label reading "Buy Centennial Vinegar." This flask was made by Owens-Illinois in 1932; the example shown is in their collection. *Owens-Illinois*

usual thirteen) stars form the arc below the eagle. The closure is a metal screw-cap. Impressed on the base of the flask is the trademark of Owens-Illinois of that date: an elongated horizontal diamond with a large O superimposed. To its left, a "7" indicates manufacture at the Alton plant; a "2" at the right represents the date 1932. Below,

A   **B**

181. The Roosevelt–TVA calabash bottle commemorating President Franklin D. Roosevelt and the building of the Norris Dam, the TVA's rural electrification program. **A**. The obverse bears a full-face view of the President above an eagle with spread wings. **B**. The reverse, dated 1936, depicts the dam, with an electrification symbol and "TVA" above it. *Private collection*

the figure "12" is the number of the mold.

3. Roosevelt–TVA calabash bottle (see GI–129 in the Charts; also Ill. 181), similar in form to GI–102 or GI–106 but, unlike them, with a short base. *Obverse:* full front view of President Franklin D. Roosevelt, with an eagle, the emblem of the USA, below. *Reverse:* at top, "TVA" with the electrification symbol of a hand with electrical energy flying from it just below; a straight line separates top from a depiction of the Norris Dam with the date "1936" beneath. Round tapered neck is finished with a broad, sloping collar. Unlike the original Jenny Lind and other mid-19th-century calabash bottles, this reproduction terminates in a low oval base. Capacity of the bottle in aquamarine colored glass is one quart.

The Roosevelt–TVA calabash was conceived and designed by Dr. J. S. Hall of Clinton, Tennessee, a medical doctor whose hobby in the 1930s was bottle collecting. The hobby had given him so much pleasure that he decided to have this commemorative bottle produced as his contribution to bottle collectors. Because the Norris Dam was not far from his own location and was of importance as well, Dr. Hall chose to commemorate its construction, the TVA's rural electrification program, and the man responsible for the entire project—President Roosevelt. The mold was

made by the T. C. Wheaton Company of Millville, New Jersey. Only 816 bottles were produced, of almost colorless glass, the order being completed in the fall of 1936. On the base of the bottle is a curiously embossed device consisting of a somewhat lopsided circle with two triangular points projecting almost opposite each other. Two-thirds of the circle is distinctly formed, the other third blurred. In a letter written to Mr. George S. McKearin in Hoosick Falls, New York, February 4, 1937, Dr. Hall indicated he was sending four dozen TVA Commemorative Bottles to Mr. McKearin's New York Antique Shop, on consignment, and suggested that they should not be sold for under $3.50 each. In 1948 the suggested sales price was $5.00 each. This bottle, one of the first 20th-century commemorative bottles, is well produced and is a worthwhile collectible.

4. General MacArthur flask (Ill. 182). *Obverse:* bust of General MacArthur facing right, wearing an Army cap; inscribed "GENERAL MAC ARTHUR" in an arc above, and "KEEP THEM FLYING" in a straight line at the base of the flask. *Reverse:* "V" for victory with the date "1942" within the "V" and the inscription "GOD BLESS AMERICA" in script in an arc above; a flag on each side of the "V," and the Morse Code symbol for the letter "V" (. . . —) below. The flask was made in amethyst, yellowish green, and a rather pale blue glass; possibly in other colors as well. The quality of the glass is fairly good. The neck was formed in the mold, but the plain lip was finished by reheating and tooling. The plain base is very slightly concave, with a scarred pontil mark. Height, 6 inches; about ½ pint capacity. Maker unknown; probably produced shortly after World War II, possibly between 1946 and 1950.

182. The obverse of the General MacArthur flask. At the base it is inscribed "KEEP THEM FLYING". The reverse bears the "V" for victory, the date "1942," the words "GOD BLESS AMERICA" in script, two flags, and the Morse code symbol for the letter "V." The maker is unknown; the flask was probably produced shortly after World War II. *Private collection*

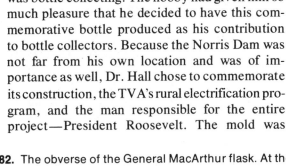

700

183. Canteen-type flask commemorating President John F. Kennedy. His portrait appears on the obverse (**A**) with the inscription "MAY 29, 1917 JOHN FITZGERALD KENNEDY NOV. 22, 1963". On the reverse (**B**) is the famous quotation from his inaugural address: "ASK NOT WHAT YOUR COUNTRY CAN DO FOR YOU . . ." *Wheaton Historical Association, Millville, N.J.*

Wheaton Commemorative Flasks and Bottles

Without doubt the Wheaton Glass Company of Millville, New Jersey, a division of Wheaton Industries, has been to date the largest producer of commemorative flasks and bottles. The year 1967 marked the beginning of their Presidential Series: 18 flasks bearing likenesses of presidents. Between then and May 1974, some 631,800 of these flasks were made by Wheaton for NULINE Products Company. Other series, initiated shortly after the Presidential Series began, included:

Great Americans	490,000
Lunar or Astronaut	194,599
Star	34,074
Christmas	96,333
Campaign	126,231
American Inventor	
Early American Patriots	
American Religious	
American Military Leaders	
American Writers	
Evangelists	
Special Series	

The total production of all these series, up to May 1974, was slightly over 1½ million. Some were marked "First Edition"—actually, they were the *only* edition—but, as can be seen above, the edition was not as limited as one tends to think an "edition"

may be. However, beginning in the fall of 1975, when the responsibility for the production of such commemorative items was turned over to the Wheaton Historical Association, for Wheaton Village in Millville, New Jersey, a policy of issuing more strictly limited editions was adopted. For example, production of the 1975 Christmas commemorative flask was limited to 5,000. In addition, these flasks were not made on an automatic bottle-making machine, but were handmade with the aid of an early semiautomatic Schiller machine. Following here are more detailed descriptions and observations about some of these bottles and flasks, several of which are illustrated:

WHEATON'S PRESIDENTIAL SERIES

5. President Kennedy Flask (Ill. 183), of cylindrical canteen shape, transparent blue glass, with an iridescent finish. *Obverse:* head of President John F. Kennedy facing left, with semicircular inscription below: "MAY 29, 1917 JOHN FITZGERALD KENNEDY NOV. 22, 1963." *Reverse:* a quotation from Kennedy's inaugural speech: "ASK NOT WHAT YOUR COUNTRY CAN DO FOR YOU; ASK WHAT YOU CAN DO FOR YOUR COUNTRY J.F.K." Entirely machine-made for the NULINE Products Company of Millville, New Jersey, by the T. C. Wheaton Manufacturing Company of Millville, New Jersey, in 1967.

One machine run of 55,300 Kennedy flasks was

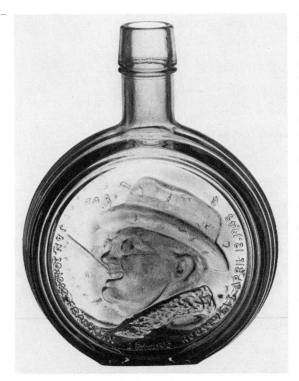

185. Washington flask from the Wheaton Presidential Series. The glass has a frosted or acid-etched finish. *Wheaton Industries, Millville, N.J.*

184. This canteen-type flask commemorating President Franklin D. Roosevelt is another in the Wheaton Presidential Series. The obverse bears his portrait; the reverse, a phrase from his first inaugural address: "WE HAVE NOTHING TO FEAR BUT FEAR ITSELF."

made to sell originally for $5.00. In 1972 these were said to be bringing as much as $100, but $35 seems a more likely price. The example illustrated is from the former Charles B. Gardner collection. It is interesting to note that already these Kennedy flasks and some others have been reproduced by a glasshouse in Italy and imported into this country by another firm.

6. Roosevelt Flask (Ill. 184), of cylindrical canteen shape; mold blown of green glass with an iridescent finish. *Obverse:* head of Roosevelt facing left, wearing a fedora, smoking a cigarette in a holder, with "JANUARY 30, 1882–FRANKLIN DELANO ROOSEVELT. APRIL 12, 1945" inscribed semicircularly below. *Reverse* bears phrase from F.D.R.'s first inaugural address: "WE HAVE NOTHING TO FEAR BUT FEAR ITSELF." This flask or bottle, issued in 1970, was the second of the Presidential Series produced. Edition of 89,700, made by automatic bottle-making machine, originally sold for $5.00.

Other flasks in the Wheaton Presidential Series include:
7. Dwight D. Eisenhower: amethyst glass, iridescent finish; 1968 (78,800).

8. Abraham Lincoln: topaz glass, iridescent finish; 1968 (92,900).

9. Woodrow Wilson: blue glass, iridescent finish; 1969 (44,600).

10. Washington (Ill. 185): colorless glass with an acid etched or "frosted" finish; 1969 (51,106).

11. Theodore Roosevelt: cobalt-blue glass, iridescent finish; 1969 (41,840).

12. Thomas Jefferson: ruby glass, iridescent finish; 1970 (30,080).

13. Andrew Jackson (Ill. 186): green glass, iridescent finish; 1971 (21,668).

186. Andrew Jackson flask from the Wheaton Presidential Series. The glass is green with an iridescent finish. 1971. *Wheaton Industries, Millville, N.J.*

14. Ulysses S. Grant (Ill. 187): topaz glass, iridescent finish; 1972 (26,266).

Other presidents represented in the series were: 15. John Adams; 16. Andrew Johnson; 17. William McKinley; 18. Herbert Hoover (Ill. 188), 1972 (16,000); 19. Harry S. Truman, 1973 (22,736); 20. Lyndon B. Johnson, 1973 (25,804); 21. Richard Nixon, 1974; and 22. Gerald R. Ford (Ill. 189), 1975.

WHEATON'S GREAT AMERICAN SERIES (490,000)

Each of these has the form of a flattened calabash bottle with broad sloping collar and an iridescent finish:

23. Martin Luther King, Jr. (Ill. 190), amber, 1969.

24. Robert E. Lee (Ill. 191)

25. Thomas Alva Edison (Ill. 192)

26. Benjamin Franklin

27. Betsy Ross (Ill. 193)

28. Billy Graham

29. Will Rogers

30. General Patton

31. Paul Revere

32. Chief Justice Hughes

33. Helen Keller

34. John Paul Jones

35. Charles Lindbergh

36. General MacArthur (Ill. 194)

37. Robert Kennedy

189. This Wheaton Presidential flask commemorating Gerald R. Ford was issued in 1975. *Wheaton Industries, Millville, N.J.*

190. Flattened calabash bottle commemorating Martin Luther King, Jr., produced in 1969, part of Wheaton's Great American Series. *Private collection*

187. Ulysses S. Grant flask from the Wheaton Presidential Series. Inscription above the portrait reads: "THE WARRIOR STATESMAN". The glass of this 1972 flask is topaz with iridescent finish. *Wheaton Industries,* Millville, N.J.

188. Herbert Clark Hoover flask from the Wheaton Presidential Series. This flask was also issued in 1972. *Wheaton Industries, Millville, N.J.*

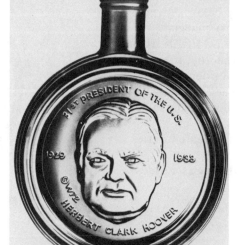

191. Robert E. Lee commemorative bottle from Wheaton's Great American Series.
Wheaton Industries, Millville, N.J.

192. Bottle commemorating Thomas Alva Edison, from Wheaton's Great American Series. *Wheaton Industries, Millville, N.J.*

193. Betsy Ross commemorative bears her name and dates: Jan. 1, 1752; Jan. 30, 1836. *Wheaton Industries, Millville, N.J.*

194. Wheaton's Great American Series also includes this commemorative honoring General MacArthur. *Private collection*

WHEATON'S ASTRONAUT OR LUNAR SERIES (194,599)

These flasks are of the same flattened calabash shape as the Great American Series; they also have an iridescent finish:

38. Apollo XI (Ill. 195), cobalt-blue, bearing portraits of astronauts Armstrong, Aldrin, and Collins

39. Apollo XII, ruby glass, bearing likenesses of astronauts Conrad, Gordon, and Dean

40. Apollo XIII (Ill. 196) of burley-colored glass, bearing likenesses of Lovell, Swigert, and Haise

41. Apollo XIV, of aqua glass, with representations of Shepard, Roosa, and Mitchell

42. Apollo XV, of green glass, showing Scott, Irwin, and Worden

Other bottles offered by T. C. Wheaton among the NULINE products, all available in amber or amethyst glass, all varying in height from 8 inches to 10 inches, and all fully machine-made, include:

43. Calabash bottle bearing Masonic emblems and the word "UNION"

195. Flattened calabash-shape flask celebrating the Apollo XI astronauts Armstrong, Aldrin, and Collins, part of Wheaton's Astronaut or Lunar Series. *Wheaton Industries, Millville, N.J.*

196. Wheaton's Apollo XIII flask bears the likenesses of Lovell, Swigert, and Haise. *Wheaton Industries, Millville, N.J.*

44. Flask bearing portrait of Washington facing left, with his name in an arch above

45. Cabin Bitters bottle

The following, also part of the NULINE series, were introduced in 1971; all were of "milk" glass and were machine-made:

46. Pint flask with three-quarter bust of Benjamin Franklin on obverse, looking toward the left, with "BENJAMIN FRANKLIN" in an arch above. *Reverse:* a glasshouse with "GLASS-HOUSE 1888" in an arch above and "WHEATON MILLVILLE, N.J." below. This commemorates the first Wheaton glasshouse. Each flask was fitted with a "gold" cannonball stopper and had a simulated pontil mark on the base in the form of an irregular indentation about ⅝ inch maximum length.

47. Horseshoe Bitters

48. Dr. Fisch's Bitters

49. Root Bitters

50. Army Drum bottle

None of these is an actual reproduction, but all are derived from 19th-century prototypes. For example,

the Army Drum bottle was inspired by McKeever's Army Bitters bottle, but the height of the adaptation is considerably less. Each of these bottles or flasks made by Wheaton was also made in green and amethyst glass with an iridescent finish; in those colors they sold for $1.50 each. Height: 7½ inches.

JAMESTOWN SERIES

A series of at least six commemorative flasks or bottles was produced at or about the time of the Jamestown Festival in 1957 on the 350th anniversary of the founding of the settlement there. All are well made, probably by Imperial Glass of Bellaire, Ohio; each was inspired by an early 19th-century prototype. The six descriptions of the Jamestown Series follow here; the first three are also pictured (Ills. 197, 198, 199).

51. Captain John Smith flask (Ill. 197). Machine-blown of pale rosy amethyst glass. *Obverse:* portrait of John Smith surrounded by "CAP-TAYNE JOHN SMITH" in a concave arc below, and—separated by a dash at each end of this inscription—the words: "SOMETYMES GOVERNOR OF VIRGINIA". *Reverse:* a ship sailing to the left, surrounded by "AMERICA'S 350TH BIRTHDAY" in a concave arc below, with the inscription "THE GOOD SHIP SUSAN CONSTANT" completing the surround. The rather long neck was blown in a mold, then tooled and finished after being reheated. Base is slightly concave and unmarked, but there are a couple of swirls near the center that may have been meant to simulate a pontil mark. Height: 8¼ inches. Approximately ¾ quart capacity.

197. Captain John Smith flask, from Wheaton's Jamestown Series. Obverse *(A)* pictures Smith. Reverse *(B)* depicts the ship *Susan Constant* and identifies the occasion as America's 350th birthday. *Private collection*

A   **B**

198. Another flask in Wheaton's Jamestown Series is this one commemorating John Rolfe, whose bust decorates the obverse (**A**). On the reverse (**B**) is a house identified as "HIS JAMESTOWN HOME." *Private collection*

52. Pint flask, in somewhat the form of the McCARTY & TORREYSON "scroll" GIX–48. *Obverse:* ¾ bust of John Rolfe facing slightly left with "JOHN ROLFE" in an arch above (Ill. 198A). *Reverse:* a house with trees behind it, a chimney on the foreground side of the house, and the words "HIS JAMESTOWN HOME" above (Ill. 198B). In the slightly concave base are several swirls near the center, somewhat simulating a pontil mark; the neck was formed in the mold and finished by tooling after being reheated. Height: 7 inches. This flask is of almost colorless glass with a pinkish or rosy tint. Background and sides have a fine pebbled surface, except for the neck, which has been tooled.

53. Colorless glass flask of cylindrical canteen form (Ill. 199). *Obverse:* three ships sailing on the left with a series of straight horizontal lines above their sails. The years "1607–1957" appear in a straight line below, with "JAMESTOWN FESTIVAL" in a concave arc underneath. *Reverse:* "AMERICA'S / 350TH / BIRTHDAY" appears in three lines of large letters. The base is marked "JAMESTOWN" with the "T" slanted at the top, "VA. 1607–1957"; between the two years is the symbol "IG" for Imperial Glass. Height: 7¼ inches.

Another flask of this same form, also colorless and marked in the same manner on the base, is part of this series. The obverse, in large letters in a circle following the exterior contour of the bottle, reads: "Gᵥ Sᵣ FRANCIS WYATT'S FORCE"; this surrounds the inscription:

199. Canteen-shape flask in the Wheaton Jamestown Series shows three ships on the obverse, the dates 1607–1957, and the words "JAMESTOWN FESTIVAL." The reverse is marked *"AMERICA'S / 350TH / BIRTHDAY." Private collection*

"MENTIONED / IN / 1625 / JAMESTOWNE / COLONIAL / CENSUS / RECORDS / FIRST / ONE / SO / LISTED".

54. Bottle in the form of a handled jug, blown of light, pale yellowish-green glass. On one side is a representation of the reconstructed Jamestown glasshouse; on the other, in five lines, the words "GLASS MAKING AT / JAMESTOWN / WAS AMERICA'S FIRST / INDUSTRY / 1608". This bottle has the same finely pebbled textured surface as Nos. 51 to 53. There is an annular ring about ½ inch from the top of the long neck. This bottle was probably blown in the mold and the whole top and neck fire-polished. Possibly, however, the ring may have been laid on and tooled. The handle was applied by hand and the lower end turned up. Height: 8⅝ inches.

55. Pumpkinseed flask of extremely pale blue, almost colorless, glass. *Obverse:* view of the ruins of the Jamestown Church, with the words "JAMESTOWN CHURCH TOWER 1639" in an arc above. *Reverse:* a monument with the words "GOVERNMENT MONUMENT JAMESTOWN 1607" in an arch above. Broad sloping collar apparently applied and tooled after removal from the mold. Base is plain, slightly concave in the form of an oval. Height: 7¾ inches.

56. Chief Powhatan–James Fort, a quart scroll flask of light yellowish-amber glass. *Obverse:* half-length portrait of an Indian with a long head-dress, facing right, with a peace pipe held in both hands."CHIEF POWHATAN" appears in a concave arc below. *Reverse:* a view of James Fort with trees beyond and the words "JAMES FORT" in two lines below; above, on the left side in a slightly curved line, is "AMERICA'S" followed by "350th" in a straight horizontal line and "BIRTHDAY" in a slight arc descending on the right. The fort is triangular, with circular bastions at each point, a cannon in each of the two forward ones and a flag flying in the center of the rear one. The whole surface, as on the John Rolfe flasks, is finely textured. The base is a plain, hollowed oval. The neck was blown in a mold and finished by hand. Height: 7⅛ inches. A knowledgeable collector has told me there is another scroll flask like the "POWHATAN," but I do not know its subject.

Miscellaneous Commemoratives

The 20th-century Figured Flasks have been made to commemorate numerous other events in various parts of the country. Among these commemoratives are

57. Colorless cylindrical canteen-shape flask with flattened bottom. *Obverse* (Ill. 200A): the seal of the State of West Virginia within a half-wreath of flowers, with a banner above reading "STATE OF WEST VIRGINIA". *Reverse* (Ill. 200B): a pebbly textured embossed map of West Virginia with the words "WHEELING/FIRST CAPI-TAL" in two lines at top left and "WEST VIRGINIA / CENTENNIAL / 1863–1963" in three lines at the lower right. The base is marked "MADE BY" (in one line) above "IMPERIAL GLASS" (in one line). This is a well-made bottle; the plain neck was partly formed in a mold and finished by hand. Height: 7¼ inches.

58. New Jersey Tercentenary flask, pint, deep amber (Ill. 201). *Obverse:* stylized pine tree with two geometric forms on each side of the trunk forming a triangle with the tree. Along the sides are "PEOPLE" and "PURPOSE"; beneath is the word "PROGRESS," and below that, in a straight line "1664–1964." "NEW JERSEY TERCENTENARY" forms an arch above the

whole. *Reverse:* a large oak tree is depicted with the inscription "SALEM OAK/1675/SALEM, N.J." in three straight lines below. The background of each side is plain and smooth. This flask was completely machine-made of good-quality glass. "ANCHOR/HOCKING/GLASS CORP." appears on the base in three straight lines. Height: 7 inches.

59. Lincoln Log Cabin flask (Ill. 202). *Obverse:* bust of Lincoln facing right surrounded by "WITH MALICE TOWARDS NONE"—the words very faintly embossed. *Reverse:* a log cabin with a fence in the foreground; "WITH CHARITY FOR ALL" appears in an arch above the cabin. These flasks of about 1½-pint capacity were made in various colors, including green, amethyst, and light yellowish amber. The base is plain and flat; the neck was blown almost entirely in a mold, except for the very upper part, which was reheated and tooled to simulate an applied sloping collar about ½ inch wide. The necks of these commemoratives vary in height just as those on 19th-century flasks did. Maker unknown; probably made in the early 1960s, undoubtedly as a Civil War centennial souvenir.

60. Quart Jefferson Davis–Robert E. Lee flask, made in numerous colors (Ill. 203). *Obverse* (an opaque white example): a full ¾-length bust of Davis facing right, with "JEFFERSON DAVIS" very lightly embossed in a slight concave arc below. *Reverse:* similar ¾-length portrait of Lee, facing left, with his name below. Each bust is surrounded by a border made up of an alternating star and conventionalized Confederate flag consisting basically of an "X." The necks of the flasks were finished by tooling, to form a slight, simulated "blob top" collar. Also made of amethyst and light yellowish amber glass, and probably other colors too, these flasks were probably made for the centennial celebration of the War Between the States; they were first sold at a centennial celebration in Gettysburg, Pennsylvania, in 1961. Which factory produced them is unknown, but they are believed to have been made in the U.S.A. The quality of the glass is good to fair, the surface of the borders around the portraits being intentionally roughened.

61. *Obverse:* "portrait"—full view of Charles B. Gardner; he is portrayed in a small three-quarter bust on a plain background, surmounted by a tripartite ribbon reading "ANTIQUE CONN. &

200. Canteen-shape flask made by Imperial Glass in honor of the West Virginia Centennial, 1863–1963. Obverse (**A**) has the state seal in the center. Reverse (**B**) features an embossed map of the state. *Private collection*

202. The maker of this Lincoln–Log Cabin flask is unknown. It doubtless is a Civil War Centennial souvenir. Obverse (**A**) bears the inscription "WITH MALICE TOWARDS NONE" along with Lincoln's likeness. **B**. Reverse shows a log cabin and is inscribed "WITH CHARITY FOR ALL." *Private collection*

201. Anchor Hocking Glass Corporation made this New Jersey Tercentenary flask. Obverse (**A**) features a stylized pine tree; reverse (**B**), an oak. Both sides bear dates and inscriptions pertinent to the state's history. *Private collection*

203. Obverse (**A**) of an opaque white flask made to commemorate Jefferson Davis and Robert E. Lee. **B**. The reverse of another example of this Davis-Lee flask, in a different color glass. No matter what the color of the glass, on each side the portrait is framed by a border consisting of stars alternating with *X*'s, suggesting the motifs of the Confederate flag. *Private collection*

DEAN OF BOTTLES" in an arc above. Below, barely visible, is the script signature "CHARLIE GARDNER" and, below that, the date "1973." *Reverse:* within a high, ridged circle is a stylized representation of a ca. 1650 bottle with the almost indecipherable word "ANTIQUES" along its lower edge, surrounded within the confines of the circle by "SOMERS CONN." and, in a concave arc below the bottle, "BOTTLE CLUB." "FBY 1971" appears in a straight line, divided on each side of the neck of the bottle. This bottle was commissioned by the Somers, Connecticut, Antique Bottle Collector's Club, on the occasion of a testimonial dinner held in honor of Charles B. Gardner, dean of bottle collectors, of New London, Connecticut. The dinner followed a full-day bottle show in Glastonbury. The original commission was for 2,500 of these bottles, all to be made in opal, or opalescent, glass, in deference to Charlie Gardner's desire. In actuality, only 900 were made, by the Pairpoint Glass Company, Inc., of Sagamore, Massachusetts. Each was inscribed with a diamond point number. The one in the author's collection is marked "#4 of 2500." Originally these flasks were offered to members at $9.00 each. The form of the flask is the same as that of the Cornucopia–Urn flask, GIII–4 (see Charts), and the Cornucopia–Grasshopper adaptation made for Old Sturbridge Village (Ill. 172). The flask was blown by hand in a mold, stuck up with a pontil, and the neck and lip entirely finished by hand. It is unfortunate that this memento to the "dean of bottle collectors" was not better conceived. For example, the rather small full-front view of what presumes to be Charlie Gardner could have been a much larger three-quarter view portraying a much more accurate portrait of him. Nevertheless, the flask was produced in such limited quantity, and so superbly that it ranks with the best of the originals. It is certainly destined to be a collector's item of the future.

62. "Spirit of '76" flask (Ill. 204). Colorless. Though an adaptation as well as a commemorative flask, this one was destined to be both a commercial container and a memento of an historical event. It is one of five flasks with designs either derived from early 19th-century flasks or inspired by them, in honor of the Bicentennial of the United States of America. It was produced also in amber glass, as were the four other designs— namely, a Cornucopia, a Liberty Bell, a Log

204. The "Spirit of '76" flask—an adaptation as well as a commemorative, and a commercial container as well as a memento of a historical event. These flasks were made in five different designs for General Foods, by several glass companies—to contain Log Cabin Syrup. *Collection of Kenneth M. Wilson*

Cabin, and an Eagle—which were made for General Foods and introduced as containers of four varieties of its Log Cabin Syrup in December 1975. They were produced by machine by the Thatcher Glass Company, the Brockway Glass Company, and Anchor Hocking. The designs were the same, but the flasks of each company differ slightly in detail from those of the other companies, for there were slight variations in the individual molds. On the base of each bottle are a depiction of a log cabin, the words "LOG CABIN SYRUP", the logo of the manufacturer, and—in some cases—a number, which probably represents the mold number. Although produced in quantity, these bottles may become "collectible" for many bottle collectors in the near future.

REFERENCE NOTES

(Full data on sources listed in the Bibliography are not given here.)

I.
NOTES FOR THE CURIOUS

1. BOTTLE COLLECTING

1. Carleton, Emma, "The Sign of the Carboy," *Century Magazine,* Vol. LXIII (Apr. 1902), p. 834.

2. Barber, Edwin Atlee, *American Glass Ware* (Philadelphia: 1900).

2. BOTTLE FAMILY NAMES

3.

(1) *Shorter Oxford English Dictionary,* 1933. "M.E. ad/aption/ of O.F. *bouteille* —a vessel with a narrow neck for holding liquids; orig. of leather."

(2) Noah Webster, in *An American Dictionary of the English Language,* 1828, deduced that if a bottle was primarily a bag, etc., the word was originally applied to bags of skins used as bottles in Asia.

(3) Botel & bottels: Geoffrey Chaucer, "The Pardoner's Tale," *The Canterbury Tales:* "And borrowed of him large botels thre." Edition edited by Alfred W. Pollard, London, 1887; ". . . his grate bottels three." Quoted in *London Encyclopaedia,* 1845, Vol. LV. Bottles.

(4) Glass Bottells, 1572: Great Britain Office of the Revels, Extracts from the accounts of the Revels at Court, in the reigns of Queen Elizabeth and King James I from the original office Books of the Masters and Yeoman. With an introduction and notes by Peter Cunningham. London, 1842, p. 28.

(5) "Leathern Bottles for wine": in passage from the will of John Wytloff, Rector of Lodiwell in the Diocese of Exeter, 1405, quoted by Ivor Noël Hume, "The Glass Wine Bottle in Colonial Virginia," note 38, p. 96.

4.

(1) Baret, John, *An Avearie or Triple Dictionary* in English, Latin and French (London: 1573, 1580).

(2) Minshew, John, *The Guide into Tongues* (London: 1617).

5.

(1) Bailey, N., *The Universal Etymological English Dictionary* (London: 1724; "generally made of glass," 1744).

(2) Johnson, S., *A Dictionary of the English Language* (London: 1755); "narrow mouth," "of glass or other matter," "a quantity of wine usually put into a bottle, a quart"; 1760: "a small vessel."

(3) Barclay, Rev. James, *A Complete and Universal English Dictionary* (London: 1782): "when of glass a glass bottle"; 1813: "Figuratively a quart." The figurative use of bottle for a quart is not surprising since quart size predominated, overwhelmingly, in the newspaper advertisements read.

(4) Webster, Noah, *An American Dictionary of the English Language,* 1828 edition: "a hollow vessel of glass, wood, leather, or other material, with a narrow mouth, for holding and carrying liquids."

6. Thorpe, W. A., "English Glassware in the XVII Century," p. 13.

7.

(1) Bailey, 1724; Johnson, 1755; Webster, 1828.

(2) Oxford, 1933: *vial* variant of *fiol, fiall,* etc.; *phial*—adaption of Old French *fiole,* also *phiole.*

8.

(1) Viole: Chaucer, "The Canon's Yeoman's Tale" (c.1380), *The Canterbury Tales*, edited by Alfred W. Pollard, 1887.

(2) Violi: Baret, 1573. *See* 4(1).

(3) Voyall: Great Britain Office of the Revels, 1576, p.119. *See* 3(4).

(4) Violl: Thorpe, *see* 6; Mansell & Co., 1628, English manufacturers of bottles.

(5) Viol: Jonson, Ben, *The Fox*, Act II, Sc. 1, 1607; Benjamine Wheat's Account Book. Connecticut Historical Society, Hartford, Conn.

(6) Foil: Digby, Sir Kenelem, *Choice and Experimental Receipts in Physick and Chirurgery* (London: 1668 [3 years after Digby's death]), p.1.

(7) Vial: Kersey, John, *Dictionarium Anglo-Britannicum or a General English Dictionary* (London: 1708). Johnson, 1755, quotes Shakespeare—"And from your small vials . . . "

(8) Violles: *The Secretes of the Reverende Maister Alexis of Piermont*, translated out of the French into English by Wyllyam Warde (London: 1558), Fol. 128.

(9) Vialls: Holm, Randle, *An Academie or Store House of Armory and Blazon*. Harley MS. 2033, c.1663, Chap. 15 Lib. 3 (London, 1905); Samuel Sewall's Diary, Apr. 16, 1703: " . . . viall of lavender Water."

9. Johnson, 1755; Webster, 1828.

10. Webster, 1828; *The Bungay Edition of Barclay's Dictionary*, 1813.

11. Philadelphia, *Pennsylvania Journal*, Apr. 21, 1755. Ad of Benjamin Jackson, Mustard Manufacturer.

12. Old English: *Shorter Oxford English Dictionary*, 1933. French flasque: Johnson, 1755, and his followers; also Webster's *New International Dictionary*, 1949, which includes also "Italian flasca," etc.

13.

(1) For powder: Minshew, *The Guide into Tongues*, (1617); Webster (1828 and later).

(2) Flasque: Blount, Thomas, *Glossographia* (1681); E. Coles, *An English Dictionary* (1685), gives "also a bottle (or pottle [2 Qts.]) of Florence Wine."

(3) Flask: Kersey, 1708, " . . . Also a sort of bottle, such as Florence-Wine is usually sold in."

14.

(1) Barclay, 1782: "thin long necked . . . "

(2) Bettée: *London Encyclopaedia*, Vol. IV (1845); *Bettie: Encyclopaedia; or a Dictionary of Arts, Sciences and Miscellaneous Literature*, first American Edition. Philadelphia, 1798. Vol. III, p. 474. Both spellings occur in late 18th- and early 19th-century advertisements in American newspapers.

15. Wall, A. J., "Proposals For Establishing a Glass Works in the City of New York in 1752," *The New-York Historical Society Quarterly Bulletin*, Vol. X (Oct. 1926), p. 97.

16.

(1) "fflint pocket bottle": Thorpe, W. A., "The Glass Sellers' Bills Woburn Abbey," p. 190.

(2) Flask: Smollett, Tobias, *Perigrine Pickle* (Bohn Library), Vol. I, p. 45.

(3) Pocket Pistol: Woodforde, *Passages from the Five Volumes of the Diary of a Country Parson, 1758–1802*, edited by John Beresford.

17.

(1) Hunting bottle: Boston, Mass., *The Weekly News Letter*, Jan. 17, 1745; New England Glass Company, Cambridge, Mass., Price List ca. 1818.

(2) Pocket bottle: *Boston Evening Post*, Apr. 30, 1750.

(3) Dram bottles: Philadelphia, *Pennsylvania Gazette*, Jan. 5, 1758; Hartford, *Connecticut Courant and Weekly Intelligencer*, July 19, 1790 and Dec. 8, 1805; English Price List, Sept. 21, 1805: green at 4s 4d per lb.

(4) Flask: New York City, *The New York Journal or General Advertiser*, Aug. 3, 1775; *Philadelphia Gazette and Universal Daily Advertiser*, Nov. 6, 1799. The latter probably were products of the Philadelphia Glass Works, Kensington, or of the New-Jersey Glass Manufactory, Glassboro, N.J.

18. Thorpe. (*See* 6. p. 15; *see* 16(1), pp. 191, 199.)

19. *New York Evening Post*, Feb. 1, 1819: "Boston manufactured sucking bottles." These must have been blown at either Boston Glass Manufactory, South Boston, or the New England Glass Company's Works, Cambridge.

20.

(1) Thorpe, "The Evolution of the Decanter," cites an advertisement in 1690 using the word *decanter*.

(2) Kersey, 1708.

21. *New York Independent Journal and the General Advertiser*, July 23, 1785: Wm. Williams, New York City merchant, imported, from London, "quart and pint decanters for Taverns." Hartford, *Connecticut Courant and Weekly Intelligencer*, Jan. 28, 1783; ad of a Middletown, Conn., merchant.

22. *The Shorter Oxford English Dictionary*, 1933; Webster's *New International Dictionary*, 1949.

23. Demi-john: Philadelphia, *Pennsylvania Journal*, Mar. 22, 1762.

Demi-jeane: Philadelphia, *Pennsylvania Packet*, July 4, 1788.

Dame John: Philadelphia, *Pennsylvania Packet*, May 14, 1790.

Dime-john: Boston, *Independent Chronicle*, Dec. 18, 1788.

Demie John: *New York Packet and the American Advertiser*, 1790.

Demi John: Hartford, *Connecticut Courant and the Weekly Intelligencer*, Aug. 18, 1788.

Demy John: Philadelphia, *Poulson's American Daily Advertiser*, Sept. 19, 1804; Apr. 19, 1814.

Dimijohn: New York, *The Diary or London Register*, Feb. 20, 1794.

Demijohn: *New York Daily Gazette*, Aug. 13, 1789.

24. Demijohns: Philadelphia, *Pennsylvania Journal*, Mar. 22, 1762; *New York Mercury*, Sept. 10, 1753; *New York Daily Advertiser*, May 9, 1792.

Carboys: Philadelphia, *Pennsylvania Chronicle*, Jan. 26, 1767; *Pennsylvania Gazette and Universal Daily Advertiser*, Jan. 24, 1794.

25. Hungary [water]: Philadelphia, *Pennsylvania Gazette*, Sept. 20, 1750.

Smelling: *The Birmingham Gazette*, July 28, 1752, cited by Francis Buckley, *History of Old English Glass* (London, 1925), p. 121.

Snuff: 1752 Day Book of John Keith, Hartford merchant (Connecticut Historical Society); *Boston News-Letter*, April 10, 1760.

Case: *Boston Gazette*, Aug. 23, 1756.

Essence: *Boston Weekly News-Letter*, June 10, 1756.

Champagne: *Boston Evening Post*, Feb. 4, 1757.

Mustard: Philadelphia, *Pennsylvania Gazette*, Feb. 2, 1758.

Lavender: *Boston News-Letter*, Feb. 5, 1761.

Beer: Philadelphia, *Pennsylvania Journal*, Apr. 13, 1769.

Spice: Philadelphia, *Pennsylvania Gazette*, Jan. 24, 1771.

Ink: *New York Journal or the General Advertiser*, Aug. 3, 1775.

Claret: Philadelphia, *Pennsylvania Gazette*, Jan. 24, 1779.

Porter: *New York Daily Gazette*, May 6, 1790.

Olive, caper, and anchovies: Philadelphia, *Pennsylvania Packet*, Apr. 13, 1798.

Seltzer: Philadelphia, *Aurora General Advertiser*, Feb. 6, 1812.

Blacking: *Philadelphia Gazette*, Jan. 23, 1813.

Cayenne: Philadelphia, *Aurora General Advertiser*, Sept. 23, 1816.

Oil: Ibid., Mar. 5, 1822.

Gin: *New York Commercial Advertiser*, June 8, 1824.

Cologne: Philadelphia, *United States Gazette*, Mar. 5, 1825.

Mineral Water: Ibid.

Varnish: Dyott's Philadelphia and Kensington Vial and Bottle Factories Price List 1825.

Castor Oil: Ibid.

Soda: New-England Glass Bottle Company's 1829 Price List.

Mead: Ibid.

26. *The Journal of Madame Knight and Rev. Mr. Buckingham from the Original Manuscripts written in 1704 and 1810* (New York: 1825), 1769/70: Stiegel's Manheim Glass Works account books, list compiled by Hunter, pp. 180, 181.

1786: *New York Packet and the American Advertiser*, Mar. 23, 1786.

1817: Hartford, Conn., *The American Mercury*, Jan. 6, 1817.

1823, 1830: Hartford, *Connecticut Courant*, Feb. 18, 1823; Apr. 13, 1830.

27. 1790: Leavenworth petition. Connecticut State Archives, Series II, Vol. 42.

1820: Hartford, *Connecticut Courant*, Mar. 21, 1820.

1828: Troy, New York, *Troy Sentinel*, Apr. 25, 1828.

1848: Bartlett, John Russell, *Dictionary of Americanisms, A Glossary of Words and Phrases usually regarded as Peculiar to the United States* (New York: 1848).

Cayenne: Hartford, *Connecticut Courant*, Oct. 6, 1797.

Anis Cordials: Ibid., Nov. 24, 1800.

Rose Water: Ibid., Dec. 18, 1805.

Macassar oil (an oil for the hair): Boston, *New England Palladium*, Mar. 13, 1829.

28. Baret, 1573 (*see* 4(1)): "a great pot to drink in."

Barclay, 1813: "large drinking vessel with a long neck, swelling out toward the bottom."

Kersey, 1708: "an earthen Pot or Pitcher to hold drink."

Bailey, 1727: "a sort of earthen pitcher or pot with a handle for drink."

Whitney Bros. Price List 1862: "jugs with handles." Illustrated p. 137, Van Rensselaer.

29. Marmelet glasses: Thorpe, *see* 16(1), p. 198.

Pickling Jars: Philadelphia, *Aurora General Advertiser*, Mar. 4, 1800; O'Hara's Letter Book, June 18, 1810.

Preserve: Philadelphia, *United States Gazette for the Country*, Dec. 8, 1817.

Fruit: *New York Commercial Advertiser*, Jan. 2, 1829.

Jelly: *The Utica Intelligencer*, Aug. 28, 1828.

3. COLORS AND COMPOSITIONS OF GLASS

30. *The Papers of Benjamin Franklin*, edited by Leonard W. Labaree (Yale University Press, 1961), Vol. 3, p. 109.

31. Dossie, Vol. II, Cap. VI, p. 284.

32.

(1) Recipes 1, 2 and 3: Dossie, Vol. II, p. 285 and p. 278.

(2) Recipe 4: Glassmaker's MS notebook, about 1815. Corning Museum of Glass.

(3) Recipe 5: *The Arcana of Arts and Sciences or Farmers' and Mechanics' Manual* (Washington, Pa.: 1824), p. 286.

(4) Recipe 6: Information obtained in an interview with Morris Holmes, 1922. Holmes, born in Saratoga in 1846, worked in the Saratoga Mountain glassworks, starting as a carrying boy when 10 years old, moved with the works to the Congressville section of Saratoga where he was a blower until the works closed around 1900.

33. First appearance of black bottles in the newspapers covered was in 1746 in the *New York Weekly Post Boy*.

34. *See* 32(4).

35. *See* 32(2).

36. Specifications for Patent 15, 665, Sept. 2, 1856. U.S. Patent Office.

37. Merret: *The Art of Glass*. Written in Italian by Antonio Neri and translated into English with some Observations on the Author (London: 1662). "To Avoid Our Authors Repetitions . . . 4 Manganese . . . " p. 22; p. 282.

38. Dossie, Vol. II, p. 278.

39. Ibid., p. 261.

40. Knittle, p. 397.

41. Dossie, Vol. II, p. 290ff.

42. Pellatt, Apsley, *Curiosities of Glassmaking* (London, 1949), p. 34.

4. FABRICATION OF FREE-BLOWN AND BLOWN-MOLDED BOTTLES AND FLASKS

43.

(1) Ravenscroft: Thorpe, W. A., *A History of English & Irish Glass* (London: 1929), Vol. I, pp. 120–22.

(2) Pots: Ibid., p. 112.

44. M[erret], C.: *The Art of Glass . . .* , p. 246.

45. Ibid., p. 247.

46. Pellatt, Apsley, *Curiosities of Glass Making*, p. 95.

47. Toulouse, Dr. Julian H., "Empontilling: a history." Reprint from *The Glass Industry* (Mar./Apr. 1968); letters.

48. Ibid.; Van Rensselaer, p. 10; Knittle, p. 40.

49. Toulouse, Dr. Julian H., letter. Patents: No. 17960 to Hiram Dillaway, Aug. 11, 1857; No. 54572 to E. McArdle, May 8, 1868.

50.

(1) "ring iron": *Encyclopaedia Britannica*, 7th edition (1842), Vol. X, p. 579.

(2) French: Diderot, *Encyclopédie des Arts et Metiers, Recueil de Planches sur les Sciences, les Arts Liberaux, et les Arts Méchaniques avec leur explication*. Verre (Art du) X, p. 466.

(3) 1662: Merret, Appendix, tools used in green glass production.

51. *See* 50(3).

II.
HISTORICAL BACKGROUND

1. ANCESTRY OF BOTTLES USED AND MADE IN AMERICA

1. Dr. Sidney M. Goldstein of The Corning Museum of Glass supplied the following references: Avigad, N., (1) "The Expedition to the Judean Desert, 1961. Expedition A," *Israel Exploration Journal* 12 (1962), pp. 180–83; (2) "Excavations in the Jewish Quarter of the Old City of Jerusalem," *Israel Exploration Journal* 22 (1972), pp. 198–200.

1a. Ancient, Egyptian and Roman Glass

(1) Petrie, W. M. Flinders, *Tell el-Amarna* (London: 1894), pp. 3, 27–30. *The Arts and Crafts of Ancient Egypt* (2nd ed., London and Edinburgh, 1910; 1st ed., 1909), pp. 119–23.

(2) Harden, D. B., "Glass of the Greeks and Romans," reprinted from *Greece and Rome*, Vol. III, No. 9 (May 1934), pp. 140–42. "Glass Ware in Roman Times" in *Catalogue of Old English Glass* (London: Arthur Churchill, Ltd., 1937), pp. 7–10.

(3) Smith, Ray Winfield, *Glass From the Ancient World* (Corn-

ing, NY., The Corning Museum of Glass, Corning Glass Center, 1957), Section II, pp. 43, 44.

(4) Engle, Anita, "3000 Years of Glass Making on the Phoenecian Coast" in *Readings in Glass History*, No. 1, pp. 14, 15.

2.

(1) Engle, *see* 1a(4).

(2) Harden, *see* 1a(2).

3. Petrie, *see* 1a(1) Tell el-Amarna.

4. *The Complete Works of Petronius*, translated by Jack Lindsay (New York: 1932), p. 36.

5.

(1) Photographs Nos. 9623–26. Museo di Napoli. The Corning Museum of Glass.

(2) Chambon, 29ff.

6.

(1) Chambon, Chaps. I, II, and III.

(2) Barrelet, *La Verrerie en France . . .*, Chaps. I–IV.

(3) Barrelet, "La Verre de Table du Moyen Age . . . "

(4) Gasparetto, Astore.

(5) Haynes, Chaps. III and IV; re "L'Altare," p. 48.

7. Gasparetto, pp. 37–44.

8.

(1) *See* 6.

(2) **Re chalices:** Barrelet. *La Verrerie en France . . .*, p. 19. Eisen, G. A., *Glass* (New York: 1927), Vol. II, p. 382.

9. *See* 6; re 1279, Haynes, p. 62, and Charleston, "The Transport of Glass."

10. Theophilus, Libre II, Chap. XII, p. 131. As translated by Robert Henrie, Theophilus was writing "of Christian Art of the 11th century." Gasparetto states that Theophilus was of the monastery of Saint Pantaleon of Cologne and wrote in the last half of the 10th century. Barrelet, *La Verrerie en France . . .*, p. 27, places the works of Theophilus at the beginning of the 12th century.

11.

(1) Table use: Chambon, p. 111.

(2) Covered: a straw- or osier-covered bottle appears in the "Nativity" by a 15th-century painter of the Venetian School of Carlo Crivelli; Barrelet, *La Verrerie en France . . .*, p. 156, states that in the 15th century (1448) there were glass bottles, generally wickered and in the form of a gourd.

(3) Betée: *London Encyclopaedia*, Vol. IV (1845); late 18th- and early 19th-century ads in American newspapers.

(4) Belgian mineral water bottles: Planche T. Chambon.

12.

(1) Chambon, pp. 51–60, 67.

(2) Gasparetto, pp. 41, 44.

(3) Barrelet: an agreement of 1328, *La Verrerie en France . . .*, p. 53; "Le Verre de Table du Moyen Age . . . ," p. 202.

13.

(1) Chambon, p. 55.

(2) Barrelet, *La Verrerie en France . . .*, p. 39; "Le Verre de Table du Moyen Age," p. 202.

(3) Hume, "Medieval Glass in London."

14.

(1) Bontemp (G.), *Guide de Verrerie* (1868), p. 496, gives 15th century.

(2) Barrelet, *La Verrerie en France . . .*, p. 71, states that bottles did not enjoy an important economic role in the 15th century and that in connection with a banquet given in Paris in 1559 by Catherine de Medici there is mention of osier-covered bottles "esquelles estoit le vin de la table."

(3) Hume, "Medieval Glass in London," p. 104, states glass of any kind was rare in London before the second half of the 15th century.

(4) Thorpe, "English Glass in the XVII Century," pp. 14, 15.

15.

(1) Haynes, Chaps. VI and VII.

(2) Perrot, Paul N., *Three Great Centuries of Venetian Glass* (The Corning Museum of Glass, 1956).

16.

(1) Hume, "Medieval Glass in London," illustrates parts of ribbed bottles excavated in London.

(2) Agricola, pp. 426, 476. Apparently Agricola's manuscript was completed in 1550 but not printed until the year after his death in 1555. The forms of glass shown in the illustration of a glasshouse interior (Fig. 2) had been produced for a long time. Laboratory vessels are among the forms. And Chambon, p. 67, states that laboratory vessels were a 15th-century form.

(3) Thorpe, "English Glass in the XVII Century," p. 15, states that "there are indications that the double-cone bottle and the pear-shaped, both forest-glass products, were so used [as decanters] occasionally in Germany, but it is uncertain how far this practice was general."

(4) Chambon, p. 65, states the pear-shaped more or less elongated bottle is relatively frequent in iconography of the 15th century and that the double-cone (to use Thorpe's term) was born in this epoch.

(5) Barrelet, *La Verrerie en France . . .*, p. 67, cites annular flasks as a 15th-century form.

17.

(1) Hawkers: Charleston, "The Transport of Glass . . . " and Barrelet, *La Verrerie en France . . .* p. 198 and Plate XXXII.

(2) 1559 covered bottles: Barrelet, p. 71.

(3) 1558 inventory: Charleston.

(4) Square and tapered bottles: Chambon, Planche R.

18. Merret, *Art of Glass*. Written in Italian by Antonio Neri, and translated into English with some Observations on the Author (London: 1662), p. 226.

19.

(1) Thorpe, "Evolution of the Decanter," and "English Glass of the XVII Century."

(2) Ruggles-Brise, 18ff.

(3) Hume, "The Glass Wine Bottle in Colonial Virginia."

(4) Hudson.

20. Thorpe, "The Glass Seller's Bills at Woburn Abbey," p. 190: "April 26th, 1690. 1 fflint pockett bottle £ 0.1.0." Mr. Thorpe said this was the only mention of a pocket bottle in all of the bills. It is the earliest of which I know at present.

21. Hume, "The Glass Wine Bottle in Colonial Virginia," p. 92.

2. THE BOTTLE INDUSTRY IN AMERICA
A. 17th Century; B. 18th Century

1. In use of "America" and "American," a long-established practice is followed here, namely, to designate the United States of North America and the colonies from which she was formed. Actually, in a strict geographical sense, glassmaking in America, the New World, began in Mexico in 1535 (*see* Alice Wilson Frothingham, *Hispanic Glass*, 1941, p. 121ff.), nearly a hundred years before the abortive trials at Jamestown, Va.

2. For full story on Jamestown, *see:*

(1) Harrington's *Glassmaking at Jamestown*, the most complete and authoritative account of the Jamestown glasshouses, including results of scientific excavation and tests of shards for composition.

(2) McKearin, *Two Hundred Years . . .*, pp. 6–9, based mainly on Captain John Smith's writings (ed. Edward Barber, 1884) and *The Records of the Virginia Company of London* (ed. Susan Myra Kingsburg, 1906, 1932, 1935), Vols. I–IV.

3. Basis of all glasshouse dates and statistics, unless otherwise noted: McKearin, *American Glass*, Chronological Chart of Glasshouses, pp. 583–613.

3a. *See* 2(1).

4. Felt, Joseph B., *The Annals of Salem* (1st ed., Salem, Mass., 1827), p. 152; (2nd ed., 1849), Vol. I, p. 186 and Vol. II, p. 168.

5.

(1) Hunter, pp. 140–42.

(2) Knittle, pp. 67–75. In the light of the known activities of the two men, Hunter's date of 1654 for Smede and 1655 for Duycking seem more probable than Knittle's date of 1645 (p. 74) as the start of their glassmaking in New York.

6.

(1) 1682: Weeks, p. 74.

(2) 1684: Pastorius, "Description of Pennsylvania, 1700," pp. 5 and 7. *Old South Leaflets*, No. 95, Vol. IV.

7. *Documentary History of New York* (Albany: 1849), Vol. I, p. 712.

8. The following, about which later research may unearth more information, are not mentioned in the text:

(1) In 1732 the census of the City of New York gave two glasshouses in operation.

(2) On March 22, 1749, William Bowdoin and Nathaniel Holmes of Boston sent a memorial to the Council and House of Representatives of Massachusetts Bay asking a grant of a "Tract of unappropriated land of the Province to enable them to prosecute the affair [glassworks] . . . where there is plenty of wood and room to settle a very Considerable Number of People who must necessarily be Employed therein." Nothing appears to have been done about the memorial until April 1750, when it was referred to a Committee to report on what it judged proper. On June 6th it was read in Council and "concur'd & Samuel Danforth & Andrew Oliver Esq. [were] joined in the affair." (*Mass. Archives*, Vol. 59, ms., pp. 355–58.) Apparently the affair remained only a plan. Hunter, p. 144, mentions only Bowdoin, giving as his source Justin Winsor's *History of Boston 1730 to 1880* (p. 461 n).

(3) According to tradition Lodewyck Bamper, partner in the Glass House Company of New York (Wall, p. 95) and one of the founders of the New Windsor Glass Works, established a works for bottles in Brooklyn (Hunter, p. 152).

(4) In 1769 Jacob Barge of Philadelphia advertised for broken flint glass to be worked up "at a new Glass-House" (*Pennsylvania Chronicle*, July 10–17 and *Pennsylvania Gazette*, July 13, 1769).

(5) In 1769 Garrit Rapalje, New York City, advertised for broken flint glass to be worked up at a new Glass-House and for a person to make red lead [an ingredient of flint or lead glass]. (*New York Gazette and Weekly Mercury*, Oct. 9, 1769.)

9.

(1) Belcher letter, Aug. 19, 1752 to Col. Alford, Boston: Van Rensselaer, pp. 125, 126, quoted from the *New Jersey Archives*, First Series, Vol. VIII, pp. 109, 110.

(2) Conn. 1747: Thomas Darling petitioned and was granted a monopoly. (*Connecticut Archives*, Industry, Series I, Vol. I, p. 160.) He also sought information from Benjamin Franklin about Wistarburgh, and problems of workmen and glassmaking. Parts of Franklin's replies may have discouraged Darling from pursuing the project. (*The Papers of Benjamin Franklin*, edited by Leonard W. Larabee, Vol. 3, pp. 109, 110.)

(3) R.I. 1752, Isaac Winslow: Van Rensselaer, p. 89. (The same Isaac Winslow as the one of Germantown, Mass.?)

10.

(1) Stiegel: Wood, Kenneth T., "A Gratuity for Baron Stiegel," *Antiques* (Jan. 1925); *Pennsylvania Gazette*, Mar. 17, 1773.

(2) Philadelphia Glass Works: Alfred Coxe Prime, *The Arts and Crafts of Pennsylvania, Maryland and South Carolina, 1721–1785*, pp. 137, 150.

11. Weeks, p. 80, from *Pennsylvania Colonial Records*, Vol. LX, p. 354.

12.

(1) Planned: *see* 8(4) and (5).

(2) Stiegel: for detailed account of his career and glasshouses, *see* Hunter, Chaps. II–X.

(3) Philadelphia Glass Works: *see* McKearin, Helen, *Bottles, Flasks, & Dr. Dyott*, Appendix C, pp. 130-36.

13. Knittle, pp. 90, 91.

14. A July 20, 1771, letter from George Washington at Mt. Vernon to Robert Cary & Co., London, mentions the end of the Virginia Association except for these categories and goes on to say: "You will please therefore be careful that none of the glass, paper &c. contained in my Invoices, are of those kinds which are subject to the duty Imposed by Parliament for the purpose of raising a Revenue in America." (*Writings of George Washington*, edited by Fitzpatrick, Vol. 3, p. 60.)

15.

(1) Wistar: *Pennsylvania Chronicle*, July 31, 1769; *New York Journal or General Advertiser*, Supplement, Aug. 17, 1769.

(2) Stiegel: *Pennsylvania Gazette* and *Pennsylvania Journal*, July 5, 1770; *New-York Gazette and Weekly Mercury*, July 29, 1771.

(3) Philadelphia Glass Works: *Pennsylvania Packet*, Mar. 22, 1773.

(1. Wistarburgh)

16. Haines, Casper Wistar, "Some Notes Concerning Casper Wistar (Immigrant) and on the Origin of the *Wistar* and *Wister* Families." Pamphlet issued May 25, 1926. For more complete information, *see* Hunter, Chap. IV., pp. 157, 163; McKearin, *Two Hundred Years . . .*, pp. 11–16.

17. I am indebted to Milo Naeve, when he was at the Henry Francis duPont Winterthur Museum, for a transcript of the part of Wistar's will pertaining to the glasshouse and glass. Hunter, pp. 160, 161, mentions the glass Richard was to give to his brother Caspar each year and on p. 159 gives the conditions of the agreement between Wistar on the one part and on the other John Wm. Wentzell, Casper Halter, John Martin Halton, and Simon Kreiszuer.

18. *See* 9(2), Franklin's letters to Darling, Feb. 10, 1746/7 and Mar. 27, 1747.

19.

(1) Provisions of Will: *see* 17.

(2) Ads of buttons & Philadelphia shop: *Pennsylvania Gazette*, July 30, 1752; *Lancaster [Pa.] Gazette*, May 11, 1752.

(3) Ads for runaway servants: $12 reward for Dutchman Philip Jacobs, stonemason, *Pennsylvania Chronicle*, Dec. 14, 1767; Adrian Brust, *Pennsylvania Gazette*, Apr. 26, 1770; Jacob Stenger and John Kindeil, *Pennsylvania Gazette*, June 14, 1770; John Godfrey Knester, carpenter, *Pennsylvania Packet*, Nov. 6, 1775.

(4) Sale ad: *Pennsylvania Journal*, Oct. 11, 1780.

20.

(1) Retail shop: *see* 19(4).

(2) Ads of bottles: *Staatsbote*, Sept. 30, 1765 (*see* Prime, 10(2), pp. 152, 153); *Pennsylvania Gazette*, Sept. 28 & *Pennsylvania Chronicle*, July 31, & *New York Journal or General Advertiser*, Supplement, Aug. 17, 1769.

(2. Germantown)

21. Hunter, pp. 144, 145. Knittle, pp. 101–4. Both use the spelling *Crellins*, but the spelling is *Crellius* in a letter he wrote to the Lieutenant Governor in Dec. 1748 and now in the *Mas-*

sachusetts Archives, Vol. 15A, ms. pp. 45–47; also in the *Journals of the House of Representatives of Massachusetts, 1749–1751, 1753* (Vol. 26, pp. 180, 183; Vol. 27, pp. 8, 28, 130; Vol. 30, pp. 16–17; also in the news item in the *Boston Weekly News Letter*, Sept. 21, 1752.

22.

(1) News item: *Boston Weekly News Letter*, Sept. 21 and 28, 1752.

(2) Palmer: Hunter & Knittle (*see* 21) state he leased the works and was joined by his brother-in-law Richard Crouch. Lura Woodside Watkins's statement (*American Glass and Glassmaking*, p. 27) that Palmer was agent or manager of the works probably refers to the later period.

23.

(1) Rev. Holyoke: Hunter, p. 145.

(2) Memorial of new Co.: *Massachusetts Archives*, Vol. 59, ms., pp. 376, 377; *Journals of the House of Representatives of Massachusetts, 1752–53*, Vol. 29, pp. 4, 53.

(3) Visitors: *Boston Weekly News Letter*, Aug. 3, 1753; *Boston Gazette*, Sept. 4, 1753.

24.

(1) Fire, 1755: *Boston Gazette*, June 2; *Boston Weekly News Letter*, June 5; *New-York Gazette and Weekly Post Boy*, July 14, 1755.

(2) Williams's ad: *Boston Evening Post*, July 14, 1755.

25.

(1) 1756 Petition: *Journals of the House of Representatives of Massachusetts*, Vol. 32, Part II 1756, p. 427 [425]; Vol. 33, Part I 1756, pp. 13, 31, 193, 214.

(2) Lottery: Ibid., Vol. 33, Part II 1757, p. 285, 293; *Acts and Resolves of the Province of Massachusetts Bay*, Vol. 3, p. 1053; *Boston News Letter*, Sept. 22, 1757, and Aug. 10, 1758.

26.

(1) 1752 Memorial: *Massachusetts Archives*, Vol. 59, ms., pp. 376, 377.

(2) Window glass and bottle production: Feb. 1754 letter from Edward Lambert (apparently general factotum at Germantown glassworks) to Thomas Flucker & Isaac Winslow, Boston, reporting on the situation at the works, window glass and bottle production, quoted by Charles Messer Stow in "A Massachusetts Glass Factory," *The Antiquarian* (Apr. 1929), pp. 27, 66, 86.

(3) Palmer's statement: according to Watkins (*see* 22(2)), a ms. letter by Joseph Palmer and owned by the Massachusetts Historical Society, Boston.

(4) Ads: *Boston Evening Post*, July 14, 1755; *Boston News Letter*, Apr. 10 & *Boston Gazette*, July 28, 1760.

(5) Williams's ad: *Boston Gazette*, Jan. 12, July 28, Aug. 23, 1756.

(3 & 4. New Windsor and Newfoundland)

27. Hunter, pp. 146–52; Knittle, pp. 107–14; Wall, pp. 95–99; McKearin, *American Glass*, pp. 96–98.

28. The draft of the agreement, quoted in full by Mr. Wall, is in the manuscript collection of the New-York Historical Society. Mr. Wall's search of "local records" failed to find any references to Greiner.

29.

(1) New Windsor, land purchase: deed dated Jan. 1, 1752; recorded Aug. 18; cited by Hunter, pp. 146, 147.

(2) To be certain about the extent of Orange County and the use of "North River" for the Hudson, I consulted the late Arthur B. Carlson, curator of the Map and Print Department of the New-York Historical Society.

(3) Bamper's ad: *New-York Gazette or Weekly Post Boy*, July 7, 1755.

(4) Will's ad: Ibid., Sept. 27, 1756.

30.

(1) The location of the Newfoundland glasshouse, later known as the Glasshouse Farm, was near the present 35th Street on the Hudson River according to Stoke's *Iconography of Manhattan Island*, or, as Mr. Wall states, on the North River between 34th & 40th streets. Mrs. Knittle (p. 107) states a "Glass House Farm" on Sir Peter Warren's land is shown on "DeWitt's Farm-Map of New York" published about 1732 and (p. 109) that the Glass-House Company "bought the old works and the ground on which it stood . . . " The location of the Newfoundland works she gave correctly, but, I was informed by Mr. Carlson, he knew of no "DeWitt's Farm-Map of New York" and that there is no record of a glassworks ever being *on* Sir Peter Warren's land, though the store run by Lepper was on Warren's Wharf.

(2) Earnest's dock: Hunter, p. 150.

(3) Earnest's ad: *New-York Gazette or Weekly Post Boy*, Oct. 30, 1758.

(4) Bayard & Earnest ad: Ibid., July 22, 1762.

(5) Place of Public Entertainment: Gottesman, Rita, *The Arts and Crafts in New York—1726–1776*, p. 93, *New-York Gazette* ad of May 23, 1762, and footnote.

(6) Gov. Moore's remarks: *The Documentary History of New York*, Vol. I, pp. 733–35.

(5. Hilltown Township)

31. Hommel, Rudolph P., "A Bucks County Glass Works," *Bucks County Traveler* (Aug. 1957), pp. 64, 65.

(6. Elizabeth Furnace and Manheim)

32. For detailed accounts, upon which the sketch is based unless another source is given, *see* Hunter, *Stiegel Glass*, and McKearin, *American Glass*, pp. 84–93, and *Two Hundred Years . . .* , pp. 16–23. Hunter, in an appendix (pp. 235–42) gives a summary of the dates of the houses, a list of employees at Elizabeth Furnace and Manheim, and a list of distributors of Stiegel's glass.

33. Hunter, p. 235, gives the starting date of the first Manheim house as Nov. 11, 1765. The ad quoted apparently was unknown to him.

34.

(1) All sorts of bottles: *Pennsylvania Chronicle*, Mar. 27, 1769; *Pennsylvania Gazette*, Mar. 23 & May 4, 1769.

(2) Hunter, list, p. 181.

(3) Phials & smelling bottles: *Pennsylvania Packet*, July 6, 1772.

(7. Philadelphia Glass Works, Kensington)

35. Towers & Leacock: Indenture of Nov. 5, 1772 (not recorded until Feb. 21, 1783), Philadelphia Land Records, Book D6, p. 266. This indenture, with the details of the Towers & Leacock purchase, etc., in 1771 and sale by them to Isaac Gray and the Elliots, gives the location as Town of Richmond, Northern Liberties. The 1772 ads (*Pennsylvania Gazette*, Jan. 23 & 30) were headed "Glass Facture in Northern Liberties." However, Gray and the Elliots in their ads used "Kensington," name of an abutting area. The Elliots' name was spelled with either one or two *t*'s.

36.

(1) Sale to Gray & Elliots: *see* 35.

(2) John Elliot's ads: Prime, 10(2), pp. 194–97.

(3) Gray's ads: *Pennsylvania Journal*, Apr. 13, 1769; *Pennsylvania Gazette*, Mar. 5, 1755 & Feb. 27, 1772; *Pennsylvania Packet*, Mar. 20 & Aug. 7, 1775.

37.

(1) 1773 ad: *Pennsylvania Gazette*, Jan. 27.

(2) Property description: Prime, 10(2), pp. 139, 140—
Pennsylvania Post, Apr. 15, 1775.

38.

(1) Philadelphia Glass Works Lottery: Prime, 10(2), pp. 136,
137—ads in *Pennsylvania Journal*, May 19, July 7 & 21, Nov. 27,
1773; *Pennsylvania Packet*, Aug. 16, 1773; *Staatsbote*, Aug. 17,
1773. The last two assert the works' claim to being the first
manufacturer of flint glass. An Aug. 30, 1773, ad in the *Pennsylvania Packet* which Prime attributes to the Philadelphia Glass
Works, I believe, because of the language and general circumstances, was one of Stiegel's ads.

(2) Stiegel lottery: Ibid., pp. 150, 151—*Pennsylvania Gazette*,
Mar. 17, 1773; *Staatsbote*, June 15, 1773, to which I would add the
Aug. 30 ad mentioned above (1). Stiegel first advertised flint glass
in 1770 (*Pennsylvania Journal*, July 5). If Towers & Leacock
produced any flint glass it was not until 1772 (*see* 35) and the white
glass of Gray and the Elliots (presumed to be flint glass because of
their claims) was not advertised until 1773. *See* 37(1).

39. *Pennsylvania Packet*, Feb. 27, 1775.

40.

(1) Ad of sales: *Pennsylvania Evening Post*, Apr. 15 & May 20,
1777.

(2) Farrell & Stiegel: *Pennsylvania Packet*, Nov. 4, 1771.

(3) Farrell & Bakeoven: *Pennsylvania Gazette*, Aug. 27, 1777.

41.

(1) Samuel Elliott to Gray; Gray, John Elliott, Jr., John Elliott,
Sr., to Leiper: Indenture, Philadelphia Land Records, Book D6,
p. 268, May 5, 1780.

(2) Accounts of the 1787 and 1788 parades with listing of partic-
ipants appeared in *The American Museum*, Vol. III, pp. 164ff. and
Vol. IV, pp. 68ff.

(3) Purchase of bottles: Letter from James Gray to Leonard
DeNeufville at Dowesborough, Dec. 20, 1788. Ms. collection,
New-York Historical Society.

42. Trippel & Co.: Philadelphia *Claypoole's American Daily
Advertiser*, Apr. 13, 1798 (ad dated Apr. 12) & Jan. 23, 1799.

43.

(1) Chronology of ownerships as given formerly: Weeks, p. 80;
Van Rensselaer, pp. 155–59, 163; Knittle, pp. 144–49; McKearin,
American Glass, pp. 93–96, 584–85.

(2) 1800 purchase: Philadelphia Land Records, Book E.F.1, pp.
320ff.

(3) 1802 & 1804: Ibid., Book E.F.18, pp. 346ff. The indenture
including the Joseph Roberts's 1802 agreement with Butland and
Rowland and the latter's Mar. 16, 1804, payment were recorded
Nov. 30, 1804; the release by Rachel Roberts was recorded Dec.
28, 1804.

44.

(1) 1815 & 1832: Butland's sale to Rowland in 1815 was in the
indenture of division of property in which James Rowland, Jr.,
paid his brother for the latter's share in "three steel furnaces" and
the lot et cetera described in previous indentures, and it was
recorded Nov. 5, 1832, Book A.M.27, pp. 542ff.

(2) Rowland to Dyott, 1833: Ibid., Book A.M.37, pp. 747ff.

45.

(1) Swerer & Bolton: General O'Hara's Letter Book, letter of
April 19, 1805, to Mr. Muhlinberg, Philadelphia; August 10, 1810,
letter to Joseph Carson, Philadelphia. Historical Society of Western Pennsylvania.

(2) Rowland ad, 1808: *Poulson's American Daily Advertiser*,
Aug. 9.

46.

(1) Philadelphia Glass-House: Philadelphia Land Records,
Book E.F.32, p. 248, indenture dated Dec. 3, 1806; ad in the
Albany Register, Nov. 8, 1808.

(2) Kensington Glass Works: *Philadelphia Gazette and Daily
Advertiser*, Aug. 2, 1816.

47.

(1) White & green glasswares: *Pennsylvania Journal*, Jan. 27,
1773, and *Pennsylvania Packet*, Mar. 22, 1773.

(2) Case & black bottles: *Pennsylvania Gazette*, July 7, 1773.

(3) Pocket, smelling & case bottles: *Pennsylvania Packet*, Feb.
27, 1775.

(4) Phials; *Pennsylvania Packet*, Feb. 27, 1775; *Pennsylvania
Gazette*, Aug. 27, 1777.

(5) *See* 42.

(6) Olives, etc., in bottles: *Boston Evening Post*, Oct. 7, 1771.

48. *Connecticut Archives*, Industry, Series I, Vol. II. Ms., pp.
168, 169, Oct. 18, 1779, petition of Elijah Hubbard of Middletown,
Isaac Mosely of Glastonbury, William Little of Lebanon, Picket
Latimer of New London; ms., pp. 173, 174, June 1780 Memorial of
Mosely and Little stating considerable sums had already been
spent and the final cost was estimated at about £3,000.

(8. The New England Glass Works of Robert Hewes)

49. Hewes's Boston business ads: *Boston Independent
Chronicle*, Sept. 3, 1766. Apr. 30, 1778, Aug. 12, 1779. No ads
were found in the 1780 papers covered, but they reappeared by
Oct. 25, 1781. However, one Apr. 6, 1780, ad sounds as though it
may have concerned Hewes: "Cash given for any quantity of
WHITE GLASS, at the Printing-office of N. Wills."

50.

(1) Accounts of Temple: Jarves, Deming, *Reminiscences of
Glassmaking* (1st ed., 1854), p. 33ff; Weeks, p. 89; Knittle, p.
166ff; Shadel, Jane, "Robert Hewes Glass Manufacturer," *Journal of Glass Studies*, Vol. XII (1970), Corning Museum of Glass;
Wilson, Kenneth M., *New England Glass and Glassmaking*
(1973).

(2) Lottery: *Boston Independent Chronicle*, May 17 & 31,
1781.

51.

(1) In an article in *Antiques*, June 1940, Lura Woodside Watkins
cites as positive evidence of Hewes's success in making crown
glass at Temple the Dec. 17, 1788, notice (Ill. 8a) of the second
exhibition of his crown glass. Since 1950 I have found a Dec. 4,
1788, notice of his crown glass made at East Hartford. Therefore
the second exhibition, Dec. 17, was of East Hartford crown glass.
However, Kenneth M. Wilson found conclusive proof that Hewes
did succeed in producing *samples* of crown glass at Temple.

(2) Mrs. Watkins gave the Smithsonian Institution,
Washington, D.C., one of the chestnut bottles having a Temple
history. Kenneth Wilson has informed me that two others, also of
darkish bubbly green glass, are now owned locally, together with
fragments and pieces of a glass pot from the site.

(3) Re shards of bottles & seals: Letters from John Gayton,
Lynn, Mass.; Richmond Morcom, Philadelphia, Pa.

(4) Sq. bottle: Letter from Mrs. Wales C. Brewster, Bradenton,
Fla. Mrs. Brewster is a descendant of John Patter, Jr., who moved
to Temple, N.H. before the Revolution. The bottle was handed
down from one generation to the next.

(9. The New-Jersey Glass Manufactory)

52.

(1) Founding: Van Rensselaer, pp. 134, 135. The research on
the Glassboro and other New Jersey houses was done by Charles
S. Boyer, President of the Camden Historical Society at the time.
In the township records he found no Stanger until May 1780,
when Soloman "Stinger" appeared on the tax list; on the 1782 list
the glasshouse was mentioned.

(2) Location: Notice in *Trenton* [*N.J.*] *Federalist*, Dec. 8, 1814.

(3) "Glassborough" appears in the obituary of Col. Heston (Philadelphia *Poulson's American Daily Advertiser*, Oct. 21, 1802), but in 1799 the nearest postal stop, Woodbury, was used (*see* ad Ill. 7a). J. E. Pfeiffer informed me that until the name Glassboro (or Glassborough) was chosen by the Fox Hunting Club the little community was known simply as The Glass House.

53.

(1) Ownership, traced by Mr. Boyer. *See* 52(1).

(2) New-Jersey Glass Manufactory: New York *Mercantile Advertiser*, Dec. 6, 1799. (*See* Ill. 7a.)

(3) Half-interest for sale: *Trenton* [*N.J.*] *Federalist*, Dec. 8, 1814 & Jan. 16, 1815; Philadelphia, *Poulson's American Daily Advertiser*, Feb. 25, 1815.

(4) Dyott, *Exposition*, p. 15 & Appendix D, p. 51.

(5) David Wolf & Co. and agent: ad dated Sept. 26 [1816], *True American & Commercial Advertiser*, Jan. 17, 1817 (Ill. 7b); *The Union*, Dec. 31, 1819 and Nov. 1820; *Aurora General Advertiser*, Mar. 12, 1821.

54.

(1) Lord Sheffield's report: Bishop, Vol. I, p. 239.

(2) White glass: *American Museum*, June 1788, Vol. III, p. 593 and *Salem* [*Mass.*] *Mercury*, July 8, 1788. The newspaper notice stated the glass was sold in Philadelphia in Front Street above Arch Street. Since *"flint glass"* was colored as well as colorless and the term connoted far finer metal than "white," it is not unlikely the reporter meant not "flint" but a good clear quality of colorless glass. I know of no documentary evidence of flint, that is, lead, glass production at Glassboro.

(3) Sales to Emlen: Jeremiah Emlen's Day Book, collection of the Henry Ford Museum.

(4) Dyott ad: *see* 53(5).

55. The splitting of the Confederation into "thirteen free republics" and its consequences were the subject of a letter signed "Casca" (*New York Packet and the American Advertiser*, Feb. 6, 1784), one of many letters to newspapers about the state of disunion and troubles of the times.

56. The Pennsylvania plan, one of the first to form a Society for the encouragement of manufactures and useful arts, was announced in Aug. 1787 (*American Museum*, Vol. II, p. 167ff.). On Jan. 18, 1788, the managers reported little progress but believed "that when by the establishment of a general government, the clandestine importation of foreign articles shall be prevented, and that preference given throughout the United States to the manufactures of America, which the common interest demands, our established manufactures will resume their former vigor and others will be found to flourish which have hitherto been little known among us." (*American Museum*, Vol. III [Feb. 1788], p. 179.)

The State tariffs were a point of argument for and against the Constitution which were widely circulated in print. Oliver Ellsworth of Connecticut pointed out that New York State raised £60,000 to £80,000 a year by imposts and added, "If we import by the medium of Massachusetts she has an impost and we must pay her tribute." (*American Museum*, report of Jan. 4, 1788, speech. Vol. I, p. 377.)

57. Petition of Boston merchants and traders, Apr. 1787, to Congress (*American Museum*, Vol. I [Apr. 1787], p. 289), typical of the many petitions sent to the U.S. Congress and also published for the public's enlightenment and support.

58. "Hints to Manufacturers" dated Hartford, November 3, 1789, and unsigned. *American Museum*, Vol. III (Aug.–Dec. 1790), p. 74.

59. *See* 10. New Bremen Glassmanufactory, 11. Dowesborough, 12. Boston Glass Manufactury, 13. East Hartford glassworks of the Pitkins, 14. New Haven Glass Works.

60. Amelung's petitions to Congress: *Annals of Congress*, 1st, Vol. II, pp. 1620–32; Ibid., Vol. III, p. 247; *American State Papers*, Class IV, Vol. II, p. 62.

61.

(1) Tariffs: *Annals of Congress*, 1st, Vol. I, p. 173; U.S. House Doc. 671, Tariff Acts; Davis, pp. 55–63 (Tariff policy 1789–1820).

(2) Petitions: *Annals of Congress*, 3rd, Vol. II, pp. 452, 453, 456; *American State Papers*, Class V, p. 492.

62.

(1) Hamilton's Report: *American Museum*, Vol. XI (Jan.–June 1790), Appendix II, Public Papers, p, 48.

(2) Philadelphia news item dated Mar. 31: *Maryland Gazette or Baltimore Advertiser*, Apr. 7, 1789.

63.

(1) Leavenworth, "Hints to Manufacturers," dated New Haven, Aug. 17, 1787, *American Museum*, Vol. V (Jan. 1789), pp. 48, 49.

(2) "Upon the Manufacture of Glass," Boston, *Massachusetts Centinel*, July 18, 1789; *Maryland Gazette or the Baltimore Advertiser*, Aug. 4, 1789; *American Museum*, Vol. VI (July–Dec. 1789), pp. 119, 120. After bottles, the writer described white glass and ended with a brief note on crown glass in which, "for particular reasons," he did not describe the method of manufacture, furnace or preparation of materials for crown glass. This last and the fact that the publication apparently appeared first in the Boston papers suggest that Robert Hewes may have been the author.

64.

(1) Pennsylvania Society: *American Museum*, Vol. II (Nov. 1787), p. 507ff.

(2) Philadelphia news item: *see* 62(2).

(3) Leavenworth's Hints: *see* 63(1).

65. Peterborough (or Peterboro) works was built about 1783 by David Goff and associates, all from Connecticut, whose hopes of supplying window glass and probably bottles to the migrants streaming into central New York were not fulfilled. The works was revived about 1804 and operated until about 1830. Window glass was the output (bottles apparently were not made as a commercial product) and advertised in the Utica and Schenectady newspapers. One which appeared in the Utica, *Columbian Gazette*, Mar. 10, 1812, was still running in 1817. For details of works *see* Mary E. Davison's "The Glass of Peterboro, New York," *Antiques* Dec. 1939.

66. One house, still little more than a statistic, is said to have been John Brown's on India Point, Providence, R.I., and to have closed after one melt in 1790. (Knittle, p. 421.)

(10. New Bremen Glassmanufactory of John Frederick Amelung)

67. For detailed accounts *see* the following:

Quynn, "John Frederick Amelung at New Bremen," *Maryland Historical Magazine* (Sept. 1948);

McKearin, *Two Hundred Years of American Blown Glass*, pp. 33ff.;

Lanmon, Dwight P., and Palmer, Arlene M., "John Frederick Amelung and the New Bremen Glassmanufactory," *Journal of Glass Studies*, Vol. XVIII (1976), pp. 20–44. Corning Museum of Glass.

Hume, Ivor Noël, "Archeological Excavations on the Site of John Frederick Amelung's New Bremen Glassmanufactory," *Journal of Glass Studies*, Vol. XVIII (1976), pp. 138–208.

68. Amelung, John Frederick: "Remarks on Manufactures Principally on the New established Glass-House, near Frederick-Town, in the State of Maryland. Printed for the Author 1787," pp. 10–13. I am fortunate enough to have a photostatic copy of the original which is in the library of the Boston Atheneum. Possibly the "Remarks" were sent to a Congressman

or to other influential persons whose interest Amelung hoped to arouse in favor of his 1790 petition to Congress for assistance; for, in the back, there is additional data in long hand and dated 1790. In this addenda he states "This pamphlet was published 2 years after my arrival here," which indicates publication late in 1786 instead of 1787 as appears on the cover. Perhaps it was *written* late in 1786.

69.

(1) Ibid., p. 12.

(2) Lanmon and Palmer (*see* 67), pp. 18, 19, 25, 26.

70.

(1) Ad: Prime (*see* 10(2)), p. 134, *Maryland Journal or Baltimore Advertiser,* Feb. 11, 1785.

(2) Petitions to Maryland: Laws of Maryland Assembly, May Session 1788, Chap. VII (Quynn, p. 13). 1790 petition quoted in full by Quynn, pp. 13–15.

71.

(1) Maryland grant: *see* 70(2).

(2) Expenditures and land: In his "Remarks" (*see* 68), p. 10, Amelung gives the sum of £15,000 — £5,000 more than £10,000 German capital. In the 1790 longhand addenda he states that £8,000 more (probably including the loan from Maryland) had been spent, thus bringing the total to £23,000 and that 1,000 more acres had been acquired. In his 1790 petitions (*see* 60 and 70(2)) he stated he had 3,000 acres of land and had spent upward of £20,000.

72.

(1) *See* Quynn, pp. 20, 21, for details of transactions.

(2) Amelung & Labes: Amelung mortgaged land to Labes in 1793 (Quynn, p. 20), but an association of Labes with Amelung or a partnership appears to have been formed earlier. Marshall Etchison of Frederick, Md., informed me that "Amelung & Labes" was among the later entries in a ledger containing the record of accounts [of a general store in Frederick] from Jan. 1, 1789 through 1792.

(3) For Sale ad: *Federal Intelligencer and Baltimore Daily Gazette,* Mar. 23, 1795.

(4) Bankruptcy: Laws of Maryland, Chap. LXXXIV, An Act for the relief of sundry insolvent debtors, No.2, folio 385, Dec. 1795.

(5) J.F.M. Amelung & James Labes: Mar. 6, 1942, letter from Marshall Etchison, who examined vital statistics, local land records, and other documentary sources, and who excavated fragments on the New Bremen glassworks' site and gathered family and local traditions.

(6) Kohlenberg, *see* 74(1) & (2)

73. Lewis Repart (Reppert): Major Craig wrote to Gen. O'Hara, Oct. 1799, that Repart, then in direction of the Johnson Works, "would gladly accept the invitation to Pittsburgh." (Daniel, p. 104.)

74.

(1) Kohlenberg Glass Works and Johnson Works: Letters, July & Dec. 1948 from E. Ralston Goldsborough; "*Maryland Products GLASS,*" *Baltimore,* Mar. 1948. pp. 41, 42.

(2) Kohlenberg & Gabler: Quynn, p. 21.

(3) 1810 figures: Annals of Congress, 13th, pp. 26, 28, Tench Coxe's "Digest of Manufactures."

75. Ads: 1785, *see* 70(1); 1788, Mar. 25, *Federal Intelligencer and Baltimore Daily Gazette;* 1789, May 22, *Maryland Journal and Baltimore Advertiser.* Of the last (1789), one was a short ad by James Labes dated May 1 and the second was a long one by John Frederick Amelung (no "& Co.") dated May 16.

76. Excavations prior to 1962: Stohlman, Martin and Elizabeth, "Excavating and Collecting Amelung Glass," *Antiques* (Oct. 1948); Millford, Harriet N., "Amelung and His New Bremen Glass Wares," *Maryland Historical Magazine* (Mar. 1952). Mrs. Millford has given to the Maryland Historical Society a large and representative number of the fragments unearthed by bulldozing a small area of the factory site.

77. Hume, Ivor Noël, "Archaeological Excavations on the Site of John Frederick Amelung's New Bremen Glassmanufactory," 1962–1963. *Journal of Glass Studies,* The Corning Museum of Glass, Vol. XVIII (1976).

(11. Dowesborough, Albany Glass-House, later Hamilton Glass Factory)

78.

(1) Elkanah Watson, ms. Journal 1821, p. 363 (expansion of 1788 Journal). New York State Library, Albany. In 1788, p. 9, Watson recorded his visit to DeNeufville in part as follows: "I took the rout to Schenectady . . . on my way I turned off to the left to view the glassworks owned by my business correspondent, Mr. DeNeufville, an opulent in Amsterdam who sacrificed an immense fortune to support our independence . . . "

(2) 1785 agreement: White, "The Albany Glass Works."

(3) Location: Watson, 1788, p. 9; Spafford, Horatio Gates, *A Gazetteer of the State of New York* (Albany: 1813).

79. Van Schaick letters, Manuscript Collection, New-York Historical Society, quoted by Lyman (p. 56), and 1786 petition (p. 57). Lyman, Susan, "The Albany Glass Works and some of their Records," *New-York Historical Society Quarterly,* Vol. 26 No. 3 (July 1942).

80. De Neufville papers, Manuscript Collection, New-York Historical Society.

81.

(1) 1789 Petition: Ibid. Also *Journals of the Assembly of the State of New York,* 12th Session, pp. 5, 93, 163.

(2) 1790 Petition: *Journals of the Assembly of the State of New York,* 13th Session, p. 87.

(3) Heefke ads: *New York Packet,* July 24–Aug. 26, 1790; Apr. 14, 1791–Jan. 20, 1792.

82.

(1) Sept. ad: Lansingburgh, *The American Spy,* Sept. 28, 1792; *Vermont Gazette,* Sept. 12, 1792 (sent to me by the late John Spargo, Old Bennington, Vt.). The members of the firm and new name of the works appeared in these for the first time in my present records. That Batterman was in charge of the works is suggested by an ad for woodcutters, *Albany Register,* Jan. 6, 1794.

(2) 1793 Loan: *Laws of the State of New York,* 16th Session, Chap. 47, p. 451.

83.

(1) New partners: On June 20, 1796, Jeremiah Van Rensselaer and Elkanah Watson, as "Committee on behalf of the present copartners," published in the *Albany Register* a notice of the dissolution of the copartnership in the Albany Glass Factory formed Feb. 27, 1793, under the firm of McClellan, McGregor & Co. In the Van Rensselaer Papers, ms. collection of the New-York Historical Society, July 12 & Dec. 7 statements list Caldwell, McClellan, & McGregor of the original company, also Van Rensselaer, Watson, the Mathers and DeZeng.

(2) Warehouse: first mentioned in ad for woodcutters, *Albany Register,* Jan. 6, 1794; headed an ad, Ibid., May 5, 1794.

84. Statements: *see* 83(1), Van Rensselaer Papers.

85.

(1) Watson letter to Lawrence: Feb. 1796. Ms. collection, New-York Historical Society.

(2) *Laws of the State of New York,* 19th Session, 1796, Chap. 54, p. 202.

86.

(1) New Society and name: Van Rensselaer Papers, Ms. collection, New-York Historical Society; ad dated Dec. 10, 1796, *Albany Register,* Jan. 16, 1797.

(2) Incorporation: *Laws of the State of New York,* 20th Session, 1797, Chap. LXVIII, pp. 296–98; 32nd Session, 1809, Private Laws, Chap. CXLVIII, p. 153.

(3) Copartnership dissolution: *see* 83(1).

(4) DeZeng and Ten Eyck: Van Rensselaer Papers (*see* (1) above); ad of Mar. 21, 1796 (Prime, *Arts and Crafts of Pennsylvania, Maryland and South Carolina,* Series II. 1786–1800, p. 151) announced that "The Business of the Glass Factory being transferred from Thomas Mather & Co. to Abraham Ten Eyck, under the firm of Abraham Ten Eyck & Co., all persons indebted to the late Firm of Thomas Mather & Co. or having any demands on them are requested to adjust the same with the said Ten Eyck." It probably was this ad which led to the assumption by some students, not knowing of the June 6, 1796, partnership dissolution, that Thomas Mather & Co. operated the glass factory itself.

87.

(1) News item dated "Albany, Apr. 22," Newfield, Conn., *American Telegraphe,* May 4, 1796.

(2) Village growth: Van Rensselaer Papers, *see* 86(1)— Inventory, Apr. 15, 1800, and Apr. 23, 1801, agreement between Society and John Van Rensselaer of the glassworks; Fessenden, Thomas Green, *The Register of Arts* (1808), pp. 299–300; Spafford, Horatio Gates, *Gazetteer of the State of New York* (1813 and 1824).

88.

(1) Van Rensselaer Papers: *see* 86(1).

(2) L. Schoolcraft letter published by White, *Antiques* (Dec. 1938).

(3) Glassblowers' defections: Among many references to the luring of blowers away from one glassworks to another was one pertaining to Henry Rowe Schoolcraft. In "People Who Work in Glasshouses," *Antiques* (May 1963), Jasena Rapplege Foley states that recently discovered documentary material reveals that in the fall of 1810, Henry, having been offered one share of stock for each blower he got for the new Ontario Glass Works at Geneva, N.Y., secured 8 who were arrested for breaking their contracts and bailed out by the company. It is likely some or all of the 8 were from Hamilton.

89.

(1) 1815 closing: Munsell, Joel, *History of Albany,* Vol. III, p. 157.

(2) 1811 Indenture: Albany County Land Records, Book 27, pp. 445–63.

(3) 1820 dividend: *New York Commercial Advertiser,* Dec. 6, 1820.

(4) 1823: *see* 88(1), Letters of Mar. 30, 1821, Mar. 17, 1823.

90.

(1) Flint glass: the Sept. 1792 ad (*see* 82(1)) stated that "great encouragement and constant employment will be given to a flint glassmaker"; also offered 10s per cwt. for broken flint glass [for cullet presumably]. In 1794 and 1796, 12s were offered (*Albany Register,* May 5, 1794, May 27, 1796). An 1800 statement in the Van Rensselaer Papers (*see* 86(1)) lists an unfinished flint glass furnace which, it had been proposed, should be torn down and replaced by another window-glass furnace. But there was no evidence as to whether or not this was done, or that the furnace was not completed. According to Fessenden's account (*see* 87(2)) flint glass was blown.

(2) Emison: Van Rensselaer Papers (*see* 86(1)). In September they blew also 8 doz. tumblers of qt. size, 23 doz. of pt., 2½ doz. ½ pt. and 4 doz. gill, 1 doz. & 8 wine glasses, 1 doz. qt. pitchers and 1 doz. milk pots [creamers].

90a.

(1) Leiper purchase of snuff bottles: *see* 41(3).

(2) Caldwell: one of his ads, among several, listed snuff, to-

bacco, chocolate and mustard. *Albany Gazette,* Apr. 14, 1790.

(3) Broken bottles: *see* 82(1).

(12. Boston Glass Manufactory)

91. Acts of 1783 and 1787: *Massachusetts Acts and Laws,* 1787, Chap. XIII, p. 642.

92.

(1) Pyramidal glasshouse: Fessenden (*see* 87(2)), p. 295.

(2) 1788: Boston, *Massachusetts Centinel,* Sept. 6; *Salem* [*Mass.*] *Mercury,* Sept. 9; Newburyport, Mass., *Essex Journal,* Sept. 10.

(3) 1789: Boston news item: *Salem* [*Mass.*] *Mercury,* Aug. 11.

(4) Kupfer: Pazaurek, Gustave E., "A German View of Early American Glass," *Antiques* (Apr. 1932); Watkins, *Antiques* (June 1940).

(5) Glassmen: Oct. 3, 1792, ad in the Boston, *Columbian Centinel* of 3 shares or 1/7 of the Glass-Manufactory for sale: "Part of the estate of a Gentleman lately deceased, and for that reason only to be sold."

93.

(1) Act of 1793: *Massachusetts Acts and Laws,* 1793, Chap. IV, p. 309.

(2) Petitions, 1794 and 1797: *see* 61(2).

(3) Expansion of project: Watkins, *Antiques* (June 1940); McKearin, *Two Hundred Years . . . ,* pp. 49, 50, 75–77.

94.

(1) 1816 announcement: Washington, D.C., *National Intelligencer,* May 16, 1816; *Boston Daily Advertiser,* Sept. 30, 1815.

(2) 1819: *Niles' Weekly Register,* Aug. 14, 1819; 1818 Price List, *see* 95(2).

(3) *See* 93(2).

95.

(1) 1812 ad: Boston, *Columbian Centinel,* Dec. 16, 1812.

(2) Price Lists: 1817(?), 1818, 1819, pasted in the back of one of Jeremiah Emlen's invoice books, collection of the Henry Ford Museum; 1822, collection of the Essex Institute.

96.

(1) Price Lists: *see* 95(2).

(2) Billhead: 1815 receipted bill, the Bella C. Landauer Collection in the New-York Historical Society.

(13. The Pitkin Glass Works)

97.

(1) East Hartford was formed from the town of Hartford, Oct. 1783, because, as John Pitkin and other inhabitants of the area stated, many lived too far from "The Place of transacting Public Business and at various seasons difficulties of crossing from the east side of the Connecticut River" often prevented attending and enjoying their legal privileges. Also they had the ability and numbers to become a distinct town. (*The Public Records of the State of Connecticut For the Year 1783 & 1784.* Leonard Woods Labaree, compiler. 1943, p. 18.)

(2) Orford changed to Manchester: Goodwin, Joseph D., *History of East Hartford* (1879), p. 95.

(3) 1783 Memorial & Act: *Connecticut Archives,* Industry, Series I, Vol. II, ms. pp. 179a, 180.

(4) Reward for services in Revolution: Van Rensselaer, p. 50. Source not given but probably a family tradition passed on to Mr. Van Rensselaer by members of the family.

(5) Proviso for monopoly not met: *see* 98(1) & (2) below and text on New Haven Glass Works.

98.

(1) Mather: *see* text No. 28. John Mather's Glassworks, East Hartford, Conn.

(2) Leavenworth, "Hints . . . ," *see* 63(1).

(3) Glasshouse described, information on capital and "Hughes" [Hewes] in an "Extract from a letter from a Gentleman in East Hartford to his friend in Boston," dated May 7, 1788. Appeared 1788 in the Boston, *Federal Gazette*, May 19; *Salem* [*Mass.*] *Mercury*, May 20; Philadelphia, *Pennsylvania Gazette* and *Freeman's Journal*, May 28.

(4) Tindsale's ad dated Aug. 8, 1787: Hartford, *Connecticut Courant*, Sept. 17, 1787.

99.

(1) Proprietors and Oct. 5, 1789, petition: *Connecticut Archives*, Industry, Series I, Vol. II, ms. pp. 239a, 240, 241.

(2) May 10, 1791, petition: Ibid., Series II, Vol. II, pp. 38a, b, c. The statement in this petition that "they have now present & under engagement an Excellent Set of Workmen well skilled in the art of making window & other kinds of Glass of various sorts" suggests to me these workmen were not obtained until early in 1791. Without giving the source of information, Knittle (pp. 193, 194) states that the head workmen and also silica for the glass were obtained from New Jersey. The writer of the 1788 letter (98(3)) wrote "The Wood in this State is large and very plenty, . . . The materials for the Glass is also plenty, and can be had on reasonable terms." He also stated that the head artificer and superintendent at the time was Robert Hewes of Boston whose last name he spelled "Hughes" as it was in the 1789 petition.

100.

(1) Petitions: *see* 99(1) & (2).

(2) 1789-lottery ads: Hartford, *Connecticut Courant*, Nov. 14, 1789, Apr. 5, 1790; New Haven, *Connecticut Journal*, Apr. 12 & June 9, 1790 (the last, the manager's notice dated June 1).

(3) 1791-lottery ads: Hartford, *Connecticut Courant*, Sept. 12, 1791; New London, *Connecticut Gazette*, Nov. 10, 1791; New Haven, *Connecticut Journal*, Dec. 14, 1791 & Jan. 11, 1792.

101. Ads: The ads of East Hartford bottles were found in the *Connecticut Courant* —the earliest in the Jan. 2, 1797, issue; the latest in that of Apr. 10, 1821.

102.

(1) J. P. Foster: Van Rensselaer, p. 50; Knittle, p. 193. Mrs. Knittle apparently was told that J. P. Foster was Joseph P. since the first page reference in the Index to Joseph P. Foster is page 193. Both writers presumably obtained information about the works from members of the Pitkin and other local families.

(2) Pitkin, Woodbridge & Co.: In the Hartford County Court manuscripts Mr. Wilson found that case 736 of the Mar. 1817 term was one in which this firm brought suit against one Stephen Cone of East Hartford who owed them for a wide variety of merchandise, including a few bottles and spirits purchased in 1815 and 1816. The credit for cutting wood was on Dec. 28, 1815; for a day's work at the glassworks, Sept. 1816.

(3) Closing ca. 1830: Van Rensselaer, p. 50; Knittle, p. 194.

103.

(1) Phrases in ads in the *Connecticut Courant* in order quoted: of Riley, Savage & Co., Jan. 2 and Isaac Bull & Isaac D. Bull, Jan. 9, 1797; of Joshua Burnham, Apr. 21, 1808. As the Bulls' ad was on page 1, whereas new ads normally appeared on the inner pages, usually page 3, and were moved to page 1 or page 4 as new ones came along, it may be inferred that possibly the Bulls' ad had been running since some time in 1796. From 1812 on the phrase was "East Hartford Bottles."

(2) Knittle, p. 195.

104.

(1) The J.P.F. attribution by Van Rensselaer (p. 50) and the Jared Spencer by Van Rensselaer (illustration p. 134) and Knittle (p. 195) was generally accepted by later writers, including myself for some years.

(2) Hartford County Land Records contain several indentures of land transactions between Jared Spencer and others between Jan. 31, 1793, and Jan. 7, 1829. One was a purchase in 1813 from Richard Pitkin. Between 1820 and 1825 there were purchases from and sales to Horace Pitkin and Dudley Woodbridge. In one instance, Mar. 10, 1824, Spencer put up land as guaranty for a $600 note payable in 4 months to Dudley Woodbridge and Horace Pitkin.

(14. New-Haven Glass Works)

105.

(1) *The Diaries of George Washington*, 1748–1799, edited by John C. Fitzpatrick, Vol. IV (1789–1799), p. 25.

(2) Leavenworth: Elected Councilman, Hartford *Connecticut Courant*, June 9, 1790; Clerk of District Court, New London, *Connecticut Gazette*, Mar. 17, 1791.

(3) Petition: *Connecticut Archives*, Industry, Series II, Vol. II, Doc. 41, pp. a, b. The petition contains also the information about building the glasshouse and fate of the March blast.

106. Report to Committee: See 105(3), Doc. 42, pp. a, b.

107.

(1) Report of Committee: Ibid., Doc. 43, p. a.

(2) Assembly resolves: Ibid., addenda to Doc. 41, p. b; Doc. 44, pp. a, b.

(3) Newspaper information on lotteries: Class First, New Haven, *Connecticut Journal*, Nov. 10 & Dec. 15, 1790; Class Second, Ibid., Jan. 26, Feb. 23, Mar. 9, 17, and 30 & Apr. 20, 1791.

108. *Connecticut Archives*, Industry, Series II, Vol. II, Doc. 45 p. a.

(15. Nicholson Glass Factory)

109.

(1) Morris & Nicholson: Weeks, p. 81, from Hagner, Charles V., *The Early History of the Falls of the Schuylkill and Lehigh Navigation Company . . .* (Philadelphia: 1869), pp. 33, 34.

(2) Eichbaum letter: Weeks, p. 81.

110. La Rochefoucauld Liancourt, Duc de, *Travels Through the United States of North America . . . in the years 1795, 1796, and 1797*, English translation (London: 1799), Vol. I, pp. 4, 5.

111.

(1) Feb. 10, 1795, ad: Prime, Alfred Coxe, *Arts and Crafts of Maryland and South Carolina*, Series II (1786–1800), p. 156, *Federal Gazette* [*Philadelphia Gazette and Universal Daily Advertiser*].

(2) Apr. 25, 1795, ad, repeated Dec. 8: Ibid.

(3) Eichbaum: Craig, Neville B., *The History of Pittsburgh* (1851), p. 276; Bishop, Vol. II, p. 165; Knittle, *Antiques* (Mar. 1927).

112.

(1) 1796 ads: *Federal Gazette* [*Philadelphia Gazette and Universal Daily Advertiser*], Jan. 25–Feb. 23 and Apr. 25–July 1, 1796.

(2) Weeks, p. 81.

(3) Philadelphia Land Records, Book E.F. 32, p. 248.

113.

(1) Eichbaum: *see* 111(3).

(2) 1795 ads: *see* 111(1) & (2), Apr. and Feb.

(3) Jan. 25–Feb. 23 ad: *see* 112 (1).

(16. Pittsburgh Glass Works)

114.

(1) O'Hara: Knittle, pp. 208, 209; Innes, p. 10.

(2) Transport: *Annals of Congress*, Vol. 15, p. 609; Fordham, Elia Pymn, *Personal Narrative of Travels in Virginia, Western Pennsylvania . . . 1817–1818* (Reprint, Cleveland, 1906), p. 59.

115.

(1) Daniel, "The First Glasshouse West of the Alleghenies," pp. 97–101, Daniel states that O'Hara's first works, 1795, was "for the purpose of making window glass but more especially to manufacture bottles for his brewery." As it seemed unlikely to me that he had established the brewery at that time and the earliest evidence I had found of his Pittsburgh Point Brewery was an 1805 advertisement, I asked the late L. Earl Dambach if he would enlighten me. Mr. Dambach informed me he found no basis for so early a date (1795) but did find that "while still a government contractor in 1798 O'Hara planned to start a brewery. He wrote in February of that year to his agent, James Henry, in Detroit, 'I intend carrying on a brewery, extensive as possible.' " My guess would be that O'Hara did not start his brewery before 1802 and after his retirement from government service.

(2) O'Hara & Craig, 1796: Neville B. Craig, in *The History of Pittsburgh* (1851), pp. 276, 277, states that arrangements were made in the spring of 1796; Daniel (p. 102) quotes a Craig letter to Eichbaum, 1796. Unless otherwise noted, references to Craig's letters are from Daniel's quotes and references to the Craig papers in the Carnegie Library, Pittsburgh.

(3) Innes, *Pittsburgh Glass*, 1791, pp. 10, 11, gives the date 1797 as that of the O'Hara and Craig glassworks and does not mention a 1795 O'Hara glasshouse. However, a footnote (p. 11) states, "Dorothy Daniel's advanced the theory that O'Hara and Craig started their house in 1795." Mr. Innes was misinformed as to Ms. Daniel's statements, namely "the first O'Hara glassworks built in 1795 in what was then the Reserve tract (p. 97) of her article and "it would appear that Craig was not a partner in the glassworks until the 1797 venture at Coal Hill . . . "

116.

(1) Col. O'Hara: Both Knittle and Daniel refer to O'Hara as General, but Craig (115(2)) quotes a June 12, 1797, letter from Major Craig which is addressed Col. James O'Hara, Detroit.

(2) Craig's interest & withdrawal: Daniel (p. 106) quotes figures from Craig's papers; Neville B. Craig (115(2)) gives reasons for withdrawal; Knittle (p. 214) gives Sept. 28, 1804, as the date of the notice of dissolution of partnership published in the *Pittsburgh Gazette*.

(3) O'Hara's investment: O'Hara's Letter Book, letter of June 25, 1805, to James Morrison, Kentucky, and July 1805 letter to P. R. Frieze, Baltimore, Md.

117.

(1) Workmen & expenses: O'Hara's Letter Book, in particular letter of Aug. 20, 1810, to Joseph Carson, Philadelphia, and of Apr. 8, 1812, to Adam Greiner.

(2) Causes of costs: I. Craig letter quoted by George H. Thurston, *Allegheny County's One Hundred Years* (Pittsburgh: 1885), p. 183.

(3) Ohio Glass Works: Daniel (p. 107) quotes from Craig letter to O'Hara, Mar. 1801—"The Ohio Glassworks have stopped and it is said have dismissed all hands"; Thurston (2) quotes from an account current of the company with the firm of Beelen & Denny in which the last entry shows a balance due as of Dec. 20, 1802, and also that " 'O'Hara' people" had taken many tools and probably would take more. O'Hara in his May 21, 1805, letter to J.F.M. Amelung mentions Falleur [La Fleur] as one of his workmen. La Fleur had been at the Ohio Glass Works.

118.

(1) Eichbaum: *see* 111(3).

(2) Craig letter: Daniel, and the June 12, 1797, letter quoted by Craig (115(2)); and Aug. 3, 1803, letter quoted by Thurston (117(2)).

(3) Re pots: O'Hara's Letter Book, June 25, 1805, letter to Morrison.

119.

(1) Local clay sent to Eichbaum: Knittle, p. 211.

(2) 1807 delay: O'Hara's Letter Book, letters of June 12 to Col. Isaac Granton, New Castle, Del., and to Gen. Henry Miller, merchant, Baltimore.

(3) Reward: ad in the *Pittsburgh Gazette*, appearing May 12 through Dec. 12, 1802.

(4) Clay sources: N.J.—Thurston (*see* 117(2)), p. 183 and O'Hara, May 21, 1805, letter to J.F.M. Amelung; Del.—O'Hara letters, May 20, June 12, 1807, to Col. Granton; German from Baltimore—O'Hara letters, Dec. 11, 1806, to J. Labes and Feb. 5, 1808, to John Holmes; Missouri—Knittle, p. 20.

120.

(1) Eichbaum, Wendt & Co., 1798–99: Weeks, p. 85; Craig letter to O'Hara, Oct. 1799; Daniels, p. 103; O'Hara reply, Oct. 18, Innes, p. 16.

(2) Eichbaum: *see* 111(3); McKearin, *Two Hundred Years . . . ,* pp. 33, 48.

121.

(1) Wendt, superintendent: Daniel, p. 102.

(2) 1800 ad: *Pittsburgh Gazette and Daily Advertiser,* Mar. 1, 1800; Philadelphia, *Aurora General Advertiser,* Mar. 4, also appearing in Apr., May, June & July; *Philadelphia Gazette and Daily Advertiser,* Mar. 10, 1801.

(3) F. Wendt & Co.: Daniel, p. 104.

122.

(1) Price: Daniel, pp. 104–7; Weeks, p. 84; Knittle, p. 213; U.S. Patent Records.

(2) 1802: Knittle, p. 213; ms. on Pittsburgh glasshouse, John Ramsey, Pittsburgh, Pa.

123.

(1) O'Hara, sole owner: O'Hara's Letter Book, 1805 letters to J.F.M. Amelung in Apr., to James Morrison in July, to P[hilip] R. Frieze in July.

(2) Re Wendt & Price: Ibid., letters Apr. 19 & May 21, 1805 to Amelung; Apr. 19, 1805 to Morrison.

(3) Expansion: Ibid., July 30, 1805, to Amelung.

(4) 1804–1806, white glass: Ibid., letter of May 21, 1805, to Amelung and Mar. 14, 1806, to Terence Campbell; *Pittsburgh Gazette*, June 8, 1804, ad dated Apr. 27.

124.

(1) Re F. M. Amelung: *see* Baltimore Glass Works (18); O'Hara Letter Book, letters to Amelung (*see* 123(2) & (3)); to Joseph Carson, Apr. 29, 1810.

(2) Wendt rehired: Ibid., letter of July 30, 1805, to Amelung.

(3) Swerer: Ibid., *see* (2); June 11, July 5 & 12 letters to Henry Muhlenburgh, Philadelphia.

125.

(1) Workmen: Ibid., letters to Joseph Carson, Aug. 20, 1810; to Robt. Smith, Frederick, Maryland, July 21, 1810; to Adolph Everhart, Mar. 31, 1812; to Adam Greiner, Apr. 18, 1812.

(2) White-glass works: Ibid., letter to Joseph Carson, Apr. 29, 1810.

(3) Output, 1803 & 1806: *Cramer's Almanac* for 1804 and 1807.

(4) Agreement, 1816: Daniel, pp. 112, 113.

(5) 1818: O'Hara's Letter Book, letter Oct. 22, 1818, to Messrs. Morgan, Dorsey & Co., New Orleans.

126.

(1) Last years: Daniel, pp. 112, 113.

(2) Lorenz: Van Rensselaer, pp. 173, 174; Knittle, p. 317.

(3) Later firms: McKearin, *American Glass,* p. 587.

127.

(1) White glass: Weeks (p. 85) and Knittle (p. 213), whom I have followed previously, state that production of flint glass was attempted by O'Hara & Craig. According to Knittle, Price was hired

at a considerable sum to come to Pittsburgh to supervise flint glass making whereas the Craig papers (quoted by Daniel, pp. 104, 105) show that it was Price who offered his services and only "white glass" was mentioned. Daniel uses the term "white glass throughout her article with two exceptions, namely "lead glass" once on p. 105 and once on p. 112. In fact "white" was the usual adjective in the primary sources. O'Hara used the term "Chrystal Glass" in an 1800 letter (Daniel, p. 107) and Edward Ensell's 1801 letter to O'Hara & Craig told of his ability to make flint glass. From O'Hara's statement to J.F.M. Amelung (letter, May 21, 1805) that white glass had been tried in the same furnace as the window glass successfully it seems unlikely he was referring to flint glass at the time. However, Price would certainly have been competent in making lead glass. Therefore, perhaps some was produced, but I doubt it was in any quantity.

(2) 1800 ad: *see* 121 (2).

(3) 1804: *Pittsburgh Gazette,* June 8, 1804, ad dated Apr. 27.

(4) Later prices: O'Hara Letter Book, letter Apr. 1, 1806, to Terrance Campbell, Bedford, Pa.; Letter Sept. 11, 1816 (Apr. 8, 1809, invoice to Wm. A. McNan(?)

128. Dates of Lorenz and later firms: *see* 126(2) and (3)

(17. New Geneva Glass Works)

129. Previous accounts: Van Rensselaer, p. 189; Knittle, pp. 202–7; McKearin, *American Glass,* pp. 117–19 and *Two Hundred Years . . . ,* pp. 45–47.

130.

(1) Tradition: Ibid.; Kramer, Leroy, *Johann Baltazar Kramer* (privately printed, Chicago); Dec. 29, 1949, letter from Cloyde R. Reppert; Ellis, *History of Fayette County,* p. 768. According to one version of the traditional and unsubstantiated accounts, one given by grandchildren of one of the blowers, Christian Kramer, Adolph Eberhart, Lewis Reitz, John G. Reppert, Baltzar Kramer, and John C. Gabler, en route to Louisville, Ky., stopped for the night and were joined by a stranger who spoke their language. He persuaded them to go to his farm on George Creek where all needed material was available. He agreed to furnish everything; the blowers were to do the blowing. Operation began in 1794. According to the account obtained from neighbors, the same group of men, crossing the mountains, stopped at Tomlinson's stand where they began making music. Albert Gallatin joined them and gave them a letter to his manager at Friendship Hill urging him to make terms with the blowers. Three of them accepted the offer. The other went on to Louisville, Ky., but, finding that location unsuitable for a glass works, returned to join the others at New Geneva.

(2) Gabler: *see* 10. New Bremen Glassmanufactory and other Frederick County glasshouses. (a) In connection with the New Geneva Glass Works, the first reference, merely "Gabler," was found in a letter of June 16, 1806, from Gallatin to Nicholson. *Albert Gallatin Autographed Letters,* collected by Albert H. Gallatin and A. E. Gallatin (New York: 1902), Vol. II, p. 28. (b) The February 1807 agreement was signed "Christian Gabeler." (Information from Cloyde R. Reppert, obtained for him by the law firm of Thompson, Baily & Montgomery, Waynesboro, Pa., from the original document.) (c) Gallatin's balance sheet for July 22, 1809, gives "John Gabler." (Balance sheet in the Gallatin Papers, New-York Historical Society.) Since no evidence has been found as yet of two Gablers being in the group which established the second works it would appear that "Christian" and "John" were the same man.

(3) Baltzar Kramer: name first appears on an 1801 account book sheet. (Gallatin Papers, New-York Historical Society.) Data on land sale and purchase supplied by Cloyde R. Reppert from Land records.

131.

(1) Badollet letter, date-lined Greensburgh: Gallatin Papers, New-York Historical Society.

132.

(1) Adams, Henry, *Life of Albert Gallatin* (Philadelphia: 1879), pp. 176, 187.

(2) July 1797 receipt: Letter, Aug. 8, 1957, from C. L. Horn.

(3) Gallatin's original copy of the Articles of Agreement: Gallatin Papers, New-York Historical Society.

133.

(1) Badollet's letter, Jan. 17, 1798: Gallatin Papers, New-York Historical Society.

(2) Gallatin to Nicholson, Mar. 9, 1798: *Albert Gallatin Autographed Letters,* collected by Albert H. Gallatin and A. E. Gallatin, Vol. I, p. 31.

134.

(1) 1816 letter, May 7, to Matthew Lyons: *Writings of Albert Gallatin,* ed. Henry Adams (Philadelphia: 1889), Vol. I, p. 701.

(2) B. F. Black & Co. reported in 1832 that "the firm a joint stock concern" had been established "two years" before. U.S. House Doc. 14 #200, p. 531.

(3) 1832 letters, Nicholson to Albert R. Gallatin: Gallatin Papers, New-York Historical Society.

135.

(1) Dissolution of Albert Gallatin & Co.: In a Feb. 7, 1799, letter to Nicholson, Gallatin referred to the "late company" (135(3) Vol. I, p. 42); also letters and account sheet indicate premature dissolution. (Gallatin Papers, New-York Historical Society.)

(2) Gallatin-Nicholson interest: (Gallatin Papers, *see above*).

(3) 1799, letters Feb. 15 & July 31 from Gallatin to Nicholson: 133(2), Vol. I, p. 46.

(4) July 14, 1799, letter from Gallatin to Bourdillon: Adams, *see* 132(1), p. 345.

136.

(1) Mussard letters to Gallatin: Nov. 20, Dec. 5 and 26, 1799; June 17, Feb. 2, 4, & 28, Apr. 12, 1800: Gallatin Papers, New-York Historical Society.

(2) Jan. 17, 1800, letter from Gallatin to Nicholson: 133(2), Vol. I, p. 55.

137.

(1) 1803 auction ad: quoted by Knittle, p. 205, from the *Pittsburgh Gazette* of May 7.

(2) Nicholson's share purchased May 20, 1803: Gallatin Papers, New-York Historical Society, Ms. Coll.

(3) Jan. 11, 1803, letter to Nicholson: 133(2), Vol. II, p. 1.

138.

(1) 1806 letters to Nicholson, June 16, Aug. 20 & Sept. 22: 133(2), Vol. II, pp. 28–29, 32, 33.

(2) Reppert land purchase: 130(2)(b). On Aug. 8, 1957, C. L. Horn of Minneapolis, Minn., wrote me that he had obtained an original indenture to Albert Gallatin from George Reppert and dated Aug. 9, 1810, for 1/7th of the Greensburgh land. This would probably be for Gallatin's share of the land purchased in 1806 for the 7 founders of the Greensburgh glasshouse, though why it should have been drawn 3 years after the Agreement of 1807 was signed is a puzzle at present.

(3) 1807 Agreement: 130(2)(b).

139.

(1) Account book sheets: Gallatin Papers, New-York Historical Society.

(2) 1810: Cramer, Spear and Eichbaum, *The Navigator* (Pittsburgh: 1814), pp. 40, 41.

(3) Coal: Aug. 8, 1957, letter from C. L. Horn.

(4) 1816 account: 134(1), p. 701.

(5) 1837: second house—Gest, Neil C. & Smith, Parke G., "The Glassmaking Kramers," *Antiques* (Mar. 1939); house rebuilt—Innes, Lowell, "Pittsburgh Glass," Part I, *Antiques* (Dec. 1949).

(6) 1847: Ms. on Pittsburgh houses, John Ramsay, Pittsburgh.

140.

(1) Metal: Gallatin Papers, New-York Historical Society.

(2) 1832 report: 134(2).

(3) Mussard's reports: *see* (1).

C. 19th Century

1. Historical background of 1800–33 period: McMasters unless otherwise noted. Statistics of glasshouses: based on McKearin, *American Glass,* Chronological Chart of American Glass Houses, p. 583 seq.

2.

(1) Non-Importation, embargoes, and non-intercourse. *Annals of Congress,* Gale & Seaton. 13th Congress, 2nd sess., Vol. II, Supplemental Journal, p. 2057ff. Feb. 1806–Dec. 1813, "catalogue of these restrictive not to say oppressive laws," in a speech against Madison's embargo, given by King, Representative of Mass. Dec. 12, 1813; also the numerous debates and acts in each session of 9th through 13th Congresses. War declared by 12th Congress, Part I, appendix, pp. 2322, 2323.

(2) Articles enumerated. Ibid. 9th Congress. Vol. II, appendix, pp. 1259–63.

(3) Quote from "The Embargo," Henry Mellen. Dover, N.H., *The Sun,* July 23, 1808.

(4) U.S. House Doc. 671, "Tariff Acts Passed by the Congress of the United States for 1789 to 1809" (Washington, Government Printing Office, 1809).

3.

(1) Perry ad. Hartford, *Connecticut Courant,* Feb. 18, 1817.

(2) Schoolcraft, Foley, Jessica Rappleye, "The Ontario Glass Manufacturing Company," *Journal of Glass Studies,* The Corning Museum of Glass, Vol. VI (1964), p. 139.

(3) Skilled craftsmen: Pears III, Thomas C., "Sidelights on the History of the Bakewell, Pears & Company from the Letters of Thomas and Sara Pears," *The Western Pennsylvania Historical Magazine,* Vol. 31 (1948), pp. 62–65; Jarves, Demming, *Reminiscences of Glass-Making,* 1854 ed., p. 44ff.

4.

(1) Tariffs: *see* 2(4).

(2) Prices: Dyott's Exposition Appendix D.

(18. Baltimore Glass Works)

5. "Maryland Products—Glass Part I," p. 63; D. A. Dressel ms.; R. H. Wood, letters, including copy of June 27, 1800, announcement, Baltimore, *Federal Gazette.*

6. Ibid. Also letters from Cloyde A. Reppert.

7. Ibid.

8.

(1) Furnival vs. Amelung: Quynn, Dorothy Mackay, "Johann Friedrick Amelung at New Bremen," *Maryland Historical Magazine* (Sept. 1948), pp. 175, 176.

(2) Furnival ad: R. H. Wood from *Federal Gazette and Baltimore Daily Advertiser,* Aug. 11, 1802.

(3) Bankruptcies: Furnival, Baltimore, *American and Commercial Daily Advertiser,* May 21, 1803; Amelung, ibid., June 11, 1803; 1800–1805, longhand notations, 1799 *Baltimore City Directory,* New-York Historical Society.

(4) *Federal Gazette and Baltimore Daily Advertiser,* Nov. 8, 1802.

9.

(1) Dissolution, Frederick M. Amelung, notice dated Nov. 2; *Federal Gazette and Baltimore Daily Advertiser,* Nov. 8, 1802.

(2) Nov. 5, 1802 lease transfer: D. A. Dressel.

10.

(1) From R. H. Wood. Repperts: Listings in Baltimore City Directories: 1807 and 1808—Lewis (Louis) and Geo. glassmakers, Fed. Hill; 1810—Lewis, manager, Geo. & Jacob glassmanufacturers; 1819—all three, glassblowers; 1824—Geo., manager, Jacob, glassblower; 1827—Geo., manufacturer, Jacob, glassblower, also Geo. & Jacob as proprietors; 1829—Geo., proprietor, Jacob, manager, "Glass House . . . proprietors J. F. Friese, George & Jacob Reppert; 1831—Geo. & Jacob, glassblowers; 1835—Geo., glassmaker; 1837—Geo., "Fed. Hill n. glass H."

(2) Amelung, superintendent: Directories 1803, 1804.

(3) Friese—O'Hara letters: O'Hara Letter Book, Historical Society of Western Pennsylvania.

(4) "Vice Master": Journal of Philip R. J. Friese, Sept. 1805 entry (D. A. Dressel).

11.

(1) John H. Friese, listed in 1799 Directory as merchant, returned to Germany 1804 or 1805. Philip, who probably lived with John for a time, was first listed in 1804. D. A. Dressel.

(2) German colony: *History of the Germans in Maryland*—Reports of the German Society—5th Report, p. 54 (Dressel); also "Maryland Products—Glass Part I," p. 63.

(3) German workmen: Ibid.

(4) Ad for apprentices dated December 25, [1810]: Baltimore, *American and Commercial Daily Advertiser,* Nov. 1, 1811.

12.

(1) Land bought: D. A. Dressel.

(2) 1811 price: Baltimore, *American and Commercial Daily Advertiser,* Apr. 15, 1811.

(3) 1820 census report showed (besides figures given in the text) that 20 men, and 10 boys and girls were employed at the glassworks. *Digest of Accounts of Manufacturing Establishments in the United States and of the Manufactures Made in pursuance of a Resolution of Congress of 30th March 1822.* Published 1823.

13.

(1) D. A. Dressel unless stated otherwise.

(2) J. F. Friese debts to Repperts, Documentary information from Cloyde A. Reppert: May 19, 1834. Wm. Tuffs and Rebecca Tuffs [widow of J. F. Friese and, with Frederick Schetter, executor of J.F. Friese] and Frederick Schetter mortgaged to Geo. and Jacob Reppert, land together with two warehouses, all other buildings, and improvements as security for "payment of 12,000 dollars part of the debt . . . " to be made June 1, 1835. Friese vs. Reppert: Feb. 1843, Philip Friese sued the Repperts [Jacob died 1837; Geo. was his executor] to recover moneys due J.F. Friese estate from the glassworks during Reppert's operation and cited payments to the Repperts of $22,640.40 covering J. F. Friese's debts to them.

(3) Bequest to Schetter: cited in 1843 Bill Friese vs. Reppert, *see* (2).

14.

(1) P. R. J. Friese & Schetter trustees: *see* 13(3).

(2) P. R. J. Friese financial troubles: D. A. Dressel.

(3) Baker warehouse: Baltimore Directory 1837.

15.

(1) D. A. Dressel, unless stated otherwise.

(2) 1842. William Baker was listed in the *Baltimore City Directory* as proprietor of the Baltimore Glass House and Works. Baker was listed in the *Baltimore Business Directory* as "Baltimore

window glass manufacturer, 2 N. Liberty, wholesale dealer in coach and window glass."

(3) Baker associates: Th. Flint, Carter A. Hall, Wm. Woodward, Th. Wm. Hall, John S. Gitting.

16. D. A. Dressel. Mr. Dressel found that (1) 1851–65 William Baker was listed without occupation at 32 & 34 Charles— warehouse and store built by his sons replacing those destroyed by fire in 1850—and (2) in the 1849/50 Directory the glassworks listing was "Baltimore Glass House, Schaum, Reitz & Co. man. 9 Hughes Street." and in 1851, "F. & L. Schaum Proprietors Baltimore Glass House Fed. Hill." Mr. Wood sent me the 1837 listings of Lewis Reitz and Lewis Schaum.

17.

(1) D. A. Dressel unless otherwise stated.

(2) Swindell at Camden and Kensington: Van Rensselaer, p. 197.

(3) Baker Bros. & Co. business: "Maryland Products—Glass Part I," p. 65.

18.

(1) Philadelphia City Directories.

(2) D. A. Dressel.

(3) Works obsolete: Ibid.

(4) Natural gas, Midwest: Davis, pp. 122–26.

19.

(1) 1800 ad: Baltimore, *Federal Gazette*, June 27, 1800. R. H. Wood.

(2) 1802 ad: Baltimore, *Telegraph & Daily Advertiser*, June 1, 1802.

(3) Window glass: *see* 17(3), Part I, pp. 64, 65; Part II pp. 42–47; reports to government in 1810 and 1820 census; among ads of sales outside Baltimore, *New York Evening Post*, July 8, 1817, Dec. 9, 1818, and Hartford, *Connecticut Courant*, Jan. 29, 1827.

(4) 1854 announcement: D. A. Dressel.

20. Philadelphia, *Aurora General Advertiser*, Sept. 2, 1815.

21.

(1) Van Rensselaer, p. 50. Note to Locomotive flask 82.

(2) Baltimore & Ohio and Camden & Amboy: Gray & Bowen, *The American Almanac and Repository of Useful Knowledge for 1833* (Boston: 1832), pp. 185, 198, 199.

(3) Cincinnati, O., *Liberty Hall & Cincinnati Gazette*, July 21, 1831.

(4) Frenchtown and New Castle: D. A. Dressel.

22. Pratt, John Horace. "An Authentic Account of all the Proceedings on the 4th of July 1815, with regard to laying the Corner Stone of the Washington Monument in the City of Baltimore" (privately published, Baltimore, 1815); Boston, *Columbian Centinel*, Nov. 25, 1829, one of the papers carrying a reprint from the *Baltimore American* on the occasion of the raising of the statue of Washington to the top of the monument.

23. White, *Antiques* (July, Sept. 1930).

24. McKearin, Helen, "The Story of American Historical Flasks" (Corning, N. Y., The Corning Museum of Glass, 1953).

25.

(1) Ad dated Nov. 28: Baltimore, *American and Commercial Daily Advertiser*, Jan. 12, 1829, and *Federal Gazette*, Mar. 24, 1829.

(2) Operation ceased 1834: D. A. Dressel.

(19. Philadelphia Glass-House, later Schuylkill Glass Works)

26.

(1) Old history: Van Rensselaer, pp. 163, 164; Knittle, p. 151.

(2) Name, etc.: *Albany [N.Y.] Register*, Nov. 8, 1808.

27.

(1) Dec. 3, 1806, indenture: Philadelphia Land Records. Book E.F. 32, p. 248.

(2) Copartnership: Ibid., Book E.F. 32, p. 226.

(3) Buildings: Weeks, p. 81; for sale ad, *Poulson's American Daily Advertiser*, July 6, 1810; to let ad, Sept. 9, 1813. Weeks gives 43′ sq. as size of glasshouse; the 1810 ad 43 x 90 for glasshouse and warehouse.

28.

(1) McIlhenney to Martin: Philadelphia Land Records. Book E.F. 32, p. 226.

(2) Encell to copartners: Ibid. Book E.F. 32, p. 250.

(3) Trevor & Encell: Pittsburgh, *Commonwealth*, Jan. 1, 1813, ad dated Dec. 23, 1812.

29. 1808 ad: *see* 26(2).

30.

(1) Auction notices: *Relf's Philadelphia Gazette*, June 17, 1809; *Poulson's American Daily Advertiser*, July 6 & 20, 1810.

(2) Harison interest: Philadelphia Land Records. Book E.F. 32, p. 248.

(3) Philip Jones & Co.: Weeks, p. 81.

(4) To let ad, dated Aug. 2: *Poulson's American Daily Advertiser*, Sept. 9, 1813.

31.

(1) Weeks, p. 81 unless otherwise noted.

(2) Richards ad: *Poulson's American Daily Advertiser*, Nov. 4, 1814; *Trenton [N.J.] Federalist*, Nov. 14, 1814, ad dated Nov. 1.

32.

(1) *See* 31(1).

(2) Peterman 1820, 1821: ad dated Sept. [1820], Philadelphia, *Aurora General Advertiser*, Mar. 12, 1821.

(3) Frank: Wilson, Thomas, *The Picture of Philadelphia for 1824*, "containing The Picture of Philadelphia for 1811 by James Mease, M.D., with all its improvements since that Period" (Philadelphia: 1823), p.9.

33. *Relf's Philadelphia Gazette and Daily Advertiser*, Jan. 28, 1813; ad dated Jan. 8.

(20. Kensington Glass Works, later Dyottville)

34.

(1) *Philadelphia Gazette and Daily Advertiser*, Aug. 2, 1816. This announcement was published in full by Van Rensselaer, p. 157. Its significance apparently escaped him as it did those who followed him. Probably one reason was that the accounts then known of Philadelphia's glassworks failed to mention this Kensington works or the firms, whereas they do trace, somewhat inaccurately, the next-door glassworks from Towars and Leacock in 1771 to Dyott in 1833 when he *did* acquire the property. Moreover the firm of Hewson, Connell & Company and Hewson & Connell were not listed in the Philadelphia City Directories.

(2) 1819: ad dated Oct. 29, *The Union*, Dec. 31, 1819.

35.

(1) John Hewson, linen printing: *Pennsylvania Journal*, July 25, 1781; *Pennsylvania Packet*, Mar. 24, 1790.

(2) John Hewson, Jr., superintendent: Dyott ad dated July 18, *The Union for the Country*, July 24, 1821 & Mar. 5, 1822; *Aurora General Advertiser*, Nov. 1, 1822.

36. For detailed account, *see* McKearin, *Bottles, Flasks and Dr. Dyott*, Chap. 1 & 2.

37.

(1) Inscribed bottle: *Federal Gazette and Baltimore Daily Advertiser*, May 17, 1809.

(2) An intimate: "Dr. Dyott," *Biographies of Philadelphians*,

Mss. Vol. 1 by Thompson Wescott comp. ca. 1866, Vol. 2, Pt. 1, pp. 7, 8. Historical Society of Pennsylvania.

(3) Olive Glass Works: Dyott's *Exposition* . . . Appendix A, p. 41; (agent) ad dated Sept. 26 [1816], *True American and Commercial Advertiser,* Jan. 17, 1817; latest ad, Mar. 5, 1822.

38.

(1) Kensington, 1818: Dyott, *Exposition* . . . , Appendix B, footnote to Jefferson letter, No. V, p. 69; 1819: "The Highly Interesting and Important Trial of Dr. T. W. Dyott, The Banker, for Fraudulent Insolvency" (Philadelphia: 1839), p. 4.

(2) Sole agent: ads—*United States Gazette for the Country,* Feb. 7, 1818 (ad dated Oct. 17 [1817]), Aug. 7, 1818; *The Union,* Apr. 4, Dec. 31, 1819; *Aurora General Advertiser,* Mar. 12, 1821—Mar. 5, 1822.

(3) Among the ads: 1821—*The Union for the Country,* Jan. 16, July 24; *The Union,* Feb. 21, Sept. 4, June 15; 1822—*Aurora General Advertiser,* Mar. 5.

(4) Rowland sale: Philadelphia Land Records. Book AM. 37, p. 747ff.

39. *Aurora General Advertiser,* Mar. 5—Nov. 1, 1822; *Connecticut Mirror,* Feb. 10, 1817.

40. Philadelphia Land Records. Book IH. 6, p. 101; Book IH. 5, p. 374.

41.

(1) Lafayette: *United States Gazette,* Sept. 10, 1824; *The American Historical Register,* Jan. 1896. p. 538.

(2) 1824 ad: *United States Gazette,* Oct. 19, 1824; still running, but without note to editors, in the *Trenton [N.J.] Federalist,* May 16, 1825.

(3) New name: Porter, Thomas, *Picture of Philadelphia* (1831), Vol. II, pp. 24, 25.

(4) Pre-1828 struggle: "Journal of the Proceedings of the Friends of Domestic Industry, in General Convention met at the City of New York. October 26, 1831" (Baltimore: 1831), p. 124.

(5) Prices Current, undated. The period from 1824 until the 1828 tariff (passed in August 1828) went into effect is indicated by the same prices for vials of all sizes and 9 patent medicine vials as those given for 1824 through 1827 in Dyott's Statistical Table p. 53, the *Exposition.*

(6) New factories: 3rd, ad dated June 13, *New York Commercial Advertiser,* Oct. 14, 1828; 4th, ad dated June 14, *Cincinnati [O.] Advertiser,* July 1, 1829; 5th—1833, Dyott's *Exposition* . . . p. 14.

(7) Land acquisitions: Philadelphia Land Records, Book AM 10 (page number missing) recorded Dec. 7, 1830, lot on which Hewson, Connell & Co. built the new Kensington Glass Works; Book AM 37, p. 747ff. July 10, 1833, land on which the original Towars and Leacock works was built 1771, acquired from James Rowland and wife.

42.

(1) Extensive scale, *see* 43 (4).

(2) Porter, *see* 43 (3).

(3) Staff, *see* 43 (4).

43.

(1) 1828 patent: *Journal of the Franklin Institute* (New Series, 1828), Vol. II, p. 405.

(2) Patent flint: ad dated Mar. 5, *Philadelphia Daily Chronicle,* Apr. 4, 1831.

(3) Lead: Dyott's *Exposition* . . . , p. 25.

(4) Michael Dyott, *see* (2).

44. Dyott, *Exposition* . . . , pp. 8–10, Appendix C.

45.

(1) Opposition: Dyott's *Exposition* . . . , Appendix A & B, Jefferson Letters and letters to the Pennsylvania Legislature.

(2) Routine: Ibid., pp. 14, 16–23, 35–38.

46. *See* 45 (2)

47. Ibid.

48. Ibid.

49. "The Highly Interesting and Important Trial of Dr. T. W. Dyott, The Banker for Fraudulent Insolvency . . . ", pp. 2, 5, 7, 13, 24; Scharf, John F., and Westcott, Thompson, *History of Philadelphia 1609–1884,* Vol. I, p. 655 and Vol. III, p. 2299.

50. "The . . . Trial . . . ," pp. 7, 8, 18, 24.

"The Late Doctor Dyott," Jan. 18, 1861. *Biographies of Philadelphians* Mss., *see* 37 (2).

"Case of Thomas W. Dyott," *Saturday Evening Post,* Mar. 16, 1839.

51. "The . . . Trial . . . ," pp. 2, 7, 16, 26.

52. "The . . . Trial . . . ," pp. 27, 28. *Saturday Evening Post,* May 15, 25, 29, 1839.

53.

(1) Trusteeship: Philadelphia Land Records, Book CS 28, p. 8.

(2) Business: Scharf & Westcott, Vol. III, p. 2299; Philadelphia City Directories.

(3) Obit: *Philadelphia Press,* Jan. 19, 1861.

54.

(1) Michael Dyott: "The . . . Trial . . . ," pp. 3, 9 and 53(2).

(2) Sheriff's sale: "The . . . Trial . . . ," pp. 5, 13, 21; *Saturday Evening Post,* May 22, 1841. Neither source gives the date or dates of the Sheriff's sale or sales, which probably were in the late fall of 1839.

(3) Lehigh . . . Co.: Scharf and Westcott, Vol. III, p. 2299.

55. Dyott's *Exposition* . . . , p. 30.

56. Scharf & Westcott, Vol. III, p. 2299; Philadelphia City Directories.

(21. The Union Glass Works, Kensington)

57. Jarves, *Reminisences* (1854 ed.), p. 39; Philadelphia Land Records, Book CWR 13, p. 1466ff.; Records of U.S. Circuit Court, 3rd District, Philadelphia, 1829. (Case of Whitney & Robinson of the New England Glass Co. against the Union Flint Glass Co.) Philadelphia Land Records, Book CWR 13, p. 466ff., Records of the U.S. Circuit Court, 3rd District, Philadelphia, 1829. McKearin, H., and Rose, J., *Antiques* (Nov. 1943). McKearin, *Two Hundred Years* . . . , p. 87.

58. *Commercial Chronicle and Baltimore Daily Advertiser,* Oct. 30, 1828.

59. *O'Brien's Wholesale Directory and United States, South America, and West Indies Free Circular for the year 1848,* p. 204.

60. Van Rensselaer, p. 148; Knittle, pp. 219, 220.

61. *Relf's Philadelphia Gazette,* Apr. 25, 1809; *The True American and Commercial Advertiser,* Jan. 18, 1817.

62. Van Rensselaer, p. 132; Knittle, p. 221.

63. Philadelphia, *United States Gazette,* Oct. 7, 1817; *Aurora General Advertiser,* Mar. 3, 1822.

64.

(1) Unless otherwise stated the information on Millville is based on Van Rensselaer, pp. 146, 147 (reference given to "Gordon's *History of New Jersey,* 1834"); McKearin, *American Glass,* p. 588.

(2) Philadelphia, *Pennsylvania Gazette,* Mar. 31, 1828.

(3) Burgin patent: *Journal of American Mechanics Magazine,* Franklin Institute, New Series, Vol. IV (1829), p. 48.

(4) Burgin Philadelphia works: Philadelphia City Directories.

(5) Toulouse, *Fruit Jars* (1969), p. 327.

(22. Harmony Glass Works; later Whitney Glass Works)

65.

(1) Unless otherwise stated, the information on the Harmony Glass Works, later Whitney Glass Works, is based mainly on

accounts by Van Rensselaer, for whom Charles S. Boyer, Pres. Camden County (N.J.) Historical Society, did the research, pp. 135–41; Knittle, pp. 155–58.

(2) Advertisements: Philadelphia, *American Centinel and Mercantile Advertiser,* Jan. 14, 1819 (ad dated Dec. 31, 1818); Trenton, N.J., *The True American,* Aug. 9, 1823.

66.

(1) Malaga: Van Rensselaer, p. 144; Knittle, p. 222.

(2) Merged with Olive Glass Works: Van Rensselaer, p. 135.

(3) Ads: *De Silver's Philadelphia Directory and Strangers' Guide,* 1829 through 1835.

67.

(1) Pepper, re. date of Whitney interest and "brothers," source not given. p. 34.

(2) *See* 65(1) and 66(1).

(3) Patents: bottle & flask, No. 31046, Jan. 1, 1861; design, No. 2652, May 14, 1867.

68.

(1) Scoville, pp. 105, 106, 110.

(2) Merger with Illinois Glass Co.; Pepper, p. 42.

69. Ads in the Philadelphia Directories for 1870, 1878, and 1880.

(23. Hammonton Glassworks and Winslow Glassworks)

70. Van Rensselaer (Boyer's research), pp. 142, 143, 153, 154; Knittle, pp. 223, 224; Pepper, pp. 94–98. Van Rensselaer gives "1817" as the year in which the Hammonton works was started; Knittle, "1817 or 1820."

(24. Waterford Glass Works)

71. Van Rensselaer, p. 150; Knittle, pp. 225–27; Pepper, pp. 109–12. Van Rensselaer gives "1834" as the year the Waterford works was started; Knittle, "between 1822 and 1824."

72. McKearin, *American Glass,* Chronological Charts of Glassworks.

(25. Mount Vernon Glass Works, Vernon; later Saratoga Mountain Glassworks)

73.

(1) Inc.: *Private Laws of the State of New York,* 33rd sess. 1810, Chap. XVI, p. 27.

(2) Assessments: Utica, N.Y., *Columbian Gazette,* Apr. 21, July, Aug., & Oct. 1810; Jan. 24, Feb. 12, 1811; June 11, 1812; Mar. 20, 1813; Sept. 20, 1814; Apr. 9, 1817.

(3) Dividends: Ibid., June 11, 1812, Jan. 10, 1821.

74. Ibid. Apr. 6, 1811.

75. Ibid. May 4, 1813; *Private Laws of the State of New York,* 38th sess, Chap. CXIII, p. 121, and 47th sess., Chap. CLXVII, p. 179.

76. *Utica [N.Y.] Observer,* Oct. 1, 1833; Buffalo City Directory, 1842, 1843; Interview with Mrs. Carr, daughter of Oscar Granger, in 1922.

77.

(1) Utica, N.Y., *Columbian Gazette,* Oct. 6, 1810, Apr. 6, 1811, Mar. 23, 1813; Jan. 11, 1814, Jan. 12, 1819.

(2) Seneca Glass Works: Ibid., Jan. 8, 1811, Aug. 12, 1812; Apr. 27, Sept. 28, Oct. 19, 1813. Utica, N.Y., *The Patrol,* Apr. 25, May 11, 1815. *Columbian Gazette,* Aug. 3, 1819.

78. 1842 and 1843 Buffalo City Directories, cited by Harry Hall White, "New York State Glass Houses," Part II, *Antiques* (Feb. 1929).

79. Unless otherwise stated, the information about the Saratoga Mount Pleasant glassworks is from McKearin, *American Glass,* pp. 185, seq., 605. Van Rensselaer, pp. 113, 114. The 1855 State Census reported a glassworks at Greenfield (the town

from which Oscar Granger's mother came), Saratoga County. In the 1860 edition of J. H. French's *Gazetteer of the State of New York,* 8th edition, Mount Pleasant is listed as having a glassworks and 140 inhabitants.

80. McKearin, *American Glass,* Chronological Charts. Wilson, Kenneth M., "The Glastenbury Glass Factory Company," *Journal of Glass Studies,* The Corning Museum of Glass, Vol. V (1963), pp. 117–32.

(26. The Keene-Marlboro-Street Glassworks)

81. Letters to H. R. Schoolcraft from Lawrence Schoolcraft and Timothy Twitchell, cited by Kay Fox. White, Harry Hall, "New York State Glass Houses," Part III, *Antiques* (Aug. 1930).

82. Twitchell letters to H. R. Schoolcraft, cited by Kay Fox; Schoolcraft letter in the "Literary and Philosophical Repository," cited by Van Rensselaer, *New Hampshire Sentinel,* Feb. 6, 1816. Lawrence Schoolcraft had been superintendent of the Hamilton Glass Factory (Albany Glass Works) 1802–18 (Van Rensselaer Papers, coll. New-York Historical Society, N.Y.) and of the Oneida Glass Works, Vernon, N.Y. (White, *see above*) 1809–12.

83. Information from Kay Fox.

84. *New Hampshire Sentinel,* Aug. 15, 1815; (dated Nov. 29) Dec. 9, 1815.

85. Ibid., Jan. 19, Apr. 6, 1816; Mar. 18, July 9, 1815.

86. Ibid. Oct. 19, Dec. 25, 1816 and information from Kay Fox.

87. Information from Kay Fox and *New Hampshire Sentinel,* Feb. 3, 1817.

88. Hartford, *Connecticut Courant,* Feb. 18, 1817; *New Hampshire Sentinel,* Mar. 29, Aug. 23 & 29, 1817, Jan. 17 & Dec. 19, 1817, Feb. 20, 1819, May 13, 1820. *Digest of Accounts of Manufacturing Establishments in the United States and of Manufactures* made in pursuance of a Resolution of Congress 30 March 1822, published 1823. (Report in 1820 census.)

89. Information from Kay Fox; *New Hampshire Sentinel,* Sept. 14, 1822, Sept. 1 and Nov. 18, 1828, ads quoted by Van Rensselaer, pp. 64, 65, 67.

90. United States Document 5, Vol. 222, p. 790.

91. Notice quoted by Van Rensselaer, p. 65; researches of Carl Flowers in contemporary newspapers and archives.

92. *New Hampshire Sentinel,* Dec. 9, 1815; Jan. 19 & Dec. 26, 1816; Jan. 17, Aug. 29, 1817; Feb. 18, 1818; May 13, 1820; Nov. 14, 1823.

93. Ibid. May 20, 1820; 1831 Directory, quote received from Kay Fox.

(27. New England Glass Company)

94. Watkins, Lura Woodside, *Cambridge Glass* (Boston, Mass.: Marshall Jones Company, 1930), pp. 7–38; McKearin, *American Glass,* p. 592.

95.

(1) Apothecaries' and chemists' wares: N. E. Glass Co. price list ca. 1818; advertisement in the Boston Annual Advertiser section of the 1829 Boston Directory.

(2) Flasks: *Columbian Centinel,* Oct. 13, 1819; Mar. 8, 1820; W. E. Mayhew Invoice May 4, 1829 in the document collection of the Maryland Historical Society, Baltimore.

96. *See* 94, p. 185.

97.

(1) Start of production: Documents Relative to the Manufactures in the U.S. 1833 [Doc. No. 308], Vol. I, Mass. Doc. 3. No. 125. East Cambridge, p. 324.

(2) Closing: Watkins, Lura Woodside, *Cambridge Glass,* p. 189.

(3) Reports: "Journal of the Proceedings of the Friends of

Domestic Industry in General Convention Met at the City of New York, October 26, 1831 (Published by order of the Convention, Baltimore, 1831), p. 124. *See* (1) pp. 324, 325.

98. Ads: *Boston Commercial Gazette,* Mar. 5, 1827; Jan. 21 & 31, 1828; June 1834, quoted by Watkins, *see* 94; *Boston Courier,* Sept. 6, 1828; *Boston Commercial Advertiser,* Mar. 5, 1829, supplied by Kenneth M. Wilson; Philadelphia, the *National Gazette,* Oct. 8, 1827; Hartford, *Connecticut Courant,* Dec. 24 & 31, 1827; Mar. 24, May 26, 1828; Hartford, *Connecticut Mirror,* May 26, 1828.

(28. John Mather's Glassworks, East Hartford)

99. Trumbull, S. Hammond, *The Memorial History of Hartford County* (Connecticut: 1635–1884; Boston: 1886), p. 252. Hammond recorded also "It required it is said 12 men to operate these works [glass factory and powder mill] . . . In 1820 Mr. Mather sold his property to Hazard-Lorrin & Bros. powder monopolists of New England." In connection with East Hartford (pp. 85–106) there was no mention of glassworks, not even the Pitkins.

100. Hartford, Conn., *American Mercury,* Dec. 30, 1802, Apr. 14, 1803, May 17, 1804.

101. Hartford County Land Records: John Mather, East Hartford, Book 7, pp. 286 & 532, May 19, 1803; Book 7, p. 539, Aug. 13, 1803 (lease) and Book 13, p. 28, Aug. 31, 1812 (purchase of leased land); Book 8, p. 523 Mar. 24, 1804; Book 9, p. 560, recorded Oct. 27, 1806; May 10, 1806, Book 8, p. 475; Jan. 9, 1807, Book 9, p. 48; John and Thomas Mather, Feb. 1811, Book 11, pp. 46, 53, 211; John Mather, Nov. 25, 1814, Book 12, p. 339; Jan. 1, 1816, Book 13, p. 34; Book 9, p. 560 indenture indicates that the agreements recorded in leases of Aug. 13, 1803, and Mar. 24, 1804, may have been made at the same time: " . . . leased to me by Nathaniel & Jason Hammond, Aug. 13th 1803 . . . "

102. Hartford, *Connecticut Courant,* Aug. 21, 1805.

103. Connecticut State Archives, Series II, Vol. II, John Mather's petition to General Assembly.

104. Hartford County Land Records Book 9, p. 560.

105. Hartford, *Connecticut Courant,* Oct. 29, 1806.

106. Ibid. dated Jan. 21, 1807; *American Mercury,* Jan. 22, 1807.

107. *See* 6. Book 8, p. 495; Book 7, p. 539; and Book 8, p. 523. Hartford, *Connecticut Courant,* Nov. 1, 1809. The latest data on John and Thomas Mather I have found was a purchase of land May 8, 1811 (Book 10, p. 454). In 1812 John Mather alone purchased the land leased Aug. 13, 1803, from Nathaniel Hammond (Book 13, p. 28).

108. Hartford County Land Records. Book 8, pp. 475 and 523 and Book 7, p. 539.

109. Hartford, *Connecticut Courant,* Jan. 10, 1810, ad dated Dec. 30, 1809.

110. McKearin, *American Glass,* p. 197.

111. Pease, John C., and Niles, John M., *A Gazeteer of the States of Connecticut and Rhode Island* (1818).

112. Hartford, *Connecticut Courant,* advertisements, by various Hartford merchants, of "East-Hartford Bottles," usually in tierces, were found from May 20, 1807, through April 10, 1821. No mention in the *Courant, Times,* or *Mirror* after 1821.

113. *Connecticut Courant,* Jan. 15, 1806.

114. Ibid., Jan. 22, 1807.

115. Ibid., July 15, 1815, ad dated July 10; *Connecticut Mirror,* Feb. 10, 1817.

116. *Hartford Conn. Times,* Mar. 28, 1820.

117. Hartford, *Connecticut Courant,* Nov. 26, 1827.

(29. Coventry Glass Works)

118. Coventry Glass Factory Company papers in the manuscript collection in the Library of the Henry Francis duPont Winterthur Museum.

119. Ibid.

120. Ibid.

121. McKearin, *American Glass,* Chronological Chart, p. 591.

122. Bottle Book B. Connecticut State Library, Hartford, Conn.

123.

(1) White. "More Light on Coventry and its Products," Parts II and III, *Antiques,* Oct. and Nov. 1940, Feb. 1941.

(2) Blown-three-mold, McKearin, *American Glass,* p. 278.

(30. Willington Glass Works)

124. Unless otherwise stated data is drawn from *American Glassware,* Edwin Atlee Barber, 1900, and from Harry Hall White, "The Willington Glass Company," *Antiques,* Aug. 1941. For the period Apr. 1849–1873 Mr. White drew on Company documents owned by Henry E. Knowlton of East Mansfield, Conn. It has been believed that all of the original stockholders were from nearby Mansfield, except Frederick Rose of Coventry. If a Belden Merriman & Co. ad in the New Haven, *Connecticut Journal,* Feb. 20, 1816, is correct, John Turner was from Coventry. And the Ebenezer Root probably was the one who was a founder of the Coventry glassworks.

125. Hartford, *Connecticut Journal,* Feb. 20, 1816.

126. White, Harry Hall, "The Willington Glass Company," *Antiques* (Aug. 1941).

127. Ibid.

128. Barrelet, James, *La Verrerie en France . . . ,* Plate LIX. Formes usuelles. Tarifs 1834 (details).

129. Pears, III, Thomas C., "Sidelights on the History of the Bakewell, Pears & Company from the letters of Thomas and Sarah Pears," *The Western Pennsylvania Historical Magazine,"* Vol. 31 (Sept.–Dec. 1948), Nos. 3 and 4, pp. 64, 65.

130. Except for some ads found in Cincinnati newspapers, date on the glassworks established by Isaac Duval is drawn from Knittle, pp. 401–3; Van Rensselaer, pp. 205–8; Weeks, p. 78.

131.

(1) 1817 and 1819 ads: *Liberty Hall and Cincinnati Gazette,* Apr. 7, 1817; dated May 14, 1819, *Cincinnati Inquisitor and Advertiser,* June 8, 1819. Though neither of these ads mentions Duval or Isaac Duval and Company the assumption that theirs was the source of the wares seems safe since there is no record as yet of any other glasshouse operating in Wellsburg at the time.

(2) 1831: Cincinnati, *Daily Gazette,* June 18, 1828.

(3) 1847: *Wellsburg Weekly Herald,* Mar. 18, 1847.

132.

(1) *Liberty Hall and Cincinnati Gazette,* Feb. 11, 1815, ad dated January 19; Feb. 26–Aug. 19, 1816, ad dated Feb. 2.

(2) Welby, Adlard, *A Visit to North America and the English Settlement in Illinois —"* (London: 1821), p. 68.

(31. Bakewells, The Pittsburgh Flint Glass Works)

133. Sources of data unless otherwise noted: *The Family Book of Bakewell * Page * Campbell,* compiled by B. G. Bakewell (Pittsburgh: 1896), pp. 45ff.
McKearin, *Two Hundred Years of American Blown Glass,* pp. 65ff; *American Glass,* Chronological Charts, p. 589.
Jarves, Deming, *Reminiscences of Glass Making* (1854).

134. Documents Relative to Manufactures in the United States 1833 [Doc. No. 308] Vol. II, Doc. 14, No. 195, pp. 525–27.

134a. 1833 ads of Bakewells & Anderson: *Cincinnati Daily*

Gazette, (1) Jan. 12–July 1; (2 & 3) June 10–Oct. 4; Oct. 28; Nov. 8–Dec. 5.

135. 1808 ads: Pittsburgh, *The Commonwealth,* Oct. 19; 1809, *Pittsburgh Gazette,* May 17; 1821, *Liberty Hall and Cincinnati Gazette,* Aug. 29–Sept. 5; 1824, Pittsburgh, *The Statesman,* Mar. 6; 1837, W. G. Lyford's *Western Address Directory.*

(32. Bridgeport Glass Works)

136.

(1) "Log cabin" (Knittle, July 1927, letter to George S. McKearin).

(2) 1811: Cramer, Spear & Eichbaum, *The Navigator* (Pittsburgh: 1814), p. 42.

(3) Joint concerns "in or about 1811": N. & P. Swearer's report, Doc. Relative to the Manufactures in the United States. 1832. Doc. No. 308, Vol. II, Doc. 14, No. 192, p. 529.

(4) Ramsey: unpublished Ms.

(5) ads: Brownsville, Pa., *American Telegraph,* Dec. 6, 1815; May 15, 1816.

(6) 1822 for sale ad: *see* (4)

(7) Kimber: Knittle, p. 252.

137.

(1) Kimber ownership: until 1837, Ramsey Ms.

(2) Swearer: *see* 1 (3)

(3) A & B Kimber: listed in Harris's *Pittsburgh Business Directory,* 1837.

(4) 1847: Ramsey Ms.

138.

(1) 1826: S. Jones, *Pittsburgh in 1826* (Directory included). 1826.

(2) 1832: *see* 1 (3).

(3) 1837: *see* 2 (2).

(33. New Boston Glass Works)

139. Van Rensselaer, p. 191; Knittle, p. 253; John Ramsey ms. 1939. Mr. Ramsey established the dates of the New Boston Glass Works as 1816–37. Van Rensselaer gave 1823 as the starting date; Knittle, the first quarter of the 19th century.

140.

(1) Sand Harris, *Pittsburgh Business Directory.*

(2) 1820: Uniontown, Pa., *The Genius of Liberty,* Feb. 2.

(3) 1826: S. Jones, *Pittsburgh in the Year 1826.*

(4) 1832 report: Document Relative to Manufacture in the U.S. 1833 [Doc. no. 308] Vol. II, Doc. 14, No. 197, pp. 528, 529. Uniontown, Pa., *Pennsylvania Democrat,* Oct. 2, 1833.

141.

(1) Baker & Martin: Uniontown, Pa., *Pennsylvania Democrat,* Oct. 2, 1833. The firm was given as Martin & Baker in the report, dated April 17, 1832, made to the Federal Government. *See* 2(4).

(2) Baker, Stewart & Co.: Harris, 1837 Pittsburgh Directory.

(34. William Ihmsen, Williamsport)

142. McCready, Jessie and Delphine, "The Ihmsen Family: Pioneer Pittsburgh Glassmakers," *Antiques* (Aug. 1938); John Ramsey ms., 1939.

143.

(1) 1795: McCready (*see* 142).

(2) 1807: Ibid.

(3) 1814: Ramsey (*see* 142).

144.

(1) 1826: Ibid. Jones (*see* 140(3)).

(2) 1814: Cramer, Spear & Eichbaum, *The Navigator,* 1814, p.

42.

(3) 1815: Ramsey (*see* 142).

144a. *See* 142.

(35. John Robinson's Stourbridge Flint Glass Works)

145. Knittle, pp. 339, 340. Mrs. Knittle apparently obtained her information from Jones, *Pittsburgh in 1826.*

146. *Liberty Hall and Cincinnati Gazette.* Bearpark, Dec. 24, 1824–Sept. 20, 1825. Pugh, Dec. 24, 1824–July 9, 1825.

147. *Cincinnati Chronicle,* June 19, 1830.

148. Ibid.

149. *Cincinnati Daily Gazette,* Jan. 23–Apr. 3, 1833; Oct. 27, 1833.

150. Report to the House of Representatives. Published 1833. Doc. 14.

151.

(1) John Robinson's death is given by Knittle as 1836 (p. 340) and by John Ramsey, who researched Pittsburgh glassworks and glassmen later, as 1835 (Ramsey Ms.)

(2) Kensington location of "new Stourbridge Glass Works" inferred from the 1837 listing in Harris's 1837 Pittsburgh Directory.

(3) Closing. Ramsey Ms.

(36. Brownsville Glass Works)

152.

(1) Location: *The Navigator* (1814), p. 42; Day, Sherman, *Historical Collections of the State of Pennsylvania.*

(2) Knittle. pp. 249–51.

153.

(1) 1829 ad: Cincinnati, O., *Daily Gazette,* May 9–July 10, 1829.

(2) 1832 report: Doc. Relative to the Manufactures in the United States 1833. Doc. No. 308, Vol. II, Doc. 14, No. 196, pp. 527, 528.

154. Knittle: *See* 152(2) above; letter to G. S. McKearin dated July 1927 traces the owners and leases up to 1873; John Ramsey in his unpublished ms. to 1900. As their findings vary somewhat as to dates of owners and operators, I have used approximate dates. Knittle gives the firm name Carter & Hogg after the latter purchased the works at a sheriff's sale; Ramsey gives Hogg & Co.

155. Ad: *see* 153(1)

156. Knittle, pp. 251, 252.

(37. Zanesville Glass Manufactory, "White Glass Works")

157. Norris F. Schneider in collaboration with Everett Greer, articles on Zanesville glassworks. Zanesville, O., *Sunday Times Signal,* July 1 and 8, Aug. 19, 1956. The accounts of Zanesville's glassworks derived not only from local histories but also from contemporary newspapers and official documents.

158. Lippitt: Ibid., July 22, 1956.

159. *Liberty Hall and Cincinnati Gazette,* July 21 through Aug. 26, 1831.

160. Schneider and Greer cite an 1816 letter referring to "flint" and an 1817 ad offering "Finest Rock or Stone for the manufacture of the most elegant Flint Glass."

(38. Muskingum Green Glass Works, "Sligo Glass Works")

161.

(1) *See* 157, July 15 and 22, Aug. 16, Sept. 6, 1956. Sligo, corrupt spelling of Slagor, the name of Martin Luther Loud Slagor who settled in Zanesville in 1800 and purchased land on the Run which was named for him.

(2) Knittle, pp. 376–77.

(39. Cincinnati Glass Works and Moscow Glass Works)

162. *Liberty Hall and Cincinnati Gazette*, Apr. 25, 1815; news item, *Chillicothe Weekly Recorder*, Aug. 11, 1815.

163. Fordham, Elias Pym, *Personal Narrative of Travels in Virginia, Maryland, Pennsylvania, Ohio, Indiana, Kentucky and a Residence in the Illinois Territory, 1817–1818.* (Reprint, Cleveland: 1906). Fearon, Henry Bradshaw, *Sketches of America.* Thomas, David. Cited by Van Rensselaer, p. 288.

164.
(1) New firm: *Liberty Hall and Cincinnati Gazette*, Apr. 8, 1816.
(2) Anthony: Ibid., Mar. 31, Apr. 21, 1817.
(3) Glass: Ibid., Aug. 12, Dec. 30, 1816–Mar. 31, 1817; Sept. 9–Oct. 14, 1816.

165. Ibid., June 4–30, July 7–Nov. 7, 1817.

166. Ibid., Feb. 25, 1818, June 30, 1818–Oct. 26, 1819.

167. Ads: Ibid., Nov. 2, 1819–Apr. 6, 1822.

168. Ibid., ads cited above; and Van Ravenswaay, Charles, "Glass in Old St. Louis," *Antiques* (Aug. 1943).

169.
(1) Information about the Jan. 25, 1823, and Mar. 31, 1825, indentures was supplied by Mrs. Lee Adams of Cincinnati who made a search of the land records.
(2) The few "facts" about the land, buildings and glassmaking were related under "Manufacturing Interests" in the *History of Clermont County Ohio* by J. L. Rockey and R. J. Bancroft, published in Philadelphia, 1880.

170. *Liberty Hall and Cincinnati Gazette* (Pugh & Teater) Oct. 21, 1813–June 15, 1823; (Kilgour, Taylor & Co.) June 11, 1824; (Rogers) Nov. 25, 1823.

171.
(1) In one announcement of the rental, Nov. 10, 1824, Pepperd's first name was given as "NATH'L" and in another, Nov. 19, 1824, as "WILLIAM."
(2) Ibid. Nov. 10, 1824, Dec. 24, 1824–Jan. 1825. June 14, 1825, Aug. 12, 1825, Sept. 16, 1826–Jan. 23, 1827, Jan. 21–Mar. 11, 1828.

172. *See* 169(2). The Teater named by the historians was Henry, whereas the ads announcing the rental give Teater's name as William.

173. *Liberty Hall and Cincinnati Gazette*, Oct. 21, 1823–June 15, 1824; June 11, July 16, Aug. 6–Nov. 19, 1824, Dec. 24, 1824, Aug. 12, 1825.

174. Ibid., July 16, 1824, Aug. 12, 1825.

175. Ibid., Aug. 12, 1825.

(40. Mantua Glass Works)

176. White's *The Story of the Mantua Glass Works.*

(41. Virginia Green Glass Works, Fairview Glass Works)

177. Jefferson, Josephine, *Wheeling Glass*, pp. 13, 16, 22; Knittle, pp. 389–391.

178. *The Pittsburgh Gazette*, Aug. 10, 1830.

179.
(1) *American Advertising Directory*, New York, 1831, 1832.
(2) *New York Commercial Advertiser*, Jan. 23, 1828.
(3) Col. McKee letter: quoted by Van Rensselaer, p. 208, and Knittle, p. 391.

180. *Pittsburgh Gazette*, Feb. 16, 1830. Ad dated Jan. 19. A similar ad appeared Jan. 12 in the *Wheeling Gazette*.

181. Jefferson, pp. 30, 33.

182. Ibid., pp. 33–44.

(42. Maryland Glass Works)

183. Dressel ms.: Van Rensselaer, p. 197.

184. *Great Exhibition of Works of Industry of All Nations*, (London: 1851), Vol. III, No. 68.

(43. Spring Garden Glass Works)

185. D. A. Dressel ms.; Van Rensselaer, p. 197.

186. Ibid.

187. U.S. Patent Records. Patent 10830.

188. *See* 185 above.

(44. Sheets & Duffy, Kensington Vial And Bottle Works)

189.
(1) Dr. Dyott: "The Highly Interesting and Important Trial of Dr. T. W. Dyott, *The Banker*, for Fraudulant Bankruptcy" (Philadelphia: 1839), p. 20.
(2) 1848 ad: *O'Brien's Philadelphia Wholesale Business Directory and Circular for the Year 1848.*

GLASSHOUSE SKETCHES
NOS. 45 THROUGH 79 BY KENNETH M. WILSON

(45. Bridgeton Glass Works)

1. Pepper, Adeline, *The Glass Gaffers of New Jersey* (New York: Charles Scribner's Sons, 1971), p. 214.

2. Original letter in the library of The Corning Museum of Glass.

3. Philadelphia Directory.

4. Toulouse, Dr. Julien H., *A Collector's Manual of Fruit Jars* (Thomas Nelson & Sons, Camden, N. J., and Everybody's Press, Hanover, Pa., 1969), pp. 69–71.

5. McKearin, George S. and Helen, *American Glass* (New York: Crown Publishers, 1941–48), p. 602.

6. Ibid.

(46. Pendleton Glass Works, Millford Glass Works)

7. *American Glass*, p. 603.

8. Van Rensselaer, Stephen, *Early American Bottles and Flasks*, p. 121.

9. Letter, Nov. 11, 1958, J. E. Pfeiffer to Helen McKearin. Additional information about J. Huffsey & Co. and Samuel Huffsey was also furnished to Helen McKearin by J. E. Pfeiffer in letters dated Nov. 20, 1957, and Nov. 17, 1962.

(47. Brooklyn Glass Works; Isabella Glass Works;
New Brooklyn Glass Works)

10. A.L.S. from J. Edward Pfeiffer to Helen McKearin, February 2, 1955.

11. Pepper, Adeline, *The Glass Gaffers of New Jersey*, p. 58.

12. Letters, J. Edward Pfeiffer to Helen McKearin, February 2, 1955, and December 9, 1961.

13. A.L.S. from J. Edward Pfeiffer to Helen McKearin, March 14, 1955.

(48. Fislerville Glass Works)

14. Van Rensselaer, Stephen, *Early American Bottles and Flasks*, pp. 131–32

15. Horner, Roy C., *Tempo*—"Clayton, N.J. Glass Houses," n.p., 1969; and Cushing, Thomas, and Sheppard, Charles, *History of the Counties of Gloucester, Salem and Cumberland, New Jersey* (Philadelphia: 1883).

16. Ibid.

(49. Crowleytown Glass Works; Atlantic Glass Works)

17. Knittle, *Early American Glass*, pp. 355–56.

18. Ibid., and also Van Rensselaer, p. 133.

19. J. E. Pfeiffer, letter dated July 18, 1971 to Helen McKearin.

20. J. E. Pfeiffer, letter dated September 9, 1962 to Helen McKearin.

21. J. E. Pfeiffer, letter dated September 7, 1962 to Helen McKearin.

(50. Bulltown Glass Works)

22. Van Rensselaer, Stephen, *Early American Bottles and Glass*, p. 130

23. Pepper, Adeline, *The Glass Gaffers of New Jersey*, p. 165.

24. Letter from J. Edward Pfeiffer to Helen McKearin, February 1, 1959.

(51. Lockport Glass Works)

25. James D. Bilotta, Ms., "The Lockport Glass Company in National Perspective 1843–72," prepared for a class at State University College of New York at Buffalo, December 21, 1970, a copy of which is deposited in the manuscript collection of the Buffalo and Erie County Historical Society, Buffalo, New York. An abridgement of that paper by Mr. Bilotta appears as "The Lockport Glass Company," in *Niagara Frontier*, Buffalo and Erie County Historical Society, Autumn 1972, pp. 76–84. Much of the material contained in the account of the Lockport Glass Works is derived from Mr. Bilotta's work, and I wish to acknowledge my indebtedness to him, as well as to Mrs. Jean W. Dunn for calling these articles to my attention and providing us with copies of them. I am also indebted to Mrs. Dunn for further information about this glassworks derived from her article, "Glass Lancaster and Lockport, New York," *Adventures in Western New York History*, XVII (1971), Buffalo and Erie County Historical Society, Buffalo, New York. In the following notes, references to the above manuscript and publications will be indicated by: Bilotta, Ms; Bilotta, *Niagara Frontier*; and Dunn, *Adventures* . . .

26. *Lockport Daily Advertiser and Democrat*, Feb. 12, 1861.

27. *Niagara Courier*, Jan. 1, 1845, and Clarence Lewis, article in *Union Sun and Journal*, Mar. 1, 1961.

28. Bilotta, Ms. pp. 7–8, fn. 28–32.

29. Bilotta, *Niagara Frontier*, p. 77.

30. Collection of the Niagara County Historical Society, Lockport, New York.

31. Bilotta, *Niagara Frontier*, p. 79.

32. Ibid., p. 79, fn. 64–65.

33. Bilotta, Ms. p. 17, fn. 64–65.

34. *New York Complete Census*, 1855.

35. Dunn, *Adventures* . . . , p. 17.

36. Ibid., p. 17.

37. Bilotta, *Niagara Frontier*, p. 78.

38. Ibid., p. 78.

39. Van Rensselaer, *Early Bottles and Flasks*, p. 111.

40. Dunn, *Adventures* . . . , p. 7.

41. Ibid., p. 18.

(52. Lancaster Glass Works)

42. *New York Tribune*, Apr. 21, 1849, article taken from the *Lexington Observer and Republican*, Apr. 14, 1849.

43. Van Rensselaer, *Early American Bottles and Flasks*, p. 100.

44. White, Harry Hall, "The Lancaster Glass Works," *Antiques* (Oct. 1927), pp. 300–302.

45. Ibid.

46. Directory, 1866.

47. Dunn, Jean W., "Glass Lancaster and Lockport, New York," *Adventures in Western New York History*, XVII, Buffalo and Erie County Historical Society, Buffalo, New York, p. 8.

(53. Albany Glass Works)

48. McKearin, George S. and Helen, *American Glass* (New York: Crown Publishers, 1941), p. 605.

49. *Hoffman's Albany Directory and City Register for 1848–49* New York: Albany, 1848), p. 60; p. 177.

50. *Hunt's Albany Commercial Directory 1848–49*, p. 20.

51. *Hoffman & Munsell's Directory and City Register, 1851–52*, p. 289.

52. *Directory to the Trades in Albany for 1853* (J. Munsell, 78 State St., Albany), p. 20.

53. McKearin, George S. and Helen, *American Glass*, p. 605.

(54. Newburgh Glass Company)

54. Usher, Kenneth F., "The Newburgh Glass Company," *The Glass Club Bulletin*, Boston, No. 71 (Sept. 1964), pp. 11–12.

55. Letter, July 21, 1966, Miss Helen Ver Nooy Gearn, City Historian, Newburgh, New York, to Kenneth M. Wilson.

56. Usher, "The Newburgh Glass Company."

57. White, Harry Hall, "The Willington Glass Company," *Antiques*, Vol. XL, No. 2 (Aug. 1941), pp. 98–101.

(55. Granite Glass Works)

58. Watkins, Laura W., "Stoddard Glass," *Antiques*, XXIV, No. 2 (Aug. 1933), pp. 52–55

59. Ibid., quoted from the *New England Mercantile Union Directory*, 1849, but Curtis is misspelled and should properly read Curtice according to the research of Miss Kay Fox, author of "Stoddard Glass," published as part of the *History of the Town of Stoddard* by the History Committee of the Stoddard Historical Society, 1974. The author is also indebted to Miss Fox for reviewing this historical sketch and furnishing additional information and corroboration.

60. Fox, "Stoddard Glass," p. 139.

61. Fox, Kay, "Stoddard Glass," *History of the Town of Stoddard*, p. 140; and Foster, John Merrill, *Old Bottle Foster and His Glass-Making Descendants* (Fort Wayne, Ind.: 1972), pp. 20–21.

62. This figure is stated in *Gould's History of Stoddard*. p. 55, as $2,500, but this must be a typographical error, since Joseph Foster's average daily expense to operate his factory in 1848 was about $52 per day (Foster and Fox).

63. Watkins, "Stoddard Glass," p. 54.

64. Foster, John M., *Old Bottle Foster* . . . , pp. 20–21.

65. Fox, "Stoddard Glass," p. 140.

(56. New London Glass Works)

66. Van Rensselaer, *Early American Bottles and Flasks*, p. 53

67. *New London Land Records*, Vol. 54, p. 455.

68. *New London City Directory for 1857–58* (New London: Starr & Co., 1857).

69. *New London City Directory for 1859–60* (New London: Starr & Co., 1859), p. 110.

70. Ibid., p. 75.

71. *New London Land Records*, Vol. 55, p. 339.

72. *Morning Chronicle*, New London, Conn., Aug. 26, 1863.

73. *New London City Director, 1865–66* (New London: Christopher Prince, 1865).

74. Van Rensselaer, *Early American Bottles and Flasks*, p. 53.

(57. Westford Glass Works)

75. Unless otherwise stated, data on Westford is from *American Glass*, p. 210, and Kenneth M. Wilson, *New England Glass*

and Glassmaking (New York: Thomas Y. Crowell Company, 1972), pp. 151–57.

76. Ms. Vital Records, Ashford, Connecticut, VI *Record of Marriages and Joint Stock Corporations,* p. 10 of Joint Stock Corporation section. Original stockholders, and their holdings are:

Theodore C. Cary	Eighty Shares
Edwin A. Buck	Eighty Shares
John S. Dean	Eighty Shares
James Richmond	One Hundred Shares
Jared D. Richmond	Sixty Shares
M. Richmond	Forty Shares
Dan Chaffee	Forty Shares
Willard Fuller	Forty Shares
Palmer Convers	Eighty Shares
Wm. D. Bicknell	Forty Shares
Ashbell Whiton	Twenty Shares
Alfred Brown	Twenty Shares
John C. Smith	Twenty Shares

77. Ms. Ashford, Connecticut, Probate Records, Book 3, p. 243 et seq., Town Hall, Ashford, Connecticut.

78. White, "The Willington Glass Company," *Antiques* (Aug. 1941).

(58. Christian Ihmsen and Sons)

79. McCready, Jesse and Delphine, "The Ihmsen Family, Pioneer Pittsburgh Glassmakers," *Antiques* (Aug. 1938); John Ramsey, ms. 1939.

80. W. & C. Ihmsen: Pittsburgh, *The Statesman,* Oct. 8, 1831.

81.

(1) Phillips: Harris's *Pittsburgh Business Directory 1837.*

(2) Young Ihmsen & Plunkett: 1846 ad in *Pittsburgh Daily Gazette and Advertiser,* quoted by Knittle, p. 338.

(3) Black wares: *see* (1).

82. Harris. 1837.

(59. William McCully & Co.)

83. *History of Allegheny County Pennsylvania* (Chicago: A. Warner & Co., 1889), Part II, p. 224.

84. Knittle, Rhea Mansfield, *Early American Glass* (New York: The Century Co.), pp. 319–20.

85. *History of Allegheny County Pennsylvania,* Part II, p. 224.

86. Edwards, Richard, ed., *Industries of Pittsburgh, Trade, Commerce and Manufacturers*: Historical and Descriptive Review for 1879–80 (Pittsburgh: 1879), p. 264.

87. Switzer, Ronald R., *The Bertrand Bottles* (Washington, D.C.: National Park Service, U.S. Department of the Interior, 1974), p. 72.

88. *History of Allegheny County Pennsylvania,* Part II, p. 392.

89. Diary of George Foster in possession of John Morrill Foster, quoted from John Morrill Foster, *Old Bottle Foster and His Glass-Making Descendants,* p. 21.

90. Ibid., p. 23.

91. AL, Thomas Stanger, Pittsburgh, August 27, 1846, to John M. Stanger, Glassboro, N.J., in library of The Corning Museum of Glass.

(60. Samuel McKee & Co., Pennsylvania Glass Works)

92. *Western Pennsylvania Historical Magazine,* Vol. 31, p. 2.

93. Van Rensselaer, p. 181.

94. Wilson, Erasmus, ed., *Standard History of Pittsburgh, Pennsylvania* (Chicago: H. R. Cornell & Co., 1898), p. 238.

95. John Ramsey, Ms. on Pittsburgh Glasshouses.

96. Edwards, Richard, ed., *Industries of Pittsburgh, Trade,*

Commerce & Manufacturers, Historical & Descriptive Review for 1879–80 (Pittsburgh: Richard Edwards, Editor and Publisher, 1879), p. 229.

97. McKearin, *American Glass,* p. 601.

98. Thurston, George H., *Pittsburgh's Progress, Industries & Resources, 1886.* Printed by A. A. Anderson & Son, 99 Fifth Ave., Pittsburgh, Pa., p. 113.

99. *Allegheny County's Hundred Years* (Pittsburgh, Pa.: A. A. Anderson & Son, 1888), p. 187.

(61. A. & D. Chambers)

100. Ramsey, Ms., "Pittsburgh Glass Houses . . ."

101. Thurston, George H., *Allegheny County's Hundred Years* (Pittsburgh: A. A. Anderson & Son, 1888), pp. 187–88.

102. White, Harry Hall, "Glass Monuments to Zebulon Pike," *Antiques* (Sept. 1932), p. 100.

(62. Cunningham & Co.)

103. Knittle, Rhea Mansfield, *Early American Glass* (New York: 1927), p. 344.

104. Edwards, Richard, ed., *Industries of Pittsburgh, Trade, Commerce and Manufacturers, Historical and Descriptive Review for 1879–1880* (Pittsburgh: 1879), p. 99; *History of Allegheny County, Pennsylvania* (Chicago: A. Warner & Co., 1889), Part II, p. 299.

105. McKearin, George S. and Helen, *American Glass* (New York: 1941), pp. 605, 607.

106. Op. cit.

107. Swetman, George, "Bottles and Blows," *Pittsburgh Press,* Sunday, December 16, 1962, pp. 8–9; and Toulouse, Julian, *Fruit Jars* Camden, N. J.: Thomas Nelson, 1969, p. 85.

108. Ibid.

(63. Adams & Co.)

109. McKearin, *American Glass,* p. 607.

110. Thurston, George H., *Allegheny County's Hundred Years* (Pittsburgh, Pa.: A. A. Anderson & Son, 1888), p. 188.

111. John Ramsey, Ms. on Pittsburgh Glasshouses.

112. *Western Pennsylvania Historical Magazine,* Vol. 41, p. 152.

113. Hopkins, *Atlas of Pittsburgh,* 1872, Directory, p. 5.

114. Thurston, Pittsburgh Directory, 1867–68, p. 86.

115. Thurston, 1888, p. 188.

(64. E. Wormser & Co.)

116. McKearin, *American Glass,* p. 609.

117. From notes compiled by Mrs. Helen Wilson, Assistant Librarian at the Historical Society of Western Pennsylvania, from the following sources: William Frank autobiography written in 1889, in possession of the Frank family, unpublished; City Business Directories; Pittsburgh Directory 1856–57 and Thurston, *Pittsburgh Progress* (1886) and *Pittsburgh As It Is.*

118. Ibid. plus interview with Joseph Wormser in the *Pittsburgh Press,* Apr. 25, 1930; deed recorded August 18, 1858, Vol. 135, p. 80.

119. Information from Mr. James Frank to Helen McKearin.

120. Joseph Wormser interview April 25, 1930; deed recorded February 2, 1864, Vol. 68, p. 283.

121. Deed recorded March 24, 1866, Vol. 200, p. 102.

122. Wormser's autobiography.

123. Deed recorded May 1, 1882, Vol. 436, p. 379, and *Pittsburgh Directory 1883.*

(65. Frankstown Glass Works)

124. William Frank, Memoirs, written in 1889, in the possession of the Frank family. In addition to these memoirs, virtually all of the information contained in this historical sketch of the Frankstown Glass Works is based upon the research of Mr. James A. Frank, great-grandson of William Frank, codified over several years by his father, William K. Frank. The authors wish to acknowledge their indebtedness and express their gratitude to them for providing this information, and to thank James A. Frank for reviewing the draft of this sketch to ensure its accuracy, as well as providing photographs of flasks and bottles made at the Frankstown Glass Works illustrated elsewhere in this book.

125. Deed, recorded August 18, 1858, Vol. 135, p. 86.

126. Deed, recorded March 24, 1866, Vol. 200, p. 102.

127. Hopkins, *Atlas of Pittsburgh* (1872), Directory, p. 5.

128. Original letterhead in the possession of James Frank.

129. William Frank, Memoirs.

130. The author is also indebted to and wishes to thank Mrs. Helen Wilson, Librarian, and the Historical Society of Western Pennsylvania, for their assistance in providing information and photocopies of materials from the Society's collections which have contributed to this historical sketch.

(66. George A. Berry & Co.)

131. McKearin, *American Glass*, p. 601, and Rhea Mansfield Knittle, "Rex Absolutus of the Monongahela," *Antiques*, Vol. 13 (Apr. 1928), p. 291.

132. Ellis, *History of Fayette County*, p. 821 says 1853; Rhea Mansfield Knittle, "Rex Absolutus of the Monongahela," p. 292 says it was in 1855.

133. McKearin, *American Glass*, p. 601.

134. Hopkins, *Atlas of Pittsburgh* (1872), p. 15.

(67. Ravenna Glass Works)

135. Harold M. Lyon, typescript, *Glass Companies of Ravenna, Ohio*, kindly furnished to the authors by Cy Plough of the Portage County Historical Society.

136. Deeds, Portage County, Ohio, Book 71, p. 47.

137. Deeds, Portage County, Ohio, Book 71, p. 29.

138. Deeds, September 8, 1857, Portage County Records, Book 71, p. 33.

139. Receipt from William D. Durham to Ebenezer Spaulding of the Ravenna Glass Company, in the possession of the Portage County Historical Society.

140. Doc. 28, p. 265, Portage County Common Pleas, November 21, 1863, William Pittman vs. the Ravenna Glass Company.

141. Doc. 28, p. 307, order of sale, Portage County Common Pleas, March 16, 1861.

142. Doc. 28, p. 500, Portage County Common Pleas, July 24, 1862. George Messenger vs. Samuel H. Terry, et al.

143. Doc. 28, p. 333, Portage County Common Pleas, May 11 and April 8, 1863; William M. Butler vs. the Ravenna Glass Company, Ebenezer Spaulding, Samuel H. Terry.

144. Doc. 29, p. 168, Portage County Common Pleas, June 24, 1863.

145. Doc. 28, p. 407, Portage County Common Pleas, Day vs. the Ravenna Glass Company, filed October 18, 1865.

146. Deed, Portage County.

147. Knittle, Rhea Mansfield, pp. 383–84.

148. Van Rensselaer, p. 224.

(68. George W. Kearns; Zanesville, Ohio, Glasshouses)

149. Schneider, Norris F., and Greer, Everett, *Sunday Times Signal*, Zanesville, O., Aug. 19, 1956; and Knittle, Rhea Mansfield, "Muskingum County, Ohio, Glass," *Antiques* (Oct. 1921), pp. 201‡2.

150. Schneider and Greer, *Sunday Times Signal*, Zanesville, O., Aug. 26, 1956.

151. Knittle, Rhea Mansfield, *Early American Glass*, p. 377.

152. Schneider and Greer, *Sunday Times Signal*, Zanesville, O., Aug. 19, 1956.

153. Knittle, *Early American Glass*, p. 377.

154. Schneider and Greer, *Sunday Times Signal*, Zanesville, O., Aug. 19, 1956.

155. Schneider and Greer, *Sunday Times Signal*, Zanesville, O., Aug. 19, 1956.

156. Schneider & Greer, *Sunday Times Signal*, Zanesville, O., Oct. 19, 1956.

157. Schneider, Norris F., *Times Recorder*, Zanesville, O., Jan. 30, 1966.

158. Schneider and Greer, *Sunday Times Signal*, Zanesville, O., Sept. 2, 1956.

159. Ibid., Sept. 2, 1956.

(69. Union Glass Works, R. Knowles & Co.)

160. Jefferson, Josephine, *Wheeling Glass*, p. 73.

161. Ibid., p. 74.

(71. Kentucky Glass Works; Louisville Glass Works)

162. Edelen, Henry Charles, "Nineteenth-century Kentucky Glass," *Antiques* (Apr. 1974), p. 825.

163. Casseday, Ben, *The History of Louisville from its Earliest Settlement Until 1852*, as quoted by Harry Hall White, "The Kentucky Glass Works," *Antiques*, IX, No. 2 (Feb. 1926), p. 85.

164. Ibid., White, p. 85.

165. *The Louisville Morning Courier*, Thursday, November 28, 1850, quoted by White; *Antiques* (Feb. 1926), pp. 85–86.

166. *The Louisville Directory and Annual Business Advertiser* for the years 1855–56, published by W. Lee White & Co.

167. Edelen, *Antiques* (Apr. 1974), p. 825.

168. White, *Antiques* (Feb. 1926), p. 86.

169. Ibid., Edelen.

170. Ibid., Edelen.

171. Van Rensselaer, Stephen, *Early American Bottles and Flasks*, p. 214.

172. Edelen, *Antiques* (Apr. 1974), p. 825.

(72. Keystone Glass Works)

173.

(1) Philadelphia Directories, 1845 through 1874.

(2) Medford: Van Rensselaer, p. 167, Knittle, p. 361.

174. Freedly, Edwin Troxell, *Philadelphia and Its Manufacturers in 1867*.

175. Toulouse, Dr. Julian H., *A Collector's Manual of Fruit Jars* (Thomas Nelson & Sons, Camden, N.J., and Everybody's Press, Hanover, Pa., 1969), p. 208.

176. Ibid., pp. 120, 176, 330.

(73. Clyde Glass Works)

177. Arreta, J., and Morrison, Wayne E., *Morrison's History of Clyde, New York* (1955) (Bel GRA Print Shop, Williamson, New York) n.p.

(74. The New Granite Glass Works)

178. Foster, John Morrill, *Old Bottle Foster and His Glass-Making Descendants* (Fort Wayne, Indiana: 1972), p. 43. Many of the details relating to the Granite Glass Works and the New

Granite Glass Works are derived from the diaries of George W. Foster, grandfather of John M. Foster, who possesses them, along with advertisements, business cards and other material related to George Foster. The authors wish to acknowledge their indebtedness to him for his interest and assistance.

179. Ibid., p. 41, Illustration 13 and p. 42, Illustration 14.

180. Ibid., p. 43, and Fox, Kay, "Stoddard Glass," *The History of the Town of Stoddard, New Hampshire,* p. 146.

181. Watkins, Lura Woodside, "Stoddard Glass," *Antiques* XXIV, No. 2 (Aug. 1933), p. 53.

(76. Tibby Brothers Glass Works)

182. This information is based upon research done by Mrs. Helen Wilson, Librarian, The Historical Society of Western Pennsylvania.

183. 1870, Pittsburgh Manuscript Census, p. 683.

184. Van Rensselaer, *Early American Bottles and Flasks,* p. 188.

185. Thurston, George H., *Pittsburgh Progress, Industries and Resources, 1886* (Pittsburgh: A. A. Anderson & Son, 1886), p. 113.

186. Van Rensselaer, p. 188.

187. *Memoirs of Allegheny County, Pa.,* Madison, Wisconsin, Northwestern Historical Association, Vol. 2 (1904), pp. 269–70.

(77. The Wheeling Glass Works)

188. Jefferson, Josephine, *Wheeling Glass,* p. 75.

189. Wheeling *Directory,* 1862–63, and Jefferson, Josephine, *Wheeling Glass,* pp. 75–76.

(78. Indianapolis Glass Works Co.)

190. *Indianapolis City Directories,* 1870–1877.

191. Letter to Miss Helen McKearin, dated August 29, 1970, from George Austin, Pine City, New York.

192. W. R. Holloway, *Indianapolis, A Historical and Statistical Sketch of the Railroad City* (1870), p. 130.

(79. Richmond Glass Works)

193. McKearin, *American Glass,* No. 3, Group C Rare Flasks, p. 507.

194. James Gergat has been curator of the York County Historical Society in York, Pennsylvania, since February 1975. Prior to that time he was curator of the Valentine Museum in Richmond, Virginia, for approximately three years. During this period in Richmond he became interested in American glass and, spurred on by an example of a marked Richmond Glassworks pint flask that was offered for sale to the Valentine Museum, he undertook a research project in search of documentary evidence of this factory. In addition, because of an urban renewal project then under way, he was able to undertake a limited amount of archaeological work at the site of this factory, which he located as a result of his documentary research. Mr. Gergat has very generously given me copies of his notes, and has permitted me to examine the glass fragments excavated at the site of the factory and to picture them in this book. Miss McKearin and I are both grateful to him for this act of generosity.

195. Publications of the *Bureau of Census,* "Report of Joseph D. Weeks, Special Agent, 1880."

196. Wirt Armistead Cate; unpublished ms. in the Archives of the Valentine Museum, Richmond, Va., p. 694, fn. 279.

197. Ibid., p. 1360, fn. 52.

198. *Virginia Patriot,* Feb. 6, 1817; *ibid.,* Jan. 12 and Jan. 24, 1817, and Mutual Assurance Society Policies Nos. 799 (1817) and 811 (1817).

199. *Daily Richmond Dispatch,* Dec. 8, 1855; *ibid.,* Feb. 4, Feb. 16, and Dec. 20, 1856.

200. Virginia Census, 1860.

201. Richmond City Deed Book, #69A, p. 506, November 20, 1855.

202. Frohlinger, Baltimore; Storm, Philadelphia—Richmond City Deed Book, #69A, p. 505.

203. Richmond City Deed Book, #69A, p. 240, July 27, 1855.

204. Richmond City Deed Book, #69A, p. 504, November 20, 1855.

205. Richmond City Deed Book, #69A, pp. 506–9, November 20, 1855.

206. Frohlinger applied for citizenship on October 7, 1856, in Baltimore. Naturalization Second Docket, State of Maryland, Common Pleas, 1856–60, p. 88.

207. *Richmond Dispatch,* Feb. 17, 1858.

208. *Richmond Dispatch,* Dec. 12, 1859.

209. Henrico County Minute Book, April 1860.

III.
WINE, SPIRIT and BEVERAGE BOTTLES

1.

(1) 15th C.: Bontemps, G., *Guide du Verrier* (1868), p. 496.

(2) 16th C.: Barrelet, *La Verrerie en France . . . ,* p. 71.

(3) 17th C.: Thorpe, "English Glass in the XVIIth Century," pp. 14, 15.

2. *The Secretes of the Reverende Maister Alexis of Piermont,* [Piedmont], translated out of French into English by Wyllyam Warde (London: 1558), Book 2, Fol. 46.

3. Star Chamber Accounts giving particulars of wines purchased for the Lords of Privy Council, 1590. Documents from the Collection of Mr. André L. Simon, *Wine Trade Loan Exhibition catalogue* (London: 1933), p. 4.
Also cited:
1602 Item for bottles to bring the Lords wine in this term 13s 4d
1605 Item for bottles to bring the Lords wine in this term 13s 4d
1635 . . . sweet wines in bottles 2s 6d
1639 . . . sweet wines and bottles from Tavern 14 16 0

4. Chambon, Planche R.

5. Barrelet, *La Verrerie en France . . . ,* Plate XXXV b and p. 171.

1. SEALED BOTTLES

6.

(1) Barrelet, *La Verrerie en France . . . ,* Plate XXXV b and p. 198.

(2) Chambon, p. 111.

(3) Thorpe, "English Glass in the XVIIth Century," pp. 14, 15; "Evolution of the Decanter," pp. 196–202.

(4) Hartshorne, Albert, *Old English Glasses* (London: 1898), p. 291, fn. 2: "the practice of impressing upon bottles and other glass vessels the initials, name or mark of the maker was of Phoenician origin." This reference was, we believe, to mold blown identifications not to applied seals of glass.

7. Unless otherwise stated the information on English sealed bottles was obtained from:

(1) *Sealed Bottles* by Sheelah Ruggles-Brise.

(2) "The Glass Wine Bottle in Colonial Virginia" by Ivor Noël Hume.

(3) "Seventeenth Century Glass Wine Bottles and Seals *Excavated at Jamestowne*" by J. Paul Hudson, *Journal of Glass Studies*, Vol. III (1961), Corning Museum of Glass.

(4) *American Glass* by George S. and Helen McKearin.

8.

(1) *Samuel Pepys' Diary*, Oct. 23, 1663.

(2) Mr. Povey: *Diary of John Evelyn*, July 1, 1664.

(3) Ruggles-Brise, p. 20.

9. "N.S." seal: found on the Wistarburgh glassworks site by J. E. Pfeiffer, and now at Corning Museum of Glass.

9a. Glasshouse Company of New York: *The New York Gazette or Weekly Post Boy*, Oct. 14, 1754.

10.

(1) John Norton, Cazenovia, New York.

(2) White, "New York State Glasshouses," Nov. 1929.

(3) New York State Legislature, 33 Session, Chap. XVI.

2. ENGLISH TYPE WINE BOTTLES . . . AND AMERICAN 19TH CENTURY VARIANTS

11. Digby, Sir Kenelm. (1) *Choice and Experimental Receipts in Physick and Chicurgery* (London: 1668); (2) *The Closet of the Eminently Learned Sir Kenelm Digby Kt. Opened* (London: 1669). Posthumous publications of Digby's collections of receipts. He was born in 1603 and died in 1665.

12.

(1) Thorpe, "English Glass in the XVIIth Century," pp. 14, 15.

(2) Ruggles-Brise, p. 18.

(3) Horridge, W., "Documents relating to the Lorraine Glassmakers in North Staffordshire with some notes Thereon," *Glass Notes*, No. 15 (London: Arthur Churchill Ltd., 1955).

13. The description of forms and dating of types of wine-bottles are based on the following:

(1) Bottles and photographs of bottles.

(2) Ruggles-Brise.

(3) Thorpe, "Evolution of the Decanter"; re "tall neck and loose sleeves," "English Glass in the XVIIth Century."

(4) Hume, "The Glass Wine Bottle in Colonial Virginia."

(5) McKearin, *American Glass*, pp. 423–25.

Hume seems definitely of the opinion that the earliest English wine bottle was made near 1650; Thorpe and Ruggles-Brise entertain the earlier possibility.

14.

(1) McKearin, *American Glass*, p. 426.

(2) White, "New Views of Old Glass, Part V. A Seventeenth Century Bottle."

(3) Hudson.

15.

(1) Salem: McKearin, *American Glass*, p. 584.

(2) New Amsterdam and New York: Knittle, Chapters X and XI.

(3) Continental: Chambon, Planche T.

16.

(1) Thorpe, *A History of English and Irish Glass 1929*, Vol. I, p. 127; "English Glass in the XVIIth Century," p. 15.

(2) Powell, H. J., *Glass-Making in England* (1923), p. 78.

17.

(1) Brannon, "Indian Trade Bottles in the South," *Antiques* (Jan. 1937).

(2) Imports: *Boston Weekly News Letter*, June 16–23, 1712; Feb. 1, 1728.

18.

(1) Ruggles-Brise, p. 19.

(2) Bacon, pp. 13–15.

19. *See* 18(1) and Thorpe, "Evolution of the Decanter."

20.

(1) *The Good Hous-wiues Treasurie* (London: 1588). Bv verso, Bvi recto, Bvi verso. "How to styll Rosewater that it may well keepe."

(2) 1558: *The Secretes of the Reverende Maister Alexis of Piermont* [Piedmont], translated out of the French into English by Wyllyam Warde (London: 1558), Book 1, Fol. 15 and 2. Bombase, according to the *Shorter Oxford English Dictionary*, was raw cotton or cotton wool.

(3) Emerson, Edward R., *Beverages Past and Present* (New York and London: 1908), Vol. I, p. 144.

21.

(1) Huguet's Last Supper from a retable (altarpiece) in Le Museo de Art de Cataluña, Spain.

(2) St. Barbara. The Prado, Madrid.

22.

(1) Pliny: *The Natural History of Pliny*, translated with copious notes and illustrations by the late John Bostoch and H. T. Riley . . . (London: 1898), Book XVI, Chap. 13, Vol. III, p. 354.

(2) 1530: *The Oxford English Dictionary*, reference: "Palsgr. 737. [Jehan Palsgrave . . .]"

(3) *See* 20(1)

23.

(1) Digby. *See* 11(2), p. 39.

(2) Worlidge, "J.W. Gent," *Vinetum Britanicum or a Treatise of Cider* (London: 1676), p. 103. It is interesting to note that Worlidge may have influenced bottling of cider since, over 100 years later, whoever wrote the section on "Bottling" for the *Encyclopaedia Britannica*, Edinburgh, 3rd ed. (1797), p. 474, and 1st American ed. (1798), stated that it was better to lay the bottles on the ground than on a frame, that sand was better than the bare ground, and "a running water, or a spring often changed was best of all."

24. Star Chamber Accounts: Catalogue of "Wine Trade Loan Exhibition of Drinking Vessels Also Books & Documents etc. etc. etc., Vintner's Hall, London, June–July 1933." Nos. X–XIV, p. 4.

The practice of bringing in bottles of wine from a tavern where the wine was drawn off from hogsheads, etc., into bottles may have originated earlier than 1639. Nos. VI–IX (accounts for 1518, 1534–35, 1567–68 and 1568) have items for wines by the hogshead, tun, gallon, and quart; hooping of hogsheads, amounts due wine porters for loading, unloading, and placing in the cellar, wines for cooking and one for fine sugar for the lords' wine.

25.

(1) Plat, Sir Hugh, *Delightes for Ladies to adorn their Persons, Tables, Closets & Distilleries with Beauties, Banquets, Perfume & Waters* (London: 1609 edition), Third Part, sig. F12v–Gn 47 (i.e., recipe No. 27, misprinted in 1609 as No. 47). According to information from the General Research and Humanities Division of the New York Public Library, the first edition listed in the catalogue of the British Museum and in the *Dictionary of National Biography* was that printed in London in 1602 by P. Short.

(2) Markham, Gervase, *The English Hus-wife* (London: 1615), p. 124.

(3) Conical corks: Bacon, John M., "Bottle-Decanters and Bottles" *Apollo* (July 1939), p. 14. " . . . It is that great writer on wine lore, M. André Simon, we must thank for the information that these first early corks [for wine bottles] were conical, and therefore easy to withdraw."

26. Digby: *See* 11(2), pp. 13–17, 61.

27.

(1) *The Receipt Book of Anne Blencowe* (London: 1694), p. 20.

(2) Pepys: *See* 8(1). Also, on July 7th 1665, he recorded the following: "at this time I have two tierces of Claret, two quarter casks of Canary, and a smaller vessel of Sack; a vessel of Tent., another of Malaga, and another of white wine, all in my wine cellar together; which I believe, none of my friends of my name now alive ever had at his owne at one time."

28.

(1) Bacon, p. 15.

(2) Ruggles-Brise, pp. 19, 21.

(3) *The Oxford English Dictionary* gives a 1720 reference for cork from Amherst's "Bottle Screw Poems:" In "Happy New Year," corkscrew is associated with a bottle of "Champaign."

(4) N. Grew, *Musaeum Regalis Societatis* (London: 1681), p. 303.

(5) G. Bernard Hughes in his "Three Centuries of Corkscrews," *Country Life* (Mar. 10, 1960), states that in his 1720 poem "The Bottle Scrue" Nicholas Amherst "has Bacchus exclaim: 'This hand a corkscrue did contain and that a bottle of Champaign!'"

29. Worlidge. *See* 23(2), pp. 103, 104, 107, 109.

30.

(1) Bacon, p. 15.

(2) Charleston, "Bottles Mainly Glass."

(3) Ruggles-Brise, pp. 19, 21.

31. Ruggles-Brise, p. 35.

32. Charleston, letter.

33. Charleston, S.C., *The City Gazette*, Jan. 2, 1744.

34.

(1) *Utica* [*N.Y.*] *Patriot*, Feb. 11, 1812. Ad dated "Vernon. Apr. 16, 1811."

(2) Utica, N.Y., *Columbian Gazette*, July 21, 1812.

35.

(1) Powell (*see* 16(2), p. 99) gives the dates of H. Ricketts & Co. as 1814 to 1853 when Powell & Ricketts was formed.

(2) Henry Ricketts patent: *British Patent Specification* A.D. 1821 No. 4623.

36. *The Book of Trades or Library of the Useful Arts.* 1st American ed., Whitall, 1807. Published by Jacob Johnson and for sale at his bookstore in Philadelphia and Richmond, Va., p. 116.

37. *See* 35 (2) and Hume, "The Glass Wine Bottle in Colonial Virginia," p. 105 and No. 23, Fig. 5, p. 101.

38.

(1) Dyott's bottle for Dr. Robertson's Family Medicine: *Federal Gazette and Baltimore Daily Advertiser*, May 17, 1809.

(2) I believe it possible that some of the flint-glass sunbursts and masonic flasks may have been blown at the Boston Glass Manufactory where Thomas Cains introduced flint-glass wares in 1813. Masonic flasks bearing the initials "HS" [Henry Schoolcraft] were blown at the Flint Glass Factory, Marlboro Street, Keene, New Hampshire, during Schoolcraft's membership in the firm, the period of which is established as Aug. 1815 to Feb. 1817 by notices in the Keene *New Hampshire Sentinel*, Aug. 10, 1815 and Feb. 3, 1817.

39. *Encyclopaedia Britannica or Dictionary of Arts, Sciences and Miscellaneous Literature*, 3rd ed., Edinburgh, 1797, Vol. III, p. 474. Appeared also in the 1st American ed., Philadelphia, 1798.

40.

(1) Dawson, C. C., *Saratoga, Its Mineral Waters* (New York: 1874), p. 49.

(2) White, "New York State Glass Houses," July, Sept., 1930.

(3) Keyes, Fenton.

(4) Dyott; *New York Commercial Advertiser*, Jan. 20, 1825.

41. Datings of factories: McKearin, *American Glass*, Chronological Charts, pp. 607, 585, 591, 584, 602, 611, 605, 600.

3. OTHER 18TH CENTURY AND COMMERCIAL WINE BOTTLES

42.

(1) Chambon, Planche T., pp. 120, 125.

(2) Barrelet, *La Verrerie en France . . .* , p. 156.

43.

(1) McKearin, *American Glass*, p. 425.

(2) Ruggles-Brise, pp. 35, 126, Plate 2.

(3) Hume, "The Glass Wine Bottle in Colonial Virginia," pp. 94, 95.

44. Champagne: Boston, *Evening Post*, Feb. 14, 1757; *Exhibition of the Works of Industry of all Times*, 1851. Report by the Juries, Vol. II, Glass XXIV, S.C.D., pp. 1169ff.

45.

(1) 1779: Philadelphia, *Pennsylvania Gazette*, Nov. 24.

(2) 1795: Philadelphia, *Gazette of the United States*, May 26.

(3) 1798: Philadelphia, *Claypoole's American Daily Advertiser*, Apr. 13.

(4) Ad dated Nov. [1798] New York, *Mercantile Advertiser*, Dec. 6, 1799.

46.

(1) 1801: Philadelphia, *Poulson's American Daily Advertiser*, July 14.

(2) French, etc.: New York, *Commercial Advertiser*, May 16, 1816; Philadelphia, *National Gazette and Literary Register*, May 10, 1834.

(3) 1804: *Pittsburgh* [*Pa.*] *Gazette*, Apr. 4.

(4) 1824: Pittsburgh, Pa., *The Statesman*, Mar. 24.

47.

(1) *Boston Courier*, Sept. 11, 1831.

(2) Child, Mrs. Lydia Maria, *The Frugal Housewife* (London: 1832), p. 17.

47a. Port: Ruggles-Brise, p. 21.

4. SQUARE OR CASE AND SPIRITS BOTTLES

48. For oil:

(1) *Boston News Letter*, Mar. 28, 1765.

(2) Philadelphia, *Pennsylvania Chronicle*, May 16, 1768.

(3) Boston, *Massachusetts Gazette*, Feb. 12, 1767; June 26, 1770.

(4) Salem, Mass., *Essex Gazette*, Oct. 8, 1771; July 13, 1773. The latter listed "Marseilles oil in 12 bottle cases, square bottles." The span of years and localities revealed by the above, a few of many, suggests a wide usage of square bottles for shipping oils. Most of them probably were of Continental manufacture since such oils came largely from the Continent.

49.

(1) Colinet: Chambon, Planche R.

(2) France: Barrelet, *La Verrerie en France . . .* , p. 71.

(3) Eng. 17th c.: Hume, "The Glass Wine Bottle in Colonial Virginia," p. 106.

(4) Eng. green-glass: Thorpe, "The Glass Sellers' Bills at Woburn Abbey," Schedule of Wholesale rates and sizes of green glass, dated January 1, 1677 (1677/78), issued by the Glass Sellers Company of London.

50.

(1) Hume: *see* 49(3), p. 106 and fn. 48.

(2) Glass Sellers' bills: *see* 49(4), p. 194.

51. Philadelphia, *Pennsylvania Gazette*, Sept. 12, 1751.

52. Byrd: *The Writings of Colonel William Byrd of Westover in Virginia, Esq.*, edited by John Spencer Basset (New York: 1901).

52a.

Sizes: pt. to gal.: *Boston Gazette*, Aug. 23, 1756.

2 to 4 gal.: *New York Mercury*, Jan. 6, 1755.

5 gal.: Hartford, *Connecticut Courant*, Dec. 18, 1805.

53.

(1) Traveling cases, 6 & 7 bottles: Philadelphia, *American Advertiser*, May 8, 1803.

9 & 12 bottles: *New York Mercury*, Feb. 20, 1759.

12 & 15 bottles: Boston *News Letter*, Nov. 1, 1761.

16 bottles: *see* 54 (1).

24 bottles: *Beckman Mercantile Papers*, edited by Philip L. White (New-York Historical Society, 1957), Vol. I, p. 22. Letter to John Channing, R.I., Aug. 6, 1747.

(2) Fine polished: Baltimore, *Maryland Gazette*, May 24, 1785.

54.

(1) *Writings of George Washington*, Fitzpatrick edition, Vol. II, p. 363.

(2) Richmond, *Virginia Argus*, Mar. 12, 1802.

55. Coles, E., *An English Dictionary* (London: 1685).

56. White, H. H., "The Willington Glass Works."

57.

(1) Palmer: Boston, *Evening Post*, July 14, 1755; *Boston Gazette*, July 28, 1760.

(2) Stiegel's Manheim Ledger No. 1, Oct. 1765–Apr. 1767; Greiner entry, Aug. 1.

(3) Wistar: Caspar Wistar's will, Will Book I, No. 310, p. 494, recorded Mar. 28, 1752 (research of Milo Naeve, Henry Francis duPont Winterthur Museum); Philadelphia, *Pennsylvania Chronicle*, July 31, 1769, and *Pennsylvania Staatbote*, Sept. 30, 1765.

(4) Bakewell: *Pittsburgh [Pa.] Gazette*, July 12, 1811.

(5) Schuylkill: Philadelphia, *Pennsylvania Gazette*, Jan. 28, 1813.

(6) Philadelphia: Ibid., July 7, 1773.

58. White: *See* 56.

5. JUNK BOTTLES—ALE, BEER, PORTER AND CIDER

59.

(1) Bottled cider: *Charleston [S.C.] Gazette*, Jan. 2, 1774.

(2) Bottled beer: Ibid., Sept. 20, 1744.

(3) Bottled ale: Philadelphia, *Pennsylvania Gazette*, Aug. 12, 1750.

(4) Bottled porter: Philadelphia, *Pennsylvania Chronicle*, Jan. 25, 1768.

(5) Bottled Lancaster, Pa., beer: Ibid., May 11, 1767.

Inasmuch as bottled ale and beer were being imported in the Barbados in 1731 (item in the *New York Gazette* for Apr. 27–May 3 of that year) it is not unlikely they were also being imported in bottles into the mainland colonies.

60.

(1) Mark Leavenworth, petition to the Connecticut Assembly, Connecticut State Archives, Industry, Series I, Vol. II, ms. Doc. 42, 1790.

(2) Winterbottom, W[illiam], *An Historical, Geographical, Commercial and Philosophical View of the United States of America* (1796), Vol. II, p. 269.

(3) Bishop, J. Leander, *A History of American Manufactures 1608–1860*, Vol. I, p. 242.

61.

(1) *Philadelphia Ledger*, Jan. 3, 1778; *Pennsylvania Gazette*, June 9, 1779, Dec. 24, 1783, and Sept. 19, 1787.

(2) Baltimore, *Maryland Journal*, June 10, 1788.

(3) *Charleston [S.C.] Gazette*, Jan. 19, 1789.

(4) Hartford, *Connecticut Courant*, May 1, 1797.

62. Oval qt. bottles: Philadelphia, *Pennsylvania Journal*, Apr.

13, 1769; and not found again until advertised in the *Pennsylvania Packet*, Apr. 13, 1789.

63. Beer bottles: *Salem [Mass.] Gazette*, Jan. 1, 1784.

Porter bottles: Philadelphia, *Pennsylvania Packet*, May 3, 1790.

Junk bottles: *New York Packet*, Mar. 28, 1786; *see also* Part I (2), Bottle Family Names.

64.

(1) Mount Vernon: *Utica Patriot*, Feb. 11, 1812. Advertisement dated "Vernon, April 6, 1811."

(2) N.–E. Glass Bottle Co.: 1829 Price List, Fig. 16; *Troy [N.Y.] Sentinel*, July 17, 1827.

65. Beer: qt. ½ gal. & gal.: Philadelphia, *Poulson's General Advertiser*, May 9, 1804.

Porter: qt. & ½ gal.: *New York Manufacturers and Farmers Journal*, Mar. 24, 1825.

London Porter in qt. and pt. bottles. *Boston Courier*, Apr. 4, 1831. Porter, Imperial Bristol and common Porter, pt., qt. and imperial: Philadelphia, *National Gazette*, May 8, 1834. Porter bottles, ½ pt.: Solomon Stanger's Blowers Book, 1848/9. Though this is the earliest reference to ½ pint porter bottles I have found, the probability is that the size had been introduced by the late 1820s as it had for mineral and soda waters.

66. *Liberty Hall and Cincinnati Gazette*, Apr. 21, 1830; *Daily Cincinnati Gazette*, May 15, 1829.

67. McKearin, *American Glass* (Honesdale), p. 613; (Lancaster), p. 606.

68. Schuylkill: Philadelphia, *Gazette and Daily Advertiser*, Jan. 28, 1813.

Th. Pears & Co.: *Cincinnati Inquisitor and Advertiser*, Mar. 19, 1819.

Bakewell, Page & Bakewell: Pittsburgh, *Liberty Hall*, June 6, 1823.

Pepperd & Teeter: *Cincinnati Gazette*, Aug. 23, 1825.

Dyott: Philadelphia, *Pennsylvania Gazette*, Oct. 1, 1827.

6. SPRING, MINERAL, AND SODA WATER BOTTLES

69. Moorman, J. J., *Mineral Springs of North America* (Philadelphia: 1873), p. 8. Moorman states that the Greeks even before the time of Hippocrates believed nature's medicated waters were a gift from the gods.

70.

(1) Chambon, Planche T., illustrates 17th- and 18th-century "bouteilles d'eau"—unstable bottles as were the flasks for Florence wines.

(2) Charleston mentions bottling of Tunbridge Wells waters in 1697 and others in the 18th century as well as waters from Continental Spa, Pyrmont and Pouhon.

(3) Spaw water, etc.: *See* 39.

(4) Seltzer water imported: *New York Packet*, July 24, 1786; Hartford, *Connecticut Courant*, Apr. 22, 1790.

(5) Pyrmont water imported: New York, *Daily Gazette*, Apr. 6, 1789; June 9, 1790.

71. Thomas, Gabriel, *Historical and Geographical Account of Pennsylvania and West New-Jersey* (London: 1698), pp. 226, 321.

72.

(1) Jackson's Spaw: Boston, *Massachusetts Gazette*, Aug. 6, 1767; *Evening Post*, Aug. 15, 1768.

(2) Harrowgate: Philadelphia, *Pennsylvania Gazette*, Apr. 28 and July 7, 1788; July 8, 1789.

(3) Ballston and Saratoga: "From the Window of the Mail Coach, A Scotsman Looks at New York State in 1811," edited by David H. Wallace, *The New-York Historical Society Quarterly* (July 1956), pp. 272, 289ff.

(4) Saratoga waters: *American Museum,* Vol. IV (1788), pp. 40–41; Monroe, (J): *The American Botanist and Family Physician* by John Monroe, compiled by S. Gaskill (Wheelock, Vt.: 1824).

(5) Steel, John H., M.D., *An Analysis of the Mineral Waters of Saratoga and Ballston* (2nd ed., Saratoga Springs: 1838), p. 42.

73.

(1) Ballston: Kenney, Alice P., "General Gansevoort's Standard of Living," *The New-York Historical Society Quarterly* (July 1964), p. 207.

(2) Saratoga: Troy, N.Y., *Troy Post,* June 20, 1815; Philadelphia, *The Democratic Press,* Nov. 20, 1816, ad dated July 15; *The Union,* Apr. 3, 1819.

74. *Pittsburgh Gazette,* Aug. 30, 1788.

75.

(1) Hartford, *Connecticut Courant,* July 23, 1827.

(2) Keyes.

(3) Dawson, *see* 40 (1), p. 49.

76. Dawson, *see* 40(1).

77. Congress Spring and owners: L. Dawson, *see* 40(1), pp. 19–22, 23–25. In the New York City Directories, Lynch & Clarke, mineral waters, was listed 1811/12–1833/34; John Clarke, 1834/35–1845/46; Clarke & Co. 1847/48–1850/51; Clarke & White, 1852/53–1864/65.

78.

(1) French, J. H., *Gazetteer of New York* (1860), p. 592.

(2) Moorman, *see* 69, p. 223.

(3) Steel, *see* 72(4), pp. 26, 27.

79.

(1) McKearin, *American Glass,* p. 185.

(2) Keyes, pp. 6–15.

(3) White, *see* 40(2).

80.

(1) White, Harry Hall, "The Willington Glass Works."

(2) Watkins, Lura Woodside, "Stoddard Glass."

(3) Van Rensselaer, pp. 289, 290.

81. Dawson, *see* 40(1), pp. 23–25.

82.

(1) Van Rensselaer, pp. 287–98.

(2) Moorman, *see* 70, Index.

83.

(1) "Soda Water in the 18th Century," *Antiques* (Apr. 1954).

(2) "A Dissertation on the Mineral Waters of Saratoga," *New York Journal and Patriotic Register* (Feb. 16, 1793).

(3) Bishop (1864 edition, Vol. II, pp. 124, 125) states: "The manufacture of artificial Carbonated Mineral Waters, was about this time [1807], first introduced in this country, at Philadelphia, by Mr. Joseph Hawkins. . . . The business was first commenced by Cohen & Hawkins, at 38 Chestnut st., and soon after, more extensively by Shaw & Hawkins at 98 Chestnut st. . . . Abraham H. Cohen established a separate business at 31 South Second st. . . . Artificial Seltzer, Soda, Pyrmont, and Ballston waters were supplied by them at six cents a glass, and from one to two dollars per dozen bottles, according to size, and from the fountain to subscribers, at $1.50 per month, or four dollars per quarter, for one glass daily." Bishop, whose account we did not find until some time after our text had been written, did not give the source or sources of his information. In checking the Philadelphia City Directories of the period for me, Carolyn Scoon, assistant curator of the New-York Historical Society, found no listing of Joseph Hawkins, of Cohen & Hawkins or Shaw & Hawkins. She did find "A. H. Cohen, manufacturer of artificial mineral waters 100 S. Second" in 1809 and 1810, "back of Jews' Synagogue Cherry" in 1811. By 1813 he was listed as a storekeeper at 13 N. Front Street. Possibly one or more of Bishop's "parties" advertised in the newspapers.

84.

(1) Sherman and Ballston waters: New Haven, *Connecticut Journal,* May 12, 1808; Hartford, *Connecticut Mirror,* Apr. 29, 1811.

(2) Rochelle water: Boston, *Evening Gazette,* Aug. 10, 1816.

(3) Magnesia waters; Boston, *Evening Gazette,* Aug. 3, 1822.

(4) Seltzer waters, bottles for: Philadelphia, *Aurora General Advertiser,* Feb. 16, 1812.

(5) Old Established Mineral & Soda Fountain: *Boston Intelligencer,* Oct. 18, 1818.

85.

(1) Dr. Darling and Thaddeus Sherman: New Haven, *Connecticut Journal,* May 12, 1808; store of S. & C. Butler: Hartford, *Connecticut Mirror,* May 14, 1810; office of Andrew Scott: New Bern, S.C., *Federal Republic,* July 8, 1816; Old Established Mineral and Soda Fountain: Boston, *Intelligencer,* Oct. 18, 1818; Pavilion Fountain of Health, Henry I. Brown: *Utica Observer,* May 22, 1832.

(2) Welby, Adlard, *A Visit To North America and the English Settlements in Illinois: with a Winter Residence at Philadelphia, etc.* (London: 1821), p. 31.

86.

(1) Flavored sodas doubtless were available at fountains, and possibly bottled, before 1832 when J. B. Marchese advertised soda water flavored with "Pineapple, Strawberry, Raspberry and the like" in the *Utica Observer,* May 22, 1832.

(2) "To Let" ad: Boston, *Columbian Centinel,* Aug. 19, 1829.

87. Philadelphia, *Aurora General Advertiser,* Feb. 16, 1812 and March 23, 1816; *United States Gazette,* Mar. 5, 1825.

88. "Egg minerals": Wyatt, Victor, "From Sand-Core to Automation" (London: Glass Manufacturers' Federation, 1965), pp. 13, 14.

88a. Thomas Stanger's letter in mss collection of the Corning Museum of Glass, Corning, N.Y.

89. *O'Brien's Philadelphia Wholesale Business Directory and United States, South American and West India Free Circular for the year 1848.*

90. "The Highly Interesting and Important Trial of Dr. T. W. Dyott, THE BANKER," Philadelphia, pp. 3, 9, 26; Scharf & Westcott, *The History of Philadelphia,* Vol. III, p. 2299.

91. McKearin, *American Glass,* p. 606.

92.

(1) Ibid, p. 609.

(2) McKearin, *Two Hundred Years of American Blown Glass,* p. 87.

93. McKearin, *American Glass,* p. 609.

7. SADDLE OR LONG-NECKED FLASKS

94. British Patent Specifications No. 386.

95. Boston, *Weekly News Letter,* Feb. 1 and Apr. 11, 1728.

IV.
UTILITARIAN and COMMERCIAL CONTAINERS

1. UTILITARIAN BOTTLES

1. Besides beverages, the following, with earliest appearance in ads covered, were advertised in bottles, presumably of glass:

(1) Hungary water at 1s.6d. per bottle: *Boston News Letter,* Sept. 27, 1708.

(2) Bottles of very good Burgamot: *New York Gazette,* Oct. 27, 1730.

(3) Florence oil: Ibid., Feb. 8, 1732.

(4) Very good Scotch Snuff: Ibid., March 22, 1731.

(5) Sweet oil by the Beteé (rush- or wicker-covered unstable bottle called *flask*): New York, *Post Boy*, Nov. 11, 1745.

(6) Mustard: Philadelphia, *Pennsylvania Journal*, Nov. 9, 1755.

(7) Pickles: Boston, *Continental Journal*, Aug. 2, 1777. (Pickle bottles from 1 quart to gallon, advertised *Boston Gazette*, Aug. 23, 1756.)

(8) Water of Beauty, qt. bottles, 10s.: Philadelphia, *Pennsylvania Journal*, Feb. 24, 1757.

(9) Red ink in phials: *Newport [R.I.] Mercury*, May 22, 1759.

(10) Bears oil: Philadelphia, *Pennsylvania Journal*, May 7, 1761.

(11) Lavender water: *Boston News Letter*, Feb. 5, 1761.

(12) Catsup: *Boston Gazette*, Apr. 5, 1762.

(13) Orange flower water in pt. bottles: Philadelphia, *Pennsylvania Journal*, Feb. 14, 1765.

(14) Mineral water from Jackson's Spaw: Boston, *Massachusetts Gazette*, Aug. 6, 1767.

(15) Anchovies, capers and olives: Boston, *Evening Post*, Oct. 7, 1771.

(16) Walnuts (pickled): New York, *Daily Gazette*, June 27, 1791. (In 1772 George Washington ordered of Robert Cary & Co., London, 2 bottles of walnuts.)

(17) Tea: Boston, *Continental Journal*, Jan. 2, 1777.

(18) Truffles in cases of 12 bottles, from France: *New Bern [N.C.] Gazette*, Aug. 14, 1778.

(19) Lemon juice: New York, *Daily Advertiser*, Sept. 24, 1789.

(20) Ketchup: *Charleston [S.C.] Gazette*, Apr. 21, 1789.

(21) Honey: Ibid., Sept. 14, 1789.

(22) Cayene: Philadelphia, *American Daily Advertiser*, Jan. 17, 1798.

(23) Presumably in bottles:
Lime juice; vinegar: Boston, *Weekly News Letter*, Aug. 28, 1740. Liquid blacking: *Newport [R.I.] Mercury*, Oct. 3, 1764. Orange juice "that will keep ten years": *Boston Gazette*, Sept. 25, 1769. Essence of peppermint: *Salem [Mass.] Mercury*, Apr. 29, 1788.

2. New York, *Mercantile Advertiser*, Dec. 6, 1799.

3. *The Journals of Madame Knight and Rev. Mr. Buckingham from the Original Manuscripts written in 1704 and 1710* (New York: 1825), p. 4.

4. *Boston Gazette*, Apr. 28, 1760.

5. Dawson, Thomas, *The Good huswivves Ievvell*, "Newly set forth with Additions" (London: 1587), Fol. 37–39.

6.

(1) Carter, Charles, *The Complete Practical Cook: or a New System of the Whole Art and Mystery of Cookery* (London: 1730).

(2) *Mrs. Eales, Confectioner to King William and Queen Mary* (3rd edition, London, 1742; 1st edition, 1718).

(3) *The County Housewifes Family Companion* (London: 1750), p. 238.

7.

(1) Yeast: *see* 6(3), p. 14.

(2) Nutt, Frederic (Esq.), *The Complete Confectioner or the Whole Art of Cookery* (London: 1790), p. 73. This book apparently was popular for a long time, in the United States as well as England. It was reprinted in New York for Richard Scott in 1807 and a "corrected and improved" edition by J. J. Macket, Distiller and Confectioner in Paris, was printed in London in 1819.

(3) *Archimagirus Anglo-Gallicus, or Excellent & Approved Receipts and Experiments in Cookery, copied from a choice manuscript of Sir Theodore Mayerne, Knight. Physician to the late K. Charles.* Printed for G. Becell & T. Collins and sold at their Shop in Fleet Street (London: 1658). Sir Theodore was born in

1573 and died in 1655. Some of his receipts may have been from the 16th century.

8. *Boston News Letter*, June 17, 1731; Boston, *Massachusetts Gazette*, July 6, 1769; Philadelphia, *Pennsylvania Gazette*, Feb. 15, 1789; *Charleston [S.C.] Gazette*, Jan. 13, 1789; New York, *Daily Advertiser*, Feb. 9, 1795 (ad dated Dec. 24, 1794).

9. English octagonal, etc: Hume, "The Glass Wine Bottle in Colonial Virginia," pp. 92, 95.

10.

(1) Bombase, parchment, cyzed cloth: *Secrets of the Reverende Maister Alexis of Piermont [Piedmont]*, translated out of the French into English by Wyllyam Warde (London: 1558), Book 1, Fol. 2 and 15.

(2) Wool: Emerson, Edward L., *Beverages Past and Present* (New York and London: 1908), Vol. I, p. 144.

(3) Wax, corke, leather, parchment: *The Good Hous-wiues Treasurie* (London: 1588), Bv1 recto, Bvi verso.

(4) Tied in: Markham, Gervase, *The English Hus-wife* (London: 1615), p. 124 (material of bottles not specified); Digby, *see* 11(2), Part III. Wine, Spirits, and Beverage Bottles.

(5) Child, Mrs. Lydia Marie, *The Frugal Housewife* (London: 1832), p. 17.

11.

(1) Robertson, Mrs. Hannah, *The Young Ladies School of Arts* (2nd ed., Edinburgh, 1767), p. 78, "To Preserve green gooseberries." "For syrup of Maiden Hair" (p. 102) she recommended "½-mutchkin bottles with bladers over the corks." This size of bottle was about ¾ of an imperial pint (*The Shorter Oxford English Dictionary*).

(2) Nutt, Frederic: *See* 7(2), p. 180.

(3) Simmons, Amelia. "An American Orphan." *American Cookery* (Hartford, Conn.: 1796), p. 46.

(4) Hog's Flair or bladder: *See* 10(4), p. 14.

12. *See* 11(3), pp. 46, 40.

2. JARS

13.

(1) "Oil" in flasks, bottles, cases and jars, first appearance in advertisements covered: Boston, *Massachusetts Gazette*, Nov. 24, 1763; "Florence oil": *New York Gazette*, Feb. 3, 1732; "Sweet oil": *New York Post Boy*, Nov. 11, 1745.

(2) Honey in jars and bottles: *Charleston [S.C.] City Gazette*, Sept. 14, 1789.

(3) Blue raisins, jars of: *Charleston Gazeteer of the State of South Carolina*, Dec. 18, 1783.

14.

(1) Stiegel: Hunter, p. 181.

(2) *Philadelphia Glass Works: Pennsylvania Evening Post*, May 20, 1777.

(3) *Pittsburgh Glass Works:* Philadelphia, *Aurora General Advertiser* and *Pittsburgh Gazette*, Mar. 4, 1800; O'Hara's Letter Book, June 18, 1810.

(4) Pickle glass: Evelyn, John, *Acetaria, A Discourse of Sallets* (London: 1600), p. 11.

(5) Thorpe: "Glass Sellers Bills at Woburn Abbey," p. 198.

15. Kalm, Peter, *Travels into North America*, translated into English by J. R. Forster (London: 1770–71), Vol. I, p. 238, Oct. 1748.

16.

(1) Pittsburgh Glass Works: *see* 13(3).

(2) Bakewell & Page of Pittsburgh, pt., qt., ½ gal. and gal.: *Pittsburgh Gazette*, July 12, 1811.

(3) Schuylkill Glass Works, pt., qt., and ½ gal.: Philadelphia, *Pennsylvania Gazette*, Jan. 28, 1813.

(4) Dyott, agt. for three glassworks—Union, Gloucester and Olive Glass Works—jars (ad. dated Dec. 8, 1817): Philadelphia, *United States Gazette for the Country,* Mar. 14, 1818; pickling & preserve jars, pt., qt., ½ gal.: Philadelphia. *The Union,* Dec. 14, 1819.

(5) Kensington Glass Works (the one estb. 1816), preserve & pickling jars: Philadelphia, *Aurora General Advertiser,* Mar. 5, 1822.

(6) Pepperd & Teater, Moscow, O., jars: *Cincinnati Gazette,* Aug. 23, 1825.

17.

(1) Mrs. Eales: *see* 6(2), p. 37.

(2) Simmons: *see* 11(3), pp. 44, 45, 43.

18. Dyott: Philadelphia, *Aurora General Advertiser,* Nov. 11, 1822 (ad dated Mar. 4, 1822); *U.S. Gazette,* Oct. 19, 1824; Price List c. 1825 (Bella Landauer Collection, New-York Historical Society), ½ pt. at 62½ᶜ a doz., pt. at 75ᶜ, qt. at $1.00, 2 qt. at $2.00, 3 qt. at $3.00, gal. at $4.00.

19. Appert: "The Canning Industry," 4th ed. (Washington, D.C.: Information Division of the National Canners Association, 1959), p. 5. Appert published his methods in "The Book for Households; or the Art of Preserving Animal and Vegetable Substances for Many Years," in June 1810 and it was translated into several languages. In England, James Durand, merchant, obtained a patent in August 1810 for "a method of Preserving Animal Food, Vegetable Food and Other Perishable Articles . . . " (Cooper, p. 5; *see* 21).

20.

(1) Underwood: *see* 19 above and "Billions of Bottles" (New York City: Glass Containers Manufacturers Institute, Inc., 1959), p. 25, giving the date as 1819. Mr. Coleman J. Barry, assistant to the President of Wm. Underwood Co., wrote to us May 16, 1963, that "The commonly accepted date at the present time is 1821" and that the first Underwood ad found to date appeared in the *Boston Daily Advertiser,* Dec. 31, 1822. Research to determine the exact date and more about the early products is still being pursued by the Company.

(2) *See* Note 1 for 18th-century bottled products.

21. Cooper, Thomas, *A Treatise of Domestic Medicine,* with a section entitled "Art of Preserving" (Reading, Pa.: 1824), pp. 111 seq. Cooper's treatise may have been first published much earlier in England. In Section 8 of the "Art of Preserving" he speaks of the year 12, presumably 1812, when he had reason to hope to be "employed to provide some nourishing provisions for the sick on board his Majesty's vessels, in consequence of some experiments which had already been made in the seaports . . . on alimentary productions preserved according to my method . . . "

22. "Mason Jar Centennial 1858–1958" and "Billions of Bottles," Glass Containers Manufacturers Institute, Inc., 1959.

23. Jan. 18, 1861. Patent No. 32,594. J. M. Whitall. Fruit Jar.

24. Toulouse, Julian H., Letters 1968 and *Fruit Jars,* p. 5.

25. Scoville, pp. 17, 155, 178–79, and Appendix B.

3. DEMIJOHNS AND CARBOYS

26.

(1) Botae: Barrelet, *La Verrerie en France* . . . , pp. 53, 156.

(2) 1677/78: Thorpe, "Glass Sellers Bills at Woburn Abbey," p. 198.

(3) Digby: *The Closet of the Eminently Learned Sir Kenelm Digby KT Opened* (London: 1669), p. 21.

(4) 2 & 4 gallons: *Boston Weekly News Letter,* Nov. 6, 1741.

(5) Wicker bottles—5 gal.: *New York Mercury,* Sept. 10, 1753.

(6) Carboys, 1 qt. to 7 gal.: Philadelphia, *Pennsylvania Chronicle,* Jan. 26, 1767.

(7) " . . . others that will hold up to 20 gal.": Philadelphia, *Pennsylvania Gazette,* Feb. 9, 1764.

27.

(1) Thomas Lepper of New York: *New York Gazette* and *Weekly Post Boy,* Nov. 4, 1754.

(2) Palmer: Boston, *News Letter,* Apr. 10, 1760.

(3) Wistar: Philadelphia, *Pennsylvania Chronicle,* July 3, 1769.

(4) Homemade, possibly Pitkin: Hartford, *Connecticut Courant,* Mar. 10, 1794.

(5) Amelung (ad of Amelung's son-in-law Andrew Keener): Baltimore, *Federal Intelligencer and Baltimore Daily Gazette,* Mar. 25, 1788.

(6) Stiegel's Manheim Ledger No. 1, Oct. 1765–Apr. 1767.

28.

(1) Hewes: Dime-Johns: Boston, *Independent Chronicle,* Dec. 18, 1788.

(2) Heefke: Demie Johns: *New York Packet,* May 4, 1790.

29.

(1) Demy Johns: Philadelphia, *Pennsylvania Packet,* Mar. 22, 1762.

(2) Carboy: Philadelphia, *Pennsylvania Chronicle,* Jan. 26, 1767.

(3) Demijohns, 8 & 9 gal.: New York, *Daily Advertiser,* May 9, 1792.

30. Demijohns, a few typical advertisements of *Sizes:*

(1) Small: New Haven, *Connecticut Mirror,* Aug. 2, 1813.

(2) Qt., ½ gal. & gal. neatly covered: Boston, *Columbian Centinel,* Feb. 24, 1821.

(3) Qt. to 5 gal.: Philadelphia, *Daily Chronicle,* Apr. 6, 1822.

(4) ¼, ½, 1, 2, 3, 4 and 5 gal.: Philadelphia, *National Gazette,* Dec. 12, 1827.

(5) All sizes, qt. to 5 gal., Dyottville: Philadelphia, *Daily Chronicle,* Apr. 6, 1829.

(6) Qt., ½ gal., gal,, & 2 gal. covered in the best manner, Dyottville: Ibid., Nov. 12, 1831.

(7) Dyott's prices: Price List, signed by Hickson W. Field, agent. The Bella C. Landauer Collection in the New-York Historical Society.

Contents (first mention found):

(1) Arrack: Philadelphia, *Pennsylvania Packet,* Mar. 22, 1762.

(2) Old & new wine (red & white): Philadelphia, *Gazette of the United States,* Mar. 20, 1797.

(3) Madeira, malmsey, brandy spirits: Philadelphia, *American Daily Advertiser,* Sept. 1, 1804.

(4) Cherry bounce, shrub, port wine, Life of man Cordial, wintergreen, lemon and peppermint cordials: *New Bedford* [*Mass.*] *Mercury,* Jan. 5, 1821.

(5) Lemon Juice: New York, *Daily Gazette,* Sept. 24, 1789.

(6) Real sweet oil: Philadelphia, *Gazette of the United States,* Sept. 13, 1797.

(7) Honey: *Diary or Evening Register,* Jan. 19, 1798.

(8) Rosewater: Philadelphia, *National Gazette,* July 2, 1827.

(9) Lentils: New York, *Daily Advertiser,* Jan. 19, 1798.

(10) Pearl barley, juniper berries, peas: Philadelphia, *Poulson's American Daily Advertiser,* Oct. 15, 1802.

(11) Sugar plums: Philadelphia, *Pennsylvania Packet,* July 4, 1788.

31. Carboys,

Sizes:

(1) 6, 8, & 10 gal.: Philadelphia, *National Gazette,* Nov. 30, 1827.

(2) 6 to 10 gal. Dyottville: Philadelphia, *Daily Chronicle,* July 1, 1831.

(3) 1 to 20 gal.: New-England Glass Bottle Company's Price List, Nov. 1, 1829, Fig. 16.

Contents (first mention found):

(1) Oil of Vitrol: Philadelphia, *Pennsylvania Gazette and Universal Advertiser*, Jan. 24, 1794.

(2) Aqua fortis, copal varnish, vitriole aether: Philadelphia, *Aurora General Advertiser*, Apr. 28, 1800.

(3) Muriatic acid, ether: Philadelphia, *American Sentinel and Mercantile Advertiser*, Sept. 16, 1806.

In all the various advertisements aqua fortis and oil of vitrol were most frequently mentioned.

32.

(1) Qt. & ½ gal. oval demijohns: Philadelphia, *Gazette of the United States*, Jan. 30, 1798.

(2) Oval demijohns: Philadelphia, *American Daily Advertiser*, Mar. 28, 1803.

33. San Francisco, Cal., City Directory 1876. Supplied by Dom Reich, Sacramento, Cal.

34. *Exhibition of the Works of Industry of All Times.* "Reports by the Juries" (1851), Vol. II, pp. 189ff.

35. *Nile's Weekly Register*, Baltimore, Md., Sept. 14, 1829.

4. COMMERCIAL CONTAINERS

(1. Snuff Bottles)

36.

(1) Snuff: *Encyclopaedia Britannica*, 1797, 1887, and 1951 editions. Lord Stanhope's remarks; 1797 edition.

(2) Aromatic: British Patent Specifications, No. 1030, Jan. 18, 1773; *Hartford [Conn.] Times*, Apr. 9, 1831.

37. *Time, The Weekly Newsmagazine*, Mar. 31, 1961.

38.

(1) Disorders of the hypochondriac . . . : British Patent Specifications, No. 650, Dec. 6, 1749.

(2) Dissolvent & alterative: Christopher Marshall's The Royal Patent Medicinal Powder or Snuff: Philadelphia, *Pennsylvania Gazette*, May 9, 1754.

(3) Eyesight: Cowdon's . . . snuff: Philadelphia, *Pennsylvania Journal*, July 31, 1760.

(4) Catarrh & headache: Aromatic snuff recommended by Dr. Waterhouse: Hartford, *Connecticut Courant*, Feb. 11, 1817.

39.

(1) Scott: *New York Gazette*, 3/22–3/29, 1731.

(2) Master workman: *Boston Weekly News Letter*, Aug. 19, 1756; Jan. 10, 1757.

40.

(1) Palmer: Boston *News Letter*, Apr. 18, 1760.

(2) Wistar: Philadelphia, *Pennsylvania Chronicle*, July 31, 1769.

(3) Stiegel's Manheim Ledger No. 1, Oct. 1765–Apr. 1767.

(4) Lieper: Philadelphia Land Records, Book D.C., p. 268; Letter written Dec. 20, 1788, by James Gray to Mr. Leonard De Deufville at the Glasshouse near Albany [Dowesborough]. New-York Historical Society.

(5) Carpenter & Heston, New Jersey Glass Manufactory: New York, *Mercantile Advertiser*, Dec. 6, 1799.

(6) Nicholson: *Pennsylvania Gazette and Universal Daily Advertiser*, Feb. 10, 1795.

(7) Trippel & Co.: *Claypoole's American Daily Advertiser*, Apr. 13, 1798.

41.

(1) O'Hara's Letter Book: Letter to James Morrison of Kentucky, June 24, 1805.

(2) Bakewell, Page & Bakewell's snuff bottles advertised by Wm. C. Rogers: Pittsburgh, *Liberty Hall*, June 6, 1823.

(3) Dyott, "Scotch, Rapee & Maccabou": *Philadelphia Gazette*, Mar. 5, 1822.

(4) Schuylkill Glass Works: Ibid., Jan. 28, 1813.

(5) Olive Glass Works: Ibid., Sept. 23, 1816.

(6) Dyott: Ibid., Nov. 9, 1824; Mar. 2, 1825.

(7) Glassboro: Solomon Stanger's Blowers Book. 1848/49; Whitney Bros. Price List 1862, illustrated by Van Rensselaer, p. 137.

(8) Millville, Whitall, Tatum & Co. Catalogue 1880. Henry Ford Museum.

42. New York, *Commercial Advertiser*, Feb. 9, 1830.

43.

(1) Maccabo Snuff in bottles and jars: Utica, N.Y., *Columbian Gazette*, Nov. 10, 1818.

(2) Jars of Maccaboy: *Albany [N.Y.] Gazette*, Sept. 28, 1822.

(3) Simmons, Amelia, *American Cookery* (Hartford, Conn.: 1796), p. 43.

(4) Trippel & Co: *see* 40(7)

(2. Mustard Bottles)

44.

(1) "It is usual in Venice to sell the meale of mustard in their markets as we doe flower and meal in England . . . this made by the addition of vinegar in two or three days becometh exceedingly good mustard." Plat, Sir Hugh, *Delightes for Ladies to adorne their Persons, Tables, Closets and Distillatories with Beauties, Banquets, Perfumes and Waters* (London: 1609 ed.), p. 25.

(2) Thorpe, "The Glass Sellers Bills at Woburn Abbey" (pp. 198, 199), concludes that the mustard glasses itemized May 9 and Dec. 15, 1682, were "Perhaps a pantry jar for storing unprepared mustard."

(3) Durham mustard: *Encyclopaedia Britannica* (1884), Vol. XV, p. 311.

(4) Benjamin Jackson: Philadelphia, *Pennsylvania Journal*, Nov. 19, 1755.

45.

(1) Benjamin Jackson: Philadelphia, *Pennsylvania Journal*, Apr. 21, 1757.

(2) Wagstaff: Philadelphia, *Pennsylvania Gazette*, Feb. 2, 1758.

(3) Wagstaff & Hunt: Ibid., July 28, 1759.

(4) Wistar: Philadelphia, *Pennsylvania Chronicle*, July 31, 1769.

46.

(1) Stiegel: Hunter's listing from the Manheim Account Books, 1769–Apr. 1, 1770.

(2) 1795: Nicholson, *see* 40(6).

(3) 1799: New Jersey Glass Manufactory, New York, *Mercantile Advertiser*, Dec. 6; Christopher Trippel & Co., Philadelphia, *Claypoole's American Daily Advertiser*, Feb. 7.

(4) Old & new: Philadelphia, *Pennsylvania Gazette*, Feb. 2, 1758.

(5) Seed or empty bottles: Boston, *Independent Chronicle*, Jan. 1, 1789.

47. Sizes: *Pound & ½ pound:* Philadelphia, *Pennsylvania Chronicle*, Jan. 25, 1768 (first of several appearances in advertisements); New-England Glass Bottle Co.'s Price List, Nov. 1, 1829; Glassboro, Solomon Stanger's Blowers Book 1848/49.

Quarter pound: Boston, *Evening Post*, July 12, 1773. (First of several.)

Quart, English: Philadelphia, *American Daily Advertiser*, Jan. 17, 1798.

48.

(1) Nicholson: *see* 40(6).

(2) London Squares: New York, *Evening Post*, Feb. 18, 1808.

(3) Squares: Boston Glass Manufactory Price List, 1818; New England Glass Co. Price List, c. 1818. Henry Ford Museum.

(4) London Mustards: T. W. Dyott's Price List, signed by Hickson W. Field, agent. The Bella C. Landauer Collection in the New-York Historical Society; Marshall & Stanger, New Brooklyn, account book 1839. Collection of J. E. Pfeiffer; Solomon Stanger's Blowers Book, 1848/49; Williamstown Price List, c. 1840–54, William Burger, agent. Collection of Charles B. Gardner.

49.

(1) Whitall, Tatum & Co. Catalogue 1880, pp. 18, 49.

(2) Dyott: Philadelphia. *United States Gazette,* Feb. 6, 1818.

(3. Blacking Bottles)

50.

(1) Agricola. Note p. 572.

(2) Harrison, Mrs. Sarah, *The Housekeeper's Pocket-Book and Compleat Family Cook* (7th edition, London, 1760), p. 160.

(3) Roberts, Robert, *The House Servant's Directory or a Monitor For Private Families* (Boston: 1828), p. 80.

(4) *Nantucket [Mass.] Inquirer,* Aug. 9, 1834.

51. *Newport [R.I.] Mercury,* Oct. 3, 1764.

52.

(1) Schuylkill Glass Works: Philadelphia, *Pennsylvania Gazette,* Jan. 23, 1813.

(2) Swabs: Boston, *Columbian Centinel,* Sept. 2, 1829.

(3) Docs. Relative to the Manufacturers of the United States, 1833. Doc. 308, Vol. I. Mass. Doc. 3, No. 198, Boston. p. 442.

53.

(1) Dyott Price List, c. 1825. *See* 30(7).

(2) New-England Glass Bottle Co. Price List, Nov. 1, 1829 (Ill. 12).

(3) Williamstown Glass Works Price List, c. 1840–54.

(4. Ink Bottles)

54.

(1) Beckman, John, *A History of Invention and Discoveries,* translated from the German by Wm. Johnston (London: 1797), p. 179.

(2) *The London Encyclopaedia or Universal Dictionary of Science, Arts & Literature & Practical Mechanics* (London: 1845), Vol. XII, pp. 19ff.

(3) Dossie, Robert, *The Handmaid to the Arts* (London: 1764), Vol. II.

(4) Fisher, Robert, *The Instructor or Youngman's Best Companion* (London: 1792), p. 46.

55. First references in sources covered:

(1) Wafers: Samuel Sewall's Diary, Jan. 13, 1721/22. Sewall asked Mrs. Mary Gibbs at Newton to accept "a Quire of Paper to write upon" and it was accompanied with "a good Leather Inkhorn, a stick of Sealing Wax, and 200 Wafers in a little Box."

(2) Powder ("ink powder and ink"): Philadelphia, *Pennsylvania Journal,* Dec. 28, 1742.

(3) Liquid: presumed from (2) "ink powder and ink"; ibid., May 4, 1760.

(4) Stick, Hugh's "new invented": Philadelphia, *Pennsylvania Packet,* July 17, 1782.

(5) Cakes: Boston, *Independent Chronicle,* May 5, 1789.

(6) Red Ink: *New York Gazette & Weekly Post Boy,* Oct. 14, 1745.

(7) India Ink: Philadelphia, *Pennsylvania Gazette,* Aug. 30, 1750.

(8) Black Ink: *New York Mercury,* Sept. 4, 1758.

(9) Japan Ink: Philadelphia, *Pennsylvania Gazette,* Nov. 2, 1785.

(10) Brooks "presses": Philadelphia, *Pennsylvania Packet,* June 19, 1775.

(11) Durable ink: Philadelphia, *Pennsylvania Packet,* June 19, 1775. It is quite possible, in fact probable, that these may have occurred earlier in advertisements not yet covered or in other sources.

56. *See* 55(6)–(11). Durable inks [bottles] appeared on the New England Glass Co. Price List ca. 1818, those of the Boston Glass Manufactory 1818–22 and Dyott's ca. 1825. They appeared also in Solomon Stanger's Blowers Book ca. 1848/49. The name *indelible* doubtless replaced durable before it appeared in Whitall, Tatum Co.'s Catalogue of 1880.

57.

(1) Red ink, in phials: *Newport [R.I.] Mercury,* May 22, 1759; in vials: Richmond, *Virginia Gazette,* Sept. 5, 1771.

(2) Japan ink in phials: Philadelphia, *Pennsylvania Gazette,* Nov. 2, 1785; *Poulson's American Daily Advertiser,* Nov. 12, 1804.

(3) Pint and quart bottles of black writing ink: New York, *Daily Advertiser,* Aug. 9, 1793.

(4) Pt., Qt. and Gallon: Lexington, Ky., *Public Advertiser,* Jan. 2, 1822 (ad dated Dec. 21, 1821).

58.

(1) Stiegel: Philadelphia, *Pennsylvania Journal,* June 4, 1772.

(2) Ball: *New York Journal and General Advertiser,* Aug. 3, 1775.

(3) Tisdale: Hartford, *Courant & Weekly Intelligencer,* Aug. 18, 1788.

59. Troy City Directories, 1838/39–1875.

60.

(1) Conical: Van Rensselaer. p. 34.

(2) Pyramid: "Pyd," Solomon Stanger's Blowers Book, 1848/49; "fluted cone," Hagerty Bros. & Co., Catalogue, 1909.

61. Fountain: John Maris & Co., Philadelphia, New York and Chicago, Catalogue, 1889.

62. U.S. Patent Office, Design No. 3871, dated March 1, 1870.

63.

(1) Durable: Price Lists of Boston Glass Manufactory, South Boston 1818; New England Glass Co. ca. 1818; Dyott ca. 1825; Williamstown Glass Works ca. 1840–54; Account book of Marshall & Stanger, New Brooklyn, N.J. 1839.

(2) Mordant: Dyott Price List ca. 1825; "Clark's Ink Mordant, Clout's do do" [Probably inscribed with ink-maker's name.]; Solomon Stanger's Blowers Book 1848/49; Williamstown Glass Works' Price List ca. 1840–54.

V.
MEDICINE and BITTERS BOTTLES

1. *Encyclopaedia Britannica* (1797) Vol. XIV, p. 359.

1. APOTHECARY VIALS

2. Among them:

(1) Samuel Sewall recorded in his diary, on April 6, 1708, taking a viall of spirits of lavender to his daughter who was ill.

(2) The stock and equipment which John Briggs, apothecary, announced for sale in 1732 (*New York Gazette,* Dec. 11) included gally pots, bottles and viols.

(3) Medicine chest for Gentlemen's families and small vessels were advertised as early as 1711. (*Boston News Letter,* July 16, 1711.)

3.

(1) Empty vials: *New York Post Boy,* July 6, 1747.

(2) Crates of: Philadelphia, *Pennsylvania Chronicle,* Feb. 2, 1767.

(3) Hogshead of: Philadelphia, *Pennsylvania Journal,* June 16, 1779.

4.

(1) Dossie, Robert, Vol. II, Sec. IV, p. 273.

(2) Green & White: Philadelphia, *Pennsylvania Journal,* June 12, 1762.

(3) Flint: *Norwich Mercury.* England, July 29, 1749, cited by Buckley, *History of Old English Glass* (London: 1925).

(4) Double flint: Philadelphia, *Pennsylvania Gazette,* Sept. 27, 1750; with ground stoppers, *Pennsylvania Journal,* Apr. 21, 1755.

(5) Sizes, as given in a few advertisements of vials and of manufacturers, were mainly ½ to 8 ounces. The earliest mention of size in the sources covered was in the Boston, *Independent Chronicle,* Jan. 30, 1777; the latest, John M. Marris & Co. Catalogue, 1889.

5. Thorpe, "English Glassware in the XVIIth Century," p. 14.

6.

(1) Hazen, Edward, *The Panorama of Professions and Trades or Every Man's Book* (Philadelphia: 1836).

(2) Patent 22,091. Mold for Glass Bottles, S. S. Shinn, Lancaster, N.Y., Nov. 16, 1858. U.S. Patent Office. This improvement formed the entire bottle.

7. "Common and Prescription vials (wide mouth) 50ᶜ advance on above prices"; Williamstown Glass Works (New Jersey), Price List ca. 1840–54. Collection of Charles B. Gardner.

8.

(1) Stiegel: Philadelphia, *Pennsylvania Packet,* July 6, 1772.

(2) Philadelphia Glass Works: Ibid., Feb. 17, 1775.

(3) Farrell & Bakeoven: Philadelphia, *Pennsylvania Gazette,* Aug. 27, 1777.

(4) New Bremen Glassmanufactory, Andrew Keener's advertisement: Baltimore, *Maryland Journal,* Mar. 25, 1788.

(5) New-Jersey Glass Manufactory: New York, *Mercantile Advertiser,* Dec. 6, 1799.

9. Philadelphia, *Pennsylvania Gazette,* July 7, 1773.

10. Dyott, p. 15.

11.

(1) Price Lists of the Boston Glass Manufactory, 1818, and New England Glass Company, ca. 1818. Henry Ford Museum.

(2) Bakewell's: Pittsburgh, Pa., *The Statesman,* June 6, 1823, and Mar. 6, 1824; *Pittsburgh Gazette,* July 12, 1811.

(3) U.S. House Doc. 671 Tariff Acts — 1789 to 1909, pp. 78, 87, 102.

12. Among them:

(1) Boston Glass Manufactory Price Lists ca. 1815, 1817, 1818, 1819 and 1822.

(2) New England Glass Co. Price List ca. 1818.

(3) Rink, Stanger & Co.: 1813, 1815, entries in account book of Jeremiah Emlen, Philadelphia druggist. Henry Ford Museum.

(4) Dyott's Philadelphia and Kensington Glass Works Price List ca. 1825.

(5) Glassboro, Solomon Stanger's Blowers Book 1848/49.

(6) Williamstown Glass Works Price List ca. 1840–54.

13. Griffenhagen and Young, p. 168. Unless otherwise indicated the information about the early English patent medicines was obtained from their "Old English Patent Medicines in America."

14. *New Bern [N.C.] Gazette,* Nov. 15, 1751.

15. "A Short Treatise of the Virtues of Dr. Bateman's Pectral Drops . . . To be sold by J. Peter Zinger, in New York," 1731. Rare Book Room, New York Public Library, Fifth Ave. and 42nd St.

16. In 1813 Rink, Stanger & Co. [Harmony Glass Works, N.J.]

supplied the Philadelphia druggist Jeremiah Emlen with "Godfrey's vials" and the following year with both "Bateman's" and "British Oil." *See* 12 (3). All three vials appear on the Boston Glass Manufactory's Price List 1818 and New England Glass Co.'s ca. 1818, from which it is safe to conclude they were blown from white, if not lead, glass. 19th- and 20th-century examples are illustrated by Griffenhagen and Young.

17.

(1) Cincinnati, O., *Liberty Hall,* Dec. 20, 1814.

(2) Child, Mrs. Lydia Maria, *The Frugal Housewife* (London: 1832), p. 14.

18. Among the 18th-century apothecaries who prepared prescriptions from "Family Receipts" was one Robert Bass in Philadelphia (*Pennsylvania Gazette,* June 7, 1790). Receipts were not only handed down from one generation to another, but popular books on cookery, medicine, and household economy contained receipts for innumerable cures which the housewife could prepare as required. Such information was needed when so many families lived far from communities where there were doctors and apothecaries. As Mrs. Harrison stated in the Preface to her 1760 London edition of *The Housekeeper's Pocket-Book or Compleat Family Cook,* if not in earlier editions: "The Country is the Place where generally Works of this Nature are best received: I have therefore added an Appendix of the most efficacious Prescriptions from the Most admired and applauded of the Faculty. When People live at a great Distance from large Towns, Things of this nature are I am sensible highly useful, and I dare be answerable for their safety."

19. Freeman, Margaret, *Herbes for the Medieval Household* (New York: The Metropolitan Museum, 1943), pp. x, 28.

20. Kalm, Peter, *Travels into North America,* translated into English by J. R. Forster (London: 1770–1771), Oct. 14, 1748.

21.

(1) *Encyclopaedia Britannica* (1797), Vol. XIV, p. 375.

(2) *London Encyclopaedia* (1845), Vol. XVII, p. 177.

(3) "Everyone His Own Physician" by Mary Morris, at the end of Mrs. Harrison's 1760 edition of *The Housekeeper's Pocket Book.*

22.

(1) Harris, Joseph N., *History of Ludlow, Vermont* (Charleston, N.H.: 1949), pp. 226, 227.

(2) *American Encyclopaedia* (1876), Vol. XVI, p. 674.

23. Caswell, Lilley B., *Athol Past and Present* (Athol, Mass.: 1899), pp. 280, 282. The Fays were one of the "old" families in Athol and the only S.E. living there when the railroad was extended to Athol was Serena E. In the *Massachusetts Register* for 1847 no railroad-stop at Athol was given, but there was one in 1852.

24. *Encyclopaedia Britannica* (1797), Vol. X, p. 670.

25.

(1) *British Patent Specifications,* No. 781, Mar. 2, 1762.

(2) Wm. Stears, Salem, Mass.: *Salem Mercury,* Apr. 29, 1788.

(3) Ebenezer Hunt, Northamptom, Mass.: *Hampshire Gazette,* Nov. 19, 1788.

(4) Griffenhagen and Young, p. 171.

26. S. Tompkins & Bros. Druggists' Apothecaries. *Medical Handbook* (1845), p. 5.

27.

(1) James Rivington: Philadelphia, *Pennsylvania Journal,* Mar. 18, 1762.

(2) Rivington & Miller: Boston, *Massachusetts Gazette and News Letter,* Jan. 24, 1763.

(3) Monroe, (J): *The American Botanist and Family Physician* by John Monroe, compiled by S. Gaskill (Wheelock, Vt.: 1824).

28.
(1) New Haven City Directories 1850–59.
(2) New Haven Advertising Directory, 1850.
29.
(1) *Encyclopaedia Britannica* (1797), Vol. IV, p. 23; Vol. X, p. 657.
(2) *American Encyclopaedia* (1858), Vol. II, p. 669.
30. *The Housekeeper's Magazine* (London: 1825–26), p. 151.

2. PATENT AND PROPRIETARY MEDICINE BOTTLES

31. Holbrook, Stewart, *The Golden Age of Quackery* (Macmillan: 1959), p. 32.
32. Griffenhagen and Young, pp. 161, 168; illustration p. 181. The authors quote Turlington's claims from a pamphlet, "Turlington's Balsam of Life," ca. 1747, and his purpose in adopting the new bottle from a brochure dating 1755–57.
33. Dyott, p. 53.
34. In an advertisement in the Philadelphia *Aurora General Advertiser*, July 18, 1814, Dyott claimed to have practiced medicine in London and the West Indies "for the last nine years," which would make 1805 the year of his Philadelphia debut. In the 1807 City Directory he was listed as having a Patent Medicine Warehouse at 57 South 2nd Street. The earliest date found with a description of his bottle was May 17, 1809, in his advertisement in the *Federal Gazette and Baltimore Daily Advertiser*. The claims for Dr. Robertson's medicines appeared also in many later advertisements, including one in the *New York Commercial Advertiser*, June 2, 1824, and M'Makin's *Model American Courier*, Philadelphia, Aug. 12, 1848.
35. *Federal Gazette and Baltimore Daily Advertiser*, May 17, 1809.
36.
(1) Dyott purchase of bottles: "Dr. Dyott," *Bibliographies of Philadelphians* mss. Vol. by Thompson Wescott comp. ca. 1866, Vol. 2 pt. 1, p. 7.
(2) Ad for flint glass manufacturer: *Albany[N.Y.] Register*, Apr. 8, 1808.
37.
(1) Skelton: *Pittsburgh Gazette*, Feb. 16, 1810.
(2) O'Hara: Daniel, p. 111.
(3) Bakewell ad including apothecary ware: Ibid., Apr. 12, 1809.
(4) Robinson: *Standard History of Pittsburgh*, p. 57, quoting *The Navigator* for 1811.
38.
(1) Dyott; McKearin, *American Glass*, p. 470.
(2) Ads: Philadelphia, *Democratic Press*, Sept. 17, 1817, and *The Union for the Country*, Feb. 9, 1822; New York, *Commercial Advertiser*, Jan. 20, 1825. *Philadelphia City Directories* 1809–1870.
39.
(1) Young, James Harvey, *The Toadstool Millionaires* (Princeton: 1961), pp. 61–65.
(2) Ad of Swaim's Laboratory in *Philadelphia City Directory*, 1876, gives date of establishment as "AD 1820."
(3) *Frederick [Md.] Political Intelligencer or Republican Gazette*, Mar. 13, 1824.
(4) Ad dated Sept. 1828 in the Utica, N.Y., *Western Recorder*, Jan. 26, 1830.
40.
(1) See 39(4).
(2) Doylestown, Pa., *Bucks County Intelligencer*, Oct. 26, 1852.

41.
(1) *Philadelphia City Directory*, 1876.
(2) White, "More Light on Coventry and Its Products" (Part III, *Antiques*, Fig. 194.)
42.
(1) Steer's Opodeldoc: Griffenhagen and Young, pp. 161, 172, 173, 177.
(2) *Salem, Mass. Mercury*, Apr. 29, 1788.
(3) *Utica [N.Y.] Intelligencer*, Nov. 20, 1829.
(4) *Boston Evening Gazette*, Feb. 2, 1822.
43.
(1) *The Mechanics Journal of the Useful Arts and Sciences* (Boston: 1834).
(2) T. Tompkins & Bros., *Medical Handbook* (New Bedford, Mass.: 1845).
(3) Mrs. Beeton, *The Book of Household Management* (1868), p. 1094.
44.
(1) Griffenhagen & Young, p. 168.
(2) Boston Glass Manufactory Price Lists ca. 1817–22.
(3) New England Glass Company Price List ca. 1818.
(4) Dyottville: Dyott, $2.60 a gross 1830–32. In the midcentury prices increased again: Williamstown Glass Works Price List ca. 1840–54, $3.75 a gross; 1880 catalogue of Whitall, Tatum & Co., Millville, N.J., $4.50 a gross; 1889 catalogue of John Maris & Co., New York, Philadelphia & Chicago, $4.50 a gross.
45.
(1) Bull: *New Haven Directory For the Year 1840, Annual Advertiser*, pp. 133, 134.
(2) Barnard: Nantucket, *The Inquirer*, Apr. 16, 1840.
(3) "Jaynes Medical Almanac," Chapman, Betty. "Bits and Pieces" (News letter of the Empire State Bottle Collectors Association), Oct. 1966.
46. *The Berkshire Courier*, July 11, 1867. "The Patent Medicine Business/How Fortunes have been made" quoted in the Pontil (News letter of the Antique Bottle Collectors Association), Mar. 1968.
47.
(1) Thomas, Gabriel, *Historical and Geographical Account of Pennsylvania and West New Jersey* (London: 1698), p. 323.
(2) Jayne's expectorant: *New Haven Directory*, see 45(3).
48.
(1) Holbrook, see 31, "The Sassaparillas," pp. 45–51.
(2) Venereal disease: see 47(1).
(3) Running gout: Kent, Elizabeth, Late Countess of, *A Choice Manuall, or Rare and Select Secrets in Physick and Chyrugery* (2nd edition, London, 1653), p. 92.
(4) With soda water: Sign of the Good Samaritan, Hartford, *Connecticut Courant*, June 23, 1829.
(5) Marshall: Philadelphia, *Daily Chronicle*, July 1, 1831.
(6) Sand: *Litchfield [Mass.] Enquirer*, Mar. 14, 1844.
49. Dyott & Townsend: *M'Makins' Model American Courier*, Aug. 12, 1848.
50.
(1) Stoddard: "120 Years of Glass Making—The Story of Foster–Forbes," *The Glass Packer*, Sept. 1962, p. 25.
(2) *New London Chronicle*, Oct. 20, 1866.
51. New London: see 50(2).
52. Holbrook, see 31, pp. 149–56.
53. *Zanesville [O.] Daily Commercial Aurora*, Jan. 11, 1851.
54.
(1) *Litchfield [Mass.] Enquirer*, Mar. 14, 1844.
(2) *Lancaster [Pa.] American Press*, June 29, 1846.
55. *New York Observer*, Apr. 28, 1864.

56.

(1) Griffenhagen and Young, p. 168.

(2) Price: Dyott, p. 53.

(3) Boston Glass Manufactory and New England Glass Co. Price Lists: *see* 12(1) and (2).

(4) 1880s: *See* 44.

57.

(1) Griffenhagen and Young, pp. 157, 161, 175.

(2) *London Encyclopedia* (1845), Vol. XVII, p. 177.

3. BITTERS BOTTLES

58.

(1) *Encyclopaedia Britannica* (1797), Vol. X, p. 650.

(2) Moffat's: Wheeling, [W.] Va., *The Daily Mirror*, Nov. 7, 1860.

(3) Druggist handbook, S. Tompkins & Bros., No. 31: *See* 26.

(4) Fithian, Philip Vickers, *Journal and Letters, 1767–1774,* edited by John Rogers Williams (1926), May 23, 1774.

59.

(1) Griffenhagen and Young, pp. 162, 167, 168, 171, 173, 177.

(2) *British Patent Specifications*, No. 390, A.D. 1712.

(3) Cincinnati, O., *The Centinel of the North West Territory,* Apr. 19, 1794.

60.

(1) Thompson, pp. 60, 61.

(2) Griffenhagen and Young, p. 171.

61.

(1) Wheeling, [W.] Va., *The Daily Union*, Nov. 7, 1860.

(2) New York City Directories, 1836–1867/68.

(3) *See* 60(1), p. 78.

62. Peterson. Arthur G., "Patent Cabin Bottles," *Hobbies The Magazine for Collectors* (June 1962), p. 68.

63.

(1) White; Frederick H. James, son of Dr. James, and John C. Lumbrix, a glassblower who started working in the Lancaster Glass Works in the fall of 1861, informed Mr. White that Wishart's Pine Tree Cordial bottles were blown in Lancaster.

(2) Philadelphia City Directories, 1856–1875.

64. Thompson, p. 26.

65. Watson, Richard, *Bitters Bottles* (1965); *Supplement to Bitters Bottles* (1968).

VI.
PATTERN-MOLDED BOTTLES, FLASKS, and JUGS

1. PATTERN-MOLDS AND PATTERN MOLDING

1. Hunter, p. 190.

2.

(1) Pazaurek, Gustave E., "A German View of Early American Glass," Part I, *Antiques* (Apr. 1932).

(2) Ribbed vessels appear in paintings by several western European artists of the 15th century. For example: tumblers in "The Last Supper" (in an altarpiece) by an unknown artist of the Amiens School, ca. 1440–ca. 1480, and a decanter in "St. Barbara reading" by the Master of Flémalle, 1375–ca. 1444, Flemish School. That rib-molds were used in Venice by the 15th century is evidenced by 15th-century vessels now in private collections and museums.

(3) Hume, "Medieval Bottles From London," pp. 104–8.

3.

(1) Agricola, Georgius, p. 592. Agricola's description of glass fabrication included the following: "then twisting the lifted blow-pipe round his head in a circle he makes a long glass, or moulds the same in a hollow copper mould, turning it round and round, then warming it again, blowing it and pressing it he widens it into the shape of a cup or vessel, or any other object he has in mind . . . " While "turning it round and round" indicates molds for symmetrical shaping of the parison, since only copper was mentioned, presumably the pattern molds shown in his illustration of a glasshouse interior, Fig. 2, were also of copper.

(2) In his *Art of Glassmaking*, Peter Mamson, a Swedish monk, living in Rome from 1508 to 1524, reported "a variety of copper moulds, ornamented inside, or with runs under ridges." Quoted by White, "Pattern Molds and Pattern Molded Glass."

(3) Haudicquer de Blancourt, Book I, Chap. III. Blancourt writing at the end of the 17th century about the glassmakers' tools stated: "There are also several moulds of Marble and Brass and also of Copper which serve to make their Forks of several Figures, according as the workman designs them in blowing, which would be too tedious here to describe."

(4) C. M.[errit], *The Art of Glass,* English translation of Antonio Neri's *De Arte Vitraria*, 1611 (London: 1662), Appendix.

4.

(1) Agricola, p. 591.

(2) De Blancourt.

(3) [Diderot] *Encyclopédie des Arts et Métiers, Recueil des Planches*, "Verrerie en bois," Plate XVIII.

5. In 1939 the molds described by Mr. White in "Pattern Molds and Pattern Molded Glass" were owned by Ralph Ross, father of Logan Ross, the present owner.

6. Smith, Miles A., p. 115; James H. Rose, Letters; Earl Seigfred, Letters.

7. White, "Pattern Molds and Pattern Molded Glass."

8.

(1) White, "The Story of the Mantua Glass Works," Part II; "Pattern Molds and Pattern Molded Glass."

(2) Logan Ross, Letters.

9. O'Hara's Letter Book, May 5, 1805.

10. For discussion of Amelung's New Bremen Glassmanufactory and of the New Geneva Glass Works: *see* Historical Background, 2. The Bottle Industry in America (17) and McKearin, *Two Hundred Years . . . ,* pp. 33–44, 45–57; and Dwight P. Lanmon, Arlene Palmer, "John Frederick Amelung and the New Bremen Glassmanufactory," *Journal of Glass Studies,* Vol. XVIII, 1976, The Corning Museum of Glass.

2. PITKIN-TYPE BOTTLES, FLASKS AND JUGS

11. Pitkin glassworks: *see* Historical Background, 2. The Bottle Industry in America, (13) and McKearin, *Two Hundred Years . . . ,* pp. 29ff.

12.

(1) White: "Keene New Hampshire"; "More Light on Coventry and Its Products," Part III.

(2) In 1926 and 1927, when data were very limited Stephen Van Rensselaer (p. 51) and Rhea Mansfield Knittle (p. 247) believed that on the Pitkin "Pitkins" the swirl or twist was invariably to the left and that on the Keene "Pitkins" it was to the right. Both mention midwestern "Pitkins."

(3) Wilson, Kenneth M., "The Glastenbury Glass Factory Company," *The Journal of Glass Studies,* The Corning Museum of Glass, Vol. V (1963).

13. Hartford, *Connecticut Courant,* Aug. 21, 1805; Jan. 15, 1806; Nov. 26, 1827. The 1805 advertisement was of John Mather's "New Glass House." At sometime before the 1827 advertisement, Merrow & Bidwell may have become the owners.

14. The small number of newspaper advertisements—only 17 between 1745 and 1800—found for "dram bottles," "pocket bottles," or "pocket flasks" suggests that the flask was not imported in large quantities. The earliest was in the *Boston Weekly News Letter,* Jan. 11, 1745—"Gentlemen's hunting bottles" (another term for pocket bottles).

15. *Philadelphia Gazette and Daily Advertiser,* Mar. 1, 1800, Mar. 10, 1801; *Aurora General Advertiser,* Mar. 4, 1800, and later issues.

16. Knittle, pp. 193, 194.

17. *See* 15.

18.

(1) Molds: Philadelphia Land Records, Book 6, p. 266.

(2) Pocket bottles: Philadelphia, *Pennsylvania Packet,* Feb. 27, 1775.

(3) Pocket bottles: Information from Caspar Wistar's will was given to me by Milo Naeve of the Henry Francis duPont Winterthur Museum. Mr. Naeve has examined this and other documents pertaining to the Wistars.

3. STIEGEL AND STIEGEL-TYPE BOTTLES AND FLASKS

19.

(1) Stiegel's Manheim Ledger No. 1, Oct. 6, 1765–Apr. 30, 1767.

(2) Hunter, pp. 180, 181.

(3) *New York Gazette and the Weekly Mercury,* Feb. 8, 1773.

20.

(1) Report to Lords of Trade from Penn. Colonial Records, IX, 354, quoted by Weeks, p. 80.

(2) American Philosophical Society Report: Boston, *News Letter,* July 11, 1771.

(3) Hunter, p. 80.

21. Hunter, p. 63.

22.

(1) Boston, *Weekly News Letter,* June 7, 1750.

(2) Boston, *Massachusetts Gazette,* Apr. 21, 1768.

(3) Boston, *Evening Post,* Nov. 4, 1774.

23. In a recent letter, this was confirmed by Dr. Robert J. Charleston of the Victoria and Albert Museum, London, but those with which he is familiar are of an early period and not pattern-molded in ribs or diamonds.

24.

(1) Bakewell's: *Pittsburgh Commonwealth,* Oct. 19, 1808.

(2) Boston: *Columbian Centinel,* Feb. 6, 1813.

(3) N. E. Glass Co.: ibid., Oct. 13, 1819.

25.

(1) White, "Migrations of Early Glassworkers."

(2) Stiegel and South Jersey Traditions: McKearin, *American Glass,* pp. 37–52.

26. Hunter, pp. 31, 32.

27. Pazaurek: *See* 2(1).

28.

(1) Stohlman, Martin and Elizabeth, "Excavating and Collecting Amelung Glass," *Antiques* (Oct. 1948).

(2) Hume, Ivor Noël, "Archaeological Excavations on the Site of John Frederick Amelung's New Bremen Glassmanufactory 1962–1963," *Journal of Glass Studies,* The Corning Museum of Glass, Vol. XVIII (1976), pp. 185 and 187, Plate 40.

29. O'Hara's Letter Book, May 5, 1805; McKearin, *Two Hundred Years . . . ,* pp. 33–44, 45–47.

30. Letters from Emil Larsen, 1962.

4. MIDWESTERN PATTERN-MOLDED FLASKS, BOTTLES AND JUGS

31.

(1) McKearin, *Two Hundred Years . . . ,* pp. 40–47.

(2) Gest, Neil C., and Smith, Parke G., "The Glassmaking Cramers," *Antiques* (Mar. 1939).

(3) *See also* Historical Background, 2. The Bottle Industry in America (17).

32.

(1) Announcement of plan for green glass: *Liberty Hall and Cincinnati Gazette,* Jan. 15, 1816; ad dated Jan. 4.

(2) Zanesville houses: Schneider, Norris F., collaborating with Everett Greer. Articles 1, 2, and 3.

33.

(1) Zanesville & Mantua: White, "The Story of the Mantua Glass Works," Part III, *Antiques* (July 1935).

(2) Maysville: *Liberty Hall and Cincinnati Gazette,* Feb. 11, 1815; ad dated Jan. 19.

(3) Cincinnati: Ibid., Apr. 25, 1815; Mar. 25, 1816, ad dated Mar. 8.

34. Smith, Miles A., pp. 118, 119; Rose, James H., Letters.

35. Rose, James H., Letters.

36. Smith, Miles A., p. 117.

37.

(1) McKearin, *American Glass,* p. 592.

(2) *Inquisitor and Cincinnati Advertiser,* June 8, 1819; ad dated May 14.

38.

(1) White, "The Story of the Mantua Glass Works," Parts I & II.

(2) McKearin, *American Glass,* pp. 227–30; *Two Hundred Years . . . ,* pp. 129, 130.

39.

(1) *Pittsburgh Gazette,* Feb. 12, 1806.

(2) Wheeling: Jefferson, pp. 12, 13.

40. *Liberty Hall and Cincinnati Gazette,* July 21, 1831.

41. White, H. H., Dec. 21, 1932, letter to George S. McKearin.

42.

(1) Maysville: Cincinnati, *Liberty Hall and Cincinnati Gazette,* Apr. 8, 1815; ad dated Jan. 19; Welby, Adlard, *A Visit to North America and the English Settlements in Illinois, with a Winter Residence at Philadelphia* (London: 1821), p. 21.

(2) Cincinnati: *Liberty Hall and Cincinnati Gazette,* Mar. 25, 1816; ad dated Mar. 8.

(3) Wares at Cincinnati: Ibid., Oct. 17–Dec. 12, 1821, and Dec. 26, 1821–Mar. 9, 1822; *National Register,* Nov. 25, 1823.

43. Smith, Miles A., p. 115.

44. McKearin, *American Glass,* p. 21 and No. 6, Plate 79.

45. *New Historical Atlas of Portage County, Ohio* (L. H. Levert & Co., 1874), p. 25.

46. Recorded Blown-three-mold patterns are illustrated in *American Glass,* Plates 84–99, pp. 247–60.

VII.
SMELLING, SCENT, AND COLOGNE BOTTLES

1. Haywood, *The Female Spectator* (ca. 1750), p. 89.

2. *New York Mercury,* Apr. 9, 1759.

3. *Pennsylvania Gazette,* Aug. 12, 1785.

4. Henshaw and Edwards, *Crisis* (1850).

5. Allegheny, Pa., *Washington Banner,* Oct. 1, 1842.

6. Buckley, Francis, *A History of Old English Glass* (London: 1925), p. 121.

7. *South Carolina Gazette,* Oct. 29, 1744.

8. Matthews, Leslie G., *The Antiques of Perfume* (London: 1973), p. 36.

9. *The Arcana of Arts & Sciences or Farmers & Mechanics Manual* (Washington, Pa.: 1824), p. 312.

10. Thickneese, Letter XII, Montpelier, 1775, pp. 86–87.

11. *Webster's New International Dictionary,* 2nd ed. (1946).

12. *Encyclopaedia Britannica* (1875).

13. *Baltimore Patriot,* Feb. 9, 1813.

14. Ms., Account Book of Jeremiah Emlen, Oct. 29, 1810–June 30, 1826, now in the collection of the Robert Tannahill Research Library, Henry Ford Museum, Dearborn, Michigan.

15. Ms. Sloar Book, Boston and Sandwich Glass Works, July 9, 1825; March 29, 1828. Now in the collection of the Robert Tannahill Research Library, Henry Ford Museum, Dearborn, Michigan.

16. Original formerly in the collection of Charles B. Gardner, now in the collection of the Wheaton Historical Association, Millville, New Jersey.

17. *Oxford English Dictionary.*

18. New York, *Daily Advertiser,* Apr. 9, 1789.

19. *The American Housewife,* 8th edition (1843).

20. Poulsons, *The American Daily Advertiser,* May 10, 1827.

21. Hartford, *Connecticut Courant,* Mar. 10, 1834.

22. Boston, *Columbian Centinel,* Dec. 4, 1819.

23. Allegheny, Pa. *Washington Banner,* October 1, 1842.

24. Ms., Goodale Letters, The Connecticut Historical Society; also Kenneth M. Wilson, "The Glastenbury Glass Factory Company," *Journal of Glass Studies,* Vol. V (1963), pp. 121–22.

25. One of several price lists pasted in the back of Jeremiah Emlen's account book. Formerly in the George S. McKearin collection, now in the Robert Tannahill Research Library, Henry Ford Museum, Dearborn, Michigan.

26. Ibid.

27. In the collection of the Robert Tannahill Research Library, Henry Ford Museum, Dearborn, Michigan.

28. McKearin, Helen, *Bottles, Flasks and Dr. Dyott,* p. 88.

29. Ibid., p. 38.

30. *Utica Observer,* July 28, 1835.

31. McKearin, Helen, *Bottles, Flasks and Dr. Dyott,* p. 88.

32. Information from J. E. Pfeiffer.

33. Solomon Stanger's Blowers Book, Prices Paid, Blasts 1848–1849, in the possession of J. E. Pfeiffer.

34. White, Harry Hall, "The Lancaster Glass Works" *Antiques* (Oct. 1927), p. 302.

35. Barber, Edwin Atlee, *American Glassware, Old and New* (Philadelphia: McKay & Co., 1900), p. 79.

36. These and many other perfume and cologne bottles, as well as a variety of other figural bottles intended to contain other substances, are described in detail by Albert Christian Revi in *American Pressed Glass and Figure Bottles,* pp. 353–411. Additional figural bottles, some originally intended to contain perfume or cologne, are illustrated and discussed in Bessie M. Lindsay's *Lore of Our Land Pictured in Glass,* pp. 314–24.

37. *Journal of the Franklin Institute . . . ,* No. 638 (Dec. 1847), p. 377.

38. Goodrich, C. R., ed. *Science and Mechanism: Illustrated by Examples in the New York Exhibition, 1853–1854* (New York: G. P. Putnam, 1854), p. 220.

VIII.
FIGURED FLASKS AND BOTTLES

1. BACKGROUND AND FABRICATION

1.

(1) Laird: Jones (S), *Pittsburgh in the year 1826; Harris' Pittsburgh Business Directory,* 1837, not in 1839; U.S. Patent Records, 1832.

(2) Robinson: That Robinson took one of his sons into the business in 1830 is indicated by a J. Robinson & Son ad, *Cincinnati Chronicle and Literary Gazette,* June 19, 1830.

2.

(1) Bartholomew: Swan, Mabel M., "Deming Jarves and His Glass Factory Village," *Antiques* (Jan. 1938), p. 25.

(2) Dillaway: Ibid.

(3) Dolfein: *see* inscription on base of GI–112, line drawing in Charts.

3. Vivian, Norma T., "Old Age, Death, Force Glass Firm to Shut Its Doors after 62 Years," Philadelphia, *Evening Bulletin,* Apr. 7, 1966.

4. Ads: 1824, *United States Gazette,* Oct. 19, 1824; Ibid., Mar. 5, 1825.

5. *See* Ref. 101 and 103, II. HISTORICAL BACKGROUND, 2. The Bottle Industry in America; also *American Glass,* Charts, pp. 457, 545, 547, and 581.

6. *See* Boston Glass Manufactory (Sketch 12)—Keene-Marlboro-Street Glassworks (Sketch 26).

7.

(1) *See* Sketch 26, The Flint Glass Factory (Keene-Marlboro-Street Glassworks . . .).

(2) Peterson, Mendel, "Underwater Thesaurus," *Antiques* (Sept. 1965), p. 324.

8. White, H. H.: Letters; "Keene, New Hampshire," "New York State Glass Houses," *Antiques.*

9. South Boston flint-glass bottles and flasks: ad., Boston, *Columbian Centinel,* Jan. 7, 1816; Price lists: ca. 1813–16, 1818, 1819 (in back of Jeremiah Emlen's invoice book, Coll. Henry Ford Museum), 1822 (Coll. Essex Institute); *see also* Boston Glass Manufactory (Sketch 12).

10. New England Glass Co. bottles and flasks: Price List ca. 1818 (back of Jeremiah Emlen's invoice book, see 9 above); ads. Boston, *Columbian Centinel,* Oct. 13, 1819 and Mar. 8, 1820; April and May invoices of glass consigned to Wm. E. Mayhew & Co., commission merchants, Baltimore, Md. (Coll. Maryland Historical Society).

11. *New Hampshire Sentinel,* Aug. 23, 1817.

12.

(1) Price List: "Prices Current. Glass Ware of the Philadelphia and Kensington Vial and Bottle Factories. . . . T. W. Dyott Proprietor or [in long hand] Hickson W. Field. agent/New York." Bella C. Landauer Collection in the New-York Historical Society. Nearly all the items listed were advertised in the newspapers but without prices. In the 18th and early 19th century, prices were rarely quoted in the newspaper ads, which seemed to be directed toward both wholesale and retail customers instead of the retail customer only.

(2) Athens, Ga., *The Hiwassean and Athens Gazette,* Jan. 2, 1826.

13.

(1) N. E. Glass Co.: Philadelphia, *The Union For the Country,* ad. dated Nov. 6, 1819; Hartford, *Connecticut Mirror,* Oct. 12, Nov. 4 and 18, 1822.

(2) Morton: 2 among many ads—Hartford, Conn., *American Mercury,* Dec. 25, 1825; *Connecticut Courant,* Dec. 24, 1827.

(3) Robinson: Cincinnati, O., *Cincinnati Daily Gazette,* Jan. 23, 1833.

(4) Hastings: Ibid., Oct. 26, 1833.

(5) Pepperd & Teater: *Liberty Hall and Cincinnati Gazette,* Aug. 12, 1825.

14.

(1) N. E. Glass Co. auction of wares: Boston, *Columbian Centinel,* Oct. 13, 1819; Mar. 8, 1820.

(2) Lafayette flasks: *Cincinnati Daily Gazette,* Jan. 21, 1828.

15.

(1) Farley & Taylor: Van Rensselaer, p. 215.

(2) Gentry Shote & Co.: N.Y. City Directory, published May 1858.

16. L. Desauque, jun. & Co.: *Philadelphia Centinel and Mercantile Advertiser,* Dec. 20, 1817.

2. DECORATIVE FLASKS

17. Cornucopia or Horn of Plenty: Bullfinch, Thomas, *The Age of Fable* (Boston: 1871), pp. 244–46.

18.

(1) *See* Sketch #31. Bakewells, Pittsburgh Flint Glass Works. . . .

(2) *See* Sketch #35. Robinson's Stourbridge Flint Glass Works . . . ; also *Cincinnati Chronicle and Literary Gazette,* June 19, 1830, and *The Daily Pittsburgh Gazette,* Aug. 31, 1834.

(3) *See* Sketch #60. Samuel McKee & Co. . . .

(4) *See* Sketch #69. Knowles & Co., Center Wheeling. . . .

(5) *See* Sketch #71. Kentucky Glass Works. . . .

(6) *See* Sketch #70. McCarty & Torreyson, Wellsburg. . . .

19. White, "The Lancaster Glass Works," *Antiques,* Oct. 1927. Mr. White's informants were Frank H. Daly, who after 1866 was associated with his father in managing the works, and John G. Luenbrix, a glassblower employed from the fall of 1861.

3. MASONIC FLASKS

20.

(1) J. Shephard & Co.: *See* Sketch #37. Zanesville Glass Manufactory. . . .

(2) Murdock & Cassel: Ibid.

21.

(1) White, H. H., *Antiques* (Dec. 1938).

(2) Foley, Jasena Rappleye, "The Ontario Glass Manufacturing Company," *Journal of Glass Studies,* The Corning Museum of Glass, Vol. VI (1964), p. 144.

22.

(1) Knox & McKee: *See* Sketch #41. Virginia Green Glass Works (Knox & McKee). . . .

(2) Mantua: White, H. H.

(3) Pepperd & Teater: *See* Sketch #39. Cincinnati Glass Works & Moscow Glass Works. . . .

23. Peterson, Mendel, "Underwater Thesaurus," *Antiques* (Sept. 1965).

24. The story of William Morgan is condensed from *McMaster,* Vol. V, pp. 109–20.

4. HISTORICAL FLASKS

25. Trollope, Frances, *Domestic Manners of the Americans,* edited by Donald Smalley (New York: 1949), pp. 102–3; Mrs. Trollope's account of her conversation with a milkman.

26. "Rise Columbia Brave and Free," lyrics by Edwin C. Hollan, Esq. Music by Jacob Eckhard Sr., organist of St. Michael's Church. 1813. Coll. New York Public Library, 42nd Street & 5th Avenue, N.Y.C.

27. Wynne, John Huddlestone, *Choice Emblems* (Philadelphia: 1790), No. 81.

28. Van Rensselaer, GII DII 14, p. 65.

29. McMaster, *History of the American People During Lincoln's Administration,* p. 231.

30.

(1) *Encyclopedic Dictionary of American Reference,* Vol. I, p. 258.

(2) "Stripes & Stars of Rebellion," *Time* (June 20, 1955).

31.

(1) Flag: *see* 30(1).

(2) Betsy Ross: Ibid., Vol. II, Appendix, p. 408.

(3) Stars & Stripes: Ibid., Vol. II, Appendix, p. 410.

32. Draker, Joseph Rodman, "The American Flag." Reprinted (without credit to the poet) from the *New York Evening Post* in the June 15, 1819 issue of the *Columbian Gazette,* Utica, N.Y.

33.

(1) "Freedom's Star," *The American Naval and Patriotic Songster* (Baltimore: P. N. Wood, 1831), pp. 62, 63. Compilation of songs, mainly of the War of 1812 period "AS SUNG AT VARIOUS PLACES OF AMUSEMENT/In honor of/Isaac Hull, John Paul Jones, Stephen Decatur, Oliver Hazard Perry, William Bainbridge, James Lawrence, &c, &c, &c." All of those mentioned, except John Paul Jones, were heroes of the Mediterranean war against the Barbary pirates and of the War of 1812.

(2) 3¢ pieces: *The Standard Catalogue of United States Coins,* compiled and published by Wayte Raymond, Inc., New York, 1954.

34. McMaster, Vol. VII. pp. 359 seq.

35.

(1) 1755: *New York Gazette,* Sept. 27, 1755.

(2) "A New Epilogue to CATO, spoken at a late Performance of that Tragedy." Unfortunately we do not have the date and title of the newspaper in which this appeared. It ended: "In vain do ye rely on foreign aid,/By her own arm Columba must be freed."

(3) Poem, Boston: Boston, *Continental Journal,* Jan. 30, 1777.

36. "Columbia a Patriotic Song: Written and Set to Music by Timothy Dwight. 1777." New Haven, printed at the press of Timothy Dwight College in Yale University, 1940.

37.

(1) Cartoon: "LIBERTY TRIUMPHANT: or the Downfall of OPPRESSION." Ca. 1774. Not in B.M. caricature engraving. Coll. of the New-York Historical Society, N.Y.

(2) Savage's Liberty: Jones, Louis C., "Liberty and considerable license," *Antiques* (July 1958).

38. "Origin and Properties of the Cap of Liberty," Lansingburgh, *Northern Budget,* July 10, 1798.

39. *See* 33(2).

40. Ibid.

41. "Ode to Columbia's Favourite Son," Song III, *Columbian Songster* (1799). Apparently the ode was composed in or by 1789. It was sung at several celebrations of Washington's inauguration as the first President of the United States. *New York Packet,* Oct. 31, 1789. Later in 1789, at Boston, it was "sung by a select choir upon the PRESIDENT appearing on the Balcony of the State-House." Boston, *Independent Chronicle,* Nov. 5, 1789.

42. White, H. H., *Antiques* (Keene), June 1927; (Coventry) Oct. & Nov. 1940, Feb. 1941. Letters to George S. McKearin.

43. Philadelphia, *United States Gazette,* Oct. 19, 1824.

44. Shankle, George Earlie, *American Nicknames and Their Significance* (New York: 1907), p. 563.

45. "Origin of The Father of His Country," *History of the*

George Washington Bicentennial Celebration, Vol. III, Literature Series (1932), p. 87. U.S. George Washington Bicentennial Celebration Commission, Washington, D.C.

46.

(1) 1789: Among many sources in which the title was found were the following:

New York Journal, Apr. 30, 1789.

Northampton (Mass.), *Hampshire Gazette,* May 3 and July 15, 1789.

New York Packet, Oct. 31, 1789. *See* 41.

(2) 1799–1800: Among many sources were the following:

Philadelphia, *Claypoole's American Daily Advertiser,* Dec. 20, 1799.

Lansingburgh, *Northern Budget,* Jan. 1, 1800.

Hartford, *Connecticut Courant,* Jan. 6, 1800.

Halsey, Wm., "An Oration delivered the 22nd February MDCCC Before the Bretheren and a Select Audience in the Hall of St. John's Lodge No.2 Newark, New Jersey."

(3) 1814: Philadelphia, *Poulson's American Daily Advertiser,* Mar. 3, 1814.

47. Linn, Wm., "A Funeral Eulogy occasioned by the death of GENERAL WASHINGTON, delivered Feb. 22, 1800, before the New York State Society of the Cincinnati" (New York: 1800).

48. Columbia's matchless son: Broadside. "Ode on the Birthday of the President of the United States" (1796). Coll. of the New-York Historical Society.

49.

(1) July 4th 1825: *Troy [N.Y.] Sentinel,* July 5, 1825.

(2) 1834: In Fall River, Mass., 13 toasts were offered after the cloth was removed at a Franklin supper to celebrate his birthday, according to an item from the *Fall River Monitor* published by the Boston, *Columbian Centinel,* Jan. 22, 1834. Printers, in particular, observed his birthday. Among others, the "Fraternity of Printers" of Concord, Mass., held a supper in 1825. Concord, *New Hampshire Patriot and State Gazette,* Jan. 24, 1825.

50. *The Columbian Harmonist* (Philadelphia: Printed by Thomas Simpson, 1814), pp. 80–81.

51.

(1) 1824 ad. *see* 43.

(2) "Where Liberty Dwells . . . ": Woods, Henry T., *American Sayings* (New York: 1945), p. 9.

52. "Erupuit . . . ": *see* 49(2), p. 8.

53. Jefferson, p. 20.

54. *Bristol Journal,* Bristol, Eng. Quoted in the New Haven, Conn., *Connecticut Gazette,* Apr. 24, 1762.

55. *Boston [Mass.] Evening Gazette,* Nov. 13, 1824.

56. Goodell, Sir Elwood Wilber, *History of Columbian Commandery to Knights Templar,* p. 12.

57. For information regarding Lafayette as a Mason we are indebted to Mr. W. K. Walker, Librarian of the Grand Lodge of New York F. & A.M., and the loan of Vol. 2, *Transactions American Lodge of Research Free & Accepted Masons.*

58. In our 1941 comments on the "ribbed Lafayette. . . . flasks" we wrote in *American Glass,* p. 465: "Just what was meant by the term ribbed in connection with the advertisement of these Moscow flasks is a matter of conjecture but possibly it referred to the vertical ribbed edges which were in contrast to the beaded edges found on most of the flasks made in the Midwest during the period from 1824 to the early 1830's." While still a matter of conjecture, the absence of a comma seems more logical to us today.

59. Knittle, Rhea Mansfield, lecture given at a meeting of the Early American Glass Club, Boston, 1940: letters to George S. McKearin, 1940–42. In 1940 Mrs. Knittle stated that Pugh &

Teeter [Teater] advertised in the June 11, 1824, issue of *Liberty Hall and Cincinnati Gazette* that among their products to be available September 1, 1824, were "ribbed Lafayette, Clay and Jackson flasks. . . . " In 1942 she wrote to Mr. McKearin saying that "Pugh" was a misprint and that "Pepperd & Teeter" advertised the flasks on August 23, 1825. The discrepancy in dates was never clarified. Mrs. Lee Jordan of the Cincinnati Historical Society has searched the 1824 issues of *Liberty Hall* . . . for me and established that, without any doubt, neither Pugh & Teater nor their successors Pepperd & Teater (Nov. 10, 1828) ever advertised these flasks in 1824. However, Mr. John Mullane, Librarian of the History and Literature Department of the Public Library of Cincinnati and Hamilton County, has sent me a photocopy of an ad by Pepperd & Teater, dated August 12, 1825, in which these flasks were among the wares to be on sale by September 1.

60. Knittle, lecture and letters, *see* 59.

61.

(1) January & April ads reported by Mrs. Knittle in 1942 letter. In the same letter she reported an ad in the January 1, 1828, *Cincinnati Daily Gazette* referring to the late works of Pepperd & Teater. Mrs. Jordan found no such ad in that issue of the paper. Nor did Mrs. Lee Adams find one during the entire year of 1828 and last half of 1827.

(2) As found by Mrs. Adams: *Cincinnati Daily Gazette,* Jan. 21, 1828, W. C. Rogers & Werth, also John Stinson & Co.; Apr. 29–June 24, 1828, John Stinson & Co.

62.

(1) Paris. July 4: *Niles Register,* Baltimore, Md., Vol. 30, p. 432, Aug. 19, 1826.

(2) Bunker Hill: *New York Commercial Advertiser,* May 21, 1829.

(3) Sale of Lands: Boston, Mass., *Columbian Centinel,* June 20, 1829; Philadelphia, Pa., *Daily Chronicle,* June 22, 1829.

63. *New York Commercial Advertiser,* Mar. 9, 12, 13, and 15, 1825.

64. Erie Canal: McMaster, Vol. IV, pp. 415–18; Vol. V, pp. 83, 132, 133.

65.

(1) *New York Commercial Advertiser,* June 8, 1825.

(2) During July and August 1825 the *New York Commercial Advertiser* published detailed reports of Clinton's tour and its events. In the June 13th issue it quoted from a letter to the editor of the *Cleaveland Herald* in which a gentleman of Portage Co., O., wrote he "would go as far to see DeWitt Clinton as to see Lafayette."

(3) Toast at Pittsburgh dinner: Pittsburgh, Pa., *The Statesman,* Aug. 16, 1825.

66. Wynne, James, M.D., "Memoir of Major Samuel Ringgold, United States Army; read before the Maryland Historical Society April 1st 1847." Published by John Murphy, 1847.

67. Ibid. (Many of the details given by Dr. Wynne appeared also in various newspaper reports and editorials following Ringgold's death in May 1846 and his final obsequies in Dec. 1846.)

68.

(1) Washington: Philadelphia, Pa., *Public Ledger,* Dec. 17, 1846.

(2) Obsequies: *Niles Register,* Baltimore, Vol. 71, Jan. 2, 1847. (Many accounts appeared in various newspapers at the time.)

69. *Baltimore American,* June 3, July 30, Aug. 13, 1846.

70. Ibid., May 26, 1846. Quoted from the Philadelphia, Pa., *North American.*

71. Werner, M. R. *Barnum,* Chaps. VI & VIII, pp. 114 seq. Unless otherwise noted the account of Jenny Lind, her American tour, and Barnum are based on Mr. Werner's account.

72.

(1) Vienna: Baltimore, *American and Commercial Advertiser,* July 13, 1846.

(2) Colman, Henry, *European Life and Manners, familiar letters to Friends* (London: 1849), Vol. II, p. 380, Letter CCXIX, London, June 29, 1848.

72a. *Struggles and Triumphants or Forty Years' Recollection of P. T. Barnum* (Author's edition, New York, 1871), p. 283.

73. New York, *The Republic,* Vol. I (June 1851), p. 281.

74. Ibid., Vol. III (June 1852), p. 313.

75.

(1) Barnum: *see* 72a, p. 290.

(2) Nantucket, *The Inquirer,* Jan. 1, 1851.

75a. Nantucket, Mass., *The Inquirer,* May 30, 1852.

76.

(1) Knittle, pp. 384, 446, 447.

(2) Van Rensselaer, Group I, Nos. 72–80, pp. 49, 50; glasshouse symbols, pp. 34.

77. Van Rensselaer, p. 11 and Group I, No. 72.

78. Unless otherwise stated, data on Kossuth up to his leaving Turkey was from the *Encyclopaedia Britannica,* 1951 ed., Vol. XIII, pp. 494ff; on his American trip and stay from McMasters, Vol. VII, pp. 143–57, and Nantucket, Mass., *The Enquirer,* 1851: Dec. 8, 10, 15, 22, 25, and 31, and 1852: Jan. 2, 5, 7, 9, 12, 14, 21, 23, 26; Feb. 6, 26; Mar. 12; Apr. 5, 28, May 3, 5, 6, 10, 26; June 16; Aug. 2.

79. Nantucket, Mass., *The Inquirer,* Apr. 21, 1850.

80. Ibid., Oct. 24, 1851. Reprint from Washington, D.C., papers of "Kossuth's Address to the United States," written by Kossuth, Mar. 27, 1850, at Bosnis, Serbia, then part of the Ottoman Empire, and made public Oct. 13, 1851.

81. Ibid., Oct. 13, 1851.

82. Ibid., Jan. 21, 1852.

83. Ibid., Jan. 7, 9, 12, 14, 1852.

84. Ibid., Feb. 25, Mar. 8, 1852.

85. *American Guide Series by Works Progress Administration in the State of Maryland,* 1933, pp. 127, 216. Philadelphia, *Poulson's American Daily Advertiser,* Mar. 3, 1814. Keene, *New Hampshire Sentinel,* Jan. 29, 1814. Troy, N.Y., *Post,* Dec. 14, 1813. Pratt, John Horace, "An authentic account of all the Proceedings on the 4th of July, 1815 with regard to laying the Corner Stone of the Washington Monument now erected in the City of Baltimore," Baltimore, 1815. Duncan, John M., Letter, Baltimore, September 1818, pp. 222, 223. *Baltimore American,* November 1829, item quoted in the *Boston Columbian Centinel,* Nov. 25, 1829.

86. *Baltimore American,* May 23, 1846, reprint from the *Philadelphia Ledger.*

87. Philadelphia, *Aurora General Advertiser,* Sept. 2, 1815. *Annals of Baltimore,* printed by Wm. Wooddy, Baltimore, 1824, p. 213; *American Guide Series (see* 85), p. 225.

88. Wood, Henry F., *American Sayings,* p. 22.

89. Nantucket, Mass., *The Inquirer,* Aug. 22, 1840.

90. *New York Herald Tribune,* Dec. 4, 1956, news item from Richmond, Va., Dec. 3.

91. Unless otherwise stated, the data on Adams and Jackson was drawn from John Bach McMaster's *History of the American People* and the *World Book Encyclopedia.*

92. Cited by McMaster, Vol. V, p. 489.

93. Trollope, Frances M., *Domestic Manners of the Americans,* Donald Smalley, ed., 1949, p. 143.

94. *See* 91.

95. Cited by McMaster, Vol. VI, p. 562.

96. Ibid.

97. *See* 91.

98. *See* 91.

99. *Liberty Hall and Cincinnati Gazette,* Aug. 12, 1825.

100. Except where noted, data on Taylor was drawn from *General Taylor* by Oliver Otis Howard, Major General U.S. Army, in "Great Commander Series" (D. Appleton & Co., 1892).

101. Baltimore, *American and Commercial Advertiser,* Apr. 5, 1845.

102. Ibid., Apr. 13, 1847, and *see* 100.

103. Troy, N.Y., *Northern Budget,* Apr. 19, 1853.

104.

(1) Shankle, George Earl, *American Nicknames* (New York: The H. W. Wilson Co., 1937).

(2) *Rough and Ready Songster* (1848) by an American Officer (New York: Nafis & Cornish Publishers).

105.

(1) Ramsay: 1853/54 was the only directory in which this wine merchant was listed at 281 8th Avenue.

(2) New Orleans: *Niles Weekly Register,* Baltimore.

(3) Bragg: Philadelphia, *Public Ledger,* Feb. 23, 1848.

106. *Encyclopedic Dictionary of American Reference* by J. Franklin Jameson, Ph.D., and J. W. Buel, Ph.D., in the *Library of American History,* Vol. I, p. 297, and *Encyclopedia Americana,* Vol. 13, pp. 135–39.

107. Adams, *The March of Democracy,* Vol. II, p. 128.

108. *Encyclopaedia Britannica* (1969), Vol. 5, pp. 907–9. Adams, Vol. II, p. 188–202, 222–33.

109. Adams, Vol. II, p. 202. "PRESIDENT CLEVELAND/ AN ILLUSTRATED POEM/By H. CLAY PREUSS/ Respectfully dedicated to the Members of the New York Delegation to the National Democratic Convention at St. Louis, June 5th, 1888, as a just tribute to a noble son of the old 'Empire State' . . ."

110. Ibid., p. 233.

111. *See* 108. *Britannica,* Vol. 14, pp. 536–38; Adams, pp. 206, 240–68.

112. *See* 108. *Britannica,* Vol. 4, pp. 316, 317; Adams, pp. 238–41; 261, 262, 311, 312, 315, 330.

113. *See* 108. *Britannica,* Vol. 9, pp. 600–616.

114. Dr. James S. Hall and Mrs. Hall's letters, Sept. 28, Oct. 6 and 31, 1961; Edward C. Wheaton's letter to Dr. Hall, Oct. 26, 1961.

5. AGRICULTURE, COMMERCE AND TRANSPORTATION

115. *Franklin:* 1815, Pittsburgh, Pa., *The Commonwealth,* Sept. 9, 1815; 1822, Troy, N.Y., *The Budget,* Nov. 26, 1822.

116. Phoenix: McKearin, *American Glass,* p. 480.

117.

(1) Quincy. *The First Railroad in America, A History of the Origin and Development of the Granite Railway Company at Quincy, Massachusetts* (Privately printed for the Granite Railway Company in Commemoration of the One Hundredth Anniversary), p. 1.

(2) Growth. *The American Almanac and Repository of Useful Knowledge for 1822* (Boston: Gray & Bowen), "Railroads." Poor, Henry V., *History of the Railroads and Canals of the United States of America* (New York: 1860).

118. Lowell: *see* 117(2); "Report of a Committee on the Boston and Lowell Railroad," Boston, 1831; "Report of the Boston and Lowell Railroad Corp.," Nov. 30, 1831; presented at the annual meeting, Jan. 3, 1835.

119.

(1) Van Rensselaer, p. 50.

(2) B. & O. engine. *Liberty Hall & Cincinnati Gazette*, July 21, 1831.

120. Henry Baldwin: Baltimore, *Niles Register*, June 3 and July 1, 1820; Pittsburgh, *The Statesman*, Apr. 21 and July 31, 1824.

6. SPORTS

121.

(1) The firm of Gentry, Shote & Co. grocers was found in only one New York City Directory, that published May 1, 1858.

(2) Flora Temple: Self, Margaret Cabell, *The Horseman's Encyclopedia* (New York: A. S. Barnes & Company, Inc., 1963). Nantucket, Mass., *The Inquirer*, Oct. 21, 1859.

122. Van Rensselaer, pp. 100, 238.

7. PIKE'S PEAK

123. Unless otherwise stated, data on the "Pike's Peak" gold rush is from McMasters, Vol. VIII, pp. 492 seq.; Hafen, Leroy R., and Rister, Carl Coke, *Western America* (New York: 1951), p. 437 seq.; Henry Villard (Special Correspondent of the *Cincinnati Daily Commercial*), *The Past and Present of the Pike's Peak Gold Regions,* with Maps and Illustrations (St. Louis: 1860).

124. Byers, Wm. N., and Kellon, John H., "A Hand Book to the Gold Fields of Nebraska and Kansas, being a complete guide to the Gold Regions of the South Platte and Cherry Creek" (Chicago: 1859), p. 12.

125.

(1) Ads: St. Louis, *Sunday Morning Republican*, Mar. 27, 1859; (Lidiard's) *Daily Missouri Republican*, Apr. 19, 1859.

126.

(1) Tools: "Guide to the Kansas Gold Mines at Pikes Peak" by Col. Wm. Gilpin of Independence, Mo.

(2) Parker & Huyett, "New Illustrated Miner's Hand-Book and Guide to Pike's Peak," St. Louis, 1859. (Facsimile reproduction from the original owned by Nolie Mumeny, Denver, Col.), pp. 38, 39.

127. McMaster, Vol. XVIII, p. 397.

128. *Leslie's Illustrated Newspaper*, Apr. 3, Aug. 30, 1859; *Harper's Weekly*, Aug. 13, 1859; McKearin, "The Story of American Historical Flasks."

129. White, "Glass Monuments to Zebulon Pike."

BIBLIOGRAPHY

Obviously this bibliography does not include the entire literature on the glass bottle. Nor, as the notes reveal, does it list all the sources used in the writing of this book. Rather it is a list of those books and articles used mainly as references in many instances.

AGRICOLA, GEORGIUS. *De Re Metallica*. Translated from the first Latin edition of 1556, by Herbert Clark Hoover and Lou Henry Hoover. 1912.

BACON. JOHN M. "Bottle-decanters and Bottles," *Apollo*, July 1939.

BARRELET. *La Verrerie en France*. Paris: Librairie Larousse, 1953. "Le Verre de Table au Moyen Age," "Cahiers de la Ceramique du Verre et Des Arts du Feu." No.16 (1959).

BISHOP, J. LEANDER. *A History of American Manufactures From 1608 to 1860*. 2 Vol. Philadelphia: Edward Young & Co., 1864

CHAMBRON, R. *L'Histoire de la Verrerie en Belgique du IIme Siècle a nos Jours*. Bruxelles: Edition de la Librairie Encyclopedique S.P.R.I., 1955.

CHARLESTON, ROBERT. "The Transport of Glass." Paper delivered before the Glass Circle, London. "Bottles, Mainly Glass." Ms. article written for Watford Brewery.

DANIEL, DOROTHY. "The First Glasshouse West of the Alleghenies." *The Western Pennsylvania Historical Magazine*, Vol. 32 (September-December 1949).

DOSSIE, ROBERT. *The Handmaid to the Arts*, 2 Vol. London: 1764.

DYOTT, M.D., T. W. *An Exposition of the System of Moral and Mental Labor Established at the Glass Factory of Dyottville . . . with the Report of the Committee chosen to Investigate the Internal Regulations of the Place . . .* Philadelphia: 1833.

GASPARETTO, ASTONE. "Aspects de la Verrerie vénitienne antérieure a la Renaissance." "Cahiers de la Ceramique du Verre et Des Arts du Feu" No.17 (1960).

HANDICQUIER DE BLANCOURT, JEAN. *The Art of Glass*. English edition. London: 1699.

HARRINGTON, JEAN C. *Glassmaking at Jamestown*. Richmond, Va.: 1952.

HAYNES, E. BARRINGTON. *Glass Through The Ages*. Pelican Books, 1959.

HUDSON, PAUL. "Seventeenth Century Glass Wine Bottles and Seals Excavated at Jamestown," *Journal of Glass Studies*, Vol. III (1961). The Corning Museum of Glass, Corning, N.Y.

HUME, IVOR NOËL, "The Glass Wine Bottle in Colonial Virginia." *Journal of Glass Studies*, Vol. III (1961). The Corning Museum of Glass, Corning, N.Y.

———— "Archaeological Excavations on the Site of John Frederick Amelung's New Bremen Glassmanufactory (1962–63)." *Journal of Glass Studies*, Vol. XVIII, 1976. The Corning Museum of Glass, Corning, N.Y.

_____ "Medieval Bottles from London." *The Connoisseur* (April 1957).

HUNTER, FREDERICK W. *Stiegel Glass*. Introduction and Notes by Helen McKearin. New York: Dover Publications, Inc., 1950.

INNES, LOWELL, *Pittsburgh Glass 1797-1891*, Houghton Mifflin Co., Boston, Mass., 1976.

JEFFERSON, JOSEPHINE. *Wheeling Glass*. Mount Vernon, Ohio: The Guide Publishing Co., 1947.

KNITTLE, RHEA MANSFIELD. *Early American Glass*. New York: The Century Company, 1927.

McKEARIN, GEORGE S. and HELEN. *American Glass*. New York: Crown Publishers, 1941.

McKEARIN, HELEN and GEORGE S. *Two Hundred Years of American Blown Glass*. Garden City, N.Y.: Doubleday & Company Inc., 1950. New York: Crown Publishers, Inc.

McKEARIN, GEORGE S. "Not For Joseph in Song and Glass." *American Collector* (July 1937).

McKEARIN, HELEN. *The Story of American Historical Flasks*. Corning, N.Y.: The Corning Museum of Glass.

_____ *Bottles, Flasks and Dr. Dyott*, New York: Crown Publishers, Inc., 1970.

C. M[ERRET]. *The Art of Glass*. Written in Italian by Antonio Neri and translated into English with some Observations on the Author. Translator, Christopher Merret.

MUNSEY, CECIL. *The Illustrated Guide to Collecting Bottles*. New York: Hawthorn Books, Inc., 1970.

PEPPER, ADELINE. *Glass Gaffers of New Jersey and Their Creations*. New York: Charles Scribner's Sons, 1971.

QUYNN, DOROTHY MACKAY. "Johann Frederick Amelung at New Bremen." *Maryland Historical Magazine* (Sept. 1948). The Maryland Historical Society, Baltimore, Md.

RUGGLES-BRISE, SHEELAH. *Sealed Bottles*. Country Life L.T.D. London. New York: Charles Scribner's Sons, 1949.

SCOVILLE, WARREN C. *Revolution in Glassmaking, Entrepreneurship and Technological Changes in American Industry 1880-1920*. Cambridge, Mass.: Harvard University Press, 1948.

SMITH, MILES A. "Zanesville Glass." *Journal of Glass Studies*, Vol. II (1960). The Corning Museum of Glass, Corning, N.Y.

THOMPSON, J. H. *Bitters Bottles*. Century House, 1947.

THORPE, W. A. "English Glassware in the XVIIth Century." *Catalogue of Old English Glass*. London: Arthur Churchill Ltd., 1937.

_____ "The Glass Seller's Bills at Woburn Abbey." The Transac-

tions of the Society of Glass Technology, Vol. 22 (1938).

_____ "The Evolution of the Decanter." *The Connoisseur*. May 1929.

TOULOUSE, JULIAN HARRISON. *A Collector's Manual, Fruit Jars*. Thomas Nelson & Sons, Camden, N.J., and Everybody's Press, Hanover, Pa., 1969.

_____ "Empontilling, A History," *The Glass Industry*, March–April, 1968.

VAN RENSSELAER, STEPHEN. *Early American Bottles and Flasks*. Revised Edition, 1926.

WALL, A. J. "Proposals For Establishing a Glass Works in the City of New York 1752." *The New-York Historical Society Quarterly Bulletin* (Oct. 1926).

WATSON, RICHARD. *Bitters Bottles*. New York: Thomas Nelson & Sons, 1965.

_____ *Supplement to Bitters Bottles*. New York: Thomas Nelson & Sons, 1968.

WEEKS, JOSEPH D. "Report on the Manufacture of Glass At the 10th Census, 1880, including a History of Glassmaking in the United States." Washington: 1883.

WHITE, HARRY HALL. Articles in *The Magazine ANTIQUES*.

"The Kentucky Glass Works," Feb. 1926.

"Keene, New Hampshire," June 1927.

"The Lancaster Glass Works," Oct. 1927.

"New York State Glasshouses," Part I, July 1930; Part II, Sept. 1929; Part III, Nov. 1929; "Mt. Pleasant," July and Sept. 1930.

"Glass Monuments to Zebulon Pike," Part I, Sept. 1932; Part II, Oct. 1932

"The Story of the Mantua Glass Works," Part I, Dec. 1934; Part II, Feb. 1935; Part III, July 1935; Part IV, Nov. 1935.

"The Albany Glass Works," July 1936.

"More Light on Coventry and its Products," Part I, Oct. 1940; Part II, Nov. 1940; Part III, Feb. 1941.

"The Willington Glass Company," Aug. 1941.

"New Views of Old Glass, Part V. A Seventeenth Century Bottle," July 1933.

"Pattern Molds and Pattern Molded Glass," Aug. 1939.

"Migrations of Early Glassworkers," Aug. 1937.

WILSON, KENNETH M. "The Glastenbury Glass Factory Company." *Journal of Glass Studies*, The Corning Museum of Glass. Vol. V (1963).

_____ *New England Glass and Glassmaking*. New York: Thomas Y. Crowell, 1972.

INDEX

Page numbers in italics refer to captions or illustrations.

BASEBALL HISTORY

BASEBALL HISTORY
An Annual of Original Baseball Research

Editor-in-Chief
PETER LEVINE
Michigan State University

Editorial Board

ELIOT ASINOF

PETER GAMMONS
Sports Illustrated

LARRY GERLACH
University of Utah

STEPHEN JAY GOULD
Harvard University

TOM HEITZ
Library, National
 Baseball Hall of Fame

FREDERICK KLEIN
The Wall Street Journal

ROBERT LIPSYTE
NBC Nightly News

LAWRENCE RITTER
New York University

DICK SCHAAP
ABC Television

ALAN STEINBERG

DAVID VOIGT
Albright College

Associate Editors
KATHERINE T. DRASKY
SHIREEN M. RUSTOM

Editorial Vice President
ANTHONY ABBOTT

Publisher
ALAN M. MECKLER

BASEBALL HISTORY

An Annual of Original Baseball Research

Premier Edition

Edited by
Peter Levine

Meckler

Cover art reproduced from the limited edition print "Fenway
Park Triptych" by Andy Jurinko, published by Bill Goff, Inc.,
P.O. Box 508 Gracie Station, NY, NY 10028.

ISBN 0-88736-288-5

Meckler Books, the Trade Division of Meckler Corporation,
    11 Ferry Lane West, Westport, CT 06880.
Meckler Ltd., Grosvenor Gardens House, Grosvenor Gardens,
    London SW1W 0BS, U.K.

Printed on acid free paper.
Manufactured in the United States of America.

Contents

EDITOR'S NOTE

Welcome to *Baseball History,* an annual of original baseball research. Old subscribers to the quarterly *Baseball History* will feel right at home with this volume. New readers will find a book that brings together original popular, scholarly pieces about the history of America's "National Game." Each fall we will bring you the best essays, interviews, personal reminiscences, and short fiction submitted during the past year. Also included are reviews and a bibliographical survey of recently published baseball books. The twelve selections for 1988 include Larry Gerlach's perceptive interview with Augie Donatelli, one of the National League's premier umpires in the 1950s and 1960s and the founder of the Major League Umpire Association; Brett Millier's moving account of her great grand-father, Cleveland pitcher "Dusty"Rhoads; Ron Briley's analysis of professional baseball and a divided America in 1968; and Larry Bowman's interesting study of the baseball career and racial views of Moses Fleetwood Walker, the first black man to play in the major leagues almost 100 years before Jackie Robinson. Our Extra Innings section includes three personal vignettes about the Yankees and the Dodgers of the 1950s—easy choices for an editor to include who spent his Saturdays at Ebbets Field while secretly rooting for the New York Yankees and Mickey Mantle. I hope you enjoy our efforts and look forward to seeing you every year at World Series time.

Peter Levine
East Lansing, Michigan

Augie Donatelli: Umpire and Union Organizer

LARRY R. GERLACH

During 24 years in the National League, August Joseph Donatelli was one of major league baseball's most respected umpires. He worked four All-Star games (1953, 1959, 1962, 1969), five World Series (1955, 1957, 1961, 1967, 1973), and two League Championship Series (1969, 1972). Moreover, he was the home-plate umpire for four no-hit games: Warren Spahn (1961), Carl Erskine (1956), Ken Johnson (1964), and Bob Moose (1969). In 1955, his fifth year in the majors, Donatelli was voted "the best National League umpire on the bases" by baseball writers. In February 1973 he received the third Al Somers award as the Outstanding Major League Umpire of 1972; that the first two Somers awards, voted on by umpires, went to Al Barlick and Nestor Chylak, universally regarded as the premier arbiters in the National and American Leagues respectively, indicates Donatelli's recognized stature within the umpiring profession.

In some ways Augie Donatelli was a typical umpire of the post-World War II era. He was a second-generation, working-class American who successfully used sport as a vehicle for socioeconomic mobility, part of a group of Italian-Americans—Babe Pinelli, Art Passarella, Joe Paparella, Frank Dascoli, Augie Guglielmo, Joe Linsalata, and Alex Salerno— whose presence was conspicuous for the first time in the ranks of umpires in the 1940s and 1950s. He was an ex-player who turned to officiating as a way of continuing his involvement with the game. And he was among the numerous war-hardened veterans who dominated college and professional sport after 1945. In other ways, Donatelli was atypical. The peculiar circumstances of his family life and experiences as a prisoner of war forged a distinctive personality—forceful, determined, and tough-minded with a strong sense of fairness and comradery. As a rapid ascent through minor leagues suggested, he was a "born" umpire, possessing that unusual combination of skill, judgment, and demeanor that marks the truly exemplary umpire. Most important, as the "founder" of the Major League Umpires Association, Augie Donatelli is one of the few men in blue to make historically important contributions to the umpiring profession as well as to major league baseball.

The following "oral autobiography" is a composite excerpt of an extended personal interview with Donatelli. It originally was to be included in my book *The Men in Blue: Conversations with Umpires* (1980), but was withheld because of his consternation that a contemporary National League arbiter would be included in the book. The interview is offered at this time for two reasons: 1) Donatelli's "story" should be a matter of record because of his demonstrable importance in baseball and umpiring history, and 2) it is an unusually comprehensive personal exegesis from an intensely private man who, like most umpires, has not sought the "limelight" and thus has not had his views widely recorded.

1

Although the material has been reorganized to present a coherent "life story" and the repetitious and incomplete statements characteristic of oral communication have been eliminated, I have tried scrupulously to preserve Donatelli's language and modes of expression in order to convey accurately a sense of the man as well as his remembrances. Excluded are his comments about memorable players, managers, and games as they conform in all essentials to what has been said ad nauseam on those subjects. We have ample testimony, for example, that Jackie Robinson was "a terrific base stealer and a great hitter." What is emphasized here is unique information pertaining to Donatelli's personal life, his umpiring career, his thoughts on the art of umpiring, and his role in organizing the umpire's union.

"I spent most of my life in coal mining towns of Cambria County in western Pennsylvania. I was born in the small town of Heilwood on August 22, 1914. When I was about two months old, my family moved over to Bakerton, where I grew up, went to high school, and joined the service during World War II. After I got married, my wife, Mary Lou, and I moved to Ebensburg, the county seat, where we raised our four children, two girls and two boys. I lived in Ebensburg even after I got to the majors, and for 16 years worked during the off-season as a goodwill representative for National Distilleries (even though I never drank whiskey). We moved to Florida a few years before I retired in 1973.

"My parents were from Italy. They immigrated over here around 1900, and my father, Tony, went to work in the coal mines. There were eight children in our family; I was number five. The oldest and youngest were girls; the rest boys. All the boys worked in the mines. It was dangerous and hard work, but what else were you going to do? I started even before graduating from high school. Times were tough then because of the Depression. Jobs were scarce, so I was glad to have the work. I did everything—worked outside as a coal dumper and inside as a loader and a spragger.[1]

"Sports was our main recreation. Two of my brothers were pretty good boxers, one was a Golden Gloves champ and the other had about 50 professional fights. I played football and basketball and ran track in high school. There was no baseball team, but we played pick-up games and after graduation I played in an industrial league while working in the mines. I was a decent, scrappy shortstop, so decided to give pro baseball a try. My father was very encouraging [about this] as a way of getting out of the mines. Tom Monaghan, the famous scout, signed me with the St. Louis Browns. I started out in the local Penn State League [Class D Pennsylvania Association], but it folded financially. Then I played in the Kitty League [Class D Kentucky–Illinois–Tennessee], and was sent back to the Penn State League with Beaver Falls. I only played 14 games [BA .266] when the league folded again in 1938, so I went back to the mines.

"I was loading coal when World War II broke out. Being single, I figured I was near to being drafted, so I enlisted in the Air Force. Like a lot of young guys, I felt it was something I had to do, not to escape the mines but because you just felt it was up to you to get into it. My basic training was at Lowry Field near Denver. When they found out I was a ballplayer, they offered me the rank of staff sergeant if I would play for the base team. So I played ball while going to armor and gunnery school. I went into combat in October 1943 and flew 18 missions as a tailgunner on a B-17 before getting shot down. I'll never forget it. We were shot down before the [June 6, 1944 D-Day] invasion, on the first daylight bomber raid on Berlin [March 6, 1944]. It was a rough mission—fighters diving at us, 20-millimeter shells exploding all around. We flew into the clouds to hide. What action! That day 68 bombers were shot down. We got hit, so the crew bailed out. I got captured and taken to Frankfurt. I spent about 15 months in prison camps. We changed camps three times; the Germans kept moving us around so the Russians couldn't liberate us.

"Early in the winter we marched from Frankfurt to the first camp, Heydekrug, about 40 miles south of Memel, Lithuania. It was no picnic. Sixty men to a barracks, ten men to a table. No food, no clothes, cold in the winter, and wait, wait, wait. Being a non-com[missioned officer], I didn't have to work. You just sat around and waited for the next meal—if you got it. We were supposed to get a slice of bread a day; sometimes we would, sometimes we wouldn't. There was no coffee, just something black like coffee made of boiled weeds of some kind. Occasionally we would get some soup with wheat and whatever vegetables the Germans could find. Turnips mostly; lots of diced turnips. Potatoes occasionally. Horsemeat if they had it. We'd fill a bucket with water, toss in the vegetables, cook it for a while, and had a water bucket of soup. It was pretty bad, but, what the hell, you ate it to keep from starving. The Germans couldn't give us much because they didn't have anything themselves. After about six months, we started getting Red Cross parcels once a week. There was supposed to be one parcel per man, but there was never enough so we shared—one package for four men. We got cigarettes, but that's when I quit smoking. I'd trade my cigarettes for food. Cliff Barker, who was later an All-American basketball player at the University of Kentucky, was in our group. He smoked, and would trade me bread for my cigarettes. He still owes me about half a loaf.

"Believe it or not, I started umpiring in the prison camp at Heydekrug. When I bailed out, I broke a bone in my ankle and couldn't do anything for a time. The guys played

Willie Mays pleads with Augie Donatelli in a 1973 World Series game. (Photo courtesy of the National Baseball Library, Cooperstown, N.Y.)

softball for recreation. There were lots of English POWs in the camp; some of them had been there for three years. They had a few softballs and bats, but almost no other equipment. Each of the barracks had a team, so there were games going on all the time. I would sit on the sidelines and watch the games—good gosh, what unbelievable rhubarbs they had over rules and judgment calls. They couldn't find any good umpires. Some of the guys found out that I had played ball and asked me if I had ever umpired. I had never umpired before and it didn't strike me that I should umpire. But I wanted to see that the games were run right and by the rules, so I started umpiring and was put on the rules committee. When you are behind the plate, they find out if you could really umpire. I must have done okay, because pretty soon the whole compound was coming after me. There was no way I could get out of it, so I umpired one game after another.

"Toward late summer my leg started healing, and I wanted to get out there and play. The guys in my barracks wanted to win the championship, so they decided we needed a manager. I took over as manager, held try-outs, and let the best guys play. There was some dissension over that, but I told them that's what we had to do to win. Barker pitched and played first base, and we won the championship. About two days after we won the championship, the Russians started a major offensive [September 1944] and the Germans started marching us again. Those who couldn't walk, the sick and wounded, were loaded into box cars.

"They took us to Stettin, a port on the North Sea, and crammed us into the hold of a ship for two days. There must have been 2,500 of us in there—hot as hell, no water, no toilet. You had to go on deck to take a leak, but no way you could have a bowel movement. When they took us off the ship, they chained two guys together at the wrists, and ran us about three miles to a place call Griefenhagen. As we went through this little town, the guards were hitting us with bayonets, the people were chasing us, the dogs were barking and chasing us—what a mess that was. After a few months, they started walking us again, this time to Neubrandenburg, north of Berlin.

"On the march to Neubrandenburg, another prisoner and I escaped. It was his idea. He said it would be easy to sneak away, and it was. On the march we were herded into barns every night. The guards couldn't take a count of prisoners because we were all split up, and guys were always going in and out of the barns because there was so much dysentery. It got dark real early, so about 6:30 one night we knocked on the barn door, went outside acting like we were going to the latrine, and took off into the woods. We were so afraid of being caught, we kept running almost all night. The next morning we were tired and cold, so we dug about 6 to 8 feet into a frozen haystack and tried to sleep. We slept for a while, but it was so cold in there that we had to crawl out and start walking again. We headed east, hoping to run into the Russians. They had started an offensive all right, but had been stopped by the Germans.

"We survived for about 10 days before being recaptured. Most of the farms in the area were worked by Polish or Russian labor and my partner, who was Polish, could speak both languages. We would approach people working on the outskirts of the farm and find out if they were being guarded or not. At one farm, two of the Polish laborers were ex-soldiers, so they let us sleep in the barn and fed us. One day we went down to where the people were working in the field, we ran into the overseer. No one told us that he would be there; it was an unpleasant surprise. He immediately recognized us as air corpsmen because of our clothes, so he pulled a gun, and took us to his home. He put us into the cellar, which was made into a jail, and called the Germans. Three or four hours later two guards picked us up and started hiking us toward Neubrandenburg.

"Neubrandenburg was a huge camp with maybe 15,000 prisoners of all the nationalities in the war. The war was coming to an end, and the Germans were rounding up prisoners from all over. Only privates, not officers, were supposed to work, but my penalty for escaping was to work for a week cutting timber for fortifications, digging trenches and burial pits and stuff like that. The burial pits were for the Russians, who didn't get a military burial like the Allies under the Geneva Convention; they were just dumped into the pit. After about three months, the Russians liberated us [April 1945].

"When I got back home, I thought about umpiring. I was 29 years old and knew the chance of making it as a player was gone. I didn't want to go back to the mines, so I thought maybe if I was lucky I could make it to the Big Time as an umpire. I talked with Elmer Daily, the president of the Penn State League, about it, and he recommended that I go to the Bill McGowan Umpire School in Cocoa Beach, Florida. My family encouraged me. You had to do something to get out of the mines, so away I went.

"I went down to McGowan's that winter on the GI bill. It was the only umpire school at that time, and there were maybe 100 guys at the school—big guys and small guys, young guys and old guys.[2] Most of them were umpires and four or five already had professional contracts. During the day we umpired games to learn proper mechanics and apply the rules. At night we had "skull" classes where McGowan would give us some pointers and tell us about umpiring in the majors. You worshipped a guy like that who was in the majors.

"I never thought I would get a job, but I got a lucky break. After about four weeks, during one of the camp games, I handled the call on a steal at second base. Al Somers, a professional umpire who was the only instructor at the school, happened to see the play and immediately went to McGowan and said 'I think the little Italian kid is a prospect. Keep your eye on him.' (I found this out later.) The next day McGowan came out to watch the students, and it was my turn on the field again. That night, during class, McGowan called Al over and said 'Hey, what's that guy's name?' Al didn't know my name, so he points and says 'That's him back there.' We were all looking around because we didn't know who in the hell he's pointing to. So McGowan says: 'I have something I have to tell you. We have a fellow in here that is going to be in the major leagues in four years.' We were all wondering 'Who in the hell is this?' McGowan kept on with his little speech: 'I watched him out there and he's doing a hell of a job. He is the most outstanding student we have.' And then he points at me. I thought, 'Jesus, he doesn't mean me.' I looked around behind me. He said, 'No, no. You. You!' I couldn't believe it: 'Me?' 'That's right, you. You've got it kid. We feel that you will be in the majors in four years.' I couldn't sleep that night. Here I was, just out of the service, at loose ends, going to umpire school on the GI bill just hoping to get a job, and the man says I can be a major leaguer some day. It was one of my biggest thrills in baseball, I'll tell you!

"So I came out of the school pretty highly rated. My first contract, 1946, was with the Pioneer League [Class C] for $150 a month and no expenses. A fellow from Pittsburgh, Pete Donett, and myself were teamed up as partners. We didn't have a car, so we rode the buses on those long trips through Idaho and Utah—Boise, Pocatello, Idaho Falls, Twin Falls, Ogden, Salt Lake City. It was pretty rough in the low minors—all kinds of rhubarbs, guys coming down to the edge of the screen and yelling and challenging you to fight them, police escorts to get you out of the ball park, things like that. When I got back home, the family didn't know what kind of a year I had. I told them, 'When you're umpiring, you're lucky if you last a season. They fire you.' They didn't fire me, and in October I got married.

"In January I went back to the school. I couldn't believe it, but McGowan made me an instructor. The minor leagues were booming after the war, and lots of veterans on the GI bill started showing up at the school. McGowan had to form two classes of about five weeks each; there must have been 300 men in both classes. After a few years it started to slack off. The boys thought it would be easy to get to the majors, but a lot of them got fired and a lot of them quit because it was hard work and no money in the minors.

"In 1947, my second year, I was promoted to the Sally League [the South Atlantic League, Class A], with a raise to $300 a month plus $6 or $7 a day for expenses. In mid-season the National League bought my contract for $2,000 and farmed me [August 15, 1947] to the International League [Class AAA]. Now I'm getting $600 a month, $350 salary and $250 expenses. There was better organization and more police protection in AAA, and the rhubarbs weren't as bad as in the low minors. But you didn't have any smooth sailing, that's for sure. It is very difficult in the minors because there are only two umpires. On the other hand, there is no better place than the minors to be scouted because there *are* only two umpires. Class will quickly show, no question about it.

"In my case, I was told that Branch Rickey was at a game one night when I was behind the plate and that he recommended somebody come down to see me. Bingo! Bill Klem got a hold of me. He saw me work a game and afterwards called me into his office. 'Look,' he said 'you use the inside protector.'[3] I had been using the outside protector, but said 'All right. I can do that.' And I did. I was in the International League for two years. I was supposed to go up the second year, but Ford Frick [president of the National League] called me into his office and told me they were bringing up Lon Warneke, the great pitcher, instead of me. But, he said, I would get the starting major league salary of $5,000. When I hit the majors in 1950—four years, just like McGowan said—I got a salary of $5,500 plus $15 a day expenses and free transportation. That was big money then.

"I broke in at the Polo Grounds with the [New York] Giants and the [Boston] Braves. Leo Durocher and Billy Southworth. My first game behind the plate was in Brooklyn, St. Louis and the Dodgers. It was a hell of a thrill being in the major leagues. I was hoping and praying that I'd get everything right, give all the ability that I could put together. My first crew was Al Barlick and Lee Ballanfant. There were three-man crews in the major leagues at the time, but in a few years they went to four umpires. It was difficult to cover plays even with three men. Hellsfire, if you couldn't move, man, you had problems. I worked with Barlick off and on for 6 or 7 years, then worked with Jocko Conlin, and then I became a crew chief myself in 1962.

"I was the first guy to come into the National League from an umpire school, and the older guys took me a little lightly at first, but there was no animosity at all.[4] When they found out that you are a decent guy and that you intended to run the game, they worked with you. They had to. After all, there are three of you out there, and if one of you is in trouble, the three of you are in trouble. Barlick and Ballanfant were real good in helping me break in. Ballanfant was the best for breaking in young fellows because he was such a nice guy—you had to like him and feel welcome on the crew. They gave me pointers, discussed the rules, and helped with mechanics a little bit. I'd also learn just by watching them. Sometimes I followed their advice and examples, sometimes I'd decide to do it another way. Actually, being at school was an advantage. You were ahead of the other fellows because you were alert on all the rules. Most umpires would read the rule book once or twice and then put it away. But when you are at the school for six weeks, you learned the rules and then applied them on the field so that they would stay with you. Umpiring is not a matter of quoting a rule, but applying it on the field.

"The best umpires I worked with were Al Barlick, Larry Goetz, and Jocko Conlan. They had what it takes to be a good umpire. First, they had the respect of the ballplayers, which is very important. They could make calls and get away with it, when another guy would get hell for the same thing. They were feared, in a way; players knew they were running the game and would toss them if they got too nasty. The more ability you had and the meaner you were, the more respect you got on the field. Also, they had very good judgment—about 1-2-3 in that respect. (I never understood how ballplayers, fans, or anyone else could question my judgment. All they had to do is look at my wife, Mary Lou, and they'd know I didn't make mistakes.) Other umpires might have judgment just as good, but didn't run the game or—I don't like to admit it—worked the political end of it. You must have respect and run the game; if you don't, when the time comes the ballplayers will cut you to pieces.

"The worst situation I was ever in happened a few years after I got to the majors. I almost got into a fight with Leo Durocher, who was managing the [New York] Giants. It was the first game of a Sunday doubleheader at the Polo Grounds [August 17, 1952]. Max Surkont was pitching for the [Boston] Braves. The whole game Durocher was screaming at Al Barlick, who was behind the plate, that Surkont was marking up the ball, spitting in his glove, and stuff like that. (At that time there weren't too many spitballs being thrown; the rules weren't relaxed as much as they have been recently.) Barlick ignored him, and Surkont kept getting them out and Durocher kept beefing. Then, in the top of the ninth, with the Braves leading [7–3], Durocher started raising hell. While waiting for his relief pitcher [Hal Gregg] to come in from the bullpen, he knelt right down on the mound, covered the ball with dirt, and started roughing it up. You can't let a man show up an umpire like that, so I ran right in from second base and asked to see the ball. But he tossed it to the pitcher instead. I said something, he said something, and I chased him. He went berserk, probably because he didn't expect it. He hadn't been into an argument with an umpire, yet I chased him. He got so mad that a couple of players and coaches grabbed him to keep him from charging me. I was waiting for him. I wasn't going to run from him; you can't be run out of the ball park. Besides, he wasn't that strong a guy, a man who couldn't be beat with fists. I knew a little bit about fighting; maybe he did too. While he was trying to get loose from the players, he was yelling some beautiful names at me. So I yelled some back at him and said 'Let him go. Let the man go.' Fortunately, they didn't let him go; he actually had to be dragged off the field. That's the closest I ever came to protecting myself. In my report I told the league president [Warren Giles] what I said to Durocher and what he said to me. Leo got fined [$100] and suspended [5 days].

"Umpiring is more than applying the rules and handling situations: you must be alert mechanically, be in the right position. That's important: you've got to be in the right position to call a tough play. If you're not in the right position and you guess at it, that is not good and you'll really catch hell. There is also a timing element involved here. You've got to wait that split second and then make the call. A split second. You can't call it too quick or too slow. You'll be wrong or look bad if your timing is bad, especially behind the plate where there are so many decisions to make. When I was working, Chris Pelekoudas was one of the best umpires—in the top ten, maybe one of the top five. Some of the boys don't want to hear that, but it's so just the same. But he waited too long. He waited so long that sometimes the broadcaster would say a pitch was a "strike" and then he would signal "ball." It was so noticeable, even the other umpires didn't like his timing. Still, he seemed to be getting the calls right.

"The mechanics in making a call are also important. You have to be decisive, and I always made a simple but very decisive motion. But no gestures, no dancing or jumping around. Toward the end of my career, some of the boys started 'showboating.' To me, showboating is out because you start taking your eyes off the ball and thinking more about how you make a particular call than the play itself. For example, Ed Sudol had the mannerisms of an acrobat; there's no room for it, no time for it. It's absolutely wrong. I don't know why he did it. Now take Ron Luciano over in the other [American] league. It appeared that he was showboating, but he was as serious as he could be. He applied a few more gestures on a call, but he was not really showboating. He was that way, so that's the way he umpired. It was natural; he never took his eye off the play or went into a dance or something like that.

"Of course, experience is the big thing. When an umpire gets to the big leagues, he is sure he knows all there is about baseball. But an umpire should improve each year. First, you learn the importance of timing on your calls. Second, you get better at running the game. Third, you can handle the difficult situations more smoothly. Fourth, constant repetition as a pitch-caller or a play-caller automatically improves a man if he keeps hustling. Fifth, you're supposed to know all the rules—and keep them in your head—but after so many years you really acquire knowledge of the laws of the game. Sixth, with greater experience comes greater execution of the rules.

"When I broke into the majors racial integration was still underway. The Dodgers had the most Negroes with Jackie Robinson, Roy Campanella, Don Newcombe, and Dan Bankhead, but there were other colored boys coming in. There weren't any real problems with Negroes coming into the majors. Of course, in spring training down South there was still the Negro section of the bleachers and separate restrooms, things like that. What I remember most is how the Negroes would flock to the games to watch the Dodgers. There would be more Negroes than whites. Wherever Jackie Robinson was, boy, how they would draw them. They used to get 10,000 people, easy, in Miami with Robinson.

"The biggest thing that happened during my career was the Major League Umpires Association, and I am proud that I helped get it organized. I started out in the majors making a pretty good salary—at least it seemed like it to me, a young guy from the coal mines. But, then, the cost of things kept getting higher and higher, and we weren't making a salary you could brag about. Also, some of the boys weren't getting raises. It wasn't right: You've got to give a major leaguer a raise to keep with the economy. Then of course there wasn't much of a pension—$100 for every year in the majors [with 15 years minimum service]. Maybe that seemed like a lot of money back when it was started in the 1930s, but didn't seem like much now. And we didn't get medical insurance or benefits like that.

"Anyway, I started talking to Jocko Conlan about it. I knew that he would be retiring pretty soon. I'd call him aside and tell him that he wasn't going to have anything after he retired except his home. Jocko was always bragging because he was the highest paid umpire in the league, but I knew he didn't have much money in the bank because he was a high liver. I told him I was also thinking about myself and the other umpires, too. Several times I said: 'Look, Jock. We can do something. You and me, we can do something about this.' I had an ace in the hole—Al Barlick, another boy from the coal mines. Barlick, like Jocko, was well respected. They were the top umpires in the league, so they were the guys I had to go to right away. I knew I couldn't go to everybody. Some of the boys were afraid of losing their jobs if they spoke up for something, and some of them were, well, liked by the league more than some of the others.

"All of a sudden, during the 1963 season, Jocko says: 'Alright. What do you want me to do?' So I told him. He said: 'What the hell are you talking about? You can't do that!' I said, 'The hell we can't. We can do it. We can form an association.' Jocko was interested, but worried. 'Half of these guys won't go along with it,' he said. I told him: 'That's right. We don't need half of them. All we need is half a dozen.' Then I went to Barlick, who said: 'Anything you do is all right with me.' Bingo!

"We started with telephone calls to every umpire in the league. Jocko, who was from Chicago, was supposed to get this judge to be our representative, but he retired or something and we couldn't get him. So Jocko got what he thought was the next best thing, his attorney, John Reynolds. We got the boys together in Chicago on an off-day and discussed an association. Barlick, Jocko, Tom Gorman, Shag Crawford, and I were elected to the board of directors. We had two or three meetings in all, and of the 24 umpires in the league, maybe eight or ten would go against us in the meetings. I remember every one of them.

"The last meeting was in May 1964, another layover day in Chicago. Reynolds did all the legal paperwork for us, and all of a sudden we have to get the guys to sign the papers forming the association. When it got down to the last day, when we wanted to meet with the owners and get them to recognize us as an association, the other guys had gone on to their games and there was only four of us left, Al Barlick's crew—Barlick, Stan Landes, Mel Steiner, and myself. Reynolds met with us at our hotel at 10 in the morning. We were supposed to be at the ball park at 11:30 for a game. 'I'll tell you fellows,' he said, 'they will fire you if you don't go along with the president of the league [Warren Giles] because the other fellows are done with it.' I thought about it, and decided that I had gone this far and was going to go the rest of the way. So, I said: 'John, I'm speaking for myself. I'm going the rest of the way. If we don't have an association, I'm going to go right to the first reporters I see and tell them what happened. That's the only way, because if I get fired, they will want to know why I got fired and I'm going to tell them.' I was hoping one or two of the other guys would speak up and do the same thing. Barlick spoke up first: 'Augie, I'm with you.' The other guys came along too. So we told Reynolds 'Go ahead and tell Giles we are standing for our rights. We are going to hold the fort. If the rest don't do it, the heck with it. Let Giles do whatever he wants.' Then we went on to the ball park and worked the game. Maybe our last one, who knows?

"What do you think happened? I don't know whether the owners called Giles, or Giles was approached by somebody else, or if Giles came to a decision on his own. Anyway, he told our attorney that he would meet with us umpires the following week. The following week we met with him and started not asking for things but *demanding* things that were right for us. We wanted a better pension, higher salaries, regular raises, fringe benefits, and more expense money. They finally agreed to all those things. That's how we started the association [National League Umpires Association].

"Of course the owners and the league president, Warren Giles, didn't like it.[5] And Giles certainly was not happy with me for getting the thing going. I had some discussions with him that he didn't like. He had just given us a raise in pension before the association came together, but I had to tell him the truth, that he wasn't helping us enough. Maybe he felt he was, but he sure wasn't generous enough. But let's face it: Giles had a job to do. He had to protect the league and his job. He was against our organization and so was his assistant, Fred Fleig. We got a lot of bad publicity in the press. The league wouldn't talk to us about it; hell, at first Giles wouldn't even meet with us. But eventually they came around.

"I don't know why Giles didn't just fire me. He could have. Maybe he respected me in a way. And I never missed a day's work—that helped a heck of a lot. But I was demoted from crew chief and assigned to Barlick's crew for the 1964 season. In fact, Giles put the four of us together because he thought we were instigators. I guess he thought he was punishing us, but actually it was the best thing he could have done for us because it kept us together all the time. Maybe he would have been better off putting each one of us on a different crew.

"The American League umpires didn't form an association at the time, so they fell far behind us in salaries, pensions, and fringe benefits. We wanted them to join the association so major league umpires would all be the same with regard to salaries and benefits.

We promised that we would back them if they wanted to join us, but they were afraid of getting fired.[6] Their league president, Joe Cronin, had them all tied up. They couldn't voice their opinion on anything. Finally, two of them, Al Salerno and Bill Valentine, tried to organize the American League umpires and got fired [September 16, 1968] for it.[7] That got the American League boys organized and they joined our association. But then Salerno and Valentine asked us to back them in suing the league. That was their downfall. We did back them, but not enough of us. We had a meeting, and about a quarter or a third of the umpires walked out when Salerno and Valentine started demanding that we should back them. I agreed with them. I got up and made a speech saying the same thing. 'Yes,' I said, 'they made a grave mistake. Sure they did. But we promised to back them and we have got to back these boys. We ought to have a vote on it.' We had a vote and there [were] only maybe nine or ten of us left—only six or seven in the National League and two or three in the American League stood up for backing them.

"Cronin later agreed to hire them back, but he wanted them to go down to the minors for a couple of months to get sharpened up or whatever, and even said they would get their major league salaries and benefits. But they wouldn't do it. I know how they felt. After all, it was embarrassing to be fired. Still, umpiring isn't too bad. I was a coal miner, and I always thought about the mines when things got tough.

"Two years later I was involved in the first umpires' strike. It was for the same thing—more money. The association was trying to negotiate a raise for the playoffs and the World Series, but the league presidents [Charles 'Chub' Feeney and Joe Cronin] wouldn't see eye-to-eye on that. So we went on strike [October 3, 1970] for the first game of the championship playoffs. I was in Pittsburgh, and instead of working the game I was pounding the cement walks with picket signs. I wasn't worried about losing my job that time, but I was worried about the public. After all, the fans pay all of us, even the league presidents and the commissioner. I didn't want to hurt the feelings of the people who went to the park that day to see the game. We got blamed because four minor league umpires were out there in our place. None of us umpires liked that; none of us wanted to be on strike. The strike only lasted one day. I was on the board of directors of the association, and the next morning we met with Feeney. A few days later, we got our raises. (The minor leaguers thought they would go to the majors because they worked out of turn. One of them [Hank Morgenweck] was brought up, but he didn't last.)[8]

"I had a great career. Twenty-four years. I am proud of the fact that I missed only one game in 24 years. I had lots of thrills, especially All-Star games and the World Series. You can't describe the feeling of excitement that pervades a World Series game. Sure, I felt the butterflies and the pressure and the responsibility. I worked with lots of great ballplayers—Stan Musial, Steve Garvey, Gil Hodges, Willie Mays; pitchers like Warren Spahn, Robin Roberts, Sandy Koufax, Bob Gibson. I have so many special memories: I was behind the plate [October 8, 1961] when Whitey Ford set the record for scoreless innings [32] in the World Series,[9] when Don Drysdale got the record [June 8, 1968] for the most consecutive shutout innings [58] in a season, when Stan Musial hit five homers in a doubleheader [May 2, 1954] and when he got his 3,000th base hit, and when Nate Colbert hit five homers and had the most RBIs [13] in a doubleheader [August 1, 1972]. I'll never forget Elroy Face winning about 20 games and losing only 3 or 4 [18–1] as a relief pitcher [1959]; even though the Pirates had a lot of power and could come from behind, that was really unusual.

"After I umpired my last game, I thought, well, I'm glad to be going home. I had a good career with lots of wonderful memories. But I missed my friends, the profession itself, and baseball—my number one game. I also missed the competitiveness. And it was hard to lose the money—hey, I was dragging down a pretty good salary when I left. I still think about it every now and then. I hope I'm remembered as a just, fair, honest umpire who called them as they were and as he saw them. And the Association was damn important to me. It went through, and it certainly is helping the boys who are in there now. It helped us a lot too, but it is too bad that we couldn't have been of the age where we could have enjoyed it more. I wanted to include the old fellows already on pension, but the boys wouldn't go for it. Today the Umpires Association is very powerful. Now the boys get just about whatever they ask for. But then we were risking our jobs just to get it organized. Things are so much better now—pension, working conditions, everything. And the boys are getting the salary. Even though they have to pay a lot of income tax, they are getting the salary. That's the important thing, isn't it?"

NOTES

1. A "spragger" controlled the speed of coal cars in mines by inserting or removing a metal rod called a "sprag" between the spokes of its wheels. Along steep sections of track the speed of the cars was slowed by inserting sprags to "lock" the wheel so that it slid instead of rolled along the track; the subsequent removal of sprags had the effect of speeding up the cars.

2. National League umpire George Barr established the first umpire school in Arkansas in 1935; American League umpire McGowan opened the second school in 1939 in Mississippi. Barr's school closed during World War II, while McGowan moved his operation to Florida.

3. Upon retiring in 1941 from years of service as a National League umpire, Klem, "The Old Arbitrator," served to his death in 1951 as the chief of umpires (i.e., supervisor and head scout) for the Senior Circuit. He made his preference for wearing a light-weight chest protector inside the jacket when umpiring behind home plate virtually mandatory for National League umpires, while his counterpart in the American League, Tommy Connolly, made the use of the large, inflated "balloon" protector held in front of the chest synonymous with Junior Circuit umpires. The distinction between the two leagues persisted until the 1970s, when the inside protector earned universal adoption.

4. William F. "Bill" McKinley, who attended both the Barr and McGowan schools, was the first graduate of an umpire school in the majors, being called up to the American League in August 1946.

5. When Ford Frick was named commissioner of baseball in 1951, Giles, then president of the Cincinnati Reds, replaced him as president of the National League. In his first year in office he increased the pension for umpires from $100 to $150 per year, and in May 1964 raised it to $200; the initial agreement with the Umpires Association increased it to $300.

6. American League umpires were hesitant to unionize in part because President Will Harridge had summarily fired umpire Ernest D. Stewart in 1945 for alleged unionizing activities. See Larry R. Gerlach, *The Men in Blue: Conversations with Umpires* (New York, 1980), 123–126.

7. Ostensibly fired for alleged "incompetence," both were veteran American League umpires—Salerno since 1961 and Valentine since 1962.

8. Although the strike affected both the Baltimore–Minnesota and the Cincinnati–Pittsburgh championship playoff games, umpires picketed only the National League park. Negotiations resulted in new pay scales for both league playoffs (from $2,500 to $4,000) and the World Series (from $6,500 to $8,000). One of the AAA arbiters who worked the Reds–Pirates game, Henry C. Morgenweck, later umpired in the American League from 1972 to 1975.

9. Ford, who left the game in the sixth inning with a sore foot, extended the record on October 4, 1962, to 33.3 innings; he had broken Babe Ruth's mark of 29.2 scoreless innings set in 1918.

Dusty Rhoads

BRETT C. MILLIER

Among the misunderstood but closely held relics my family moved from house to house during my childhood were a pair of baseballs, real hard balls, autographed in a thin, wavering hand by my great-grandfather, Dusty Rhoads. We held a dim collective memory that Dusty had been a major league baseball player, but we were neither athletes nor fans and anyway the major leagues hadn't much reality for little kids in southeastern Kansas in the early 1960s. The baseballs were inscribed to my brothers, but enjoyed somewhat inconsistent protection from my mother, who saw that they never made it into so much as a game of catch. This wasn't a problem; they hardly played.

Dusty was an old man by the time we knew him—79 when I was born, mostly deaf, and slowed by the tuberculosis he'd contracted many years before. He was so old I was afraid of him. His house smelled old. I crept around him, stealing glances at his long form curved into a rocking chair, plaid-shirted and dimly visible in the house darkened against the desert heat. His long arms and huge hands dwarfed the sturdy slats of the chair, and his chin rested on his chest. He had a hearing aid that he kept turned off; indeed he seemed impenetrable. He died when I was nine, leaving behind my much more vivid great-grandmother, some photographs of men identified in her careful script as Stan Musial, Honus Wagner, Connie Mack, and Ty Cobb, and several more autographed baseballs.

Twelve years later I found Dusty quite by accident in a baseball encyclopedia. I had become the lone fan in the family and was working as an intern at a sports magazine where someone advised me to familiarize myself with this valuable research tool. When I opened it up, there he was. To my uninitiated eyes, the account seemed dry and statistical, as remote as Dusty himself. He played eight years in the majors, six-and-a-half with Cleveland—"Cle A." He was a good pitcher, I discerned, with a lifetime 2.61 ERA, a .545 winning percentage, and 21 shutouts. He was 21–10, 1.80 in 1906; 18–12, 1.77 in 1908. He worked hard, 1,691.2 career innings with 154 complete games in 185 starts. He struck out more guys than he walked (522 to 494) and even hit .188 for his career. He was a right-hander, apparently strapping—6'1", 215.

Perhaps because my family is otherwise spectacularly devoid of athletes, perhaps because I needed a hook, a personal connection to legitimate my growing and unfeminine interest in baseball—for whatever reason, I suddenly wanted to know who this man was, what his entry in the baseball encyclopedia signified, why someone else had found him important when we had not. The encyclopedia entry was just enough to enliven my memory of the dim and gnarled figure in the rocking chair, to make me want to know what his life had been.

Perhaps grandiosely, I began at Cooperstown. The Hall of Fame has a baseball autographed by Dusty in 1960, a Pacific Coast League ball just like the ones he gave to my brothers at about the same time. Five or six photographs show him in stylized poses in the uniforms of St. Louis and Cleveland—mid-motion, peering in for the sign, standing at attention. A questionnaire signed by Dusty gives the dates and places of his major league career. In the space following the question "If you had it all to do over, would you play professional baseball?" he wrote, "Yes." He was nominated to the Hall of Fame three times, but never made it, because, I was told, he played only eight years in the majors instead of the requisite ten.

A collector friend of mine found Dusty in the T-206 series of tobacco issue baseball cards, "Piedmont" and "Sweet Caporal" brands. He has the smooth boyish face that all the players of that era seemed to have, though his nose is bigger than most. He also appears in the various histories of the formation of the American League, and of the Cleveland Indians, known as the "Blues" and "Naps" when he played. Biographies of other more famous players refer to particular games he played and pitches he threw. The standard record books show him on various lists; his accomplishments are considered "modern." All of these accounts are confused about the spelling of his name—Rhodes, Rhoades, Roades. In the little town where he lived, the local paper chronicled his public life. My great-grandmother, grandmother, great-aunt and mother remember his masculine and fatherly charm; my great-uncle, his son, remembers the baseball stories.

Uncle Bob recalls his father's version of the beginning. At the age of 16, Barton Emery Rhoads was proving to be a disruptive force in the farming life of his Amish parents and their Wooster, Ohio, community. He wanted to play baseball. Some scout had come to town looking for talent, had seen Barton pitch and wanted him to go up to Cleveland for a tryout. Although in 1896 baseball seemed far from a fit occupation for his son, Barton's father took him to the tryout under duress. He didn't make the Blues that year, but was "shang-haied" into a contract with the Chicago Cubs, who sent him to Memphis of the Southern League. In 1902, he came up for the Cubs and pitched in 16 games, using the name "Bob Rhoads" to protect his family's reputation. He hated Chicago, he said, and at the end of the year was traded to St. Louis, which traded him home to Cleveland at midseason, 1903.

Bob Rhoads was near the heart of a truly great pitching staff in Cleveland in these early years of modern baseball. Addie Joss, Red Donohue, Bill Bernhard, Earl Moore, and Otto Hess were all in their primes. The team never won a pennant and was best known for its regular and intense midseason slumps, but it had pitching. In 1906 Joss, Hess, and Rhoads all won 20 games and had 27 shutouts and a 1.90 ERA between them. In 1908, when the Naps were knocked out of the race on the last day of the season by last place St. Louis, Dusty, as he was known by then, assured himself a measure of immortality by pitching a no-hitter against Frank Arellanes and the Red Sox, a 2–1 win ("I walked in the run") on September 18th. He gave up "nothing that even resembled a hit," the historians say. Two weeks later, Joss pitched a perfect game to cement his team's hold on first place. Dusty attributed his no-hitter to a new pitch he'd developed called the "Merry Widow Curve," but claimed he got more thrills that year by defeating St. Louis 6–5 while giving up 23 hits.

In 1909, Dusty had a bad year. He went 5 and 8 and at the end of that season, the Naps attributed his no-hitter to a new pitch he developed called the "Merry Widow Curve," Wrigley's Cubs. Dusty was furious; he belonged in Cleveland with his friends Joss and the great Napoleon Lajoie, player–manager of the team. He jumped the contract and headed for Canada. In 1910 he returned to play a few very successful minor league seasons in Kansas City, then wandered in the West for several years before finally settling in the desert of southern California, where he'd spent off-seasons tending cattle.

The "fashionplate righthander," as the papers called him, was an anomaly among ballplayers of his day. He "seemed rich," my grandmother told me. He dressed well and had a reputation as a man-about-several-towns. No one knew where his money came from in these days when baseball players made about $1,200 a season. The explanation became apparent during one of the club's several financial crises. It was near the end of spring training in 1904 and the Cleveland Blues were preparing to leave their San Antonio camp for a game in Dallas. Owner Charley Somers was flat broke and counting on gate receipts from two exhibition games to pay hotel bills and buy the team's train tickets. The weekend was rained out; there was no money for bills or food or train fare. So, the story goes, Dusty offered to help. That night at a crap table in the infamous Crystal Palace Casino in San Antonio, 23-year-old Dusty Rhoads parlayed Somers' $180 into the requisite $1,600, plus $200 more. He gave Somers the money for the bill and split the rest among his hungry teammates. The legend lives in the annals of the Cleveland Indians.

Having missed World War I because he was already going deaf, Dusty settled permanently near the Mojave Desert town of Barstow, California, in 1919. While tending a herd of Holstein cattle on a ranch near there, he met and fell in love with the cook, my great-grandmother, who had been widowed in the 1918 flu epidemic. Barstow grew pleased to have a famous baseball player in its midst, and he eventually cut a large figure in the small town. In 1937, 28 years after this last major league victory, they paid tribute by raising

Dusty Rhoads and granddaughter Frances in Barstow, California, c.1931. (Photo courtesy of Brett Millier.)

RHOADES, CLEVELAND

T-206 Tobacco Series Baseball Card, "Sweet Caporal" Brand, c.1909. (Photo courtesy of Brett Millier.)

enough money to send him to New York to see the Yankees–Giants World Series. Dusty hadn't seen a major league game in nearly 30 years and the trip was enormously important both to him and to his proud community. Years later he remembered it as one of the three great thrills of his life. The second was his first big league victory, and the third was "when Connie Mack rushed to meet me on his arrival in Barstow . . . although it had been more than 30 years since we met, after the first greetings it seemed only yesterday that we were, well, let's say, friendly enemies on the diamond." Mack came to Barstow in 1938 with the Pittsburgh Pirates, who had been so impressed with the town's generosity in the World Series trip that they drove out from their spring training site in San Bernardino to play an exhibition game. They stayed at the Beacon Tavern and the next day met a team of locals that Dusty and his friends had put together, the Barstow All-Stars. It had been a wet year on the desert, and the game was played on an old landing field because the park in town was still flooded. Dusty threw out the first pitch to his old friend Honus Wagner, but let the Pirates win, 7–2. Twenty years later, in 1958, the town again rallied to send Dusty to Cleveland for the 50th anniversary of his no-hitter. His relationship to California baseball after that year consisted of a fierce, transplanted hatred of O'Malley's Dodgers and enthusiastic, if distant, support of the San Francisco Giants. The Dodgers and Giants moved west the year I was born; in these prejudices I am indeed Dusty's descendant.

Dusty served the town of Barstow in a variety of capacities. He was a talented, if unlicensed, veterinarian. He had a gift for getting along with the crews of Mexican and Indian workers he managed in his career as a ranch foreman. He moved furniture, hauled mail, worked at the local supply depot during the war, painted boxcars for the Southern Pacific Railroad, whose "hump" yard and majestic station house still dominate Barstow's geography. He "built something," he said, "on Roosevelt's make work thing." My grandmother remembers that he maintained his easygoing air even when there was no money. "There'd be a pile of hot and sweaty kids in the back of the pick-up, then he'd come along and suddenly we'd all have soda pops. And this was during the Depression!" He was an unyielding umpire for the town's softball league and said he was fond of ending disputes by picking up the dissenter by the collar and the seat of his pants and tossing him back into the dugout. The town remembers him for the American flag and "Honor Board" he erected at the train station, on which were inscribed the names of local boys killed in battle since World War II.

Dusty liked himself best as the author of a column in the old *Barstow Printer* called "Dustin' 'em Off," which he began in 1938. There he took on whatever was news in Barstow, and applied his wisdom and gift for plain speech to problems of philosophy, baseball, and local affairs. He once noted that while visiting the local high school football practice, he saw boys sneaking puffs on cigarettes between workouts. "Football and cigarettes don't mix," he cautioned, "and anyhow, better wait until you're dry behind the ears before you start smokin'." He advised aspiring pitchers to "run or walk six to eight miles every day. . . . A pitcher lasts just as long as his legs." In chastising a local minister's grim suggestion that his congregation contemplate their lives as if they had only one day to live, he said righteously if not accurately, " . . . am under the impression that Christianity teaches the joy of living, rather than the fear of death."

Barstowers loved Dusty especially for the famous ballplayers he brought to town— Mack and Wagner, Stan Musial, and his best baseball buddy, Ty Cobb. Cobb had retired to Southern California and while the rest of the world frowned on his ill temper, he and Dusty were friends for nearly 30 years. My great-grandmother recalled that each of their several-times-yearly trips to the mountains to hunt or to Las Vegas to play ended violently, with Dusty storming off the train at the station after the inevitable falling out. A month or so later they'd be back together. Dusty was proud that Cobb had batted only .266 in 64 at-bats against him, and to have served as best man at Cobb's second wedding in 1949. Cobb called Dusty "crooked arm" to honor his distinguished screwball, and called him stupid for refusing to buy Coca Cola stock when Cobb married into that family.

Dusty lived the rest of his life in Barstow. He grew old and deaf and irascible. The tuberculosis made it hard for him to get around; more and more he retreated into the silence he created by shutting off the hearing aid. I'm sure he didn't know me from any of the other great-granddaughters. After all, I threw, and still throw, like a girl. But I no longer think of him bent in the rocking chair in the darkened house. Instead, he's pitching at Cleveland Stadium, pitching to Honus Wagner and the Pirates on a muddy landing field in Barstow, pitching a softball on a patch of green grass in the brown little desert town. He's shooting craps for train fare in the Crystal Palace in 1904. He's handing out soda pops to a pick-up load of dusty kids in 1930. He's expostulating in his elliptical style in the old *Barstow Printer*. He's running down the Southern Pacific platform in front of the big old stationhouse waving at Connie Mack, Ty Cobb, my great-grandmother, or Uncle Bob, just home from the war in the Pacific in 1945.

Baseball at Salisbury Prison Camp

JIM SUMNER

One of the best known and most intriguing portraits of 19th-century baseball is a sketch of a game between Union prisoners at the Salisbury, North Carolina Confederate prison. Drawn by Union Major Otto Boetticher, a New York artist who spent part of 1862 in the prison, the picture shows a pastoral, almost idyllic scene. Two teams of well-dressed, apparently well-fed teams square off in front of dozens of equally well-off spectators. Off to one side a group of men engage in what appears to be learned discourse, while dogs frolic around their feet. The spacious grounds, filled with trees and grass, resemble a park or college campus more than a prison.

It would be easy for skeptics to question the validity of the picture drawn by Major Boetticher. Although not as well-known as Richmond's Libby Prison or the notorious Andersonville Prison, the Salisbury facility exacted a gruesome toll on those held within its confines. According to the best modern estimates, approximately one-quarter of Salisbury's 15,000 total prisoners died while held there; victims of neglect, disease, malnutrition, and violence. Given these figures how accurate can Boetticher's famous portrait be? How widespread was baseball at the Salisbury Prison Camp and under what conditions was it played? More importantly how did this activity affect the lives and well-being of the prisoners and what does it say about prison life?[1]

By the advent of the Civil War baseball had evolved from a variety of children's bat and ball games to become a widely popular and surprisingly sophisticated sport, particularly in and around New York City. The National Association of Baseball Players boasted 54 teams at the highest level of competition in 1860 while countless less formal teams were spread throughout the North. Contrary to popular belief baseball was played in the antebellum South, although not to the same extent as in the North. It was particularly popular in New Orleans, which had seven organized teams in 1860. Such modern rules as the nine-inning game and the three-out inning were in place by that year.[2] Undoubtedly many Union soldiers had some exposure to the sport in the late antebellum period.

Both Civil War historians and sport historians agree that baseball was enormously popular in the Civil War with troops of both armies. Bell Irvin Wiley, the noted chronicler of the life of the everyday soldier, wrote that "baseball . . . appears to have been the most popular of all competitive sports" in the Union Army. On the other side of the lines Wiley notes, "Next to music Johnny Reb probably found more frequent and satisfactory diversion in sports than in anything else. When leisure and weather permitted, soldiers turned out in large numbers for baseball."[3] Other historians give accounts, perhaps exaggerated, of games witnessed by tens of thousands of soldier-spectators.[4] Yet these were games played behind the lines, in times of relative leisure and security. Could these circumstances be duplicated in the considerably less hospitable environment of a prison camp such as the one at Salisbury?

Salisbury is located in the western piedmont of North Carolina. At the beginning of the Civil War it was the largest city in that part of the state, with a population in 1860 of about 2,400. The core of the 11-acre prison grounds was a cotton factory built in 1840. It was adapted for prison use in late 1861 and began receiving prisoners in December of that year when 120 Union prisoners arrived. This modest trickle became a flood during the spring of 1862. By April over 1,400 prisoners occupied the camp, not all of whom were Union military prisoners of war. Salisbury always had varying numbers of Confederate prisoners, deserters, and civilians. The majority of 1862 prisoners were captured troops, however, many were already veterans of other Confederate prisons.[5]

According to contemporary sources baseball was played at the prison during the spring and summer of 1862 on an almost daily basis, weather permitting. It was one of a number of recreational pursuits, organized by and for the benefit of the prisoners during this period. There were several factors that allowed such activity. Despite the influx of prisoners into Salisbury, the prison was far from overcrowded. Indeed the facility, designed to hold about 3,000, seemed almost spacious in its early years. Prison food was bland and unappetizing but relatively abundant. The crude prison hospitals provided minimally competent medical care. Perhaps most importantly prisoners were exchanged on a fairly frequent basis, promoting a feeling of relative well-being.[6]

The best accounts of baseball in 1862 come from the diary of Charles Carrol Gray, a young Union physician from New York. Gray was only 23 when he was captured in the early days of the war at First Manassas (Bull Run). By the time he arrived at Salisbury, on May 17, 1862, Gray was a hardened veteran of prison life in Richmond, Charleston, and Columbia.[7] On May 22nd, less than a week after his arrival, he wrote, "Took a little walk in the evening and watched some of the officers play ball."[8] On June 6th Gray observed: "A good state of cheerfullness [sic], thanks to the open space is fairly prevailing. Ball play for those who like it and are able, walking, card playing as keep us in employment; but reading matter is about used up."[9] There are numerous other references to ball games in the Gray diary. Unfortunately for future historians Gray was a spectator not a participant and his entries are usually brief and uninformative. The absence of Gray from the camp ball games was possibly a result of disinterest but more likely can be blamed on a persistent stomach problem that forced him to bed on several occasions and led to his frequent use of opium for pain relief.[10]

Also captured at First Manassas was William Crossley, a Union soldier from Rhode Island. Crossley, like Gray, was shuttled in and out of several prisons prior to his arrival at Salisbury from Tuscaloosa, Alabama on March 13, 1862. On May 8th Crossley wrote in his diary that rumors were rampant that the prisoners would be paroled and "maybe that accounts for Johnnie [Reb] allowing us to have a concert in the big yard this afternoon."[11] On May 21 Crossley gives an account of a game matching newly arrived prisoners from Tuscaloosa and prisoners transferred from a prison in New Orleans:

> And to-day the great game of baseball came off between the Orleanists and Tuscaloosans with apparently as much enjoyment to the Rebs as the Yanks, for they came in hundreds to see the sport, and I have seen more smiles to-day on their oblong faces than before since I came to Rebeldom, for they have been the most doleful looking set of men I ever saw and that Confederate gray uniform really adds to their mournful appearance. The game was a tie, eleven each but the factory fellows were skunked three times, and we but twice.[12]

It is not clear what Crossley means by his reference to the "factory fellows." Since the prison was located at the site of an abandoned factory it is tempting to infer that he was referring to games involving Confederate guards. However, there are no other references to Confederates playing at this prison and it is likely Crossley was referring to a group of prisoners. It is clear, however, that the Confederates watched the games in large numbers and with some enthusiasm.

Other narratives confirm that prisoners formed teams along lines of previous imprisonment. Gray distinguishes some games as "match games," but typically fails to elaborate.[13] Some of the New Orleans prisoners who arrived in Salisbury in the early part of 1862 were paroled so quickly that one observer reported "it is much to be regretted that we have no official report of the match-games played in Salisbury between the New Orleans and Tuscaloosa boys, resulting in the triumph of the latter; the cells of the Parish Prison were unfavorable to the development of the skill of the 'New Orleans Nine.' "[14] These may have been the same games described by Crossley.

The papers of some of these prisoners who were moved from New Orleans to Salisbury were published in 1862 under the title *The Stars and Stripes in Rebeldom.* They further illuminate the nature of recreational activity in the latter prison. One paper tells of sophisticated theatrical productions put on by the prisoners: "Three of the rooms (containing 250 men each) had each a nicely arranged stage, with all the paraphernalia of theatrical accompaniment." Actors, machinists, carpenters, and decorators combined forces to put on a fare that ranged from pantomime to Shakespeare. Prisoners concluded that "friends at home might be setting down to poorer entertainments than those we were giving in that rebel prison."[15] As for outdoor activities one prisoner ironically credits the bad food with opening up recreational opportunities. Finding the food "most unhealthy and repulsive" this observer wrote that because of the diet "the privileges of the yard were extended only after the most urgent representations from the physician in charge, that more room was absolutely required for the existence of the men, that they must get out of

Union Major Otto Boetticher's rendition of life at Salisbury, c.1862.

doors." Once done the prisoners found that "since the men have the liberty of the yard [the quarters] are more endurable than at any other point in Rebeldom."[16]

What did the Confederates make of all this ballplaying? It is difficult to tell. In April 1865, during the dying days of the war and after the prison had been emptied of its prisoners, Salisbury was visited by the troops of Union General George Stoneman on his famous raid. Not surprisingly Stoneman allowed his troops to burn the prison. This destruction, as justified as it may have been, unfortunately resulted in the loss of prison records.[17] The one Confederate recollection we do have is by Adolphus W. Mangum. A native of Salisbury, Mangum served as prison chaplain in the later part of the war. In 1862, however, he visited the prison while on a trip home. Mangum tells of attending a dress parade:

> . . . with a number of ladies. When it was finished the officers among the prisoners came out and presented truly a beautiful scene in their recreation. A number of the younger and less dignified ran like schoolboys to the play ground and were soon joining in high glee in a game of ball. Others . . . sat down side by side with the prison officials and witnessed the sport.[18]

Mangum's account confirms the relatively benign picture painted by Union prisoners. It also confirms that Confederates both watched and enjoyed the ball games.

This summer of activity in Salisbury peaked on Independence Day, July 4, 1862. Prison officials forbade their charges from engaging in formal oratory on the holiday but apparently prohibited little else. In the morning the prisoners participated in a reading of both the Declaration of Independence and Washington's Farewell Address, augmented by prayer, music, and poetry readings. In the afternoon their celebrations were more physical and less cerebral. A pig race failed to come off when the swine, borrowed from the Confederates, "wouldn't run for Yankees." However, sack races, foot races, and blind-folded wheelbarrow races set the stage for the main event: a match game of baseball. The contest, in Gray's words:

> . . . excited much interest and . . . considerable money (theoretically) was staked. I lost to Fish a set of Kingsley's novels; knowing when I bet that the odds were much against me; but as I have always won of him before I gave him choice of sides. These trifles served to pass the day quite pleasantly. . . . The cheers given in the grove were a sort never before heard in Salisbury.[19]

Gray's reference to betting implies that it was a regular occurrence and indicates that the relative skill levels of the players were common knowledge in the prison.

During 1862 prisoners were exchanged from Salisbury on a frequent if irregular basis, depending on the inclinations of field commanders of both sides. Increased pressure to formalize these exchange procedures led to the Dix–Hill Cartel. The agreement, painstakingly negotiated between Union Major John Dix and Confederate Major D.H. Hill, set out formal terms of exchange. Its adoption in the summer of 1862 led to the wholesale exchange of prisoners. By the end of August Salisbury had been emptied of all Union military prisoners.[20]

Despite this removal of Union prisoners Salisbury was far from empty. From the fall of 1862 until the fall of 1864 the prison contained "Rebel convicts, Northern deserters, hostages, Southern Union men, and all persons that the enemy [the Confederacy] designed to hold."[21] It is not certain whether any of these prisoners engaged in baseball games. The best known prisoners during this period were Albert Richardson and Junius Henri Browne, both war correspondents for the *New York Tribune*. They were captured at Vicksburg, Mississippi, in July 1863, and transferred from Richmond to Salisbury in

February 1864. After their daring escape from Salisbury in December of that year both men published lengthy and popular memoirs of their war adventures.[22]

Both men agreed that prisoners had unusually frequent access to outdoor activities. In the words of Browne: "we preferred . . . [Salisbury] to the Castle or Libby, because we had the privilege of the yard, and had a daily opportunity to breathe the external atmosphere, and behold the overarching sky."[23] Richardson's account agrees with that of his compatriot:

> We found Salisbury comparatively endurable . . . the yard . . . , like some old college grounds, with great oak trees and a well of sweet, pure water, was open to us during the whole day. There the first time for nine months our feet pressed the mother earth, and the blessed open air fanned our cheeks."[24]

Other diarists agree that during this period Salisbury was a relatively comfortable prison, in large part because of its open spaces.[25] However, none of these men give any details on how this open space was used. Baseball may have been played but there is no firsthand evidence of any organized recreational activity. If indeed baseball was not played during this period it is an indication of how intimately associated the sport was with the Northern fighting man, who was largely absent from Salisbury at this time.

In October 1864 Salisbury changed again, this time much for the worse. The formal

Another 1862 view of Salisbury drawn by Sgt. Fred Will of the 20th Massachusetts volunteers. Note Will's signature and "prisoner of war" notation in the lower right-hand corner.

exchange cartel, so laboriously worked out in the summer of 1862, had broken down the next summer, largely over the question of Confederate treatment of captured black soldiers. However, some field exchanges took place through the end of 1863. The battles in the spring and summer of 1864 sent an unusually large number of captives into the prison systems of both combatants. Negotiations to resume exchanges were held but proved fruitless, due to the race question and the increasing Northern perception that the South stood to benefit from the proposed exchanges. It was this general overcrowding that resulted in the overcrowding of the Andersonville Prison and the subsequent decision to again send large numbers of military prisoners to Salisbury.[26]

In the early part of October 1864 about 7,500 prisoners were sent to Salisbury to join the approximately 800 political and civilian prisoners already there. From this time until February 1865 the prison was grotesquely overcrowded. Shortages of shelter, food, medicine, clothes, fuel, and other necessities of life, combined with severe winter weather and a total breakdown of prison control by the authorities led to a tragically high loss of life.[27]

Prisoners in this period agree that at this point Salisbury "changed into a scene of cruelty and horror."[28] Junius Henri Browne writes: "Imagine nine or ten thousand scantily clad, emaciated, woe-begone soldiers . . . in an inclosure of five or six acres, half of them without other shelter than holes they had dug in the earth, or under the small buildings employed as hospitals."[29]

With the prison overcrowded, the prisoners in poor health, and morale at an absolute low it is no surprise that formal recreation gave way to the more basic struggle for survival. None of the many accounts of Salisbury during this period mention any attempt at recreation. Albert Richardson alludes directly to their absence: " . . . no song, no athletic game, few rounds of laughter broke the silence of the garrison."[30] The most detailed account of this period was by an Iowa soldier, Benjamin Booth. Extremely bitter, the Booth recollection recounts the horror of these days in unusual detail but fails to give even a hint of organized recreational activity.[31] It seems safe to assume that there was no baseball played at Salisbury in late 1864 or early 1865.

In February 1865 a prisoner exchange agreement was reached that led to the exchange of all Union prisoners from Salisbury by early March. The prison was burned by General Stoneman on April 13, 1865, unmourned by both sides. Confederate Major John Gee, one of the last prison commandants, was later tried on several charges but was acquitted. The Salisbury National Cemetery now holds the remains of Salisbury's dead.[32]

The history of Salisbury prison camp can be divided into three distinct periods. During the second period, from September 1862 through September 1864, the opportunity for baseball and other outdoor activities clearly existed. However, the prison population was composed of several disparate groups who have left no clear record of any such activity. In the absence of such evidence the best that can be concluded is that baseball might have been played during this period. The brief but tragic third period was from October 1864 through February 1865. The best known memoirs of the prison come from this period and make it apparent that outdoor activities such as baseball were totally out of the question. Thus we are left with the first period, the spring and summer of 1862, when baseball was a major source of recreation for both officers and enlisted men.

What can we make of this activity? One of the long standing myths of Civil War baseball is that Southerners learned the game from the Yankee invaders and spread it throughout the South after the war, in the manner of sporting Johnny Appleseeds. Although the existence of baseball in certain portions of the antebellum South has been established it appears that baseball was played little if at all in prewar North Carolina and that the sport quickly attained a statewide popularity in the years after the war.[33] We know that

Confederates watched the games with some enthusiasm in 1862 and it is logical to assume that at least some of these men maintained this enthusiasm after the war. At the very least the ease with which these varied groups of prisoners organized games of baseball is an indication of how popular it had become in the antebellum North.

These Union prisoners weren't baseball evangelists of course, at least not in a conscious sense. More important is the question of how baseball affected the lives of these men. John Carrol Gray felt that baseball and other activities were "trifles" that served little more purpose than passing the time.[34] Other prisoners, however, felt that future generations "will judge the character of the prisoners of war by their occupations, and will find them to have been a thoughtful, energetic body of men . . . intelligent, hardy, and faithful; forming as it does probably an army of the highest character the world has ever seen."[35] The truth undoubtedly lies somewhere between. Trifles though they may have been, the baseball games played in the Salisbury prison camp during the spring and summer of 1862 were a means by which Union prisoners exerted some control over their environment and coped with their captivity.

1. Louis A. Brown, *The Salisbury Prison: A Case Study of Confederate Military Prisons, 1861–1865* (Wendell, NC: Avera Press, 1980), 162–166. The portrait is best seen, in color, in *The American Heritage Picture History of the Civil War* (New York: American Heritage Publishing Company, 1960), 382–383. Boetticher was born in Prussia around 1816 and established a studio in New York City in 1851. He served in the Sixty-eighth New York volunteers during the war. He was captured in 1862 and was briefly imprisoned in

"Bird's Eye View" of Salisbury by C.A. Kraus, 1864. The addition of the tents in this drawing may indicate the severe overcrowding that was plaguing the prison at this time.

Richmond's Libby Prison before being moved to Salisbury. Mark E. Neely, Jr., Harold Holzer, and Gabor S. Boritt, *The Confederate Image: Prints of the Lost Cause* (Chapel Hill, NC: University of North Carolina Press, 1987), 207.

2. Melvin L. Adelman, *A Sporting Time: New York City and the Rise of Modern Athletics, 1820–1870* (Urbana and Chicago: University of Illinois Press, 1986), 121–142; Harold Seymour, *Baseball: The Early Years* (New York: Oxford University Press, 1960), 3–39; David Quentin Voigt, *American Baseball: From Gentleman's Sport to the Commissioner System* (Norman, OK: University of Oklahoma Press, 1966), 3–13; Dale A. Somers, *The Rise of Sports in New Orleans, 1850–1900* (Baton Rouge: Louisiana State University Press, 1977), 49–51..

3. Bell Irwin Wiley, *The Life of Billy Yank: The Common Soldier of the Union* (Indianapolis and New York: The Bobbs-Merrill Company, 1952), 170; Bell Irwin Wiley, *The Life of Johnny Reb: The Common Soldier of the Confederacy* (Baton Rouge: Louisiana State University Press, 1943), 159. Also see Lawrence W. Fielding, "War and Trifles: The Meter Stick of the Civil War Soldier," *Journal of Sport History* 4 (Summer, 1977).

4. Voigt, *American Baseball,* 11; Seymour, *Baseball: The Early Years,* 40–41.

5. James S. Brawley, *The Rowan Story, 1753–1953: A Narrative History of Rowan County, North Carolina* (Salisbury, NC: Rowan Printing Company, 1953), 171–175.

6. Brown, *The Salisbury Prison,* 135–140; William Best Hesseltine, *Civil War Prisons: A Study in War Psychology* (Columbus, OH: Ohio State University, 1930), 65–66.

7. Finding aid for the John Carrol Gray Diary, Southern Historical Collection, University of North Carolina, Chapel Hill. After the war Gray recopied the diary for improved legibility. The page numbers cited are from the recopy.

8. Gray Diary, 174.

9. *Ibid.,* 182.

10. *Ibid.,* 183, 199.

11. William J. Crossley, *Personal Narratives of Events in the War of the Rebellion,* Series 6, No. 4 (Providence: Rhode Island Soldiers and Sailors Historical Society, 1903), 43.

12. Crossley, *Personal Narratives,* 43–44.

13. Gray Diary, 200, 212.

14. W.G. Bates (Ed.), *The Stars and Stripes in Rebeldom: A Series of Papers Written by Federal Prisoners (Privates) in Richmond, Tuscaloosa, New Orleans, and Salisbury, N.C.* (Boston: T.O.H.P. Burnham, 1862), 127.

15. *Ibid.,* 130–131. This *Stars and Stripes* should not be confused with the later military newspaper of the same name. See Herbert Mitgang, "At War With the *Stars and Stripes*," *American Heritage,* XXII, No. 3. April, 1971.

16. *Ibid.,* 134–135.

17. Brown, *The Salisbury Prison,* 150–154; John G. Barrett, *The Civil War in North Carolina* (Chapel Hill, NC: University of North Carolina Press, 1963), 357–359.

18. A.W. Mangum, "Salisbury Prison," in Walter Clark (Ed.), *Histories of the Several Regiments and Battalions from North Carolina in the Great War, 1861–1865* (Raleigh, NC: The State of North Carolina, 5 volumes, 1901), IV, 74; Finding aid: A.W. Mangum Papers, Southern Historical Collection, University of North Carolina, Chapel Hill, NC.

19. Gray Diary, 204–205.

20. Hesseltine, *Civil War Prisons,* 7–32; James M. McPherson, *Ordeal by Fire: The Civil War and Reconstruction* (New York: Alfred Knopf, 1982), 451–455; Brown, *The Salisbury Prison,* 4–6.

21. Junius Henri Browne, *Four Years in Secessia* (Hartford, CT: O.D. Case and Co., 1865), 315.

22. See also Albert D. Richardson, *The Secret Service, The Field, The Dungeon, and Escape* (Hartford, CT: The American Publishing Co., 1865).

23. Browne, *Four Years in Secessia,* 315–316.

24. Richardson, *The Secret Service, The Field, The Dungeon, and Escape,* 401.

25. See also Homer B. Sprague, *Lights and Shadows in Confederate Prisons: A Personal Experience, 1864–1865* (New York and London: G.P. Putnam's Sons, 1915); Willard W. Glazier, *The Capture, the Prison Pen, and the Escape* (New York: United States Publishing Co., 1868); Robert L. Drummond, "Personal Reminiscences of Prison Life During the War of the Rebellion," Southern Historical Collection, University of North Carolina, Chapel Hill. For a Confederate perspective see Louis A. Brown (Ed.), "The Correspondence of David Orlando McRaven and Amanda Nance McRaven," *North Carolina Historical Review,* XXVI, No. 1 (January, 1949). McRaven was a Confederate guard in 1864 and 1865.

26. McPherson, *Ordeal By Fire,* 455–456.

27. Hesseltine, *Civil War Prisons*, 169–170; Brown, *The Salisbury Prison*, 107–108.

28. Glazier, *The Capture, the Prison Pen, and the Escape*, 138.

29. Browne, *Four Years in Secessia*, 322.

30. Richardson, *The Secret Service, The Field, The Dungeon, and Escape*, 416.

31. Benjamin F. Booth, *Dark Days of the Rebellion, or Life in Southern Military Prisons Giving a Correct and Thrilling History of Unparalleled Suffering, Narrow Escapes, Heroic Encounters, Bold Achievement, Cold-Blooded Murders, Severe Test of Loyalty and Patriotism* (Indianola, Iowa), 1897.

32. Brown, *The Salisbury Prison*, 149–166.

33. See Jim Sumner, "The North Carolina State Professional Baseball League, 1902," *North Carolina Historical Review*, LXIV, No. 3 (July, 1987).

34. Gray Diary, 205.

35. Bates (Ed.), *The Stars and Stripes in Rebeldom*, 131.

Under Pallor, Under Shadow

BILL FELBER

There's never been a pennant race like the battle for the 1920 American League title. It was a contest waged against a gathering backdrop of black. Suspicion and grief, not anticipation, comprised its dominant elements. The struggle claimed the life of one player, the reputations of seven others, including some of the game's most popular names. And when it was over and the champion crowned, fans everywhere did not cheer the triumph so much as they breathed a sigh of relief at the resolution.

No, there's never been a pennant race like the battle for the 1920 American League title. And if there's never another like it in the future, baseball will be blessed.

Through most of that summer, Cleveland Indians partisans, deprived of a pennant through the American League's first two decades, could hardly have imagined a doleful denouement. The home team claimed first place in April, and stayed there for months at a time. League Park was a place to which fans flocked and a setting where heroes held sway.

Those heroes included Jim Bagby, a sturdy, fastball-throwing Southern gentleman and Stanley Coveleski, the raw Polish spitball-hurling son of a Pennsylvania coal miner. Together they won 31 and 24 games respectively. Fans gloried in player–manager Tris Speaker's batting (which peaked at a .407 average in mid-August), and in his breathtaking outfield feats. They marveled at bemuscled right fielder Elmer Smith, a war veteran and native of nearby Sandusky, who slugged balls off of—and over—a right field wall that theretofore had seemed a formidable barrier. They took confidence from the field gener-alship of smooth catcher Steve O'Neill, the mature abilities of slick third baseman Larry Gardner (like Speaker a veteran of championship seasons with Boston), and of second sacker Bill Wambsganss from nearby Garfield Heights. Many could not spell his name—to the masses he was simply 'Wamby'—but even the least educated appreciated his infield play.

Above all, they doted on the competitive consistency of Ray Chapman, the team's shortstop. They thrilled as Chapman's average soared above .300 early in the season and stayed there. Proud fathers took their sons to the park to learn from Chapman's place-hitting artistry, to envy his quick hands and glove, to draw from his nervelessness.

Chapman was something of an adopted son in the city, and in 1920 the club's senior representative. He had joined the team as a 21-year-old in 1912, quickly won the regular shortstop's job, and in October 1919 further endeared himself by taking as his bride the beautiful socialite, Katherine Daly, daughter of one of the city's most prominent busi-nessmen. The marriage was said to fortell a business future for Chapman, although others wondered whether he might harbor political aspirations. At the wedding, Chapman was asked whether he planned to retire that winter to pursue one of those career options. He acknowledged the talk, but added his desire to play through 1920. "I want to bring a pennant to the fans of this city," he explained.[1]

A single pitch eternally shattered that dream. On Monday, August 16th, the Indians came to New York to face the Yankees at the start of a vital 2-week eastern road swing. Cleveland was in first place at the time, but New York stood only one-and-a-half games back, with Chicago close in third. Chapman, a notorious plate crowder, opened the fifth inning with the Indians leading 2–0. On the mound for New York was Carl Mays, a brusque right-hander with a submarine delivery and a reputation for giving no quarter. Mays threw the first pitch high and inside, intent on forcing Chapman back off the plate. The batter instinctively started to stride into the pitch, then, too late, saw that the missile was bound directly for him. He attempted to duck, but only had time to turn his head.

The ball struck Chapman with such force and so resonant a crack that Mays, believing it must have hit the bat, fielded it and threw to first base. Chapman lay motionless for several minutes, then was revived and helped to the clubhouse, and finally to a nearby hospital. It was to no avail. Hemorrhaging resulting from a skull fracture ended his life before dawn the following morning. He remains the only major leaguer ever to die as the result of an on-field accident.

For the Chicago White Sox, the treachery was more insidious. Following the team's pennant in 1919, the heavily favored Sox lost the World Series to Cincinnati 5 games to 3, an outcome that shocked knowledgeable sportsmen. Almost immediately, rumors circulated of a conspiracy involving gamblers and several Sox players. No proof was offered, but all during the winter of 1919–1920 the stories gained in general circulation, so that by the start of the 1920 season the names of the suspects were widely known: pitchers Eddie Cicotte and Lefty Williams, first baseman Chick Gandil, shortstop Swede Risberg, third baseman Buck Weaver, outfielders Joe Jackson and Happy Felsch, and reserve Fred McMullin. Gandil refused to report to spring training because of a salary dispute and announced his retirement. But the others did come back, and several—among them Cicotte, Jackson and Felsch—ranked among the game's premier stars.

The building excitement of the 1920 race gradually eclipsed interest in discussion of a 1919 Series fix. Certainly the players seemed to have forgotten. Cicotte and Williams accumulated victories at 20-win paces. Jackson hit over .400 for much of the summer, while Weaver and Felsch stayed well above .350 into mid-season. Still it was said by insiders that the Chicago team was a house divided: that the so-called "Black Sox" had been ostracized by the "Clean Sox," firebrand catcher Ray Schalk, second baseman Eddie Collins, and pitchers Dickie Kerr and Red Faber. "There's been a division among the players for months," wrote one observer, close to the team, in September. "Gruff words, dirty looks, suspicions, rumors . . . made team harmony a non-existent virtue."[2]

Then in early September a grand jury was impaneled in Chicago to investigate the alleged influence of gambling in professional baseball. Oddly, the initial directive was aimed not at the Sox but at the cross-town Cubs, who had been implicated in a suspicious game in late August. But the probe also rekindled suspicions which had never quite died about the previous autumn.

If the White Sox were dissension-riddled, they never showed it on their play in the field. Chicago stayed close to New York and Cleveland through the first two weeks of September, then delivered a crushing blow to the Yankees' hopes, sweeping them in three games at Comiskey Park.

That the Indians had been able to remain in contention following Chapman's death was every bit as amazing an achievement as was the curious determination of the cliquish Sox. Speaker's bereaved club stumbled through two weeks of lackluster play in late August, briefly falling to third place. But two critical acquisitions saved them. Dunn purchased the contract of 21-year-old shortstop Joe Sewell from New Orleans of the Southern League to take Chapman's place, and he batted .329 over the final 22 games. Dunn's other purchase was at least as important, for although Bagby, Coveleski, and right-hander Ray Caldwell (20–10) formed a first-rate triad of pitchers, the staff was woefully weak behind them. Speaker especially needed a left-hander, and Dunn got him one in late August when he bought Walter "Duster" Mails from Sacramento of the Pacific Coast League. Mails performed shakily in his debut, then won his next five starts. The performances of those two newcomers stabilized the Indians so that they held a one-and-a-half game lead over the Sox as the teams prepared for their final and decisive meeting of the season, a three-game series scheduled in Cleveland for September 23–25, in the season's final 10 days.

Yet with each passing day it was becoming less and less certain that the champion would be decided on the field. In Chicago, the focus of the grand jury, meeting in secret, was rumored to be shifting toward an inquiry into the World Series. On September 22nd, the very eve of the Sox–Indians showdown, Illinois Assistant States Attorney Hartley Replogle, the man in charge of the probe, flatly told the *Chicago Herald and Examiner,* that "the last World's Series . . . was not on the square. From five to seven players of the Chicago White Sox are involved."[3] The *New York Times,* noting the swell of leaks emanating from the grand jury room, cautioned that "unless all early signs fail, it is

The scandal-plagued Chicago White Sox, 1919. (Photo courtesy of the National Baseball Library, Cooperstown, N.Y.)

probable that some major league players will be expelled for all time."[4] The esteemed Damon Runyon, writing in the *New York American,* asserted that "someone knows something, or someone lies."[5]

It seemed inevitable that, if players were indicted, public opinion would demand their immediate suspension, an action which, if coming in the final stages of so taut a pennant race, almost inevitably would be decisive. White Sox owner Charles Comiskey was among witnesses called to testify. Emerging to face reporters, he remained close-mouthed about what he had said in the jury room. His only comment: "The White Sox are going to clean up on those Indians."[6]

SEPTEMBER 23

Whatever the grand jury was pondering was of no interest to the nearly 30,000 who tested the limits of League Park for the first game of the most important series of baseball games in Cleveland's history. "Fans here are literally mad to have Speaker's splendid team annex the championship," one Chicago observer wired home.[7] "Reserved seats are not to be had, and have not been for several days," another cabled.[8] Those who could not crowd into seats spilled onto the playing field, penned behind ropes in deep left and center. Speaker selected Bagby, the 29-game winner from Georgia, to meet Chicago left-hander Kerr, 19–9, and any League Park delirium was abetted early when Risberg fumbled Smith's grounder, allowing Joe Evans to score a first-inning run. But the Sox drew even in the fourth when Risberg, who had reached on a fielder's choice, moved to third on Schalk's base hit and scored on a two-out double steal.

The afternoon's key play occurred in the home half of the fourth, an act of raw courage that not only stymied the Indians but established beyond any question Kerr's toughness. Cleveland's Doc Johnston drilled a smash right through the middle of the diamond that the bantam pitcher, only 5'6", instinctively attempted to knock down with his bare hand. The force of the blow was reported in newspapers to actually have dislocated one of Kerr's fingers, yet he still maintained the presence of mind to dash to the ball, pick it up in his damaged hand and throw Johnston out.[9] Then Kerr calmly trotted to the Sox bench, had the injury treated, and returned to the mound to complete the inning and the game!

Chicago dented Bagby in the sixth, but only with an assist from the ground rules stipulating that any ball hit into the overflow of fans should go as a double. Jackson lofted such a fly to start the inning. A frustrated Evans, who ordinarily would have settled easily under the ball, could only stand with his back to the rope and watch it settle just beyond his reach. Bagby threw wild to first on Felsch's bunt attempt, allowing Jackson to score the lead run, and after Felsch continued to second John Collins tried a repeat of the bunt strategy. An error by Wambsganss left Collins safe at first and Felsch at third. Risberg singled the inning's second run across, and Kerr's bounce out made it 4–1.

Kerr provided the home team no further chance to get back in the game, Cleveland did add two runs, but only after the visitors had scored five times in the seventh. The 10–3 final lifted the Sox to within one-half game of first place.

Hearkening to the fateful sixth, one frustrated Cleveland wit summed up the afternoon's disappointments in doggerel.

> A pop fly falls among the throng.
> On measly bunts the Tribe goes wrong.

One untamed heave and one dropped throw
And Bagby's cake all turns to dough.[10]

SEPTEMBER 24

For a second day, the attention of the baseball world was divided between indoor and outdoor scenarios.

In Chicago, grand jury foreman Henry Brigham met with representatives of the press. He would not discuss the evidence, but he did assert the jury's intention to go "to the limit on this inquiry." Added Brigham, "I am shocked at the rottenness thus far revealed."[11] Reports surfaced that famed showman George M. Cohan, rumored to have been a "heavy loser" in the 1919 Series, would be called by the grand jury.[12] American League president Ban Johnson testified in private, then issued a baseless statement to the effect that gamblers were seeking to blackmail Chicago players into losing the 1920 pennant. "I heard several weeks ago . . . that the White Sox would not dare win," Johnson said.[13]

In Cleveland, an audience of 20,000 assembled to watch the battle which, for the winner, would carry first place. Sox manager Kid Gleason gave the ball to Faber, already a 21-game winner, while Speaker—his best pitchers all needing rest—pondered his options. He could gamble on a second-liner, which seemed close to futility against the savvy Faber. Or he could entrust the outcome to the brilliant but inexperienced Mails. Speaker selected Mails.

Rarely has a rookie, less than one month out of the minors, more generously justified the faith of his boss. Cleveland scored single runs off Faber in each of the first two innings, then placed all of the stifling burden of protecting that cushion—and the lead in the pennant race itself—on the shoulders of the fresh-faced Californian. And he did it, shutting out the White Sox on a mere three hits.

But not without at least one moment of travail sufficient to steel the hearts of all of the assembled Tribe fans. The moment of deepest drama occurred in the Chicago fifth, which Mails opened by striking out Risberg. But he walked Schalk, and when the feeble-hitting Faber also drew a base on balls the rookie appeared to be losing his composure. After two more balls to Sox leadoff man Amos Strunk, Speaker called time and trotted in from center to confer with his young pitcher. He also motioned to three Indian pitchers to dash to the bullpen and warm up. Speaker resumed his position . . . and Mails walked Strunk as well!

Now the bases were full with just one out, the tying run in scoring position, and the very heart of the Sox juggernaut due next: Weaver, Collins, and Jackson, each batting well above .330. Weaver, a slashing switch-hitter, smiled menacingly out at Mails from the right side of the plate. The first pitch was a ball, then followed a strike. The batter fouled a second strike into the seats. Another ball, and the count was 2 and 2. Thousands too nervous to sit or breathe stood as Mails delivered the fifth pitch. Weaver swung and the crack of the ball against O'Neill's mitt prompted a spontaneous mass exhalation.

But the fans' relief was brief, for Weaver's was only the second out. Collins, even more dangerous, came next. Not only did the veteran second baseman boast a .369 average, but unlike Weaver he was considered virtually impossible to strike out, having done so fewer than 20 times all season. The first pitch glanced off Collins' bat into the grandstand. A second did likewise. Mails aimed the third at the outside corner and it was called a ball. His fourth split the plate and Collins turned on it with all the fury inside his 175-pound physique. The ball careened down the left field line, menacing the chalk dividing fair and foul territories before colliding with the turf just to the foul side.

Ball two followed, then a second shot ricocheted among the fandom gathered beyond the ropes in left barely to the foul side of the line. Those blows, neither of which had missed dropping for extra base hits by more than inches, haunted the by-now hysterical fans as Mails wound and threw another fastball. It bore toward the inside corner. Collins lashed out again . . . and missed!

Proper women jumped from their seats, men flung their straw hats skyward. Such a din arose that Cleveland players returning to the dugout were obliged to put their fingers to their ears to protect themselves from the oppressive sound.[14] Mails found it a comparative snap to retire the Sox through the final four innings, complete the 2–0 shutout, and record his sixth victory of the pennant race without defeat. Cleveland remained in first place.

SEPTEMBER 25

Eddie Cicotte sneered into the telephone connecting his hotel room with Chicago. On this, the morning of the final game of the most important series of the season, Cicotte had just been advised that the names of the eight players under investigaton by the grand jury for their alleged roles in fixing the 1919 World Series had been published. Cicotte's name was prominent on the list.

The news embittered him. He denied ever having bet on a game, called the Series scandal talk "idle gossip," and rejected the notion that the grand jury could have any evidence implicating him. Just before hanging up the phone, Cicotte snarled, "I'm going to pitch against Cleveland, and we'll beat the hell out of them."[15]

But Gleason did not give the right-hander his chance at immediate vindication, selecting fellow suspect—and fellow 21-game winner—Williams instead. His opponent was to be Coveleski, who as a child had worked 21-hour days in the mines, and who had won 23 games that season.

News of the impending indictments beat the visitors to the ball park, and further incited the Saturday audience of nearly 30,000, which was presented with the disgusting prospect of the city's pure heroes being denied a pennant by a band of crooks. The thought was more than most could bear. Jackson took the field for warm-ups to a furious round of boos and catcalls. Some fans, mindful that the star outfielder had dodged military service in 1918 by taking a naval shipbuilding assignment, taunted him with calls of "Shipyard" and "Slacker." Others used megaphones to hurl abuse to the Sox starting pitcher, a three-time loser in the 1919 Series. They reviled him as "Cincinnati Williams," and urged him to "Go on down to Cincinnati, where you belong."[16]

The contest itself lingered in the balance only for three innings. Chicago scored twice in the first on a pair of hits and an equal number of fumbles. The Indians got one run back in the third thanks to Sewell's double.

But two more Chicago runs in the fourth fractured the relative peace of the 2–1 game. Then after Weaver and Collins were retired to open the fifth, Jackson drove a Coveleski pitch high and far over the right field wall for a fifth run. Thousands stood and booed the accused traitor as he wended his way around the bases, and Jackson incited further abuse by conspicuously raising his finger to his nose and authoring a pointed gesture of derision.[17]

Williams finished with a five-hitter and a 5–1 victory that returned the Sox to within a half game of first place. Their remaining games included two with the seventh-place Tigers and three with the fourth-place Browns. Cleveland, too, faced the Browns and Tigers for four games each. Chicago left Cleveland openly confident of making up that slight margin of difference over the final week . . . if only the grand jury would permit it.

AFTERMATH

The following day in Chicago, a Sunday, 25,000 disbelieving Sox fans turned out to watch Cicotte defeat the Tigers. The victory, the great pitcher's 21st of the year and 219th of a lengthy career, was also his last. On Monday, as Mails won his seventh straight for Cleveland, Cicotte and his accused teammates issued denials of their complicity in any 1919 misdeeds. For his part, Comiskey was quoted variously. Several publications reported his promise of swift action against any indicted players. But in at least one instance he was said to have insisted that, even if the grand jury did indict members of his team, he would stand by them and not issue suspensions until their guilt was proven in court. "This entire matter looks to me now as propaganda designed to disturb the morale of the team and thereby cause it to lose the championship," Comiskey said.[18]

But there was no waffling and there were no denials the following day. That morning, Cicotte walked into a grand jury room and confessed. Indictments followed within hours. Jackson implicated himself that same afternoon. Williams and Felsch followed the next day. Comiskey no sooner received word of Cicotte's confession and of the indictments than he suspended all seven, leaving his team, although just a game out of first place, in tatters.

What was left of the Sox bravely traveled to St. Louis for their final weekend series, still hopeful of somehow winning the pennant, for whatever it was worth. Employing a lineup replete with reserves and minor leaguers, Chicago won one of the three games, but the Indians defeated the Tigers on the next to last day to clinch the title. Already, Jackson and Felsch had repudiated their confessions; Weaver, McMullin, Risberg, and Gandil staunchly denied their guilt.[19] A year later, when the case finally came to trial, all eight were acquitted. But none of them ever played another game in the major leagues. Baseball's new commissioner, Judge Landis, as one of his first acts in office, issued permanent suspensions.

Almost overlooked in the purple glare of the Chicago developments, Speaker led his Indians into the World Series against the Brooklyn Dodgers. The Cleveland club dedicated its performance to Chapman, wore black armbands, and voted his widow a full share of the winnings. With Coveleski winning three games, with Smith hitting a grand slam home run, and with Wambsganss completing the only unassisted triple play in World Series history, the Indians defeated the Dodgers five games to two.

NOTES

1. *Cleveland Plain Dealer,* August 18, 1920.
2. *Chicago Daily News,* September 29, 1920.
3. *Chicago Herald and Examiner,* September 23, 1920.
4. *New York Times,* September 27, 1920.
5. *New York American,* September 22, 1920.
6. *Chicago Tribune,* September 22, 1920.
7. *Chicago Herald and Examiner,* September 23, 1920.
8. *Chicago Daily News,* September 23, 1920.
9. *Cleveland Press,* September 24, 1920.
10. *Cleveland Press,* September 24, 1920.

11. *Chicago Tribune,* September 24, 1920.
12. *Chicago Tribune,* September 25, 1920.
13. *New York American,* September 25, 1920.
14. *Cleveland Plain Dealer,* September 25, 1920.
15. *Chicago Herald and Examiner,* September 25, 1920.
16. *Chicago Herald and Examiner,* September 26, 1920.
17. *Cleveland Press,* September 27, 1920.
18. *Chicago Herald and Examiner,* September 27, 1920.
19. *Chicago Herald and Examiner,* October 2, 1920.

Joe and Luke: The Sewell Story

EUGENE MURDOCK

EDITOR'S NOTE

This article is based on in-person interviews conducted by the author with the Sewell brothers. He talked with Luke at his Akron, Ohio, home on March 31, 1974, and with Joe at his Tuscaloosa, Alabama home on August 4, 1977. Each ran a little over two hours. Incidental, non-interview material has been incorporated in the article. These interviews are two of the 75 the author was privileged to have conducted with ballplayers of the 1910–1940 era, between 1973 and 1982.

It was an unforgettable day at the Polo Grounds, that August 16, 1920. The top half of the fifth inning was beginning. Carl Mays, the Yankees' rough, tough, submarine right-hander, was facing Cleveland's classy shortstop Ray Chapman. "Chappie," a notorious plate-crowder, was in his familiar crouch in the right-hand batter's box. Mays' knuckles scraped the ground as he fired the first pitch plateward. A sharp crack echoed throughout the stadium and the ball rolled back to Mays. The pitcher picked it up and tossed to Wally Pipp at first base. Meanwhile, crumpled at home plate, Ray Chapman lay dying.

Little doubt remains that Mays, who had a reputation for throwing at batters, had killed Chapman with a strike. Yankee shortstop Roger Peckinpaugh, who had a clear view of the pitch, said "Chappie's head was over the plate; he simply froze."[1] Yankee catcher "Muddy" Ruel agreed. "His head was in the strike zone; he must have been paralyzed, fascinated like the rabbit by the snake."[2] The Boston and Detroit players, who hated Mays, demanded that American League president Ban Johnson expel him from the game. Johnson, however, who had no love for Mays himself, investigated the incident and ruled quite fairly that the fatal beaning was an accident. Although Mays deeply regretted what had happened, it did not bother his pitching. He finished the 1920 season with the best record of his career, 26 wins and 11 losses.

Accident or not, the death of Chapman devastated the Cleveland club. It had the finest team in its 20-year history and was a strong favorite to win the American League pennant. Wheeler "Doc" Johnston, Bill Wamby, Chapman, and Larry Gardner gave them a solid infield, while Elmer Smith, Manager Tris Speaker, and Charlie Jamieson comprised one of the best outfields in the league. Steve O'Neill was an old-hand behind the plate. Pitchers Jim Bagby (31–12), Stan Coveleski (24–14), and Ray Caldwell (20–10) would account for 75 of the team's 96 victories. But there was no one to replace Chapman. The *New York Times* aptly summed it up:

> The Cleveland players are so badly affected by the loss of one of their star players that their chances of winning this year's pennant have received a severe setback. Manager Speaker has

no seasoned player to put in the vacant position and grief among the players over Chapman's death is sure to affect their playing for some time to come.[3]

But help was only 1,000 miles away. A few days after Chapman's passing, Colonel Heinemann, owner of the New Orleans Pelicans of the Southern Association, summoned to his office his rookie shortstop. Joseph Wheeler Sewell, a senior at the University of Alabama, had joined the team in June when the college season was over. He had been recommended to Heinemann by Ward McDowell, for whom Joe had played several seasons in the Tennessee Coal and Iron League (TCI), a rugged semi-pro circuit in northern Alabama. He was batting .289 in 92 games since signing with New Orleans.

As he entered the club's office, Sewell was greeted by manager Johnny Dobbs. "Say, it looks like you're going to the major leagues sooner than we thought," he said.

"When I heard this," Sewell recalled, "I knew I would be going up to replace Ray Chapman. Cleveland had a working agreement with New Orleans, and both Chapman and I were shortstops, so I knew that was where I was headed."

But he did not think he was ready. "I had only played half a season of professional ball. Although the TCI was a fast league, I still wondered if they might not be rushing me. I asked them about that during this interview and Johnny Dobbs saw at once that I needed to be "peppered up."

"Oh, you can do it all right," he said. "Look at so-and-so and such-and-such. They're up there and you're as good as they are." After a pause Dobbs went on. "Son, the Cleveland club is trying to win the pennant and they need help. You're just the man that can give it to them. Now no more of this 'not ready' talk. You leave tonight."

That was all Sewell needed. He rode the Southern Railroad all night and the next day, which took him to Cincinnati. Missing his connection to Cleveland, he spent the night in Cincinnati and arrived in Cleveland in the middle of the next afternoon and went directly to the Hollenden Hotel. When he told the desk clerk his name was 'Joe Sewell,' he was suddenly swarmed over by local reporters. The word was in the paper that he was coming from New Orleans and they were lying in wait for him.

After freeing himself from the press, Sewell got a cab and rode out to League Park, or Dunn Field, as it was then called, at the corner of East 66th Street and Lexington Avenue. It was an off day so most of the players were at the racetrack. (This was before the Landis era.) The concessions managers showed him around. "I was lost," Sewell said, "I didn't know anybody, I was out of place, all by myself. That gentleman made me feel right at home." The newcomer was taken up to the office where he met owner Jimmy Dunn and manager Tris Speaker.

The next day, September 9th, the Yankees were in town. Speaker thought it best to let the rookie sit out his first game. He saw Elmer Smith make a sensational running, over-the-shoulder catch in right-center field, while Speaker "made some of the most remarkable catches you ever saw." "Doc" Johnston went five-for-five and stole home as the Indians routed New York, 10–4. As Joe observed Cleveland go about its business in style, he shrank farther and farther back into his little corner of the dugout bench. "Pshaw," he thought to himself, "this is no place for me. I know I can't play here."

On September 10th, Joe Evans and Sewell split the shortstop chores as the Yankees triumphed 6–1. Sewell, in his first appearance, went 0-for-2, and made one error. Speaker decided to rest him the following day and New York won again, 6–2. On September 12th, Connie Mack's Philadelphia Athletics arrived in Cleveland, and Speaker told Joe, "You're playing shortstop today." The "butterflies" were now flitting back and forth. When he came to bat for the first time, facing ancient Scott Perry, Joe hit a bullet to left center. "An extra-baser, for sure," he thought. But Tillie Walker, the A's center fielder, coasted over easily for the routine catch. "Pshaw, I'll never hit a lick up here."

On Sewell's next at-bat, Perry threw a curve which just broke across the outside corner to the left-handed hitter. He reached out and lined the ball over the third base bag down into the left-field corner. "Boy, I flew around the bases," Sewell chuckled. "Nothing touched the ground but the tips of my toes." When he reached third base with his first major league hit, he stood there and looked the scene over. "Pshaw, this isn't so much." From that moment throughout the rest of his career, "I was never excited or nervous. I would get keyed up, as at World Series time, but I was never nervous. I was not as good as some of the superstars of the day, but I was good enough to be up there with them. I had my confidence from that moment on."

Did Joe Sewell make a difference to the Indians in those waning weeks of the 1920 season? Cleveland played 20 games after Chapman was killed and before Sewell arrived on September 10th. With Harry Lunte playing shortstop in most of those games—and batting .203—the club won 11 and lost 9, turning first place over to the White Sox in the last ten days of August. They regained it in early September, but relinquished it again, this time to the Yankees, in the second week of the month.

Sewell entered the lineup for good on September 12th. From that day through the end of

Joe and Luke Sewell during their time with Cleveland. (Photo courtesy of the National Baseball Library, Cooperstown, N.Y.)

the season on October 3rd, the Indians won 16 and lost 6. On September 15th they destroyed the Athletics, 14–0, and went on to win the next six games which put them in first place to stay. Sewell collected 23 hits in 70 at bats in 22 games for a nifty .329 average.

However, Joe made 16 errors in that stretch, three in one game twice. An error on October 1st against Detroit cost Cleveland the game and delayed clinching the pennant until the next day. But the errors played a small part in the larger picture. The Indians won 7 and lost 3 in games where Sewell made errors. Joe explained the problem:

> I could cover the ground and I had a good arm. Practically all of those errors were on bad throws. I was not used to those big double-deck grandstands and the white shirts in the seats. The trouble was that I could not pick out the first baseman quickly enough against that background and my throws were pulling him off the bag. Once I got settled that difficulty cleared up.

Sewell's bat helped—his glove did not hurt that much—to stabilize the Cleveland club after the loss of Chapman. More important, however, was the arrival of pitcher Walter "Duster" Mails, who came from the West Coast in late August and won seven straight games. Mails accounted for over one-fourth of the team's victories after Chapman. Between Sewell and Mails, Cleveland's pennant aspirations were revived and fulfilled. But the team still needed help.

This came from Chicago where on September 28th eight key members of the White Sox, who were close behind Cleveland in the pennant chase, were suspended for throwing the 1919 World Series to Cincinnati. This marked the beginning of the so-called "Black Sox Scandal." At this moment Chicago was one-half game behind Cleveland (two in the lost column) with three games to play, all against the .500 St. Louis Browns. Cleveland, however, had six games remaining, two against St. Louis and four with the second division Detroit Tigers. It was problematical whether the absence of its eight starters would make a difference to Chicago's pennant hopes in the final outcome. But it did. Cleveland won four of its last six games that week, while Chicago won one of its three games. Had they won all three of those games they would have finished in a dead heat for first place necessitating a playoff game. So it was not just Sewell, it was not just Sewell and Mails; it was Sewell, Mails, and the Black Sox who salvaged the 1920 flag for Cleveland.

Technically, Joe was not eligible for the World Series because he had come to Cleveland after September 1st, the cut-off date. However, because of the unusual circumstances of the case, Brooklyn waived the rule thus allowing him to play. He did not star as he had in the last weeks of the season, batting only .174 and making six errors, but the Indians won the series, taking five of the seven games played. Sewell did participate in one of the most unusual World Series games ever played. It was the fifth game in Cleveland on October 10th. The Indians got off to a big lead with Elmer Smith's grand-slam home run in the first inning and Jim Bagby's three-run shot in the fourth. In the top of the fifth the "Robins," as they were occasionally called because of Manager Wilbert Robinson, tried to get something going. Second baseman Pete Kilduff led off with a single to center. Catcher Otto Miller also singled to center, Kilduff being held at second by a strong throw from Speaker. Clarence Mitchell, a good hitting pitcher who had relieved starter Burleigh Grimes the previous inning, was up next. Sewell described what happened:

> Mitchell hit a hard line drive just to Wamby's side of second base. Bill ran over and jumped just as high as he could—he was a little over six feet tall—it looked to me like he jumped three or four feet in the air. He came down only a step or two from second base since he had been moving in that direction. I was only a few steps away at shortstop and thought the ball was a sure hit. Well, Bill made this great catch, came down and touched second base, and turned

preparing to fire the ball to first. But I saw old Otto Miller chugging down the baseline so I called out to Bill, "tag him!", "tag him!" So Bill just stepped over and tagged him. Otto looked around like he was lost. He couldn't believe Bill had the ball. We walked off the field together and I congratulated him on his great play. The fans sat in stunned silence. Suddenly they realized that they had witnessed an unassisted triple play and they broke out in wild cheers. Then they began tossing their straw hats out on the field. There was a huge crowd there and it seemed like everyone was wearing a straw hat. The game had to be delayed quite awhile in order to pick up all the straw hats.

A remarkable beginning for the rookie shortstop, who remained a Cleveland fixture for the next decade. The advent of younger brother Luke on the major league scene was not quite so dramatic. In fact, some people were not sure he was on the team. Nearly three years younger than Joe, Luke also attended the University of Alabama and played semi-pro ball. Thus his minor league experience was similarly abbreviated. He played for two years with the Crimson Tide, and in 1920 split time between the Delta League in Mississippi and the Million Dollar League in Georgia. These were fast semi-pro circuits, much like the TCI. Fourteen players came out of the Delta League in that period who made it to the majors and stayed. Among others, in addition to Luke, were Hughie Critz, Riggs Stephenson, and Bill Terry.

By 1921 Cleveland's catching situation was becoming serious. Steve O'Neill was over 30 while back-up catchers Leslie Nunamaker and Chet Thomas were not first-line players. As for Thomas, Luke recalled, "Chet couldn't do much. He couldn't catch and he couldn't run." O'Neill caught over 100 games in 1921, 1922, and 1923 when he was traded to Boston with Wamby. Luke was brought up at the tail end of the 1921 season but was used only sparingly while O'Neill was around. He played in 41 games in 1922 and only 10 in 1923. In the latter year, O'Neill's last, the Indians acquired Glenn Myatt, a catcher, from Milwaukee. With O'Neill gone in 1924, Speaker began to platoon Sewell and Myatt. "Glenn was a left-handed hitter," explained Sewell, "and we had that short right field wall in Cleveland. I hit right-handed, so when we went on the road I caught. When we returned to Cleveland Glenn caught."

In 1926, however, Speaker decided to go with Sewell behind the plate. Myatt had trouble with men on base. "When men got on base," Luke said, "he would seldom call for a curve ball. He wanted fast balls so he could get his throw to second base off quicker. Of course, the other team knew he would call for a fast ball and then laid into it." Beginning with that year Sewell caught over 100 games in 9 of his remaining 12 seasons as an active player.

Joe was noted even more than Luke for his durability. He had a consecutive streak of 1,103 games played and was closing in on the current record of 1,307 set a few years before by Everett "Deacon" Scott when he was felled by the flu in St. Louis. From September 1, 1922, until April 30, 1930, he never missed a game.

They both also had strong arms. Unlike Myatt, Luke had no trouble with base runners. But before he became the regular catcher, he was put out on waivers several times. Detroit claimed him each time so the waivers were withdrawn. "Why did Detroit claim you?" he was asked. "Well, the first game I ever caught was against Detroit. Ty Cobb was their manager and although it was late in his career, he was still an excellent base runner. He tried to steal second base twice in that game and I threw him out both times. He claimed me, I suppose, so I wouldn't throw him out anymore."

Cobb never did cause too many problems on the bases for Sewell. "You knew he was going to run," Luke said. "Every time Ty got on you figured he was going to run on every pitch, so you were always ready. It seemed that he would take a lot of people by surprise, but I was always ready for him." Testimony to Sewell's throwing strength and accuracy is the American League record he held for many years: most years leading catchers in assists. He led the league in this category in 1926, 1927, 1928, and in 1936 when he was 35 years old.

Reminded of this achievement, he quickly remarked, "But look at all those errors." Indeed, a check revealed that he also led the American League catchers in errors in 1927 and 1929. "But you know," he went on, "about half of those errors were on throws directly over second base. One time they were working on a new method of breaking up the hit-and-run play. The players at second base and shortstop held their positions longer to prevent the ball from getting by them and then would break late for the base. I was throwing to beat the runners and by the time the fielders got to the base my throw was in center field and I got an error as the runner went to third. In addition to that our pitchers weren't very good at holding runners on first. I would have had more assists if they could have done that better."

Speaking of errors, do not be misled by Joe's six miscues in the 1920 World Series. He was right when he said that once he got settled the problem would disappear. In fact, he became one of the best fielding shortstops in the American League. He led the league in shortstop putouts in 1924, 1925, 1926, and 1927. He was the shortstop assist leader in 1924, 1925, 1927, and 1928, and the third base assist leader in 1929. He led all shortstops in fielding percentage in 1927 and 1928. He had a league-leading 59 errors in 1923, but the time for "settling down" had arrived and he never approached that figure again.

Along with center fielder–manager Tris Speaker and first baseman "Doc" Johnston, Sewell worked out a clever double-play routine. Speaker, of course, was a fine hitter, but he was also noted for his excellent fielding skills. He played a short center field, which cut down the chances for a base runner to get an extra base when the ball was hit to him. His speed enabled him to go deep for balls hit over his head. The double-play trick could not be used against experienced players, but with green rookies it was often successful. Sewell explained how it worked:

We'll say a young fellow is on first base with a bunt in order. Being the shortstop, I'd run to second base until I saw how the play was going to develop. If the play was going to be a force at second I would stay there. If the play was going to be at first base, I would stay at second until the runner was about five or ten feet from the bag. At that moment I would take off like a son-of-a-gun for third base, as if I thought there was going to be a play there. In the meantime, Speaker would be easing in from center field. Not running, but just sort of drifting in. The first baseman would not be looking at second base, but he knew Speaker would be there. The base runner would make his turn at second and follow me to third. Then the first baseman would throw the ball—wham!—to second base to Speaker and the runner would be caught trying to get back to the base. We used to catch a lot of them that way. I made a trip to the Ralph Edwards program in Los Angeles on that one play. They had Tris on the "This is Your Life" program. I stayed out there a week just to tell them what I've said here."

*   *   *

Joe and Luke Sewell were two of six children who grew up in the rural community of Titus, Alabama. Their father was a country doctor who had received his medical degree from the Alabama Medical School in Mobile in 1890. He served Titus and its environs for over 40 years. One of the most important things Dr. Sewell instilled in his children was the value of an education. As a result, every one of them went to college and earned a degree. The oldest of the six was a boy, Toxie, who graduated from the University of Alabama, served in World War I, and then completed his medical education at Vanderbilt. He practiced medicine until his untimely death from sleeping sickness on December 5, 1932. Joe and Luke agree that Toxie was the best athlete in the family. He had an outstanding record at the University and no doubt would have done well in professional sports.

Joe and Luke also planned to follow their father and older brother into medicine and had taken pre-med programs at Alabama. But unlike Toxie's experience, baseball overtook their medical aspirations. Had they not been successful on the diamond they probably would have attended medical school. The youngest brother, Tommy, had baseball rather than medical ambitions from the start, but unfortunately, he lacked the ability of his brothers. He had a brief tryout with the Cubs in the late 1920s and then drifted off to the minors.

"It was a happy, healthy, normal life—growing up in Titus. We didn't realize it until later," remembered Joe, "just how nice it really was." Titus had a grammar school through the ninth grade, but no high school. After grammar school they had to travel to Wetumpka High, about 15 miles away, to continue their education. It was a regular procession of Sewell boys through the school system. Starting with Toxie, then Joe, Luke, Tommy, each went in turn from grammar school to Wetumpka and then to the University of Alabama.

It is not clear how Toxie got to Wetumpka High each day, but by the time it was Joe's turn, the Sewells had a Model T Ford. They were the only family for miles with such a luxury—this was in 1912—which certainly elevated their status within local social circles. Joe was the first to drive—he was only 14 years old—and he later passed on the secrets of the new science to his father and brother Luke. "How did you learn to drive?" a curious visitor inquired. "When they sold you the car they sent a tutor along with the car to teach someone to drive. They sent us a fellow who was crippled. He had lost his foot, but he was still a good driver. He stayed right in your house until you were qualified. It was like a 'driver education' course today."

Wetumpka had no baseball team, but the boys played baseball most of the time. "While school was in session," Joe said, "we played during the 30-minute recess and after school all winter long. In the summer it was baseball all day." Equipment was sometimes hard to come by. "We generally had usable balls and bats, but not always," said Joe. "One day we lost our baseball so I sat down and unraveled a new stocking my mother had just knitted for me and made a baseball out of it. When she found out what I had done with that sock, she got the 'peach tree limb' out and went to work. She did a pretty good job, too."

Most of the bats they used were homemade, fashioned from branches of willow trees. The limbs were normally straight, but if left out in the sun too long they warped. "We would just turn the warped side to the ball and really hit it," laughed Joe. The first real catcher's glove they ever saw was one Toxie had ordered from Sears and Roebuck. It was black and everyone in the countryside wanted to look at it. When they played a game both catchers would use that mitt. Joe's first fielding glove was made from one of his father's driving gloves. He stuck a little bit of cotton in it to serve as a pad.

Old baseball fans, that is those who followed the game in the 1920s and 1930s, remember what was perhaps Joe's most remarkable achievement as a major league ballplayer: how rarely he struck out. His record in this regard is incredible. From the day he broke in on September 10, 1920 until he hung up his spikes at the close of the 1933 season, playing in 1,902 games and going to bat 7,132 times, Sewell struck out only 114 times! That averages out at 0.016 strikeouts for every time at bat! He was slow in perfecting this batting skill. He struck out four times in his brief stint in 1920, 17 times in 1921, 20 times in 1922, 12 times in 1923, and 13 times in 1924. Thus 66, nearly 60 percent of his strikeouts, occurred in the first four-and-a-fraction seasons of his career.

Beginning in 1925 when he was right in the middle of his consecutive game streak, he struck out nine or less times in each of his remaining years. He fanned only four times each in 1925 and 1929, and in 1933, when he played in only 135 games. He struck out three times in 1930 (109 games) and 1932 (124 games). "How do you explain these unbelievable figures?" It was the inquisitive visitor again. "I never remember when I couldn't hit," Joe began to explain. "As a boy I used to gather up a handful of rocks or Coca Cola bottle caps, toss them in the air, and swing at them with an old broomstick. I could knock the 'lightning arresters' off the tops of telephone poles. Right now I think that helped me all the way through with my reflexes. You've got to look at the rock or bottle top before you can hit it. It develops your reflexes, your coordination, and your timing."

Joe brought out his favorite bat. It was one of the first bats he had when he broke in in 1920. It was a 40-ounce Louisville Slugger with George Burns' name printed on it. He used it in the early part of the season, but as the weather got warmer he dropped back to a 36-ounce bat. It was darkened from years of usage, but well preserved. Joe pointed to a six-inch section near the end where the wood was somewhat lighter. "This is where I hit the ball most of the time. I always made contact with the ball and usually at about the same place."

Students of the game have always challenged statements that a batter can actually see the ball as it makes contact with the bat. No doubt exists in Joe Sewell's mind. "All through my career in baseball," he said, "I could see the ball leave my bat. That's how closely I followed the ball. I played on teams with some great hitters, like Speaker, Ruth, Gehrig, and others. They used to stand across the plate from me during batting practice to watch me just as I would hit the ball. They wanted to see if they could see me see the ball as I hit it. Finally one day old Babe said, 'I think he does see it'."

While Joe made a study of the science of batting, Luke made a study of the science of pitching and catching. They should have written manuals on those subjects. As for the hit-and-run play which caused Luke so many errors, his theory was to call for a curve ball when he suspected the hit-and-run was on. Even though the ball gets to the plate more slowly, it is more difficult to hit, thus reducing the chance of executing the play successfully. "Of course," he said, "if you had stolen the sign and knew it was the hit-and-run, you would pitch out. But if you weren't sure, call for a curve. If you called for a pitch out and the play was not on, you merely put your pitcher in a deeper hole."

"Did you get tipped off on the play very often?" he was asked.

"Oh, yes," was the reply. "One good way was to bribe the opposing team's batboy. He would hear what they were saying and then tell us. His reward was a brand new baseball. I remember on one eastern swing I called for pitch-outs on every hit-and-run play that was attempted on the trip. They couldn't understand it. You were guessing part of the time, but mostly we knew it because we knew the players and managers—and batboys. Players, rather than managers, put on the hit-and-run. And that is the only correct way to do it. Because if the player does not have confidence that he can hit the ball on that pitch the play is no good. They had better hit-and-run players in the early days because they weren't always going for home runs."

Speaking of home runs, how was Ruth pitched to? "We pitched him hard," was the laconic reply.

In Luke's opinion, the most effective pitcher against Ruth was Hub Pruett of the St. Louis Browns. If he was correct in this, Pruett must have been mighty ineffective against everyone else. His career record was 29 and 48 in seven seasons. At any rate, next to Pruett was George Uhle of Cleveland, whom he caught many times. Sometimes, when Uhle was pitching, they would even walk the man ahead of him to get to Ruth. Uhle had just an average fastball, but he had a good assortment of changes of speed. And when the hitter was set for the "average" fastball he would put a little extra on it and throw it by the hitter. He also had a spinning curveball which, when he bore down on it, would just drop off like falling off a table. "Uhle," said Sewell, "would throw Ruth a three-quarters curveball and break it in right around his knees. Ruth would swing from Port Arthur and I don't ever recall him hitting that pitch off of Uhle."

But make no mistake, everyone, including Joe and Luke, respected the Babe. "I honestly believe," said Luke, "that if Ruth had gone for a batting average rather than home runs, he could have hit .500. I thought he had the greatest eye at the plate." When asked about his brother Joe, he replied "He had great control of the bat and great balance at the plate, too."

Even George Uhle had his doubts at times. Joe Sewell recalled a game with the Yankees in Cleveland when Uhle was pitching. The Indians were ahead in the ninth inning, 7–6. Two men were out, a man was on first base, and Ruth was coming to bat. He had already hit four or five home runs in the series. A conference was called on the pitcher's mound. "Let's walk him," suggested first baseman George Burns. Uhle agreed. "I think I can get Gehrig (the next hitter) better than I can Ruth. I'll 'dink' him," meaning he would throw that little curveball on the outside corner. "Well," said Joe chuckling, "while we were walking Ruth, everyone was watching Gehrig. Lou was walking back and forth, charging around the on-deck circle like a lion in a cage. The idea of walking Ruth to get to him was driving him crazy. Well, when Gehrig got up there, Uhle tossed that little dinky curveball which you could have caught in your bare hand. Lou couldn't wait until it got up there and jumped at the thing. He hit a little dribbler to me and I threw to second to end the game. The newspapers gave us fits the next day for going against all baseball strategy in walking the winning run on base, but we got away with it." The Indians had a standing rule to walk Ruth whenever he was at bat with no one on base.

Joe Sewell, who played with Ruth for three years in the early 1930s, commented on the Babe's tremendous arm. Of course, he was an outstanding pitcher before he became an outfielder. "In my years with the Babe," he said, "I never saw him make a bad play in the field, or throw to the wrong base, or drop the ball once he got his hands on it. He was the greatest thrower I ever played with. With a runner on first and a base hit to right field I would go over to third base, stand with my feet straddling the bag, and the Babe would throw the ball to me on the first hop every time. It was like picking cherries."

"Would Ruth have been better had he taken better care of himself?"

"Ruth could not have been any better than he was," was Sewell's quick response.

While Joe and Luke respect the ability of most modern players, they have a problem with the attitudes of some of them. Joe chuckles when he hears a player say today that he is getting mentally prepared to play. "Pshaw! When I rolled out of bed in the morning I was mentally ready. We had our recreation, but we spent a lot of time in hotel lobbies talking over the game that day and planning for tomorrow's game. We'd talk about the next day's pitcher and things like that. We couldn't wait to get out on the field again." Luke speaks of the different philosophies of today's players. "When I was playing you had to be ready mentally or somebody else had your job. I asked one young fellow once in February what he was doing to get in shape and he said without blushing, 'I'm getting ready mentally.' We were always ready mentally and spent the winter staying in shape physically."

Humor on the field is part of the fun of the going to the old ball park. One can almost count on something amusing occurring every time he is at a game. Joe and Luke had plenty of such stories to tell. Joe's favorite took place in a game with the White Sox in Cleveland. Good-natured Smead Jolley, the huge and powerful slugger—but clumsy fielder—was on duty in right field. The Indians' catcher Glenn Myatt drilled a hit to right center. Jolley ambled over to the ball and bent over to scoop it up. He failed to bend far enough, however, and the ball passed through his legs toward the fence. Myatt rounded first and headed for second. Jolley turned and pursued the ball, but it struck hard against the fence and came back through his legs once more. He turned again and went trotting after the elusive pellet as Myatt rounded second and headed for third. Jolley finally corralled the ball, righted himself and fired it 15 rows back into the third base seats. Myatt rounded third and came in to score on this, the third error on the play. By now players from both dugouts were out on the field roaring with laughter, the spectators were convulsed with mirth, while Jolley himself was standing in short right field, hands on hips, grinning sheepishly. At length he was heard to mutter, "My Gawd, I never knew I could throw the ball so far."

Luke's best story came on a bunt play down the third base line. Normally, he covered such plays with ease, charging the ball quickly, pivoting and firing it to first base in one motion. On this occasion Frank Brower, Cleveland's 6'4" first baseman, also charged the ball. However, when he saw that Sewell would get it, he turned back to first base and bent over to be out of the line of the throw. But like Smead Jolley, he failed to bend far enough and the throw caught him right in "the seater," as Luke delicately put it. "You never heard such a yell as Brower let out! I just had to sit down and laugh." In the future, Brower said, he would lie flat on the ground.

*　*　*

Both Joe and Luke left Cleveland within two years of each other and enjoyed successful careers with their new clubs. And they each got into a World Series. Joe was released after the 1930 season. He had slowed down by this time and had been shifted to third base. He was still hitting over .300 each year, but Cleveland concluded that he was no longer worth the high salary he was drawing—in the neighborhood of $13,000. As a ten-year man he could not be traded, so the Indians put him on waivers. No club claimed him because of his salary, which would have to be assumed. In January 1931 he was released. "When the news got out," Joe chuckled, "the other teams came after me like a bunch of bees. The Yankees made the best offer so I signed with them. I still felt I had some good baseball left in me."

He was right. He had three good years with the Yankees (1931, 1932, and 1933), playing 130 games each season. His batting did fall off a bit, however, and he had his two poorest years in 1932 (.272) and 1933 (.273), although those figures would be quite respectable by modern standards. Joe helped the Yankees win the 1932 pennant and batted .333 in the World Series, as New York swept the Cubs in four straight games.

He was an eyewitness to Babe Ruth's "called shot" home run in the top of the fifth inning in game three. He insists that Ruth clearly indicated that he was going to hit one over the right-center field fence. "It was bravado," Joe said, "but he was mad—we were all mad—that the Cubs voted our old teammate Mark Koenig only half a World Series share after he had helped them win the pennant." On the other hand, Woody English, the Chicago third baseman that day, told the author that Ruth was yelling at the Cub dugout and held up two fingers, saying he still had another pitch left. (Incidentally, English said that all but two of the Chicago players voted for giving Koenig a full share, but that the vote had to be unanimous.) Whatever the truth of the matter, the "called shot" remains one of baseball's hardiest and most romantic legends.

In the clubhouse after the game, while the players were congratulating him, the Bambino said, "I told that little kid in the hospital this morning that I was going to hit a home run for him." This was the first news any of the players had of the "promised" home run.

Mrs. Sewell happened to be sitting in the grandstands with Mrs. Ruth when Babe called his shot. She recalls her calling out, just before he hit the homer, "Remember the kid, remember the kid." The only difficulty with this last story is that Ruth had already hit one home run, a three-run blast in the first inning. The "called shot" was his second homer of the game. Anyhow, "the kid" was well-remembered.

Luke was traded to Washington on January 7, 1933, for Roy Spencer. To many Clevelanders it was a bad trade. Spencer hit only .203 in 1933 and was let go in 1934 after appearing in only five games. But it was a good deal for Sewell. He caught 141 games and helped the Senators win the pennant just as Joe had helped the Yankees the previous year. His most-remembered play occurred while Washington was in New York late in the season. The Yankees were their closest challenger for the title. The home team came to bat in the last of the ninth trailing the Senators by three runs. Gehrig opened against Monte Weaver with a single. Dixie Walker then walked, bringing the tying run to the plate in the person of Tony Lazzeri. Lazzeri ripped a line drive over "Goose" Goslin's head in right-center field. But the ball caromed cleanly back to Goslin who threw it to Joe Cronin in short center field. Cronin relayed the ball to Sewell who tagged Gehrig sliding into home. The next thing Luke knew there was Walker coming in fast on the heels of Gehrig. He got Dixie as well. The double play saved the game and may have had a bearing on the pennant race as well.

Luke was injured in 1934 and traded to the St. Louis Browns after the season was over. He never played for the Browns, however, being acquired by the White Sox before the 1935 season began. He had three good years in Chicago, but 1935 was his best. "Yes," he reflected, "it was 1935. I had a better year than Al Simmons. You look up his 1935 season and you'll see that I outhit him. You see, he came out of the small park in Philadelphia into our spacious Comiskey Park. He was still trying to hit home runs and it didn't work there." Sewell hit .285 and Simmons .267 in 1935. "I'll never forget," Luke went on, "in September of that year he said to me 'the league is upside down when you're outhitting me'."

Luke played 65 games with the White Sox in 1938 and in 1939 joined his old team, the Indians, as a catcher–coach. He became a full-time coach in 1940, a year made memorable by manager Oscar Vitt's "crybaby" troupe. "Oscar was a fine fellow," Sewell said, "but he talked too much. He would say things, promise things, which he forgot he ever said or promised. Players resented this because they thought he did it on purpose. But he didn't." After citing an example or two of this, Luke went on. "But it was not all Oscar's fault. The players were to blame, too. They picked on one another, blamed each other when things went wrong, and blew a pennant they should have won."

During the players' "rebellion" against Vitt, Cleveland owner Alva Bradley offered Luke Sewell the managerial job on three different occasions. The plan was to merely relieve, not fire, Vitt, alleging ill-health, and replace him with Sewell. Luke would not buy this. "They must have been crazy," he said, "to come with a scheme like that. Oscar hired me and I was not going to take his place under those circumstances. If they dismissed him, that would have been different and I would have been available. But they didn't do that and I turned the position down all three times."

The irony of it all was that when the 1940 season was history and Detroit had eased past Cleveland to win the American League title by one game, Vitt was fired. Who was the new manager? Roger Peckinpaugh! "Maybe they figured that since I had rejected the job three times before," Sewell said, "that I didn't want it now. But I did."

Luke did get the chance to manage that very same year. Maybe Bradley gave the St. Louis Browns owner, Donald Barnes, the idea—because he liked Sewell—or maybe he did not. However, a month into the 1941 season, Barnes hired Luke to replace Fred Haney as the Browns' manager. A new career had opened up for him and he made the most of it. He led the club to the 1944 American League title. And even though it was wartime, and even though the hometown Cardinals defeated his team in the World Series, it was one of his best years in baseball.

While Luke was outhitting Al Simmons and going on to greater things, Joe was at the end of the line. His last year as an active player was 1933. He helped break in his successor, Robert "Red" Rolfe, and stayed on as a Yankee coach in 1934 and 1935. After that he left baseball to operate a hardware store in Tuscaloosa. He returned to scout for the Indians from 1952 to 1962 and for the neophyte Mets in 1963. But by this time most people had forgotten about Joe Sewell. Then in 1977 his name reappeared in the sport pages of America. He was elected to baseball's Hall of Fame.

NOTES

1. Roger Peckinpaugh interview with author, July 9, 1973.
2. *Sporting News,* March 24, 1948.
3. *New York Times,* August 18, 1920.

Baseball and the Great Depression

BILL RABINOWITZ

In October 1929 the United States plunged into an economic depression the length and severity of which were unparalleled in its history. During the first few months of the crisis, few people considered the slump to be more than a recession, albeit a severe one. After all, there had been panics in 1837 and 1893 and a severe recession as recently as 1921–1922. As late as January 1931, 14 months after the crash, the prominent National Economic League voted the economic troubles as the United States' fourth most pressing issue, behind prohibition, administration of justice, and lawlessness.[1] Baseball as it approached the 1930s was in the best shape in its history. Spurred by the rise of Babe Ruth, the game had rebounded from the Black Sox scandal to unprecedented popularity in the 1920s. In 1929, regular season attendance in the major leagues topped 9 million for a record sixth straight year. Though profits totaling $1.33 million were down about $1 million from the record of 1926, there was a good reason: the pennant races in 1926 were much closer than those in 1929. Still, the profit picture looked bright and baseball owners looked forward to even better numbers in the coming decade.

But this time, instead of improving, the economy worsened, with only brief, deceptive remissions. By 1933, the Gross National Product (GNP) had fallen to $55.76 billion, down from the 1929 GNP of $103.83 billion. The unemployment rate, 3.6 percent in 1929, reached 25 percent in 1933. That same year marked the nadir of the Depression, but the recovery, under newly elected President Franklin Delano Roosevelt, was painfully slow. Not until 1941 did the GNP reach the 1929 level or unemployment subside substantially.[2]

Major league baseball, like virtually every industry, severely felt the effects of the Depression, though not immediately. In 1930, the first full year of the economic collapse, the combined net income of major league clubs was $1,965,000, exceeding that of 1929 by $629,000. In fact, combined net income for 1930 was the highest since 1926. The profit margin increased as well, from 11.3 percent in 1929 to 16.4 percent in 1930. This increase can be attributed largely to the closer National League pennant race of 1930. In 1929, when the Chicago Cubs won the crown by ten games, the league's income was $750,000. The 1930 NL pennant race, in which the top four teams finished within six games of each other, was mostly responsible for the major leagues' net income of $1,462,000.[3]

By 1931, however, baseball began to feel the effects of the economy's slump. Net income fell to $217,000 and the profit margin dwindled to 2.3 percent. Most clubs lost money. The American League finished more than $56,000 in the red. Though the National League showed a combined profit of $373,121, only three of the eight clubs finished in the black. The St. Louis Cardinals profited on the strength of their World Series championship, and the Cubs ended up on the plus side of the ledger because of their third place finish and because they had the benefit of playing in a large city, with its generally larger attendance. The third team showing a profit, the Pittsburgh Pirates, finished in the black probably because of revenue from their affiliated baseball real estate company.[4] Still, while the economy in general was falling apart, major league baseball as a whole had managed to register a net profit.

That baseball, despite its reputation as a working-class avocation, held its own during the first two years of the Depression should not seem surprising. Baseball had always done well in years of economic recession and high unemployment. "Poor business years are good baseball years," was the popular saying.[5] Indeed, during the 1921–1922 recession, profit margins for major league teams hovered above 20 percent.[6] During previous recessions, an unemployed man had usually saved enough money to live on for a while and was able to afford the dollar or less to buy a ticket for a ball game.

By 1932, however, the unemployed man who "thought he was laid off for a few weeks two summers ago in many cases still [was] unemployed. Whereas in July, 1930, it was a case of scaring up four bits for a bleacher seat at the Stadium, [in 1932] it [was] a matter of getting enough for a cheap meal."[7] In other words, what was different during the economic depression in the 1930s was its duration. The Depression had finally hit baseball.

The worst financial years for major league baseball were 1932 and 1933. In 1932, club owners lost a combined $1,201,000. Their "loss" margin was 15 percent. The next year was even worse. Net losses totaled $1,651,000, and the "loss" margin was 23.9 percent. Attendance plunged to just over 6 million fans in 1933, down from the 1930 record high of more than 10 million. Only two major league teams, both in the National League, reported profits. The World Series' champion New York Giants earned $59,416, and the Philadelphia Phillies profited a grand sum of $3,184, only finishing in the black by selling many of their players to other teams.[8]

After the heavy losses of 1932 and 1933, major league baseball's financial fortunes improved as the economy began a slow, erratic recovery. In 1934 the owners lost almost $290,000, a large amount, but a far cry from the $1,650,000 loss sustained the year before. In 1935, major league baseball owners reported an income of $565,906, the first net profit in four years. For each succeeding year for the rest of the decade, with the exception of 1937, the year of the Roosevelt recession, owners' profits increased. However, even though the net losses of 1932–1934 did not return, neither did the boom years of 1920–1930. Not until after World War II did net profits exceed those of 1930.[9]

Despite baseball's financial ills during the Depression, its officials were convinced and consoled themselves in their belief that baseball's troubles were external in cause. In other words, baseball was not to blame for its problems; the Depression was. Kenesaw Mountain Landis, who was appointed commissioner after the Black Sox scandal of 1919 and who ruled major league baseball with almost total authority for 25 years, stated his belief in 1934 that the only thing that ailed baseball was the Depression. "Steel, factories, railroads, newspapers, agriculture, baseball—we rode down together, and we'll ride back together. The American people love baseball. They will return as paying customers as soon as they have money."[10]

Other voices were not so willing to take such a passive view. An editorial in the *Sporting News,* the self-proclaimed "Bible of Baseball," lambasted baseball officials after they refused to change the 1932 World Series policy of selling tickets in three-game allotments only, a practice that resulted in large numbers of unsold seats.

This is a new era, demanding new treatment, and baseball must get in step with the times. Talking about innovations as being 'bad for precedent,' that they hadn't been 'attempted before' and that what was 'good enough yesterday is good enough today,' won't get the game anywhere. The officials of Organized Ball, both high and low, must adjust themselves to the new order, or make way for others not so shackled by precedent.[11]

Baseball was indeed slow to adjust to the changing times, but the Depression was responsible nonetheless for a number of proposed measures. Though not all were actually adopted, such proposals would have been unheard of five years earlier.

One of the ideas not accepted was a profit-sharing plan. Even in the prosperous 1920s, a large disparity existed between the haves and the have-nots. For example, while the Yankees earned more than $2,600,000 between 1923 and 1930, the Boston Red Sox lost more than $300,000 during the same period.[12] When the Depression hit the majors in full force, the have-nots united in favor of a profit-sharing plan. The scheme was rejected by unsympathetic richer owners. Yankee owner Jacob Ruppert made the argument for the majority. "I found out a long time ago that there is no charity in baseball, and that every club owner must make his own fight for existence."[13]

Around the same time, Bill Veeck, then president of the Chicago Cubs, proposed a series of inter-league games to keep the interest of the fans during the so-called "dog days" lasting between July 5th and the middle of August. Veeck's proposal received the support of four other National League clubs. John Heydler, the league president, supported Veeck's proposal, saying, "We cannot afford to stand pat . . . and rely on a return to the good old days."[14]

The American League clubs, except for the Cleveland Indians, which even then showed the ability to side with a losing cause, would not, however, agree to the plan. The American League was the stuffier of the two leagues, partly because of the dominance that its

Franklin D. Roosevelt opens the 1937 season at Washington, D.C. (Photo courtesy of the National Baseball Library, Cooperstown, N.Y.)

Yankees possessed over the rest of the baseball world. Clark Griffith, the Washington Senators' president, expressed his distaste at Veeck's proposition. "Our business has held up at least as well as any other. We're going on just the way we are."[15] In the end, Griffith's corps prevailed and the profit-sharing plan was abandoned.

This reluctance to make changes based on the times was reflected also in the debate over ticket prices. Despite the drop in attendance, owners were unwilling to cut the price for admission to games to increase the number of customers. Their rationale was that they had not raised ticket prices during the 1920s and should not be expected to reduce them during poor economic times. Only Philip Wrigley, owner of the Chicago Cubs, bucked the trend by offering a special price to children of 25 cents for bleacher tickets in 1935.

Based on similar experiments in the minor leagues, the reluctance of the major league magnates to cut prices may have been a wise decision. When bleacher ticket prices were halved in the American Association minor league in 1932, bleacher sales did not double. One reason for the experiment's failure was that in 1932, a year of high unemployment, minor league attendance in general fell off sharply. Moreover, many fans who would have bought the more expensive box seats decided to save their money and purchase bleacher tickets.[16]

Though fans had to pay the same ticket prices as in more prosperous times, they found that one of the recently accepted customs was being called into question. In earlier times, it was tradition for fans to return foul balls to the playing field. However, when a St. Louis Cardinals fan refused to turn over a ball to the usher one day during the 1920s, the usher responded by dragging him to owner Sam Breadon's office—dragging him, that is, by the feet. The Cardinals eventually settled with the man out of court for $1,200. From then on, fans catching foul balls were given the option of exchanging the ball for a free admission to another game. If they refused to part with the ball, owners decided it was easier just to let the fan keep it.[17]

By the late 1920s, then, it was common for fans to keep the ball. When the Depression struck, the practice became criticized. The *Sporting News* asked why baseball fans should be allowed to keep balls when patrons of other sports did not enjoy the same privilege. And in fact, the cost of balls was not negligible. Balls cost $1.25 each and teams used between 6,000 and 10,000 balls each year.[18] Perhaps because owners reasoned that the loss of goodwill would outweigh the savings in balls, no formal motion disallowing fans from keeping foul balls was ever brought forward. This change, after all, had been initiated by fans and not by clubs.

Though owners may have wished that they could continue unaffected by the Depression, they eventually had no choice except make changes or suffer serious economic consequences. Not surprisingly, the changes introduced first were targeted at player salaries. These and other measures sought to meet the difficulties of "hard times" by cutting costs.

By the end of 1930, with the economy slipping steadily, it became clear that player salaries were going to be reduced. Baseball players, classified as skilled laborers at best, were told that their salaries were "out of proportion if compared with what skilled labor receives for an all-year around occupation."[19] An editorial in the *Sporting News* informed players that they should be prepared to expect as much as a 25 percent cut in pay and if that happened they "would not have been treated more harshly than men have been treated in other employments."[20]

The next year, with baseball's finances approaching the red, baseball magnates, during their annual winter meeting, formally resolved to substantially reduce player salaries.

Unlike what happened in the minor leagues, though, the big leagues did not adopt a salary limit, nor did owners name a specific percentage of how much wages would be cut.[21]

In fact, though salaries were indeed lower for the next two years, the reductions were not as severe as many had anticipated. Salaries for major leaguers averaged just over $6,000, down $1,500 from the 1929 level, a significant drop but hardly a draconian one. By contrast, the average earnings for employees for all industries had fallen to $1,064 by 1933, only 75 percent of the 1929 level. Player salaries looked even better when compared with what had happened to their minor league brethren. Wages for players in the Class D leagues, the lowest minor league classification, had plunged to an average of $330, only 40 percent of the average in 1929.[22]

Though economic conditions would have undoubtedly precipitated salary cuts anyway, the process was aided by the decline of baseball's greatest star. Babe Ruth had earned as much as $80,000 during his prime, but by the time the Depression hit, he was in his mid-30s and could no longer command the same wages. When he signed his contract for $35,000 in January 1934 for the upcoming season, it represented a cut of $45,000 from his salary of three years earlier. Because Ruth's salary was regarded as the yardstick by which most owners paid their players, the magnates were able to use the Ruth example to justify cuts to their players.[23]

1937 All-Stars, from left to right: Gehrig, Cronin, Dickey, DiMaggio, Gehringer, Foxx, and Greenberg. (Photo courtesy of the National Baseball Library, Cooperstown, N.Y.)

Though players were not happy about the scaling down of salaries, they generally accepted the cuts without much of a hassle. The widely anticipated holdouts did not materialize. Pitcher Burleigh Grimes summed up the prevailing view of the time. "The ball player . . . is a fortunate man. In other occupations, there has been a shrinkage in salaries and lack of employment. The ball player, under terms of his contract has gone on daily and been paid in full."[24]

Besides, even if a player was displeased with his salary he had little choice but to accept it anyway. The reserve clause binding a player to one team was still very much in existence. Few ballplayers could find more financially rewarding jobs in the outside world, if they could find any jobs at all.

To further impress upon their players the importance of cutting salaries to meet the times, baseball officials themselves took pay reductions. National League president John Heydler told owners upon his re-election to another term that he insisted on having his salary reduced to set an example for the players. The same year, Commissioner Landis took a pay cut of $25,000, a reduction of 40 percent. Though the cut was voluntary, had Landis not reduced his salary there was some evidence to suggest he would not have been re-elected to another term.[25]

Reduction of player salaries was not the only measure by the owners to cut operating expenses. At the December 1931 winter meetings, owners reduced the active player rosters from 25 to 23 men. The American League favored a reduction to 22 players but the National League decided against it. The *Sporting News* insisted that a 20-man roster would be more than adequate.[26] Coaching staffs were pared to a minimum as were front office personnel. Umpires' salaries were trimmed also. The Depression years saw an increase in player–managers, not because owners suddenly came to the conclusion that they were more qualified than non-playing managers, but because it was cheaper to pay one man to do two jobs.[27]

To save further on operating expenses, owners voted to adopt a standardized ball, beginning with the 1934 season. This action was taken partly because major league teams for years had spent large sums for players whose averages had been inflated by an extraordinarily lively ball. (Because there were so many minor leagues, it sometimes was difficult to determine always which leagues used the jackrabbit balls.) When teams in higher classifications purchased these players, it became clear that often a player's high batting average resulted more from the juiced-up ball than from real talent. During the Depression, owners had to be more financially cautious and could not afford to take excessive risks on players who might not pan out.[28]

The adoption of a lively ball as the standard also reflected owners' attempts to try to generate revenue as well as to cut back on expenses. The decision to use a lively ball, patterned after the American League model, was based on the theory that fans prefer home runs to pitching duels. Also, owners agreed to the new ball with the hope that the weaker teams would gain most from the change, thus increasing competitiveness and therefore, attendance.

Though the Depression struck baseball later than most other industries, clearly the sport had cut back pay and personnel as business in general had done. Just as American workers had to take pay cuts—U.S. Steel set the standard for the time by cutting wages 10 percent—most baseball players had to accept less than they had received in better economic times.[29] However, while corporations found it necessary to lay-off workers with little notice, ballplayers had much more security. Though rosters were reduced from 25 to 23 men, those men who did make the major league roster were paid their entire salaries.

Both baseball and industry leaders resisted the temptation to cut the price of goods.

Baseball owners refused to cut ticket prices; industry leaders, even after the National Recovery Act (NRA) was declared unconstitutional in 1935, generally held prices firm. However, while the Supreme Court's ruling against the NRA ended President Roosevelt's most ambitious early New Deal program to improve conditions during the Depression, baseball officials had no such barriers as the Supreme Court to hamper experimentation.

Some changes were relatively insignificant, but others were not. Several innovations instituted during the Depression, for example, changed the sport of baseball forever. One was the advent of public address systems. Because many teams, especially those in the National League, were inexplicably reluctant to follow the Yankees' example of numbering players, and the megaphones used to relay information to fans were often not loud enough for many fans to hear, many spectators had a difficult time knowing who was playing or exactly what was going on. For example, in a late-season game in 1933 when the New York Giants, just after the Cardinals had taken a four-run lead, broke into a wild celebration, fans at Sportsman's Park in St. Louis probably thought the visiting team had gone berserk. Unbeknown to most fans, the Giants were celebrating having clinched the National League pennant after receiving word that the second-place Pittsburgh Pirates had been eliminated after a loss.

Though it is difficult, if not impossible, to determine whether the Depression's impact on attendance led to the installation of loudspeakers or whether it was simply a natural development that would have happened anyway, the fact is that by the end of the 1930s, almost every owner had installed public address systems and the change was advertised as a means of attracting fans.

Another development of the Depression era was the inauguration of the All-Star game. Though perhaps not technically a Depression-inspired measure either, the All-Star game nonetheless reflected baseball's attempt to aid the poverty-stricken, both ex-players and the needy in general, during the period. The All-Star game was the brainchild of Arch Ward, sports editor of the *Chicago Tribune*. After watching an exhibition baseball game at the 1932 Chicago World's Fair, Ward came up with the idea of a game pitting the stars of each league against each other. He solicited and received the support of the two league presidents and Commissioner Landis. In 1933 the first game, held in Chicago's Comiskey Park, was played. Much of the proceeds from the game went to a fund of which some were given to needy ex-ballplayers. Because of the favorable response the game received, the owners decided to make the exhibition an annual event.[30]

The All-Star game may have been the most publicized example of baseball's contributions to charity, but it was not the only one. In 1931 Landis extended the deadline prohibiting exhibition games from October 31st to November 15th so as to allow the playing of contests "from which the entire receipts go to relief or charity funds."[31] That year, charity games netted approximately $250,000 to funds aiding the unemployed.[32]

Linking baseball to technology (loudspeakers) or to charity (the All-Star game) and simultaneously attracting a wider viewer audience were non-controversial developments and coincidental with the Depression's impact upon the game of baseball. The argument about the continuation of radio broadcasting of baseball games, on the other hand, was both controversial and directly a consequence of the Depression.

The debate during the Depression about the merits of radio broadcasting illustrated how easy it can be to perceive what are in reality strengths as liabilities. It also shows the constraints which a depression mentality exercised upon perceptions.

The issue of radio broadcasting had been controversial ever since 1921, when Harold Arlin broadcast the first game for station KDKA in Pittsburgh. Many owners feared that potential paying customers would stay at home and listen to radio broadcasts. Given the

Depression environment, the fears were exacerbated and not unreasonable, even if un-founded. During almost every year's winter meetings, a proposal to ban broadcasts would be brought up, though no ban was ever enacted. Each owner decided whether or not to allow broadcasts. Many owners were convinced that radio broadcasts harmed attendance. But as the experience of the St. Louis Cardinals in 1934 showed, owners who thought radio broadcasts hurt attendance were wrong. Though the Cards were one of the first teams to broadcast games in the 1920s, team owner Sam Breadon wasn't sure of its benefits after dismal attendance figures in 1932 and 1933. Before the 1934 season, Breadon announced in a statement with St. Louis Browns owner Phil Ball that broadcasts from Sportsman's Park would be barred.

"There, no doubt, was a time when the microphones did us some good," Breadon said. "That was in the high times. But now we are at a point where we are willing to experiment a season without the 'mikes.' "[33]

As the attendance figures from 1934 showed, however, the ban backfired. The decision not to allow broadcasts was almost certainly the major cause for the disappointing attendance in 1934. The 325,000 fans the eventual World Champions attracted in 1934 were 283,000 fewer than the 1931 championship team had drawn, despite the fact that the 1934 pennant race was much tighter than the one in 1931. Furthermore, while the 1931 Cardinals garnered 13.28 percent of the National League's attendance—14 percent was the average for a pennant winner—the 1934 Gashouse Gang, regarded by baseball historians as one of the most colorful ever, lured only 10.16 percent of the league's crowds.[34]

Slowly, the obstinance of most owners faded, though pockets of resistance remained. The three New York teams—the Yankees, Dodgers, and Giants—barred radio broadcasts in 1934, a ban that continued until 1939.[35] Gradually, though, resistance melted away, perhaps because radio was producing an increasing amount of revenue for those teams which continued broadcasts. In 1933, broadcast rights sold to radio stations accounted for just .3 percent of revenue; six years later the percentage had increased to 7.3 percent.[36] In 1936, Commissioner Landis signed a contract selling the exclusive broadcast rights to the World Series for $100,000.[37]

If there was any other single thing that had a more influential long-term effect than the widespread use of radio, it was the introduction of what one owner erroneously predicted would be "the ruination of baseball"—night games.[38] Night baseball was not a new development. In fact, baseball had been played under lights a half century earlier, one year after Thomas Edison perfected the light bulb.[39] In 1909, a lighting system devised by George Cahill was tried in Cincinnati with the hope that the system could one day be suitable for major league use. Though witnesses were impressed by the system, it was clear that further development was needed. A similar experiment was done in Chicago ten years later, but nothing materialized from it.[40]

When the Depression struck, minor league clubs, which had often struggled in the best of economic times, were quick to try night ball. Minor league club owners knew that most people could not take off work early to see afternoon games, and they saw no reason why night ball should not be attempted. There is some debate about where the first minor league night game was played. The general belief is that the inaugural contest was held in Independence, Kansas, in 1930, though a game in Des Moines, Iowa, a few days later, received more publicity.[41]

Wherever its origin, night ball was an immediate success. Though at first the quality of lighting was spotty, in time the kinks were worked out and visibility proved to be almost the equal of play during the daytime. Owners in every major league classification rushed to install lights. The cost of installation ranged from under $5,000 for a spartan system with lights mounted on wooden telephone poles to $25,000 for more elaborate systems using steel towers. The electricity cost per game varied from $10 for inexpensive systems to $50 for more elaborate set-ups. The benefits proved to be well worth the costs. As the owners hoped, attendance (and therefore revenue) shot up dramatically, giving many minor leagues at least a temporary respite from the Depression's impact.[42]

Still, many remained unconvinced that night ball had a future. In 1933, noting that night game attendance had subsided, the *Sporting News* stated that baseball under the lights "had run its course" and the publication reaffirmed its notion that "baseball is essentially a daytime game."[43] *The Literary Digest* cited the attendance decline to question the long-term usefulness of nocturnal play. The magazine quoted an executive from the Louisville minor league team who declared that the future of night ball would be as a novelty rather than as an everyday occurrence.[44] However, the drop in attendance no doubt occurred because of a worsening of the Depression and not because night ball was a fad whose time had come and gone.

By 1934, with the economy slowly recovering and minor league attendance on the upswing, it became clear that night ball was indeed proving its worth. Even the *Sporting News* changed its tune. "Times are changing and baseball must keep step . . . Men are not going to quit their tasks during the week to go to ballgames, for their jobs are too precious and the time is too short. But a vast majority of them would welcome a chance to go in the evenings to relax," read one editorial. At the year-end winter meetings, the National League, reeling from a loss of $243,000 for the 1934 season, reluctantly accepted a plan at the urging of Cincinnati Reds general manager Larry MacPhail and new owner Powell Crosley to permit teams to play seven night ball games.

This decision was met with immediate and virulent criticism by the American League, which had lost only one-fifth as much money as the senior circuit in 1934 and whose owners were not as desperate to experiment. Night ball in the minor leagues was one thing, opponents declared, but to play ball after dark in the majors bordered on sacrilege. "A cowardly surrender to commercialism," protested one critic. "The National League has become a burlesque circuit," declared Washington Senators' president Clark Griffith.[45]

Despite the criticism, night ball would get its chance in the major leagues. The first nocturnal game was played on May 24, 1935, in Cincinnati between the Reds and the Philadelphia Phillies. By all accounts, the experiment was a resounding success. The $50,000 lighting system replete with 616 1,500-watt bulbs "literally turned night into day."[46] Neither the players nor the fans had problems picking up the ball. Twenty thousand fans, ten times the number of fans the lowly Reds were accustomed to playing for, witnessed the event. Even American League president Will Harridge admitted that the game was "the best spectacle I've seen in years. Nothing is lost by playing at night."[47]

The success at Cincinnati did not send critics or night ball into wild retreat. They still maintained that nocturnal games cheapened the sport. They insisted that the novelty would soon wear off. They were wrong. Attendance in Cincinnati doubled in 1935 over the previous year, in no small part to the seven night games. For the first time since 1926, the Reds turned a profit, earning almost $50,000 for the season.[48]

But night baseball, for all the exaggerated claims of its success, did not, in truth, bring prosperity back to the major leagues during the Depression itself. Rather it was, as Judge Landis had predicted in 1934, the slow but general recovery of the economy as a whole which produced the revival. By 1935, baseball had turned the corner. The economy had begun to recover and the Depression-caused adjustments, namely salary cuts, were already in place. Owners felt that they did not need nocturnal games to earn a profit.

Cincinnati was the only team with lights until 1938. But by then, night ball had proven itself over the long haul. The lasting significance of night ball in the 1930s was that the Depression had given night ball a chance to be tried. Had Cincinnati not been in such deep financial difficulties, it seems highly unlikely that the other, highly tradition-conscious owners would have granted permission to the Reds to play night games. Before the end of the decade, however, enough owners had night ball to realize that it could be profitable. By 1941, nine of the 16 major league teams were hosting nocturnal games.

By that year, however, a new external force was just beginning to force its way onto the national pastime. The Depression was soon to be yesterday's nightmare. World War II was to be the new one. Two months after the Yankees defeated the Dodgers to capture the 1941 World Series, the Japanese bombed Pearl Harbor. Not until 1946 would baseball return to a normal state. But those wartime years were another and different story.

NOTES

1. Frederick Lewis Allen, *Since Yesterday*. (New York: Harper & Row, 1939), 24.
2. U.S. House of Representatives report, *Organized Baseball*, 1615.
3. *Ibid.*, 1599.
4. *Ibid.*, 1599, 1600.
5. "Hard Times Hit the Minors," *Literary Digest*, July 30, 1932, 37.
6. U.S. House of Representatives report, *Organized Baseball*, 1615.
7. "Hard Times Hit the Minors," 37.
8. U.S. House of Representatives report, *Organized Baseball*, 1600.
9. *Ibid.*
10. G.H. Fleming (Ed.), *The Dizziest Season*, (New York: William Morrow, 1984), 19.
11. The *Sporting News*, October 3, 1932.
12. U.S. House of Representatives report, *Organized Baseball*, 1599.
13. David Q. Voigt, *American Baseball*, (Norman, OK: University of Oklahoma Press, 1970), 251.
14. The *New York Times*, August 24, 1933.
15. *Ibid.*
16. The *Sporting News*, December 19, 1932.
17. John Kieran, "Big-League Business," *Saturday Evening Post*, May 31, 1930, 16.
18. *Ibid.*
19. The *Sporting News*, February 5, 1931.
20. *Ibid.*
21. The *New York Times*, December 11, 1931.
22. U.S. House of Representatives report, *Organized Baseball*, 1610.
23. G.H. Fleming (Ed.), *The Dizziest Season*, 30.
24. The *Sporting News*, February 5, 1931.
25. David Q. Voigt, *American Baseball*, 149.
26. The *Sporting News*, July 29, 1932.
27. G.H. Fleming (Ed.), *The Dizziest Season*, 31.
28. *St. Louis Post-Dispatch*, December 6, 1932; a lively ball is one that is wound extremely tightly, thus making the ball's core much harder and therefore the ball goes further and faster when hit.
29. Robert Smith, *Baseball*. (New York: Simon & Schuster, 1970), 228.
30. David Q. Voigt, *American Baseball*, 222.
31. The *New York Times*, October 23, 1931.
32. The *Sporting News*, October 1, 1931.
33. *Ibid.*, February 8, 1934.
34. U.S. House of Representatives report, *Organized Baseball*, 1600, 1617.
35. Red Barber, *The Broadcasters*. (New York: Dial Press, 1970), 92.
36. U.S. House of Representatives report, *Organized Baseball*, 1610.
37. David Q. Voigt, *American Baseball*, 233.
38. The *Sporting News*, February 21, 1952.
39. "The First Night Baseball Game—Ever," *Yankee Magazine*, August 1975.

40. Oscar Eddleton, "Under the Lights," in *Insider's Baseball*, L. Robert Davids (Ed.). (New York: Charles Scribner's Sons, 1983), 160.

41. *Ibid.*

42. The *Sporting News,* January 24, 1935.

43. *Ibid.*, January 26, 1933.

44. "Dark Side of Night Baseball," *Literary Digest,* February 16, 1932, 40.

45. *St. Louis Post-Dispatch,* December 12, 1934.

46. The *Sporting News,* May 30, 1935.

47. *Ibid.*

48. U.S. House of Representatives report, *Organized Baseball,* 1600.

Moses Fleetwood Walker: The First Black Major League Baseball Player

LARRY BOWMAN

In the spring of 1947 as the baseball season opened, Branch Rickey and his Brooklyn Dodgers commenced what Rickey called the "noble experiment."[1] The "noble experiment" Rickey referred to was in reality a revolution. Rickey's "experiment" concerned the inclusion of John Roosevelt ("Jackie") Robinson on the Dodgers' roster for the 1947 season and heralded an end to the ban on black ballplayers in the major leagues. Informed observers who followed the black Dodger's progress through spring training and the opening of the 1947 season understood that the euphemism "noble experiment" actually meant the arrival of a long overdue change in the composition of baseball teams and a change for American society in general. Baseball was finally expelling Jim Crow. As all manner of publicity and controversy followed Robinson's pioneering efforts to break down the color line in the big leagues, the "experiment" gained a convert. In July 1947, Bill Veeck, the owner of the Cleveland Indians, announced he had purchased the contract of Larry Doby, a powerful hitter, from the Newark Eagles.[2] When Doby joined the Indians' roster in the summer of 1947, the color line in the American League was also breached. Organized baseball leagues went through the often unpleasant process of ending racial exclusion while Robinson, Doby, and a handful of talented black athletes in the minor leagues proved themselves as players, endured slights and insults, found white friends, and steadily ensured that the "noble experiment" was indeed a revolution.

Throughout the late 1940s and early 1950s as more and more of the major league teams installed blacks in their lineups, the media reported this monumental change in baseball in great detail. The names of Robinson, Doby, Dan Bankhead, Roy Campanella, Luke Easter, Don Newcombe, Samuel Jethroe, and others became familiar to baseball fans everywhere, but Jackie Robinson occupied the forefront of the "noble experiment." In the eyes of millions of Americans, Robinson became an important symbol and hero, and, unfortunately, to other millions of Americans, he became a villain. Regardless of the reactions to Robinson, he was widely perceived by the general public as being the first black to compete in the big leagues. Robinson proved himself as a courageous man and as an exciting performer and he deserved all the praise he received, but, as knowledgeable baseball fans then knew, he was not the first of his race to make the roster of a major league baseball team. That honor belonged to Moses Fleetwood Walker who had a brief major league career 63 years before Robinson made his historic debut with the Brooklyn Dodgers.

In spite of the distinction of being the first black in the major leagues, Moses Fleetwood Walker died on May 11, 1924, a nearly forgotten and embittered man.[3] At the time of his death, Walker was a resident of Cleveland, Ohio, where in the final years of his life he lived in quiet retirement. Although he was a discernible figure in Cleveland's black community, it was his baseball career of 40 years earlier that won him a bit of local notoriety and probably contributed to his deep-seated disillusionment with American society that became so manifest in the last two decades of his life.

During the summer of 1884, Walker played in 61 games for the Toledo club of the American Association. In the formative days of organized professional baseball, the American Association was considered a major league from 1882 to 1891, and Toledo, which was a new member of the American Association in 1884, signed Walker as one of the club's catchers.[4] Walker subsequently made his first appearance in the league on May 1, 1884, when Toledo opened its season in Kentucky against the Louisville team.[5] The game drew about 3,000 spectators who caused no incident while witnessing an historic event. Walker's debut was, however, unspectacular. Louisville defeated Toledo 5–1 and Walker went hitless in four times at bat and was charged with five errors.[6] He was not, in all likelihood, pleased with his first game, but Walker probably realized that he was the first black to appear in the major leagues and that, in and of itself, must have made May 1, 1884, something of a memorable day for him.

Details concerning Moses' early life are sparse. He was born on October 7, 1857, in the little eastern Ohio town of Mount Pleasant into what appears to have been an unusual family.[7] Little is known about his father, Moses W. Walker, who was a practicing physician and less is known about his mother, Caroline O'Hara Walker.[8] Historical evidence clearly suggests, however, that the Walkers were prudent people, good parents, and keenly interested in the welfare of their children. All the Walker children did well in life, served as community leaders, and, in general, proved themselves to be worthy people.

Even though Mount Pleasant was a tiny village, it did have one distinction that may have made it attractive to the Walkers. A sizeable number of Quakers lived in and around Mount Pleasant and they were active in the Underground Railroad that smuggled slaves northward to freedom in the years prior to the Civil War.[9] It is unknown if the Walkers were involved in the Underground Railroad's crusade, but they probably approved of its activities and found the local environment an acceptable one.

A few years after young Moses was born, the senior Walker moved his family to nearby Steubenville, established a medical practice, and there reared his growing family. Until he was about 20 years old, little of young Moses' life can be accurately reconstructed. He probably lived a comfortable, protected childhood while being imbued with his parents' values and expectations. Then, at the age of 20, Moses arrived on the campus of Oberlin College, and, at that point, the circumstances and events that shaped his life became a bit easier to locate, identify, and assess.

After several months of study in Oberlin College's Preparatory School, Moses, who was now nearly 21 years old, was admitted to the college's freshman class in the fall of 1878.[10] Moses enrolled in such classes as Latin, Greek, French, German, geometry, algebra, trigonometry, botany, chemistry, zoology, and others and compiled a competent but undistinguished record as a student.[11] Although he was black and a bit older than most of his classmates, Walker apparently never observed that his unique status ever had anything but an acceptable effect upon his life as an undergraduate at Oberlin. During his three years at Oberlin, Moses proved himself to be a sociable, competent student who possessed better than average talent as an athlete. Even though he found his fare at Oberlin relatively agreeable, he never really settled into the school's academic mainstream. One clue may indicate that the fruits of academia may have become increasingly less important to him during his sojourn there. Transcripts at Oberlin in 1870s not only recorded students' grades, they also recorded their class attendance. During his freshman year,

Moses Fleetwood Walker. (Photo courtesy of the National Baseball Library, Cooperstown, N.Y.)

Moses missed only 26 classes and failed to attend 47 classes his sophomore year. Almost 23 years old when his junior year began, he missed a total of 116 classes during his last two terms at Oberlin.[12]

His conduct may not have been unusual for an undergraduate at Oberlin in the 1870s and 1880s, but his grade average also declined as a consequence of his waning class participation. On the other hand, however, he had begun to develop a new interest outside the realm of academic pursuits. Baseball became a popular sport in post-Civil War America, and Moses began to pursue his interest in the game in an active fashion while he was enrolled at Oberlin.

If Oberlin College did not motivate Walker to high academic achievement, it did nurture his growing fascination with baseball. The *Oberlin Review* reported in the fall of 1880 that a new baseball diamond, paid for by faculty and student subscription, had been dedicated and that the campus facility was to be the site of intramural competition.[13] Walker was among the group of students who formed the teams using the new diamond that fall, and, when a varsity team was established in the spring of 1881, he joined that team and became its catcher.

With the creation of a varsity baseball team, Oberlin sought other teams to challenge, and played a brief schedule during Walker's last term on campus. Among the opponents the Oberlin team played in 1881 was the also newly formed team from the University of Michigan. Moses performed well in Oberlin's encounters with Michigan and drew attention to himself.[14] He caught, fielded, and hit with authority and ran the bases with above average skill. He was, apparently, a natural ballplayer. Moses' involvement with baseball for the next decade clearly indicated he enjoyed the game, and he obviously possessed noticeable athletic skills.

In 1881 Walker left Oberlin without finishing his course of study and eventually decided to enroll at the University of Michigan to attend law school and to play baseball the following spring. He played in five games for the University of Michigan in 1882, hit .308, and drew praise for his catching, throwing, and base running.[15] By the time Moses had completed the 1882 baseball season he apparently had earned quite a reputation as a ballplayer because, even though he returned to classes at Michigan for the academic year of 1882–1883, he became a professional ballplayer when he joined the Toledo club in the spring of 1883.[16] At that point, Toledo was a member of the Northwestern League, a good, minor league franchise.[17]

So far as the records will reveal, Walker, who now was often referred to as "Fleet," did not publicly discuss why he decided to leave the University of Michigan in 1883 to become a professional ballplayer. Most likely among the reasons for turning to baseball, in view of his mild interest in academic pursuits, was that he was a 25-year-old man who possessed obvious skills as an athlete and a career as a professional athlete offered excitement and financial reward. Whatever his motivations may have been, Walker left the University of Michigan, abandoned his law studies, and moved to nearby Toledo to begin his baseball career.

His choice, as far as baseball was concerned, was a good one. The Toledo team was composed of a number of good, young ballplayers who immediately made their club a contender for the league's title. Moses did his share in contributing to Toledo's successful season. He hit .251 and established a reputation for himself as a durable catcher.[18]

Moses had a good season but not a great one. He was, for example, fourth among league catchers in hitting, tenth in fielding percentage, and first only in the number of games caught.[19] Injuries undoubtedly hindered his performance; overall, Walker's statistics as a catcher ranked him as a durable, competent, but scarcely spectacular player. Six of his teammates had higher batting averages and seven of his teammates stood higher in their positions' rankings for fielding averages.[20] Even though he endured the ordeal of catching in an era when a catcher's equipment was in a primitive state, Moses could not be termed a star player. He simply did not have the statistics to support that status even though later generations of writers have often attempted to elevate him to that level.

Sporting Life did not report a single racially-motivated incident involving Walker during the 1883 season. In fact, *Sporting Life* treated him as something of a curiosity. In the "Notes and Comments" section of the July 22, 1883 edition, the editor, who commented on some of the oddities of professional baseball and its salary structure, wrote:

> Columbus has a deaf mute and Cleveland a one-armed pitcher, Toledo a colored catcher and Providence a deaf centre-fielder; and yet these men can earn about $2,000 per annum apiece.[21]

Apparently, Walker found playing baseball in small, midwestern towns a racially uncomplicated experience even though he may have been viewed as something of an oddity and treated accordingly. If the estimate of players' salaries was relatively accurate, Moses certainly must have found his first year in professional baseball a financially rewarding one. In any event, Moses' first year was spent with a winning team, playing in a relatively benign environment, and probably fulfilling his desire for excitement and financial gain. Toledo won the league's title in 1883 and there was talk that the club would join the American Association in 1884. That meant that Walker and his teammates would move to a higher level of competition.[22] All this speculation about Toledo's potential change in leagues must have pleased Moses. He had proved himself to be a sturdy catcher and he soon would have the opportunity to match his skills against better opponents than he had faced in the Northwestern League.

In 1884, the eight-team American Association, which was then considered to be a major league equal to the older National League, admitted five new members in an expansion movement that did not pay much attention to the new members' financial condition, personnel, or playing facilities.[23] It was sort of a helter-skelter expansion for the Association and, rather suddenly, several teams, Toledo among them, found themselves thrust into a new, faster level of competition.[24] In 1883, before joining the American Association, Moses and his teammates had competed in a league whose teams never travelled more than a couple of hundred miles from home. Now, a year later in the American Association, they would play as far east as Brooklyn and as far west as St. Louis with ten other stops between those termini. The American Association was truly national in its geographical scope and its talented teams played well against non-league rivals. In those early and formative days of professional baseball, the American Association, along with the National League, deserved the designation of being major, professional baseball leagues.

Moses opened the season as Toledo's regular catcher on May 7, 1884, and *Sporting Life* reported that Toledo ". . . suffered greatly through the errors of Walker who made three terrible throws . . ." in its 5–1 loss to Louisville.[25] Toledo lost its first six games while playing Louisville, St. Louis, and Cincinnati. Finally, against Cincinnati, Toledo won its first game of the season. Walker was in the lineup in six of the first seven games and had five hits in 20 at-bats for a .227 average. He committed seven errors, and was charged with six passed balls.[26] Even though he got off to an inauspicious start, Walker's manager, Charles Morton, apparently had great confidence in his catcher since Morton kept Moses in the fourth spot in the lineup and rested the catcher sparingly.

A rugged man who had his manager's respect, nevertheless the 1884 season was something of a disappointment to Walker. Injuries didn't help. Moses had coped with injuries during the 1883 season, but 1884 brought more numerous and serious injuries for him to surmount. Several factors, aside from bad luck, conspired against him. For one thing, catchers' equipment was just evolving in the 1880s, and Moses, as did other catchers, had little means of protection from the ravages of the baseball as it abruptly arrived in his hands or against his body. Catchers' gloves, chest protectors, and shin guards were virtually unknown in the early 1880s, and Walker usually caught wearing only a mask. An article by William A. Brewer in the *Negro Digest,* documents Walker's lack of protection:

> G.L. Mercerau, a former Toledo baseball mascot, served as bat boy part of Walker's tenure with that club. Reminiscing gently about the great catcher, Mercerau, who was about 10 years old at the time he saw Fleet in action, said the only catching paraphernalia regularly used by the catcher was a mask. On occasion, Mercerau recalled, Walker used an ordinary glove of lambskin fabric with the forefinger split and a small padding in the palm of his hand.[27]

In spite of the fact that catchers routinely took their positions six feet or more behind the hitters, they were, with so little protective gear available to them, extremely vulnerable. By July, both Walker and fellow catcher and teammate James McGuire were hampered by painful hand bruises and a variety of minor injuries.[28] American Association catchers, in general, were victimized, *Sporting Life* asserted, by the fact that the league permitted pitchers to deliver to the plate while their arms rose above the line of their shoulders.[29] Allowing pitchers to throw overhand probably did not cause that many problems for Walker, but, regardless of *Sporting Life*'s point of view, Walker and McGuire, who took the catcher's position deep behind the hitters, could scarcely avoid suffering hand injuries.

Another factor which surely contributed to Walker's woes that season was his relationship with Anthony Mullane, Toledo's leading pitcher. Mullane was a hard-throwing, mean-spirited man who disliked Walker for no other reason than that the catcher was black. Years later Mullane admitted that Walker was:

> . . . the best catcher I ever worked with, but I disliked a Negro and whenever I had to pitch to him I used to pitch anything I wanted without looking at his signals. One day he signalled me for a curve and I shot a fast ball at him. He caught it and walked down to me. 'Mr. Mullane,' he said, 'I'll catch you without signals, but I won't catch you if you are going to cross me when I give you a signal.' And all the rest of that season he caught everything I pitched without knowing what was coming.[30]

Mullane's conduct certainly did nothing to help Walker to try to avoid injury and in July he was struck by a foul tip and suffered a fractured rib.[31] After July 12, 1884, when Moses was seriously hurt, he played only a few games in August and early September before he was released. During his last five games Moses was dropped to ninth in the batting order and had only three hits. The season's toll of injuries, minor and major, finally rendered Moses nearly ineffective as a hitter and as a catcher.

One of Moses' better recollections about the 1884 season was that his brother, Welday, joined the club and played in the outfield. Welday played in only six games and hit .222, but his arrival on the team must certainly have afforded Moses some companionship and solace as he saw his season ending prematurely.[32]

On a far less attractive plane, Walker encountered overt harassment by racists that summer as the team played on the road. Moses was treated well by the spectators at home when he played in Toledo's League Park, but on the road, especially in Louisville, he was frequently threatened, insulted, and distracted by ugly, mean-spirited fans.[33] He was never assaulted, and he was never barred from a playing field, but all the tension surrounding his appearances may well have affected his performances and his emotional well-being. While playing in the Northwestern League in 1883, Moses had no difficulties rising above race, but in 1884, in Louisville and elsewhere, cruel epithets stung him; a teammate openly expressed his contempt; and each game held the prospect of another unwanted incident. Nevertheless, Moses persevered until injuries forced him out of the lineup. When he returned, he was only partly recovered and the quality of his play was poor. Finally, in early September, he was released. The *Toledo Daily Blade* reported that Walker ". . . has been released by the Toledo Association on account of bad health. He was a conscientious player and very popular with the Toledo audience."[34] His career with the Toledo team was finished as were his major league playing days.

Considering the facts that he had an injury-plagued season and played under discernible stress, Moses acquitted himself relatively well. According to *Sporting Life,* which published the American Association's season statistics in the November 26, 1884 issue, Moses did not rank highly in any category. His batting average was .251 which was 45th among the league's hitters and his fielding average of .888 ranked him 25th among catchers.[35] There is no evidence that Walker openly demonstrated bitterness or resentment over his treatment while at Toledo or when he was released. His forbearance was remarkable in view of the fact that, among other unhappy experiences, he had witnessed firsthand the disheartening consequences of racist conduct by at least one teammate and by opposing players and spectators. Moses behaved honorably, played as best he could, and accepted his release without creating any sort of incident.

After the 1884 season Moses remained in organized baseball for another five years. He played on four different teams (Cleveland, Waterbury, Newark, and Syracuse) in four different leagues (the Western League, the Southern New England League, the Eastern League, and the International Association) and compiled a record as a competent yet undistinguished hitter and catcher.[36] His best year was in 1887 with Newark when he hit .263 and led the International Association in putouts.[37] In the other post-Toledo years, Moses' batting averages hovered around .200; it was his defensive work that kept him in the lineup.[38] By 1883, he was one of few blacks competing in the organized professional leagues and by 1889, he was the only black player in the International Association.[39] Then, after the 1889 season with Syracuse when he hit .216 and finished 17th among the league's 18 catchers in fielding, Moses, who would be 32 that coming December, left organized baseball.[40] After six years with minor league teams and most of one season with a major league team, Moses' career as a professional baseball player came to an end.

When Walker retired from baseball, he left a rather unimpressive set of career statistics. True, he played under a type of stress that only black players could comprehend and he was frequently hampered by injuries, but, overall, Walker did not perform in a fashion that set him apart from his contemporaries. His cumulative hitting statistics for those seven years in professional baseball were 303 hits in 1,330 at-bats for a career average of .228.[41] As a catcher, he was tenacious, but he never excelled in fielding percentages when compared to other catchers who competed against him. Contemporary sportswriters did not mention a powerful throwing arm, blazing speed on the base paths, or any other special characteristic of his play; writers, however, sooner or later noted that Moses was a dependable member of his team. In other words, Moses, who was often injured, was a reliable, average ballplayer. The game was developing rapidly, and new, talented players were emerging while Walker failed to mature into anything other than a journeyman catcher.

After retiring from baseball, Moses continued to live in Syracuse, where he was well-known after having played two seasons for the Syracuse Stars and, as events were later to demonstrate, well-liked. In early 1891, Moses was married and supporting his wife, Mary, and their growing family by working as a railroad mail clerk.[42] His work regularly took him to and from New York City and, while his job was not a demanding one, he apparently earned an adequate income. Little information about his years with Mary, who died in 1893 leaving him with two sons and a daughter, has survived. But, in April 1891, their lives were nearly shattered by a frightening incident.[43]

One afternoon, Moses, who had the day off from work, had become intoxicated and was walking through a tough section of Syracuse. As he passed by a saloon, a group of men accosted him, and one of the group, a local hoodlum named Patrick Murray who had a reputation as a petty criminal, got into an argument with Walker and struck him. Walker thereupon drew a knife and stabbed Murray in the groin and then fled the scene before Murray's companions could retaliate. Walker was later arrested and, when Murray died, charged with first degree murder.[44] Fortunately for Walker, Murray's escapades prior to his death were locally notorious and, when his case came before a court, Moses got a fair hearing. On June 3, 1891, Walker's case, which was now reduced to murder in the second degree, was taken before a Court of Oyer and Terminer and the facts of the tragic altercation were presented to a jury. After hearing the evidence, the jury acquitted Walker on the grounds of self-defense.[45] According to the account of the trial printed in *Sporting Life* the jury's verdict was greeted by applause from the spectators. The correspondent also reported that:

> After the tumult had subsided the jury requested that some good advice be given to Walker, and the court complied, telling him that, if he had been addicted to the use of liquor, this was a good time for him to swear off. An order for his formal discharge was then entered by the clerk.[46]

Sporting Life's Syracuse correspondent also observed that public sentiment had favored the prisoner throughout the whole episode and that most people had expected that the charge would be reduced to manslaughter and that Walker would be set free.[47]

Moses was a fortunate man; he had endured a frightening incident that few people experience and he emerged a free man. The legal system and public opinion had protected a black man's rights even though he had killed a white man who probably provoked the incident. A few years later, when Moses wrote a treatise on how blacks could never expect justice from whites, he must have conveniently forgotten the fact that he had stood before the bar of justice accused of killing a white man and that a white-dominated legal system had properly set him free. Even though Moses eventually lost any faith he ever had in the legal system of the nation and in white peoples' capacity to render justice to blacks, once in his lifetime he found himself in need of a fair and impartial hearing before a jury of his peers; he got his hearing and he was vindicated.

Between 1891 when he was residing in Syracuse and 1904 when he settled in Cadiz, Ohio, Walker's life underwent several discernible changes.[48] First of all, his professional baseball career was clearly at an end and his wife had died leaving him a widower with three small children. Moses returned to Ohio, and, in 1898, he married Edna Jane Mason who was a graduate of Oberlin College and a schoolteacher.[49] When he first returned to Ohio, Moses lived in Steubenville until he and his second wife relocated in Cadiz where he was employed as the manager of the local opera house. Then, in 1905, he leased the opera house and soon began running motion pictures once they became a popular form of entertainment.[50] Moses apparently earned a comfortable income from his business and lived a quiet and relatively prosperous life in rural, small-town Ohio.

On the surface it appeared that Moses, whose life had been an eventful one, had found a placid life-style that insulated him from the disturbing, racially-motivated incidents he had experienced as a young man. Moses did find life in Cadiz acceptable; he lived there until 1922, but he did not overlook the fact that black Americans were being oppressed nearly everywhere in America. He was not, for example, unaware of how Ohio was in a state of ferment on the race question and he undoubtedly was disheartened by its social and political consequences.[51] So, with his brother Welday's encouragement, Moses prepared a statement in which he expressed his views on the relationship of blacks and whites and what he thought must be the ultimate solution to the entire situation.

In 1908, as he approached his 51st birthday, Walker publicly set forth his views on the race question when his treatise, *Our Home Colony,* was printed by the Herald Publishing Company of Steubenville, Ohio. His 48-page essay was divided into three unequal parts entitled "The Dark Period," "The Colonial Period," and "The Destined Period."[52] The first two sections of *Our Home Colony* were devoted to an analysis of the past and present of black–white race relations in America, and in the third segment Walker proposed what he believed to be the only solution to end the ongoing racial strife in the United States. Walker was clearly distressed and disillusioned by the persistence of racism in earlier American history and his own times, and he was wholly pessimistic about the likelihood of an accommodation between the black and white races in the foreseeable future. The history of the Negro's role in America, as Walker read it, was one of coercion, sacrifice, and misery. *Our Home Colony* was his protest over an unconscionable wrong done to generations of Americans.

In his discussion of what he called "The Dark Period" Walker indicated he made no pretense of discussing fully the dire impact of slavery upon the American Negro but he did, he believed, point out the worst consequences of two-and-a-half centuries of bondage. Slavery, Walker correctly asserted, brutally oppressed Negroes and denied them opportunities to advance morally, socially, and intellectually.[53] The Negro family was vitiated while, using Walker's phraseology, the Anglo-Saxon master engaged in a mad scramble for profits extracted from the sufferings of an innocent and victimized people. Right, truth, and justice, the goals of any civilized society, were dethroned by avarice, Walker wrote, and generations of Americans, black and white, were debased by a reprehensible exploitation of Negroes.[54]

After delivering a succinct and scathing indictment of the system of slavery and its smothering effects upon its victims, Walker developed a second focus in "The Dark Period." He offered his views on the Civil War and Abraham Lincoln as an emancipator. According to Walker's analysis of the Civil War, it came as a logical consequence to a nation that condoned a monstrous, prolonged exploitation of an enslaved people. He wrote that ". . . national happiness is the direct result of obedience to Justice, Truth and Right; and that National calamities are but punishment for the century."[55] There was no necessity for the war had the principles of right, truth, and justice been promoted for all, but, since those glowing principles were subverted by greedy Anglo-Saxon masters who were abetted by a timid or insensitive society, the war came as punishment for the misdoings of generations of people who directly or indirectly profited from slavery. Walker did not openly state that he believed the Civil War was divine retribution upon a wicked nation, but it is difficult to read *Our Home Colony* and fail to sense that Walker saw the wrath of God on the Civil War battlefields.

Walker also argued that liberty for the slaves was not the issue at stake in the Civil War and that emancipation was a "military necessity" to weaken the Confederate States of America.[56] Rather than viewing Lincoln as a great moral figure, he saw the embattled president as a practical wartime politician seeking means to end a titanic military struggle. Part one of *Our Home Colony* concluded on a somber note. Walker wrote that the

". . . Negro race in America has never during the Dark Period received moral treatment at the hands of the white man, nor has it been able to perform one move for its own improvement."[57]

If the tragic events of "The Dark Period" disturbed him, the second section of *Our Home Colony,* which was entitled "The Colonial Period," clearly expressed Walker's resentment of how race relations had developed in post-Civil War America. In this section of his essay, Walker analyzed events affecting the well-being of black Americans' place in society during the years between the Emancipation Proclamation and the first decade of the 20th century.

Walker conceded that "The Colonial Period" began on proper and hopeful notes. The Emancipation Proclamation, the Civil Rights Act of 1866, and the Thirteenth, Fourteenth, and Fifteenth Amendments to the Constitution put into place the means to establish social and political justice for black Americans.[58] The years between the Emancipation Proclamation and 1870, when the Fifteenth Amendment was added to the Constitution, were, in Walker's opinion, an era in which an end to the uncivilized treatment of American blacks appeared to dawn. History revealed, Walker observed, that Negroes were fated to disappointment as new forms of enforced subservience to their white contemporaries began to emerge as the impetus of Reconstruction began to wane. Then, in 1883, the United States Supreme Court declared much of the Civil Rights Act of 1875 to be unconstitutional and a new, grim reality descended upon an abused and defenseless people.[59] As the effort to establish blacks in the mainstream of American life was gradually abandoned and as Jim Crow cast his intimidating shadow across the nation, Walker correctly observed that the few opportunities recently created for blacks to better themselves began to disappear. In the late 19th century, blacks were systematically placed upon the bottom rung of the socioeconomic ladder and no one, even supposed black leaders, cried out effectively for justice.[60] Black Americans of his day were, Walker reasoned, treated as a subjugated colonial population and they were being placed in a quasi-caste system. The caste system, as he termed the emerging social order, was designed to revive and perpetuate forms of exploitation that were tragically familiar to black Americans.

In the space of time between the repeal of the Civil Rights Act in 1883 and the publication of *Our Home Colony* in 1908, Walker personally experienced the painful and formal reappearance of oppression visited upon blacks by an apparently uncaring society. It is also evident that Walker believed the subjugation of blacks would become more extensive, and, if necessary, more vicious as white Americans condoned the reconquest of their recently liberated black contemporaries.[61] By 1908, Walker was a thoroughly disillusioned man who somehow managed to remain calmly defiant in the face of an overwhelming tide of racism that undeniably swept through the nation. The Negroes of America were, Walker sorrowfully predicted, certain to live as an exploited subculture dominated by a ruthless, greedy, and fundamentally flawed white society.[62]

"The Destined Period" was Walker's final section in *Our Home Colony.* Here he advanced his views on how American Negroes could realistically expect to rebuild their lives and regain their dignity and independence. The only workable solution to the race question, he wrote, ". . . is entire separation of the races by Emigration of the Negro from America."[63] There was no other answer; the association of the races in America began in crime and was unnatural, Walker asserted, and the only means available to blacks to cleanse themselves of the degradation visited upon them by generations of slavery and abuse was to return to "old Africa."[64]

In his conclusion to *Our Home Colony,* Walker rejected the possibilities of intermarriage, education, thrift, industry or the passing of time as avenues to an equitable redress of the plight of his people.[65] Immigration from America and separation from the white man was the only answer to the black man's dilemma of racism in the United States. Walker cited the example of Liberia as proof that black Americans had been successfully repatriated to Africa and he passionately urged his readers to accept the notion of voluntary emigration, as drastic a proposal as that appeared to be, as the only certain means for Negroes to throw off the yoke of racial injustice.

Walker's separationist argument was considered both undesirable and unrealistic by most recognized black leaders in 1908. Men such as Booker T. Washington, W.E.B. DuBois, and other black spokesmen vigorously disagreed on the means Negroes should employ to reach parity with whites, but all opposed emigration to Africa. Walker's *Our Home Colony* amply indicates that he was familiar with the writings of most of the men who spoke out on the race issue, and he was unquestionably conversant with the works of both Washington and DuBois. He also was aware of the controversy aroused in 1903 when DuBois charged that industrial education, Washington's strategy for elevating black Americans' status, had been unwisely emphasized at the expense of liberal arts education. DuBois argued that Negroes needed to prepare themselves for political and cultural advancement if they expected to salvage their hopes for the future, and that, while vocational training was helpful, young leaders were needed for the struggle and they were not produced in the Washington plan. DuBois' point of view fostered a vitriolic quarrel among black leaders in the early 1900s and Walker seemed disheartened by the schism. Walker apparently concluded that not only were Washington, DuBois, and other black spokesman who sought assimilation for blacks into the mainstream of American life on the wrong path but that they were hopelessly divided as well.[66] No matter how skilled, how educated, or cultured black men became, they would never, Walker believed, be accepted as an equal by white men. The only answer for blacks was to leave America.

Our Home Colony was a straightforward presentation of Walker's opinions concerning race relations, and, for the most part, his historical perspective was balanced and accurate. He used historical evidence to support his arguments carefully, and the only major criticism one can level at his essay is that he occasionally omitted evidence that would have strengthened his case. On the whole, however, he did an acceptable job in presenting his views to his readers. In fact, a reader of *Our Home Colony* gains the distinct impression that Walker labored diligently to present the Negro's odyssey in American history in a factual, well-ordered fashion. If any emotion dominated his treatise, it was pessimism. Walker's pessimism concerning the past and future of race relations is not at all difficult to comprehend. He had experienced alarming encounters with racial discrimination, and he had lived through what C. Vann Woodward in *The Strange Career of Jim Crow* termed an era of "capitulation to racism."[67] Political events, social practice, economic deprivation, and, most of all, court decisions all convinced Walker that racial injustice was irrevocably institutionalized by 1908. His points of view would have been difficult to dispute in the early 1900s; the next civil rights legislation of any consequence was nearly 60 years in the future. Africa was home, and it was the only salvation Walker could imagine as he witnessed the oppression of blacks intensify.

In spite of his plea for American blacks to emigrate home to Africa, Walker remained in the United States until he died in 1924. As best as now can be determined, he never seriously considered relocating in his ancestoral homeland. Between 1908 and 1924, conditions for black Americans steadily worsened and one can only guess how much emotional turmoil Walker experienced as he remained inactive and did not leave for

Africa. Even though he was named for a prophet who led his people out of oppression, Walker never stepped forward and led or set an example by departing for Africa. He simply could not bring himself to act in accordance with his viewpoint.

Moses' second wife died in 1918 and he continued to live in Cadiz until 1922, when, in March 1922, he sold his theater business to a company owned by R.H. Minteer and O.C. Gray.[68] After severing his ties to Cadiz, Moses first moved to Steubenville and then finally relocated in Cleveland where he resided at 2284 East 49th Street. Once he settled in Cleveland in the latter part of 1922, Moses went into retirement. Walker was now almost 65 years old, and he was apparently able to live comfortably on his financial resources.[69] Except for injuries associated with his days as a ballplayer, he had consistently enjoyed good health, and he may have contemplated new business ventures of one sort or another, but that was not to be.

On May 11, 1924, Moses was admitted to Cleveland's City Hospital. When he arrived at the hospital he was desperately ill and died of lobar pneumonia only six hours after he was admitted.[70] The old catcher's end came quickly. An obituary noting his passing appeared in Cleveland's black newspaper, *The Gazette*, and reminded its readers that years ago Walker had been recognized as one of the better ballplayers in the Midwest and that he had been a "... wonderful batter, runner, thrower and heady player."[71] While the obituary may have exaggerated his exploits a bit, it concluded correctly that he had been an affable, intelligent, and deservedly popular player.

Moses' remains were claimed by his son, Thomas, who took them to Steubenville to be buried in Union Cemetery.[72] Moses then slipped into obscurity until the 1940s when Jackie Robinson arrived on the baseball scene and rekindled interest in Walker's career as a ballplayer. Then, when the civil rights movement gained momentum in the 1960s, another generation of writers renewed the public's acquaintance with the man who by now had become something of a legend. Each time Moses' exploits were re-examined, his prowess as a player was magnified.

The assertions that Walker was a good, genial man who played baseball well were unquestionable, but the claims that he was a great baseball player are debatable. During the 1960s Walker was awarded stardom by well-meaning writers who did not critically assess his achievements compared to those of his contemporaries. Moses, nevertheless was a pioneer in baseball's early days; he was also a competent, journeyman catcher and a worthy man. And, if nothing else, he compiled an interesting record while competing for recognition in times difficult to all black Americans.

NOTES

1. Jules Tygiel, *Baseball's Great Experiment: Jackie Robinson and His Legacy* (New York: Vintage Books, 1984), 211.

2. *Ibid.*

3. Robert Peterson, *Only the Ball Was White* (Englewood Cliffs, NJ: Prentice-Hall, Inc., 1970), 46. The *Oberlin News–Tribune* [Oberlin, OH], November 14, 1946.

4. Ocania Chalk, *Pioneers of Black Sport* (New York: Dodd, Mead, and Co., 1975), 6. Hy Turkin and S.C. Thompson, *The Official Encyclopedia of Baseball* (New York: A.S. Barnes and Co., 1973), 39, 43–44.

5. *Ibid.*

6. *Sporting Life,* May 7, 1884, 6.

7. Robert Peterson, *Only the Ball Was White,* 21. *Oberlin News–Tribune* [Oberlin, OH], November 14, 1946.

8. *Harrison News–Herald* (Cadiz, Ohio, May 16, 1985). Almost nothing is known of Moses' mother. In fact, Moses' son, Thomas, did not know his grandmother's maiden name when he supplied information for his

father's death certificate; Division of Vital Statistics, Death Certificate, Department of Health, State of Ohio, File No. 27001, Moses Fleetwood Walker, May 11, 1924.

9. Peterson, *Only the Ball Was White*, 21–22. William Henry Siebert, *The Mysteries of Ohio's Underground Railroad* (Columbus, OH: Long's College Book Co., 1951), 129. For a map placing Mount Pleasant on the network of the Underground Railroad in Ohio, see William Henry Siebert, *The Underground Railroad: From Slavery to Freedom* (New York: Arno Press, 1968), 112–113.

10. *Oberlin News–Tribune* [Oberlin, OH], November 14, 1946.

11. Moses Fleetwood Walker transcript, College Archives, Oberlin College, Oberlin, OH.

12. *Ibid.*

13. *Oberlin News–Tribune* [Oberlin, OH], November 14, 1946.

14. *Ibid.*

15. Moses Fleetwood Walker, Statistics Sheet, National Baseball Library, National Baseball Hall of Fame and Museum, Inc., Cooperstown, New York. Cited hereafter as Statistics sheet.

16. *Sporting Life,* April 22, 1883. A. S. "Doc" Young, *Great Negro Baseball Stars* (New York: A. S. Barnes, 1953), 6. Ocania Chalk, *Pioneers of Black Sport* (New York: Dodd, Mead and Company, 1975), 8.

17. *Sporting Life,* April 22, 1883. The Northwestern League was formed in the autumn of 1882 and was composed of teams located in Bay City, Michigan, Grand Rapids, Michigan, East Saginaw, Michigan, Fort Wayne, Indiana, Springfield, Illinois, Peoria, Illinois, Quincy, Illinois, and Toledo.

18. Statistics sheet. Moses played in 60 of Toledo's games in 1883. He suffered a broken thumb early in the season and missed nearly a month's worth of games before he returned to the lineup. *Sporting Life,* May 27, 1883.

19. *Sporting Life,* November 11, 1883, 2.

20. *Ibid.*

21. *Ibid.,* July 22, 1882, 7.

22. *Ibid.,* October 15, 1883, 6. The Toledo team was owned by a group of stockholders who had formed the Toledo Baseball Association. *Toledo Daily Blade,* July 29, 1884.

23. The thirteen teams, in the order of their standing at the end of the season were the: New York Metropolitans, Columbus Buckeyes, Louisville Eclipses, St. Louis Browns, Cincinnati Reds, Baltimore Orioles, Philadelphia Athletics, Toledo Mudhens, Brooklyn Atlantics, Richmond Virginians, Pittsburgh Alleghenys, Indianapolis Hoosiers, and the Washington Nationals. Turkin and Thompson, *The Official Encyclopedia of Baseball,* 43, 55–56. Also see Chalk, *Pioneers of Black Sport,* 11. The Richmond and Washington teams did not finish the season and played only 42 and 63 games respectively; the other teams played slightly more than 100 games.

24. *Ibid.* All the new teams in the American Association (Toledo, Brooklyn, Richmond, Indianapolis, and Washington) finished in the bottom half of the league's final standings for 1884.

25. *Sporting Life,* May 7, 1884, 6.

26. *Ibid.* May 3, 5, 7, 9, 10, and 11, 1884.

27. William A. Brewer, "Barehanded Catcher," *Negro Digest,* IX (1951), 85–87. Chalk, *Pioneers of Black Sport,* 7. For a brief account of the introduction of catchers' masks and chest protectors in the early days of baseball see Richard E. Noble, "Saving Face: The Genesis of the Catcher's Mask," *Baseball History* Fall (1987), 46–49.

28. *Toledo Daily Blade,* July 22, 1884.

29. *Sporting Life,* September 17, 1884, 5.

30. *The New York Age,* January 11, 1919.

31. Peterson, *Only the Ball Was White, 24. Sporting Life,* August 6, 1884.

32. *Sporting Life,* July 23, 1884, 3.

33. Peterson, *Only the Ball Was White, 23. Toledo Daily Blade,* September 24, 1884.

34. *Toledo Daily Blade,* September 24, 1884. *Sporting Life,* September 20, 1884, 6.

35. *Sporting Life,* November 26, 1884, 4.

36. Peterson, *Only the Ball Was White,* 24–25. *Oberlin News–Tribune,* September 12, 1963. The Cleveland team disbanded on June 6, 1885, and Moses moved on to the Waterbury, Connecticut club that was a member of the Southern New England League. Then, in September, when Norfolk dropped out of the Eastern League, Waterbury joined the Eastern League. *Sporting Life,* June 17, 1885 and September 9, 1885.

37. Statistics sheet. Among the reasons Moses led the league in putouts in 1887, was the fact he caught for George Stovey, a hard-throwing black pitcher, who won 34 games for Newark. Peterson, *Only the Ball Was White,* 25. Also see Chalk, *Pioneers of Black Sport,* 281.

38. *Ibid.*

39. Peterson, *Only the Ball Was White,* 44.

40. Statistics sheet. *Sporting Life,* October 9 and 16, 1889. Syracuse did not place Moses on its reserve list in the fall of 1889, and he, as a consequence, became a free agent. He never signed with another professional baseball club after he was released in 1889.

41. Statistics sheet.

42. *Sporting Life,* April 11, 1891. "Fleetwood Walker," *Black Sports* I (1971), 49. Peterson, *Only the Ball Was White,* 45.

43. *The Gazette* [Cleveland, OH], May 17, 1924, 2.

44. Syracuse Police Record, Syracuse, New York, April 9, 1891.

45. *Sporting Life,* June 6, 1891. *The Gazette* [Cleveland, OH], April 18, 1891.

46. *Sporting Life,* June 6, 1891.

47. *Ibid.*

48. *Cadiz Republican* [Cadiz, OH], March 2, 1922.

49. "Fleetwood Walker," *Black Sports* I (1971), 49. *The Gazette* [Cleveland, OH], May 17, 1924.

50. *Harrison News–Herald* [Cadiz, OH], May 16, 1985. Cadiz had a good-sized black community when Moses settled there. According to an article in the *Cadiz Republican* that appeared on its front page on September 14, 1905, Cadiz's "colored population" was 405 out of the town's total population of 2,244 residents.

51. For an excellent account of racial tensions in Ohio at the time Walker returned to his home state, see David A. Gerber, *Black Ohio and the Color Line, 1860–1915* (Urbana, IL: University of Illinois Press, 1976), 374, 417–418, 425–427.

52. M.F. Walker, *Our Home Colony: A Treatise on the Past, Present and Future of the Negro Race in America* (Steubenville, OH: The Herald Printing Company, 1908), 5.

53. *Ibid.,* 6–7.

54. *Ibid.,* 8.

55. *Ibid.,* 10.

56. *Ibid.,* 10–11.

57. *Ibid.,* 12.

58. *Ibid.,* 15–16. Walker did not mention the Civil Rights Act of 1870 or the Civil Rights Act of 1875. Both acts were designed to clarify the status of blacks during the turmoil of Reconstruction. For good discussions of the various civil rights acts and other issues affecting the rights of Negroes in the aftermath of the Civil War, see C. Herman Prichett, *The American Constitution* (New York: McGraw-Hill Book Company, 1968), 398–410.

59. Stanley I. Kutler, *Judicial Power and Reconstruction Politics* (Chicago: The University of Chicago Press, 1968), 29, 148–49, 159, 166. Albert P. Blaustein and Clarence Clyde Ferguson, Jr., *Desegregation and the Law* (New Brunswick, NJ: Rutgers University Press, 1957), 87–100.

60. Walker, *Our Home Colony,* 18–19, 40–42. Walker, for example, clearly disapproved of Booker T. Washington's views on how Negroes would combat racial oppression. In his famous address in Atlanta, in 1895, Washington admonished black Americans to cast down their buckets and befriend the white man and earn his respect through thrift and hard work. "Atlanta Exposition Address," in Louis R. Harlan (Ed.), *The Booker T. Washington Papers* (Urbana, IL: University of Illinois Press, 1974), III, 583–587. Also Howard Brotz (Ed.), *Negro Social and Political Thought, 1850–1920* (New York: Basic Books, Inc., 1966), 356–359.

61. Walker, *Our Home Colony,* 18–21.

62. *Ibid.,* 31.

63. *Ibid.,* 31–34.

64. *Ibid.,* 31–32, 34–37. Walker also rejected the assimilationist views of Archibald H. Grimke who argued that blacks could prove their worth as laborers in the burgeoning industrial revolution in America and thereby gain acceptance by the white man. See "Modern Industrialization and the Negroes of the United States," by Grimke in Brotz, *Negro Social and Political Thought, 1850–1920,* 464–480.

65. Walker, *Our Home Colony,* 34–44.

66. *Ibid.,* 41–43. Also see William E.B. DuBois, *The Souls of Black Folk* (Chicago: McClurg and Co., 1903), 88–109, 166–188.

67. C. Vann Woodward, *The Strange Career of Jim Crow* (New York: Oxford University Press, 1966) 67–109.

68. *Harrison News-Herald* [Cadiz, OH], May 16, 1985. *The Gazette* [Cleveland, OH], May 17, 1922.

69. Division of Vital Statistics, Certificate of Death, File Number 27001, Moses Fleetwood Walker.

70. *The Gazette* [Cleveland, OH], May 17, 1922.

71. *Ibid.*

72. *Ibid.*

Reminiscing with Riggs Stephenson

WALTER LANGFORD

For 14 seasons in the major leagues, five with the Cleveland Indians and nine with the Chicago Cubs, Riggs Stephenson specialized in whacking the old horsehide to all corners of whatever ball park he happened to be playing in. He did this better than nearly all players in the history of baseball.

The list of lifetime batting leaders in *The Baseball Encyclopedia* places Riggs in the 18th spot among players who had at least 4,000 official at bats. This says that Stephenson was quite a hitter. He hit over .300 in every season except his last one in Cleveland and his final one with the Cubs. In two World Series he slugged the ball at a .378 clip.

All but two of the players ahead of Riggs on the all-time list are comfortably ensconced in the Hall of Fame. Of the two who aren't, one is Shoeless Joe Jackson, who forfeited his right to be third on the list when he became a part of the Black Sox in 1919. The other is Pete Browning from the 19th century.

Stephenson's career average of .336 is better than loads of players who may be better known but weren't better hitters. He stands, for instance, above the likes of Al Simmons, Paul Waner, Eddie Collins, Stan Musial, Honus Wagner, Jimmie Foxx, Joe DiMaggio, Joe Medwick, and innumerable others. All of those just listed are in the Hall of Fame. It seems that Stephenson, like Rodney Dangerfield, "don't get no respect."

Riggs Stephenson was always a quiet, mild-mannered man with the gentle accent of the old South. During his baseball career he was not a showman or a colorful character in the manner of Dizzy Dean or Babe Ruth. He was not a practical joker like Pepper Martin. Though quite adequate in the outfield, he was no Willie Mays. And his throwing arm did not strike terror into base runners. But there is no way you can forget his booming bat and the endless stream of line drives it produced.

In June 1982 I went to Tuscaloosa, Alabama, and talked with Riggs Stephenson. I'm awfully glad now that I did, for Riggs died on November 15, 1985, only seven weeks before his 88th birthday. Affectionately known to his teammates as "Old Hoss," Riggs was by nature not in the least garrulous or even talkative. He always preferred to let his bat do the talking for him. But here is the way he remembered some of the moments and people connected with his sterling career.

"I was born in Akron, down in Hale County, Alabama, on January 5, 1898. My father was a rural mail carrier and I had one sister and two brothers, both of whom played baseball. One pitched for the University of Alabama team and the other played in the Georgia–Alabama League. When I was about 15 years old, I played semipro ball up and down the railroad line. All the little towns around there had baseball teams in those days— Greensboro, Livingston, Eutaw, Marion. That was about the only recreation we had during the summertime.

"After my brother who pitched for Alabama graduated there, he got a job teaching and coaching in Guntersville High School. So I went to that same high school and played football, baseball, and a little basketball.

"Then I started at the University of Alabama in 1917 and played my freshman year on the football team. And when spring came I played baseball. In 1918 we didn't have a football team because of World War I, so I played two more years of football later and kept on playing baseball.

"Our coach was Zinn Scott from Cleveland, and in the spring of 1920 he took me down to New Orleans to try out with the Cleveland Indians. They signed me for $300 a month, and I went back to the University and played baseball. In those days you could sign with a pro team and still play in college if you hadn't played in any pro games.

"In the spring of 1921 the Indians came through the South playing exhibition games. At that time Bill Wambsganss had a broken arm, and Harry Lunte, a reserve infielder, had a charley horse or something. They didn't have anyone else to play second base except Joe Evans, who was an outfielder. So Tris Speaker, the Indian manager, wired me and asked if I could come and play second at the opening of the season. I saw Dean Barnwell at the University and he told me I could finish up my studies later. So I went and joined the Indians.

"We opened the season against the Browns, who had a very good team at that time, with George Sisler, Ken Williams, Baby Doll Jacobson, and Urban Shocker, a great pitcher. I just worked out the first day, but I played second base the next day. Got two hits and didn't have a single fielding chance.

"After Wambsganss got well and back into the lineup, I was used as a utility man and pinch hitter. I had a try at third base for a few games, but I guess I wasn't a very good third baseman. So it went on that way until early in the 1925 season, when Speaker said he wanted to send me down to Kansas City to learn to play the outfield.

"So I went to Kansas City, and while I was there Cleveland had a chance to get a second baseman from Indianapolis named Johnny Hodapp. So they sent me and four or five other fellows to Indianapolis for Hodapp. I think I hit .325 at Indianapolis for the rest of the season.

"In 1926 the Indianapolis team trained at Hot Springs, Arkansas, with Donie Bush as our manager. I hit good that spring and was batting something like .370 early in the season when the Chicago Cubs bought me. They sent a shortstop named Shannon, an outfielder, and some cash to Indianapolis for me. I stayed with the Cubs through the 1934 season. My first year with them I signed for $6,500, with the promise that I might get more the next year if I did well."

It's worth pausing here for a moment to point out that Riggs was a teammate at Alabama of Joe and Luke Sewell, both of whom (through Zinn Scott's warm recommendations) also were signed by the Cleveland Indians. Joe, of course, went on to hit .312 in 14 major league seasons and is now in the Hall of Fame. More than that, he holds the major league record (and probably always will) for fewest strikeouts in a career and in a season. He averaged just over eight strikeouts per year and in 608 at bats for 1925 he whiffed just four times. Luke was a standout catcher for 20 seasons, most of them with Cleveland, and managed the St. Louis Browns to their only pennant in 1944.

Joe Sewell says that Stephenson didn't make it as a second baseman for the Indians because he had hurt his right elbow playing football and had a stiff arm. This kept him from turning the double play properly. But with our hindsight advantage we can conclude that Cleveland made a big mistake in letting Riggs get away in the Johnny Hodapp deal.

Riggs Stephenson. (Photo courtesy of the National Baseball Library, Cooperstown, N.Y.)

Hodapp played well in the majors, but the Indians certainly could have used his big bat for the next several years.

Joe McCarthy, then in his first year as manager of the Cubs, told his bosses early in the 1926 season to buy Stephenson from Indianapolis. The previous year Joe had managed in the American Association and saw enough of Riggs to know he could hit well in the majors.

"McCarthy was the best manager I ever played under," Stephenson recalled. "He was the best strategist and had the best baseball mind, by far. Hornsby was pretty strict and a little bit rough. Charlie Grimm was a good-natured fellow and hardly ever got on anybody.

"Joe Sewell entered the University of Alabama a year before I did, and we met when we both went out for football practice. You know, in the 63 years since we met I think maybe we've had only one argument. I missed the sign once when I was on first base and he was hitting behind me. He got on me a little bit and we jawed awhile, but it didn't last and we went on home together."

The Cubs had finished in the cellar in 1925, but under McCarthy's leadership the improvement was steady. In 1926 they advanced to fourth place, remained there in 1927, then moved to third in 1928 prior to capturing the National League pennant in 1929. But when they barely lost out to St. Louis in 1930, McCarthy was dropped in favor of Rogers Hornsby. Stephenson enjoyed recalling his teammates on the Cubs during his nine years on the club.

"Old Hack Wilson was a real good ballplayer. A lot of people just dwell on his night life, but he was a good outfielder, had a good arm, could go back for a ball, and could come in and slide on his stomach to catch those little pop flies. He had good speed, too. And, as you know, in 1930 he hit 56 home runs and batted in 190. He still holds the National League record for home runs and the major league record for RBIs.

"And Gabby Hartnett was the best catcher I saw in the majors. He was good at handling pitchers, and his arm was so good that hardly anybody ever tried to run on him. Except in 1929 when his arm was hurt and he could only be used as a pinch hitter. That year the Cubs bought Zack Taylor from the Boston Braves and we went on to win the pennant.

"Charlie Root was a real fine pitcher and won 26 games the year after I joined the Cubs. He had a sidearm fastball and a pretty fair curve, and he was a nice fellow. Guy Bush was from Mississippi and when I first got there he only had a fastball. He developed a screwball later and became quite a pitcher.

"Pat Malone was awfully wild when I played against him down in the American Association. Later he got control and had a good fastball and good curve. He was a winning pitcher, but he and Hack Wilson ran around together in their nighttime activities. They got into more than a few skirmishes.

"And Burleigh Grimes, 'Old Stubblebeard' as they called him, was a spitball pitcher and a mighty good one. He'd knock you down, so you couldn't take a toehold on him. He's in the Hall of Fame now and also on the Old-Timers Committee for voting older players into the Hall of Fame.

"Billy Herman came up from Louisville while I was there. He got to be a great second baseman with a fine arm, and he was mighty good too as a hit-and-run man at the plate. Lon Warneke came up from down in Arkansas while I was with the Cubs and got to be one of the top pitchers in the league. After he was through playing he became an umpire.

"And, of course, Charlie Grimm. Besides being our manager the last three years I was there, he had been one of the best first basemen in the league and a really funny guy. He was very original in what he would do. For instance, he'd pick up the canvas bag that held the practice balls and play it like an accordion while he sang some song or other.

"There was a lot of bitterness between the Cubs and Yankees in the 1932 World Series, and I've been asked a lot of times if Babe Ruth really called his home run shot in the fifth inning of the third game. Our bench got on Ruth mighty hard and he and other Yankees responded. It was all because we had voted to give Mark Koenig just half a share of the Series money. Babe and the Yankees were mad because Koenig had played shortstop for them previously. As far as the 'called' home run goes, Joe Sewell was sitting close to where Ruth was and says Babe pointed to center field. He did put up his fingers and I don't know whether he pointed or not, but I do know that he hit it over the scoreboard. I was out in left field, and I really couldn't tell if he was pointing or not.

"The toughest pitcher to hit? Well, for me it was Dazzy Vance. Most pitchers seemed to think I could hit the high outside pitch into right center, but I thought I was a better low ball hitter. At first I had some trouble with the curveball, but I got some pitchers on our team to go out with me a lot of mornings and just throw curveball after curveball to me until I got tired. Finally I got to where I could hit the curve pretty good to right field.

"I never could see the stitches on the ball and I didn't see it leave the bat when I hit it, but I had a pretty good eye. The spitball was a hard thing for me to hit. And Eddie Rommel was one of the few pitchers in my time to throw the knuckler. I had trouble with that pitch.

"We didn't swing at the 3 and 0 pitch very much in my day. Some fellows like Babe Ruth would swing at it sometimes. I only remember swinging at it once, and I bounced it right back to the pitcher.

"And, naturally, knowing a pitcher's style wasn't any guarantee you could hit him well. We had a little infielder with us on the Cubs named Clyde Beck who used to boast that he had something on every pitcher in the league. One day he was talking about that and I asked him, 'How much you hitting, Clyde?' And he said, 'Oh, I'm hitting .240 now.'

"And in those days when you first came into the league the pitchers would test you by throwing at you or mighty close to you, trying to back you off the plate. When I first came to Cleveland I got hit several times on the left arm. One time Walter Johnson, who supposedly didn't throw at anyone, hit me with one of his fastballs right on the hard part of my head. That was the only time I ever got hit bad. I just lay there a few minutes, then got up and trotted down to first. And I never had any aftereffects from it.

"Another time, when I was with the Cubs, we were playing the Phillies and the first time up I hit a home run into the left field stands. Then the next time at bat I put one in the right field seats. As I came up the third time I heard the Philly manager holler out to his pitcher, 'Knock that big so-and-so down!' Only he didn't say so-and-so.

"You want to know how much I made playing baseball? Well, my first year in the majors I signed with Cleveland for $300 a month, or $1,800 for the year. The next year I got a total of $3,000. My first year with the Cubs I reported to them in June and signed for $6,500 a year. I had my best season in 1929, when I hit .362 with 17 home runs and 110 runs batted in. But my best salary didn't come until about my next to last year, and then I got $14,000. That was pretty good in those times.

"The club furnished our uniforms and bats. The player had to get his own shoes and glove. The team paid all expenses on the road—hotel bills and everything. Sometimes we signed for meals in the hotel, but most of the time they'd give us $3.50 a day to eat on."

"Riggs," I cut in, "what did baseball mean to the players in your day?"

"It meant having that uniform to put on every day," he responded. "There was always somebody standing behind you wanting to take your job away. Wally Pipp, a fine first baseman, found that out when he took a day off in 1925 and let Lou Gehrig play and never got back in. There was more competition in those days. Some clubs had nearly three dozen minor league teams, while nowadays they have maybe five or six. And not so many players went right from college to the majors, so most people got more experience playing in the minors before going up."

"Are you disappointed at not being voted into the Hall of Fame so far?" I asked him.

"Well, of course everybody would like to get into the Hall of Fame. But I watched the induction proceedings this year, and if all the ones who get voted in talk as long as Happy Chandler and Frank Robinson did, I don't know whether I'd want to go up there or not. Anyway, I'm not worrying about it at all."

"After you finished playing in the majors," I wanted to know, "what did you do?"

"I went to Indianapolis and played one year there. I hit about .340. Then Birmingham offered me a job as manager. So I went there and managed for two years. The first year we finished third, and in a [championship] series with Tulsa of the Texas League they beat us. The next year we finished fifth and they fired me. I would much rather play than manage.

"I always wanted to be a coach in the majors but never did get a job as one. After leaving Birmingham I coached the high school baseball team for two years down in Akron, Alabama, the little place where I was born. Then I went into the lumber business with another fellow. And I did coach a semipro team here in Tuscaloosa, and we went to the annual tournament in Wichita and came within one game of winning the championship.

"I also coached a little football at Akron High School, but we didn't have many players. When we scrimmaged I'd have to play against the first team. One time the football coach at Marion Institute, a college prep school, called me up and wanted to arrange a game with our team. I told him, 'Heck, we ain't got but 13 men.' So he said, 'I'll tell you what we'll do. I'll play with my team and you play with yours.' So I said, 'All right. Come on over.' They came to Akron to play us and we beat them 20 to 7, or maybe it was 30 to 7, and I played the whole game."

"Who were the best players you saw at each position in the majors?"

"Well," he said slowly, "for pitchers I'd take Lefty Grove and Walter Johnson. George Sisler or maybe Gehrig on first base. Eddie Collins would be at second base. I'll put Joe Sewell at shortstop and Pie Traynor on third. In the outfield I like Cobb, Speaker, and Ruth. And Gabby Hartnett for catcher. I didn't see fellows like Warren Spahn or Bob Feller pitch, so I can't name them."

Then I asked Riggs what he thought about such present-day aspects of baseball as artificial surfaces, night baseball, the emergence of relief specialists, and free agency.

"I didn't play on any artificial surfaces, but it seems like they're a lot faster. I think the batter gets more hits on that stuff. The balls really got through the infield in a hurry. I did play night baseball for two years in the minors. I thought it made it harder to see and to hit, but nowadays maybe the lights are a lot better.

"There weren't as many relief pitchers in my day, because the starters usually pitched complete games. The good relief pitchers, like Elroy Face of Pittsburgh some time back and Bruce Sutter today, are no doubt better than any we had. The relief specialists have changed the game a good deal from the way it was when I started out. As a whole, the players today are bigger and stronger than we were. But I don't think they play as hard as we did.

"With regard to free agency, I'm sorry I'm not in there for that big money, though I'm not going to worry about that, either. I think free agency has been a blow to the owners, and I don't know how they're going to get along with it. Of course, I'm always for the ballplayer most of all, because after all he's the one that makes baseball what it is."

I'll always remember a remark Charlie Grimm made to me once when Stephenson's name came up. He said, "Riggs, the Old Hoss. He was a great clutch hitter. He never left a man in scoring position that I know of."

Obviously, that's something of an overstatement, but it speaks to us eloquently of Riggs Stephenson's dependability and how he played the game.

It Was 20 Years Ago Today: Baseball Responds to the Unrest of 1968

RON BRILEY

On February 17, 1968 columnist Dick Young observed that Baltimore Orioles' out-fielder and future Hall-of-Famer Frank Robinson was complaining that Boston Red Sox star Carl Yastrzemski received more acclaim for his 1967 American League triple crown than Robinson had gained for accomplishing the same feat in 1966. Robinson believed the difference in public reaction was due simply to the fact that he was black and Yastrzemski white. Young concurred with Robinson's analysis as the columnist observed that blacks had done so well in baseball of late and that there had been few white heroes. For some fans Yastrzemski's achievements were really something about which to crow. But Young downplayed this apparent racism in baseball, commenting, "It's nothing to get excited about. We'll outgrow this stuff in another 20 years or so."[1]

Twenty years have passed and allegations of racism continue to plague American society, as well as the baseball establishment. Before the breakdown of the liberal consensus in the mid-to-late 1960s, the so-called national pastime had apparently mirrored American faith in the nation's values and institutions. The two cornerstones of the post-World War II liberal consensus were anticommunism and a belief that social and racial inequities in American life could be surmounted by an expanding economy and gross national product.[2] Accordingly, there was no need to resort to violence to bring about change. Problems would be solved through the application of reason and orderly expansion. Baseball in the 1950s and early 1960s apparently well exemplified these consensus values. Through barnstorming tours by major league clubs and generous outlays of baseball equipment the State Department often used the sport as a diplomatic tool to indoctrinate wayward Asians and Latins with the benefits of American civilization and values. On the domestic front, baseball's experience with integration following the appearance of Jackie Robinson in a Dodgers' uniform was often touted as fulfilling the American dream of social mobility in which an individual is judged by talent rather than skin color or social origins.

But the liberal consensus was shattered in the late 1960s with racial violence, campus unrest, assassinations, and the war in Vietnam. The baseball consensus, which often viewed itself as America in microcosm, was, in turn, disrupted by player unionization, accusations of racial prejudice, and questions of free expression. The sport's status as the national pastime was also challenged by professional football, supposedly more in touch with the values of the 1960s.[3] Perhaps no single year presented a greater challenge to American beliefs in reason and progress than 1968 in which Americans witnessed an escalating Vietnam War with the Tet offensive; student uprisings on major college campuses such as Columbia University; assassinations of Dr. Martin Luther King, Jr. and Robert Kennedy; racial violence in many of America's major cities; street protest and a violent police reaction at the Democratic National Convention in Chicago; and a growing counterculture movement which questioned the moral and economic values comprising the American consensus. An examination of baseball's response to this most troubled and turbulent year should provide some insight into how Americans and American institutions persevered in a time when everything was falling apart and nothing seemed to work.

The new year of 1968 found baseball in somewhat of a defensive posture. In 1967, the American League had enjoyed one of the best pennant races in major league baseball history with four teams in contention during the final weekend of the season. Yet, a league record attendance figure of 11,336,936 was only some 130,000 above the 1948 record. While drawing 12,971,430 fans, the National League gate was off 13 percent from the 1966 pace. The *Sporting News* cited racial fears as a key factor in disappointing attendance figures. The paper observed that too many major league parks were located in ghetto areas, and "the problem had grown acute in recent years with stories of racial violence all over the country making people exceedingly wary of venturing into slum areas, especially at night."[4] This editorial comment sounds almost like a statement presidential candidate Richard Nixon might have made about the crime problem in America, but it does reflect the increasing economic and racial polarization in 1968 as fear and misunderstanding guided the assumptions of many Americans. The exodus of the middle class and businesses from the inner city had left a crumbling infrastructure and ball parks which symbolized the optimism of a different time.

If assumptions about racial violence were undermining the liberal consensus in baseball and American society, certainly one of the other disruptive questions of the 1960s was the Vietnam War. On this issue baseball sought to maintain its posture as a cornerstone of the anticommunist consensus. As with World Wars I and II, as well as the Korean War, baseball would continue during the conflict, seeking to provide an important morale factor for soldiers at the front and civilians at home. The *Sporting News* offered a program in which patriotic baseball fans could purchase subscriptions for servicemen stationed in Vietnam. In return, the paper relished printing the gratitude of soldiers such as private J.B. Yanulavich who stated, "Mainly what I want to say is that its nice to know that most of the people in the U.S. are really proud of us, like I am proud to be an American myself." The *Official Baseball Guide* was also offered, compliments of the major leagues, to servicemen. Colonel E. Parmly, IV, Commanding Officer, Company C, 5th Special Forces Group, asserted that only a small percentage of the 500 Green Berets under his command could use the book at any one time, but it always remained by the radio for Sunday games. Baseball commissioner William Eckert received a Pentagon citation for contributing to morale in Vietnam, and, just as in previous military engagements, baseball sponsored visits by athletes to military hospitals to lift the spirits of wounded servicemen.[5]

Los Angeles Angels' shortstop Jim Fregosi, visiting hospitals in Guam, Okinawa, Japan, and the Philippines, noted that strains of American dissent intruded upon his mission. Some servicemen were upset that newspaper coverage of demonstrations against the war was crowding out sports stories, and one burly Marine commented, "Just give me two more good Marines and we'll stop all that nonsense." But not all the personnel in the hospital were ready to go back to America and crack some heads. The Vietnam experience had raised doubts in the minds of many young men, such as an 18-year-old veteran who had both of his legs blown off. He asked Fregosi how it was possible that he could return to America and still not be able to buy a drink or cast a vote. Fregosi, an athlete rather than a diplomat, simply had no reply, insisting, "What could I say? It really hit me. You just can't answer it."[6]

In previous conflicts the morale boosting hospital visit had solidified baseball's contribution to the formation of a wartime consensus, but in 1968 for athletes, such as Fregosi, it could be a reminder of the divisions in American society. Of course, the Vietnam War, which was shredding the fabric of the American consensus, was not an issue which baseball usually confronted directly. Morale and the draft status of players were baseball's main contacts with the war, but no major institution in America could completely escape the forces of dissent and division unleashed by this conflict which contributed so much to the breakdown of consensus values in America. In 1968, baseball's version of the American dream in which a young man, regardless of skin color or social background, could achieve success through talent and be appreciative of this opportunity was shattered by more militant players willing to question the assumptions of management. Certainly, baseball has a long history of players disputing the reserve clause and ownership, but the difference in 1968 was that players, operating in a milieu which was more supportive of challenges to tradition, enjoyed greater success than their discontented brethren in previous player–management confrontations.

The Baseball Players Association under the aggressive leadership of former steelworker representative Marvin Miller demanded that baseball owners raise the minimum salary of players. Rumors of a strike swirled through the baseball world prior to the 1968 season. A settlement was reached and a strike averted as the minimum salary was raised from $7,000 to $10,000, effective for a two-year period. But the controversial reserve clause, under

DETROIT TIGERS - 1968 American League Champions

The 1968 Detroit Tigers. (Photo courtesy of the National Baseball Library, Cooperstown, N.Y.)

which a player was bound to the team which originally signed him until traded or released, was left on the negotiating table for further study. Disgruntled players such as Oakland A's pitcher Jack Aker made evident their distaste for management and the reserve clause. Aker who served as player representative for the A's had several difficult encounters with owner Charles Finley during the 1967 season and was rewarded with a pay cut. Aker complained that the reserve clause left him with no choice but to accept a reduction in salary for the 1968 campaign. He needed a job and still required a couple of years to qualify for baseball's pension plan. Aker reluctantly concluded, "I'm going to play in spite of Mr. Finley and do the best job I can."[7]

As players openly questioned baseball ownership on issues of salary, benefits, and the reserve clause, the baseball establishment also had to consider allegations of racism in its hiring practices. With the civil rights movement challenging the consensus claim of equal opportunity, baseball could point to the increasing presence of blacks on the playing field. But on the executive level in 1968 there were no black managers, only two black coaches (Jim Gilliam of the Dodgers and Ernie Banks of the Cubs), and only one black individual in baseball's front offices (Bill Lucas of the Braves who was related to slugger Hank Aaron). The *Sporting News* called upon baseball management to address the situation, editorializing, "A policy statement would seem very much in order to emphasize that a color line does not exist to bar Negroes from coaching and front office jobs in sports."[8]

But many in the sports world were impatient with liberal promises and demanded action. Harry Edwards, a sociology professor at San Jose State, attracted headlines in 1968 when he organized the Olympic Project for Human Rights to boycott the Mexico City Olympic games. The articulate Edwards argued that sports such as baseball were not realistic avenues of social mobility for minorities in America. Black youth who spent their time playing games in order to become superstars were missing out on important educational opportunities which would qualify them for jobs in a modern technological society. Edwards concluded, "Big-name athletes who tell Black kids to 'practice and work hard and one day you can be just like me' are playing games with the future of Black society." Jack Scott, director of the Institute for the Study of Sport and Society, concurred with Edwards' assessment regarding sports and social mobility. Scott labeled the assertion that sports could serve as an excellent means of social advancement for blacks as myth. He insisted, "for every white youth lifted out of a coal-mining town and every black person taken from the ghetto by an athletic scholarship, there are hundreds of other lower-class youths who have wasted their lives futilely preparing to be a sports star."[9] While critics like Edwards and Scott were leveling most of their criticism at collegiate athletics, it was, indeed, difficult for professional sports such as baseball to ignore the questions being raised regarding the consensus view of athletics as a path to the American dream.

Although criticism of sports was on the increase and the defensive baseball establishment issued nondiscriminatory statements, few management positions for minorities were forthcoming. Reflecting divisions in the civil rights movement between militants and those advocating less confrontational tactics, blacks in baseball disagreed as to how vocal they should be in pushing for racial advances within the game. Jackie Robinson who had to silently endure racial indignities in his early playing days was a very proud man. After his status as a player was assured, he wasted few opportunities to confront racism in baseball. Recognizing that he was an important symbol for black Americans, Robinson continued to speak out following his playing days. Robinson criticized black superstar Willie Mays for not living up to his responsibilities in the black community. Using the rhetoric of more militant blacks who sometimes labeled black liberals as "Uncle Toms," Robinson referred to Mays as a "do nothing Negro." The San Francisco Giants' center fielder, who was a favorite of many whites, resented Robinson's allegations. Mays observed that he had worked for the Jobs Corps and addressed many black youth organizations, while he maintained faith in the American consensus and that room for blacks could be made in the American dream. Militance was not required, as Mays asserted, "There has been progress made and we've all been a part of making it so, and it will continue to get better. But even when I get out of baseball, I'm not going to stand on a soap box or preach or picket or carry banners. I have my own way of getting our message across."[10] This exchange between such important symbols to the black community as Robinson and Mays was indicative of the increasing division among blacks regarding the pace of racial progress under such liberal leaders as Lyndon Johnson.

Faced with questions regarding its racial practices, and with voices of dissent challenging such traditional practices as the reserve clause, baseball management sought to reiterate the views of consensus America and the 1950s organization man. Baseball Commissioner William Eckert, a former general known more for his organizing rather than his fighting talents, sought to placate malcontents such as Aker and Robinson with refrains similar to President Johnson's, "Come, let us reason together." Thus, in response to baseball critics Eckert proclaimed, "I believe in cooperation and the creation of good will on all levels. I believe in the most effective organization possible, with progressive working committees, proper delegation of authority and responsibility and extensive, meaningful discussion."[11] Eckert advocated the values of the American consensus in which discussion, organization, and reason would bring orderly change and expansion.

But America in 1968 was becoming an increasingly violent society in which Eckert's values appeared out of place. On April 4th, Martin Luther King, Jr. was gunned down by a sniper in Memphis. Rioting erupted in over a hundred cities, and 21,000 federal troops and 34,000 state guardsmen were dispatched to restore order. Given the chaos in America's major cities, there was little that big league baseball clubs could do but postpone home openers. The postponement also gave major league baseball the opportunity to honor Dr. King and appear as a champion of racial harmony, perhaps getting some of its critics off its back. Announcing the altered schedule, Commissioner Eckert dispatched a telegram to Mrs. King conveying baseball's condolences, as well as pledging that the sport would continue to "carry out the goals of Dr. King." The *Sporting News* lauded Eckert's decision to alter the schedule, as it "put baseball on the side of social justice." The publication went on to insist that baseball's unprecedented action was in "keeping with baseball's position as a pioneer in granting the Negro the opportunities which his skills demand."[12]

The *Sporting News* was making an effort to maintain baseball's position within the crumbling consensus of values. According to the paper, protest was not necessary when the opportunity to achieve on the athletic field could lead to acceptance and financial success. In pursuit of this editorial policy, the paper presented interviews with several black players in the wake of the assassination of Dr. King. The black players selected by the paper extolled the virtues of racial progress in baseball. Willie Mays insisted that it was pointless to discuss racism in the sport's past. Baseball had been great to him, and he believed that he owed the sport everything.

If Mays, the star, was reluctant to criticize the hand that fed him so well, what about black players who were not so well known and paid? Tommy Harper of the Cleveland Indians asserted that there was no racial antagonism between the players. The lack of interracial roommates was not evidence of prejudice. Blacks just naturally like to hang out with blacks, and whites preferred to be with whites. Harper was hardly advocating black separatism when he concluded, "But why make two guys uncomfortable? I think the relationship is great all the way."

Other players picked for the interview did express some reservations. Leon "Daddy Wags" Wagner of the Indians commented upon the fact that many blacks believed teams maintained racial quotas limiting the number of black athletes. He confessed that he had no proof, "just a feeling." Lee May of the Senators complained that white players were able to obtain more commercial endorsements than blacks. May alleged that Roger Maris had received over a million dollars in endorsements for hitting 61 home runs, and he argued, "no Negro boy could have done that well on the side." Despite these disclaimers from Wagner and May, the basic portrait which the *Sporting News* sought to paint was that of the liberal consensus in which cooperation and compromise brought progress.[13]

But the reality of racial relations in America was perhaps more evident when the baseball season did open in Washington, D.C., on April 10, 1968. The Senators had sold over 45,000 tickets for the game, but only slightly over 32,000 fans showed up to watch the Twins defeat the Senators 2–0. D.C. Stadium was only a few blocks from the scene of some of the worst rioting in American history, and the crowd constituted the smallest opening day figure since the Senators moved into their new stadium for the 1961 season. Fearing further violence, President Johnson was not available to throw out the first ball, and that somewhat dubious honor, under the circumstances, was bestowed upon Vice-President Hubert Humphrey. National guardsmen who had been bivouacked in the stadium were given free tickets to the game. But their presence provided an eerie reminder of the turbulence through which the nation had just passed. The guardsmen watched the game in uniform as they were told that if they were needed to quell any further disorder they would be notified over the public address system. Fortunately, the guardsmen were not called upon, and for a change conflict was confined to the playing field.[14]

Despite problems of curfews and crowd control in many cities, the 1968 baseball season did get under way. But the decision to postpone opening day out of respect for Dr. King was not without its critics. A vigorous debate occurred in the pages of the *Sporting News* as many irate readers voiced their displeasure over baseball's honoring of Dr. King. Representative of this view was the comment by a man from Vienna, West Virginia, who observed, "I feel that if they needed a reason to postpone the opening of the baseball season, they could have done it for two Memphis police who, in trying to uphold the law were killed by rioters." Other readers supported the decision reached by Commissioner Eckert and baseball management. Bernard Winkler of Washington, D.C., argued that the baseball establishment was following the recommendations of the police and military authorities. Besides, "the players wanted to honor Dr. King and not the rioters." Although the King assassination and its aftermath had been divisive, Robert Lipsyte in the *New York Times* hoped that the birth of a new baseball season would help the healing process. Lipsyte suggested that the sport offered a "comfort zone" for Americans as, "its petty detail and endless speculation holds no import nor danger, and so is balm. And in a world of sharp edges and cruel aftereffects, baseball is slow and soft and sleepy as a fat old dog in the sun."[15]

Lipsyte's desire for a comfort zone was only a dream, for baseball and American society were barely able to deal with some of the scars left by the King assassination before the nation was traumatized by the assassination of presidential candidate Robert Kennedy in June following his victory in the California Democratic primary. Failure by Commissioner Eckert to take a decisive position on baseball's response to the assassination resulted in considerable controversy and antagonism which seemed to exacerbate growing player criticisms of management and decline of the baseball consensus. Instead of postponing all games on Saturday, June 8th, the day of Kennedy's funeral, Eckert announced that games in New York and Washington, the site of funeral observances for the slain Senator, would be cancelled, while all other games would not start until after the funeral. As for June 9th, which had been declared by President Johnson as the official day of mourning for Kennedy, Eckert stated that playing would be up to the individual clubs. Only the Red Sox and Orioles cancelled their home games. However, the huge crowds which turned out to view the funeral train making its way from California delayed the funeral ceremonies and played havoc with baseball's schedule. Why was there no outright cancellation of games as with the King assassination? Although denied by Eckert, reports persisted that the commissioner had contacted the owners before announcing his decision, and since there was no rioting in the streets which would discourage fans from attending games the owners advised against any mass cancellation.

Regardless of its source, Eckert's ambiguous ruling created considerable confusion and hard feelings, especially in Cincinnati and Houston. The June 8th contest between the St. Louis Cardinals and Cincinnati Reds had been changed from a day to evening game, but the Kennedy rites were running considerably behind schedule. After waiting 45 minutes past the rescheduled starting time, Reds' management decided to begin the game. General Manager Bob Howsam defended this action, maintaining, "Our position was that we had scheduled this game in good faith about an hour and a half after the burial was scheduled. We would have waited if the delay had been a short one." To deflect criticism, Howsam also engaged in a little buck passing, asserting that he called the commissioner to inform him of the situation, and Eckert "felt the only thing to do was go ahead and play." Management's decision to play the contest did not sit well with many players who viewed the decision as placing profit over moral concerns. Consensus values of cooperation were not apparent as Reds' pitcher and player representative Milt Pappas led the struggle to cancel the game. Cardinal players did not want to play but insisted that the final determination belonged to the home team. With Reds' manager Dave Bristol lobbying in favor of conducting the contest, the Reds took two votes on playing. The first poll was a 12 to 12 stalemate with one abstention. On a second vote the total was 13 to 12 in favor of going on with the game. Pappas believed his teammates had caved in to management pressure, and he shouted to them as they filed onto the field, "You guys are wrong. I'm telling you you're all wrong. If you guys play you'll have to find another player rep." Pappas did not have to worry about resigning as Reds' management had no desire to deal with a malcontent, dispatching the pitcher to Atlanta shortly after the incident in a six-man deal.[16]

Meanwhile, a player revolt was brewing in Houston. Astro players voted unanimously not to play the June 9th contest with the visiting Pittsburgh Pirates. Houston General Manager Spec Richardson was intent upon maintaining management control over the players. The game would be played as scheduled and any players refusing to participate would face heavy fines. Astro pitcher and player representative Dave Giusti announced that the players would reluctantly play the game, stating, "We changed our position after the strongest economic pressures had been brought to bear against us by the general manager." However, Houston stars Rusty Staub and Bob Aspromonte decided to sit the game out and, reportedly, were fined by Richardson. Maury Wills of the Pirates also refused to play, explaining, "I was out of uniform when Dr. King died and if I didn't respect Senator Kennedy's memory, too, I felt I would be hypocritical." Initially, star Pittsburgh outfielder Roberto Clemente was going to join Wills, but after a meeting with manager Larry Shepard he agreed to play. In a statement following his discussion with Shepard, Clemente made it clear that he preferred not to participate and blasted teammates who were indifferent to events such as the Kennedy assassination. The aftermath of the aborted player revolt in Houston was that Richardson sought to prevent any dissent among the Astros, imposing a gag rule on players repeating to reporters anything said in the clubhouse. Breaking the gag rule would result in a $500 fine and suspension or both.[17] While Richardson may have won a temporary battle in quelling player discontent, management would tend to lose the war as players would become more assertive later in the year with the pension plan and throughout the late 1960s and 1970s with their challenge to the reserve system.

Baseball's experience with racial tensions and the impact of the King and Kennedy assassinations certainly indicated that the sport could not escape the forces undermining the American consensus. Baseball's place among the chaos and confusion engulfing American society in 1968 was carefully analyzed in a July *Sporting News* editorial which still viewed the sport as a positive symbol of American values, even in the worst of times. The editorial argued that the nation was beset by assassinations, rebellious youth, racial violence, and a challenge to traditional values which were lowering moral standards. And baseball was not mere escapism during this crisis of values, as the sport's continued popularity was evidence that consensus values of "fair play, sportsmanship, and teamwork" were still alive in the country. In a bit of a rhetorical excess, the paper proclaimed, "If you believe that working in harmony with your fellow man is dull stuff, if your kicks are psychedelic, if Bonnie and Clyde are your heroes, then baseball and Willie Mays and Mickey Mantle will be dull." The editorial concluded that baseball might be dull for a radical with a gun, but it would take a man with a bat to provide Americans with "confidence that our country can and will pull together like a championship team." Thus, despite controversies such as the sport's response to the Kennedy assassination, some believed baseball could shun radical change and maintain its position as a bastion of traditional values.[18]

This stance was apparent in baseball's somewhat cosmetic approach to the issue of black hiring. The American League employed former Olympic star Jesse Owens as a troubleshooter to improve racial relations. Essentially, his job was to keep the channels of communication open with black players. As Owens described it, "I'm going to sit down and talk to them. Then, I'll take it from there. If necessary, I'll go to the managers or owners." The hiring of the conservative Owens, who had been very active in attempting to head off black protests and boycotts in track and field, seemed to be just an effort to prevent further criticism of baseball's racial policies. This apparent policy of co-option was further displayed when Commissioner Eckert appointed the respected former black player Monte Irvin to a position in the Commissioner's office. Despite these efforts at conciliation and window dressing, few other blacks were able to find employment in baseball's executive ranks.[19] And 20 years later this issue still continues to plague the sport.

If the baseball consensus was to some degree successful in muting black protest in 1968, the same certainly cannot be said for a more union-oriented approach by white, black, and Latin players to the economic status of the major league athlete. Baseball management had always taken great pride in the alleged consensus of values between management and players who worked together to achieve financial success and make the sport the great democratic game in which through talent, not protest, one could enhance his status. Accordingly, in 1963, Judge Robert Cannon, legal counsel to the Major League Players Association, gave credit to the owners for their "cooperative and generous dealings with the players." In exchange for these favors Cannon insisted that the players owed loyalty to the owners as well as the great game. It was the duty of players "to get out and preach the baseball gospel, spread good will and improve public relations toward the game."[20]

However, by 1968, Cannon's paternalistic approach was no longer appropriate to baseball or American society. Professional athletes were hardly immune to the protests dealing with freedom of speech, individual liberties, and equal economic opportunity sweeping the nation. In 1966, Marvin Miller replaced Cannon, and a new era in player–management relations was ushered in for the sport. The extent of this change from the 1950s' cooperation to the 1960s' confrontation became apparent in the second half of the 1968 season as Miller and the players demanded that a larger portion of the increasing television revenues be allocated to the players' pension fund. The issue was one of power as well as money. It was evident that television would play a prominent role in the future of the game, and players were determined to establish the principle that they were guaranteed a slice of this lucrative pie. To ensure good faith bargaining on the part of management, Miller urged players not to sign their 1969 contracts until the pension issue was resolved.[21]

Management protested that Miller was introducing the confrontational tactics of labor into the consensus world of baseball. Owners perceived the strategy of not signing a contract as a strike threat, and they attempted to portray Miller as an outside agitator who was misleading players and diverting their attention from the game itself. Thus, like the Old South before the introduction of such so-called agitators as the freedom riders, baseball was tranquil before the arrival of union man Miller. Of course, this was not actually the case as management had often provoked criticism and player challenges to the reserve clause. This provision of the player contract was protected under a 1922 Supreme Court decision written by Oliver Wendell Holmes in which baseball was exempted from the antitrust laws. A challenge to the reserve clause during the 1940s resulted in an out-of-court cash settlement between owners and New York Giants' outfielder Danny Gardella. A 1953 Supreme Court decision reaffirmed, by a seven to two vote, the Holmes' ruling of 30 years earlier. However, the climate of opinion in America during the late 1960s seemed to provide an opportune time in which players might again assault the privileges of baseball ownership. With authority and tradition being openly confronted on the streets and campuses of America in 1968, the time seemed right for players to assert their position under a more aggressive leader such as Miller.

Nevertheless, the *Sporting News,* supporting management, sought to ridicule Miller and appeal to the players' pride by insisting that the players' representative had not adjusted to the fact that "he now represents a group of professionals who take pride in their work (as most do). All too often, Miller acts as if he still is employed by the clock-punching members of the Steelworkers." Players were professionals with high standards and, thus, above blue-collar unionization. But athletes who were bound to service contracts with one club believed that they were not always treated as professionals by team owners. And player representatives such as pitcher Steve Hamilton of the Yankees rushed to the defense of Miller, exclaiming that, "the Players Association is fortunate indeed to have a man of Marvin Miller's caliber who is 100 percent behind the players, and I assure you the players are 100 percent behind him." Hamilton also rejected the consensus values of cooperation, arguing that players had only been able to gain a decent pension system because they had fought for their rights. Miller also struck back at what he perceived to be the paternalistic nature of owners who believed players could not negotiate and concentrate on their play at the same time. The players' representative asserted, "The players wonder if they think they should shut their eyes to the war in Vietnam, the demonstrations in Chicago and other current events and think only about the game. They are insulted by the owners' entire line of reasoning."[22] Miller's comments document the fact that baseball management and players were not immune to the forces of dissent sweeping through America. Players could not escape the influence of the "real" world and changes taking place in American society.

A players' strike was not the only threat hanging over baseball in the latter months of

1968. Umpires were also on the warpath regarding the decision by American League President Joe Cronin to fire umpires Al Salerno and Bill Valentine shortly before the conclusion of the season. Cronin accused both arbiters of "incompetence." However, Salerno and Valentine insisted they were let go because of their efforts to organize American League umpires whose pay and benefits were below those of the already unionized National League umpires. Arbiters maintained solidarity and threatened a strike as veteran National League umpire Augie Donatelli stated, "We'll stand by the American leaguers if Salerno and Valentine aren't reinstated."[23] Intransigent owners such as Finley of Oakland asserted that the umpires and players were out of line, and should they strike, the sport should simply shut down.[24] After all, players and umpires were dependent upon the owners. Sounding somewhat like a college president who believed the school could exist without students, Finley did not seem to notice that power relations in America were in a state of flux and that players might be on the verge of enhancing their position within the game.

As the World Series approached, baseball's establishment was beset with questions of unionization and individual rights when the repercussions of the Vietnam War again placed the sport in a controversial position. Before the October 7, 1968 Series contest between the St. Louis Cardinals and Detroit Tigers folksinger Jose Feliciano was asked to sing the national anthem. Feliciano responded with a blues rendition of the anthem which let loose a storm of protest. The Tiger Stadium switchboard received over 2,000 complaints in less than an hour. To many, Feliciano's experimentation was representative of a society in which tradition was under attack and patriotism was no longer viewed as a virtue. Reflecting this perspective was Murphy L. Tamkersley who was recovering from Vietnam wounds in a Houston veterans' hospital. Tamkersley lamented, "Some of us have seen people die in Vietnam, soldiers singing part of the National Anthem as they gave their lives for our country. Then to be in a hospital with injuries and illnesses we got in the service and to hear that Anthem sung in such a dishonorable fashion." Feliciano expressed surprise that anyone was so insecure as to feel threatened by his singing, but reaffirmed that he meant no disrespect, explaining, "I owe everything I have to this country."[25]

Organized baseball was also urged to do more to boost morale in Vietnam, and Commissioner Eckert responded by planning more trips by baseball celebrities there. A delegation led by Ernie Banks, "Mr. Cub", was dispatched to Vietnam in December 1968. Banks, a gifted black athlete, was not one to criticize the baseball establishment or American society. Banks believed that he had achieved the American dream through hard work and perseverance, and he had little use for those who were not willing to labor diligently within the system. Banks told reporters that in the U.S. "you see a lot of young people complaining, people who hang out in the streets, and who don't want to work." But in Vietnam young men only 19 and 20 years of age are piloting helicopters, and young 21-year-old lieutenants were leading men into combat. Banks concluded, "It really proved to me that young people, when they're called upon, can do the job. It was a pleasure meeting them."[26] With players like Banks, baseball was still able to provide its morale boost and support of the consensus even amidst the agitation unleashed by the conflict in Vietnam. Yet, trotting out Ernie Banks to utter support for traditional values was not going to stem the tide of racial, legal, and union issues confronting the sport.

At organized baseball's annual winter meeting, held in December 1968 in San Francisco, baseball owners moved to dump Eckert as commissioner. Eckert had been selected for the post in 1965, even though he professed to have little knowledge of the game. Owners extolled his experience as an able administrator and organizer within the military, representing the 1950s values of the organization man. Also Eckert was viewed as an individual over whom the owners might be able to exert considerable influence due to his lack of experience with the game. But if this was the primary motivation, it certainly backfired as after only three years in the job owners were screaming for the scalp of baseball's unknown soldier and calling for strong leadership in the sport. Yankee President Mike Burke, who feared that baseball was losing its hold on young people, argued, "We recognize our problem. It's the attitude of the public at large that baseball is not with it, that it's not as contemporary as football, hockey and basketball, the contact sports. It's an attitude that exists and we've got to decide what to do about it. We need strong, courageous, intelligent leadership." The *Sporting News* believed that the sport's difficulties could be traced back to Ford Frick's long tenure as commissioner from 1951 to 1965. The paper argued that Frick had not been assertive enough as "problems piled up on the surface, baseball lost ground to the rapid growth of professional football and the game's entire structure began to weaken."[27] Interestingly enough, this line of reasoning seems to parallel the thinking that many of the social problems in America which came to the surface during the 1960s had been quietly simmering throughout the 1950s, but under the unassuming leadership of President Eisenhower these problems were not dealt with in their early stages.

But if baseball owners really believed they needed new dynamic leadership to find a fresh position for the sport in the late 1960s, they did not demonstrate this perspective when a new commissioner was selected. Stodgy Bowie Kuhn, attorney for the National League, was chosen by the owners to represent baseball.[28] This selection was viewed as an effort to use the commissionership to support the owners in negotiations with Miller and the players. However, in 1968 the tide had turned in baseball as well as in American society. Bowie Kuhn and Richard Nixon might become chief executives, but they could not always have their way. Black players would continue to be more assertive about race relations, and Marvin Miller would obtain an increased pension compensation plan, while players would persist in their assault upon the reserve system throughout the 1970s. Umpires would also develop a strong union, and Salerno and Valentine would finally gain reinstatement. For better or worse, individual rights would be emphasized over the corporate image of the game.

The changing nature of baseball was also noted in the fall of 1968 by a somewhat nostalgic Senator Eugene McCarthy whose bid to gain the Democratic presidential nomination on an antiwar platform had been defeated at the violent Chicago convention. Instead of campaigning for his fellow Democrat Hubert Humphrey against Richard Nixon, a bitter McCarthy agreed to cover the World Series for *Life* magazine. McCarthy's comments on the nature of baseball reveal a great deal of ambivalence about the sport and American society. The Senator lamented the fact that baseball (which he had played on a semi-pro basis), like America, had lost some of its pastoral innocence. Issues of unionization, monopoly, and racism in the sport led the disillusioned Senator to despair for the future of baseball. McCarthy mused about the sport, "It really isn't the national pastime any more. We start kids out in the Little Leagues, and right away the whole thing is very serious. They get too much too soon. The whole thing is overengineered and the only place people want to go is to the top. There's no room in the middle for fun. Perhaps we should abolish organized baseball—the Little Leagues as well as the majors. Then we could just leave a few balls and bats lying around and see if people picked them up."[29]

But McCarthy was wrong in assuming that all the fun had departed from organized baseball. Despite allegations of racism, labor confrontations, and the controversy surrounding its response to the King and Kennedy assassinations, major league baseball was still an exciting spectator sport as pitching dominated during the 1968 season. In the

American League, Detroit right-hander Denny McClain became the first pitcher in over 30 years to win 30 games, while in the National League, St. Louis Cardinals' ace Bob Gibson set a record by establishing a 1.12 ERA. The World Series was also suspenseful, with the Tigers triumphing over the Cards in seven games with chunky Tiger left-hander Mickey Lolich emerging as the Series hero. In responding to the turmoil of 1968 the liberal consensus in baseball and American society had been altered. The faith of players, both black and white, that the expanding corporate economy and baseball management would look out for their interest was undermined. Players who were coerced into performing during the Kennedy funeral sought a more labor-oriented association under the strong leadership of Marvin Miller which would assert their economic position and individual liberties.

American society in 1968 appeared to be almost coming apart under the strains of racism, violence, assassination, protest, and war, but the nation persevered. The "play" world of professional baseball was also affected by these forces of change, and the 1968 season helped further a shift in the balance of power from the owners to the players. Racial conflicts in American society encouraged debate on the role of blacks in baseball, and a climate of opinion in which dissent was tolerated certainly contributed to player assertiveness on issues of pay and expression. But baseball persevered because in the midst of the chaos of 1968 it retained certain traditional values of fair play and teamwork which had meaning to Americans on both sides of the barricades in the 1960s. In his collection of essays, *Baseball the Beautiful,* Marvin Cohen has well captured the place baseball holds in the hearts of many Americans. Cohen writes, "Fashions come and go, and wars, and social problems, economic crises, political climates. Baseball outlives them all—in our midst. A steady constant that retains its own slow unfolding patterns, while convulsions grip the land outside and tear out the old to plant the new. Baseball serenely glides by— permanent, beautiful, ever itself: insular, yet mildly reflecting, in a peaceful way, in its own terms, the changes going on outside."[30]

The nation and the sport of baseball, which has often so well reflected America, were stronger in 1968 than many observers thought. Yet, baseball which was able to accommodate, under coercion of course, many of the demands made by players has yet to satisfactorily deal with the issue of black hiring in the higher echelons of the game. Commissioner Peter Ueberroth has brought the 1960s' militant Harry Edwards into the commissioner's office to help with minority recruitment. According to Ueberroth's figures, the percentage of minorities in front office jobs has increased from 2 percent in 1986 to 10 percent in 1987, but as we approach the 1988 baseball season there are still no black managers in the major leagues.[31] Although many of the events of 1968 may seem recent in our collective memories, it was 20 years ago, and it is high past time to deal with the issue of racial hiring and employment. We do not need to again disprove Dick Young's prophecy that "we'll outgrow this stuff in another 20 years or so."

NOTES

1. *Sporting News,* February 17, 1968. For the key role played by the *Sporting News,* in baseball see *Sporting News, First Hundred Years, 1886–1986* (St. Louis: Sporting News, 1986). The "Bible of Baseball" will constitute a primary source for this investigation into the sport during 1968.

2. For the development of the liberal consensus and its breakdown see Geoffrey Hodgson, *America in Our Time* (New York: Doubleday, 1976); Allen J. Matusow, *The Unraveling of America: A History of Liberalism in the 1960s* (New York: Harper and Row, 1984); and William L. O'Neil, *Coming Apart: An Informal History of America in the 1960s* (New York: Quadrangle, 1971).

3. Studies which have used baseball to investigate American values include Richard Crepeau, *Baseball: America's Diamond Mind, 1919–1941* (Orlando, FL: University Presses of Florida, 1980); Peter Levine, *A.G. Spalding and the Rise of Baseball: The Promise of American Sport* (New York: Oxford University Press, 1985); Steven A. Riess, *Touching Base: Professional Baseball and American Culture in the Progressive Era* (Westport, CT: Greenwood Press, 1980); Leverett T. Smith, Jr., *The American Dream and the National Game* (Bowling Green, Ohio: Bowling Green University Popular Press, 1975); and Jules Tygiel, *Baseball's Great Experiment: Jackie Robinson and His Legacy* (New York: Oxford University Press, 1983).

4. *Sporting News*, January 6, 1968. For a background history of baseball during the 1960s see David Quentin Voigt, *American Baseball* (Vol. III): *From Postwar Expansion to the Electronic Age* (University Park, PA: Penn State University Press, 1983).

5. *Sporting News*, May 13 and November 18, 1967. For a comparison with baseball activities during World War II see William B. Mead, *Even the Browns: The Zany, True Story of Baseball in the Early Forties* (Chicago: Contemporary Books, 1978); and Richard Goldstein, *Spartan Seasons: How Baseball Survived the Second World War* (New York: MacMillan, 1980).

6. *Sporting News*, January 6, 1968. For an interesting discussion of the connection between American culture and the Vietnam War see Loren Baritz, *Backfire: A History of How American Culture Led Us into Vietnam and Made Us Fight the Way We Did* (New York: William Morrow and Co., 1985).

7. *Sporting News*, February 10, 1968. For background information on Marvin Miller see Robert Boyle, "This Miller Admits He's a Grind," *Sports Illustrated*, 40 (March 11, 1974), 22; Robin Roberts, "The Game Deserves the Best: Marvin Miller as Executive Director of the Baseball Players' Association," *Sports Illustrated*, 30 (February 24, 1969), 46–47; and David Q. Voigt, "They Shaped the Game: Nine Innovators of Major League Baseball," *Baseball History*, 1 (Spring 1986), 5–21.

8. *Sporting News*, April 13, 1968. For background information on racism in baseball and sport during the 1950s and 1960s see Richard Bardalph, *The Negro Vanguard* (New York: Vintage Books, 1961); Robert Boyle, "The Negro in Baseball," *Sports Illustrated*, 12 (March 21, 1960), 16–21; Myron Cope, "The Frustration of the Negro Athlete," *Sport*, 41 (January 1966), 24–25; William B. Furlong, "A Negro Ballplayer's Life Today," *Sport*, 38 (May 1962), 38–39; Jack Olsen, *The Black Athlete: A Shameful Story, the Myth of Integration in American Sport* (New York: Time-Life Books, 1968); Art Rust, Jr., *Get That Nigger Off the Field* (New York: Delacorte, 1976); and Jules Tygiel, "Beyond the Point of No Return: Those Who Came After," *Sports Illustrated*, 58 (June 27, 1983), 40–42.

9. Harry Edwards, *The Revolt of the Black Athlete* (New York: Free Press, 1970); Edwards, *The Struggle That Must Be: An Autobiography* (New York: Macmillan, 1980), 242; and Jack Scott, *The Athletic Revolution* (New York: Free Press, 1971), 181.

10. *Sporting News*, March 30 and April 6, 1968. For Mays and racial issues see Charles Einstein, *Willie's Time: A Memoir* (New York: J.B. Lippincott, 1979); and Ed Linn, "Trials of a Negro Idol," *Saturday Evening Post*, 236 (June 22, 1963), 70–72. For background on Robinson see Tygiel, *Baseball's Great Experiment;* and Jackie Robinson, *I Never Had It Made: An Autobiography* (New York: G.P. Putnam's Sons, 1972).

11. *Sporting News*, April 13, 1968. On Eckert see Barry Kremenko, "The General Takes Command," *Baseball Digest*, 25 (February 1966), 23–25; and John Underwood, "Progress Report on the Unknown Soldier," *Sports Illustrated*, 24 (April 4, 1966), 40–42.

12. *Sporting News*, April 20, 1968. For the King assassination and the ensuing violence see David L. Lewis, *King: A Biography* (Urbana, IL: University of Illinois Press, 1978); and Stephen B. Oates, *Let the Trumpet Sound: The Life of Martin Luther King, Jr.* (New York: New American Library, 1982).

13. *Sporting News*, April 20, 1968. None of the players in this interview were noted for being outspoken on racial issues, with the possible exception of Leon Wagner. For additional information on Wagner see Robert Creamer, "A Free-Swinging Angel Who Never Fears to Tread," *Sports Illustrated*, 19 (August 12, 1963), 46.

14. *Sporting News*, April 27, 1968; and *New York Times*, April 11, 1968.

15. *Sporting News*, April 27 and May 11, 1968: and *New York Times*, April 11, 1968.

16. For detailed coverage of baseball's response to the Kennedy assassination see *Sporting News*, June 22, 1968. For the national response to the assassination and the details of the Kennedy funeral see Arthur Schlesinger, Jr., *Robert Kennedy and His Times* (New York: Ballantine Books, 1978).

17. *Sporting News*, June 29, 1968.

18. *Ibid.*, July 20, 1968. For a discussion of the 1960s counterculture which threatened the baseball and American consensus see Charles Reich, *The Greening of America* (New York: Random House, 1970).

19. *Sporting News*, August 3 and September 7, 1968. For a fine biography which explains Jesse Owens' conservative politics see William J. Baker, *Jesse Owens: An American Life* (New York: The Free Press, 1986). For Monte Irvin see Jackie Robinson, *Baseball Has Done It* (Philadelphia: Lippincott, 1964), 87–96; and Rust, *Get That Nigger off the Field*, 112–119.

20. *Sporting News,* January 26, 1963.

21. For information on the pension question see Bob Broeg, "$12,000 Pensions Near, Pre-'46 Stars Get Nothing," *Baseball Digest,* 25 (November 1966), 79–81; and Richard Dozer, "After the Cheers Have Faded," *Baseball Digest,* 25 (November 1966), 35–39.

22. For *Sporting News* coverage of the pension issue see August 17, August 31, and September 21, 1986.

23. *Ibid.,* December 21, 1968. For information on umpires in the mid-1960s see John Hall, "The New Breed of Umpire," *Baseball Digest,* 26 (June 1967), 20–23.

24. *Sporting News,* December 28, 1968. For the intransigent Finley see Bill Libby, *Charlie O. and the Angry A's* (New York: Doubleday, 1975); and Herbert Mitchelson, *Charlie O.: Charlie Finley vs. the Baseball Establishment* (New York: Bobbs-Merrill, 1975).

25. *Sporting News,* October 19 and 26, 1968. For the 1968 Series see Roger Angell, "World Series: Detroit Tigers vs. St. Louis Cardinals," *New Yorker,* 44 (October 26, 1968), 171–174.

26. *Sporting News,* December 7, 1968. On the irrepressible Banks see Ernie Banks with Jim Enright, *Mr. Cub* (Chicago: Follett Publishing Co., 1971); William Furlong, "Ernie Banks' Life with a Loser," *Sport,* 35 (April 1963), 64–95; and Bill Libby, *Ernie Banks, Mr. Cub* (New York: G.P. Putnam, 1971).

27. On the firing of Eckert see *Sporting News,* December 21 and 28, 1968; Mickey Herskowitz, "A Farewell to General Eckert," *Baseball Digest,* 27 (April 1969), 12–15; and William Leggett, "Court Martial for a General," *Sports Illustrated,* 29 (December 16, 1968), 24–25.

28. On Bowie Kuhn see Kuhn, *Hardball: The Education of a Baseball Commissioner* (New York: Times Books, 1987); and John J. Smith, "Why the Owners Chose Bowie Kuhn," *Baseball Digest,* 27 (April 1969), 5–12.

29. Eugene McCarthy, "Confessions of a Fair Country Ballplayer," *Life,* 65 (October 18, 1968), 67–72.

30. Marvin Cohen, *Baseball the Beautiful: Decoding the Diamond* (New York: Links Books, 1974), 120.

31. *Sporting News,* December 21, 1987.

Whiskey Jack Bishop:
The Sinner Redeemed

MERRITT CLIFTON

AUTHOR'S NOTE

Except where otherwise attributed, my knowledge of Jack Bishop comes from countless conversations with the older residents of Richford, Vermont, and surrounding communities. Most of these conversations were quite informal, taking place at the post office, the ball park, over the hoods of pick-up trucks, and twice, at dying men's bedsides. Only three of my many sources personally knew Bishop; two of the three are now deceased. The rest repeated fragments of a legend given them in their distant youth. Reassembling the fragments is somewhat like reassembling potsherds, in that one can only put together what one finds, and must guess from that about what's missing.

"It was at the turn of the century that the great American game of baseball suddenly became popular in Richford," town historian Jack Salisbury recently wrote.[1]

"The Richford team was a strong one," giving the perennially impoverished Vermont–Quebec border milltown a source of community pride other than the success of smugglers. "Her ace player was one Jack Bishop, a former southern hobo who had been bounced from a train at Richford. A heavy drinker but a gifted pitcher, in February he married a local girl, Maud Whaley, and tried, with varying success, to settle down. He found a job in the local feed store. . . ."

Joining a cellar ball club in June, that had just lost a big home game to arch-rival Enosburg Falls 17–10, Bishop made his debut by shutting out Enosburg 8–0 in their own park. A crowd of 200 Richford residents carried him much of the 10 miles home on their shoulders, then treated the whole team to dinner at the town's best hotel. By season's end, Richford had won the Franklin County League pennant, while Bishop had become an enduring legend, remaining larger than life over 60 years after his death.

No one alive ever faced him. Only a dwindling few old-timers ever saw him. Salisbury never did. Salisbury never even liked baseball, he'll admit, or thought it important in itself. Jack Bishop was important enough to make the town history, Salisbury judged, simply because his name still brings instant recognition from fellow citizens. Start talking baseball in the Richford post office or the Hour Bar or the coffee shop, where Bishop's photo hung on the wall until a recent change of ownership, and they'll tell you: Whiskey Jack

Bishop was the best pitcher Richford ever had, when baseball was important. He was also the longtime rum-running capital's most popular drunk. He was the swaggering character who characterized the town when the town was most prosperous, when Richford was ready to take on anyone over anything, with just a little bet, say ten bucks or so, on the side. Bishop was Casey who didn't strike out. He was the typical small-town American hero, half Huck Finn and half Jack Armstrong, who challenged the mores of his time and place, but conformed just enough at just the right time to win praise from the pulpit—even as he was ducking out the door with a dozen other rebels to prepare for the Sunday ball game.

W.R. "Dig" Rowley, at 83, will take anyone interested up the hill overlooking the international border to show off Bishop's grave. Rowley was only a year old when Bishop won his lasting reputation. But Rowley was a batboy toward the end of Bishop's career, witnessing strikeout feats still recalled with awe. Later, during the 1930s, Rowley captained the Richford Rabbits, twice winners of the Vermont state semi-pro championship. The Rabbits had some well-remembered pitchers themselves: A.C. "Shorty" Coderre, who once trained with the Red Sox; Benny Benoit, 29–14 career; Ken Bailey, 10–6; and Dick Rowse, 8–6. The latter two are still alive. Getting together with Rowley, they agree Bishop was probably the best. They were good themselves, they allow, maybe just as good on certain days, but somehow Bishop above all others had the stuff of legend.

It isn't only old-timers in Richford who speak of Bishop. Chris O'Shea, age 40, edits the Enosburg Falls *County Courier,* which some years ago absorbed the Richford *Standard.* O'Shea has editorially argued that the Whiskey Jack Bishop story has the right tragic qualities to make a made-for-TV movie. Bishop's local reputation even exceeds that of three authentic major leaguers who faced Bishop in the Franklin County League, and later, in the Quebec-based Sovereign League.

The late Larry Gardner of Enosburg Falls started out as a pitcher but switched to shortstop while at the University of Vermont from 1905 to 1908. He played summer ball for the Enosburg town team. He seems to have given up pitching after Bishop jumped from Richford to Enosburg circa 1906. As a third baseman, Gardner batted .289 in 17 seasons with the Red Sox and Indians. Ty Cobb reportedly called him "the best third baseman I ever played against."[2]

Gardner is still remembered with reverence. Old-timers show off his house, across the street from the baseball diamond. Yet they don't tell Gardner stories the way they tell Bishop stories, probably because Gardner left the region when he joined the Red Sox toward the end of 1908.

Jean "Frenchy" Dubuc of St. Johnsbury is totally forgotten, despite an 85–75 record and 3.05 ERA in nine big league seasons with the Reds, Tigers, and Giants. He also was instrumental in organizing one of Vermont's few ventures into organized baseball, the Quebec–Ontario–Vermont League of 1924. Also forgotten is George Lewis "Luckless" LaClaire, of Milton, a regular starter for two years with three different teams in the short-lived Federal League. He joined Farnham, Quebec of the Sovereign League in 1918, but influenza swiftly cut him down, annihilating his entire family.

Old Whiskey Jack beat them all. Whiskey Jack, actually already in the twilight of his erratic career, was reputedly the only northern Vermont pitcher who could strike men out at will.

"He used to stand out on the mound," recalls Dig Rowley, "and ask how much somebody would give him if he'd strike this man out, or that one, or the whole side. He'd run the bet up to ten bucks or so," with equivalent buying power to $100 today, "and then he'd bear down and he'd usually do it. He was a terrible boozer, though, and that was probably his undoing."

Rowley has made a point of at least taking batting practice against all Richford's town team pitching aces, up to and including those of 1987. He laments that he never faced Bishop, not even in fun. "I was still just a boy when he was pitching," Rowley explains. Bishop didn't pitch to boys, and he didn't pitch easy, though he did encourage young Rowley and others to play ball.

Probably the last living batsman who did face Bishop was the late Kenneth "Tup" Tree of Stanbridge East, Quebec, who died at age 94 in July 1987. A teenaged utility infielder and relief pitcher in the Sovereign League, Tree tried unsuccessfully to hit Bishop circa World War I. Bishop was then close to 40, but still the undisputed king of the local mounds.

"He certainly wasn't a very young player," Tree remembered in 1984. But Bishop was big, over six feet tall, with blond hair, usually a mustache, perhaps a bit of rough beard, and an overpowering fastball. He combined the fastball with a sharp-breaking curve, was said to have had pinpoint control when sober, and didn't mind giving the hitters a shave.

"He was a rough-talking fellow," Tree added, but he had a sense of humor, too. "The fellows on the other teams, they used to razz him something awful. He used to swear something awful, and give them right back just as good as he got."

Tree also recalled the weakness that did him in. "I know he drank quite heavily," Tree grinned, "because after the games here in Stanbridge East, the boys would always go over to the hotel, and he'd almost always get loaded. But he wasn't drinking during or before the games, no sir. When he came to pitch, he pitched first and drank after."

Had Bishop been able to maintain as much discipline as a young professional prospect, he'd almost certainly have made the major leagues, and perhaps become a star. "Unfortunately, Bishop's stats are very incomplete due to unpublished averages," notes Bob Hoie of the Society for American Baseball Research's minor league committee. But what stats can be found are impressive.

The son of a Civil War veteran, Bishop was born on the family farm in southern Virginia in 1876. He was named John Lee Bishop, with the middle name in honor of Confederate general Robert E. Lee. Little is known of his early years, but it's a cinch they weren't easy, since the region had been the principal no-man's-land of the war and had been thoroughly devastated. Even 12 years after Lee's surrender, most former Confederates were still barely scratching out a living.

Most young men in Virginia at that time became coal miners, dirt farmers, drifted west, or went to sea. But Jack Bishop had another option: he could throw a ball harder than just about anyone. Said to have starred for local semi-pro teams from his early teens on, Bishop probably worked at nominal tasks for mills and factories during the week and was paid primarily for wearing the company colors when he pitched on Sunday.

His exploits eventually impressed professional scouts. In 1897, at age 21, Bishop signed with Norfolk of the Atlantic League, which at that time was just two steps away from the big leagues. He hurled 20 games, with an unrecorded won–lost mark. But boozing was already getting him into trouble.

As a semi-pro, the Richford legend runs, Bishop had often been paid in Virginia moonshine. He'd come to like strong drink, and now he was making enough money pitching to have as much as he wanted. Early in 1898, Norfolk had enough of him and traded him to Richmond, their perennial rival.

That was a big mistake. In 36 games, Bishop compiled a 23–12 record, either leading the league or coming close to it in all pitching departments. He opened 1899 still with Richmond, but by mid-season was sold to Syracuse of the Eastern League. The Eastern League of that era is today's International League—today's Eastern League wasn't founded until 1923. Then, as now, Syracuse was one step below the major leagues. In fact, Syracuse had been a major league team for one season in 1890. Most of Bishop's teammates had either been to the majors or were going there.

Bishop pitched only a few games for Syracuse in 1899, but was counted upon as a regular starter in 1900. That's when he drank himself into trouble and possibly hurt his arm pitching with insufficient rest. Ineffective in 17 games, he was released and wound up the year back with town teams.

From then on, Bishop's professional career was mostly downhill, though much of his best pitching lay ahead of him. He resumed his pro career with Richmond in 1901, managing just a 6 and 10 record in 17 games. A brief stint with Charlotte of the North Carolina League and a 3 and 3 record with Manchester of the New England League followed, in 1902.

At Manchester, Bishop was able to shake his hard-drinking reputation, for a time. He moved on to the championship Schenectady club of the New York State League in 1903. Now twenty-nine, Bishop knew he was running out of time to impress the scouts. But that knowledge wasn't enough to keep him sober. He returned to boozing and was soon released. Schenectady baseball historian Frank M. Keetz reports that some time afterward Bishop's mother appealed to readers of the *Schenectady Gazette* with "a touching letter" seeking any knowledge of her son's whereabouts.

During the off-seasons, Bishop had never really developed any marketable skill. He merely did whatever work his strong back could obtain and awaited baseball season. With nothing to turn toward after Schenectady dumped him, Bishop became a hobo, drifting through odd jobs and town-team pitching stints wherever he could find them.

He was headed for Montreal one night, the story goes, when a railroad bull tossed him off a train into the Missisquoi River, just south of Richford. Unknown to himself, Bishop had come home—at least to as much of a home as he ever had. However, even after finding a steady job, a bride, and winning Richford the pennant in 1905, Bishop felt inclined to roam. He visited Virginia in 1906, achieving reconciliation with his family, and earning a final chance at pitching professionally, with Danville of the Virginia League. Only after booze got the better of him again did he return to Richford, a dry town by ordinance if anything but in actuality.

Mostly, Bishop pitched for Richford. But often he'd pitch for Enosburg Falls and nearby Frelighsburg on the same weekend, hopping trains to get from one town to the next. Usually, he capped the weekend with a bender. Surprisingly, despite his rough language, rougher habits, and Confederate background, there's no record of anyone hating his guts. Instead, Bishop was praised whenever he quit drinking, pitied when he resumed, lauded and emulated for his feats on the diamond.

Bishop's Confederate background could have become an obstacle to community acceptance, but it didn't. Northern Vermont and southern Quebec had been terminus for the Underground Railroad that helped thousands of runaway slaves escape before the Civil War. As of the early 1900s, many blacks still lived in Sovereign League territory. Old photos show several blacks playing for the Bedford town team, and since Frelighsburg had enough blacks to support an all-black cemetery, it's a good bet some were among Bishop's teammates there.

This may have influenced Bishop's most impressive deed of all, or rather non-deed, uncharacteristically quietly done, not on the mound or the barstool but behind closed doors among men sworn to secrecy.

Though nobody ever publicized Ku Klux Klan identities, Bishop was thought by many Richford citizens to have been a sometime Klan member, or at least associate. This wouldn't have been remarkable for any young southern man of Bishop's rowdy nature in that particular era. The First Klan was actually in decline at the turn of the century, as Bishop came of age. Nonetheless, Bishop grew up in a center of Klan activity, coming from within an hour's walk of Lynchburg, Virginia, for which the crime of lynching is named. Whether or not he personally participated in Klan activities and lynchings, he certainly kept the sort of rough, idle company who did participate. The very frequency of lynchings in his time and place suggests he must have been at least a witness after the fact.[3]

Bishop never spoke of lynchings to the knowledge of acquaintances still living in the mid-1980s; but those acquaintances were children when they knew him, while lynchings during Bishop's youth tended to be particularly brutal, with the victims being burned alive more often than hanged, usually after prolonged beatings and torture.[4]

Bishop was already long settled in Richford by the time the Second Klan formed, in 1915. Adding anti-Catholicism to anti-black and anti-immigrant sentiments, the Second Klan spread rapidly into the Northeast, where Catholic Quebecois flooded over the border to compete for jobs much as Hispanics flood into the Southwest from Mexico today. By the mid-1920s the Klan claimed from 4 to 5 million members nationwide, and controlled the Maine state legislature.

Vermont, with the second-longest border on Quebec after Maine, had also been among the Klan's organizing targets. As a border town, with a Catholic church established in 1840, Richford grew anxious. Simultaneously with the formation of the Second Klan, the D.W. Griffith film *Birth of a Nation,* based on Thomas Dixon's novel *The Clansman,* "drew hundreds of people" to Richford screenings, according to Salisbury. "The crowds were so great that a special police officer was required to keep order." Community leaders are said to have worried that Jack Bishop might work to promote the Klan, increasing civic unrest already stirred by Prohibition, which began in Richford by local ordinance in 1914, five years before the Volstead Act imposed prohibition nationally. The local prohibition had provoked a nightly contest between mostly Protestant lawmen and vigilantes on the one hand, and mostly Catholic Quebecois bottleggers on the other. After the Volstead Act, the contest expanded to include professional rumrunners from Boston and Chicago. Of mostly Irish and Italian ancestry, the professionals also tended to be Catholic, while the outside reinforcements assigned to the border by the federal government tended to be Protestants. Their encounters often turned violent. Richford's most notorious linehouse, a saloon with doors on either side of the border, was aptly named The Bucket O' Blood.[5]

But perhaps because Bishop's boozing had made him a good friend of many Catholics, he left the Klan alone. That Bishop was a Mason probably also had a lot to do with it. Bishop had joined the local Masons during one of his attempts to sober up and make friends in Richford. The Masons are a Protestant order, but the Vermont Masons nonetheless opposed the Klan, as a violent secret society. The Klan opposed the Masons on the same grounds. The result was territorial warfare. "An interesting story is related," wrote Richford historian Rhoda Berger in 1980, "concerning the closing of most of the Masonic Lodges in Vermont. This happened about the year 1913 [the date is incorrect], when the Ku Klux Klan was getting a foothold. . . . Fear of fires, and other wreckage caused most of the Lodges to close up. Richford," with Bishop an active member, "was one that defiantly never closed its doors. Historical records are vague as to whether there was any violence here."[6]

The Masonic emblem on Bishop's gravestone shows which organization received his strongest loyalty. The mere fact that it appears there, with the Klan still nationally prominent at his death, seems a statement of values. Maybe Bishop was only protecting his source of liquor, but whatever the case, without his support, the Klan was forced back south.

Did Bishop's position really make a difference? Men and boys reputedly followed him down the street. He was a public hero. Perhaps he'd have been repudiated if he had become a Klan advocate. But again, there was already the pro-temperance vigilante committee, a potential Klan foundation.

Bishop, however, did maintain ties to Virginia throughout the rest of his life and in 1925 he died at Marion, Virginia, of an aneurism of the ascending aorta—a heart attack, perhaps brought on by too much moonshine during a visit to the homefolks. Then again, it might have come about from one last fling at pitching. He was 48, plus ten months and seven days. Wife Martha brought him back to Richford to be buried. His hillside plot overlooked that era's town baseball diamond.

As an athlete, Bishop was strictly a community hero. His achievements in the minor leagues have been duplicated by thousands. Even his ability to strike out town team players at will is scarcely unique. As an individual, Bishop is difficult to portray in a flattering light—an irresponsible braggart, at best, a brawling drunk who couldn't hold a job by every living acquaintance's testimony. As a symbol, though, Bishop suited Richford perfectly. Richford too briefly rose to prosperity by rebelling against the work ethic. After the Volstead Act, the town flourished through bootlegging as never before, until disaster struck with the flood of 1927, devastating downtown and obliterating the diamond where Bishop had pitched. To townspeople, Catholics or Protestant fundamentalists, the flood, like Bishop's death, was God's punishment for indulgence. The lesson that indulgence shall be punished is still recalled among the religious on the anniversaries of the flood, in sermons, reminiscences, and letters to the editor of the *County Courier;* while the lesson that excessive logging brings erosion and flooding often seems little heard.

Though Dig Rowley and the other old-timers don't audibly think about social symbolism, Bishop's character and demise probably gained greater legendary significance during the post-flood era than in his own. In telling Bishop's story, townspeople—reticent, like other Vermonters, about themselves—were in a sense recounting their own history, shielded from self-incrimination. Bishop and his 1905 champions became symbolic ancestors of the Rabbits, who lacked real stars, but who persevered despite poverty, and through exemplary teamwork compiled the best overall percentage (.629) of any northern Vermont club between 1932 and 1940.

Told together, as the stories are in the post office, the Hour Bar, and the coffee shop, the legends of Whiskey Jack Bishop and the Rabbits are an unconscious local parallel of Christian myth. Bishop died for Richford's sins, as well as his own. He left behind an ideal that redeemed Richford, through the disciples who formed the Rabbits, and if the town didn't go to heaven then, that was only because World War II broke the comeback momentum supplied by the WPA, but represented by Benny Benoit, Ken Bailey, Dick and Mugs Rouse, slugger Paul Conger, and all the rest.

NOTES

1. Jack C. Salisbury, *Richford, Vermont: Frontier Town. The First 150 Years* (Canaan, NH: Phoenix Publishing, 1987), p. 94.

2. Phil Lotane, "The Larry Gardner Story." University of Vermont Alumni Magazine, Spring 1986.

3. Editor Sam Clark of *Jim Jam Jems,* a radical journal based in Bismarck, North Dakota, in July 1921 counted 2,701 lynchings in the 13 southern states over the preceding 34 years. Another radical editor, Ralph Ginzburg of *Eros,* tallied over 5,000 in his Dell paperback *100 Years of Lynching,* published 1965. Both Clark and Ginzburg worked from newspaper accounts of lynchings. Ginzburg estimated that the actual total was probably much higher, believing most lynchings were not reported.

4. Both Clark and Ginzburg quote detailed newspaper accounts.

5. Salisbury gives details of Richford rumrunning on pages 107–109, 117–119, and 123 of his history. Many other accounts exist.

6. Rhoda Berger, *Glimpses of Richford 1780–1980.* Self-published.

Judge Kenesaw Mountain Landis and the Art of Cartel Enforcement

CLARK NARDINELLI

Judge Kenesaw Mountain Landis, commissioner of organized baseball from 1921 until his death in 1944, was one of the most respected public figures in the United States. Viewed from today, it is difficult to comprehend the place baseball once occupied in American life. Baseball was indeed the national pastime before and during the Landis years. The importance of the game was reflected in the positions of the men who were under consideration for commissioner before the appointment of Landis; the list of candidates included former President William Howard Taft, former Secretary of the Treasury William McAdoo, Generals John J. Pershing and Leonard Wood, and Senator (and Presidential hopeful) Hiram Johnson.[1] Landis himself was a federal judge at the time of his appointment; his salary as commissioner was to be almost seven times what he had earned as a judge.[2] Although the commissioner is still important, the baseball owners of today would be unlikely to be able to hire a person of similar importance (or have an incentive to do so). In 1920, however, the executive branch of baseball could compete for candidates with major government departments.

During his tenure as baseball "czar," the public believed that Landis represented the interests of fans and players against rapacious owners. His long-time critic, J.G. Taylor Spink, wrote that Landis

> . . . was the friend of the ball player, and while he was Commissioner of all baseball, he always felt he was the ball player's man and the fan's man on baseball's supreme body.
> "The clubowners have their league presidents to look out for their interests," he once said.[3]

The image of the stern old man protecting the players and fans still remains. A recent popular work of baseball history put it as follows:

> The autocrat of the federal bench knew where his constituency lay, too. He ran roughshod over the men who paid him—many club owners came to regret the sweeping powers they had given him—but the players idolized him and the fans respected him, and any attempt to remove him from office might well have been interpreted that something, again, was amiss with the game.[4]

Frequent battles between Landis and individual owners fostered the belief that he represented fans and players. Yet, neither fans nor players appointed Landis to his job. The owners of the 16 major league teams hired him, paid his salary, and could have removed him at any time by buying up his contract.[5] Despite the public's impression that he was baseball's dictator, when the owners opposed Landis on a major issue—the farm system—he was forced to give way.[6]

The perception of Landis differed from the reality in that the supposed nemesis of the owners was also their valued employee, continually reappointed to his job. Lance Davis demonstrated that the discrepancy between the image and the reality of Landis can be explained by an application of the economic model of a cartel.[7] Organized baseball was a cartel designed to create monopsony in the market for the services of players. Monopsony is a labor market dominated by a single employer. Because the owners of professional baseball teams agreed not to compete among each other for players, each player faced (effectively) only one possible employer—his current team.

Although the bargaining advantage created by monopsony generates profits for employers, most economists believe it to be extremely difficult to maintain a private cartel without government protection.[8] The problem is that private cartels create incentives for members to chisel on the agreement.[9] Only government or some other outside agency can force the existing firms in an industry to obey the agreement and prevent new firms from entering the industry if profits are above average.

The hypothesis that baseball was a monopsony created by a private cartel of the owners explains the apparently paradoxical relationship between Landis and the owners. To maintain the cartel, all teams had to conform to the rules and spirit of the cartel contract, known as the National Agreement.[10] The owners hired Landis to manage the cartel agreement and to prevent outside challenges to the cartel. The conflicts between the commissioner and individual owners originated in attempts to violate the cartel agreement. The same owners nevertheless voted to retain Landis as commissioner because to vote against him could damage and possibly destroy the cartel.

The long success of the baseball cartel is exceptional. Most private cartels—OPEC is a recent example—are successful for at most a few years. The remarkable success of the baseball cartel lies in a combination of fortuitous circumstances, absence of legal sanction, and Landis' extraordinary effectiveness as the cartel enforcer. The effectiveness of Landis can best be demonstrated by considering the history of monopsony in baseball.

THE BASEBALL MONOPSONY

In 1975 pitchers Andy Messersmith and Dave McNally successfully challenged baseball's reserve clause, a contractual provision that gave a single baseball team the perpetual exclusive right to purchase the services of a particular player.[11] Under the reserve clause the baseball players' labor market had been a monopsony.[12] Although it is possible that profits from the monopsony may have been competed away, star players clearly were subject to monopsonistic exploitation. Monopsonistic exploitation is said to exist when the marginal revenue product exceeds the wage rate. A baseball player's marginal revenue product is defined as the increase in his team's revenue attributable to that player. For example, Gerald Scully estimated that in 1966 Sandy Koufax produced a marginal revenue product equal to $725,000, far more than his salary of $125,000.[13] With the near abolition of the reserve clause after 1975, the average real salary of major league baseball players jumped 8.99 percent in 1976, 38.75 percent in 1977, and a further 21.95 percent in 1978.[14] In 1973, 1974, and 1975 the increase in average salaries had been less than 1 percent per year. The monopsony, despite some lingering remnants, broke down after 1975. An attempt by owners to reintroduce a de facto reserve clause in 1981 failed, as the players struck to preserve their bargaining positions.

The high salaries and complicated contracts of current players now dominate the baseball news. The ease of transition into the new era has caused many to forget the most remarkable circumstance of the former monopsony: its long survival. During most of the period from 1876 to 1975 baseball was the most popular spectator sport in America. The great popularity of the game generated profits that created incentives for new firms to enter the market and for individual players to attempt to break free from the reserve clause. Although casual observers often consider the era before 1975 to have been one of unchallenged monopsony, many attempts were made to break the power of the cartel; some of the more important are listed in the chart. The most common challenge was the entry (or attempted entry) of new leagues. Organized baseball dealt with potential entry in various ways, including expanding to allow the entrants into the cartel, buying out potential entrants, or driving competitors out of business.[15] The most important threats in the early years of baseball were the American Association and the American League; the National League countered both threats by bringing the new team owners into the cartel. The most serious threat in the later years came in 1960 in the form of Branch Rickey's proposed Continental League. In response, the American and National Leagues both expanded, bringing the potential competitors into the cartel. The history of the baseball monopsony was therefore stormy; players and potential entrants made continual attempts to break it up.[16] Only one period corresponds to the image of organized baseball as the secure, unchallenged monopsony: the years 1921 to 1944. These years marked the tenure of Judge Kenesaw Mountain Landis as commissioner of baseball.

Several factors account for the relative peace of the Landis years. In 1922, Supreme

Judge Kenesaw Mountain Landis, Commissioner for 23 years, shown beginning another season. (Photo courtesy of the National Baseball Library, Cooperstown, N.Y.)

Court Justice Oliver Wendell Holmes wrote the decision that held baseball was not interstate commerce and was therefore not subject to antitrust laws.[17] This ruling prevented players and potential entrants from challenging the cartel in court. However, exemption from antitrust laws might not have been sufficient to protect the cartel. Monopsony profits would induce entry into the baseball market or attempts by insiders to appropriate a larger share. Such attempts did not occur because the powers of the commissioner, and the way Landis used them, maintained and enforced the cartel agreement so completely that no serious challenges arose after his first few years in office. A principal reason Landis proved so successful in enforcing the cartel agreement was his early establishment and use of severe punishment for any player within organized baseball who challenged the monopsony. His willingness and ability to do so was in turn the combined outcome of his earlier career (and inclinations) and the public reaction to the fixing of the 1919 World Series.

ESTABLISHING THE CREDIBLE THREAT

In March 1905 President Theodore Roosevelt appointed Landis to the federal judgeship for the Northern District of Illinois (including Chicago and the surrounding area). While on the bench he became known as an ardent trust-buster, mainly as a result of fining Standard Oil $29,240,000 in a rebate case.[18] He also tended to render harsh judgments against union organizers. In a famous case involving the Industrial Workers of the World (IWW), he sentenced their leader to 20 years in prison on vague charges of obstructing the war effort. Most of his severe judgments were either overturned (Standard Oil) or commuted (IWW), but these decisions helped to make Landis a public character.[19]

The antitrust case that was to make Landis' fortune was one in which he failed to reach a decision. In 1915, the Federal Baseball League brought suit against the National and American Leagues for violating the Sherman and Clayton antitrust acts.[20] After hearing the arguments, Landis delayed ruling on the suit. While he stalled, organized baseball reached a peace settlement with the Federal League, which allowed the dismissal of the suit.

The major league club owners were suitably impressed with the handling of the case and the judge's pronouncement that "any blows at the thing called baseball would be regarded by this court as a blow to a national institution."[21] With the breakdown of the ruling National Commission in 1918–1919, Landis was one of those considered for the new position of chairman of the commission.[22] In the wake of the scandal over the 1919 World Series, which broke in September 1920, Landis was appointed to the new position of commissioner and given wide discretionary powers to clean up baseball. His first task was to establish his discretionary power.

The full story of the 1919 World Series will never be known. The basic facts are that various gamblers met with eight members of the American League champion Chicago White Sox and offered them bribes to throw the Series. What happened next differs across accounts. The most plausible reconstruction of the events is that at least some players deliberately tried to throw the first two and the eighth games of the Series, won by the Cincinnati Reds, five games to three.[23] Seven White Sox received payoffs from gamblers. An eighth, Buck Weaver, met with the gamblers but refused to participate and received no payoff. A Chicago jury acquitted the accused players in August 1921, after a farcical trial for conspiracy to defraud the public, but Landis immediately issued a statement that the eight Black Sox were banned from organized baseball for life, "regardless of the verdict of juries. . . ."[24]

Banning the Black Sox has rightly been regarded as the most significant act of Landis' career. The emphasis, however, has usually been placed on his regard for the integrity of the game and his hatred for gamblers and their influence.[25] Historians have overlooked the importance of his actions with respect to the economic viability of the baseball cartel and to his own position as cartel enforcer. On one level, throwing games was a form of shirking, a common problem under conditions of monopsony. Because owners paid players only a part of their marginal revenue products, players often played at less than maximum capacity. Shirking often took the form of indifferent play, or "letting up" against certain opponents. It was common for players on teams involved in pennant races to send cash gifts to other teams, if those teams defeated key rivals. At times, players apparently sent cash to defeated opponents, an activity suspiciously close to paying players to throw games.

The most serious form of shirking was, of course, throwing games. Although the mythology of baseball asserts that throwing baseball games was invented by gamblers on the eve of the 1919 World Series, the practice had been common since the early days of the game.[26] Deliberately losing after placing bets allowed players to increase their incomes while shirking. Several players, most notably Hal Chase, bet against their own team and then took actions to protect their investment.[27] Circumstantial evidence indicates that the practice was widespread before 1920.[28] Throwing games could even be pure shirking, occurring even though no bets were involved. Rumors persisted that the Philadelphia Athletics deliberately lost the 1914 World Series in a protest over niggardly salaries.

Landis' banishment of the Black Sox reduced the expected payoff from throwing games as a form of shirking. On another level, his handling of the scandal established his ability to ban players, whatever the judgment of juries. The absolute power over a player's eligibility could be used not only to punish shirking, but to punish any other form of attack on the cartel's monopsony power. Once the credible threat was firmly established, Landis used it in a skillful manner to solidify the cartel's power and his position as cartel manager.

USING THE CREDIBLE THREAT

The reserve clause underlaid the baseball monopsony; the job of the commissioner of baseball was to protect it. New leagues, potential competitors for players, posed the main outside threat to the reserve clause. Disputes between club owners over players could also threaten the monopsony. In addition to policing the monopsony, Landis wished to protect his own position as commissioner. How he accomplished both tasks can best be seen in his handling of various cases during his early years in office.[29]

The case of Shufflin' Phil Douglas demonstrated to players that Landis would offer no second chances.[30] Douglas, an alcoholic pitcher, had been fined by the New York Giants and placed in a sanatarium for five days after going on a binge. Once out, angry and possibly drunk, he wrote a letter to Leslie Mann, perhaps the most straight-laced member of the St. Louis Cardinals, offering to disappear and thereby possibly prevent the Giants from winning the pennant. The letter could not possibly have been a serious proposal to throw games; the choice of Mann as the recipient was itself probably a joke. As Douglas could have expected, Mann immediately turned the letter over to his manager, who forwarded it to Landis. Landis banned Douglas for life. The harsh treatment of a pathetic drunk established that Landis would show no mercy in such cases. The players no doubt got the message.

Landis also let players know that they, and not their superiors, would be punished for their actions. In late 1924, Jimmy O'Connell, an outfielder for the New York Giants, attempted to bribe the shortstop of the Philadelphia Phillies.[31] When Landis questioned O'Connell, he explained that he had simply followed the instructions of Giant coach Cozy Dolan. O'Connell also implied three other Giant players had known of the attempted bribe. The three other players were cleared by Landis, but O'Connell and Dolan were banned. The most curious part of the O'Connell–Dolan investigation was its limited scope. Dolan served as assistant, or flunky, to John J. McGraw, Giant manager and part owner. Many of the scandals that had occurred in the previous several years had involved Giants and ex-Giants; the trail obviously led to McGraw, but Landis made no attempt to follow it.[32] McGraw was part owner of the franchise that had dominated the National League for 20 years in attendance and performance. Landis chose to expel the pawns without investigating who may have been behind the bribe. The players' commissioner never forgot who paid his salary.

From the standpoint of the baseball cartel, the decision rendered by Landis in the Ray Fisher case proved highly significant.[33] Fisher, a pitcher for the Cincinnati Reds, had signed a contract for the 1921 season for a salary of $4,500, $1,000 less than he had been paid in 1920. Unhappy with the terms of his contract, Fisher applied for and was offered a job as baseball coach at the University of Michigan. When he informed owner August Herrmann of the Michigan offer, Hermann offered to restore the $1,000 pay cut if Fisher would remain with the Reds. Fisher, 33 years old and beginning to worry about his financial future, then requested a three-year contract. When Herrmann refused, he asked to be placed on the voluntary retired list. Permission granted, Fisher accepted the coaching job, though he let Cincinnati know he might be willing to return to the team after the college baseball season. Herrmann, perhaps because he was angry at Fisher's refusal of his offer, placed him on the permanent ineligible list rather than the voluntary retired list. A team from a Pennsylvania outlaw league contacted Fisher, informing him that rumors were circulating that he was to be blacklisted from organized baseball. If the rumors were true, they offered him a contract to play in the outlaw league after the college season.

Fisher applied to Judge Landis for a ruling on his status. After receiving information from Fisher and the Reds, Landis banned him permanently from organized baseball in June 1921. The harsh judgment of Landis has been explained many different ways. J.G. Taylor Spink regarded it as an example of Landis' tendency (frequently displayed as a federal judge) to be arbitrarily lenient or severe as the mood hit him.[34] Donald Proctor attributed the decision to Landis' unwillingness to believe Fisher rather than Herrmann and the Reds.[35] Fisher himself believed that Landis was not sufficiently acquainted with the evidence and would have reinstated him had he appealed.[36] Seymour simply found the permanent ban "incomprehensible."[37]

There is another explanation for the ban. Landis knew that the profits in organized baseball arose largely from its ability to expropriate economic rents from players. Economic rent, in turn, was equal to the difference between the marginal revenue product of an individual as a baseball player and his marginal revenue product in some other occupation. The existence of these rents made monopsony profits possible. In contract negotiations with the Reds, Fisher used his ability to sell his services as a baseball player or coach elsewhere as a bargaining chip in his negotiations with the Reds. One of the strongest factors in the ability of club owners to extract rents was that if the player did not sign, he would lose all rent. For the typical player, this left the advantage with the ball club, which could always purchase or trade for a replacement. By taking away part of the club's advantage, Fisher's bargaining tactics undermined the monopsony, something Landis could not allow. The extraordinarily harsh treatment of Fisher, coming as it did soon after Landis took office, served notice to baseball players that no attempt—either of the Fisher variety or some other—to undermine the monopsony would be tolerated by the commissioner.

One of Fisher's Cincinnati teammates, third baseman Heinie Groh, was involved in another of Landis' important early decisions. Teams often cheated on the baseball cartel by tampering with players on other teams. The methods was as follows. New York might want a particular Boston player and be willing to pay him a higher salary than he was earning with Boston. The New York team might secretly convince the player to hold out or perhaps even walk out on Boston. After a few weeks of the contract dispute, New York would then offer to purchase the player's contract from Boston, who usually preferred cash in hand to the recalcitrant player.

In 1921, Heinie Groh refused to sign with Cincinnati and remained a holdout well into the season. In June, the Reds and Giants agreed to a deal whereby the Giants would trade three players and cash in return for Groh, who agreed to sign a contract only on condition of being traded. Landis vetoed the trade, saying that it was an "unhealthy situation if a dissatisfied player could dictate his transfer to a strong contender before he agreed to sign a contract."[38] After being told by Landis that he would play for Cincinnati or not at all, Groh signed his contract and returned to the Reds. Although the Giants eventually acquired Groh, Landis' action served to close off an important method of cheating on the cartel.

The interpretation of Landis' actions as an astute cartel enforcer can also explain his harsh decision in the Benny Kauff case. Kauff, the center fielder of the Giants, was indicted and tried for automobile theft and receiving stolen goods.[39] In May 1921, he was acquitted. Landis, however, declared the acquittal a mistake and banned Kauff from baseball. His ignoring the jury's decision has been taken as further evidence of his arbitrariness. Another explanation may be in order.

Kauff had come to the Giants after the dissolution of the Federal League (he had been that league's batting champion in 1914 and 1915). Landis may have treated him harshly because of his background in the "outlaw" league. The implicit message was that the judge did not take kindly to those who had challenged the monopsony by signing with an outside league. The terms of organized baseball's settlement with the Federal League prevented Landis, except as the opportunity arose (the Kauff case), from punishing players who had joined the Federals in the 1914 and 1915 seasons. His action in the case of Kauff may have been intended to tell players what would happen to anyone who joined a competing league. It may be significant that no outside league attempted to challenge the monopsony until after Landis' death.

The most ironic instance of Landis' treatment of outlaws was in the case of Dickie Kerr. Kerr was one of the pitching heroes of the 1919 World Series, winning two games for the White Sox despite what may have been mixed support from his teammates. The same low pay, however, that had helped cause the scandal drove Kerr from the White Sox after the 1921 season. Finding that he could make more money playing outside of organized baseball than in the American League, he did not sign for 1922 and played for an independent team in Texas. Kerr's team, however, played against some of the banned players that year. Landis banned Kerr for a season and effectively ended his major league career.[40]

WHEN LANDIS WAS LENIENT

The cases of the Black Sox, Douglas, Kauff, Fisher, O'Connell, and Dolan demonstrate that Landis could mete out harsh punishments, not being afraid to destroy a player's career. Such behavior is consistent with the hypothesis that Landis was a skillful and ruthless cartel enforcer. His behavior might also simply be interpreted as evidence that Landis was the dedicated protector of the integrity of the game, reacting harshly to any challenge. The problem with the Landis as protector thesis is that in many instances, he was unaccountably lenient. The leniency can be explained if one accepts the cartel manager hypothesis. I will consider two cases in which Landis displayed leniency: the Benton case, and the Cobb–Speaker affair.

Rube Benton, a pitcher of dubious character, had admitted knowing about the 1919 World Series plot. Benton had also openly associated with gamblers and other undesirables. Despite his admission and connections, Benton remained in organized baseball, playing for the St. Paul minor league team in 1922. Because Benton pitched well in St. Paul, August Herrmann, owner of the Cincinnati Reds, purchased his contract. National League president John Heydler and a majority of owners ruled that Benton should not be allowed to play in the National League. Landis supported Herrmann and Benton, ruling that if the player was eligible to play in the minor leagues, he was eligible to play in the major leagues.[41] Landis' lenient decision was wholly inconsistent with his rulings in the cases of Benny Kauff and Buck Weaver (banned for life because of his knowledge of the 1919 fix).

The most famous example of Landis' leniency was the scandal involving Ty Cobb and Tris Speaker, two of the game's greatest players.[42] Cobb and Speaker were accused of betting on and then fixing a game on September 25, 1919. After the 1926 season, both players were permitted to retire from baseball. Apparently, they "voluntarily" retired in order to avoid publicity. Landis, however, made the accusations and arrangement public. Cobb and Speaker then withdrew their resignations. After a hearing in which their chief accuser—perhaps because he was afraid of the ferocious Cobb—refused to appear, Landis acquitted the two players and ordered them reinstated. Seymour speculated that the reinstatement of Cobb and Speaker came about because of the popularity and public support for the two players.[43] Also, the accusations against Cobb and Speaker unleashed a flood of charges about past fixes involving as many as 40 players. Landis complained that he was tired of old scandals; he established a five-year statute of limitations on baseball offenses to stem the tide.

The reinstatements of Cobb, Speaker, and Benton can be explained in another way. All three had been banned by someone other than Landis. Landis wanted to make it clear that only he had the authority to ban players from the game. In the Benton case, he overruled National League president John Heydler. In the Cobb–Speaker case, he overruled Ban Johnson, the American League president. Indeed, the real battle during the Cobb–Speaker case was between Landis and Johnson. Johnson had announced that Cobb and Speaker would never again play baseball in the American League. When he reinstated them, Landis insisted that the two players play in the American League. Cobb signed with the Philadelphia Athletics, Speaker with the Washington Senators. A humiliated Ban Johnson retired shortly thereafter and Landis' position as the exclusive guardian of the baseball cartel was secure.[44]

THE QUIET YEARS

After the Cobb–Speaker case and the accompanying flood of accusations had been disposed of, baseball experienced a long respite from scandal. More importantly, no new challenges to the cartel arose. Landis had established his ability to summarily ban players who signed with outlaw leagues. His power made it extraordinarily costly for a potential rival league to do what the American League had done—lure players away from the established leagues by paying higher salaries. The risk, especially for individuals whose skills were so specialized and careers so short, would be immense.

The position of Landis as the exclusive keeper of the cartel also contributed mightily to his effectiveness. In the years before Landis, a player blacklisted by one league could often find employment in another (major or minor) league. With Landis, this option disappeared. Furthermore, the cost of joining an outlaw league rose drastically. Violating the cartel now meant swift and sure punishment, without possibility of redress. Backed by the Supreme Court's decision that antitrust laws did not apply to baseball, Landis could effectively stop any internal or external threats to cartel stability. No such threats appeared after 1927. Cartel stability was also helped by the Depression. Average annual attendance fell from 9.6 million in 1921 through 1930 to 7.6 million in 1931 through 1935. The decline in minor league attendance was even more severe.[45] From 1936 attendance revived but the cartel remained stable. No one openly challenged Landis.

One possible threat to the cartel deserves mention: black players. The Negro Leagues by the 1930s were competitive with the major leagues. Indeed, the best players in black baseball were as good or better than the best players in white baseball. Yet, teams in organized baseball signed no black players. It is clear that, despite public protestations to the contrary, Landis privately policed the policy of racism.[46] Within a year of his death the Brooklyn Dodgers began scouting the Negro Leagues for players, finally signing Jackie Robinson in August 1945.

The racism of Landis and the owners is undeniable. It is nevertheless true that economic motives may have supplemented racism; a policy of opening up baseball could have threatened the monopsony. Black players would have been free agents. Bidding wars for their services could have erupted.[47] Moreover, the Negro Leagues themselves could have bid to retain some of their stars. Furthermore, the Negro Leagues had never been able to maintain a strict monopsony. Stars such as Satchel Paige were used to selling their services to the highest bidder. When baseball was finally integrated, the piecemeal manner in which it occurred posed no threat to the monopsony.[48] The owners of the 1930s, however, could not have known that integration would not threaten their position. Landis made sure that they did not have to find out.

The latter years of the Landis regime, then, saw no serious challenge to the monopsony. That rare creation, a stable private cartel, held. In a series of decisions, Landis had established a harsh and arbitrary enforcement policy that effectively kept the cartel in place. The key was the fear he inspired in players. No player dared risk his career in order to challenge the monopsony. With players unwilling to jump to a new league, no league could hope to compete with organized baseball. None tried. The seeming arbitrariness of Landis' rulings probably enhanced his effectiveness, as uncertainty raised the expected costs of defiance.

The circumstances of the time—Black Sox scandal, antitrust decision, Depression, World War II—may well have made the control of baseball by a cartel inevitable. The contribution of Landis was to ensure that the cartel's control was absolute and unchallenged. The best testimony to Landis' effectiveness came with his death. Within two years, a rival league—the Mexican League—appeared. Other challenges soon followed. The monopsony survived another 30 years through geographic relocation and expansion to bring potential entrants into the cartel. Bonuses paid to young players and other extra expenditures no doubt dissipated part of the monopsony rents of the postwar era. Then came the Curt Flood case, strikes, arbitration, and, finally, Messersmith–McNally. The stability of the cartel died with Landis and his ruthless enforcement of the reserve clause.

111

SOME CHALLENGES TO THE BASEBALL MONOPSONY

Year	Event
1882	American Association. New league competes with National League.
1884	Union Association. A third league. Folds after one season.
1885	Brotherhood of Professional Ball Players. Union of players.
1890	Players' League. New league formed by the Brotherhood. Folds after one season.
1891	War between National League and American Association. American Association folds after the season. Stronger teams join National League.
1901	American League. New league successfully competes for players and fans. Unites with National League to form new cartel in 1903.
1901	Players Protective Association. Attempted union.
1912	Baseball Players Fraternity. Short-lived union. Disappeared after 1920.
1914	Federal League. Competing league. Folds after 1915 season.
1922	*Federal Baseball Club of Baltimore v. National League,* 259 U.S. 200. Antitrust suit. Supreme Court rules baseball not subject to Sherman and Clayton Acts.
1946	Mexican League. New league signs several major league players. Folds during first season.
1946	American Baseball Guild. Another attempt to form union. Owners establish pensions and minimum salaries in return for disbanding union.
1949	*Gardella v. Chandler,* 172 F.2d 402. Appellate court rules that player can sue under antitrust laws. Settled out of court.
1953	*Toolson v. New York Yankees,* 346 U.S. 356. Supreme Court reaffirms *Federal Baseball.*
1960	Continental League. Proposed new league. Expansion of existing major leagues kills new league before it is launched.
1966	Major League Baseball Players' Association. First successful union.
1972	*Curtis C. Flood v. Bowie K. Kuhn et al.,* 407 U.S. 258. Baseball's exemption from antitrust laws upheld once again by the Supreme Court.
1972	Major league strike. Players strike for 13 days at beginning of season. Owners agree to increase contributions to pension fund.
1973	Arbitration. Owners agree to outside arbitration in salary disputes in order to avert strike.
1975	Messersmith and McNally cases. Arbitrator overturns the reserve clause, effectively ending monopsony in major league baseball.

NOTES

1. Harold Seymour, *Baseball: The Golden Age* (New York: Oxford University Press, 1971), 312.
2. *Ibid.,* 311–323; J.G. Taylor Spink, *Judge Landis and 25 Years of Baseball* (St. Louis, 1974), 71. Landis earned $7,500 per year as a federal judge, $50,000 (over $400,000 in 1988 prices) as commissioner of baseball. For several months he served as both federal judge and commissioner. He resigned his judgeship in 1922 under pressure from Congress, the press, and the American Bar association, all of whom believed that he could not perform both jobs.
3. Spink, *Judge Landis and 25 Years of Baseball,* 244–245.
4. Donald Honig, *Baseball America* (New York: Macmillan, 1985), 115.
5. At intervals, they could also have simply not renewed his contract. The owners disposed of A.B. Chandler, Landis' successor, by not renewing his contract.

6. Seymour, *Baseball: The Golden Age,* 400–422; U.S. Congress, *Organized Baseball.* Hearings Before the Subcommittee on Study of Monopoly Power. House of Representatives, 82nd Congress, 1st Session, Part 6 (Washingon, DC, 1952), 652–690.

7. Lance E. Davis, "Self-Regulation in Baseball, 1909–1971," in Roger E. Noll (ed.), *Government and the Sports Business* (Washington, DC, 1974), 349–386.

8. For example, see Yale Brozen, *Concentration, Mergers, and Public Policy* (New York: Free Press, 1982), 130–185).

9. Davis, "Self-Regulation in Baseball, 1909–1971," 350–359.

10. On the origin and early history of the National Agreement, see Harold Seymour, *Baseball: The Early Years* (New York: Oxford University Press, 1960), 135–161 and 307–324. The agreements of 1903, 1921, and 1946 are printed in U.S. Congress, *Organized Baseball,* 521–525, 1263–1265, 1121–1125.

11. For a summary of the facts and implications of the Messersmith case, see *Official Baseball Guide for 1976,* (St. Louis: Sporting News, 1976), 284–292 and *Official Baseball Guide for 1977* (St. Louis: Sporting News, 1977), 283–304.

12. Simon Rottenberg, "The Baseball Players' Labor Market," *Journal of Political Economy* 64 (June 1956), 242–258.

13. Gerald W. Scully, "Pay and Performance in Major League Baseball," *American Economic Review* 64 (December 1974): 915–930. Scully estimated the value of Koufax with two statistical equations. One equation related the strikeout to walk ratio and innings pitched to the team's winning percentage. The other related the team's winning percentage to its revenues. Combining the two equations produced an estimate of the contribution Koufax made to Dodger revenues. Although the more sophisticated measures of player performance developed in recent years would no doubt make it possible to estimate the marginal revenue product more precisely, Scully's general conclusion would certainly continue to hold.

14. Kenneth Lehn, "Property Rights, Risk Sharing, and Player Disability in Major League Baseball," *Journal of Law and Economics* 25 (October 1982): 343–366.

15. Organized baseball used all three methods to deal with the Federal League. Two owners of Federal League teams purchased existing franchises in the American and National leagues. Two owners received cash settlements. The other four teams, deserted by the financially stronger franchises, simply folded. The Baltimore franchise unsuccessfully sought redress in the courts. See Gary Hailey, "Anatomy of a Murder: The Federal League and the Courts," *The National Pastime* 4 (Spring 1985): 62–73.

16. The best history of the cartel is Davis, "Self-Regulation in Baseball, 1909–1971." For two useful overviews of developments in the 19th century, see U.S. Congress, *Organized Baseball,* 126–157 and Jack Selzer, *Baseball in the Nineteenth Century: An Overview* (Cooperstown, New York, 1986).

17. *Federal Baseball Club of Baltimore v. National League,* 259 U.S. 200 (1922). For a general discussion of antitrust law in baseball and other sports, see Steven R. Rivkin, "Sports Leagues and the Federal Antitrust Laws," in Noll, *Government and the Sports Business,* 387–410.

18. Spink, *Judge Landis and 25 Years of Baseball,* 31–36.

19. Seymour, *Baseball: The Golden Age,* 368–372.

20. *Ibid.,* 196–234; Spink, *Judge Landis and 25 Years of Baseball,* 37–44.

21. Seymour, *Baseball: The Golden Age,* 212.

22. Before Landis, a National Commission governed baseball. The commission consisted of the presidents of the two major leagues and a third member chosen by them to serve as chairman. The only chairman the National Commission ever had was August Herrmann, president of the Cincinnati club. The commission was frequently criticized for favoring one league or the other. Bitter feuds between the two league presidents also hampered its effectiveness. At first, the owners planned to bring in a chairman from outside organized baseball. Events soon led them to create the new, more powerful position of commissioner.

23. Eliot Asinof, *Eight Men Out* (New York: Holtzman Press, 1963).

24. *Ibid.,* 273. For some other accounts of the scandal, see Lewis Thompson and Charles Boswell, "Say It Ain't So, Joe!" *American Heritage* 11 (June 1960): 24–27, 88–93; Fred Lieb, *Baseball As I Have Known It* (New York, 1977), 115–125; and Seymour, *Baseball: The Golden Age,* 294–310.

25. In what follows I emphasize other motives behind the behavior of Landis. In doing so, I do not mean to suggest that his concern for the integrity of the game was not genuine. It was.

26. In 1865 two players were expelled from the amateur National Association of Baseball Players for fixing games. See Selzer, *Baseball in the Nineteenth Century: An Overview,* 6.

27. Lieb, *Baseball As I Have Known It,* 105–113.

28. Seymour, *Baseball: The Golden Age,* 274–293; 367–399.

29. For a list of banned (and nearly banned) players and brief summaries of their cases, see Bill James, *The Bill James Historical Baseball Abstract* (New York: Ballantine, 1988), 134–139.

30. Spink, *Judge Landis and 25 Years of Baseball,* 101–104.

31. Seymour, *Baseball: The Golden Age,* 377–382; Lowell Blaisdell, "The O'Connell–Dolan Scandal," *Baseball Research Journal* 11 (1982): 44–49.

32. *Ibid.,* 47.

33. Donald J. Proctor, "The Blacklisting of Ray Fisher," *Baseball Research Journal* 10 (1981): 34–45, 182–188.

34. Spink, *Judge Landis and 25 Years of Baseball,* 93.

35. Proctor, "The Blacklisting of Ray Fisher."

36. U.S. Congress, *Organized Baseball,* 438.

37. Seymour, *Baseball: The Golden Age,* 374.

38. Spink, *Judge Landis and 25 Years of Baseball,* 90.

39. *Ibid.,* 88–89.

40. Seymour, *Baseball: The Golden Age,* 334. Kerr did not suffer alone. Landis banned several other players for playing in outlaw leagues. See U.S. Congress, *Organized Baseball,* 625–630.

41. Spink, *Judge Landis and 25 Years of Baseball,* 111–113.

42. The principal evidence against the two players was two letters, obtained by Ban Johnson, in which Cobb and Joe Wood discussed the distribution of the winnings from a betting proposition. The original recipient of the letters, retired pitcher Dutch Leonard, charged that the bets were on a game fixed by Cobb and Speaker. Historians have been reluctant to pronounce the two players guilty or innocent, though the evidence against Speaker was particularly weak. For a sample of opinions on the affair, see Spink, *Judge Landis and 25 Years of Baseball,* 135–141, 155–158; Charles C. Alexander, *Ty Cobb* (New York: Oxford University Press, 1984), 183–195; and Lieb, *Baseball As I Have Known It,* 60–63.

43. Seymour, *Baseball: The Golden Age,* 383–384.

44. Eugene C. Murdock, *Ban Johnson: Czar of Baseball* (Westport, CT: Greenwood Press, 1982), 205–225.

45. Minor league attendance declined from an annual average of 12.6 million in 1921–1930 to 7.9 million in 1931–1935. See U.S. Congress, *Organized Baseball,* 1616.

46. Jules Tygiel, *Baseball's Great Experiment: Jackie Robinson and His Legacy* (New York: Oxford University Press, 1983), 30–32.

47. Bidding wars were not inevitable; the owners could have organized a draft to bring black players into organized baseball. At the time, however, players entered organized baseball as free agents. Owners consistently rejected proposals for a draft.

48. *Ibid.,* 285–302.

Baseball Literature 1987–1988:
A Survey

JOSEPH LAWLER

"Some books are to be tasted, others to be swallowed, and some few to be chewed and digested." So said Francis Bacon nearly 400 years ago. In applying his words to the latest in baseball books it would be appropriate to add a line, ". . . still others are to be spit out." Apologies are tendered to the great English philosopher to whom a hit-and-run was as unknown as his *Novum Organum* is to the average bleacherite.

A recent survey by *Publisher's Weekly* showed that sports publishing is flourishing. In quantity and quality, baseball leads the pack. The continued growth of interest in baseball history, and its illegitimate offspring, trivia, is responsible for the proliferation of titles on the old ball game. The literary menu for 1987–1988 was full but just as Mrs. Boggs has discovered dozens of ways to prepare chicken so too have writers learned to dress up the same dish over and over again. How many more paeans to the Brooklyn Dodgers or Joe DiMaggio will the market allow? Can anything more be said about the New York Mets? Or the Yankees? We've had inside views on both clubs from nearly every quarter. Let's not forget the Cubs. How can we when each year brings another crop of rhapsodic ramblings on the lovable Chicagoans or their hallowed ball park.

This list, covering the period from January 1987 to March 1988, contains two books on the 1961 New York Yankees, three on baseball's great or greatest moments, five that deal in great part with the 1986 New York Mets, and two spring training guides by way of example.

To be fair, publishing is a business and, as such, must obey the market. A "hot" property, team or individual, who makes headlines one year will likely crowd bookshelves the next. Likely, but not certainly. The Minnesota Twins, despite their position as world champions, are conspicuously absent from this list. "It helps to play in New York," runs an old baseball chestnut.

It is not this writer's intent to condemn the repetition which seems to increase each year but to ask why so many other worthy topics are ignored. Enough of Pete Rose, disgruntled Yankees, Mickey, Willie, and Duke. Where are the biographies of Grover Cleveland Alexander, Honus Wagner, or Tris Speaker? The public thrives on colorful, slightly tarnished celebrities. Where, outside of show business or politics, can one find more eccentric, outrageous, or outright disreputable characters than Rube Waddell, Pepper Martin, Hal Chase, and Rabbit Maranville? Umpires have been largely ignored, except for Ron Luciano's annual joke book, and there are scores of books on the minors, collegiate, semi-pro, and amateur baseball to be written.

Major publishing houses, alas, are loathe to gamble on such topics. It is left to those dedicated authors with enough capital to self publish to provide serious fans with the unusual. The Society for American Baseball Research makes tremendous contributions through its publications and if the resources were available would do even more.

All is not lost however. Each year a number of out-of-the-ordinary titles appear to the delight of baseball bibliophiles. Examples from this list include biographies of Dick Bartell and Larry Doby, Harvey Frommer's look at baseball's development during the closing decades of the last century, and Charles Alexander's treatment of John McGraw. Diamond Communications has added greatly to the field with a steady run of books on broadcasters and their trade topped by Curt Smith's massive history, *Voices of the Game*. Such works are to be applauded; let there be more.

As always, there is something for every taste; the man who orders nothing but vanilla ice cream must be served too. The choice is up to the individual. Bacon was a quality starter and for a strong closer let us turn to Miguel de Cervantes, "There is no book so bad that something good may not be found in it." Agreed.

The following list is presented as a guide to recently published baseball books. There are, no doubt, omissions; none were intentional. Most entries are annotated but many titles are self-explanatory. While great effort was made to verify the existence of each title there may be a "ghost" or two. Prices may vary in some cases.

Note: A (P) after a book title denotes paperback. Several of the books listed here are reviewed in depth in the Book Review section at the back of this volume.

1987

ANTHOLOGIES

The Armchair Book of Baseball II. John Thorn, ed. Macmillan. $19.95.

Sixty selections from such luminaries as Zane Grey, Bill Veeck, Philip Roth, Chaim Potok, and Leo Durocher. Drawings by Bernie Fuchs.

Diamonds Are Forever: Artists and Writers on Baseball. Peter H. Gordon, ed. Chronicle. $30.00; $18.95 (P).

Writers from Malamud to Hemingway and artists from 19th-century craftsmen to Warhol cover all aspects of the game.

The Fireside Book of Baseball, 4th ed. Charles Einstein, ed. Fireside/Simon & Schuster. $10.95. (P).

Latest edition of classic series features fact and fiction from Angell, Boswell, Runyan, Gallico, Updike, Kahn among others.

The National Pastime. John Thorn, ed. Warner. $3.95 (P).

The best from SABR's annual contains 30 articles.

The Red Sox Reader: Thirty Years of Musings on Baseball's Most Amusing Team. Dan Dailey, ed. Ventura Arts. $12.95.

The best of Boston baseball from Red Smith, Peter Gammons, Bill Lee, and others. Includes Updike's "Hub Fans Bid Kid Adieu."

BIOGRAPHY

Bill Veeck: A Baseball Legend. Gerald Eskenazi. McGraw-Hill. $16.95.

The baseball iconoclast and his midget, exploding scoreboards, outlandish uniforms as well as pennants, personal life, and physical hardships.

Billyball. Billy Martin with Phil Pepe. Doubleday. $16.95.

The man who will not go away ponders, life, baseball, and those whose lives he has touched.

Biographical Dictionary of American Sport: Baseball. David L. Porter, ed. Greenwood Press. $75.

Detailed profiles of 500 players, managers, umpires, and administrators from all major leagues, Negro Leagues, 1871–1986. Inclusion based on record and impact on the game.

Cincinnati Seasons: My 34 Years with the Reds. Earl Lawson. Diamond. $16.95.

Hall-of-Fame baseball writer recalls his days covering the Reds, 1951–1984.

Dandy, Day, and The Devil: A Trilogy of Negro League Biographies. Jim Riley. TK Publishers. $12.95 (P).

Biographies and career details of black superstars Ray Dandridge, Leon Day, and Willie Wells.

A Dream Season. Gary Carter and John Hough, Jr. Harcourt Brace Jovanovich. $17.95.

The Mets from behind the plate: All-Star catcher recounts his career and team's climactic 1986 season.

Hardball: The Education of a Baseball Commissioner. Bowie Kuhn. Times. $19.95.

Controversial boss tells of his life in baseball during tumultuous years of expansion, free agency, and drugs.

Jackie Robinson: A Life Remembered. Maury Allen. Franklin Watts. $16.95.

Author goes to Robinson's family, teammates, and opponents for a look at the life and career of black pioneer.

The Jewish Baseball Hall of Fame: A Who's Who of Baseball Stars. Erwin Lynn. Shapolsky. $7.95 (P).

Profiles and photos of Jewish big leaguers along with lifetime records and 600 related trivia questions.

Joe DiMaggio: Baseball's Yankee Clipper. Jack B. Moore. Praeger. $9.95 (P).

Fully documented biography of a baseball legend in a social and cultural context.

Kiner's Korner: My Quarter Century with the New York Mets. Ralph Kiner with Joe Gergen. Arbor House. $16.95.

The Mets from the broadcast box: team's history, development, and comments on major personalities from original member of Mets family.

The Legends of Baseball: An Oral History of the Game's Golden Age. Walter Langford. Diamond. $16.95; $8.95 (P).

Sixteen subjects from the 1930s and 1940s talk baseball. Group includes Johnny Vander Meer, Al Lopez, Marty Marion, and Charley Grimm.

Mays, Mantle, and Snider: A Celebration. Donald Honig. Macmillan. $19.95.

Photos, stats, and narrative on New York's centerfield trio of the 1950s.

Nails: The Inside Story of an Amazin' Season. Lenny Dykstra with Marty Noble. Doubleday. $15.95.

The Mets from center field: expletive saturated account of 1986 season.

Off the Record. Buzzie Bavasi with John Strege. Contemporary. $16.95.

Account of executive's almost 50 years in baseball.

Oh Baby, I Love It! Tim McCarver with Ray Robinson. Villard. $16.95.

The Mets, again. Four-decade major league player and respected broadcaster recounts his career on the field and in the booth.

Orlando Cepeda, the Baby Bull. Woodford. $6 (P).

First in a monographic series on baseball greats. Career overview with photos.

The Roaring Redhead: Larry McPhail, Baseball's Great Innovator. Don Warfield. Diamond. $16.95.

Life of dynamic and controversial team owner who brought the major leagues into the 20th century with lights, planes, and television.

Rocket Man: The Roger Clemens Story. Roger Clemens with Peter Gammons. Stephen Greene. $15.95.

The Cy Young and MVP winner tells all about himself and the Red Sox 1986 American League championship campaign.

Rowdy Richard: A Firsthand Account of the National League Baseball Wars of the 1930s and the Men Who Fought Them. Dick Bartell and Norman Macht. North Atlantic. $18.95.

Personal recollections of Bartell's two rowdy decades in baseball as a top shortstop.

Slick: My Years In and Around Baseball. Whitey Ford with Phil Pepe. Morrow. $16.95.

Yankees foremost lefty includes, along with his life story, a primer on successful cheating through creative doctoring of baseballs.

White Rat: A Life in Baseball. Whitey Herzog and Kevin Horrigan. Harper & Row. $16.95.

From journeyman player to managerial genius, Herzog, the White Rat, expounds on the game.

CHILDREN'S

Ask Dale Murphy. Dale Murphy with Curtis Patton. Algonquin. $8.95 (P).

School children follow the title and question Braves star on the game.

Red Foley's Best Baseball Book Ever. Red Foley. Simon & Schuster. $6.95 (P).

Fun book with peel-off stickers, puzzles, and trivia quiz for each team.

Steve Garvey's Hitting System: Raise Your Batting Average, Hit in Game Situations, and Solve All Your Hitting Problems. Steve Garvey with Bob Cluck. Contemporary. $9.95.

Title says it all. All aspects of hitting from bat selection to mental strategy.

Winning Edge Series: Baserunning; Catching; Shortstop; Hitting. Bob Cluck. Contemporary. $4.95 each (P).

Four individual titles discuss skills, equipment, and strategy for youngsters in grades 5 through 8.

The Winning Pitcher: Baseball's Top Pitchers Demonstrate What it Takes to Be an Ace. Tom House. Contemporary. $9.95 (P).

Innovative big league pitching coach's program for physical conditioning and mental positiveness.

HISTORY

70 Years with the Pelicans. Art Schott. Sirgo Links. $6 (P).

History and records of minor league New Orleans Pelicans 1887–1957.

The All-Star Game: A Pictorial History, 1933–1987. Donald Honig. The Sporting News. $19.95.

Box scores and descriptions of every game enhanced by 500 photos.

Baseball: An Illustrated History. David Q. Voigt. Penn State. $32.50.

The game from colonial days through the 1986 World Series. Covers majors, minors, college, semi-pro, and amateur.

Baseball in Cincinnati: A History. Harry Ellard. Ohio Book Store. $22.95.

Reprint of 1907 classic covers Cincy baseball from earliest days to early 1900s while also giving attention to other National League teams.

Baseball in the Fifties: A Decade of Transition. Donald Honig. Crown. $19.95.

Lavishly illustrated with season-by-season overview and sketches of individual stars.

Baseball: The Startling Stories Behind the Records. Jim Benagh. Sterling. $8.95 (P).

Includes Clemens 20-K game, Tovar and Campaneris at all nine positions in single games, Pruett's hex on Babe Ruth.

The Cubbies: Quotations on the Chicago Cubs. Bob Chieger. Atheneum. $10.95 (P).

Coverage begins with the team's birth over a century ago.

Daily News Scrapbook History of the New York Mets 1986 Season. Bill Madden. Edited by Mike Aronstein. New York Daily News. $10.95 (P).

The Mets yet again: every box score and game story for regular season, League Championship Series, and World Series.

The Dodgers Move West. Neil Sullivan. Oxford. $17.95.

Detailed study shows Walter O'Malley in new light and proposes that move was worthwhile for fans in the long run.

Explosion! Mickey Mantle's Legendary Home Runs. Mark Gallagher. Arbor House. $17.95.

Exhaustive study of Mantle's blasts. Appendixes include table of every home run with date, place, score, etc.

Giant Orange and Dodger Blue: Where Were You in '62? Ed Oiseth. Dungeon Printing. $6.75 (P).

Poetic title introduces San Francisco Giants fan's personal memories of 1962 National League pennant race and World Series.

Giants Diary: A Century of Giants Baseball in New York and San Francisco. Fred Stein and Nick Peters. North Atlantic. $12.95 (P).

Overview and season highlights, 1883–1986. Capsule data on every Giants player, ball park, and World Series.

Great Baseball Feats, Facts, and Firsts. David Nemec. NAL. $12.95 (P).

Eclectic assortment of unusual, amusing, and outstanding: list includes tallest and shortest players, pinch-hitting records, and leading losers.

Great Moments in Baseball. George L. Flynn. Gallery. $9.98.

Covers 1903–1986: Haddix's perfecto, Mazeroski's homer, Brett's pine tar, and many more.

The Greatest Game Ever Played. Jerry Izenberg. Holt. $14.95.

Game 6 of the 1986 National League Championship Series is the one. Previous five games and profiles of key personnel involved also covered.

Greatest Moments in Baseball. Joel Zoss. Bison. $9.98.

Arranged by decades from 1900. World Series and regular season.

The Impossible Dream Remembered: The 1967 Red Sox. Ken Coleman with Dan Valenti. Stephen Greene. $18.95.

The underdog Red Sox and their drive to a pennant are reviewed on occasion of its 20th anniversary. Game-by-game survey and World Series insights by Bobby Doerr included.

Innings Ago: Recollections by Kansas City Ballplayers of Their Days in the Game. Jack Etkin. Normandy Square. $9.95 (P).

Seventeen oral histories by players whose roots are in Kansas City or who played for the city's major, minor, and Negro teams.

One Strike Away: The Story of the 1986 Red Sox. Dan Shaughnessy. Beaufort. $15.95.

Boston Globe writer's inside coverage of heart-breaking World Series loss.

The Pitcher. John Thorn and John Holway. Prentice-Hall, $19.95.
Art of pitching explained through stats, analyses, and anecdotes. Role of catchers and coaches discussed along with such factors as ball parks, relief pitching, and illegal pitches.

Player's Choice: Major League Baseball Players Vote on the All Time Greats. Eugene V. and Roger A. McCaffrey. Facts on File. $16.95.

Based on poll of 600 major leaguers and covers every decade of this century: best all-time teams and best of various categories of play.

Playing the Field: Why Defense is the Most Fascinating Art in Major League Baseball. Jim Kaplan, Algonquin. $12.95 (P).

Inside, in-depth look at great glovemen position-by-position.

Runs, Hits, and Errors: A Treasury of Cub History and Humor. Jim Langford, comp. Diamond. $14.95.

Collection of columns by the likes of George Will, Mike Royko, and Warren Brown.

Sandlot Seasons: Sport in Black Pittsburgh. Rob Ruck. Illinois. $21.95.

Study of sport as symbol of civic pride in 1930s and 1940s. Emphasis on baseball and football, particularly the success of the Crawfords, a great black professional team.

Sixty-One: The Team, the Record, the Men. Tony Kubek and Terry Pluto. Macmillan. $19.95.

The 1961 world champion Yankees through the eyes of team shortstop. First section devoted to Roger Maris's pursuit of Ruth's record. Interviews with team members and review of pennant race and Series.

The Sporting News Selects Baseball's 25 Greatest Pennant Races. Lowell Reidenbaugh. TSN. $19.95.

Selections include National League: 1908, 1946, 1951, 1962; American League: 1948, 1978, 1980. Profiles of key players, photos, and graphs accompany narrative.

Sports Illustrated Great Moments in Baseball. Bill Gutman. Pocket Books. $2.50 (P).

Sports Illustrated Strange and Amazing Baseball Stories. Bill Gutman. Pocket Books. $2.50 (P).

The Texas League: A Century of Baseball. Bill O'Neal. Eakin. $15.

Decade by decade account, 1887–1987. History, stats, players.

Voices of the Game: The First Full-Scale Overview of Baseball Broadcasting, 1921 to the Present. Curt Smith. Diamond. $22.95.

Comprehensive history of all major and many lesser known broadcasters in context of world and baseball events.

HOBBY

1987 Baseball Cards: 120 of the Hottest Players. Signet. $4.95 (P).

Photos of Topps, Fleers, and Donruss cards with stats and biographies.

Classic Baseball Cards: The Golden Years, 1886–1956. Frank Slocum. Warner. $79.95.

Full size reproductions of 9,000 cards with comments on individual sets and baseball history.

Collecting Baseball Cards: Dimes to Dollars. Donn Pearlman. Bonus. $6.95 (P).

Hygrade Catalog and Price Guide of Topps, Donruss, Fleer, and Sportflics Baseball Cards. Hygrade. $4.95 (P).

Checklists, prices, photos for each company from first issue through 1987.

HUMOR / TRIVIA

Baseball: A Laughing Matter. Warner Fusselle, Brian Zevnik, and Rick Wolff. TSN. $9.95.

Anecdotes, insults, funny facts and figures, and bloopers.

The Baseball Hall of Shame III. Bruce Nash and Allen Zullo. Pocket Books. $6.95 (P).

Latest assortment of blunders and diamond embarrassments uncovers many new laughables.

Baseball Trivia II. The Sporting News. TSN. $10.95 (P).

Los Angeles Dodgers Trivia. John Grabowski. Quinlan. $7.95 (P).

New York Mets Trivia: The Silver Anniversary Book. Mike Getz. Quinlan. $7.95 (P).

New York Yankees Trivia. Mike Getz. Quinlan. $7.95 (P).

Playing the Field: Dodgers Trivia. Mike Getz. Quinlan. $7.95 (P).

INSTRUCTION / FITNESS / RULES

Baseball by the Rules: Pine Tar, Spitballs, and Midgets, An Anecdotal Guide to America's Oldest and Most Complex Sport. Glen Waggoner and Hugh Howard. Taylor. $12.95 (P).

Based on official rules, annotated with lively examples involving many baseball stars.

Baseball Players Guide to Sports Medicine. Pat Croce. Leisure. $9.95 (P).

Professional trainer and sports therapist explains prevention and treatment of baseball injuries and offers conditioning and diet tips.

Baseball Signs and Signals. Tom Petroff with Jack Clary. Taylor. $9.95 (P).

For players, coaches, and fans. Explanation of introduction, practice, and use of signs during game situations.

POETRY

Adam's At Bat. Paul Weinmen. Samisdat. $1.50 (P).

A game in free verse from locker room to final out.

The Illustrated Casey at the Bat; The Immortal Baseball Ballad. Keith Bendis. Workman. $5.95 (P).

New drawings bring Thayer's classic to life. Poem's history is traced in introduction by Roger Kahn.

Pete Rose Agonistes. Mike Shannon. Third Lung Press. $3 (P).

Fourteen poetic monologues tell of a team's personalities and turmoil. Unidentified speakers are members of Reds organization; allusions to Rose connect them.

REFERENCE / STATISTICS

The Baseball Record Companion. Joseph L. Reichler. Macmillan. $13.95 (P).

Revised and updated version of author's *Great All-Time Baseball Record Book.* Lists major league records with related performances. Players indexed by name for quick reference.

The Baseball Research Handbook. Gerald Tomlinson. SABR. $6 (P).

A-to-Z instruction on how and where to do research for beginners and veterans.

Bill James Presents the Great American Baseball Stat Book. Bill James and John Dewan. Ballantine. $12.95 (P).

Includes three years of work by Project Scoresheet; covers every major league game during the period. Numerous categories of information. Also essays on top players.

Fungoes, Floaters, and Fork Balls: A Colorful Baseball Dictionary. Patrick Ercolano. Prentice-Hall. $6.95 (P).

Contains derivation of common words and sayings, e.g., why next batter is considered to be "on deck."

How to Talk Baseball. Mike Whitford. Dembner. $8.95 (P).

Words and slang of the game explained.

How to Watch Baseball: A Fan's Guide to Savoring the Fine Points of the Game. Steve Fiffer. Facts on File. $16.95.

Detailed examination of inside doings with comments from Tom Lasorda, Ted Williams, and others.

How to Win at Rotisserie Baseball: The Strategic Guide to America's New National (Armchair) Pastime. Peter Golenbock, Vintage. $6.95 (P).

Tips on researching, scouting, buying, and selling players for patrons of the popular sit-down version of baseball.

Jays Jazz. David Driscoll. Driscoll. $11.95 (P).

Detailed analysis of Toronto's 1986 season. Statistics promise surprising revelations.

Rotisserie League Baseball. Glen Waggoner and Robert Sklar, eds. Bantam. $8.95 (P). Assessment of current major league players and their worth in Rotisserie league accompanies rule book and how-to-play guide.

Spalding Baseball Guides. Ralph Horton, ed. Horton. $14.95 each (P).

Exact reprints of popular annual guides. Contain official rules, standings, averages, etc. Guides for 1884, 1885, 1886 available.

SOCIOLOGY

Saying It Ain't So: American Values as Revealed in Children's Baseball Stories. Debra Dagavarian. Peter Lang. $32.50.

Study of children's literature on baseball and how it reflects the game's values of responsibility, supportiveness, and fairness.

With the Boys: Little League Baseball and Preadolescent Culture. Gary Alan Fine. Chicago. $37.50; $12.95 (P).

Boyhood culture, its formation and dissemination and how boys deal with it in the context of little league baseball.

1988 (January–March)

ANTHOLOGIES

The Best of Spitball Magazine. Mike Shannon, ed. Pocket Books. $5.95 (P).

Potpourri from baseball's literary magazine.

BIOGRAPHY

Ballplayer! The Headfirst Life of Peter Edward Rose. Pete Rose and Roger Kahn. Warner. $18.95.

Latest biography of future Hall-of-Famer includes 16 pages of color photos.

Baseball's Hot New Stars. Bill Gutman. Archway. $2.50 (P).

Profiles of eight current major league stars.

Between the Lines. Steve Howe with Jim Greenfield. Contemporary. $17.95.

Story of a left-hander's struggle with drugs and baseball.

Blackball Stars: Negro League Pioneers. John Holway. Meckler. $22.50.

Detailed stories of 26 major figures with individual stats, photos.

Bleep! Larry Bowa Manages. Larry Bowa with Barry Bloom. Bonus. $15.95.

A look at former Padres manager during his rookie season.

Catfish: My Life in Baseball. Jim Hunter and Armen Keteyan. McGraw-Hill. $16.95.

From North Carolina to Cooperstown, the story of hick/slick Hunter.

Cleveland Baseball Winners: Who Was Who in 1946–1956. John Philips. Capital. $15 (P).

Profiles of every Indians player during successful decade.

Diamond Greats. Rich Westcott. Meckler. $22.50.

A living history of baseball presented through interviews with 65 of the game's best players.

The Duke of Flatbush. Duke Snider with Bill Gilbert. Zebra.

Willie and Mickey and now the Duke; his life story.

Extra Innings. Frank Robinson with Berry Stainback. McGraw-Hill. $16.95.

Baseball's first black manager tells his story and discusses racism in baseball.

Jack of All Trades. Jack McKeon with Tom Friend. Contemporary. $16.95.

Loquacious baseball veteran's life as player, scout, coach, and noted general manager.

The Jock's Itch: The Fast-Track Private World of the Professional Ballplayer. Tom House. Contemporary. $16.95.

Former pitcher, now a pitching coach, House offers an inside look at the private society of pro players.

John McGraw. Charles C. Alexander. Viking. $19.95.

Biographer of Ty Cobb turns to McGraw, another dominant personality from baseball's early years.

Legends: Conversations with Baseball Greats. Art Rust, Jr. and Michael Marley. McGraw-Hill. $16.95.

Candid discussions with the old and the new, e.g., Mattingly and Steinbrenner; DiMaggio, Campanella, and Newcombe.

My Dad, the Babe: Growing Up with an American Hero. Dorothy Ruth Pirone with Chris Martens. Quinlan. $16.95.

Personal look at all-time great by his daughter.

The Niekro Files: The Uncensored Letters of Baseball's Most Notorious Brothers. Phil and Joe Niekro with Ken Picking. Contemporary. $16.95.

A year's correspondence between the knuckle-balling Niekros.

Pride Against Prejudice: The Biography of Larry Doby. Joseph Thomas Moore. Praeger. $12.95.

Life and career of American League's pioneering black player.

Say Hey: The Autobiography of Willie Mays. Willie Mays with Lou Sahadi. Simon & Schuster. $17.95.

The "Say Hey Kid" by the kid himself.

Strikeout: The Story of Denny McLain. Denny McLain. TSN. $16.95.

Baseball's last 30-game winner, from Cy Young to federal prison.

Throwing Heat. Nolan Ryan and Harvey Frommer. Doubleday. $16.95.

Baseball's hardest throwing "senior" citizen writes of his two decades in baseball.

Winfield: A Player's Life. Dave Winfield with Tom Parker. Norton. $16.95.

The story of a multi-talented athlete and his rise to multi-millionaire major leaguer.

Wizard. Ozzie Smith with Bob Rains. Contemporary. $16.95.

Fielding magician talks about his career, teammates, and the game.

Yesterday's Heroes: Revisiting the Old Time Stars. Marty Appel. Morrow. $16.95.

Baseball through the eyes of the greats of the past.

HISTORY

The '69 Mets. Stanley Cohen. Harcourt Brace Jovanovich. $16.95.

Account of team's miracle season and those responsible.

Baseball Fathers, Baseball Sons. Dick Wimmer. Morrow. $15.95.

Musial, Williams, DiMaggio, and others discuss the tradition of baseball.

Baseball From a Different Angle. Bob Broeg and Bill Miller. Diamond. $19.95.

The history, humor, and appeal of baseball.

Before the Game. Louis D. Rubin, Jr. Photos by Scott Mlyn. Taylor. $13.95 (P).

The flavor of baseball in those moments before a game are captured in words and pictures.

Bleachers: A Summer in Wrigley Field. Lonnie Wheeler. Contemporary. $16.95.

Observations on the game, players, and fans during a season at Wrigley.

Bob Broeg's Redbirds: A Century of Cardinal Baseball. Bob Broeg. River City. $21.95.

History of St. Louis club includes 250 photos.

Breaking into the Big Leagues. Al Goldis and Rick Wolff. Human Kinetics. $13.95.

Inside look at baseball scouting system plus stories of several pro players.

Cleveland Blues 1901. John Philips. Capital. $13.50 (P).

Day-by-day account of Cleveland's inaugural American League season. Has all scores, winning pitchers, player transactions.

The Game for All America. John Thorn. TSN. $35.

Baseball from T-ball to the majors, the color and excitement which surrounds it is portrayed through narrative and 400 full-color photos.

The Giants of the Polo Grounds. Noel Hynd. Doubleday. $17.95.

The story of the New York Giants, their times, their players.

The Greatest First Basemen of All Time. Donald Honig. Crown. $14.95.

Individual chapters for author's choices which include McCovey, Hodges, and 17 others. First in a new "Greatest Position" series.

The Greatest Pitchers of All Time. Donald Honig. Crown. $14.95.

Facts and photos on the likes of Marichal, Mathewson, Young, Palmer.

Notes from Fenway Park. John Hough, Jr. Harcourt Brace Jovanovich. $17.95.

Baseball and the Boston Red Sox: an insider's view.

Primitive Baseball: The First Quarter Century of the National Pastime. Harvey Frommer. Atheneum. $17.95.

The growth of baseball from local activity to prominent position in American society and culture in the years before 1900.

Season of Glory: The Amazing Saga of the 1961 New York Yankees. Ralph Houk and Robert W. Creamer. Putnam. $18.95.

The man who replaced Casey Stengel as manager tells the story of the team and its record-breaking season.

Season Ticket: A Baseball Companion. Roger Angell. Houghton Mifflin. $18.95.

A compilation of the author's New Yorker articles on spring training, field, dugout, and clubhouse activity.

The Series: An Illustrated History of Baseball's Postseason Showcase. The Sporting News. TSN. $12.95 (P).

Every World Series and League Championship Series game from Day 1 in words, pictures, and numbers.

Sports Illustrated: Baseball's Record Breakers. Bill Gutman. Archway. $2.50 (P).

Inside dope on famous records and those who broke them.

Streak: Joe DiMaggio and the Summer of '41. Michael Seidel. McGraw-Hill. $17.95.

DiMaggio's 56-game hitting streak is discussed along with the nation's mood in the last summer before World War II.

Sweet Seasons: Baseball's Top Teams Since 1920. Howard Siner. Pharos. $8.95 (P).

Author chooses 25 championship clubs based on season winning percentages. Playoffs and World Series records also. Included are 1927 Yankees, 1942 Cardinals, 1975 Reds, and 1986 Mets.

When Lajoie Came to Town: The 1902 Cleveland Blues. John Philips. Capital. $15 (P).

Day-by-day account of 1902 season, Napolean Lajoie's first in Cleveland.

HOBBY

Baseball Card and Collectibles Dealer Directory. Jim Wright and Jean-Paul Emard. Meckler. $10.95 (P).

Listing of over 1,000 dealers nationwide.

Sports Collectors Digest Baseball Card Prices. Dan Albaugh. Krause. $12.95.

Values for over 200,000 items, sets and singles.

HUMOR / TRIVIA

Baseball Confidential. Bruce Nash and Allan Zullo. Pocket Books. $6.95 (P).

Hall-of-Shamers present anecdotes on all big league teams.

It's Anybody's Game. Joe Garagiola. Contemporary. $17.95.

Baseball pundit continues with his premise that baseball is a funny game made more so by plastic grass, domed stadia, and the like.

Remembrance of Swings Past. Ron Luciano and David Fisher. Bantam. $16.95.

Prolific duo offers laughs from baseball's "good old days."

So You Think You're a Baseball Fan. Jack Clary. Quinlan. $7.95 (P).

Q's and A's for fans and fanatics.

The Ultimate Baseball Quiz Book. Dom Forker. Signet. $3.95 (P).

Contains 3,500 questions on latest baseball topics.

INSTRUCTION / FITNESS / RULES

A Hitting Clinic: The Walt Hriniak Way. Walt Hriniak with Henry Horenstein and Mark Starr. Perennial. $9.95.

Red Sox hitting coach goes public with his method and philosophy.

Professional Baseball Trainer's Fitness Book. Lee Lowenfish. Warner. $12.95.

Major league baseball trainers show part-time athletes the way.

Warmup for Little League Baseball. Morris A. Shirts. Archway. $2.50 (P).

Tips for both little league beginners and vets.

REFERENCE / STATISTICS

"96 Years of Hope" Cleveland Baseball Transactions, 1892–1987. John Philips. Capital. $15 (P).

A list of every signing, sale, purchase, release, and trade by Cleveland's major league teams.

The Baseball Fan's Guide to Spring Training. Mike Shatzkin and Jim Charlton. Addison-Wesley. $9.95.

Offers a history of spring training along with maps and information on parking, hotels, game tickets, and nearby attractions for every major league training site.

The Complete Handbook of Baseball. Zander Hollander, ed. Signet. $4.95 (P).

Scouting reports for all major league teams plus schedules, player profiles, and photos.

Dodger Dogs to Fenway Franks: The Ultimate Guide to America's Top Baseball Parks. Robert Wood. McGraw-Hill. $16.95.

Author rates major league parks for atmosphere, service, and convenience.

Grapefruit League Road Trip: A Guide to Spring Training in Florida. Ken Coleman with Dan Valenti. Stephen Greene. $7.95 (P).

Baseball Baedeker for the 18 teams that train in Florida. Has data on each complex, maps, anecdotes, and scoring instructions.

Give Me Back My Bums!

ROBERT A. FRAUENGLAS

The 1988 baseball season is upon us. It presents another opportunity for the New York Yankees to play the Los Angeles Dodgers in the World Series again. There have already been 11 World Series between these two penultimate rivals. But even if Yankees versus Dodgers #12 takes place, something won't be right.

No subway will carry Dodger fans to the borders of upstate New York—the Bronx. Brooklyn's Flatbush Avenue won't be bumper-to-bumper with cars, as the Bums' fanatical fans jostle their way to Ebbets Field to root and pray for their beloved Bums. Those times are long past. I still mourn them.

I was only seven when Walter O'Malley (he of hated memory) and his infamous band of blood-sucking, cold-hearted, money-worshiping traitors deserted the Bums' true home and the people who loved them.

I hated the Los Angeles Dodgers. I became a rabid Yankee fan. It was the not-too-rare-case of an old Brooklyn Dodger fan rooting for the ancient enemy who stayed. Mickey, Whitey, Yogi, Billy, Clete, Moose, Ellie, Bobby, Maris, and The Sheriff became my heroes. The Los Angeles Dodgers were not forgotten. They were despised.

Then came 1963. Sandy Koufax and Don Drysdale handcuffed my Yanks in just four games. The Dodgers were World Champs again. They had beaten the Yankees again.

I was thirteen and confused. The Dodgers were back. They were beating the pants off the ancient enemy—the Yankees. I was feeling strange stirrings. Emotions held in check since 1956. Could these Dodgers of the golden sun still stir the blood of the Brooklynites who birthed them?

After all, Sandy was still one of ours. He was still Brooklyn. Don was still one of us. But Mickey Mantle . . . Mickey was my hero. I ached when he struck out. But it was Sandy pitching those strikeouts. Sandy Koufax, one of the last of the Brooklyn Bums. This was all too much for a 13-year-old. I couldn't be all happy or all sad—1963 left me feeling cheated.

I still can't cheer unabashedly for the Dodgers. They're not mine anymore. They belong to a glamorous, Hollywood, movie star culture I'll never know nor understand. I don't hate them anymore, but. . . .

Recently, my friend of 34 years was in a reminiscing mood. He told his wife of the summers we shared. Summers spent on the beach in Far Rockaway, New York. In particular, the long gone summers of '55 and '56 caught his attention. They were the summers of Brooklyn's only World Championship and of Don Larsen's perfect game to spoil the Bums' bid for two-in-a-row.

He told his wife about my Brooklyn Dodger t-shirt and cap. They were the religious garments of my childhood summers. He also told his wife of his Yankee t-shirt and cap. I remember our arguments. They were constant.

It was inconceivable to me that anyone could think there were better players than Duke, Pee Wee, Campy, Preacher Roe, Jackie, Hodges, Newk, Cookie, Furillo, and any other human being wearing a Brooklyn Dodger uniform. The arguments ended in 1957. The friendship endures.

In 1977 and 1978 I lived in Scotland. Baseball was not the national pastime. Everybody, everywhere wasn't talking about the Dodgers versus the Yankees.

I rooted for the Yankees. Three thousand miles from Brooklyn and 6,000 miles from Los Angeles helped moot the confusion I felt in 1963. I was older and Sandy and Don were gone. These were the Dodgers of the golden sun and golden hair. These Dodgers even complained about the New York home crowd. These were not my Dodgers.

In 1981, the Yankees faced the L.A. Dodgers in the World Series again. Why did this confrontation stir long-dormant, but never dead emotions? Some of the old L.A. crowd of '77 and '78 were back. Those were not true Dodgers. But Fernando Valenzuela . . . yes, Fernando would have fit in just fine with the old Bums. And even crazy Lasorda could have easily meshed with those Bums.

It was dilemma time again. I was home, in Brooklyn, for this '81 series. My adopted Yankees were fighting against my forcibly removed birthright Dodgers. Why couldn't I root crazily for just one? Why can't I still have the chance to root for Dem Bums the way my father did? Will I ever be able to tell my young children, to be, about the times I snuck into Ebbets Field (II) to watch Dem Bums play for God and Brooklyn, the way my father told me?

GIVE ME BACK MY BUMS!!!

Call me a dreamer. Others have shared these dreams. New York State Senator Thomas Bartosiewicz, from Brooklyn of course, introduced the bill which created the Brooklyn Sports Authority. This is the first step in building a new stadium and bringing a baseball team back to Brooklyn.

A novel by David Ritz, *The Man Who Brought the Dodgers Back to Brooklyn* (Simon and Schuster, 1981), has Dem Bums coming home by 1988. A fantasy novel or a book ahead of its time?

It's 1988. It's over 30 years since the Dodgers deserted Brooklyn for L.A. I'm 37 and too old for boyish pipe dreams. But I want to wear my Brooklyn Dodger t-shirt and cap again. It's a sin that Brooklyn, the fourth largest city in the United States, has no professional baseball team.

GIVE ME BACK MY BUMS!!!

EPILOGUE

My mother, a Brooklyn Dodger fan for many more years than I, also became a Yankee fan after the Great Desertion. All during the sixth and final game of the 1981 World Series, she was nervously cleaning the house and bemoaning the fate of the Yankees. Yet, she stayed up way past her usual bedtime and wouldn't leave until the final out. As I glanced over, at that moment, she had a huge grin on her face and was quietly clapping. I could sense my Dad grinning with approval from up in heaven.

That *was* next year.

Sandy Koufax, of the 'wayward' Los Angeles Dodgers. (Photo courtesy of the National Baseball Library, Cooperstown, N.Y.)

A Day at The Stadium

ALEX HOLZMAN

I have never wanted to be anything so much as I wanted to be a Yankee. Partly this was because the Yanks introduced me to baseball and provided heroes like Roger Maris, Mickey Mantle, Yogi Berra, and Whitey Ford. But it was mostly because baseball provided common ground for my father and me, the only common ground we shared for much of my childhood. Being a Yankee would have been a way to please him and play a game I loved in and of itself.

My awareness of baseball began in 1954, when my father took me to a Yankee–Indians game at The Stadium. I was only four and didn't understand the game at all, but I did notice that it relaxed Dad in a way that his 70-hour work week didn't usually allow. This in turn offered me a chance to be relaxed around him, a rare event. A stern, quiet father and a timid, equally quiet boy—at least around him—were not exactly Ward and Beaver Cleaver, but at the ball game we could enjoy each other without the usual barriers. Add to this my amazement at finding such vast expanses of green in a place like the Bronx and at the crowd's excitement when Mickey Mantle beat out a drag bunt, and my interest in the game seems almost inevitable.

We didn't immediately follow up on this new source of friendship, though. Family finances improved enough for us to move from Manhattan to New Jersey, but that increased my father's work week still more, as a one-block walk to his dry cleaning store became a one-hour commute. Every so often we'd watch a game together on TV; even less often we'd have a catch in the backyard, but by and large we spent what time we had together doing chores in the yard on his one day off. Neither one of us much cared for that.

The move to New Jersey did give me my first chance to play the game, and I found it immediately addictive. Some subconscious urge surely must have wanted to please my father and work on developing our possible friendship, but my pleasure was more elemental and immediately physical. I simply loved trying to hit a baseball.

Which is not to say I had much success at it. Though I was right-handed, hitting left-handed somehow felt better, even as I suffered an entire summer of consistently missing the ball. My new friends giggled at first, then started to insist that I bat righty. No way; in what was the first indication of an emergent stubbornness not unlike my father's, I suffered through an entire summer of futility as I kept swinging lefty and missing lefty.

Finally, by some miracle of eye-hand coordination in the seven-year-old child, my brain and body got their signals straight. I suddenly learned the joy of hitting a ball hard, catching it on the sweet spot between the trademark and the end of the bat, hitting it past infielders, past outfielders, farther than I had ever thought possible. My new hitting prowess quickly made me an early choice in pickup games and even got me into games against older boys.

Still, I never did make Little League. Whenever tryouts were held in front of adult

135

coaches, I choked. Yogi Berra once said you can't think and hit at the same time; it's even harder to hit when your entire body is trembling and a lump the size of the proverbial apple is caught in your throat. Throughout my childhood and adolescence I was to be a great pickup player in stickball, hardball, or softball, but a terrible performer before adults.

This included, of course, my father, who would hear me brag about my hitting and then watch me not do it on those rare occasions when we could play together. I could see the disappointment in his face, but he never got angry or sarcastic. Knowing that I was beginning to dream about growing up to be center-fielder for the Yankees and knowing that kids take their dreams quite seriously, he would quietly and devastatingly advise me to consider alternative careers. He was right of course, but I hated him for his honesty.

Still, even as he critiqued my performance, baseball continued to give us common ground, a little more each year as I learned the game better and followed the Yankees more closely. I began to develop the spectator part of my fandom in 1959, when the team lost the pennant for the first time in five years. An odd time to get interested, perhaps, but looking back on it, I think losing made the Yankees seem more human. At the same time, their sudden fall from perfection startled many people, including my father, causing them to pay closer attention to the team as they tried to figure out what had gone wrong.

My growing interest continued during the 1960 season, reaching a new peak in the Yanks' World Series loss to Pittsburgh. I was thoroughly captivated by alternating close Pirate victories and Yankee blowouts until Bill Mazeroski broke my heart with his ninth-inning, seventh-game homer to beat my heroes.

This World Series brought about my first school rebellion. A shy, good student who knew just how far I could push without getting into real trouble, I risked all in that era of daytime baseball by smuggling a transistor radio to class. The radio went into my pants pocket and a cord earplug attached to it threaded under my shirt, up my chest, down my sleeve, and into my palm. While teachers droned, I could occasionally cradle my head sideways into my hand to pick up a few words of Mel Allen's play-by-play.

The sense of danger such nefarious behavior gave me just added to baseball's thrills. And by now, though rarely talking about anything else, my father and I often talked about the Yanks. We were both captivated immediately by the 1961 team, as Mantle and Roger Maris launched their assault on Babe Ruth's home run record and the team engaged the Tigers in a tough, close pennant race. It took a family effort, but my father allowed himself to be talked into our first return to the Stadium since '54 and we ordered tickets for a September 1st showdown with Detroit.

The three-game series began with the Yanks only a game-and-a-half ahead of Detroit and I knew it could well decide the pennant. The first game—our game—would pit Whitey Ford, already a 20-game winner for the first time in his career, against Don Mossi, a left-hander so far enjoying a 16–2 year.

The day became a personal odyssey as I left our house in Bergenfield around 2:00 P.M. to meet my father at his Columbus Avenue cleaning store, then got stuck with him in a traffic jam caused by the start of the Labor Day weekend and near-capacity crowd game jam-ups. We didn't get to our seats until just before the 8 o'clock start. Even though we'd sent for tickets in June, our seats were in the upper deck, way out in left field. We didn't care—we were in the Stadium for the biggest game of the year.

We expected lots of scoring in this record-setting year for hitters, but Mossi and Ford thwarted the offenses. The tension of a scoreless game in the middle of a pennant race became the first new baseball experience I learned about that night. Scoreless hardly meant devoid of action, and Dad and I kept very busy discussing all that happened before us. When Ford picked Tiger catcher Mike Roarke off first base, my father taught me about a left-hander's "balk" move, and explained that Ford's skill in that department was legendary.

When a hip injury forced the Yankee ace from the game in the fifth inning, we shared our anxieties about relief pitcher Bud Daley's ability to keep the Tigers at bay. And when Daley proceeded to pick *another* Tiger runner off base, we laughed and told each other how crafty those Yanks were.

By the eighth the tension in the ball park was palpable and the crowd transformed itself on every pitch from 60,000 individuals to a single voice, cheering the good things, groaning or gasping at the bad. When Al Kaline followed a Billy Bruton lead-off walk with a smash down the left-field line, you could hear that gigantic gasp as we realized the situation about to confront us. Runners on second and third, no out. But wait. Yogi Berra, transformed this season from a catcher to an outfielder, grabbed the ball cleanly off the wall, turned, and in a burst of inspired creativity, threw behind lead runner Bruton to get Kaline going into second.

The gasping died, replaced for a split second by almost complete silence, then changed into a single roar that seemed to last ten minutes. As Daley then routinely—and to us inevitably after Berra's genius—retired the next two batters to preserve the tie, my father explained how fielders must envision situations before they occur so that they know what to do once they actually get the ball. What made this play so wondrous, Dad explained, was that Berra was playing an essentially new position and had still known what to do. What a game.

Mickey Mantle. (Photo courtesy of the National Baseball Library, Cooperstown, N.Y.)

Now came the bottom of the ninth. Mossi had been brilliant for the Tigers, limiting the Yanks to two hits. When he set down Maris and Mantle to start the inning, the crowd started settling back, anticipating the extra innings that now seemed surely necessary to settle this battle.

Suddenly, almost too quickly for me to absorb, Elston Howard singled and the ubiquitous Berra followed with another base hit, moving Howard to third. As Bill Skowron approached the plate, the collective voice screamed, "Mooooooooooose!" drawing out his nickname. Again the voice stopped in mid-sound and transformed itself into its loudest roar yet on this incredible evening, as Skowron grounded the ball through the hole between short and third and Howard trotted home. The Yanks had won.

My father and I stood cheering with the rest of the crowd, yelling, laughing, exchanging nods and exclamations with our neighbors as we watched thousands of others toss their hats on the field in sheer joy. Standing there in a stadium full of fans, exultant at the bounce of a small white ball skipping its way through a piece of real estate in the Bronx, we had for the first time become friends.

Memories of Growing Up a Brooklyn Dodger Fan

ANN GREENBERG

Why was I a Dodger fan? Perhaps it was because our father was born in Brooklyn and that had something to do with it. I have to use the plural as this is my twin sister Dody's growing up as well. Daddy had no sons to carry on the family name or share his interest in baseball, so Dody and I received the bats and mitts for birthdays. We also went to our first baseball game as a present for our 11th birthday. The date was May 30, 1941 and even though our birthday wasn't for another three days it was Memorial Day and there was no school. Our father's friend Reg Gosling worked for the Brooklyn bank that handled the Dodgers business affairs and he bought the tickets for Daddy. After all, a doubleheader with the Giants needed tickets in advance.

Johnny Rizzo won the first game with a home run in the eighth. By the time we were leaving the ball park after the second game (that one they lost) the papers were on the street—I guess it was the *Brooklyn Eagle*—with the headlines of the victory and we came home with printed souvenirs of that day.

The 1940s. My best Dodger memorabilia was the natural wood mechanical pencil shaped like a baseball bat. The coupons to send for it were scarce, and for a quarter you had a pencil which you didn't take to school. Dody and I wore the mandatory teenage kerchiefs with our pea coats from the Hempstead Army & Navy store, but ours had Dodgers hand-embroidered on one corner, just like our pillowcases. We had our set of facsimile autographed pictures bought at the ball park. We would prop our little sister Carolyn up and make her show off her intelligence for Lillie Neimeyer across the street by giving a name to each face. "Kirby . . ." we would lead her on . . . and she would say . . . (hopefully) . . . "Higbie." "Frenchy . . ." "Bor-dar-gar-ay. . . ."

We would send birthday cards to the players in care of Ebbetts Field and sent get well cards to Pete Reiser when he hit his head at Sportsman's Park. We listened to Fred Allen when he had Leo Durocher on as a foil with the Brooklyn "Pinafore" and we reeled with delight. Our next door neighbor, Mrs. Osborne, would sometimes take us to Ladies' Day on summer afternoons. We never went by car; it was always the railroad from Mineola which would take us to Flatbush Avenue and then the subway ride. There was a short walk from the subway to Ebbetts Field, and it intensified as you got closer to the field; the crowd would grow and you would be enveloped in a happy stream of Brooklyn Dodger fans. By the time we were 15 we were allowed to go to games by ourselves. You could buy the tickets at the park on the spur of the moment.

In the early 1950s Dody and I went away to college together and baseball became a secondary interest. We couldn't listen to the early spring games in Maryland—so it became only a game of summer for us when we returned home to Long Island. But in the

Jackie Robinson acknowledging fans. (Photo courtesy of the National Baseball Library, Cooperstown, N.Y.)

fall of 1951, the Negro All-Stars were playing Gil Hodges' All-Stars in the then-segregated ball field on the other side of town in Frederick. Dody, our friend Mary, and I cut the afternoon class to find the rather ramshackle field. Mary even found Suitcase Simpson from her hometown of Cleveland sitting in the bus waiting for game time. It was wonderful! Roy Campanella and Don Newcombe talked to us, but Dody never felt kindly to Gil Hodges after that day because he wouldn't say hello. He didn't have the time.

In the fall of 1955 Dody and I were going to our jobs in the Rockefeller Center area of Manhattan. It was 8:00 A.M. and on a near empty 49th Street we met a group of five Dodgers, Johnny Padres and his pals, who just the day before had won the World Series from the Yankees. They were on their way to be on the "Today" show and they shone with grace and wonder. Dody and I were speechless and could only blurt out one word, "Congratulations." That was a priceless moment in our lives. The Series had been unbelievable in itself and now this. But our father had died in 1954 and would never know what his daughters had done.

In 1957 I married a Yankee fan. After all these years it does seem peculiar. But Gerry was—and is—a baseball fan in the best sense. He rattles off seeing DiMaggio and Henrich and Mantle when I do my Reese and Reiser routine. I was most impressed with his family when he told me his Uncle Ben was a good friend of Abe Stark. I mean, *The* Abe Stark— HIT SIGN WIN SUIT on the bottom of the scoreboard at Ebbets Field. . . .

By the time our first child was born in 1958, the Brooklyn Dodgers were no more. I had sad emotions when Roy Campanella had his tragic accident not more than two miles from where we were living. He was part of the old boys feeling in my heart. I began to take an interest in the new team in Flushing and I slowly grew to be a Met fan. It wasn't the same but it was baseball. *The Boys of Summer* by Roger Kahn came out and I had something in my hand to reinforce the memories. I wrote Red Barber a note when the Yankees let him go, and he said on a card that he sent back to me that he was thankfully released from "Burke's peerage." This man had such a lasting way with words and a gift to make the field come alive for us all out there. He was our mentor to the listening of the ball games and the keeper of the facts. I remember that during the war years, 1941–1945, you couldn't mention weather on the broadcasts, just in case it might help the enemy. Torrents could be washing away the play but nothing could be said. Whether you were at the ball park, in person, or listening to Red Barber or his staff, you were on the edge of the green waiting for the next pitch. You were swishing for Bill Nicholson of the competition or seeing the ephus (now how do I spell it?) pitch of Rip Sewell. Dody met up with Pee Wee Reese in a San Francisco gift shop. He was charming she said, and as gracious as in his shortstop days.

In the early 1970s I was substitute teaching a 6th grade class the day after Jackie Robinson's death. I tried to tell the students what he meant to me, to sports, to the black athlete, the black person. My eyes filled up and I rambled on, seeing in my head Jackie playing his heart and soul out. I am probably the only one in the classroom who remembers that day. The kids were too young to know what I was talking about.

Now it's well into the 1980s. The newspapers occasionally mention a bit of Dodger history, an obituary notice of someone from the Brooklyn era—I remember them easily, quietly in my heart.

I'm thankful for the day I walked past the scoreboard on our way out over the turf and I stopped and grabbed some green grass. I came home and enshrined it with cotton in an old watch case. It's there still in a hand carved watch holder which belonged to a great, great-grandfather. It's in my bureau drawer upstairs with a 1940s practice baseball. It didn't have official printing on it but it does have to this day two very real autographs. The first,

Whitlow Wyatt's, was obtained by my cousin Alan Brown who was killed in World War II, and the ball came to the twins. For the second we thank the second wife of Uncle Rebe who had friends next door who had friends in Rockville Centre who knew Dixie Walker. The ball was out of our sight for some weeks, but it came back with his name on the side opposite Wyatt's.

It's been many years since I saw my first big league game. You had to go to a ball park then to see the game and feel it and smell it.

Back and forth from the subway to the park you could buy your peanuts and your scorecards—or get a free scorecard with your paper. The pace quickened as you got to the field, climbed the ramparts and the thrill was always there each time you saw the green revealed. The real sod . . . from Long Island. The names return . . . hello Ducky Medwick, Dolph Camilli, Billy Herman, Augie Galan . . . goodbye child of summer, she who can sing along with the Gladys Gooding pipe organ rendering of "Leave us go root for the Dodgers, Rodgers, that's the team for me!" I can't give credit for a song I never saw in print. The words may not be recalled exactly right, but that song in my heart is there forever. Oh, is it there!

Red Barber. (Photo courtesy of the National Baseball Library, Cooperstown, N.Y.)

Angell, Roger. *Season Ticket: A Baseball Companion*. Boston: Houghton Mifflin, 1988. 406 pp.

Season Ticket is the fourth volume of the collected baseball chronicles Roger Angell has been providing *New Yorker* readers with for over two decades. His first baseball book, *The Summer Game,* began with his observations on the 1962 season, and it has been followed by *Five Seasons* and *Late Innings.*

When I was asked to review *Season Ticket,* I almost declined. It seemed like a conflict of interest. How objective could I be about a good friend's work? This, I quickly realized, was an odd response: I have never met or corresponded with Roger Angell. Nor, do I think, he is even a friend of a friend of a friend. But since my first reading of *The Summer Game,* I liked Roger Angell, as a person, and, given the chance, felt he might like me.

From the time the Dodgers left Brooklyn until 1972, baseball had played little or no part in my life. Partially, this was a bitter aftermath of the Bums' desertion of my home town; partially, it reflected the self-involved/self-important lifestyle of my college and graduate school years. But, above all, this inattention came from a feeling that baseball was a kid's game, something you grew out of, like acne. Also, I was never a particularly good player, and it was nice to be able to ignore a world where athletic skills were the measure of success and move to one where the intellect (presumably my stronger point) was.

Ironically, it was precisely at the moment when I was most challenged intellectually—when my wife and I were both writing our Ph.D. dissertation proposals—that I rediscovered baseball. After long hot days in the library and frustrating hours at the typewriter playing complex intellectual games, to our surprise, we found ourselves relaxing and regaining our sanity by sitting in front of the television watching the Mets or the Yankees play.

Out of guilt or just a natural scholarly inclination, I began to spend part of my library time reading about baseball. I was uneasy at first. From boyhood I remembered baseball books as mindless hero worship or cliché-ridden "as-told-to" autobiographies. But, fortunately, my renewed interest coincided with the emergence of a different type of baseball book—Jim Bouton's iconoclastic *Ball Four,* Roger Kahn's "bittersweet" *Boys of Summer,* and, of course, Roger Angell's *The Summer Game.*

The Summer Game taught me a most valuable lesson about baseball: it was, in some ways, wasted on the young. Part of growing up was to leave behind disappointed childhood fantasies of being a great player, a hero, and to turn to the less narcissistic and more realistic task of being a good fan, appreciating others' skills. And I discovered that would take work, because like many other American kids, I had played the game without ever realizing how the game was played. Angell turned me into a "born again" baseball fan, and I felt the kind of personal warmth toward him that you have toward the few people whose wisdom or example have occasionally changed your life for the better.

The major theme of Angell's latest book, *Season Ticket,* is a reminder to fans of the sheer difficulty of major league baseball. Angell's epigram is, appropriately, from Ted Williams: "Don't you know how hard this all is?" This sentiment, repeated time and again in different ways and in different contexts unites what is otherwise a potpourri: chronicles of seasons, League playoffs and World Series; character sketches (e.g., of Kansas City relief pitcher Dan Quisenberry and of Roy Eisenhardt, then Oakland A's president); meditations on perplexing elements of the game (some eternal—like the role of chance or fortuity in baseball—and some, we hope, more fleeting—like player drug abuse); and inquiries into what it takes to hit, pitch, catch, and play infield on a major league level.

Season Ticket, in fact, closes with Angell's long-delayed first trip to the Hall of Fame in 1987. His visit to Cooperstown reminds him of how fans' "infatuations are ferociously battered and eroded by various forces . . . most of all, by the wearisome, heartbreaking difficulty of the sport, which inexorably throws down last year's champions, exposes rookie marvels as disappointing journeymen, and turns lithe young stars into straining old men, all in a very short space of time." Yet, Angell concludes that the Hall of Fame also reminds us that there exists a handful of baseball players ". . . [who] played so well and so long, succeeding eventually at this almost impossible game. . . ."

While Angell, himself, might object to comparing the difficulty of playing consistently great baseball with consistently great writing about baseball, the publication of *Season Ticket* seems an especially appropriate moment for this Angell fan to ponder how his hero has stood up to the rigors of time. Much of what began so long ago with *The Summer Game* comes to an end or a climax in *Season Ticket.* Angell has never hidden his loyalty to the Mets and the Red Sox, and in *Season Ticket* he is faced with the ultimate choice—the two teams actually meet each other in the World Series. On a more melancholy note, Angell records the end of the long baseball careers of men like Tom Seaver and Carl Yastrzemski, who were the young heroes of Angell's first book 26 years ago.

When I started reading *Season Ticket,* I began to wonder whether perhaps Angell the writer had, at last, begun to show the wear and tear of too many seasons. In fact my notes on the first few chapters are sparse, and, at least judging from the scorecard I was keeping in the margins of the book, Angell seemed to have lost his stuff. Comments like "pretentious," "overwriting," or "too cute" pop up again and again.

I was annoyed by Angell's description of the 1983 Billy Martin–George Brett pine-tar debate: "Brett, in demurral, attempted thuggee upon the arbiters and was excused for the rest of the day. . . ." Did Angell really have to describe the standings in the American League as "less parlous?" Did he have to offer us an "apothegm" from a fellow writer instead of just a witty saying. Was I reading about baseball or getting practice for a Scrabble match?

I was disappointed by his chapters on baseball's technical skills. In part, I didn't feel I was learning much that was new to me. But, also, I was irritated by the overly cute guiding images Angell had chosen to structure those chapters. For example "In the Fire," where Angell examines the undervalued trade of a catcher, is treated like a colloquium. Talking to Tom Haller, a former catcher for the Giants, Dodgers, and Tigers, Angell turns his other informants into an imaginary audience: "leaning forward in the chairs a little restlessly over there as they wait to be heard from. . . . The long lanky one is Carlton Fisk, and the intense fellow, smoking a cigarette, is Ted Simmons. In a *minute,* you guys—all right?" In "Taking Infield" Angell talks of beginning his "tutorials." Having read *A Day in the Life of Roger Angell,* I knew that in his other life, as a nonbaseball writer, he is a master of parody. I began to wonder if out of boredom Angell had begun to put on his innocent baseball readers.

Yet as the book went on I found my interest increasing. I felt like I was watching an old pro who had been struggling for a few innings but was beginning to find his rhythm. Again and again I was struck by Angell's marvelous eye: "Weaver is the only mid-size, middle-aged executive I know who can sit behind a desk with no clothes on, as naked as a trout, and never lose the thread of his thinking." In *The Summer Game,* Angell observed that one of the reasons baseball is remembered so intensely is that "only baseball is so intensely watched," and Angell's ability to capture the essence of what is or can be seen on the field begins to dominate *Season Ticket.* The chapter on Dan Quisenberry includes the type of miniature portrait that has been an Angell trademark: "Barely pausing between pitches, he leaned, sank, bobbed, threw, hopped sidewise, got the ball back, and did it all over again. His work was funny-looking and profoundly undramatic, and he went about it like a man sweeping out a kitchen."

In fact, the chapter on Quisenberry contains much of the secret of Angell's continuing success. Written initially at the height of Quisenberry's fame, in 1985, it includes an afterword reflecting on the Quis's subsequent difficulties on the mound. Angell obviously likes Quisenberry very much as a person. Yet, in the wake of Quis's baseball problems, Angell confesses to beginning, like other people around him, to disparage the Quis: ". . . part of me would think, maybe he isn't so good, after all." Angell tells himself that "this is bitterly *unfair,* but what are *we* to do about it? *We* want our favorites to be great out there, and when that stops *we* feel betrayed a little." Angell sees this as what divides the pros from the bystanders, the players from the fans. "All players know that at any moment things can go horribly wrong for them. . . . It's part of the game. They are prepared to lose out there in plain sight, while the *rest of us* do it in private and then pretend it hasn't happened."

What has kept Angell special has been this continuing commitment to remain a fan (to think in terms of "we" and "the rest of us") as well as a writer. In the foreword to *The Summer Game,* Angell described himself as "a part-time, nonprofessional baseball watcher." Over 25 years later, in the Preface to *Season Ticket,* Angell rejects other characterizations of his work (baseball "historian," "essayist," "even . . . a poet") for "autobiography: the story of myself as a fan." Somehow Angell has managed to maintain a creative tension between the increasing access to baseball people his fame and skill have gained for him (how else could he get to know the Quis?) and his sense of being, above all, a fan.

It is the extraordinary type of fan he is that ultimately makes me still feel that writing about Roger Angell is like writing about a friend. Although Angell's work is his story as a fan, it is not full of himself. Angell is intense and partisan about the game, but he is never shrill or sanctimonious. He has strong opinions without seeming opinionated. Although they cover five years, all the chapters of *Season Ticket* are left in the present tense, and when later events prove one of Angell's predictions or judgments to be wrong, he points that out in footnotes. Fair-minded would seem to be the most apt description of Angell as a writer–fan.

Angell's basic decency leaves me wanting to be fair, too. Looking back on my initial reaction to *Season Ticket,* I wonder whether I was being just. So what if I'm not going to learn too much more from Angell about catching or throwing a split-finger fastball? If that's the case, it's probably because years ago Angell inspired me to go out and learn about such things on my own. What is a great teacher, but someone who inspires his students to learn to teach themselves? Besides, I strongly suspect that I will soon reread those chapters, trying hard to follow Angell's example and suppress a smug sense of my own knowledge. I'm sure to discover how much I missed. And, finally, I must admit that even Angell's occasional overwriting appeals to me, like the mannerisms of a favorite veteran player, who has earned the right to his oddities by the sparkling quality of his play season after season after season.

Fred Roberts
Department of Social Science
Michigan State University

Bowen, Michael. *Can't Miss*. New York: Harper & Row, 1987. 378 pp. $16.95.

It seems impossible to contemplate a boring book about a natural hitter. It further seems difficult to envision reading a boring account about the first female in the majors. But Michael Bowen has accomplished this feat. Chris Tilden, a Minnesota farmgirl who hit .641 in her senior year at Macalester College is offered a try out by the American League's Denver Marshalls. Already we're talking improbable. While a half dozen recent college stars have gone immediately to the "bigs," the more usual route is through an apprenticeship in the minors. Since there are no female minor leagues where Tilden could have honed her already considerable skills, lets grant Bowen his scheme. The question still arises: where is the excitement of Branch Rickey's noble experiment as related in Jules Tygiel's *Baseball's Great Experiment: Jackie Robinson and His Legacy*? Nowhere in *Can't Miss* is the excitement currently generated by the possibility of Pam Postema becoming the first female umpire in the majors. So you say Rickey and Postema are life, *Can't Miss* is art, right? Wrong. The tension, character development, and plot resolutions that are hallmarks of literature are nowhere to be found in this novel.

Bowen never gets beyond offering us cardboard characters, contrived actions, juvenile dialogue, and situations that never fully develop. His best developed figure is not Chris Tilden but Mace Dickson, a good field, no hit utility man. Even here the reader would be hard-pressed to empathize with Dickson, or even care that he is the only character with more than one dimension. And, what is the reader to make of Cindy Briggs, publicity director and daughter of the owner of the Marshalls? Is she as hard-drinking and as whoring as her male ballplayers? Or is she a dedicated baseball executive better than one might think because she is the boss's daughter? What happens to Cindy's relationship with the volatile star left-handed pitcher? Bowen leaves more loose ends than a baseball with busted seams.

Chris Tilden's brief tryout would have been turned into high drama or sharp satire by the likes of I.B. Singer, James Alan McPherson, or Joe Durso. When Bowen finally gets Tilden romantically involved with an older sportswriter, the depiction of this relationship is as flat and wooden as everything else in the novel. *Can't Miss* unfortunately does miss—all the bases.

Harry Reed
Michigan State University

Eskenazi, Gerald. *Bill Veeck: A Baseball Legend*. New York: McGraw-Hill, 1988. 182 pp., $16.95.

In 1968 Paul Zimmerman, then of the *New York Post* and now of *Sports Illustrated*, interviewed Bill Veeck, then in retirement from baseball and now among the ultimate bleacher bums. This would be Zimmerman's one and only meeting with Veeck. Having interviewed the interviewer, Gerald Eskenazi notes the "clarity and emotion" that Zimmerman can still summon when he thinks about his subject. "I'd say it was the most memorable interview I've ever conducted in my life . . . I knew that whatever I was going to write was going to be inadequate because there was no way I could cover this man in one column or a magazine piece or even one book, unless it was a real fat one."

Well, Mr. Zimmerman, you're right. A Bill Veeck biography ought to be a "real fat one." This "baseball legend" deserves as much. And maybe some day Paul Zimmerman or someone else will write such a book. Two years and one biography after Veeck's death there is still room for a hefty tome on the life and times of Bill Veeck—as in Spec(tator)—for that, after all, is just what Bill Veeck was, whether he happened to own a ball team or not.

On a plus side, this is a brief and breezy book, and Veeck was nothing if not a breezy sort of guy—at least on the outside. There are, however, hints between these covers of another Veeck, a Veeck who did not frequent front offices or bleachers, ranches or night clubs. This was a Bill Veeck who was neither scheming to explode baseball traditions by sending rockets into the air or diminishing the game itself by sending midgets to the plate.

This was a Veeck with barely concealed anger over his treatment at the hands (and feet) of the baseball establishment, a Veeck with well-concealed guilt over his own treatment of his first family, and a Veeck increasingly frightened by the absence of successful treatment for either his fast-disappearing leg or his smoke-clogged lungs. This is not, however, a psycho-biography of a man who was never able to stay in one place (let alone lay on one couch—or bleacher) long enough for friend, foe, or shrink to get a real fix on him.

Eskenazi is more friend than foe, and, as such, he doesn't even pretend to be a shrink. But there are those tantalizing hints that behind his subject's open face and equally open collar were countless secrets and not a few resentments.

Why, then, has Eskenazi chosen to peek ever so gingerly behind the Bill Veeck mask? And why has he poked at all into the labyrinthian finances of Bill Veeck, wheeler-dealer manipulator, or pulled back the curtain, ever so briefly, to reveal the private drama of one Bill Veeck, unloving husband to his first wife and absent father to their three children? Is it to pull down one more "baseball legend," to pulverize another once-sacred icon?

Eskenazi's intentions are not so base as all that. But neither are they very grand. The truth of the matter is that this is not a very ambitious book about a baseball man whose ambitions were at once simple and grandiose. Bill Veeck wanted to see smiling faces filling his ball parks from Milwaukee to Cleveland, from St. Louis to Chicago, and from Chicago to Chicago. And if he could make money and tweak the hated Yankees at the same time, so much the better.

But if that is all there was to the career of one Bill Veeck, why bother writing his biography at all? Of course, that was far from all there was to Veeck's baseball life. This, after all, was the man who would have integrated major league baseball before Branch Rickey had not Commissioner Kenesaw Mountain Landis foiled his effort to purchase the Philadelphia Phillies and stock the club with black players in 1943. This was the man who challenged more baseball traditions than there have been balk calls during the first weeks of the 1988 "de-balkle" of a season. And this was the man who won pennants in Cleveland and Chicago (the latter's first in 40 years, which ought to have been sufficient penance for the Black Sox scandal), not to mention a World Series for Cleveland (its only such triumph in the 40 years since that 1948 campaign).

Yes, Bill Veeck is a worthy subject for a biography—and a "fat one" at that. So why did Gerald Eskenazi write a very thin book about a very full life? Why indeed!

In one sense, the book isn't thin at all. In fact, parts of it have actually been *padded*. There are digressions on the Black Sox scandal, on Satchel Paige's vagabond career, on the Comiskey family, and on the doings of the first Bill Veeck family. (The second set of children, six in all, is virtually absent.)

Absent as well is any informed argument to the book. A scholarly biography this is not. Perhaps such an approach would have been inappropriate given who Bill Veeck was—and who he was not. Behind those horn-rimmed glasses was a baseball man and a promoter, not necessarily in that order. Then again, behind those same glasses was an inveterate reader, who read five books a week—all while soaking that damnable stump.

Perhaps the career of Bill Veeck does deserve the scholarly treatment after all. At least it ought to be subjected to a few searching questions. To his credit, reporter Eskenazi has asked questions. He has done his legwork, if not his head work. He has interviewed everyone from Veeck players, Bob Feller and Larry Doby, to Veeck pals, Skitch Henderson and Bob Hope. He even tracked down Bob Cain, who . . . oh hell, every baseball fan knows why Bill Veeck made Bob Cain the answer to a baseball trivia question.

But Eskenazi hasn't asked himself enough questions. He has taken us on the roller-coaster ride that was Bill Veeck's career. But then Veeck himself did that. Both of his autobiographies make for a great read, whether consumed in one gulp or two. This biography has replaced neither of them.

In fairness to Eskenazi, Veeck was not famous for his public introspection. Eskenazi has tried to fill in some of the gaps in the private Veeck. But again, to what end? This is not a muckraking exposé of a tyrannical and tight-fisted owner. I liked Bill Veeck before I read this book, and I still like him—even though I now know that he went 20 years without speaking to his eldest son. Moreover, I think Eskenazi wants his readers to like Bill Veeck, even if they learn that his life included a few errors among the hits and runs.

The real question, I think, is this: why do baseball fans like Bill Veeck? Was it because he was an anti-establishmentarian in a game too full of establishment types? Was it because he was a baseball populist in a game crowded with millionaires on and off the field? Or was it because he was not only a players' owner, but the fans' owner as well? No doubt all of the above qualify as partial answers.

Perhaps the question ought to be rephrased slightly to: why do baseball purists like Bill Veeck? Having struggled mightily (and unsuccessfully) to come to terms with such monstrosities as the designated hitter and the domed stadium, I include myself among the ranks of at least the semi-pure, if not the simon-pure (whoever they are). And yet I liked Bill Veeck even though I knew he was far from a baseball purist before I picked up this book. After all, this was the man who once suggested going to a three-ball walk and a two-strike out in the name of speeding up the game! If the DH is an abomination, what in the name of John McGraw can be said about that kind of tampering with tradition?

Bill Veeck was no Cornelius Vanderbilt. Never would he have said—or so much as thought—"The public be damned." But tradition was another matter entirely. In fact, the reason that he often damned tradition was in the name of appeasing the public.

Sure, Bill Veeck did revere some traditions. He loved outdoor baseball and day baseball under the sun and in the bleachers. (In fact, his one baseball regret was his failure to follow his father and run the Cubs.) But the same Bill Veeck could wheel and deal with the best of them, when not concocting franchise shifts at will. His recurring problem was that he lacked the necessary wheels to make those desired deals. Maybe, just maybe, Veeck would have stayed in one place long enough to reap financial rewards and to honor baseball traditions had he only had the big bucks to make a go of it in a big way. And then again, maybe not.

As matters stand, we'll never know. He was forced to be a perpetual carpetbagger, because his bag was never full. And he could, at times, be a resentful carpetbagger at that. Still, he had a good time trying to live out his version of the American dream. Maybe that's why baseball fans of all varieties like him. This, after all, was a man who lived his life the way he wanted to live it.

He may have been a peripatetic vagabond on that one good leg, but he did take the time to smell those roses, when not thumbing his nose at those off-the-field baseball powers or watching in awe and delight the prowess of those other baseball powers who played their games on the field, where it still really matters most.

John C. Chalberg
Normandale Community College

Herzog, Whitey, and Kevin Horrigan. *White Rat: A Life in Baseball*. New York: Harper & Row, 1987. 228 pp. $16.95.

"I never stand still," says Whitey Herzog. "If you're standing still, you're losing ground." This assertion sets the tone of Herzog's autobiography, *White Rat: A Life in Baseball,* written with Kevin Horrigan of the *St. Louis Post-Dispatch. White Rat* mirrors the personality of its subject—brash, opinionated, shrewd, and uncompromising. Herzog's admirers will undoubtedly like this book, his critics may not. Herzog could probably care less either way. He calls the game the way he sees it.

Whether he is discussing August A. Busch, Jr., Gene Autry ("The Cowboy"), Charles O. Finley, or Ewing Kauffman, Herzog is not bashful about setting forth his views of the magnates who control the game. Anecdotes concerning Autry, Herzog's former employer with the California Angels, are alone almost worth the purchase price of the book. He does not hesitate to criticize aspects of the St. Louis Cardinals' organization, his current employers, though he has nothing but praise for beer baron Gussie Busch. ("I've worked for a lot of owners and a lot of good people, but I don't think anyone ever appreciated me or my talents until I met Gussie Busch. . . . The smartest people are those who hire good people and then just get the hell out of the way.")

Herzog offers little insight into those aspects of his youth that shaped his personality and outlook on life, although he does talk briefly about growing up in New Athens, Illinois, a German community 40 miles from St. Louis. Punctuality, order, and knowing the value of a dollar: all these Herzog attributes stem, he tells the reader, from New Athens, where people "do the same things at the same time, every week, every year."

There is surprisingly little in the book concerning the Cardinals' World Series appearances in 1982 and 1985. But the 1986 season—an extremely frustrating one for Herzog and the Cardinals—is discussed in much greater detail. One quickly realizes that when the players do not play well no manager looks like a genius. Herzog is brutally candid on this point, concerning both himself and his players. He frankly acknowledges that some situations have no solutions, and that a manager can only do so much. At one point during the dismal 1986 campaign he reflects: "I've held a couple of meetings in the clubhouse, but you really can't rant and rave at the guys. That kind of thing never does any good . . . the more I talk . . . the more they just go out and screw it up worse. I really don't know what to do. It's got me buffaloed."

Buffaloed perhaps, but never without opinions and insights about the unique sport-business of baseball in all its aspects, from little league playing fields to corporate offices,

Herzog offers plenty of stimulating ideas about ways to improve the game. This is the strength of his book. For example, he opposes further expansion of the major leagues at the present time and advocates the elimination of two franchises and the creation of two 12-team leagues with four six-team divisions. He wants uniform agreement on the designated hitter rule: make everyone use it or drop it. He thinks the World Series should be played in a neutral domed stadium every year. He calls for using the same umpiring crews in both major leagues. ("This is one of those problems that has an easy solution and wouldn't cost anything to fix.")

Always a realist, Herzog acknowledges that many of his suggestions will never be adopted, but he has no patience with hidebound conservatives who cite tradition as a substitute for fresh thinking. One quality stands out about Herzog—he is always thinking. That is a rare quality not only in baseball circles but in other sectors of modern American society as well, as the corporate mindset continues to encroach upon the province of individual initiative and creativity. Whatever else he may or may not be, the White Rat is no corporate animal, and that is why his story is well worth reading.

Rodney M. Sievers
Humboldt State University

Holway, John. *Blackball Stars: Negro League Pioneers.* Westport, CT: Meckler Books, 1988. 374 pp. $22.50.

Remembering John B. Holway's 1975 classic *Voices from the Great Black Baseball Leagues* I initially was wary when I encountered his new book. This new work seemed to promise more of the same, although much has been published to illuminate the experiences of the "invisible men." *Voices* offered 18 profiles of black professionals playing between 1890 and 1945. *Blackball Stars* carries on the technique of biographical sketches of outstanding players in black baseball history. The narratives are informative, lively, vary in length, and include portraits of Louis Santop, Oscar Charleston, "Biz" Mackey, Martin Dihigo, and 21 others.

Holway puts some flesh on the old myths about black baseball. He has searched out box scores and has computed the averages of black stars against white major leaguers and has verified that blacks more than held their own. Norman "Turkey" Stearnes the slugging Detroit Stars' outfielder and leading home run hitter in black baseball history hit .313 against white major league pitchers. Stearnes appeared in 14 games with white pros between 1923 and 1934. In 48 at bats he collected 15 hits including 4 home runs. The stats have been verified by the Society for American Baseball Research.

Although the stories are entertaining the work has several flaws. While the subjects are different than in the 1975 work much of the writing has appeared elsewhere in the *SABR Research Journal* and newspapers. Given that Holway has done so much writing and research about black baseball it would have been more desirable to discuss the historical significance of the men and their pursuits rather than continuing to duplicate the interesting but Sunday supplement-like articles.

Holway ends the work without a conclusion. This is a particular failing since he makes an important observation at the end of his brief introduction. He states, for example, that blacks have deserted the game they once loved and thronged to see. A more substantial work would have speculated why this is so. And, perhaps, a more adventurous writer would have explored the dangerous but significant topic of prescriptions for possible change.

Harry A. Reed
Michigan State University

Honig, Donald. *The New York Mets: The First Quarter Century.* New York: Crown, 1987. 160 pp. $17.95.

In *The New York Mets: The First Quarter Century,* author and baseball historian Donald Honig hones his writing skills to a fine edge as he skillfully guides the reader through the first 25 years of the franchise. The resulting book is not only very interesting and well researched; but makes for most delightful reading.

The book is divided into ten chronological sections. The first "A New Team in Town" relates how Donald Shea and Branch Rickey used the leverage of the proposed Continental League to land another National League team in New York to replace the departed Giants.

"The Opening Years" depicts how the initial team of the expansion franchise was put together player by player; while Section Three, "Casey and the Amazin's" deals with the trials and tribulations of an expansion team from 1960 through 1965.

"The Pre-Miracle Years" shows how the new franchise continued to struggle first under Wes Westrum who replaced Stengel and then Gil Hodges, one of the most popular and respected men to ever wear a baseball uniform. In this section Honig tells the fascinating story of the fluke incident that enabled the Mets to get Tom Seaver.

This book is liberally filled with magnificent photos, both black and white and colored. Not only are all the great and near great Mets shown; but such little knowns as Larry Stahl, Don Hahn, Hank Webb, Roy Staiger, and many others.

"The Miracle" will definitely please the true Met fan as all the crucial points of the first pennant in 1969 are relived. "After the Miracle" shows how the team regrouped with the eventual house cleaning of the 1969 squad in 1972. Included in this section is the inside story of why Nolan Ryan, one of the fastest pitchers the game has ever seen, was traded.

"Another Pennant" relives the second pennant year (1973); while "The Quiet Years" chronicles another regrouping. Told here is the unpopular and disastrous trade of Tom Seaver.

Honig resists the opportunity to mire you in baseball statistics as do so many baseball writers. He does have a neat table at the end with the more important figures.

"Resurgence" heralds the arrival of Dave Johnson; while the final section "The Cup Runneth Over" guides us through the most recent pennant season.

While *The New York Mets* might be described as a gloss coffee-table tome for browsing, even the most casual baseball fan will be unable to put it down until the entire volume has been consumed page by page.

In critically looking for mistakes I could find but one. On page 27 the photo of southpaw hitter, Tim Harkness has been reversed to show him hitting right-handed. This *E* must be scored against the publisher and not Donald Honig. Highly recommended for both pleasure and a reference source for your library.

Stanley Grosshandler
University of North Carolina

151

Honig, Donald. *The New York Yankees: An Illustrated History* (rev. ed.). New York: Crown, 1987. 352 pp. Index. $22.50.

This is a revised and updated edition of one of Donald Honig's distinctive photo albums. The genre now includes, besides this one, volumes on each major league, the World Series, the Red Sox, and Brooklyn's Dodgers. Honig calls them illustrated histories, or "tributes;" I prefer to think of them as biographical photography. For while each edition has a crisp and serviceable text of some 35,000 words, it is the author's painstaking picture research and astute picture editing that makes these books the unique contributions to baseball history that they are.

The New York Yankees was first published in 1981. This expanded and revised edition continues through the 1986 season and follows the others in format and design. Honig has divided *Yankees* into eight time periods, beginning each one with a double-spread "theme" photograph followed by a swatch of text, and then letting the pictures run. In Chapter 3, "Gehrig and Two Guys Named Joe," there are 47 pages of photos. If I counted correctly, there is a total of 598 photos altogether.

While some of Honig's choices are familiar, they are welcome ones—Willie Keeler as a Highlander bunting, the up-from-under shot of high-kicking Lefty Gomez—and almost none is a cliché. The time-honored sideline poses are, of course, inevitable, particularly those from the days of the Graflex view cameras and the Speed Graphics with their slow shutters and film.

Whatever their technical limitations, many of the photos are remarkable. The Chapter 1 opener is a panorama of Hilltop Park circa 1909 with the White Sox at bat against the Yankees. The caption reconstructing the game situation is Honig at his best. Although third base cannot be seen, Hal Chase is playing far off first and on the grass; the right fielder is in right center and the other outfielders are shifted so far left that they are out of the frame. Probably bases full, Honig surmises, with a dead pull hitter at bat and Chase looking for a play at the plate.

Most pictures repay study of their fascinating detail: Evolving catcher's gear, Miller Huggins in his playing days choking his bat halfway, Home Run Baker as a Yankee with his two little daughters for whom he sat out the 1920 season after his wife died and he could not arrange for their care, a rare shot of Dazzy Vance trying out with the Yankees years before his success with Brooklyn, and an odd one of Ping Bodie with holes snipped in his cap. For ventilation? Old pictures show that this was Buck Weaver's habit, too.

Stare into the faces of the special men who played baseball. Those of long ago strike me as grittier than today's, perhaps tougher, not necessarily more mature, but certainly less young. Honig has been scrupulous about finding pictures appropriate to his time zones. Young Urban Shocker in Chapter 1, and Shocker two years from death in Chapter 2. Babe Ruth's progress is clearly marked from the trim pitcher-turned-outfielder of 1921 to the fat, worn-out old slugger with the Braves in 1935; as is Gehrig's from muscular power hitter of 1925 to poignant bystander at the 1939 World Series, Iron Horse no longer.

Chapter by chapter the team evolves. "Always the young strangers," said photographer Edward Steichen. Year by year they emerge, replacing their elders and ultimately being replaced. Little Rizzuto fresh from Kansas City—is it possible that 32 years have passed since we last saw him at short? DiMag and Mantle in 1951: an ending for the man, a beginning for the boy; and now it's 20 seasons since Mickey last swung the bat.

The stars are first to catch the eye, but many lesser Yankees helped to keep the organism intact and flourishing. Remember Lyn Lary, Atley Donald, Joe Page, Gene Woodling, Clete Boyer, Roy White? And their opponents. Honig reminds us of the generations of Yankee foes: McGraw and his Giants, including an unshaven, hard-faced Casey Stengel, Alex as he looked when he fanned Lazzeri in 1926, Wes Ferrell, Hubbell, Koufax, Brett.

The book is printed offset on a decently calendared sheet, black only. The best photographs are richly textured. Lesser ones, perhaps from copy negatives, second-generation prints, or high-contrast playing-field shots, are less well served. I like the brown-black sepia ink of the National and American League books better. Those, of course, unlike the Yankee book with its required cast of players, had the luxury of simply selecting the finest photos available of eight teams' all-time rosters.

To my eye, the oldest and most recent time periods provide the finest Yankee photographs. The 1950s and 1960s are least satisfactory as to picture quality and photographic interest. The early ones glow with the charm of what seems a simpler time; and for the present day, Honig has had access to a number of talented professionals whose fast film and zoom lenses have caught an array of outstanding action portraits.

I could wish that Honig's captions were more "atmospheric," like the Chapter 1 opener, and less statistical. But he has covered the ground thoroughly and well. Even if your admiration for the Yankees is restrained, this album of their long and splendid 85-year life span belongs on your baseball shelf.

A.D. Suehsdorf
Sonoma, California

Hoppel, Joe and Craig Carter. *The Sporting News Baseball Trivia 2*. St. Louis: The Sporting News Publishing Co., 1987. 288 pp. $10.95.

Barnidge, Tom. (Ed.), *Best Sports Stories 1987*. St. Louis: The Sporting News Publishing Co., 1987. 288 pp. $10.95.

Just what the world needs, another baseball trivia book, I thought to myself as I opened *The Sporting News Baseball Trivia 2*. Its chapters were cleverly numbered for the first through tenth innings. Not a good sign.

Before I shut the book, though, I randomly opened to Chapter 4, "No Hitters and Perfect Games." There, leading off, was Grover Cleveland Alexander. Old Pete, I soon learned, is the pitcher with the most career major league wins who never pitched a no-hitter. In fact, there was a list of the other eight 300-game winners—Alexander led with 373—who had not pitched no-hitters. There was another list in the same section, too. This one named those pitchers with the fewest wins who had pitched no-hitters. No, it wasn't the Browns' Bobo Holloman—he had three major league wins, though his photo did make the book, one of 132 black-and-white photographs, plus 10 drawings by Bill Wilson that illustrate the book.

Now if you want the answer to that or to other questions about no-hit games—such as the name of the shortstop who played in 11 no-hitters, the team that went the most seasons without a no-hitter, or the umpire who called and pitched no-hitters—you'll have to obtain your own copy of *Trivia 2*.

After I had finished the no-hitter chapter, I picked another one. Before I knew it, I was hooked. One chapter called "A Family Affair," then another entitled "The Trading Season," until I was finished and wondering if I should start calling used book stores to find where I might locate a copy of *Trivia 1*, which came out in 1983.

I've read my share of trivia books over the years, and this one might just be the best one ever. Nearly every page had a surprise or two. Again and again, I found myself saying, "Wow, I didn't know that," or "They really did their homework to find out this one."

They, in this case, are co-editor and writer Joe Hoppel and co-editor and researcher Craig Carter. You can appreciate the archival records TSN has accumulated in its long publishing history, and Hoppel and Carter have given them a long, hard look to put together this volume.

I was enjoying this healthy diet of information about the great American game. And, surprisingly enough, I took time out to notice that the season was still on. Had it been the dead of winter, *Trivia 2* might well have gotten me through a whole week without baseball. Where else could I have learned, for instance, the identity of the only "Z" battery in major league history, the name of the pitcher who gave up 24 runs in his only major league game and later became a Catholic priest, the name of the major leaguer who played every inning of every All-Star game for seven straight seasons (no, not Willie Mays, but a good guess), and the future governor who played 81 games for a Pirates' farm club in 1952?

Even if you like movies more than baseball, you can try Chapter 9, "Actors and Their Roles," which highlights the stars and lesser lights of baseball movies. Reading here, you will find out that Gary Cooper had to learn to hit left-handed to play Lou Gehrig in *The Pride of the Yankees,* and you will also learn the names of his two illustrious tutors. You will also learn that William Frawley, who played Fred Mertz on "I Love Lucy," played in five different baseball movies, including *The Babe Ruth Story* and *Safe at Home,* the forgettable 1962 turkey starring Mickey Mantle and Roger Maris.

What a great book! Find it, enjoy it, and have as good a time with it as I did.

* * *

Best Sports Stories 1987 is just that, a "sports" book. Editing and publishing its fifth edition of this anthology, TSN keeps alive a yearly collection of stories and photographs that was first brought out in 1944. Five professors from the University of Missouri's journalism education program selected the winning entries.

There is at least some hope for the baseball fan, however, for the summer game is represented with some quality contributions drawn from a number of different magazines and newspapers. But baseball and baseball-related stories only occupy about one-third of the entire volume. Since many of these works will probably not appear in another anthology, you could gain access to stories you might otherwise have missed altogether.

Let me at least give you the baseball "highlights" from *Best Sports Stories 1987.* I particularly enjoyed reading two stories again—"'The Natural'—Live!" by Glenn Dickey for *Inside Sports* and "The Silence" by Glenn Duffy for *Philadelphia Magazine.* In both cases, it was the subject matter, though both pieces were well written, that kept me reading. Give me a young Cuban-born slugger from Miami with movie star good looks who has been compared to both Willie Mays and Mickey Mantle or a closed-mouth southpaw who kept writers at bay almost as much as he did opposing hitters as he came to be known as "the Greatest Lefthander of his Day."

Some of the other baseball stories stand out, especially Rick Reilly's "King of the Sports Page," a profile of *Los Angeles Times* sports columnist Jim Murray, Malcolm Moran's "Bob Feller Still Pitches Coast to Coast." I also liked several others very much, among them William Gildea's "Donovan Still Casts a Big Shadow," a profile of ex-Baltimore Colt Art Donovan's life after football, and Richard Hoffer's "The Black Pioneers," which describes how Earl Lloyd, Chuck Cooper, and Nat (Sweetwater) Clifton became the first three black men to play NBA basketball in 1950.

Fans of other sports have a lot of reading to catch up on here, including a full selection of professional, college, and high school sports, along with golf, track and field, tennis, triathlons, horse racing, cycling, and boxing and sports-related pieces of the dangers of alcohol and drug abuse. And the good thing is, if you can't find what you want in this year's anthology, you can—with apologies to Casey Stengel and anyone else who ever said it— wait until next year.

There's something here for almost everyone—drama, pain, humor, passion—all portrayed with style, intelligence, and wit.

Denis Telgemeier
San Francisco

Kaplan, Jim. *Playing the Field: Why Defense is the Most Fascinating Art in Major League Baseball.* Chapel Hill, NC: Algonquin Books, 1987. 167 pp. $13.95.

Yogi Berra said that you can't think and hit at the same time, and that goes for fielding, too. Catching a baseball traveling at over 120 miles per hour requires sublimation of the intellect. Positioning before the play and throwing to the right base require thinking, but the intermediary step of getting the ball into the glove represents the triumph of practiced response over instinctive fear.

Perhaps it's the anti-intellectual nature of fielding that makes it resist written examination as fervently as the weekend third baseman shies from a grass-cutter down the line. Additionally, inculcated with nightly highlights—a treat which may end with this season's encoding of major league satellite signals—we've become accustomed to appreciating the grace of Ozzie Smith visually. Prose is bound to finish a poor second.

Attempts to write about fielding generally stand up as well as Lonnie Smith in pursuit of a drive to the warning track. William Curran's *Mitts* deteriorated from a chatty reminiscence into a mind-numbing procession of names of great and near-great fielders. Jim Kaplan's *Playing the Field* seeks a more analytical approach and succeeds moderately, cataloging great plays and opinions from a hodgepodge of major league sources.

Playing the Field perpetuates the premise that fans don't appreciate fielding, a condescending view that should be put to rest. There's hardly a scorecard scribbler in the stands who doesn't have a symbol for a great play. Listen to any post-game discussion among fans and you're likely to hear more about backhand stops than clever pitching patterns. Fans do admire fielding, and they don't need a report from the clubhouse to embellish what they've seen.

Kaplan's best efforts examine the diverse defensive demands of the positions. Profiles of the game's greatest executors and innovators at each position only once reach beyond the 1960s. The volume of great plays, one example including Kelvin Chapman and Howard Johnson, grows overwhelming. Welcome, but insufficient, attention is given to the often stunning mechanics of making plays.

There's too little said about team defensive concepts, information found in instructional manuals but rarely presented for fans in the context of watching the game. What are those nine players supposed to do when a batter singles to right with one out and runners on first and second?

Kaplan's selection for the greatest fielding moment in history turns out to be an extremely unsatisfying example of the book's clubby, "that's-rich-old-chap" tone. Kaplan too often chooses cleverness over information, making the book more of a prose clinic than a celebration of the persistence, intelligence, and, above all, courage that it takes to be a great gloveman.

Eliot Cohen
Jamaica, New York

Klein, Frederick C. *On Sports*. Chicago: Bonus Books, 1987. 270 pp. $15.95.

Since I happen to suffer from a chronic allergy to most *Wall Street Journal* editorials, I have rarely encountered Fred Klein's essays and musings hot off the griddle. However, Klein has now collected some 60 or so of his *WSJ* columns (a weekly feature since 1983), thus saving me the trouble of reading the editorial page.

It's been said that yesterday's sports columns are as perishable as one-run leads in the 7th inning at Fenway Park. Red Smith's anthology of obituaries was more durable than most in this genre and I can recall being pleased by an old Jimmy Cannon collection. But Klein's gallimaufry, with only about 20 percent of the contents devoted to baseball (in a chapter entitled "Hardball," also the title of a recent Bowie Kuhn book), is not apt to survive next year's World Series winner in very good shape.

Despite Klein's slyly irreverent style and his freedom from sports jargon, the material, for the most part, has already become dated. Thus, topicality and enduring insights are somewhat limited.

Take, for example, his October 1983 column about how the Baltimore Orioles' pitching staff bamboozled the Philadelphia Phillies in five World Series games. Within 5 years that assemblage of pitchers—Boddicker, McGregor, Flanagan, Palmer, etc.—has depreciated in value faster than last October's stock market. So, the suggestion by Klein that "the care and feeding of Baltimore pitchers" is somewhat unique in baseball circles appears, by 1988, as a highly dubious assertion. Perhaps Klein's paean to the Oriole pitchers should serve as a careful reminder of how fast and far that mound operation has plummeted in only a few years.

An essay on the renascent Chicago Cubs (the author admits to being a lifelong Cubs aficionado) also proves, if any proof is necessary, how quickly a sports column opts for the dustbin of history. There is chatter about Dallas Green in the front office, Lee Elia and Jim Frey managing, and Lee Smith doing the relief-pitching, while now all are gone with the Chicago wind, a tribute to baseball's evanescent glories.

Klein is at his breezy best when he goes beyond the box scores and performs an "exhumation" of the body, as Jerome Holtzman suggests in his foreword to the book. There are a couple of pieces that emerge in pretty fresh condition, even though they were written over 8 years ago.

In 1912, someone named John Owen Wilson, hit 36 three-baggers for the Pittsburgh Pirates, a mark that has never been equalled. Remarkably, no player has ever socked more than 26 triples since Wilson's banner year. Klein dug down to tell us why this has happened—changes in ball park structure, today's outfielders positioning themselves deeper in the outfield, and the contemporary ballplayer obsession with hitting home runs.

In another yarn Klein chronicles the adventures of Marvin J. Rotblatt, a southpaw who had a cup of coffee with the White Sox in the early 1950s (4 wins, 3 losses). Rotblatt was sufficiently obscure so that a group of Carleton College students in Northfield, Minnesota, named a slow-pitch softball league after him. In a game in his honor, Rotblatt pitched and hit home runs batting left-handed and right-handed. (Unfortunately, Klein misses the opportunity to reveal to us that in 15 times at bat as a major leaguer Rotblatt never connected for a single hit, thus leaving him with a lifetime batting average of .000.)

An amusing interview with WABC's Art Rust, Jr., who is a walking encyclopedia on sports, with a heavy accent on baseball inconsequentia, closes out the book. "I'm a brilliant black SOB," Rust tells Klein, "but I never got to do play-by-play for any big league team. There was no way they were gonna have a black in the booth." Rust goes on to tell Klein that he'd never done a bad show on radio, "I can make cockroaches running across the floor sound like the Kentucky Derby," he boasts.

More funny folks like Art Rust, Jr. and less stuff on the Olympics, boxing, football, tennis, and mountain climbing might have made this book more appealing to readers of *Baseball History*. And I wish that when Klein wrote his piece on sports loyalties that he remembered to point out that players rarely come from the cities that they represent. Tom Seaver and Billy Martin are native Californians. Why do they love 'em in New York? Klein doesn't tell us.

Ray Robinson
New York City

Murphy, Dale with Curtis Patton. *Ask Dale Murphy*. Chapel Hill, NC: Algonquin Books, 1987. 102 pp. $8.95 (pbk.).

In the introduction to *Ask Dale Murphy*, Furman Bisher, the long-time Georgia sportswriter, states that the book's origin was a weekly column of "advice to young baseball players" in the *Atlanta Constitution and Journal*. The column itself was directly inspired by one in the Cincinnati area written by Pat McInally, the former Harvard and Bengal football star. Thus *Ask Dale Murphy* is a collection of questions asked over a period of several years by the star Atlanta outfielder's numerous fans in the South. The book is profusely illustrated with 50 black and white photographs arranged chronologically.

Although one question was asked by a grandfather ("Is my three-year-old grandson too young to play ball?"), most of the book's approximately 150 questions are, not surprisingly, asked by youngsters ranging in age from 5 to 17. What *is* surprising is that about a third of Murphy's respondents are female, a tribute either to the ballplayer's sex appeal or the fact that a large number of girls in the Atlanta area are interested in playing baseball or at least following the game.

The book is in part a "how-to" manual with sections dealing with "Hitting a Baseball," "The Defensive Game," and "It's How You Play the Game: The Right Attitude." The reader learns, among many things, how to strengthen one's throwing arm, how to overcome "ball-shyness," and how to respond to teammates "who give me a hard time after I strike out." Murphy's response—"Ignore the bad times and encourage those who discourage you . . . eventually that will change their outlook"—has a decidedly Biblical cast.

A large number of the questions in other sections, however, deal with the Atlanta slugger's own career: how he decided upon baseball, his early experiences in youth baseball, his years in the minors, his major league debut, etc. We learn that Murphy's favorite team in his youth was San Francisco, his favorite player Willie Mays, that former Houston star J.R. Richard was the toughest pitcher he's ever faced, and that he was headed for college at Arizona State before he signed a professional contract with the Braves.

It shouldn't come as a surprise to most that Dale Murphy, a devout Mormon, is a traditionalist who likes grass fields, older ball parks, and "traditional-looking" uniforms. Murphy's dislikes include traveling and playing baseball on Sundays, "objectionable" language, tobacco chewing, dipping snuff, and female sportswriters in locker rooms. But as Bisher points out reassuringly in his introduction, Murphy "seldom speaks a discouraging word" and "rarely is he without a smile on his face."

As far as books of this type go, it does have value and interest for baseball-loving youngsters, especially if they follow the career of the Braves' star. Murphy's answers to his readers are both serious and honest, for he is particularly concerned about young people being pushed athletically by parents who are trying to relive their own youth. And as Dale Murphy himself says, "If some of those readers are adults who played the summer game when they were young and who still watch it, so much the better."

W.G. Nicholson
Watertown, Connecticut

Pearlman, Donn. *Dimes to Dollars: Collecting Baseball Cards.* Chicago: Bonus Books, 1987. 108 pp. $6.95.

Almost every baseball fan retains a soft spot for the baseball bubble gum cards which provided endless entertainment and wonder on hot summer afternoons and evenings. But in *Dimes to Dollars: Collecting Baseball Cards,* Donn Pearlman reminds us that cards of player records and pictures have become something more than just nostalgia. Baseball card collecting is more than just a hobby for youngsters, it has become a profitable business and investment opportunity for baseball fans of all ages.

Although Pearlman concentrates primarily upon the business aspects of baseball card collecting, he does provide an interesting historical overview of the baseball card. The first cards were produced in the 1880s by cigarette companies. Among these first cards perhaps the most valuable today is that of Hall-of-Famer Honus Wagner who asked for his card to be withdrawn because of his aversion to tobacco products. In the first two decades of the 20th century candy companies such as Cracker Jacks replaced the tobacco companies, but the modern era of baseball cards began in the Depression when the Goudey Gum Company of Boston produced a series of over 200 color cards. Due to a paper shortage, card production was discontinued during World War II. Production was resumed in 1948 by the Bowman Gum Company which was eventually absorbed by Topps Chewing Gum, Inc. in 1956. After lawsuits alleging monopolistic control, the Fleer Corporation and the Donruss Company have entered the baseball card market, offering full sets.

Following his fascinating history of baseball card production, Pearlman devotes the bulk of his study to discussing baseball cards as an investment. But he does stress that one should be a collector first and enjoy the cards for their intrinsic value. Pearlman's work is very loosely constructed. Around chapters interviewing key figures in baseball card marketing, he weaves chapters discussing grading cards, card auctions, autographing cards, cards with errors, and baseball card publications.

Although there is a great deal of repetition in Pearlman's approach, certain key themes do emerge. Almost all the collectors/investors interviewed by Pearlman insist that anyone wishing to get into the business should begin by purchasing a complete set of cards, but these heavy hitters, as Pearlman calls them, also point out that so many cards are published each year that it is impossible to collect everything. Perhaps one of the most interesting descriptions of baseball card collecting comes from Dr. James Beckett who publishes the annual *Official Price Guide to Baseball Cards.* Beckett argues that "it [buying a baseball card] is like buying a fine painting. There is a pride of ownership. If it goes up in value, that's great. On the other hand, even if it doesn't you still have the enjoyment of the painting. But then again people usually don't take a painting down off the wall and read the back of it, or trade their paintings with other owners of paintings." (p. 32)

Although a little disorganized and simplistic in style, this volume is full of practical suggestions for the baseball fan who wants to go into, or return to, the pursuit of acquiring baseball cards. Pearlman makes numerous analogies between the collecting of baseball cards and the hobbies / businesses of collecting stamps and coins. This is most apparent in the grading of baseball cards and the importance of mint condition. Pearlman devotes an entire chapter to the proper care of baseball cards. He also demolishes a few myths about the value of cards. Autographed cards may be viewed as defaced by some collectors, and cards containing mistakes are not necessarily worth more in the market. In fact, the card correcting a mistake may be worth more depending on how many are printed. Pearlman also offers his readers a service by describing, in some detail, how to purchase cards through the mail auction houses. And Pearlman concludes his work by listing hobby publications where readers may gain additional information about the phenomenon of baseball card collecting / investing.

In conclusion, Pearlman has produced a very useful volume for the baseball fan who would like to go into card collecting. Yet in this business discussion one does miss some of the common pleasures delivered by the cards. As a young boy fondling the cards, sleeping with them under the pillow, and inventing countless numbers of baseball card games to play with photos of my heroes, I, of course, ruined the mint condition of my cards. But really there is no monetary value I can place on the pleasure those cards brought me on hot summer afternoons in West Texas. Thus, Pearlman's volume often misses the nostalgic and spiritual values of the cards. But it did stir some memories, and I have just ordered my first set of cards in many years. Thank you, Donn Pearlman.

Ron Briley
Albuquerque, New Mexico

Plimpton, George. *The Curious Case of Sidd Finch.* New York: Macmillan, 1987. 275 pp. $14.95.

This enjoyable book is not about baseball history. It is instead a spin-off of an article that appeared in *Sports Illustrated,* which itself made baseball history. The article detailed the arrival in the New York Mets organization of a new super phenom, a gangling Buddhist monk ballplayer from Tibet named Sidd Finch, who pitched the baseball, barefooted, at 168 miles per hour with unerring accuracy. The resultant stir created by the April Fool's Day piece in 1985 led to massive reader mail, cancellations of some subscriptions, and, no doubt, numerous convulsions in barbershops, beauty parlors, and medical and dental waiting rooms around the nation.

In this book version, Robert Temple, a Vietnam reporter–veteran paralyzed by writer's block, is called upon by the Mets' management to promote baseball to the English-born Tibetan tiger. Rather than calling in the great baseball commentators (Red Barber or Mel Allen come to mind), showing Finch Cooperstown, or taking him to see Robert Redford in *The Natural,* the Mets look to Temple to persuade Finch that the American pastime is a holy tradition worthy of the mind-matter that he has expended perfecting his craft pegging stones at snow leopards high in the Himalayas. Finch, however, unlike any other rookie candidate in baseball history, is searching for special meaning and purpose in his pitching. He proves an enigmatic, elusive student. Temple tells Finch of the titans of baseball—Ruth, DiMaggio, Mantle, Mays; he tells him of the great fastball pitchers, including Ryan, Gossage, Feller, and Koufax. He takes Sidd Finch and Sidd's friend, Debby Sue, a mermaid windsurfer and lady-of-the-lake figure, into his home and life; he even relates the grim story of the great Polish-American phenom, Steve Dalkowski, whose career in the Orioles chain was cut short by his uncontrolled speedball.

Soon after *Sports Illustrated* runs its feature article on the Buddhist ballplayer, creating great public attention, Finch, too, loses control, senses forebodingly that the "Perfect Pitch, once a thing of Harmony, is now potentially an instrument of Chaos and Cruelty," and runs off to a monastery. Most Americans hence come to believe that the story was a grandiose, practical joke. In *The Curious Case of Sidd Finch,* however, Finch returns to New York's Shea Stadium in August 1985 to pitch for the Mets against the St. Louis Cardinals. He strikes out 27 men in succession in a perfect, perfect game, and he transforms the national pastime immediately into an American Little League, dominated by a tall, gangling (alien) pitcher. The explosive response reveals much about American sport. There is talk of scouting other players in the Himalayas; there develops speculation about changing the rules and moving back the mound to redress the imbalance between pitcher and batter; there even arises talk about barring the Buddhist ballplayer from the national pastime. An underworld figure, Al "Big Cakes" Caporetto, bungles an effort against Finch's life. Before American baseball can concert its efforts, however, before even Finch's signature can appear on a single baseball card, the Buddhist monk walks off the mound after 26 straight outs in his second rotation, abandons the game (Jesse Orosco finishes up), and flees to London with his paramour. The reader is left to ponder why. The reader is also left to wonder about the peculiarities of America's national pastime, the sociology of teams, the vagaries of absorbing diverse new players in each season's new renewal, and about Plimpton's meaning.

American baseball has been historically a great assimilation machine, absorbing diverse newcomers from varied backgrounds. Yet it cannot absorb Sidd Finch, a foreign-born seeker after holy perfection. Why not? This is the puzzle Plimpton ultimately puts before his readers. The novel's true subject may perhaps be the writer, Temple, affectionately dubbed "Owl" by Debby Sue, who in writing about Sidd Finch, cures his own Vietnam-induced paralysis. Or it may be the search for timeless perfection and balance in baseball and Buddhism alike and the simultaneous search for personal liberation. This reader, and many other readers, however, will marvel at the failed effort by baseball to absorb a speedball rookie phenom who would radically transform the national game. Why this can't be done is open to speculation. Perhaps no greater insight is offered, though, than that by Davey Johnson, the Mets' manager, at the outset of the book. Confronted by the challenge of taking in, training, and harnessing a Zen master, Johnson quips, "Give me a Presbyterian any old time."

Kenneth Waltzer
James Madison College
Michigan State University

Riley, Dan (Ed.) *The Red Sox Reader*. Thousand Oaks, CA: Ventura Arts, 1987. xvi + 224 pp. $9.95.

"I don't understand why people expect us to fail," Charles Pierce quotes Red Sox second baseman Marty Barrett in his essay "History's Sad Lesson." "We're playing real good ball right now. Why can't people just enjoy that?" They can't, Pierce makes clear, because Red Sox fans know their history. For the New Englander, history isn't random events; it is—as it has been since the winds carried the Mayflower safely into Cape Cod Bay—a record of signs and portents, lessons for our instruction and warning. "Baseball is not a life and death matter," Peter Gammons quotes *Boston Globe* columnist Mike Barnicle in another essay, "but the Red Sox are."

First baseman Bill Buckner marveled that the throng who turned out to honor the Sox after their 1986 World Series defeat cheered him even though he had let the ball roll through his legs to lose Game 6. But John Updike presciently explained the cheers in an essay published just before the Series: "All men are mortal, and therefore all men are losers; our profoundest loyalty goes out to the fallible." More, to lose is to win, as Michael Blowen argues in "The Perfect Ending to a Perfect Season:"

> Although, as fans, we often think that winning brings eternal gratification, it doesn't. James Dickey, the poet-novelist, was once asked why he wrote so many depressing poems. "Some of them are depressing," he replied, "but I hope it's the type of depression you leap up from, renewed."

The Red Sox renew their fans through their failure. Their effect on their supporters is the catharsis of Greek tragedy. As Blowen points out, the Sox "represent the kind of classicism that Aristotle might envy." Harvard classicist Emily Vermeule (writing about the Sox' 1978 playoff loss to the Yankees) explains the team's tragic majesty:

> They were . . . actors in traditional and poignant myth, in the long conflict between the larger-than-life hero and inexorable time, native brilliance and predestined ruin, the flukiness of luck, tyche, set against the hardest stirring of the individual.

Dan Riley, editor of this intriguing collection of essays, calls the Red Sox "the greatest *what if* team in sports . . . What if Buckner makes the play at first? What if Piniella doesn't come up with Remy's drive to right? . . . What if Frazee doesn't sell the Babe?" Riley should know these are idle questions. What if Oedipus doesn't slay his father? But he does, and that's it.

History, like tragedy, knows no "what ifs." Seen in retrospect, everything that happens is inevitable. It is this inevitability that gives classical tragedy and Red Sox history their power to move us. Its inevitability is what makes the Sox' perennial stumble at the threshhold of victory so poignant and so productive of memorable writing.

Riley brings together in *The Red Sox Reader* much of the finest writing about the Sox and their players. Updike's "Hub Fans Bid Kid Adieu" (that classic narrative of the individual hero's triumph amid team failure that salves Sox fans' hurt) is here, as are Roger Angell's moving reflections on the 1975 World Series and the 1978 Sox–Yankee playoff. Although to include, as Riley does, eight of eleven essays from a *Boston Globe* supplement—*Literati on the Red Sox*—is a lazy way of bulking up an anthology, most of the pieces are worthy of inclusion, and one—Doris Kearns Goodwin's "From Father, With Love"—shines among baseball literature's crown jewels. Other gems in Riley's collection: Leonard Shecter's "Baseball: The Great American Myth," an insightful look at the disintegration of the Red Sox in 1968, a year after they won the pennant; Thomas Boswell's

"The Greatest Game Ever Played" (the 1978 playoff), one of the greatest game stories ever written; Updike's personal testament "Loving the Sox;" and the brief essays by Pierce, Gammons, Blowen, and Vermeule, cited earlier, which conclude the book and establish the Red Sox as Myth.

Not every piece is a masterpiece. Red Smith's "Ted Williams Spits" is a labored trifle, and Ray Fitzgerald's goodbye to Bill Lee represents the sports column at its most ordinary. Editor Riley's two short stories, lame as literature, seem out of place as the sole works of fiction in the book.

Some Red Sox enthusiasts will regret the absence of personal favorites. (I would like to have seen George V. Higgins's "Ballpark: Fenway, with Tears.") And one wishes the editor had searched more diligently for out-of-the-way pieces, and for a sampling of early writing about the club and its players. Overall, however, Riley has assembled a fine collection.

Not so fine is the book's appearance. It is as drab as the Sox' road uniforms, typeset on a Macintosh computer by someone with no sense of printing aesthetics. (Slightly smaller type and leading between the lines would work wonders.) Further, the compositor was unable to master the machine: in many places dashes are divided between lines. More annoying are the numerous typographical errors (a few of which were corrected in the book's second printing).

Riley subtitles his book "30 Years of Musings on Baseball's Most Amusing Team," but although he calls on archaic and obsolete definitions to make "amuse" mean "bemuse," "absorb," "distract," and "bewilder," "amusing" nevertheless suggests a shallowness at odds with the underlying seriousness (not solemnity) of most of the pieces he has brought together. There is an ambivalence in Riley's introduction; he checks himself part way through with a shift in tone that seems to warn: "Hey, let's not get carried away—baseball's just a game, after all."

But life itself is a kind of game, and if we find in baseball and its stories insight for living and uplift for the spirit, shall we be denied? Readers have long been moved and edified by sullen Achilles, and waffling Hamlet, and monomaniacal Ahab. The writers represented in *The Red Sox Reader* persuade us that the team of Ted Williams, and Carl Yastrzemski, and Wade Boggs is as fully rewarding of our absorption.

Frederick Ivor-Campbell
Warren, Rhode Island

Tullius, John, *I'd Rather Be a Yankee: An Oral History of America's Most Loved and Most Hated Baseball Team*. New York: Macmillan, 1986. 364 pp. $19.95.

Ever since Lawrence Ritter's pioneering *The Glory of Their Times* (1966), "oral history"—edited transcriptions of oral remembrances—has become an increasingly popular method of recording sport history. That the great majority of such works treat baseball testifies to the sport's popularity and long-standing traditions. We've "heard" from great and not-so-great players, managers, broadcasters, umpires, and, most recently, members of individual teams. What began as a novel literary form has become a conventional genre dedicated to capturing the invaluable personal insights usually missing in traditional studies of the baseball industry.

Subtitle notwithstanding, *I'd Rather Be a Yankee* is not really an "oral history." While

John Tullius has interviewed an indeterminable number of unidentified Yankees past and present, the volume is primarily a pastiche of quotations assembled scissors-and-paste fashion from magazines, newspapers, tape recordings in the Baseball Hall of Fame Library, and, most notably, previously published oral histories. Besides being largely derivative, the book is flawed both in substance and execution.

Weaknesses in content stem from the fact that this is at best a "passive oral history." The commentaries extracted from periodical literature, especially prior to the 1960s, are predictably banal as interviewees invariably gave the kinds of guarded, clichéd responses that met the interviewer's objective—obtaining quotable quotes about personalities and performances to entertain fans rather than probing into matters of significance in Yankee or baseball history. Consequently, such important topics as racism, personnel management, relations between team officials and the press, and the workings of the farm system are ignored or superficially discussed. Even when Tullius appears to have conducted personal interviews, the results indicate that he is unfamiliar with the techniques of critical oral interviewing. Significantly, much of the best material in the collection is taken from other oral histories and thus is familiar to Yankeephiles. For example, seven of the nine Whitey Ford quotes are reprints, two-thirds from Joseph Durso's *Whitey and Mickey* (1977).

Moreover, Tullius fails to compensate for the unavoidable limitations of much of the material by maximizing the contribution of the compendium. A compiler rather than an editor, he neither explains nor corrects texts and is content to provide cursory commentary to connect the disparate quotes. Symptomatically, by providing a superficial introduction and allowing two patently circumspect statements by Elston Howard to stand unchallenged as the lone commentary on racial integration (pp. 277–278), Tullius downplays the depths of racism on the Yankees and ignores Casey Stengel's penchant for publicly referring to blacks derogatorily as "niggers" and "jungle bunnies." Baseball historians will find numerous nits to pick, whether misspellings (e.g., Cy Rigler p. 181, Bill Dinneen p. 9, and Billy Hoeft p. 184), mistakes (e.g., Mickey Mantle was *not* a "quintessential farm boy" p. 222), or inaccurate judgments (e.g., Ralph Houk was "a perennial loser" p. 22, Lou Gehrig "didn't have great talent, he had great strength" p. 72, and Earl Combs is "the greatest lead-off man in Yankee history" p. 91). The index is grossly incomplete, a deficiency all the more troubling because there is no discernible pattern for inclusions and omissions.

Most annoying is the inexcusable decision to offer a "history" sans attribution for quoted material. Tullius exults that "some of the real gems" in the book were unearthed from "the mother lode—a dusty, uncatalogued, lost-in-the-archives library of hundreds of hours of old tapes" (p. xvi) in the Hall of Fame Library, but does not explain who did the recordings, when, and for what reason. Footnotes are provided only (but not always) for excerpts from copyrighted published works; other quotes, whether from newspapers, magazines, recordings, or personal interviews, are undocumented. In oral history, context and time are critical considerations.

To be fair, Tullius has assembled a lot of interesting material concerning the Yankees from the team's humble beginnings as the Highlanders in 1903 through the glory days as the Bronx Bombers on to the present "Bronx Zoo" era. The problem is that he compiled a scrapbook of quotes instead of an oral history. Inveterate Yankee fans may enjoy this catalogue of comments from and about their diamond heroes, but serious readers will find it of limited interest and usefulness. For one who stood alone in his neighborhood in the early 1950s rooting for the Yankees, it is difficult for me to admit that as a "team oral history," *I'd Rather Be a Yankee* is decidedly inferior to Peter Golenbock's *Bums: An Oral History of the Brooklyn Dodgers* (1984).

Larry R. Gerlach
University of Utah

CONTRIBUTORS

Larry Bowman, a professor of history at the University of North Texas, has long held baseball as a special interest. He hopes to begin work soon on the biography of Cap Anson.

Ron Briley is Assistant Headmaster and Chairman of the History Department at Sandia Preparatory School in Albuquerque, New Mexico. He took his graduate work in history at West Texas State University and the University of New Mexico, and is currently working on a book examining baseball as a symbol of post World War II American values. This is his second appearance in *Baseball History*.

Merritt Clifton owns and operates Samisdat press. He is currently working on *Townball,* a history of New England and Quebec town team baseball during the first half of the 20th century. Merritt's essay is from this work-in-progress and this is his second appearance in *Baseball History*.

Bill Felber is Editor of the *Manhattan Mercury,* in Manhattan, Kansas, and is appearing in *Baseball History* for the second time.

Robert Frauenglas is a freelance writer and third-generation Brooklynite. He co-founded the Brooklyn Book Fair and founded SOMRIE Press and Brooklyn Publishing Company, Ltd.. Robert still mourns the loss of the Dodgers, 31 years post-desertion.

Larry Gerlach is professor of history at the University of Utah, Salt Lake City. He is the author of *The Men in Blue: Conversations With Umpires* (1980) and is presently writing a history of baseball umpiring.

Ann Greenberg has been employed with the corporate offices of Merrill Lynch Realty for nine years. Born and raised on Long Island, she makes her home in Northport with her husband. This is her first published work.

Alex Holzman is an editor at Ohio State University Press and is still a follower of the New York Yankees.

Walter Langford is a retired Notre Dame professor of modern languages who last year published *Legends of Baseball*. His interviews have become a regular feature of *Baseball History*.

Joseph Lawler is a freelance writer, SABR member, and librarian who lives and works in Kingston, Rhode Island.

Brett Millier is an assistant professor of American Literature at Middlebury College, Vermont. She recalls reaching "such an acute limited excellence" as scoreboard operator for the San Francisco Giants, "that everything afterward savors of anti-climax."

Gene Murdock, professor emeritus of history at Marietta College and past president of SABR, is the author of several books on the Civil War, business, and baseball, including the fine *Ban Johnson: Czar of Baseball* and *Mighty Casey: All-American*. His work appeared in the very first issue of Baseball History and he continues to do historical research and writing.

Clark Nardinelli is an associate professor of economics at Clemson University. Most of his scholarly work has been devoted to British and American economic history; labor history in particular.

Bill Rabinowitz is a sportswriter for the Jamestown, New York *Post Journal* and has worked for the *Sporting News.* He holds a master's degree in journalism from Northwestern University.

Jim Sumner is employed by the North Carolina Division of Archives and History as staff historian for the North Carolina State Historic Preservation Office. His sport history articles have been published in, among others, *The Journal of Sport History* and a variety of SABR publications. Jim is an active member of SABR.